A Merriam-Webster
REG. U.S. PAT. OFF.

REG. U.S. PAT. OFF.

THE NEW
MERRIAM-WEBSTER
POCKET
DICTIONARY

A POCKET CARDINAL EDITION
PUBLISHED BY POCKET BOOKS · NEW YORK

THE NEW
MERRIAM-WEBSTER
POCKET DICTIONARY

A POCKET **CARDINAL** EDITION

1st printing........June, 1964
17th printing....October, 1966

This POCKET **CARDINAL®** EDITION
of THE NEW MERRIAM-WEBSTER
POCKET DICTIONARY
has been printed from brand-new plates.

Pocket CARDINAL editions are published by Pocket Books, Inc., and are printed and distributed in the U.S.A. by Affiliated Publishers, a division of Pocket Books, Inc., 630 Fifth Avenue, New York 20, N. Y.

Trademarks registered in the United States and other countries.

MERRIAM-WEBSTER PRONUNCIATION SYMBOLS

ə .....alone, silent, capital, collect, suppose
ˈə, ˌə ..humdrum, abut
ᵊ .....(in ᵊl, ᵊn) battle, cotton; (in lᵊ, mᵊ, rᵊ) French table, prisme, titre
ər ....operation, further
a ....map, patch
ā ....day, fate
ä ....bother, cot, father
ȧ ....a sound between \a\ and \ä\, as in an Eastern New England pronunciation of aunt, ask
au̇ ...now, out
b ....baby, rib
ch ...chin, catch
d ....did, adder
e .....set, red
ē .....beat, nosebleed, easy
f .....fifty, cuff
g ....go, big
h ....hat, ahead
hw ...whale
i .....tip, banish
ī .....site, buy
j .....job, edge
k ....kin, cook
k̲ ....loch as commonly pronounced in Scotland (it is \k\ without actual contact between tongue and palate)
l .....lily, cool
m ....murmur, dim
n ....nine, own
ⁿ .....indicates that a preceding vowel or diphthong is pronounced through both nose and mouth, as in French bon \bōⁿ\
ŋ ....sing, singer, finger, ink
ō ....bone, hollow
ȯ ....saw, cork
œ ....\e\ with lip rounding, as in French bœuf, German Hölle
œ̄ ....\ā\ with lip rounding, as in French feu, German Höhle
ȯi ....toy, sawing
p ....pepper, lip
r .....rarity
s .....source, less
sh ....shy, mission
t .....tie, attack
th ....thin, ether
th̲ ....then, either
ü ....boot, few \ˈfyü\
u̇ ....put, pure \ˈpyu̇r\
ue ...\i\ with lip rounding, as in German füllen
ue̅ ....\ē\ with lip rounding, as in French rue, German fühlen
v ....vivid, give
w ....we, away
y ....yard, cue \ˈkyü\
ʸ .....indicates that a preceding \l\, \n\, or \w\ is modified by the placing of the tongue tip against the lower front teeth, as in French digne \dēnʸ\
z .....zone, raise
zh ...vision, pleasure
\ .....slant line used in pairs to mark the beginning and end of a transcription: \ˈpen\
ˈ .....mark at the beginning of a syllable that has primary (strongest) stress: \ˈpen-mən-ˌship\
ˌ .....mark at the beginning of a syllable that has secondary (next-strongest) stress: \ˈpen-mən-ˌship\
- .....mark of syllable division in pronunciations (the mark of syllable division in entries is a centered dot •)
( )....indicate that what is symbolized between sometimes occurs and sometimes does not occur in the pronunciation of the word: factory \ˈfak-t(ə-)rē\ = \ˈfak-tə-rē, ˈfak-trē\

PREFACE

The first MERRIAM-WEBSTER POCKET DICTIONARY was published in 1947. Its reception over the years has been such that after the appearance of a new Merriam-Webster unabridged, *Webster's Third New International Dictionary*, in 1961, a new pocket dictionary became necessary and inevitable to serve the needs of present-day users. This NEW MERRIAM-WEBSTER POCKET DICTIONARY has been completely revised, enlarged, and reset in a new typeface (Times Roman) and with a larger page. Like the large unabridged dictionary from which it is drawn, it is a citation dictionary. This means that every definition is based on examples in the Merriam-Webster files of actual use, examples that cover the range of Modern English from Shakespeare and the Bible down to living authors writing and publishing today. It means also that the selection of words and senses for inclusion is based on actual recorded use or on users' highly probable need.

To get satisfactory and pleasing rewards from looking into a dictionary one must learn how to use it, that is, how to interpret the information that is contained at each entry. This knowledge involves mainly an ability to recognize different typefaces, a small number of abbreviations that occur over and over, and a few traditional dictionary devices. Every user is, therefore, urged to find time to read this preface carefully.

THE ENTRY

The entries in this dictionary begin on page 1 and continue in alphabetical order from A to Z on page 592. Each page contains, set off at the top, a pair of guide words to the entries contained alphabetically between them on the page. The entries are printed in heavy black letters (**boldface type**) set flush with the left-hand margin or run on after a dash. The left-hand words (like **abide**) are MAIN ENTRIES and determine the alphabetical order. Those following dashes (like **absolutely** at **absolute**) are DERIVATIVE ENTRIES, derived from or formed on the main entry.

Most English words, especially nouns and verbs, change their forms to agree with their varying roles in context. Nouns have plural forms (as *boys* and *houses*). Verbs have past forms (as *walked* and *amplified*) and participial forms (as *walking, amplifying,* and *shown*). Adjectives and adverbs have comparative forms (like *cheaper* and *happier*) and superlative forms (like *cheapest* and *happiest*). When these forms are made regularly like thousands of other words, the forms are not shown in this dictionary because every native speaker of English is able to form them himself by repeated use of similar forms. If, however, these forms are irregular, they appear in boldface type and are called INFLECTIONAL ENTRIES. Examples: **mice** at **mouse, beeves** *or* **beefs** at **beef, beaux** *or* **beaus** at **beau, fungi** *or* **funguses** at **fungus, saw** and **seen** at **see, abetted** and **abetting** at **abet**, **bivouacked** at **bivouac**, **worse** and **worst** at **bad**. Occasionally these inflectional forms are shown only as parts of words preceded by a hyphen (like **-horred** and **-horring** for *abhorred* and *abhorring* at **abhor**) which indicates that the user can supply the missing syllable or syllables from the main entry.

CENTERED PERIODS in boldface within entry words (as in **an·ti·bi·ot·ic**) indicate division points at which a hyphen may be put at the end of a line of handwriting, typewriting, or printing. In accordance with widespread practice among publishers in making syllabic divisions at the end of a line, this book does not show a division after a single initial letter of a word, before a single final letter of a word, before a single final letter of an English prefix, or after a single initial letter of an English suffix. Examples: **ane·mia**, **Pass·over**, **semi·fi·nal**, **read·able** rather than *a·ne·mi·a*, *Pass·o·ver*, *sem·i·fi·nal*, *read·a·ble*. A single hyphen in a boldface word at the end of a line (as **fa-** in **fatherless** at **father**) replaces a centered period.

In entries no division mark is placed after the second of two vowels that might be taken as a digraph (**pi·ety** rather than *pi·e·ty*).

The syllabic division of an entry is based on the pronunciation variant shown first in this book if another variant requires a different division.

Words taken over unchanged into English from a foreign language are often divided in accordance with the practices of the foreign language (as **cause cé·lè·bre**).

A DOUBLE HYPHEN ⸗ at the end of a line in this dictionary (as at **bungalow**) stands for a hyphen that belongs at that point in a hyphened word and should be retained when the word is written as a unit on one line of writing or type.

Boldface words in parentheses (like **coca** at **cocaine** and **coconut palm** at **coconut**) are RUN-IN ENTRIES.

When one main entry has exactly the same written form as another that follows it, they are distinguished by SUPERIOR NUMBERS preceding each word (like **¹chase**, **²chase**, **³chase**, and **⁴chase**). Such words are called homographs. Some homographs are related to each other through being derived from the same root. Others have no relationship beyond the accident of spelling.

PRONUNCIATION

A set of reversed virgules \ \ usually follows the boldface entries. The symbols within these slant lines indicate pronunciation. A tabular key to the Merriam-Webster pronunciation symbols appears on the page immediately preceding this preface. Also a simplified key for quick reference is shown in the three lines at the bottom of every other page throughout the vocabulary.

A high-set mark ' indicates that the syllable following has primary (strongest) stress; a low-set mark ˌ indicates that the syllable following has secondary (next-strongest) stress (as \'ded-ˌlīn\ at **deadline**).

A syllable with neither a high-set mark nor a low-set mark is unstressed (as the middle syllable of \'ab-di-ˌkāt\ at abdicate)

Parentheses mean that whatever is indicated within them is (1) present in the pronunciation of some speakers and absent from the pronunciation of other speakers, (2) present in some utterances and absent from other utterances of the same speaker, or (3) simply sometimes heard and sometimes not heard. The pronunciation \'fak-t(ə-)rē\ at factory shows that the pronunciation may be in three syllables \'fak-tə-rē\ or two syllables \'fak-trē\.

The placement of syllable divisions in the pronunciation transcriptions is based only on phonetic considerations. Thus *miner* and *minor* are identical in pronunciation and the two transcriptions are identically syllabified. (In syllabifying the boldface entry, however other considerations may prevail, for the sole purpose of this division is to indicate desirable places to insert a hyphen at the end of a line of print or writing. Thus the entry *miner*, which is composed of the verb *mine* and the suffix *-er*, is divided after the *n*, whereas the identically pronounced entry *minor*. which does not contain two meaningful English elements, is divided before the *n*.)

An entry is usually not pronounced if it is identical in spelling, division, and pronunciation with a preceding entry (as ²meet and ³meet are like ¹meet and megaphone *verb* is like megaphone *noun*). An entry is often not pronounced if it consists of a preceding entry and a suffix that is entered at its alphabetical place with pronunciation (as the pronunciation of implicitly is that at implicit plus that at -ly). Open compounds of two or more words usually have no pronunciation indicated (as at cable car).

A syllable or syllable sequence at the beginning of a pronunciation may be omitted if it is identical with the beginning of a pronunciation for a closely preceding entry (as the pronunciation of multiplicity gets its first two syllables from the pronunciation at multiplication and that of multiplier from multiply).

VARIANTS

Variant entries are joined by an italicized *or* (as caddie *or* caddy, -celed *or* -celled at cancel, and baldachin *or* baldachino) or by an italicized *also* (as woolly *also* wooly, although *also* altho, -bra *also* -brums at candelabrum). Once *also* has been used, additional variants joined by *or* are also-variants (as at ²cleave the past cleaved has two also-variants which are cleft or clove, and the past participle also has two also-variants, cleft or cloven). The italicized *or* joins equal variants. This means that neither is to be preferred to the other as a matter of correctness. The individual may use one or the other. The italicized *also* joins a secondary variant to a spelling or form that is more common but it does not mean that the secondary variant is wrong or even less appropriate. In either case (*or* or *also*) ordinarily no one should be induced by its dictionary entry alone, apart from other considerations not indicated in the dictionary, to change from one form to the other. The form one has always used or the form prevailing in one's community is likely to be the preferred form for the individual.

Variant pronunciations are separated within the pronunciation virgules by a comma. The presence of variant pronunciations simply indicates that not all educated speakers pronounce the word the same way. A second-place variant is not to be regarded as per se a less desirable variant than the one given first. In fact, it may be used by as many educated speakers as the first variant. A variant which our records indicate is appreciably less frequent than that or those preceding may be preceded by *also*. Some variant pronunciations (as \'ak-,sent, ak-'sent\ for the verb **accent**, \ə-'brā-siv, -ziv\ at **abrasive**) are the kind that one speaker uses but another does not for the reason that their dialects are different and that the speech habits of one are different from those of the other.

ITALIC LABELS

An italic label following the pronunciation or, if no pronunciation is given, following the entry itself, indicates the part of speech. The eight traditional parts of speech are thus abbreviated:

ac·tive . . . *adj*	(adjective)
¹across . . . *adv*	(adverb)
al·though . . . *conj*	(conjunction)
ahoy . . . *interj*	(interjection)
¹act . . . *n*	(noun)
²across *prep*	(preposition)
he . . . *pron*	(pronoun)
²act *vb*	(verb)

These labels are sometimes combined [as at **awash** *adv (or adj)*] and especially at undefined derivatives (like **billionth** *adj or n*).

Other italic labels sometimes occurring in the same position as the part-of-speech label and signaled by an initial or final hyphen are:

an·ti- . . . *prefix*
-ness . . . *n suffix*
²-ant *adj suffix*

The label *pl* means PLURAL. This occurs after a comma to introduce the boldface plural form of a singular entry (as at **abacus** . . . *n, pl* -ci . . .) or without a comma to indicate that the preceding boldface is a plural (as **environs** *n pl*).

(No italic labels are regularly used to indicate inflectional verb parts since their position after the infinitive of the entry form is regular. At ¹**dive** the past, in second position, is **dived** or **dove**; the past participle, in third position, is **dived**; and the present participle, in fourth position, is **diving**. For similar reasons the comparative and superlative forms of adjectives and adverbs, when shown, are not labeled.)

Still other labels occurring infrequently are *archaic*, *slang*, and *dial* (meaning "dialect"):

be·seem . . . *archaic*
¹sire . . . *archaic*
va·moose . . . *slang*
crit·ter . . . *dial*

and also regional labels:

pet·rol . . . *Brit*
pone . . . *n, South and Midland*

7a

CAPITALIZATION

Words nearly always capitalized are capitalized in the boldface entry (as **Al·ex·an·dri·an**) unless it is the second or third or fourth sense of a lowercase word. In the latter situation it is labeled *cap* (as at dem·o·crat . . . 3 *cap* . . .). Sometimes the letters to be capitalized are specified (as at **union jack** . . . 2 *cap U & J* . . .).

Words entered with an initial boldface lowercase letter sometimes bear a label to indicate that it is not always written lowercase:

> **al·ex·an·drine** . . . *often cap*
> ¹**word** . . . 4 *often cap*

Words entered with an initial capital but having a sense often lowercased have at the relevant sense a label *often not cap* (as at **Mass** . . . 2 *often not cap*).

ETYMOLOGY

The matter in boldface square brackets preceding the definition is the etymology. Meanings given in roman type within these brackets are not definitions of the main entry but meanings of the non-English words within the brackets. No attempt has been made to give etymologies for all the vocabulary entries, but a sufficient number is provided to show the varied origins of the English vocabulary:

> **alms** . . . [OE *ælmesse.* fr LL *eleemosyna,* fr. Gk *eleēmosynē* pity, alms, fr *eleēmōn* merciful, fr. *eleos* pity]
> **as·sas·sin** . . . [Ar *hashshāshīn* members of a medieval Muslim order who committed murder under the influence of hashish, fr *hashīsh* hashish]
> **ba·bel** . . . [fr. the Tower of *Babel* Gen 11:4–9]
> **bed·lam** . . . [fr. *Bedlam,* popular name for the Hospital of St. Mary of Bethlehem, London insane asylum]

SYMBOLIC COLON

This dictionary uses a boldface character recognizably distinct from the usual roman colon as a linking symbol between the main entry and a definition. It stands for an unexpressed simple predicate that may be read "is being here defined as (or by)". It indicates that the supporting orientation immediately after the main entry is over and thus facilitates a visual jumping from word to definition:

> **de·bil·i·tate** . . . **:** to impair the health or strength of
> **tac·tic** . . . **:** a device for accomplishing an end

Words that have two or more definitions have two or more symbolic colons. The signal for another definition is another colon:

> **ab·bre·vi·a·tion** . . . **1 :** the act or result of abbreviating **2 :** a shortened form of a word or phrase used for brevity esp. in writing

SENSE DIVISION

Boldface arabic numerals within an entry separate the senses of a word that has more than a single sense:

> **ap·peal** . . . *vb* **1 :** to take steps to have (a case) reheard in a higher court **2 :** to plead for help, corroboration, or decision **3 :** to arouse a sympathetic response

8a

No one of the senses, as defined, is better or more important than another, but one may have more appropriate meaning in a specific context. Senses closely related, as two aspects of the same sense, are usually joined by a semicolon plus *also* or *esp:*

> **all·spice** . . . **:** the berry of the pimento tree; *also* **:** a spice made from it
> **all–Amer·i·can** . . . **:** representative of the U. S. as a whole; *esp* **:** selected as the best in the U. S.

VERBAL ILLUSTRATIONS

The matter enclosed in a pair of angle brackets illustrates an appropriate use of the word in context. The word being illustrated is replaced by a swung dash which stands for the same form of the word as the main entry or by a swung dash plus an italicized suffix which can be added without any change of letters to the form of the main entry. Otherwise the word is written in full and italicized:

> **er·satz** . . . *adj* . . . ⟨~ flour⟩
> **¹be·tween** . . . *prep* **1 :** . . . ⟨earned $10,000 ~ the two of them⟩
> **2 :** . . . ⟨an alley ~ two buildings⟩ **3 :** . . . ⟨choose ~ two cars⟩ **4 :** . . . ⟨hostility ~ nations⟩ ⟨a bond ~ brothers⟩
> **–ance** . . . *n suffix* **1 :** . . . ⟨further*ance*⟩ **2 :** . . . ⟨protuber*ance*⟩
> **3 :** . . . ⟨conduct*ance*⟩

USAGE NOTES

A usage note is introduced by a lightface dash. A usage note provides information about the use of the word being defined and so always modifies the word that is the main entry. It may be in the form of a comment on idiom, syntax, semantic relationship, status, or various other matters:

> **¹al·le·gro** . . . — used as a direction in music
> **be·lay** . . . — used in the imperative
> **jaw** . . . — usu. used in pl.
> **sir** . . . — used as a title before the given name of a knight or baronet

A usage note may stand in place of a definition and without the symbolic colon. Some function words have little or no semantic content, and most interjections express feelings but otherwise are untranslatable into a meaning that can be substituted. Many other words (as some oaths and imprecations, calls to animals, specialized signals, song refrains, and honorific titles), though genuinely a part of the language, have a usage note instead of a definition:

> **fie** . . . *interj* — used to express disgust or shock
> **be·hold** . . . *vb* . . . — used imperatively to direct the attention
> **and/or** . . . — used as a function word to indicate that either *and* or *or* may apply
> **¹at** . . . *prep* . . . — used to indicate a point in time or space
> **may** . . . — used as an auxiliary to express a wish or desire, purpose or expectation, or contingency or concession

CROSS-REFERENCES

A sequence of lightface SMALL CAPITALS used in a definition is identical letter-by-letter with a boldface entry (or with one of its inflectional forms) at its own alphabetical place. This sequence is a cross-reference. It is not a definition but an indication that a definition at its boldface equivalent can be substituted at the place where the small capitals are used. It appears sometimes with a full definition, sometimes by itself:

> ׀aban·don . . . : to give up : FORSAKE, DESERT
> ab·bey . . . : MONASTERY, CONVENT
> abet . . . : ASSIST

Sometimes the small capitals simply direct the user to another place in the vocabulary:

> ran *past of* RUN
> mice *pl of* MOUSE
> ׀bet·ter . . . *comparative of* GOOD
> disc *var of* DISK
> di·nar . . . — see MONEY table
> gaol . . . *chiefly Brit var of* JAIL
> him . . . *objective case of* HE

SYNONYMS

The boldface symbol **syn** near the end of an entry introduces words that are synonymous with the word being defined in some uses. Synonyms are not definitions, although they may often be substituted for each other in context. Examples:

> ben·e·fi·cial . . . **syn** advantageous, profitable
> bel·li·cose . . . **syn** belligerent, quarrelsome

ABBREVIATIONS

Abbreviations are not included as main entries in the vocabulary but they are classed as vocabulary entries. They are separately alphabetized in a section of back matter titled "Abbreviations".

Symbols for chemical elements are included alphabetically among the abbreviations in the back matter.

OTHER BACK MATTER

A section on the population follows the abbreviations. Cities of the U. S. are arranged by numerical groups from places over 1,000,000 down to places from 10,000 to 25,000. The names in each group are, however, alphabetical rather than numerical.

The population of U. S. states and dependencies is summarized on page 617.

Places in Canada having 10,000 or more inhabitants are grouped alphabetically by provinces. Canadian population is summarized on page 619.

A section of foreign words (as **monde**) and phrases (as **ad extremum**) often seen in English context follows. It includes state and national mottoes (as **ad astra per aspera** and **semper fidelis**). They are entries mostly from Latin and French, with a sprinkling of Italian, Spanish, German, and Greek.

A
DICTIONARY
OF
THE ENGLISH LANGUAGE

1a \'ā\ *n, often cap* : the 1st letter of the English alphabet

2a \ə, (')ā\ *indefinite article* : ONE, SOME — used to indicate an unspecified or unidentified individual ⟨there's ~ man outside⟩

aard·vark \'ärd-,värk\ *n* : a large burrowing ant-eating African mammal

aback \ə-'bak\ *adv* : by surprise ⟨taken ~⟩

ab·a·cus \'ab-ə-kəs\ *n, pl* -ci \-,sī, -,kē\ *or* -cus·es : an instrument for performing calculations by sliding counters along rods or grooves

1abaft \ə-'baft\ *adv* : toward or at the stern : AFT

2abaft *prep* : to the rear of

ab·a·lo·ne \,ab-ə-'lō-nē\ *n* : a large edible sea mollusk with an ear-shaped shell

1aban·don \ə-'ban-dən\ *vb* : to give up : FORSAKE, DESERT — **aban·don·ment** *n*

2abandon *n* **1** : a thorough yielding to natural impulses **2** : ENTHUSIASM, EXUBERANCE

aban·doned *adj* **1** : FORSAKEN **2** : morally unrestrained **syn** profligate, dissolute

abase \ə-'bās\ *vb* : HUMBLE, DEGRADE — **abase·ment** *n*

abash \ə-'bash\ *vb* : to destroy the composure of : EMBARRASS — **abash·ment** *n*

abate \ə-'bāt\ *vb* **1** : to put an end to ⟨~ a nuisance⟩ **2** : to decrease in amount, number, or degree

abate·ment *n* **1** : DECREASE **2** : an amount abated; *esp* : a deduction from the full amount of a tax

ab·a·tis \'ab-ə-,tē, 'ab-ət-əs\ *n, pl* -tis \-,tēz\ *or* -tis·es \-əs-oz\ : a defensive barrier of felled trees with sharpened branches turned outward

ab·at·toir \'ab-ə-,twär\ *n* : SLAUGHTERHOUSE

ab·ba·cy \'ab-ə-sē\ *n* : the office or term of office of an abbot or abbess

ab·bé \a-'bā, 'ab-,ā\ *n* : a member of the French secular clergy — used as a title

ab·bess \'ab-əs\ *n* : the superior of an abbey for women

ab·bey \'ab-ē\ *n* **1** : MONASTERY, CONVENT **2** : an abbey church

ab·bot \'ab-ət\ *n* : the superior of an abbey for men

ab·bre·vi·ate \ə-'brē-vē-,āt\ *vb* : SHORTEN, CURTAIL; *esp* : to reduce to an abbreviation

ab·bre·vi·a·tion \ə-,brē-vē-'ā-shən\ *n*

1 : the act or result of abbreviating **2** : a shortened form of a word or phrase used for brevity esp. in writing

ab·di·cate \'ab-di-,kāt\ *vb* : to give up (as a throne) formally — **ab·di·ca·tion** \,ab-di-'kā-shən\ *n*

ab·do·men \'ab-də-mən, ab-'dō-mən\ *n* : the cavity in or area of the body between the chest and the pelvis — **ab·dom·i·nal** \ab-'däm-ən-ᵊl\ *adj*

ab·duct \ab-'dəkt\ *vb* : to take away (a person) by force : KIDNAP — **ab·duc·tion** \-'dək-shən\ *n* — **ab·duc·tor** \-'dək-tər\ *n*

abeam \ə-'bēm\ *adv* : on a line at right angles to a ship's keel

abe·ce·dar·i·an \,ā-bē-sē-'der-ē-ən\ *n* : one learning the rudiments of something (as the alphabet)

abed \ə-'bed\ *adv (or adj)* : in bed

ab·er·ra·tion \,ab-ə-'rā-shən\ *n* **1** : deviation from normal or usual : DERANGEMENT **2** : failure of a mirror or lens to produce exact point-to-point correspondence between an object and its image — **ab·er·rant** \a-'ber-ənt\ *adj*

abet \ə-'bet\ *vb* **abet·ted; abet·ting** **1** : INCITE, ENCOURAGE **2** : ASSIST — **abet·tor** *or* **abet·ter** *n*

abey·ance \ə-'bā-əns\ *n* : a condition of suspended activity

ab·hor \ab-'hȯr, əb-\ *vb* **-horred; -horring** : LOATHE, DETEST — **ab·hor·rence** \-'hȯr-əns\ *n*

ab·hor·rent \-'hȯr-ənt\ *adj* : LOATHSOME, DETESTABLE

abide \ə-'bīd\ *vb* **abode** \-'bōd\ *or* **abid·ed; abid·ing** **1** : DWELL, REMAIN, LAST **2** : BEAR, ENDURE, TOLERATE

abil·i·ty \ə-'bil-ət-ē\ *n* : the quality of being able : POWER, SKILL

ab·ject \'ab-,jekt, ab-'jekt\ *adj* : low in spirit or hope : CRINGING — **ab·jec·tion** \ab-'jek-shən\ *n* — **ab·ject·ly** \'ab-jekt-lē, ab-'jekt\ *adv* — **ab·ject·ness** *n*

ab·jure \ab-'jür\ *vb* **1** : to renounce solemnly : RECANT **2** : to abstain from — **ab·ju·ra·tion** \,ab-jə-'rā-shən\ *n*

ab·late \a-'blāt\ *vb* : to remove or become removed by cutting, erosion, melting, or vaporization — **ab·la·tion** \-'blā-shən\ *n*

ab·la·tive \'ab-lət-iv\ *adj* : of, relating to, or constituting a grammatical case (as in Latin) expressing typically the relation of separation and source — **ablative** *n*

ə abut; ᵊ kitten; ər further; a back; ā bake; ä cot, cart; aů out; ch chin; e less; ē easy; g gift; i trip; ī life; j joke; ŋ sing; ō flow; ȯ flaw; ȯi coin; th thin; t͟h this; ü loot; ů foot; y yet; yü few; yů furious; zh vision

ablaze \ə-'blāz\ *adj* **:** being on fire **:** BLAZING

able \'ā-bəl\ *adj* **1 :** having sufficient power, skill, or resources to accomplish an object **2 :** marked by skill or efficiency — **ably** \-blē\ *adv*

-able *also* **-ible** \ə-bəl\ *adj suffix* **1 :** capable of, fit for, or worthy of (being so acted upon or toward) ⟨break*able*⟩ ⟨collect*ible*⟩ **2 :** tending, given, or liable to ⟨knowledge*able*⟩ ⟨perish*able*⟩ — **-ably** *also* **-ibly** \ə-blē\ *adv suffix*

able-bod·ied \ˌā-bəl-'bäd-ēd\ *adj* **:** having a sound strong body

abloom \ə-'blüm\ *adj* **:** BLOOMING

ab·lu·tion \a-'blü-shən\ *n* **:** a washing or cleansing of the body

ab·ne·gate \'ab-ni-ˌgāt\ *vb* **1 :** SURRENDER, RELINQUISH **2 :** DENY, RENOUNCE — **ab·ne·ga·tion** \ˌab-ni-'gā-shən\ *n*

ab·nor·mal \ab-'nòr-məl\ *adj* **:** deviating from the normal or average — **ab·nor·mal·i·ty** \ˌab-nòr-'mal-ət-ē\ *n* — **ab·nor·mal·ly** \ab-'nòr-mə-lē\ *adv*

1aboard \ə-'bōrd\ *adv* **1 :** on, onto, or within a conveyance (as a ship) **2 :** ALONGSIDE

2aboard *prep* **:** ON, ONTO, WITHIN

abode \ə-'bōd\ *n* **1 :** STAY, RESIDENCE **2 :** the place where one abides **:** HOME

abol·ish \ə-'bäl-ish\ *vb* **:** to do away with **:** ANNUL — **ab·o·li·tion** \ˌab-ə-'lish-ən\ *n*

ab·o·li·tion·ist \ˌab-ə-'lish-(ə-)nəst\ *n* **:** one in favor of the abolition of slavery

A-bomb \'ā-ˌbäm\ *n* **:** ATOM BOMB — **A-bomb** *vb*

abom·i·na·ble \ə-'bäm-(ə-)nə-bəl\ *adj* **:** ODIOUS, LOATHSOME, DETESTABLE

abom·i·nate \ə-'bäm-ə-ˌnāt\ *vb* **:** LOATHE, DETEST, ABHOR

abom·i·na·tion \ə-ˌbäm-ə-'nā-shən\ *n* **1 :** something abominable **2 :** DISGUST, LOATHING

ab·orig·i·nal \ˌab-ə-'rij-(ə-)nəl\ *adj* **:** ORIGINAL, INDIGENOUS, PRIMITIVE

ab·orig·i·ne \ˌab-ə-'rij-ə-nē\ *n* **:** a member of the original race of inhabitants of a region **:** NATIVE

aborn·ing \ə-'bòr-niŋ\ *adv* **:** while being born or produced

abor·tion \ə-'bòr-shən\ *n* **:** a premature birth occurring before the fetus can survive; *also* **:** an induced expulsion of a fetus — **abort** \ə-'bòrt\ *vb* — **abor·tive** \-'bòrt-iv\ *adj*

abor·tion·ist \-ist\ *n* **:** a producer of illegal abortions

abound \ə-'baund\ *vb* **1 :** to be plentiful **:** TEEM **2 :** to be fully supplied

1about \ə-'baut\ *adv* **1 :** on all sides **2 :** AROUND **3 :** NEARBY

2about *prep* **1 :** on every side of **2 :** near to **3 :** on the verge of beginning **:** GOING ⟨he was just ~ to go⟩ **4 :** CONCERNING

about-face \-'fās\ *n* **:** a reversal of direction or attitude — **about-face** *vb*

1above \ə-'bəv\ *adv* **1 :** in the sky; *also* **:** in or to heaven **2 :** in or to a higher place; *also* **:** higher on the same page or on a preceding page

2above *prep* **1 :** in or to a higher place than **:** OVER ⟨storm clouds ~ the bay⟩ **2 :** superior to ⟨he thought her far ~ him⟩ **3 :** more than **:** EXCEEDING ⟨men ~ 35⟩

above·board \-ˌbōrd\ *adv* (*or adj*) **:** without concealment or deception **:** OPENLY

ab·ra·ca·dab·ra \ˌab-rə-kə-'dab-rə\ *n* **1 :** a magical charm or incantation against calamity **2 :** JARGON

abrade \ə-'brād\ *vb* **:** to wear away by rubbing — **abra·sion** \-'brā-zhən\ *n*

abra·sive \ə-'brā-siv\ *n* **:** a substance (as emery, pumice, or fine sand) for grinding, smoothing, or polishing

abreast \ə-'brest\ *adv* (*or adj*) **1 :** side by side **2 :** up to a standard or level esp. of knowledge

abridge \ə-'brij\ *vb* [MF *abregier*, fr. LL *abbreviare*, fr. L *ad* to + *brevis* brief] **:** to lessen in length or extent **:** SHORTEN — **abridg·ment** *or* **abridge·ment** *n*

abroad \ə-'bròd\ *adv* (*or adj*) **1 :** over a wide area **2 :** out of doors **3 :** outside one's country

ab·ro·gate \'ab-rə-ˌgāt\ *vb* **:** ANNUL, REVOKE — **ab·ro·ga·tion** \ˌab-rə-'gā-shən\ *n*

abrupt \ə-'brəpt\ *adj* **1 :** broken or as if broken off **2 :** SUDDEN, HASTY **3 :** so quick as to seem rude **4 :** DISCONNECTED **5 :** STEEP — **abrupt·ly** *adv*

ab·scess \'ab-ˌses\ *n* **:** a collection of pus surrounded by inflamed tissue

ab·scond \ab-'skänd\ *vb* **:** to depart secretly and hide oneself

ab·sence \'ab-səns\ *n* **1 :** failure to be present **2 :** WANT, LACK **3 :** lack of attention

1ab·sent \'ab-sənt\ *adj* **1 :** not present **2 :** LACKING **3 :** INATTENTIVE

2ab·sent \ab-'sent\ *vb* **:** to keep (oneself) away

ab·sen·tee \ˌab-sən-'tē\ *n* **:** one that is absent or absents himself

ab·sen·tee·ism \-ˌiz-əm\ *n* **:** chronic absence from work

ab·sent-mind·ed \ˌab-sənt-'mīn-dəd\ *adj* **:** unaware of one's surroundings or action **:** INATTENTIVE — **ab·sent-mind·ed·ly** *adv*

ab·sinthe \'ab-ˌsinth\ *n* **:** a liqueur flavored esp. with wormwood and anise

ab·so·lute \'ab-sə-ˌlüt\ *adj* **1 :** free from imperfection **2 :** free from mixture **3 :** free from control, restriction, or qualification **4 :** lacking grammatical connection with any other word in a sentence ⟨~ construction⟩ **5 :** POSITIVE ⟨~ proof⟩ **6 :** FUNDAMENTAL, ULTIMATE — **ab·so·lute·ly** \'ab-sə-ˌlüt-lē, ˌab-sə-'lüt-\ *adv*

ab·so·lu·tion \ˌab-sə-'lü-shən\ *n* **:** the act of absolving; *esp* **:** a remission of sins pronounced by a priest in the sacrament of penance

ab·so·lut·ism \'ab-sə-ˌlüt-ˌiz-əm\ *n* **1 :** the theory that a sovereign should have unlimited power **2 :** government by an absolute ruler

ab·solve \ab-'sälv, -'zälv\ *vb* **1 :** to set free from an obligation or the consequences of guilt **2 :** ACQUIT *syn* pardon, confess, shrive

ab·sorb \əb-'sòrb, -'zòrb\ *vb* **1 :** ASSIMILATE, INCORPORATE **2 :** to suck up or take in in the manner of a sponge **3 :** to engage (one's attention) **:** ENGROSS **4 :** to receive without recoil or echo ⟨a ceiling that ~s sound⟩ — **ab·sorb·ing** *adj*

ab·sor·bent \-'sòr-bənt, -'zòr-\ *adj* **:** able to absorb ⟨~ cotton⟩ — **ab·sorbent** *n*

ab·sorp·tion \-'sòrp-shən, -'zòrp-\ *n* **1 :** a process of absorbing or being absorbed **2 :** concentration of attention

— **ab·sorp·tive** \-'sòrp-tiv, -'zòrp-\ adj

ab·stain \ob-'stān\ vb : to restrain oneself : leave off syn refrain, forbear — **ab·sten·tion** \-'sten-chon\ n

ab·ste·mi·ous \ab-'stē-mē-os\ adj: sparing in use of food or drink : TEMPERATE — **ab·ste·mi·ous·ly** adv

ab·sti·nence \'ab-sto-nons\ n : voluntary refraining esp. from eating certain foods or drinking liquor

1ab·stract \ab-'strakt, 'ab-,strakt\ adj 1 : considered apart from any specific embodiment 2 : expressing a quality apart from an object ⟨whiteness is an ∼ word⟩ 3 : having only intrinsic form with little or no pictorial representation ⟨∼ painting⟩ — **ab·stract·ly** adv — **ab·stract·ness** n

2ab·stract \'ab-,strakt\ n 1 : SUMMARY, EPITOME 2 : an abstract thing, state, or word

3ab·stract \ab-'strakt, esp for 2 'ab-,strakt\ vb 1 : REMOVE, SEPARATE; also : STEAL 2 : to make an abstract of : SUMMARIZE 3 : to draw away the attention of

ab·strac·tion \ab-'strak-shon\ n 1 : the act of abstracting : the state of being abstracted 2 : an abstract idea 3 : an abstract work of art

ab·struse \ob-'strüs, ab-\ adj : hard to understand : RECONDITE — **ab·struse·ly** adv — **ab·struse·ness** n

ab·surd \ob-'sord, -'zord\ adj : RIDICULOUS, UNREASONABLE — **ab·sur·di·ty** \-ot-ē\ n — **ab·surd·ly** adv

abun·dant \o-'bon-dont\ adj : more than enough : amply sufficient syn copious, plentiful — **abun·dance** \-dons\ n — **abun·dant·ly** adv

1abuse \o-'byüz\ vb 1 : to put to a wrong use : MISUSE 2 : MISTREAT 3 : to blame or scold rudely : REVILE — **abu·sive** \-'byü-siv\ adj — **abu·sive·ly** adv

2abuse \-'byüs\ n 1 : MISUSE 2 : MISTREATMENT 3 : a corrupt practice 4 : coarse and insulting speech

abut \o-'bot\ vb **abut·ted; abut·ting** : to touch along a border : border on

abut·ment n : a structure that supports weight or withstands lateral pressure (as at either end of a bridge or arch)

abut·tals \o-'bot-ºlz\ n pl : the boundaries of lands with respect to other contiguous lands or highways by which they are bounded

abysm \o-'biz-om\ n : ABYSS

abys·mal \o-'biz-mol\ adj : immeasurably deep : BOTTOMLESS — **abys·mal·ly** adv

abyss \o-'bis\ n 1 : the bottomless pit of old accounts of the universe 2 : an immeasurable depth

aca·cia \o-'kā-sho\ n : any of numerous leguminous trees or shrubs with round white or yellow flower clusters

ac·a·deme \'ak-o-,dēm\ n : SCHOOL; also : academic environment

ac·a·dem·ic \,ak-o-'dem-ik\ adj 1 : of or relating to schools or colleges 2 : literary or general rather than technical 3 : theoretical rather than practical — **ac·a·dem·i·cal·ly** adv

ac·a·de·mi·cian \,ak-od-o-'mish-on, o-,kad-o-\ n : a member of a society of scholars or artists

ac·a·dem·i·cism \,ak-o-'dem-o-,siz-om\ n : manner, style, or content conforming to the traditions or rules of a school or an official academy

acad·e·my \o-'kad-o-mē\ n [Gk Akadēmeia, school of philosophy founded by Plato, fr. Akadēmeia, gymnasium where Plato taught, fr. Akadēmos Academus, Greek mythological hero] 1 : a school above the elementary level; esp : a private secondary school 2 : a society of scholars, artists, or learned men

acan·thus \o-'kan-thos\ n : an ornamentation (as on a column) representing the leaves of a prickly herb of the Mediterranean region

a cap·pel·la \,äk-o-'pel-o\ adv (or adj) : without instrumental accompaniment ⟨the choir sang a cappella⟩

ac·cede \ak-'sēd\ vb 1 : to adhere to an agreement 2 : to express approval 3 : to enter upon an office syn acquiesce, assent, consent, subscribe

ac·ce·le·ran·do \ä-,chel-o-'rän-dō\ adv (or adj) : gradually faster — used as a direction in music

ac·cel·er·ate \ik-'sel-o-,rāt, ak-\ vb 1 : to bring about earlier 2 : to speed up : QUICKEN — **ac·cel·er·a·tion** \-,sel-o-'rā-shon\ n — **ac·cel·er·a·tor** \-'sel-o-,rāt-or\ n

1ac·cent \'ak-,sent\ n 1 : a distinctive manner of pronunciation ⟨a foreign ∼⟩ 2 : prominence given to one syllable of a word esp. by stress 3 : a mark (as ´, `, ˆ) over a vowel in writing or printing used usu. to indicate a difference in pronunciation (as stress) from a vowel not so marked — **ac·cen·tu·al** \ak-'sench-(o-)wol\ adj

2ac·cent \'ak-,sent, ak-'sent\ vb : STRESS, EMPHASIZE

ac·cen·tu·ate \ak-'sen-cho-,wāt\ vb : ACCENT — **ac·cen·tu·a·tion** \-,sen-cho-'wā-shon\ n

ac·cept \ik-'sept, ak-\ vb 1 : to receive or take willingly 2 : to agree to 3 : to acknowledge as binding and promise to pay — **ac·cept·abil·i·ty** \-,sep-to-'bil-ot-ē\ n — **ac·cept·able** \-'sep-to-bol\ adj

ac·cep·tance \ik-'sep-tons, ak-\ n 1 : the act of accepting 2 : the state of being accepted or acceptable 3 : an accepted bill of exchange

ac·cep·ta·tion \,ak-,sep-'tā-shon\ n : the meaning in which a word is generally understood

ac·cess \'ak-,ses\ n 1 : ATTACK, FIT 2 : APPROACH, ADMITTANCE 3 : a way of approach : ENTRANCE

ac·ces·si·ble \ik-'ses-o-bol, ak-\ adj : easy to approach — **ac·ces·si·bil·i·ty** \-,ses-o-'bil-ot-ē, ik-\ n

ac·ces·sion \ik-'sesh-on, ak-\ n 1 : something added 2 : increase by something added 3 : the act of acceding (as to a throne)

ac·ces·so·ry \ik-'ses-(o-)rē, ak-\ n 1 : something helpful but not essential 2 : a person who though not present abets or assists in the commission of an offense syn appurtenance, adjunct, appendage — **accessory** adj

ac·ci·dence \'ak-sod-ons\ n : the part of grammar that deals with inflections

ac·ci·dent \'ak-sod-ont\ n 1 : something occurring by chance or without intention **2** : CHANCE **3** : a nonessential property

¹ac·ci·den·tal \,ak-sə-'dent-ᵊl\ *adj* : happening unexpectedly or by chance **syn** casual, fortuitous, incidental, adventitious — **ac·ci·den·tal·ly** \-(ᵊ-)lē\ *adv*

²accidental *n* : a note (as a sharp or flat) not belonging to the key indicated by the signature of a musical composition

ac·claim \ə-'klām\ *vb* **1** : APPLAUD, PRAISE **2** : to welcome or proclaim with applause **syn** extol, laud — **acclaim** *n*

ac·cla·ma·tion \,ak-lə-'mā-shən\ *n* : an overwhelming affirmative vote by shouting or applause rather than by ballot

ac·cli·mate \ə-'klī-mət, 'ak-lə-,māt\ *vb* : to accustom to a new climate or new conditions

ac·cli·ma·tize \ə-'klī-mə-,tīz\ *vb* **1** : ACCLIMATE **2** : to become acclimated — **ac·cli·ma·ti·za·tion** \-,klī-mət-ə-'zā-shən\ *n*

ac·cliv·i·ty \ə-'kliv-ət-ē\ *n* : a steep upward slope

ac·co·lade \'ak-ə-,lād\ *n* : a recognition of merit : AWARD

ac·com·mo·date \ə-'käm-ə-,dāt\ *vb* **1** : to make fit or suitable : ADAPT, ADJUST **2** : HARMONIZE, RECONCILE **3** : to provide with something needed **4** : to hold without crowding

ac·com·mo·dat·ing *adj* : OBLIGING

ac·com·mo·da·tion \ə-,käm-ə-'dā-shən\ *n* **1** : something supplied to satisfy a need **2** : the act of accommodating : ADJUSTMENT

ac·com·pa·ni·ment \ə-'kəmp-(ə-)nē-mənt\ *n* : something that accompanies something else; *esp* : subordinate music to support a principal voice or instrument

ac·com·pa·ny \ə-(ə)-nē\ *vb* **1** : to go or occur along with : ESCORT, ATTEND **2** : to play an accompaniment for — **ac·com·pa·nist** \-(ə-)nəst\ *n*

ac·com·plice \ə-'käm-pləs, -'kəm-\ *n* : an associate in crime

ac·com·plish \ə-'käm-plish, -'kəm-\ *vb* : to bring to completion **syn** achieve, effect, fulfill, discharge, execute, perform

ac·com·plished *adj* **1** : COMPLETED **2** : EXPERT, SKILLED

ac·com·plish·ment *n* **1** : COMPLETION **2** : something completed or effected **3** : an acquired excellence or skill : ATTAINMENT

¹ac·cord \ə-'kord\ *vb* **1** : GRANT, CONCEDE **2** : AGREE, HARMONIZE — **ac·cor·dant** \-'kord-ᵊnt\ *adj*

²accord *n* : AGREEMENT, HARMONY

ac·cor·dance \ə-'kord-ᵊns\ *n* **1** : ACCORD **2** : the act of granting

ac·cord·ing·ly *adv* **1** : in accordance **2** : CONSEQUENTLY, SO

according to *prep* **1** : in conformity with ⟨they're paid *according to* ability⟩ **2** : as stated or attested by ⟨*according to* the paper, his trial starts today⟩

¹ac·cor·di·on \ə-'kord-ē-ən\ *n* : a portable musical instrument with a bellows, keys, and reeds

²accordion *adj* : folding like the bellows of an accordion ⟨~ pleats⟩

ac·cost \ə-'kost\ *vb* : to approach and speak to : ADDRESS

¹ac·count \ə-'kaunt\ *n* **1** : RECKONING **2** : a statement of business transactions **3** : an arrangement with a vendor to supply credit **4** : NARRATIVE, REPORT **5** : WORTH, VALUE **6** : a sum of money deposited in a bank and subject to withdrawal by the depositor — **on account of** : because of — **on no account** : under no circumstances — **on one's account** : for one's benefit — **in one's behalf**

²account *vb* **1** : CONSIDER ⟨I ~ him lucky⟩ **2** : to give an explanation — used with *for*

ac·count·able *adj* **1** : ANSWERABLE, RESPONSIBLE **2** : EXPLICABLE — **ac·count·abil·i·ty** \-,kaunt-ə-'bil-ət-ē\ *n*

ac·coun·tant \ə-'kaunt-ᵊnt\ *n* : a person skilled in accounting — **ac·coun·tan·cy** \-ᵊn-sē\ *n*

ac·count·ing *n* **1** : the art or system of keeping financial records **2** : an explanation of one's behavior

ac·cou·ter *or* **ac·cou·tre** \ə-'küt-ər\ *vb* : to equip esp. for military service — **ac·cou·ter·ment** *or* **ac·cou·tre·ment** \-'küt-ər-mənt, -'kü-trə-mənt\ *n*

ac·cred·it \ə-'kred-ət\ *vb* **1** : to authorize officially : APPROVE, ENDORSE **2** : CREDIT

ac·cre·tion \ə-'krē-shən\ *n* **1** : growth esp. by addition from without **2** : a product of accretion

ac·crue \ə-'krü\ *vb* **1** : to come by way of increase **2** : to be added by regular growth over a period of time — **ac·cru·al** \-əl\ *n*

ac·cul·tur·a·tion \ə-,kəl-chə-'rā-shən\ *n* : a process of intercultural borrowing between diverse peoples resulting in new and blended patterns

ac·cu·mu·late \ə-'kyü-myə-,lāt\ *vb* : to heap or pile up **syn** amass, gather, collect — **ac·cu·mu·la·tion** \ə-,kyü-myə-'lā-shən\ *n* — **ac·cu·mu·la·tor** \-'kyü-myə-,lāt-ər\ *n*

ac·cu·ra·cy \'ak-yə-rə-sē\ *n* : freedom from mistake : EXACTNESS, PRECISION

ac·cu·rate \'ak-yə-rət\ *adj* : free from error : EXACT, PRECISE — **ac·cu·rate·ly** *adv* — **ac·cu·rate·ness** *n*

ac·cursed \ə-'kərsəd, -'kərst\ *or* **ac·curst** \-'kərst\ *adj* **1** : being under a curse **2** : DAMNABLE, EXECRABLE

ac·cus·al \ə-'kyü-zəl\ *n* : ACCUSATION

ac·cu·sa·tive \ə-'kyü-zət-iv\ *adj* : of, relating to, or constituting a grammatical case marking the direct object of a verb or the object of a preposition — **accusative** *n*

ac·cuse \ə-'kyüz\ *vb* : to charge with an offense : BLAME — **ac·cu·sa·tion** \,ak-yə-'zā-shən\ *n* — **ac·cus·er** \ə-'kyü-zər\ *n*

ac·cus·tom \ə-'kəs-təm\ *vb* : FAMILIARIZE, HABITUATE

ac·cus·tomed *adj* : USUAL, CUSTOMARY

¹ace \'ās\ *n* **1** : a playing card bearing a single large pip in its center **2** : a point (as in tennis) won by a single stroke **3** : a golf score of one stroke on a hole **4** : an aviator who has brought down 5 or more enemy planes **5** : one that excels

²ace *vb* : to score an ace against (an opponent)

³ace *adj* : of first rank or quality

acer·bi·ty \ə-'sər-bət-ē\ *n* : SOURNESS, BITTERNESS — **acerb** \-'sorb\ *adj*

ac·et·an·i·lide \,as-ə-'tan-ᵊl-,īd\ *n* : a drug used to relieve pain or fever

ac·e·tate \'as-ə-,tāt\ *n* **1** : a salt or ester of acetic acid **2** : a fast-drying fabric made of fiber derived from cellulose and acetic acid; *also* : a plastic of similar composition used for wrapping film and phonograph records

ace·tic \ə-'sēt-ik\ *adj* : of, relating to, or producing acetic acid or vinegar

acetic acid *n* : a colorless biting liquid that is familiar as the chief acid of vinegar and is usu. manufactured

ac·e·tone \'as-ə-ˌtōn\ *n* : a volatile flammable liquid of pleasing odor used as a solvent

acet·y·lene \ə-'set-ᵊl-ən, -ᵊl-ˌēn\ *n* : a colorless flammable gas used for lighting and as a fuel in welding and soldering

ache \'āk\ *vb* 1 : to suffer a usu. dull persistent pain 2 : LONG, YEARN — **ache** *n*

achieve \ə-'chēv\ *vb* [MF *achever* to finish, fr. *a* to (fr. L *ad*) + *chef* head, fr. L *caput*] : to gain by work or effort **syn** accomplish, fulfill, effect — **achievement** *n*

ach·ro·mat·ic \ˌak-rə-'mat-ik\ *adj* : giving an image almost free from colors not in the object (~ lens)

¹ac·id \'as-əd\ *adj* 1 : sour or biting to the taste; *also* : sharp or sour in manner 2 : of or relating to an acid — **acid·i·ty** \ə-'sid-ət-ē\ *n*

²acid *n* 1 : a sour substance , 2 : a usu. water-soluble chemical compound that has a sour taste, reacts with a base to form a salt, and reddens litmus — **acid·ic** \ə-'sid-ik\ *adj*

ac·i·do·sis \ˌas-ə-'dō-səs\ *n* : an abnormal state of reduced alkalinity of the blood and body tissues

acid·u·lous \ə-'sij-ə-ləs\ *adj* : slightly acid : SOURISH

ack-ack \'ak-ˌak\ *n* : an antiaircraft gun; *also* : its fire

ac·knowl·edge \ik-'nil-ij, ak-\ *vb* 1 : to admit as true 2 : to admit the authority of 3 : to express thanks for; *also* : to report receipt of 4 : to recognize as valid — **ac·knowl·edg·ment** *also* **ac·knowl·edge·ment** *n*

ac·me \'ak-mē\ *n* : the highest point : PEAK

ac·ne \'ak-nē\ *n* : a skin disorder marked by inflammation of skin glands and hair follicles and by pimple formation esp. on the face

ac·o·lyte \'ak-ə-ˌlīt\ *n* : a man or boy who assists the clergyman in a liturgical service

ac·o·nite \'ak-ə-ˌnīt\ *n* 1 : any of several blue-flowered or purple-flowered poisonous plants related to the buttercups 2 : a drug obtained from a common Old World aconite

acorn \'ā-ˌkȯrn, -kərn\ *n* : the nut of the oak

acous·tic \ə-'kü-stik\ *adj* 1 : of or relating to the sense or organs of hearing, to sound, or to the science of sounds 2 : deadening sound (~ tile) 3 : operated by or utilizing sound waves — **acous·ti·cal** *adj* — **acous·ti·cal·ly** *adv*

acous·tics \-stiks\ *n sing or pl* 1 : the science dealing with sound 2 : the qualities in a room that make it easy or hard for a person in it to hear distinctly

ac·quaint \ə-'kwānt\ *vb* 1 : INFORM, NOTIFY 2 : to make familiar : cause to know

ac·quaint·ance \-ᵊns\ *n* 1 : personal knowledge 2 : a person with whom one is acquainted — **ac·quaint·ance·ship** \-ˌship\ *n*

ac·qui·esce \ˌak-wē-'es\ *vb* : to accept a plan or statement without open opposition **syn** consent, agree, assent, accede — **ac·qui·es·cence** \-'es-ᵊns\ *n* — **ac·qui·es·cent** \-ᵊnt\ *adj* — **ac·qui·es·cent·ly** *adv*

ac·quire \ə-'kwī(ə)r\ *vb* : to come into possession of : GET

ac·quire·ment *n* 1 : the act of acquiring 2 : ATTAINMENT, ACCOMPLISHMENT

ac·qui·si·tion \ˌak-wə-'zish-ən\ *n* 1 : ACQUIREMENT 2 : something acquired

ac·quis·i·tive \ə-'kwiz-ət-iv\ *adj* : eager to acquire : GREEDY — **ac·quis·i·tive·ly** *adv* — **ac·quis·i·tive·ness** *n*

ac·quit \ə-'kwit\ *vb* **-quit·ted; -quit·ting** 1 : to pronounce not guilty 2 : to conduct (oneself) usu. satisfactorily : BEHAVE — **ac·quit·tal** \-ᵊl\ *n*

acre \'ā-kər\ *n* 1 *pl* : LANDS, ESTATE 2 : a unit of area equal to 4840 square yards

acre·age \'ā-k(ə-)rij\ *n* : area in acres : ACRES

ac·rid \'ak-rəd\ *adj* 1 : sharp and biting in taste or odor 2 : bitterly irritating : CAUSTIC — **acrid·i·ty** \a-'krid-ət-ē, ə-\ *n*

ac·ri·mo·ny \'ak-rə-ˌmō-nē\ *n* : harsh or biting sharpness of language or feeling : ASPERITY — **ac·ri·mo·ni·ous** \ˌak-rə-'mō-nē-əs\ *adj*

ac·ro·bat \'ak-rə-ˌbat\ *n* : a performer of gymnastic feats — **ac·ro·bat·ic** \ˌak-rə-'bat-ik\ *adj*

ac·ro·bat·ics \ˌak-rə-'bat-iks\ *n sing or pl* : the performances of an acrobat

ac·ro·nym \'ak-rə-ˌnim\ *n* : a word (as *radar*) formed from the initial letter or letters of each of the successive parts or major parts of a compound term

ac·ro·pho·bia \ˌak-rə-'fō-bē-ə\ *n* : abnormal dread of being at a great height

acrop·o·lis \ə-'kräp-ə-ləs\ *n* : the upper fortified part of an ancient Greek city

¹across \ə-'krȯs\ *adv* 1 : to or on the opposite side 2 : so as to be understandable or acceptable : OVER (get the point ~)

²across *prep* 1 : to or on the opposite side of (ran ~ the street) (standing ~ the street) 2 : on at an angle (slapped him ~ the face); *esp* : on so as to cross (there's a log ~ the road)

across-the-board *adj* 1 : placed in combination to win, place, or show (an ~ bet) 2 : including all classes or categories (an ~ wage increase)

acros·tic \ə-'krȯ-stik\ *n* 1 : a composition usu. in verse in which the initial or final letters of the lines taken in order form a word or phrase 2 : a series of words of equal length arranged to read the same horizontally or vertically — **acros·ti·cal·ly** *adv*

¹act \'akt\ *n* 1 : a thing done : DEED 2 : STATUTE, DECREE 3 : a main division of a play; *also* : an item on a variety program 4 : an instance of insincere behavior : PRETENSE

ə abut; ᵊ kitten; ər further; a back; ā bake; ä cot, cart; aú out; ch chin; e less; ē easy; g gift; i trip; ī life; j joke; ŋ sing; ō flow; ȯ flaw; ȯi coin; th thin; t͟h this; ü loot; u̇ foot; y yet; yü few; yu̇ furious; zh vision

²**act** vb 1 : to perform by action esp. on the stage; also : FEIGN, SIMULATE, PRETEND 2 : to conduct oneself : BEHAVE 3 : to perform a specified function : produce an effect

act·ing adj : doing duty temporarily or for another ⟨~ president⟩

ac·tin·ic \ak-'tin-ik\ adj : relating to the property of radiant energy (as light) whereby chemical changes are produced (as in a photographic film)

ac·tin·i·um \ak-'tin-ē-əm\ n : a radioactive metallic chemical element

ac·tion \'ak-shən\ n 1 : a legal proceeding 2 : the manner or method of performing 3 : ACTIVITY 4 : ACT 5 pl : CONDUCT 6 : COMBAT, BATTLE 7 : the events of a literary plot 8 : an operating mechanism ⟨~ of a gun⟩; also : the way it operates ⟨stiff ~⟩

ac·tion·able adj : subject to or affording ground for an action or suit at law

ac·ti·vate \'ak-tə-ˌvāt\ vb 1 : to spur into action; also : to make active, reactive, or radioactive 2 : to aerate (sewage) to favor the growth of organisms that cause decomposition 3 : to set up (a military unit) formally

ac·tive \'ak-tiv\ adj 1 : causing action or change 2 : asserting that the grammatical subject performs the action represented by the verb ⟨~ voice⟩ 3 : BRISK, LIVELY 4 : marked by present operation or use — active n — ac·tive·ly adv

ac·tiv·i·ty \ak-'tiv-ət-ē\ n 1 : the quality or state of being active 2 : an occupation in which one is engaged

ac·tor \'ak-tər\ n : one that acts in a play or motion picture — **ac·tress** \-trəs\ n

ac·tu·al \'ak-ch(ə-w)əl\ adj : really existing : REAL — **ac·tu·al·i·ty** \ˌak-chə-'wal-ət-ē\ n — **ac·tu·al·ly** \'ak-ch(ə-w)ə-lē\ adv

ac·tu·ary \'ak-chə-ˌwer-ē\ n : an expert who calculates insurance risks and premiums — **ac·tu·ar·i·al** \ˌak-chə-'wer-ē-əl\ adj

ac·tu·ate \'ak-chə-ˌwāt\ vb 1 : to put into action 2 : to incite to action : MOTIVATE

acu·i·ty \ə-'kyü-ət-ē\ n : keenness of perception esp. visually

acu·men \ə-'kyü-mən\ n : mental keenness and penetration syn discernment, insight

acute \ə-'kyüt\ adj 1 : SHARP, POINTED 2 : containing less than 90 degrees ⟨~ angle⟩ 3 : sharply perceptive; esp : mentally keen 4 : SEVERE ⟨~ distress⟩; also : rising rapidly to a peak and then subsiding ⟨~ inflammation⟩ 5 : of, marked by, or being an accent mark having the form ' — **acute·ly** adv — **acute·ness** n

ad \'ad\ n : ADVERTISEMENT

ad·age \'ad-ij\ n : an old familiar saying : PROVERB, MAXIM

¹**ada·gio** \ə-'däj-ō, -'däj-ē-ō, -'däzh-\ adv (or adj) : in slow time — used as a direction in music

²**adagio** n 1 : an adagio movement 2 : a ballet duet or trio displaying feats of lifting and balancing

¹**ad·a·mant** \'ad-ə-mənt\ n : a stone believed to be of impenetrable hardness — **ad·a·man·tine** \ˌad-ə-'man-ˌtēn, -ˌtīn\ adj

²**adamant** adj : INFLEXIBLE, UNYIELDING — **ad·a·mant·ly** adv

Ad·am's apple \ˌad-əmz-\ n : the projection in front of the neck formed by the largest cartilage of the larynx

adapt \ə-'dapt\ vb : to make suitable or fit (as for a new use or for different conditions) syn adjust, accommodate — **adapt·abil·i·ty** \ə-ˌdap-tə-'bil-ət-ē\ n — **adapt·able** adj — **ad·ap·ta·tion** \ˌad-ˌap-'tā-shən\ n

add \'ad\ vb 1 : to join to something else so as to increase in number or amount 2 : to combine (numbers) into one sum

ad·den·dum \ə-'den-dəm\ n, pl -da \-də\ : something to be added

¹**ad·der** \'ad-ər\ n 1 : a poisonous European viper or a related snake 2 : any of various harmless No. American snakes (as the puff adder)

²**add·er** n : one that adds

¹**ad·dict** \ə-'dikt\ vb : to devote or surrender (oneself) to something habitually or excessively — **ad·dic·tive** \-'dik-tiv\ adj

²**ad·dict** \'ad-(ˌ)ikt\ n : one who is addicted (as to a drug)

ad·dic·tion \ə-'dik-shən\ n : the quality or state of being addicted; esp : compulsive use of habit-forming drugs

ad·di·tion \ə-'dish-ən\ n 1 : the act or process of adding; also : something added 2 : the adding of numbers to obtain their sum syn accretion, increment, accession — **ad·di·tive** \'ad-ət-iv\ adj or n

ad·di·tion·al \ə-'dish-(ə-)nəl\ adj : coming by way of addition : ADDED, EXTRA — **ad·di·tion·al·ly** adv

ad·dle \'ad-ᵊl\ vb 1 : to throw into confusion : MUDDLE 2 : to become rotten ⟨addled eggs⟩

¹**ad·dress** \ə-'dres\ vb 1 : to direct the attention of (oneself) 2 : to direct one's remarks to : deliver an address to 3 : to mark directions for delivery on

²**ad·dress** \ə-'dres, 'ad-ˌres\ n 1 : skillful management 2 : a formal speech : LECTURE 3 : the place where a person or organization may be communicated with 4 : the directions for delivery placed on mail

ad·dress·ee \ˌad-ˌres-'ē, ə-ˌdres-'ē\ n : one to whom something is addressed

ad·duce \ə-'d(y)üs\ vb : to bring forward as an argument, reason, or proof syn advance, allege, cite

-ade \'ād\ n suffix 1 : act : action ⟨blockade⟩ 2 : product; esp : sweet drink (limeade)

ad·e·noid \'ad-(ᵊ-)ˌnoid\ n : an enlarged mass of tissue near the opening of the nose into the throat — usu. used in pl.

¹**ad·ept** \'ad-ˌept\ n : EXPERT

²**adept** \ə-'dept\ adj : highly skilled : EXPERT — **adept·ly** adv — **adept·ness** n

ad·e·quate \'ad-i-kwət\ adj : equal to or sufficient for a specific requirement — **ad·e·qua·cy** \-kwə-sē\ n — **ad·e·quate·ly** adv

ad·here \ad-'hiər, əd-\ vb 1 : to give support : maintain loyalty 2 : to stick fast : CLING — **ad·her·ence** \-'hir-əns\ n — **ad·her·ent** \-ənt\ adj or n

ad·he·sion \ad-'hē-zhən, əd-\ n 1 : the act or state of adhering 2 : bodily tissues abnormally grown together after inflammation

¹**ad·he·sive** \-'hē-siv\ adj 1 : tending to adhere : STICKY 2 : prepared for

adhering (~ tape) — **ad·he·sive·ness** n
²adhesive n : an adhesive substance
adieu \ə-'d(y)ü\ n, pl adieus or adieux \-'d(y)üz\ : FAREWELL — often used interjectionally
ad in·fi·ni·tum \ˌad-ˌin-fə-'nīt-əm\ adv (or adj) : without end or limit
ad in·ter·im \ˌad-'in-tə-rəm\ adv (or adj) : for the intervening time
adi·os \ˌad-ē-'ōs, ˌäd-\ interj — used to express farewell
ad·i·pose \'ad-ə-ˌpōs\ adj : of or relating to animal fat : FATTY — **ad·i·pos·i·ty** \ˌad-ə-'päs-ət-ē\ n
ad·ja·cent \ə-'jās-ᵊnt\ adj : situated near or next syn adjoining, contiguous, abutting, juxtaposed
ad·jec·tive \'aj-ik-tiv\ n : a word that typically serves as a modifier of a noun — **ad·jec·ti·val** \ˌaj-ik-'tī-vəl\ adj — **ad·jec·ti·val·ly** adv
ad·join \ə-'join\ vb : to be situated next to
ad·join·ing adj : touching or bounding at a point or line
ad·journ \ə-'jərn\ vb 1 : to suspend indefinitely or until a stated time 2 : to transfer a session to another place — **ad·journ·ment** n
ad·judge \ə-'jəj\ vb 1 : JUDGE, ADJUDICATE 2 : to hold or pronounce to be : DEEM 3 : to award by judicial decision
ad·ju·di·cate \ə-'jüd-i-ˌkāt\ vb : to settle judicially — **ad·ju·di·ca·tion** \ə-ˌjüd-i-'kā-shən\ n
ad·junct \'aj-ˌəŋkt\ n : something joined or added to another thing but not essentially a part of it syn appendage, appurtenance, accessory
ad·jure \ə-'jür\ vb : to command solemnly : entreat earnestly syn beg, beseech, implore — **ad·ju·ra·tion** \ˌaj-ə-'rā-shən\ n
ad·just \ə-'jəst\ vb 1 : to bring to agreement : SETTLE 2 : to cause to conform : ADAPT, FIT 3 : REGULATE (~ a watch) — **ad·just·able** adj — **ad·just·er** or **ad·jus·tor** n — **ad·just·ment** n
ad·ju·tant \'aj-ət-ənt\ n : one who assists; esp : an officer who assists a commanding officer by handling correspondence and keeping records
¹ad·ju·vant \'aj-ə-vənt\ adj : serving to aid or contribute : AUXILIARY
²adjuvant n : something that enhances the effectiveness of medical treatment
ad lib \ad-'lib\ adv : at one's pleasure : to any desired extent
ad-lib \ad-'lib\ vb -libbed; -lib·bing : IMPROVISE
ad·man \'ad-ˌman\ n : one who writes, solicits, or places advertisements
ad·min·is·ter \əd-'min-ə-stər\ vb 1 : MANAGE, SUPERINTEND 2 : to mete out : DISPENSE 3 : to give usu. ritually or remedially (~ quinine for malaria) 4 : to perform the office of administrator — **ad·min·is·tra·ble** \-strə-bəl\ adj — **ad·min·is·trant** \-strənt\ n
ad·min·is·tra·tion \ˌmin-ə-'strā-shən, ad-\ n 1 : the act or process of administering 2 : MANAGEMENT 3 : the body of persons directing the government of a country 4 : the term of office of an administrative officer or

body — **ad·min·is·tra·tive** \əd-'min-ə-ˌstrāt-iv\ adj
ad·min·is·tra·tor \əd-'min-ə-ˌstrāt-ər\ n : one that administers; esp : one who settles an intestate estate
ad·mi·ra·ble \'ad-m(ə-)rə-bəl\ adj : worthy of admiration : EXCELLENT — **ad·mi·ra·bly** adv
ad·mi·ral \'ad-m(ə-)rəl\ n : a commissioned officer in the navy ranking next below a fleet admiral
ad·mi·ral·ty \-tē\ adj : relating to or having jurisdiction over maritime questions (~ law) (~ court)
Admiralty n : the British government department having authority over naval affairs
ad·mire \əd-'mī(ə)r\ vb : to regard with high esteem — **ad·mi·ra·tion** \ˌad-mə-'rā-shən\ n — **ad·mir·er** \əd-'mīr-ər\ n
ad·mis·si·ble \əd-'mis-ə-bəl\ adj : that can be or is worthy to be admitted or allowed : ALLOWABLE (~ evidence) — **ad·mis·si·bil·i·ty** \-ˌmis-ə-'bil-ət-ē\ n — **ad·mis·si·bly** \-'mis-ə-blē\ adv
ad·mis·sion \əd-'mish-ən\ n 1 : the granting of an argument 2 : the acknowledgment of a fact 3 : the act of admitting 4 : the privilege of being admitted 5 : a fee paid for admission
ad·mit \əd-'mit\ vb -mit·ted; -mit·ting 1 : to allow to enter 2 : PERMIT, ALLOW 3 : to recognize as genuine or valid — **ad·mit·ted·ly** adv
ad·mit·tance \əd-'mit-ᵊns\ n : permission to enter
ad·mix \ad-'miks\ vb : MINGLE, MIX (~ soil and gravel)
ad·mix·ture \ad-'miks-chər\ n 1 : MIXTURE 2 : something added in mixing
ad·mon·ish \əd-'män-ish\ vb : to warn gently : reprove with a warning syn chide, reproach, rebuke, reprimand — **ad·mo·ni·tion** \ˌad-mə-'nish-ən\ n — **ad·mon·i·to·ry** \əd-'män-ə-ˌtōr-ē\ adj
ad nau·se·am \ad-'nȯ-zē-əm\ adv : to a sickening length or degree
ado \ə-'dü\ n 1 : bustling excitement : FUSS 2 : TROUBLE
ado·be \ə-'dō-bē\ n [Sp, fr. Ar aṭ-ṭūb the brick, fr. Coptic tōbe brick] 1 : sun-dried brick; also : clay for making such bricks 2 : a structure made of adobe bricks — adobe adj
ad·o·les·cence \ˌad-ᵊl-'es-ᵊns\ n : the process or period of growth between childhood and maturity — **ad·o·les·cent** \-ᵊnt\ adj or n
adopt \ə-'däpt\ vb 1 : to take (a child of other parents) as one's own child 2 : to take up and practice as one's own 3 : to accept formally and put into effect — **adop·tion** \-'däp-shən\ n
adop·tive \ə-'däp-tiv\ adj : made or acquired by adoption (~ father) — **adop·tive·ly** adv
ador·able \ə-'dȯr-ə-bəl\ adj 1 : worthy of adoration 2 : extremely charming — **ador·ably** \-blē\ adv
adore \ə-'dȯr\ vb [L adorare, fr. L ad- to + orare to pray] 1 : WORSHIP 2 : to regard with reverent admiration 3 : to be extremely fond of — **ad·o·ra·tion** \ˌad-ə-'rā-shən\ n
adorn \ə-'dȯrn\ vb : to decorate with ornaments : BEAUTIFY — **adorn·ment** n
adre·nal \ə-'drēn-ᵊl\ adj [L ad to, at

+ *renes* kidneys] **:** of, relating to, or being a pair of endocrine organs (adrenal glands) located near the kidneys that produce several hormones of which one (adren•a•line \-'dren-°l-ən\ *or* adre•nin \-'drē-nən\) acts on smooth muscle and raises blood pressure

adrift \ə-'drift\ *adv (or adj)* **1 :** afloat without motive power or moorings **2 :** without guidance or purpose

adroit \ə-'dròit\ *adj* **1 :** dexterous with one's hands **2 :** SHREWD, RESOURCEFUL **syn** deft, clever, cunning, ingenious — adroit•ly *adv* — adroit•ness *n*

ad•sorb \ad-'sórb, -'zórb\ *vb* **:** to take up (as molecules of gases) and hold on the surface of a solid or liquid — ad•sorp•tion \-'sórp-shən, -'zórp-\ *n* — ad•sorp•tive \-'sórp-tiv,-'zórp-\ *adj*

ad•u•la•tion \,aj-ə-'lā-shən\ *n* **:** excessive or servile praise **:** FLATTERY

¹adult \ə-'dəlt, 'ad,əlt\ *adj* **:** fully developed and mature

²adult *n* **:** one that is adult; *esp* **:** a human being past an age (as 21) specified by law

adul•ter•ant \ə-'dəl-tə-rənt\ *n* **:** something used to adulterate another thing

adul•ter•ate \ə-'dəl-tə-,rāt\ *vb* **:** to make impure by mixing in a foreign or inferior substance — adul•ter•a•tion \-,dəl-tə-'rā-shən\ *n*

adul•tery \ə-'dəl-t(ə-)rē\ *n* **:** sexual unfaithfulness of a married person — adul•ter•er \-t(ə)r-ər\ *n* — adul•ter•ess \-t(ə-)rəs\ *n* — adul•ter•ous \-t(ə-)rəs\ *adj*

adult•hood \ə-'dəlt-,hùd\ *n* **:** the state or time of being an adult

ad•um•brate \'ad-əm-,brāt\ *vb* **1 :** to foreshadow vaguely **:** INTIMATE **2 :** to suggest or disclose partially **3 :** SHADE, OBSCURE — ad•um•bra•tion \,ad-əm-'brā-shən\ *n*

¹ad•vance \əd-'vans\ *vb* **1 :** to bring or move forward **2 :** to assist the progress of **3 :** to promote in rank **4 :** to make earlier in time **5 :** PROPOSE **6 :** to raise in rate **:** INCREASE **7 :** LEND — ad•vance•ment *n*

²advance *n* **1 :** a forward movement **2 :** IMPROVEMENT **3 :** a rise esp. in price or value **4 :** OFFER

³advance *adj* **:** made, sent, or furnished ahead of time

ad•van•tage \əd-'vant-ij\ *n* **1 :** superiority of position **2 :** BENEFIT, GAIN **3 :** the first point won in tennis after deuce — ad•van•ta•geous \,ad-,van-'tā-jəs\ *adj*

ad•vent \'ad-,vent\ *n* **1** *cap* **:** a penitential season beginning four Sundays before Christmas **2 :** ARRIVAL; *esp, cap* **:** the coming of Christ

ad•ven•ti•tious \,ad-vən-'tish-əs\ *adj* **:** ACCIDENTAL, INCIDENTAL — ad•ven•ti•tious•ly *adv* — ad•ven•ti•tious•ness *n*

¹ad•ven•ture \əd-'ven-chər\ *n* **1 :** a risky undertaking **2 :** a remarkable and exciting experience **3 :** a business venture — ad•ven•tur•ous \-'vench-(ə-)rəs\ *adj*

²adventure *vb* **:** RISK, HAZARD

ad•ven•tur•er \-'ven-chər-ər\ *n* **1 :** a person who engages in new and risky undertakings **2 :** a person who follows a military career for adventure or profit **3 :** a person who tries to advance his fortunes by questionable means — ad•ven•tur•ess \-'vench-(ə-)rəs\ *n*

ad•ven•ture•some \-'ven-chər-səm\ *adj* **:** inclined to take risks **:** DARING

ad•verb \'ad-,vərb\ *n* **:** a word that typically serves as a modifier of a verb, an adjective, or another adverb — ad•ver•bi•al \ad-'vər-bē-əl\ *adj* — ad•ver•bi•al•ly *adv*

ad•ver•sary \'ad-və(r),ser-ē\ *n* **:** FOE

ad•ver•sa•tive \əd-'vər-sət-iv\ *adj* **:** expressing opposition or adverse circumstance — ad•ver•sa•tive•ly *adv*

ad•verse \(')ad-'vərs\ *adj* **1 :** acting against or in a contrary direction **2 :** UNFAVORABLE — ad•verse•ly *adv*

ad•ver•si•ty \əd-'vər-sət-ē\ *n* **:** hard times **:** MISFORTUNE

ad•vert \ad-'vərt\ *vb* **:** REFER

ad•ver•tise \'ad-vər-,tīz\ *vb* **1 :** INFORM, NOTIFY **2 :** to call public attention to esp. in order to arouse a desire to purchase — ad•ver•tis•er *n*

ad•ver•tise•ment \,ad-vər-'tīz-mənt, ad-'vərt-əz-\ *n* **1 :** the act of advertising **2 :** a public notice intended to advertise something

ad•ver•tis•ing \'ad-vər-,tī-ziŋ\ *n* **:** the business of preparing advertisements

ad•vice \əd-'vīs\ *n* **1 :** recommendation with regard to a course of action **:** COUNSEL **2 :** INFORMATION, REPORT

ad•vis•able \əd-'vī-zə-bəl\ *adj* **:** proper to be done **:** EXPEDIENT — ad•vis•abil•i•ty \-,vī-zə-'bil-ət-ē\ *n*

ad•vise \əd-'vīz\ *vb* **1 :** to give advice to **:** COUNSEL **2 :** INFORM, NOTIFY **3 :** CONSULT, CONFER — ad•vis•er *or* ad•vi•sor *n*

ad•vise•ment \əd-'vīz-mənt\ *n* **:** careful consideration

ad•vi•so•ry \əd-'vīz-(ə-)rē\ *adj* **1 :** having or exercising power to advise **2 :** containing advice

ad•vo•cate \'ad-və-kət, -,kāt\ *n* **1 :** one who pleads another's cause **2 :** one who argues or pleads for a cause or proposal — ad•vo•ca•cy \-və-kə-sē\ *n*

adz *or* adze \'adz\ *n* **:** a cutting tool that has a curved blade set at right angles to the handle and is used in shaping wood

ae•gis \'ē-jəs\ *n* **1 :** SHIELD, PROTECTION **2 :** PATRONAGE, SPONSORSHIP

ae•o•li•an harp \e-,ō-lē-ən-\ *n* **:** a box having stretched strings that produce varying musical sounds when the wind blows on them

ae•on \'ē-ən, 'ē-,än\ *n* **:** an indefinitely long time **:** AGE

aer•ate \'a-(ə)r-,āt\ *vb* **1 :** to supply (blood) with oxygen by respiration **2 :** to supply or impregnate with air **3 :** to combine or charge with gas — aer•a•tion \,a-(ə)r-'ā-shən\ *n*

¹aer•i•al \'ar-ē-əl, ā-'ir-ē-əl\ *adj* **1 :** inhabiting, produced by, or done in the air **2 :** AIRY **3 :** of or relating to aircraft

²aer•i•al \'ar-ē-əl\ *n* **:** a radio or television antenna

aer•i•al•ist \'ar-ē-ə-ləst\ *n* **:** a performer of feats above the ground esp. on a flying trapeze

aer•ie \'a(ə)r-ē, 'i(ə)r-ē\ *n* **:** a highly placed nest (as of an eagle)

aero \'a(ə)r-ō\ *adj* **1 :** of or relating to aircraft **2 :** designed for aerial use

aer•o•bic \,a-(ə)r-'ō-bik\ *adj* **:** living or active only in the presence of oxygen (~bacteria) — aer•obe \'a(-ə)r-,ōb\ *n*

aer•o•drome \'ar-ə-,drōm\ *n, Brit* **:** AIRFIELD, AIRPORT

aer·o·naut \'ar-ə-,nȯt\ *n* **:** one who operates or travels in an airship or balloon

aer·o·nau·tics \,ar-ə-'nȯt-iks\ *n* **:** a science dealing with the operation of aircraft or with their design and manufacture — **aer·o·nau·tic** *or* **aer·o·nau·ti·cal** *adj*

aero·plane \'ar-ə-,plān\ *n, chiefly Brit var of* AIRPLANE

aer·o·sol \'ar-ə-,sȯl, -,säl\ *n* **:** a suspension of fine solid or liquid particles in a gas; *esp* **:** a substance (as an insecticide, medicine, or cosmetic) in a liquid sprayed from the valve of a special container

aero·space \'ar-ə-,spās\ *n* **:** the earth's atmosphere and the space beyond

aery \'a(ə)r-ē\ *adj* **:** having an aerial quality **:** ETHEREAL

aes·thete \'es-,thēt\ *n* **:** a person having or affecting sensitivity to beauty esp. in art

aes·thet·ic \es-'thet-ik\ *adj* **1 :** of or relating to aesthetics **:** ARTISTIC **2 :** appreciative of the beautiful — **aes·thet·i·cal·ly** *adv*

aes·thet·ics \-'thet-iks\ *n* **:** a branch of philosophy dealing with beauty and the beautiful

aes·ti·vate \'es-tə-,vāt\ *vb* **:** to pass the summer in a state of torpor — **aes·ti·va·tion** \,es-tə-'vā-shən\ *n*

afar \ə-'fär\ *adv* **:** from, at, or to a great distance

af·fa·ble \'af-ə-bəl\ *adj* **:** courteous and agreeable in conversation — **af·fa·bil·i·ty** \,af-ə-'bil-ət-ē\ *n* — **af·fa·bly** \'af-ə-blē\ *adv*

af·fair \ə-'faər\ *n* **1 :** something that relates to or involves one **:** CONCERN **2 :** a romantic or sexual attachment of limited duration

1af·fect \ə-'fekt, a-\ *vb* **1 :** to be fond of using or wearing **2 :** SIMULATE, ASSUME, PRETEND

2affect *vb* **:** to produce an effect on **:** INFLUENCE, IMPRESS

af·fec·ta·tion \,af-,ek-'tā-shən\ *n* **:** an attitude or mode of behavior assumed by a person in an effort to impress others

af·fect·ed *adj* **1 :** pretending to some trait which is not natural **2 :** artificially assumed to impress others 〈~ mannerisms〉 — **af·fect·ed·ly** *adv*

af·fect·ing *adj* **:** arousing pity, sympathy, or sorrow 〈an ~ story〉 — **af·fect·ing·ly** *adv*

1af·fec·tion \ə-'fek-shən\ *n* **:** tender attachment **:** LOVE — **af·fec·tion·ate** \-sh(ə-)nət\ *adj* — **af·fec·tion·ate·ly** *adv*

2affection *n* **:** DISEASE, DISORDER 〈an ~ of the brain〉

af·fer·ent \'af-ə-rənt\ *adj* **:** bearing or conducting inward toward a more central part 〈~ nerves〉

af·fi·ance \ə-'fī-əns\ *vb* **:** BETROTH, ENGAGE

af·fi·da·vit \,af-ə-'dā-vət\ *n* **:** a sworn statement in writing

1af·fil·i·ate \ə-'fil-ē-,āt\ *vb* **:** to associate as a member or branch — **af·fil·i·a·tion** \-,fil-ē-'ā-shən\ *n*

2af·fil·i·ate \-'fil-ē-ət\ *n* **:** an affiliated person or organization

af·fin·i·ty \ə-'fin-ət-ē\ *n* **1 :** KINSHIP,

RELATIONSHIP **2 :** attractive force **:** ATTRACTION, SYMPATHY

af·firm \ə-'fərm\ *vb* **1 :** CONFIRM, RATIFY **2 :** to assert positively **:** aver, avow, avouch, declare, assert — **af·fir·ma·tion** \,af-ər-'mā-shən\ *n*

af·fir·ma·tive \ə-'fər-mət-iv\ *adj* **:** asserting that the fact is so **:** POSITIVE

2affirmative *n* **1 :** an expression of affirmation or assent **2 :** the side that upholds the proposition stated in a debate

1af·fix \ə-'fiks\ *vb* **:** ATTACH, FASTEN, ADD

2af·fix \'af-,iks\ *n* **:** one or more sounds or letters attached to the beginning or end of a word and serving to produce a derivative word or an inflectional form

af·fla·tus \ə-'flāt-əs\ *n* **:** divine inspiration

af·flict \ə-'flikt\ *vb* **:** to cause pain and distress to **:** trouble grievously **:** try, torment, torture — **af·flic·tion** \-'flik-shən\ *n*

af·flic·tive \-'flik-tiv\ *adj* **:** causing affliction **:** DISTRESSING — **af·flic·tive·ly** *adv*

af·flu·ence \'af-,lü-əns\ *n* **:** abundant supply; *also* **:** WEALTH, RICHES — **af·flu·ent** \-ənt\ *adj*

af·ford \ə-'fōrd\ *vb* **1 :** to manage to bear or bear the cost of without serious harm or loss **2 :** PROVIDE, FURNISH

af·fray \ə-'frā\ *n* **:** FIGHT, FRAY

af·fright \ə-'frīt\ *vb* **:** FRIGHTEN, ALARM — **affright** *n*

af·front \ə-'frənt\ *vb* **1 :** INSULT **2 :** CONFRONT — **affront** *n*

af·ghan \'af-,gan, -gən\ *n* **:** a blanket or shawl of colored wool knitted or crocheted in sections

af·ghani \af-'gan-ē\ *n* — see MONEY table

afi·cio·na·do \ə-,fis-ē-ə-'näd-ō, -,fish-ə-'näd-\ *n* **:** DEVOTEE, FAN

afield \ə-'fēld\ *adv* **1 :** to, in, or on the field **2 :** away from home **3 :** out of the way **:** ASTRAY

afire \ə-'fī(ə)r\ *adj* **:** being on fire **:** BURNING

aflame \ə-'flām\ *adj* **:** FLAMING

afloat \ə-'flōt\ *adv (or adj)* **1 :** being on board ship **2 :** FLOATING, ADRIFT **3 :** flooded with water

aflut·ter \ə-'flət-ər\ *adj* **1 :** FLUTTERING **2 :** nervously excited

afoot \ə-'fut\ *adv (or adj)* **1 :** on foot **2 :** in action **:** in progress

afore·men·tioned \ə-'fōr-,men-chənd\ *adj* **:** mentioned previously

afore·said \ə-'fōr-,sed\ *adj* **:** said or named before

afore·thought \-,thȯt\ *adj* **:** PREMEDITATED 〈with malice ~〉

a for·ti·o·ri \,ä-,fȯrt-ē-'ōr-ē\ *adv* **:** with even greater reason

afoul \ə-'faul\ *adj* **:** FOULED, TANGLED

afoul of *prep* **1 :** in or into collision or entanglement with **2 :** in or into conflict with

afraid \ə-'frād, *South also* -'fre(ə)d\ *adj* **:** FRIGHTENED, FEARFUL

afresh \ə-'fresh\ *adv* **:** ANEW, AGAIN

Af·ri·can \'af-ri-kən\ *n* **1 :** a native or inhabitant of Africa **2 :** NEGRO — **African** *adj*

Af·ri·kaans \,af-ri-'käns\ *n* **:** a language

ə abut; ᵊ kitten; ər further; a back; ā bake; ä cot, cart; au̇ out; ch chin; e less; ē easy; g gift; i trip; ī life; j joke; ŋ sing; ō flow; ȯ flaw; ȯi coin; th thin; th this; ü loot; u̇ foot; y yet; yü few; yu̇ furious; zh vision

developed from 17th century Dutch that is one of the official languages of the Republic of South Africa

Af·ro-Amer·i·can \ˌaf-rō-ə-ˈmer-ə-kən\ *adj* **:** of or relating to Americans of African and esp. of negroid descent — **Afro-American** *n*

aft \ˈaft\ *adv* **:** near, toward, or in the stern of a ship or the tail of an aircraft

¹af·ter \ˈaf-tər\ *adv* **:** AFTERWARD, SUBSEQUENTLY

²after *prep* **1 :** behind in place **2 :** later than **3 :** intent on the seizure, mastery, or achievement of ⟨go ~ an escaped prisoner⟩ ⟨he's ~ your job⟩

³after *conj* **:** following the time when

⁴after *adj* **1 :** LATER **2 :** located toward the rear

af·ter·birth \ˈaf-tər-ˌbərth\ *n* **:** structures and membranes expelled from the uterus after the birth of young

af·ter·care \-ˌkeər\ *n* **:** the care, nursing, or treatment of a convalescent patient

af·ter·deck \-ˌdek\ *n* **:** the rear half of the deck of a ship

af·ter·ef·fect \-ə-ˌfekt\ *n* **1 :** an effect that follows its cause after some time has passed **2 :** a secondary effect coming on after the first or immediate effect has subsided ⟨a medicine with no noticeable ~s⟩

af·ter·glow \-ˌglō\ *n* **:** a glow remaining (as in the sky after sunset) where a light has disappeared

af·ter·life \-ˌlīf\ *n* **:** an existence after death

af·ter·math \ˈaf-tər-ˌmath\ *n* **1 :** a second-growth crop esp. of hay **2 :** CONSEQUENCES, EFFECTS *syn* sequel, result, outcome

af·ter·noon \ˌaf-tər-ˈnün\ *n* **:** the time between noon and evening

af·ter·taste \-ˌtāst\ *n* **:** a sensation (as of flavor) continuing after the stimulus causing it has ended

af·ter·thought \ˈaf-tər-ˌthȯt\ *n* **:** a later thought; *also* **:** something thought of later

af·ter·ward \ˈaf-tə-(r)-wərd\ *or* **af·ter·wards** \-wərdz\ *adv* **:** at a later time

again \ə-ˈgen\ *adv* **1 :** once more **:** ANEW **2 :** on the other hand **3 :** FURTHER, MOREOVER **4 :** in addition

against \ə-ˈgenst\ *prep* **1 :** directly opposite to **:** FACING **2 :** in opposition to **3 :** as defense from **4 :** so as to touch or strike ⟨threw him ~ the wall⟩; *also* **:** TOUCHING

¹agape \ə-ˈgāp\ *adj* **:** having the mouth open in wonder or surprise **:** GAPING

²aga·pe \ä-ˈgäp-ā, ˈäg-ə-ˌpā\ *n* **:** self-giving loyal concern that freely accepts another and seeks his good

ag·ate \ˈag-ət\ *n* **1 :** a striped or clouded quartz **2 :** a child's marble of agate or of glass resembling agate

aga·ve \ə-ˈgäv-ē\ *n* **:** any of several spiny-leaved plants related to the amaryllis

¹age \ˈāj\ *n* **1 :** the length of time during which a being or thing has lived or existed **2 :** the time of life at which some particular qualification is achieved; *esp* **:** MAJORITY **3 :** the latter part of life **4 :** the quality of being old **5 :** a long time **6 :** a period in history

²age *vb* **1 :** to grow old or cause to grow old **2 :** to become or cause to become mature or mellow

-age \ij\ *n suffix* **1 :** aggregate **:** collec-

tion ⟨track*age*⟩ **2 a :** action **:** process ⟨haul*age*⟩ **b :** cumulative result of ⟨break*age*⟩ **c :** rate of ⟨dos*age*⟩ **3 :** house or place of ⟨orphan*age*⟩ **4 :** state **:** rank ⟨vassal*age*⟩ **5 :** fee **:** charge ⟨post*age*⟩

aged \ˈā-jəd *for 1,* ˈājd *for 2*\ *adj* **1 :** of advanced age **2 :** having attained a specified age ⟨a man ~ forty years⟩

age·less \ˈāj-ləs\ *adj* **1 :** not growing old or showing the effects of age **2 :** TIMELESS, ETERNAL ⟨an ~ story⟩

agen·cy \ˈā-jən-sē\ *n* **1 :** one through which something is accomplished **:** INSTRUMENTALITY **2 :** the office or function of an agent **3 :** an establishment doing business for another **4 :** an administrative division of a government *syn* means, medium

agen·da \ə-ˈjen-də\ *n* **:** a list of things to be done **:** PROGRAM

agent \ˈā-jənt\ *n* **1 :** one that acts **2 :** MEANS, INSTRUMENT **3 :** a person acting or doing business for another *syn* attorney, deputy, proxy

age-old \ˈāj-ˈōld\ *adj* **:** having existed for ages **:** ANCIENT

ag·glom·er·ate \ə-ˈgläm-ə-ˌrāt\ *vb* **:** to gather into a mass **:** CLUSTER — **agglom·er·a·tion** \-ˌgläm-ə-ˈrā-shən\ *n*

ag·glu·ti·nate \ə-ˈglüt-ᵊn-ˌāt\ *vb* **:** to cause to adhere **:** gather into a group or mass — **ag·glu·ti·na·tion** \-ˌglüt-ᵊn-ˈā-shən\ *n*

ag·gran·dize \ə-ˈgran-ˌdīz, ˈag-rən-\ *vb* **:** to make great or greater — **ag·gran·dize·ment** \ə-ˈgran-dəz-mənt, -ˌdīz-; ˌag-rən-ˈdīz-mənt\ *n*

ag·gra·vate \ˈag-rə-ˌvāt\ *vb* **1 :** to make more severe **:** INTENSIFY **2 :** IRRITATE — **ag·gra·va·tion** \ˌag-rə-ˈvā-shən\ *n*

¹ag·gre·gate \ˈag-ri-gət\ *adj* **:** formed by the gathering of units into one mass

²ag·gre·gate \-ˌgāt\ *vb* **:** to collect into one mass

³ag·gre·gate \-gət\ *n* **:** a mass or body of units or parts somewhat loosely associated with one another; *also* **:** the whole amount

ag·gre·ga·tion \ˌag-ri-ˈgā-shən\ *n* **1 :** the collecting of units or parts into a mass or whole **2 :** a group, body, or mass composed of many distinct parts **:** ASSEMBLAGE

ag·gres·sion \ə-ˈgresh-ən\ *n* **1 :** an unprovoked attack **2 :** the practice of making attacks — **ag·gres·sive** \-ˈgres-iv\ *adj* — **ag·gres·sive·ly** *adv* — **ag·gres·sive·ness** *n* — **ag·gres·sor** \-ˈgres-ər\ *n*

ag·grieve \ə-ˈgrēv\ *vb* **1 :** to cause grief to **2 :** to inflict injury on **:** WRONG

aghast \ə-ˈgast\ *adj* **:** struck with amazement or horror

ag·ile \ˈaj-əl\ *adj* **:** able to move quickly and easily **:** NIMBLE — **agil·i·ty** \ə-ˈjil-ət-ē\ *n*

ag·i·tate \ˈaj-ə-ˌtāt\ *vb* **1 :** to move with an irregular rapid motion **2 :** to stir up **3 :** EXCITE **3 :** to discuss earnestly **4 :** to attempt to arouse public feeling — **ag·i·ta·tion** \ˌaj-ə-ˈtā-shən\ *n* — **ag·i·ta·tor** \ˈaj-ə-ˌtāt-ər\ *n*

agleam \ə-ˈglēm\ *adj* **:** GLEAMING

aglit·ter \ə-ˈglit-ər\ *adj* **:** GLITTERING

aglow \ə-ˈglō\ *adj* **:** GLOWING

ag·nos·tic \ag-ˈnäs-tik\ *adj* [Gk *agnōstos* unknown, unknowable, fr. *a-* un- + *gignōskein* to know] **:** of or relating to the belief that the existence of any ultimate reality (as God) is unknown

and prob. unknowable — **agnostic** n —
ag·nos·ti·cism \-'näs-tə-,siz-əm\ n

ago \ə-'gō\ adj (or adv) : earlier than the present time

agog \ə-'gäg\ adj : full of excitement : EAGER

ag·o·nize \'ag-ə-,nīz\ vb : to suffer or cause to suffer agony — **ag·o·niz·ing·ly** adv

ag·o·ny \'ag-ə-nē\ n : extreme pain of mind or body   syn suffering, distress

ago·ra \,äg-ə-'rä\ n, pl **ago·rot** \-'rōt\ — see MONEY table

ag·o·ra·pho·bia \,ag-ə-rə-'fō-bē-ə\ n : abnormal fear of being in open spaces — **ag·o·ra·pho·bic** \-'fō-bik, -'fäb-ik\ adj

agrar·i·an \ə-'grer-ē-ən\ adj 1 : of or relating to land or its ownership ⟨~ reforms⟩ 2 : of or relating to farmers or farming interests

agree \ə-'grē\ vb 1 : ADMIT, CONCEDE 2 : to settle by common consent 3 : to express agreement or approval 4 : to be in harmony 5 : to be similar : CORRESPOND 6 : to be fitting or healthful : SUIT ⟨the climate ~s with him⟩

agree·able adj 1 : PLEASING, PLEASANT 2 : ready to consent 3 : SUITABLE — **agree·able·ness** n — **agree·ably** adv

agree·ment n 1 : harmony of opinion or action 2 : mutual understanding or arrangement; also : a document containing such an arrangement

ag·ri·cul·ture \'ag-ri-,kəl-chər\ n : FARMING, HUSBANDRY — **ag·ri·cul·tur·al** \,ag-ri-'kəlch-(ə)-rəl\ adj — **ag·ri·cul·tur·ist** \-rəst\ n

aground \ə-'graund\ adv (or adj) : with the bottom lodged on the ground : STRANDED

ague \'ā-gyü\ n : a fever with recurrent chills and sweating; esp : MALARIA

ahead \ə-'hed\ adv (or adj) 1 : in or toward the front 2 : into or for the future ⟨plan ~⟩ 3 : in or toward a more advantageous position

ahead of prep 1 : in front or advance of 2 : in excess of : ABOVE

ahoy \ə-'hȯi\ interj — used in hailing ⟨ship ~⟩

¹**aid** \'ād\ vb : to provide with what is useful in achieving an end : ASSIST

²**aid** n 1 : ASSISTANCE 2 : ASSISTANT

aide \'ād\ n : a person who acts as an assistant; esp : a military officer assisting a superior

aide-de-camp \,ād-di-'kamp, -'käⁿ\ n, pl **aides-de-camp** \,ādz-di-\ : AIDE

ai·grette \ā-'gret, 'ā-,gret\ n : a plume or decorative tuft for the head

ail \'āl\ vb 1 : to be the matter with : TROUBLE 2 : to be unwell

ai·le·ron \'ā-lə-,rän\ n : a movable part of an airplane wing or of an airfoil external to the wing

ail·ment \'āl-mənt\ n : a bodily disorder

¹**aim** \'ām\ vb 1 : to point (a weapon) toward some object 2 : to direct one's efforts : ASPIRE 3 : to direct to or toward a specified object or goal

²**aim** n 1 : the direction of a weapon 2 : OBJECT, PURPOSE

aim·less \-ləs\ adj : lacking purpose : RANDOM — **aim·less·ly** adv

¹**air** \'aər\ n 1 : the gaseous mixture

surrounding the earth 2 : a light breeze 3 : compressed air ⟨~ sprayer⟩ 4 : AIRCRAFT ⟨~ patrol⟩ 5 : AVIATION ⟨~ safety⟩ 6 : the medium of transmission of radio waves; also : RADIO, TELEVISION 7 : the outward appearance of a person or thing : MANNER 8 : an artificial manner ⟨put on ~s⟩ 9 : MELODY, TUNE

²**air** vb 1 : to expose to the air 2 : to expose to public view

air·borne \-,bȯrn\ adj : supported or transported by air

air·brush \-,brəsh\ n : a device for applying a fine spray (as of paint) by compressed air

air conditioning n : the process of washing and controlling the temperature and humidity of air before it enters a room — **air·con·di·tioned** \,aər-kən-'dish-ənd\ adj

air·craft \'aər-,kraft\ n : a weight-carrying machine (as an airplane, glider, helicopter, or balloon) for navigation of the air

air·drome \-,drōm\ n : AIRPORT

air·drop \-,dräp\ n : delivery of cargo or personnel by parachute from an airplane in flight — **air·drop** vb

air·field \-,fēld\ n 1 : the landing field of an airport 2 : AIRPORT

air·foil \-,fȯil\ n : an airplane surface (as a wing or rudder) designed to produce reaction from the air

air force n : the military organization of a nation for air warfare

air gun n 1 : a pistol-shaped hand tool that works by compressed air 2 : AIRBRUSH

air·lift \'aər-,lift\ n : a supply line operated by aircraft — **airlift** vb

air line n 1 : a straight line 2 **air·line** : a system of transportation by aircraft; also : a company operating such a system

air·lin·er \'aər-,lī-nər\ n : a large passenger airplane operating over an airline

air·mail \'aər-,māl\ n : the system of transporting mail by airplane; also : mail transported by air — **airmail** vb

air·man \-mən\ n 1 : an enlisted man in the air force in one of the four ranks next below a staff sergeant 2 : AVIATOR

air·mind·ed \-'mīn-dəd\ adj : interested in aviation or in air travel

air·plane \-,plān\ n : a fixed-wing aircraft heavier than air that is driven by a propeller or by a rearward jet and supported by the reaction of the air against its wings

air·port \-,pȯrt\ n : a place maintained for the landing and takeoff of airplanes and for receiving and discharging passengers and cargo

air·post \-,pōst\ n : AIRMAIL

air·ship \-,ship\ n : an aircraft lighter than air that is borne in the air by a gas-filled container and has an engine, propeller, and rudder

air·sick \-,sik\ adj : affected with motion sickness associated with flying — **air·sick·ness** n

air·space \-,spās\ n : the space lying above a nation and coming under its jurisdiction

air·speed \-,spēd\ n : the speed of an

ə abut; ə kitten; ər further; a back; ā bake; ä cot, cart; aú out; ch chin; e less; ē easy; g gift; i trip; ī life; j joke; ŋ sing; ō flow; ȯ flaw; ȯi coin; th thin; th this; ü loot; ủ foot; y yet; yü few; yủ furious; zh vision

airplane with relation to the air as distinguished from its speed relative to the earth

air·strip \-,strip\ *n* : a runway without normal airport facilities

air·tight \-'tīt\ *adj* **1** : so tightly sealed that no air can enter or escape **2** : leaving no opening for attack

air·wave \-,wāv\ *n* : the medium of radio and television transmission — usu. used in pl.

air·way \-,wā\ *n* **1** : a regular route for airplanes **2** : AIRLINE

air·wor·thy \-,wər-thē\ *adj* : fit or safe for operation in the air ⟨a very ~ plane⟩ — **air·wor·thi·ness** *n*

airy \'a(ə)r-ē\ *adj* **1** : LOFTY **2** : lacking in reality : EMPTY **3** : DELICATE **4** : BREEZY

aisle \'īl\ *n* **1** : the side of a church nave separated by piers from the nave proper **2** : a passage between sections of seats

ajar \ə-'jär\ *adv (or adj)* : partly open ⟨the door was ~⟩

akim·bo \ə-'kim-bō\ *adv (or adj)* : with hand on hip and elbow turned outward

akin \ə-'kin\ *adj* **1** : related by blood **2** : similar in kind

1-al \əl\ *adj suffix* : of, relating to, or characterized by ⟨directional⟩ ⟨fictional⟩

2-al *n suffix* : action : process ⟨rehearsal⟩

al·a·bas·ter \'al-ə-,bas-tər\ *n* : a compact fine-textured usu. white and translucent gypsum mineral often carved into objects (as vases)

a la carte \,al-ə-'kärt, ,äl-\ *adv (or adj)* : with a separate price for each item on the menu

alac·ri·ty \ə-'lak-rət-ē\ *n* : cheerful readiness : BRISKNESS

a la mode \,al-ə-'mōd, ,äl-\ *adj* **1** : FASHIONABLE, STYLISH **2** : topped with ice cream

1alarm \ə-'lärm\ *n* [MF *alarme*, fr. It *all' arme* to arms] **1** : a warning signal **2** : the terror caused by sudden danger

2alarm *vb* **1** : to warn of danger **2** : to arouse to a sense of danger : FRIGHTEN

alarm·ist *n* : a person who is given to alarming others esp. needlessly

al·ba·core \'al-bə-,kōr\ *n* : any of several tunas

Al·ba·ni·an \al-'bā-nē-ən\ *n* : a native or inhabitant of Albania

al·ba·tross \'al-bə-,trós, -,träs\ *n* : a large web-footed seabird related to the petrels

al·be·it \al-'bē-ət, ól-\ *conj* : even though : ALTHOUGH

al·bi·no \al-'bī-nō\ *n* : a person or lower animal lacking coloring matter in the skin, hair, and eyes — **al·bi·nism** \'al-bə-,niz-əm\ *n*

al·bum \'al-bəm\ *n* **1** : a book with blank pages in which to insert photographs, stamps, or autographs **2** : one or more phonograph records or tape recordings carrying a major musical work or a group of related selections

al·bu·men \al-'byü-mən\ *n* **1** : the white of an egg **2** : ALBUMIN

al·bu·min \al-'byü-mən\ *n* : any of various water-soluble proteins of blood, milk, egg white, and plant and animal tissues

al·bu·min·ous \-mə-nəs\ *adj* : containing or resembling albumen or albumin

al·cal·de \al-'käl-dē\ *n* : the chief administrative and judicial officer of a

Spanish or Spanish-American town

al·ca·zar \al-'kaz-ər\ *n* : a Spanish fortress or palace

al·che·my \'al-kə-mē\ *n* : medieval chemistry chiefly concerned with efforts to turn base metals into gold — **al·chem·i·cal** \al-'kem-i-kəl\ *adj* — **al·che·mist** \'al-kə-məst\ *n*

al·co·hol \'al-kə-,hól\ *n* **1** : the liquid that is the intoxicating element in fermented and distilled liquors **2** : any of various carbon compounds similar to alcohol **3** : beverages containing alcohol — **alcoholic** *adj*

al·co·hol·ic \,al-kə-'hól-ik, -'häl-\ *n* : a person addicted to excessive use of alcoholic liquors or affected with alcoholism

al·co·hol·ism \'al-kə-,hól-,iz-əm\ *n* : continued excessive and usu. uncontrollable use of alcoholic drinks; *also* : the abnormal state associated with such use

al·cove \'al-,kōv\ *n* **1** : a nook or small recess opening off a larger room **2** : a niche or arched opening (as in a wall)

al·der \'ól-dər\ *n* : a tree or shrub related to the birches and growing in wet areas

al·der·man \'ól-dər-mən\ *n* : a member of a city legislative body

ale \'āl\ *n* : an alcoholic beverage brewed from malt and hops that is usu. more bitter than beer

alee \ə-'lē\ *adv (or adj)* : on or toward the lee

ale·house \'āl-,haùs\ *n* : a place where ale is sold to be drunk on the premises

alem·bic \ə-'lem-bik\ *n* : an apparatus formerly used in distillation

1alert \ə-'lórt\ *adj* **1** : watchful against danger **2** : quick to perceive and act — **alert·ly** *adv* — **alert·ness** *n*

2alert *n* **1** : a signal given to warn of danger **2** : the period during which an alert is in effect

3alert *vb* : WARN

Al·ex·an·dri·an \,al-ig-'zan-drē-ən\ *adj* **1** : of or relating to Alexander the Great **2** : HELLENISTIC

al·ex·an·drine \-'zan-drən\ *n, often cap* : a line of six iambic feet

al·fal·fa \al-'fal-fə\ *n* : a leguminous plant widely grown for hay and forage

al·fres·co \al-'fres-kō\ *adv (or adj)* : in the open air

al·ga \'al-gə\ *n, pl* **al·gae** \'al-(,)jē\ : any of a group of lower plants having chlorophyll but no vascular system and including seaweeds and related freshwater plants

al·ge·bra \'al-jə-brə\ *n* : a branch of mathematics using symbols (as letters) in calculating — **al·ge·bra·ic** \,al-jə-'brā-ik\ *adj*

Al·ge·ri·an \al-'jir-ē-ən\ *n* : a native or inhabitant of Algeria

1alias \'ā-lē-əs, 'āl-yəs\ *adv* : otherwise called

2alias *n* : an assumed name

1al·i·bi \'al-ə-,bī\ *n* **1** : a plea offered by an accused person of having been elsewhere than at the scene of commission of an offense **2** : a plausible excuse (as for failure or negligence)

2alibi *vb* **1** : to offer an excuse **2** : to make an excuse for

1alien \'ā-lē-ən, 'āl-yən\ *adj* : FOREIGN

2alien *n* : a foreign-born resident who has not been naturalized

alien·able \'āl-yə-nə-bəl, 'ā-lē-ə-nə-\ *adj*

: transferable to the ownership of another ⟨~ property⟩

alien·ate \'āl-ē-ə-ˌnāt, -yə-ˌnāt\ *vb* **1** : to transfer (property) to another **2** : to make hostile where previously friendship had existed : ESTRANGE — **alien·ation** \ˌā-lē-ə-'nā-shən, ˌāl-yə-\ *n*

alien·ist \'ā-lē-ə-nəst, 'āl-yə-\ *n* : PSYCHIATRIST; *esp* : one testifying in legal proceedings

¹alight \ə-'līt\ *vb* **alight·ed** *also* **alit** \ə-'lit\ **alight·ing 1** : to get down (as from a vehicle) **2** : to come to rest from the air **syn** dismount, land, perch

²alight *adj* : lighted up

align *also* **aline** \ə-'līn\ *vb* **1** : to bring into line **2** : to array on the side of or against a cause — **align·ment** *also* **aline·ment** *n*

¹alike \ə-'līk\ *adj* : LIKE **syn** similar, comparable

²alike *adv* : EQUALLY

al·i·ment \'al-ə-mənt\ *n* : FOOD, NUTRIMENT

al·i·men·ta·ry \ˌal-ə-'men-t(ə-)rē\ *adj* : of, relating to, or functioning in nourishment or nutrition

alimentary canal *n* : a tube that extends from the mouth to the anus and functions in the digestion and absorption of food and the elimination of residues

al·i·mo·ny \'al-ə-ˌmō-nē\ *n* : an allowance paid by a man to a woman after her legal separation or divorce from him

alive \ə-'līv\ *adj* **1** : having life : LIVING **2** : being in force or operation **3** : SENSITIVE **4** : ANIMATED

al·ka·li \'al-kə-ˌlī\ *n* **1** : a substance (as carbonate of sodium, carbonate of potassium, or hydroxide of sodium) that has marked basic properties (as an acrid taste and the power to neutralize acids, form salts, and turn red litmus blue) **2** : a mixture of salts in the soil of some dry regions in such amount as to make virtuous farming impossible — **al·ka·line** \-kə-lən, -ˌlīn\ *adj* — **al·ka·lin·i·ty** \ˌal-kə-'lin-ət-ē\ *n*

al·ka·lin·ize \'al-kə-lə-ˌnīz\ *also* **al·ka·lize** \'al-kə-ˌlīz\ *vb* : to make alkaline

al·ka·loid \'al-kə-ˌlȯid\ *n* : any of various usu. basic and bitter organic compounds found esp. in seed plants

al·kyd \'al-kəd\ *n* : any of numerous synthetic resins used for protective coatings

¹all \'ȯl\ *adj* **1** : the whole of **2** : the greatest possible **3** : every one of

²all *adv* **1** : WHOLLY **2** : so much ⟨~ the better for it⟩ **3** : for each side ⟨the score is two ~⟩

³all *pron* **1** : every one : the whole number ⟨~ of you are welcome⟩ **2** : the whole : every bit ⟨~ of the money is gone⟩ **3** : EVERYTHING

Al·lah \'al-ə, ä-'lä\ *n* : the supreme being of the Muslims

all-Amer·i·can \ˌȯl-ə-'mer-ə-kən\ *adj* **1** : composed wholly of American elements **2** : representative of the U.S. as a whole; *esp* : selected as the best in the U.S.

all-around \ˌȯl-ə-'raund\ *also* **all-round** \'ȯl-'raund\ *adj* : having ability in many fields : VERSATILE

al·lay \ə-'lā\ *vb* **1** : to reduce in severity **2** : to put at rest **syn** alleviate, lighten

al·lege \ə-'lej\ *vb* **1** : to state as a fact without proof **2** : to bring forward as a reason or excuse — **al·le·ga·tion** \ˌal-i-'gā-shən\ *n* — **al·leg·ed·ly** \ə-'lej-əd-lē\ *adv*

al·le·giance \ə-'lē-jəns\ *n* **1** : loyalty owed by a citizen to his government **2** : loyalty to a person or cause

al·le·go·ry \'al-ə-ˌgōr-ē\ *n* : the expression through symbolic figures and actions of truths or generalizations about human conduct or experience — **al·le·gor·i·cal** \ˌal-ə-'gȯr-i-kəl\ *adj*

¹al·le·gro \ə-'leg-rō, -'lā-grō\ *adv* (*or adj*) : in a brisk lively tempo — used as a direction in music

²allegro *n* : an allegro movement

al·le·lu·ia \ˌal-ə-'lü-yə\ *interj* : HALLELUJAH

al·ler·gen \'al-ər-jən\ *n* : something that causes allergy — **al·ler·gen·ic** \ˌal-ər-'jen-ik\ *adj*

al·ler·gist \'al-ər-jəst\ *n* : a specialist in allergy

al·ler·gy \'al-ər-jē\ *n* **1** : exaggerated or abnormal reaction to substances, situations, or physical states harmless to most people **syn** susceptibility — **al·ler·gic** \ə-'lər-jik\ *adj*

al·le·vi·ate \ə-'lē-vē-ˌāt\ *vb* : to make easier to be endured **syn** LIGHTEN, MITIGATE — **al·le·vi·a·tion** \ə-ˌlē-vē-'ā-shən\ *n*

al·ley \'al-ē\ *n* **1** : a narrow passage between buildings **2** : a place for bowling; *esp* : a hardwood lane

al·ley·way \-ˌwā\ *n* **1** : a narrow passageway **2** : a narrow street giving access to the rear of buildings

All·hal·lows \ȯl-'hal-ōz\ *n* : ALL SAINTS' DAY

al·li·ance \ə-'lī-əns\ *n* : a union to promote common interests **syn** league, coalition, confederacy, federation

al·lied \ə-'līd, 'al-ˌīd\ *adj* : joined in alliance

al·li·ga·tor \'al-ə-ˌgāt-ər\ *n* [Sp *el lagarto* the lizard, fr. L *lacertus* lizard] : a large aquatic reptile related to the crocodiles but having a shorter and broader snout

al·lit·er·ate \ə-'lit-ə-ˌrāt\ *vb* **1** : to form an alliteration **2** : to arrange so as to make alliteration

al·lit·er·a·tion \ə-ˌlit-ə-'rā-shən\ *n* : the repetition of initial sounds in adjacent words or syllables — **al·lit·er·a·tive** \-'lit-ə-ˌrāt-iv\ *adj*

al·lo·cate \'al-ə-ˌkāt\ *vb* : ALLOT, ASSIGN — **al·lo·ca·tion** \ˌal-ə-'kā-shən\ *n*

al·lot \ə-'lät\ *vb* **-lot·ted; -lot·ting** : to distribute as a share or portion **syn** assign, apportion, allocate — **al·lot·ment** *n*

all-out \'ȯl-'aut\ *adj* : using maximum energy or resources ⟨an ~ offensive⟩

all over *adv* : EVERYWHERE ⟨looked *all over* for the book⟩

al·low \ə-'lau\ *vb* **1** : to assign as a share ⟨~ time for rest⟩ **2** : to reckon as a deduction **3** : ADMIT, CONCEDE **4** : PERMIT **5** : to make allowance ⟨~ for expansion⟩ — **al·low·able** *adj*

al·low·ance \-əns\ *n* **1** : an allotted share **2** : money given regularly as a bounty **3** : the taking into account of mitigating circumstances or possible contingencies ⟨make ~ for his youth⟩

al·loy \'al-,ȯi, ə-'lȯi\ *n* **1** : a substance composed of metals fused together **2** : an admixture of something that debases — **alloy** *vb*

all right *adv* **1** : YES **2** : beyond doubt : CERTAINLY

All Saints' Day *n* : a church feast observed November 1 in honor of all the saints

All Souls' Day *n* : a day of supplication for the souls in purgatory observed in some churches

all·spice \'ȯl-,spīs\ *n* : the berry of the pimento tree; *also* : a spice made from it

all told *adv* : with everything counted : in all

al·lude \ə-'lüd\ *vb* : to refer indirectly or by suggestion — **al·lu·sion** \-'lü-zhən\ *n* — **al·lu·sive** \-'lü-siv\ *adj* — **al·lu·sive·ly** *adv* — **al·lu·sive·ness** *n*

al·lure \ə-'lu̇r\ *vb* : to entice by charm or attraction : ATTRACT — **al·lure·ment** *n*

al·lu·vi·um \ə-'lü-vē-əm\ *n* : soil material (as clay or gravel) deposited by running water — **al·lu·vi·al** \-vē-əl\ *adj*

¹al·ly \ə-'lī, 'al-,ī\ *vb* [OF *alier*, fr. L *alligare* to bind to, fr. *ad-* to + *ligare* to bind] : to unite in alliance

²al·ly \'al-,ī, ə-'lī\ *n* : a person or state united with another in an alliance

-al·ly \(ə-)lē\ *adv suffix* : ²-LY ⟨terrifically⟩

al·ma ma·ter \,al-mə-'mät-ər\ *n* : a school, college, or university that one has attended

al·ma·nac \'ȯl-mə-,nak, 'al-\ *n* : a calendar containing astronomical and meteorological data and often a miscellany of other information

al·mighty \ȯl-'mīt-ē\ *adj* **1** *often cap* : having absolute power over all ⟨*Almighty* God⟩ **2** : relatively unlimited in power

Almighty *n* : ²GOD

al·mond \'äm-ənd, 'am-; 'al-mənd\ *n* : a small tree related to the peach; *also* : the edible nutlike kernel of its fruit

al·mo·ner \'al-mə-nər, 'äm-ə-\ *n* : an officer who distributes alms

al·most \'ȯl-,mōst, ȯl-'mōst\ *adv* : only a little less than : NEARLY

alms \'ämz\ *n, pl* **alms** [OE *ælmesse*, fr. LL *eleemosyna*, fr. Gk *eleēmosynē* pity, alms, fr. *eleēmōn* merciful, fr. *eleos* pity] : something given freely to relieve the poor

alms·house \-,hau̇s\ *n, Brit* : a privately financed home for the poor

al·oe \'al-ō\ *n* **1** : any of various succulent mostly African plants related to the lilies **2** *pl* : the dried tonic and purgative juice of the leaves of an aloe

aloft \ə-'lȯft\ *adv* **1** : high in the air **2** : on or to the higher rigging of a ship

alo·ha \ə-'lō-ə, ä-'lō-hä\ *interj* — used to express greeting or farewell

alone \ə-'lōn\ *adj* **1** : separated from others **2** : not including anyone or anything else : ONLY **syn** lonely, lonesome, lone, forlorn — **alone** *adv*

¹alon· \ə-'lȯŋ\ *prep* **1** : on or near in a lengthwise direction ⟨walk ~ the street⟩ ⟨sail ~ the coast⟩ **2** : at a point on or during ⟨stopped ~ the way⟩

²along *adv* **1** : FORWARD, ON **2** : as a companion or associate ⟨bring her ~⟩ **3** : all the time ⟨knew it all ~⟩

along·shore \ə-'lȯŋ-'shȯr\ *adv* (*or adj*) : along the shore or coast

¹along·side \ə-'lȯŋ-,sīd\ *adv* : along or by the side

²alongside *prep* **1** : to, along, or at the side of ⟨came ~ the dock⟩ ⟨swimming ~ the dock⟩ ⟨anchored the dock⟩ **2** : WITH ⟨working ~ his colleagues⟩

alongside of *prep* : ALONGSIDE

aloof \ə-'lüf\ *adj* : removed or distant in interest or feeling : RESERVED — **aloof·ness** *n*

aloud \ə-'lau̇d\ *adv* : using the voice so as to be clearly heard

alp \'alp\ *n* : a high mountain

al·paca \al-'pak-ə\ *n* : a So. American mammal related to the llama; *also* : its wool or cloth made from this

al·pen·horn \'al-pən ,hȯrn\ *or* **alp·horn** \'alp-,hȯrn\ *n* : a long wooden horn used by Swiss herdsmen

al·pen·stock \'al-pən-,stäk\ *n* : a long iron-pointed staff used in mountain climbing

al·pha·bet \'al-fə-,bet, -bət\ *n* : the set of letters used in writing a language arranged in a conventional order

al·pha·bet·ic \,al-fə-'bet-ik\ *or* **al·pha·bet·i·cal** \-'bet-i-kəl\ *adj* **1** : of or employing an alphabe **2** : arranged in the order of the letters of the alphabet — **al·pha·bet·i·cal·ly** *adv*

al·pha·bet·ize \'al-fə-bə-,tīz\ *vb* : to arrange in alphabetic orde

al·pha particle \,al-fə\ *n* : a positively charged particle that is ejected at high speed in various radioactive transformations

alpha ray *n* : a stream of alpha particles

Al·pine \'al-,pīn\ *adj* : relating to, located in, or resembling the Alps

al·ready \ȯl-'red-ē\ *adv* **1** : prior to a specified or implied time : PREVIOUSLY **2** : so soon

al·so \'ȯl-sō\ *adv* : in addition : TOO

al·so-ran \-,ran\ *n* **1** : a horse or dog that finishes out of the money in a race **2** : a contestant that does not win

al·tar \'ȯl-tər\ *n* **1** : a structure on which sacrifices are offered or incense is burned in worship **2** : a table used as a center of ritual

al·tar·piece \-,pēs\ *n* : a work of art to decorate the space above and behind the altar

al·ter \'ȯl-tər\ *vb* : to make or become different : CHANGE, MODIFY — **al·ter·ation** \,ȯl-tə-'rā-shən\ *n*

al·ter·ca·tion \,ȯl-tər-'kā-shən\ *n* : a noisy or angry dispute

al·ter ego \,ȯl-tər-'ē-gō\ *n* : a second self; *esp* : a trusted friend

¹al·ter·nate \'ȯl-tər-nət, 'al-\ *adj* **1** : arranged or succeeding by turns **2** : every other — **al·ter·nate·ly** *adv*

²al·ter·nate \-,nāt\ *vb* : to occur or cause to occur by turns — **al·ter·na·tion** \,ȯl-tər-'nā-shən, ,al-\ *n*

³al·ter·nate \'ȯl-tər-nət, 'al-\ *n* : SUBSTITUTE

alternating current *n* : an electric current that reverses its direction at regular short intervals

al·ter·na·tive \ȯl-'tər-nət-iv, al-\ *adj* : that may be chosen in place of something else — **alternative** *n*

al·though *also* **al·tho** \ȯl-'thō\ *conj* : in spite of the fact that : even though

al·tim·e·ter \al-'tim-ət-ər, 'al-tə-,mēt-ər\ *n* : an instrument for measuring altitudes

al·ti·tude \'al-tə-,t(y)üd\ *n* **1** : vertical

elevation : HEIGHT   **2** : angular distance above the horizon

al·to \'al-tō\ n : the lowest female voice; also : a singer or instrument having the range of such a voice

al·to·geth·er \ˌȯl-tə-'geth-ər\ adv **1** : WHOLLY   **2** : on the whole

al·tru·ism \'al-trü-ˌiz-əm\ n : unselfish interest in the welfare of others — **al·tru·ist** \-trü-əst\ n — **al·tru·is·tic** \ˌal-trü-'is-tik\ adj — **al·tru·is·ti·cal·ly** adv

al·um \'al-əm\ n **1** : either of two colorless crystalline compounds containing aluminum that have a sweetish-sour taste and are used (as to stop bleeding) in medicine   **2** : a colorless aluminum salt used in purifying water and in tanning and dyeing

alu·mi·na \ə-'lü-mə-nə\ n : the oxide of aluminum occurring in nature as corundum, emery, and ruby

al·u·min·i·um \ˌal-yə-'min-ē-əm\ n, chiefly Brit : ALUMINUM

alu·mi·num \ə-'lü-mə-nəm\ n : a whitish light malleable metal used in articles where lightness and strength are desirable

alum·na \ə-'ləm-nə\ n, pl -nae \-ˌ(ˌ)nē\ : a woman graduate or former student of a college or school

alum·nus \ə-'ləm-nəs\ n, pl -ni \-ˌnī\ : a graduate or former student of a college or school

al·ways \'ȯl-wēz, -wəz\ adv **1** : at all times   **2** : FOREVER   **3** : without exception

am pres 1st sing of BE

amah \'äm-ə, -ˌä\ n : a female servant typically Chinese; esp : NURSE

amain \ə-'mān\ adv : with full force or speed

amal·gam \ə-'mal-gəm\ n **1** : an alloy of mercury with another metal used in making dental cements and in silvering mirrors   **2** : a compound made up of different things

amal·ga·mate \ə-'mal-gə-ˌmāt\ vb : to unite into one body or organization — **amal·ga·ma·tion** \-ˌmal-gə-'mā-shən\ n

aman·u·en·sis \ə-ˌman-yə-'wen-səs\ n, pl -en·ses \-ˌsēz\ : one employed to write from dictation or to copy what another has written : SECRETARY

am·a·ranth \'am-ə-ˌranth\ n **1** : an imaginary flower held never to fade   **2** : any of various coarse herbs sometimes grown for their showy flowers — **am·a·ran·thine** \ˌam-ə-'ran-thən, -ˌthīn\ adj

am·a·ryl·lis \ˌam-ə-'ril-əs\ n : any of various mostly bulbous herbs with clusters of lilylike often bright-colored flowers

amass \ə-'mas\ vb : to heap up : ACCUMULATE

am·a·teur \'am-ə-ˌtər, -ˌter, -ə-ˌt(y)ur\ n [F, fr. L amator lover, fr. amare to love] **1** : a person who engages in a pursuit for pleasure and not as a profession   **2** : a person who is not expert — **am·a·teur·ish** \ˌam-ə-'tər-ish, -'t(y)ur-ish\ adj — **am·a·teur·ism** \'am-ə-ˌtər-ˌiz-əm, -ə-ˌt(y)ur-, n

am·a·to·ry \'am-ə-ˌtōr-ē\ adj : of or expressing sexual love

amaze \ə-'māz\ vb : to overwhelm with wonder : ASTOUND   syn astonish, surprise — **amaze·ment** n — **amaz·ing·ly** adv

am·a·zon \'am-ə-ˌzän, -zən\ n **1** cap : a member of a race of female warriors repeatedly warring with the ancient Greeks of mythology   **2** : a tall strong masculine woman — **am·a·zo·ni·an** \ˌam-ə-'zō-nē-ən\ adj, often cap

am·bas·sa·dor \am-'bas-əd-ər\ n : a person accredited to a foreign government as an official representative of his own government — **am·bas·sa·dor·ship** \-ˌship\ n

am·ber \'am-bər\ n : a yellowish fossil resin used esp. for ornamental objects; also : the color of this resin

am·ber·gris \'am-bər-ˌgris, -ˌgrēs\ n : a waxy substance from the sperm whale used in making perfumes

am·bi·dex·trous \ˌam-bi-'dek-strəs\ adj : using both hands with equal ease — **am·bi·dex·trous·ly** adv

am·bi·ence \ä⁻-byä⁻s, 'an -bē-əns\ n : a surrounding or pervading atmosphere

am·bi·ent \'am-bē-ənt\ adj : SURROUNDING

am·big·u·ous \am-'big-yə-wəs\ adj : capable of being understood in more than one way — **am·bi·gu·i·ty** \ˌam-bə-'gyü-ət-ē\ n

am·bi·tion \am-'bish-ən\ n : eager desire for success, honor, or power

am·bi·tious \am-'bish-əs\ adj : characterized by ambition — **am·bi·tious·ly** adv

am·biv·a·lence \am-'biv-ə-ləns\ n : simultaneous attraction toward and repulsion from a person, object, or action — **am·biv·a·lent** \-lənt\ adj

¹am·ble \'am-bəl\ vb : to go at an amble : SAUNTER

²amble n : an easy gait esp. of a horse

am·bro·sia \am-'brō-zh(ē-)ə\ n : the food of the Greek and Roman gods — **am·bro·sial** \-zh(ē-)əl\ adj

am·bu·lance \'am-byə-ləns\ n : a vehicle equipped for carrying the injured or sick

am·bu·lant adj : moving about : AMBULATORY

¹am·bu·la·to·ry \'am-byə-lə-ˌtōr-ē\ adj **1** : of, relating to, or adapted to walking   **2** : able to walk about

²ambulatory n : a sheltered place (as a cloister) for walking

am·bus·cade \'am-bə-ˌskād\ n : AMBUSH

am·bush \'am-ˌbush\ n : a trap by which concealed persons attack an enemy by surprise — **ambush** vb

ame·ba, ame·bic var of AMOEBA, AMOEBIC

ame·lio·rate \ə-'mēl-yə-ˌrāt\ vb : to make or grow better : IMPROVE — **ame·lio·ra·tion** \-ˌmēl-yə-'rā-shən\ n

amen \(')ā-'men, (')ä-\ interj — used esp. at the end of prayers to express solemn ratification or approval

ame·na·ble \ə-'mē-nə-bəl, -'men-ə-\ adj **1** : ANSWERABLE   **2** : easily managed : TRACTABLE

amend \ə-'mend\ vb **1** : to change for the better : IMPROVE   **2** : to alter formally in phraseology

amend·ment \ə-'men(d)-mənt\ n **1**

ə abut; ᵊ kitten; ər further; a back; ā bake; ä cot, cart; au out; ch chin; e less; ē easy; g gift; i trip; ī life; j joke; ŋ sing; ō flow; ȯ flaw; ȯi coin; th thin; th this; ü loot; u̇ foot; y yet; yü few; yu̇ furious; zh vision

: correction of faults **2** : the process of amending a parliamentary motion or a constitution; *also* : the alteration so proposed or made

amends \ə-'men(d)z\ *n sing or pl* : compensation for injury or loss

amen·i·ty \ə-'men-ət-ē, -'mē-nət-\ *n* **1** : AGREEABLENESS **2** : something conducing to comfort or convenience **3** *pl* : the conventions observed in social intercourse

amerce \ə-'mərs\ *vb* **1** : to penalize by a fine determined by the court **2** : PUNISH — **amerce·ment** *n*

Amer·i·can \ə-'mer-ə-kən\ *n* **1** : a native or inhabitant of No. or So. America **2** : a citizen of the U.S. — **American** *adj* — **Amer·i·can·ism** \-ə-kə-.niz-əm\ *n* — **Amer·i·can·iza·tion** \ə-.mer-ə-kə-nə-'zā-shən\ *n* — **amer·i·can·ize** \ə-'mer-ə-kə-.nīz\ *vb, often cap*

am·er·i·ci·um \.am-ə-'ris(h)-ē-əm\ *n* : a radioactive metallic chemical element artificially produced from uranium

am·e·thyst \'am-ə-thəst\ *n* : a gemstone consisting of clear purple or bluish violet quartz

ami·a·ble \'ā-mē-ə-bəl\ *adj* **1** : AGREEABLE **2** : having a friendly and sociable disposition — **ami·a·bil·i·ty** \.ā-'bil-ət-ē\ *n* — **ami·a·bly** \'ā-mē-ə-blē\ *adv*

am·i·ca·ble \'am-i-kə-bəl\ *adj* : FRIENDLY, PEACEABLE — **am·i·ca·bly** *adv*

amid \ə-'mid\ *or* **amidst** \-'midst\ *prep* : in or into the middle of : AMONG

amid·ships \-'mid-.ships\ *adv* : in or toward the part of a ship midway between the bow and the stern

ami·no acid \ə-.mē-nō-, .am-ə-.nō-\ *n* : any of numerous nitrogen-containing acids that include some which are the building blocks of proteins

¹amiss \ə-'mis\ *adv* **1** : FAULTILY **2** : IMPROPERLY

²amiss *adj* **1** : WRONG **2** : out of place

am·i·ty \'am-ət-ē\ *n* : FRIENDSHIP; *esp* : friendly relations between nations

am·me·ter \'am-.ēt-ər\ *n* : an instrument for measuring electric current in amperes

am·mo \'am-ō\ *n* : AMMUNITION

am·mo·nia \ə-'mō-nyə\ *n* **1** : a colorless gaseous compound of nitrogen and hydrogen used in refrigeration and in the making of fertilizers and explosives **2** : a solution (**ammonia water**) of ammonia in water

am·mo·nite \'am-ə-.nīt\ *n* : any of various ancient flat spiral fossil mollusk shells

am·mu·ni·tion \.am-yə-'nish-ən\ *n* **1** : projectiles fired from guns **2** : explosive items used in war **3** : material for use in attack or defense

am·ne·sia \am-'nē-zhə\ *n* : abnormal loss of memory — **am·ne·si·ac** \-z(h)ē-.ak\ *or* **am·ne·sic** \-'nē-zik, -sik\ *adj or n*

am·nes·ty \'am-nə-stē\ *n* : an act granting a pardon to a group of individuals

amoe·ba \ə-'mē-bə\ *n, pl* **-bas** *or* **-bae** \-(.)bē\ : any of various tiny one-celled animals that lack permanent cell organs and occur esp. in water and soil — **amoe·bic** \-bik\ *adj*

amok \ə-'mək, -'mäk\ *or* **amuck** *adv* : in a murderously frenzied manner

among \ə-'məŋ\ *also* **amongst** \-'məŋst\ *prep* **1** : in or through the midst of **2** : in the number or class of **3** : in

shares to each of **4** : by common action of

amon·til·la·do \ə-.män-tə-'läd-ō\ *n* : a pale dry sherry

amor·al \ā-'mor-əl\ *adj* : neither moral nor immoral; *esp* : being outside the sphere to which moral judgments apply — **amor·al·ly** *adv*

am·o·rous \'am-(ə-)rəs\ *adj* **1** : inclined to love **2** : being in love — **am·o·rous·ly** *adv* — **am·o·rous·ness** *n*

amor·phous \ə-'mor-fəs\ *adj* **1** : SHAPELESS, FORMLESS **2** : not crystallized

am·or·tize \'am-ər-.tīz, ə-'mor-.tīz\ *vb* : to extinguish (as a mortgage) usu. by payment on the principal at the time of each periodic interest payment — **amor·ti·za·tion** \.am-ərt-ə-'zā-shən, ə-.mort-ə-\ *n*

¹amount \ə-'maunt\ *vb* **1** : to reach as a total ⟨the bill ~ed to $10⟩ **2** : to be equivalent

²amount *n* **1** : the total number or quantity **2** : a principal sum plus the interest on it

amour \ə-'mur, a-, ä-\ *n* : a love affair esp. when illicit

amour pro·pre \.am-.ùr-'propr'\ *n* : SELF-ESTEEM

am·pere \'am-.piər\ *n* : a unit of intensity of electric current equivalent to a steady current produced by one volt applied across a resistance of one ohm — **am·per·age** \-p(ə-)rij\ *n*

am·per·sand \'am-pər-.sand\ *n* : a character & standing for the word *and*

am·phib·i·an \am-'fib-ē-ən\ *n* **1** : an amphibious organism; *esp* : any of a group of animals (as frogs and newts) intermediate between fishes and reptiles **2** : an airplane designed to take off from and land on either land or water

am·phib·i·ous \-ē-əs\ *adj* [Gk *amphibios*, fr. *amphi*- on both sides + *bios* life] **1** : able to live both on land and in water **2** : adapted for both land and water **3** : made by joint action of land, sea, and air forces invading from the sea; *also* : trained for such action ⟨~ forces⟩

am·phi·the·ater \'am-fə-.thē-ət-ər\ *n* : an oval or circular building with rising tiers of seats around an arena

am·pho·ra \'am-fə-rə\ *n, pl* **-rae** \-.rē\ *or* **-ras** : an ancient Greek jar or vase with two handles that rise almost to the level of the mouth

am·ple \'am-pəl\ *adj* **1** : LARGE, CAPACIOUS **2** : enough to satisfy : ABUNDANT — **am·ply** \-plē\ *adv*

am·pli·fy \'am-plə-.fī\ *vb* **1** : to expand by extended treatment **2** : to increase (voltage, current, or power) in magnitude or strength (as by the use of a vacuum tube) **3** : to make louder — **am·pli·fi·ca·tion** \.am-plə-fə-'kā-shən\ *n* — **am·pli·fi·er** \'am-plə-.fī(-ə)r\ *n*

am·pli·tude \'am-plə-.t(y)üd\ *n* **1** : ample extent : FULLNESS **2** : the extent of a vibratory movement (as of a pendulum) or of an oscillation (as of an alternating current or a radio wave)

amplitude modulation *n* : modulation of the amplitude of a transmitting radio wave in accordance with the strength of the signal; *also* : a broadcasting system using such modulation

am·pul *or* **am·poule** \'am-p(y)ül\ *n* : a small sealed bulbous glass vessel used to hold a solution for hypodermic injection

am·pu·tate \'am-pyə-.tāt\ *vb* : to cut off

⟨~ a leg⟩ — am·pu·ta·tion \,am-pyə-'tā-shən\ n

am·pu·tee \,am-pyə-'tē\ n : one who has had a limb amputated

am·u·let \'am-yə-lət\ n : an ornament worn as a charm against evil

amuse \ə-'myüz\ vb : to entertain in a light or playful manner — DIVERT — amuse·ment n

an \ən, (')an\ indefinite article : A — used before words beginning with a vowel sound

¹-an \ən\ or -ian \(ē-)ən\ also -ean \(ē-)ən, ¸ē-ən\ n suffix 1 : one that belongs to ⟨American⟩ ⟨Bostonian⟩ ⟨crustacean⟩ 2 : one skilled in or specializing in ⟨phonetician⟩

²-an or -ian also -ean adj suffix 1 : of or belonging to ⟨American⟩ ⟨Floridian⟩ 2 : characteristic of : resembling ⟨Mozartean⟩

anach·ro·nism \ə-'nak-rə-,niz-əm\ n 1 : the error of placing a person or thing in a period to which he or it does not belong 2 : a person or thing that is chronologically out of place — anach·ro·nis·tic \ə-,nak-rə-'nis-tik\ adj

an·a·con·da \,an-ə-'kän-də\ n : a large So. American snake that crushes its prey

an·a·dem \'an-ə-,dem\ n : GARLAND, CHAPLET

anaemia var of ANEMIA

an·aer·o·bic \,an-ə-'rō-bik\ adj : living, active, or occurring in the absence of free oxygen

an·aes·the·sia, an·aes·thet·ic var of ANESTHESIA, ANESTHETIC

ana·gram \'an-ə-,gram\ n : a word or phrase made by transposing the letters of another word or phrase

anal \'ān-ⁿl\ adj : of, relating to, or situated near the anus

an·al·ge·sia \,an-ⁿl-'jē-zhə\ n : insensibility to pain — an·al·ge·sic \-'jē-zik, -sik\ adj or n

anal·o·gous \ə-'nal-ə-gəs\ adj : similar in one or more respects but not homologous

an·a·logue or an·a·log \'an-ⁿl-,òg\ n : something that is analogous or similar to something else

anal·o·gy \-ə-jē\ n 1 : inference that if two or more things agree in some respects they will prob. agree in others 2 : a likeness in one or more ways between things otherwise unlike — an·a·log·i·cal \,an-ⁿl-'äj-i-kəl\ adj — an·a·log·i·cal·ly adv

anal·y·sis \ə-'nal-ə-səs\ n, pl -y·ses \-ə-,sēz\ 1 : separation of a thing into the parts or elements of which it is composed 2 : an examination of a thing to determine its parts or elements; also : a statement showing the results of such an examination 3 : PSYCHOANALYSIS — an·a·lyst \'an-ⁿl-əst\ n — an·a·lyt·ic \,an-ⁿl-'it-ik\ or an·a·lyt·i·cal \-i-kəl\ adj — an·a·lyt·i·cal·ly adv

an·a·lyze \'an-ⁿl-,īz\ vb : to make an analysis of

an·a·pest \'an-ə-,pest\ n : a metrical foot of two unaccented syllables followed by one accented syllable — an·a·pes·tic \,an-ə-'pes-tik\ adj

an·ar·chism \'an-ər-,kiz-əm\ n 1 : the theory that all government is an evil 2 : TERRORISM — an·ar·chist \-kəst\ n — an·ar·chis·tic \,an-ər-'kis-tik\ adj

an·ar·chy \'an-ər-kē\ n 1 : a social structure without government or law and order 2 : utter confusion — an·ar·chic \a-'när-kik\ also an·ar·chi·cal \-ki-kəl\ adj

anath·e·ma \ə-'nath-ə-mə\ n 1 : a solemn curse 2 : a person or thing accursed; also : one intensely disliked

anath·e·ma·tize \-mə-,tīz\ vb : to pronounce an anathema against : CURSE

anat·o·mize \ə-'nat-ə-,mīz\ vb : to dissect so as to examine the structure and parts; also : ANALYZE

anat·o·my \ə-'nat-ə-mē\ n 1 : a branch of science dealing with the structure of organisms 2 : a separating into parts for detailed study : ANALYSIS, ANATOMIZING — an·a·tom·ic \,an-ə-'täm-ik\ or an·a·tom·i·cal \-i-kəl\ adj — anat·o·mist \ə-'nat-ə-məst\ n

-ance \əns\ n suffix 1 : action or process ⟨furtherance⟩ : instance of an action or process ⟨performance⟩ 2 : quality or state : instance of a quality or state ⟨protuberance⟩ 3 : amount or degree ⟨conductance⟩

an·ces·tor \'an-,ses-tər\ n : one from whom an individual is descended — an·ces·tress \-trəs\ n

an·ces·try \-,ses-trē\ n 1 : line of descent : LINEAGE 2 : ANCESTORS — an·ces·tral \an-'ses-trəl\ adj

¹an·chor \'aŋ-kər\ n : a heavy metal device attached to a boat and so made that when thrown overboard it catches hold of the earth and holds the boat in place

²anchor vb : to hold or become held in place by or as if by an anchor

an·chor·age \'aŋ-k(ə-)rij\ n : a place suitable for ships to anchor

an·cho·rite \'aŋ-kə-,rīt\ n : one who lives in seclusion esp. for religious reasons — an·cho·ress \-k(ə-)rəs\ n

an·cho·vy \'an-,chō-vē, an-'chō-\ n : a small herringlike fish used esp. for sauces and relishes

an·cien ré·gime \ᵉn²ä-syaⁿ-rā-zhēm\ n 1 : the political and social system of France before the Revolution of 1789 2 : a system no longer prevailing

¹an·cient \'ān-shənt, 'āŋ-\ adj 1 : having existed for many years 2 : belonging to times long past; esp : belonging to the period before the Middle Ages

²ancient n 1 : an aged person 2 pl : the peoples of ancient Greece and Rome

an·cil·lary \'an-sə-,ler-ē\ adj 1 : SUBORDINATE, SUBSIDIARY 2 : AUXILIARY, SUPPLEMENTARY

-an·cy \ən-sē\ n suffix : quality or state ⟨flamboyancy⟩

and \ən(d), (')an(d)\ conj — used as a function word to indicate connection or addition esp. of items within the same class or type or to join words or phrases of the same grammatical rank or function

¹an·dan·te \än-'dän-,tā, an-'dant-ē\ adv (or adj) : moderately slow — used as a direction in music

²andante n : an andante movement

and·iron \'an-,dī(-ə)rn\ n : one of a pair of metal supports for firewood in a fireplace

and/or conj — used as a function word to indicate that either and or or may apply

⟨men ~ women means men *and* women or men *or* women⟩

an·dro·gen \'an-drə-jən\ *n* **:** a male sex hormone

an·ec·dote \'an-ik-,dōt\ *n* **:** a brief story of an interesting usu. biographical incident

ane·mia \ə-'nē-mē-ə\ *n* **1 :** a condition in which blood is deficient in quantity, in red cells, or in hemoglobin and which is marked by pallor, weakness, and irregular heart action **2 :** lack of vitality — **ane·mic** \-mik\ *adj*

an·e·mom·e·ter \,an-ə-'mäm-ət-ər\ *n* **:** an instrument for measuring the force or speed of the wind

anem·o·ne \ə-'nem-o-nē\ *n* **:** a small herb related to the buttercups that has showy usu. white flowers

anent \ə-'nent\ *prep* **:** ABOUT, CONCERNING

an·es·the·sia \,an-əs-'thē-zhə\ *n* **:** loss of bodily sensation

¹an·es·thet·ic \-'thet-ik\ *adj* **:** of, relating to, or capable of producing anesthesia

²anesthetic *n* **:** an agent (as ether) that produces anesthesia — **anes·the·tist** \ə-'nes-thət-əst\ *n* — **anes·the·tize** \-thə-,tīz\ *vb*

anew \ə-'n(y)ü\ *adv* **:** over again **:** from a new start

an·gel \'ān-jəl\ *n* [LL *angelus*, fr. Gk *angelos*, lit., messenger] **1 :** a spiritual being superior to man **2 :** an attendant spirit ⟨guardian ~⟩ **3 :** a winged figure of human form in art **4 :** MESSENGER, HARBINGER **5 :** a person held to resemble an angel — **an·gel·ic** \an-'jel-ik\ *or* **an·gel·i·cal** \-i-kəl\ *adj* — **an·gel·i·cal·ly** *adv*

¹an·ger \'aŋ-gər\ *n* **:** a strong feeling of displeasure **syn** wrath, ire, rage, fury, indignation

²anger *vb* **:** to make angry

an·gi·na \an-'jī-nə\ *n* **:** a disorder (as of the heart) marked by attacks of intense pain — **an·gi·nal** \-'jīn-ᵊl\ *adj*

¹an·gle \'aŋ-gəl\ *n* **1 :** the figure formed by the meeting of two lines in a point **2 :** a sharp projecting corner **3 :** a point of view

²angle *vb* **:** to turn, move, or direct at an angle

³angle *vb* **:** to fish with a hook and line — **an·gler** \-glər\ *n* — **an·gling** \-gliŋ\ *n*

an·gle·worm \'aŋ-gəl-,wərm\ *n* **:** EARTHWORM

An·gli·can \'aŋ-gli-kən\ *n* **:** a member of the Church of England; *also* **:** EPISCOPALIAN

an·gli·cize \'aŋ-glə-,sīz\ *vb*, *often cap* **1 :** to make English (as in habits, speech, character, or outlook) **2 :** to borrow (a foreign word or phrase) into English without changing form or spelling and sometimes without changing pronunciation — **an·gli·ci·za·tion** \,aŋ-glə-sə-'zā-shən\ *n*, *often cap*

an·glo·phile \'aŋ-glə-,fīl\ *n*, *often cap* **:** one who greatly admires England

an·glo·phobe \-,fōb\ *n*, *often cap* **:** one who is averse to England and things English

An·glo-Sax·on \,aŋ-glō-'sak-sən\ *n* **1 :** a member of any of the Germanic peoples who invaded England in the 5th century A.D. **2 :** a member of the English people **3 :** OLD ENGLISH — **Anglo-Saxon** *adj*

an·go·ra \aŋ-'gŏr-ə, an-\ *n* **1** *cap* **:** a cat, goat, or rabbit with a long silky coat **2 :** yarn or cloth made from the hair of an Angora goat or rabbit

an·gry \'aŋ-grē\ *adj* **:** feeling or showing anger **syn** enraged, wrathful, irate, indignant — **an·gri·ly** *adv*

angst \'äŋst\ *n* **:** a feeling of anxiety **:** DREAD

an·guish \'aŋ-gwish\ *n* **:** extreme pain or distress esp. of mind

an·guished *adj* **:** full of anguish **:** TORMENTED ⟨an ~ call for help⟩

an·gu·lar \'aŋ-gyə-lər\ *adj* **1 :** having one or more angles **2 :** sharp-cornered **3 :** being thin and bony — **an·gu·lar·i·ty** \,aŋ-gyə-'lar-ət-ē\ *n*

an·hy·drous \an-'hī-drəs\ *adj* **:** free from water

an·i·line \'an-ᵊl-ən\ *n* **:** an oily poisonous liquid used in making dyes, medicines and explosives

an·i·mad·vert \,an-ə-,mad-'vərt\ *vb* **:** to remark critically **:** express censure — **an·i·mad·ver·sion** \-'vər-zhən\ *n*

¹an·i·mal \'an-ə-məl\ *n* **1 :** a living being capable of feeling and voluntary motion **2 :** a lower animal as distinguished from man; *also* **:** MAMMAL

²animal *adj* **1 :** of, relating to, or derived from animals **2 :** of or relating to the physical as distinguished from the mental or spiritual **syn** carnal

an·i·mal·cule \,an-ə-'mal-kyül\ *n* **:** a tiny animal usu. invisible to the naked eye

an·i·mal·ism \'an-ə-mə-,liz-əm\ *n* **:** SENSUALITY

¹an·i·mate \'an-ə-mət\ *adj* **:** having life

²an·i·mate \-,māt\ *vb* **1 :** to impart life to **2 :** to give spirit and vigor to **3 :** to make appear to move ⟨~ a cartoon for motion pictures⟩ — **an·i·mat·ed** *adj*

an·i·ma·tion \,an-ə-'mā-shən\ *n* **1 :** LIVELINESS, VIVACITY **2 :** an animated cartoon

an·i·mism \'an-ə-,miz-əm\ *n* **:** attribution of conscious life to nature as a whole or to inanimate objects — **an·i·mist** *n* — **an·i·mis·tic** \,an-ə-'mis-tik\ *adj*

an·i·mos·i·ty \,an-ə-'mäs-ət-ē\ *n* **:** ILL WILL, RESENTMENT

an·i·mus \'an-ə-məs\ *n* **:** deep-seated resentment and hostility

an·ise \'an-əs\ *n* **:** an herb related to the carrot with aromatic seeds (**ani·seed** \-ə(s)-,sēd\) used in flavoring

ankh \'aŋk\ *n* **:** a cross having a loop for its upper vertical arm and serving esp. in ancient Egypt as an emblem of life

an·kle \'aŋ-kəl\ *n* **:** the joint or region between the foot and the leg

an·klet \'aŋ-klət\ *n* **1 :** something (as an ornament) worn around the ankle **2 :** a short sock reaching slightly above the ankle

an·nals \'an-ᵊlz\ *n pl* **1 :** a record of events in chronological order **2 :** HISTORY — **an·nal·ist** \-ᵊl-əst\ *n*

an·neal \ə-'nēl\ *vb* **:** to soften and toughen (as glass or steel) by subjecting to heat and then cooling

¹an·nex \ə-'neks, 'an-,eks\ *vb* **1 :** to attach as an addition **2 :** to incorporate (as a territory) within a political domain — **an·nex·a·tion** \,an-,ek-'sā-shən\ *n*

²an·nex \'an-,eks, -iks\ *n* **:** a subsidiary or supplementary structure ⟨his room is in the ~ to the hotel⟩

an·ni·hi·late \ə-'nī-ə-,lāt\ *vb* **:** to destroy completely : wipe out — **an·ni·hi·la·tion** \-ˌnī-ə-'lä-shən\ n

an·ni·ver·sa·ry \ˌan-ə-'vərs-(ə-)rē\ n : the annual return of the date of some notable event and esp. a wedding

an·no Do·mi·ni \ˌan-ō-'däm-ə-nē, -ˌnī\ adv, often cap A — used to indicate that a time division falls within the Christian era

an·no·tate \'an-ə-ˌtāt\ vb : to furnish with notes — **an·no·ta·tion** \ˌan-ə-'tā-shən\ n — **an·no·ta·tor** \'an-ə-ˌtāt-ər\ n

an·nounce \ə-'naůns\ vb 1 : to make known publicly 2 : to give notice of the arrival or presence of — **an·nounce·ment** n

an·nounc·er n : a person who introduces radio or television programs, reads commercials and news summaries, and gives station identification

an·noy \ə-'nȯi\ vb : to disturb or irritate esp. by repeated acts : VEX SYN irk, bother, pester, tease, harass — **an·noy·ing·ly** adv

an·noy·ance \-'nȯi-əns\ n 1 : the act of annoying : the state of being annoyed 2 : NUISANCE

¹**an·nu·al** \'an-y(ə-w)əl\ adj 1 : covering the period of a year 2 : occurring once a year : YEARLY 3 : completing the life cycle in one growing season (~ plants) — **an·nu·al·ly** adv

²**annual** n 1 : a publication appearing once a year 2 : an annual plant

an·nu·i·tant \ə-'n(y)ü-ət-ənt\ n : a beneficiary of an annuity

an·nu·i·ty \ə-'n(y)ü-ət-ē\ n : an amount payable annually; also : the right to receive such a payment

an·nul \ə-'nəl\ vb -nulled; -nul·ling : to make legally void — **an·nul·ment** n

an·nu·lar \'an-yə-lər\ adj : ring-shaped

an·nun·ci·ate \ə-'nən-sē-ˌāt\ vb : ANNOUNCE — **an·nun·ci·a·tor** n — **an·nun·ci·a·to·ry** \-sē-ə-ˌtōr-ē\ adj

an·nun·ci·a·tion \ə-ˌnən-sē-'ā-shən\ n 1 : the act of announcing : ANNOUNCEMENT 2 cap : a church feast commemorating the announcement of the Incarnation and celebrated on March 25

an·ode \'an-ˌōd\ n 1 : the positive electrode of an electrolytic cell 2 : the negative terminal of a battery 3 : the electron-collecting electrode of an electron tube — **an·od·ic** \a-'näd-ik\ adj

an·o·dyne \'an-ə-ˌdīn\ n : something that relieves pain : a soothing agent

anoint \ə-'nȯint\ vb 1 : to apply oil to esp. as a sacred rite 2 : CONSECRATE — **anoint·ment** n

anom·a·lous \ə-'näm-ə-ləs\ adj : deviating from a general rule : ABNORMAL

anom·a·ly \ə-'näm-ə-lē\ n : something anomalous : IRREGULARITY

anon \ə-'nän\ adv, archaic : SOON, PRESENTLY

anon·y·mous \ə-'nän-ə-məs\ adj : of unknown or undeclared origin or authorship — **an·o·nym·i·ty** \ˌan-ə-'nim-ət-ē\ n — **anon·y·mous·ly** \ə-'nän-ə-məs-lē\ adv

anoph·e·les \ə-'näf-ə-ˌlēz\ n : a mosquito that transmits malaria to man

¹**an·oth·er** \ə-'nəth-ər\ adj 1 : any or some other 2 : being one in addition : one more

²**another** pron 1 : an additional one : one more 2 : one that is different from the first or present one

¹**an·swer** \'an-sər\ n 1 : something spoken or written in return to or satisfying a question 2 : a solution of a problem

²**answer** vb 1 : to speak or write in reply to 2 : to be responsible 3 : to be adequate — **an·swer·er** n

an·swer·able \'ans-(ə-)rə-bəl\ adj 1 : liable to be called to give an explanation or satisfaction : RESPONSIBLE 2 : capable of being refuted

ant \'ant\ n : any of various small insects related to the bees and living in communities usu. in earth or wood

ant- — see ANTI-

¹**-ant** \ənt\ n suffix 1 : one that performs or promotes (a specified action) (coolant) (expectorant) 2 : thing that is acted upon (in a specified manner) (inhalant)

²**-ant** adj suffix 1 : performing (a specified action) or being (in a specified condition) (propellant) 2 : promoting (a specified action or process) (expectorant)

ant·ac·id \ant-'as-əd\ n : a substance that counteracts acidity

an·tag·o·nism \an-'tag-ə-ˌniz-əm\ n 1 : active opposition or hostility 2 : opposition in physiological action — **an·tag·o·nis·tic** \-ˌtag-ə-'nis-tik\ adj

an·tag·o·nist \an-'tag-ə-nəst\ n : ADVERSARY, OPPONENT

an·tag·o·nize \-ə-ˌnīz\ vb : to provoke the hostility of

ant·arc·tic \ant-'är(k)t-ik\ adj, often cap : of or relating to the south pole or the region near it

antarctic circle n, often cap A&C : a circle of the earth parallel to its equator approximately 23°27' from the south pole

¹**an·te** \'ant-ē\ n : a poker stake put up by each player before he sees his hand; also : an amount paid : PRICE

²**ante** vb 1 : to put up (an ante) 2 : PAY

an·te·bel·lum \ˌant-i-'bel-əm\ adj : existing before a war; esp : existing before the U.S. Civil War of 1861-65

an·te·ced·ent \ˌant-ə-'sēd-ənt\ n 1 : a noun, pronoun, phrase, or clause referred to by a personal or relative pronoun 2 : a preceding event or cause 3 pl : the significant conditions of one's earlier life 4 pl : ANCESTORS — **antecedent** adj

an·te·cham·ber \'ant-i-ˌchām-bər\ n : an outer chamber leading to another room

an·te·choir \-ˌkwī(ə)r\ n : a space enclosed or reserved for the clergy and choristers at the entrance to a choir

an·te·date \-ˌdāt\ vb 1 : to date (a paper) as of an earlier day than that on which the actual writing or signing is done 2 : to precede in time

an·te·di·lu·vi·an \ˌant-i-də-'lü-vē-ən, -dī-\ adj 1 : of the period before the biblical flood 2 : ANTIQUATED, OBSOLETE

an·te·lope \'ant-ᵊl-ˌōp\ n : any of various mammals related to the oxen but with smaller lighter bodies and horns that extend upward and backward

---

ə abut; ᵊ kitten; ər further; a back; ā bake; ä cot, cart; aů out; ch chin; e less; ē easy; g gift; i trip; ī life; j joke; ŋ sing; ō flow; ȯ flaw; ȯi coin; th thin; th̲ this; ü loot; ů foot; y yet; yü few; yů furious; zh vision

an·te me·ri·di·em \,ant-i-mə-'rid-ē-əm\ *adj* : being before noon

an·te·mor·tem \-'mȯrt-əm\ *adj* : preceding death

an·te·na·tal \-'nāt-ᵊl\ *adj* **1** : of or relating to an unborn child **2** : occurring during pregnancy

an·ten·na \an-'ten-ə\ *n* **1** *pl usu* **-nae** \-'ten-(,)ē\ : one of the long slender paired sensory organs on the head of an arthropod (as an insect or crab) **2** *pl usu* **-nas** : a metallic device (as a rod or wire) for sending out or receiving radio waves

an·te·pe·nult \,ant-i-'pē-,nəlt\ *n* : the 3d syllable of a word counting from the end — **an·te·pen·ul·ti·mate** \-pi-'nəl-tə-mət\ *adj or n*

an·te·ri·or \an-'tir-ē-ər\ *adj* : located before in place or time **syn** preceding, previous, prior

an·te·room \'ant-i-,rüm, -,rùm\ *n* : a room forming the entrance to another and often used as a waiting room

an·them \'an-thəm\ *n* **1** : a sacred composition usu. sung by a church choir **2** : a song or hymn of praise or gladness

an·ther \'an-thər\ *n* : the part of the stamen of a seed plant that contains pollen

ant·hill \'ant-,hil\ *n* : a mound thrown up by ants or termites in digging their nest

an·thol·o·gy \an-'thäl-ə-jē\ *n* : a collection of literary selections

an·thra·cite \'an-thrə-,sīt\ *n* : a hard glossy coal that burns without much smoke

an·thrax \'an-,thraks\ *n* : a destructive bacterial disease of warm-blooded animals (as cattle and sheep)

an·thro·po·cen·tric \,an-thrə-pə-'sen-trik\ *adj* : interpreting or regarding the world in terms of human values and experiences

¹**an·thro·poid** \'an-thrə-,pȯid\ *adj* **1** : resembling man **2** : resembling an ape

²**anthropoid** *n* : any of several large higher apes (as a gorilla)

an·thro·pol·o·gy \,an-thrə-'päl-ə-jē\ *n* : a science dealing with man and esp. his origin, development, and culture — **an·thro·po·log·i·cal** \-pə-'läj-i-kəl\ *adj* — **an·thro·pol·o·gist** \-'päl-ə-jəst\ *n*

an·thro·po·mor·phism \,an-thrə-pə-'mȯr-,fiz-əm\ *n* : the conception of God or gods as possessing human qualities — **an·thro·po·mor·phic** \-'fik\ *adj*

an·ti \'an-,tī, 'ant-ē\ *n* : one who is opposed

an·ti- \,ant-i, -,ē; ,an-,tī\ *or* **ant-** *prefix* **1** : opposite in kind, position, or action **2** : opposing : hostile toward **3** : counteractive **4** : preventive of : curative of

antiaircraft   antifascist
anti-American   anti-imperialism
antibacterial   anti-imperialist
anticapitalist   antilabor
anti-Catholic   antimalarial
anticlerical   antimicrobial
anticoagulant   antislavery
anticolonial   antispasmodic
anti-Communism   antisubmarine
anti-Communist   antitank
antidemocratic   antitrust

an·ti·bi·ot·ic \,ant-i-bī-'ät-ik, ,an-,tī-, -bē-\ *n* : a substance produced by an organism (as a fungus or bacteria) that in dilute solution inhibits or kills harmful microorganisms — **antibiotic** *adj*

an·ti·body \'ant-i-,bäd-ē\ *n* : a bodily substance that specifically counteracts the effects of a disease-producing microorganism

¹**an·tic** \'ant-ik\ *n* : a ludicrous act : CAPER

²**antic** *adj* **1** *archaic* : GROTESQUE **2** : PLAYFUL

an·ti·christ \'ant-i-,krīst\ *n* **1** : one who denies or opposes Christ **2** : a false Christ

an·tic·i·pate \an-'tis-ə-,pāt\ *vb* **1** : to foresee and provide for beforehand **2** : to look forward to — **an·tic·i·pa·tion** \-,tis-ə-'pā-shən\ *n* — **an·tic·i·pa·to·ry** \-'tis-ə-pə-,tōr-ē\ *adj*

an·ti·cli·max \,ant-i-'klī-,maks\ *n* : an event or statement esp. closing a series that is strikingly less important than what has preceded it — **an·ti·cli·mac·tic** \-klī-'mak-tik\ *adj*

an·ti·dote \'ant-i-,dōt\ *n* : a remedy to counteract the effects of poison

an·ti·freeze \-,frēz\ *n* : a substance added to the liquid in an automobile radiator to prevent its freezing

an·ti·his·ta·mine \,ant-i-'his-tə-,mēn\ *n* : any of various drugs used in treating allergies and colds

an·ti-in·tel·lec·tu·al·ism \,ant-ē-,int-ᵊl-'ek-ch(ə-w)ə-,liz-əm, ,an-,tī-\ *n* : hostility toward or suspicion of intellectuals or intellectual traits and activities

an·ti·knock \,ant-i-'näk\ *n* : a substance that when added to the fuel of an internal-combustion engine helps to prevent knocking

an·ti·log·a·rithm \,ant-i-'lȯg-ə-,rith-əm, ,an-,tī-, -'läg-\ *n* : the number corresponding to a given logarithm

an·ti·ma·cas·sar \,ant-i-mə-'kas-ər\ *n* : a cover to protect the back or arms of furniture

an·ti·mo·ny \'ant-ə-,mō-nē\ *n* : a brittle silvery white metallic chemical element used in alloys

an·ti·pas·to \,ant-i-'pas-tō, -'päs-\ *n* : HORS D'OEUVRE

an·tip·a·thy \an-'tip-ə-thē\ *n* **1** : settled aversion or dislike **2** : an object of aversion

an·ti·per·son·nel \,ant-i-,pərs-ᵊn-'el, ,an-,tī-\ *adj* : designed for use against military personnel (~ mine)

an·tiph·o·nal \an-'tif-ən-ᵊl\ *adj* : performed by two alternating groups : ANSWERING — **an·tiph·o·nal·ly** *adv*

an·tip·o·des \an-'tip-ə-,dēz\ *n pl* : the parts of the earth diametrically opposite — **an·tip·o·dal** \-'tip-əd-ᵊl\ *adj*

an·ti·quar·i·an \,ant-ə-'kwer-ē-ən\ *adj* **1** : of or relating to antiquities **2** : dealing in old or rare books — **an·ti·quar·i·an·ism** \-,iz-əm\ *n*

an·ti·quary \'ant-ə-,kwer-ē\ *n* : a person who collects or studies antiquities

an·ti·quat·ed \'ant-ə-,kwāt-əd\ *adj* : OUT-OF-DATE, OLD-FASHIONED (~ economic theories)

¹**an·tique** \an-'tēk\ *adj* **1** : belonging to antiquity **2** : OLD-FASHIONED **3** : of a bygone style or period

²**antique** *n* : an object made in a bygone period

an·tiq·ui·ty \an-'tik-wət-ē\ *n* **1** : ancient times **2** : great age **3** *pl* : relics of ancient times **4** *pl* : matters relating to the culture of ancient times

an·ti-Sem·i·tism \,ant-i-'sem-ə-,tiz-əm, ,an-,tī-\ *n* : hostility toward Jews as a religious or social minority — **an·ti·Se·mit·ic** \-sə-'mit-ik\ *adj*

an·ti·sep·tic \,ant-ə-'sep-tik\ *adj* : killing or checking the growth of germs that cause decay or infection — **antiseptic** *n* — **an·ti·sep·ti·cal·ly** *adv*

an·ti·so·cial \,ant-i-'sō-shəl, ,an-,tī-\ *adj* 1 : contrary or hostile to the well-being of society (crime is ~) 2 : disliking the society of others

an·tith·e·sis \an-'tith-ə-səs\ *n, pl* **-e·ses** \-ə-,sēz\ 1 : the opposition or contrast of ideas 2 : the direct opposite

an·ti·tox·in \,ant-I-'täk-sən\ *n* : an antibody able to neutralize a particular toxin that is formed when the toxin is introduced into the body and is produced in lower animals for use in treating human diseases (as diphtheria)

an·ti·viv·i·sec·tion·ist \,ant-i-,viv-ə-'sek-sh(ə-)nəst, ,an-,tī-\ *n* : a person opposed to vivisection

ant·ler \'ant-lər\ *n* : the solid usu. branched horn of deer — **ant·lered** \-lərd\ *adj*

ant·onym \'an-tə-,nim\ *n* : a word of opposite meaning

an·trum \'an-trəm\ *n, pl* **-tra** \-trə\ : the cavity of a hollow organ or a sinus

anus \'ā-nəs\ *n* : the posterior opening of the alimentary canal

an·vil \'an-vəl\ *n* : a heavy iron block on which metal is shaped (as by hammering)

anx·i·ety \aŋ-'zī-ət-ē\ *n* : painful uneasiness of mind usu. over an anticipated ill

anx·ious \'aŋk-shəs\ *adj* 1 : uneasy in mind : WORRIED 2 : earnestly wishing : EAGER — **anx·ious·ly** *adv*

¹**any** \'en-ē\ *adj* 1 : one chosen at random 2 : of whatever number or quantity

²**any** *pron* 1 : any one or ones (take ~ of the books you like) 2 : any amount (~ of the money not used is to be returned)

³**any** *adv* : to any extent or degree : at all (could not walk ~ farther)

any·body \-,bäd-ē\ *pron* : ANYONE

any·how \-,haù\ *adv* 1 : in any way 2 : NEVERTHELESS; *also* : in any case

any·more \,en-ē-'mōr\ *adv* : at the present time

any·one \'en-ē-(,)wən\ *pron* : any person

any·place \-,plās\ *adv* : in any place

any·thing \-,thiŋ\ *pron* : any thing whatever

any·way \'en-ē-,wā\ *adv* : ANYHOW

any·where \-,hweər\ *adv* : in or to any place

any·wise \-,wīz\ *adv* : in any way whatever

aor·ta \ā-'òrt-ə\ *n, pl* **-tas** *or* **-tae** \-'òr-,tē\ : the main artery that carries blood from the heart — **aor·tic** \-'òrt-ik\ *adj*

apace \ə-'pās\ *adv* : SWIFTLY

ap·a·nage *var of* APPANAGE

apart \ə-'pärt\ *adv* 1 : separately in place or time 2 : ASIDE 3 : to pieces : ASUNDER

apart·heid \ə-'pär-,tāt\ *n* : a policy of racial segregation practiced in the Republic of So. Africa

apart·ment \ə-'pärt-mənt\ *n* : a room or set of rooms esp. occupied as a dwelling; *also* : a building divided into individual dwelling units

ap·a·thy \'ap-ə-thē\ *n* 1 : lack of emotion 2 : lack of interest : INDIFFERENCE — **ap·a·thet·ic** \,ap-ə-'thet-ik\ *adj* — **ap·a·thet·i·cal·ly** *adv*

¹**ape** \'āp\ *n* 1 : any of the larger tailless primates (as a baboon or gorilla); *also* : MONKEY 2 : MIMIC, IMITATOR; *also* : a large uncouth person

²**ape** *vb* : IMITATE, MIMIC

apeak \ə-'pēk\ *adv* (*or adj*) : in a vertical position (oars ~)

aper·i·tif \,äp-,er-ə-'tēf\ *n* : an alcoholic drink taken before a meal as an appetizer

ap·er·ture \'ap-ə(r)-,chùr, -chər\ *n* : OPENING, HOLE

apex \'ā-,peks\ *n, pl* **apex·es** *or* **api·ces** \'ā-pə-,sēz, 'ap-ə-\ : the highest point : PEAK

apha·sia \ə-'fā-zh(ē-)ə\ *n* : loss of power to use or understand speech

aphid \'ā-fəd, 'af-əd\ *n* : a small insect that sucks the juices of plants

aphis \'ā-fəs, 'af-əs\ *n, pl* **aphi·des** \'ā-fə-,dēz, 'af-ə-\ : APHID

aph·o·rism \'af-ə-,riz-əm\ *n* : a short saying stating a general truth : MAXIM — **aph·o·ris·tic** \,af-ə-'ris-tik\ *adj*

aph·ro·dis·i·ac \,af-rə-'diz-ē-,ak\ *adj* : exciting sexual desire — **aphrodisiac** *n*

api·ary \'ā-pē-,er-ē\ *n* : a place where bees are kept — **api·a·rist** \-ə-rəst\ *n*

apiece \ə-'pēs\ *adv* : for each one

aplomb \ə-'pläm, -'pləm\ *n* : complete composure or self-assurance : POISE

apoc·a·lypse \ə-'päk-ə-,lips\ *n* : a writing prophesying a cataclysm in which evil forces are destroyed — **apoc·a·lyp·tic** \-,päk-ə-'lip-tik\ *or* **apoc·a·lyp·ti·cal** *adj*

Apoc·ry·pha \ə-'päk-rə-fə\ *n* 1 *not cap* : writings of dubious authenticity 2 : books included in the Septuagint and Vulgate but excluded from the Jewish and Protestant canons of the Old Testament 3 : early Christian writings not included in the New Testament

apoc·ry·phal \-rə-fəl\ *adj* 1 : of or resembling the Apocrypha 2 : not canonical : SPURIOUS (an ~ anecdote) — **apoc·ry·phal·ly** *adv*

apo·gee \'ap-ə-(,)jē\ *n* [fr. *apogee* point at which the moon is farthest from the earth, fr. F *apogée*, fr. NL *apogaeum*, fr. Gk *apogaion*, fr. *apo* away from + *gē, gaia* earth] : the point at which an orbiting object is farthest from the body (as the earth or moon) being orbited

apol·o·get·ic \ə-,päl-ə-'jet-ik\ *adj* : expressing apology — **apol·o·get·i·cal·ly** *adv*

apo·lo·gia \,ap-ə-'lō-j(ē-)ə\ *n* : APOLOGY; *esp* : an argument in support or justification

apol·o·gize \ə-'päl-ə-,jīz\ *vb* : to make an apology : express regret — **apol·o·gist** \-ə-jəst\ *n*

apol·o·gy \ə-'päl-ə-jē\ *n* 1 : a formal justification : DEFENSE 2 : an expression of regret for a discourteous remark or act

ap·o·plexy \'ap-ə-,plek-sē\ *n* : sudden loss of consciousness caused by rupture or obstruction of an artery of the brain — **ap·o·plec·tic** \,ap-ə-'plek-tik\ *adj*

ə abut; ᵉ kitten; ər further; a back; ā bake; ä cot, cart; aù out; ch chin; e less; ē easy; g gift; i trip; ī life; j joke; ŋ sing; ō flow; ò flaw; òi coin; th thin; t͟h this; ü loot; ù foot; y yet; yü few; yù furious; zh vision

aport \ə-'pōrt\ *adv (or adj)* **:** on or toward the left side of a ship

apos·ta·sy \ə-'päs-tə-sē\ *n* **:** a renunciation or abandonment of a former loyalty (as to a religious faith) — **apos·tate** \ə-'päs-ˌtāt, -tət\ *adj or n*

a pos·te·ri·o·ri \ˌ,ä-pō-ˌstir-ē-'ōr-ē\ *adj* **:** characterized by or derived by reasoning from observed facts — **a posteriori** *adv*

apos·tle \ə-'päs-əl\ *n* **1 :** one of the group composed of Jesus' 12 original disciples and Paul **2 :** the first prominent missionary to a region or group **3 :** one who initiates or first advocates a great reform — **apos·tle·ship** \-ˌship\ *n*

ap·os·tol·ic \ˌap-ə-'stäl-ik\ *adj* **1 :** of or relating to an apostle or to the New Testament apostles **2 :** of or relating to a succession of spiritual authority from the apostles **3 :** PAPAL

¹apos·tro·phe \ə-'päs-trə-(ˌ)fē\ *n* **:** the rhetorical addressing of an absent person as if present or of an abstract idea or inanimate object as if capable of understanding (as in "O grave, where is thy victory?")

²apostrophe *n* **:** a punctuation mark ' used esp. to indicate the possessive case or the omission of a letter or figure

apos·tro·phize \ə-'träs-trə-ˌfīz\ *vb* **:** to address as if present or as if capable of understanding

apoth·e·cary \ə-'päth-ə-ˌker-ē\ *n* **:** DRUGGIST

ap·o·thegm \'ap-ə-ˌthem\ *n* **:** APHORISM, MAXIM

apoth·e·o·sis \ə-ˌpäth-ē-'ō-səs, ˌap-ə-'thē-ə-səs\ *n, pl* **-o·ses** \-'ō-ˌsēz, -ə-ˌsēz\ **1 :** DEIFICATION **2 :** the perfect example

ap·pall *also* **ap·pal** \ə-'pól\ *vb* **-palled; -pall·ing :** to overcome with horror **:** DISMAY

ap·pa·nage \'ap-ə-nij\ *n* **1 :** provision (as a grant of land) made by a sovereign or legislative body for dependent members of the royal family **2 :** a rightful adjunct

ap·pa·rat·us \ˌap-ə-'rat-əs, -'rät-\ *n, pl* **-rat·us** *or* **-rat·us·es :** a set of materials or equipment for a particular use **2 :** a complex machine or device **:** MECHANISM **3 :** the organization of a political party or underground movement

¹ap·par·el \ə-'par-əl\ *n* **:** CLOTHING, DRESS

²apparel *vb* **-eled** *or* **-elled; -el·ing** *or* **-el·ling 1 :** CLOTHE, DRESS **2 :** ADORN

ap·par·ent \ə-'par-ənt\ *adj* **1 :** open to view **:** VISIBLE **2 :** EVIDENT, OBVIOUS **3 :** appearing as real or true **:** SEEMING — **ap·par·ent·ly** *adv*

ap·pa·ri·tion \ˌap-ə-'rish-ən\ *n* **:** a supernatural appearance **:** GHOST

ap·peal \ə-'pēl\ *vb* **1 :** to take steps to have (a case) reheard in a higher court **2 :** to plead for help, corroboration, or decision **3 :** to arouse a sympathetic response — **appeal** *n*

ap·pear \ə-'piər\ *vb* **1 :** to become visible **2 :** to come formally before an authority **3 :** SEEM **4 :** to become evident **5 :** to come before the public

ap·pear·ance \ə-'pir-əns\ *n* **1 :** the act of appearing **2 :** outward aspect **:** LOOK **3 :** PHENOMENON

ap·pease \ə-'pēz\ *vb* **1 :** to cause to subside **:** ALLAY **2 :** PACIFY, CONCILIATE; *esp* **:** to buy off by concessions — **ap·pease·ment** *n*

ap·pel·lant \ə-'pel-ənt\ *n* **:** one who appeals esp. from a judicial decision

ap·pel·late \ə-'pel-ət\ *adj* **:** having power to review decisions of a lower court

ap·pel·la·tion \ˌap-ə-'lā-shən\ *n* **:** NAME, DESIGNATION

ap·pel·lee \ˌap-ə-'lē\ *n* **:** one against whom an appeal is taken

ap·pend \ə-'pend\ *vb* **:** to attach esp. as something additional **:** AFFIX

ap·pend·age \ə-'pen-dij\ *n* **:** something appended to a principal or greater thing **syn** accessory, adjunct

ap·pen·dec·to·my \ˌap-ən-'dek-tə-mē\ *n* **:** surgical removal of the intestinal appendix

ap·pen·di·ci·tis \ə-ˌpen-də-'sīt-əs\ *n* **:** inflammation of the intestinal appendix

ap·pen·dix \ə-'pen-diks\ *n, pl* **-dix·es** *or* **-di·ces** \-də-ˌsēz\ **1 :** supplementary matter added at the end of a book **2 :** a small tubular outgrowth from the intestinal cecum

ap·per·tain \ˌap-ər-'tān\ *vb* **:** to belong as a rightful part or privilege

ap·pe·tite \'ap-ə-ˌtīt\ *n* **1 :** natural desire for satisfying some want or need esp. for food **2 :** TASTE, PREFERENCE

ap·pe·tiz·er \'ap-ə-ˌtī-zər\ *n* **:** a food or drink taken just before a meal to stimulate the appetite

ap·pe·tiz·ing \-ˌziŋ\ *adj* **:** tempting to the appetite — **ap·pe·tiz·ing·ly** *adv*

ap·plaud \ə-'plód\ *vb* **:** to show approval esp. by clapping

ap·plause \ə-'plóz\ *n* **:** approval publicly expressed (as by clapping)

ap·ple \'ap-əl\ *n* **:** a rounded fruit with firm white flesh and a seedy core; *also* **:** a tree related to the roses that bears this fruit

ap·ple·jack \-ˌjak\ *n* **:** a liquor distilled from fermented cider

ap·pli·ance \ə-'plī-əns\ *n* **1 :** INSTRUMENT, DEVICE **2 :** a piece of household equipment (as a stove, toaster, or vacuum cleaner) operated by gas or electricity

ap·pli·ca·ble \'ap-li-kə-bəl, ə-'plik-ə-\ *adj* **:** capable of being applied **:** RELEVANT — **ap·pli·ca·bil·i·ty** \ˌap-li-kə-'bil-ət-ē, ə-ˌplik-ə-\ *n*

ap·pli·cant \'ap-li-kənt\ *n* **:** one who applies — **ap·pli·can·cy** \-kən-sē\ *n*

ap·pli·ca·tion \ˌap-lə-'kā-shən\ *n* **1 :** the act of applying **2 :** assiduous attention **3 :** REQUEST; *also* **:** a form used in making a request **4 :** something placed or spread on a surface **5 :** capacity for use

ap·pli·ca·tor \'ap-lə-ˌkāt-ər\ *n* **:** one that applies; *esp* **:** a device for applying a substance (as medicine or polish)

ap·plied \ə-'plīd\ *adj* **:** put to practical use

ap·pli·qué \ˌap-lə-'kā\ *n* **:** a fabric decoration cut out and fastened to a larger piece of material — **appliqué** *vb*

ap·ply \ə-'plī\ *vb* **1 :** to place in contact **:** put or spread on a surface **2 :** to put to practical use **3 :** to employ with close attention **4 :** to submit a request personally or by letter

ap·point \ə-'point\ *vb* **1 :** to fix or set officially ⟨~ a day for trial⟩ **2 :** to name officially (∼ a committee) **8 :** to fit out **: EQUIP**

ap·poin·tee \ə-ˌpȯin-ˈtē, ˌap-ˌȯin-\ n **:** a person appointed

ap·point·ive \ə-ˈpȯint-iv\ adj **:** subject to appointment

ap·point·ment \ə-ˈpȯint-mənt\ n **1 :** the act of appointing **2 :** a nonelective office or position **3 :** an arrangement for a meeting **4** pl **:** FURNISHINGS, EQUIPMENT

ap·por·tion \ə-ˈpōr-shən\ vb **:** to distribute proportionately **: ALLOT —** **ap·por·tion·ment** n

ap·po·site \ˈap-ə-zət\ adj **:** APPROPRIATE, RELEVANT **— ap·po·site·ly** adv **— ap·po·site·ness** n

ap·po·si·tion \ˌap-ə-ˈzish-ən\ n **:** a grammatical construction in which a noun or pronoun is followed by another that explains it (as *the poet* and *Burns* in "a biography of the poet Burns")

ap·pos·i·tive \ə-ˈpäz-ət-iv\ n **:** the second of a pair of nouns or noun equivalents in apposition **— appositive** adj

ap·praise \ə-ˈprāz\ vb **:** to set a value on **— ap·prais·al** \-ˈprā-zəl\ n **— ap·prais·er** n

ap·pre·cia·ble \ə-ˈprē-shə-bəl\ adj **:** large enough to be recognized and measured **— ap·pre·cia·bly** adv

ap·pre·ci·ate \ə-ˈprē-shē-ˌāt\ vb **1 :** to value justly **2 :** to be aware of **3 :** to be grateful for **4 :** to increase in value **— ap·pre·ci·a·tion** \-ˌprē-shē-ˈā-shən\ n

ap·pre·cia·tive \ə-ˈprē-shət-iv, -shē-ˌāt-iv\ adj **:** having or showing appreciation

ap·pre·hend \ˌap-ri-ˈhend\ vb **1 :** ARREST **2 :** to become aware of **3 :** to look forward to with dread **4 :** UNDERSTAND **— ap·pre·hen·sion** \-ˈhen-chən\ n

ap·pre·hen·sive \ˌap-ri-ˈhen-siv\ adj **:** viewing the future with anxiety **— ap·pre·hen·sive·ly** adv **— ap·pre·hen·sive·ness** n

¹ap·pren·tice \ə-ˈprent-əs\ n **1 :** a person learning a craft under a skilled worker **2 :** BEGINNER **— ap·pren·tice·ship** \-ˌship\ n

²apprentice vb **:** to bind or set at work as an apprentice

ap·prise *also* **ap·prize** \ə-ˈprīz\ vb **:** INFORM

ap·proach \ə-ˈprōch\ vb **1 :** to move nearer to **2 :** to take preliminary steps toward **— approach** n **— ap·proach·able** adj

ap·pro·ba·tion \ˌap-rə-ˈbā-shən\ n **:** APPROVAL

¹ap·pro·pri·ate \ə-ˈprō-prē-ˌāt\ vb **1 :** to take possession of **2 :** to set apart for a particular use

²ap·pro·pri·ate \-prē-ət\ adj **:** fitted to a purpose or use **: SUITABLE** **syn** proper, fit, apt **— ap·pro·pri·ate·ly** adv **— ap·pro·pri·ate·ness** n

ap·pro·pri·a·tion \ə-ˌprō-prē-ˈā-shən\ n **:** money set aside by formal action for a specific use

ap·prov·al \ə-ˈprüi-vəl\ n **:** an act of approving **— on approval :** subject to a prospective buyer's acceptance or refusal

ap·prove \ə-ˈprüv\ vb **1 :** to have or

express a favorable opinion of **2 :** to accept as satisfactory **: RATIFY**

¹ap·prox·i·mate \ə-ˈpräk-sə-mət\ adj **:** nearly correct or exact **— ap·prox·i·mate·ly** adv

²ap·prox·i·mate \-sə-ˌmāt\ vb **:** to come near **:** APPROACH **— ap·prox·i·ma·tion** \ə-ˌpräk-sə-ˈmā-shən\ n

ap·pur·te·nance \ə-ˈpərt-(ə-)nəns\ n **:** something that belongs to or goes with another thing **syn** accessory, adjunct, appendage **— ap·pur·te·nant** adj

apri·cot \ˈap-rə-ˌkät, ˈā-prə-\ n **:** an oval orange-colored fruit resembling the related peach in flavor; *also* **:** the tree bearing it

April \ˈā-prəl\ n **:** the 4th month of the year having 30 days

a pri·o·ri \ˌä-prē-ˈōr-ē\ adj **1 :** characterized by or derived by reasoning from self-evident propositions **2 :** independent of experience **— a priori** adv

apron \ˈā-prən, -pərn\ n [ME; alter. of *napron* (the phrase *a napron* being understood as *an apron*), fr. MF *naperon*, dim. of *nape* cloth, modif. of L *mappa* napkin] **1 :** a garment tied over the front of the body to protect the clothes **2 :** a paved area for parking or handling airplanes

¹ap·ro·pos \ˌap-rə-ˈpō, ˈap-rə-ˌpō\ adv **1 :** OPPORTUNELY **2 :** SUITABLY

²apropos adj **:** being to the point **:** PERTINENT

apropos of prep **:** with regard to **:** CONCERNING

apse \ˈaps\ n **:** a projecting usu. semicircular and vaulted part of a building (as a church)

apt \ˈapt\ adj **1 :** well adapted **:** SUITABLE **2 :** having an habitual tendency **:** LIKELY **3 :** quick to learn **— apt·ly** adv **— apt·ness** n

ap·ti·tude \ˈap-tə-ˌt(y)üd\ n **1 :** capacity for learning **2 :** natural ability **:** TALENT **3 :** APPROPRIATENESS

aq·ua·cade \ˈak-wə-ˌkād, ˈäk-\ n **:** an elaborate water spectacle consisting of exhibitions of swimming, diving, and acrobatics accompanied by music

aq·ua·lung \ˈak-wə-ˌləŋ, ˈäk-\ n **:** an underwater breathing device

aq·ua·ma·rine \ˌak-wə-mə-ˈrēn, ˌäk-\ n **:** a bluish green gem

aq·ua·plane \ˈak-wə-ˌplān, ˈäk-\ n **:** a board towed behind a speeding motorboat and ridden by a person standing on it **— aquaplane** vb

aquar·i·um \ə-ˈkwer-ē-əm\ n, pl **-i·ums** or **-ia** \-ē-ə\ **1 :** a container in which living aquatic animals and plants are kept **2 :** a place where aquatic animals and plants are kept and shown

aquat·ic \ə-ˈkwät-ik, -ˈkwat-\ adj **1 :** growing or living in or frequenting water **2 :** performed in or on water

aq·ue·duct \ˈak-wə-ˌdəkt\ n **1 :** a conduit for carrying running water **2 :** a structure carrying a canal over a river or hollow **3 :** a passage in a bodily part

aque·ous \ˈā-kwē-əs, ˈak-wē-\ adj **1 :** WATERY **2 :** made of, by, or with water

aqu·i·line \ˈak-wə-ˌlīn, -lən\ adj **1 :** of or resembling an eagle **2 :** hooked like an eagle's beak (an ∼ nose)

-ar \ər\ adj suffix **:** of or relating to

(molecu*lar*) : being (spectacu*lar*) : resembling (orac*ular*)

Ar·ab \'ar-əb\ *n* **1** : a member of a Semitic people of the Arabian peninsula **2** : a member of an Arabic-speaking people — **Arab** *adj* — **Ara·bi·an** \ə-'rā-bē-ən\ *adj or n*

ar·a·besque \,ar-ə-'besk\ *n* : a design of interlacing lines forming figures of flowers, foliage, and sometimes animals

1Ar·a·bic \'ar-ə-bik\ *adj* : of or relating to Arabia, the Arabs, or Arabic

2Arabic *n* : a Semitic language of southwest Asia and north Africa

arabic numeral *n, often cap A* : one of the number symbols 1, 2, 3, 4, 5, 6, 7, 8, 9, and 0

ar·a·ble \'ar-ə-bəl\ *adj* : fit for or cultivated by plowing : suitable for crops

ar·ba·lest *or* **ar·ba·list** \'är-bə-ləst\ : a medieval crossbow with a steel bow

ar·bi·ter \'är-bət-ər\ *n* : one having power to decide : JUDGE

ar·bit·ra·ment \är-'bit-rə-mənt\ *n* **1** : the act of deciding a dispute **2** : the judgment given by an arbitrator

ar·bi·trary \'är-bə-,trer-ē\ *adj* **1** : determined by will or caprice : selected at random **2** : AUTOCRATIC, DESPOTIC — **ar·bi·trar·i·ly** \,är-bə-'trer-ə-lē\ *adv* — **ar·bi·trar·i·ness** \'är-bə-,trer-ē-nəs\ *n*

ar·bi·trate \'är-bə-,trāt\ *vb* **1** : to act as arbitrator **2** : to act on as arbitrator **3** : to submit for decision to an arbitrator — **ar·bi·tra·tion** \,är-bə-'trā-shən\ *n*

ar·bi·tra·tor \'är-bə-,trāt-ər\ *n* : one chosen to settle differences between two parties in a controversy

ar·bor \'är-bər\ *n* : a bower formed of or covered with vines or branches

ar·bo·re·al \är-'bōr-ē-əl\ *adj* **1** : of, relating to, or resembling a tree **2** : living in trees

ar·bo·re·tum \,är-bə-'rēt-əm\ *n, pl* -tums *or* -ta \-'rēt-ə\ : a place where trees and plants are grown for scientific and educational purposes

ar·bor·vi·tae \,är-bər-'vīt-ē\ *n* : any of various scale-leaved evergreen trees related to the pines

ar·bu·tus \är-'byüt-əs\ *n* : a trailing spring-blossoming plant with fragrant pink or white flowers; *also* : its flower

arc \'ärk\ *n* **1** : a part of a curved line (as of a circle) **2** : a sustained luminous discharge of electricity (as between two electrodes)

ar·cade \är-'kād\ *n* **1** : a row of arches with their supporting columns **2** : an arched or covered passageway; *esp* : one lined with shops

ar·cane \är-'kān\ *adj* : SECRET, MYSTERIOUS

1arch \'ärch\ *n* **1** : a curved structure spanning an opening (as a door or window) **2** : something resembling an arch **3** : ARCHWAY

2arch *vb* **1** : to cover with an arch **2** : to form or bend into an arch

3arch *adj* **1** : CHIEF, EMINENT **2** : ROGUISH, MISCHIEVOUS — **arch·ly** *adv* — **arch·ness** *n*

ar·chae·ol·o·gy \,är-kē-'äl-ə-jē\ *n* : the study of past human life as revealed by relics left by ancient peoples — **ar·chae·o·log·i·cal** \-kē-ə-'läj-i-kəl\ *adj* — **ar·chae·ol·o·gist** \-kē-'äl-ə-jəst\ *n*

ar·cha·ic \är-'kā-ik\ *adj* **1** : belonging to an earlier time : ANTIQUATED (~ customs) **2** : having the characteristics

of the language of the past and surviving chiefly in specialized uses (~ words) — **ar·cha·i·cal·ly** *adv*

arch·an·gel \'ärk-,ān-jəl\ *n* : an angel of high rank

arch·bish·op \ärch-'bish-əp\ *n* : a bishop of high rank — **arch·bish·op·ric** \-'bish-ə-(,)prik\ *n*

arch·dea·con \-'dē-kən\ *n* **1** : an ecclesiastical dignitary usu. ranking below a bishop **2** : an Anglican priest who often supervises the missionary work of a diocese

arch·di·o·cese \-'dī-ə-səs, -,sēz\ *n* : the diocese of an archbishop

arch·duke \ärch-'d(y)ük\ *n* : a prince of the imperial family of Austria

arch·en·e·my \ärch-'en-ə-mē\ *n* : a principal enemy

ar·chery \'ärch-(ə-)rē\ *n* : the art or practice of shooting with bow and arrows — **ar·cher** \'är-chər\ *n*

ar·che·type \'är-ki-,tīp\ *n* : the original pattern or model of all things of the same type

arch·fiend \'ärch-'fēnd\ *n* : a chief fiend; *esp* : SATAN

ar·chi·epis·co·pal \,är-kē-ə-'pis-kə-pəl\ *adj* : of or relating to an archbishop

ar·chi·man·drite \,är-kə-'man-,drīt\ *n* : a church dignitary in an Eastern church ranking below a bishop

ar·chi·pel·a·go \,är-kə-'pel-ə-,gō, ,är-chə-\ *n, pl* -goes *or* -gos **1** : a sea dotted with islands **2** : a group of islands

ar·chi·tect \'är-kə-,tekt\ *n* : a person who plans buildings and oversees their construction

ar·chi·tec·ton·ic \,är-kə-,tek-'tän-ik\ *adj* : of, relating to, or according with the principles of architecture

ar·chi·tec·ton·ics \-iks\ *n sing or pl* : structural design

ar·chi·tec·ture \'är-kə-,tek-chər\ *n* **1** : the art or science of planning and building structures **2** : method or style of building — **ar·chi·tec·tur·al** \,är-kə-'tek-chə-rəl, -'tek-shrəl\ *adj*

ar·chi·trave \'är-kə-,trāv\ *n* : the supporting horizontal member just above the columns in a building in the classical style of architecture

ar·chive \'är-,kīv\ *n* : a place for keeping public records; *also* : public records — usu. used in pl.

ar·chi·vist \'är-kə-vəst, -,kī-\ *n* : a person in charge of archives

ar·chon \'är-,kän, -kən\ *n* : a chief magistrate of ancient Athens

arch·way \'ärch-,wā\ *n* : a passageway under an arch; *also* : an arch over a passage

1arc·tic \'är(k)t-ik\ *adj* [Gk *arktikos*, fr. *arktos* bear, Ursa Major] **1** *often cap* : of or relating to the north pole or the region near it **2** : FRIGID

2arctic *n* : a rubber overshoe reaching to the ankle or above

arctic circle *n, often cap A & C* : a circle of the earth parallel to its equator approximately 23°27′ from the north pole

-ard \ərd\ *also* **-art** \ərt\ *n suffix* : one that is characterized by performing some action, possessing some quality, or being associated with some thing esp. conspicuously or excessively (bragg*ard*) (dull*ard*) : a large one of its kind

ar·dent \'ärd-ᵊnt\ *adj* **1** : characterized by warmth of feeling : PASSIONATE

2 : FIERY, HOT   3 : GLOWING — **ar·dent·ly** adv

ar·dor \'ärd-ər\ n 1 : warmth of feeling : ZEAL   2 : burning heat

ar·du·ous \'är-jə-wəs\ adj : DIFFICULT, LABORIOUS — **ar·du·ous·ly** adv — **ar·du·ous·ness** n

are pres 2d sing or pres pl of BE

ar·ea \'ar-ē-ə\ n 1 : a flat surface or space   2 : the amount of surface included (as within the lines of a geometric figure)   3 : REGION   4 : range or extent of some thing or concept : FIELD ⟨~s of experience⟩ ⟨~ of foreign policy⟩

ar·ea·way \-,wā\ n : a sunken space for giving access, air, and light to a basement

are·na \ə-'rē-nə\ n 1 : an enclosed area used for public entertainment   2 : a sphere of activity

ar·gent \'är-jənt\ adj : of or resembling silver : SILVERY

Ar·gen·tine \'är-jən-,tēn\ n : a native or inhabitant of Argentina — **Argentine** adj

ar·gon \'är-,gän\ n : a colorless odorless gaseous chemical element found in the air and used for filling electric light bulbs

ar·go·sy \'är-gə-sē\ n 1 : a large ship   2 : FLEET

ar·got \'är-gət, -,gō\ n : the language of a particular group or class esp. of the underworld

ar·gu·able \'är-gyə-wə-bəl\ adj : open to argument, dispute, or question

ar·gue \'är-gyü\ vb 1 : to give reasons for or against something   2 : to contend in words : DISPUTE   3 : DEBATE   4 : to persuade by giving reasons

ar·gu·ment \-gyə-mənt\ n 1 : a reason offered in proof   2 : discourse intended to persuade   3 : DISCUSSION, DEBATE

ar·gu·men·ta·tion \,är-gyə-mən-'tā-shən\ n : the art of formal discussion

ar·gu·men·ta·tive \,är-gyə-'ment-ət-iv\ adj : inclined to argue

ar·gyle \'är-,gīl\ n : a geometric knitting pattern of varicolored diamonds on a single background color; also : a sock knit in this pattern

aria \'är-ē-ə\ n : an accompanied elaborate vocal solo forming part of a larger work

ar·id \'ar-əd\ adj 1 : DRY, BARREN   2 : having insufficient rainfall to support agriculture — **arid·i·ty** \ə-'rid-ət-ē\ n

aright \ə-'rīt\ adv : RIGHTLY, CORRECTLY

arise \ə-'rīz\ vb **arose** \-'rōz\ **aris·en** \-'riz-ᵊn\ **aris·ing** \-'rī-ziŋ\ 1 : to get up   2 : ORIGINATE   3 : ASCEND syn rise, mount, spring, issue

ar·is·toc·ra·cy \,ar-ə-'stäk-rə-sē\ n 1 : government by a noble or privileged class; also : a state so governed   2 : the governing class of an aristocracy   3 : UPPER CLASS — **aris·to·crat** \ə-'ris-tə-,krat\ n — **aris·to·crat·ic** \ə-,ris-tə-'krat-ik\ adj

arith·me·tic \ə-'rith-mə-,tik\ n : mathematics that deals with computations with numbers — **ar·ith·met·i·cal** \,ar-ith-'met-i-kəl\ adj — **arith·me·ti·cian** \ə-,rith-mə-'tish-ən\ n

ark \'ärk\ n : a boat held to resemble that of Noah at the time of the Deluge

2 : the sacred chest in which the ancient Hebrews kept the tablets of the Law

¹**arm** \'ärm\ n 1 : a human upper limb   2 : something resembling or corresponding to the human upper limb   3 : POWER, MIGHT ⟨the ~ of the law⟩

²**arm** vb : to furnish or equip with weapons

³**arm** n 1 : WEAPON   2 : a branch of the military forces   3 pl : the hereditary heraldic devices of a family

ar·ma·da \är-'mäd-ə, -'mād-\ n : a fleet of armed ships

ar·ma·dil·lo \,är-mə-'dil-ō\ n : a small burrowing mammal with head and body protected by an armor of bony plates

Ar·ma·ged·don \,är-mə-'ged-ᵊn\ n : a final conclusive battle between the forces of good and evil; also : the site or time of this

ar·ma·ment \'är-mə-mənt\ n 1 : military strength   2 : supply of materials for war   3 : the process of preparing for war

ar·ma·ture \'är-mə-chər, -,chu̇r\ n 1 : protective covering   2 : the part including the conductors in an electric generator or motor in which the current is induced; also : the movable part in an electromagnetic device (as an electric bell or a loudspeaker)

arm·chair \'ärm-,cheər\ n : a chair with supports for the arms

armed forces n pl : the combined military, naval, and air forces of a nation

arm·hole \'ärm-,hōl\ n : an opening for the arm in a garment

ar·mi·stice \'är-mə-stəs\ n : temporary suspension of hostilities by mutual agreement : TRUCE

arm·let \'ärm-lət\ n : a band worn around the upper arm

ar·mor \'är-mər\ n : protective covering — **ar·mored** \-mərd\ adj

ar·mor·er \-mər-ər\ n 1 : one that makes arms and armor   2 : one that services firearms

ar·mo·ri·al \är-'mōr-ē-əl\ adj : of or bearing heraldic arms

ar·mo·ry \'ärm-(ə-)rē\ n 1 : a place where arms are stored   2 : a factory where arms are made

arm·pit \'ärm-,pit\ n : the hollow under the junction of the arm and shoulder

arm·rest \-,rest\ n : a support for the arm

ar·my \'är-mē\ n 1 : a body of men organized for war   2 often cap : the complete military organization of a country for land warfare   3 : a great number   4 : a body of persons organized to advance a cause

ar·ni·ca \'är-ni-kə\ n 1 : any of several herbs related to the daisies   2 : a soothing preparation of arnica flowers or roots used on bruises and sprains

aro·ma \ə-'rō-mə\ n : a usu. pleasing odor : FRAGRANCE — **ar·o·mat·ic** \,ar-ə-'mat-ik\ adj

¹**around** \ə-'rȧund\ adv 1 : in or along a circuit   2 : on all sides   3 : NEARBY   4 : in various places   5 : in an opposite direction

²**around** prep 1 : ENVELOPING ⟨trees ~ the house⟩   2 : along the circuit of ⟨go ~ the world⟩   3 : to or on the other

ə abut; ᵊ kitten; ər further; a back; ā bake; ä cot, cart; au̇ out; ch chin; e less; ē easy; g gift; i trip; ī life; j joke; ŋ sing; ō flow; ȯ flaw; ȯi coin; th thin; t͟h this; ü loot; u̇ foot; y yet; yü few; yu̇ furious; zh vision

side of ⟨~ the corner⟩ **4 :** NEAR ⟨stayed right ~ home⟩

arouse \ə-'rauz\ vb **1 :** to awaken from sleep **2 :** to stir up **:** rouse to action — **arous·al** \-'rau-zəl\ n

ar·peg·gio \är-'pej-ō, -ē-ō\ n **:** a chord whose notes are performed in succession and not simultaneously

ar·raign \ə-'rān\ vb **1 :** to call before a court to answer to an indictment **2 :** to accuse of wrong or imperfection — **ar·raign·ment** n

ar·range \ə-'rānj\ vb **1 :** to put in order **2 :** to come to an agreement about **:** SETTLE **3 :** to adapt (a musical composition) to voices or instruments other than those for which it was orig. written — **ar·range·ment** n

ar·rant \'ar-ənt\ adj **1 :** THOROUGHGOING **2 :** notoriously bad

ar·ras \'ar-əs\ n, pl **arras** **1 :** TAPESTRY **2 :** a wall hanging or screen of tapestry

¹**ar·ray** \ə-'rā\ vb **1 :** to arrange in order **2 :** to dress esp. in splendid attire

²**array** n **1 :** a regular arrangement **2 :** rich apparel **3 :** an imposing group

ar·rears \ə-'riərz\ n pl **1 :** a state of being behind in the discharge of obligations (three months in ~) **2 :** overdue debts

¹**ar·rest** \ə-'rest\ vb **1 :** STOP, CHECK **2 :** to take into legal custody

²**arrest** n **:** the act of taking into custody by legal authority

ar·ri·ere·pen·sée \,ar-ē-,er-pän-'sā\ n **:** a mental reservation

ar·riv·al \ə-'rī-vəl\ n **1 :** the act of arriving **2 :** one that arrives

ar·rive \-'rīv\ vb **1 :** to reach a destination **2 :** to be near or at hand ⟨the time to go finally *arrived*⟩ **:** COME **3 :** to attain success

ar·ro·gant \'ar-ə-gənt\ adj **:** offensively exaggerating one's own importance — **ar·ro·gance** \-gəns\ n — **ar·rogant·ly** adv

ar·ro·gate \'ar-ə-,gāt\ vb **:** to claim or seize without justification as one's right

ar·row \'ar-ō\ n **1 :** a missile shot from a bow and usu. having a slender shaft, a pointed head, and feathers at the butt **2 :** a pointed mark used to indicate direction

ar·row·head \-,hed\ n **:** the pointed end of an arrow

ar·row·root \-,rüt, -,rut\ n **:** an edible starch from the roots of a tropical American plant

ar·royo \ə-'rói-ə, -'rói-ō\ n **1 :** WATERCOURSE **2 :** a water-carved gully or channel

ar·se·nal \'ärs-nəl, -ᵊn-əl\ n **1 :** a place for making and storing arms and military equipment **2 :** STORE, REPERTORY

ar·se·nic \'ärs-nik, -ᵊn-ik\ n **1 :** a solid brittle poisonous chemical element of grayish color and metallic luster whose compounds are used as insecticides and in drug preparations **2 :** a very poisonous oxygen compound of arsenic used in making glass and in-secticides — **ar·sen·i·cal** \är-'sen-i-kəl\ adj or n — **ar·se·ni·ous** \är-'sē-nē-əs\ adj

ar·son \'ärs-ᵊn\ n **:** the malicious burning of property

art \'ärt\ n **1 :** skill acquired by ex-

perience or study **:** KNACK **2 :** a branch of learning; esp **:** one of the humanities **3 :** systematic use of knowledge or skill in making or doing things **4 :** the use of skill and imagination in the production of things of beauty; also **:** works so produced **5 :** ARTFULNESS

-art — see **-ARD**

ar·te·ri·al \är-'tir-ē-əl\ n **:** a through street or arterial highway

ar·te·rio·scle·ro·sis \är-,tir-ē-ō-sklə-'rō-səs\ n **:** a chronic disease in which arterial walls are abnormally thickened and hardened — **ar·te·rio·scle·rot·ic** \-'rät-ik\ adj or n

ar·te·ry \'ärt-ə-rē\ n **1 :** one of the tubular vessels that carry the blood from the heart **2 :** a main channel of communication; esp **:** a principal road with through-traffic facilities — **ar·te·ri·al** \är-'tir-ē-əl\ adj

ar·te·sian well \är-,tē-zhən-\ n **1 :** a bored well gushing water like a fountain **2 :** a relatively deep-bored well

art·ful \'ärt-fəl\ adj **1 :** INGENIOUS **2 :** CRAFTY — **art·ful·ly** adv — **art·ful·ness** n

ar·thri·tis \är-'thrīt-əs\ n **:** inflammation of the joints — **ar·thrit·ic** \-'thrit-ik\ adj or n

ar·thro·pod \'är-thrə-,päd\ n **:** any of a major group of invertebrate animals comprising those (as insects, spiders, or crabs) with segmented bodies and jointed limbs — **arthropod** adj

ar·ti·choke \'ärt-ə-,chōk\ n **:** a tall herb related to the daisies; also **:** its edible flower head

ar·ti·cle \'ärt-i-kəl\ n **1 :** a distinct part of a written document **2 :** a non-fictional prose composition forming an independent part of a publication **3 :** a word (as *an, the*) used with a noun to limit or give definiteness to its application **4 :** a member of a class of things; esp **:** COMMODITY

ar·tic·u·lar \är-'tik-yə-lər\ adj **:** of or relating to a joint

¹**ar·tic·u·late** \är-'tik-yə-lət\ adj **1 :** divided into meaningful parts **:** INTELLIGIBLE **2 :** able to speak; also **:** expressing oneself readily and effectively **3 :** JOINTED — **ar·tic·u·late·ly** adv — **ar·tic·u·late·ness** n

²**ar·tic·u·late** \-,lāt\ vb **1 :** to utter distinctly **2 :** to unite by joints — **ar·tic·u·la·tion** \,tik-yə-'lā-shən\ n

ar·ti·fact or **ar·te·fact** \'ärt-ə-,fakt\ n **:** a usu. simple object (as a tool or ornament) showing human workmanship or modification

ar·ti·fice \'ärt-ə-fəs\ n **1 :** TRICK; also **:** TRICKERY **2 :** an ingenious device; also **:** INGENUITY

ar·tif·i·cer \är-'tif-ə-sər\ n **:** a skilled workman

ar·ti·fi·cial \,ärt-ə-'fish-əl\ adj **1 :** produced by art rather than nature; also **:** made by man to imitate nature **2 :** not genuine **:** FEIGNED — **ar·ti·fi·ci·al·i·ty** \-,fish-ē-'al-ət-ē\ n — **ar·ti·fi·cial·ly** \-'fish-(ə-)lē\ adv — **ar·ti·fi·cial·ness** \-'fish-əl-nəs\ n

ar·til·lery \är-'til-(ə-)rē\ n **1 :** large-caliber mounted firearms **:** ORDNANCE **2 :** a branch of the army armed with artillery — **ar·til·ler·ist** \-rəst\ n

ar·ti·san \'ärt-ə-zən\ n **:** a skilled manual workman

art·ist \'ärt-əst\ n **1 :** one who practices an art; esp **:** one who creates objects of beauty **2 :** a skilled public performer

ar·tiste \är-'tēst\ n **:** a skilled public performer

ar·tis·tic \är-'tis-tik\ adj **:** showing taste and skill — **ar·tis·ti·cal·ly** adv

ar·tist·ry \'ärt-ə-strē\ n **:** artistic quality or ability

art·less \'ärt-ləs\ adj **1 :** lacking art or skill **2 :** free from artificiality **:** NATURAL **3 :** free from guile **:** SINCERE — **art·less·ly** adv — **art·less·ness** n

arty \'ärt-ē\ adj **:** showily imitative of art **2 :** pretentiously artistic — **art·i·ly** adv — **art·i·ness** n

ar·um \'ar-əm\ n **:** any of a genus of plants with flowers in a fleshy enclosed spike including many grown for their showy foliage

1-ary \,er-ē\ n suffix, pl **-ar·ies :** thing or person belonging to or connected with ⟨function*ary*⟩

2-ary adj suffix **:** of, relating to, or connected with ⟨budget*ary*⟩

Ar·y·an \'ar-ē-ən\ adj **1 :** INDO-EURO-PEAN **2 :** NORDIC **3 :** GENTILE — **Aryan** n

1as \əz, (,)az\ conj **1 :** in the same amount or degree in which ⟨green ~ grass⟩ **2 :** the same way that ⟨farmed ~ his father before him had farmed⟩ **3 :** WHILE, WHEN ⟨spoke to me ~ I was leaving⟩ **4 :** THOUGH ⟨improbable ~ it seems, it's true⟩ **5 :** SINCE, BE-CAUSE ⟨~ I'm not wanted, I'll leave⟩ **6 :** that the result is ⟨so guilty ~ to leave no doubt⟩

2as adv **1 :** to the same degree or amount **:** EQUALLY ⟨~ green as grass⟩ **2 :** for instance ⟨various trees, ~ oak or pine⟩ **3 :** when considered in a specified relation ⟨my opinion ~ distinguished from his⟩

3as pron **1 :** THAT — used after *same* or *such* ⟨it's the same price ~ before⟩ **2 :** a fact that ⟨he is rich, ~ everyone knows⟩

4as prep **:** in the capacity or character of ⟨this will serve ~ a substitute⟩

as·a·fet·i·da or **as·a·foe·ti·da** \,as-ə-'fit-əd-ē, -'fet-əd-ə\ n **:** an ill-smelling plant gum formerly used in medicine

as·bes·tos also **as·bes·tus** \as-'bes-təs, az-\ n **:** a nonburning grayish mineral that occurs in fibrous form and is used as a fireproof material

as·cend \ə-'send\ vb **1 :** to move upward **:** MOUNT, CLIMB **2 :** to succeed to **:** OCCUPY ⟨he ~ed the throne⟩

as·cen·dan·cy or **as·cen·den·cy** \ə-'sen-dən-sē\ n **:** controlling influence **:** DOMI-NATION

1as·cen·dant or **as·cen·dent** \ə-'sen-dənt\ n **:** a position of dominant power ⟨radicals were in the ~⟩

2ascendant or **ascendent** adj **1 :** moving upward **:** DOMINANT

as·cen·sion \ə-'sen-chən\ n **1 :** the act of ascending **2** cap **:** the ascending of Christ into heaven commemorated as **Ascension Day** on the Thursday 40 days after Easter

as·cent \ə-'sent\ n **1 :** the act of mounting upward **:** CLIMB **2 :** degree of upward slope

as·cer·tain \,as-ər-'tān\ vb **:** to find out **:** learn by inquiry — **as·cer·tain·able** adj

as·cet·ic \ə-'set-ik\ adj **:** practicing self-denial esp. for religious reasons **:** AUS-TERE — **ascetic** n — **as·cet·i·cism**

ascor·bic acid \ə-,skor-bik-\ n **:** VITA-MIN C

as·cot \'as-kət, -,kät\ n **:** a broad neck scarf that is looped under the chin and sometimes pinned

as·cribe \ə-'skrīb\ vb **:** to refer to a supposed cause, source, or author **:** ATTRIBUTE — **as·crib·able** adj — **as·crip·tion** \-'skrip-shən\ n

asep·tic \ā-'sep-tik\ adj **:** free or freed from disease-causing germs

asex·u·al \ā-'sek-sh(ə-w)əl\ adj **:** lack-ing sex **:** involving no sexual action ⟨an ~ spore⟩

as for prep **:** with regard to **:** CONCERN-ING ⟨*as for* your other request, you had better take it up with the manager⟩

1ash \'ash\ n **:** a tree related to the olives; also **:** its tough elastic wood

2ash n **1 :** the solid matter left when material is burned **2 :** fine mineral particles from a volcano **3** pl **:** the re-mains of the dead human body

ashamed \ə-'shāmd\ adj **1 :** feeling shame **2 :** restrained by anticipation of shame ⟨~ to say anything⟩ — **asham-ed·ly** \-'shā-məd-lē\ adv

ash·en \'ash-ən\ adj **1 :** of or re-sembling ashes; esp **:** ash-colored **2 :** deadly pale

ash·lar \'ash-lər\ n **:** hewn or squared stone; **:** masonry of such stone

ashore \ə-'shōr\ adv (or adj) **:** on or to the shore

Ash Wednesday n **:** the 1st day of Lent

ashy \'ash-ē\ adj **:** ASHEN

Asian \'ā-zhən, -shən\ n **:** a native or inhabitant of Asia — **Asian** adj

1aside \ə-'sīd\ adv **1 :** to or toward the side **2 :** out of the way **:** AWAY

2aside n **:** an actor's words heard by the audience but supposedly not by other characters on stage

aside from prep **1 :** BESIDES ⟨*aside from* being pretty, she's intelligent⟩ **2 :** with the exception of **:** EXCLUDING ⟨*aside from* one D his grades have been ex-cellent⟩

as if conj **1 :** as it would be if ⟨it's as if nothing had changed⟩ **2 :** as one would if ⟨he acts *as if* he'd never been away⟩ **3 :** THAT ⟨it seems *as if* nothing ever happens around here⟩

as·i·nine \'as-əⁿ,īn\ adj **:** STUPID, FOOLISH — **as·i·nin·i·ty** \,as-əⁿ-'in-ət-ē\ n

ask \'ask\ vb **1 :** to call on for an answer **2 :** UTTER ⟨~ a question⟩ **3 :** to make a request of ⟨~ him for help⟩ **4 :** to make a request for ⟨~ help of him⟩ **5 :** to set as a price **6 :** INVITE ⟨~ them to a party⟩

askance \ə-'skans\ adv **1 :** with a side glance **2 :** with distrust

askew \ə-'skyü\ adv (or adj) **:** out of line **:** AWRY

1aslant \ə-'slant\ adv **:** in a slanting direction

2aslant prep **:** over or across in a slanting direction

asleep \ə-'slēp\ adv (or adj) **1 :** in or into a state of sleep **2 :** DEAD **3 :** NUMBED **4 :** INACTIVE

as long as conj **1 :** on condition that

ə abut; ᵊ kitten; ər further; a back; ā bake; ä cot, cart; aù out; ch chin; e less; ē easy; g gift; i trip; ī life; j joke; ŋ sing; ō flow; ò flaw; òi coin; th thin; t̲h̲ this; ü loot; ù foot; y yet; yü few; yù furious; zh vision

⟨can do as they like *as long as* they have a B average⟩ **2** : inasmuch as : SINCE ⟨*as long as* you're up, turn on the light⟩

as of *prep* : AT, DURING, FROM, ON ⟨takes effect *as of* July 1⟩

asp \'asp\ *n* : a small poisonous African snake

as·par·a·gus \ə-'spar-ə-gəs\ *n* : a tall perennial herb related to the lilies; *also* : its edible young stalks

as·pect \'as-,pekt\ *n* **1** : a position facing a particular direction **2** : AP-PEARANCE, LOOK **3** : PHASE

as·pen \'as-pən\ *n* : any of several poplars with leaves that flutter in the slightest breeze

as·per·i·ty \a-'sper-ət-ē, ə-\ *n* **1** : ROUGHNESS **2** : harshness of temper

as·per·sion \ə-'spər-zhən\ *n* : the act of calumniating; *also* : a calumnious re-mark

¹**as·phalt** \'as-,fȯlt\ *n* : a dark solid or somewhat plastic substance that is found in natural beds or obtained as a residue in petroleum or coal-tar refining and is used in paving streets, in roofing houses, and in paints

²**asphalt** *vb* : to cover or impregnate with asphalt

as·pho·del \'as-fə-,del\ *n* : any of several Old World herbs (as daffodil or narcissus) related to the lilies

as·phyx·i·ate \as-'fik-sē-,āt\ *vb* : SUFFO-CATE — **as·phyx·i·a·tion** \-,fik-sē-'ā-shən\ *n*

as·pic \'as-pik\ *n* : a savory meat jelly

as·pi·rant \'as-p(ə-)rənt, ə-'spī-rənt\ *n* : one who aspires   syn candidate, applicant

as·pi·ra·tion \,as-pə-'rā-shən\ *n* : a strong desire to achieve something noble; *also* : an object of this desire

as·pire \ə-'spī(ə)r\ *vb* **1** : to have a noble desire or ambition **2** : to rise aloft

as·pi·rin \'as-p(ə-)rən\ *n* : a white crystalline drug used to relieve pain and fever

as regards *or* **as respects** *prep* : in re-gard to : with respect to

ass \'as\ *n* **1** : a long-eared animal smaller than the related horse : DONKEY **2** : a stupid person

as·sail \ə-'sāl\ *vb* : to attack violently — **as·sail·able** *adj* — **as·sail·ant** \-'sā-lənt\ *n*

as·sas·sin \ə-'sas-ᵊn\ *n* [Ar *hashshāshīn* members of a medieval Muslim order who committed murder under the in-fluence of hashish, fr. *hashīsh* hashish] : a murderer esp. for hire or fanatical reasons

as·sas·si·nate \-ᵊn-,āt\ *vb* : to murder by sudden or secret attack — **as·sas·si·na·tion** \-,sas-ᵊn-'ā-shən\ *n*

as·sault \ə-'sȯlt\ *n* **1** : a violent attack **2** : an unlawful attempt or offer to do hurt to another — **assault** *vb*

¹**as·say** \a-'sā, 'as-,ā\ *n* **1** : TRY, ATTEMPT **2** : to subject (as an ore or drug) to an assay **3** : to make a critical estimate of **4** : to prove to be of a particular nature by means of an assay

²**as·say** \'as-,ā, a-'sā\ *n* **1** : a test (as of gold) to determine characteristics (as weight or quality) **2** : analysis (as of an ore or drug) to determine presence of one or more ingredients

as·sem·blage \ə-'sem-blij\ *n* **1** : a collection of persons or things : GATHER-ING **2** : the act of assembling

as·sem·ble \ə-'sem-bəl\ *vb* **1** : to collect into one place : CONGREGATE **2** : to fit together the parts of **3** : to meet together : CONVENE

as·sem·bly \ə-'sem-blē\ *n* **1** : a gather-ing of persons : MEETING **2** *cap* : a legislative body; *esp* : the lower house of a legislature **3** : a signal for troops to assemble **4** : the fitting together of parts (as of a machine)

as·sem·bly·man \-mən\ *n* : a member of a legislative assembly

as·sent \ə-'sent\ *vb* **1** : CONSENT **2** : AGREE, CONCUR — **assent** *n*

as·sert \ə-'sərt\ *vb* **1** : to state posi-tively **2** : to maintain against opposi-tion : DEFEND   syn declare, affirm, pro-test,   avow,   claim — **as·ser·tive** \-'sərt-iv\ *adj* — **as·sert·ive·ness** *n*

as·ser·tion \ə-'sər-shən\ *n* : a positive statement

as·sess \ə-'ses\ *vb* **1** : to fix the rate or amount of **2** : to impose (as a tax) at a specified rate **3** : to evaluate for taxa-tion — **as·sess·ment** *n* — **as·ses·sor** *n*

as·set \'as-,et\ *n* **1** *pl* : the entire prop-erty of a person or company that may be used to pay debts **2** : ADVANTAGE, RESOURCE

as·sev·er·ate \ə-'sev-ə-,rāt\ *vb* : to assert earnestly — **as·sev·er·a·tion** \-,sev-ə-'rā-shən\ *n*

as·sid·u·ous \ə-'sij-ə-wəs\ *adj* : steadily attentive : DILIGENT — **as·si·du·i·ty** \,as-ə-'d(y)ü-ət-ē\ *n* — **as·sid·u·ous·ly** \ə-'sij-ə-wəs-lē\ *adv* — **as·sid·u·ous·ness** *n*

as·sign \ə-'sīn\ *vb* **1** : to transfer (property) to another **2** : to appoint to a duty **3** : PRESCRIBE ⟨~ a lesson⟩ **4** : FIX, SPECIFY ⟨~ a limit⟩ **5** : ASCRIBE ⟨~ a reason⟩ — **as·sign·able** *adj*

as·sig·na·tion \,as-ig-'nā-shən\ *n* : an appointment for a lovers' meeting; *also* : the resulting meeting

as·sign·ment \ə-'sīn-mənt\ *n* **1** : the act of assigning **2** : something assigned : TASK

as·sim·i·late \ə-'sim-ə-,lāt\ *vb* **1** : to take up and absorb as nourishment; *also* : to absorb into a cultural tradition **2** : COMPREHEND **3** : to make or become similar — **as·sim·i·la·tion** \-,sim-ə-'lā-shən\ *n*

¹**as·sist** \ə-'sist\ *vb* : HELP, AID — **as·sis·tance** *n*

²**assist** *n* **1** : an act of assistance **2** : the act of a player who enables a teammate to make a putout (as in baseball) or score a goal (as in hockey)

as·sis·tant \ə-'sis-tənt\ *n* : one who assists : HELPER

as·size \ə-'sīz\ *n* **1** : a judicial inquest **2** *pl* : the regular sessions of certain superior courts of the various counties of England

¹**as·so·ci·ate** \ə-'sō-s(h)ē-,āt\ *vb* **1** : to join in companionship or partnership **2** : to connect in thought

²**as·so·ciate** \-s(h)ē-ət, -,shət\ *n* **1** : a fellow worker : PARTNER **2** : COM-PANION — **associate** *adj*

as·so·ci·a·tion \ə-,sō-s(h)ē-'ā-shən\ *n* **1** : the act of associating **2** : an organ-ization of persons : SOCIETY

as·so·cia·tive \ə-'sō-s(h)ē-,āt-iv, -shət-iv\ *adj* : of, relating to, or involved in association and esp. mental association

as·so·nance \'as-ə-nəns\ *n* : repetition of vowels esp. as an alternative to rhyme in verse

as soon as conj : immediately at or just after the time that 〈we'll start as soon as he comes〉

as·sort \ə-'sȯrt\ vb 1 : to distribute into like groups : CLASSIFY 2 : HARMONIZE

as·sort·ed adj : consisting of various kinds

as·sort·ment \-'sȯrt-mənt\ n : a collection of assorted things or persons

as·suage \ə-'swāj\ vb 1 : to make (as pain or grief) less 2 : EASE 2 : SATISFY syn alleviate, relieve, lighten

as·sume \ə-'süm\ vb 1 : to take upon oneself 2 : to pretend to have 3 : to take as granted though not proved

as·sump·tion \ə-'səmp-shən\ n 1 : the taking up of a person into heaven 2 cap : a church feast commemorating the Assumption of Mary and celebrated on August 15 3 : a taking upon oneself 4 : PRETENSION 5 : SUPPOSITION

as·sur·ance \ə-'shu̇r-əns\ n 1 : PLEDGE 2 : CERTAINTY 3 : INSURANCE 4 : SELF-CONFIDENCE 5 : AUDACITY

as·sure \ə-'shu̇r\ vb 1 : INSURE 2 : to give confidence to 3 : to state confidently to 4 : to make certain the attainment of

as·sured \ə-'shu̇rd\ n, pl assured or assureds : the beneficiary of an insurance policy

as·ta·tine \'as-tə-,tēn\ n : an unstable radioactive chemical element

as·ter \'as-tər\ n : any of various mostly fall-blooming leafy-stemmed herbs with daisylike purple, white, pink, or yellow flower heads

as·ter·isk \'as-tə-,risk\ n : a character used as a reference mark or as an indication of the omission of letters or words

astern \ə-'stərn\ adv 1 : behind a ship or airplane : in the rear 2 : at or toward the stern of a ship or aircraft 3 : BACKWARD

as·ter·oid \'as-tə-,rȯid\ n : one of thousands of small planets between Mars and Jupiter with diameters under 500 miles

asth·ma \'az-mə\ n : an often allergic disorder marked by difficulty in breathing and a cough — **asth·mat·ic** \az-'mat-ik\ adj or n

as though conj : as if

astig·ma·tism \ə-'stig-mə-,tiz-əm\ n : a defect in a lens or an eye causing improper focusing

astir \ə-'stər\ adj : being in action : MOVING

as to prep 1 : ABOUT, CONCERNING 〈at a loss as to what went on that night〉 2 : according to 〈graded as to size and color〉

as·ton·ish \ə-'stän-ish\ vb : to strike with sudden wonder : AMAZE — **as·ton·ish·ing·ly** adv — **as·ton·ish·ment** n

as·tound \ə-'staund\ vb : to fill with bewildered wonder — **as·tound·ing·ly** adv

¹astrad·dle \ə-'strad-°l\ adv : on or above and extending onto both sides

²astraddle prep : ASTRIDE

as·tra·khan \'as-trə-kən, -,kan\ n : KARAKUL

as·tral \'as-trəl\ adj : of or relating to the stars

astray \ə-'strā\ adv 1 : off the right way or route 2 : into error

¹astride \ə-'strīd\ adv 1 : with one leg on each side 2 : with legs apart

²astride prep : with one leg on each side of

¹as·trin·gent \ə-'strin-jənt\ adj : able or tending to shrink body tissues — **as·trin·gen·cy** \-jən-sē\ n

²astringent n : an astringent agent or substance

as·tro·labe \'as-trə-,lāb\ n : an instrument for observing the positions of celestial bodies

as·trol·o·gy \ə-'sträl-ə-jē\ n : divination based on the supposed influence of the stars upon human events — **as·trol·o·ger** \-ə-jər\ n — **as·tro·log·i·cal** \,as-trə-'läj-i-kəl\ adj

as·tro·naut \'as-trə-,nȯt\ n : a traveler in a spaceship — **as·tro·nau·ti·cal** \,as-trə-'nȯt-i-kəl\ adj — **as·tro·nau·tics** \-'nȯt-iks\ n

as·tro·nom·i·cal \,as-trə-'näm-i-kəl\ or **as·tro·nom·ic** \-ik\ adj 1 : of or relating to astronomy 2 : extremely large 〈an ~ amount of money〉

as·tron·o·my \ə-'strän-ə-mē\ n : the science of the celestial bodies and of their magnitudes, motions, and constitution — **as·tron·o·mer** \ə-mər\ n

as·tro·phys·ics \,as-trə-'fiz-iks\ n : astronomy dealing with the physical and chemical constitution of the celestial bodies — **as·tro·phys·i·cist** \-'fiz-ə-səst\ n

as·tute \ə-'st(y)üt, a-\ adj : shrewdly discerning; also : WILY — **as·tute·ly** adv — **as·tute·ness** n

asun·der \ə-'sən-dər\ adv (or adj) 1 : into separate pieces 2 : separated in position

as well adv : in addition : TOO

as well as prep : in addition to : BESIDES

as yet adv : so far : YET 〈have not changed as yet〉

asy·lum \ə-'sī-ləm\ n 1 : a place of refuge 2 : protection given to esp. political fugitives 3 : an institution for the care of the needy or afflicted and esp. of the insane

asym·met·ric \,ā-sə-'met-rik\ or **asym·met·ri·cal** \-ri-kəl\ adj : not symmetrical

¹at \ət, (')at\ prep 1 — used to indicate a point in time or space 〈be here ~ 3 o'clock〉 〈he is ~ the hotel〉 2 — used to indicate a goal 〈swung ~ the ball〉 〈laugh ~ him〉 3 — used to indicate position or condition 〈~ rest〉 4 — used to indicate means, cause, or manner 〈sold ~ auction〉

²at \'ät\ n, pl at — see MONEY table

at all adv 1 : in all ways : without restriction 〈will go anywhere at all〉 2 : in any way : in any circumstances 〈not at all likely〉

at·a·vism \'at-ə-,viz-əm\ n : appearance in an individual of a remotely ancestral character; also : such an individual or character — **at·a·vis·tic** \,at-ə-'vis-tik\ adj

ate past of EAT

¹-ate n suffix 1 : one acted upon (in a specified way) 〈distillate〉 2 : chemical compound or element derived from a

ə abut; ᵊ kitten; ər further; a back; ā bake; ä cot, cart; au̇ out; ch chin; e less; ē easy; g gift; i trip; ī life; j joke; ŋ sing; ō flow; ȯ flaw; ȯi coin; th thin; t͟h this; ü loot; u̇ foot; y yet; yü few; yu̇ furious; zh vision

(specified) compound or element 〈phen*olate*〉; *esp* : salt or ester of an acid with a name ending in *-ic* 〈acet*ate*〉

²-ate *n suffix* : office : function : rank : group of persons holding a (specified) office or rank 〈professor*ate*〉

³-ate *adj suffix* **1** : acted on (in a specified way) : brought into or being in a (specified) state 〈temper*ate*〉 **2** : marked by having 〈chord*ate*〉

⁴-ate *vb suffix* : cause to be modified or affected by 〈camphor*ate*〉 : cause to become 〈activ*ate*〉 : furnish with 〈aer*ate*〉

ate·lier \ˌat-ˀl-'yā\ *n* **1** : an artist's studio **2** : WORKSHOP

athe·ist \'ā-thē-əst\ *n* : one who denies the existence of God — **athe·ism** \'ā-thē-ˌiz-əm\ *n* — **athe·is·tic** \ˌā-thē-'is-tik\ *adj*

ath·e·nae·um *or* **ath·e·ne·um** \ˌath-ə-'nē-əm\ *n* : a building where books, magazines, and newspapers are kept for use : LIBRARY

athirst \ə-'thərst\ *adj* **1** : THIRSTY **2** : EAGER, LONGING

ath·lete \'ath-ˌlēt\ *n* : one trained to compete in athletics

ath·let·ic \ath-'let-ik\ *adj* **1** : of or relating to athletes or athletics **2** : VIGOROUS, ACTIVE **3** : STURDY, MUSCULAR

ath·let·ics \-iks\ *n sing or pl* : exercises and games requiring physical skill, strength, and endurance

¹athwart \ə-'thwòrt\ *adv* : obliquely across

²athwart *prep* **1** : ACROSS **2** : in opposition to

atilt \ə-'tilt\ *adj* (*or adv*) **1** : TILTED **2** : with lance in hand

at·las \'at-ləs\ *n* : a book of maps

at·mo·sphere \'at-mə-ˌsfiər\ *n* **1** : the mass of air surrounding the earth **2** : a surrounding influence **3** : pressure of air at sea level used as a unit in physics **4** : a dominant effect — **at·mo·spher·ic** \ˌat-mə-'sfi(ə)r-ik, -'sfer-\ *adj*

atoll \'a-ˌtòl, 'ā-, -ˌtäl\ *n* : a ring-shaped coral island surrounding a lagoon

at·om \'at-əm\ *n* [Gk *atomos*, fr. *atomos* indivisible, fr. *a-* un- + *tom-*, *temnein* to cut] **1** : a tiny particle : BIT **2** : the smallest particle of a chemical element that can exist alone or in combination

atom bomb *or* **atomic bomb** *n* : a very destructive bomb utilizing the energy released by splitting the atom

atom·ic \ə-'täm-ik\ *adj* **1** : of or relating to atoms, atomic energy, or atomic bombs **2** : extremely small

atomic energy *n* : energy that can be liberated by changes (as by fission or fusion) in the nucleus of an atom

atom·ics \ə-'täm-iks\ *n* : the science of atoms esp. when involving atomic energy

at·om·ize \'at-ə-ˌmīz\ *vb* : to subject to atom bomb attack

at·om·iz·er *n* : a device for reducing a liquid to a very fine spray (as for spraying the throat)

aton·al \ā-'tōn-ˀl\ *adj* : characterized by avoidance of traditional musical tonality — **ato·nal·i·ty** \ˌā-tō-'nal-ət-ē\ *n* — **aton·al·ly** \ā-'tōn-ˀl-ē\ *adv*

atone \ə-'tōn\ *vb* **1** : to make amends **2** : EXPIATE

atone·ment \-mənt\ *n* **1** : RECONCILIATION; *esp* : the reconciliation of God and man through the death of Jesus Christ **2** : reparation for an offense

atop \ə-'täp\ *prep* : on top of

atri·um \'ā-trē-əm\ *n, pl* **atria** \-trē-ə\ *also* **atri·ums 1** : the central hall of a Roman house **2** : an anatomical cavity or passage; *esp* : one of the parts of the heart that receives blood from the veins — **atri·al** \-trē-əl\ *adj*

atro·cious \ə-'trō-shəs\ *adj* **1** : savagely brutal, cruel, or wicked **2** : very bad : ABOMINABLE — **atro·cious·ly** *adv* — **atro·cious·ness** *n*

atroc·i·ty \ə-'träs-ət-ē\ *n* **1** : ATROCIOUSNESS **2** : an atrocious act or object

¹at·ro·phy \'at-rə-fē\ *n* : decrease in size or wasting away of a bodily part or tissue

²atrophy *vb* : to cause or undergo atrophy

at·ro·pine \'at-rə-ˌpēn, -pən\ *n* : a poisonous drug from belladonna and related plants used to relieve spasms and to dilate the pupil of the eye

at·tach \ə-'tach\ *vb* **1** : to seize legally in order to force payment of a debt **2** : to bind by personal ties **3** : FASTEN, CONNECT **4** : to be fastened or connected

at·ta·ché \ˌat-ə-'shā, ˌa-ˌta-, ə-ˌta-\ *n* : a technical expert on the diplomatic staff of an ambassador

at·ta·ché case \ə-'tash-ē-, ˌat-ə-'shā-\ *n* : a small suitcase used esp. for carrying papers and documents

at·tach·ment \ə-'tach-mənt\ *n* **1** : legal seizure of property **2** : connection by ties of affection and regard **3** : a device attached to a machine or implement **4** : a connection by which one thing is attached to another

¹at·tack \ə-'tak\ *vb* **1** : to set upon with force or words : ASSAIL, ASSAULT **2** : to set to work on

²attack *n* **1** : an offensive action **2** : a fit of sickness

at·tain \ə-'tān\ *vb* **1** : ACHIEVE, ACCOMPLISH **2** : to arrive at : REACH — **at·tain·abil·i·ty** \ə-ˌtā-nə-'bil-ət-ē\ *n* — **at·tain·able** \-'tā-nə-bəl\ *adj*

at·tain·der \ə-'tān-dər\ *n* : extinction of the civil rights of a person upon sentence of death or outlawry

at·tain·ment \ə-'tān-mənt\ *n* **1** : the act of attaining **2** : something attained : ACCOMPLISHMENT

at·taint \ə-'tānt\ *vb* : to condemn to loss of civil rights

at·tar \'at-ər\ *n* : a fragrant floral oil

at·tempt \ə-'tempt\ *vb* : to make an effort toward : TRY — **attempt** *n*

at·tend \ə-'tend\ *vb* **1** : to look after : TEND **2** : to be present with : ACCOMPANY **3** : to be present at **4** : to pay attention **5** : to apply oneself **6** : to take charge

at·ten·dance \ə-'ten-dəns\ *n* **1** : the act or fact of attending **2** : the number of persons present

¹at·ten·dant \ə-'ten-dənt\ *adj* : ACCOMPANYING 〈~ circumstances〉

²attendant *n* : one that attends another to render a service

at·ten·tion \ə-'ten-chən\ *n* **1** : the act or state of applying the mind to an object **2** : CONSIDERATION **3** : an act of courtesy **4** : a position of readiness for further orders assumed on command by a soldier — **at·ten·tive** \-'tent-iv\ *adj* — **at·ten·tive·ly** *adv*

at·ten·u·ate \ə-'ten-yə-ˌwāt\ *vb* **1** : to make or become thin **2** : WEAKEN — **at·ten·u·a·tion** \ə-ˌten-yə-'wā-shən\ *n*

at·test \ə-'test\ *vb* **1** : to certify as genuine by signing as a witness **2** : MANIFEST **3** : TESTIFY — **at·tes·ta·tion** \ₐ-ₜes-'tā-shən\ *n*

at·tic \'at-ik\ *n* : the space or room in a building next below the roof

¹**at·tire** \ə-'tī(ə)r\ *vb* : DRESS, ARRAY

²**attire** *n* : DRESS, CLOTHES

at·ti·tude \'at-ə-ₜt(y)üd\ *n* **1** : the arrangement of the parts of a body : POSTURE **2** : a mental position or feeling with regard to an object **3** : the position of something in relation to something else

at·ti·tu·di·nize \ₐat-ə-'t(y)üd-ªn-ₜīz\ *vb* : to assume an affected mental attitude : POSE

at·tor·ney \ə-'tər-nē\ *n* : a legal agent qualified to act for persons in legal proceedings

at·tract \ə-'trakt\ *vb* **1** : to draw to or toward oneself : cause to approach **2** : to draw by emotional or aesthetic appeal   *syn* charm, fascinate, allure — **at·trac·tive** \-'trak-tiv\ *adj* — **at·trac·tive·ly** *adv* — **at·trac·tive·ness** *n*

at·trac·tion \ə-'trak-shən\ *n* **1** : the act or power of attracting; *esp* : personal charm **2** : an attractive quality, object, or feature **3** : a force tending to draw particles together

¹**at·tri·bute** \'at-rə-ₜbyüt\ *n* **1** : an inherent characteristic : QUALITY **2** : a word ascribing a quality; *esp* : ADJECTIVE

²**at·trib·ute** \ə-'trib-yət\ *vb* **1** : to explain as to cause or origin ⟨~ the illness to fatigue⟩ **2** : to regard as a characteristic   *syn* ascribe, credit, charge — **at·trib·ut·able** \ə-'trib-yət-ə-bəl\ *adj* — **at·tri·bu·tion** \ₐat-rə-'byü-shən\ *n*

at·trib·u·tive \ə-'trib-yət-iv\ *adj* : joined directly to a modified noun without a copulative verb ⟨red in red hair is an ~ adjective⟩ — **attributive** *n*

at·tri·tion \ə-'trish-ən\ *n* : the act of wearing away as if by rubbing

at·tune \ə-'t(y)ün\ *vb* : to bring into harmony : TUNE

atyp·i·cal \ā-'tip-i-kəl\ *adj* : not typical : IRREGULAR

au·burn \'ȯ-bərn\ *adj* : reddish brown — **auburn** *n*

au cou·rant \ₐō-kü-'räⁿ\ *adj* : fully informed : UP-TO-DATE

¹**auc·tion** \'ȯk-shən\ *n* : public sale of property to the highest bidder

²**auction** *vb* : to sell at auction

auc·tion·eer \ₐȯk-shə-'ni^ər\ *n* : an agent who conducts an auction

auc·to·ri·al \ȯk-'tōr-ē-əl\ *adj* : of or relating to an author

au·da·cious \ȯ-'dā-shəs\ *adj* **1** : DARING, BOLD **2** : INSOLENT — **au·da·cious·ly** *adv* — **au·da·cious·ness** *n* — **au·dac·i·ty** \ȯ-'das-ət-ē\ *n*

au·di·ble \'ȯd-ə-bəl\ *adj* : capable of being heard — **au·di·bil·i·ty** \ₐȯd-ə-'bil-ət-ē\ *n* — **au·di·bly** \'ȯd-ə-blē\ *adv*

au·di·ence \'ȯd-ē-əns\ *n* **1** : a formal interview **2** : an opportunity of being heard **3** : an assembly of listeners or spectators

au·dio \'ȯd-ē-ₜō\ *adj* **1** : of or relating to frequencies (as of radio waves) corresponding to those of audible sound waves **2** : of or relating to sound or its reproduction and esp. high-fidelity reproduction **3** : relating to or used in the transmission or reception of sound

au·dio·phile \'ȯd-ē-ə-ₜfīl\ *n* : one who is enthusiastic about high-fidelity sound reproduction

au·dio·vi·su·al \ₐȯd-ē-ō-'vizh-(ə-w)əl\ *adj* : of, relating to, or making use of both hearing and sight ⟨~ teaching aids⟩

¹**au·dit** \'ȯd-ət\ *n* : a formal examination and verification of financial accounts

²**audit** *vb* **1** : to make an audit of **2** : to attend (a course) without expecting formal credit

¹**au·di·tion** \ȯ-'dish-ən\ *n* : HEARING; *esp* : a trial performance to appraise an entertainer's merits

²**audition** *vb* : to give an audition to

au·di·tor \'ȯd-ət-ər\ *n* **1** : LISTENER **2** : a person who audits

au·di·to·ri·um \ₐȯd-ə-'tōr-ē-əm\ *n* **1** : the part of a public building where an audience sits **2** : a hall or building used for public gatherings

au·di·to·ry \'ȯd-ə-ₜtōr-ē\ *adj* : of or relating to hearing or the sense or organs of hearing

auf Wie·der·seh·en \aúf-'vēd-ər-ₜzän\ *interj* — used to express farewell

au·ger \'ȯ-gər\ *n* : a boring tool

aught \'ȯt, 'ät\ *n* : ZERO, CIPHER

aug·ment \ȯg-'ment\ *vb* : ENLARGE, INCREASE — **aug·men·ta·tion** \ₐȯg-mən-'tā-shən\ *n*

au gra·tin \ō-'grat-ªn, -'grat-\ *adj* : covered with bread crumbs, butter, and cheese and browned

¹**au·gur** \'ȯ-gər\ *n* : DIVINER, SOOTHSAYER

²**augur** *vb* **1** : to foretell esp. from omens **2** : to give promise of : PRESAGE

au·gu·ry \'ȯ-g(y)ə-rē\ *n* **1** : divination from omens **2** : OMEN, PORTENT

au·gust \ȯ-'gəst\ *adj* : marked by majestic dignity or grandeur — **au·gust·ly** *adv* — **au·gust·ness** *n*

Au·gust \'ȯ-gəst\ *n* : the 8th month of the year having 31 days

auk \'ȯk\ *n* : a stocky black-and-white diving seabird that breeds in arctic regions

auld \'ȯl(d), 'äl(d)\ *adj, chiefly Scot* : OLD

aunt \'ant, 'änt\ *n* **1** : the sister of one's father or mother **2** : the wife of one's uncle

au·ra \'ȯr-ə\ *n* **1** : a distinctive atmosphere surrounding a given source **2** : a luminous radiation

au·ral \'ȯr-əl\ *adj* : of or relating to the ear or to the sense of hearing

aurar *pl of* EYRIR

au·re·ate \'ȯr-ē-ət\ *adj* **1** : of a golden color or brilliance **2** : RESPLENDENT, ORNATE

au·re·ole \'ȯr-ē-ₜōl\ *n* : HALO, NIMBUS

au re·voir \ₐȯr-əv-'wär\ *n* : GOOD-BYE

au·ri·cle \'ȯr-i-kəl\ *n* **1** : the external ear **2** : an earlike lobe (as of the heart)

au·ric·u·lar \ȯ-'rik-yə-lər\ *adj* **1** : AURAL **2** : told privately **3** : known by the sense of hearing **4** : of or relating to an auricle

au·rif·er·ous \ȯ-'rif-(ə-)rəs\ *adj* : goldbearing

au·ro·ra \ə-'rōr-ə\ *n, pl* **-rae** \-'rōr-(,)ē\ *or* **-ras 1** : AURORA BOREALIS **2** : AURORA AUSTRALIS

aurora aus·tra·lis \-ȯ-'strā-ləs\ *n* : a display of light in the southern hemisphere corresponding to the aurora borealis

aurora bo·re·al·is \-ˌbōr-ē-'al-əs\ *n* : streamers or arches of light in the night sky that are held to be of electrical origin and appear esp. in the arctic regions

aus·pice \'ȯ-spəs\ *n* **1** : observation in augury **2** : a prophetic sign or omen **3** *pl* : kindly patronage and protection

aus·pi·cious \ȯ-'spish-əs\ *adj* **1** : affording a favorable auspice **2** : FORTUNATE, PROSPEROUS — **aus·pi·cious·ly** *adv*

aus·tere \ȯ-'stiər\ *adj* **1** : STERN, SEVERE, STRICT **2** : ABSTEMIOUS **3** : UNADORNED 〈~ style〉 — **aus·tere·ly** *adv* — **aus·ter·i·ty** \ȯ-'ster-ət-ē\ *n*

aus·tral \'ȯ-strəl\ *adj* : SOUTHERN

Aus·tra·lian \ȯ-'strāl-yən\ *n* : a native or inhabitant of Australia — **Australian** *adj*

Aus·tri·an \'ȯ-strē-ən\ *n* : a native or inhabitant of Austria — **Austrian** *adj*

au·then·tic \ə-'thent-ik, ȯ-\ *adj* : GENUINE, REAL — **au·then·ti·cal·ly** *adv* — **au·then·tic·i·ty** \ˌȯ-ˌthen-'tis-ət-ē\ *n*

au·then·ti·cate \ə-'thent-i-ˌkāt, ȯ-\ *vb* : to prove genuine — **au·then·ti·ca·tion** \-ˌthent-i-'kā-shən\ *n*

au·thor \'ȯ-thər\ *n* **1** : one that writes or composes a literary work **2** : one that originates or creates — **au·thor·ess** \-th(ə-)rəs\ *n*

au·thor·i·tar·i·an \ə-ˌthȯr-ə-'ter-ē-ən, ȯ-\ *adj* **1** : characterized by or favoring the principle of blind obedience to authority **2** : characterized by or favoring concentration of political power in an authority not responsible to the people

au·thor·i·ta·tive \ə-'thȯr-ə-ˌtāt-iv, ȯ-\ *adj* : supported by or proceeding from authority : TRUSTWORTHY — **au·thor·i·ta·tive·ly** *adv*

au·thor·i·ty \ə-'thȯr-ət-ē, ȯ-\ *n* **1** : a citation used in support of a statement or in defense of an action; *also* : the source of such a citation **2** : one appealed to as an expert **3** : power to influence thought or behavior **4** : freedom granted : RIGHT **5** : persons in command; *esp* : GOVERNMENT

au·tho·rize \'ȯ-thə-ˌrīz\ *vb* **1** : to give legal power to **2** : SANCTION **3** : JUSTIFY — **au·tho·ri·za·tion** \ˌȯ-th(ə-)rə-'zā-shən\ *n*

au·thor·ship \'ȯ-thər-ˌship\ *n* **1** : the state of being an author **2** : the origin of a piece of writing

au·to \'ȯt-ō\ *n* : AUTOMOBILE

au·to·bahn \'ȯt-ō-ˌbän, 'aut-\ *n* : a German expressway

au·to·bi·og·ra·phy \ˌȯt-ə-bī-'äg-rə-fē\ *n* : the biography of a person narrated by himself — **au·to·bi·og·ra·pher** \-rə-fər\ *n* — **au·to·bi·o·graph·i·cal** \-ˌbī-ə-'graf-i-kəl\ *adj*

au·toch·tho·nous \ȯ-'täk-thə-nəs\ *adj* : INDIGENOUS, NATIVE

au·toc·ra·cy \ȯ-'täk-rə-sē\ *n* : government by one person having unlimited power — **au·to·crat** \'ȯt-ə-ˌkrat\ *n* — **au·to·crat·ic** \ˌȯt-ə-'krat-ik\ *adj* — **au·to·crat·i·cal·ly** *adv*

1au·to·graph \'ȯt-ə-ˌgraf\ *n* **1** : an original manuscript **2** : a person's signature written by hand

2autograph *vb* : to write one's signature on

au·to·in·tox·i·ca·tion \ˌȯt-ō-in-ˌtäk-sə-'kā-shən\ *n* : a state of being poisoned by substances produced within the body

au·to·mate \'ȯt-ə-ˌmāt\ *vb* **1** : to operate by automation **2** : to convert to automatic operation

1au·to·mat·ic \ˌȯt-ə-'mat-ik\ *adj* **1** : INVOLUNTARY **2** : made so that certain parts act in a desired manner at the proper time : SELF-ACTING — **au·to·mat·i·cal·ly** *adv*

2automatic *n* : an automatic device; *esp* : an automatic firearm

au·to·ma·tion \ˌȯt-ə-'mā-shən\ *n* **1** : the technique of making an apparatus, a process, or a system operate automatically **2** : the state of being operated automatically **3** : automatically controlled operation of an apparatus, process, or system by mechanical or electronic devices that take the place of human operators

au·tom·a·tize \ȯ-'täm-ə-ˌtīz\ *vb* : to make automatic — **au·tom·a·ti·za·tion** \-ˌtäm-ət-ə-'zā-shən\ *n*

au·tom·a·ton \ȯ-'täm-ət-ən, -ə-ˌtän\ *n* **1** : an automatic machine; *esp* : one made to imitate the motions of a person **2** : a creature who acts in a mechanical manner

au·to·mo·bile \ˌȯt-ə-mō-'bēl, -'mō-ˌbēl\ *n* : a usu. 4-wheeled self-propelling vehicle for passenger transportation on streets and roadways — **au·to·mo·bil·ist** \-mō-'bē-ləst\ *n*

au·to·mo·tive \ˌȯt-ə-'mōt-iv\ *adj* **1** : SELF-PROPELLING **2** : of or relating to self-propelling vehicles and esp. automobiles and motorcycles

au·ton·o·mous \ȯ-'tän-ə-məs\ *adj* : having the right or power of self-government : INDEPENDENT — **au·ton·o·mous·ly** *adv* — **au·ton·o·my** \-mē\ *n*

au·top·sy \'ȯ-ˌtäp-sē, 'ȯt-əp-\ *n* : examination of a dead body usu. to determine the cause of death

au·tumn \'ȯt-əm\ *n* : the season between summer and winter — **au·tum·nal** \ȯ-'təm-nəl\ *adj*

1aux·il·ia·ry \ȯg-'zil-yə-rē\ *adj* **1** : providing help **2** : functioning in a subsidiary capacity **3** : accompanying a verb form to express person, number, mood, or tense 〈~ verbs〉

2auxiliary *n* **1** : an auxiliary person, group, or device **2** : an auxiliary verb

aux·in \'ȯk-sən\ *n* : a plant hormone; *esp* : one stimulating growth in length

1avail \ə-'vāl\ *vb* : to be of use or advantage : HELP, BENEFIT

2avail *n* : USE 〈effort was of no ~〉

avail·able \ə-'vā-lə-bəl\ *adj* **1** : that may be utilized **2** : ACCESSIBLE — **avail·abil·i·ty** \-ˌvā-lə-'bil-ət-ē\ *n*

av·a·lanche \'av-ə-ˌlanch\ *n* : a mass of snow, ice, earth, or rock sliding down a mountainside

avant–garde \ˌäv-ˌän(t)-'gärd, -ˌän-\ *n* : those esp. in the arts who create or apply new or experimental ideas and techniques — **avant–garde** *adj*

av·a·rice \'av-(ə-)rəs\ *n* : excessive desire for wealth : GREED — **av·a·ri·cious** \ˌav-ə-'rish-əs\ *adj*

avast \ə-'vast\ *vb* — a nautical command to stop or cease

av·a·tar \'av-ə-,tär\ *n* : INCARNATION

avaunt \ə-'vont\ *adv, archaic* : AWAY, HENCE

ave \'äv-,ā\ *n* : an expression of greeting or parting

Ave Ma·ria \,äv-,ä-mə-'rē-ə\ *n* : a salutation and prayer to the Virgin Mary

avenge \ə-'venj\ *vb* : to take vengeance for — aveng·er *n*

av·e·nue \'av-ə-,n(y)ü\ *n* 1 : PASSAGEWAY 2 : a way of attaining something 3 : a broad street esp. when bordered by trees

aver \ə-'vər\ *vb* averred; aver·ring : to declare positively

1av·er·age \'av-(ə-)rij\ *n* 1 : ³MEAN 4 2 : a ratio (as a rate per thousand) of successful tries to total tries ⟨batting ~ of .303⟩

2average *adj* 1 : equaling or approximating an average 2 : being about midway between extremes 3 : being not out of the ordinary : COMMON ⟨the ~ man⟩

3average *vb* 1 : to be at or come to an average 2 : to be usually 3 : to find the average of

aver·ment \ə-'vər-mənt\ *n* : AFFIRMATION

averse \ə-'vərs\ *adj* : having an active feeling of dislike or reluctance ⟨~ from publicity⟩ ⟨~ to exercise⟩

aver·sion \ə-'vər-zhən\ *n* 1 : a feeling of repugnance for something with a desire to avoid it 2 : something decidedly disliked

avert \ə-'vərt\ *vb* 1 : to turn aside or away ⟨~ the eyes⟩ 2 : to ward off : prevent the occurrence of

avi·an \'ā-vē-ən\ *adj* : of, relating to, or derived from birds

avi·ary \'ā-vē-,er-ē\ *n* : a place where live birds are kept usu. for exhibition

avi·a·tion \,ā-vē-'ā-shən, ,av-ē-\ *n* 1 : the operation of heavier-than-air airplanes 2 : aircraft manufacture, development, and design — avi·a·tor \'ā-vē-,āt-ər, 'av-ē-\ *n*

avi·a·trix \,ā-vē-'ā-triks, ,av-ē-\ *n* : a woman airplane pilot

av·id \'av-əd\ *adj* 1 : craving eagerly : GREEDY 2 : enthusiastic in pursuit of an interest — avid·i·ty \ə-'vid-ət-ē, a-\ *n* — av·id·ly \'av-əd-lē\ *adv*

avi·on·ics \,ā-vē-'än-iks, ,av-ē-\ *n* : the production of electrical devices for use in aviation, missilery, and astronautics — avi·on·ic \-ik\ *adj*

avi·ta·min·osis \,ā-,vīt-ə-mə-'nō-səs\ *n* : disease resulting from vitamin deficiency — avi·ta·min·ot·ic \-mə-'nät-ik\ *adj*

av·o·ca·do \,av-ə-'käd-ō\ *n* : the soft oily edible fruit of a tropical American tree; *also* : this tree

av·o·ca·tion \,av-ə-'kā-shən\ *n* : a subordinate occupation pursued esp. for pleasure : HOBBY

avoid \ə-'void\ *vb* 1 : to keep away from : SHUN 2 : to prevent the occurrence of 3 : to refrain from — avoid·able *adj* — avoid·ance \-'n(t)s\ *n*

1av·oir·du·pois \,av-ərd-ə-'poiz\ *n* 1 : avoirdupois weight 2 : WEIGHT, HEAVINESS; *esp* : personal weight

2avoirdupois *adj* : of or relating to a system of weights (avoirdupois weights) based on the pound of 16 ounces and the ounce of 16 drams

avouch \ə-'vauch\ *vb* 1 : to declare positively : AVER 2 : GUARANTEE

avow \ə-'vau\ *vb* : to declare openly : ACKNOWLEDGE — avow·al \-'vau(-ə)l\ *n*

avun·cu·lar \ə-'vəŋ-kyə-lər\ *adj* : of, relating to, or resembling an uncle

await \ə-'wāt\ *vb* 1 : to wait for : EXPECT 2 : to be ready for

1awake \ə-'wāk\ *vb* awoke \-'wōk\ *also* awaked; awaked *also* awoke or awoken \-'wō-kən\ awak·ing : to bring back to consciousness after sleep : wake up

2awake *adj* : not asleep; *also* : ALERT

awak·en \ə-'wā-kən\ *vb* : AWAKE

1award \ə-'word\ *vb* 1 : to give by judicial decision ⟨~ damages⟩ 2 : to give in recognition of merit or achievement ⟨~ a prize⟩

2award *n* 1 : a final decision : JUDGMENT 2 : something awarded : PRIZE

aware \ə-'waər\ *adj* : having perception or knowledge : CONSCIOUS, INFORMED — aware·ness *n*

awash \ə-'wosh, -'wäsh\ *adv (or adj)* 1 : washed by waves or tide 2 : AFLOAT 3 : FLOODED

1away \ə-'wā\ *adv* 1 : from this or that place ⟨go ~⟩ 2 : out of the way ⟨lay ~⟩ 3 : in another direction ⟨turn ~⟩ 4 : out of existence ⟨fade ~⟩ 5 : from one's possession ⟨give ~⟩ 6 : without interruption ⟨chatter ~⟩ 7 : without hesitation ⟨fire ~⟩ 8 : at a distance in space or time ⟨far ~⟩ ⟨~ back in 1910⟩

2away *adj* 1 : ABSENT 2 : DISTANT ⟨a lake 10 miles ~⟩

1awe \'o\ *n* 1 : profound and reverent dread of the supernatural 2 : respectful fear inspired by authority

2awe *vb* : to inspire with awe

awea·ry \ə-'wi(ə)r-ē\ *adj* : WEARIED

aweigh \ə-'wā\ *adj* : just clear of the bottom and hanging perpendicularly ⟨anchors ~⟩

awe·some \'o-səm\ *adj* 1 : expressive of awe 2 : inspiring awe

awe·strick·en \'o-,strik-ən\ *or* awe·struck \-,strək\ *adj* : filled with awe

aw·ful \'o-fəl\ *adj* 1 : inspiring awe 2 : extremely disagreeable 3 : very great

aw·ful·ly *usu* 'o-fə-lē *for* 1, 'o-flē *for* 2\ *adv* 1 : in an awful manner 2 : EXCEEDINGLY

awhile \ə-'hwīl\ *adv* : for a while

awhirl \ə-'hwərl\ *adv (or adj)* : in a whirl : WHIRLING

awk·ward \'o-kwərd\ *adj* 1 : CLUMSY 2 : UNGRACEFUL 3 : difficult to explain : EMBARRASSING 4 : difficult to deal with — awk·ward·ly *adv* — awk·ward·ness *n*

awl \'ol\ *n* : a pointed instrument for making small holes

awn \'on\ *n* : one of the bristles on a spike of grass

aw·ning \'o-niŋ\ *n* : a rooflike cover (as of canvas) extended over or in front of a place as a shelter

AWOL \'ā-,wol, ,ā-,dəb-əl-yü-,ō-'el\ *n* : a person who is absent without permission — AWOL *adv (or adj)*

awry \ə-'rī\ *adv (or adj)* 1 : twisted to

ə abut; ᵉ kitten; ər further; a back; ā bake; ä cot, cart; aú out; ch chin; e less; ē easy; g gift; i trip; ī life; j joke; ŋ sing; ō flow; ò flaw; òi coin; th thin; t͟h this; ü loot; ủ foot; y yet; yü few; yủ furious; zh vision

one side **:** ASKEW **2 :** out of the right course **:** AMISS

ax or **axe** \'aks\ n **:** a chopping or cutting tool with an edged head fitted parallel to a handle

ax·i·al \'ak-sē-əl\ adj **1 :** of, relating to, or functioning as an axis **2 :** situated around, in the direction of, on, or along an axis

ax·i·om \'ak-sē-əm\ n **1 :** a statement generally accepted as true **:** MAXIM **2 :** a proposition regarded as a self-evident truth — **ax·i·om·at·ic** \,ak-sē-ə-'mat-ik\ adj

ax·is \'ak-səs\ n, pl **ax·es** \-,sēz\ **1 :** a real or imaginary straight line passing through a body that actually or supposedly revolves upon it ⟨the earth's ~⟩ **2 :** a lengthwise central line or part (as a plant stem) around which parts of a body are symmetrically arranged **3 :** an alliance between major powers to show solidarity of interest and to insure mutual support

ax·le \'ak-səl\ n **:** a spindle on which a wheel revolves

axle·tree \-,(,)trē\ n **:** a fixed bar with bearings at its ends on which wheels (as of a cart) revolve

ayah \'ī-ə, 'ä-yə\ n **:** a native nurse or maid in India

1aye also **ay** \'ā\ adv **:** ALWAYS, EVER

2aye also **ay** \'ī\ adv **:** YES

3aye \'ī\ n **:** an affirmative vote

aza·lea \ə-'zāl-yə\ n **:** any of various rhododendrons with funnel-shaped blossoms and usu. deciduous leaves

az·i·muth \'az-ə-məth\ n **1 :** an arc of the horizon measured between a fixed point and the vertical circle passing through the center of an object **2 :** horizontal direction

Az·tec \'az-,tek\ n **:** a member of an Indian people that founded the Mexican empire and were conquered by Cortes in 1519 — **Az·tec·an** adj

azure \'azh-ər\ n **:** the blue of the clear sky — **azure** adj

---

b \'bē\ n, often cap **:** the 2d letter of the English alphabet

bab·ble \'bab-əl\ vb **1 :** to utter meaningless sounds **2 :** to talk foolishly or excessively — **babble** n — **bab·bler** \-(ə-)lər\ n

babe \'bāb\ n **:** BABY

ba·bel \'bab-əl, 'bab-\ n, often cap [fr. the Tower of Babel, Gen 11:4–9] **:** a place or scene of noise and confusion; also **:** a confused sound (as of voices) syn hubbub, racket, din, uproar

ba·boon \ba-'bün\ n **:** a large ape of Asia and Africa with a doglike muzzle

ba·bush·ka \bə-'büsh-kə\ n **:** a kerchief for the head usu. folded triangularly

1ba·by \'bā-bē\ n **1 :** a very young child **:** INFANT **2 :** the youngest or smallest of a group **3 :** a childish person — **baby** adj — **ba·by·hood** n — **ba·by·ish** adj

2baby vb **:** to use with great care or consideration **:** HUMOR

ba·by·sit \-,sit\ vb **:** to care for children usu. during a short absence of the parents — **ba·by-sit·ter** n

bac·ca·lau·re·ate \,bak-ə-'lòr-ē-ət\ n **1 :** the degree of bachelor conferred by colleges and universities **2 :** a sermon (baccalaureate sermon) delivered to a graduating class

bac·cha·na·lia \,bak-ə-'nāl-yə\ n, pl **-lia :** a drunken orgy — **bac·cha·na·lian** adj or n

bach·e·lor \'bach-(ə-)lər\ n **1 :** a person holding the first or lowest academic degree **2 :** a man who has not married — **bach·e·lor·hood** n

ba·cil·lus \bə-'sil-əs\ n, pl **-cil·li** \-'sil-,ī\ **:** any of numerous rod-shaped bacteria; also **:** a disease-producing bacterium — **bac·il·lary** \'bas-ə-,ler-ē\ adj

1back \'bak\ n **1 :** the rear or dorsal part of the human body; also **:** the corresponding part of a lower animal **2 :** the part or surface opposite the front **:** REAR, REVERSE **3 :** a player in the backfield in football — **back·less** adj

2back adv **1 :** to, toward, or at the rear **2 :** AGO **3 :** so as to be restrained or

retarded **4 :** to, toward, or in a former place or state **5 :** in return or reply

3back adj **1 :** located at or in the back; also **:** REMOTE **2 :** OVERDUE **3 :** moving or operating backward **4 :** not current syn posterior

4back vb **1 :** SUPPORT, UPHOLD **2 :** to go or make go backward or in reverse **3 :** to furnish with a back **:** form the back of

back·ache \-,āk\ n **:** pain in the back; esp **:** a dull persistent pain in the lower back

back·bench·er \-'ben-chər\ n **:** a rank-and-file member of a British legislature

back·bite \-,bīt\ vb **:** to say mean or spiteful things about someone who is absent — **back·bit·er** n

back·board \-,bōrd\ n **:** a board or construction placed at the back or serving as a back

back·bone \-'bōn\ n **1 :** the bony column in the back of a vertebrate that encloses the spinal cord and is the chief support of the trunk **2 :** firm resolute character

back·drop \-,dräp\ n **:** a painted cloth hung across the rear of a stage

back·er n **:** one that supports (as a policy) syn upholder, champion, sponsor, patron

back·field \'bak-,fēld\ n **:** the football players whose positions are behind the line

back·fire \-,fī(ə)r\ n **:** a premature explosion in the cylinder or an explosion in the intake or exhaust passages of an internal-combustion engine — **backfire** vb

back·gam·mon \'bak-,gam-ən\ n **:** a game played with pieces on a double board in which the moves are determined by throwing dice

back·ground \-,graùnd\ n **1 :** the scenery behind something seen or represented **2 :** the conditions that form the setting within which something is experienced; also **:** the sum of a person's experience, training, and understanding

back·hand \-,hand\ n **:** a stroke made

with the back of the hand turned in the direction in which the hand is moving; *also* : the side on which such a stroke is made

back·ing \-iŋ\ *n* **1** : a material back **2** : SUPPORT, AID; *also* : a body of supporters

back·log \-,lȯg, -,läg\ *n* **1** : a large log at the back of a hearth fire **2** : a reserve esp. of unfilled orders **3** : an accumulation of unperformed tasks

back of *prep* : BEHIND

back·rest \'bak-,rest\ *n* : a rest at or for the back

back·side \'bak-'sīd\ *n* : BUTTOCKS

back·slap \-,slap\ *vb* : to display excessive cordiality — **back·slap·per** *n*

back·slide \-,slīd\ *vb* : to lapse morally or in the practice of religion — **back·slid·er** *n*

back·spin \'bak-,spin\ *n* : a backward rotary motion of a ball

back·stop \-,stäp\ *n* : something serving as a stop behind something else; *esp* : a screen or fence used in a game (as baseball) to keep a ball from leaving the field of play

back·stretch \-,strech\ *n* : the side opposite the homestretch on a racecourse

back·stroke \-,strōk\ *n* : a swimming stroke executed by a swimmer lying on his back

back·track \-,trak\ *vb* **1** : to retrace one's course **2** : to reverse a position or stand

1back·ward \-word\ *or* **back·wards** \-wordz\ *adv* **1** : toward the back **2** : with back foremost **3** : in a reverse or contrary direction or way **4** : toward the past; *also* : toward a worse state

2backward *adj* **1** : directed, turned, or done backward **2** : DIFFIDENT, SHY **3** : retarded in development — **back·ward·ness** *n*

back·wash \'bak-,wȯsh, -,wäsh\ *n* : backward movement (as of water or air) produced by motion of oars or other propelling force

back·woods \-'wu̇dz\ *n pl* **1** : wooded or partly cleared frontier areas **2** : a remote or isolated place

ba·con \'bā-kən\ *n* : salted and smoked meat from the sides or back of a pig

bac·te·ri·ol·o·gy \bak-,tir-ē-'äl-ə-jē\ *n* **1** : a science dealing with bacteria **2** : bacterial life and phenomena — **bac·te·ri·o·log·i·cal** \-ē-ə-'läj-i-kəl\ *adj* — **bac·te·ri·ol·o·gist** \-ē-'äl-ə-jəst\ *n*

bac·te·ri·um \bak-'tir-ē-əm\ *n*, *pl* **-ria** \-ē-ə\ : any of a large group of microscopic plants including some that are disease producers and others valued esp. for their fermentations — **bac·te·ri·al** *adj* — **bac·te·ri·cid·al** \-,tir-ə-'sīd-ə'l\ *adj*

bad \'bad\ *adj* **worse** \'wərs\ **worst** \'wȯrst\ **1** : below standard : POOR; *also* : UNFAVORABLE (a ~ report) **2** : WICKED; *also* : not well-behaved : NAUGHTY **3** : DISAGREEABLE (a ~ taste); *also* : HARMFUL **4** : DEFECTIVE, FAULTY (~ wiring); *also* : not valid (a ~ check) **5** : SPOILED, DECAYED **6** : UNWELL, ILL **7** : SORRY, REGRETFUL **syn** evil, wrong, putrid — **bad·ly** *adv* — **bad·ness** *n*

bade *past of* BID

badge \'baj\ *n* : a device or token usu. worn as a sign of status (as of membership, office, or authority)

1bad·ger \'baj-ər\ *n* : a sturdy burrowing mammal with long claws on the forefeet

2badger *vb* : to harass or annoy persistently

bad·i·nage \,bad-ə'n-'äzh\ *n* : playful talk back and forth : BANTER

bad·min·ton \'bad-,mint-ə'n\ *n* : a court game played with light rackets and a shuttlecock volleyed over a net

1baf·fle \'baf-əl\ *vb* : FRUSTRATE, THWART, FOIL; *also* : PERPLEX

2baffle *n* : a device (as a wall or screen) to deflect, check, or regulate flow (as of liquid or sound)

1bag \'bag\ *n* : a flexible usu. closable container (as for storing or carrying)

2bag *vb* **bagged; bag·ging 1** : DISTEND, BULGE **2** : to get possession of; *esp* : to take in hunting (~ a partridge) **syn** trap, snare, catch

ba·gasse \bə-'gas\ *n* : plant residue (as of sugarcane) left after a product (as juice) has been extracted

bag·a·telle \,bag-ə-'tel\ *n* : TRIFLE

ba·gel \'bā-gəl\ *n* : a hard glazed doughnut-shaped roll

bag·gage \'bag-ij\ *n* **1** : the traveling bags and personal belongings of a traveler : LUGGAGE **2** : a saucy, worthless, or immoral woman

bag·gy \'bag-ē\ *adj* : puffed out or hanging like a bag — **bag·gi·ly** *adv*

ba·gnio \'ban-yō\ *n* : BROTHEL

bag·pipe \'bag-,pīp\ *n* : a musical wind instrument consisting of a bag, a tube with valves, and sounding pipes — often used in pl.

baht \'bät\ *n*, *pl* **bahts** *or* **baht** — see MONEY table

1bail \'bāl\ *n* : security given to guarantee a prisoner's appearance when legally required; *also* : one giving such security or the release secured

2bail *vb* : to release under bail; *also* : to procure the release of by giving bail

3bail *n* : a container for ladling water out of a boat

4bail *vb* : to dip and throw out water from a boat

5bail *n* : the arched handle of a pail or kettle

bai·liff \'bā-ləf\ *n* **1** : an aide of a British sheriff employed esp. in serving writs and making arrests; *also* : a minor officer of a U.S. court **2** : an estate or farm manager esp. in Britain : STEWARD

bai·li·wick \'bā-li-,wik\ *n* : one's special province or domain **syn** territory, field, sphere

bails·man \'bālz-mən\ *n* : one who gives bail for another

bairn \'baȯrn\ *n*, *Scot* : CHILD

1bait \'bāt\ *vb* **1** : to persecute by continued attacks **2** : to harass with dogs usu. for sport (~ a bear) **3** : ALLURE, ENTICE **4** : to furnish (as a hook) with bait **5** : to give food and drink to (as an animal) **syn** badger, heckle, hound

2bait *n* **1** : a lure for catching animals (as fish) **2** : LURE, TEMPTATION **syn** snare, trap, decoy

baize \'bāz\ *n* : a coarse feltlike fabric

¹**bake** \'bāk\ vb **1** : to cook or become cooked in dry heat esp. in an oven **2** : to dry and harden by heat (~ bricks) — **bak·er** n

²**bake** n : a social gathering featuring baked food

bak·ery \'bā-k(ə-)rē\ n : a place for baking or selling baked goods

bak·sheesh \'bak-ˌshēsh\ n : a gift of money esp. in the Near East

¹**bal·ance** \'bal-əns\ n [OF, fr. (assumed) VL *bilancia*, fr. LL *bilanc-, bilanx* having two scalepans, fr. L *bi-* two + *lanx* plate] **1** : a weighing device : SCALE **2** : a weight, force, or influence counteracting the effect of another **3** : a vibrating wheel used to regulate a watch or clock **4** : a state of equilibrium **5** : REMAINDER, REST; *esp* : an amount in excess esp. on the credit side of an account

²**balance** vb **1** : to compute the balance of an account **2** : to arrange so that one set of elements equals another; *also* : to equal or equalize in weight, number, or proportions **3** : WEIGH **4** : to bring or come to a state or position of equipoise; *also* : to bring into harmony or proportion

bal·boa \bal-'bō-ə\ n — see MONEY table

bal·brig·gan \bal-'brig-ən\ n : a knitted cotton fabric used esp. for underwear

bal·co·ny \'bal-kə-nē\ n **1** : a platform projecting from the side of a building and enclosed by a railing **2** : a gallery inside a building (as a theater)

bald \'bȯld\ adj **1** : lacking a natural or usual covering (as of hair) **2** : UNADORNED, PLAIN **syn** bare, barren, naked, nude — **bald·ness** n

bal·da·chin \'bȯl-də-kən, 'bal-\ or **bal·da·chi·no** \ˌbal-də-'kē-nō\ n : a canopylike structure over an altar

bal·der·dash \'bȯl-dər-ˌdash\ n : NONSENSE

bal·dric \'bȯl-drik\ n : a belt worn over the shoulder to carry a sword or bugle

¹**bale** \'bāl\ n : a large bundle or closely packed package

²**bale** vb : to pack in a bale — **bal·er** n

ba·leen \bə-'lēn\ n : WHALEBONE

bale·ful \'bāl-fəl\ adj : DEADLY, HARMFUL; *also* : OMINOUS **syn** sinister

¹**balk** \'bȯk\ n : HINDRANCE, CHECK, SETBACK

²**balk** vb **1** : CHECK, BLOCK, THWART **2** : to stop short and refuse to go on **syn** frustrate

balky adj : likely to balk

¹**ball** \'bȯl\ n **1** : a rounded body or mass (as at the base of the thumb or for use as a missile or in a game) **2** : a game played with a ball **3** : PITCH ⟨curve ~⟩ **4** : a pitched baseball that misses the strike zone and is not swung at by the batter

²**ball** vb : to form into a ball

³**ball** n : a large formal dance

bal·lad \'bal-əd\ n **1** : a simple song : AIR **2** : a narrative poem of strongly marked rhythm suitable for singing **3** : a slow romantic dance song

¹**bal·last** \'bal-əst\ n **1** : heavy material put in the hold of a ship to steady it or in the car of a balloon to steady it or control its ascent **2** : crushed stone used in making roadbeds firm

²**ballast** vb : to provide with ballast **syn** balance

ball·car·ri·er \'bȯl-ˌkar-ē-ər\ n : the football player carrying the ball in an offensive play

bal·le·ri·na \ˌbal-ə-'rē-nə\ n : a female ballet dancer

bal·let \'bal-ˌā, bal-'ā\ n **1** : dancing in which fixed poses and steps are combined with light flowing movements often to convey a story or theme; *also* : a theatrical art form using ballet dancing **2** : a company of ballet dancers

bal·lis·tic \bə-'lis-tik\ adj **1** : of or relating to ballistics **2** : being a missile that is self-powered during most of its ascent, travels in a high arch, and descends as a free-falling object

bal·lis·tics \-tiks\ n *sing or pl* **1** : the science dealing with the motion of projectiles (as bullets) or of bombs dropped from aircraft **2** : the flight characteristics of a missile

bal·loon \bə-'lün\ n **1** : a bag filled with gas or heated air so as to rise and float in the atmosphere **2** : a toy consisting of a rubber bag that can be inflated — **bal·loon·ist** n

¹**bal·lot** \'bal-ət\ n **1** : a piece of paper used to cast a vote **2** : the action or a system of voting; *also* : the right to vote **3** : the number of votes cast in an election

²**ballot** vb : to decide by ballot : VOTE

ball·room \'bȯl-ˌrüm, -ˌrum\ n : a large room for dances

bal·ly·hoo \'bal-ē-ˌhü\ n **1** : a noisy attention-getting demonstration or talk **2** : grossly exaggerated or sensational advertising or propaganda

balm \'bäm\ n **1** : a fragrant healing or soothing lotion or ointment **2** : any of several spicy fragrant herbs **3** : something that comforts or soothes

balmy adj : gently soothing : MILD **syn** soft, bland

bal·sa \'bȯl-sə\ n : the extremely light strong wood of a tropical American tree

bal·sam \'bȯl-səm\ n **1** : a fragrant aromatic and usu. resinous substance oozing from various plants; *also* : a preparation containing or smelling like balsam **2** : a balsam-yielding plant; *also* : any of several showy garden plants

bal·us·ter \'bal-ə-stər\ n : an upright support of a rail (as of a staircase)

bal·us·trade \-ə-ˌstrād\ n : a row of balusters topped by a rail

bam·boo \bam-'bü\ n : any of various woody mostly tall tropical grasses including some with strong hollow stems used for building, furniture, or utensils

bam·boo·zle \bam-'bü-zəl\ vb : TRICK, HOODWINK

¹**ban** \'ban\ vb **banned**; **ban·ning** : PROHIBIT, FORBID

²**ban** n **1** : CURSE **2** : a legal or official prohibiting

³**ban** \'bän\ n, pl **ba·ni** \'bän-ē\ — see MONEY table

ba·nal \bə-'näl, -'nal; 'bān-ᵊl\ adj : COMMONPLACE, TRITE — **ba·nal·i·ty** \bā-'nal-ət-ē\ n

ba·nana \bə-'nan-ə\ n : a treelike tropical plant bearing thick clusters of yellow or reddish fruit; *also* : this fruit

¹**band** \'band\ n **1** : something (as a fetter or an obligation) that constrains or restrains **2** : a strip serving to bring or hold together; *also* : one used to cover, protect, or finish something **3** : a range of wavelengths (as in radio)

²**band** vb 1 : to tie up, finish, or enclose with a band   2 : to gather or unite in a company or for some common end

³**band** n : a group of persons, animals, or things; esp : a company of musicians organized for playing together

¹**ban·dage** \'ban-dij\ n : a strip of material used esp. in dressing wounds

²**bandage** vb : to dress or cover with a bandage

ban·dan·na or **ban·dana** \ban-'dan-ə\ n : a large colored figured handkerchief

band·box \'ban(d)-,bäks\ n : a light box for carrying articles of attire

ban·de·role or **ban·de·rol** \'ban-də-,rōl\ n : a long narrow forked flag or streamer

ban·dit \'ban-dət\ n, pl **bandits** also **ban·dit·ti** \ban-'dit-ē\ : BRIGAND, GANGSTER — **ban·dit·ry** \'ban-də-trē\ n

ban·do·lier or **ban·do·leer** \,ban-də-'liər\ n : a belt slung over the shoulder and used esp. to carry ammunition

band·stand \'ban(d)-,stand\ n : a usu. roofed outdoor stand or platform on which a band or orchestra performs

band·wag·on \'band-,wag-ən\ n 1 : a wagon carrying musicians in a parade   2 : a candidate, side, or movement that attracts open support or approval because it seems to be winning or gaining popularity — used in phrases like *climb on the bandwagon*

¹**ban·dy** \'ban-dē\ vb 1 : to exchange (as blows or quips) in rapid succession   2 : to use in a glib or offhand way

²**bandy** adj : curved outward ⟨~ legs⟩

bane \'bān\ n 1 : POISON   2 : WOE, HARM; also : a source of this — **bane·ful** adj

¹**bang** \'baŋ\ vb 1 : BUMP   2 : to strike, thrust, or move usu. with a loud noise

²**bang** n 1 : BLOW   2 : a sudden loud noise

³**bang** adv : DIRECTLY, RIGHT

⁴**bang** n : a fringe of hair cut short (as across the forehead)

⁵**bang** vb : to cut a bang or a bang in

ban·gle \'baŋ-gəl\ n : BRACELET; also : a loose-hanging ornament

bang-up \'baŋ-,əp\ adj : FIRST-RATE, EXCELLENT ⟨a ~ job⟩

ban·ish \'ban-ish\ vb 1 : to require by authority to leave a country   2 : to drive out : EXPEL syn exile, ostracize, deport — **ban·ish·ment** n

ban·is·ter \'ban-ə-stər\ n 1 : a baluster of a stair rail   2 : the handrail of a staircase

ban·jo \'ban-,jō\ n : a musical instrument with a long neck, a drumlike body, and usu. 5 strings — **ban·jo·ist** n

¹**bank** \'baŋk\ n 1 : a piled-up mass (as of cloud or earth)   2 : an undersea elevation   3 : rising ground bordering a lake, river, or sea   4 : the sidewise slope of a surface along a curve or of a vehicle as it rounds a curve

²**bank** vb 1 : to form a bank about   2 : to build (a curve) with the roadbed or track inclined laterally upward from the inside edge   3 : to pile or heap in a bank; also : to arrange in a tier   4 : to incline (an airplane) laterally

³**bank** n 1 : a tier of oars   2 : a group of objects arranged near together (as in a row or tier)

⁴**bank** n 1 : an establishment concerned esp. with the custody, loan, exchange, or issue of money, the extension of credit, and the transmission of funds   2 : a stock of or a place for holding something in reserve ⟨a blood ~⟩

⁵**bank** vb 1 : to conduct the business of a bank   2 : to deposit money or have an account in a bank — **bank·er** n — **bank·ing** n

bank·book \-,bùk\ n : the depositor's book in which a bank records his deposits and withdrawals

bank note n : a promissory note issued by a bank and circulating as money

bank·roll \'baŋk-,rōl\ n : supply of money : FUNDS

¹**bank·rupt** \'baŋk-(,)rəpt\ n : an insolvent person; esp : one whose property is turned over by court action to a trustee to be handled for the benefit of his creditors — **bankrupt** vb

²**bankrupt** adj 1 : reduced to financial ruin; esp : legally declared a bankrupt   2 : wholly lacking in or deprived of some essential ⟨~ soils⟩ ⟨~ of natural emotion⟩ — **bank·rupt·cy** n

¹**ban·ner** \'ban-ər\ n 1 : a piece of cloth attached to a staff and used by a ruler or commander as his standard   2 : FLAG

²**banner** adj : distinguished from all others esp. in excellence ⟨a ~ year for apple growers⟩

ban·nock \'ban-ək\ n : a flat oatmeal or barley cake usu. cooked on a griddle

banns \'banz\ n pl : public announcement esp. in church of a proposed marriage

ban·quet \'baŋ-kwət\ n : a ceremonial dinner — **banquet** vb

ban·quette \baŋ-'ket\ n 1 : a raised way along the inside of a parapet or trench for gunners or guns   2 : a long upholstered seat esp. along a wall

ban·shee \'ban-shē\ n : a female spirit in Gaelic folklore whose wailing warns a family of an approaching death

ban·tam \'bant-əm\ n 1 : a small domestic fowl that is often a miniature of a standard breed   2 : a small but pugnacious person

¹**ban·ter** \'bant-ər\ vb : to ridicule playfully : CHAFF, RALLY

²**banter** n : RAILLERY

bant·ling \'bant-liŋ\ n : a young child

Ban·tu \'ban-,tü\ n : a member of a family of negroid peoples occupying equatorial and southern Africa — **Bantu** adj

ban·yan \'ban-yən\ n : a large East Indian tree whose aerial roots grow downward to the ground and form new trunks

bao·bab \'baù-,bab, 'bā-ə-\ n : an Old World tropical tree with short swollen trunk and sour edible gourdlike fruits

bap·tism \'bap-,tiz-əm\ n 1 : a Christian sacrament signifying spiritual rebirth and symbolized by the ritual use of water   2 : an act of baptizing — **bap·tis·mal** \bap-'tiz-məl\ adj

Bap·tist \'bap-təst\ n : a member of a Protestant denomination emphasizing baptism of believers by immersion

bap·tis·tery \-tə-strē\ n : a place esp. in a church used for baptism

bap·tize \bap-'tīz\ vb [Gk *baptizein*, fr.

baptos dipped, fr. *baptein* to dip] **1** : to administer baptism to; *also* : CHRISTEN **2** : to purify esp. by an ordeal

1bar \'bär\ *n* **1** : a long narrow piece of material (as wood or metal) used esp. for a lever, fastening, or support **2** : BARRIER, OBSTACLE **3** : the railing in a law court at which prisoners are stationed; *also* : the legal profession or the whole body of lawyers **4** : a stripe, band, or line much longer than wide **5** : a counter at which food or esp. drink is served; *also* : BARROOM **6** : a vertical line across the musical staff

2bar *vb* barred; bar·ring **1** : to fasten, confine, or obstruct with or as if with a bar or bars **2** : to mark with bars : STRIPE **3** : to shut or keep out : EX-CLUDE **4** : FORBID, PREVENT

3bar *prep* : EXCEPT

barb \'bärb\ *n* : a sharp usu. hooked or back-extending projection (as on an arrowhead, a fishhook, or a plant process) — **barbed** \'bärbd\ *adj*

bar·bar·i·an \bär-'ber-ē-ən\ *n* : an in-completely civilized person — **barbarian** *adj*

bar·bar·ic \bär-'bar-ik\ *adj* **1** : BAR-BARIAN **2** : WILD **3** : PRIMITIVE, UN-SOPHISTICATED

bar·ba·rism \'bär-bə-,riz-əm\ *n* **1** : a word or expression that offends current standards of correctness or purity **2** : the social level of barbarians; *also* : the use or display of barbarian or barbarous cultural attributes

bar·ba·rous \'bär-b(ə-)rəs\ *adj* **1** : us-ing linguistic barbarisms **2** : deficient in culture or refinement **3** : mercilessly harsh or cruel — **bar·bar·i·ty** \bär-'bar-ət-ē\ *n* — **bar·ba·rous·ly** *adv*

1bar·be·cue \'bär-bi-,kyü\ *n* : a large animal (as an ox) roasted whole over an open fire; *also* : a social gathering at which barbecued food is served

2barbecue *vb* : to cook over hot coals or on a revolving spit usu. with a highly seasoned vinegar sauce

bar·bell \'bär-,bel\ *n* : a bar with ad-justable weights attached to each end used for exercise and in weight-lifting competition

bar·ber \'bär-bər\ *n* : one whose busi-ness is cutting and dressing hair or shaving and trimming beards

bar·ber·ry \'bär-,ber-ē\ *n* : a spiny shrub bearing sour oblong red berries

bar·bi·can \'bär-bi-kən\ *n* : an outer defensive work

bar·bit·u·rate \bär-'bich-ə-rət\ *n* : a salt or ester of an organic acid (**bar-bi·tu·ric acid** \,bär-bə-,t(y)ùr-ik-\); *esp* : one used as a sedative or hyp-notic

bar·ca·role *or* **bar·ca·rolle** \'bär-kə-,rōl\ *n* : a Venetian boat song charac-terized by a beat suggesting a rowing rhythm; *also* : a piece of music imitating this

bard \'bärd\ *n* : POET

1bare \'baər\ *adj* **1** : NAKED **2** : UNCON-CEALED, EXPOSED **3** : EMPTY **4** : leav-ing nothing to spare : MERE **5** : PLAIN, UNADORNED syn nude, bald — **bare-ness** *n*

2bare *vb* : to make or lay bare : REVEAL

bare·back \-,bak\ *or* **bare·backed** \-'bakt\ *adv (or adj)* : without a saddle

bare·faced \-'fāst\ *adj* **1** : having the face uncovered; *esp* : BEARDLESS **2** : not concealed : OPEN

bare·foot \-,fût\ *or* **bare·foot·ed** \-'füt-əd\ *adv (or adj)* : with the feet bare

bare·hand·ed \-'han-dəd\ *adv (or adj)* **1** : without gloves **2** : without tools or weapons

bare·head·ed \-'hed-əd\ *adv (or adj)* : without a hat

bare·ly *adv* **1** : by a narrow margin : SCARCELY **2** : with nothing to spare : SPARSELY syn hardly

1bar·gain \'bär-gən\ *n* **1** : AGREEMENT **2** : something of which the value ex-ceeds the cost **3** : a transaction, situ-ation, or event with important good or bad results

2bargain *vb* **1** : to talk over the terms of an agreement : CHAFFER, HAGGLE; *also* : to come to terms : BARTER

1barge \'bärj\ *n* **1** : a broad flat-bot-tomed boat for river or canal use usu. moved by towing **2** : a powerboat sup-plied to a flagship (as for use by an ad-miral) **3** : a ceremonial boat elegantly furnished — **barge·man** \-mən\ *n*

2barge *vb* **1** : to carry by barge **2** : to move or thrust oneself clumsily or rudely

bar·i·tone \'bar-ə-,tōn\ *n* [It *baritono*, fr. Gk *barytonos* having a deep sound, fr. *barys* heavy + *tonos* tone] : a male voice between bass and tenor; *also* : a man with such a voice

bar·i·um \'bar-ē-əm\ *n* : a silver-white metallic chemical element that occurs only in combination and is used in the form of its sulfate as a pigment and as a substance that is opaque to X rays

1bark \'bärk\ *vb* **1** : to make the charac-teristic short sharp cry of a dog : to speak or utter in a curt loud tone : SNAP

2bark *n* : the sound made by a barking dog

3bark *n* : the tough corky outer covering of a woody stem or root

4bark *vb* **1** : to strip the bark from **2** : to rub the skin from : ABRADE

5bark *n* : a 3-masted ship with foremast and mainmast square-rigged

bar·keep·er \'bär-,kē-pər\ *n* : one that keeps or tends a bar for the sale of liquors

bark·er \'bär-kər\ *n* : a person who stands at the entrance esp. to a show and tries to attract customers to it

bar·ley \'bär-lē\ *n* : a cereal grass with seeds used as food and in making malt liquors; *also* : its seed

bar mitz·vah \bär-'mits-və\ *n* **1** : a Jewish boy who at about 13 years of age assumes religious responsibilities **2** : the ceremony recognizing a boy as a bar mitzvah

barn \'bärn\ *n* : a building used esp. for storing hay and grain and for hous-ing livestock and often adjoined by a fenced enclosure (**barn·yard** \-,yärd\)

bar·na·cle \'bär-ni-kəl\ *n* : a marine crustacean free-swimming when young but fixed (as to rocks) when adult

barn·storm \'bärn-,störm\ *vb* **1** : to tour through rural districts staging theatrical performances usu. in one-night stands **2** : to travel from place to place making brief stops (as in political campaigning)

barn·yard \-,yärd\ *n* : a usu. fenced area adjoining a barn

ba·rom·e·ter \bə-'räm-ət-ər\ *n* : an in-strument for measuring atmospheric pressure and so predicting weather changes — **baro·met·ric** \,bar-ə-'met-rik\ *adj*

bar·on \'bar-ən\ *n* 1 : a member of the lowest grade of the British peerage — **ba·ro·ni·al** \bə-'rō-nē-əl\ *adj* — **bar·ony** \'bar-ə-nē\ *n*

bar·on·age \-ij\ *n* : PEERAGE

bar·on·ess \'bar-ə-nəs\ *n* 1 : the wife or widow of a baron 2 : a woman holding a baronial title in her own right

bar·on·et \-nət\ *n* : a man holding a rank of honor below a baron but above a knight — **bar·on·et·cy** *n*

ba·roque \bə-'rōk, -'räk\ *adj* : marked by elaborate and sometimes grotesque ornamentation and esp. by curved and plastic figures

ba·rouche \bə-'rüsh\ *n* : a 4-wheeled carriage with a high driver's seat in front and a folding top

bar·racks \'bar-əks\ *n sing or pl* : a building or group of buildings for lodging soldiers

bar·ra·cu·da \,bar-ə-'küd-ə\ *n* : any of several large fierce sea fishes related to the gray mullets

bar·rage \bə-'räzh, -'räj\ *n* : a barrier laid down by machine-gun or artillery fire directed against a narrow strip of ground

bar·ra·try \'bar-ə-trē\ *n* 1 : the purchase or sale of office or preferment in church or state 2 : a fraudulent breach of duty by the master or crew of a ship intended to harm the owner or cargo 3 : the practice of inciting lawsuits or quarrels

barred \'bärd\ *adj* : STRIPED

¹**bar·rel** \'bar-əl\ *n* 1 : a round bulging cask with flat ends of equal diameter 2 : the amount contained in a barrel 3 : a cylindrical or tubular part ⟨gun ~⟩

²**barrel** *vb* -reled *or* -relled; -rel·ing *or* -rel·ling 1 : to pack in a barrel 2 : to travel at high speed

¹**bar·ren** \'bar-ən\ *adj* 1 : STERILE, UNFRUITFUL 2 : lacking interest or charm 3 : UNPROFITABLE 4 : DULL, STUPID — **bar·ren·ness** *n*

²**barren** *n* : a tract of barren land

bar·rette \bä-'ret\ *n* : a clasp for holding a woman's hair in place

¹**bar·ri·cade** \'bar-ə-,kād\ *vb* : to block, obstruct, or fortify with a barricade

²**barricade** *n* 1 : a hastily thrown-up obstruction or fortification 2 : BARRIER, OBSTACLE

bar·ri·er \'bar-ē-ər\ *n* : something material that separates, demarcates, or serves as a barricade; *also* : an immaterial obstacle ⟨racial ~s⟩

bar·ris·ter \'bar-ə-stər\ *n* : a British counselor admitted to plead in the higher courts **syn** lawyer, attorney

bar·room \'bär-,rüm, -,rum\ *n* : an establishment whose main feature is a bar for the sale of liquor

¹**bar·row** \'bar-ō\ *n* : a large burial mound of earth and stones

²**barrow** *n* : a male hog castrated while young

³**barrow** *n* 1 : a frame that has handles and sometimes a wheel and is used for carrying things 2 : a cart with boxlike body and two shafts for pushing

bar·tend·er \'bär-,ten-dər\ *n* : one that serves liquor at a bar

bar·ter \'bärt-ər\ *vb* : to trade by exchange of goods — **barter** *n*

bas·al \'bā-səl\ *adj* : BASIC

ba·salt \bə-'sȯlt, 'bā-,sȯlt\ *n* : a dark fine-grained igneous rock — **ba·sal·tic** \bə-'sȯl-tik\ *adj*

¹**base** \'bās\ *n* 1 : BOTTOM, FOUNDATION 2 : a main ingredient or fundamental part 3 : the point of beginning an act or operation 4 : any of the four stations at the corners of a baseball diamond 5 : a place on which a force depends for supplies 6 : a chemical compound (as lime or ammonia) that reacts with an acid to form a salt, has a salty taste, and turns litmus blue **syn** basis, ground

²**base** *vb* 1 : to form or serve as a base for 2 : ESTABLISH

³**base** *adj* 1 : of inferior quality : DEBASED, ALLOYED 2 : CONTEMPTIBLE, IGNOBLE 3 : MENIAL, DEGRADING 4 : of little value **syn** low, vile — **base·ly** *adv* — **base·ness** *n*

base·ball \'bās-,bȯl\ *n* : a game played with a bat and ball by 2 teams on a field with 4 bases arranged in a diamond; *also* : the ball used in this game

base·board \-,bōrd\ *n* : a line of boards or molding covering the joint of a wall and the adjoining floor

base·less \-ləs\ *adj* : having no base or basis : GROUNDLESS

base·ment \-mənt\ *n* 1 : the part of a building that is wholly or partly below ground level 2 : the lowest or fundamental part of something

base on balls : an advance to first base given to a baseball player who receives four balls

bash \'bash\ *vb* 1 : to strike violently : BEAT 2 : to smash by a blow

bash·ful \'bash-fəl\ *adj* : inclined to shrink from public attention — **bash·ful·ness** *n*

ba·sic \'bā-sik\ *adj* 1 : of, relating to, or forming the base or essence : FUNDAMENTAL 2 : of, relating to, or having the character of a chemical base (a ~ substance) **syn** underlying — **ba·si·cal·ly** *adv*

bas·il \'baz-əl, 'bās-\ *n* : an aromatic mint used in cookery

ba·sil·i·ca \bə-'sil-i-kə, -'zil-\ *n* 1 : an early Christian church of simple design 2 : a church or cathedral given ceremonial privileges

bas·i·lisk \'bas-ə-,lisk, 'baz-\ *n* : a legendary reptile with fatal breath and glance

ba·sin \'bās-ᵊn\ *n* 1 : a wide hollow vessel for holding liquid (as water) 2 : a hollow or enclosed place containing water; *also* : the region drained by a river

ba·sis \'bā-səs\ *n, pl* **ba·ses** \-,sēz\ 1 : FOUNDATION, BASE 2 : a fundamental principle

bask \'bask\ *vb* 1 : to expose oneself to comfortable heat 2 : to enjoy something as if comforting warmth ⟨~ing in his friends' admiration⟩

bas·ket \'bas-kət\ *n* : a container of woven material (as twigs or grasses); *also* : any of various lightweight usu. wood containers — **bas·ket·ful** *n*

bas·ket·ball \-,bȯl\ *n* : a game played on a court by 2 teams who try to throw an inflated ball through a raised goal; *also* : the ball used in this game

bas mitz·vah \bäs-'mits-və\ *n* **1** : a Jewish girl who at about 13 years of age assumes religious responsibilities **2** : the ceremony recognizing a girl as a bas mitzvah

Basque \'bask\ *n* : a member of a people inhabiting a region bordering on the Bay of Biscay in northern Spain and southwestern France — **Basque** *adj*

bas-re·lief \,bä-ri-'lēf\ *n* : a sculpture in relief with the design raised very slightly from the background

¹**bass** \'bas\ *n* : any of several spiny-finned sport and food fishes of eastern No. America

²**bass** \'bās\ *adj* : deep or grave in tone : of low pitch

³**bass** \'bās\ *n* **1** : a deep sound or tone **2** : the lowest part in harmonic or polyphonic music **3** : the lowest male singing voice **4** : a singer or instrument having a bass voice or part

bas·si·net \,bas-ə-'net\ *n* : a basket hooded at one end for use as a cradle

bas·so \'bas-ō\ *n* : a bass singer

bas·soon \ba-'sün, bə-\ *n* : a musical wind instrument lower in pitch than the oboe

bass·wood \'bas-,wud\ *n* **1** : a linden tree; *also* : its wood **2** : TULIP TREE

bast \'bast\ *n* : strong woody plant fiber used esp. in making ropes

¹**bas·tard** \'bas-tərd\ *n* : an illegitimate child

²**bastard** *adj* **1** : ILLEGITIMATE **2** : of an inferior or nontypical kind, size, or form; *also* : SPURIOUS — **bas·tardy** *n*

¹**baste** \'bāst\ *vb* : to sew with long stitches so as to keep temporarily in place

²**baste** *vb* : to moisten (as roasting meat) at intervals with liquid while cooking

bas·ti·na·do \,bas-tə-'nād-ō, -'näd-\ *n*, *pl* **-does 1** : a blow or beating esp. with a stick **2** : a punishment consisting of beating the soles of the feet

bas·tion \'bas-chən\ *n* : a projecting part of a fortification; *also* : a fortified area or position — **bas·tioned** *adj*

¹**bat** \'bat\ *n* **1** : a stout stick : CLUB **2** : a sharp blow **3** : an implement (as of wood) used to hit the ball (as in baseball) **4** : a turn at batting — usu. used with *at*

²**bat** *vb* **bat·ted; bat·ting** : to hit with or as if with a bat

³**bat** *n* : any of a large group of flying mammals with forelimbs modified to form wings

batch \'bach\ *n* **1** : a quantity (as of bread) baked at one time **2** : a quantity of material for use at one time or produced at one operation

bate \'bāt\ *vb* : MODERATE, REDUCE

ba·teau *also* **bat·teau** \ba-'tō\ *n*, *pl* **ba·teaux** \-'tōz\ : any of various small craft

bath \'bath, 'bàth\ *n*, *pl* **baths** \'bathz, 'baths, 'bàthz, 'bàths\ **1** : a washing of the body **2** : water for washing the body **3** : a liquid in which objects are immersed so that it can act on them **4** : BATHROOM

bathe \'bāth\ *vb* **1** : to wash in liquid and esp. water; *also* : to apply water or a medicated liquid to ⟨bathed her eyes⟩ **2** : to wash along, over, or against so as to wet **3** : to suffuse with or as if with

light **4** : to take a bath; *also* : to take a swim — **bath·er** *n*

bath·house \'bath-,haus, 'bàth-\ *n* **1** : a building equipped for bathing **2** : a building containing dressing rooms for bathers

ba·thos \'bā-,thäs\ *n* **1** : the sudden appearance of the commonplace in otherwise elevated matter or style **2** : insincere or overdone pathos — **ba·thet·ic** \bə-'thet-ik\ *adj*

bath·robe \-,rōb\ *n* : a loose usu. absorbent robe worn before and after bathing or as a dressing gown

bath·room \-,rüm, -,rum\ *n* **1** : a room with facilities for bathing **2** : TOILET

bath·tub \-,təb\ *n* : a usu. fixed tub for bathing

ba·tiste \bə-'tēst\ *n* : a fine sheer fabric of plain weave

bat·man \'bat-mən\ *n* : an orderly of a British military officer

ba·ton \bə-'tän\ *n* : STAFF, ROD; *esp* : a stick with which the leader directs an orchestra or band

ba·tra·chi·an \bə-'trā-kē-ən\ *n* : a tailless leaping amphibian : FROG, TOAD — **ba·tra·chi·an** *adj*

bats·man \'bats-mən\ *n* : a batter esp. in cricket

bat·tal·ion \bə-'tal-yən\ *n* **1** : a large body of troops organized to act together : ARMY **2** : a military unit composed of a headquarters and two or more units (as companies)

¹**bat·ten** \'bat-ᵊn\ *vb* **1** : to grow or make fat **2** : THRIVE

²**batten** *n* : a strip of wood for nailing across other pieces to cover a crack or strengthen parts

³**batten** *vb* : to fasten with battens

¹**bat·ter** \'bat-ər\ *vb* : to beat or damage with repeated blows

²**batter** *n* : a soft mixture (as for cake) basically of flour and liquid

³**batter** *n* : one that bats; *esp* : the player whose turn it is to bat

battering ram *n* : an ancient military machine for battering down walls

bat·tery \'bat-(ə-)rē\ *n* **1** : BEATING; *esp* : unlawful beating of or use of force on a person **2** : a grouping of artillery pieces for tactical purposes; *also* : the guns of a warship **3** : a group of electric cells for furnishing electric current; *also* : a single electric cell ⟨a flashlight ∼⟩ **4** : a number of similar items grouped or used as a unit ⟨a ∼ of tests⟩ **5** : the pitcher and the catcher of a baseball team

bat·ting \'bat-iŋ\ *n* : layers or sheets of cotton or wool (as for lining quilts)

¹**bat·tle** \'bat-ᵊl\ *n* : a general military engagement; *also* : an extended contest or controversy

²**battle** *vb* : to engage in battle : CONTEND, FIGHT

bat·tle-ax \-,aks\ *n* : a long-handled ax formerly used as a weapon

bat·tle·dore \-,dōr\ *n* : a light flat bat or racket used in striking a shuttlecock

bat·tle·field \-,fēld\ *n* : a place where a battle is fought

bat·tle·ment \-mənt\ *n* : a decorative or defensive parapet on top of a wall

bat·tle·ship \-,ship\ *n* : a warship of the most heavily armed and armored class

bau·ble \'bò-bəl\ *n* : a trifling bit of finery : TRINKET

baux·ite \'bòk-,sīt\ *n* : a clayey substance that is the chief ore of aluminum

bawdy \'bȯd-ē\ *adj* : OBSCENE, LEWD — **bawd·i·ly** *adv* — **bawd·i·ness** *n*

¹**bawl** \'bȯl\ *vb* : to cry or cry out loudly; *also* : to scold harshly

²**bawl** *n* : a long loud cry : BELLOW

¹**bay** \'bā\ *adj* : reddish brown

²**bay** *n* **1** : a bay-colored animal **2** : a moderate brown

³**bay** *n* : the Old World laurel; *also* : a shrub or tree resembling this

⁴**bay** *n* **1** : a compartment of a building set off from other parts (as by pillars) **2** : a compartment projecting outward from the wall of a building and containing a window

⁵**bay** *vb* : to bark with deep long tones

⁶**bay** *n* **1** : the position of one unable to escape and forced to face danger **2** : a baying bark

⁷**bay** *n* : an inlet of a body of water (as the sea) usu. smaller than a gulf

bay·ber·ry \'bā-,ber-ē\ *n* **1** : a West Indian tree related to the allspice **2** : the American wax myrtle; *also* : its fruit

¹**bay·o·net** \'bā-ə-nət, ,bā-ə-'net\ *n* : a daggerlike weapon made to fit on the muzzle end of a rifle

²**bayonet** *vb* **-net·ed** *also* **-net·ted**; **-net·ing** *also* **-net·ting** : to use or stab with a bayonet

bay·ou \'bī-ō, -ü\ *n* : a minor or secondary stream that is tributary to a larger body of water; *also* : a marshy or sluggish body of water

ba·zaar \bə-'zär\ *n* **1** : a group of shops : MARKETPLACE **2** : a fair usu. for charity

ba·zoo·ka \bə-'zü-kə\ *n* : a weapon consisting of a tube and launching an explosive rocket able to pierce armor

be \(')bē\ *vb*, *past 1st & 3rd sing* **was** \(')wəz, 'wäz\ *2nd sing* **were** \(')wər\ *pl sing* **were**; *past subjunctive* **were**; *past part* **been** \(')bin\ *pres part* **be·ing** \'bē-iŋ\ *pres 1st sing* **am** \(ə)m, (')am\ *2nd sing* **are** \ər, (')är\ *3rd sing* **is** \'iz, əz\ *pl* **are**; *pres subjunctive* **be 1** : to equal in meaning or symbolically ⟨*God is* love⟩; *also* : to have a specified qualification or relationship ⟨leaves *are* green⟩ ⟨this fish *is* a trout⟩ **2** : to have objective existence ⟨there *was* once an old woman⟩; *also* : to have or occupy a particular place ⟨here *is* your pen⟩ **3** : to take place : OCCUR ⟨the meeting *is* tonight⟩ **4** — used with the past participle of transitive verbs as a passive voice auxiliary ⟨the door *was* opened⟩ **5** — used as the auxiliary of the present participle in expressing continuous action ⟨he *is* sleeping⟩ **6** — used as an auxiliary with the past participle of some intransitive verbs to form archaic perfect tenses **7** — used as an auxiliary with *to* and the infinitive to express futurity, prearrangement, or obligation ⟨he *is* to come when called⟩

¹**beach** \'bēch\ *n* : the shore of the sea or of a lake

²**beach** *vb* : to run or drive ashore

beach·comb·er \-,kō-mər\ *n* **1** : a drifter, loafer, or casual worker along the seacoast **2** : one who searches along a shore for useful or salable flotsam and refuse

beach flea *n* : any of various small leaping crustaceans common on beaches

beach·head \'bēch-,hed\ *n* : an area on an enemy-held shore occupied by an advance attacking force to protect the later landing of troops or supplies

bea·con \'bē-kən\ *n* **1** : a signal fire **2** : a signal mark (as a lighthouse) for guidance **3** : a radio transmitter emitting signals for guidance of airplanes

bead \'bēd\ *n* [OE *bed* prayer] **1** *pl* : a series of prayers and meditations made with a rosary **2** : a small piece of material pierced for threading on a line (as in a rosary) **3** : a small globular body **4** : a narrow projecting rim or band — **bead·ing** *n* — **beady** *adj*

bea·dle \'bēd-ᵊl\ *n* : a usu. English parish officer whose duties include keeping order in church

bea·gle \'bē-gəl\ *n* : small short-legged smooth-coated hound

beak \'bēk\ *n* : the bill of a bird and esp. of a bird of prey; *also* : a pointed projecting part — **beaked** \'bēkt\ *adj*

bea·ker \'bē-kər\ *n* **1** : a large drinking cup with a wide mouth **2** : a thin-walled laboratory vessel with a wide mouth

¹**beam** \'bēm\ *n* **1** : a large long piece of timber or metal **2** : the bar of a balance from which the scales hang **3** : the breadth of a ship at its widest part **4** : a ray or shaft of light **5** : a collection of nearly parallel rays (as X rays) or streams of particles (as electrons) **6** : a directed flow of radio signals for the guidance of pilots; *also* : the course indicated by this flow

²**beam** *vb* **1** : to send out light **2** : to smile with joy **3** : to aim (a radio broadcast) by directional antennas

bean \'bēn\ *n* : the edible seed borne in pods by some leguminous plants; *also* : a plant or a pod bearing these seeds

bean·ie \'bē-nē\ *n* : a small round tight-fitting skullcap worn esp. by schoolboys and collegians

¹**bear** \'baər\ *n* **1** *or pl* **bear** : a large heavy mammal with shaggy hair and a very short tail **2** : a surly uncouth person **3** : one who sells securities or commodities in expectation of a price decline — **bear·ish** *adj*

²**bear** *vb* **bore** \'bōr\ **borne** \'bōrn\ *also* **born** \'bȯrn\ **bear·ing 1** : CARRY **2** : to be equipped with **3** : to give testimony ⟨~ witness to the facts of the case⟩ **4** : to give birth to; *also* : PRODUCE, YIELD ⟨a tree that ~s regularly⟩ **5** : ENDURE, SUSTAIN ⟨~ pain⟩ ⟨*bore* the weight on piles⟩; *also* : to exert pressure or influence **6** : to be or become directed ⟨~ to the right⟩ — **bear·able** *adj* — **bear·er** *n*

¹**beard** \'biərd\ *n* **1** : the hair that grows on the face of a man **2** : a growth of bristly hairs (as on rye or the chin of a goat) — **beard·less** *adj*

²**beard** *vb* : to confront boldly

bear·ing \'ba(ə)r-iŋ\ *n* **1** : manner of carrying oneself : COMPORTMENT **2** : a supporting object, purpose, or point **3** : an emblem in a coat of arms **4** : connection with or influence on something; *also* : SIGNIFICANCE **5** : a machine part in which another part (as an axle or pin) turns **6** : the position or direction of one point with respect to another or to the compass; *also* : a determination of

---

ə abut; ᵉ kitten; ər further; a back; ā bake; ä cot, cart; aȯ out; ch chin; e less; ē easy; g gift; i trip; ī life; j joke; ŋ sing; ō flow; ȯ flaw; ȯi coin; th thin; t̲h̲ this; ü loot; u̇ foot; y yet; yü few; yu̇ furious; zh vision

position **7** *pl* **:** comprehension of one's position or situation

bear·skin \'baər-,skin\ *n* **:** an article (as a military hat) made of the skin of a bear

beast \'bēst\ *n* **1 :** ANIMAL; *esp* **:** a 4-footed animal **2 :** a contemptible person **syn** brute — **beast·ly** *adj*

¹**beat** \'bēt\ *vb* beat; beat·en \'bēt-ᵊn\ *or* beat; beat·ing **1 :** to strike repeatedly **2 :** TREAD **3 :** to affect or alter by beating (~ metal into sheets) **4 :** OVERCOME; *also* **:** SURPASS **5 :** to sound (as an alarm) on a drum **6 :** to act or arrive before (~ his brother home) **7 :** THROB — **beat·er** *n*

²**beat** *n* **1 :** a single stroke or blow esp. of a series; *also* **:** PULSATION **2 :** a rhythmic stress in poetry or music or the rhythmic effect of these **3 :** a regular course

be·atif·ic \,bē-ə-'tif-ik\ *adj* **:** giving or indicative of great joy or bliss

be·at·i·fy \bē-'at-ə-,fī\ *vb* **1 :** to make supremely happy **2 :** to declare to have attained the blessedness of heaven and authorize the title "Blessed" — **be·at·i·fi·ca·tion** \-,at-ə-fə-'kā-shən\ *n*

be·at·i·tude \-'at-ə-,t(y)üd\ *n* **1 :** a state of utmost bliss **2 :** a declaration made in the Sermon on the Mount (Mt 5: 3-12) beginning "Blessed are"

beat·nik \'bēt-nik\ *n* **:** a person who behaves and dresses unconventionally and is inclined to exotic philosophizing and extreme self-expression

beau \'bō\ *n, pl* beaux \'bōz\ *or* beaus **1 :** a man of fashion **:** DANDY **2 :** SUITOR, LOVER

Beau·jo·lais \,bō-zhə-'lā\ *n* **:** a French red table wine

beau monde \bō-'mänd\ *n* **:** the world of high society and fashion

beau·te·ous \'byüt-ē-əs\ *adj* **:** BEAUTIFUL — **beau·te·ous·ly** *adv*

beau·ti·cian \byü-'tish-ən\ *n* **:** COSMETOLOGIST

beau·ti·ful \'byüt-i-fəl\ *adj* **:** characterized by beauty **:** LOVELY **syn** pretty, fair — **beau·ti·ful·ly** *adv*

beau·ti·fy \'byüt-ə-,fī\ *vb* **:** to make more beautiful — **beau·ti·fi·er** *n*

beau·ty \'byüt-ē\ *n* **:** qualities that give pleasure to the senses or exalt the mind **:** LOVELINESS; *also* **:** something having such qualities

bea·ver \'bē-vər\ *n* **:** a large fur-bearing rodent that builds dams and underwater houses of mud and sticks; *also* **:** its fur

be·calm \bi-'käm\ *vb* **:** to keep (a ship) motionless by lack of wind

be·cause \bi-'kòz\ *conj* **:** for the reason that

because of *prep* **:** by reason of

beck \'bek\ *n* **:** a beckoning gesture; *also* **:** SUMMONS

beck·on \'bek-ən\ *vb* **:** to summon or signal esp. by a nod or gesture; *also* **:** ATTRACT

be·cloud \bi-'klaùd\ *vb* **:** OBSCURE

be·come \bi-'kəm\ *vb* **1 :** to come to be (~ tired) **2 :** to suit or be suitable to (her dress ~s her)

be·com·ing \bi-'kəm-iŋ\ *adj* **:** SUITABLE, FIT; *also* **:** ATTRACTIVE — **be·com·ing·ly** *adv*

¹**bed** \'bed\ *n* **1 :** an article of furniture to sleep on **2 :** a plot of ground prepared for plants **3 :** FOUNDATION, BOTTOM (river ~) **4 :** LAYER, STRATUM (~ of sandstone)

²**bed** *vb* bed·ded; bed·ding **1 :** to put or go to bed **2 :** to fix in a foundation **:** EMBED **3 :** to plant in a bed or beds **4 :** to lay or set flat or in layers

be·daub \bi-'dòb\ *vb* **:** SMEAR

be·daz·zle \-'daz-əl\ *vb* **:** to confuse by or as if by a strong light — **be·daz·zle·ment** *n*

bed·bug \-,bəg\ *n* **:** a wingless blood-sucking insect infesting houses and esp. beds

bed·clothes \-,klō(th)z\ *n* **:** BEDDING

bed·ding *n* **1 :** materials for making up a bed **2 :** FOUNDATION

be·deck \bi-'dek\ *vb* **:** ADORN

be·dev·il \bi-'dev-əl\ *vb* **1 :** HARASS, TORMENT **2 :** CONFUSE, MUDDLE

be·dew \bi-'d(y)ü\ *vb* **:** to wet with or as if with dew

bed·fel·low \'bed-,fel-ō\ *n* **:** one sharing the bed of another

be·di·zen \bi-'dīz-ᵊn, -'diz-\ *vb* **:** to dress or adorn with showy or vulgar finery

bed·lam \'bed-ləm\ *n* [fr. *Bedlam*, popular name for the Hospital of St. Mary of Bethlehem, London insane asylum] **1** *archaic* **:** an insane asylum **2 :** a scene of uproar and confusion

bed·ou·in \'bed-ə-wən\ *n, often cap* **:** a nomadic Arab of the Arabian, Syrian, or No. African deserts

be·drag·gled \bi-'drag-əld\ *adj* **:** soiled and disordered as if by being drenched

bed·rid·den \'bed-,rid-ᵊn\ *adj* **:** kept in bed by illness or weakness

bed·rock \-'räk\ *n* **:** the solid rock underlying surface materials (as soil)

bed·roll \-,rōl\ *n* **:** bedding rolled up for carrying

bed·room \-,rüm, -,rùm\ *n* **:** a room containing a bed and used esp. for sleeping

bed·side \-,sīd\ *n* **:** the place beside a bed esp. of a sick or dying person

bed·spread \-,spred\ *n* **:** a usu. ornamental outer cover for a bed

bed·stead \-,sted\ *n* **:** the framework of a bed

bed·time \-,tīm\ *n* **:** time to go to bed

bee \'bē\ *n* **1 :** a colonial 4-winged insect often kept in hives for the honey it produces; *also* **:** any of various related insects **2 :** a neighborly gathering for work

beech \'bēch\ *n* **:** a deciduous hardwood tree with smooth gray bark and small sweet triangular nuts (beech·nuts \-,nəts\) — **beech·en** \'bē-chən\ *adj*

beef \'bēf\ *n, pl* beeves \'bēvz\ *or* beefs **1 :** the flesh of a steer, cow, or bull; *also* **:** the dressed carcass of a beef animal **2 :** a steer, cow, or bull esp. when fattened for food **3 :** MUSCLE, BRAWN

beef·steak \-,stāk\ *n* **:** a slice of beef suitable for broiling or frying

beefy *adj* **:** THICKSET, BRAWNY

bee·hive \'bē-,hīv\ *n* **:** HIVE

bee·keep·er \-,kē-pər\ *n* **:** a raiser of bees — **bee·keep·ing** *n*

bee·line \-,līn\ *n* **:** a straight direct course

been *past part of* BE

beer \'biər\ *n* **:** an alcoholic beverage brewed from malt and hops — **beery** *adj*

bees·wax \'bēz-,waks\ *n* **:** wax that bees secrete and use in making honeycomb

beet \'bēt\ *n* **:** a garden plant with edible leaves and a thick sweet root used as a vegetable, as a source of sugar, or as forage; *also* : its root

1bee·tle \'bēt-ºl\ *n* : an insect with 4 wings of which the stiff outer pair covers the membranous inner pair when not in flight

2beetle *n* : a heavy tool for hammering or ramming

3beetle *vb* : to jut out : PROJECT

be·fall \bi-'fol\ *vb* : to happen to : OCCUR

be·fit \bi-'fit\ *vb* : to be suitable to : BECOME

be·fog \bi-'fog, -'fäg\ *vb* : OBSCURE; *also* : CONFUSE

1be·fore \bi-'fōr\ *adv* 1 : in front 2 : EARLIER

2before *prep* 1 : in front of (stood ~ him) 2 : earlier than (got there ~ me) 3 : in a more important category than (put quality ~ quantity)

3before *conj* 1 : earlier than the time when (he got here ~ I did) 2 : more willingly than (he will starve ~ he will steal)

be·fore·hand \-,hand\ *adv (or adj)* : in advance

be·foul \bi-'faul\ *vb* : SOIL

be·friend \bi-'frend\ *vb* : to act as friend to

be·fud·dle \bi-'fəd-ºl\ *vb* : MUDDLE, CONFUSE

beg \'beg\ *vb* begged; beg·ging 1 : to ask as a charity; *also* : ENTREAT 2 : EVADE 3 : to seek or live by asking charity

be·get \bi-'get\ *vb* -got \-'gät\ -gotten \-'gät-ºn\ *or* -got; -get·ting : to become the father of : SIRE

1beg·gar \'beg-ər\ *n* : one that begs esp. as a way of living

2beggar *vb* : IMPOVERISH

beg·gar·ly *adj* 1 : marked by unrelieved poverty (a ~ life) 2 : contemptibly mean or inadequate (a ~ wage)

beg·gary *n* 1 : extreme poverty 2 : the class or occupation of beggars

be·gin \bi-'gin\ *vb* be·gan \-'gan\ be·gun \-'gən\ be·gin·ning 1 : to do the first part of an action; *also* : to undertake or undergo initial steps : COMMENCE 2 : to come into being : ARISE *also* : FOUND 3 : ORIGINATE, INVENT — be·gin·ner *n*

be·gone \bi-'gon\ *vb* : to go away : DEPART — used esp. in the imperative

be·go·nia \bi-'gōn-yə\ *n* : any of a genus of tropical herbs widely grown for their showy leaves and waxy flowers

be·grime \bi-'grīm\ *vb* : to make dirty with grime : SOIL

be·grudge \-'grəj\ *vb* : GRUDGE

be·guile \-'gīl\ *vb* 1 : DECEIVE, CHEAT 2 : to while away 3 : to coax by wiles : CHARM

be·guine \-'gēn\ *n* : a vigorous popular dance of the islands of Saint Lucia and Martinique

be·gum \'bē-gəm\ *n* : a Muslim woman of high rank

be·half \bi-'haf, -'hàf\ *n* : BENEFIT, SUPPORT, DEFENSE

be·have \bi-'hāv\ *vb* 1 : to bear, comport, or conduct oneself in a particular and esp. a proper way 2 : to act, function, or react in a particular way

be·hav·ior \bi-'hāv-yər\ *n* : way of behaving; *esp* : personal conduct — be·hav·ior·al *adj*

be·head \bi-'hed\ *vb* : to cut off the head of

be·he·moth \bi-'hē-məth, 'bē-ə-,mòth\ *n* : a huge powerful animal described in Job 40:15–24 that is prob. the hippopotamus

be·hest \bi-'hest\ *n* : COMMAND, INJUNCTION

1be·hind \-'hīnd\ *adv* 1 : BACK, BACKWARD 2 : LATE, SLOW

2behind *prep* 1 : in a former place, situation, or time of (stayed ~ the troops) 2 : to or at the back or farther side or part of (ran ~ the house) (stood ~ a tree) 3 : inferior to (as in rank) : BELOW (three games ~ the first-place team) 4 : in support of : SUPPORTING (we're ~ you all the way)

be·hind·hand \-,hand\ *adv (or adj)* 1 : in arrears : BEHIND 2 : behind the times *syn* tardy, late, overdue

be·hold \bi-'hōld\ *vb* 1 : to have in sight : SEE 2 — used imperatively to direct the attention *syn* view, observe, notice, contemplate — be·hold·er *n*

be·hold·en \-'hōl-dən\ *adj* : OBLIGATED, INDEBTED

be·hoof \-'hüf\ *n* : ADVANTAGE, PROFIT

be·hoove \-'hüv\ *or* be·hove \-'hōv\ *vb* : to be necessary, proper, or advantageous for

beige \'bāzh\ *n* : a pale dull yellowish brown — beige *adj*

be·ing \'bē-iŋ\ *n* 1 : EXISTENCE; *also* : LIFE 2 : the qualities or constitution of an existent thing 3 : a living thing; *esp* : PERSON

be·la·bor \bi-'lā-bər\ *vb* 1 : to beat soundly : DRUB 2 : to assail (as with words) tiresomely or at length

be·lat·ed \-'lāt-əd\ *adj* : DELAYED, LATE

be·lay \-'lā\ *vb* 1 : to wind (a rope) around a pin or cleat in order to hold secure 2 : QUIT, STOP — used in the imperative

belch \'belch\ *vb* 1 : to expel (gas) from the stomach through the mouth 2 : to gush forth (a volcano ~ing lava)

bel·dam *or* bel·dame \'bel-dəm\ *n* : an old woman; *esp* : HAG

be·lea·guer \bi-'lē-gər\ *vb* 1 : BESET, BESIEGE 2 : HARASS

bel·fry \'bel-frē\ *n* : a tower for a bell (as on a church); *also* : the part of the tower in which the bell hangs

Bel·gian \'bel-jən\ *n* : a native or inhabitant of Belgium — Belgian *adj*

be·lie \bi-'lī\ *vb* 1 : MISREPRESENT 2 : to give the lie to : be false to; *also* : to run counter to

be·lief \ba-'lēf\ *n* 1 : CONFIDENCE, TRUST 2 : something (as a tenet or creed) believed *syn* conviction, opinion

be·lieve \ba-'lēv\ *vb* 1 : to have religious convictions 2 : to have a firm conviction about something : accept as truly such as indicated 3 : to hold an opinion : SUPPOSE — be·liev·able *adj* — be·liev·er *n*

be·like \bi-'līk\ *adv, archaic* : PROBABLY

be·lit·tle \-'lit-ºl\ *vb* 1 : to make seem little or less; *also* : DISPARAGE

1bell \'bel\ *n* 1 : a hollow metallic device that makes a ringing sound when

ə abut; ᵉ kitten; ər further; a back; ā bake; ä cot, cart; aù out; ch chin; e less; ē easy; g gift; i trip; ī life; j joke; ŋ sing; ō flow; ò flaw; òi coin; th thin; t̲h̲ this; ü loot; ù foot; y yet; yü few; yù furious; zh vision

struck **2** : the sounding or stroke of a bell (as on shipboard to tell the time); *also* : time so indicated **3** : something with the flared form of a typical bell

2bell *vb* : to provide with a bell

bel·la·don·na \,bel-ə-'dän-ə\ *n* [It, lit., beautiful lady; fr. its cosmetic use] **a** : a poisonous herb related to the potato that yields a drug used esp. to relieve spasms and pain or to dilate the eye; *also* : this drug

bell·boy \'bel-,bȯi\ *n* : a hotel or club employee who escorts guests to rooms, assists them with luggage, and runs errands

belle \'bel\ *n* : an attractive and popular girl or woman

belles lettres \bel-letrᵊ\ *n pl* : literature of aesthetic rather than utilitarian value

bell·hop \'bel-,häp\ *n* : BELLBOY

bel·li·cose \'bel-i-,kōs\ *adj* : WARLIKE, PUGNACIOUS **syn** belligerent, quarrelsome — **bel·li·cos·i·ty** \,bel-i-'käs-ət-ē\ *n*

bel·lig·er·en·cy \bə-'lij-(ə-)rən-sē\ *n* **1** : the status of a nation engaged in war **2** : BELLIGERENCE, TRUCULENCE

bel·lig·er·ent \-rənt\ *adj* **1** : waging war **2** : TRUCULENT **syn** bellicose, pugnacious — **bel·lig·er·ence** \-rəns\ *n* — belligerent *n*

bel·low \'bel-ō\ *vb* **1** : to make the deep hollow sound characteristic of a bull **2** : to call or utter in a loud deep voice — bellow *n*

bel·lows \-,ōz, -əz\ *n sing or pl* : a closed boxlike device with sides that can be spread apart or pressed together thereby drawing in air and then expelling it through a tube

bell·weth·er \'bel-'weth-ər\ *n* : one that takes the lead or initiative : LEADER

1bel·ly \'bel-ē\ *n* **1** : ABDOMEN; *also* : STOMACH **2** : the under part of an animal's body

2belly *vb* : BULGE

belly button *n* : NAVEL

be·long \bi-'lȯŋ\ *vb* **1** : to be suitable or appropriate; *also* : to be properly situated ⟨shoes ~ in the closet⟩ **2** : to be the property ⟨this ~s to me⟩; *also* : to be attached (as through birth or membership) ⟨~ to a club⟩ **3** : to form an attribute or part ⟨this wheel ~s to the cart⟩ **4** : to be classified ⟨whales ~ among the mammals⟩

be·long·ings \-'lȯŋ-iŋz\ *n pl* : GOODS, EFFECTS, POSSESSIONS

be·loved \-'ləv-(ə)d\ *adj* : dearly loved — beloved *n*

1be·low \-'lō\ *adv* **1** : in or to a lower place or rank **2** : on earth **3** : in hell **syn** under, beneath, underneath

2below *prep* **1** : in or to a lower place than : UNDER ⟨swimming ~ the surface⟩ **2** : inferior to (as in rank)

1belt \'belt\ *n* **1** : a strip (as of leather) worn about the waist **2** : an endless band passing around pulleys or cylinders to communicate motion or convey material **3** : a region marked by some distinctive feature; *esp* : one suited to a particular crop

2belt *vb* **1** : to encircle or secure with a belt **2** : to beat with or as if with a belt **3** : to mark with an encircling band

bel·ve·dere \'bel-və-,diər\ *n* : a structure (as a summerhouse) designed to command a view

be·mire \bi-'mī(ə)r\ *vb* : to cover or soil with or sink in mire

be·moan \bi-'mōn\ *vb* : LAMENT, DEPLORE **syn** bewail

be·mock \-'mäk\ *vb* : MOCK

be·muse \-'myüz\ *vb* : BEWILDER, CONFUSE

bench \'bench\ *n* **1** : a long seat for two or more persons **2** : a table for holding work and tools ⟨a carpenter's ~⟩ **3** : the seat of a judge in court; *also* : the office or dignity of a judge **4** : COURT; *also* : JUDGES

1bend \'bend\ *n* : a knot by which a rope is fastened (as to another rope)

2bend *vb* **bent** \'bent\ **bend·ing** **1** : to draw (as a bow) taut **2** : to turn or cause to turn : CURVE; *also* : TREND **3** : to make fast : SECURE **4** : SUBDUE **5** : RESOLVE, DETERMINE; *also* : APPLY ⟨*bent* themselves to the task⟩ **6** : DEFLECT **7** : to curve downward : STOOP **8** : YIELD, SUBMIT

3bend *n* **1** : an act or process of bending **2** : something bent; *esp* : CURVE **3** *pl* : a painful and dangerous disorder resulting from too sudden removal (as of a diver) from a compressed atmosphere

1be·neath \bi-'nēth\ *adv* : BELOW, UNDERNEATH **syn** under

2beneath *prep* **1** : BELOW, UNDER ⟨stood ~ a tree⟩ **2** : unworthy of ⟨considered such behavior ~ contempt⟩

ben·e·dict \'ben-ə-,dikt\ *n* : a newly married man who has long been a bachelor

ben·e·dic·tion \,ben-ə-'dik-shən\ *n* : the invocation of a blessing esp. at the close of a public worship service

ben·e·fac·tion \-'fak-shən\ *n* : a charitable donation **syn** contribution, alms

ben·e·fac·tor \'ben-ə-,fak-tər\ *n* : one that confers a benefit and esp. a benefaction

ben·e·fac·tress \-trəs\ *n* : a female benefactor

ben·e·fice \'ben-ə-fəs\ *n* : an ecclesiastical office to which the revenue from an endowment is attached

be·nef·i·cence \bə-'nef-ə-səns\ *n* **1** : beneficent quality **2** : BENEFACTION

be·nef·i·cent \-sənt\ *adj* : doing or producing good (as by acts of kindness or charity); *also* : productive of benefit

ben·e·fi·cial \,ben-ə-'fish-əl\ *adj* : being of benefit or help : HELPFUL **syn** advantageous, profitable — **ben·e·fi·cial·ly** *adv*

ben·e·fi·ci·ary \-'fish-ē-,er-ē, -'fish-(ə)-rē\ *n* : one that receives some benefit (as the income of a trust or the proceeds of an insurance)

1ben·e·fit \'ben-ə-,fit\ *n* **1** : ADVANTAGE, PROFIT **2** : useful aid : HELP; *also* : material aid provided or due (as in sickness or unemployment) as a right **3** : a performance or event to raise funds for some person or cause

2benefit *vb* **-fit·ed** *or* **-fit·ted; -fit·ing** *or* **-fit·ting** **1** : to be useful or profitable to **2** : to receive benefit

be·nev·o·lence \bə-'nev(-ə)-ləns\ *n* **1** : charitable nature **2** : an act of kindness : CHARITY — **be·nev·o·lent** \-lənt\ *adj*

be·night·ed \bi-'nīt-əd\ *adj* **1** : overtaken by darkness or night **2** : living in ignorance

be·nign \bi-'nīn\ *adj* **1** : kindly disposed : GRACIOUS **2** : of a mild kind; *esp* : not malignant ⟨~ tumors⟩ **syn** benignant, kind — **be·nig·ni·ty** \-'nig-nət-ē\ *n*

be·nig·nant \-'nig-nənt\ *adj* **:** BENIGN 1 **syn** kind, kindly

ben·i·son \'ben-ə-sən\ *n* **:** BLESSING, BENEDICTION

bent \'bent\ *n* 1 **:** tendency of mind **:** BIAS 2 **:** power of endurance **syn** talent, aptitude, gift

be·numb \bi-'nəm\ *vb* 1 **:** DULL, DEADEN 2 **:** to make numb esp. by cold

ben·zene \'ben-ˌzēn\ *n* **:** a colorless highly flammable liquid obtained chiefly in the distillation of coal and used as a solvent and in making dyes and drugs

ben·zine \'ben-ˌzēn\ *n* **:** any of various flammable petroleum distillates used as solvents for fats or as motor fuels

ben·zo·ate \'ben-zə-ˌwāt\ *n* **:** a salt or ester of benzoic acid

ben·zo·ic acid \ben-ˌzō-ik-\ *n* **:** a white crystalline acid that occurs in benzoin and cranberries and is used as a preservative and antiseptic

ben·zo·in \'ben-zə-wən\ *n* **:** a balsamlike resin from trees of southern Asia used esp. in medicine and perfumes

ben·zol \'ben-ˌzól\ *n* **:** BENZENE

be·queath \bi-'kwēth, -'kwēth\ *vb* 1 **:** to leave by will 2 **:** to hand down

be·quest \-'kwest\ *n* 1 **:** the action of bequeathing 2 **:** LEGACY

be·rate \-'rāt\ *vb* **:** to scold harshly

Ber·ber \'bər-bər\ *n* **:** a member of a Caucasoid people of northwestern Africa

ber·ceuse \beər-'sə(r)z\ *n* 1 **:** LULLABY 2 **:** a musical composition of a tranquil nature

be·reave \-'rēv\ *vb* **be·reaved** *or* **be·reft** \-'reft\ **be·reav·ing** **:** to deprive esp. by death **:** STRIP ⟨bereaved of hope⟩ — **be·reave·ment** *n*

be·ret \bə-'rā\ *n* **:** a round soft cap with no visor

berg \'bərg\ *n* **:** ICEBERG

beri·beri \ˌber-ē-'ber-ē\ *n* **:** a deficiency disease marked by weakness, wasting, and nerve damage and caused by lack of thiamine

berke·li·um \'bər-klē-əm, ˌbər-'kē-lē-əm\ *n* **:** an artificially prepared radioactive chemical element

ber·ry \'ber-ē\ *n* 1 **:** a small pulpy fruit; *esp* **:** a simple fruit (as a grape, tomato, or banana) with the wall of the ripened ovary thick and pulpy 2 **:** the dry seed of some plants (as coffee)

ber·serk \bə(r)-'sərk, -'zərk\ *adj* **:** FRENZIED, CRAZED — **berserk** *adv*

¹berth \'bərth\ *n* 1 **:** room enough for a ship to maneuver 2 **:** the place where a ship lies at anchor 3 **:** a place to sit or sleep esp. on a ship or vehicle 4 **:** JOB, POSITION **syn** post, situation

²berth *vb* 1 **:** to bring or come into a berth 2 **:** to allot a berth to

ber·yl \'ber-əl\ *n* **:** a hard silicate mineral occurring as green, yellow, pink, or white crystals

be·ryl·li·um \bə-'ril-ē-əm\ *n* **:** a light strong metallic chemical element used as a hardener in alloys

be·seech \bi-'sēch\ *vb* **be·sought** \-'sót\ *or* **be·seeched**; **be·seech·ing** **:** to ask earnestly **:** ENTREAT **syn** implore, beg

be·seem \-'sēm\ *vb*, *archaic* **:** to be seemly or fitting **:** BEFIT

be·set \-'set\ *vb* 1 **:** TROUBLE, HARASS 2 **:** ASSAIL; *also* **:** to hem in **:** SURROUND

be·set·ting *adj* **:** persistently present or assailing

be·shrew \bi-'shrü\ *vb*, *archaic* **:** CURSE

¹be·side \-'sīd\ *adv*, *archaic* **:** BESIDES

²beside *prep* 1 **:** by the side of ⟨sit ∼ me⟩ 2 **:** in addition to ⟨∼ being pretty, she's intelligent⟩ 3 **:** other than ⟨there's nobody here ∼ me⟩

¹be·sides \-'sīdz\ *prep* **:** ²BESIDE 2, 3

²besides *adv* 1 **:** in addition **:** ALSO 2 **:** MOREOVER

be·siege \bi-'sēj\ *vb* **:** to lay siege to; *also* **:** IMPORTUNE — **be·sieg·er** *n*

be·smear \-'smiər\ *vb* **:** SMEAR

be·smirch \-'smərch\ *vb* **:** SMIRCH, SOIL

be·som \'bē-zəm\ *n* **:** BROOM

be·sot·ted \bi-'sät-əd\ *adj* **:** DULL, STUPID; *esp* **:** muddled with drink

be·span·gle \-'spaŋ-gəl\ *vb* **:** to adorn with or as if with spangles

be·spat·ter \-'spat-ər\ *vb* **:** SPATTER

be·speak \-'spēk\ *vb* 1 **:** to hire or arrange for beforehand 2 **:** INDICATE, SIGNIFY 3 **:** FORETELL

be·sprin·kle \-'spriŋ-kəl\ *vb* **:** SPRINKLE

¹best \'best\ *adj*, *superlative of* GOOD 1 **:** excelling all others 2 **:** most productive (as of good or satisfaction) 3 **:** LARGEST, MOST

²best *adv*, *superlative of* WELL 1 **:** in the best way 2 **:** to the highest degree **:** MOST

³best *n* **:** something that is best

⁴best *vb* **:** to get the better of **:** OUTDO

bes·tial \'bes-chəl\ *adj* 1 **:** of or relating to beasts 2 **:** resembling a beast esp. in lack of intelligence or reason **:** BEASTLY

bes·ti·al·i·ty \ˌbes-chē-'al-ət-ē\ *n* 1 **:** the condition or status of a lower animal 2 **:** display or gratification of bestial traits or impulses

be·stir \bi-'stər\ *vb* **:** to rouse to action

be·stow \-'stō\ *vb* 1 **:** PUT, PLACE, STOW 2 **:** to present as a gift **:** CONFER — **be·stow·al** *n*

be·stride \-'strīd\ *vb* **:** to ride, sit, or stand astride

bet \'bet\ *n* **:** WAGER — **bet** *n*

be·take \bi-'tāk\ *vb* **:** to cause (oneself) to go

be·ta particle \'bāt-ə-\ *n* **:** an electron or positron ejected from an atomic nucleus during radioactive transformation

beta ray *n* **:** a stream of beta particles

be·tel \'bēt-ᵊl\ *n* **:** a climbing pepper whose leaves are chewed together with lime and the astringent seed (betel nut) of a palm esp. by southern Asians

bête noire \bāt-'nwär\ *n*, *pl* **bêtes noires** \bāt-'nwär(z)\ **:** one that is an object of strong fear or aversion

beth·el \'beth-əl\ *n* **:** a place of worship esp. for seamen

be·think \bi-'thiŋk\ *vb* **:** to cause (oneself) to call to mind or consider

be·tide \-'tīd\ *vb* **:** to happen to **:** BEFALL

be·times \-'tīmz\ *adv* **:** in good time **:** EARLY **syn** soon, beforehand

be·to·ken \-'tō-kən\ *vb* 1 **:** to give evidence of 2 **:** PRESAGE **syn** indicate, signify

be·tray \-'trā\ *vb* 1 **:** to lead astray;

ə abut; **ᵊ** kitten; **ər** further; **a** back; **ā** bake; **ä** cot, cart; **au̇** out; **ch** chin; **e** less; **ē** easy; **g** gift; **i** trip; **ī** life; **j** joke; **ŋ** sing; **ō** flow; **ȯ** flaw; **ȯi** coin; **th** thin; **t͟h** this; **ü** loot; **u̇** foot; **y** yet; **yü** few; **yu̇** furious; **zh** vision

esp : SEDUCE **2** : to deliver to an enemy by treachery **3** : to prove unfaithful to **4** : to reveal unintentionally; *also* : SHOW, INDICATE **syn** mislead, delude, deceive, disclose, divulge — **be·tray·al** *n* — **be·tray·er** *n*

be·troth \-'trōth, -'trōth\ *vb* : to promise to marry : AFFIANCE — **be·troth·al** *n*

be·trothed *n* : the person to whom one is betrothed

¹bet·ter \'bet-ər\ *adj, comparative of* GOOD **1** : more than half **2** : improved in health **3** : of higher quality

²better *adv, comparative of* WELL **1** : in a superior manner **2** : to a higher or greater degree; *also* : MORE

³better *n* **1** : something better; *also* : a superior esp. in merit or rank **2** : ADVANTAGE

⁴better *vb* **1** : to make or become better **2** : SURPASS, EXCEL

bet·ter·ment \'bet-ər-mənt\ *n* : IMPROVEMENT

bet·tor *or* **bet·ter** \'bet-ər\ *n* : one that bets

¹be·tween \bi-'twēn\ *prep* **1** : by the common action of ⟨earned $10,000 ~ the two of them⟩ **2** : in the interval separating ⟨an alley ~ two buildings⟩ **3** : in point of comparison of ⟨choose ~ two cars⟩ **4** : marking or constituting the interrelation or interaction of ⟨hostility ~ nations⟩ ⟨a bond ~ brothers⟩

²between *adv* : in an intervening space or interval

be·twixt \-'twikst\ *adv or prep, archaic* : BETWEEN

¹bev·el \'bev-əl\ *n* **1** : the angle or slant that one surface or line makes with another when not at right angles **2** : a device for adjusting the slant of the surfaces of a piece of work

²bevel *vb* **-eled** *or* **-elled; -el·ing** *or* **-el·ling 1** : to cut or shape (as an edge or surface) to a bevel **2** : INCLINE, SLANT

bev·er·age \'bev-(ə-)rij\ *n* : liquid for drinking; *esp* : a liquid (as milk or coffee) other than water

bevy \'bev-ē\ *n* : a group (as of women or quail) together

be·wail \bi-'wāl\ *vb* : LAMENT **syn** deplore, bemoan

be·ware \-'waər\ *vb* : to be on one's guard : be wary of

be·wil·der \-'wil-dər\ *vb* : PERPLEX, CONFUSE **syn** mystify, distract, puzzle — **be·wil·der·ment** *n*

be·witch \-'wich\ *vb* **1** : to affect by witchcraft **2** : CHARM, FASCINATE **syn** enchant, attract

bey \'bā\ *n* **1** : a former Turkish provincial governor **2** : the former ruler of Tunis or Tunisia

¹be·yond \bē-'änd\ *adv* **1** : FARTHER **2** : BESIDES

²beyond *prep* **1** : on or to the farther side of **2** : out of the reach or sphere of **3** : BESIDES

bez·el \'bez-əl\ *n* **1** : a sloping edge on a cutting tool **2** : the top part of a ring setting **3** : the faceted part of a cut gem that rises above the setting **4** : a usu. grooved rim holding the glass on a watch, clock dial, or headlight

be·zoar \'bē-,zōr\ *n* : a concretion found in animal intestines

bhang \'baŋ\ *n* : a narcotic and intoxicant product of the hemp plant

bi·an·nu·al \bī-'an-y(ə-w)əl\ *adj* : occurring twice a year — **bi·an·nu·al·ly** *adv*

¹bi·as \'bī-əs\ *n* **1** : a line diagonal to the grain of a fabric **2** : PREJUDICE, BENT

²bias *adv* : on the bias : DIAGONALLY

³bias *vb* **bi·ased** *or* **bi·assed; bi·as·ing** *or* **bi·as·sing** : PREJUDICE

bib \'bib\ *n* : a protective cover tied under a child's chin over the clothes at meals

bi·be·lot \,bib-ə-'lō, ,bēb-\ *n* : a small household ornament or decorative object

Bi·ble \'bī-bəl\ *n* [ML *biblia*, fr. Gk. pl. of *biblion* book, fr. *byblos* papyrus, fr. *Byblos*, ancient Phoenician city from which papyrus was exported] **1** : the sacred scriptures of Christians comprising the Old and New Testaments **2** : the sacred scriptures of Judaism or of some other religion — **bib·li·cal** \'bib-li-kəl\ *adj, sometimes cap*

bib·li·og·ra·phy \,bib-lē-'äg-rə-fē\ *n* **1** : the history or description of writings or publications **2** : a list of writings (as on a subject or of an author) — **bib·li·og·ra·pher** \-fər\ *n* — **bib·li·o·graph·ic** \-lē-ə-'graf-ik\ *or* **bib·li·o·graph·i·cal** *adj*

bib·lio·phile \'bib-lē-ə-,fīl\ *n* : a lover of books

bib·u·lous \'bib-yə-ləs\ *adj* **1** : highly absorbent **2** : inclined to drink esp. to excess

bi·cam·er·al \'bī-'kam-(ə-)rəl\ *adj* : having or consisting of two legislative branches

bi·car·bon·ate of soda \bī-,kär-bə-nət-, -,nāt-\ : a white crystalline salt used in cooking and in medicine

bi·ceps \'bī-,seps\ *n* : a muscle (as in the front of the upper arm) having two points of origin

bi·chlo·ride \bī-'klōr-,īd\ *n* : any of several chlorides; *esp* : one (**mercuric chloride** *or* **bichloride of mercury**) that is a poisonous compound of mercury and chlorine used as an antiseptic and fungicide

¹bick·er \'bik-ər\ *n* : WRANGLING, ALTERCATION

²bicker *vb* : to contend in petty altercation : SQUABBLE

bi·cus·pid \bī-'kəs-pəd\ *n* : either of 2 double-pointed teeth next to the canine on each side of each jaw in man

bi·cy·cle \'bī-,sik-əl\ *n* : a light 2-wheeled vehicle with a steering handle, saddle, and pedals by which it is propelled

¹bid \'bid\ *vb* **bade** \'bad, 'bād\ *or* **bid; bid·den** \'bid-ᵊn\ *or* **bid** *also* **bade; bid·ding 1** : COMMAND, ORDER **2** : INVITE **3** : to give expression to **4** : to make a bid : OFFER — **bid·der** *n*

²bid *n* **1** : an act of bidding; *also* : a chance or turn to bid **2** : an offer (as at an auction) of what one will give for something; *also* : the thing or sum offered **3** : an announcement by a player in a card game of what he proposes to accomplish; *also* : an attempt to win or gain **4** : INVITATION

bide \'bīd\ *vb* **bode** \'bōd\ *or* **bid·ed; bid·ed; bid·ing 1** : WAIT, TARRY **2** : DWELL **3** : to wait for ⟨*bided* his time⟩

bi·en·ni·al \bī-'en-ē-əl\ *adj* **1** : taking place once in two years **2** : lasting two years **3** : producing leaves the first year and fruiting and dying the second year — biennial *n* — bi·en·ni·al·ly *adv*

bier \'biər\ *n* : a stand bearing a coffin or corpse

bi·fo·cals \bī-'fō-kəlz\ *n pl* : eyeglasses with lenses that have one part that corrects for near vision and one for distant vision

bi·fur·cate \'bī-fər-ˌkāt\ *vb* : to divide into two branches or parts — **bi·fur·ca·tion** \ˌbī-fər-'kā-shən\ *n*

big \'big\ *adj* 1 : large in size, amount, or scope 2 : PREGNANT; *also* : SWELLING 3 : IMPORTANT, IMPOSING syn great — **big·ness** *n*

big·a·my \'big-ə-mē\ *n* : the act of marrying one person while still legally married to another — **big·a·mist** *n* — **big·a·mous** *adj*

Big Dipper *n* : the seven principal stars in the constellation of Ursa Major arranged in a form resembling a dipper

big·horn \'big-ˌhôrn\ *n* : a wild sheep of mountainous western No. America

bight \'bīt\ *n* 1 : the slack part of a rope fastened at both ends 2 : a curve in a coast; *also* : the bay formed by such a curve

big·ot \'big-ət\ *n* : one intolerantly devoted to his own church, party, or opinion syn fanatic, enthusiast, zealot — **big·ot·ed** *adj* — **big·ot·ry** *n*

big·wig \'big-ˌwig\ *n* : an important person

bike \'bīk\ *n* : BICYCLE

bi·ki·ni \bə-'kē-nē\ *n* : a woman's brief 2-piece bathing suit

bi·lat·er·al \bī-'lat-(ə-)rəl\ *adj* 1 : having or involving 2 sides 2 : affecting reciprocally 2 sides or parties — **bi·lat·er·al·ly** *adv*

bile \'bīl\ *n* 1 : a bitter greenish fluid secreted by the liver that aids in the digestion of fats 2 : ill-humored state : SURLINESS

bilge \'bilj\ *n* 1 : the part of a ship that lies between the bottom and the point where the sides go straight up 2 : foul water that collects in the bottom of a ship

bi·lin·gual \bī-'liŋ-gwəl\ *adj* : expressed in, knowing, or using two languages

bil·ious \'bil-yəs\ *adj* 1 : marked by or suffering from disordered liver function 2 : IRRITABLE, CHOLERIC

bilk \'bilk\ *vb* : to cheat out of what is due : SWINDLE

¹bill \'bil\ *n* : the jaws of a bird together with their horny covering; *also* : a mouth structure (as of a turtle) resembling these

²bill *vb* : to caress fondly

³bill *n* 1 : a written document (as a memorandum); *esp* : a draft of a law presented to a legislature for enactment 2 : a written statement of a legal wrong suffered or of some breach of law 3 : a paper bearing a statement of particulars (as of a ship's crew members and their duties) 4 : a list of items (as of goods and their costs or of moneys due) 5 : an advertisement (as a poster or handbill) displayed or distributed 6 : a piece of paper money

⁴bill *vb* 1 : to enter in or prepare a bill; *also* : to submit a bill or account to

2 : to advertise by bills or posters

bill·board \-ˌbôrd\ *n* : a flat surface on which advertising bills are posted

¹bil·let \'bil-ət\ *n* 1 : an order requiring a person to provide lodging for a soldier; *also* : quarters assigned by or as if by such an order 2 : POSITION, APPOINTMENT

²billet *vb* : to assign lodging to by billet

bil·let-doux \ˌbil-ā-'dü\ *n, pl* **bil·lets-doux** \-'dü(z)\ : a love letter

bill·fold \'bil-ˌfōld\ *n* : WALLET

bill·head \'bil-ˌhed\ *n* : a printed form on which a commercial bill may be made out

bil·liards \'bil-yərdz\ *n* : any of several games played on a rectangular table (billiard table) by driving balls against each other or into pockets with a cue

bil·lings·gate \'bil-iŋz-ˌgāt\ *n* [fr. *Billingsgate*, old gate and fish market in London] : coarsely abusive language

bil·lion \'bil-yən\ *n, pl* **billions** *or* **billion** 1 : a thousand millions 2 *Brit* : a million millions — **billion** *adj* — **bil·lionth** \-yənth\ *adj or n*

bill of exchange : a written order from one party to another to pay to a person named in the bill a specified sum of money

¹bil·low \'bil-ō\ *n* 1 : WAVE; *esp* : a great wave 2 : a rolling mass (as of fog or flame) like a great wave — **bil·lowy** *adj*

²billow *vb* : to rise and roll in waves; *also* : to swell out (~*ing* sails)

bil·ly \'bil-ē\ *n* : a heavy usu. wooden club; *esp* : a policeman's club

bi·met·al·lism \bī-'met-ᵊl-ˌiz-əm\ *n* : the policy of using two metals at fixed ratios to form a standard of value for a monetary system

bin \'bin\ *n* : a box, crib, or enclosure used for storage

bi·na·ry \'bī-nə-rē\ *adj* : consisting of two things or parts : DOUBLE — **binary** *n*

bin·au·ral \bī-'nôr-əl\ *adj* : of or relating to sound transmission, recording, or reproduction techniques that provide two separate transmission or recording paths to achieve an effect of hearing sound sources in their original positions

bind \'bīnd\ *vb* **bound** \'baùnd\ **binding** 1 : TIE; *also* : to restrain as if by tying 2 : to put under an obligation; *also* : to constrain with legal authority 3 : to unite in a mass 4 : BANDAGE 5 : CONSTIPATE 6 : to strengthen or decorate with a band 7 : to fasten together and enclose in a cover (~ books) 8 : to compel as if by a pledge 9 : to exert a tying, restraining, or compelling effect — **bind·er** *n*

bind·ing *n* : something (as a ski fastening, a cover, or an edging fabric) used to bind

binge \'binj\ *n* : SPREE

bin·na·cle \'bin-i-kəl\ *n* : a container holding a ship's compass

¹bin·oc·u·lar \bī-'näk-yə-lər, bə-\ *adj* : of, relating to, or adapted to the use of both eyes

²bin·oc·u·lar \bə-, bī-\ *n* 1 : a binocular optical instrument (as a microscope) 2 : FIELD GLASS — usu. used in pl.

bi·no·mi·al \bī-'nō-mē-əl\ *n* 1 : a mathematical expression consisting of two terms connected by the sign plus (+) or minus (—) **2** : a biological species name consisting of two terms — **binomial** adj

bio·chem·is·try \,bī-ō-'kem-ə-strē\ n : chemistry that deals with the chemical compounds and processes in organisms — **bio·chem·i·cal** \-'kem-i-kəl\ adj — **bio·chem·ist** \-'kem-əst\ n

bio·ge·og·ra·phy \-jē-'äg-rə-fē\ n : a branch of biology that deals with the distribution of plants and animals — **bio·ge·og·ra·pher** \-fər\ n — **bio·ge·o·graph·ic** \-,jē-ə-'graf-ik\ adj

bi·og·ra·phy \bī-'äg-rə-fē\ n : a written history of a person's life; also : such writings in general — **bi·og·ra·pher** \-fər\ n — **bi·o·graph·i·cal** \,bī-ə-'graf-i-kəl\ or **bi·o·graph·ic** adj

biological warfare n : warfare in which living organisms (as bacteria) are used to harm the enemy or his livestock and crops

bi·ol·o·gy \bī-'äl-ə-jē\ n **1** : a science that deals with living beings and life processes **2** : the laws and phenomena of life (as of a kind of organism) — **bi·o·log·i·cal** \,bī-ə-'läj-i-kəl\ adj — **bi·ol·o·gist** \bī-'äl-ə-jəst\ n

bi·op·sy \'bī-,äp-sē\ n : the removal of cells or tissue from the living body for examination

bi·o·tin \'bī-ə-tən\ n : a member of the vitamin B complex found esp. in yeast, liver, and egg yolk and active in growth promotion

bi·pa·ren·tal \,bī-pə-'rent-ᵊl\ adj : involving or derived from 2 parents ⟨~ inheritance⟩

bi·par·ti·san \bī-'pärt-ə-zən\ adj : representing or composed of members of two parties

bi·par·tite \-'pär-,tīt\ adj **1** : being in two parts **2** : shared by two ⟨~ treaty⟩

bi·ped \'bī-,ped\ n : a 2-footed animal

bi·plane \'bī-,plān\ n : an airplane with two main supporting surfaces placed one above the other

bi·ra·cial \bī-'rā-shəl\ adj : of, relating to, or involving members of two races

¹**birch** \'bərch\ n **1** : any of a genus of mostly short-lived deciduous shrubs and trees with membranous outer bark and pale close-grained wood; also : this wood **2** : a birch rod or bundle of twigs for flogging — **birch·en** adj

²**birch** vb : WHIP, FLOG

bird \'bərd\ n : a warm-blooded egg-laying vertebrate having the body feathered and the forelimbs modified to form wings

bird·bath \-,bath, -,bàth\ n : a usu. ornamental basin set up for birds to bathe in

bird·house \-,haùs\ n : an artificial nesting place for birds

bird·ie \'bərd-ē\ n : a score of one under par on a hole in golf

bird·lime \-,līm\ n : a sticky substance smeared on twigs to snare small birds

bird·seed \-,sēd\ n : a mixture of small seeds (as of hemp or millet) used chiefly for feeding cage birds

bird's-eye \'bərd-,zī\ adj **1** : seen from above as if by a flying bird ⟨~ view⟩; also : CURSORY **2** : marked with spots resembling birds' eyes ⟨~ maple⟩; also : made of bird's-eye wood

bi·ret·ta \bə-'ret-ə\ n : a square cap with three ridges on top worn esp. by Roman Catholic clergymen

birth \'bərth\ n **1** : the act or fact of being born or of bringing forth young **2** : LINEAGE, DESCENT **3** : ORIGIN, BEGINNING

birth·day \-,dā\ n : the day or anniversary of one's birth

birth·mark \-,märk\ n : an unusual mark or blemish on the skin at birth

birth·place \-,plās\ n : place of birth or origin

birth·rate \-,rāt\ n : the number of births for every hundred or every thousand persons in a given area or group during a given time

birth·right \-,rīt\ n : a right, privilege, or possession to which one is entitled by birth **syn** prerogative, heritage, inheritance

birth·stone \-,stōn\ n : a precious stone associated symbolically with the month of one's birth

bis·cuit \'bis-kət\ n [MF *bescuit*, fr. *pain bescuit* twice-cooked bread] : an unraised bread formed into flat cakes and baked hard and crisp; also : a bread made with a leavening agent other than yeast baked in small cakes

bi·sect \'bī-,sekt\ vb : to divide into two usu. equal parts; also : CROSS, INTERSECT

bi·sex·u·al \bī-'sek-sh(ə-w)əl\ adj **1** : possessing characters of or sexually oriented toward both sexes **2** : of, relating to, or involving two sexes

bish·op \'bish-əp\ n [OE *biscop*, fr. LL *episcopus*, fr. Gk *episkopos*, lit., overseer, fr. *epi-* on, over + *skeptesthai* to look] **1** : a clergyman ranking above a priest and typically governing a diocese **2** : any of various Protestant church officials who superintend other clergy **3** : a chess piece that can move diagonally across any number of unoccupied squares

bish·op·ric \-ə-prik\ n **1** : DIOCESE **2** : the office of bishop

bis·muth \'biz-məth\ n : a heavy brittle grayish white metallic chemical element used in alloys and medicine

bi·son \'bīs-ᵊn, 'bīz-\ n, pl **bison** : a large shaggy-maned hump-shouldered wild ox formerly abundant on the plains of central U.S.

bisque \'bisk\ n **1** : a thick cream soup **2** : ice cream containing powdered nuts or macaroons

bis·tro \'bis-trō\ n **1** : a small or unpretentious European wineshop or restaurant **2** : BAR; also : NIGHTCLUB

¹**bit** \'bit\ n **1** : the part of a bridle that is placed in a horse's mouth **2** : a drilling or boring tool used in a brace

²**bit** n **1** : a morsel of food; also : a small piece or quantity of something **2** : a small coin; also : a unit of value equal to 12½ cents **3** : something small or trivial; also : some degree or extent ⟨a ~ tired⟩

bitch \'bich\ n : the female of the dog

¹**bite** \'bīt\ vb **bit** \'bit\ **bit·ten** \'bit-ᵊn\ also **bit**; **bit·ing** \'bīt-iŋ\ **1** : to grip with teeth or jaws; also : to wound or sting with or as if with fangs **2** : to cut or pierce as if with a sharp-edged instrument **3** : to cause to smart or sting **4** : CORRODE **5** : to take bait ⟨fish are *biting* well⟩

²**bite** n **1** : the act or manner of biting **2** : MORSEL, SNACK **3** : a wound made by biting; also : a biting sensation : STING

bit·ing \'bīt-iŋ\ *adj* : producing bodily or mental distress ⟨~ winds⟩ ⟨a ~ speech⟩

bit·ter \'bit-ər\ *adj* 1 : having the acrid lingering taste suggestive of wormwood or hops that is one of the basic taste sensations 2 : marked by intensity or severity (as of distress or hatred) 3 : extremely harsh or cruel — **bit·ter·ly** *adv* — **bit·ter·ness** *n*

bit·tern \'bit-ərn\ *n* : a small heron with a loud booming call

bit·ters \'bit-ərz\ *n sing or pl* : a usu. alcoholic solution of bitter and often aromatic plant products used in mixing drinks and as a mild tonic

bit·ter·sweet \'bit-ər-,swēt\ *n* 1 : a poisonous nightshade with purple flowers and orange-red berries 2 : a woody vine with yellow capsules that open when ripe and disclose scarlet seed coverings

bi·tu·men \bə-'t(y)ü-mən, bī-\ *n* : any of various mixtures of hydrogen-and-carbon-containing substances (as asphalt, tar, or petroleum)

bi·tu·mi·nous \-mə-nəs\ *adj* 1 : resembling, mixed with, or containing bitumen 2 : being coal that when heated yields considerable volatile bituminous matter

bi·valve \'bī-,valv\ *n* : an animal (as a clam) with a shell composed of 2 separate parts that open and shut — **bi·valve** *adj*

¹**biv·ouac** \'biv-(ə-),wak\ *n* : a temporary encampment or shelter

²**bivouac** *vb* **biv·ouacked; biv·ouack·ing** : to form a bivouac : CAMP

bi·zarre \bə-'zär\ *adj* : ODD, ECCENTRIC, FANTASTIC — **bi·zarre·ly** *adv*

blab \'blab\ *vb* **blabbed; blab·bing** : TATTLE, GOSSIP

¹**black** \'blak\ *adj* 1 : of the color black; *also* : very dark 2 : SWARTHY; *also* : of or relating to a group of dark-haired dark-skinned people 3 : SOILED, DIRTY 4 : lacking light ⟨a ~ night⟩ 5 : WICKED, EVIL ⟨~ deeds⟩ ⟨~ magic⟩ 6 : DISMAL, GLOOMY ⟨a ~ outlook⟩ 7 : SULLEN ⟨a ~ mood⟩ — **black·ish** *adj* — **black·ness** *n*

²**black** *n* 1 : a black pigment or dye; *also* : something (as clothing) that is black 2 : the color of least lightness that characterizes objects which neither reflect nor transmit light : the opposite of white 3 : a person of a dark-skinned race

³**black** *vb* : BLACKEN

black·a·moor \'blak-ə-,mu̇r\ *n* : NEGRO

black art *n* : MAGIC, WITCHCRAFT

black·ball \'blak-,bȯl\ *n* : a black object used to cast a negative vote; *also* : such a vote — **black·ball** *vb*

black·ber·ry \-,ber-ē\ *n* : the usu. black or purple juicy but seedy edible fruit of various brambles; *also* : a plant bearing this fruit

black·bird \-,bərd\ *n* : any of various birds (as the redwing blackbird) of which the male is largely or wholly black

black·board \-,bȯrd\ *n* : a dark smooth surface (as of slate) used for writing or drawing on usu with chalk

black·en \'blak-ən\ *vb* 1 : to make or become black 2 : DEFAME, SULLY

black·guard \'blag-ərd, -,ärd\ *n* : SCOUNDREL, RASCAL

black·head \'blak-,hed\ *n* : a small oily mass plugging the outlet of a skin gland

¹**black·jack** \-,jak\ *n* 1 : a leather-covered club with a flexible handle 2 : a card game in which the object is to be dealt cards having a higher count than the dealer but not exceeding 21

²**blackjack** *vb* : to hit with or as if with a blackjack

black·list \'blak-,list\ *n* : a list of persons who are disapproved of and are to be punished (as by refusal of jobs or a boycott) — **blacklist** *vb*

black·mail \-,māl\ *n* : extortion by threats esp. of public exposure; *also* : something so extorted — **blackmail** *vb* — **black·mail·er** *n*

black·out \-,au̇t\ *n* : a transitory loss or dulling of vision or consciousness — **black out** \'au̇t\ *vb*

black sheep *n* : a discreditable member of an otherwise respectable group ⟨the *black sheep* of the family⟩

black·smith \-,smith\ *n* : a workman who shapes heated iron by hammering it

black·thorn \-,thȯrn\ *n* : a European thorny plum; *also* : an American hawthorn

black·top \-,täp\ *n* : a blackish bituminous material used esp. for surfacing roads

blad·der \'blad-ər\ *n* : a sac in which liquid is stored; *esp* : one in a vertebrate into which urine passes from the kidneys

blade \'blād\ *n* 1 : a leaf of a plant and esp. of a grass; *also* : the flat part of a leaf as distinguished from its stalk 2 : something (as the flat part of an oar or an arm of a propeller) resembling the blade of a leaf 3 : the cutting part of an instrument or tool 4 : SWORD; *also* : SWORDSMAN 5 : a dashing fellow ⟨a group of gay young ~s⟩

blain \'blān\ *n* : an inflammatory swelling or sore

¹**blame** \'blām\ *vb* 1 : to find fault with 2 : to hold responsible or responsible for **syn** charge, condemn, criticize

²**blame** *n* 1 : CENSURE, REPROOF 2 : responsibility for fault or error **syn** guilt — **blame·less** *adj* — **blame·less·ness** *n*

blame·wor·thy \-,wər-thē\ *adj* : deserving blame — **blame·wor·thi·ness** *n*

blanch \'blanch\ *vb* 1 : BLEACH 2 : to make or become white or pale

blanc·mange \blə-'mänj\ *n* : a dessert made from gelatin or a starchy substance and milk usu. sweetened and flavored

bland \'bland\ *adj* 1 : smooth in manner 2 : SUAVE 3 : gently soothing ⟨a ~ diet⟩; *also* : INSIPID **syn** diplomatic, mild, soft, balmy — **bland·ly** *adv* — **bland·ness** *n*

blan·dish·ment \'blan-dish-mənt\ *n* : flattering or coaxing speech or action : CAJOLERY

¹**blank** \'blaŋk\ *adj* 1 : showing or causing an appearance of dazed dismay; *also* : EXPRESSIONLESS 2 : DULL, COLORLESS ⟨~ moments⟩ 3 : EMPTY; *esp* : free from writing or marks 4 : ABSOLUTE, DOWNRIGHT ⟨a ~ refusal⟩ 5 : not

ə abut; ᵊ kitten; ər further; a back; ā bake; ä cot, cart; au̇ out; ch chin; e less; ē easy; g gift; i trip; ī life; j joke; ŋ sing; ō flow; ȯ flaw; ȯi coin; th thin; th̲ this; ü loot; u̇ foot; y yet; yü few; yu̇ furious; zh vision

shaped in final form — **blank·ly** adv — **blank·ness** n

²**blank** n **1** : an empty space **2** : a form with spaces for the entry of data **3** : the center of a target **4** : a cartridge with powder but no bullet

³**blank** vb **1** : to cover or close up : OBSCURE, OBSTRUCT **2** : to keep from scoring

¹**blan·ket** \'blaŋ-kət\ n **1** : a heavy woven often woolen covering ⟨an extra ~ for the bed⟩ **2** : a covering layer ⟨a ~ of snow⟩

²**blanket** vb : to cover with a blanket

³**blanket** adj : covering a group or class ⟨~ insurance⟩; also : applicable in all instances ⟨~ rules⟩

blank verse n : unrhymed iambic pentameter

¹**blare** \'blaər\ vb : to sound loud and harsh; also : to proclaim loudly — **blare** n

²**blar·ney** \'blär-nē\ n : skillful flattery : BLANDISHMENT

bla·sé \blä-'zā\ adj : not responsive to pleasure or excitement as a result of excessive indulgence; also : SOPHISTICATED

blas·pheme \blas-'fēm\ vb **1** : to speak of or address with irreverence **2** : to utter blasphemy

blas·phe·my \'blas-fə-mē\ n **1** : the act of expressing lack of reverence for God **2** : irreverence toward something considered sacred — **blas·phe·mous** adj

¹**blast** \'blast\ n **1** : a violent gust of wind; also : its effect **2** : sound made by a wind instrument **3** : a sudden withering esp. of plants : BLIGHT **4** : a current of air forced at high pressure through a hole (as in a bellows, organ, or furnace) **5** : EXPLOSION; also : the often destructive wave of increased air pressure that moves outward from an explosion

²**blast** vb **1** : to shrivel up : BLIGHT **2** : to shatter by or as if by an explosive

blast off vb : to take off — used esp. of rocket-propelled devices

bla·tant \'blāt-ᵊnt\ adj : offensively obtrusive : vulgarly showy **syn** vociferous, boisterous — **bla·tan·cy** \-ᵊn-sē\ n

blath·er \'blath-ər\ vb : to talk foolishly — **blather** n

blath·er·skite \-,skīt\ n : a blustering talkative person

¹**blaze** \'blāz\ n **1** : FIRE **2** : intense direct light (as of the sun at noon) **3** : something (as a dazzling display or sudden outburst) suggesting fire ⟨a ~ of autumn leaves⟩ **syn** glare, glow

²**blaze** vb **1** : to burn brightly; also : to flare up **2** : to be conspicuously bright : GLITTER

³**blaze** vb : to make public

⁴**blaze** n **1** : a white mark on the face of an animal **2** : a mark made on a tree by chipping off a piece of bark

⁵**blaze** vb : to mark (as a tree or trail) with blazes

blaz·er \'blā-zər\ n : a light single-breasted jacket for sport wear

¹**bla·zon** \'blāz-ᵊn\ n **1** : COAT OF ARMS **2** : ostentatious display

²**blazon** vb **1** : to publish abroad **2** : DECK, ADORN

¹**bleach** \'blēch\ vb : to whiten or become white : BLANCH

²**bleach** n : a preparation used in bleaching

bleach·ers \'blē-chərz\ n sing or pl : a usu. uncovered stand containing lower-priced tiered seats for spectators

bleak \'blēk\ adj **1** : desolately barren and windswept **2** : lacking warm or cheering qualities ⟨~ weather⟩ ⟨~ prospects⟩ — **bleak·ly** adv — **bleak·ness** n

blear \'bliər\ adj : dim with water or tears ⟨~ eyes⟩

bleary \'bli(ə)r-ē\ adj **1** : dull or dimmed esp. from fatigue or sleep **2** : poorly outlined or defined

bleat \'blēt\ n : the cry of a sheep or goat or a sound like it — **bleat** vb

bleed \'blēd\ vb **bled** \'bled\ **bleed·ing 1** : to lose or shed blood **2** : to be wounded; also : to feel pain or distress **3** : to flow or ooze from a wounded surface; also : to draw fluid from ⟨a patient⟩ ⟨~ a tire⟩ **4** : to extort money from

bleed·er n : one that bleeds; esp : HEMOPHILIAC

¹**blem·ish** \'blem-ish\ vb : to spoil by a flaw : MAR

²**blemish** n : a noticeable flaw (as a pimple on the skin)

¹**blench** \'blench\ vb : FLINCH, QUAIL **syn** shrink, recoil, wince

²**blench** vb : to grow or make pale

¹**blend** \'blend\ vb **1** : to mix thoroughly **2** : to prepare (as coffee) by mixing different varieties **3** : to combine into an integrated whole **4** : HARMONIZE **syn** fuse, merge, mingle

²**blend** n : a product of blending **syn** compound, composite

bless \'bles\ vb **blessed** \'blest\ also **blest** \'blest\ **bless·ing 1** : to hallow or consecrate by religious rite or word **2** : to make the sign of the cross over **3** : to invoke divine care for **4** : PRAISE, GLORIFY **5** : to confer happiness upon

bless·ed \'bles-əd\ adj **1** : HOLY **2** : BEATIFIED **3** : DELIGHTFUL — **blessed·ness** n

bless·ing n **1** : the act of one who blesses **2** : a thing conducive to happiness **3** : grace said at a meal

blew past of BLOW

¹**blight** \'blīt\ n **1** : a plant disorder marked by withering; also : an organism causing a blight **2** : an impairing or frustrating influence; also : an impaired condition

²**blight** vb : to affect with or suffer from blight

blimp \'blimp\ n : a small airship without a rigid framework

¹**blind** \'blīnd\ adj **1** : lacking or grossly deficient in ability to see; also : intended for blind persons ⟨~ schools⟩ **2** : not based on reason, evidence, or knowledge ⟨~ faith⟩ ⟨a ~ choice⟩ **3** : not intelligently controlled or directed ⟨~ chance⟩ **4** : performed solely by the aid of instruments within an airplane and without looking outside ⟨a ~ landing⟩ **5** : hard to discern or make out : HIDDEN ⟨a ~ seam⟩ **6** : lacking an opening or outlet ⟨a ~ alley⟩ — **blind·ly** adv — **blind·ness** n

²**blind** vb **1** : to make blind **2** : DAZZLE **3** : DARKEN; also : HIDE

³**blind** n **1** : something (as a shutter) to hinder vision or keep out light **2** : AMBUSH **3** : SUBTERFUGE

blind date n : a date between persons of opposite sex not previously acquainted; also : either of the persons

blind·fold \'blīn(d)-ˌfōld\ *vb* : to cover the eyes of with or as if with a bandage — **blindfold** *n*

¹**blink** \'bliŋk\ *vb* **1** : WINK **2** : TWINKLE **3** : EVADE, SHIRK

²**blink** *n* **1** : GLIMMER, SPARKLE **2** : a usu. involuntary shutting and opening of the eyes

blink·er \'bliŋ-kər\ *n* : a blinking light used as a signal

blin·tze \'blint-sə\ *or* **blintz** \'blints\ *n* : a thin rolled pancake with a filling usu. of cream cheese

bliss \'blis\ *n* **1** : complete happiness **2** : HEAVEN, PARADISE **syn** felicity — **bliss·ful** \-fəl\ *adj* : full of or causing bliss — **bliss·ful·ly** *adv*

¹**blis·ter** \'blis-tər\ *n* **1** : a raised area of skin containing watery fluid; *also* : an agent that causes blisters **2** : something (as a raised spot in paint) suggesting a blister

²**blister** *vb* : to develop a blister; *also* : to cause blisters

blithe \'blīth, 'blīth\ *adj* : happily lighthearted : CHEERFUL **syn** merry, jovial, jolly — **blithe·ly** *adv* — **blithe·some** \-səm\ *adj*

¹**blitz** \'blits\ *n* **1** : an intensive series of air raids **2** : a fast intensive campaign — **blitz** *vb*

blitz·krieg \'blits-ˌkrēg\ *n* : war conducted with great speed and force

bliz·zard \'bliz-ərd\ *n* : a long severe snowstorm esp. with wind-driven snow and intense cold

bloat \'blōt\ *vb* : to swell by or as if by filling with water or air

bloat·er \'blōt-ər\ *n* : a fat herring or mackerel lightly salted and smoked

blob \'bläb\ *n* : a small lump or drop (as of paste or paint) of a thick consistency

bloc \'bläk\ *n* : a combination of individuals or groups (as nations) working for a common purpose

¹**block** \'bläk\ *n* **1** : a solid piece of substantial material (as wood or stone) **2** : a frame enclosing one or more pulleys and having a hook or strap by which it may be attached to objects **3** : a quantity of things considered as a unit ⟨a ~ of seats⟩ **4** : a large building divided into separate units (as apartments or offices) **5** : a row of houses or shops **6** : a city square; *also* : the distance along one of the sides of such a square **7** : HINDRANCE, OBSTRUCTION; *also* : interruption of normal function of body or mind ⟨heart ~⟩ **8** : an engraved stamp from which impressions are made

²**block** *vb* **1** : OBSTRUCT, CHECK **2** : to outline roughly ⟨~ out a statue⟩ **3** : to provide or support with a block ⟨~ up a wheel⟩ **syn** bar, impede, hinder

¹**block·ade** \blä-'kād\ *n* : the shutting off of a place usu. by troops or ships to prevent entrance or exit

²**blockade** *vb* : to subject to a blockade

block·bust·er \'bläk-ˌbəs-tər\ *n* : a very large high-explosive demolition bomb

block·head \'bläk-ˌhed\ *n* : DOLT, DUNCE

block·house \-ˌhaús\ *n* : a small strong building used as a shelter (as from

enemy fire) or observation post (as of operations producing blast or radiation)

¹**blond** *also* **blonde** \'bländ\ *adj* : fair in complexion; *also* : of a light or bleached color ⟨~ mahogany⟩

²**blond** *also* **blonde** \-\ *n* : a blond person

blood \'bləd\ *n* **1** : the red liquid that circulates in the heart, arteries, and veins of animals **2** : LIFEBLOOD; *also* : LIFE **3** : LINEAGE, STOCK **4** : KINSHIP; *also* : KINDRED **5** : the taking of life **6** : TEMPER, PASSION **7** : a gay fellow — **blood·less** \-ləs\ *adj* — **blood-stained** \-ˌstānd\ *adj* — **bloody** *adj*

blood·cur·dling \-ˌkərd-(ᵊ-)liŋ\ *adj* : seeming to have the effect of congealing the blood through fear or horror : TERRIFYING ⟨~ screams⟩

blood·ed \'bləd-əd\ *adj* **1** : entirely or largely of pure stock ⟨~ horses⟩ **2** : having blood of a specified kind ⟨warm-*blooded* animals⟩

blood·hound \-ˌhaùnd\ *n* : a large powerful hound noted for keenness of smell

blood·mo·bile \-mō-ˌbēl\ *n* : an automobile equipped for collecting blood from donors

blood pressure *n* : pressure of the blood on the walls of blood vessels and esp. arteries

blood·shed \'bləd-ˌshed\ *n* : wounding or taking of life : SLAUGHTER, CARNAGE

blood·shot \-ˌshät\ *adj* : inflamed to redness ⟨~ eyes⟩

blood·stain \-ˌstān\ *n* : a discoloration caused by blood — **blood·stained** *adj*

blood·stone \-ˌstōn\ *n* : a green quartz sprinkled with red spots

blood·stream \-ˌstrēm\ *n* : the flowing blood in a circulatory system

blood·suck·er \-ˌsək-ər\ *n* : an animal that sucks blood; *esp* : LEECH — **blood-suck·ing** *adj*

blood·thirsty \-ˌthər-stē\ *adj* : eager to shed blood : CRUEL — **blood·thirst·i·ly** *adv*

bloody mary \-'me(ə)r-ē\ *n* : a drink made of vodka and tomato juice

¹**bloom** \'blüm\ *n* **1** : FLOWER; *also* : flowers or amount of flowers (as of a plant) **2** : the period or state of flowering **3** : a state or time of beauty and vigor **4** : a powdery coating esp. on fruits and leaves **5** : rosy color; *also* : an appearance of freshness or health — **bloomy** *adj*

²**bloom** *vb* **1** : to produce or yield flowers **2** : to glow esp. with healthy color **syn** flower, blossom

bloo·mers \'blü-mərz\ *n pl* : a woman's garment of short loose trousers gathered at the knee

bloop·er \'blü-pər\ *n* **1** : an embarrassing blunder made in public **2** : a fly ball hit barely beyond a baseball infield

¹**blos·som** \'bläs-əm\ *n* : the flower of a plant : BLOOM

²**blossom** *vb* : FLOWER, BLOOM

¹**blot** \'blät\ *n* **1** : SPOT, STAIN ⟨ink ~s⟩ **2** : BLEMISH **syn** stigma, brand

²**blot** *vb* **blot·ted**; **blot·ting 1** : SPOT, STAIN **2** : OBSCURE, ECLIPSE **3** *obs* : MAR; *also* : DISGRACE **4** : to dry or remove with or as if with blotting papers **5** : to make a blot

blotch \'bläch\ *n* : a usu. large and

irregular spot or mark (as of ink or color) — **blotch** *vb* — **blotchy** *adj*

blot·ter \'blät-ər\ *n* 1 : a piece of blotting paper 2 : a book for preliminary records (as of sales or arrests)

blot·ting paper *n* : a soft spongy paper used to absorb excess ink on freshly written manuscript

blouse \'blaús, 'blaúz\ *n* 1 : a loose outer garment like a smock 2 : the uniform coat of the U. S. Army 3 : a usu. loose garment reaching from the neck to about the waist level

¹blow \'blō\ *vb* **blew** \'blü\ **blown** \'blōn\ **blow·ing** 1 : to move forcibly (the wind *blew*) 2 : to send forth a current of gas (as air) 3 : to sound or cause to sound (~ a horn) 4 : PANT, GASP; *also* : to expel moist air in breathing (the whale *blew*) 5 : BOAST; *also* : BLUSTER 6 : MELT — used of an electrical fuse 7 : to act on with a current of gas or vapor; *esp* : to drive with such a current 8 : to shape or form by blown or injected air (~ glass) 9 : to shatter or destroy by or as if by explosion 10 : to make breathless by exertion 11 : to spend recklessly — **blow·er** *n*

²blow *n* 1 : a usu. strong blowing of air : GALE 2 : BOASTING, BRAG 3 : a blowing from the mouth or nose or through or from an instrument (a ~ of his whistle)

³blow *vb* **blew** \'blü\ **blown** \'blōn\ **blow·ing** : FLOWER, BLOOM

⁴blow *n* 1 : a forcible stroke (a ~ to the jaw) 2 *pl* : COMBAT (come to ~s) 3 : a severe and usu. unexpected calamity (a ~ to his hopes)

blow-by-blow *adj* : minutely detailed (~ account)

blow·gun \'blō-,gən\ *n* : a tube from which an arrow or a dart may be shot by the force of the breath

blow·out \-,aút\ *n* : a bursting of something (as a tire) because of pressure of the contents (as air)

blow·pipe \-,pīp\ *n* : an instrument for blowing gas (as air) into a flame in such a way as to concentrate and increase the heat

blow·sy \'blaú-zē\ *adj* : DISHEVELED, SLOVENLY

blow·torch \'blō-,tórch\ *n* : a small portable burner in which combustion is intensified by means of a blast of air or oxygen

blowy \'blō-ē\ *adj* : WINDY

¹blub·ber \'bləb-ər\ *n* 1 : the fat of large sea mammals (as whales) 2 : a noisy crying

²blubber *vb* : to cry noisily

blu·cher \'blü-chər, -kər\ *n* : a shoe with the tongue and vamp in one piece

blud·geon \'bləj-ən\ *n* : a short often loaded club

²bludgeon *vb* : to strike with or as if with a bludgeon

¹blue \'blü\ *adj* 1 : of the color blue; *also* : BLUISH 2 : MELANCHOLY; *also* : DEPRESSING 3 : PURITANICAL 4 : INDECENT

²blue *n* 1 : a color between green and violet in the spectrum : the color of the clear daytime sky 2 : something (as clothing or the sky) that is blue

blue baby *n* : a baby with bluish skin usu. due to a congenital heart defect

blue·bell \'blü-,bel\ *n* : a plant with blue bell-shaped flowers

blue·ber·ry \-,ber-ē, -b(ə-)rē\ *n* : the edible blue or blackish berry of various shrubs related to the heaths; *also* : one of these shrubs

blue·bird \-,bərd\ *n* : any of several small songbirds related to the robin and more or less blue above

blue cheese *n* : cheese marked with veins of greenish blue mold

blue·fish \-,fish\ *n* : a marine sport and food fish bluish above and silvery below

blue·grass \-,gras\ *n* : a valuable pasture and lawn grass with bluish green stems

blue·jack·et \-,jak-ət\ *n* : an enlisted man in the navy : SAILOR

blue jay *n* : an American crested jay with upper parts bright blue

blue·nose \'blü-,nōz\ *n* : one who advocates a rigorous moral code

blue·point \'blü-,póint\ *n* : a small delicate oyster orig. from Long Island

blue·print \-,print\ *n* 1 : a photographic print in white on a blue ground used esp. for copying mechanical drawings and architects' plans 2 : a detailed plan of action — **blueprint** *vb*

blues \'blüz\ *n pl* 1 : MELANCHOLY 2 : music in a style of American Negro origin marked by recurrent minor intervals and melancholy lyrics

blue·stock·ing \'blü-,stäk-iŋ\ *n* : a woman having intellectual interests

blu·et \'blü-ət\ *n* : a low American herb with dainty solitary bluish flowers

¹bluff \'bləf\ *adj* 1 : having a broad flattened front 2 : rising steeply with a broad flat front 3 : OUTSPOKEN, FRANK **syn** blunt, brusque, curt, gruff

²bluff *n* : a high steep bank : CLIFF

³bluff *vb* : to frighten or deceive by a show of confidence

⁴bluff *n* : an act or instance of bluffing; *also* : one who bluffs

blu·ing *or* **blue·ing** \'blü-iŋ\ *n* : a preparation of blue or violet dyes used in laundering to counteract yellowing of white fabrics

blu·ish \'blü-ish\ *adj* : somewhat blue

¹blun·der \'blən-dər\ *vb* 1 : to move clumsily or unsteadily 2 : to make a stupid or needless mistake

²blunder *n* : an avoidable and usu. serious mistake

blun·der·buss \-,bəs\ *n* [by folk etymology fr. obs. D *donderbus*, lit., thunder gun] : an obsolete short-barreled firearm with a flaring muzzle

¹blunt \'blənt\ *adj* 1 : not sharp : DULL 2 : lacking in tact : BLUFF **syn** brusque, curt, gruff — **blunt·ly** *adv* — **blunt·ness** *n*

²blunt *vb* : to make or become dull

¹blur \'blər\ *n* 1 : a blot or cloud that obscures 2 : something vaguely seen or perceived — **blur·ry** *adj*

²blur *vb* **blurred; blur·ring** : DIM, CLOUD, OBSCURE

blurb \'blərb\ *n* : a brief notice praising a product extravagantly

blurt \'blərt\ *vb* : to utter suddenly and impulsively

blush \'bləsh\ *n* : a reddening of the face (as from modesty or confusion) : FLUSH — **blush** *vb*

blus·ter \'bləs-tər\ *vb* 1 : to blow in noisy gusts 2 : to talk or act with noisy violence — **bluster** *n* — **blus·tery** *adj*

boa \'bō-ə\ *n* 1 : a large snake (as the **boa con·stric·tor** \-,bō-ə-kən-'strik-tər\ or the related anaconda) that crushes its prey in its coils **2 :** a fluffy scarf usu. of fur or feathers

boar \'bōr\ *n* **:** a male swine; *also* **:** the Old World wild hog from which domestic swine are descended

1board \'bōrd\ *n* **1 :** the side of a ship **2 :** a thin flat length of sawed lumber; *also* **:** material (as cardboard) or a piece of material formed as a thin flat firm sheet **3** *pl* STAGE 1 **4 :** a table spread with a meal; *also* **:** daily meals esp. when furnished for pay **5 :** a table at which a council or magistrates sit **6 :** a group or association of persons organized for a special responsibility (as the management of a business or institution); *also* **:** an organized commercial exchange

2board *vb* **1 :** to go aboard (~ a boat) **2 :** to cover with boards **3 :** to provide or be provided with meals and often lodging — **board·er** *n*

board·ing·house \-iŋ-,haùs\ *n* **:** a house at which persons are boarded

board·walk \-,wòk\ *n* **:** a promenade (as of planking) along a beach

boast \'bōst\ *vb* **1 :** to vaunt oneself **2 :** to mention or assert with undue pride **3 :** to prize as a possession; *also* **:** HAVE (the house ~s a fireplace) — **boast** *n* — **boast·er** *n*

boast·ful \-fəl\ *adj* **:** given to or marked by boasting (~ speeches) — **boast·ful·ly** *adv*

boat \'bōt\ *n* **:** a vessel (as a canoe or ship) for traveling through water

boat hook *n* **:** a pole-handled hook used esp. to pull or push a boat, log, or raft into place

boat·house \'bōt-,haùs\ *n* **:** a house or shelter for boats

boat·ing *n* **:** the action, fact, or pastime of cruising or racing in a boat

boat·man \'bōt-mən\ *n* **:** a man who manages, works on, or deals in boats

boat·swain \'bōs-ʾn\ *n* **:** a subordinate officer of a ship in charge of the hull and related matters (as rigging and anchors)

1bob \'bäb\ *vb* **bobbed; bob·bing 1 :** to move up and down jerkily or repeatedly **2 :** to come or go suddenly or unexpectedly

2bob *n* **:** a bobbing movement

3bob *n* **1 :** a knob, bunch, or tuft esp. of hair or angling bait **2 :** FLOAT 3 **3 :** a short haircut of a woman or child **4 :** a small usu. pendent weight (as on a pendulum or plumb line)

4bob *vb* **bobbed; bob·bing :** to cut hair in a bob

5bob *n*, *pl* **bob** *slang* **:** SHILLING

bob·bin \'bäb-ən\ *n* **:** a cylinder or spindle for holding or dispensing thread (as in a sewing machine)

bob·ble \'bäb-əl\ *vb* **:** FUMBLE — **bobble** *n*

bob·by \'bäb-ē\ *n*, *Brit* **:** POLICEMAN

bob·by-sox·er \-,säk-sər\ *n* **:** an adolescent girl

bob·cat \'bäb-,kat\ *n* **:** a small usu. rusty-colored American lynx

bob·o·link \'bäb-ə-,liŋk\ *n* **:** an American migratory songbird related to the meadowlarks

bob·sled \'bäb-,sled\ *n* **1 :** a short sled usu. used as one of a joined pair **2 :** a compound sled formed of two bobsleds

and a coupling — **bobsled** *vb*

bob·white \(')bäb-'hwīt\ *n* **:** QUAIL

boc·cie \'bäch-ē\ *n* **:** Italian lawn bowling played on a long narrow court

bock \'bäk\ *n* **:** a dark heavy beer usu. sold in early spring

1bode \'bōd\ *vb* **:** to indicate by signs **:** PRESAGE

2bode *past of* BIDE

bod·ice \'bäd-əs\ *n* **:** the usu. close-fitting part of a dress above the waist

bodi·less \'bäd-ē-ləs\ *adj* **:** lacking a body or material form

bodi·ly \'bäd-ʾl-ē\ *adj* **:** of or relating to the body (~ welfare)

bod·kin \'bäd-kən\ *n* **1 :** DAGGER **2 :** a pointed implement for punching holes in cloth **3 :** a blunt needle for drawing tape or ribbon through a loop or hem

body \'bäd-ē\ *n* **1 :** the physical whole of a living or dead organism; *also* **:** the trunk or main mass of an organism as distinguished from its appendages **2 :** a human being **:** PERSON **3 :** the main part of something **4 :** a mass of matter distinct from other masses **5 :** GROUP **6 :** VISCOSITY, FIRMNESS **7 :** richness of flavor — used esp. of wines

body·guard \-,gärd\ *n* **:** a personal guard; *also* **:** RETINUE

Boer \'bōr, 'bùr\ *n* **:** a South African of Dutch or Huguenot descent

1bog \'bäg, 'bòg\ *n* **:** wet spongy and usu. acid ground — **bog·gy** *adj*

2bog *vb* **bogged; bog·ging :** to sink into or as if into a bog

bo·gey *or* **bo·gy** *or* **bo·gie** *n* **1 :** \'bùg-ē, 'bō-gē\ **:** SPECTER, HOBGOBLIN; *also* **:** a source of annoyance **2 :** \'bō-gē\ **:** a score of one over par on a hole in golf

bo·gey·man \'bùg-ē-,man, 'bō-gē-\ *n* **:** a terrifying person or thing; *esp* **:** an imaginary figure used in threatening children

bo·gus \'bō-gəs\ *adj* **:** SPURIOUS, SHAM

Bo·he·mi·an \bō-'hē-mē-ən\ *n* **1 :** a native or inhabitant of Bohemia **2** *often not cap* **:** VAGABOND, WANDERER **3** *often not cap* **:** a writer or artist living an unconventional life — **bohemian** *adj*, *often cap*

1boil \'bòil\ *n* **:** an inflamed swelling on the skin containing pus

2boil *vb* **1 :** to heat or become heated to a temperature (boiling point) at which vapor is formed and rises in bubbles (water ~s and changes to steam); *also* **:** to act on or be acted on by a boiling liquid (~ eggs) **2 :** to be in a state of seething agitation (~ with rage) (the tide ~*ing* over rocks)

3boil *n* **:** the action or state of boiling

boil·er *n* **1 :** a container in which something is boiled **2 :** the part of a steam-generating plant in which water is heated until it becomes steam **3 :** a tank holding hot water

boil·er·mak·er \-,mā-kər\ *n* **:** whiskey with a beer chaser

bois·ter·ous \'bòi-st(ə-)rəs\ *adj* **:** noisily turbulent or exuberant — **bois·ter·ous·ly** *adv*

bold \'bōld\ *adj* **1 :** COURAGEOUS, INTREPID **2 :** IMPUDENT **3 :** STEEP **4 :** DARING *syn* dauntless, brave — **bold·ly** *adv* — **bold·ness** *n*

bold·face \-,fās\ *n* **:** a heavy-faced type;

also : printing in boldface — **bold-faced** \-'fāst\ *adj*

bole \'bōl\ *n* : the trunk of a tree

bo·le·ro \bə-'le(ə)r-ō\ *n* **1** : a Spanish dance or its music **2** : a short loose jacket open at the front

bo·li·var \bə-'lē-,vär, 'bäl-ə-vər\ *n, pl* **bolivars** *or* **bo·li·va·res** \,bäl-ə-'vär-,ās\ — see MONEY table

bo·li·vi·a·no \bə-,liv-ē-'än-ō\ *n* — see MONEY table

boll \'bōl\ *n* : a seed pod (as of cotton)

bo·lo \'bō-lō\ *n* : a long heavy single-edged knife used in the Philippines

bo·lo·gna \bə-'lō-nē\ *n* : a large smoked sausage of beef, veal, and pork

Bol·she·vik \'bōl-shə-,vik\ *n* **1** : a member of the party that seized power in Russia during the revolution of 1917–20 **2** : COMMUNIST — **Bolshevik** *adj*

Bol·she·vism \'bōl-shə-,viz-əm\ *n* : the doctrine or program of the Bolsheviks advocating esp. violent overthrow of capitalism

¹bol·ster \'bōl-stər\ *n* : a long pillow or cushion extending from side to side of a bed

²bolster *vb* : to support with or as if with a bolster; *also* : REINFORCE

¹bolt \'bōlt\ *n* **1** : a usu. short stout blunt missile for a crossbow or catapult **2** : a flash of lightning : THUNDERBOLT **3** : a sliding bar to fasten a door **4** : a roll of cloth or wallpaper of specified length **5** : a rod with a head at one end and a screw thread at the other used to hold objects in place **6** : a short length or block of timber

²bolt *vb* **1** : to move suddenly (as in fright or hurry) : START, DASH **2** : to break away (as from control or association) (~ a political convention) **3** : to secure or fasten with a bolt **4** : to swallow hastily or without chewing

³bolt *n* : an act of bolting (made a ~ for the door)

⁴bolt *vb* : SIFT (~ flour)

bo·lus \'bō-ləs\ *n* : a rounded mass (as of chewed food or medicine)

¹bomb \'bäm\ *n* **1** : an explosive-filled case that may be dropped (as from a plane) or projected (as by hand) and is designed to detonate under specified conditions (as impact) **2** : a container of material (as insecticide) under pressure for release in a fine spray

²bomb *vb* : to attack with bombs

bom·bard \bäm-'bärd, bəm-\ *vb* **1** : to attack with artillery **2** : to assail persistently **3** : to subject to the impact of rapidly moving particles (as electrons) — **bom·bard·ment** *n*

bom·bar·dier \,bäm-bə(r)-'diər\ *n* : a bomber-crew member who releases the bombs

bom·bast \'bäm-,bast\ *n* : pretentious wordy utterance — **bom·bas·tic** \bäm-'bas-tik\ *adj*

bom·ba·zine \,bäm-bə-'zēn\ *n* **1** : a silk fabric in twill weave dyed black **2** : a twilled fabric with silk warp and worsted filling

bomb·er \'bäm-ər\ *n* : one that bombs; *esp* : an airplane for dropping bombs

bomb·proof \'bäm-'prüf\ *adj* : safe against the explosive force of bombs

bomb·shell \'bäm-,shel\ *n* **1** : BOMB 1 **2** : something wholly unanticipated

bomb·sight \-,sīt\ *n* : a sighting device on an airplane for aiming bombs

bo·na fide \'bō-nə-,fīd, ,bō-nə-'fīd-ē\ *adj* **1** : made in good faith (a *bona fide* agreement); *also* : legally valid **2** : GENUINE, REAL (a *bona fide* bargain) syn authentic

bo·nan·za \bə-'nan-zə\ *n* : something yielding a rich return

bon·bon \'bän-,bän\ *n* : a candy usu. with a creamy center in a cover (as of chocolate)

¹bond \'bänd\ *n* **1** *pl* : FETTERS **2** : a binding or uniting force or tie (~s of friendship) **3** : an agreement or obligation often made binding by a pledge of money or goods **4** : a person who acts as surety for another **5** : an interest-bearing certificate of public or private indebtedness **6** : the state of goods subject to supervision pending payment of taxes or duties due (imports held in ~)

²bond *vb* **1** : to assure payment of duties or taxes on (goods) by giving a bond **2** : to insure against losses caused by the acts of (~ a salesman) **3** : to make or become firmly united as if by bonds (~ iron to copper)

bond·age \'bän-dij\ *n* : SLAVERY, SERVITUDE

bond·hold·er \'bänd-,hōl-dər\ *n* : one that owns a government or corporation bond

bond·man \'bän(d)-mən\ *n* : SLAVE, SERF

¹bonds·man \'bän(d)z-mən\ *n* : BONDMAN

²bondsman *n* : SURETY

bond·wom·an \'bänd-,wùm-ən\ *n* : a female slave or serf

bone \'bōn\ *n* **1** : a hard largely calcareous tissue forming most of the skeleton of a vertebrate animal; *also* : one of the pieces in which bone naturally occurs **2** : a hard animal substance (as ivory or whalebone) similar to true bone **3** : something made of bone — **bone·less** \-ləs\ *adj* — **bony** *adj*

²bone *vb* : to free from bones (~ a chicken)

bon·er \'bō-nər\ *n* : a stupid and ridiculous blunder

bon·fire \'bän-,fī(ə)r\ *n* : a large fire built in the open air

bon·go \'bäŋ-gō\ *n* : one of a pair of small tuned drums played with the hands

bon·ho·mie \,bän-ə-'mē\ *n* : good-natured easy friendliness : GENIALITY

bo·ni·to \bə-'nēt-ō\ *n* : any of several medium-sized tunas

bon mot \bōⁿ-'mō\ *n, pl* **bons mots** \bōⁿ-'mō(z)\ *or* **bon mots** \-'mō(z)\ : a clever remark

bon·net \'bän-ət\ *n* : a covering (as a cap) for the head; *esp* : a hat for a woman or infant tied under the chin

bon·ny *also* **bon·nie** \'bän-ē\ *adj*, *chiefly Brit* : HANDSOME, PRETTY, FINE

bon·sai \bōn-'sī\ *n* : a potted plant (as a tree) dwarfed by special methods of culture

bo·nus \'bō-nəs\ *n* : something added and esp. money given in addition to what is usual or due syn bounty, premium, reward

bon vi·vant \,bän-vē-'vänt, ,bōⁿ-vē-'väⁿ\ *n, pl* **bons vivants** *or* **bon vivants** \,bän-vē-'vänts, ,bōⁿ-vē-'väⁿ(z)\ : a person having cultivated or refined tastes esp. in food and drink

bon voy·age \,bōⁿv-,wī-'äzh\ *n* : a good

trip : FAREWELL — often used as an interjection

boo \'bü\ n : a shout of disapproval or contempt — **boo** vb

boo·by \'bü-bē\ n : an awkward ineffective person : DOLT

boo·dle \'büd-ᵊl\ n : bribe money; also : LOOT

1book \'bùk\ n 1 : a set of sheets bound into a volume 2 : a long written or printed narrative or record 3 : a subdivision of a long literary work 4 cap : BIBLE

2book vb : to engage, reserve, or schedule by or as if by writing in a book ⟨~ seats on a plane⟩

book·case \-,kās\ n : a piece of furniture consisting of shelves to hold books

book·end \-,end\ n : a support placed at the end of a row of books to hold them up

book·ie \-ē\ n : BOOKMAKER

book·ish adj 1 : fond of books and reading 2 : inclined to rely unduly on book knowledge

book·keep·ing \-,kē-piŋ\ n : the art or practice of keeping a systematic record of business transactions and accounts — **book·keep·er** n

book·let \'bùk-lət\ n : PAMPHLET

book·mak·er \-,mā-kər\ n : one who determines odds and receives and pays off bets — **book·mak·ing** n

book·mark \-,märk\ n : a marker for finding a place in a book

book·mo·bile \-mō-,bēl\ n : a truck that serves as a traveling library

book·plate \-,plāt\ n : a label placed in a book to show who owns it

book·sell·er \-,sel-ər\ n : the proprietor of a bookstore

book·shelf \-,shelf\ n : a shelf for books

1boom \'büm\ n 1 : a long spar used to extend the bottom of a sail 2 : a beam projecting from the upright pole of a derrick to support or guide the object lifted 3 : a line of floating timbers used to hold logs in a restricted water area

2boom vb 1 : to make a deep hollow sound : RESOUND 2 : to grow or cause to grow rapidly esp. in value, esteem, or importance

3boom n 1 : a booming sound or cry 2 : a rapid expansion or increase

boo·mer·ang \'bü-mə-,raŋ\ n : a bent or angular club that can be so thrown as to return near the starting point

boom·town \'büm-,taùn\ n : a town undergoing a sudden growth in economic activity and population

1boon \'bün\ n : BENEFIT, BLESSING syn favor, gift

2boon adj : INTIMATE, CONGENIAL

boon·dog·gling \'bün-,dȯg-(ə-)liŋ\ n : a trivial, useless, or wasteful activity

boor \'bùr\ n : a rude or clownish person syn churl, lout, bumpkin — **boor·ish** adj

boost \'büst\ vb 1 : to push up from below 2 : INCREASE, RAISE ⟨~ prices⟩ 3 : AID, PROMOTE ⟨voted a bonus to ~ morale⟩ — **boost** n — **boost·er** n

1boot \'büt\ n : something given to equalize an exchange

2boot vb, archaic : AVAIL, PROFIT

3boot n 1 : a covering for the foot and leg 2 : a protective sheath (as of a

flower) or liner (as in a tire) 3 Brit : an automobile trunk 4 : KICK; also : a discharge from employment

4boot vb 1 : KICK 2 : to eject or discharge summarily

boot·black \-,blak\ n : a person who shines boots and shoes

boo·tee or **boo·tie** \'büt-ē\ n : an infant's knitted or crocheted sock

booth \'büth\ n, pl booths \'büthz, 'büths\ 1 : a small enclosed stall (as at a fair) 2 : a restaurant accommodation having a table between backed benches

boot·leg \'büt-,leg\ vb : to make, transport, or sell (as liquor) illegally — **bootleg** adj or n — **boot·leg·ger** n

boot·less \'büt-ləs\ adj : USELESS syn futile, vain — **boot·less·ly** adv

boo·ty \'büt-ē\ n : PLUNDER, SPOIL

1booze \'büz\ vb : to drink liquor to excess — **booz·er** n

2booze n : intoxicating liquor — **boozy** adj

bo·rac·ic acid \bə-,ras-ik-\ n : BORIC ACID

bo·rax \'bōr-,aks\ n : a crystalline compound of boron that occurs as a mineral and is used as a flux and cleanser and in glass and ceramics

1bor·der \'bȯrd-ər\ n 1 : EDGE, MARGIN 2 : BOUNDARY, FRONTIER syn rim, brim, brink

2border vb 1 : to put a border on 2 : ADJOIN 3 : VERGE

bor·der·land \-,land\ n 1 : territory at or near a border 2 : an outlying or intermediate region often not clearly defined ⟨the ~ between sleeping and waking⟩

1bore \'bōr\ vb 1 : to make a hole in usu. with a rotary tool 2 : to make (as a well) by piercing or drilling syn perforate, drill — **bor·er** n

2bore n 1 : a hole made by boring 2 : a lengthwise cylindrical cavity 3 : the diameter of a hole or tube; esp : the interior diameter of a gun barrel or engine cylinder

3bore past of BEAR

4bore n : one that causes boredom

5bore vb : to weary with tedious dullness

bo·re·al \'bōr-ē-əl\ adj : of, relating to, or located in northern regions

bore·dom \'bȯrd-əm\ n : the condition of being bored

bo·ric acid \,bōr-ik-\ n : a white crystalline weak acid that contains boron and is used as an antiseptic

born \'bȯrn\ adj : produced by or acquired at birth ⟨native-born citizens⟩

borne past part of BEAR

bo·ron \'bȯr-,än\ n : a chemical element that occurs in nature only in combination and is used esp. in metallurgy

bor·ough \'bər-ō\ n 1 : a British town that sends one or more members to parliament; also : an incorporated British urban area 2 : an incorporated town or village in some U.S. states; also : any of the 5 political divisions of New York City

bor·row \'bär-ō\ vb 1 : to take or receive (something) temporarily and with intent to return 2 : to take into possession or use from another source : DERIVE, APPROPRIATE ⟨~ a metaphor⟩ ⟨~ed rites⟩

ə abut; ⁹ kitten; ər further; a back; ā bake; ä cot, cart; aù out; ch chin; e less; ē easy; g gift; i trip; ī life; j joke; ŋ sing; ō flow; ȯ flaw; ȯi coin; th thin; t͟h this; ü loot; ù foot; y yet; yü few; yù furious; zh vision

borsch *or* borscht \'bȯrsh(t)\ *n* : a soup made esp. from beets

bosh \'bäsh\ *n* : foolish talk : NONSENSE

bosky \'bäs-kē\ *adj* : covered with trees or shrubs

1bos·om \'bùz-əm\ *n* 1 : the front of the human chest; *esp* : the female breasts 2 : the part of a garment covering the breast 3 : the seat of secret thoughts and feelings

2bosom *adj* : CLOSE, INTIMATE

1boss \'bäs, 'bȯs\ *n* : a knoblike ornament : STUD

2boss *vb* : to ornament with bosses : EMBOSS

3boss \'bȯs\ *n* 1 : one (as a foreman or manager) exercising control or supervision 2 : a politician who controls votes or dictates policies — bossy *adj*

4boss \'bȯs\ *vb* : to act as a boss : SUPERVISE

bo·sun \'bōs-ᵊn\ *var of* BOATSWAIN

bot·a·ny \'bät-(ᵊ-)nē\ *n* : a branch of biology dealing with plant and plant life — bo·tan·i·cal \bə-'tan-i-kəl\ *or* bo·tan·ic \-ik\ *adj* — bot·a·nist \'bät-(ᵊ-)nəst\ *n* — bot·a·nize \-ᵊn-,īz\ *vb*

botch \'bäch\ *vb* 1 : to patch clumsily 2 : BUNGLE — botch *n*

1both \'bōth\ *adj* : the one and the other

2both *pron* : both ones : the one and the other

3both *conj* : both or all of the following, namely : INCLUSIVELY — used with following *and* (he was ~ hungry and tired)

both·er \'bäth-ər\ *vb* : WORRY, PESTER, TROUBLE *syn* vex, annoy, irk — bother *n* — both·er·some \-səm\ *adj*

1bot·tle \'bät-ᵊl\ *n* 1 : a container (as of glass) with a narrow neck and no handles 2 : the quantity held by a bottle 3 : intoxicating liquor

2bottle *vb* : to put into a bottle

bot·tle·neck \-,nek\ *n* 1 : a narrow passage or point of congestion 2 : something that obstructs or impedes

bot·tom \'bät-əm\ *n* 1 : an under or supporting surface; *also* : BUTTOCKS 2 : the bottom of a body of water 3 : the lowest part or place; *also* : an inferior position (start at the ~) — bottom *adj* — bot·tom·less \-ləs\ *adj*

bou·doir \'bü-,dwär\ *n* : a woman's private room

bouf·fant \bü-'fänt, -'fäⁿ\ *adj* : puffed out (~ hairdos)

bough \'baù\ *n* : a usu. large or main branch of a tree

bought *past of* BUY

bouil·lon \'bù-,yän; 'bùl-,yän, -,yən\ *n* : a clear soup made usu. from beef

boul·der \'bōl-dər\ *n* : a large detached rounded or worn mass of rock

bou·le·vard \'bùl-ə-,värd, 'bül-\ *n* [F, modif. of MD *bolwerc* bulwark; so called because the first boulevards were laid out on the sites of razed city fortifications] : a broad often landscaped thoroughfare

bounce \'baùns\ *vb* : BOUND, REBOUND — bounce *n*

bounc·er *n* : a man employed in a public place to remove disorderly persons

1bound \'baùnd\ *adj* : intending to go : GOING

2bound *n* : LIMIT, BOUNDARY — boundless \-ləs\ *adj* — bound·less·ness *n*

3bound *vb* 1 : to set limits to 2 : to form the boundary of 3 : to name the boundaries of

4bound *adj* 1 : constrained by or as if by bonds : CONFINED, OBLIGED; *also* : held in combination (~ water) 2 : enclosed in a binding or cover 3 : RESOLVED, DETERMINED; *also* : SURE (~ to rain)

5bound *n* 1 : LEAP, JUMP 2 : REBOUND, BOUNCE

6bound *vb* : SPRING, BOUNCE

bound·a·ry \'baùn-d(ə-)rē\ *n* : something that marks or fixes a limit (as of territory) *syn* border, frontier

bound·en \'baùn-dən\ *adj* : BINDING (his ~ duty)

boun·te·ous \'baùnt-ē-əs\ *adj* 1 : GENEROUS 2 : ABUNDANT — boun·te·ous·ly *adv*

boun·ti·ful \'baùnt-i-fəl\ *adj* 1 : giving freely 2 : PLENTIFUL — boun·ti·ful·ly *adv*

boun·ty \'baùnt-ē\ *n* 1 : GENEROSITY 2 : something given liberally 3 : a reward, premium, or subsidy given usu. for doing something *syn* award, prize, bonus

bou·quet \bō-'kā, bù-\ *n* 1 : a bunch of flowers 2 : distinctive aroma (as of wine) *syn* scent, fragrance

bour·bon \'bər-bən\ *n* : a whiskey distilled from a corn mash

bour·geois \'bùrzh-,wä\ *n, pl* bourgeois \-,wä(z)\ [MF, lit., citizen of a town, fr. OF *borc* town, borough, fr. L *burgus* fortified place, of Gmc origin] : a middle-class person — bourgeois *adj*

bour·geoi·sie \,bùrzh-,wä-'zē\ *n* : a social order dominated by bourgeois

bourn *or* bourne \'bōrn, 'bùrn\ *n, archaic* : BOUNDARY; *also* : DESTINATION

bourse \'bùrs\ *n* : a European stock exchange

bout \'baùt\ *n* 1 : CONTEST, MATCH 2 : OUTBREAK, ATTACK (a ~ of measles) 3 : SESSION

bou·tique \bü-'tēk\ *n* : a small retail store; *esp* : a fashionable specialty shop for women

bou·ton·niere \,büt-ᵊn-'iər\ *n* : a flower or bouquet worn in a buttonhole

bo·vine \'bō-,vīn, -,vēn\ *adj* : of, related to, or resembling the ox or cow — bovine *n*

1bow \'baù\ *vb* 1 : SUBMIT, YIELD 2 : to bend the head or body (as in submission, courtesy, or assent)

2bow *n* : an act or posture of bowing

3bow \'bō\ *n* 1 : BEND, ARCH; *esp* : RAINBOW 2 : a weapon for shooting arrows; *also* : ARCHER 3 : a knot formed by doubling a line into two or more loops 4 : a wooden rod strung with horsehairs for playing esp. a violin

4bow \'bō\ *vb* 1 : BEND, CURVE 2 : to play (an instrument) with a bow

5bow \'baù\ *n* : the forward part of a ship — bow *adj*

bowd·ler·ize \'bōd-lə-,rīz, 'baùd-\ *vb* : to expurgate with prudish care

bow·el \'baù-(ə)l\ *n* 1 *pl* : INTESTINES 2 : one of the divisions of the intestine 3 *pl* : the inmost parts (the ~s of the earth)

bow·er \'baù-(ə)r\ *n* : a shelter of boughs or vines : ARBOR

1bowl \'bōl\ *n* 1 : a concave vessel to hold liquids 2 : a drinking vessel 3 : a bowl-shaped part or structure — bowl·ful \-,fùl\ *n*

2bowl *n* 1 : a ball for rolling on a level

surface in bowling **2 :** a cast of the ball in bowling

³**bowl** *vb* **1 :** to play a game of bowling; *also* **:** to roll a ball in bowling **2 :** to travel in a vehicle rapidly and smoothly **3 :** to strike or knock down with a moving object; *also* **:** to overwhelm with surprise

bowl·der *var of* BOULDER

bow·leg \'bō-,leg, -'leg\ *n* **:** a leg bowed outward usu. at or below the knee — **bow·leg·ged** \-'leg-əd\ *adj*

¹**bowl·er** \'bō-lər\ *n* **:** one that bowls

²**bowl·er** \'bō-lər\ *n* **:** DERBY 3

bowl·ing *n* **:** any of various games in which balls are rolled on a green (**bowling green**) or alley (**bowling alley**) at an object or a group of objects; *esp* **:** TENPINS

bow·man \'bō-mən\ *n* **:** ARCHER

bow·sprit \'baù-,sprit\ *n* **:** a spar projecting forward from the prow of a ship

bow·string \'bō-,striŋ\ *n* **:** the cord connecting the two ends of a bow

¹**box** \'bäks\ *n* **:** an evergreen shrub or small tree used esp. for hedges — **box·wood** \-,wùd\ *n*

²**box** *n* **1 :** a rigid typically rectangular receptacle often with a cover; *also* **:** the quantity held by a box **2 :** a small compartment (as for a group of theater patrons); *also* **:** a boxlike receptacle or division **3 :** any of 6 spaces on a baseball diamond where the batter, pitcher, coaches, and catcher stand **4 :** PREDICAMENT

³**box** *vb* **:** to furnish with or enclose in or as if in a box

⁴**box** *n* **:** SLAP, CUFF

⁵**box** *vb* **1 :** to strike with the hand **2 :** to engage in boxing with **:** fight with the fists   *syn* smite, strike, slap

box·car \-,kär\ *n* **:** a roofed freight car usu. with sliding doors in the sides

¹**box·er** *n* **:** PUGILIST

²**boxer** *n* **:** a compact short-haired usu. fawn or brindle dog of German origin

box·ing *n* **:** the sport of fighting with the fists

¹**boy** \'bòi\ *n* **1 :** a male child **:** YOUTH **2 :** a male servant — **boy·hood** \-,hùd\ *n* — **boy·ish** *adj* — **boy·ish·ness** *n*

boy·cott \'bòi-,kät\ *vb* **:** to refrain from having any dealings with — **boycott** *n*

bra \'brä\ *n* **:** BRASSIERE

¹**brace** \'brās\ *n* **1 :** a crank-shaped device for turning a bit **2 :** something (as a tie, prop, or clamp) that distributes, directs, or resists pressure or weight; *also* **:** an appliance for supporting a body part **3** *pl* **:** SUSPENDERS **4 :** a mark { or } or — used to connect words or items to be considered together

²**brace** *vb* **1** *archaic* **:** to make fast **:** BIND **2 :** to tighten preparatory to use; *also* **:** to get ready for **:** prepare oneself **3 :** INVIGORATE **4 :** to furnish or support with a brace; *also* **:** STRENGTHEN **5 :** to set firmly (~ your feet); *also* **:** to gain courage or confidence

brace·let \-lət\ *n* **:** an ornamental band or chain worn around the arm

brack·en \'brak-ən\ *n* **:** a large coarse fern; *also* **:** a growth of such ferns

¹**brack·et** \'brak-ət\ *n* **1 :** a projecting framework or arm designed to support weight; *also* **:** a shelf on such framework

2 : one of a pair of punctuation marks [ ] used esp. to enclose interpolated matter **3 :** a continuous section of a series; *esp* **:** one of a graded series of income groups

²**bracket** *vb* **1 :** to furnish or fasten with brackets **2 :** to place within brackets; *also* **:** to separate or group with or as if with brackets

brack·ish \'brak-ish\ *adj* **:** somewhat salty

bract \'brakt\ *n* **:** an often modified leaf on or at the base of a flower stalk

brad \'brad\ *n* **:** a slender nail with a small head

brae \'brā\ *n*, *chiefly Scot* **:** a hillside esp. along a river

brag \'brag\ *vb* **bragged; brag·ging :** to talk or assert boastfully — **brag** *n*

brag·ga·do·cio \,brag-ə-'dō-sh(ē-,)ō\ *n* **1 :** BRAGGART, BOASTER **2 :** empty boasting **3 :** arrogant pretension

brag·gart \'brag-ərt\ *n* **:** one who brags

Brah·man *or* **Brah·min** \'bräm-ən\ *n* **:** a Hindu of the highest caste traditionally assigned to the priesthood

Brah·man·ism \-,iz-əm\ *n* **:** orthodox Hinduism

Brah·min \'bräm-ən\ *n* **:** an intellectually and socially cultivated and exclusive person

¹**braid** \'brād\ *vb* **1 :** to form (strands) into a braid **:** PLAIT; *also* **:** to make by braiding **2 :** to ornament with braid

²**braid** *n* **1 :** a cord or ribbon of three or more interwoven strands **2 :** a narrow ornamental fabric of intertwined threads

braille \'brāl\ *n*, *often cap* **:** a system of writing for the blind that uses characters made up of raised dots

¹**brain** \'brān\ *n* **1 :** the part of the vertebrate nervous system that is the organ of thought and nervous coordination, is made up of nerve cells and their fibers, and is enclosed in the skull; *also* **:** a centralized mass of nerve tissue in an invertebrate **2 :** INTELLECT, INTELLIGENCE — often used in pl. — **brain·less** \-ləs\ *adj* — **brainy** *adj*

²**brain** *vb* **:** to kill by smashing the skull

brain·child \-,chīld\ *n* **:** a product of one's creative imagination

brain·storm \-,stòrm\ *n* **:** a sudden burst of inspiration

brain·wash·ing \-,wòsh-iŋ, -,wäsh-\ *n* **1 :** a forcible attempt by indoctrination to induce someone to give up his basic political, social, or religious beliefs and attitudes and to accept contrasting regimented ideas **2 :** persuasion by propaganda or salesmanship

braise \'brāz\ *vb* **:** to cook (meat) slowly in fat and little moisture in a covered dish

¹**brake** \'brāk\ *n* **:** a large coarse fern **:** BRACKEN

²**brake** *n* **:** a device for slowing up or checking motion (as of a wheel)

³**brake** *vb* **1 :** to slow or stop by or as if by a brake **2 :** to apply a brake

⁴**brake** *n* **:** rough or wet land heavily overgrown (as with thickets or reeds)

brake·man \-mən\ *n* **:** a train crew member whose duties include operating hand brakes and switches and checking the train personnel

bram·ble \'bram-bəl\ *n* : any of a large genus of prickly shrubs of the rose family

bran \'bran\ *n* : broken husks of cereal grain sifted from flour or meal

1branch \'branch\ *n* 1 : a natural subdivision (as a bough or twig) of a plant stem 2 : a division (as of an antler or a river) related to a whole like a plant branch to its stem 3 : a discrete unit or element of a complex system (as of knowledge, people, or business); *esp* : a division of a family descended from a particular ancestor

2branch *vb* 1 : to develop branches 2 : DIVERGE

1brand \'brand\ *n* 1 : a piece of charred or burning wood 2 : a mark made (as by burning) usu. to identify; *also* : a mark of disgrace : STIGMA 3 : a class of goods identified as the product of a particular firm or producer 4 : a distinctive kind (his own ∼ of humor)

2brand *vb* 1 : to mark with a brand 2 : STIGMATIZE

bran·dish \'bran-dish\ *vb* : to shake or wave menacingly **syn** flourish, swing

brand-new \'bran-'n(y)ü\ *adj* : conspicuously new and unused

bran·dy \'bran-dē\ *n* : a liquor distilled from wine or fermented fruit juice — **brandy** *vb*

brash \'brash\ *adj* 1 : IMPETUOUS 2 : aggressively self-assertive : IMPUDENT

brass \'bras\ *n* 1 : an alloy of copper and zinc; *also* : an object of brass 2 : bold assurance — **brassy** *adj*

bras·siere \brə-'zir\ *n* : a woman's close-fitting undergarment designed to support the breasts

brat \'brat\ *n* : a usu. ill-behaved child

bra·va·do \brə-'väd-ō\ *n* : swaggering pretense of courage

1brave \'brāv\ *adj* 1 : showing courage 2 : EXCELLENT, SPLENDID **syn** bold, intrepid — **brave·ly** *adv*

2brave *vb* : to face or endure bravely

3brave *n* : a No. American Indian warrior

brav·ery \'brāv-(ə-)rē\ *n* : COURAGE

bra·vo \'brä-vō\ *n* : a shout of approval — often used as an interjection in applauding

bra·vu·ra \brə-'v(y)ùr-ə\ *n* 1 : a florid brilliant musical style 2 : self-assured brilliant performance

brawl \'brol\ *n* : a noisy quarrel **syn** fracas, row, rumpus, scrap — **brawl** *vb* — **brawl·er** *n*

brawn \'bron\ *n* : strong muscles; *also* : muscular strength — **brawny** *adj*

bray \'brā\ *n* : the characteristic harsh cry of a donkey — **bray** *vb*

braze \'brāz\ *vb* : to solder with a relatively infusible alloy (as brass)

bra·zen \'brāz-ʰn\ *adj* 1 : made of brass 2 : sounding harsh and loud 3 : of the color of brass 4 : SHAMELESS, IMPUDENT — **bra·zen·ly** *adv*

1bra·zier \'brā-zhər\ *n* : a worker in brass

2brazier *n* : a vessel holding burning coals (as for heating); *also* : a device on which food is exposed to heat through a wire grill

Bra·zil·ian \brə-'zil-yən\ *n* : a native or inhabitant of Brazil — **Brazilian** *adj*

1breach \'brēch\ *n* 1 : a breaking of a law, obligation, tie (as of friendship), or standard (as of conduct) 2 : an

interruption or opening made by or as if by breaking through **syn** violation, transgression, infringement

2breach *vb* : to make a breach in

1bread \'bred\ *n* 1 : baked food made basically of flour or meal 2 : FOOD

2bread *vb* : to cover with bread crumbs before cooking

bread·bas·ket \-,bas-kət\ *n* : a major cereal-producing region

bread·stuff \-,stəf\ *n* : GRAIN, FLOUR

breadth \'bredth\ *n* 1 : WIDTH 2 : SPACIOUSNESS; *also* : liberality of taste or views

bread·win·ner \'bred-,win-ər\ *n* : a member of a family whose wages supply its livelihood

break \'brāk\ *vb* broke \'brōk\ broken \'brō-kən\ break·ing 1 : to separate into parts usu. suddenly or violently : come or force apart 2 : TRANSGRESS (∼ a law) 3 : to force a way into, out of, or through 4 : to disrupt the order or unity of (∼ ranks) (∼ up a gang); *also* : to bring to submission or helplessness 5 : EXCEED, SURPASS (∼ a record) 6 : RUIN 7 : to make known 8 : HALT, INTERRUPT; *also* : to act or change abruptly (as a course or activity) 9 : to come esp. suddenly into being or notice (as day ∼s) 10 : to fail under stress 11 : HAPPEN, DEVELOP — **break·able** *adj or n*

2break *n* 1 : an act of breaking 2 : a result of breaking; *esp* : an interruption of continuity 3 : an awkward social blunder 4 : a stroke of good luck

break·age \'brā-kij\ *n* 1 : the action of breaking 2 : articles or amount broken 3 : allowance for things broken

break·down \'brāk-,daùn\ *n* 1 : functional failure; *esp* : a physical, mental, or nervous collapse 2 : DISINTEGRATION (∼ of communications) 3 : DECOMPOSITION (∼ of stored fruit) 4 : ANALYSIS, CLASSIFICATION

break·er *n* 1 : one that breaks 2 : a wave that breaks into foam (as when nearing shore)

break·fast \'brek-fast\ *n* : the first meal of the day — **breakfast** *vb*

break·out \'brāk-,aùt\ *n* : a military attack to break from encirclement

break·through \-,thrü\ *n* 1 : an act or point of breaking through an obstruction or defensive line 2 : a sudden advance in knowledge or technique

break·wa·ter \'brāk-,wòt-ər, -,wät-\ *n* : a structure built to break the force of waves

bream \'brim\ *n* : any of various small freshwater sunfishes

breast \'brest\ *n* 1 : either of two milk-producing glandular organs situated on the front of the chest esp. in the human female; *also* : the front part of the chest 2 : something resembling a breast

breast·bone \'bres(t)-,bōn, -,bòn\ *n* : STERNUM

breast·plate \-,plāt\ *n* : a metal plate of armor for protecting the breast

breast·stroke \-,strōk\ *n* : a swimming stroke executed by extending the arms in front of the head while drawing the knees forward and outward and then sweeping the arms back with palms out while kicking backward and outward

breast·work \'brest-,wərk\ *n* : a temporary or improvised fortification

breath \'breth\ *n* 1 : the act or power of breathing 2 : a slight breeze 3 : air inhaled or exhaled in breathing **4 :** spoken sound **:** UTTERANCE **5 :** SPIRIT — **breath·less** \-ləs\ adj — **breath·less·ly** adv

breathe \'brēth\ vb **1 :** to draw air into and expel it from the lungs in respiration **2 :** LIVE **3 :** to halt for rest **4 :** to utter softly or secretly

breath·tak·ing \'breth-,tā-kiŋ\ adj **1 :** making one out of breath ⟨a ~ climb⟩ **2 :** EXCITING, THRILLING ⟨~ beauty⟩

breech \'brēch\ n **1** pl \usu 'brich-əz\ **:** trousers ending near the knee; also **:** PANTS **2 :** BUTTOCKS, RUMP **3 :** the rear part of a firearm behind the bore

¹breed \'brēd\ vb bred \'bred\ **breed·ing 1 :** BEGET; also **:** ORIGINATE **2 :** to propagate sexually; also **:** MATE **3 :** to bring up **:** NURTURE **syn** generate, reproduce — **breed·er** n

²breed n **1 :** a strain of similar and presumably related plants or animals usu. developed under the influence of man **2 :** KIND, SORT, CLASS ⟨a different ~ of courage⟩

breed·ing n **1 :** ANCESTRY **2 :** training in polite social intercourse **3 :** sexual propagation of plants or animals

breeze \'brēz\ n **:** a light wind — **breezy** adj

breeze·way \'brēz-,wā\ n **:** a roofed open passage usu. connecting two buildings (as a house and garage)

breth·ren \'breth-(ə-)rən, 'breth-ərn\ pl of BROTHER — used esp. in formal or solemn address

Brethren n pl **:** members of one of several Protestant denominations originating chiefly in a German religious movement and stressing Bible study and personal religious experience

bre·vet \brə-'vet\ n **:** a commission giving a military officer higher nominal rank than that for which he receives pay — **brevet** vb

bre·via·ry \'brē-v(y)ə-rē, -vē-,er-ē\ n **:** a book of prayers, hymns, psalms, and readings used by Roman Catholic priests

brev·i·ty \'brev-ət-ē\ n **1 :** shortness of duration **2 :** CONCISENESS

brew \'brü\ vb **:** to prepare (as beer) by steeping, boiling, and fermenting — **brew·er** n — **brew·ery** n

¹bribe \'brīb\ vb **:** to corrupt or influence (one in a position of trust) by favors or gifts — **brib·ery** n

²bribe n **:** something offered or given in bribing

bric-a-brac \'brik-ə-,brak\ n **:** small ornamental articles

¹brick \'brik\ n **:** a block molded from moist clay and hardened by heat used esp. for building

²brick vb **:** to close, cover, or pave with bricks

brick·bat \-,bat\ n **1 :** a piece of a broken brick esp. when thrown as a missile **2 :** an uncomplimentary remark

brick·lay·er \-,lā-ər\ n **:** a person who builds or paves with bricks — **brick·lay·ing** n

¹brid·al \'brīd-ᵊl\ n **:** MARRIAGE, WEDDING

²bridal adj **:** of or relating to a bride or a wedding

bride \'brīd\ n **:** a woman newly married or about to be married

bride·groom \-,grüm, -,grum\ n **:** a man newly married or about to be married

brides·maid \'brīdz-,mād\ n **:** a woman who attends a bride at her wedding

¹bridge \'brij\ n **1 :** a structure built over a depression or obstacle for use as a passageway **2 :** something (as the upper part of the nose) resembling a bridge in form or function; esp **:** a platform over the deck of a ship **3 :** an artificial replacement for missing teeth

²bridge vb **:** to build a bridge over — **bridge·able** adj

³bridge n **:** a card game for 4 players developed from whist and usu. played as either **contract bridge** or **auction bridge**

bridge·head \-,hed\ n **:** an advanced position seized in enemy territory as a foothold

bridge·work \-,wərk\ n **:** the dental bridges in a mouth

¹bri·dle \'brīd-ᵊl\ n **1 :** headgear with which a horse is controlled **2 :** CURB, RESTRAINT

²bridle vb **1 :** to put a bridle on; also **:** to restrain with or as if with a bridle **2 :** to show hostility or scorn usu. by tossing the head

¹brief \'brēf\ adj **1 :** short in duration or extent **2 :** CONCISE; also **:** CURT — **brief·ly** adv — **brief·ness** n

²brief n **1 :** a concise statement or document; esp **:** one summarizing a law client's case or a legal argument **2** pl **:** short snug drawers

³brief vb **:** to give final instructions or essential information to ⟨~ a bombing crew⟩

brief·case \-,kās\ n **:** a flat flexible case usu. of leather for carrying papers

bri·er or **bri·ar** \'brī-(ə)r\ n **:** a plant (as a bramble or rose) with a thorny or prickly woody stem; also **:** a group or mass of brier bushes — **bri·ery** adj

¹brig \'brig\ n **:** a 2-masted square-rigged sailing ship

²brig n **:** the place of confinement for offenders on a naval ship

bri·gade \brig-'ād\ n **1 :** a military unit composed of a headquarters, one or more units of infantry or armored forces, and supporting units **2 :** a group organized for a particular purpose (as fire-fighting)

brig·a·dier general \,brig-ə-,diər-\ n **:** a commissioned officer (as in the army) ranking next below a major general

brig·and \'brig-ənd\ n **:** BANDIT — **brig·and·age** \-ən-dij\ n

brig·an·tine \'brig-ən-,tēn\ n **:** a 2-masted square-rigged ship not carrying a square mainsail

bright \'brīt\ adj **1 :** SHINING, RADIANT **2 :** ILLUSTRIOUS, GLORIOUS **3 :** INTELLIGENT, CLEVER; also **:** LIVELY, CHEERFUL **syn** brilliant, lustrous, beaming, smart — **bright·ly** adv — **bright·ness** n

bright·en \'brīt-ᵊn\ vb **:** to make or become bright or brighter

bril·liant \'bril-yənt\ adj **1 :** very bright **2 :** DISTINGUISHED, SPLENDID **3 :** very intelligent **syn** radiant, lustrous, beaming, clever, bright, smart — **bril·liance** n

---

ə abut; ᵊ kitten; ər further; a back; ā bake; ä cot, cart; aù out; ch chin; e less; ē easy; g gift; i trip; ī life; j joke; ŋ sing; ō flow; ò flaw; òi coin; th thin; t̲h̲ this; ü loot; ù foot; y yet; yü few; yù furious; zh vision

\-yəns\ or **bril·lian·cy** \-yən-sē\ n —
bril·liant·ly adv

bril·lian·tine \'bril-yən-‚tēn\ n : a usu.
oily dressing for the hair

brim \'brim\ n : EDGE, RIM **syn** brink,
border, verge — **brim·less** adj

brim·ful \-'ful\ adj : full to the brim

brim·stone \'brim-‚stōn\ n : SULFUR

brin·dled \'brin-d°ld\ adj : having dark
streaks or flecks on a gray or tawny
ground

brine \'brīn\ n 1 : water saturated with
salt 2 : OCEAN — **briny** adj

bring \'briŋ\ vb **brought** \'brȯt\
bring·ing 1 : to cause to come with
one 2 : INDUCE, PERSUADE, LEAD
3 : PRODUCE, EFFECT 4 : to fetch in
exchange : sell for — **bring·er** n

bring up vb 1 : to give a parent's foster-
ing care to 2 : to come or bring to a
sudden halt 3 : to call to notice

brink \'briŋk\ n 1 : an edge at the top
of a steep place 2 : the point of onset
: VERGE

brio \'brē-ō\ n : VIVACITY, SPIRIT

bri·oche \brē-'ōsh\ n : a roll baked
from light yeast dough rich with eggs
and butter

bri·quette or **bri·quet** \brik-'et\ n : a
consolidated often brick-shaped mass of
fine material ⟨a charcoal ~⟩

brisk \'brisk\ adj 1 : ALERT, LIVELY
2 : INVIGORATING **syn** agile, spry —
brisk·ly adv — **brisk·ness** n

bris·ket \'bris-kət\ n : the breast or
lower chest of a quadruped

bris·ling or **bris·tling** \'briz-liŋ, 'bris-\
n : a small sardinelike herring

¹**bris·tle** \'bris-əl\ n : a short stiff coarse
hair — **bris·tly** \-(ə-)lē\ adj

²**bristle** vb 1 : to stand stiffly erect
2 : to show angry defiance 3 : to appear as if covered with bristles

Bri·tan·nic \bri-'tan-ik\ adj : BRITISH

Brit·ish \'brit-ish\ n pl : the people of
Great Britain or the British Commonwealth — **British** adj

Brit·on \'brit-°n\ n 1 : a member of a
people inhabiting Britain before the
Anglo-Saxon invasion 2 : a native or
inhabitant of Great Britain

brit·tle \'brit-°l\ adj : easily broken or
snapped : FRAGILE **syn** crisp

¹**broach** \'brōch\ n 1 : a pointed tool
(as for opening casks) 2 : a bitlike tool
for enlarging or shaping a hole

²**broach** vb 1 : to pierce (as a cask) in
order to draw the contents 2 : to shape
or enlarge a hole with a broach 3 : to
introduce as a topic of conversation

broad \'brȯd\ adj 1 : WIDE 2 : SPA-
CIOUS 3 : CLEAR, OPEN 4 : OBVIOUS
5 : COARSE, CRUDE ⟨~ stories⟩ 6 : liberal in outlook 7 : GENERAL 8 : dealing with essential points — **broad·ly**
adv

¹**broad·cast** \-‚kast\ adj 1 : cast in all
directions 2 : made public by means
of radio or television — **broadcast** adv

²**broadcast** n 1 : the transmitting of
sound or images by radio waves 2 : a
single radio or television program

³**broadcast** vb -cast also -cast·ed;
-cast·ing 1 : to scatter or sow broadcast; also : to make widely known
2 : to send out or speak or perform on
a radio or television broadcast —
broad·cast·er n

broad·cloth \-‚klȯth\ n 1 : a smooth
dense woolen cloth 2 : a fine soft cloth
of cotton, silk, or synthetic fiber

broad·en \'brȯd-°n\ vb : WIDEN

broad–mind·ed \-'mīn-dəd\ adj : free
from prejudice : TOLERANT

broad·side \-‚sīd\ n 1 : the part of a
ship's side above the waterline 2 : simultaneous discharge of all the guns
on one side of a ship; also : a volley of
abuse or denunciation

broad–spectrum : having a wide
range esp. of effectiveness ⟨~ anti-
biotics⟩

broad·sword \'brȯd-‚sȯrd\ n : a broad-
bladed sword

bro·cade \brō-'kād\ n : a usu. silk fabric
with a raised design

broc·co·li \'bräk-(ə-)lē\ n : an open
branching cauliflower whose young
flowering shoots are used as a vegetable

bro·chette \brō-'shet\ n : a small spit
: SKEWER

bro·chure \brō-'shȯr\ n : PAMPHLET,
BOOKLET

bro·gan \'brō-gən, brō-'gan\ n : a
heavy shoe; esp : a work shoe reaching
to the ankle

brogue \'brōg\ n : a dialect or regional
pronunciation; esp : an Irish accent

broi·der \'brȯid-ər\ vb : EMBROIDER
— **broi·dery** n

broil \'brȯil\ vb : to cook by exposure
to radiant heat : GRILL — **broil** n

broil·er n 1 : a utensil for broiling
2 : a young chicken fit for broiling

broke past of BREAK

bro·ken \'brō-kən\ adj 1 : SHATTERED
2 : having gaps or breaks : INTERRUPTED,
DISRUPTED 3 : SUBDUED, CRUSHED
4 : BANKRUPT 5 : imperfectly spoken
— **bro·ken·ly** adv

bro·ken·heart·ed \‚brō-kən-'härt-əd\
adj : shattered by grief or despair

bro·ker \'brō-kər\ n : an agent who
negotiates contracts of purchase and
sale for a fee or commission; also
: DEALER

bro·ker·age \-k(ə-)rij\ n 1 : the business of a broker 2 : the fee or commission on business transacted through
a broker

bro·mide \'brō-‚mīd\ n 1 : a compound of bromine and another element
or a radical including some (as potassium bromide) used as sedatives 2 : a
trite remark or notion

bro·mid·ic \brō-'mid-ik\ adj : DULL,
TIRESOME ⟨~ remarks⟩

bro·mine \-‚mēn\ n [F brome bromine,
fr. Gk brōmos stink] : a deep red liquid
corrosive chemical element that gives
off an irritating vapor and occurs
naturally only in combination

bron·chi·al \'bräŋ-kē-əl\ adj : of, relating to, or affecting the bronchi or their
branches

bron·chi·tis \brän-'kīt-əs, bräŋ-\ n
: inflammation of the bronchi and their
branches — **bron·chit·ic** \-'kit-ik\ adj

bron·chus \'bräŋ-kəs\ n, pl **bron·chi**
\'bräŋ-‚kī, 'bräŋ-‚-‚kē\ : either of the
main divisions of the windpipe each
leading to a lung

bron·co \'bräŋ-kō, brän-\ n : a small
half-wild horse of western No. America

¹**bronze** \'bränz\ vb : to give the appearance of bronze

²**bronze** n 1 : an alloy basically of copper and tin; also : something (as a
sculpture) of bronze 2 : a yellowish
brown color

brooch \'brōch, 'brüch\ n : an ornamental clasp or pin

¹**brood** \'brüd\ *n* : a family of young animals or children and esp. of birds

²**brood** *vb* 1 : to sit on eggs to hatch them; *also* : to shelter (hatched young) with the wings 2 : PONDER

³**brood** *adj* : kept for breeding ⟨a ~ mare⟩

brood·er *n* 1 : one that broods 2 : a heated structure for raising young birds

¹**brook** \'brúk\ *vb* : TOLERATE, BEAR

²**brook** *n* : a small natural stream of water

brook·let \-lət\ *n* : a small brook

broom \'brüm, 'brúm\ *n* 1 : a shrub of the pea group with long slender branches and yellow flowers 2 : an implement for sweeping orig. made from twigs — **broom·stick** \-,stik\ *n*

broth \'bróth\ *n* : liquid in which meat or sometimes vegetable food has been cooked

broth·el \'bräth-əl, 'bróth-\ *n* : an establishment housing prostitutes

broth·er \'brəth-ər\ *n* 1 : a male having one or both parents in common with another individual; *also* : KINSMAN 2 : a kindred human being 3 : a man who is a religious but not a priest — **broth·er·li·ness** *n* — **broth·er·ly** *adj*

broth·er·hood \-,húd\ *n* 1 : the state of being brothers or a brother 2 : ASSOCIATION, FRATERNITY 3 : the whole body of persons in a business or profession

brother-in-law *n, pl* **brothers-in-law** : the brother of one's spouse; *also* : the husband of one's sister or one's spouse's sister

brougham \'brü(-ə)m, 'brō(-ə)m\ *n* 1 : a light closed horse-drawn carriage with the driver outside in front 2 : a coupe automobile; *esp* : one electrically driven 3 : a sedan having no roof over the driver's seat

brought *past of* BRING

brou·ha·ha \brü-'hä-hä\ *n* : HUBBUB, FURORE

brow \'braù\ *n* 1 : the eyebrow or the ridge on which it grows; *also* : FOREHEAD 2 : the projecting upper part of a steep place

brow·beat \-,bēt\ *vb* : to disconcert by abuse : BULLY **syn** intimidate

¹**brown** \'braùn\ *adj* : of the color brown; *also* : of dark or tanned complexion

²**brown** *n* 1 : a pigment or dye that colors brown 2 : a color like that of coffee or chocolate that is a blend of red and yellow darkened by black — **brown·ish** *adj*

³**brown** *vb* : to make or become brown

brown·ie \'braù-nē\ *n* : a cheerful goblin supposed to do good deeds at night

brown·stone \'braùn-,stōn\ *n* : a dwelling faced with reddish brown sandstone

¹**browse** \'braùz\ *n* : tender shoots, twigs, and leaves fit for food for cattle

²**browse** *vb* 1 : to feed on browse; *also* : GRAZE 2 : to read bits at random in a book or collection of books

bru·in \'brü-ən\ *n* : BEAR

¹**bruise** \'brüz\ *n* : a surface injury to flesh : CONTUSION

²**bruise** *vb* 1 : to inflict a bruise on; *also* : to become bruised 2 : to break down

by pounding : CRUSH ⟨~ garlic for a salad⟩

bruit \'brüt\ *vb* : to noise abroad : RUMOR

brunch \'brənch\ *n* : a late breakfast, an early lunch, or a combination of the two

bru·net *or* **bru·nette** \brü-'net\ *adj* : of dark or relatively dark pigmentation; *esp* : having brown or black hair and eyes — **brunet** *n*

brunt \'brənt\ *n* : the main shock, force, or stress esp. of an attack

¹**brush** \'brəsh\ *also* **brush·wood** \-,wúd\ *n* 1 : small branches lopped from trees or shrubs 2 : THICKET; *also* : coarse shrubby vegetation

²**brush** *n* 1 : a device composed of bristles set in a handle and used esp. for cleaning or painting 2 : a bushy tail (as of a fox) 3 : a light rubbing or touching

³**brush** *vb* 1 : to treat (as in cleaning or painting) with a brush 2 : to remove with or as if with a brush; *also* : to dispose of in an offhand manner 3 : to touch gently in passing

⁴**brush** *n* : SKIRMISH **syn** encounter

brush-off \-,óf\ *n* : an abrupt or offhand dismissal

brusque \'brəsk\ *adj* : CURT, BLUNT, ABRUPT **syn** gruff, bluff — **brusque·ly** *adv*

brus·sels sprout \,brəs-əl(z)-\ *n* : one of the edible small heads borne on the stalk of a cabbagelike plant; *also* : this plant

bru·tal \'brüt-ºl\ *adj* : resembling or befitting a brute (as in coarseness or cruelty) : RUTHLESS, BRUTISH — **bru·tal·i·ty** \brü-'tal-ət-ē\ *n* — **bru·tal·ly** \'brüt-ºl-ē\ *adv*

¹**brute** \'brüt\ *adj* 1 : of, relating to, or typical of beasts 2 : BRUTAL 3 : UNREASONING; *also* : purely physical

²**brute** *n* 1 : BEAST 1 2 : a brutal person **syn** animal

brut·ish *adj* 1 : BRUTE 1 2 : stupidly cruel or sensual; *also* : UNREASONING

bub·ble \'bəb-əl\ *vb* : to form, rise in, or give off bubbles

²**bubble** *n* 1 : a globule of gas in a liquid 2 : a thin film of liquid filled with gas 3 : something lacking firmness or solidity — **bub·bly** \-(ə-)lē\ *adj*

bu·bon·ic plague \b(y)ü-,bän-ik-\ *n* : a bacterial plague transmitted to man by flea bites and marked esp. by chills and fever and by inflammatory swellings (**bu·boes** \'b(y)ü-bōz\) usu. in the groin

buc·ca·neer \,bək-ə-'niər\ *n* : PIRATE

¹**buck** \'bək\ *n* 1 : a male animal (as a deer or antelope) 2 : DANDY 3 *slang* : DOLLAR

²**buck** *vb* 1 : to spring with a quick plunging leap ⟨a ~ing horse⟩ 2 : to charge against something; *also* : to strive for advancement sometimes without regard to ethical behavior 3 : to charge into (the opponents' line) in football

buck·board \-,bōrd\ *n* : a 4-wheeled vehicle with a springy platform carrying the seat

buck·et \'bək-ət\ *n* 1 : PAIL 2 : an object resembling a bucket in collecting, scooping, or carrying something — **buck·et·ful** \-,fúl\ n

¹buck·le \'bƏk-Əl\ n : a clasp (as on a belt) for two loose ends

²buckle vb **1** : to fasten with a buckle **2** : to apply oneself with vigor **3** : to crumple up : BEND, COLLAPSE

³buckle n : BEND, FOLD, KINK

buck·ler \'bƏk-lƏr\ n : SHIELD

buck·ram \'bƏk-rƏm\ n : a coarse stiff cloth used esp. for binding books

buck·saw \'bƏk-,sò\ n : a saw set in a deep often H-shaped frame and used for sawing wood on a sawhorse

buck·shot \-,shät\ n : coarse lead shot used in shotgun shells

buck·skin \-,skin\ n **1** : the skin of a buck **2** : a soft usu. suede-finished leather

buck·wheat \-,hwēt\ n : an herb grown for its triangular seeds which are used as a cereal grain; also : these seeds

bu·col·ic \byü-'käl-ik\ adj : RURAL, RUSTIC

¹bud \'bƏd\ n **1** : an undeveloped plant shoot (as of a leaf or a flower); also : a partly opened flower **2** : an asexual reproductive structure **3** : something not yet mature

²bud vb **bud·ded; bud·ding 1** : to form or put forth buds; also : to reproduce by asexual buds **2** : to be or develop like a bud **3** : to propagate a desired variety (as of peach) by inserting a bud in a plant of a different variety

Bud·dhism \'bü-,diz-Əm, 'búd-,iz-\ n : a religion of eastern and central Asia growing out of the teachings of Gautama Buddha — **Bud·dhist** \'büd-Əst, 'búd-\ n or adj

bud·dy \'bƏd-ē\ n : COMPANION; esp : a fellow soldier

budge \'bƏj\ vb : MOVE, STIR, SHIFT

bud·ger·i·gar \'bƏj-(Ə-)rē-,gär\ n : a small Australian parrot raised in many colors for a pet

¹bud·get \'bƏj-Ət\ n **1** : STOCK, SUPPLY **2** : a financial report containing estimates of income and expenses; also : a plan for coordinating income and expenses

²budget vb **1** : to allow for in a budget **2** : to draw up a budget

¹buff \'bƏf\ n **1** : a fuzzy-surfaced usu. oil-tanned leather; also : a garment of this **2** : a dull yellow-orange color **3** : FAN, ENTHUSIAST

²buff adj : of the color buff

³buff vb : POLISH, SHINE

buf·fa·lo \'bƏf-Ə-,lō\ n, pl **-lo** or **-loes** : any of several wild oxen; esp : BISON

¹buff·er \'bƏf-Ər\ n : one that buffs

²buffer n : something that lessens shock (as from a physical or financial blow)

¹buf·fet \'bƏf-Ət\ n : BLOW, SLAP

²buffet vb **1** : to strike with the hand or repeatedly **2** : to struggle against or on syn beat

³buf·fet \(,)bƏ-'fā, bü-\ n **1** : SIDEBOARD **2** : a counter for refreshments; also : a meal at which people serve themselves (as from a buffet)

buf·foon \(,)bƏ-'fün\ n : CLOWN syn fool, jester — **buf·foon·ery** \-(Ə-)rē\ n

bug \'bƏg\ n **1** : a small usu. obnoxious creeping or crawling creature (as a louse or spider); esp : any of a group of 4-winged sucking insects that includes many serious plant pests **2** : a disease-producing germ

bug·a·boo \'bƏg-Ə-,bü\ n : BOGEY

bug·bear \'bƏg-,baƏr\ n : BOGEY; also : a source of dread

bug·gy \'bƏg-ē\ n : a light carriage

bu·gle \'byü-gƏl\ n : a brass wind instrument resembling a trumpet but shorter — **bu·gler** \-glƏr\ n

¹build \'bild\ vb **built** \'bilt\ **build·ing 1** : to form or have formed by ordering and uniting materials (~ a house); also : to bring into being or develop **2** : ESTABLISH, FOUND (~ an argument on facts) **3** : INCREASE, ENLARGE; also : ENHANCE (~ up one's reputation) **4** : to engage in building — **build·er** n

²build n : form or mode of structure; esp : PHYSIQUE

build·ing n **1** : a usu. roofed and walled structure (as a house) for permanent use **2** : the art or business of constructing buildings

built-in \'bil-'tin\ adj **1** : forming an integral part of a structure **2** : INHERENT

bulb \'bƏlb\ n **1** : a large underground plant bud or bud group from which a new plant (as a lily or onion) can grow; also : a fleshy plant structure (as a tuber) resembling a bud **2** : a plant having or growing from a bulb **3** : a rounded, spheroidal, or pear-shaped object or part (as an electric lamp) — **bul·bous** \'bƏl-bƏs\ adj

bul·bul \'bùl-,bùl\ n : a Persian songbird

Bul·gar·i·an \,bƏl-'gar-ē-Ən, bùl-\ n : a native or inhabitant of Bulgaria — **Bulgarian** adj

¹bulge \'bƏlj\ n : a swelling projecting part

²bulge vb : to become or cause to become protuberant

¹bulk \'bƏlk\ n **1** : MAGNITUDE, VOLUME **2** : a large mass **3** : the major portion — **bulky** adj

²bulk vb **1** : to give a bulky effect : LOOM **2** : to be impressive or important

bulk·head \'bƏlk-,hed\ n **1** : a partition separating compartments on a ship **2** : a retaining wall along a waterfront **3** : a structure built to cover a mine shaft or a descending stairway

¹bull \'bùl\ n **1** : the adult male of an animal of the cattle kind or of some other large animals (as the elephant or walrus) **2** : one who buys securities or commodities in expectation of a price increase — **bull·ish** adj

²bull adj **1** : MALE **2** : large of its kind **3** : RISING (a ~ market)

³bull n [ML bulla papal seal, bull, fr. L. amulet] **1** : a papal letter **2** : EDICT

⁴bull n **1** : a grotesque blunder **2** slang : NONSENSE

¹bull·dog \-,dòg\ n : a compact muscular short-haired dog of English origin

²bulldog vb : to throw (a steer) by seizing the horns and twisting the neck

bull·doze \-,dōz\ vb **1** : to move, clear, gouge out, or level off with a tractor-driven machine (**bull·doz·er**) having a broad blade or a ram for pushing **2** : to force as if by using a bulldozer

bul·let \'bùl-Ət\ n : a missile to be shot from a firearm — **bul·let·proof** \,bùl-Ət-'prüf\ adj

bul·le·tin \'bùl-Ət-°n\ n **1** : a brief public report of a matter of public interest **2** : a periodical publication (as of a college) — **bulletin** vb

bull·fight \'bùl-,fīt\ n : a spectacle in which men ceremonially excite and kill bulls in an arena — **bull·fight·er** *n*

bull·finch \-,finch\ *n* **:** a red-breasted English songbird often kept as a pet

bull·frog \-,frog, -,fräg\ *n* **:** FROG; *esp* **:** a large deep-voiced frog

bull·head \-,hed\ *n* **:** a large-headed fish (as a catfish)

bull·head·ed \-'hed-əd\ *adj* **:** stupidly stubborn **:** HEADSTRONG

bul·lion \'bul-yən\ *n* **:** gold or silver metal

bul·lock \'bul-ək\ *n* **:** a young bull; *also* **:** STEER

¹**bul·ly** \'bul-ē\ *n* **:** a blustering fellow oppressive to others weaker than himself

²**bully** *adj* **:** EXCELLENT, FIRST-RATE — often used interjectionally

³**bully** *vb* **:** to behave as a bully toward **:** DOMINEER **syn** browbeat, intimidate

bul·rush \'bul-,rəsh\ *n* **:** a tall coarse rush or sedge

bul·wark \'bul-(,)wərk, -,wȯrk, 'bəl-(,)wərk\ *n* **1 :** a wall-like defensive structure **2 :** a strong support or protection in danger

¹**bum** \'bəm\ *vb* **bummed; bum·ming 1 :** to wander as a tramp; *also* **:** LOAF **2 :** to seek or gain by begging (~ a meal)

²**bum** *n* **:** an idle worthless fellow **:** LOAFER

³**bum** *adj* **1 :** WORTHLESS **2 :** DISABLED (a ~ knee)

bum·ble·bee \'bəm-bəl-,bē\ *n* **:** a large hairy social bee that makes a loud humming sound in flight

¹**bump** \'bəmp\ *vb* **1 :** to strike or knock forcibly; *also* **:** to move or alter by bumping **2 :** to collide with

²**bump** *n* **1 :** a sudden forceful blow or impact **2 :** a local bulge; *esp* **:** a swelling of tissue — **bumpy** *adj*

¹**bump·er** *n* **1 :** a cup or glass filled to the brim **2 :** something unusually large — **bumper** *adj*

²**bumper** *n* **:** a device for absorbing shock or preventing damage in collision; *esp* **:** a metal bar at either end of an automobile

bump·kin \'bəmp-kən\ *n* **:** a country lout

bump·tious \'bəmp-shəs\ *adj* **:** obtusely and often noisily self-assertive

bun \'bən\ *n* **:** a sweet biscuit or roll

¹**bunch** \'bench\ *n* **1 :** SWELLING **2 :** CLUSTER, GROUP — **bunchy** *adj*

²**bunch** *vb* **:** to form or form into a bunch

bun·co *or* **bun·ko** \'bəŋ-kō\ *n* **:** a swindling scheme — **bunco** *vb*

¹**bun·dle** \'bən-d²l\ *n* **1 :** several items bunched and fastened together; *also* **:** something wrapped for carrying **:** PARCEL **2 :** a considerable amount **:** LOT **3 :** GROUP

²**bundle** *vb* **:** to gather or tie in a bundle

bung \'bəŋ\ *n* **:** the stopper in the bunghole of a cask

bun·ga·low \'bəŋ-gə-,lō\ *n* **:** a one-storied dwelling with low sweeping lines and a wide veranda

bung·hole \'bəŋ-,hōl\ *n* **:** a hole for emptying or filling a cask

bun·gle \'bəŋ-gəl\ *vb* **:** to do badly **:** BOTCH — **bungle** *n* — **bun·gler** \-g(ə-)lər\ *n*

bun·ion \'bən-yən\ *n* **:** an inflamed swelling of the first joint of the big toe

¹**bunk** \'bəŋk\ *n* **:** a built-in bed (as on a ship) that is often one of a tier

²**bunk** *n* **:** BUNKUM, NONSENSE

bun·ker \'bəŋ-kər\ *n* **1 :** a bin or compartment for storage (as for coal on a ship) **2 :** a protective embankment or dugout; *also* **:** an embankment constituting a hazard on a golf course

bun·kum *or* **bun·combe** \'bəŋ-kəm\ *n* **:** NONSENSE, TWADDLE

¹**bunt** \'bənt\ *vb* **1 :** BUTT **2 :** to push or tap a baseball lightly without swinging the bat

²**bunt** *n* **:** an act or instance of bunting; *also* **:** a bunted ball

bun·ting \'bənt-iŋ\ *n* **:** any of numerous small stout-billed finches

bunting *n* **:** a thin fabric used esp. for flags; *also* **:** FLAGS

¹**buoy** \'bü-ē, 'bȯi\ *n* **1 :** a floating object anchored in water to mark something (as a channel, shoal, or rock) **2 :** a float consisting of a ring of buoyant material to support a person who has fallen into the water

²**buoy** *vb* **1 :** to mark by a buoy **2 :** to keep afloat **3 :** to raise the spirits of

buoy·an·cy \'bȯi-ən-sē, 'bü-yən-\ *n* **1 :** the quality of being able to float **2 :** upward force exerted by a liquid or gas upon a body in or on it **3 :** resilience of spirit — **buoy·ant** \-ənt, -yənt\ *adj*

bur \'bər\ *var of* BURR

bur·den \'bərd-²n\ *n* **1 :** LOAD; *also* **:** CARE, RESPONSIBILITY **2 :** something oppressive **:** ENCUMBRANCE **3 :** CARGO; *also* **:** capacity for cargo

²**burden** *vb* **:** LOAD, OPPRESS — **bur·den·some** \-səm\ *adj*

³**burden** *n* **1 :** REFRAIN, CHORUS **2 :** a main theme or idea **:** GIST

bur·dock \'bər-,däk\ *n* **:** a tall coarse herb with prickly flower heads

bu·reau \'byur-ō\ *n, pl* **-reaus** *also* **-reaux** \-ōz\ **1 :** a chest of drawers for bedroom use **2 :** an administrative unit (as of a government department) **3 :** a business office (news ~)

bu·reau·cra·cy \byu-'räk-rə-sē\ *n* **1 :** a body of appointive government officials **2 :** administration characterized by specialization of functions under fixed rules and a hierarchy of authority; *also* **:** an unwieldy administrative system deficient in initiative and flexibility — **bu·reau·crat** \'byur-ə-,krat\ *n* — **bu·reau·crat·ic** \,byur-ə-'krat-ik\ *adj*

bur·gee \,bər-'jē, 'bər-jē\ *n* **:** a swallow-tailed flag used esp. by ships for signals or identification

bur·geon \'bər-jən\ *vb* **:** to put forth fresh growth (as from buds) **:** grow vigorously **:** FLOURISH

bur·gess \'bər-jəs\ *n* **1 :** a citizen of a borough **2 :** an official or representative usu. of a borough

burgh \'bər-ō\ *n* **:** a Scottish town

bur·gher \'bər-gər\ *n* **1 :** TOWNSMAN **2 :** a prosperous solid citizen

bur·glary \'bər-glə-rē\ *n* **:** forcible entry into a building and esp. a dwelling with intent to steal — **bur·glar** \-glər\ *n* — **bur·glar·i·ous** \,bər-'glar-ē-əs\ *adj* — **bur·glar·ize** \'bər-glə-,rīz\ *vb*

bur·go·mas·ter \'bər-gə-,mas-tər\ *n*

: the chief magistrate of a town in some European countries

Bur·gun·dy \'bər-gən-dē\ *n* : a dry usu. red table wine

buri·al \'ber-ē-əl\ *n* : the act or process of burying

bur·lap \'bər-ˌlap\ *n* : a coarse fabric usu. of jute or hemp used esp. for bags

¹**bur·lesque** \(ˌ)bər-'lesk\ *n* **1** : witty or derisive usu. literary imitation **2** : broadly humorous theatrical entertainment consisting of several items (as songs, skits, or dances)

²**burlesque** *vb* : to make ludicrous by burlesque **syn** MOCK, caricature, parody

bur·ly \'bər-lē\ *adj* : strongly and heavily built : HUSKY **syn** muscular, brawny

Bur·mese \ˌbər-'mēz\ *n, pl* **Burmese** : a native or inhabitant of Burma — **Burmese** *adj*

¹**burn** \'bərn\ *vb* **burned** \'bərnd\ *or* **burnt** \'bərnt\ **burn·ing** **1** : to be on fire **2** : to feel or look as if on fire **3** : to alter or become altered by or as if by the action of fire or heat : SCORCH, CHAR, SCALD ⟨clay ∼ed to brick⟩ **4** : to use as fuel ⟨∼ coal⟩; *also* : to destroy by fire ⟨∼ trash⟩ **5** : to cause or make by fire ⟨∼ a hole⟩; *also* : to affect as if by heat ⟨*burnt* out by overwork⟩ — **burn·er** *n*

²**burn** *n* : an injury or effect produced by burning

bur·nish \'bər-nish\ *vb* : to polish usu. with something hard and smooth — **bur·nish·er** *n*

bur·noose *or* **bur·nous** \(ˌ)bər-'nüs\ *n* : a hooded cloak worn by Arabs and Moors

burp \'bərp\ *n* : an act of belching — **burp** *vb*

burr \'bər\ *n* **1** *usu* **bur** : a rough or prickly envelope of a fruit; *also* : a plant that bears burs **2** : a roughness left on metal that has been cut or shaped (as by a drill or lathe) **3** : WHIR — **bur·ry** *adj*

bur·ro \'bər-ō, 'bùr-\ *n* : a usu. small donkey

¹**bur·row** \'bər-ō\ *n* : a hole in the ground made by an animal (as a rabbit)

²**burrow** *vb* **1** : to form by tunneling ⟨∼ a way through the snow⟩; *also* : to make a burrow **2** : to progress by or as if by digging ⟨clams ∼ing into the sand⟩ — **bur·row·er** *n*

bur·sar \'bər-sər\ *n* : a treasurer esp. of a college

bur·si·tis \(ˌ)bər-'sīt-əs\ *n* : inflammation of the serous sac (**bur·sa** \'bər-sə\) of a joint (as the elbow or shoulder)

¹**burst** \'bərst\ *vb* **burst** *or* **burst·ed**; **burst·ing** **1** : to fly apart or into pieces **2** : suddenly to give vent to : PLUNGE ⟨∼ into song⟩ **3** : to enter or emerge suddenly : SPRING **4** : to be filled to the breaking point

²**burst** *n* **1** : a sudden outbreak or effort : SPURT **2** : EXPLOSION **3** : an act or result of bursting

bury \'ber-ē\ *vb* **1** : to deposit in the earth; *also* : to inter with funeral ceremonies **2** : CONCEAL, HIDE

bus \'bəs\ *n, pl* **bus·es** *or* **bus·ses** : a large motor-driven passenger vehicle

bus·boy \'bəs-ˌbói\ *n* : a waiter's helper

bus·by \'bəz-bē\ *n* : a military full-dress fur hat with a bag hanging down on one side

bush \'bùsh\ *n* **1** : SHRUB **2** : rough uncleared country **3** : a thick tuft or mat — **bushy** *adj*

bush·el \'bùsh-əl\ *n* : a dry measure equal to 4 pecks or 32 quarts

bush·ing \'bùsh-iŋ\ *n* : a metal lining used esp. as a bearing (as for an axle or shaft)

bush·whack \'bùsh-ˌhwak\ *vb* **1** : to live or hide out in the woods **2** : AMBUSH — **bush·whack·er** *n*

busi·ly \'biz-ə-lē\ *adv* : in a busy manner

busi·ness \'biz-nəs, -nəz\ *n* **1** : OCCUPATION, CALLING; *also* : TASK, MISSION **2** : a commercial or industrial enterprise; *also* : TRADE ⟨∼ is good⟩ **3** : AFFAIR, MATTER **4** : personal concerns ⟨minds his own ∼⟩ **syn** work, commerce, industry

busi·ness·man \-ˌman\ *n* : a man engaged in business esp. as an executive

bus·kin \'bəs-kən\ *n* **1** : a laced half boot **2** : tragic drama

buss \'bəs\ *n* : KISS — **buss** *vb*

bust \'bəst\ *n* **1** : sculpture representing the upper part of the human figure **2** : the part of the human torso between the neck and the waist; *esp* : the breasts of a woman

¹**bus·tle** \'bəs-əl\ *vb* : to move or work in a brisk fussy way

²**bustle** *n* : briskly energetic activity : STIR

³**bustle** *n* : a pad or frame formerly worn to swell out the fullness at the back of a woman's skirt

busy \'biz-ē\ *adj* **1** : engaged in action : not idle **2** : being in use ⟨∼ telephones⟩ **3** : full of activity ⟨∼ streets⟩ **4** : OFFICIOUS **syn** industrious, diligent

²**busy** *vb* : to make or keep busy : OCCUPY

busy·body \'biz-ē-ˌbäd-ē\ *n* : MEDDLER

¹**but** \(ˌ)bət\ *conj* **1** : except for the fact ⟨would have protested ∼ that he was afraid⟩ **2** : as to the following, namely ⟨there's no doubt ∼ he's the guilty one⟩ **3** : without the concomitant that ⟨never rains ∼ it pours⟩ **4** : on the contrary, rather ⟨not one, ∼ two job offers⟩ **5** : yet nevertheless ⟨would like to go, ∼ I can't⟩; *also* : while on the contrary ⟨would like to go ∼ he is busy⟩ **6** : yet also ⟨came home sadder ∼ wiser⟩ ⟨poor ∼ proud⟩

²**but** *prep* : other than : EXCEPT ⟨there's no one here ∼ me⟩ ⟨who ∼ George would do such a thing⟩

¹**butch·er** \'bùch-ər\ *n* **1** : one who slaughters animals or dresses their flesh; *also* : a dealer in meat **2** : one who kills brutally or needlessly — **butch·ery** \-(ə-)rē\ *n*

²**butcher** *vb* **1** : to slaughter and dress for meat ⟨∼ hogs⟩ **2** : to kill barbarously

but·ler \'bət-lər\ *n* : the chief male servant of a household

¹**butt** \'bət\ *vb* : to strike with the head or horns

²**butt** *n* : a blow or thrust with the head or horns

³**butt** *n* **1** : TARGET **2** : an object of abuse or ridicule

⁴**butt** *vb* **1** : ABUT **2** : to place or join edge to edge without overlapping

⁵**butt** *n* : a large, thicker, or bottom end of something

⁶**butt** *n* **1** : a large cask **2** : a varying measure for liquid

butte \'byüt\ *n* : an isolated steep-sided hill

¹**but·ter** \'bət-ər\ *n* [OE *butere*, fr. L *butyrum*, fr. Gk *boutyron*, fr. *bous* cow + *tyros* cheese] : a solid edible emulsion of fat obtained from cream by churning 2 : a substance resembling butter — **but·tery** *adj*

²**butter** *vb* : to spread with butter

but·ter·cup \-ˌkəp\ *n* : a usu. 5-petaled yellow-flowered herb

but·ter·fat \-ˌfat\ *n* : the natural fat of milk and chief constituent of butter

but·ter·fin·gered \ˌbət-ər-'fiŋ-gərd\ *adj* : likely to let things fall or slip through the fingers — **but·ter·fin·gers** \'bət-ər-ˌfiŋ-gərz\ *n sing or pl*

but·ter·fly \'bət-ər-ˌflī\ *n* : any of a group of slender day-flying insects with 4 broad wings covered with bright-colored scales

but·ter·milk \-ˌmilk\ *n* : the liquid remaining after butter is churned

but·ter·nut \-ˌnət\ *n* : the edible oily nut of an American tree related to the walnut; *also* : this tree

but·ter·scotch \-ˌskäch\ *n* : a candy made from sugar, corn syrup, and water; *also* : the flavor of such candy

but·tocks \'bət-əks\ *n pl* : the seat of the body : RUMP

¹**but·ton** \'bət-ᵊn\ *n* 1 : a small knob secured to an object and usu. passed through an opening (**but·ton·hole** \-ˌhōl\) in another part of the object to act as a fastener 2 : a buttonlike part, object, or device

²**button** *vb* : to close or fasten with buttons

but·ton·hook \-ˌhůk\ *n* : a hook for drawing small buttons through button-holes

¹**but·tress** \'bət-rəs\ *n* 1 : a projecting structure to support a wall 2 : PROP, SUPPORT

²**buttress** *vb* : PROP, SUPPORT

bux·om \'bək-səm\ *adj* : healthily plump

¹**buy** \'bī\ *vb* **bought** \'bòt\ **buy·ing** : to obtain for a price : PURCHASE; *also* : BRIBE — **buy·er** *n*

²**buy** *n* 1 : PURCHASE 1, 2 2 : an exceptional value

¹**buzz** \'bəz\ *vb* 1 : to make a buzz 2 : to fly low and fast over in an airplane

²**buzz** *n* : a low humming sound (as of bees in flight)

buz·zard \'bəz-ərd\ *n* 1 : a heavy slow-flying hawk 2 : an American vulture

buzz·er *n* : a device that signals with a buzzing sound

¹**by** \(')bī, bə\ *prep* 1 : NEAR ⟨stood ~ the window⟩ 2 : through or through the medium of : VIA ⟨left ~ the door⟩ 3 : PAST ⟨drove ~ the house⟩ 4 : DURING, AT ⟨studied ~ night⟩ 5 : no later than ⟨get here ~ 3 p.m.⟩ 6 : through the means or direct agency of ⟨got it ~ fraud⟩ ⟨was seen ~ the others⟩ 7 : in conformity with : according to ⟨did it ~ the book⟩ 8 : with respect to ⟨an electrician ~ trade⟩ 9 : to the amount or extent of ⟨his horse won ~ a nose⟩ ⟨was overpaid ~ three dollars⟩

²**by** \'bī\ *adv* 1 : near at hand; *also* : IN ⟨stopped ~ to chat⟩ 2 : PAST 3 : ASIDE, APART

bye \'bī\ *n* : a position of a participant in a tournament who has no opponent after pairs are drawn and advances to the next round without playing

by·gone \'bī-ˌgòn\ *adj* : gone by : PAST — **bygone** *n*

by·law *or* **bye·law** \'bī-ˌlò\ *n* : a rule adopted by an organization for managing its internal affairs

by·line \-ˌlīn\ *n* : a line at the head of a newspaper or magazine article giving the writer's name

¹**by·pass** \'bī-ˌpas\ *n* : a way around something; *esp* : an alternate route

²**bypass** *vb* : to avoid by means of a bypass

by·path \-ˌpath, -ˌpàth\ *n* : BYWAY

by·play \-ˌplā\ *n* : action engaged in at the side of a stage while the main action proceeds

by·prod·uct \-ˌpräd-(ˌ)əkt\ *n* : something produced (as in manufacturing) in addition to the main product

by·stand·er \-ˌstan-dər\ *n* : one present but not participating **syn** onlooker, witness, spectator

by·way \-ˌwā\ *n* : a side road; *also* : a secondary aspect

by·word \-ˌwərd\ *n* 1 : PROVERB 2 : an object of scorn

---

c \'sē\ *n, often cap* : the 3d letter of the English alphabet

cab \'kab\ *n* 1 : a light closed horse-drawn carriage 2 : TAXICAB 3 : the covered compartment for the engineer and operating controls of a locomotive; *also* : a similar structure on a truck, tractor, or crane — **cab·man** \-mən\ *n*

¹**ca·bal** \kə-'bal\ *n* : a secret group of plotters or political conspirators

²**cabal** *vb* **-balled; -bal·ing** : to unite in or form a cabal

ca·ba·na \kə-'ban-(y)ə\ *n* : a beach shelter with an open side facing the sea

cab·a·ret \ˌkab-ə-'rā\ *n* : a restaurant providing liquor and entertainment; *also* : the show provided

cab·bage \'kab-ij\ *n* : a vegetable related to the turnip and grown for its dense head of leaves

cab·by *or* **cab·bie** \'kab-ē\ *n* : a driver of a cab

cab·in \'kab-ən\ *n* 1 : a private room on a ship; *also* : a compartment below deck on a small boat for passengers or crew 2 : a small one-story house of simple construction 3 : an airplane compartment for passengers, crew, or cargo

cabin boy *n* : a boy acting as servant on a ship

cabin class *n* : a class of accommodations on a passenger ship superior to tourist class and inferior to first class

cab·i·net \'kab-(ə-)nət\ *n* 1 : a case or

cupboard for holding or displaying articles (as jewels, specimens, or documents) **2** : an upright case housing a radio or television receiver **3** *archaic* : a private room for consultations **4** : the advisory council of a sovereign, president, or other head of state

cab·i·net·mak·er \-,mā-kər\ *n* : a skilled woodworker who makes fine furniture — **cab·i·net·mak·ing** *n*

cab·i·net·work \-,work\ *n* : the finished work of a cabinetmaker

¹ca·ble \'kā-bəl\ *n* **1** : a very strong rope, wire, or chain **2** : CABLEGRAM **3** : a bundle of insulated wires to carry electric current

²cable *vb* : to telegraph by submarine cable

cable car *n* : a car moved along rails by an endless cable operated by a stationary engine or along an overhead cable

ca·ble·gram \'kā-bəl-,gram\ *n* : a message sent by a submarine telegraph cable

ca·boose \kə-'büs\ *n* : a car usu. at the rear of a freight train for the use of the train crew and railroad workmen

cab·ri·o·let \,kab-rē-ə-'lā\ *n* **1** : a light 2-wheeled one-horse carriage **2** : a convertible coupe

cab·stand \'kab-,stand\ *n* : a place for cabs to park while waiting for passengers

ca·cao \kə-'kaù, 'kā-ō\ *n* : a So. American tree whose seeds (**cacao beans**) are the source of cocoa and chocolate

¹cache \'kash\ *n* : a hiding place esp. for concealing and preserving provisions; *also* : something hidden or stored in a cache

²cache *vb* : to place or store in a cache

ca·chet \ka-'shā\ *n* **1** : a seal used esp. as a mark of official approval **2** : a feature or quality conferring prestige; *also* : PRESTIGE **3** : a flour paste capsule for medicine **4** : a design, inscription, or advertisement printed or stamped on mail

cack·le \'kak-əl\ *n* **1** : a sharp broken cry esp. of a hen **2** : a laugh suggestive of a hen's cackle **3** : noisy chatter — **cackle** *vb* — **cack·ler** \-(ə-)lər\ *n*

ca·coph·o·ny \ka-'käf-ə-nē\ *n* : harsh or discordant sound : DISSONANCE — **ca·coph·o·nous** *adj*

cac·tus \'kak-təs\ *n, pl* **-ti** \-,tī\ *or* **-tus·es** : any of a large group of drought-resistant flowering plants with fleshy usu. jointed stems and with leaves replaced by scales or prickles

cad \'kad\ *n* : a person without gentlemanly instincts — **cad·dish** *adj* — **cad·dish·ly** *adv* — **cad·dish·ness** *n*

ca·dav·er \kə-'dav-ər\ *n* : a dead body : CORPSE

ca·dav·er·ous \kə-'dav-(ə-)rəs\ *adj* : suggesting a corpse esp. in gauntness or pallor *syn* wasted — **ca·dav·er·ous·ly** *adv*

cad·die *or* **cad·dy** \'kad-ē\ *n* : one that assists a golfer esp. by carrying his clubs — **caddie** *or* **caddy** *vb*

cad·dy \'kad-ē\ *n* : a small box or chest; *esp* : one to keep tea in

ca·dence \'kād-°ns\ *n* : the measure or beat of a rhythmical flow (as of sound or motion) : RHYTHM — **ca·denced** *adj*

ca·den·za \kə-'den-zə\ *n* : a brilliant sometimes improvised passage usu. toward the close of a musical composition

ca·det \kə-'det\ *n* **1** : a younger son or brother **2** : a student military officer

cadge \'kaj\ *vb* : SPONGE, BEG

cad·mi·um \'kad-mē-əm\ *n* : a grayish metallic chemical element used in protective platings and bearing metals

cad·re \'kad-rē\ *n* **1** : FRAMEWORK **2** : a nucleus esp. of trained personnel capable of assuming control and training others

ca·du·ce·us \kə-'d(y)ü-sē-əs, -sē-,i\ *n, pl* **-cei** \-sē-,ī\ *n* **1** : the staff of a herald; *esp* : a representation of a staff with two entwined snakes and two wings at the top **2** : an insignia bearing a caduceus and symbolizing a physician

cae·cum *var of* CECUM

Cae·sar \'sē-zər\ *n* **1** : any of the Roman emperors succeeding Augustus Caesar — used as a title **2** *often not cap* : a powerful ruler : AUTOCRAT, DICTATOR; *also* : the civil or temporal power as such

cae·su·ra \si-'z(h)ür-ə\ *n* : a break in the flow of sound usu. in the middle of a line of verse

ca·fé \ka-'fā\ *n* **1** : RESTAURANT **2** : BARROOM **3** : CABARET

ca·fé au lait \,kaf-,ā-ō-'lā\ *n* : coffee with usu. hot milk in about equal parts

caf·e·te·ria \,kaf-ə-'tir-ē-ə\ *n* : a self-service restaurant or lunchroom

caf·feine \ka-'fēn\ *n* : a stimulating alkaloid found esp. in coffee and tea

caf·tan \kaf-'tan\ *n* : an ankle-length garment with long sleeves worn in the Levant

¹cage \'kāj\ *n* **1** : an openwork enclosure for confining an animal **2** : something resembling a cage

²cage *vb* : to put or keep in or as if in a cage

cage·ling \-liŋ\ *n* : a caged bird

ca·gey *also* **ca·gy** \'kā-jē\ *adj* : wary of being trapped or deceived : SHREWD, CAUTIOUS, CALCULATING — **ca·gi·ly** *adv* — **cag·i·ness** *n*

ca·hoot \kə-'hüt\ *n* : PARTNERSHIP, LEAGUE — usu. used in pl. ⟨in ~s with the devil⟩

cairn \'kaərn\ *n* : a heap of stones serving as a memorial or a landmark

cais·son \'kās-,än, -°n\ *n* **1** : an ammunition chest mounted on two wheels and joined as a trailer to form an ammunition wagon **2** : a watertight chamber used for carrying on construction under water or as a foundation

cai·tiff \'kāt-əf\ *adj* : being base, cowardly, or despicable — **caitiff** *n*

ca·jole \kə-'jōl\ *vb* : to persuade or coax esp. with flattery or false promises : WHEEDLE — **ca·jole·ment** \-'jōl-mənt\ *n* — **ca·jol·ery** \-'jōl-(ə-)rē\ *n*

Ca·jun \'kā-jən\ *n* : a Louisianian descended from French-speaking immigrants from Acadia

¹cake \'kāk\ *n* **1** : any of various usu. small round flat breads **2** : any of various fancy sweetened breads often coated with an icing **3** : a flattened round mass of baked or fried food **4** : a block of compacted matter **5** : CRUST

²cake *vb* **1** : to form or harden into a cake **2** : ENCRUST

cal·a·bash \'kal-ə-,bash\ *n* : a gourd fruit

cal·a·boose \-,büs\ *n, dial* : JAIL

cal·a·mine \'kal-ə-,mīn\ *n* : a mixture of oxides of zinc and iron used in lotions and ointments

ca·lam·i·ty \kə-'lam-ət-ē\ *n* **1** : great distress or misfortune **2** : an event causing great harm or loss and affliction : DISASTER — **ca·lam·i·tous** *adj*

— ca·lam·i·tous·ly *adv* — ca·lam·i·tous·ness *n*

cal·car·e·ous \kal-'kar-ē-əs\ *adj* **:** containing calcium or a calcium compound (as calcium carbonate or lime); *also* **:** resembling calcium carbonate in hardness

cal·ci·fy \'kal-sə-,fī\ *vb* **:** to make or become calcareous — cal·ci·fi·ca·tion \,kal-sə-fə-'kā-shən\ *n*

cal·ci·mine \'kal-sə-,mīn\ *n* **:** a thin water paint for plastering — calcimine *vb*

cal·cine \kal-'sīn\ *vb* **:** to heat to a high temperature but without fusing to drive off volatile matter and often to reduce to powder — cal·ci·na·tion \,kal-sə-'nā-shən\ *n*

cal·ci·um \'kal-sē-əm\ *n* **:** a silver-white soft metallic chemical element occurring in combination (as in limestone and bones)

calcium carbonate *n* **:** a substance found in nature as limestone and marble and in plant ashes, bones, and shells

cal·cu·late \'kal-kyə-,lāt\ *vb* [L *calculare*, fr. *calculus* small stone, pebble used in reckoning] **1: :** to determine by mathematical processes **:** COMPUTE **2 :** to reckon by exercise of practical judgment **:** ESTIMATE **3 :** to design or adapt for a purpose **:** COUNT, RELY — cal·cu·la·ble \-lə-bəl\ *adj* — cal·cu·la·bly *adv* — cal·cu·la·tive \'kal-kyə-,lāt-iv\ *adj* — cal·cu·la·tor \-ər\ *n*

cal·cu·lat·ed *adj* **:** undertaken after estimating the probability of success or failure ⟨a ~ risk⟩

cal·cu·lat·ing *adj* **:** marked by shrewd consideration esp. of self-interest **:** SCHEMING

cal·cu·la·tion \,kal-kyə-'lā-shən\ *n* **1 :** the process or an act of calculating **2 :** the result of an act of calculating **3 :** studied care in analyzing or planning **:** CAUTION

cal·cu·lus \'kal-kyə-ləs\ *n* **:** a process or system of usu. mathematical reasoning through the use of symbols; *esp* **:** one dealing with rate of change and integrals of functions

cal·dron \'kȯl-drən\ *n* **:** a large kettle or boiler

¹cal·en·dar \'kal-ən-dər\ *n* **1 :** an arrangement of time into days, weeks, months, and years; *also* **:** a sheet or folder containing such an arrangement for a period (as a year) **2 :** an orderly list **:** SCHEDULE

²calendar *vb* **:** to enter in a calendar

¹cal·en·der \-dər\ *vb* **:** to press (as cloth or paper) between rollers or plates so as to make smooth or glossy or to thin into sheets

²calender *n* **:** a machine for calendering

cal·ends \'kal-əndz\ *n sing or pl* **:** the first day of the ancient Roman month

calf \'kaf, 'kȧf\ *n, pl* calves \'kavz, 'kȧvz\ **1 :** the young of the domestic cow or of some related large mammals (as the whale) **2 :** leather made from the skin of a calf **3 :** the fleshy back part of the leg below the knee

calf·skin \-,skin\ *n* **:** leather made of the skin of a calf

cal·i·ber *or* cal·i·bre \'kal-ə-bər\ *n* **1 :** the diameter of a projectile **2 :** the diameter of the bore of a gun **3 :** de-

gree of mental capacity or moral quality **:** measure of excellence or importance

cal·i·brate \'kal-ə-,brāt\ *vb* **1 :** to measure the caliber of **2 :** to determine, correct, or put the measuring marks on ⟨~ a thermometer⟩ — cal·i·bra·tion \,kal-ə-'brā-shən\ *n* — cal·i·bra·tor \-ər\ *n*

cal·i·co \'kal-i-,kō\ *n, pl* -coes *or* -cos **:** cotton cloth; *esp* **:** a cheap cotton printed fabric — calico *adj*

cal·i·for·ni·um \,kal-ə-'fȯr-nē-əm\ *n* **:** an artificially prepared radioactive chemical element

cal·i·per *or* cal·li·per \'kal-ə-pər\ *n* **:** an instrument with two adjustable legs used to measure the thickness of objects or distances between surfaces — usu. used in pl. ⟨a pair of ~s⟩

ca·liph *or* ca·lif \'kāl-əf, 'kal-\ *n* **:** a successor of Muhammad as head of Islam — used as a title — ca·liph·ate \-,āt\ *n*

cal·is·then·ics \,kal-əs-'then-iks\ *n sing or pl* **:** systematic bodily exercises without apparatus or with light hand apparatus — cal·is·then·ic *adj*

calk \'kȯk\ *var of* CAULK

¹call \'kȯl\ *vb* **1 :** SHOUT, CRY; *also* **:** to utter a characteristic cry **2 :** to utter in a loud clear voice **3 :** to announce authoritatively **4 :** SUMMON **5 :** to make a request or demand ⟨~ for an investigation⟩ **6 :** to get or try to get into communication by telephone **7 :** to demand payment of (a loan); *esp* **:** to demand surrender of (a bond issue) for redemption **8 :** to make a brief visit **9 :** to speak of or address by name **:** give a name to **10 :** to estimate or consider for practical purposes ⟨~ it ten miles⟩ — call·er *n*

²call *n* **1 :** SHOUT **2 :** the cry of an animal (as a bird) **3 :** a request or a command to come or assemble **:** INVITATION, SUMMONS **4 :** DEMAND, CLAIM; *also* **:** REQUEST **5 :** ROLL CALL **6 :** a brief usu. formal visit **7 :** an act of calling on the telephone

cal·la \'kal-ə\ *n* **:** a plant whose flowers form a fleshy yellow spike surrounded by a lilylike usu. white or pink leaf

call·board \'kȯl-,bȯrd\ *n* **:** a board for posting notices (as of rehearsal calls in a theater)

call down \'kȯl-'daùn\ *vb* **:** REPRIMAND

cal·lig·ra·phy \kə-'lig-rə-fē\ *n* **1 :** beautiful or elegant handwriting; *also* **:** the art of producing such writing **2 :** PENMANSHIP — cal·lig·ra·pher *n*

call·ing \'kȯ-liŋ\ *n* **1 :** a strong inner impulse toward a particular vocation **2 :** the activity in which one customarily engages as an occupation

cal·li·o·pe \kə-'lī-ə-(,)pē, 'kal-ē-,ōp\ *n* **:** a musical instrument consisting of a series of whistles played by keys arranged as in an organ

cal·los·i·ty \ka-'läs-ət-ē\ *n* **1 :** the quality or state of being callous **2 :** CALLUS 1

¹cal·lous \'kal-əs\ *adj* **1 :** being thickened and usu. hardened ⟨~ skin⟩ **2 :** hardened in feeling **:** UNFEELING — cal·lous·ly *adv*

²callous *vb* **:** to make callous

³cal·low \'kal-ō\ *adj* **:** lacking adult so-

phistication : IMMATURE, INEXPERIENCED — **cal·low·ness** n

¹cal·lus \'kal-əs\ n 1 : a callous area on skin or bark 2 : tissue that is converted into bone in the healing of a bone fracture

²callus vb : to form a callus

¹calm \'käm\ n 1 : a period or a condition of freedom from storms, high winds, or turbulent water 2 : complete or almost complete absence of wind 3 : a state of freedom from turmoil or agitation

²calm adj : marked by calm : STILL, PLACID, SERENE — **calm·ly** adv — **calm·ness** n

³calm vb : to make or become calm

cal·o·mel \'kal-ə-məl, -,mel\ n : a chloride of mercury used esp. as a purgative and fungicide

ca·lor·ic \kə-'lȯr-ik\ adj 1 : of or relating to heat 2 : of or relating to calories

cal·o·rie \'kal-(ə-)rē\ n : a unit for measuring heat; esp : one for measuring the value of foods for producing heat and energy in the human body equivalent to the amount of heat required to raise the temperature of one kilogram of water one degree centigrade

cal·o·rif·ic \,kal-ə-'rif-ik\ adj : CALORIC

cal·o·rim·e·ter \,kal-ə-'rim-ət-ər\ n : an apparatus for measuring quantities of heat

cal·u·met \'kal-yə-,met, -ə-\ n : an ornamented ceremonial pipe of the American Indians

ca·lum·ni·ate \kə-'ləm-nē-,āt\ vb : to accuse falsely and maliciously : SLANDER syn defame, malign, libel — **ca·lum·ni·a·tion** \-,ləm-nē-'ā-shən\ n — **ca·lum·ni·a·tor** \-'ləm-nē-,āt-ər\ n

cal·um·ny \'kal-əm-nē\ n : false and malicious accusation — SLANDER — **ca·lum·ni·ous** \kə-'ləm-nē-əs\ adj — **ca·lum·ni·ous·ly** adv

calve \'kav, 'kav\ vb : to give birth to a calf

calves pl of CALF

Cal·vin·ism \'kal-və-,niz-əm\ n : the theological system of Calvin and his followers — **Cal·vin·ist** n — **Cal·vin·is·tic** \,kal-və-'nis-tik\ adj

ca·lyp·so \kə-'lip-sō\ n : an improvised ballad usu. satirizing current events in a rhythmic style originating in the British West Indies

ca·lyx \'kā-liks, 'kal-\ n : the outside usu. green or leaflike part of a flower

cam \'kam\ n : a rotating or sliding projection (as on a wheel) for receiving or imparting motion

cam·a·rad·e·rie \,kam-(ə-)'rad-ə-rē, ,käm-(ə-)'räd-\ n : friendly feeling and goodwill between comrades

cam·ber \'kam-bər\ n : a slight convexity or arching (as of a road surface) — **camber** vb

cam·bi·um \'kam-bē-əm\ n : a thin cellular layer between xylem and phloem of most higher plants from which new tissues develop

cam·bric \'kām-brik\ n : a fine thin white linen fabric or a cotton cloth resembling this

came past of COME

cam·el \'kam-əl\ n : a large hoofed cud-chewing mammal used esp. in desert regions of Asia and Africa for carrying burdens and for riding

cam·el·back \-,bak\ n : an uncured compound chiefly of reclaimed or synthetic rubber used for retreading or recapping pneumatic tires

ca·mel·lia also **ca·me·lia** \kə-'mēl-yə\ n : any of several shrubs or trees related to the tea plant and grown in warm regions for their showy roselike flowers

ca·mel·o·pard \kə-'mel-ə-,pärd\ n : GIRAFFE

cam·eo \'kam-ē-,ō\ n : a gem carved in relief; also : a small medallion with a profiled head in relief

cam·era \'kam-(ə-)rə\ n : a closed light-proof box with an aperture through which the image of an object can be recorded on a surface sensitive to light; also : the part of a television transmitter in which the image to be transmitted is formed — **in camera** : PRIVATELY, SECRETLY

cam·i·sole \'kam-ə-,sōl\ n : a short sleeveless undergarment for women

cam·o·mile var of CHAMOMILE

cam·ou·flage \'kam-ə-,fläzh\ n 1 : the disguising of military equipment or installations with paint, nets, or foliage; also : the disguise itself 2 : a deceptive expedient — **camouflage** vb

¹camp \'kamp\ n 1 : a place where tents or buildings are erected for usu. temporary shelter (as for an army) 2 : a collection of tents or other shelters 3 : a body of persons encamped

²camp vb 1 : to make or occupy a camp 2 : to live in a camp or outdoors — **camp·er** n

cam·paign \kam-'pān\ n 1 : a series of military operations forming one distinct stage in a war 2 : a series of activities designed to bring about a particular result (advertising ~) — **campaign** vb — **cam·paign·er** n

cam·pa·ni·le \,kam-pə-'nē-lē\ n : a usu. freestanding bell tower

cam·pa·nol·o·gy \,kam-pə-'näl-ə-jē\ n : the art of bell ringing — **cam·pa·nol·o·gist** n

cam·phor \'kam-fər\ n : a gummy volatile fragrant compound obtained from an evergreen Asiatic tree (**camphor tree**) and used esp. in medicine and the chemical industry

cam·phor·ate \-,āt\ vb : to impregnate with camphor (camphorated oil)

camp meeting n : a series of evangelistic meetings held outdoors or in a tent

cam·po·ree \,kam-pə-'rē\ n : a gathering of boy scouts or girl scouts from a given geographic area

camp·stool \'kamp-,stül\ n : a folding backless seat

cam·pus \'kam-pəs\ n : the grounds and buildings of a college or school; also : a central grassy part of the grounds

cam·shaft \'kam-,shaft\ n : a shaft to which a cam is fastened

¹can \kən, (')kan\ vb, past could \kəd, (')kůd\ 1 : to be able to 2 : may perhaps (~ he still be alive) 3 : be permitted by conscience or feeling to (you ~ hardly blame him) 4 : have permission or liberty to (you ~ go now)

²can \'kan\ n 1 : a typically cylindrical metal container or receptacle (garbage ~) (coffee ~) 2 slang : JAIL

³can \'kan\ vb canned; can·ning 1 : to put in a can : preserve by sealing in airtight cans or jars 2 slang : to discharge from employment 3 slang : to put a stop or an end to 4 : to record on discs or tape

Ca·na·di·an \kə-'nād-ē-ən\ n : a native

or inhabitant of Canada — **Canadian** *adj*

ca·naille \kə-'nī, -'nāl\ *n* : RABBLE, RIFFRAFF

ca·nal \kə-'nal\ *n* **1** : a tubular passage in the body : DUCT **2** : a channel dug and filled with water (as for passage of boats or irrigation of land)

ca·nal·ize \kə-'nal-,īz\ *vb* **1** : to provide with a canal or make into or like a channel **2** : to provide with an outlet; *esp* : to direct into preferred channels — **ca·nal·iza·tion** \-,nal-ə-'zā-shən\ *n*

can·a·pé \'kan-ə-pē\ *n* : a piece of bread or toast or a cracker topped with a savory food

ca·nard \kə-'närd\ *n* : a false or unfounded report or story circulated to deceive the public

ca·nary \kə-'ne(ə)r-ē\ *n* [fr. the *Canary* islands] **1** : a usu. sweet wine similar to Madeira **2** : a usu. yellow or greenish finch often kept as a cage bird **3** : a bright yellow

ca·nas·ta \kə-'nas-tə\ *n* : rummy played with two full decks of cards plus four jokers

can·can \'kan-,kan\ *n* : a woman's dance of French origin characterized by high kicking

¹can·cel \'kan-səl\ *vb* **-celed** *or* **-celled**; **-cel·ing** *or* **-cel·ling** **1** : to cross out : DELETE **2** : to destroy the force or validity of : ANNUL **3** : to match in force or effect : OFFSET **4** : to remove (a common divisor) from a numerator and denominator; *also* : to remove (equivalents) on opposite sides of an equation or account **5** : to cross (a postage stamp) with lines to invalidate for reuse **6** : to neutralize each other's strength or effect — **can·cel·la·tion** \,kan-sə-'lā-shən\ *n*

²cancel *n* **1** : CANCELLATION **2** : a deleted part **3** : a part (as a page) from which something has been deleted

can·cer \'kan-sər\ *n* **1** : a malignant tumor that tends to spread in the body **2** : a malignant evil that corrodes slowly and fatally — **can·cer·ous** \'kans-(ə)-rəs\ *adj*

can·de·la·bra \,kan-də-'läb-rə, -'lab-\ *n* : CANDELABRUM

can·de·la·brum \-'läb-rəm, -'lab-\ *n, pl* **-bra** \-rə\ *also* **-brums** : an ornamental branched candlestick or lamp with several lights

can·des·cent \kan-'des-ᵊnt\ *adj* : glowing or dazzling esp. from great heat — **can·des·cence** *n*

can·did \'kan-dəd\ *adj* **1** : FRANK, STRAIGHTFORWARD **2** : relating to the informal recording (as in photography or television) of human subjects acting naturally or spontaneously without being posed — **can·did·ly** *adv* — **can·did·ness** *n*

can·di·da·cy \'kan-(d)əd-ə-sē\ *n* : the state of being a candidate

can·di·date \'kan-(d)ə-,dāt, -(d)əd-ət\ *n* [L *candidatus*, fr. *candidatus* clothed in white; so called fr. the white toga worn by candidates in ancient Rome] : one who seeks or is proposed by others for an office, honor, or membership

can·di·da·ture \-(d)əd-ə-,chùr\ *n, chiefly Brit* : CANDIDACY

can·died \'kan-dēd\ *adj* : preserved in or encrusted with sugar

¹can·dle \'kan-dᵊl\ *n* : a slender mass of tallow or wax molded around a wick and burned to give light

²candle *vb* : to examine (as eggs) by holding between the eye and a light — **can·dler** \-d(ᵊ-)lər\ *n*

can·dle·light \'kan-dᵊl-,līt\ *n* **1** : the light of a candle; *also* : any soft artificial light **2** : time for lighting up : DUSK

Can·dle·mas \-məs\ *n* : the church feast celebrated on February 2 in commemoration of the presentation of Christ in the temple

can·dle·pin \-,pin\ *n* : a slender bowling pin tapering toward top and bottom used in a bowling game (**candlepins**) with a smaller ball than that used in tenpins

can·dle·stick \-,stik\ *n* : a holder with a socket for a candle

can·dle·wick \-,wik\ *n* : a soft cotton yarn; *also* : embroidery made with this yarn usu. in tufts

can·dor \'kan-dər\ *n* : FRANKNESS, OUTSPOKENNESS

¹can·dy \'kan-dē\ *n* : a confection made from sugar often with flavoring and filling

²candy *vb* **1** : to encrust in sugar often by cooking in a syrup **2** : to crystallize into sugar **3** : to make seem attractive : SWEETEN (**candied** words)

¹cane \'kān\ *n* **1** : a slender hollow or pithy stem (as of a reed or bramble) **2** : a tall woody grass or reed (as sugarcane) **3** : a walking stick; *also* : a rod for flogging

²cane *vb* **1** : to beat with a cane **2** : to weave or make with cane — **can·er** *n*

cane·brake \-,brāk\ *n* : a thicket of cane

¹ca·nine \'kā-,nīn\ *adj* **1** : of or relating to dogs or to the natural group to which they belong **2** : being the pointed tooth next to the incisors

²canine *n* **1** : a canine tooth **2** : DOG

can·is·ter \'kan-ə-stər\ *n* **1** : a small box for holding a dry product (as tea) **2** : a shell for close-range artillery fire **3** : a perforated box containing material to absorb or filter a harmful substance in the air

can·ker \'kaŋ-kər\ *n* : a spreading sore that eats into tissue — **can·ker·ous** *adj*

can·ker·worm \-,wərm\ *n* : an insect larva (as a caterpillar) that injures plants

canned \'kand\ *adj* **1** : preserved in cans or jars **2** : recorded for radio or television reproduction

can·nel coal \,kan-ᵊl-\ *n* : a bituminous coal containing much volatile matter that burns brightly

can·ner \'kan-ər\ *n* : one who cans foods

can·nery \'kan-(ə-)rē\ *n* : a factory for the canning of foods

can·ni·bal \'kan-ə-bəl\ *n* **1** : a human being who eats human flesh **2** : an animal that eats its own kind — **can·ni·bal·ism** \-,iz-əm\ *n* — **can·ni·bal·is·tic** \,kan-ə-bə-'lis-tik\ *adj*

can·ni·bal·ize \'kan-ə-bə-,līz\ *vb* **1** : to dismantle (a machine) for parts for other machines **2** : to practice cannibalism

can·non \'kan-ən\ *n, pl* **cannons** *or*

ə abut; ᵊ kitten; ər further; a back; ā bake; ä cot, cart; aú out; ch chin; e less; ē easy; g gift; i trip; ī life; j joke; ŋ sing; ō flow; ò flaw; òi coin; th thin; t̲h̲ this; ü loot; ù foot; y yet; yü few; yù furious; zh vision

cannon 1 : an artillery piece supported on a carriage or mount 2 : a heavy-caliber automatic gun on an airplane 3 *Brit* : a carom in billiards

can·non·ade \,kan-ə-'nād\ n : a heavy fire of artillery — **cannonade** vb

¹**can·non·ball** \'kan-ən-,bȯl\ n : a usu. round solid missile for firing from a cannon

²**cannonball** vb : to travel at great speed

can·non·eer \,kan-ə-'niər\ n : an artilleryman who tends and fires cannon : GUNNER

can·not \'kan-,ät, kə-'nät\ : can not — **cannot but** : to be bound to : MUST

can·ny \'kan-ē\ adj : PRUDENT, FAR-SIGHTED, SHREWD — **can·ni·ly** adv — **can·ni·ness** n

ca·noe \kə-'nü\ n : a small long narrow boat with sharp ends and curved sides that is usu. propelled by paddles — **canoe** vb — **ca·noe·ist** n

¹**can·on** \'kan-ən\ n 1 : a regulation decreed by a church council; also : a provision of ecclesiastical law (canon law) 2 : an accepted principle (the ~s of good taste) 3 : an official or authoritative list (as of the saints or the books of the Bible)

²**canon** n : a clergyman on the staff of a cathedral — **can·on·ry** \-rē\ n

ca·ñon \'kan-yən\ var of CANYON

ca·non·i·cal \kə-'nän-i-kəl\ adj 1 : of, relating to, or conforming to a canon 2 : conforming to a general rule : OR-THODOX 3 : of or relating to a clergyman who is a canon — **ca·non·i·cal·ly** adv

ca·non·i·cals \-kəlz\ n pl : the vestments prescribed by canon for an officiating clergyman

can·on·ize \'kan-ə-,nīz\ vb 1 : to declare an officially recognized saint 2 : GLORIFY, EXALT — **can·on·iza·tion** \,kan-ə-nə-'zā-shən\ n

canon regular n, pl **canons regular** : a member of one of several Roman Catholic religious institutes of regular priests living in community

can·o·py \'kan-ə-pē\ n : an overhanging cover, shelter, or shade — **canopy** vb

¹**cant** \'kant\ n 1 : an oblique or slanting surface 2 : an inclination from a given line : TILT, SLANT

²**cant** vb 1 : to tip or tilt up or over 2 : to pitch to one side : LEAN 3 : SLOPE

³**cant** vb 1 : to whine like a beggar 2 : to talk hypocritically

⁴**cant** n 1 : the special idiom of a profession or trade : JARGON 2 : insincere conventional mode of speech; esp : insincere use of pious phraseology

can't \kant, kȧnt, känt\ : can not

can·ta·bi·le \kän-'täb-ə-,lā\ adv (or adj) : in a singing manner — used as a direction in music

can·ta·loupe \'kant-ᵊl-,ōp\ n : MUSK-MELON; esp : one with orange flesh and rough skin

can·tan·ker·ous \kan-'taŋ-k(ə-)rəs\ adj : ILL-NATURED, CROTCHETY, QUAR-RELSOME — **can·tan·ker·ous·ly** adv — **can·tan·ker·ous·ness** n

can·ta·ta \kən-'tät-ə\ n : a choral composition arranged in a somewhat dramatic manner and usu. accompanied by organ, piano, or orchestra

can·teen \kan-'tēn\ n 1 : a store (as in a camp or factory) in which food, drinks, and small supplies are sold 2 : a place of recreation and entertainment for servicemen 3 : a flask for water carried by soldiers and travelers

can·ter \'kant-ər\ n : a horse's 3-beat gait resembling but easier and slower than a gallop — **canter** vb

can·ti·cle \'kant-i-kəl\ n : SONG; esp : any of several liturgical songs taken from the Bible

can·ti·le·ver \'kant-ᵊl-,ē-vər, -,ev-ər\ n : a projecting beam or structure supported only at one end; also : either of a pair of such structures projecting toward each other so that when joined they form a bridge

can·tle \'kant-ᵊl\ n : the upwardly projecting rear part of a saddle

can·to \'kan-tō\ n : one of the major divisions of a long poem

¹**can·ton** \'kant-ᵊn, 'kan-,tän\ n : a small territorial division of a country; esp : one of the political divisions of Switzerland — **can·ton·al** \'kant-ᵊn-əl, kan-'tän-ᵊl\ adj

²**canton** \same for 1; for 2 usu kan-'tōn, -'tän\ vb 1 : to divide into cantons 2 : to allot quarters to (as to troops) : QUARTER

can·ton·ment \kan-'tōn-mənt, -'tän-\ n 1 : the quartering of troops 2 : a group of more or less temporary structures for housing troops

can·tor \'kant-ər\ n : a synagogue official who sings liturgical music and leads the congregation in prayer

can·vas also **can·vass** \'kan-vəs\ n 1 : a strong cloth used esp. for making tents and sails 2 : a set of sails 3 : a group of tents 4 : a surface prepared to receive oil paint; also : an oil painting 5 : the floor of a boxing or wrestling ring

can·vas·back \-,bak\ n : a No. American wild duck with red head and gray back

¹**can·vass** also **can·vas** \'kan-vəs\ vb : to go through (a district) or to go to (persons) to solicit votes or orders for goods or to determine public opinion or sentiment — **can·vass·er** n

²**canvass** also **canvas** n : an act of canvassing (as the solicitation of votes or orders or an examination into public opinion)

can·yon \'kan-yən\ n : a deep valley with high steep slopes

caou·tchouc \kaù-'chük\ n : RUBBER 3

¹**cap** \'kap\ n 1 : a usu. tight-fitting covering for the head; also : something resembling such a covering (bottle ~) 2 : a paper or metal container holding an explosive charge

²**cap** vb **capped; cap·ping** 1 : to provide or protect with or as if with a cap 2 : to form a cap over : CROWN 3 : OUTDO, SURPASS 4 : CLIMAX

ca·pa·ble \'kā-pə-bəl\ adj : having ability, capacity, or power to do something : ABLE, COMPETENT — **ca·pa·bil·i·ty** \,kā-pə-'bil-ət-ē\ n — **ca·pa·bly** \-blē\ adv

ca·pa·cious \kə-'pā-shəs\ adj : able to contain much — **ca·pa·cious·ly** adv — **ca·pa·cious·ness** n

ca·pac·i·tate \kə-'pas-ə-,tāt\ vb : to make capable : QUALIFY

ca·pac·i·ty \kə-'pas-ət-ē\ n 1 : the ability to contain, receive, or accommodate 2 : extent of space : VOLUME 3 : legal qualification or fitness 4 : ABILITY 5 : position or character assigned or assumed (served in the ~ of manager) cap·a·pie *or* cap·â·pie \,kap-ə-'pē\ *adv* : from head to foot : at all points

ca·par·i·son \kə-'par-ə-sən\ *n* **1** : an ornamental covering for a horse **2** : TRAPPINGS, ADORNMENT — cap·ari·son *vb*

¹cape \'kāp\ *n* : a point of land jutting out into water

²cape *n* : a sleeveless garment hanging from the neck over the shoulders

¹ca·per \'kā-pər\ *n* : the flower bud of a Mediterranean shrub pickled for use as a relish; *also* : this shrub

²caper *vb* : to leap about in a gay frolicsome way : PRANCE

³caper *n* **1** : a frolicsome leap or spring **2** : a capricious escapade **3** *slang* : an illegal escapade

cape·skin \'kāp-,skin\ *n* : a light flexible leather made from sheepskins

cap·il·lar·i·ty \,kap-ə-'lar-ət-ē\ *n* : the action by which the surface of a liquid where (as in a slender tube) it is in contact with a solid is raised or lowered depending on the relative attraction of the molecules of the liquid for each other and for those of the solid

¹cap·il·lary \'kap-ə-,ler-ē\ *adj* **1** : resembling a hair; *esp* : having a very small bore (~ tube) **2** : of or relating to capillaries or to capillarity

²capillary *n* : any of the tiny thin-walled tubes that carry blood between the smallest arteries and their corresponding veins

¹cap·i·tal \'kap-ət-ʾl\ *adj* **1** : punishable by death (~ offense) **2** : most serious (~ error) **3** : first in importance or position : CHIEF (~ city) **4** : conforming to the series A, B, C rather than a, b, c (~ letters) (~ G) **5** : of or relating to capital (~ expenditures) **6** : FIRST-RATE, EXCELLENT (a ~ dinner)

²capital *n* **1** : a letter larger than the ordinary small letter and often different in form **2** : the capital city of a state or country; *also* : a city preeminent in some activity (the fashion ~ of the world) **3** : accumulated wealth esp. as used to produce more wealth **4** : the total face value of shares of stock issued by a company **5** : capitalists considered as a group **6** : ADVANTAGE, GAIN

³capital *n* : the top part or piece of an architectural column

capital goods *n pl* : machinery, tools, factories, and commodities used in the production of goods

cap·i·tal·ism \'kap-ət-ʾl-,iz-əm\ *n* : an economic system characterized by private or corporation ownership of capital goods and by prices, production, and distribution of goods that are determined mainly in a free market

¹cap·i·tal·ist \-əst\ *n* **1** : a person who has capital esp. invested in business **2** : a person of great wealth : PLUTOCRAT **3** : a believer in capitalism

²capitalist *or* cap·i·tal·is·tic \,kap-ət-ʾl-'is-tik\ *adj* **1** : owning capital **2** : practicing or advocating capitalism **3** : marked by capitalism — cap·i·tal·is·ti·cal·ly *adv*

cap·i·tal·iza·tion \,kap-ət-ʾl-ə-'zā-shən\ *n* **1** : the act or process of capitalizing **2** : the total amount of money

used as capital in a business

cap·i·tal·ize \'kap-ət-ʾl-,īz\ *vb* **1** : to write or print with an initial capital or in capitals **2** : to convert into or use as capital **3** : to supply capital for **4** : to gain by turning something to advantage : PROFIT (~ on another's error)

cap·i·tal·ly \'kap-ət-ʾl-ē\ *adv* **1** : in a way involving sentence of death **2** : ADMIRABLY, EXCELLENTLY

capital ship *n* : a warship (as a battleship or aircraft carrier) of the greatest size or offensive power

cap·i·ta·tion \,kap-ə-'tā-shən\ *n* : a direct uniform tax levied on each person

cap·i·tol \'kap-ət-ʾl\ *n* : the building in which a legislature holds its sessions

ca·pit·u·late \kə-'pich-ə-,lāt\ *vb* **1** : to surrender esp. on conditions agreed upon **2** : to cease resisting : ACQUIESCE syn surrender, yield, succumb, relent — ca·pit·u·la·tion \-,pich-ə-'lā-shən\ *n*

ca·pon \'kā-,pän\ *n* : a castrated male chicken — ca·pon·ize \-pə-,nīz\ *vb*

ca·pric·cio \kə-'prēch-(ē-,)ō\ *n* : an instrumental piece in free form usu. lively in tempo and brilliant in style

ca·price \kə-'prēs\ *n* **1** : a sudden whim or fancy **2** : an instrumental piece in free form and usu. lively tempo — ca·pri·cious \kə-'prish-əs\ *adj* — ca·pri·cious·ly *adv* — ca·pri·cious·ness *n*

cap·ri·ole \'kap-rē-,ōl\ *n* : CAPER; *esp* : an upward leap of a horse without forward motion — capriole *vb*

cap·size \'kap-,sīz, kap-'sīz\ *vb* : UPSET, OVERTURN

cap·stan \'kap-stən\ *n* : an upright revolving drum used on ships to lift weights by use of a rope wound around it

cap·su·lar \'kap-sə-lər\ *adj* : of, relating to, or resembling a capsule

cap·su·late \-,lāt\ *or* cap·su·lat·ed *adj* : enclosed in a capsule

cap·sule \'kap-səl, -,sül\ *n* **1** : an enveloping cover (as of a bodily joint) (a spore ~); *esp* : an edible shell enclosing medicine to be swallowed **2** : a dry fruit made of two or more united carpels that splits open when ripe **3** : a small pressurized compartment for an aviator or astronaut for flight or emergency escape

¹cap·tain \'kap-tən\ *n* **1** : a commander of a body of troops **2** : an officer in charge of a ship **3** : a commissioned officer in the navy ranking next below a rear admiral or a commodore **4** : a commissioned officer (as in the army) ranking next below a major **5** : a leader of a side or team **6** : a dominant figure — cap·tain·cy *n* — cap·tain·ship *n*

²captain *vb* : to be captain of : LEAD

cap·tion \'kap-shən\ *n* **1** : a heading esp. of an article or document : TITLE **2** : a legend accompanying an illustration **3** : a motion-picture subtitle — caption *vb*

cap·tious \'kap-shəs\ *adj* : marked by an inclination to find fault : CRITICAL — cap·tious·ly *adv* — cap·tious·ness *n*

cap·ti·vate \'kap-tə-,vāt\ *vb* : to attract and hold irresistibly by some special charm or art : FASCINATE, CHARM — cap·ti·va·tion \,kap-tə-'vā-shən\ *n* — cap·ti·va·tor \'kap-tə-,vāt-ər\ *n*

¹cap·tive \'kap-tiv\ n 1 : a prisoner esp. of war 2 : one captivated or controlled

²captive adj 1 : made prisoner esp. in war 2 : kept within bounds : CONFINED 3 : held under control 4 : of or relating to bondage — cap·tiv·i·ty \kap-'tiv-ət-ē\ n

cap·tor \'kap-tər\ n : one that captures

¹cap·ture \'kap-chər\ n 1 : seizure by force or trickery 2 : one that has been taken; esp : a prize ship

²capture vb 1 : to take captive : WIN, GAIN 2 : to preserve in a relatively permanent form ⟨historic moment captured on film⟩

Cap·u·chin \'kap-yə-shən, kə-'p(y)ü-\ n : a member of an austere branch of the first order of St. Francis of Assisi engaged in missionary work and preaching

car \'kär\ n 1 : a vehicle moved on wheels 2 : the cage of an elevator 3 : the part of a balloon or airship which carries passengers or equipment

car·a·bao \,kar-ə-'baů\ n : the water buffalo of the Philippines

car·a·bi·neer or car·a·bi·nier \,kar-ə-bə-'niər\ n : a soldier armed with a carbine

car·a·cole \'kar-ə-,kōl\ n : a half turn to right or left executed by a mounted horse — caracole vb

ca·rafe \kə-'raf\ n : a water bottle with a flaring lip

car·a·mel \'kar-ə-məl, 'kär-məl\ n 1 : burnt sugar used for flavoring and coloring 2 : a firm chewy candy

car·a·pace \'kar-ə-,pās\ n : a protective case or shell on the back of an animal (as a turtle or crab)

¹carat var of KARAT

²car·at \'kar-ət\ n : a unit of weight for precious stones equal to 200 milligrams

car·a·van \'kar-ə-,van\ n 1 : a group of travelers journeying together through desert or hostile regions 2 : a group of vehicles traveling together in a file 3 : VAN

car·a·van·sa·ry \,kar-ə-'van-sə-rē\ or car·a·van·se·rai \-sə-,rī\ n : an inn in eastern countries where caravans rest at night 2 : HOTEL, INN

car·a·vel \'kar-ə-,vel\ n : a small 15th and 16th century ship with broad bows, high narrow poop, and lateen sails

car·a·way \'kar-ə-,wā\ n : an aromatic herb related to the carrot with seeds used in seasoning and medicine

car·bine \'kär-,bīn, -,bēn\ n : a short-barreled lightweight rifle

car·bo·hy·drate \,kär-bō-'hī-,drāt\ n : any of various compounds composed of carbon, hydrogen, and oxygen including the sugars and starches

car·bo·lat·ed \'kär-bə-,lāt-əd\ adj : impregnated with carbolic acid

car·bol·ic acid \,kär-,bäl-ik-\ n : a caustic crystalline compound usu. obtained from coal tar or by synthesis and used in solution as an antiseptic and disinfectant and in making plastics

car·bon \'kär-bən\ n 1 : a chemical element occurring in nature as the diamond and graphite and forming a constituent of coal, petroleum, and limestone 2 : a piece of carbon paper; also : a copy made with carbon paper

¹car·bon·ate \'kär-bə-,nāt, -nət\ n : a salt or ester of carbonic acid

²car·bon·ate \-,nāt\ vb : to impregnate with carbon dioxide ⟨a carbonated beverage⟩ — car·bon·ation \,kär-bə-'nā-shən\ n

carbon copy n 1 : a copy made by carbon paper 2 : DUPLICATE

carbon dioxide n : a heavy colorless gas that does not support combustion but is formed by the combustion and decomposition of organic substances

carbon 14 n : a heavy radioactive form of carbon used for determining the age of old specimens of formerly living materials

car·bon·ic acid \kär-,bän-ik-\ n : a weak acid that decomposes readily into water and carbon dioxide

car·bon·if·er·ous \,kär-bə-'nif-(ə-)rəs\ adj : producing or containing carbon or coal

carbon monoxide n : a colorless odorless very poisonous gas formed by the incomplete burning of carbon

carbon paper n : a thin paper coated with a waxy substance containing pigment and used in making copies of written or printed matter

car·boy \'kär-,bói\ n : a large specially cushioned cylindrical container for liquids

car·bun·cle \'kär-,bəŋ-kəl\ n : a painful inflammation of the skin and underlying tissue that discharges pus from several openings

car·bu·re·tor \'kär-b(y)ə-,rāt-ər\ n : an apparatus for supplying an internal-combustion engine with vaporized fuel mixed with air in an explosive mixture

car·cass \'kär-kəs\ n : a dead body; esp : one of an animal dressed for food

car·cin·o·gen \kär-'sin-ə-jən\ n : an agent causing or inciting cancer — car·cin·o·gen·ic \,sin-ə-'jen-ik\ adj — car·cin·o·ge·nic·i·ty \,sin-ə-jə-'nis-ət-ē\ n

¹card \'kärd\ vb : to comb with a card : cleanse and untangle before spinning — card·er n

²card n 1 : an implement for raising a nap on cloth 2 : a toothed instrument for combing wool, cotton, or flax before spinning

³card n 1 : PLAYING CARD 2 pl : a game played with playing cards; also : card playing 3 : a usu. clownishly amusing person : WAG 4 : a small piece of pasteboard for various purposes 5 : PROGRAM; esp : a sports program

⁴card vb 1 : to place or fasten on a card 2 : to list or record on a card 3 : SCORE

card·board \-,bôrd\ n : a stiff moderately thick board made of paper

car·di·ac \'kärd-ē-,ak\ adj 1 : of, relating to, or located near the heart 2 : of, relating to, or being the part of the stomach into which the esophagus opens

car·di·gan \'kärd-i-gən\ n : a sweater or jacket usu. without a collar and with a full-length opening in the front

¹car·di·nal \'kärd-(ᵊ-)nəl\ adj 1 : of basic importance : CHIEF, MAIN, PRIMARY 2 : of cardinal red color — car·di·nal·ly adv

²cardinal n 1 : an ecclesiastical official of the Roman Catholic Church ranking next below the pope 2 : a bright red 3 : any of several American finches of which the male is bright red

car·di·nal·ate \-ət, -,āt\ n 1 : the office, rank, or dignity of a cardinal 2 : CARDINALS

cardinal number n : a number (as 1, 5,

82, 357) that is used in simple counting and answers the question "how many?"

car·dio·vas·cu·lar \,kärd-ē-ō-'vas-kyə-lər\ adj : of or relating to the heart and blood vessels

¹**care** \'keər\ n 1 : a heavy sense of responsibility : WORRY, ANXIETY 2 : watchful attention : HEED 3 : CHARGE, SUPERVISION 4 : a person or thing that is an object of anxiety or solicitude

²**care** vb 1 : to feel anxiety 2 : to feel interest 3 : to have a liking, fondness, taste, or inclination 4 : to give care ⟨~ for the sick⟩ 5 : to be concerned about ⟨~ what happens⟩

ca·reen \kə-'rēn\ vb 1 : to cause (as a boat) to lean over on one side 2 : to heel over 3 : to sway from side to side : LURCH

¹**ca·reer** \kə-'riər\ n 1 : a course of action or events; esp : a person's progress in his chosen occupation 2 : an occupation or profession followed as a life's work

²**career** vb : to go at top speed esp. in a headlong manner

care·free \'keər,frē\ adj : free from care or worry

care·ful \-fəl\ adj 1 : using or taking care : WATCHFUL, VIGILANT 2 : marked by solicitude, caution, or prudence — **care·ful·ly** adv — **care·ful·ness** n

care·less \-ləs\ adj 1 : free from care : UNTROUBLED 2 : UNCONCERNED, INDIFFERENT 3 : not taking care 4 : not showing or receiving care — **care·less·ly** adv — **care·less·ness** n

¹**ca·ress** \kə-'res\ n : a tender or loving touch or embrace

²**caress** vb : to touch or stroke tenderly or lovingly — **ca·ress·er** n

car·et \'kar-ət\ n [L, is missing, fr. carēre to be lacking] : a mark ∧ used to indicate the place where something is to be inserted

care·tak·er \'keər-,tā-kər\ n 1 : one in charge usu. as occupant in place of an absent owner : CUSTODIAN 2 : one temporarily fulfilling the functions of an office

care·worn \-,wōrn\ adj : showing effects of grief or anxiety

car·fare \'kär-,faər\ n : passenger fare (as on a streetcar or bus)

car·go \'kär-gō\ n, pl -goes or -gos : the goods carried in a ship, airplane, or vehicle : FREIGHT

car·hop \-,häp\ n : one who serves customers at a drive-in restaurant

car·i·bou \'kar-ə-,bü\ n : a large No. American deer related to the reindeer

car·i·ca·ture \'kar-i-kə-,chür\ n 1 : distorted representation of parts or features to produce a ridiculous effect 2 : a representation esp. in literature or art having the qualities of caricature — **car·i·ca·ture** vb — **car·i·ca·tur·ist** \-,chür-əst\ n

car·ies \'ka(ə)r-ēz\ n : tooth decay

car·il·lon \'kar-ə-,län\ n : a set of bells tuned to the chromatic scale and sounded by hammers controlled by a keyboard

car·il·lon·neur \,kar-ə-lä-'nər\ n : a carillon player

car·load \'kär-,lōd\ n : a load that fills a car

car·min·a·tive \kär-'min-ət-iv\ adj : expelling gas from the alimentary canal

car·mine \'kär-mən, -,mīn\ n : a vivid red

car·nage \'kär-nij\ n : great destruction of life : SLAUGHTER

car·nal \'kärn-ᵊl\ adj 1 : of or relating to the body 2 : SENSUAL — **car·nal·i·ty** \kär-'nal-ət-ē\ n — **car·nal·ly** \'kärn-ᵊl-ē\ adv

car·na·tion \kär-'nā-shən\ n : a cultivated usu. double-flowered pink

car·nau·ba \kär-'nó-bə, ,kär-nə-'ü-bə\ n : a Brazilian palm that yields a brittle yellowish wax used esp. in polishes; also : this wax

car·ne·lian \kär-'nēl-yən\ n : a hard tough reddish quartz used as a gem

car·ni·val \'kär-nə-vəl\ n 1 : a season of merrymaking just before Lent 2 : a boisterous merrymaking 3 : a traveling enterprise offering a variety of amusements 4 : an organized program of entertainment

car·niv·o·ra \kär-'niv-(ə-)rə\ n pl : carnivorous mammals

car·ni·vore \'kär-nə-,vōr\ n : a flesh-eating animal; esp : any of a large group of mammals that feed mostly on flesh and include the dogs, cats, bears, minks, and seals — **car·niv·o·rous** \kär-'niv-(ə-)rəs\ adj — **car·niv·o·rous·ly** adv — **car·niv·o·rous·ness** n

car·ol \'kar-əl\ n : a song of joy, praise, or devotion — **carol** vb

car·om \'kar-əm\ n 1 : a shot in billiards in which the cue ball strikes each of two object balls 2 : a striking and rebounding esp. at an angle — **carom** vb

car·o·tene \'kar-ə-,tēn\ n : any of several orange to red pigments formed esp. in plants and used as a source of vitamin A

ca·rous·al \kə-'rau̇-zəl\ n : CAROUSE

ca·rouse \kə-'rau̇z\ n : a drunken revel — **carouse** vb — **ca·rous·er** n

carousel var of CARROUSEL

¹**carp** \'kärp\ vb : to find fault : CAVIL, COMPLAIN — **carp·er** n

²**carp** n : a long-lived soft-finned freshwater fish of sluggish waters

car·pe di·em \,kär-pē-'dē-,em\ n : enjoyment of the present without concern for the future

car·pel \'kär-pəl\ n : one of the highly modified leaves that together form the ovary of a flower

car·pen·ter \'kär-pən-tər\ n : one who builds or repairs wooden structures — **carpenter** vb — **car·pen·try** \-trē\ n

¹**car·pet** \'kär-pət\ n : a heavy fabric used esp. as a floor covering

²**carpet** vb : to cover with or as if with a carpet

car·pet·bag \-,bag\ n : a traveling bag common in the 19th century

car·pet·bag·ger n : a Northerner in the South during the reconstruction period seeking private gain by taking advantage of unsettled conditions and political corruption

car·pet·ing n : material for carpets; also : CARPETS

car·port \'kär-,pōrt\ n : an open-sided automobile shelter

car·rel \'kar-əl\ n : a table with bookshelves often partitioned or enclosed for individual study in a library

---

ə abut; ᵉ kitten; ər further; a back; ā bake; ä cot, cart; au̇ out; ch chin; e less; ē easy; g gift; i trip; ī life; j joke; ŋ sing; ō flow; ȯ flaw; ȯi coin; th thin; t̲h̲ this; ü loot; u̇ foot; y yet; yü few; yu̇ furious; zh vision

car·riage \'kar-ij\ n 1 : conveyance esp. of goods 2 : manner of holding or carrying oneself : BEARING 3 : a wheeled vehicle 4 Brit : a railway passenger coach 5 : a movable part of a machine for supporting some other moving part

carriage trade n : trade from well-to-do or upper-class people

car·ri·er \'kar-ē-ər\ n 1 : one that carries something; esp : one that spreads germs while remaining well himself 2 : a person or corporation in the transportation business 3 : a wave whose characteristic (as amplitude or frequency) is varied in order to transmit a radio or television signal

car·ri·on \'kar-ē-ən\ n : dead and decaying flesh

car·rot \'kar-ət\ n : a vegetable widely grown for its elongated orange-red root; also : this root

car·rou·sel or **car·ou·sel** \,kar-ə-'sel\ n : MERRY-GO-ROUND

¹car·ry \'kar-ē\ vb 1 : to move while supporting : TRANSPORT, CONVEY, TAKE 2 : to influence by mental or emotional appeal 3 : to get possession or control of : CAPTURE, WIN 4 : to have or wear upon one's person; also : to bear within one 5 : INVOLVE, IMPLY 6 : to hold or bear (oneself) in a specified way 7 : to sustain the weight or burden of : SUPPORT 8 : to keep in stock for sale 9 : to prolong in space, time, or degree 10 : to reach or penetrate to a distance 11 : to win adoption (as in a legislature) 12 : to succeed in (an election) 13 : PUBLISH, PRINT 14 : to keep on one's books as a debtor

²carry n 1 : the range of a gun or projectile or of a struck or thrown ball 2 : an act or method of carrying ⟨fireman's ~⟩ 3 : a portage esp. between two bodies of navigable water

carry away vb : to arouse to a high and often excessive degree of emotion or enthusiasm

carry on vb 1 : CONDUCT, MANAGE 2 : to behave in a foolish, excited, or improper manner 3 : to continue in spite of hindrance or discouragement

carry out vb 1 : to put into execution ⟨carry out a plan⟩ 2 : to bring to a successful conclusion

¹cart \'kärt\ n 1 : a 2-wheeled wagon 2 : a small wheeled vehicle

²cart vb : to convey in or as if in a cart — **cart·er** n

cart·age \'kärt-ij\ n : the act of or rate charged for carting

carte blanche \'kärt-'bläⁿsh\ n : full discretionary power

car·tel \kär-'tel\ n : a combination of independent business enterprises designed to limit competition **syn** pool, syndicate, monopoly

car·ti·lage \'kärt-ᵊl-ij\ n : an elastic tissue composing most of the skeleton of embryonic and very young vertebrates and later mostly turning into bone — **car·ti·lag·i·nous** \,kärt-ᵊl-'aj-ə-nəs\ adj

car·tog·ra·phy \kär-'täg-rə-fē\ n : the making of maps — **car·tog·ra·pher** n

car·ton \'kärt-ᵊn\ n : a cardboard box or container

car·toon \kär-'tün\ n 1 : a preparatory sketch (as for a painting) 2 : a satirical drawing commenting on public affairs 3 : COMIC STRIP — **cartoon** vb — **cartoon·ist** n

car·tridge \'kär-trij\ n 1 : a tube containing a complete charge for a firearm 2 : a container of material for insertion into an apparatus 3 : a phonograph part that translates stylus motion into electrical voltage

cart·wheel \'kärt-,hwēl\ n 1 : a large coin (as a silver dollar) 2 : a lateral handspring with arms and legs extended

carve \'kärv\ vb 1 : to cut with care or precision : shape by cutting 2 : to cut into pieces or slices 3 : to slice and serve meat at table 4 : to work as a sculptor or engraver — **carv·er** n — **carv·ing** n

car·y·at·id \,kar-ē-'at-əd\ n, pl **-atids** or **-at·i·des** \-'at-ə-,dēz\ : a sculptured draped female figure used as an architectural column

ca·sa·ba \kə-'säb-ə\ n : any of several winter melons with yellow rind and sweet flesh

¹cas·cade \kas-'kād\ n 1 : a steep usu. small waterfall 2 : something arranged in a series or succession of stages so that each stage derives from or acts upon the product of the preceding

²cascade vb : to fall, pass, or connect in or as if in a cascade

cas·cara \kas-'kar-ə\ n : the dried bark of a small Pacific coastal tree used as a laxative; also : this tree

¹case \'kās\ n 1 : a particular instance or situation 2 : a convincing argument 3 : an inflectional form esp. of a noun or pronoun indicating its grammatical relation to other words; also : such a relation whether indicated by inflection or not 4 : what actually exists or happens : FACT 5 : a suit or action in law : CAUSE 6 : an instance of disease or injury; also : PATIENT 7 : INSTANCE, EXAMPLE

²case n 1 : a receptacle (as a box) for holding something 2 : SET (a ~ of instruments); esp : PAIR 3 : an outer covering 4 : a shallow divided tray for holding printing type 5 : the frame of a door or window : CASING

³case vb 1 : to enclose in or cover with a case 2 slang : to inspect esp. with intent to rob

ca·sein \kā-'sēn, 'kā-sē-ən\ n : a whitish phosphorous-containing protein occurring in milk

case·ment \'kās-mənt\ n : a window sash opening on hinges at the side like a door; also : a window having such a sash

¹cash \'kash\ n 1 : ready money 2 : money or its equivalent paid at the time of purchase or delivery

²cash vb : to pay or obtain cash for ⟨~ a check⟩

cash·ew \'kash-ü, kə-'shü\ n : a tropical American tree related to the sumac; also : its edible nut

¹cash·ier \kash-'iər\ vb : to dismiss from service; esp : to dismiss in disgrace

²cashier n : a bank official responsible for moneys received and paid out 2 : an employee (as of a store or restaurant) who receives and records payments to customers

cashier's check n : a check drawn by a bank upon its own funds and signed by its cashier

cash·mere \'kazh-,miər, 'kash-\ n : fine wool from the undercoat of an Indian goat or a yarn spun of this; also : a soft twilled fabric orig. woven from this yarn

cas·ing \'kā-siŋ\ *n* : something that encases

ca·si·no \kə-'sē-nō\ *n* 1 : a building or room for social amusements; *esp* : one used for gambling 2 *or* **cas·si·no** : a card game

cask \'kask\ *n* : a barrel-shaped container usu. for liquids; *also* : the quantity held by such a container

cas·ket \'kas-kət\ *n* 1 : a small box (as for jewels) 2 : COFFIN

casque \'kask\ *n* : HELMET

cas·sa·va \kə-'säv-ə\ *n* : a tropical spurge whose rootstock yields a nutritious starch from which tapioca is prepared

cas·se·role \'kas-ə-,rōl\ *n* 1 : a glass or earthenware dish in which food may be baked and served 2 : a dish cooked and served in a casserole

cas·sette \kə-'set\ *n* : a lightproof container of films or plates for use in a camera

cas·sia \'kash-ə\ *n* 1 : a coarse cinnamon bark 2 : any of various East Indian leguminous herbs, shrubs, and trees of which several yield senna

cas·sock \'kas-ək\ *n* : an ankle-length garment worn by the clergy of certain churches

¹**cast** \'kast\ *vb* **cast; cast·ing** 1 : THROW, FLING 2 : DIRECT (~ a glance) 3 : to deposit (a ballot) formally 4 : to throw off, out, or away : DISCARD, SHED 5 : COMPUTE; *esp* : add up 6 : to assign the parts of (a play) to actors; *also* : to assign to a role or part 7 : MOLD 8 : to make (as a knot or stitch) by looping or catching up

²**cast** *n* 1 : THROW, FLING 2 : a throw of dice 3 : something formed in or as if in a mold; *also* : a rigid surgical dressing (as for protecting and supporting a fractured bone) 4 : TINGE, HUE 5 : APPEARANCE, LOOK 6 : something thrown out or off, shed, or expelled (worm ~s) 7 : the group of actors to whom parts in a play are assigned

cas·ta·nets \,kas-tə-'nets\ *n pl* [Sp *castañetas*, fr. *castaña* chestnut, fr. L *castanea*] : a rhythm instrument consisting of two small ivory or wooden shells held in the hand and clicked in accompaniment with music and dancing

cast·away \'kas-tə-,wā\ *adj* 1 : thrown away : REJECTED 2 : cast adrift or ashore as a survivor of a shipwreck — **castaway** *n*

caste \'kast\ *n* 1 : one of the hereditary social classes in Hinduism 2 : a division of society based upon wealth, inherited rank, or occupation 3 : social position : PRESTIGE 4 : a system of rigid social stratification

cas·tel·lat·ed \'kas-tə-,lāt-əd\ *adj* : having battlements like a castle

cast·er *or* **cas·tor** \'kas-tər\ *n* 1 : a small container to hold salt or pepper at the table 2 : a small wheel usu. free to swivel used to support and move furniture, trucks, and machines

cas·ti·gate \'kas-tə-,gāt\ *vb* : to punish, reprove, or criticize severely — **cas·ti·ga·tion** \,kas-tə-'gā-shən\ *n* — **cas·ti·ga·tor** \'kas-tə-,gāt-ər\ *n*

cast·ing *n* 1 : something cast in a mold 2 : something cast off or out

cast iron *n* : a hard brittle alloy of iron, carbon, and silicon cast in a mold

cas·tle \'kas-əl\ *n* 1 : a large fortified building or set of buildings 2 : a large or imposing house 3 : ³ROOK

cas·tled \'kas-əld\ *adj* : CASTELLATED

cast-off \'kas-,tof\ *adj* : thrown away or aside : DISCARDED

cast off *n* : a cast-off person or thing

cas·tor oil \'kas-tər-\ *n* : a thick yellowish oil extracted from the poisonous seeds of an herb and used as a lubricant and cathartic

cas·trate \'kas-,trāt\ *vb* : to deprive of sex glands and usu. testes — **cas·tra·tion** \kas-'trā-shən\ *n*

ca·su·al \'kazh-(ə-w)əl\ *adj* 1 : resulting from or occurring by chance 2 : OCCASIONAL, INCIDENTAL 3 : showing or feeling little concern : OFFHAND, NONCHALANT 4 : designed for informal use (~ clothing) — **ca·su·al·ly** *adv* — **ca·su·al·ness** *n*

ca·su·al·ty \'kazh-(ə-w)əl-tē\ *n* 1 : serious or fatal accident : DISASTER 2 : a military person lost through death, injury, sickness, or capture or through being missing in action 3 : a person or thing injured, lost, or destroyed

ca·su·ist·ry \'kazh-ə-wə-strē\ *n* : adroit but false or misleading argument or reasoning esp. about morals — **ca·su·ist** \-wəst\ *n* — **ca·su·is·tic** \,kazh-ə-'wis-tik\ *or* **ca·su·is·ti·cal** *adj*

ca·sus bel·li \,käs-əs-'bel-,ē\ *n* : an event or action that justifies or allegedly justifies war

cat \'kat\ *n* 1 : a common domestic mammal long kept by man as a pet or for catching rats and mice 2 : any of various animals (as the lion, lynx, or leopard) that are related to the domestic cat 3 : a spiteful woman 4 : CAT-O'-NINE-TAILS

cat·a·clysm \'kat-ə-,kliz-əm\ *n* : a violent change or upheaval — **cat·a·clys·mic** \,kat-ə-'kliz-mik\ *adj*

cat·a·comb \'kat-ə-,kōm\ *n* : an underground burial place with galleries and recesses for tombs

cat·a·falque \-,falk, -,fò(l)k\ *n* : an ornamental structure sometimes used in solemn funerals to hold the body

cat·a·lep·sy \'kat-ʲl-,ep-sē\ *n* : a trancelike state of suspended animation — **cat·a·lep·tic** \,kat-ʲl-'ep-tik\ *adj or n*

¹**cat·a·log** *or* **cat·a·logue** \'kat-ʲl-,òg\ *n* 1 : LIST, REGISTER 2 : a systematic list of items with descriptive details; *also* : a book containing such a list

²**catalog** *or* **catalogue** *vb* 1 : to make a catalog of 2 : to enter in a catalog — **cat·a·log·er** *or* **cat·a·logu·er** *n*

ca·tal·pa \kə-'tal-pə\ *n* : a broad-leaved tree with showy flowers and long slim pods

ca·tal·y·sis \kə-'tal-ə-səs\ *n* : the change and esp. increase in the rate of a chemical reaction brought about by a substance (**cat·a·lyst** \'kat-ʲl-əst\) that is itself unchanged at the end

cat·a·ma·ran \,kat-ə-mə-'ran\ *n* 1 : a raft propelled by paddles or sails 2 : a boat with twin hulls

cat·a·mount \'kat-ə-,maùnt\ *n* : COUGAR; *also* : LYNX

cat·a·pult \'kat ə-,pəlt, -,pùlt\ *n* 1 : an

ancient military machine for hurling missiles (as stones and arrows) **2** : a device for launching an airplane from the deck of a ship — **catapult** vb

cat·a·ract \'kat-ə-,rakt\ n **1** : a large waterfall; also : steep rapids in a river **2** : a cloudiness of the lens of the eye obstructing vision

ca·tarrh \kə-'tär\ n : inflammation of a mucous membrane esp. of the nose and throat — **ca·tarrh·al** adj

ca·tas·tro·phe \kə-'tas-trə-(,)fē\ n **1** : a sudden calamity : great disaster or misfortune **2** : utter failure : FIASCO — **cat·a·stroph·ic** \,kat-ə-'sträf-ik\ adj

cat·bird \'kat-,bərd\ n : an American songbird with a call like the cry of a cat

cat·boat \-,bōt\ n : a sailboat with a single mast set far forward and a single large sail extended by a long boom

cat·call \-,kòl\ n : a sound like the cry of a cat; also : a noise made to express disapproval (as at a sports event) — **catcall** vb

¹**catch** \'kach, 'kech\ vb **caught** \'kòt\ **catch·ing** **1** : to capture esp. after pursuit **2** : TRAP **3** : to discover esp. unexpectedly : SURPRISE, DETECT **4** : to become suddenly aware of **5** : to take hold of : SEIZE, GRASP **6** : SNATCH ⟨~ at a straw⟩ **7** : INTERCEPT **8** : to get entangled **9** : to become affected with or by ⟨~ fire⟩ ⟨~ cold⟩ **10** : to seize and hold firmly; also : FASTEN **11** : to take in and retain **12** : OVERTAKE **13** : to be in time for ⟨~ a train⟩ **14** : to look at or listen to ⟨~ a TV show⟩

²**catch** n **1** : the act of catching; also : a game in which a ball is thrown and caught **2** : something caught **3** : something that catches or checks or holds immovable ⟨a door ~⟩ **4** : one worth catching esp. in marriage **5** : FRAGMENT, SNATCH **6** : a concealed difficulty

catch·all \-,òl\ n : something to hold a variety of odds and ends

catch·er n : one that catches; esp : a player stationed behind home plate in baseball

catch·ing adj **1** : INFECTIOUS, CONTAGIOUS **2** : ALLURING, CATCHY

catch on vb **1** : UNDERSTAND **2** : to become popular

catch up vb : to travel or work fast enough to overtake or complete

catch·up var of CATSUP

catchy \'kach-ē, 'kech-\ adj **1** : apt to catch the interest or attention **2** : tending to mislead : TRICKY **3** : FITFUL, IRREGULAR

cat·e·chism \'kat-ə-,kiz-əm\ n : a summary or test (as of religious doctrine) usu. in the form of questions and answers — **cat·e·chist** \-,kist\ n — **cat·e·chize** \-,kīz\ vb

cat·e·chu·men \,kat-ə-'kyü-mən\ n : a religious convert receiving training before baptism

cat·e·gor·i·cal \,kat-ə-'gòr-i-kəl\ adj **1** : ABSOLUTE, UNQUALIFIED **2** : of, relating to, or constituting a category — **cat·e·gor·i·cal·ly** adv

cat·e·go·rize \'kat-i-gə-,rīz\ vb : to put into a category : CLASSIFY

cat·e·go·ry \-,gōr-ē\ n : a division used in classification; also : CLASS, GROUP, KIND

ca·ter \'kāt-ər\ vb **1** : to provide a supply of food **2** : to supply what is wanted — **ca·ter·er** n

ca·ter·cor·ner \,kat-ē-'kòr-nər, ,kàt-ə-, ,kit-ē-\ or **cat·er·cor·nered** adv (or adj) : in a diagonal or oblique position

cat·er·pil·lar \'kat-ə(r)-,pil-ər\ n : a wormlike often hairy insect esp. of a butterfly or moth

cat·er·waul \'kat-ər-,wòl\ vb : to make the characteristic harsh cry of a rutting cat — **caterwaul** n

cat·fish \'kat-,fish\ n : any of several big-headed gluttonous fishes with fleshy sensory processes around the mouth

cat·gut \-,gət\ n : a tough cord made usu. from sheep intestines

ca·thar·tic \kə-'thärt-ik\ adj or n : PURGATIVE

ca·the·dral \kə-'thē-drəl\ n : the principal church of a diocese

cath·e·ter \'kath-ət-ər\ n : a tube for insertion into a bodily passage or cavity esp. for drawing off material (as urine)

cath·ode \'kath-,ōd\ n **1** : the negative electrode of an electrolytic cell **2** : the positive terminal of a battery **3** : the electron-emitting electrode of an electron tube — **ca·thod·ic** \ka-'thäd-ik\ adj

cath·o·lic \'kath-(ə-)lik\ adj **1** : GENERAL, UNIVERSAL ⟨a man of ~ interests⟩ **2** cap : of or relating to Catholics and esp. Roman Catholics

Cath·o·lic n : a member of a church claiming historical continuity from the ancient undivided Christian church; esp : a member of the Roman Catholic Church — **Ca·thol·i·cism** \kə-'thäl-ə-,siz-əm\ n

cath·o·lic·i·ty \,kath-ə-'lis-ət-ē\ n **1** cap : the character of being in conformity with a Catholic church **2** : liberality of sentiments or views **3** : comprehensive range

cat·kin \'kat-kən\ n : a long flower cluster (as of a willow) bearing crowded flowers and prominent bracts

cat·like \-,līk\ adj : resembling a cat; esp : STEALTHY

cat·nap \-,nap\ n : a very short light nap — **catnap** vb

cat·nip \-,nip\ n : an aromatic mint relished by cats

cat-o'-nine-tails \,kat-ə-'nīn-,tālz\ n, pl **cat-o'-nine-tails** : a whip made of usu. 9 knotted cords fastened to a handle

cat's cradle n : a game played with a string looped on the fingers in such a way as to resemble a small cradle

cat's-paw \'kats-,pó\ n : one used by another as a tool : DUPE

cat·sup \'kech-əp, 'kach-əp, 'kat-səp\ n : a seasoned sauce of puree consistency usu. made of tomatoes

cat·tail \'kat-,tāl\ n : a tall reedlike marsh herb with furry brown spikes of tiny flowers

cat·tle \'kat-ᵊl\ n, pl **cattle** : LIVESTOCK; esp : domestic bovines (as cows, bulls, or calves) — **cat·tle·man** \-mən\ n

cat·ty \'kat-ē\ adj : slyly spiteful : MALICIOUS — **cat·ti·ly** adv — **cat·ti·ness** n

cat·ty-cor·ner or **cat·ty-cor·nered** var of CATERCORNER

cat·walk \'kat-,wòk\ n : a narrow walk (as along a bridge or around a large machine)

Cau·ca·sian \kò-'kāzh-ən, -'kazh-\ n : a member of the white race — **Caucasian** adj — **Cau·ca·soid** \'kò-kə-,sòid\ adj or n

cau·cus \'kò-kəs\ n : a meeting of

leaders of a party or faction usu. to decide upon policies and candidates — **caucus** vb

cau·dal \'kȯd-ᵊl\ adj : of, relating to, or located near the tail or the hind end of the body — **cau·dal·ly** adv

caught past of CATCH

cauldron var of CALDRON

cau·li·flow·er \'kȯ-li-ˌflaù(-ə)r\ n : a vegetable closely related to cabbage and grown for its compact head of undeveloped flowers; also : this head

cauliflower ear n : an ear deformed from injury and excessive growth of scar tissue

caulk \'kȯk\ vb : to make the seams of (a boat) watertight by filling with waterproofing material; also : to make tight against leakage by a sealing substance ⟨~ a pipe joint⟩ — **caulk·er** n

caus·al \'kȯ-zəl\ adj 1 : expressing or indicating cause 2 : relating to or acting as a cause 3 : showing interaction of cause and effect — **cau·sal·i·ty** \kȯ-'zal-ət-ē\ n — **caus·al·ly** \'kȯ-zə-lē\ adv

cau·sa·tion \kȯ-'zā-shən\ n 1 : the act or process of causing 2 : the means by which an effect is produced

¹**cause** \'kȯz\ n 1 : something that brings about a result; esp : a person or thing that is the agent of bringing something about 2 : REASON, MOTIVE 3 : a question or matter to be decided 4 : a suit or action in court : CASE 5 : a principle or movement earnestly supported — **cause·less** adj

²**cause** vb : to be the cause or occasion of — **caus·ative** \'kȯ-zat-iv\ adj — **caus·er** n

cause cé·lè·bre \ˌkȯz-sā-'lebrᵊ\ n, pl **causes célèbres** \same\ 1 : a legal case that excites widespread interest 2 : a notorious incident or episode

cause·way \'kȯz-ˌwā\ n : a raised way or road across wet ground or water

¹**caus·tic** \'kȯ-stik\ adj 1 : CORROSIVE 2 : SHARP, INCISIVE ⟨~ wit⟩ — **caus·ti·cal·ly** adv

²**caustic** n : a caustic substance

cau·ter·ize \'kȯt-ə-ˌrīz\ vb : to burn or sear usu. to prevent infection or bleeding — **cau·ter·i·za·tion** \ˌkȯt-ə-rə-'zā-shən\ n

¹**cau·tion** \'kȯ-shən\ n 1 : a word or act that conveys a warning 2 : prudent forethought to minimize risk : WARINESS 3 : one that arouses astonishment : an extreme or grotesque example

²**caution** vb : to advise caution to : WARN

cau·tion·ary \'kȯ-shə-ˌner-ē\ adj : serving as or offering a caution

cau·tious \'kȯ-shəs\ adj : marked by or given to caution : CAREFUL, PRUDENT — **cau·tious·ly** adv — **cau·tious·ness** n

cav·al·cade \ˌkav-əl-'kād\ n 1 : a procession of persons on horseback; also : a procession of vehicles 2 : a dramatic sequence or procession : PARADE, PAGEANT

¹**cav·a·lier** \ˌkav-ə-'liər\ n [MF, fr. It cavaliere, fr. Old Provençal cavalier, fr. LL caballarius groom, fr. L caballus horse] 1 : a mounted soldier : KNIGHT 2 cap : a Royalist in the time of Charles I of England 3 : a debonair person : GALLANT

²**cavalier** adj 1 : gay and easy in manner : DEBONAIR 2 : DISDAINFUL, HAUGHTY — **cav·a·lier·ly** adv — **cav·a·lier·ness** n

cav·al·ry \'kav-əl-rē\ n : troops mounted on horseback or moving in motor vehicles — **cav·al·ry·man** \-mən\ n

cave \'kāv\ n : a natural underground chamber with an opening to the surface

cave·at \'kā-vē-ˌat\ n : WARNING

caveat emp·tor \ˌkā-vē-ˌat-'emp-tər, -ˌtȯr\ n : a warning principle in trading that the buyer should be alert to see that he gets the quantity and quality paid for

cave-in \'kāv-ˌin\ n 1 : the action of caving in 2 : a place where earth has caved in

cave·man \-ˌman\ n 1 : one who lives in a cave; esp : a man of the Stone Age 2 : a man who acts with rough or violent directness esp. toward women

cav·ern \'kav-ərn\ n : a hollowed-out space in the earth; esp : an underground chamber of large extent — **cav·ern·ous** adj — **cav·ern·ous·ly** adv

cav·i·ar or **cav·i·are** \'kav-ē-ˌär\ n : the salted roe of a large fish (as sturgeon) used as an appetizer

cav·il \'kav-əl\ vb -iled or -illed; -il·ing or -il·ling : to find fault without good reason : make frivolous objections — **cavil** n — **cav·il·er** or **cav·il·ler** n

cav·i·ty \'kav-ət-ē\ n : an unfilled space within a mass : a hollow place

ca·vort \kə-'vȯrt\ vb : PRANCE, CAPER

ca·vy \'kā-vē\ n : GUINEA PIG

caw \'kȯ\ vb : to utter the harsh raucous natural call of the crow or a similar cry — **caw** n

cay \'kē, 'kā\ n : a small low island or emergent reef of sand or coral : ISLET, KEY

cay·enne pepper \ˌkī-ˌen-, ˌkā-\ n : a pungent condiment consisting of ground dried fruits or seeds of a hot pepper

horse·use \'kī-ˌ(y)üs\ n : a native range horse of the western U.S.

cease \'sēs\ vb : to come or bring to an end : STOP

cease-fire \-'fī(ə)r\ n : a suspension of active hostilities

cease·less \-ləs\ adj : being without pause or stop : CONTINUOUS — **cease·less·ly** adv — **cease·less·ness** n

ce·cum \'sē-kəm\ n, pl **ce·ca** \-kə\ or **cecums** : the blind pouch at the beginning of the large intestine into one side of which the small intestine opens — **ce·cal** \-kəl\ adj

ce·dar \'sēd-ər\ n : any of various cone-bearing trees noted for their fragrant durable wood; also : this wood

cede \'sēd\ vb 1 : to yield or give up esp. by treaty 2 : ASSIGN, TRANSFER — **ced·er** n

ceil·ing \'sē-liŋ\ n 1 : the overhead inside surface of a room 2 : the greatest height at which an airplane can operate efficiently 3 : the height above the ground of the base of the lowest layer of clouds 4 : an upper prescribed limit ⟨price ~⟩

cel·an·dine \'sel-ən-ˌdīn, -ˌdēn\ n : a

yellow-flowered herb related to the poppies

cel·e·brate \'sel-ə-ˌbrāt\ vb 1 : to perform (as a sacrament) with appropriate rites 2 : to honor (as a holy day) by solemn ceremonies or by refraining from ordinary business 3 : to observe a notable occasion with festivities 4 : to hold up for public acclaim : EXTOL — **cel·e·brant** \-brənt\ n — **cel·e·bra·tion** \ˌsel-ə-'brā-shən\ n

cel·e·brat·ed \'sel-ə-ˌbrāt-əd\ adj : widely known and often referred to syn distinguished, renowned, noted, famous, illustrious, notorious

ce·leb·ri·ty \sə-'leb-rət-ē\ n 1 : the state of being celebrated : RENOWN 2 : a celebrated person

ce·ler·i·ty \sə-'ler-ət-ē\ n : SPEED, RAPIDITY

cel·ery \'sel-(ə-)rē\ n : an herb related to the carrot and widely grown for crisp edible petioles

ce·les·tial \sə-'les-chəl\ adj 1 : of or relating to the sky ⟨a star is a ~ body⟩ 2 : HEAVENLY, DIVINE — **ce·les·tial·ly** adv

celestial navigation n : navigation by observation of the positions of celestial bodies

celestial sphere n : an imaginary sphere of infinite radius against which the celestial bodies appear to be projected

cel·i·ba·cy \'sel-ə-bə-sē\ n 1 : the state of being unmarried; esp : abstention by vow from marriage 2 : CHASTITY

cel·i·bate \-bət\ n : one who lives in celibacy — **celibate** adj

cell \'sel\ n 1 : a small room (as in a convent or prison) usu. for use of a single person; also : a small compartment, cavity, or bounded space 2 : a tiny mass of protoplasm that contains a nucleus, is enclosed by a membrane, and forms the fundamental unit of living matter 3 : a container holding an electrolyte either for generating electricity or use in electrolysis 4 : a device for converting radiant energy into electrical energy or for varying an electric current in accordance with radiation received

cel·lar \'sel-ər\ n 1 : a room or group of rooms below the surface of the ground and usu. under a building 2 : a stock of wines

cel·lar·ette or **cel·lar·et** \ˌsel-ə-'ret\ n : a case or cabinet for a few bottles of wine or liquor

cel·list \'chel-əst\ n : one that plays the cello

cel·lo \'chel-ō\ n : a bass member of the violin family tuned an octave below the viola

cel·lo·phane \'sel-ə-ˌfān\ n : a thin transparent material made from cellulose and used as a wrapping

cel·lu·lar \'sel-yə-lər\ adj 1 : of, relating to, or consisting of cells 2 : porous in texture

cel·lu·lose \-ˌlōs\ n : a complex carbohydrate of the cell walls of plants used esp. in making paper or rayon — **cel·lu·los·ic** \ˌsel-yə-'lō-sik\ adj or n

Cel·si·us \'sel-sē-əs\ adj : CENTIGRADE ⟨10° ~⟩

Celt \'selt, 'kelt\ n : a member of any of a group of peoples (as the Irish or Welsh) of western Europe — **Celt·ic** adj

cel·tuce \'sel-təs\ n : a vegetable related to lettuce but grown for its leafstalks

that combine the flavor of celery and lettuce

cem·ba·lo \'chem-bə-ˌlō\ n, pl -los or -li \-ˌlē\ : HARPSICHORD

¹ce·ment \si-'ment\ n 1 : a powder that is produced from a burned mixture chiefly of clay and limestone, that with water forms a paste that hardens into a stonelike mass, and that is used in mortars and concretes; also : CONCRETE 2 : a binding element or agency 3 : a substance for filling cavities in teeth

²cement vb : to unite or cover with cement

cem·e·tery \'sem-ə-ˌter-ē\ n : a burial ground : GRAVEYARD

cen·o·bite \'sen-ə-ˌbīt\ n : a member of a religious group living together — **cen·o·bit·ic** \ˌsen-ə-'bit-ik\ adj

cen·o·taph \'sen-ə-ˌtaf\ n : a tomb or a monument erected in honor of a person whose body is elsewhere

cen·ser \'sen-sər\ n : a vessel for burning incense (as in religious ritual)

¹cen·sor \'sen-sər\ n 1 : one of two early Roman magistrates whose duties included taking the census 2 : an official who inspects printed matter or sometimes motion pictures with power to suppress anything objectionable — **cen·so·ri·al** \sen-'sōr-ē-əl\ adj

²censor vb : to subject to censorship

cen·so·ri·ous \sen-'sōr-ē-əs\ adj : marked by or given to censure : CRITICAL — **cen·so·ri·ous·ly** adv — **cen·so·ri·ous·ness** n

cen·sor·ship \'sen-sər-ˌship\ n 1 : the office of a Roman censor 2 : the action of a censor esp. in stopping the transmission or publication of matter considered objectionable

¹cen·sure \'sen-chər\ n 1 : the act of blaming or condemning sternly 2 : an official reprimand

²censure vb : to find fault with and criticize as blameworthy — **cen·sur·able** adj — **cen·sur·er** n

cen·sus \'sen-səs\ n 1 : a periodic governmental count of population 2 : COUNT, TALLY

cent \'sent\ n 1 : a unit of value equal to 100th part of a basic unit in various monetary systems 2 : a coin, token, or note representing one cent — see MONEY table

cen·taur \'sen-ˌtòr\ n : one of a race of creatures in Greek mythology half man and half horse

cen·ta·vo \sen-'täv-ō\ n — see MONEY table

cen·te·nar·i·an \ˌsent-ᵊn-'er-ē-ən\ n : a person who is 100 or more years old

cen·ten·a·ry \sen-'ten-ə-rē, 'sent-ᵊn-ˌer-ē\ adj or n : CENTENNIAL

cen·ten·ni·al \sen-'ten-ē-əl\ n : a 100th anniversary or its celebration — **centennial** adj — **cen·ten·ni·al·ly** adv

¹cen·ter \'sent-ər\ n 1 : the point equally distant or at the average distance from the outside points of a figure or body 2 : the point about which an activity concentrates or from which something originates 3 : a region of concentrated population 4 : a middle part 5 often cap : political figures holding moderate views esp. between those of conservatives and liberals 6 : a player occupying a middle position (as in football or basketball)

²center vb 1 : to place or fix at or around a center or central area 2 : to gather to a center : CONCENTRATE **3** : to have a center

cen·ter·board \-,bōrd\ *n* : a retractable keel used esp. in sailboats

cen·ter·piece \-,pēs\ *n* : an object occupying a central position; *esp* : an adornment in the center of a table

1cen·tes·i·mo \chen-'tez-ə-,mō\ *n*, *pl* **cen·tes·i·mi** \-,(,)mē\ — see MONEY table

2cen·tes·i·mo \sen-'tes-ə-,mō\ *n* — see MONEY table

cen·ti·grade \'sent-ə-,grād, 'sänt-\ *adj* : relating to, conforming to, or having a thermometer scale on which the interval between the freezing and boiling points of water is divided into 100 degrees with 0° representing the freezing point and 100° the boiling point ⟨10° ~⟩

cen·ti·gram \-,gram\ *n* : a weight of ⅟₁₀₀ gram

cen·time \'sän-,tēm\ *n* — see MONEY table

cen·ti·me·ter \'sent-ə-,mēt-ər, 'sänt-\ *n* : a measure of length equal to ⅟₁₀₀ meter

cen·ti·mo \'sent-ə-,mō\ *n* — see MONEY table

cen·ti·pede \'sent-ə-,pēd\ *n* : a long flat many-legged arthropod

1cen·tral \'sen-trəl\ *adj* **1** : constituting a center **2** : ESSENTIAL, PRINCIPAL **3** : relating to, at, or near the center **4** : centrally placed and superseding separate units ⟨~ heating⟩ — **cen·tral·ly** *adv*

2central *n* : a telephone exchange or an operator handling calls there

cen·tral·ize \'sen-trə-,līz\ *vb* : to bring to a central point or under central control — **cen·tral·i·za·tion** \,sen-trə-lə-'zā-shən\ *n* — **cen·tral·iz·er** \'sen-trə-,lī-zər\ *n*

cen·tre \'sent-ər\ *chiefly Brit var of* CENTER

cen·trif·u·gal \sen-'trif-yə-gəl\ *adj* **1** : proceeding or acting in a direction away from a center or axis **2** : using centrifugal force or acting or separated by it — **cen·trif·u·gal·ly** *adv*

centrifugal force *n* : the force that tends to impel a thing or parts of a thing outward from a center of rotation

cen·tri·fuge \'sen-trə-,fyüj, 'sän-\ *n* : a machine using centrifugal force (as for separating substances of different densities or for removing moisture)

cen·trip·e·tal \sen-'trip-ət-°l\ *adj* : proceeding or acting in a direction toward a center or axis — **cen·trip·e·tal·ly** *adv*

cen·trist \'sen-trəst\ *n* **1** *often cap* : a member of a center party **2** : one that holds moderate views

cen·tu·ri·on \sen-'t(y)ùr-ē-ən\ *n* : an officer commanding a Roman century

cen·tu·ry \'sench-(ə-)rē\ *n* **1** : a subdivision of a Roman legion **2** : a group or sequence of 100 like things **3** : a period of 100 years esp. of the Christian era or the preceding period

ce·phal·ic \sə-'fal-ik\ *adj* **1** : of or relating to the head **2** : directed toward or situated on or in or near the head

cephalic index *n* : the ratio multiplied by 100 of the maximum breadth of the head to its maximum length

ce·ram·ic \sə-'ram-ik\ *n* **1** *pl* : the art or process of making articles from clay by shaping and hardening by firing; *also* : the process of making any product (as earthenware, brick, tile, or glass) from a nonmetallic mineral by firing **2** : a product produced by ceramics — **ceramic** *adj*

ce·ram·ist \sə-'ram·əst\ *or* **ce·ram·i·cist** \-'ram-ə-səst\ *n* : one that engages in ceramics

ce·re·al \'sir-ē-əl\ *n* **1** : a grass (as wheat) yielding grain suitable for food; *also* : its grain **2** : cereal grain prepared for use as a breakfast food

cer·e·bel·lum \,ser-ə-'bel-əm\ *n* : a part of the brain that projects over the medulla and is concerned esp. with coordination of muscular action and with bodily equilibrium — **cer·e·bel·lar** *adj*

ce·re·bral palsy \sə-,rē-brəl-, ,ser-ə-\ *n* : a disorder caused by brain damage usu. before or during birth and marked esp. by defective muscle control

cer·e·brate \'ser-ə-,brāt\ *vb* : THINK — **cer·e·bra·tion** \,ser-ə-'brā-shən\ *n*

ce·re·brum \sə-'rē-brəm 'ser-ə-\ *n* : the enlarged front and upper part of the brain that contains the higher nervous centers — **ce·re·bral** *adj*

cere·cloth \'sir-,klòth\ *n* : cloth treated with melted wax or gummy matter and formerly used esp. for wrapping a dead body

cere·ment \'ser-ə-mənt, 'sìr-mənt\ *n* : a shroud for the dead

1cer·e·mo·ni·al \,ser-ə-'mō-nē-əl\ *adj* : of, relating to, or forming a ceremony — **cer·e·mo·ni·al·ly** *adv* — **cer·e·mo·ni·al·ness** *n*

2ceremonial *n* : a ceremonial act or system : RITUAL, FORM

cer·e·mo·ni·ous \,ser-ə-'mō-nē-əs\ *adj* **1** : CEREMONIAL **2** : devoted to forms and ceremony **3** : according to formal usage or procedure **4** : marked by ceremony — **cer·e·mo·ni·ous·ly** *adv* — **cer·e·mo·ni·ous·ness** *n*

cer·e·mo·ny \'ser-ə-,mō-nē\ *n* **1** : a formal act or series of acts prescribed by law, ritual, or convention **2** : a conventional act of politeness **3** : a mere outward form **4** : FORMALITY

ce·rise \sə-'rēs\ *n* : a moderate red

ce·ri·um \'sir-ē-əm\ *n* : a malleable metallic chemical element

cer·tain \'sərt-°n\ *adj* **1** : FIXED, SETTLED **2** : proved to be true **3** : of a specific but unspecified character ⟨~ people in authority⟩ **4** : DEPENDABLE, RELIABLE **5** : INDISPUTABLE, UNDENIABLE **6** : assured in mind or action — **cer·tain·ly** *adv*

cer·tain·ty \-tē\ *n* **1** : something that is certain **2** : the quality or state of being certain — **for a certainty** : beyond doubt — **certainly**

cer·tif·i·cate \sər-'tif-i-kət\ *n* **1** : a document testifying to the truth of a fact **2** : a document testifying that one has fulfilled certain requirements (as of a course or school) **3** : a document evidencing ownership or debt

cer·ti·fi·ca·tion \,sərt-ə-fə-'kā-shən\ *n* **1** : the act of certifying : the state of

ə abut; ᵊ kitten; ər further; a back; ā bake; ä cot, cart; aù out, ch chin; e less; ē easy; g gift; i trip; ī life; j joke; ŋ sing; ō flow; ò flaw, òi coin; th thin; th̶ this; ü loot; ù foot; y yet; yü few; yù furious; zh vision

being certified **2 :** a certified statement
certified check \ *n* **:** a check certified to be good by the bank upon which it is drawn

cer·ti·fy \'sərt-ə-ˌfī\ *vb* **1 :** VERIFY, CONFIRM **2 :** to endorse officially **3 :** to guarantee (a bank check) as good by a statement to that effect stamped on its face **4 :** to attest officially to the insanity of **syn** attest, witness, accredit, approve, sanction — **cer·ti·fi·er** *n*

cer·ti·tude \'sərt-ə-ˌt(y)üd\ *n* **:** the state of being or feeling certain **:** CERTAINTY

ce·ru·le·an \sə-'rü-lē-ən\ *adj* **:** AZURE

ce·sar·e·an or **ce·sar·i·an** \si-'zar-ē-ən\ *n* **:** surgical incision of the walls of the abdomen and uterus for delivery of offspring — **cesarean** or **cesarian** *adj*

ce·si·um \'sē-zē-əm\ *n* **:** a silver-white soft ductile chemical element

ces·sa·tion \se-'sā-shən\ *n* **:** a temporary or final ceasing (as of action) **:** STOP

ces·sion \'sesh-ən\ *n* **:** a yielding (as of property or rights) to another

cess·pool \'ses-ˌpül\ *n* **:** an underground pit or tank for receiving household sewage

Cha·blis \'shab-ˌlē\ *n* **:** a dry white table wine

cha–cha \'chä-ˌchä\ *n* **:** a fast rhythmic ballroom dance originating in Latin America

chafe \'chāf\ *vb* **1 :** IRRITATE, VEX **2 :** FRET **3 :** to warm by rubbing esp. with the hands **4 :** to rub so as to wear away; *also* **:** to make sore by rubbing

cha·fer \'chā-fər\ *n* **:** any of various large beetles

1chaff \'chaf\ *n* **1 :** debris (as husks) separated from grain in threshing **2 :** something light and worthless — **chaffy** *adj*

2chaff *n* **:** light jesting talk **:** BANTER

3chaff *vb* **:** to tease in a good-natured manner

chaf·fer \'chaf-ər\ *vb* **:** BARGAIN, HAGGLE — **chaf·fer·er** *n*

chaf·finch \'chaf-ˌinch\ *n* **:** a finch with a cheerful song often kept as a cage bird

chaf·ing dish \'chā-fiŋ-\ *n* **:** a utensil for cooking food at the table

1cha·grin \shə-'grin\ *n* **:** mental uneasiness or annoyance caused by failure, disappointment, or humiliation

2chagrin *vb* **cha·grined; cha·grin·ing :** to cause to feel chagrin

1chain \'chān\ *n* **1 :** a flexible series of connected links **2** *pl* **:** BONDS, FETTERS; *also* **:** BONDAGE **3 :** a series of things linked together **4 :** a chainlike measuring instrument 66 feet long; *also* **:** a unit of measurement equal to 66 feet **syn** train, string, set, sequence, succession

2chain *vb* **:** to fasten, bind, or connect with a chain; *also* **:** FETTER

chain gang *n* **:** a gang of convicts chained together

chain mail *n* **:** flexible armor of interlocking metal rings

chain reaction *n* **1 :** a series of events in which each event initiates the succeeding one **2 :** a chemical or nuclear reaction giving products that cause further reactions of the same kind

chain store *n* **:** one of numerous usu. retail stores under the same ownership

and general management and selling the same lines of goods

1chair \'cheər\ *n* **1 :** a seat with four legs and a back for one person **2 :** an official seat; *also* **:** an office or position of authority or dignity **3 :** CHAIRMAN **4 :** a sedan chair **5 :** ELECTRIC CHAIR

2chair *vb* **:** to act as chairman of

chair·man \-mən\ *n* **1 :** the presiding officer of a meeting or of a committee **2 :** a carrier of a sedan chair — **chair·man·ship** *n*

chaise \'shāz\ *n* **1 :** a 2-wheeled carriage with a folding top **2 :** a light carriage or pleasure cart

chaise longue \'shāz-'lôŋ\ *or* **chaise lounge** \-'laúnj\ *n* **:** a long couchlike chair

chal·ced·o·ny \kal-'sed-ᵊn-ē\ *n* **:** a translucent pale blue or gray quartz

cha·let \sha-'lā\ *n* **1 :** a herdsman's cabin in the Swiss mountains **2 :** a building in the style of a Swiss cottage with a wide roof overhang and balconies

chal·ice \'chal-əs\ *n* **:** a drinking cup; *esp* **:** the eucharistic cup

1chalk \'chók\ *n* **1 :** a soft limestone **2 :** chalk or chalky material used as a crayon — **chalky** *adj*

2chalk *vb* **1 :** to rub or mark with chalk **2 :** to record (an account) with or as if with chalk

chalk·board \'chók-ˌbōrd\ *n* **:** BLACKBOARD

1chal·lenge \'chal-ənj\ *vb* **1 :** to halt and demand the countersign of **2 :** to take exception to **:** DISPUTE **3 :** to issue an invitation to compete against one esp. in single combat **:** DARE, DEFY — **chal·leng·er** *n*

2challenge *n* **1 :** a calling into question **:** PROTEST **2 :** an exception taken to a juror **3 :** a sentry's command to halt and prove identity **4 :** a summons to a duel **5 :** an invitation to compete in a sport

chal·lis \'shal-ē\ *also* **chal·lie** *n* **:** a lightweight clothing fabric of wool, cotton, or synthetic yarns

cham \'kam\ *var of* KHAN

cham·ber \'chām-bər\ *n* **1 :** ROOM; *esp* **:** BEDROOM **2 :** an enclosed space or compartment **3 :** a hall for meetings of a legislative body **4** *pl, chiefly Brit* **:** a set of rooms arranged for business or personal use **5 :** a judge's consultation room — usu. used in pl. **6 :** a legislative or judicial body; *also* **:** a council for a business purpose **7 :** a compartment in the cartridge cylinder of a revolver — **cham·bered** *adj*

cham·ber·lain \'chām-bər-lən\ *n* **1 :** a high court dignitary (as the chief household officer of a king) **2 :** a treasurer or receiver of public money (as for a city)

cham·ber·maid \-ˌmād\ *n* **:** a maid who takes care of bedrooms

chamber music *n* **:** music intended for performance by a few musicians before a small audience

cham·bray \'sham-ˌbrā\ *n* **:** a lightweight clothing fabric of white and colored threads

cha·me·leon \kə-'mēl-yən\ *n* **:** a small lizard whose skin changes color esp. according to the surroundings

cham·ois \'sham-ē\ *n, pl* **cham·ois** \-ē(z)\ **1 :** a small goatlike antelope of Europe and the Caucasus **2** *also*

cham·my : a soft leather made esp. from the skin of the sheep or goat

cham·o·mile \'kam-ə-ˌmīl\ n : any of a genus of strong-scented herbs related to the daisy whose flower heads yield a bitter medicinal substance

¹**champ** \'champ, 'chämp\ vb 1 : to chew noisily 2 : to show impatience or delay or restraint

²**champ** \'champ\ n : CHAMPION

cham·pagne \sham-'pān\ n : a sparkling white wine

cham·paign \-'pān\ n : a stretch of flat open country

¹**cham·pi·on** \'cham-pē-ən\ n 1 : a militant advocate or defender 2 : one that wins first prize or place in a contest 3 : one that is acknowledged to be better than all others

²**champion** vb : to protect or fight for as a champion syn back, advocate, uphold, support

cham·pi·on·ship \-ˌship\ n 1 : the position or title of a champion 2 : a defending as a champion 3 : a contest held to determine a champion

¹**chance** \'chans\ n 1 : something that happens without apparent cause 2 : the unpredictable element in existence : LUCK, FORTUNE 3 : OPPORTUNITY 4 : the likelihood of a particular outcome in an uncertain situation : PROBABILITY 5 : RISK 6 : a ticket in a raffle — chance adj

²**chance** vb 1 : to take place by chance : HAPPEN 2 : to come by chance — used with upon 3 : to leave to chance 4 : to accept the risk of

chan·cel \'chan-səl\ n : the part of a church including the altar and choir

chan·cel·lery or **chan·cel·lory** \'chans-(ə-)lə-rē\ n 1 : the position or office of a chancellor 2 : the building or room housing a chancellor's office 3 : the office or staff of an embassy or consulate

chan·cel·lor \'chans-(ə-)lər\ n 1 : a high state official in various countries 2 : a judge in the equity court in various states of the U.S. 3 : the head of various universities 4 : the chief minister of state in some European countries — **chan·cel·lor·ship** \-ˌship\ n

chan·cery \'chans-(ə-)rē\ n 1 : any of various courts of equity in the U.S. and Britain 2 : a record office for public or diplomatic archives 3 : a chancellor's court or office 4 : the office of an embassy 5 : a wrestling hold that imprisons the head

chan·cre \'shaŋ-kər\ n : a primary sore or ulcer at the site of entry of an infective agent (as of syphilis)

chancy \'chan-sē\ adj 1 Scot : AUSPICIOUS 2 : RISKY

chan·de·lier \ˌshan-də-'liər\ n : a branched lighting fixture hanging from a ceiling

chan·dler \'chan-dlər\ n : a dealer in provisions and supplies of a specified kind ⟨ship's ∼⟩ — **chan·dlery** n

¹**change** \'chānj\ vb 1 : to make or become different : ALTER 2 : to replace with another 3 : EXCHANGE 4 : to give or receive an equivalent sum in notes or coins of usu. smaller denominations or of another currency 5 : to

put fresh clothes or covering on ⟨∼ a bed⟩ 6 : to put on different clothes — **change·able** adj — **chang·er** n

²**change** n 1 : the act, process, or result of changing : ALTERATION, TRANSFORMATION, SUBSTITUTION 2 : a fresh set of clothes to replace those being worn 3 : surplus money returned to a person who offers payment exceeding the sum due 4 : money given in exchange for other money of higher denomination 5 : coins esp. of small denominations — **change·ful** adj — **change·less** adj

change·ling \'chānj-liŋ\ n : a child secretly exchanged for another in infancy

change of life : MENOPAUSE

change ringing n : the art or practice of ringing a set of tuned bells in continually varying order

¹**chan·nel** \'chan-ᵊl\ n 1 : the bed of a stream 2 : the deeper part of a waterway 3 : DUCT, TUBE; also : PASSAGEWAY 4 : a long narrow depression (as a groove or furrow) 5 : STRAIT 6 : a means of passage or transmission 7 : a range of frequencies of sufficient width for a single radio or television transmission

²**channel** vb -neled or -nelled; -nel·ing or -nel·ling 1 : to make a channel in 2 : to direct into or through a channel

chan·nel·ize \'chan-ᵊl-ˌīz\ vb : CHANNEL — **chan·nel·iza·tion** \ˌchan-ᵊl-ə-'zā-shən\ n

chan·son \shäⁿ-sōⁿ\ n : SONG; esp : a cabaret song

¹**chant** \'chant\ vb 1 : SING; esp : to sing a chant 2 : to sing or speak in the manner of a chant 3 : to celebrate or praise in song — **chant·er** n

²**chant** n 1 : SONG : a repetitive melody in which several words are sung to one tone; esp : a liturgical melody 2 : a manner of singing or speaking in musical monotones

chan·teuse \shäⁿ-'tə(r)z, shan-'tüz\ n : a female concert or nightclub singer

chan·tey or **chan·ty** \'shant-ē, 'chant-\ n : a song sung by sailors in rhythm with their work

chan·ti·cleer \ˌchant-ə-'kliər\ n : COCK 1

chan·try \'chan-trē\ n 1 : an endowment for the chanting of masses 2 : a chapel endowed by a chantry

Cha·nu·kah \'kän-ə-kə, 'hän-\ var of HANUKKAH

cha·os \'kā-ˌäs\ n often cap : the confused unorganized state existing before the creation of distinct forms 2 : complete disorder syn confusion, jumble, snarl, muddle — **cha·ot·ic** \kā-'ät-ik\ adj — **cha·ot·i·cal·ly** adv

¹**chap** \'chap\ n : FELLOW

²**chap** vb chapped; chap·ping : to dry and crack open usu. from wind and cold ⟨chapped lips⟩

³**chap** \'chap, 'chap\ n : a jaw with its fleshy covering — usu. used in pl.

chap·book \'chap-ˌbúk\ n : a small book containing ballads, tales, or tracts

chap·el \'chap-əl\ n 1 : a private or subordinate place of worship 2 : an assembly at an educational institution usu. including devotional exercises 3 : a place of worship used by a Christian group other than the established church

¹chap·er·on or **chap·er·one** \'shap-ə-,rōn\ n 1 : a matron who accompanies young unmarried women in public for propriety 2 : an older person who accompanies young people at a social gathering to ensure proper behavior

²chaperon or **chaperone** vb \: ESCORT, GUIDE 2 : to act as a chaperon to or for — **chap·er·on·age** n

chap·fall·en \'chap-,fȯ-lən, 'chāp-\ adj 1 : having the lower jaw hanging loosely 2 : DEJECTED, DEPRESSED

chap·lain \'chap-lən\ n 1 : a clergyman officially attached to a special group (as the army) 2 : a person chosen to conduct religious exercises (as for a club) — **chap·lain·cy** n

chap·let \'chap-lət\ n 1 : a wreath for the head 2 : a string of beads : NECKLACE — **chap·let·ed** adj

chap·man \'chap-mən\ n, Brit : an itinerant dealer : PEDDLER

chaps \'shaps\ n pl : leather leggings resembling trousers without a seat that are worn esp. by western ranch hands

chap·ter \'chap-tər\ n 1 : a main division of a book 2 : a body of canons (as of a cathedral) 3 : a local branch of a society or fraternity

¹char \'chär\ n : any of a genus of small-scaled trouts (as the brook trout of eastern No. America)

²char vb charred; char·ring 1 : to burn to charcoal 2 : SCORCH 3 : to burn to a cinder

³char vb charred; char·ring : to work as a charwoman

char·a·banc \'shar-ə-,baŋ\ n Brit : a sight-seeing motor coach

char·ac·ter \'kar-ik-tər\ n 1 : a graphic symbol (as a letter) used in writing or printing 2 : a distinguishing feature : ATTRIBUTE 3 : the complex of mental and ethical traits marking a person or a group 4 : a person marked by conspicuous often peculiar traits 5 : one of the persons in a novel or play 6 : REPUTATION 7 : moral excellence

¹char·ac·ter·is·tic \,kar-ik-tə-'ris-tik\ adj : serving to mark individual character syn individual, peculiar, distinctive — **char·ac·ter·is·ti·cal·ly** adv

²characteristic n : a distinguishing trait, quality, or property

char·ac·ter·ize \'kar-ik-tə-,rīz\ vb 1 : to describe the character or quality of 2 : to be a quality or feature of : be characteristic of — **char·ac·ter·i·za·tion** \,kar-ik-tə-rə-'zā-shən\ n

char·ac·tery \'kar-ik-t(ə-)rē\ n : written letters or symbols

cha·rades \shə-'rādz\ n sing or pl : a guessing game in which contestants act out the syllables of a word to be guessed

char·coal \'chär-,kōl\ n 1 : a dark porous carbon made by partly burning wood in such a way that little air gets to it during the burning 2 : a piece of fine charcoal used in drawing; also : a drawing made with charcoal

chard \'chärd\ n : a beet lacking the enlarged root but having leaves and stalks often cooked as a vegetable

¹charge \'chärj\ vb 1 : to load or fill to capacity; also : IMPREGNATE 2 : to give an electric charge to; also : to restore the activity of (a storage battery) by means of an electric current 3 : to impose a task or responsibility on 4 : COMMAND, ORDER 5 : ACCUSE 6 : to rush against : rush forward in assault 7 : to make liable for payment; also : to record a debt or liability against 8 : to fix as a price — **chargeable** adj

²charge n 1 : a quantity (as of fuel or ammunition) required to fill something to capacity 2 : a store or accumulation of force 3 : an excess or deficiency of electrons in a body 4 slang : THRILL, KICK 5 : a task or duty imposed 6 : one given into another's care 7 : CARE, RESPONSIBILITY 8 : ACCUSATION, INDICTMENT 9 : instructions from a judge to a jury 10 : COST, EXPENSE, PRICE; also : a debit to an account 11 : ATTACK, ASSAULT

char·gé d'af·faires \shär-,zhäd-ə-'faer\ n, pl **char·gés d'af·faires** \-,zhā(z)d-ə-\ : a diplomat who substitutes for an absent ambassador or minister

¹charg·er \'chär-jər\ n : a large platter

²charg·er n 1 : a device or a workman that charges something 2 : WAR-HORSE

char·i·ot \'char-ē-ət\ n : a 2-wheeled vehicle of ancient times used in war and in races and processions — **char·i·o·teer** \,char-ē-ə-'tiər\ n

char·is·mat·ic \,kar-əz-'mat-ik\ adj : having or showing a personal quality of leadership that arouses special popular loyalty or enthusiasm

char·i·ta·ble \'char-ət-ə-bəl\ adj 1 : liberal in giving to the poor 2 : merciful or lenient in judging others syn benevolent, philanthropic — **char·i·ta·ble·ness** n — **char·i·ta·bly** adv

char·i·ty \'char-ət-ē\ n [OF charité, fr. LL caritat-, caritas, fr. L, affection, fr. carus dear] 1 : Christian love for God and men 2 : an act or feeling of generosity 3 : the giving of aid to the poor; also : ALMS 4 : an institution engaged in relief of the poor 5 : leniency in judging others syn mercy, clemency, philanthropy

char·la·tan \'shär-lə-tən\ n : a person pretending to knowledge or ability that he lacks : QUACK

char·ley horse \'chär-lē-,hȯrs\ n : pain and stiffness from muscular strain in an arm or leg

¹charm \'chärm\ n 1 : an act or expression believed to have magic power 2 : something worn about the person to ward off evil or bring good fortune : AMULET 3 : a trait that fascinates or allures 4 : physical grace or attraction 5 : a small ornament worn on a bracelet or chain

²charm vb 1 : to affect by or as if by a magic spell 2 : FASCINATE, ENCHANT 3 : to protect by or as if by charms (a ~ed life) syn allure, captivate, bewitch, attract

charm·er n : one that pleases or fascinates; esp : an attractive woman

charm·ing adj : greatly pleasing to the mind or senses : DELIGHTFUL — **charm·ing·ly** adv

char·nel \'chärn-ᵊl\ n : a building or chamber in which bodies or bones are deposited — **charnel** adj

¹chart \'chärt\ n 1 : MAP 2 : a sheet giving information in the form of a table, list, or diagram; also : GRAPH 2 : PLAN

²chart vb 1 : to make a chart of 2 : PLAN

¹char·ter \'chärt-ər\ n 1 : an official

document granting rights or privileges (as to a colony, town, or college) from a sovereign or a governing body 2 : CONSTITUTION 3 : an instrument from a society creating a branch 4 : a mercantile lease of a ship

²**charter** vb 1 : to establish, enable, or convey by charter 2 Brit : CERTIFY ⟨~ed engineer⟩ 3 : to hire, rent, or lease for temporary use ⟨~ed bus⟩ — **char·ter·er** n

char·treuse \shär-ˈtrüz, -ˈtrüs\ n 1 : a usu. green or yellow liqueur 2 : a variable color averaging a brilliant yellow green

char·wom·an \ˈchär-ˌwu̇m-ən\ n : a woman who does cleaning (as of houses and offices) by the hour or day

chary \ˈcha(ə)r-ē\ adj 1 : CAUTIOUS, CIRCUMSPECT 2 : SPARING — **char·i·ly** adv — **char·i·ness** n

¹**chase** \ˈchās\ vb 1 : to follow rapidly : PURSUE 2 : HUNT 3 : to seek out ⟨salesmen chasing orders⟩ 4 : to cause to depart or flee : drive away 5 : RUSH, HASTEN ⟨~ off to school⟩

²**chase** n 1 : PURSUIT; also : HUNTING 2 : QUARRY 3 : a tract of unenclosed land used as a game preserve

³**chase** vb : to decorate (a metal surface) by embossing or engraving

⁴**chase** n : FURROW, GROOVE

chas·er \ˈchā-sər\ n 1 : one that chases 2 : a mild drink taken after hard liquor

chasm \ˈkaz-əm\ n : a narrow steep-walled valley : GORGE

chas·sis \ˈshas-ē, ˈchas-\ n : a supporting framework (as for the body of an automobile or the parts of a radio set)

chaste \ˈchāst\ adj 1 : innocent of unlawful sexual intercourse : VIRTUOUS, PURE 2 : CELIBATE 3 : pure in thought : MODEST 4 : severe or simple in design — **chaste·ly** adv — **chaste·ness** n

chas·ten \ˈchās-ⁿn\ vb : to correct through punishment or suffering : DISCIPLINE; also : PURIFY — **chas·ten·er** n

chas·tise \chas-ˈtīz\ vb : to punish esp. bodily (as by whipping) — **chas·tise·ment** \-mənt, ˈchas-təz-\ n

chas·ti·ty \ˈchas-tət-ē\ n : the quality or state of being chaste; esp : sexual purity

chas·u·ble \ˈchaz-ə-bəl, ˈchas-\ n : the outer vestment of the celebrant at the Eucharist

chat \ˈchat\ n : light familiar informal talk — **chat** vb

châ·teau \sha-ˈtō\ n, pl **châ·teaus** \-ˈtōz\ or **châ·teaux** \-ˈtō(z)\ [F, fr. L castellum castle, dim. of castra camp] 1 : a feudal castle in France 2 : a large country house 3 : a French vineyard estate

chat·e·laine \ˈshat-ⁿl-ˌān\ n 1 : the mistress of a chateau 2 : a clasp or hook worn by women for holding a watch, purse, or bunch of keys

chat·tel \ˈchat-ⁿl\ n 1 : an item of tangible property other than real estate 2 : SLAVE, BONDMAN

chat·ter \ˈchat-ər\ vb 1 : to utter speechlike but meaningless sounds 2 : to talk idly, incessantly, or fast : JABBER, BABBLE 3 : to click repeatedly or uncontrollably ⟨~ing teeth⟩ —

chatter n — **chat·ter·er** n

chat·ter·box \ˈchat-ər-ˌbäks\ n : one that talks incessantly

chat·ty \ˈchat-ē\ adj : TALKATIVE — **chat·ti·ly** adv — **chat·ti·ness** n

¹**chauf·feur** \ˈshō-fər, shō-ˈfər\ n : a person employed to drive an automobile

²**chauffeur** vb 1 : to do the work of a chauffeur 2 : to transport in the manner of a chauffeur

chaunt \ˈchȯnt, ˈchänt\ archaic var of CHANT

chau·vin·ism \ˈshō-və-ˌniz-əm\ n : excessive or blind patriotism — **chau·vin·ist** n — **chau·vin·is·tic** \ˌshō-və-ˈnis-tik\ adj — **chau·vin·is·ti·cal·ly** adv

cheap \ˈchēp\ adj 1 : costing little money : INEXPENSIVE 2 : costing little effort to obtain 3 : worth little 4 : SHODDY, TAWDRY 5 : worthy of scorn — **cheap** adv — **cheap·ly** adv — **cheap·ness** n

cheap·en \ˈchē-pən\ vb 1 : to make or become cheap or cheaper in price or value 2 : to make tawdry or vulgar

cheap·skate \ˈchēp-ˌskāt\ n : a niggardly person; esp : one seeking to avoid his share of costs

¹**cheat** \ˈchēt\ n 1 : the act of deceiving : FRAUD, DECEPTION 2 : a means of cheating : a deceitful trick 3 : one that cheats : a dishonest person — **cheat·er** n

²**cheat** vb 1 : to deprive of something through fraud or deceit 2 : to practice fraud or trickery 3 : to violate rules (as of a game) dishonestly

¹**check** \ˈchek\ n 1 : a sudden stoppage of progress 2 : a sudden pause or break 3 : something that stops or restrains : CURB, RESTRAINT 4 : a standard for testing or evaluation 5 : EXAMINATION, INSPECTION, INVESTIGATION 6 : the act of testing or verifying 7 : a written order to a bank to pay money 8 : a ticket or token showing ownership or identity 9 : a slip indicating an amount due 10 : a pattern in squares; also : a fabric in such a pattern 11 : a mark typically √ placed beside an item to show that it has been noted 12 : CRACK, SPLIT

²**check** vb 1 : to slow down or stop : BRAKE 2 : to restrain the action or force of : CURB 3 : to compare with a source, original, or authority : VERIFY 4 : to correspond point by point : TALLY 5 : to inspect or test for satisfactory condition 6 : to mark with a check as examined 7 : to leave or accept for safekeeping in a checkroom 8 : to consign for shipment for one holding a passenger ticket 9 : to mark into squares 10 : CRACK, SPLIT

check·book \-ˌbu̇k\ n : a book containing blank checks to be drawn on a bank

¹**check·er** \ˈchek-ər\ n : a piece in the game of checkers

²**checker** vb 1 : to variegate with different colors or shades 2 : to mark into squares

³**checker** n : one that checks

check·ers \ˈchek-ərz\ n : a game for two played on a board (**check·er·board** \-ər-ˌbȯrd\) of 64 squares of alternate colors with each player having 12 pieces

check in vb : to report one's presence (as at a hotel)

---

check·list \'chek-,list\ *n* **:** a list of items that may easily be referred to

check·mate \'chek-,māt\ *vb* **1 :** to thwart completely **:** DEFEAT, FRUSTRATE **2 :** to attack (an opponent's king) in chess so that escape is impossible — **checkmate** *n*

check·off \-,of\ *n* **:** the deduction of union dues from a worker's paycheck by the employer

check out *vb* **:** to settle one's account (as at a hotel) and leave

check·point \'chek-,point\ *n* **:** a point at which vehicular traffic is halted for inspection or clearance

check·room \'chek-,rüm, -,rùm\ *n* **:** a room for temporary safekeeping of baggage, parcels, or clothing

check·up \-,əp\ *n* **:** EXAMINATION; *esp* **:** a general physical examination

ched·dar \'ched-ər\ *n, often cap* **:** a hard-pressed standard factory cheese of smooth texture

cheek \'chēk\ *n* **1 :** the fleshy side part of the face **2 :** IMPUDENCE, BOLDNESS, AUDACITY

cheek·bone \-'bōn\ *n* **:** the bone or bony projection below the eye

cheeky \'chē-kē\ *adj* **:** IMPUDENT, SAUCY — **cheek·i·ly** *adv* — **cheek·i·ness** *n*

cheep \'chēp\ *vb* **:** to utter faint shrill sounds **:** PEEP — **cheep** *n*

1cheer \'chior\ *n* **1 :** state of mind or heart **:** SPIRIT **2 :** ANIMATION, GAIETY **3 :** hospitable entertainment **:** WELCOME **4 :** food and drink for a feast **5 :** something that gladdens **6 :** a shout of applause or encouragement

2cheer *vb* **1 :** to give hope or courage to **:** COMFORT **2 :** to make glad **3 :** to urge on esp. by shouts **4 :** to applaud with shouts **5 :** to grow or be cheerful —usu. used with *up* — **cheer·er** *n*

cheer·ful \'chior-fəl\ *adj* **1 :** having or showing good spirits **2 :** conducive to good spirits **:** pleasant and bright — **cheer·ful·ly** *adv* — **cheer·ful·ness** *n*

cheer·lead·er \-,lēd-ər\ *n* **:** a person who directs organized cheering esp. at a sports event

cheer·less \-ləs\ *adj* **:** BLEAK, DISPIRITING — **cheer·less·ly** *adv* — **cheer·less·ness** *n*

cheery \'chi(ə)r-ē\ *adj* **:** LIVELY, BRIGHT, GAY — **cheer·i·ly** *adv* — **cheer·i·ness** *n*

cheese \'chēz\ *n* **:** the curd of milk usu. pressed into cakes and cured for use as food — **cheesy** *adj*

cheese·burg·er \-,bər-gər\ *n* **:** a hamburger with a slice of toasted cheese

cheese·cloth \-,klòth\ *n* **:** a lightweight coarse cotton gauze

cheese·par·ing \-,pa(ə)r-iŋ\ *n* **:** miserly or petty economizing — **cheeseparing** *adj*

chef \'shef\ *n* [F, head, chief, fr. L *caput* head] **1 :** a male head cook **2 :** COOK

chef d'oeu·vre \shā-dœvr*\ *n, pl* **chefs d'oeuvre** *same*\ **:** a masterpiece esp. in art or literature

che·la \'kē-lə\ *n* **:** a large pincerlike organ on a limb of a crustacean — **che·late** \-,lāt\ *adj*

1chem·i·cal \'kem-i-kəl\ *adj* **1 :** of or relating to chemistry **2 :** acting or operated or produced by chemicals — **chem·i·cal·ly** *adv*

2chemical *n* **:** a substance obtained by a process involving the use of chemistry;

also **:** a substance used for producing a chemical effect

che·mise \shə-'mēz\ *n* **1 :** a woman's one-piece undergarment **2 :** a loose straight-hanging dress

chem·ist \'kem-əst\ *n* **1 :** one trained or engaged in chemistry **2** *Brit* **:** PHARMACIST

chem·is·try \-ə-strē\ *n* **1 :** a science that deals with the composition, structure, and properties of substances and of the changes they undergo **2 :** chemical composition or properties (the ~ of gasoline)

chemo·ther·a·py \,kem-ō-'ther-ə-pē, ,kē-mō-\ *n* **:** the use of chemicals in the treatment or control of disease

chem·ur·gy \'kem-(,)ər-jē\ *n* **:** chemistry that deals with industrial utilization of organic raw materials esp. from farm products — **chem·ur·gic** \ke-'mər-jik\ *adj*

che·nille \shə-'nēl\ *n* **:** a wool, cotton, silk, or rayon yarn with protruding pile; *also* **:** a fabric of such yarn

cheque \'chek\ *chiefly Brit var of* **1CHECK 7**

cher·ish \'cher-ish\ *vb* **1 :** to hold dear **:** treat with care and affection **2 :** to keep deeply in mind (as a memory or purpose)

che·root \shə-'rüt\ *n* **:** a cigar cut square at both ends

cher·ry \'cher-ē\ *n* **1 :** the small fleshy fruit of a tree related to the peaches and plums **2 :** a variable color averaging a moderate red

chert \'chərt, 'chat\ *n* **:** a rock resembling flint and consisting essentially of fine crystalline quartz or fibrous chalcedony

cher·ub \'cher-əb\ *n, pl* **cherubs** *or* **cher·u·bim** \'cher-(y)ə-,bim\ **1 :** an angel of the second highest rank **2 :** a chubby rosy child

chess \'ches\ *n* **:** a game for two played on a board of 64 squares of alternate colors with each player having 16 pieces (**chess·men** \-,men, -mən\)

chest \'chest\ *n* **1 :** a box, case, or boxlike receptacle for storage or shipping **2 :** the part of the body enclosed by the ribs and breastbone

ches·ter·field \'ches-tər-,fēld\ *n* **:** an overcoat with a velvet collar

chest·nut \'ches-(,)nət\ *n* **1 :** the edible nut of a tree related to the beech and oak; *also* **:** this tree **2 :** a grayish brown **3 :** an old joke or story

che·val glass \shə-'val-\ *n* **:** a full-length mirror that may be tilted in a frame

chev·a·lier \,shev-ə-'liər\ *n* **:** a member of one of various orders of knighthood or of merit

chev·i·ot \'shev-ē-ət\ *n* **1 :** a twilled fabric with a rough nap used for coats and suits **2 :** a sturdy soft-finished cotton fabric used for shirts

chev·ron \'shev-rən\ *n* **:** a sleeve badge of one or more bars or stripes worn to indicate rank or service (as in the armed forces)

1chew \'chü\ *vb* **:** to crush or grind with the teeth — **chew·able** *adj* — **chew·er** *n*

2chew *n* **1 :** an act of chewing **2 :** something that is chewed or is suitable for chewing

chewy *adj* **:** requiring chewing (~ candy)

Chi·an·ti \kē-'änt-ē\ *n* **:** a dry usu. red table wine

chiao \'tyaů\ *n, pl* **chiao** — see MONEY table

chiar·oscu·ro \kē-,är-ə-'sk(y)ůr-ō\ *n* **1 :** pictorial representation in terms of light and shade without regard to color **2 :** the arrangement or treatment of light and dark parts in a pictorial work of art

1chic \'shēk\ *n* : STYLISHNESS

2chic *adj* : cleverly stylish : SMART; *also* : currently fashionable

chi·ca·nery \shik-'ān-(ə-)rē\ *n* : TRICK-ERY, DECEPTION

chick \'chik\ *n* : a young chicken; *also* : a young bird

chick·a·dee \'chik-ə-(,)dē\ *n* : a small grayish American bird with a black cap

chick·en \'chik-ən\ *n* : a common domestic fowl esp. when young; *also* : its flesh used as food

chick·en-heart·ed \,chik-ən-'härt-əd\ *adj* : TIMID, COWARDLY

chick·weed \'chik-,wēd\ *n* : a low small-leaved weed related to the pinks that has seeds relished by birds

chic·o·ry \'chik-(ə-)rē\ *n* : an herb related to the thistles and used as a salad; *also* : its dried ground root used for flavoring or adulterating coffee

chide \'chīd\ *vb* **chid** \'chid\ *or* **chid·ed** \'chīd-əd\ **chid** *or* **chid·den** \'chid-ⁿn\ *or* **chid·ed; chid·ing** \'chīd-in\ : to voice disapproval to : speak out in rebuke or displeasure **syn** reproach, reprove, reprimand, admonish, scold, rebuke

1chief \'chēf\ *n* **1 :** the leader of a body or organization : HEAD **2 :** the principal or most valuable part

2chief *adj* **1 :** highest in rank **2 :** most eminent or important **syn** principal, main, leading — **chief·ly** *adv*

chief master sergeant *n* : a noncommissioned officer of the highest rank in the air force

chief petty officer *n* : an enlisted man in the navy ranking next below a senior chief petty officer

chief·tain \'chēf-tən\ *n* : a chief esp. of a band, tribe, or clan — **chief·tain·cy** *n* — **chief·tain·ship** *n*

chief warrant officer *n* : a warrant officer of senior rank

chif·fon \shif-'än\ *n* : a sheer fabric esp. of silk

chif·fo·nier \,shif-ə-'niơr\ *n* : a high narrow chest of drawers

chig·ger \'chig-ər\ *n* **1 :** a tropical flea that burrows under the skin **2 :** a blood-sucking larval mite that irritates the skin

chi·gnon \'shēn-,yän\ *n* : a knot of hair worn at the back of the head

chil·blain \'chil-,blān\ *n* : a sore or inflamed swelling (as on the feet or hands) caused by cold

child \'chīld\ *n, pl* **chil·dren** \'chil-drən\ **1 :** an unborn or recently born person **2 :** a young person between the periods of infancy and youth **3 :** one strongly influenced by another or by a place or state of affairs — **child·ish** \'chīl-dish\ *adj* — **child·ish·ly** *adv* — **child·ish·ness** *n* — **child·less** \'chīld-ləs\ *adj* — **child·less·ness** *n* — **child-like** *adj*

child·birth \'chīld-,bərth\ *n* : the act or process of giving birth to offspring

child·hood *n* : the state or time of being a child

1chill \'chil\ *vb* **1 :** to make or become cold or chilly **2 :** to make cool esp. without freezing **3 :** to harden the surface of (as metal) by sudden cooling — **chill·er** *n*

2chill *adj* **1 :** moderately cold **2 :** COLD, RAW **3 :** DISTANT, FORMAL (a ~ reception) **4 :** DEPRESSING, DISPIRITING

3chill *n* **1 :** a feeling of coldness attended with shivering **2 :** moderate coldness **3 :** a check to warmth of feeling

chilly *adj* **1 :** noticeably cold **2 :** unpleasantly affected by cold **3 :** lacking warmth of feeling — **chill·i·ness** *n*

1chime \'chīm\ *n* **1 :** a set of bells musically tuned **2 :** the sound of a set of bells — usu. used in pl. **3 :** a sound suggesting bells

2chime *vb* **1 :** to make bell-like sounds **2 :** to indicate (as the time of day) by chiming **3 :** to be or act in accord : be in harmony

chime in *vb* : to break into or join in a conversation

chi·me·ra *or* **chi·mae·ra** \kī-'mir-ə, kə-\ *n* **1 :** an imaginary monster made up of incongruous parts **2 :** a frightful or foolish fancy

chi·mer·i·cal \-'mer-i-kəl\ *adj* **1 :** FANTASTIC, IMAGINARY **2 :** inclined to fantastic schemes

chim·ney \'chim-nē\ *n* **1 :** a passage for smoke that is usu. made of bricks, stone, or metal and often rises above the roof of a building **2 :** a glass tube around a lamp flame

chimp \'chimp, 'shimp\ *n* : CHIMPANZEE

chim·pan·zee \,chim-,pan-'zē, ,shim-, -'pan-zē\ *n* : an African manlike ape

1chin \'chin\ *n* : the part of the face below the mouth including the prominence of the lower jaw

2chin *vb* **chinned; chin·ning :** to raise (oneself) while hanging by the hands until the chin is level with the support

chi·na \'chī-nə\ *n* : porcelain ware; *also* : domestic pottery in general

chinch bug \'chinch-\ *n* : a small black and white bug destructive to cereal grasses

chin·chil·la \chin-'chil-ə\ *n* **1 :** a small So. American rodent with soft pearly gray fur; *also* : its fur **2 :** a heavy long-napped woolen cloth

Chi·nese \chī-'nēz\ *n, pl* **Chinese 1 :** a native or inhabitant of China **2 :** any of a group of related languages of China — **Chinese** *adj*

Chinese wall *n* : a strong barrier; *esp* : a serious obstacle to understanding

1chink \'chiŋk\ *n* : a small crack or fissure

2chink *vb* : to fill the chinks of : stop up

3chink *n* : a slight sharp metallic sound

4chink *vb* : to make a slight sharp metallic sound

chi·no \'chē-nō\ *n* **1 :** a usu. khaki cotton twill **2 :** an article of clothing made of chino — usu. used in pl.

chintz \'chints\ *n* : a usu. glazed printed cotton cloth

chintzy *adj* **1 :** decorated with or as if with chintz **2 :** GAUDY, CHEAP

1chip \'chip\ *n* **1 :** a small usu. thin and

flat piece (as of wood) cut or broken off **2** : a thin crisp morsel of food **3** : a counter used in games (as poker) **4** *pl, slang* : MONEY **5** : a flaw left after a chip is removed

2chip *vb* **chipped; chip·ping 1** : to cut or break chips from **2** : to break off in small pieces at the edges **3** : to play a chip shot

chip in *vb* : CONTRIBUTE

chip·munk \'chip-,məŋk\ *n* : a small striped American ground-dwelling squirrel

chipped beef \'chip(t)-\ *n* : smoked dried beef sliced thin

1chip·per \'chip-ər\ *n* : one that chips

2chipper *adj* : LIVELY, CHEERFUL, SPRIGHTLY

chip shot *n* : a short usu. low shot to the green in golf

chi·rog·ra·phy \kī-'räg-rə-fē\ *n* : HANDWRITING, PENMANSHIP — **chi·rog·ra·pher** *n* — **chi·ro·graph·ic** \,kī-rə-'graf-ik\ *adj*

chi·rop·o·dy \kə-'räp-əd-ē, shə-\ *n* : professional care and treatment of the human foot — **chi·rop·o·dist** *n*

chi·ro·prac·tic \'kī-rə-,prak-tik\ *n* : a system of healing based esp. on manipulation of body structures — **chi·ro·prac·tor** \-tər\ *n*

chirp \'chərp\ *n* : a short sharp sound characteristic of a small bird or cricket — **chirp** *vb*

1chis·el \'chiz-əl\ *n* : a sharp-edged metal tool used in cutting away and shaping wood, stone, or metal

2chisel *vb* **-eled** *or* **-elled; -el·ing** *or* **-el·ling 1** : to work with or as if with a chisel **2** : to obtain by shrewd often unfair methods; *also* : CHEAT — **chis·el·er** *n*

1chit \'chit\ *n* **1** : CHILD **2** : a pert young woman

2chit *n* : a signed voucher for a small debt (as for food or drink)

chit-chat \'chit-,chat\ *n* : casual or trifling conversation

chit·ter·lings *or* **chit·lings** *or* **chit·lins** \'chit-lənz\ *n pl* : the intestines of hogs esp. prepared as food

chi·val·ric \shə-'val-rik\ *adj* : relating to chivalry : CHIVALROUS

chiv·al·rous \'shiv-əl-rəs\ *adj* **1** : of or relating to chivalry **2** : marked by honor, courtesy, and generosity **3** : marked by especial courtesy to women — **chiv·al·rous·ly** *adv* — **chiv·al·rous·ness** *n*

chiv·al·ry \-rē\ *n* **1** : a body of knights **2** : the system or practices of knighthood **3** : the spirit or character of the ideal knight

chive \'chīv\ *n* : an herb related to the onion that has leaves used for flavoring

chlo·ral \'klōr-əl\ *n* : a white crystalline compound used as a narcotic

chlor·dane \'klōr-,dān\ *n* : a viscous liquid insecticide

chlo·ride \'klōr-,īd\ *n* : a compound of chlorine with another element or a radical

chlo·ri·nate \'klōr-ə-,nāt\ *vb* : to treat or cause to combine with chlorine or a chlorine-containing compound esp. for purifying — **chlo·ri·na·tion** \,klōr-ə-'nā-shən\ *n*

chlo·rine \'klōr-,ēn\ *n* : a chemical element that is a heavy strong-smelling greenish yellow irritating gas used as a bleach, oxidizing agent, and disinfectant

1chlo·ro·form \'klōr-ə-,fòrm\ *n* : a colorless heavy fluid with etherlike odor used as a solvent and anesthetic

2chloroform *vb* : to treat with chloroform so as to produce anesthesia or death

chlo·ro·phyll \-,fil\ *n* : the green coloring matter of plants that functions in photosynthesis

chock \'chäk\ *n* : a wedge for steadying something or for blocking the movement of a wheel — **chock** *vb*

chock·a·block \-ə-,bläk\ *adj* : very full : CROWDED

chock-full \-'fùl\ *adj* : full to the limit

choc·o·late \'chäk-(ə-)lət, 'chòk-\ *n* [Sp. fr. Nahuatl *xocoatl*] **1** : processed ground and roasted cacao beans; *also* : a drink prepared from this **2** : a candy made of or with a coating of chocolate **3** : a dark brown color

1choice \'chòis\ *n* **1** : the act of choosing : SELECTION **2** : the power or opportunity of choosing : OPTION **3** : a person or thing selected **4** : the best part : CREAM **5** : a variety offered for selection

2choice *adj* **1** : worthy of being chosen **2** : selected with care : well chosen **3** : of high quality

choir \'kwī(ə)r\ *n* **1** : an organized company of singers esp. in a church **2** : the part of a church occupied by the singers

choir·boy \-,bòi\ *n* : a boy member of a church choir

choir·mas·ter \-,mas-tər\ *n* : the director of a choir (as in a church)

1choke \'chōk\ *vb* **1** : to hinder breathing (as by obstructing the windpipe) : STRANGLE **2** : to check the growth or action of **3** : CLOG, OBSTRUCT **4** : to decrease or shut off the air intake of the carburetor of a gasoline engine to make the fuel mixture richer

2choke *n* **1** : a choking or sound of choking **2** : a narrowing in size toward the muzzle in the bore of a gun **3** : a valve for choking a gasoline engine

chol·er \'käl-ər, 'kō-lər\ *n* : tendency toward anger : IRASCIBILITY

chol·era \'käl-ə-rə\ *n* : a disease marked by severe vomiting and dysentery; *esp* : an often fatal epidemic disease (Asiatic cholera) chiefly of southeastern Asia

chol·er·ic \'käl-ə-rik, kə-'ler-ik\ *adj* **1** : IRASCIBLE : hot-tempered **2** : ANGRY, IRATE

cho·les·ter·ol \kə-'les-tə-,ròl\ *n* : a physiologically important waxy substance in animal tissues

chon \'chän\ *n, pl* **chon** — see MONEY table

choose \'chüz\ *vb* **chose** \'chōz\ **cho·sen** \'chōz-ᵊn\ **choos·ing 1** : to select esp. after consideration **2** : to think proper : see fit : PLEASE **3** : DECIDE ⟨*chose* to go by train⟩ — **choos·er** *n*

choosy *or* **choos·ey** \'chü-zē\ *adj* : very particular in making choices

1chop \'chäp\ *vb* **chopped; chop·ping 1** : to cut by repeated blows **2** : to cut into small pieces : MINCE **3** : to strike (a ball) with a short quick downward stroke — **chop·per** *n*

2chop *n* **1** : a sharp downward blow or stroke **2** : a small cut of meat often including part of a rib **3** : a short abrupt motion (as of waves)

3chop *n* **1** : an official seal or stamp or its impression **2** : a mark on goods to indicate quality or kind; *also* **:** QUALITY, GRADE

chop·house \-ˌhau̇s\ *n* **:** RESTAURANT

chop·py \'chäp-ē\ *adj* **:** CHANGEABLE, VARIABLE ⟨a ~ wind⟩ — **chop·pi·ly** *adv* — **chop·pi·ness** *n*

choppy *adj* **1 :** rough with small waves **2 :** JERKY, DISCONNECTED — **chop·pi·ly** *adv* — **chop·pi·ness** *n*

chops \'chäps\ *n pl* **:** the fleshy covering of the jaws

chop·stick \'chäp-ˌstik\ *n* **:** one of a pair of sticks used in oriental countries for lifting food to the mouth

chop su·ey \chäp-'sü-ē\ *n* **:** a dish made typically of bean sprouts, bamboo shoots, celery, onions, mushrooms, and meat or fish and served with rice

cho·ral \'kōr-əl\ *adj* **:** of, relating to, or sung by a choir or chorus or in chorus — **cho·ral·ly** *adv*

cho·rale also **cho·ral** \kə-'ral\ *n* **1 :** a hymn or psalm sung in church; *also* **:** a hymn tune or a harmonization of a traditional melody **2 :** CHORUS, CHOIR

¹chord \'kȯrd\ *n* **:** a combination of tones that blend harmoniously when sounded together

²chord *n* **1 :** CORD, STRING; *esp* **:** a cord-like anatomical structure **2 :** a straight line joining two points on a curve

chore \'chōr\ *n* **1** *pl* **:** the daily light work of a household or farm **2 :** a routine task or job **3 :** a difficult or disagreeable task

cho·rea \kə-'rē-ə\ *n* **:** a nervous disorder marked by spasmodic uncontrolled movements

cho·re·og·ra·phy \ˌkōr-ē-'äg-rə-fē\ *n* **:** the art of dancing or of arranging dances and esp. ballets — **cho·re·og·ra·pher** *n*

cho·ris·ter \'kōr-ə-stər\ *n* **:** a singer in a choir

chor·tle \'chȯrt-ᵊl\ *vb* **:** to laugh or chuckle esp. in satisfaction or exultation — **chortle** *n*

¹cho·rus \'kōr-əs\ *n* **1 :** an organized company of singers **:** CHOIR **2 :** a group of dancers and usu. singers supporting the featured players in a revue **3 :** a part of a song repeated at intervals **4 :** a composition to be sung by a number of voices in concert; *also* **:** group singing **5 :** sounds uttered by a number of persons or animals together

²chorus *vb* **:** to sing or utter in chorus

cho·sen \'chōz-ᵊn\ *adj* **:** selected or marked for special favor or privilege ⟨the ~ few⟩

chow \'chau̇\ *n* **:** a thick-coated straight-legged muscular dog with a blue-black tongue and a short tail curled close to the back

chow-chow \-ˌchau̇\ *n* **:** chopped mixed pickles in mustard sauce

chow·der \'chau̇d-ər\ *n* **:** a thick soup made from seafood and usu. containing milk

chow mein \'chau̇-'mān\ *n* **1 :** fried noodles **2 :** a thick stew of shredded or diced meat, mushrooms, vegetables, and seasonings that is served with fried noodles

chrism \'kriz-əm\ *n* **:** consecrated oil used esp. in baptism and confirmation

Christ \'krīst\ *n* [L *Christus*, fr. Gk

Christos, lit., anointed, trans. of Heb *māshīaḥ*] **:** Jesus esp. in his character as the Messiah

chris·ten \'kris-ᵊn\ *vb* **1 :** BAPTIZE **2 :** to name at baptism **3 :** to name or dedicate (as a ship) by a ceremony suggestive of baptism — **chris·ten·ing** *n*

Chris·ten·dom \'kris-ᵊn-dəm\ *n* **1 :** the entire body of Christians **2 :** the part of the world in which Christianity prevails

¹Chris·tian \'kris-chən\ *n* **1 :** an adherent of Christianity **2 :** a member of one of several Protestant religious bodies dedicated to the restoration of a united New Testament Christianity

²Christian *adj* **1 :** of, relating to, or professing a belief in Christianity **2 :** of or relating to Jesus Christ **3 :** based on or conforming with Christianity **4 :** of or relating to a Christian

Chris·ti·an·i·ty \ˌkris-chē-'an-ət-ē\ *n* **1 :** CHRISTENDOM **2 :** the religion derived from Jesus Christ, based on the Bible as sacred scripture, and professed by Christians

Chris·tian·ize \'kris-chə-ˌnīz\ *vb* **:** to make Christian

Christian Scientist *n* **:** one who practices the teachings of Christian Science

Christ·mas \'kris-məs\ *n* **:** December 25 celebrated as a church festival in commemoration of the birth of Christ and observed as a legal holiday

Christ·mas·tide \-ˌtīd\ *n* **:** the season of Christmas

chro·mat·ic \krō-'mat-ik\ *adj* **1 :** of or relating to color **2 :** proceeding by half steps of the musical scale

chrome \'krōm\ *n* **1 :** CHROMIUM **2 :** a chromium pigment **3 :** plating of a chromium alloy

chro·mi·um \'krō-mē-əm\ *n* **:** a bluish white hard brittle metallic chemical element used in alloys for lustrous rust-resistant platings in automobiles

chro·mo \'krō-mō\ *n* **:** a colored picture printed from lithographic surfaces

chro·mo·some \'krō-mə-ˌsōm\ *n* **:** one of the usu. elongated bodies in a cell nucleus that contains the genes

chron·ic \'krän-ik\ *adj* **:** marked by long duration or frequent recurrence ⟨a ~ disease⟩; *also* **:** affected by a chronic condition ⟨a ~ grumbler⟩ — **chron·i·cal·ly** *adv*

¹chron·i·cle \'krän-i-kəl\ *n* **:** HISTORY; NARRATIVE

²chronicle *vb* **:** to record in or as if in a chronicle — **chron·i·cler** \-k-(ə-)lər\ *n*

chron·o·graph \'krän-ə-ˌgraf\ *n* **:** an instrument for measuring and recording time intervals with accuracy

chro·nol·o·gy \krə-'näl-ə-jē\ *n* **1 :** the science that deals with measuring time and dating events **2 :** a chronological list or table **3 :** arrangement of events in the order of their occurrence — **chron·o·log·i·cal** \ˌkrän-ᵊl-'äj-i-kəl\ *adj* — **chron·o·log·i·cal·ly** *adv* — **chro·nol·o·gist** \krə-'näl-ə-jəst\ *n*

chro·nom·e·ter \krə-'näm-ət-ər\ *n* **:** TIMEPIECE; *esp* **:** a very accurate timepiece

chrys·a·lis \'kris-ə-ləs\ *n* **:** an insect pupa quiescent in a firm case

chry·san·the·mum \kris-'an-thə-məm\

n : any of a genus of plants related to the daisies including some grown for their showy bloom or for medicinal products or insecticides; *also* : a chrysanthemum bloom

chrys·o·lite \'kris-ə-ˌlīt\ *n* : an olive-green mineral sometimes used as a gem

chub \'chəb\ *n* : a small freshwater fish related to the carp

chub·by \'chəb-ē\ *adj* : PLUMP — **chub·bi·ness** *n*

1**chuck** \'chək\ *vb* 1 : to give a pat or tap 2 : to toss or throw with a short motion of the arms 3 : DISCARD; *also* : EJECT 4 : to have done with 〈~ed his job〉

2**chuck** *n* 1 : a light pat under the chin 2 : TOSS

3**chuck** *n* 1 : a part of a side of dressed beef 2 : a device for holding work or a tool (as in a lathe)

chuck·hole \-ˌhōl\ *n* : a hole or rut in a road

chuck·le \'chək-əl\ *vb* : to laugh in a quiet hardly audible manner — **chuckle** *n*

chuck wagon *n* : a wagon equipped with a stove and provisions for cooking

1**chug** \'chəg\ *n* : a dull explosive sound made by or as if by a laboring engine

2**chug** *vb* chugged; chug·ging : to move or go with chugs (a locomotive *chugging* along)

chuk·ka \'chək-ə\ *n* : a short usu. ankle-length leather boot with two pairs of eyelets

chuk·ker \-ər\ *or* **chuk·ka** \-ə\ *n* : a playing period of a polo game

1**chum** \'chəm\ *n* : an intimate friend

2**chum** *vb* chummed; chum·ming 1 : to room together 2 : to go about with as a friend

chum·my \'chəm-ē\ *adj* : INTIMATE, SOCIABLE — **chum·mi·ly** *adv* — **chum·mi·ness** *n*

chump \'chəmp\ *n* : FOOL, BLOCKHEAD

chunk \'chəŋk\ *n* 1 : a short thick piece 2 : a sizable amount

chunky *adj* : STOCKY

church \'chərch\ *n* [OE *cirice*, fr. LGk *kyriakon*, short for *kyriakon dōma*, lit., the Lord's house, fr. Gk *Kyrios* Lord + *dōma* house] 1 : a building esp. for Christian public worship 2 : the whole body of Christians 3 : DENOMINATION 4 : CONGREGATION 5 : public divine worship

church·go·er \-ˌgō-(ə)r\ *n* : one that goes to church esp. habitually — **church·go·ing** \-ˌgō-iŋ\ *adj or n*

church·less \-ləs\ *adj* : not affiliated with a church

church·man \-mən\ *n* 1 : CLERGYMAN 2 : a member of a church — **church·wom·an** *n*

church·war·den \-ˌwȯrd-ᵊn\ *n* : WARDEN 5

church·yard \-ˌyärd\ *n* : a yard that belongs to a church and is often used as a burial ground

churl \'chərl\ *n* 1 : a medieval peasant 2 : RUSTIC 3 : a surly fellow : a rude ill-bred person — **churl·ish** *adj* — **churl·ish·ly** *adv* — **churl·ish·ness** *n*

1**churn** \'chərn\ *n* : a container in which milk or cream is violently stirred in making butter

2**churn** *vb* 1 : to stir in a churn; *also* : to make (butter) by such stirring 2 : to shake around violently

chute \'shüt\ *n* 1 : an inclined surface,

trough, or passage down or through which something may pass (a coal ~) (a mail ~) 2 : PARACHUTE

chut·ney \'chət-nē\ *n* : a condiment of acid fruits with raisins, dates, and onions

ci·ca·da \sə-'kād-ə\ *n* : a stout large-winged insect related to the true bugs

cic·a·trix \'sik-ə-ˌtriks\ *n, pl* **cic·a·tri·ces** \ˌsik-ə-'trī-ˌsēz\ : a scar resulting from formation and contraction of fibrous tissue in a flesh wound

ci·ce·ro·ne \ˌsis-ə-'rō-nē\ *n* : a guide who conducts sightseers

ci·der \'sīd-ər\ *n* : juice pressed from fruit (as apples) and used as a beverage, vinegar, or flavoring

ci·gar \sig-'är\ *n* : a roll of tobacco for smoking

cig·a·rette \ˌsig-ə-'ret\ *n* : a small tube of cut tobacco enclosed in paper for smoking

cinch \'sinch\ *n* 1 : a strong strap for holding a saddle or a pack in place 2 : a sure or an easy thing — **cinch** *vb*

cin·cho·na \siŋ-'kō-nə\ *n* : a So. American tree; *also* : its bitter quinine-containing bark

cinc·ture \'siŋk-chər\ *n* : BELT, GIRDLE

cin·der \'sin-dər\ *n* 1 : SLAG 2 : a hot piece of partly burned wood or coal 3 *pl* : ASHES

cin·e·ma \'sin-ə-mə\ *n* 1 : a motion-picture theater 2 : MOVIES — **cin·e·mat·ic** \ˌsin-ə-'mat-ik\ *adj*

cin·e·mat·o·graph \ˌsin-ə-'mat-ə-ˌgraf\ *n* : a motion-picture projector, camera, theater, or show

cin·e·ma·tog·ra·phy \-mə-'täg-rə-fē\ *n* : motion-picture photography — **cin·e·ma·tog·ra·pher** \-fər\ *n* — **cin·e·mat·o·graph·ic** \-ˌmat-ə-'graf-ik\ *adj*

cin·na·bar \'sin-ə-ˌbär\ *n* : a red mineral that is the only important ore of mercury

cin·na·mon \'sin-ə-mən\ *n* : the aromatic inner bark of a tropical Asiatic tree related to the true laurel that is used as a spice

1**ci·pher** \'sī-fər\ *n* [MF *cifre*, fr. ML *cifra*, fr. Ar *sifr* empty, zero] 1 : ZERO, NAUGHT 2 : a method of secret writing : CODE

2**cipher** *vb* : to compute arithmetically

cir·ca \'sər-kə\ *prep* : ABOUT 〈born ~ 1600〉

cir·cle \'sər-kəl\ *n* 1 : a closed curve every point of which is equally distant from a point within it 2 : something in the form of a circle 3 : an area of action or influence 4 : CYCLE, ROUND 5 : a group bound by a common tie

2**circle** *vb* 1 : to enclose in a circle 2 : to move or revolve around; *also* : to move in a circle

cir·clet \'sər-klət\ *n* : a small circle; *esp* : a circular ornament

cir·cuit \'sər-kət\ *n* 1 : a boundary around an enclosed space 2 : a moving or revolving around (as in an orbit) 3 : a regular tour (as by a judge)around an assigned territory 4 : LEAGUE; *also* : a chain of theaters 5 : the path of an electric current

cir·cu·itous \ˌsər-'kyü-ət-əs\ *adj* 1 : marked by a circular or winding course 2 : ROUNDABOUT, INDIRECT

cir·cuit·ry \'sər-kə-trē\ *n* : the plan or the components of an electric circuit

cir·cu·ity \ˌsər-'kyü-ət-ē\ *n* : INDIRECTION

cir·cu·lar \'sər-kyə-lər\ *adj* 1 : having

the form of a circle : ROUND 2 : moving in or around a circle 3 : CIRCUITOUS 4 : sent around to a number of persons ⟨a ~ letter⟩ — cir·cu·lar·i·ty \,sər-kyə-'lar-ət-ē\ n

²circular n : a paper (as an advertising leaflet) intended for wide distribution

cir·cu·lar·ize \'sər-kyə-lə-,rīz\ vb 1 : to send circulars to 2 : to poll by questionnaire

cir·cu·late \'sər-kyə-,lāt\ vb 1 : to move or cause to move in a circle, circuit, or orbit 2 : to pass from place to place or from person to person — cir·cu·la·tion \,sər-kyə-'lā-shən\ n — cir·cu·la·to·ry \'sər-kyə-lə-,tōr-ē\ adj

cir·cum·am·bu·late \,sər-kəm-'am-byə-,lāt\ vb : to circle on foot esp. ritualistically

cir·cum·cise \'sər-kəm-,sīz\ vb : to cut off the foreskin of — cir·cum·ci·sion \,sər-kəm-'sizh-ən\ n

cir·cum·fer·ence \sər-'kəm-f(ə-)rəns\ n 1 : the perimeter of a circle 2 : the external boundary or surface of a figure or object

cir·cum·flex \'sər-kəm-,fleks\ n : a mark (as ^) used chiefly to indicate length, contraction, or a specific vowel quality

cir·cum·lo·cu·tion \,sər-kəm-lō-'kyü-shən\ n : the use of an unnecessarily large number of words to express an idea

cir·cum·nav·i·gate \-'nav-ə-,gāt\ vb : to go completely around esp. by water — cir·cum·nav·i·ga·tion \-,nav-ə-'gā-shən\ n

cir·cum·scribe \'sər-kəm-,skrīb\ vb 1 : to draw a line around 2 : to limit narrowly the range or activity of — cir·cum·scrip·tion \,sər-kəm-'skrip-shən\ n

cir·cum·spect \'sər-kəm-,spekt\ adj : careful to consider all circumstances and consequences : PRUDENT — cir·cum·spec·tion \,sər-kəm-'spek-shən\ n

cir·cum·stance \'sər-kəm-,stans\ n 1 : a fact or event that must be considered along with another fact or event 2 pl : surrounding conditions 3 pl : situation with regard to wealth 4 : CEREMONY ⟨pomp and ~⟩ 5 : CHANCE, FATE

cir·cum·stan·tial \,sər-kəm-'stan-chəl\ adj 1 : consisting of or depending on circumstances ⟨~ evidence⟩ 2 : INCIDENTAL 3 : containing full details — cir·cum·stan·tial·ly adv

cir·cum·vent \,sər-kəm-'vent\ vb : to check or defeat esp. by ingenuity or stratagem

cir·cus \'sər-kəs\ n 1 : an often tent-covered arena used for shows featuring feats of physical skill and daring, wild animal acts, and performances by clowns 2 : a circus performance; also : the physical plant, livestock, and personnel of a circus

cir·rus \'sir-əs\ n : a filmy white cloud usu. of minute ice crystals at high altitudes

cis·tern \'sis-tərn\ n : an often underground artificial tank for storing water

cit·a·del \'sit-əd-ºl\ n 1 : a fortress commanding a city 2 : STRONGHOLD

ci·ta·tion \sī-'tā-shən\ n 1 : an official summons to appear (as before a court) 2 : QUOTATION 3 : a formal statement of the achievements of a person; also : a specific reference in a military dispatch to meritorious performance of duty

cite \'sīt\ vb 1 : to summon to appear before a court 2 : QUOTE 3 : to refer to esp. in commendation or praise

cit·i·fy \'sit-i-,fī\ vb : to stamp with or accustom to urban ways

cit·i·zen \'sit-ə-zən\ n 1 : an inhabitant of a city or town 2 : a person who owes allegiance to a government and is entitled to protection from it — cit·i·zen·ship n

cit·i·zen·ry \-rē\ n : CITIZENS

cit·ric acid \,sit-rik-\ n : a sour acid substance obtained from lemon and lime juices or by fermentation of sugars and used as a flavoring

cit·ron \'sit-rən\ n 1 : the oval lemon-like fruit of an Asiatic citrus tree 2 : a small hard-fleshed watermelon used esp. in pickles and preserves

cit·ro·nel·la \,sit-rə-'nel-ə\ n : a fragrant Asiatic grass that yields an oil used esp. as an insect repellent

cit·rus \'sit-rəs\ n : any of a genus of often thorny evergreen trees or shrubs grown in warm regions for their fruits (as the orange, lemon, lime, citron, and grapefruit)

city \'sit-ē\ n 1 : an inhabited place larger or more important than a town 2 : a municipality in the U.S. governed under a charter granted by the state; also : an incorporated municipal unit of the highest class in Canada

civ·et \'siv-ət\ n : a yellowish strong-smelling substance obtained from a cat-like African mammal (civet cat) and used in making perfumes

civ·ic \'siv-ik\ adj : of or relating to a city, a citizen, citizenship, or civil affairs

civ·ics \-iks\ n : a social science dealing with the rights and duties of citizens

civ·il \'siv-əl\ adj 1 : of or relating to citizens or to the state as a political body 2 : of or relating to the general population : not military or ecclesiastical 3 : COURTEOUS, POLITE 4 : of or relating to legal proceedings in connection with private rights and obligations ⟨the ~ code⟩

civil engineering n : engineering dealing chiefly with design and construction of public works (as roads or harbors) — civil engineer n

ci·vil·ian \sə-'vil-yən\ n : a person not on active duty in a military, police, or fire-fighting force

ci·vil·i·ty \sə-'vil-ət-ē\ n : POLITENESS, COURTESY

civ·i·li·za·tion \,siv-ə-lə-'zā-shən\ n 1 : a relatively high level of cultural and technological development 2 : the culture characteristic of a time or place

civ·i·lize \'siv-ə-,līz\ vb 1 : to raise from a primitive state to an advanced and ordered stage of cultural development 2 : REFINE — civ·i·lized adj

civ·il·ly \-ə(l)-lē\ adv 1 : in a civil manner : POLITELY 2 : in terms of civil rights, matters, or law ⟨~ dead⟩

¹clack \'klak\ vb 1 : CHATTER, PRATTLE 2 : to make or cause to make a clatter

²clack n : rapid continuous talk : CHAT-

TER **2** : a sound of clacking (the ~ of a typewriter)

clad \'klad\ *adj* : CLOTHED, COVERED

¹claim \'klām\ *vb* **1** : to ask for as one's own; *also* : to take as the rightful owner **2** : to call for : REQUIRE **3** : to state as a fact : MAINTAIN

²claim *n* **1** : a demand for something due **2** : a right to something usu. in another's possession **3** : an assertion open to challenge **4** : something claimed

claim·ant \'klā-mənt\ *n* : a person making a claim

clair·voy·ant \klaər-'vȯi-ənt\ *adj* **1** : unusually perceptive **2** : having the power of discerning objects not present to the senses — **clair·voy·ance** *n* — **clairvoyant** *n*

clam \'klam\ *n* : any of numerous bivalve mollusks including many that are edible

clam·bake \-,bāk\ *n* : a party or gathering (as at the seashore) at which food (as clams or potatoes) is cooked usu. on heated rocks covered by seaweed

clam·ber \'klam-bər\ *vb* : to climb awkwardly

clam·my \'klam-ē\ *adj* : being damp, soft, sticky, and usu. cool — **clam·mi·ness** *n*

¹clam·or \'klam-ər\ *n* **1** : a noisy shouting; *also* : a loud continuous noise **2** : vigorous protest or demand — **clam·or·ous** *adj*

²clamor *vb* : to make a clamor

¹clamp \'klamp\ *n* : a device for holding things together

²clamp *vb* : to fasten with or as if with a clamp

clan \'klan\ *n* : a group (as in the Scottish Highlands) made up of households whose heads claim descent from a common ancestor — **clan·nish** *adj*

clan·des·tine \klan-'des-tən\ *adj* : held in or conducted with secrecy

clang \'klaŋ\ *n* : a loud metallic ringing sound — **clang** *vb*

clan·gor \'klaŋ-(g)ər\ *n* : a resounding clang or medley of clangs

clank \'klaŋk\ *n* : a sharp brief metallic ringing sound (the ~ of chains) — **clank** *vb*

¹clap \'klap\ *vb* **clapped; clap·ping 1** : to strike noisily **2** : APPLAUD

²clap *n* **1** : a loud noisy crash (a ~ of thunder) **2** : APPLAUSE

³clap *n* : GONORRHEA

clap·board \'klab-ərd, 'kla(p)-,bȯrd\ *n* : a narrow board thicker at one edge than the other used for covering wooden buildings

clap·per \'klap-ər\ *n* : one that makes a clapping sound; *esp* : the tongue of a bell

clap·trap \'klap-,trap\ *n* : pretentious nonsense

claque \'klak\ *n* : a group hired to applaud at a performance

clar·et \'klar-ət\ *n* : a dry red table wine

clar·i·fy \'klar-ə-,fī\ *vb* : to make or become clear or clearer — **clar·i·fi·ca·tion** \,klar-ə-fə-'kā-shən\ *n*

clar·i·net \,klar-ə-'net\ *n* : a single-reed woodwind instrument in the form of a cylindrical tube with moderately flaring end — **clar·i·net·ist** *n*

clar·i·on \'klar-ē-ən\ *adj* : brilliantly clear (a ~ call to action)

clar·i·ty \'klar-ət-ē\ *n* : CLEARNESS

¹clash \'klash\ *vb* **1** : to make or cause

to make a clash **2** : CONFLICT, COLLIDE

²clash *n* **1** : a noisy usu. metallic sound of collision **2** : a hostile encounter; *also* : a conflict of opinion

¹clasp \'klasp\ *n* **1** : a device (as a hook) for holding objects or parts together **2** : EMBRACE, GRASP (the warm ~ of his hand)

²clasp *vb* **1** : to fasten with a clasp **2** : EMBRACE **3** : GRASP

¹class \'klas\ *n* **1** : a group of the same general status or nature **2** : social rank; *also* : high quality **3** : a course of instruction; *also* : the period when such a course is taught **4** : a group of students meeting regularly in a course; *also* : a group graduating together **5** : a division or rating based on grade or quality — **class·less** *adj*

²class *vb* : CLASSIFY

¹clas·sic \'klas-ik\ *adj* **1** : serving as a standard of excellence; *also* : TRADITIONAL **2** : CLASSICAL **3** : notable esp. as the best example **4** : AUTHENTIC

²classic *n* **1** : a work of enduring excellence and esp. of ancient Greece or Rome; *also* : its author **2** : a traditional event

clas·si·cal \'klas-i-kəl\ *adj* **1** : CLASSIC **2** : of or relating to the ancient Greek and Roman classics **3** : of or relating to a form or system of first significance before modern times (~ economics) **4** : concerned with a general study of the arts and sciences

clas·si·cism \'klas-ə-,siz-əm\ *n* **1** : the principles or style of the literature or art of ancient Greece and Rome **2** : adherence to traditional standards believed to be universally valid — **clas·si·cist** \-səst\ *n*

clas·si·fied \'klas-ə-,fīd\ *adj* : withheld from general circulation for reasons of national security (~ information)

clas·si·fy \-,fī\ *vb* : to arrange in or assign to classes — **clas·si·fi·ca·tion** \,klas-ə-fə-'kā-shən\ *n*

class·mate \'klas-,māt\ *n* : a member of the same class (as in a college)

class·room \-,rüm, -,rum\ *n* : a room (as in a school) in which classes meet

clat·ter \'klat-ər\ *n* : a rattling sound (the ~ of dishes) — **clatter** *vb*

clause \'klȯz\ *n* **1** : a separate part of an article or document **2** : a group of words having its own subject and predicate but forming only part of a compound or complex sentence

claus·tro·pho·bia \,klȯs-trə-'fō-bē-ə\ *n* : abnormal dread of being in closed or narrow spaces

clav·i·chord \'klav-ə-,kȯrd\ *n* : an early keyboard instrument in use before the piano

clav·i·cle \'klav-i-kəl\ *n* [NL *clavicula*, fr. L, dim. of *clavis* key] : COLLARBONE

cla·vier \klə-'vir, 'klā-vē-ər\ *n* **1** : the keyboard of a musical instrument **2** : an early keyboard instrument

¹claw \'klȯ\ *n* **1** : a sharp usu. curved nail on the toe of an animal **2** : a sharp curved process (as on the foot of an insect); *also* : CHELA

²claw *vb* : to rake, seize, or dig with or as if with claws

clay \'klā\ *n* **1** : plastic earthy material used in making pottery that consists largely of silicates of aluminum and becomes permanently hardened by firing; *also* : finely divided soil consisting largely of such clay **2** : EARTH, MUD

8 : the mortal human body — **clay·ey** *adj*

clay·more \-ˌmōr\ *n* **:** a large 2-edged sword formerly used by Scottish Highlanders

clay pigeon *n* **:** a saucer-shaped target thrown from a trap in trapshooting

¹**clean** \'klēn\ *adj* **1 :** free from dirt or disease **2 :** PURE; *also* **:** HONORABLE **3 :** THOROUGH ⟨made a ~ sweep⟩ **4 :** TRIM ⟨a ship with ~ lines⟩; *also* **:** EVEN **5 :** habitually neat — **clean** *adv* — **clean·ly** \'klēn-lē\ *adv* — **clean·ness** *n*

²**clean** *vb* **:** to make or become clean — **clean·er** *n*

clean–cut \'klēn-'kət\ *adj* **1 :** cut so that the surface or edge is smooth and even **2 :** sharply defined or outlined ⟨~ decision⟩ **3 :** giving an effect of wholesomeness ⟨a ~ young man⟩

clean·ly \'klen-lē\ *adj* **1 :** careful to keep clean **2 :** habitually kept clean — **clean·li·ness** *n*

cleanse \'klenz\ *vb* **:** to make clean — **cleans·er** *n*

¹**clear** \'kliər\ *adj* **1 :** BRIGHT, LUMINOUS; *also* **:** UNTROUBLED, SERENE **2 :** CLEAN, PURE; *also* **:** TRANSPARENT **3 :** easily heard, seen, or understood **4 :** capable of sharp discernment; *also* **:** free from doubt **5 :** INNOCENT **6 :** free from restriction, obstruction, or entanglement — **clear** *adv* — **clear·ly** *adv* — **clear·ness** *n*

²**clear** *vb* **1 :** to make or become clear **2 :** to go away **:** DISPERSE **3 :** to free from accusation or blame; *also* **:** to certify as trustworthy **4 :** EXPLAIN **5 :** to get free from obstruction **6 :** SETTLE **7 :** NET **8 :** to get rid of **:** REMOVE **9 :** to jump or go by without touching; *also* **:** PASS

³**clear** *n* **:** a clear space or part

clear·ance \'klir-əns\ *n* **1 :** an act or process of clearing **2 :** the distance by which one object clears another

clear–cut \'kliər-'kət\ *adj* **1 :** sharply outlined **2 :** DEFINITE, UNEQUIVOCAL

clear·head·ed \-'hed-əd\ *adj* **:** having a clear understanding **:** PERCEPTIVE

clear·ing \'kli(ə)r-iŋ\ *n* **1 :** a tract of land cleared of wood **2 :** the passage of checks and claims through a clearinghouse

clear·ing·house \-ˌhaus\ *n* **:** an institution maintained by banks for making an exchange of checks and claims held by each bank against other banks

cleat \'klēt\ *n* **:** a strip of wood or metal fastened on or projecting from something to give strength, provide a grip, or prevent slipping

cleav·age \'klē-vij\ *n* **:** a splitting apart **:** SPLIT

¹**cleave** \'klēv\ *vb* **cleaved** *or* **clove** \'klōv\ **cleav·ing :** ADHERE, CLING

²**cleave** *vb* **cleaved** *also* **cleft** \'kleft\ *or* **clove** \'klōv\ **cleaved** *also* **cleft** *or* **clo·ven** \'klō-vən\ **cleav·ing 1 :** to divide by force **:** split asunder **2 :** DIVIDE ⟨~ a group into two camps⟩

cleav·er *n* **:** a heavy chopping knife used by butchers in cutting meat

clef \'klef\ *n* **:** a sign placed on the staff in music to show what pitch is represented by each line and space

cleft \'kleft\ *n* **:** FISSURE, CRACK

clem·a·tis \'klem-ət-əs, klə-'mat-\ *n* **:** a vine related to the buttercups that has showy usu. white or purple flowers

clem·en·cy \'klem-ən-sē\ *n* **1 :** disposition to be merciful **2 :** mildness of weather

clem·ent \-ənt\ *adj* **1 :** MERCIFUL, LENIENT **2 :** TEMPERATE, MILD ⟨~ weather⟩

clench \'klench\ *vb* **1 :** CLINCH **2 :** to hold fast **3 :** to set or close tightly

clere·sto·ry *or* **clear·sto·ry** \'kliər-ˌstōr-ē\ *n* **:** an outside wall of a room or building that rises above an adjoining roof and contains windows

cler·gy \'klər-jē\ *n* **:** a body of religious officials authorized to conduct services

cler·gy·man \-mən\ *n* **:** a member of the clergy

cler·ic \'kler-ik\ *n* **:** CLERGYMAN

cler·i·cal \'kler-i-kəl\ *adj* **1 :** of or relating to the clergy or a clergyman **2 :** of or relating to a clerk or office worker

cler·i·cal·ism *n* **:** a policy of maintaining or increasing the power of a religious hierarchy

clerk \'klərk\ *n* **1 :** CLERIC **2 :** an official responsible for correspondence, records, and accounts; *also* **:** a person employed to perform general office work **3 :** a store salesman — **clerk·ship** *n*

clev·er \'klev-ər\ *adj* **1 :** showing skill or resourcefulness **2 :** marked by wit or ingenuity — **clev·er·ly** *adv* — **clev·er·ness** *n*

¹**clew** \'klü\ *n* **1 :** CLUE **2 :** a metal loop on a lower corner of a sail to hold ropes

²**clew** *vb* **:** to haul a sail up or down by ropes through the clews

cli·ché \klē-'shā\ *n* **:** a trite phrase or expression

¹**click** \'klik\ *n* **:** a slight sharp noise

²**click** *vb* **1 :** to make or cause to make a click **2 :** to fit or work together smoothly

cli·ent \'klī-ənt\ *n* **1 :** DEPENDENT **2 :** a person who engages the professional services of another; *also* **:** PATRON, CUSTOMER

cli·en·tele \ˌklī-ən-'tel\ *n* **:** a body of clients and esp. customers

cliff \'klif\ *n* **:** a high steep face of rock

cliff–hang·er \-ˌhaŋ-ər\ *n* **1 :** an adventure serial or melodrama usu. presented in installments each of which ends in suspense **2 :** a contest whose outcome is in doubt up to the very end

cli·mate \'klī-mət\ *n* **:** the average weather conditions at a place over a period of years — **cli·mat·ic** \klī-'mat-ik\ *adj*

¹**cli·max** \'klī-ˌmaks\ *n* [LL, fr. Gk, lit., staircase, ladder] **1 :** a series of ideas or statements so arranged that they increase in force and power from the first to the last; *also* **:** the last member of such a series **2 :** the highest point **:** CULMINATION — **cli·mac·tic** \klī-'mak-tik\ *adj*

²**climax** *vb* **:** to come or bring to a climax

¹**climb** \'klīm\ *vb* **1 :** to go up or down esp. by use of hands and feet; *also* **:** to ascend in growing **2 :** to rise to a higher point — **climb·er** *n*

ə abut; ᵊ kitten; ər further; a back; ā bake; ä cot, cart; au̇ out; ch chin; e less; ē easy; g gift; i trip; ī life; j job; ŋ sing; ō flow; ȯ flaw; ȯi coin; th thin; t̲h̲ this; ü loot; u̇ foot; y yet; yü few; yu̇ furious; zh vision

²**climb** n 1 : a place where climbing is necessary 2 : the act of climbing : ascent by climbing

clime \'klīm\ n : CLIMATE

¹**clinch** \'klinch\ vb 1 : to fasten securely (as by driving a nail through boards and bending its point over) 2 : to make final : SETTLE 3 : to hold fast or firmly

²**clinch** n 1 : a fastening by means of a clinched nail, rivet, or bolt 2 : an act or instance of clinching in boxing

clinch·er n : one that clinches; esp : a decisive fact, argument, act, or remark

cling \'klin\ vb **clung** \'klən\ **cling·ing** 1 : to adhere as if glued firmly; also : to hold or hold on tightly 2 : to have a strong emotional attachment

clin·ic \'klin-ik\ n 1 : medical instruction featuring the examination and discussion of actual cases 2 : a facility (as of a hospital) for diagnosis and treatment of outpatients

clin·i·cal \'klin-i-kəl\ adj 1 : of, relating to, or typical of a clinic; esp : involving direct observation of the patient 2 : scientifically detached and dispassionate — **clin·i·cal·ly** adv

¹**clink** \'klink\ vb : to make or cause to make a slight sharp short metallic sound

²**clink** n : a clinking sound

clin·ker \'klin-kər\ n : stony matter fused by fire (as in a furnace from impurities in coal)

¹**clip** \'klip\ vb **clipped**; **clip·ping** 1 : to clasp or fasten with a clip 2 : to block an opponent in football by hitting with the body from behind

²**clip** n 1 : a device that grips, clasps, or hooks 2 : a cartridge holder for a rifle

³**clip** vb **clipped**; **clip·ping** 1 : to cut or cut off with shears 2 : CURTAIL, DIMINISH 3 : HIT, PUNCH

⁴**clip** n 1 : a 2-bladed instrument for cutting esp. the nails 2 : a sharp blow 3 : a rapid pace

clip·board \'klip-,bōrd\ n : a small writing board with a spring clip at the top for holding papers

clip·per n : an implement for clipping esp. the hair or nails — usu. used in pl. 2 : a fast sailing ship

clip·ping n : a piece clipped from something (as a newspaper)

clique \'klēk, 'klik\ n : a small exclusive group of people : COTERIE

¹**cloak** \'klōk\ n 1 : a loose outer garment 2 : something that conceals or covers

²**cloak** vb : to cover or hide with a cloak

cloche \'klōsh\ n : a woman's small helmetlike hat

¹**clock** \'kläk\ n : a timepiece not intended to be carried on the person

²**clock** vb 1 : to time (a person or a performance) by a timing device 2 : to register (as time, distance, rate, or speed) on a recording device

³**clock** n : an ornamental figure on a stocking or sock

clock·wise \-,wīz\ adv : in the direction in which the hands of a clock move

clock·work \-,wərk\ n : machinery containing a train of wheels of small size

clod \'kläd\ n 1 : a lump esp. of earth or clay 2 : a dull or insensitive person

clod·hop·per \-,häp-ər\ n 1 : an uncouth rustic 2 : a large heavy shoe

¹**clog** \'kläg\ n 1 : a weight so attached as to impede motion 2 : a thick-soled shoe

²**clog** vb **clogged**; **clog·ging** 1 : to impede with a clog : HINDER 2 : to obstruct passage through 3 : to become filled with extraneous matter

cloi·son·né \,kloiz-ᵊn-'ā\ n : a colored decoration made of enamels poured into the divided areas in a design outlined with bent wire or metal strips

¹**clois·ter** \'kloi-stər\ n 1 : a monastic establishment 2 : a covered usu. colonnaded passage on the side of a court — **clois·tral** \-strəl\ adj

²**cloister** vb : to shut away from the world

clop \'kläp\ n : a sound made by or as if by a hoof or wooden shoe against pavement

¹**close** \'klōz\ vb 1 : to bar passage through : SHUT 2 : to suspend the operations (as of a school) 3 : END, TERMINATE 4 : to bring together the parts or edges of; also : to fill up 5 : GRAPPLE ⟨~ with the enemy⟩ 6 : to enter into an agreement — **clos·able** adj

²**close** n : CONCLUSION, END

³**close** \'klōs\ n : an enclosed area

⁴**close** \'klōs\ adj 1 : having no openings 2 : narrowly restricting or restricted 3 : limited to a privileged class 4 : SECLUDED; also : SECRETIVE 5 : RIGOROUS 6 : SULTRY, STUFFY 7 : STINGY 8 : having little space between 9 : fitting tightly; also : SHORT ⟨~ haircut⟩ 10 : NEAR 11 : INTIMATE ⟨~ friends⟩ 12 : ACCURATE 13 : decided by a narrow margin ⟨a ~ game⟩ — **close·ly** adv — **close·ness** n

closed circuit n : television in which the signal is transmitted by wire

close-fist·ed \'klōs-'fis-təd\ adj : STINGY

close-mouthed \-'mauthd, -'mautht\ adj : cautious in speaking

¹**clos·et** \'kläz-ət\ n 1 : a small room for privacy 2 : a small compartment for household utensils or clothing 3 : WATER CLOSET

²**closet** vb : to take into a private room for an interview

close-up \'klōs-,əp\ n 1 : a photograph or movie shot taken at close range 2 : an intimate view or examination of something

clo·sure \'klō-zhər\ n 1 : an act of closing : the condition of being closed 2 : something that closes : CLOTURE

clot \'klät\ n : a mass formed by a portion of liquid (as blood or cream) thickening and sticking together — **clot** vb

cloth \'klòth\ n 1 : a pliable fabric made usu. by weaving or knitting natural or synthetic fibers and filaments 2 : TABLECLOTH 3 : distinctive dress of a profession and esp. of the clergy; also : CLERGY

clothe \'klōth\ vb **clothed** or **clad** \'klad\ **cloth·ing** 1 : DRESS 2 : to express by suitably significant language

clothes \'klō(th)z\ n pl 1 : CLOTHING 2 : BEDCLOTHES

clothes·horse \-,hòrs\ n 1 : a frame on which to hang clothes 2 : a conspicuously dressy person

clothes·pin \-,pin\ n : a device (as of wood or plastic) for fastening clothes on a line

clothes·press \-,pres\ n : a receptacle for clothes

cloth·ier \'klōth-yər\ *n* : a maker or seller of cloth or clothing

cloth·ing \'klō-thiŋ\ *n* : garments in general

clo·ture \'klō-chər\ *n* : the closing or limitation by closure by calling for a vote) of debate in a legislative body

¹**cloud** \'klaúd\ *n* 1 : a visible mass of water or ice particles in the air above the earth's surface; *also* : a visible mass of particles (as of dust) in the air 2 : CROWD, SWARM ⟨a ~ of mosquitoes⟩ 3 : something having a dark or threatening look — **cloud·i·ness** *n* — **cloud·less** *adj* — **cloudy** *adj*

²**cloud** *vb* 1 : to darken or hide with or as if with a cloud 2 : OBSCURE 3 : TAINT, SULLY

cloud·burst \-,bərst\ *n* : a sudden heavy rainfall

cloud·let \-lət\ *n* : a small cloud

¹**clout** \'klaút\ *n* : a blow esp. with the hand

²**clout** *vb* : to hit forcefully

¹**clove** *past of* CLEAVE

²**clove** \'klōv\ *n* [OF *clou* nail, fr. L *clavus*] : the dried flower bud of an East Indian tree used esp. as a spice

clo·ver \'klō-vər\ *n* : any of numerous leguminous herbs with usu. 3-parted leaves and dense flower heads

¹**clown** \'klaún\ *n* 1 : BOOR 2 : a fool or comedian in an entertainment (as a play or circus) — **clown·ish** *adj* — **clown·ish·ly** *adv*

²**clown** *vb* : to act like a clown

cloy \'klói\ *vb* : to surfeit with an excess of something orig. pleasing

¹**club** \'kləb\ *n* 1 : a heavy wooden stick or staff used as a weapon; *also* : BAT 2 : any of a suit of playing cards marked with a black figure resembling a clover leaf 3 : a group of persons associated for a common purpose; *also* : the meeting place of such a group

²**club** *vb* **clubbed; club·bing** 1 : to strike with a club 2 : to unite or combine for a common cause

club·foot \-'fút\ *n* : a misshapen foot twisted out of position from birth — **club·foot·ed** *adj*

club·house \-,haús\ *n* 1 : a house occupied by a club 2 : locker rooms used by an athletic team

cluck \'klək\ *n* : the call of a hen esp. to her chicks — **cluck** *vb*

¹**clue** \'klü\ *n* : a guide through an intricate procedure or maze; *esp* : a piece of evidence leading to the solution of a problem

²**clue** *vb* : to provide with a clue

¹**clump** \'kləmp\ *n* 1 : a group of things clustered together 2 : a heavy tramping sound

²**clump** *vb* : to tread clumsily and noisily

clum·sy \'kləm-zē\ *adj* 1 : lacking dexterity, nimbleness, or grace 2 : not tactful or subtle — **clum·si·ly** *adv* — **clum·si·ness** *n*

clung *past of* CLING

¹**clus·ter** \'kləs-tər\ *n* : GROUP, BUNCH

²**cluster** *vb* : to grow or gather in a cluster

¹**clutch** \'kləch\ *vb* : to grasp with or as if with the hand

²**clutch** *n* 1 : the claws or a hand in the act of grasping; *also* : CONTROL, POWER 2 : a device (as a coupling for connecting two working parts in machinery) for gripping an object 3 : a crucial situation

¹**clut·ter** \'klət-ər\ *vb* : to fill with scattered things that impede movement or reduce efficiency

²**clutter** *n* : crowded confusion

¹**coach** \'kōch\ *n* 1 : a closed 2-door 4-wheeled carriage with an elevated outside front seat for the driver 2 : a railroad passenger car esp. for day travel 3 : BUS 4 : an automobile body; *also* : a closed 2-door automobile 5 : a private tutor; *also* : one who instructs or trains a team of performers ⟨debating ~⟩ ⟨football ~⟩

²**coach** *vb* 1 : to go in a horse-drawn coach 2 : to instruct, direct, or prompt as a coach — **coach·er** *n*

coach·man \-mən\ *n* : a man whose business is driving a coach or carriage

co·ad·ju·tor \,kō-ə-'jüt-ər\ *n* : ASSISTANT; *esp* : an assistant bishop having the right of succession

co·ag·u·lant \kō-'ag-yə-lənt\ *n* : something that produces coagulation

co·ag·u·late \-,lāt\ *vb* : CLOT — **co·ag·u·la·tion** \-,ag-yə-'lā-shən\ *n*

¹**coal** \'kōl\ *n* 1 : EMBER 2 : a black solid combustible mineral used as fuel

²**coal** *vb* 1 : to supply with coal 2 : to take in coal

co·alesce \,kō-ə-'les\ *vb* : to grow together; *also* : FUSE **syn** merge, blend, mingle, mix — **co·ales·cence** \,kō-ə-'les-ᵊns\ *n*

coal·field \'kōl-,fēld\ *n* : a region where deposits of coal occur

co·ali·tion \,kō-ə-'lish-ən\ *n* : UNION; *esp* : a temporary union for a common purpose — **co·ali·tion·ist** *n*

coal oil *n* : KEROSENE

coal tar *n* : tar distilled from bituminous coal and used in dyes, explosives, and drugs

coarse \'kōrs\ *adj* 1 : of ordinary or inferior quality 2 : composed of large parts or particles ⟨~ sand⟩ 3 : ROUGH, HARSH 4 : CRUDE ⟨~ manners⟩ — **coarse·ly** *adv* — **coarse·ness** *n*

coars·en \'kōrs-ᵊn\ *vb* : to make or become coarse

¹**coast** \'kōst\ *n* 1 : SEASHORE 2 : a slide down a slope — **coast·al** *adj*

²**coast** *vb* 1 : to sail along the shore 2 : to move (as downhill on a sled or as on a bicycle while not pedaling) without effort — **coast·er** *n*

coast guard *n* : a military force employed in guarding or patrolling a coast

coast·line \'kōst-,līn\ *n* : the outline or shape of a coast

¹**coat** \'kōt\ *n* 1 : an outer garment for the upper part of the body 2 : an external growth (as of fur or feathers) on an animal 3 : a covering layer ⟨a ~ of paint⟩

²**coat** *vb* : to cover usu. with a finishing or protective coat

coat·ing *n* : COAT, COVERING ⟨a ~ of ice⟩

coat of arms : the heraldic bearings (as of a person) usu. depicted on an escutcheon

coat of mail : a garment of metal scales or rings worn as armor

---

ə abut; ᵊ kitten; ər further; a back; ā bake; ä cot, cart; aú out; ch chin; e less; ē easy; g gift; i trip; ī life; j joke; ŋ sing; ō flow; ȯ flaw; ȯi coin; th thin; t̲h̲ this; ü loot; u̇ foot; y yet; yü few; yu̇ furious; zh vision

co·au·thor \'kō-'ò-thər\ *n* **:** a joint or associate author

coax \'kōks\ *vb* **:** WHEEDLE; *also* **:** to gain by gentle urging or flattery — **coax·er** *n*

co·ax·i·al \kō-'ak-sē-əl\ *adj* **1 :** having coincident axes **2 :** being an electrical cable that consists of a tube of conducting material surrounding a central conductor

cob \'käb\ *n* **1 :** a male swan **2 :** CORN COB **3 :** a short-legged stocky horse

co·balt \'kō-,bòlt\ *n* **:** a tough shiny silver-white magnetic metallic chemical element found with iron and nickel

cob·ble \'käb-əl\ *vb* **:** to make or put together roughly or hastily

cob·bler \'käb-lər\ *n* **1 :** a mender or maker of shoes **2 :** a deep-dish fruit pie with a thick crust

cob·ble·stone \'käb-əl-,stōn\ *n* **:** a naturally rounded stone larger than a pebble and smaller than a boulder

co·bra \'kō-brə\ *n* **:** a venomous snake of Asia and Africa that when excited expands the skin of the neck into a broad hood

cob·web \'käb-,web\ *n* **1 :** the network spun by a spider; *also* **:** a thread of insect or spider silk **2 :** something flimsy or entangling

co·caine \kō-'kān\ *n* **:** an addictive drug obtained from the leaves of a So. American shrub (**co·ca** \'kō-kə\) and sometimes used as a local anesthetic

coch·i·neal \'käch-ə-,nēl\ *n* **:** a red dye made from the dried bodies of a tropical American insect (**cochineal insect**)

coch·lea \'käk-lē-ə\ *n* **:** the usu. spiral part of the inner ear that is the seat of the organ of hearing

¹cock \'käk\ *n* **1 :** the male of a bird and esp. of the common domestic fowl **2 :** VALVE, FAUCET **3 :** LEADER **4 :** the hammer of a firearm; *also* **:** the position of the hammer when drawn back ready for firing

²cock *vb* **1 :** to draw back the hammer of a firearm **2 :** to set erect **3 :** to turn or tilt usu. to one side

³cock *n* **:** a small conical pile (as of hay)

cock·ade \kä-'kād\ *n* **:** an ornament (as a rosette) worn on the hat as a badge

cock·a·tiel \,käk-ə-'tēl\ *n* **:** a small crested parrot often kept as a cage bird

cock·a·too \'käk-ə-,tü\ *n* **:** a large crested brilliantly colored Australian parrot

cock·a·trice \'käk-ə-trəs, -,trīs\ *n* **:** a legendary serpent with a deadly glance

cock·crow \'käk-,krō\ *n* **:** early morning

cock·er·el \'käk-(ə-)rəl\ *n* **:** a young cock

cock·eye \'käk-,ī\ *n* **:** a squinting eye — **cock·eyed** \-'īd\ *adj*

cock·fight \-,fīt\ *n* **:** a contest of gamecocks usu. heeled with metal spurs

¹cock·le \'käk-əl\ *n* **:** any of several weeds found in fields where grain is grown

²cockle *n* **:** a bivalve mollusk with a heart-shaped shell

cock·le·shell \-,shel\ *n* **1 :** the shell of a cockle **2 :** a small shallow boat

cock·ney \'käk-nē\ *n, often cap* **:** a native of London and esp. of the East End of London; *also* **:** the dialect of a cockney

cock·pit \-,pit\ *n* **1 :** a pit for cockfights **2 :** an open space aft of a decked area from which a small boat is steered **3 :** a space in an airplane fuselage for the pilot, pilot and passengers, or pilot and crew

cock·roach \-,rōch\ *n* **:** an active nocturnal insect often infesting houses and ships

cock·sure \-'shùr\ *adj* **1 :** CERTAIN **2 :** COCKY

cock·tail \-,tāl\ *n* **1 :** an iced drink made of liquor and flavoring ingredients **2 :** an appetizer (as tomato juice) served as a first course of a meal

cocky \'käk-ē\ *adj* **:** PERT, CONCEITED — **cock·i·ly** *adv* — **cock·i·ness** *n*

co·co \'kō-kō\ *n* **:** the coconut palm or its fruit

co·coa \'kō-kō\ *n* **1 :** CACAO **2 :** chocolate deprived of some of its fat and powdered; *also* **:** a drink made of this cooked with water or milk

co·co·nut \'kō-kə-(,)nət\ *n* **:** a large edible nut produced by a tall tropical palm (**coconut palm**)

co·coon \kə-'kün\ *n* **:** a case which an insect larva forms and in which it passes the pupal stage

cod \'käd\ *n* **:** a soft-finned large-mouthed food fish of the No. Atlantic

co·da \'kōd-ə\ *n* **:** a closing section in a musical composition that is formally distinct from the main structure

cod·dle \'käd-⁷l\ *vb* **1 :** to cook slowly in water below the boiling point **2 :** PAMPER

code \'kōd\ *n* [MF, fr. LL *codex* written collection of laws, fr. L, book] **1 :** a systematic statement of a body of law **2 :** a system of principles or rules {moral ∼} **3 :** a system of signals **4 :** a system of letters or symbols used (as in secret communication or in a computing machine) with special meanings

co·deine \'kō-,dēn, 'kōd-ē-ən\ *n* **:** a narcotic drug obtained from opium and used in cough remedies

co·dex \'kō-,deks\ *n, pl* **co·di·ces** \'kōd-ə-,sēz, 'käd-\ **:** a manuscript book (as of the Scriptures or classics)

cod·fish \'käd-,fish\ *n* **:** COD

codg·er \'käj-ər\ *n* **:** an odd or cranky fellow

cod·i·cil \'käd-ə-səl\ *n* **:** a legal instrument modifying an earlier will

cod·i·fy \'käd-ə-,fī, 'kōd-\ *vb* **:** to arrange in a systematic form — **cod·i·fi·ca·tion** \,käd-ə-fə 'kā-shən, ,kōd-\ *n*

cod·ling \'käd-liŋ\ *n* **1 :** a young cod **2 :** HAKE

co·ed \'kō-,ed\ *n* **:** a female student in a coeducational institution — **co·ed** *adj*

co·ed·u·ca·tion \,kō-,ej-ə-'kā-shən\ *n* **:** the education of male and female students at the same institution — **co·ed·u·ca·tion·al** *adj* — **co·ed·u·ca·tion·al·ly** *adv*

co·ef·fi·cient \,kō-ə-'fish-ənt\ *n* **1 :** any of the factors of a product considered in relation to a specific factor **2 :** a number that serves as a measure of some property or characteristic (as of a substance or device)

co·equal \kō-'ē-kwəl\ *adj* **:** equal with another — **co·equal·i·ty** \,kō-ē-'kwäl-ət-ē\ *n* — **co·equal·ly** \kō-'ē-kwə-lē\ *adv*

co·erce \kō-'ərs\ *vb* **1 :** REPRESS **2 :** COMPEL **3 :** ENFORCE — **co·er·cion** *n*

\-'ər-zhən, -shən\ *n* — **co·er·cive** \-'ər-siv\ *adj*

co·eval \kō-'ē-vəl\ *adj* : of the same age — **coeval** *n*

co·ex·ist \,kō-ig-'zist\ *vb* 1 : to exist together or at the same time 2 : to live in peace with each other — **co·ex·is·tence** \-'zis-təns\ *n*

co·ex·ten·sive \,kō-ik-'sten-siv\ *adj* : having the same scope or extent in space or time

cof·fee \'kȯ-fē\ *n* : a drink made from the roasted and ground seeds of a fruit of a tropical shrub or tree; *also* : these seeds (**coffee beans**) or a plant producing them

cof·fee·house \-,haús\ *n* : CAFE

cof·fee·pot \-,pät\ *n* : a utensil for preparing or serving coffee

coffee shop *n* : a small restaurant esp. for light refreshments

cof·fer \'kȯ-fər\ *n* : a chest or box used esp. for valuables

cof·fer·dam \-,dam\ *n* : a watertight enclosure from which water is pumped to expose the bottom of a body of water and permit construction

cof·fin \'kȯ-fən\ *n* : a box or chest for a corpse to be buried in

cog \'käg\ *n* : a tooth on the rim of a wheel in a machine

co·gent \'kō-jənt\ *adj* : having power to compel or constrain : CONVINCING — **co·gen·cy** *n*

cog·i·tate \'käj-ə-,tāt\ *vb* : THINK, PONDER — **cog·i·ta·tion** \,käj-ə-'tā-shən\ *n*

co·gnac \'kōn-,yak\ *n* : a French brandy

cog·nate \'käg-,nāt\ *adj* 1 : RELATED; *esp* : related by descent from the same ancestral language 2 : of the same or similar nature — **cognate** *n*

cog·ni·tion \käg-'nish-ən\ *n* : the act or process of knowing — **cog·ni·tion·al** *adj* — **cog·ni·tive** \'käg-nət-iv\ *adj*

cog·ni·zance \'käg-nə-zəns\ *n* 1 : apprehension by the mind : AWARENESS 2 : NOTICE, HEED — **cog·ni·zant** *adj*

cog·no·men \käg-'nō-mən\ *n* : NAME; *esp* : NICKNAME

cog·wheel \'käg-,hwēl\ *n* : a wheel with cogs on the rim

co·hab·it \kō-'hab-ət\ *vb* : to live together as husband and wife — **co·hab·i·ta·tion** \-,hab-ə-'tā-shən\ *n*

co·heir \'kō-'aər\ *n* : a joint heir

co·here \kō-'hiər\ *vb* : to stick together

co·her·ent \-'hir-ənt\ *adj* 1 : having the quality of cohering 2 : logically consistent — **co·her·ence** *n* — **co·her·ent·ly** *adv*

co·he·sion \-'hē-zhən\ *n* 1 : a sticking together 2 : a molecular attraction by which the particles of a body are united — **co·he·sive** \-siv\ *adj*

co·hort \'kō-,hȯrt\ *n* 1 : a group of warriors or followers 2 : COMPANION, ACCOMPLICE

coif \'kȯif\ *n* 1 : a close-fitting hat 2 : COIFFURE

coif·feur \kwä-'fər\ *n* : HAIRDRESSER

coif·fure \kwä-'fyùr\ *n* : a manner of arranging the hair

¹**coil** \'kȯil\ *vb* : to wind in a spiral shape

²**coil** *n* : a series of rings or loops (as of coiled rope, wire, or pipe) : RING, LOOP

¹**coin** \'kȯin\ *n* : a piece of metal issued by government authority as money

²**coin** *vb* 1 : to make (a coin) esp. by stamping : MINT 2 : CREATE, INVENT ⟨~ a phrase⟩ — **coin·er** *n*

coin·age \-ij\ *n* 1 : the act or process of coining 2 : COINS

co·in·cide \,kō-ən-'sīd\ *vb* 1 : to occupy the same place in space 2 : to correspond or agree exactly — **co·in·ci·dence** \kō-'in-səd-əns\ *n*

co·in·ci·dent \kō-'in-səd-ənt\ *adj* 1 : occupying the same space or time 2 : of similar nature — **co·in·ci·den·tal** \-,in-sə-'dent-ᵊl\ *adj*

co·itus \'kō-ət-əs\ *n* : sexual intercourse

coke \'kōk\ *n* : a hard gray porous fuel made by heating soft coal to drive off most of its volatile material

co·la \'kō-lə\ *n* : a carbonated soft drink

col·an·der \'kəl-ən-dər, 'käl-\ *n* : a perforated utensil for draining food

¹**cold** \'kōld\ *adj* 1 : having a low or decidedly subnormal temperature 2 : lacking warmth of feeling 3 : suffering or uncomfortable from lack of warmth — **cold·ly** *adv* — **cold·ness** *n*

²**cold** *n* 1 : a condition marked by low temperature; *also* : cold weather 2 : a chilly feeling 3 : a bodily disorder (as a respiratory inflammation) popularly associated with chilling

cold–blood·ed \-'bləd-əd\ *adj* 1 : lacking normal human feelings 2 : sensitive to cold

cole·slaw \'kōl-,slȯ\ *n* : a salad made of raw cabbage

col·ic \'käl-ik\ *n* : sharp sudden abdominal pain

col·i·se·um \,käl-ə-'sē-əm\ *n* : a large structure (as a stadium) esp. for athletic contests

col·lab·o·rate \kə-'lab-ə-,rāt\ *vb* 1 : to work jointly with others (as in writing a book) 2 : to cooperate with an enemy force occupying one's country — **col·lab·o·ra·tion** \-,lab-ə-'rā-shən\ *n* — **col·lab·o·ra·tor** \-'lab-ə-,rāt-ər\ *n*

col·lage \kə-'läzh\ *n* : an artistic composition of fragments (as of printed matter) pasted on a picture surface

¹**col·lapse** \kə-'laps\ *vb* 1 : DISINTEGRATE; *also* : to fall in : give way 2 : to shrink together abruptly 3 : to break down physically or mentally; *esp* : to fall helpless or unconscious — **col·laps·ible** *adj*

²**collapse** *n* : BREAKDOWN

¹**col·lar** \'käl-ər\ *n* 1 : a band, strip, or chain worn around the neck or the neckline of a garment 2 : something resembling a collar — **col·lar·less** *adj*

²**collar** *vb* : to seize by the collar; *also* : CAPTURE, GRAB

col·lar·bone \-,bōn\ *n* : the bone of the shoulder that joins the breastbone and the shoulder blade

col·lard \'käl-ərd\ *n* : a stalked smooth-leaved kale — usu. used in pl.

col·late \kə-'lāt\ *vb* : to compare (as two texts) carefully and critically

¹**col·lat·er·al** \kə-'lat-(ə-)rəl\ *adj* 1 : associated but of secondary importance 2 : descended from the

same ancestors but not in the same line **3 :** PARALLEL **4 :** of, relating to, or being collateral used as security; *also* **:** secured by collateral

²**collateral** *n* **:** property (as stocks) used as security for the repayment of a loan

col·la·tion \kə-'lā-shən\ *n* **1 :** a light meal **2 :** the act, process, or result of collating

col·league \'käl-ˌēg\ *n* **:** an associate esp. in a profession

¹**col·lect** \'käl-ikt\ *n* **:** a short prayer comprising an invocation, petition, and conclusion

²**col·lect** \kə-'lekt\ *vb* **1 :** to bring or come together into one body or place **:** ASSEMBLE **2 :** to gather from numerous sources (~ stamps) **3 :** to gain control of (~ his thoughts) **4 :** to receive payment for — **col·lect·ible** *or* **col·lect·able** *adj* — **col·lec·tion** \-'lek-shən\ *n* — **col·lec·tor** \-'lek-tər\ *n*

³**col·lect** \kə-'lekt\ *adv (or adj)* **:** to be paid for by the receiver

col·lect·ed \kə-'lek-təd\ *adj* **:** SELF-POSSESSED, CALM

¹**col·lec·tive** \kə-'lek-tiv\ *adj* **1 :** of, relating to, or denoting a group of individuals considered as a whole **2 :** formed by collecting **3 :** shared or assumed by all members of the group — **col·lec·tive·ly** *adv*

²**collective** *n* **1 :** GROUP **2 :** a cooperative unit or organization

col·lec·tiv·ism \-'ti-ˌviz-əm\ *n* **:** a political or economic theory advocating collective control esp. over production and distribution

col·leen \käl-ˌēn\ *n* **:** an Irish girl

col·lege \'käl-ij\ *n* **1 :** a building used for an educational or religious purpose **2 :** an institution of higher learning granting a bachelor's degree; *also* **:** an institution offering instruction esp. in a vocational or technical field (barber ~) **3 :** an organized body of persons having common interests or duties (~ of cardinals) — **col·le·giate** \kə-'lē-jət\ *adj*

col·le·gian \kə-'lē-jən\ *n* **:** a college student

col·le·gium \-j(ē-)əm\ *n* **:** a governing group in which each member has approximately equal power and authority

col·lide \kə-'līd\ *vb* **1 :** to come together with solid impact **2 :** CLASH — **col·li·sion** \-'lizh-ən\ *n*

col·lie \'käl-ē\ *n* **:** a large usu. long-haired dog of a breed developed in Scotland for herding sheep

col·lier \'käl-yər\ *n* **1 :** a coal dealer or coal miner **2 :** a ship for carrying coal

col·liery \-yə-rē\ *n* **:** a coal mine

col·lo·ca·tion \ˌkäl-ə-'kā-shən\ *n* **:** a placing together or side by side; *also* **:** the result of such placing

col·lo·di·on \kə-'lōd-ē-ən\ *n* **:** a sticky substance that hardens in the air and is used to cover wounds and coat photographic films

col·loid \'käl-ˌóid\ *n* **:** a substance in the form of very fine particles that are not visible in an ordinary microscope and that when in solution or suspension do not settle out; *also* **:** such a substance together with the gaseous, liquid, or solid substance in which it is dispersed — **col·loi·dal** \kə-'lóid-ᵊl\ *adj*

col·lo·qui·al \kə-'lō-kwē-əl\ *adj* **:** of, relating to, or characteristic of con-

versation and esp. of familiar and informal conversation

col·lo·qui·al·ism *n* **:** a colloquial expression

col·lo·qui·um \kə-'lō-kwē-əm\ *n* **:** CONFERENCE, SEMINAR

col·lo·quy \'käl-ə-kwē\ *n* **:** a usu. formal conversation or conference

col·lu·sion \kə-'lü-zhən\ *n* **:** secret agreement or cooperation for a fraudulent or deceitful purpose — **col·lu·sive** \-'lü-siv\ *adj*

co·logne \kə-'lōn\ *n* **:** a perfumed liquid consisting of alcohol and various aromatic oils

¹**co·lon** \'kō-lən\ *n* **:** the part of the large intestine extending from the cecum to the rectum

²**colon** *n* **:** a punctuation mark **:** used esp. to direct attention to following matter (as a list, explanation, or quotation)

³**co·lon** \kə-'lōn\ *n, pl* **co·lo·nes** \-'lō-ˌnäs\ — see MONEY table

col·o·nel \'kərn-ᵊl\ *n* [alter. of earlier *coronel*, fr. MF, modif. of It *colonnello*, fr. *colonna* column, fr. L *columna*] **:** a commissioned officer (as in the army) ranking next below a brigadier general

¹**co·lo·ni·al** \kə-'lō-nē-əl\ *adj* **1 :** of, relating to, or characteristic of a colony; *also* **:** possessing or composed of colonies **2** *often cap* **:** of or relating to the original 13 colonies forming the U.S.

²**colonial** *n* **:** a member or inhabitant of a colony

co·lo·ni·al·ism *n* **:** control by one power over a dependent area or people; *also* **:** a policy advocating or based on such control

col·o·nist \'käl-ə-nəst\ *n* **1 :** COLONIAL **2 :** one who takes part in founding a colony

col·o·nize \-ˌnīz\ *vb* **1 :** to establish a colony in or on **2 :** to settle in a colony — **col·o·niz·er** \-ˌnī-zər\ *n*

col·on·nade \ˌkäl-ə-'nād\ *n* **:** a row of columns usu. supporting the base of the roof structure

col·o·ny \'käl-ə-nē\ *n* **1 :** a body of people sent out by a state to a new territory; *also* **:** the territory inhabited by these people **2 :** a localized population of organisms (a ~ of bees) **3 :** a group with common interests (a writers' ~); *also* **:** the section occupied by such a group

col·o·phon \-fən, -ˌfän\ *n* **:** an inscription placed at the end of a book with facts relative to its production

¹**col·or** \'kəl-ər\ *n* **1 :** a phenomenon of light (as red or blue) or visual perception that enables one to differentiate otherwise identical objects; *also* **:** a hue as contrasted with black, white, or gray **2 :** APPEARANCE **3 :** complexion tint **4** *pl* **:** FLAG; *also* **:** military service (a call to the ~s) **5 :** VIVIDNESS, INTEREST — **col·or·ful** *adj* — **col·or·less** *adj*

²**color** *vb* **1 :** to give color to (as by painting); *also* **:** to change the color of **2 :** BLUSH

col·or·ation \ˌkəl-ə-'rā-shən\ *n* **:** use or arrangement of colors

col·or·a·tu·ra \ˌkəl-ə-rə-'t(y)ùr-ə\ *n* **1 :** florid ornamentation in vocal music **2 :** a soprano specializing in coloratura

col·ored \'kəl-ərd\ *adj* **1 :** having color **2 :** SLANTED, BIASED **3 :** of a race other than the white; *esp* **:** NEGRO

col·or·fast \'kəl-ər-,fast\ *adj* : having color that does not fade or run — **col·or·fast·ness** *n*

co·los·sal \kə-'läs-əl\ *adj* : of very great size or degree

co·los·sus \kə-'läs-əs\ *n* : a gigantic statue; *also* : one resembling a colossus esp. in size

col·por·teur \'käl-,pōrt-ər\ *n* : a peddler of religious books

colt \'kōlt\ *n* : FOAL; *also* : a young male horse, ass, or zebra

col·um·bine \'käl-əm-,bīn\ *n* : a plant related to the buttercups that has showy spurred flowers

col·umn \'käl-əm\ *n* 1 : one of two or more vertical sections of a printed page; *also* : a special department (as in a newspaper) 2 : a pillar supporting a roof or gallery; *also* : something resembling such a column (a ~ of water) 3 : a long row (as of soldiers) — **co·lum·nar** \kə-'ləm-nər\ *adj*

col·um·nist \'käl-əm-(n)əst\ *n* : one who writes a newspaper column

co·ma \'kō-mə\ *n* : a state of deep unconsciousness caused by disease, injury, or poison — **co·ma·tose** \-,tōs\ *adj*

comb \'kōm\ *n* 1 : a toothed instrument for arranging the hair or for separating and cleaning textile fibers 2 : a fleshy crest on the head of a fowl 3 : HONEYCOMB — **comb** *vb*

com·bat \kəm-'bat, 'käm-,bat\ *vb* 1 : FIGHT, CONTEND 2 : to struggle or work against : OPPOSE — **com·bat** \'käm-,bat\ *n* — **com·bat·ant** \kəm-'bat-ʰnt, 'käm-bət-ənt\ *n* — **com·bat·ive** \kəm-'bat-iv\ *adj*

comb·er \'kō-mər\ *n* 1 : one that combs 2 : a long curling oceanic wave

com·bi·na·tion \,käm-bə-'nā-shən\ *n* 1 : the process of combining or being combined 2 : a union or aggregation made by combining 3 : a series of symbols which when dialed by a disk on a lock will open the lock

1**com·bine** \kəm-'bīn\ *vb* : to become one : UNITE, JOIN

2**com·bine** \'käm-,bīn\ *n* 1 : COMBINATION; *esp* : one made to secure business or political advantage 2 : a machine that harvests and threshes grain while moving over the field

comb·ings \'kō-miŋz\ *n pl* : loose hairs or fibers removed by a comb

combining form *n* : a linguistic form that occurs only in compounds or derivatives

com·bo \'käm-bō\ *n, pl* **combos** : a small jazz or dance band

com·bus·ti·ble \kəm-'bəs-tə-bəl\ *adj* : apt to catch fire : FLAMMABLE — **com·bustible** *n*

com·bus·tion \-'bəs-chən\ *n* 1 : the process of burning 2 : slow oxidation (as in the animal body)

come \(')kəm\ *vb* **came** \'kām\ **come; com·ing** \'kəm-iŋ\ 1 : APPROACH 2 : ARRIVE 3 : to reach the point of being or getting (~ to a boil) 4 : to have a place in a series, calendar, or scale 5 : ORIGINATE, ARISE 6 : to be available 7 : REACH, EXTEND 8 : AMOUNT

come·back \'kəm-,bak\ *n* 1 : RETORT 2 : a return to a former position or condition (as of health or prosperity)

co·me·di·an \kə-'mēd-ē-ən\ *n* 1 : an actor in comedy 2 : an amusing person

co·me·di·enne \-,mēd-ē-'en\ *n* : an actress who plays comedy

come·down \'kəm-,daún\ *n* : a descent in rank or dignity

com·e·dy \'käm-əd-ē\ *n* 1 : a light amusing play with a happy ending 2 : a literary work treating a comic theme or written in a comic style

come·ly \'kəm-lē\ *adj* : good-looking : HANDSOME — **come·li·ness** *n*

come-on \-,ôn, -,än\ *n* : INDUCEMENT, LURE

1**co·mes·ti·ble** \kə-'mes-tə-bəl\ *adj* : EDIBLE

2**comestible** *n* : FOOD — usu. used in pl.

com·et \'käm-ət\ *n* [Gk *komētēs*, lit., long-haired, fr. *komē* hair] : a fuzzy heavenly body that often when in the part of its orbit near the sun develops a cloudy tail and that moves in an orbit around the sun in a period from three to thousands of years

come·up·pance \kə-'məp-əns\ *n* : a deserved rebuke or penalty

com·fit \'kəm-fət\ *n* : a candied fruit or nut

1**com·fort** \'kəm-fərt\ *n* 1 : CONSOLATION 2 : freedom from pain, trouble, or anxiety; *also* : something that gives such freedom — **com·fort·less** *adj*

2**comfort** *vb* 1 : to give strength and hope to 2 : CONSOLE

com·fort·able \'kəm(f)t-ə-bəl, 'kəm-fort-\ *adj* 1 : providing comfort 2 : more than adequate 3 : feeling at ease : enjoying comfort — **com·fort·ably** *adv*

com·fort·er \'kəm-fə(r)t-ər\ *n* 1 : one that comforts 2 : QUILT

com·fy \-fē\ *adj* : COMFORTABLE

1**com·ic** \'käm-ik\ *adj* 1 : relating to comedy 2 : provoking laughter : LUDICROUS **syn** laughable, funny — **com·i·cal** *adj*

2**comic** *n* 1 : COMEDIAN 2 : a magazine composed of comic strips

comic strip *n* : a group of cartoons in narrative sequence

com·ing \'kəm-iŋ\ *adj* 1 : APPROACHING, NEXT 2 : gaining importance

com·i·ty \'käm-ət-ē\ *n* : friendly civility : COURTESY

com·ma \'käm-ə\ *n* : a punctuation mark, used esp. as a mark of separation within the sentence

1**com·mand** \kə-'mand\ *vb* 1 : to direct authoritatively : ORDER 2 : DOMINATE, CONTROL, GOVERN 3 : to overlook from a strategic position

2**command** *n* 1 : the act of commanding 2 : an order given 3 : ability to control : MASTERY 4 : a body of troops under a commander; *also* : an area or position that one commands 5 : a position of highest authority

com·man·dant \'käm-ən-,dant, -,dänt\ *n* : an officer in command

com·man·deer \,käm-ən-'diər\ *vb* : to seize for military purposes

com·mand·er \kə-'man-dər\ *n* 1 : LEADER, CHIEF; *esp* : an officer commanding an army or subdivision of an army 2 : a commissioned officer in the navy ranking next below a captain

commander in chief : one who holds supreme command of the armed forces of a nation

com·mand·ment \kə-'man(d)-mənt\ n : COMMAND, ORDER; esp : any of the Ten Commandments

com·man·do \kə-'man-dō\ n, pl -dos or -does : a member of a military unit trained for surprise raids

com·mem·o·rate \kə-'mem-ə-,rāt\ vb 1 : to call or recall to mind 2 : to serve as a memorial of — **com·mem·o·ra·tion** \-,mem-ə-'rā-shən\ n

com·mem·o·ra·tive \-'mem-ə-,rāt-iv\ adj : intended to commemorate an event ⟨a ~ stamp⟩

com·mence \kə-'mens\ vb : BEGIN, START

com·mence·ment \-mənt\ n 1 : the act or time of a beginning 2 : the graduation exercises of a school or college

com·mend \kə-'mend\ vb 1 : to commit to one's care 2 : RECOMMEND 3 : PRAISE — **com·mend·able** adj — **com·men·da·tion** \,käm-ən-'dā-shən\ n

com·men·su·rate \kə-'mens(-ə)-rət, -'mench(-ə)-\ adj : equal in measure or extent; also : PROPORTIONATE, CORRESPONDING

com·ment \'käm-,ent\ n 1 : an expression of opinion 2 : an explanatory, illustrative, or critical note or observation : REMARK — **comment** vb

com·men·tary \'käm-ən-,ter-ē\ n : a systematic series of comments

com·men·ta·tor \-,tāt-ər\ n : one who comments; esp : one who gives talks on news events on radio or television

com·merce \'käm-(,)ərs\ n : the buying and selling of commodities : TRADE

¹com·mer·cial \kə-'mər-shəl\ adj : having to do with commerce; also : designed for profit or for mass appeal — **com·mer·cial·ly** adv

²commercial n : an advertisement broadcast on radio or television

com·mer·cial·ism n : a spirit, method, or practice characteristic of business

com·mer·cial·ize vb : to treat in a business way esp. so as to yield profit

com·mi·na·tion \,käm-ə-'nā-shən\ n : DENUNCIATION — **com·mi·na·to·ry** \'käm-ə-nə-,tōr-ē\ adj

com·min·gle \kə-'miŋ-gəl\ vb : MINGLE, BLEND

com·mis·er·ate \kə-'miz-ə-,rāt\ vb : to feel or express pity : SYMPATHIZE — **com·mis·er·a·tion** \-,miz-ə-'rā-shən\ n

com·mis·sar \'käm-ə-,sär\ n : a Communist party official assigned to a military unit to teach and enforce party principles and policy

com·mis·sar·i·at \,käm-ə-'ser-ē-ət\ n 1 : a system for supplying troops with food 2 : a department headed by a commissar

com·mis·sary \'käm-ə-,ser-ē\ n : a store for equipment and provisions esp. for military personnel

¹com·mis·sion \kə-'mish-ən\ n 1 : a warrant granting certain powers and imposing certain duties 2 : authority to act as agent for another; also : something to be done by an agent 3 : a body of persons charged with performing a duty 4 : the doing of some act; also : the thing done 5 : the allowance made to an agent for transacting business for another 6 : a certificate conferring military rank and authority

²commission vb 1 : to give a commission to 2 : to order to be made 3 : to put (a ship) into a state of readiness for service

commissioned officer n : a military or naval officer holding the rank of second lieutenant or ensign or a higher rank

com·mis·sion·er n 1 : a person given a commission 2 : a member of a commission 3 : an official in charge of a department of public service — **com·mis·sion·er·ship** n

com·mit \kə-'mit\ vb -mit·ted; -mit·ting 1 : to put into charge or trust : ENTRUST ⟨committed the children to the care of a friend⟩ 2 : TRANSFER, CONSIGN 3 : to put in a prison or mental institution 4 : PERPETRATE ⟨~ a crime⟩ 5 : to pledge or assign to some particular course or use — **com·mit·ment** n — **com·mit·tal** n

com·mit·tee \kə-'mit-ē\ n : a body of persons selected to consider and act or report on some matter — **com·mit·tee·man** \-mən\ n

com·mode \kə-'mōd\ n : a movable washstand with cupboard underneath

com·mo·di·ous \-'mōd-ē-əs\ aaj : comfortably spacious : ROOMY

com·mod·i·ty \-'mäd-ət-ē\ n 1 : a product of agriculture or mining 2 : an article of commerce

com·mo·dore \'käm-ə-,dōr\ n 1 : a commissioned officer in the navy ranking next below a rear admiral 2 : an officer commanding a group of merchant ships; also : the chief officer of a yacht club

¹com·mon \'käm-ən\ adj 1 : belonging to or serving the community : PUBLIC 2 : shared by a number in a group 3 : widely or generally known, found, or observed : FAMILIAR 4 : ORDINARY, USUAL 5 : not above the average esp. in social status syn universal, mutual, popular, vulgar — **com·mon·ly** adv

²common n 1 pl : the mass of people as distinguished from the nobility 2 : a piece of land held in common by a community 3 pl : a dining hall 4 pl, cap : the lower house of the British and Canadian parliaments — **in common** : shared together

com·mon·al·ty \-'l-tē\ n : the common people

com·mon·er n : one of the common people : one having no rank of nobility

¹com·mon·place \'käm-ən-,plās\ n : something (as a remark) that is ordinary or trite

²commonplace adj : not remarkable : ORDINARY

com·mon·weal \-,wēl\ n 1 : the general welfare 2 archaic : COMMONWEALTH

com·mon·wealth \-,welth\ n 1 : the body of people politically organized into a state 2 : STATE; also : an association or federation of autonomous states

com·mo·tion \kə-'mō-shən\ n 1 : AGITATION 2 : DISTURBANCE, UPRISING

com·mu·nal \kə-'myün-'l, 'käm-yən-\ adj 1 : relating to a commune or to organization in communes 2 : of or belonging to a community 3 : marked by collective ownership and use of property

¹com·mune \kə-'myün\ vb : to communicate intimately syn consult, negotiate

²com·mune \'käm-,yün\ n 1 : the common people 2 : the smallest administrative district in some European countries

com·mu·ni·ca·ble \kə-'myü-ni-kə-bəl\ *adj* : capable of being communicated ⟨~ diseases⟩

com·mu·ni·cant \-kənt\ *n* 1 : a church member entitled to receive Communion 2 : one who communicates; *esp* : INFORMANT

com·mu·ni·cate \kə-'myü-nə-,kāt\ *vb* 1 : TRANSMIT, IMPART 2 : to make known 3 : to receive Communion 4 : to be in communication 5 : JOIN, CONNECT ⟨the rooms ~⟩

com·mu·ni·ca·tion \-,myü-nə-'kā-shən\ *n* 1 : an act of transmitting 2 : exchange of information or opinions 3 : MESSAGE 4 : a means of communicating — **com·mu·ni·ca·tive** \-'myü-nə-,kāt-iv, -ni-kət-\ *adj*

com·mu·nion \kə-'myü-nyən\ *n* 1 : a sharing of something with others 2 : mutual intercourse 3 *cap* : a Christian sacrament in which bread and wine are partaken of 4 *cap* : a commemoration of the death of Christ 4 *cap* : the act of receiving the sacrament 5 : a body of Christians having a common faith and discipline

com·mu·ni·qué \kə-'myü-nə-,kā\ *n* : an official communication

com·mu·nism \'käm-yə-,niz-əm\ *n* 1 : social organization in which goods are held in common 2 : a theory of social organization advocating common ownership of means of production and an equal distribution of products of industry 3 *cap* : a political doctrine based upon revolutionary Marxian socialism that is the official ideology of the U.S.S.R. and some other countries — **com·mu·nist** \n *or adj, often cap* — **com·mu·nis·tic** \,käm-yə-'nis-tik\ *adj, often cap*

com·mu·ni·ty \kə-'myü-nət-ē\ *n* 1 : a body of people living in the same place under the same laws; *also* : a natural population of plants and animals occupying a common area 2 : society at large 3 : joint ownership 4 : AGREEMENT, CONCORD

com·mu·ta·tion \,käm-yə-'tā-shən\ *n* : substitution of one form of payment or penalty for another

commutation ticket *n* : a transportation ticket sold at a reduced rate for a fixed number of trips over the same route

com·mu·ta·tor \'käm-yə-,tāt-ər\ *n* : a device (as on a generator or motor) for changing the direction of electric current

com·mute \kə-'myüt\ *vb* 1 : EXCHANGE 2 : to substitute a less severe penalty for (one more severe) 3 : to travel back and forth regularly — **com·mut·er** *n*

¹**com·pact** \kəm-'pakt, (')käm-\ *adj* 1 : SOLID, DENSE 2 : BRIEF, SUCCINCT 3 : filling a small space or area — **com·pact·ly** *adv* — **com·pact·ness** *n*

²**compact** *vb* : to pack together — COMPRESS

³**com·pact** \'käm-,pakt\ *n* 1 : a small case for cosmetics 2 : a small automobile

⁴**com·pact** \'käm-,pakt\ *n* : AGREEMENT, COVENANT

¹**com·pan·ion** \kəm-'pan-yən\ *n* [OF *compagnon*, fr. LL *companion-*, *com-*

panio, lit., one who shares bread, fr. L *com-* together + *panis* bread] 1 : an intimate friend or associate : COMRADE 2 : one of a pair of matching things — **com·pan·ion·able** *adj* — **com·pan·ion·less** *adj* — **com·pan·ion·ship** *n*

²**companion** *n* : COMPANIONWAY

com·pan·ion·way \-,wā\ *n* : a ship's stairway or ladder leading from one deck to another

com·pa·ny \'kəmp-(ə-)nē\ *n* 1 : association with others : FELLOWSHIP; *also* : COMPANIONS 2 : RETINUE 3 : an association of persons for carrying on a business 4 : a group of musical or dramatic performers 5 : GUESTS 6 : an infantry unit normally commanded by a captain 7 : the officers and crew of a ship *syn* party, band, troupe, troop, troupe

com·pa·ra·ble \'käm-p(ə-)rə-bəl\ *adj* : capable of being compared *syn* parallel, similar, like, alike

¹**com·par·a·tive** \kəm-'par-ət-iv\ *adj* 1 : of, relating to, or constituting the degree of grammatical comparison that denotes increase in quality, quantity, or relation 2 : RELATIVE ⟨a ~ stranger⟩ — **com·par·a·tive·ly** *adv*

²**comparative** *n* : the comparative degree or a comparative form in a language

¹**com·pare** \kəm-'paər\ *vb* 1 : to represent as like something : LIKEN 2 : to examine for likenesses and differences 3 : to inflect or modify (an adjective or adverb) according to the degrees of comparison

²**compare** *n* : COMPARISON

com·par·i·son \-'par-ə-sən\ *n* 1 : act of comparing : relative estimate 2 : change in the form of an adjective or adverb to show different levels of quality, quantity, or relation

com·part·ment \-'pärt-mənt\ *n* 1 : a section of an enclosed space : ROOM 2 : a separate division

com·part·men·tal·ize \-,pärt-'ment-°l-,īz\ *vb* : to separate into compartments

¹**com·pass** \kəm-pəs, 'käm-\ *vb* 1 : CONTRIVE, PLOT 2 : to bring about : ACHIEVE 3 : to make a circuit of; *also* : SURROUND

²**compass** *n* 1 : BOUNDARY, CIRCUMFERENCE 2 : an enclosed space 3 : RANGE, SCOPE 4 *usu pl* : an instrument for drawing circles or transferring measurements consisting of two legs joined at the top by a pivot 5 : a device for determining direction by means of a magnetic needle swinging freely and pointing to the magnetic north; *also* : a nonmagnetic device that indicates direction

com·pas·sion \kəm-'pash-ən\ *n* : sympathetic feeling : PITY, MERCY — **com·pas·sion·ate** \-(ə-)nət\ *adj*

com·pat·i·ble \kəm-'pat-ə-bəl\ *adj* : able to exist or act together harmoniously ⟨~ colors⟩ ⟨~ drugs⟩ *syn* consonant, congenial, sympathetic — **com·pat·i·bil·i·ty** \-,pat-ə-'bil-ət-ē\ *n*

com·pa·tri·ot \kəm-'pā-trē-ət, -,ät\ *n* : a fellow countryman

com·peer \'käm-,piər\ *n* : EQUAL, PEER

com·pel \kəm-'pel\ *vb* : to drive or urge with force : CONSTRAIN

com·pen·di·um \kəm-'pen-dē-əm\ *n, pl* **-di·ums** *or* **-dia** \-dē-ə\ : a brief sum-

---

mary of a larger work or of a field of knowledge

com·pen·sate \'käm-pən-ˌsāt\ *vb* 1 : to be equivalent to in value or effect : COUNTERBALANCE 2 : PAY, REMUNERATE *syn* balance, offset, recompense, repay, satisfy — **com·pen·sa·tion** \ˌkäm-pən-'sā-shən\ *n* — **com·pen·sa·to·ry** \kəm-'pen-sə-ˌtōr-ē\ *adj*

com·pete \kəm-'pēt\ *vb* : CONTEND, VIE

com·pe·tence \'käm-pət-əns\ *n* 1 : adequate means for subsistence 2 : FITNESS, ABILITY

com·pe·ten·cy *n* : COMPETENCE

com·pe·tent \-pət-ənt\ *adj* : CAPABLE, FIT, QUALIFIED

com·pe·ti·tion \ˌkäm-pə-'tish-ən\ *n* 1 : the act of competing : RIVALRY 2 : CONTEST, MATCH — **com·pet·i·tive** \kəm-'pet-ət-iv\ *adj* — **com·pet·i·tive·ly** *adv*

com·pet·i·tor \kəm-'pet-ət-ər\ *n* : one that competes; *esp* : a rival in selling or buying

com·pile \kəm-'pīl\ *vb* 1 : to collect (literary materials) into a volume 2 : to compose out of materials from other documents — **com·pi·la·tion** \ˌkäm-pə-'lā-shən\ *n* — **com·pil·er** \kəm-'pī-lər\ *n*

com·pla·cence \kəm-'plās-ᵊns\ *n* : SATISFACTION; *esp* : SELF-SATISFACTION — **com·pla·cent** *adj* — **com·pla·cent·ly** *adv*

com·pla·cen·cy *n* : COMPLACENCE

com·plain \kəm-'plān\ *vb* 1 : to express grief, pain, or discontent 2 : to make a formal accusation — **com·plain·ant** *n*

com·plaint \-'plānt\ *n* 1 : expression of grief or discontent 2 : a bodily ailment or disease 3 : a formal accusation against a person

com·plai·sance \kəm-'plās-ᵊns, ˌkäm-plā-,zans\ *n* : disposition to please : AFFABILITY — **com·plai·sant** *adj*

¹com·ple·ment \'käm-plə-mənt\ *n* 1 : a quantity needed to make a thing complete 2 : full quantity, number, or amount 3 : an added word by which a predication is made complete — **com·ple·men·ta·ry** \ˌkäm-plə-'men-t(ə-)rē\ *adj*

²com·ple·ment \'käm-plə-ˌment\ *vb* : to be complementary to : fill out

¹com·plete \kəm-'plēt\ *adj* 1 : having no part lacking 2 : ENDED 3 : fully realized : THOROUGH — **com·plete·ly** *adv* — **com·plete·ness** *n* — **com·ple·tion** \-'plē-shən\ *n*

²complete *vb* : to make whole or perfect 2 : FINISH, CONCLUDE

¹com·plex \(')käm-'pleks, kəm-\ *adj* 1 : composed of two or more parts 2 : consisting of a main clause and one or more subordinate clauses (~ sentence) 3 : COMPLICATED, INTRICATE — **com·plex·i·ty** \kəm-'plek-sət-ē, käm-\ *n*

²com·plex \'käm-ˌpleks\ *n* : something made up of or involving an often intricate combination of elements; *esp* : a system of repressed desires and memories that modify the personality or the individual's response to a subject or situation

com·plex·ion \kəm-'plek-shən\ *n* 1 : the hue or appearance of the skin esp. of the face 2 : general appearance : ASPECT

com·pli·ance \kəm-'plī-əns\ *n* 1 : the act of complying to a demand or pro-

posal 2 : a disposition to yield — **com·pli·ant** *adj*

com·pli·an·cy *n* : COMPLIANCE

com·pli·cate \'käm-plə-ˌkāt\ *vb* : to make or become complex or intricate — **com·pli·ca·tion** \ˌkäm-plə-'kā-shən\ *n*

com·pli·cat·ed *adj* 1 : consisting of parts intricately combined 2 : difficult to analyze, understand, or explain — **com·pli·cat·ed·ly** *adv* — **com·pli·cat·ed·ness** *n*

com·plic·i·ty \kəm-'plis-ət-ē\ *n* : state of being an accomplice : PARTICIPATION

¹com·pli·ment \'käm-plə-mənt\ *n* 1 : an expression of approval or courtesy; *esp* : a flattering remark 2 *pl* : formal greeting

²com·pli·ment \-ˌment\ *vb* : to pay a compliment to

com·pli·men·ta·ry \ˌkäm-plə-'men-t(ə-)rē\ *adj* 1 : containing or expressing a compliment 2 : given free as a courtesy (~ ticket)

com·ply \kəm-'plī\ *vb* : ACQUIESCE, YIELD

¹com·po·nent \kəm-'pō-nənt, 'käm-ˌpō-\ *n* : a component part *syn* ingredient, element

²component *adj* : serving to form a part of : CONSTITUENT

com·port \kəm-'pōrt\ *vb* 1 : AGREE, ACCORD 2 : CONDUCT (~ed himself honorably) *syn* behave

com·port·ment *n* : BEHAVIOR, BEARING

com·pose \kəm-'pōz\ *vb* 1 : to form by putting together : FASHION 2 : ADJUST, ARRANGE 3 : CALM, QUIET 4 : to set type for printing 5 : to practice composition (~ music) — **com·posed** \-'pōzd\ *adj* — **com·pos·ed·ly** \-'pō-zəd-lē\ *adv* — **com·pos·er** *n*

¹com·pos·ite \käm-'päz-ət, kəm-\ *adj* 1 : made up of distinct parts or elements 2 : of, relating to, or being a large group of flowering plants (as the daisy) that bear many small flowers united into compact heads resembling single flowers *syn* blend, compound, mixture

²composite *n* 1 : something composed 2 : a plant of the composite group

com·po·si·tion \ˌkäm-pə-'zish-ən\ *n* 1 : the act of composing; *esp* : arrangement of elements in artistic form 2 : the art or practice of writing 3 : MAKEUP, CONSTITUTION 4 : COMBINATION 5 : a literary, musical, or artistic product; *esp* : ESSAY 6 : the composing of type

com·pos·i·tor \kəm-'päz-ət-ər\ *n* : one who sets type

com·post \'käm-ˌpōst\ *n* : a fertilizing material consisting largely of decayed organic matter

com·po·sure \kəm-'pō-zhər\ *n* : CALMNESS, SELF-POSSESSION

com·pote \'käm-ˌpōt\ *n* 1 : fruits cooked in syrup 2 : a bowl (as of glass) usu. with a base and stem from which compotes, fruits, nuts, or sweets are served

¹com·pound \(')käm-'paund, kəm-\ *vb* 1 : COMBINE 2 : to form by combining parts (~ a medicine) 3 : SETTLE (~ a dispute) 4 : to increase (as interest) by an amount that itself increases; *also* : to add to 5 : to forbear prosecution of (an offense) in return for some reward

²com·pound \'käm-ˌpaund\ *adj* 1 : made up of two or more parts 2 : formed by the combination of two or more other-

wise independent elements ⟨~ sentence⟩
³com·pound \'käm-,paúnd\ n 1 : a compound substance; esp : one formed by the union of two or more chemical elements 2 : a solid or hyphenated word made up of two or more distinct words or word elements syn mixture, composite, blend

⁴com·pound \'käm-,paúnd\ n : an enclosure of European residences and commercial buildings esp. in the Orient

com·pre·hend \,käm-pri-'hend\ vb 1 : UNDERSTAND 2 : INCLUDE — **com·pre·hen·si·ble** \-'hen-sə-bəl\ adj — **com·pre·hen·sion** \-'hen-chən\ n — **com·pre·hen·sive** \-'hen-siv\ adj

¹com·press \kəm-'pres\ vb : to squeeze together : CONDENSE syn constrict, contract, shrink — **com·pressed** adj — **com·pres·sion** \-'presh-ən\ n — **com·pres·sor** \-'pres-ər\ n

²com·press \'käm-,pres\ n : a soft often wet or medicated pad used to press upon an injured bodily part

compressed air n : air under pressure greater than that of the atmosphere

com·prise \kəm-'prīz\ vb 1 : INCLUDE, CONTAIN 2 : to be made up of 3 : to make up : CONSTITUTE

¹com·pro·mise \'käm-prə-,mīz\ n : a settlement of differences reached by mutual concessions; also : the agreement thus made

²compromise vb 1 : to settle by compromise 2 : to endanger the reputation of : expose to discredit

comp·trol·ler \kən-'trō-lər, 'kämp-,trō-\ n : an official who audits and supervises expenditures and accounts

com·pul·sion \kəm-'pəl-shən\ n 1 : COERCION 2 : an irresistible impulse syn constraint, force, violence, restraint — **com·pul·sive** \-'pəl-siv\ adj — **com·pul·so·ry** \-'pəls-(ə-)rē\ adj

com·punc·tion \kəm-'pəŋk-shən\ n : anxiety arising from guilt : REMORSE

com·pute \kəm-'pyüt\ vb : CALCULATE, RECKON — **com·pu·ta·tion** \,käm-pyü-'tā-shən\ n

com·put·er \kəm-'pyüt-ər\ n : an automatic electronic machine for calculating

com·rade \'käm-,rad, -rəd\ n [MF camarade group of soldiers sleeping in one room, roommate, companion, fr. Sp camarada, fr. cámara room, fr. LL camera] : COMPANION, ASSOCIATE — **com·rade·ship** n

¹con \'kän\ vb conned; con·ning 1 : STUDY 2 : MEMORIZE

²con adv : in opposition : AGAINST

³con n : an opposing argument, person, or position

⁴con vb conned; con·ning 1 : SWINDLE 2 : COAX, CAJOLE

con brio \kän-'brē-ō\ adv : with spirit : VIGOROUSLY — used as a direction in music

con·cat·e·na·tion \(,)kän-,kat-ə-'nā-shən\ n : a series connected like links in a chain

con·cave \(')kän-'kāv\ : curved or rounded inward like the inside of a bowl — **con·cav·i·ty** \kän-'kav-ət-ē\ n

con·ceal \kən-'sēl\ vb : to place out of sight : HIDE — **con·ceal·ment** n

con·cede \kən-'sēd\ vb 1 : to admit to

be true 2 : GRANT, YIELD syn allow, accord, award

con·ceit \kən-'sēt\ n 1 : excessively high opinion of oneself, one's appearance, or ability : VANITY 2 : an elaborate or strained metaphor — **con·ceit·ed** adj

con·ceive \kən-'sēv\ vb 1 : to become pregnant 2 : to form an idea of : THINK, IMAGINE — **con·ceiv·able** adj — **con·ceiv·ably** adv

con·cen·trate \'kän-sən-,trāt\ vb 1 : to gather into one body, mass, or force 2 : to make less dilute 3 : to fix one's powers, efforts, or attentions on one thing

con·cen·tra·tion \,kän-sən-'trā-shən\ n 1 : the act or process of concentrating : the state of being concentrated; esp : direction of attention on a single object 2 : the relative content of a component : STRENGTH ⟨the ~ of salt in a solution⟩

con·cen·tric \kən-'sen-trik\ adj 1 : having a common center ⟨~ circles drawn one within another⟩ 2 : COAXIAL

con·cept \'kän-,sept\ n : THOUGHT, NOTION, IDEA — **con·cep·tu·al** \kən-'sep-ch(ə-w)əl\ adj

con·cep·tion \kən-'sep-shən\ n 1 : the act of conceiving or being conceived; also : BEGINNING 2 : the power to form ideas or concepts 3 : IDEA, CONCEPT

¹con·cern \kən-'sərn\ vb 1 : to relate to 2 : to be the business of : INVOLVE 3 : ENGAGE, OCCUPY

²concern n 1 : AFFAIR, MATTER 2 : INTEREST, ANXIETY 3 : a business organization syn business, care, worry

con·cerned adj : ANXIOUS, TROUBLED

con·cern·ing prep : relating to : REGARDING

con·cern·ment n 1 : something in which one is concerned 2 : IMPORTANCE, CONSEQUENCE

¹con·cert \kən-'sərt\ vb 1 : to plan together 2 : to act in conjunction or harmony

²con·cert \'kän-(,)sərt\ n 1 : agreement in a plan or design 2 : a concerted action 3 : a musical performance by several instruments or voices

con·cert·ed \kən-'sərt-əd\ adj : mutually agreed on

con·cer·ti·na \,kän-sər-'tē-nə\ n : an instrument of the accordion family

con·cert·mas·ter \'kän-sərt-,mas-tər\ n : the leader of the first violins and assistant conductor of an orchestra

con·cer·to \kən-'chert-ō\ n, pl -ti \-(,)ē\ or -tos : a symphonic piece for one or more solo instruments and orchestra

con·ces·sion \kən-'sesh-ən\ n 1 : an act of conceding or yielding 2 : something yielded : ADMISSION, ACKNOWLEDGMENT 3 : a grant by a government of land or of a right to use it 4 : a grant of a portion of premises for some specific purpose — **con·ces·sion·aire** \-,sesh-ə-'naer\ n

con·ces·sive \-'ses-iv\ adj : tending toward, expressing, or being a concession

conch \'käŋk, 'känch\ n, pl **conchs** \'käŋks\ or **conch·es** \'kän-chəz\ : a large spiral-shelled marine mollusk

con·cierge \kō⁽ⁿ⁾-'syerzh\ n : an attendant at the entrance of a building esp. in France who observes those entering and leaving, handles mail, and acts as a janitor or porter

con·cil·i·ate \kən-'sil-ē-ˌāt\ vb 1 : to win over from a state of hostility 2 : to gain the goodwill of — con·cil·i·a·tion \-ˌsil-ē-'ā-shən\ n — con·cil·ia·to·ry \-'sil-yə-ˌtōr-ē\ adj

con·cise \kən-'sīs\ adj : expressing much in few words : TERSE, SUCCINCT — con·cise·ness n

con·clave \'kän-ˌklāv\ n [ML, fr. L, room that can be locked, fr. com- together + clavis key] : a private gathering (as of Roman Catholic cardinals); also : CONVENTION

con·clude \kən-'klüd\ vb 1 : to bring to a close : END 2 : DECIDE, JUDGE 3 : to bring about as a result (~ an agreement) syn close, finish, terminate, complete, gather, infer

con·clu·sion \kən-'klü-zhən\ n 1 : the logical consequence of a reasoning process : INFERENCE 2 : TERMINATION, END 3 : OUTCOME, RESULT — con·clu·sive \-'klü-siv\ adj — con·clu·sive·ly adv

con·coct \kən-'käkt, kän-\ vb 1 : to prepare by combining diverse ingredients 2 : DEVISE (~ a scheme) — con·coc·tion \-'käk-shən\ n

con·com·i·tant \-'käm-ət-ənt\ adj : ACCOMPANYING, ATTENDING — concomitant n

con·cord \'kän-ˌkȯrd, 'käŋ-\ n : AGREEMENT, HARMONY

con·cor·dance \kən-'kȯrd-°ns\ n 1 : AGREEMENT 2 : an alphabetical index of words in a book or in an author's works with the passages in which they occur

con·cor·dant \-°nt\ adj : HARMONIOUS, AGREEING

con·cor·dat \kən-'kȯr-ˌdat\ n : AGREEMENT, COVENANT

con·course \'kän-ˌkōrs\ n 1 : a flocking together of people : GATHERING 2 : an open place where roads meet or crowds may gather

con·cres·cence \kən-'kres-°ns\ n : a growing together — con·cres·cent adj

¹con·crete \'kän-ˌkrēt, kän-'krēt\ adj 1 : united in solid form 2 : naming a real thing or class of things : not abstract 3 : not theoretical : ACTUAL 4 : made of or relating to concrete syn specific, particular, special

²con·crete \'kän-ˌkrēt, kän-'krēt\ n : a hard building material made by mixing cement, sand, and gravel with water \'kän-'krēt, kän-'krēt\

³con·crete \'kän-ˌkrēt, kän-'krēt\ vb 1 : SOLIDIFY 2 : to cover with concrete

con·cre·tion \kən-'krē-shən\ n : a hard mass esp. when formed abnormally in the body

con·cu·bine \'käŋ-kyə-ˌbīn\ n : a woman who is not legally a wife but lives with a man and has a recognized position in his household — con·cu·bi·nage \kän-'kyü-bə-nij\ n

con·cu·pis·cence \kän-'kyü-pə-səns\ n : ardent sexual desire : LUST

con·cur \kən-'kər\ vb -curred; -curring 1 : COINCIDE 2 : to act together 3 : AGREE syn unite, combine, cooperate

con·cur·rence \-'kər-əns\ n 1 : CONJUNCTION, COINCIDENCE 2 : agreement in action or opinion

con·cur·rent adj 1 : happening or operating at the same time 2 : joint and equal in authority

con·cus·sion \kən-'kəsh-ən\ n 1 : SHOCK, SHAKING 2 : a sharp sudden blow or collision; also : bodily injury (as to the brain) resulting from a sudden jar

con·demn \kən-'dem\ vb 1 : to declare to be wrong 2 : to convict of guilt 3 : to sentence judicially 4 : to pronounce unfit for use (~ a building) 5 : to declare forfeited or taken for public use syn denounce, censure, blame, criticize, doom, damn — con·dem·na·tion \ˌkän-ˌdem-'nā-shən\ n — con·dem·na·to·ry \kən-'dem-nə-ˌtōr-ē\ adj

con·dense \kən-'dens\ vb 1 : to make or become more compact or dense : CONCENTRATE 2 : to change from vapor to liquid syn contract, shrink, deflate — con·den·sa·tion \ˌkän-ˌden-'sā-shən\ n — con·dens·er \kən-'den-sər\ n

con·de·scend \ˌkän-di-'send\ vb 1 : to assume an air of superiority syn stoop, deign — con·de·scend·ing·ly adv — con·de·scen·sion \-'sen-chən\ n

con·dign \kən-'dīn, 'kän-ˌdīn\ adj : DESERVED, APPROPRIATE (~ punishment)

con·di·ment \'kän-də-mənt\ n : something used to make food savory; esp : a pungent seasoning (as pepper)

¹con·di·tion \kən-'dish-ən\ n 1 : something essential to the occurrence of some other thing 2 pl : state of affairs : CIRCUMSTANCES 3 : state of being 4 : station in life : social rank 5 : state in respect to fitness (as for action or use); esp : state of health

²condition vb 1 : to limit or modify by a condition 2 : to put into proper condition for action or use

con·di·tion·al \-'(ə-)nəl\ adj : containing, implying, or depending upon a condition

con·dole \kən-'dōl\ vb : to express sympathetic sorrow — con·do·lence \kən-'dō-ləns, 'kän-də-\ n

con·do·min·i·um \ˌkän-də-'min-ē-əm\ n 1 : joint sovereignty (as by two or more nations) 2 : a politically dependent territory under condominium 3 : individual ownership of a unit in a multi-unit structure (as an apartment)

con·done \kən-'dōn\ vb : to overlook or forgive (an offense) by treating the offender as if he had done nothing wrong syn excuse, pardon — con·do·na·tion \ˌkän-dō-'nā-shən\ n

con·dor \'kän-dər\ n : a very large western American vulture

con·duce \kən-'d(y)üs\ vb : to lead or contribute to a result — con·du·cive adj

¹con·duct \'kän-(ˌ)dəkt\ n 1 : MANAGEMENT, DIRECTION 2 : BEHAVIOR

²con·duct \kən-'dəkt\ vb 1 : GUIDE, ESCORT 2 : MANAGE, DIRECT 3 : to serve as a channel for : CONVEY, TRANSMIT 4 : BEHAVE, BEAR (~ himself honorably) — con·duc·tion \-'dək-shən\ n

con·duc·tive \kən-'dək-tiv\ adj : having the power to conduct (as heat or electricity) — con·duc·tance n — con·duc·tiv·i·ty \ˌkän-ˌdək-'tiv-ət-ē\ n

con·duc·tor \kən-'dək-tər\ n 1 : one that conducts 2 : a collector of fares in a public conveyance 3 : the leader of a musical ensemble

con·duit \'kän-ˌd(y)ü-ət, -dət\ *n* **1** : a channel (as a pipe or aqueduct) for conveying fluid **2** : a tube or trough for protecting electric wires or cables

cone \'kōn\ *n* **1** : the scaly fruit of trees of the pine family **2** : a solid figure whose base is a circle and whose sides taper evenly up to an apex; *also* : something having a similar shape

Con·es·to·ga \ˌkän-ə-'stō-gə\ *n* : a broad-wheeled covered wagon usu. drawn by six horses and formerly used esp. for transporting freight across the prairies

co·ney \'kō-nē\ *n* : a rabbit or its fur

con·fab·u·la·tion \kən-ˌfab-yə-'lā-shən\ *n* : familiar talk : CHAT; *also* : CONFERENCE

con·fec·tion \kən-'fek-shən\ *n* : a fancy dish or sweet; *also* : CANDY

con·fec·tion·er \-sh(ə-)nər\ *n* : a maker of or dealer in confections (as candies)

con·fec·tion·ery \-shə-ˌner-ē\ *n* **1** : CANDIES **2** : a confectioner's place of business

con·fed·er·a·cy \kən-'fed-(ə-)rə-sē\ *n* **1** : LEAGUE, ALLIANCE **2** *cap* : the 11 southern states that seceded from the U. S. in 1860 and 1861

¹con·fed·er·ate \-(ə-)rət\ *adj* **1** : united in a league : ALLIED **2** *cap* : of or relating to the Confederacy

²confederate *n* **1** : ALLY; *also* : ACCOMPLICE **2** *cap* : an adherent of the Confederacy

³con·fed·er·ate \kən-'fed-ə-ˌrāt\ *vb* : to unite in a confederacy or a conspiracy

con·fed·er·a·tion \-ˌfed-ə-'rā-shən\ *n* **1** : act of confederating **2** : ALLIANCE, LEAGUE

con·fer \kən-'fər\ *vb* -ferred; -fer·ring **1** : GRANT, BESTOW **2** : to exchange views : CONSULT — **con·fer·ee** \ˌkän-fə-'rē\ *n*

con·fer·ence \'kän-f(ə-)rəns\ *n* : an interchange of views; *also* : a meeting for this purpose

con·fess \kən-'fes\ *vb* **1** : to acknowledge or disclose one's misdeed, fault, or sin **2** : to acknowledge one's sins to God or to a priest **3** : to receive the confession of (a penitent) *syn* admit, own

con·fess·ed·ly \-'fes-əd-lē\ *adv* : by confession : ADMITTEDLY

con·fes·sion \-'fesh-ən\ *n* **1** : an act of confessing (as in the sacrament of penance) **2** : an acknowledgment of guilt **3** : a formal statement of religious beliefs **4** : a religious body having a common creed — **con·fes·sion·al** *adj*

con·fes·sion·al *n* : a place where a priest hears confessions

con·fes·sor \kən-'fes-ər\ *n* **1** : one that confesses **2** : a priest who hears confessions

con·fet·ti \kən-'fet-ē\ *n* : bits of colored paper or ribbon for throwing about in celebration

con·fi·dant \'kän-fə-ˌdant\ *n* : one to whom secrets are confided

con·fide \kən-'fīd\ *vb* **1** : to have or show faith : TRUST (~ in a friend) **2** : to tell confidentially (~ a secret) **3** : ENTRUST

con·fi·dence \'kän-fəd-əns\ *n* **1** : TRUST,

RELIANCE **2** : SELF-ASSURANCE, BOLDNESS **3** : a state of trust or intimacy — **con·fi·dent** \-dənt\ *adj* — **con·fi·dent·ly** *adv*

con·fi·den·tial \ˌkän-fə-'den-chəl\ *adj* **1** : SECRET, PRIVATE **2** : enjoying or treated with confidence (~ clerk) — **con·fi·den·tial·ly** \-'dench-(ə-)lē\ *adv*

con·fig·u·ra·tion \kən-ˌfig-yə-'rā-shən\ *n* : structural arrangement of parts : SHAPE

con·fine \kən-'fīn\ *vb* **1** : to keep within limits : RESTRAIN **2** : IMPRISON **3** : to restrict to a particular place or situation (as from illness or duties) — **con·fine·ment** *n* — **con·fin·er** *n*

con·firm \kən-'fərm\ *vb* **1** : to make firm or firmer **2** : RATIFY **3** : VERIFY, CORROBORATE **4** : to administer the rite of confirmation to — **con·fir·ma·to·ry** \-'fər-mə-ˌtōr-ē\ *adj* — **con·firmed** *adj*

con·fir·ma·tion \ˌkän-fər-'mā-shən\ *n* **1** : an act of ratifying or corroborating; *also* : PROOF **2** : a religious ceremony admitting a person to full membership in a church or synagogue

con·fis·cate \'kän-fə-ˌskāt\ *vb* : to take possession of by or as if by public authority — **con·fis·ca·tion** \ˌkän-fə-'skā-shən\ *n* — **con·fis·ca·to·ry** \kən-'fis-kə-ˌtōr-ē\ *adj*

con·fla·gra·tion \ˌkän-flə-'grā-shən\ *n* : FIRE; *esp* : a large disastrous fire

¹con·flict \'kän-ˌflikt\ *n* **1** : WAR **2** : clash between hostile or opposing elements or ideas

²con·flict \kən-'flikt\ *vb* : to show antagonism or irreconcilability : CLASH

con·flu·ence \'kän-ˌflü-əns\ *n* **1** : the meeting or place of meeting of two or more streams **2** : a flocking together **3** : CROWD — **con·flu·ent** *adj*

con·flux \'kän-ˌfləks\ *n* **1** : CONFLUENCE

con·form \kən-'fȯrm\ *vb* **1** : to make or be like : AGREE, ACCORD **2** : to obey customs or standards — **con·form·able** *adj*

con·for·mance \-'fȯr-məns\ *n* : CONFORMITY

con·for·ma·tion \ˌkän-fȯr-'mā-shən\ *n* : arrangement and congruity of parts : FORM

con·for·mi·ty \kən-'fȯr-mət-ē\ *n* **1** : HARMONY, AGREEMENT **2** : COMPLIANCE, OBEDIENCE

con·found \kən-'faùnd, kän-\ *vb* **1** : to throw into disorder or confusion : DISMAY **2** : to mix up : CONFUSE *syn* bewilder, puzzle, perplex, mistake

con·fra·ter·ni·ty \ˌkän-frə-'tər-nət-ē\ *n* : a society devoted to a religious or charitable cause

con·frere \'kōⁿ-ˌfreər, 'kän-\ *n* : COLLEAGUE, COMRADE

con·front \kən-'frənt\ *vb* **1** : to face esp. in challenge : OPPOSE **2** : to cause to face or meet

Con·fu·cian·ism \kən-'fyü-shən-ˌiz-əm\ *n* : a religion growing out of the teachings of the Chinese philosopher Confucius — **Con·fu·cian** *n or adj*

con·fuse \kən-'fyüz\ *vb* : to make mentally unclear or uncertain; *also* : to disturb the composure of **2** : to mix up : JUMBLE *syn* muddle, befuddle, mistake, confound — **con·fus·ed·ly** \-'fyü-zəd-lē\ *adv* con·fu·sion \-'fyü-zhən\ n 1 : turmoil or uncertainty of mind 2 : DISORDER, JUMBLE

con·fute \kən-'fyüt\ vb : to overwhelm by argument : REFUTE — con·fu·ta·tion \,kän-fyù-'tā-shən\ n

con·ga \'käŋ-gə\ n : a Cuban dance of African origin performed by a group usu. in single file

con·geal \kən-'jēl\ vb 1 : FREEZE 2 : to make or become hard or thick as if by freezing

con·ge·ner \'kän-jə-nər\ n : one related to another

con·ge·nial \kən-'jē-nyəl\ adj 1 : KIN-DRED, SYMPATHETIC 2 : suited to one's taste or nature : AGREEABLE

con·gen·i·tal \kən-'jen-ət-ʾl\ adj : existing at or dating from birth but usu. not hereditary syn inborn, innate

con·ger eel \,käŋ-gər-\ n : a large edible marine eel

con·ge·ries \'kän-jə-(,)rēz\ n : AGGRE-GATION, COLLECTION

con·gest \kən-'jest\ vb 1 : to cause excessive fullness of the blood vessels of (as a lung) 2 : to obstruct by overcrowding — con·ges·tion \-'jes-chən\ n

¹con·glom·er·ate \kən-'gläm-(ə-)rət\ adj 1 : made up of parts from various sources 2 : densely massed or clustered

²con·glom·er·ate \-ə-,rāt\ vb : to form into a ball or mass — con·glom·er·a·tion \-,gläm-ə-'rā-shən\ n

³con·glom·er·ate \-'gläm-(ə-)rət\ n : a mass formed of fragments from various sources; esp : a rock composed of fragments varying from pebbles to boulders held together by a cementing material

con·grat·u·late \kən-'grach-ə-,lāt\ vb : to express sympathetic pleasure to on account of success or good fortune : FELICITATE — con·grat·u·la·tion \-,grach-ə-'lā-shən\ n — con·grat·u·la·to·ry \-'grach-(ə-)lə-,tōr-ē\ adj

con·gre·gate \'käŋ-gri-,gāt\ vb : AS-SEMBLE

con·gre·ga·tion \,käŋ-gri-'gā-shən\ n 1 : an assembly of persons met esp. for worship; also : a group that habitually so meets 2 : a company or order of religious persons under a common rule 3 : the act or an instance of congregating

con·gre·ga·tion·al \-sh(ə-)nəl\ adj 1 : of or relating to a congregation 2 cap : observing the faith and practice of certain Protestant churches which recognize the independence of each congregation in church matters

Con·gre·ga·tion·al·ist n : a member of one of several Protestant denominations that emphasize the autonomy of the local congregation — Con·gre·ga·tion·al·ism n

con·gress \'käŋ-grəs\ n 1 : an assembly esp. of delegates for discussion and usu. action on some question 2 : the body of senators and representatives constituting a nation's legislature — con·gres·sio·nal \kən-'gresh-(ə-)nəl\ adj

con·gress·man \'käŋ-grəs-mən\ n : a member of a congress

con·gru·ence \kən-'grü-əns, 'käŋ-grə-wəns\ n : the quality of according or coinciding : CONGRUITY — con·gru·ent adj

con·gru·en·cy \n : CONGRUENCE

con·gru·i·ty \kən-'grü-ət-ē\ n : corre-

spondence between things : AGREEMENT, HARMONY — con·gru·ous \'käŋ-grə-wəs\ adj

con·ic \'kän-ik\ adj : relating to or resembling a cone — con·i·cal adj

con·i·fer \'kän-ə-fər, 'kōn-\ n : a cone-bearing tree or shrub (as a pine) — co·nif·er·ous \kō-'nif-(ə-)rəs\ adj

con·jec·ture \kən-'jek-chər\ n : GUESS, SURMISE — con·jec·tur·al adj — conjecture vb

con·join \kən-'jóin\ vb : to join together : UNITE — con·joint \-'jóint\ adj

con·ju·gal \'kän-ji-gəl, kən-'jü-\ adj : of or relating to marriage : MATRI-MONIAL

¹con·ju·gate \'kän-ji-gət\ adj 1 : united esp. in pairs : COUPLED 2 : of kindred origin and meaning ⟨sing and song are ~⟩

²con·ju·gate \-jə-,gāt\ vb 1 : INFLECT ⟨~ a verb⟩ 2 : to join together : COUPLE

con·ju·ga·tion \,kän-jə-'gā-shən\ n 1 : the act of conjugating 2 : the state of being conjugated 2 : a schematic arrangement of the inflectional forms of a verb

con·junct \kən-'jəŋkt\ adj : JOINED, UNITED

con·junc·tion \kən-'jəŋk-shən\ n 1 : UNION, COMBINATION 2 : occurrence at the same time 3 : a word that joins together sentences, clauses, phrases, or words

con·junc·tive \-'jəŋk-tiv\ adj 1 : CON-NECTIVE 2 : CONJUNCT 3 : being or functioning like a conjunction

con·junc·ture \-'jəŋk-chər\ n 1 : CON-JUNCTION, UNION 2 : a combination of circumstances or events esp. producing a crisis

con·jure \'kän-jər, kən-; 3 is kən-'jür\ vb 1 : to practice magic; esp : to summon (as a devil) by sorcery 2 : to practice sleight of hand 3 : to implore earnestly or solemnly — con·ju·ra·tion \,kän-jə-'rā-shən, ,kən-\ n — con·jur·er or con·ju·ror \see verb\ n

conk \'käŋk\ vb : to break down; esp : STALL ⟨the motor ~ed out⟩

con·nect \kə-'nekt\ vb 1 : JOIN, LINK 2 : to associate in one's mind — con·nec·tor n

con·nec·tion \kə-'nek-shən\ n 1 : JUNC-TION, UNION 2 : logical relationship : COHERENCE; esp : relation of a word to other words in a sentence 3 : BOND, LINK 4 : family relationship 5 : relationship in social affairs or in business 6 : a person related by blood or marriage 7 : an association of persons; esp : a religious denomination

¹con·nec·tive \-'nek-tiv\ adj : connecting or functioning in connecting : JOIN-ING

²connective n : a word (as a conjunction) that connects words or word groups

con·nip·tion \kə-'nip-shən\ n : a fit of rage, hysteria, or alarm

con·nive \kə-'nīv\ vb [L conivēre, lit., to close the eyes, wink] 1 : to pretend ignorance of something one ought to oppose as wrong 2 : to cooperate secretly : give secret aid — con·niv·ance n

con·nois·seur \,kän-ə-'sər\ n : a critical judge in matters of art or taste

con·no·ta·tion \,kän-ə-'tā-shən\ n : a meaning in addition to or apart from the thing explicitly named or described by a word

con·no·ta·tive \'kän-ə-ˌtāt-iv, kə-'nōt-ət-\ *adj* **1** : connoting or tending to connote **2** : relating to connotation

con·note \kə-'nōt\ *vb* **1** : to suggest or mean along with or in addition to the exact explicit meaning **2** : to be associated with as a consequence or concomitant (guilt usually ~s suffering)

con·nu·bi·al \kə-'n(y)ü-bē-əl\ *adj* : of or relating to marriage : CONJUGAL

con·quer \'käŋ-kər\ *vb* **1** : to gain by force of arms : WIN **2** : to get the better of : OVERCOME **syn** defeat, subjugate, subdue, overthrow — **con·quer·or** *n*

con·quest \'kän-ˌkwest, 'käŋ-\ *n* **1** : an act of conquering : VICTORY **2** : something conquered

con·quis·ta·dor \kȯn-'kēs-tə-ˌdȯr\ *n, pl* **-do·res** \-ˌkēs-tə-'dȯr-ēz\ *or* **-dors** \-'kēs-tə-ˌdȯrz\ : CONQUEROR; *esp* : a leader in the Spanish conquest of America and esp. of Mexico and Peru in the 16th century

con·san·guin·i·ty \ˌkän-ˌsan-'gwin-ət-ē, -ˌsaŋ-\ *n* : blood relationship — **con·san·guin·e·ous** \-'gwin-ē-əs\ *adj*

con·science \'kän-chəns\ *n* : consciousness of the moral right and wrong of one's own acts or motives — **science·less** *adj*

con·sci·en·tious \ˌkän-chē-'en-chəs\ *adj* : guided by one's own sense of right and wrong **syn** scrupulous, honorable, honest, upright, just — **con·sci·en·tious·ly** *adv*

con·scious \'kän-chəs\ *adj* **1** : AWARE **2** : mentally awake or alert : not asleep or unconscious **3** : known or felt by one's inner self **4** : INTENTIONAL — **con·scious·ly** *adv* — **con·scious·ness** *n*

con·script \kən-'skript\ *vb* : to enroll by compulsion for military or naval service — **con·script** \'kän-ˌskript\ *n* — **con·scrip·tion** \kən-'skrip-shən\ *n*

con·se·crate \'kän-sə-ˌkrāt\ *vb* **1** : to induct (as a bishop) into an office with a religious rite **2** : to make or declare sacred (~ a church) **3** : to devote solemnly to a purpose — **con·se·cra·tion** \ˌkän-sə-'krā-shən\ *n*

con·sec·u·tive \kən-'sek-(y)ət-iv\ *adj* : following in regular order : SUCCESSIVE —**con·sec·u·tive·ly** *adv*

con·sen·sus \kən-'sen-səs\ *n* **1** : agreement in opinion, testimony, or belief : UNANIMITY **2** : collective opinion

1con·sent \kən-'sent\ *vb* : to give assent or approval

2consent *n* : approval or acceptance of something done or proposed by another

con·se·quence \'kän-sə-ˌkwens, -kwəns\ *n* **1** : RESULT **2** : IMPORTANCE **syn** effect, outcome, significance

con·se·quent \-ˌkwent, -ˌkwent\ *adj* : following as a result or effect — **con·se·quent·ly** *adv*

con·se·quen·tial \ˌkän-sə-'kwen-chəl\ *adj* **1** : having significant consequences **2** : showing self-importance

con·ser·va·tion \ˌkän-sər-'vā-shən\ *n* : PRESERVATION, PROTECTION; *esp* : planned management of natural resources

con·ser·va·tion·ist *n* : one who advocates conservation esp. of natural resources

con·ser·va·tism \kən-'sər-və-ˌtiz-əm\ *n* : disposition to keep to established ways : opposition to change

1con·ser·va·tive \-vət-iv\ *adj* **1** : PRE-SERVATIVE **2** : disposed to maintain existing views, conditions, or institutions **3** : MODERATE, CAUTIOUS — **con·ser·va·tive·ly** *adv*

2conservative *n* : one who adheres to traditional methods or views

con·ser·va·tor \kən-'sər-vət-ər, 'kän-sər-ˌvāt-\ *n* **1** : PROTECTOR, GUARDIAN **2** : one named by a court to protect the interests of an incompetent (as a child)

con·ser·va·to·ry \kən-'sər-və-ˌtōr-ē\ *n* **1** : GREENHOUSE **2** : a place of instruction in one of the fine arts (as music)

1con·serve \kən-'sərv\ *vb* : to keep from losing or wasting : PRESERVE

2con·serve \'kän-ˌsərv\ *n* **1** : CONFECTION; *esp* : a candied fruit **2** : PRESERVE; *esp* : one prepared from a mixture of fruits

con·sid·er \kən-'sid-ər\ *vb* **1** : THINK, PONDER **2** : HEED, REGARD **3** : JUDGE, BELIEVE — **con·sid·ered** *adj*

con·sid·er·able \-'sid-ər-(ə-)bəl\ *adj* **1** : IMPORTANT **2** : large in extent, amount, or degree — **con·sid·er·ably** *adv*

con·sid·er·ate \-'sid-(ə-)rət\ *adj* : observant of the rights and feelings of others **syn** thoughtful, attentive

con·sid·er·a·tion \-ˌsid-ə-'rā-shən\ *n* **1** : careful thought : DELIBERATION **2** : thoughtful attention **3** : MOTIVE, REASON **4** : JUDGMENT, OPINION **5** : RECOMPENSE

con·sid·er·ing *prep* : in view of : taking into account

con·sign \kən-'sīn\ *vb* **1** : to deliver formally **2** : ENTRUST, COMMIT **3** : ALLOT **4** : to send (goods) to an agent for sale — **con·sign·ee** \ˌkän-sə-'nē, ˌkän-ˌsī-, kən-ˌsī-\ *n* — **con·sign·or** \kən-'sī-nər; ˌkän-sə-'nȯr, ˌkän-ˌsī-, kən-ˌsī-\ *n*

con·sign·ment \kən-'sīn-mənt\ *n* : a shipment of goods consigned to an agent

con·sist \kən-'sist\ *vb* **1** : to be inherent : LIE — used with *in* **2** : to be composed or made up (coal ~s chiefly of carbon)

con·sis·tence \-'sis-təns\ *n* : CONSISTENCY

con·sis·ten·cy \-tən-sē\ *n* **1** : COHESIVENESS, FIRMNESS **2** : agreement or harmony in parts or of different things **3** : UNIFORMITY (~ of behavior) — **con·sis·tent** \-tənt\ *adj* — **con·sis·tent·ly** *adv*

con·sis·to·ry \kən-'sis-t(ə-)rē\ *n* : a solemn assembly (as of Roman Catholic cardinals)

1con·sole \kən-'sōl\ *vb* : to soothe the grief of : COMFORT, SOLACE — **con·so·la·tion** \ˌkän-sə-'lā-shən\ *n* — **con·so·la·to·ry** \kən-'sōl-ə-ˌtōr-ē, -'säl-\ *adj*

2con·sole \'kän-ˌsōl\ *n* **1** : the desklike part of an organ at which the organist sits **2** : a panel or cabinet for the controls of an electrical or mechanical device **3** : a cabinet for a radio or television set resting directly on the floor

con·sol·i·date \kən-'säl-ə-ˌdāt\ *vb* **1** : to

unite or become united into one whole : COMBINE 2 : to make firm or secure 3 : to form into a compact mass — **con·sol·i·da·tion** \-ˌsäl-ə-ˈdā-shən\ n

con·som·mé \ˌkän-sə-ˈmā\ n : a clear soup that is essentially a well-seasoned meat broth

con·so·nance \ˈkän-s(ə-)nəns\ n 1 : AGREEMENT, HARMONY 2 : repetition of consonants esp. as an alternative to rhyme in verse

¹**con·so·nant** \-s(ə-)nənt\ adj : having consonance, harmony, or agreement **syn** consistent, compatible, congruous, congenial, sympathetic

²**consonant** n 1 : a speech sound (as \p\, \g\, \n\, \l\, \s\, \r\) characterized by constriction or closure at one or more points in the breath channel 2 : a letter other than a, e, i, o, and u — **con·so·nan·tal** \ˌkän-sə-ˈnant-ᵊl\ adj

¹**con·sort** \ˈkän-ˌsȯrt\ n 1 : SPOUSE, MATE 2 : a ship accompanying another for protection

²**con·sort** \kən-ˈsȯrt\ vb 1 : to keep company : ASSOCIATE 2 : ACCORD, HARMONIZE

con·sor·tium \-ˈsȯr-sh(ē-)əm\ n, pl **-tia** \-sh(ē-)ə\ : an international business or banking agreement or combination

con·spec·tus \kən-ˈspek-təs\ n 1 : a brief survey or summary 2 : OUTLINE, SYNOPSIS

con·spic·u·ous \kən-ˈspik-yə-wəs\ adj : attracting attention : PROMINENT, STRIKING **syn** noticeable, remarkable, outstanding — **con·spic·u·ous·ly** adv

con·spir·a·cy \kən-ˈspir-ə-sē\ n : an agreement among conspirators : PLOT

con·spire \kən-ˈspī(ə)r\ vb : to plan secretly an unlawful act : PLOT — **con·spir·a·tor** \-ˈspir-ət-ər\ n

con·sta·ble \ˈkän-stə-bəl, ˈkən-\ n [ME conestable chief officer of a nobleman's household, fr. OF, fr. LL comes stabuli companion or officer of the stable] : POLICEMAN

con·stab·u·lary \kən-ˈstab-yə-ˌler-ē\ n 1 : the police of a particular district or country 2 : an armed police force organized on military lines but distinct from the regular army

con·stan·cy \ˈkän-stən-sē\ n 1 : firmness of mind : STEADFASTNESS 2 : STABILITY

¹**con·stant** \-stənt\ adj 1 : STEADFAST, FAITHFUL 2 : FIXED, UNCHANGING 3 : continually recurring : REGULAR — **con·stant·ly** adv

²**constant** n : something unchanging

con·stel·la·tion \ˌkän-stə-ˈlā-shən\ n : any of 88 groups of stars forming patterns

con·ster·na·tion \ˌkän-stər-ˈnā-shən\ n : amazed dismay and confusion

con·sti·pa·tion \ˌkän-stə-ˈpā-shən\ n : abnormally delayed or infrequent passage of usu. hard dry feces — **con·sti·pate** \ˈkän-stə-ˌpāt\ vb

con·stit·u·en·cy \kən-ˈstich-ə-wən-sē\ n : a body of constituents; also : an electoral district

¹**con·stit·u·ent** \-wənt\ adj 1 : COMPONENT 2 : having power to elect 3 : having power to frame or revise a constitution

²**constituent** n 1 : a component part 2 : one entitled to vote for a representative for a district

con·sti·tute \ˈkän-stə-ˌt(y)üt\ vb 1 : to appoint to an office or duty 2 : to set

up : ESTABLISH ⟨~ a law⟩ 3 : to make up : COMPOSE

con·sti·tu·tion \ˌkän-stə-ˈt(y)ü-shən\ n 1 : an established law or custom 2 : the physical makeup of the individual 3 : the structure, composition, or make-up of something ⟨~ of the sun⟩ 4 : the basic law in a politically organized body; also : a document containing such law — **con·sti·tu·tion·al** \-sh(ə-)nəl\ adj

con·sti·tu·tion·al n : an exercise (as a walk) taken for one's health

con·sti·tu·tion·al·i·ty \-ˌt(y)ü-shə-ˈnal-ət-ē\ n : the condition of being in accordance with the constitution of a nation or state

con·sti·tu·tive \ˈkän-stə-ˌt(y)üt-iv, kən-ˈstich-ət-\ adj : CONSTITUENT, ESSENTIAL

con·strain \kən-ˈstrān\ vb 1 : COMPEL, FORCE 2 : CONFINE 3 : RESTRAIN

con·straint \-ˈstrānt\ n 1 : COMPULSION; also : RESTRAINT 2 : unnaturalness of manner produced by a repression of one's natural feelings : EMBARRASSMENT

con·strict \kən-ˈstrikt\ vb : to draw together : SQUEEZE — **con·stric·tion** \-ˈstrik-shən\ n — **con·stric·tive** \-ˈstrik-tiv\ adj

con·struct \kən-ˈstrəkt\ vb : BUILD, MAKE — **con·struc·tor** n

con·struc·tion \kən-ˈstrək-shən\ n 1 : the art, process, or manner of building; also : something built : STRUCTURE 2 : INTERPRETATION 3 : syntactical arrangement of words in a sentence — **con·struc·tive** \-ˈstrək-tiv\ adj

con·struc·tion·ist n : one who construes an instrument (as the U.S. Constitution) in a specific way ⟨a strict ~⟩

con·strue \kən-ˈstrü\ vb 1 : to explain the mutual relations of words in a sentence; also : TRANSLATE 2 : EXPLAIN, INTERPRET

con·sub·stan·ti·a·tion \ˌkän-səb-ˌstan-chē-ˈā-shən\ n : the actual substantial presence and combination of the body of Christ with the eucharistic bread and wine

con·sul \ˈkän-səl\ n 1 : a chief magistrate of the Roman republic 2 : an official appointed by a government to reside in a foreign country to care for the commercial interests of citizens of his own country — **con·su·lar** \-sə-lər\ adj — **con·su·late** \-lət\ n — **con·sul·ship** \-səl-ˌship\ n

con·sult \kən-ˈsəlt\ vb 1 : to ask the advice or opinion of 2 : CONFER — **con·sul·tant** \-ᵊnt\ n — **con·sul·ta·tion** \ˌkän-səl-ˈtā-shən\ n

con·sume \kən-ˈsüm\ vb 1 : DESTROY ⟨consumed by fire⟩ 2 : to spend wastefully 3 : to eat up : DEVOUR 4 : to absorb the attention of : ENGROSS — **con·sum·er** n

¹**con·sum·mate** \kən-ˈsəm-ət\ adj : COMPLETE, PERFECT **syn** finished, accomplished

²**con·sum·mate** \ˈkän-sə-ˌmāt\ vb : to make complete : FINISH, ACHIEVE — **con·sum·ma·tion** \ˌkän-sə-ˈmā-shən\ n

con·sump·tion \kən-ˈsəmp-shən\ n 1 : the act of consuming or using up 2 : the use of economic goods 3 : progressive bodily wasting away; also : TUBERCULOSIS

¹**con·sump·tive** \-ˈsəmp-tiv\ adj 1 : DESTRUCTIVE, WASTEFUL 2 : relating to or affected with bodily consumption

²**consumptive** n : a consumptive person

¹**con·tact** \ˈkän-ˌtakt\ n 1 : a touching

or meeting of bodies **2 :** ASSOCIATION, RELATIONSHIP; *also :* CONNECTION, COMMUNICATION

²contact *vb* **1 :** to come or bring into contact **:** TOUCH **2 :** to get in communication with

contact lens *n* **:** a thin lens fitting over the cornea

con·ta·gion \kən-'tā-jən\ *n* **1 :** the passing of disease by contact **2 :** a contagious disease; *also :* its causative agent **3 :** transmission of an influence on the mind or emotions

con·ta·gious \-jəs\ *adj* **:** communicable by contact; *also :* relating to contagion or to contagious diseases

con·tain \kən-'tān\ *vb* **1 :** ENCLOSE, INCLUDE **2 :** to have within **:** HOLD **3 :** RESTRAIN

con·tain·er *n* **:** RECEPTACLE; *esp :* one for shipment of goods

con·tam·i·nant \kən-'tam-ə-nənt\ *n* **:** something that contaminates

con·tam·i·nate \kən-'tam-ə-ˌnāt\ *vb* **:** to soil, stain, or infect by contact or association — **con·tam·i·na·tion** \-ˌtam-ə-'nā-shən\ *n*

con·temn \kən-'tem\ *vb* **:** to view or treat with contempt

con·tem·plate \'känt-əm-ˌplāt\ *vb* **1 :** to view or consider with continued attention **2 :** INTEND — **con·tem·pla·tion** \ˌkänt-əm-'plā-shən\ *n* — **con·tem·pla·tive** \kən-'tem-plət-iv, 'känt-əm-ˌplāt-\ *adj*

con·tem·po·ra·ne·ous \kən-ˌtem-pə-'rā-nē-əs\ *adj* **:** CONTEMPORARY

con·tem·po·rary \kən-'tem-pə-ˌrer-ē\ *adj* **1 :** occurring or existing at the same time **2 :** being of the same age **3 :** marked by characteristics of the present period **:** MODERN — **contemporary** *n*

con·tempt \kən-'tempt\ *n* **1 :** the act of despising **:** the state of mind of one who despises **:** DISDAIN **2 :** DISGRACE **3 :** disobedience to or open disrespect of a court or legislative body

con·tempt·ible *adj* **:** deserving contempt **:** DESPICABLE — **con·tempt·ibly** *adv*

con·temp·tu·ous \kən-'temp-ch(ə-w)əs\ *adj* **:** feeling or expressing contempt — **con·temp·tu·ous·ly** *adv*

con·tend \kən-'tend\ *vb* **1 :** to strive against rivals or difficulties; *also :* ARGUE, DEBATE **2 :** MAINTAIN, CLAIM — **con·tend·er** *n*

¹con·tent \kən-'tent\ *adj* **:** SATISFIED

²content *vb* **:** SATISFY; *esp :* to limit (oneself) in requirements or actions

³content *n* **:** CONTENTMENT

⁴con·tent \'kän-ˌtent\ *n* **1 :** something contained (~s of a room) (~s of a bottle) **2 :** subject matter or topics treated (as in a book or course of study) **3 :** essential meaning **4 :** proportion contained

con·tent·ed \kən-'tent-əd\ *adj* **:** SATISFIED — **con·tent·ed·ly** *adv* — **con·tent·ed·ness** *n*

con·ten·tion \kən-'ten-chən\ *n* **:** CONTEST, STRIFE — **con·ten·tious** \-chəs\ *adj*

con·tent·ment \kən-'tent-mənt\ *n* **:** ease of mind **:** SATISFACTION

con·ter·mi·nous \kən-'tər-mə-nəs, kän-\ *adj* **:** having the same or a common

boundary — **con·ter·mi·nous·ly** *adv*

¹con·test \kən-'test\ *vb* **1 :** to engage in strife **:** FIGHT, STRUGGLE **2 :** CHALLENGE, DISPUTE — **con·tes·tant** \-'tes-tənt\ *n*

²con·test \'kän-ˌtest\ *n* **1 :** STRUGGLE, FIGHT **2 :** COMPETITION

con·text \'kän-ˌtekst\ *n* **:** the part of a discourse surrounding a word or group of words that helps to explain the meaning of the word or word group; *also :* the circumstances surrounding an act or event

con·tig·u·ous \kən-'tig-yə-wəs\ *adj* **:** being in contact **:** TOUCHING; *also :* NEXT, ADJOINING — **con·ti·gu·i·ty** \ˌkänt-ə-'gyü-ət-ē\ *n*

con·ti·nence \'känt-ⁿn-əns\ *n* **1 :** SELF-RESTRAINT; *esp :* voluntary refraining from sexual intercourse **2 :** ability to retain a bodily discharge — **con·ti·nent** \-ⁿn-ənt\ *adj*

con·ti·nent \'känt-(ⁿ-)nənt\ *n* **1 :** one of the grand divisions of land on the globe **2** *cap :* the continent of Europe as distinguished from the British Isles

¹con·ti·nen·tal \ˌkänt-ⁿn-'ent-ⁿl\ *adj* **1 :** of or relating to a continent; *esp :* of or relating to the continent of Europe as distinguished from the British Isles **2** *often cap :* of or relating to the colonies later forming the U.S. ⟨*Continental* Congress⟩

²continental *n* **1** *often cap :* a soldier in the Continental army **2 :** the least bit ⟨not worth a ~⟩

con·tin·gen·cy \kən-'tin-jən-sē\ *n* **:** a chance or possible event

¹con·tin·gent \kən-'tin-jənt\ *adj* **1 :** liable but not certain to happen **:** POSSIBLE **2 :** happening by chance **:** not planned **3 :** CONDITIONAL **4 :** dependent on something that may or may not occur **syn** accidental, casual, incidental

²contingent *n* **:** a quota (as of troops) supplied from an area or group

con·tin·u·al \kən-'tin-y(ə-w)əl\ *adj* **1 :** CONTINUOUS, UNBROKEN **2 :** steadily recurring — **con·tin·u·al·ly** *adv*

con·tin·u·ance \-yə-wəns\ *n* **1 :** a continuing in a state or course of action **:** DURATION **2 :** unbroken succession **3 :** adjournment of legal proceedings

con·tin·u·a·tion \kən-ˌtin-yə-'wā-shən\ *n* **1 :** extension or prolongation of a state or activity **:** resumption after an interruption; *also :* something that carries on after a pause or break

con·tin·ue \kən-'tin-yü\ *vb* **1 :** to remain in a place or condition **:** ABIDE, STAY **2 :** ENDURE, LAST **3 :** PERSEVERE **4 :** to resume (as a story) after an intermission **5 :** EXTEND; *also :* to persist in **6 :** to allow to remain **7 :** to keep (a legal case) on the calendar or undecided

con·ti·nu·i·ty \ˌkänt-ⁿn-'(y)ü-ət-ē\ *n* **1 :** the condition of being continuous **2 :** something that continues without a break; *esp :* a motion-picture scenario

con·tin·u·ous \kən-'tin-yə-wəs\ *adj* **:** continuing without interruption **:** UNBROKEN — **con·tin·u·ous·ly** *adv*

con·tin·u·um \-yə-wəm\ *n*, *pl* **-ua** \-yə-wə\ *also* **-uums** **1 :** something that is the same throughout **2 :** something consisting of a series of variations or of a sequence of things in regular order

---

ə abut; ᵊ kitten; ər further; a back; ā bake; ä cot, cart; aů out; ch chin; e less; ē easy; g gift; i trip; ī life; j joke; ŋ sing; ō flow; ȯ flaw; ȯi coin; th thin; ṯh this; ü loot, ů foot; y yet; yü few; yů furious; zh vision

con·tort \kən-'tȯrt\ vb : to twist out of shape : DEFORM, DISTORT — **con·tor·tion** \-'tȯr-shən\ n

con·tor·tion·ist \-'tȯr-sh(ə-)nəst\ n : an acrobat who puts himself into unusual postures

con·tour \'kän-ˌtu̇r\ n 1 : OUTLINE ⟨~ of a mountain against the sky⟩ 2 : SHAPE, FORM — usu. used in pl. ⟨the ~s of a statue⟩

con·tra·band \'kän-trə-ˌband\ n : goods legally prohibited in trade; also : smuggled goods

con·tra·cep·tion \ˌkän-trə-'sep-shən\ n : intentional prevention of conception — **con·tra·cep·tive** \-'sep-tiv\ adj or n

¹**con·tract** \'kän-ˌtrakt\ n 1 : a binding agreement : COVENANT 2 : an undertaking to win a specified number of tricks in contract bridge — **con·trac·tu·al** \kən-'trak-ch(ə-w)əl\ adj — **con·trac·tu·al·ly** adv

²**con·tract** \kən-'trakt, 1 usu 'kän-ˌtrakt\ vb 1 : to establish or undertake by contract 2 : CATCH ⟨~ a disease⟩ 3 : SHRINK, LESSEN; esp : to draw together esp. so as to shorten ⟨~ a muscle⟩ 4 : to shorten (a word) by omitting letters or sounds in the middle — **con·trac·tion** \kən-'trak-shən\ n — **con·trac·tor** \'kän-ˌtrak-tər\ n

con·trac·tile \kən-'trak-tᵊl\ adj : able to contract — **con·trac·til·i·ty** \ˌkän-ˌtrak-'til-ət-ē\ n

con·tra·dict \ˌkän-trə-'dikt\ vb : to state the contrary of : deny the truth of — **con·tra·dic·tion** \-'dik-shən\ n — **con·tra·dic·to·ry** \-'dik-t(ə-)rē\ adj

con·tra·dis·tinc·tion \-dis-'tiŋk-shən\ n : distinction by contrast ⟨painting in ~ to sculpture⟩

con·trail \'kän-ˌtrāl\ n : streaks of condensed water vapor created in the air by an airplane or rocket at high altitudes

con·tral·to \kən-'tral-tō\ n 1 : the lowest female voice; also : a singer having such a voice

con·trap·tion \kən-'trap-shən\ n : CONTRIVANCE, DEVICE

con·tra·pun·tal \ˌkän-trə-'pənt-ᵊl\ adj : of or relating to counterpoint

con·tra·ri·e·ty \ˌkän-trə-'rī-ət-ē\ n : the state of being contrary : DISAGREEMENT, INCONSISTENCY

con·trari·wise \'kän-ˌtrer-ē-ˌwīz\ adv 1 : on the contrary : NO 2 : OPPOSITELY, CONVERSELY

con·trary \'kän-ˌtrer-ē, 4 often kən-'tre(ə)r-\ adj 1 : opposite in nature or position 2 : UNFAVORABLE 3 : COUNTER, OPPOSED 4 : tending to oppose or find fault : PERVERSE — **con·trar·i·ly** \'kän-ˌtrer-ə-lē, kən-'trer-\ adv — **con·trary** \n 'kän-ˌtrer-ē, adv like adj\ n or adv

¹**con·trast** \'kän-ˌtrast\ n 1 : unlikeness as shown when things are compared : DIFFERENCE 2 : diversity of adjacent parts in color, emotion, tone, or brightness ⟨a photograph with good ~⟩

²**con·trast** \kən-'trast\ vb 1 : to show differences when compared 2 : to compare in such a way as to show differences

con·tra·vene \ˌkän-trə-'vēn\ vb 1 : to go or act contrary to ⟨~ a law⟩ 2 : CONTRADICT ⟨a proposition that is not likely to be contravened⟩

con·tre·temps \'kän-trə-ˌtäⁿ\ n, pl con·tre·temps \-ˌtäⁿ(z)\ : an inopportune embarrassing occurrence

con·trib·ute \kən-'trib-yət\ vb : to give along with others (as to a fund) : supply or furnish a share to : HELP, ASSIST — **con·tri·bu·tion** \ˌkän-trə-'byü-shən\ n — **con·trib·u·tor** \kən-'trib-yət-ər\ n — **con·trib·u·to·ry** \-yə-ˌtōr-ē\ adj

con·trite \'kän-ˌtrīt, kən-'trīt\ adj : PENITENT, REPENTANT — **con·tri·tion** \kən-'trish-ən\ n

con·triv·ance \kən-'trī-vəns\ n 1 : SCHEME, PLAN 2 : a mechanical device : APPLIANCE

con·trive \kən-'trīv\ vb 1 : PLAN, DEVISE 2 : FRAME, MAKE 3 : to bring about with difficulty : EFFECT — **con·triv·er** n

¹**con·trol** \kən-'trōl\ vb -trolled; -trol·ling 1 : to exercise restraining or directing influence over : REGULATE 2 : DOMINATE, RULE

²**control** n 1 : power to direct or regulate 2 : RESERVE, RESTRAINT 3 : a device for regulating a mechanism ⟨the ~s of an airplane⟩

con·trol·ler n 1 : COMPTROLLER 2 : one that controls

con·tro·ver·sy \'kän-trə-ˌvər-sē\ n : a clash of opposing views : DISPUTE — **con·tro·ver·sial** \ˌkän-trə-'vər-shəl, -sē-əl\ adj

con·tro·vert \'kän-trə-ˌvərt, ˌkän-trə-'vərt\ vb : DENY, CONTRADICT — **con·tro·vert·ible** adj

con·tu·ma·cious \ˌkän-t(y)ə-'mā-shəs\ adj : stubbornly resisting or disobeying authority syn rebellious, insubordinate — **con·tu·ma·cy** \kən-'t(y)ü-mə-sē, 'kän-t(y)ə-\ n

con·tu·me·li·ous \ˌkän-t(y)ə-'mē-lē-əs\ adj : insolently abusive and humiliating

con·tu·me·ly \kən-'t(y)ü-mə-lē, 'kän-t(y)ə-ˌmē-lē\ n : contemptuous treatment : INSULT

con·tu·sion \kən-'t(y)ü-zhən\ n : BRUISE — **con·tuse** \-'t(y)üz\ vb

co·nun·drum \kə-'nən-drəm\ n : RIDDLE

con·ur·ba·tion \ˌkän-ˌər-'bā-shən\ n : a continuous network of urban communities

con·va·lesce \ˌkän-və-'les\ vb : to recover health gradually — **con·va·les·cence** \-'les-ᵊns\ n — **con·va·les·cent** \-ᵊnt\ adj or n

con·vec·tion \kən-'vek-shən\ n : a circulatory motion in fluids due to warmer portions rising and colder denser portions sinking; also : the transfer of heat by such motion

con·vene \kən-'vēn\ vb : ASSEMBLE, MEET

con·ve·nience \kən-'vē-nyəns\ n 1 : SUITABLENESS 2 : personal comfort : EASE 3 : a labor-saving device 4 : a suitable time

con·ve·nient adj 1 : suited to one's comfort or ease 2 : placed near at hand — **con·ve·nient·ly** adv

con·vent \'kän-vənt, -ˌvent\ n : a local community or house of a religious order esp. of nuns — **con·ven·tu·al** \kən-'ven-chə-wəl\ adj

con·ven·ti·cle \kən-'vent-i-kəl\ n : MEETING; esp : a secret meeting for worship

con·ven·tion \kən-'ven-chən\ n 1 : an agreement esp. between states on a matter of common concern 2 : MEETING, ASSEMBLY 3 : a body of delegates convened for some purpose 4 : fixed usage : accepted way of acting 5 : a social form sanctioned by general custom

con·ven·tion·al \-'vench-(ə-)nəl\ adj

1 : sanctioned by general custom **2** : COMMONPLACE, ORDINARY **syn** formal, ceremonial — con·ven·tion·al·i·ty \-ˌven-chə-ˈnal-ət-ē\ n

con·ven·tion·al·ize \-ˈvench-(ə-)nə-ˌlīz\ vb : to make conventional

con·verge \kən-ˈvərj\ vb : to approach one common center or single point — con·ver·gence or con·ver·gen·cy n — con·ver·gent adj

con·ver·sant \kən-ˈvərs-ᵊnt\ adj : having knowledge and experience

con·ver·sa·tion \ˌkän-vər-ˈsā-shən\ n : an informal talking together — con·ver·sa·tion·al \-sh(ə-)nəl\ adj

¹con·verse \kən-ˈvərs\ vb : to engage in conversation — con·verse \ˈkän-ˌvərs\ n

²con·verse \ˈkän-ˌvərs\ n : CONVERSATION

³con·verse \kən-ˈvərs, ˈkän-ˌvərs\ adj : reversed in order or relation — con·verse·ly adv

⁴con·verse \ˈkän-ˌvərs\ n **1** : a statement related to another statement by having the parts reversed or interchanged **2** : OPPOSITE, REVERSE

con·ver·sion \kən-ˈvər-zhən\ n **1** : a change in nature or form **2** : an experience associated with a decisive adoption of religion **3** : illegal seizure and use of property of another person

¹con·vert \kən-ˈvərt\ vb **1** : to turn from one belief or party to another **2** : TRANSFORM, CHANGE **3** : MISAPPROPRIATE **4** : EXCHANGE — con·vert·er or con·ver·tor n — con·vert·ible adj

²con·vert \ˈkän-ˌvərt\ n : one who has undergone religious conversion

con·vert·ible \kən-ˈvərt-ə-bəl\ n : an automobile with a top that may be lowered or removed

con·vex \(ˈ)kän-ˈveks\ adj : curved or rounded like the exterior of a sphere or circle — con·vex·i·ty \kən-ˈvek-sət-ē\ n

con·vey \kən-ˈvā\ vb **1** : CARRY, TRANSPORT **2** : TRANSMIT, TRANSFER — con·vey·er or con·vey·or n

con·vey·ance \-ˈvā-əns\ n **1** : the act of conveying **2** : VEHICLE **3** : a legal paper transferring ownership of property

¹con·vict \kən-ˈvikt\ n : a person convicted of a serious crime

²con·vict \kən-ˈvikt\ vb : to prove or find guilty

con·vic·tion \kən-ˈvik-shən\ n **1** : the act of convicting esp. in a court **2** : a being convinced : strong belief **3** : positive opinion

con·vince \kən-ˈvins\ vb : to bring by demonstration or argument to a sure belief — con·vinc·ing adj — con·vinc·ing·ly adv

con·viv·ial \kən-ˈviv-yəl\ adj [LL convivialis, fr. L convivium feast, fr. com- together + vivere to live] : enjoying companionship and the pleasures of feasting and drinking : JOVIAL, FESTIVE — con·viv·i·al·i·ty \-ˌviv-ē-ˈal-ət-ē\ n — con·viv·ial·ly \-ˈviv-yə-lē\ adv

con·vo·ca·tion \ˌkän-və-ˈkā-shən\ n **1** : a ceremonial assembly (as of clergymen) **2** : the act of convoking

con·voke \kən-ˈvōk\ vb : to call together to a meeting

con·vo·lut·ed \ˈkän-və-ˌlüt-əd\ adj

1 : folded in curved or tortuous windings **2** : INVOLVED, INTRICATE

con·vo·lu·tion \ˌkän-və-ˈlü-shən\ n **1** : a winding or coiling together **2** : a tortuous or sinuous structure; esp : one of the ridges of the brain

¹con·voy \ˈkän-ˌvói, kən-ˈvói\ vb : to accompany for protection

²con·voy \ˈkän-ˌvói\ n : one that convoys; esp : a protective escort for ships, persons, or goods

con·vulse \kən-ˈvəls\ vb : to agitate violently

con·vul·sion \kən-ˈvəl-shən\ n **1** : an abnormal and violent involuntary contraction or series of contractions of muscle **2** : a violent disturbance — con·vul·sive \-ˈvəl-siv\ adj — con·vul·sive·ly adv

cony var of CONEY

coo \ˈkü\ n : a soft low sound made by doves or pigeons; also : a sound like this — coo vb

¹cook \ˈkúk\ n : one who prepares food for eating

²cook vb **1** : to prepare food for eating **2** : to subject to heat or fire

cook·book \-ˌbúk\ n : a book of cooking directions and recipes

cook·ery \ˈkúk-(ə-)rē\ n : the art or practice of cooking

cook·ie or cooky \ˈkúk-ē\ n : a small sweet flat cake

cook·out \-ˌaút\ n : an outing at which a meal is cooked and served in the open

cook·stove \-ˌstōv\ n : a stove for cooking

¹cool \ˈkül\ adj **1** : moderately cold **2** : protecting from heat **3** : not excited : CALM **4** : not ardent **5** : indicating dislike **6** : IMPUDENT **7** : stated without exaggeration **syn** chilly, composed, collected, unruffled, nonchalant — cool·ly \ˈkül-(l)ē\ adv — cool·ness n

²cool vb : to make or become cool

cool·ant \ˈkü-lənt\ n : a usu. fluid cooling agent

cool·er n **1** : REFRIGERATOR **2** : JAIL, PRISON

coo·lie \ˈkü-lē\ n : an unskilled laborer in the Far East

coon \ˈkün\ n : RACCOON

¹coop \ˈküp, ˈkúp\ n : a small enclosure or building usu. for poultry

²coop vb : to confine in or as if in a coop

co-op \ˈkō-ˌäp\ n : COOPERATIVE

coop·er \ˈküp-ər, ˈkúp-\ n : one who makes or repairs barrels or casks — cooper vb — coop·er·age n

co·op·er·ate \kō-ˈäp-ə-ˌrāt\ vb : to act jointly with another or others — co·op·er·a·tion \-ˌäp-ə-ˈrā-shən\ n — co·op·er·a·tor \-ˈäp-ə-ˌrāt-ər\ n

¹co·op·er·a·tive \kō-ˈäp-(ə-)rət-iv, -ə-ˌrāt-\ adj **1** : willing to work with others **2** : of or relating to an association formed to enable its members to buy or sell to better advantage by eliminating middlemen's profits

²cooperative n : a cooperative association

co-opt \kō-ˈäpt\ vb : to choose or elect as a fellow member or colleague

¹co·or·di·nate \kō-ˈórd-(ᵊ-)nət\ adj **1** : equal in rank or order **2** : of equal rank in a compound sentence (∼ clause)

3 : joining words or word groups of the same rank

²**coordinate** n : one of a set of numbers used in specifying the location of a point on a surface or in space

³**co·or·di·nate** \-'òrd-ᵊn-,āt\ vb **1** : to make or become coordinate **2** : to work or act together harmoniously — **co·or·di·na·tion** \-,òrd-ᵊn-'ā-shən\ n

coot \'küt\ n : a dark-colored ducklike bird of the rail group

coo·tie \'küt-ē\ n : a body louse

cop \'käp\ n : POLICEMAN

co·part·ner \'kō-'pärt-nər\ n : PARTNER

¹**cope** \'kōp\ n : a long cloaklike ecclesiastical vestment

²**cope** vb : to struggle to overcome problems or difficulties

co·pi·lot \'kō-,pī-lət\ n : an assistant airplane pilot

cop·ing \'kō-piŋ\ n : the top layer of a wall

co·pi·ous \'kō-pē-əs\ adj : LAVISH, ABUNDANT — **co·pi·ous·ly** adv — **co·pi·ous·ness** n

cop·per \'käp-ər\ n **1** : a malleable reddish metallic chemical element that is one of the best conductors of heat and electricity **2** : something made of copper; esp : PENNY — **cop·pery** adj

cop·per·as \'käp-(ə-)rəs\ n : a green sulfate of iron used in dyeing and in making inks

cop·per·head \'käp-ər-,hed\ n : a largely coppery brown venomous snake of upland eastern U.S.

cop·pice \'käp-əs\ n : THICKET

co·pra \'kō-prə\ n : dried coconut meat yielding coconut oil

copse \'käps\ n : THICKET

cop·u·la \'käp-yə-lə\ n : a verb (as be, seem, feel, grow, turn) that links a subject with its predicate — **cop·u·la·tive** \-,lāt-iv\ adj

cop·u·late \'käp-yə-,lāt\ vb : to engage in sexual intercourse — **cop·u·la·tion** \,käp-yə-'lā-shən\ n

¹**copy** \'käp-ē\ n **1** : an imitation or reproduction of an original work **2** : PATTERN **3** : material (as manuscript) to be set up for printing **syn** duplicate

²**copy** vb **1** : to make a copy of **2** : IMITATE — **cop·y·ist** n

copy·book \-,bùk\ n : a book containing copies esp. of penmanship for learners to imitate

copy·boy \-,bòi\ n : one that carries copy and runs errands (as in a newspaper office)

copy·cat \-,kat\ n : a sedulous imitator

copy·desk \-,desk\ n : the desk at which newspaper copy is edited

copy·read·er \-,rēd-ər\ n : one who edits and writes headlines for newspaper copy; also : one who reads and corrects manuscript copy in a publishing house

¹**copy·right** \-,rīt\ n : the sole right to reproduce, publish, and sell a literary or artistic work

²**copyright** vb : to secure a copyright on

co·quet or **co·quette** \kō-'ket\ vb -**quet·ted**; -**quet·ting** : FLIRT — **co·quet·ry** \'kō-kə-trē\ n

co·quette \kō-'ket\ n : FLIRT — **co·quett·ish** adj

cor·a·cle \'kòr-ə-kəl\ n : a boat made of hoops covered with horsehide or tarpaulin

cor·al \'kòr-əl\ n **1** : a stony or horny material that forms the skeleton of colonies of tiny sea polyps and includes a red form used in jewelry; also : a coral-forming polyp or polyp colony **2** : a deep pink color

cor·bel \'kòr-bəl\ n : a bracket-shaped architectural member that projects from a wall and supports a weight

¹**cord** \'kòrd\ n **1** : a usu. heavy string consisting of several strands woven or twisted together **2** : a long slender anatomical structure (as a tendon or nerve) **3** : a cubic measure used esp. for firewood and equal to a stack 4x4x8 feet **4** : a rib or ridge on cloth

²**cord** vb **1** : to tie or furnish with a cord **2** : to pile (wood) in cords

cord·age n : ROPES, CORDS; esp : ropes in the rigging of a ship

¹**cor·dial** \'kòr-jəl\ adj : warmly receptive or welcoming : HEARTFELT, HEARTY — **cor·di·al·i·ty** \,kòr-jē-'al-ət-ē\ n — **cor·dial·ly** \'kòr-jə-lē\ adv

²**cordial** n **1** : a stimulating medicine or drink **2** : LIQUEUR

cor·dil·le·ra \,kòrd-ᵊl-'(y)er-ə, kòr-'dil-ə-rə\ n : a group of mountain ranges

cor·do·ba \'kòrd-ə-bə, -və\ n — see MONEY table

cor·don \'kòrd-ᵊn\ n **1** : an ornamental cord **2** : an encircling line composed of individual units

cor·do·van \'kòrd-ə-vən\ n : a soft fine-grained leather

cor·du·roy \'kòrd-ə-,ròi\ n : a heavy ribbed fabric; also, pl : trousers of this material

cord·wain·er \'kòrd-,wā-nər\ n : SHOEMAKER

¹**core** \'kòr\ n **1** : the central usu. inedible part of some fruits (as the apple); also : an inmost part of something **2** : GIST, ESSENCE

²**core** vb : to take out the core of

co·re·spon·dent \,kō-ri-'spän-dənt\ n : a person named as guilty of adultery with the defendant in a divorce suit

cork \'kòrk\ n **1** : the tough elastic bark of a European oak (**cork oak**) used for stoppers and insulation; also : a stopper of this **2** : a tissue making up most of the bark of a woody plant — **cork** vb — **corky** adj

cork·screw \-,skrü\ n : a device for drawing corks from bottles

cor·mo·rant \'kòrm-(ə-)rənt\ n : a greedy dark seabird used in the Orient to catch fish

¹**corn** \'kòrn\ n **1** : the seeds of a cereal grass and esp. of the chief cereal crop of a region; also : a cereal grass **2** : MAIZE **3** : sweet corn served as a vegetable

²**corn** vb : to salt (as beef) in brine and preservatives

³**corn** n : a local hardening and thickening of skin (as on a toe)

corn·cob \-,käb\ n : the axis on which the kernels of Indian corn are arranged

corn·crib \-,krib\ n : a crib for storing ears of Indian corn

cor·nea \'kòr-nē-ə\ n : the transparent part of the coat of the eyeball covering the iris and the pupil — **cor·ne·al** adj

¹**cor·ner** \'kòr-nər\ n **1** : the point or angle formed by the meeting of lines, edges, or sides **2** : the place where two streets come together **3** : a quiet secluded place **4** : a position from which retreat or escape is impossible **5** : control of enough of the available supply (as of a commodity) to permit manipulation of the price

²**cor·ner** vb **1** : to drive into a corner **2** : to turn a corner

cor·ner·stone \-ˌstōn\ n **1** : a stone forming part of a corner in a wall; esp : such a stone laid with special ceremonies **2** : something of basic importance

cor·net \kȯr-ˈnet\ n : a brass band instrument resembling the trumpet

corn flour \ˈkȯrn-ˌflau̇(ə)r\ n, Brit : CORNSTARCH

corn·flow·er \-ˌflau̇(-ə)r\ n : a pink-, blue-, or white-flowered garden plant related to the daisies

cor·nice \ˈkȯr-nəs\ n : the horizontal projecting part crowning the wall of a building

corn·meal \ˈkȯrn-ˈmēl\ n : meal ground from corn

corn·stalk \-ˌstȯk\ n : a stalk of Indian corn

corn·starch \-ˌstärch\ n : a starch made from corn and used in cookery as a thickening agent

corn syrup n : a syrup obtained by partial hydrolysis of cornstarch

cor·nu·co·pia \ˌkȯr-n(y)ə-ˈkō-pē-ə\ n : a goat's horn shown filled with fruits and grain emblematic of abundance

corny \ˈkȯr-nē\ adj : mawkishly old-fashioned or countrified : tiresomely simple or sentimental ⟨~ music⟩

co·rol·la \kə-ˈräl-ə\ n : the petals of a flower

cor·ol·lary \ˈkȯr-ə-ˌler-ē\ n **1** : a deduction from a proposition already proved true **2** : CONSEQUENCE, RESULT

co·ro·na \kə-ˈrō-nə\ n : a colored ring surrounding the sun or moon; esp : a shining ring around the sun seen during eclipses

cor·o·nach \ˈkȯr-ə-nək\ n : DIRGE

cor·o·nal \ˈkȯr-ən-ᵊl\ n : a circlet for the head

¹**cor·o·nary** \ˈkȯr-ə-ˌner-ē\ adj : of or relating to the heart or its blood vessels

²**coronary** n : coronary disease

cor·o·na·tion \ˌkȯr-ə-ˈnā-shən\ n : the ceremony attending the crowning of a monarch

cor·o·ner \ˈkȯr-ə-nər\ n : a public official whose chief duty is to investigate the causes of deaths possibly not due to natural causes

cor·o·net \ˌkȯr-ə-ˈnet\ n **1** : a small crown indicating rank lower than sovereignty **2** : an ornamental band worn around the temples

¹**cor·po·ral** \ˈkȯr-p(ə-)rəl\ adj : BODILY, PHYSICAL ⟨~ punishment⟩

²**corporal** n : a noncommissioned officer (as in the army) ranking next below a sergeant

cor·po·rate \ˈkȯr-p(ə-)rət\ adj **1** : combined into one body : INCORPORATED; also : belonging to an incorporated body

cor·po·ra·tion \ˌkȯr-pə-ˈrā-shən\ n **1** : a political body legally authorized to act as a person **2** : a legal creation authorized to act with the rights and liabilities of a person ⟨a business ~⟩

cor·po·re·al \kȯr-ˈpōr-ē-əl\ adj **1** : PHYSICAL, MATERIAL **2** : BODILY

corps \ˈkōr\ n, pl corps \ˈkōrz\ **1** : an organized subdivision of a country's military forces ⟨the Marine Corps⟩ **2** : a group acting under common direction

corpse \ˈkȯrps\ n : a dead body

cor·pu·lence \ˈkȯr-pyə-ləns\ or **cor·pu·len·cy** n : excessive fatness — **cor·pu·lent** adj

cor·pus \ˈkȯr-pəs\ n, pl **cor·po·ra** \-pə-rə\ **1** : BODY; esp : CORPSE **2** : a body of writings

cor·pus·cle \ˈkȯr-(ˌ)pəs-əl\ n **1** : a minute particle **2** : a living cell; esp : one (as in blood or cartilage) not aggregated into continuous tissues

cor·pus de·lic·ti \ˌkȯr-pəs-di-ˈlik-ˌtī, -tē\ n : the substantial fact establishing that a crime has been committed; also : the body of a victim of murder

cor·ral \kə-ˈral\ n : an enclosure for confining or capturing animals; also : an enclosure for defense — **corral** vb

¹**cor·rect** \kə-ˈrekt\ vb **1** : to make right **2** : REPROVE, CHASTISE — **cor·rec·tion** \-ˈrek-shən\ n — **cor·rec·tive** \-ˈrek-tiv\ adj

²**correct** adj **1** : agreeing with fact or truth **2** : conforming to a conventional standard — **cor·rect·ly** adv — **cor·rect·ness** n

cor·re·late \ˈkȯr-ə-ˌlāt\ vb : to connect in a systematic way : establish the mutual relations existing between — **cor·re·la·tion** \ˌkȯr-ə-ˈlā-shən\ n

cor·rel·a·tive \kə-ˈrel-ət-iv\ adj **1** : reciprocally related **2** : regularly used together (as either and or) — **correlative** n

cor·re·spond \ˌkȯr-ə-ˈspänd\ vb **1** : to be in agreement : SUIT, MATCH **2** : to communicate by letter

cor·re·spon·dence \-ˈspän-dəns\ n **1** : agreement between particular things **2** : communication by letters; also : the letters exchanged

¹**cor·re·spon·dent** \-dənt\ adj **1** : SIMILAR **2** : FITTING, CONFORMING

²**correspondent** n **1** : something that corresponds to some other thing **2** : a person with whom one communicates by letter **3** : a person employed to contribute news regularly from a place

cor·ri·dor \ˈkȯr-əd-ər\ n **1** : a passageway into which compartments or rooms open (as in a hotel or school) **2** : a narrow strip of land esp. through foreign-held territory

cor·ri·gen·dum \ˌkȯr-ə-ˈjen-dəm\ n, pl -da \-də\ : an error in a printed work discovered after printing and shown with its correction on a separate sheet

cor·rob·o·rate \kə-ˈräb-ə-ˌrāt\ vb : to support with evidence : CONFIRM — **cor·rob·o·ra·tion** \-ˌräb-ə-ˈrā-shən\ n — **cor·rob·o·ra·tive** \-ˈräb-ə-ˌrāt-iv\ adj — **cor·rob·o·ra·to·ry** \-rə-ˌtōr-ē\ adj

cor·rode \kə-ˈrōd\ vb : to eat or be eaten away gradually (as by action of rust or of a chemical) — **cor·ro·sion** \-ˈrō-zhən\ n — **cor·ro·sive** \-ˈrō-siv\ adj or n

cor·ru·gate \ˈkȯr-ə-ˌgāt\ vb : to form into wrinkles or ridges and grooves — **cor·ru·gat·ed** adj — **cor·ru·ga·tion** \ˌkȯr-ə-ˈgā-shən\ n

¹**cor·rupt** \kə-ˈrəpt\ vb **1** : to make evil : DEPRAVE; esp : BRIBE **2** : TAINT — **cor·rupt·ible** adj — **cor·rup·tion** \-ˈrəp-shən\ n

²**corrupt** adj : DEPRAVED, DEBASED

cor·sage \kȯr-ˈsäzh, -ˈsäj\ n **1** : the

waist of a woman's dress **2 :** a bouquet worn or carried by a woman

cor·sair \'kȯr-ˌsaər\ *n* **1 :** PIRATE **2 :** a pirate's ship

cor·set \'kȯr-sət\ *n* **:** a stiffened undergarment worn by women to give shape to the waist and hips

cor·tege \kȯr-ˈtezh\ *n* **:** PROCESSION; *esp* **:** a funeral procession

cor·tex \'kȯr-ˌteks\ *n, pl* **cor·ti·ces** \'kȯrt-ə-ˌsēz\ *or* **cor·tex·es :** an outer or covering layer of an organism or one of its parts ⟨the kidney ~⟩ ⟨~ of a plant stem⟩; *esp* **:** the outer layer of gray matter of the brain — **cor·ti·cal** \'kȯrt-i-kəl\ *adj*

cor·ti·sone \'kȯrt-ə-ˌsōn, -ˌzōn\ *n* **:** a steroid adrenal hormone used in treating arthritis

co·run·dum \kə-ˈrən-dəm\ *n* **:** a very hard aluminum-containing mineral used as an abrasive or in some crystalline forms as a gem

cor·us·cate \'kȯr-ə-ˌskāt\ *vb* **:** FLASH, SPARKLE — **cor·us·ca·tion** \ˌkȯr-ə-ˈskā-shən\ *n*

cor·vette \kȯr-ˈvet\ *n* **1 :** a naval sailing ship smaller than a frigate **2 :** a lightly armed escort ship smaller than a destroyer

co·ry·za \kə-ˈrī-zə\ *n* **:** an inflammatory disorder of the upper respiratory tract **:** the common cold

co·sig·na·to·ry \kō-ˈsig-nə-ˌtōr-ē\ *n* **:** a joint signer

[1]**cos·met·ic** \käz-ˈmet-ik\ *n* **:** an external application intended to beautify the complexion

[2]**cosmetic** *adj* [Gk *kosmētikos* of adornment, fr. *kosmein* to adorn, fr. *kosmos* orderly arrangement, ornament, universe] **:** relating to beautifying the physical appearance

cos·me·tol·o·gist \ˌkäz-mə-ˈtäl-ə-jəst\ *n* **:** one who gives beauty treatments (as to skin and hair) — **cos·me·tol·o·gy** *n*

cos·mic \'käz-mik\ *adj* **1 :** of or relating to the cosmos **2 :** VAST, GRAND

cosmic ray *n* **:** a stream of very penetrating and high speed atomic nuclei that enter the earth's atmosphere from outer space

cos·mog·o·ny \käz-ˈmäg-ə-nē\ *n* **:** the origin or creation of the world or universe

cos·mol·o·gy \-ˈmäl-ə-jē\ *n* **:** a study dealing with the origin and structure of the universe — **cos·mo·log·i·cal** \ˌkäz-mə-ˈläj-i-kəl\ *adj*

cos·mo·naut \'käz-mə-ˌnȯt\ *n* **:** ASTRONAUT

cos·mo·pol·i·tan \ˌkäz-mə-ˈpäl-ət-ˀn\ *adj* **:** belonging to all the world **:** not local **syn** universal — **cosmopolitan** *n*

cos·mos \'käz-məs\ *n* **1 :** UNIVERSE **2 :** a tall garden herb related to the daisies

cos·sack \'käs-ˌak, -ək\ *n* **:** a member of a group of frontiersmen of southern Russia organized as cavalry in the czarist army

[1]**cost** \'kȯst\ *n* **1 :** the amount paid or asked for a thing **:** PRICE **2 :** the loss or penalty incurred in gaining something **3 :** OUTLAY

[2]**cost** *vb* **cost; cost·ing 1 :** to require a specified amount in payment **2 :** to cause to pay, suffer, or lose

cost·ly *adj* **:** of great cost or value **:** not cheap **syn** dear, valuable — **cost·li·ness** *n*

cos·tume \'käs-ˌt(y)üm\ *n* **:** CLOTHES, ATTIRE; *also* **:** a suit or dress characteristic of a period or country — **cos·tum·er** \'käs-ˌt(y)ü-mər\ *n* — **cos·tu·mi·er** \käs-ˈt(y)ü-mē-ər\ *n*

cosy *var of* COZY

[1]**cot** \'kät\ *n* **:** a small house **:** COTTAGE

[2]**cot** \'kät\ *n* **:** a small often collapsible bed (as of canvas stretched on a frame)

cote \'kōt, 'kät\ *n* **:** a small shed or coop (as for sheep or doves)

co·te·rie \'kōt-ə-ˌrē\ *n* **:** an intimate often exclusive group of persons with a common interest

co·ter·mi·nal \kō-ˈtər-mən-ˀl\ *adj* **:** having the same or coincident boundaries

co·ter·mi·nous \-mə-nəs\ *adj* **:** coextensive in scope or duration

co·til·lion \kō-ˈtil-yən\ *n* **1 :** an elaborate dance with frequent changing of partners executed under the leadership of one couple at formal balls **2 :** a formal ball

cot·tage \'kät-ij\ *n* **:** a small house — **cot·tag·er** *n*

cot·ter *or* **cot·tar** \'kät-ər\ *n* **:** a farm laborer occupying a cottage and often a small holding

cot·ter pin \'kät-ər-\ *n* **:** a metal strip bent into a pin whose ends can be flared after insertion through a hole

cot·ton \'kät-ˀn\ *n* **:** a soft fibrous usu. white substance composed of hairs attached to the seeds of a plant related to the mallow; *also* **:** thread or cloth made of cotton — **cot·tony** *adj*

cot·ton·seed \'kät-ˀn-ˌsēd\ *n* **:** the seed of the cotton plant yielding a protein-rich meal and a fixed oil (**cottonseed oil**) used esp. in cooking

cot·ton·tail \-ˌtāl\ *n* **:** an American rabbit with a white-tufted tail

cot·ton·wood \-ˌwu̇d\ *n* **:** a poplar with cottony hair on its seed

cot·y·le·don \ˌkät-ˀl-ˈēd-ˀn\ *n* **:** the first leaf or one of the first pair or whorl of leaves developed by a seed plant

[1]**couch** \'kau̇ch\ *vb* **1 :** to lie or place on a couch **2 :** to phrase in a certain manner

[2]**couch** *n* **:** a bed or sofa for resting or sleeping

couch·ant \'kau̇-chənt\ *adj* **:** lying down with the head raised ⟨coat of arms with lion ~⟩

cou·gar \'kü-gər, -ˌgär\ *n* **:** a large tawny wild American cat

cough \'kȯf\ *vb* **:** to force air from the lungs with short sharp noises; *also* **:** to expel by coughing — **cough** *n*

could \kəd, (ˈ)ku̇d\ *past of* CAN — used as an auxiliary in the past or as a polite or less forceful alternative to *can* in the present

coun·cil \'kau̇n-səl\ *n* **1 :** ASSEMBLY, MEETING **2 :** an official body of lawmakers ⟨a city ~⟩ — **coun·cil·lor** *or* **coun·cil·or** *n* — **coun·cil·man** \-səl-mən\ *n*

[1]**coun·sel** \'kau̇n-səl\ *n* **1 :** ADVICE **2 :** deliberation together **3 :** a plan of action **4 :** LAWYER

[2]**counsel** *vb* **-seled** *or* **-selled; -sel·ing** *or* **-sel·ling 1 :** ADVISE, RECOMMEND **2 :** to consult together

coun·sel·or *or* **coun·sel·lor** *n* **1 :** ADVISER **2 :** LAWYER

[1]**count** \'kau̇nt\ *vb* **1 :** to name one by one in order to find the total number **2 :** to recite numbers in order **3 :** CONSIDER, ESTEEM **4 :** RELY ⟨you can ~ on

him〉 **5 :** to be of value or account — **count·a·ble** *adj*

²**count** *n* **1 :** the act of counting; *also* **:** the total obtained by counting **2 :** a particular charge in an indictment or legal declaration

³**count** *n* **:** a European nobleman whose rank corresponds to that of a British earl

count·down \-‚daùn\ *n* **:** an audible backward counting off (as in seconds) to indicate the time remaining before an event (as the launching of a rocket)

¹**coun·te·nance** \'kaùnt-(°-)nəns\ *n* **1 :** the human face esp. as an indicator of mood or character **2 :** FAVOR, APPROVAL

²**countenance** *vb* **:** SANCTION, TOLERATE

¹**count·er** \'kaùnt-ər\ *n* **1 :** a device used in counting or in games **2 :** a level surface (as a board) over which business is transacted, food is served, or work is conducted

²**coun·ter** *vb* **:** to act in opposition to **:** OPPOSE, OFFSET

³**coun·ter** *adv* **:** in an opposite direction **:** CONTRARY

⁴**coun·ter** *adj* **:** CONTRARY, OPPOSITE

⁵**coun·ter** *n* **1 :** OPPOSITE, CONTRARY **2 :** an answering or offsetting force or blow

coun·ter·act \‚kaùnt-ər-'akt\ *vb* **:** to lessen the force of **:** OFFSET 〈~ the effect of poison〉 〈~ an evil influence〉 — **coun·ter·ac·tive** *adj*

coun·ter·at·tack \'kaùnt-ər-ə-‚tak\ *n* **:** an attack made to oppose an enemy's attack — **counterattack** *vb*

¹**coun·ter·bal·ance** \'kaùnt-ər-‚bal-əns\ *n* **:** a weight or influence that balances another

²**coun·ter·bal·ance** \‚kaùnt-ər-'bal-əns\ *vb* **:** to oppose with equal weight or influence

coun·ter·claim \'kaùnt-ər-‚klām\ *n* **:** an opposing claim esp. in law

coun·ter·clock·wise \‚kaùnt-ər-'kläk-‚wiz\ *adv (or adj)* **:** in a direction opposite to that in which the hands of a clock rotate

coun·ter·es·pi·o·nage \-'es-pē-ə-‚näzh, -nij\ *n* **:** the attempt to discover and defeat enemy espionage

¹**coun·ter·feit** \'kaùnt-ər-‚fit\ *vb* **1 :** to copy or imitate in order to deceive **2 :** PRETEND, FEIGN — **coun·ter·feit·er** *n*

²**counterfeit** *adj* **:** SHAM, SPURIOUS; *also* **:** FORGED

³**counterfeit** *n* **:** something made to imitate another thing with a view to defraud **syn** fraud, sham, fake, imposture, deceit, deception

coun·ter·in·tel·li·gence \‚kaùnt-ər-in-'tel-ə-jəns\ *n* **:** organized activities of an intelligence service designed to counter the activities of an enemy's intelligence service

count·er·man \'kaùnt-ər-‚man\ *n* **:** one who tends a counter (as in a lunchroom)

coun·ter·mand \'kaùnt-ər-‚mand\ *vb* **:** to withdraw (an order already given) by a contrary order

coun·ter·mea·sure \-‚mezh-ər\ *n* **:** an action undertaken to counter another

coun·ter·of·fen·sive \-ə-‚fen-siv\ *n* **:** a large-scale military offensive undertaken

by a force previously on the defensive

coun·ter·pane \-‚pān\ *n* **:** BEDSPREAD

coun·ter·part \-‚pärt\ *n* **:** a person or thing very closely like or corresponding to another person or thing

coun·ter·point \-‚point\ *n* **:** music in which one melody is accompanied by one or more other melodies all woven into a harmonious whole

coun·ter·poise \-‚pòiz\ *n* **:** COUNTERBALANCE

coun·ter·rev·o·lu·tion \‚kaùnt-ə-(r)‚rev-ə-'lü-shən\ *n* **:** a revolution opposed to a former revolution

¹**coun·ter·sign** \'kaùnt-ər-‚sīn\ *n* **1 :** a confirmatory signature added to a writing already signed by another person **2 :** a secret signal that must be given by a person who wishes to pass a guard

²**countersign** *vb* **:** to add a confirmatory signature to — **coun·ter·sig·na·ture** \‚kaùnt-ər-'sig-nə-‚chùr\ *n*

coun·ter·sink \'kaùnt-ər-‚sink\ *vb* **:** to form a flaring depression around the top of (a hole in wood or metal made to receive a screw or bolt); *also* **:** to sink (a screw or bolt) in such a depression — **countersink** *n*

coun·ter·ten·or \-‚ten-ər\ *n* **:** a tenor with an unusually high range

coun·ter·weight \-‚wāt\ *n* **:** COUNTERBALANCE

count·ess \'kaùnt-əs\ *n* **1 :** the wife or widow of a count or an earl **2 :** a woman holding the rank of a count or an earl in her own right

count·ing·house \'kaùnt-iŋ-‚haùs\ *n* **:** a building or office for keeping books and conducting business

count·less \'kaùnt-ləs\ *adj* **:** INNUMERABLE

coun·tri·fied *or* **coun·try·fied** \'kən-tri-‚fīd\ *adj* **:** looking or acting like a person from the country **:** RUSTIC

coun·try \'kən-trē\ *n* **1 :** REGION, DISTRICT **2 :** the territory of a nation **3 :** FATHERLAND **4 :** NATION **5 :** rural regions as opposed to towns and cities

coun·try·dance \-‚dans\ *n* **:** an English dance in which partners face each other esp. in rows

coun·try·man \-mən\ *n* **1 :** an inhabitant of a certain country; *also* **:** COMPATRIOT **2** \-‚man, -mən\ **:** one raised in the country **:** RUSTIC

coun·try·side \-‚sīd\ *n* **:** a rural area or its people

coun·ty \'kaùnt-ē\ *n* **1 :** the domain of a count or earl **2 :** a territorial division of a country or state for purposes of local government

coup \'kü\ *n* **:** a brilliant sudden stroke or stratagem

coup de grace \‚küd-ə-'gräs\ *n* **:** a death-blow or final decisive stroke or event

coup d'etat \‚küd-ə-'tä\ *n* **:** a sudden violent overthrow of a government by a small group

cou·pé *or* **coupe** \kü-'pā, *2 often* 'küp\ *n* **1 :** a closed carriage for two persons inside with an outside seat for the driver in front **2** *usu* **coupe :** a 2-door automobile with an enclosed body and separate luggage compartment

¹**cou·ple** \'kəp-əl\ *vb* **:** to link together **:** JOIN, CONNECT, PAIR

²**couple** *n* **1 :** BOND, TIE **2 :** PAIR

3 : two persons closely associated; *esp* : a man and a woman married or otherwise paired

cou·plet \'kəp-lət\ *n* : two successive rhyming lines of verse

cou·pling \'kəp-(ə-)liŋ\ *n* 1 : CONNECTION 2 : a device for connecting two parts or things

cou·pon \'k(y)ü-,pän\ *n* 1 : a certificate attached to a bond showing interest due and designed to be cut off and presented for payment 2 : a certificate given to a purchaser of goods and redeemable in merchandise or cash

cour·age \'kər-ij\ *n* : ability to conquer fear or despair : BRAVERY, VALOR — **cou·ra·geous** \kə-'rā-jəs\ *adj* — **cou·ra·geous·ly** *adv*

cou·ri·er \'kur-ē-ər, 'kər-\ *n* 1 : one who bears messages or information for the diplomatic or military services 2 : a tourists' guide

¹**course** \'kōrs\ *n* 1 : PROGRESS, PASSAGE; *also* : direction of progress 2 : the ground or path over which something moves 3 : the part of a meal served at one time 4 : an ordered series of acts or proceedings : sequence of events 5 : method of procedure : CONDUCT, BEHAVIOR 6 : a series of instruction periods dealing with a subject 7 : the series of studies leading to graduation from a school or college

²**course** *vb* 1 : to hunt with dogs (~ a rabbit) 2 : to run or go speedily ‹*coursing* over the fields›

cours·er *n* : a swift or spirited horse

¹**court** \'kōrt\ *n* 1 : the residence of a sovereign or similar dignitary 2 : a sovereign and his officials and advisers as a governing power 3 : an assembly of the retinue of a sovereign 4 : an open space enclosed by a building or buildings 5 : a space walled or marked off for playing a game (as tennis or basketball) 6 : the place where justice is administered; *also* : the judicial body 7 : HOMAGE, COURTSHIP

²**court** *vb* 1 : to try to gain the favor of 2 : WOO 3 : ATTRACT, TEMPT (~ danger)

cour·te·ous \'kərt-ē-əs\ *adj* : marked by respect for others : CIVIL, POLITE — **cour·te·ous·ly** *adv*

cour·te·san \'kōrt-ə-zən, 'kərt-\ *n* : PROSTITUTE

cour·te·sy \'kərt-ə-sē\ *n* 1 : courteous behavior : POLITENESS 2 : a favor courteously performed

court·house \'kōrt-,haus\ *n* 1 : a building in a town or city for holding courts of law 2 : a building for housing county offices

court·ier \'kōrt-ē-ər\ *n* : a person in attendance at a royal court

court·ly \'kōrt-lē\ *adj* : REFINED, ELEGANT, POLITE **syn** courteous, civil — **court·li·ness** *n*

court-mar·tial \'kōrt-,mär-shəl\ *n, pl* **courts-martial** : a military or naval court for trial of offenses against military or naval law; *also* : a trial by this court — **court-martial** *vb*

court·room \-,rüm, -,rum\ *n* : a room in which a court of law is held

court·ship \'kōrt-,ship\ *n* : the act of courting

court·yard \-,yärd\ *n* : an enclosure attached to a house or palace

cous·in \'kəz-ᵊn\ *n* [OF, fr. L *consobrinus*, lit., child of a mother's sister, fr.

com- together + *soror* sister] : a child of one's uncle or aunt

cove \'kōv\ *n* 1 : a trough for lights at the upper part of a wall 2 : a small sheltered inlet or bay

cov·en \'kəv-ən, 'kō-vən\ *n* : an assembly or band of witches

cov·e·nant \'kəv-ə-nənt\ *n* : a formal binding agreement : COMPACT — **cov·e·nant** \-nənt, -,nant\ *vb*

¹**cov·er** \'kəv-ər\ *vb* 1 : to place something over or upon 2 : CLOTHE 3 : to bring or hold within range of a firearm 4 : PROTECT, SHIELD 5 : INCLUDE, COMPRISE 6 : HIDE, CONCEAL 7 : to have as one's field of activity 8 : to buy (stocks) in order to have them for delivery on a previous short sale

²**cover** *n* 1 : something that protects or shelters 2 : LID, TOP 3 : CASE, BINDING 4 : SCREEN, DISGUISE 5 : TABLECLOTH 6 : a cloth used on a bed 7 : an envelope or wrapper for mail

cov·er·age \-(ə-)rij\ *n* 1 : the act or fact of covering 2 : the total group covered : SCOPE

cov·er·all \'kəv-ər-,ȯl\ *n* : a one-piece outer garment worn to protect one's clothes — usu. used in pl.

cov·er·let \-lət\ *n* : BEDSPREAD

¹**cov·ert** \'kəv-ərt, 'kōv-\ *adj* 1 : HIDDEN, SECRET 2 : SHELTERED — **cov·ert·ly** *adv*

²**covert** *n* 1 : a secret or sheltered place; *esp* : a thicket sheltering game 2 : a feather covering the bases of the quills of the wings and tail of a bird 3 : a wool or silk-and-wool cloth usu. of mixed-color yarns

cov·et \'kəv-ət\ *vb* : to desire enviously : long for — **cov·et·ous** \-əs\ *adj* — **cov·et·ous·ness** *n*

cov·ey \'kəv-ē\ *n* 1 : a bird with her brood of young 2 : a small flock (as of quail)

¹**cow** \'kau\ *n* 1 : the mature female of cattle or of an animal (as the moose) of which the male is called *bull* 2 : a domestic bovine animal irrespective of sex or age

²**cow** *vb* : INTIMIDATE, DAUNT, OVERAWE

cow·ard \'kau-(ə)rd\ *n* : one who lacks courage or shows shameful fear or timidity — **coward** *adj* — **cow·ard·ice** \-əs\ *n* — **cow·ard·ly** *adv* or *adj*

cow·boy \'kau-,bȯi\ *n* : one (as a mounted ranch hand) who tends or drives cattle

cow·er \'kau-(ə)r\ *vb* : to shrink or crouch down from fear or cold : QUAIL

cow·hide \'kau-,hīd\ *n* 1 : the hide of a cow; *also* : leather made from it 2 : a coarse whip of braided rawhide

cowl \'kaul\ *n* 1 : a monk's hood 2 : the top part of the front of the body of an automobile to which the windshield is attached

cow·lick \'kau-,lik\ *n* : a turned-up tuft of hair that resists control

cowl·ing \'kau-liŋ\ *n* : a usu. metal covering over the engine or another part of an airplane

co-work·er \'kō-,wər-kər\ *n* : a fellow worker

cow·poke \'kau-,pōk\ *n* : COWBOY

cow·punch·er \-,pən-chər\ *n* : COWBOY

cow·slip \'kau-,slip\ *n* 1 : a yellow-flowered swamp plant 2 : a yellow-flowered European primrose

cox·comb \'käks-,kōm\ *n* : a conceited silly man : FOP

cox·swain \'käk-sən, -,swān\ *n* : the steersman of a ship's boat or a racing shell

coy \'kȯi\ *adj* : BASHFUL, SHY; *esp* : pretending shyness — **coy·ly** *adv* — **coy·ness** *n*

coy·ote \'kī-,ōt, kī-'ōt-ē\ *n* : a small wolf native to western No. America

coy·pu \'kȯi-pü\ *n* 1 : a So. American aquatic rodent with webbed feet and dorsal mammary glands 2 : NUTRIA 2

coz·en \'kəz-ʰn\ *vb* : CHEAT, DEFRAUD — **coz·en·age** *n*

¹**co·zy** \'kō-zē\ *adj* : SNUG, COMFORTABLE — **co·zi·ly** *adv* — **co·zi·ness** *n*

²**cozy** *n* : a padded covering for a vessel (as a teapot) to keep the contents hot

crab \'krab\ *n* : a crustacean with a short broad shell and small abdomen

crab apple *n* : a small sour apple

crab·bed \'krab-əd\ *adj* 1 : MOROSE, PEEVISH 2 : CRAMPED, IRREGULAR (~ handwriting)

crab·by \'krab-ē\ *adj* : ILL-NATURED

¹**crack** \'krak\ *vb* 1 : to break with a sharp sudden sound 2 : to fail in tone or become harsh (his voice ~*ed*) 3 : to break without completely separating into parts 4 : to subject (as a petroleum oil) to heat for breaking down into lighter products (as gasoline)

²**crack** *n* 1 : a sudden sharp noise 2 : a witty or sharp remark 3 : a narrow break or opening : FISSURE 4 : a sharp blow 5 : ATTEMPT, TRY

crack·down \-,daün\ *n* : an act or instance of taking positive disciplinary action (a ~ on gambling)

crack·er \'krak-ər\ *n* 1 : FIRECRACKER 2 : a dry thin crisp bakery product made of flour and water 3 *cap* : a native of Georgia or Florida

crack·er·jack \-,jak\ *n* : something very excellent — **crackerjack** *adj*

crack·le \'krak-əl\ *vb* 1 : to make small sharp snapping noises 2 : to develop fine cracks in a surface — **crackle** *n*

crack·pot \'krak-,pät\ *n* : an eccentric person

crack·up \'krak-,əp\ *n* : CRASH, WRECK; *also* : BREAKDOWN

¹**cra·dle** \'krād-ʰl\ *n* 1 : a baby's bed or cot 2 : a place of origin and early development 3 : a scythe for mowing grain

²**cradle** *vb* 1 : to place in or as if in a cradle 2 : NURSE, REAR

cra·dle·song \-,sȯŋ\ *n* : LULLABY

craft \'kraft\ *n* 1 : ART, SKILL; *also* : an occupation requiring special skill 2 : CUNNING, GUILE 3 *pl usu* **craft** : a boat esp. of small size; *also* : AIRCRAFT

crafts·man \'krafts-mən\ *n* : a skilled artisan — **crafts·man·ship** *n*

crafty \'kraf-tē\ *adj* : CUNNING, DECEITFUL, SUBTLE — **craft·i·ness** *n*

¹**crag** \'krag\ *n* : a steep rugged cliff or point of rock — **crag·gy** *adj*

cram \'kram\ *vb* **crammed; cram·ming** 1 : to eat greedily : stuff with food 2 : to pack in tight : JAM 3 : to study rapidly under pressure for an examination

¹**cramp** \'kramp\ *n* 1 : a sudden painful contraction of muscle 2 : sharp abdominal pains

²**cramp** *vb* 1 : to affect with cramp 2 : to restrain from free action : HAMPER 3 : to turn (the front wheels) sharply to the side

cran·ber·ry \'kran-,ber-ē, -b(ə-)rē\ *n* : the red acid berry of a trailing plant related to the heaths; *also* : this plant

¹**crane** \'krān\ *n* 1 : a tall wading bird related to the rails 2 : a machine for lifting and carrying heavy objects

²**crane** *vb* : to stretch one's neck to see better

cra·ni·um \'krā-nē-əm\ *n, pl* **-ni·ums** *or* **-nia** \-nē-ə\ : SKULL; *esp* : the part enclosing the brain — **cra·ni·al** *adj*

¹**crank** \'kraŋk\ *n* 1 : a bent part of an axle or shaft or an arm at right angles to the end of a shaft by which circular motion is imparted to or received from it 2 : a person with a mental twist esp. on some one subject 3 : a bad-tempered person : GROUCH

²**crank** *vb* : to start or operate by turning a crank

crank·case \-,kās\ *n* : the housing of a crankshaft

crank·shaft \-,shaft\ *n* : a shaft turning or driven by a crank

cranky \'kraŋ-kē\ *adj* 1 : operating uncertainly or imperfectly 2 : IRRITABLE

cran·ny \'kran-ē\ *n* : CREVICE, CHINK

crape \'krāp\ *n* : CREPE; *esp* : black crepe used in mourning

craps \'kraps\ *n* : a gambling game played with 2 dice

crap·shoot·er \'krap-,shüt-ər\ *n* : a person who plays craps

¹**crash** \'krash\ *vb* 1 : to break noisily : SMASH 2 : to bring down an airplane in such a way that it is damaged

²**crash** *n* 1 : a loud sound (as of things smashing) 2 : SMASH; *also* : COLLISION 3 : a sudden failure (as of a business) 4 : the crashing of an airplane

³**crash** *n* : coarse linen fabric used for towels and draperies

crash·land \-'land\ *vb* : to land an airplane under emergency conditions usu. with damage to the craft

crass \'kras\ *adj* : STUPID, GROSS — **crass·ly** *adv*

crate \'krāt\ *n* : a container with spaces for ventilation — **crate** *vb*

cra·ter \'krāt-ər\ *n* : the depression around the opening of a volcano; *also* : a bowl-shaped depression

cra·vat \krə-'vat\ *n* : NECKTIE

crave \'krāv\ *vb* 1 : to ask earnestly : BEG 2 : to long for : DESIRE

cra·ven \'krā-vən\ *adj* : COWARDLY — **craven** *n*

crav·ing \'krā-viŋ\ *n* : an urgent or abnormal desire

craw·fish \'krȯ-,fish\ *n* : CRAYFISH; *also* : the spiny lobster

¹**crawl** \'krȯl\ *vb* 1 : to move slowly by drawing the body along the ground 2 : to advance feebly or cautiously 3 : to swarm with or as if with creeping things 4 : to feel as if crawling creatures were swarming over one

²**crawl** *n* 1 : a very slow pace or advance 2 : a speed swimming stroke

cray·fish \'krā-,fish\ *n* : a freshwater crustacean like a lobster but smaller

cray·on \'krā-,än, -ən\ *n* : a stick of chalk or wax used for writing, drawing,

---

or coloring; *also* : a drawing made with such material — **crayon** *vb*

¹**craze** \'krāz\ *vb* : to make or become insane

²**craze** *n* : FAD, MANIA

cra·zy \'krā-zē\ *adj* **1** : mentally disordered : INSANE **2** : wildly impractical; *also* : ERRATIC — **cra·zi·ly** *adv*

creak \'krēk\ *vb* : to make a prolonged squeaking or grating sound — **creak** *n* — **creaky** *adj*

¹**cream** \'krēm\ *n* **1** : the yellowish fat-rich part of milk **2** : a thick smooth sauce, confection, or cosmetic **3** : the choicest part **4** : a pale yellow color — **creamy** *adj*

²**cream** *vb* **1** : to prepare with a cream sauce **2** : to beat or blend (butter) into creamy consistency

cream cheese *n* : a cheese made from sweet milk enriched with cream

cream·ery \'krēm-(ə-)rē\ *n* : an establishment where butter and cheese are made or milk and cream are prepared for sale

crease \'krēs\ *n* : a mark or line made by or as if by folding — **crease** *vb*

cre·ate \krē-'āt\ *vb* : to bring into being : cause to exist : MAKE, PRODUCE — **cre·ative** \-'āt-iv\ *adj*

cre·ation \krē-'ā-shən\ *n* **1** : the act of creating or producing ⟨~ of the world⟩ **2** : something that is created **3** : all created things : WORLD

cre·ator \krē-'āt-ər\ *n* : one that creates : MAKER, AUTHOR

crea·ture \'krē-chər\ *n* : a lower animal; *also* : a human being

crèche \'kresh\ *n* : a representation of the Nativity scene in the stable at Bethlehem

cre·dence \'krēd-²ns\ *n* : BELIEF

cre·den·tial \kri-'den-chəl\ *n* : something that gives a basis for credit or confidence

cred·i·ble \'kred-ə-bəl\ *adj* : TRUSTWORTHY, BELIEVABLE — **cred·i·bil·i·ty** \,kred-ə-'bil-ət-ē\ *n*

¹**cred·it** \'kred-ət\ *n* **1** : the balance (as in a bank) in a person's favor **2** : time given for payment for goods sold on trust **3** : an accounting entry of payment received **4** : BELIEF, FAITH **5** : financial trustworthiness **6** : ESTEEM **7** : a source of honor or distinction **8** : a unit of academic work

²**credit** *vb* **1** : BELIEVE **2** : to give credit to

cred·it·able \'kred-ət-ə-bəl\ *adj* : worthy of esteem or praise — **cred·it·ably** *adv*

cred·i·tor \'kred-ət-ər\ *n* : a person to whom money is owed

cre·do \'krēd-ō, 'krād-\ *n* : CREED

cred·u·lous \'krej-ə-ləs\ *adj* : inclined to believe esp. on slight evidence — **cre·du·li·ty** \kri-'d(y)ü-lət-ē\ *n*

creed \'krēd\ *n* [OE *crēda*, fr. L *credo* I believe, first word of the Apostles' and Nicene Creeds] : a statement of the essential beliefs of a religious faith

creek \'krēk, 'krik\ *n* **1** : a small inlet **2** : a stream smaller than a river and larger than a brook

creel \'krēl\ *n* : a wickerwork basket esp. for carrying fish

creep \'krēp\ *vb* **crept** \'krept\ **creep·ing** **1** : CRAWL **2** : to grow over a surface like ivy **3** : to feel as though insects were crawling on the skin — **creep** *n* — **creep·er** *n*

creepy \'krē-pē\ *adj* : having or produc-

ing a nervous shivery fear

cre·mate \'krē-,māt\ *vb* : to reduce (a dead body) to ashes with fire — **cre·ma·tion** \kri-'mā-shən\ *n*

cre·ma·to·ry \'krēm-ə-,tōr-ē, 'krem-\ *n* : a furnace for cremating; *also* : a structure containing such a furnace

cren·el·late *or* **cren·el·ate** \'kren-²l-,āt\ *vb* : to furnish with battlements — **cren·el·la·tion** \,kren-²l-'ā-shən\ *n*

Cre·ole \'krē-,ōl\ *n* : a descendant of early French or Spanish settlers of the U.S. Gulf states preserving their speech and culture; *also* : a person of mixed French or Spanish and Negro descent speaking a dialect of French or Spanish

cre·o·sote \'krē-ə-,sōt\ *n* : an oily fluid obtained by distillation of coal tar and used in preserving wood

crepe *or* **crêpe** \'krāp\ *n* : a light crinkled fabric of silk, rayon, wool, or cotton

cre·pus·cu·lar \kri-'pəs-kyə-lər\ *adj* **1** : of, relating to, or resembling twilight **2** : active in the twilight ⟨~ insects⟩

cre·scen·do \kri-'shen-dō\ *adv (or adj)* : increasing in loudness — used as a direction in music — **crescendo** *n*

cres·cent \'kres-²nt\ *n* : the moon at any stage between new moon and first quarter and between last quarter and new moon; *also* : something shaped like the figure of the crescent moon with a convex and a concave edge

cress \'kres\ *n* : any of several salad plants related to the mustards

¹**crest** \'krest\ *n* **1** : a tuft or process on the head of an animal (as a bird) **2** : the ridge at the top of a hill or a billow **3** : a heraldic device — **crest·ed** *adj* — **crest·less** *adj*

²**crest** *vb* **1** : CROWN **2** : to reach the crest of **3** : to rise to a crest ⟨the river ~ed at eight feet⟩

crest·fall·en \'krest-,fò-lən\ *adj* : DISPIRITED, DEJECTED

cre·ta·ceous \kri-'tā-shəs\ *adj* : having the nature of or abounding in chalk

cre·tonne \'krē-,tän\ *n* : a strong unglazed cotton cloth for curtains and upholstery

cre·vasse \kri-'vas\ *n* **1** : a deep fissure esp. in a glacier **2** : a break in a levee

crev·ice \'krev-əs\ *n* : a narrow fissure : CRACK

¹**crew** \'krü\ *chiefly Brit past of* CROW

²**crew** *n* **1** : a body of men trained to work together for certain purposes **2** : the body of seamen who man a ship **3** : the persons who man an airplane in flight

¹**crib** \'krib\ *n* **1** : a manger for feeding animals **2** : a building or bin for storage (as of grain) **3** : a small bedstead for a child **4** : a translation prepared to aid a student in preparing a lesson

²**crib** *vb* **cribbed; crib·bing 1** : CONFINE, CRAMP **2** : to put in a crib **3** : STEAL; *esp* : PLAGIARIZE — **crib·ber** *n*

crib·bage \'krib-ij\ *n* : a card game usu. played by 2 players and scored on a board (**cribbage board**)

crick \'krik\ *n* : a painful spasm of muscles (as of the neck)

¹**crick·et** \'krik-ət\ *n* : a leaping insect noted for the chirping notes of the males

²**cricket** *n* : a game played with a bat and ball by 2 teams on a field with 2 wickets each defended by a batsman

cri·er \'krī-(ə)r\ *n* : one who calls out proclamations and announcements

crime \'krīm\ *n* **:** a serious offense against the public law

1crim·i·nal \'krim-ən-ˀl\ *adj* **1 :** involving or being a crime **2 :** relating to crime or its punishment — **crim·i·nal·i·ty** \ˌkrim-ə-'nal-ət-ē\ *n* — **crim·i·nal·ly** \'krim-ən-ˀl-ē\ *adv*

2criminal *n* **:** one who has committed a crime

crim·i·nol·o·gy \ˌkrim-ə-'näl-ə-jē\ *n* **:** the scientific study of crime and criminals — **crim·i·no·log·i·cal** \-ˌnä-'läj-i-kəl\ *adj* — **crim·i·nol·o·gist** \-'näl-ə-jəst\ *n*

1crimp \'krimp\ *vb* **:** to cause to become crinkled, wavy, or bent (~ hair) — **crimp·er** *n*

2crimp *n* **:** something (as a curl in hair) produced by or as if by crimping

1crim·son \'krim-zən\ *n* **:** a deep purplish red — **crimson** *adj*

2crimson *vb* **:** to make or become crimson

cringe \'krinj\ *vb* **:** to shrink in fear **:** WINCE, COWER, QUAIL

crin·kle \'kriŋ-kəl\ *vb* **:** to turn or wind in many short bends or curves; *also* **:** WRINKLE, RIPPLE — **crinkle** *n* — **crin·kly** \-k(ə-)lē\ *adj*

crin·o·line \'krin-ˀl-ən\ *n* **1 :** an open-weave cloth used for stiffening and lining **2 :** a full stiff skirt

1crip·ple \'krip-əl\ *n* **:** a lame or disabled person

2cripple *vb* **:** to make lame **:** DISABLE

cri·sis \'krī-səs\, *n, pl* **cri·ses** \-ˌsēz\ **1 :** the turning point for better or worse in an acute disease or fever **2 :** a decisive or critical moment

crisp \'krisp\ *adj* **1 :** CURLY, WAVY **2 :** BRITTLE **3 :** being sharp and clear **4 :** LIVELY, SPARKLING **5 :** FIRM, FRESH (~ lettuce) **6 :** FROSTY, SNAPPY; *also* **:** BRACING — **crisp** *vb* — **crisp·ly** *adv* — **crisp·ness** *n* — **crispy** *adj*

1criss·cross \'kris-ˌkrös\ *n* **:** a pattern of crossed lines

2crisscross *vb* **1 :** to mark with crossed lines **2 :** to go or pass back and forth

3crisscross *adv* **:** CONTRARY, AWRY

cri·te·ri·on \krī-'tir-ē-ən\ *n* **:** STANDARD, TEST

crit·ic \'krit-ik\ *n* **1 :** one skilled in judging literary or artistic works **2 :** one inclined to find fault or complain

crit·i·cal \'krit-i-kəl\ *adj* **1 :** inclined to criticize **2 :** requiring careful judgment **3 :** being a crisis **4 :** UNCERTAIN **5 :** relating to criticism or critics — **crit·i·cal·ly** *adv*

crit·i·cism \'krit-ə-ˌsiz-əm\ *n* **1 :** the act of criticizing; *esp* **:** CENSURE **2 :** a critical judgment or review **3 :** the art of judging expertly works of literature or art

crit·i·cize \-ˌsīz\ *vb* **1 :** to judge as a critic **:** EVALUATE **2 :** to find fault **:** express criticism *syn* blame, censure, condemn

cri·tique \krə-'tēk\ *n* **:** a critical estimate or discussion

crit·ter \'krit-ər\ *n, dial* **:** CREATURE

croak \'krōk\ *n* **:** a hoarse harsh cry (as of a frog) — **croak** *vb*

cro·chet \krō-'shā\ *n* **:** needlework done with a single thread and hooked needle — **crochet** *vb*

crock \'kräk\ *n* **:** a thick earthenware pot or jar

crock·ery \-(ə-)rē\ *n* **:** EARTHENWARE

croc·o·dile \'kräk-ə-ˌdīl\ *n* **:** a thick-skinned long-bodied reptile of tropical and subtropical waters

cro·cus \'krō-kəs\ *n* **:** a low herb related to the irises with brightly colored flowers borne singly in early spring

crois·sant \krə-ˌwä-'säⁿ\ *n* **:** a rich crescent-shaped roll

crone \'krōn\ *n* **:** a withered old woman

cro·ny \'krō-nē\ *n* **:** an intimate companion

1crook \'kruk\ *n* **1 :** a bent or curved implement **2 :** a bent or curved part; *also* **:** BEND, CURVE **3 :** SWINDLER, THIEF

2crook *vb* **:** to curve or bend sharply

crook·ed \'kruk-əd\ *adj* **1 :** having a crook **:** BENT, CURVED **2 :** DISHONEST

croon \'krün\ *vb* **1 :** to sing in a low soft voice **2 :** to sing in half voice — **croon·er** *n*

1crop \'kräp\ *n* **1 :** a pouch in the throat of many birds and insects where food is received **2 :** the handle of a whip; *also* **:** a short riding whip **3 :** something that can be harvested; *also* **:** the yield at harvest

2crop *vb* **cropped; crop·ping 1 :** to remove the tips of **:** cut off short; *also* **:** to feed on by cropping **2 :** to devote (land) to crops **3 :** to appear unexpectedly

crop·land \'kräp-ˌland\ *n* **:** land devoted to the production of plant crops

crop·per *n* **:** a raiser of crops; *esp* **:** SHARECROPPER

cro·quet \krō-'kā\ *n* **:** a game in which mallets are used to drive wooden balls through a series of wickets set out on a lawn

cro·quette \krō-'ket\ *n* **:** a roll or ball of hashed meat, fish, or vegetables fried in deep fat

cro·sier \'krō-zhər\ *n* **:** a staff carried by bishops and abbots

1cross \'krös\ *n* **1 :** a structure consisting of an upright beam and a crossbar used esp. by the ancient Romans for execution **2** *often cap* **:** a figure of the cross on which Christ was crucified used as a Christian symbol **3 :** a hybridizing of unlike individuals or strains; *also* **:** a product of this **4 :** a punch delivered with a circular motion over an opponent's lead

2cross *vb* **1 :** to lie or place across; *also* **:** INTERSECT **2 :** to cancel by marking a cross on or by lining through **:** strike out **3 :** THWART, OBSTRUCT **4 :** to go or extend across **:** TRAVERSE **5 :** HYBRIDIZE **6 :** to meet and pass on the way

3cross *adj* **1 :** lying across **2 :** CONTRARY, OPPOSED **3 :** marked by bad temper **4 :** HYBRID — **cross·ly** *adv*

cross·bar \-ˌbär\ *n* **:** a transverse bar or piece

cross·bones \-ˌbōnz\ *n pl* **:** two leg or arm bones placed or depicted crosswise

cross·bow \-ˌbō\ *n* **:** a medieval weapon consisting of a strong bow mounted crosswise on a stock

cross·breed \-ˌbrēd\ *vb* **:** HYBRIDIZE

cross·coun·try \-ˌkən-trē\ *adj* **1 :** proceeding over the countryside (as fields and woods) rather than by roads 2 : of or relating to cross-country sports — **cross-country** adv

cross·cur·rent \-'kər-ənt\ n 1 : a current running counter to another 2 : a conflicting tendency

¹**cross·cut** \-,kət\ vb : to cut or saw crosswise esp. of the grain of wood

²**crosscut** adj 1 : made or used for crosscutting 2 : cut across the grain

³**crosscut** n : something that cuts through transversely ⟨a ~ through the park⟩

cross-ex·am·ine \,krös-ig-'zam-ən\ vb : to examine with questions as a check to answers to previous examination — **cross-ex·am·i·na·tion** \-,zam-ə-'nā-shən\ n

cross-eye \'krös-,ī\ n : an abnormality in which the eye turns toward the nose — **cross-eyed** \-'īd\ adj

cross·hatch \-,hach\ vb : to mark with a series of parallel lines that cross esp. obliquely — **cross·hatch·ing** n

cross·ing n 1 : a point of intersection (as of a street and a railroad track) 2 : a place for crossing something (as a street or river)

cross·piece \'krös-,pēs\ n : a crosswise member (as of a figure or a structure)

cross-pol·li·na·tion \,krös-,päl-ə-'nā-shən\ n : transfer of pollen from one flower to the stigma of another — **cross-pol·li·nate** \'krös-'päl-ə-,nāt\ vb

cross-ques·tion \'krös-'kwes-chən\ vb : CROSS-EXAMINE

cross-re·fer \,krös-ri-'fər\ vb : to refer by a notation or direction from one place to another (as in a book or list) — **cross-ref·er·ence** \'krös-'ref-(ə-)rəns\ n

cross·road \'krös-,röd\ n 1 : a road that crosses a main road or runs between main roads 2 : a place where roads meet — usu. used in pl.

cross section n 1 : a section cut across something; also : a representation made by or as if from such cutting 2 : a number of persons or things selected from an entire group to show the general nature of the whole group

cross·walk \'krös-,wök\ n : a specially marked path for pedestrians crossing a street

cross·wise \-,wīz\ also **cross·ways** \-,wāz\ adv : so as to cross something : ACROSS — **crosswise** adj

crotch \'kräch\ n : an angle formed by the parting of two legs, branches, or members

crotch·et \'kräch-ət\ n : an odd notion : WHIM — **crotch·ety** adj

crouch \'kraúch\ vb 1 : to stoop over 2 : CRINGE, COWER — **crouch** n

croup \'krüp\ n : laryngitis esp. of infants marked by a hoarse ringing cough and difficult breathing

crou·pi·er \'krü-pē-ər, -pē-,ā\ n : an employee of a gambling casino who collects and pays bets at a gaming table

crou·ton \'krü-,tän\ n : a small piece of toast

¹**crow** \'krö\ n : a large glossy black bird

²**crow** vb crowed; crow·ing 1 : to make the loud shrill sound characteristic of the rooster 2 : to utter a sound expressive of pleasure 3 : EXULT, GLOAT; also : BRAG, BOAST

³**crow** n : the cry of the cock

crow·bar \'krö-,bär\ n : a metal bar usu. wedge-shaped at the end for use as a pry or lever

¹**crowd** \'kraúd\ vb 1 : to collect in numbers : THRONG 2 : to press close 3 : CRAM, STUFF

²**crowd** n : a large number of people gathered together at random : THRONG

crow·foot \'krö-,fút\ n : BUTTERCUP

¹**crown** \'kraún\ n 1 : GARLAND; also : the title of champion in a sport 2 : a royal headdress 3 cap : sovereign power; also : MONARCH 4 : the top of the head 5 : a British silver coin 6 : something resembling a crown in shape, position, or use; esp : a top part (as of a tree or tooth)

²**crown** vb 1 : to place a crown upon 2 : HONOR 3 : TOP, SURMOUNT 4 : to fit (a tooth) with an artificial crown

cru·cial \'krü-shəl\ adj : DECISIVE; also : SEVERE, TRYING

cru·ci·ble \'krü-sə-bəl\ n : a container used to hold a substance (as metal or ore) treated under great heat

cru·ci·fix \'krü-sə-,fiks\ n : a representation of Christ on the cross

cru·ci·fix·ion \,krü-sə-'fik-shən\ n : the act of crucifying; esp, cap : the execution of Christ on the cross

cru·ci·form \'krü-sə-,förm\ adj : cross-shaped

cru·ci·fy \'krü-sə-,fī\ vb 1 : to put to death by nailing or binding the hands and feet to a cross 2 : MORTIFY ⟨~ the flesh⟩ 3 : TORTURE, PERSECUTE

crude \'krüd\ adj 1 : not refined : RAW ⟨~ oil⟩ ⟨~ statistics⟩ 2 : lacking grace, taste, tact, or polish : RUDE — **crude·ly** adv — **cru·di·ty** \'krüd-ət-ē\ n

cru·el \'krü-əl\ adj : causing pain and suffering to others : MERCILESS — **cru·el·ly** adv — **cru·el·ty** n

cru·et \'krü-ət\ n : a glass bottle for oil or vinegar at the table

cruise \'krüz\ vb 1 : to sail about touching at a series of ports 2 : to travel for enjoyment 3 : to travel about the streets at random 4 : to travel at the most efficient operating speed ⟨the cruising speed of an airplane⟩ — **cruise** n

cruis·er \'krü-zər\ n 1 : a fast moderately armored and gunned warship 2 : a motorboat equipped for living aboard 3 : a police car equipped with radio to maintain communication with headquarters

crul·ler \'krəl-ər\ n 1 : a sweet cake made of egg batter fried in deep fat 2 North & Midland : an unraised doughnut

¹**crumb** \'krəm\ n : a small fragment (as of bread)

²**crumb** vb 1 : to break into crumbs 2 : to cover with crumbs

crum·ble \'krəm-bəl\ vb : to break into small pieces : DISINTEGRATE — **crum·bly** \-b(ə-)lē\ adj

crum·pet \'krəm-pət\ n : a small round cake made of unsweetened batter cooked on a griddle

crum·ple \'krəm-pəl\ vb 1 : to crush together : RUMPLE 2 : COLLAPSE

crunch \'krənch\ vb : to chew with a grinding noise; also : to grind or press with a crushing noise — **crunch** n

cru·sade \krü-'sād\ n 1 cap : any of the expeditions in the 11th, 12th, and 13th centuries undertaken by Christian countries to recover the Holy Land from the Turks 2 : a reforming enterprise undertaken with zeal — **crusade** vb — **cru·sad·er** n

cruse \'krüz, 'krüs\ n : a jar for water or oil

¹**crush** \'krəsh\ vb 1 : to squeeze out of shape 2 : HUG, EMBRACE 3 : to grind or pound to small bits 4 : OVERWHELM, SUPPRESS

²**crush** n 1 : an act of crushing 2 : a violent crowding 3 : INFATUATION

crust \'krəst\ n 1 : the outside part of bread; also : a piece of old dry bread 2 : the cover of a pie 3 : a hard surface layer — **crust·al** adj — **crusty** adj

crus·ta·cean \krəs-'tā-shən\ n : any of a large group of mostly aquatic arthropods (as lobsters or crabs) having a firm crustlike shell

crutch \'krəch\ n : a supporting device; esp : a staff with a cross-piece at the top to fit under the armpit used by lame persons

crux \'krəks, 'krùks\ n 1 : a puzzling or difficult problem 2 : a crucial point

cru·zei·ro \krü-'zā-rō, -rü\ n — see MONEY table

¹**cry** \'krī\ vb 1 : to call out : SHOUT 2 : WEEP 3 : to proclaim publicly; also : to advertise wares by calling out

²**cry** n 1 : a loud outcry 2 : APPEAL, ENTREATY 3 : a fit of weeping 4 : the characteristic sound uttered by an animal

cry·ba·by \-,bā-bē\ n : one who cries easily or often

crypt \'kript\ n : a chamber wholly or partly underground

cryp·tic \'krip-tik\ adj : MYSTERIOUS, ENIGMATIC

cryp·to·gram \'krip-tə-,gram\ n : a writing in cipher or code

cryp·tog·ra·phy \krip-'täg-rə-fē\ n : the enciphering and deciphering of messages in secret code — **cryp·tog·ra·pher** n

crys·tal \'kris-t°l\ n 1 : transparent quartz 2 : something resembling crystal (as in transparency); esp : a clear glass used for table articles 3 : a body that is formed by solidification of a substance and has a regular repeating arrangement of atoms and often of external plane faces ⟨a snow ∼⟩ ⟨a salt ∼⟩ 4 : the transparent cover of a watch dial — **crys·tal·line** \-tə-lən\ adj

crys·tal·lize \-tə-,līz\ vb : to assume or cause to assume a crystalline structure or a fixed and definite shape — **crys·tal·li·za·tion** \,kris-tə-lə-'zā-shən\ n

cub \'kəb\ n : a young individual of some animals (as a fox, bear, or lion)

cub·by·hole \'kəb-ē-,hōl\ n 1 : a snug or confined place (as for hiding) 2 : a small closet, cupboard, or compartment for storing things

¹**cube** \'kyüb\ n 1 : a solid having 6 equal square sides 2 : the product obtained by taking a number 3 times as a factor ⟨27 is the ∼ of 3⟩

²**cube** vb 1 : to raise to the third power ⟨∼ 3 to get 27⟩ 2 : to form into a cube 3 : to cut into cubes

cu·bic \'kyü-bik\ adj 1 : having the form of a cube 2 : having three dimensions 3 : being the volume of a cube whose edge is a specified unit — **cu·bi·cal** adj

cu·bi·cle \'kyü-bi-kəl\ n 1 : a sleeping compartment partitioned off from a

large room 2 : a small partitioned space

cu·bit \-bət\ n : an ancient measure of length equal to about 18 inches

cuck·old \'kək-əld, 'kük-\ n : a man whose wife is unfaithful

cuck·oo \'kük-ü, 'kük-\ n : a European bird that lays its eggs in the nests of other birds for them to hatch

cu·cum·ber \'kyü-(,)kəm-bər\ n : a fleshy fruit related to the gourds and eaten as a vegetable

cud \'kəd\ n : food brought up into the mouth by ruminating animals (as cows) from the first stomach to be chewed again

cud·dle \'kəd-°l\ vb : to lie close : SNUGGLE

cud·gel \'kəj-əl\ n : a short heavy club — **cudgel** vb

¹**cue** \'kyü\ n 1 : words or stage business serving as a signal for an entrance or for the next speaker to speak 2 : HINT

²**cue** n : a tapered rod for striking the balls in billiards

¹**cuff** \'kəf\ n 1 : a part (as of a sleeve or glove) encircling the wrist 2 : the folded hem of a trouser leg

²**cuff** vb : to strike esp. with the open hand : SLAP

³**cuff** n : a blow with the hand esp. when open

cui·sine \kwi-'zēn\ n : manner of cooking; also : the food so prepared

cul·de·sac \'kəl-di-'sak\ n, pl **culs·de·sac** \kəl(z)-di-\ also **cul·de·sacs** \,kəl-di-'saks\ : a street or passage closed at one end

cu·li·nary \'kəl-ə-,ner-ē, 'kyü-lə-\ adj : relating to cookery

¹**cull** \'kəl\ vb : to pick out from a group : CHOOSE

²**cull** n : something rejected from a group or lot as worthless or inferior

cul·len·der var of COLANDER

cul·mi·nate \'kəl-mə-,nāt\ vb : to form a summit : rise to the highest point — **cul·mi·na·tion** \,kəl-mə-'nā-shən\ n

cul·pa·ble \'kəl-pə-bəl\ adj : deserving blame

cul·prit \'kəl-prət\ n : one accused or guilty of a crime : OFFENDER

cult \'kəlt\ n 1 : formal religious veneration 2 : a religious system; also : its adherents 3 : faddish devotion; also : a group of persons showing such devotion — **cult·ist** n

cul·ti·vate \'kəl-tə-,vāt\ vb 1 : to prepare for the raising of crops 2 : to foster the growth of ⟨∼ vegetables⟩ 3 : REFINE, IMPROVE 4 : ENCOURAGE, FURTHER — **cul·ti·va·ble** \-və-bəl\ adj — **cul·ti·vat·able** \-,vāt-ə-bəl\ adj — **cul·ti·va·tion** \,kəl-tə-'vā-shən\ n — **cul·ti·va·tor** \'kəl-tə-,vāt-ər\ n

cul·ture \'kəl-chər\ n 1 : TILLAGE, CULTIVATION; also : the growing of a particular crop ⟨grape ∼⟩ 2 : the act of developing by education and training 3 : a stage of advancement in civilization — **cul·tur·al** adj — **cul·tur·al·ly** adv — **cul·tured** adj

cul·vert \'kəl-vərt\ n : a drain crossing under a road or railroad

cum·ber \'kəm-bər\ vb : to weigh down : HAMPER, BURDEN — **cum·ber·some** adj — **cum·brous** \'kəm-brəs\ adj

cum·mer·bund \'kəm-ər-,bənd\ *n* : a broad sash worn as a waistband

cu·mu·la·tive \'kyü-myə-lət-iv, -,lāt-\ *adj* : increasing in force or value by successive additions

cu·mu·lus \'kyü-myə-ləs\ *n* : a massive cloud having a flat base and rounded outlines

cu·ne·i·form \kyü-'nē-ə-,fȯrm\ *adj* 1 : wedge-shaped 2 : composed of wedge-shaped characters ⟨~ alphabet⟩

¹**cun·ning** \'kən-iŋ\ *adj* 1 : contrived with skill 2 : CRAFTY, SLY 3 : CLEVER 4 : prettily appealing — **cun·ning·ly** *adv*

²**cunning** *n* 1 : SKILL 2 : CRAFTINESS, SLYNESS

cup \'kəp\ *n* 1 : a small bowl-shaped drinking vessel 2 : the contents of a cup 3 : communion wine 4 : something resembling a cup : a small bowl or hollow — **cup·ful** *n*

cup·bear·er \-,bar-ər\ *n* : one who has the duty of filling and serving cups of wine

cup·board \'kəb-ərd\ *n* : a small storage closet

cup·cake \'kəp-,kāk\ *n* : a small cake baked in a cuplike mold

cu·pid \'kyü-pəd\ *n* : a winged naked figure of an infant often with a bow and arrow that represents the god Cupid

cu·pid·i·ty \kyü-'pid-ət-ē\ *n* : excessive desire for money : AVARICE

cu·po·la \'kyü-pə-lə, -,lō\ *n* : a small structure on top of a roof or building (as to complete a design or to serve as a lookout)

cur \'kər\ *n* : a mongrel dog

cu·rate \'kyùr-ət\ *n* 1 : a clergyman in charge of a parish 2 : a clergyman who assists a rector or vicar — **cu·ra·cy** \-ə-sē\ *n*

cu·ra·tive \'kyùr-ət-iv\ *adj* : relating to or used in the cure of diseases

cu·ra·tor \kyù-'rāt-ər\ *n* : CUSTODIAN; *esp* : one in charge of a place of exhibit (as a museum or zoo)

¹**curb** \'kərb\ *n* 1 : a chain or strap on a bit used to check a horse 2 : CHECK, RESTRAINT 3 : a raised stone edging along a paved street 4 : a market for trading in securities not listed on the stock exchange

²**curb** *vb* : to hold in or back : RESTRAIN

curb·ing *n* 1 : the material for a curb 2 : CURB

curd \'kərd\ *n* : the thick protein-rich part of coagulated milk

cur·dle \'kərd-ᵊl\ *vb* : to form curds; *also* : SPOIL, SOUR

¹**cure** \'kyùr\ *n* 1 : spiritual care 2 : recovery or relief from disease 3 : a curative agent : REMEDY 4 : a course or period of treatment — **cure·less** *adj*

²**cure** *vb* 1 : to restore to health : HEAL, REMEDY 2 : to process for storage or use ⟨~ bacon⟩; *also* : to become cured ⟨sun-*cured* hay⟩ — **cur·able** *adj*

³**cu·ré** \kyù-'rā\ *n* : a parish priest

cure-all \'kyùr-,ȯl\ *n* : a remedy for all ill : PANACEA

cur·few \'kər-,fyü\ *n* [MF *covrefeu* curfew signal, fr. *covrir* to cover + *jeu* fire] : a regulation that specified persons (as children) be off the streets at a set hour of the evening; *also* : the sounding of a signal (as a bell) at this hour

cu·ria \'k(y)ùr-ē-ə\ *n*, *often cap* : the body of congregations, tribunals, and offices through which the pope governs the Roman Catholic Church

cu·rio \'kyùr-ē-,ō\ *n* : a small object valued for its rarity or beauty; *also* : an unusual or strange thing

cu·ri·ous \'kyùr-ē-əs\ *adj* 1 : having a desire to investigate and learn : INQUISITIVE, PRYING 2 : STRANGE, UNUSUAL 3 : ODD, ECCENTRIC — **cu·ri·os·i·ty** \,kyùr-ē-'äs-ət-ē\ — **cu·ri·ous·ly** \'kyùr-ē-əs-lē\ *adv*

¹**curl** \'kərl\ *vb* 1 : to form into ringlets 2 : CURVE, COIL — **curl·er** *n*

²**curl** *n* 1 : a lock of hair that coils : RINGLET 2 : something having a spiral or twisted form — **curly** *adj*

cur·lew \'kər-(y)ü\ *n* : a long-legged brownish bird with a down-curved bill

curl·i·cue \'kər-lē-,kyü\ *n* : a fancifully curved or spiral figure

cur·rant \'kər-ənt\ *n* 1 : a small seedless raisin 2 : the acid berry of a shrub related to the gooseberry; *also* : this plant

cur·ren·cy \'kər-ən-sē\ *n* 1 : general use or acceptance 2 : something that is in circulation as a medium of exchange : MONEY

¹**cur·rent** \'kər-ənt\ *adj* 1 : occurring in or belonging to the present 2 : used as a medium of exchange 3 : generally accepted or practiced

²**current** *n* 1 : continuous onward movement of a fluid; *also* : the swiftest part of a stream 2 : a movement of electricity analogous to the flow of a stream of water

cur·ric·u·lum \kə-'rik-yə-ləm\ *n*, *pl* **-u·la** \-yə-lə\ *also* **-ulums** [L, racecourse, fr. *currere* to run] : a course of study offered by a school or one of its divisions

¹**cur·ry** \'kər-ē\ *vb* 1 : to dress the coat of (a horse) with a metal-toothed comb (**cur·ry·comb**) 2 : to scrape (leather) until clean

²**curry** *n* : a powder of blended spices used in cooking; *also* : a food seasoned with curry

¹**curse** \'kərs\ *n* 1 : a prayer for harm to come upon one 2 : something that is cursed 3 : something that comes as if in response to a curse : SCOURGE

²**curse** *vb* 1 : to call on divine power to send injury upon 2 : BLASPHEME 3 : AFFLICT **syn** execrate, damn, anathematize

cur·sive \'kər-siv\ *adj* : written or formed with the strokes of the letters joined together and the angles rounded ⟨~ handwriting⟩

cur·so·ry \'kərs-(ə)-rē\ *adj* : hastily and often superficially done : HASTY — **cur·so·ri·ly** \-ə-rē-lē\ *adv*

curt \'kərt\ *adj* : rudely short or abrupt — **curt·ly** *adv*

cur·tail \(,)kər-'tāl\ *vb* : to cut off the end of : SHORTEN — **cur·tail·ment** *n*

cur·tain \'kərt-ᵊn\ *n* 1 : a hanging screen that can be drawn back esp. at a window 2 : the screen between the stage and auditorium of a theater — **curtain** *vb*

curt·sy *or* **curt·sey** \'kərt-sē\ *n* : a courteous bow made by women chiefly by bending the knees — **curtsy** *vb*

cur·va·ture \'kər-və-,chùr\ *n* : a measure or amount of curving : BEND

¹**curve** \'kərv\ *vb* : to bend from a straight line or course

²**curve** *n* 1 : a bending without angles 2 : something curved 3 : a ball thrown

so that it swerves from its normal course

cur·vet \(,)kər-'vet\ *n* **:** a prancing leap of a horse — **curvet** *vb*

¹cush·ion \'kush-ən\ *n* **1 :** a stuffed bag or case for sitting on or lying against in comfort **2 :** the springy pad inside the rim of a billiard table

²cushion *vb* **1 :** to provide (as a seat) with a cushion **2 :** to soften or lessen the force or shock of

cusp \'kəsp\ *n* **:** a pointed end (as of a tooth)

cus·pi·dor \'kəs-pə-,dȯr\ *n* **:** SPITTOON

cus·tard \'kəs-tərd\ *n* **:** a sweetened mixture of milk and eggs cooked until it is set

cus·to·di·an \,kəs-'tōd-ē-ən\ *n* **:** one who has custody (as of a public building) **:** KEEPER

cus·to·dy \'kəs-təd-ē\ *n* **:** immediate care or charge

¹cus·tom \'kəs-təm\ *n* **1 :** habitual course of action **:** recognized usage **2** *pl* **:** taxes levied on imports **3 :** business patronage

²custom *adj* **1 :** made to personal order **2 :** doing work only on order

cus·tom·ary \'kəs-tə-,mer-ē\ *adj* **1 :** based on or established by custom ⟨~ rent⟩ **2 :** commonly practiced or observed **:** HABITUAL ⟨~ courtesy⟩ — **cus·tom·ar·i·ly** \,kəs-tə-'mer-ə-lē\ *adv*

cus·tom-built \,kəs-təm-'bilt\ *adj* **:** built to individual order

cus·tom·er \'kəs-tə-mər\ *n* **:** BUYER, PURCHASER; *esp* **:** a regular or frequent buyer

cus·tom·house \'kəs-təm-,haus\ *n* **:** the building where customs are paid

cus·tom-made \,kəs-təm-'mād\ *adj* **:** made to individual order

¹cut \'kət\ *vb* **cut; cut·ting 1 :** to penetrate or divide with a sharp edge **:** CLEAVE, GASH; *also* **:** to experience the growth of (a tooth) through the gum **2 :** SHORTEN, REDUCE **3 :** to remove by severing or paring **4 :** INTERSECT, CROSS **5 :** to strike sharply **6 :** to divide into parts **7 :** to go quickly or change direction abruptly **8 :** to cause to stop ⟨~ a motor⟩

²cut *n* **1 :** something made by cutting **:** GASH, CLEFT **2 :** an excavated channel or roadway **3 :** SHARE **4 :** a customary segment of a meat carcass **5 :** a sharp stroke or blow **6 :** the shape or manner in which a thing is cut **7 :** REDUCTION ⟨~ in wages⟩ **8 :** an engraved surface for printing; *also* **:** a picture printed from it

cut-and-dried \,kət-ᵊn-'drīd\ *adj* **:** according to a plan, set procedure, or formula

cu·ta·ne·ous \kyu̇-'tā-nē-əs\ *adj* **:** of or relating to the skin

cut·back \'kət-,bak\ *n* **1 :** something cut back **2 :** REDUCTION

cute \'kyüt\ *adj* **1 :** CLEVER, SHREWD **2 :** daintily attractive **:** PRETTY

cu·ti·cle \'kyüt-i-kəl\ *n* **:** an outer layer (as of skin)

cut·lass \'kət-ləs\ *n* **:** a short heavy curved sword

cut·lery \'kət-lə-rē\ *n* **:** edged or cutting tools; *esp* **:** implements for cutting and eating food — **cut·ler** *n*

cut·let \'kət-lət\ *n* **:** a slice (as of veal)

cut from the leg or ribs

cut·off \-,ȯf\ *n* **1 :** the channel formed when a stream cuts through the neck of an oxbow; *also* **:** SHORTCUT **2 :** a device for cutting off

cut·ter \'kət-ər\ *n* **1 :** a tool or a machine for cutting **2 :** a ship's boat for carrying stores and passengers **3 :** a small armed powerboat (coast guard ~) **4 :** a light sleigh

¹cut·throat \'kət-,thrōt\ *n* **:** MURDERER

²cutthroat *adj* **1 :** MURDEROUS, CRUEL **2 :** MERCILESS, RUTHLESS ⟨~ competition⟩

cut·ting \'kət-iŋ\ *n* **:** a piece of a plant able to grow into a new plant

cut·tle·fish \'kət-ᵊl-,fish\ *n* **:** a 10-armed mollusk related to the squid with an internal shell (**cut·tle·bone** \-,bōn\) used in cage-bird feeding

cut·up \'kət-,əp\ *n* **:** one that clowns or acts boisterously

cut·worm \'kət-,wərm\ *n* **:** a smooth-bodied moth larva that feeds on plants at night

-cy \sē\ *n suffix* **:** action **:** practice ⟨mendancy⟩ **:** rank **:** office ⟨chaplaincy⟩ **:** body **:** class ⟨magistracy⟩ **:** state **:** quality ⟨accuracy⟩ ⟨bankruptcy⟩

cy·a·nide \'sī-ə-,nīd\ *n* **:** a very poisonous potassium-containing or sodium-containing substance used esp. in electroplating

cy·cla·men \'sī-klə-mən\ *n* **:** an herb related to the primroses and grown for its showy nodding flowers

cy·cle \'sī-kəl, 5 & 6 also 'sik-əl\ *n* **1 :** a period of time occupied by a series of events that repeat themselves regularly and in the same order **2 :** a recurring round of operations or events **3 :** one complete series of changes of value of an alternating current or an electromagnetic wave; *also* **:** the number of such changes per second ⟨a current of 60 ~s⟩ **4 :** a long period of time **5 :** AGE **6 :** BICYCLE **6 :** MOTORCYCLE — **cy·clic** \'sī-klik, 'sik-ik\ *adj*

cy·clist \'sī-k-(ə-)ləst, 'sik-\ *n* **:** one who rides a cycle

cy·clom·e·ter \sī-'kläm-ət-ər\ *n* **:** a device that records the revolutions of a wheel and the distance covered

cy·clone \'sī-,klōn\ *n* **1 :** a storm or system of winds that rotates about a center of low atmospheric pressure and advances at 20 to 30 miles an hour **2 :** TORNADO — **cy·clon·ic** \sī-'klän-ik\ *adj*

cy·clo·pe·dia *or* **cy·clo·pae·dia** \,sī-klə-'pēd-ē-ə\ *n* **:** ENCYCLOPEDIA

cy·clo·tron \'sī-klə-,trän\ *n* **:** a device for giving high speed to charged particles by magnetic and electrical means

cyg·net \'sig-nət\ *n* **:** a young swan

cyl·in·der \'sil-ən-dər\ *n* **1 :** the solid figure formed by turning a rectangle about one side as an axis; *also* **:** a body of this form **2 :** the rotating chamber in a revolver **3 :** the piston chamber in an engine — **cy·lin·dri·cal** \sə-'lin-dri-kəl\ *adj*

cym·bal \'sim-bəl\ *n* **:** one of a pair of concave brass plates clashed together to make a ringing sound

cyn·ic \'sin-ik\ *n* **:** one who attributes all actions to selfish motives — **cyn-**

---

i·cal \-i-kəl\ adj — cyn·i·cism \'sin-ə-,siz-əm\ n

cy·no·sure \'sī-nə-,shùr, 'sin-ə-\ n : a center of attraction

cy·press \'sī-prəs\ n : a scaly-leaved evergreen tree related to the pines

cyst \'sist\ n : an abnormal closed bodily sac usu. containing liquid — cys·tic \'sis-tik\ adj

czar \'zär\ n : the ruler of Russia until 1917; also : one having great authority — czar·ist n or adj

cza·ri·na \zä-'rē-nə\ n : the wife of a czar

Czech \'chek\ n 1 : a native or inhabitant of Czechoslovakia 2 : the language of the Czechs — Czech adj

---

d \'dē\ n, often cap : the 4th letter of the English alphabet

¹dab \'dab\ n 1 : a sudden blow or thrust : POKE; also : PECK 2 : a gentle touch or stroke : PAT

²dab vb dabbed; dab·bing 1 : to strike or touch gently : PAT 2 : to apply lightly or irregularly : DAUB

³dab n 1 : DAUB 2 : a small amount

dab·ble \'dab-əl\ vb 1 : to wet by splashing : SPATTER 2 : to paddle or play in or as if in water 3 : to work or concern oneself lightly or without serious effort ⟨~s in politics⟩ — dab·bler n

dace \'dās\ n, pl dace : a small freshwater fish related to the carp

da·cha \'däch-ə\ n : a Russian country house

dachs·hund \'däks-,hùnt\ n : a small dog of a breed of German origin with a long body, short legs, and long drooping ears

dac·tyl \'dak-t⁹l\ n : a metrical foot of one accented syllable followed by two unaccented syllables — dac·tyl·ic \dak-'til-ik\ adj

dad \'dad\ n : FATHER

dad·dy \'dad-ē\ n : FATHER

dae·mon var of DEMON

daf·fo·dil \'daf-ə-,dil\ n : a narcissus with usu. large flowers having a trumpetlike center

daft \'daft\ adj : FOOLISH; also : INSANE — daft·ness n

dag·ger \'dag-ər\ n 1 : a short knifelike weapon used for stabbing 2 : a character † used as a reference mark or to indicate a death date

da·guerre·o·type \də-'ger-(ē-)ə-,tīp\ n : an early photograph produced on a silver or a silver-covered copper plate

dahl·ia \'dal-yə\ n : a tuberous herb related to the daisies and widely grown for its showy flowers

¹dai·ly \'dā-lē\ adj 1 : occurring, done, or used every day or every weekday 2 : of or relating to every day ⟨~ visitors⟩ 3 : computed in terms of one day ⟨~ wages⟩ — daily adv

²daily n : a newspaper published every weekday

¹dain·ty \'dānt-ē\ n : something delicious or pleasing to the taste : DELICACY

²dainty adj 1 : pleasing to the taste 2 : delicately pretty 3 : having or showing delicate taste; also : FASTIDIOUS — dain·ti·ly adv — dain·ti·ness n

dai·qui·ri \'dī-kə-rē\ n : a cocktail made of rum, lime juice, and sugar

dairy \'de(ə)r-ē\ n 1 : CREAMERY 2 : a farm specializing in milk production

dairy·maid \-,mād\ n : a woman employed in a dairy

dairy·man \-mən\ n : one who operates a dairy farm or works in a dairy

da·is \'dā-əs, 'dī-\ n : a raised platform usu. above the floor of a hall or large room

dai·sy \'dā-zē\ n [OB dægeseage, lit., day's eye] : any of numerous composite plants having flower heads in which the marginal flowers resemble petals

dale \'dāl\ n : VALLEY

dal·ly \'dal-ē\ vb 1 : to act playfully; esp : to play amorously 2 : to waste time 3 : LINGER, DAWDLE — dal·li·ance n

dal·ma·tian \dal-'mā-shən\ n, often cap : a large dog of a breed characterized by a white short-haired coat with black or brown spots

¹dam \'dam\ n : a female parent — used esp. of a domestic animal

²dam n : a barrier (as across a stream) to prevent the flow of water — dam vb

¹dam·age \'dam-ij\ n 1 : loss or harm due to injury to persons, property, or reputation 2 pl : compensation in money imposed by law for loss or injury ⟨bring a suit for ~s⟩

²damage vb : to cause damage to

dam·a·scene \'dam-ə-,sēn\ vb : to ornament (as iron or steel) with wavy patterns or with inlaid work of precious metals

dam·ask \'dam-əsk\ n 1 : a firm lustrous reversible figured fabric used esp. for household linen 2 : a tough steel (damask steel or Da·mas·cus steel \də-,mas-kəs-\) formerly valued for sword blades

dame \'dām\ n 1 : a woman of rank, station, or authority 2 : an elderly woman 3 slang : WOMAN

damn \'dam\ vb 1 : to condemn esp. to hell 2 : CURSE — damned \'damd\ adj

dam·na·ble \'dam-nə-bəl\ adj 1 : liable to or deserving punishment 2 : EXECRABLE ⟨~ weather⟩ — dam·na·bly adv

dam·na·tion \dam-'nā-shən\ n 1 : the act of damning 2 : the state of being damned

¹damp \'damp\ n 1 : a noxious gas 2 : MOISTURE

²damp vb 1 : DEPRESS 2 : CHECK, RESTRAIN 3 : DAMPEN

³damp adj : MOIST — damp·ness n

damp·en \'dam-pən\ vb 1 : to check or diminish in activity or vigor 2 : to make or become damp

damp·er n : one that damps; esp : a valve or movable plate (as in the flue of a stove, furnace, or fireplace) to regulate the draft

dam·sel \'dam-zəl\ n : GIRL, MAIDEN

dam·son \'dam-zən\ n : a plum with acid purple fruit; also : its fruit

¹dance \'dans\ vb 1 : to glide, step, or move through a set series of movements usu. to music 2 : to move quickly up and down or about 3 : to perform or

take part in as a dancer — **danc·er** n

²dance n **1** : an act or instance of dancing **2** : a social gathering for dancing **3** : a piece of music (as a waltz) by which dancing may be guided **4** : the art of dancing

dan·de·li·on \'dan-d°l-,ī-ən\ n : a common yellow-flowered herb related to the chicory

dan·der \'dan-dər\ n : ANGER, TEMPER (got his ~ up)

dan·di·fy \'dan-di-,fī\ vb : to make characteristic of a dandy

dan·dle \'dan-d°l\ vb : to move up and down in one's arms or on one's knee in affectionate play

dan·druff \'dan-drəf\ n : a whitish scurf on the scalp that comes off in small scales

¹dan·dy \'dan-dē\ n **1** : a man unduly attentive to dress **2** : something excellent in its class

²dandy adj : very good : FIRST-RATE

Dane \'dān\ n : a native or inhabitant of Denmark

dan·ger \'dān-jər\ n **1** : exposure or liability to injury, harm, or evil **2** : something that may cause injury or harm syn peril, hazard

dan·ger·ous \'dānj-(ə-)rəs\ adj **1** : HAZARDOUS, PERILOUS **2** : able or likely to inflict injury — **dan·ger·ous·ly** adv

dan·gle \'daŋ-gəl\ vb **1** : to hang loosely esp. with a swinging motion : SWING **2** : to be a hanger-on or dependent **3** : to be left without proper grammatical connection in a sentence (dangling participle) **4** : to keep hanging uncertainly

Dan·ish \'dā-nish\ n : the language of the Danes — **Danish** adj

Danish pastry n : a rich pastry made of dough raised with yeast with the shortening rolled in

dank \'daŋk\ adj : disagreeably wet or moist : DAMP

dan·seuse \däⁿ-'sə(r)z, -'süz\ n : a fe male ballet dancer

dap·per \'dap-ər\ adj **1** : SPRUCE, TRIM **2** : being alert and lively in movement and manners : JAUNTY

dap·ple \'dap-əl\ vb : to mark with different-colored spots

¹dare \'daər\ vb **1** : to have sufficient courage : be bold enough to **2** : CHALLENGE **3** : to confront boldly

²dare n : an invitation to contend : CHALLENGE

dare·dev·il \-,dev-əl\ n : a recklessly bold person

dar·ing \'da(ə)r-iŋ\ n : venturesome boldness — **daring** adj — **dar·ing·ly** adv

¹dark \'därk\ adj **1** : being without light or without much light **2** : not light in color (a ~ suit) **3** : GLOOMY (looks on the ~ side of life) **4** : being without knowledge and culture (the Dark Ages) **5** : SECRETIVE — **dark·ly** adv — **dark·ness** n

²dark n **1** : absence of light : DARKNESS; esp : NIGHT **2** : a dark or deep color **3** : IGNORANCE; also : SECRECY

dark·en \'där-kən\ vb **1** : to make or grow dark or darker **2** : DIM **3** : BESMIRCH, TARNISH (~ a reputation) **4** : to make or become gloomy or forbidding

dark·ling \'där-kliŋ\ adv : in the dark

dark·room \'därk-,rüm, -,rúm\ n : a room protected from rays of light that are harmful in the process of developing sensitive photographic plates and film

dark·some \'därk-səm\ adj : DARK

¹dar·ling \'där-liŋ\ n **1** : a dearly loved person **2** : FAVORITE

²darling adj **1** : dearly loved : FAVORITE **2** : very pleasing : CHARMING

darn \'därn\ vb : to mend with interlacing stitches — **darn** n — **darn·er** n

dar·nel \'därn-ªl\ n : a weedy grass with bristly flower clusters

darning needle n **1** : a needle for darning **2** : DRAGONFLY

¹dart \'därt\ n **1** : a small pointed missile thrown at a target in a game (darts) **2** : something projected with sudden speed; esp : a sharp glance **3** : something causing a sudden pain **4** : a stitched tapering fold in a garment **5** : a quick movement

²dart vb **1** : to throw with a sudden movement **2** : to thrust or move suddenly or rapidly (hundreds of minnows ~ing about in the creek)

dart·er n : a small freshwater fish related to the perches

¹dash \'dash\ vb **1** : to knock, hurl, or thrust violently **2** : SMASH **3** : SPLASH, SPATTER **4** : RUIN **5** : DEPRESS, SADDEN **6** : to perform or finish hastily (~ off a letter) **7** : to move with sudden speed (~ed upstairs)

²dash n **1** : a sudden burst or splash **2** : a stroke of a pen **3** : a punctuation mark — used esp. to indicate a break in the thought or structure of a sentence **4** : a small addition (add a ~ of salt) **5** : conspicuous display **6** : animation in style and action **7** : a sudden rush or attempt (made a ~ for the door) **8** : a short foot race

dash·board \-,bōrd\ n : an instrument panel below the windshield in an automobile or airplane

dash·er n : a device (as in a churn) that agitates or stirs up something

dash·ing adj **1** : marked by vigorous action **2** : marked by smartness esp. in dress and manners

das·tard \'das-tərd\ n : COWARD; esp : one who sneakingly commits malicious acts — **das·tard·ly** adj

da·ta \'dāt-ə, 'dat-\ n sing or pl **1** : factual information (as measurements or statistics) used as a basis for reasoning, discussion, or calculation **2** : DATUM

¹date \'dāt\ n : the edible fruit of a tall Old World palm; also : this plant

²date n **1** : the day, month, or year of an event **2** : a statement giving the time of execution or making (as of a coin or check) **3** : the period to which something belongs **4** : APPOINTMENT; esp : a social engagement between two persons of opposite sex **5** : a person of the opposite sex with whom one has a social engagement — **to date** : up to the present moment

³date vb **1** : to determine the date of **2** : to record the date of or on **3** : to mark or reveal the date, age, or period of (the architecture ~s the house) **4** : to make or have a date with **5** : ORIGINATE (~s from ancient times) **6** : EXTEND

⟨*dating* back to childhood⟩ **7** : to show qualities typical of a past period

date·less adj **1** : ENDLESS **2** : having no date **3** : too ancient to be dated **4** : TIMELESS

date·line \'dāt-₁līn\ n : a line in a publication giving the date and place of composition or issue

da·tive \'dāt-iv\ adj : of, relating to, or constituting a grammatical case marking typically the indirect object of a verb — **dative** n

da·tum \'dāt-əm, 'dat-\ n, pl **da·ta** \-ə\ or **datums** : a single piece of data : FACT

¹**daub** \'dòb\ vb **1** : to cover with soft adhesive matter : PLASTER **2** : SMEAR, SMUDGE **3** : to paint crudely — **daub·er** n

²**daub** n **1** : something daubed on : SMEAR **2** : a crude picture

daugh·ter \'dòt-ər\ n **1** : a female offspring esp. of human beings **2** : a human female having a specified ancestor or belonging to a group of common ancestry — **daugh·ter·ly** adj

daughter-in-law n, pl **daughters-in-law** : the wife of one's son

daunt \'dònt\ vb : to lessen the courage of : INTIMIDATE

daunt·less adj : FEARLESS, UNDAUNTED

dau·phin \'dò-fən\ n : the eldest son of a king of France

dav·en·port \'dav-ən-₁pòrt\ n : a large upholstered sofa

da·vit \'dāv-ət, 'dav-\ n : either of a pair of small cranes for raising and lowering small boats

daw·dle \'dòd-ᵊl\ vb **1** : to spend time wastefully or idly : LINGER **2** : LOITER — **daw·dler** \'dòd-(ᵊ-)lər\ n

¹**dawn** \'dòn\ vb **1** : to begin to grow light as the sun rises **2** : to begin to appear or develop **3** : to begin to be understood ⟨the solution ~ed on him⟩

²**dawn** n **1** : the first appearance of light in the morning **2** : a first appearance : BEGINNING ⟨the ~ of a new era⟩

day \'dā\ n **1** : the period of light between one night and the next : DAYLIGHT **2** : the period of the earth's revolution on its axis **3** : a period of 24 hours beginning at midnight **4** : a specified day or date ⟨wedding ~⟩ **5** : a specified time or period : AGE ⟨in olden ~s⟩ **6** : the conflict or contention of the day ⟨carried the ~⟩ **7** : the time set apart by usage or law for work ⟨the 8-hour ~⟩

day·bed \-₁bed\ n : a couch with low head and foot pieces

day·book \-₁bùk\ n : DIARY, JOURNAL

day·break \-₁brāk\ n : DAWN

day·dream \-₁drēm\ n : a pleasant reverie — **daydream** vb

day·light \-₁līt\ n **1** : the light of day **2** : DAWN **3** : understanding of something that has been obscure **4** pl : CONSCIOUSNESS; also : WITS

daylight saving time n : time usu. one hour ahead of standard time

Day of Atonement : YOM KIPPUR

day·time \-₁tīm\ n : the period of daylight

¹**daze** \'dāz\ vb **1** : to stupefy esp. by a blow : STUN **2** : DAZZLE

²**daze** n : the state of being dazed

daz·zle \'daz-əl\ vb **1** : to overpower with light **2** : to impress greatly or confound with brilliance ⟨*dazzled* the audience with his oratory⟩ — **dazzle** n

DDT \₁dē-(₁)dē-'tē\ n : an insecticide widely used against lice, flies, mosquitoes, and agricultural pests

dea·con \'dē-kən\ n [OE *dēacon*, fr. LL *diaconus*, fr. Gk *diakonos* servant, attendant, deacon] : a subordinate officer in a Christian church — **dea·con·ess** n

de·ac·ti·vate \dē-'ak-tə-₁vāt\ vb : to make inactive or ineffective

¹**dead** \'ded\ adj **1** : LIFELESS **2** : DEATHLIKE, DEADLY ⟨in a ~ faint⟩ **3** : NUMB **4** : very tired **5** : UNRESPONSIVE **6** : EXTINGUISHED ⟨~ coals⟩ **7** : INANIMATE, INERT **8** : no longer active or functioning : EXHAUSTED, EXTINCT ⟨a ~ battery⟩ ⟨a ~ volcano⟩ **9** : lacking power, significance, or effect ⟨a ~ custom⟩ **10** : OBSOLETE ⟨a ~ language⟩ **11** : lacking in gaiety or animation ⟨a ~ party⟩ **12** : QUIET, IDLE, UNPRODUCTIVE ⟨~ capital⟩ **13** : lacking elasticity ⟨a ~ tennis ball⟩ **14** : not circulating : STAGNANT ⟨~ air⟩ **15** : lacking warmth, vigor, or taste ⟨~ wine⟩ **16** : absolutely uniform ⟨~ level⟩ **17** : UNERRING, EXACT ⟨a ~ shot⟩ **18** : ABRUPT ⟨a ~ stop⟩ **19** : COMPLETE ⟨a ~ loss⟩

²**dead** n, pl **dead 1** : one that is dead — usu. used collectively ⟨the living and the ~⟩ **2** : the time of greatest quiet ⟨the ~ of the night⟩

³**dead** adv **1** : UTTERLY ⟨~ right⟩ **2** : in a sudden and complete manner ⟨stopped ~⟩ **3** : DIRECTLY ⟨~ ahead⟩

dead·beat \-₁bēt\ n : one who persistently fails to pay his debts or his way

dead·en \'ded-ᵊn\ vb **1** : to impair in force, activity, or sensation : BLUNT ⟨~ pain⟩ **2** : to lessen the luster or spirit of **3** : to make (as a wall) soundproof

dead·line \'ded-₁līn\ n : a date or time before which something must be done

dead·lock \'ded-₁läk\ n : a stoppage of action because neither of two equally strong factions in a struggle will give in — **deadlock** vb

¹**dead·ly** \'ded-lē\ adj **1** : likely to cause or capable of causing death **2** : HOSTILE, IMPLACABLE **3** : very accurate : UNERRING **4** : fatal to spiritual progress ⟨~ sin⟩ **5** : tending to deprive of force or vitality ⟨a ~ habit⟩ **6** : suggestive of death **7** : very great : EXTREME — **dead·li·ness** n

²**deadly** adv **1** : suggesting death ⟨~ pale⟩ **2** : EXTREMELY ⟨~ dull⟩

dead·weight \'ded-'wāt\ n : the unrelieved weight of an inert mass

dead·wood \-₁wùd\ n **1** : wood dead on the tree **2** : useless personnel or material

deaf \'def\ adj **1** : unable to hear **2** : unwilling to hear or listen ⟨~ to all suggestions⟩ — **deaf·ness** n

deaf·en \'def-ən\ vb : to make deaf

deaf-mute \'def-'myüt\ n : a deaf person who cannot speak

¹**deal** \'dēl\ n **1** : an indefinite quantity or degree ⟨a great ~⟩; also : a large quantity ⟨a ~ of money⟩ **2** : the act or right of distributing cards to players in a card game; also : HAND

²**deal** vb **dealt** \'delt\ **deal·ing** \'dē-liŋ\ **1** : DISTRIBUTE **2** : ADMINISTER, DELIVER ⟨*dealt* him a blow⟩ **3** : to have to do : TREAT ⟨the book ~s with crime⟩ **4** : to take action in regard to something ⟨~ with offenders⟩ **5** : TRADE; also : to sell or distribute something as a business ⟨~ in used cars⟩ — **deal·er** \'dē-lər\ n

³**deal** n 1 : BARGAINING, NEGOTIATION; also : TRANSACTION 2 : treatment received ⟨a raw ∼⟩ 3 : a secret or underhand agreement 4 : BARGAIN

⁴**deal** n : wood or a board of fir or pine

deal·ing n 1 pl : INTERCOURSE, TRAFFIC; esp : business transactions 2 : a way of acting or of doing business ⟨fair in his ∼⟩

dean \'dēn\ n 1 : a clergyman who is head of a group of canons or of joint pastors of a church 2 : the head of a division, faculty, college, or school of a university 3 : a college or secondary school administrator in charge of counseling and disciplining students 4 : the senior member of a group ⟨the ∼ of a diplomatic corps⟩ — **dean·ship** n

dean·ery \-(ə-)rē\ n : the office, jurisdiction, or official residence of a clerical dean

¹**dear** \'dior\ adj 1 : highly valued : PRECIOUS 2 : AFFECTIONATE, FOND 3 : EXPENSIVE 4 : HEARTFELT — **dear·ly** adv — **dear·ness** n

²**dear** n : a loved one : DARLING

dearth \'dərth\ n : SCARCITY, FAMINE

death \'deth\ n 1 : the end of life 2 : the cause of loss of life 3 : the state of being dead 4 : DESTRUCTION, EXTINCTION 5 : SLAUGHTER — **death·like** adj

death·bed \-'bed\ n 1 : the bed in which a person dies 2 : the last hours of life

death·blow \-'blō\ n : a destructive or killing stroke or event

death·less adj : IMMORTAL, IMPERISHABLE ⟨∼ fame⟩

death·ly adj 1 : FATAL 2 : of, relating to, or suggestive of death ⟨a ∼ pallor⟩ — **deathly** adv

death's-head \'deths-,hed\ n : a human skull emblematic of death

¹**death·watch** \'deth-,wäch\ n : a small insect that makes a ticking sound

²**deathwatch** n : a vigil kept with the dead or dying

deb \'deb\ n : DEBUTANTE

de·ba·cle \di-'bäk-əl, -'bak-\ n : BREAKDOWN, COLLAPSE ⟨stock market ∼⟩

de·bar \di-'bär\ vb : to bar from having or doing something : PRECLUDE

de·bark \-'bärk\ vb : DISEMBARK — **de·bar·ka·tion** \,dē-,bär-'kā-shən\ n

de·base \di-'bās\ vb : to lower in character, dignity, quality, or value syn degrade, corrupt, deprave — **de·base·ment** n

de·bate \-'bāt\ vb 1 : to discuss or examine a question by presenting and considering arguments on both sides 2 : to take part in a debate — **de·bat·able** adj — **debate** n — **de·bat·er** n

de·bauch \-'bòch\ vb : SEDUCE, CORRUPT — **de·bauch·ery** \-(ə-)rē\ n

de·ben·ture \-'ben-chər\ n : a certificate of indebtedness; esp : a bond secured only by the general assets of the issuing government or corporation

de·bil·i·tate \di-'bil-ə-,tāt\ vb : to impair the health or strength of

de·bil·i·ty \-'bil-ət-ē\ n : an infirm or weakened state

¹**deb·it** \'deb-ət\ n 1 : an entry in an account showing money paid out or owed 2 : a disadvantageous or un-

favorable quality or character

²**debit** vb : to enter as a debit : charge with or as a debt

deb·o·nair \,deb-ə-'naər\ adj : gaily and gracefully charming : LIGHTHEARTED

de·bouch \di-'büsh, -'bauch\ vb : to march or issue out into an open area

de·brief \di-'brēf\ vb : to question (as a pilot back from a mission) in order to obtain useful information

de·bris \də-'brē, 'dā-,brē\ n, pl **debris** \-'brēz, -,brēz\ 1 : the remains of something broken down or destroyed : RUINS 2 : an accumulation of fragments of rock

debt \'det\ n 1 : SIN, TRESPASS 2 : something owed : OBLIGATION 3 : a condition of owing; esp : the state of owing money in amounts greater than one can pay

debt·or \'det-ər\ n 1 : SINNER 2 : one that owes a debt

de·bunk \dē-'bəŋk\ vb : to expose the sham or falseness in ⟨∼ a rumor⟩

de·but \'dā-,byü\ n 1 : a first public appearance 2 : a formal entrance into society

deb·u·tante \'deb-yu-,tänt\ n : a young woman making her formal entrance into society

dec·ade \'dek-,ād, -əd\ n : a period of 10 years

dec·a·dence \'dek-əd-əns, di-'kād-²ns\ n : DETERIORATION, DECLINE — **dec·a·dent** adj or n

de·cal \'dē-,kal\ n : DECALCOMANIA

de·cal·co·ma·nia \di-,kal-kə-'mā-nē-ə\ n : a transferring (as to glass) of designs from specially prepared paper; also : a design prepared for such transferring

dec·a·logue \'dek-ə-,lòg\ n, often cap : the ten commandments of God given to Moses on Mount Sinai

de·camp \di-'kamp\ vb 1 : to break up a camp 2 : to depart suddenly : ABSCOND

de·cant \-'kant\ vb : to pour (liquor) gently

de·cant·er n : an ornamental glass bottle for serving wine

deca·syl·lab·ic \,dek-ə-sə-'lab-ik\ adj : having or composed of verses having 10 syllables — **decasyllabic** n

de·cath·lon \di-'kath-lən\ n : an athletic contest in which each competitor participates in each of a series of 10 track-and-field events

de·cay \di-'kā\ vb 1 : to decline from a sound, prosperous, or healthy condition ⟨a ∼ing neighborhood⟩ ⟨∼ed teeth⟩ 2 : to cause or undergo decomposition ⟨radium ∼s slowly⟩; esp : to break down in the course of spoiling : ROT — **decay** n

de·cease \-'sēs\ n : DEATH — **decease** vb

de·ce·dent \-'sēd-²nt\ n : a deceased person

de·ceit \-'sēt\ n 1 : DECEPTION 2 : TRICK 3 : DECEITFULNESS

de·ceit·ful adj 1 : practicing or tending to practice deceit 2 : MISLEADING, DECEPTIVE ⟨a ∼ answer⟩ — **de·ceit·ful·ly** adv — **de·ceit·ful·ness** n

---

ə abut; ə kitten; ər further; a back; ā bake; ä cot, cart; au̇ out; ch chin; e less; ē easy; g gift; i trip; ī life; j joke; ŋ sing; ō flow; ȯ flaw; ȯi coin; th thin; tẖ this; ü loot; u̇ foot; y yet; yü few; yu̇ furious; zh vision

de·ceive \di-'sēv\ vb 1 : to cause to believe an untruth 2 : to deal with dishonestly 3 : to use or practice dishonesty — de·ceiv·er n

de·cel·er·ate \dē-'sel-ə-,rāt\ vb : to slow down

De·cem·ber \di-'sem-bər\ n : the 12th month of the year having 31 days

de·cen·cy \'dēs-°n-sē\ n 1 : PROPRIETY 2 : conformity to standards of taste, propriety, or quality 3 : standard of propriety — usu. used in pl.

de·cent \'dēs-°nt\ adj 1 : conforming to standards of propriety, good taste, or morality 2 : modestly clothed 3 : free from immodesty or obscenity 4 : ADEQUATE (~ housing) — de·cent·ly adv

de·cen·tral·iza·tion \dē-,sen-trə-lə-'zā-shən\ n 1 : the dispersion or distribution of functions and powers from a central authority to regional and local authorities 2 : the redistribution of population and industry from urban centers to outlying areas — de·cen·tral·ize \-'sen-trə-,līz\ vb

de·cep·tion \di-'sep-shən\ n 1 : the act of deceiving 2 : the fact or condition of being deceived 3 : FRAUD, TRICK — de·cep·tive \-'sep-tiv\ adj — de·cep·tive·ly adv

deci·bel \'des-ə-,bel\ n 1 : a unit for expressing the ratio of two amounts of electric or acoustic signal power 2 : a unit for measuring the relative loudness of sounds equal to about the smallest degree of difference detectable by the human ear whose range includes about 130 such units

de·cide \di-'sīd\ vb 1 : to arrive at a solution that ends uncertainty or dispute about 2 : to bring to a definitive end (one blow decided the fight) 3 : to induce to come to a choice 4 : to make a choice or judgment

de·cid·ed adj 1 : CLEAR, UNMISTAKABLE (a ~ smell of gas) 2 : FIRM, DETERMINED — de·cid·ed·ly adv

de·cid·u·ous \di-'sij-ə-wəs\ adj 1 : falling off usu. at the end of a period of growth or function (~ leaves) (a ~ tooth) 2 : having deciduous parts (~ trees)

¹dec·i·mal \'des-ə-məl\ adj : based on the number 10 ; reckoning by tens

²decimal n : a fraction in which the denominator is a power of 10 usu. not expressed but signified by a point placed at the left of the numerator (as .2 = 2/10, .25 = 25/100, .025 = 25/1000)

dec·i·mate \'des-ə-,māt\ vb 1 : to take or destroy the 10th part of 2 : to destroy a large part of

de·ci·pher \di-'sī-fər\ vb 1 : to translate from secret writing (as code) 2 : to make out the meaning of despite indistinctness — de·ci·pher·able adj

de·ci·sion \di-'sizh-ən\ n 1 : the act or result of deciding esp. by giving judgment 2 : promptness and firmness in deciding : DETERMINATION

de·ci·sive \-'sī-siv\ adj 1 : having the power to decide (the ~ vote) 2 : CONCLUSIVE (a ~ victory) 3 : marked by or showing decision (a ~ manner) — de·ci·sive·ly adv — de·ci·sive·ness n

¹deck \'dek\ n 1 : a floorlike platform of a ship; also : something resembling the deck of a ship 2 : a pack of playing cards

²deck vb 1 : ARRAY 2 : DECORATE 3 : to furnish with a deck

deck·hand \-,hand\ n : a seaman who performs manual duties

de·claim \di-'klām\ vb : to speak or deliver loudly or impressively — dec·la·ma·tion \,dek-lə-'mā-shən\ n — de·clam·a·to·ry \di-'klam-ə-,tōr-ē\ adj

de·clar·a·tive \di-'klar-ət-iv\ adj : making a declaration (~ sentence)

de·clare \di-'klaer\ vb 1 : to make known formally or explicitly : ANNOUNCE (~ war) 2 : to state emphatically : AFFIRM 3 : to make a full statement of — dec·la·ra·tion \,dek-lə-'rā-shən\ n — de·clar·a·to·ry \di-'klar-ə-,tōr-ē\ adj — de·clar·er \-'klar-ər\ n

de·clas·si·fy \dē-'klas-ə-,fī\ vb 1 : to remove or reduce the security classification of

de·clen·sion \di-'klen-chən\ n 1 : a schematic arrangement of the inflectional forms esp. of a noun or pronoun 2 : DECLINE, DETERIORATION 3 : DESCENT, SLOPE

¹de·cline \di-'klīn\ vb 1 : to slope downward : DESCEND 2 : DROOP 3 : RECEDE 4 : WANE 5 : to withhold consent; also : REFUSE, REJECT 6 : INFLECT (~ a noun) — de·clin·able adj — dec·li·na·tion \,dek-lə-'nā-shən\ n

²decline n 1 : a gradual sinking and wasting away 2 : a change to a lower state or level 3 : the time when something is approaching its end 4 : a descending slope 5 : a wasting disease; esp : pulmonary tuberculosis

de·cliv·i·ty \di-'kliv-ət-ē\ n : a steep downward slope

de·code \dē-'kōd\ vb : to convert (a coded message) into ordinary language

dé·col·le·té \dā-,käl-ə-'tā\ adj 1 : wearing a strapless or low-necked gown 2 : having a low-cut neckline

de·com·mis·sion \,dē-kə-'mish-ən\ vb : to take out of commission (~ a battleship)

de·com·pose \,dē-kəm-'pōz\ vb 1 : to separate into its constituent parts 2 : to break down in decay : ROT — de·com·po·si·tion \dē-,käm-pə-'zish-ən\ n

de·com·press \,dē-kəm-'pres\ vb : to release (as a diver) from pressure or compression — de·com·pres·sion \-'presh-ən\ n

de·con·tam·i·nate \,dē-kən-'tam-ə-,nāt\ vb : to rid of contamination — de·con·tam·i·na·tion \-,tam-ə-'nā-shən\ n

de·cor or dé·cor \dā-'kor\ n : DECORATION; esp : the arrangement of accessories in interior decoration

dec·o·rate \'dek-ə-,rāt\ vb 1 : to make more attractive by adding something beautiful or becoming : ADORN, EMBELLISH 2 : to award a mark of honor (as a medal) to

dec·o·ra·tion \,dek-ə-'rā-shən\ n 1 : the act or process of decorating 2 : ORNAMENT 3 : a badge of honor

dec·o·ra·tive \'dek-(ə-)rət-iv\ adj : ORNAMENTAL

dec·o·ra·tor \'dek-ə-,rāt-ər\ n : one that decorates; esp : a person who designs or executes the interiors of buildings and their furnishings

dec·o·rous \'dek-ə-rəs, di-'kōr-əs\ adj : PROPER, SEEMLY, CORRECT

de·co·rum \di-'kōr-əm\ n 1 : conformity to accepted standards of conduct : proper behavior 2 : ORDERLINESS, PROPRIETY

¹de·coy \'di-'koi, 'dē-,koi\ n : something

that lures or entices; *esp* : an artificial bird used to attract live birds within shot

²**decoy** *vb* : to lure by or as if by a decoy : ENTICE

¹**de·crease** \di-'krēs\ *vb* : to grow or cause to grow less : DIMINISH

²**decrease** *n* **1** : DIMINISHING, LESSENING ⟨a ~ in accidents⟩ **2** : REDUCTION ⟨a ~ in prices⟩

¹**de·cree** \di-'krē\ *n* **1** : ORDER, EDICT **2** : a judicial decision

²**decree** *vb* **1** : COMMAND **2** : to determine or order judicially

de·crep·it \di-'krep-ət\ *adj* : broken down with age : worn out — **de·crep·i·tude** \-ə-,t(y)üd\ *n*

de·cry \di-'krī\ *vb* **1** : to belittle publicly **2** : to find fault with : CONDEMN

ded·i·cate \'ded-i-,kāt\ *vb* **1** : to devote to the worship of a divine being esp. with sacred rites **2** : to set apart for a definite purpose; *also* : to give over : COMMIT **3** : to inscribe or address as a compliment ⟨a ~ a book to a teacher⟩ — **ded·i·ca·tion** \,ded-i-'kā-shən\ *n* — **ded·i·ca·to·ry** \'ded-i-kə-,tōr-ē\ *adj*

de·duce \di-'d(y)üs\ *vb* **1** : to trace the course of ⟨~ their lineage⟩ **2** : to derive by reasoning : INFER — **de·duc·ible** *adj*

de·duct \-'dəkt\ *vb* : SUBTRACT — **de·duct·ible** *adj*

de·duc·tion \-'dək-shən\ *n* **1** : SUBTRACTION **2** : the deriving of a conclusion by reasoning : the conclusion so reached **3** : something that is or may be subtracted : ABATEMENT — **de·duc·tive** \-'dək-tiv\ *adj*

¹**deed** \'dēd\ *n* **1** : something done **2** : FEAT, EXPLOIT **3** : a document containing some legal transfer, bargain, or contract

²**deed** *vb* : to convey or transfer by deed

deem \'dēm\ *vb* : THINK, JUDGE, SUPPOSE

¹**deep** \'dēp\ *adj* **1** : extending far down, back, within, or outward **2** : having a specified extension downward or backward **3** : difficult to understand; *also* : MYSTERIOUS, OBSCURE ⟨a ~ dark secret⟩ **4** : WISE **5** : ENGROSSED, INVOLVED ⟨~ in thought⟩ **6** : INTENSE, PROFOUND ⟨~ sleep⟩ **7** : high in saturation and low in lightness ⟨a ~ red⟩ **8** : having a low musical pitch or range ⟨a ~ voice⟩ **9** : coming from or situated well within ⟨a ~ sigh⟩ **10** : covered, enclosed, or filled often to a specified degree ⟨knee-*deep* in snow⟩ — **deep·ly** *adv*

²**deep** *adv* **1** : DEEPLY **2** : far on : LATE ⟨~ in the night⟩

³**deep** *n* **1** : an extremely deep place or part; *esp* : OCEAN **2** : the middle or most intense part ⟨the ~ of winter⟩

deep·en *vb* : to make or become deep or deeper

deep-root·ed \-'rüt-əd, -'rüt-\ *adj* : deeply implanted or established ⟨~ loyalty⟩

deep-sea \-,sē\ *adj* : of, relating to, or occurring in the deeper parts of the sea ⟨~ fishing⟩

deep-seat·ed \-'sēt-əd\ *adj* **1** : situated far below the surface **2** : firmly established ⟨~ convictions⟩

deep-set \-'set\ *adj* : set far in ⟨~ eyes⟩

deer \'diər\ *n, pl* **deer** [OE *dēor* wild animal] : any of a group of ruminant

mammals with cloven hoofs and antlers in the males

deer·skin \-,skin\ *n* : leather made from the skin of a deer; *also* : a garment of such leather

de·face \di-'fās\ *vb* : to destroy or mar the face or surface of — **de·face·ment** *n*

de fac·to \di-'fak-tō, dā-\ *adj* (*or adv*) **1** : actually exercising power ⟨*de facto* government⟩ **2** : actually existing ⟨*de facto* state of war⟩

de·fal·ca·tion \,dē-,fal-'kā-shən, ,dē-,fòl-, ,def-əl-\ *n* : EMBEZZLEMENT

de·fame \di-'fām\ *vb* : to injure or destroy the reputation of by libel or slander — **def·a·ma·tion** \,def-ə-'mā-shən\ *n* — **de·fam·a·to·ry** \di-'fam-ə-,tōr-ē\ *adj*

de·fault \di-'fòlt\ *n* : failure to do something required by duty or law ⟨the defendant failed to appear and was held in ~⟩; *also* : failure to compete in or to finish an appointed contest ⟨lose a race by ~⟩ — **default** *vb* — **de·fault·er** *n*

¹**de·feat** \di-'fēt\ *vb* **1** : FRUSTRATE, NULLIFY **2** : to win victory over : BEAT

²**defeat** *n* **1** : FRUSTRATION **2** : an overthrow of an army in battle **3** : loss of a contest

de·feat·ism *n* : acceptance of or resignation to defeat — **de·feat·ist** *n or adj*

¹**de·fect** \'dē-,fekt, di-'fekt\ *n* : BLEMISH, FAULT, IMPERFECTION

²**de·fect** \di-'fekt\ *vb* : to desert a cause or party esp. in order to espouse another — **de·fec·tion** \-'fek-shən\ *n* — **de·fec·tor** \-'fek-tər\ *n*

de·fec·tive \di-'fek-tiv\ *adj* : FAULTY, DEFICIENT

defence *chiefly Brit var of* DEFENSE

de·fend \di-'fend\ *vb* **1** : to repel danger or attack from **2** : to act as attorney for **3** : to oppose the claim of another in a lawsuit : CONTEST **4** : to maintain against opposition ⟨~ an idea⟩ — **de·fend·er** *n*

de·fen·dant \-'fen-dənt\ *n* : a person required to make answer in a legal action or suit

de·fense \di-'fens\ *n* **1** : the act of defending : resistance against attack **2** : capability of resisting attack **3** : means or method of defending **4** : an argument in support or justification **5** : a defending party or group **6** : the answer made by the defendant in a legal action — **de·fense·less** *adj* — **de·fen·si·ble** *adj* — **de·fen·sive** *adj*

¹**de·fer** \-'fər\ *vb* **de·ferred; de·fer·ring** : to put off : DELAY

²**defer** *vb* **de·ferred; de·fer·ring** : to submit or yield to the opinion or wishes of another

def·er·ence \'def-(ə-)rəns\ *n* : courteous, respectful, or ingratiating regard for another's wishes — **def·er·en·tial** \,def-ə-'ren-chəl\ *adj*

de·fer·ment \di-'fər-mənt\ *n* : the act of delaying; *esp* : official postponement of military service

de·fi·ance \-'fī-əns\ *n* **1** : CHALLENGE **2** : a willingness to resist : contempt of opposition

de·fi·ant \-ənt\ *adj* : full of defiance : BOLD, INSOLENT — **de·fi·ant·ly** *adv*

de·fi·cient \di-'fish-ənt\ *adj* : lacking in something necessary (as for complete-

---

ə abut; ᵊ kitten; ər further; a back; ā bake; ä cot, cart; aù out; ch chin; e less; ē easy; g gift; i trip; ī life; j joke; ŋ sing; ō flow; ò flaw; òi coin; th thin; <u>th</u> this; ü loot; ù foot; y yet; yü few; yù furious; zh vision

ness or health) : DEFECTIVE — **de·fi·cien·cy** n

def·i·cit \'def-ə-sət\ n : a deficiency in amount; *esp* : an excess of expenditures over revenue

¹**de·file** \di-'fīl\ vb 1 : to make filthy 2 : CORRUPT 3 : RAVISH, VIOLATE 4 : to make ceremonially unclean : DESECRATE 5 : DISHONOR — **de·file·ment** n

²**defile** n : a narrow passage or gorge

de·fine \di-'fīn\ vb 1 : to fix or mark the limits of 2 : to clarify in outline or character 3 : to discover and set forth the meaning of ⟨~ a word⟩ — **de·fin·able** adj — **de·fin·er** n

def·i·nite \'def-(ə-)nət\ adj 1 : having distinct limits : FIXED 2 : clear in meaning : EXACT, IMPLICIT 3 : typically designating an identified or immediately identifiable person or thing — **def·i·nite·ly** adv — **def·i·nite·ness** n

def·i·ni·tion \,def-ə-'nish-ən\ n 1 : an act of determining or settling 2 : a statement of the meaning of a word or word group; *also* : the action or process of stating such a meaning 3 : the action or the power of making definite and clear : CLARITY, DISTINCTNESS

de·fin·i·tive \di-'fin-ət-iv\ adj 1 : DECISIVE, CONCLUSIVE 2 : being authoritative and apparently exhaustive ⟨~ studies⟩ 3 : serving to define or specify precisely

de·flate \di-'flāt\ vb 1 : to release air or gas from 2 : to cause to contract from an abnormally high level : reduce from a state of inflation 3 : to become deflated : COLLAPSE

de·fla·tion \-'flā-shən\ n 1 : an act or instance of deflating : the state of being deflated 2 : reduction in the volume of available money or credit resulting in a decline of the general price level

de·flect \-'flekt\ vb : to turn aside — **de·flec·tion** \-'flek-shən\ n

de·form \di-'fôrm\ vb 1 : MISSHAPE, DISTORT 2 : DISFIGURE, DEFACE — **de·for·ma·tion** \,dē-,fôr-'mā-shən\ n

de·for·mi·ty \di-'fôr-mət-ē\ n 1 : the state of being deformed 2 : DISFIGUREMENT

de·fraud \-'frôd\ vb : CHEAT

de·fray \-'frā\ vb : to provide for the payment of : PAY — **de·fray·al** n

de·frost \-'frôst\ vb 1 : to thaw out 2 : to free from ice

deft \'deft\ adj : quick and neat in action : SKILLFUL — **deft·ly** adv — **deft·ness** n

de·funct \di-'fəŋkt\ adj : DEAD, EXTINCT ⟨a ~ organization⟩

de·fy \di-'fī\ vb 1 : CHALLENGE, DARE 2 : to refuse boldly to obey or to yield to : DISREGARD ⟨~ the law⟩ 3 : WITHSTAND, BAFFLE ⟨a scene that *defies* description⟩

¹**de·gen·er·ate** \-'jen-(ə-)rət\ adj : fallen from a former, higher, or normal condition — **de·gen·er·a·cy** \-rə-sē\ n — **de·gen·er·a·tion** \-,jen-ə-'rā-shən\ n — **de·gen·er·a·tive** \-'jen-ə-,rāt-iv\ adj

²**degenerate** n : a degenerate person; *esp* : a sexual pervert

³**de·gen·er·ate** \-'jen-ə-,rāt\ vb : to become degenerate : DETERIORATE

de·grade \di-'grād\ vb 1 : to reduce from a higher to a lower rank or degree 2 : DEBASE, CORRUPT — **deg·ra·da·tion** \,deg-rə-'dā-shən\ n

de·gree \di-'grē\ n 1 : a step in a series

2 : the extent, intensity, or scope of something esp. as measured by a graded series 3 : one of the forms or sets of forms used in the comparison of an adjective or adverb 4 : a rank or grade of official, ecclesiastical, or social position; *also* : the civil condition of a person 5 : a title conferred upon students by a college, university, or professional school upon completion of a unified program of study 6 : a 360th part of the circumference of a circle 7 : a line or space of the musical staff; *also* : a note or tone of a musical scale

de·horn \dē-'hôrn\ vb : to deprive of horns

de·hu·man·ize \dē-'(h)yü-mə-,nīz\ vb : to divest of human qualities or personality — **de·hu·man·iza·tion** \-,(h)yü-mə-nə-'zā-shən\ n

de·hu·mid·i·fy \,dē-(h)yü-'mid-ə-,fī\ vb : to remove moisture from (as the air)

de·hy·drate \dē-'hī-,drāt\ vb 1 : to remove liquid (as water) from ⟨*dehydrated* by fever⟩ ⟨~ fruits⟩; *also* : to lose liquid — **de·hy·dra·tion** \,dē-,hī-'drā-shən\ n

de·ice \dē-'īs\ vb : to keep free of ice — **de·ic·er** n

de·ify \'dē-ə-,fī\ vb 1 : to make a god of 2 : WORSHIP, GLORIFY — **de·ifi·ca·tion** \,dē-ə-fə-'kā-shən\ n

deign \'dān\ vb : CONDESCEND

de·ism \'dē-,iz-əm\ n : a system of thought advocating natural religion based on human reason rather than revelation — **de·ist** n — **de·is·tic** \dē-'is-tik\ adj

de·ity \'dē-ət-ē\ n 1 : the rank or nature of a god or supreme being 2 cap : ²GOD 3 : GOD; *also* : GODDESS

de·ject·ed \di-'jek-təd\ adj : low-spirited : SAD, DEPRESSED — **de·ject·ed·ly** adv

de·jec·tion \-'jek-shən\ n : lowness of spirits : DEPRESSION

de ju·re \dē-'jür-ē\ adj (or adv) : existing or exercising power by legal right ⟨*de jure* government⟩

¹**de·lay** \di-'lā\ n 1 : the act of delaying : the state of being delayed 2 : the time during which something is delayed

²**delay** vb 1 : to put off : POSTPONE 2 : to stop, detain, or hinder for a time 3 : to move or act slowly

de·le \'dē-lē\ vb : to remove (as a word) from typeset matter : ERASE, DELETE

de·lec·ta·ble \di-'lek-tə-bəl\ adj 1 : highly pleasing : DELIGHTFUL 2 : DELICIOUS

de·lec·ta·tion \,dē-,lek-'tā-shən\ n : DELIGHT, PLEASURE, DIVERSION

¹**del·e·gate** \'del-i-gət\ n 1 : DEPUTY, REPRESENTATIVE 2 : a member of the lower house of the legislature of Maryland, Virginia, or West Virginia

²**del·e·gate** \-,gāt\ vb 1 : to entrust to another ⟨*delegated* his authority⟩ 2 : to appoint as one's delegate

del·e·ga·tion \,del-i-'gā-shən\ n 1 : the act of delegating 2 : one or more persons chosen to represent others

de·lete \di-'lēt\ vb : to eliminate esp. by blotting out, cutting out, or erasing — **de·le·tion** \-'lē-shən\ n

del·e·te·ri·ous \,del-ə-'tir-ē-əs\ adj : HARMFUL, NOXIOUS

delft \'delft\ n 1 : a Dutch brown pottery covered with an opaque white glaze upon which the predominantly blue decoration is painted 2 : glazed pottery esp. when blue and white

delft·ware \-ˌwaȯr\ *n* : DELFT

¹de·lib·er·ate \di-'lib-(ə-)rət\ *adj* **1** : determined after careful thought **2** : weighing facts and arguments : careful and slow in deciding **3** : UNHURRIED, SLOW — **de·lib·er·ate·ly** *adv* — **de·lib·er·ate·ness** *n*

²de·lib·er·ate \-'lib-ə-ˌrāt\ *vb* **1** : to consider carefully — **de·lib·er·a·tion** \-ˌlib-ə-'rā-shən\ *n*

de·lib·er·a·tive \-'lib-ə-ˌrāt-iv, -'lib-(ə-)rət-\ *adj* : of, relating to, or marked by deliberation ⟨~ assembly⟩ — **de·lib·er·a·tive·ly** *adv*

del·i·ca·cy \'del-i-kə-sē\ *n* **1** : something pleasing to eat because it is rare or luxurious **2** : FINENESS, DAINTINESS; *also* : FRAILTY **3** : nicety or expressiveness of touch **4** : precise perception and discrimination : SENSITIVITY **5** : sensibility in feeling or conduct; *also* : SQUEAMISHNESS **6** : the quality or state of requiring delicate treatment

del·i·cate \-kət\ *adj* **1** : pleasing to the senses of taste or smell esp. in a mild or subtle way **2** : marked by daintiness or charm : EXQUISITE **3** : FASTIDIOUS, SQUEAMISH, SCRUPULOUS **4** : marked by minute precision : very sensitive **5** : marked by or requiring meticulous technique or fine skill **6** : easily damaged : FRAGILE; *also* : SICKLY **7** : SUBTLE **8** : marked by or requiring tact — **del·i·cate·ly** *adv*

del·i·ca·tes·sen \ˌdel-i-kə-'tes-ᵊn\ *n pl* [G, pl. of *delicatesse* delicacy, fr. F *délicatesse*, prob. fr. It *delicatezza*, fr. *delicato* delicate] **1** : ready-to-eat food products (as cooked meats and prepared salads) **2** *sing, pl* **delicatessens** : a store where delicatessen are sold

de·li·cious \di-'lish-əs\ *adj* : affording great pleasure : DELIGHTFUL; *esp* : very pleasing to the taste or smell — **de·li·cious·ly** *adv*

¹de·light \-'līt\ *n* **1** : great pleasure or satisfaction : JOY **2** : something that gives great pleasure — **de·light·ful** *adj* — **de·light·ful·ly** *adv*

²delight *vb* **1** : to take great pleasure **2** : to satisfy greatly : PLEASE

de·light·ed *adj* : highly pleased : GRATIFIED, JOYOUS — **de·light·ed·ly** *adv*

de·lim·it \di-'lim-ət\ *vb* : to fix the limits of : BOUND

de·lin·e·ate \di-'lin-ē-ˌāt\ *vb* **1** : SKETCH, PORTRAY **2** : to picture in words : DESCRIBE — **de·lin·ea·tion** \-ˌlin-ē-'ā-shən\ *n*

de·lin·quen·cy \di-'liŋ-kwən-sē\ *n* : the quality or state of being delinquent

¹de·lin·quent \-kwənt\ *n* : a delinquent person

²delinquent *adj* **1** : offending by neglect or violation of duty or of law **2** : being in arrears in payment

del·i·quesce \ˌdel-i-'kwes\ *vb* **1** : to become liquid by absorbing moisture from the air **2** : MELT — **del·i·ques·cent** \-'kwes-ᵊnt\ *adj*

de·lir·i·um \di-'lir-ē-əm\ *n* : mental disturbance marked by confusion, disordered speech, and hallucinations; *also* : violent excitement — **de·lir·i·ous** *adj* — **de·lir·i·ous·ly** *adv*

de·liv·er \di-'liv-ər\ *vb* **1** : to set free : SAVE **2** : to hand over : CONVEY, SURRENDER **3** : to assist in giving birth or at the birth of **4** : UTTER, RELATE, COMMUNICATE **5** : to send to an intended target or destination ⟨~ a blow⟩ — **de·liv·er·ance** *n* — **de·liv·er·er** *n*

de·liv·ery \-'liv-(ə-)rē\ *n* **1** : a freeing from restraint **2** : the act of handing over : something delivered at one time or in one unit **3** : PARTURITION **4** : UTTERANCE; *also* : manner of speaking or singing **5** : the act or manner of discharging or throwing

dell \'del\ *n* : a small secluded valley

de·louse \dē-'laȯs\ *vb* : to remove lice from

del·phin·i·um \del-'fin-ē-əm\ *n* : any of a genus of mostly perennial herbs related to the buttercups and grown for their tall branching spikes of irregular flowers

del·ta \'del-tə\ *n* [Gk, fr. delta, fourth letter of the Gk alphabet, Δ, which an alluvial delta resembles in shape] : triangular silt-formed land at the mouth of a river

de·lude \di-'lüd\ *vb* : MISLEAD, DECEIVE, TRICK

¹del·uge \'del-ˌyüj\ *n* **1** : a flooding of land by water **2** : a drenching rain **3** : an irresistible rush ⟨a ~ of Easter mail⟩

²deluge *vb* **1** : INUNDATE, FLOOD **2** : to overwhelm as if with a deluge

de·lu·sion \di-'lü-zhən\ *n* : a deluding or being deluded; *esp* : a persistent belief in something false typical of some mental disorders — **de·lu·sive** \-'lü-siv\ *adj*

de·luxe \di-'lu̇ks, -'lə̇ks\ *adj* : notably luxurious or elegant ⟨a ~ edition⟩

delve \'delv\ *vb* **1** : DIG **2** : to seek laboriously for information in written records (as books)

de·mag·ne·tize \dē-'mag-nə-ˌtīz\ *vb* : to deprive of magnetic properties

dem·a·gogue *or* **dem·a·gog** \'dem-ə-ˌgäg\ *n* : a person who appeals to the emotions and prejudices of people esp. in order to advance his own political ends — **dem·a·gog·uery** \-ˌgäg-(ə-)rē\ *n* — **dem·a·gogy** \-ˌgäj-ē, -ˌgäg-\ *n*

¹de·mand \di-'mand\ *n* **1** : an act of demanding or asking esp. with authority; *also* : something claimed as due **2** : an expressed desire to own or use something (the ~ for new cars) **3** : the ability and desire to buy goods or services; *also* : the quantity of goods wanted at a stated price **3** : a seeking or being sought after : urgent need **4** : a pressing need or requirement ⟨~s that taxed his energy⟩

²demand *vb* **1** : to ask for with authority : claim as due **2** : to ask earnestly or in the manner of a command **3** : REQUIRE, NEED ⟨an illness that ~s care⟩

de·mar·cate \di-'mär-ˌkāt, 'dē-ˌmär-\ *vb* **1** : to mark the limits of **2** : SEPARATE — **de·mar·ca·tion** \ˌdē-ˌmär-'kā-shən\ *n*

de·marche \dā-'märsh\ *n* : a course of action : MANEUVER

¹de·mean \di-'mēn\ *vb* : to behave or conduct (oneself) usu. in a proper manner

²demean *vb* : DEGRADE, DEBASE

de·mea·nor \di-'mē-nər\ *n* : CONDUCT, BEARING

de·ment·ed \di-'ment-əd\ *adj* : MAD, INSANE — **de·ment·ed·ly** *adv*

de·men·tia \-'men-chə\ n : mental deterioration : INSANITY

de·mer·it \dē-'mer-ət\ n 1 : FAULT 2 : a mark placed against a person's record for some fault or offense

de·mesne \di-'mān, -'mēn\ n 1 : manorial land actually possessed by the lord and not held by free tenants 2 : ESTATE 3 : REGION 4 : REALM

demi·god \'dem-ē-,gäd\ n : a mythological being with more power than a mortal but less than a god

demi·john \-,jän\ n : a large glass or hard pottery bottle enclosed in wickerwork

de·mil·i·ta·rize \dē-'mil-ə-tə-,rīz\ vb : to strip of military forces, weapons, or fortifications — **de·mil·i·ta·ri·za·tion** \-,mil-ə-tə-rə-'zā-shən\ n

demi·mon·daine \,dem-ē-,män-'dān\ n : a woman of the demimonde

demi·monde \'dem-ē-,mänd\ n 1 : a class of women on the fringes of respectable society supported by wealthy lovers 2 : a group engaged in activity of doubtful legality or propriety

de·mise \di-'mīz\ n 1 : LEASE 2 : transfer of sovereignty to a successor ⟨~ of the crown⟩ 3 : DEATH

demi·tasse \'dem-ē-,tas\ n : a small cup of black coffee; also : the cup used to serve it

de·mo·bi·lize \di-'mō-bə-,līz\ vb 1 : to disband from military service 2 : to change from a state of war to a state of peace — **de·mo·bi·li·za·tion** \-,mō-bə-lə-'zā-shən\ n

de·moc·ra·cy \di-'mäk-rə-sē\ n 1 : government by the people; esp : rule of the majority 2 : a government in which the supreme power is held by the people 3 : a political unit that has a democratic government 4 cap : the principles and policies of the Democratic party in the U.S. 5 : the common people esp. when constituting the source of political authority 6 : the absence of hereditary or arbitrary class distinctions or privileges

dem·o·crat \'dem-ə-,krat\ n 1 : an adherent of democracy 2 : one who practices social equality 3 cap : a member of the Democratic party of the U.S.

dem·o·crat·ic \,dem-ə-'krat-ik\ adj 1 : of, relating to, or favoring democracy 2 often cap : of or relating to one of the two major political parties in the U.S. associated in modern times with policies of broad social reform and internationalism 3 : of, relating to, or appealing to the common people ⟨~ art⟩ 4 : not snobbish

de·moc·ra·tize \di-'mäk-rə-,tīz\ vb : to make democratic

de·mog·ra·phy \di-'mäg-rə-fē\ n : the statistical study of human populations and esp. their size and distribution and the number of births and deaths — **de·mog·ra·pher** n — **de·mo·graph·ic** \,dē-mə-'graf-ik, ,dem-\ adj — **de·mo·graph·i·cal·ly** adv

dem·oi·selle \,dem-(w)ə-'zel\ n : a young woman

de·mol·ish \di-'mäl-ish\ vb 1 : to tear down : RAZE 2 : SMASH 3 : to put an end to

dem·o·li·tion \,dem-ə-'lish-ən, ,dē-mə-\ n : the act of demolishing; esp : destruction in war by means of explosives

de·mon or **dae·mon** \'dē-mən\ n 1 usu **daemon** : an attendant power or spirit 2 : an evil spirit : DEVIL 3 : one that has unusual drive or effectiveness ⟨he is a ~ for work⟩

de·mon·e·tize \dē-'män-ə-,tīz, -'mən-\ vb : to stop using as money or as a monetary standard ⟨~ silver⟩ — **de·mon·e·ti·za·tion** \-,män-ət-ə-'zā-shən, -,mən-\ n

de·mo·ni·ac \di-'mō-nē-,ak\ adj 1 : possessed or influenced by a demon 2 : DEVILISH, FIENDISH — **de·mo·ni·a·cal** \,dē-mə-'nī-ə-kəl\ adj

de·mon·ol·o·gy \,dē-mə-'näl-ə-jē\ n 1 : the study of demons 2 : belief in demons

de·mon·stra·ble \di-'män-strə-bəl\ adj 1 : capable of being demonstrated or proved 2 : APPARENT, EVIDENT

dem·on·strate \'dem-ən-,strāt\ vb 1 : to show clearly 2 : to prove or make clear by reasoning or evidence 3 : to explain esp. with many examples 4 : to show publicly ⟨~ a new car⟩ 5 : to make a public display (as of feelings or military force) ⟨citizens *demonstrated* in protest⟩ — **dem·on·stra·tion** \,dem-ən-'strā-shən\ n — **dem·on·stra·tor** \'dem-ən-,strāt-ər\ n

1de·mon·stra·tive \di-'män-strət-iv\ adj 1 : demonstrating as real or true 2 : characterized by demonstration 3 : pointing out the one referred to and distinguishing it from others of the same class ⟨~ pronoun⟩ ⟨~ adjective⟩ 4 : marked by display of feeling : EFFUSIVE ⟨a ~ greeting⟩

2demonstrative n : a demonstrative word and esp. a pronoun

de·mor·al·ize \di-'mor-ə-,līz\ vb 1 : to corrupt in morals 2 : to weaken in discipline or spirit : DISORGANIZE — **de·mor·al·iza·tion** \-,mor-ə-lə-'zā-shən\ n

de·mote \-'mōt\ vb : to reduce to a lower grade or rank

de·mot·ic \-'mät-ik\ adj : of or relating to the people : POPULAR ⟨~ Greek⟩

de·mul·cent \-'məl-sənt\ n : a usu. oily or somewhat thick and gelatinous preparation used to soothe or protect an irritated mucous membrane

de·mur \-'mər\ vb or **de·murred; de·mur·ring** : to take exception : OBJECT — **de·mur** n

de·mure \-'myūr\ adj 1 : quietly modest : DECOROUS 2 : affectedly modest, reserved, or serious : PRIM — **de·mure·ly** adv

de·mur·rage \-'mər-ij\ n : the detention of a ship by the shipper or receiver beyond the time allowed for loading, unloading, or sailing; also : a charge for detaining a ship, freight car, or truck for such a delay

de·mur·rer \-'mər-ər\ n : a claim by the defendant in a legal action that the pleadings of the plaintiff are defective

den \'den\ n 1 : a shelter or resting place of a wild animal 2 : a hiding place (as for thieves) 3 : a dirty wretched place in which people live or gather ⟨~ of misery⟩ 4 : a cozy private little room

de·na·ture \dē-'nā-chər\ vb : to change the nature of; esp : to make (alcohol) unfit for drinking

den·gue \'deŋ-gē\ n : an acute infectious disease characterized by headache, severe joint pain, and rash

de·ni·al \di-'nī-(ə)l\ n 1 : rejection of a request 2 : refusal to admit the truth of a statement or charge : CONTRADICTION; also : assertion that something alleged is false 3 : DISAVOWAL 4 : restriction on one's own activity or desires

den·ier \'den-yər\ n : a unit of fineness for silk, rayon, or nylon yarn equal to the fineness of a yarn weighing one gram for each 9000 meters

den·i·grate \'den-ə-ˌgrāt\ vb : to cast aspersions on : DEFAME

den·im \'den-əm\ n [F serge de Nîmes serge of Nîmes, France] 1 : a firm durable twilled usu. cotton fabric woven with colored warp and white filling threads 2 pl : overalls or trousers of usu. blue denim

den·i·zen \'den-ə-zən\ n : INHABITANT ⟨~s of the forest⟩

de·nom·i·nate \di-'näm-ə-ˌnāt\ vb : to give a name to : DESIGNATE

de·nom·i·na·tion \-ˌnäm-ə-'nā-shən\ n 1 : an act of denominating 2 : NAME, DESIGNATION; esp : a general name for a class of things 3 : a religious body comprising a number of local congregations having similar beliefs 4 : a value or size of a series of related values (as of money) — **de·nom·i·na·tion·al** \-'nā-sh(ə-)nəl\ adj

de·nom·i·na·tor \-'näm-ə-ˌnāt-ər\ n : the part of a fraction that is below the line

de·note \di-'nōt\ vb 1 : to mark out plainly : INDICATE 2 : to make known : SHOW ⟨smiled to ~ approval⟩ 3 : MEAN, NAME — **de·no·ta·tion** \ˌdē-nō-'tā-shən\ n

de·noue·ment \ˌdā-ˌnü-'mäⁿ\ n : the final outcome of the dramatic complications in a literary work

de·nounce \di-'nauns\ vb 1 : to point out as deserving blame or punishment 2 : to inform against : ACCUSE 3 : to announce formally the termination of (as a treaty) — **de·nounce·ment** n

dense \'dens\ adj 1 : marked by compactness or crowding together of parts ⟨a ~ forest⟩ : THICK, COMPACT ⟨a ~ fog⟩ 2 : DULL, STUPID — **dense·ly** adv — **dense·ness** n

den·si·ty \'den-sət-ē\ n 1 : the quality or state of being dense 2 : the quantity of something per unit volume, unit area, or unit length ⟨~ of a substance in grams per cubic centimeter⟩ ⟨population ~⟩

dent \'dent\ n 1 : a small depressed place made by a blow or by pressure 2 : an impression or effect made usu. against resistance 3 : initial progress — **dent** vb

den·tal \'dent-ᵊl\ adj : of or relating to the teeth or dentistry — **den·tal·ly** adv

den·tate \'den-ˌtāt\ adj : having pointed projections : NOTCHED

den·ti·frice \'dent-ə-frəs\ n : a powder, paste, or liquid for cleaning the teeth

den·tist \'dent-əst\ n : one whose profession is the care and replacement of teeth — **den·tist·ry** n

den·ti·tion \den-'tish-ən\ n : the number, kind, and arrangement of teeth (as of a person)

den·ture \'den-chər\ n : an artificial replacement for teeth

de·nude \di-'n(y)üd\ vb : to strip the covering from — **de·nu·da·tion** \ˌdē-n(y)ü-'dā-shən\ n

de·nun·ci·a·tion \di-ˌnən-sē-'ā-shən\ n

: the act of denouncing; esp : a public accusation

de·ny \di-'nī\ vb 1 : to declare untrue : CONTRADICT 2 : to refuse to recognize or acknowledge : DISAVOW ⟨denied his faith⟩ 3 : to refuse to grant ⟨~ a request⟩ 4 : to reject as false ⟨~ the theory of evolution⟩

de·odor·ant \dē-'ōd-ə-rənt\ n : a preparation that destroys or masks unpleasant odors

de·odor·ize \-'īz\ vb : to eliminate or prevent the offensive odor of

de·oxy·ri·bo·nu·cle·ic acid \dē-ˌäk-sē-'rī-bō-n(y)ü-ˌklē-ik-\ n : any of various acids found esp. in cell nuclei

de·part \di-'pärt\ vb 1 : to go away : go away from : LEAVE 2 : DIE 3 : to turn aside : DEVIATE

de·part·ment \-mənt\ n 1 : a distinct sphere : PROVINCE 2 : a functional or territorial division (as of a government, business, or college) — **de·part·men·tal** \di-ˌpärt-'ment-ᵊl, ˌdē-\ adj

de·par·ture \di-'pär-chər\ n 1 : the act of going away 2 : a starting out (as on a journey) 3 : DIVERGENCE

de·pend \di-'pend\ vb 1 : to hang down ⟨a vine ~ing from a tree⟩ 2 : to rely for support 3 : to be determined by or based on some action or condition 4 : TRUST, RELY

de·pend·able \-'pen-də-bəl\ adj : TRUSTWORTHY, RELIABLE — **de·pend·abil·i·ty** \-ˌpen-də-'bil-ət-ē\ n

de·pen·dence also **de·pen·dance** \-'pen-dəns\ n 1 : the quality or state of being dependent; esp : the quality or state of being influenced by or subject to another 2 : RELIANCE, TRUST 3 : something on which one relies

de·pen·den·cy \-dən-sē\ n 1 : DEPENDENCE 2 : a territory under the jurisdiction of a nation but not formally annexed by it

¹**de·pen·dent** \-dənt\ adj 1 : hanging down 2 : determined or conditioned by another 3 : relying on another for support 4 : subject to another's jurisdiction 5 : SUBORDINATE 4

²**de·pen·dent** also **de·pen·dant** \-dənt\ n : one that is dependent; esp : a person who relies on another for support

de·pict \di-'pikt\ vb 1 : to represent by a picture 2 : to describe in words — **de·pic·tion** \-'pik-shən\ n

de·pil·a·to·ry \-'pil-ə-ˌtōr-ē\ n : an agent for removing hair, wool, or bristles

de·plane \dē-'plān\ vb : to get off an airplane

de·plete \di-'plēt\ vb : to exhaust esp. of strength or resources — **de·ple·tion** \-'plē-shən\ n

de·plor·able \-'plōr-ə-bəl\ adj 1 : LAMENTABLE 2 : WRETCHED — **de·plor·ably** adv

de·plore \-'plōr\ vb 1 : to feel or express grief for 2 : to regret strongly 3 : to consider unfortunate or deserving of disapproval

de·ploy \-'ploi\ vb : to spread out (as troops or ships) in order for battle

de·po·nent \-'pō-nənt\ n : one who gives evidence esp. in writing

de·pop·u·late \dē-'päp-yə-ˌlāt\ vb : to reduce greatly the population of by destroying or driving away the inhabitants ⟨a city *depopulated* by an epidemic⟩ — **de·pop·u·la·tion** \-ˌpäp-yə-ˈlā-shən\ *n*

de·port \di-ˈpōrt\ *vb* 1 : CONDUCT, BEHAVE 2 : BANISH, EXILE — **de·por·ta·tion** \ˌdē-ˌpōr-ˈtā-shən\ *n*

de·port·ment \di-ˈpōrt-mənt\ *n* : BEHAVIOR, BEARING

de·pose \-ˈpōz\ *vb* 1 : to remove from a high office (as of king) 2 : to testify under oath or by affidavit

¹**de·pos·it** \-ˈpäz-ət\ *vb* 1 : to place for safekeeping or as a pledge; *esp* : to put money in a bank 2 : to lay down : PUT 3 : to let fall or sink ⟨sand and silt ~*ed* by a flood⟩ — **de·pos·i·tor** *n*

²**deposit** *n* 1 : the state of being deposited ⟨money on ~⟩ 2 : something placed for safekeeping; *esp* : money deposited in a bank 3 : money given as a pledge 4 : an act of depositing 5 : something laid or thrown down ⟨a ~ of silt by a river⟩ 6 : an accumulation of mineral matter (as ore, oil, or gas) in nature

dep·o·si·tion \ˌdep-ə-ˈzish-ən, ˌdēp-\ *n* 1 : an act of removing from a position of authority 2 : TESTIMONY 3 : the process of depositing 4 : DEPOSIT

de·pos·i·to·ry \di-ˈpäz-ə-ˌtōr-ē\ *n* : a place where something is deposited esp. for safekeeping

de·pot \1, 3 *usu* ˈdep-ō, 2 *usu* ˈdēp-\ *n* 1 : STOREHOUSE 2 : a building for railroad, bus, or airplane passengers : STATION 3 : a place where military supplies are kept or where troops are assembled and trained

de·prave \di-ˈprāv\ *vb* : CORRUPT, PERVERT — **de·praved** *adj* — **de·prav·i·ty** \-ˈprav-ət-ē\ *n*

dep·re·cate \ˈdep-ri-ˌkāt\ *vb* 1 : to express disapproval of 2 : DEPRECIATE — **dep·re·ca·tion** \ˌdep-ri-ˈkā-shən\ *n*

dep·re·ca·to·ry \ˈdep-ri-kə-ˌtōr-ē\ *adj* 1 : serving to deprecate 2 : expressing deprecation : APOLOGETIC

de·pre·ci·ate \di-ˈprē-shē-ˌāt\ *vb* 1 : to lessen in price or value 2 : UNDERVALUE, BELITTLE, DISPARAGE — **de·pre·ci·a·tion** \-ˌprē-shē-ˈā-shən\ *n*

dep·re·da·tion \ˌdep-rə-ˈdā-shən\ *n* : a laying waste or plundering ⟨the ~*s* of rodents⟩

de·press \di-ˈpres\ *vb* 1 : to press down : cause to sink to a lower position 2 : to lessen the activity or force of 3 : SADDEN, DISCOURAGE 4 : to lessen in price or value

de·pres·sant *n* : one that depresses; *esp* : an agent that reduces bodily functional activity

de·pres·sion \-ˈpresh-ən\ *n* 1 : an act of depressing : a state of being depressed 2 : a pressing down : LOWERING 3 : DEJECTION, MELANCHOLY 4 : a depressed area or part : HOLLOW 5 : a period of low general economic activity with widespread unemployment

dep·ri·va·tion \ˌdep-rə-ˈvā-shən\ *n* : an act or instance of depriving : LOSS; *also* : PRIVATION

de·prive \di-ˈprīv\ *vb* 1 : to take something away from ⟨~ a king of his power⟩ 2 : to stop from having something

depth \ˈdepth\ *n* 1 : something that is deep; *esp* : the deep part of a body of water 2 : a part that is far from the outside or surface ⟨the ~*s* of the woods⟩ 3 : ABYSS 4 : the middle or innermost part ⟨the ~ of winter⟩ 5 : an extreme state (as of misery); *also* : the worst part

⟨the ~*s* of despair⟩ 6 : the perpendicular distance downward from a surface; *also* : the distance from front to back 7 : the quality of being deep 8 : degree of intensity ⟨the ~ of a color⟩

dep·u·ta·tion \ˌdep-yə-ˈtā-shən\ *n* 1 : the act of appointing a deputy 2 : DELEGATION

de·pute \di-ˈpyüt\ *vb* : DELEGATE

dep·u·tize \ˈdep-yə-ˌtīz\ *vb* : to appoint as deputy

dep·u·ty \ˈdep-yət-ē\ *n* 1 : a person appointed to act for or in place of another 2 : an assistant empowered to act as a substitute in the absence of his superior 3 : a member of a lower house of a legislative assembly

de·rail \di-ˈrāl\ *vb* 1 : to cause to run off the rails ⟨a train ~*ed* by heavy snow⟩ — **de·rail·ment** *n*

de·range \di-ˈrānj\ *vb* 1 : DISARRANGE, UPSET 2 : to make insane — **de·range·ment** *n*

der·by \ˈdər-bē, *Brit* ˈdär-\ *n* 1 : a horse race usu. for three-year-olds held annually 2 : a race or contest open to all 3 : a man's stiff felt hat with dome-shaped crown and narrow brim

¹**der·e·lict** \ˈder-ə-ˌlikt\ *adj* 1 : abandoned by the owner or occupant ⟨a ~ ship⟩ 2 : NEGLECTFUL, NEGLIGENT ⟨~ in his duty⟩

²**derelict** *n* 1 : something voluntarily abandoned; *esp* : a ship abandoned on the high seas 2 : one that is not a responsible or acceptable member of society

der·e·lic·tion \ˌder-ə-ˈlik-shən\ *n* 1 : the act of abandoning : the state of being abandoned 2 : a failure in duty : DELINQUENCY

de·ride \di-ˈrīd\ *vb* : to laugh at scornfully : make fun of : RIDICULE — **de·ri·sion** \-ˈrizh-ən\ *n* — **de·ri·sive** \-ˈrī-siv\ *adj* — **de·ri·sive·ly** *adv*

de ri·gueur \də-rē-ˈgər\ *adj* : prescribed or required by fashion, etiquette, or custom

der·i·va·tion \ˌder-ə-ˈvā-shən\ *n* 1 : the formation of a word from an earlier word or root; *also* : an act of ascertaining or stating the derivation of a word 2 : ETYMOLOGY 3 : SOURCE, ORIGIN; *also* : DESCENT 4 : an act or process of deriving

¹**de·riv·a·tive** \di-ˈriv-ət-iv\ *adj* : derived from something else : not original or fundamental

²**derivative** *n* 1 : a word formed by derivation 2 : something derived

de·rive \di-ˈrīv\ *vb* 1 : to receive or obtain from a source 2 : to obtain from a parent substance 3 : to trace the origin, descent, or derivation of 4 : to come from a certain source 5 : INFER, DEDUCE

der·ma·ti·tis \ˌdər-mə-ˈtīt-əs\ *n* : skin inflammation

der·ma·tol·o·gy \-ˈtäl-ə-jē\ *n* : a branch of knowledge concerned with the skin and its disorders — **der·ma·tol·o·gist** *n*

der·o·gate \ˈder-ə-ˌgāt\ *vb* 1 : to cause to seem inferior : DISPARAGE 2 : DETRACT — **der·o·ga·tion** \ˌder-ə-ˈgā-shən\ *n*

de·rog·a·to·ry \di-ˈräg-ə-ˌtōr-ē\ *adj* : intended to lower the reputation of a person or thing : DISPARAGING ⟨~ remarks⟩

der·rick \ˈder-ik\ *n* 1 : a hoisting apparatus : CRANE 2 : a framework over a drill hole (as for oil) supporting the tackle for boring and hoisting

der·ri·ere or **der·ri·ère** \,der-ē-'eər\ n : BUTTOCKS

der·ring–do \,der-iŋ-'dü\ n : daring action : DARING

der·rin·ger \'der-ən-jər\ n : a short-barreled pocket pistol

der·ris \'der-əs\ n : an insecticide obtained from several Old World legumes; also : one of these plants

der·vish \'dər-vish\ n : a member of a Muslim religious order noted for devotional exercises (as bodily movements leading to a trance)

des·cant \'des-,kant, des-'kant\ vb 1 : to sing or play part music : SING, WARBLE 2 : to discourse or write at length

de·scend \di-'send\ vb 1 : to pass from a higher to a lower place or level : pass, move, or climb down or down along 2 : DERIVE ⟨~ed from royalty⟩ 3 : to pass by inheritance or transmission 4 : to incline, lead, or extend downward ⟨the road ~s to the river⟩ 5 : to swoop down in a sudden attack

¹de·scen·dant or **de·scen·dent** \-'sendənt\ adj 1 : DESCENDING 2 : proceeding from an ancestor or source

²descendant or **descendent** n 1 : one descended from another or from a common stock 2 : one deriving directly from a precursor or prototype

de·scent \di-'sent\ n 1 : the act or process of descending 2 : a downward step (as in station or value) : DECLINE 3 : ANCESTRY, BIRTH, LINEAGE 4 : SLOPE 5 : a descending way (as a downgrade or stairway) 6 : a sudden hostile raid or assault

de·scribe \-'skrīb\ vb 1 : to represent or give an account of in words 2 : to trace the outline of — **de·scrib·able** adj

de·scrip·tion \-'skrip-shən\ n 1 : an account of something; esp : an account that presents a picture to a person who reads or hears it 2 : KIND, SORT — **de·scrip·tive** \-'skrip-tiv\ adj

de·scry \-'skrī\ vb 1 : to catch sight of 2 : to discover by observation or investigation

des·e·crate \'des-i-,krāt\ vb : PROFANE — **des·e·cra·tion** \,des-i-'krā-shən\ n

de·seg·re·gate \dē-'seg-ri-,gāt\ vb : to eliminate segregation in; esp : to free of any law, provision, or practice requiring isolation of the members of a particular race in separate units — **de·seg·re·ga·tion** \-,seg-ri-'gā-shən\ n

¹des·ert \'dez-ərt\ n : a dry barren region incapable of supporting a population without an artificial water supply

²desert adj : of, relating to, or resembling a desert; esp : being barren and without life ⟨a ~ island⟩

³de·sert \di-'zərt\ n 1 : worthiness of reward or punishment 2 : a just reward or punishment

⁴de·sert \di-'zərt\ vb 1 : to withdraw from : LEAVE, ABANDON 2 : FORSAKE — **de·sert·er** n — **de·ser·tion** \-'zər-shən\ n

de·serve \di-'zərv\ vb : to be worthy of : MERIT — **de·serv·ing** adj

de·serv·ed·ly \-'zər-vəd-lē\ adv : according to merit : JUSTLY

des·ic·cant \'des-i-kənt\ n : a drying agent

des·ic·cate \'des-i-,kāt\ vb : DRY, DEHY-

DRATE — **des·ic·ca·tion** \,des-i-'kā-shən\ n

de·sid·er·a·tum \di-,sid-ə-'rät-əm\ n, pl **-er·a·ta** \-'rät-ə\ : something desired as essential or needed

¹de·sign \di-'zīn\ vb 1 : to conceive and plan out in the mind; also : DEVOTE, CONSIGN 2 : INTEND 3 : to devise for a specific function or end 4 : to make a pattern or sketch of 5 : to conceive and draw the plans for ⟨~ an airplane⟩ — **de·sign·er** n

²design n 1 : a mental project or scheme : PLAN 2 : a particular purpose : deliberate planning 3 : a secret project or scheme : PLOT 4 pl : aggressive or evil intent — used with on or against 5 : a preliminary sketch or plan : DELINEATION 6 : an underlying scheme that governs functioning, developing, or unfolding : MOTIF 7 : the arrangement of elements that make up a structure or a work of art 8 : a decorative pattern

¹des·ig·nate \'dez-ig-,nāt, -nət\ adj : chosen for an office but not yet installed ⟨ambassador ~⟩

²des·ig·nate \'dez-ig-,nāt\ vb 1 : to mark or point out : INDICATE; also : SPECIFY, STIPULATE 2 : to appoint or choose by name for a special purpose 3 : to call by a name or title — **des·ig·na·tion** \,dez-ig-'nā-shən\ n

de·sign·ing \di-'zī-niŋ\ adj : CRAFTY, SCHEMING

de·sir·able \-'zī-rə-bəl\ adj 1 : PLEASING, ATTRACTIVE ⟨a ~ woman⟩ ⟨a ~ location⟩ 2 : ADVISABLE ⟨~ legislation⟩ — **de·sir·abil·i·ty** \-,zī-rə-'bil-ət-ē\ n

¹de·sire \-'zī(ə)r\ vb 1 : to long, hope, or wish for : COVET 2 : REQUEST

²desire n 1 : a strong wish : LONGING, CRAVING 2 : an expressed wish : REQUEST 3 : something desired

de·sir·ous \di-'zī-rəs\ adj : eagerly wishing : DESIRING

de·sist \-'zist\ vb : to cease to proceed or act

desk \'desk\ n 1 : a table, frame, or case esp. for writing and reading 2 : a counter, stand, or booth at which a person performs his duties 3 : a specialized division of an organization (as a newspaper) ⟨city ~⟩

¹des·o·late \'des-ə-lət\ adj 1 : DESERTED, ABANDONED 2 : FORSAKEN, LONELY 3 : DILAPIDATED 4 : BARREN, LIFELESS 5 : CHEERLESS, GLOOMY — **des·o·late·ly** adv

²des·o·late \-,lāt\ vb : to make desolate : lay waste : make wretched

des·o·la·tion \,des-ə-'lā-shən\ n 1 : the action of desolating 2 : DEVASTATION, RUIN 3 : barren wasteland 4 : GRIEF, SADNESS 5 : LONELINESS

¹de·spair \di-'spaər\ vb : to lose all hope or confidence — **de·spair·ing** adj — **de·spair·ing·ly** adv

²despair n 1 : utter loss of hope 2 : a cause of hopelessness

des·patch var of DISPATCH

des·per·a·do \,des-pə-'räd-ō, -'rād-\ n, pl **-does** or **-dos** : a bold or reckless criminal

des·per·ate \'des-p(ə-)rət\ adj 1 : being beyond or almost beyond hope : causing despair 2 : RASH 3 : OVERPOWERING — **des·per·ate·ly** adv

des·per·a·tion \,des-pə-'rā-shən\ n
1 : a loss of hope and surrender to misery or dread **2 :** a state of hopelessness leading to rashness

de·spic·a·ble \di-'spik-ə-bəl, 'des-pi-kə-\ adj **:** deserving to be despised **:** CONTEMPTIBLE — **des·pi·ca·bly** adv

de·spise \di-'spīz\ vb **1 :** to look down on with contempt or aversion **:** DISDAIN, DETEST **2 :** to regard as negligible, worthless, or distasteful

de·spite \-'spīt\ prep **:** in spite of

de·spoil \-'spȯil\ vb **:** to strip of belongings, possessions, or value **:** PLUNDER, PILLAGE — **de·spoil·er** n — **de·spoil·ment** n

de·spo·li·a·tion \-,spō-lē-'ā-shən\ n **:** the act of plundering **:** the state of being despoiled

¹de·spond \di-'spänd\ vb **:** to become discouraged or disheartened

²despond n **:** DESPONDENCY

de·spon·den·cy \-'spän-dən-sē\ n **:** DEJECTION, HOPELESSNESS — **de·spon·dent** adj

des·pot \'des-pət\ n [Gk despotēs master] **1 :** a ruler with absolute power and authority **:** AUTOCRAT, TYRANT **2 :** a person exercising power abusively, oppressively, or tyrannously — **des·pot·ic** \des-'pät-ik\ adj — **des·po·tism** \'des-pə-,tiz-əm\ n

des·sert \di-'zərt\ n **:** a course of sweet food, fruit, or cheese served at the close of a meal

des·ti·na·tion \,des-tə-'nā-shən\ n **1 :** an act of appointing, setting aside for a purpose, or predetermining **2 :** purpose for which something is destined **3 :** a place set for the end of a journey or to which something is sent

des·tine \'des-tən\ vb **1 :** to settle in advance **2 :** to designate, assign, or dedicate in advance **3 :** to be bound or directed ⟨a ship destined for Gulf ports⟩

des·ti·ny \'des-tə-nē\ n **1 :** something to which a person or thing is destined **:** FATE, FORTUNE **2 :** a predetermined course of events

des·ti·tute \'des-tə-,t(y)üt\ adj **1 :** lacking something needed or desirable **2 :** extremely poor — **des·ti·tu·tion** \,des-tə-'t(y)ü-shən\ n

de·stroy \di-'strȯi\ vb **1 :** to put an end to **:** RUIN **2 :** KILL

de·stroy·er n **1 :** one that destroys **2 :** a small speedy warship

de·struc·ti·ble \di-'strək-tə-bəl\ adj **:** capable of being destroyed — **de·struc·ti·bil·i·ty** \-,strək-tə-'bil-ət-ē\ n

de·struc·tion \-'strək-shən\ n **1 :** the action or process of destroying something **2 :** RUIN **3 :** a destroying agency — **de·struc·tive** \-'strək-tiv\ adj — **de·struc·tive·ly** adv — **de·struc·tive·ness** n

des·ue·tude \'des-wi-,t(y)üd\ n **:** DISUSE

des·ul·to·ry \'des-əl-,tōr-ē\ adj **:** passing aimlessly from one thing or subject to another **:** DISCONNECTED

de·tach \di-'tach\ vb **1 :** to separate esp. from a larger mass **2 :** DISENGAGE, WITHDRAW — **de·tach·able** adj

de·tached adj **1 :** not joined or connected **:** SEPARATE **2 :** ALOOF, UNCONCERNED, IMPARTIAL ⟨a ~ attitude⟩

de·tach·ment \di-'tach-mənt\ n **1 :** SEPARATION **2 :** the dispatching of a body of troops or part of a fleet from the main body for special service; also **:** the portion so dispatched **3 :** a small permanent military unit different in composition from normal units **4 :** indifference to worldly concerns **:** ALOOFNESS, UNWORLDLINESS **5 :** IMPARTIALITY

¹de·tail \di-'tāl, 'dē-,tāl\ n **1 :** a dealing with something item by item ⟨go into ~⟩; also **:** ITEM, PARTICULAR ⟨the ~s of a story⟩ **2 :** selection (as of soldiers) for special duty; also **:** the persons thus selected

²detail vb **1 :** to report in detail **2 :** ENUMERATE, SPECIFY **3 :** to select for some special duty

de·tain \di-'tān\ vb **1 :** to hold in or as if in custody **2 :** STOP, DELAY

de·tect \-'tekt\ vb **:** to discover the nature, existence, presence, or fact of ⟨~smoke⟩ — **de·tect·able** adj — **de·tec·tion** \-'tek-shən\ n — **de·tec·tor** n

¹de·tec·tive \di-'tek-tiv\ adj **1 :** fitted for, employed for, or concerned with detection ⟨a ~ device for coal gas⟩ **2 :** of or relating to detectives ⟨a ~ story⟩

²detective n **:** a person employed or engaged in detecting lawbreakers or getting information that is not readily accessible

dé·tente \dā-'tänt\ n **:** a relaxation of strained relations or tensions (as between nations)

de·ten·tion \di-'ten-chən\ n **1 :** the act or fact of detaining **:** CONFINEMENT; esp **:** temporary custody awaiting trial **2 :** a forced delay

de·ter \-'tər\ vb **-terred; -ter·ring 1 :** to turn aside, discourage, or prevent from acting (as by fear) **2 :** INHIBIT

de·ter·gent \-'tər-jənt\ n **:** a cleansing agent; esp **:** any of numerous synthetic preparations chemically different from soap

de·te·ri·o·rate \-'tir-ē-ə-,rāt\ vb **:** to make or grow worse **:** DEGENERATE — **de·te·ri·o·ra·tion** \-,tir-ē-ə-'rā-shən\ n

de·ter·min·able \di-'tər-mə-nə-bəl\ adj **:** capable of being determined; esp **:** ASCERTAINABLE

de·ter·mi·nant \-nənt\ n **1 :** something that determines or conditions **:** FACTOR **2 :** a hereditary factor **:** GENE

de·ter·mi·nate \-nət\ adj **1 :** having fixed limits **:** DEFINITE **2 :** definitely settled

de·ter·mi·na·tion \di-,tər-mə-'nā-shən\ n **1 :** the act of coming to a decision; also **:** the decision or conclusion reached **2 :** the act of fixing the extent, position, or character of something **3 :** accurate measurement (as of length or volume) **4 :** firm or fixed purpose

de·ter·mine \di-'tər-mən\ vb **1 :** to fix conclusively or authoritatively **2 :** to come to a decision **:** SETTLE, RESOLVE **3 :** to fix the form or character of beforehand **:** ORDAIN; also **:** REGULATE **4 :** to find out the limits, nature, dimensions, or scope of ⟨~ a position at sea⟩ **5 :** to be the cause of or reason for **:** DECIDE

de·ter·mined adj **1 :** DECIDED, RESOLVED **2 :** FIRM, RESOLUTE — **de·ter·mined·ly** adv — **de·ter·mined·ness** n

de·ter·min·ism \-mə-,niz-əm\ n **:** a doctrine that acts of the will, natural events, or social changes are determined by preceding causes — **de·ter·min·ist** n or adj

de·ter·rence \di-'tər-əns\ n **:** the act, process, or capacity of deterring

de·ter·rent \-ənt\ adj **1 :** serving to

deter 2 : relating to deterrence — **de·ter·rent** *n*

de·test \di-'test\ *vb* : LOATHE, HATE — **de·test·able** *adj* — **de·tes·ta·tion** \ˌdē-ˌtes-'tā-shən\ *n*

de·throne \di-'thrōn\ *vb* : to remove from a throne : DEPOSE — **de·throne·ment** *n*

det·o·nate \'det-ᵊn-ˌāt\ *vb* : to explode with violence — **det·o·na·tion** \ˌdet-ᵊn-'ā-shən\ *n*

¹de·tour \'dē-ˌtùr\ *n* : a roundabout way temporarily replacing part of a route

²detour *vb* : to go by detour

de·tract \di-'trakt\ *vb* 1 : to take away : WITHDRAW, SUBTRACT 2 : DISTRACT — **de·trac·tion** \-'trak-shən\ *n* — **de·trac·tor** *n*

de·train \dē-'trān\ *vb* : to leave or cause to leave a railroad train

det·ri·ment \'det-rə-mənt\ *n* : injury or damage or its cause : HURT — **det·ri·men·tal** \ˌdet-rə-'ment-ᵊl\ *adj* — **det·ri·men·tal·ly** *adv*

de·tri·tus \di-'trīt-əs\ *n* : fragments resulting from disintegration (as of rocks acted on by frost)

deuce \'d(y)üs\ *n* 1 : a two in cards or dice 2 : a tie in tennis with both sides at 40 3 : DEVIL — used chiefly as a mild oath

deu·te·ri·um \d(y)ü-'tir-ē-əm\ *n* : a form of hydrogen that is of twice the mass of ordinary hydrogen

deut·sche mark \ˌdòi-chə-'märk\ *n* — see MONEY table

de·val·ue \dē-'val-yü\ *vb* : to reduce the international exchange value of (~ a currency) — **de·val·u·a·tion** \-ˌval-yə-'wā-shən\ *n*

dev·as·tate \'dev-ə-ˌstāt\ *vb* 1 : to reduce to ruin : lay waste 2 : to shatter completely : DEMOLISH — **dev·as·ta·tion** \ˌdev-ə-'stā-shən\ *n*

de·vel·op \di-'vel-əp\ *vb* 1 : to unfold gradually or in detail 2 : to place (exposed photographic material) in chemicals in order to make the image visible 3 : to bring out the possibilities of 4 : to make more available or usable (~ natural resources) 5 : to acquire gradually (~ a taste for olives) 6 : to go through a natural process of growth and differentiation : EVOLVE 7 : to become apparent — **de·vel·op·er** *n* — **de·vel·op·ment** *n*

de·vi·ant \'dē-vē-ənt\ *adj* : deviating esp. from some accepted norm 2 : characterized by deviation

de·vi·ate \'dē-vē-ˌāt\ *vb* : to turn aside from a course, standard, principle, or topic — **de·vi·a·tion** \ˌdē-vē-'ā-shən\ *n*

de·vice \di-'vīs\ *n* 1 : SCHEME, STRATAGEM 2 : a piece of equipment or a mechanism for a special purpose 3 : WILL, DESIRE (left to his own ~*s*) 4 : an emblematic design (as on a coat of arms)

¹dev·il \'dev-əl\ *n* [OE *dēofol*, fr. LL *diabolus*, fr. Gk *diabolos*, lit., slanderer, fr. *diaballein* to slander] 1 *often cap* : the personal supreme spirit of evil 2 : DEMON 3 : a wicked person 4 : a reckless or dashing person 5 : a pitiable person (poor ~) 6 : a printer's apprentice

²devil *vb* -iled *or* -illed; -il·ing *or* -il·ling 1 : TEASE, ANNOY 2 : to chop fine and season highly (~*ed* eggs)

dev·il·ish \-(ə-)lish\ *adj* 1 : characteristic of or resembling the devil (~ tricks) 2 : EXTREME, EXCESSIVE (in a ~ hurry) — **dev·il·ish·ly** *adv* — **dev·il·ish·ness** *n*

dev·il·ment \'dev-əl-mənt, -ˌment\ *n* : MISCHIEF

dev·il·ry \-rē\ *or* dev·il·try \-trē\ *n* 1 : action performed with the help of the devil : WITCHCRAFT 2 : reckless mischievousness

de·vi·ous \'dē-vē-əs\ *adj* 1 : deviating from a straight line : ROUNDABOUT 2 : ERRING 3 : TRICKY

¹de·vise \di-'vīz\ *vb* 1 : INVENT 2 : PLOT 3 : to give (real estate) by will

²devise *n* 1 : a disposing of real property by will 2 : a will or clause of a will disposing of real property 3 : property given by will

de·vi·tal·ize \dē-'vīt-ᵊl-ˌīz\ *vb* : to deprive of life or vitality

de·void \di-'vòid\ *adj* : entirely lacking : DESTITUTE (a book ~ of interest)

de·voir \dəv-'wär\ *n* 1 : DUTY 2 : a formal act of civility or respect — usu. used in pl.

de·volve \di-'välv\ *vb* : to pass from one person to another by succession or transmission — **dev·o·lu·tion** \ˌdev-ə-'lü-shən\ *n*

de·vote \di-'vōt\ *vb* 1 : to set apart for a special purpose : DEDICATE 2 : to give up to wholly or chiefly (*devoted* his time to sports)

de·vot·ed *adj* 1 : ZEALOUS, ARDENT, DEVOUT 2 : AFFECTIONATE, LOVING (a ~ husband)

dev·o·tee \ˌdev-ə-'tē\ *n* 1 : an esp. ardent adherent of a religion or deity 2 : a zealous follower, supporter, or enthusiast (a ~ of sports)

de·vo·tion \di-'vō-shən\ *n* 1 : religious fervor 2 : an act of prayer or supplication — usu. used in pl. 3 *pl* : prayers or service of worship for private use 4 : the act of devoting or quality of being devoted (~ to music) 5 : strong love or affection — **de·vo·tion·al** *adj*

de·vour \di-'vaù(ə)r\ *vb* 1 : to eat up greedily or ravenously 2 : WASTE, ANNIHILATE 3 : to take in eagerly by the senses or mind (~ a book) — **de·vour·er** *n*

de·vout \di-'vaùt\ *adj* 1 : devoted to religion : PIOUS 2 : expressing devotion : SINCERE — **de·vout·ly** *adv* — **de·vout·ness** *n*

dew \'d(y)ü\ *n* : moisture condensed on the surfaces of cool bodies at night — **dewy** *adj*

dew·ber·ry \'d(y)ü-ˌber-ē\ *n* : any of several sweet edible berries related to and resembling blackberries

dew·drop \-ˌdräp\ *n* : a drop of dew

dew·lap \-ˌlap\ *n* : a hanging fold of skin under the neck esp. of a bovine animal

dex·ter·i·ty \dek-'ster-ət-ē\ *n* 1 : readiness and grace in physical activity; *esp* : skill and ease in using the hands 2 : mental skill or quickness

dex·ter·ous \'dek-st(ə-)rəs\ *or* dex·trous \-strəs\ *adj* 1 : skillful and competent with the hands 2 : EXPERT

ə abut; ᵉ kitten; ər further; a back; ā bake; ä cot, cart; aù out; ch chin; e less; ē easy; g gift; i trip; ī life; j joke; ŋ sing; ō flow; ò flaw; òi coin; th thin; t͟h this; ü loot; ù foot; y yet; yü few; yù furious; zh vision

3 : done with skillfulness — **dex·ter·ous·ly** *adv*

dex·trose \'dek-ˌstrōs\ *n* : a sugar that occurs in plants and blood and may be made from starch

dhow \'daù\ *n* : an Arab sailing ship usu. having a long overhang forward and a high poop

di·a·be·tes \ˌdī-ə-'bēt-ēz, -'bēt-əs\ *n* : an abnormal state marked by passage of excessive amounts of urine; *esp* : one in which insulin is deficient and the urine and blood contain excess sugar — **di·a·bet·ic** \-'bet-ik\ *adj or n*

di·a·bol·ic \-'bäl-ik\ *adj* : DEVILISH, FIENDISH — **di·a·bol·i·cal** *adj* — **di·a·bol·i·cal·ly** *adv*

di·a·crit·ic \-'krit-ik\ *n* : a mark accompanying a letter and indicating a sound value different from that of the same letter when unmarked — **diacritic** *or* **di·a·crit·i·cal** *adj*

di·a·dem \'dī-ə-ˌdem\ *n* : CROWN; *esp* : a band worn on or around the head as a badge of royalty

di·aer·e·sis \dī-'er-ə-səs\ *n, pl* **di·aer·e·ses** \-ˌsēz\ : a mark ¨ placed over a vowel to show that it is pronounced in a separate syllable (as in *naïve*)

di·ag·no·sis \ˌdī-ig-'nō-səs\ *n, pl* **-no·ses** \-ˌsēz\ : the art or act of identifying a disease from its signs and symptoms — **di·ag·nose** \'dī-ig-ˌnōs\ *vb* — **di·ag·nos·tic** \ˌdī-ig-'näs-tik\ *adj* — **di·ag·nos·ti·cian** \-ˌnäs-'tish-ən\ *n*

¹**di·ag·o·nal** \dī-'ag-ən-ᵊl\ *adj* **1** : extending from one corner to the opposite corner in a 4-sided figure **2** : running in a slanting direction ⟨~ stripes⟩ **3** : having slanting markings or parts ⟨a ~ weave⟩ — **di·ag·o·nal·ly** *adv*

²**diagonal** *n* **1** : a diagonal line **2** : a diagonal direction **3** : a diagonal row, arrangement, or pattern

¹**di·a·gram** \'dī-ə-ˌgram\ *n* : a drawing, sketch, plan, or chart that makes something easier to understand — **di·a·gram·mat·ic** \ˌdī-ə-grə-'mat-ik\ *or* **di·a·gram·mat·i·cal** *adj* — **di·a·gram·mat·i·cal·ly** *adv*

²**diagram** *vb* **-gramed** *or* **-grammed**; **-gram·ing** *or* **-gram·ming** : to represent by a diagram

¹**di·al** \'dī(-ə)l\ *n* **1** : SUNDIAL **2** : the face of a timepiece **3** : a plate or face with a pointer and numbers that indicate something ⟨the ~ of a pressure gauge⟩ **4** : a disk with a knob or slots that is turned for making connections (as on a telephone) or for regulating operation (as of a radio)

²**dial** *vb* **-aled** *or* **-alled**; **-al·ing** *or* **-al·ling** **1** : to manipulate a telephone dial so as to call **2** : to manipulate a dial so as to operate or select ⟨~ a radio program⟩

di·a·lect \'dī-ə-ˌlekt\ *n* : a regional variety of a language

di·a·lec·tic \ˌdī-ə-'lek-tik\ *n* : the process or art of reasoning correctly

di·a·logue *or* **di·a·log** \'dī-ə-ˌlòg\ *n* **1** : a conversation between two or more persons **2** : the parts of a literary or dramatic composition that represent conversation

di·am·e·ter \dī-'am-ət-ər\ *n* [Gk *diametros*, fr. *dia-* through + *metron* measure] **1** : a straight line that passes through the center of a circle and divides it in half **2** : THICKNESS ⟨~ of a rope⟩

di·a·met·ri·cal·ly \ˌdī-ə-'met·ri·

k(ə-)lē\ *adv* : as if at opposite ends of a diameter ⟨~ opposed⟩

di·a·mond \'dī-(ə-)mənd\ *n* **1** : a hard brilliant mineral that consists of crystalline carbon and is used as a gem **2** : a flat figure having four equal sides, two acute angles, and two obtuse angles **3** : any of a suit of playing cards marked with a red diamond **4** : INFIELD; *also* : the entire playing field in baseball

di·a·mond·back \-ˌbak\ *n* : a large and very deadly rattlesnake

di·a·pa·son \ˌdī-ə-'pāz-ᵊn\ *n* **1** : the range of notes sounded by a voice or instrument **2** : an organ stop covering the range of the organ

¹**di·a·per** \'dī-(ə-)pər\ *n* **1** : a cotton or linen fabric woven in a simple geometric pattern **2** : a piece of folded cloth drawn up between the legs of a baby and fastened about the waist

²**diaper** *vb* **1** : to ornament with diaper designs **2** : to put a diaper on

di·aph·a·nous \dī-'af-ə-nəs\ *adj* : so fine of texture as to be transparent

di·a·phragm \'dī-ə-ˌfram\ *n* **1** : a muscular bodily partition; *esp* : one between the chest and abdominal cavities of a mammal **2** : a vibrating disk (as in a telephone receiver) — **di·a·phrag·mat·ic** \ˌdī-ə-ˌfrag-'mat-ik\ *adj*

di·a·rist \'dī-ə-rəst\ *n* : one who keeps a diary

di·ar·rhea *or* **di·ar·rhoea** \ˌdī-ə-'rē-ə\ *n* : abnormal looseness of the bowels

di·a·ry \'dī-(ə-)rē\ *n* : a daily record esp. of personal experiences and observations; *also* : a book for keeping such private notes and records

di·as·to·le \dī-'as-tə-(ˌ)lē\ *n* : a rhythmically recurrent expansion; *esp* : the dilatation of the cavities of the heart during which they fill with blood

dia·ther·my \'dī-ə-ˌthər-mē\ *n* : the generation of heat in tissue for medical or surgical purposes by electric currents

di·a·tribe \'dī-ə-ˌtrīb\ *n* : a bitter or violent attack in speech or writing : an angry criticism or denunciation

dib·ble \'dib-əl\ *n* : a pointed hand tool for making holes (as for planting bulbs) in the ground — **dibble** *vb*

¹**dice** \'dīs\ *n, pl* **dice** : a small cube marked on each face with one to six spots and used usu. in pairs in various games and in gambling

²**dice** *vb* **1** : to cut into small cubes ⟨~ carrots⟩ **2** : to play games with dice

di·chot·o·my \dī-'kät-ə-mē\ *n* : a division or the process of dividing into two esp. mutually exclusive or contradictory groups

dick·er \'dik-ər\ *vb* : BARGAIN, HAGGLE

dick·ey *or* **dicky** \'dik-ē\ *n* **1** : a small fabric insert worn to fill in the neckline **2** *chiefly Brit* : the driver's seat in a carriage; *also* : a seat at the back of a carriage or automobile

di·cot·y·le·don \ˌdī-ˌkät-ᵊl-'ēd-ᵊn\ *n* : a seed plant having two cotyledons — **di·cot·y·le·don·ous** *adj*

¹**dic·tate** \'dik-ˌtāt\ *vb* **1** : to speak or read for a person to transcribe or for a machine to record **2** : COMMAND, ORDER — **dic·ta·tion** \dik-'tā-shən\ *n*

²**dictate** *n* : an authoritative rule, prescription, or injunction : COMMAND ⟨the ~s of conscience⟩

dic·ta·tor \'dik-ˌtāt-ər\ *n* **1** : a person ruling absolutely and often brutally and oppressively **2** : one that dictates

dic·ta·to·ri·al \,dik-tə-'tōr-ē-əl\ *adj* **1** : of, relating to, or characteristic of a dictator or a dictatorship : AUTOCRATIC, IMPERIOUS, DESPOTIC

dic·ta·tor·ship \dik-'tāt-ər-,ship\ *n* **1** : the office or term of office of a dictator **2** : autocratic rule, control, or leadership **3** : a government or country in which absolute power is held by a dictator or a small clique

dic·tion \'dik-shən\ *n* **1** : choice of words esp. with regard to correctness, clearness, or effectiveness : WORDING **2** : ENUNCIATION

dic·tio·nary \'dik-shə-,ner-ē\ *n* : a reference book containing words usu. alphabetically arranged along with information about their forms, pronunciations, functions, etymologies, meanings, and syntactical and idiomatic uses

dic·tum \'dik-təm\ *n, pl* **-ta** \-tə\ *also* **-tums** **1** : an authoritative statement : PRONOUNCEMENT **2** : a formal statement of an opinion

did *past of* DO

di·dac·tic \dī-'dak-tik\ *adj* **1** : intended primarily to instruct; *esp* : intended to teach a moral lesson **2** : having or showing a tendency to instruct or lecture others ⟨a ~ manner⟩

di·do \'dīd-ō\ *n, pl* **-does** *or* **-dos** : a foolish or mischievous act

¹**die** \'dī\ *vb* **died; dy·ing** **1** : to stop living : EXPIRE **2** : to pass out of existence ⟨a *dying* race⟩ **3** : to disappear or subside gradually ⟨the wind *died* down⟩ **4** : to long keenly ⟨*dying* to go⟩ **5** : STOP ⟨the motor *died*⟩

²**die** \'dī\ *n, pl* **dice** \'dīs\ *or* **dies** \'dīz\ **1** *pl* **dice** : DICE **2** *pl usu* **dice** : something determined as if by a cast of dice : FATE ⟨the *dice* appear to be loaded against a victory this year⟩ **3** *pl* **dies** : a device used in shaping or stamping an object or material

die-hard \-,härd\ *n* : one who resists against hopeless odds

di·elec·tric \,dī-ə-'lek-trik\ *n* : an electrically nonconducting material

die·sel engine \,dē-zəl-, -səl-\ *n* : an engine in which air is compressed to a temperature sufficiently high to ignite the fuel in the cylinder

¹**di·et** \'dī-ət\ *n* **1** : the food and drink regularly consumed (as by a person or group) : FARE **2** : an allowance of food prescribed with reference to a particular state (as ill health) — **di·etary** \'dī-ə-,ter-ē\ *adj or n*

²**diet** *vb* : to eat or cause to eat less or according to a prescribed rule — **di·et·er** *n*

di·etet·ics \,dī-ə-'tet-iks\ *n pl* : the science or art of applying the principles of nutrition to diet — **di·etet·ic** *adj* — **di·eti·tian** *or* **di·eti·cian** \-'tish-ən\ *n*

dif·fer \'dif-ər\ *vb* **1** : to be unlike **2** : DISAGREE

dif·fer·ence \'dif-(ə)-rəns\ *n* **1** : UNLIKENESS ⟨~ in their looks⟩ **2** : distinction or discrimination in preference **3** : DISAGREEMENT, DISSENSION; *also* : an instance or cause of disagreement ⟨unable to settle their ~s⟩ **4** : the amount by which one number or quantity differs from another

dif·fer·ent \-rənt\ *adj* **1** : UNLIKE, DISSIMILAR **2** : not the same : DISTINCT, VARIOUS, ANOTHER, SEPARATE ⟨~ age groups⟩ (seen at ~ times) ⟨try a ~ book⟩ **3** : UNUSUAL, SPECIAL — **dif·fer·ent·ly** *adv*

¹**dif·fer·en·tial** \,dif-ə-'ren-chəl\ *adj* : showing, creating, or relating to a difference

²**differential** *n* **1** : the amount or degree by which things differ **2** : an arrangement of gears in an automobile that allows one wheel to go faster than another (as in rounding curves)

dif·fer·en·ti·ate \-'ren-chē-,āt\ *vb* **1** : to make or become different **2** : to recognize or state the difference ⟨~ between two plants⟩ — **dif·fer·en·ti·a·tion** \-,ren-chē-'ā-shən\ *n*

dif·fi·cult \'dif-i-(,)kəlt\ *adj* **1** : hard to do or make : ARDUOUS **2** : hard to understand or deal with ⟨~ reading⟩ ⟨a ~ child⟩

dif·fi·cul·ty \-,kəl-tē\ *n* **1** : difficult nature ⟨the ~ of a task⟩ **2** : great effort **3** : OBSTACLE ⟨overcome *difficulties*⟩ **4** : TROUBLE ⟨in financial *difficulties*⟩ **5** : DISAGREEMENT ⟨settled their *difficulties*⟩ *syn* hardship, rigor, vicissitude

dif·fi·dent \'dif-əd-ənt\ *adj* **1** : lacking confidence : TIMID **2** : RESERVED, UNASSERTIVE — **dif·fi·dence** *n* — **dif·fi·dent·ly** *adv*

¹**dif·fuse** \dif-'yüs\ *adj* **1** : not concentrated ⟨~ light⟩ **2** : VERBOSE, WORDY ⟨~ writing⟩ **3** : SCATTERED

²**dif·fuse** \-'yüz\ *vb* : to pour out or spread widely : SCATTER — **dif·fu·sion** \-'yü-zhən\ *n*

dig \'dig\ *vb* **dug** \'dəg\; **dig·ging** **1** : to turn up the soil (as with a spade) **2** : to hollow out or form by removing earth ⟨~ a hole⟩ **3** : to uncover or seek by turning up earth ⟨~ potatoes⟩ **4** : DISCOVER ⟨~ up information⟩ **5** : POKE, THRUST ⟨~ a person in the ribs⟩ **6** : to work hard

²**dig** *n* **1** : THRUST, POKE **2** : a cutting remark : GIBE

¹**di·gest** \'dī-,jest\ *n* : a summation or condensation of a body of information or of a literary work

²**di·gest** \dī-'jest, də-\ *vb* **1** : to think over and arrange in the mind **2** : to convert (food) into a form that can be absorbed **3** : to compress into a short summary — **di·gest·ible** *adj* — **di·ges·tion** \-'jes-chən\ *n* — **di·ges·tive** \-'jes-tiv\ *adj*

dig·it \'dij-ət\ *n* **1** : any of the figures 1 to 9 inclusive and usu. the symbol 0 **2** : FINGER, TOE

dig·i·tal·is \,dij-ə-'tal-əs\ *n* : a drug from the common foxglove that is a powerful heart stimulant

dig·ni·fied \'dig-nə-,fīd\ *adj* : showing or expressing dignity

dig·ni·fy \-,fī\ *vb* : to give dignity or distinction to : HONOR

dig·ni·tary \-,ter-ē\ *n* : a person of high position or honor ⟨*dignitaries* of the church⟩

dig·ni·ty \'dig-nət-ē\ *n* **1** : the quality or state of being worthy, honored, or esteemed : true worth : EXCELLENCE **2** : high rank, office, or position

3 : formal reserve of manner or language

di·graph \'dī-,graf\ n : a group of 2 successive letters whose phonetic value is a single sound

di·gress \dī-'gres\ vb : to turn aside esp. from the main subject in writing or speaking — **di·gres·sion** \-'gresh-ən\ n — **di·gres·sive** \-'gres-iv\ adj

dike \'dīk\ n : a bank of earth to control water : LEVEE

di·lap·i·dat·ed \də-'lap-ə-,dāt-əd\ adj : fallen into partial ruin or decay — **di·lap·i·da·tion** \-,lap-ə-'dā-shən\ n

di·late \dī-'lāt\ vb : SWELL, DISTEND, EXPAND \~ the nostrils\ — **di·la·ta·tion** \,dil-ə-'tā-shən\ n — **di·la·tion** \dī-'lā-shən\ n

dil·a·to·ry \'dil-ə-,tōr-ē\ adj 1 : DELAYING 2 : TARDY, SLOW

di·lem·ma \də-'lem-ə\ n : a choice between equally undesirable alternatives

dil·et·tante \,dil-ə-'tänt(-ē), -'tant(-ē)\ n, pl **-tantes** or **-tan·ti** \-'tänt-ē, -'tant-\ : a person who follows an art or study superficially though with interest

dil·i·gent \'dil-ə-jənt\ adj : characterized by steady, earnest, and energetic application and effort : PAINSTAKING — **dil·i·gence** n — **dil·i·gent·ly** adv

dill \'dil\ n : an herb related to the carrot with aromatic leaves and seeds used in pickles

dil·ly·dal·ly \'dil-ē-,dal-ē\ vb : to waste time by loitering or delay : DAWDLE

di·lute \dī-'lüt, də-\ vb : to lessen the consistency or strength of by mixing with something else \~ wine with water\ — **di·lu·tion** \-'lü-shən\ n

²dilute adj : DILUTED, WEAK

¹dim \'dim\ adj 1 : not bright or distinct : OBSCURE, FAINT 2 : LUSTERLESS, DULL 3 : not seeing or understanding clearly — **dim·ly** adv — **dim·ness** n

²dim vb dimmed; dim·ming 1 : to make or become dim or lusterless 2 : to reduce the light from \~ the headlights\

dime \'dīm\ n [MF, tenth part, fr. L decima, fr. fem. of decimus tenth, fr. decem ten] : a U.S. silver coin worth ¹⁄₁₀ dollar

di·men·sion \də-'men-chən\ n 1 : measurement of extension (as in length, height, or breadth) 2 : EXTENT, SCOPE, PROPORTIONS — **di·men·sion·al** adj

di·min·ish \də-'min-ish\ vb 1 : to make less or cause to appear less 2 : BELITTLE 3 : DWINDLE 4 : TAPER — **dim·i·nu·tion** \,dim-ə-'n(y)ü-shən\ n

¹di·min·u·tive \də-'min-yət-iv\ n 1 : a diminutive word or affix 2 : a diminutive object or individual

²diminutive adj 1 : indicating small size and sometimes the state or quality of being lovable, pitiable, or contemptible (the \~ suffixes -ette and -ling) 2 : extremely small : TINY

dim·i·ty \'dim-ət-ē\ n : a thin usu. corded cotton fabric

dim·mer \'dim-ər\ n 1 : one that dims 2 pl : automobile headlights that have been dimmed

¹dim·ple \'dim-pəl\ n : a small depression esp. in the cheek or chin

²dimple vb : to form dimples (as in smiling)

din \'din\ n : loud, confused, or clanging noise

di·nar \di-'när\ n — see MONEY table

dine \'dīn\ vb 1 : to eat dinner 2 : to give a dinner to : FEED

din·er \'dī-nər\ n 1 : one that dines 2 : a railroad dining car; also : a restaurant in the shape of a railroad car

di·nette \dī-'net\ n : an alcove or small room used for dining

din·ghy \'diŋ-(k)ē\ n 1 : a light rowboat 2 : a rubber life raft

din·gle \'diŋ-gəl\ n : a narrow wooded valley

din·gus \'diŋ-(g)əs\ n : something whose proper name is unknown or forgotten

din·gy \'din-jē\ adj 1 : DARK, DULL 2 : not fresh or clean : GRIMY — **din·gi·ness** n

din·ky \'din-kē\ adj : SMALL, INSIGNIFICANT

din·ner \'din-ər\ n : the main meal of the day; also : a formal banquet

din·ner·ware \-,waər\ n : china, glassware, or tableware used in table service

di·no·saur \'dī-nə-,sȯr\ n : any of a group of extinct long-tailed reptiles often of huge size

dint \'dint\ n 1 archaic : BLOW, STROKE 2 : FORCE, POWER (he reached the top by \~ of sheer grit) 3 : DENT

di·o·cese \'dī-ə-səs, -,sēz\ n : the territorial jurisdiction of a bishop — **di·oc·e·san** \dī-'äs-ə-sən\ adj or n

¹dip \'dip\ vb dipped; dip·ping 1 : to plunge temporarily or partially under the surface (as of a liquid) so as to moisten, cool, or coat 2 : to thrust in a way to suggest immersion \~ water to scoop up or out : LADLE 4 : to lower and then raise quickly (\~ a flag in salute) 5 : to drop or slope down or out of sight esp. suddenly (the moon dipped below the crest) 6 : to decrease moderately and usu. temporarily (prices dipped) 7 : to reach down inside or as if inside or below a surface (dipped into their savings) 8 : to delve casually into something; esp : to read superficially (\~ into a book)

²dip n 1 : an act of dipping; esp : a brief plunge into the water for sport or exercise 2 : inclination downward : DROP 3 : something obtained by or used in dipping 4 : a liquid into which something may be dipped

diph·the·ria \dif-'thir-ē-ə, dip-\ n : an acute contagious bacterial disease marked by fever and by coating of the air passages with a membrane that interferes with breathing

diph·thong \'dif-,thȯŋ, 'dip-\ n : two vowel sounds joined in one syllable to form one speech sound (as ou in out, oi in oil)

di·plo·ma \də-'plō-mə\ n : an official paper bearing record of graduation from or of a degree conferred by an educational institution

di·plo·ma·cy \-mə-sē\ n 1 : the art and practice of conducting negotiations between nations 2 : TACT — **dip·lo·mat** \'dip-lə-,mat\ n — **dip·lo·mat·ic** \,dip-lə-'mat-ik\ adj

di·plo·ma·tist \də-'plō-mət-əst\ n : DIPLOMAT

dip·per \'dip-ər\ n 1 : something (as a ladle or scoop) that dips or is used for dipping 2 cap : BIG DIPPER 3 cap : LITTLE DIPPER 4 : any of several birds skilled in diving

dip·stick \'dip-,stik\ n : a graduated rod for indicating depth

dip·ter·ous \'dip-tə-rəs\ adj : having two wings; also : of or relating to the two-winged flies — **dip·ter·an** adj or n

dire \'dī(ə)r\ *adj* **1** : very horrible : DREADFUL **2** : warning of disaster ⟨a ~ forecast⟩ **3** : EXTREME ⟨~ need⟩

¹di·rect \də-'rekt, dī-\ *vb* **1** : ADDRESS ⟨~ a letter⟩; *also* : to impart orally : AIM ⟨~ a remark to the gallery⟩ **2** : to cause to turn, move, or point or to follow a certain course **3** : to point, extend, or project in a specified line or course **4** : to show or point out the way **5** : to regulate the activities or course of : guide the supervision, organizing, or performance of **6** : to request or instruct with authority ⟨the court ~ed the jury to bring in a verdict⟩

²direct *adj* **1** : leading from one point to another in time or space without turn or stop : STRAIGHT **2** : stemming immediately from a source, cause, or reason ⟨~ result⟩ **3** : operating without an intervening agency or step ⟨~ action⟩ **4** : being or passing in a straight line of descent : LINEAL ⟨~ ancestor⟩ **5** : NATURAL, STRAIGHTFORWARD ⟨a ~ manner⟩ **6** : effected by the action of the people or the electorate and not by representatives ⟨~ legislation⟩ **7** : consisting of or reproducing the exact words of a speaker ⟨~ discourse⟩ — **di·rect·ly** *adv* — **di·rect·ness** *n*

di·rec·tion \-'rek-shən\ *n* **1** : MANAGEMENT, GUIDANCE **2** *archaic* : SUPERSCRIPTION **3** : COMMAND, ORDER, INSTRUCTION **4** : the course or line along which something moves, lies, or points; *also* : TREND — **di·rec·tion·al** *adj*

di·rec·tive \-'rek-tiv\ *n* : a general instruction as to procedure ⟨a ~ from the main office⟩

di·rec·tor \-tər\ *n* **1** : one that directs : MANAGER, SUPERVISOR, CONDUCTOR **2** : one of a group of persons who direct the affairs of an organized body (as a corporation) — **di·rec·tor·ship** *n*

di·rec·to·ry \-t(ə-)rē\ *n* : an alphabetical or classified list of names and addresses

dire·ful \'dī(ə)r-fəl\ *adj* **:** producing dire effects

dirge \'dərj\ *n* : a song or hymn of lamentation; *also* : a slow mournful piece of music

dir·ham \də-'ram\ *n* — see MONEY table

dir·i·gi·ble \'dir-ə-jə-bəl\ *n* : AIRSHIP

dirk \'dərk\ *n* : DAGGER

dirndl \'dərn-d⁰l\ *n* : a full skirt with a tight waistband

dirt \'dərt\ *n* **1** : a filthy or soiling substance (as mud, dust, or grime) **2** : loose or packed earth : SOIL **3** : moral uncleanness **4** : scandalous gossip

¹dirty *adj* **1** : SOILED, FILTHY **2** : BASE, UNFAIR ⟨a ~ trick⟩ **3** : INDECENT, SMUTTY ⟨~ talk⟩ **4** : STORMY, FOGGY ⟨~ weather⟩ **5** : not clear in color : DULL ⟨a ~ red⟩ — **dirt·i·ness** *n*

²dirty *vb* : to make or become dirty

dis·able \dis-'ā-bəl\ *vb* **1** : to incapacitate by or as if by illness, injury, or wounds : CRIPPLE **2** : to disqualify legally — **dis·abil·i·ty** \dis-ə-'bil-ət-ē\ *n*

dis·abuse \dis-ə-'byüz\ *vb* : to free from error or fallacy

dis·ad·van·tage \dis-əd-'vant-ij\ *n* **1** : loss or damage esp. to reputation or finances **2** : an unfavorable, inferior, or prejudicial condition; *also* : HANDICAP — **dis·ad·van·ta·geous** \dis-,ad-van-'tā-jəs\ *adj*

dis·af·fect \dis-ə-'fekt\ *vb* : to alienate the affection or loyalty of : cause discontent in ⟨the troops were ~ed⟩ — **dis·af·fec·tion** \-'fek-shən\ *n*

dis·agree \dis-ə-'grē\ *vb* **1** : to fail to agree ⟨the accounts ~⟩ **2** : to differ in opinion **3** : to be unsuitable ⟨fried foods ~ with her⟩ — **dis·agree·ment** *n*

dis·agree·able *adj* **1** : causing discomfort : UNPLEASANT, OFFENSIVE **2** : ill-tempered : PEEVISH — **dis·agree·ably** *adv*

dis·al·low \dis-ə-'lau̇\ *vb* : to refuse to admit or recognize : REJECT ⟨~ a claim⟩ — **dis·al·low·ance** *n*

dis·ap·pear \-ə-'piər\ *vb* **1** : to pass out of sight **2** : to cease to be : become lost — **dis·ap·pear·ance** *n*

dis·ap·point \-ə-'pȯint\ *vb* : to fail to fulfill the expectation or hope of — **dis·ap·point·ment** *n*

dis·ap·pro·ba·tion \dis-,ap-rə-'bā-shən\ *n* : DISAPPROVAL

dis·ap·prov·al \dis-ə-'prü-vəl\ *n* : adverse judgment : CENSURE

dis·ap·prove \-ə-'prüv\ *vb* **1** : CONDEMN **2** : REJECT **3** : to feel or express disapproval ⟨~s of smoking⟩

dis·arm \dis-'ärm\ *vb* **1** : to take arms or weapons from **2** : DISBAND; *esp* : to reduce the size and strength of the armed forces of a country **3** : to make harmless, peaceable, or friendly : win over ⟨a ~ing smile⟩ — **dis·ar·ma·ment** \-'är-mə-mənt\ *n*

dis·ar·range \dis-ə-'rānj\ *vb* : to disturb the arrangement or order of — **dis·ar·range·ment** *n*

dis·ar·ray \-ə-'rā\ *n* **1** : DISORDER, CONFUSION **2** : disorderly or careless dress

dis·as·sem·ble \dis-ə-'sem-bəl\ *vb* : to take apart

dis·as·so·ci·ate \-sō-s(h)ē-,āt\ *vb* : to detach from association : DISSOCIATE

di·sas·ter \diz-'as-tər\ *n* : a sudden or great misfortune : CALAMITY — **di·sas·trous** \-'as-trəs\ *adj* — **di·sas·trous·ly** *adv*

dis·avow \dis-ə-'vau̇\ *vb* : to deny responsibility for : REPUDIATE — **dis·avow·al** *n*

dis·band \dis-'band\ *vb* : to break up the organization of : DISPERSE

dis·bar \-'bär\ *vb* : to expel from the bar or the legal profession — **dis·bar·ment** *n*

dis·be·lieve \dis-bi-'lēv\ *vb* **1** : to hold not to be true or real ⟨disbelieved his testimony⟩ **2** : to withhold or reject belief ⟨disbelieved in his sincerity⟩ — **dis·be·lief** \-'lēf\ *n* — **dis·be·liev·er** *n*

dis·bur·den \dis-'bərd-⁰n\ *vb* : to rid of a burden

dis·burse \dis-'bərs\ *vb* : to pay out : EXPEND — **dis·burse·ment** *n*

disc *var of* DISK

dis·card \dis-'kärd\ *vb* **1** : to let go a playing card from one's hand; *also* : to play (a card) from a suit other than a trump but different from the one led **2** : to get rid of as useless or unwanted — **dis·card** \'dis-,kärd\ *n*

dis·cern \dis-'ərn, diz-\ *vb* **1** : to detect with the eyes : DISTINGUISH

ə abut; ᵊ kitten; ər further; a back; ā bake; ä cot, cart; au̇ out; ch chin; e less; ē easy; g gift; i trip; ī life; j joke; ŋ sing; ō flow; ȯ flaw; ȯi coin; th thin; th this; ü loot; u̇ foot; y yet; yü few; yu̇ furious; zh vision

2 : to come to know or recognize mentally **3 :** DISCRIMINATE — **dis·cern·ible** adj — **dis·cern·ment** n

dis·cern·ing adj : revealing insight and understanding : DISCRIMINATING

1dis·charge \dis-'chärj\ vb **1 :** to relieve of a charge, load, or burden : UNLOAD **2 :** SHOOT ⟨~ a gun⟩ ⟨~ an arrow⟩ **3 :** to set free ⟨~ a prisoner⟩ **4 :** to dismiss from service or employment ⟨~ a soldier⟩ **5 :** to let go or let off ⟨~ passengers⟩ **6 :** to give forth fluid ⟨the river ~s into the ocean⟩ **7 :** to get rid of by paying or doing ⟨~ a debt⟩ ⟨~ a duty⟩ **8 :** to remove the electrical energy from ⟨~ a storage battery⟩

2dis·charge \'dis-,chärj, dis-'chärj\ n **1 :** the act of discharging, unloading, or releasing **2 :** something that discharges; esp : a certification of release or payment **3 :** a firing off (as of a gun) **4 :** a flowing out (as of blood from a wound); also : a flow of electricity through a gas **5 :** release or dismissal esp. from an office or employment; also : complete separation from military service

dis·ci·ple \dis-'ī-pəl\ n **1 :** a pupil or follower who helps to spread his master's teachings; also : a convinced adherent **2** cap : a member of the Disciples of Christ

dis·ci·pli·nar·i·an \,dis-ə-plə-'ner-ē-ən\ n : one who disciplines or enforces order

dis·ci·plin·ary \'dis-ə-plə-,ner-ē\ n : of or relating to discipline : CORRECTIVE ⟨~ problems⟩

1dis·ci·pline \'dis-ə-plən\ n **1 :** a field of study : SUBJECT **2 :** training that corrects, molds, or perfects **3 :** PUNISHMENT **4 :** control gained by obedience or training : orderly conduct **5 :** a system of rules governing conduct

2discipline vb **1 :** PUNISH **2 :** to train or develop by instruction and exercise esp. in self-control **3 :** to bring under control ⟨~ troops⟩; also : to impose order upon

disc jockey n : a person who conducts a radio or television program of musical recordings

dis·claim \dis-'klām\ vb : to deny having a connection with or responsibility for : DISAVOW — **dis·claim·er** n

dis·close \-'klōz\ vb : to expose to view : REVEAL — **dis·clo·sure** \-'klō-zhər\ n

dis·col·or \-'kəl-ər\ vb : to alter or change in hue or color : STAIN, FADE — **dis·col·or·a·tion** \-,kəl-ə-'rā-shən\ n

dis·com·bob·u·late \,dis-kəm-'bäb-(y)ə-,lāt\ vb : UPSET, CONFUSE

dis·com·fit \dis-'kəm-fət, ,dis-kəm-'fit\ vb : UPSET, FRUSTRATE — **dis·com·fi·ture** \dis-'kəm-fə-,chùr\ n

1dis·com·fort \dis-'kəm-fərt\ vb : to make uncomfortable or uneasy

2discomfort n : lack of comfort : uneasiness of mind or body : DISTRESS

dis·com·mode \,dis-kə-'mōd\ vb : INCONVENIENCE, TROUBLE

dis·com·pose \-kəm-'pōz\ vb **1 :** AGITATE **2 :** DISARRANGE — **dis·com·po·sure** \-'pō-zhər\ n

dis·con·cert \-kən-'sərt\ vb : CONFUSE, UPSET

dis·con·nect \-kə-'nekt\ vb : to undo the connection of — **dis·con·nec·tion** \-'nek-shən\ n

dis·con·nect·ed adj : not connected

: RAMBLING, INCOHERENT — **dis·con·nect·ed·ly** adv

dis·con·so·late \dis-'kän-sə-lət\ adj **1 :** hopelessly sad **2 :** CHEERLESS — **dis·con·so·late·ly** adv

dis·con·tent \,dis-kən-'tent\ n : uneasiness of mind : DISSATISFACTION — **dis·con·tent·ed** adj

dis·con·tin·ue \-'tin-yü\ vb **1 :** to break the continuity of : cease to operate, use, or take **2 :** END — **dis·con·tin·u·ance** \-yə-wəns\ n — **dis·con·ti·nu·i·ty** \dis-,känt-ᵊn-'(y)ü-ət-ē\ n — **dis·con·tin·u·ous** \,dis-kən-'tin-yə-wəs\ adj

dis·cord \'dis-,kòrd\ n **1 :** lack of agreement or harmony : DISSENSION, CONFLICT, OPPOSITION **2 :** a harsh combination of musical sounds : DISSONANCE **3 :** a harsh or unpleasant sound — **dis·cor·dant** \dis-'kòrd-ᵊnt\ adj

1dis·count \'dis-,kaúnt\ n **1 :** a reduction made from a regular or list price **2 :** a deduction of interest in advance when lending money

2discount \'dis-,kaúnt, dis-'kaúnt\ vb **1 :** to deduct from the amount of a bill, debt, or charge usu. for cash or prompt payment; also : to sell or offer for sale at a discount **2 :** to lend money after deducting the discount ⟨~ a note⟩ **3 :** DISREGARD; also : MINIMIZE **4 :** to make allowance for bias or exaggeration ⟨~ a romantic tale⟩; also : DISBELIEVE **5 :** to take into account (as a future event) in present calculations — **dis·count·able** adj

dis·coun·te·nance \dis-'kaúnt-(ᵊ)nəns\ vb **1 :** EMBARRASS, DISCONCERT **2 :** to look with disfavor on

dis·cour·age \dis-'kər-ij\ vb **1 :** to deprive of courage or confidence : DISHEARTEN **2 :** to hinder by inspiring fear of consequences : DETER ⟨laws that ~ speeding⟩ **3 :** to attempt to dissuade — **dis·cour·age·ment** n

1dis·course \'dis-,kōrs\ n **1 :** CONVERSATION **2 :** formal and orderly and usu. extended expression of thought on a subject

2dis·course \dis-'kōrs\ vb **1 :** to express oneself in esp. oral discourse **2 :** TALK, CONVERSE

dis·cour·te·ous \dis-'kərt-ē-əs\ adj : lacking courtesy : UNCIVIL, RUDE — **dis·cour·te·ous·ly** adv

dis·cour·te·sy \-'kərt-ə-sē\ n : RUDENESS; also : a rude act

dis·cov·er \dis-'kəv-ər\ vb **1 :** to make known or visible **2 :** to obtain sight or knowledge of for the first time : FIND — **dis·cov·er·er** n — **dis·cov·ery** \-(ə-)rē\ n

1dis·cred·it \-'kred-ət\ vb **1 :** DISBELIEVE **2 :** to cause disbelief in the accuracy or authority of : DISGRACE — **dis·cred·it·able** adj

2discredit n **1 :** loss of credit or reputation **2 :** lack or loss of belief or confidence

dis·creet \dis-'krēt\ adj : showing good judgment : PRUDENT; esp : capable of observing prudent silence — **dis·creet·ly** adv

dis·crep·an·cy \-'krep-ən-sē\ n **1 :** DIFFERENCE, DISAGREEMENT **2 :** an instance of being discrepant : VARIATION, INCONSISTENCY

dis·crep·ant \-ənt\ adj : being at variance : DISAGREEING

dis·crete \dis-'krēt, 'dis-,krēt\ adj

1 : individually distinct **2 :** NONCON-
TINUOUS
dis·cre·tion \dis-'kresh-ən\ *n* **1 :** the
quality of being discreet **:** PRUDENCE
2 : individual choice or judgment
3 : power of free decision or latitude
of choice ⟨reached the age of ~⟩ —
dis·cre·tion·ary *adj*
dis·crim·i·nate \-'krim-ə-,nāt\ *vb*
1 : DISTINGUISH, DIFFERENTIATE **2 :** to
make a distinction in favor of or against
one person or thing as compared with
others — **dis·crim·i·na·tion** \-,krim-ə-
'nā-shən\ *n*
dis·crim·i·nat·ing *adj* **:** marked by discrimination; *esp* **:** DISCERNING, JUDI-
CIOUS
dis·crim·i·na·to·ry \dis-'krim-ə-nə-
,tōr-ē\ *adj* **:** marked by esp. unjust discrimination ⟨~ treatment⟩
dis·cur·sive \-'kər-siv\ *adj* **:** passing
from one topic to another **:** RAMBLING —
dis·cur·sive·ly *adv*
dis·cus \'dis-kəs\ *n* **:** a disk (as of wood
or rubber) that is hurled for distance in
a track-and-field contest
dis·cuss \dis-'kəs\ *vb* **1 :** to argue or
consider carefully by presenting the various sides **2 :** to talk about — **dis·cus-
sion** \-'kəsh-ən\ *n*
dis·cus·sant \-'kəs-ənt\ *n* **:** one who
takes part in a formal discussion or
symposium
¹dis·dain \dis-'dān\ *n* **:** CONTEMPT,
SCORN — **dis·dain·ful** *adj* — **dis·dain-
ful·ly** *adv*
²disdain *vb* **1 :** to look upon with scorn
2 : to reject or refrain from because of
disdain
dis·ease \diz-'ēz\ *n* **:** an alteration of a
living body that impairs its functioning;
also **:** a particular instance or kind of
this — **dis·eased** *adj*
dis·em·bark \,dis-əm-'bärk\ *vb* **:** to go
or put ashore from a ship — **dis·em-
bar·ka·tion** \dis-,em-,bär-'kā-shən\ *n*
dis·em·body \,dis-əm-'bäd-ē\ *vb* **:** to divest of bodily existence ⟨disembodied
spirits⟩
dis·em·bow·el \-'baü-(ə)l\ *vb* **:** EVIS-
CERATE — **dis·em·bow·el·ment** *n*
dis·en·chant \,dis-ⁿn-'chant\ *vb* **:** to
free from enchantment **:** DISILLUSION —
dis·en·chant·ment *n*
dis·en·cum·ber \-'kəm-bər\ *vb* **:** to free
from something that burdens or obstructs
dis·en·gage \-'gāj\ *vb* **:** RELEASE, EXTRI-
CATE, DISENTANGLE
dis·en·tan·gle \-'taŋ-gəl\ *vb* **:** to free
from entanglement **:** UNRAVEL
dis·es·tab·lish \,dis-ə-'stab-lish\ *vb* **:** to
end the establishment of; *esp* **:** to deprive of the status of an established
church — **dis·es·tab·lish·ment** *n*
dis·es·teem \-ə-'stēm\ *n* **:** lack of esteem **:** DISFAVOR, DISREPUTE
di·seuse \dē-'zᵫz(r)z, -'zᵫz\ *n* **:** a skilled
and usu. professional woman reciter
dis·fa·vor \dis-'fā-vər\ *n* **1 :** DISAP-
PROVAL, DISLIKE **2 :** the state or fact of
being deprived of favor
dis·fig·ure \-'fig-yər\ *vb* **:** to spoil the
appearance of ⟨disfigured by a scar⟩ —
dis·fig·ure·ment *n*
dis·fran·chise \-'fran-,chīz\ *vb* **:** to deprive of a franchise, a legal right, or a

privilege; *esp* **:** to deprive of the right to
vote
dis·gorge \-'gȯrj\ *vb* **:** VOMIT; *also* **:** to
discharge forcefully or confusedly
¹dis·grace \-'grās\ *vb* **:** to bring reproach or shame to
²disgrace *n* **1 :** the condition of being
out of favor **:** loss of respect **2 :** SHAME,
DISHONOR; *also* **:** a cause of shame —
dis·grace·ful *adj* — **dis·grace·ful·ly**
adv
dis·grun·tle \dis-'grənt-ⁿl\ *vb* **:** to put
in bad humor
¹dis·guise \-'gīz\ *vb* **:** to change the
dress or looks of so as to conceal the
identity or so as to resemble another
: ALTER **2 :** HIDE, CONCEAL
²disguise *n* **1 :** clothing put on to conceal one's identity or counterfeit another's **2 :** an outward form hiding or
misrepresenting the true nature or identity of a person or thing **:** PRETENSE
¹dis·gust \dis-'gəst\ *n* **:** AVERSION, RE-
PUGNANCE
²disgust *vb* **:** to provoke to loathing,
repugnance, or aversion **:** be offensive to
— **dis·gust·ed·ly** *adv*
¹dish \'dish\ *n* [OE *disc*, fr. L *discus*
quoit, disk, dish, fr. Gk *diskos*] **1 :** a
vessel used for serving food **2 :** the
food served in a dish ⟨a ~ of berries⟩
3 : food prepared in a particular way
4 : something resembling a dish esp. in
being shallow and concave
²dish *vb* **1 :** to put into a dish ⟨~ up the
dinner⟩ **2 :** to make concave like a
dish
dis·har·mo·ny \dis-'här-mə-nē\ *n* **:** lack
of harmony
dish·cloth \'dish-,klȯth\ *n* **:** a cloth for
washing dishes
dis·heart·en \dis-'härt-ⁿn\ *vb* **:** DIS-
COURAGE, DEJECT
di·shev·el \dish-'ev-əl\ *vb*-eled *or* -elled;
-el·ing *or* -el·ling **:** to let hang or
fall loosely in disorder **:** DISARRAY —
di·shev·eled *or* **di·shev·elled** *adj*
dis·hon·est \dis-'än-əst\ *adj* **1 :** not
honest **:** UNTRUSTWORTHY **2 :** DECEIT-
FUL, CORRUPT — **dis·hon·est·ly** *adv* —
dis·hon·es·ty \-ə-stē\ *n*
¹dis·hon·or \-'än-ər\ *n* **1 :** lack or loss
of honor **:** SHAME, DISGRACE **2 :** something dishonorable **:** a cause of disgrace
3 : the act of dishonoring a negotiable
instrument when presented for payment
— **dis·hon·or·able** *adj* — **dis·hon·or-
ably** *adv*
²dishonor *vb* **1 :** DISGRACE **2 :** to refuse
to accept or pay ⟨~ a check⟩
dish·rag \'dish-,rag\ *n* **:** DISHCLOTH
dish·wash·er \-,wȯsh-ər, -,wäsh-\ *n*
: a person or a machine that washes
dishes
dish·wa·ter \-,wȯt-ər, -,wät-\ *n* **:** water
in which dishes have been or are to be
washed
dis·il·lu·sion \,dis-ə-'lü-zhən\ *vb* **:** to
free from or deprive of illusion — **dis·il-
lu·sion·ment** *n*
dis·in·cli·na·tion \dis-,in-klə-'nā-shən\
n **:** a feeling of unwillingness or aversion
: DISTASTE
dis·in·cline \,dis-ⁿn-'klīn\ *vb* **:** to make
or be unwilling
dis·in·fect \-'fekt\ *vb* **:** to free from infection esp. by destroying disease germs

---

ə abut; ᵊ kitten; ər further; a back; ā bake; ä cot, cart; aú out; ch chin;
e less; ē easy; g gift; i trip; ī life; j joke; ŋ sing; ō flow; ȯ flaw; ȯi coin;
th thin; t̶h this; ü loot; ú foot; y yet; yü few; yú furious; zh vision

— dis·in·fec·tant adj or n — dis·in·fec·tion \-'fek-shən\ n

dis·in·gen·u·ous \-'jen-yə-wəs\ adj : lacking in candor : not frank or naïve

dis·in·her·it \-'her-ət\ vb : to prevent from inheriting property that would naturally be passed on

dis·in·te·grate \dis-'int-ə-,grāt\ vb 1 : to break or decompose into constituent parts or small particles 2 : to destroy the unity or integrity of — dis·in·te·gra·tion \-,int-ə-'grā-shən\ n

dis·in·ter \,dis-'n-'tər\ vb 1 : to take from the grave or tomb 2 : UNEARTH

dis·in·ter·est·ed \dis-'in-t(ə-)rəs-təd, -tə-,res-\ adj 1 : not interested 2 : free from selfish motive or interest : UNBIASED — dis·in·ter·est·ed·ness n

dis·join \dis-'join\ vb : SEPARATE

dis·joint \-'joint\ vb : to separate the parts of : DISCONNECT; also : to separate at the joints

dis·joint·ed adj 1 : separated at or as if at the joint 2 : DISCONNECTED; esp : INCOHERENT (~ conversation)

disk or disc \'disk\ n 1 : something round and flat; esp : a flat rounded anatomical structure (as the central part of the flower head of a composite plant or a pad of cartilage between vertebrae) 2 usu disc : a phonograph record

¹dis·like \dis-'līk\ vb : to regard with dislike : DISAPPROVE

²dislike n : a feeling of distaste or disapproval

dis·lo·cate \'dis-lō-,kāt, dis-'lō-\ vb 1 : to put out of place; esp : to displace (a joint) from normal connections (~ a shoulder) 2 : DISRUPT — dis·lo·ca·tion \,dis-lō-'kā-shən\ n

dis·lodge \dis-'läj\ vb 1 : to force out of a place 2 : to drive out from a place of hiding or defense

dis·loy·al \-'lói-əl\ adj : lacking in loyalty — dis·loy·al·ty n

dis·mal \'diz-məl\ adj 1 : gloomy to the eye or ear : DREARY, DEPRESSING 2 : DEPRESSED — dis·mal·ly adv

dis·man·tle \dis-'mant-ªl\ vb 1 : to strip of furniture and equipment 2 : to take apart

dis·may \-'mā\ vb : to cause to lose courage or resolution from alarm or fear : DAUNT — dismay n

dis·mem·ber \-'mem-bər\ vb 1 : to cut off or separate the limbs, members, or parts of 2 : to break up or tear into pieces — dis·mem·ber·ment n

dis·miss \-'mis\ vb 1 : to send away 2 : to send or remove from office, service, or employment 3 : to put aside or out of mind 4 : to refuse further judicial hearing or consideration to (the judge ~ed the charge) — dis·miss·al n

dis·mount \-'maunt\ vb 1 : to get down from something (as a horse or bicycle) 2 : UNHORSE 3 : to take (as a cannon) from the carriage or mountings 4 : to take apart (as a machine)

dis·obe·di·ence \,dis-ə-'bēd-ē-əns\ n : neglect or refusal to obey — dis·o·be·di·ent adj

dis·obey \-'bā\ vb : to fail to obey : be disobedient

¹dis·or·der \dis-'òrd-ər\ vb 1 : to disturb the order of 2 : to cause disorder in (a ~ed digestion)

²disorder n 1 : lack of order : CONFUSION 2 : breach of the peace or public order : TUMULT 3 : an abnormal state of body or mind : AILMENT

dis·or·der·ly adj 1 : UNRULY, TURBULENT 2 : offensive to public order or decency; also : guilty of disorderly conduct 3 : marked by disorder : DISARRANGED (a ~ desk)

dis·or·ga·nize \dis-'òr-gə-,nīz\ vb : to break up the regular system of : throw into disorder : CONFUSE — dis·or·ga·ni·za·tion \-,òr-gə-nə-'zā-shən\ n

dis·own \dis-'ōn\ vb : REPUDIATE, RENOUNCE, DISCLAIM

dis·par·age \-'par-ij\ vb 1 : to lower in rank or reputation : DEGRADE 2 : BELITTLE — dis·par·age·ment n — dis·par·ag·ing·ly adv

dis·pa·rate \'dis-'par-ət, 'dis-pə-rət\ adj : distinct in quality or character : DISSIMILAR — dis·par·i·ty \dis-'par-ət-ē\ n

dis·pas·sion·ate \dis-'pash-(ə-)nət\ adj : not influenced by strong feeling : CALM, IMPARTIAL — dis·pas·sion·ate·ly adv

¹dis·patch \dis-'pach\ vb 1 : to send off or away with promptness or speed esp. on official business 2 : to put to death 3 : to attend to (as a task) rapidly or efficiently — dis·patch·er n

²dispatch n 1 : the sending of a message or messenger 2 : the shipment of goods 3 : MESSAGE 4 : the act of putting to death 5 : a news item sent in by a correspondent to a newspaper 6 : promptness and efficiency in performing a task

dis·pel \dis-'pel\ vb -pelled; -pel·ling : to drive away by scattering : DISSIPATE

dis·pens·able \-'pen-sə-bəl\ adj : capable of being dispensed with : NONESSENTIAL

dis·pen·sa·ry \-'pens-(ə-)rē\ n : a place where medicine or medical or dental aid is dispensed

dis·pen·sa·tion \,dis-pən-'sā-shən\ n 1 : a system of rules for ordering affairs; esp : a system of revealed commands and promises regulating human affairs 2 : a particular arrangement or provision esp. of nature 3 : an exemption from a rule or from a vow or oath 4 : the act of dispensing 5 : something dispensed or distributed

dis·pense \dis-'pens\ vb 1 : to portion out 2 : ADMINISTER (~ justice) 3 : EXEMPT 4 : to make up and give out (remedies) — dis·pens·er n

dis·perse \-'pərs\ vb 1 : to break up and scatter about : SPREAD 2 : DISSEMINATE, DISTRIBUTE — dis·per·sal n — dis·per·sion \-'pər-zhən\ n

dis·pir·it \'pir-ət\ vb : DEPRESS, DISCOURAGE, DISHEARTEN

dis·place \-'plās\ vb 1 : to remove from the usual or proper place; esp : to expel or force to flee from home or native land (displaced persons) 2 : to remove from an office 3 : to take the place of : REPLACE

dis·place·ment n 1 : the act of displacing : the state of being displaced 2 : the volume or weight of a fluid displaced by a floating body (as a ship) 3 : the difference between the initial position of an object and a later position

¹dis·play \dis-'plā\ vb : to present to view

²display n : a displaying of something : EXHIBITION

dis·please \dis-'plēz\ vb 1 : to arouse the disapproval and dislike of 2 : to be offensive to : give displeasure

dis·plea·sure \-'plezh-ər\ n : a feeling of annoyance and dislike accompanying disapproval : DISSATISFACTION

dis·port \dis-'pōrt\ *vb* **1** : DIVERT, AMUSE ⟨~ themselves on the beach⟩ **2** : FROLIC **3** : DISPLAY

dis·pos·al \dis-'pō-zəl\ *n* **1** : ARRANGEMENT **2** : a getting rid of ⟨trash ~⟩ **3** : MANAGEMENT, ADMINISTRATION **4** : the transfer of something into new hands **5** : CONTROL, COMMAND

dis·pose \-'pōz\ *vb* **1** : to give a tendency to : INCLINE ⟨*disposed* to accept⟩ **2** : PREPARE ⟨troops *disposed* for withdrawal⟩ **3** : ARRANGE **4** : SETTLE — **dis·pos·able** *adj* — **dis·pos·er** *n* — **dispose of 1** : to settle or determine the fate, condition, or use of **2** : to get rid of ⟨*dispose of* rubbish⟩ **3** : to transfer to the control of another

dis·po·si·tion \,dis-pə-'zish-ən\ *n* **1** : the act or power of disposing : DISPOSAL ⟨funds at their ~⟩ **2** : RELINQUISHMENT **3** : ARRANGEMENT **4** : TENDENCY, INCLINATION **5** : natural attitude toward things ⟨a cheerful ~⟩

dis·pos·sess \,dis-pə-'zes\ *vb* : to put out of possession or occupancy : OUST — **dis·pos·ses·sion** \ -'zesh-ən\ *n*

dis·praise \dis-'prāz\ *vb* : DISPARAGE — **dispraise** *n*

dis·pro·por·tion \,dis-prə-'pōr-shən\ *n* : lack of proportion, symmetry, or proper relation — **dis·pro·por·tion·ate** \-sh(ə-)nət\ *adj*

dis·prove \dis-'prüv\ *vb* : to prove to be false : REFUTE — **dis·proof** \-'prüf\ *n*

dis·pu·tant \dis-'pyüt-ənt, 'dis-pyət-ənt\ *n* : DISPUTER

dis·pu·ta·tion \,dis-pyə-'tā-shən\ *n* **1** : DEBATE **2** : an oral defense of an academic thesis

dis·pu·ta·tious \-shəs\ *adj* : inclined to dispute : ARGUMENTATIVE

¹**dis·pute** \dis-'pyüt\ *vb* **1** : ARGUE, DEBATE **2** : WRANGLE **3** : to deny the truth or rightness of **4** : to struggle against or over : CONTEST — **dis·put·able** \dis-'pyüt-ə-bəl, 'dis-pyət-ə-bəl\ *adj* — **dis·put·er** \dis-'pyüt-ər\ *n*

²**dispute** *n* **1** : DEBATE **2** : QUARREL

dis·qual·i·fy \dis-'kwäl-ə-,fī\ *vb* **1** : to make or declare unfit or ineligible **2** : to deprive of necessary qualifications — **dis·qual·i·fi·ca·tion** \-,kwäl-ə-fə-'kā-shən\ *n*

¹**dis·qui·et** \dis-'kwī-ət\ *vb* : to make uneasy or restless : DISTURB

²**disquiet** *n* : lack of peace or tranquillity : ANXIETY

dis·qui·etude \dis-'kwī-ə-,t(y)üd\ *n* : AGITATION, ANXIETY

dis·qui·si·tion \,dis-kwə-'zish-ən\ *n* : a formal inquiry or discussion : DISCOURSE

¹**dis·re·gard** \,dis-ri-'gärd\ *vb* : to pay no attention to : treat as unworthy of notice or regard

²**disregard** *n* : the act of disregarding : the state of being disregarded : NEGLECT — **dis·re·gard·ful** *adj*

dis·re·pair \,dis-ri-'paər\ *n* : the state of being in need of repair

dis·rep·u·ta·ble \dis-'rep-yət-ə-bəl\ *adj* : not reputable : DISCREDITABLE, DISGRACEFUL; *esp* : having a bad reputation

dis·re·pute \,dis-ri-'pyüt\ *n* : loss or lack of reputation : low esteem : DISCREDIT

dis·re·spect \-'spekt\ *n* : DISCOURTESY — **dis·re·spect·ful** *adj*

dis·robe \dis-'rōb\ *vb* : UNDRESS

dis·rupt \-'rəpt\ *vb* **1** : to break apart **2** : to throw into disorder : break up — **dis·rup·tion** \-'rəp-shən\ *n* — **dis·rup·tive** *adj*

dis·sat·is·fac·tion \dis-,at-əs-'fak-shən\ *n* : DISCONTENT

dis·sat·is·fy \dis-'at-əs-,fī\ *vb* : to fail to satisfy : DISPLEASE — **dis·sat·is·fied** *adj*

dis·sect \dis-'ekt, dī-'sekt\ *vb* **1** : to divide into parts esp. for examination and study **2** : ANALYZE — **dis·sec·tion** \-'ek-shən, -'sek-\ *n*

dis·sect·ed *adj* : cut deeply into narrow lobes ⟨a ~ leaf⟩

dis·sem·ble \dis-'em-bəl\ *vb* **1** : to hide under or put on a false appearance : conceal facts, intentions, or feelings under some pretense **2** : SIMULATE — **dis·sem·bler** \-b(ə-)lər\ *n*

dis·sem·i·nate \dis-'em-ə-,nāt\ *vb* : to spread abroad as though sowing seed ⟨~ ideas⟩ — **dis·sem·i·na·tion** \-,em-ə-'nā-shən\ *n*

dis·sen·sion \dis-'en-chən\ *n* : disagreement in opinion : DISCORD, QUARRELING

¹**dis·sent** \dis-'ent\ *vb* **1** : to withhold assent **2** : to differ in opinion

²**dissent** *n* **1** : difference of opinion; *esp* : religious nonconformity **2** : a written statement in which a justice disagrees with the opinion of the majority — **dis·sen·tient** \-'en-chənt\ *adj or n*

dis·sent·er *n* **1** : one that dissents **2** *cap* : an English Nonconformist

dis·ser·ta·tion \,dis-ər-'tā-shən\ *n* : an extended usu. written treatment of a subject; *esp* : one submitted for a doctorate

dis·ser·vice \dis-'ər-vəs\ *n* : INJURY, HARM, MISCHIEF

dis·sev·er \dis-'ev-ər\ *vb* : SEPARATE, DISUNITE

dis·si·dent \'dis-əd-ənt\ *adj* : openly and violently differing with an opinion or a group — **dis·si·dence** *n* — **dissident** *n*

dis·sim·i·lar \dis-'im-ə-lər\ *adj* : UNLIKE — **dis·sim·i·lar·i·ty** \-,im-ə-'lar-ət-ē\ *n*

dis·sim·u·late \dis-'im-yə-,lāt\ *vb* : to hide under a false appearance : DISSEMBLE — **dis·sim·u·la·tion** \-,im-yə-'lā-shən\ *n*

dis·si·pate \'dis-ə-,pāt\ *vb* **1** : to break up and drive off : DISPERSE, SCATTER ⟨~ a crowd⟩ **2** : DISPEL, DISSOLVE ⟨the breeze *dissipated* the fog⟩ **3** : SQUANDER **4** : to break up and vanish **5** : to be dissolute; *esp* : to drink alcoholic beverages to excess — **dis·si·pat·ed** *adj* — **dis·si·pa·tion** \,dis-ə-'pā-shən\ *n*

dis·so·ci·ate \dis-'ō-s(h)ē-,āt\ *vb* : DISCONNECT, DISUNITE — **dis·so·ci·a·tion** \-,ō-s(h)ē-'ā-shən\ *n*

dis·so·lute \'dis-ə-,lüt\ *adj* : loose in morals or conduct — **dis·so·lute·ly** *adv* — **dis·so·lute·ness** *n*

dis·so·lu·tion \,dis-ə-'lü-shən\ *n* **1** : separation of a thing into its parts **2** : DECAY; *esp* : DEATH **3** : the termination or breaking up of an assembly or a partnership

dis·solve \diz-'älv\ *vb* **1** : to separate into component parts **2** : to pass or cause to pass into solution ⟨sugar ~s

ə abut; ᵊ kitten; ər further; a back; ā bake; ä cot, cart; aú out; ch chin; e less; ē easy; g gift; i trip; I life; j joke; ŋ sing; ō flow; ó flaw; oi coin; th thin; t͟h this; ü loot; ủ foot; y yet; yü few; yủ furious; zh vision

in water⟩ **3** : TERMINATE, DISPERSE ⟨~ parliament⟩ **4** : to waste or fade away ⟨his strength *dissolved*⟩ **5** : to appear or fade out gradually **6** : to be overcome emotionally ⟨~ in tears⟩ **7** : to resolve itself as if by dissolution

dis·so·nance \'dis-ə-nəns\ *n* : DISCORD — **dis·so·nant** *adj*

dis·suade \dis-'wād\ *vb* : to advise against a course of action : persuade or try to persuade not to do something

dis·taff \'dis-ˌtaf\ *n* **1** : a staff for holding the flax, tow, or wool in spinning **2** : a woman's work or domain **3** : the female branch or side of a family

¹dis·tance \'dis-təns\ *n* **1** : measure of separation in space or time **2** : EXPANSE **3** : a full course ⟨go the ~⟩ **4** : spatial remoteness **5** : COLDNESS, RESERVE **6** : DIFFERENCE, DISPARITY **7** : a distant point

²distance *vb* : to leave far behind : OUTSTRIP

dis·tant \-tənt\ *adj* **1** : separate in space **2** : AWAY **3** : FAR-OFF **3** : being far apart **4** : not close in relationship ⟨a ~ cousin⟩ **5** : different in kind **6** : RESERVED, ALOOF, COLD ⟨~ politeness⟩ **7** : coming from or going to a distance

dis·taste \dis-'tāst\ *n* : DISINCLINATION, DISLIKE, AVERSION — **dis·taste·ful** *adj*

dis·tem·per \-'tem-pər\ *n* : a bodily disorder usu. of a domestic animal; *esp* : a contagious often fatal virus disease of dogs

dis·tend \-'tend\ *vb* : EXPAND, SWELL — **dis·ten·sion** or **dis·ten·tion** \-'ten-chən\ *n*

dis·tich \'dis-(ˌ)tik\ *n* : a strophic unit of two lines

dis·till *also* **dis·til** \dis-'til\ *vb* **1** : to fall or let fall drop by drop **2** : to obtain or extract by distillation — **dis·till·er** *n* — **dis·till·ery** \-(ə-)rē\ *n*

dis·til·la·tion \ˌdis-tə-'lā-shən\ *n* : the driving off of gas or vapor from liquids or solids by heat into a retort and then condensing to a liquid product

dis·tinct \dis-'tiŋkt\ *adj* **1** : distinguished from others : SEPARATE, INDIVIDUAL **2** : clearly seen, heard, or understood : PLAIN, UNMISTAKABLE — **dis·tinct·ly** *adv* — **dis·tinct·ness** *n*

dis·tinc·tion \-'tiŋk-shən\ *n* **1** : the act of distinguishing a difference **2** : DIFFERENCE **3** : a distinguishing quality or mark **4** : a special recognition; *also* : a mark or sign of such recognition **5** : HONOR

dis·tinc·tive \-'tiŋk-tiv\ *adj* **1** : clearly marking a person or a thing as different from others **2** : CHARACTERISTIC **3** : having or giving style or distinction

dis·tin·guish \-'tiŋ-gwish\ *vb* **1** : to recognize by some mark or characteristic **2** : to hear or see clearly : DISCERN **3** : to make distinctions ⟨~ between right and wrong⟩ **4** : to set apart : mark as different **5** : to make outstanding — **dis·tin·guish·able** *adj*

dis·tin·guished *adj* **1** : marked by eminence, distinction, or excellence **2** : befitting an eminent person

dis·tort \dis-'tort\ *vb* **1** : to twist out of the true meaning **2** : to twist out of a natural, normal, or original shape or condition **3** : to reproduce improperly ⟨a radio *distorting* sound⟩ — **dis·tor·tion** \-'tor-shən\ *n*

dis·tract \-'trakt\ *vb* **1** : DIVERT; *esp* : to draw (the attention or mind) to a

different object **2** : to stir up or confuse with conflicting emotions or motives : HARASS — **dis·trac·tion** \-'trak-shən\ *n*

dis·trait \di-'strā\ *adj* : ABSENTMINDED, DISTRAUGHT

dis·traught \dis-'trot\ *adj* : PERPLEXED, CONFUSED; *also* : CRAZED

¹dis·tress \dis-'tres\ *n* **1** : suffering of body or mind : PAIN, ANGUISH **2** : TROUBLE, MISFORTUNE **3** : a condition of danger or desperate need — **dis·tress·ful** *adj*

²distress *vb* **1** : to subject to great strain or difficulties **2** : UPSET

dis·trib·ute \dis-'trib-yət\ *vb* **1** : to divide among several or many : APPORTION **2** : to spread out : SCATTER; *also* : DELIVER **3** : CLASSIFY **4** : to market in a particular area usu. as a wholesaler — **dis·tri·bu·tion** \ˌdis-trə-'byü-shən\ *n* — **dis·trib·u·tor** \dis-'trib-yət-ər\ *n*

dis·trict \'dis-(ˌ)trikt\ *n* **1** : a fixed territorial division (as for administrative or electoral purposes) **2** : an area, region, or section with a distinguishing character

district attorney *n* : the prosecuting attorney for a state or federal government

¹dis·trust \dis-'trəst\ *vb* : to feel no confidence in : SUSPECT

²distrust *n* : a lack of trust or confidence : SUSPICION, WARINESS — **dis·trust·ful** *adj* — **dis·trust·ful·ly** *adv*

dis·turb \dis-'tərb\ *vb* **1** : to interfere with : INTERRUPT **2** : to alter the position or arrangement of **3** : to destroy the tranquillity or composure of : make uneasy **4** : to throw into disorder **5** : INCONVENIENCE — **dis·tur·bance** \-'tər-bəns\ *n* — **dis·turb·er** *n*

dis·turbed *adj* : showing symptoms of mental or emotional illness

dis·unite \ˌdis-yü-'nīt\ *vb* : DIVIDE, SEPARATE

dis·uni·ty \dis-'yü-nət-ē\ *n* : lack of unity; *esp* : DISSENSION

dis·use \-'yüs\ *n* : a cessation of use or practice

ditch \'dich\ *n* : a trench dug in the earth

dith·er \'dith-ər\ *n* : a highly nervous, excited, or agitated state

dit·to \'dit-ō\ *n* **1** : the same or more of the same : ANOTHER — used to avoid repeating a word ⟨lost: one book (new); ~ (old)⟩ **2** : a mark composed of a pair of inverted commas or apostrophes used as a symbol for the word *ditto*

dit·ty \'dit-ē\ *n* : a short simple song

di·uret·ic \ˌdī-yə-'ret-ik\ *adj* : tending to increase urine flow — **diuretic** *n*

di·ur·nal \dī-'ərn-ᵊl\ *adj* **1** : DAILY **2** : of, relating to, or occurring in the daytime

di·va \'dē-və\ *n, pl* **divas** or **di·ve** \-ˌvā\ : PRIMA DONNA

di·va·gate \'dī-və-ˌgāt\ *vb* **1** : to wander about **2** : DIVERGE — **di·va·ga·tion** \ˌdī-və-'gā-shən\ *n*

di·van \'dī-ˌvan\ *n* : COUCH, SOFA

¹dive \'dīv\ *vb* **dived** or **dove** \'dōv\ **dived**; **div·ing** **1** : to plunge into water headfirst **2** : SUBMERGE **3** : to descend or fall precipitously **4** : to descend in an airplane at a steep angle with or without power **5** : to plunge into some matter or activity **6** : DART, LUNGE — **div·er** *n*

²dive *n* **1** : the act or an instance of

diving 2 : a sharp decline 3 : a disreputable bar or place of amusement

di·verge \də-'vərj, dī-\ vb 1 : to move or extend in different directions from a common point : draw apart 2 : to differ in character, form, or opinion 3 : DEVIATE 4 : DEFLECT — di·ver·gence n — di·ver·gent adj

di·vers \'dī-vərz\ adj : VARIOUS

di·verse \dī-'vərs, də-\ adj 1 : UNLIKE 2 : having various forms or qualities ⟨the ~ nature of man⟩ — di·verse·ly adv

di·ver·si·fy \də-'vər-sə-,fī, dī-\ vb : to make different or various in form or quality — di·ver·si·fi·ca·tion \-,vər-sə-fə-'kā-shən\ n

di·ver·sion \-'vər-zhən\ n 1 : a turning aside from a course, activity, or use : DEVIATION 2 : something that diverts or amuses : PASTIME

di·ver·si·ty \-'vər-sət-ē\ n 1 : the condition of being different or having differences : VARIETY 2 : an instance or a point of difference

di·vert \-'vərt\ vb 1 : to turn from a course or purpose : DEFLECT, DEVIATE 2 : DISTRACT 3 : ENTERTAIN, AMUSE

di·vest \dī-'vest, də-\ vb 1 : to strip esp. of clothing, ornament, or equipment 2 : to deprive or dispossess esp. of property, authority, or rights

1di·vide \də-'vīd\ vb 1 : SEPARATE; also : CLASSIFY 2 : CLEAVE, PART 3 : DISTRIBUTE, APPORTION 4 : to possess or make use of in common : share in ⟨~ the blame⟩ 5 : to cause to be separate, distinct, or apart from one another 6 : to separate into opposing sides or parties 7 : to mark divisions on 8 : to subject to mathematical division 9 : to branch out

2divide n : WATERSHED

div·i·dend \'div-ə-,dend\ n 1 : a sum or amount to be divided and distributed; also : an individual share of such a sum 2 : BONUS 3 : a number to be divided by another

di·vid·ers \də-'vīd-ərz\ n pl : COMPASSES

div·i·na·tion \,div-ə-'nā-shən\ n 1 : the art or practice that seeks to foresee or foretell future events or discover hidden knowledge usu. by the study of omens or by the aid of supernatural powers 2 : unusual insight or intuitive perception

1di·vine \də-'vīn\ adj 1 : of, relating to, or being deity 2 : supremely good : SUPERB; also : HEAVENLY — di·vine·ly adv

2divine n 1 : CLERGYMAN 2 : THEOLOGIAN

3divine vb 1 : INFER, CONJECTURE 2 : PROPHESY — di·vin·er n

di·vin·i·ty \də-'vin-ət-ē\ n 1 : the quality or state of being divine 2 : a divine being; esp : GOD 3 : THEOLOGY

di·vis·i·ble \də-'viz-ə-bəl\ adj : capable of being divided

di·vi·sion \də-'vizh-ən\ n 1 : DISTRIBUTION, SEPARATION 2 : one of the parts, sections, or groupings into which a whole is divided 3 : a large self-contained military unit 4 : a naval unit or subdivision 5 : an administrative or operating unit of a governmental,

business, or educational organization 6 : something that divides or separates 7 : DISAGREEMENT, DISUNITY 8 : the process of finding how many times one number or quantity is contained in another — di·vi·sion·al adj

di·vi·sive \də-'vī-siv\ adj : creating disunity or dissension — di·vi·sive·ly adv — di·vi·sive·ness n

di·vi·sor \də-'vī-zər\ n : the number by which a dividend is divided

di·vorce \də-'vōrs\ n 1 : a complete legal breaking up of a marriage 2 : SEPARATION, SEVERANCE — divorce vb — di·vorce·ment n

di·vor·cée \,də-,vōr-'sā\ n : a divorced woman

div·ot \'div-ət\ n : a piece of turf dug from a golf fairway in making a stroke

di·vulge \də-'vəlj, dī-\ vb : REVEAL, DISCLOSE

diz·zy \'diz-ē\ adj 1 : having a sensation of whirling : GIDDY 2 : causing or caused by giddiness — diz·zi·ly adv — diz·zi·ness n

do \(')dü\ vb did \(')did\ done \'dən\ do·ing \'dü-iŋ\ does \(')dəz\ 1 : to bring to pass : ACCOMPLISH 2 : ACT, BEHAVE ⟨~ as I say⟩ 3 : to be active or busy ⟨up and ~ing⟩ 4 : HAPPEN ⟨what's ~ing?⟩ 5 : to work at ⟨he does tailoring⟩ 6 : PREPARE ⟨did his homework⟩ 7 : to put in order (as by cleaning or arranging) ⟨~ the dishes⟩ 8 : DECORATE ⟨did the hall in blue⟩ 9 : to get along ⟨he does well⟩ 10 : to carry on 11 : to feel or function better ⟨could ~ with some food⟩ 12 : RENDER 13 : FINISH ⟨when he had done⟩ 14 : EXERT ⟨did my best⟩ 15 : PRODUCE ⟨did a poem⟩ 16 : to play the part of 17 : CHEAT ⟨did him out of his share⟩ 18 : TRAVERSE, TOUR 19 : TRAVEL 20 : to serve out in prison 21 : to serve the needs or purpose of : SUIT 22 : to be fitting or proper 23 — used as an auxiliary verb (1) before the subject in an interrogative sentence ⟨does he work?⟩ and after some adverbs ⟨never did he say so⟩, (2) in a negative statement ⟨I don't know⟩, (3) for emphasis ⟨he does know⟩, and (4) as a substitute for a preceding predicate ⟨he works harder than I ~⟩ — do away with 1 : to get rid of 2 : DESTROY, KILL — do by : to act toward in a specified way : TREAT ⟨did right by her⟩ — do for : to bring about the death or ruin of ⟨he's done for if you don't help⟩

dob·bin \'däb-ən\ n 1 : a farm horse 2 : a quiet plodding horse

do·cent \'dōs-°nt, dō(t)-'sent\ n : TEACHER, LECTURER

doc·ile \'däs-əl\ adj [L docilis teachable, fr docēre to teach] : easily taught, led, or managed : TRACTABLE — do·cil·i·ty \dä-'sil-ət-ē\ n

1dock \'däk\ n : a weedy herb related to buckwheat

2dock vb 1 : to cut off the end of : cut short 2 : to take away a part of : deduct from ⟨~ a man's wages⟩

3dock n 1 : an artificial basin to receive ships 2 : a slip between two piers to receive ships 3 : a wharf or platform for loading or unloading materials

4dock vb : to bring or come into dock

⁵dock n : the place in a court where a prisoner stands or sits during trial

dock·age \-ij\ n : the provision or use of a dock; also : the charge for using a dock

dock·et \'däk-ət\ n 1 : a formal abridged record of the proceedings in a legal action; also : a register of such records **2** : a list of legal causes to be tried **3** : a calendar of matters to be acted on : AGENDA **4** : a label attached to a parcel containing identification or directions — **docket** vb

dock·hand \'däk-,hand\ n : LONGSHOREMAN

dock·yard \'däk-,yärd\ n : a storage place for naval supplies or materials used in building ships

¹doc·tor \'däk-tər\ n 1 : a person holding one of the highest academic degrees (as a PhD) conferred by a university **2** : one skilled in healing arts; esp : an academically and legally qualified physician, surgeon, dentist, or veterinarian — **doc·tor·al** \-t(ə-)rəl\ adj

²doctor vb **1** : to give medical treatment to **2** : to practice medicine **3** : REPAIR **4** : to adapt or modify for a desired end **5** : to alter deceptively

doc·tor·ate \'däk-t(ə-)rət\ n : the degree, title, or rank of a doctor

doc·tri·naire \,däk-trə-'naer\ n : one who attempts to put an abstract theory into effect without regard to practical difficulties — **doctrinaire** adj

doc·trine \'däk-trən\ n 1 : something that is taught **2** : DOGMA, TENET — **doc·tri·nal** \-trən-ᵊl\ adj

doc·u·ment \'däk-yə-mənt\ n : a paper that furnishes information, proof, or support of something else — **doc·u·ment** \-,ment\ vb — **doc·u·men·ta·tion** \,däk-yə-mən-'tā-shən\ n

doc·u·men·ta·ry \,däk-yə-'men-t(ə-)rē\ adj 1 : of or relating to documents **2** : giving a factual presentation in artistic form ⟨a ~ movie⟩ — **documentary** n

dod·der \'däd-ər\ vb : to become feeble and shaky usu. from age

¹dodge \'däj\ vb 1 : to move suddenly aside; also : to avoid or evade by so doing **2** : to avoid by trickery or evasion

²dodge n 1 : an act of evading by sudden bodily movement **2** : an artful device to evade, deceive, or trick **3** : TECHNIQUE, METHOD

do·do \'dōd-ō\ n, pl **-does** or **-dos** **1** : a heavy flightless extinct bird related to the pigeons but larger than a turkey and formerly found on some of the islands of the Indian ocean **2** : one hopelessly behind the times

doe \'dō\ n : an adult female deer; also : the female of a mammal of which the male is called buck — **doe·skin** \-,skin\ n

doff \'däf\ vb 1 : to take off ⟨~ed his clothes⟩; esp : to take off or lift up ⟨he ~ed his hat⟩ **2** : to rid oneself of

¹dog \'dóg\ n 1 : a flesh-eating domestic mammal related to the wolves; esp : a male of this animal **2** : a worthless fellow **3** : FELLOW, CHAP ⟨a gay ~⟩ **4** : a mechanical device for holding something **5** : affected stylishness or dignity ⟨put on the ~⟩ **6** pl : RUIN ⟨gone to the ~s⟩

²dog vb **dogged; dog·ging 1** : to hunt or track like a hound **2** : to worry as if by dogs : HOUND

dog·bane \-,bān\ n : any of a genus of mostly poisonous herbs with milky juice and often showy flowers

dog·cart \-,kärt\ n : a light one-horse carriage with two seats back to back

dog·catch·er \-,kach-ər, -,kech-\ n : a community official assigned to catch and dispose of stray dogs

doge \'dōj\ n : the chief magistrate in the republics of Venice and Genoa

dog-ear \'dóg-,iər\ n : the turned-down corner of a leaf of a book — **dog-eared** adj

dog·fight \-,fīt\ n : a fight between two or more fighter planes usu. at close quarters

dog·fish \-,fish\ n : any of various small sharks

dog·ged \'dóg-əd\ adj : stubbornly determined : TENACIOUS — **dog·ged·ly** adv — **dog·ged·ness** n

dog·ger·el \-(ə-)rəl\ n : verse that is loosely styled and irregular in measure esp. for comic effect

dog·house \'dóg-,haús\ n : a shelter for a dog — **in the doghouse** : in a state of disfavor

dog·ma \'dóg-mə\ n 1 : a tenet or code of tenets **2** : a doctrine or body of doctrines formally proclaimed by a church

dog·ma·tism \-,tiz-əm\ n : positiveness in stating matters of opinion esp. when unwarranted or arrogant — **dog·mat·ic** \dóg-'mat-ik\ adj — **dog·mat·i·cal·ly** adv

dog·trot \'dóg-,trät\ n : a gentle trot — **dogtrot** vb

doi·ly \'dói-lē\ n : a small often decorative mat

do·ings \'dü-iŋz\ n pl : ACTS, DEEDS, EVENTS

dol·drums \'dōl-drəmz, 'däl-\ n pl **1** : a spell of listlessness or despondency **2** : a part of the ocean near the equator abounding in calms **3** : a state of inactivity, stagnation, or slump ⟨business is in the ~⟩

¹dole \'dōl\ n 1 : a distribution esp. of food, money, or clothing to the needy; also : something so distributed **2** : a grant of government funds to the unemployed

²dole vb **1** : to give or distribute as a charity **2** : to give in small portions : PARCEL ⟨~ out food⟩

dole·ful \-fəl\ adj : full of grief : SAD — **dole·ful·ly** adv

doll \'däl, 'dól\ n 1 : a small figure of a human being used esp. as a child's plaything **2** : a pretty but sometimes empty-headed young woman

dol·lar \'däl-ər\ n 1 : a basic monetary unit; esp : a U.S. silver coin of the legal value of 100 cents — see MONEY table **2** : a coin, note, or token representing one dollar

dol·lop \'däl-əp\ n : LUMP, BLOB

dol·ly \'däl-ē\ n : a small wheeled truck used in moving heavy loads; also : a wheeled platform for a television or movie camera

dol·men \'dōl-mən, 'däl-\ n : a prehistoric monument consisting of two or more upright stones supporting a horizontal stone slab

do·lor \'dō-lər, 'däl-ər\ n : mental suffering or anguish : SORROW — **do·lor·ous** adj — **do·lor·ous·ly** adv — **do·lor·ous·ness** n

dol·phin \'däl-fən\ n : a sea mammal related to the whales

dolt \'dōlt\ n : a stupid fellow — **dolt·ish** adj

-dom \dəm\ n suffix 1 : dignity : office ⟨duke**dom**⟩ 2 : realm : jurisdiction ⟨king**dom**⟩ 3 : geographical area 4 : state or fact of being ⟨free**dom**⟩ 5 : those having a (specified) office, occupation, interest, or character ⟨official**dom**⟩

do·main \dō-'mān\ n 1 : complete and absolute ownership of land 2 : land completely owned 3 : a territory over which dominion is exercised 4 : a sphere of influence or action ⟨the ~ of science⟩

dome \'dōm\ n : a large hemispherical roof or ceiling

1do·mes·tic \də-'mes-tik\ adj 1 : of or relating to the household or the family 2 : relating and limited to one's own country or the country under consideration 3 : INDIGENOUS 4 : living near or about the habitations of man 5 : TAME, DOMESTICATED 6 : devoted to home duties and pleasures — **do·mes·ti·cal·ly** adv

2domestic n : a household servant

do·mes·ti·cate \də-'mes-ti-ˌkāt\ vb : to adapt to life in association with and to the use of man ⟨the dog was domesticated in prehistoric times⟩ — **do·mes·ti·ca·tion** \-ˌmes-ti-'kā-shən\ n

do·mes·tic·i·ty \ˌdō-ˌmes-'tis-ət-ē, də-\ n 1 : the quality or state of being domestic or domesticated 2 : domestic activities or life

dom·i·cile \'däm-ə-ˌsīl\ n : a dwelling place : ABODE, HOME, RESIDENCE — **domicile** vb — **dom·i·cil·i·ary** \ˌdäm-ə-'sil-ē-ˌer-ē\ adj

dom·i·nance \'däm-ə-nəns\ n : AUTHORITY, CONTROL — **dom·i·nant** adj

dom·i·nate \-ˌnāt\ vb 1 : RULE, CONTROL 2 : to have a commanding position or controlling power over 3 : to rise high above in a position suggesting power to dominate ⟨a mountain range dominated by a single peak⟩

dom·i·na·tion \ˌdäm-ə-'nā-shən\ n 1 : supremacy or preeminence over another 2 : exercise of mastery or preponderant influence

dom·i·neer \ˌdäm-ə-'niər\ vb 1 : to rule in an arrogant manner 2 : to be overbearing

dom·i·nie \'däm-ə-nē, 'dō-mə-\ n 1 chiefly Scot : PEDAGOGUE 2 : CLERGYMAN

do·min·ion \də-'min-yən\ n 1 : supreme authority : SOVEREIGNTY 2 : DOMAIN 3 often cap : a self-governing nation of the British Commonwealth

dom·i·no \'däm-ə-ˌnō\ n, pl **-noes** or **-nos** 1 : a long loose hooded cloak usu. worn with a half mask as a masquerade costume 2 : a half mask worn with a masquerade costume 3 : a person wearing a domino 4 : a flat rectangular block used as a piece in a game ⟨dominoes⟩

1don \'dän\ n [Sp, fr. L dominus lord, master] 1 : a Spanish nobleman or gentleman—used as a title prefixed to the Christian name 2 : a head, tutor, or fellow in an English university

2don vb donned; **don·ning** : to put on (as clothes)

do·ña \'dō-nyə\ n : a Spanish woman of rank—used as a title prefixed to the Christian name

do·nate \'dō-ˌnāt\ vb 1 : to make a gift of : CONTRIBUTE 2 : to make a donation

do·na·tion \dō-'nā-shən\ n 1 : the action of making a gift esp. to a charity 2 : a free contribution : GIFT

1done \'dən\ past part of DO

2done adj 1 : conformable to social convention 2 : gone by : OVER ⟨when day is ~⟩ 3 : doomed to failure, defeat, or death ⟨industry is ~ in this area⟩ 4 : cooked sufficiently ⟨the meat is ~⟩

don·key \'däŋ-kē, 'dəŋ-\ n 1 : the domestic ass 2 : a stupid or obstinate person

don·ny·brook \'dän-ē-ˌbrůk\ n, often cap : an uproarious brawl

do·nor \'dō-nər\ n : one that gives, donates, or presents

doo·dad \'dü-ˌdad\ n : a small article whose common name is unknown or forgotten

doo·dle \'düd-ˀl\ vb : to draw or scribble aimlessly while occupied with something else — **doodle** n — **doo·dler** \-(ə-)lər\ n

doom \'düm\ n 1 : JUDGMENT, SENTENCE; esp : a judicial condemnation or sentence 2 : DESTINY, FATE 3 : RUIN, DEATH — **doom** vb

dooms·day \'dümz-ˌdā\ n : the day of the Last Judgment

door \'dōr\ n 1 : the movable frame by which a passageway for entrance can be opened or closed 2 : a passage for entrance 3 : a means of access ⟨the ~ to success⟩

door·jamb \-ˌjam\ n : an upright piece forming the side of a door opening

door·keep·er \-ˌkē-pər\ n : one that tends a door

door·knob \-ˌnäb\ n : a knob that when turned releases a door latch

door·man \-ˌman\ n 1 : DOORKEEPER 2 : one who tends a door (as of a hotel) and assists people by calling taxis and helping them in and out of cars

door·mat \-ˌmat\ n : a mat placed before or inside a door for wiping dirt from the shoes

door·plate \-ˌplāt\ n : a plate or plaque bearing a name (as of a resident) on a door

door·step \-ˌstep\ n : a step or series of steps before an outer door

door·way \-ˌwā\ n 1 : the opening that a door closes 2 : a means of gaining access

door·yard \-ˌyärd\ n : a yard outside the door of a house

1dope \'dōp\ n 1 : a preparation for giving a desired quality 2 : a narcotic preparation 3 : a stupid person 4 : INFORMATION

2dope vb 1 : to treat with dope; esp : to give a narcotic to 2 slang : PREDICT, FIGURE ⟨~ out which team will win⟩

dorm \'dȯrm\ n : DORMITORY

dor·mant \'dȯr-mənt\ adj : INACTIVE; esp : not actively growing or functioning ⟨~ buds⟩ — **dor·man·cy** n

dor·mer \-mər\ n : a window (dormer window) built upright in a sloping roof

dor·mi·to·ry \'dȯr-mə-ˌtōr-ē\ n 1 : a

room for sleeping; *esp* **:** a large room containing a number of beds **2 :** a residence hall providing sleeping rooms

dor·mouse \'dȯr-ˌmaús\ *n, pl* **dor·mice** \-ˌmīs\ **:** an Old World squirrellike rodent

dor·sal \'dȯr-səl\ *adj* **:** of, relating to, or located near or on the surface of the body that in man is the back but in most other animals is the upper surface — **dor·sal·ly** *adv*

do·ry \'dȯr-ē\ *n* **:** a flat-bottomed boat with flaring sides

1dose \'dōs\ *n* **1 :** a quantity (as of medicine) to be taken or administered at one time **2 :** the quantity of radiation administered or absorbed — **dos·age** \'dō-sij\ *n*

2dose *vb* **1 :** to give medicine to **2 :** to give in doses

dos·sier \'dȯs-ˌyā\ *n* **:** a file of papers containing a detailed report or detailed information.

1dot \'dät\ *n* **1 :** a small spot **:** SPECK **2 :** a small round mark made with or as if with a pen **3 :** a precise point in time or space ⟨be here on the ∼⟩

2dot *vb* **dot·ted; dot·ting 1 :** to mark with a dot ⟨∼ an *i*⟩ **2 :** to cover with or as if with dots ⟨a lake *dotted* with boats⟩

dot·age \'dōt-ij\ *n* **:** feebleness of mind esp. in old age **:** SENILITY

dot·ard \-ərd\ *n* **:** a person in dotage

dote \'dōt\ *vb* **1 :** to be feebleminded esp. from old age **2 :** to show excessive or foolish affection or fondness ⟨*doted* on her only niece⟩ — **dot·ing** *adj*

dot·tle \'dät-ᵊl\ *n* **:** unburned and partially burned tobacco caked in the bowl of a pipe

1dou·ble \'dəb-əl\ *adj* **1 :** TWOFOLD, DUAL **2 :** consisting of two members or parts **3 :** being twice as great or as many **4 :** folded in two **5 :** having more than one whorl of petals ⟨∼ roses⟩

2double *n* **1 :** something twice another in size, strength, speed, quantity, or value **2 :** a hit in baseball that enables the batter to reach second base **3 :** COUNTERPART, DUPLICATE; *esp* **:** a person who closely resembles another **4 :** UNDERSTUDY, SUBSTITUTE **5 :** a sharp turn **:** REVERSAL **6 :** FOLD **7 :** a combined bet placed on two different contests **8** *pl* **:** a tennis match with two players on each side **9 :** an act of doubling in a card game

3double *adv* **1 :** DOUBLY **2 :** two together ⟨sleep ∼⟩

4double *vb* **1 :** to make, be, or become twice as great or as many **2 :** to make a call in bridge that increases the trick values and penalties of (an opponent's bid) **3 :** FOLD **4 :** CLENCH **5 :** BEND **6 :** to sail around (as a cape) by reversing direction **7 :** to take the place of another **8 :** to hit a double **9 :** to turn sharply and suddenly; *esp* **:** to turn back on one's course

dou·ble-cross \ˌdəb-əl-'krȯs\ *vb* **:** to deceive by double-dealing — **dou·ble-cross·er** *n*

dou·ble-deal·ing \-'dē-liŋ\ *n* **:** action contradictory to a professed attitude **:** DUPLICITY — **dou·ble-deal·er** *n* — **double-dealing** *adj*

dou·ble-deck·er \-'dek-ər\ *n* **1 :** something (as a ship or bed) having two decks **2 :** a sandwich having two layers

dou·ble en·ten·dre \ˌdüb-(ə-)ˌläⁿ-

'täⁿdr\, ˌdəb-\ *n* **:** a word or expression capable of two interpretations one of which is usu. risqué

dou·ble-head·er \ˌdəb-əl-'hed-ər\ *n* **:** two games played consecutively on the same day by the same teams or by different pairs of teams

dou·blet \'dəb-lət\ *n* **1 :** a man's close-fitting jacket worn in Europe esp. in the 16th century **2 :** one of two similar or identical things

dou·ble-talk \'dəb-əl-ˌtȯk\ *n* **:** language that appears to be meaningful but in fact is a mixture of sense and nonsense

dou·bloon \ˌdə-'blün\ *n* **:** a former gold coin of Spain and Spanish America

dou·bly \'dəb-lē\ *adv* **1 :** to twice the degree **2 :** in a twofold manner

1doubt \'daút\ *vb* **1 :** to be uncertain about **2 :** to lack confidence in **:** DISTRUST, FEAR **3 :** to consider unlikely

2doubt *n* **1 :** uncertainty of belief or opinion **2 :** the condition of being uncertain ⟨the outcome was in ∼⟩ **3 :** DISTRUST **4 :** an inclination not to believe or accept

doubt·ful \-fəl\ *adj* **1 :** not clear or certain as to fact **2 :** QUESTIONABLE **3 :** UNDECIDED **4 :** not certain in outcome ⟨a ∼ battle⟩ — **doubt·ful·ly** *adv*

1doubt·less \-ləs\ *adv* **1 :** without doubt **2 :** PROBABLY

2doubtless *adj* **:** free from doubt **:** CERTAIN

douche \'düsh\ *n* **:** a jet of fluid (as water) directed against a part or into a cavity of the body; *also* **:** a cleansing with a douche

dough \'dō\ *n* **1 :** a mixture of flour and other ingredients stiff enough to knead or roll **2 :** something resembling dough esp. in consistency **3 :** MONEY — **doughy** *adj*

dough·boy \-ˌbȯi\ *n* **:** an infantry soldier

dough·nut \-(ˌ)nət\ *n* **:** a small usu. ring-shaped cake fried in fat

dough·ty \'daút-ē\ *adj* **:** ABLE, STRONG, VALIANT

dour \'daú(ə)r, 'dúr\ *adj* **1 :** STERN, HARSH **2 :** GLOOMY, SULLEN

douse \'daús\ *vb* **1 :** to plunge into water **2 :** DRENCH **3 :** EXTINGUISH

1dove \'dəv\ *n* **:** PIGEON; *esp* **:** a small wild pigeon — **dove·cote** \-ˌkōt\ or **dove·cot** \-ˌkät\ *n*

2dove \'dōv\ *past of* DIVE

1dove·tail \'dəv-ˌtāl\ *n* **:** something that resembles a dove's tail; *esp* **:** a flaring tenon and a mortise into which it fits tightly

2dovetail *vb* **1 :** to join (as timbers) by means of dovetails **2 :** to fit skillfully together to form a whole ⟨our plans ∼ perfectly⟩

dow·a·ger \'daú-i-jər\ *n* **1 :** a widow owning property or a title received from her deceased husband **2 :** a dignified elderly woman

dowdy \'daúd-ē\ *adj* **:** lacking neatness and charm **:** SHABBY, UNTIDY; *also* **:** lacking smartness

dow·el \'daú(-ə)l\ *n* **:** a pin used for fastening together 2 pieces (as of board) — **dowel** *vb*

1dow·er \'daú(-ə)r\ *n* **1 :** the part of a deceased husband's real estate which the law gives for life to his widow **2 :** DOWRY

2dower *vb* **:** to supply with a dower or dowry **:** ENDOW

¹**down** \'daŭn\ *n* : a rolling usu. treeless upland with sparse soil ⟨the ~s of southern England⟩

²**down** *adv* 1 : toward or in a lower physical position 2 : to a lying or sitting position 3 : toward or to the ground, floor, or bottom 4 : in cash ⟨paid $5 ~⟩ 5 : on paper ⟨put ~ what he says⟩ 6 : to a source or place of concealment ⟨tracked him ~⟩ 7 : FULLY, COMPLETELY 8 : in a direction that is the opposite of up 9 : SOUTH 10 : toward or in the center of a city; *also* : away from a center 11 : to or in a lower or worse condition or status 12 : from a past time ⟨heirlooms handed ~⟩ 13 : to or in a state of less activity 14 : from a thinner to a thicker consistency

³**down** *adj* 1 : occupying a low position; *esp* : lying on the ground 2 : directed or going downward 3 : being at a lower level ⟨sales were ~⟩ 4 : being in a state of reduced or low activity 5 : DEPRESSED, DEJECTED 6 : SICK ⟨~ with a cold⟩ 7 : having a low opinion or dislike ⟨~ on the boy⟩ 8 : FINISHED, DONE 9 : being the part of a price paid at the time of purchase or delivery ⟨a ~ payment⟩

⁴**down** *prep* : in a descending direction in, on, along, or through : to or toward the lower end or bottom of

⁵**down** *n* 1 : a low or falling period (as in activity, emotional life, or fortunes) ⟨the ups and ~s of business⟩ 2 : one of a series of attempts to advance a football

⁶**down** *vb* : to go or cause to go or come down

⁷**down** *n* 1 : a covering of soft fluffy feathers; *also* : such feathers 2 : a downlike covering or material

down·beat \'daŭn-,bēt\ *n* : the downward stroke of a conductor indicating the principally accented note of a measure of music

down·cast \'daŭn-,kast\ *adj* 1 : DEJECTED ⟨a ~ manner⟩ 2 : directed down ⟨a ~ glance⟩

down·fall \-,fol\ *n* 1 : a sudden fall (as from high rank) : RUIN 2 : a fall (as of rain) esp. when sudden or heavy 3 : something that causes a downfall — **down·fal·len** \-,fo-lən\ *adj*

¹**down·grade** \-,grād\ *n* 1 : a downward grade or slope (as of a road) 2 : a decline toward a worse condition

²**downgrade** *vb* : to lower in grade, rank, position, or status

down·heart·ed \-'härt-əd\ *adj* : DEJECTED

down·hill \-'hil\ *adv* : toward the bottom of a hill

down·pour \-,pōr\ *n* : a heavy rain

down·range \-'rānj\ *adv (or adj)* : toward the target area of a firing range

¹**down·right** \-,rīt\ *adv* : THOROUGHLY ⟨~ mean⟩

²**downright** *adj* 1 : ABSOLUTE, THOROUGH ⟨a ~ lie⟩ 2 : PLAIN, BLUNT ⟨a ~ man⟩

down·stage \'daŭn-'stāj\ *adv (or adj)* : toward or at the front of a theatrical stage

down·stairs \-'staərz\ *adv* : on or to a lower floor and, the main or ground floor — **downstairs** *adj or n*

down·stream \-'strēm\ *adv (or adj)* : in the direction of flow of a stream

down·stroke \-,strōk\ *n* : a stroke made in a downward direction

down·swing \-,swiŋ\ *n* 1 : a swing downward 2 : DOWNTURN

down-to-earth *adj* : PRACTICAL, REALISTIC

¹**down·town** \'daŭn-'taŭn\ *adv* : to, toward, or in the lower part or business center of a town or city

²**downtown** *n* : an urban business center — **downtown** *adj*

down·trod·den \-'träd-ᵊn\ *adj* : abused by superior power : OPPRESSED

¹**down·turn** \-,tərn\ *n* 1 : a turning downward 2 : a decline esp. in business activity

¹**down·ward** \-wərd\ *also* **down·wards** \-wərdz\ *adv* 1 : from a higher to a lower place or condition 2 : from an earlier time 3 : from an ancestor or predecessor

²**downward** *adj* : directed toward or situated in a lower place or condition : DESCENDING

down·wind \'daŭn-'wind\ *adv (or adj)* : in the direction toward which the wind is blowing

downy \'daŭ-nē\ *adj* : resembling or covered with down

dow·ry \'daŭ(ə)r-ē\ *n* : the property that a woman brings to her husband in marriage

dowse \'daŭz\ *vb* : to use a divining rod esp. to find water — **dows·er** *n*

dox·ol·o·gy \däk-'säl-ə-jē\ *n* : a usu. short hymn of praise to God

doze \'dōz\ *vb* : to sleep lightly — **doze** *n*

doz·en \'dəz-ᵊn\ *n, pl* **dozens** *or* **dozen** [OF *dozaine*, fr. *doze* twelve, fr. L *duodecim*, fr. *duo* two + *decem* ten] : a group of twelve — **doz·enth** \-ᵊnth\ *adj*

drab \'drab\ *adj* 1 : being of a light olive-brown color 2 : DULL, MONOTONOUS, CHEERLESS

drach·ma \'drak-mə\ *n, pl* **-mas** *or* **-mae** \-(,)mē\ *or* **-mai** \-,mī\ — see MONEY table

¹**draft** \'draft, 'dräft\ *n* 1 : the act of drawing or hauling : the thing or amount that is drawn 2 : the force required to pull an implement 3 : the act or an instance of drinking or inhaling; *also* : the portion drunk or inhaled in one such act 4 : DOSE, POTION 5 : DELINEATION, PLAN, DESIGN; *also* : a preliminary sketch, outline, or version ⟨a rough ~ of a speech⟩ 6 : the act of drawing (as from a cask); *also* : a portion of liquid so drawn 7 : the depth of water a ship draws esp. when loaded 8 : the selection of a person esp. for compulsory military service; *also* : the persons so selected 9 : an order for the payment of money drawn by one person or bank on another 10 : a heavy demand : STRAIN 11 : a current of air; *also* : a device to regulate air supply (as to a fire) — **on draft** : ready to be drawn from a receptacle ⟨beer on draft⟩

²**draft** *adj* 1 : used for drawing loads ⟨~ animals⟩ 2 : constituting a preliminary or tentative version, sketch, or

outline ⟨a ~ treaty⟩ **3 :** being on draft; *also :* DRAWN ⟨~ beer⟩

³draft *vb* **1 :** to select usu. on a compulsory basis; *esp :* to conscript for military service **2 :** to draw the preliminary sketch, version, or plan of **3 :** COMPOSE, PREPARE **:** to draw up, off, or away

draft·ee \draf-'tē, dräf-\ *n :* a person who is drafted esp. into the armed forces

drafts·man \'drafts-mən, 'dräfts-\ *n* **:** one who draws plans (as for buildings or machinery)

drafty *adj :* relating to or exposed to a draft ⟨a ~ hall⟩

¹drag \'drag\ *n* **1 :** something (as a harrow, grapnel, sledge, or clog) that is dragged along over a surface **2 :** something that hinders progress **3 :** the act or an instance of dragging

²drag *vb* dragged; drag·ging **1 :** HAUL **2 :** to move with painful slowness or difficulty **3 :** to force into or out of some situation, condition, or course of action **4 :** to pass (time) in pain or tedium **5 :** PROTRACT ⟨~ a story out⟩ **6 :** to hang or lag behind **7 :** to trail along on the ground **8 :** to explore, search, or fish with a drag **9 :** DRAW, PUFF ⟨~ on a cigarette⟩

drag·net \-,net\ *n* **1 :** NET, TRAWL **2 :** a network of planned actions for pursuing and catching ⟨a police ~⟩

drag·o·man \'drag-ə-mən\ *n, pl* -mans *or* -men \-mən\ **:** an interpreter esp. of Arabic employed esp. in the Near East

drag·on \'drag-ən\ *n* **:** a fabulous animal usu. represented as a huge winged scaly serpent with a crested head and large claws

drag·on·fly \-,flī\ *n* **:** any of a group of large harmless 4-winged insects

¹dra·goon \drə-'gün\ *n* **:** a heavily armed mounted soldier

²dragoon *vb* **:** to force or attempt to force into submission by violent measures

¹drain \'drān\ *vb* **1 :** to draw off or flow off gradually or completely **2 :** to exhaust physically or emotionally **3 :** to make or become gradually dry or empty **4 :** to carry away the surface water of **:** discharge surface or surplus water **5 :** EMPTY, EXHAUST — **drain·er** *n*

²drain *n* **1 :** a means (as a channel or sewer) of draining **2 :** the act of draining **3 :** DEPLETION **4 :** BURDEN, STRAIN ⟨a ~ on his savings⟩

drain·age \-ij\ *n* **1 :** the act or process of draining; *also :* something that is drained off **2 :** a means for draining **:** DRAIN, SEWER **3 :** an area drained

drain·pipe \-,pīp\ *n* **:** a pipe for drainage

drake \'drāk\ *n* **:** a male duck

dram \'dram\ *n* **1 :** an avoirdupois weight equal to 1/16 ounce **2 :** an apothecaries' weight equal to 1/8 ounce **3 :** a measure of liquid capacity equal to 1/8 ounce **4 :** a small drink

dra·ma \'dräm-ə, 'dram-\ *n* [Gk *drama*, *drama*, lit., action, fr. *dran* to do, act] **1 :** a literary composition designed for theatrical presentation **2 :** PLAYS **3 :** a series of events involving conflicting forces — **dra·mat·ic** \drə-'mat-ik\ *adj* — **dra·mat·i·cal·ly** *adv* — **dram·a·tist** \'dram-ət-əst\ *n*

dram·a·tize \'dram-ə-,tīz\ *vb* **1 :** to adapt for or be suitable for theatrical presentation **2 :** to present or represent

in a dramatic manner — **dram·a·ti·za·tion** \,dram-ət-ə-'zā-shən\ *n*

drank *past of* DRINK

¹drape \'drāp\ *vb* **1 :** to cover or adorn with or as if with folds of cloth **2 :** to cause to hang or stretch out loosely or carelessly **3 :** to arrange or become arranged in flowing lines or folds

²drape *n* **1 :** CURTAIN **2 :** arrangement in or of folds **3 :** the cut or hang of clothing

drap·er \'drā-pər\ *n, Brit :* a dealer in cloth and sometimes in clothing and dry goods

drap·ery \-p(ə-)rē\ *n* **1** *Brit :* DRY GOODS **2** *Brit :* the occupation of a draper **3 :** a decorative fabric esp. when hung loosely and in folds **:** HANGINGS **4 :** the draping or arranging of materials

dras·tic \'dras-tik\ *adj :* HARSH, RIGOROUS, SEVERE ⟨~ punishment⟩ — **dras·ti·cal·ly** *adv*

draught, draughts *chiefly Brit var of* DRAFT **:** CHECKERS

¹draw \'dro\ *vb* drew \'drü\ drawn \'dron\ draw·ing **1 :** HAUL, DRAG **2 :** to cause to go in a certain direction ⟨drew him aside⟩ **3 :** to move or go steadily or gradually ⟨night ~s near⟩ **4 :** ATTRACT, ENTICE **5 :** PROVOKE, ROUSE ⟨drew enemy fire⟩ **6 :** INHALE ⟨~ a deep breath⟩ **7 :** to bring or pull out **8 :** to force out from cover or possession ⟨~ trumps⟩ **9 :** to extract the essence from ⟨~ tea⟩ **10 :** EVISCERATE **11 :** to require (a specified depth) to float in **12 :** ACCUMULATE, GAIN ⟨~ing interest⟩ **13 :** to take money from a place of deposit **:** WITHDRAW **14 :** to receive regularly from a source ⟨~ a salary⟩ **15 :** to take (cards) from a stack or the dealer **16 :** to receive or take at random ⟨~ a winning number⟩ **17 :** to bend (a bow) by pulling back the string **18 :** WRINKLE, SHRINK **19 :** to change shape by or as if by pulling or stretching ⟨a face drawn with sorrow⟩ **20 :** to leave (a contest) undecided **:** TIE **21 :** DELINEATE, SKETCH **22 :** to write out in due form **:** DRAFT ⟨~ up a will⟩ **23 :** FORMULATE ⟨~ comparisons⟩ **24 :** DEDUCE **25 :** to spread or elongate (metal) by hammering or by pulling through dies **26 :** to produce or allow a draft or current of air ⟨the furnace ~s well⟩ **27 :** to swell out in a wind ⟨all sails ~ing⟩

²draw *n* **1 :** the act, process, or result of drawing **2 :** a lot or chance drawn at random **3 :** TIE **4 :** ATTRACTION

draw·back \-,bak\ *n* **:** HINDRANCE, HANDICAP

draw·bridge \-,brij\ *n* **:** a bridge made to be drawn up, down, or aside

draw·er \'dro(-ə)r\ *n* **1 :** one that draws **2 :** a sliding boxlike compartment (as in a table or desk) **3** *pl :* an undergarment for the lower part of the body

draw·ing *n* **1 :** an act or instance of drawing; *esp :* an occasion when something is decided by drawing lots **2 :** the act or art of making a figure, plan, or sketch by means of lines **3 :** SKETCH, representation made by drawing

drawing room *n* **1 :** a formal reception room **2 :** a private room on a railroad car with three berths

drawl \'drol\ *vb* **:** to speak or utter

slowly with vowels greatly prolonged — **drawl** *n*

draw-string \'drȯ-striŋ\ *n* : a string, cord, or tape for use in closing a bag or controlling fullness in garments or curtains

dray \'drā\ *n* : a strong low cart for carrying heavy loads

1dread \'dred\ *vb* 1 : to fear greatly 2 : to feel extreme reluctance to meet face to face

2dread *n* 1 : great fear esp. of some harm to come

3dread *adj* 1 : causing great fear or anxiety 2 : inspiring awe

dread-ful \-fəl\ *adj* 1 : inspiring dread or awe : FRIGHTENING 2 : extremely distasteful, unpleasant, or shocking — **dread-ful-ly** *adv*

dread-nought \-,nȯt\ *n* : a battleship with big guns all of one caliber

1dream \'drēm\ *n* 1 : a series of thoughts, images, or emotions occurring during sleep 2 : a dreamlike vision : DAYDREAM, REVERIE 3 : something notable for its beauty, excellence, or enjoyable quality 4 : IDEAL — **dream-like** *adj* — **dreamy** *adj*

2dream *vb* **dreamed** \'drēmd\ *or* **dreamt** \'dremt\ **dream-ing** \'drē-miŋ\ 1 : to have a dream of 2 : to indulge in daydreams or fantasies : pass (time) in reverie or inaction 3 : IMAGINE — **dream-er** \'drē-mər\ *n*

dream-land \-,land\ *n* : an unreal delightful country that exists in imagination or in dreams

dream-world \-,wərld\ *n* : DREAMLAND; *also* : a world of illusion or fantasy

drear \'driər\ *adj* : DREARY

dreary \'dri(ə)-rē\ *adj* 1 : DOLEFUL, SAD 2 : DISMAL, GLOOMY — **drear-i-ly** *adv*

1dredge \'drej\ *n* : a machine or ship for scooping up and removing earth or silt

2dredge *vb* : to gather or search with or as if with a dredge — **dredg-er** *n*

3dredge *vb* : to coat (food) by sprinkling (as with flour)

dregs \'dregz\ *n pl* 1 : LEES, SEDIMENT 2 : the most worthless part of something

drench \'drench\ *vb* : to wet through : SOAK

1dress \'dres\ *vb* 1 : to make or set straight : ALIGN 2 : to put clothes on : CLOTHE; *also* : to put on or wear formal or fancy clothes 3 : TRIM, EMBELLISH ⟨~ a store window⟩ 4 : to prepare for use; *esp* : BUTCHER 5 : to apply dressings or remedies to 6 : to arrange (the hair) by combing or curling 7 : to apply fertilizer to 8 : SMOOTH, FINISH ⟨~ leather⟩

2dress *n* 1 : APPAREL, CLOTHING 2 : FROCK, GOWN — **dress-mak-er** \-,mā-kər\ *n* — **dress-mak-ing** *n*

3dress *adj* : suitable for a formal occasion; *also* : requiring formal dress

dres-sage \drə-'säzh\ *n* : the execution by a horse of complex maneuvers in response to barely perceptible movements of a rider's hands, legs, and weight

1dress-er \'dres-ər\ *n* : a chest of drawers or bureau with a mirror

2dresser *n* : one that dresses

dress-ing *n* 1 : the act or process of one

who dresses 2 : a sauce or similar mixture for adding to a dish 3 : a seasoned mixture usu. used as a stuffing (as for poultry) 4 : material used to cover an injury

dressing gown *n* : a loose robe worn esp. while dressing or resting

dressy *adj* 1 : showy in dress 2 : STYLISH, SMART

drew *past of* DRAW

1drib-ble \'drib-əl\ *vb* 1 : to fall or flow in drops : TRICKLE 2 : DROOL 3 : to propel by successive slight taps or bounces

2dribble *n* 1 : a small trickling stream or flow 2 : a drizzling shower 3 : the dribbling of a ball or puck

drib-let \'drib-lət\ *n* 1 : a trifling sum or part 2 : a small amount 2 : a falling drop

dri-er *also* **dry-er** \'drī-(ə)r\ *n* 1 : a substance dissolved in paints, varnishes, or inks to speed drying 2 *usu dryer* : a device for drying

1drift \'drift\ *n* 1 : the motion or course of something drifting 2 : a mass of matter (as snow or sand) blown up by wind 3 : earth, gravel, and rock deposited by a glacier or by running water 4 : a general underlying design or tendency : MEANING — **drift-wood** \-,wùd\ *n*

2drift *vb* 1 : to float or be driven along by wind, waves, or currents 2 : to pile up under the force of the wind and water

drift-er *n* : a person without aim, ambition, or initiative

1drill \'dril\ *vb* 1 : to bore with a drill 2 : to instruct and exercise by repetition — **drill-er** *n*

2drill *n* 1 : a boring tool 2 : the training of soldiers 3 : strict training and instruction in a subject

3drill *n* : an agricultural implement for making furrows and dropping seed into them

4drill *n* : a firm cotton fabric in twill weave

drill-mas-ter \-,mas-tər\ *n* : one who drills; *esp* : an instructor in military drill

dri-ly *var of* DRYLY

1drink \'driŋk\ *vb* **drank** \'draŋk\ **drunk** \'drəŋk\ *or* **drank; drink-ing** 1 : to swallow liquid : IMBIBE 2 : ABSORB 3 : to take in through the senses ⟨~ in the beautiful scenery⟩ 4 : to give or join in a toast 5 : to drink alcoholic beverages esp. to excess — **drink-able** *adj* — **drink-er** *n*

2drink *n* 1 : BEVERAGE 2 : alcoholic liquor 3 : a draft or portion of liquid 4 : excessive consumption of alcoholic beverages

1drip \'drip\ *vb* **dripped** *or* **dript; drip-ping** 1 : to fall or let fall in drops 2 : to let fall drops of moisture or liquid ⟨a *dripping* faucet⟩ 3 : to overflow with or as if with moisture ⟨a coat *dripping* with gold braid⟩

2drip *n* 1 : a falling in drops 2 : liquid that falls, overflows, or is extruded in drops 3 : the sound made by or as if by falling drops

1drive \'drīv\ *vb* **drove** \'drōv\ **driv-en** \'driv-ən\ **driv-ing** \'drī-viŋ\ 1 : to urge, push, or force onward 2 : to direct the movement or course of 3 : to convey in a vehicle **4 :** to set or keep in motion or operation **5 :** to carry through strongly ⟨~ a bargain⟩ **6 :** FORCE, COMPEL ⟨*driven* by hunger to steal⟩ **7 :** to project, inject, or impress forcefully ⟨*drove* the lesson home⟩ **8 :** to bring into a specified condition ⟨the noise ~*s* me crazy⟩ **9 :** to produce by opening a way ⟨~ a well⟩ **10 :** to rush and press with violence **11 :** to propel an object of play (as a golf ball) by a hard blow — **driv·er** \'drī-vər\ *n*

²**drive** *n* **1 :** a trip in a carriage or automobile **2 :** a driving together of animals (as for capture or slaughter) **3 :** the guiding of logs downstream to a mill **4 :** the act of driving a ball; *also :* the flight of a ball **5 :** DRIVEWAY **6 :** a public road for driving (as in a park) **7 :** an offensive or aggressive move **8 :** an intensive campaign ⟨membership ~⟩ **9 :** the state of being hurried and under pressure **10 :** NEED, LONGING **11 :** dynamic quality **12 :** the apparatus by which motion is imparted to a machine

drive-in \'drīv-,in\ *adj* **:** accommodating patrons while they remain in their automobiles ⟨a ~ theater⟩ — **drive-in** *n*

¹**driv·el** \'driv-əl\ *vb* **-eled** *or* **-elled**; **-el·ing** *or* **-el·ling 1 :** DROOL, SLAVER **2 :** to talk or utter stupidly, carelessly, or in an infantile way — **driv·el·er** *or* **driv·el·ler** \-(ə-)lər\ *n*

²**drivel** *n archaic* **:** saliva trickling from the mouth **2 :** NONSENSE

drive·way \'drīv-,wā\ *n* **1 :** a road or way along which animals are driven **2 :** a short private road leading from the street to a house, garage, or parking lot

¹**driz·zle** \'driz-əl\ *vb* **:** to rain in very small drops

²**drizzle** *n* **:** a fine misty rain

drogue \'drōg\ *n* **:** a small attached parachute for slowing down or stabilizing something (as an astronaut's capsule in landing)

droll \'drōl\ *adj* **:** having a humorous, whimsical, or odd quality ⟨a ~ expression⟩ — **droll·ery** \-(ə-)rē\ *n* — **drol·ly** \'drō(l)-lē\ *adv*

drom·e·dary \'dräm-ə-,der-ē\ *n* **:** CAMEL; *esp* **:** a usu. speedy one-humped camel used esp. for riding

¹**drone** \'drōn\ *n* **1 :** a male honeybee **2 :** one that lives on the labors of others **:** PARASITE **3 :** a pilotless airplane or ship controlled by radio

²**drone** *vb* **:** to sound with a low dull monotonous murmuring sound **:** speak monotonously

³**drone** *n* **:** a deep monotonous sound **:** HUM

drool \'drül\ *vb* **1 :** to let liquid flow from the mouth **2 :** to talk foolishly **:** express in a sentimental or effusive manner

droop \'drüp\ *vb* **1 :** to hang or incline downward **2 :** to sink gradually **3 :** LANGUISH — **droop** *n*

¹**drop** \'dräp\ *n* **1 :** the quantity of fluid that falls in one spherical mass **2** *pl* **:** a dose of medicine measured by drops **3 :** a small quantity of drink **4 :** the smallest practical unit of liquid measure **5 :** something (as a pendant or a small round candy) that resembles a liquid drop in quantity or quality **6 :** FALL **7 :** a decline in quantity or quality **8 :** a descent by parachute

9 : the distance through which something drops

²**drop** *vb* **dropped; drop·ping 1 :** to fall or let fall in drops **2 :** to let fall ⟨~ a glove⟩ **:** LOWER ⟨*dropped* his voice⟩ **3 :** SEND ⟨~ me a note⟩ **4 :** to let go **:** DISMISS ⟨~ the subject⟩ **5 :** to knock down **:** cause to fall **6 :** to go lower **:** become less ⟨prices *dropped*⟩ **7 :** to come or go unexpectedly or informally ⟨~ in to call⟩ **8 :** to pass from one state into a less active one ⟨~ off to sleep⟩ **9 :** to move downward or with a current **10 :** QUIT ⟨*dropped* out of the race⟩

drop-kick \'dräp-'kik\ *n* **:** a kick made by dropping a football to the ground and kicking it at the moment it starts to rebound — **drop-kick** *vb*

drop·let \-lət\ *n* **:** a tiny drop

drop·out \-,aůt\ *n* **:** one who drops out (as from school) before achieving his goal

drop·per \-ər\ *n* **1 :** one that drops **2 :** a short glass tube with a rubber bulb used to measure out liquids by drops

drop·sy \'dräp-sē\ *n* **:** an abnormal accumulation of serous fluid in the body — **drop·si·cal** *adj*

dross \'dräs\ *n* **1 :** the scum that forms on the surface of a molten metal **2 :** waste matter **:** REFUSE

drought *or* **drouth** \'draůth, 'draůt\ *n* **:** a long spell of dry weather

drove \'drōv\ *n* **1 :** a group of animals driven or moving in a body **2 :** a crowd of people moving or acting together

drov·er \'drō-vər\ *n* **:** one that drives domestic animals usu. to market; *also* **:** a dealer in cattle

drown \'draůn\ *vb* **1 :** to suffocate by submersion esp. in water **2 :** to become drowned **3 :** to cover with water **:** INUNDATE **4 :** OVERCOME, OVERPOWER

drowse \'draůz\ *vb* **:** DOZE — **drowse** *n*

drow·sy \'draů-zē\ *adj* **1 :** ready to fall asleep **2 :** making one sleepy — **drows·i·ly** *adv* — **drows·i·ness** *n*

drub \'drəb\ *vb* **drubbed; drub·bing 1 :** to beat severely **:** PUMMEL, THRASH **2 :** to defeat decisively

drudge \'drəj\ *vb* **:** to do hard, menial, or monotonous work — **drudge** *n* — **drudg·ery** \-(ə-)rē\ *n*

¹**drug** \'drəg\ *n* **1 :** a substance used as or in medicine **2 :** NARCOTIC

²**drug** *vb* **drugged; drug·ging 1 :** to affect with drugs; *esp* **:** to stupefy with a narcotic

drug·gist \-əst\ *n* **:** a dealer in drugs and medicines **:** PHARMACIST

drug·store \-,stōr\ *n* **:** a retail shop where medicines and miscellaneous articles are sold

dru·id \'drü-əd\ *n, often cap* **:** one of an ancient Celtic priesthood of Gaul, Britain, and Ireland appearing in legends as magicians and wizards

¹**drum** \'drəm\ *n* **1 :** a musical percussion instrument usu. consisting of a hollow cylinder with a skin head stretched over each end that is beaten with sticks in playing **2 :** EARDRUM **3 :** the sound of a drum; *also :* a similar sound **4 :** a drum-shaped object

²**drum** *vb* **drummed; drum·ming 1 :** to beat a drum **2 :** to sound rhythmically **:** THROB, BEAT **3 :** to summon or assemble by or as if by beating a drum ⟨~ up customers⟩ **4 :** EXPEL ⟨*drummed* out of camp⟩ **5 :** to drive or force by

steady effort ⟨∼ a lesson into his head⟩ **6 :** to strike or tap repeatedly so as to produce rhythmic sounds

drum·beat \'drəm-‚bēt\ *n* **:** a stroke on a drum or its sound

drum·mer *n* **1 :** one that plays a drum **2 :** a traveling salesman

drum·stick \'drəm-‚stik\ *n* **1 :** a stick for beating a drum **2 :** the lower segment of a fowl's leg

1drunk \'drəŋk\ *adj* **1 :** having the faculties impaired by alcohol **2 :** controlled by some feeling as if under the influence of alcohol ⟨∼ with power⟩ **3 :** of, relating to, or caused by intoxication

2drunk *n* **1 :** a period of excessive drinking **2 :** a drunken person **:** DRUNKARD

drunk·ard \-ərd\ *n* **:** one who is habitually drunk

drunk·en *adj* **1 :** DRUNK **2 :** given to habitual excessive use of alcohol **3 :** of, relating to, or resulting from intoxication **4 :** unsteady or lurching as if from intoxication — **drunk·en·ness** *n*

1dry \'drī\ *adj* **1 :** free or freed from water or liquid **2 :** characterized by loss or lack of water or moisture **3 :** lacking freshness **:** WITHERED; *also* **:** low in or deprived of succulence ⟨∼ fruits⟩ **4 :** not being in or under water ⟨∼ land⟩ **5 :** THIRSTY **6 :** marked by the absence of alcoholic beverages **7 :** no longer liquid or sticky ⟨the ink is ∼⟩ **8 :** containing or employing no liquid **9 :** not giving milk ⟨a ∼ cow⟩ **10 :** lacking natural lubrication ⟨a ∼ cough⟩ **11 :** solid as opposed to liquid ⟨∼ groceries⟩ **12 :** SEVERE **13 :** not productive **:** BARREN **14 :** marked by a matter-of-fact, ironic, or terse manner of expression ⟨∼ humor⟩ **15 :** UNINTERESTING, WEARISOME **16 :** not sweet ⟨∼ wine⟩ **17 :** relating to, favoring, or practicing prohibition of alcoholic beverages — **dry·ly** *adv* — **dry·ness** *n*

2dry *vb* **:** to make or become dry

3dry *n, pl* **drys :** PROHIBITIONIST

dry·ad \'drī-əd\ *n* **:** WOOD NYMPH

dry-clean *vb* **:** to clean (fabrics) chiefly with solvents (as naphtha) other than water — **dry cleaning** *n*

dry·er *var of* DRIER

dry goods \-‚gudz\ *n pl* **:** textiles, ready-to-wear clothing, and notions as distinguished from other goods

du·al \'d(y)ü-əl\ *adj* **1 :** TWOFOLD, DOUBLE **2 :** having a double character or nature — **du·al·ism** *n* — **du·al·i·ty** \d(y)ü-'al-ət-ē\ *n*

1dub \'dəb\ *vb* **dubbed; dub·bing 1 :** to confer knighthood upon **2 :** NAME, NICKNAME

2dub *vb* **dubbed; dub·bing :** to add (sound effects) to a motion picture or to a radio or television production

dub·bin \'dəb-ən\ *n* **:** a dressing of oil and tallow for leather

du·bi·e·ty \d(y)ü-'bī-ət-ē\ *n* **:** UNCERTAINTY **2 :** a matter of doubt

du·bi·ous \'d(y)ü-bē-əs\ *adj* **1 :** occasioning doubt **:** UNCERTAIN **2 :** feeling doubt **:** UNDECIDED **3 :** QUESTIONABLE ⟨resorted to ∼ measures⟩ — **du·bi·ous·ly** *adv* — **du·bi·ous·ness** *n*

du·cal \'d(y)ü-kəl\ *adj* **:** of or relating to a duke or dukedom

duc·at \'dək-ət\ *n* **:** a gold coin of various European countries

duch·ess \'dəch-əs\ *n* **1 :** the wife or widow of a duke **2 :** a woman holding a ducal title in her own right

duchy \'dəch-ē\ *n* **:** the territory of a duke or duchess **:** DUKEDOM

1duck \'dək\ *n* **:** any of various swimming birds related to but smaller than geese and swans

2duck *vb* **1 :** to thrust or plunge under water **2 :** to lower the head or body suddenly **3 :** BOW, BOB **4 :** DODGE **5 :** to evade a duty, question, or responsibility ⟨∼ the issue⟩

3duck *n* **1 :** a durable closely woven usu. cotton fabric **2** *pl* **:** clothes made of duck

duck·bill \-‚bil\ *n* **:** PLATYPUS

duck·board \-‚bōrd\ *n* **:** a boardwalk or slatted flooring laid on a wet, muddy, or cold surface — usu. used in pl.

duck·ling \-liŋ\ *n* **:** a young duck

duck·pin \-‚pin\ *n* **:** a small bowling pin shorter and wider in the middle than a tenpin bowled at in a game ⟨duck·pins⟩

duct \'dəkt\ *n* **:** a tube or canal for conveying a fluid; *also* **:** a pipe or tube for electrical conductors — **duct·less** *adj*

duc·tile \'dək-t²l\ *adj* **1 :** capable of being drawn out (as into wire) or hammered thin **2 :** DOCILE — **duc·til·i·ty** \‚dək-'til-ət-ē\ *n*

dud \'dəd\ *n* **1** *pl* **:** CLOTHES; *also* **:** personal belongings **2 :** one that fails completely **3 :** a missile that fails to explode

dude \'d(y)üd\ *n* **1 :** FOP, DANDY **2 :** a city man; *esp* **:** an Easterner in the West

dud·geon \'dəj-ən\ *n* **:** ill humor **:** RESENTMENT ⟨in high ∼⟩

1due \'d(y)ü\ *adj* **1 :** owed or owing as a debt **2 :** owed or owing as a right **3 :** APPROPRIATE, FITTING **4 :** SUFFICIENT, ADEQUATE **5 :** REGULAR, LAWFUL ⟨∼ process of law⟩ **6 :** ATTRIBUTABLE, ASCRIBABLE ⟨∼ to negligence⟩ **7 :** PAYABLE ⟨a bill ∼ today⟩ **8 :** required or expected to happen **:** SCHEDULED ⟨∼ to arrive soon⟩

2due *n* **1 :** DEBT ⟨pay him his ∼⟩ **2** *pl* **:** a regular or legal charge or fee ⟨membership ∼s⟩

3due *adv* **:** DIRECTLY, EXACTLY ⟨∼ north⟩

du·el \'d(y)ü-əl\ *n* **:** a combat between two persons; *esp* **:** one fought with weapons in the presence of witnesses — **duel** *vb* — **du·el·ist** *or* **du·el·list** *n*

du·en·na \d(y)ü-'en-ə\ *n* **1 :** an elderly woman in charge of the younger ladies in a Spanish or Portuguese family **2 :** GOVERNESS, CHAPERON

du·et \d(y)ü-'et\ *n* **:** a musical composition for 2 performers

duf·fer \'dəf-ər\ *n* **:** an incompetent or clumsy person

dug *past of* DIG

dug·out \'dəg-‚aut\ *n* **1 :** a boat made by hollowing out a log **2 :** a shelter dug in a hillside or in the ground or in the side of a trench **3 :** a low shelter facing a baseball diamond and containing the players' bench

ə abut; ə kitten; ər further; a back; ā bake; ä cot, cart; au̇ out; ch chin; e less; ē easy; g gift; i trip; ī life; j joke; ŋ sing; ō flow; ȯ flaw; ȯi coin; th thin; t̲h̲ this; ü loot; u̇ foot; y yet; yü few; yu̇ furious; zh vision

duke \\'d(y)ük\ *n* [OF *duc,* fr. L *duc-, dux* leader, commander] **1 :** a sovereign ruler of a continental European duchy **2 :** a nobleman of the highest rank; *esp* **:** a member of the highest grade of the British peerage — **duke·dom** *n*

dul·cet \\'dəl-sət\ *adj* **1 :** sweet to the ear **:** MELODIOUS **2 :** AGREEABLE, SOOTHING

dul·ci·mer \\'dəl-sə-mər\ *n* **:** a wire-stringed instrument of trapezoidal shape played with light hammers held in the hands

1dull \\'dəl\ *adj* **1 :** mentally slow **:** STUPID **2 :** slow in perception or sensibility **3 :** LISTLESS **4 :** slow in action **:** SLUGGISH ⟨a ~ market⟩ **5 :** BLUNT **6 :** lacking brilliance or luster **7 :** DIM, INDISTINCT **8 :** not resonant or ringing **9 :** CLOUDY, OVERCAST **10 :** TEDIOUS, UNINTERESTING **11 :** low in saturation and lightness ⟨~ color⟩ — **dull·ness** *or* **dul·ness** *n* — **dul·ly** \\'dəl-(l)ē\ *adv*

2dull *vb* **:** to make or become dull

dull·ard \\'dəl-ərd\ *n* **:** a stupid person

du·ly \\'d(y)ü-lē\ *adv* **:** in a due manner, time, or degree

du·ma \\'dü-mə\ *n* **:** the principal legislative assembly in czarist Russia

dumb \\'dəm\ *adj* **1 :** lacking the power of speech **2 :** SILENT **3 :** STUPID — **dumb·ly** *adv*

dumb·bell \\'dəm-,bel\ *n* **1 :** a weight of 2 rounded ends connected by a short bar and usu. used in pairs for gymnastic exercises **2 :** one who is dull or stupid **:** DUMMY

dumb·found *or* **dum·found** \\,dəm-'faûnd\ *vb* **:** to strike dumb with astonishment **:** AMAZE

dumb·wait·er \\'dəm-'wāt-ər\ *n* **:** a small elevator for conveying food and dishes or small goods from one story of a building to another

dum·dum \\'dəm-,dəm\ *n* **:** a soft-nosed bullet that expands upon hitting an object

dum·my \\'dəm-ē\ *n* **1 :** a dumb person **2 :** the exposed hand in bridge played by the declarer in addition to his own hand; *also* **:** a bridge player whose hand is a dummy **3 :** an imitation or copy of something used as a substitute **4 :** one who seems to be acting for himself but is really acting for another **5 :** something usu. mechanically operated that serves to replace or aid a human being's work **6 :** a pattern arrangement of matter to be reproduced esp. by printing

1dump \\'dəmp\ *vb* **:** to let fall in a mass **:** UNLOAD ⟨~ coal⟩

2dump *n* **1 :** a place for dumping something (as refuse) **2 :** a reserve supply; *esp* **:** one of military materials stored at one place ⟨an ammunition ~⟩ **3 :** a slovenly or dilapidated place

dump·ling \\-liŋ\ *n* **1 :** a small mass of dough cooked by boiling or steaming **2 :** a dessert of fruit baked in biscuit dough

dumps \\'dəmps\ *n pl* **:** a dull gloomy state of mind **:** low spirits ⟨in the ~⟩

dumpy \\'dəm-pē\ *adj* **:** short and thick in build

1dun \\'dən\ *adj* **:** having a variable color averaging a nearly neutral slightly brownish dark gray

2dun *vb* **dunned; dun·ning 1 :** to ask repeatedly (as for payment of a debt) **2 :** PLAGUE, PESTER — **dun** *n*

dunce \\'dəns\ *n* **:** a dull-witted and stupid person

dun·der·head \\'dən-dər-,hed\ *n* **:** DUNCE, BLOCKHEAD

dune \\'d(y)ün\ *n* **:** a hill or ridge of sand piled up by the wind

1dung \\'dəŋ\ *n* **:** MANURE

2dung *vb* **:** to dress (land) with dung

dun·ga·ree \\,dəŋ-gə-'rē\ *n* **1 :** a heavy coarse cotton twill; *esp* **:** blue denim **2** *pl* **:** trousers or work clothes made of dungaree

dun·geon \\'dən-jən\ *n* **:** a close dark prison commonly underground

dung·hill \\'dəŋ-,hil\ *n* **:** a manure pile

dunk \\'dəŋk\ *vb* **1 :** to dip (as bread) into liquid (as coffee) while eating **2 :** to dip or submerge temporarily in liquid **3 :** to submerge oneself in water

duo \\'d(y)ü-ō\ *n* **1 :** DUET **2 :** PAIR

du·o·de·num \\,d(y)ü-ə-'dēn-əm, d(y)u̇-'äd-ʰn-\ *n* **:** the part of the small intestine immediately below the stomach — **du·o·de·nal** \\-'dēn-ʰl, -ʰn-əl\ *adj*

1dupe \\'d(y)üp\ *n* **:** one who is easily deceived or cheated **:** FOOL

2dupe *vb* **:** to make a dupe of **:** DECEIVE, FOOL

1du·plex \\'d(y)ü-,pleks\ *adj* **:** DOUBLE, TWOFOLD

2duplex *n* **:** something duplex; *esp* **:** a 2-family house

1du·pli·cate \\'d(y)ü-pli-kət\ *adj* **1 :** consisting of or existing in 2 corresponding or identical parts or examples **2 :** being the same as another

2duplicate *n* **:** a thing that exactly resembles another in appearance, pattern, or content **:** COPY

3du·pli·cate \\-,kāt\ *vb* **1 :** to make double or twofold **2 :** to make an exact copy of — **du·pli·ca·tion** \\,d(y)ü-pli-'kā-shən\ *n*

du·pli·ca·tor \\'d(y)ü-pli-,kāt-ər\ *n* **:** a machine for making copies of typed, drawn, or printed matter

du·plic·i·ty \\d(y)ü-'plis-ət-ē\ *n* **:** deception by pretending to feel and act one way while acting another

du·ra·ble \\'d(y)ur-ə-bəl\ *adj* **:** able to endure **:** LASTING ⟨~ clothing⟩ — **du·ra·bil·i·ty** \\,d(y)ur-ə-'bil-ət-ē\ *n*

du·rance \\'d(y)ur-əns\ *n* **:** IMPRISONMENT

du·ra·tion \\d(y)u̇-'rā-shən\ *n* **1 :** continuance in time **2 :** the time during which something exists or lasts

du·ress \\d(y)u̇-'res\ *n* **1 :** forcible restraint or restriction **2 :** compulsion by threat ⟨confession made under ~⟩

dur·ing \\,d(y)ur-iŋ\ *prep* **1 :** throughout the course of ⟨there was rationing ~ the war⟩ **2 :** at some point in the course of ⟨broke in ~ the night⟩

dusk \\'dəsk\ *n* **1 :** the darker part of twilight esp. at night **2 :** GLOOM

dusky *adj* **1 :** somewhat dark in color; *esp* **:** having dark skin **2 :** SHADOWY — **dusk·i·ness** *n*

1dust \\'dəst\ *n* **1 :** powdery particles (as of earth) **2 :** the earthy remains of bodies once alive; *esp* **:** the human corpse **3 :** something worthless **4 :** a state of humiliation **5 :** the surface of the ground — **dust·less** *adj* — **dust·y** *adj*

2dust *vb* **1 :** to make free of dust **:** remove dust **2 :** to sprinkle with fine particles **3 :** to sprinkle in the form of dust

dust·er *n* **1 :** one that removes dust

2 : a lightweight garment to protect clothing from dust **3** : a dress-length housecoat **4** : one that scatters fine particles

dust·pan \'dəst-,pan\ n : a shovel-shaped pan for sweepings

Dutch \'dəch\ n **1** Dutch pl : the people of the Netherlands **2** : the language of the Netherlands — **Dutch** adj — **Dutch-man** \-mən\ n

du·te·ous \'d(y)üt-ē-əs\ adj : DUTIFUL, OBEDIENT

du·ti·able \'d(y)üt-ē-ə-bəl\ adj : subject to a duty ⟨~ imports⟩

du·ti·ful \'d(y)üt-i-fəl\ adj **1** : filled with or motivated by a sense of duty ⟨a ~ son⟩ **2** : proceeding from or expressive of a sense of duty ⟨~ affection⟩ — **du·ti·ful·ly** adv — **du·ti·ful·ness** n

du·ty \'d(y)üt-ē\ n **1** : conduct due to parents or superiors : RESPECT **2** : the action required by one's occupation or position **3** : assigned service or business; esp : active military service **4** : a moral or legal obligation **5** : TAX **6** : the service required (as of a machine) : USE ⟨a heavy-duty tire⟩

¹dwarf \'dwórf\ n, pl **dwarfs** or **dwarves** \'dwórvz\ : a person, animal, or plant much below normal size — **dwarf** adj — **dwarf·ish** adj

²dwarf vb **1** : to restrict the growth or development of : STUNT **2** : to cause to appear smaller

dwell \'dwel\ vb **dwelt** \'dwelt\ or **dwelled** \'dweld\ **dwell·ing 1** : ABIDE, REMAIN **2** : RESIDE, EXIST **3** : to keep the attention directed : LINGER **4** : to write or speak at length or insistently — **dwell·er** n

dwell·ing n : ABODE, RESIDENCE, HOUSE

dwin·dle \'dwin-d²l\ vb : to make or become steadily less : DIMINISH, SHRINK

dyb·buk \'dib-ək\ n : a wandering soul believed in Jewish folklore to enter and possess a person

¹dye \'dī\ n **1** : color produced by dyeing **2** : material used for coloring or staining

²dye vb **dyed; dye·ing 1** : to impart a new color to esp. by impregnating with a dye **2** : to take up or impart color in dyeing

dye·stuff \-,stəf\ n : DYE 2

dying pres part of DIE

dyke var of DIKE

dy·nam·ic \dī-'nam-ik\ adj : of or relating to physical force producing motion : ENERGETIC, FORCEFUL

¹dy·na·mite \'dī-nə-,mīt\ n : an explosive made of nitroglycerin absorbed in a porous material; also : a blasting explosive

²dynamite vb : to blow up with dynamite

dy·na·mo \'dī-nə-,mō\ n : a machine for converting mechanical energy into electrical energy

dy·nas·ty \'dī-nəs-tē, -,nas-\ n **1** : a succession of rulers of the same line of descent **2** : a powerful group or family that maintains its position for a considerable time — **dy·nas·tic** \dī-'nas-tik\ adj

dys·en·tery \'dis-²n-,ter-ē\ n : a disorder marked by diarrhea with blood and mucus in the feces

dys·pep·sia \dis-'pep-shə, -sē-ə\ n : INDIGESTION — **dys·pep·tic** \-'pep-tik\ adj or n — **dys·pep·ti·cal·ly** adv

dys·pro·si·um \dis-'prō-zē-əm\ n : a metallic chemical element that forms highly magnetic compounds

---

e \'ē\ n, often cap : the 5th letter of the English alphabet

¹each \'ēch\ adj : being one of the class named ⟨~ man⟩ ⟨~ grape in the bunch⟩

²each pron : each one : every individual one

³each adv : APIECE ⟨cost five cents ~⟩

ea·ger \'ē-gər\ adj : marked by urgent or enthusiastic desire or interest ⟨~ to learn⟩ syn avid, anxious — **ea·ger·ly** adv — **ea·ger·ness** n

ea·gle \'ē-gəl\ n **1** : a large bird of prey related to the hawks **2** : a U.S. 10-dollar gold coin **3** : a score of two under par on a hole in golf

ea·glet \'ē-glət\ n : a young eagle

-ean — see -AN

¹ear \'iər\ n **1** : the organ of hearing; also : the outer part of this in a vertebrate **2** : something resembling a mammal's ear in shape or position **3** : sympathetic attention

²ear n : the fruiting spike of a cereal (as wheat)

ear·ache \-,āk\ n : an ache or pain in the ear

ear·drum \-,drəm\ n : a thin membrane that transmits sound waves to the receptors of the ear

earl \'ərl\ n : a member of the British peerage ranking below a marquess and above a viscount

earl·dom \-dəm\ n : the rank, dignity, or lands of an earl or countess

ear·lobe \'iər-,lōb\ n : the pendent part of the ear

¹ear·ly \'ər-lē\ adv : at an early time (as in a period or series)

²early adj **1** : of, relating to, or occurring near the beginning (as of a period, series, or development) **2** : ANCIENT, PRIMITIVE **3** : occurring before the usual time ⟨an ~ breakfast⟩; also : occurring in the near future ⟨looked for an ~ improvement in prices⟩

ear·mark \'iər-,märk\ n : a mark of identification orig. on the ear of an animal — **earmark** vb

ear·muff \-,məf\ n : one of a pair of ear coverings connected by a flexible band and worn as protection against cold

earn \'ərn\ vb **1** : to receive as a return for service **2** : DESERVE, MERIT syn gain, secure, get, obtain

¹ear·nest \'ər-nəst\ n : an intensely serious state of mind

²earnest adj **1** : seriously intent and sober ⟨an ~ face⟩ ⟨an ~ attempt to understand⟩ **2** : GRAVE, IMPORTANT

ə abut; ᵊ kitten; ər further; a back; ā bake; ä cot, cart; aú out; ch chin; e less; ē easy; g gift; i trip; ī life; j joke; ŋ sing; ō flow; ò flaw; òi coin; th thin; ṯh this; ü loot; ù foot; y yet; yü few; yù furious; zh vision

syn solemn, sedate, staid — **ear·nest·ly** *adv* — **ear·nest·ness** *n*

³earnest *n* **1** : something of value given by a buyer to a seller to bind a bargain **2** : PLEDGE

earn·ings \'ər-niŋz\ *n pl* : something earned : WAGES, PROFIT

ear·phone \'iər-‚fōn\ *n* : a device that converts electrical energy into sound and is worn over or in the ear

ear·ring \'iər-‚riŋ\ *n* : an ornament for the earlobe

ear·shot \-‚shät\ *n* : range of hearing

earth \'ərth\ *n* **1** : SOIL, DIRT **2** : LAND, GROUND **3** : the planet inhabited by man : WORLD

earth·en \'ər-thən\ *adj* : made of earth or baked clay

earth·en·ware \-‚waər\ *n* : slightly porous opaque pottery fired at low heat

earth·ly *adj* : typical of or belonging to this earth esp. as distinguished from heaven ⟨~ affairs⟩

earth·quake \'ərth-‚kwāk\ *n* : a shaking or trembling of a portion of the earth

earth·work \-‚wərk\ *n* : an embankment or fortification of earth

earth·worm \-‚wərm\ *n* : a long segmented worm found in damp soil

earthy \'ər-thē\ *adj* **1** : consisting of or resembling soil **2** : PRACTICAL **3** : COARSE, GROSS ⟨~ remarks⟩

¹ease \'ēz\ *n* **1** : comfort of body or mind **2** : naturalness of manner **3** : freedom from difficulty or effort **syn** relaxation, rest, repose, comfort, leisure

²ease *vb* **1** : to relieve from something (as pain or worry) that distresses **2** : to lessen the pressure or tension of **3** : to make or become less difficult ⟨~ credit⟩

ea·sel \'ē-zəl\ *n* : a frame to hold a painter's canvas or a picture

¹east \'ēst\ *adv* : to or toward the east

²east *adj* **1** : situated toward or at the east **2** : coming from the east

³east *n* **1** : the general direction of sunrise **2** : the compass point directly opposite to west **3** *cap* : regions or countries east of a specified or implied point — **east·er·ly** \-ər-lē\ *adv or adj* — **east·ward** *adv or adj* — **east·wards** *adv*

Eas·ter \'ēs-tər\ *n* : a church festival observed on a Sunday in March or April in commemoration of Christ's resurrection

east·ern \'ēst-ərn\ *adj* **1** *often cap* : of, relating to, or characteristic of a region conventionally designated East **2** : lying toward or coming from the east **3** *cap* : of, relating to, or being the Christian churches originating in the church of the Eastern Roman Empire — **East·ern·er** *n*

easy \'ē-zē\ *adj* **1** : marked by ease ⟨an ~ life⟩; *esp* : not causing distress or difficulty ⟨~ tasks⟩ **2** : MILD, LENIENT ⟨be ~ on him⟩ **3** : TRANQUIL ⟨an ~ calm⟩ **4** : not less than ⟨weighs an ~ 200 pounds⟩ **5** : GRADUAL ⟨an ~ slope⟩ **syn** comfortable, restful, facile, simple, effortless — **eas·i·ly** *adv* — **eas·i·ness** *n*

easy·go·ing \‚ē-zē-'gō-iŋ\ *adj* : taking life easily

eat \'ēt\ *vb* ate \'āt\ eat·en \'ēt-ᵊn\ eat·ing **1** : to take in as food : take food **2** : to use up : DEVOUR **3** : CORRODE — **eat·able** *adj or n* — **eat·er** *n*

eaves \'ēvz\ *n pl* : the overhanging lower edge of a roof

eaves·drop \-‚dräp\ *vb* : to listen secretly — **eaves·drop·per** *n*

¹ebb \'eb\ *n* **1** : the flowing back of water brought in by the tide **2** : a point or state of decline

²ebb *vb* **1** : to recede from the flood state **2** : DECLINE ⟨as his fortunes ~ed⟩

¹eb·o·ny \'eb-ə-nē\ *n* : a hard heavy wood of Old World tropical trees (ebony trees) related to the persimmon

²ebony *adj* **1** : made of or resembling ebony **2** : BLACK, DARK

ebul·lient \i-'búl-yənt, -'bəl-\ *adj* **1** : BOILING, AGITATED **2** : EXUBERANT — **ebul·lience** *n*

eb·ul·li·tion \‚eb-ə-'lish-ən\ *n* **1** : a boiling or bubbling up **2** : a seething excitement or outburst

ec·cen·tric \ik-'sen-trik\ *adj* **1** : deviating from a usual or accepted pattern : ODD, STRANGE **2** : deviating from a circular path ⟨~ orbits⟩ **3** : set with axis or support off center ⟨an ~ cam⟩; *also* : being off center **syn** erratic, queer, singular, curious — **eccentric** *n* — **ec·cen·tri·cal·ly** *adv* — **ec·cen·tric·i·ty** \‚ek-‚sen-'tris-ət-ē\ *n*

ec·cle·si·as·tic \ik-‚lē-zē-'as-tik\ *n* : CLERGYMAN

ec·cle·si·as·ti·cal *adj* : of or relating to a church esp. as an institution ⟨~ art⟩ — **ecclesiastic** *adj*

ech·e·lon \'esh-ə-‚län\ *n* **1** : a steplike arrangement (as of troops or airplanes) **2** : a level (as of authority or responsibility) within a hierarchy

echo \'ek-ō\ *n, pl* **ech·oes** : repetition of a sound caused by a reflection of the sound waves; *also* : the reflection of a radar signal by an object — **echo** *vb*

éclair \ā-'klaər\ *n* : an oblong shell of light pastry with whipped cream or custard filling

éclat \ā-'klä\ *n* **1** : a dazzling effect or success **2** : ACCLAIM

eclec·tic \e-'klek-tik, i-\ *adj* : selecting or made up of what seems best of varied sources

¹eclipse \i-'klips\ *n* **1** : the total or partial obscuring of one heavenly body by another; *also* : a passing into the shadow of a heavenly body **2** : a falling into obscurity, decline, or disgrace

²eclipse *vb* : to cause an eclipse of

eclip·tic \i-'klip-tik\ *n* : the great circle of the celestial sphere that is the apparent path of the sun

ec·logue \'ek-‚lóg\ *n* : a pastoral poem

ecol·o·gy \i-'käl-ə-jē\ *n* : a branch of science concerned with the interaction of organisms and their environments — **ec·o·log·ic** \‚ek-ə-'läj-ik, ‚ēk-\ *or* **ec·o·log·i·cal** *adj* — **ecol·o·gist** \i-'käl-ə-jəst\ *n*

ec·o·nom·ic \‚ek-ə-'näm-ik, ‚ēk-\ *adj* : of or relating to the satisfaction of man's material needs

ec·o·nom·i·cal *adj* : THRIFTY **syn** frugal, sparing — **ec·o·nom·i·cal·ly** *adv*

ec·o·nom·ics *n* : a branch of knowledge dealing with the production, distribution, and consumption of goods and services — **econ·o·mist** \i-'kän-ə-məst\ *n*

econ·o·mize \i-'kän-ə-‚mīz\ *vb* : to practice economy : be frugal

econ·o·my \i-'kän-ə-mē\ *n* **1** : thrifty management or use of resources; *also* : an instance of this ⟨petty *economies*⟩ **2** : manner of arrangement or functioning : ORGANIZATION ⟨the bodily ~⟩

3 : an economic system ⟨a money ~⟩

ec·sta·sy \'ek-stə-sē\ *n* : extreme and usu. rapturous emotional excitement — **ec·stat·ic** \ek-'stat-ik\ *adj* — **ec·stat·i·cal·ly** *adv*

ec·u·men·i·cal \,ek-yə-'men-i-kəl\ *adj* [LL *oecumenicus* worldwide, fr. LGk *oikoumenikos*, fr. Gk *oikoumenē* world, fr. fem. of *oikoumenos*, prp. passive of *oikein* to inhabit, fr. *oikos* house, home] **1** : general in extent or influence; *esp* : promoting or tending toward worldwide Christian unity — **ec·u·men·i·cal·ly** *adv* — **ec·u·me·nic·i·ty** \-mə-'nis-ət-ē\ *n*

ec·ze·ma \ig-'zē-mə, 'ek-sə-\ *n* : an itching skin inflammation with crusted lesions — **ec·zem·a·tous** \ig-'zem-ət-əs\ *adj*

1-ed \d *after a vowel or b, g, j, l, m, n, ŋ, r, th, v, z, zh; əd *after d, t;* t *after other sounds*\ *vb suffix or adj suffix* **1** — used to form the past participle of regular weak verbs ⟨end*ed*⟩ ⟨fad*ed*⟩ ⟨tri*ed*⟩ ⟨patt*ed*⟩ **2** — used to form adjectives of identical meaning from Latin-derived adjectives ending in *-ate* ⟨pinnat*ed*⟩ **3** : having : characterized by ⟨cultur*ed*⟩ ⟨two-legg*ed*⟩; *also* : having the characteristics of ⟨bigot*ed*⟩

2-ed *vb suffix* — used to form the past tense of regular weak verbs ⟨judg*ed*⟩ ⟨deni*ed*⟩ ⟨dropp*ed*⟩

Edam \'ēd-əm, 'ē-,dam\ *n* : a Dutch pressed cheese of yellow color and mild flavor made in balls

ed·dy \'ed-ē\ *n* : WHIRLPOOL; *also* : a contrary or circular current — **eddy** *vb*

edel·weiss \'ād-°l-,wīs\ *n* : a small perennial woolly herb that is related to the thistles and grows high in the Alps

Eden \'ēd-°n\ *n* : PARADISE 2

1edge \'ej\ *n* **1** : the cutting side of a blade **2** : power to cut or penetrate : SHARPNESS **3** : the line where something begins or ends; *also* : the area adjoining such an edge

2edge *vb* **1** : to give or form an edge **2** : to move or force gradually ⟨~ into a crowd⟩

edge·ways \-,wāz\ *or* **edge·wise** \-,wīz\ *adv* : SIDEWAYS

edg·ing *n* : something that forms an edge or border ⟨a lace ~⟩

edgy *adj* **1** : SHARP ⟨an ~ tone⟩ **2** : TENSE, NERVOUS — **edg·i·ness** *n*

ed·i·ble \'ed-ə-bəl\ *adj* : fit or safe to be eaten — **ed·i·bil·i·ty** \,ed-ə-'bil-ət-ē\ *n* — **edible** *n*

edict \'ē-,dikt\ *n* : DECREE

ed·i·fi·ca·tion \,ed-ə-fə-'kā-shən\ *n* : instruction and improvement esp. in morality — **ed·i·fy** \-,fī\ *vb*

ed·i·fice \'ed-ə-fəs\ *n* : a usu. large building

ed·it \'ed-ət\ *vb* **1** : to revise and prepare for publication **2** : to direct the publication and policies of (as a newspaper) — **ed·i·tor** *n* — **ed·i·tor·ship** *n*

edi·tion \i-'dish-ən\ *n* **1** : the form in which a text is published **2** : the total number of copies (as of a book) published at one time **3** : VERSION

1ed·i·to·ri·al \,ed-ə-'tōr-ē-əl\ *adj* **1** : of, relating to, or functioning as an editor **2** : being an editorial; *also* : expressing opinion — **ed·i·to·ri·al·ly** *adv*

2editorial *n* : an article (as in a newspaper) expressing the views of an editor or publisher

ed·u·ca·ble \'ej-ə-kə-bəl\ *adj* : capable of being educated

ed·u·cate \'ej-ə-,kāt\ *vb* **1** : to provide with schooling **2** : to develop and cultivate mentally and morally **syn** train, discipline, school, instruct — **ed·u·ca·tor** *n*

ed·u·ca·tion \,ej-ə-'kā-shən\ *n* **1** : the action or process of educating or being educated **2** : a field of knowledge dealing with technical aspects of teaching — **ed·u·ca·tion·al** *adj*

educe \i-'d(y)üs\ *vb* **1** : ELICIT, EVOKE **2** : to arrive at usu. through reasoning ⟨~ a conclusion⟩ **syn** extract

eel \'ēl\ *n* : a snakelike fish with a smooth slimy skin

ee·rie *also* **ee·ry** \'i(ə)r-ē\ *adj* : WEIRD, UNCANNY — **ee·ri·ly** *adv*

ef·face \i-'fās\ *vb* : to obliterate or obscure by or as if by rubbing out **syn** erase, delete — **ef·face·able** *adj*

1ef·fect \i-'fekt\ *n* **1** : RESULT **2** : MEANING, INTENT **3** : APPEARANCE **4** : FULFILLMENT **5** : REALITY **6** : INFLUENCE **7** *pl* : GOODS, POSSESSIONS **8** : the quality or state of being operative : OPERATION **syn** consequence, outcome, upshot

2effect *vb* **1** : ACCOMPLISH ⟨~ repairs⟩ **2** : PRODUCE ⟨~ changes⟩

ef·fec·tive \-'fek-tiv\ *adj* **1** : producing a decided, decisive, or desired effect **2** : IMPRESSIVE, STRIKING **3** : ready for service or action **4** : being in effect — **ef·fec·tive·ly** *adv* — **ef·fec·tive·ness** *n*

ef·fec·tu·al \-'fek-ch(ə-w)əl\ *adj* : producing an intended effect : ADEQUATE — **ef·fec·tu·al·ly** *adv*

ef·fec·tu·ate \-chə-,wāt\ *vb* : to bring about : EFFECT

ef·fem·i·nate \ə-'fem-ə-nət\ *adj* : marked by qualities more typical of and suitable to women than men : UNMANLY — **ef·fem·i·na·cy** \-nə-sē\ *n*

ef·fen·di \e-'fen-dē\ *n* : a man of property, authority, or education in an eastern Mediterranean country

ef·fer·ent \'ef-ə-rant\ *adj* : bearing or conducting outward from a more central part ⟨~ nerves⟩

ef·fer·vesce \,ef-ər-'ves\ *vb* : to bubble and hiss as gas escapes; *also* : to be exhilarated — **ef·fer·ves·cence** *n* — **ef·fer·ves·cent** *adj*

ef·fete \e-'fēt\ *adj* : worn out : EXHAUSTED; *also* : DECADENT

ef·fi·ca·cious \,ef-ə-'kā-shəs\ *adj* : producing an intended effect ⟨~ remedies⟩ **syn** effectual, effective — **ef·fi·ca·cy** \'ef-i-kə-sē\ *n*

ef·fi·cient \i-'fish-ənt\ *adj* : productive of desired effects esp. without loss or waste : COMPETENT — **ef·fi·cien·cy** *n* — **ef·fi·cient·ly** *adv*

ef·fi·gy \'ef-ə-jē\ *n* : IMAGE, REPRESENTATION; *esp* : a crude figure of a hated person

ef·flo·resce \,ef-lə-'res\ *vb* : to burst forth : BLOOM

ef·flo·res·cence *n* **1** : the period or state of flowering **2** : the action or process of developing **3** : fullness of manifestation : CULMINATION

ef·flu·vi·um \e-'flü-vē-əm\ *n*, *pl* -**via**

\-vē-ə\ *or* -vi·ums : a usu. unpleasant emanation

ef·fort \'ef-ərt\ *n* 1 : EXERTION, EN-DEAVOR; *also* : a product of effort ⟨literary ~s⟩ 2 : active or applied force — ef·fort·less *adj* — ef·fort·less·ly *adv*

ef·fron·tery \i-'frənt-ə-rē\ *n* : shameless boldness : IMPUDENCE **syn** temerity, audacity

ef·ful·gence \i-'ful-jəns, -'fəl-\ *n* : radiant splendor : BRILLIANCE — ef·ful·gent *adj*

ef·fu·sion \i-'fyü-zhən\ *n* : a gushing forth; *also* : unrestrained utterance — ef·fuse \i-'fyüz\ *vb* — ef·fu·sive \-'fyü-siv\ *adj*

eft \'eft\ *n* : NEWT

egal·i·tar·i·an·ism \i-,gal-ə-'ter-ē-ə-,niz-əm\ *n* : a belief in human equality esp. in social, political, and economic affairs — egal·i·tar·i·an *adj or n*

¹egg \'eg\ *vb* : to urge to action

²egg *n* 1 : a rounded shelled reproductive body esp. of birds and reptiles from which the young hatches; *also* : the egg of domestic poultry as an article of food ⟨allergic to ~s⟩ 2 : a female germ cell

egg·beat·er \-,bēt-ər\ *n* : a rotary beater operated by hand for beating eggs or liquids (as cream)

egg·head \-,hed\ *n* : INTELLECTUAL, HIGHBROW

egg·nog \-,näg\ *n* : a drink consisting of eggs beaten up with sugar, milk or cream, and often alcoholic liquor

egg·plant \-,plant\ *n* : the edible usu. large and purplish fruit of a plant related to the potato

egg·shell \-,shel\ *n* : the hard exterior covering of an egg

egis \'ē-jəs\ *var of* AEGIS

eg·lan·tine \'eg-lən-,tīn, -,tēn\ *n* : SWEETBRIER

ego \'ē-gō\ *n* 1 : the self as distinguished from others 2 : the conscious part of the personality derived from the id through contact with reality

ego·cen·tric \,ē-gō-'sen-trik\ *adj* : concerned or overly concerned with the self; *esp* : SELF-CENTERED

ego·ism \'ē-gō-,iz-əm\ *n* 1 : a doctrine holding self-interest to be the motive or the valid end of action 2 : EGOTISM — ego·ist \-əst\ *n* — ego·is·tic \,ē-gō-'tis-tik\ *also* ego·is·ti·cal \,ē-gō-'tis-ti-kəl\ — ego·is·ti·cal·ly *adv*

ego·tism \'ē-gə-,tiz-əm\ *n* : too frequent reference to oneself; *also* : excessive self-awareness : CONCEIT — ego·tist \-təst\ *n* — ego·tis·tic \,ē-gə-'tis-tik\ *or* ego·tis·ti·cal *adj* — ego·tis·ti·cal·ly *adv*

egre·gious \i-'grē-jəs\ *adj* [L egregius outstanding from the herd, fr. *ex, e* out of + *greg-, grex* flock, herd] : notably bad : FLAGRANT

egress \'ē-,gres\ *n* : a way out : EXIT

egret \'ē-grət, i-'gret, 'eg-rət\ *n* : any of various herons that bear long plumes (aigrettes) during the breeding season

Egyp·tian \i-'jip-shən\ *n* : a native or inhabitant of Egypt — **Egyptian** *adj*

ei·der \'īd-ər\ *n* : a northern sea duck that yields a soft down (eider down)

ei·do·lon \ī-'dō-lən\ *n, pl* -lons *or* -la \-lə\ 1 : an unsubstantial image : PHANTOM 2 : IDEAL

eight \'āt\ *n* 1 : one more than seven 2 : the 8th in a set or series 3 : something having eight units; *esp* : an 8-cylinder engine or automobile — **eight**

adj or pron — eighth \'ātth\ *adj or adv or n*

eigh·teen \'ā(t)-'tēn\ *n* : one more than 17 — **eighteen** *adj or pron* — eigh·teenth *adj or n*

eighty \'āt-ē\ *n* : eight times 10 — eight·i·eth *adj or n* — **eighty** *adj or n*

ein·stei·ni·um \īn-'stī-nē-əm\ *n* : an artificially produced radioactive element

ei·stedd·fod \ī-'steth-,vȯd\ *n* : a Welsh competitive festival of the arts esp. in singing

¹ei·ther \'ē-thər, 'ī-\ *adj* 1 : both the one and the other ⟨trees on ~ side of the drive⟩ 2 : the first or the second : this or that ⟨take ~ one of the two⟩

²either *pron* : one of two or more

³either *conj* — used as a function word before the first of two or more words or word groups of which the last is preceded by *or* to indicate that they represent alternatives ⟨a statement is ~ true or false⟩

ejac·u·late \i-'jak-yə-,lāt\ *vb* 1 : to utter suddenly : EXCLAIM 2 : to eject a fluid (as semen) — ejac·u·la·tion \-,jak-yə-'lā-shən\ *n*

eject \i-'jekt\ *vb* : to drive or throw out or off **syn** expel, oust, evict — ejec·tion \-'jek-shən\ *n*

eke \'ēk\ *vb* : to gain, supplement, or extend usu. with effort — usu. used with *out* ⟨~ out a living⟩

¹elab·o·rate \i-'lab-(ə-)rət\ *adj* 1 : planned or carried out with care and in detail 2 : being complex and usu. ornate — elab·o·rate·ly *adv* — elab·o·rate·ness *n*

²elab·o·rate \-'lab-ə-,rāt\ *vb* 1 : to work out in detail : develop fully 2 : to build up from simpler ingredients — elab·o·ra·tion \i-,lab-ə-'rā-shən\ *n*

élan \ā-'läⁿ\ *n* : ARDOR, SPIRIT

elapse \i-'laps\ *vb* : to slip by (as time) : PASS

¹elas·tic \i-'las-tik\ *adj* 1 : SPRINGY 2 : FLEXIBLE, PLIABLE 3 : ADAPTABLE **syn** resilient, supple — elas·tic·i·ty \-,las-'tis-ət-ē\ *n*

²elastic *n* 1 : elastic material 2 : a rubber band

elate \i-'lāt\ *vb* : to fill with joy or pride — ela·tion \-'lā-shən\ *n*

¹el·bow \'el-,bō\ *n* 1 : the joint of the arm; *also* : the outer curve of the bent arm 2 : a bend or joint resembling an elbow in shape

²elbow *vb* : to push or shove aside with the elbow; *also* : to make a way by elbowing

el·bow·room \-,rüm, -,rum\ *n* 1 : room for moving the elbows freely 2 : enough space for work or operation

¹el·der \'el-dər\ *n* : a shrub related to the honeysuckles; *also* : its small black or red fruit (el·der·ber·ry \-,ber-ē\)

²elder *adj* 1 : OLDER 2 : EARLIER, FORMER 3 : of higher ranking : SENIOR

³elder *n* 1 : an older individual : SENIOR 2 : one having authority by reason of age and experience 3 : a church officer

el·der·ly \'el-dər-lē\ *adj* 1 : rather old; *esp* : past middle age 2 : of, relating to, or characteristic of later life

el·dest \'el-dəst\ *adj* : OLDEST

El Do·ra·do \,el-də-'räd-ō, -'räd-\ *n* : a place of vast riches or abundance

¹elect \i-'lekt\ *adj* 1 : CHOSEN, SELECT 2 : elected but not yet installed in office

²elect *vb* 1 : to select by vote (as for

office or membership) **2** : CHOOSE, PICK syn designate, name

elec·tion \i-'lek-shən\ n **1** : an act or process of electing **2** : the fact of being elected

elec·tion·eer \i-,lek-shə-'niər\ vb : to work for the election of a candidate or party

1elec·tive \i-'lek-tiv\ adj **1** : chosen or filled by election **2** : permitting a choice : OPTIONAL

2elective n : an elective course or subject of study

elec·tor \i-'lek-tər\ n **1** : one qualified to vote in an election **2** : one elected to a body (electoral college) and entitled to vote for the president and vice-president — **elec·tor·al** \-'lek-t(ə-)rəl\ adj

elec·tor·ate \i-'lek-t(ə-)rət\ n : a body of persons entitled to vote

elec·tric \i-'lek-trik\ or **elec·tri·cal** adj **1** : of, relating to, operated by, or produced by electricity **2** : ELECTRIFYING, THRILLING (an ~ performance) — **elec·tri·cal·ly** adv — **elec·tri·cal·ness** n

electric chair n : a chair used in legal electrocution

electric eye n : a photoelectric cell with accessories that does something (as opening a door) automatically

elec·tri·cian \i-,lek-'trish-ən\ n : one who designs, installs, operates, or repairs electrical equipment

elec·tric·i·ty \i-,lek-'tris-(ə-)tē\ n : a fundamental phenomenon of nature observable in the attractions and repulsions of bodies electrified by friction and in natural phenomena (as lightning) and utilized as a source of energy in the form of electric currents; also : such a current

electric wave n : an electromagnetic wave

elec·tri·fy \i-'lek-trə-,fī\ vb **1** : to charge with electricity **2** : to equip for use of electrical power **3** : THRILL — **elec·tri·fi·ca·tion** \-,lek-trə-fə-'kā-shən\ n

elec·tro·cute \i-'lek-trə-,kyüt\ vb : to kill by an electric shock — **elec·tro·cu·tion** \-,lek-trə-'kyü-shən\ n

elec·trode \i-'lek-,trōd\ n : a conductor used to establish electrical contact with a nonmetallic part of a circuit (as in a storage battery or electron tube)

elec·trol·y·sis \i-,lek-'träl-ə-səs\ n : the production of chemical changes by passage of an electric current through an electrolyte — **elec·tro·lyt·ic** \-trə-'lit-ik\ adj

elec·tro·lyte \i-'lek-trə-,līt\ n : a nonmetallic electric conductor (as a liquid) in which current is carried by the movement of ions with matter liberated at electrodes; also : a substance whose solution or molten form is such a conductor

elec·tro·mag·net \i-,lek-trō-'mag-nət\ n : a core of magnetic materials (as soft iron) surrounded by wire through which an electric current is passed to magnetize the core

elec·tro·mag·net·ic \-mag-'net-ik\ adj **1** : of or relating to magnetism (electro·mag·ne·tism \-'mag-nə-,tiz-əm\) developed by a current of electricity

2 : being a wave (as a light wave) propagated by regular variations of the intensity of an associated electric and magnetic effect

elec·tro·mo·tive force \i-,lek-trə-,mōt-iv-\ n **1** : something that moves or tends to move electricity **2** : the amount of energy derived from an electrical source per unit quantity of electricity passing through the source (as a generator)

elec·tron \i-'lek-,trän\ n : a negatively charged particle that singly or in numbers forms the part of an atom outside the nucleus and is of the kind whose flow along a conductor forms an electric current

elec·tron·ic \i-,lek-'trän-ik\ adj : of or relating to electrons or electronics — **elec·tron·i·cal·ly** adv

elec·tron·ics n : the physics of electrons and their utilization

electron tube n : a device in which electrical conduction by electrons takes place within a container and which is used for the controlled flow of electrons (as in radio)

elec·tro·plate \i-'lek-trə-,plāt\ vb : to coat (as with metal) by electrolysis

elec·tio·type \-,tīp\ n : a plate for use in printing made by covering a mold made from typeset matter with a thin shell of metal by an electric process and then putting on a heavier backing (as of metal)

el·ee·mos·y·nary \,el-i-'mäs-ᵊn-,er-ē\ adj : CHARITABLE

el·e·gance \'el-i-gəns\ n **1** : refined gracefulness; also : tasteful richness (as of design) **2** : something marked by elegance — **el·e·gant** adj — **el·e·gant·ly** adv

el·e·gi·ac \,el-ə-'jī-ak, i-'lē-jē-,ak\ adj : of, relating to, or constituting an elegy; esp : expressing grief

el·e·gy \'el-ə-jē\ n : a poem expressing grief for one who is dead; also : a reflective poem usu. melancholy in tone

el·e·ment \'el-ə-mənt\ n **1** : a constituent part **2** pl : the simplest principles (as of an art or science) : RUDIMENTS **3** : a substance not separable by ordinary chemical means into substances different from itself syn component, ingredient, factor — **el·e·men·tal** \,el-ə-'ment-ᵊl\ adj

el·e·men·ta·ry \,el-ə-'men-t(ə-)rē\ adj **1** : SIMPLE, RUDIMENTARY; also : of, relating to, or teaching the basic subjects of education **2** : of or relating to an element; also : consisting of a single chemical element : UNCOMBINED

el·e·phant \'el-ə-fənt\ n : a huge mammal with the snout prolonged as a trunk and two long ivory tusks

el·e·phan·tine \,el-ə-'fan-,tēn, -,tīn\ adj **1** : of great size or strength : MASSIVE **2** : CLUMSY, PONDEROUS

el·e·vate \'el-ə-,vāt\ vb **1** : to lift up : RAISE **2** : EXALT, ENNOBLE **3** : ELATE

el·e·va·tion \,el-ə-'vā-shən\ n **1** : the height to which something is raised (as above sea level) **2** : a lifting up **3** : something (as a hill or swelling) that is elevated syn altitude

el·e·va·tor \'el-ə-,vāt-ər\ n **1** : a cage or platform for conveying something from one level to another **2** : a building for storing and discharging grain **3** : a movable surface on an airplane to produce motion up or down

elev·en \i-'lev-ən\ *n* **1** : one more than 10 **2** : the 11th in a set or series **3** : something having 11 units; *esp* : a football team — **eleven** *adj or pron* — **elev·enth** *adj or n*

elf \'elf\ *n, pl* **elves** \'elvz\ : a mischievous fairy — **elf·in** \'el-fən\ *adj* — **elf·ish** *adj*

elic·it \i-'lis-ət\ *vb* : to draw out or forth **syn** evoke, educe, extract, extort

elide \i-'līd\ *vb* : to suppress or alter by elision

el·i·gi·ble \'el-i-jə-bəl\ *adj* : qualified to be chosen — **el·i·gi·bil·i·ty** \,el-i-jə-'bil-ət-ē\ *n* — **eligible** *n*

elim·i·nate \i-'lim-ə-,nāt\ *vb* **1** : EXCLUDE, EXPEL; *esp* : to pass (wastes) from the body **2** : to leave out : IGNORE — **elim·i·na·tion** \-,lim-ə-'nā-shən\ *n*

eli·sion \i-'lizh-ən\ *n* : the omission of a final or initial sound of a word; *esp* : the omission of an unstressed vowel or syllable in a verse to achieve a uniform rhythm

elite \ā-'lēt\ *n* : the choice part; *also* : a superior group

elix·ir \i-'lik-sər\ *n* **1** : a substance held capable of prolonging life indefinitely; *also* : PANACEA **2** : a sweetened alcoholic medicinal solution

Eliz·a·be·than \i-,liz-ə-'bē-thən\ *adj* : of, relating to, or characteristic of Elizabeth I of England or her times

elk \'elk\ *n* : a very large deer; *esp* : WAPITI

¹ell \'el\ *n* : a unit of length; *esp* : a former English cloth measure of 45 inches

²ell *n* : an extension at right angles to a building **syn** wing, annex

el·lipse \i-'lips\ *n* : a closed curve of oval shape — **el·lip·tic** \-'lip-tik\ *or* **el·lip·ti·cal** *adj*

el·lip·sis \i-'lip-səs\ *n, pl* **-lip·ses** \-,sēz\ **1** : omission from an expression of a word clearly implied **2** : marks (as . . . or ∗∗∗) to show omission

elm \'elm\ *n* : a tall shade tree with spreading branches and broad top; *also* : its wood

el·o·cu·tion \,el-ə-'kyü-shən\ *n* : the art of effective public speaking — **el·o·cu·tion·ist** *n*

elon·gate \i-'lŏ[ng]-gāt\ *vb* : to make or grow longer **syn** extend, lengthen — **elon·ga·tion** \-,lŏ[ng]-'gā-shən\ *n*

elope \i-'lōp\ *vb* : to run away esp. to be married — **elope·ment** *n*

el·o·quent \'el-ə-kwənt\ *adj* **1** : speaking with ease and force **2** : of a kind to move the hearers **syn** articulate, fluent, glib — **el·o·quence** *n* — **el·o·quent·ly** *adv*

¹else \'els\ *adv* **1** : so as to differ (as in manner, place, or time) ⟨where ~ can we meet⟩ **2** : OTHERWISE ⟨obey or ~ regret⟩

²else *adj* : OTHER; *esp* : being in addition ⟨what ~ do you want⟩

else·where \-,hwer\ *adv* : in or to another place

elu·ci·date \i-'lü-sə-,dāt\ *vb* : to make clear usu. by explanation **syn** interpret — **elu·ci·da·tion** \-,lü-sə-'dā-shən\ *n*

elude \i-'lüd\ *vb* **1** : EVADE **2** : to escape the notice of

elu·sive \i-'lü-siv\ *adj* : tending to

elude : EVASIVE — **elu·sive·ly** *adv* — **elu·sive·ness** *n*

el·ver \'el-vər\ *n* : a young eel

elves *pl of* ELF

Ely·si·um \i-'liz(h)-ē-əm\ *n* : PARADISE — **Ely·sian** \-'lizh-ən\ *adj*

ema·ci·ate \i-'mā-shē-,āt\ *vb* : to become or cause to become very thin — **ema·ci·a·tion** \-,mā-s(h)ē-'ā-shən\ *n*

em·a·nate \'em-ə-,nāt\ *vb* : to come out from a source **syn** proceed, spring, rise, arise, originate — **em·a·na·tion** \,em-ə-'nā-shən\ *n*

eman·ci·pate \i-'man-sə-,pāt\ *vb* : to set free **syn** enfranchise, liberate, release, deliver, discharge — **eman·ci·pa·tion** \-,man-sə-'pā-shən\ *n* — **eman·ci·pa·tor** \-'man-sə-,pāt-ər\ *n*

emas·cu·late \i-'mas-kyə-,lāt\ *vb* : CASTRATE, GELD; *also* : WEAKEN — **emas·cu·la·tion** \-,mas-kyə-'lā-shən\ *n*

em·balm \im-'bäm\ *vb* : to treat (a corpse) with preservative preparations — **em·balm·er** *n*

em·bank \im-'ba[ng]k\ *vb* : to enclose or confine by an embankment

em·bank·ment \im-'ba[ng]k-mənt\ *n* : a raised structure (as of earth) to hold back water or carry a roadway

em·bar·go \im-'bär-gō\ *n, pl* **-goes** : a prohibition on commerce — **embargo** *vb*

em·bark \im-'bärk\ *vb* **1** : to put or go on board a ship or airplane **2** : to make a start — **em·bar·ka·tion** \,em-,bär-'kā-shən\ *n*

em·bar·rass \im-'bar-əs\ *vb* **1** : HINDER **2** : CONFUSE, DISCONCERT **3** : to involve in financial difficulties — **em·bar·rass·ment** *n*

em·bas·sy \'em-bə-sē\ *n* **1** : the function or position of an ambassador; *also* : an official mission esp. of an ambassador **2** : a group of diplomatic representatives usu. headed by an ambassador **3** : the official residence and offices of an ambassador

em·bat·tle \im-'bat-ᵊl\ *vb* : to arrange in order of battle

em·bed \-'bed\ *vb* : to enclose closely in a surrounding mass

em·bel·lish \-'bel-ish\ *vb* : ADORN, DECORATE **syn** beautify, deck, bedeck, garnish, ornament — **em·bel·lish·ment** *n*

em·ber \'em-bər\ *n* **1** : a glowing or smoldering fragment from a fire **2** *pl* : smoldering remains of a fire

em·bez·zle \im-'bez-əl\ *vb* : to take (as money) fraudulently by breach of trust — **em·bez·zle·ment** *n*

em·bit·ter \-'bit-ər\ *vb* **1** : to make bitter **2** : to arouse bitter feelings in

em·bla·zon \-'blāz-ᵊn\ *vb* **1** : to adorn with heraldic devices **2** : to make bright with color **3** : EXTOL

em·blem \'em-bləm\ *n* : something (as an object or picture) suggesting another object or an idea : SYMBOL — **em·blem·at·ic** \,em-blə-'mat-ik\ *also* **em·blem·at·i·cal** *adj*

em·body \im-'bäd-ē\ *vb* **1** : INCARNATE **2** : to express in definite form **3** : to incorporate into a system or body **syn** materialize, assimilate, identify — **em·bod·i·ment** *n*

em·bold·en \-'bōl-dən\ *vb* : to inspire with courage

em·bo·lism \'em-bə-,liz-əm\ *n* : obstruction of a blood vessel by a foreign or abnormal particle (as an air bubble or blood clot) during life — **em·bol·ic** \em-'bäl-ik\ *adj*

em·bon·point \äⁿ-bōⁿ-'pwaⁿ\ *n* : plumpness of person : STOUTNESS

em·boss \im-'bäs, -'bòs\ *vb* **1** : to ornament with raised work **2** : to raise in relief from a surface (as a head on a coin)

em·bou·chure \,äm-bù-'shùr\ *n* : the position and use of the lips in producing a musical tone on a wind instrument

em·bow·er \im-'baú(-ə)r\ *vb* : to shelter or enclose in a bower

¹em·brace \-'brās\ *vb* [MF *embracer*, fr. *en* in + *brace* the two arms, fr. L *bracchia*, pl. of *bracchium* arm] **1** : to clasp in the arms; *also* : CHERISH, LOVE **2** : ENCIRCLE **3** : to take up : ADOPT; *also* : WELCOME **4** : INCLUDE **5** : to participate in an embrace **syn** comprehend, involve

²embrace *n* : an encircling with the arms

em·bra·sure \im-'brā-zhər\ *n* **1** : a recess of a door or window **2** : an opening in a wall through which cannon are fired

em·bro·cate \'em-brə-,kāt\ *vb* : to moisten and rub (a part of the body) with a medicinal lotion or liniment — **em·bro·ca·tion** \,em-brə-'kā-shən\ *n*

em·broi·der \im-'bròid-ər\ *vb* **1** : to ornament with or do needlework **2** : to elaborate with florid detail

em·broi·dery *n* **1** : the forming of decorative designs with needlework **2** : something embroidered

em·broil \im-'bròil\ *vb* : to throw into confusion or strife — **em·broil·ment** *n*

em·bryo \'em-brē-,ō\ *n* : a living being in its earliest stages of development — **em·bry·on·ic** \,em-brē-'än-ik\ *adj*

em·bry·ol·o·gy \,em-brē-'äl-ə-jē\ *n* : a branch of biology dealing with embryos and their development — **em·bry·o·log·i·cal** \-brē-ə-'läj-i-kəl\ *adj* — **em·bry·ol·o·gist** \-brē-'äl-ə-jəst\ *n*

em·cee \'em-'sē\ *n* : MASTER OF CEREMONIES — **emcee** *vb*

emend \ē-'mend\ *vb* : to correct or alter usu. by altering the text of **syn** rectify, revise, amend — **emen·da·tion** \,ē-,men-'dā-shən, ,em-ən-\ *n*

¹em·er·ald \'em-(ə-)rəld\ *n* : a green beryl prized as a gem

²emerald *adj* : brightly or richly green

emerge \i-'mərj\ *vb* : to rise, come forth, or come out into view **syn** appear, loom — **emer·gence** *n* — **emer·gent** *adj*

emer·gen·cy \i-'mər-jən-sē\ *n* : an unforeseen happening or state of affairs requiring prompt action **syn** exigency, contingency, crisis

emer·i·tus \i-'mer-ət-əs\ *adj* : retired from active duty

em·ery \'em-(ə-)rē\ *n* : a dark granular corundum used esp. for grinding

emet·ic \i-'met-ik\ *n* : an agent that induces vomiting — **emetic** *adj*

em·i·grate \'em-ə-,grāt\ *vb* : to leave a place (as a country) to settle elsewhere — **em·i·grant** \-grənt\ *n* — **em·i·gra·tion** \,em-ə-'grā-shən\ *n*

émi·gré *or* **em·i·gré** \,em-ə-'grā\ *n* : a person who emigrates esp. because of political conditions

em·i·nence \'em-ə-nəns\ *n* **1** : high

rank or position; *also* : a person of high rank or attainments **2** : a lofty place

em·i·nent *adj* **1** : CONSPICUOUS, EVIDENT **2** : LOFTY, HIGH **3** : DISTINGUISHED, PROMINENT ⟨~ men⟩ — **em·i·nent·ly** *adv*

emir \i-'miər\ *n* : a native ruler in parts of Africa and Asia

em·is·sary \'em-ə-,ser-ē\ *n* : AGENT; *esp* : a secret agent

emit \ē-'mit\ *vb* **emit·ted**; **emit·ting** **1** : to give off or out ⟨~ light⟩; *also* : EJECT **2** : to put (as money) into circulation **3** : EXPRESS, UTTER — **emis·sion** \-'mish-ən\ *n*

emol·lient \i-'mäl-yənt\ *adj* : making soft or supple; *also* : soothing esp. to the skin or mucous membrane — **emol·lient** *n*

emol·u·ment \i-'mäl-yə-mənt\ *n* : the product (as salary or fees) of an employment

emote \i-'mōt\ *vb* : to give expression to emotion in or as if in a play

emo·tion \i-'mō-shən\ *n* : a usu. intense feeling (as of love, hate, or despair) — **emo·tion·al** *adj* — **emo·tion·al·ly** *adv*

em·pa·thy \'em-pə-thē\ *n* : capacity for participating in the feelings or ideas of another — **em·path·ic** \em-'path-ik\ *n*

em·per·or \'em-pər-ər\ *n* : the sovereign ruler of an empire

em·pha·sis \'em-fə-səs\ *n*, *pl* **-pha·ses** \-,sēz\ : particular stress or prominence given (as to a phrase in speaking or to a phase of action)

em·pha·size \-,sīz\ *vb* : STRESS

em·phat·ic \im-'fat-ik\ *adj* : uttered with emphasis : STRESSED — **em·phat·i·cal·ly** *adv*

em·pire \'em-,pī(ə)r\ *n* **1** : a group of states under a single sovereign who is usu. an emperor **2** : imperial sovereignty or dominion

em·pir·i·cal \im-'pir-i-kəl\ *or* **em·pir·ic** *adj* : depending or based on experience or observation; *also* : subject to verification by observation or experiment ⟨~ laws⟩ — **em·pir·i·cal·ly** *adv*

em·pir·i·cism \-'pir-ə-,siz-əm\ *n* : the practice of relying upon experience and experiment esp. in the natural sciences — **em·pir·i·cist** \-,sist\ *n*

em·place·ment \im-'plās-mənt\ *n* : a prepared position for weapons or military equipment **2** : PLACEMENT

¹em·ploy \im-'plòi\ *vb* **1** : USE **2** : to use the services of **3** : OCCUPY, DEVOTE

²employ *n* : EMPLOYMENT

em·ploy·ee \im-,plòi-'ē, -em-\ *n* : a person who works for another

em·ploy·er \im-'plòi(-ə)r\ *n* : one that employs

em·ploy·ment \im-'plòi-mənt\ *n* **1** : the act of employing : the condition of being employed **2** : OCCUPATION, ACTIVITY

em·po·ri·um \im-'pōr-ē-əm\ *n*, *pl* **-ri·ums** *also* **-ria** \-ē-ə\ : a commercial center; *esp* : a store carrying varied articles

em·pow·er \im-'paú(-ə)r\ *vb* : AUTHORIZE

em·press \'em-prəs\ *n* **1** : the wife or widow of an emperor **2** : a woman holding an imperial title in her own right

---

ə abut; ⁰ kitten; ər further; a back; ā bake; ä cot, cart; aú out; ch chin; e less; ē easy; g gift; i trip; ī life; j joke; ŋ sing; ō flow; ò flaw; òi coin; th thin; th̲ this; ü loot; ù foot; y yet; yü few; yù furious; zh vision

1emp·ty \\'emp-tē\\ *adj* **1** : containing nothing **2** : UNOCCUPIED, UNINHABITED **3** : lacking value, force, sense, or purpose **syn** vacant, blank, void, idle, hollow, vain — **emp·ti·ness** *n*

2empty *vb* **1** : to make or become empty **2** : to discharge its contents; *also* : to transfer by emptying

emp·ty-hand·ed \\,emp-tē-'han-dəd\\ *adj* **1** : having nothing in the hands **2** : having acquired or gained nothing

em·py·re·an \\,em-,pī-'rē-ən, -pī-\\ *n* : the highest heaven; *also* : HEAVENS, FIRMAMENT

emu \\'ē-myü\\ *n* : a flightless Australian bird smaller than the related ostrich

em·u·late \\'em-yə-,lāt\\ *vb* : to strive to equal or excel : RIVAL — **em·u·la·tion** \\,em-yə-'lā-shən\\ *n* — **em·u·lous** \\'em-yə-ləs\\ *adj*

emul·si·fi·er \\i-'məl-sə-,fī(-ə)r\\ *n* : something (as a soap) that promotes the formation and stabilizing of an emulsion

emul·si·fy \\-,fī\\ *vb* : to convert into or become an emulsion — **emul·si·fi·able** *adj* — **emul·si·fi·ca·tion** \\-,məl-sə-fə-'kā-shən\\ *n*

emul·sion \\i-'məl-shən\\ *n* **1** : a mixture of mutually insoluble liquids in which one is dispersed in droplets throughout the other (an ~ of oil in water) **2** : a light-sensitive coating on photographic film or paper

1-en \\ən, ᵊn\\ *also* **-n** \\n\\ *adj suffix* : made of : consisting of (earthen) (woolen) (leathern)

2-en *vb suffix* **1** : become or cause to be (sharpen) **2** : cause or come to have (lengthen)

en·able \\in-'ā-bəl\\ *vb* **1** : to make able or feasible **2** : to give legal power, capacity, or sanction to

en·act \\-'akt\\ *vb* **1** : to make into law **2** : to act out — **en·act·ment** *n*

enam·el \\in-'am-əl\\ *n* **1** : a glasslike substance used for coating the surface of metal or pottery **2** : the hard outer layer of a tooth **3** : a usu. glossy paint that forms a hard coat — **enamel** *vb*

enam·el·ware \\-,waər\\ *n* : metal utensils (as pots and pans) coated with enamel

en·am·or \\in-'am-ər\\ *vb* : to inflame with love

enamour *chiefly Brit var of* ENAMOR

en bloc \\äⁿ-'bläk\\ *adv* (*or adj*) : as a whole : in a mass

en·camp \\in-'kamp\\ *vb* : to make camp — **en·camp·ment** *n*

en·cap·su·late \\-'kap-sə-,lāt\\ *vb* : to encase or become encased in a capsule

en·case \\-'kās\\ *vb* : to enclose in or as if in a case

-ence \\əns, ᵊns\\ *n suffix* **1** : action or process (emergence) : instance of an action or process (reference) **2** : quality or state (dependence)

en·ceinte \\äⁿ-'sant\\ *adj* : PREGNANT

en·ceph·a·li·tis \\en-,sef-ə-'līt-əs\\ *n* : inflammation of the brain — **en·ceph·a·lit·ic** \\-'lit-ik\\ *adj*

en·chain \\in-'chān\\ *vb* : FETTER, CHAIN

en·chant \\-'chant\\ *vb* **1** : BEWITCH **2** : ENRAPTURE, FASCINATE — **en·chant·er** *n* — **en·chant·ment** *n* — **en·chant·ress** \\'chan-trəs\\ *n*

en·chant·ing *adj* : CHARMING

en·chi·la·da \\,en-chə-'läd-ə\\ *n* : a tortilla rolled with meat filling and served with tomato sauce seasoned with chili

en·ci·pher \\in-'sī-fər\\ *vb* : to convert (a message) into cipher

en·cir·cle \\in-'sər-kəl\\ *vb* : to pass completely around : SURROUND — **en·cir·cle·ment** *n*

en·clave \\'en-,klāv, 'än-\\ *n* : a territorial or culturally distinct unit enclosed within foreign territory

en·close \\in-'klōz\\ *vb* **1** : to shut up or in; *esp* : to surround with a fence **2** : to put in a cover along with a parcel or letter (~ a check) — **en·clo·sure** \\-'klō-zhər\\ *n*

en·code \\-'kōd\\ *vb* : to convert (a message) into code

en·co·mi·um \\en-'kō-mē-əm\\ *n, pl* **-mi·ums** *or* **-mia** \\-mē-ə\\ : high or glowing praise

en·com·pass \\in-'kəm-pəs, -'käm-\\ *vb* **1** : ENCIRCLE **2** : ENVELOP, INCLUDE, CONTAIN

1en·core \\'än-,kōr\\ *n* : a demand for repetition or reappearance; *also* : a further performance (as of a singer) in response

2encore *vb* : to request an encore from

1en·coun·ter \\in-'kaunt-ər\\ *vb* **1** : to meet as an enemy : FIGHT **2** : to meet usu. unexpectedly

2encounter *n* **1** : a hostile meeting; *esp* : COMBAT **2** : a chance meeting

en·cour·age \\in-'kər-ij\\ *vb* **1** : to inspire with courage and hope **2** : STIMULATE, INCITE; *also* : FOSTER — **en·cour·age·ment** *n*

en·croach \\-'krōch\\ *vb* : to enter or force oneself gradually upon another's property or rights : TRESPASS — **en·croach·ment** *n*

en·crust \\-'krəst\\ *vb* : to provide with or form a crust

en·cum·ber \\-'kəm-bər\\ *vb* **1** : to weigh down : BURDEN **2** : to hinder the function or activity of — **en·cum·brance** \\-brəns\\ *n*

-en·cy \\ən-sē, ᵊn-\\ *n suffix, pl* **-encies** : quality or state (despondency)

1en·cyc·li·cal \\in-'sik-li-kəl\\ *adj* : addressed to all the individuals of a group

2encyclical *n* : an encyclical letter; *esp* : a papal letter to the bishops of the church

en·cy·clo·pe·dia \\in-,sī-klə-'pēd-ē-ə\\ *n* : a work treating the various branches of learning — **en·cy·clo·pe·dic** *adj*

1end \\'end\\ *n* **1** : the part of an area that lies at the boundary; *also* : a point which marks the extent or limit of something or at which something ceases to exist **2** : a ceasing of a course (as of action or activity); *also* : DEATH **3** : an ultimate state; *also* : RESULT, ISSUE **4** : REMNANT **5** : PURPOSE, OBJECTIVE **6** : a share or phase esp. of an undertaking **7** : a player stationed at the extremity of a line (as in football)

2end *vb* **1** : to bring or come to an end **2** : to put to death; *also* : DIE **3** : to form or be at the end of (*syn* close, conclude, terminate, finish

en·dan·ger \\in-'dān-jər\\ *vb* : to bring into danger : IMPERIL, RISK

en·dear \\-'diər\\ *vb* : to cause to become an object of affection

en·dear·ment *n* : a sign of affection : CARESS

en·deav·or \\in-'dev-ər\\ *vb* : TRY, ATTEMPT — **endeavor** *n*

en·dem·ic \\en-'dem-ik\\ *adj* : restricted or peculiar to a particular place (~ plants) (an ~ disease)

end·ing n : something that forms an end; esp : SUFFIX

en·dive \'en-,dīv\ n : an herb related to chicory and grown as a salad plant; also : the blanched shoot of chicory

end·less \'end-ləs\ adj 1 : having no end : ETERNAL 2 : united at the ends : CONTINUOUS ⟨an ∼ belt⟩ syn interminable, everlasting, unceasing — **end·less·ly** adv

end man n : a man at each end of the line of performers in a minstrel show who engages in comic repartee with the interlocutor

end·most \'en(d)-,mōst\ adj : situated at the very end

en·do·crine \'en-də-krən, -,krīn, -,krēn\ adj : producing secretions that are distributed by way of the bloodstream ⟨∼ glands⟩; also : HORMONAL ⟨∼ effects⟩ — **endocrine** n — **en·do·cri·nol·o·gy** \,en-də-kri-'näl-ə-jē\ n

en·dorse \in-'dors\ vb 1 : to sign one's name on the back of (as a check) for some purpose 2 : APPROVE, SANCTION syn accredit — **en·dorse·ment** n

en·dow \-'daù\ vb 1 : to furnish with funds for support ⟨∼ a school⟩ 2 : to furnish with something freely or naturally ⟨∼ed with beauty⟩ — **en·dow·ment** n

en·due \-'d(y)ü\ vb : to provide with some quality or power

en·dur·ance \-'d(y)ùr-əns\ n 1 : DURATION 2 : ability to withstand hardship or stress : FORTITUDE

en·dure \-'d(y)ùr\ vb 1 : LAST, PERSIST 2 : to suffer firmly or patiently : BEAR 3 : TOLERATE syn continue, abide — **en·dur·able** adj

end·ways \'end-,wāz\ or **end·wise** \-,wīz\ adv (or adj) 1 : with the end forward 2 : LENGTHWISE 3 : on end

en·e·ma \'en-ə-mə\ n : injection of liquid into the rectum; also : material so injected

en·e·my \'en-ə-mē\ n [OF enemi, fr. L inimicus personal enemy, fr. in- un- + amicus friend, fr. amare to love] : one that attacks or tries to harm another : FOE; esp : a military opponent

en·er·get·ic \,en-ər-'jet-ik\ adj : marked by energy : ACTIVE, VIGOROUS syn strenuous, lusty — **en·er·get·i·cal·ly** adv

en·er·gize \'en-ər-,jīz\ vb : to give energy to : make energetic

en·er·gy \-jē\ n 1 : vitality of expression 2 : capacity for action : VIGOR; also : vigorous action 3 : capacity for performing work syn strength, might

en·er·vate \'en-ər-,vāt\ vb : to lessen the strength or vigor of : weaken in mind or body

en·fee·ble \in-'fē-bəl\ vb : to make feeble syn weaken, debilitate, sap, undermine — **en·fee·ble·ment** n

en·fi·lade \'en-fə-,lād\ n : gunfire directed along the length of an enemy battle line

en·fold \in-'fōld\ vb 1 : ENVELOP 2 : EMBRACE

en·force \-'fōrs\ vb 1 : COMPEL ⟨∼ obedience by threats⟩ 2 : to execute with vigor ⟨∼ the law⟩ — **en·force·able** adj — **en·force·ment** n

en·fran·chise \-'fran-,chīz\ vb 1 : to set free (as from slavery) 2 : to admit to citizenship; also : to grant the vote to — **en·fran·chise·ment** \-,chīz-mənt, -,chəz-\ n

en·gage \-'gāj\ vb 1 : to offer as security : PLEDGE 2 : to attract and hold esp. by interesting ⟨engaged his friend's attention⟩; also : to cause to participate 3 : to connect or interlock with : MESH; also : to cause to mesh 4 : BETROTH 5 : EMPLOY, HIRE 6 : to bring or enter into conflict 7 : to commence or take part in a venture (as in business)

en·gage·ment n 1 : BETROTHAL 2 : EMPLOYMENT 3 : a hostile encounter 4 : APPOINTMENT

en·gag·ing adj : ATTRACTIVE — **en·gag·ing·ly** adv

en·gen·der \in-'jen-dər\ vb 1 : BEGET 2 : to bring into being : CREATE, PRODUCE syn generate, breed, sire

en·gine \'en-jən\ n 1 : a mechanical device; esp : a machine used in war 2 : a machine by which physical power is applied to produce a physical effect 3 : LOCOMOTIVE

¹en·gi·neer \,en-jə-'niər\ n 1 : a member of a military group devoted to engineering work 2 : a designer or builder of engines 3 : one trained in engineering 4 : one that operates an engine

²engineer vb 1 : to lay out or manage as an engineer syn guide, pilot, lead, steer

en·gi·neer·ing n : a science by which the properties of matter and sources of energy are made useful to man in structures, machines, and products

En·glish \'iŋ-glish\ n 1 English pl : the people of England 2 : the language of England, the U.S., and many areas now or formerly under British rule — **English** adj — **En·glish·man** \-mən\ n

en·graft \in-'graft\ vb : GRAFT 1; also : IMPLANT

en·grave \-'grāv\ vb 1 : to produce (as letters or lines) by incising a surface 2 : to incise (as stone or metal) to produce a representation (as of letters or figures) esp. that may be printed from; also : to print from such a plate 3 : PHOTOENGRAVE — **en·grav·er** n

en·grav·ing n 1 : the art of one who engraves 2 : an engraved plate; also : a print made from it

en·gross \in-'grōs\ vb 1 : to copy or write in a large hand; also : to prepare the final text of (an official document) 2 : to occupy fully (the scene ⟨∼ed his interest⟩ syn monopolize, absorb

en·gulf \-'gəlf\ vb : to flow over and enclose

en·hance \-'hans\ vb : to make greater (as in value or desirability) syn heighten, intensify — **en·hance·ment** n

enig·ma \i-'nig-mə\ n : something obscure or hard to understand : PUZZLE

en·ig·mat·ic \,en-ig-'mat-ik, ,ēn-\ also **en·ig·mat·i·cal** \-i-kəl\ adj : resembling an enigma : CRYPTIC, PUZZLING syn obscure, ambiguous, equivocal — **en·ig·mat·i·cal·ly** adv

en·isle \in-'īl\ vb 1 : ISOLATE 2 : to make an island of

en·jamb·ment or **en·jambe·ment** \in-'jam-mənt\ n : the running over of a sentence from one verse or couplet into another so that closely related words fall in different lines

en·join \in-'join\ *vb* **1** : COMMAND, ORDER **2** : FORBID *syn* direct, bid, charge, prohibit

en·joy \-'joi\ *vb* **1** : to take pleasure or satisfaction in ⟨~ed the concert⟩ : have and use with satisfaction **2** : to have for one's benefit, use, or lot ⟨~ good health⟩ *syn* like, love, relish, fancy, possess, own — **en·joy·able** *adj* — **en·joy·ment** *n*

en·large \-'lärj\ *vb* **1** : to make or grow larger **2** : to set free **3** : to speak or write at length *syn* increase, augment, multiply — **en·large·ment** *n*

en·light·en \-'līt-ᵊn\ *vb* **1** : INSTRUCT, INFORM **2** : to give spiritual insight to *syn* illuminate — **en·light·en·ment** *n*

en·list \-'list\ *vb* **1** : to engage for service in the armed forces **2** : to secure the aid or support of — **en·list·ment** *n*

en·liv·en \-'lī-vən\ *vb* : to give life, action, or spirit to : ANIMATE

en masse \än-'mas\ *adv* : in a body : as a whole

en·mesh \in-'mesh\ *vb* : to catch or entangle in or as if in meshes

en·mi·ty \'en-mət-ē\ *n* : ILL WILL; *esp* : mutual hatred *syn* hostility, antipathy, animosity, rancor

en·no·ble \in-'ō-bəl\ *vb* : ELEVATE, EXALT; *esp* : to raise to noble rank — **en·no·ble·ment** *n*

en·nui \'än-'wē\ *n* : BOREDOM

enor·mi·ty \i-'nòr-mət-ē\ *n* **1** : great wickedness **2** : an outrageous act **3** : huge size

enor·mous \-məs\ *adj* **1** : exceedingly wicked **2** : great in size, number, or degree : HUGE *syn* immense, vast, gigantic, giant, colossal, mammoth, elephantine

¹enough \i-'nəf\ *adj* : SUFFICIENT *syn* adequate

²enough *adv* **1** : SUFFICIENTLY **2** : TOLERABLY

³enough *n* : SUFFICIENCY

en·plane \in-'plān\ *vb* : to board an airplane

en·quire \in-'kwī(ə)r\, **en·qui·ry** \in-'kwī(ə)r-ē, 'in-kwə-rē\ *var of* INQUIRE, INQUIRY

en·rage \in-'rāj\ *vb* : to fill with rage : ANGER

en·rap·ture \-'rap-chər\ *vb* : DELIGHT

en·rich \-'rich\ *vb* **1** : to make rich or richer **2** : ORNAMENT, ADORN — **en·rich·ment** *n*

en·roll *or* **en·rol** \-'rōl\ *vb* **-rolled; -roll·ing 1** : to enter or register on a roll or list **2** : to offer (oneself) for enrolling — **en·roll·ment** *n*

en route \än-'rüt, en-\ *adv* : on or along the way

en·sconce \in-'skäns\ *vb* **1** : SHELTER, CONCEAL **2** : to settle snugly or securely *syn* secrete, hide

en·sem·ble \än-'säm-bəl\ *n* **1** : SET, WHOLE **2** : integrated music of two or more parts **3** : a complete costume of harmonizing garments **4** : a group of persons (as musicians) acting together to produce a particular effect or end

en·sheathe \in-'shēth\ *vb* : to cover with or as if with a sheath

en·shrine \in-'shrīn\ *vb* **1** : to enclose in or as if in a shrine **2** : to cherish as sacred

en·shroud \-'shraud\ *vb* : SHROUD, OBSCURE

en·sign \'en-sən, *1 also* -,sīn\ *n* **1** : FLAG; *also* : BADGE, EMBLEM **2** : a commissioned officer in the navy ranking next below a lieutenant junior grade

en·si·lage \'en-sə-lij\ *n* : SILAGE

en·sile \en-'sīl\ *vb* : to prepare and store (fodder) for silage

en·slave \in-'slāv\ *vb* : to make a slave of — **en·slave·ment** *n*

en·snare \-'snaər\ *vb* : SNARE, TRAP *syn* entrap, bag, catch, capture

en·sue \-'sü\ *vb* : to follow as a consequence or in time : RESULT

en·sure \-'shùr\ *vb* : INSURE, GUARANTEE *syn* assure, secure

¹-ent \ənt, ᵊnt\ *n suffix* : one that performs (a specified action) ⟨regent⟩ ⟨tangent⟩

²-ent *adj suffix* : doing, behaving, or existing (in the way specified) : -ING ⟨apparent⟩ ⟨reverent⟩

en·tail \in-'tāl\ *vb* **1** : to limit the inheritance of (property) to the owner's lineal descendants or to a class thereof **2** : to include or involve as a necessary result

en·tan·gle \-'taŋ-gəl\ *vb* : TANGLE, CONFUSE — **en·tan·gle·ment** *n*

en·tente \än-'tänt\ *n* : an understanding providing for joint action; *also* : parties linked by such an entente

en·ter \'ent-ər\ *vb* **1** : to go or come in or into **2** : to become a member of : JOIN ⟨~ the ministry⟩ **3** : BEGIN **4** : to take part in : CONTRIBUTE **5** : to set down (as in a list) : REGISTER **6** : to place (a complaint) before a court; *also* : to put on record ⟨~ed his objections⟩ **7** : to go into or upon and take possession ⟨~ rented premises⟩

en·ter·i·tis \,ent-ə-'rīt-əs\ *n* : intestinal inflammation

en·ter·prise \'ent-ər-prīz\ *n* **1** : UNDERTAKING, PROJECT **2** : a business organization **3** : readiness for daring action : INITIATIVE

en·ter·pris·ing *adj* : bold and vigorous in action : ENERGETIC

en·ter·tain \,ent-ər-'tān\ *vb* **1** : to treat or receive as a guest **2** : to hold in mind **3** : AMUSE, DIVERT *syn* harbor, shelter, lodge, house — **en·ter·tain·er** *n* — **en·ter·tain·ment** *n*

en·thrall *or* **en·thral** \in-'thròl\ *vb* **-thralled; -thrall·ing 1** : ENSLAVE **2** : to hold spellbound

en·throne \-'thrōn\ *vb* **1** : to seat on or as if on a throne **2** : EXALT

en·thuse \in-'th(y)üz\ *vb* **1** : to make enthusiastic **2** : to show enthusiasm

en·thu·si·asm \in-'th(y)ü-zē-,az-əm\ *n* **1** : strong warmth of feeling : keen interest : FERVOR **2** : a cause of fervor — **en·thu·si·ast** \-,ast, -əst\ *n* — **en·thu·si·as·tic** \-,th(y)ü-zē-'as-tik\ *adj* — **en·thu·si·as·ti·cal·ly** *adv*

en·tice \in-'tīs\ *vb* : ALLURE, TEMPT — **en·tice·ment** *n*

en·tire \-'tī(ə)r\ *adj* : COMPLETE, WHOLE *syn* total, all, gross, perfect, intact — **en·tire·ly** *adv*

en·tire·ty \-'tī-rət-ē, -'tī(ə)rt-ē\ *n* **1** : COMPLETENESS **2** : WHOLE, TOTALITY

en·ti·tle \-'tīt-ᵊl\ *vb* **1** : NAME, DESIGNATE **2** : to give a right or claim to

en·ti·ty \'ent-ət-ē\ *n* **1** : EXISTENCE, BEING **2** : something with separate and real existence

en·tomb \in-'tüm\ *vb* : to place in a

tomb : BURY — **en·tomb·ment** \-'tüm-mənt\ n

en·to·mol·o·gy \,ent-ə-'mäl-ə-jē\ n : a branch of zoology that deals with insects — **en·to·mo·log·i·cal** \-mə-'läj-i-kəl\ adj — **en·to·mol·o·gist** \-'mäl-ə-jəst\ n

en·tou·rage \,änt-ə-'räzh\ n : RETINUE

en·tr'acte \än-'trakt\ n 1 : the interval between two acts of a play   2 : something (as a dance) performed between two acts of a play

en·trails \'en-trəlz -,trālz\ n pl : VISCERA; esp : INTESTINES

en·train \in-'trān\ vb : to put or go aboard a railroad train

¹**en·trance** \'en-trəns\ n 1 : the act of entering   2 : a means or place of entry   3 : permission or right to enter

²**en·trance** \in-'trans\ vb : CHARM, DELIGHT

en·trant \'en-trənt\ n : one that enters esp. as a competitor

en·trap \in-'trap\ vb : ENSNARE, TRAP — **en·trap·ment** n

en·treat \in-'trēt\ vb : to ask earnestly or urgently : BESEECH syn beg, implore — **en·treaty** \-'trēt-ē\ n

en·trée or **en·tree** \'än-,trā\ n 1 : ENTRANCE   2 : a dish served before the roast or between the chief courses; also : the principal dish of a meal syn entry, access

en·trench \in-'trench\ vb 1 : to surround with a trench; also : to establish in a strong defensive position ⟨~ed customs⟩   2 : ENCROACH, TRESPASS — **en·trench·ment** n

en·tre·pre·neur \,än-trə-prə-'nər\ n : an organizer or promoter of an activity; esp : one that manages and assumes the risk of a business

en·tro·py \'en-trə-pē\ n 1 : a measure of the unavailable energy of a system   2 : an ultimate state of inert uniformity

en·trust \in-'trəst\ vb 1 : to commit something to as a trust   2 : to commit to another with confidence syn confide, consign, relegate

en·try \'en-trē\ n 1 : ENTRANCE 1, 2; also : VESTIBULE   2 : an entering in a record; also : an item so entered   3 : a headword with its definition or identification; also : VOCABULARY ENTRY   4 : one entered for a contest

en·twine \in-'twīn\ vb : to twine together or around

enu·mer·ate \i-'n(y)ü-mə-,rāt\ vb 1 : to determine the number of : COUNT   2 : LIST — **enu·mer·a·tion** \-,n(y)ü-mə-'rā-shən\ n

enun·ci·ate \ē-'nən-sē-,āt\ vb 1 : to state definitely; also : ANNOUNCE, PROCLAIM   2 : PRONOUNCE, ARTICULATE — **enun·ci·a·tion** \-,nən-sē-'ā-shən\ n

en·vel·op \in-'vel-əp\ vb : to enclose completely with or as if with a covering — **en·vel·op·ment** n

en·ve·lope \'en-və-,lōp, 'än-\ n 1 : WRAPPER, COVERING   2 : a usu. paper container for a letter   3 : the bag containing the gas in a balloon or airship

en·ven·om \in-'ven-əm\ vb 1 : to taint or fill with poison   2 : EMBITTER

en·vi·able \'en-vē-ə-bəl\ adj : highly desirable — **en·vi·ably** adv

en·vi·ous \'en-vē-əs\ adj : feeling or

showing envy — **en·vi·ous·ly** adv — **en·vi·ous·ness** n

en·vi·ron·ment \in-'vī-rən-mənt\ n : SURROUNDINGS — **en·vi·ron·men·tal** \-,vī-rən-'ment-ᵊl\ adj

en·vi·rons \in-'vī-rənz\ n pl 1 : SUBURBS   2 : ENVIRONMENT; also : VICINITY

en·vis·age \in-'viz-ij\ vb : to have a mental picture of : VISUALIZE

en·voi or **en·voy** \'en-,vȯi, 'än-\ n : the concluding remarks to a poem, essay, or book

en·voy \'en-,vȯi, 'än-\ n 1 : a diplomatic agent   2 : REPRESENTATIVE, MESSENGER

¹**en·vy** \'en-vē\ n : grudging desire for or discontent at the sight of another's excellence or advantages; also : an object of envy

²**envy** vb : to feel envy toward or on account of

en·wreathe \in-'rēth\ vb : WREATHE, ENVELOP

en·zyme \'en-,zīm\ n : a complex mostly protein product of living cells that induces or speeds chemical reactions in plants and animals without being itself permanently altered — **en·zy·mat·ic** \,en-zə-'mat-ik\ adj

eon \'ē-ən, 'ē-,än\ var of AEON

ep·au·let also **ep·au·lette** \,ep-ə-'let\ n : a shoulder ornament esp. on a uniform

épée \'ep-,ā, ā-'pā\ n : a fencing or dueling sword having a bowl-shaped guard and a tapering rigid blade with no cutting edge

eper·gne \i-'pərn\ n : a composite centerpiece of silver or glass used esp. on a dinner table

ephed·rine \i-'fed-rən\ n : a drug used in relieving hay fever, asthma, and nasal congestion

ephem·er·al \i-'fem-(ə-)rəl\ adj : SHORT-LIVED, TRANSITORY syn passing, fleeting

ep·ic \'ep-ik\ n : a long poem in elevated style narrating the deeds of a hero — **epic** adj

ep·i·cure \'ep-i-,kyur\ n [after Epicurus d270 B.C. Greek hedonistic philosopher] : a person with sensitive and fastidious tastes esp. in food and wine — **ep·i·cu·re·an** \,ep-i-kyu-'rē-ən\ n : EPICURE — **epicurean** adj

¹**ep·i·dem·ic** \,ep-ə-'dem-ik\ adj : affecting many persons at one time ⟨~ disease⟩; also : excessively prevalent

²**epidemic** n : an epidemic outbreak esp. of disease

epi·der·mis \,ep-ə-'dər-məs\ n : an outer layer esp. of skin — **epi·der·mal** \-məl\ adj

epi·glot·tis \,ep-ə-'glät-əs\ n : a thin plate of flexible tissue protecting the tracheal opening during swallowing

ep·i·gram \'ep-ə-,gram\ n : a short witty poem or saying — **ep·i·gram·mat·ic** \,ep-ə-grə-'mat-ik\ adj

epig·ra·phy \i-'pig-rə-fē\ n : the study of inscriptions and esp. of ancient inscriptions

ep·i·lep·sy \'ep-ə-,lep-sē\ n : a nervous disorder marked typically by convulsive attacks with loss of consciousness — **ep·i·lep·tic** \,ep-ə-'lep-tik\ adj or n

ep·i·logue \'ep-ə-,lȯg\ n : a speech often

ə abut; ᵊ kitten; ər further; a back; ā bake; ä cot, cart; aù out; ch chin; e less; ē easy; g gift; i trip; ī life; j joke; ŋ sing; ō flow; ȯ flaw; ȯi coin; th thin; th this; ü loot; ù foot; y yet; yü few; yù furious; zh vision

in verse addressed to the spectators by an actor at the end of a play

Epiph·a·ny \i-'pif-ə-nē\ n : a feast on January 6 commemorating the coming of the Magi to Jesus at Bethlehem

epis·co·pa·cy \i-'pis-kə-pə-sē\ n 1 : government of a church by bishops 2 : EPISCOPATE

epis·co·pal \-pəl\ adj 1 : of or relating to a bishop 2 : of, having, or constituting government by bishops 3 cap : of or relating to the Protestant Episcopal Church

Epis·co·pa·lian \i-,pis-kə-'pāl-yən\ n : a member of the Protestant Episcopal Church

epis·co·pate \i-'pis-kə-pət\ n 1 : the rank, office, or term of bishop 2 : a body of bishops

ep·i·sode \'ep-ə,sōd\ n 1 : a unit of action in a dramatic or literary work 2 : an incident in a course of events : OCCURRENCE (a feverish ~) — **ep·i·sod·ic** \,ep-ə-'säd-ik\ adj

epis·tle \i-'pis-əl\ n 1 cap : one of the letters of the New Testament 2 : LETTER — **epis·to·lary** \'pis-tə-,ler-ē\ adj

ep·i·taph \'ep-ə,taf\ n : an inscription (as on a tomb) in memory of a dead person

ep·i·tha·la·mi·um \,ep-ə-thə-'lā-mē-əm\ or **ep·i·tha·la·mi·on** \-mē-ən\ n, pl **-mi·ums** or **-mia** \-mē-ə\ : a song or poem in honor of a bride and bridegroom

ep·i·the·li·um \,ep-ə-'thē-lē-əm\ n : a cellular membrane covering a bodily surface or lining a cavity — **ep·i·the·li·al** adj

ep·i·thet \'ep-ə-,thet\ n : a characterizing and often abusive word or phrase

epit·o·me \i-'pit-ə-mē\ n 1 : ABSTRACT, SUMMARY 2 : EMBODIMENT — **epit·o·mize** \-,mīz\ vb

ep·och \'ep-ək, -,äk\ n : a usu. extended period : ERA, AGE — **ep·och·al** adj

ep·oxy resin \(,)ep-,äk-sē-\ n : a synthetic resin used in coatings and adhesives

eq·ua·ble \'ek-wə-bəl, 'ēk-\ adj : UNIFORM, EVEN; esp : free from unpleasant extremes — **eq·ua·bil·i·ty** \,ek-wə-'bil-ət-ē, ,ēk-\ n — **eq·ua·bly** \'ek-wə-blē, 'ēk-\ adv

¹equal \'ē-kwəl\ adj 1 : of the same measure, quantity, value, quality, number, or degree as another : EVEN, EQUIVALENT 2 : IMPARTIAL 3 : free from extremes 4 : able to cope with a situation or task syn same, identical — **equal·i·ty** \i-'kwäl-ət-ē\ n — **equal·ly** \'ē-kwə-lē\ adv

²equal n : one that is equal; esp : a person of like rank, abilities, or age

³equal vb **equaled** or **equalled**; **equal·ing** or **equal·ling** : to be or become equal to : MATCH

equal·ize \'ē-kwə-,līz\ vb : to make equal, uniform, or constant — **equal·iza·tion** \,ē-kwə-lə-'zā-shən\ n — **equal·iz·er** \'ē-kwə-,lī-zər\ n

equa·nim·i·ty \,ek-wə-'nim-ət-e, ,ēk-\ n : evenness of mind : COMPOSURE

equate \i-'kwāt\ vb : to make, treat, or regard as equal or comparable

equa·tion \i-'kwā-zhən, -shən\ n 1 : an act of equating 2 : the state of being equated 2 : a usu. formal statement of equivalence (as between mathematical or logical expressions) with the relation

typically symbolized by the sign =

equa·tor \i-'kwāt-ər\ n : an imaginary circle around the earth that is everywhere equally distant from the two poles and divides the earth's surface into the northern and southern hemispheres — **equa·to·ri·al** \,ēk-wə-'tōr-ē-əl, ,ek-\ adj

eq·uer·ry \'ek-wə-rē, i-'kwer-ē\ n 1 : an officer in charge of the horses of a prince or nobleman 2 : a personal attendant of a member of the British royal family

¹eques·tri·an \i-'kwes-trē-ən\ adj 1 : of or relating to horses, horsemen, or horsemanship 2 : representing a person on horseback

²equestrian n : one that rides on horseback

eques·tri·enne \i-,kwes-trē-'en\ n : a female equestrian

equi·dis·tant \,ē-kwə-'dis-tənt\ adj : equally distant

equi·lat·er·al \-'lat-(ə-)rəl\ adj : having equal sides

equi·lib·ri·um \-'lib-rē-əm\ n, pl **-ri·ums** or **-ria** \-rē-ə\ : a state of balance between opposing forces or actions syn poise

equine \'ē-,kwīn\ adj : of or relating to the horse — **equine** n

equi·nox \'ē-kwə-,näks\ n : either of the two times each year when the sun crosses the equator and day and night are everywhere of equal length that occur about March 21 and September 23 — **equi·noc·tial** \,ē-kwə-'näk-shəl\ adj

equip \i-'kwip\ vb **equipped**; **equip·ping** : to supply with needed resources : fit out : PREPARE

equi·page \'ek-wə-pij\ n : a horse-drawn carriage usu. with its attendant servants

equip·ment \i-'kwip-mənt\ n 1 : the equipping of a person or thing : the state of being equipped 2 : things used in equipping : SUPPLIES, OUTFIT, PARAPHERNALIA

equi·poise \'ek-wə-,pȯiz, 'ēk-\ n 1 : BALANCE, EQUILIBRIUM 2 : COUNTERPOISE

equi·ta·ble \'ek-wət-ə-bəl\ adj : JUST, FAIR — **equi·ta·bly** adv

equi·ta·tion \,ek-wə-'tā-shən\ n : the act or art of riding on horseback

equi·ty \'ek-wət-ē\ n 1 : JUSTNESS, IMPARTIALITY 2 : a legal system developed into a body of rules supplementing the common law 3 : value of a property or of an interest in it in excess of claims against it

equiv·a·lent \i-'kwiv-(ə)-lənt\ adj : EQUAL; also : virtually identical syn same — **equiv·a·lence** n — **equiva·lent** n

equiv·o·cal \i-'kwiv-ə-kəl\ adj 1 : AMBIGUOUS 2 : UNCERTAIN 3 : SUSPICIOUS, DUBIOUS (~ behavior) syn obscure, dark, vague, enigmatic — **equiv·o·cal·ly** adv

equiv·o·cate \-,kāt\ vb : to use misleading language; also : PREVARICATE — **equiv·o·ca·tion** \-,kwiv-ə-'kā-shən\ n

¹-er \ər\ adj suffix or adv suffix — used to form the comparative degree of adjectives and adverbs of one syllable ⟨hotter⟩ ⟨drier⟩ and of some adjectives and adverbs of two syllables ⟨completer⟩ and sometimes of longer ones

²-er also **-ier** \ē-ər, yər\ or **-yer** \yər\ n suffix 1 : a person occupationally connected with ⟨*batter*⟩ ⟨*lawyer*⟩ **2** : a person or thing belonging to or associated with ⟨*old-timer*⟩ **3** : a native of : resident of ⟨New *Yorker*⟩ **4** : one that has ⟨*three-decker*⟩ **5** : one that produces or yields ⟨*porker*⟩ **6** : one that does or performs (a specified action) ⟨*reporter*⟩ ⟨builder-*upper*⟩ **7** : one that is a suitable object of (a specified action) ⟨*broiler*⟩ **8** : one that is ⟨*foreigner*⟩

era \\'ir-ə, 'er-ə\\ *n* **1** : a chronological order or system of notation reckoned from a given date as basis **2** : a period typified by some special feature **syn** age, epoch, aeon

erad·i·cate \\i-'rad-ə-ˌkāt\\ *vb* [L *eradicare*, fr. *ex-*, *e-* out + *radic-*, *radix* root] : UPROOT, ELIMINATE **syn** exterminate — **erad·i·ca·ble** \\-'rad-i-kə-bəl\\ *adj*

erase \\i-'rās\\ *vb* **1** : to rub or scratch out (as written words); *also* : OBLITERATE **syn** cancel, efface, delete — **eras·er** *n* — **era·sure** \\-'rā-shər\\ *n*

ere \\(ˌ)eər\\ *prep or conj* : BEFORE

¹erect \\i-'rekt\\ *adj* : not leaning or lying down : UPRIGHT

²erect *vb* **1** : BUILD **2** : to fix or set in an upright position **3** : to set up; *also* : ESTABLISH, DEVELOP — **erec·tion** \\-'rek-shən\\ *n*

ere·long \\eər-'lȯŋ\\ *adv* : before long : SOON

er·e·mite \\'er-ə-ˌmīt\\ *n* : HERMIT

er·mine \\'ər-mən\\ *n* **1** : a weasel with winter fur mostly white; *also* : its fur **2** : a rank or office whose official robe is ornamented with ermine

erode \\i-'rōd\\ *vb* : to diminish or destroy by degrees; *esp* : to gradually eat into or wear away ⟨soil *eroded* by wind and water⟩ — **ero·sion** \\i-'rō-zhən\\ *n*

erot·ic \\i-'rät-ik\\ *adj* : relating to or dealing with sexual love : AMATORY

err \\'eər, 'ər\\ *vb* : to be or do wrong

er·rand \\'er-ənd\\ *n* : a short trip taken to do something esp. for another; *also* : the object or purpose of this trip

er·rant \\'er-ənt\\ *adj* **1** : WANDERING **2** : going astray; *esp* : doing wrong **3** : moving aimlessly

er·ra·ta \\e-'rät-ə\\ *n* : a list of corrigenda

er·rat·ic \\ir-'at-ik\\ *adj* **1** : IRREGULAR, CAPRICIOUS **2** : ECCENTRIC, QUEER — **er·rat·i·cal·ly** *adv*

er·ra·tum \\e-'rät-əm\\ *n, pl* **-ta** \\-ə\\ : CORRIGENDUM

er·ro·ne·ous \\ir-'ō-nē-əs\\ *adj* **1** : INCORRECT, MISTAKEN — **er·ro·ne·ous·ly** *adv*

er·ror \\'er-ər\\ *n* **1** : a usu. ignorant or unintentional deviating from accuracy or rectitude : MISTAKE, BLUNDER ⟨made an ~ in adding⟩ **2** : the state of one that errs ⟨to be in ~⟩ **3** : a product of mistake ⟨a typographical ~⟩ **4** : a defensive misplay in baseball

er·satz \\'er-ˌzäts\\ *adj* : SUBSTITUTE, SYNTHETIC ⟨~ flour⟩

erst \\'ərst\\ *adv, archaic* : FORMERLY

erst·while \\-ˌhwīl\\ *adv (or adj)* : in the past : HERETOFORE

er·u·di·tion \\ˌer-(y)ə-'dish-ən\\ *n* : LEARNING, SCHOLARSHIP — **er·u·dite** \\'er-(y)ə-ˌdīt\\ *adj*

erupt \\i-'rəpt\\ *vb* **1** : to force out or release usu. suddenly and violently ⟨~

steam⟩ : become suddenly or violently active ⟨an ~*ing* volcano⟩ ⟨~ into sudden anger⟩ **2** : to break out with or as if with a skin rash — **erup·tion** \\-'rəp-shən\\ *n* — **erup·tive** \\-'rəp-tiv\\ *adj*

-ery \\(ə-)rē\\ *n suffix* **1** : qualities collectively : character **:** -NESS ⟨snobb*ery*⟩ **2** : art : practice ⟨cook*ery*⟩ **3** : place of doing, keeping, producing, or selling (the thing specified) ⟨fish*ery*⟩ ⟨bak*ery*⟩ **4** : collection : aggregate ⟨fin*ery*⟩ **5** : state or condition ⟨slav*ery*⟩

er·y·sip·e·las \\ˌer-ə-'sip-(ə-)ləs, ˌir-\\ *n* : an acute bacterial disease marked by fever and severe skin inflammation

¹-es \\əz *after* s, z, sh, ch; z *after* v *or a vowel*\\ *n pl suffix* **1** — used to form the plural of most nouns that end in *s* ⟨glass*es*⟩, *z* ⟨fuzz*es*⟩, *sh* ⟨bush*es*⟩, *ch* ⟨peach*es*⟩, or a final *y* that changes to *i* ⟨lad*ies*⟩ and of some nouns ending in *f* that changes to *v* ⟨loav*es*⟩ **2** : **¹-s 2**

²-es *vb suffix* — used to form the third person singular present of most verbs that end in *s* ⟨bless*es*⟩, *z* ⟨fizz*es*⟩, *sh* ⟨hush*es*⟩, *ch* ⟨catch*es*⟩, or a final *y* that changes to *i* ⟨defi*es*⟩

es·ca·la·tor \\'es-kə-ˌlāt-ər\\ *n* : a power-driven set of stairs arranged to ascend or descend continuously

es·cal·lop \\is-'käl-əp, -'kal-\\ *var of* SCALLOP

es·ca·pade \\'es-kə-ˌpād\\ *n* : a mischievous adventure : PRANK

¹es·cape \\is-'kāp\\ *vb* **1** : to get away **2** : to avoid a threatening evil **3** : to miss or succeed in averting ⟨~ injury⟩ **4** : ELUDE ⟨his name ~s me⟩ **5** : to be produced or uttered involuntarily by ⟨let a sob ~ him⟩

²escape *n* **1** : flight from or avoidance of something unpleasant **2** : LEAKAGE **3** : a means of escape

³escape *adj* : providing a means or way of escape

es·cap·ee \\ˌes-ˌkā-'pē, is-ˌ\\ *n* : one that has escaped esp. from prison

es·cap·ism \\is-'kā-ˌpiz-əm\\ *n* : diversion of the mind to imaginative activity as an escape from routine — **es·cap·ist** \\-pəst\\ *adj or n*

es·carp·ment \\is-'kärp-mənt\\ *n* **1** : a steep slope in front of a fortification **2** : a long cliff

es·chew \\is-'chü\\ *vb* : SHUN, AVOID

¹es·cort \\'es-ˌkȯrt\\ *n* : one (as a person or warship) accompanying another esp. as a protection or courtesy

²es·cort \\is-'kȯrt, es-\\ *vb* : to accompany as an escort

es·cri·toire \\'es-krə-ˌtwär\\ *n* : a writing table or desk

es·cu·do \\is-'küd-ō\\ *n* — see MONEY table

es·cutch·eon \\is-'kəch-ən\\ *n* : the surface on which armorial bearings are displayed

Es·ki·mo \\'es-kə-ˌmō\\ *n* **1** : a member of a group of peoples of northern Canada, Greenland, Alaska, and eastern Siberia

esoph·a·gus \\i-'säf-ə-gəs\\ *n, pl* **-gi** \\-ˌgī, -ˌjī\\ : a muscular tube connecting the mouth and stomach — **esoph·a·geal** \\-ˌsäf-ə-'jē-əl\\ *adj*

es·o·ter·ic \\ˌes-ə-'ter-ik\\ *adj* **1** : designed for or understood by the specially

ə abut; ᵊ kitten; ər further; a back; ā bake; ä cot, cart; aú out; ch chin; e less; ē easy; g gift; i trip; ī life; j joke; ŋ sing; ō flow; ȯ flaw; ȯi coin; th thin; <u>th</u> this; ü loot; ù foot; y yet; yü few; yu̇ furious; zh vision

initiated alone 2 : PRIVATE, SECRET

es·pa·drille \'es-pə-‚dril\ n : a flat sandal usu. having a fabric upper and a flexible sole

es·pal·ier \is-'pal-yər, -‚yā\ n : a plant (as a fruit tree) trained to grow flat against a support (as a wall or trellis) — espalier vb

es·pe·cial \is-'pesh-əl\ adj : SPECIAL, PARTICULAR — es·pe·cial·ly adv

Es·pe·ran·to \‚es-pə-'rant-ō\ n : an artificial international language based as far as possible on words common to the chief European languages

es·pi·o·nage \'es-pē-ə-‚näzh, -‚nij\ n : the practice of spying

es·pla·nade \'es-plə-‚näd, -‚nād\ n : a level open stretch or area; esp : one designed for walking or driving along a shore

es·pous·al \is-'pau̇-zəl\ n 1 : BETROTHAL; also : WEDDING 2 : a taking up (as of a cause) as a supporter — es·pouse \-'pau̇z\ vb

espres·so \is-'pres-ō\ n : coffee brewed by forcing steam through finely ground darkly roasted coffee beans

es·prit \is-'prē\ n : sprightly wit

es·prit de corps \-‚prēd-ə-'kȯr\ n : the common spirit existing in the members of a group

es·py \is-'pī\ vb : to catch sight of syn behold, see, perceive, discern, notice

es·quire \'es-‚kwī(ə)r\ n [MF esquier squire to a knight, fr. LL scutarius shield bearer, fr. L scutum shield] 1 : a man of the English gentry ranking next below a knight 2 : a candidate for knighthood serving as attendant to a knight 3 — used as a title of courtesy

-ess \əs\ n suffix : female ⟨authoress⟩

1es·say \e-'sā, 'es-‚ā\ vb : ATTEMPT, TRY

2es·say \'es-‚ā\ n 1 : ATTEMPT 2 : a literary composition usu. dealing with a subject from a limited or personal point of view — es·say·ist n

es·sence \'es-ᵊns\ n 1 : fundamental nature or quality 2 : a substance distilled or extracted from another substance (as a plant or drug) and having the special qualities of the original substance ⟨~ of peppermint⟩ 3 : PERFUME

1es·sen·tial \i-'sen-chəl\ adj 1 : containing or constituting an essence 2 : of the utmost importance : INDISPENSABLE syn requisite, needful — es·sen·tial·ly adv

2essential n : something essential

1-est \əst\ adj suffix or adv suffix — used to form the superlative degree of adjectives and adverbs of one syllable ⟨fattest⟩ ⟨latest⟩, of some adjectives and adverbs of two syllables ⟨luckiest⟩ ⟨oftenest⟩, and less often of longer ones ⟨beggarliest⟩

2-est \əst\ or -st \st\ vb suffix — used to form the archaic second person singular of English verbs (with thou) ⟨gettest⟩ ⟨didst⟩

es·tab·lish \is-'tab-lish\ vb 1 : to make firm or stable 2 : ORDAIN 3 : FOUND ⟨~ a settlement⟩; also : EFFECT 4 : to put on a firm basis : set up ⟨~ a son in business⟩ 5 : to gain acceptance or recognition of (as a claim or fact) ⟨~ed his right to help⟩; also : PROVE

es·tab·lish·ment n 1 : an organized force for carrying on public or private business 2 : a place of residence and business with its furnishings and staff

3 : an establishing or being established

es·ta·mi·net \‚es-tȧ-mē-nā\ n : a small café

es·tate \is-'tāt\ n 1 : STATE, CONDITION; also : social standing : STATUS 2 : a social or political class (the three ~s of nobility, clergy, and commons) 3 : a person's possessions : FORTUNE 4 : a landed property

1es·teem \i-'tēm\ n : high regard

2esteem vb 1 : REGARD 2 : to set a high value on : PRIZE syn respect, admire

es·ter \'es-tər\ n : an often fragrant organic compound formed by the reaction of an acid and an alcohol

esthete, esthetic, esthetics var of AESTHETE, AESTHETIC, AESTHETICS

es·ti·ma·ble \'es-tə-mə-bəl\ adj : worthy of esteem

1es·ti·mate \'es-tə-‚māt\ vb 1 : to give or form an approximation (as of the value, size, or cost of something) 2 : to form an opinion of : CONCLUDE, JUDGE syn evaluate, value, rate, calculate

2es·ti·mate \-mət\ n 1 : OPINION, JUDGMENT 2 : a rough or approximate calculation 3 : a statement of the cost of a job

es·ti·ma·tion \‚es-tə-'mā-shən\ n 1 : JUDGMENT, OPINION 2 : ESTIMATE 3 : ESTEEM, HONOR

Es·to·ni·an \es-'tō-nē-ən\ n : a native or inhabitant of Estonia

es·trange \is-'trānj\ vb : to alienate the affections or confidence of — es·trange·ment n

es·tro·gen \'es-trə-jən\ n : a substance (as a hormone) that promotes development of various female characteristics

es·tu·ary \'es-chə-‚wer-ē\ n : an arm of the sea at the mouth of a river

etch \'ech\ vb 1 : to make lines on (as metal) usu. by the action of acid; also : to produce (as a design) by etching 2 : to delineate clearly — etch·er n

etch·ing n 1 : the act, process, or art of etching 2 : a design produced on or print made from an etched plate

eter·nal \i-'tərn-ᵊl\ adj : EVERLASTING, PERPETUAL — eter·nal·ly adv

eter·ni·ty \i-'tər-nət-ē\ n 1 : infinite duration 2 : IMMORTALITY

1-eth \əth\ or -th \th\ vb suffix — used to form the archaic third person singular present of verbs ⟨goeth⟩ ⟨doth⟩

2-eth — see -TH

ether \'ē-thər\ n 1 : the upper regions of space; also : the gaseous element formerly held to fill these regions 2 : a light flammable liquid used as an anesthetic and solvent

ethe·re·al \i-'thir-ē-əl\ adj 1 : CELESTIAL, HEAVENLY 2 : exceptionally delicate : AIRY, DAINTY — ethe·re·al·ly adv

eth·i·cal \'eth-i-kəl\ adj 1 : of or relating to ethics 2 : conforming to accepted and esp. professional standards of conduct syn virtuous, honorable, upright — eth·i·cal·ly adv

eth·ics \-iks\ n sing or pl 1 : a discipline dealing with good and evil and with moral duty 2 : moral principles or practice

Ethi·o·pi·an \‚ē-thē-'ō-pē-ən\ n : a native or inhabitant of Ethiopia — Ethiopian adj

eth·nic \'eth-nik\ adj : of or relating to races or large groups of people classed according to common traits and customs — eth·ni·cal·ly \-ni-k(ə-)lē\ adv eth·nol·o·gy \eth-'näl-ə-jē\ n : a science dealing with the races of man, their origin, distribution, characteristics, and relations — eth·no·log·ic \,eth-nə-'läj-ik\ adj — eth·nol·o·gist \eth-'näl-ə-jəst\ n

eth·yl \'eth-əl\ n : a carbon and hydrogen radical occurring in alcohol and ether

eti·ol·o·gy \,ēt-ē-'äl-ə-jē\ n : CAUSE, ORIGIN; also : the study of causes — eti·o·log·ic \,ēt-ē-ə-'läj-ik\ adj

et·i·quette \'et-i-kət, -,ket\ n : the forms prescribed by custom or authority to be observed in social, official, or professional life syn propriety, decorum

étude \'ā-,t(y)üd\ n : a musical composition for practice to develop technical skill

et·y·mol·o·gy \,et-ə-'mäl-ə-jē\ n 1 : the history of a linguistic form (as a word) shown by tracing its development and relationships 2 : a branch of linguistics dealing with etymologies — et·y·mo·log·i·cal \-mə-'läj-i-kəl\ adj — et·y·mol·o·gist \-'mäl-ə-jəst\ n

eu·ca·lyp·tus \,yü-kə-'lip-təs\ n : any of a genus of mostly Australian evergreen trees widely grown for shade or useful products

Eu·cha·rist \'yü-k(ə-)rəst\ n : COMMUNION 3 — eu·cha·ris·tic \,yü-kə-'ris-tik\ adj, often cap

eu·chre \'yü-kər\ n : a card game in which the side naming the trump must take 3 of 5 tricks to win

eu·gen·ics \yü-'jen-iks\ n : a science dealing with the improvement (as by selective breeding) of hereditary qualities esp. of human beings — eu·gen·ic adj

eu·lo·gy \'yü-lə-jē\ n 1 : a speech in praise of some person or thing 2 : high praise — eu·lo·gis·tic \,yü-lə-'jis-tik\ adj — eu·lo·gize \'yü-lə-,jīz\ vb

eu·nuch \'yü-nək\ n : a castrated man

eu·phe·mism \'yü-fə-,miz-əm\ n : the substitution of a pleasant expression for one offensive or unpleasant; also : the expression substituted

eu·pho·ni·ous \yù-'fō-nē-əs\ adj : pleasing to the ear

eu·pho·ny \'yü-fə-nē\ n : the effect produced by words so combined as to please the ear

eu·pho·ria \yù-'fōr-ē-ə\ n : a marked feeling of well-being or elation — euphor·ic \-'fòr-ik\ adj

Eur·asian \yù-'rā-zhən, -shən\ adj : of or relating to Europe and Asia — Eurasian n

eu·re·ka \yù-'rē-kə\ interj — used to express triumph on a discovery

Eu·ro·pe·an \,yùr-ə-'pē-ən\ n : a native or inhabitant of Europe — European adj

eu·ro·pi·um \yù-'rō-pē-əm\ n : a metallic chemical element

eu·tha·na·sia \,yü-thə-'nā-zh(ē-)ə\ n : an easy death; also : the act or practice of killing (as an aged animal or incurable invalid) for reasons of mercy

eu·then·ics \yü-'then-iks\ n : a science dealing with the improvement of human qualities by changes in environment — eu·then·ic adj

evac·u·ate \i-'vak-yə-,wāt\ vb 1 : EMPTY

2 : to discharge wastes from the body 3 : to remove or withdraw from : VACATE — evac·u·a·tion \-,vak-yə-'wā-shən\ n

evac·u·ee \i-,vak-yə-'wē\ n : an evacuated person

evade \i-'vād\ vb : to manage to avoid esp. by dexterity or slyness : ELUDE, ESCAPE

eval·u·ate \i-'val-yə-,wāt\ vb : APPRAISE, VALUE — eval·u·a·tion \-,val-yə-'wā-shən\ n

ev·a·nes·cent \,ev-ə-'nes-ᵊnt\ adj : tending to vanish like vapor : FLEETING syn passing, transient, transitory, momentary — ev·a·nes·cence n

evan·gel·i·cal \,ē-,van-'jel-i-kəl, ,ev-ən-\ adj [LL evangelium gospel, fr. Gk evangelion, fr. eu- good + angelos messenger] 1 : of or relating to the Christian gospel esp. as presented in the four Gospels 2 : of or relating to certain Protestant churches emphasizing the authority of Scripture and the importance of preaching as contrasted with ritual 3 : ZEALOUS (~ fervor) — Evangelical n — Evan·gel·i·cal·ism n — evan·gel·i·cal·ly adv

evan·ge·lism \i-'van-jə-,liz-əm\ n 1 : the winning or revival of personal commitments to Christ 2 : militant or crusading zeal

evan·ge·list \i-'van-jə-ləst\ n 1 often cap : the writer of any of the four Gospels 2 : one who evangelizes; esp : a preacher who conducts revival services — evan·ge·lis·tic \-,van-jə-'lis-tik\ adj — evan·ge·lis·ti·cal·ly adv

evan·ge·lize \i-'van-jə-,līz\ vb 1 : to preach the gospel 2 : to convert to Christianity

evap·o·rate \i-'vap-ə-,rāt\ vb 1 : to pass off in vapor 2 : to convert into vapor 3 : to drive out the moisture from (as by heat) — evap·o·ra·tion \-,vap-ə-'rā-shən\ n — evap·o·ra·tor \-'vap-ə-,rāt-ər\ n

eva·sion \i-'vā-zhən\ n 1 : an act or instance of evading 2 : a means of evading; esp : an equivocal statement used in evading — eva·sive \-'vā-siv\ adj

eve \'ēv\ n 1 : EVENING 2 : the period just before some important event

¹even \'ē-vən\ adj 1 : LEVEL, FLAT 2 : REGULAR, SMOOTH 3 : EQUAL 4 : FAIR 5 : BALANCED; also : fully revenged 6 : divisible by two 7 : EXACT syn flush, uniform, steady, constant — even·ly adv — even·ness \-vən-nəs\ n

²even adv 1 : as well : PRECISELY, JUST 2 : FULLY, QUITE 3 : at the very time : ALREADY 4 — used as an intensive to stress identity or the comparative degree (~ we know that) (gold and ~ more precious treasures)

³even vb : to make or become even

even·hand·ed \,ē-vən-'han-dəd\ adj : FAIR, IMPARTIAL

eve·ning \'ēv-niŋ\ n : the end of the day and early part of the night

even·song \'ē-vən-,sòŋ\ n, often cap 1 : VESPERS 2 : evening prayer esp. when sung

event \i-'vent\ n 1 : OCCURRENCE 2 : a noteworthy happening 3 : CON-

ə abut; ᵊ kitten; ər further; a back; ā bake; ä cot, cart; aù out; ch chin; e less; ē easy; g gift; i trip; ī life; j joke; ŋ sing; ō flow; ò flaw; òi coin; th thin; th this; ü loot; ù foot; y yet; yü few; yù furious; zh vision

TINGENCY **4** : a contest in a program of sports — **event·ful** adj

even·tide \'ē-vən-ˌtīd\ n : EVENING

even·tu·al \i-'ven-ch(ə-w)əl\ adj : LATER; also : ULTIMATE — **even·tu·al·ly** adv

even·tu·ate \-chə-ˌwāt\ vb : to come to pass

ev·er \'ev-ər\ adv **1** : ALWAYS **2** : at any time **3** : in any case

ev·er·bloom·ing \ˌev-ər-'blü-miṇ\ adj : blooming more or less continuously throughout the growing season

ev·er·glade \'ev-ər-ˌglād\ n : a lowlying tract of swampy or marshy land

ev·er·green \-ˌgrēn\ adj : having foliage that remains green ⟨coniferous trees are mostly ~⟩ — **evergreen** n

[1]**ev·er·last·ing** \ˌev-ər-'las-tiṇ\ adj : enduring forever : ETERNAL — **ev·er·last·ing·ly** adv

[2]**everlasting** n **1** : ETERNITY ⟨from ~⟩ **2** : a plant whose flowers may be dried without loss of form or color

ev·er·more \-'mōr\ adv : FOREVER

ev·ery \'ev-rē\ adj **1** : being one of the total of members of a group or class **2** : all possible ⟨given ~ chance⟩; also : COMPLETE

ev·ery·body \'ev-ri-ˌbäd-ē\ pron : every person

ev·ery·day \'ev-rē-ˌdā\ adj : used or fit for daily use : ORDINARY

ev·ery·one \-(ˌ)wən\ pron : every person

ev·ery·thing \-ˌthiṇ\ pron : all that exists; also : all that is relevant

ev·ery·where \-ˌhwear\ adv : in every place or part

evict \i-'vikt\ vb : to put (a person) out from a property by legal process; also : EXPEL syn eject, oust — **evic·tion** \-'vik-shən\ n

ev·i·dence \'ev-əd-əns\ n **1** : an outward sign : INDICATION **2** : PROOF, TESTIMONY; esp : matter submitted in court to determine the truth of alleged facts

ev·i·dent \'ev-əd-ənt\ adj : clear to the vision and understanding syn manifest, distinct, obvious, apparent, plain — **ev·i·dent·ly** \-ˌdent-lē\ adv

[1]**evil** \'ē-vəl\ adj **1** : WICKED **2** : causing or threatening distress or harm : PERNICIOUS — **evil·ly** adv

[2]**evil** n **1** : SIN **2** : a source of sorrow or distress : CALAMITY — **evil·do·er** \ˌē-vəl-'dü-ər\ n

evil–mind·ed \ˌē-vəl-'mīn-dəd\ adj : having an evil disposition or evil thoughts

evince \i-'vins\ vb : SHOW, REVEAL

evis·cer·ate \i-'vis-ə-ˌrāt\ vb **1** : to remove the entrails of **2** : to deprive of vital content or force

evoke \i-'vōk\ vb : to call forth or up — **evo·ca·tion** \ˌē-vō-'kā-shən, ˌev-ə-\ n

ev·o·lu·tion \ˌev-ə-'lü-shən\ n **1** : a process of change in a particular direction **2** : one of a series of prescribed movements (as in a dance or military exercise) **3** : the process by which through a series of steps something (as an organism) attains its distinctive character; also : a theory that existent types of animals and plants have developed from previously existing kinds — **ev·o·lu·tion·ary** adj — **ev·o·lu·tion·ist** n

evolve \i-'välv\ vb : to develop by or as if by evolution

ewe \'yü\ n : a female sheep

ew·er \'yü-ər\ n : a vase-shaped jug

ex·ac·er·bate \ig-'zas-ər-ˌbāt\ vb : to make more violent, bitter, or severe — **ex·ac·er·ba·tion** \-ˌzas-ər-'bā-shən\ n

[1]**ex·act** \ig-'zakt\ vb **1** : to compel to furnish : EXTORT **2** : to call for as suitable or necessary — **ex·ac·tion** \-'zak-shən\ n

[2]**exact** adj : precisely accurate or correct syn right, precise — **ex·act·ly** adv — **ex·act·ness** n

ex·act·ing adj **1** : greatly demanding ⟨an ~ taskmaster⟩ **2** : requiring close attention and precision ⟨~ studies⟩

ex·ac·ti·tude \ig-'zak-tə-ˌt(y)üd\ n : the quality or an instance of being exact

ex·ag·ger·ate \ig-'zaj-ə-ˌrāt\ vb [L exaggerare, lit., to heap up, fr. ex- out + agger heap, rampart] : to enlarge (as a statement) beyond bounds : OVERSTATE — **ex·ag·ger·a·tion** \-ˌzaj-ə-'rā-shən\ n

ex·alt \ig-'zolt\ vb **1** : to raise up esp. in rank, power, or dignity **2** : GLORIFY **3** : to elate the mind or spirits — **ex·al·ta·tion** \ˌeg-ˌzol-'tā-shən\ n

ex·am \ig-'zam\ n : EXAMINATION

ex·am·ine \ig-'zam-ən\ vb **1** : to inspect closely : SCRUTINIZE, INVESTIGATE **2** : QUESTION; esp : to test by questioning syn scan, audit, quiz, catechize — **ex·am·i·na·tion** \-ˌzam-ə-'nā-shən\ n

ex·am·ple \ig-'zam-pəl\ n **1** : a representative sample **2** : something forming a model to be followed or avoided **3** : a problem to be solved in order to show the application of some rule

ex·as·per·ate \ig-'zas-pə-ˌrāt\ vb : VEX, IRRITATE — **ex·as·per·a·tion** \-ˌzas-pə-'rā-shən\ n

ex·ca·vate \'ek-skə-ˌvāt\ vb **1** : to hollow out; also : to form by hollowing out **2** : to dig out and remove (as earth) **3** : to reveal to view by digging away a covering — **ex·ca·va·tion** \ˌek-skə-'vā-shən\ n — **ex·ca·va·tor** \'ek-skə-ˌvāt-ər\ n

ex·ceed \ik-'sēd\ vb **1** : to go or be beyond the limit of **2** : SURPASS

ex·ceed·ing·ly adv : EXTREMELY, VERY

ex·cel \ik-'sel\ vb : SURPASS, OUTDO

ex·cel·lence \'eks-(ə)-ləns\ n **1** : the quality of being excellent **2** : an excellent or valuable quality : VIRTUE **3** : EXCELLENCY 2

ex·cel·len·cy n **1** : EXCELLENCE **2** — used as a title of honor

ex·cel·lent adj : very good of its kind : FIRST-CLASS — **ex·cel·lent·ly** adv

ex·cel·si·or \ik-'sel-sē-ər\ n : fine curled wood shavings used esp. for packing fragile items

[1]**ex·cept** \ik-'sept\ vb **1** : to take or leave out **2** : OBJECT

[2]**except** also **ex·cept·ing** prep **1** : not including ⟨daily ~ Sundays⟩ **2** : other than : BUT ⟨saw no one ~ him⟩

[3]**except** also **ex·cept·ing** conj : ONLY ⟨I'd go, ~ it's too far⟩

ex·cep·tion \ik-'sep-shən\ n **1** : the act of excepting **2** : something excepted **3** : OBJECTION

ex·cep·tion·able adj : liable to exception : OBJECTIONABLE

ex·cep·tion·al adj : UNUSUAL; esp : SUPERIOR — **ex·cep·tion·al·ly** adv

ex·cerpt \'ek-ˌsərpt\ n : a passage selected or copied : EXTRACT

ex·cess \ik-'ses, 'ek-ˌses\ n **1** : SUPERFLUITY, SURPLUS **2** : the amount by which one quantity exceeds another **3** : INTEMPERANCE — **excess** adj — **ex-**

ces·sive \ik-'ses-iv\ *adj* — ex·ces·sive·ly *adv*

¹ex·change \iks-'chānj, 'eks-,chānj\ *n* 1 : the giving or taking of one thing in return for another : TRADE 2 : a substituting of one thing for another 3 : interchange of valuables and esp of business orders or drafts (bills of exchange) or money of different countries 4 : a place where things and services are exchanged; *esp* : a marketplace esp. for securities 5 : a central office in which telephone lines are connected for communication

²exchange *vb* : to transfer in return for some equivalent : BARTER, SWAP — ex·change·able *adj*

ex·che·quer \'eks-,chek-ər\ *n* : TREASURY; *esp* : a national treasury

¹ex·cise \'ek-,sīz, -,sīs\ *n* : a tax on the manufacture, sale, or consumption of goods within a country

²ex·cise \ek-'sīz\ *vb* : to remove by cutting out — ex·ci·sion \-'sizh-ən\ *n*

ex·cite \ik-'sīt\ *vb* 1 : to rouse to activity : stir up 2 : to kindle the emotions of : STIMULATE **syn** provoke, stimulate, pique — ex·cit·abil·i·ty \-,sīt-ə-'bil-ət-ē\ *n* — ex·cit·able \-'sīt-ə-bəl\ *adj* — ex·cit·ed·ly *adv*

ex·cite·ment \ik-'sīt-mənt\ *n* : AGITATION, STIR

ex·claim \iks-'klām\ *vb* : to cry out, speak, or utter sharply or vehemently — ex·cla·ma·tion \,eks-klə-'mā-shən\ *n* — ex·clam·a·to·ry \iks-'klam-ə-,tōr-ē\ *adj*

exclamation point *n* : a punctuation mark ! used esp. after an interjection or exclamation

ex·clude \iks-'klüd\ *vb* 1 : to shut out (as from using or participating) : BAR 2 : EJECT — ex·clu·sion \-'klü-zhən\ *n*

ex·clu·sive \iks-'klü-siv\ *adj* 1 : reserved for particular persons 2 : snobbishly aloof; *also* : STYLISH 3 : SOLE 〈~ rights〉; *also* : UNDIVIDED 〈your ~ attention〉 **syn** select, elect, fashionable — ex·clu·sive·ly *adv* — ex·clu·sive·ness *n*

exclusive of *prep* : not taking into account

ex·cog·i·tate \eks-'käj-ə-,tāt\ *vb* : to think out : DEVISE

ex·com·mu·ni·cate \,eks-kə-'myü-nə-,kāt\ *vb* 1 : to cut off officially from communion with the church 2 : to exclude from fellowship — ex·com·mu·ni·ca·tion \-,myü-nə-'kā-shən\ *n*

ex·co·ri·ate \ek-'skōr-ē-,āt\ *vb* : to censure with harsh severity

ex·cre·ment \'ek-skrə-mənt\ *n* : waste discharged from the body and esp. from the alimentary canal

ex·cres·cence \ek-'skres-'ns\ *n* : OUTGROWTH; *esp* : an abnormal outgrowth (as a wart) — ex·cres·cent *adj*

ex·crete \ek-'skrēt\ *vb* : to separate and eliminate wastes from the body esp. in urine — ex·cre·tion \-'skrē-shən\ *n* — ex·cre·to·ry \'ek-skrə-,tōr-ē\ *adj*

ex·cru·ci·at·ing \ik-'skrü-shē-,āt-iŋ\ *adj* : intensely painful or distressing **syn** agonizing

ex·cul·pate \'ek-(,)skəl-,pāt\ *vb* : to clear from alleged fault or guilt **syn** absolve, exonerate, acquit, vindicate

ex·cur·sion \ik-'skər-zhən\ *n* 1 : EXPEDITION; *esp* : a pleasure trip 2 : DIGRESSION 3 : an outward movement or a cycle of movement (as of a pendulum) — ex·cur·sion·ist *n*

ex·cur·sive \ik-'skər-siv\ *adj* : constituting or characterized by digression

ex·cur·sus \-səs\ *n* : an appendix or a digression containing further exposition of some point or topic

¹ex·cuse \ik-'skyüz\ *vb* 1 : to offer excuse for 2 : PARDON 3 : to release from an obligation 4 : JUSTIFY — ex·cus·able *adj*

²ex·cuse \-'skyüs\ *n* 1 : an act of excusing 2 : grounds for being excused : JUSTIFICATION 3 : APOLOGY

ex·e·cra·ble \'ek-si-krə-bəl\ *adj* 1 : DETESTABLE 2 : very bad 〈~ spelling〉

ex·e·crate \'ek-sə-,krāt\ *vb* : to denounce as evil or detestable; *also* : DETEST — ex·e·cra·tion \,ek-sə-'krā-shən\ *n*

ex·e·cute \'ek-sə-,kyüt\ *vb* 1 : to carry to completion : PERFORM 2 : to do what is called for by (as a law) 3 : to put to death in accordance with a legal sentence 4 : to produce in accordance with a plan or design 5 : to do what is needed to give legal force to (as a deed) — ex·e·cu·tion \,ek-sə-'kyü-shən\ *n* — ex·e·cu·tion·er *n*

¹ex·ec·u·tive \ig-'zek-(y)ət-iv\ *adj* 1 : designed for or related to carrying out plans or purposes 2 : of or relating to the enforcement of laws and the conduct of affairs

²executive *n* 1 : the branch of government with executive duties 2 : one constituting the controlling element of an organization 3 : one working as a manager or administrator

ex·ec·u·tor \ig-'zek-(y)ət-ər\ *n* : the person named by a testator to execute his will

ex·ec·u·trix \-(y)ə-,triks\ *n* : a female executor

ex·e·ge·sis \,ek-sə-'jē-səs\ *n*, *pl* -ge·ses \-,sēz\ : explanation or critical interpretation of a text

ex·e·gete \'ek-sə-,jēt\ *n* : one who practices exegesis

ex·em·plar \ig-'zem-,plär, -,plər\ *n* 1 : one that serves as a model or pattern; *esp* : an ideal model 2 : a typical instance or example

ex·em·pla·ry \ig-'zem-plə-rē\ *adj* : serving as a pattern; *also* : COMMENDABLE

ex·em·pli·fy \ig-'zem-plə-,fī\ *vb* : to illustrate by example : serve as an example of — ex·em·pli·fi·ca·tion \-,zem-plə-fə-'kā-shən\ *n*

¹ex·empt \ig-'zempt\ *adj* : free from some liability to which others are subject

²exempt *vb* : to make exempt : EXCUSE — ex·emp·tion \-'zemp-shən\ *n*

ex·e·quies \'ek-sə-kwēz\ *n pl* : funeral rites

¹ex·er·cise \'ek-sər-,sīz\ *n* 1 : EMPLOYMENT, USE 〈~ of authority〉 2 : exertion made for the sake of training 3 : a task or problem done to develop skill 4 *pl* : a public exhibition or ceremony 〈graduation ~s〉

²exercise *vb* 1 : to EXERT 〈~ control〉 2 : to train by or engage in exercise 〈~

muscles⟩ ⟨~ troops⟩ **3** : WORRY, DISTRESS

ex·ert \ig-'zərt\ vb : to bring or put into action ⟨~ a skill⟩ ⟨~ed himself⟩ — **ex·er·tion** \-'zər-shən\ n

ex·hale \eks-'hāl\ vb **1** : to breathe out **2** : to give or pass off in the form of vapor — **ex·ha·la·tion** \,eks-(h)ə-'lā-shən\ n

¹**ex·haust** \ig-'zȯst\ vb **1** : to draw out completely (as air from a jar); also : EMPTY **2** : to use up wholly **3** : to tire or wear out **4** : to develop (a subject) completely

²**exhaust** n : the escape of used steam or gas from an engine; also : the matter that escapes

ex·haus·tion \ig-'zȯs-chən\ n : extreme weariness : FATIGUE

ex·haus·tive \-'zȯ-stiv\ adj : covering all possibilities : THOROUGH

ex·haust·less \-'zȯst-ləs\ adj : INEXHAUSTIBLE

¹**ex·hib·it** \ig-'zib-ət\ vb **1** : to display esp. publicly **2** : to present to a court in legal form syn expose, show, parade, flaunt — **ex·hi·bi·tion** \,ek-sə-'bish-ən\ n — **ex·hib·i·tor** \ig-'zib-ət-ər\ n

²**exhibit** n **1** : an act or instance of exhibiting; also : something exhibited **2** : something produced and identified in court for use as evidence

ex·hi·bi·tion·ism \,ek-sə-'bish-ə-,niz-əm\ n : the act or practice of so behaving as to attract undue attention sometimes by indecent exposure — **ex·hi·bi·tion·ist** n

ex·hil·a·rate \ig-'zil-ə-,rāt\ vb : to ENLIVEN, CHEER, STIMULATE — **ex·hil·a·ra·tion** \-,zil-ə-'rā-shən\ n

ex·hort \ig-'zȯrt\ vb : to urge, advise, or warn earnestly — **ex·hor·ta·tion** \,eks-,ȯr-'tā-shən, ,egz-\ n

ex·hume \igz-'(y)üm\ vb : DISINTER — **ex·hu·ma·tion** \,eks-yü-'mā-shən\ n

ex·i·gen·cy \'ek-sə-jən-sē, ig-'zij-ən-\ n **1** : urgent need **2** pl : REQUIREMENTS — **ex·i·gent** \'ek-sə-jənt\ adj

ex·ig·u·ous \eg-'zig-yə-wəs\ adj : scanty in amount — **ex·i·gu·i·ty** \,ek-sə-'gyü-ət-ē\ n

¹**ex·ile** \'eg-,zīl, 'ek-,sīl\ n **1** : BANISHMENT **2** : a person driven from his native place

²**exile** vb : BANISH, EXPEL syn expatriate, deport

ex·ist \ig-'zist\ vb **1** : to have being **2** : to continue to be : LIVE

ex·is·tence \ig-'zis-təns\ n **1** : continuance in living **2** : actual occurrence **3** : something existing — **ex·is·tent** adj

ex·is·ten·tial·ism \,eg-zis-'ten-chə-,liz-əm\ n : a philosophy centered upon the analysis of existence and stressing the freedom, responsibility, and usu. the isolation of the individual — **ex·is·ten·tial·ist** adj or n

ex·it \'egz-ət, 'eks-\ n **1** : a departure from a stage **2** : a going out or away; also : DEATH **3** : a way out of an enclosed space — **exit** vb

ex·o·dus \'ek-səd-əs\ n : a mass departure : EMIGRATION

ex of·fi·cio \,ek-sə-'fish-ē-,ō\ adv (or adj) : by virtue or because of an office ⟨ex officio chairman⟩

ex·on·er·ate \ig-'zän-ə-,rāt\ vb [L exonerare to unburden, fr. ex- out + oner-, onus load] : to free from blame syn acquit, absolve, exculpate — **ex·on·-**

er·a·tion \-,zän-ə-'rā-shən\ n

ex·or·bi·tant \ig-'zȯr-bət-ənt\ adj : exceeding what is usual or proper : EXCESSIVE

ex·or·cise \'ek-,sȯr-,sīz, -sər-\ vb **1** : to get rid of by or as if by solemn command **2** : to free of an evil spirit — **ex·or·cism** \-,siz-əm\ n — **ex·or·cist** \-,sist\ n

ex·or·di·um \eg-'zȯrd-ē-əm\ n : a beginning or introduction esp. to a discourse or composition

ex·ot·ic \ig-'zät-ik\ adj : FOREIGN, STRANGE — **exotic** n — **ex·ot·i·cal·ly** adv — **ex·ot·i·cism** \-'zät-ə-,siz-əm\ n

ex·pand \ik-'spand\ vb **1** : to spread out **2** : ENLARGE **3** : to develop in detail syn amplify, swell, distend, inflate, dilate — **ex·pand·er** n

ex·panse \-'spans\ n : a broad extent (as of land or sea)

ex·pan·sion \-'span-chən\ n **1** : the act or process of expanding **2** : the state or degree of being expanded **3** : an expanded part or thing

ex·pan·sive \-'span-siv\ adj : tending to expand or to cause expansion **2** : warmly benevolent or emotional **3** : of large extent or scope — **ex·pan·sive·ly** adv

ex parte \eks-'pärt-ē\ adj (or adv) : from a one-sided or partisan point of view

ex·pa·ti·ate \ek-'spā-shē-,āt\ vb : to talk or write at length — **ex·pa·ti·a·tion** \-,spā-shē-'ā-shən\ n

ex·pa·tri·ate \ek-'spā-trē-,āt\ vb : EXILE — **ex·pa·tri·ate** \-,āt, -ət\ n

ex·pect \ik-'spekt\ vb **1** : to look forward to **2** : to consider (one) in duty bound **3** : SUPPOSE, ASSUME

ex·pec·tan·cy \-'spek-tən-sē\ n **1** : EXPECTATION **2** : something expected

ex·pec·tant adj : EXPECTING — **ex·pec·tant·ly** adv

ex·pec·ta·tion \,ek-,spek-'tā-shən\ n **1** : the act or state of expecting **2** : anticipation of future good **3** : something expected

ex·pec·to·rant \ik-'spek-tə-rənt\ adj : tending to promote discharge of mucus from the respiratory tract

ex·pec·to·rate \ik-'spek-tə-,rāt\ vb : SPIT — **ex·pec·to·ra·tion** \-,spek-tə-'rā-shən\ n

ex·pe·di·en·cy \ik-'spēd-ē-ən-sē\ or **ex·pe·di·ence** n **1** : fitness to some end **2** : use of expedient means and methods; also : something expedient

¹**ex·pe·di·ent** adj **1** : adapted for achieving a particular end **2** : marked by concern with what is advantageous without regard to fairness or rightness

²**expedient** n : something that is expedient; also : a means devised or used for want of something better

ex·pe·dite \'ek-spə-,dīt\ vb : to carry out promptly; also : FACILITATE

ex·pe·dit·er n : one that expedites; esp : one employed to ensure adequate supplies of raw materials and equipment or to coordinate the flow of materials, tools, parts, and processed goods within a plant

ex·pe·di·tion \,ek-spə-'dish-ən\ n **1** : a journey for a particular purpose; also : the persons making it **2** : efficient promptness — **ex·pe·di·tion·ary** adj

ex·pe·di·tious \-'dish-əs\ adj : marked by or acting with prompt efficiency syn swift, fast, rapid

ex·pel \ik-'spel\ vb -**pelled; -pel·ling**

: to drive or force out : EJECT — **ex-pel·lant** \-'spel-ənt\ *adj or n*

ex·pend \ik-'spend\ *vb* 1 : to pay out : SPEND 2 : to consume by use : use up — **ex·pend·able** *adj*

ex·pen·di·ture \-'spen-di-chər\ *n* 1 : the act or process of expending 2 : something (as money) expended

ex·pense \-'spens\ *n* 1 : EXPENDITURE 2 : COST 3 : a cause of expenditure 4 : SACRIFICE

ex·pen·sive \-'spen-siv\ *adj* : COSTLY, DEAR — **ex·pen·sive·ly** *adv*

¹**ex·pe·ri·ence** \ik-'spir-ē-əns\ *n* 1 : observation or practice resulting in or tending toward knowledge; *also* : the resulting state of enhanced comprehension and efficiency 2 : a state of being affected from without (as by events); *also* : an affecting event (a startling ~) 3 : something or the totality experienced (as by a person or community) (human ~)

²**experience** *vb* 1 : to know as an experience : SUFFER, UNDERGO (~ hunger) (~ conversion) 2 : to find out : DISCOVER

ex·pe·ri·enced *adj* : made capable by repeated experience (~ workmen)

¹**ex·per·i·ment** \ik-'sper-ə-mənt\ *n* : a controlled procedure carried out to discover, test, or demonstrate something; *also* : the practice of experiments — **ex·per·i·men·tal** \-,sper-ə-'ment-'l\ *adj*

²**ex·per·i·ment** \-'sper-ə-,ment\ *vb* : to make experiments — **ex·per·i·men·ta·tion** \-,sper-ə-mən-'tā-shən\ *n* — **ex·per·i·ment·er** \-'sper-ə-,ment-ər\ *n*

¹**ex·pert** \'ek-,spərt\ *adj* : thoroughly skilled — **ex·pert·ly** *adv* — **ex·pert·ness** *n*

²**expert** *n* : an expert person : SPECIALIST

ex·per·tise \,ek-,spər-'tēz\ *n* : EXPERTNESS

ex·pi·ate \'ek-spē-,āt\ *vb* : to make amends : ATONE — **ex·pi·a·tion** \,ek-spē-'ā-shən\ *n*

ex·pi·a·to·ry \'ek-spē-ə-,tōr-ē\ *adj*: serving to expiate

ex·pire \ik-'spī(ə)r, ek-\ *vb* 1 : to breathe out from or as if from the lungs; *also* : to emit the breath 2 : DIE 3 : to come to an end — **ex·pi·ra·tion** \,ek-spə-'rā-shən\ *n*

ex·plain \ik-'splān\ *vb* 1 : to make clear or plain 2 : to give the reason for or cause of — **ex·pla·na·tion** \,ek-splə-'nā-shən\ *n* — **ex·plan·a·to·ry** \ik-'splan-ə-,tōr-ē\ *adj*

ex·ple·tive \'ek-splət-iv\ *n* : a usu profane exclamation

ex·pli·ca·ble \ek-'splik-ə-bəl, 'ek-(,)splik-\ *adj* : capable of being explained

ex·pli·cate \'ek-splə-,kāt\ *vb* : to give a detailed explanation of

ex·plic·it \ik-'splis-ət\ *adj* : clearly and precisely expressed — **ex·plic·it·ly** *adv*

ex·plode \ik-'splōd\ *vb* 1 : DISCREDIT (~ a belief) 2 : to affect or be affected (as by driving or shattering) by or as if by the pressure of expanding gas (~ a bomb) (the boiler *exploded*) 3 : to cause or undergo a rapid chemical or nuclear reaction with production of heat and violent expansion of gas (~ dynamite) (material that ~s when

jarred); *also* : to react violently (ready to ~ with rage)

¹**ex·ploit** \'ek-,splóit\ *n* : a usu. heroic act : DEED

²**ex·ploit** \ik-'splóit, 'ek-,splóit\ *vb* 1 : to turn to economic account (~ resources); *also* : UTILIZE 2 : to use unfairly for one's own advantage — **ex·ploi·ta·tion** \,ek-,splói-'tā-shən\ *n*

ex·plore \ik-'splōr\ *vb* : to range over (a region) in order to discover facts about it; *also* : to examine in careful detail (~ a wound) — **ex·plo·ra·tion** \,ek-splə-'rā-shən\ *n* — **ex·plor·er** \ik-'splōr-ər\ *n*

ex·plo·sion \ik-'splō-zhən\ *n* : the process or an instance of exploding

ex·plo·sive \-'splō-siv\ *adj* 1 : relating to or prepared to cause explosion 2 : tending to explode — **explosive** *n* — **ex·plo·sive·ly** *adv*

ex·po·nent \ik-'spō-nənt, 'ek-,spō-\ *n* 1 : a symbol written above and to the right of a mathematical expression to signify how many times it is to be repeated as a factor 2 : INTERPRETER, EXPOUNDER 3 : ADVOCATE, CHAMPION — **ex·po·nen·tial** \,ek-spə-'nen-chəl\ *adj*

¹**ex·port** \ek-'spōrt\ *vb* : to send (as merchandise) to foreign countries — **ex·por·ta·tion** \,ek-,spōr-'tā-shən, -spər-\ *n* — **ex·port·er** \ek-'spōrt-ər\ *n*

²**ex·port** \'ek-,spōrt\ *n* 1 : something exported esp. for trade 2 : an act or the business of exporting

¹**ex·pose** \ik-'spōz\ *vb* 1 : to deprive of shelter or protection 2 : to submit or subject to an action or influence; *esp* : to subject (a sensitive photographic film, plate, or paper) to the action of radiant energy (as light) 3 : to display esp. for sale 4 : to bring to light : DISCLOSE

²**ex·po·sé** \,ek-spō-'zā\ *n* : an exposure of something discreditable

ex·po·si·tion \,ek-spə-'zish-ən\ *n* 1 : a setting forth of the meaning or purpose (as of a writing); *also* : discourse designed to convey information 2 : a public exhibition

ex·pos·i·tor \ik-'späz-ət-ər\ *n* : one that explains or expounds

ex·pos·tu·late \ik-'späs-chə-,lāt\ *vb* : to reason earnestly with a person esp. in dissuading : REMONSTRATE — **ex·pos·tu·la·tion** \-,späs-chə-'lā-shən\ *n*

ex·po·sure \ik-'spō-zhər\ *n* 1 : an exposing or being exposed 2 : a section of a photographic film for one picture 3 : the time during which a film is subjected to the action of light

ex·pound \ik-'spaund\ *vb* 1 : STATE 2 : INTERPRET, EXPLAIN — **ex·pound·er** *n*

¹**ex·press** \ik-'spres\ *adj* 1 : EXPLICIT; *also* : EXACT, PRECISE 2 : SPECIFIC (his ~ purpose) 3 : traveling at high speed and usu. with few stops (~ train); *also* : adapted to high speed use (~ roads) 4 : being or relating to special transportation of goods at premium rates (~ delivery) (~ rates) — **ex·press·ly** *adv*

²**express** *n* : an express system or vehicle

³**express** *vb* 1 : to make known : SHOW,

ə abut; ⁹ kitten; ər further; a back; ā bake; ä cot, cart; aú out; ch chin; e less; ē easy; g gift; i trip; ī life; j joke; ŋ sing; ō flow; ó flaw; ói coin; th thin; ṯh this; ü loot; ú foot; y yet; yü few; yú furious; zh vision

STATE (~ regret) (~ed himself through art); also : SYMBOLIZE 2 : to squeeze out : extract by pressing 3 : to send by express

ex·pres·sion \ik-'spresh-ən\ n 1 : UT-TERANCE 2 : something that represents or symbolizes : SIGN; esp : a mathematical symbol or symbol group representing a quantity or operation 3 : a significant word or phrase; also : manner of expressing (as in writing or music) 4 : facial aspect or vocal intonation indicative of feeling (an ~ of disgust) — ex·pres·sion·less adj — ex·pres·sive \-'spres-iv\ adj — ex·pres·sive·ness n

ex·pres·sion·ism n : a theory or practice in art of seeking to depict the artist's subjective responses to objects and events — ex·pres·sion·ist n or adj — ex·pres·sion·is·tic \ik-,spresh-ə-'nis-tik\ adj

ex·press·man \ik-'spres-,man\ n : a person employed in the express business

ex·press·way \ik-'spres-,wā\ n : a high-speed divided highway for through traffic with grade separations at intersections

ex·pro·pri·ate \ek-'sprō-prē-,āt\ vb : to take away from a person the possession of or right to (property) — ex·pro·pri·a·tion \-,sprō-prē-'ā-shən\ n

ex·pul·sion \ik-'spəl-shən\ n : an expelling or being expelled : EJECTION

ex·punge \ik-'spənj\ vb : OBLITERATE, ERASE

ex·pur·gate \'ek-spər-,gāt\ vb : to clear (as a book) of objectionable passages — ex·pur·ga·tion \,ek-spər-'gā-shən\ n

1ex·qui·site \ek-'skwiz-ət, 'ek-(,)skwiz-\ adj 1 : excellent in form or workmanship 2 : keenly appreciative 3 : pleasingly beautiful or delicate 4 : INTENSE

2exquisite n : an overly fastidious individual

ex·tant \'ek-stənt, ek-'stant\ adj : EXISTENT; esp : not lost or destroyed

ex·tem·po·ra·ne·ous \ek-,stem-pə-'rā-nē-əs\ adj : not planned beforehand : IMPROMPTU — ex·tem·po·ra·ne·ous·ly adv

ex·tem·po·rary \ik-'stem-pə-,rer-ē\ adj : EXTEMPORANEOUS

ex·tem·po·re \-pə-(,)rē\ adv : EXTEM-PORANEOUSLY — extempore adj

ex·tem·po·rize \-pə-,rīz\ vb : to do something extemporaneously

ex·tend \ik-'stend\ vb 1 : to spread or stretch forth or out (as in reaching or straightening) 2 : to exert or make exert to capacity 3 : PROLONG (~ a note) 4 : PROFFER (~ credit) 5 : to make greater or broader (~ knowledge) (~ a business) 6 : to spread over (as space) or through (as time) (the town ~ed northward) (the sale ~s through tomorrow) syn lengthen, elongate

ex·ten·sion \-'sten-chən\ n 1 : an extending or being extended 2 : an additional part (~ on a house)

ex·ten·sive \-'sten-siv\ adj : of considerable extent : far-reaching : BROAD (~ changes) (an ~ property) — ex·ten·sive·ly adv

ex·tent \-'stent\ n 1 : the size, length, or bulk of something (a property of large ~) 2 : the degree or measure of something (the ~ of his guilt)

ex·ten·u·ate \ik-'sten-yə-,wāt\ vb : to treat (as a fault) as of less importance

than is real or apparent : EXCUSE — ex·ten·u·a·tion \-,sten-yə-'wā-shən\ n

1ex·te·ri·or \ek-'stir-ē-ər\ adj 1 : EX-TERNAL 2 : suitable for use on an outside surface (~ paint)

2exterior n : an exterior part or surface : OUTSIDE

ex·ter·mi·nate \ik-'stər-mə-,nāt\ vb : to destroy utterly syn extirpate, eradicate — ex·ter·mi·na·tion \-,stər-mə-'nā-shən\ n

ex·tern \'ek-,stərn\ n : a person (as a doctor) professionally connected with an institution but not living in it

1ex·ter·nal \ek-'stərn-ºl\ adj 1 : outwardly perceivable; also : SUPERFICIAL 2 : of, relating to, or located on the outside or an outer part 3 : arising or acting from without; also : FOREIGN (~ affairs) — ex·ter·nal·ly adv

2external n : something that is external

ex·tinct \ik-'stiŋkt, 'ek-,stiŋkt\ adj 1 : EXTINGUISHED (with hope ~) 2 : no longer existing (as a kind of plant) or active (as a volcano) or in use (as a language) — ex·tinc·tion \ik-'stiŋk-shən\ n

ex·tin·guish \ik-'stiŋ-gwish\ vb : to put out (as a fire); also : to bring to an end (as by destroying, checking, eclipsing, or nullifying) — ex·tin·guish·able adj — ex·tin·guish·er n

ex·tir·pate \'ek-stər-,pāt\ vb : UPROOT syn exterminate, eradicate — ex·tir·pa·tion \,ek-stər-'pā-shən\ n

ex·tol also ex·toll \ik-'stōl\ vb -tolled; -tol·ling : to praise highly : GLORIFY syn laud, eulogize, acclaim

ex·tort \ik-'stȯrt\ vb : to obtain by force or improper pressure (~ a bribe) — ex·tor·tion \-'stȯr-shən\ n — ex·tor·tion·er n

ex·tor·tion·ate \ik-'stȯr-sh(ə-)nət\ adj : EXCESSIVE, EXORBITANT — ex·tor·tion·ate·ly adv

1ex·tra \'ek-strə\ adj 1 : ADDITIONAL 2 : SUPERIOR syn spare, surplus, superfluous

2extra n 1 : something (as a charge) added 2 : a special edition of a newspaper 3 : an additional worker or performer (as in a group scene)

3extra adv : beyond what is usual (~ good)

1ex·tract \ik-'strakt\ vb 1 : to draw out; esp : to pull out forcibly (~ a tooth) 2 : to withdraw (as a juice or a constituent) by a physical or chemical process 3 : to select for citation : QUOTE — ex·tract·able adj — ex·trac·tion \-'strak-shən\ n — ex·trac·tor \-'strak-tər\ n

2ex·tract \'ek-,strakt\ n 1 : EXCERPT, CITATION 2 : a product (as a juice or concentrate) obtained by extracting

ex·tra·cur·ric·u·lar \,ek-strə-kə-'rik-yə-lər\ adj : lying outside the regular curriculum; esp : of or relating to school-connected activities (as sports) carrying no academic credit

ex·tra·dite \'ek-strə-,dīt\ vb : to obtain by or deliver up to extradition

ex·tra·di·tion \,ek-strə-'dish-ən\ n : a surrendering of an alleged criminal to a different jurisdiction for trial

ex·tra·dos \'ek-strə-,däs, ek-'strā-\ n : the exterior curve of an arch

ex·tra·mu·ral \,ek-strə-'myùr-əl\ adj : relating to or taking part in informal contests between teams of different schools other than varsity teams ex·tra·ne·ous \ek-'strā-nē-əs\ *adj* 1 : coming from without ⟨~ moisture⟩ 2 : not intrinsic ⟨~ incidents in a story⟩; *also* : IRRELEVANT ⟨~ digressions⟩ — ex·tra·ne·ous·ly *adv*

ex·traor·di·nary \ik-'strȯrd-ᵊn-ˌer-ē, ˌek-strə-'ȯrd-\ *adj* 1 : notably unusual or exceptional 2 : employed on a special service — ex·traor·di·nar·i·ly \ik-ˌstrȯrd-ᵊn-'er-ə-lē, ˌek-strə-ˌȯrd-\ *adv*

ex·trap·o·late \ik-'strap-ə-ˌlāt\ *vb* : to infer (unknown data) from known data — ex·trap·o·la·tion \-ˌstrap-ə-'lā-shən\ *n*

ex·tra·sen·so·ry \ˌek-strə-'sens-(ə-)rē\ *adj* : occurring beyond the known senses ⟨~ perception⟩

ex·tra·ter·ri·to·ri·al \-ˌter-ə-'tȯr-ē-əl\ *adj* 1 : located outside the territorial limits of a jurisdiction 2 : of or relating to extraterritoriality ⟨~ rights⟩

ex·tra·ter·ri·to·ri·al·i·ty \-ˌtȯr-ē-'al-ət-ē\ *n* : exemption from the application or jurisdiction of local law or tribunals ⟨diplomats enjoy ~⟩

ex·trav·a·gant \ik-'strav-i-gənt\ *adj* 1 : EXCESSIVE ⟨~ claims⟩ 2 : unduly lavish : WASTEFUL 3 : too costly *syn* immoderate, exorbitant, extreme — ex·trav·a·gance *n* — ex·trav·a·gant·ly *adv*

ex·trav·a·gan·za \ik-ˌstrav-ə-'gan-zə\ *n* 1 : a literary or musical work marked by extreme freedom of style and structure 2 : a lavish or spectacular show or event

¹ex·treme \ik-'strēm\ *adj* 1 : very great or intense ⟨~ cold⟩ 2 : very severe or drastic ⟨~ measures⟩ 3 : going to great lengths or beyond normal limits ⟨politically ~⟩ 4 : most remote ⟨~ end⟩ 5 : UTMOST; *also* : MAXIMUM ⟨an ~ effort⟩ — ex·treme·ly *adv*

²extreme *n* 1 : an extreme state 2 : something located at one end or the other of a range or series 3 : EXTREMITY 4

ex·trem·ist \-'strē-məst\ *n* : one who advocates or practices extreme measures esp. in politics — ex·trem·ism \-ˌmiz-əm\ *n*

ex·trem·i·ty \-'strem-ət-ē\ *n* 1 : the most remote part or point 2 : a limb of the body; *esp* : a human hand or foot 3 : the greatest need or danger 4 : the utmost degree; *also* : a drastic or desperate measure

ex·tri·cate \'ek-strə-ˌkāt\ *vb* : to free from an entanglement or difficulty *syn* disentangle, untangle

ex·trin·sic \ek-'strin-zik, -sik\ *adj* 1 : not forming part of or belonging to a thing : EXTRANEOUS 2 : EXTERNAL — ex·trin·si·cal·ly *adv*

ex·tro·vert \'ek-strə-ˌvərt\ *n* : a person more interested in the world about him than in his inner self — ex·tro·ver·sion

\ˌek-strə-'vər-zhən\ *n* — ex·tro·vert·ed \'ek-strə-ˌvərt-əd\ *or* extrovert *adj*

ex·trude \ik-'strüd\ *vb* : to force, press, or push out; *esp* : to form (as plastic) by forcing through a die — ex·tru·sion \-'strü-zhən\ *n*

ex·u·ber·ant \ig-'zü-b(ə-)rənt\ *adj* 1 : joyously unrestrained 2 : PROFUSE — ex·u·ber·ance *n* — ex·u·ber·ant·ly *adv*

ex·ude \ig-'züd\ *vb* [L *exsudare*, fr. *ex-* out + *sudare* to sweat] 1 : to discharge slowly through pores or cuts 2 : to spread out in all directions — ex·u·date \'eks-ə-ˌdāt, 'egz-\ *n* — ex·u·da·tion \ˌeks-ə-'dā-shən, ˌegz-\ *n*

ex·ult \ig-'zəlt\ *vb* : to rejoice in triumph : GLORY — ex·ul·tant \-'zəlt-ᵊnt\ *adj* — ex·ul·tant·ly *adv* — ex·ul·ta·tion \ˌeks-ˌəl-'tā-shən, ˌegz-\ *n*

ex·urb \'ek-ˌsərb\ *n* : a region or district outside a city and usu. beyond its suburbs inhabited chiefly by well-to-do families — ex·ur·bia \ek-'sər-bē-ə\ *n*

ex·ur·ban·ite \ek-'sər-bə-ˌnīt\ *n* : one who lives in an exurb

-ey — see -Y

¹eye \'ī\ *n* 1 : an organ of sight typically consisting of a globular structure (eye·ball \-ˌbȯl\) in a socket of the skull with thin movable covers (eye·lids \-ˌlidz\) bordered with hairs (eye·lash·es \-ˌlash-əz\) 2 : VISION, PERCEPTION; *also* : faculty of discrimination ⟨a good ~ for bargains⟩ 3 : something suggesting an eye ⟨the ~ of a needle⟩; *esp* : an undeveloped bud (as of a potato)

²eye *vb* : to look at : WATCH

eye·brow \-ˌbrau̇\ *n* : the bony arch forming the upper edge of the eye socket; *also* : the hairs growing on this

eye·glass \-ˌglas\ *n* 1 : a lens variously mounted for personal use as an aid to vision 2 *pl* : GLASS 3

eye·let \-lət\ *n* 1 : a small reinforced hole in material intended for ornament or for passage of something (as a cord or lace) 2 : a metal ring for reinforcing an eyelet

eye·sight \-ˌsīt\ *n* : SIGHT, VISION

eye·sore \-ˌsȯr\ *n* : something displeasing to the sight ⟨that old building is an ~⟩

eye·strain \'ī-ˌstrān\ *n* : weariness or a strained state of the eye

eye·tooth \-'tüth\ *n* : a canine tooth of the upper jaw

eye·wash \-ˌwȯsh, -ˌwäsh\ *n* 1 : an eye lotion 2 : misleading or deceptive statements, actions, or procedures

eye·wit·ness \-'wit-nəs\ *n* : a person who sees an occurrence with his own eyes and is able to give a firsthand account of it

ey·rie \'ī(ə)r-ē, 'a(ə)r-, 'i(ə)r-\ *n* : AERIE

ey·rir \'ā-ˌriȯr\ *n, pl* au·rar \'au̇-ˌrär\ — see MONEY table

---

1 \\'ef\\ *n, often cap* **:** the 6th letter of the English alphabet

Fa·bi·an \\'fā-bē-ən\\ *adj* **:** of, relating to, or being a society of socialists organized in England in 1884 to spread socialist principles gradually — **Fabian** *n* — **Fa·bi·an·ism** *n*

fa·ble \\'fā-bəl\\ *n* **1 :** a legendary story of supernatural happenings **2 :** a narration intended to teach a lesson; *esp* **:** one in which animals speak and act like people **3 :** FALSEHOOD

fa·bled *adj* **1 :** FICTITIOUS **2 :** told or celebrated in fable

fab·ric \\'fab-rik\\ *n* **1 :** STRUCTURE, FRAMEWORK ⟨the ~ of society⟩ **2 :** CLOTH; *also* **:** a material that resembles cloth

fab·ri·cate \\'fab-ri-ˌkāt\\ *vb* **1 :** CONSTRUCT, MANUFACTURE **2 :** INVENT, CREATE **3 :** to make up for the sake of deception — **fab·ri·ca·tion** \\ˌfab-ri-'kā-shən\\ *n*

fab·u·lous \\'fab-yə-ləs\\ *adj* **1 :** resembling a fable **:** LEGENDARY **2 :** told in or based on fable **3 :** INCREDIBLE, MARVELOUS — **fab·u·lous·ly** *adv*

fa·cade *also* **fa·çade** \\fə-'säd\\ *n* **1 :** the principal face or front of a building **2 :** a false, superficial, or artificial appearance ⟨a ~ of composure⟩

1face \\'fās\\ *n* **1 :** the front part of the head **2 :** PRESENCE ⟨in the ~ of danger⟩ **3 :** facial expression **:** LOOK ⟨put a sad ~ on⟩ **4 :** GRIMACE ⟨made a ~⟩ **5 :** outward appearance ⟨looks easy on the ~ of it⟩ **6 :** BOLDNESS **7 :** DIGNITY, PRESTIGE ⟨afraid to lose ~⟩ **8 :** the surface of something; *esp* **:** the front or principal surface — **faced** *adj*

2face *vb* **1 :** to confront brazenly **2 :** to line near the edge esp. with a different material; *also* **:** to cover the front or surface of ⟨~ a building with marble⟩ **3 :** to bring face to face ⟨*faced* him with the proof⟩ **4 :** to stand or sit with the face toward ⟨~ the sun⟩ **5 :** to front on ⟨a house *facing* the park⟩ **6 :** to oppose firmly ⟨*faced* up to his foe⟩ **7 :** to turn the face or body in a specified direction

face·down \\'fās-'daùn\\ *adv* **:** with the face downward

face-lift·ing \\-ˌlif-tiŋ\\ *n* **1 :** a plastic operation for removal of facial defects (as wrinkles or sagging) usu. associated with aging **2 :** MODERNIZATION

fac·et \\'fas-ət\\ *n* **1 :** one of the small plane surfaces of a cut gem **2 :** ASPECT, PHASE

fa·ce·tious \\fə-'sē-shəs\\ *adj* **1 :** COMICAL **2 :** JOCULAR **3 :** FLIPPANT — **fa·ce·tious·ly** *adv* — **fa·ce·tious·ness** *n*

1fa·cial \\'fā-shəl\\ *adj* **:** of or relating to the face

2facial *n* **:** a facial treatment or massage

fac·ile \\'fas-əl\\ *adj* **1 :** easily accomplished, handled, or attained **2 :** SUPERFICIAL **3 :** readily manifested and often insincere ⟨~ tears⟩ **4 :** mild or yielding in disposition **:** PLIANT **5 :** READY, FLUENT ⟨a ~ writer⟩

fa·cil·i·tate \\fə-'sil-ə-ˌtāt\\ *vb* **:** to make easier

fa·cil·i·ty \\-ət-ē\\ *n* **1 :** the quality of being easily performed **2 :** ease in per-formance **:** APTITUDE **3 :** PLIANCY **4 :** something that makes easier an action, operation, or course of conduct ⟨*facilities* for further study⟩ **5 :** something (as a hospital or plumbing) built, installed, or established to serve a purpose

fac·ing \\'fā-siŋ\\ *n* **1 :** a lining at the edge esp. of a garment **2** *pl* **:** the collar, cuffs, and trimmings of a uniform coat **3 :** an ornamental or protective covering; *esp* **:** one on the face of something **4 :** material for facing

fac·sim·i·le \\fak-'sim-ə-lē\\ *n* **1 :** an exact copy **2 :** the transmitting of printed matter or pictures by wire or radio for reproduction

fact \\'fakt\\ *n* **1 :** DEED; *esp* **:** CRIME ⟨accessory after the ~⟩ **2 :** the quality of being actual **3 :** something that exists or occurs **:** ACTUALITY, EVENT; *also* **:** a piece of information about such a fact

fac·tion \\'fak-shən\\ *n* **1 :** a group or combination (as in a state or church) acting together within and usu. against a larger body **:** CLIQUE **2 :** party spirit esp. when marked by dissension

fac·tious \\-shəs\\ *adj* **1 :** of, relating to, or caused by faction **2 :** inclined to faction or the formation of factions **:** causing dissension

fac·ti·tious \\fak-'tish-əs\\ *adj* **:** ARTIFICIAL, SHAM ⟨a ~ display of grief⟩

1fac·tor \\'fak-tər\\ *n* **1 :** AGENT **2 :** something that actively contributes to a result **:** INGREDIENT **3 :** GENE **4 :** a number or symbol in mathematics that when multiplied with another forms a product

2factor *vb* **1 :** to resolve into factors **2 :** to work as a factor

fac·to·ry \\-t(ə-)rē\\ *n* **1 :** a trading post where resident factors trade **2 :** a building or group of buildings used for manufacturing

fac·to·tum \\fak-'tōt-əm\\ *n* **:** an employee with numerous varied duties

fac·tu·al \\'fak-ch(ə-w)əl\\ *adj* **:** of or relating to facts; *also* **:** based on fact — **fac·tu·al·ly** *adv*

fac·ul·ty \\'fak-əl-tē\\ *n* **1 :** ability to act or do **:** POWER; *also* **:** natural aptitude **2 :** one of the powers of the mind or body ⟨the ~ of hearing⟩ **3 :** the teachers in a school or college **4 :** a department of instruction in an educational institution **5 :** the members of a profession

fad \\'fad\\ *n* **:** a practice or interest followed for a time with exaggerated zeal **:** CRAZE — **fad·dish** *adj* — **fad·dist** *n*

1fade \\'fād\\ *vb* **1 :** WITHER **2 :** to lose or cause to lose freshness or brilliance of color **3 :** to grow dim or faint **4 :** to sink away **:** VANISH

2fade *n* **:** fading

fade·less \\-ləs\\ *adj* **:** not susceptible to fading

fae·cal, fae·ces *var of* FECAL, FECES

fa·er·ie *also* **fa·ery** \\'fā-(ə-)rē, 'fa(ə)r-ē\\ *n* **1 :** FAIRYLAND **2 :** FAIRY

1fag \\'fag\\ *vb* **fagged; fag·ging 1 :** DRUDGE **2 :** to act as a fag **3 :** TIRE, EXHAUST

2fag *n* **1 :** an English public-school boy who acts as servant to another **2 :** MENIAL, DRUDGE

³fag n : CIGARETTE

fag end n 1 : the last part or coarser end of a web of cloth 2 : the untwisted end of a rope 3 : REMNANT 4 : the extreme end

fag·ot or **fag·got** \'fag-ət\ n : a bundle of sticks or twigs esp. as used for fuel

fag·ot·ing or **fag·got·ing** n : an embroidery produced by tying threads in hourglass-shaped clusters

Fahr·en·heit \'far-ən-ˌhīt\ adj [after Gabriel *Fahrenheit* d1736 German physicist] : relating to, conforming to, or having a thermometer scale on which the boiling point of water is at 212 degrees and the freezing point at 32 degrees above its zero point

fa·ience or **fa·ience** \fā-'äns\ n : earthenware decorated with opaque colored glazes

¹fail \'fāl\ vb 1 : to become feeble; esp : to decline in health 2 : to die away 3 : to stop functioning 4 : to fall short ⟨~ed in his duty⟩ 5 : to be or become absent or inadequate 6 : to be unsuccessful 7 : to become bankrupt 8 : DISAPPOINT, DESERT ⟨~ a friend in need⟩ 9 : NEGLECT

²fail n : FAILURE ⟨without ~⟩

¹fail·ing n : WEAKNESS, SHORTCOMING

²failing prep : in the absence or lack of

faille \'fīl\ n : a somewhat shiny closely woven ribbed silk, rayon, or cotton fabric

fail·ure \'fāl-yər\ n 1 : a failing to do or perform 2 : a state of inability to perform a normal function adequately ⟨heart ~⟩ 3 : a lack of success 4 : BANKRUPTCY 5 : DEFICIENCY 6 : DETERIORATION, BREAKDOWN 7 : one that has failed

¹fain \'fān\ adj, archaic 1 : GLAD 2 : INCLINED 3 : OBLIGED

²fain adv, archaic 1 : WILLINGLY 2 : RATHER

¹faint \'fānt\ adj 1 : COWARDLY, SPIRITLESS 2 : weak and dizzy nearly to the loss of consciousness 3 : lacking vigor or strength : FEEBLE ⟨~ praise⟩ 4 : INDISTINCT, DIM — **faint·ly** adv — **faint·ness** n

²faint vb : to lose consciousness

³faint n : an act or condition of fainting ⟨fell in a ~⟩

faint·heart·ed \-'härt-əd\ adj : lacking courage : TIMID

¹fair \'faər\ adj 1 : attractive in appearance : BEAUTIFUL; also : FEMININE 2 : superficially pleasing : SPECIOUS 3 : CLEAN, PURE 4 : CLEAR, LEGIBLE 5 : not stormy or cloudy ⟨~ weather⟩ 6 : JUST 7 : conforming with the rules : ALLOWED; also : being within the foul lines ⟨~ ball⟩ 8 : open to legitimate pursuit or attack ⟨~ game⟩ 9 : PROMISING, LIKELY ⟨a ~ chance of winning⟩ 10 : favorable to a ship's course ⟨a ~ wind⟩ 11 : light in coloring : BLOND 12 : ADEQUATE — **fair·ness** n

²fair adv : FAIRLY

³fair n 1 : a gathering of buyers and sellers at a stated time and place for trade 2 : a competitive exhibition (as of farm products) 3 : a sale of a collection of articles usu. for a charitable purpose

fair·ground \-ˌgraůnd\ n : an area set aside for the holding of fairs and similar gatherings

fair·ly adv 1 : HANDSOMELY, FAVORABLY ⟨~ situated⟩ 2 : QUITE, COMPLETELY 3 : in a fair manner : JUSTLY 4 : MODERATELY, TOLERABLY ⟨a ~ easy job⟩

fair·spo·ken \'faər-'spō-kən\ adj : using fair speech : COURTEOUS

fair–trade \-'trād\ adj : of, relating to, or being an agreement between a producer and a seller that branded merchandise will be sold at or above a specified price ⟨~ items⟩ — **fair–trade** vb

fair·way \-ˌwā\ n : the mowed part of a golf course between tee and green

fairy \'fa(ə)r-ē\ n : an imaginary being of folklore and romance usu. having diminutive human form and magic powers — **fairy tale** n

fairy·land \-ˌland\ n 1 : the land of fairies 2 : a place of delicate beauty or magical charm

fait ac·com·pli \fā-tà-kōⁿ-plē\ n, pl **faits accompli** ⟨same⟩ : a thing accomplished and presumably irreversible

faith \'fāth\ n 1 : allegiance to duty or a person : LOYALTY 2 : belief and trust in God 3 : CONFIDENCE 4 : a system of religious beliefs — **faith·ful** adj — **faith·ful·ly** adv — **faith·ful·ness** n — **faith·less** adj — **faith·less·ly** adv — **faith·less·ness** n

¹fake \'fāk\ vb 1 : to treat so as to falsify : DOCTOR 2 : COUNTERFEIT 3 : PRETEND, SIMULATE — **fak·er** n

²fake n 1 : IMITATION, FRAUD, COUNTERFEIT 2 : IMPOSTOR

³fake adj : COUNTERFEIT, SHAM

fa·kir \fə-'kiər\ n 1 : a Muslim mendicant : DERVISH 2 : a wandering beggar of India who performs tricks

fal·chion \'fól-chən\ n : a broad-bladed slightly curved medieval sword

fal·con \'fal-kən, 'fó(l)-\ n : a hawk trained to pursue game birds; also : any of various long-winged hawks — **fal·con·er** n — **fal·con·ry** n

¹fall \'fól\ vb **fell** \'fel\ **fall·en** \'fó-lən\ **fall·ing** 1 : to descend freely by the force of gravity 2 : to hang freely 3 : to come as if by descending ⟨darkness *fell*⟩ 4 : to become uttered 5 : to lower or become lowered : DROP ⟨her eyes *fell*⟩ 6 : to leave an erect position suddenly and involuntarily 7 : STUMBLE, STRAY 8 : to drop down wounded or dead : die in battle 9 : to become captured or defeated 10 : to suffer ruin or failure 11 : to commit an immoral act 12 : to move or extend in a downward direction 13 : SUBSIDE, ABATE 14 : to decline in quality, activity, quantity, or value 15 : to assume a look of shame or dejection ⟨her face *fell*⟩ 16 : to occur at a certain time 17 : to come by chance 18 : DEVOLVE 19 : to have the proper place or station ⟨the accent ~s on the first syllable⟩ 20 : to come within the scope of something 21 : to pass from one condition to another ⟨*fell* ill⟩ 22 : to set about heartily or actively ⟨~ to work⟩ — **fall flat** : to produce no response or result — **fall for** 1 : to fall in love with 2 : to become a victim of — **fall foul** 1 : to have a collision 2 : to have a quarrel : CLASH ⟨*fell* foul of one another⟩

— **fall from grace 1 :** SIN **2 :** BACK-SLIDE — **fall into line :** to comply with a certain course of action — **fall over oneself :** to display excessive eagerness — **fall short 1 :** to be deficient **2 :** to fail to attain

²**fall** n **1 :** the act of falling **2 :** a falling out, off, or away **:** DROPPING **3 :** AUTUMN **4 :** a thing or quantity that falls ⟨a light ∼ of snow⟩ **5 :** COLLAPSE, DOWNFALL **6 :** the surrender or capture of a besieged place **7 :** departure from virtue **8 :** SLOPE **9 :** WATERFALL — usu. used in pl. **10 :** a decrease in size, quantity, activity, or value ⟨a ∼ in price⟩ **11 :** the distance which something falls **:** DROP **12 :** an act of forcing a wrestler's shoulders to the mat; also **:** a bout of wrestling

fal·la·cious \fə-'lā-shəs\ adj **1 :** embodying a fallacy ⟨a ∼ argument⟩ **2 :** MISLEADING, DECEPTIVE

fal·la·cy \'fal-ə-sē\ n **1 :** a false or mistaken idea **2 :** false or illogical reasoning; also **:** an instance of such reasoning

fall guy n **1 :** one that is easily duped **2 :** SCAPEGOAT

fal·li·ble \'fal-ə-bəl\ adj **1 :** liable to be erroneous **2 :** capable of making a mistake

fall·ing-out \,fȯl-iŋ-'aȯt\ n, pl **fallings-out :** QUARREL

falling star n **:** METEOR

fall·out \'fȯl-,aȯt\ n **:** the often radioactive particles that result from a nuclear explosion and descend through the air

fal·low \'fal-ō\ n **:** usu. cultivated land left idle during a growing season **:** land plowed but not tilled or sowed — **fallow** vb — **fallow** adj

fallow deer n **:** a small European deer with broad antlers and a pale yellow coat spotted white in the summer

false \'fȯls\ adj **1 :** not true **:** ERRONEOUS, INCORRECT **2 :** intentionally untrue **3 :** DISHONEST, DECEITFUL **4 :** adjusted or made so as to deceive ⟨∼ scales⟩ **5 :** inaccurate in pitch **6 :** tending to mislead **:** DECEPTIVE ⟨∼ promises⟩ **7 :** not faithful or loyal **:** TREACHEROUS **8 :** SHAM, ARTIFICIAL **9 :** not essential or permanent ⟨∼ front⟩ **10 :** based on mistaken ideas — **false·ly** adv — **false-ness** n — **fal·si·ty** \'fȯl-sət-ē\ n

false·hood \'fȯls-,hȯd\ n **1 :** LIE **2 :** absence of truth or accuracy **3 :** the practice of lying

fal·set·to \fȯl-'set-ō\ n **:** an artificially high voice; esp **:** an artificial singing voice that overlaps and extends above the range of the full voice esp. of a tenor

fal·si·fy \'fȯl-sə-,fī\ vb **1 :** to make false **:** change so as to deceive ⟨∼ accounts⟩ **2 :** LIE **3 :** MISREPRESENT **4 :** to prove to be false — **fal·si·fi·ca·tion** \,fȯl-sə-fə-'kā-shən\ n

falt·boat \'fält-,bōt\ n **:** a small collapsible canoe made of rubberized cloth stretched over a framework

fal·ter \'fȯl-tər\ vb **1 :** to move unsteadily **:** STUMBLE, TOTTER **2 :** to hesitate in speech **:** STAMMER **3 :** to hesitate in purpose or action **:** WAVER, FLINCH — **fal·ter·ing·ly** adv

fame \'fām\ n **:** public reputation **:** RENOWN — **famed** \'fāmd\ adj

fa·mil·ial \fə-'mil-yəl\ adj **:** of, relating to, or characteristic of a family ⟨a ∼ disease⟩

¹**fa·mil·iar** \fə-'mil-yər\ n **1 :** COMPANION **2 :** a spirit held to attend and serve or guard a person **3 :** one that frequents a place

²**familiar** adj **1 :** closely acquainted **:** INTIMATE **2 :** of or relating to a family **3 :** INFORMAL ⟨a ∼ essay⟩ **4 :** FORWARD, PRESUMPTUOUS **5 :** frequently seen or experienced **6 :** being of everyday occurrence — **fa·mil·iar·ly** adv

fa·mil·iar·i·ty \fə-,mil-'yar-ət-ē\ n **1 :** close friendship **:** INTIMACY **2 :** close acquaintance with or knowledge of something **3 :** INFORMALITY **4 :** an unduly bold or forward act or expression **:** IMPROPRIETY

fa·mil·iar·ize \fə-'mil-yə-,rīz\ vb **1 :** to make known or familiar **2 :** to make thoroughly acquainted **:** ACCUSTOM

fam·i·ly \'fam-(ə-)lē\ n **1 :** a group of persons of common ancestry **:** CLAN **2 :** a group of individuals living under one roof and under one head **:** HOUSEHOLD **3 :** a social group composed of parents and their children **4 :** a group of related persons, lower animals, or plants; also **:** a group of things having common characteristics

fam·ine \'fam-ən\ n **1 :** an extreme general scarcity of food **2 :** a great shortage

fam·ish \'fam-ish\ vb **1 :** STARVE **2 :** to suffer or cause to suffer from extreme hunger

fa·mous \'fā-məs\ adj **1 :** widely known **2 :** honored for achievement **3 :** EXCELLENT, FIRST-RATE   syn renowned, celebrated, noted, notorious, distinguished, eminent, illustrious

fa·mous·ly adv **:** SPLENDIDLY, EXCELLENTLY

¹**fan** \'fan\ n **:** a device (as a hand-waved triangular piece or a mechanism with blades) for producing a current of air

²**fan** vb **fanned; fan·ning 1 :** to drive away the chaff from grain by winnowing **2 :** to move (air) with or as if with a fan **3 :** to direct a current of air upon ⟨∼ a fire⟩ **4 :** to stir up to activity **:** STIMULATE **5 :** to spread like a fan **6 :** to strike out in baseball

³**fan** n **1 :** an enthusiastic follower of a sport or entertainment **2 :** an enthusiastic admirer (as of a celebrity)

fa·nat·ic \fə-'nat-ik\ adj **:** marked or moved by excessive enthusiasm and intense uncritical devotion — **fanatic** n — **fa·nat·i·cal** adj — **fa·nat·i·cism** \-'nat-ə-,siz-əm\ n

fan·ci·er \'fan-sē-ər\ n **:** a person who breeds or grows some kind of animal or plant for points of excellence

fan·ci·ful \-si-fəl\ adj **1 :** full of fancy **:** guided by fancy **:** WHIMSICAL **2 :** coming from the fancy rather than from the reason **3 :** curiously made or shaped ⟨∼ forms of ice on a windowpane⟩ — **fan·ci·ful·ly** adv

¹**fan·cy** \'fan-sē\ n **1 :** LIKING, INCLINATION; also **:** LOVE **2 :** NOTION, IDEA, WHIM ⟨a passing ∼⟩ **3 :** IMAGINATION **4 :** TASTE, JUDGMENT

²**fancy** vb **1 :** LIKE **2 :** IMAGINE **3 :** to believe without any evidence

³**fancy** adj **1 :** WHIMSICAL **2 :** not plain **:** ORNAMENTAL **3 :** of particular excellence **4 :** bred for special qualities **5 :** above real value **:** EXTRAVAGANT **6 :** executed with technical skill and superior grace — **fan·ci·ly** adv

fancy dress n : a costume (as for a masquerade) chosen to suit the wearer's fancy

fan·cy-free \'fan-sē-‚frē\ adj : not centering the attention on any one person or thing; esp : not in love

fan·cy·work \-‚wərk\ n : ornamental needlework (as embroidery)

fan·dan·go \fan-'dan-gō\ n : a lively Spanish or Spanish-American dance

fane \'fān\ n : TEMPLE

fan·fare \'fan-‚faər\ n 1 : a flourish of trumpets 2 : a showy outward display

fang \'fan\ n : a long sharp tooth; esp : a grooved or hollow tooth of a venomous snake

fan·light \'fan-‚līt\ n : a semicircular window with radiating sash bars like the ribs of a fan placed over a door or window

fan·tail \-‚tāl\ n 1 : a fan-shaped tail or end 2 : a fancy goldfish with the tail fins double 3 : an overhang at the stern of a ship

fan·ta·sia \fan-'tā-zh(ē-)ə, ‚fant-ə-'zē-ə\ n : a musical composition free and fanciful in form

fan·tas·tic \fan-'tas-tik\ also **fan·tas·ti·cal** adj 1 : IMAGINARY, UNREAL, UNREALISTIC 2 : conceived by unrestrained fancy : GROTESQUE 3 : exceedingly or unbelievably great 4 : extremely individual : ECCENTRIC — **fan·tas·ti·cal·ly** adv

fan·ta·sy \'fant-ə-sē\ n 1 : IMAGINATION, FANCY 2 : a product of the imagination : ILLUSION 3 : FANTASIA

¹**far** \'fär\ adv **far·ther** \-thər\ or **fur·ther** \'fər-\; **far·thest** \-thəst\ or **fur·thest** 1 : at or to a considerable distance in space or time (~ from home) 2 : by a broad interval : WIDELY, MUCH (~ better) 3 : to or at a definite distance, point, or degree (as ~ as I know) 4 : to an advanced point or extent : a long way (go ~ in his field) — **by far** : GREATLY — **far and away** : DECIDEDLY

²**far** adj **farther** or **further**; **farthest** or **furthest** 1 : remote in space or time : DISTANT 2 : DIFFERENT (a ~ cry from former methods) 3 : LONG (a ~ journey) 4 : being the more distant of two (on the ~ side of the lake)

far·away \'fär-ə-‚wä\ adj 1 : DISTANT, REMOTE 2 : DREAMY

farce \'färs\ n 1 : a play marked by broadly satirical comedy and improbable plot 2 : the broad humor characteristic of farce or pretense : MOCKERY 3 : a ridiculous action, display, or pretense — **far·ci·cal** adj

¹**fare** \'faər\ vb 1 : GO, TRAVEL 2 : to get along : SUCCEED 3 : EAT, DINE

²**fare** n 1 : the price charged to transport a person 2 : a person paying a fare : PASSENGER 3 : range of food : DIET; also : material provided for use, consumption, or enjoyment

¹**fare-well** \faər-'wel\ imperative verb : get along well — used interjectionally to or by one departing

²**farewell** n 1 : a wish of welfare at parting : GOOD-BYE 2 : LEAVE-TAKING

³**farewell** adj : PARTING, FINAL (a ~ concert)

far-fetched \'fär-'fecht\ adj : not easily or naturally deduced or introduced : IMPROBABLE

far-flung \-'flən\ adj : widely spread or distributed

fa·ri·na \fə-'rē-nə\ n : a fine meal (as of wheat) used in puddings or as a breakfast cereal

¹**farm** \'färm\ n : a tract of land used for raising crops or livestock

²**farm** vb : to use (land) as a farm (~ed 200 acres); also : to raise crops or livestock esp. as a business — **farm·er** n

farm·hand \'färm-‚hand\ n : a farm laborer

farm·house \-‚haús\ n : a dwelling on a farm

farm·ing n : the occupation or business of a person who farms : AGRICULTURE

farm·land \'färm-‚land\ n : land used or suitable for farming

farm·stead \-‚sted\ n : the buildings and adjacent service areas of a farm

farm·yard \-‚yärd\ n : space around or enclosed by farm buildings

far-off \'fär-'óf\ adj : remote in time or space : DISTANT

far·rouche \fə-'rüsh\ adj : marked by shyness and lack of polish; also : WILD

far·ra·go \fə-'räg-ō\ n, pl **-goes** : a confused collection : MIXTURE

far-reach·ing \'fär-'rē-chin\ adj : having a wide range, influence, or effect

far·ri·er \'far-ē-ər\ n : a blacksmith who shoes horses; also : VETERINARIAN

¹**far·row** \'far-ō\ vb : to give birth to a farrow

²**farrow** n : a litter of pigs

far·see·ing \'fär-'sē-in\ adj : FARSIGHTED

far·sight·ed \'fär-'sīt-əd\ adj 1 : able to see distant things more clearly than near 2 : JUDICIOUS, WISE, SHREWD — **far·sight·ed·ness** n

¹**far·ther** \'fär-thər\ adv 1 : at or to a greater distance or more advanced point 2 : more completely

²**farther** adj 1 : more distant 2 : ²**FURTHER** 2

¹**far·thest** \-thəst\ adj : most distant

²**farthest** adv 1 : to or at the greatest distance : REMOTEST 2 : to the most advanced point 3 : by the greatest degree or extent : MOST

far·thing \'fär-thin\ n : a British monetary unit equal to ¼ of a penny; also : a coin representing this unit

far·thin·gale \'fär-thən-‚gāl\ n : a support (as of hoops) worn esp. in the 16th century to swell out a skirt

fas·ci·cle \'fas-i-kəl\ n 1 : a small bundle or cluster (as of flowers or roots) 2 : one of the divisions of a book published in parts

fas·ci·nate \'fas-ʰn-‚āt\ vb 1 : to transfix and hold spellbound by an irresistible power 2 : ALLURE 3 : to be irresistibly attractive — **fas·ci·na·tion** \‚fas-ʰn-'ā-shən\ n

fas·cism \'fash-‚iz-əm\ n 1 often cap : the body of principles held by Fascisti 2 : a political philosophy, movement, or regime that exalts nation and race and stands for a centralized autocratic government headed by a dictatorial leader, severe economic and social regimentation, and forcible suppression of opposition — **fas·cist** \-əst\ n or adj, *often cap* — **fas·cis·tic** \fash-'is-tik\ *adj, often cap*

Fa·sci·sta \fä-'shē-stä\ *n, pl* **-sti** \-stē\ : a member of an Italian political organization under Mussolini governing Italy 1922–43 according to the principles of fascism

¹**fash·ion** \'fash-ən\ *n* 1 : the make or form of something 2 : MANNER, WAY 3 : a prevailing custom, usage, or style 4 : the prevailing style (as in dress) during a particular time *syn* mode, vogue

²**fashion** *vb* 1 : MOLD, CONSTRUCT 2 : FIT, ADAPT

fash·ion·able \'fash-(ə-)nə-bəl\ *adj* 1 : dressing or behaving according to fashion : STYLISH 2 : of or relating to the world of fashion (~ resorts) — **fash·ion·ably** *adv*

¹**fast** \'fast\ *adj* 1 : firmly fixed or bound 2 : tightly shut 3 : adhering firmly : STUCK 4 : UNCHANGEABLE (hard and ~ rules) 5 : STAUNCH (~ friends) 6 : characterized by quick motion, operation, or effect (a ~ trip) (a ~ track) 7 : indicating ahead of the correct time (the clock is ~) 8 : not easily disturbed : SOUND (a ~ sleep) 9 : permanently dyed; *also* : being proof against fading (colors ~ to sunlight) 10 : DISSIPATED, WILD 11 : daringly unconventional esp. in sexual matters *syn* rapid, swift, fleet, quick, speedy, hasty

²**fast** *adv* 1 : in a fast or fixed manner (stuck ~ in the mud) 2 : SOUNDLY, DEEPLY (~ asleep) 3 : SWIFTLY 4 : RECKLESSLY

³**fast** *vb* 1 : to abstain from food 2 : to eat sparingly or abstain from some foods

⁴**fast** *n* 1 : the act or practice of fasting 2 : a time of fasting

fas·ten \'fas-ᵊn\ *vb* 1 : to attach or join by or as if by pinning, tying, or nailing 2 : to make fast : fix securely 3 : to fix or set steadily (~ed his eyes on her) 4 : to become fixed or joined — **fas·ten·er** \'fas-(ᵊ-)nər\ *n*

fas·ten·ing \'fas-(ᵊ-)niŋ\ *n* : something that fastens : FASTENER

fas·tid·i·ous \fas-'tid-ē-əs\ *adj* 1 : overly difficult to please 2 : showing or demanding excessive delicacy or care — **fas·tid·i·ous·ness** *n*

fast·ness \'fas(t)-nəs\ *n* 1 : the quality or state of being fast 2 : a fortified or secure place : STRONGHOLD

¹**fat** \'fat\ *adj* 1 : FLESHY, PLUMP 2 : OILY, GREASY 3 : well filled out : BIG 4 : well stocked : ABUNDANT 5 : PROFITABLE — **fat·ness** *n*

²**fat** *n* 1 : animal tissue rich in greasy or oily matter 2 : any of numerous energy-rich esters that occur naturally in animal fats and in plants and are soluble in organic solvents (as ether) but not in water 3 : the best or richest portion (lived on the ~ of the land) 4 : excess matter

fa·tal \'fāt-ᵊl\ *adj* 1 : MORTAL, DEADLY, DISASTROUS 2 : FATEFUL — **fa·tal·ly** *adv*

fa·tal·ism \-,iz-əm\ *n* : the belief that events are determined by fate — **fa·tal·ist** *n* — **fa·tal·is·tic** \,fāt-ᵊl-'is-tik\ *adj*

fa·tal·i·ty \fā-'tal-ət-ē\ *n* 1 : DEADLINESS 2 : the quality or state of being destined for disaster 3 : FATE 4 : death resulting from a disaster or accident

fat·back \'fat-,bak\ *n* : a fatty strip from the back of the hog usu. cured by salting and drying

fate \'fāt\ *n* 1 : the cause beyond man's control that is held to determine events : DESTINY 2 : LOT, FORTUNE 3 : END, OUTCOME 4 : DISASTER; *esp* : DEATH 5 *cap, pl* : the three goddesses of classical mythology who determine the course of human life

fat·ed \'fāt-əd\ *adj* : decreed, controlled, or marked by fate

fate·ful \'fāt-fəl\ *adj* 1 : IMPORTANT 2 : OMINOUS, PROPHETIC 3 : determined by fate 4 : DEADLY, DESTRUCTIVE — **fate·ful·ly** *adv*

¹**fa·ther** \'fäth-ər\ *n* 1 : a male parent 2 *cap* : God esp. as the first person of the Trinity 3 : ANCESTOR, FOREFATHER 4 : one deserving the respect and love given to a father 5 *often cap* : an early Christian writer accepted by the church as an authoritative witness to its teaching and practice 6 : ORIGINATOR (the ~ of modern radio); *also* : SOURCE 7 : PRIEST — used esp. as a title 8 : one of the leading men (city ~s) — **fa·ther·land** \-,land\ *n* — **fa·ther·less** *adj* — **fa·ther·ly** *adj*

²**father** *vb* 1 : BEGET 2 : to be the founder, producer, or author of 3 : to treat or care for as a father

fa·ther·hood \-,hûd\ *n* : the state of being a father

father-in-law *n, pl* **fathers-in-law** : the father of one's husband or wife

¹**fath·om** \'fath-əm\ *n* [OE *fæthm* outstretched arms, fathom] : a nautical unit of length equal to 6 feet

²**fathom** *vb* 1 : to measure by a sounding line 2 : PROBE 3 : to get to the bottom of and come to understand — **fath·om·able** *adj*

fa·thom·less \-ləs\ *adj* : incapable of being fathomed

¹**fa·tigue** \fə-'tēg\ *n* 1 : weariness from labor or use 2 : manual or menial work performed by military personnel 3 *pl* : the uniform or work clothing worn on fatigue and in the field

²**fatigue** *vb* : WEARY, TIRE

fat·ten \'fat-ᵊn\ *vb* : to make or grow fat

fat·ty \'fat-ē\ *adj* : containing fat or having the qualities of fat

fa·tu·i·ty \fə-'t(y)ü-ət-ē\ *n* : FOOLISHNESS, STUPIDITY

fat·u·ous \'fach-ə-wəs\ *adj* : FOOLISH, INANE, SILLY — **fat·u·ous·ly** *adv*

fau·bourg \fō-'bûr\ *n* 1 : SUBURB; *esp* : a suburb of a French city 2 : a city quarter

fau·cet \'fòs-ət, 'fäs-\ *n* : a fixture for drawing off a liquid (as from a pipe) : TAP

¹**fault** \'fòlt\ *n* 1 : a weakness in character : FAILING 2 : IMPERFECTION, IMPAIRMENT 3 : an error in a racket game 4 : MISDEMEANOR; *also* : MISTAKE 5 : responsibility for something wrong 6 : a fracture in the earth's crust — **fault·i·ly** *adv* — **fault·less** *adj* — **fault·less·ly** *adv* — **faulty** *adj*

²**fault** *vb* 1 : to commit a fault : ERR 2 : to fracture so as to produce a geologic fault 3 : to find a fault in (could not ~ his argument)

fault·find·er \-,fīn-dər\ *n* : a person who is inclined to find fault or complain — **fault·find·ing** *n or adj*

faun \'fòn\ *n* : an ancient Italian deity

of fields and herds represented as part goat and part man

fau·na \'fȯ-nə\ n, pl **-nas** also **-nae** \-,nē, -,nī\ : animals or animal life esp. of a region or period — **fau·nal** adj

faux pas \'fō-'pä\ n, pl **faux pas** \-'pä(z)\ : BLUNDER; esp : a social blunder

1fa·vor \'fā-vər\ n 1 : friendly regard shown toward another esp. by a superior 2 : APPROVAL 3 : PARTIALITY 4 : POPULARITY 5 : gracious kindness; also : an act of such kindness 6 pl : effort in one's behalf : ATTENTION 7 : a token of love (as a ribbon) usu. worn conspicuously 8 : a small gift or decorative item given out at a party 9 : a special privilege 10 archaic : LETTER 11 : BEHALF, INTEREST

2favor vb 1 : to regard or treat with favor 2 : OBLIGE 3 : ENDOW (~ed by nature) 4 : to treat gently or carefully : SPARE (~ a lame leg) 5 : PREFER 6 : SUPPORT, SUSTAIN 7 : FACILITATE (darkness ~s attack) 8 : RESEMBLE (he ~s his father)

fa·vor·able \'fāv-(ə-)rə-bəl\ adj 1 : APPROVING 2 : HELPFUL, PROMISING, ADVANTAGEOUS (~ weather) — **fa·vor·ably** adv

fa·vor·ite \-(ə-)rət\ n 1 : a person or a thing that is favored above others 2 : a competitor (as a horse in a race) regarded as most likely to win — **favorite** adj

favorite son n : a candidate supported by the delegates of his state at a presidential nominating convention

fa·vor·it·ism \-,iz-əm\ n : PARTIALITY, BIAS

favour chiefly Brit var of FAVOR

1fawn \'fȯn\ vb 1 : to show affection (a dog ~ing on its master) 2 : to court favor by a cringing or flattering manner : GROVEL

2fawn n 1 : a young deer 2 : a variable color toward a light grayish brown

fay \'fā\ n : FAIRY, ELF

faze \'fāz\ vb : to disturb the composure or courage of : DAUNT

fe·al·ty \'fē-(ə)l-tē\ n : LOYALTY, ALLEGIANCE

1fear \'fiər\ n 1 : an unpleasant often strong emotion caused by expectation or awareness of danger; also : an instance of or a state marked by this emotion 2 : anxious concern : SOLICITUDE 3 : profound reverence esp. toward God syn dread, fright, alarm, panic, terror, trepidation

2fear vb 1 : to have a reverent awe of (~ God) 2 : to be afraid of : have fear 3 : to be apprehensive

fear·ful adj 1 : causing fear 2 : filled with fear 3 : showing or caused by fear 4 : extremely bad, intense, or large — **fear·ful·ly** adv

fear·less adj : free from fear : BRAVE — **fear·less·ly** adv — **fear·less·ness** n

fear·some adj 1 : causing fear 2 : TIMID

fea·si·ble \'fē-zə-bəl\ adj 1 : capable of being done or carried out (a ~ plan) 2 : SUITABLE 3 : REASONABLE, LIKELY — **fea·si·bil·i·ty** \,fē-zə-'bil-ət-ē\ n — **fea·si·bly** \'fē-zə-blē\ adv

1feast \'fēst\ n 1 : an elaborate meal : BANQUET 2 : FESTIVAL 1

2feast vb 1 : to eat plentifully : partielpate in a feast 2 : to entertain with rich and plentiful food 3 : DELIGHT, GRATIFY

feat \'fēt\ n : DEED, EXPLOIT, ACHIEVEMENT; esp : an act notable for courage, skill, endurance, or ingenuity

1feath·er \'feth-ər\ n 1 : one of the light horny outgrowths that form the external covering of the body of a bird 2 : PLUME 3 : PLUMAGE 4 : KIND, NATURE (men of the same ~) 5 : ATTIRE, DRESS (fine ~s) 6 : CONDITION, MOOD (feeling in good ~) 7 : a feathery tuft or fringe of hair (as on the leg of a dog) — **feath·er·less** adj — **feath·ery** adj — a feather in one's cap : a mark of distinction : HONOR

2feather vb 1 : to furnish with a feather (~ an arrow) 2 : to cover, clothe, line, or adorn with feathers — **feather one's nest** : to provide for oneself esp. reprehensibly while in a position of trust

feath·er·bed·ding \-,bed-iŋ\ n : the requiring of an employer usu. under a union rule or safety statute to employ more workers than are needed or to limit production

feath·er·edge \-,ej\ n : a very thin sharp edge; esp : one that is easily broken or bent over

feath·er·weight \-,wāt\ n 1 : a very light weight 2 : one that is very light in weight; esp : a boxer weighing more than 118 but not over 126 pounds

fea·ture \'fē-chər\ n 1 : the shape or appearance of the face or its parts 2 : a part of the face : LINEAMENT 3 : a specially prominent characteristic 4 : a special attraction (as in a motion picture or newspaper) 5 : something offered to the public or advertised as particularly attractive

2feature vb 1 : to outline or mark the features of 2 : to give special prominence to (~ a story in a newspaper) 3 : to play an important part

feaze \'fēz, 'fāz\ var of FAZE

feb·rile \'feb-rəl, 'fēb-, -,ril\ adj : FEVERISH

Feb·ru·ary \'feb-(yə)-,wer-ē, 'feb-rə-\ n : the 2d month of the year having 28 and in leap years 29 days

fe·ces \'fē-,sēz\ n pl : bodily waste discharged from the intestine — **fe·cal** \-kəl\ adj

feck·less \'fek-ləs\ adj 1 : INEFFECTUAL, WEAK 2 : WORTHLESS, IRRESPONSIBLE

fe·cund \'fek-ənd, 'fek-\ adj : FRUITFUL, PROLIFIC — **fe·cun·di·ty** \fi-'kən-dət-ē\ n

fec·un·date \'fek-ən-,dāt\ vb : FERTILIZE — **fec·un·da·tion** \,fek-ən-'dā-shən\ n

fed·er·al \'fed-(ə-)rəl\ adj 1 : formed by a compact between political units that surrender individual sovereignty to a central authority but retain certain limited powers 2 : of or constituting a form of government in which power is distributed between a central authority and constituent territorial units 3 : of or relating to the central government of a federation 4 often cap : FEDERALIST 5 often cap : of, relating to, or loyal to the federal government or the Union

ə abut; ᵊ kitten; ər further; a back; ā bake; ä cot, cart; au̇ out; ch chin; e less; ē easy; g gift; i trip; ī life; j joke; ŋ sing; ō flow; ȯ flaw; ȯi coin; th thin; th̷ this; ü loot; u̇ foot; y yet; yü few; yu̇ furious; zh vision

armies of the U.S. in the American Civil War

Federal n : a supporter of the U.S. government in the Civil War; esp : a soldier in the federal armies

federal district n : a district (as the District of Columbia) set apart as the seat of the central government of a federation

fed·er·al·ism \ n 1 often cap : the federal principle of organization 2 : support or advocacy of federalism 3 cap : the principles of the Federalists

fed·er·al·ist n 1 : an advocate of federalism; esp, often cap : an advocate of a federal union between the American colonies after the Revolution and of the adoption of the U.S. Constitution 2 cap : a member of a major political party in the early years of the U.S. favoring a strong centralized national government — **federalist** adj, often cap

fed·er·al·ize \'fed-(ə-)rə-,līz\ vb 1 : to unite in or under a federal system 2 : to bring under the jurisdiction of a federal government

fed·er·ate \'fed-ə-,rāt\ vb : to join in a federation

fed·er·a·tion \,fed-ə-'rā-shən\ n 1 : the act of federating; esp : the formation of a federal union 2 : a federal government 3 : a union of organizations

fe·do·ra \fi-'dōr-ə\ n : a low soft felt hat with the crown creased lengthwise

fed up adj : satiated, tired, or disgusted beyond endurance

fee \'fē\ n 1 : an estate in land held from a feudal lord 2 : an inherited or heritable estate in land 3 : a fixed charge; also : a charge for a professional service 4 : TIP

fee·ble \'fē-bəl\ adj [OF feble, fr. L flebilis lamentable, wretched, fr. flēre to weep] 1 : DECREPIT, FRAIL 2 : INEFFECTIVE, INADEQUATE ⟨a ~ protest⟩ — **fee·ble·ness** n — **fee·bly** adv

fee·ble·mind·ed \,fē-bəl-'mīn-dəd\ adj : lacking normal intelligence : mentally deficient — **fee·ble·mind·ed·ness** n

¹**feed** \'fēd\ vb fed \'fed\ feed·ing 1 : to give food to; also : to give as food 2 : to consume food; also : PREY ⟨fleas ~ing on a dog⟩ 3 : to furnish what is necessary to the growth or function of — **feed·er** n

²**feed** n 1 : a usu. large meal; also : food for livestock 2 : material supplied (as to a furnace) 3 : a mechanism for feeding material to a machine

feed·back \'fēd-,bak\ n : the return to the input of a part of the output of a machine, system, or process

¹**feel** \'fēl\ vb felt \'felt\ feel·ing 1 : to perceive or examine through physical contact : TOUCH, HANDLE 2 : EXPERIENCE; also : to suffer from 3 : to ascertain by cautious trial ⟨~ out public sentiment⟩ 4 : to be aware of 5 : BELIEVE, THINK 6 : to search for something with the fingers : GROPE 7 : to be conscious of an inward impression, state of mind, or physical condition 8 : to seem esp. to the touch 9 : to have sympathy or pity

²**feel** n 1 : the sense of touch 2 : SENSATION, FEELING 3 : a quality of a thing as imparted through touch

feel·er n 1 : a tactile organ (as on the head of an insect) 2 : a proposal or remark made to find out the views of other people

¹**feel·ing** n 1 : the sense of touch; also : a sensation perceived by this 2 : an often indefinite state of mind ⟨a ~ of loneliness⟩ 3 : EMOTION; also, pl : SENSIBILITIES 4 : mental awareness 5 : OPINION, BELIEF 6 : unreasoned attitude : SENTIMENT 7 : capacity to respond emotionally : SYMPATHY

²**feeling** adj : SENSITIVE; esp : easily moved emotionally — **feel·ing·ly** adv

feet pl of FOOT

feign \'fān\ vb 1 : to give a false appearance of : SHAM ⟨~ illness⟩ 2 : to assert as if true : PRETEND

feint \'fānt\ n : something feigned; esp : a mock blow or attack at one point in order to distract attention from the point one really intends to attack — **feint** vb

fe·lic·i·tate \fi-'lis-ə-,tāt\ vb : CONGRATULATE — **fe·lic·i·ta·tion** \-,lis-ə-'tā-shən\ n

fe·lic·i·tous \fi-'lis-ət-əs\ adj 1 : suitably expressed : APT 2 : possessing a talent for apt expression ⟨a ~ speaker⟩ — **fe·lic·i·tous·ly** adv

fe·lic·i·ty \-ət-ē\ n 1 : the quality or state of being happy; esp : great happiness 2 : something that causes happiness 3 : a pleasing faculty esp. in art or language : APTNESS 4 : an apt expression

¹**fe·line** \'fē-,līn\ adj 1 : of or relating to cats or their kin 2 : SLY, TREACHEROUS, STEALTHY

²**feline** n : a feline animal

¹**fell** \'fel\ n : SKIN, HIDE, PELT

²**fell** vb 1 : to cut, beat, or knock down ⟨~ trees⟩; also : KILL 2 : to sew (a seam) by folding one raw edge under the other

³**fell** past of FALL

⁴**fell** adj : CRUEL, FIERCE; also : DEADLY

fel·lah \'fel-ə\ n, pl fel·la·hin \,fel-ə-'hēn\ : a peasant or agricultural laborer in Arab countries (as Egypt or Syria)

fel·low \'fel-ō\ n 1 : COMRADE, ASSOCIATE 2 : EQUAL, PEER 3 : one of a pair : MATE 4 : a member of an incorporated literary or scientific society 5 : MAN, BOY 6 : BEAU 7 : a person granted a stipend for advanced study

fel·low·man \,fel-ō-'man\ n : a kindred human being

fel·low·ship \'fel-ō-,ship\ n 1 : the condition of friendly relationship existing among persons : COMPANIONSHIP, COMRADESHIP 2 : a community of interest or feeling 3 : a group with similar interests : ASSOCIATION 4 : the position of a fellow (as of a university) 5 : the stipend granted a fellow; also : a foundation granting such a stipend

fellow traveler n : a person who sympathizes with and often furthers the ideals and program of an organized group (as the Communist party) without joining it or regularly participating in its activities

fel·ly \'fel-ē\ or **fel·loe** \'fel-ō\ n : the outside rim or a part of the rim of a wheel supported by the spokes

¹**fel·on** \'fel-ən\ n : CRIMINAL; esp : one who has committed a felony

²**felon** n : a deep inflammation on a finger or toe

fel·o·ny \'fel-ə-nē\ n : a serious crime punishable by a heavy sentence — **fe·lo·ni·ous** \fə-'lō-nē-əs\ adj

¹**felt** \'felt\ n 1 : a cloth made of wool and fur often mixed with natural or

synthetic fibers **2 :** a material resembling felt

²felt *past of* FEEL

fe·male \'fē-ˌmāl\ *adj* **:** of, relating to, or being the sex that bears young; *also* **:** PISTILLATE **syn** feminine, womanly, womanlike, womanish, effeminate, ladylike — **female** *n*

¹fem·i·nine \'fem-ə-nən\ *adj* **1 :** of the female sex; *also* **:** characteristic of or appropriate or peculiar to women **2 :** of, relating to, or constituting the gender that includes most words or grammatical forms referring to females — **fem·i·nin·i·ty** \ˌfem-ə-'nin-ət-ē\ *n*

²feminine *n* **1 :** the female principle **2 :** a noun, pronoun, adjective, or inflectional form or class of the feminine gender; *also* **:** the feminine gender

fem·i·nism \'fem-ə-ˌniz-əm\ *n* **1 :** the theory of the political, economic, and social equality of the sexes **2 :** organized activity on behalf of women's rights and interests — **fem·i·nist** *n or adj*

fe·mur \'fē-mər\ *n, pl* **femurs** *or* **fem·o·ra** \'fem-ə-rə\ **:** the long bone of the thigh

¹fen \'fen\ *n* **:** low swampy land

²fen \'fən\ *n, pl* **fen** — see MONEY table

¹fence \'fens\ *n* **1 :** a barrier intended to prevent escape or intrusion or to mark a boundary; *esp* **:** such a barrier made of posts and wire or boards **2 :** a person who receives stolen goods; *also* **:** a place where stolen goods are disposed of — **on the fence :** in a state of indecision or neutrality

²fence *vb* **1 :** to enclose with a fence **2 :** to keep in or out with a fence **3 :** to practice fencing **4 :** to use tactics of attack and defense esp. in debate — **fenc·er** *n*

fenc·ing *n* **1 :** the art or practice of attack and defense with the sword or foil **2 :** the fences of a property or region **3 :** material used for building fences

fend \'fend\ *vb* **1 :** to keep or ward off **:** REPEL **2 :** SHIFT ⟨~ for himself⟩

fend·er *n* **:** a protective device (as a guard over the wheel of an automobile or as a screen before a fire)

fen·es·tra·tion \ˌfen-ə-'strā-shən\ *n* **:** the arrangement, proportioning, and design of windows and doors in a building

Fe·ni·an \'fē-nē-ən\ *n* **:** a member of a secret 19th century Irish and Irish-American organization dedicated to the overthrow of British rule in Ireland

fen·nel \'fen-ᵊl\ *n* **:** an herb related to the carrot and grown for its aromatic seeds

¹fer·ment \fər-'ment\ *vb* **1 :** to cause or undergo fermentation **2 :** to be or cause to be in a state of agitation **:** SEETHE, FOMENT

²fer·ment \'fər-ˌment\ *n* **1 :** an agent (as yeast) that causes fermentation **2 :** AGITATION, TUMULT

fer·men·ta·tion \ˌfər-mən-'tā-shən\ *n* **1 :** chemical decomposition of an organic substance (as milk or fruit juice) by enzymatic action often with formation of gas **2 :** AGITATION, UNREST

fer·mi·um \'fer-mē-əm, 'fər-\ *n* **:** an

artificially produced radioactive metallic chemical element

fern \'fərn\ *n* **:** any of a group of flowerless seedless vascular green plants

fern·ery *n* **1 :** a place for growing ferns **2 :** a collection of growing ferns

fe·ro·cious \fə-'rō-shəs\ *adj* **1 :** FIERCE, SAVAGE **2 :** unbearably intense **:** EXTREME ⟨~ heat⟩ — **fe·ro·cious·ly** *adv* — **fe·ro·cious·ness** *n*

fe·roc·i·ty \fə-'räs-ət-ē\ *n* **:** the quality or state of being ferocious

¹fer·ret \'fer-ət\ *n* **:** a usu. white European polecat used esp. for hunting rodents

²ferret *vb* **1 :** to hunt game with ferrets **2 :** to drive out of a hiding place **3 :** to find and bring to light by searching ⟨~ out the truth⟩

fer·ric \'fer-ik\ *adj* **:** of, relating to, or containing iron

Fer·ris wheel \'fer-əs-\ *n* **:** an amusement device consisting of a large upright power-driven wheel carrying seats that remain horizontal around its rim

fer·rous \'fer-əs\ *adj* **:** of, relating to, or containing iron

fer·rule \'fer-əl\ *n* **:** a metal ring or band around the end of a cane or a tool handle to prevent splitting

¹fer·ry \'fer-ē\ *vb* **1 :** to carry by boat over a body of water **2 :** to cross by a ferry **3 :** to convey from one place to another

²ferry *n* **1 :** a place where persons or things are carried across a body of water (as a river) in a boat **2 :** FERRY-BOAT **3 :** an organized service and route for flying airplanes

fer·ry·boat \-ˌbōt\ *n* **:** a boat used in ferrying

fer·tile \'fərt-ᵊl\ *adj* **1 :** producing plentifully **:** PRODUCTIVE ⟨~ soils⟩ **2 :** capable of developing or reproducing ⟨~ eggs⟩ ⟨a ~ family⟩ **syn** fruitful, prolific — **fer·til·i·ty** \ˌfər-'til-ət-ē\ *n*

fer·til·ize \-ᵊl-ˌīz\ *vb* **1 :** to make fertile; *esp* **:** to apply fertilizer to **2 :** to interact with to form a zygote ⟨one sperm ~s each egg⟩ — **fer·til·iza·tion** \ˌfərt-ᵊl-ə-'zā-shən\ *n*

fer·til·iz·er \'fərt-ᵊl-ˌī-zər\ *n* **:** material (as manure or a chemical mixture) for enriching land

fer·ule \'fer-əl\ *n* **:** a rod or ruler used to punish children

fer·ven·cy \'fər-vən-sē\ *n* **:** FERVOR

fer·vent \-vənt\ *adj* **1 :** very hot **:** GLOWING **2 :** marked by great warmth of feeling **:** ARDENT — **fer·vent·ly** *adv*

fer·vid \-vəd\ *adj* **1 :** very hot **:** BURNING **2 :** ARDENT, ZEALOUS — **fer·vid·ly** *adv*

fer·vor \-vər\ *n* **1 :** intense heat **2 :** intensity of feeling or expression **:** PASSION, ENTHUSIASM

fes·tal \'fest-ᵊl\ *adj* **:** FESTIVE

¹fes·ter \'fes-tər\ *n* **:** a pus-filled sore

²fester *vb* **1 :** to form pus; *also* **:** to become inflamed **2 :** RANKLE

fes·ti·val \'fes-tə-vəl\ *n* **1 :** a time of celebration marked by special observances; *esp* **:** an occasion marked with religious ceremonies **2 :** a periodic season or program of cultural events or entertainment ⟨a dance ~⟩ **3 :** CONVIVIALITY, GAIETY

ə abut; ᵊ kitten; ər further; a back; ā bake; ä cot, cart; aú out; ch chin; e less; ē easy; g gift; i trip; ī life; j joke; ŋ sing; ō flow; ó flaw; ói coin; th thin; th̲ this; ü loot; ù foot; y yet; yü few; yù furious; zh vision

fes·tive \-tiv\ *adj* **1** : of, relating to, or suitable for a feast or festival **2** : JOYOUS, GAY — **fes·tive·ly** *adv*

fes·tiv·i·ty \fes-'tiv-ət-ē\ *n* **1** : FESTIVAL **2** : the quality or state of being festive **3** : festive activity

¹fes·toon \fes-'tün\ *n* **1** : a decorative chain or strip hanging in a curve between two points **2** : a carved, molded, or painted ornament representing a decorative chain

²festoon *vb* **1** : to hang or form festoons on **2** : to shape into festoons

fetch \'fech\ *vb* **1** : to go or come after and bring or take back (teach a dog to ~ a stick) **2** : to cause to come : bring out (~ed tears from the eyes) **3** : DRAW (~ing her breath); *also* : HEAVE (~ a sigh) **4** : to sell for **5** : to give by striking (~ him a blow)

fetch·ing *adj* : ATTRACTIVE, PLEASING — **fetch·ing·ly** *adv*

¹fete or fête \'fāt\ *n* **1** : FESTIVAL **2** : a lavish often outdoor entertainment **3** : a lavish usu. large party

²fete or fête *vb* **1** : to honor or commemorate with a fete **2** : to pay high honor to

fet·id \'fet-əd\ *adj* : having an offensive smell : STINKING

fet·ish or fet·ich \'fet-ish\ *n* **1** : an object (as an idol or image) believed to have magical powers (as in curing disease) **2** : an object of unreasoning devotion or concern : PREPOSSESSION (made a ~ of discipline)

fet·lock \'fet-,läk\ *n* : a projection on the back of a horse's leg above the hoof; *also* : a tuft of hair on this

fet·ter \'fet-ər\ *n* **1** : a chain or shackle for the feet **2** : something that confines : RESTRAINT — **fetter** *vb*

fet·tle \'fet-ᵊl\ *n* : a state of fitness or order : CONDITION (in fine ~)

fe·tus \'fēt-əs\ *n* : an unborn or unhatched vertebrate esp. after its basic structure is laid down — **fe·tal** \-ᵊl\ *adj*

feud \'fyüd\ *n* : a prolonged quarrel; *esp* : a lasting conflict between families or clans marked by violent attacks undertaken for revenge — **feud** *vb*

feu·dal \'fyüd-ᵊl\ *adj* **1** : of, relating to, or having the characteristics of a medieval fee **2** : of, relating to, or characteristic of feudalism

feu·dal·ism *n* : a system of political organization prevailing in medieval Europe in which a vassal renders service to a lord and receives protection and land in return; *also* : a similar political or social system — **feu·dal·is·tic** \,fyüd-ᵊl-'is-tik\ *adj*

¹feu·da·to·ry \'fyüd-ə-,tōr-ē\ *adj* : owing feudal allegiance : being in the relation of a vassal to his lord

²feudatory *n* **1** : a person who holds lands by feudal law or usage **2** : FIEF

fe·ver \'fē-vər\ *n* **1** : a rise in body temperature above the normal; *also* : a disease of which this is a chief symptom **2** : a state of heightened emotion or activity **3** : a contagious transient enthusiasm : CRAZE — **fe·ver·ish** *adj* — **fe·ver·ish·ly** *adv*

¹few \'fyü\ *pron* : not many : a small number

²few *adj* **1** : consisting of or amounting to a small number **2** : not many but some (caught a ~ fish) — **few·ness** *n*

³few *n* **1** : a small number of units or individuals (a ~ of them) **2** : a special limited number (among the ~)

fey \'fā\ *adj* **1** *chiefly Scot* : fated to die; *also* : marked by a foreboding of death or calamity **2** : ELFIN

fez \'fez\ *n, pl* **fez·zes** : a round flat-crowned hat that usu. has a tassel, is made of red felt, and is worn by men in eastern Mediterranean countries

fi·an·cé \,fē-,än-'sā\ *n* : a man engaged to be married

fi·an·cée \-'sā\ *n* : a woman engaged to be married

fi·as·co \fē-'as-kō\ *n, pl* **-coes** : a complete failure

fi·at \'fī-,at, 'fē-\ *n* : an authoritative and often arbitrary order or decree

¹fib \'fib\ *n* : a lie about some trivial matter

²fib *vb* **fibbed**; **fib·bing** : to tell a fib — **fib·ber** *n*

fi·ber or fi·bre \'fī-bər\ *n* **1** : a thread-like substance or structure (as a muscle cell or fine root); *esp* : a natural (as wool or flax) or artificial (as rayon) filament capable of being spun or woven **2** : an element that gives texture or substance **3** : basic toughness : STRENGTH — **fi·brous** \-brəs\ *adj*

fi·ber·board \'fī-bər-,bōrd\ *n* : a material made by compressing fibers (as of wood) into stiff sheets

fiber glass *n* : glass in fibrous form used in making various products (as yarn and insulation)

fi·broid \'fī-,brȯid\ *adj* : resembling, forming, or consisting of fibrous tissue (~ tumors)

fi·chu \'fish-ü\ *n* : a woman's light triangular scarf draped over the shoulders and fastened in front

fick·le \'fik-əl\ *adj* : not firm or steadfast in disposition or character : INCONSTANT — **fick·le·ness** *n*

fic·tion \'fik-shən\ *n* **1** : something (as a story) invented by the imagination **2** : fictitious literature (as novels and short stories) — **fic·tion·al** *adj*

fic·ti·tious \fik-'tish-əs\ *adj* **1** : of, relating to, or characteristic of fiction : IMAGINARY **2** : FEIGNED *syn* fabulous, legendary, mythical

¹fid·dle \'fid-ᵊl\ *n* : VIOLIN

²fiddle *vb* **1** : to play on a fiddle **2** : to move the hands or fingers restlessly **3** : PUTTER **4** : MEDDLE, TAMPER — **fid·dler** \-(ᵊ-)lər\ *n*

fid·dle·stick \'fid-ᵊl-,stik\ *n* **1** : a violin bow **2** *pl* : NONSENSE — used as an interjection

fi·del·i·ty \fə-'del-ət-ē, fī-\ *n* **1** : the quality or state of being faithful **2** : ACCURACY (~ of a news report) (~ in sound reproduction) *syn* allegiance, loyalty, devotion

¹fid·get \'fij-ət\ *n* **1** *pl* : uneasiness or restlessness as shown by nervous movements **2** : one that fidgets — **fid·gety** *adj*

²fidget *vb* : to move or cause to move or act restlessly or nervously

fi·du·ci·ary \fə-'d(y)ü-shē-,er-ē, fī-\ *adj* **1** : involving a confidence or trust (employed in a ~ capacity) **2** : held or holding in trust for another (~ accounts) — **fiduciary** *n*

fie \'fī\ *interj* — used to express disgust or shock

fief \'fēf\ *n* : a feudal estate : FEE

¹field \'fēld\ *n* **1** : open country **2** : a piece of cleared land for tillage or pasture **3 :** a piece of land yielding some special product **4 :** the place where a battle is fought; *also* **:** BATTLE **5 :** an area, division, or sphere of activity (the ~ of science) ⟨salesmen in the ~⟩ **6 :** an area for military exercises **7 :** an area for sports **8 :** a background on which something is drawn or projected ⟨a flag with white stars on a ~ of blue⟩ — **field** *adj*

²**field** *vb* **1 :** to handle a batted or thrown baseball while on defense **2 :** to put into the field — **field·er** *n*

field glass *n* **:** a hand-held binocular telescope — usu. used in pl.

field marshal *n* **:** an officer (as in the British army) of the highest rank

field-piece \'fēld-ˌpēs\ *n* **:** a gun or howitzer for use in the field

fiend \'fēnd\ *n* [OB *féond, fiend,* lit., enemy] **1 :** DEVIL, DEMON **2 :** an extremely wicked or cruel person **3 :** a person excessively devoted to a pursuit **:** FANATIC ⟨golf ~⟩ **4 :** ADDICT ⟨dope ~⟩ — **fiend·ish** *adj*

fierce \'fiərs\ *adj* **1 :** violently hostile or aggressive in temperament **2 :** PUGNACIOUS **3 :** INTENSE **4 :** furiously active or determined **5 :** wild or menacing in aspect *syn* ferocious, barbarous, savage, cruel — **fierce·ly** *adv* — **fierce·ness** *n*

fi·ery \'fī-(ə-)rē\ *adj* **1 :** consisting of fire **2 :** BURNING, BLAZING **3 :** FLAMMABLE **4 :** hot like a fire **:** INFLAMED, FEVERISH **5 :** RED **6 :** full of emotion or spirit **7 :** IRRITABLE

fi·es·ta \fē-'es-tə\ *n* **:** FESTIVAL

fife \'fīf\ *n* **:** a small shrill flutelike musical instrument

fif·teen \fif-'tēn\ *n* **:** one more than 14 — **fifteen** *adj or pron* — **fif·teenth** *adj or n*

¹**fifth** \'fifth\ *adj* **1 :** being number five in a countable series **2 :** next after the fourth — **fifth** *adv*

²**fifth** *n, pl* **fifths** **1 :** one that is fifth **2 :** one of five equal parts of something **3 :** a unit of measure for liquor equal to ⅕ U.S. gallon

fifth column *n* **:** a group of secret sympathizers or supporters of a nation's enemy that engage in espionage or sabotage within the country — **fifth columnist** *n*

fif·ty \'fif-tē\ *n* **:** five times 10 — **fif·ti·eth** *adj or n* — **fifty** *adj or pron*

fif·ty-fif·ty \ˌfif-tē-'fif-tē\ *adj* **1 :** shared equally ⟨a ~ proposition⟩ **2 :** half favorable and half unfavorable ⟨a ~ chance to live⟩

fig \'fig\ *n* **:** a usu. pear-shaped edible fruit of warm regions; *also* **:** a tree related to the mulberry that bears this fruit

¹**fight** \'fīt\ *vb* **fought** \'fȯt\ **fight·ing** **1 :** to contend against another in battle or physical combat **2 :** BOX **3 :** to put forth a determined effort **4 :** STRUGGLE, CONTEND **5 :** to attempt to prevent the success or effectiveness of **6 :** WAGE **7 :** to gain by struggle

²**fight** *n* **1 :** a hostile encounter **2 :** a boxing match **3 :** a verbal disagreement **4 :** a struggle for a goal or an objective **5 :** strength or disposition for fighting ⟨full of ~⟩

fight·er *n* **1 :** one that fights; *esp* **:** WARRIOR **2 :** BOXER **3 :** an airplane of high speed and maneuverability with armament for destroying enemy aircraft

fig·ment \'fig-mənt\ *n;* something imagined or made up ⟨a ~ of the imagination⟩

fig·u·ra·tive \'fig-yə-rət-iv\ *adj* **1 :** EMBLEMATIC **2 :** SYMBOLIC, METAPHORICAL ⟨~ language⟩ **3 :** characterized by figures of speech or elaborate expression ⟨a ~ description⟩ — **fig·u·ra·tive·ly** *adv*

¹**fig·ure** \'fig-yər\ *n* **1 :** a symbol representing a number **:** NUMERAL **2** *pl* **:** arithmetical calculations **3 :** a written or printed character **4 :** PRICE, AMOUNT **5 :** SHAPE, FORM, OUTLINE **6 :** the graphic representation of a form and esp. of a person **7 :** a diagram or pictorial illustration **8 :** an expression (as in metaphor) that uses words in other than a plain or literal way **9 :** PATTERN, DESIGN **10 :** appearance made or impression produced ⟨they cut quite a ~⟩ **11 :** a series of movements (as in a dance) **12 :** PERSONAGE

²**figure** *vb* **1 :** to represent by or as if by a figure or outline **:** PORTRAY **2 :** to decorate with a pattern **3 :** to indicate or represent by numerals **4 :** REGARD, CONSIDER **5 :** to be or appear important or conspicuous **6 :** COMPUTE, CALCULATE

fig·ure·head \-ˌhed\ *n* **1 :** a carved figure on the bow of a ship **2 :** a person who has the title but not the powers of the head or chief

fig·u·rine \ˌfig-yə-'rēn\ *n* **:** a small carved or molded figure

fil·a·ment \'fil-ə-mənt\ *n* **:** a fine thread or threadlike object, part, or process — **fil·a·men·tous** \ˌfil-ə-'ment-əs\ *adj*

fil·bert \'fil-bərt\ *n* **:** the oblong edible nut of a European hazel; *also* **:** this plant

filch \'filch\ *vb* **:** to steal furtively **:** PILFER

¹**file** \'fīl\ *n* **:** a steel instrument with ridged surface used for rubbing down a hard substance

²**file** *vb* **:** to rub, smooth, or cut away with a file

³**file** *vb* **1 :** to arrange in order for preservation or reference **2 :** to enter or record officially or as prescribed by law ⟨~ a lawsuit⟩ **3 :** to send (copy) to a newspaper

⁴**file** *n* **1 :** a device (as a folder or cabinet) by means of which papers or records may be kept in order **2 :** a collection of papers usu. arranged or classified

⁵**file** *n* **:** a row of persons, animals, or things arranged one behind the other

⁶**file** *vb* **:** to march or proceed in file

fil·er *n* **:** one that files

fi·let mi·gnon \ˌfil-ā-mēn-'yōⁿ\ *n, pl* **filets mignons** \-ā-mēn-'yō(z)\ **:** a fillet of beef cut from the thick end of a beef tenderloin

fil·i·al \'fil-ē-əl\ *adj* **:** of, relating to, or befitting a son or daughter

fil·i·bus·ter \'fil-ə-ˌbəs-tər\ *n* **1 :** a military adventurer; *esp* **:** an American engaged in fomenting insurrections in Latin America in the mid-19th century

ə abut; ᵊ kitten; ər further; a back; ā bake; ä cot, cart; au̇ out; ch chin; e less; ē easy; g gift; i trip; ī life; j joke; ŋ sing; ō flow; ȯ flaw; ȯi coin; th thin; t͟h this; ü loot; u̇ foot; y yet; yü few; yu̇ furious; zh vision

2 : the use of delaying tactics (as extremely long speeches) esp. in a legislative assembly; *also* : an instance of this practice — **filibuster** *vb* — **fil·i·bus·ter·er** *n*

fil·i·gree \'fil-ə-ˌgrē\ *n* : ornamental openwork (as of fine wire)

fil·ing \'fī-liŋ\ *n* **1** : the act of one who files **2** : a small piece scraped off by a file ⟨iron ∼s⟩

Fil·i·pi·no \ˌfil-ə-'pē-nō\ *n* : a native or inhabitant of the Philippines — **Filipino** *adj*

1fill \'fil\ *vb* **1** : to make or become full **2** : to stop up : PLUG ⟨∼ a cavity⟩ **3** : FEED, SATIATE **4** : SATISFY, FULFILL ⟨∼ all requirements⟩ **5** : to occupy fully **6** : to spread through ⟨laughter ∼ed the room⟩ **7** : OCCUPY ⟨∼ the office of president⟩ **8** : to put a person in ⟨∼ a vacancy⟩ **9** : to supply as directed ⟨∼ a prescription⟩

2fill *n* **1** : a full supply; *esp* : a quantity that satisfies or satiates **2** : material used esp. for filling a ditch or hollow in the ground

1fill·er \'fil-ər\ *n* : one that fills

2fill·er \'fil-ˌeər\ *n, pl* **fillers** *or* **filler** — see MONEY table

1fil·let \'fil-ət, 2 also fi-'lā, 'fil-ā\ *also* **fi·let** \fi-'lā, 'fil-ā\ *n* **1** : a narrow band, strip, or ribbon **2** : a piece or slice of boneless meat or fish; *esp* : the tenderloin of beef

2fillet *vb* **1** : to bind or adorn with or as if with a fillet **2** : to cut into fillets

fill·ing \'fil-iŋ\ *n* **1** : material used to fill something ⟨a ∼ for a tooth⟩ **2** : the yarn interlacing the warp in a fabric **3** : a food mixture used to fill pastry or sandwiches

filling station *n* : an outdoor retail establishment for servicing motor vehicles esp. with gasoline and oil

fil·lip \'fil-əp\ *n* **1** : a blow or gesture made by a flick or snap of the finger across the thumb **2** : something that serves to arouse or stimulate — **fillip** *vb*

fil·ly \'fil-ē\ *n* : a young female horse

1film \'film\ *n* **1** : a thin skin or membrane **2** : a thin coating or layer **3** : a flexible strip of chemically treated material used in taking pictures **4** : MOTION PICTURE — **filmy** *adj*

2film *vb* **1** : to cover with a film **2** : PHOTOGRAPH **3** : to make a motion picture of

film·dom *n* **1** : the motion-picture industry **2** : the personnel of the motion-picture industry

fils \'fils\ *n, pl* **fils** — see MONEY table

1fil·ter \'fil-tər\ *n* **1** : a porous material through which a fluid is passed to separate out matter in suspension; *also* : a device containing such material **2** : a device for suppressing waves or oscillations of certain frequencies; *esp* : one (as on a camera lens) that absorbs light of certain colors

2filter *vb* **1** : to pass through a filter **2** : to remove by means of a filter — **fil·ter·able** *also* **fil·tra·ble** \-t(ə-)rə-bəl\ *adj* — **fil·tra·tion** \fil-'trā-shən\ *n*

filth \'filth\ *n* **1** : foul matter; *esp* : loathsome dirt or refuse **2** : moral corruption **3** : OBSCENITY — **filth·i·ness** *n* — **filthy** *adj*

fil·trate \'fil-ˌtrāt\ *n* : the fluid that has passed through a filter

fin \'fin\ *n* **1** : one of the thin external processes by which an aquatic animal

(as a fish) moves through water **2** : a fin-shaped part (as on an airplane) **3** : FLIPPER 2

fi·na·gle \fə-'nā-gəl\ *vb* **1** : to arrange for **2** : to obtain by trickery **3** : to use devious dishonest methods to achieve one's ends — **fi·na·gler** \-g(ə-)lər\ *n*

1fi·nal \'fīn-ºl\ *adj* **1** : not to be altered or undone : CONCLUSIVE **2** : ULTIMATE ⟨the ∼ climax⟩ ⟨the ∼ goal of life⟩ **3** : relating to or occurring at the end or conclusion — **fi·nal·i·ty** \fī-'nal-ət-ē\ *n* — **fi·nal·ly** \'fīn-(º-)lē\ *adv*

2final *n* **1** : a deciding match, game, or trial **2** : the last examination in a course

fi·na·le \fə-'nal-ē\ *n* : the close or termination of something; *esp* : the last section of a musical composition

fi·nal·ist \'fīn-ºl-əst\ *n* : a contestant in the finals of a competition

fi·nal·ize \-ˌīz\ *vb* : to put in final or finished form

1fi·nance \fə-'nans, 'fī-ˌnans\ *n* **1** *pl* : money resources available esp. to a government or business **2** : management of money affairs

2finance *vb* **1** : to raise or provide funds for **2** : to furnish with necessary funds **3** : to sell or supply on credit

finance company *n* **1** : a company that pays to the seller the cost of an article (as an automobile) purchased on the installment plan and is reimbursed with interest in installments by the purchaser **2** : a company that makes small loans to individuals usu. at high rates of interest

fi·nan·cial \fə-'nan-chəl, fī-\ *adj* : having to do with finance or financiers ⟨in ∼ circles⟩ — **fi·nan·cial·ly** *adv*

fin·an·cier \ˌfin-ən-'siər, ˌfī-ˌnan-\ *n* **1** : a person skilled in managing large funds **2** : a person who invests large sums of money

finch \'finch\ *n* : any of a group of songbirds (as sparrows, linnets, or buntings) with strong conical bills

1find \'fīnd\ *vb* **found** \'faůnd\ **finding** **1** : to come upon either by chance or by searching or study : ENCOUNTER, DISCOVER **2** : to obtain by effort or management ⟨∼ time to read⟩ **3** : to arrive at : REACH ⟨the bullet *found* its mark⟩ **4** : EXPERIENCE, DETECT, PERCEIVE, FEEL **5** : to gain or regain the use of ⟨*found* his voice again⟩ **6** : PROVIDE, SUPPLY ⟨∼ room for a guest⟩ **7** : to settle upon and make a statement about ⟨∼ a verdict⟩

2find *n* **1** : an act or instance of finding **2** : something found; *esp* : a valuable item of discovery

find·er *n* : one that finds; *esp* : a device on a camera showing the view being photographed

fin de siè·cle \ˌfanⁿ-də-'syeklº\ *adj* : of, relating to, or characteristic of the close of the 19th century

find·ing \'fīn-diŋ\ *n* **1** : the act of finding **2** : FIND 2 **3** : the result of a judicial proceeding or inquiry

1fine \'fīn\ *n* : money exacted as a penalty for an offense

2fine *vb* : to impose a fine on : punish by a fine

3fine *adj* **1** : free from impurity **2** : very thin in gauge or texture **3** : not coarse **4** : SUBTLE, SENSITIVE ⟨a ∼ distinction⟩ **5** : superior in quality, conception, or appearance **6** : ELEGANT, REFINED

— **fine·ly** *adv* — **fine·ness** *n*

⁴**fine** *adv* : FINELY

fine art *n* : art (as painting, sculpture, or music) concerned primarily with the creation of beautiful objects ⟨majored in *fine arts*⟩

fin·ery \'fīn-(ə-)rē\ *n* : ORNAMENT, DECORATION; *esp* : showy clothing and jewels

fi·nesse \fə-'nes\ *n* **1** : delicate skill **2** : CUNNING, STRATAGEM, TRICK — *finesse vb*

¹**fin·ger** \'fiŋ-gər\ *n* **1** : one of the five divisions at the end of the hand; *esp* : one other than the thumb **2** : something that resembles or does the work of a finger **3** : a part of a glove into which a finger is inserted

²**finger** *vb* **1** : to touch with the fingers : HANDLE **2** : to perform with the fingers or with a certain fingering **3** : to mark the notes of a piece of music as a guide in playing **4** : to point out : IDENTIFY

fin·ger·board \-,bôrd\ *n* : the part of a stringed instrument against which the fingers press the strings to vary the pitch

finger bowl *n* : a basin to hold water for rinsing the fingers at table

fin·ger·ing \'fiŋ-g(ə-)riŋ\ *n* **1** : the act or process of handling or touching with the fingers **2** : the act or method of using the fingers in playing an instrument **3** : the marking of the method of fingering

fin·ger·nail \'fiŋ-gər-,nāl\ *n* : the nail of a finger

fin·ger·print \-,print\ *n* : the pattern of marks made by pressing the tip of a finger or thumb on a surface; *esp* : an ink impression of such a pattern taken for the purpose of identification — **fingerprint** *vb*

fin·ger·tip \-,tip\ *n* : the tip of a finger

fin·ick·ing \'fin-i-kiŋ\ *adj* : FINICKY

fin·icky \'fin-i-kē\ *adj* : excessively particular in taste or standards

fin·is \'fin-əs, 'fī-nəs\ *n* : END, CONCLUSION

¹**fin·ish** \'fin-ish\ *vb* **1** : TERMINATE **2** : to use or dispose of entirely **3** : to bring to completion : ACCOMPLISH; *also* : PERFECT **4** : to put a final coat or surface on **6** : to come to the end of a course or undertaking — **fin·ish·er** *n*

²**finish** *n* **1** : END, CONCLUSION **2** : something that completes or perfects **3** : the treatment given a surface; *also* : the result or product of a finishing process ⟨a shiny ∼ on a new car⟩ **4** : social polish

fi·nite \'fī-,nīt\ *adj* **1** : having definite or definable limits **2** : having a limited nature or existence **3** : being neither infinite nor infinitesimal

Finn \'fin\ *n* : a native or inhabitant of Finland

fin·nan had·die \,fin-ən-'had-ē\ *n* : smoked haddock

¹**Finn·ish** \'fin-ish\ *adj* : of or relating to Finland, the Finns, or Finnish

²**Finnish** *n* : the language of Finland

fin·ny \'fin-ē\ *adj* **1** : resembling or having fins **2** : of, relating to, or full of fish

fiord *var of* **fjord**

fir \'fər\ *n* : an erect evergreen tree related to the pines; *also* : its light soft wood

¹**fire** \'fī(ə)r\ *n* **1** : the light or heat and esp. the flame of something burning **2** : fuel that is burning (as in a stove or fireplace) **3** : destructive burning of something (as a house) **4** : ENTHUSIASM, ZEAL **5** : the discharge of firearms — **fire·less** *adj* — **fire·proof** \-'prüf\ *adj or vb*

²**fire** *vb* **1** : KINDLE, IGNITE ⟨∼ a house⟩ **2** : STIR, ENLIVEN ⟨∼ the imagination⟩ **3** : to dismiss from employment **4** : SHOOT ⟨∼ a gun⟩ ⟨∼ an arrow⟩ **5** : to apply fire or fuel to something ⟨∼ a furnace⟩ **6** : BAKE ⟨∼ing pottery in a kiln⟩

fire·arm \-,ärm\ *n* : a weapon (as a rifle or pistol) from which a shot is discharged by an explosion of gunpowder

fire·ball \-,bôl\ *n* **1** : a ball of fire **2** : a brilliant meteor that may trail bright sparks **3** : the highly luminous cloud of vapor and dust created by a nuclear explosion (as of an atom bomb)

fire·boat \-,bōt\ *n* : a ship equipped with apparatus (as pumps) for fighting fire

fire·brand \-,brand\ *n* **1** : a piece of burning wood **2** : a person who creates unrest or strife : AGITATOR

fire·break \-,brāk\ *n* : a barrier of cleared or plowed land intended to check a forest or grass fire

fire·brick \-,brik\ *n* : a brick capable of withstanding great heat and used for lining furnaces or fireplaces

fire·bug \-,bəg\ *n* : a person who deliberately sets destructive fires

fire·crack·er \'fī(ə)r-,krak-ər\ *n* : a paper tube containing an explosive to be fired for noise during celebrations

fire·dog \-,dôg\ *n* : ANDIRON

fire·fly \-,flī\ *n* : a small night-flying beetle that produces a soft light

fire irons *n pl* : implements for tending a fire esp. in a fireplace

fire·man \'fī(ə)r-mən\ *n* **1** : a member of a company organized to put out fires **2** : STOKER; *also* : a locomotive crew member who services motors and assists the engineer

fire·place \-,plās\ *n* **1** : a framed rectangular opening made in a chimney to hold an open fire : HEARTH **2** : an outdoor structure of brick or stone made for an open fire

fire·pow·er \-,paů(-ə)r\ *n* : the relative ability to deliver gunfire or warheads on a target

fire·trap \-,trap\ *n* : a building or place apt to catch on fire or difficult to escape from in case of fire

fire·wa·ter \-,wôt-ər, -,wät-\ *n* : intoxicating liquor

fire·wood \-,wůd\ *n* : wood cut for fuel

fire·work \-,wərk\ *n* : a device designed to be lighted and produce a display of light, noise, and smoke (as for a celebration)

¹**firm** \'fərm\ *adj* **1** : securely fixed in place **2** : SOLID, VIGOROUS ⟨a ∼ handshake⟩ **3** : having a solid or compact texture ⟨∼ flesh⟩ **4** : not subject to change or fluctuation : STEADY ⟨∼ prices⟩ **5** : STEADFAST **6** : indicating

firmness or resolution ⟨a ~ mouth⟩ — **firm·ly** adv — **firm·ness** n

²**firm** vb : to make or become firm

³**firm** n 1 : the name under which a company transacts business 2 : a business partnership of two or more persons 3 : a business enterprise

fir·ma·ment \'fər-mə-mənt\ n : the arch of the sky : HEAVENS

¹**first** \'fərst\ adj 1 : being number one in a countable series 2 : preceding all others

²**first** adv 1 : before any other 2 : for the first time 3 : in preference to something else

³**first** n 1 : number one in a countable series 2 : one that is first 3 : the lowest forward gear in an automotive vehicle

first aid n : emergency care or treatment given an injured or ill person — **first-aid** adj

first-born \'fərst-'bórn\ adj : ELDEST — **firstborn** n

first class n : the best or highest group in a classification — **first-class** adj or adv

first-hand \-'hand\ adj : coming directly from the original source ⟨~ knowledge⟩ — **firsthand** adv

first lady n, often cap F&L : the wife or hostess of the chief executive of a political unit (as a country)

first lieutenant n : a commissioned officer (as in the army) ranking next below a captain

first·ling \'fərst-liŋ\ n 1 : the first of a class or kind 2 : the first produce or result

first·ly adv : in the first place : FIRST

first-rate \'fərst-'rāt\ adj : of the first order of size, importance, or quality — **first-rate** adv

first sergeant n : MASTER SERGEANT 1

firth \'fərth\ n : a narrow arm of the sea

fis·cal \'fis-kəl\ adj 1 : of or relating to taxation, public revenues, or public debt 2 : of or relating to financial matters

¹**fish** \'fish\ n, pl **fish** or **fish·es** 1 : a water animal; esp : any of a large group of cold-blooded water-breathing vertebrates with fin, gills, and usu. scales 2 : the flesh of fish used as food

²**fish** vb 1 : to attempt to catch fish 2 : to seek something by roundabout means ⟨~ for praise⟩ 3 : to search (as with a hook) for something underwater 4 : to engage in a search by groping 5 : to draw forth — **fish·er** n

fish-and-chips n pl : fried fish and french fried potatoes

fish·er·man \'fish-ər-mən\ n : a person engaged in fishing; also : a fishing boat

fish·ery \-(ə-)rē\ n : the business of catching fish; also : a place for catching fish

fish·hook \'fish-,hủk\ n : a usu. barbed hook for catching fish

fish·ing n : the business or sport of catching fish

fish ladder n : an arrangement of pools by which fish can pass around a dam

fish·wife \'fish-,wif\ n 1 : a woman who sells fish 2 : an abusive woman

fishy adj 1 : of, relating to, or resembling fish 2 : QUESTIONABLE

fis·sion \'fish-ən\ n [L fission-, fissio, fr. fiss-, findere to split] 1 : a cleaving into parts 2 : the splitting of an atomic nucleus resulting in the release of large amounts of energy — **fis·sion·able** adj

fis·sure \'fish-ər\ n : a narrow opening or crack

fist \'fist\ n 1 : the hand with fingers doubled into the palm 2 : INDEX 6

fist·i·cuffs \'fis-ti-,kəfs\ n pl : a fight with usu. bare fists

fis·tu·la \'fis-chə-lə\ n, pl -las or -lae \-,lē\ : an abnormal passage leading from an abscess or hollow organ — **fis·tu·lous** adj

¹**fit** \'fit\ n 1 : a sudden violent attack (as of bodily disorder) 2 : a sudden outburst (as of laughter)

²**fit** adj 1 : adapted to a purpose : APPROPRIATE 2 : PROPER, RIGHT, BECOMING 3 : PREPARED, READY 4 : QUALIFIED, COMPETENT 5 : physically and mentally sound — **fit·ly** adv — **fit·ness** n

³**fit** vb **fit·ted; fit·ting** 1 : to be suitable for or to : BEFIT 2 : to be correctly adjusted to or shaped for 3 : to insert or adjust until correctly in place 4 : to make a place or room for 5 : to be in agreement or accord with 6 : PREPARE 7 : ADJUST 8 : SUPPLY, EQUIP 9 : BELONG — **fit·ter** n

⁴**fit** n 1 : the state or manner of fitting or being fitted 2 : a piece of clothing that fits

fit·ful \-fəl\ adj : RESTLESS ⟨~ sleep⟩ — **fit·ful·ly** adv

¹**fit·ting** adj : APPROPRIATE, SUITABLE — **fit·ting·ly** adv

²**fit·ting** n 1 : the action or act of one that fits; esp : a trying on of clothes being made or altered 2 : a small accessory part ⟨a plumbing ~⟩ ⟨an airplane ~⟩

five \'fīv\ n 1 : one more than four 2 : the 5th in a set or series 3 : something having five units; esp : a male basketball team — **five** adj or pron

¹**fix** \'fiks\ vb 1 : to make firm, stable, or fast 2 : to give a permanent or final form to 3 : AFFIX, ATTACH 4 : to hold or direct steadily ⟨~es his eyes on the stars⟩ 5 : ESTABLISH ⟨~ a date⟩ 6 : ASSIGN ⟨~ blame⟩ 7 : to set in order : ADJUST 8 : PREPARE 9 : to make whole or sound again 10 : to get even with 11 : to influence by improper or illegal methods ⟨~ a horse race⟩

²**fix** n : PREDICAMENT

fix·a·tion \fik-'sā-shən\ n : an obsessive or unhealthy preoccupation or attachment

fix·a·tive \'fik-sət-iv\ n : something (as a varnish for crayon drawings) that stabilizes or sets

fixed \'fikst\ adj 1 : securely placed or fastened : STATIONARY 2 : not volatile 3 : SETTLED, FINAL 4 : INTENT, CONCENTRATED ⟨a ~ stare⟩ 5 : supplied with a definite amount of something needed (as money) — **fix·ed·ly** \'fik-səd-lē\ adv — **fix·ed·ness** \'fik-səd-nəs\ n

fix·i·ty \'fik-sət-ē\ n : the quality or state of being fixed or stable

fix·ture \'fiks-chər\ n : something firmly attached as a permanent part of some other thing ⟨an electrical ~⟩ ⟨a plumbing ~⟩

¹**fizz** \'fiz\ vb : to make a hissing or sputtering sound

²**fizz** n : an effervescent beverage

¹**fiz·zle** \'fiz-əl\ vb 1 : FIZZ 2 : to fail after a good start

²fizzle n : FAILURE

fjord \fē-'ȯrd\ n : a narrow inlet of the sea between cliffs or steep slopes

flab·ber·gast \'flab-ər-ˌgast\ vb : ASTOUND

flab·by \'flab-ē\ adj : lacking firmness and substance : FLACCID ⟨~ muscles⟩

flac·cid \'flak-səd\ adj : deficient in firmness : FLABBY ⟨~ plant stems⟩

flac·on \'flak-ən\ n : a small usu. ornamental bottle with a tight cap

¹flag \'flag\ n : a usu. wild iris or a related plant

²flag n : a hard flat stone (**flag·stone** \-ˌstōn\) suitable for paving

³flag n 1 : a usu. rectangular piece of fabric of distinctive design that is used as a symbol (as of nationality) or as a signaling device 2 : something used like a flag to signal or attract attention 3 : one of the cross strokes of a musical note less than a quarter note in value —

⁴flag vb **flagged; flag·ging** 1 : to put a flag on 2 : to signal with or as if with a flag; esp : to signal to stop ⟨~ a taxi⟩

⁵flag vb **flagged; flag·ging** 1 : to be loose, yielding, or limp : DROOP 2 : to become suspended, feeble, or spiritless ⟨his interest flagged⟩ 3 : to decline in interest or attraction ⟨the topic flagged⟩

flag·el·late \'flaj-ə-ˌlāt\ vb : to punish by whipping : WHIP

fla·geo·let \ˌflaj-ə-'let, -'lā\ n : a small woodwind instrument belonging to the flute class

fla·gi·tious \flə-'jish-əs\ adj 1 : grossly wicked : VILLAINOUS

flag·on \'flag-ən\ n : a container for liquids usu. with a handle, spout, and lid

flag·pole \'flag-ˌpōl\ n : a pole to raise a flag on

fla·grant \'flā-grənt\ adj : conspicuously bad : OUTRAGEOUS, NOTORIOUS — **fla·grant·ly** adv

flag·ship \-ˌship\ n : the ship that carries the commander of a fleet or subdivision thereof and flies his flag

flag·staff \-ˌstaf\ n : FLAGPOLE

¹flail \'flāl\ n : a tool for threshing grain by hand

²flail vb : to beat with or as if with a flail

flair \'flaər\ n 1 : discriminating sense 2 : natural aptitude : BENT ⟨a ~ for acting⟩

flak \'flak\ n : antiaircraft guns or bursting shells fired from them

¹flake \'flāk\ n 1 : a small loose mass or bit 2 : a thin flattened piece or layer : CHIP — **flaky** adj

² flake vb : to form or separate into flakes

flam·beau \'flam-ˌbō\ n, pl **flam·beaus** \-ˌbōz\ or **flambeaux** : a flaming torch

flam·boy·ant \flam-'bȯi-ənt\ adj : FLORID, ORNATE, SHOWY — **flam·boy·ance** also **flam·boy·an·cy** n — **flam·boy·ant·ly** adv

flame \'flām\ n 1 : the glowing gaseous part of a fire 2 : a state of blazing combustion 3 : a flamelike condition or appearance 4 : BRILLIANCE 5 : burning zeal or passion 6 : SWEETHEART — **flame** vb — **flam·ing** adj

fla·men·co \flə-'meŋ-kō\ n : a vigorous rhythmic dance style of the Andalusian gypsies

flame·throw·er \'flām-ˌthrō-(ə)r\ n : a device that expels from a nozzle a burning stream of liquid or semiliquid fuel under pressure

fla·min·go \flə-'miŋ-gō\ n : a long-legged long-necked tropical water bird with scarlet wings and a broad bill bent downward

flam·ma·ble \'flam-ə-bəl\ adj : easily ignited

flange \'flanj\ n : a rim used for strengthening or guiding something or for attachment to another object

¹flank \'flaŋk\ n 1 : the fleshy part of the side between the ribs and the hip; also : the side of a quadruped 2 : SIDE 3 : the right or left of a formation (as a line of battle)

²flank vb 1 : to attack or threaten the flank of 2 : to get around the flank of 3 : BORDER

flank·er n 1 : one that flanks 2 : a football player stationed wide of the end who serves chiefly as a pass receiver

flan·nel \'flan-ᵊl\ n 1 : a soft twilled wool or worsted fabric with a napped surface 2 : a stout cotton fabric napped on one side 3 pl : flannel underwear or trousers

flan·nel·ette \ˌflan-ᵊl-'et\ n : a cotton flannel napped on one or both sides

¹flap \'flap\ n 1 : a stroke with something broad : SLAP 2 : something broad, limber, or flat and usu. thin that hangs loose ⟨the ~ of a pocket⟩ 3 : the motion or sound of something broad and limber as it swings to and fro

²flap vb **flapped; flap·ping** 1 : to beat with something broad and flat 2 : FLING 3 : to move (as wings) with a beating motion 4 : to sway loosely usu. with a noise of striking

flap·jack \'flap-ˌjak\ n : PANCAKE

flap·per n 1 : one that flaps 2 : a young woman esp. of the 1920s who shows bold freedom from conventions in conduct and dress

¹flare \'flaər\ vb 1 : to flame with a sudden unsteady light 2 : to become suddenly excited or angry ⟨~ up⟩ 3 : to spread outward

²flare n 1 : an unsteady glaring light 2 : a blaze of light used to signal or illuminate; also : a device for producing such a blaze

flare–up \-ˌəp\ n : a sudden outburst or intensification

¹flash \'flash\ vb 1 : to break forth in or like a sudden flame 2 : to appear or pass suddenly or with great speed 3 : to send out in or as if in flashes ⟨~ a message⟩ 4 : to make a sudden display (as of brilliance or feeling) 5 : to gleam or glow intermittently 6 : to fill by a sudden rush of water 7 : to expose to view very briefly ⟨~ a badge⟩ syn glance, glint, sparkle

²flash n 1 : a sudden burst of light 2 : a movement of a flag or light in signaling 3 : a sudden and brilliant burst (as of wit) 4 : a brief time 5 : SHOW, DISPLAY; esp : ostentatious display 6 : one that attracts notice; esp : an outstanding athlete 7 : GLIMPSE, LOOK 8 : a first brief news report 9 : FLASHLIGHT 10 : a quick-spreading flame or momentary intense outburst of radiant heat

³flash adj 1 : of sudden origin and usu. short duration ⟨a ~ fire⟩ ⟨a ~ flood⟩

2 : involving brief exposure to an intense agent (as heat or cold) ⟨~ freezing of food⟩

flash·back \-,bak\ n : injection into the chronological sequence of events in a literary or theatrical work of an event of earlier occurrence

flash·bulb \-,bolb\ n : an electric lamp burning metal to produce an intense flash of light for photography

flash·gun \-,gən\ n : a device for holding and operating a flashbulb

flash·ing \-iŋ\ n : sheet metal used in waterproofing roof valleys or the angle between a chimney and a roof

flash·light \-,līt\ n **1** : a sudden bright artificial light used in photography; also : a photograph made by such a light **2** : a small battery-operated portable electric light

flashy adj **1** : momentarily dazzling **2** : BRIGHT **3** : SHOWY — **flash·i·ness** n

flask \'flask\ n : a bottle-shaped container ⟨a whiskey ~⟩

¹flat \'flat\ adj **1** : having a smooth, level, or even surface **2** : spread out along a surface **3** : having a broad smooth surface and little thickness **4** : DOWNRIGHT, POSITIVE ⟨a ~ refusal⟩ **5** : FIXED, UNCHANGING ⟨charge a ~ rate⟩ **6** : EXACT, PRECISE **7** : DULL, UNINTERESTING ⟨a ~ story⟩; also : INSIPID ⟨a ~ taste⟩ **8** : DEFLATED **9** : lower than the true pitch; also : lower by a half step ⟨a ~ note⟩ **10** : lacking contrast ⟨a ~ photographic negative⟩ **11** : free from gloss — **flat·ly** adv — **flat·ness** n

²flat n **1** : a level surface of land : PLAIN **2** : a flat part or surface **3** : a flat note or tone in music; also : a character ♭ indicating a half step drop in pitch **4** : something (as a shoe having a flat heel) flat **5** : a deflated tire

³flat adv **1** : FLATLY **2** : EXACTLY ⟨in one minute ~⟩ **3** : below the true musical pitch

⁴flat vb **flat·ted; flat·ting 1** : FLATTEN **2** : to lower in pitch esp. by a half step **3** : to sing or play below the true pitch

⁵flat n **1** : a floor or story in a building **2** : an apartment on one floor

flat·boat \'flat-,bōt\ n : a flat-bottomed boat used esp. for carrying bulky freight

flat·car \-,kär\ n : a railroad freight car without permanent raised sides, ends, or covering

flat·fish \-,fish\ n : any of a group of flattened bony sea fishes with both eyes on the upper side

flat·iron \-,ī(-ə)rn\ n : an iron for pressing clothes

flat·ten \'flat-ᵊn\ vb : to make or become flat

flat·ter \-ər\ vb **1** : to praise too much or without sincerity **2** : to represent too favorably ⟨the picture ~s her⟩ **3** : to judge (oneself) favorably or too favorably ⟨~ed himself on his skill as a dancer⟩ — **flat·ter·er** n

flat·tery \-ə-rē\ n : flattering speech or attentions : insincere or excessive praise

flat·u·lent \'flach-ə-lənt\ adj **1** : full of gas ⟨a ~ stomach⟩ **2** : TURGID ⟨~ oratory⟩ — **flat·u·lence** n

flat·ware \'flat-,waər\ n : tableware (as silver) more or less flat and usu. formed or cast in a single piece

flaunt \'flȯnt\ vb **1** : to wave or flutter showily **2** : to display oneself to public

notice **3** : to display ostentatiously or impudently : PARADE — **flaunt** n

flau·tist \'flȯt-əst, 'flaut-\ n : FLUTIST

¹fla·vor \'flā-vər\ n **1** : the quality of something that affects the sense of taste or of taste and smell; also : the resulting sensation **2** : something (as a condiment or extract) that adds flavor **3** : characteristic or predominant quality — **fla·vor·ful** adj — **fla·vor·less** adj — **fla·vor·some** adj

²flavor vb : to give or add flavor to

fla·vor·ing \'flāv-(ə-)riŋ\ n : FLAVOR 2

flavour chiefly Brit var of FLAVOR

flaw \'flȯ\ n : an imperfect part : CRACK, FAULT, DEFECT — **flawed** adj — **flaw·less** adj

flax \'flaks\ n : a blue-flowered plant grown for its fiber and its oily seeds; also : its fiber that is the source of linen

flax·en adj **1** : made of flax **2** : resembling flax esp. in pale soft straw color

flay \'flā\ vb **1** : to strip off the skin or surface of **2** : to criticize harshly : SCOLD

flea \'flē\ n : any of a group of small wingless leaping bloodsucking insects

flea·bane \-,bān\ n : any of various plants of the daisy family believed to drive away fleas

flea market n : a street market for cheap or secondhand articles

¹fleck \'flek\ vb : STREAK, SPOT

²fleck n **1** : SPOT, MARK **2** : FLAKE, PARTICLE

fledg·ling \'flej-liŋ\ n : a young bird with feathers newly developed

flee \'flē\ vb **fled** \'fled\ **flee·ing 1** : to run away from danger or evil : FLY **2** : to run away from : SHUN **3** : VANISH

¹fleece \'flēs\ n **1** : the coat of wool covering a sheep **2** : a soft or woolly covering — **fleecy** adj

²fleece vb **1** : SHEAR **2** : to strip of money or property by fraud or extortion

fleer \'fliər\ vb : to laugh or grimace in a coarse manner : SNEER

¹fleet \'flēt\ vb : to fly swiftly : pass rapidly ⟨time is ~ing⟩

²fleet n **1** : a group of warships under one command **2** : a group of ships or vehicles (as trucks or airplanes) under one management

³fleet adj **1** : SWIFT, NIMBLE **2** : not enduring : FLEETING — **fleet·ness** n

fleet admiral n : a commissioned officer of the highest rank in the navy

fleet·ing adj : passing swiftly : TRANSITORY

Flem·ing \'flem-iŋ\ n : a member of a Germanic people inhabiting chiefly northern Belgium

Flem·ish \-ish\ n **1** : the Germanic language of the Flemings **2** Flemish pl : FLEMINGS — **Flemish** adj

flesh \'flesh\ n **1** : the soft parts of an animal's body; esp : muscular tissue **2** : MEAT **3** : the physical being of man as distinguished from the soul **4** : human beings; also : living beings **5** : STOCK, KINDRED **6** : fleshy plant tissue (as fruit pulp)

flesh·ly adj **1** : CORPOREAL, BODILY **2** : CARNAL, SENSUAL **3** : not spiritual : WORLDLY

fleshy adj : consisting of or resembling animal flesh; also : PLUMP, FAT

flew past of FLY

flex \'fleks\ vb : to bend esp. repeatedly

flex·i·ble \'flek-sə-bəl\ adj **1** : capable of being flexed : PLIANT, PLIABLE

2 : yielding to influence : TRACTABLE 3 : readily changed or changing : ADAPTABLE **syn** elastic, supple, resilient, springy — **flex·i·bil·i·ty** \,flek-sə-'bil-ət-ē\ n

flex·ure \'flek-shər\ n 1 : TURN, FOLD, BEND

flib·ber·ti·gib·bet \,flib-ərt-ē-'jib-ət\ n : a silly restless person

¹**flick** \'flik\ n 1 : a light sharp jerky stroke or movement 2 : a sound produced by a flick 3 : DAUB, SPLOTCH

²**flick** vb 1 : to strike lightly with a quick sharp motion 2 : FLUTTER, DART, FLIT

¹**flick·er** \'flik-ər\ vb 1 : to waver unsteadily; also : FLUTTER 2 : FLIT, DART 3 : to burn fitfully or with a fluctuating light ⟨a ~ing candle⟩

²**flicker** n 1 : an act of flickering 2 : a sudden brief movement ⟨a ~ of an eyelid⟩ 3 : a momentary stirring ⟨a ~ of interest⟩ 4 : a brief interval of brightness 5 : a wavering light

flied past of FLY

fli·er \'flī(-ə)r\ n 1 : one that flies; esp : AVIATOR 2 : something (as an express train) that travels fast 3 : a reckless or speculative undertaking 4 : an advertising circular for mass distribution

¹**flight** \'flīt\ n 1 : an act or instance of flying 2 : the ability to fly 3 : a passing through the air or through space ⟨a balloon ~⟩ ⟨a rocket ~ to the moon⟩ 4 : the distance covered in a flight 5 : swift movement 6 : a trip made by or in an airplane 7 : a group of similar individuals (as birds or airplanes) flying as a unit 8 : a passing (as of the imagination) beyond ordinary limits ⟨a series of stairs from one landing to another — **flight·less** adj

²**flight** n : an act or instance of running away

flighty adj 1 : subject to flights of fancy or sudden change of mind : CAPRICIOUS 2 : SKITTISH 3 : not stable : IRRESPONSIBLE; also : SILLY

flim·flam \'flim-,flam\ n : DECEPTION, FRAUD

flim·sy \'flim-zē\ adj 1 : lacking strength or substance 2 : of inferior materials and workmanship 3 : having little worth or plausibility ⟨a ~ excuse⟩ — **flim·si·ly** adv — **flim·si·ness** n

flinch \'flinch\ vb : to shrink from or as if from physical pain : WINCE

¹**fling** \'fliŋ\ vb **flung** \'fləŋ\ **fling·ing** 1 : to move hastily, brusquely, or violently ⟨flung out of the room⟩ 2 : to kick or plunge vigorously 3 : to throw with force or recklessness : HURL 4 : DISCARD, DISREGARD 5 : to put suddenly into a state or condition

²**fling** n 1 : an act or instance of flinging 2 : a casual try : ATTEMPT 3 : a period of self-indulgence

flint \'flint\ n 1 : a hard quartz that strikes fire with steel 2 : an alloy used for striking fire in cigarette lighters — **flinty** adj

flint·lock \'flint-,läk\ n 1 : a lock for a 17th and 18th century firearm using a flint to ignite the charge 2 : a firearm fitted with a flintlock

¹**flip** \'flip\ vb **flipped**; **flip·ping** 1 : to turn by tossing ⟨~ a coin⟩ 2 : to turn

quickly ⟨~ the pages of a book⟩ 3 : FLICK, JERK ⟨~ a light switch⟩ — flip n

²**flip** adj : FLIPPANT, IMPERTINENT

flip·pant \'flip-ənt\ adj : treating lightly something serious or worthy of respect : SAUCY — **flip·pan·cy** n

flip·per \'flip-ər\ n 1 : a broad flat limb (as of a seal) adapted for swimming 2 : a paddlelike shoe used in swimming

¹**flirt** \'flərt\ vb 1 : to move erratically : FLIT 2 : to behave amorously without serious intent 3 : to deal lightly : TRIFLE ⟨~ with death⟩ — **flir·ta·tion** \,flor-'tā-shən\ n — **flir·ta·tious** adj

²**flirt** n 1 : an act or instance of flirting 2 : a person who flirts

flit \'flit\ vb **flit·ted**; **flit·ting** : to pass or move quickly or abruptly from place to place : DART

flitch \'flich\ n : a side of pork cured and smoked as bacon

fliv·ver \'fliv-ər\ n : a small cheap usu. old automobile

¹**float** \'flōt\ n 1 : something (as a raft) that floats 2 : a cork buoying up the baited end of a fishing line 3 : a hollow ball that floats at the end of a lever in a cistern or tank and regulates the level of the liquid 4 : a vehicle with a platform to carry an exhibit

²**float** vb 1 : to rest on the surface of or be suspended in a fluid 2 : to move gently on or through a fluid 3 : to cause to float 4 : WANDER 5 : FLOOD 6 : to offer (securities) in order to finance an enterprise 7 : to finance (an enterprise) by floating an issue of stocks or bonds 8 : to arrange for ⟨~ a loan⟩ — **float·er** n

¹**flock** \'fläk\ n 1 : a group of birds or mammals assembled or herded together 2 : a group of people under the guidance of a leader; esp : CONGREGATION 3 : a large number

²**flock** vb : to gather or move in a crowd

floe \'flō\ n : a flat mass of floating ice

flog \'fläg\ vb **flogged**; **flog·ging** : to beat severely with a rod or whip : LASH — **flog·ger** n

¹**flood** \'fləd\ n 1 : a great flow of water over the land 2 : the flowing in of the tide 3 : an overwhelming volume

²**flood** vb 1 : to cover or become filled with a flood 2 : to fill abundantly or excessively 3 : to pour forth in a flood

flood·light \-,līt\ n : a lamp that throws a broad beam of light; also : the beam itself — **floodlight** vb

¹**floor** \'flōr\ n 1 : the bottom of a room on which one stands 2 : a ground surface 3 : a story of a building 4 : a main level space (as in a legislative chamber) distinguished from a platform or gallery 5 : AUDIENCE 6 : the right to speak from one's place in an assembly — **floor·ing** n

²**floor** vb 1 : to furnish with a floor 2 : to knock down 3 : SHOCK, OVERWHELM 4 : DEFEAT

floor·board \-,bōrd\ n 1 : a board in a floor 2 : the floor of an automobile

floor leader n : a member of a legislative body chosen by his party to have charge of its organization and strategy on the floor

floor show n : a series of acts presented in a nightclub

floor-walk-er \'flȯr-,wȯk-ər\ n : a man employed in a retail store to oversee the sales force and aid customers

floo-zy \'flü-zē\ n : a tawdry or immoral woman

flop \'fläp\ vb **flopped; flop-ping** **1** : FLAP **2** : to throw oneself down heavily, clumsily, or in a relaxed manner ⟨*flopped* into a chair⟩ **3** : FAIL — **flop** n

flop-py adj : tending to flop; esp : soft and flexible ⟨a ~ hat brim⟩

flo-ra \'flȯr-ə\ n, pl **floras** also **flo-rae** \-,ē, -,ī\ : plants or plant life esp. of a region or period

flo-ral \-əl\ adj : of or relating to flowers

flo-res-cence \flȯ-'res-ᵊns, flə-\ n : a state or period of being in bloom or flourishing — **flo-res-cent** adj

flor-id \'flȯr-əd\ adj **1** : excessively flowery in style : ORNATE ⟨~ writing⟩ **2** : tinged with red : RUDDY

flor-in \'flȯr-ən\ n **1** : an old gold coin first struck at Florence in 1252 **2** : gold coin of a European country patterned after the Florentine florin **3** : a modern silver coin in the Netherlands and in Great Britain

flo-rist \'flȯr-əst\ n : one who deals in flowers

floss \'fläs\ n **1** : waste or short silk fibers that cannot be reeled **2** : soft thread of silk or mercerized cotton used for embroidery **3** : a lightweight wool knitting yarn **4** : a fluffy filamentous mass esp. of plant fiber ⟨milkweed ~⟩

flossy adj **1** : of, relating to, or having the characteristics of floss; also : DOWNY **2** : STYLISH, GLAMOROUS

flo-til-la \flō-'til-ə\ n : a small fleet or a fleet of small ships

flot-sam \'flät-səm\ n : floating wreckage of a ship or its cargo

¹flounce \'flaůns\ vb **1** : to move with exaggerated jerky motions **2** : to go with sudden determination **3** : FLOUNDER, STRUGGLE

²flounce n : an act or instance of flouncing

³flounce n : a strip of fabric attached by one edge ⟨a wide ~ at the bottom of her skirt⟩

floun-der \'flaůn-dər\ n : FLATFISH; esp : one important as food

²flounder vb **1** : to struggle to move or obtain footing **2** : to proceed clumsily ⟨~ed through his speech⟩

¹flour \'flaů(-ə)r\ n [ME, flower, the best of anything, flour, fr. OF, fr. L flōr-, flos] : finely ground and sifted meal of a cereal (as wheat); also : a fine soft powder — **floury** adj

²flour vb : to coat with or as if with flour

¹flour-ish \'flər-ish\ vb **1** : THRIVE, PROSPER **2** : to be in a state of activity or production ⟨~ed about 1850⟩ **3** : to reach a height of development or influence **4** : to make bold and sweeping gestures **5** : BRANDISH

²flourish n **1** : a florid embellishment or passage ⟨handwriting with ~es⟩ ⟨a ~ of drums⟩ **2** : WAVE ⟨with a ~ of his cane⟩ **3** : a dramatic action ⟨introduced her with a ~⟩

¹flout \'flaůt\ vb **1** : SCORN **2** : to indulge in scornful behavior : jeer at : MOCK

²flout n : INSULT, MOCKERY

¹flow \'flō\ vb **1** : to issue or move in a stream **2** : RISE ⟨the tide ebbs and ~s⟩

3 : ABOUND **4** : to proceed smoothly and readily **5** : to have a smooth uninterrupted continuity **6** : to hang loose and billowing **7** : COME, ARISE **8** : MENSTRUATE

²flow n **1** : an act or manner of flowing **2** : FLOOD 1, 2 **3** : a smooth uninterrupted movement **4** : STREAM **5** : the quantity that flows in a certain time **6** : MENSTRUATION **7** : YIELD, PRODUCTION **8** : a continuous flow of energy ⟨a ~ of electricity⟩

¹flow-er \'flaů(-ə)r\ n **1** : a plant branch modified for seed production and bearing leaves specialized into floral organs (as petals); also : a flowering plant **2** : the best part or example **3** : the finest most vigorous period **4** : a state of blooming or flourishing — **flow-er-less** adj

²flower vb **1** : to produce flowers : BLOOM **2** : DEVELOP; also : FLOURISH

flow-ered adj **1** : having or bearing flowers **2** : decorated with flowers or flowerlike figures ⟨~ silk⟩

flower girl n : a little girl who carries flowers at a wedding

flower head n : a very short compact flower cluster suggesting a single flower

flow-er-pot \-,pät\ n : a pot in which to grow plants

flow-ery adj **1** : full of or covered with flowers **2** : full of fine words or phrases : FLORID ⟨~ language⟩ — **flow-er-i-ness** n

flown past part of FLY

flu \'flü\ n **1** : INFLUENZA **2** : a minor virus ailment usu. with respiratory symptoms

fluc-tu-ate \'flək-chə-,wāt\ vb **1** : to move up and down or back and forth like a wave **2** : WAVER, VACILLATE — **fluc-tu-a-tion** \,flək-chə-'wā-shən\ n

flue \'flü\ n : a passage (as in a chimney) for gases, smoke, flame, or air

flu-ent \'flü-ənt\ adj **1** : capable of flowing ⟨FLUID⟩ **2** : ready or facile in speech ⟨~ in French⟩ **3** : effortlessly smooth and rapid : POLISHED ⟨~ speech⟩ — **flu-en-cy** n — **flu-ent-ly** adv

¹fluff \'fləf\ n **1** : NAP, DOWN ⟨~ from a pillow⟩ **2** : something fluffy **3** : something inconsequential **4** : BLUNDER; esp : an actor's lapse of memory

²fluff vb **1** : to make or become fluffy ⟨~ up a pillow⟩ **2** : to make a mistake : BOTCH

fluffy adj **1** : having, covered with, or resembling fluff or down **2** : being light and soft or airy ⟨a ~ omelet⟩ **3** : FATUOUS, SILLY

¹flu-id \'flü-əd\ adj **1** : capable of flowing like a liquid or gas **2** : likely to change or move **3** : FLOWING, FLUENT ⟨~ speech⟩ **4** : available for various uses ⟨~ capital⟩ **5** : easily converted into cash ⟨~ assets⟩ — **flu-id-i-ty** \flü-'id-ət-ē\ n

²fluid n : a substance tending to conform to the outline of its container ⟨liquids and gases are ~s⟩

fluke \'flük\ n **1** : the part of an anchor that fastens in the ground **2** : a barbed head (as of a harpoon) **3** : a lobe of a whale's tail

²fluke n : a stroke of luck ⟨won by a ⟩

flume \'flüm\ n **1** : a ravine or gorge with a stream running through it **2** : an inclined channel for carrying water (as for power)

flung past of FLING

flunk \'flənk\ *vb* : to fail esp. in an examination or recitation

flun·ky *or* **flun·key** \'flən-kē\ *n* 1 : a liveried servant; *esp* : FOOTMAN 2 : TOADY

flu·o·res·cence \flu̇(-ə)r-'es-ᵊns\ *n* : emission of radiation usu. as visible light from and only during the absorption of radiation from some other source; *also* : the emitted radiation — **flu·o·resce** \-'es\ *vb* — **flu·o·res·cent** *adj*

fluorescent lamp *n* : a tubular electric lamp in which light is produced on the inside special coating by the action of invisible radiation

flu·o·ri·date \'flu̇r-ə-,dāt\ *vb* : to add a compound of fluorine to — **flu·o·ri·da·tion** \,flu̇r-ə-'dā-shən\ *n*

flu·o·rine \'flu̇(-ə)r-,ēn, -ən\ *n* : a pale yellowish flammable irritating toxic gaseous chemical element

flu·o·ro·scope \'flu̇r-ə-,skōp\ *n* : an instrument for observing the internal structure of an opaque object (as the living body) by means of X rays

¹**flur·ry** \'flər-ē\ *n* 1 : a gust of wind 2 : a brief light snowfall 3 : COMMOTION, BUSTLE 4 : a brief outburst of activity ⟨a ~ of trading⟩

²**flurry** *vb* : AGITATE, EXCITE, FLUSTER

¹**flush** \'fləsh\ *vb* : to cause (as a bird) to take wing suddenly

²**flush** *n* 1 : a sudden flow (as of water) 2 : a surge esp. of emotion ⟨a ~ of triumph⟩ 3 : a tinge of red : BLUSH 4 : a fresh and vigorous state ⟨in the ~ of youth⟩ 5 : a passing sensation of extreme heat

³**flush** *vb* 1 : to flow and spread suddenly and freely : RUSH 2 : to glow brightly 3 : BLUSH 4 : to wash out with a rush of liquid 5 : INFLAME, EXCITE 6 : to make red or hot ⟨~ed by fever⟩

⁴**flush** *adj* 1 : filled to overflowing 2 : fully supplied esp. with money 3 : full of life and vigor 4 : of a ruddy healthy color 5 : readily available : ABUNDANT 6 : having an unbroken or even surface 7 : being on a level with an adjacent surface 8 : directly abutting : immediately adjacent 9 : set even with the left edge of the type page or column 10 : DIRECT

⁵**flush** *adv* 1 : in a flush manner 2 : SQUARELY ⟨a blow ~ on the chin⟩

⁶**flush** *vb* : to make flush

⁷**flush** *n* : a hand of cards all of the same suit

flus·ter \'fləs-tər\ *vb* : to put into a state of agitated confusion : UPSET — **fluster** *n*

¹**flute** \'flüt\ *n* 1 : a hollow pipelike musical instrument 2 : a grooved pleat 3 : CHANNEL, GROOVE ⟨one of the vertical ~s in an architectural column⟩ — **flut·ed** *adj* — **flut·ing** *n*

flut·ist \'flüt-əst\ *n* : a flute player

¹**flut·ter** \'flət-ər\ *vb* 1 : to flap the wings rapidly without flying or in short flights 2 : to move with quick wavering or flapping motions 3 : to vibrate in irregular spasms 4 : to move about or behave in an agitated aimless manner — **flut·tery** *adj*

²**flutter** *n* 1 : an act of fluttering 2 : a

state of nervous confusion 3 : FLURRY, COMMOTION

¹**flux** \'fləks\ *n* 1 : an excessive fluid discharge esp. from the bowels 2 : an act of flowing 3 : a state of continuous change 4 : a substance used to aid in fusing metals

²**flux** *vb* : FUSE

¹**fly** \'flī\ *vb* **flew** \'flü\ **flown** \'flōn\ **fly·ing** 1 : to move in or pass through the air with wings 2 : to move through the air or before the wind 3 : to float or cause to float, wave, or soar in the air 4 : FLEE; *also* : AVOID, SHUN 5 : to fade and disappear : VANISH 6 : to move or pass swiftly 7 : to become expended or dissipated rapidly 8 : to pursue or attack in flight 9 : *past or past part* **flied** : to hit a fly in baseball 10 : to operate or travel in an airplane 11 : to journey over by flying 12 : to transport by flying

²**fly** *n* 1 : the action or process of flying : FLIGHT 2 : a horse-drawn public coach or delivery wagon; *also, chiefly Brit* : a light covered carriage or cab 3 *pl* : the space over a theater stage 4 : a garment closing concealed by a fold of cloth extending over the fastener 5 : the outer canvas of a tent with double top 6 : the length of an extended flag from its staff or support 7 : a baseball hit high into the air

³**fly** *n* : a winged insect; *esp* : any of a large group of typically stout-bodied mostly 2-winged insects 2 : a fishhook dressed to suggest an insect

fly·able *adj* : suitable for flying or being flown

fly·blown \'flī-,blōn\ *adj* : TAINTED, SPOILED ⟨a ~ reputation⟩

fly casting *n* : the act or practice of throwing the lure in angling with artificial flies — **fly·cast·er** *n*

fly·catch·er \'flī-,kach-ər, -,kech-\ *n* : a small bird that feeds on insects caught in flight

fly·er *var of* FLIER

flying buttress *n* : a projecting arched structure to support a wall or building

flying colors *n pl* : complete success ⟨passed his exams with *flying colors*⟩

flying saucer *n* : any of various unidentified moving objects repeatedly reported as seen in the air and usu. alleged to be saucer-shaped or disk-shaped

fly·leaf \'flī-,lēf\ *n* : a blank leaf at the beginning or end of a book

fly·pa·per \-,pā-pər\ *n* : paper poisoned or coated with a sticky substance for killing or catching flies

fly·speck \-,spek\ *n* 1 : a speck of fly dung 2 : something small and insignificant — **flyspeck** *vb*

fly·wheel \-,hwēl\ *n* : a heavy wheel that rotates steadily and thus regulates the speed of the machinery to which it is connected

foal \'fōl\ *n* : the young of an animal of the horse group — **foal** *vb*

¹**foam** \'fōm\ *n* 1 : a light mass of fine bubbles formed in or on the surface of a liquid : FROTH, SPUME 2 : material (as rubber) in a lightweight cellular form — **foamy** *adj*

²**foam** *vb* : to form foam : FROTH

fob \'fäb\ *n* 1 : a short strap, ribbon,

or chain attached to a watch worn esp. in the watch pocket **2** : a small ornament worn on a fob

fob off \fäb-'òf\ *vb* **1** : to put off with a trick or excuse **2** : to pass or offer as genuine **3** : to put aside

fo'c'sle *var of* FORECASTLE

¹**fo·cus** \'fō-kəs\ *n, pl* **fo·cus·es** *or* **fo·ci** \'fō-,sī\ **1** : a point at which rays (as of light, heat, or sound) meet or appear to meet after being reflected or refracted **2** : the distance from a lens or mirror to the point where the rays from it meet **3** : adjustment (as of eyes or eyeglasses) that gives clear vision **4** : central point : CENTER — **fo·cal** \-kəl\ *adj*

²**focus** *vb* **-cused** *also* **-cussed**; **-cus·ing** *also* **-cus·sing 1** : to bring or come to a focus (~ rays of light) **2** : CENTER (~ attention on a problem) **3** : to adjust the focus of

fod·der \'fäd-ər\ *n* : coarse dry food (as cornstalks) for livestock

foe \'fō\ *n* : ENEMY

foe·man \-mən\ *n* : an enemy in war : FOE

foe·tal, foe·tus *var of* FETAL, FETUS

¹**fog** \'fòg, 'fäg\ *n* **1** : fine particles of water that are suspended in the lower air and obscure vision **2** : mental confusion — **fog·gy** *adj*

²**fog** *vb* **fogged; fog·ging** : to obscure or become obscured with or as if with fog

fog·horn \-,hòrn\ *n* : a horn sounded in a fog to give warning

fo·gy *also* **fo·gey** \'fō-gē\ *n* : a person with old-fashioned ideas (he's an old ~)

foi·ble \'fòi-bəl\ *n* : a minor failing or weakness in personal character or behavior

¹**foil** \'fòil\ *vb* **1** : to prevent from attaining an end : DEFEAT **2** : to bring to naught

²**foil** *n* : a fencing weapon with a light flexible blade tapering to a blunt point

³**foil** *n* [ME *foil*, *foille* leaf, fr. L *folium*] **1** : a very thin sheet of metal **2** : something that by contrast sets off another thing to advantage

foist \'fòist\ *vb* : to pass off (something false or worthless) as genuine

¹**fold** \'fōld\ *n* **1** : an enclosure for sheep **2** : a group of people with a common faith, belief, or interest

²**fold** *vb* : to house (sheep) in a fold

³**fold** *vb* **1** : to double or become doubled over itself **2** : to clasp together **3** : to lay one part over or against another part of something **4** : to enclose in or as if in a fold **5** : EMBRACE **6** : to incorporate into a mixture by repeated overturnings without stirring or beating (~ in whites of eggs) **7** : FAIL, COLLAPSE

⁴**fold** *n* **1** : a doubling or folding over **2** : a part doubled or laid over another part

fold·er *n* **1** : one that folds **2** : a printed circular of folded sheets **3** : a folded cover or large envelope for loose papers

fol·de·rol \'fäl-də-,räl\ *n* **1** : a useless trifle **2** : NONSENSE

fo·liage \'fō-l(ē-)ij\ *n* : a mass of leaves (as of a plant or forest)

fo·lio \'fō-lē-,ō\ *n* **1** : a leaf of a book; *also* : a page number **2** : the size of a piece of paper cut two from a sheet **3** : a book printed on folio pages

¹**folk** \'fōk\ *n* **1** : a group of people forming a tribe or nation; *also* : the largest number or most characteristic part of such a group **2** : PEOPLE, PERSONS (country ~) (old ~s) **3** : the persons of one's own family

²**folk** *adj* : of, relating to, or originating among the common people (~ music)

folk·lore \-,lōr\ *n* : customs, beliefs, stories, and sayings of a people handed down from generation to generation — **folk·lor·ist** *n*

folk song *n* : a song traditional among the common people — **folk singer** *n*

folk·sy \'fōk-sē\ *adj* **1** : SOCIABLE, FRIENDLY **2** : informal, casual, or familiar in manner or style

folk·way \'fōk-,wā\ *n* : a way of thinking, feeling, or acting common to a people or to a social group

fol·li·cle \'fäl-i-kəl\ *n* : a small anatomical cavity or gland (a hair ~)

fol·low \'fäl-ō\ *vb* **1** : to go or come after **2** : PURSUE **3** : OBEY **4** : to proceed along **5** : to attend upon steadily (~ the sea) (~ a profession) **6** : to keep one's attention fixed on (~ a speech) **7** : to result from syn succeed, ensue — **fol·low·er** *n* — **follow suit 1** : to play a card of the same suit as the card led **2** : to follow an example

¹**fol·low·ing** *adj* **1** : next after : SUCCEEDING **2** : that immediately follows

²**following** *n* : a group of followers, adherents, or partisans

³**following** *prep* : subsequent to : AFTER

fol·low-up \'fäl-ō-,əp\ *n* : a system or instance of pursuing an initial effort by supplementary action

fol·ly \'fäl-ē\ *n* **1** : lack of good sense **2** : a foolish act or idea : FOOLISHNESS **3** : an excessively costly or unprofitable undertaking

fo·ment \fō-'ment\ *vb* **1** : to treat with moist heat (as for easing pain) **2** : to stir up : INSTIGATE — **fo·men·ta·tion** \,fō-mən-'tā-shən\ *n*

fond \'fänd\ *adj* **1** : FOOLISH, SILLY (~ pride) **2** : prizing highly : DESIROUS (~ of praise) **3** : strongly attracted or predisposed (~ of music) **4** : foolishly tender : INDULGENT; *also* : LOVING, AFFECTIONATE **5** : CHERISHED, DEAR (his ~est hopes) — **fond·ly** *adv* — **fond·ness** *n*

fon·dant \'fän-dənt\ *n* : a creamy preparation of sugar used as a basis for candies or icings

fon·dle \'fän-d'l\ *vb* : to touch or handle lovingly : CARESS, PET

fon·due *also* **fon·du** \fän-'d(y)ü\ *n* : a preparation of melted cheese usu. flavored with wine or brandy

¹**font** \'fänt\ *n* **1** : a receptacle for baptismal or holy water **2** : FOUNTAIN, SOURCE

²**font** *n* : an assortment of printing type of one size and style

food \'füd\ *n* **1** : material taken into an organism and used for growth, repair, and vital processes and as a source of energy; *also* : organic material produced by green plants and used by them as food **2** : solid nutritive material as distinguished from drink **3** : something that nourishes, sustains, or supplies (~ for thought)

food poisoning *n* : illness caused by food contaminated with bacteria or their products or with chemical residues

food·stuff \'füd-,stəf\ *n* : something

with food value; *esp* **:** a specific nutrient (as fat or protein)

¹fool \ˈfül\ *n* **1 :** a person who lacks sense or judgment **2 :** JESTER **3 :** DUPE ⟨he's nobody's ∼⟩ **4 :** IDIOT

²fool *vb* **1 :** to spend time idly or aimlessly **2 :** to meddle or tamper thoughtlessly or ignorantly **3 :** JOKE **4 :** DECEIVE **5 :** FRITTER ⟨∼ed away his time⟩

fool·ery \ˈfül-(ə-)rē\ *n* **1 :** the habit of fooling **:** the behavior of a fool **2 :** a foolish act **:** HORSEPLAY

fool·har·dy \-ˌhärd-ē\ *adj* **:** foolishly daring **:** RASH — **fool·har·di·ness** *n*

fool·ish *adj* **1 :** showing or arising from folly or lack of judgment **2 :** ABSURD, RIDICULOUS **3 :** ABASHED — **fool·ish·ly** *adv* — **fool·ish·ness** *n*

fool·proof \ˈfül-ˈprüf\ *adj* **:** so simple or reliable as to leave no opportunity for error, misuse, or failure

fools·cap \ˈfül-ˌskap\ *n* **:** a size of paper typically 16x13 inches

fool's errand *n* **:** a needless or profitless errand

¹foot \ˈfut\ *n, pl* **feet** \ˈfēt\ *also* **foot 1 :** the terminal part of a leg on which one stands **2 :** a measure of length equal to 12 inches **3 :** a group of syllables forming the basic unit of verse meter **4 :** something resembling an animal's foot in position or use **5** *foot pl, chiefly Brit* **:** INFANTRY **6 :** the lowest part **:** BOTTOM **7 :** the part at the opposite end from the head

²foot *vb* **1 :** DANCE **2 :** to go on foot **3 :** to make speed **:** MOVE **4 :** to add up **5 :** to pay or provide for paying ⟨∼ the bill⟩

foot·age \ˈfut-ij\ *n* **:** length expressed in feet

foot·ball \-ˌbol\ *n* **1 :** any of several games played by two teams on a rectangular field with goalposts at each end; *esp* **:** one in which the ball is in possession of one team at a time and is advanced by running or passing **2 :** the ball used in football

foot·board \-ˌbord\ *n* **1 :** a narrow platform on which to stand or brace the feet **2 :** a board forming the foot of a bed

foot·bridge \-ˌbrij\ *n* **:** a bridge for pedestrians

foot·ed \-əd\ *adj* **1 :** having a foot or feet ⟨a ∼ stand⟩ ⟨∼ creatures⟩ **2 :** having such or so many feet ⟨flat-*footed*⟩ ⟨four-*footed*⟩

foot·fall \-ˌfol\ *n* **:** FOOTSTEP; *also* **:** the sound of a footstep

foot·hill \-ˌhil\ *n* **:** a hill at the foot of higher hills

foot·hold \-ˌhōld\ *n* **1 :** a hold for the feet **:** FOOTING **2 :** a position usable as a base for further advance

foot·ing \ˈfut-iŋ\ *n* **1 :** the placing of one's foot in a position to secure a firm stand **2 :** a place for the foot to rest on **:** FOOTHOLD **3 :** a moving on foot **:** WALK, TREAD, DANCE **4 :** position with respect to one another **:** STATUS **5 :** BASIS **6 :** the adding up of a column of figures; *also* **:** the total amount of such a column

foot·less \-ləs\ *adj* **1 :** having no feet **2 :** UNSUBSTANTIAL **3 :** STUPID, INEPT

foot·lights \-ˌlīts\ *n pl* **:** a row of lights along the front of a stage floor **2 :** the stage as a profession

foot·ling \-liŋ\ *adj* **1 :** INEPT **2 :** TRIVIAL

foot·lock·er \-ˌläk-ər\ *n* **:** a small flat trunk designed to be placed at the foot of a bed (as in barracks)

foot·loose \-ˌlüs\ *adj* **:** having no ties **:** FREE, UNTRAMMELED

foot·man \ˈfut-mən\ *n* **:** a male servant who attends a carriage, waits on table, admits visitors, and runs errands

foot·note \-ˌnōt\ *n* **1 :** a note of reference, explanation, or comment placed usu. at the bottom of a page **2 :** COMMENTARY

foot·pad \-ˌpad\ *n* **:** a highwayman or robber on foot

foot·path \-ˌpath, -ˌpath\ *n* **:** a narrow path for pedestrians

foot·print \-ˌprint\ *n* **:** an impression of the foot

foot·race \-ˌrās\ *n* **:** a race run on foot

foot·rest \-ˌrest\ *n* **:** a support for the feet

foot·sore \-ˌsōr\ *adj* **:** having sore or tender feet (as from much walking)

foot·step \-ˌstep\ *n* **1 :** TREAD **2 :** distance covered by a step **:** PACE **3 :** the mark of the foot **:** TRACK **4 :** a step on which to ascend or descend

foot·stool \-ˌstül\ *n* **:** a low stool to support the feet

foot·work \-ˌwərk\ *n* **:** the management of the feet (as in boxing)

fop \ˈfäp\ *n* **:** DANDY — **fop·pery** \-(ə-)rē\ *n* — **fop·pish** *adj*

¹for \fər, (ˈ)for\ *prep* **1 :** as a preparation toward ⟨dress ∼ dinner⟩ **2 :** toward the purpose or goal of ⟨need time ∼ study⟩ ⟨money ∼ a trip⟩ **3 :** so as to reach or attain ⟨run ∼ cover⟩ **4 :** as being ⟨took him ∼ a fool⟩ **5 :** because of ⟨cry ∼ joy⟩ **6** — used to indicate a recipient ⟨a letter ∼ you⟩ **7 :** in support of ⟨fought ∼ his country⟩ **8 :** directed at **:** AFFECTING ⟨a cure ∼ what ails you⟩ **9** — used with a noun or pronoun followed by an infinitive to form the equivalent of a noun clause ⟨∼ you to go would be silly⟩ **10 :** in exchange as equal to **:** so as to return the value of ⟨a lot of trouble ∼ nothing⟩ ⟨pay $10 ∼ a hat⟩ **11 :** CONCERNING ⟨a stickler ∼ detail⟩ **12 :** CONSIDERING ⟨tall ∼ his age⟩ **13 :** through the period of ⟨served ∼ three years⟩ **14 :** in honor of

²for *conj* **:** BECAUSE

fora *pl of* FORUM

¹for·age \ˈfor-ij\ *n* **1 :** food for animals esp. when taken by browsing or grazing **2 :** a search for provisions

²forage *vb* **1 :** to collect forage from **2 :** to wander in search of provisions **3 :** to get by foraging **4 :** RAVAGE, RAID **5 :** to make a search **:** RUMMAGE

for·ay \ˈfor-ˌā\ *vb* **:** to raid esp. in search of plunder **:** PILLAGE — **foray** *n*

¹for·bear \for-ˈbaər\ *vb* **-bore** \-ˈbor\ **-borne** \-ˈborn\ **-bear·ing 1 :** to refrain from **:** ABSTAIN **2 :** to be patient — **for·bear·ance** *n*

²for·bear \ˈfor-ˌbaər\ *var of* FOREBEAR

for·bid \fər-ˈbid\ *vb* **-bade** \-ˈbad, -ˈbād⟩ *or* **-bad** \-ˈbad\ **-bid·den** \-ˈbid-ᵊn\ **-bid·ding 1 :** to command against **:** PROHIBIT **2 :** to exclude or warn off by express command **3 :** to bar from use **4 :** HINDER, PREVENT syn enjoin, interdict, inhibit

for·bid·ding adj **:** DISAGREEABLE, REPELLENT

1force \'fȯrs\ n **1 :** strength or energy esp. of an exceptional degree **:** active power **2 :** capacity to persuade or convince **3 :** military strength; also, pl **:** the whole military strength (as of a nation) **4 :** a body (as of persons or ships) assigned to or available for a particular purpose **5 :** VIOLENCE, COMPULSION **6 :** an influence (as a push or pull) that causes motion or a change of motion — **force·ful** adj — **force·ful·ly** adv

2force vb **1 :** COMPEL, COERCE **2 :** to cause through necessity ⟨forced to admit defeat⟩ **3 :** to press, attain to, or effect against resistance or inertia ⟨~ your way through⟩ **4 :** to achieve or win by strength in struggle or violence **5 :** to raise or accelerate to the utmost ⟨~ the pace⟩ **6 :** to produce with unnatural or unwilling effort ⟨forced laughter⟩ **7 :** to hasten (as in growth) by artificial means

for·ceps \'fȯr-səps\ n, pl **forceps :** a hand-held instrument for grasping, holding, or pulling objects esp. for delicate operations

forc·ible \'fȯr-sə-bəl\ adj **1 :** obtained or done by force **2 :** showing force or energy **:** POWERFUL — **forc·ibly** adv

1ford \'fȯrd\ n **:** a place where a stream may be crossed by wading

2ford vb **:** to cross by a ford

1fore \'fȯr\ adv **:** in, toward, or adjacent to the front **:** FORWARD

2fore adj **:** being or coming before in time, order, or space

3fore n **1 :** FRONT **2 :** something that occupies a front position

4fore interj — used by a golfer to warn anyone within range of the probable line of flight of his ball

fore-and-aft adj **:** running in the line of the length (as of a ship) **:** LONGITUDINAL

1fore·arm \'fȯr-'ärm\ vb **:** to arm in advance **:** PREPARE

2fore·arm \'fȯr-,ärm\ n **:** the part of the arm between the elbow and the wrist

fore·bear \'fȯr-,baər\ or **for·bear** \'fȯr-\ n **:** ANCESTOR, FOREFATHER

fore·bode also **for·bode** \fȯr-'bōd, fȯr-\ vb **1 :** FORETELL, PORTEND **2 :** to have a premonition esp. of misfortune syn augur, predict — **fore·bod·ing** n

fore·cast \'fȯr-,kast\ vb **-cast** or **-cast·ed; -cast·ing 1 :** PREDICT, CALCULATE ⟨~ weather conditions⟩ **2 :** to indicate as likely to occur **:** FORESEE — **forecast** n — **fore·cast·er** n

fore·cas·tle \'fōk-səl\ n **1 :** the upper deck of a ship in front of the foremast **2 :** the forward part of a merchant ship where the sailors live

fore·close \fȯr-'klōz\ vb **1 :** to shut out **:** DEBAR **2 :** to take legal measures to terminate a mortgage and take possession of the mortgaged property

fore·clo·sure \-'klō-zhər\ n **:** the act of foreclosing; esp **:** the legal procedure of foreclosing a mortgage

fore·doom \-'düm\ vb **:** to doom beforehand

fore·fa·ther \'fȯr-,fä̇th-ər\ n **1 :** ANCESTOR **2 :** a person of an earlier period and common heritage

fore·fin·ger \-,fiŋ-gər\ n **:** the finger next to the thumb

fore·foot \-,fu̇t\ n **:** either of the front feet of a quadruped

fore·front \-,frənt\ n **:** the foremost part or place **:** VANGUARD

fore·gath·er var of FORGATHER

1fore·go \fȯr-'gō\ vb **:** PRECEDE

2forego var of FORGO

fore·go·ing adj **:** PRECEDING ⟨the ~ paragraphs⟩

fore·gone \-'gȯn\ adj **:** determined in advance **:** PREVIOUS, PAST ⟨a ~ conclusion⟩

fore·ground \'fȯr-,grau̇nd\ n **1 :** the part of a scene or representation that appears nearest to and in front of the spectator **2 :** a position of prominence

fore·hand \-,hand\ n **:** a stroke made with the palm of the hand turned in the direction in which the hand is moving; also **:** the side on which such a stroke is made — **forehand** adj

fore·hand·ed \-'han-dəd\ adj **:** mindful of the future **:** THRIFTY, PRUDENT

fore·head \'fȯr-əd, 'fȯr-,hed\ n **:** the part of the face above the eyes

for·eign \'fȯr-ən\ adj [OF forein, fr. LL foranus situated outside, fr. L foris outside] **1 :** situated outside a place or country and esp. one's own country **2 :** born in, belonging to, or characteristic of some place or country other than the one under consideration ⟨~ language⟩ **3 :** not connected or pertinent **4 :** related to or dealing with other nations ⟨~ affairs⟩ **5 :** occurring in an abnormal situation in the living body ⟨a ~ body in the eye⟩

for·eign·er \-ər\ n **:** a person belonging to or owing allegiance to a foreign country **:** ALIEN

foreign minister n **:** a governmental minister for foreign affairs

fore·know \fȯr-'nō\ vb **:** to have previous knowledge of **:** know beforehand — **fore·knowl·edge** \-'näl-ij\ n

fore·la·dy \'fȯr-,lād-ē\ n **:** a woman who acts as a foreman

fore·land \-lənd\ n **:** PROMONTORY, HEADLAND

fore·leg \-,leg\ n **:** either of the front legs of a quadruped

fore·limb \-,lim\ n **:** either of an anterior pair of limbs (as wings, arms, or fins)

fore·lock \-,läk\ n **:** a lock of hair growing from the front part of the head

fore·man \'fȯr-mən\ n **1 :** a spokesman of a jury **2 :** a workman in charge of a group of workers

fore·mast \-,mast, -məst\ n **:** the mast nearest the bow of a ship

fore·most \-,mōst\ adj **:** first in time, place, or order **:** most important **:** PREEMINENT — **foremost** adv

fore·name \-,nām\ n **:** a first name

fore·named \-,nāmd\ adj **:** previously named **:** AFORESAID

fore·noon \-,nün\ n **:** the period from morning to noon **:** MORNING

1fo·ren·sic \fə-'ren-sik\ adj [L forensic, lit., of the forum, fr. forum, where the lawcourts of ancient Rome were located] **:** belonging to, used in, or suitable to courts of law or to public speaking or debate ⟨~ eloquence⟩

2forensic n **1 :** an argumentative exercise **2** pl **:** the art or study of argumentative discourse

fore·or·dain \,fȯr-ȯr-'dān\ vb **:** to ordain or decree beforehand **:** PREDESTINE fore·quar·ter \'fōr-ˌkwȯrt-ər\ n : the front half of a lateral half of the body or carcass of a quadruped ⟨a ~ of beef⟩

fore·run·ner \-ˌrən-ər\ n 1 : one that goes or is sent before to give notice of the approach of others : HARBINGER 2 : PREDECESSOR, ANCESTOR syn precursor, herald

fore·sail \-ˌsāl, -səl\ n 1 : the lowest sail on the foremast of a square-rigged ship 2 : the lower sail set toward the stern on the foremast of a schooner

fore·see \fōr-'sē\ vb : to see or realize beforehand : EXPECT syn foreknow, divine, apprehend, anticipate — fore·see·able adj

fore·shad·ow \-'shad-ō\ vb : to give a hint or suggestion of beforehand : represent beforehand

fore·sheet \'fōr-ˌshēt\ n 1 : one of the sheets of a foresail 2 pl : the forward part of an open boat

fore·shore \-ˌshōr\ n : the part of a seashore between high-water and low-water marks

fore·short·en \fōr-'shȯrt-ᵊn\ vb : to shorten (a detail) in a drawing or painting so that the composition appears to have depth

fore·sight \'fōr-ˌsīt\ n 1 : the act or power of foreseeing 2 : an act of looking forward; also : a view forward 3 : care or provision for the future : PRUDENCE — fore·sight·ed adj — fore·sight·ed·ness n

fore·skin \-ˌskin\ n : a fold of skin enclosing the end of the penis

for·est \'fȯr-əst\ n : a large thick growth of trees and underbrush — for·est·ed adj

fore·stall \fȯr-'stȯl\ vb 1 : to keep out, hinder, or prevent by measures taken in advance 2 : ANTICIPATE

for·est·ry \'fȯr-ə-strē\ n : the science of growing and caring for forests — for·est·er n

¹fore·taste \'fōr-ˌtāst\ n : an advance indication, warning, or notion

²fore·taste \fōr-'tāst\ vb : to taste beforehand : ANTICIPATE

fore·tell \fōr-'tel\ vb : to tell of beforehand : PREDICT syn forecast, prophesy, prognosticate

fore·thought \'fōr-ˌthȯt\ n 1 : PREMEDITATION 2 : consideration for the future

fore·to·ken \fōr-'tō-kən\ vb : to indicate in advance ⟨the bright sunset ~ed good weather⟩

fore·top \'fōr-ˌtäp, 'fōrt-əp\ n : the platform at the head of a ship's foremast

for·ev·er \fər-'ev-ər\ adv 1 : for a limitless time 2 : at all times : ALWAYS

for·ev·er·more \-ˌev-ər-'mōr\ adv : FOREVER

fore·warn \fōr-'wȯrn\ vb : to warn beforehand

fore·wom·an \'fōr-ˌwum-ən\ n : FORELADY

fore·word \-ˌwərd\ n : PREFACE

¹for·feit \'fȯr-fət\ n 1 : something forfeited : PENALTY, FINE 2 : FORFEITURE 3 : something deposited and then redeemed on payment of a fine 4 pl : a game in which forfeits are exacted

²forfeit vb : to lose or lose the right to by some error, offense, or crime

for·fei·ture \'fȯr-fə-ˌchúr\ n 1 : the act of forfeiting 2 : something forfeited : PENALTY

for·fend \fȯr-'fend\ vb 1 : to ward off 2 : PROTECT, PRESERVE

for·gath·er or fore·gath·er \fȯr-'gath-ər, fōr-\ vb 1 : to come together : ASSEMBLE 2 : to meet someone usu. by chance

¹forge \'fȯrj\ n [OF, fr. L fabrica, fr. faber smith] : SMITHY

²forge vb 1 : to form (metal) by heating and hammering 2 : FASHION, SHAPE ⟨~ an agreement⟩ 3 : to make or imitate falsely esp. with intent to defraud ⟨~ a signature⟩ — forg·er n — forg·ery n

³forge vb : to move ahead steadily but gradually

for·get \fər-'get\ vb -got; -got·ten or -got; -get·ting 1 : to be unable to think of or recall 2 : to fail to become mindful of at the proper time : NEGLECT, DISREGARD ⟨forgot his old friends⟩ — for·get·ful adj — for·get·ful·ness n

forg·ing \'fȯr-jiŋ\ n : a piece of forged work

for·give \fər-'giv\ vb -gave; -giv·en; -giv·ing 1 : PARDON, ABSOLVE 2 : to give up resentment of 3 : to grant relief from payment of — for·giv·able adj — for·give·ness n

for·giv·ing adj : showing forgiveness : inclined or ready to forgive

for·go or fore·go \fȯr-'gō, fōr-\ vb : to give up : abstain from : RENOUNCE

fo·rint \'fō-ˌrint\ n — see MONEY table

¹fork \'fȯrk\ n 1 : an implement with two or more prongs for taking up (as in eating), piercing, pitching, or digging 2 : a forked part, tool, or piece of equipment 3 : a dividing into branches or a place where something branches; also : a branch of such a fork

²fork vb 1 : to divide into two or more branches 2 : to give the form of a fork to ⟨~ing her fingers⟩ 3 : to raise or pitch with a fork ⟨~ hay⟩

forked \'fȯrkt, 'fȯr-kəd\ adj : having a fork; shaped like a fork ⟨~ lightning⟩

fork·lift \'fȯrk-ˌlift\ n : a machine for hoisting heavy objects by means of steel fingers inserted under the load

for·lorn \fər-'lȯrn\ adj 1 : DESERTED, FORSAKEN 2 : WRETCHED 3 : nearly hopeless — for·lorn·ly adv

forlorn hope n 1 : a body of men selected to perform a perilous service 2 : a desperate or extremely difficult enterprise

¹form \'fȯrm\ n 1 : SHAPE, STRUCTURE 2 : a body esp. of a person : FIGURE 3 : the essential nature of a thing 4 : established manner of doing or saying something 5 : FORMULA 6 : a printed or typed document with blank spaces for insertion of requested information ⟨tax ~⟩ 7 : CEREMONY, CONVENTIONALITY 8 : manner or style of performing according to recognized standards 9 : a long seat : BENCH 10 : a frame model of the human figure used for displaying clothes 11 : MOLD ⟨a ~ for concrete⟩ 12 : type or plates in a frame ready for printing 13 : MODE, KIND, VARIETY ⟨coal is a ~ of carbon⟩ 14 : orderly method of arrangement;

ə abut; ᵊ kitten; ər further; a back; ā bake; ä cot, cart; au̇ out; ch chin; e less; ē easy; g gift; i trip; ī life; j joke; ŋ sing; ō flow; ȯ flaw; ȯi coin; th thin; t͟h this; ü loot; u̇ foot; y yet; yü few; yu̇ furious; zh vision

also : a particular kind or instance of such arrangement ⟨the sonnet ~ in poetry⟩ **15** : the structural element, plan, or design of a work of art **16** : a bounded surface or volume **17** : a grade in a British secondary school or in some American private schools **18** : a table with information on the past performances of racehorses **19** : known ability to perform; *also* : condition (as of an athlete) suitable for performing **20** : one of the ways in which a word is changed to show difference in use ⟨the plural ~ of a noun⟩

²**form** *vb* **1** : to give form or shape to : FASHION, MAKE **2** : to give a particular shape to : ARRANGE **3** : TRAIN, IN-STRUCT **4** : DEVELOP, ACQUIRE ⟨~ a habit⟩ **5** : to make up : CONSTITUTE **6** : to arrange in order ⟨~ a battle line⟩ **7** : to take form : ARISE ⟨clouds are ~ing⟩ **8** : to take a definite form, shape, or arrangement — **form·er** *n*

¹**for·mal** \'for-məl\ *adj* **1** : CONVEN-TIONAL **2** : done in due or lawful form ⟨a ~ contract⟩ **3** : based on conventional forms and rules ⟨a ~ reception⟩ **4** : CEREMONIOUS, PRIM ⟨a ~ manner⟩ **5** : NOMINAL — **for·mal·ly** *adv*

²**formal** *n* : something (as a social event) formal in character

form·al·de·hyde \for-'mal-də-,hīd\ *n* : a colorless pungent gas used in water solution as a preservative and disinfectant

for·mal·ism \'for-mə-,liz-əm\ *n* : strict adherence to set forms

for·mal·i·ty \for-'mal-ət-ē\ *n* **1** : the quality or state of being formal **2** : compliance with formal or conventional rules : CEREMONY **3** : an established form that is required or conventional

for·mal·ize \'for-mə-,līz\ *vb* **1** : to give a certain or definite form to : SHAPE **2** : to make formal; *also* : to give formal status or approval to

for·mat \'for-,mat\ *n* **1** : the general composition or style of a publication **2** : the general plan or arrangement of something

for·ma·tion \for-'mā-shən\ *n* **1** : a giving form to something : DEVELOP-MENT **2** : something that is formed **3** : STRUCTURE, SHAPE **4** : an arrangement of persons, ships, or airplanes

for·ma·tive \'for-mət-iv\ *adj* **1** : giving or capable of giving form : CONSTRUC-TIVE **2** : of, relating to, or characterized by important growth or formation ⟨a child's ~ years⟩

for·mer \'for-mər\ *adj* **1** : PREVIOUS, EARLIER **2** : FOREGOING **3** : being first mentioned or in order of two things

for·mer·ly *adv* : in time past : HERETO-FORE, PREVIOUSLY

form-fit·ting \'form-,fit-iŋ\ *adj* : conforming to the outline of the body : close-fitting

for·mi·da·ble \'for-məd-ə-bəl\ *adj* **1** : exciting fear, dread, or awe **2** : imposing serious difficulties

form·less \'form-ləs\ *adj* : having no definite shape or form

for·mu·la \'for-myə-lə\ *n, pl* **-las** *also* **-lae** \-,lē\ **1** : a set form of words for ceremonial use **2** : a conventionalized statement intended to express some fundamental truth **3** : RECIPE **4** : a milk mixture or substitute for a baby **5** : a group of symbols or figures joined to express a single rule or idea **6** : a

prescribed or set form or method

for·mu·late \-,lāt\ *vb* **1** : to express in a formula **2** : to state definitely and clearly ⟨~ a plan⟩ **3** : to prepare according to a formula — **for·mu·la·tion** \,for-myə-'lā-shən\ *n*

for·ni·ca·tion \,for-nə-'kā-shən\ *n* : human sexual intercourse other than between a man and his wife

for·sake \fər-'sāk, for-\ *vb* **-sook** \-'sùk\ **-sak·en** \-'sā-kən\ **-sak·ing 1** : to give up : RENOUNCE **2** : to quit or leave entirely : ABANDON — **for·sak·en** *adj*

for·sooth \fər-'sùth\ *adv* : in truth : INDEED

for·swear *or* **fore·swear** \for-'swaər, for-\ *vb* **1** : to renounce earnestly or upon oath **2** : to deny upon oath **3** : to swear falsely : commit perjury

¹**forte** \'fort, 'for-,tā\ *n* : something in which a person excels ⟨cooking is her ~⟩

²**for·te** \'for-,tā\ *adv (or adj)* : LOUDLY, POWERFULLY — used as a direction in music

forth \'forth\ *adv* **1** : FORWARD, ON-WARD ⟨from that day ~⟩ **2** : out into view ⟨put ~ leaves⟩

forth·com·ing \'forth-'kəm-iŋ\ *adj* **1** : APPROACHING, COMING ⟨the ~ holi-days⟩ **2** : readily available or approachable ⟨the funds will be ~⟩

forth·right \'forth-,rīt\ *adj* : DIRECT, STRAIGHTFORWARD ⟨a ~ answer⟩

forth·with \'forth-'with, -'with\ *adv* : IMMEDIATELY

for·ti·fy \'fort-ə-,fī\ *vb* **1** : to strengthen and secure by military defenses **2** : to give physical strength, courage, or endurance to **3** : ENCOURAGE **4** : EN-RICH ⟨~ bread with vitamins⟩ — **for·ti·fi·ca·tion** \,fort-ə-fə-'kā-shən\ *n*

for·ti·tude \'fort-ə-,t(y)üd\ *n* : strength of mind that enables a person to meet danger or bear pain or adversity with courage *syn* grit, backbone, pluck

fort·night \'fort-,nīt\ *n* [ME *fourtenight* fourteen nights] : the space of 14 days : two weeks

fort·night·ly *adj* : occurring or appearing once in a fortnight — **fortnightly** *adv*

for·tress \'for-trəs\ *n* : FORT 1

for·tu·i·tous \for-'t(y)ü-ət-əs\ *adj* : happening by chance : ACCIDENTAL

for·tu·i·ty \-ət-ē\ *n* **1** : the quality or state of being fortuitous **2** : a chance event or occurrence

for·tu·nate \'forch-(ə-)nət\ *adj* **1** : coming by good luck **2** : LUCKY — **for·tu·nate·ly** *adv*

for·tune \'for-chən\ *n* **1** : CHANCE, LUCK **2** : good or bad luck **3** : FATE, DESTINY **4** : RICHES, WEALTH

fortune hunter *n* : a person who seeks wealth esp. by marriage

for·tune-tel·ler *n* : a person who professes to tell future events — **fortune-tell·ing** *n or adj*

for·ty \'fort-ē\ *n* : four times 10 — **for·ti·eth** *adj or n* — **forty** *adj or pron*

for·ty-nin·er \,fort-ē-'nī-nər\ *n* : a person in the rush to California for gold in 1849

forty winks *n sing or pl* : a short sleep : NAP

fo·rum \'for-əm\ *n, pl* **forums** *also*

fo·ra \-ə\ *n* 1 : the marketplace or central meeting place of an ancient Roman city 2 : a medium (as a publication) of open discussion 3 : COURT 4 : a public assembly, lecture, or program involving audience or panel discussion

¹**for·ward** \'fȯr-wərd\ *adj* 1 : being near or at or belonging to the front 2 : EAGER, READY 3 : BRASH, BOLD 4 : notably advanced or developed : PRECOCIOUS 5 : moving, tending, or leading toward a position in front (a ~ movement) 6 : EXTREME, RADICAL 7 : of, relating to, or getting ready for the future — **for·ward·ness** *n*

²**forward** *adv* : to or toward what is before or in front

³**forward** *n* : a player stationed near the front of his team (as in basketball)

⁴**forward** *vb* 1 : to help onward : ADVANCE 2 : to send forward : TRANSMIT 3 : to send or ship onward

for·ward·er *n* : one that forwards; *esp* : an agent who forwards goods (a freight ~) — **for·ward·ing** *n*

for·wards *adv* : FORWARD

¹**fos·sil** \'fäs-əl\ *n* 1 : a trace or impression or the remains of a plant or animal preserved in the earth's crust from past ages 2 : a person whose ideas are out-of-date — **fos·sil·ize** *vb*

²**fossil** *adj* 1 : extracted from the earth (~ fuels such as coal) 2 : being or resembling a fossil (~ plants)

¹**fos·ter** \'fȯs-tər\ *adj* : affording, receiving, or sharing nourishment or parental care though not related by blood or legal ties (~ parent) (~ child)

²**foster** *vb* 1 : to give parental care to : NURTURE 2 : to promote the growth or development of : ENCOURAGE

fos·ter·ling \-liŋ\ *n* : a foster child

fought *past of* FIGHT

¹**foul** \'faul\ *adj* 1 : offensive to the senses : LOATHSOME; *also* : clogged with dirt 2 : ODIOUS, DETESTABLE 3 : OBSCENE, ABUSIVE 4 : DISAGREEABLE, STORMY (~ weather) 5 : TREACHEROUS, DISHONORABLE, UNFAIR 6 : marking the bounds of a playing field (~ lines); *also* : being outside the foul line (~ ball) (~ territory) 7 : marked up or defaced by changes (~ manuscript) 8 : ENTANGLED — **foul·ly** \'faul-(l)ē\ *adv* — **foul·ness** *n*

³**foul** *n* 1 : ENTANGLEMENT, COLLISION 2 : an infraction of the rules in a game or sport; *also* : a baseball hit outside the foul line

³**foul** *adv* : FOULLY

⁴**foul** *vb* 1 : to make or become foul or filthy 2 : DISGRACE, DISHONOR 3 : to make or hit a foul 4 : to entangle or become entangled 5 : OBSTRUCT, BLOCK 6 : to collide with

fou·lard \fu̇-'lärd\ *n* : a lightweight silk of plain or twill weave usu. decorated with a printed pattern

foul-mouthed \'faul-'mau̇thd, -'mau̇tht\ *adj* : given to the use of obscene, profane, or abusive language

foul play *n* : unfair play or dealing : dishonest conduct; *esp* : VIOLENCE (the dead man was a victim of *foul play*)

¹**found** \'faund\ *past of* FIND

²**found** *vb* 1 : to take the first steps in

building (~ a colony) 2 : to set or ground on something solid : BASE 3 : to establish and often to provide for the future maintenance of (~ a college) — **found·er** *n*

³**found** *vb* 1 : to melt (metal) and pour into a mold 2 : to make by founding metal — **found·er** *n*

foun·da·tion \faun-'dā-shən\ *n* 1 : the act of founding 2 : the base or basis upon which something stands or is supported (suspicions without ~) 3 : funds given for the permanent support of an institution : ENDOWMENT; *also* : an institution so endowed 4 : supporting structure : BASE 5 : CORSET — **foun·da·tion·al** *adj*

foun·der \'faun-dər\ *vb* 1 : to make or become lame (~ a horse) 2 : to give way : COLLAPSE 3 : to sink below the surface of the water (a ~*ing* ship) 4 : FAIL

found·ling \'faund-liŋ\ *n* : an infant found after its unknown parents have abandoned it

found·ry \'faun-drē\ *n* : a building or works where metal is cast

fount \'faunt\ *n* : FOUNTAIN, SOURCE

foun·tain \'faunt-ᵊn\ *n* 1 : a spring of water 2 : SOURCE 3 : an artificial jet of water 4 : a container for liquid that can be drawn off as needed

foun·tain·head \-,hed\ *n* : SOURCE

fountain pen *n* : a pen with a reservoir that feeds the writing point with ink

four \'fȯr\ *n* 1 : one more than three 2 : the 4th in a set or series 3 : something having four units — **four** *adj or pron*

four-flush \-,fləsh\ *vb* : to make a false claim : BLUFF — **four-flush·er** *n*

four·fold \-'fōld\ *adj* 1 : having four units or members 2 : of or amounting to 400 percent — **fourfold** *adv*

Four Hundred *or* **400** *n* : the exclusive social set of a community — used with *the*

four-in-hand \'fȯr-ən-,hand\ *n* 1 : a team of four horses driven by one person; *also* : a vehicle drawn by such a team 2 : a necktie tied in a slipknot with long ends overlapping vertically in front

four-post·er \-'pō-stər\ *n* : a bed with tall corner posts orig. designed to support curtains or a canopy

four·score \-,skȯr\ *adj* : being four times twenty : EIGHTY

four·some \-səm\ *n* 1 : a group of four persons or things 2 : a golf match between two pairs of partners

four·square \-'skwa(ə)r\ *adj* 1 : SQUARE 2 : marked by boldness and conviction; *also* : FORTHRIGHT — **foursquare** *adv*

four·teen \-'tēn\ *n* : one more than 13 — **fourteen** *adj or pron* — **four·teenth** \-'tēnth\ *adj or n*

¹**fourth** \'fȯrth\ *adj* 1 : being number four in a countable series 2 : next after the third — **fourth** *adv*

²**fourth** *n* 1 : one that is fourth 2 : one of four equal parts of something 3 : the 4th forward gear in an automotive vehicle

fourth estate *n, often cap F & E* : the public press

¹**fowl** \'faul\ *n* 1 : BIRD 2 : a domestic

cock or hen; *also* : the flesh of these used as food

²fowl *vb* : to hunt wildfowl — **fowl·er** *n*

¹fox \\ˈfäks\\ *n* **1** : a mammal related to the wolves but smaller and with shorter legs and pointed muzzle **2** : a clever crafty person

²fox *vb* : TRICK, OUTWIT

foxed \\ˈfäkst\\ *adj* : discolored with yellowish brown stains ⟨an old book with some pages ~⟩

fox·glove \\-ˌgləv\\ *n* : a plant grown for its showy spikes of dotted white or purple tubular flowers and as a source of digitalis

fox·hole \\-ˌhōl\\ *n* : a pit dug for protection against enemy fire

fox·hound \\-ˌhaůnd\\ *n* : any of various large swift powerful hounds used in hunting foxes

foxy *adj* : WILY; *also* : CLEVER

foy·er \\ˈfói-ər, ˈfói-ˌ(y)ā\\ *n* : LOBBY; *also* : an entrance hallway

fra·cas \\ˈfrāk-əs, ˈfrak-\\ *n* : BRAWL

frac·tion \\ˈfrak-shən\\ *n* **1** : a numerical representation of one or more equal parts of a unit ⟨½, ⅝, .256 are ~s⟩ **2** : FRAGMENT **3** : PORTION — **frac·tion·al** *adj*

frac·tious \\-shəs\\ *adj* **1** : tending to be troublesome : hard to handle or control **2** : QUARRELSOME, IRRITABLE

frac·ture \\ˈfrak-chər\\ *n* **1** : a breaking of something and esp. a bone **2** : CRACK, CLEFT — **fracture** *vb*

frag·ile \\ˈfraj-əl\\ *adj* : easily broken : DELICATE — **fra·gil·i·ty** \\frə-ˈjil-ət-ē\\ *n*

frag·ment \\ˈfrag-mənt\\ *n* : a part broken off, detached, or incomplete

frag·men·tary \\-mən-ˌter-ē\\ *adj* : made up of fragments : INCOMPLETE

fra·grant \\ˈfrā-grənt\\ *adj* : sweet or agreeable in smell — **fra·grance** *n* — **fra·grant·ly** *adv*

frail \\ˈfrāl\\ *adj* **1** : morally or physically weak **2** : FRAGILE, DELICATE

frail·ty \\ˈfrā(-ə)l-tē\\ *n* **1** : the quality or state of being frail **2** : a fault due to weakness ⟨as of character⟩

¹frame \\ˈfrām\\ *vb* **1** : PLAN, CONTRIVE **2** : FORMULATE **3** : SHAPE, CONSTRUCT **4** : to draw up ⟨~ a constitution⟩ **5** : to fit or adjust for a purpose : ARRANGE **6** : to provide with or enclose in a frame **7** : to make appear guilty ⟨~ an innocent man⟩ — **fram·er** *n*

²frame *n* **1** : something made of parts fitted and joined together **2** : the physical makeup of the body **3** : an arrangement of structural parts that gives form or support **4** : a supporting or enclosing border or open case ⟨as for a window or picture⟩ **5** : a particular state or disposition ⟨as of mind⟩ : MOOD

frame-up \\-ˌəp\\ *n* : a scheme to cause an innocent person to be accused of a crime; *also* : the action resulting from such a scheme

frame·work \\-ˌwərk\\ *n* **1** : a skeletal, openwork, or structural frame **2** : a basic structure ⟨as of ideas⟩

franc \\ˈfraŋk\\ *n* — see MONEY table

fran·chise \\ˈfran-ˌchīz\\ *n* **1** : a special privilege granted to an individual or group ⟨a ~ to operate a ferry⟩ **2** : a constitutional or statutory right or privilege; *esp* : the right to vote

fran·ci·um \\ˈfran-sē-əm\\ *n* : a radioactive metallic chemical element

¹frank \\ˈfraŋk\\ *adj* : marked by free, forthright, and sincere expression : OUTSPOKEN — **frank·ly** *adv* — **frank·ness** *n*

²frank *vb* : to mark ⟨a piece of mail⟩ with an official signature or sign indicating that it can be mailed free; *also* : to mail in this manner

³frank *n* **1** : a signature, mark, or stamp on a piece of mail indicating that it can be mailed free **2** : the privilege of sending mail free of charge

Fran·ken·stein \\ˈfraŋ-kən-ˌstīn, -ˌstēn\\ *n* **1** : a work or agency that ruins its originator **2** : a monster in the shape of a man

frank·furt·er or **frank·fort·er** \\ˈfraŋk-fə(r)t-ər\\ or **frank·furt** or **frank·fort** \\-fərt\\ *n* : a seasoned beef or beef and pork sausage

frank·in·cense \\ˈfraŋ-kən-ˌsens\\ *n* : a fragrant resin burned as incense

fran·tic \\ˈfrant-ik\\ *adj* : wildly excited : FRENZIED — **fran·ti·cal·ly** *adv*

frap·pé \\fra-ˈpā\\ or **frappe** \\ˈfrap\\ *n* **1** : an iced or frozen mixture or drink **2** : a thick milk shake — **frap·pé** *adj*

fra·ter·nal \\frə-ˈtərn-ᵊl\\ *adj* **1** : of, relating to, or involving brothers **2** : of, relating to, or being a fraternity or society **3** : FRIENDLY, BROTHERLY — **fra·ter·nal·ly** *adv*

fra·ter·ni·ty \\-ˈtər-nət-ē\\ *n* **1** : a social, honorary, or professional organization; *esp* : a social club of male college students **2** : BROTHERLINESS, BROTHERHOOD **3** : men of the same class, profession, or tastes ⟨the legal ~⟩

frat·er·nize \\ˈfrat-ər-ˌnīz\\ *vb* **1** : to associate or mingle as brothers or friends **2** : to associate on intimate terms with citizens or troops of a hostile nation — **frat·er·ni·za·tion** \\ˌfrat-ər-nə-ˈzā-shən\\ *n*

fraud \\ˈfród\\ *n* **1** : DECEIT, TRICKERY **2** : TRICK **3** : IMPOSTOR, CHEAT

fraud·u·lent \\ˈfrój-ə-lənt\\ *adj* : characterized by, based on, or done by fraud : DECEITFUL — **fraud·u·lent·ly** *adv*

fraught \\ˈfrót\\ *adj* : ACCOMPANIED ⟨~ with memories⟩ **2** : bearing promise or menace

¹fray \\ˈfrā\\ *n* : BRAWL, FIGHT; *also* : DISPUTE

²fray *vb* **1** : to wear ⟨as an edge of cloth⟩ by rubbing **2** : to separate the threads at the edge of **3** : to wear out or into shreds **4** : STRAIN, IRRITATE ⟨~ed nerves⟩

fraz·zle \\ˈfraz-əl\\ *vb* **1** : FRAY **2** : to put in a state of extreme physical or nervous fatigue

freak \\ˈfrēk\\ *n* **1** : WHIM, CAPRICE **2** : a strange, abnormal, or unusual person or thing — **freak·ish** *adj*

freck·le \\ˈfrek-əl\\ *n* : a brownish spot on the skin — **freckle** *vb*

free \\ˈfrē\\ *adj* **1** : having liberty **2** : not controlled by others : INDEPENDENT; *also* : not allowing slavery **3** : not subject to a duty, tax, or other charge **4** : released or not suffering from something unpleasant **5** : given without charge **6** : made or done voluntarily : SPONTANEOUS **7** : LAVISH **8** : PLENTIFUL **9** : OPEN, FRANK **10** : not restricted by conventional forms **11** : not literal or exact **12** : not obstructed : CLEAR **13** : not being used or occupied **14 :** not fastened or bound — **free·ly** adv

²**free** adv **1 :** FREELY **2 :** without charge

³**free** vb **free** **1 :** to set free **2 :** RELIEVE, RID **3 :** DISENTANGLE, CLEAR syn release, liberate, discharge

free·board \'frē-ˌbōrd\ n **:** the vertical distance between the waterline and the deck of a ship

free·boot·er \-ˌbüt-ər\ n **:** PLUNDERER, PIRATE

free·born \-'bȯrn\ adj **1 :** not born in vassalage or slavery **2 :** relating to or befitting one that is freeborn

freed·man \'frēd-mən\ n **:** a man freed from slavery

free·dom \'frēd-əm\ n **1 :** the quality or state of being free **2 :** INDEPENDENCE **2 :** EXEMPTION, RELEASE **3 :** EASE, FACILITY **4 :** FRANKNESS **5 :** unrestricted use **6 :** a political right; also **:** FRANCHISE, PRIVILEGE

free·hand \'frē-ˌhand\ adj **:** done without mechanical aids or devices **:** FREE ⟨~ drawing⟩

free·hold \'frē-ˌhōld\ n **:** ownership of an estate for life usu. with the right to bequeath it to one's heirs; also **:** an estate thus owned — **free·hold·er** n

free·man \-mən\ n **1 :** one who has civil or political liberty **2 :** one having the full rights of a citizen

Free·ma·son \-'mās-ᵊn\ n **:** a member of a secret fraternal society called Free and Accepted Masons — **Free·ma·son·ry** n

free·stand·ing \-'stan-diŋ\ adj **:** standing alone or on its own foundation

free·stone \-ˌstōn\ n **1 :** a stone that may be cut freely without splitting **2 :** a fruit stone to which the flesh does not cling; also **:** a fruit (as a peach or cherry) having such a stone

free·think·er \-'thiŋ-kər\ n **:** one who forms opinions on the basis of reason independently of authority; esp **:** one who doubts or denies religious dogma — **free·think·ing** n or adj

free trade n **:** trade based upon the unrestricted international exchange of goods with tariffs used only as a source of revenue

free verse n **:** verse whose meter is irregular or whose rhythm is not metrical

free·way \'frē-ˌwā\ n **:** an expressway with fully controlled access

free·wheel \-'hwēl\ vb **:** to move, live, or drift along freely or irresponsibly

free will n **:** the power to choose without restraint of physical or divine necessity or causal law

free·will \ˌfrē-ˌwil\ adj **:** VOLUNTARY ⟨a ~ offering⟩

¹**freeze** \'frēz\ vb **froze** \'frōz\ **fro·zen** \'frōz-ᵊn\ **freez·ing** **1 :** to harden into ice or a like solid by loss of heat **2 :** to chill or become chilled with cold **3 :** to act or become coldly formal in manner **4 :** to act toward in a stiff and formal way **5 :** to damage by frost **6 :** to adhere solidly by freezing **7 :** to cause to grip tightly or remain in immovable contact **8 :** to clog with ice **9 :** to become fixed or motionless **10 :** to fix at a certain stage or level ⟨~ rents⟩

²**freeze** n **1 :** a state of weather marked by low temperature **2 :** an act or instance of freezing **3 :** the state of being frozen

freez·er n **:** one that freezes or keeps something cool; esp **:** a compartment for keeping food at a subfreezing temperature or for freezing perishable food rapidly

¹**freight** \'frāt\ n **1 :** payment for carrying goods **2 :** LOAD, CARGO **3 :** the carrying of goods by some common carrier **4 :** a train that carries freight

²**freight** vb **1 :** to load with goods for transportation **2 :** BURDEN, CHARGE **3 :** to ship or transport by freight — **freight·er** n

French \'french\ n **1 French** pl **:** the people of France **2 :** the language of France — **French** adj — **French·man** \-mən\ n

french fry vb, often cap 1st F **:** to fry (as strips of potato) in deep fat until brown — **french fries** n pl, often cap 1st F

fre·net·ic \fri-'net-ik\ adj **:** FRENZIED, FRANTIC — **fre·net·i·cal·ly** adv

fren·zy \'fren-zē\ n **:** temporary madness or a violently agitated state — **fren·zied** adj

fre·quen·cy \'frē-kwən-sē\ n **1 :** the fact or condition of occurring frequently **2 :** rate of occurrence **3 :** the number of cycles per second of an alternating electric current **4 :** the number of waves per second produced by a sounding body **5 :** the number of complete oscillations per second of an electromagnetic wave

frequency modulation n **:** modulation of the frequency of a transmitting radio wave in accordance with the strength of the audio or video signal; also **:** a broadcasting system using such modulation

¹**fre·quent** \'frē-kwənt\ adj **1 :** happening often or at short intervals **2 :** HABITUAL, CONSTANT — **fre·quent·ly** adv

²**fre·quent** \frē-'kwent\ vb **:** to visit often **:** associate with, be in, or resort to habitually — **fre·quent·er** n

fres·co \'fres-kō\ n, pl **-coes** or **-cos** **:** the art of painting on fresh plaster; also **:** a painting done by this method

fresh \'fresh\ adj **1 :** not salt ⟨~ water⟩ **2 :** PURE, INVIGORATING **3 :** fairly strong **:** BRISK ⟨~ breeze⟩ **4 :** not altered by processing (as freezing or canning) **5 :** VIGOROUS, REFRESHED **6 :** not stale, sour, or decayed ⟨~ bread⟩ **7 :** not faded **8 :** not worn or rumpled **:** SPRUCE **9 :** experienced, made, or received newly or anew **10 :** ADDITIONAL, ANOTHER ⟨made a ~ start⟩ **11 :** ORIGINAL, VIVID **12 :** INEXPERIENCED **13 :** newly come or arrived ⟨~ from school⟩ **14 :** IMPUDENT — **fresh·ly** adv — **fresh·ness** n

fresh·en \-ən\ vb **:** to make, grow, or become fresh

fresh·et \-ət\ n **:** an overflowing of a stream caused by heavy rains or melted snow

fresh·man \-mən\ n **1 :** NOVICE, NEWCOMER **2 :** a student in his first year (as in college)

fresh·wa·ter \-'wȯt-ər, -'wät-\ adj **1 :** of, relating to, or living in water that is not salt **2 :** accustomed to navigation

ə abut; ᵊr kitten; ər further; a back; ā bake; ä cot, cart; aù out; ch chin; e less; ē easy; g gift; i trip; ī life; j joke; ŋ sing; ō flow; ȯ flaw; ȯi coin; th thin; t͟h this; ü loot; ù foot; y yet; yü few; yù furious; zh vision

only on fresh water; *also* **:** UNSKILLED ⟨a ~ sailor⟩

¹**fret** \'fret\ *vb* **fret·ted; fret·ting 1 :** to become irritated **:** WORRY, VEX **2 :** WEAR, CORRODE **3 :** FRAY **4 :** to cause by wearing away **5 :** GRATE, RUB, CHAFE **6 :** AGITATE, RIPPLE

²**fret** *n* **1 :** EROSION **2 :** a worn or eroded spot **3 :** IRRITATION

³**fret** *n* **:** ornamental work esp. of straight lines in symmetrical patterns

⁴**fret** *n* **:** a metal or ivory ridge across the fingerboard of a stringed musical instrument

fret·ful *adj* **1 :** IRRITABLE **2 :** TROUBLED ⟨~ waters⟩ **3 :** GUSTY ⟨a ~ wind⟩ — **fret·ful·ly** *adv* — **fret·ful·ness** *n*

fret·work \'fret-,wərk\ *n* **1 :** decoration consisting of work adorned with frets **2 :** ornamental openwork or work in relief

fri·a·ble \'frī-ə-bəl\ *adj* **:** easily pulverized

fri·ar \'frī-(-ə)r\ *n* [OF *frere*, lit., brother, fr. L *fratr-, frater*] **:** a member of a mendicant religious order

fri·ary \-ē\ *n* **:** a monastery of friars

¹**fric·as·see** \'frik-ə-,sē\ *n* **:** a dish made of meat ⟨as chicken or veal⟩ cut into pieces and stewed in a gravy

²**fricassee** *vb* **:** to cook as a fricassee

fric·tion \'frik-shən\ *n* **1 :** the rubbing of one body against another **2 :** the resistance to motion between two surfaces that are touching each other in machinery **3 :** clash in opinions between persons or groups **:** DISAGREEMENT — **fric·tion·al** *adj*

friction tape *n* **:** a usu. cloth tape impregnated with insulating material and an adhesive and used esp. to protect and insulate electrical conductors

Fri·day \'frīd-ē\ *n* **:** the 6th day of the week

fried·cake \'frīd-,kāk\ *n* **:** DOUGHNUT, CRULLER

friend \'frend\ *n* **1 :** a person attached to another by respect or affection **:** ACQUAINTANCE **2 :** one who is not hostile **3 :** one who supports or favors something ⟨a ~ of art⟩ **4** *cap* **:** a member of the Society of Friends **:** QUAKER — **friend·less** *adj* — **friend·li·ness** *n* — **friend·ly** *adj* — **friend·ship** *n*

frieze \'frēz\ *n* **:** an ornamental often sculptured band extending around something ⟨as a building or room⟩

frig·ate \'frig-ət\ *n* **1 :** a square-rigged warship **2 :** a British or Canadian escort ship between a corvette and a destroyer in size **3 :** a U.S. warship smaller than a cruiser and larger than a destroyer

fright \'frīt\ *n* **1 :** sudden terror **:** ALARM **2 :** something that is ugly or shocking

fright·en \-ᵊn\ *vb* **1 :** to make afraid **:** TERRIFY **2 :** to drive away or out by frightening **3 :** to become frightened

fright·ful *adj* **1 :** TERRIFYING **2 :** STARTLING **3 :** EXTREME ⟨~ thirst⟩ — **fright·ful·ly** *adv* — **fright·ful·ness** *n*

frig·id \'frij-əd\ *adj* **1 :** intensely cold **2 :** lacking warmth or ardor **:** INDIFFERENT — **fri·gid·i·ty** \frij-'id-ət-ē\ *n*

frigid zone *n* **:** the area or region between the arctic circle and the north pole or between the antarctic circle and the south pole

frill \'fril\ *n* **1 :** a gathered, pleated, or ruffled edging **2 :** an ornamental addition **:** something unessential — **frilly** *adj*

fringe \'frinj\ *n* **1 :** an ornamental border consisting of short threads or strips hanging from cut or raveled edges or from a separate band **2 :** something that resembles a fringe **:** BORDER **3 :** something on the margin of an activity, process, or subject matter — **fringe** *vb*

fringe area *n* **:** a region in which reception from a broadcasting station is weak or subject to serious distortion

fringe benefit *n* **:** an employment benefit paid for by an employer without affecting basic wage rates

frip·pery \'frip-(ə-)rē\ *n* **1 :** cheap showy finery **2 :** pretentious display

frisk \'frisk\ *vb* **1 :** to leap, skip, or dance in a lively or playful way **:** GAMBOL **2 :** to search ⟨a person⟩ esp. for concealed weapons by running the hand rapidly over the clothing

frisky *adj* **:** FROLICSOME

¹**frit·ter** \'frit-ər\ *n* **:** a small quantity of fried or sautéed batter often containing fruit or meat

²**fritter** *vb* **1 :** to reduce or waste piecemeal **:** DISSIPATE **2 :** to break into small fragments

friv·o·lous \'friv-ə-ləs\ *adj* **1 :** of little importance **:** TRIVIAL **2 :** lacking in seriousness **:** PLAYFUL — **fri·vol·i·ty** \friv-'äl-ət-ē\ *n* — **friv·o·lous·ly** \'friv-ə-ləs-lē\ *adv*

frizz \'friz\ *vb* **:** to curl in small tight curls — **frizz** *n* — **frizzy** *adj*

¹**friz·zle** \'friz-əl\ *vb* **:** FRIZZ, CURL — **frizzle** *n* — **friz·zly** \-(ə-)lē\ *adj*

²**frizzle** *vb* **1 :** to fry until crisp and curled **2 :** to cook with a sizzling noise

fro \'frō\ *adv* **:** BACK, AWAY — used in the phrase *to and fro*

frock \'fräk\ *n* **1 :** an outer garment worn by monks and friars **2 :** an outer garment worn esp. by men **3 :** a woolen jersey worn esp. by sailors **4 :** a woman's or child's dress

frock coat *n* **:** a man's usu. double-breasted coat with knee-length skirts

frog \'frog, 'fräg\ *n* **1 :** a largely aquatic smooth-skinned tailless leaping amphibian **2 :** a soreness in the throat causing hoarseness **3 :** an ornamental braiding for fastening the front of a garment by a loop through which a button passes **4 :** an arrangement of rails where one railroad track crosses another

frog·man \-,man\ *n* **:** a swimmer having equipment ⟨as oxygen helmet and flippers⟩ that permits an extended stay under water usu. for observation or demolition

¹**frol·ic** \'fräl-ik\ *vb* **-icked; -ick·ing 1 :** to make merry **:** ROMP **2 :** to play about happily

²**frolic** *n* **1 :** a playful mischievous action **2 :** FUN, MERRIMENT — **frol·ic·some** *adj*

from \(')frəm, 'främ\ *prep* **:** forth out of — used to indicate a physical or abstract point of origin or beginning

frond \'fränd\ *n* **:** a usu. large divided leaf ⟨as of a fern⟩

¹**front** \'frənt\ *n* **1 :** FOREHEAD; *also* **:** the whole face **:** DEMEANOR, BEARING **2 :** external **3 :** external and often feigned appearance **4 :** a region of active fighting; *also* **:** a sphere of activity **5 :** the

side of a building containing the main entrance 6 : the forward part or surface 7 : FRONTAGE 8 : a position directly before or ahead of something else 9 : a person, group, or thing used to mask the identity or true character or activity of the actual controlling agent — front·al \'frənt-ᵊl\ adj

²front vb 1 : FACE 2 : to serve as a front 3 : CONFRONT

front·age \'frənt-ij\ n 1 : the front face (as of a building) 2 : the direction in which something faces 3 : the front boundary line of a lot on a street; also : the length of such a line

fron·tier \,frən-'tiər\ n 1 : a border between two countries 2 : a region that forms the margin of settled territory in a country being populated 3 : the outer limits of knowledge or achievement (the ~s of science) — fron·tiers·man \-'tiərz-mən\ n

fron·tis·piece \'frənt-ə-,spēs\ n : an illustration preceding and usu. facing the title page of a book

front man \'frənt-,man\ n : a person serving as a front or figurehead

¹frost \'frȯst\ n 1 : freezing temperature 2 : a covering of minute ice crystals formed on a cold surface from atmospheric vapor — frosty adj

²frost vb 1 : to cover with frost 2 : to put icing on (as a cake) 3 : to produce a slightly roughened surface on (as glass) 4 : to injure or kill by frost 5 : QUICK-FREEZE (~ed food)

frost·bite \'frȯs(t)-,bīt\ n : the freezing or the local effect of a partial freezing of some part of the body

frost·ing \'frȯs-tiŋ\ n 1 : ICING 2 : dull finish on metal or glass

froth \'frȯth\ n 1 : bubbles formed in or on a liquid by fermentation or agitation 2 : something light or frivolous — frothy adj

frou-frou \'frü-frü\ n 1 : a rustling esp. of a woman's skirts 2 : frilly ornamentation esp. in women's clothing

fro·ward \'frō-(w)ərd\ adj : PERVERSE, DISOBEDIENT, WILLFUL

frown \'fraun\ vb 1 : to wrinkle the forehead (as in anger, displeasure, or thought) 2 : SCOWL 2 : to look with disapproval 3 : to express with a frown — frown n

frow·zy or frow·sy \'frau-zē\ adj : having a slovenly or uncared-for appearance

froze past of FREEZE

fro·zen \'frōz-ᵊn\ adj 1 : affected or crusted over by freezing 2 : subject to long and severe cold 3 : CHILLED, REFRIGERATED 4 : expressing or characterized by cold unfriendliness 5 : incapable of being changed, moved, or undone : FIXED (~ wages) 6 : not available for present use (~ capital)

fruc·ti·fy \'frək-tə-,fī\ vb 1 : to bear fruit 2 : to make fruitful or productive

fru·gal \'frü-gəl\ adj : ECONOMICAL, THRIFTY — fru·gal·i·ty \frü-'gal-ət-ē\ n — fru·gal·ly adv

¹fruit \'früt\ n [OF, fr. L fructus fruit, profit, fr. frui to enjoy, have the use of] 1 : a usu. useful product of plant growth; esp : a usu. edible and sweet reproductive body of a seed plant 2 : a product of fertilization in a plant;

esp : the ripe ovary of a seed plant with its contents and appendages 3 : CONSEQUENCE, RESULT 4 : fruit·ful adj — fruit·ful·ness n — fruit·less adj

²fruit vb : to bear or cause to bear fruit

fruit·cake \-,kāk\ n : a rich cake containing nuts, dried or candied fruits, and spices

fruit·er·er \-ər-ər\ n : one that deals in fruit

fru·i·tion \frü-'ish-ən\ n 1 : ENJOYMENT 2 : the state of bearing fruit 3 : REALIZATION, ACCOMPLISHMENT

frus·trate \'frəs-,trāt\ vb 1 : to balk in an endeavor : BLOCK 2 : to bring to nothing : NULLIFY — frus·tra·tion \,frəs-'trā-shən\ n

¹fry \'frī\ vb 1 : to cook in a pan or on a griddle over a fire esp. with the use of fat 2 : to undergo frying

²fry n 1 : a dish of something fried 2 : a social gathering where fried food is eaten

³fry n, pl fry 1 : a young or tiny fish 2 : a young or insignificant individual (small ~)

fry·er \'frī(-ə)r\ n : something (as a pan) for frying; esp : a young chicken somewhat larger than a broiler

fuch·sia \'fyü-shə\ n : a shrub grown for its showy nodding often red or purple flowers

fud·dle \'fəd-ᵊl\ vb : MUDDLE, CONFUSE

fudge \'fəj\ n 1 : NONSENSE 2 : a soft creamy candy of milk, sugar, butter, and flavoring

¹fu·el \'fyü-əl\ n : a substance (as coal) used to produce heat or power by combustion; also : a substance from which atomic energy can be liberated

²fuel vb -eled or -elled; -el·ing or -el·ling : to provide with or take in fuel

fu·gi·tive \'fyü-jət-iv\ adj 1 : running away or trying to escape 2 : likely to vanish suddenly : not fixed or lasting

²fugitive n 1 : one who flees or tries to escape 2 : something elusive or hard to find

fugue \'fyüg\ n : a musical composition in which different parts successively repeat the theme

füh·rer or fueh·rer \'fyùr-ər, 'fir-\ n : LEADER — used chiefly of the leader of the German Nazis

¹-ful \fəl\ adj suffix 1 : full of (eventful) 2 : characterized by (peaceful) 3 : having the qualities of (masterful) 4 : -ABLE (mournful)

²-ful \,fùl\ n suffix : number or quantity that fills or would fill (roomful)

ful·crum \'fùl-krəm, 'fəl-\ n, pl -crums or -cra \-krə\ : the support on which a lever turns

ful·fill or ful·fil \fùl-'fil\ vb -filled; -fill·ing 1 : to put into effect 2 : to bring to an end 3 : SATISFY (~ requirements) — ful·fill·ment n

¹full \'fùl\ adj 1 : FILLED 2 : COMPLETE 3 : having all the distinguishing characteristics (a ~ member) 4 : MAXIMUM 5 : rounded in outline 6 : having an abundance of material (a ~ skirt) 7 : possessing or containing an abundance (~ of wrinkles) 8 : rich in detail (a ~ report) 9 : satisfied esp. with food or drink 10 : having volume or depth of sound 11 : completely occu-

pied with a thought or plan — **full·ness** also **ful·ness** n

²**full** adv **1** : VERY, EXTREMELY **2** : ENTIRELY **3** : EXACTLY **4** : STRAIGHT, SQUARELY ⟨hit him ∼ in the face⟩

³**full** n **1** : the utmost extent **2** : the highest or fullest state or degree **3** : the requisite or complete amount

⁴**full** vb **:** to shrink and thicken (woolen cloth) by moistening, heating, and pressing — **full·er** n

full·back \-ˌbak\ n **:** a football back stationed between the halfbacks

full-blood·ed \-ˈbləd-əd\ adj **:** of unmixed ancestry : PUREBRED

full-blown \-ˈblōn\ adj **1** : being at the height of bloom **2** : fully mature or developed

full-bod·ied \-ˈbäd-ēd\ adj **:** marked by richness and fullness

full dress n **:** the style of dress prescribed for ceremonial or formal social occasions

full-fledged \-ˈflejd\ adj **1** : fully developed **:** MATURE **2** : having full plumage

full moon n **:** the moon with its whole disk illuminated

full-scale \ˈful-ˈskāl\ adj **1** : identical to an original in proportion and size ⟨∼ drawing⟩ **2** : involving full use of available resources ⟨a ∼ biography⟩

full tilt adv **:** at high speed

ful·ly \ˈful-(l)ē\ adv **1** : in a full manner or degree **:** COMPLETELY **2** : at least ⟨∼ nine tenths of us⟩

ful·mi·nate \ˈful-mə-ˌnāt, ˈfəl-\ vb **1** : to utter or send out censure or invective **:** condemn severely **2** : EXPLODE — **ful·mi·na·tion** \ˌful-mə-ˈnā-shən, ˌfəl-\ n

ful·some \ˈful-səm\ adj **:** offensive esp. from insincerity or baseness of motive **:** DISGUSTING

fum·ble \ˈfəm-bəl\ vb **1** : to grope about clumsily **2** : to fail to hold, catch, or handle properly ⟨∼ a baseball⟩ — **fumble** n

¹**fume** \ˈfyüm\ n **:** a usu. irritating smoke, vapor, or gas

²**fume** vb **1** : to treat with fumes **2** : to give off fumes **3** : to express anger or annoyance

fu·mi·gant \ˈfyü-mi-gənt\ n **:** a substance used for fumigation

fu·mi·gate \ˈfyü-mə-ˌgāt\ vb **:** to treat with fumes to disinfect or destroy pests — **fu·mi·ga·tion** \ˌfyü-mə-ˈgā-shən\ n

fun \ˈfən\ n **1** : something that provides amusement or enjoyment **2** : AMUSEMENT, ENJOYMENT

¹**func·tion** \ˈfəŋk-shən\ n **1** : OCCUPATION **2** : special purpose **3** : a formal ceremony or social affair **4** : an action contributing to a larger action; esp **:** the normal contribution of a bodily part to the economy of the organism **5** : a mathematical quantity so related to another quantity that any change in the value of one is associated with a corresponding change in the other — **func·tion·al** adj — **func·tion·less** adj

²**function** vb **1** : SERVE **2** : OPERATE, WORK

func·tion·ary \ˈfəŋk-shə-ˌner-ē\ n **:** one who performs a certain function; esp **:** OFFICIAL

function word n **:** a word expressing primarily grammatical relationship

¹**fund** \ˈfənd\ n **1** : STORE, SUPPLY

2 : a sum of money or resources the income from which is set apart for a special purpose **3** pl **:** available money **4** : an organization administering a special fund

²**fund** vb **:** to convert (a short-term obligation) into a long-term interest-bearing debt

fun·da·men·tal \ˌfən-də-ˈment-ᵊl\ adj **:** PRIMARY, BASIC, RADICAL, PRINCIPAL — **fundamental** n — **fun·da·men·tal·ly** adv

fun·da·men·tal·ism \-ˌiz-əm\ n, often cap **:** a Protestant religious movement emphasizing the literal infallibility of the Scriptures — **fun·da·men·tal·ist** \-ist\ adj or n

¹**fu·ner·al** \ˈfyün-(ə-)rəl\ adj **1** : of, relating to, or constituting a funeral **2** : FUNEREAL **2**

²**funeral** n **:** the ceremonies held for a dead person usu. before burial

fu·ner·ary \ˈfyü-nə-ˌrer-ē\ adj **:** of, used for, or associated with burial

fu·ne·re·al \fyü-ˈnir-ē-əl\ adj **1** : of or relating to a funeral **2** : suggesting a funeral

fun·gi·cide \ˈfən-jə-ˌsīd\ n **:** an agent that kills or checks the growth of fungi — **fun·gi·cid·al** \ˌfən-jə-ˈsīd-ᵊl\ adj

fun·gus \ˈfəŋ-gəs\ n, pl **fun·gi** \ˈfən-ˌjī, ˈfəŋ-ˌgī\ also **fun·gus·es :** any of a large group of lower plants that lack chlorophyll and include molds, mildews, mushrooms, and bacteria — **fungous** \ˈfəŋ-gəs\ adj

fu·nic·u·lar \f(y)ü-ˈnik-yə-lər, fə-\ n **:** a cable railway ascending a mountain; esp **:** one in which an ascending car counterbalances a descending car

funk \ˈfəŋk\ n **:** a state of paralyzed fear **:** PANIC

¹**fun·nel** \ˈfən-ᵊl\ n **1** : a cone-shaped utensil with a tube used for catching and directing a downward flow (as of liquid) **2** : FLUE, SMOKESTACK

²**funnel** vb -neled also -nelled; -nel·ing also -nel·ling **1** : to pass through or as if through a funnel **2** : to move to a central point or into a central channel

¹**fun·ny** \ˈfən-ē\ adj **1** : AMUSING **2** : FACETIOUS **3** : QUEER **4** : UNDERHANDED **5** : COMIC

²**funny** n **:** a comic strip or a comic section of a newspaper or periodical ⟨let's look at the funnies⟩

funny bone n **:** a place at the back of the elbow where a blow compresses a nerve and causes a painful tingling sensation

fur \ˈfər\ n **1** : the hairy coat of a mammal esp. when fine, soft, and thick; also **:** this coat dressed for human use **2** : an article of clothing made of or with fur — **fur** adj

fur·be·low \ˈfər-bə-ˌlō\ n **1** : FLOUNCE, RUFFLE **2** : showy trimming

fur·bish \ˈfər-bish\ vb **1** : POLISH **2** : RENOVATE, REVIVE

fu·ri·ous \ˈfyur-ē-əs\ adj **1** : FIERCE, ANGRY, VIOLENT **2** : BOISTEROUS **3** : INTENSE — **fu·ri·ous·ly** adv

furl \ˈfərl\ vb **1** : to wrap or roll (as a sail or a flag) close to or around something **2** : to curl or fold in furls — **furl** n

fur·long \ˈfər-ˌlóŋ\ n **:** a unit of length equal to 220 yards

fur·lough \ˈfər-lō\ n **:** a leave of absence from duty granted esp. to a soldier — **furlough** vb

fur·nace \ˈfər-nəs\ n **:** an enclosed

structure in which heat is produced

fur·nish \'fər-nish\ *vb* 1 : to provide with what is needed : EQUIP 2 : SUPPLY, GIVE

fur·nish·ings *n pl* 1 : articles or accessories of dress (men's ~) 2 : FURNITURE

fur·ni·ture \'fər-ni-chər\ *n* : equipment that is necessary, useful, or desirable; *esp* : movable articles (as chairs, tables, or beds) for a room

fu·ror \'fyùr-,ór\ *n* 1 : ANGER, RAGE 2 : FURORE

fu·rore \-,ór\ *n* 1 : a contagious excitement; *esp* : a fashionable craze 2 : UPROAR

fur·ri·er \'fər-ē-ər\ *n* : one who prepares or deals in fur — **fur·ri·ery** *n*

fur·ring \'fər-iŋ\ *n* : wood or metal strips applied to a wall or ceiling to form a level surface or an air space

fur·row \'fər-ō\ *n* 1 : a trench in earth made by or as if by a plow 2 : a narrow groove (as a wrinkle) — **furrow** *vb*

fur·ry \'fər-ē\ *adj* 1 : resembling or consisting of fur 2 : covered with fur

¹fur·ther \'fər-thər\ *adv* 1 : ¹FARTHER 1 2 : in addition : MOREOVER 3 : to a greater extent or degree

²further *adj* 1 : ²FARTHER 1 2 : ADDITIONAL

³further *vb* : to help forward : PROMOTE — **fur·ther·ance** *n*

fur·ther·more \-,mór, -,mōr\ *adv* : in addition to what precedes : BESIDES

fur·ther·most \-,mōst\ *adj* : most distant : FARTHEST

fur·thest \'fər-thəst\ *adv (or adj)* : FARTHEST

fur·tive \'fərt-iv\ *adj* : done by stealth SLY, SECRET — **fur·tive·ly** *adv* — **fur·tive·ness** *n*

fu·ry \'fyùr-ē\ *n* 1 : violent anger : RAGE 2 : extreme fierceness or violence 3 : FRENZY

furze \'fərz\ *n* : a common spiny evergreen Old World shrub with yellow flowers

¹fuse \'fyüz\ *n* 1 : a tube filled with something flammable and lighted to transmit fire to an explosive 2 *usu* **fuze** : a mechanical or electrical device for exploding the bursting charge of a projectile, bomb, or torpedo

²fuse *or* **fuze** *vb* : to equip with a fuse

³fuse *vb* 1 : MELT 2 : to unite by or as if by melting together — **fus·ible** *adj*

⁴fuse *n* : an electrical safety device in which metal melts and interrupts the circuit when the current becomes too strong

fu·see \fyù-'zē\ *n* 1 : a friction match with a bulbous head not easily blown out 2 : a red signal flare used esp. for protecting stalled trains and trucks

fu·se·lage \'fyü-sə-,läzh, -zə-\ *n* : the central body portion of an airplane that holds the crew, passengers, and cargo

fu·sil·lade \'fyü-sə-,läd, -zə-\ *n* : a discharge or a succession of discharges of a number of firearms at one time

fu·sion \'fyü-zhən\ *n* 1 : the process of melting or melting together 2 : a merging (as of diverse elements) by or as if by melting : COALITION 3 : the union of atomic nuclei to form heavier nuclei with the release of huge quantities of energy

¹fuss \'fəs\ *n* 1 : needless bustle or excitement : COMMOTION 2 : effusive praise 3 : a state of agitation 4 : OBJECTION, PROTEST 5 : DISPUTE

²fuss *vb* 1 : to create or be in a state of restless activity; *esp* : to shower flattering attentions 2 : to pay undue attention to small details 3 : WORRY

fuss·bud·get \-,bəj-ət\ *n* : one who fusses about trifles

fussy *adj* 1 : IRRITABLE 2 : requiring or giving close attention to details 3 : FASTIDIOUS — **fuss·i·ly** *adv* — **fuss·i·ness** *n*

fus·tian \'fəs-chən\ *n* 1 : a strong cotton and linen cloth 2 : pretentious writing or speech

fus·ty \'fəs-tē\ *adj* 1 : MOLDY, MUSTY 2 : OLD-FASHIONED

fu·tile \'fyüt-ʾl\ *adj* 1 : USELESS, VAIN 2 : FRIVOLOUS, TRIVIAL — **fu·til·i·ty** \fyü-'til-ət-ē\ *n*

¹fu·ture \'fyü-chər\ *adj* 1 : coming after the present 2 : of, relating to, or constituting a verb tense that expresses time yet to come

²future *n* 1 : time that is to come 2 : what is going to happen 3 : an expectation of advancement or progressive development 4 : the future tense; *also* : a verb form in it

fu·tur·ism \-chə-,riz-əm\ *n* : a modern movement in art, music, and literature that tries esp. to express the energy and activity of contemporary life — **fu·tur·ist** *n*

fu·tur·is·tic \,fyü-chə-'ris-tik\ *adj* : of or relating to the future or to futurism

fu·tu·ri·ty \fyü-'t(y)ùr-ət-ē\ *n* 1 : FUTURE 2 : the quality or state of being future 3 *pl* : future events or prospects

fuze *var of* FUSE

fu·zee *var of* FUSEE

fuzz \'fəz\ *n* : fine light particles or fibers (as of down or fluff)

fuzzy *adj* 1 : covered with or resembling fuzz 2 : INDISTINCT

-fy \,fī\ *vb suffix* 1 : make : form into (dandify) 2 : invest with the attributes of : make similar to (citify) — **-fi·er** \,fī(-ə)r\ *n suffix*

---

g \'jē\ *n, often cap* 1 : the 7th letter of the English alphabet 2 : a unit of force equal to the force exerted by gravity on a body at rest and used to indicate the force to which a body is subjected when accelerated

gab \'gab\ *vb* **gabbed; gab·bing** : to talk in a rapid or thoughtless manner : CHATTER — **gab** *n*

gab·ar·dine \'gab-ər-,dēn\ *n* 1 : GABERDINE 2 : a firm durable twilled fabric having diagonal ribs and made of

---

various fibers; *also* **:** a garment of gabardine

gab·ble \'gab-əl\ *vb* **:** JABBER, BABBLE

gab·by \'gab-ē\ *adj* **:** TALKATIVE, GARRULOUS

gab·er·dine \'gab-ər-ˌdēn\ *n* **1 :** a long coat or smock worn chiefly by Jews in medieval times **2 :** an English laborer's smock **3 :** GABARDINE

gab·fest \'gab-ˌfest\ *n* **1 :** an informal gathering for general talk **2 :** an extended conversation

ga·ble \'gā-bəl\ *n* **:** the triangular part of the end of a building formed by the sides of the roof sloping from the ridgepole down to the eaves — **ga·bled** *adj*

gad \'gad\ *vb* **gad·ded; gad·ding :** to roam about **:** wander restlessly and without purpose — **gad·der** *n*

gad·about \'gad-ə-ˌbaut\ *n* **:** a person who flits about in social activity

gad·fly \'gad-ˌflī\ *n* **:** a fly that bites or harasses (as livestock)

gad·get \'gaj-ət\ *n* **:** DEVICE, CONTRIVANCE — **gad·ge·teer** \ˌgaj-ə-'tiər\ *n* — **gad·get·ry** \'gaj-ə-trē\ *n*

gad·o·lin·i·um \ˌgad-ʲl-'in-ē-əm\ *n* **:** a magnetic metallic chemical element

Gael \'gāl\ *n* **:** a Celtic inhabitant of Ireland or Scotland

Gael·ic \'gā-lik\ *adj* **:** of or relating to the Gaels or their languages — **Gaelic** *n*

gaff \'gaf\ *n* **1 :** a spear used in taking fish or turtles; *also* **:** a metal hook for holding or lifting heavy fish **2 :** the spar along the top of a fore-and-aft sail **3 :** rough treatment **:** ABUSE

gaffe \'gaf\ *n* **:** a social blunder

gaf·fer \'gaf-ər\ *n* **:** an old man

¹gag \'gag\ *vb* **gagged; gag·ging 1 :** to prevent from speaking or crying out by stopping up the mouth **2 :** to prevent from speaking freely **3 :** to cause to retch **:** RETCH **4 :** OBSTRUCT, CHOKE **5 :** BALK **6 :** to make quips

²gag *n* **1 :** something thrust into the mouth esp. to prevent speech or outcry **2 :** a check to free speech **3 :** a laugh-provoking remark or act **4 :** HOAX, TRICK

¹gage \'gāj\ *n* **1 :** a token of defiance; *esp* **:** a glove or cap cast on the ground as a pledge of combat **2 :** SECURITY

²gage *var of* GAUGE

gai·ety \'gā-ət-ē\ *n* **1 :** MERRYMAKING **2 :** MERRIMENT **3 :** FINERY

gai·ly \'gā-lē\ *adv* **:** in a gay manner

¹gain \'gān\ *n* **1 :** PROFIT, ADVANTAGE **2 :** ACQUISITION, ACCUMULATION **3 :** INCREASE — **gain·ful** *adj*

²gain *vb* **1 :** to get possession of **:** EARN **2 :** WIN (~ a victory) **3 :** ACHIEVE (~ strength) **4 :** to arrive at **5 :** PERSUADE **6 :** to increase in (~ momentum) **7 :** to run fast (the watch ~s a minute a day) **8 :** PROFIT **9 :** INCREASE **10 :** to improve in health — **gain·er** *n*

gain·say \gān-'sā\ *vb* **gain·said** \-'sād, -'sed\ **gain·say·ing 1 :** DENY, DISPUTE **2 :** to speak against **:** CONTRADICT — **gain·say·er** *n*

gait \'gāt\ *n* **:** manner of moving on foot; *also* **:** a particular pattern or style of such moving — **gait·ed** *adj*

gai·ter \'gāt-ər\ *n* **1 :** a leather or cloth leg covering reaching from the instep to ankle, mid calf, or knee **2 :** an ankle-high shoe with elastic gores in the sides **3 :** an overshoe with a fabric upper

ga·la \'gā-lə, 'gal-ə\ *n* **:** a gay celebration **:** FESTIVITY — **gala** *adj*

gal·axy \'gal-ək-sē\ *n* **1 :** often cap **:** MILKY WAY GALAXY **2 :** one of billions of systems each including stars, nebulae, and dust that make up the universe **3 :** an assemblage of brilliant or famous persons or things — **ga·lac·tic** \gə-'lak-tik\ *adj*

gale \'gāl\ *n* **1 :** a strong wind **2 :** an emotional outburst (as of laughter)

ga·le·na \gə-'lē-nə\ *n* **:** a bluish gray mineral with metallic luster consisting of sulfide of lead

¹gall \'gòl\ *n* **1 :** BILE **2 :** something bitter to endure **3 :** RANCOR **4 :** IMPUDENCE

²gall *n* **:** a sore on the skin caused by chafing

³gall *vb* **1 :** CHAFE; *esp* **:** to become sore or worn by rubbing **2 :** VEX, HARASS

⁴gall *n* **:** a swelling of plant tissue caused by parasites (as fungi or mites)

¹gal·lant \gə-'lant, -'länt\ *n* **1 :** a young man of fashion **2 :** a man who shows a marked fondness for the company of women and who is esp. attentive to them **3 :** SUITOR

²gal·lant \'gal-ənt (*usual for 3, 4*); gə-'lant, -'länt\ *adj* **1 :** showy in dress or bearing **2 :** SMART **3 :** SPLENDID, STATELY **3 :** SPIRITED, BRAVE **4 :** CHIVALROUS, NOBLE **5 :** polite and attentive to women — **gal·lant·ly** *adv*

gal·lant·ry \'gal-ən-trē\ *n* **1 :** archaic **:** gallant appearance **2 :** an act of marked courtesy **3 :** courteous attention to a woman **4 :** conspicuous bravery

gall·blad·der \'gòl-ˌblad-ər\ *n* **:** a pouch attached to the liver in which bile is stored

gal·le·on \'gal-ē-ən\ *n* **:** a former sailing vessel used for war or commerce esp. by the Spanish

gal·lery \'gal-(ə-)rē\ *n* **1 :** an outdoor balcony; *also* **:** PORCH, VERANDA **2 :** a balcony in a theater, auditorium, or church; *esp* **:** the highest one in a theater **3 :** a body of spectators (as at a tennis match) **4 :** a long narrow room or hall; *esp* **:** one with windows along one side **5 :** a narrow passage (as one made underground by a miner or through wood by an insect) **6 :** a room where works of art are exhibited; *also* **:** an organization dealing in works of art **7 :** an artist's studio — **gal·ler·ied** *adj*

gal·ley \'gal-ē\ *n* **1 :** a former ship propelled by both oars and sails **2 :** the kitchen of a ship, airplane, or train **3 :** a tray to hold printer's type that has been set; *also* **:** proof from type in such a tray

Gal·lic \'gal-ik\ *adj* **:** of or relating to Gaul or France

gal·li·mau·fry \ˌgal-ə-'mò-frē\ *n* **:** MEDLEY, JUMBLE

gal·li·um \'gal-ē-əm\ *n* **:** a rare bluish white metallic chemical element

gal·li·vant \'gal-ə-ˌvant\ *vb* **:** to go roaming about for pleasure

gal·lon \'gal-ən\ *n* **:** a unit of liquid capacity equal to four quarts

gal·lop \'gal-əp\ *n* **:** a springing gait of a quadruped; *esp* **:** a fast 3-beat gait of a horse — **gallop** *vb* — **gal·lop·er** *n*

gal·lows \'gal-ōz\ *n* **1 :** a frame usu. of two upright posts and a crosspiece from which criminals are hanged **2 :** a structure consisting of an upright frame with a crossbar

gall·stone \'gòl-ˌstōn\ *n* **:** an abnormal

concretion occurring in the gallbladder or bile passages

ga·lore \gə-'lōr\ *adj* [IrGael *go leor* in plenty, fr. *go* to + *leor* sufficiency] : ABUNDANT, PLENTIFUL ⟨gifts ~⟩

ga·losh \gə-'läsh\ *n* : a high overshoe worn esp. in snow and slush

gal·va·nism \'gal-və-ˌniz-əm\ *n* : electricity produced by chemical action in a battery — gal·van·ic \gal-'van-ik\ *adj*

gal·va·nize \'gal-və-ˌnīz\ *vb* **1** : to stimulate as if by an electric shock **2** : to coat (iron or steel) with zinc for protection against rust

gam·bit \'gam-bət\ *n* **1** : a chess opening in which a player risks one or more minor pieces to gain an advantage in position **2** : a calculated move : STRATAGEM

¹gam·ble \'gam-bəl\ *vb* **1** : to play a game for money or other stakes **2** : SPECULATE, BET, WAGER **3** : VENTURE, HAZARD — gam·bler *n*

²gamble *n* : a risky undertaking

gam·bol \'gam-bəl\ *vb* -boled *or* -bolled; -bol·ing *or* -bol·ling : to skip about in play : FRISK — gambol *n*

¹game \'gām\ *n* **1** : AMUSEMENT, DIVERSION **2** : SPORT, FUN **3** : SCHEME, PROJECT **4** : a line of work : PROFESSION **5** : CONTEST **6** : animals hunted for sport or food; *also* : the flesh of a game animal

²game *vb* : to play for a stake : GAMBLE

³game *adj* : PLUCKY — game·ly *adv* — game·ness *n*

⁴game *adj* : LAME ⟨a ~ leg⟩

game·cock \'gām-ˌkäk\ *n* : a male game fowl

game·keep·er \-ˌkē-pər\ *n* : one that has charge of the breeding and protection of game animals or birds on a private preserve

game·some \-səm\ *adj* : GAY, FROLICSOME

game·ster \-stər\ *n* : GAMBLER

ga·mete \gə-'mēt, 'gam-ˌēt\ *n* : a matured germ cell — ga·met·ic \gə-'met-ik\ *adj*

gam·in \'gam-ən\ *n* **1** : a boy who roams the streets : URCHIN **2** : GAMINE

ga·mine \ga-'mēn\ *n* **1** : a girl who roams the streets : TOMBOY **2** : a girl of elfin appeal

gam·ma glob·u·lin \ˌgam-ə-'gläb-yə-lən\ *n* : a blood protein fraction rich in antibodies

gamma rays *n pl* : penetrating radiation of the same nature as X rays but of shorter wavelength

gam·mer \'gam-ər\ *n* : an old woman

¹gam·mon \'gam-ən\ *n* : a cured ham or side of bacon

²gammon *n* : deceptive talk : HUMBUG

gam·ut \'gam-ət\ *n* : an entire range or series

gamy \'gā-mē\ *adj* **1** : GAME, PLUCKY **2** : having the flavor of game esp. when slightly tainted ⟨~ meat⟩ — gam·i·ness *n*

¹gan·der \'gan-dər\ *n* : a male goose

²gander *n, slang* : LOOK, GLANCE

¹gang \'gaŋ\ *n* **1** : a group of persons working, going about, or associated together **2** : a set of implements or devices arranged to operate together

²gang *vb* **1** : to attack in a gang — usu.

used with *up* **2** : to form into or move or act as a gang

gang·land \-ˌland\ *n* : the world of organized crime

gan·gling \'gaŋ-gliŋ\ *adj* : LANKY, SPINDLING

gan·gli·on \'gaŋ-glē-ən\ *n, pl* -glia \-glē-ə\ *also* -gli·ons : a mass of nerve cells : a nerve center either in or outside of the brain — gan·gli·on·ic \ˌgaŋ-glē-'än-ik\ *adj*

gang·plank \'gaŋ-ˌplaŋk\ *n* : a movable platform used in boarding or leaving a ship

gan·grene \'gaŋ-ˌgrēn, 'gaŋ-\ *n* : the dying of a part of the body due to interference with its nutrition — gangrene *vb* — gan·gre·nous \'gaŋ-grə-nəs\ *adj*

gang·ster \'gaŋ-stər\ *n* : a member of a gang of criminals : RACKETEER

gang·way \'gaŋ-ˌwā\ *n* **1** : a passage into, through, or out of an enclosed place **2** : GANGPLANK

gan·net \'gan-ət\ *n* : a large fish-eating seabird

gant·let \'gónt-lət\ *var of* GAUNTLET

gan·try \'gan-trē\ *n* : a frame structure on side supports over or around something ⟨a ~ for servicing a rocket⟩

gaol \'jāl\ *chiefly Brit var of* JAIL

gap \'gap\ *n* **1** : BREACH, CLEFT **2** : a mountain pass **3** : a break or separation in continuity : a blank space

gape \'gāp\ *vb* **1** : to open the mouth wide **2** : to open or part widely **3** : to stare with mouth open **4** : YAWN — gape *n*

ga·rage \gə-'räzh, -'räj\ *n* : a building for housing or repairing automobiles

¹garb \'gärb\ *n* **1** : style of dress **2** : CLOTHING, DRESS

²garb *vb* : CLOTHE, ARRAY

gar·bage \'gär-bij\ *n* : food waste

gar·ble \'gär-bəl\ *vb* : to distort the meaning or sound of ⟨~ a story⟩ ⟨~ words⟩ : REFUSE

gar·çon \gär-'sōⁿ\ *n* : WAITER

¹gar·den \'gärd-ᵊn\ *n* **1** : a plot for growing fruits, flowers, or vegetables **2** : a fertile region **3** : a public recreation area; *esp* : one for displaying plants or animals

²garden *vb* : to develop or work in a garden — gar·den·er *n*

gar·de·nia \gär-'dē-nyə\ *n* : a leathery-leaved tree or shrub with fragrant white or yellow flowers; *also* : its flower

gar·gle \'gär-gəl\ *vb* : to rinse the throat with liquid agitated by air forced through it from the lungs — gargle *n*

gar·goyle \'gär-ˌgóil\ *n* **1** : a waterspout in the form of a grotesque human or animal figure projecting from the roof or eaves of a building **2** : a grotesquely carved figure

gar·ish \'ga(ə)r-ish\ *adj* : FLASHY, GLARING, SHOWY, GAUDY

gar·land \'gär-lənd\ *n* : a wreath or rope of leaves or flowers

gar·lic \'gär-lik\ *n* : an herb related to the lilies and grown for its pungent bulbs used in cooking

gar·ment \'gär-mənt\ *n* : an article of clothing

gar·ner \'gär-nər\ *vb* **1** : to gather into

ə abut; ᵊ kitten; ər further; a back; ā bake; ä cot, cart; aú out; ch chin; e less; ē easy; g gift; i trip; ī life; j joke; ŋ sing; ō flow; ò flaw; òi coin; th thin; th̲ this; ü loot; ú foot; y yet; yü few; yú furious; zh vision

storage **2** : to acquire by effort : EARN **3** : ACCUMULATE, COLLECT

gar·net \'gär-nət\ n : a transparent deep red mineral sometimes used as a gem

gar·nish \'gär-nish\ vb **1** : DECORATE, EMBELLISH **2** : to add decorative or savory touches to (food) — **garnish** n — **gar·ni·ture** \-ni-chər\ n

gar·ret \'gar-ət\ n : the part of a house just under the roof : ATTIC

gar·ri·son \'gar-ə-sən\ n **1** : a military post; esp : a permanent military installation **2** : the troops stationed at a garrison — **garrison** vb

gar·rote or **ga·rotte** \gə-'rät, -'rōt\ n **1** : a method of execution by strangling with an iron collar; also : the iron collar used **2** : strangulation esp. for the purpose of robbery; also : an implement for this purpose — **garrote** or **garotte** vb

gar·ru·lous \'gar-ə-ləs\ adj : CHATTERING, TALKATIVE, WORDY — **gar·ru·li·ty** \gə-'rü-lət-ē\ n — **gar·ru·lous·ly** \'gar-ə-ləs-lē\ adv — **gar·ru·lous·ness** n

gar·ter \'gärt-ər\ n : a band or strap worn to hold up a stocking or sock

gas \'gas\ n **1** : a fluid (as hydrogen or air) that tends to expand indefinitely **2** : a gas or mixture of gases used as a fuel or anesthetic **3** : a substance that can be used to produce a poisonous, asphyxiating, or irritant atmosphere **4** : GASOLINE — **gas** vb — **gas·eous** \-ē-əs\ adj

gash \'gash\ n : a deep long cut — **gash** vb

gas·ket \'gas-kət\ n : material (as asbestos, rubber, or metal) used to seal a joint against leakage of fluid

gas·light \'gas-,līt\ n **1** : light made by burning illuminating gas **2** : a gas flame; also : a gas lighting fixture

gas·o·line or **gas·o·lene** \,gas-ə-'lēn\ n : a flammable liquid made esp. by blending products from natural gas and petroleum and used as a motor fuel and cleaning fluid

gasp \'gasp\ vb **1** : to catch the breath with emotion (as shock) **2** : to breathe laboriously : PANT **3** : to utter in a gasping manner — **gasp** n

gas·tric \'gas-trik\ adj : of, relating to, or located near the stomach

gastric juice n : the acid digestive secretion of the stomach

gas·tri·tis \gas-'trīt-əs\ n : inflammatory disorder of the stomach

gas·tron·o·my \gas-'trän-ə-mē\ n : the art of good eating — **gas·tro·nom·ic** \,gas-trə-'näm-ik\ adj — **gas·tro·nom·i·cal** adj

gas·tro·pod \'gas-trə-,päd\ n : any of a large group of mollusks (as snails, whelks, and slugs) with a muscular foot and a shell of one valve

gas·works \'gas-,wərks\ n pl : a plant for manufacturing gas

gate \'gāt\ n **1** : an opening for passage in a wall or fence **2** : a city or castle entrance often with defensive structures **3** : the frame or door that closes a gate **4** : a device (as a door or valve) for controlling the flow of a fluid **5** : the total admission receipts or the number of spectators at a sports event

gate–crash·er \-,krash-ər\ n : one who enters without paying admission or

attends without invitation

gate·post \-,pōst\ n : the post to which a gate is hung or the one against which it closes

gate·way \-,wā\ n **1** : an opening for a gate in a wall or fence **2** : a passage into or out of a place or state

¹gath·er \'gath-ər\ vb **1** : to bring together **2** : COLLECT **2** : PICK, HARVEST **3** : to pick up little by little **4** : to gain or win by gradual increase (~ speed) **5** : ACCUMULATE **6** : to summon up (~ courage to dive) **7** : to draw about or close to something **8** : to pull (fabric) along a line of stitching into puckers **9** : GUESS, DEDUCE, INFER **10** : ASSEMBLE **11** : to swell out and fill with pus **12** : GROW, INCREASE — **gath·er·er** n — **gath·er·ing** n

²gather n : a puckering in cloth made by gathering

gauche \'gōsh\ adj : lacking social experience or grace : AWKWARD, CRUDE

gau·che·rie \,gōsh-(ə-)'rē\ n : a tactless or awkward action

gau·cho \'gaü-chō\ n : a cowboy of the So. American pampas

gaud \'gód\ n : ORNAMENT, TRINKET

gaudy adj : ostentatiously or tastelessly ornamented syn garish, flashy — **gaud·i·ly** adv — **gaud·i·ness** n

¹gauge \'gāj\ n **1** : measurement according to some standard or system **2** : DIMENSIONS, SIZE **3** : an instrument for measuring, testing, or registering

²gauge vb **1** : MEASURE **2** : to determine the capacity or contents of **3** : ESTIMATE, JUDGE

gaunt \'gónt\ adj **1** : being thin and angular : LANK, HAGGARD **2** : GRIM, BARREN, DESOLATE — **gaunt·ness** n

¹gaunt·let \'gónt-lət\ n **1** : a protective glove **2** : a challenge to combat **3** : a dress glove extending above the wrist

²gauntlet n **1** : a double file of men armed with weapons (as clubs) with which to strike at an individual who is made to run between them **2** : ORDEAL

gauze \'góz\ n : a very thin often transparent fabric used chiefly for clothing, draperies, or surgical dressings — **gauzy** adj

gave past of GIVE

gav·el \'gav-əl\ n : the mallet of a presiding officer or auctioneer

ga·votte \gə-'vät\ n : a dance of French peasant origin marked by the raising of the feet

gawk \'gók\ vb : to gape or stare stupidly

gawky \'gó-kē\ adj : AWKWARD, CLUMSY

gay \'gā\ adj **1** : MERRY **2** : BRIGHT, LIVELY **3** : brilliant in color **4** : given to social pleasures; also : LICENTIOUS

gay·ety, gay·ly var of GAIETY, GAILY

gaze \'gāz\ vb : to fix the eyes in a steady intent look — **gaze** n — **gaz·er** n

ga·ze·bo \gə-'zā-bō, -'zē-\ n : BELVEDERE

ga·zelle \gə-'zel\ n : a small swift graceful antelope

¹ga·zette \gə-'zet\ n **1** : NEWSPAPER **2** : an official journal

²gazette vb, chiefly Brit : to announce or publish in a gazette

gaz·et·teer \,gaz-ə-'tər\ n **1** archaic : JOURNALIST, PUBLICIST **2** : a geographical dictionary

gear \'giər\ n **1** : CLOTHING **2** : EQUIPMENT (fishing ~) (photographic ~) **3** : movable property **4** : a mechanism that performs a specific function ⟨steering ~⟩ **5** : a toothed wheel that interlocks with another toothed wheel or shaft for transmitting motion **6** : working adjustment of gears ⟨in ~⟩ **7** : one of several adjustments of automobile transmission gears that determine direction of travel and relative speed between engine and motion of vehicle ⟨reverse ~⟩ ⟨first ~⟩ — **gear** vb — **gear·ing** n

gear·shift \-,shift\ n : a mechanism by which automobile transmission gears are engaged or disengaged

geese pl of GOOSE

Gei·ger counter \'gī-gər-\ or **Geiger-Mül·ler counter** \-'myül-ər-\ n : an electronic instrument for indicating (as by clicks) the presence of cosmic rays or radioactive substances

gei·sha \'gā-shə, 'gē-\ n, pl **geisha** or **geishas** : a Japanese girl who is trained to provide entertaining company for men

gel·a·tin also **gel·a·tine** \'jel-ət-ᵊn\ n : a glutinous substance obtained from animal tissues by boiling and used as a food, in dyeing, and in photography — **ge·lat·i·nous** \jə-'lat-(ᵊ-)nəs\ adj

geld \'geld\ vb : CASTRATE

geld·ing n : a gelded individual; esp : a castrated male horse

gel·id \'jel-əd\ adj : extremely cold

gem \'jem\ n **1** : JEWEL **2** : a more or less valuable stone cut and polished for ornament **3** : something valued for beauty or perfection

gem·i·nate \'jem-ə-,nāt\ vb : DOUBLE — **gem·i·na·tion** \,jem-ə-'nā-shən\ n

gem·stone \'jem-,stōn\ n : a mineral or petrified material that when cut and polished can be used in jewelry

gen·darme \'zhän-,därm, 'jän-\ n [F, soldier, gendarme, back-formation fr. gens d'armes, lit., people of arms] : one of a body of soldiers esp. in France serving as an armed police force

gen·dar·mer·ie \jän-'där-mə-rē, zhän-\ n : a body of gendarmes

gen·der \'jen-dər\ n **1** : SEX **2** : any of two or more divisions within a grammatical class that determine agreement with and selection of other words or grammatical forms

gene \'jēn\ n : one of the complex chemical units of a chromosome that are the actual carriers of heredity — **gen·ic** \'jē-nik\ adj

ge·ne·al·o·gy \,jēn-ē-'äl-ə-jē, ,jen-, -'al-\ n : PEDIGREE, LINEAGE; also : the study of family pedigrees — **ge·ne·a·log·i·cal** \-ē-ə-'läj-i-kəl\ adj

genera pl of GENUS

¹gen·er·al \'jen-(ə-)rəl\ adj **1** : of or relating to the whole : not local **2** : taken as a whole **3** : relating to or covering all instances or individuals of a class or group ⟨a ~ conclusion⟩ **4** : not limited in meaning : not specific ⟨a ~ outline⟩ **5** : common to many : PREVALENT ⟨a ~ custom⟩ **6** : not special or specialized **7** : not precise or definite **8** : holding superior rank : CHIEF ⟨inspector ~⟩ — **gen·er·al·ly** adv

²general n **1** : something that involves or is applicable to the whole **2** : a commissioned officer ranking next below a general of the army or a general of the

air force **3** : a commissioned officer of the highest rank in the marine corps

gen·er·a·lis·si·mo \,jen-(ə-)rə-'lis-ə-,mō\ n : the chief commander of an army : COMMANDER IN CHIEF

gen·er·al·i·ty \,jen-ə-'ral-ət-ē\ n **1** : the quality or state of being general **2** : GENERALIZATION **2 3** : a vague or inadequate statement **4** : the greatest part : BULK

gen·er·al·iza·tion \,jen-(ə-)rə-lə-'zā-shən\ n **1** : the act or process of generalizing **2** : a general statement, law, principle, or proposition

gen·er·al·ize \'jen-(ə-)rə-,līz\ vb **1** : to make general **2** : to draw general conclusions from **3** : to reach a general conclusion esp. on the basis of particular instances **4** : to extend throughout the body

general of the air force : a commissioned officer of the highest rank in the air force

general of the army : a commissioned officer of the highest rank in the army

gen·er·al·ship n **1** : office or tenure of office of a general **2** : military skill as a high commander **3** : LEADERSHIP

gen·er·ate \'jen-ə-,rāt\ vb : to bring into existence : PRODUCE; esp : to originate (as electricity) by a vital or chemical process

gen·er·a·tion \,jen-ə-'rā-shən\ n **1** : a body of living beings constituting a single step in the line of descent from an ancestor; also : the average period between generations **2** : PRODUCTION ⟨~ of electric current⟩ — **gen·er·a·tive** \'jen-ə-,rāt-iv, -(ə-)rət-\ adj

gen·er·a·tor \'jen-ə-,rāt-ər\ n : one that generates; esp : a machine by which mechanical energy is changed into electrical energy

ge·ner·ic \jə-'ner-ik\ adj **1** : not specific : GENERAL **2** : of or relating to a genus

gen·er·ous \'jen-(ə-)rəs\ adj **1** : free in giving or sharing : UNSELFISH **2** : HIGH-MINDED, NOBLE **3** : ABUNDANT, AMPLE, COPIOUS — **gen·er·os·i·ty** \,jen-ə-'räs-ət-ē\ n — **gen·er·ous·ly** \'jen-(ə-)rəs-lē\ adv — **gen·er·ous·ness** n

gen·e·sis \'jen-ə-səs\ n, pl **-e·ses** \-,sēz\ : the origin or coming into existence of something

ge·net·ic \jə-'net-ik\ adj : of or relating to the origin, development, or causes of something; also : of or relating to genetics — **ge·net·i·cal·ly** adv

ge·net·ics n : a branch of biology dealing with heredity and variation

ge·nial \'jē-nyəl\ adj **1** : favorable to growth or comfort ⟨~ sunshine⟩ **2** : CHEERFUL, CHEERING, KINDLY ⟨a ~ host⟩ — **ge·ni·al·i·ty** \,jē-nē-'al-ət-ē, jēn-'yal-\ n — **ge·nial·ly** \'jē-nyə-lē\ adv

-gen·ic \'jen-ik\ adj comb form **1** : producing : forming **2** : produced by : formed from **3** : suitable for production or reproduction by (such) a medium

ge·nie \'jē-nē\ n, pl **genies** also **ge·nii** \-nē-,ī\ : a supernatural spirit that often takes human form

gen·i·tal \'jen-ə-tᵊl\ adj : concerned with reproduction ⟨~ organs⟩ — **geni·tal** n

---

ə abut; ᵊ kitten; ər further; a back; ā bake; ä cot, cart; aů out; ch chin; e less; ē easy; g gift; i trip; ī life; j joke; ŋ sing; ō flow; ȯ flaw; ȯi coin; th thin; t͟h this; ü loot; ů foot; y yet; yü few; yů furious; zh vision

gen·i·ta·lia \,jen-ə-'tā-lē-ə\ *n pl* : reproductive organs; *esp* : the external genital organs

gen·i·tive \'jen-ət-iv\ *adj* : of, relating to, or constituting a grammatical case marking typically a relationship of possessor or source — **genitive** *n*

ge·nius \'jē-nyəs\ *n, pl* **ge·nius·es** *or esp in 1 & 5* **ge·nii** \-nē-,ī\ 1 : an attendant spirit of a person or place 2 : a strong leaning or inclination 3 : a peculiar or distinctive character or spirit (as of a nation or a language) 4 : the associations and traditions of a place 5 : a nature spirit; *also* : a person who influences another for good or evil 6 : a single strongly marked capacity or aptitude 7 : extraordinary intellectual power; *also* : a person having such power

gen·o·cide \'jen-ə-,sīd\ *n* : the deliberate and systematic destruction of a racial, political, or cultural group

-ge·nous \j-ə-nəs\ *adj comb form* 1 : producing : yielding 2 : having (such) an origin

genre \'zhä(ⁿ)n-rə, 'zhän(-ə)r\ *n* 1 : a style of painting in which everyday subjects are treated realistically 2 : a distinctive type or category of literary composition

gens \'jenz, 'gens\ *n, pl* **gen·tes** \'jen-,tēz, 'gen-,tās\ : a Roman clan embracing the families of the same stock in the male line

gent \'jent\ *n* : MAN, FELLOW

gen·teel \jen-'tēl\ *adj* 1 : ARISTOCRATIC 2 : ELEGANT, STYLISH 3 : POLITE, REFINED 4 : maintaining the appearance of superior or middle-class social status or respectability 5 : marked by false delicacy, prudery, or affectation

gen·tian \'jen-chən\ *n* : a fall-flowering herb with blue flowers

gen·tile \'jen-,tīl\ *n* [LL *gentilis* heathen, pagan, lit., belonging to the nations, fr. L *gent-, gens* family, clan, nation] 1 *often cap* : a person who is not Jewish 2 : HEATHEN, PAGAN — **gentile** *adj, often cap*

gen·til·i·ty \jen-'til-ət-ē\ *n* 1 : good birth and family 2 : the qualities characteristic of a well-bred person 3 : good manners 4 : maintenance of the appearance of superior or middle-class social status

¹**gen·tle** \'jent-ᵊl\ *adj* 1 : belonging to a family of high social station 2 : of, relating to, or characteristic of a gentleman 3 : KIND, AMIABLE 4 : TRACTABLE, DOCILE 5 : not harsh, stern, or violent : MILD 6 : SOFT, DELICATE 7 : MODERATE — **gent·ly** \'jent-lē\ *adv*

²**gentle** *vb* 1 : to make mild, docile, soft, or moderate 2 : MOLLIFY, PLACATE

gen·tle·folk \'jent-ᵊl-,fōk\ *also* **gen·tle·folks** *n pl* : persons of good family and breeding

gen·tle·man \-mən\ *n* 1 : a man of good family 2 : a well-bred man 3 : MAN — used in pl. as a form of address — **gen·tle·man·ly** *adj*

gen·tle·wom·an \-,wům-ən\ *n* 1 : a woman of good family or breeding 2 : a woman attending a lady of rank

gen·try \'jen-trē\ *n* 1 : people of good birth, breeding, and education : ARISTOCRACY 2 : the class of English people between the nobility and the yeomanry 3 : PEOPLE; *esp* : persons of a designated class

gen·u·flect \'jen-yə-,flekt\ *vb* : to bend the knee esp. in worship — **gen·u·flec·tion** *or* **gen·u·flex·ion** \,jen-yə-'flek-shən\ *n*

gen·u·ine \'jen-yə-wən\ *adj* 1 : AUTHENTIC, REAL 2 : SINCERE, HONEST — **gen·u·ine·ly** *adv* — **gen·u·ine·ness** *n*

ge·nus \'jē-nəs\ *n, pl* **gen·era** \'jen-ə-rə\ : a category of biological classification comprising related organisms and usu. consisting of several species

ge·og·ra·phy \jē-'äg-rə-fē\ *n* 1 : a science that deals with the natural features of the earth and the climate, products, and inhabitants 2 : the natural features of a region — **ge·og·ra·pher** \-fər\ *n* — **geo·graph·ic** \,jē-ə-'graf-ik\ *or* **geo·graph·i·cal** *adj* — **geo·graph·i·cal·ly** *adv*

ge·ol·o·gy \jē-'äl-ə-jē\ *n* 1 : a science that deals with the history of the earth and its life esp. as recorded in rocks 2 : the geologic features of an area — **geo·log·ic** \,jē-ə-'läj-ik\ *or* **geo·log·i·cal** *adj* — **ge·ol·o·gist** \jē-'äl-ə-jəst\ *n*

ge·om·e·try \jē-'äm-ə-trē\ *n* : a branch of mathematics dealing with the relations, properties, and measurements of solids, surfaces, lines, and angles — **geo·met·ric** \,jē-ə-'me-trik\ *or* **geo·met·ri·cal** *adj*

geo·pol·i·tics \,jē-ō-'päl-ə-,tiks\ *n* : a science based on the theory that domestic and foreign politics of a country are dependent on physical geography

ge·ra·ni·um \jə-'rā-nē-əm\ *n* 1 : a purple or pink wild flower with deeply cut leaves 2 : a garden plant with clusters of usu. white, pink, or scarlet flowers

ger·i·at·ric \,jer-ē-'at-rik\ *adj* : of or relating to aging, the aged, or geriatrics

ger·i·at·rics *n* : a branch of medicine dealing with the aged and the problems of aging

germ \'jərm\ *n* 1 : a bit of living matter capable of growth and development (as into an organism); *also* : MICROBE 2 : SOURCE, RUDIMENT

Ger·man \'jər-mən\ *n* 1 : a native or inhabitant of Germany 2 : the language of Germany — **German** *adj* — **Ger·man·ic** \(,)jər-'man-ik\ *adj*

ger·mane \(,)jər-'mān\ *adj* : RELEVANT, PERTINENT

ger·ma·ni·um \(,)jər-'mā-nē-əm\ *n* : a grayish white hard chemical element used as a semiconductor

ger·mi·cide \'jər-mə-,sīd\ *n* : an agent that destroys microbes — **ger·mi·cid·al** \,jər-mə-'sīd-ᵊl\ *adj*

ger·mi·nate \'jər-mə-,nāt\ *vb* : to begin to develop : SPROUT — **ger·mi·na·tion** \,jər-mə-'nā-shən\ *n*

ger·on·tol·o·gy \,jer-ən-'täl-ə-jē\ *n* : a scientific study of aging and the problems of the aged — **ger·on·tol·o·gist** *n*

ger·ry·man·der \,jer-ē-'man-dər, 'jer-\ *vb* : to divide (as a state or county) into election districts so as to give one political party an advantage over its opponents — **gerrymander** *n*

ger·und \'jer-ənd\ *n* : a word having the characteristics of both verb and noun

ge·sta·po \gə-'stäp-ō\ *n* : a secret police organization operating esp. against suspected political criminals

ges·ta·tion \jes-'tā-shən\ *n* : PREGNANCY, INCUBATION — **ges·tate** \'jes-,tāt\ *vb*

ges·tic·u·late \jes-'tik-yə-ˌlāt\ vb : to make gestures esp. when speaking — **ges·tic·u·la·tion** \-ˌtik-yə-'lā-shən\ n

ges·ture \'jes-chər\ n 1 : the use of motions of the body or limbs as a means of expression 2 : a movement usu. of the body or limbs that expresses or emphasizes an idea, sentiment, or attitude 3 : something said or done by way of formality or courtesy, as a symbol or token, or for its effect on the attitudes of others — **gesture** vb

ge·sund·heit \gə-'zunt-ˌhīt\ interj — used to wish good health esp. to one who has just sneezed

¹**get** \'get\ vb \got \'gät\ got or got·ten \'gät-ᵊn\ get·ting 1 : to gain possession of (as by receiving, acquiring, earning, buying, or winning) : PROCURE, OBTAIN, FETCH 2 : to succeed in coming or going 3 : to cause to come or go 4 : BEGET 5 : to cause to be in a certain condition or position 6 : BECOME (~ sick) 7 : PREPARE 8 : SEIZE 9 : to move emotionally; also : IRRITATE 10 : BAFFLE, PUZZLE 11 : HIT 12 : KILL 13 : to be subjected to (~ the measles) 14 : to receive as punishment 15 : to find out by calculation 16 : HEAR; also : UNDERSTAND 17 : PERSUADE, INDUCE 18 : HAVE (he's got no money) 19 : to have as an obligation or necessity (he has got to go) 20 : to establish communication with 21 : to be able : CONTRIVE, MANAGE 22 : to leave at once

²**get** n : OFFSPRING, PROGENY

get·away \'get-ə-ˌwā\ n 1 : ESCAPE 2 : the action of starting or getting under way (as by an automobile starting from a dead stop)

get-to·geth·er \'get-tə-ˌgeth-ər\ n : MEETING; esp : an informal social gathering

get-up \'get-ˌəp\ n 1 : general composition or structure 2 : OUTFIT, COSTUME

gew·gaw \'g(y)ü-ˌgo\ n : a showy trifle : BAUBLE, TRINKET

gey·ser \'gī-zər\ n [fr. Geysir, a geyser in Haukadal, Iceland, fr. Icelandic geysa to gush] : a spring that from time to time shoots up hot water and steam

Gha·na·ian \gä-'nä-(y)ən, gə-\ n : a native or inhabitant of Ghana — **Ghanaian** adj

ghast·ly \'gast-lē\ adj 1 : HORRIBLE, SHOCKING 2 : resembling a ghost : DEATHLIKE, PALE syn gruesome, grim, lurid

ghat \'gót\ n : a landing place with stairs descending to a river in India

gher·kin \'gər-kən\ n : a small spiny pale cucumber used for pickling; also : a young common cucumber similarly used

ghet·to \'get-ō\ n, pl -tos or -toes : a quarter of a city in which members of a minority group (as Jews) live because of social, legal, or economic pressure

ghost \'gōst\ n 1 : the seat of life : SOUL 2 : a disembodied soul; esp : the soul of a dead person believed to be an inhabitant of the unseen world or to appear in bodily form to living people 3 : SPIRIT, DEMON 4 : a faint trace or suggestion (a ~ of a smile) — **ghost·ly** adv

ghost·write \-ˌrīt\ vb : to write for and

in the name of another — **ghost–writ·er** n

ghoul \'gül\ n : a legendary evil being that robs graves and feeds on corpses — **ghoul·ish** adj

¹**GI** \(')jē-'ī\ adj 1 : provided by an official U.S. military supply department (GI shoes) 2 : of, relating to, or characteristic of U.S. military personnel 3 : conforming to military regulations or customs (a GI haircut)

²**GI** n : a member or former member of the U.S. armed forces; esp : an enlisted man

gi·ant \'jī-ənt\ n 1 : a huge legendary manlike being of great strength 2 : a living being or thing of extraordinary size or powers — **giant** adj — **gi·ant·ess** n

gib·ber \'jib-ər\ vb : to speak rapidly, inarticulately, and often foolishly : CHATTER

gib·ber·ish n : unintelligible, confused, or meaningless speech or language

¹**gib·bet** \'jib-ət\ n : GALLOWS

²**gibbet** vb 1 : to hang on a gibbet 2 : to expose to public scorn 3 : to execute by hanging

gib·bon \'gib-ən\ n : a manlike ape of southeastern Asia and the East Indies

gibe \'jīb\ vb : to utter taunting words : SNEER — **gibe** n

gib·let \'jib-lət\ n : the edible inner organs of a bird (as a fowl) (chicken ~s)

Gib·son \'gib-sən\ n : a cocktail made of gin and dry vermouth and garnished with a small onion

gid·dy \'gid-ē\ adj 1 : DIZZY 2 : causing dizziness 3 : not serious : FRIVOLOUS, FICKLE — **gid·di·ness** n

gift \'gift\ n 1 : the act or power of giving 2 : something given : PRESENT 3 : a special ability : TALENT

gift·ed adj : TALENTED

¹**gig** \'gig\ n 1 : a long light ship's boat 2 : a light 2-wheeled carriage

²**gig** n : a pronged spear for catching fish — **gig** vb

³**gig** n : a military demerit — **gig** vb

gi·gan·tic \jī-'gant-ik\ adj : resembling a giant : IMMENSE, HUGE

gig·gle \'gig-əl\ vb : to laugh with repeated short catches of the breath : laugh in a silly manner — **giggle** n — **gig·gly** \-(ə-)lē\ adj

gig·o·lo \'jig-ə-ˌlō\ n 1 : a man living on the earnings of a woman 2 : a professional dancing partner or male escort

¹**gild** \'gild\ vb gild·ed or gilt \'gilt\ gild·ing 1 : to overlay with or as if with a thin covering of gold 2 : to give an attractive but often deceptive outward appearance to — **gild·ing** n

²**gild** var of GUILD

¹**gill** \'jil\ n : a U.S. liquid unit equal to ¼ of a liquid pint

²**gill** \'gil\ n : an organ (as of a fish) for obtaining oxygen from water

¹**gilt** \'gilt\ adj : of the color of gold

²**gilt** n : gold or a substance resembling gold laid on the surface of an object

³**gilt** n : a young female swine

gim·crack \'jim-ˌkrak\ n : a showy object of little use or value

gim·let \'gim-lət\ n : a small tool with screw point and cross handle for boring

gim·mick \'gim-ik\ n 1 : CONTRIVANCE,

GADGET; *esp* : one used secretly or illegally **2** : an important feature that is not immediately apparent : CATCH **3** : a new and ingenious scheme

gimpy \'gim-pē\ *adj* : CRIPPLED, LAME

¹**gin** \'jin\ *n* **1** : TRAP, SNARE **2** : a machine to separate seeds from cotton — **gin** *vb*

²**gin** *n* : a liquor distilled from a grain mash and flavored with juniper berries

gin·ger \'jin-jər\ *n* : the pungent aromatic rootstock of a tropical plant used esp. as a spice and in medicine; *also* : this plant

gin·ger·bread \-,bred\ *n* **1** : a cake made with molasses and flavored with ginger **2** : tawdry, gaudy, or superfluous ornament

gin·ger·ly \jə-\lē\ *adj* : very cautious or careful — **gingerly** *adv*

gin·ger·snap \-,snap\ *n* : a thin brittle molasses cookie flavored with ginger

ging·ham \'giŋ-əm\ *n* : a clothing fabric usu. of yarn-dyed cotton in plain weave

Gipsy *var of* GYPSY

gi·raffe \jə-'raf\ *n* : an African ruminant mammal with an extraordinarily long neck

gird \'gərd\ *vb* **gird·ed** *or* **girt** \'gərt\ **gird·ing 1** : to encircle or fasten with or as if with a belt : GIRDLE ⟨~ on a sword⟩ **2** : SURROUND **3** : to clothe or invest esp. with power or authority **4** : PREPARE, BRACE ⟨~ed themselves for a struggle⟩

gird·er \'gərd-ər\ *n* : a strong horizontal beam on which the weight of a floor or partition is carried

gir·dle \'gərd-ᵊl\ *n* **1** : something (as a belt or sash) that encircles or confines **2** : a woman's supporting undergarment that extends from the waist to below the hips — **girdle** *vb*

girl \'gərl\ *n* **1** : a female child : a young unmarried woman; *also* : a woman of any age **2** : a female servant or employee **3** : SWEETHEART — **girl·hood** \-,húd\ *n* — **girl·ish** \-ish\ *adj*

girth \'gərth\ *n* **1** : a band around an animal by which something (as a saddle) may be fastened on its back **2** : a measure around something (as the waist)

gist \'jist\ *n* : the main point of a matter : ESSENCE

¹**give** \'giv\ *vb* **gave** \'gāv\ **giv·en** \'giv-ən\ **giv·ing 1** : to make a present of **2** : to bestow by formal action **3** : to accord or yield to another **4** : to put into the possession or keeping of another **5** : PROFFER **6** : DELIVER; *esp* : to deliver in exchange **7** : PAY **8** : to present in public performance or to view **9** : PROVIDE **10** : ATTRIBUTE **11** : PRODUCE **12** : to deliver by some bodily action ⟨~ him a push⟩ : EXECUTE **13** : UTTER, PRONOUNCE **14** : DEVOTE **15** : to cause to have or receive ⟨*gave* us pleasure⟩ **16** : CONTRIBUTE, DONATE **17** : to yield to force, strain, or pressure

²**give** *n* **1** : capacity or tendency to yield to force or strain **2** : the quality or state of being springy

give-and-take *n* : an exchange (as of remarks or ideas) esp. on fair or equal terms

give·away \'giv-ə-,wā\ *n* **1** : an unintentional revelation or betrayal **2** : something given away free; *esp* : PREMIUM

giv·en \'giv-ən\ *adj* **1** : DISPOSED,

INCLINED ⟨~ to swearing⟩ **2** : SPECIFIED, FIXED ⟨at a ~ time⟩ **3** : granted as true : ASSUMED **4** : EXECUTED, DATED ⟨~ under my hand and seal⟩

giz·mo *or* **gis·mo** \'giz-mō\ *n* : GADGET

giz·zard \'giz-ərd\ *n* : a muscular usu. horny-lined enlargement following the crop of a bird

gla·brous \'glā-brəs\ *adj* : SMOOTH; *esp* : having a surface without hairs or projections

gla·cial \'glā-shəl\ *adj* **1** : extremely cold **2** : of or relating to glaciers **3** : being or relating to a past period of time when a large part of the earth was covered by glaciers

gla·cier \'glā-shər\ *n* : a large body of ice moving slowly down a slope or valley or spreading outward on a land surface

¹**glad** \'glad\ *adj* **1** : experiencing pleasure, joy, or delight **2** : PLEASED **3** : very willing **4** : PLEASANT, JOYFUL **5** : CHEERFUL — **glad·ly** *adv* — **glad·ness** *n*

²**glad** *n* : GLADIOLUS

glad·den \'glad-ᵊn\ *vb* : to make glad

glade \'glād\ *n* : a grassy open space in a forest

glad·i·a·tor \'glad-ē-,āt-ər\ *n* **1** : a person engaged in a fight to the death for public entertainment in ancient Rome **2** : a person engaging in a fierce fight or controversy — **glad·i·a·to·ri·al** \,glad-ē-ə-'tōr-ē-əl\ *adj*

glad·i·o·lus \,glad-ē-'ō-ləs\ *n, pl* **-li** \-(,)lē, -,lī\ *or* **-lus** *or* **-lus·es** : a plant related to the irises and widely grown for its spikes of brilliantly colored flowers

glad·some \'glad-səm\ *adj* : giving or showing joy : CHEERFUL

glad·stone \-,stōn\ *n, often cap* : a traveling bag with flexible sides on a rigid frame that opens flat into two compartments

glam·or·ize *also* **glam·our·ize** \'glam-ə-,rīz\ *vb* **1** : to make glamorous **2** : GLORIFY

glam·our *or* **glam·or** \'glam-ər\ *n* : a romantic, exciting, and often illusory attractiveness; *esp* : alluring personal attraction — **glam·or·ous** *also* **glam·our·ous** *adj*

¹**glance** \'glans\ *vb* **1** : to strike and fly off to one side **2** : FLASH, GLEAM **3** : to give a quick look

²**glance** *n* **1** : a quick intermittent flash or gleam **2** : a glancing impact or blow **3** : a quick look

gland \'gland\ *n* : a cell or group of cells that prepares and secretes a substance (as saliva or sweat) for further use in or discharge from the body — **glan·du·lar** \'glan-jə-lər\ *adj*

¹**glare** \'glaər\ *vb* **1** : to shine with a harsh dazzling light **2** : to gaze fiercely or angrily — **glar·ing** \'gla(ə)r-iŋ\ *adj* — **glar·ing·ly** *adv*

²**glare** *n* **1** : a harsh uncomfortably brilliant light **2** : an angry or fierce stare

glass \'glas\ *n* **1** : a hard brittle usu. transparent or translucent substance made by melting sand and other materials and used for windows and lenses; *also* : a substance (as rock produced by cooling of molten minerals) resembling glass **2** : something made of glass **3** *pl* : a pair of lenses used to correct defects of vision : SPECTACLES **4** : GLASS-

FUL — glass *adj* — glass·ware \-,waər\ *n* — glassy *adj*

glass·blow·ing \'glas-,blō-ig\ *n* : the art of shaping a mass of glass that has been softened by heat by blowing air into it through a tube — **glass·blow·er** \-,blō-(-ə)r\ *n*

glass·ful \-,fúl\ *n* : the quantity held by a glass

¹glaze \'glāz\ *vb* 1 : to furnish (as a window frame) with glass 2 : to apply glaze to

²glaze *n* 1 : a smooth coating of thin ice 2 : a glassy coating (as on food or pottery)

gla·zier \'glā-zhər\ *n* : a person who sets glass in window frames

¹gleam \'glēm\ *n* 1 : a transient subdued or partly obscured light 2 : GLINT 3 : a faint trace ⟨a ~ of hope⟩

²gleam *vb* 1 : to shine with subdued light or moderate brightness 2 : to appear briefly or faintly

glean \'glēn\ *vb* 1 : to gather grain left by reapers 2 : to collect little by little or with patient effort ⟨~ knowledge from books⟩ — **glean·able** *adj* — **glean·er** *n*

glean·ings *n pl* : things acquired by gleaning

glebe \'glēb\ *n* : land belonging or yielding revenue to a parish church or ecclesiastical benefice

glee \'glē\ *n* 1 : JOY, HILARITY 2 : an unaccompanied song for three or more solo vcs. male voices — **glee·ful** *adj*

glee·man \-,mən\ *n* : MINSTREL

glen \'glen\ *n* : a secluded narrow valley

glen·gar·ry \glen-'gar-ē\ *n, often cap* : a woolen cap of Scottish origin

glib \'glib\ *adj* : speaking or spoken with careless ease — **glib·ly** *adv*

¹glide \'glīd\ *vb* 1 : to move smoothly and effortlessly 2 : to descend smoothly without engine power ⟨~ in an airplane⟩

²glide *n* 1 : smooth sliding motion 2 : smooth descent without engine power

glid·er *n* 1 : one that glides 2 : an aircraft resembling an airplane but having no engine 3 : a porch seat suspended from an upright framework by short chains or straps

¹glim·mer \'glim-ər\ *vb* : to shine faintly or unsteadily

²glimmer *n* 1 : a faint unsteady light 2 : INKLING 3 : a small amount : BIT ⟨a ~ of hope⟩

¹glimpse \'glimps\ *vb* : to take a brief look : see momentarily or incompletely

²glimpse *n* 1 : a faint idea : GLIMMER 2 : a short hurried look

¹glint \'glint\ *vb* 1 : to shine by reflection : SPARKLE, GLITTER, GLEAM 2 : to appear briefly or faintly — **glint** *n*

¹glis·ten \'glis-ⁿn\ *vb* : to shine by reflection with a soft luster or sparkle

²glisten *n* : GLITTER, SPARKLE

glis·ter \'glis-tər\ *vb* : GLISTEN

¹glit·ter \'glit-ər\ *vb* 1 : to shine with brilliant or metallic luster ⟨~ing sequins⟩ 2 : SPARKLE 3 : to shine with a cold glassy brilliance ⟨eyes that ~ed cruelly⟩ 4 : to be brilliantly attractive esp. in a superficial way

²glitter *n* 1 : sparkling brilliancy, showiness, or attractiveness 2 : small glit-

tering objects used for ornamentation — **glit·tery** *adj*

gloam·ing \'glō-mig\ *n* : TWILIGHT, DUSK

gloat \'glōt\ *vb* 1 : to gaze at or think about with great self-satisfaction or joy 2 : to linger over or dwell upon something with malicious pleasure

glob \'gläb\ *n* : a small drop

glob·al \'glō-bəl\ *adj* : WORLDWIDE — **glob·al·ly** *adv*

globe \'glōb\ *n* 1 : BALL, SPHERE; *also* : something nearly spherical 2 : EARTH; *also* : a spherical representation of the earth

globe-trot·ter \-,trät-ər\ *n* : one that travels widely

glob·ule \'gläb-yül\ *n* : a tiny globe or ball ⟨~s of fat⟩ — **glob·u·lar** \-yə-lər\ *adj*

glock·en·spiel \'gläk-ən-,s(h)pēl\ *n* : a percussion musical instrument consisting of a series of graduated metal bars tuned to the chromatic scale and played with two hammers

gloom \'glüm\ *n* 1 : partial or total darkness 2 : lowness of spirits : DEJECTION 3 : an atmosphere of despondency — **gloomy** *adj*

glo·ri·fy \'glōr-ə-,fī\ *vb* 1 : to raise to celestial glory 2 : to shed splendor on 3 : to make glorious by presentation in a favorable aspect 4 : to give glory to (as in worship) — **glo·ri·fi·ca·tion** \,glōr-ə-fə-'kā-shən\ *n*

glo·ri·ous \'glōr-ē-əs\ *adj* 1 : possessing or deserving glory : ILLUSTRIOUS, PRAISEWORTHY 2 : conferring glory 3 : RESPLENDENT, MAGNIFICENT 4 : DELIGHTFUL, WONDERFUL — **glo·ri·ous·ly** *adv*

¹glory \'glōr-ē\ *n* 1 : RENOWN 2 : honor and praise rendered in worship 3 : something that secures praise or renown 4 : a brilliant asset 5 : RESPLENDENCE, MAGNIFICENCE 6 : celestial bliss 7 : a height of prosperity or achievement

²glory *vb* : to rejoice proudly : EXULT

¹gloss \'gläs, 'glòs\ *n* 1 : LUSTER, SHEEN, BRIGHTNESS 2 : outward show — **glossy** *adj*

²gloss *vb* 1 : to give a deceptive appearance to 2 : to pass over quickly in an attempt to ignore ⟨~ over inadequacies⟩

³gloss *n* [L *glossa* unusual word requiring explanation, fr. Gk *glōssa, glōtta*, lit., tongue, language] 1 : an explanatory note (as in the margin of a text) 2 : GLOSSARY 3 : an interlinear translation 4 : a continuous commentary accompanying a text

⁴gloss *vb* : to furnish glosses for : ANNOTATE

glos·sa·ry \'gläs-(ə-)rē, 'glòs-\ *n* : a dictionary of the special terms found in a particular area of knowledge or usage — **glos·sar·i·al** \glä-'sar-ē-əl, glò-\ *adj*

glot·tis \'glät-əs\ *n, pl* **glot·tis·es** *or* **glot·ti·des** \-ə-,dēz\ : the slitlike opening between pharynx and windpipe — **glot·tal** *adj*

glove \'gləv\ *n* 1 : a covering for the hand having separate sections for each finger 2 : a padded leather covering for the hand for use in a sport

¹glow \'glō\ *vb* 1 : to shine with or as

ə abut; ° kitten; ər further; a back; ā bake; ä cot, cart; aú out; ch chin; e less; ē easy; g gift; i trip; ī life; j joke; ŋ sing; ō flow; ò flaw; òi coin; th thin; <u>th</u> this; ü loot; ú foot; y yet; yü few; yú furious; zh vision

if with intense heat **2 :** to have a rich warm usu. ruddy color **:** FLUSH, BLUSH **3 :** to feel hot **4 :** to show exuberance or elation ⟨~ with pride⟩

²**glow** n **1 :** brightness or warmth of color; *esp* **:** REDNESS **2 :** warmth of feeling or emotion **3 :** a sensation of warmth **4 :** light such as is emitted from a heated substance

glow·er \'glau̇-(ə)r\ vb **:** to look or stare with sullen annoyance or anger — **glower** n

glow-worm \'glō-,wȯrm\ n **:** an insect or insect larva that gives off light

gloze \'glōz\ vb **:** to make appear right or acceptable **:** GLOSS ⟨~ over a person's faults⟩

glu·cose \'glü-,kōs\ n **1 :** a sugar known in three different forms; *esp* **:** DEXTROSE **2 :** a light-colored syrup obtained chiefly from cornstarch and used as a sweetening agent

glue \'glü\ n **:** a jellylike protein substance made from animal materials and used for sticking things together; *also* **:** any of various other strong adhesives — **glue** vb — **gluey** adj

glum \'gləm\ adj **1 :** MOROSE, SULLEN **2 :** DREARY, GLOOMY

¹**glut** \'glət\ vb **glut·ted**; **glut·ting 1 :** to fill esp. with food to satiety **:** SATIATE **2 :** OVERSUPPLY

²**glut** n **:** an excessive quantity **:** OVER-SUPPLY

glu·ten \'glüt-ᵊn\ n **:** a gluey protein substance that causes dough to be sticky

glu·ti·nous \'glüt-(ᵊ-)nəs\ adj **:** STICKY

glut·ton \'glət-ᵊn\ n **:** one that eats to excess — **glut·ton·ous** adj — **glut·tony** n

glyc·er·in or **glyc·er·ine** \'glis-(ə-)rən\ n **:** a sweet colorless syrupy liquid obtained from fats or synthesized and used as a solvent, moistener, and lubricant

glyc·er·ol \'glis-ə-,rȯl\ n **:** GLYCERIN

G-man \'jē-,man\ n **:** a special agent of the Federal Bureau of Investigation

gnarl \'närl\ n **:** a hard enlargement with twisted grain on a tree — **gnarled** adj

gnash \'nash\ vb **:** to grind (as teeth) together

gnat \'nat\ n **:** any of various small usu. biting two-winged flies

gnaw \'nȯ\ vb **1 :** to consume, wear away, or make by persistent biting or nibbling ⟨~ a bone⟩ ⟨rats ~ed holes in the wall⟩ **2 :** to affect as if by gnawing ⟨a dull ~ing pain⟩

gneiss \'nīs\ n **:** a granitelike rock in layers

gnome \'nōm\ n **:** a dwarf of folklore living inside the earth who guards precious ore or treasure — **gnom·ish** adj

gnu \'n(y)ü\ n **:** a large African antelope with oxlike head and horns and horselike mane and tail

¹**go** \'gō\ vb **went** \'went\ **gone** \'gȯn\ **go·ing** \'gō-iŋ\ **1 :** to move on a course **:** PROCEED ⟨~ slow⟩ **2 :** LEAVE, DEPART **3 :** to take a certain course **:** follow a certain procedure **4 :** EXTEND, RUN ⟨his land ~es to the river⟩; *also* **:** LEAD ⟨that door ~es to the cellar⟩ **5 :** to be habitually in a certain state ⟨~es armed after dark⟩ **6 :** to become lost, consumed, or spent; *also* **:** DIE **7 :** ELAPSE, PASS **8 :** to pass by sale ⟨went for a good price⟩ **9 :** to become

impaired or weakened **10 :** to give way under force or pressure **:** BREAK **11 :** HAPPEN ⟨what's ~ing on⟩ **12 :** to be in general or on an average ⟨cheap, as yachts ~⟩ **13 :** to become esp. as the result of a contest ⟨the decision went against him⟩ **14 :** to put or subject oneself ⟨~ to great expense⟩ **15 :** RESORT ⟨went to court to recover damages⟩ **16 :** to begin or maintain an action or motion ⟨here ~es⟩ **17 :** to function properly ⟨the clock doesn't ~⟩ **18 :** to have currency **:** CIRCULATE ⟨the report ~es⟩ **19 :** to be or act in accordance ⟨a good rule to ~ by⟩ **20 :** to come to be applied **21 :** to pass by award, assignment, or lot **22 :** to contribute to a result ⟨qualities that ~ to make a hero⟩ **23 :** to be about, intending, or expecting something ⟨is ~ing to leave town⟩ **24 :** to arrive at a certain state or condition ⟨~ to sleep⟩ **25 :** to come to be ⟨the tire went flat⟩ **26 :** to be capable of being sung or played ⟨the tune ~es like this⟩ **27 :** to be suitable or becoming **:** HARMONIZE **28 :** to be capable of passing, extending, or being contained or inserted ⟨this coat will ~ in the trunk⟩ **29 :** to have a usual or proper place or position **:** BELONG ⟨these books ~ on the top shelf⟩ **30 :** to be capable of being divided ⟨3 ~es into 6 twice⟩ **31 :** to have a tendency ⟨that ~es to show that he is honest⟩ **32 :** to be acceptable, satisfactory, or adequate ⟨any kind of dress ~es here⟩ **33 :** to proceed along or according to **:** FOLLOW ⟨he's ~ing my way⟩ **34 :** TRAVERSE **35 :** BET, BID ⟨willing to ~ $50⟩ **36 :** to assume the function or obligation of ⟨~ bail for a friend⟩ **37 :** to participate to the extent of ⟨~ halves⟩ **38 :** WEIGH **39 :** ENDURE, TOLERATE **40 :** AFFORD ⟨can't ~ the price⟩ — **go at 1 :** ATTACK, ATTEMPT **2 :** UNDERTAKE — **go back on 1 :** ABANDON **2 :** BETRAY **3 :** FAIL — **go by the board :** to be discarded — **go down the line :** to give wholehearted support — **go for 1 :** to pass for or serve as **2 :** to try to secure **3 :** FAVOR — **go one better :** OUTDO, SURPASS — **go over 1 :** EXAMINE **2 :** REPEAT **3 :** STUDY, REVIEW — **go places :** to be on the way toward success

²**go** n, pl **goes 1 :** the act or manner of going **2 :** the height of fashion ⟨boots are all the ~⟩ **3 :** a turn of affairs **:** OCCURRENCE **4 :** ENERGY, VIGOR **5 :** ATTEMPT, TRY **6 :** a spell of activity — **no go :** USELESS, HOPELESS — **on the go :** constantly or restlessly active

goad \'gōd\ n **1 :** a pointed rod used to urge on an animal **2 :** something that urges **:** SPUR — **goad** vb

goal \'gōl\ n **1 :** the mark set as limit to a race **2 :** AIM, PURPOSE **3 :** an area or object toward which play is directed in order to score; *also* **:** a successful attempt to score

goal·ie \'gō-lē\ n **:** a player who defends the goal (as in soccer or hockey)

goal·keep·er \'gōl-,kē-pər\ n **:** GOALIE

goal·post \'gōl-,pōst\ n **:** one of the two vertical posts with a crossbar that constitute the goal (as in soccer)

goat \'gōt\ n **:** a hollow-horned ruminant mammal related to the sheep that has backward-curving horns, short tail, and usu. straight hair

goa·tee \gō-'tē\ n **:** a small trim pointed

or tufted beard on a man's chin

goat·skin \'gōt-,skin\ *n* : the skin of a goat used for making leather

¹gob \'gäb\ *n* : LUMP, MASS

²gob *n* : SAILOR

gob·bet \'gäb-ət\ *n* : LUMP, MASS

¹gob·ble \'gäb-əl\ *vb* 1 : to swallow or eat greedily 2 : to take eagerly : GRAB

²gobble *vb* : to make the natural guttural noise of a turkey cock

gob·ble·dy·gook *or* **gob·ble·de·gook** \,gäb-əl-dē-'gook\ *n* : wordy and generally unintelligible jargon

gob·bler \'gäb-lər\ *n* : a male turkey

go·be·tween \'gō-bə-,twēn\ *n* : a person who acts as a messenger or an intermediary between two parties

gob·let \'gäb-lət\ *n* : a drinking glass with a foot and stem

gob·lin \'gäb-lən\ *n* : an ugly grotesque sprite with mischievous and sometimes evil ways

¹god \'gäd\ *n* 1 : a being or object believed to have more than natural attributes and powers and to require man's worship 2 : a person or thing of supreme value

²God *n* : the supreme reality; *esp* : the Being whom men worship as the creator and ruler of the universe

god·child \-,chīld\ *n* : a person (**god·daugh·ter, god·son**) for whom one stands as sponsor (**god·fa·ther, god·moth·er**) at baptism

god·dess \-əs\ *n* 1 : a female god 2 : a woman whose charm or beauty arouses adoration

god·head \-,hed\ *n* 1 : divine nature or essence 2 *often cap* : DEITY; *also* : the nature of God esp. as existing in three persons

god·hood \-,hud\ *n* : DIVINITY

god·less \-ləs\ *adj* : not acknowledging a deity or divine law — **god·less·ness** *n*

god·like \-,līk\ *adj* : resembling or having the qualities of God or a god : DIVINE

god·ly \-lē\ *adj* 1 : DIVINE 2 : PIOUS, DEVOUT — **god·li·ness** *n*

god·par·ent \-,par-ənt\ *n* : a sponsor at baptism

god·send \-,send\ *n* : a desirable or needed thing that comes unexpectedly as if sent by God

go·get·ter \'gō-,get-ər\ *n* : an aggressively enterprising person

gog·gle \'gäg-əl\ *vb* : to stare with wide or protuberant eyes

gog·gles \-əlz\ *n pl* : large eyeglasses to protect the eyes (as from bright light or dust)

go·ings-on \,gō-iŋz-'ón, -'än\ *n pl* : ACTIONS, EVENTS

goi·ter *also* **goi·tre** \'gòit-ər\ *n* : an abnormally enlarged thyroid gland visible as a swelling at the base of the neck — **goi·trous** \-(ə-)rəs\ *adj*

gold \'gōld\ *n* 1 : a malleable yellow metallic chemical element used esp. for coins and jewelry 2 : gold coins; *also* : MONEY 3 : a yellow color

gold·beat·er \'gōl(d)-,bēt-ər\ *n* : one that beats gold into gold leaf

gold·brick \-,brik\ *n* : a person (as a soldier) who shirks assigned work — **goldbrick** *vb*

gold·en \'gōl-dən\ *adj* 1 : made of or relating to gold 2 : abounding in gold 3 : having the color of gold; *also* : BLOND 4 : SHINING, LUSTROUS 5 : SUPERB 6 : FLOURISHING, PROSPEROUS 7 : radiantly youthful and vigorous 8 : FAVORABLE, ADVANTAGEOUS (a ~ opportunity) 9 : MELLOW, RESONANT (a ~ tenor)

gold·en·rod \-,räd\ *n* : any of numerous herbs related to the daisies but having tall slender stalks with many tiny usu. yellow flower heads

gold·field \'gōl(d)-,fēld\ *n* : a goldmining district

gold·finch \'gōl(d)-,finch\ *n* : an American finch the male of which becomes bright yellow and black in summer

gold·fish \-,fish\ *n* : a small usu. yellow or golden carp often kept as an aquarium fish

gold·smith \-,smith\ *n* : one who makes or deals in articles of gold

golf \'gälf, 'gólf\ *n* : a game played with a small ball and various clubs on a course having 9 or 18 holes

-gon \,gän\ *n comb form* : figure having (so many) angles ⟨hexagon⟩

go·nad \'gō-,nad\ *n* : a sex gland : OVARY, TESTIS

gon·do·la \'gän-də-lə (*usual for* 1), gän-'dō-\ *n* 1 : a long narrow boat used on the canals of Venice 2 : a railroad car with no top designed for bulky materials 3 : an enclosure attached to the undersurface of an airship or balloon

gon·do·lier \,gän-də-'liər\ *n* : one who propels a gondola

gone \'gón\ *adj* 1 : PAST 2 : ADVANCED, ABSORBED 3 : INFATUATED 4 : PREGNANT 5 : DEAD 6 : LOST, RUINED 7 : SINKING, WEAK

gon·er \'gón-ər\ *n* : one whose case is hopeless

gon·fa·lon \'gän-fə-,län\ *n* : a flag that hangs from a crosspiece or frame

gong \'gäŋ, 'góŋ\ *n* : a metallic disk that produces a resounding tone when struck

gon·or·rhea \,gän-ə-'rē-ə\ *n* : a bacterial inflammatory disease of the genital tract — **gon·or·rhe·al** *adj*

goo \'gü\ *n* 1 : a viscid or sticky substance 2 : sickly sentimentality

¹good \'gud\ *adj* **bet·ter** \'bet-ər\ **best** \'best\ 1 : of a favorable character or tendency 2 : BOUNTIFUL, FERTILE 3 : COMELY, ATTRACTIVE 4 : SUITABLE, FIT 5 : SOUND, WHOLE 6 : AGREEABLE, PLEASANT 7 : SALUTARY, WHOLESOME 8 : CONSIDERABLE, AMPLE 9 : FULL 10 : WELL-FOUNDED 11 : TRUE ⟨holds ~ for everybody⟩ 12 : REAL 13 : recognized or valid esp. in law 14 : ADEQUATE, SATISFACTORY 15 : conforming to a standard 16 : DISCRIMINATING 17 : COMMENDABLE, VIRTUOUS 18 : KIND 19 : UPPER-CLASS 20 : COMPETENT 21 : LOYAL — **good-heart·ed** \-'härt-əd\ *adj* — **good·ish** *adj* — **good-look·ing** \'gud-'lük-iŋ\ *adj* — **good-na·tured** \-'nā-chərd\ *adj* — **good-tem·pered** \-'tem-pərd\ *adj*

²good *n* 1 : something good 2 : GOODNESS 3 : BENEFIT, WELFARE (for the ~ of mankind) 4 : something that has economic utility 5 *pl* : personal property 6 *pl* : CLOTH 7 *pl* : WARES, COMMOD-

ITIES 8 : good persons ⟨the ~ die young⟩

good–bye *or* **good–by** \ˌgu̇d-ˈbī\ *n* **:** a concluding remark at parting — often used interjectionally

Good Friday *n* **:** the Friday before Easter observed as the anniversary of the crucifixion of Christ

good·ly \ˈgu̇d-lē\ *adj* **1 :** of pleasing appearance **2 :** LARGE, CONSIDERABLE

good·man \ˈgu̇d-mən\ *n, archaic* **:** MISTER

good·ness *n* **:** EXCELLENCE, VIRTUE

good·wife \ˈgu̇d-ˌwīf\ *n, archaic* — used as a title equivalent to *Mrs.* ⟨~ Brown⟩

good·will \-ˈwil\ *n* **1 :** BENEVOLENCE **2 :** the value of the trade a business has built up over a considerable time **3 :** cheerful consent **4 :** willing effort

goody \ˈgu̇d-ē\ *n* **:** something that is good to eat

goody–goody \ˌgu̇d-ē-ˈgu̇d-ē\ *adj* **:** affectedly good — **goody–goody** *n*

goof \ˈgüf\ *vb* **:** BLUNDER — **goof** *n*

goofy *adj* **:** CRAZY, SILLY — **goof·i·ness** *n*

goose \ˈgüs\ *n, pl* **geese** \ˈgēs\ **1 :** a large web-footed bird related to the swans and ducks; *esp* **:** a female goose as distinguished from a gander **2 :** a foolish person **3** *pl* **goos·es :** a tailor's smoothing iron

goose·ber·ry \ˈgüs-ˌber-ē, ˈgüz-\ *n* **:** the acid berry of a shrub related to the currant and used esp. in jams and pies

goose·flesh \ˈgüs-ˌflesh\ *n* **:** a roughening of the skin caused usu. by cold or fear

go·pher \ˈgō-fər\ *n* **1 :** a burrowing American land tortoise **2 :** any of various American burrowing rodents (as a ground squirrel) that mostly have cheek pouches

¹gore \ˈgōr\ *n* **:** BLOOD

²gore *n* **:** a tapering or triangular piece (as of cloth in a skirt)

³gore *vb* **:** to pierce or wound with a horn or tusk

¹gorge \ˈgȯrj\ *n* **1 :** THROAT **2 :** a narrow ravine **3 :** a mass of matter that chokes up a passage

²gorge *vb* **:** to eat greedily **:** stuff to capacity **:** GLUT

gor·geous \ˈgȯr-jəs\ *adj* **:** resplendently beautiful

Gor·gon·zo·la \ˌgȯr-gən-ˈzō-lə\ *n* **:** a blue cheese of Italian origin

go·ril·la \gə-ˈril-ə\ *n* **:** an African manlike ape related to but much larger than the chimpanzee

gor·man·dize \ˈgȯr-mən-ˌdīz\ *vb* **:** to eat ravenously — **gor·man·diz·er** *n*

gorse \ˈgȯrs\ *n* **1 :** FURZE **2 :** JUNIPER

gory \ˈgōr-ē\ *adj* **1 :** BLOODSTAINED **2 :** HORRIBLE, SENSATIONAL

gos·ling \ˈgäz-liŋ, ˈgȯz-\ *n* **:** a young goose

gos·pel \ˈgäs-pəl\ *n* **1 :** the teachings of Christ and the apostles **2** *cap* **:** any of the first four books of the New Testament **3 :** something accepted as infallible truth

gos·sa·mer \ˈgäs-ə-mər, ˈgäz-\ *n* **1 :** a film of floating cobweb **2 :** a thin sheer fabric **3 :** something light, delicate, or tenuous

¹gos·sip \ˈgäs-əp\ *n* **1 :** a person who habitually reveals personal or sensational facts **2 :** a rumor or report of an intimate nature **3 :** an informal conversation — **gos·sipy** *adj*

²gossip *vb* **:** to spread gossip

got *past of* GET

Goth \ˈgäth\ *n* **:** a member of a Germanic race that early in the Christian era overran the Roman Empire

¹Goth·ic \ˈgäth-ik\ *adj* **1 :** of or relating to the Goths **2 :** of or relating to a style of architecture prevalent in western Europe from the middle 12th to the early 16th century

²Gothic *n* **1 :** the Germanic language of the Goths **2 :** the Gothic architectural style or decoration

gotten *past part of* GET

Gou·da \ˈgau̇d-ə\ *n* **:** a mild Dutch milk cheese shaped in balls and usu. covered with a red protective coating

¹gouge \ˈgau̇j\ *n* **1 :** a rounded troughlike chisel **2 :** a hole or groove made with or as if with a gouge

²gouge *vb* **1 :** to cut holes or grooves in with or as if with a gouge **2 :** DEFRAUD, CHEAT

gou·lash \ˈgü-ˌläsh, -ˌlash\ *n* **:** a beef stew with onion, paprika, and caraway

gourd \ˈgōrd, ˈgu̇rd\ *n* **1 :** any of a group of tendril-bearing vines including the cucumber, squash, and melon **2 :** the fruit of a gourd; *esp* **:** any of various inedible hard-shelled fruits used esp. for ornament or implements

gourde \ˈgu̇rd\ *n* — see MONEY table

gour·mand \ˈgu̇r-ˌmänd\ *n* **1 :** one who is excessively fond of eating and drinking **2 :** GOURMET

gour·met \ˈgu̇r-ˌmā\ *n* **:** a connoisseur in eating and drinking

gout \ˈgau̇t\ *n* **:** a disease marked by painful inflammation and swelling of the joints — **gouty** *adj*

gov·ern \ˈgəv-ərn\ *vb* [OF *governer*, fr. L *gubernare* to steer, govern, fr. Gk *kybernan*] **1 :** to control and direct the making and administration of policy in **:** RULE **2 :** CONTROL, DIRECT, INFLUENCE **3 :** DETERMINE, REGULATE **4 :** RESTRAIN — **gov·er·nance** *n*

gov·ern·ess *n* **:** a woman who teaches and trains a child esp. in a private home

gov·ern·ment \ˈgəv-ər(n)-mənt\ *n* **1 :** authoritative direction or control **:** RULE **2 :** the making of policy **3 :** the organization or agency through which a political unit exercises authority **4 :** the institutions, laws, and customs through which a political unit is governed **5 :** the governing body — **gov·ern·men·tal** \ˌgəv-ər(n)-ˈment-əl\ *adj*

gov·er·nor \ˈgəv-ə(r)-nər\ *n* **1 :** one that governs; *esp* **:** a ruler, chief executive, or head of a political unit (as a state) **2 :** an attachment to a machine for automatic control of speed — **gov·er·nor·ship** *n*

gown \ˈgau̇n\ *n* **1 :** a loose flowing outer garment **2 :** an official robe worn esp. by a judge, clergyman, or teacher **3 :** a woman's dress (evening ~*s*) **4 :** a loose robe (as a dressing gown) — **gown** *vb*

grab \ˈgrab\ *vb* **grabbed; grab·bing :** to take hastily **:** CLUTCH, SNATCH — **grab** *n*

¹grace \ˈgrās\ *n* **1 :** help given man by God (as in overcoming temptation) **2 :** freedom from sin through divine grace **3 :** a virtue coming from God **4 :** a short prayer before or after a meal **5 :** a temporary respite (as from the payment of a debt) **6 :** APPROVAL, ACCEPTANCE ⟨in his good ~*s*⟩ **7 :** CHARM **8 :** ATTRACTIVENESS, BEAUTY **9 :** fitness or proportion of line or expression **10 :** ease of movement **11 :** a musical trill or or-

nament **12** — used as a title for a duke, a duchess, or an archbishop —
grace·ful *adj* — **grace·ful·ly** *adv* — **grace·ful·ness** *n* — **grace·less** *adj*

²grace *vb* **1** : HONOR **2** : ADORN, EMBELLISH

gra·cious \'grā-shəs\ *adj* **1** : marked by kindness and courtesy **2** : GRACEFUL **3** : characterized by charm and good taste **4** : MERCIFUL ⟨His Most *Gracious* Majesty⟩ — **gra·cious·ly** *adv* — **gra·cious·ness** *n*

grack·le \'grak-əl\ *n* **1** : an Old World starling **2** : an American blackbird with glossy iridescent plumage

gra·da·tion \grā-'dā-shən\ *n* **1** : a series forming successive stages **2** : a step, degree, or stage in a series **3** : an advance by regular degrees **4** : the act or process of grading

¹grade \'grād\ *n* **1** : a degree or stage in a series, order, or ranking **2** : a position in a scale of rank, quality, or order **3** : a class of persons or things of the same rank or quality **4** : a division of the school course representing one year's work; *also* : the pupils in such a division **5** *pl* : the elementary school system **6** : a mark or rating esp. of accomplishment in school **7** : the degree of slope (as of a road); *also* : SLOPE

²grade *vb* **1** : to arrange in grades : SORT **2** : to make level or evenly sloping ⟨~ a highway⟩ **3** : to give a grade to ⟨~ a pupil in history⟩ **4** : to assign to a grade

grade school *n* : a public school including the first six or the first eight grades

gra·di·ent \'grād-ē-ənt\ *n* : SLOPE, GRADE

grad·u·al \'graj-(ə-w)əl\ *adj* : proceeding or changing by steps or degrees — **grad·u·al·ly** *adv*

grad·u·al·ism *n* : the policy of approaching a desired end by gradual stages

¹grad·u·ate \'graj-ə-wət, -,wāt\ *n* **1** : a holder of an academic degree or diploma **2** : a receptacle marked with figures for measuring contents

²graduate *adj* **1** : holding an academic degree or diploma **2** : of or relating to studies beyond the first or bachelor's degree ⟨~ school⟩

³grad·u·ate \-,wāt\ *vb* **1** : to grant or receive an academic degree or diploma **2** : to admit to a particular standing or grade **3** : to mark with degrees of measurement **4** : to divide into grades, classes, or intervals

grad·u·a·tion \,graj-ə-'wā-shən\ *n* **1** : a mark that graduates something **2** : an act or process of graduating **3** : COMMENCEMENT

graf·fi·to \grə-'fēt-ō\ *n*, *pl* **-ti** \-(,)ē\ : a rude inscription or drawing found on rocks or walls

¹graft \'graft\ *vb* **1** : to insert a shoot from one plant into another so that they join and grow; *also* : to join one thing to another as in plant grafting ⟨~ skin over a burn⟩ **2** : to get (as money) by dishonest means — **graft·er** *n*

²graft *n* **1** : a grafted plant; *also* : the point of union in this **2** : material (as skin or a plant shoot) used in grafting **3** : the getting of money or advantage

by dishonest means; *also* : the money or advantage gained dishonestly

gra·ham flour \'grā-əm-\ *n* : whole wheat flour

Grail \'grāl\ *n* : the cup or platter used according to medieval legend by Christ at the Last Supper and thereafter the object of knightly quests

grain \'grān\ *n* **1** : a seed or fruit of a cereal grass **2** : seeds or fruits of various food plants and esp. cereal grasses; *also* : a plant producing grain **3** : a small hard particle **4** : a unit of weight equal to .0648 gram **5** : TEXTURE; *also* : the arrangement of fibers in wood **6** : natural disposition

grain·field \-,fēld\ *n* : a field where grain is grown

grainy *adj* **1** : GRANULAR **2** : resembling the grain of wood

gram *or* **gramme** \'gram\ *n* : a unit of weight in the metric system equal to ⅟₁₀₀₀ kilogram

-gram \,gram\ *n comb form* : drawing : writing : record ⟨tele*gram*⟩

gram·mar \'gram-ər\ *n* **1** : the study of the classes of words, their inflections, and their functions and relations in the sentence **2** : a study of what is to be preferred and what avoided in inflection and syntax; *also* : speech or writing evaluated according to its conformity to the principles of grammar — **gram·mar·i·an** \grə-'mer-ē-ən\ *n* — **gram·mat·i·cal** \'mat-i-kəl\ *adj* — **gram·mat·i·cal·ly** *adv*

grammar school *n* **1** : a British secondary school emphasizing Latin and Greek in preparation for college; *also* : a British college preparatory school **2** : a school intermediate between the primary grades and high school

gra·na·ry \'grān-(ə-)rē, 'gran-\ *n* : a storehouse for grain

grand \'grand\ *adj* **1** : higher in rank or importance : FOREMOST, CHIEF **2** : great in size **3** : INCLUSIVE, COMPLETE ⟨a ~ total⟩ **4** : MAGNIFICENT, SPLENDID **5** : showing wealth or high social standing **6** : IMPRESSIVE, STATELY — **grand·ly** *adv* — **grand·ness** *n*

gran·dam \'gran-,dam, -dəm\ *n* : an old woman

grand·child \'gran(d)-,chīld\ *n* : a child of one's son or daughter

grand·daugh·ter \'gran-,dȯt-ər\ *n* : a daughter of one's son or daughter

gran·dee \gran-'dē\ *n* : a high-ranking Spanish or Portuguese nobleman

gran·deur \'gran-jər\ *n* **1** : the quality or state of being grand : awe-inspiring magnificence **2** : something grand or conducive to grandness

grand·fa·ther \'gran(d)-,fäth-ər\ *n* : the father of one's father or mother; *also* : ANCESTOR

gran·dil·o·quence \gran-'dil-ə-kwəns\ *n* : pompous eloquence — **gran·dil·o·quent** *adj*

gran·di·ose \'gran-dē-,ōs\ *adj* : IMPRESSIVE, IMPOSING; *also* : affectedly splendid

grand·moth·er \'gran(d)-,məth-ər\ *n* : the mother of one's father or mother; *also* : a female ancestor

grand·par·ent \-,par-ənt\ *n* : a parent of one's father or mother

---

ə abut; ᵊ kitten; ər further; a back; ā bake; ä cot, cart; aú out; ch chin; e less; ē easy; g gift; i trip; ī life; j joke; ŋ sing; ō flow; ȯ flaw; ȯi coin; th thin; th̲ this; ü loot; ü̇ foot; y yet; yü few; yu̇ furious; zh vision

grand piano *n* : a piano with horizontal frame and strings

grand·son \'gran(d)-ˌsən\ *n* : a son of one's son or daughter

grand·stand \-ˌstand\ *n* : a usu. roofed stand for spectators at a racecourse or stadium

grange \'grānj\ *n* : a farm or farmhouse with its various buildings

gran·ite \'gran-ət\ *n* : a hard igneous rock that takes a polish and is used for building

gran·ite·ware \-ˌwaər\ *n* : enameled ironware

¹**grant** \'grant\ *vb* **1** : to consent to : ALLOW, PERMIT **2** : GIVE, BESTOW **3** : to admit as true : CONCEDE — **grant·er** *n* — **grant·or** *n*

²**grant** *n* **1** : the act of granting **2** : something granted; *esp* : a gift for a particular purpose ⟨a ~ for study abroad⟩ **3** : a transfer of property by deed or writing; *also* : the instrument by which such a transfer is made **4** : the property transferred by grant

gran·tee \grant-'ē\ *n* : one to whom a grant is made

gran·u·lar \'gran-yə-lər\ *adj* : consisting of or appearing to consist of granules

gran·u·late \-ˌlāt\ *vb* : to form into grains or crystals — **gran·u·lat·ed** *adj* — **gran·u·la·tion** \ˌgran-yə-'lā-shən\ *n*

gran·ule \'gran-yül\ *n* : a small particle; *esp* : one of numerous particles forming a larger unit

grape \'grāp\ *n* : a smooth juicy edible berry that is the chief source of wine **2** : a woody vine widely grown for its clustered grapes

grape·fruit \-ˌfrüt\ *n* : a large edible yellow-skinned citrus fruit

grape·shot \-ˌshät\ *n* : a cluster of small iron balls used as a cannon charge

grape·vine \-ˌvīn\ *n* **1** : GRAPE **2 2** : RUMOR, REPORT; *also* : an informal means of circulating information or gossip

graph \'graf\ *n* : a diagram that by means of dots and lines shows a system of relationships between things

-graph \ˌgraf\ *n comb form* **1** : something written ⟨autograph⟩ **2** : instrument for making or transmitting records ⟨seismograph⟩

graph·ic \'graf-ik\ *adj* **1** : being written, drawn, or engraved **2** : vividly described **3** : of or relating to the arts (**graphic arts**) of representation, decoration, and printing on flat surfaces — **graph·i·cal·ly** *adv*

graph·ite \'graf-ˌīt\ *n* [G *graphit*, fr. Gk *graphein* to write] : soft carbon used esp. for lead pencils and lubricants

grap·nel \'grap-n²l\ *n* : a small anchor with two or more claws used in dragging or grappling operations and for anchoring a small boat

¹**grap·ple** \'grap-əl\ *n* **1** : GRAPNEL **2** : a hand-to-hand struggle

²**grapple** *vb* **1** : to seize or hold with or as if with a hooked implement **2** : to seize one another **3** : WRESTLE **4** : COPE ⟨~ with a problem⟩

¹**grasp** \'grasp\ *vb* **1** : to make the motion of seizing **2** : to take or seize firmly **3** : to enclose and hold with the fingers or arms **4** : COMPREHEND

²**grasp** *n* **1** : HANDLE **2** : EMBRACE **3** : HOLD, CONTROL **4** : the reach of the arms **5** : the power of seizing and hold-

ing **6** : COMPREHENSION ⟨a good ~ of the subject⟩

grass \'gras\ *n* **1** : herbage for grazing animals **2** : any of a large group of plants with jointed stems and narrow leaves **3** : grass-covered land — **grassy** *adj*

grass·hop·per \-ˌhäp-ər\ *n* : any of a group of leaping plant-eating insects

grass·land \-ˌland\ *n* : land covered naturally or under cultivation with grasses and low-growing herbs

¹**grate** \'grāt\ *n* **1** : a framework with bars across it (as in a window) **2** : a frame of iron bars for holding fuel while it is burning

²**grate** *vb* **1** : to pulverize by rubbing against something rough **2** : to grind or rub against with a rasping noise **3** : IRRITATE — **grat·er** *n* — **grat·ing·ly** *adv*

grate·ful \'grāt-fəl\ *adj* **1** : THANKFUL, APPRECIATIVE; *also* : expressing gratitude **2** : PLEASING — **grate·ful·ly** *adv* — **grate·ful·ness** *n*

grat·i·fy \'grat-ə-ˌfī\ *vb* : to afford pleasure to : FAVOR, OBLIGE — **grat·i·fi·ca·tion** \ˌgrat-ə-fə-'kā-shən\ *n*

grat·ing \'grāt-iŋ\ *n* : a frame with bars : GRATE

gra·tis \'grāt-əs, 'grat-\ *adv* (*or adj*) : without charge or recompense : FREE

grat·i·tude \'grat-ə-ˌt(y)üd\ *n* : THANKFULNESS

gra·tu·i·tous \grə-'t(y)ü-ət-əs\ *adj* **1** : done or provided without recompense : FREE **2** : UNWARRANTED

gra·tu·i·ty \-ət-ē\ *n* : TIP

gra·va·men \grə-'väm-ən, -'väm-\ *n, pl* **-mens** *or* **-mi·na** \-ə-nə\ : the basic or significant part of a grievance or complaint

¹**grave** \'grāv\ *vb* : SCULPTURE, ENGRAVE — **grav·er** *n*

²**grave** *n* : an excavation in the earth as a place of burial; *also* : TOMB

³**grave** *adj* **1** : IMPORTANT **2** : threatening great harm or danger **3** : DIGNIFIED, SOLEMN **4** : drab in color : SOMBER **5** : of, marked by, or being an accent mark having the form ` — **grave·ly** *adv* — **grave·ness** *n*

grave·clothes \-ˌklō(th)z\ *n pl* : the clothes in which a dead person is buried

grav·el \'grav-əl\ *n* : loose rounded fragments of rock — **grav·el·ly** *adj*

grave·stone \'grāv-ˌstōn\ *n* : a burial monument

grave·yard \-ˌyärd\ *n* : CEMETERY

grav·id \'grav-əd\ *adj* : PREGNANT

grav·i·tate \'grav-ə-ˌtāt\ *vb* **1** : to move or tend to move under the influence of gravitation **2** : to move toward something

grav·i·ta·tion \ˌgrav-ə-'tā-shən\ *n* : a natural force of attraction that tends to draw bodies together — **grav·i·ta·tion·al** *adj*

grav·i·ty \'grav-ət-ē\ *n* **1** : IMPORTANCE; *esp* : SERIOUSNESS **2** : WEIGHT **3** : the attraction of bodies toward the center of the earth

gra·vy \'grā-vē\ *n* **1** : a sauce made from the thickened and seasoned juices of cooked meat **2** : unearned or illicit gain : GRAFT

¹**gray** \'grā\ *adj* **1** : of the color gray; *also* : dull in color **2** : having gray hair **3** : CHEERLESS, DISMAL — **gray·ish** *adj* — **gray·ness** *n*

²**gray** *n* **1** : something of a gray color

2 : a neutral color ranging between black and white

³**gray** *vb* **:** to make or become gray

gray·beard \'grā-,bi͝erd\ *n* **:** an old man

gray·ling \'grā-liŋ\ *n* **:** any of several slender freshwater food and sport fishes related to the trouts

gray matter *n* **:** the grayish part of nervous tissue consisting mostly of nerve cell bodies

¹**graze** \'grāz\ *vb* **1 :** to feed (livestock) on grass or pasture **2 :** to feed on herbage or pasture

²**graze** *vb* **1 :** to touch lightly in passing **2 :** SCRATCH

gra·zier \'grā-zhər\ *n* **:** a person who grazes cattle; *also* **:** RANCHER

¹**grease** \'grēs\ *n* **:** rendered and usu. solid animal fat; *also* **:** oily material — **greasy** \'grē-sē, -zē\ *adj*

²**grease** \'grēs, 'grēz\ *vb* **:** to smear or lubricate with grease

grease·paint \'grēs-,pānt\ *n* **:** theater makeup

great \'grāt, *South also* 'gre(ə)t\ *adj* **1 :** large in size **:** BIG **2 :** ELABORATE, AMPLE **3 :** large in number **:** NUMEROUS **4 :** being beyond the average **:** MIGHTY, INTENSE ⟨a ~ weight⟩ ⟨in ~ pain⟩ **5 :** EMINENT, DISTINGUISHED, GRAND **6 :** long continued ⟨a ~ while⟩ **7 :** MAIN, PRINCIPAL **8 :** more distant in a family relationship by one generation ⟨a *great*-grandfather⟩ **9 :** markedly superior in character or quality; *also* **:** remarkably skilled ⟨~ at bridge⟩ **10 :** EXCELLENT, FINE ⟨had a ~ time⟩ — **great·ly** *adv* — **great·ness** *n*

great·coat \-,kōt\ *n* **:** a heavy overcoat

great-heart·ed \-'härt-əd\ *adj* **1 :** COURAGEOUS **2 :** MAGNANIMOUS

grebe \'grēb\ *n* **:** any of a group of lobe-toed diving birds related to the loons

Gre·cian \'grē-shən\ *adj* **:** GREEK

greed \'grēd\ *n* **:** acquisitive or selfish desire beyond reason **:** AVARICE — **greed·i·ly** *adv* — **greed·i·ness** *n* — **greedy** *adj*

¹**Greek** \'grēk\ *n* **1 :** a native or inhabitant of Greece **2 :** the ancient or modern language of Greece

²**Greek** *adj* **1 :** of, relating to, or characteristic of Greece, the Greeks, or Greek **2 :** ORTHODOX **3**

¹**green** \'grēn\ *adj* **1 :** of the color green **2 :** covered with verdure; *also* **:** consisting of green plants or of the leafy parts of plants ⟨a ~ salad⟩ **3 :** UNRIPE; *also* **:** IMMATURE **4 :** having a sickly appearance ⟨~ with envy⟩ **5 :** not fully processed or treated ⟨~ liquor⟩ ⟨~ hides⟩ **6 :** INEXPERIENCED; *also* **:** NAÏVE — **green·ish** *adj* — **green·ness** \'grēn-nəs\ *n*

²**green** *n* **1 :** a color between blue and yellow in the spectrum **:** the color of growing fresh grass or of the emerald **2 :** something of a green color **3** *pl* **:** leafy parts of plants (as for ornament or food) **4 :** a grassy plot; *esp* **:** a grassy area at the end of a golf fairway containing the hole into which the ball must be played

green·back \-,bak\ *n* **:** a legal-tender note issued by the U.S. government

green·belt \-,belt\ *n* **:** a belt of parkways or farmlands that encircles a community and is designed to prevent undesirable encroachments

green·ery \-(ə-)rē\ *n* **:** green foliage or plants

green·gro·cer \-,grō-sər\ *n, chiefly Brit* **:** a retailer of fresh vegetables and fruit

green·horn \-,hȯrn\ *n* **:** an inexperienced person; *esp* **:** one easily tricked or cheated

green·house \-,hau̇s\ *n* **:** a glass structure for the growing of tender plants

green·room \-,rüm, -,ru̇m\ *n* **:** a room in a theater or concert hall where actors or musicians relax before, between, or after appearances

green·sward \-,swȯrd\ *n* **:** turf green with growing grass

green·wood \-,wu̇d\ *n* **:** a forest green with foliage

greet \'grēt\ *vb* **1 :** to address with expressions of kind wishes **:** HAIL **2 :** to meet or react to in a specified manner ⟨~ed him with cheers⟩ **3 :** to be perceived by — **greet·er** *n*

greet·ing *n* **1 :** a salutation on meeting **2** *pl* **:** best wishes **:** REGARDS

gre·gar·i·ous \gri-'gar-ē-əs\ *adj* **1 :** SOCIAL, COMPANIONABLE **2 :** tending to flock together — **gre·gar·i·ous·ly** *adv* — **gre·gar·i·ous·ness** *n*

grem·lin \'grem-lən\ *n* **:** a small gnome held to be responsible for malfunction of equipment esp. in an airplane

gre·nade \grə-'nād\ *n* [MF, lit., pomegranate, fr. LL *granata*, fr. L *granatus* seedy, fr. *granum* grain, seed] **:** a case filled with a destructive agent (as an explosive) and designed to be hurled against an enemy

gren·a·dier \,gren-ə-'di͝er\ *n* **:** a member of a European regiment formerly armed with grenades

gren·a·dine \,gren-ə-'dēn\ *n* **:** a syrup flavored with pomegranates and used in mixed drinks

grew *past of* GROW

grey *var of* GRAY

grey·hound \'grā-,hau̇nd\ *n* **:** a tall slender dog noted for speed and keen sight

grid \'grid\ *n* **1 :** GRATING, GRIDIRON **2 :** a ridged or perforated metal plate for conducting current in a storage battery; *also* **:** an electron tube electrode with openings used for controlling the flow of electrons between other electrodes

grid·dle \'grid-ᵊl\ *n* **:** a flat usu. metal surface on which food is placed for cooking

griddle cake *n* **:** PANCAKE

grid·iron \'grid-,ī(-ə)rn\ *n* **1 :** a grate (as of parallel bars) for broiling food **2 :** something resembling a gridiron in appearance; *esp* **:** a football field

grief \'grēf\ *n* **1 :** emotional suffering caused by or as if by bereavement; *also* **:** a cause of such suffering **2 :** MISHAP, DISASTER

griev·ance \'grē-vəns\ *n* **1 :** a cause of distress affording reason for complaint or resistance **2 :** COMPLAINT

grieve \'grēv\ *vb* **1 :** to cause grief or sorrow to **:** DISTRESS **2 :** to feel grief **:** SORROW

griev·ous \'grē-vəs\ *adj* **1 :** OPPRESSIVE, ONEROUS **2 :** causing suffering **:** SEVERE ⟨a ~ wound⟩ **3 :** causing grief or sorrow 4 : SERIOUS, GRAVE — **griev·ous·ly** adv

¹grill \'gril\ vb 1 : to broil on a grill; also : to fry or toast on a griddle 2 : to question intensely

²grill n 1 : GRIDIRON; also : GRIDDLE 2 : an informal restaurant esp. in a hotel

grille or **grill** \'gril\ n : a grating that forms a barrier or screen

grill·work \'gril-,wərk\ n : work constituting or resembling a grille

grim \'grim\ adj 1 : CRUEL, SAVAGE, FIERCE 2 : harsh and forbidding in appearance 3 : RELENTLESS 4 : ghastly, repellent, or sinister in character — **grim·ly** adv — **grim·ness** n

grim·ace \'grim-əs, grim-'ās\ n : a facial expression usu. of disgust or disapproval — **grimace** vb

grime \'grīm\ n : soot, smut, or dirt adhering to or embedded in a surface; also : accumulated dirtiness and disorder — **grimy** adj

grin \'grin\ vb grinned; grin·ning : to draw back the lips so as to show the teeth esp. in amusement or laughter — **grin** n

¹grind \'grīnd\ vb ground \'graund\; grind·ing 1 : to reduce to small particles 2 : to wear down, polish, or sharpen by friction 3 : to press with a grating noise : GRIT ⟨~ the teeth⟩ 4 : OPPRESS 5 : to operate or produce by turning a crank 6 : to move with difficulty or friction ⟨gears ~ing⟩ 7 : DRUDGE; esp : to study hard

²grind n 1 : monotonous labor or routine; esp : intensive study 2 : a student who studies excessively

grind·er \'grīn-dər\ n 1 : MOLAR 2 pl : TEETH 3 : one that grinds 4 : a large sandwich usu. consisting of a long roll split lengthwise with various fillings

grind·stone \'grīn-,stōn\ n : a flat circular stone of natural sandstone that revolves on an axle and is used for grinding, shaping, or smoothing

¹grip \'grip\ vb gripped; grip·ping 1 : to seize firmly 2 : to hold strongly the interest of

²grip n 1 : GRASP; also : strength in gripping 2 : CONTROL, MASTERY 3 : UNDERSTANDING 4 : a device for grasping and holding 5 : SUITCASE

gripe \'grīp\ vb 1 : SEIZE, GRIP 2 : DISTRESS; also : VEX 3 : to cause or experience spasmodic pains in the bowels 4 : COMPLAIN — **gripe** n

grippe \'grip\ n : INFLUENZA

gris-gris \'grē-,grē\ n, pl gris-gris \-,grēz\ : an amulet or incantation used chiefly by people of African Negro ancestry

gris·ly \'griz-lē\ adj : HORRIBLE, GRUESOME

grist \'grist\ n : grain to be ground or already ground

gris·tle \'gris-əl\ n : CARTILAGE — **gris·tly** adj

grist·mill \'grist-,mil\ n : a mill for grinding grain

¹grit \'grit\ n 1 : a hard sharp granule (as of sand); also : material composed of such granules 2 : firmness of mind or spirit : unyielding courage — **grit·ty** adj

²grit vb grit·ted; grit·ting : GRIND, GRATE

grits \'grits\ n pl : coarsely ground hulled grain

griz·zled \'griz-əld\ adj : streaked or mixed with gray

¹griz·zly \'griz-lē\ adj : GRIZZLED

²grizzly n : GRIZZLY BEAR

grizzly bear n : a large pale-coated bear of western No. America

groan \'grōn\ vb 1 : MOAN 2 : to make a harsh sound under sudden or prolonged strain ⟨the chair ~ed under his weight⟩ — **groan** n

groat \'grōt\ n : a former British coin worth four pennies

gro·cer \'grō-sər\ n [MF grossier wholesaler, fr. gros coarse, gross, wholesale, fr. L grossus coarse] : a dealer esp. in staple foodstuffs — **gro·cery** \'grōs-(ə-)rē\ n

grog \'gräg\ n 1 : alcoholic liquor; esp : liquor (as rum) mixed with water

grog·gy \'gräg-ē\ adj : weak and dazed and unsteady on the feet or in action

groin \'groin\ n 1 : the fold marking the juncture of abdomen and thigh; also : the region of this fold 2 : the curved line in a building formed by the meeting of two vaults

grom·met \'gräm-ət\ n 1 : a ring of rope 2 : an eyelet of firm material to strengthen or protect an opening

¹groom \'grüm, 'grum\ n 1 : a male servant; esp : one in charge of horses 2 : BRIDEGROOM

²groom vb 1 : to attend to the cleaning of (an animal) 2 : to make neat, attractive, or acceptable : POLISH

grooms·man \'grümz-mən, 'grumz-\ n : a male friend who attends a bridegroom at his wedding

groove \'grüv\ n 1 : a long narrow channel 2 : a fixed routine — **groove** vb

grope \'grōp\ vb 1 : to feel about blindly or uncertainly in search ⟨~ for the right word⟩ 2 : to feel one's way by groping

gro·schen \'grō-shən\ n, pl groschen — see MONEY table

gros·grain \'grō-,grān\ n : a silk or rayon fabric with crosswise cotton ribs

gross \'grōs\ adj 1 : glaringly noticeable 2 : OUT-AND-OUT, UTTER 3 : BIG, BULKY; esp : excessively fat 4 : excessively luxuriant 5 : RANK 5 : GENERAL, BROAD 6 : consisting of an overall total exclusive of deductions ⟨~ earnings⟩ 7 : EARTHY, CARNAL ⟨~ pleasures⟩ 8 : UNDISCRIMINATING 9 : lacking knowledge or culture : UNREFINED 10 : OBSCENE — **gross·ly** adv — **gross·ness** n

²gross n 1 : an overall total exclusive of deductions 2 archaic : main body : MASS — **gross** vb

³gross n, pl gross : a total of 12 dozen things ⟨a ~ of pencils⟩

grosz \'grōsh\ n, pl gro·szy \'grō-shē\ — see MONEY table

grot \'grät\ n : GROTTO

gro·tesque \grō-'tesk\ adj 1 : FANCIFUL, BIZARRE 2 : absurdly incongruous 3 : ECCENTRIC — **gro·tesque·ly** adv

grot·to \'grät-ō\ n, pl -toes also -tos 1 : CAVE 2 : an artificial cavelike structure

grouch \'grauch\ n 1 : a fit of bad temper 2 : an habitually irritable or complaining person — **grouch** vb — **grouchy** adj

¹ground \'graund\ n 1 : the bottom of a body of water 2 pl : sediment at the bottom of a liquid : DREGS, LEES

3 : a basis for belief, action, or argument ⟨*~s* for divorce⟩ **4** : BACKGROUND **5** : FOUNDATION **6** : the surface of the earth; *also* : SOIL **7** : an area of land with a particular use ⟨parade *~s*⟩ **8** *pl* : the area about and pertaining to a building **9** : a conductor that makes electrical connection with the earth or a large body of zero potential — **ground·less** *adj*

²ground *vb* **1** : to bring to or place on the ground **2** : to provide a reason or justification for **3** : to instruct in fundamental principles **4** : to connect with an electrical ground **5** : to restrict to the ground ⟨*~* a pilot⟩ **6** : to run aground

³ground *past of* GRIND

ground cover *n* : low plants that grow over and cover the soil; *also* : a plant suitable for this use

ground·er *n* : a baseball hit on the ground

ground·hog \'graŭnd-,hóg, -,häg\ *n* : WOODCHUCK

ground·ling \'graŭnd-liŋ\ *n* **1** : a spectator in the cheaper part of a theater **2** : a person of inferior judgment or taste

ground·sheet \'graŭn(d)-,shēt\ *n* : a waterproof sheet placed on the ground for protection from moisture

ground·wa·ter \'graŭnd-,wót-ər, -,wät-\ *n* : water within the earth that supplies wells and springs

ground·work \-,wərk\ *n* : FOUNDATION, BASIS

¹group \'grüp\ *n* : a number of individuals related by a common factor (as physical association, community of interests, or blood)

²group *vb* : to associate in groups : CLUSTER, AGGREGATE

¹grouse \'graŭs\ *n, pl* **grouse** : a ground-dwelling game bird related to the pheasants

²grouse *vb* : COMPLAIN, GRUMBLE

grove \'grōv\ *n* : a small wood usu. without underbrush

grov·el \'gräv-əl, 'grəv-\ *vb* **-eled** *or* **-elled; -el·ing** *or* **-el·ling 1** : to creep or lie with the body prostrate in fear or humility **2** : CRINGE

grow \'grō\ *vb* **grew** \'grü\ **grown** \'grōn\ **grow·ing 1** : to spring up and come to maturity **2** : to be able to grow : THRIVE **3** : to unite by or as if by growth **4** : INCREASE, EXPAND **5** : RESULT, ORIGINATE **6** : to come into existence : ARISE **7** : BECOME **8** : to obtain influence ⟨habit *~s* on a man⟩ **9** : to cause to grow : CULTIVATE — **grow·er** *n*

growl \'graŭl\ *vb* **1** : RUMBLE **2** : to utter a deep throaty threatening sound ⟨the dog *~ed* at the stranger⟩ **3** : GRUMBLE — **growl** *n*

grown-up \'grōn-,əp\ *adj* : ADULT ⟨*~* books⟩ — **grown-up** *n*

growth \'grōth\ *n* **1** : stage or condition attained in growing **2** : a process of growing : progressive development or increase **3** : a result or product of growing ⟨a fine *~* of hair⟩; *also* : an abnormal mass of tissue (as a tumor)

¹grub \'grəb\ *vb* **grubbed; grub·bing 1** : to clear or root out by digging

2 : DRUDGE **3** : to dig in the ground usu. for a hidden object **4** : RUMMAGE

²grub *n* **1** : a soft thick wormlike larva ⟨beetle *~s*⟩ **2** : DRUDGE; *also* : a slovenly person **3** : FOOD

grub·by \'grəb-ē\ *adj* : DIRTY, SLOVENLY — **grub·bi·ness** *n*

grub·stake \'grəb-,stāk\ *n* : supplies or funds furnished a mining prospector in return for a promise of a share in his finds

¹grudge \'grəj\ *vb* : to be reluctant to give : BEGRUDGE

²grudge *n* : a feeling of deep-seated resentment or ill will

gru·el \'grü-əl\ *n* : a thin porridge

gru·el·ing *or* **gru·el·ling** \-ə-liŋ\ *adj* : requiring extreme effort : EXHAUSTING ⟨a *~* race⟩

grue·some \'grü-səm\ *adj* : inspiring horror or repulsion : GRISLY

gruff \'grəf\ *adj* **1** : rough in speech or manner **2** : being deep and harsh : HOARSE — **gruff·ly** *adv*

grum·ble \'grəm-bəl\ *vb* **1** : to mutter in discontent **2** : GROWL **3** : RUMBLE — **grum·bler** \-b(ə-)lər\ *n*

grumpy \'grəm-pē\ *adj* : moodily cross : SURLY

grunt \'grənt\ *n* : a deep throaty sound (as that of a hog) — **grunt** *vb*

gua·no \'gwän-ō\ *n* : a substance composed chiefly of the excrement of seabirds and used as a fertilizer

gua·ra·ni \,gwär-ə-'nē\ *n, pl* **guaranis** *or* **guaranies** — *see* MONEY table

¹guar·an·tee \,gar-ən-'tē\ *n* **1** : GUARANTOR **2** : GUARANTY 1 **3** : an agreement by which one person undertakes to secure another in the possession or enjoyment of something **4** : an assurance of the quality of or of the length of use to be expected from a product offered for sale **5** : GUARANTY 3

²guarantee *vb* **1** : to undertake to answer for the debt, failure to perform, or faulty performance of (another) **2** : to undertake an obligation to establish, perform, or continue ⟨*guaranteed* wage⟩ **3** : to give security to : SECURE

guar·an·tor \,gar-ən-'tór\ *n* : a person who gives a guarantee

¹guar·an·ty \'gar-ən-tē\ *n* **1** : an undertaking to answer for another's failure to pay a debt or perform a duty **2** : GUARANTEE **3** : PLEDGE, SECURITY **4** : GUARANTOR

²guaranty *vb* : GUARANTEE

¹guard \'gärd\ *n* **1** : a posture of defense **2** : the act or duty of protecting or defending : PROTECTION **3** : a man or a body of men on sentinel duty **4** *pl* : troops attached to the person of the sovereign **5** : BRAKEMAN **6** *Brit* : CONDUCTOR **7** : a football lineman playing between center and tackle; *also* : a basketball player stationed toward the rear **8** : a protective or safety device

²guard *vb* **1** : PROTECT, DEFEND **2** : to watch over **3** : to be on guard

guard·house \-,haŭs\ *n* **1** : a building occupied by a guard or used as a headquarters by soldiers on guard duty **2** : a military jail

guard·ian \'gärd-ē-ən\ *n* **1** : CUSTODIAN **2** : one who has the care of the person

---

ə abut; ᵊ kitten; ər further; a back; ā bake; ä cot, cart; aŭ out; ch chin; e less; ē easy; g gift; i trip; ī life; j joke; ŋ sing; ō flow; ó flaw; ói coin; th thin; t͟h this; ü loot; ŭ foot; y yet; yü few; yu̇ furious; zh vision

or property of another — **guard·ian·ship** *n*

guard·room \'gärd-,rüm, -,rùm\ *n* 1 : a room used by a military guard while on duty   2 : a room where military prisoners are confined

guards·man \'gärdz-mən\ *n* : a member of the guards

gu·ber·na·to·ri·al \,g(y)ü-bə(r)-nə-'tōr-ē-əl\ *adj* : of or relating to a governor

guer·don \'gord-ᵊn\ *n* : REWARD, RECOMPENSE

guer·ril·la *or* **gue·ril·la** \gə-'ril-ə\ *n* : a person who carries on irregular warfare esp. as a member of an independent unit

guess \'ges\ *vb* 1 : to form an opinion from little or no evidence   2 : to conjecture correctly about : DISCOVER   3 : BELIEVE, SUPPOSE — **guess** *n*

guest \'gest\ *n* 1 : a person to whom hospitality (as of a house or a club) is extended   2 : a patron of a commercial establishment (as a hotel or restaurant)

guf·faw \(,)gə-'fò\ *n* : a loud burst of laughter — **guffaw** *vb*

guid·ance \'gïd-ᵊns\ *n* 1 : the act or process of guiding   2 : ADVICE, DIRECTION

¹guide \'gïd\ *n* 1 : one who leads or directs another in his way or course   2 : one who exhibits and explains points of interest   3 : something that provides a person with guiding information; *also* : SIGNPOST   4 : a device on a machine to direct the motion of something

²guide *vb* 1 : CONDUCT   2 : MANAGE, DIRECT   3 : SUPERINTEND

guide·book \-,bùk\ *n* : a book of information for travelers

guided missile *n* : a missile whose course toward a target may be altered during flight

gui·don \'gïd-,än, -ᵊn\ *n* : a small flag usu. borne by a military unit as a unit marker

guild \'gild\ *n* : an association of men with common aims and interests; *esp* : a medieval association of merchants or craftsmen — **guild·hall** \-,hòl\ *n*

guil·der \'gil-dər\ *n* : GULDEN

guile \'gïl\ *n* : deceitful cunning : DUPLICITY — **guile·ful** *adj* — **guile·less** \'gïl-ləs\ *adj* — **guile·less·ness** *n*

guil·lo·tine \'gil-ə-,tēn, 'gē-(y)ə-\ *n* : a machine for beheading persons — **guillotine** *vb*

guilt \'gilt\ *n* 1 : the fact of having committed an offense esp. against the law   2 : BLAMEWORTHINESS   3 : a feeling of responsibility for offenses — **guilt·less** *adj*

guilty *adj* 1 : having committed a breach of conduct   2 : suggesting or involving guilt   3 : aware of or suffering from guilt — **guilt·i·ness** *n*

guin·ea \'gin-ē\ *n* : a British gold coin no longer issued worth 21 shillings

guinea pig *n* : a small stocky short-eared and nearly tailless So. American rodent

guise \'gïz\ *n* 1 : a form or style of dress : COSTUME   2 : external appearance : SEMBLANCE

gui·tar \gə-'tär\ *n* : a musical instrument with six strings plucked with a plectrum or with the fingers

gulch \'gəlch\ *n* : RAVINE

gul·den \'gül-dən\ *n, pl* **guldens** *or* **gulden** — see MONEY table

gulf \'gəlf\ *n* 1 : an extension of an ocean or a sea into the land   2 : ABYSS, CHASM   3 : a wide separation

¹gull \'gəl\ *n* : a usu. white or gray long-winged web-footed seabird

²gull *vb* : to make a dupe of : DECEIVE — **gull·ible** *adj*

³gull *n* : DUPE

gul·let \'gəl-ət\ *n* : ESOPHAGUS; *also* : THROAT

gul·ly \'gəl-ē\ *n* : a trench worn in the earth by running water after rains

gulp \'gəlp\ *vb* 1 : to swallow hurriedly or greedily   2 : SUPPRESS (~ down a sob)   3 : to catch the breath as if in taking a long drink — **gulp** *n*

¹gum \'gəm\ *n* : the tissue along the jaw that surrounds the necks of the teeth

²gum *n* 1 : a sticky plant exudate; *esp* : one that hardens on drying and is soluble in or swells in water and that includes substances used as emulsifiers, adhesives, and thickeners and in inks   2 : a sticky substance   3 : a preparation usu. of a plant gum sweetened and flavored and used as a chew — **gum·my** *adj*

gum arabic *n* : a water-soluble gum obtained from several acacias and used esp. in adhesives, in confectionery, and in pharmacy

gum·bo \'gəm-bō\ *n* : a rich thick soup (as of vegetables) with meat or seafood) usu. thickened with okra

gum·boil \'gəm-,bòil\ *n* : an abscess in the gum

gum·drop \-,dräp\ *n* : a candy made usu. from corn syrup with gelatin and coated with sugar crystals

gump·tion \'gəmp-shən\ *n* 1 : shrewd common sense   2 : ENTERPRISE, INITIATIVE

¹gun \'gən\ *n* 1 : CANNON   2 : a portable firearm   3 : a discharge of a gun   4 : something suggesting a gun in shape or function   5 : THROTTLE

²gun *vb* **gunned**; **gun·ning** 1 : to hunt with a gun   2 : SHOOT   3 : to open up the throttle of so as to increase speed ⟨~ the engine⟩

gun·boat \-,bōt\ *n* : a small lightly armed ship for use in shallow waters

gun·fight \-,fït\ *n* : a duel with guns

gun·fire \-,fï(ə)r\ *n* : the firing of guns

gun·man \-mən\ *n* : a man armed with a gun; *esp* : an armed bandit or gangster

gun·ner *n* 1 : a soldier or airman who operates or aims a gun   2 : one that hunts with a gun

gun·nery \'gən-(ə-)rē\ *n* : the use of guns; *esp* : the science of the flight of projectiles and of the effective use of guns

gunnery sergeant *n* : a noncommissioned officer in the marine corps ranking next below a first sergeant

gun·ny \'gən-ē\ *n* 1 : coarse jute material for making sacks   2 : BURLAP

gun·ny·sack \-,sak\ *n* : a sack made of gunny or burlap

gun·point \'gən-,pòint\ *n* : the point of a gun — **at gunpoint** : under a threat of death by being shot

gun·pow·der \'gən-,paùd-ər\ *n* : explosive powder used in guns and blasting

gun·shot \-,shät\ *n* 1 : shot or a projectile fired from a gun   2 : the range of a gun ⟨within ~⟩

gun-shy \-,shï\ *adj* 1 : afraid of a loud noise (as of a gun)   2 : markedly distrustful

gun·smith \-ˌsmith\ *n* : one whose business is the making and repair of firearms
gun·wale *or* **gun·nel** \'gən-ᵊl\ *n* : the upper edge of a ship's side
gup·py \'gəp-ē\ *n* : a tiny brightly colored tropical fish
gur·gle \'gər-gəl\ *vb* **1** : to flow in a broken irregular current **2** : to make a sound like that of a gurgling liquid — **gurgle** *n*
gush \'gəsh\ *vb* **1** : to issue or pour forth copiously or violently : SPOUT **2** : to make an effusive display of affection or enthusiasm
gush·er *n* : one that gushes; *esp* : an oil well with a large natural flow
gushy *adj* : marked by effusive sentimentality
gus·set \'gəs-ət\ *n* : a triangular insert (as in a seam of a sleeve) to give width or strength
gust \'gəst\ *n* **1** : a sudden brief rush of wind **2** : a sudden outburst : SURGE — **gusty** *adj*
gus·ta·to·ry \'gəs-tə-ˌtōr-ē\ *adj* : of, relating to, or being the sense or sensation of taste
gus·to \'gəs-tō\ *n* : RELISH, ZEST
¹**gut** \'gət\ *n* **1** *pl* : BOWELS, ENTRAILS **2** : the alimentary canal or a part of it (as the intestine); *also* : BELLY, ABDOMEN **3** *pl* : the inner essential parts **4** *pl* : COURAGE, STAMINA
²**gut** *vb* **gut·ted; gut·ting 1** : EVISCERATE **2** : to destroy the inside of ⟨*fire* *gutted* the building⟩
gut·ter \'gət-ər\ *n* : a channel for carrying off waste water (as at the eaves of a house or at the sides of a road)
gut·ter·snipe \-ˌsnīp\ *n* : a street urchin
gut·tur·al \'gət-ə-rəl\ *adj* **1** : of or relating to the throat **2** : sounded in the throat **3** : being or marked by an utterance that is strange, unpleasant, or disagreeable — **guttural** *n*
gut·ty \'gət-ē\ *adj* : being vital, bold, and challenging ⟨∼ realism⟩
¹**guy** \'gī\ *n* : a rope, chain, or rod attached to something to steady it

²**guy** *vb* : to steady or reinforce with a guy
³**guy** *n* : MAN, FELLOW
⁴**guy** *vb* : to make fun of : RIDICULE
guz·zle \'gəz-əl\ *vb* : to drink greedily
gym \'jim\ *n* : GYMNASIUM
gym·kha·na \jim-'kän-ə\ *n* : a meet featuring sports contests (as horseback-riding events)
gym·na·si·um \jim-'nā-zē-əm *for 1*, gim-'nä- *for 2*\ *n*, *pl* **-si·ums** *or* **-sia** \-zē-ə\ [L, fr. Gk *gymnasion*, fr. *gymnazein* to exercise naked, fr. *gymnos* naked] **1** : a place or building for sports activities **2** : a German secondary school that prepares students for the university
gym·nas·tics \jim-'nas-tiks\ *n* : physical exercises performed in or adapted to performance in a gymnasium — **gym·nast** \'jim-ˌnast\ *n*
gyn·e·col·o·gy \ˌjin-i-'käl-ə-jē, ˌgīn-\ *n* : a branch of medicine dealing with women and diseases peculiar to women — **gyn·e·co·log·i·cal** \-kə-'läj-i-kəl\ *adj* — **gyn·e·col·o·gist** \-'käl-ə-jəst\ *n*
gyp \'jip\ *n* **1** : CHEAT, SWINDLER **2** : FRAUD, SWINDLE — **gyp** *vb*
gyp·sum \'jip-səm\ *n* : a calcium-containing mineral used in making plaster of paris
Gyp·sy \'jip-sē\ *n* : one of a dark Caucasian race coming orig. from India and living chiefly in Europe and the U.S.; *also* : the language of this race
gy·rate \'jī-ˌrāt\ *vb* **1** : to revolve around a point or axis **2** : to oscillate with or as if with a circular or spiral motion — **gy·ra·tion** \jī-'rā-shən\ *n*
gy·ro·com·pass \'jī-rō-ˌkəm-pəs, -ˌkäm-\ *n* : a compass in which the axis of a spinning gyroscope points to the north
gy·ro·scope \'jī-rə-ˌskōp\ *n* : a wheel or disk mounted to spin rapidly about an axis that is free to turn in various directions
gyve \'jīv\ *n* : FETTER — usu. used in pl. — **gyve** *vb*

---

h \'āch\ *n*, *often cap* : the 8th letter of the English alphabet
ha·ba·ne·ra \ˌ(h)äb-ə-'ner-ə\ *n* : a Cuban dance in slow time; *also* : the music for this dance
ha·be·as cor·pus \ˌhā-bē-əs-'kȯr-pəs\ *n* : a writ issued to bring a party before a court
hab·er·dash·er \'hab-ə(r)-ˌdash-ər\ *n* : a dealer in men's furnishings
hab·er·dash·ery \-ˌdash-(ə-)rē\ *n* **1** : goods sold by a haberdasher **2** : a haberdasher's shop
ha·bil·i·ment \hə-'bil-ə-mənt\ *n* **1** *pl* : TRAPPINGS, EQUIPMENT **2** : DRESS; *esp* : the dress characteristic of an occupation or occasion — usu. used in pl.
hab·it \'hab-ət\ *n* **1** : DRESS, GARB **2** : BEARING, CONDUCT **3** : PHYSIQUE **4** : mental makeup **5** : a usual manner of behavior : CUSTOM **6** : a behavior pattern acquired by frequent repetition

7 : ADDICTION **8** : mode of growth or occurrence
hab·it·a·ble \'hab-ət-ə-bəl\ *adj* : capable of being lived in — **hab·it·abil·i·ty** \ˌhab-ət-ə-'bil-ət-ē\ *n* — **hab·it·able·ness** \'hab-ət-ə-bəl-nəs\ *n* — **hab·it·ably** *adv*
hab·i·tant \'hab-ət-ənt\ *n* : INHABITANT, RESIDENT
hab·i·tat \'hab-ə-ˌtat\ *n* [L, it inhabits] : the place or kind of place where a plant or animal naturally occurs
hab·i·ta·tion \ˌhab-ə-'tā-shən\ *n* **1** : OCCUPANCY **2** : a dwelling place : RESIDENCE **3** : SETTLEMENT
hab·it-form·ing \'hab-ət-ˌfȯr-miŋ\ *adj* : inducing the formation of an addiction
ha·bit·u·al \hə-'bich-(ə-w)əl\ *adj* **1** : CUSTOMARY **2** : doing, practicing, or acting in some manner by force of habit **3** : inherent in an individual — **ha·bit·u·al·ly** *adv* — **ha·bit·u·al·ness** *n*

---

ha·bit·u·ate \hə-'bich-ə-ˌwāt\ vb : AC-CUSTOM — **ha·bit·u·a·tion** \-ˌbich-ə-'wā-shən\ n

ha·bi·tué \hə-'bich-ə-ˌwā\ n : one who frequents a place or class of places

ha·ci·en·da \ˌ(h)äs-ē-'en-də\ n 1 : a landed estate in a Spanish-speaking country 2 : the main building of a farm or ranch

¹hack \'hak\ vb 1 : to cut with re-peated irregular blows : CHOP 2 : to cough in a short dry manner — **hack·er** n

²hack n 1 : an implement for hacking; also : a hacking blow 2 : a short dry cough

³hack n 1 : a horse let out for hire or used for varied work; also : a horse worn out in service 2 : a light easy often 3-gaited saddle horse 3 : HACK-NEY 2 : a writer who works mainly for hire

hack·le \'hak-əl\ n 1 : one of the long feathers on the neck or lower back of a bird 2 pl : hairs (as on the neck of a dog) that can be erected 3 pl : TEMPER, DANDER

hack·man \'hak-mən\ n : a driver of a cab

¹hack·ney \'hak-nē\ n 1 : a horse for riding or driving 2 : a carriage or automobile kept for hire

²hackney vb : to make trite or common-place

hack·neyed adj : worn out from too long or too much use : COMMONPLACE

hack·saw \'hak-ˌsò\ n : a fine-tooth saw in a bow-shaped frame for cutting metal

hack·work \-ˌwòrk\ n : work done on order usu. according to a formula and in conformity with commercial stan-dards

had past of HAVE

had·dock \'had-ək\ n : an Atlantic food fish usu. smaller than the related cod

Ha·des \'hād-(ˌ)ēz\ n 1 : the abode of the dead in Greek mythology 2 often not cap : HELL

haem·or·rhage \'hem-(ə-)rij\ var of HEMORRHAGE

haf·ni·um \'haf-nē-əm\ n : a gray metallic chemical element

haft \'haft\ n : the handle of a weapon or tool

hag \'hag\ n 1 : WITCH 2 : an ugly, slatternly, or evil-looking old woman

hag·gard \'hag-ərd\ adj : having a worn or emaciated appearance : GAUNT syn careworn, wasted — **hag·gard·ly** adv

hag·gis \'hag-əs\ n : a pudding esp. popular in Scotland made of the heart, liver, and lungs of a sheep or a calf minced with suet, onions, oatmeal, and seasonings and boiled in the stomach of the animal

hag·gle \'hag-əl\ vb : to argue in bar-gaining : WRANGLE — **hag·gler** \-(ə-)lər\ n

hag·i·og·ra·phy \ˌhag-ē-'äg-rə-fē, ˌhā-jē-\ n 1 : biography of saints or vener-ated persons 2 : idealizing or idolizing biography — **hag·i·og·ra·pher** n

¹hail \'hāl\ n 1 : small lumps of ice that fall from the clouds esp. during thunderstorms 2 : something that gives the effect of falling hail ⟨a ~ of bullets⟩

²hail vb 1 : to precipitate hail 2 : to hurl forcibly

³hail interj — used to express acclama-tion

⁴hail vb : SALUTE, GREET

⁵hail n 1 : an expression of greeting, approval, or praise 2 : hearing distance

hail·stone \-ˌstōn\ n : a pellet of hail

hail·storm \-ˌstòrm\ n : a storm accom-panied by hail

hair \'haər\ n : a threadlike outgrowth esp. of the skin of a mammal; also : a covering (as of the head) consisting of such hairs — **hair·less** adj

hair·breadth \-ˌbredth\ or **hairs-breadth** \'haərz-\ n : a very small distance or margin

hair·brush \-ˌbrəsh\ n : a brush for the hair

hair·cloth \'haər-ˌklòth\ n : a stiff wiry fabric (as of horsehair) used esp. for upholstery

hair·cut \-ˌkət\ n : the act, process, or style of cutting and shaping the hair

hair·do \-ˌdü\ n : a way of dressing a woman's hair

hair·dress·er \-ˌdres-ər\ n : one who dresses or cuts women's hair

hair·line \'haər-ˌlīn\ n 1 : a very slender line 2 : the outline of the scalp or of the hair on the head

hair·pin \-ˌpin\ n : a U-shaped pin to hold the hair in place

hair·rais·ing \'haər-ˌrā-ziŋ\ adj : caus-ing terror or astonishment

hair·split·ter \-ˌsplit-ər\ n : a person who makes unnecessarily fine distinc-tions in reasoning or argument — **hair·split·ting** adj or n

hairy \'ha(ə)r-ē\ adj : covered with or as if with hair — **hair·i·ness** n

hake \'hāk\ n : a marine food fish re-lated to the cod

hal·berd \'hal-bərd, 'hòl-\ or **hal·bert** \-bərt\ n : a weapon esp. of the 15th and 16th centuries consisting of a battle-ax and pike mounted on a long handle

hal·cy·on \'hal-sē-ən\ adj : CALM, PEACEFUL

¹hale \'hāl\ adj : free from defect, dis-ease, or infirmity syn healthy, sound, robust, well

²hale vb 1 : HAUL, PULL 2 : to compel to go ⟨haled him into court⟩

ha·ler \'häl-ər\ n — see MONEY table

¹half \'haf, 'hàf\ n, pl **halves** \'havz, 'hàvz\ 1 : one of two equal parts into which something is divisible 2 : one of a pair

²half adj 1 : being one of two equal parts; also : amounting to nearly half 2 : of half the usual size or extent 3 : PARTIAL, IMPERFECT — **half** adv

half·back \-ˌbak\ n : a football back stationed on or near the flank

half·baked \-'bākt\ adj 1 : not thor-oughly baked 2 : poorly planned; also : lacking intelligence or common sense

half boot n : a boot with a top reaching above the ankle

half·breed \'haf-ˌbrēd, 'hàf-\ n : the offspring of parents of different races

half brother n : a brother by one parent only

half·caste \'haf-ˌkast, 'hàf-\ n : one of mixed racial descent

half·heart·ed \'haf-'härt-əd, 'hàf-\ adj : lacking spirit or interest — **half·heart·ed·ly** adv — **half·heart·ed·ness** n

half·mast \-'mast\ n : a point some distance but not necessarily halfway down below the top of a mast or staff or the peak of a gaff (flags hanging at ~)

half·pen·ny \'hāp-(ə-)nē\ *n, pl* **-pence** \'hā-pəns\ *or* **-pennies** : a British coin representing one half of a penny

half sister *n* : a sister by one parent only

half step *n* : a pitch interval between any two adjacent keys on a keyboard instrument

half-track \'haf-ˌtrak, 'hȧf-\ *n* **1** : an endless chain-track drive system that propels a vehicle supported in front by a pair of wheels **2** : a motor vehicle propelled by half-tracks; *esp* : such a vehicle lightly armored for military use

half-truth \-ˌtrüth\ *n* : a statement that is only partially true; *esp* : one that mingles truth and falsehood and is deliberately intended to deceive

half·way \-'wā\ *adj* **1** : midway between two points **2** : PARTIAL — **half·way** *adv*

half-wit \-ˌwit\ *n* : a foolish or imbecilic person — **half-wit·ted** \-'wit-əd\ *adj*

hal·i·but \'hal-ə-bət\ *n* : a large edible marine flatfish

hal·i·to·sis \ˌhal-ə-'tō-səs\ *n* : a condition of having fetid breath

hall \'hȯl\ *n* **1** : the residence of a medieval king or noble; *also* : the house of a landed proprietor **2** : a large public building **3** : a college or university building **4** : LOBBY; *also* : CORRIDOR **5** : AUDITORIUM

hal·le·lu·jah \ˌhal-ə-'lü-yə\ *interj* — used to express praise, joy, or thanks

hall·mark \'hȯl-ˌmärk\ *n* **1** : a mark put on an article to indicate origin, purity, or genuineness **2** : a distinguishing characteristic

hal·lo \hə-'lō, ha-\ *or* **hal·loo** \-'lü\ *var of* HOLLO

hal·low \'hal-ō\ *vb* **1** : CONSECRATE **2** : REVERE — **hal·lowed** \-ōd, -ə-wəd\ *adj*

Hal·low·een \ˌhal-ə-'wēn, ˌhäl-\ *n* : the evening of October 31 observed esp. by children in merrymaking and masquerading

hal·lu·ci·na·tion \hə-ˌlüs-ᵊn-'ā-shən\ *n* : a perceiving of objects with no reality usu. arising from disorder of the nervous system; *also* : something so perceived **syn** DELUSION, ILLUSION, MIRAGE — **hal·lu·ci·nate** \-'lüs-ᵊn-ˌāt\ *vb* — **hal·lu·ci·na·tion·al** \-ˌlüs-ᵊn-'ā-sh(ə-)nəl\ *adj* — **hal·lu·ci·na·tive** \-'lüs-ᵊn-ˌāt-iv\ *adj* — **hal·lu·ci·na·to·ry** \-ᵊn-ə-ˌtōr-ē\ *adj*

hall·way \'hȯl-ˌwā\ *n* : an entrance hall; *also* : CORRIDOR

ha·lo \'hā-lō\ *n, pl* **-los** *or* **-loes 1** : a circle of light appearing to surround a shining body (as the sun or moon) **2** : the aura of glory surrounding an idealized person or thing

hal·o·gen \'hal-ə-jən\ *n* : any of the five chemical elements fluorine, chlorine, bromine, iodine, and astatine

¹halt \'hȯlt\ *adj* : LAME

²halt *n* : STOP

³halt *vb* **1** : to stop marching or traveling **2** : DISCONTINUE, END

¹hal·ter \'hȯl-tər\ *n* **1** : a rope or strap for leading or tying an animal; *also* : HEADSTALL **2** : NOOSE; *also*

: death by hanging **3** : a brief blouse held in place by straps around the neck and across the back

²halter *vb* **1** : to catch with or as if with a halter; *also* : to put a halter on (as a horse) **2** : HAMPER, RESTRAIN

halt·ing *adj* **1** : LAME, LIMPING **2** : UNCERTAIN, FALTERING — **halt·ing·ly** *adv*

halve \'hav, 'hȧv\ *vb* **1** : to divide into two equal parts; *also* : to share equally **2** : to reduce to one half

halv·ers \'hav-ərz, 'hȧv-\ *n pl* : half shares

halves *pl of* HALF

hal·yard *or* **hal·liard** \'hal-yərd\ *n* : a rope or tackle for hoisting and lowering

¹ham \'ham\ *n* **1** : a buttock with its associated thigh; *also* : a cut of meat and esp. pork from this region **2** : an inept actor esp. in a highly theatrical style **3** : an operator of an amateur radio station

²ham *vb* **hammed; ham·ming** : to overplay a part **:** OVERACT

hama·dry·ad \ˌham-ə-'drī-əd\ *n* : a nymph living in the woods

ham·burg·er \'ham-ˌbər-gər\ *or* **hamburg** \-ˌbərg\ *n* **1** : ground beef **2** : a sandwich consisting of a ground-beef patty in a round roll

ham·let \'ham-lət\ *n* : a small group of houses in the country

¹ham·mer \'ham-ər\ *n* **1** : a hand tool used for pounding; *also* : something resembling a hammer in form or function **2** : the part of a gun whose striking action causes explosion of the charge **3** : a metal sphere with a flexible wire handle that is hurled for distance in a track-and-field event (**hammer throw**)

²hammer *vb* **1** : to beat, drive, or shape with repeated blows of a hammer **:** POUND **2** : to produce or bring about as if by repeated blows (~ out a policy)

ham·mer·lock \-ˌläk\ *n* : a wrestling hold in which an opponent's arm is held bent behind his back

ham·mer·toe \-ˌtō\ *n* : a deformed toe with the second and third joints permanently flexed

ham·mock \'ham-ək\ *n* [Sp *hamaca*, of AmerInd origin] : a swinging couch hung by cords at each end

¹ham·per \'ham-pər\ *vb* **1** : IMPEDE **syn** trammel, clog, fetter, shackle

²hamper *n* : a large basket

ham·ster \'ham-stər\ *n* : a stocky short-tailed Old World rodent with large cheek pouches

ham·string \'ham-ˌstriŋ\ *vb* **1** : to cripple by cutting the leg tendons **2** : to make ineffective or powerless **:** CRIPPLE

¹hand \'hand\ *n* **1** : the end of a front limb when modified (as in man) for grasping **2** : personal possession — usu. used in pl; *also* : CONTROL **3** : SIDE **4** : a pledge esp. of betrothal **5** : HANDWRITING **6** : SKILL, ABILITY; *also* : a significant part **7** : SOURCE **8** : ASSISTANCE; *also* : PARTICIPATION **9** : an outburst of applause **10** : a single round in a card game; *also* : the cards held by a player after a deal **11** : WORKER, EMPLOYEE; *also* : a member of a ship's crew — **hand·less** *adj* — **at hand** : near in time or place

²**hand** *vb* **1 :** to lead, guide, or assist with the hand **2 :** to give, pass, or transmit with the hand

hand-bag \'han(d)-ˌbag\ *n* **:** a woman's bag for carrying small personal articles and money

hand-ball \-ˌbȯl\ *n* **:** a game played by striking a small rubber ball against a wall with the hand

hand-bar-row \-ˌbar-ō\ *n* **:** a flat rectangular frame with handles at both ends that is carried by two persons

hand-bill \-ˌbil\ *n* **:** a small printed sheet for distribution by hand

hand-book \-ˌbu̇k\ *n* **:** a concise reference book **:** MANUAL

hand-car \'han(d)-ˌkär\ *n* **:** a small 4-wheeled railroad car propelled by a hand-operated mechanism or by a small motor

hand-clasp \-ˌklasp\ *n* **:** HANDSHAKE

²**hand-cuff** \-ˌkəf\ *vb* **:** MANACLE

²**handcuff** *n* **:** a metal fastening that can be locked around a wrist and is usu. connected with another such fastening

hand-ful \-ˌfu̇l\ *n* **1 :** as much or as many as the hand will grasp **2 :** a small number ⟨a ~ of people⟩

hand-gun \-ˌgən\ *n* **:** a firearm held and fired with one hand

¹**hand-i-cap** \'han-di-ˌkap\ *n* **1 :** a contest in which an artificial advantage is given or disadvantage imposed on a contestant to equalize chances of winning; *also* **:** the advantage given or disadvantage imposed **2 :** a disadvantage that makes achievement difficult

²**handicap** *vb* **-capped; -cap-ping 1 :** to give a handicap to **2 :** to put at a disadvantage

hand-i-craft \-ˌkraft\ *n* **1 :** manual skill **2 :** an occupation requiring manual skill **3 :** the articles fashioned by those engaged in handicraft — **hand-i-craft-er** *n* — **hand-i-crafts-man** \-ˌkrafts-mən\ *n*

hand-i-work \-ˌwərk\ *n* **:** work done personally

hand-ker-chief \'haŋ-kər-chəf, -ˌchēf\ *n*, *pl* **-chiefs** \-chəfs, -ˌchēfs\ *also* **-chieves** \-ˌchēvz\ **:** a small piece of cloth esp. for various personal purposes (as the wiping of the face)

¹**han-dle** \'han-dᵊl\ *n* **:** a part (as of a tool) designed to be grasped by the hand

²**handle** *vb* **1 :** to touch, hold, or manage with the hands **2 :** to deal with **3 :** to deal or trade in

han-dle-bar \-ˌbär\ *n* **:** a straight or bent bar with a handle (as for steering a bicycle) at each end

hand-made \'han(d)-ˌmād\ *adj* **:** made by hand or a hand process

hand-maid \-ˌmād\ *or* **hand-maid-en** \-ˌᵊn\ *n* **:** a female attendant

hand-out \'hand-ˌau̇t\ *n* **1 :** a portion (as of food) given to a beggar **2 :** a press release from a news service; *also* **:** a prepared statement released to the press

hand-pick \'han(d)-ˌpik\ *vb* **:** to select personally

hand-rail \'hand-ˌrāl\ *n* **:** a narrow rail for grasping as a support

hand-sel *also* **han-sel** \'han-səl\ *n* **1 :** a gift made as a token of good luck **2 :** a first installment

hand-shake \'han(d)-ˌshāk\ *n* **:** a clasping of right hands by two people (as in greeting)

hand-some \'han-səm\ *adj* **1 :** SIZABLE, AMPLE **2 :** GENEROUS, LIBERAL **3 :** pleasing and usu. impressive in appearance *syn* beautiful, lovely, pretty, comely, fair — **hand-some-ly** *adv* — **hand-some-ness** *n*

hand-spike \'han(d)-ˌspīk\ *n* **:** a bar used as a lever

hand-spring \-ˌspriŋ\ *n* **:** a feat of tumbling in which the body turns forward or backward in a full circle from a standing position and lands first on the hands and then on the feet

hand-to-hand \ˌhan-tə-'hand\ *adj* **:** being at very close quarters

hand-wo-ven \'hand-ˌwō-vən\ *adj* **:** produced on a hand-operated loom

hand-writ-ing \-ˌrīt-iŋ\ *n* **:** writing done by hand; *also* **:** the form of writing peculiar to a person — **hand-writ-ten** \-ˌrit-ᵊn\ *adj*

handy \'han-dē\ *adj* **1 :** conveniently near **2 :** easily used or managed **3 :** DEXTEROUS — **hand-i-ly** *adv* — **hand-i-ness** *n*

handy-man \-ˌman\ *n* **:** one who does odd jobs

¹**hang** \'haŋ\ *vb* **hung** \'həŋ\ *also* **hanged** \'haŋd\ **hang-ing 1 :** to fasten or remain fastened to an elevated point without support from below; *also* **:** to fasten or be fastened so as to allow free motion on the point of suspension ⟨~ a door⟩ **2 :** to put or come to death by suspension (as from a gallows) **3 :** to fasten to a wall ⟨~ wallpaper⟩ **4 :** to prevent (a jury) from coming to a decision **5 :** to display (pictures) in a gallery **6 :** to remain stationary in the air **7 :** to be imminent **8 :** DEPEND **9 :** to take hold for support **10 :** to be burdensome **11 :** to undergo delay **12 :** to incline downward; *also* **:** to fit or fall from the figure in easy lines **13 :** to be rapidly attentive **14 :** LINGER, LOITER — **hang-er** *n*

²**hang** *n* **1 :** the manner in which a thing hangs **2 :** peculiar and significant meaning **3 :** KNACK

hang-ar \'haŋ-ər\ *n* **:** a covered and usu. enclosed area for housing and repairing airplanes

hang-dog \'haŋ-ˌdȯg\ *adj* **1 :** ASHAMED, GUILTY **2 :** ABJECT, COWED

hang-er-on \ˌhaŋ-ər-'ȯn, -'än\ *n*, *pl* **hangers-on :** one who hangs around a person or place esp. for personal gain

hang-ing \'haŋ-iŋ\ *n* **1 :** an execution by strangling or snapping the neck by a suspended noose **2 :** something hung — **hanging** *adj*

hang-man \-mən\ *n* **:** a public executioner

hang-nail \-ˌnāl\ *n* **:** a bit of skin hanging loose at the side or base of a fingernail

hang-out \'haŋ-ˌau̇t\ *n* **:** a favorite or usual place of resort

hang-over \-ˌō-vər\ *n* **1 :** something (as a surviving custom) that remains from what is past **2 :** disagreeable physical effects following heavy drinking

hank \'haŋk\ *n* **:** COIL, LOOP

han-ker \'haŋ-kər\ *vb* **:** to desire strongly or persistently **:** LONG — **han-ker-ing** *n*

han-ky-pan-ky \ˌhaŋ-kē-'pan-kē\ *n* **:** questionable or underhand activity

han-som \'han-səm\ *n* **:** a 2-wheeled covered carriage with the driver's seat elevated at the rear

Ha·nuk·kah \'kän-ə-kə, 'hän-\ *n* : an 8-day Jewish holiday commemorating the rededication of the Temple

hap \'hap\ *n* 1 : HAPPENING 2 : CHANCE, FORTUNE

¹hap·haz·ard \hap-'haz-ərd\ *n* : CHANCE

²haphazard *adj* : marked by lack of plan or order : AIMLESS — **hap·haz·ard·ly** *adv* — **hap·haz·ard·ness** *n*

hap·less \'hap-ləs\ *adj* : UNFORTUNATE — **hap·less·ly** *adv* — **hap·less·ness** *n*

hap·ly \-lē\ *adv* : by chance

hap·pen \'hap-ən\ *vb* 1 : to occur by chance 2 : to take place 3 : CHANCE

hap·pen·ing \-(ə-)niŋ\ *n* : OCCURRENCE

hap·pi·ly \'hap-ə-lē\ *adv* 1 : LUCKILY 2 : in a happy manner or state 3 : APTLY, SUCCESSFULLY

hap·pi·ness \'hap-ē-nəs\ *n* 1 : a state of well-being and contentment; *also* : a pleasurable satisfaction 2 : APTNESS

hap·py \'hap-ē\ *adj* 1 : FORTUNATE 2 : APT, FELICITOUS 3 : enjoying well-being and contentment 4 : PLEASANT; *also* : PLEASED, GRATIFIED **syn** glad, cheerful, lighthearted, joyful, joyous

hap·py-go-lucky *adj* : CAREFREE

hara-kiri \,har-i-'ki(ə)r-ē\ *n* : suicide by disembowelment

ha·rangue \hə-'raŋ\ *n* 1 : a bombastic ranting discourse 2 : LECTURE — **harangue** *vb* — **ha·rangu·er** *n*

ha·rass \hə-'ras, 'har-əs\ *vb* 1 : to worry and impede by repeated raids 2 : EXHAUST, FATIGUE 3 : to annoy continually **syn** harry, plague, pester, tease, tantalize — **ha·rass·ment** *n*

har·bin·ger \'här-bən-jər\ *n* : one that announces or foreshadows what is coming : PRECURSOR; *also* : PORTENT

¹har·bor \'här-bər\ *n* 1 : a place of security and comfort 2 : a part of a body of water protected and deep enough to furnish anchorage : PORT

²harbor *vb* 1 : to give or take refuge : SHELTER 2 : to be the home or habitat of; *also* : LIVE 3 : to hold a thought or feeling (~ a grudge)

har·bor·age \-ij\ *n* : SHELTER, HARBOR

harbour *chiefly Brit var of* HARBOR

hard \'härd\ *adj* 1 : not easily penetrated 2 : having an alcoholic content of more than 22.5 percent; *also* : containing salts that prevent lathering with soap 3 : stable in value (~ currency) 4 : physically fit; *also* : free from flaw 5 : FIRM, DEFINITE (~ agreement) 6 : CLOSE, SEARCHING (~ look) 7 : REALISTIC (good ~ sense) 8 : OBDURATE, UNFEELING (~ heart) 9 : difficult to bear (~ times); *also* : HARSH, SEVERE 10 : RESENTFUL (~ feelings) 11 : STRICT, UNRELENTING (~ bargain) 12 : INCLEMENT (~ winter) 13 : intense in force or manner (~ blow) 14 : ARDUOUS, STRENUOUS (~ work) 15 : TROUBLESOME (~ problem) 16 : having difficulty in doing something (~ of hearing) — **hard** *adv* — **hard·ness** *n*

hard-and-fast \,härd-ⁿ-'fast\ *adj* : rigidly binding : STRICT (a ~ rule)

hard·back \'härd-,bak\ *n* : a book bound in hard covers

hard·ball \-,ból\ *n* : BASEBALL

hard-bit·ten \-'bit-ⁿn\ *adj* : SEASONED, TOUGH (~ campaigners)

hard-boiled \-'bóild\ *adj* 1 : boiled until both white and yolk have solidified 2 : lacking sentiment : CALLOUS; *also* : HARDHEADED

hard·en \-ⁿn\ *vb* 1 : to make or become hard or harder 2 : to confirm or become confirmed in disposition or feelings — **hard·en·er** *n*

hard·head·ed \-'hed-əd\ *adj* 1 : STUBBORN, WILLFUL 2 : SOBER, REALISTIC — **hard·head·ed·ly** *adv* — **hard·head·ed·ness** *n*

hard·heart·ed \-'härt-əd\ *adj* : UNFEELING, PITILESS — **hard·heart·ed·ly** *adv* — **hard·heart·ed·ness** *n*

har·di·hood \'härd-ē-,hůd\ *n* 1 : resolute courage and fortitude 2 : VIGOR, ROBUSTNESS

hard·ly \'härd-lē\ *adv* 1 : with force 2 : SEVERELY 3 : with difficulty 4 : not quite : SCARCELY

hard·pan \-,pan\ *n* : a compact often clayey layer in soil that roots scarcely penetrate

hard-shell \-,shel\ *adj* : CONFIRMED, UNCOMPROMISING (a ~ conservative)

hard·ship \-,ship\ *n* 1 : SUFFERING, PRIVATION 2 : something that causes suffering or privation

hard·stand \-,stand\ *n* : a hard-surfaced area for parking an airplane

hard-sur·face \-'sər-fəs\ *vb* : to provide (as a road) with a paved surface

hard·tack \-,tak\ *n* : a hard biscuit made of flour and water without salt

hard·top \'härd-,täp\ *n* : an automobile resembling a convertible but having a rigid top

hard·ware \-,waər\ *n* : ware (as cutlery, tools, or utensils) made of metal

hard·wood \-,wůd\ *n* : the wood of a broad-leaved usu. deciduous tree as distinguished from that of a conifer; *also* : such a tree

hard-work·ing \-'wər-kiŋ\ *adj* : INDUSTRIOUS

har·dy \'härd-ē\ *adj* 1 : BOLD, BRAVE 2 : AUDACIOUS, BRAZEN 3 : ROBUST; *also* : able to withstand adverse conditions (as of weather) (~ shrubs) — **har·di·ly** *adv* — **har·di·ness** *n*

hare \'haər\ *n* : a swift timid long-eared mammal distinguished from the related rabbit by being open-eyed and furry at birth

hare·bell \-,bel\ *n* : a slender herb with blue bell-shaped flowers

hare·brained \-'brānd\ *adj* : FLIGHTY

hare·lip \-'lip\ *n* : a deformity in which the upper lip is vertically split — **hare·lipped** *adj*

har·em \'har-əm\ *n* 1 : a house or part of a house allotted to women in a Muslim household 2 : the wives, concubines, female relatives, and servants occupying a harem

hark \'härk\ *vb* : LISTEN

harken *var of* HEARKEN

har·le·quin \'här-li-k(w)ən\ *n* 1 *cap* : a character (as in comedy) with a shaved head, masked face, variegated tights, and wooden sword 2 : BUFFOON

har·lot \'här-lət\ *n* : PROSTITUTE

¹harm \'härm\ *n* 1 : physical or mental damage : INJURY 2 : MISCHIEF, HURT — **harm·ful** *adj* — **harm·ful·ly** *adv*

ə abut; ᵉ kitten; ər further; a back; ā bake; ä cot, cart; aů out; ch chin; e less; ē easy; g gift; i trip; ī life; j joke; ŋ sing; ō flow; ȯ flaw; ȯi coin; th thin; t͟h this; ü loot; ů foot; y yet; yü few; yů furious; zh vision

harm•ful•ness n — **harm•less** adj — **harm•less•ly** adv — **harm•less•ness** n

¹**harm** vb 1 : to cause harm to : INJURE

¹**har•mon•ic** \härˈmän-ik\ adj 1 : of or relating to musical harmony or harmonics 2 : pleasing to the ear — **har•mon•i•cal•ly** adv

²**harmonic** n : a musical overtone

har•mon•i•ca \-i-kə\ n : a small wind instrument played by breathing in and out through metallic reeds

har•mon•ics \-iks\ n sing or pl : the study of the physical characteristics of musical sounds

har•mo•ni•ous \härˈmō-nē-əs\ adj 1 : musically concordant 2 : CONGRUOUS 3 : marked by accord in sentiment or action — **har•mo•ni•ous•ly** adv — **har•mo•ni•ous•ness** n

har•mo•ni•um \härˈmō-nē-əm\ n : a keyboard wind instrument in which the wind acts on a set of metal reeds

har•mo•nize \ˈhär-mə-ˌnīz\ vb 1 : to play or sing in harmony 2 : to be in harmony 3 : to bring into consonance or accord — **har•mo•ni•za•tion** \ˌhär-mə-nə-ˈzā-shən\ n

har•mo•ny \-nē\ n 1 : musical agreement of sounds; esp : the combination of tones into chords and progressions of chords 2 : a pleasing arrangement of parts; also : CORRESPONDENCE, ACCORD 3 : internal calm

¹**har•ness** \ˈhär-nəs\ n 1 : the gear other than a yoke of a draft animal 2 : occupational routine

²**harness** vb 1 : to put a harness on; also : YOKE 2 : UTILIZE

¹**harp** \ˈhärp\ n : a musical instrument consisting of a triangular frame set with strings plucked by the fingers — **harp•ist** n

²**harp** vb 1 : to play on a harp 2 : to dwell on a subject tiresomely — **harp•er** n

har•poon \härˈpün\ n : a barbed spear used esp. in hunting large fish or whales — **harpoon** vb — **har•poon•er** n

harp•si•chord \ˈhärp-si-ˌkȯrd\ n : a keyboard instrument resembling a grand piano

har•py \ˈhär-pē\ n 1 : a predatory person : LEECH 2 : a shrewish woman

har•ri•dan \ˈhar-əd-ᵊn\ n : a scolding old woman

¹**har•ri•er** \ˈhar-ē-ər\ n 1 : a small hound used esp. in hunting rabbits 2 : a runner on a cross-country team

²**harrier** n : a slender long-legged hawk

¹**har•row** \ˈhar-ō\ n : an implement set with spikes, spring teeth, or disks and used esp. to pulverize and smooth the soil

²**harrow** vb 1 : to cultivate with a harrow 2 : TORMENT, VEX

har•ry \ˈhar-ē\ vb 1 : RAID, PILLAGE 2 : to torment by or as if by constant attack syn worry, annoy, plague, pester

harsh \ˈhärsh\ adj 1 : disagreeably rough 2 : causing discomfort or pain 3 : unduly exacting : SEVERE — **harsh•ly** adv — **harsh•ness** n

hart \ˈhärt\ n : STAG

harts•horn \ˈhärts-ˌhȯrn\ n : a preparation of ammonia used as smelling salts

har•um-scar•um \ˌhar-əm-ˈskar-əm\ adj : RECKLESS, IRRESPONSIBLE

¹**har•vest** \ˈhär-vəst\ n 1 : the season for gathering in crops; also : the act of gathering in a crop 2 : a mature crop (as of grain or fruit) 3 : the product or reward of exertion

²**harvest** vb 1 : to gather in a crop : REAP — **har•vest•er** n

has pres 3d sing of HAVE

has-been \ˈhaz-ˌbin\ n : one that has passed the peak of ability, power, effectiveness, or popularity

¹**hash** \ˈhash\ vb 1 : to chop into small pieces 2 : to talk about

²**hash** n 1 : chopped meat mixed with potatoes and browned 2 : HODGE-PODGE, JUMBLE

hash•ish \ˈhash-ˌēsh\ n : a narcotic and intoxicating preparation from the hemp plant

hasp \ˈhasp\ n : a fastener (as for a door) consisting of a hinged metal strap that fits over a staple and is secured by a pin or padlock

has•sle \ˈhas-əl\ n 1 : WRANGLE; also : FIGHT — **hassle** vb

has•sock \ˈhas-ək\ n : a cushion that serves as a seat or leg rest; also : a cushion to kneel on in prayer

haste \ˈhāst\ n 1 : rapidity of motion or action : SPEED 2 : rash or headlong action 3 : undue eagerness to act : URGENCY — **hast•i•ly** adv — **hast•i•ness** n — **hasty** adj

has•ten \ˈhās-ᵊn\ vb 1 : to urge on 2 : to move or act quickly : HURRY syn speed, accelerate, quicken

hat \ˈhat\ n : a covering for the head

hat•box \-ˌbäks\ n : a round piece of luggage esp. for carrying hats

¹**hatch** \ˈhach\ n 1 : a small door or opening 2 : a door or grated cover for access down into a compartment of a ship

²**hatch** vb 1 : to produce young by incubation; also : to emerge from an egg or chrysalis 2 : ORIGINATE — **hatch•ery** \-(ə-)rē\ n

hatch•et \ˈhach-ət\ n 1 : a short-handled ax with a hammerlike part opposite the blade 2 : TOMAHAWK

hatchet man n : a person hired for murder, coercion, or unscrupulous attack

hatch•ing \ˈhach-iŋ\ n : the engraving or drawing of fine lines in close proximity chiefly to give an effect of shading; also : the pattern so created

hatch•ment \-mənt\ n : a panel on which a coat of arms of a deceased person is temporarily displayed

hatch•way \-ˌwā\ n : an opening having a hatch

¹**hate** \ˈhāt\ n 1 : intense hostility and aversion 2 : an object of hatred — **hate•ful** adj — **hate•ful•ly** adv — **hate•ful•ness** n

²**hate** vb 1 : to express or feel extreme enmity 2 : to find detestable or distasteful syn detest, abhor, abominate, loathe — **hat•er** n

ha•tred \ˈhā-trəd\ n : HATE; also : prejudiced hostility or animosity

hat•ter \ˈhat-ər\ n : one that makes, sells, or cleans and repairs hats

hau•berk \ˈhȯ-bərk\ n : a coat of mail

haugh•ty \ˈhȯt-ē\ adj : disdainfully proud : ARROGANT syn insolent, lordly, overbearing — **haugh•ti•ly** adv — **haugh•ti•ness** n

¹**haul** \ˈhȯl\ vb 1 : to exert traction on : DRAW, PULL 2 : to furnish transportation : CART — **haul•er** n

²**haul** n 1 : PULL, TUG 2 : the result of an effort to collect : TAKE 3 : the

distance over which a load is transported; *also* : LOAD

haul·age \-ij\ *n* 1 : the act or process of hauling 2 : a charge made for hauling

haunch \'hȯnch\ *n* 1 : HIP 1 2 : HINDQUARTER 2 — usu. used in pl. 3 : HINDQUARTER 1

¹**haunt** \'hȯnt\ *vb* 1 : FREQUENT 2 : to recur constantly to; *also* : to reappear continually in 3 : to visit or inhabit as a ghost — **haunt·er** *n* — **haunt·ing·ly** *adv*

²**haunt** *n* 1 : a place habitually frequented 2 *chiefly dial* : GHOST

haut·bois *or* **haut·boy** \'(h)ō-,bȯl\ *n*, *pl* **-bois** \-,bȯiz\ *or* **-boys** : OBOE

hau·teur \hō-'tər\ *n* : HAUGHTINESS

¹**have** \(')hav, (h)əv\ *vb* **had** \(')had, (h)əd\ **hav·ing** \'hav-iŋ\ **has** \(')haz, (h)əz\ 1 : to hold in possession; *also* : to hold in one's use, service, or affection 2 : to be compelled or forced to 3 : to stand in relationship to 4 : OBTAIN; *also* : RECEIVE, ACCEPT 5 : to be marked by 6 : SHOW; *also* : USE, EXERCISE 7 : EXPERIENCE; *also* : TAKE ⟨~ a look⟩ 8 : to entertain in the mind; *also* : MAINTAIN 9 : to cause to 10 : ALLOW 11 : to be competent in 12 : to hold in a disadvantageous position; *also* : TRICK 13 : BEGET 14 : to partake of 15 — used as an auxiliary with the past participle to form the present perfect, past perfect, or future perfect

²**have** \'hav\ *n* : one that has material wealth as distinguished from one that is poor

ha·ven \'hā-vən\ *n* 1 : HARBOR, PORT 2 : a place of safety

have-not \'hav-,nät, -'nät\ *n* : one that is poor in material wealth as distinguished from one that is rich

hav·er·sack \'hav-ər-,sak\ *n* : a bag or case worn over one shoulder and used to carry supplies (as on a hike)

hav·oc \'hav-ək\ *n* 1 : wide and general destruction 2 : great confusion and disorder

haw \'hȯ\ *n* : a hawthorn berry; *also* : HAWTHORN

hawk \'hȯk\ *n* : any of numerous mostly small or medium-sized day-flying birds of prey (as a falcon or kite)

hawk·er \'hȯ-kər\ *n* : one who offers goods for sale by calling out in the street

haw·ser \'hȯ-zər\ *n* : a large rope for towing, mooring, or securing a ship

haw·thorn \'hȯ-,thȯrn\ *n* : a spiny shrub or tree related to the apple and noted for its white or pink fragrant flowers

¹**hay** \'hā\ *n* 1 : herbage (as grass) mowed and cured for fodder 2 : REWARD; *also* : a small amount of money

²**hay** *vb* : to cut, cure, and store herbage for hay

hay·cock \-,käk\ *n* : a conical pile of hay

hay fever *n* : an acute allergic catarrh

hay·fork \'hā-,fȯrk\ *n* : a hand or mechanically operated fork for loading or unloading hay

hay·loft \-,lȯft\ *n* : a loft for hay

hay·mow \-,maú\ *n* : a mow of or for hay

hay·rick \-,rik\ *n* : a large sometimes

thatched outdoor stack of hay

hay-seed \'hā-,sēd\ *n* 1 : clinging bits of straw or chaff from hay 2 : BUMPKIN, YOKEL

¹**haz·ard** \'haz-ərd\ *n* [ME, a dice game, fr. MF *hasard*, fr. Ar *az-zahr* the die] 1 : a source of danger 2 : CHANCE; *also* : ACCIDENT 3 : an obstacle on a golf course — **haz·ard·ous** *adj*

²**hazard** *vb* : VENTURE, RISK

¹**haze** \'hāz\ *n* 1 : fine dust, smoke, or light vapor causing lack of transparency in the air 2 : vagueness of mind or perception

²**haze** *vb* : to harass by abusive and humiliating tricks

ha·zel \'hā-zəl\ *n* 1 : any of a genus of shrubs or small trees related to the birches and bearing edible nuts (**ha·zel·nuts** \-,nəts\) 2 : a light brown

hazy \'hā-zē\ *adj* 1 : obscured or darkened by haze 2 : VAGUE, INDEFINITE 3 : CLOUDED — **haz·i·ly** *adv* — **haz·i·ness** *n*

he \(')hē, ē\ *pron* 1 : that male one 2 : a or the person ⟨~ who hesitates is lost⟩ ⟨if a student fails ~ must take the course over again⟩

¹**head** \'hed\ *n* 1 : the front or upper part of the body containing the brain, the chief sense organs, and the mouth 2 : MIND; *also* : natural aptitude 3 : POISE 4 : the obverse of a coin 5 : INDIVIDUAL; *also, pl* **head** : a unit of number (as of cattle) 6 : an upper or higher end; *also* : either end of something (as a drum) whose two ends need not be distinguished 7 : DIRECTOR, LEADER; *also* : a leading element (as of a procession) 8 : a projecting part; *also* : the striking part of a weapon 9 : the place of leadership or honor 10 : a separate part or topic 11 : the foam on a fermenting or effervescing liquid 12 : CRISIS — **head·less** *adj*

²**head** *adj* 1 : PRINCIPAL, CHIEF 2 : coming from in front ⟨~ sea⟩

³**head** *vb* 1 : to cut back the upper growth of 2 : to provide with or form a head; *also* : to form the head of 3 : LEAD, CONDUCT 4 : to get in front of esp. so as to stop; *also* : SURPASS 5 : to put or stand at the head 6 : to point or proceed in a certain direction 7 : ORIGINATE

head·ache \-,āk\ *n* 1 : pain in the head 2 : a baffling situation or problem

head·band \-,band\ *n* : a band worn on or around the head

head·board \-,bȯrd\ *n* : a board forming the head (as of a bed)

head·dress \'hed-,dres\ *n* : an often elaborate covering for the head

head-first \-'fərst\ *adv* (*or adj*) : HEADLONG

head·gear \-,giər\ *n* : a covering or protective device for the head

head·ing \-iŋ\ *n* 1 : the compass direction in which the longitudinal axis of a ship or airplane points 2 : something that forms or serves as a head (as of a letter)

head·land \-lənd\ *n* : PROMONTORY

head·light \-,līt\ *n* : a light with a reflector and special lens mounted on the front of an automotive vehicle

head·line \-,līn\ *n* : a head of a newspaper story or article usu. printed in large type

head·lock \-ˌläk\ n : a wrestling hold in which one encircles his opponent's head with one arm

¹head·long \-ˈloŋ\ adv 1 : with the head foremost 2 : RECKLESSLY 3 : without delay

²headlong adj 1 : PRECIPITATE, RASH 2 : plunging with the head foremost

head·man \ˈhed-ˈman, -ˌman\ n : one who is a leader (as of a tribe, clan, or village) : CHIEF

head·mas·ter \-ˌmas-tər\ n : a man heading the staff of a private school

head·mis·tress \-ˌmis-trəs\ n : a woman heading the staff of a private school

head·phone \-ˌfōn\ n : an earphone held over the ear by a band worn on the head

head·piece \-ˌpēs\ n 1 : a covering for the head 2 : a ornament esp. at the beginning of a chapter

head·pin \-ˌpin\ n : the front pin in the triangular formation of pins in tenpins

head·quar·ters \-ˌkwȯrt-ərz\ n sing or pl 1 : a place from which a commander performs the functions of command 2 : the administrative center of an enterprise

head·rest \ˈhed-ˌrest\ n : a support for the head

head·set \-ˌset\ n : a pair of headphones

head·ship \-ˌship\ n : the position, office, or dignity of a head

heads·man \ˈhedz-mən\ n : EXECUTIONER

head·stall \ˈhed-ˌstȯl\ n : an arrangement of straps or rope encircling the head of an animal and forming part of a bridle or halter

head·stone \-ˌstōn\ n : a stone at the head of a grave

head·strong \-ˌstrȯŋ\ adj 1 : not easily restrained 2 : directed by ungovernable will syn unruly, intractable, willful

head·wait·er \-ˈwāt-ər\ n : the head of the dining-room staff of a restaurant or hotel

head·wa·ter \-ˌwȯt-ər, -ˌwät-\ n : the source and upper part of a stream — usu. used in pl.

head·way \-ˌwā\ n 1 : forward motion; also : PROGRESS 2 : clear space (as under an arch)

head·word \-ˌwərd\ n 1 : a word or term placed at the beginning (as of a chapter or entry) 2 : a word qualified by a modifier

head·work \-ˌwərk\ n : mental work or effort : THINKING

heady \ˈhed-ē\ adj 1 : WILLFUL, RASH; also : IMPETUOUS 2 : INTOXICATING 3 : SHREWD

heal \ˈhēl\ vb 1 : to make or become sound or whole; also : to restore to health 2 : CURE, REMEDY — heal·er n

health \ˈhelth\ n 1 : sound physical or mental condition; also : general functional condition (in poor ∼) 2 : WELL-BEING 3 : TOAST

health·ful adj 1 : beneficial to health 2 : HEALTHY — health·ful·ly adv — health·ful·ness n

healthy adj 1 : enjoying or typical of good health : WELL 2 : evincing or conducive to health 3 : PROSPEROUS; also : CONSIDERABLE — health·i·ly adv — health·i·ness n

¹heap \ˈhēp\ n : PILE; also : LOT

²heap vb 1 : to throw or lay in a heap 2 : to fill more than full

hear \ˈhior\ vb heard \ˈhərd\ hear·ing \ˈhi(ə)r-iŋ\ 1 : to perceive by the ear 2 : HEED; also : ATTEND 3 : to give a legal hearing to or take testimony from 4 : LEARN — hear·er n

hear·ing n 1 : the process, function, or power of perceiving sound; esp : the special sense by which noises and tones are received as stimuli 2 : EARSHOT 3 : opportunity to be heard 4 : a listening to arguments (as in a court); also : a session in which witnesses are heard (as by a legislative committee)

hear·ken \ˈhär-kən\ vb : to give attention : LISTEN syn hear, hark

hear·say \ˈhiər-ˌsā\ n : RUMOR

hearse \ˈhərs\ n : a vehicle for carrying the dead to the grave

heart \ˈhärt\ n 1 : a hollow muscular organ that by rhythmic contraction keeps up the circulation of the blood in the body 2 : any of a suit of playing cards marked with a red heart; also, pl : a card game in which the object is to avoid taking tricks containing hearts 3 : the whole personality; also : the emotional or moral as distinguished from the intellectual nature 4 : COURAGE 5 : one's innermost being 6 : CENTER; also : the essential part 7 : MEMORY, ROTE (learn by ∼)

heart·ache \-ˌāk\ n : anguish of mind

heart·beat \-ˌbēt\ n : one complete pulsation of the heart

heart·break \-ˌbrāk\ n : crushing grief — heart·bro·ken adj

heart·burn \-ˌbərn\ n : a burning distress behind the lower sternum usu. due to spasm of the esophagus or upper stomach

heart·en \ˈhärt-ᵊn\ vb : ENCOURAGE

heart·felt \-ˌfelt\ adj : deeply felt : EARNEST

hearth \ˈhärth\ n 1 : an area (as of brick) in front of a fireplace; also : the floor of a fireplace 2 : HOME

hearth·side \-ˌsīd\ n : FIRESIDE

hearth·stone \-ˌstōn\ n 1 : a stone forming a hearth 2 : HOME

heart·less \ˈhärt-ləs\ adj : CRUEL

heart·rend·ing \-ˌren-diŋ\ adj : causing intense grief, anguish, or distress (a ∼ experience)

heart·sick \-ˌsik\ adj : very despondent — heart·sick·ness n

heart·strings \-ˌstriŋz\ n pl : the deepest emotions or affections (pulled at his ∼)

heart·throb \-ˌthräb\ n 1 : the throb of a heart 2 : sentimental emotion 3 : SWEETHEART

heart-to-heart adj : SINCERE, FRANK (a ∼ talk)

¹hearty \ˈhärt-ē\ adj 1 : THOROUGHGOING; also : JOVIAL 2 : vigorously healthy 3 : ABUNDANT; also : NOURISHING syn sincere, wholehearted, unfeigned — heart·i·ly adv — heart·i·ness n

²hearty n : COMRADE; also : SAILOR

¹heat \ˈhēt\ vb : to make or become warm or hot 2 : EXCITE — heat·ed·ly adv — heat·er n

²heat n 1 : a condition of being hot : WARMTH 2 : a form of energy that causes a body to rise in temperature, to fuse, to evaporate, or to expand 3 : high temperature 4 : intensity of feeling; also : sexual excitement esp.

in a female mammal **5 :** pungency of flavor **6 :** a single continuous effort; *also* **:** a preliminary race for eliminating less competent contenders **7 :** PRESSURE — **heat·less** *adj*

heat engine *n* **:** a mechanism for converting heat energy into mechanical energy

heath \'hēth\ *n* **1 :** any of a large group of often evergreen shrubby plants (as a blueberry or heather) of wet acid soils **2 :** a tract of wasteland — **heath·less** *adj* — **heathy** *adj*

hea·then \'hē-thən\ *n, pl* **heathens** *or* **heathen 1 :** an unconverted member of a people or nation that does not acknowledge the God of the Bible **2 :** an uncivilized or irreligious person — **heathen** *adj* — **hea·then·dom** *n* — **hea·then·ish** *adj* — **hea·then·ism** *n*

heath·er \'heth-ər\ *n* **:** a northern evergreen heath with lavender flowers — **heath·ery** *adj*

heat·stroke \'hēt-,strōk\ *n* **:** a disorder marked esp. by high body temperature without sweating and by collapse that follows prolonged exposure to excessive heat

¹heave \'hēv\ *vb* **heaved** *or* **hove** \'hōv\ **heav·ing 1 :** to rise or lift upward **2 :** THROW **3 :** to rise and fall rhythmically; *also* **:** PANT **4 :** PULL, PUSH **5 :** RETCH — **heav·er** *n*

²heave *n* **1 :** an effort to lift or raise **2 :** THROW, CAST **3 :** an upward motion **4** *pl* **:** a chronic lung disease of horses marked by difficult breathing and persistent cough

heav·en \'hev-ən\ *n* **1 :** FIRMAMENT — usu. used in pl. **2** *often cap* **:** the abode of the Deity and of the blessed dead; *also* **:** a spiritual state of everlasting communion with God **3** *cap* **:** ²GOD **4 :** a place of supreme happiness — **heav·en·ly** *adj* — **heav·en·ward** *adv (or adj)*

¹heavy \'hev-ē\ *adj* **1 :** having great weight **2 :** hard to bear **3 :** SERIOUS **4 :** DEEP, PROFOUND **5 :** burdened with something oppressive; *also* **:** PREGNANT **6 :** SLUGGISH **7 :** DRAB; *also* **:** DOLEFUL **8 :** DROWSY **9 :** greater than the average of its kind or class **10 :** digested with difficulty; *also* **:** not properly raised or leavened **11 :** producing goods (as steel) used in the production of other goods **12 :** heavily armed or armored — **heav·i·ly** *adv* — **heav·i·ness** *n*

²heavy *n* **:** a theatrical role representing a dignified or imposing person; *also* **:** a villain in a story or a play

heavy-du·ty \,hev-ē-'d(y)üt-ē\ *adj* **:** able or designed to withstand unusual strain

heavy-hand·ed \,hev-ē-'han-dəd\ *adj* **1 :** CLUMSY, UNGRACEFUL **2 :** OPPRESSIVE

heavy-heart·ed \-'härt-əd\ *adj* **:** SADDENED, DESPONDENT

heavy-set \-'set\ *adj* **:** stocky and compact in build

heavy·weight \'hev-ē-,wāt\ *n* **:** one above average in weight; *esp* **:** a boxer weighing over 175 pounds

He·bra·ism \'hē-brā-,iz-əm\ *n* **:** the thought, spirit, or practice characteristic of the Hebrews — **He·bra·ic** \hi-'brā-ik\ *adj* — **He·bra·ist** \'hē-,brā-əst\ *n*

He·brew \'hē-brü\ *n* **1 :** a member of or descendant from a group of Semitic peoples; *esp* **:** ISRAELITE **2 :** the language of the Hebrews — **Hebrew** *adj*

hec·a·tomb \'hek-ə-,tōm\ *n* **:** an ancient Greek and Roman sacrifice of 100 oxen or cattle

heck·le \'hek-əl\ *vb* **:** to harass with questions or gibes **:** BADGER — **heck·ler** \-(ə-)lər\ *n*

hect·are \'hek-,taər\ *n* **:** a metric unit of area equal to about 2.47 acres

hec·tic \'hek-tik\ *adj* **1 :** characteristic of a wasting disease esp. in being fluctuating but persistent (a ~ fever); *also* **:** FLUSHED **2 :** RESTLESS — **hec·ti·cal·ly** *adv*

hec·tor \'hek-tər\ *vb* **1 :** SWAGGER **2 :** to intimidate by bluster or personal pressure

¹hedge \'hej\ *n* **1 :** a fence or boundary formed of shrubs or small trees **2 :** BARRIER

²hedge *vb* **1 :** ENCIRCLE **2 :** HINDER **3 :** to protect oneself financially by a counterbalancing transaction **4 :** to evade the risk of commitment — **hedg·er** *n*

hedge·hog \-,hòg, -,häg\ *n* **:** a small Old World insect-eating mammal covered with spines; *also* **:** PORCUPINE

hedge·hop \-,häp\ *vb* **:** to fly an airplane very close to the ground

hedge·row \-,rō\ *n* **:** a row of shrubs or trees bounding or separating fields

he·do·nism \'hēd-°n-,iz-əm\ *n* **:** the doctrine that pleasure is the chief good in life; *also* **:** a way of life based on this — **he·do·nist** *n* — **he·do·nis·tic** \,hēd-°n-'is-tik\ *adj*

¹heed \'hēd\ *vb* **:** to pay attention **:** MIND

²heed *n* **:** ATTENTION, NOTICE — **heed·ful** *adj* — **heed·ful·ly** *adv* — **heed·ful·ness** *n* — **heed·less** *adj* — **heed·less·ly** *adv* — **heed·less·ness** *n*

¹heel \'hēl\ *n* **1 :** the hind part of the foot **2 :** one of the crusty ends of a loaf of bread **3 :** a solid attachment forming the back of the sole of a shoe **4 :** a rear, low, or bottom part **5 :** a contemptible person — **heel·less** \'hēl-ləs\ *adj*

²heel *vb* **:** to tilt to one side **:** LIST

¹heft \'heft\ *n* **:** WEIGHT, HEAVINESS

²heft *vb* **:** to test the weight of by lifting

hefty \'hef-tē\ *adj* **1 :** marked by bigness, bulk, and usu. strength **2 :** impressively large

he·gem·o·ny \hi-'jem-ə-nē\ *n* **:** preponderant influence or authority esp. of one nation over others

he·gi·ra \hi-'jī-rə\ *n* **:** a journey esp. when undertaken to seek refuge away from a dangerous or undesirable environment

heif·er \'hef-ər\ *n* **:** a young cow; *esp* **:** one that has not had a calf

height \'hīt, 'hītth\ *n* **1 :** the highest part or point **:** SUMMIT, ZENITH **2 :** the distance from the bottom to the top of something standing upright **3 :** ALTITUDE

height·en \'hīt-°n\ *vb* **1 :** to increase in amount or degree **:** AUGMENT

2 : to make or become high or higher : ELEVATE syn enhance, intensify

hei·nous \'hā-nəs\ adj : hatefully or shockingly evil : ATROCIOUS — **hei·nous·ly** adv — **hei·nous·ness** n

heir \'aər\ n : one who inherits or is entitled to inherit property — **heir·ship** n

heir·ess \'ar-əs\ n : a female heir esp. to great wealth

heir·loom \'aər-ˌlüm\ n **1** : a piece of personal property that descends by inheritance **2** : something handed on from one generation to another

heist \'hīst\ vb, slang : to commit armed robbery on; also : STEAL

held past of HOLD

hel·i·cal \'hel-i-kəl, 'hēl-\ adj : SPIRAL

hel·i·cop·ter \'hel-ə-ˌkäp-tər\ n : an aircraft that is supported in the air by one or more rotors revolving on substantially vertical axes

he·lio·trope \'hēl-yə-ˌtrōp\ n : a hairy-leaved garden herb grown for its clusters of small fragrant white or purple flowers

heli·port \'hel-ə-ˌpōrt\ n : a landing and takeoff place for a helicopter

he·li·um \'hē-lē-əm\ n [NL, fr. Gk hēlios sun; so called from the fact that its existence in the sun's atmosphere was inferred before it was identified on the earth] : a very light nonflammable gaseous chemical element occurring in various natural gases

he·lix \'hē-liks\ n, pl **hel·i·ces** \'hel-ə-ˌsēz, 'hē-lə-\ also **he·lix·es** : something spiral

hell \'hel\ n **1** : a nether world in which the dead continue to exist **2** : the realm of the devil in which the damned suffer everlasting punishment **3** : a place or state of torment or destruction — **hell·ish** adj

hell-bent \-ˌbent\ adj **1** : stubbornly determined **2** : going full speed

hel·le·bore \'hel-ə-ˌbōr\ n **1** : a plant related to the buttercup; also : its roots used formerly in medicine **2** : a poisonous plant related to the lilies; also : its dried roots used in medicine and as insecticides

Hel·lene \'hel-ˌēn\ n : GREEK

Hel·le·nism \'hel-ə-ˌniz-əm\ n : a body of humanistic and classical ideals associated with ancient Greece — **Hel·len·ic** \he-'len-ik\ adj — **Hel·le·nist** \'hel-ə-nəst\ n

Hel·le·nis·tic \ˌhel-ə-'nis-tik\ adj : of or relating to Greek history, culture, or art after Alexander the Great

hell·gram·mite \'hel-grə-ˌmīt\ n : an aquatic insect larva used as bait in fishing

hel·lion \'hel-yən\ n : a troublesome or mischievous person

hel·lo \hə-'lō, he-\ n : an expression of greeting — used interjectionally

helm \'helm\ n **1** : a lever or wheel for steering a ship **2** : a position of control

hel·met \'hel-mət\ n : a protective covering for the head

helms·man \'helmz-mən\ n : the man at the helm : STEERSMAN

hel·ot \'hel-ət\ n : SLAVE, SERF

1help \'help\ vb **1** : AID, ASSIST **2** : REMEDY, RELIEVE **3** : to be of use; also : PROMOTE **4** : to change for the better **5** : to refrain from; also : PREVENT **6** : to serve with food or drink — **help·er** n

2help n **1** : AID, ASSISTANCE; also : a source of aid **2** : REMEDY, RELIEF **3** : one who assists another **4** : the services of a paid worker — **help·ful** adj — **help·ful·ly** adv — **help·ful·ness** n — **help·less** adj — **help·less·ly** adv — **help·less·ness** n

help·ing n : a portion of food ⟨asked for a second ~ of potatoes⟩

help·mate \'help-ˌmāt\ n **1** : HELPER **2** : WIFE

help·meet \-ˌmēt\ n : HELPMATE

hel·ter-skel·ter \ˌhel-tər-'skel-tər\ adv **1** : in headlong disorder **2** : HAPHAZARDLY

helve \'helv\ n : a handle of a tool or weapon

Hel·ve·tian \hel-'vē-shən\ adj : SWISS — **Helvetian** n

1hem \'hem\ n **1** : a border of a cloth article doubled back and stitched down **2** : RIM, MARGIN

2hem vb hemmed; hem·ming **1** : to make a hem in sewing; also : BORDER, EDGE **2** : to surround restrictively : CONFINE

he-man \'hē-'man\ n : an obviously strong virile man

hemi·sphere \'hem-ə-ˌsfiər\ n **1** : one of the halves of the earth as divided by the equator into northern and southern parts (northern hemisphere, southern hemisphere) or by a meridian into two parts so that one half (eastern hemisphere) to the east of the Atlantic ocean includes Europe, Asia, and Africa and the half (western hemisphere) to the west includes No. and So. America and surrounding waters **2** : either of two half spheres formed by a plane through the sphere's center — **hemi·spher·i·cal** \ˌhem-ə-'sfir-i-kəl, -'sfer-\ adj

hemi·stich \'hem-i-ˌstik\ n : half a poetic line usu. divided by a caesura

hem·line \'hem-ˌlīn\ n : the line formed by the lower edge of a dress, skirt, or coat

hem·lock \'hem-ˌläk\ n **1** : any of several poisonous herbs related to the carrot **2** : an evergreen tree related to the pines; also : its soft light wood

he·mo·glo·bin or **hae·mo·glo·bin** \'hē-mə-ˌglō-bən\ n : an iron-containing compound found in red blood cells that carries oxygen from the lungs to the body tissues

he·mol·y·sis \hi-'mäl-ə-səs\ n : a breaking down of red blood cells — **he·mo·lyt·ic** \ˌhē-mə-'lit-ik\ adj

he·mo·phil·ia \ˌhē-mə-'fil-ē-ə\ n : a usu. hereditary tendency to severe prolonged bleeding — **he·mo·phil·i·ac** \-ē-ˌak\ adj or n

hem·or·rhage \'hem-(ə-)rij\ n : a large discharge of blood from the blood vessels — **hemorrhage** vb — **hem·or·rhag·ic** \ˌhem-ə-'raj-ik\ adj

hem·or·rhoid \'hem-(ə-)ˌroid\ n : a swollen mass of dilated veins situated at or just within the anus — usu. used in pl.

hemp \'hemp\ n : a tall Asiatic herb related to the mulberry and grown for its tough fiber used in cordage and its flowers and leaves used in drugs — **hemp·en** adj

hem·stitch \'hem-ˌstich\ vb : to embroider (fabric) by drawing out parallel threads and stitching the exposed threads in groups to form various designs

hen \'hen\ *n* **:** a female domestic fowl esp. over a year old; *also* **:** a female bird

hence \'hens\ *adv* **1 :** AWAY **2 :** from this time **3 :** CONSEQUENTLY **4 :** from this source or origin

hence·forth \-,fōrth\ *adv* **:** from this point on

hence·for·ward \hens-'fōr-wərd\ *adv* **:** HENCEFORTH

hench·man \'hench-mən\ *n* **1 :** a trusted follower **2 :** a political follower whose support is chiefly for personal advantage

hen·na \'hen-ə\ *n* **1 :** an Old World tropical shrub with fragrant white flowers; *also* **:** a reddish brown dye obtained from its leaves and used esp. for the hair **2 :** the color of henna dye

hen·peck \'hen-,pek\ *vb* **:** to subject (one's husband) to persistent nagging and domination

hep \'hep\ *adj* **1 :** keenly aware of or interested in the newest developments **2 :** WISE, ALERT

hep·a·ti·tis \,hep-ə-'tīt-əs\ *n* **:** inflammation of the liver; *also* **:** an acute virus disease of which this is a feature

hep·cat \'hep-,kat\ *n* **:** HIPSTER

¹**her** \(h)ər, ,hər\ *adj* **:** of or relating to her or herself

²**her** *pron, objective case of* SHE

¹**her·ald** \'her-əld\ *n* **1 :** an official crier or messenger **2 :** HARBINGER **3 :** ANNOUNCER, SPOKESMAN

²**herald** *vb* **1 :** to give notice of **2 :** PUBLICIZE; *also* **:** HAIL

he·ral·dic \he-'ral-dik\ *adj* **:** of or relating to heralds or heraldry

her·ald·ry \'her-əl-drē\ *n* **1 :** the practice of devising, blazoning, and granting armorial insignia and of tracing and recording genealogies **2 :** an armorial ensign; *also* **:** INSIGNIA **3 :** PAGEANTRY

herb \'(h)ərb\ *n* **1 :** a seed plant that lacks woody tissue and dies to the ground at the end of a growing season **2 :** a plant or plant part valued for medicinal or savory qualities — **her·ba·ceous** \,(h)ər-'bā-shəs\ *adj*

herb·age \'(h)ər-bij\ *n* **:** green plants esp. when used or fit for grazing

herb·al·ist \-bə-ləst\ *n* **:** one that collects, grows, or deals in herbs

her·bi·cide \'(h)ər-bə-,sīd\ *n* **:** an agent used to destroy unwanted plants — **her·bi·cid·al** \,(h)ər-bə-'sīd-ᵊl\ *adj*

her·biv·o·rous \,(h)ər-'biv-ə-rəs\ *adj* **:** feeding on plants — **her·bi·vore** \'(h)ər-bə-,vōr\ *n* — **her·biv·o·rous·ly** \,(h)ər-'biv-ə-rəs-lē\ *adv*

her·cu·le·an \,hər-kyə-'lē-ən, ,hər-'kyli-lē-\ *adj, often cap* **:** of extraordinary power, size, or difficulty

¹**herd** \'hərd\ *n* **1 :** a group of animals of one kind kept or living together **2 :** a group of people with a common bond **3 :** MOB

²**herd** *vb* **:** to assemble or move in a herd — **herd·er** *n*

herds·man \'hərdz-mən\ *n* **:** one who manages, breeds, or tends livestock

¹**here** \'hiər\ *adv* **1 :** in or at this place; *also* **:** NOW **2 :** at or in this point or particular **3 :** in the present life or state **4 :** HITHER

²**here** *n* **:** this place ⟨get away from ∼⟩

here·about \'hir-ə-,baut\ *or* **here·abouts** \-,bauts\ *adv* **:** in this vicinity **:** about or near this place

¹**here·af·ter** \hir-'af-tər\ *adv* **1 :** after this in sequence or in time **2 :** in some future time or state

²**hereafter** *n* **1 :** FUTURE **2 :** an existence beyond earthly life

here·by \hiər-'bī\ *adv* **:** by means of this

he·red·i·tary \hə-'red-ə-,ter-ē\ *adj* **1 :** genetically passed or passable from parent to offspring **2 :** passing by inheritance; *also* **:** having title or possession through inheritance **3 :** of a kind established by tradition   *syn* innate, inborn, inbred

he·red·i·ty \-ət-ē\ *n* **:** the qualities and potentialities genetically derived from one's ancestors; *also* **:** the passing of these from ancestor to descendant

here·in \hir-'in\ *adv* **:** in this

here·of \-'əv, -'äv\ *adv* **:** of this

here·on \-'ȯn, -'än\ *adv* **:** on this document

her·e·sy \'her-ə-sē\ *n* [OF *heresie,* fr. Gk *hairesis* choice, sect, fr. *hairesthai* to choose] **1 :** adherence to a religious opinion contrary to church dogma **2 :** an opinion or doctrine contrary to church dogma **3 :** dissent from a dominant theory or opinion — **her·e·tic** \-ə-,tik\ *n* — **he·ret·i·cal** \hə-'ret-i-kəl\ *adj*

here·to \hir-'tü\ *adv* **:** to this document

here·to·fore \'hirt-ə-,fōr\ *adv* **:** up to this time

here·un·der \hir-'ən-dər\ *adv* **:** under this

here·un·to \hir-'ən-tü\ *adv* **:** to this

here·upon \'hir-ə-,pȯn, -,pän\ *adv* **:** on this

here·with \hiər-'with, -'with\ *adv* **1 :** with this **2 :** HEREBY

her·i·ta·ble \'her-ət-ə-bəl\ *adj* **:** capable of being inherited

her·i·tage \'her-ət-ij\ *n* **1 :** property that descends to an heir **2 :** LEGACY **3 :** BIRTHRIGHT

her·met·ic \hər-'met-ik\ *adj* **1 :** RECONDITE **2 :** tightly sealed **:** AIRTIGHT — **her·met·i·cal** *adj* — **her·met·i·cal·ly** *adv*

her·mit \'hər-mət\ *n* **:** one who lives in solitude esp. for religious reasons **:** RECLUSE

her·mit·age \-ij\ *n* **1 :** the dwelling of a hermit **2 :** a secluded dwelling

her·nia \'hər-nē-ə\ *n* **:** a protruding of a bodily part (as a loop of intestine) into a pouch of the weakened wall of a cavity in which it is normally enclosed; *also* **:** the protruded mass — **her·ni·al** *adj* — **her·ni·ate** \-nē-,āt\ *vb* — **her·ni·a·tion** \,hər-nē-'ā-shən\ *n*

he·ro \'hē-rō\ *n, pl* **-roes 1 :** a mythological or legendary figure of great strength or ability **2 :** a man admired for his achievements and qualities **3 :** the chief male character in a literary or dramatic work — **he·ro·ic** \hi-'rō-ik\ *adj* — **he·ro·i·cal·ly** *adv*

heroic couplet *n* **:** a rhyming couplet in iambic pentameter

he·ro·ics \hi-'rō-iks\ *n pl* **:** extravagant display of heroic attitudes in action or expression

---

ə abut; ᵊ kitten; ər further; a back; ā bake; ä cot, cart; aủ out; ch chin; e less; ē easy; g gift; i trip; ī life; j joke; ŋ sing; ō flow; ȯ flaw; ȯi coin; th thin; t͟h this; ü loot; ủ foot; y yet; yü few; yủ furious; zh vision

her·o·in \'her-ə-wən\ *n* **:** an addictive narcotic drug made from morphine

her·o·ine \-wən\ *n* **:** a woman of heroic achievements or qualities

her·o·ism \'her-ə-,wiz-əm\ *n* **1 :** heroic conduct **2 :** the qualities of a hero **syn** valor, prowess, gallantry

her·on \'her-ən\ *n* **:** a long-legged long-billed wading bird with soft plumage

her·ring \'her-iŋ\ *n* **:** a soft-finned narrow-bodied food fish of the north Atlantic; *also* **:** any of various similar or related fishes

her·ring·bone \-,bōn\ *n* **:** a pattern made up of rows of parallel lines with adjacent rows slanting in reverse directions; *also* **:** a twilled fabric with this pattern

hers \'hərz\ *pron* **:** one or the ones belonging to her

her·self \(h)ər-'self\ *pron* **:** SHE, HER — used reflexively, for emphasis, or in absolute constructions ⟨she hurt ~⟩ ⟨she ~ did it⟩ ⟨~ busy, she sent me⟩

hes·i·tant \'hez-ə-tənt\ *adj* **:** tending to hesitate — **hes·i·tan·cy** \-tan-sē\ *n* — **hes·i·tant·ly** *adv*

hes·i·tate \-,tāt\ *vb* **1 :** to hold back (as in doubt) **2 :** PAUSE **syn** waver, vacillate, falter — **hes·i·ta·tion** \,hez-ə-'tā-shən\ *n*

het·er·o·dox \'het-(ə-)rə-,däks\ *adj* **1 :** differing from an acknowledged standard **2 :** holding unorthodox opinions — **het·er·o·doxy** *n*

het·er·o·ge·ne·ous \,het-(ə-)rə-'jē-nē-əs\ *adj* **:** consisting of dissimilar ingredients or constituents **:** MIXED — **het·er·o·ge·ne·ous·ly** *adv* — **het·er·o·ge·ne·ous·ness** *n*

het·er·o·sex·u·al \,het-ə-rō-'sek-sh(ə-w)əl\ *adj* **:** involving two sexes; *also* **:** oriented toward the opposite sex — **het·er·o·sex·u·al·i·ty** \-,sek-shə-'wal-ət-ē\ *n*

hew \'hyü\ *vb* **hewed; hewed** *or* **hewn** \'hyün\ **hew·ing 1 :** to cut or fell with blows (as of an ax) **2 :** to give shape to with or as if with an ax **3 :** to conform strictly — **hew·er** *n*

¹hex \'heks\ *vb* **1 :** to practice witchcraft **2 :** JINX

²hex *n* **:** SPELL, JINX

hexa·gon \'hek-sə-,gän\ *n* **:** a polygon having 6 angles and 6 sides — **hex·ag·o·nal** \hek-'sag-ən-ᵊl\ *adj*

hex·am·e·ter \hek-'sam-ət-ər\ *n* **:** a line consisting of six metrical feet

hexa·pod \'hek-sə-,päd\ *n* **:** INSECT

hey·day \'hā-,dā\ *n* **:** a period of greatest strength, vigor, or prosperity

hi·a·tus \hī-'āt-əs\ *n* **1 :** a break in an object **:** GAP **2 :** a lapse in continuity

hi·ba·chi \hē-'bäch-ē\ *n* **:** a charcoal brazier

hi·ber·nate \'hī-bər-,nāt\ *vb* **:** to pass the winter in a torpid or resting state — **hi·ber·na·tion** \,hī-bər-'nā-shən\ *n* — **hi·ber·na·tor** \'hī-bər-,nāt-ər\ *n*

hi·bis·cus \hī-'bis-kəs, hə-\ *n* **:** any of a genus of herbs, shrubs, and trees related to the mallows and noted for large showy flowers

hic·cup *also* **hic·cough** \'hik-(,)əp\ *n* **:** a spasmodic breathing movement checked by sudden closing of the glottis accompanied by a peculiar sound; *also* **:** this sound — **hiccup** *vb*

hick \'hik\ *n* **:** an awkward provincial person

hick·o·ry \'hik-(ə-)rē\ *n* **:** any of a genus of No. American hardwood trees related to the walnuts; *also* **:** the wood of a hickory

hi·dal·go \hid-'al-gō\ *n, often cap* [Sp. fr. earlier *fijo dalgo*, lit., son of something, son of property] **:** a member of the lower nobility of Spain

¹hide \'hīd\ *vb* **hid** \'hid\ **hid·den** \'hid-ᵊn\ *or* **hid; hid·ing** \'hīd-iŋ\ **1 :** to put or remain out of sight **2 :** to conceal for shelter or protection; *also* **:** to seek protection **3 :** to keep secret **4 :** to turn (as the face) away in shame or anger

²hide *n* **:** the skin of an animal

hide-and-seek \,hīd-ᵊn-'sēk\ *n* **:** a children's game in which one player covers his eyes and after giving the others time to hide goes looking for and tries to catch them

hide·away \'hīd-ə-,wā\ *n* **:** a place of retreat or concealment

hide·bound \-,baúnd\ *adj* **:** obstinately conservative

hid·eous \'hid-ē-əs\ *adj* **1 :** offensive to one of the senses **:** UGLY **2 :** morally offensive **:** SHOCKING — **hid·eous·ly** *adv* — **hid·eous·ness** *n*

hide·out \'hīd-,aút\ *n* **:** a place of refuge or concealment

hie \'hī\ *vb* **hied; hy·ing** *or* **hie·ing** **:** HASTEN

hi·er·ar·chy \'hī-(ə-)rär-kē\ *n* **1 :** a ruling body of clergy organized into ranks **2 :** persons or things arranged in a graded series — **hi·er·ar·chi·cal** \,hī-ə-'rär-ki-kəl\ *adj*

hi·er·o·glyph·ic \,hī-(ə-)rə-'glif-ik\ *n* **1 :** a character in a system of picture writing (as of the ancient Egyptians) **2 :** a symbol or sign difficult to decipher

hi·er·o·phant \'hī-(ə-)rə-,fant\ *n* **1 :** a priest in ancient Greece **2 :** EX-POSITOR; *also* **:** ADVOCATE

hi-fi \'hī-'fī\ *n* **1 :** HIGH FIDELITY **2 :** equipment for reproduction of sound with high fidelity

hig·gle·dy-pig·gle·dy \,hig-əl-dē-'pig-əl-dē\ *adv* **:** in confusion

¹high \'hī\ *adj* **1 :** ELEVATED; *also* **:** TALL **2 :** advanced toward fullness or culmination; *also* **:** slightly tainted **3 :** long past **4 :** SHRILL, SHARP **5 :** far from the equator ⟨~ latitudes⟩ **6 :** exalted in character **7 :** of greater degree, size, or amount than average **8 :** of relatively great importance **9 :** FORCIBLE, STRONG ⟨~ winds⟩ **10 :** BOASTFUL, ARROGANT **11 :** showing elation or excitement; *also* **:** INTOXICATED **12 :** COSTLY, DEAR **13 :** advanced esp. in complexity ⟨~er mathematics⟩ — **high·ly** *adv*

²high *adv* **1 :** at or to a high place or degree **2 :** LUXURIOUSLY ⟨living ~⟩

³high *n* **1 :** an elevated place **2 :** a high point or level **3 :** the arrangement of gears in an automobile that gives the highest speed

high·ball \-,bòl\ *n* **:** a usu. tall drink of liquor mixed with water or a carbonated beverage

high·born \-'bòrn\ *adj* **:** of noble birth

high·boy \-,bòi\ *n* **:** a high chest of drawers mounted on a base with long legs

high·bred \-'bred\ *adj* **:** coming from superior stock

high·brow \-,braú\ *n* **:** a person of superior learning or culture

high·er–up \,hī-ər-'əp\ n : a superior officer or official

high explosive n : an explosive (as TNT) that generates gas with extreme rapidity and has a shattering effect

high–fa·lu·tin \,hī-fə-'lüt-ᵊn\ adj : PRETENTIOUS, POMPOUS

high fidelity n : the reproduction of sound with a high degree of faithfulness to the original

high–flown \'hī-'flōn\ adj 1 : EXALTED 2 : BOMBASTIC

high frequency n : a frequency of a radio wave between 3 and 30 megacycles

high–hand·ed \'hī-'han-dəd\ adj : OVERBEARING — **high–hand·ed·ly** adv — **high–hand·ed·ness** n

high–hat \-'hat\ vb : to treat in a supercilious or snobbish manner

high·land \-lənd\ n : elevated or mountainous land

high·land·er n 1 : an inhabitant of a highland 2 cap : an inhabitant of the Highlands of Scotland

¹**high·light** \'hī-,līt\ n : an event or detail of major importance

²**highlight** vb 1 : EMPHASIZE 2 : to constitute a highlight of

high–mind·ed \-'mīn-dəd\ adj : marked by elevated principles and feelings — **high–mind·ed·ness** n

high·ness n : the quality or state of being high — used as a title (as for kings or princes)

high·road \'hī-,rōd\ n, chiefly Brit : HIGHWAY

high school n : a secondary school usu. comprising the 9th to 12th or 10th to 12th years of study

high sea n : the open sea outside territorial waters — usu. used in pl.

high–sound·ing \'hī-'saun-diŋ\ adj : POMPOUS, IMPOSING

high–spir·it·ed \-'spir-ət-əd\ adj : characterized by a bold or lofty spirit

high–strung \'hī-'strəŋ\ adj : marked by an extremely nervous or sensitive temperament

high·tail \,-tāl\ vb : to retreat at full speed

high–tension adj : having, using, or relating to high voltage

high·way \'hī-,wā\ n : a public road

high·way·man \-mən\ n : a person who robs travelers on a road

hi·jack or **high–jack** \'hī-,jak\ vb : to steal esp. by stopping a vehicle on the highway — **hi·jack·er** n

¹**hike** \'hīk\ vb 1 : to move or raise with a sudden effort 2 : to take a long walk — **hik·er** n

²**hike** n 1 : a long walk 2 : RISE

hi·lar·i·ous \hil-'ar-ē-əs, hī-'lar-\ adj : marked by or providing boisterous merriment — **hi·lar·i·ous·ly** adv — **hi·lar·i·ty** \-ət-ē\ n

hill \'hil\ n 1 : a usu. rounded elevation of land 2 : a little heap or mound (as of earth) — **hilly** adj

hill·bil·ly \-,bil-ē\ n : a person from a backwoods area

hill·ock \'hil-ək\ n : a small hill

hill·side \-,sīd\ n : the part of a hill between the summit and the foot

hill·top \-,täp\ n : the highest part of a hill

hilt \'hilt\ n : a handle esp. of a sword or dagger

him \im, (ᵊ)him\ pron, objective case of HE

him·self \(h)im-'self\ pron : HE, HIM — used reflexively, for emphasis, or in absolute constructions ⟨he hurt ~⟩ ⟨he ~ did it⟩ ⟨~ busy, he sent me⟩

¹**hind** \'hīnd\ n : a female deer : DOE

²**hind** n : a British farmhand

³**hind** adj : REAR

hin·der \'hin-dər\ vb 1 : to impede the progress of : HAMPER 2 : to hold back : CHECK syn obstruct, block, bar

²**hind·er** \'hīn-dər\ adj : HIND

Hin·di \'hin-dē\ n : a literary and official language of northern India

hind·most \'hīn(d)-,mōst\ adj : farthest to the rear

hind·quar·ter \-,kwȯrt-ər\ n 1 : the back half of a lateral half of the body or carcass of a quadruped 2 pl : the part of the body of a quadruped behind the junction of hind limbs and trunk

hin·drance \'hin-drəns\ n 1 : the state of being hindered; also : the action of hindering 2 : IMPEDIMENT

hind·sight \'hīn(d)-,sīt\ n : understanding of an event after it has happened

Hin·du·ism \'hin-dü-,iz-əm\ n : a body of religious beliefs and practices native to India — **Hin·du** n or adj

¹**hinge** \'hinj\ n : a jointed piece on which one piece (as a door, gate, or lid) turns or swings on another

²**hinge** vb 1 : to attach by or furnish with hinges 2 : to be contingent on a single consideration

hint \'hint\ n 1 : an indirect or summary suggestion 2 : CLUE 3 : a very small amount — **hint** vb

hin·ter·land \'hint-ər-,land\ n 1 : a region behind a coast 2 : a region remote from cities

¹**hip** \'hip\ n : the fruit of a rose

²**hip** n : the part of the body on either side below the waist consisting of the side of the pelvis and the upper thigh; also : the joint between pelvis and femur

³**hip** var of HEP

hip·po·drome \'hip-ə-,drōm\ n : an arena for equestrian performances

hip·po·pot·a·mus \,hip-ə-'pät-ə-məs\ n, pl **-mus·es** or **-mi** \-,mī\ : a large thick-skinned African river animal related to the swine

hip·ster \'hip-stər\ n : one who is esp. hep (as to new patterns in jazz)

¹**hire** \'hī(ə)r\ n 1 : PAY, WAGES 2 : EMPLOYMENT

²**hire** vb 1 : to employ for pay 2 : to engage the temporary use of for pay

hire·ling \-liŋ\ n : a hired person whose motives are chiefly mercenary

hir·sute \'hər-,süt, 'hiər-\ adj : HAIRY

¹**his** \(h)iz, ,hiz\ adj : of or relating to him or himself

²**his** \'hiz\ pron : one or the ones belonging to him

hiss \'his\ vb : to make a sharp sibilant sound; also : to condemn by hissing — **hiss** n

his·ta·mine \'his-tə-,mēn\ n : a chemical compound widespread in animal tissues and believed to play a role in allergic reactions

---

ə abut; ᵊ kitten; ər further; a back; ā bake; ä cot, cart; aù out; ch chin; e less; ē easy; g gift; i trip; ī life; j joke; ŋ sing; ō flow; ȯ flaw; ȯi coin; th thin; <u>th</u> this; ü loot; ù foot; y yet; yü few; yù furious; zh vision

his·to·ri·an \his-'tōr-ē-ən\ *n* : a student or writer of history

his·to·ric·i·ty \,his-tə-'ris-ət-ē\ *n* : historical actuality

his·to·ri·og·ra·pher \his-,tōr-ē-'äg-rə-fər\ *n* : a usu. official writer of history : HISTORIAN

his·to·ry \'his-t(ə-)rē\ *n* [L *historia,* fr. Gk. investigation, research, history, fr. *histōr* judge] 1 : a chronological record of significant events usu. with an explanation of their causes 2 : a branch of knowledge that records and explains past events — **his·tor·ic** \his-'tōr-ik\ *adj* — **his·tor·i·cal** *adj* — **his·tor·i·cal·ly** *adv*

his·tri·on·ic \,his-trē-'än-ik\ *adj* 1 : of or relating to actors, acting, or the theater 2 : deliberately affected : THEATRICAL — **his·tri·on·i·cal·ly** *adv*

his·tri·on·ics *n pl* 1 : theatrical performances 2 : deliberate display of emotion for effect

¹hit \'hit\ *vb* hit; **hit·ting** 1 : to reach with a blow : STRIKE 2 : to come or cause to come in contact : COLLIDE 3 : to affect detrimentally 4 : to make a request of 5 : to come upon 6 : SUIT 7 : REACH, ATTAIN 8 : to indulge in often to excess — **hit·ter** *n*

²hit *n* 1 : BLOW; *also* : COLLISION 2 : something highly successful 3 : a stroke in an athletic contest; *esp* : one that enables a baseball player to reach base

¹hitch \'hich\ *vb* 1 : to move by jerks 2 : to catch or fasten esp. by a hook or knot 3 : HITCHHIKE

²hitch *n* 1 : JERK 2 : a sudden halt 3 : a connection between a vehicle or implement and a detachable source of power 4 : KNOT

hitch·hike \-,hīk\ *vb* 1 : to travel by securing free rides from passing vehicles — **hitch·hik·er** *n*

¹hith·er \'hith-ər\ *adv* : to this place

²hither *adj* : being on the near or adjacent side

hith·er·to \-,tü\ *adv* : up to this time

hive \'hīv\ *n* 1 : a container for housing honeybees 2 : a colony of bees 3 : a place swarming with busy occupants — **hive** *vb*

hives \'hīvz\ *n, pl* **hives** : an allergic disorder marked by the presence of itching wheals

hoard \'hōrd\ *n* : a hidden store or accumulation — **hoard** *vb* — **hoard·er** *n*

hoard·ing \'hōrd-iŋ\ *n* 1 : a temporary board fence put about a building being erected or repaired 2 *Brit* : BILLBOARD

hoar·frost \'hōr-,frȯst\ *n* : FROST 2

hoarse \'hōrs\ *adj* 1 : rough and harsh in sound 2 : having a grating voice — **hoarse·ly** *adv* — **hoarse·ness** *n*

hoary \'hōr-ē\ *adj* 1 : gray or white with age 2 : ANCIENT — **hoar·i·ness** *n*

hoax \'hōks\ *n* : an act intended to trick or dupe; *also* : something accepted or established by fraud — **hoax** *vb* — **hoax·er** *n*

¹hob \'häb\ *n* : MISCHIEF, TROUBLE ⟨raise ∼⟩

²hob *n* : a projection at the back or side of a fireplace on which something may be kept warm

¹hob·ble \'häb-əl\ *vb* 1 : to limp along; *also* : to make lame 2 : FETTER

²hobble *n* 1 : a hobbling movement 2 : something used to hobble an animal

hob·by \'häb-ē\ *n* : a pursuit or interest engaged in for relaxation

hob·by·horse \-,hȯrs\ *n* 1 : a stick sometimes with a horse's head on which children pretend to ride 2 : a toy horse mounted on rockers 3 : something (as a favorite topic) to which one constantly reverts

hob·gob·lin \'häb-,gäb-lən\ *n* 1 : a mischievous goblin 2 : BOGEY

hob·nail \-,nāl\ *n* : a short large-headed nail for studding shoe soles

hob·nob \-,näb\ *vb* **-nobbed; -nob·bing** : to associate familiarly

ho·bo \'hō-bō\ *n, pl* **-boes** *also* **-bos** : TRAMP

¹hock \'häk\ *n* : a joint or region in the hind limb of a quadruped corresponding to the human ankle

²hock *n* : PAWN — **hock** *vb*

hock·ey \'häk-ē\ *n* : a game played on ice or on a field by 2 teams using curved sticks to drive a puck or ball

ho·cus-po·cus \,hō-kəs-'pō-kəs\ *n* 1 : SLEIGHT OF HAND 2 : nonsense or sham used to conceal deception

hod \'häd\ *n* 1 : a long-handled tray or trough for carrying a load esp. of mortar or bricks 2 : SCUTTLE

hodge·podge \'häj-,päj\ *n* : a heterogeneous mixture

hoe \'hō\ *n* : a long-handled implement with a thin flat blade used esp. for cultivating, weeding, or loosening the earth around plants — **hoe** *vb*

hoe·cake \-,kāk\ *n* : a cornmeal cake often baked on a griddle

hog \'hȯg, 'häg\ *n* 1 : a domestic swine esp. when grown 2 : a selfish, gluttonous, or filthy person — **hog·gish** *adj*

hogs·head \'hȯgz-,hed, 'hägz-\ *n* 1 : a large cask; *esp* : one holding from 63 to 140 gallons 2 : a liquid measure equal to 63 U.S. gallons

hog-tie \'hȯg-,tī, 'häg-\ *vb* 1 : to tie together the feet of ⟨∼ a calf⟩ 2 : to make helpless ⟨operations *hogtied* by red tape⟩

hog·wash \-,wȯsh, -,wäsh\ *n* 1 : SWILL 1, SLOP 2 2 : worthless or nonsensical language

hoi pol·loi \,hȯi-pə-'lȯi\ *n* : the general populace

¹hoist \'hȯist\ *vb* : RAISE, LIFT

²hoist *n* 1 : LIFT 2 : an apparatus for hoisting 3 : the height of a flag when viewed flying

ho·kum \'hō-kəm\ *n* : NONSENSE

¹hold \'hōld\ *vb* held \'held\ **hold·ing** 1 : POSSESS; *also* : KEEP 2 : RESTRAIN 3 : to have or maintain a grasp on 4 : to remain or cause to remain in a particular situation or position 5 : SUSTAIN; *also* : RESERVE 6 : BEAR, COMPORT 7 : to maintain in being or action : PERSIST 8 : CONTAIN, ACCOMMODATE 9 : HARBOR, ENTERTAIN; *also* : CONSIDER, REGARD 10 : to carry on by concerted action; *also* : CONVOKE 11 : to occupy esp. by appointment or election 12 : to be valid 13 : HALT, PAUSE — **hold·er** *n*

²hold *n* 1 : STRONGHOLD 2 : CONFINEMENT; *also* : PRISON 3 : the act or manner of holding or clasping : GRIP 4 : a nonphysical bond which attaches or restrains or by which something is affected 5 : something that may be grasped as a support

³hold *n* 1 : the interior of a ship below decks; *esp* : a ship's cargo deck 2 : an airplane's cargo compartment

hold·ing \ n **1 :** land held esp. of a superior; *also* **:** property owned **2 :** a ruling of a court esp. on an issue of law

hold-up \'hōld-,əp\ n **1 :** robbery at the point of a gun **2 :** DELAY

hole \'hōl\ n **1 :** an opening into or through something **2 :** a hollow place (as a pit or cave) **3 :** DEN, BURROW **4 :** a unit of play from tee to cup in golf **5 :** a mean or dingy place **6 :** an awkward position — **hole** vb

hol·i·day \'häl-ə-,dā\ n **1 :** a day observed in Judaism with commemorative ceremonies **2 :** a day of freedom from work; *esp* **:** one in commemoration of an event **3 :** VACATION

ho·li·ness \'hō-lē-nəs\ n **:** the quality or state of being holy — used as a title esp. for the pope

hol·lo \hä-'lō, hä-'lō\ or **hol·la** \'häl-ə\ *interj* — used esp. to attract attention

¹**hol·low** \'häl-ō\ adj **1 :** CONCAVE, SUNKEN **2 :** having a cavity within **3 :** MUFFLED (a ~ sound) **4 :** devoid of value or significance; *also* **:** FALSE, DECEITFUL — **hol·low·ness** n

²**hollow** vb **:** to make or become hollow

³**hollow** n **1 :** a surface depression **2 :** CAVITY

hol·ly \'häl-ē\ n **:** a tree or shrub with usu. evergreen glossy leaves and red berries

hol·ly·hock \-,häk, -,hôk\ n **:** a tall perennial herb widely grown for its showy flowers

hol·mi·um \'hōl-mē-əm\ n **:** a metallic chemical element

hol·o·caust \'häl-ə-,kóst, 'hō-lə-\ n **:** a thorough destruction esp. by fire

hol·o·graph \-,graf\ n **:** a document wholly in the handwriting of the purported author

hol·ster \'hōl-stər\ n **:** a usu. leather case for a pistol

ho·ly \'hō-lē\ adj **1 :** SACRED **2 :** commanding absolute devotion **3 :** spiritually pure **syn** divine, godly, hallowed, blessed, religious

ho·ly·stone \-,stōn\ n **:** a soft sandstone used to scrub a ship's decks — **holystone** vb

hom·age \'(h)äm-ij\ n **:** reverential regard **:** RESPECT

hom·burg \'häm-,bərg\ n **:** a man's felt hat with a stiff curled brim and a high crown creased lengthwise

home \'hōm\ n **1 :** one's residence; *also* **:** HOUSE **2 :** the social unit formed by a family living together **3 :** a congenial environment; *also* **:** HABITAT **4 :** a place of origin **5 :** the objective in various games (as baseball) — **home·less** adj

home·body \-,bäd-ē\ n **:** one whose life centers in the home

home·bred \-'bred\ adj **:** produced at home

home·com·ing \-,kəm-iŋ\ n **1 :** a return home **2 :** the return of a group of people esp. on a special occasion to a place formerly frequented

home·grown \-'grōn\ adj **1 :** grown domestically (~ corn) **2 :** LOCAL, INDIGENOUS

home·land \-,land\ n **:** native land

home·ly \'hōm-lē\ adj **1 :** FAMILIAR **2 :** KINDLY **3 :** unaffectedly natural **:** PLAIN **4 :** lacking beauty or propor-

tion — **home·li·ness** n

home·made \hōm-'mād\ adj **:** made in the home, on the premises, or by one's own efforts

home·mak·er \-,mā-kər\ n **:** one who manages a household esp. as a wife and mother

home plate n **:** a slab at the apex of a baseball diamond that a base runner must touch in order to score

home·room \'hōm-,rüm, -,rùm\ n **:** a schoolroom where pupils of the same class report at the opening of school

home run n **:** a hit in baseball that enables the batter to make a circuit of the bases and score a run

home·sick \'hōm-,sik\ adj **:** longing for home and family while absent from them — **home·sick·ness** n

home·spun \-,spən\ adj **1 :** spun or made at home; *also* **:** made of a loosely woven usu. woolen or linen fabric **2 :** SIMPLE, HOMELY

home·stead \-,sted\ n **:** the home and adjoining land occupied by a family

home·stead·er n **:** one who acquires a tract of land from U.S. public lands by filing a record and living on and cultivating the tract

home·stretch \-'strech\ n **1 :** the part of a racecourse between the last curve and the winning post **2 :** a final stretch

home·ward \-wərd\ adv (or adj) **:** in the direction of home

home·work \-,wərk\ n **:** an assignment given a student to be completed outside the classroom

hom·i·cide \'häm-ə-,sīd\ n [L *homicida* manslayer & *homicidium* manslaughter; both fr. *homo* man + *caedere* to cut, kill] **1 :** a person who kills another **2 :** a killing of one human being by another — **hom·i·cid·al** \,häm-ə-'sīd-°l\ adj

hom·i·ly \'häm-ə-lē\ n **:** SERMON — **hom·i·let·ic** \,häm-ə-'let-ik\ adj

hom·i·ny \'häm-ə-nē\ n **:** hulled corn with the germ removed

ho·mo·ge·ne·ous \,hō-mə-'jē-nē-əs\ adj **:** of the same or a similar kind; *also* **:** of uniform structure — **ho·mo·ge·ne·i·ty** \-jə-'nē-ət-ē\ n — **ho·mo·ge·ne·ous·ly** \-'jē-nē-əs-lē\ adv — **ho·mo·ge·ne·ous·ness** n

ho·mog·e·nize \hō-'mäj-ə-,nīz\ vb **1 :** to make homogeneous **2 :** to reduce the particles in (as milk or paint) to uniform size and distribute them evenly throughout the liquid — **ho·mog·e·nized** adj

homo·graph \'häm-ə-,graf\ n **:** one of two or more words spelled alike but different in origin or meaning or pronunciation (the adjective *fair* and the noun *fair* are ~)

ho·mol·o·gous \hō-'mäl-ə-gəs\ adj **:** corresponding in structure usu. because of community of origin (wings and arms are ~ organs) — **ho·mol·o·gy** \-ə-jē\ n

hom·o·nym \'häm-ə-,nim\ n **1 :** HOMOPHONE, HOMOGRAPH **2 :** one of two or more words spelled and pronounced alike but different in meaning (*pool* of water and *pool* the game are ~s)

homo·phone \'häm-ə-,fōn\ n **1 :** one of two or more words (as *to, too, two*) pronounced alike but different in meaning or derivation or spelling

ho·mo sa·pi·ens \ˌhō-mō-'sap-ē-ənz, -'sāp-\ n : MAN, MANKIND

ho·mo·sex·u·al \ˌhō-mō-'sek-shə-wəl\ adj : of, relating to, or exhibiting sexual desire toward a member of one's own sex — **homosexual** n — **ho·mo·sex·u·al·i·ty** \-ˌsek-shə-'wal-ət-ē\ n

hone \'hōn\ n : a fine-grit stone for sharpening a cutting implement — **hone** vb — **hon·er** n

hon·est \'än-əst\ adj 1 : free from deception : TRUTHFUL; also : GENUINE, REAL 2 : REPUTABLE 3 : CREDITABLE 4 : marked by integrity 5 : FRANK syn upright, just, conscientious, honorable — **hon·est·ly** adv — **hon·esty** \-ə-stē\ n

hon·ey \'hən-ē\ n : a sweet sticky substance made by bees (**hon·ey·bees** \-ˌbēz\) from the nectar of flowers

1hon·ey·comb \-ˌkōm\ n : a mass of 6-sided wax cells built by honeybees; also : something of similar structure or appearance

2honeycomb vb : to make or become full of cavities like a honeycomb

hon·ey·dew melon \ˌhən-ē-ˌd(y)ü-\ n : a smooth-skinned muskmelon with sweet green flesh

hon·ey·moon \'hən-ē-ˌmün\ n 1 : a holiday taken by a newly married couple 2 : a period of harmony esp. just after marriage — **honeymoon** vb

hon·ey·suck·le \-ˌsək-əl\ n : any of various shrubs, vines, or herbs with tubular flowers rich in nectar

honk \'häŋk\ n : the cry of a goose; also : a similar sound (as of a horn) — **honk** vb — **honk·er** n

hon·ky-tonk \'häŋ-kē-ˌtäŋk\ n : a cheap nightclub or dance hall

1hon·or \'än-ər\ n 1 : good name : REPUTATION; also : outward respect 2 : PRIVILEGE 3 : a person of superior standing — used esp. as a title 4 : one whose worth brings respect or fame 5 : an evidence or symbol of distinction 6 : CHASTITY, PURITY 7 : INTEGRITY syn homage, reverence, deference, obeisance

2honor vb 1 : to regard or treat with honor 2 : to confer honor on 3 : to fulfill the terms of (as by accepting and paying when due) — **hon·or·er** n

hon·or·able \'än-(ə-)rə-bəl\ adj 1 : deserving of honor 2 : accompanied with marks of honor 3 : of great renown 4 : doing credit to the possessor 5 : characterized by integrity — **hon·or·able·ness** n — **hon·or·ably** adv

hon·o·rar·i·um \ˌän-ə-'rer-ē-əm\ n, pl -ia \-ē-ə\ also -i·ums : a reward usu. for services on which custom or propriety forbids a price to be set

hon·or·ary \'än-ə-ˌrer-ē\ adj 1 : having or conferring distinction 2 : conferred in recognition of achievement without the usual prerequisites (~ degree) 3 : UNPAID, VOLUNTARY — **hon·or·ar·i·ly** \ˌän-ə-'rer-ə-lē\ adv

honour chiefly Brit var of HONOR

hood \'hud\ n 1 : a covering for the head and neck and sometimes the face 2 : an ornamental fold (as at the back of an ecclesiastical vestment) 3 : a cover for parts of mechanisms; esp : the metal covering over an automobile engine — **hood·ed** adj

-**hood** \ˌhud\ n suffix 1 : state : condition : quality : character (boyhood) (hardihood) 2 : instance of a (specified) state or quality (falsehood) 3 : individuals sharing a (specified) state or character (brotherhood)

hood·lum \'hud-ləm\ n 1 : THUG 2 : a young ruffian

hoo·doo \'hud-ü\ n 1 : VOODOO 2 : something that brings bad luck — **hoodoo** vb

hood·wink \'hud-ˌwiŋk\ vb : to deceive by false appearance

hoo·ey \'hü-ē\ n : NONSENSE

hoof \'huf, 'huf\ n, pl **hooves** \'huvz, 'huvz\ or **hoofs** : a horny covering that protects the ends of the toes of some mammals (as horses or cattle); also : a hoofed foot — **hoofed** adj

1hook \'huk\ n 1 : a curved or bent device for catching, holding, or pulling 2 : something curved or bent like a hook 3 : a flight of a ball (as in golf) that curves in a direction opposite to the dominant hand of the player propelling it 4 : a short punch delivered with a circular motion and with the elbow bent and rigid

2hook vb 1 : CURVE, CROOK 2 : to seize or make fast with a hook 3 : STEAL

hook·ah \'huk-ə\ n : a pipe for smoking that has a long flexible tube whereby the smoke is cooled by passing through water

hook-up \'huk-ˌəp\ n : an assemblage (as of apparatus or circuits) used for a specific purpose (as in radio)

hook·worm \-ˌwərm\ n : a parasitic intestinal worm having hooks or plates around the mouth

hoo·li·gan \'hü-li-gən\ n : RUFFIAN, HOODLUM

hoop \'hup, 'hup\ n 1 : a circular strip used esp. for holding together the staves of a container (as a barrel) 2 : a circular figure or object : RING 3 : a circle of flexible material for expanding a woman's skirt

hoop·la \'hup-ˌlä\ n 1 : TO-DO 2 : utterances designed to bewilder or confuse

hoot \'hut\ vb 1 : to utter a loud shout usu. in contempt 2 : to make the characteristic cry of an owl — **hoot** n — **hoot·er** n

hoo·te·nan·ny \'hut-ˌn-ˌan-ē\ n : a gathering at which folk singers entertain often with the audience joining in

1hop \'häp\ vb hopped; hop·ping 1 : to move by quick springy leaps 2 : to make a quick trip esp. by air

2hop n 1 : a short brisk leap esp. on one leg 2 : DANCE 3 : a short trip esp. by air

3hop n : a vine related to the mulberry whose ripe dried cones are used in medicine and in flavoring malt liquors; also : its cone

4hop vb hopped; hop·ping : to increase the power of beyond an original rating (~ up an engine)

1hope \'hōp\ vb : to desire with expectation of fulfillment

2hope n 1 : TRUST, RELIANCE 2 : desire accompanied by expectation of fulfillment; also : something hoped for 3 : one that gives promise for the future — **hope·ful** adj — **hope·ful·ly** adv — **hope·ful·ness** n — **hope·less** adj — **hope·less·ly** adv — **hope·less·ness** n

hop·per n 1 : a usu. immature hopping insect 2 : a receptacle holding material to be passed on in a subsequent operation

hop·scotch \'häp-,skäch\ *n* : a child's game in which a player tosses an object (as a stone) consecutively into areas of a figure outlined on the ground and hops through the figure and back to regain the object

horde \'hōrd\ *n* : THRONG, SWARM

hore·hound \'hōr-,haùnd\ *n* : an aromatic bitter mint with downy leaves used esp. in candy

ho·ri·zon \hə-'rīz-°n\ *n* [Gk *horizont-, horizōn,* fr. prp. of *horizein* to bound, fr. *horos* limit, boundary] **1** : the line marking the apparent junction of earth and sky **2** : range of outlook or experience

hor·i·zon·tal \,hȯr-ə-'zänt-°l\ *adj* : parallel to the horizon : LEVEL — **hor·i·zon·tal·ly** *adv*

hor·mon·al \'hȯr-,mōn-°l\ *adj* : of, relating to, or resembling a hormone

hor·mone \'hȯr-,mōn\ *n* : a product of living cells that circulates in body fluids and has a specific effect on some other cells; *esp* : the secretion of an endocrine gland

horn \'hȯrn\ *n* **1** : one of the hard bony projections on the head of many hoofed animals **2** : something resembling or suggesting a horn **3** : a brass wind instrument **4** : a usu. electrical device that makes a noise ⟨automobile ∼⟩ — **horn·less** *adj* — **horny** *adj*

horn·book \'hȯrn-,bùk\ *n* **1** : a child's primer **2** : a rudimentary treatise

hor·net \'hȯr-nət\ *n* : any of the larger social wasps

horn·pipe \'hȯrn-,pīp\ *n* : a lively folk dance of the British Isles

ho·rol·o·gy \hə-'räl-ə-jē\ *n* : the science of measuring time or constructing time-indicating instruments — **hor·o·log·i·cal** \,hȯr-ə-'läj-i-kəl\ *adj* — **ho·rol·o·gist** \hə-'räl-ə-jəst\ *n*

hor·o·scope \'hȯr-ə-,skōp\ *n* : a diagram of the relative positions of planets and signs of the zodiac at a particular time for use by astrologers to foretell events of a person's life

hor·ren·dous \hȯ-'ren-dəs\ *adj* : DREADFUL, HORRIBLE

hor·ri·ble \'hȯr-ə-bəl\ *adj* **1** : marked by or conducive to horror **2** : highly disagreeable — **hor·ri·ble·ness** *n* — **hor·ri·bly** *adv*

hor·rid \'hȯr-əd\ *adj* **1** : HIDEOUS **2** : REPULSIVE — **hor·rid·ly** *adv*

hor·ri·fy \'hȯr-ə-,fī\ *vb* : to cause to feel horror **syn** appall, daunt, dismay

hor·ror \'hȯr-ər\ *n* **1** : painful and intense fear, dread, or dismay **2** : intense aversion or repugnance **3** : something that horrifies

hors de com·bat \,ȯrd-ə-kōⁿ-'bä\ *adv* (*or adj*) : in a disabled condition

hors d'oeuvre \ȯr-'dərv\ *n* : an appetizer usu. served with crackers or toast

horse \'hȯrs\ *n* **1** : a large solid-hoofed herbivorous mammal domesticated as a draft and saddle animal **2** : a supporting framework usu. with legs — **horse·less** *adj*

¹horse·back \-,bak\ *n* : the back of a horse

²horseback *adv* : on horseback

horse·flesh \-,flesh\ *n* : horses for riding, driving, or racing

horse·fly \-,flī\ *n* : any of a group of large two-winged flies with bloodsucking females

horse·hair \-,haər\ *n* **1** : the hair of a horse esp. from the mane or tail **2** : cloth made from horsehair

horse·hide \-,hīd\ *n* : the dressed or raw hide of a horse

horse·laugh \-,laf, -,läf\ *n* : a loud boisterous laugh

horse·man \-mən\ *n* **1** : one who rides horseback; *also* : one skilled in managing horses **2** : a breeder or raiser of horses — **horse·man·ship** *n*

horse·play \-,plā\ *n* : rough boisterous play

horse·pow·er \-,paù(-ə)r\ *n* : a unit of power equal to the power necessary to raise 33,000 pounds one foot in one minute

horse·rad·ish \-,rad-ish\ *n* : a tall white-flowered herb related to the mustards whose pungent root is used as a condiment

horse·shoe \'hȯrs(h)-,shü\ *n* **1** : a protective metal plate fitted to the rim of a horse's hoof **2** *pl* : a game in which horseshoes are pitched at a fixed object — **horse·sho·er** *n*

horse·whip \'hȯrs-,hwip\ *vb* : to flog with a whip made to be used on a horse

horse·wom·an \-,wùm-ən\ *n* : a woman skilled in riding horseback or in caring for or managing horses

hors·ey *or* **horsy** \'hȯr-sē\ *adj* **1** : of, relating to, or suggesting a horse **2** : having to do with horses or horse racing

hor·ta·tive \'hȯrt-ət-iv\ *adj* : giving exhortation

hor·ta·to·ry \'hȯrt-ə-,tōr-ē\ *adj* : HORTATIVE

hor·ti·cul·ture \'hȯrt-ə-,kəl-chər\ *n* : the science and art of growing fruits, vegetables, flowers, and ornamental plants — **hor·ti·cul·tur·al** \,hȯrt-ə-'kəlch-(ə-)rəl\ *adj* — **hor·ti·cul·tur·ist** \-'kəlch-(ə-)rəst\ *n*

ho·san·na \hō-'zan-ə\ *interj* — used as a cry of acclamation or adoration

¹hose \'hōz\ *n, pl* **hose** *or* **hos·es** **1** *pl* **hose** : STOCKING, SOCK; *also* : a close-fitting garment covering the legs and waist **2** : a flexible tube for conveying fluids (as from a faucet)

²hose *vb* : to spray, water, or wash with a hose

ho·siery \'hōz(h)-ə-rē\ *n* : STOCKINGS, SOCKS

hos·pice \'häs-pəs\ *n* : a lodging for travelers or for young persons or the underprivileged

hos·pit·a·ble \häs-'pit-ə-bəl, 'häs-(,)pit-\ *adj* **1** : given to generous and cordial reception of guests **2** : readily receptive — **hos·pit·a·bly** *adv*

hos·pi·tal \'häs-,pit-°l\ *n* : an institution where the sick or injured receive medical or surgical care

hos·pi·tal·i·ty \,häs-pə-'tal-ət-ē\ *n* : hospitable treatment, reception, or disposition

hos·pi·tal·ize \'häs-,pit-°l-,īz\ *vb* : to place in a hospital for care and treatment — **hos·pi·tal·iza·tion** \ˌhäs-ˌpit-°l-ə-ˈzā-shən\ n

¹host \ˈhōst\ n **1** : ARMY **2** : MULTITUDE

²host n **1** : one who receives or entertains guests socially or commercially **2** : an animal or plant on or in which a parasite lives

³host n, often cap : the eucharistic bread

hos·tage \ˈhäs-tij\ n : a person kept as a pledge pending the fulfillment of an agreement

hos·tel \ˈhäst-ᵊl\ n **1** : INN **2** : a supervised lodging for youth — **hos·tel·er** n

hos·tel·ry \-rē\ n : INN, HOTEL

host·ess \ˈhō-stəs\ n : a woman who acts as host

hos·tile \ˈhäs-tᵊl, -ˌtīl\ adj : marked by usu. overt antagonism : UNFRIENDLY — **hos·tile·ly** adv — **hos·til·i·ty** \häs-ˈtil-ət-ē\ n

hos·tler \ˈ(h)äs-lər\ n : one who takes care of horses or mules

hot \ˈhät\ adj **1** : marked by a high temperature or an uncomfortable degree of body heat **2** : giving a sensation of heat or of burning **3** : ARDENT, FIERY **4** : LUSTFUL **5** : EAGER **6** : newly made or received **7** : PUNGENT **8** : unusually lucky or favorable **9** : recently and illegally obtained ⟨~ jewels⟩ — hot adv — **hot·ly** adv — **hot·ness** n

hot·bed \-ˌbed\ n **1** : a glass-covered bed of soil heated (as by fermenting manure) and used esp. for raising seedlings **2** : an environment that favors rapid growth or development

hot-blood·ed \-ˈbləd-əd\ adj : easily roused or excited

hot·box \-ˌbäks\ n : a journal bearing (as of a railroad car) overheated by friction

hot dog \-ˌdȯg\ n : a cooked frankfurter usu. served in a long split roll

ho·tel \hō-ˈtel\ n : a building where lodging and usu. meals, entertainment, and various personal services are provided to the public

hot·foot \ˈhät-ˌfu̇t\ n, pl -**foots** : a practical joke in which a match is surreptitiously inserted into the side of a victim's shoe and lighted

hot·head·ed \ˈhät-ˈhed-əd\ adj : FIERY, IMPETUOUS — **hot·head·ed·ly** adv — **hot·head·ed·ness** n

hot·house \-ˌhau̇s\ n : a heated glass-enclosed house for raising plants

hot plate n : a simple portable appliance for heating or for cooking

hot rod n : an automobile rebuilt or modified esp. for high speed — **hot-rod·der** n

hot·shot \ˈhät-ˌshät\ n : a showily skillful person

¹hound \ˈhau̇nd\ n : a long-eared hunting dog that follows its prey by scent

²hound vb : to pursue constantly and relentlessly

hour \ˈau̇(ə)r\ n **1** : the 24th part of a day **2** : the time of day **3** : a particular or customary time **4** : a class session — **hour·ly** adv

hour·glass \-ˌglas\ n : an instrument for measuring time consisting of a glass vessel with two compartments from the uppermost of which a quantity of sand, water, or mercury runs in an hour into the lower one

hou·ri \ˈhu̇r-ē\ n : one of the beautiful maidens of the Muslim paradise

¹house \ˈhau̇s\ n, pl **hous·es** \ˈhau̇-zəz\ **1** : a building for human habitation **2** : a shelter for an animal **3** : a building in which something is stored **4** : HOUSEHOLD; also : FAMILY **5** : a legislative body **6** : a place of business or entertainment **7** : a business organization **8** : the audience in a theater or concert hall — **house·less** \ˈhau̇s-ləs\ adj

²house \ˈhau̇z\ vb **1** : to provide with or take shelter : LODGE **2** : STORE

house·boat \ˈhau̇s-ˌbōt\ n : a barge fitted for use as a dwelling or for leisurely cruising

house·boy \-ˌbȯi\ n : a boy or man hired to act as a general household servant

house·break·ing \-ˌbrā-kiŋ\ n : the act of breaking into and entering a person's dwelling house with the intent of committing a felony

house·clean \-ˌklēn\ vb : to clean a house and its furniture — **house·clean·ing** n

house·coat \ˈhau̇s-ˌkōt\ n : a woman's usu. long-skirted informal garment for wear around the house

house·fly \-ˌflī\ n : a two-winged fly that is common about human habitations and acts as a vector of diseases (as typhoid fever)

¹house·hold \ˈhau̇s-ˌhōld\ n : those who dwell as a family under the same roof — **house·hold·er** n

²household adj **1** : DOMESTIC **2** : FAMILIAR

house·keep·er \-ˌkē-pər\ n : a woman employed to take care of a house — **house·keep·ing** n

house·lights \-ˌlīts\ n pl : the lights that illuminate the parts of a theater occupied by the audience

house·maid \-ˌmād\ n : a female servant employed to do housework

house·moth·er \-ˌməth-ər\ n : a woman acting as hostess, chaperon, and often housekeeper in a residence for young people

house·top \-ˌtäp\ n : ROOF

house·warm·ing \-ˌwȯr-miŋ\ n : a party to celebrate the taking possession of a house or premises

house·wife \ˈhau̇s-ˌwīf, 2 often ˈhəz-əf, ˈhəs-\ n **1** : a married woman in charge of a household **2** : a small container (as for needles and thread) — **house·wife·li·ness** n — **house·wife·ly** adj or adv — **house·wif·ery** \-ˌwīf-(ə-)rē\ n

house·work \ˈhau̇s-ˌwərk\ n : the work of housekeeping

¹hous·ing \ˈhau̇-ziŋ\ n **1** : SHELTER **2** : something that covers or protects ⟨~ for a machine⟩

²housing n **1** : an ornamental cover for a saddle **2** pl : TRAPPINGS

hove past of HEAVE

hov·el \ˈhəv-əl, ˈhäv-\ n : a small mean house : HUT

hov·er \ˈhəv-ər\ vb **1** : FLUTTER; also : to move to and fro **2** : to be in an uncertain state

how \(ˈ)hau̇\ adv **1** : in what way or manner ⟨~ was it done⟩ **2** : with what meaning ⟨~ do we interpret such behavior⟩ **3** : for what reason ⟨~ could you have done such a thing⟩ **4** : to what extent or degree ⟨~ deep is it⟩ **5** : in what state or condition ⟨~ are you⟩ — **how about** : what do you say to or think of ⟨how about coming with me⟩

— **how come** : why is it that ⟨*how come you are here*⟩

¹how·be·it \haù-'bē-ət\ *adv* : NEVERTHELESS

²howbeit *conj* : ALTHOUGH

how·dah \'haùd-ə\ *n* : a seat or covered pavilion on the back of an elephant or camel

how·ev·er \haù-'ev-ər\ *conj* : in whatever manner

²however *adv* **1** : to whatever degree; *also* : in whatever manner **2** : in spite of that

how·it·zer \'haù-ət-sər\ *n* : a short cannon that shoots shells at a high angle of fire

howl \'haùl\ *vb* **1** : to emit a loud long doleful sound characteristic of dogs **2** : to cry loudly — **howl** *n*

howl·er *n* **1** : one that howls **2** : a stupid and ridiculous blunder

how·so·ev·er \,haù-sə-'wev-ər\ *adv* : HOWEVER 1

hoy·den \'hòid-ᵊn\ *n* : a girl or woman of saucy, boisterous, or carefree behavior

hua·ra·che \wə-'rāch-ē\ *n* : a low-heeled sandal having an upper made of interwoven leather thongs

hub \'həb\ *n* **1** : the central part of a wheel, propeller, or fan **2** : a center of activity

hub·bub \'həb-ᵊb\ *n* **1** : UPROAR; *also* : TURMOIL

hu·bris \'hyü-brəs\ *n* : overweening pride or self-confidence

huck·le·ber·ry \'hək-əl-ber-ē\ *n* **1** : an American shrub related to the blueberry; *also* : its edible dark blue berry **2** : BLUEBERRY

huck·ster \'hək-stər\ *n* : PEDDLER, HAWKER

¹hud·dle \'həd-ᵊl\ *vb* **1** : to crowd together **2** : CONFER

²huddle *n* **1** : a closely packed group **2** : MEETING, CONFERENCE

hue \'hyü\ *n* **1** : a color as distinct from white, gray, and black; *also* : gradation of color **2** : the attribute of colors that permits them to be classed as red, yellow, green, blue, or an intermediate color

hue and cry *n* : a clamor of pursuit or protest

huff \'həf\ *n* : a fit of anger or pique — **huffy** *adj*

hug \'həg\ *vb* **hugged; hug·ging** **1** : EMBRACE **2** : to stay close to ⟨the road ∼*s* the river⟩ — **hug** *n*

huge \'hyüj\ *adj* : very large or extensive — **huge·ly** *adv* — **huge·ness** *n*

Hu·gue·not \'hyü-gə-,nät\ *n* : a French Protestant of the 16th and 17th centuries

hu·la \'hü-lə\ *n* : a sinuous Polynesian dance usu. accompanied by chants and rhythmic drumming

hulk \'həlk\ *n* **1** : a heavy clumsy ship **2** : a bulky or unwieldy person or thing **3** : the body of an old ship unfit for service

hulk·ing \'həl-kiŋ\ *adj* : HUSKY, MASSIVE

¹hull \'həl\ *n* **1** : the outer covering of a fruit or seed **2** : the frame or body esp. of a ship

²hull *vb* : to remove the hulls of — **hull·er** *n*

hul·la·ba·loo \'həl-ə-bə-,lü\ *n* : a confused noise

hum \'həm\ *vb* **hummed; hum·ming** **1** : to utter a prolonged *m*-like sound **2** : DRONE **3** : to be busily active **4** : to sing with closed lips — **hum** *n* — **hum·mer** *n*

hu·man \'(h)yü-mən\ *adj* **1** : of, relating to, being, or characteristic of man **2** : having human form or attributes — **human** *n* — **hu·man·ly** *adv* — **hu·man·ness** *n*

hu·mane \(h)yü-'mān\ *adj* **1** : marked by compassion, sympathy, or consideration for others **2** : HUMANISTIC — **hu·mane·ly** *adv* — **hu·mane·ness** *n*

hu·man·ism \'(h)yü-mə-,niz-əm\ *n* **1** : the revival of classical letters characteristic of the Renaissance **2** : a doctrine or way of life centered on human interests or values — **hu·man·ist** *n* — **hu·man·is·tic** \,(h)yü-mə-'nis-tik\ *adj*

hu·man·i·tar·i·an \(h)yü-,man-ə-'ter-ē-ən\ *n* : one who practices philanthropy — **humanitarian** *adj* — **hu·man·i·tar·i·an·ism** *n*

hu·man·i·ty \(h)yü-'man-ət-ē\ *n* **1** : the quality or state of being human or humane **2** *pl* : the branches of learning having primarily a cultural character **3** : MANKIND

hu·man·ize \'(h)yü-mə-,nīz\ *vb* : to make human or humane — **hu·man·iza·tion** \,(h)yü-mə-nə-'zā-shən\ *n*

hu·man·kind \-mən-,kīnd\ *n* : MANKIND

¹hum·ble \'(h)əm-bəl\ *adj* [OF, fr. L *humilis* low, humble, fr. *humus* earth, ground] **1** : not proud or haughty **2** : not pretentious : UNASSUMING **3** : INSIGNIFICANT **syn** meek, modest, lowly — **hum·ble·ness** *n* — **hum·bly** *adv*

²humble *vb* **1** : to make humble **2** : to destroy the power or prestige of — **hum·bler** \-b(ə-)lər\ *n*

¹hum·bug \'həm-,bəg\ *n* **1** : HOAX, FRAUD **2** : NONSENSE

²humbug *vb* : DECEIVE

hum·ding·er \'həm-'diŋ-ər\ *n* : a person or thing of striking excellence

hum·drum \-,drəm\ *adj* : MONOTONOUS, DULL

hu·mer·us \'hyüm-(ə-)rəs\ *n* : the long bone extending from elbow to shoulder — **hu·mer·al** *adj*

hu·mid \'(h)yü-məd\ *adj* : containing or characterized by perceptible moisture : DAMP — **hu·mid·i·ty** \(h)yü-'mid-ət-ē\ *n* — **hu·mid·ly** \'(h)yü-məd-lē\ *adv*

hu·mid·i·fy \(h)yü-'mid-ə-,fī\ *vb* : to make humid — **hu·mid·i·fi·ca·tion** \-,mid-ə-fə-'kā-shən\ *n* — **hu·mid·i·fi·er** \-'mid-ə-,fī(-ə)r\ *n*

hu·mi·dor \'(h)yü-mə-,dòr\ *n* : a case usu. for storing cigars in which the air is kept properly humidified

hu·mil·i·ate \(h)yü-'mil-ē-,āt\ *vb* : to injure the self-respect of : MORTIFY — **hu·mil·i·a·tion** \-,mil-ē-'ā-shən\ *n*

hu·mil·i·ty \-'mil-ət-ē\ *n* : the quality or state of being humble

hum·ming·bird \'həm-iŋ-,bərd\ *n* : a tiny American bird related to the swifts

hum·mock \'həm-ək\ *n* : a rounded mound : KNOLL

¹hu·mor \'(h)yü-mər\ *n* **1** : TEMPERA-

ə abut; ᵊ kitten; ər further; a back; ā bake; ä cot, cart; aù out; ch chin; e less; ē easy; g gift; i trip; ī life; j joke; ŋ sing; ō flow; ò flaw; òi coin; th thin; th̲ this; ü loot; ù foot; y yet; yü few; yù furious; zh vision

MENT 2 : MOOD 3 : WHIM 4 : a quality that appeals to a sense of the ludicrous or incongruous (the ~ of his plight); *also* : a keen perception of the ludicrous or incongruous 5 : something designed to be comical or amusing — hu·mor·ist \'(h)yüm-(ə-)rəst\ *n* — hu·mor·less \'(h)yü-mər-ləs\ *adj* — hu·mor·less·ly *adv* — hu·mor·less·ness *n* — hu·mor·ous \'(h)yüm-(ə-)rəs\ *adj* — hu·mor·ous·ly *adv* — hu·mor·ous·ness *n*

²humor *vb* : INDULGE

humour *chiefly Brit var of* HUMOR

hump \'həmp\ *n* 1 : a rounded protuberance (as on the back of a camel) 2 : a difficult phase (as of an undertaking)

hump·back \-,bak\ *n* : HUNCHBACK — hump·backed *adj*

hu·mus \'(h)yü-məs\ *n* : the dark organic part of soil formed from decaying matter

Hun \'hən\ *n* : a member of an Asian people that invaded Europe in the 5th century A.D.

¹hunch \'hənch\ *vb* 1 : to thrust oneself forward 2 : to assume or cause to assume a bent or crooked posture

²hunch *n* 1 : PUSH 2 : a strong intuitive feeling as to how something will turn out

hunch·back \-,bak\ *n* : a back with a hump; *also* : a person with a crooked back — hunch·backed *adj*

hun·dred \'hən-drəd\ *n* : 10 times 10 — hundred *adj* — hun·dredth *adj or n*

hun·dred·weight \-,wāt\ *n* 1 : a unit of weight equal to 100 avoirdupois pounds 2 *Brit* : a unit of weight equal to 112 avoirdupois pounds

hung *past of* HANG

Hun·gar·i·an \,həŋ-'ger-ē-ən\ *n* 1 : a native or inhabitant of Hungary 2 : the language of Hungary — Hungarian *adj*

hun·ger \'həŋ-gər\ *n* 1 : a craving or urgent need for food 2 : a strong desire — hunger *vb* — hun·gri·ly \-grə-lē\ *adv* — hun·gry *adj*

hunk \'həŋk\ *n* : a large piece

hun·ker \'həŋ-kər\ *vb* : CROUCH, SQUAT

hun·kers \-kərz\ *n pl* : HAUNCHES

hun·ky-do·ry \,həŋ-kē-'dōr-ē\ *adj* : quite satisfactory : FINE

¹hunt \'hənt\ *vb* 1 : to pursue for food or in sport; *also* : to take part in a hunt 2 : to try to find : SEEK 3 : to drive or chase esp. by harrying ⟨~ a criminal out of town⟩ 4 : to traverse in search of prey — hunt·er *n*

²hunt *n* 1 : an act, practice, or instance of hunting 2 : an association of huntsmen

hunt·ress \'hən-trəs\ *n* : a female hunter

hunts·man \'hənts-mən\ *n* 1 : HUNTER 2 : one who manages a hunt and looks after the hounds

hur·dle \'hərd-ᵊl\ *n* 1 : a movable frame for enclosing land or livestock 2 : an artificial barrier over which men or horses leap in a race 3 : OBSTACLE — hurdle *vb*

hur·dy-gur·dy \,hərd-ē-'gərd-ē\ *n* : a musical instrument in which the sound is produced by turning a crank

hurl \'hərl\ *vb* 1 : to move or cause to move vigorously 2 : to throw down with violence 3 : FLING; *also* : PITCH — hurl *n* — hurl·er *n*

hur·ly-bur·ly \,hər-lē-'bər-lē\ *n* : UPROAR, TUMULT

hur·rah \hu-'rȯ, -'rä\ *interj* — used to express joy, approval, or encouragement

hur·ri·cane \'hər-ə-,kān\ *n* [Sp *huracán*, of AmerInd origin] : a cyclone that originates over tropical oceans, has winds of 73 miles per hour or greater, and is usu. accompanied by rain, thunder, and lightning

hur·ry \'hər-ē\ *vb* 1 : to carry or cause to go with haste 2 : to speed up 3 : to move or act with haste — hur·ried·ly *adv* — hur·ried·ness *n*

hurry *n* : extreme haste or eagerness

¹hurt \'hərt\ *vb* hurt; hurt·ing 1 : to feel or cause to feel pain 2 : to do harm to : DAMAGE 3 : OFFEND 4 : HAMPER

²hurt *n* 1 : a bodily injury or wound 2 : SUFFERING 3 : HARM, WRONG — hurt·ful *adj*

hur·tle \'hərt-ᵊl\ *vb* 1 : to move with a rushing sound 2 : HURL, FLING

¹hus·band \'həz-bənd\ *n* : a married man

²husband *vb* : to manage prudently

hus·band·man \-bən(d)-mən\ *n* : FARMER

hus·band·ry \-bən-drē\ *n* 1 : the control or judicious use of resources 2 : AGRICULTURE

hush \'həsh\ *vb* 1 : to make or become quiet or calm 2 : SUPPRESS

²hush *n* : SILENCE, QUIET

hush-hush \'həsh-,həsh\ *adj* : SECRET, CONFIDENTIAL

¹husk \'həsk\ *n* 1 : a usu. thin dry outer covering of a seed or fruit 2 : an outer layer : SHELL

²husk *vb* : to strip the husk from — husk·er *n*

husk·ing *n* : a gathering of farm families to husk corn

¹husky \'həs-kē\ *adj* : HOARSE — husk·i·ly *adv* — husk·i·ness *n*

²husky *adj* 1 : BURLY, ROBUST 2 : LARGE — husk·i·ness *n*

hus·sar \hə-'zär\ *n* : a member of any of various European cavalry units

hus·sy \'həz-ē, 'həs-\ *n* 1 : a lewd or brazen woman 2 : a pert or mischievous girl

hus·tings \'həs-tiŋz\ *n pl* : a place where political campaign speeches are made; *also* : the proceedings in an election campaign

¹hus·tle \'həs-əl\ *vb* 1 : JOSTLE, SHOVE 2 : HASTEN, HURRY 3 : to work energetically — hus·tler \-(ə-)lər\ *n*

²hustle *n* : energetic activity

hut \'hət\ *n* : a small and often temporary dwelling : SHACK

hutch \'həch\ *n* 1 : a chest or compartment for storage 2 : a low cupboard usu. surmounted with open shelves 3 : a pen or coop for an animal 4 : HUT, SHACK

hut·ment \'hət-mənt\ *n* 1 : a collection of huts 2 : HUT

huz·zah or huz·za \hə-'zä\ *interj* — used to express joy or approbation

hy·a·cinth \'hī-ə-(,)sinth\ *n* : a bulbous herb related to the lilies and widely grown for its spikes of fragrant bell-shaped flowers

hy·ae·na *var of* HYENA

hy·brid \'hī-brəd\ *n* 1 : an offspring of genetically differing parents (as members of different breeds or species) 2 : one of mixed origin or composition — hybrid *adj* — hy·brid·iza·tion \,hī-brəd-ə-'zā-shən\ *n* — hy·brid·ize \'hī-brəd-,īz\ *vb*

hy·dran·gea \hī-'drān-jə\ n : any of a genus of shrubs related to the currants and grown for their large clusters of white or tinted flowers

hy·drant \'hī-drənt\ n : a pipe with a valve and spout at which water may be drawn from a main pipe

hy·drate \'hī-,drāt\ n 1 : a compound formed by union of water with some other substance 2 HYDROXIDE ⟨calcium ∼⟩

hy·drau·lic \hī-'drò-lik\ adj 1 : operated, moved, or effected by means of water 2 : of or relating to hydraulics 3 : operated by the resistance offered or the pressure transmitted when a quantity of liquid is forced through a small orifice or through a tube ⟨∼ brake⟩ 4 : hardening or setting under water ⟨∼ cement⟩

hy·drau·lics n : a science that deals with practical applications of liquids (as water) in motion

hy·dro \'hī-drō\ adj : HYDROELECTRIC

hy·dro·car·bon \,hī-drə-'kär-bən\ n : a compound (as acetylene) containing only carbon and hydrogen

hy·dro·chlo·ric acid \,hī-drə-,klòr-ik-\ n : a sharp-smelling corrosive acid used in the laboratory and in industry

hy·dro·elec·tric \,hī-drō-i-'lek-trik\ adj : of, relating to, or used in the production of electricity by waterpower

hy·dro·gen \'hī-drə-jən\ n : a gaseous colorless odorless highly flammable chemical element that is the lightest of the elements — **hy·drog·e·nous** \hī-'dräj-ə-nəs\ adj

hydrogen bomb n : a bomb whose violent explosive power is due to the sudden release of atomic energy resulting from the union of light nuclei (as of hydrogen atoms)

hydrogen peroxide n : an unstable liquid compound of hydrogen and oxygen used as an oxidizing and bleaching agent, an antiseptic, and a propellant

hy·drol·y·sis \hī-'dräl-ə-səs\ n : a chemical decomposition involving the addition of the elements of water

hy·drom·e·ter \hī-'dräm-ət-ər\ n : a floating instrument for determining specific gravities of liquids and hence the strength (as of alcoholic liquors)

hy·dro·pho·bia \,hī-drə-'fō-bē-ə\ n : RABIES

hy·dro·plane \'hī-drə-,plān\ n 1 : a speedboat with fins or a stepped bottom so that the hull is raised wholly or partly out of the water 2 : SEAPLANE

hy·dro·pon·ics \,hī-drə-'pän-iks\ n : the growing of plants in nutrient solutions — **hy·dro·pon·ic** \-ik\ adj

hy·dro·stat·ic \-'stat-ik\ adj : of or relating to liquids at rest or to the pressures they exert or transmit

hy·dro·ther·a·py \,hī-drō-'ther-ə-pē\ n : the external application of water in the treatment of disease or disability

hy·drous \'hī-drəs\ adj : containing water

hy·drox·ide \hī-'dräk-,sīd\ n : a compound of an oxygen-and-hydrogen group with an element or radical

hy·e·na \hī-'ē-nə\ n : a large nocturnal carnivorous mammal of Asia and Africa

hy·giene \'hī-,jēn\ n 1 : a science dealing with the establishment and maintenance of health 2 : conditions or practices conducive to health — **hy·gien·ic** \,hī-jē-'en-ik, hī-'jen-\ adj — **hy·gien·i·cal·ly** adv — **hy·gien·ist** \'hī-jē-nəst\ n

nying pres part of HIE

hy·me·ne·al \,hī-mə-'nē-əl\ adj : NUPTIAL

hymn \'him\ n : a song of praise esp. to God — **hymn** vb — **hym·nal** \'him-nºl\ n

hym·no·dy \'him-nəd-ē\ n 1 : hymn singing or writing 2 : the hymns of a time, place, or church

hy·per·acid·i·ty \,hī-pər-ə-'sid-ət-ē\ n : excessive stomach acidity

hy·per·bo·le \hī-'pər-bə-(,)lē\ n : extravagant exaggeration used as a figure of speech

hy·per·bo·re·an \,hī-pər-'bōr-ē-ən\ adj : of, relating to, or inhabiting a remote northern region

hy·per·crit·i·cal \,hī-pər-'krit-i-kəl\ adj : excessively critical — **hy·per·crit·i·cal·ly** adv

hy·per·sen·si·tive \-'sen-sət-iv\ adj : excessively or abnormally sensitive — **hy·per·sen·si·tiv·i·ty** \-,sen-sə-'tiv-ət-ē\ n

hy·per·son·ic \-'sän-ik\ adj 1 : of or relating to speed five or more times that of sound in air 2 : moving, capable of moving, or utilizing air currents that move at hypersonic speed

hy·per·ten·sion \-'ten-chən\ n : abnormally high blood pressure — **hy·per·ten·sive** \-'ten-siv\ adj or n

hy·per·tro·phy \hī-'pər-trə-fē\ n : excessive growth or development of a body part — **hy·per·tro·phic** \,hī-'pər-trə-fik, ,hī-pər-'träf-ik\ adj — **hypertrophy** vb

hy·phen \'hī-fən\ n : a punctuation mark - used to divide or to compound words or word elements — **hyphen** vb

hy·phen·ate \'hī-fə-,nāt\ vb : HYPHEN — **hy·phen·ation** \,hī-fə-'nā-shən\ n

hyp·no·sis \hip-'nō-səs\ n : an induced state which resembles sleep and in which the subject is responsive to suggestions of the inducer (**hyp·no·tist** \'hip-nə-təst\) — **hyp·no·tism** \-,tiz-əm\ n — **hyp·no·tize** \hip-nə-,tīz\ vb

¹**hyp·not·ic** \hip-'nät-ik\ adj 1 : inducing sleep : SOPORIFIC 2 : of or relating to hypnosis or hypnotism — **hyp·not·i·cal·ly** adv

²**hypnotic** n : a sleep-inducing drug

hy·po·chon·dria \,hī-pə-'kän-drē-ə\ n : depression of mind usu. centered on imaginary physical ailments — **hy·po·chon·dri·ac** \-drē-,ak\ adj or n

hy·poc·ri·sy \hip-'äk-rə-sē\ n : a feigning to be what one is not or to believe what one does not; esp : the false assumption of an appearance of virtue or religion — **hyp·o·crite** \'hip-ə-,krit\ n — **hyp·o·crit·i·cal** \,hip-ə-'krit-i-kəl\ adj — **hyp·o·crit·i·cal·ly** adv

hy·po·der·mic \,hī-pə-'dər-mik\ n : a small syringe with a hollow needle for injecting material into or through the skin; also : an injection made with this

hy·pot·e·nuse \hī-'pät-ºn-,(y)üs, -,(y)üz\ n : the side of a right-angled triangle that is opposite the right angle

ə abut; ᵊ kitten; ər further; a back; ā bake; ä cot, cart; aù out; ch chin; e less; ē easy; g gift; i trip; ī life; j joke; ŋ sing; ō flow; ò flaw; òi coin; th thin; th̲ this; ü loot; ù foot; y yet; yü few; yù furious; zh vision

hy·poth·e·cate \hī-'päth-ə-ˌkāt\ *vb* : HYPOTHESIZE

hy·poth·e·sis \hī-'päth-ə-səs\ *n* : an assumption made esp. in order to draw out and test its logical or empirical consequences — **hy·po·thet·i·cal** \ˌhī-pə-'thet-i-kəl\ *adj* — **hy·po·thet·i·cal·ly** *adv*

hy·poth·e·size \hī-'päth-ə-ˌsīz\ *vb* : to adopt as a hypothesis

hys·sop \'his-əp\ *n* : a European mint used in medicine

hys·ter·ec·to·mize \ˌhis-tə-'rek-tə-ˌmīz\ *vb* : to perform a hysterectomy on

hys·ter·ec·to·my \ˌhis-tə-'rek-tə-mē\ *n* : surgical removal of the uterus

hys·te·ria \his-'tir-ē-ə\ *n* 1 : a nervous disorder marked esp. by defective emotional control 2 : uncontrollable fear or emotion — **hys·ter·ic** \-'ter-ik\ *or* **hys·ter·i·cal** *adj* — **hys·ter·i·cal·ly** *adv*

hys·ter·ics \-'ter-iks\ *n* : a fit of uncontrollable laughter or crying

---

i \'ī\ *n, often cap* : the 9th letter of the English alphabet

I \(')ī, ə\ *pron* : the one speaking or writing

iamb \'ī-ˌam\ *n* : a metrical foot of one unaccented syllable followed by one accented syllable — **iam·bic** \ī-'am-bik\ *adj*

-ian — see -AN

ibex \'ī-ˌbeks\ *n* : an Old World wild goat with large curved horns

ibi·dem \'ib-ə-ˌdem, ib-'īd-əm\ *adv* : in the same place

ibis \'ī-bəs\ *n* : any of several wading birds related to the herons but having a down-curved bill

-ible — see -ABLE

1-ic \ik\ *adj suffix* 1 : having the character or form of : being 〈panoram*ic*〉 : consisting of 2 : of or relating to 〈alderman*ic*〉 3 : related to, derived from, or containing 〈alcohol*ic*〉 4 : in the manner of : like that of : characteristic of 5 : associated or dealing with : utilizing 〈electron*ic*〉 6 : characterized by : exhibiting 〈nostalg*ic*〉 : affected with 〈allerg*ic*〉 7 : caused by 8 : tending to produce

2-ic *n suffix* : one having the character or nature of : one belonging to or associated with : one exhibiting or affected by : one that produces

-i·cal \i-kəl\ *adj suffix* : -IC 〈symmetr*ical*〉 〈geolog*ical*〉 — **-i·cal·ly** \i-k(ə-)lē\ *adv suffix*

1ice \'īs\ *n* 1 : water frozen 2 : a state of coldness (as from formality or reserve) 3 : a substance resembling ice 4 : a frozen dessert; *esp* : one containing no milk or cream

2ice *vb* 1 : FREEZE 2 : CHILL 3 : to cover with or as if with icing — **iced** *adj*

ice bag *n* : a waterproof bag to hold ice for local application of cold to the body

ice·berg \-ˌbərg\ *n* : a huge mass of ice broken off from a glacier; *also* : an emotionally cold person

ice·boat \-ˌbōt\ *n* 1 : a boatlike frame on runners propelled on ice usu. by sails 2 : ICEBREAKER 2

ice·bound \-ˌbaund\ *adj* : surrounded or obstructed by ice

ice·box \-ˌbäks\ *n* 2 : REFRIGERATOR

ice·break·er \'īs-ˌbrā-kər\ *n* 1 : a structure that protects a bridge pier from floating ice 2 : a ship equipped to make and maintain a channel through ice

ice cap *n* : a cover of perennial ice and snow; *esp* : a glacier forming on relatively level land and flowing outward from its center

ice cream *n* : a frozen food containing cream or butterfat, flavoring, sweetening, and usu. eggs

ice·house \'īs-ˌhaus\ *n* : a building for storing ice

Ice·land·er \-ˌlan-dər, -lən-\ *n* : a native or inhabitant of Iceland

Ice·lan·dic \īs-'lan-dik\ *adj* : of, relating to, or characteristic of Iceland, the Icelanders, or their language

ice·man \īs-ˌman\ *n* : one who sells or delivers ice

ice pick *n* : a hand tool ending in a spike for chipping ice

ice sheet *n* : ICE CAP

ice-skate \'īs-ˌskāt\ *vb* : to skate on ice — **ice skater** *n*

ice water *n* : chilled or iced water esp. for drinking

ichor \'īk-ˌor, -ər, 'ik-\ *n* : an ethereal fluid taking the place of blood in the veins of the ancient Greek gods

ich·thy·ol·o·gy \ˌik-thē-'äl-ə-jē\ *n* : a branch of zoology dealing with fishes — **ich·thy·ol·o·gist** \-jəst\ *n*

ici·cle \'ī-ˌsik-əl\ *n* : a hanging mass of ice formed by the freezing of dripping water

ic·ing *n* : a coating for baked goods usu. made from sugar and butter combined with water, milk, egg white, and flavoring

icon \'ī-ˌkän\ *n* : IMAGE; *esp* : a religious image painted on a small wood panel

icon·o·clasm \ī-'kän-ə-ˌklaz-əm\ *n* : the doctrine, practice, or attitude of an iconoclast

icon·o·clast \ī-'kän-ə-ˌklast\ *n* [MGk *eikonoklastēs*, fr. Gk *eikōn* image + *klan* to break] 1 : one who destroys religious images or opposes their veneration 2 : one who attacks cherished beliefs or institutions

-ics \iks\ *n sing or pl suffix* 1 : study : knowledge : skill : practice 〈linguist*ics*〉 〈electron*ics*〉 2 : characteristic actions or activities 〈acrobat*ics*〉 3 : characteristic qualities, operations, or phenomena 〈mechan*ics*〉

ic·tus \'ik-təs\ *n* : the recurring stress or beat in a rhythmic or metrical series of sounds

icy \'ī-sē\ *adj* 1 : covered with, abounding in, or consisting of ice 2 : intensely cold 3 : being cold and unfriendly : FRIGID 〈an ~ stare〉 — **ic·i·ly** *adv* — **ic·i·ness** *n*

id \'id\ *n* : the primitive undifferentiated part of the psychic apparatus which is the seat of psychic energy and from which the higher psychic components (as ego and superego) derive

idea \ī-'dē-ə\ *n* 1 : a plan for action : DESIGN, PROJECT 2 : something imagined or pictured in the mind **3** : a central meaning or purpose ⟨the ~ of the game is to keep from getting caught⟩ **syn** concept, conception, notion, impression

¹ide·al \ī-'dē(-ə)l\ *adj* **1** : existing only in the mind : IMAGINARY; *also* : lacking practicality **2** : of or relating to an ideal or to approach to perfection : PERFECT ⟨~ weather⟩

²ideal *n* **1** : a standard of perfection, beauty, or excellence **2** : one regarded as exemplifying an ideal and often taken as a model for imitation **3** : GOAL

ide·al·ism \ī-'dē-(ə-)liz-əm\ *n* **1** : the practice of forming or living according to ideals **2** : the ability or tendency to see things as they should be rather than as they are — **ide·al·ist** \-(ə-)ləst\ *n* — **ide·al·is·tic** \ī-dē-(ə-)'lis-tik\ *adj*

ide·al·ize \ī-'dē-(ə-)līz\ *vb* : to think of or represent as ideal — **ide·al·iza·tion** \ī-dē-(ə-)lə-'zā-shən\ *n*

ide·al·ly \ī-'dē-(ə-)lē\ *adv* **1** : in idea or imagination : MENTALLY **2** : in agreement with an ideal : PERFECTLY

idem \'īd-,em, 'ēd-\ *pron* : something previously mentioned

iden·ti·cal \ī-'dent-i-kəl\ *adj* **1** : being the same **2** : exactly or essentially alike **syn** equivalent, equal

iden·ti·fi·ca·tion \ī-,dent-ə-fə-'kā-shən\ *n* **1** : an act of identifying : the state of being identified **2** : evidence of identity

iden·ti·fy \ī-'dent-ə-,fī\ *vb* **1** : to be or cause to be or become identical **2** : ASSOCIATE ⟨*identified* himself with no church group⟩ **3** : to establish the identity of ⟨*identified* the watch as his⟩

iden·ti·ty \ī-'dent-ət-ē\ *n* **1** : sameness of essential character **2** : INDIVIDUALITY **3** : the fact of being the same person or thing as one described

ide·ol·o·gy \,īd-ē-'äl-ə-jē, ,id-\ *n* **1** : the body of ideas characteristic of a particular individual, group, or culture **2** : the assertions, theories, and aims that constitute a political, social, and economic program — **ide·o·log·i·cal** \,īd-ē-ə-'läj-i-kəl, ,id-\ *adj*

ides \'īdz\ *n sing or pl* : the 15th day of March, May, July, or October or the 13th day of any other month in the ancient Roman calendar

id·i·o·cy \'id-ē-ə-sē\ *n* **1** : extreme mental deficiency **2** : something notably stupid or foolish

id·i·om \'id-ē-əm\ *n* **1** : the language peculiar to an individual, a group, a class, or a district ⟨DIALECT ⟨Shakespeare's ~⟩ ⟨doctors speaking in their professional ~⟩ **2** : the characteristic form or structure of a language ⟨know the vocabulary of a foreign language but not its ~⟩ **3** : an expression in the usage of a language that is peculiar to itself either grammatically (as *it wasn't me*) or that cannot be understood from the meanings of its separate words (as *take cold*) — **id·i·om·at·ic** \,id-ē-ə-'mat-ik\ *adj*

id·i·o·syn·cra·sy \,id-ē-ə-'siŋ-krə-sē\ *n* : personal peculiarity (as of habit or of response to a drug)

id·i·ot \'id-ē-ət\ *n* **1** : a feebleminded person requiring complete custodial care **2** : a silly or foolish person — **id·i·ot·ic**

\,id-ē-'ät-ik\ *adj* — **id·i·ot·i·cal·ly** *adv*

¹idle \'īd-ºl\ *adj* **1** : GROUNDLESS, WORTHLESS, USELESS ⟨~ rumor⟩ ⟨~ talk⟩ **2** : not occupied or employed : INACTIVE **3** : LAZY ⟨~ fellows⟩ — **idle·ness** — **idly** \'īd-lē\ *adv*

²idle *vb* **1** : to spend time doing nothing **2** : to pass in idleness **3** : to make idle **4** : to run without being connected so that power is not used for useful work ⟨the engine is *idling*⟩ — **idler** \-(ᵊ-)lər\ *n*

idol \'īd-ºl\ *n* **1** : a representation of a deity used as an object of worship **2** : a false god **3** : an object of passionate devotion

idol·a·ter \ī-'däl-ət-ər\ *n* : a worshiper of idols

idol·a·try \-ə-trē\ *n* **1** : the worship of a physical object as a god **2** : immoderate devotion — **idol·a·trous** \-ə-trəs\ *adj*

idol·ize \'īd-ºl-,īz\ *vb* : to make an idol of : love or admire to excess

idyll or **idyl** \'īd-ºl\ *n* **1** : a simple descriptive or narrative composition; *esp* : a poem about country life **2** : a fit subject for an idyll **3** : a romantic interlude — **idyl·lic** \ī-'dil-ik\ *adj*

-ier — see -ER

if \(,)if, əf\ *conj* **1** : in the event that ⟨~ he stays, I leave⟩ **2** : WHETHER ⟨ask ~ he left⟩ **3** : even though ⟨an interesting ~ untenable argument⟩

if·fy \'if-ē\ *adj* : abounding in contingencies or unknown qualities or conditions

-i·fy \ə-,fī\ *vb suffix* : -FY

ig·loo \'ig-lü\ *n* : an Eskimo house or hut often made of snow blocks and in the shape of a dome

ig·ne·ous \'ig-nē-əs\ *adj* **1** : FIERY **2** : formed by solidification of molten rock

ig·nite \ig-'nīt\ *vb* : to set afire or catch fire

ig·ni·tion \ig-'nish-ən\ *n* **1** : a setting on fire **2** : the process or means (as an electric spark) of igniting the fuel mixture in an engine

ig·no·ble \ig-'nō-bəl\ *adj* **1** : of low birth : PLEBEIAN **2** : not honorable : BASE, MEAN, DESPICABLE — **ig·no·bly** \-blē\ *adv*

ig·no·min·i·ous \,ig-nə-'min-ē-əs\ *adj* **1** : DISHONORABLE **2** : DESPICABLE **3** : HUMILIATING, DEGRADING — **ig·no·min·i·ous·ly** *adv* — **ig·no·mi·ny** \'ig-nə-,min-ē, ig-'näm-ə-nē\ *n*

ig·no·ra·mus \,ig-nə-'rā-məs\ *n* : an utterly ignorant person : DUNCE

ig·no·rance \'ig-nə-rəns\ *n* : the state of being ignorant : lack of knowledge

ig·no·rant \-rənt\ *adj* **1** : lacking knowledge : UNEDUCATED **2** : resulting from or showing lack of knowledge or intelligence **3** : UNAWARE, UNINFORMED — **ig·no·rant·ly** *adv*

ig·nore \ig-'nōr\ *vb* : to refuse to take notice of : DISREGARD **syn** overlook, slight, neglect

igua·na \i-'gwän-ə\ *n* : a large edible tropical American lizard

ikon *var of* ICON

ilk \'ilk\ *n* : SORT, FAMILY — used chiefly in the phrase *of that ilk*

¹ill \'il\ *adj* **worse** \'wərs\ **worst** \'wərst\ **1** : not normal or sound ⟨~

health); *also* : suffering ill health (an ~ child) : SICK   2 : BAD, UNLUCKY (~ omen)   3 : not meeting an accepted standard (~ manners)   4 : UNFRIENDLY, HOSTILE (~ feeling)   5 : HARSH, CRUEL (~ treatment)

²ill *adv* worse; worst   1 : with displeasure or hostility   2 : in a harsh manner   3 : HARDLY, SCARCELY (can ~ afford it)   4 : BADLY, UNLUCKILY   5 : in a faulty or inefficient manner

³ill *n*   1 : EVIL   2 : MISFORTUNE, DISTRESS   3 : AILMENT, SICKNESS; *also* : TROUBLE

ill-ad-vised \,il-əd-ˈvīzd\ *adj* : not well counseled : UNWISE, RASH (~ efforts) — ill-ad-vis-ed-ly \-ˈvī-zəd-lē\ *adv*

ill-bred \ˈil-ˈbred\ *adj* : badly brought up : IMPOLITE

il-le-gal \(ˈ)il-ˈ(l)ē-gəl\ *adj* : not lawful; *also* : not sanctioned by official rules — il-le-gal-i-ty \,il-ē-ˈgal-ət-ē\ *n* — il-le-gal-ly \(ˈ)il-ˈ(l)ē-gə-lē\ *adv*

il-leg-i-ble \il-ˈ(l)ej-ə-bəl\ *adj* : not legible : impossible or difficult to read or decipher — il-leg-i-bil-i-ty \-,ej-ə-ˈbil-ət-ē\ *n* — il-leg-i-bly \il-ˈ(l)ej-ə-blē\ *adv*

il-le-git-i-mate \,il-i-ˈjit-ə-mət\ *adj*   1 : born of parents not married to each other   2 : ILLOGICAL   3 : ERRATIC   4 : ILLEGAL — il-le-git-i-mate-ly *adv* — il-le-git-i-ma-cy \-ˈjit-ə-mə-sē\ *n*

ill-fat-ed \ˈil-ˈfāt-əd\ *adj* : having or destined to an evil fate : UNFORTUNATE (an ~ voyage)

ill-fa-vored \-ˈfā-vərd\ *adj*   1 : unattractive in physical appearance; *esp* : having an ugly face   2 : OFFENSIVE, OBJECTIONABLE

ill-got-ten \ˈgät-ᵊn\ *adj* : acquired by evil means (~ gains)

ill-hu-mored \-ˈ(h)yü-mərd\ *adj* : SURLY, IRRITABLE

il-lib-er-al \il-ˈ(l)ib-(ə-)rəl\ *adj* : not liberal : NARROW, BIGOTED

il-lic-it \il-ˈ(l)is-ət\ *adj* : not permitted : UNLAWFUL — il-lic-it-ly *adv*

il-lim-it-able \il-ˈ(l)im-ət-ə-bəl\ *adj* : BOUNDLESS, MEASURELESS — il-lim-it-ably *adv*

il-lit-er-ate \il-ˈ(l)it-ə-rət\ *adj*   1 : having little or no education; *esp* : unable to read or write   2 : showing a lack of familiarity with language and literature or with the fundamentals of a particular field of knowledge — il-lit-er-a-cy \-rə-sē\ *n* — illiterate *n*

ill-man-nered \ˈil-ˈman-ərd\ *adj* : marked by bad manners : RUDE

ill-na-tured \-ˈnā-chərd\ *adj* : CROSS, SURLY — ill-na-tured-ly *adv*

ill-ness *n* : SICKNESS

il-log-i-cal \il-ˈ(l)äj-i-kəl\ *adj* : not according to good reasoning; *also* : SENSELESS — il-log-i-cal-ly *adv*

ill-starred \ˈil-ˈstärd\ *adj* : ILL-FATED, UNLUCKY

ill-tem-pered \ˈil-ˈtem-pərd\ *adj* : ILL-NATURED, QUARRELSOME

ill-treat \ˈil-ˈtrēt\ *vb* : to treat cruelly or improperly : MALTREAT — ill-treat-ment *n*

il-lume \il-ˈüm\ *vb* : ILLUMINATE

il-lu-mi-nate \il-ˈü-mə-,nāt\ *vb*   1 : to supply or brighten with light : make luminous or shining   2 : to make clear : ELUCIDATE   3 : to decorate (as a manuscript) with gold or silver or brilliant colors or with often elaborate designs or pictures — il-lu-mi-na-tion

\-,ü-mə-ˈnā-shən\ *n* — il-lu-mi-na-tor \-ˈü-mə-,nāt-ər\ *n*

il-lu-mine \-ˈü-mən\ *vb* : ILLUMINATE

ill-us-age \ˈil-ˈyü-sij, -zij\ *n* : harsh, unkind, or abusive treatment

ill-use \-ˈyüz\ *vb* : MALTREAT, ABUSE — ill-use \-ˈyüs\ *n*

il-lu-sion \il-ˈü-zhən\ *n*   1 : a mistaken idea : MISAPPREHENSION, MISCONCEPTION, FANCY   2 : a misleading image presented to the vision : HALLUCINATION; *esp* : APPARITION

il-lu-sive \il-ˈü-siv\ *adj* : ILLUSORY

il-lu-so-ry \il-ˈüs-(ə-)rē, -ˈüz-\ *adj* : based on or producing illusion : DECEPTIVE

il-lus-trate \ˈil-ə-,strāt\ *vb*   1 : to make clear or explain (as by use of examples) : CLARIFY; *also* : DEMONSTRATE   2 : to provide with pictures or figures intended to explain or decorate (~ a book)   3 : to serve to explain or decorate — il-lus-tra-tor *n*

il-lus-tra-tion \,il-ə-ˈstrā-shən\ *n*   1 : the action of illustrating : the condition of being illustrated   2 : an example or instance that helps make something (as a statement or article) clear   3 : a picture, drawing, or diagram intended to explain or decorate a book or article

il-lus-tra-tive \il-ˈəs-trət-iv\ *adj* : serving, tending, or designed to illustrate (an ~ diagram) (a definition with ~ examples) — il-lus-tra-tive-ly *adv*

il-lus-tri-ous \il-ˈəs-trē-əs\ *adj* : notably outstanding because of rank or achievement : EMINENT, DISTINGUISHED — il-lus-tri-ous-ness *n*

ill will *n* : unfriendly feeling

¹im-age \ˈim-ij\ *n*   1 : a likeness or imitation of a person or thing; *esp* : STATUE   2 : a visual counterpart of an object formed by a device (as a mirror or lens)   3 : a mental picture or conception : IMPRESSION, IDEA, CONCEPT   4 : a vivid representation or description   5 : a person strikingly like another person : COUNTERPART, COPY (he is the ~ of his father)

²image *vb*   1 : to describe or portray in words   2 : to bring up before the imagination : IMAGINE, FANCY   3 : REFLECT, MIRROR (a face *imaged* in a mirror)   4 : to make appear : PROJECT   5 : to create a representation of

im-ag-ery \ˈij-(ə-)rē\ *n*   1 : IMAGES; *also* : the art of making images   2 : figurative language   3 : mental images; *esp* : the products of imagination

imag-in-able \im-ˈaj-(ə-)nə-bəl\ *adj* : capable of being imagined : CONCEIVABLE — imag-in-ably *adv*

imag-i-nary \im-ˈaj-ə-,ner-ē\ *adj* : existing only in the imagination : FANCIED

imag-i-na-tion \im-,aj-ə-ˈnā-shən\ *n*   1 : the act or power of forming a mental image of something not present to the senses or not previously known or experienced   2 : creative ability   3 : RESOURCEFULNESS   4 : a mental image : a creation of the mind   5 : popular or traditional belief or conception — imag-i-na-tive \im-ˈaj-(ə-)nət-iv, -ə-,nāt-iv\ *adj* — imag-i-na-tive-ly *adv*

imag-ine \im-ˈaj-ən\ *vb*   1 : to form a mental picture of something not present : FANCY   2 : PLAN, SCHEME   3 : THINK, SUPPOSE, GUESS (I ~ it will rain)

im-ag-ism \ˈim-ij-,iz-əm\ *n* : a movement in poetry advocating free verse and the expression of ideas and emotions through clear precise images — **im·ag·ist** n

ima·go \im-'ā-gō, -'äg-ō\ n, pl **imagoes** or **ima·gi·nes** \-'ā-gə-,nēz, -'äg-ə-\ : an insect in its final adult stage — **ima·gi·nal** \im-'ā-gən-ºl, -'äg-ən-\ adj

im·bal·ance \(')im-'bal-əns\ n : lack of balance : the state of being out of equilibrium or out of proportion ⟨∼ of exports and imports⟩

im·be·cile \'im-bə-səl\ n 1 : a feebleminded person; esp : one capable of performing routine personal care under supervision 2 : FOOL, IDIOT — **imbecile** or **im·be·cil·ic** \,im-bə-'sil-ik\ adj — **im·be·cil·i·ty** \,im-bə-'sil-ət-ē\ n

im·bed \im-'bed\ var of EMBED

im·bibe \im-'bīb\ vb 1 : DRINK 2 : to receive and retain in the mind 3 : ASSIMILATE 4 : to drink in : ABSORB — **im·bib·er** n

im·bri·ca·tion \,im-brə-'kā-shən\ n 1 : an overlapping of edges (as of tiles) 2 : a decoration or pattern showing imbrication — **im·bri·cate** \'im-brə-,kāt\ adj

im·bro·glio \im-'brōl-yō\ n 1 : a confused mass 2 : a difficult, complicated, or embarrassing situation; also : a serious or embarrassing misunderstanding

im·brue \im-'brü\ vb : DRENCH, STAIN ⟨a nation imbrued with the blood of executed men⟩

im·bue \im-'byü\ vb 1 : to tinge or dye deeply 2 : to cause to become penetrated : PERMEATE ⟨imbued with a desire to help⟩

im·i·ta·ble \'im-ət-ə-bəl\ adj : capable or worthy of being imitated or copied

im·i·tate \'im-ə-,tāt\ vb 1 : to follow as a pattern or model : COPY 2 : REPRODUCE 3 : RESEMBLE 4 : MIMIC, COUNTERFEIT — **im·i·ta·tor** n

im·i·ta·tion \,im-ə-'tā-shən\ n 1 : an act of imitating or mimicking 2 : COPY, COUNTERFEIT 3 : a literary work designed to reproduce the style of another author — **imitation** adj

im·i·ta·tive \'im-ə-,tāt-iv\ adj 1 : marked by imitation 2 : exhibiting mimicry 3 : inclined to imitate or copy 4 : COUNTERFEIT

im·mac·u·late \im-'ak-yə-lət\ adj 1 : being without stain or blemish : PURE 2 : spotlessly clean ⟨∼ linen⟩ — **im·mac·u·late·ly** adv

im·ma·nent \'im-ə-nənt\ adj 1 : INDWELLING; esp : having existence only in the mind 2 : dwelling in nature and the souls of men — **im·ma·nence** or **im·ma·nen·cy** n

im·ma·te·ri·al \,im-ə-'tir-ē-əl\ adj 1 : not consisting of matter : SPIRITUAL 2 : UNIMPORTANT, TRIFLING

im·ma·ture \,im-ə-'t(y)ùr\ adj : lacking complete development : not yet mature — **im·ma·tu·ri·ty** \-'t(y)ùr-ət-ē\ n

im·mea·sur·able \(')im-'ezh-(ə-)rə-bəl\ adj : not capable of being measured : indefinitely extensive : ILLIMITABLE — **im·mea·sur·ably** adv

im·me·di·a·cy \im-'ēd-ē-ə-sē\ n 1 : the quality or state of being immediate; esp : lack of an intervening object, place, time, or agent 2 : URGENCY 3 : something that is of immediate importance ⟨the immediacies of life⟩

im·me·di·ate \im-'ēd-ē-ət\ adj 1 : acting directly and alone : DIRECT ⟨the ∼ cause of death⟩ 2 : INTUITIVE ⟨∼ awareness⟩ 3 : being next in line or relation ⟨members of the ∼ family attended⟩ 4 : made or done at once : INSTANT ⟨an ∼ response⟩ 5 : near to or related to the present time ⟨the ∼ future⟩ 6 : not distant : CLOSE ⟨the ∼ neighborhood⟩ — **im·me·di·ate·ly** adv

im·me·mo·ri·al \,im-ə-'mōr-ē-əl\ adj : extending beyond the reach of memory, record, or tradition

im·mense \im-'ens\ adj [L immensus, lit., unmeasured, fr. in- in- + mensus, pp. of metiri to measure] 1 : marked by greatness esp. in size or degree : VAST, HUGE 2 : EXCELLENT — **im·mense·ly** adv — **im·men·si·ty** \-'en-sət-ē\ n

im·merse \im-'ərs\ vb 1 : to plunge or dip esp. into a fluid 2 : to baptize by immersing 3 : ENGROSS, ABSORB ⟨immersed in a book⟩ — **im·mer·sion** \im-'ər-zhən\ n

im·mi·grant \'im-i-grənt\ n 1 : a person who immigrates 2 : a plant or animal that becomes established where it was previously unknown

im·mi·grate \'im-ə-,grāt\ vb : to come into a foreign country and take up permanent residence there — **im·mi·gra·tion** \,im-ə-'grā-shən\ n

im·mi·nent \'im-ə-nənt\ adj : ready to take place; esp : hanging threateningly over one's head ⟨∼ danger⟩ — **im·mi·nence** \-nəns\ n — **im·mi·nent·ly** adv

im·mis·ci·ble \(')im-'is-ə-bəl\ adj : incapable of mixing

im·mit·i·ga·ble \(')im-'it-i-gə-bəl\ adj : not capable of being mitigated

im·mo·bile \(')im-'ō-bəl\ adj : incapable of being moved : IMMOVABLE, FIXED, MOTIONLESS — **im·mo·bil·i·ty** \,im-ō-'bil-ət-ē\ n

im·mo·bi·lize \im-'ō-bə-,līz\ vb : to make immobile ⟨∼ an injured joint with splints⟩

im·mod·er·ate \(')im-'äd-(ə-)rət\ adj : lacking in moderation : having no limit : EXCESSIVE — **im·mod·er·a·cy** \-(ə-)rə-sē\ n — **im·mod·er·ate·ly** adv

im·mod·est \(')im-'äd-əst\ adj : not modest : BRAZEN, INDECENT ⟨an ∼ dress⟩ ⟨∼ conduct⟩ — **im·mod·est·ly** adv — **im·mod·es·ty** n

im·mo·late \'im-ə-,lāt\ vb : to offer in sacrifice; esp : to kill as a sacrificial victim — **im·mo·la·tion** \,im-ə-'lā-shən\ n

im·mor·al \(')im-'òr-əl\ adj : inconsistent with purity or good morals : WICKED, LICENTIOUS — **im·mor·al·ly** adv

im·mo·ral·i·ty \,im-,ò-'ral-ət-ē, ,im-ə-'ral-\ n 1 : WICKEDNESS; esp : UNCHASTITY 2 : an immoral act or practice

¹im·mor·tal \(')im-'òrt-ºl\ adj 1 : not mortal : exempt from death ⟨∼ gods⟩ 2 : exempt from oblivion : IMPERISHABLE, ABIDING ⟨those ∼ words⟩ ⟨∼ fame⟩ — **im·mor·tal·ly** adv

²immortal n 1 : one exempt from death 2 pl, often cap : the gods in Greek and Roman mythology 3 : a person whose fame is lasting ⟨one of the ∼s of baseball⟩

ə abut; ᵉ kitten; ər further; a back; ā bake; ä cot, cart; aù out; ch chin; e less; ē easy; g gift; i trip; ī life; j joke; ŋ sing; ō flow; ò flaw; òi coin; th thin; th this; ü loot; ù foot; y yet; yü few; yù furious; zh vision

im·mor·tal·i·ty \,im-,ôr-'tal-ət-ē\ n : the quality or state of being immortal; *esp* : unending existence

im·mor·tal·ize \im-'ort-ᵊl-,īz\ vb : to make immortal

im·mov·able \(')im-'ü-və-bəl\ adj 1 : firmly fixed, settled, or fastened : FAST, STATIONARY ⟨~ mountains⟩ 2 : STEADFAST, UNYIELDING 3 : IMPASSIVE — **im·mov·abil·i·ty** \(,)im-,ü-və-'bil-ət-ē\ n — **im·mov·ably** \(')im-'ü-və-blē\ adv

im·mune \im-'yün\ adj : EXEMPT; *esp* : having a special capacity for resistance (as to a disease) — **im·mu·ni·ty** \im-'yü-nət-ē\ n

im·mu·nize \'im-yə-,nīz\ vb : to make immune — **im·mu·ni·za·tion** \,im-yə-nə-'zā-shən\ n

im·mure \im-'yůr\ vb 1 : to enclose within or as if within walls : IMPRISON 2 : to build into a wall; *esp* : to entomb in a wall

im·mu·ta·ble \(')im-'yüt-ə-bəl\ adj : UNCHANGEABLE, UNCHANGING — **im·mu·ta·bil·i·ty** \(,)im-,yüt-ə-'bil-ət-ē\ n — **im·mu·ta·bly** \(')im-'yüt-ə-blē\ adv

imp \'imp\ n 1 : a small demon : FIEND 2 : a mischievous child

¹**im·pact** \im-'pakt\ vb 1 : to press close : wedge in; *also* : to fill with impacted material 2 : to have an impact on

²**im·pact** \'im-,pakt\ n 1 : a forceful contact, collision, or onset; *also* : the impetus communicated in or as if in a collision 2 : EFFECT

im·pact·ed \im-'pak-təd\ adj : wedged between the jawbone and another tooth

im·pair \im-'paər\ vb : to diminish in quantity, value, excellence, or strength : DAMAGE, LESSEN ⟨health ~ed by overwork⟩ — **im·pair·ment** n

im·pale \im-'pāl\ vb : to pierce with or as if with something pointed; *esp* : to torture or kill by fixing on a sharp stake — **im·pale·ment** n

im·pal·pa·ble \(')im-'pal-pə-bəl\ adj 1 : incapable of being felt by the touch : INTANGIBLE 2 : not readily discerned or apprehended : IMPERCEPTIBLE ⟨an ~ difference between 2 shades of red⟩

im·pan·el \im-'pan-ᵊl\ vb : to enter in or on a panel : ENROLL ⟨~ a jury⟩

im·part \im-'pärt\ vb 1 : to give, grant, or bestow from one's store or abundance : TRANSMIT ⟨the sun ~s warmth⟩ 2 : to make known : DISCLOSE ⟨~ information⟩

im·par·tial \(')im-'pär-shəl\ adj : not partial : UNBIASED, JUST — **im·par·tial·i·ty** \(,)im-,pärsh-(ē-)'al-ət-ē\ n — **im·par·tial·ly** \(')im-'pärsh-(ə-)lē\ adv

im·pass·able \(')im-'pas-ə-bəl\ adj : incapable of being passed, traversed, or circulated ⟨~ roads⟩ ⟨~ counterfeit money⟩

im·passe \'im-,pas\ n 1 : an impassable road or way 2 : a predicament from which there is no obvious escape : DEADLOCK

im·pas·si·ble \(')im-'pas-ə-bəl\ adj : UNFEELING, IMPASSIVE ⟨a hardened ~ criminal⟩

im·pas·sioned \im-'pash-ənd\ adj : filled with passion or zeal : showing great warmth or intensity of feeling ⟨an ~ plea⟩ **syn** passionate, ardent, fervent, fervid

im·pas·sive \(')im-'pas-iv\ adj : showing no signs of feeling, emotion, or interest : EXPRESSIONLESS, INDIFFERENT **syn** stoic, phlegmatic, apathetic, stolid — **im·pas·sive·ly** adv — **im·pas·siv·i·ty** \,im-,pas-'iv-ət-ē\ n

im·pa·tience \im-'pā-shəns\ n 1 : restlessness of spirit esp. under irritation, delay, or opposition 2 : restless or eager desire or longing

im·pa·tient \im-'pā-shənt\ adj 1 : not patient : restless or short of temper esp. under irritation, delay, or opposition 2 : INTOLERANT ⟨~ of poverty⟩ 3 : prompted or marked by impatience 4 : ANXIOUS — **im·pa·tient·ly** adv

im·peach \im-'pēch\ vb 1 : to charge (a public official) before an authorized tribunal with misbehavior in office 2 : to challenge the credibility or validity of ⟨~ a person's honesty⟩ — **im·peach·ment** n

im·pearl \im-'pərl\ vb : to form into pearls; *also* : to form of or adorn with pearls

im·pec·ca·ble \(')im-'pek-ə-bəl\ adj 1 : not capable of sinning or wrongdoing 2 : FAULTLESS, FLAWLESS, IRREPROACHABLE ⟨a man of ~ character⟩ — **im·pec·ca·bly** adv

im·pe·cu·nious \,im-pi-'kyü-nyəs, -nē-əs\ adj : having little or no money : PENNILESS

im·pede \im-'pēd\ vb : to interfere with the progress of : HINDER, BLOCK

im·ped·i·ment \im-'ped-ə-mənt\ n : HINDRANCE, OBSTRUCTION; *esp* : a speech defect

im·ped·i·men·ta \im-,ped-ə-'ment-ə\ n pl : things (as baggage or supplies) that impede

im·pel \im-'pel\ vb -pelled; -pel·ling : to urge or drive forward or on : FORCE; *also* : PROPEL

im·pend \im-'pend\ vb 1 : to hover or hang over threateningly : MENACE 2 : to be about to occur

im·pend·ing adj : threatening to occur soon : IMMINENT, APPROACHING ⟨~ danger⟩

im·pen·e·tra·ble \(')im-'pen-ə-trə-bəl\ adj 1 : incapable of being penetrated or pierced ⟨an ~ jungle⟩ 2 : incapable of being comprehended : INSCRUTABLE ⟨an ~ mystery⟩ — **im·pen·e·tra·bil·i·ty** \(,)im-,pen-ə-trə-'bil-ət-ē\ n — **im·pen·e·tra·bly** \(')im-'pen-ə-trə-blē\ adv

im·pen·i·tent \(')im-'pen-ə-tənt\ adj : not penitent : not repenting of sin

im·per·a·tive \im-'per-ət-iv\ adj 1 : expressing a command, entreaty, or exhortation ⟨~ sentence⟩ 2 : URGENT, OBLIGATORY, BINDING, COMPULSORY — **imperative** n — **im·per·a·tive·ly** adv

im·per·cep·ti·ble \,im-pər-'sep-tə-bəl\ adj : not perceptible by the senses or by the mind : extremely slight, gradual, or subtle ⟨~ changes⟩ — **im·per·cep·ti·bly** adv

im·per·cep·tive \-'sep-tiv\ adj : not perceptive

im·per·cip·i·ent \-'sip-ē-ənt\ adj : UNPERCEPTIVE

¹**im·per·fect** \(')im-'pər-fikt\ adj 1 : not perfect : DEFECTIVE, INADEQUATE, INCOMPLETE 2 : of, relating to, or constituting a verb tense used to designate a continuing state or an incomplete action esp. in the past — **im·per·fect·ly** adv

²**im·per·fect** n : the imperfect tense; *also* : a verb form in it

im·per·fec·tion \,im-pər-'fek-shən\ n : the quality or state of being imperfect;

also : DEFICIENCY, FAULT, BLEMISH

im·pe·ri·al \im-'pir-ē-əl\ *adj* [L *im-perialis*, fr. *imperium* command, sovereign power, empire] **1** : of, relating to, or befitting an empire or an emperor; *also* : of or relating to the United Kingdom or to the British Commonwealth or Empire **2** : ROYAL, SOVEREIGN; *also* : REGAL, IMPERIOUS **3** : of superior or unusual size or excellence

²imperial *n* : a pointed beard growing below the lower lip

im·pe·ri·al·ism \-ē-ə-,liz-əm\ *n* **1** : imperial government, authority, or system **2** : the policy of seeking to extend the power, dominion, or territories of a nation — **im·pe·ri·al·ist** \-ē-ə-ləst\ *adj or n* — **im·pe·ri·al·is·tic** \(,)im-,pir-ē-ə-'lis-tik\ *adj*

im·per·il \im-'per-əl\ *vb* **-iled** *or* **-illed; -il·ing** *or* **-il·ling** : ENDANGER

im·pe·ri·ous \im-'pir-ē-əs\ *adj* **1** : COMMANDING, LORDLY **2** : ARROGANT, DOMINEERING **3** : IMPERATIVE, URGENT — **im·pe·ri·ous·ly** *adv*

im·per·ish·able \(')im-'per-ish-ə-bəl\ *adj* : not perishable or subject to decay : INDESTRUCTIBLE ⟨~ glory⟩

im·per·ma·nent \(')im-'pər-mə-nənt\ *adj* : not permanent : TRANSIENT — **im·per·ma·nent·ly** *adv*

im·per·me·able \(')im-'pər-mē-ə-bəl\ *adj* : not permitting passage (as of a fluid) through its substance : IMPERVIOUS

im·per·son·al \(')im-'pərs-(ə-)nəl\ *adj* : not referring to any particular person or thing — **im·per·son·al·ly** *adv*

im·per·son·ate \im-'pərs-'n-,āt\ *vb* : to assume or act the character of ⟨caught trying to ~ an officer⟩ — **im·per·son·ation** \(,)im-,pərs-'n-'ā-shen\ *n* — **im·per·son·ator** \im-'pərs-'n-,āt-ər\ *n*

im·per·ti·nent \(')im-'pərt-'n-ənt\ *adj* **1** : IRRELEVANT **2** : not restrained within due or proper bounds : RUDE, INSOLENT, SAUCY — **im·per·ti·nence** \-'n-əns\ *n* — **im·per·ti·nent·ly** *adv*

im·per·turb·able \,im-pər-'tər-bə-bəl\ *adj* : marked by extreme calm, impassivity, and steadiness : SERENE

im·per·vi·ous \(')im-'pər-vē-əs\ *adj* **1** : incapable of being penetrated (as by moisture) **2** : not capable of being affected or disturbed ⟨~ to criticism⟩

im·pe·ti·go \,im-pə-'tē-gō, -'tī-\ *n* : a contagious skin disease

im·pet·u·ous \im-'pech-(ə-)wəs\ *adj* **1** : marked by force and violence ⟨with ~ speed⟩ **2** : marked by impulsive vehemence ⟨~ temper⟩ — **im·pet·u·os·i·ty** \(,)im-,pech-ə-'wäs-ət-ē\ *n* — **im·pet·u·ous·ly** *adv*

im·pe·tus \'im-pət-əs\ *n* **1** : a driving force : IMPULSE **2** : INCENTIVE **3** : the tendency of a moving body to keep moving after the force which has kept it in motion ceases to act

im·pi·ety \(')im-'pī-ət-ē\ *n* **1** : the quality or state of being impious **2** : an impious act

im·pinge \im-'pinj\ *vb* **1** : to strike or dash esp. with a sharp collision **2** : ENCROACH, INFRINGE ⟨~ on another person's rights⟩

im·pi·ous \'im-pē-əs, (')im-'pī-əs\ *adj*

: not pious : IRREVERENT, PROFANE

imp·ish \'im-pish\ *adj* : of, relating to, or befitting an imp; *esp* : MISCHIEVOUS — **imp·ish·ly** *adv* — **imp·ish·ness** *n*

im·plac·a·ble \(')im-'plak-ə-bəl, -'plā-kə-\ *adj* : not capable of being appeased, pacified, mitigated, or changed ⟨an ~ enemy⟩ — **im·plac·a·bly** *adv*

im·plant \im-'plant\ *vb* **1** : to fix or set firmly or deeply : INCULCATE **2** : to insert in a living site

im·plau·si·ble \(')im-'plȯ-zə-bəl\ *adj* : not plausible — **im·plau·si·bil·i·ty** \(,)im-,plȯ-zə-'bil-ət-ē\ *n*

¹im·ple·ment \'im-plə-mənt\ *n* : TOOL, UTENSIL, INSTRUMENT

²im·ple·ment \-,ment\ *vb* **1** : to carry out : FULFILL; *esp* : to put into practice **2** : to provide implements for

im·pli·cate \'im-plə-,kāt\ *vb* **1** : IMPLY **2** : INVOLVE ⟨*implicated* in a crime⟩ — **im·pli·ca·tion** \,im-plə-'kā-shən\ *n*

im·plic·it \im-'plis-ət\ *adj* **1** : understood though not directly stated or expressed : IMPLIED; *also* : POTENTIAL **2** : COMPLETE, UNQUESTIONING, ABSOLUTE ⟨~ faith⟩ — **im·plic·it·ly** *adv*

im·plode \im-'plōd\ *vb* : to burst inward — **im·plo·sion** \-'plō-zhən\ *n* — **im·plo·sive** \-'plō-siv\ *adj*

im·plore \im-'plōr\ *vb* : BESEECH, ENTREAT **syn** supplicate, beg

im·ply \im-'plī\ *vb* **1** : to involve or indicate by inference, association, or necessary consequence rather than by direct statement ⟨war *implies* fighting⟩ **2** : to express indirectly : hint at : SUGGEST ⟨remarks that *implied* consent⟩

im·po·lite \,im-po-'līt\ *adj* : not polite : RUDE, DISCOURTEOUS

im·pol·i·tic \(')im-'päl-ə-,tik\ *adj* : not politic : UNWISE

im·pon·der·a·ble \(')im-'pän-d-(ə-)rə-bəl\ *adj* : incapable of being weighed or evaluated with exactness — **imponderable** *n*

¹im·port \im-'pōrt\ *vb* **1** : MEAN, SIGNIFY **2** : to bring (as merchandise) into a place or country from a foreign or external source — **im·port·er** *n*

²im·port \'im-,pōrt\ *n* **1** : MEANING, SIGNIFICATION **2** : IMPORTANCE, SIGNIFICANCE **3** : something (as merchandise) brought in from another country

im·por·tance \im-'pōrt-'ns\ *n* : the quality or state of being important : MOMENT, SIGNIFICANCE **syn** consequence, import, weight

im·por·tant \-'nt\ *adj* **1** : marked by importance : SIGNIFICANT **2** : giving an impression of importance — **im·por·tant·ly** *adv*

im·por·ta·tion \,im-,pōr-'tā-shən, -pər-\ *n* **1** : the act or practice of importing **2** : something imported : IMPORT

im·por·tu·nate \im-'pȯrch-(ə-)nət\ *adj* **1** : BURDENSOME, TROUBLESOME **2** : troublesomely urgent : overly persistent ⟨an ~ beggar⟩

im·por·tune \,im-pər-'t(y)ün, im-'pȯrchən\ *vb* : to urge or beg with troublesome persistence — **im·por·tu·ni·ty** \,im-pər-'t(y)ü-nət-ē\ *n*

im·pose \im-'pōz\ *vb* **1** : to establish or apply as compulsory : LEVY ⟨~ a tax⟩; *also* : INFLICT ⟨*imposed* himself as leader\ 2 : to palm off ⟨~ fake antiques on buyers⟩ 3 : OBTRUDE ⟨*imposed* herself upon others⟩ 4 : to take unwarranted advantage of something ⟨~ upon his good nature⟩ 5 : to practice deception ⟨~ on the public⟩ — **im·po·si·tion** \,im-pə-'zish-ən\ n

im·pos·ing adj : impressive because of size, bearing, dignity, or grandeur : COMMANDING ⟨an ~ appearance⟩

im·pos·si·ble \(')im-'päs-ə-bəl\ adj 1 : incapable of being or of occurring 2 : HOPELESS 3 : extremely undesirable : UNACCEPTABLE 4 : OBJECTIONABLE — **im·pos·si·bil·i·ty** \(,)im-,päs-ə-'bil-ət-ē\ n — **im·pos·si·bly** \(')im-'päs-ə-blē\ adv

im·post \'im-,pōst\ n : TAX, DUTY

im·pos·tor or **im·pos·ter** \im-'päs-tər\ n : one that assumes an identity or title not his own for the purpose of deception : PRETENDER

im·pos·ture \im-'päs-chər\ n : DECEPTION; esp : fraudulent impersonation

im·po·tent \'im-pət-ənt\ adj 1 : lacking in power, strength, or vigor : HELPLESS 2 : lacking the power of procreation : STERILE — **im·po·tence** \-pət-əns\ also **im·po·ten·cy** \-ən-sē\ n

im·pound \im-'paúnd\ vb 1 : CONFINE, ENCLOSE ⟨~ stray dogs⟩ 2 : to seize and hold in legal custody 3 : to collect in a reservoir ⟨~ water for irrigation⟩ — **im·pound·ment** \-'paún(d)-mənt\ n

im·pov·er·ish \im-'päv-(ə-)rish\ vb : to make poor; also : to deprive of strength, richness, or fertility — **im·pov·er·ish·ment** n

im·prac·ti·ca·ble \(')im-'prak-ti-kə-bəl\ adj : not practicable : incapable of being put into practice or use ⟨an ~ plan⟩

im·prac·ti·cal \(')im-'prak-ti-kəl\ adj 1 : not practical 2 : IMPRACTICABLE

im·pre·cate \'im-pri-,kāt\ vb : to invoke evil upon : CURSE — **im·pre·ca·tion** \,im-pri-'kā-shən\ n

im·preg·na·ble \im-'preg-nə-bəl\ adj : able to resist attack : INCONQUERABLE, UNASSAILABLE — **im·preg·na·bil·i·ty** \(,)im-,preg-nə-'bil-ət-ē\ n

im·preg·nate \im-'preg-,nāt\ vb 1 : to make pregnant; also : to make fertile or fruitful 2 : to saturate, fill, or charge with some other substance ⟨~ wood with a preservative⟩ — **im·preg·na·tion** \,im-,preg-'nā-shən\ n

im·pre·sa·rio \,im-prə-'sär-ē-,ō\ n 1 : the promoter, manager, or conductor of an opera or concert company 2 : one who puts on or sponsors an entertainment 3 : MANAGER, PRODUCER

¹**im·press** \im-'pres\ vb 1 : to apply with pressure so as to imprint 2 : to produce (as a mark) by pressure : IMPRINT 3 : to press, stamp, or print in or upon 4 : to produce a vivid impression of 5 : to affect esp. forcibly or deeply : INFLUENCE ⟨favorably ~ed⟩ — **im·press·ible** adj

²**im·press** \'im-,pres\ n 1 : a mark made by pressure : IMPRINT 2 : an image of something formed by or as if by pressure; esp : SEAL 3 : a product of pressure or influence 4 : a characteristic or distinctive mark : STAMP 5 : IMPRESSION, EFFECT

³**im·press** \im-'pres\ vb 1 : to enlist forcibly into public service; esp : to force into naval service 2 : to get the aid or services of by forcible argument

or persuasion — **im·press·ment** n

im·pres·sion \im-'presh-ən\ n 1 : a stamp, form, or figure made by impressing : IMPRINT 2 : an esp. marked influence or effect on feeling, sense, or mind 3 : a characteristic trait or feature resulting from influence : IMPRESS 4 : a single print or copy (as from type or from an engraved plate or book) 5 : all the copies of a publication (as a book) printed for one issue : PRINTING 6 : a usu. vague notion, recollection, belief, or opinion ⟨a first ~ of the place⟩ ⟨under a mistaken ~⟩ 7 : an imitation in caricature of a noted personality as a form of entertainment

im·pres·sion·able \-'presh-(ə-)nə-bəl\ adj : capable of being easily impressed : easily molded or influenced

im·pres·sion·ism \-'presh-ə-,niz-əm\ n 1 often cap : a theory or practice in modern art of depicting the natural appearances of objects by dabs or strokes of primary unmixed colors in order to simulate actual reflected light 2 : the depiction of scene, emotion, or character by details intended to achieve a vividness or effectiveness esp. by evoking subjective and sensory impression — **im·pres·sion·ist** \-'presh-(ə-)nəst\ n or adj — **im·pres·sion·is·tic** \(,)im-,presh-ə-'nis-tik\ adj

im·pres·sive \im-'pres-iv\ adj : making or tending to make a marked impression : stirring deep feeling esp. of awe or admiration ⟨an ~ speech⟩ ⟨~ mountains⟩ — **im·pres·sive·ly** adv

im·pri·ma·tur \,im-prə-'mät-ər\ n 1 : a license to print or publish; also : official approval of a publication by a censor 2 : SANCTION, APPROVAL

¹**im·print** \im-'print\ vb 1 : to stamp or mark by or as if by pressure : IMPRESS 2 archaic : PRINT

²**im·print** \'im-,print\ n 1 : something imprinted or printed : IMPRESS 2 : a publisher's name often with place and date of publication printed at the foot of a title page 3 : an indelible distinguishing effect or influence

im·pris·on \im-'priz-ᵊn\ vb : to put in or as if in prison : CONFINE — **im·pris·on·ment** n

im·prob·a·ble \(')im-'präb-ə-bəl\ adj : unlikely to be true or to occur — **im·prob·a·bil·i·ty** \(,)im-,präb-ə-'bil-ət-ē\ n — **im·prob·a·bly** \(')im-'präb-ə-blē\ adv

im·promp·tu \im-'prämp-t(y)ü\ adj 1 : made or done on or as if on the spur of the moment : IMPROVISED 2 : EXTEMPORANEOUS, UNREHEARSED — **impromptu** adv or n

im·prop·er \(')im-'präp-ər\ adj 1 : not proper, fit, or suitable 2 : INCORRECT, INACCURATE 3 : not in accord with propriety, modesty, or good manners : INDECOROUS, INDECENT — **im·prop·er·ly** adv

improper fraction n : a fraction whose numerator is equal to or larger than the denominator

im·pro·pri·e·ty \,im-prə-'prī-ət-ē\ n 1 : the quality or state of being improper 2 : an improper act or remark; esp : an unacceptable use of a word or of language

im·prove \im-'prüv\ vb 1 : INCREASE, AUGMENT ⟨his chances *improved* his chances⟩ 2 : to enhance or increase in value or quality : make better ⟨~ farmlands by cultivation⟩ ⟨*improved* his grades⟩ **3 :** to grow or become better ⟨~ in health⟩ **4 :** to make good use of ⟨~ the time by reading⟩

im·prove·ment n **1 :** the act or process of improving **2 :** increased value or excellence of something **3 :** something that adds to the value or appearance of a thing ⟨add a number of ~*s* to an old house⟩

im·prov·i·dent \(')im-'präv-əd-ənt\ *adj* **:** not providing for the future **:** THRIFTLESS — **im·prov·i·dence** n

im·pro·vise \'im-prə-'vīz\ vb **1 :** to compose, recite, or sing on the spur of the moment **:** EXTEMPORIZE ⟨~ on the piano⟩ **2 :** to make, invent, or arrange offhand ⟨~ a sail out of shirts⟩— **im·pro·vi·sa·tion** \im-ˌpräv-ə-'zā-shən, ˌim-prə-və-\ n — **im·pro·vis·er** or **im·pro·vi·sor** \ˌim-prə-'vī-zər\ n

im·pru·dent \(')im-'prüd-ᵊnt\ adj **:** not prudent **:** lacking discretion — **im·pru·dence** \-ᵊns\ n

im·pu·dent \'im-pyəd-ənt\ adj **:** marked by contemptuous or cocky boldness or disregard of others **:** INSOLENT, DISRESPECTFUL — **im·pu·dence** \-əns\ n — **im·pu·dent·ly** adv

im·pugn \im-'pyün\ vb **:** to attack by words or arguments **:** oppose or attack as false ⟨~ the motives of an opponent⟩

im·pulse \'im-ˌpəls\ n **1 :** a force that starts a body into motion; *also* **:** the motion produced by such a force **2 :** an arousing of the mind and spirit to action; *also* **:** a wave of nervous excitation **3 :** a natural tendency

im·pul·sion \im-'pəl-shən\ n **1 :** the act of impelling **:** the state of being impelled **2 :** a force that impels **3 :** a sudden inclination **:** IMPULSE **4 :** IMPETUS

im·pul·sive \im-'pəl-siv\ adj **:** having the power of or actually driving or impelling ⟨an ~ force⟩ **2 :** acting or prone to act on impulse ⟨~ buying⟩ — **im·pul·sive·ly** adv

im·pu·ni·ty \im-'pyü-nət-ē\ n [L *impunitas*, fr. *impune* without punishment, fr. *in-* in- + *poena* punishment, penalty] **:** exemption or freedom from punishment, harm, or loss

im·pure \(')im-'pyùr\ adj **1 :** not pure **:** UNCHASTE, OBSCENE **2 :** DIRTY, FOUL **3 :** ADULTERATED, MIXED — **im·pu·ri·ty** \-'pyùr-ət-ē\ n

im·pute \im-'pyüt\ vb **1 :** to lay the responsibility or blame for **:** CHARGE ⟨~ a mistake to ignorance⟩ **2 :** to credit to a person or a cause **:** ATTRIBUTE — **im·pu·ta·tion** \ˌim-pyə-'tā-shən\ n

¹**in** \(')in, ən, ᵊn\ prep **1 —** used to indicate physical surroundings ⟨swim ~ the lake⟩ **2 :** INTO 1 ⟨ran ~ the house⟩ **3 :** DURING ⟨~ the summer⟩ **4 :** WITH ⟨written ~ pencil⟩ **5 —** used to indicate one's situation or state of being ⟨~ luck⟩ ⟨~ love⟩ ⟨~ trouble⟩ **6 —** used to indicate manner ⟨~ a hurry⟩ or purpose ⟨said ~ reply⟩ **7 :** INTO 2 ⟨broke ~ pieces⟩

²**in** \'in\ adv **1 :** to or toward the inside ⟨come ~⟩ **:** to or toward some destination or place ⟨flew ~ from the South⟩ **2 :** at close quarters **:** NEAR ⟨the enemy closed ~⟩ **3 :** into the midst of some-

thing ⟨mix ~ the flour⟩ **4 :** to or at its proper place ⟨fit a piece ~⟩ **5 :** WITH-IN ⟨locked ~⟩ **6 :** in vogue or season; *also* **:** at hand **7 :** in a completed or terminated state ⟨the harvest is ~⟩

³**in** \'in\ adj **1 :** located inside or within **2 :** that is in position, connection, operation, or power ⟨the ~ party⟩ **3 :** directed inward **:** INCOMING ⟨the ~ train⟩

⁴**in** \'in\ n **1 :** one who is in office or power or on the inside **2 :** INFLUENCE, PULL ⟨he has an ~ with the owner⟩

in- \(')in, ˌin\ prefix **:** not **:** NON-, UN-

inacceptable
inaccuracy
inaccurate
inaction
inactive
inactivity
inadmissible
inadvisability
inadvisable
inapplicable
inapposite
inappreciative
inapproachable
inappropriate
inapt
inartistic
inattentive
inauspicious
incalculable
incautious
incombustible
incomprehension
inconceivable
inconclusive
inconsistency
inconsistent
incoordination

indefensible
indemonstrable
indeterminable
indiscernible
indistinguishable
inedible
inefficacious
inelastic
inelasticity
inequitable
inequity
ineradicable
inexpedient
inexpensive
inexpressive
inextinguishable
infeasible
inharmonious
inhospitable
injudicious
inoffensive
insanitary
insensitive
insignificant
insuppressible
insusceptible

in·abil·i·ty \ˌin-ə-'bil-ət-ē\ n **:** the quality or state of being unable **:** lack of ability, power, or means

in ab·sen·tia \ˌin-ab-'sen-ch(ē-)ə\ adv **:** in one's absence ⟨was awarded the degree *in absentia*⟩

in·ac·ces·si·ble \ˌin-ik-'ses-ə-bəl, ˌin-ak-\ adj **:** not accessible — **in·ac·ces·si·bil·i·ty** \-ˌses-ə-'bil-ət-ē\ n

in·ac·ti·vate \(')in-'ak-tə-ˌvāt\ vb **:** to make inactive — **in·ac·ti·va·tion** \(ˌ)in-ˌak-tə-'vā-shən\ n

in·ad·e·quate \(')in-'ad-i-kwət\ adj **:** not adequate **:** INSUFFICIENT — **in·ad·e·qua·cy** \-kwə-sē\ n — **in·ad·e·quate·ly** adv — **in·ad·e·quate·ness** n

in·ad·ver·tent \ˌin-əd-'vərt-ᵊnt\ adj **1 :** HEEDLESS, INATTENTIVE **2 :** UNINTENTIONAL — **in·ad·vert·ent·ly** adv

in·alien·able \(')in-'āl-yə-nə-bəl, -'ā-lē-ə-nə-\ adj **:** incapable of being alienated, surrendered, or transferred ⟨~ rights of a citizen⟩ — **in·alien·abil·i·ty** \(ˌ)in-ˌāl-yə-nə-'bil-ət-ē, -ˌā-lē-ə-nə-\ n — **in·alien·ably** \(')in-'āl-yə-nə-blē, -'ā-lē-ə-nə-\ adv

in·amo·ra·ta \ˌin-ˌam-ə-'rät-ə\ n **:** a woman with whom one is in love

inane \in-'ān\ adj **:** EMPTY, INSUBSTANTIAL; *also* **:** SHALLOW, SILLY ⟨an ~ remark⟩ — **inan·i·ty** \in-'an-ət-ē\ n

in·an·i·mate \(')in-an-ə-mət\ adj **:** not animate or animated **:** lacking the special qualities of living things

in·a·ni·tion \ˌin-ə-'nish-ən\ n **:** a weak state from or as if from lack of food and water

in·ap·pre·cia·ble \,in-ə-'prē-shə-bəl\ *adj* : too small to be perceived ⟨an ~ change⟩ — **in·ap·pre·cia·bly** *adv*

in·ap·ti·tude \(')in-'ap-tə-,t(y)üd\ *n* : lack of aptitude

in·ar·tic·u·late \,in-är-'tik-yə-lət\ *adj* **1 :** uttered or formed without the definite articulations of intelligible speech **2 :** MUTE **3 :** incapable of being expressed by speech; *also* : UNSPOKEN **4 :** not having the power of distinct utterance or effective expression — **in·ar·tic·u·late·ly** *adv*

in·as·much as \,in-əz-,məch-əz\ *conj* : seeing that : SINCE

in·at·ten·tion \,in-ə-'ten-chən\ *n* : failure to pay attention : DISREGARD

in·au·di·ble \(')in-'ȯd-ə-bəl\ *adj* : not audible — **in·au·di·bly** *adv*

¹in·au·gu·ral \in-'ȯ-gyə-rəl, -g(ə-)rəl\ *adj* **1 :** of or relating to an inauguration **2 :** marking a beginning

²inaugural *n* **1 :** an inaugural address **2 :** INAUGURATION

in·au·gu·rate \in-'ȯ-g(y)ə-,rāt\ *vb* **1 :** to introduce into an office with suitable ceremonies : INSTALL **2 :** to dedicate ceremoniously ⟨~ a new library⟩ **3 :** BEGIN, INITIATE ⟨~ a new system⟩ — **in·au·gu·ra·tion** \-,ȯ-g(y)ə-'rā-shən\ *n*

in·board \'in-,bȯrd\ *adv* **1 :** inside the hull of a ship **2 :** toward, facing, or closer to the center line of a ship or airplane fuselage — **inboard** *adj*

in·born \'in-'bȯrn\ *adj* : present from birth rather than acquired : NATURAL **syn** innate, congenital, inbred

in·bound \'in-,baůnd\ *adj* : inward bound ⟨~ traffic⟩

in·bred \'in-'bred\ *adj* **1 :** INBORN, INNATE **2 :** produced by breeding closely related individuals together ⟨a feeble and ~ stock⟩

in·breed·ing \'in-,brēd-iṇ\ *n* **1 :** the interbreeding of closely related individuals esp. to preserve and fix desirable characters of and to eliminate unfavorable characters from a stock **2 :** confinement to a narrow range or a local or limited field of choice

In·ca \'iṇ-kə\ *n* : a noble or a member of the ruling family of an Indian empire of Peru, Bolivia, and Ecuador until the Spanish conquest

in·cal·cu·la·ble \(')in-'kal-kyə-lə-bəl\ *adj* : not capable of being calculated; *esp* : too large or numerous to be calculated — **in·cal·cu·la·bly** *adv*

in·can·des·cent \,in-kən-'des-ᵊnt\ *adj* **1 :** glowing with heat **2 :** SHINING, BRILLIANT — **in·can·des·cence** \-'des-ᵊns\ *n*

in·can·ta·tion \,in-,kan-'tā-shən\ *n* **:** a use of spells or verbal charms spoken or sung as a part of a ritual of magic; *also* : a formula of words chanted or recited in or as if in such a ritual

in·ca·pa·ble \(')in-'kā-pə-bəl\ *adj* : lacking capacity, ability, or qualification for the purpose or end in view : INCOMPETENT; *also* : UNQUALIFIED — **in·ca·pa·bil·i·ty** \(,)in-,kā-pə-'bil-ət-ē\ *n*

in·ca·pac·i·tate \,in-kə-'pas-ə-,tāt\ : to make incapable or unfit : DISQUALIFY, DISABLE

in·ca·pac·i·ty \,in-kə-'pas-ət-ē\ *n* : the quality or state of being incapable

in·car·cer·ate \in-'kär-sə-,rāt\ *vb* : IMPRISON, CONFINE — **in·car·cer·a·tion** \(,)in-,kär-sə-'rā-shən\ *n*

in·car·na·dine \in-'kär-nə-,dīn, -,dēn\ *vb* : REDDEN

in·car·nate \in-'kär-nət, -,nāt\ *adj* **1 :** having bodily and esp. human form and substance **2 :** PERSONIFIED — **in·car·nate** \-,nāt\ *vb*

in·car·na·tion \,in-,kär-'nā-shən\ *n* **1 :** the act of incarnating : the state of being incarnate **2 :** the embodiment of a deity or spirit in an earthly form **3 :** a person showing a trait or typical character to a marked degree

incase *var of* ENCASE

in·cen·di·ary \in-'sen-dē-,er-ē\ *adj* **1 :** of or relating to a deliberate burning of property **2 :** tending to excite or inflame : INFLAMMATORY **3 :** designed to kindle fires ⟨an ~ bomb⟩ — **incendiary** *n*

¹in·cense \'in-,sens\ *n* **1 :** material used to produce a fragrant odor when burned **2 :** the perfume or smoke from some spices and gums when burned

²in·cense \in-'sens\ *vb* : to make extremely angry

in·cen·tive \in-'sent-iv\ *n* : something that incites or has a tendency to incite to determination or action : INDUCEMENT

in·cep·tion \in-'sep-shən\ *n* : BEGINNING, COMMENCEMENT ⟨a success from the moment of its ~⟩

in·cer·ti·tude \(')in-'sərt-ə-,t(y)üd\ *n* **1 :** UNCERTAINTY, DOUBT, INDECISION **2 :** INSECURITY, INSTABILITY

in·ces·sant \(')in-'ses-ᵊnt\ *adj* : continuing or flowing without interruption : UNCEASING ⟨~ rains⟩ — **in·ces·sant·ly** *adv*

in·cest \'in-,sest\ *n* : sexual intercourse between persons so closely related that marriage is illegal — **in·ces·tu·ous** \in-'ses-chə-wəs\ *adj*

¹inch \'inch\ *n* [OE *ynce, ince*, fr. L *uncia* twelfth part, inch, ounce] : a measure of length that equals the 12th part of a foot

²inch *vb* : to advance or retire a little at a time : move slowly ⟨cars ~ing along the slippery road⟩

in·cho·ate \in-'kō-ət, 'in-kə-,wāt\ *adj* : being recently begun or only partly in existence : INCOMPLETE, INCIPIENT

in·ci·dence \'in-səd-əns\ *n* : rate of occurrence or effect

¹in·ci·dent \-səd-ənt\ *n* **1 :** OCCURRENCE, HAPPENING **2 :** an action likely to lead to grave consequences esp. in matters diplomatic

²incident *adj* **1 :** occurring or likely to occur esp. in connection with some other happening **2 :** falling or striking on ⟨~ light rays⟩

in·ci·den·tal \,in-sə-'dent-ᵊl\ *adj* **1 :** subordinate, nonessential, or attendant in position or significance ⟨~ expenses⟩ **2 :** CASUAL, CHANCE ⟨~ traveling companions⟩ — **in·ci·den·tal·ly** \-(ᵊ-)lē\ *adv*

²incidental *n* **1 :** something that is incidental **2** *pl* : minor items (as of expense) that are not individually accounted for

in·cin·er·ate \in-'sin-ə-,rāt\ *vb* : to burn to ashes — **in·cin·er·a·tor** *n*

in·cip·i·ent \in-'sip-ē-ənt\ *adj* : beginning to be or become apparent

in·cise \in-'sīz\ *vb* : to cut into : CARVE, ENGRAVE

in·ci·sion \in-'sizh-ən\ *n* : CUT, GASH; *esp* : a surgical wound

in·ci·sive \in-'sī-siv\ *adj* **1** : CUTTING, PENETRATING **2** : ACUTE, CLEAR-CUT ⟨~ comments⟩ — in·ci·sive·ly *adv*

in·ci·sor \in-'sī-zər\ *n* : a tooth adapted for cutting; *esp* : one of the cutting teeth in front of the canines of a mammal

in·cite \in-'sīt\ *vb* : to arouse to action : stir up — in·cite·ment *n*

in·ci·vil·i·ty \,in-sə-'vil-ət-ē\ *n* **1** : DISCOURTESY, RUDENESS **2** : a rude or discourteous act

in·clem·ent \(')in-'klem-ənt\ *adj* **1** : SEVERE, STORMY ⟨~ weather⟩ **2** : UNMERCIFUL, RIGOROUS ⟨an ~ judge⟩ — in·clem·en·cy \-ən-sē\ *n*

in·clin·able \in-'klī-nə-bəl\ *adj* : having a tendency or inclination : DISPOSED; *also* : FAVORABLE

in·cli·na·tion \,in-klə-'nā-shən\ *n* **1** : BOW, NOD ⟨an ~ of the head⟩ **2** : a tilting of something **3** : PROPENSITY, BENT; *esp* : LIKING ⟨an ~ for sports⟩ **4** : SLANT, SLOPE

¹in·cline \in-'klīn\ *vb* **1** : BOW, BEND **2** : to lean, tend, or become drawn toward an opinion or course of conduct **3** : to deviate from the vertical or horizontal : SLOPE, SLANT **4** : INFLUENCE, PERSUADE

²in·cline \'in-,klīn\ *n* : SLOPE

inclose, inclosure *var of* ENCLOSE, ENCLOSURE

in·clude \in-'klüd\ *vb* : to take in or comprise as a part or parts of a whole ⟨the price ~s tax⟩ — in·clu·sion \-'klü-zhən\ *n* — in·clu·sive \-'klü-siv\ *adj*

¹in·cog·ni·to \,in-,käg-'nēt-ō, in-'käg-nə-,tō\ *adv (or adj)* : with one's identity concealed (as under an assumed name or title) ⟨the prince traveled ~⟩

²incognito *n* **1** : one appearing or living incognito **2** : the state or disguise of an incognito

in·co·her·ent \,in-kō-'hir-ənt, -'her-\ *adj* **1** : not sticking closely or compactly together : LOOSE **2** : not clearly or logically connected : RAMBLING — in·co·her·ence \-əns\ *n* — in·co·her·ent·ly *adv*

in·come \'in-,kəm\ *n* : a gain usu. measured in money that comes in to a person from his labor, business, or property

income tax *n* : a tax on the net income of an individual or business concern

in·com·ing \'in-,kəm-iŋ\ *adj* : coming in ⟨the ~ tide⟩ ⟨~ freshmen⟩ ⟨~ orders⟩

in·com·men·su·rate \,in-kə-'mens-(ə-)rət, -'mench-(ə-)rət\ *adj* : not commensurate; *esp* : not adequate ⟨funds that are ~ with their needs⟩

in·com·mode \,in-kə-'mōd\ *vb* : INCONVENIENCE, DISTURB

in·com·mu·ni·ca·ble \,in-kə-'myü-ni-kə-bəl\ *adj* : not communicable : not capable of being communicated or imparted; *also* : UNCOMMUNICATIVE

in·com·mu·ni·ca·do \,in-kə-,myü-nə-'käd-ō\ *adv (or adj)* : without means of communication; *also* : in solitary confinement ⟨a prisoner held ~⟩

in·com·pa·ra·ble \(')in-'käm-p(ə-)rə-bəl\ *adj* **1** : eminent beyond comparison : MATCHLESS **2** : not suitable for comparison

in·com·pat·i·ble \,in-kəm-'pat-ə-bəl\ *adj* : incapable of or unsuitable for association ⟨~ colors⟩ ⟨~ drugs⟩ ⟨temperamentally ~⟩ — in·com·pat·i·bil·i·ty \,in-kəm-,pat-ə-'bil-ət-ē\ *n*

in·com·pe·tent \(')in-'käm-pət-ənt\ *adj* **1** : not competent : lacking sufficient knowledge, skill, strength, or ability **2** : not legally qualified — in·com·pe·tence \-pət-əns\ *also* in·com·pe·ten·cy \-ən-sē\ *n* — incompetent *n*

in·com·plete \,in-kəm-'plēt\ *adj* : lacking a part or parts : UNFINISHED, IMPERFECT — in·com·plete·ly *adv*

in·com·pre·hen·si·ble \,in-,käm-prē-'hen-sə-bəl\ *adj* : impossible to comprehend : UNINTELLIGIBLE, UNFATHOMABLE

in·com·press·ible \,in-kəm-'pres-ə-bəl\ *adj* : not capable of or resistant to compression

in·con·gru·ent \,in-kən-'grü-ənt, (')in-'kän-grə-wənt\ *adj* : not congruent

in·con·gru·ous \(')in-'käŋ-grə-wəs\ *adj* : not consistent with or suitable to the surroundings or associations : not harmonious, appropriate, or proper ⟨colors⟩ ⟨sports costumes look ~ at a formal dance⟩ — in·con·gru·i·ty \,in-kən-'grü-ət-ē, -käŋ-\ *n* — in·con·gru·ous·ly \(')in-'käŋ-grə-wəs-lē\ *adv*

in·con·se·quen·tial \,in-,kän-sə-'kwen·chəl\ *adj* **1** : ILLOGICAL; *also* : IRRELEVANT **2** : of no significance : UNIMPORTANT — in·con·se·quen·tial·ly *adv*

in·con·sid·er·able \,in-kən-'sid-ər-(ə-)bəl\ *adj* : SLIGHT, TRIVIAL

in·con·sid·er·ate \,in-kən-'sid-(ə-)rət\ *adj* : HEEDLESS, THOUGHTLESS; *esp* : not duly respecting the rights or feelings of others — in·con·sid·er·ate·ly *adv* — in·con·sid·er·ate·ness *n*

in·con·sol·able \,in-kən-'sō-lə-bəl\ *adj* : incapable of being consoled : DISCONSOLATE — in·con·sol·ably *adv*

in·con·spic·u·ous \,in-kən-'spik-yə-wəs\ *adj* : not readily noticeable — in·con·spic·u·ous·ly *adv*

in·con·stant \(')in-'kän-stənt\ *adj* : not constant : CHANGEABLE ⟨syn fickle, capricious, mercurial, unstable⟩ — in·con·stan·cy \-stən-sē\ *n* — in·con·stant·ly *adv*

in·con·test·able \,in-kən-'tes-tə-bəl\ *adj* : not contestable : INDISPUTABLE — in·con·test·ably *adv*

in·con·ti·nent \(')in-'känt-ᵊn-ənt\ *adj* **1** : lacking self-restraint **2** : unable to contain, keep, or restrain : UNCONTROLLED — in·con·ti·nence \-ᵊn-əns\ *n*

in·con·tro·vert·ible \,in-,kän-trə-'vərt-ə-bəl\ *adj* : not open to question : INDISPUTABLE ⟨~ evidence⟩ — in·con·tro·vert·ibly *adv*

¹in·con·ve·nience \,in-kən-'vē-nyəns\ *n* **1** : DISCOMFORT ⟨the ~ of his quarters⟩ **2** : something that is inconvenient : DISADVANTAGE, HANDICAP

²inconvenience *vb* : to subject to inconvenience

in·con·ve·nient \,in-kən-'vē-nyənt\ *adj* : not convenient : causing trouble or annoyance : INOPPORTUNE — in·con·ve·nient·ly *adv*

in·cor·po·rate \in-'kòr-pə-,rāt\ *vb* **1** : to unite closely or so as to form one body : BLEND **2** : to form, form into, or become a corporation **3** : to give material form to : EMBODY — in·cor·po·rat·ed adj — in·cor·po·ra·tion \(,)in-,kôr-pə-'rā-shən\ n

in·cor·po·re·al \,in-kôr-'pōr-ē-əl\ adj : having no material body or form : IMMATERIAL ⟨~ spirits⟩ — in·cor·po·re·al·ly adv

in·cor·rect \,in-kə-'rekt\ adj 1 : INACCURATE, FAULTY 2 : not true : WRONG 3 : UNBECOMING, IMPROPER — in·cor·rect·ly adv — in·cor·rect·ness n

in·cor·ri·gi·ble \(')in-'kôr-ə-jə-bəl\ adj : incapable of being corrected, amended, or reformed : DEPRAVED, DELINQUENT, UNMANAGEABLE, UNALTERABLE — in·cor·ri·gi·bil·i·ty \(,)in-,kôr-ə-jə-'bil-ət-ē\ n — in·cor·ri·gi·bly \(')in-'kôr-ə-jə-blē\ adv

in·cor·rupt·ible \,in-kə-'rəp-tə-bəl\ adj 1 : not subject to decay or dissolution 2 : incapable of being bribed or morally corrupted ⟨an ~ judge⟩ — in·cor·rupt·ibil·i·ty \,in-kə-,rəp-tə-'bil-ət-ē\ n — in·cor·rupt·ibly \,in-kə-'rəp-tə-blē\ adv

¹in·crease \in-'krēs, 'in-,krēs\ vb 1 : to become greater : GROW 2 : to multiply by the production of young ⟨rabbits ~ rapidly⟩ 3 : to make greater : AUGMENT — in·creas·ing·ly adv

²in·crease \'in-,krēs\ n 1 : addition or enlargement in size, extent, or quantity : GROWTH 2 : something (as offspring, produce, or profit) that is added to the original stock by augmentation or growth

in·cred·i·ble \(')in-'kred-ə-bəl\ adj : too extraordinary and improbable to be believed; also : hard to believe — in·cred·i·bil·i·ty \(,)in-,kred-ə-'bil-ət-ē\ n — in·cred·i·bly \(')in-'kred-ə-blē\ adv

in·cred·u·lous \(')in-'krej-ə-ləs\ adj : SKEPTICAL; also : expressing disbelief — in·cre·du·li·ty \,in-kri-'d(y)ü-lət-ē\ n — in·cred·u·lous·ly \(')in-'krej-ə-ləs-lē\ adv

in·cre·ment \'in-krə-mənt, 'in-\ n 1 : an increase esp. in quantity or value : ENLARGEMENT; also : QUANTITY 2 : something gained or added; esp : one of a series of regular consecutive additions

in·crim·i·nate \in-'krim-ə-,nāt\ vb : to charge with or involve in a crime or fault : ACCUSE — in·crim·i·na·tion \-,krim-ə-'nā-shən\ n — in·crim·i·na·to·ry \-'krim-ə-nə-,tōr-ē\ adj

incrust var of ENCRUST

in·crus·ta·tion \,in-,krəs-'tā-shən\ n 1 : the act of encrusting 2 : the state of being encrusted 3 : a hard coating : CRUST; also : something resembling a crust

in·cu·bate \'iŋ-kyə-,bāt, 'in-\ vb : to sit upon eggs to hatch them; also : to keep (as eggs) under conditions favorable for development — in·cu·ba·tion \,iŋ-kyə-'bā-shən, ,in-\ n

in·cu·ba·tor \'iŋ-kyə-,bāt-ər, 'in-\ n : one that incubates; esp : an apparatus providing suitable conditions (as of warmth and moisture) for incubating something

in·cu·bus \'iŋ-kyə-bəs, 'in-\ n, pl -bi \-,bī, -,bē\ also -bus·es 1 : a spirit supposed to work evil on persons in their sleep 2 : NIGHTMARE 3 : a person or thing that oppresses or burdens like a nightmare

in·cul·cate \in-'kəl-,kāt, 'in-(,)kəl-\ vb : to teach and impress upon the mind by frequent repetitions or admonitions — in·cul·ca·tion \,in-(,)kəl-'kā-shən\ n

in·cul·pa·ble \(')in-'kəl-pə-bəl\ adj : free from guilt : BLAMELESS

in·cul·pate \in-'kəl-,pāt, 'in-(,)kəl-\ vb : to involve or implicate in guilt : INCRIMINATE

in·cum·ben·cy \in-'kəm-bən-sē\ n 1 : the quality or state of being incumbent 2 : something that is incumbent 3 : the office or period of office of an incumbent

¹in·cum·bent \in-'kəm-bənt\ n : the holder of an office or position

²incumbent adj 1 : lying or resting on something else 2 : imposed as a duty : OBLIGATORY ⟨it is ~ on us to help⟩ 3 : occupying a specified office

incumber var of ENCUMBER

in·cu·nab·u·lum \,in-kyə-'nab-yə-ləm, ,iŋ-\ n, pl -la \-lə\ : a book printed before 1501

in·cur \in-'kər\ vb -curred; -cur·ring 1 : to meet with (as an inconvenience) 2 : to become liable or subject to : bring down upon oneself

in·cur·able \(')in-'kyùr-ə-bəl\ adj : not subject to cure — in·cur·abil·i·ty \(,)in-,kyùr-ə-'bil-ət-ē\ n — incurable n

in·cu·ri·ous \(')in-'kyùr-ē-əs\ adj : not curious or inquisitive : UNINTERESTED

in·cur·sion \in-'kər-zhən\ n : a sudden usu. temporary invasion : RAID

in·debt·ed \in-'det-əd\ adj 1 : owing money 2 : owing gratitude or recognition to another : BEHOLDEN — in·debt·ed·ness n

in·de·cent \in-'dēs-ªnt\ adj : not decent : UNBECOMING, UNSEEMLY; also : morally offensive — in·de·cen·cy \-ⁿ-sē\ n — in·de·cent·ly adv

in·de·ci·pher·able \,in-di-'sī-f(ə-)rə-bəl\ adj : that cannot be deciphered

in·de·ci·sion \,in-di-'sizh-ən\ n : a wavering between two or more possible courses of action : IRRESOLUTION

in·de·ci·sive \,in-di-'sī-siv\ adj 1 : not decisive : INCONCLUSIVE 2 : marked by or prone to indecision : HESITATING, UNCERTAIN 3 : INDEFINITE — in·de·ci·sive·ly adv — in·de·ci·sive·ness n

in·de·clin·able \,in-di-'klī-nə-bəl\ adj : having no grammatical inflections

in·dec·o·rous \(')in-'dek-ə-rəs, ,in-di-'kōr-əs\ adj : not decorous syn improper, unseemly, indecent, unbecoming, indelicate — in·dec·o·rous·ly adv — in·dec·o·rous·ness n

in·deed \in-'dēd\ adv 1 : without any question : TRULY — often used interjectionally to express irony, disbelief, or surprise 2 : in reality 3 : all things considered 4 : ADMITTEDLY, UNDENIABLY

in·de·fat·i·ga·ble \,in-di-'fat-i-gə-bəl\ adj : UNTIRING — in·de·fat·i·ga·bly adv

in·de·fea·si·ble \,in-di-'fē-zə-bəl\ adj : not capable of or not liable to being annulled, made void, or forfeited — in·de·fea·si·bly adv

in·de·fin·able \,in-di-'fī-nə-bəl\ adj : incapable of being precisely described or analyzed

in·def·i·nite \(')in-'def-(ə-)nət\ adj 1 : not defining or identifying ⟨an is an ~ article⟩ 2 : not precise : VAGUE 3 : having no fixed limit or amount — in·def·i·nite·ly adv — in·def·i·nite·ness n

in·del·i·ble \in-'del-ə-bəl\ *adj* [L *indelebilis*, fr. *in-* in- + *delēre* to destroy] **1** : not capable of being removed, washed away, or erased **2** : making marks that cannot easily be removed ⟨an ~ pencil⟩ — **in·del·i·bly** *adv*

in·del·i·cate \(')in-'del-i-kət\ *adj* : not delicate; *esp* : IMPROPER, COARSE, TACTLESS **syn** indecent, unseemly, indecorous, unbecoming — **in·del·i·ca·cy** \-kə-sē\ *n*

in·dem·ni·fy \in-'dem-nə-,fī\ *vb* **1** : to secure against hurt, loss, or damage **2** : to make compensation for some loss or damage **3** : to make compensation for : make good ⟨~ a loss⟩ — **in·dem·ni·fi·ca·tion** \-,dem-nə-fə-'kā-shən\ *n*

in·dem·ni·ty \in-'dem-nət-ē\ *n* **1** : security against hurt, loss, or damage; *also* : exemption from incurred penalties or liabilities **2** : something that indemnifies

¹in·dent \in-'dent\ *vb* **1** : to make a toothlike cut on the edge of : make jagged : NOTCH **2** : to bind by a contract : INDENTURE **3** : to space in (as the first line of a paragraph) from the margin

²indent *vb* **1** : to force inward so as to form a depression : IMPRESS ⟨~ a pattern in metal⟩ **2** : to form a depression on the surface of

in·den·ta·tion \,in-,den-'tā-shən\ *n* **1** : NOTCH; *also* : a usu. deep recess (as in a coastline) **2** : the action of indenting : the condition of being indented **3** : DENT **4** : INDENTION 2

in·den·tion \in-'den-chən\ *n* **1** : the action of indenting : the condition of being indented **2** : the blank space produced by indenting

¹in·den·ture \in-'den-chər\ *n* **1** : a written certificate or agreement; *esp* : a contract binding one person (as an apprentice) to work for another for a given period of time — usu. used in pl. **2** : INDENTATION 1 **3** : DENT

²indenture *vb* : to bind (as an apprentice) by indentures

in·de·pen·dence \,in-də-'pen-dəns\ *n* : the quality or state of being independent : FREEDOM

Independence Day *n* : July 4 observed as a legal holiday in commemoration of the adoption of the Declaration of Independence in 1776

in·de·pen·dent \,in-də-'pen-dənt\ *adj* **1** : SELF-GOVERNING; *also* : not affiliated with a larger controlling unit **2** : not requiring or relying on something else or somebody else ⟨an ~ conclusion⟩ ⟨an ~ source of income⟩ **3** : not easily influenced : showing self-reliance ⟨an ~ mind⟩ **4** : not committed to a political party ⟨an ~ voter⟩ **5** : refusing or disliking to look to others for help ⟨too ~ to accept charity⟩; *also* : marked by impatience with or annoyance at restriction ⟨a bold and ~ manner of acting⟩ **6** : MAIN ⟨an ~ clause⟩ — **independent** *n* — **in·de·pen·dent·ly** *adv*

in·de·scrib·able \,in-di-'skrī-bə-bəl\ *adj* **1** : that cannot be described ⟨an ~ sensation⟩ **2** : surpassing description ⟨~ horror⟩ — **in·de·scrib·ably** *adv*

in·de·struc·ti·ble \,in-di-'strək-tə-bəl\ *adj* : not destructible — **in·de·struc·ti-**

bil·i·ty \,in-di-,strək-tə-'bil-ət-ē\ *n*

in·de·ter·mi·nate \,in-di-'tər-mə-nət\ *adj* **1** : VAGUE; *also* : not known in advance **2** : not limited in advance; *also* : not leading to a definite end or result — **in·de·ter·mi·nate·ly** *adv*

¹in·dex \'in-,deks\ *n*, *pl* **in·dex·es** *or* **in·di·ces** \-də-,sēz\ **1** : a guide for facilitating references; *esp* : an alphabetical list of items (as topics or names) treated in a printed work with the page number where each item may be found **2** : POINTER, INDICATOR **3** : SIGN, TOKEN ⟨an ~ of character⟩ **4** : a list of restricted or prohibited material ⟨an ~ of forbidden books⟩ **5** *pl usu* **indices** : a number or symbol or expression (as an exponent) associated with another to indicate a mathematical operation or use or position in an arrangement or expansion **6** : a character ☞ used to direct particular attention to a note or paragraph : FIST

²index *vb* **1** : to provide with or put into an index **2** : to serve as an index of

index finger *n* : FOREFINGER

In·dia·man \'in-dē-ə-mən\ *n* : a large sailing ship formerly used in trade with India

In·di·an \'in-dē-ən\ *n* **1** : a native or inhabitant of the Republic or the peninsula of India **2** : a member of any of the aboriginal peoples of No. and So. America except the Eskimo — **Indian** *adj*

Indian corn *n* : a tall widely grown American cereal grass bearing seeds on long ears; *also* : its ears or seeds

Indian meal *n* : CORNMEAL

Indian summer *n* : a period of warm or mild weather in late autumn or early winter

In·dia paper \,in-dē-ə-\ *n* **1** : a thin absorbent paper used esp. for taking impressions (as of steel engravings) **2** : a thin tough opaque printing paper

in·di·cate \'in-də-,kāt\ *vb* **1** : to point out or to **2** : to state briefly : show indirectly : SUGGEST, INTIMATE, HINT — **in·di·ca·tion** \,in-də-'kā-shən\ *n* — **in·di·ca·tor** \'in-də-,kāt-ər\ *n*

¹in·dic·a·tive \in-'dik-ət-iv\ *adj* **1** : of, relating to, or constituting a verb form that represents a denoted act or state as an objective fact ⟨~ mood⟩ **2** : serving to indicate : SUGGESTIVE ⟨actions ~ of fear⟩

²indicative *n* **1** : the indicative mood of a language **2** : a form in the indicative mood

in·di·cia \in-'dish-(ē-)ə\ *n pl* **1** : distinctive marks **2** : postal markings often imprinted on mail or on labels to be affixed to mail

in·dict \in-'dīt\ *vb* **1** : to charge with an offense : ACCUSE **2** : to charge with a crime by the finding of a grand jury ⟨~ed for murder⟩ — **in·dict·ment** \-mənt\ *n*

in·dif·fer·ent \in-'dif-(ə-)rənt\ *adj* **1** : UNBIASED, UNPREJUDICED **2** : of no importance one way or the other **3** : marked by no special liking for or dislike of something : APATHETIC **4** : being neither excessive nor defective **5** : MODERATE, AVERAGE **5** : PASSABLE, MEDIOCRE **6** : being neither right nor

ə abut; ᵊ further; ə̇r further; a back; ā bake; ä cot, cart; au̇ out; ch chin; e less; ē easy; g gift; i trip; ī life; j joke; ŋ sing; ō flow; ȯ flaw; ȯi coin; th thin; t͟h this; ü loot; u̇ foot; y yet; yü few; yu̇ furious; zh vision

wrong — **in·dif·fer·ence** *n* — **in·dif·fer·ent·ly** *adv*

in·dig·e·nous \in-'dij-ə-nəs\ *adj* : NATIVE

in·di·gent \'in-di-jənt\ *adj* : IMPOVERISHED, NEEDY — **in·di·gence** *n*

in·di·gest·ible \,in-dī-'jes-tə-bəl, -də-\ *adj* : not readily digested

in·di·ges·tion \-'jes-chən\ *n* : inadequate or difficult digestion : DYSPEPSIA

in·dig·nant \in-'dig-nənt\ *adj* : filled with or marked by indignation — **in·dig·nant·ly** *adv*

in·dig·na·tion \,in-dig-'nā-shən\ *n* : anger aroused by something unjust, unworthy, or mean

in·dig·ni·ty \in-'dig-nət-ē\ *n* : an offense against personal dignity or self-respect : INSULT; *also* : humiliating treatment

in·di·go \'in-di-,gō\ *n, pl* **-gos** *or* **-goes** 1 : a blue dye obtained from plants or synthesized 2 : a color between blue and violet

in·di·rect \,in-də-'rekt, -dī-\ *adj* 1 : not straight (an ~ route) 2 : not straightforward and open (~ methods) 3 : not having a plainly seen connection (an ~ cause) 4 : not directly to the point (an ~ answer) — **in·di·rec·tion** \-'rek-shən\ *n* — **in·di·rect·ly** *adv*

in·dis·creet \,in-dis-'krēt\ *adj* : not discreet : IMPRUDENT — **in·dis·cre·tion** \-dis-'kresh-ən\ *n*

in·dis·crim·i·nate \in-dis-'krim-ə-nət\ *adj* 1 : not marked by discrimination or careful distinction (~ reading habits) 2 : HAPHAZARD, RANDOM 3 : UNRESTRAINED 4 : JUMBLED, CONFUSED; *also* : HETEROGENEOUS — **in·dis·crim·i·nate·ly** *adv*

in·dis·pens·able \,in-dis-'pen-sə-bəl\ *adj* : absolutely essential : REQUISITE — **in·dis·pens·abil·i·ty** \,in-dis-,pen-sə-'bil-ət-ē\ *n* — **indispensable** *n* — **in·dis·pens·ably** \-'pen-sə-blē\ *adv*

in·dis·posed \,in-dis-'pōzd\ *adj* 1 : slightly ill 2 : AVERSE — **in·dis·po·si·tion** \(,)in-,dis-pə-'zish-ən\ *n*

in·dis·put·able \,in-dis-'pyüt-ə-bəl, (')in-'dis-pyət-ə-bəl\ *adj* : not disputable : UNQUESTIONABLE (~ proof) — **in·dis·put·ably** *adv*

in·dis·sol·u·ble \,in-dis-'äl-yə-bəl\ *adj* : not capable of being dissolved, undone, or broken : PERMANENT (an ~ contract)

in·dis·tinct \,in-dis-'tiŋkt\ *adj* 1 : not sharply outlined or separable : BLURRED, FAINT, DIM 2 : not readily distinguishable : UNCERTAIN — **in·dis·tinct·ly** *adv* — **in·dis·tinct·ness** *n*

in·dite \in-'dīt\ *vb* : COMPOSE (~ a poem); *also* : to put in writing (~ a letter)

in·di·um \'in-dē-əm\ *n* : a malleable tarnish-resistant silvery metallic chemical element

¹**in·di·vid·u·al** \,in-də-'vij-(ə-w)əl\ *adj* 1 : of, relating to, or used by an individual (~ traits) 2 : being an individual : existing as an indivisible whole 3 : intended for one person (an ~ serving) 4 : SEPARATE (~ copies) 5 : having marked individuality (an ~ style) — **in·di·vid·u·al·ly** *adv*

²**individual** *n* 1 : a single member of a category : a particular person, animal, or thing 2 : PERSON (a disagreeable ~)

in·di·vid·u·al·ism \-'vij-ə-(wə-),liz-əm\ *n* 1 : EGOISM 2 : a doctrine that the chief end of society is to promote the welfare of its individual members 3 : a doctrine holding that the individual has certain political or economic rights with which the state must not interfere

in·di·vid·u·al·ist \-'ləst\ *n* 1 : one that pursues a markedly independent course in thought or action 2 : one that advocates or practices individualism — **in·di·vid·u·al·is·tic** \-,vij-ə-(wə-)'lis-tik\ *adj*

in·di·vid·u·al·i·ty \,in-də-,vij-ə-'wal-ət-ē\ *n* 1 : the sum of qualities that characterize and distinguish an individual from all others; *also* : PERSONALITY 2 : INDIVIDUAL, PERSON 3 : separate or distinct existence

in·di·vid·u·al·ize \-'vij-ə-(wə-),līz\ *vb* 1 : to make individual in character 2 : to treat or notice individually : PARTICULARIZE (the teacher ~s each student's problems) 3 : to adapt to the needs of an individual

in·di·vis·i·ble \,in-də-'viz-ə-bəl\ *adj* : not divisible : not separable into parts — **in·di·vis·i·bil·i·ty** \-,viz-ə-'bil-ət-ē\ *n* — **in·di·vis·i·bly** \-'viz-ə-blē\ *adv*

in·doc·tri·nate \in-'däk-trə-,nāt\ *vb* 1 : to instruct esp. in fundamentals or rudiments : TEACH 2 : to imbue with a usu. partisan or sectarian opinion, point of view, or principle — **in·doc·tri·na·tion** \-,däk-trə-'nā-shən\ *n*

In·do-Eu·ro·pe·an \,in-dō-,yùr-ə-'pē-ən\ *adj* : of, relating to, or constituting a family of languages comprising those spoken in most of Europe and in the parts of the world colonized by Europeans since 1500 and also in Persia, the subcontinent of India, and some other parts of Asia

in·do·lent \'in-də-lənt\ *adj* 1 : slow to develop or heal (~ ulcers) 2 : LAZY — **in·do·lence** \-ləns\ *n*

in·dom·i·ta·ble \in-'däm-ət-ə-bəl\ *adj* : UNCONQUERABLE (~ courage) — **in·dom·i·ta·bly** *adv*

In·do·ne·sian \,in-də-'nē-zhən\ *n* : a native or inhabitant of the Republic of Indonesia — **Indonesian** *adj*

in·door \,in-,dōr\ *adj* 1 : of or relating to the interior of a building 2 : done, living, or belonging within doors

in·doors \in-'dōrz\ *adv* : in or into a building

indorse *var of* ENDORSE

in·du·bi·ta·ble \(')in-'d(y)ü-bət-ə-bəl\ *adj* : UNQUESTIONABLE — **in·du·bi·ta·bly** *adv*

in·duce \in-'d(y)üs\ *vb* 1 : to prevail upon : PERSUADE, INFLUENCE 2 : to bring on or bring about : EFFECT, CAUSE (illness *induced* by overwork) 3 : to produce (as an electric current or charge) by induction 4 : to determine by induction; *esp* : to infer from particulars — **in·duc·er** *n*

in·duce·ment *n* 1 : the act or process of inducing 2 : something that induces : MOTIVE

in·duct \in-'dəkt\ *vb* 1 : to place in office : INSTALL 2 : to admit as a member : INTRODUCE, INITIATE 3 : to enroll for military training or service (as under a selective-service act)

in·duc·tance \-'dək-təns\ *n* : a property of an electric circuit by which a varying current produces an electromotive force in that circuit or in a nearby circuit

in·duc·tion \in-'dək-shən\ *n* 1 : IN-

STALLATION; *also* : INITIATION **2** : the formality by which a civilian is inducted into military service **3** : reasoning from a part to a whole or from particular instances to a general conclusion; *also* : the conclusion so reached **4** : the process by which an electric current, an electric charge, or magnetism is produced in a body by the proximity of an electric or magnetic field

in·duc·tive \in-'dək-tiv\ *adj* **1** : of, relating to, or employing reasoning by induction **2** : of or relating to inductance or electrical induction

indue *var of* ENDUE

in·dulge \in-'dəlj\ *vb* **1** : to give free rein to : take unrestrained pleasure in : GRATIFY (~ a taste for exotic dishes) **2** : to yield to the desire of : treat leniently or generously : HUMOR (~ a sick child) **3** : to gratify one's taste or desire for (~ in alcohol)

in·dul·gence \in-'dəl-jəns\ *n* **1** : remission of temporal punishment due in Roman Catholic doctrine for sins whose eternal punishment has been remitted by reception of the sacrifice of penance **2** : the act of indulging : the state of being indulgent **3** : an indulgent act : a favor granted **4** : the thing indulged in **5** : SELF-INDULGENCE — **in·dul·gent** \-jənt\ *adj* — **in·dul·gent·ly** *adv*

in·dus·tri·al \in-'dəs-trē-əl\ *adj* : of, relating to, or having to do with industry — **in·dus·tri·al·ly** *adv*

in·dus·tri·al·ist \-ə-ləst\ *n* : a person owning or engaged in the management of an industry : MANUFACTURER

in·dus·tri·al·ize \-trē-ə-ˌlīz\ *vb* : to make or become industrial (~ a rural area) — **in·dus·tri·al·iza·tion** \in-ˌdəs-trē-ə-lə-'zā-shən\ *n*

in·dus·tri·ous \in-'dəs-trē-əs\ *adj* : DILIGENT, BUSY — **in·dus·tri·ous·ly** *adv* — **in·dus·tri·ous·ness** *n*

in·dus·try \'in-(ˌ)dəs-trē\ *n* **1** : DILIGENCE **2** : a department or branch of a craft, art, business, or manufacture; *esp* : one that employs a large personnel and capital **3** : a distinct group of productive enterprises (the automobile ~) **4** : manufacturing activity as a whole

in·dwell \(ˈ)in-'dwel\ *vb* : to exist within as an activating spirit, force, or principle

¹ine·bri·ate \in-'ē-brē-ˌāt\ *vb* : to make drunk : INTOXICATE — **ine·bri·a·tion** \-ˌē-brē-'ā-shən\ *n*

²ine·bri·ate \in-'ē-brē-ət\ *n* : one that is drunk; *esp* : an habitual drunkard

in·ed·it·ed \(ˈ)in-'ed-ət-əd\ *adj* : UNPUBLISHED

in·ed·u·ca·ble \-'ej-ə-kə-bəl\ *adj* : incapable of being educated

in·ef·fa·ble \(ˈ)in-'ef-ə-bəl\ *adj* **1** : incapable of being expressed in words : INDESCRIBABLE (~ joy) **2** : UNSPEAKABLE (~ disgust) **3** : not to be uttered : TABOO (the ~ name of Jehovah) — **in·ef·fa·bly** *adv*

in·ef·face·able \ˌin-ə-'fā-sə-bəl\ *adj* : not effaceable : INERADICABLE

in·ef·fec·tive \ˌin-ə-'fek-tiv\ *adj* **1** : not effective : INEFFECTUAL **2** : INCAPABLE — **in·ef·fec·tive·ly** *adv*

in·ef·fec·tu·al \ˌin-ə-'fek-ch(ə-w)əl\ *adj* : not producing the proper or usual effect : FUTILE — **in·ef·fec·tu·al·ly** *adv*

in·ef·fi·cient \ˌin-ə-'fish-ənt\ *adj* **1** : not producing the effect intended or desired **2** : INCAPABLE, INCOMPETENT — **in·ef·fi·cien·cy** \-'fish-ən-sē\ *n* — **in·ef·fi·cient·ly** *adv*

in·el·e·gant \(ˈ)in-'el-i-gənt\ *adj* : lacking in refinement, grace, or good taste — **in·el·e·gance** \-gəns\ *n*

in·el·i·gi·ble \(ˈ)in-'el-ə-jə-bəl\ *adj* : not qualified to be chosen for an office : not worthy to be chosen or preferred — **in·el·i·gi·bil·i·ty** \(ˌ)in-ˌel-ə-jə-'bil-ət-ē\ *n* — **ineligible** *n*

in·eluc·ta·ble \ˌin-i-'lək-tə-bəl\ *adj* : not to be avoided, changed, or resisted : INEVITABLE

in·ept \in-'ept\ *adj* **1** : lacking in fitness or aptitude : UNFIT **2** : being out of place : INAPPROPRIATE **3** : FOOLISH **4** : generally incompetent : BUNGLING — **in·ep·ti·tude** \in-'ep-tə-ˌt(y)üd\ *n* — **in·ept·ly** *adv* — **in·ept·ness** *n*

in·equal·i·ty \ˌin-i-'kwäl-ət-ē\ *n* **1** : the quality of being unequal or uneven; *esp* : UNEVENNESS, DISPARITY, CHANGEABLENESS **2** : an instance of being unequal (as in position, proportion, evenness, or regularity)

in·ert \in-'ərt\ *adj* **1** : powerless to move itself **2** : lacking in active properties (chemically ~) **3** : SLUGGISH — **in·ert·ly** *adv* — **in·ert·ness** *n*

in·er·tia \in-'ər-sh(ē-)ə\ *n* **1** : a property of matter whereby it remains at rest or continues in uniform motion unless acted upon by some outside force **2** : INERTNESS, SLUGGISHNESS — **in·er·tial** \-shəl\ *adj*

in·es·cap·able \ˌin-ə-'skā-pə-bəl\ *adj* : incapable of being escaped : INEVITABLE — **in·es·cap·ably** *adv*

in·es·ti·ma·ble \(ˈ)in-'es-tə-mə-bəl\ *adj* **1** : incapable of being estimated or computed (~ errors) **2** : too valuable or excellent to be fully appreciated (an ~ service to his country) — **in·es·ti·ma·bly** *adv*

in·ev·i·ta·ble \in-'ev-ət-ə-bəl\ *adj* : incapable of being avoided or evaded : bound to happen — **in·ev·i·ta·bil·i·ty** \-ˌev-ət-ə-'bil-ət-ē\ *n* — **in·ev·i·ta·bly** \-'ev-ət-ə-blē\ *adv*

in·ex·act \ˌin-ig-'zakt\ *adj* **1** : not precisely correct or true : INACCURATE **2** : not rigorous and careful — **in·ex·act·ly** *adv*

in·ex·cus·able \ˌin-ik-'skyü-zə-bəl\ *adj* : being without excuse or justification — **in·ex·cus·ably** *adv*

in·ex·haust·ible \ˌin-ig-'zö-stə-bəl\ *adj* **1** : incapable of being used up (an ~ supply) **2** : UNTIRING — **in·ex·haust·ibly** *adv*

in·ex·o·ra·ble \(ˈ)in-'eks-(ə-)rə-bəl\ *adj* : not to be moved by entreaty : UNYIELDING, RELENTLESS — **in·ex·o·ra·bly** *adv*

in·ex·pe·ri·ence \ˌin-ik-'spir-ē-əns\ *n* : lack of experience or of knowledge or proficiency gained by experience — **in·ex·pe·ri·enced** *adj*

in·ex·pert \(ˈ)in-'ek-ˌspərt\ *adj* **1** : INEXPERIENCED **2** : not expert : UNSKILLED — **in·ex·pert·ly** *adv*

in·ex·pi·a·ble \(ˈ)in-'ek-spē-ə-bəl\ *adj*

: not capable of being atoned for ⟨an ~ crime⟩

in·ex·plic·a·ble \,in·ik-'splik-ə-bəl, (')in-'ek-(,)splik-\ *adj* : incapable of being explained, interpreted, or accounted for — **in·ex·plic·a·bly** *adv*

in·ex·press·ible \,in·ik-'spres-ə-bəl\ *adj* : not capable of being expressed : INDESCRIBABLE — **in·ex·press·ibly** *adv*

in ex·tre·mis \,in-ik-'strā-məs\ *adv* : in extreme circumstances; *esp* : at the point of death

in·ex·tric·a·ble \,in-ik-'strik-ə-bəl, (')in-'ek-(,)strik-\ *adj* **1** : forming a maze or tangle from which it is impossible to get free **2** : incapable of being disentangled or untied : UNSOLVABLE — **in·ex·tric·a·bly** *adv*

in·fal·li·ble \(')in-'fal-ə-bəl\ *adj* **1** : incapable of error : UNERRING **2** : SURE, CERTAIN ⟨an ~ remedy⟩ — **in·fal·li·bil·i·ty** \(,)in,fal-ə-'bil-ət-ē\ *n* — **in·fal·li·bly** \(')in-'fal-ə-blē\ *adv*

in·fa·mous \'in-fə-məs\ *adj* **1** : having a reputation of the worst kind **2** : DISGRACEFUL ⟨an ~ crime⟩ — **in·fa·mous·ly** *adv*

in·fa·my \'in-fə-mē\ *n* **1** : evil reputation brought about by something grossly criminal, shocking, or brutal **2** : an extreme and publicly known criminal or evil act **3** : the state of being infamous

in·fan·cy \'in-fən-sē\ *n* **1** : early childhood **2** : a beginning or early period of existence ⟨in the ~ of our country⟩

in·fant \'in-fənt\ *n* [L *infant-, infans* not talking, young, fr. *in-* + *fant-, fans*, prp. of *fari* to speak] : BABY; *also* : a person who is a legal minor

in·fan·tile \'in-fən-,tīl, -t'l, -,tēl\ *adj* : of or relating to infants; *also* : CHILDISH

infantile paralysis *n* : POLIOMYELITIS

in·fan·try \'in-fən-trē\ *n* : soldiers trained, armed, and equipped for service on foot

in·fat·u·ate \in-'fach-ə-,wāt\ *vb* : to inspire with a foolish and unrestrained love or admiration — **in·fat·u·a·tion** \-,fach-ə-'wā-shən\ *n*

in·fect \in-'fekt\ *vb* **1** : to contaminate with disease-producing matter **2** : to communicate a germ or disease to **3** : to influence so as to induce sympathy, belief, or support ⟨~ed the audience with his own enthusiasm⟩

in·fec·tion \in-'fek-shən\ *n* **1** : an act of infecting : the state of being infected **2** : a communicable disease; *also* : an infective agent (as a germ) — **in·fec·tious** \-shəs\ *adj* — **in·fec·tive** \-'fek-tiv\ *adj*

in·fe·lic·i·tous \,in-fi-'lis-ət-əs\ *adj* **1** : UNHAPPY, UNFORTUNATE **2** : not apt in application or expression : AWKWARD ⟨an ~ phrase⟩ — **in·fe·lic·i·ty** \-ət-ē\ *n*

in·fer \in-'fər\ *vb* **-ferred; -fer·ring** **1** : to derive as a conclusion from facts or premises **2** : GUESS, SURMISE **3** : to lead to as a conclusion or consequence : point out : INDICATE **4** : HINT, SUGGEST **syn** deduce, conclude, judge, gather — **in·fer·ence** \'in-f(ə-)rəns\ *n*

in·fe·ri·or \in-'fir-ē-ər\ *adj* : situated lower (as in position, degree, rank, or merit) — **inferior** *n* — **in·fe·ri·or·i·ty** \(,)in,fir-ē-'ȯr-ət-ē\ *n*

in·fer·nal \in-'fərn-'l\ *adj* **1** : of or relating to hell ⟨~ fires⟩ **2** : HELLISH, FIENDISH ⟨~ schemes⟩ **3** : DAMNABLE,

DAMNED ⟨an ~ nuisance⟩ — **in·fer·nal·ly** *adv*

in·fer·no \in-'fər-nō\ *n* : a place or a state that resembles or suggests hell

in·fer·tile \(')in-'fərt-'l\ *adj* : not fertile or productive : BARREN

in·fest \in-'fest\ *vb* : to trouble by spreading or swarming in or over; *also* : to live in or on as a parasite — **in·fes·ta·tion** \,in-,fes-'tā-shən\ *n*

in·fi·del \'in-fəd-'l, -fə-,del\ *n* **1** : one who is not a Christian or opposes Christianity **2** : an unbeliever esp. in respect to a particular religion

in·fi·del·i·ty \,in-fə-'del-ət-ē, -fī-\ *n* **1** : lack of belief in a religion **2** : UNFAITHFULNESS, DISLOYALTY

in·field \'in-,fēld\ *n* : the part of a baseball field inside the base lines — **in·field·er** *n*

in·fight·ing \'in-,fīt-iŋ\ *n* : fighting or boxing at close quarters

in·fil·trate \in-'fil-,trāt, 'in-(,)fil-\ *vb* **1** : to enter or filter into or through something **2** : to pass into or through by or as if by filtering or permeating — **in·fil·tra·tion** \,in-(,)fil-'trā-shən\ *n*

in·fi·nite \'in-fə-nət\ *adj* **1** : LIMITLESS, BOUNDLESS, ENDLESS ⟨~ space⟩ ⟨~ patience⟩ **2** : VAST, IMMENSE; *also* : INEXHAUSTIBLE ⟨~ wealth⟩ — **infinite** *n* — **in·fi·nite·ly** *adv*

in·fin·i·tes·i·mal \(,)in-,fin-ə-'tes-ə-məl\ *adj* : immeasurably or incalculably small : very minute — **in·fin·i·tes·i·mal·ly** *adv*

in·fin·i·tive \in-'fin-ət-iv\ *n* : a verb form having the characteristics of both verb and noun and in English usu. being used with *to*

in·fin·i·tude \in-'fin-ə-,t(y)üd\ *n* **1** : the quality or state of being infinite **2** : something that is infinite esp. in extent

in·fin·i·ty \in-'fin-ət-ē\ *n* **1** : the quality of being infinite **2** : unlimited extent of time, space, or quantity : BOUNDLESSNESS **3** : an indefinitely great number or amount

in·firm \in-'fərm\ *adj* **1** : deficient in vitality; *esp* : feeble from age **2** : not solid or stable : INSECURE

in·fir·ma·ry \in-'fərm-(ə-)rē\ *n* : a place for the care of the infirm or sick

in·fir·mi·ty \in-'fər-mət-ē\ *n* **1** : FEEBLENESS **2** : DISEASE, AILMENT **3** : a personal failing : FOIBLE

in·flame \in-'flām\ *vb* **1** : KINDLE **2** : to excite to excessive or unnatural action or feeling; *also* : INTENSIFY **3** : to affect or become affected with inflammation

in·flam·ma·ble \in-'flam-ə-bəl\ *adj* **1** : FLAMMABLE **2** : easily inflamed, excited, or angered : IRASCIBLE

in·flam·ma·tion \,in-flə-'mā-shən\ *n* : a bodily response to injury in which an affected area becomes red, hot, and painful and congested with blood

in·flam·ma·to·ry \in-'flam-ə-,tōr-ē\ *adj* **1** : tending to excite the senses or to arouse anger, disorder, or tumult : SEDITIOUS ⟨an ~ speech⟩ **2** : causing or accompanied by inflammation ⟨an ~ disease⟩

in·flate \in-'flāt\ *vb* **1** : to swell with air or gas ⟨~ a balloon⟩ **2** : to puff up : ELATE ⟨*inflated* with pride⟩ **3** : to expand or increase abnormally ⟨*inflated* prices⟩ — **in·flat·able** *adj*

in·fla·tion \in-'flā-shən\ *n* **1** : an act

of inflating : the state of being inflated
2 : empty pretentiousness : POMPOSITY
3 : an abnormal increase in the volume of money and credit resulting in a substantial and continuing rise in the general price level

in·fla·tion·ary \-shə-‚ner-ē\ adj : of, characterized by, or productive of inflation

in·fla·tion·ism \-'flā-shə-‚niz-əm\ n : the policy of economic inflation — **in·fla·tion·ist** \-shə(-ə)nəst\ n or adj

in·flect \in-'flekt\ vb **1** : to turn from a direct line or course : CURVE **2** : to vary a word by inflection **3** : to change or vary the pitch of the voice : MODULATE

in·flec·tion \in-'flek-shən\ n **1** : the act or result of curving or bending **2** : a change in pitch or loudness of the voice **3** : the change of form that words undergo to mark case, gender, number, tense, person, mood, or voice — **in·flec·tion·al** \-sh(ə-)nəl\ adj

in·flex·i·ble \(')in-'flek-sə-bəl\ adj **1** : RIGID **2** : UNYIELDING **3** : UNALTERABLE — **in·flex·i·bil·i·ty** \(‚)in-‚flek-sə-'bil-ət-ē\ n — **in·flex·i·bly** \(')in-'flek-sə-blē\ adv

in·flex·ion \in-'flek-shən\ chiefly Brit var of INFLECTION

in·flict \in-'flikt\ vb **1** : to give or deliver (as blows, pain, or penalty) by or as if by striking : IMPOSE, AFFLICT — **in·flic·tion** \-'flik-shən\ n

in·flo·res·cence \‚in-flə-'res-ᵊns\ n : the manner of development and arrangement of flowers on its stem; also : a flowering stem with its appendages : a flower cluster

in·flow \'in-‚flō\ n : INFLUX

¹in·flu·ence \'in-‚flü-əns\ n **1** : the act or power of producing an effect without apparent force or direct authority **2** : the power or capacity of causing an effect in indirect or intangible ways ⟨under the ~ of liquor⟩ **3** : a person or thing that exerts influence — **in·flu·en·tial** \‚in-flü-'en-chəl\ adj

²influence vb **1** : to affect or alter by influence : SWAY **2** : to have an effect on the condition or development of : MODIFY

in·flu·en·za \‚in-flü-'en-zə\ n : an acute and very contagious virus disease marked by fever, prostration, aches and pains, and respiratory inflammation; also : any of various feverish usu. virus diseases typically with respiratory symptoms

in·flux \'in-‚fləks\ n : a flowing in ⟨the ~ of holiday visitors⟩

in·fold vb **1** \in-'fōld\ : ENFOLD **2** \'in-‚fōld\ : to fold inward or toward one another

in·form \in-'fórm\ vb **1** : to communicate knowledge to : TELL **2** : to give information or knowledge **3** : to act as an informer syn acquaint, apprise, advise, notify

in·for·mal \(')in-'fór-məl\ adj **1** : conducted or carried out without formality or ceremony ⟨an ~ party⟩ **2** : characteristic of or appropriate to ordinary, casual, or familiar use ⟨~ clothes⟩ — **in·for·mal·i·ty** \‚in-fór-'mal-ət-ē,-fər-\ n — **in·for·mal·ly** \(')in-'fór-mə-lē\ adv

in·for·mant \in-'fór-mənt\ n : one who gives information : INFORMER

in·for·ma·tion \‚in-fər-'mā-shən\ n **1** : the communication or reception of knowledge or intelligence **2** : knowledge obtained from investigation, study, or instruction : INTELLIGENCE, NEWS, FACTS, DATA — **in·for·ma·tion·al** \-'mā-sh(ə-)nəl\ adj

in·for·ma·tive \in-'fór-mət-iv\ adj : imparting knowledge : INSTRUCTIVE

in·formed \in-'fórmd\ adj : EDUCATED, INTELLIGENT

in·form·er n : one that informs; esp : a person who informs against someone else

in·frac·tion \in-'frak-shən\ n : the act of infringing : VIOLATION ⟨~ of the rules⟩

in·fra dig \‚in-frə-'dig\ adj : being beneath one's dignity

in·fra·red \‚in-frə-'red\ adj : being or relating to invisible heat rays having wavelengths longer than those of red light

in·fra·son·ic \-'sän-ik\ adj : having a frequency below the audibility range of the human ear ⟨~ vibration⟩

in·fre·quent \(')in-'frē-kwənt\ adj **1** : seldom happening : RARE **2** : placed or occurring at considerable distances or intervals : OCCASIONAL syn uncommon, scarce, rare, sporadic — **in·fre·quent·ly** adv

in·fringe \in-'frinj\ vb **1** : VIOLATE, TRANSGRESS ⟨~ a treaty⟩ **2** : ENCROACH, TRESPASS ⟨~ upon a person's rights⟩ — **in·fringe·ment** n

in·fu·ri·ate \in-'fyùr-ē-‚āt\ vb : to make furious : ENRAGE

in·fuse \in-'fyüz\ vb **1** : to instill a principle or quality in : INTRODUCE **2** : INSPIRE, ANIMATE **3** : to steep (as tea) without boiling — **in·fu·sion** \-'fyü-zhən\ n

in·fus·ible \(')in-'fyü-zə-bəl\ adj : incapable or very difficult of fusion

¹-ing \iŋ\ vb suffix or adj suffix — used to form the present participle ⟨sailing⟩ and sometimes to form an adjective resembling a present participle but not derived from a verb ⟨swashbuckling⟩

²-ing n suffix : one of a (specified) kind

³-ing n suffix **1** : action or process ⟨sleeping⟩ : instance of an action or process ⟨a meeting⟩ **2** : product or result of an action or process ⟨an engraving⟩ ⟨earnings⟩ **3** : something used in an action or process ⟨a bed covering⟩ **4** : something connected with, consisting of, or used in making ⟨a specified thing⟩ ⟨scaffolding⟩ **5** : something related to ⟨a specified concept⟩ ⟨offing⟩

in·gath·er·ing \'in-‚gath-(ə-)riŋ\ n **1** : COLLECTION, HARVEST **2** : ASSEMBLY

in·ge·nious \in-'jēn-yəs\ adj **1** : marked by special aptitude at discovering, inventing, or contriving **2** : marked by originality, resourcefulness, and cleverness in conception or execution — **in·ge·nious·ly** adv — **in·ge·nious·ness** n

in·ge·nue or **in·gé·nue** \'an-jə-‚nü, 'aⁿ-zhə-\ n : a naïve girl or young woman; esp : an actress representing such a person

in·ge·nu·i·ty \‚in-jə-'n(y)ü-ət-ē\ n : skill

ə abut; ᵊ kitten; ər further; a back; ā bake; ä cot, cart; aù out; ch chin; e less; ē easy; g gift; i trip; ī life; j joke; ŋ sing; ō flow; ò flaw; òi coin; th thin; th this; ü loot; ù foot; y yet; yü few; yù furious; zh vision

or cleverness in planning or inventing
: INVENTIVENESS

in·gen·u·ous \in-'jen-yə-wəs\ adj
1 : STRAIGHTFORWARD, FRANK 2 : NAÏVE
— in·gen·u·ous·ly adv — in·gen·u·ous·ness n

in·gest \in-'jest\ vb : to take in for or
as if for digestion : ABSORB — in·ges·tion \-'jes-chən\ n

in·gle \'iŋ-gəl\ n 1 : FLAME, BLAZE
2 : FIREPLACE

in·gle·nook \'iŋ-gəl-ˌnúk\ n 1 : a
corner by the fire or chimney 2 : a
high-backed wooden settee placed close
to a fireplace

in·glo·ri·ous \(')in-'glōr-ē-əs\ adj
1 : not glorious : lacking fame or honor
2 : SHAMEFUL — in·glo·ri·ous·ly adv

in·got \'iŋ-gət\ n : a mass of metal cast
in a form convenient for storage or
transportation

ingraft var of ENGRAFT

¹in·grain \(')in-'grān\ vb : to work
indelibly into the natural texture or
mental or moral constitution : IMBUE
— in·grained adj

²in·grain \'in-ˌgrān\ adj 1 : made of fiber that is dyed before being spun into
yarn 2 : made of yarn that is dyed
before being woven or knitted 3 : IN-
NATE — in·grain \'in-ˌgrān\ n

in·grate \'in-ˌgrāt\ n : an ungrateful
person

in·gra·ti·ate \in-'grā-shē-ˌāt\ vb : to
gain favor by deliberate effort

in·gra·ti·at·ing adj 1 : capable of
winning favor : PLEASING ⟨an ~ smile⟩
2 : FLATTERING ⟨an ~ manner⟩

in·grat·i·tude \(')in-'grat-ə-ˌt(y)üd\ n
: lack of gratitude : UNGRATEFULNESS

in·gre·di·ent \in-'grēd-ē-ənt\ n : one
of the substances that make up a mixture or compound : CONSTITUENT, COM-
PONENT

in·gress \'in-ˌgres\ n : ENTRANCE,
ACCESS

in·grow·ing \'in-ˌgrō-iŋ\ adj : grown
in; esp : having the free tip or edge embedded in the flesh ⟨~ toenail⟩

in·grown \'in-ˌgrōn\ adj : grown in
and esp. into the flesh ⟨an ~ toenail⟩

in·hab·it \in-'hab-ət\ vb : to live or
dwell in — in·hab·it·able adj

in·hab·i·tant \in-'hab-ət-ənt\ n : a
permanent resident in a place

in·hal·ant \in-'hā-lənt\ n : something
(as a medicine) that is inhaled

in·hale \in-'hāl\ vb : to draw in in
breathing : breathe in — in·ha·la·tion
\ˌin-(h)ə-'lā-shən\ n

in·hal·er \in-'hā-lər\ n : a device by
means of which material can be inhaled

in·here \in-'hiər\ vb : to be inherent
: BELONG ⟨power to make laws ~s in
the state⟩

in·her·ent \in-'hir-ənt, -'her-\ adj : established as an essential part of something : INTRINSIC — in·her·ent·ly adv

in·her·it \in-'her-ət\ vb : to receive esp.
from one's ancestors — in·her·i·tance
\-ət-əns\ n — in·her·i·tor n

in·hib·it \in-'hib-ət\ vb 1 : PROHIBIT,
FORBID 2 : to hold in check : RESTRAIN,
REPRESS

in·hi·bi·tion \ˌin-(h)ə-'bish-ən\ n
1 : PROHIBITION, RESTRAINT 2 : a usu.
inner check on free activity, expression,
or functioning

in·hu·man \(')in-'(h)yü-mən\ adj
1 : lacking pity or kindness : CRUEL,
SAVAGE 2 : COLD, IMPERSONAL 3 : not

worthy of or conforming to the needs
of human beings 4 : of or suggesting
a nonhuman class of beings — in·hu·man·ly adv

in·hu·mane \ˌin-(h)yü-'mān\ adj : not
humane : INHUMAN 1

in·hu·man·i·ty \ˌin-(h)yü-'man-ət-ē\ n
1 : the quality or state of being cruel or
barbarous 2 : a cruel or barbarous act

in·hume \in-'hyüm\ vb : BURY, INTER —
in·hu·ma·tion \ˌin-hyü-'mā-shən\ n

in·im·i·cal \in-'im-i-kəl\ adj 1 : HOSTILE,
UNFRIENDLY 2 : HARMFUL, ADVERSE
⟨habits ~ to health⟩ — in·im·i·cal·ly adv

in·im·i·ta·ble \(')in-'im-ət-ə-bəl\ adj
: not capable of being imitated : MATCH-
LESS

in·iq·ui·ty \in-'ik-wət-ē\ n 1 : WICKED-
NESS 2 : a wicked act : SIN — in·iq·ui·tous \-wət-əs\ adj

¹ini·tial \in-'ish-əl\ adj 1 : of or relating to the beginning : INCIPIENT
2 : FIRST — ini·tial·ly adv

²initial n : the first letter of a word or
name

³initial vb -tialed or -tialled; -tial·ing
or -tial·ling : to affix an initial to

¹ini·ti·ate \in-'ish-ē-ˌāt\ vb 1 : START,
BEGIN 2 : to instruct in the first
principles of something : INTRODUCE
⟨~ a city boy into the mysteries of
farming⟩ 3 : to induct into membership by or as if by special ceremonies —
ini·ti·a·tion \-ˌish-ē-'ā-shən\ n

²ini·ti·ate \in-'ish-(ē-)ət\ n 1 : a person
who is undergoing or has passed an
initiation 2 : a person who is instructed
or adept in some special field

ini·tia·tive \in-'ish-ət-iv\ n 1 : an
introductory step 2 : self-reliant
enterprise 3 : a process by which laws
may be introduced or enacted directly
by vote of the people

ini·tia·to·ry \in-'ish-(ē-)ə-ˌtōr-ē\ adj
1 : INTRODUCTORY 2 : tending or
serving to initiate ⟨~ rites⟩

in·ject \in-'jekt\ vb 1 : to force into
something ⟨~ serum with a needle⟩
2 : to introduce (as by way of suggestion or interruption) into some situation
or subject ⟨~ a note of suspicion⟩ —
in·jec·tion \-'jek-shən\ n

in·junc·tion \in-'jəŋk-shən\ n 1 : OR-
DER, ADMONITION 2 : a court writ
whereby one is required to do or to
refrain from doing a specified act

in·jure \'in-jər\ vb : WRONG, DAMAGE,
HURT syn harm, impair, mar, spoil

in·ju·ry \'inj-(ə-)rē\ n 1 : an act that
damages or hurts : WRONG 2 : hurt,
damage, or loss sustained — in·ju·ri·ous \in-'jür-ē-əs\ adj

in·jus·tice \(')in-'jəs-təs\ n : viola-
tion of a person's rights : UNFAIRNESS,
WRONG 2 : an unjust act or deed

¹ink \'iŋk\ n : a usu. liquid and colored
material for writing and printing

²ink vb : to put ink on

ink·blot \-ˌblät\ n : any of several plates
showing blots of ink for use in psychological testing

ink·horn \-ˌhȯrn\ n : a small bottle (as
of horn) for holding ink

in·kling \'iŋ-kliŋ\ n 1 : HINT, INTIMA-
TION 2 : a vague idea

ink·stand \'iŋk-ˌstand\ n : INKWELL;
also : a pen and ink stand

ink·well \-ˌwel\ n : a container for
writing ink

inky \'iŋ-kē\ adj : consisting of, using

or resembling ink **:** soiled with or as if with ink **:** BLACK

in·laid \'in-ˌlād\ *adj* **:** decorated with material set into a surface

¹in·land \'in-ˌland, -lənd\ *n* **:** the interior of a country

²inland *adj* **1** *chiefly Brit* **:** not foreign **:** DOMESTIC ⟨~ revenue⟩ **2 :** of or relating to the interior of a country

³inland *adv* **:** into or toward the interior

in-law \'in-ˌlò\ *n* **:** a relative by marriage

¹in·lay \(')in-'lā\ *vb* **:** to set (one material into another) by way of decoration

²in·lay \'in-ˌlā\ *n* **1 :** inlaid work **2 :** a shaped filling cemented into a tooth

in·let \'in-ˌlet, -lət\ *n* **1 :** a bay in the shore of a sea, lake, or river **2 :** a narrow strip of water running into the land

in·mate \'in-ˌmāt\ *n* **:** a person who lives in the same house or institution with another; *esp* **:** a person confined to an asylum, prison, or poorhouse

in me·di·as res \in-ˌmād-ē-ˌäs-'räs\ *adv* **:** in or into the middle of a narrative or plot

in me·mo·ri·am \ˌin-mə-'mōr-ē-əm\ *prep* **:** in memory of

in·most \'in-ˌmōst\ *adj* **:** deepest within **:** INNERMOST

inn \'in\ *n* **:** HOTEL, TAVERN

in·nards \'in-ərdz\ *n pl* **1 :** the internal organs of a man or animal; *esp* **:** VISCERA **2 :** the internal parts of a structure or mechanism

in·nate \in-'āt\ *adj* **1 :** existing in or belonging to an individual from birth **:** NATIVE **2 :** belonging to the essential nature of something **:** INHERENT — **in·nate·ly** *adv*

in·ner \'in-ər\ *adj* **1 :** situated farther in ⟨the ~ ear⟩ **2 :** near a center esp. of influence ⟨the ~ circle⟩ **3 :** of or relating to the mind or spirit ⟨~ thoughts⟩

in·ner·most \'in-ər-ˌmōst\ *adj* **:** farthest inward **:** INMOST

in·ner·sole \ˌin-ər-'sōl\ *n* **:** INSOLE

in·ning \'in-iŋ\ *n* **:** a baseball team's turn at bat; *also* **:** a division of a baseball game consisting of a turn at bat for each team

in·nings \'in-iŋz\ *n sing or pl* **:** a division of a cricket match

inn·keep·er \'in-ˌkē-pər\ *n* **:** the landlord of an inn

in·no·cence \'in-ə-səns\ *n* **1 :** BLAMELESSNESS; *also* **:** freedom from legal guilt **2 :** GUILELESSNESS, SIMPLICITY; *also* **:** IGNORANCE

in·no·cent \-sənt\ *adj* **1 :** free from guilt or sin **:** BLAMELESS **2 :** harmless in effect or intention; *also* **:** CANDID **3 :** free from legal guilt or fault **:** LAWFUL **4 :** DESTITUTE **5 :** ARTLESS, IGNORANT — **innocent** *n* — **in·no·cent·ly** *adv*

in·noc·u·ous \in-'äk-yə-wəs\ *adj* **1 :** HARMLESS **2 :** INOFFENSIVE, INSIPID

in·nom·i·nate \in-'äm-ə-nət\ *adj* **:** having no name; *also* **:** ANONYMOUS

in·no·vate \'in-ə-ˌvāt\ *vb* **:** to introduce as or as if new **:** make changes — **in·no·va·tor** *n*

in·no·va·tion \ˌin-ə-'vā-shən\ *n* **1 :** the introduction of something new **2 :** a new idea, method, or device **:** NOVELTY

in·nu·en·do \ˌin-yə-'wen-dō\ *n, pl* **-dos** *or* **-does :** HINT, INSINUATION; *esp* **:** a veiled reflection on character or reputation

in·nu·mer·a·ble \in-'(y)üm-(ə-)rə-bəl\ *adj* **:** too many to be numbered — COUNTLESS

in·oc·u·late \in-'äk-yə-ˌlāt\ *vb* **:** to introduce something into; *esp* **:** to treat usu. with a serum or antibody to prevent or cure a disease — **in·oc·u·la·tion** \-ˌäk-yə-'lā-shən\ *n*

in·op·er·a·ble \(')in-'äp-(ə-)rə-bəl\ *adj* **1 :** not suitable for surgery **2 :** not operable

in·op·er·a·tive \-'äp-(ə-)rət-iv, -ə-ˌrāt-iv\ *adj* **:** not functioning **:** producing no effect

in·op·por·tune \(ˌ)in-ˌäp-ər-'t(y)ün\ *adj* **:** INCONVENIENT, UNSEASONABLE — **in·op·por·tune·ly** *adv*

in·or·di·nate \in-'òrd-(°-)nət\ *adj* **1 :** UNREGULATED, DISORDERLY **2 :** EXTRAORDINARY, IMMODERATE ⟨an ~ curiosity⟩ — **in·or·di·nate·ly** *adv*

in·or·gan·ic \ˌin-òr-'gan-ik\ *adj* **:** being or composed of matter of other than plant or animal origin **:** MINERAL

in·pa·tient \'in-ˌpā-shənt\ *n* **:** a hospital patient who receives lodging and food as well as treatment

in pet·to \in-'pet-ō\ *adv (or adj)* **:** in private **:** SECRETLY

in·put \'in-ˌpùt\ *n* **:** something put in; *esp* **:** power or energy put into a machine or system

in·quest \'in-ˌkwest\ *n* **1 :** an official inquiry or examination esp. before a jury (coroner's ~) **2 :** INQUIRY, INVESTIGATION

in·qui·etude \(')in-'kwī-ə-ˌt(y)üd\ *n* **:** UNEASINESS, RESTLESSNESS

in·quire \in-'kwī(ə)r\ *vb* **1 :** to ask about **:** ASK **2 :** INVESTIGATE, EXAMINE — **in·quir·er** *n* — **in·quir·ing·ly** *adv*

in·qui·ry \in-'kwī(ə)r-ē, 'in-ˌkwə-rē\ *n* **1 :** a request for information; *also* **:** a search for truth or knowledge **2 :** a systematic investigation of a matter of public interest

in·qui·si·tion \ˌin-kwə-'zish-ən\ *n* **1 :** a judicial or official inquiry usu. before a jury **2** *cap* **:** a former Roman Catholic tribunal for the discovery and punishment of heretics **3 :** a severe questioning — **in·quis·i·tor** \in-'kwiz-ət-ər\ *n*

in·quis·i·tive \in-'kwiz-ət-iv\ *adj* **1 :** given to examination or investigation ⟨an ~ mind⟩ **2 :** unduly curious — **in·quis·i·tive·ly** *adv* — **in·quis·i·tive·ness** *n*

in re \in-'rē, -'rā\ *prep* **:** in the matter of **:** CONCERNING

in·road \'in-ˌrōd\ *n* **1 :** INVASION, RAID **2 :** ENCROACHMENT

in·rush \'in-ˌrəsh\ *n* **:** a crowding or flooding in **:** INFLUX

in·sa·lu·bri·ous \ˌin-sə-'lü-brē-əs\ *adj* **:** UNWHOLESOME, NOXIOUS

in·sane \(')in-'sān\ *adj* **1 :** not mentally sound **:** MAD; *also* **:** used by or for the insane **2 :** FOOLISH, WILD — **in·sane·ly** *adv* — **in·san·i·ty** \in-'san-ət-ē\ *n*

in·sa·tia·ble \(')in-'sā-shə-bəl\ *adj* **:** incapable of being satisfied ⟨an ~ appetite⟩

in·sa·tiate \-'sā-sh(ē-)ət\ *adj* **:** not

ə abut; ᵉ kitten; ər further; a back; ā bake; ä cot, cart; aù out; ch chin; e less; ē easy; g gift; i trip; ī life; j joke; ŋ sing; ō flow; ò flaw; òi coin; th thin; t͟h this; ü loot; ù foot; y yet; yü few; yù furious; zh vision

satiated or satisfied; *also* **:** INSATIABLE

in·scribe \in-'skrīb\ *vb* **1 :** to write, engrave, or print esp. as a lasting record **2 :** ENROLL **3 :** to write, engrave, or print characters upon **4 :** to dedicate to someone (~ a poem to a friend) **5 :** to stamp deeply or impress esp. on the memory — **in·scrip·tion** \-'skrip-shən\ *n*

in·scru·ta·ble \in-'skrüt-ə-bəl\ *adj* **1 :** not readily comprehensible **:** MYSTERIOUS (an ~ smile) **2 :** impossible to see or see through physically (an ~ fog) — **in·scru·ta·bly** *adv*

in·seam \'in-,sēm\ *n* **:** an inner seam of a garment or shoe

in·sect \'in-,sekt\ *n* **:** any of a major group of small usu. winged animals with three pairs of legs including the flies, bees, beetles, and moths

in·sec·ti·cide \in-'sek-tə-,sīd\ *n* **:** a preparation for destroying insects

in·sec·tiv·o·rous \,in-,sek-'tiv-(ə-)rəs\ *adj* **:** using insects as food

in·se·cure \,in-si-'kyúr\ *adj* **1 :** UNCERTAIN **2 :** UNPROTECTED, UNSAFE **3 :** LOOSE, SHAKY **4 :** INFIRM **5 :** beset by fear or anxiety — **in·se·cure·ly** *adv* — **in·se·cu·ri·ty** \-'kyúr-ət-ē\ *n*

in·sen·sate \(')in-'sen-,sāt\ *adj* **1 :** INANIMATE **2 :** lacking sense or understanding; *also* **:** FOOLISH **3 :** BRUTAL, INHUMAN (~ rage)

in·sen·si·ble \(')in-'sen-sə-bəl\ *adj* **1 :** INANIMATE **2 :** UNCONSCIOUS **3 :** lacking sensory perception or ability to react (~ to pain) (~ from cold) **4 :** IMPERCEPTIBLE; *also* **:** SLIGHT, GRADUAL **5 :** APATHETIC, INDIFFERENT; *also* **:** UNAWARE (~ of their danger) **6 :** MEANINGLESS **7 :** lacking delicacy or refinement — **in·sen·si·bil·i·ty** \(,)in-,sen-sə-'bil-ət-ē\ *n* — **in·sen·si·bly** \(')in-'sen-sə-blē\ *adv*

in·sen·tient \(')in-'sen-ch(ē-)ənt\ *adj* **:** lacking perception, consciousness, or animation — **in·sen·tience** *n*

in·sep·a·ra·ble \(')in-'sep-(ə-)rə-bəl\ *adj* **:** incapable of being separated or disjoined — **in·sep·a·ra·bil·i·ty** \(,)in-'sep-(ə-)rə-'bil-ət-ē\ *n* — **in·sep·a·ra·bly** \(')in-'sep-(ə-)rə-blē\ *adv*

¹in·sert \in-'sərt\ *vb* **1 :** to put or thrust in **:** INTRODUCE (~ a key in a lock) (~ a comma) **2 :** INTERPOLATE (~ed a few words of description) **3 :** to set in (as a piece of fabric) and make fast (~ a patch)

²in·sert \'in-,sərt\ *n* **:** something that is inserted or is for insertion; *esp* **:** written or printed material inserted (as between the leaves of a book)

in·ser·tion \in-'sər-shən\ *n* **1 :** the act or process of inserting **2 :** something that is inserted

in·set \'in-,set\ *vb* **-set** *or* **-set·ted; -set·ting :** to set in **:** INSERT — **inset** *n*

¹in·shore \'in-'shór, -,shór\ *adj* **1 :** situated or carried on near shore **2 :** moving toward shore

²inshore *adv* **:** to or toward shore

¹in·side \in-'sīd, 'in-,sīd\ *n* **1 :** an inner side or surface **:** INTERIOR **2 :** inward nature, thoughts, or feeling **3** *pl* **:** VISCERA, ENTRAILS **4 :** a position of power or confidence — **inside** *adj*

²inside *prep* **1 :** in or into the inside of **2 :** before the end of **:** WITHIN (~ an hour)

³inside *adv* **1 :** on the inner side **2 :** in or into the interior

inside of *prep* **:** INSIDE

in·sid·er \in-'sīd-ər\ *n* **:** a person who is in a position of power or has access to confidential information

in·sid·i·ous \in-'sid-ē-əs\ *adj* **1 :** SLY, TREACHEROUS **2 :** SEDUCTIVE **3 :** having a gradual and cumulative effect **:** SUBTLE

in·sight \'in-,sīt\ *n* **:** the power or act of seeing into a situation **:** UNDERSTANDING, PENETRATION; *also* **:** INTUITION

in·sig·nia \in-'sig-nē-ə\ *or* **in·sig·ne** \-(,)nē\ *n, pl* **-nia** *or* **-ni·as :** a distinguishing mark esp. of authority, office, or honor **:** BADGE, EMBLEM

in·sin·cere \,in-sin-'siər\ *adj* **:** not sincere **:** HYPOCRITICAL — **in·sin·cere·ly** *adv* — **in·sin·cer·i·ty** \-'ser-ət-ē\ *n*

in·sin·u·ate \in-'sin-yə-,wāt\ *vb* **1 :** to introduce (as an idea) gradually or in a subtle or indirect way **2 :** HINT, IMPLY **3 :** to introduce (as oneself) by stealthy, smooth, or artful means (*insinuate* himself into their confidence) — **in·sin·u·a·tion** \(,)in-,sin-yə-'wā-shən\ *n*

in·sin·u·at·ing *adj* **1 :** tending gradually to cause doubt, distrust, or change of outlook (~ remarks) **2 :** winning favor and confidence by imperceptible degrees (~ voice)

in·sip·id \in-'sip-əd\ *adj* **1 :** lacking savor **:** TASTELESS, FLAT **2 :** DULL, UNINTERESTING — **in·si·pid·i·ty** \,in-sə-'pid-ət-ē\ *n*

in·sist \in-'sist\ *vb* **:** to take a resolute stand **:** PERSIST

in·sis·tence \-'sis-təns\ *n* **:** the act of insisting; *also* **:** an insistent attitude or quality **:** URGENCY

in·sis·tent \-'sis-tənt\ *adj* **:** disposed to insist **:** PERTINACIOUS — **in·sis·tent·ly** *adv*

in si·tu \in-'sī-tü\ *adv* (*or adj*) **:** in the natural or original position

in·so·far as \,in-sə-,fär-əz\ *conj* **:** to the extent or degree that

in·sole \'in-,sōl\ *n* **1 :** an inside sole of a shoe **2 :** a loose thin strip (as of felt or leather) placed inside a shoe for warmth or ease

in·so·lent \'in-sə-lənt\ *adj* **:** contemptuous, rude, disrespectful, or brutal in behavior or language **:** OVERBEARING, BOLD — **in·so·lence** \-ləns\ *n*

in·sol·u·ble \(')in-'säl-yə-bəl\ *adj* **1 :** having or admitting of no solution or explanation **2 :** that cannot readily be dissolved in a liquid — **in·sol·u·bil·i·ty** \(,)in-,säl-yə-'bil-ət-ē\ *n*

in·solv·able \(')in-'säl-və-bəl\ *adj* **:** admitting no solution — **in·solv·ably** *adv*

in·sol·vent \(')in-'säl-vənt\ *adj* **1 :** unable to pay one's debts **2 :** insufficient to pay all debts charged against it (an ~ estate) **3 :** IMPOVERISHED, DEFICIENT — **in·sol·ven·cy** \-'säl-vən-sē\ *n*

in·som·nia \in-'säm-nē-ə\ *n* **:** prolonged or abnormal sleeplessness

in·so·much \,in-sə-'məch\ *adv* **:** so much **:** to such a degree **: so —** used with *as or that*

in·sou·ci·ance \in-'sü-sē-əns\ *n* **:** a lighthearted unconcern — **in·sou·ci·ant** *adj*

in·spect \in-'spekt\ *vb* **:** to view closely and critically **:** EXAMINE — **in·spec·tion** \-'spek-shən\ *n* — **in·spec·tor** \-tər\ *n*

in·spi·ra·tion \,in-spə-'rā-shən\ *n* **1 :** INHALATION **2 :** the act or power of moving the intellect or emotions **3 :** the quality or state of being inspired; *also* : something that is inspired 4 : an inspiring agent or influence — **in·spi·ra·tion·al** \-sh(ə-)nəl\ *adj*

in·spire \in-'spī(ə)r\ *vb* 1 : INHALE 2 : to influence, move, or guide by divine or supernatural inspiration : exert an animating, enlivening, or exalting influence upon : AFFECT 3 : to communicate to an agent supernaturally; *also* : CREATE 4 : to bring about; *also* : INCITE 5 : to spread by indirect means or through another ⟨a rumor *inspired* by interested parties⟩ — **in·spir·er** *n*

in·spir·it \in-'spir-ət\ *vb* : ANIMATE, HEARTEN

in·sta·bil·i·ty \,in-stə-'bil-ət-ē\ *n* : lack of firmness or steadiness

in·stall *or* **in·stal** \in-'stól\ *vb* **-stalled**; **-stall·ing** 1 : to place formally in office : induct into an office, rank, or order 2 : to establish in an indicated place, condition, or status 3 : to set up for use or service — **in·stal·la·tion** \,in-stə-'lā-shən\ *n*

¹**in·stall·ment** *or* **in·stal·ment** \in-'stól-mənt\ *n* : INSTALLATION

²**installment** *also* **instalment** *n* 1 : one of the parts into which a debt or sum is divided for payment 2 : one of several parts presented at intervals ⟨the last ~ of a serial story⟩

¹**in·stance** \'in-stəns\ *n* 1 : INSTIGATION, REQUEST ⟨entered the contest at the ~ of friends⟩ 2 : EXAMPLE ⟨an ~ of heroism⟩ ⟨for ~⟩ 3 : an event or step that is part of a process or series : OCCASION ⟨in the last ~⟩ *syn* case, illustration, sample, specimen

²**instance** *vb* : to mention as a case or example : CITE

¹**in·stant** \'in-stənt\ *n* 1 : MOMENT ⟨the ~ we met⟩ 2 : the present or current month ⟨your letter of the 10th ~⟩

²**instant** *adj* 1 : URGENT 2 : PRESENT, CURRENT 3 : IMMEDIATE ⟨~ relief⟩ 4 : partially prepared by the manufacturer to make final preparation easy ⟨~ cake mix⟩; *also* : immediately soluble in water ⟨~ coffee⟩

in·stan·ta·ne·ous \,in-stən-'tā-nē-əs\ *adj* : done or occurring in an instant or without delay — **in·stan·ta·ne·ous·ly** *adv*

in·stan·ter \in-'stant-ər\ *adv* : at once : INSTANTLY

in·stant·ly \'in-stənt-lē\ *adv* : at once : IMMEDIATELY

in·state \in-'stāt\ *vb* : to establish in a rank or office : INSTALL

in sta·tu quo \in-,stā-tü-'kwō, -,sta-\ : in the former or same state

in·stead \in-'sted\ *adv* 1 : as a substitute or equivalent 2 : as an alternative : RATHER

instead of *prep* : as a substitute for or alternative to

in·step \'in-,step\ *n* : the arched part of the human foot in front of the ankle joint

in·sti·gate \'in-stə-,gāt\ *vb* : to goad or urge forward : PROVOKE, INCITE ⟨~ a revolt⟩ — **in·sti·ga·tion** \,in-stə-'gā-shən\ *n* — **in·sti·ga·tor** \'in-stə-,gāt-ər\ *n*

in·still *also* **in·stil** \in-'stil\ *vb* **-stilled**; **-still·ing** 1 : to cause to enter drop by

drop 2 : to impart gradually

¹**in·stinct** \'in-,stiŋkt\ *n* 1 : a natural aptitude 2 : complex but largely hereditary and unalterable response of an organism to stimuli; *also* : behavior originating below the conscious level — **in·stinc·tive** \in-'stiŋk-tiv\ *adj* — **in·stinc·tive·ly** *adv*

²**in·stinct** \in-'stiŋkt, 'in-,stiŋkt\ *adj* : IMBUED, INFUSED

¹**in·sti·tute** \'in-stə-,t(y)üt\ *vb* 1 : to establish in a position or office 2 : to originate and get established : ORGANIZE 3 : INAUGURATE, INITIATE

²**institute** *n* 1 : an elementary principle recognized as authoritative; *also, pl* : a collection of such principles and precepts 2 : an organization for the promotion of a cause : ASSOCIATION 3 : an educational institution 4 : a meeting for instruction or a brief course of such meetings

in·sti·tu·tion \,in-stə-'t(y)ü-shən\ *n* 1 : an act of originating, setting up, or founding 2 : an established practice, law, or custom 3 : a society or corporation esp. of a public character ⟨a charitable ~⟩; *also* : the building which houses it — **in·sti·tu·tion·al** \-'t(y)ü-sh(ə-)nəl\ *adj* — **in·sti·tu·tion·al·ize** \-,īz\ *vb* — **in·sti·tu·tion·al·ly** *adv*

in·struct \in-'strəkt\ *vb* 1 : TEACH 2 : INFORM 3 : to give directions or commands to

in·struc·tion \in-'strək-shən\ *n* 1 : LESSON, PRECEPT 2 : COMMAND, ORDER 3 *pl* : DIRECTIONS 4 : the action, practice, or profession of a teacher

in·struc·tive \in-'strək-tiv\ *adj* : carrying a lesson : ENLIGHTENING

in·struc·tor \in-'strək-tər\ *n* : one that instructs; *esp* : a college teacher below professorial rank — **in·struc·tor·ship** *n*

in·stru·ment \'in-strə-mənt\ *n* 1 : a means by which something is done 2 : TOOL, UTENSIL 3 : a device used to produce music 4 : a legal document ⟨as a deed⟩ 5 : a device used in navigating an airplane

in·stru·men·tal \,in-strə-'ment-ᵊl\ *adj* 1 : acting as an agent or means 2 : of, relating to, or done with an instrument 3 : relating to, composed for, or performed on a musical instrument

in·stru·men·tal·ist *n* : a player on a musical instrument

in·stru·men·tal·i·ty \,in-strə-mən-'tal-ət-ē, -,men-\ *n* 1 : the quality or state of being instrumental 2 : MEANS, AGENCY

in·stru·men·ta·tion \,in-strə-mən-'tā-shən, -,men-\ *n* 1 : the use or application of instruments 2 : the arrangement or composition of music for instruments esp. for a band or orchestra

in·sub·or·di·nate \,in-sə-'bórd-(ᵊ-)nət\ *adj* : unwilling to submit to authority : DISOBEDIENT — **in·sub·or·di·na·tion** \-,bórd-ᵊn-'ā-shən\ *n*

in·sub·stan·tial \,in-səb-'stan-chəl\ *adj* 1 : lacking substance or reality : IMAGINARY 2 : lacking firmness or solidity

in·suf·fer·able \(')in-'səf-(ə-)rə-bəl\ *adj* : incapable of being endured : INTOLERABLE ⟨an ~ bore⟩ — **in·suf·fer·ably** *adv*

ə abut; ᵊ kitten; ər further; a back; ā bake; ä cot, cart; aù out; ch chin; e less; ē easy; g gift; i trip; ī life; j joke; ŋ sing; ō flow; ó flaw; ói coin; th thin; t͟h this; ü loot; ù foot; y yet; yü few; yù furious; zh vision in·suf·fi·cient \,in-sə-'fish-ənt\ adj : not sufficient : INADEQUATE; also : INCOMPETENT — in·suf·fi·cien·cy \-'fishən-sē\ n — in·suf·fi·cient·ly adv

in·su·lar \'ins-(y)ə-lər, 'in-shə-lər\ adj 1 : of, relating to, or forming an island 2 : ISOLATED, DETACHED 3 : of or relating to island people 4 : NARROW, PREJUDICED — in·su·lar·i·ty \,ins-(y)ə-'lar-ət-ē, ,in-shə-\ n

in·su·late \'in-sə-,lāt\ vb [L insula island] : ISOLATE; esp : to separate a conductor of electricity, heat, or sound from something that will not conduct electricity, heat, or sound — in·su·la·tion \,in-sə-'lā-shən\ n — in·su·la·tor \'in-sə-,lāt-ər\ n

in·su·lin \'in-s(ə-)lən\ n : a pancreatic hormone essential for bodily use of sugars and used in the control of diabetes

¹in·sult \in-'səlt\ vb : to treat with insolence or contempt : AFFRONT

²in·sult \'in-,səlt\ n : a gross indignity : INSOLENCE

in·su·per·a·ble \(')in-'sü-p(ə-)rə-bəl\ adj : incapable of being surmounted, overcome, or passed over — in·su·per·a·bly adv

in·sup·port·able \,in-sə-'pōrt-ə-bəl\ adj 1 : UNENDURABLE 2 : UNJUSTIFIABLE

in·sur·able \in-'shůr-ə-bəl\ adj : capable of being or proper to be insured against loss, damage, or death

in·sur·ance \in-'shůr-əns\ n 1 : the action or process of insuring : the state of being insured; also : means of insuring 2 : the business of insuring persons or property 3 : coverage by contract whereby one party agrees to indemnify or guarantee another against loss by a specified contingent event or peril 4 : the sum for which something is insured

in·sure \in-'shůr\ vb 1 : to give, take, or procure an insurance on or for : UNDERWRITE 2 : to make certain : ENSURE

in·sured n : a person whose life or property is insured

in·sur·er n : one that insures; esp : a company issuing insurance

in·sur·gent \in-'sər-jənt\ n 1 : a person who revolts against civil authority or an established government : REBEL 2 : one who acts contrary to the policies and decisions of his political party — in·sur·gence \-jəns\ n — in·sur·gent adj

in·sur·mount·able \,in-sər-'maůnt-ə-bəl\ adj : INSUPERABLE (~ disadvantages) — in·sur·mount·ably adv

in·sur·rec·tion \,in-sə-'rek-shən\ n : an act or instance of revolting against civil authority or an established government — in·sur·rec·tion·ist n

in·tact \in-'takt\ adj : untouched esp. by anything that harms or diminishes : ENTIRE, UNINJURED

in·ta·glio \in-'tal-yō\ n : an engraving or incised figure in a hard material (as stone) depressed below the surface of the material

in·take \'in-,tāk\ n 1 : an opening through which fluid enters an enclosure 2 : the act of taking in 3 : the amount taken in

in·tan·gi·ble \(')in-'tan-jə-bəl\ adj 1 : incapable of being touched : not tangible : IMPALPABLE 2 : incapable of being defined or determined with

certainty or precision : VAGUE — in·tangi·ble n — in·tan·gi·bly adv

in·te·ger \'int-i-jər\ n : a number (as 1, 2, 3, 12, 432) that is not a fraction and does not include a fraction, is the negative of such a number, or is 0

¹in·te·gral \'int-i-grəl\ adj 1 : essential to completeness : CONSTITUENT 2 : formed as a unit with another part 3 : composed of parts that make up a whole 4 : ENTIRE

²integral n : a whole number

in·te·grate \'int-ə-,grāt\ vb 1 : to form into a whole : UNITE 2 : to incorporate into a larger unit 3 : to end the segregation of and bring into common and equal membership in society or an organization; also : DESEGREGATE — in·te·gra·tion \,int-ə-'grā-shən\ n

in·teg·ri·ty \in-'teg-rət-ē\ n 1 : SOUNDNESS 2 : adherence to a code of values (as moral or artistic) : utter sincerity, honesty, and candor 3 : COMPLETENESS

in·teg·u·ment \in-'teg-yə-mənt\ n : a covering layer (as a skin or cuticle) of an organism

in·tel·lect \'int-ᵊl-,ekt\ n 1 : the power of knowing : the capacity for knowledge 2 : the capacity for rational or intelligent thought esp. when highly developed 3 : a person of notable intellect

in·tel·lec·tu·al \,int-ᵊl-'ek-ch(ə-w)əl\ adj 1 : of, relating to, or performed by the intellect : RATIONAL 2 : given to study, reflection, and speculation 3 : engaged in activity requiring the creative use of the intellect — intellectual n — in·tel·lec·tu·al·ly adv

in·tel·lec·tu·al·ism n : devotion to the exercise of intellect or to intellectual pursuits

in·tel·li·gence \in-'tel-ə-jəns\ n 1 : ability to learn and understand or to deal with new or trying situations 2 : relative intellectual capacity 3 : INFORMATION, NEWS 4 : an agency engaged in obtaining information esp. concerning an enemy or possible enemy

intelligence quotient n : a number expressing the intelligence of a person determined by dividing his mental age by his chronological age and multiplying by 100

in·tel·li·gent \in-'tel-ə-jənt\ adj : having or showing intelligence or intellect — in·tel·li·gent·ly adv

in·tel·li·gen·tsia \in-,tel-ə-'jent-sē-ə, -'gent-\ n : intellectual people as a group : the educated class

in·tel·li·gi·ble \in-'tel-ə-jə-bəl\ adj : capable of being understood or comprehended — in·tel·li·gi·bil·i·ty \-,tel-ə-jə-'bil-ət-ē\ n — in·tel·li·gi·bly \-'tel-ə-jə-blē\ adv

in·tem·per·ance \(')in-'tem-p(ə-)rəns\ n : lack of moderation esp. in satisfying an appetite or passion; esp : habitual or excessive drinking of intoxicants — in·tem·per·ate \-p(ə-)rət\ adj — in·tem·per·ate·ness n

in·tend \in-'tend\ vb 1 : to have in mind as a purpose or aim : PLAN 2 : to design for a specified use or future

in·ten·dant \in-'ten-dənt\ n : a governor or similar administrative official esp. under the French, Spanish, or Portuguese monarchies

¹in·tend·ed adj 1 : PROPOSED; esp : BETROTHED 2 : INTENTIONAL

²**intended** *n* **:** an affianced person **:** BETROTHED

in·tense \in-'tens\ *adj* **1 :** existing in an extreme degree **2 :** very large **:** CONSIDERABLE **3 :** strained or straining to the utmost **4 :** feeling deeply; *also* **:** deeply felt — **in·tense·ly** *adv*

in·ten·si·fy \in-'ten-sə-ˌfī\ *vb* **1 :** to make or become intense or more intensive **2 :** to make more acute **:** SHARPEN *syn* aggravate, heighten, enhance — **in·ten·si·fi·ca·tion** \-ˌten-sə-fə-'kā-shən\ *n*

in·ten·si·ty \in-'ten-sət-ē\ *n* **:** the quality or state of being intense **2 :** degree of strength, energy, or force ⟨~ of light⟩ ⟨~ of an electric current⟩ ⟨~ of a sound⟩

¹**in·ten·sive** \in-'ten-siv\ *adj* **1 :** involving or marked by special effort **:** THOROUGH, EXHAUSTIVE **2 :** serving to give emphasis (the ~ adverb *very* in "very cold") — **in·ten·sive·ly** *adv*

²**intensive** *n* **:** an intensive word, particle, or prefix

¹**in·tent** \in-'tent\ *n* **1 :** PURPOSE **2 :** the state of mind with which an act is done **:** VOLITION **3 :** AIM **4 :** MEANING, SIGNIFICANCE

²**intent** *adj* **1 :** directed with keen or eager attention **:** CONCENTRATED ⟨an ~ gaze⟩ **2 :** ENGROSSED; *also* **:** DETERMINED ⟨~ on having fun⟩ — **in·tent·ly** *adv* — **in·tent·ness** *n*

in·ten·tion \in-'ten-chən\ *n* **1 :** a determination to act in a certain way **2 :** PURPOSE, AIM, END *syn* intent, design, object, objective, goal

in·ten·tion·al \in-'tench-(ə-)nəl\ *adj* **:** done by intention or design **:** INTENDED — **in·ten·tion·al·ly** *adv*

in·ter \in-'tər\ *vb* **-terred; -ter·ring** [L *in* in + *terra* earth] **:** BURY

in·ter·ac·tion \ˌint-ər-'ak-shən\ *n* **:** mutual or reciprocal action or influence — **in·ter·act** \-'akt\ *vb*

in·ter alia \ˌint-ər-'ā-lē-ə, -'äl-ē-\ *adv* **:** among other things

in·ter·breed \ˌin-tər-'brēd\ *vb* **:** to breed together

in·ter·ca·lary \in-'tər-kə-ˌler-ē\ *adj* **1 :** INTERCALATED ⟨February 29 is an ~ day⟩ **2 :** INTERPOLATED

in·ter·ca·late \-ˌlāt\ *vb* **1 :** to insert (as a day) in a calendar **2 :** to insert between or among existing elements or layers — **in·ter·ca·la·tion** \-ˌtər-kə-'lā-shən\ *n*

in·ter·cede \ˌint-ər-'sēd\ *vb* **:** to act between parties with a view to reconciling differences **:** MEDIATE

in·ter·cept \ˌint-ər-'sept\ *vb* **1 :** to stop or interrupt the progress or course of **2 :** to cut through **:** INTERSECT — **in·ter·cep·tion** \-'sep-shən\ *n*

in·ter·ces·sion \ˌint-ər-'sesh-ən\ *n* **1 :** MEDIATION **2 :** prayer or petition in favor of another — **in·ter·ces·sor** \-'ses-ər\ *n* — **in·ter·ces·so·ry** \-'ses-(ə-)rē\ *adj*

¹**in·ter·change** \ˌint-ər-'chānj\ *vb* **1 :** to put each in the place of the other **2 :** EXCHANGE **3 :** to change places mutually — **in·ter·change·able** *adj*

²**in·ter·change** \'int-ər-ˌchānj\ *n* **1 :** EXCHANGE **2 :** a highway junction that by

separated levels permits passage between highways without crossing traffic streams

in·ter·col·le·giate \ˌint-ər-kə-'lē-j(ē-)ət\ *adj* **:** existing, carried on, or participating in activities between colleges

in·ter·com \'int-ər-ˌkäm\ *n* **:** INTERCOMMUNICATION SYSTEM

in·ter·com·mu·ni·ca·tion system \ˌint-ər-kə-ˌmyü-nə-'kā-shən-\ *n* **:** a two-way communication system with microphone and loudspeaker at each station for localized use

in·ter·con·ti·nen·tal \-ˌkänt-ᵊn-'ent-ᵊl\ *adj* **1 :** extending among or carried on between continents ⟨~ trade⟩ **2 :** capable of traveling between continents ⟨~ missile⟩

in·ter·course \'int-ər-ˌkōrs\ *n* **1 :** connection or dealings between persons or nations **:** COMMUNICATION **2 :** COPULATION

in·ter·cul·tur·al \ˌint-ər-'kʌlch-(ə-)rəl\ *adj* **:** occurring between or relating to two or more cultures

in·ter·de·nom·i·na·tion·al \-ˌnäm-ə-'nā-sh(ə-)nəl\ *adj* **:** involving or occurring between different denominations

in·ter·de·part·men·tal \ˌint-ər-di-ˌpärt-'ment-ᵊl, -ˌdē-\ *adj* **:** carried on between or involving different departments (as of a college)

in·ter·de·pen·dent \ˌint-ər-di-'pen-dənt\ *adj* **:** dependent upon one another — **in·ter·de·pen·dence** \-dəns\ *n*

in·ter·dict \ˌint-ər-'dikt\ *vb* **:** to prohibit by decree — **in·ter·dic·tion** \-'dik-shən\ *n*

in·ter·dis·ci·plin·ary \-'dis-ə-plə-ˌner-ē\ *adj* **:** involving two or more academic disciplines

¹**in·ter·est** \'in-t(ə-)rəst, -tə-ˌrest\ *n* **1 :** right, title, or legal share in something **2 :** WELFARE, BENEFIT; *esp* **:** SELF-INTEREST **3 :** a charge for borrowed money that is generally a percentage of the amount borrowed **:** the return received by capital on its investment **4** *pl* **:** a group financially interested in an industry or enterprise ⟨oil ~s⟩ **5 :** readiness to be concerned with or moved by an object or class of objects **6 :** the quality in a thing that arouses interest

²**interest** *vb* **1 :** AFFECT, CONCERN **2 :** to persuade or participate or engage **3 :** to engage the attention of

in·ter·est·ing *adj* **:** holding the attention **:** capable of arousing interest

in·ter·faith \ˌint-ər-'fāth\ *adj* **:** involving persons of different religious faiths

in·ter·fere \ˌint-ə(r)-'fiər\ *vb* **1 :** to come in collision or be in opposition **:** CLASH **2 :** to enter into the affairs of others **3 :** to affect one another **4 :** to run ahead of and provide blocking for the ballcarrier in football; *also* **:** to hinder illegally an attempt of a football player to receive a pass — **in·ter·fer·ence** \-'fir-əns\ *n*

in·ter·fuse \ˌint-ər-'fyüz\ *vb* **1 :** to combine by fusing **:** BLEND **2 :** INFUSE **3 :** PERVADE, PERMEATE

in·ter·im \'in-tə-rəm\ *n* **:** a time intervening **:** INTERVAL

ə abut; ᵊ kitten; ər further; a back; ā bake; ä cot, cart; aủ out; ch chin; e less; ē easy; g gift; i trip; ī life; j joke; ŋ sing; ō flow; ȯ flaw; ȯi coin; th thin; t͟h th's; ü loot; u̇ foot; y yet; yü few; yu̇ furious; zh vision

¹in·te·ri·or \in-'tir-ē-ər\ adj 1 : lying, occurring, or functioning within the limits : INSIDE, INNER 2 : remote from the surface, border, or shore : INLAND

²interior n 1 : INSIDE 2 : the inland part (as of a country) 3 : the internal affairs of a state or nation 4 : a scene or view of the interior of a building

in·ter·ject \,int-ər-'jekt\ vb : to throw in between or among other things : INSERT ⟨~ a remark⟩

in·ter·jec·tion \,int-ər-'jek-shən\ n : an exclamatory word (as ouch) — in·ter·jec·tion·al·ly adv

in·ter·lace \,int-ər-'lās\ vb 1 : to unite by or as if by lacing together : INTERWEAVE, INTERTWINE 2 : INTERSPERSE

in·ter·lard \,int-ər-'lärd\ vb : to insert or introduce at intervals : INTERSPERSE ⟨English ~ed with Spanish terms⟩

in·ter·leaf \'int-ər-,lēf\ n : a usu. blank leaf inserted between two leaves of a book

in·ter·leave \,int-ər-'lēv\ vb : to equip with an interleaf

¹in·ter·line \,int-ər-'līn\ vb : to insert between lines already written or printed; also : to insert something between the lines of ⟨~ a page⟩

²interline vb : to provide (as a coat) with an interlining

in·ter·lin·ear \,int-ər-'lin-ē-ər\ adj : inserted between lines already written or printed ⟨an ~ translation of a text⟩

in·ter·lin·ing \'int-ər-,lī-niŋ\ n : a lining (as of a coat) between the ordinary lining and the outside fabric

in·ter·link \,int-ər-'liŋk\ vb : to link together

in·ter·lock \,int-ər-'läk\ vb 1 : to engage or interlace together : lock together : UNITE 2 : to connect in such a way that action of one part affects action of another part or parts — in·ter·lock \'int-ər-,läk\ n

in·ter·loc·u·tor \,int-ər-'läk-yət-ər\ n 1 : one who takes part in dialogue or conversation 2 : a man in a minstrel show who questions the end men

in·ter·loc·u·to·ry \,int-ər-'läk-yə-,tōr-ē\ adj : pronounced during the progress of a legal action and having only provisional force ⟨an ~ decree⟩

in·ter·lop·er \,int-ər-'lō-pər, 'int-ər-,lō-\ n : INTRUDER

in·ter·lude \'int-ər-,lüd\ n 1 : a performance given between the acts of a play 2 : an intervening period, space, or event : INTERVAL ⟨an ~ of peace between wars⟩ 3 : a short piece of music inserted between the parts of a longer composition or a religious service

in·ter·lu·nar \,int-ər-'lü-nər\ adj : relating to the interval between the old and new moon when the moon is invisible

in·ter·mar·riage \,int-ər-'mar-ij\ n : marriage between members of different groups; also : marriage within one's own group

in·ter·mar·ry \-'mar-ē\ vb 1 : to marry each other 2 : to marry within a group 3 : to become connected by intermarriage

in·ter·med·dle \,int-ər-'med-ᵊl\ vb : MEDDLE, INTERFERE

¹in·ter·me·di·ary \,int-ər-'mēd-ē-,er-ē\ adj 1 : INTERMEDIATE 2 : acting as a mediator

²intermediary n : MEDIATOR, GO-BETWEEN

¹in·ter·me·di·ate \,int-ər-'mēd-ē-ət\ adj : being or occurring at the middle place or degree or between extremes

²intermediate n 1 : an intermediate term, object, or class 2 : MEDIATOR, GO-BETWEEN

in·ter·ment \in-'tər-mənt\ n : BURIAL

in·ter·mez·zo \,int-ər-'met-sō, -'med-zō\ n, pl -zi \-,sē, -,zē\ or -zos : a short movement connecting major sections of an extended musical work (as a symphony); also : a short independent instrumental composition

in·ter·mi·na·ble \(')in-'tərm-(ə-)nə-bəl\ adj : ENDLESS; esp : wearisomely protracted — in·ter·mi·na·bly adv

in·ter·min·gle \,int-ər-'miŋ-gəl\ vb : to mingle or mix together

in·ter·mis·sion \,int-ər-'mish-ən\ n 1 : INTERRUPTION, BREAK 2 : a temporary halt esp. in a public performance : PAUSE

in·ter·mit \,int-ər-'mit\ vb -mit·ted; -mit·ting : DISCONTINUE; also : to be intermittent

in·ter·mit·tent \,int-ər-'mit-ᵊnt\ adj : coming and going at intervals : repeatedly starting and stopping syn recurrent, periodic, alternate — in·ter·mit·tent·ly adv

in·ter·mix \,int-ər-'miks\ vb : to mix together : INTERMINGLE — in·ter·mix·ture \-'miks-chər\ n

¹in·tern \'in-,tərn, in-'tərn\ vb : to confine or impound esp. during a war

²in·tern or in·terne \'in-,tərn\ n : an advanced student or recent graduate (as in medicine) gaining supervised practical experience — in·tern·ship n

³in·tern \'in-,tərn\ vb : to act as an intern

in·ter·nal \in-'tərn-ᵊl\ adj 1 : INWARD, INTERIOR 2 : having to do with or situated in the inside of the body ⟨~ pain⟩ ⟨~ medicine⟩ 3 : relating or belonging to or existing within the mind : SUBJECTIVE 4 : INTRINSIC, INHERENT 5 : of or relating to the domestic affairs of a country or state ⟨~ revenue⟩ — in·ter·nal·ly adv

internal–combustion engine n : a heat engine in which combustion takes place (as in an automobile) instead of in a furnace

¹in·ter·na·tion·al \,int-ər-'nash-(ə-)nᵊl\ adj 1 : common to or affecting two or more nations ⟨~ trade⟩ 2 : of, relating to, or constituting a group having members in two or more nations ⟨~ movement⟩ — in·ter·na·tion·al·ly adv

²in·ter·na·tion·al \same, or -,nash-ə-'näl for 1\ n 1 : one of several socialist or communist organizations of international scope 2 : a labor union having locals in more than one country

in·ter·na·tion·al·ism n : a policy of political and economic cooperation among nations; also : an attitude favoring such a policy

in·ter·na·tion·al·ize vb : to make international; esp : to place under international control

in·ter·ne·cine \,int-ər-'nes-,ēn, -'nē-,sīn\ adj 1 : DEADLY; esp : mutually destructive 2 : of, relating to, or involving conflict within a group ⟨~ feuds⟩

in·tern·ee \,in-,tər-'nē\ n : an interned person

in·ter·nist \in-'tər-nəst\ *n* : a specialist in internal medicine esp. as distinguished from a surgeon

in·tern·ment \in-'tərn-mənt\ *n* : the act of interning : the state of being interned

in·ter·nun·cio \,int-ər-'nən-sē-,ō, -'nün-\ *n* : a papal legate of lower rank than a nuncio

in·ter·of·fice \-'of-əs\ *adj* : functioning or communicating between the offices of an organization ⟨an ∼ memo⟩

in·ter·plan·e·tary \-'plan-ə,ter-ē\ *adj* : existing, carried on, or operating between planets ⟨∼ space⟩ ⟨∼ travel⟩

in·ter·play \'int-ər-,plā\ *n* : INTERACTION

in·ter·po·late \in-'tər-pə-,lāt\ *vb* 1 : to change (as a text) by inserting new or foreign matter 2 : to insert (as words) into a text or into a conversation — **in·ter·po·la·tion** \-,tər-pə-'lā-shən\ *n*

in·ter·pose \,int-ər-'pōz\ *vb* 1 : to place between 2 : to thrust in : INTRUDE, INTERRUPT 3 : to inject between parts of a conversation or argument 4 : to be or come between : INTERVENE, MEDIATE **syn** interfere, intercede — **in·ter·po·si·tion** \-pə-'zish-ən\ *n*

in·ter·pret \in-'tər-prət\ *vb* 1 : to explain the meaning of; *also* : to act as an interpreter : TRANSLATE 2 : to understand according to individual belief, judgment, or interest : CONSTRUE 3 : to represent artistically ⟨∼s a role⟩ — **in·ter·pret·er** *n* — **in·ter·pre·tive** \-'tər-prət-iv\ *adj*

in·ter·pre·ta·tion \in-,tər-prə-'tā-shən\ *n* 1 : EXPLANATION 2 : an instance of artistic interpretation in performance or adaptation — **in·ter·pre·ta·tive** \-'tər-prə-,tāt-iv\ *adj*

in·ter·ra·cial \,int-ə(r)-'rā-shəl\ *adj* : of, involving, or designed for members of different races

in·ter·reg·num \,int-ə-'reg-nəm\ *n, pl* -nums *or* -na \-nə\ 1 : the time during which a throne is vacant between two successive reigns or regimes 2 : a pause in a continuous series

in·ter·re·late \,int-ə(r)-ri-'lāt\ *vb* : to bring into or have a mutual relationship — **in·ter·re·la·tion** \-ri-'lā-shən\ *n* — **in·ter·re·la·tion·ship** *n*

in·ter·ro·gate \in-'ter-ə-,gāt\ *vb* : to question esp. formally and systematically : ASK — **in·ter·ro·ga·tion** \-,ter-ə-'gā-shən\ *n* — **in·ter·ro·ga·tor** \-'ter-ə-,gāt-ər\ *n*

in·ter·rog·a·tive \,int-ə-'räg-ət-iv\ *adj* : asking a question ⟨∼ sentence⟩ — **interrogative** *n*

in·ter·rog·a·to·ry \,int-ə-'räg-ə-,tōr-ē\ *adj* : INTERROGATIVE

in·ter·rupt \,int-ə-'rəpt\ *vb* 1 : to stop or hinder by breaking in 2 : to break the uniformity or continuity of 3 : to break in upon an action; *esp* : to break in with questions or remarks while another is speaking — **in·ter·rup·tion** \-'rəp-shən\ *n* — **in·ter·rup·tive** \-'rəp-tiv\ *adj*

in·ter·scho·las·tic \,int-ər-skə-'las-tik\ *adj* : existing or carried on between schools

in·ter·school \-'skül\ *adj* : INTERSCHOLASTIC

in·ter·sect \,int-ər-'sekt\ *vb* : to cut or

divide by passing through : cut across : meet and cross : OVERLAP — **in·ter·sec·tion** \-'sek-shən\ *n*

in·ter·sperse \,int-ər-'spərs\ *vb* 1 : to insert at intervals among other things 2 : to place something at intervals in or among — **in·ter·sper·sion** \-'spər-zhən\ *n*

in·ter·state \,int-ər-'stāt\ *adj* : relating to, including, or connecting two or more states esp. of the U.S.

in·ter·stel·lar \-'stel-ər\ *adj* : located or taking place among the stars

in·ter·stice \in-'tər-stəs\ *n* : a space that intervenes between things : CHINK, CREVICE, INTERVAL : **in·ter·sti·tial** \,int-ər-'stish-əl\ *adj*

in·ter·tid·al \,int-ər-'tīd-ᵊl\ *adj* : of, relating to, or being the area that is above low-tide mark but exposed to tidal flooding

in·ter·twine \,int-ər-'twīn\ *vb* : to twine or twist together one with another : INTERLACE

in·ter·twist \-'twist\ *vb* : INTERTWINE

in·ter·ur·ban \,int-ər-'ər-bən\ *adj* : going between or connecting cities or towns

in·ter·val \'int-ər-vəl\ *n* 1 : a space of time between events or states : PAUSE 2 : a space between objects, units, or states 3 : the difference in pitch between two tones

in·ter·vene \,int-ər-'vēn\ *vb* 1 : to enter or appear as an unrelated feature or circumstance ⟨rain *intervened* and we postponed the trip⟩ 2 : to occur, fall, or come between points of time or between events 3 : to come in or between in order to stop, settle, or modify ⟨∼ in a quarrel⟩ 4 : to occur or lie between ⟨*intervening* mountains⟩ — **in·ter·ven·tion** \-ər-'ven-chən\ *n*

in·ter·ven·tion·ism *n* : interference by one country in the political affairs of another — **in·ter·ven·tion·ist** *n or adj*

in·ter·view \'int-ər-,vyü\ *n* 1 : a formal consultation 2 : a meeting at which a writer or reporter obtains information from a person; *also* : the written account of such a meeting — **interview** *vb* — **in·ter·view·er** *n*

in·ter·weave \,int-ər-'wēv\ *vb* : to weave or blend together : INTERTWINE, INTERMINGLE — **in·ter·wo·ven** \-'wō-vən\ *adj*

in·tes·tate \in-'tes-,tāt, -tət\ *adj* 1 : having made no valid will ⟨died ∼⟩ 2 : not disposed of by will ⟨∼ estate⟩

in·tes·tine \in-'tes-tən\ *n* : the tubular part of the alimentary canal that extends from stomach to anus and consists of a long narrow upper part (**small in·testine**) followed by a broader shorter lower part (**large intestine**) — **in·tes·ti·nal** \-tən-ᵊl\ *adj*

¹in·ti·mate \'int-ə-,māt\ *vb* 1 : ANNOUNCE, NOTIFY 2 : to communicate indirectly : HINT — **in·ti·ma·tion** \,int-ə-'mā-shən\ *n*

²in·ti·mate \'int-ə-mət\ *adj* 1 : INTRINSIC; *also* : INNERMOST 2 : marked by very close association, contact, or familiarity 3 : marked by a warm friendship 4 : suggesting informal warmth or privacy ⟨a small ∼ theater⟩ 5 : of a very personal or private nature

— in·ti·ma·cy \'int-ə-mə-sē\ n — in·ti·mate·ly adv

³in·ti·mate \'int-ə-mət\ n : an intimate friend, associate, or confidant

in·tim·i·date \in-'tim-ə-,dāt\ vb : to make timid or fearful : FRIGHTEN; esp : to compel or deter by or as if by threats syn cow, bulldoze, bully, browbeat — in·tim·i·da·tion \-,tim-ə-'dā-shən\ n

in·tinc·tion \in-'tiŋk-shən\ n : the administration of the sacrament of Communion by dipping the bread in the wine and giving it to the communicant

in·to \'in-tə, -tü\ prep 1 : to the inside of ⟨ran ~ the house⟩ 2 : to the state, condition, or form of ⟨got ~ trouble⟩ 3 : AGAINST ⟨ran ~ a wall⟩

in·tol·er·a·ble \(')in-'täl-(ə-)rə-bəl\ adj 1 : UNBEARABLE 2 : EXCESSIVE — in·tol·er·a·bly adv

in·tol·er·ant \(')in-'täl-ə-rənt\ adj 1 : unable to endure 2 : unwilling to endure 3 : unwilling to grant equal freedom of expression esp. in religious matters or social, political, or professional rights : BIGOTED — in·tol·er·ance n

in·to·na·tion \,in-tə-'nā-shən\ n 1 : the act of intoning and esp. of chanting 2 : something that is intoned 3 : the manner of singing, playing, or uttering tones 4 : the rise and fall in pitch of the voice in speech

in·tone \in-'tōn\ vb : to utter in musical or prolonged tones : CHANT

in to·to \in-'tōt-ō\ adv : TOTALLY, ENTIRELY ⟨accepted the plan in toto⟩

in·tox·i·cant \in-'täk-si-kənt\ n : something that intoxicates; esp : an alcoholic drink — intoxicant adj

in·tox·i·cate \in-'täk-sə-,kāt\ vb 1 : to make drunk 2 : to excite or elate to the point of enthusiasm or frenzy ⟨intoxicated with joy⟩ — in·tox·i·ca·tion \-,täk-sə-'kā-shən\ n

in·trac·ta·ble \(')in-'trak-tə-bəl\ adj : not easily controlled : OBSTINATE

in·tra·dos \in-'trā-,däs, in-'trā-\ n : the interior curve of an arch

in·tra·mu·ral \,in-trə-'myùr-əl\ adj : being or occurring within the walls or limits (as of a city or college) ⟨~ sports⟩

in·tran·si·geance \in-'tran-sə-jəns, -'tranz-\ n : INTRANSIGENCE

in·tran·si·gence \-jəns\ n : the quality or state of being intransigent

in·tran·si·gent \-jənt\ adj : UNCOMPROMISING; also : IRRECONCILABLE

in·tran·si·tive \(')in-'tran-sət-iv, -'tranz-\ adj : not transitive; esp : not having or containing an object required to complete its meaning — in·tran·si·tive·ly adv — in·tran·si·tive·ness n

in·tra·state \,in-trə-'stāt\ adj : existing or occurring within a state

in·tra·ve·nous \,in-trə-'vē-nəs\ adj : being within or entering by way of the veins — in·tra·ve·nous·ly adv

in·trench var of ENTRENCH

in·trep·id \in-'trep-əd\ adj : characterized by resolute fearlessness, fortitude, and endurance — in·tre·pid·i·ty \,in-trə-'pid-ət-ē\ n

in·tri·cate \'in-tri-kət\ adj 1 : COMPLICATED 2 : difficult to follow, understand, or solve — in·tri·ca·cy \-tri-kə-sē\ n — in·tri·cate·ly adv

¹in·trigue \in-'trēg\ vb 1 : to accomplish by intrigue 2 : to carry on an intrigue; esp : PLOT, SCHEME 3 : to arouse the

interest, desire, or curiosity of ⟨the story ~s me⟩

²in·trigue \in-,trēg, in-'trēg\ n 1 : a secret and involved stratagem : MACHINATION 2 : a clandestine love affair

in·trin·sic \in-'trin-zik, -sik\ adj : belonging to the essential nature or constitution of a thing 2 : REAL, ACTUAL — in·trin·si·cal adj — in·trin·si·cal·ly adv

in·tro·duce \,in-trə-'d(y)üs\ vb 1 : to lead or bring in esp. for the first time 2 : to bring into practice or use : INSTITUTE 3 : to cause to be acquainted 4 : to bring to notice : PRESENT 5 : to put in : INSERT syn insinuate, interpolate, interpose, interject — in·tro·duc·tion \-trə-'dək-shən\ n — in·tro·duc·to·ry \,in-trə-'dək-t(ə-)rē\ adj

in·tro·mit \,in-trə-'mit\ vb -mit·ted; -mit·ting : to send or put in : INSERT — in·tro·mis·sion \-'mish-ən\ n

in·tro·spec·tion \,in-trə-'spek-shən\ n : a reflective looking inward : an examination of one's own thoughts or feelings — in·tro·spec·tive \-'spek-tiv\ adj — in·tro·spec·tive·ly adv

in·tro·vert \'in-trə-,vərt\ n : a person more interested in his own mental life than in the world about him — in·tro·ver·sion \,in-trə-'vər-zhən\ n — introvert adj — in·tro·vert·ed \'in-trə-,vərt-əd\ adj

in·trude \in-'trüd\ vb 1 : to thrust, enter, or force in or upon 2 : ENCROACH, TRESPASS — in·trud·er n — in·tru·sion \-'trü-zhən\ n — in·tru·sive \-'trü-siv\ adj

intrust var of ENTRUST

in·tu·it \in-'t(y)ü-ət\ vb : to apprehend by intuition

in·tu·i·tion \,in-t(y)ü-'ish-ən\ n 1 : the power or faculty of knowing things without conscious reasoning 2 : quick and ready insight — in·tu·i·tive \in-'t(y)ü-ət-iv\ adj — in·tu·i·tive·ly adv

in·tu·mesce \,in-t(y)ü-'mes\ vb : ENLARGE, SWELL — in·tu·mes·cence n — in·tu·mes·cent adj

in·un·date \'in-ən-,dāt\ vb : to cover with or as if with a flood : OVERFLOW — in·un·da·tion \,in-ən-'dā-shən\ n

in·ure \in-'(y)ùr\ vb 1 : to accustom to accept something undesirable : HABITUATE, HARDEN 2 : to become of advantage : ACCRUE

in·urn \in-'ərn\ vb 1 : to enclose in an urn 2 : ENTOMB

in vac·uo \in-'vak-yə-,wō\ adv : in a vacuum

in·vade \in-'vād\ vb 1 : to enter for conquest or plunder 2 : to encroach upon 3 : to spread through and usu. harm ⟨germs ~ the tissues⟩ — in·vad·er n

¹in·val·id \(')in-'val-əd\ adj : being without foundation or force in fact, truth, or law : not valid

²in·va·lid \'in-və-ləd\ adj : defective in health : SICKLY

³in·va·lid \'in-və-ləd\ n : a person in usu. chronic ill health — in·va·lid·ism \-,iz-əm\ n

⁴in·va·lid \'in-və-ləd, -,lid\ vb 1 : to make sickly or disabled 2 : to remove from active duty by reason of sickness or disability

in·val·i·date \(')in-'val-ə-,dāt\ vb : to make invalid; esp : to weaken or make valueless

in·val·u·able \(')in-'val-yə-(wə-)bəl\ adj

: valuable beyond estimation : PRICE-LESS

in·vari·able \(')in-'ver-ē-ə-bəl\ *adj* : not changing or capable of change : CONSTANT — **in·vari·ably** *adv*

in·va·sion \in-'vā-zhən\ *n* : an act or instance of invading; *esp* : entry of an army into a country for conquest or plunder

in·vec·tive \in-'vek-tiv\ *n* **1** : an abusive expression or speech **2** : insulting or abusive language — **invective** *adj*

in·veigh \in-'vā\ *vb* : to protest or complain bitterly or vehemently : RAIL

in·vei·gle \in-'vā-gəl, -'vē-\ *vb* **1** : to win over by flattery : ENTICE **2** : to acquire by ingenuity or flattery

in·vent \in-'vent\ *vb* **1** : to think up : IMAGINE, FABRICATE ⟨~ an excuse⟩ **2** : to create or produce for the first time : DEVISE — **in·ven·tor** *n*

in·ven·tion \in-'ven-chən\ *n* **1** : INVENTIVENESS **2** : a creation of the imagination; *esp* : a false conception **3** : a device, contrivance, or process originated after study and experiment **4** : the act or process of inventing

in·ven·tive \in-'vent-iv\ *adj* **1** : CREATIVE, INGENIOUS ⟨an ~ composer⟩ **2** : characterized by invention ⟨an ~ turn of mind⟩ — **in·ven·tive·ness** *n*

in·ven·to·ry \'in-vən-ˌtōr-ē\ *n* **1** : an itemized list of current goods or assets **2** : SURVEY, SUMMARY **3** : STOCK, SUPPLY **4** : the act or process of taking an inventory — **inventory** *vb*

in·ver·ness \ˌin-vər-'nes\ *n* : a loose belted coat having a cape with a close round collar

in·verse \(')in-'vərs, 'in-ˌvərs\ *adj* : opposite in order, nature, or effect : REVERSED — **in·verse·ly** *adv*

in·ver·sion \in-'vər-zhən\ *n* **1** : the act or process of inverting **2** : a reversal of position, order, or relationship

in·vert \in-'vərt\ *vb* **1** : to turn upside down or inside out **2** : to turn inward **3** : to reverse in position, order, or relationship

¹in·ver·te·brate \(')in-'vərt-ə-brət, -ˌbrāt\ *adj* : lacking a spinal column; *also* : of or relating to invertebrates

²invertebrate *n* : an invertebrate animal

¹in·vest \in-'vest\ *vb* **1** : to install formally in an office or honor **2** : to furnish with power or authority : VEST **3** : to cover completely : ENVELOP **4** : CLOTHE, ADORN **5** : BESIEGE **6** : to endow with a quality or characteristic : INFUSE

²invest *vb* **1** : to commit money in order to earn a financial return **2** : to make use of for future benefits or advantages **3** : to make an investment — **in·ves·tor** *n*

in·ves·ti·gate \in-'ves-tə-ˌgāt\ *vb* : to observe or study by close examination and systematic inquiry — **in·ves·ti·ga·tion** \-ˌves-tə-'gā-shən\ *n* — **in·ves·ti·ga·tor** \-'ves-tə-ˌgāt-ər\ *n*

in·ves·ti·ture \in-'ves-tə-ˌchùr, -chər\ *n* **1** : the act of ratifying or establishing in office : CONFIRMATION **2** : something that covers or adorns

in·vest·ment \in-'ves(t)-mənt\ *n* **1** : an outer layer : ENVELOPE **2** : INVESTITURE **3** : BLOCKADE, SIEGE

²investment *n* : the outlay of money for income or profit; *also* : the sum invested or the property purchased

in·vet·er·ate \in-'vet-(ə-)rət\ *adj* **1** : firmly established by age or long persistence **2** : confirmed in a habit : HABITUAL ⟨an ~ smoker⟩ — **in·vet·er·a·cy** *n*

in·vid·i·ous \in-'vid-ē-əs\ *adj* **1** : tending to cause discontent, animosity, or envy **2** : ENVIOUS **3** : INJURIOUS — **in·vid·i·ous·ly** *adv*

in·vig·o·rate \in-'vig-ə-ˌrāt\ *vb* : to give life and energy to : ANIMATE — **in·vig·o·ra·tion** \-ˌvig-ə-'rā-shən\ *n*

in·vin·ci·ble \(')in-'vin-sə-bəl\ *adj* : incapable of being conquered, overcome, or subdued — **in·vin·ci·bil·i·ty** \(ˌ)in-ˌvin-sə-'bil-ət-ē\ *n* — **in·vin·ci·bly** \(')in-'vin-sə-blē\ *adv*

in·vi·o·la·ble \(')in-'vī-ə-lə-bəl\ *adj* **1** : safe from violation or profanation **2** : UNASSAILABLE — **in·vi·o·la·bil·i·ty** \(ˌ)in-ˌvī-ə-lə-'bil-ət-ē\ *n*

in·vi·o·late \(')in-'vī-ə-lət\ *adj* : not violated or profaned : PURE

in·vis·i·ble \(')in-'viz-ə-bəl\ *adj* **1** : incapable of being seen ⟨~ to the naked eye⟩ **2** : HIDDEN **3** : IMPERCEPTIBLE, INCONSPICUOUS — **in·vis·i·bil·i·ty** \(ˌ)in-ˌviz-ə-'bil-ət-ē\ *n* — **in·vis·i·bly** \(')in-'viz-ə-blē\ *adv*

in·vite \in-'vīt\ *vb* **1** : ENTICE, TEMPT **2** : to increase the likelihood of ⟨behavior that ~s criticism⟩ **3** : to request the presence or participation of : ASK **4** : to request formally ⟨*invited* them to be their leader⟩ **5** : ENCOURAGE ⟨~ bids on a contract⟩ — **in·vi·ta·tion** \ˌin-və-'tā-shən\ *n*

in·vit·ing \in-'vīt-iŋ\ *adj* : ATTRACTIVE, TEMPTING

in·vo·ca·tion \ˌin-və-'kā-shən\ *n* **1** : SUPPLICATION; *esp* : a prayer at the beginning of a service **2** : a formula for conjuring : INCANTATION

¹in·voice \'in-ˌvòis\ *n* **1** : an itemized list of goods shipped usu. specifying the price and the terms of sale : BILL **2** : a consignment of merchandise

²invoice *vb* : to make an invoice of : BILL

in·voke \in-'vōk\ *vb* **1** : to petition for help or support **2** : to appeal to or cite as authority ⟨~ a law⟩ **3** : to call forth by incantation : CONJURE ⟨~ spirits⟩ **4** : to make an earnest request for : SOLICIT **5** : to put into effect or operation **6** : to bring about : CAUSE

in·vol·un·tary \(')in-'väl-ən-ˌter-ē\ *adj* **1** : done contrary to or without choice **2** : COMPULSORY **3** : not subject to control by the will ⟨~ muscles⟩ — **in·vol·un·tar·i·ly** \(ˌ)in-ˌväl-ən-'ter-ə-lē\ *adv*

in·vo·lute \'in-və-ˌlüt\ *adj* **1** : curled spirally and usu. closely ⟨~ shell⟩ **2** : INVOLVED, INTRICATE

in·vo·lu·tion \ˌin-və-'lü-shən\ *n* **1** : the act or an instance of enfolding or entangling **2** : COMPLEXITY, INTRICACY

in·volve \in-'välv\ *vb* **1** : to draw in as a participant : ENGAGE, IMPLICATE **2** : ENVELOP **3** : to relate closely : CONNECT **4** : INCLUDE **5** : ENTAIL, IMPLY **6** : AFFECT **7** : to occupy fully : ABSORB, ENGROSS ⟨*involved* in a game of chess⟩

in·vul·ner·a·ble \(')in-'vəl-nə-rə-bəl\

ə abut; ᵊ kitten; ər further; a back; ā bake; ä cot, cart; aù out; ch chin; e less; ē easy; g gift; i trip; ī life; j joke; ŋ sing; ō flow; ò flaw; òi coin; th thin; th̲ this; ü loot; ù̇ foot; y yet; yü few; yù̇ furious; zh vision *adj* **1** : incapable of being wounded, injured, or damaged   **2** : immune to or proof against attack — **in·vul·ner·a·bil·i·ty** \(,)in-,vəl-nə-rə-'bil-ət-ē\ *n* — **in·vul·ner·a·bly** \(')in-'vəl-nə-rə-blē\ *adv*

¹**in·ward** \'in-wərd\ *adj* **1** : situated on the inside : INNER   **2** : MENTAL; *also* : SPIRITUAL ⟨~ peace⟩   **3** : directed toward the interior

²**inward** *or* **in·wards** \-wərdz\ *adv* **1** : toward the inside, center, or interior   **2** : toward the inner being

in·ward·ly \'in-wərd-lē\ *adv* **1** : MENTALLY, SPIRITUALLY   **2** : INTERNALLY ⟨bled ~⟩   **3** : to oneself : PRIVATELY ⟨cursed ~⟩   **4** : toward the center or interior

in·wards \'in-ərdz, -wərdz\ *n pl* : INNARDS

in·wrought \(')in-'rȯt\ *adj* : having a decorative element worked or woven in : ORNAMENTED

io·dide \'ī-ə-,dīd\ *n* : a compound of iodine with another element or a radical

io·dine \'ī-ə-,dīn, -əd-ʰn\ *n* [F *iode* iodine, fr. Gk *ioeidēs* violet-colored, fr. *ion* violet; so called fr. its violet-colored vapor] : a nonmetallic chemical element used in medicine and photography

ion \'ī-ən, 'ī-,än\ *n* : an electrically charged particle or group of atoms — **ion·ic** \ī-'än-ik\ *adj*

io·ta \ī-'ōt-ə\ *n* : a very small quantity ⟨JOT ⟨not an ~ of truth in the story⟩

ip·so fac·to \,ip-sō-'fak-tō\ *adv* : by the very nature of the case

Ira·ni·an \ir-'ā-nē-ən\ *n* : a native or inhabitant of Iran — **Iranian** *adj*

Iraqi \i-'räk-ē\ *n* : a native or inhabitant of Iraq — **Iraqi** *adj*

iras·ci·ble \ir-'as-ə-bəl, ī-'ras-\ *adj* : marked by hot temper and easily provoked anger **syn** choleric, testy, touchy, cranky, cross — **iras·ci·bil·i·ty** \ir-,as-ə-'bil-ət-ē, ī-,ras-\ *n*

irate \ī-'rāt\ *adj* **1** : roused to or given to ire : INCENSED   **2** : arising from anger ⟨~ words⟩ — **irate·ly** *adv*

ire \'ī(ə)r\ *n* : ANGER, WRATH — **ire·ful** \-fəl\ *adj*

iren·ic \ī-'ren-ik\ *adj* : conducive to or operating toward peace or conciliation

ir·i·des·cence \,ir-ə-'des-ʰns\ *n* : a rainbowlike play of colors — **ir·i·des·cent** \-ʰnt\ *adj*

irid·i·um \ir-'id-ē-əm\ *n* : a hard brittle very heavy metallic chemical element used in alloys

iris \'ī-rəs\ *n, pl* **iris·es** *or* **iri·des** \'ī-rə-,dēz, 'ir-ə-\ **1** : the colored part around the pupil of the eye   **2** : a plant with linear basal leaves and large showy flowers

Irish \'ī(ə)r-ish\ *n* **1** Irish *pl* : the people of Ireland   **2** : the Celtic language of Ireland — **Irish** *adj* — **Irish·man** \-mən\ *n*

irk \'ərk\ *vb* : to make weary, irritated, or bored : ANNOY

irk·some \-səm\ *adj* : tending to irk : TEDIOUS, ANNOYING — **irk·some·ly** *adv*

¹**iron** \'ī(ə)rn\ *n* **1** : a metallic chemical element that rusts easily, is attracted by magnets, can be readily shaped, and is vital to biological processes   **2** : something (as a utensil) made of metal and esp. iron; *also* : something (as handcuffs) used to bind or restrain ⟨put them in ~s⟩   **3** : STRENGTH, HARDNESS

²**iron** *vb* **1** : to press or smooth with or as if with a heated flatiron   **2** : to remove by ironing ⟨~ out wrinkles⟩

iron-bound \-'baund\ *adj* **1** : HARSH, RUGGED   **2** : STERN, RIGOROUS

¹**iron-clad** \-'klad\ *adj* **1** : sheathed in iron armor   **2** : RIGOROUS, EXACTING

²**iron-clad** \-,klad\ *n* : an armored naval vessel

iron curtain *n* : a political, military, or ideological barrier that cuts off and isolates an area; *esp* : one between an area under Soviet Russian control and other areas

iron·ic \ī-'rän-ik\ *adj* **1** : of, relating to, or marked by irony   **2** : given to irony — **iron·i·cal** *adj* — **iron·i·cal·ly** *adv*

iron lung *n* : a device for artificial respiration (as in polio) that encloses the chest or body in a chamber in which changes of pressure force air into and out of the lungs

iron·ware \'ī(-ə)rn-,waər\ *n* : articles made of iron

iron·work \-,wərk\ *n* **1** : work in iron   **2** *pl* : a mill or building where iron or steel is smelted or heavy iron or steel products are made

iro·ny \'ī-rə-nē\ *n* **1** : the use of words to express the opposite of what one really means   **2** : incongruity between the actual result of a sequence of events and the expected result

ir·ra·di·ate \ir-'ād-ē-,āt\ *vb* **1** : ILLUMINATE   **2** : ENLIGHTEN   **3** : to treat by exposure to radiation   **4** : RADIATE — **ir·ra·di·a·tion** \-,ād-ē-'ā-shən\ *n*

ir·ra·tio·nal \(')ir-'ash-(ə-)nəl\ *adj* **1** : incapable of reasoning ⟨~ beasts⟩; *also* : defective in mental power ⟨~ with fever⟩   **2** : not based on reason ⟨~ fears⟩ — **ir·ra·tio·nal·ly** *adv*

ir·re·claim·able \,ir-i-'klā-mə-bəl\ *adj* : incapable of being reclaimed

ir·rec·on·cil·able \(')ir-'ek-ən-,sī-lə-bəl\ *adj* : impossible to reconcile, adjust, or harmonize — **ir·rec·on·cil·abil·i·ty** \(,)ir-,ek-ən-,sī-lə-'bil-ət-ē\ *n*

ir·re·cov·er·able \,ir-i-'kəv-(ə-)rə-bəl\ *adj* : not capable of being recovered or rectified : IRREPARABLE

ir·re·deem·able \,ir-i-'dē-mə-bəl\ *adj* **1** : not redeemable; *esp* : not terminable by payment of the principal ⟨an ~ bond⟩   **2** : not convertible into gold or silver at the will of the holder   **3** : admitting of no change or reform : HOPELESS

ir·re·den·tism \,ir-i-'den-,tiz-əm\ *n* : a principle or policy directed toward the incorporation of a territory historically or ethnically part of another into that other — **ir·re·den·tist** \-'dent-əst\ *n or adj*

ir·re·duc·ible \,ir-i-'d(y)ü-sə-bəl\ *adj* : not reducible

ir·ref·ra·ga·ble \(')ir-'ef-rə-gə-bəl\ *adj* : impossible to deny or refute : INVIOLABLE

ir·re·fut·able \,ir-i-'fyüt-ə-bəl, (')ir-'ef-yət-\ *adj* : impossible to refute : INDISPUTABLE, INCONTROVERTIBLE

ir·reg·u·lar \(')ir-'eg-yə-lər\ *adj* **1** : not regular : not natural or uniform   **2** : not conforming to the normal or usual manner of inflection ⟨~ verbs⟩ — **ir·reg·u·lar·i·ty** \(,)ir-,eg-yə-'lar-ət-ē\ *n* — **ir·reg·u·lar·ly** \(')ir-'eg-yə-lər-lē\ *adv*

ir·rel·e·vant \(')ir-'el-ə-vənt\ *adj* : not relevant : INAPPLICABLE, FOREIGN — **ir·rel·e·vance** \-vəns\ *n*

ir·re·li·gious \ˌir-i-'lij-əs\ *adj* : lacking religious emotions, doctrines, or practices

ir·re·me·di·a·ble \ˌir-i-'mēd-ē-ə-bəl\ *adj* : impossible to remedy or correct : INCURABLE

ir·re·mov·able \ˌir-i-'mü-və-bəl\ *adj* : not removable

ir·rep·a·ra·ble \(')ir-'ep-(ə-)rə-bəl\ *adj* : impossible to make good, undo, repair, or remedy : IRRETRIEVABLE ⟨~ damage⟩

ir·re·place·able \ˌir-i-'plā-sə-bəl\ *adj* : not replaceable

ir·re·press·ible \ˌir-i-'pres-ə-bəl\ *adj* : impossible to repress, restrain, or control ⟨~ laughter⟩

ir·re·proach·able \ˌir-i-'prō-chə-bəl\ *adj* : not reproachable : BLAMELESS

ir·re·sist·ible \ˌir-i-'zis-tə-bəl\ *adj* : impossible to successfully resist — **ir·re·sist·ibly** *adv*

ir·res·o·lute \(')ir-'ez-ə-ˌlüt\ *adj* : uncertain how to act or proceed : VACILLATING — **ir·res·o·lute·ly** *adv* — **ir·res·o·lu·tion** \(ˌ)ir-ˌez-ə-'lü-shən\ *n*

ir·re·spec·tive of \ˌir-i-'spek-tiv-\ *prep* : without regard to

ir·re·spon·si·ble \ˌir-i-'spän-sə-bəl\ *adj* : not responsible — **ir·re·spon·si·bil·i·ty** \-ˌspän-sə-'bil-ət-ē\ *n* — **ir·re·spon·si·bly** \-'spän-sə-blē\ *adv*

ir·re·triev·able \ˌir-i-'trē-və-bəl\ *adj* : not retrievable : IRRECOVERABLE

ir·rev·er·ence \(')ir-'ev-(ə-)rəns\ *n* 1 : lack of reverence 2 : an irreverent act or utterance — **ir·rev·er·ent** *adj*

ir·re·vers·ible \ˌir-i-'vər-sə-bəl\ *adj* : incapable of being reversed

ir·rev·o·ca·ble \(')ir-'ev-ə-kə-bəl\ *adj* : incapable of being revoked or recalled : UNALTERABLE — **ir·rev·o·ca·bly** *adv*

ir·ri·gate \'ir-ə-ˌgāt\ *vb* : to supply (as land) with water by artificial means; *also* : to flush with liquid — **ir·ri·ga·tion** \ˌir-ə-'gā-shən\ *n*

ir·ri·ta·ble \'ir-ət-ə-bəl\ *adj* : capable of being irritated; *esp* : readily or easily irritated — **ir·ri·ta·bil·i·ty** \ˌir-ət-ə-'bil-ət-ē\ *n* — **ir·ri·ta·bly** \-ət-ə-blē\ *adv*

ir·ri·tate \'ir-ə-ˌtāt\ *vb* 1 : to excite to anger : EXASPERATE 2 : to act as a stimulus toward : STIMULATE; *also* : to make sore or inflamed — **ir·ri·tant** \'ir-ə-tənt\ *adj or n* — **ir·ri·ta·tion** \ˌir-ə-'tā-shən\ *n*

ir·rupt \(')ir-'əpt\ *vb* 1 : to rush in forcibly or violently : INTRUDE 2 : to increase suddenly in numbers ⟨rabbits ~ in cycles⟩ — **ir·rup·tion** \-'əp-shən\ *n*

is *pres 3d sing of* BE

-ish \ish\ *adj suffix* 1 : of, relating to, or being (Finn*ish*) 2 : characteristic of (boy*ish*) : having the undesirable qualities of (mul*ish*) 3 : having a touch or trace of : somewhat (purpl*ish*) 4 : having the approximate age of (forty*ish*) 5 : being or occurring at the approximate time of (eight*ish*)

isin·glass \'īz-ⁿn-ˌglas, 'ī-zin-\ *n* 1 : a gelatin obtained from the air bladders of various fish 2 : MICA

Is·lam \is-'läm, iz-, -'lam\ *n* : the religious faith of Muslims; *also* : the civilization built on this faith — **Is·lam·ic** \is-'läm-ik, iz-, -'lam-\ *adj*

is·land \'ī-lənd\ *n* 1 : a body of land surrounded by water and smaller than a continent 2 : something resembling an island by its isolated or surrounded position

is·land·er *n* : a native or inhabitant of an island

isle \'īl\ *n* : ISLAND; *esp* : a small island

is·let \'ī-lət\ *n* : a small island

ism \'iz-əm\ *n* : a distinctive doctrine, cause, or theory

-ism \ˌiz-əm\ *n suffix* 1 : act : practice : process (critic*ism*) 2 : manner of action or behavior characteristic of a (specified) person or thing 3 : state : condition : property (barbarian*ism*) 4 : abnormal state or condition resulting from excess of a (specified) thing (alcohol*ism*) or marked by resemblance to (such) a person or thing (mongol*ism*) 5 : doctrine : theory : cult (Buddh*ism*) 6 : adherence to a system or a class of principles (stoic*ism*) 7 : characteristic or peculiar feature or trait (colloquial*ism*)

iso·bar \'ī-sə-ˌbär\ *n* : a line on a map connecting places of equal barometric pressure

iso·late \'ī-sə-ˌlāt, 'is-ə-\ *vb* : to place or keep by itself : separate from others — **iso·la·tion** \ˌī-sə-'lā-shən, ˌis-ə-\ *n*

iso·la·tion·ism \ˌī-sə-'lā-shə-ˌniz-əm, ˌis-ə-\ *n* : a policy of national isolation by abstention from international political and economic relations (as alliances) — **iso·la·tion·ist** \-sh(ə-)nəst\ *n or adj*

iso·mer \'ī-sə-mər\ *n* : any of two or more chemical compounds that contain the same numbers of atoms of the same elements but differ in structural arrangement and properties — **iso·mer·ic** \ˌī-sə-'mer-ik\ *adj*

isos·ce·les \ī-'säs-ə-ˌlēz\ *adj* : having two equal sides (an ~ triangle)

iso·tope \'ī-sə-ˌtōp\ *n* : any of two or more species of atoms of the same chemical element nearly identical in chemical behavior but differing in the number of neutrons — **iso·top·ic** \ˌī-sə-'täp-ik, -'tōp-\ *adj*

Is·rae·li \iz-'rā-lē\ *n* : a native or inhabitant of the Republic of Israel — **Is·rae·li** *adj*

Is·ra·el·ite \'iz-rē-ə-ˌlīt\ *n* : a member of the Hebrew people descended from Jacob — **Israelite** *adj*

is·su·ance \'ish-ù-əns\ *n* : the act of issuing or giving out esp. officially

¹is·sue \'ish-ü\ *n* 1 *pl* : proceeds from a source of revenue (as an estate) 2 : the action of going, coming, or flowing out : EGRESS, EMERGENCE 3 : EXIT, OUTLET, VENT 4 : OFFSPRING, PROGENY 5 : OUTCOME, RESULT 6 : a point of debate or controversy; *also* : the point at which an unsettled matter is ready for a decision 7 : a discharge (as of blood) from the body 8 : something coming forth from a specified source ⟨~s of a disordered imagination⟩ 9 : the act of officially giving out or printing : PUBLICATION; *also* : the quantity of things given out at one time ⟨a new ~ of stamps⟩

²issue *vb* 1 : to go, come, or flow out 2 : to come forth or cause to come forth : EMERGE, DISCHARGE, EMIT 3 : ACCRUE 4 : to descend from a speci-

---

ə abut; ᵊ kitten; ər further; a back; ā bake; ä cot, cart; aù out; ch chin; e less; ē easy; g gift; i trip; ī life; j joke; ŋ sing; ō flow; ò flaw; òi coin; th thin; t̲h̲ this; ü loot; ù foot; y yet; yü few; yù furious; zh vision

fied parent or ancestor **5 :** EMANATE, RESULT **6 :** to appear through issuance or publication **7 :** to have an outcome **:** result in **8 :** to put forth or distribute officially ⟨~ rifles to soldiers⟩ **9 :** PUBLISH

¹**-ist** \əst\ *n suffix* **1 :** one that performs a (specified) action ⟨cycl*ist*⟩ **:** one that makes or produces ⟨novel*ist*⟩ **2 :** one that plays a (specified) musical instrument ⟨harp*ist*⟩ **3 :** one that operates a (specified) mechanical instrument or contrivance ⟨automobil*ist*⟩ **4 :** one that specializes in a (specified) art or science or skill ⟨geolog*ist*⟩ **5 :** one that adheres to or advocates a (specified) doctrine or system or code of behavior ⟨social*ist*⟩ or that of a (specified) individual ⟨Darwin*ist*⟩

²**-ist** *adj suffix* **:** of, relating to, or characteristic of ⟨dilettant*ist*⟩

isth·mi·an \'is-mē-ən\ *adj* **:** of, relating to, or situated in or near an isthmus

isth·mus \'is-məs\ *n* **:** a narrow strip of land connecting two larger portions of land

-is·tic \'is-tik\ *also* **-is·ti·cal** \-ti-kəl\ *adj suffix* **:** of, relating to, or characteristic of ⟨altru*istic*⟩

¹**it** \(')it, ət\ *pron* **1 :** that one — used of a lifeless thing, a plant, a person or animal, or an abstract entity ⟨~'s a big building⟩ ⟨~'s a shade tree⟩ ⟨who is ~⟩ ⟨beauty is everywhere and ~ is a source of joy⟩ **2 :** — used as an anticipatory subject or object ⟨~'s good to see you⟩ ⟨I find ~ odd that you should mention that⟩

²**it** \'it\ *n* **:** the player in a game who performs a function (as trying to catch others in a game of tag) essential to the nature of the game

Ital·ian \ə-'tal-yən, i-\ *n* **1 :** a native or inhabitant of Italy **2 :** the language of Italy — **Italian** *adj*

ital·ic \ə-'tal-ik, i-, I-\ *adj* **:** relating to type in which the letters slope up toward the right (as in "*italic*") — **italic** *n*

ital·i·cize \-'tal-ə-‚sīz\ *vb* **:** to print in italics

itch \'ich\ *n* **1 :** an uneasy irritating skin sensation related to pain **2 :** a skin disorder accompanied by an itch **3 :** a

troublesome persistent desire — **itch** *vb* — **itchy** *adj*

-ite \‚īt\ *n suffix* **1 :** native **:** resident ⟨Brooklyn*ite*⟩ **2 :** descendant ⟨Ishmael*ite*⟩ **3 :** adherent **:** follower ⟨Lenin*ite*⟩ **4 :** product ⟨vulcan*ite*⟩ **5 :** mineral **:** rock ⟨quartz*ite*⟩

item \'īt-əm\ *n* [L, likewise, also] **1 :** a separate particular in a list, account, or series **:** ARTICLE **2 :** a separate piece of news (as in a newspaper)

item·ize \'īt-ə-‚mīz\ *vb* **:** to set down in detail or by particulars **:** LIST

it·er·ate \'it-ə-‚rāt\ *vb* **:** REITERATE, REPEAT — **it·er·a·tion** \‚it-ə-'rā-shən\ *n*

itin·er·ant \ī-'tin-ə-rənt, ə-\ *adj* **:** traveling from place to place; *esp* **:** covering a circuit ⟨an ~ preacher⟩

itin·er·ary \ī-'tin-ə-‚rer-ē, ə-\ *n* **1 :** the route of a journey or the proposed outline of one **2 :** a travel diary **3 :** a traveler's guidebook

its \(‚)its, əts\ *adj* **:** of or relating to it or itself

it·self \it-'self, ət-\ *pron* **:** its self **:** IT — used reflexively, for emphasis, or in absolute constructions

-i·ty \ət-ē\ *n suffix* **:** quality **:** state **:** degree ⟨alkalin*ity*⟩

-ive \iv\ *adj suffix* **:** that performs or tends toward an (indicated) action ⟨correct*ive*⟩

ivo·ry \'īv-(ə-)rē\ *n* **1 :** the hard creamy-white material composing elephants' tusks **2 :** a variable color averaging a pale yellow **3 :** something (as dice or piano keys) made of ivory or of a similar substance

ivy \'ī-vē\ *n* **:** a trailing woody vine with evergreen leaves and small black berries

-ize \‚īz\ *vb suffix* **1 :** cause to be or conform to or resemble ⟨system*ize*⟩ **:** cause to be formed into ⟨union*ize*⟩ **2 :** subject to a (specified) action ⟨satir*ize*⟩ **3 :** saturate, treat, or combine with ⟨macadam*ize*⟩ **4 :** treat like ⟨idol*ize*⟩ **5 :** become **:** become like ⟨crystall*ize*⟩ **6 :** be productive in or of **:** engage in a (specified) activity ⟨philosoph*ize*⟩ **7 :** adopt or spread the manner of activity or the teaching of ⟨calvin*ize*⟩ — **-iza·tion** \ə-'zā-shən, (*not shown elsewhere in vocabulary*) ī-'zā-\ *n suffix*

---

j \'jā\ *n, often cap* **:** the 10th letter of the English alphabet

¹**jab** \'jab\ *vb* **jabbed; jab·bing :** to thrust quickly or abruptly **:** POKE

²**jab** *n* **:** a usu. short straight punch

jab·ber \'jab-ər\ *vb* **:** to talk rapidly, indistinctly, or unintelligibly **:** CHATTER — **jabber** *n*

jab·ber·wocky \-‚wäk-ē\ *n* **:** meaningless speech or writing

ja·bot \zha-'bō\ *n* **:** a ruffle (as of lace) worn down the front of a dress or shirt

ja·cinth \'jās-‚nth\ *n* **:** HYACINTH

¹**jack** \'jak\ *n* **1 :** a mechanical device; *esp* **:** one used to raise a heavy body a short distance **2 :** a small national flag flown by a ship **3 :** a playing card bearing the figure of a man **4 :** a small target ball in lawn bowling **5 :** a small 6-pointed metal object used in a game (jacks) **6 :** an electrical socket into which a plug is inserted for making

connection **7 :** a male donkey

²**jack** *vb* **1 :** to raise by means of a jack **2 :** INCREASE ⟨~ up prices⟩

jack·al \'jak-əl, -‚ól\ *n* **:** an Old World wild dog smaller than the related wolves

jack·a·napes \-ə-‚nāps\ *n* **1 :** MONKEY, APE **2 :** an impudent or conceited person

jack·ass \-‚as\ *n* **1 :** a male ass; *also* **:** DONKEY **2 :** a stupid person **:** FOOL

jack·boot \-‚büt\ *n* **:** a heavy military boot of glossy black leather extending above the knee

jack·daw \-‚dó\ *n* **:** a black and gray Eurasian crowlike bird

jack·et \'jak-ət\ *n* **1 :** a garment for the upper body usu. having a front opening, collar, and sleeves **2 :** an outer covering or casing ⟨a book ~⟩ — **jack·et·ed** *adj*

Jack Frost *n* **:** frost or frosty weather personified

¹jack·knife \'jak-ˌnīf\ n 1 : a large strong pocketknife 2 : a dive in which the diver bends from the waist and touches his ankles before straightening out

²jackknife vb : to turn or rise and form an angle of 90 degrees or less with each other — used esp. of a pair of connected vehicles

jack·leg \'jak-ˌleg\ adj 1 : lacking skill or training (~ carpenter) 2 : MAKESHIFT

jack-of-all-trades n, pl **jacks-of-all-trades** : one who is able to do passable work at various trades

jack·pot \-ˌpät\ n 1 : a large sum of money formed by the accumulation of stakes from previous play (as in poker) 2 : an impressive and often unexpected success or reward

jack·rab·bit \-ˌrab-ət\ n : a large hare of western No. America with very long hind legs

jac·quard \'jak-ˌärd\ n, often cap : a fabric of intricate variegated weave or pattern

¹jade \'jād\ n 1 : a broken-down, vicious, or worthless horse 2 : a disreputable woman

²jade vb 1 : to wear out by overwork or abuse 2 : to become weary syn exhaust, fatigue, tire

³jade n : a usu. green gemstone that takes a high polish

jag \'jag\ n : a sharp projecting part (as of rock)

jag·ged \'jag-əd\ adj : sharply notched (a ~ edge)

jag·uar \'jag-ˌwär\ n : a black-spotted tropical American cat that is larger and stockier than the Old World leopard

jai alai \'hī-ˌlī\ n : a court game played by two or four players with a ball and a curved wicker basket strapped to the right wrist

¹jail \'jāl\ n : PRISON; esp : one for persons held in temporary custody

²jail vb : to confine in a jail

jail·bird \-ˌbərd\ n : a person confined in jail

jail·break \-ˌbrāk\ n : a forcible escape from jail

jail·er or **jail·or** \'jā-lər\ n : a keeper of a jail

jal·ap \'jal-əp, 'jäl-\ n : a purgative drug from the root of a Mexican plant related to the morning glory; also : this root or plant

ja·lopy \jə-'läp-ē\ n : a dilapidated automobile

jal·ou·sie \'jal-ə-sē\ n : a blind, window, or door with adjustable horizontal slats or louvers for control of light and air

¹jam \'jam\ vb **jammed; jam·ming** 1 : to press into a close or tight position 2 : to push forcibly (~ on the brakes) 3 : CRUSH, BRUISE 4 : to cause to become wedged so as to be unworkable; also : to become unworkable through the jamming of a movable part 5 : to make unintelligible by sending out interfering signals or messages

²jam n 1 : a crowded mass that impedes or blocks (traffic ~) 2 : a difficult state of affairs

³jam n : a food made by boiling fruit and sugar to a thick consistency

jamb \'jam\ n : an upright piece forming the side of an opening (as of a door)

jam·bo·ree \ˌjam-bə-'rē\ n : a large festive gathering

jan·gle \'jaŋ-gəl\ vb : to make a harsh or discordant sound — **jangle** n

jan·i·tor \'jan-ət-ər\ n : a person who has the care of a building (as a school or an apartment)

Jan·u·ary \'jan-yə-ˌwer-ē\ n : the 1st month of the year having 31 days

Jap·a·nese \ˌjap-ə-'nēz\ n, pl **Japanese** 1 : a native or inhabitant of Japan 2 : the language of Japan — **Japanese** adj

¹jape \'jāp\ vb 1 : JOKE 2 : MOCK

²jape n : JEST, GIBE

¹jar \'jär\ vb **jarred; jar·ring** 1 : to make a harsh or discordant sound 2 : to have a harsh or disagreeable effect 3 : VIBRATE, SHAKE

²jar n 1 : a harsh discordant sound 2 : JOLT 3 : QUARREL, DISPUTE 4 : a painful effect : SHOCK

³jar n : a broad-mouthed container usu. of glass or earthenware

jar·di·niere \ˌjärd-ᵊn-'ir\ n : an ornamental stand or pot for plants or flowers

jar·gon \'jär-gən, -ˌgän\ n 1 : confused unintelligible language 2 : the special vocabulary of a particular group or activity 3 : obscure and often pretentious language

jas·mine \'jaz-mən\ n : any of various climbing shrubs with fragrant flowers

jas·per \'jas-pər\ n : an opaque quartz that is red, green, or yellow in color

¹jaun·dice \'jón-dəs\ n : yellowish discoloration of skin, tissues, and body fluids by bile pigments; also : a disorder marked by jaundice

²jaundice vb : PREJUDICE

jaunt \'jónt\ n : a short trip usu. for pleasure

jaun·ty \'jónt-ē\ adj : sprightly in manner or appearance : LIVELY syn debonair, perky, cocky — **jaun·ti·ly** adv — **jaun·ti·ness** n

jav·e·lin \'jav-(ə-)lən\ n 1 : a light spear 2 : a slender metal-tipped shaft of wood thrown for distance in a track-and-field contest

jaw \'jó\ n 1 : either of the bony or cartilaginous structures that support the soft tissues enclosing the mouth and usu. bear teeth; also : the parts forming the walls of the mouth and serving to open and close it — usu. used in pl. 2 : one of a pair of movable parts for holding or crushing something — **jaw·bone** \-ˌbōn, -ˌbōn\ n

jaw·break·er \-ˌbrā-kər\ n 1 : a word difficult to pronounce 2 : a round hard candy

jay \'jā\ n : any of various noisy brightly colored birds smaller than the related crows

jay·walk \'jā-ˌwók\ vb : to cross a street carelessly without regard to traffic regulations — **jay·walk·er** n

¹jazz \'jaz\ vb : ENLIVEN (~ things up)

²jazz n 1 : American music characterized by improvisation, syncopated rhythms, and contrapuntal ensemble playing 2 : empty talk : STUFF

jazzy adj 1 : having the characteristics

of jazz **2** : marked by unrestraint, animation, or flashiness

jeal·ous \'jel-əs\ adj **1** : demanding complete devotion **2** : suspicious of a rival or of one believed to enjoy an advantage **3** : VIGILANT ⟨~ of his rights⟩ **4** : distrustfully watchful — **jeal·ous·ly** adv — **jeal·ou·sy** \-ə-sē\ n

jeans \'jēnz\ n pl : pants made of durable twilled cotton cloth

1jeer \'jiər\ vb **1** : to speak or cry out in derision **2** : RIDICULE

2jeer n : TAUNT

Je·ho·vah \ji-'hō-və\ n : 2GOD

je·hu \'jē-h(y)ü\ n : a driver of a coach or cab

je·june \ji-'jün\ adj **1** : lacking interest or significance — **2** : DULL **2** : CHILDISH ⟨~ remarks⟩

jell \'jel\ vb **1** : to come to the consistency of jelly **2** : to take shape ⟨his opinions slowly ~ed⟩

jel·ly \'jel-ē\ n **1** : a food with a soft somewhat elastic consistency due usu. to the presence of gelatin or pectin; esp : a fruit product made by boiling sugar and the juice of a fruit **2** : a substance resembling jelly in consistency — **jelly** vb

jel·ly·fish \-,fish\ n : a sea animal with a saucer-shaped jellylike body

jen·net \'jen-ət\ n **1** : a small Spanish horse **2** : a female donkey

jeop·ar·dy \'jep-ərd-ē\ n : exposure to death, loss, or injury syn peril, hazard, risk, danger — **jeop·ar·dize** \-ər-,dīz\ vb — **jeop·ar·dous** \-ərd-əs\ adj

jer·e·mi·ad \,jer-ə-'mī-əd\ n : a prolonged lamentation or complaint

1jerk \'jərk\ vb **1** : to give a sharp quick push, pull, or twist **2** : to move in short abrupt motions

2jerk n **1** : a short quick pull or twist **2** : TWITCH **2** : a stupid, foolish, or eccentric person — **jerk·i·ly** adv — **jerky** adj

jer·kin \'jər-kən\ n : a close-fitting sleeveless jacket

jerk·wa·ter \'jərk-,wôt-ər, -,wät-\ adj : of minor importance : INSIGNIFICANT ⟨~ towns⟩

jer·ry-built \'jer-ē-,bilt\ adj **1** : built cheaply and flimsily **2** : carelessly or hastily put together

jer·sey \'jər-zē\ n [fr. Jersey, one of the Channel islands] **1** : a plain weft-knitted fabric **2** : a close-fitting knitted garment for the upper body **3** : any of a breed of small usu. fawn-colored dairy cattle

jess \'jes\ n : a leg strap to which the leash of a falconer's hawk is attached

jes·sa·mine \'jes-ə-mən\ var of JASMINE

1jest \'jest\ n **1** : an act intended to provoke laughter **2** : a witty remark **3** : a frivolous mood ⟨spoken in ~⟩

2jest vb : JOKE, BANTER

jest·er n : a retainer formerly kept to provide casual entertainment ⟨a king's

1jet \'jet\ n : a compact velvet-black coal that takes a good polish and is used for jewelry

2jet vb **jet·ted; jet·ting 1** : to spout or emit in a stream : SPURT **2** : to travel by jet

3jet n **1** : a forceful rush (as of liquid or gas) through a narrow opening; also : a nozzle for a jet of fluid **2** : a jet-propelled airplane

jet-pro·pelled \,jet-prə-'peld\ adj

: driven by an engine (jet engine) that produces motion as a result of the rearward discharge of a jet of fluid (as heated air and exhaust gases)

jet·sam \'jet-səm\ n : goods thrown overboard to lighten a ship in distress; esp : such goods when washed ashore

jet·ti·son \'jet-ə-sən\ vb **1** : to throw (goods) overboard to lighten a ship in distress **2** : DISCARD — **jettison** n

jet·ty \'jet-ē\ n **1** : a pier built to influence the current or to protect a harbor **2** : a landing wharf

jeu d'es·prit \zhœ-des-prē\ n, pl **jeux d'esprit** ⟨same⟩ : a witty comment or composition

Jew \'jü\ n **1** : ISRAELITE **2** : one whose religion is Judaism — **Jew·ish** adj

1jew·el \'jü-əl\ n **1** : an ornament of precious metal worn as an accessory of dress **2** : GEMSTONE, GEM

2jewel vb : to adorn or equip with jewels

jew·el·er or **jew·el·ler** \-l-ər\ n : a person who makes or deals in jewelry and related articles

jew·el·ry \-əl-rē\ n : JEWELS; esp : objects of precious metal set with gems and worn for personal adornment

Jew·ry \'jü-rē\ n : the Jewish people

jib \'jib\ n : a triangular sail extending forward from the foremast of a ship

jibe \'jīb\ vb : to be in accord : AGREE ⟨their stories of what happened do not ~⟩

jif·fy \'jif-ē\ n : MOMENT, INSTANT ⟨I'll be ready in a ~⟩

1jig \'jig\ n **1** : a lively dance in triple rhythm **2** : TRICK, GAME ⟨the ~ is up⟩ **3** : a device used to hold work while being fabricated or assembled

2jig vb **jigged; jig·ging** : to dance a jig

jig·ger \'jig-ər\ n : a measure usu. holding 1½ ounces used in mixing drinks

jig·gle \'jig-əl\ vb **1** : to move with quick little jerks

jig·saw \'jig-,sò\ n : a machine saw with a narrow vertical blade esp. for cutting up a picture on rigid material into curved and irregular pieces that are fitted together to form a puzzle (jigsaw puzzle)

1jilt \'jilt\ n : a woman who jilts a man

2jilt vb : to cast (as a lover) aside unfeelingly

jim-dan·dy \'jim-'dan-dē\ n : something excellent of its kind

jim·my \'jim-ē\ vb : to force open with a short crowbar

jim·son·weed \'jim-sən-,wēd\ n : a coarse poisonous weed of the nightshade group sometimes grown for its large trumpet-shaped white or violet flowers

1jin·gle \'jin-gəl\ vb : to make a light clinking or tinkling sound

2jingle n **1** : a light clinking or tinkling sound **2** : a short verse or song with catchy repetition

jin·go·ism \'jin-gō-,iz-əm\ n : extreme chauvinism or nationalism marked esp. by a belligerent foreign policy — **jin·go·ist** \-,gō-əst\ n — **jin·go·is·tic** \,jin-gō-'is-tik\ adj

jin·rik·i·sha \jin-'rik-,shò\ n : a small 2-wheeled covered vehicle pulled by one man and used orig. in Japan

1jinx \'jinks\ n : one that brings bad luck

2jinx vb : to foredoom to failure or misfortune

jit·ney \'jit-nē\ n : a small bus that carries passengers over a regular route according to a flexible schedule

jit·ter·bug \'jit-ər-,bəg\ n 1 : a dance in which couples two-step, balance, and twirl vigorously in standardized patterns 2 : one who dances the jitterbug — **jitterbug** vb

jit·ters \'jit-ərz\ n pl : extreme nervousness — **jit·tery** \-ə-rē\ adj

¹**job** \'jäb\ n 1 : a piece of work 2 : something that has to be done : DUTY 3 : a regular remunerative position — **job·less** \'jäb-ləs\ adj

²**job** vb **jobbed**; **job·bing** 1 : to do occasional pieces of work for hire 2 : to hire or let by the job

job·ber \'jäb-ər\ n 1 : MIDDLEMAN 2 : a person who does work by the job

job·hold·er \'jäb-,hōl-dər\ n : one having a regular job

¹**jock·ey** \'jäk-ē\ n : one who rides or drives a horse esp. as a professional in a race

²**jockey** vb : to maneuver or manipulate by adroit or devious means

jo·cose \jō-'kōs\ adj : MERRY, HUMOROUS **syn** jocular, facetious, witty

joc·u·lar \'jäk-yə-lər\ adj : marked by jesting : PLAYFUL — **joc·u·lar·i·ty** \,jäk-yə-'lar-ət-ē\ n

joc·und \'jäk-ənd\ adj : marked by mirth or cheerfulness : GAY

jodh·pur \'jäd-pər\ n 1 pl : riding breeches loose above the knee and tight-fitting below 2 : an ankle-high boot fastened with a strap

¹**jog** \'jäg\ vb **jogged**; **jog·ging** 1 : to give a slight shake or push to 2 : to go at a slow monotonous pace ⟨~ around the track⟩

²**jog** n 1 : a slight shake 2 : a jogging movement or pace

³**jog** n 1 : a projecting or retreating part of a line or surface 2 : a brief abrupt change in direction

jog·gle \'jäg-əl\ vb : to shake slightly — **joggle** n

john·ny \'jän-ē\ n : a short gown opening in the back that is used by hospital bed patients

joie de vi·vre \,zhwäd-ə-'vēvrᵊ\ n : keen enjoyment of life

join \'jȯin\ vb 1 : to come or bring together so as to form a unit 2 : to come or bring into close association 3 : to become a member of ⟨~ a church⟩ 4 : to take part in a collective activity 5 : ADJOIN

join·er n 1 : a worker who constructs articles by joining pieces of wood 2 : a gregarious person who joins many organizations

¹**joint** \'jȯint\ n 1 : the point of contact between bones of an animal skeleton with the parts that surround and support it 2 : a cut of meat suitable for roasting 3 : a place where two things or parts are connected 4 : ESTABLISHMENT

²**joint** adj 1 : UNITED ⟨a ~ effort⟩ 2 : common to two or more ⟨a ~ account⟩ — **joint·ly** adv

³**joint** vb 1 : to unite by or provide with a joint 2 : to separate the joints of

joist \'jȯist\ n : any of the small timbers or metal beams ranged parallel from wall to wall in a building to support the floor or ceiling

¹**joke** \'jōk\ n : something said or done

to provoke laughter; esp : a brief narrative with a humorous climax

²**joke** vb : to speak or act without seriousness

jok·er n 1 : a person who jokes 2 : an extra card used in some card games 3 : a part (as of an agreement) meaning something quite different from what it seems to mean and changing the apparent intention of the whole

jol·li·fi·ca·tion \,jäl-i-fə-'kā-shən\ n : a festive celebration

jol·li·ty \'jäl-ət-ē\ n : GAIETY, MERRIMENT

jol·ly \'jäl-ē\ adj : full of high spirits : MERRY

¹**jolt** \'jōlt\ vb 1 : to move with a sudden jerky motion 2 : to give a quick hard knock or blow to

²**jolt** n 1 : an abrupt jerky blow or movement 2 : a sudden shock

jon·gleur \zhōⁿ-'glər\ n : an itinerant medieval minstrel providing entertainment chiefly by song or recitation

jon·quil \'jän-kwəl\ n : a narcissus with fragrant clustered white or yellow flowers

josh \'jäsh\ vb : TEASE, JOKE

joss \'jäs\ n : a Chinese idol or cult image

jos·tle \'jäs-əl\ vb 1 : to come in contact or into collision 2 : to make one's way by pushing and shoving

¹**jot** \'jät\ n : the least bit : IOTA

²**jot** vb **jot·ted**; **jot·ting** : to write briefly and hurriedly

jounce \'jauns\ vb : JOLT — **jounce** n

jour·nal \'jərn-ᵊl\ n 1 : a brief account of daily events 2 : a record of proceedings (as of a legislative body) 3 : a periodical (as a newspaper) dealing esp. with current events 4 : the part of a rotating axle or spindle that turns in a bearing

jour·nal·ese \,jərn-ᵊl-'ēz\ n : a style of writing held to be characteristic of newspapers

jour·nal·ism \'jərn-ᵊl-,iz-əm\ n 1 : the business of writing for, editing, or publishing periodicals (as newspapers) 2 : writing designed for or characteristic of newspapers — **jour·nal·ist** \-əst\ n — **jour·nal·is·tic** \,jərn-ᵊl-'is-tik\ adj

¹**jour·ney** \'jər-nē\ n : travel or passage from one place to another

²**journey** vb : to go on a journey : TRAVEL

jour·ney·man \-mən\ n 1 : a worker who has learned a trade and works for another person 2 : an experienced reliable workman

¹**joust** \'jaust\ vb : to engage in a joust

²**joust** n : a combat on horseback between two knights with lances esp. as part of a tournament

jo·vi·al \'jō-vē-əl\ adj : marked by good humor : full of fun — **jo·vi·al·i·ty** \,jō-vē-'al-ət-ē\ n — **jo·vi·al·ly** \'jō-vē-ə-lē\ adv

¹**jowl** \'jaul\ n 1 : the lower jaw 2 : CHEEK

²**jowl** n : loose flesh about the lower jaw or throat

¹**joy** \'jȯi\ n [OF joie, fr. L gaudium] 1 : a feeling of happiness that comes from success, good fortune, or a sense of well-being ⟨a ~ to behold⟩ 2 : a source or cause of happiness **syn** bliss,

delight, enjoyment, pleasure — **joy·less** \-ləs\ adj

²**joy** vb : REJOICE

joy·ful \-fəl\ adj : experiencing, causing, or showing joy — **joy·ful·ly** adv

joy·ous \'jȯi-əs\ adj : JOYFUL — **joy·ous·ly** adv — **joy·ous·ness** n

joy·ride \-ˌrīd\ n : a ride taken for pleasure — **joy·rid·er** n

ju·bi·lant \'jü-bə-lənt\ adj : expressing great joy : EXULTANT — **ju·bi·lant·ly** adv

ju·bi·la·tion \ˌjü-bə-'lā-shən\ n : EXULTATION

ju·bi·lee \'jü-bə-ˌlē\ n 1 : a 50th anniversary 2 : a season or occasion of celebration

Ju·da·ism \'jüd-ə-ˌiz-əm\ n : a religion developed among the ancient Hebrews and marked by belief in one God and by the moral and ceremonial laws of the Old Testament and the rabbinic tradition

¹**judge** \'jəj\ vb 1 : to form an authoritative opinion 2 : to decide as a judge : TRY 3 : to determine or pronounce after inquiry and deliberation : CONSIDER 4 : to form an estimate, conclusion, or evaluation about something : THINK syn adjudge, adjudicate, arbitrate, conclude, deduce, gather

²**judge** n 1 : a public official authorized to decide questions brought before a court 2 : UMPIRE 3 : one who gives an authoritative opinion : CRITIC

judg·ment or **judge·ment** \'jəj-mənt\ n 1 : a decision or opinion given after judging ; esp : a formal decision given by a court 2 cap : the final judging of mankind by God 3 : the process of forming an opinion by discerning and comparing 4 : the capacity for judging : DISCERNMENT

ju·di·ca·ture \'jüd-i-kə-ˌchùr\ n 1 : the administration of justice 2 : JUDICIARY 1

ju·di·cial \jù-'dish-əl\ adj 1 : of or relating to the administration of justice or the judiciary 2 : ordered or enforced by a court 3 : CRITICAL — **ju·di·cial·ly** adv

ju·di·ci·ary \jù-'dish-ē-ˌer-ē\ n 1 : a system of courts of law; also : the judges of these courts 2 : a branch of government in which judicial power is vested — **judiciary** adj

ju·di·cious \jù-'dish-əs\ adj : having, exercising, or characterized by sound judgment : DISCREET syn prudent, sage, sane, sensible, wise — **ju·di·cious·ly** adv

ju·do \'jüd-ō\ n : a form of jujitsu that uses special applications of the principles of movement, balance, and leverage

jug \'jəg\ n : a large deep usu. earthenware or glass container with a narrow mouth and a handle

jug·ger·naut \'jəg-ər-ˌnȯt\ n : a massive inexorable force or object that crushes everything in its path

jug·gle \'jəg-əl\ vb 1 : to keep several objects in motion in the air at the same time 2 : to manipulate esp. in order to achieve a desired and often fraudulent end — **jug·gler** \'jəg-lər\ n

jug·u·lar \'jəg-yə-lər\ adj : of, relating to, or situated in or on the throat or neck (the ~ veins return blood from the head)

juice \'jüs\ n 1 : the extractable fluid contents of cells or tissues 2 pl : the natural fluids of an animal body 3 : a medium (as electricity) that supplies power

juicy \'jü-sē\ adj 1 : SUCCULENT 2 : rich in interest; also : RACY

ju·jit·su or **ju·jut·su** \jü-'jit-sü\ n : the Japanese art of defending oneself by grasping or striking an opponent so that his own strength and weight are used against him

ju·jube \'jü-ˌjüb\ n : a candy made from corn syrup with gelatin or gum arabic

juke·box \'jük-ˌbäks\ n : a cabinet containing an automatic player of phonograph records that is started by inserting a coin in a slot

ju·lep \'jü-ləp\ n : a drink made of bourbon, sugar, and mint served over crushed ice in a tall glass

Ju·ly \jù-'lī\ n : the 7th month of the year having 31 days

¹**jum·ble** \'jəm-bəl\ vb : to mix in a confused mass

²**jumble** n : a disorderly mass or pile

jum·bo \'jəm-bō\ n : a very large specimen of its kind

¹**jump** \'jəmp\ vb 1 : to spring into the air : leap over 2 : to give a start 3 : to rise or increase suddenly or sharply 4 : to make a sudden attack 5 : ANTICIPATE (~ the gun) 6 : to leave hurriedly and often furtively (~ town)

²**jump** n 1 : a spring into the air; esp : one made for height or distance in a track meet 2 : a sharp sudden increase 3 : an initial advantage (get the ~ on him)

¹**jump·er** n : one that jumps

²**jumper** n 1 : a loose blouse 2 : a sleeveless one-piece dress worn usu. with a blouse 3 pl : a child's sleeveless coverall

jumpy adj : NERVOUS, JITTERY

jun·co \'jəŋ-kō\ n, pl -cos or -coes : any of several small common pink-billed American finches that are largely gray or with conspicuous white feathers in the tail

junc·tion \'jəŋk-shən\ n 1 : an act of joining 2 : a place or point of meeting (a railroad ~)

junc·ture \'jəŋk-chər\ n 1 : UNION 2 : JOINT, CONNECTION 3 : a critical time or state of affairs

June \'jün\ n : the 6th month of the year having 30 days

jun·gle \'jəŋ-gəl\ n 1 : a thick tangled mass of tropical vegetation; also : a tract overgrown with rank vegetation 2 : a place of ruthless struggle for survival

¹**ju·nior** \'jü-nyər\ n [L, fr. junior younger, compar. of juvenis young] 1 : a person who is younger or of lower rank than another 2 : a student in his next-to-last year (as at a college)

²**junior** adj 1 : YOUNGER 2 : lower in rank 3 : of or relating to juniors (~ class)

ju·ni·per \'jü-nə-pər\ n : any of various evergreen shrubs or trees related to the pines

¹**junk** \'jəŋk\ n 1 : old iron, glass, paper, or waste; also : discarded articles 2 : a shoddy product

²**junk** vb : DISCARD, SCRAP

³**junk** n : a ship of Chinese waters

Jun·ker \'yùn-kər\ n : a member of the Prussian landed aristocracy

jun·ket \'jəŋ-kət\ n 1 : a dessert of sweetened flavored milk set in a jelly

2 : a trip made by an official at public expense

jun·ta \'hün-tə, 'jənt-ə\ *n* **:** a group of persons controlling a government esp. after a revolutionary seizure of power

Ju·pi·ter \'jü-pət-ər\ *n* **:** the largest of the planets and the one 5th in order of distance from the sun

ju·rid·i·cal \jü-'rid-i-kəl\ *adj* **1 :** of or relating to the administration of justice **2 :** LEGAL

ju·ris·dic·tion \jür-əs-'dik-shən\ *n* **1 :** the power, right, or authority to interpret and apply the law **2 :** the authority of a sovereign power **3 :** the sphere of authority — **ju·ris·dic·tion·al** *adj*

ju·ris·pru·dence \-'prüd-ᵊns\ *n* **1 :** a system of laws **2 :** the science or philosophy of law

ju·rist \'jür-əst\ *n* **:** one having a thorough knowledge of law

ju·ror \'jür-ər\ *n* **:** a member of a jury

ju·ry \'jür-ē\ *n* **1 :** a body of persons sworn to inquire into and test a matter submitted to them and to give their verdict according to the evidence presented **2 :** a committee for judging and awarding prizes (as at a contest) — **ju·ry·man** \-mən\ *n*

¹just \'jəst\ *adj* **1 :** REASONABLE ⟨~ comment⟩ **2 :** CORRECT, PROPER ⟨~ proportions⟩ **3 :** morally or legally right (a ~ title) **4 :** DESERVED, MERITED ⟨~ punishment⟩ **syn** upright, honor-

able, conscientious, honest — **just·ly** *adv* — **just·ness** *n*

²just \(,)jəst, (,)jist\ *adv* **1 :** EXACTLY ⟨~ right⟩ **2 :** very recently ⟨has ~ left⟩ **3 :** BARELY ⟨lives ~ outside the city⟩ **4 :** DIRECTLY ⟨~ across the street⟩ **5 :** ONLY ⟨~ a note⟩ **6 :** VERY ⟨~ wonderful⟩

jus·tice \'jəs-təs\ *n* **1 :** the administration of what is just (as by assigning merited rewards or punishments) **2 :** JUDGE **3 :** the administration of law **4 :** FAIRNESS; *also* **:** RIGHTEOUSNESS

jus·ti·fy \'jəs-tə-,fī\ *vb* **1 :** to prove to be just, right, or reasonable **2 :** to pronounce free from guilt or blame **3 :** to adjust or arrange exactly — **jus·ti·fi·able** \-,fī-ə-bəl\ *adj* — **jus·ti·fi·ca·tion** \,jəs-tə-fə-'kā-shən\ *n*

jut \'jət\ *vb* **jut·ted; jut·ting :** PROJECT, PROTRUDE

jute \'jüt\ *n* **:** a strong glossy fiber from a tropical herb used esp. for making sacks and twine

¹ju·ve·nile \'jü-və-,nīl, -nᵊl\ *adj* **1 :** showing incomplete development **:** IMMATURE **2 :** of, relating to, or characteristic of children or young people

²juvenile *n* **1 :** a young person or lower animal **2 :** an actor or actress who plays youthful parts

jux·ta·pose \'jək-stə-,pōz\ *vb* **:** to place side by side — **jux·ta·po·si·tion** \,jək-stə-pə-'zish-ən\ *n*

---

k \'kā\ *n, often cap* **:** the 11th letter of the English alphabet

ka·bob \'kā-,bäb, kə-'bäb\ *n* **:** cubes of meat cooked with vegetables usu. on a skewer

kaf·fee·klatsch \'kȯf-ē-,klach, 'käf-\ *n, often cap* **:** an informal social gathering for coffee and talk

kai·ser \'kī-zər\ *n* **:** EMPEROR; *esp* **:** the ruler of Germany from 1871 to 1918

kale \'kāl\ *n* **:** a hardy cabbage with curled leaves that do not form a head

ka·lei·do·scope \kə-'līd-ə-,skōp\ *n* **:** an instrument containing loose bits of colored glass between two flat plates and two plane mirrors so placed that changes of position of the bits of glass are reflected in an endless variety of patterns — **ka·lei·do·scop·ic** \kə-,līd-ə-'skäp-ik\ *adj*

ka·mi·ka·ze \,käm-i-'käz-ē\ *n* **:** a member of a corps of Japanese pilots assigned to make a crash on a target; *also* **:** an airplane flown in such an attack

kan·ga·roo \,kaŋ-gə-'rü\ *n* **:** a large leaping marsupial mammal of Australia with powerful hind legs and a long thick tail

ka·o·lin \'kā-ə-lən\ *n* **:** a fine usu. white clay used in ceramics and refractories and as an absorbent

ka·pok \'kā-,päk\ *n* **:** silky fiber from the seeds of a tropical tree used esp. as a filling (as for cushions and life preservers)

ka·put \kä-'pùt\ *adj* **1 :** utterly de-

feated or destroyed **2 :** made useless or unable to function

kar·a·kul \'kar-ə-kəl\ *n* **:** the dark tightly curled pelt of the newborn lamb of an Asiatic fat-tailed sheep valued as fur

kar·at \'kar-ət\ *n* **:** a unit for expressing proportion of gold in an alloy equal to ¹⁄₂₄ part of pure gold ⟨16-*karat* gold is ¹⁶⁄₂₄ pure gold⟩

ka·ra·te \kə-'rät-ē\ *n* **:** a Japanese system of self-defense without a weapon

kar·ma \'kär-mə\ *n, often cap* **:** the force generated by a person's actions held in Hinduism and Buddhism to perpetuate transmigration and to determine his destiny in his next existence — **kar·mic** \-mik\ *adj, often cap*

ka·ty·did \'kāt-ē-,did\ *n* **:** any of several large green tree-dwelling American grasshoppers

kay·ak \'kī-,ak\ *n* **:** a decked-in Eskimo canoe made of skin and propelled by a double-bladed paddle; *also* **:** a similar canvas-covered portable canoe

kayo \kā-'ō\, *n* **:** KNOCKOUT — **kayo** *vb*

ka·zoo \kə-'zü\ *n* **:** a toy musical instrument consisting of a tube with a membrane sealing one end and a side hole into which one sings or hums

ke·bab *or* **ke·bob** \kə-'bäb\ *var of* KABOB

¹kedge \'kej\ *vb* **:** to move a ship by hauling on a line attached to a small anchor dropped at the distance and in the direction desired

²**kedge** n : a small anchor

keel \'kēl\ n 1 : a timber or plate running lengthwise along the center of the bottom of a ship 2 : something (as the breastbone of a bird) like a ship's keel in form or use

keel over vb 1 : OVERTURN, CAPSIZE 2 : FAINT, SWOON

¹**keen** \'kēn\ adj 1 : SHARP (a ~ knife) 2 : SEVERE (a ~ wind) 3 : ENTHUSIASTIC (~ about swimming) 4 : mentally alert (a ~ mind) 5 : STRONG, ACUTE (~ eyesight) — **keen·ly** adv — **keen·ness** n

²**keen** n : a lamentation for the dead uttered in a loud wailing voice or in a wordless cry — **keen** vb

¹**keep** \'kēp\ vb **kept** \'kept\ **keep·ing** 1 : FULFILL, OBSERVE (~ a promise) (~ a holiday) 2 : GUARD (~ us from harm); also : to take care of (~ a neighbor's children) 3 : MAINTAIN (~ silence) 4 : to have in one's service or at one's disposal (~ a horse) 5 : to preserve a record in (~ a diary) 6 : to have in stock for sale 7 : to retain in one's possession (~ what you find) 8 : to carry on (as a business) : CONDUCT 9 : HOLD DETAIN (~ him in jail) 10 : to refrain from revealing (~ a secret) 11 : to continue in good condition (meat will ~ in a freezer) 12 : ABSTAIN (couldn't ~ from laughing) — **keep·er** n

²**keep** n 1 : FORTRESS 2 : the means or provisions by which one is kept

keep·sake \-,sāk\ n : MEMENTO

keg \'keg\ n : a small cask or barrel

keg·ler \'keg-lər\ n : BOWLER

kelp \'kelp\ n : any of various coarse brown seaweeds; also : a mass of these or their ashes often used as fertilizer

Kelt \'kelt\ var of CELT

ken \'ken\ n 1 : range of vision : SIGHT 2 : range of understanding

ken·nel \'ken-ᵊl\ n : a shelter for a dog; also : an establishment for the breeding or boarding of dogs — **kennel** vb

ke·pi \'kā-pē, 'kep-ē\ n : a military cap with a round flat top sloping toward the front and a visor

kerb n, Brit : CURB

ker·chief \'kər-chəf\ n [OF couvrechef, fr. couvrir to cover + chef head] 1 : a square of cloth worn by women esp. as a head covering 2 : HANDKERCHIEF

ker·nel \'kərn-ᵊl\ n 1 : the inner softer part of a seed, fruit stone, or nut 2 : a whole seed of a cereal 3 : a central or essential part : CORE

ker·o·sene or **ker·o·sine** \'ker-ə-,sēn\ n : a thin oil produced from petroleum and used for a fuel and as a solvent

ketch \'kech\ n : a fore-and-aft rigged ship with 2 masts

ketch·up var of CATSUP

ket·tle \'ket-ᵊl\ n : a metallic vessel for boiling liquids

ket·tle·drum \-,drəm\ n : a brass or copper drum with parchment stretched across the top

¹**key** \'kē\ n 1 : a usu. metal instrument by which the bolt of a lock is turned; also : a device having the form or function of a key 2 : a means of gaining or preventing entrance possession, or control 3 : EXPLANATION, SOLUTION 4 : one of the levers pressed by a finger in operating or playing an instrument 5 : a leading individual or principle 6 : a system of seven tones based on their relationship to a tonic; also : the tone or pitch of a voice 7 : a small switch for opening or closing an electric circuit

²**key** vb 1 : SECURE, FASTEN 2 : to regulate the musical pitch of; also : ATTUNE 3 : to make nervous — usu. used with up

³**key** n : a low island or reef (as off the southern coast of Florida)

key·board \-,bȯrd\ n 1 : a row of keys (as on a piano) 2 : an assemblage of keys for operating a machine

key·hole \-,hōl\ n : a hole for receiving a key

¹**key·note** \-,nōt\ n 1 : the first and harmonically fundamental tone of a scale 2 : the central fact, idea, or mood

²**keynote** vb 1 : to set the keynote of 2 : to deliver the major address (as at a convention) — **key·not·er** n

key·stone \-,stōn\ n : the wedge-shaped piece at the crown of an arch that locks the other pieces in place

khaki \'kak-ē, 'käk-\ n 1 : a light yellowish brown 2 : a khaki-colored cloth; also : a military uniform of this cloth

khan \'kän, 'kan\ n : a Mongol leader; esp : a successor of Genghis Khan

khe·dive \kə-'dēv\ n : a ruler of Egypt from 1867 to 1914 governing as a viceroy of the sultan of Turkey

kib·butz \kib-'ùts\ n : a collective farm or settlement in Israel

kib·itz·er \'kib-ət-sər\ n : one who looks on and usu. offers unwanted advice esp. at a card game — **kib·itz** \-əts\ vb

ki·bosh \'kī-,bäsh\ n : something that serves as a check or stop (put the ~ on his plan)

¹**kick** \'kik\ vb 1 : to strike out or hit with the foot; also : to score by kicking a ball 2 : to object strongly : PROTEST 3 : to recoil when fired (these guns ~) — **kick·er** n

²**kick** n 1 : a blow or thrust with the foot; esp : a prop.lling of a ball with the foot 2 : the recoil of a gun 3 : a feeling or expression of objection 4 : a stimulating effect esp. of pleasure

kick·back \'kik-,bak\ n 1 : a sharp violent reaction 2 : a secret return of a part of a sum received

kick·off \-,ȯf\ n 1 : a kick that puts the ball in play (as in football) 2 : COMMENCEMENT

kick·shaw \-,shȯ\ n 1 : DELICACY 2 : BAUBLE

¹**kid** \'kid\ n 1 : a young goat 2 : the flesh, fur, or skin of a young goat; also : something (as leather) made of kid 3 : CHILD, YOUNGSTER — **kid·dish** adj

²**kid** vb **kid·ded; kid·ding** 1 : FOOL 2 : TEASE

kid·nap \-,nap\ vb **-napped** or **-naped** \-,napt\ **-nap·ping** or **-nap·ing** 1 : to carry a person away by unlawful force or by fraud and against his will — **kid·nap·per** or **kid·nap·er** n

kid·ney \'kid-nē\ n 1 : either of a pair of organs lying near the spinal column that excrete waste products of the body in the form of urine 2 : TEMPERAMENT; also : SORT

kid·skin \'kid-,skin\ n : the skin of a

young goat used in making leather goods

¹**kill** \'kil\ *vb* **1 :** to deprive of life **2 :** to put an end to (~ competition); *also* : DEFEAT (~ a proposed amendment) **3 :** to use up (~ time) **4 :** to mark for omission (~ a news story) **syn** SLAY, MURDER, ASSASSINATE, EXECUTE — **kill·er** *n*

²**kill** *n* **1 :** an act of killing **2 :** an animal killed (as in a hunt)

kill·ing \'kil-iŋ\ *n* **:** a sudden notable gain or profit (made a ~ in the stock market)

kill·joy \-,jȯi\ *n* **:** one who spoils the pleasures of others

kiln \'kil(n)\ *n* **:** a heated enclosure (as an oven) for processing a substance by burning, firing, or drying

ki·lo \'kē-lō, 'kil-ō\ *n* **1 :** KILOGRAM **2 :** KILOMETER

kilo·cy·cle \'kil-ə-,sī-kəl\ *n* **:** one thousand cycles per second — used as a unit of radio frequency

kilo·gram \-,gram\ *n* **:** a metric unit of weight equal to 1000 grams (2.2046 lbs.)

ki·lo·me·ter \kil-'äm-ət-ər, 'kil-ə-,mēt-\ *n* **:** a metric unit of length equal to 1000 meters (3280.8 ft. or about .62 mile)

kilo·watt \'kil-ə-,wät\ *n* **:** a unit of electric power equal to 1000 watts

kilt \'kilt\ *n* **:** a knee-length pleated skirt usu. of tartan worn by men in Scotland

kil·ter \'kil-tər\ *n* **:** proper condition (out of ~)

ki·mo·no \kə-'mō-nə\ *n* **1 :** a loose robe with wide sleeves and a broad sash traditionally worn as an outer garment by the Japanese **2 :** a loose dressing gown worn esp. by women

kin \'kin\ *n* **1 :** an individual's relatives **2 :** KINSMAN

¹**kind** \'kīnd\ *n* **1 :** essential quality or character **2 :** a group united by common traits or interests **:** CATEGORY (different ~*s* of insects); *also* : VARIETY (all ~*s* of people) **3 :** goods or commodities as distinguished from money

²**kind** *adj* **1 :** of a sympathetic, forbearing, or pleasant nature (~ friends) **2 :** arising from sympathy or forbearance (~ deeds) **syn** BENEVOLENT, BENIGN, BENIGNANT, GRACIOUS — **kind·ness** *n*

kin·der·gar·ten \'kin-dər-,gärt-ᵊn\ *n* **:** a school or class for children of the 4 to 6 age group

kind-heart·ed \'kīnd-'härt-əd\ *adj* **:** marked by a sympathetic nature

kin·dle \'kin-dᵊl\ *vb* **1 :** to set on fire **:** start burning **2 :** to stir up **:** AROUSE (~ his anger) **3 :** ILLUMINATE, GLOW

kin·dling \'kin-dliŋ\ *n* **:** easily combustible material for starting a fire

¹**kind·ly** \'kīn-dlē\ *adj* **1 :** of an agreeable or beneficial nature (a ~ climate) **2 :** of a sympathetic or generous nature (~ men) — **kind·li·ness** *n*

²**kindly** *adv* **1 :** READILY (does not take ~ to criticism) **2 :** SYMPATHETICALLY **3 :** COURTEOUSLY, OBLIGINGLY

¹**kin·dred** \'kin-drəd\ *n* **1 :** a group of related individuals **2 :** one's relatives

²**kindred** *adj* **:** of a like nature or character

kine \'kīn\ *archaic pl of* COW

ki·net·ic \kə-'net-ik, kī-\ *adj* [Gk *kinētikos,* fr. *kinein* to move] **:** of or relating to the motion of material bodies and the forces and energy associated therewith

kin·folk \'kin-,fōk\ *or* **kins·folk** \'kinz-\ *n* **:** RELATIVES

king \'kiŋ\ *n* **1 :** a male sovereign **2 :** a chief among competitors (home-run ~) **3 :** the principal piece in the game of chess **4 :** a playing card bearing the figure of a king **5 :** a checker that has been crowned — **king·less** \-ləs\ *adj* — **king·ly** *adj* — **king·ship** \-,ship\ *n*

king·dom \-dəm\ *n* **1 :** a country whose head is a king or queen **2 :** a realm or region in which something or someone is dominant (a cattle ~) **3 :** one of the three primary divisions of lifeless material, plants, and animals (**mineral kingdom, plant kingdom, animal kingdom**) into which natural objects are grouped

king·fish·er \-,fish-ər\ *n* **:** a bright-colored crested bird that feeds chiefly on fish

king·pin \-,pin\ *n* **1 :** any of several bowling pins **2 :** the leader in a group or undertaking

king-size \-,sīz\ *or* **king-sized** \-,sīzd\ *adj* **1 :** longer than the regular or standard size **2 :** unusually large

kink \'kiŋk\ *n* **1 :** a short tight twist or curl **2 :** CRAMP (a ~ in the back) **3 :** an imperfection likely to cause difficulties in operation — **kinky** *adj*

kin·ship \'kin-,ship\ *n* **:** RELATIONSHIP

kins·man \'kinz-mən\ *n* **:** RELATIVE; *esp* **:** a male relative

kins·wom·an \-,wu̇m-ən\ *n* **:** a female relative

ki·osk \'kē-,äsk\ *n* **:** a small structure with one or more open sides (telephone ~)

¹**kip** \'kip\ *n* **:** the undressed hide of a young or small animal

²**kip** *n, pl* **kip** *or* **kips** — see MONEY table

kip·per \'kip-ər\ *n* **:** a fish (as a herring) preserved by salting and drying or smoking — **kipper** *vb*

kirk \'kiǝrk, 'kərk\ *n, chiefly Scot* **:** CHURCH

kir·tle \'kərt-ᵊl\ *n* **:** a long gown or dress worn by women

kis·met \'kiz-,met\ *n, often cap* **:** FATE

¹**kiss** \'kis\ *vb* **1 :** to touch with the lips as a mark of affection or greeting **2 :** to touch gently or lightly

²**kiss** *n* **1 :** a caress with the lips **2 :** a gentle touch or contact **3 :** a bite-size candy

kit \'kit\ *n* **1 :** a set of articles for personal use; *also* : a set of tools or implements or of parts to be assembled **2 :** a container (as a case) for a kit

kitch·en \'kich-ən\ *n* **1 :** a room with cooking facilities **2 :** the personnel that prepares, cooks, and serves food

kitch·en·ette \,kich-ən-'et\ *n* **:** a small kitchen or an alcove containing cooking facilities

kitch·en·ware \'kich-ən-,waǝr\ *n* **:** implements and vessels used in the storage, preparation, and cooking of food

kite \'kīt\ *n* **1 :** any of several small

hawks **2** : a light frame covered with paper or cloth and designed to be flown in the air at the end of a long string

kith \'kith\ *n* : familiar friends, neighbors, or relatives ⟨~ and kin⟩

kit·ten \'kit-ᵊn\ *n* : a young cat — **kit·ten·ish** *adj*

¹kit·ty \'kit-ē\ *n* : CAT; *esp* : KITTEN

²kitty *n* : a fund in a poker game made up of contributions from each pot; *also* : POOL

kit·ty-cor·ner \,kit-ē-'kȯr-nər\ *or* **kit·ty-cor·nered** *var of* CATERCORNER

klep·to·ma·nia \,klep-tə-'mā-nē-ə\ *n* : a persistent neurotic impulse to steal esp. without economic motive — **klep·to·ma·ni·ac** \-nē-,ak\ *adj or n*

knack \'nak\ *n* **1** : a clever way of doing something **2** : natural aptitude

knap·sack \'nap-,sak\ *n* : a usu. canvas or leather bag or case strapped on the back and used esp. for carrying supplies (as on a hike)

knave \'nāv\ *n* **1** : ROGUE **2** : JACK 3 — **knav·ery** \'nāv-(ə-)rē\ *n* — **knav·ish** \'nā-vish\ *adj*

knead \'nēd\ *vb* : to work and press into a mass with the hands; *also* : MASSAGE

knee \'nē\ *n* : the joint in the middle part of the leg

knee·hole \-,hōl\ *n* : a space (as under a desk) for the knees

kneel \'nēl\ *vb* **knelt** \'nelt\ *or* **kneeled** \'nēld\ **kneel·ing** : to bend the knee : fall or rest on the knees

¹knell \'nel\ *vb* **1** : to ring esp. for a death or disaster **2** : to summon, announce, or proclaim by a knell

²knell *n* **1** : a stroke of a bell esp. when tolled (as for a funeral) **2** : an indication (as a sound) of the end or failure of something

knew *past of* KNOW

knick·ers \'nik-ərz\ *n pl* : loose-fitting short pants gathered at the knee

knick·knack \'nik-,nak\ *n* : a small trivial article intended for ornament

¹knife \'nīf\ *n, pl* **knives** \'nīvz\ **1** : a cutting instrument consisting of a sharp blade fastened to a handle **2** : a sharp cutting blade or tool in a machine

²knife *vb* : to stab, slash, or wound with a knife

knight \'nīt\ *n* **1** : a mounted warrior of feudal times serving a king **2** : a man honored by a sovereign for merit and in Great Britain ranking below a baronet **3** : a man devoted to the service of a lady as her attendant or champion **4** : a member of any of various orders or societies **5** : a chess piece having a move of two squares to a square of the opposite color — **knight·ly** *adj*

knight·hood \-,hu̇d\ *n* **1** : the rank, dignity, or profession of a knight **2** : CHIVALRY **3** : knights as a class or body

knit \'nit\ *vb* **knit** *or* **knit·ted**; **knit·ting** **1** : to link firmly or closely **2** : WRINKLE ⟨~ her brows⟩ **3** : to form a fabric by interlacing yarn or thread in connected loops with needles **4** : to grow together — **knit·ter** *n*

knit·wear \-,waər\ *n* : knitted clothing

knob \'näb\ *n* **1** : a rounded protuberance; *also* : a small rounded ornament or handle **2** : a rounded usu. isolated hill or mountain —

knobbed \'näbd\ *adj* — **knob·by** \'näb-ē\ *adj*

¹knock \'näk\ *vb* **1** : to strike with a sharp blow **2** : BUMP, COLLIDE **3** : to make a pounding noise esp. as a result of abnormal ignition **4** : to find fault with

²knock *n* **1** : a sharp blow **2** : a pounding noise; *esp* : one caused by abnormal ignition

knock·er *n* : one that knocks; *esp* : a device hinged to a door for use in knocking

knock·out \'näk-,au̇t\ *n* **1** : a blow that fells and immobilizes an opponent (as in boxing) **2** : something sensationally striking or attractive

knoll \'nōl\ *n* : a small round hill

¹knot \'nät\ *n* **1** : an interlacing (as of string or ribbon) that forms a lump or knob **2** : PROBLEM **3** : a bond of union; *esp* : the marriage bond **4** : a protuberant lump or swelling in tissue; *also* : the base of a woody branch enclosed in the stem from which it arises **5** : GROUP, CLUSTER **6** : an ornamental bow of ribbon **7** : one nautical mile per hour; *also* : one nautical mile — **knot·ty** *adj*

²knot *vb* **knot·ted**; **knot·ting** **1** : to tie in or with a knot : form knots in **2** : ENTANGLE

knot·hole \-,hōl\ *n* : a hole in a board or tree trunk where a knot has come out

know \'nō\ *vb* **knew** \'n(y)ü\ **known** \'nōn\ **know·ing** **1** : to perceive directly : have understanding or direct cognition of; *also* : to recognize the nature of **2** : to be acquainted or familiar with **3** : to be aware of the truth of **4** : to have a practical understanding of ⟨~s how to write⟩ — **know·able** \'nō-ə-bəl\ *adj*

know-how \-,hau̇\ *n* : knowledge of how to do something smoothly and efficiently

know·ing *adj* **1** : having or reflecting knowledge, intelligence, or information **2** : shrewdly and keenly alert **3** : DELIBERATE, INTENTIONAL **syn** astute, bright, smart — **know·ing·ly** *adv*

knowl·edge \'näl-ij\ *n* **1** : understanding gained by actual experience ⟨a ~ of carpentry⟩ **2** : range of information ⟨within my ~⟩ **3** : clear perception of truth **4** : something learned and kept in the mind : LEARNING ⟨a man of great ~⟩

knowl·edge·able *adj* : having or showing knowledge or intelligence

knuck·le \'nək-əl\ *n* : the rounded knob at a joint and esp. at a finger joint

ko·bold \'kō-,bȯld\ *n* : a gnome or spirit of German folklore

kohl·ra·bi \kōl-'rab-ē, -'räb-\ *n* : a cabbage that forms no head but has a swollen fleshy edible stem

ko·lin·sky \kə-'lin-skē\ *n* : the fur of various Asiatic minks

ko·peck \'kō-,pek\ *n* — see MONEY table

Ko·ran \kə-'ran\ *n* : a book of writings accepted by Muslims as revelations made to Muhammad by Allah

Ko·re·an \kə-'rē-ən\ *n* : a native or inhabitant of Korea — **Korean** *adj*

ko·ru·na \'kȯr-ə-nə\ *n, pl* **ko·ru·ny** \-nē\ *or* **korunas** — see MONEY table

ko·sher \'kō-shər\ *adj* : ritually fit for use according to Jewish law; *also* : selling or serving such food

kow·tow \kau̇-'tau̇\ *vb* **1** : to kneel and

touch the forehead to the ground as a sign of homage or deep respect **2** : to show obsequious deference

kraal \\'kröl\ *n* **1** : a village of southern African natives **2** : an enclosure for domestic animals in southern Africa

kraut \\'kraůt\ *n* : SAUERKRAUT

Krem·lin \\'krem-lən\ *n* : the Russian government

¹kro·na \\'krō-nə\ *n, pl* **kro·nur** \-nər\ — see MONEY table

²krona *n, pl* **kro·nor** \-nor\ — see MONEY table

kro·ne \\'krō-nə\ *n, pl* **kro·ner** \-nər\ — see MONEY table

ku·dos \\'k(y)ü-,däs\ *n, pl* **ku·dos** \-,döz\ : fame and renown resulting from an act or achievement : GLORY

ku·lak \k(y)ü-'lak\ *n* **1** : a wealthy peasant farmer in 19th century Russia **2** : a farmer characterized by Communists as having excessive wealth

kum·quat \\'kəm-,kwät\ *n* : a small citrus fruit with sweet spongy rind and acid pulp

ky·at \kē-'(y)ät\ *n* — see MONEY table

l \\'el\ *n, often cap* : the 12th letter of the English alphabet

lab \\'lab\ *n* : LABORATORY

¹la·bel \\'lā-bəl\ *n* **1** : a slip (as of paper or cloth) attached to something for identification or description **2** : a descriptive or identifying word or phrase

²label *vb* **-beled** *or* **-belled; -bel·ing** *or* **-bel·ling** **1** : to affix a label to **2** : to describe or designate with a label

la·bi·al \\'lā-bē-əl\ *adj* : of or relating to the lips

la·bile \\'lā-,bīl, -bəl\ *adj* **1** : ADAPTABLE **2** : UNSTABLE

¹la·bor \\'lā-bər\ *n* **1** : expenditure of physical or mental effort; *also* : human activity that provides the goods or services in an economy **2** : the physical activities involved in parturition **3** : TASK **4** : those who do manual labor or work for wages; *also* : labor unions or their officials

²labor *vb* **1** : WORK **2** : to move with great effort **3** : to be in the labor of giving birth **4** : to suffer from some disadvantage or distress (~ under a delusion) **5** : to treat or work out laboriously (~ the obvious) — **la·bor·er** *n*

lab·o·ra·to·ry \\'lab-(ə-)rə-,tōr-ē\ *n* : a place equipped for experimental study in a science or for testing and analysis

Labor Day *n* : the 1st Monday in September observed as a legal holiday in recognition of the workingman

la·bored *adj* : not freely or easily done (~ breathing)

la·bo·ri·ous \lə-'bōr-ē-əs\ *adj* **1** : INDUSTRIOUS **2** : requiring great effort — **la·bo·ri·ous·ly** *adv*

la·bor·sav·ing \\'lā-bər-,sā-viŋ\ *adj* : designed to replace or decrease labor

la·bour *chiefly Brit var of* LABOR

la·bur·num \lə-'bər-nəm\ *n* : a leguminous shrub or tree with hanging clusters of yellow flowers

lab·y·rinth \\'lab-ə-,rinth\ *n* : a place constructed of or filled with confusing intricate passageways : MAZE — **lab·y·rin·thine** \lab-ə-'rin-thən\ *adj*

lac \\'lak\ *n* : a resinous substance secreted by a scale insect and used in the manufacture of shellac, lacquers, and sealing wax

¹lace \\'lās\ *n* [OF *laz*, fr. L *laqueus* noose, snare] **1** : a cord or string used for drawing together two edges (as of a shoe) **2** : an ornamental braid (as for trimming a uniform) **3** : a fine openwork usu. figured fabric made of thread — **lacy** \\'lā-sē\ *adj*

²lace *vb* **1** : TIE **2** : INTERTWINE **3** : to adorn with lace **4** : BEAT, LASH **5** : to give zest or savor to

lac·er·ate \\'las-ə-,rāt\ *vb* : to tear roughly — **lac·er·a·tion** \,las-ə-'rā-shən\ *n*

lach·ry·mose \\'lak-rə-,mōs\ *adj* **1** : TEARFUL **2** : MOURNFUL

¹lack \\'lak\ *vb* **1** : to be wanting or missing **2** : to be deficient in

²lack *n* : the fact or state of being wanting or deficient : NEED

lack·a·dai·si·cal \lak-ə-'dā-zi-kəl\ *adj* : lacking life, spirit, or zest — **lack·a·dai·si·cal·ly** *adv*

lack·ey \\'lak-ē\ *n* **1** : a liveried retainer **2** : TOADY

lack·lus·ter \\'lak-,ləs-tər\ *adj* : DULL

la·con·ic \lə-'kän-ik\ *adj* : sparing of words : TERSE — **la·con·i·cal·ly** *adv*

lac·quer \\'lak-ər\ *n* : a clear or colored usu. glossy and quick-drying surface coating that contains natural or synthetic substances (as shellac or a cellulose substance) and dries by evaporation of the solvent

lac·ri·mal *also* **lach·ry·mal** \\'lak-rə-məl\ *adj* : of, relating to, or being the glands (lacrimal glands) that produce tears

la·crosse \lə-'krós\ *n* : a game played on a field by two teams with a hard ball and long-handled rackets

lac·tate \\'lak-,tāt\ *vb* : to secrete milk — **lac·ta·tion** \lak-'tā-shən\ *n*

lac·te·al \\'lak-tē-əl\ *adj* : consisting of, producing, or resembling milk : MILKY

lac·tic \-tik\ *adj* **1** : of or relating to milk **2** : formed in the souring of milk

lactic acid *n* : a syrupy acid present in blood and muscle tissue, produced by bacterial fermentation of carbohydrates, and used in food and medicine

la·cu·na \lə-'k(y)ü-nə\ *n, pl* **-nae** \-,(,)nē\ *or* **-nas** : a blank space or missing part : GAP

lad \\'lad\ *n* : YOUTH; *also* : FELLOW

lad·der \\'lad-ər\ *n* : a structure for climbing up or down that consists of two long parallel sidepieces joined at intervals by crosspieces

lad·die \\'lad-ē\ *n* : a young lad

lad·en \\'lād-ᵊn\ *adj* : LOADED, BURDENED

lad·ing \\'lād-iŋ\ *n* : CARGO, FREIGHT

la·dle \\'lād-ᵊl\ *n* : a deep-bowled long-

ə abut; ᵉ kitten; ər further; a back; ā bake; ä cot, cart; aů out; ch chin; e less; ē easy; g gift; i trip; ī life; j joke; ŋ sing; ō flow; ȯ flaw; ȯi coin; th thin; ṯh this; ü loot; ů foot; y yet; yü few; yů furious; zh vision

handled spoon used in taking up and conveying liquids — **ladle** vb

la·dy \'lād-ē\ n **1 :** a woman of property, rank, or authority; also **:** a woman of superior social position or of refinement and gentle manners **2 :** WOMAN **3 :** WIFE

la·dy·bug \-‚bəg\ n **:** any of various small nearly hemispherical and usu. brightly colored beetles that mostly feed on other insects

la·dy·fin·ger \-‚fiŋ-gər\ n **:** a small finger-shaped sponge cake

la·dy·in-wait·ing n, pl **la·dies-in-wait·ing :** a lady appointed to attend or wait on a queen or princess

la·dy·like \'lād-ē-‚līk\ adj **:** WELL-BRED

la·dy·love \-‚ləv\ n **:** SWEETHEART

la·dy·ship \-‚ship\ n **:** the condition of being a lady **:** rank of lady

¹lag \'lag\ vb **lagged**; **lag·ging 1 :** to fail to keep up **:** stay behind **:** LOITER, LINGER **2 :** to slacken gradually **:** FLAG
syn dawdle

²lag n **1 :** a slowing up or falling behind; also **:** the amount by which one lags **2 :** INTERVAL

la·ger \'läg-ər\ n **:** a light-colored usu. dry beer

lag·gard \'lag-ərd\ adj **:** DILATORY, SLOW — **laggard** n

la·gniappe \'lan-‚yap\ n **:** something given without charge or by way of good measure

la·goon \lə-'gün\ n **:** a shallow sound, channel, or pond near or communicating with a larger body of water

laid *past of* LAY

lain *past part of* LIE

lair \'laər\ n **:** the resting or living place of a wild animal **:** DEN

laird \'laərd\ n, Scot **:** a landed proprietor

lais·sez-faire \‚les-‚ā-'faər\ n [F *laissez faire* let do] **:** a doctrine opposing governmental interference in economic affairs beyond the minimum necessary to maintain peace and property rights

la·ity \'lā-ət-ē\ n **1 :** the people of a religious faith who are distinguished from its clergy **2 :** the mass of the people who are distinguished from those of a particular profession or those specially skilled

lake \'lāk\ n **:** an inland body of standing water of considerable size; also **:** a pool of liquid (as lava or pitch)

¹lamb \'lam\ n **1 :** a young sheep; also **:** its flesh used as food **2 :** an innocent or gentle person

²lamb vb **:** to bring forth a lamb

lam·baste or **lam·bast** \lam-'bāst, -'bast\ vb **1 :** BEAT **2 :** EXCORIATE

lam·bent \'lam-bənt\ adj **1 :** FLICKERING **2 :** softly radiant ⟨~ eyes⟩ **3 :** marked by lightness or brilliance ⟨~ humor⟩ — **lam·ben·cy** \-bən-sē\ n — **lam·bent·ly** adv

lamb·skin \'lam-‚skin\ n **:** a lamb's skin or a small fine-grade sheepskin or the leather made from either

¹lame \'lām\ adj **1 :** having a body part and usu. a limb so disabled as to impair freedom of movement; also **:** marked by stiffness and soreness **2 :** lacking substance **:** WEAK ⟨a ~ excuse⟩ — **lame·ly** adv — **lame·ness** n

²lame vb **:** to make lame **:** CRIPPLE

³la·mé \lä-'mā, la-\ n **:** a brocaded clothing fabric made from any of various fibers combined with tinsel filling

threads (as of gold or silver)

¹la·ment \lə-'ment\ vb **1 :** to mourn aloud **:** WAIL **2 :** to express sorrow for **:** BEWAIL — **lam·en·ta·ble** \'lam-ən-tə-bəl\ adj — **lam·en·ta·bly** adv — **lam·en·ta·tion** \‚lam-ən-'tā-shən\ n

²lament n **1 :** a crying out in grief **:** WAIL **2 :** DIRGE, ELEGY

la·mia \'lā-mē-ə\ n **:** a female demon

lam·i·na \'lam-ə-nə\ n, pl **-nae** \-‚nē\ or **-nas :** a thin plate or scale

lam·i·nar \-nər\ adj **:** arranged in or consisting of laminae

lam·i·nat·ed \-‚nāt-əd\ adj **:** consisting of laminae; esp **:** composed of layers of firmly united material — **lam·i·nate** \-‚nāt\ vb — **lam·i·nate** \-nət\ n — **lam·i·nate** \-nət\ adj — **lam·i·na·tion** \‚lam-ə-'nā-shən\ n

lamp \'lamp\ n **1 :** a vessel with a wick for burning a flammable liquid (as oil) to produce artificial light **2 :** a device for producing light or heat

lamp·light·er \-‚līt-ər\ n **:** a person employed to go about lighting street lights that burn gas

lam·poon \lam-'pün\ n **:** SATIRE; esp **:** one that is harsh and usu. directed against an individual — **lampoon** vb

lam·prey \'lam-prē\ n **:** an eellike water animal with sucking mouth and no jaws

la·nai \lə-'nī\ n **:** a porch furnished for use as a living room

¹lance \'lans\ n **1 :** a steel-headed spear **2 :** any of various sharp-pointed implements; esp **:** LANCET

²lance vb **:** to pierce or open with a lance ⟨~ a boil⟩

lance corporal n **:** a noncommissioned officer in the marine corps ranking next below a corporal

lanc·er \'lan-sər\ n **:** a cavalryman armed with a lance

lan·cet \'lan-sət\ n **:** a sharp-pointed and usu. 2-edged surgical instrument

¹land \'land\ n **1 :** the solid part of the surface of the earth; also **:** a part of the earth's surface in some way distinguishable (as by political boundaries or physical quality) **2 :** the people of a country; also **:** REALM, DOMAIN **3** pl **:** territorial possessions — **land·less** \-ləs\ adj

²land vb **1 :** DISEMBARK; also **:** to touch at a place on shore **2 :** to bring to or arrive at a destination **3 :** to catch with a hook and bring in ⟨~ a fish⟩; also **:** GAIN, SECURE ⟨~ a job⟩ **4 :** to strike or meet the ground (as after a fall) **5 :** to alight or cause to alight on a surface ⟨~ an airplane⟩

lan·dau \'lan-‚daù\ n **1 :** a 4-wheeled carriage with a top divided into two sections that can be lowered, thrown back, or removed **2 :** an enclosed automobile with a top whose rear quarter can be opened or folded down

land·ed \'lan-dəd\ adj **:** having an estate in land ⟨~ gentry⟩

land·fall \'lan(d)-‚fòl\ n **:** a sighting or making of land (as after a voyage); also **:** the land first sighted

land·hold·er \'land-‚hōl-dər\ n **:** a holder or owner of land — **land·hold·ing** n

land·ing \'lan-diŋ\ n **1 :** the action of one that lands; also **:** a place for discharging or taking on passengers and cargo **2 :** a level part of a staircase

land·locked \'land-‚läkt\ adj **1 :** enclosed or nearly enclosed by land ⟨a ~

harbor⟩ **2** : confined to fresh water by some barrier ⟨~ salmon⟩

land·lord \'-,lȯrd\ *n* **1** : the owner of property leased or rented to another **2** : a man who rents lodgings — INN-KEEPER — **land·la·dy** *n*

land·lub·ber \-,lᴧb-ər\ *n* : one who knows little of the sea or seamanship

land·mark \'lan(d)-,märk\ *n* **1** : an object that marks the boundary of land **2** : a conspicuous object on land that marks a course or serves as a guide **3** : an event that marks a turning point

land·mass \-,mas\ *n* : a large area of land

land·own·er \'land-,ō-nər\ *n* : an owner of land

¹land·scape \'lan(d)-,skāp\ *n* **1** : a picture representing a view of natural inland scenery **2** : a portion of land that the eye can see in one glance

²landscape *vb* : to improve the natural beauties of a tract of land by grading, clearing, or decorative planting

land·slide \-,slīd\ *n* **1** : the slipping down of a mass of rocks or earth on a steep slope; *also* : the mass of material that slides **2** : an overwhelming victory esp. in a political contest

lands·man \'lan(d)z-mən\ *n* : a person who lives or works on land

land·ward \'land-wərd\ *adj* : lying or being toward the land — **landward** *adv*

lane \'lān\ *n* **1** : a narrow passageway (as between fences) **2** : a relatively narrow way or track ⟨traffic ~⟩ ⟨ocean ~⟩

lan·guage \'laŋ-gwij\ *n* **1** : the words, their pronunciation, and the methods of combining them used and understood by a considerable community **2** : form or manner of verbal expression; *esp* : STYLE

lan·guid \'laŋ-gwəd\ *adj* **1** : WEAK **2** : sluggish in character or disposition : LISTLESS **3** : SLOW — **lan·guid·ly** *adv* — **lan·guid·ness** *n*

lan·guish \'laŋ-gwish\ *vb* **1** : to become languid **2** : to become dispirited : PINE **3** : to appeal for sympathy by assuming an expression of grief or emotion

lan·guor \'laŋ-(g)ər\ *n* **1** : a languid feeling **2** : listless indolence **syn** lethargy, lassitude — **lan·guor·ous** \-əs\ *adj* — **lan·guor·ous·ly** *adv*

lank \'laŋk\ *adj* **1** : not well filled out : SLENDER **2** : hanging straight and limp ⟨~ hair⟩

lanky \'laŋ-kē\ *adj* : ungracefully tall and thin

lan·o·lin \'lan-ᵊl-ən\ *n* : the fatty coating of sheep's wool esp. when refined for use in ointments and cosmetics

lan·tern \'lant-ərn\ *n* **1** : a usu. portable light with a protective transparent or translucent covering **2** : the chamber in a lighthouse containing the light **3** : a projector for slides

lan·yard \'lan-yərd\ *n* : a piece of rope for fastening something in ships

Lao·tian \lā-'ō-shən, 'laú-shən\ *n* : a member of a Buddhist people living in Laos and northeastern Thailand

¹lap \'lap\ *n* **1** : a loose panel or hanging flap of a garment **2** : the clothing that lies on the knees, thighs, and lower part of the trunk when one sits; *also*

: the front part of the lower trunk and thighs of a seated person **3** : an environment of nurture ⟨the ~ of luxury⟩ **4** : CHARGE, CONTROL ⟨in the ~ of the gods⟩

²lap *vb* **lapped**; **lap·ping 1** : FOLD **2** : WRAP **3** : to lay over or near so as to partly cover

³lap *n* **1** : the amount by which an object overlaps another; *also* : the part of an object that overlaps another **2** : one circuit around a racecourse **3** : one complete turn of a rope around a drum⟩

⁴lap *vb* **1** : to scoop up food or drink with the tip of the tongue; *also* : DEVOUR — usu. used with *up* **2** : to splash gently ⟨*lapping* waves⟩

⁵lap *n* **1** : an act or instance of lapping **2** : a gentle splashing sound

lap·board \'lap-,bȯrd\ *n* : a board used on the lap as a table or desk

lap·dog \-,dȯg\ *n* : a small dog that may be held in the lap

la·pel \lə-'pel\ *n* : the fold of the front of a coat that is usu. a continuation of the collar

¹lap·i·dary \'lap-ə-,der-ē\ *n* : one who cuts, polishes, and engraves precious stones

²lapidary *adj* **1** : of or relating to precious stones or the art of cutting them **2** : of, relating to, or suitable for engraved inscriptions

lap·in \'lap-ən\ *n* : rabbit fur usu. sheared and dyed

la·pis la·zu·li \,lap-əs-'laz(h)-ə-lē\ *n* : a usu. blue semiprecious stone often having sparkling bits of an iron compound

Lapp \'lap\ *n* : a member of a people of northern Scandinavia, Finland, and the Kola peninsula of Russia

lap·pet \'lap-ət\ *n* : a fold or flap on a garment

¹lapse \'laps\ *n* **1** : a slight error **2** : a fall from a higher to a lower state **3** : the termination of a right or privilege through failure to meet requirements **4** : a passage of time; *also* : INTERVAL

²lapse *vb* **1** : to commit apostasy **2** : to sink or slip gradually : SUBSIDE **3** : CEASE

lap·wing \'lap-,wiŋ\ *n* : an Old World crested plover

lar·board \'lär-bərd\ *n* : PORT

lar·ce·ny \'lärs-(ᵊ)-nē\ *n* : THEFT — **lar·ce·nous** \-nəs\ *adj*

larch \'lärch\ *n* : a conical tree related to the pines that sheds its needles in the fall

¹lard \'lärd\ *vb* **1** : to insert strips of usu. pork fat into (meat) before cooking; *also* : GREASE **2** : ENRICH

²lard *n* : a soft white fat obtained by rendering fatty tissue of the hog

lar·der \'lärd-ər\ *n* : a place where foods (as meat) are kept

lar·es and pe·na·tes \,lar-ēz-ən-pə-'nāt-ēz\ *n pl* **1** : household gods **2** : personal or household effects

large \'lärj\ *adj* : having more than usual power, capacity, or scope : exceeding most other things of like kind in quantity or size **syn** big, great — **large·ly** *adv* — **large·ness** *n*

lar·gess *or* **lar·gesse** \lär-'jes\ *n* **1** : liberal giving **2** : a generous gift

¹lar·go \'lär-gō\ *adv* (*or adj*) : in a very

slow and broad manner — used as a direction in music

²largo n : a largo movement

lar·i·at \'lar-ē-ət\ n [Sp *la riata* the rope] : a long light rope used esp. to catch or tether livestock

¹lark \'lärk\ n : any of various small songbirds; esp : SKYLARK

²lark vb : FROLIC, SPORT

³lark n : FROLIC; also : PRANK

lark·spur \-,spər\ n : any of various mostly annual delphiniums

lar·va \'lär-və\ n, pl **lar·vae** \-(,)vē\ also **-vas** : the wingless often wormlike form in which insects hatch from the egg; also : any young animal (as a tadpole) that is fundamentally unlike its parent — **lar·val** \-vəl\ adj

lar·yn·gi·tis \,lar-ən-'jīt-əs\ n : inflammation of the larynx

lar·ynx \'lar-iŋks\ n, pl **la·ryn·ges** \lə-'rin-,jēz\ or **lar·ynx·es** : the upper part of the trachea containing the vocal cords — **la·ryn·ge·al** \lə-'rin-jē-əl, ,lar-ən-'jē-əl\ adj

las·car \'las-kər\ n : an East Indian sailor

las·civ·i·ous \lə-'siv-ē-əs\ adj : LEWD, LUSTFUL — **las·civ·i·ous·ness** n

¹lash \'lash\ vb 1 : to move vigorously 2 : WHIP 3 : to attack or retort verbally

²lash n 1 : a stroke esp. with a whip; also : the flexible part of a whip 2 : a verbal blow 3 : EYELASH

³lash vb : to bind with a rope, cord, or chain

lass \'las\ n : GIRL

lass·ie \-ē\ n : LASS

las·si·tude \'las-ə-,t(y)üd\ n 1 : WEARINESS, FATIGUE 2 : LISTLESSNESS, LANGUOR

las·so \'las-ō, la-'sü\ n, pl **lassos** or **lassoes** : a rope or long leather thong with a running noose used for catching livestock — **lasso** vb

¹last \'last\ vb 1 : to continue in existence or operation 2 : to remain valid, valuable, or important : ENDURE 3 : to be enough for the needs of

²last adj 1 : following all the rest : FINAL 2 : next before the present ⟨~ week⟩ 3 : least likely ⟨the ~ thing he wants⟩ 4 : CONCLUSIVE; also : SUPREME — **last·ly** adv

³last adv 1 : at the end 2 : most recently 3 : in conclusion

⁴last n : something that is last : END

⁵last n : a foot-shaped form on which a shoe is shaped or repaired

⁶last vb : to shape with a last

lat·a·kia \,lat-ə-'kē-ə\ n : an aromatic Turkish smoking tobacco

¹latch \'lach\ vb : to catch or get hold ⟨~ onto a pass⟩

²latch n : a catch that holds a door or gate closed

³latch vb : CATCH, FASTEN

latch·et \'lach-ət\ n : a strap, thong, or lace for fastening a shoe or sandal

latch·key \'lach-,kē\ n : a key by which a door latch may be opened from the outside

latch·string \-,striŋ\ n : a string on a latch that may be left hanging outside the door for raising the latch

¹late \'lāt\ adj 1 : coming or remaining after the due, usual, or proper time : TARDY 2 : far advanced toward the close or end 3 : recently deceased ⟨her ~ husband⟩; also : holding a position

recently but not now 4 : made, appearing, or happening just previous to the present : RECENT — **late·ly** adv — **late·ness** n

²late adv 1 : after the usual or proper time; also : at or to an advanced point in time 2 : RECENTLY

late·com·er \-,kəm-ər\ n : one who arrives late

la·tent \'lāt-ᵊnt\ adj : present but not visible or active syn dormant, quiescent, potential — **la·ten·cy** \-ᵊn-sē\ n

lat·er·al \'lat-(ə-)rəl\ adj : situated on, directed toward, or coming from the side — **lat·er·al·ly** adv

la·tex \'lā-,teks\ n : a milky plant juice esp. of members of the milkweed group ⟨rubber is made from a ~⟩

lath \'lath\ n : a thin narrow strip of wood used esp. as a base for plaster; also : a building material in sheets used for the same purpose

lathe \'lāth\ n : a machine in which a piece of material is held and turned while being shaped by a tool

¹lath·er \'lath-ər\ n 1 : a foam or froth formed when a detergent is agitated in water; also : foam from profuse sweating (as by a horse) 2 : DITHER

²lather vb : to spread lather over; also : to form a lather

Lat·in \'lat-ᵊn\ n 1 : the language of ancient Rome 2 : a member of any of the peoples (as the French or Spanish) whose languages derive from Latin — **Latin** adj

Latin American n : a native or inhabitant of any of the countries of No., Central, or So. America whose official language is Spanish or Portuguese — **Latin-American** adj

lat·i·tude \'lat-ə-,t(y)üd\ n 1 : angular distance north or south from the earth's equator measured in degrees 2 : a region marked by its latitude 3 : freedom of action or choice

lat·i·tu·di·nar·i·an \,lat-ə-,t(y)üd-ᵊn-'er-ē-ən\ n : a person who is broad and liberal in his standards of religious belief and conduct

la·trine \lə-'trēn\ n : TOILET

lat·ter \'lat-ər\ adj 1 : more recent; also : FINAL 2 : of, relating to, or being the second of two things referred to — **lat·ter·ly** adv

lat·ter-day adj 1 : of a later or subsequent time 2 : of present or recent time

lat·tice \'lat-əs\ n : a framework of crossed wood or metal strips; also : a window, door, or gate having a lattice

lat·tice·work \-,wərk\ n : LATTICE; also : work made of lattices

Lat·vi·an \'lat-vē-ən\ n : a native or inhabitant of Latvia

¹laud \'lȯd\ n 1 : ACCLAIM, PRAISE

²laud vb : EXTOL, PRAISE — **laud·able** \-ə-bəl\ adj — **laud·ably** adv

lau·da·num \'lȯd-(ᵊ-)nəm\ n : OPIATE; esp : a tincture of opium

lau·da·to·ry \'lȯd-ə-,tōr-ē\ adj : of, relating to, or expressive of praise

¹laugh \'laf, 'lȧf\ vb : to show mirth, joy, or scorn with a smile and chuckle or explosive sound; also : to become amused or derisive — **laugh·able** \-ə-bəl\ adj

²laugh n 1 : the act of laughing 2 : JOKE; also : JEER

laugh·ing·stock \-iŋ-,stäk\ n : an object of ridicule

laugh·ter \-tər\ *n* : the action or sound of laughing

¹launch \'lȯnch\ *vb* **1** : THROW, HURL; *also* : to send off (~ a rocket) **2** : to set afloat **3** : to set in operation : START

²launch *n* : an act or instance of launching

³launch *n* : a small open or half-decked motorboat

launching pad *n* : a platform from which a rocket is launched

laun·der \'lȯn-dər\ *vb* : to wash or wash and iron clothing and household linens — **laun·der·er** *n* — **laun·dress** \-drəs\ *n*

laun·dry \-drē\ *n* [fr. obs. *launder* launderer, fr. MF *lavandier*, fr. ML *lavandarius*, fr. L *lavandus* needing to be washed, fr. *lavare* to wash] **1** : clothes or linens that have been or are to be laundered **2** : a place where laundering is done — **laun·dry·man** \-mən\ *n*

lau·re·ate \'lȯr-ē-ət\ *n* : the recipient of honor for achievement in an art or science — **lau·re·ate·ship** \-,ship\ *n*

lau·rel \'lȯr-əl\ *n* **1** : any of several trees or shrubs related to the sassafras and cinnamon; *esp* : a small evergreen tree of southern Europe **2** : a crown of laurel leaves **3** : HONOR, DISTINCTION

la·va \'läv-ə, 'lav-\ *n* : melted rock coming from a volcano; *also* : such rock that has cooled and hardened

la·vage \lə-'väzh\ *n* : WASHING; *esp* : the washing out (as of an organ) for medicinal reasons

la·va·liere *or* **la·val·liere** \,läv-ə-'liər\ *n* : a pendant on a fine chain that is worn as a necklace

lav·a·to·ry \'lav-ə-,tōr-ē\ *n* **1** : a fixed bowl or basin with running water and drainpipe for washing **2** : BATHROOM

lave \'lāv\ *vb* : WASH

lav·en·der \'lav-ən-dər\ *n* **1** : a European mint or its dried leaves and flowers used to perfume clothing and bed linen **2** : a pale purple

¹lav·ish \'lav-ish\ *adj* **1** : expending or bestowing profusely : PRODIGAL **2** : expended or produced in abundance — **lav·ish·ly** *adv*

²lavish *vb* : to expend or give freely

law \'lȯ\ *n* **1** : a rule of conduct or action established by custom or laid down and enforced by a governing authority; *also* : the whole body of such rules **2** : the control brought about by enforcing rules (forces of ~ and order) **3** : a rule or principle of construction or procedure (~s of poetry) **4** : a rule or principle stating something that always works in the same way under the same conditions; *also* : the observed regularity of nature **5** *cap* : the revelation of the divine will set forth in the Old Testament; *also* : the first part of the Jewish scriptures **6** : trial in a court to determine what is just and right **7** : the science that deals with laws and their interpretation and application **8** : the profession of a lawyer

law·break·er \-,brā-kər\ *n* : one who violates the law

law·ful \-fəl\ *adj* **1** : permitted by law **2** : RIGHTFUL — **law·ful·ly** *adv*

law·giv·er \-,giv-ər\ *n* : LEGISLATOR

law·less \-ləs\ *adj* **1** : having no laws **2** : UNRULY, DISORDERLY (a ~ mob) — **law·less·ness** *n*

law·mak·er \-,mā-kər\ *n* : LEGISLATOR

¹lawn \'lȯn\ *n* : a fine sheer linen or cotton fabric

²lawn *n* : ground (as around a house) covered with closely mowed grass

law·ren·ci·um \lȯ-'ren-sē-əm\ *n* : a short-lived radioactive element

law·suit \'lȯ-,süt\ *n* : a suit in law

law·yer \'lȯ-yər\ *n* : one who conducts lawsuits for clients or advises as to legal rights and obligations in other matters

lax \'laks\ *adj* **1** : LOOSE, OPEN **2** : not strict (~ discipline) **3** : not tense **4** : SLACK **syn** remiss, negligent, neglectful — **lax·i·ty** \'lak-sət-ē\ *n* — **lax·ly** *adv*

lax·a·tive \'lak-sət-iv\ *adj* : relieving constipation

²laxative *n* : a usu. mild laxative drug

¹lay \'lā\ *vb* **laid** \'lād\ **lay·ing 1** : to beat or strike down **2** : to put on or against a surface : PLACE **3** : to produce and deposit eggs **4** : SETTLE; *also* : ALLAY **5** : WAGER **6** : SPREAD **7** : to set in order or position **8** : to impose esp. as a duty or burden **9** : PREPARE, CONTRIVE **10** : to bring to a specified condition **11** : to put forward : SUBMIT

²lay *n* : the way in which something lies or is laid in relation to something else

³lay *past of* LIE

⁴lay *n* **1** : a simple narrative poem **2** : SONG

⁵lay *adj* : of or relating to the laity

lay·er \'lā-ər\ *n* **1** : one that lays **2** : one thickness, course, or fold laid or lying over or under another

lay·ette \lā-'et\ *n* : an outfit of clothing and equipment for a newborn infant

lay·man \'lā-mən\ *n* : a member of the laity

lay·off \'lā-,of\ *n* **1** : the act of dismissing an employee temporarily **2** : a period of inactivity

lay·out \-,aut\ *n* **1** : ARRANGEMENT **2** : SET, OUTFIT

laz·ar \'laz-ər\ *n* : LEPER

laze \'lāz\ *vb* : to pass time in idleness or relaxation

la·zy \'lā-zē\ *adj* : disliking activity or exertion : INDOLENT **2** : SLUGGISH (a ~ stream) — **la·zi·ly** *adv* — **la·zi·ness** *n*

la·zy·bones \'lā-zē-,bōnz\ *n* : a lazy person

lazy Su·san \,lā-zē-'süz-ᵊn\ *n* : a revolving tray placed on a dining table (as for serving condiments or relishes)

lea \'lē\ *n* : PASTURE, MEADOW

leach \'lēch\ *vb* : to pass a liquid (as water) through to carry off the soluble components; *also* : to dissolve out by such means (~ alkali from ashes)

¹lead \'lēd\ *vb* **led** \'led\ **lead·ing 1** : to guide on a way; *also* : to run in a specified direction **2** : LIVE (~ a quiet life) **3** : to direct the operations, activity, or performance of (~ an orchestra) **4** : to go at the head of : be first (~ a parade) **5** : to begin play with; *also* : BEGIN, OPEN **6** : to tend toward a definite result (study ~ing to a degree) — **lead·er** *n* — **lead·er·less** *adj* — **lead·er·ship** *n*

²**lead** \'lēd\ *n* **1** : a position at the front; *also* : a margin by which one leads **2** : one that leads **3** : the privilege of leading in cards; *also* : the card or suit led **4** : a principal role (as in a play); *also* : one who plays such a role **5** : EXAMPLE, PRECEDENT **6** : INDICATION, CLUE

³**lead** \'led\ *n* **1** : a heavy bluish white chemical element that is easily bent and shaped **2** : an article made of lead; *esp* : a weight for sounding at sea **3** : a thin strip of metal used to separate lines of type in printing **4** : a thin stick of marking substance in or for a pencil

⁴**lead** \'led\ *vb* **1** : to cover, line, or weight with lead **2** : to fix (glass) in position with lead

lead·en \'led-ªn\ *adj* **1** : made of lead; *also* : of the color of lead **2** : low in quality **3** : SLUGGISH, DULL

¹**leaf** \'lēf\ *n, pl* **leaves** \'lēvz\ **1** : a usu. flat and green outgrowth of a plant stem that is a unit of foliage and functions esp. in photosynthesis; *also* : FOLIAGE **2** : PETAL **3** : something (as a single sheet of a book, the movable part of a table top, or a thin sheet of gold) that is suggestive of a leaf — **leaf·less** \'lēf-lǝs\ *adj* — **leafy** *adj*

²**leaf** *vb* **1** : to produce leaves **2** : to turn the pages of a book

leaf·age \'lē-fij\ *n* : FOLIAGE

leaf·let \'lēf-lǝt\ *n* **1** : a division of a compound leaf **2** : PAMPHLET, FOLDER

leaf·stalk \-,stȯk\ *n* : PETIOLE

¹**league** \'lēg\ *n* : a measure of distance equal to about 3 miles

²**league** *n* **1** : an association or alliance (as of nations or persons) for a common purpose **2** : CLASS, CATEGORY — **league** *vb*

¹**leak** \'lēk\ *vb* **1** : to enter or escape through a leak **2** : to become or make known

²**leak** *n* **1** : a crack or hole that accidentally admits a fluid or light or lets it escape; *also* : something that secretly or accidentally permits the admission or escape of something else **2** : LEAKAGE — **leaky** *adj*

leak·age \'lē-kij\ *n* **1** : the act of leaking **2** : the thing or amount that leaks

leal \'lēl\ *adj, chiefly Scot* : LOYAL

¹**lean** \'lēn\ *vb* **1** : to bend from a vertical position : INCLINE **2** : to cast one's weight to one side for support **3** : to rely on for support or inspiration **4** : to incline in opinion, taste, or desire

²**lean** *adj* **1** : lacking or deficient in flesh and esp. in fat **2** : lacking richness or productiveness — **lean·ness** *n*

lean-to \'lēn-,tü\ *n* : a wing or extension of a building having a roof of only one slope; *also* : a rough shed or shelter with a similar roof

¹**leap** \'lēp\ *vb* **leaped** *or* **leapt** \'lēpt, 'lept\ **leap·ing** \'lē-piŋ\ : to spring free from the ground : JUMP

²**leap** *n* : JUMP

leap·frog \'lēp-,frȯg, -,fräg\ *n* : a game in which one player bends down and another leaps over him

leap year *n* : a year containing 366 days with February 29 as the extra day

learn \'lǝrn\ *vb* **1** : to gain knowledge, understanding, or skill by study or experience; *also* : MEMORIZE **2** : to find out : ASCERTAIN — **learn·er** *n*

learn·ed \'lǝr-nǝd\ *adj* : SCHOLARLY, ERUDITE

learn·ing \'lǝr-niŋ\ *n* : KNOWLEDGE, ERUDITION

¹**lease** \'lēs\ *n* : a contract by which one party conveys real estate to another for a term of years or at will usu. for a specified rent

²**lease** *vb* **1** : to grant by lease **2** : to hold under a lease syn let, charter, hire, rent

lease·hold \-,hōld\ *n* **1** : a tenure by lease **2** : land held by lease — **lease·hold·er** *n*

leash \'lēsh\ *n* : a line for leading or restraining an animal — **leash** *vb*

¹**least** \'lēst\ *adj* **1** : lowest in importance or position **2** : smallest in size or degree **3** : SLIGHTEST

²**least** *n* : one that is least : the smallest amount or degree

³**least** *adv* : in the smallest or lowest degree

least·wise \-,wīz\ *adv* : at least

leath·er \'leth-ǝr\ *n* : animal skin dressed for use — **leather** *adj* — **leath·ern** \-ǝrn\ *adj* — **leath·ery** *adj*

leath·er·neck \-ǝr-,nek\ *n* : MARINE

leave \'lēv\ *vb* **left** \'left\ **leav·ing** **1** : BEQUEATH **2** : to allow or cause to remain behind; *also* : DELIVER **3** : to have as a remainder **4** : to let stay without interference **5** : to go away : depart from **6** : to give up : ABANDON

²**leave** *n* **1** : PERMISSION; *also* : authorized absence from duty **2** : DEPARTURE

³**leave** *vb* : LEAF

leav·en \'lev-ǝn\ *n* **1** : a substance (as yeast) used to produce fermentation (as in dough) **2** : something that modifies or lightens a mass or aggregate

²**leaven** *vb* : to raise (dough) with a leaven; *also* : to permeate with a modifying or vivifying element

leav·en·ing *n* : LEAVEN

leaves *pl of* LEAF

leave-tak·ing \'lēv-,tā-kiŋ\ *n* : DEPARTURE, FAREWELL

leav·ings \'lē-viŋz\ *n pl* : REMNANT, RESIDUE

lech·ery \'lech-ǝ-rē\ *n* : inordinate indulgence in sexual activity — **lech·er** \-ǝr\ *n* — **lech·er·ous** *adj* — **lech·er·ous·ness** *n*

lec·tern \'lek-tǝrn\ *n* : a desk to support a book in a convenient position for a standing reader

lec·tor \-tǝr\ *n* : one whose chief duty is to read the lessons in a church service

lec·ture \'lek-chǝr\ *n* **1** : a discourse given before an audience or a class esp. for instruction **2** : REPRIMAND — **lecture** *vb* — **lec·tur·er** *n*

led *past of* LEAD

le·der·ho·sen \'lād-ǝr-,hōz-ªn\ *n pl* : knee-length leather trousers worn esp. in Bavaria

ledge \'lej\ *n* **1** : a shelflike projection from a top or an edge **2** : REEF

led·ger \'lej-ǝr\ *n* : a book containing accounts to which debits and credits are transferred in final form

lee \'lē\ *n* **1** : a protecting shelter **2** : the side (as of a ship) that is sheltered from the wind

leech \'lēch\ *n* **1** : any of various segmented usu. freshwater worms related to the earthworms; *esp* : one formerly used by physicians to draw blood **2** : a hanger-on who seeks advantage or gain

leek \'lēk\ *n* : an onionlike herb grown for its mildly pungent leaves and stalk

leer \'liər\ *n* **:** a suggestive, knowing, or malicious look — **leer** *vb*

leery \'li(ə)r-ē\ *adj* **:** SUSPICIOUS, WARY

lees \'lēz\ *n pl* **:** DREGS

lee·ward \'lē-wərd, 'lü-ərd\ *adj* **:** situated away from the wind — **leeward** *adv*

lee·way \'lē-,wā\ *n* **1 :** off-course lateral movement of a ship when under way **2 :** an allowable margin of freedom or variation

¹left \'left\ *adj* **1 :** of, relating to, or being the side of the body in which the heart is mostly located; *also* **:** located nearer to this side than to the right **2** *often cap* **:** of, adhering to, or constituted by the political Left — **left** *adv*

²left *n* **1 :** the left hand; *also* **:** the location or direction of or part on the left side **2** *cap* **:** those professing political views characterized by desire to reform the established order and to give greater freedom to the common man

³left *past of* LEAVE

left-hand \,left-'hand\ *adj* **1 :** situated on the left **2 :** LEFT-HANDED

left-hand·ed \'left-'han-dəd\ *adj* **1 :** using the left hand habitually **2 :** CLUMSY, AWKWARD

left·ist \'lef-təst\ *n* **:** one who advocates or adheres to the policies of the Left

left·over \'left-,ō-vər\ *n* **:** an unused or unconsumed residue

¹leg \'leg\ *n* **1 :** a limb of an animal used esp. for supporting the body and in walking; *esp* **:** the part of the vertebrate leg between knee and foot **2 :** something resembling an animal leg in shape or use (table ~) **3 :** the part of an article of clothing that covers the leg — **leg·less** *adj*

²leg *vb* **legged** \'legd\ **leg·ging :** to use the legs in walking or esp. in running

leg·a·cy \'leg-ə-sē\ *n* **:** INHERITANCE, BEQUEST; *also* **:** something that has come from an ancestor or predecessor or the past

le·gal \'lē-gəl\ *adj* **1 :** of or relating to law or lawyers **2 :** LAWFUL; *also* **:** STATUTORY **3 :** enforced in courts of law — **le·gal·i·ty** \li-'gal-ət-ē\ *n* — **le·gal·ize** \'lē-gə-,līz\ *vb* — **le·gal·ly** *adv*

le·gal·ism \'lē-gə-,liz-əm\ *n* **:** strict, literal, or excessive conformity to the law or to a religious or moral code — **le·gal·is·tic** \,lē-gə-'lis-tik\ *adj*

le·gate \'leg-ət\ *n* **:** an official representative; *esp* **:** AMBASSADOR

leg·a·tee \,leg-ə-'tē\ *n* **:** a person to whom a legacy is bequeathed

le·ga·tion \li-'gā-shən\ *n* **1 :** a diplomatic mission headed by a minister **2 :** the official residence and office of a minister to a foreign government

leg·end \'lej-ənd\ *n* [ML *legenda,* lit., something to be read, fr. L *legere* to read] **1 :** a story coming down from the past; *esp* **:** one popularly accepted as historical though not verifiable **2 :** an inscription on an object; *also* **:** CAPTION

leg·end·ary \'lej-ən-,der-ē\ *adj* **:** of, relating to, or characteristic of a legend **:** FABULOUS

leg·er·de·main \,lej-ərd-ə-'mān\ *n* **:** SLEIGHT OF HAND

leg·ging *or* **leg·gin** \'leg-ən, -in\ *n* **:** a covering for the leg — usu. used in pl.

leg·horn \'leg-,(h)órn, 'leg-ərn\ *n* **1 :** a fine plaited straw; *also* **:** a hat made of this straw **2 :** any of a Mediterranean breed of small hardy fowls

leg·i·ble \'lej-ə-bəl\ *adj* **:** capable of being read **:** CLEAR — **leg·i·bil·i·ty** \,lej-ə-'bil-ət-ē\ *n* — **leg·i·bly** \'lej-ə-blē\ *adv*

le·gion \'lē-jən\ *n* **1 :** a unit of the Roman army comprising 3000 to 6000 soldiers **2 :** MULTITUDE **3 :** an association of ex-servicemen — **le·gion·ary** \-,er-ē\ *n* — **le·gion·naire** \,lē-jən-'aər\ *n*

leg·is·late \'lej-ə-,slāt\ *vb* **:** to make or enact laws; *also* **:** to bring about by legislation — **leg·is·la·tor** \-,slāt-ər\ *n*

leg·is·la·tion \,lej-ə-'slā-shən\ *n* **1 :** the action of legislating **2 :** laws made by a legislative body

leg·is·la·tive \'lej-ə-,slāt-iv\ *adj* **1 :** having the power of legislating **2 :** of or relating to a legislature

leg·is·la·ture \-,slā-chər\ *n* **:** an organized body of persons having the authority to make laws for a political unit

le·git·i·mate \li-'jit-ə-mət\ *adj* **1 :** lawfully begotten **2 :** GENUINE **3 :** LAWFUL **4 :** conforming to recognized principles or accepted rules or standards — **le·git·i·ma·cy** \-mə-sē\ *n* — **le·git·i·mate·ly** *adv*

leg·man \'leg-,man\ *n* **1 :** a newspaperman assigned usu. to gather information **2 :** an assistant who gathers information and runs errands

leg·ume \'leg-,yüm, li-'gyüm\ *n* **1 :** any of a large group of plants having fruits that are dry pods and split when ripe and including important food and forage plants (as beans and clover) **2 :** the part (as seeds or pods) of a legume used as food; *also* **:** VEGETABLE **2** — **le·gu·mi·nous** \li-'gyü-mə-nəs\ *adj*

¹lei \'lā(-,ē)\ *n* **:** a wreath or necklace usu. of flowers

²lei \'lā\ *pl of* leu

lei·sure \'lē-zhər, 'lezh-ər\ *n* **1 :** time free from work or duties **2 :** EASE; *also* **:** CONVENIENCE syn relaxation, rest, repose — **lei·sure·ly** *adj*

leit·mo·tiv *or* **leit·mo·tif** \'līt-mō-,tēf\ *n* **:** a dominant recurring theme

lek \'lek\ *n* — see MONEY table

lem·ming \'lem-iŋ\ *n* **:** any of several short-tailed northern rodents

lem·on \'lem-ən\ *n* **:** an acid yellow usu. nearly oblong citrus fruit

lem·on·ade \,lem-ə-'nād\ *n* **:** a beverage of lemon juice, sugar, and water

lem·pi·ra \lem-'pir-ə\ *n* — see MONEY table

lend \'lend\ *vb* **lent** \'lent\ **lend·ing 1 :** to give for temporary use on condition that the same or its equivalent be returned **2 :** AFFORD, FURNISH **3 :** ACCOMMODATE — **lend·er** *n*

lend-lease \-'lēs\ *n* **:** the transfer of goods and services to an ally to aid in a common cause with payment being made by a return of the original items or their use in the common cause or by a similar transfer of other goods and services

length \'leŋth\ *n* **1 :** the longer or longest dimension of an object; *also* **:** a measured distance or dimension **2** : duration or extent in time or space **3** : the length of something taken as a unit of measure ⟨the horse won by a ~⟩ **4** : PIECE; *esp* : one in a series of pieces designed to be joined ⟨a ~ of pipe⟩ — **lengthy** *adj*

length·en \'leŋ-thən\ *vb* : to make or become longer **syn** extend, elongate, prolong, protract

length·wise \'leŋth-wīz\ *adv (or adj)* : in the direction of the length

le·ni·ent \'lē-nē-ənt\ *adj* : of mild and tolerant disposition or effect **syn** soft, gentle, indulgent, forbearing — **le·ni·en·cy** \-ən-sē\ *n* — **le·ni·ent·ly** *adv*

len·i·tive \'len-ət-iv\ *adj* : alleviating pain or acrimony

len·i·ty \'len-ət-ē\ *n* : LENIENCY, MILDNESS

lens \'lenz\ *n* [L *lent-*, *lens* lentil; so called fr. the shape of a convex lens] **1** : a curved piece of glass or plastic used singly or combined in an optical instrument (as spectacles, a telescope, or a projector) for forming an image; *also* : a device for focusing radiations other than light **2** : a transparent body in the eye that focuses light rays on receptors at the back of the eye

Lent \'lent\ *n* : a 40-day period of penitence and fasting observed from Ash Wednesday to Easter by many churches — **Lent·en** \-ᵊn\ *adj*

len·til \'lent-ᵊl\ *n* : an Old World legume grown for its flat edible seeds and for fodder; *also* : its seed

le·o·nine \'lē-ə-‚nīn\ *adj* : of, relating to, or resembling a lion

leop·ard \'lep-ərd\ *n* : a large strong usu. tawny and black-spotted cat of southern Asia and Africa

le·o·tard \'lē-ə-‚tärd\ *n* : a close-fitting garment worn esp. by dancers and acrobats

lep·er \'lep-ər\ *n* **1** : a person affected with leprosy **2** : OUTCAST

lep·re·chaun \'lep-rə-‚kän\ *n* : a mischievous elf of Irish folklore

lep·ro·sy \'lep-rə-sē\ *n* : a chronic bacterial disease marked esp. by slow-growing swellings with deformity and loss of sensation of affected parts — **lep·rous** \-rəs\ *adj*

lep·ton \'lep-‚tän\ *n*, *pl* **lep·ta** \-‚tä\ — see MONEY table

les·bi·an \'lez-bē-ən\ *n* : a female homosexual — **lesbian** *adj* — **les·bi·an·ism** \-‚iz-əm\ *n*

le·sion \'lē-zhən\ *n* : an abnormal structural change in the body due to injury or disease

¹less \'les\ *adj* **1** : FEWER ⟨~ than six⟩ **2** : of lower rank, degree, or importance **3** : SMALLER; *also* : more limited in quantity

²less *adv* : to a lesser extent or degree

³less *prep* : diminished by : MINUS

⁴less *n* : a smaller portion **2** : something of less importance

-less \ləs\ *adj suffix* **1** : destitute of : not having ⟨child*less*⟩ **2** : unable to be acted on or to act (in a specified way) ⟨daunt*less*⟩

les·see \le-'sē\ *n* : a tenant under a lease

less·en \'les-ᵊn\ *vb* : to make or become less **syn** decrease, diminish, dwindle

less·er \-ər\ *adj* **1** : SMALLER **2** : INFERIOR

les·son \'les-ᵊn\ *n* **1** : a passage from sacred writings read in a service of

worship **2** : a reading or exercise to be studied by a pupil; *also* : something learned **3** : a period of instruction **4** : an instructive example

les·sor \'les-‚ór, le-'sór\ *n* : one who conveys property by a lease

lest \'lest\ *conj* : for fear that

¹let \'let\ *n* [ME *lette*, fr. *letten* to delay, hinder, fr. OE *lettan*] **1** : HINDRANCE, OBSTACLE **2** : a stroke in racket games that does not count

²let *vb* **let**; **let·ting** [OE *lǣtan*] **1** : to cause to : MAKE ⟨~ it be known⟩ **2** : RENT, LEASE; *also* : to assign esp. after bids **3** : ALLOW, PERMIT ⟨~ him go⟩

-let \lət\ *n suffix* **1** : small one ⟨book*let*⟩ **2** : article worn on ⟨wrist*let*⟩

let·down \'let-‚daun\ *n* **1** : DISAPPOINTMENT **2** : a slackening of effort

le·thal \'lē-thəl\ *adj* : DEADLY, FATAL — **le·thal·ly** *adv*

leth·ar·gy \'leth-ər-jē\ *n* **1** : abnormal drowsiness **2** : the quality or state of being lazy or indifferent **syn** languor, lassitude — **le·thar·gic** \li-'thär-jik\ *adj*

Lett \'let\ *n* : LATVIAN

¹let·ter \'let-ər\ *n* **1** : a symbol that stands for a speech sound and constitutes a unit of an alphabet **2** : a written or printed communication **3** *pl* : LITERATURE; *also* : LEARNING **4** : the literal meaning ⟨the ~ of the law⟩ **5** : a single piece of type

²letter *vb* : to mark with letters: INSCRIBE — **let·ter·er** *n*

let·ter·head \-‚hed\ *n* : stationery with a printed or engraved heading; *also* : the heading itself

let·ter-per·fect \‚let-ər-'pər-fikt\ *adj* : correct to the smallest detail; *esp* : VERBATIM

let·ter·press \'let-ər-‚pres\ *n* **1** : printing done directly by impressing the paper on an inked raised surface **2** : TEXT

letters patent *n pl* : a written grant from a government to a person in a form readily open for inspection by all

let·tuce \'let-əs\ *n* : a garden plant with crisp leaves used esp. in salads

let·up \'let-‚əp\ *n* : a lessening of effort

leu \'leü\ *n*, *pl* **lei** \'lā\ — see MONEY table

leu·ke·mia \lü-'kē-mē-ə\ *n* : a cancerous disease in which white blood cells increase greatly

leu·ko·cyte \'lü-kə-‚sīt\ *n* : WHITE BLOOD CELL

lev \'lef\ *n*, *pl* **le·va** \'lev-ə\ — see MONEY table

¹lev·ee \'lev-ē, lə-'vē\ *n* : a reception held by a person of distinction

²lev·ee \'lev-ē\ *n* : an embankment to prevent flooding (as by a river); *also* : a river landing place

lev·el \'lev-əl\ *n* **1** : a device for establishing a horizontal line or plane **2** : horizontal condition **3** : a horizontal position, line, or surface often taken as an index of altitude; *also* : a flat area of ground **4** : height, position, rank, or size in a scale

²level *vb* **-eled** *or* **-elled**; **-el·ing** *or* **-el·ling 1** : to make flat or level; *also* : to come to a level **2** : AIM, DIRECT **3** : EQUALIZE **4** : RAZE — **lev·el·er** *n*

³level *adj* **1** : having a flat even surface **2** : HORIZONTAL **3** : of the same height or rank; EVEN; *also* : UNIFORM **4** : steady

and cool in judgment — **lev·el·ly** *adv*
— **lev·el·ness** *n*

lev·el·head·ed \,lev-əl-'hed-əd\ *adj*
: having sound judgment : SENSIBLE

lev·er \'lev-ər, 'lē-vər\ *n* **1** : a bar used
for prying or dislodging something;
also : a means for achieving one's
purpose (a ~ to gain votes) **2** : a rigid
piece turning about an axis and used for
transmitting and changing force and
motion

lev·er·age \-ij\ *n* : the action or mechanical effect of a lever

le·vi·a·than \li-'vī-ə-thən\ *n* **1** : a large
sea animal **2** : something very large or
formidable of its kind

lev·i·tate \'lev-ə-,tāt\ *vb* : to rise or
cause to rise in the air in seeming defiance of gravitation — **lev·i·ta·tion**
\,lev-ə-'tā-shən\ *n*

lev·i·ty \'lev-ət-ē\ *n* : lack of earnestness : FRIVOLITY **syn** lightness, flip-
pancy

¹levy \'lev-ē\ *n* **1** : the imposition or collection of an assessment; *also* : an
amount levied **2** : the enlistment of
men for military service; *also* : troops
raised by levy

²levy *vb* **1** : to impose or collect by
legal authority (~ a tax) **2** : to enlist
for military service **3** : WAGE (~ war)
4 : to seize property in satisfaction of a
legal claim

lewd \'lüd\ *adj* **1** : sexually unchaste
: LASCIVIOUS **2** : OBSCENE, SALACIOUS
— **lewd·ly** *adv* — **lewd·ness** *n*

lex·i·cog·ra·phy \,lek-sə-'käg-rə-fē\ *n*
1 : the editing or making of a dictionary
2 : the principles and practices of dictionary making — **lex·i·cog·ra·pher**
\-fər\ *n* — **lex·i·co·graph·ic** \-kō-
'graf-ik\ *or* **lex·i·co·graph·i·cal** *adj*

lex·i·con \'lek-sə-,kän\ *n* : DICTIONARY

li·a·bil·i·ty \,lī-ə-'bil-ət-ē\ *n* **1** : the
quality or state of being liable **2** *pl*
: DEBTS **3** : DRAWBACK, DISADVANTAGE

li·a·ble \'lī-ə-bəl\ *adj* **1** : legally obligated : RESPONSIBLE **2** : LIKELY, APT
(~ to fall) **3** : SUSCEPTIBLE (~ to disease)

li·ai·son \'lē-ə-,zän, lē-'ā-\ *n* **1** : a close
bond : INTERRELATIONSHIP **2** : an illicit
sexual relationship **3** : communication
esp. between parts of an armed force

li·ar \'lī-ər\ *n* : a person who lies

li·ba·tion \lī-'bā-shən\ *n* **1** : an act of
pouring a liquid as a sacrifice (as to a
god); *also* : the liquid poured **2** : DRINK
— **li·ba·tion·ary** *adj*

¹li·bel \'lī-bəl\ *n* **1** : the action or crime
of injuring a person's reputation by
something printed or written or by a
visible representation **2** : a spoken or
written statement or a representation
that gives an unjustly unfavorable impression of a person or thing — **li·bel-
ous** *or* **li·bel·lous** \-bə-ləs\ *adj*

²libel *vb* **-beled** *or* **-belled; -bel·ing** *or*
-bel·ling : to make or publish a libel
— **li·bel·er** *or* **li·bel·ler** *n*

¹lib·er·al \'lib-(ə-)rəl\ *adj* **1** : of, relating to, or based on studies designed to
provide general knowledge and to develop the general intellectual capacities
(~ arts) **2** : GENEROUS, BOUNTIFUL
3 : not literal **4** : not narrow in
opinion or judgment : TOLERANT; *also*

: not orthodox **5** : not conservative
— **lib·er·al·ly** \'lib-ə-'ral-ət-ē\ *n* —

lib·er·al·ize \'lib-(ə-)rə-,līz\ *vb* —
lib·er·al·ly \'lib-(ə-)rə-lē\ *adv*

²liberal *n* : a person who holds liberal
views

lib·er·al·ism \'lib-(ə-)rə-,liz-əm\ *n* : liberal principles and theories

lib·er·ate \'lib-ə-,rāt\ *vb* **1** : to free
from bondage or restraint **2** : to free
(as a gas) from combination — **lib·er·a-
tion** \,lib-ə-'rā-shən\ *n* — **lib·er·a·tor**
\'lib-ə-,rāt-ər\ *n*

lib·er·tar·i·an \,lib-ər-'ter-ē-ən\ *n* **1** : an
advocate of the doctrine of free will
2 : one who upholds the principles of
liberty esp. of thought and action

lib·er·tine \'lib-ər-,tēn\ *n* : one who
leads a life of dissoluteness

lib·er·ty \-ərt-ē\ *n* **1** : FREEDOM **2** : an
action going beyond normal limits;
esp : FAMILIARITY **3** : a short authorized absence from naval duty

li·bid·i·nous \lə-'bid-ᵊn-əs\ *adj* **1** : LAS-
CIVIOUS **2** : LIBIDINAL

li·bi·do \lə-'bēd-ō, -'bīd-\ *n* : psychic
energy derived from basic biological
urges; *also* : sexual drive — **li·bid·i·nal**
\lə-'bid-ᵊn-əl\ *adj*

li·brar·i·an \lī-'brer-ē-ən\ *n* : a specialist in the care or management of a
library

li·brary \'lī-,brer-ē\ *n* **1** : a place in
which books are kept for use but not for
sale **2** : a collection of books

li·bret·to \lə-'bret-ō\ *n, pl* **-tos** *or* **-ti**
\-ē\ : the text of a work (as an opera)
for the musical theater; *also* : a book
containing such a text — **li·bret·tist**
\-əst\ *n*

Lib·y·an \'lib-ē-ən\ *n* : a native or
inhabitant of Libya

lice *pl of* LOUSE

li·cense *or* **li·cence** \'līs-ᵊns\ *n* **1** : permission to act; *esp* : legal permission to
engage in a business, occupation, or
activity **2** : a document, plate, or tag
evidencing a license granted **3** : freedom used irresponsibly — **license** *vb*

li·cens·ee \,līs-ᵊn-'sē\ *n* : a licensed
person

li·cen·ti·ate \lī-'sen·chē-ət\ *n* : one
licensed (as by a university) to practice
a profession

li·cen·tious \lī-'sen-chəs\ *adj* : LEWD,
LASCIVIOUS — **li·cen·tious·ly** *adv* — **li-
cen·tious·ness** *n*

li·chen \'lī-kən\ *n* : any of various
complex lower plants made up of an
alga and a fungus growing as a unit on a
solid surface (as of a stone or tree
trunk) — **li·chen·ous** \-əs\ *adj*

lic·it \'lis-ət\ *adj* : LAWFUL

¹lick \'lik\ *vb* **1** : to draw the tongue
over; *also* : to flicker over like a tongue
2 : THRASH; *also* : DEFEAT

²lick *n* **1** : a stroke of the tongue **2** : a
small amount **3** : a hasty careless effort
4 : BLOW **5** : a place (as a spring)
having a deposit of salt that animals
regularly lick

lick·e·ty-split \,lik-ət-ē-'split\ *adv* : at
great speed

lic·o·rice \'lik-(ə-)rish, -rəs\ *n* [LL liqui-
ritia, alter. of L glycyrrhiza, fr. Gk
glykyrrhiza, fr. glykys sweet + rhiza
root] **1** : a European leguminous plant;

ə abut; ᵊ kitten; ər further; a back; ā bake; ä cot, cart; aú out; ch chin;
e less; ē easy; g gift; i trip; ī life; j joke; ŋ sing; ō flow; ò flaw; òi coin;
th thin; t̲h̲ this; ü loot; ù foot; y yet; yü few; yù furious; zh vision

also : its dried root or an extract from it used esp. as a flavoring and in medicine **2** : a confection flavored with licorice extract

lid \\'lid\\ *n* **1** : a movable cover **2** : EYELID

li·do \\'lēd-ō\\ *n* : a fashionable beach resort

¹lie \\'lī\\ *vb* **lay** \\'lā\\ **lain** \\'lān\\ **ly·ing** \\'lī-iŋ\\ **1** : to be in, stay at rest in, or assume a horizontal position; *also* : to be in a helpless or defenseless state (~ in prison) **2** : EXTEND **3** : to occupy a certain relative position **4** : to have an effect esp. through mere presence (grief ~s heavily on him)

²lie *n* : the position in which something lies

³lie *vb* **lied; ly·ing** \\'lī-iŋ\\ : to tell a lie

⁴lie *n* : an untrue statement made with intent to deceive

lied \\'lēt\\ *n*, *pl* **lie·der** \\'lēd-ər\\ : a German song esp. of the 19th century

lief \\'lēv, 'lēf\\ *adv* : GLADLY, WILLINGLY

¹liege \\'lēj\\ *adj* : LOYAL, FAITHFUL

²liege *n* **1** : VASSAL **2** : a feudal superior

lien \\'lēn, 'lē-ən\\ *n* : a legal claim on the property of another for the satisfaction of a debt or the fulfillment of a duty

lieu \\'lü\\ *n*, *archaic* : PLACE, STEAD -- **in lieu of** : in the place of

lieu·ten·ant \\lü-'ten-ənt\\ *n* **1** : a representative of another in the performance of duty **2** : a commissioned officer (as in the army) ranking next below a captain **3** : a commissioned officer in the navy ranking next below a lieutenant commander — **lieu·ten·an·cy** \\-ən-sē\\ *n*

lieutenant colonel *n* : a commissioned officer (as in the army) ranking next below a colonel

lieutenant commander *n* : a commissioned officer in the navy ranking next below a commander

lieutenant general *n* : a commissioned officer (as in the army) ranking next below a general

lieutenant junior grade *n* : a commissioned officer in the navy ranking next below a lieutenant

life \\'līf\\ *n*, *pl* **lives** \\'līvz\\ **1** : the quality that distinguishes a vital and functional being from a dead body or inanimate matter; *also* : a state of an organism characterized esp. by capacity for metabolism, growth, reaction to stimuli, and reproduction **2** : the physical and mental experiences of an individual **3** : BIOGRAPHY **4** : the period of existence **5** : manner of living **6** : PERSON **7** : ANIMATION, SPIRIT; *also* : LIVELINESS **8** : animate activity (signs of ~) **9** : one providing interest and vigor (~ of the party) — **life·less** \\'līf-ləs\\ *adj* — **life·like** \\-,līk\\ *adj*

life·blood \\-'bləd\\ *n* : a basic source of strength and vitality

life·boat \\'līf-,bōt\\ *n* : a strong boat designed for use in saving lives at sea

life·guard \\-,gärd\\ *n* : a usu. expert swimmer employed to safeguard bathers

life·line \\-,līn\\ *n* **1** : a line to which persons may cling to save or protect their lives **2** : a land, sea, or air route considered indispensable

life·long \\'līf-,lòŋ\\ *adj* : continuing through life

life preserver *n* : a device designed to save a person from drowning by buoying up the body while in the water

lif·er \\'lī-fər\\ *n* : a person sentenced to life imprisonment

life·sav·ing \\'līf-,sā-viŋ\\ *n* : the art or practice of saving or protecting lives esp. of drowning persons

life·time *n* : the duration of an individual's existence

life·work \\-'wərk\\ *n* : the entire or principal work of one's lifetime; *also* : a work extending over a lifetime

¹lift \\'lift\\ *vb* **1** : RAISE, ELEVATE; *also* : RISE, ASCEND **2** : to put an end to : STOP **3** : to pay off (~ a mortgage)

²lift *n* **1** : LOAD **2** : the action or an instance of lifting **3** : HELP; *also* : a ride along one's way **4** : RISE, ADVANCE **5** *chiefly Brit* : ELEVATOR **6** : the upward force that is developed by a moving airplane and that opposes the pull of gravity **7** : an elevation of the spirits

lig·a·ment \\'lig-ə-mənt\\ *n* : a band of tough tissue that holds bones together

lig·a·ture \\'lig-ə-,chùr, -chər\\ *n* **1** : something that binds or ties : BAND, BOND; *also* : a thread used in surgery esp. for tying blood vessels **2** : a printed or written character consisting of two or more letters or characters (as æ) united

¹light \\'līt\\ *n* **1** : something that makes vision possible : electromagnetic radiation visible to the human eye; *also* : BRIGHTNESS **2** : DAYLIGHT **3** : a source of light (as a candle) **4** : ENLIGHTENMENT; *also* : TRUTH **5** : public knowledge **6** : WINDOW **7** : STANDARDS (according to his ~s) **8** : CELEBRITY **9** : a lighthouse beacon; *also* : a traffic signal **10** : a flame for lighting something

²light *adj* **1** : BRIGHT **2** : PALE (~ blue) — **light·ness** *n*

³light *vb* **light·ed** *or* **lit** \\'lit\\ **light·ing** **1** : to make or become light **2** : to cause to burn : BURN **3** : to conduct with a light **4** : ILLUMINATE

⁴light *adj* **1** : not heavy **2** : not serious (~ reading) **3** : SCANTY (~ rain) **4** : GENTLE (a ~ blow) **5** : easily endurable (~ cold); *also* : requiring little effort (~ exercise) **6** : SWIFT, NIMBLE **7** : FRIVOLOUS **8** : DIZZY **9** : producing goods for direct consumption by the consumer (~ industry) — **light·ly** *adv* — **light·ness** *n*

⁵light *vb* **light·ed** *or* **lit** \\'lit\\ **light·ing** **1** : SETTLE, ALIGHT **2** : to fall unexpectedly **3** : HAPPEN (~ upon a solution)

¹light·en \\'līt-°n\\ *vb* **1** : ILLUMINATE, BRIGHTEN **2** : to give out flashes of lightning

²lighten *vb* **1** : to relieve of a burden **2** : GLADDEN **3** : to become lighter

¹light·er \\'līt-ər\\ *n* : a barge used esp. in loading or unloading ships

²light·er *n* : a device for lighting (cigarette ~)

light·face \\'līt-,fās\\ *n* : a type having light thin lines (as in this) — **light·faced** \\-'fāst\\ *adj*

light·heart·ed \\'līt-'härt-əd\\ *adj* : GAY — **light·heart·ed·ly** *adv* — **light·heart·ed·ness** *n*

light·house \\-,haùs\\ *n* : a structure with a powerful light for guiding mariners

light·ning \\'līt-niŋ\\ *n* : the flashing of light produced by a discharge of atmospheric electricity from one cloud to another or between a cloud and the earth

light·proof \-'prüf\ *adj* : impenetrable by light

lights \'līts\ *n pl* : the lungs esp. of a slaughtered animal

light·ship \'līt-,ship\ *n* : a ship equipped with a brilliant light and moored at a place dangerous to navigation

light·some \'līt-səm\ *adj* **1** : NIMBLE **2** : CHEERFUL

light·weight \-,wāt\ *n* : one of less than average weight; *esp* : a boxer weighing more than 126 but not over 135 pounds

lig·ne·ous \'lig-nē-əs\ *adj* : WOODY

lig·nite \-,nīt\ *n* : brownish black soft coal of a slightly woody texture

1like \'līk\ *vb* **1** : ENJOY ⟨~s baseball⟩ **2** : WANT **3** : CHOOSE ⟨does he ~s⟩ — **lik·able** *or* **like·able** \-ə-bəl\ *adj*

2like *n* : PREFERENCE

3like *adj* : SIMILAR **syn** alike, identical, comparable, parallel, uniform

4like *prep* **1** : similar or similarly to **2** : typical of **3** : inclined to ⟨looks ~ rain⟩ **4** : such as ⟨a subject ~ physics⟩

5like *n* : COUNTERPART

6like *conj* : in the same way that

-like \,līk\ *adj suffix* **1** : of a form, kind, appearance, or effect resembling or suggesting ⟨a life*like* statue⟩ ⟨bell*like* tones⟩ **2** : of the kind befitting or characteristic of ⟨lady*like* behavior⟩ ⟨dog*like* devotion⟩

like·li·hood \'lī-klē-,hùd\ *n* : PROBABILITY

1like·ly \'lī-klē\ *adj* **1** : PROBABLE **2** : BELIEVABLE **3** : PROMISING ⟨a ~ place to fish⟩

2likely *adv* : in all probability

lik·en \'lī-kən\ *vb* : COMPARE

like·ness \'līk-nəs\ *n* **1** : RESEMBLANCE **2** : APPEARANCE, GUISE **3** : COPY, PORTRAIT

like·wise \-,wīz\ *adv* **1** : in like manner **2** : in addition : ALSO

lik·ing \'lī-kiŋ\ *n* : favorable regard; *also* : TASTE

li·lac \'lī-lək, -,lak\ *n* **1** : a shrub with large clusters of fragrant grayish pink, purple, or white flowers **2** : a moderate purple

1lilt \'lilt\ *n* **1** : a gay lively song or tune **2** : a rhythmical swing, flow, or cadence

lily \'lil-ē\ *n* : any of numerous tall bulbous herbs with leafy stems and usu. funnel-shaped flowers; *also* : any of various related plants (as the onion, amaryllis, or iris)

limb \'lim\ *n* : one of the projecting paired appendages (as legs, arms, or wings) that an animal uses esp. in moving or grasping **2** : a large branch of a tree : BOUGH — **limb·less** \'lim-ləs\ *adj*

lim·beck \'lim-,bek\ *n* : ALEMBIC

1lim·ber \'lim-bər\ *adj* **1** : FLEXIBLE, SUPPLE **2** : LITHE, NIMBLE

2limber *vb* : to make or become limber

lim·bo \'lim-bō\ *n* **1** *often cap* : an abode of souls barred from heaven through no fault of their own **2** : a place or state of confinement or oblivion

1lime \'līm\ *n* : a caustic infusible white substance that consists of calcium and oxygen, is obtained by heating lime-

stone or shells until they crumble to powder, and is used in making cement and in fertilizer — **limy** \'lī-mē\ *adj*

2lime *n* : a small lemonlike greenish yellow citrus fruit with juicy acid pulp

lime·ade \lī-'mād\ *n* : a beverage of lime juice, sugar, and water

lime·kiln \'līm-,kil(n)\ *n* : a kiln or furnace for making lime by burning limestone or shells

lime·light \-,līt\ *n* **1** : a device in which flame is directed against a cylinder of lime formerly used in the theater to cast a strong white light on the stage **2** : the center of public attention

lim·er·ick \'lim-(ə-)rik\ *n* : a light or humorous poem of five lines

lime·stone \'līm-,stōn\ *n* : a rock that is formed by accumulation of organic remains (as shells), is used in building, and yields lime when burned

1lim·it \'lim-ət\ *n* **1** : BOUNDARY; *also*, *pl* : BOUNDS **2** : something that restrains or confines; *also* : the utmost extent **3** : a prescribed maximum or minimum — **lim·it·less** \-ləs\ *adj*

2limit *vb* **1** : to set limits to **2** : to reduce in quantity or extent — **lim·i·ta·tion** \,lim-ə-'tā-shən\ *n*

lim·it·ed \'lim-ət-əd\ *adj* **1** : confined within limits : RESTRICTED **2** : offering superior and faster service and transportation

limn \'lim\ *vb* **1** : DRAW; *also* : PAINT **2** : DELINEATE, DESCRIBE

lim·ou·sine \'lim-ə-,zēn\ *n* : a large luxurious often chauffeur-driven sedan

1limp \'limp\ *vb* **1** : to walk lamely; *also* : to proceed with difficulty

2limp *n* : a limping movement or gait

3limp *adj* **1** : having no defined shape; *also* : not stiff or rigid **2** : lacking in strength or firmness — **limp·ly** *adv* — **limp·ness** *n*

lim·pet \'lim-pət\ *n* : a sea mollusk with a conical shell that clings to rocks or timbers

lim·pid \-pəd\ *adj* : CLEAR, TRANSPARENT

lin·age \'lī-nij\ *n* : the number of lines of written or printed matter

linch·pin \'linch-,pin\ *n* : a locking pin inserted crosswise (as through the end of an axle)

lin·den \'lin-dən\ *n* : a large tree with heart-shaped leaves and yellow flowers

1line \'līn\ *vb* : to cover the inner surface of

2line *n* **1** : CORD, ROPE, WIRE; *also* : a length of material used in measuring and leveling **2** : pipes for conveying a fluid ⟨a gas ~⟩ **3** : a horizontal row of written or printed characters; *also* : VERSE **4** : NOTE **5** *pl* : the words making up a part in a drama **6** : something distinct, long, and narrow; *also* : ROUTE **7** : a state of agreement **8** : a course of conduct, action, or thought; *also* : OCCUPATION **9** : LIMIT **10** : an arrangement (as of cars) in or as if in a row or sequence; *also* : the football players who are stationed on the line of scrimmage **11** : a transportation system **12** : a long narrow mark; *also* : EQUATOR **13** : CONTOUR **14** : a general plan **15** : an indication (as of intention) based on insight or investigation

³line *vb* **1** : to mark with a line **2** : to place or form a line along **3** : ALIGN

lin·eage \'lin-ē-ij\ *n* : lineal descent from a common progenitor; *also* : FAMILY

lin·eal \'lin-ē-əl\ *adj* **1** : LINEAR **2** : consisting of or being in a direct line of ancestry; *also* : HEREDITARY

lin·ea·ment \'lin-ē-ə-mənt\ *n* : an outline, feature, or contour of a body or figure and esp. of a face — usu. used in pl.

lin·ear \'lin-ē-ər\ *adj* **1** : of, relating to, or consisting of a line : STRAIGHT **2** : being long and uniformly narrow

line drive *n* : a baseball hit in a nearly straight line and typically not far above the ground

line·man \'līn-mən\ *n* **1** : one who sets up or repairs communication or power lines **2** : a player in the line in football

lin·en \'lin-ən\ *n* **1** : cloth made of flax; *also* : thread or yarn spun from flax **2** : clothing or household articles made of linen cloth or similar fabric

lin·er \'lī-nər\ *n* : a ship or airplane belonging to a regular transportation line

lines·man \'līnz-mən\ *n* **1** : LINEMAN **2** : an official who assists a referee (as in football)

line·up \'līn-əp\ *n* **1** : a line of persons arranged for inspection or identification **2** : a list of players taking part in a game (as of baseball)

ling \'liŋ\ *n* : any of several fishes related to the cod

lin·ger \'liŋ-gər\ *vb* : TARRY; *also* : PROCRASTINATE

lin·ge·rie \,län-jə-'rā, -'rē\ *n* : women's intimate apparel (as underwear)

lin·go \'liŋ-gō\ *n, pl* **lingoes** : usu. strange or incomprehensible language

lin·gual \-gwəl\ *adj* : of, relating to, or produced by the tongue

lin·guist \'liŋ-gwist\ *n* [L *lingua* tongue, language] **1** : a person skilled in languages **2** : one who specializes in linguistics

lin·guis·tics \liŋ-'gwis-tiks\ *n* : the study of human speech including the units, nature, structure, and development of language or a language — **lin·guis·tic** *adj*

lin·i·ment \'lin-ə-mənt\ *n* : a liquid preparation rubbed on the skin esp. to relieve pain

lin·ing \'lī-niŋ\ *n* : material used to line esp. an inner surface (as of a garment)

link \'liŋk\ *n* **1** : a connecting structure; *esp* : a single ring of a chain **2** : BOND, TIE — **link** *vb*

link·age *n* **1** : the manner or style of being united **2** : the quality or state of being linked **3** : a system of links

links \'liŋks\ *n pl* : a golf course

link·up \'liŋk-əp\ *n* **1** : MEETING **2** : something that serves as a linking device or factor

lin·net \'lin-ət\ *n* : an Old World finch

li·no·le·um \lə-'nō-lē-əm\ *n* : a floor covering with a canvas back and a surface of hardened linseed oil and a filler (as cork dust)

lin·seed \'lin-,sēd\ *n* : the seeds of flax yielding a yellowish drying oil (**linseed oil**) used esp. in paints, printing inks, and linoleum

lin·sey-wool·sey \,lin-zē-'wul-zē\ *n* : a coarse sturdy fabric of wool and linen or cotton

lint \'lint\ *n* **1** : linen made into a soft fleecy substance for use in surgical dressings **2** : fine ravels, fluff, or loose short fibers from yarn or fabrics **3** : the fibers that surround cotton seeds and form the cotton staple

lin·tel \'lint-ᵊl\ *n* : a horizontal piece across the top of an opening (as of a door) that carries the weight of the structure above it

li·on \'lī-ən\ *n* : a large flesh-eating cat of Africa and southern Asia with a shaggy mane in the male — **li·on·ess** \-ə-nəs\ *n*

li·on·heart·ed \,lī-ən-'härt-əd\ *adj* : having a courageous heart : BRAVE

li·on·ize \'lī-ə-,nīz\ *vb* : to treat as an object of great interest or importance — **li·on·iza·tion** \,lī-ə-nə-'zā-shən\ *n*

lip \'lip\ *n* **1** : either of the two fleshy folds that surround the mouth; *also* : a part or projection suggesting such a lip **2** : the edge of a hollow vessel or cavity — **lipped** \'lipt\ *adj*

lip·read·ing \'lip-,rēd-iŋ\ *n* : the interpreting of a speaker's words without hearing his voice by watching his lip and facial movements

lip·stick \'lip-,stik\ *n* : a waxy solid colored cosmetic in stick form for the lips

liq·ue·fy \'lik-wə-,fī\ *vb* : to reduce to a liquid state : become liquid — **liq·ue·fac·tion** \,lik-wə-'fak-shən\ *n*

li·queur \li-'kər\ *n* : a distilled alcoholic liquor flavored with aromatic substances and usu. sweetened

¹liquid \'lik-wəd\ *adj* **1** : flowing freely like water **2** : neither solid nor gaseous **3** : shining clear (large ~ eyes) **4** : smooth and musical in tone; *also* : smooth and unconstrained in movement **5** : consisting of or capable of ready conversion into cash (~ assets)

²liquid *n* : a liquid substance

liq·ui·date \'lik-wə-,dāt\ *vb* **1** : to pay off (~ a debt) **2** : to settle the accounts and distribute the assets of (as a business) **3** : to get rid of; *esp* : KILL — **liq·ui·da·tion** \,lik-wə-'dā-shən\ *n*

li·quor \'lik-ər\ *n* : a liquid substance; *esp* : a distilled alcoholic beverage

li·ra \'lir-ə\ *n* — see MONEY table

lisle \'līl\ *n* : a smooth tightly twisted thread usu. made of long-staple cotton

lisp \'lisp\ *vb* : to pronounce *s* and *z* imperfectly esp. by giving them the sound of *th*; *also* : to speak childishly — **lisp** *n*

lis·some \'lis-əm\ *adj* : LITHE; *also* : NIMBLE

¹list \'list\ *vb* : PLEASE; *also* : WISH

²list *vb* : LISTEN

³list *n* **1** : a simple series of names; *also* : an official roster **2** : INDEX, CATALOG

⁴list *vb* : to make a list of; *also* : to include on a list

⁵list *vb* : TILT

⁶list *n* : a heeling over : TILT

lis·ten \'lis-ᵊn\ *vb* **1** : to pay attention in order to hear **2** : HEED — **lis·ten·er** *n*

list·less \'list-ləs\ *adj* : LANGUID, SPIRITLESS — **list·less·ly** *adv* — **list·less·ness** *n*

lists \'lists\ *n pl* : an arena for jousting or for combat

lit *past of* LIGHT

lit·a·ny \'lit-ᵊn-ē\ *n* : a prayer consisting of a series of supplications and responses said alternately by a leader and a group

li·ter or **li·tre** \'lēt-ər\ n : a metric unit of capacity equal to 1.0567 liquid quarts

lit·er·al \'lit-(ə-)rəl\ adj 1 : adhering to fact or to the ordinary or usual meaning (as of a word) 2 : UNADORNED; also : PROSAIC 3 : VERBATIM — **lit·er·al·ly** adv

lit·er·al·ism \'lit-(ə-)rə-,liz-əm\ n 1 : adherence to the explicit substance (as of an idea) 2 : fidelity to observable fact — **lit·er·al·is·tic** \,lit-(ə-)rə-'lis-tik\ adj

lit·er·ary \'lit-ə-,rer-ē\ adj 1 : of or relating to literature 2 : versed in literature : WELL-READ

lit·er·ate \'lit-ə-rət\ adj 1 : EDUCATED; also : able to read and write 2 : LITERARY; also : POLISHED, LUCID — **lit·er·a·cy** \-rə-sē\ n

li·te·ra·ti \,lit-ə-'rät-ē\ n pl 1 : the educated class 2 : men of letters

lit·er·a·tim \,lit-ə-'rät-əm\ adv (or adj) : letter for letter

lit·er·a·ture \'lit-(ə-)rə-,chùr, -chər\ n 1 : the production of written works having excellence of form or expression and dealing with ideas of permanent or universal interest 2 : writings in prose or verse

lithe \'līth, 'lïth\ adj 1 : SUPPLE, RESILIENT 2 : characterized by effortless grace

lithe·some adj : LISSOME

lith·i·um \'lith-ē-əm\ n : a light silver-white chemical element

li·thog·ra·phy \lith-'äg-rə-fē\ n : the process of printing from a plane surface (as a smooth stone or metal plate) on which the image to be printed is ink-receptive and the blank area ink-repellent — **lith·o·graph** \'lith-ə-,graf\ vb — **lithograph** n — **li·thog·ra·pher** \lith-'äg-rə-fər, 'lith-ə-,graf-ər\ n — **lith·o·graph·ic** \,lith-ə-'graf-ik\ adj

Lith·u·a·ni·an \,lith-(y)ə-'wā-nē-ən\ n 1 : a native or inhabitant of Lithuania 2 : the language of the Lithuanians — **Lithuanian** adj

lit·i·gant \'lit-i-gənt\ n : a party to a lawsuit

lit·i·gate \'lit-ə-,gāt\ vb : to carry on a legal contest by judicial process; also : to contest at law — **lit·i·ga·tion** \,lit-ə-'gā-shən\ n

li·ti·gious \lə-'tij-əs\ adj 1 : CONTENTIOUS 2 : prone to engage in lawsuits 3 : of or relating to litigation — **li·ti·gious·ness** n

lit·mus \'lit-məs\ n : a coloring matter from lichens that turns red in acid solutions and blue in alkaline

¹**lit·ter** \'lit-ər\ n 1 : a covered and curtained couch with shafts used to carry a single passenger; also : a device (as a stretcher) for carrying a sick or injured person 2 : material used as bedding for animals; also : the uppermost layer of organic debris on the forest floor 3 : the offspring of an animal at one birth 4 : RUBBISH

²**litter** vb 1 : to give birth to young 2 : to strew with litter

lit·ter·bug \-,bəg\ n : one who litters a public area

¹**lit·tle** \'lit-ºl\ adj 1 : not big 2 : not much 3 : not important 4 : NARROW, MEAN — **lit·tle·ness** n

²**little** adv 1 : SLIGHTLY; also : not at all 2 : INFREQUENTLY

³**little** n 1 : a small amount or quantity 2 : a short time or distance

Little Dipper n : the seven principal stars in the constellation of Ursa Minor arranged in a form resembling a dipper with the North Star forming the outer end of the handle

lit·to·ral \'lit-ə-rəl, ,lit-ə-'ral\ adj : of, relating to, or growing on or near a shore esp. of the sea — **littoral** n

lit·ur·gy \'lit-ər-jē\ n : a rite or body of rites prescribed for public worship — **li·tur·gi·cal** \lə-'tər-ji-kəl\ adj — **li·tur·gi·cal·ly** adv — **lit·ur·gist** \'lit-ər-jəst\ n

liv·able also **live·able** \'liv-ə-bəl\ adj 1 : suitable for living in or with 2 : ENDURABLE — **liv·a·bil·i·ty** \,liv-ə-'bil-ət-ē\ n

¹**live** \'liv\ vb 1 : to be or continue alive 2 : SUBSIST 3 : to conduct one's life 4 : RESIDE 5 : to remain in human memory or record

²**live** \'līv\ adj 1 : having life 2 : abounding with life 3 : BURNING, GLOWING (a ~ cigar) 4 : connected to electric power (a ~ wire) 5 : UNEXPLODED (a ~ bomb) 6 : of continuing interest (a ~ issue) 7 : being in play (a ~ ball) 8 : of or involving the actual presence of real people (~ audience); also : broadcast directly at the time of production (a ~ radio program)

live·li·hood \'līv-lē-,hùd\ n : means of support or subsistence

live·long \,liv-,lóŋ\ adj : WHOLE, ENTIRE (the ~ day)

live·ly \'līv-lē\ adj 1 : full of life 2 : KEEN, VIVID (~ interest) 3 : ANIMATED (~ debate) 4 : showing activity or vigor (a ~ manner) 5 : quick to rebound (~ ball) syn vivacious, sprightly, gay — **live·li·ness** n

liv·en \'lī-vən\ vb : ENLIVEN

liv·er \'liv-ər\ n : a large glandular organ of vertebrates that secretes bile and is a center of metabolic activity

liv·er·ish \'liv-(ə-)rish\ adj 1 : resembling liver esp. in color 2 : BILIOUS 3 : MELANCHOLY

liv·er·wort \'liv-ər-,wərt\ n : any of various plants resembling the related mosses

liv·er·wurst \-,wərst, -,wù(r)st\ n : a sausage consisting chiefly of liver

liv·ery \'liv-(ə)-rē\ n 1 : a special uniform worn by the servants of a wealthy household; also : distinctive dress 2 : the feeding, care, and stabling of horses for pay; also : the keeping of horses and vehicles for hire — **liv·er·ied** \-rēd\ adj

liv·ery·man \-rē-mən\ n : the keeper of a livery stable

lives pl of LIFE

live·stock \'līv-,stäk\ n : farm animals kept for use and profit

liv·id \'liv-əd\ adj 1 : discolored by bruising 2 : ASHEN, PALLID

¹**liv·ing** \'liv-iŋ\ adj 1 : having life 2 : NATURAL 3 : full of life and vigor; also : VIVID

²**living** n 1 : the condition of being alive; also : manner of life 2 : LIVELIHOOD

living room *n* : a room in a residence used for the common social activities of the occupants

liz·ard \'liz-ərd\ *n* : a 4-legged scaly reptile with a long tapering tail

lla·ma \'läm-ə\ *n* : any of several wild or domesticated So. American mammals related to the camel but smaller and without a hump

lla·no \'län-ō\ *n* : an open grassy plain esp. of Spanish America

lo \'lō\ *interj* — used esp. to call attention

¹load \'lōd\ *n* **1** : PACK; *also* : CARGO **2** : a mass of weight supported by something **3** : something that burdens the mind or spirits **4** : a large quantity — usu. used in pl.

²load *vb* **1** : to put a load in or on; *also* : to receive a load **2** : BURDEN **3** : to increase the weight of by adding something **4** : to supply abundantly **5** : to put a charge in (as a firearm)

load·stone *var of* LODESTONE

¹loaf \'lōf\ *n, pl* **loaves** \'lōvz\ : a shaped or molded mass esp. of bread

²loaf *vb* : to spend time in idleness : LOUNGE — **loaf·er** *n*

loam \'lōm, 'lüm\ *n* : SOIL; *esp* : a loose soil of mixed clay, sand, and silt — **loamy** *adj*

¹loan \'lōn\ *n* **1** : money let out at interest; *also* : something furnished for the borrower's temporary use **2** : the grant of temporary use

²loan *vb* : LEND

loan·word \-,wərd\ *n* : a word taken from another language and at least partly naturalized

loath \'lōth, 'lōth\ *adj* : RELUCTANT

loathe \'lōth\ *vb* : to dislike greatly **syn** abominate, abhor, detest

loath·ing \'lō-thiŋ\ *n* : extreme disgust

loath·ly \'lōth-lē, 'lōth-\ *adj* : LOATHSOME

loath·some \'lōth-səm, 'lōth-\ *adj* : exciting loathing : REPULSIVE

¹lob \'läb\ *vb* **lobbed; lob·bing** : to throw, hit, or propel something in a high arc — **lob** *n*

¹lob·by \'läb-ē\ *n* **1** : a corridor or hall used esp. as a passageway or waiting room **2** : a group of persons engaged in lobbying

²lobby *vb* : to try to influence public officials and esp. legislators — **lob·by·ist** \-əst\ *n*

lobe \'lōb\ *n* : a curved or rounded projection or division ⟨the ~ of the ear⟩ — **lo·bar** \'lō-bər\ *adj*

lob·ster \'läb-stər\ *n* : an edible marine crustacean with 2 large pincerlike claws and 4 other pairs of legs; *also* : a related crustacean (the **spiny lobster**) with small claws and many spines

¹lo·cal \'lō-kəl\ *adj* **1** : of, relating to, or occupying a particular place **2** : affecting a small part of the body ⟨~ infection⟩ **3** : serving a particular limited district ⟨~ government⟩; *also* : making all stops ⟨a ~ train⟩ — **lo·cal·ly** *adv*

²local *n* : one that is local

lo·cale \lō-'kal\ *n* : a place that is the setting for a particular event

lo·cal·i·ty \lō-'kal-ət-ē\ *n* : a particular spot, situation, or place

lo·cal·ize \'lō-kə-,līz\ *vb* : to fix in or confine to a definite place or locality — **lo·cal·i·za·tion** \,lō-kə-lə-'zā-shən\ *n*

lo·cate \'lō-,kāt\ *vb* **1** : STATION, SETTLE

2 : to determine the site of **3** : to find or fix the place of in a sequence

lo·ca·tion \lō-'kā-shən\ *n* **1** : the process of locating **2** : SITUATION, PLACE **3** : a place outside a studio where a motion picture is filmed

loch \'läk, 'läḵ\ *n, Scot* : LAKE; *also* : a bay or arm of the sea esp. when nearly landlocked

¹lock \'läk\ *n* : a tuft, strand, or ringlet of hair; *also* : a cohering bunch (as of wool or flax)

²lock *n* **1** : a fastening in which a bolt is operated (as by a key) **2** : an enclosure (as in a canal) used in raising or lowering boats from level to level **3** : the mechanism of a firearm by which the charge is exploded

³lock *vb* **1** : to fasten the lock of; *also* : to make fast with a lock **2** : to confine or exclude by means of a lock **3** : INTERLOCK

lock·er \'läk-ər\ *n* **1** : a drawer, cupboard, or compartment for individual storage use **2** : an insulated compartment for storing frozen food

lock·et \'läk-ət\ *n* : a small usu. metal case for a memento worn suspended from a chain or necklace

lock·jaw \'läk-,jȯ\ *n* : TETANUS

lock·out \-,aut\ *n* : the suspension of work or closing of a plant by an employer during a labor dispute in order to make his employees accept his terms

lock·smith \-,smith\ *n* : one who makes or repairs locks

lock·step \-,step\ *n* : a mode of marching in step by a body of men moving in a very close single file

lock·up \-,əp\ *n* : JAIL

lo·co·mo·tion \,lō-kə-'mō-shən\ *n* **1** : the act or power of moving from place to place **2** : TRAVEL

¹lo·co·mo·tive \-'mōt-iv\ *adj* : of or relating to locomotion or a locomotive

²locomotive *n* : a self-propelled vehicle used to move railroad cars

lo·co·mo·tor \,lō-kə-,mōt-ər\ *adj* : of or relating to locomotion

lo·cus \'lō-kəs\ *n, pl* **lo·ci** \'lō-,sī\ : PLACE, LOCALITY

lo·cust \'lō-kəst\ *n* **1** : a usu. destructive migratory grasshopper **2** : CICADA **3** : any of various hard-wooded leguminous trees

lo·cu·tion \lō-'kyü-shən\ *n* : a particular form of expression; *also* : PHRASEOLOGY

lode \'lōd\ *n* : a deposit of a mineral (as gold ore) that fills a crack in rock

lode·star \-,stär\ *n* : a guiding star; *esp* : NORTH STAR

lode·stone \-,stōn\ *n* : an iron-containing rock with magnetic properties

¹lodge \'läj\ *vb* **1** : to provide quarters for; *also* : to settle in a place **2** : CONTAIN; *also* : to come to a rest and remain **3** : to deposit for safekeeping **5** : to vest (as authority) in an agent **6** : FILE ⟨~ a complaint⟩

²lodge *n* **1** : a house set apart for residence in a special season or by an employee on an estate ⟨hunting ~⟩ ⟨caretaker's ~⟩; *also* : INN **2** : a den or lair esp. of gregarious animals **3** : the meeting place of a branch of a fraternal organization; *also* : the members of such a branch

lodg·er \'läj-ər\ *n* : a person who occupies a rented room in another's house

lodg·ing \-iŋ\ *n* **1** : DWELLING **2** : a

room or suite of rooms in another's house rented as a dwelling place — usu. used in pl.

lodg·ment or **lodge·ment** \'läj-mənt\ n 1 : a lodging place 2 : the act or manner of lodging 3 : DEPOSIT

¹loft \'lȯft\ n 1 : ATTIC 2 : GALLERY ⟨organ ~⟩ 3 : an upper floor (as in a warehouse or barn) esp. when not partitioned

²loft vb : to strike or throw a ball so that it rises high in the air

lofty \'lȯf-tē\ adj 1 : extremely proud 2 : NOBLE; also : SUPERIOR 3 : HIGH, TALL — **loft·i·ly** \-tə-lē\ adv — **loft·i·ness** n

¹log \'lȯg, 'läg\ n 1 : a bulky piece of unshaped timber 2 : an apparatus for measuring the rate of a ship's motion through the water 3 : the daily record of a ship's progress; also : a regularly kept record of performance (as of an airplane)

²log vb **logged; log·ging 1** : to cut trees for lumber 2 : to enter in a log 3 : to sail a ship or fly an airplane for an indicated distance or period of time — **log·ger** n

log·a·rithm \'lȯg-ə-,rith-əm, 'läg-\ n : the exponent that indicates the power to which a base number is raised to produce a given number ⟨the ~ of 100 to the base number 10 is 2⟩ — **log·a·rith·mic** \,lȯg-ə-'rith-mik, ,läg-\ adj

loge \'lōzh\ n 1 : a small compartment; also : a box in a theater 2 : a small partitioned area; also : the forward section of a theater mezzanine

log·ger·head \'lȯg-ər-,hed, 'läg-\ n : a large sea turtle of the warmer parts of the Atlantic — **at loggerheads** : in a state of quarrelsome disagreement

log·gia \'läj-(ē-)ə, 'lȯ-,jä\ n : a roofed open gallery

log·ic \'läj-ik\ n 1 : a science that deals with the rules and tests of sound thinking and proof by reasoning 2 : sound reasoning — **log·i·cal** \-i-kəl\ adj — **log·i·cal·ly** \-i-k(ə-)lē\ adv — **lo·gi·cian** \lō-'jish-ən\ n

lo·gis·tics \lō-'jis-tiks\ n sing or pl : the procurement, maintenance, and transportation of matériel, facilities, and personnel — **lo·gis·tic** adj

log·jam \'lȯg-,jam, 'läg-\ n 1 : a deadlocked jumble of logs in a watercourse 2 : DEADLOCK

log·roll·ing \'lȯg-,rō-liŋ, 'läg-\ n : the trading of votes by legislators to secure favorable action on projects of individual interest

lo·gy \'lō-gē\ adj : deficient in vitality : SLUGGISH

loin \'lȯin\ n 1 : the part of the body on each side of the spinal column and between the hip and the lower ribs; also : a cut of meat from this part of a meat animal 2 pl : the upper and lower abdominal regions and the region about the hips

loin·cloth \-,klȯth\ n : a cloth worn about the loins often as the sole article of clothing in warm climates

loi·ter \'lȯit-ər\ vb 1 : LINGER 2 : to hang around idly syn dawdle, dally, procrastinate — **loi·ter·er** n

¹loll \'läl\ vb 1 : DROOP, DANGLE 2 : LOUNGE

lol·li·pop or **lol·ly·pop** \'läl-ē-,päp\ n : a lump of hard candy on a stick

lone \'lōn\ adj 1 : SOLITARY ⟨a ~ sentinel⟩ 2 : SOLE, ONLY ⟨the ~ theater in town⟩ 3 : ISOLATED ⟨a ~ tree⟩

lone·ly \-lē\ adj 1 : being without company 2 : UNFREQUENTED ⟨a ~ spot⟩ 3 : LONESOME — **lone·li·ness** n

lone·some \-səm\ adj 1 : sad from lack of companionship 2 : REMOTE; also : SOLITARY

¹long \'lȯŋ\ adj **lon·ger** \'lȯŋ-gər\ **lon·gest** \-gəst\ 1 : extending for a considerable distance; also : TALL, ELONGATED 2 : having a specified length 3 : extending over a considerable time; also : TEDIOUS 4 : containing many items in a series 5 : being a syllable or speech sound of relatively great duration 6 : extending far into the future 7 : well furnished with something — used with on

²long adv : for or during a long time

³long n : a long period of time

⁴long vb : to feel a strong desire or wish syn yearn, hanker, pine

long·bow \-,bō\ n : a wooden bow drawn by hand and usu. 5 to 6 feet long

lon·gev·i·ty \län-'jev-ət-ē\ n : a long duration of individual life; also : length of life

long·hand \'lȯŋ-,hand\ n : HANDWRITING

long·ing \'lȯŋ-iŋ\ n : an eager desire esp for something unattainable — **long·ing·ly** adv

lon·gi·tude \'län-jə-,t(y)üd\ n : angular distance due east or west from a meridian and esp. from the meridian that runs between the north and south poles and passes through Greenwich, England, expressed in degrees or in time

lon·gi·tu·di·nal \,län-jə-'t(y)üd-(ə-)nəl\ adj 1 : of or relating to length 2 : extending lengthwise — **lon·gi·tu·di·nal·ly** adv

long·shore·man \'lȯŋ-'shōr-mən\ n : a laborer at a wharf who loads and unloads cargo

long-suf·fer·ing \-'səf-(ə-)riŋ\ n : long and patient endurance of offense

long-term \'lȯŋ-'tərm\ adj 1 : extending over or involving a long period of time 2 : constituting a financial obligation based on a term usu. of more than 10 years ⟨~ mortgage⟩

lon·gueur \lōⁿ-gœr\ n : a dull tedious passage or section

¹look \'lùk\ vb 1 : to exercise the power of vision : SEE 2 : EXPECT 3 : to have an appearance that befits ⟨~s the part⟩ 4 : SEEM ⟨~s thin⟩ 5 : to direct one's attention : HEED 6 : POINT, FACE 7 : to show a tendency

²look n 1 : the action of looking : GLANCE 2 : EXPRESSION; also : physical appearance 3 : ASPECT

looking glass n : MIRROR

look·out \'lùk-,aùt\ n 1 : a person assigned to watch (as on a ship) 2 : a careful watch 3 : VIEW 4 : a matter of concern

¹loom \'lüm\ n : a frame or machine for weaving together threads or yarns into cloth

²loom vb 1 : to come into sight in an unnaturally large, indistinct, or dis-

ə abut; ᵊ kitten; ər further; a back; ā bake; ä cot, cart; aù out; ch chin; e less; ē easy; g gift; i trip; ī life; j joke; ŋ sing; ō flow; ȯ flaw; ȯi coin; th thin; t͟h this; ü loot; ù foot; y yet; yü few; yù furious; zh vision

torted form **2 :** to appear in an impressively exaggerated form

loon \'lün\ *n* **:** a web-footed black-and-white fish-eating diving bird

loo·ny *or* **loo·ney** \'lü-nē\ *adj* **:** CRAZY, FOOLISH

loop \'lüp\ *n* **1 :** a fold or doubling of a line leaving an aperture between the parts through which another line can be passed; *also* **:** a loop-shaped figure or course (a ~ in a river) **2 :** a circular airplane maneuver involving flying upside down — **loop** *vb*

loop·hole \-,hōl\ *n* **1 :** a small opening in a wall through which small firearms may be discharged **2 :** a means of escape

¹**loose** \'lüs\ *adj* **1 :** not rigidly fastened **2 :** free from restraint or obligation **3 :** not dense or compact in structure **4 :** not chaste **:** LEWD **5 :** SLACK **6 :** not precise or exact — **loose·ly** *adv* — **loose·ness** *n*

²**loose** *vb* **1 :** RELEASE **2 :** UNTIE **3 :** DETACH **4 :** DISCHARGE **5 :** RELAX, SLACKEN

³**loose** *adv* **:** LOOSELY

loos·en \'lüs-ᵊn\ *vb* **1 :** FREE **2 :** to make or become loose **3 :** to relax the severity of

¹**loot** \'lüt\ *n* **:** goods taken in war **:** PLUNDER — **loot** *vb* — **loot·er** *n*

¹**lop** \'läp\ *vb* **lopped; lop·ping :** to cut branches or twigs from **:** TRIM; *also* **:** to cut off

²**lop** *vb* **lopped; lop·ping :** to hang downward; *also* **:** to flop or sway loosely

lope \'lōp\ *n* **:** an easy bounding gait — **lope** *vb*

lop·sid·ed \'läp-'sīd-əd\ *adj* **1 :** leaning to one side **2 :** UNSYMMETRICAL — **lop·sid·ed·ly** *adv* — **lop·sid·ed·ness** *n*

lo·qua·cious \lō-'kwā-shəs\ *adj* **:** excessively talkative — **lo·quac·i·ty** \-'kwas-ət-ē\ *n*

lord \'lȯrd\ *n* [OE *hlāford*, fr. *hlāf* loaf, bread + *weard* keeper, guard] **1 :** one having power and authority over others; *esp* **:** a person from whom a feudal fee or estate is held **2 :** a man of rank or high position; *esp* **:** a British nobleman **3** *pl, cap* **:** the upper house of the British parliament

lord·ly \-lē\ *adj* **1 :** DIGNIFIED; *also* **:** NOBLE **2 :** HAUGHTY

lord·ship \-,ship\ *n* **1 :** the rank or dignity of a lord — used as a title **2 :** the authority, power, or territory of a lord

Lord's Supper *n* **:** COMMUNION

lore \'lōr\ *n* **:** KNOWLEDGE; *esp* **:** traditional knowledge or belief

lor·gnette \lȯrn-'yet\ *n* **:** a pair of eyeglasses or opera glasses with a handle

lorn \'lȯrn\ *adj* **:** FORSAKEN, DESOLATE

lor·ry \'lȯr-ē\ *n* **:** a large low horse-drawn wagon without sides **2** *Brit* **:** MOTORTRUCK

lose \'lüz\ *vb* **lost** \'lȯst\ **los·ing** \'lü-ziŋ\ **1 :** DESTROY **2 :** to miss from a customary place **:** MISLAY **3 :** to suffer deprivation of **4 :** to fail to use **:** WASTE **5 :** to fail to win or obtain (~ the game) **6 :** to fail to keep or maintain (~ his balance) **7 :** to wander from (~ his way) **8 :** to get rid of (~ weight) — **los·er** *n*

loss \'lȯs\ *n* **1 :** the harm resulting from losing **2 :** something that is lost **3** *pl* **:** killed, wounded, or captured soldiers **4 :** failure to win **5 :** an

amount by which the cost exceeds the selling price **6 :** decrease in amount or degree **7 :** RUIN

lost \'lȯst\ *adj* **1 :** not used, won, or claimed **2 :** unable to find the way; *also* **:** HELPLESS **3 :** ruined or destroyed physically or morally **4 :** no longer possessed or known **5 :** DENIED; *also* **:** HARDENED **6 :** ABSORBED, RAPT

lot \'lät\ *n* **1 :** an object used in deciding something by chance; *also* **:** the use of lots to decide something **2 :** SHARE, PORTION; *also* **:** FORTUNE, FATE **3 :** a plot of land **4 :** a group of individuals **:** SET **5 :** a considerable quantity

loth \'lōth, 'lȯth\ *var of* LOATH

lo·tion \'lō-shən\ *n* **:** a liquid preparation for cosmetic and external medicinal use

lot·tery \'lät-ə-rē\ *n* **1 :** a drawing of lots in which prizes are given to the winning names or numbers **2 :** a matter determined by chance

lo·tus *or* **lot·os** \'lōt-əs\ *n* **1 :** a fruit held in Greek legend to cause dreamy content and forgetfulness **2 :** a water lily used in ancient Egyptian and Hindu art and religious symbolism **3 :** any of several forage plants related to the clovers

loud \'laud\ *adj* **1 :** marked by intensity or volume of sound **2 :** CLAMOROUS, NOISY **3 :** obtrusive or offensive in color or pattern (a ~ suit) — **loud** *adv* — **loud·ly** *adv* — **loud·ness** *n*

loud·mouthed \-'mauthd, -'mautht\ *adj* **1 :** having an offensively loud voice or a noisy manner **2 :** TACTLESS

loud·speak·er \-'spē-kər\ *n* **:** a device similar to a telephone receiver in operation but amplifying sound

¹**lounge** \'launj\ *vb* **:** to act or move lazily or listlessly **:** LOAF

²**lounge** *n* **1 :** a room with comfortable furniture; *also* **:** a room (as in a theater) with lounging, smoking, and toilet facilities **2 :** a long couch

lour \'lau̇(-ə)r\ *var of* LOWER

louse \'laus\ *n, pl* **lice** \'līs\ **1 :** a small wingless insect parasitic on warm-blooded animals **2 :** a plant pest (as an aphid)

lousy \'lau̇-zē\ *adj* **1 :** infested with lice **2 :** POOR, INFERIOR **3 :** amply supplied (~ with money) — **lous·i·ly** *adv* — **lous·i·ness** *n*

lout \'laut\ *n* **:** a stupid awkward fellow — **lout·ish** *adj* — **lout·ish·ly** *adv*

lou·ver *or* **lou·vre** \'lü-vər\ *n* **1 :** an opening having parallel slanted slats to allow flow of air but to exclude rain or sun or to provide privacy; *also* **:** a slat in such an opening **2 :** a device with fins, vanes, or a grating for controlling a flow of air or the radiation of light

¹**love** \'ləv\ *n* **1 :** strong affection **2 :** warm attachment **:** ENTHUSIASM (~ of the sea) **3 :** attraction based on sexual desire **4 :** a beloved person **5 :** a score of zero in tennis — **love·less** \-ləs\ *adj*

²**love** *vb* **1 :** CHERISH **2 :** to feel a passion, devotion, or tenderness for **3 :** CARESS **4 :** to take pleasure in (~s to play bridge) — **lov·able** \'ləv-ə-bəl\ *adj* — **lov·er** *n*

love·ly \-lē\ *adj* **:** BEAUTIFUL — **love·li·ness** *n*

love·sick \'ləv-,sik\ *adj* **1 :** YEARNING **2 :** expressing a lover's longing — **love·sick·ness** *n*

lov·ing \'lǝv-iŋ\ adj : AFFECTIONATE — **lov·ing·ly** adv

1low \'lō\ vb : MOO

2low n : MOO

3low adj **1** : not high or tall (~ wall); also : DÉCOLLETÉ **2** : situated or passing below the normal level or surface (~ ground); also : marking a nadir **3** : STRICKEN, PROSTRATE **4** : not loud (~ voice) **5** : being near the equator **6** : humble in status **7** : WEAK; also : DEPRESSED **8** : less than usual (as in degree, amount, or value) **9** : falling short of a standard **10** : UNFAVORABLE — **low** adv — **low·ness** n

4low n **1** : something that is low **2** : a region of low barometric pressure **3** : an adjustment of gears in an automobile transmission that gives the slowest speed and greatest power

low-brow \'lō-,braü\ n : a person without intellectual interests or culture

low-down \-,daün\ n : pertinent and esp. guarded information

1low·er \'laü-(-ǝ)r\ vb **1** : FROWN **2** : to become dark, gloomy, and threatening

2low·er \'lō-(-ǝ)r\ adj **1** : relatively low (as in rank) **2** : constituting the popular and more representative branch of a bicameral legislative body **3** : situated beneath the earth's surface

3low·er \'lō-(-ǝ)r\ vb **1** : DROP; also : DIMINISH **2** : to let descend by its own weight; also : to reduce the height of **3** : to reduce in value or amount **4** : DEGRADE; also : HUMBLE

low·er·case \,lō-(-ǝ)r-'kās\ adj : being a letter that belongs to or conforms to the series a, b, c, etc., rather than A, B, C, etc. — **lowercase** n

lower class n : a social class occupying a position below the middle class and having the lowest status in a society — **lower-class** adj

low frequency n : a frequency of a radio wave in the range between 30 and 300 kilocycles

low·land \'lō-lǝnd\ n : low and usu. level country

low·ly \-lē\ adj **1** : HUMBLE, MEEK **2** : ranking low in some hierarchy — **low·li·ness** n

lox \'läks\ n : liquid oxygen

2lox n, pl **lox** or **lox·es** : smoked salmon

loy·al \'lȯi-ǝl\ adj **1** : faithful in allegiance to one's government **2** : faithful esp. to a cause or ideal : CONSTANT — **loy·al·ly** adv — **loy·al·ty** \-ǝl-tē\ n

loy·al·ist \-ǝst\ n : one who is or remains loyal to a political party, government, or sovereign

loz·enge \'läz-°nj\ n **1** : a diamond-shaped figure **2** : a small flat often medicated candy

lu·au \'lü-,aü\ n : a Hawaiian feast

lub·ber \'lǝb-ǝr\ n **1** : LOUT **2** : an unskilled seaman

lu·bri·cant \'lü-bri-kǝnt\ n : a material (as grease) used between moving parts of machinery to make the surfaces slippery and reduce friction

lu·bri·cate \-brǝ-,kāt\ vb : to apply a lubricant to — **lu·bri·ca·tion** \,lü-brǝ-'kā-shǝn\ n — **lu·bri·ca·tor** \'lü-brǝ-,kāt-ǝr\ n

lu·bri·cious \lü-'brish-ǝs\ adj **1** : LECHEROUS; also : SALACIOUS **2** : SMOOTH,

SLIPPERY; also : SHIFTY — **lu·bric·i·ty** \-'bris-ǝt-ē\ n

lu·cent \'lüs-°nt\ adj **1** : LUMINOUS **2** : CLEAR, LUCID

lu·cerne \lü-'sǝrn\ n, chiefly Brit : ALFALFA

lu·cid \'lü-sǝd\ adj **1** : SHINING **2** : clear-minded **3** : easily understood — **lu·cid·i·ty** \lü-'sid-ǝt-ē\ n — **lu·cid·ly** \'lü-sǝd-lē\ adv — **lu·cid·ness** n

Lu·ci·fer \'lü-sǝ-far\ n : DEVIL, SATAN

luck \'lǝk\ n **1** : CHANCE, FORTUNE **2** : good fortune : SUCCESS — **luck·less** \-lǝs\ adj

lucky \'lǝk-ē\ adj **1** : favored by luck : FORTUNATE **2** : FORTUITOUS **3** : seeming to bring good luck — **luck·i·ly** adv

lu·cra·tive \'lü-krǝt-iv\ adj : PROFITABLE — **lu·cra·tive·ly** adv — **lu·cra·tive·ness** n

lu·cre \'lü-kǝr\ n : PROFIT; also : MONEY

lu·cu·bra·tion \,lü-k(y)ǝ-'brā-shǝn\ n : laborious study : MEDITATION

lu·di·crous \'lüd-ǝ-krǝs\ adj : LAUGHABLE, RIDICULOUS — **lu·di·crous·ly** adv — **lu·di·crous·ness** n

luff \'lǝf\ vb : to sail a ship closer to the wind — **luff** n

1lug \'lǝg\ vb **lugged**; **lug·ging 1** : DRAG, PULL **2** : to carry laboriously

2lug n : a projecting piece (as for fastening or support)

lug·gage \'lǝg-ij\ n **1** : BAGGAGE **2** : containers (as suitcases) for carrying personal belongings

lu·gu·bri·ous \lu·'gü-brē-ǝs\ adj : mournful often to an exaggerated degree — **lu·gu·bri·ous·ly** adv — **lu·gu·bri·ous·ness** n

luke·warm \'lük-'wȯrm\ adj **1** : moderately warm : TEPID **2** : not enthusiastic

1lull \'lǝl\ vb **1** : SOOTHE, CALM **2** : to cause to relax vigilance

2lull n **1** : a temporary calm (as during a storm) **2** : a temporary drop in activity

lul·la·by \'lǝl-ǝ-,bī\ n : a song to lull children to sleep

lum·ba·go \,lǝm-'bā-gō\ n : rheumatic pain in the lower back and loins

1lum·ber \'lǝm-bǝr\ vb : to move heavily or clumsily

2lumber n **1** : surplus or disused articles that are stored away **2** : timber esp. when dressed for use

3lumber vb : to cut logs; also : to saw logs into lumber — **lum·ber·man** \-mǝn\ n

lum·ber·jack \-,jak\ n : LOGGER

lum·ber·yard \-,yärd\ n : a place where lumber is kept for sale

lu·mi·nary \'lü-mǝ-,ner-ē\ n **1** : a very famous person **2** : a source of light; esp : a heavenly body

lu·mi·nous \'lü-mǝ-nǝs\ adj **1** : emitting light; also : LIGHTED **2** : CLEAR, INTELLIGIBLE — **lu·mi·nos·i·ty** \,lü-mǝ-'näs-ǝt-ē\ n — **lu·mi·nous·ly** \'lü-mǝ-nǝs-lē\ adv

lum·mox \'lǝm-ǝks\ n : a clumsy person

1lump \'lǝmp\ n **1** : a piece or mass of irregular shape **2** : AGGREGATE, TOTALITY **3** : a usu. abnormal swelling — **lump·ish** adj — **lumpy** adj

2lump vb **1** : to heap together in a lump **2** : to form into lumps

lu·na·cy \'lü-nə-sē\ n 1 : INSANITY 2 : extreme folly

lu·nar \-nər\ adj : of or relating to the moon

¹**lu·na·tic** \'lü-nə-,tik\ adj 1 : INSANE; also : used for insane persons 2 : extremely foolish

²**lunatic** n : an insane person

¹**lunch** \'lənch\ n 1 : a light meal usu. eaten in the middle of the day 2 : the food prepared for a lunch

²**lunch** vb : to eat lunch

lun·cheon \'lən-chən\ n : a usu. formal lunch

lun·cheon·ette \,lən-chə-'net\ n : a place where light lunches are sold

lunch·room \'lənch-,rüm, -,rûm\ n : a restaurant specializing in food that is ready to serve or that can be quickly prepared

lu·nette \lü-'net\ n : something shaped like a crescent or half-moon

lung \'ləŋ\ n : one of the usu. paired baglike breathing organs in the chest of an air-breathing vertebrate

lunge \'lənj\ n 1 : a sudden stretching thrust or pass (as with a sword) 2 : a sudden forward stride or leap — **lunge** vb

lu·pine \'lü-pən\ n : a leguminous plant with long clusters of pealike flowers

lurch \'lərch\ n : a sudden swaying or tipping movement — **lurch** vb

¹**lure** \'lür\ n 1 : ENTICEMENT; also : APPEAL 2 : an artificial bait for catching fish

²**lure** vb : to draw on with a promise of pleasure or gain : lead astray

lu·rid \'lür-əd\ adj 1 : LIVID 2 : shining with the red glow of fire seen through smoke or cloud 3 : GRUESOME; also : SENSATIONAL syn ghastly, grisly — **lu·rid·ly** adv

lurk \'lərk\ vb 1 : to move furtively : SNEAK 2 : to lie concealed

lus·cious \'ləsh-əs\ adj 1 : having a pleasingly sweet taste or smell 2 : sensually appealing — **lus·cious·ly** adv — **lus·cious·ness** n

lush \'ləsh\ adj : having or covered with abundant growth 〈~ pastures〉

lust \'ləst\ n 1 : sexual desire often to an intense or unrestrained degree 2 : an intense longing — **lust** vb — **lust·ful** \-fəl\ adj

lus·ter or **lus·tre** \'ləs-tər\ n 1 : a shine or sheen esp. from reflected light 2 : BRIGHTNESS, GLITTER 3 : GLORY, SPLENDOR — **lus·ter·less** \-tər-ləs\ adj — **lus·trous** \-trəs\ adj

lus·tral \'ləs-trəl\ adj : PURIFICATORY

lusty \'ləs-tē\ adj : full of vitality : VIGOROUS, ROBUST — **lust·i·ly** adv — **lust·i·ness** n

lute \'lüt\ n : a stringed musical instrument with a pear-shaped body and a fretted fingerboard

Lu·ther·an \'lü-th(ə-)rən\ n : a member of a Protestant denomination adhering to the doctrines of Martin Luther — **Lu·ther·an·ism** \-,iz-əm\ n

lux·u·ri·ant \,ləg-'zhûr-ē-ənt, ,lək-'shûr-\ adj 1 : yielding or growing abundantly : LUSH, PRODUCTIVE 2 : exuberantly rich and varied; also : FLORID — **lux·u·ri·ance** \-ē-əns\ n — **lux·u·ri·ant·ly** adv

lux·u·ri·ate \-ē-,āt\ vb 1 : to grow profusely 2 : REVEL

lux·u·ry \'ləksh-(ə-)rē, 'ləgzh-\ n 1 : great ease or comfort 2 : something desirable but costly or hard to get 3 : something adding to pleasure or comfort but not absolutely necessary — **lux·u·ri·ous** \,ləg-'zhûr-ē-əs, ,lək-'shûr-\ adj — **lux·u·ri·ous·ly** adv

¹**-ly** \lē\ adj suffix 1 : like in appearance, manner, or nature 〈queenly〉 2 : characterized by regular recurrence in (specified) units of time : every 〈hourly〉

²**-ly** \lē\ (corresponding adjectives may end in əl, as "double"); -ically is i-k(ə-)lē\ adv suffix 1 : in a (specified) manner 〈slowly〉 2 : from a (specified) point of view 〈grammatically〉

ly·ce·um \lī-'sē-əm\ n 1 : a hall for public lectures 2 : an association providing public lectures, concerts, and entertainments

lye \'lī\ n : a white crystalline corrosive alkaline substance used in making rayon and soap

¹**lying** pres part of LIE

²**ly·ing** \'lī-iŋ\ adj : UNTRUTHFUL, FALSE

ly·ing-in \,lī-iŋ-'in\ n : the state attending and consequent to childbirth : CONFINEMENT

lymph \'limf\ n : a pale liquid consisting chiefly of blood plasma and white blood cells, circulating in thin-walled tubes (lymphatic vessels), and bathing the body tissues — **lym·phat·ic** \lim-'fat-ik\ adj

lynch \'linch\ vb : to put to death by mob action without legal sanction or due process of law — **lynch·er** n

lynx \'links\ n : a wildcat with a short tail, long legs, and usu. tufted ears

lyre \'lī(ə)r\ n : a stringed musical instrument of the harp class used by the ancient Greeks

¹**lyr·ic** \'lir-ik\ adj 1 : suitable for singing : MELODIC 2 : expressing direct and usu. intense personal emotion

²**lyric** n 1 : a lyric poem 2 pl : the words of a popular song — **lyr·i·cal** \-i-kəl\ adj

---

m \'em\ n, often cap : the 13th letter of the English alphabet

ma \'mä, 'mó\ n : MOTHER

ma'am \'mam\ n : MADAM

ma·ca·bre \mə-'käbr\ adj 1 : having death as a subject 2 : GRISLY, GRUESOME 3 : HORRIBLE

mac·ad·am \mə-'kad-əm\ n 1 : a roadway or pavement constructed of small closely packed broken stone usu. cemented with stone dust or bituminous material 2 : the broken stone used in macadamizing — **mac·ad·am·ize** \-,īz\ vb

ma·caque \mə-'kak\ n : any of several short-tailed Asiatic and East Indian monkeys

mac·a·ro·ni \,mak-ə-'rō-nē\ n, pl -nis or -nies 1 : a food made chiefly of wheat flour dried in the form of usu. slender tubes 2 : FOP, DANDY

mac·a·roon \,mak-ə-'rün\ n : a small

cake made chiefly of egg whites, sugar, and ground almonds or coconut

ma·caw \mə-'kȯ\ *n* **:** a large long-tailed parrot of Central and So. America

Mc·Coy \mə-'kȯi\ *n* **:** something that is neither imitation nor substitute 〈the real ~〉

1mace \'mās\ *n* **1 :** a heavy often spiked club used as a weapon esp. in the Middle Ages **2 :** an ornamental staff carried as a symbol of authority esp. before a public official

2mace *n* **:** a spice from the fibrous coating of the nutmeg

mac·er·ate \'mas-ə-,rāt\ *vb* **1 :** to cause to waste away **2 :** to soften by steeping or soaking so as to separate the parts — **mac·er·a·tion** \,mas-ə-'rā-shən\ *n*

ma·chete \mə-'shet-ē\ *n* **:** a large heavy knife used esp. in So. America and the West Indies for cutting sugarcane and underbrush

ma·chic·o·la·tion \mə-,chik-ə-'lā-shən\ *n* **:** an opening between the corbels of a projecting parapet (as of a medieval castle) or in the floor of a gallery or roof of a portal for discharging missiles upon assailants below

mach·i·na·tion \,mak-ə-'nā-shən\ *n* **1 :** an act of planning esp. to do harm **2 :** PLOT — **mach·i·nate** \'mak-ə-,nāt\ *vb*

1ma·chine \mə-'shēn\ *n* **1 :** CONVEYANCE, VEHICLE; *esp* **:** AUTOMOBILE **2 :** a combination of mechanical parts that transmit forces, motion, and energy one to another to some desired end (as for sewing, printing, or hoisting) **3 :** an instrument (as a pulley or lever) for transmitting or modifying force or motion **4 :** a highly organized political group under the leadership of a boss or small clique

2machine *vb* **:** to shape or finish by machine-operated tools

machine gun *n* **:** an automatic gun using small-arms ammunition for rapid continuous firing

ma·chine·ry \mə-'shēn-(ə-)rē\ *n* **1 :** MACHINES; *also* **:** the working parts of a machine **2 :** the means by which something is done or kept going

ma·chin·ist \-'shē-nəst\ *n* **:** a person who makes or works on machines and engines

mack·er·el \'mak-(ə-)rəl\ *n* **:** a No. Atlantic food fish greenish above and silvery below

mack·i·naw \'mak-ə-,nȯ\ *n* **:** a short heavy plaid coat

mack·in·tosh \'mak-ən-,täsh\ *n* **1** *chiefly Brit* **:** RAINCOAT **2 :** a lightweight waterproof fabric

mac·ro·cosm \'mak-rə-,käz-əm\ *n* **:** the great world **:** UNIVERSE

ma·cron \'māk-,rän, 'mak-\ *n* **:** a mark ‾ placed over a vowel (as in \māk\) to show that the vowel is long

mac·ro·scop·ic \,mak-rə-'skäp-ik\ *adj* **:** visible to the naked eye

mad \'mad\ *adj* **1 :** disordered in mind **:** INSANE **2 :** being rash and foolish **3 :** FURIOUS, ENRAGED **4 :** FRANTIC **5 :** carried away by enthusiasm **6 :** wildly gay **7 :** RABID — **mad·ly** *adv* — **mad·ness** *n*

mad·am \'mad-əm\ *n* **1** *pl* **mes·dames** \mā-'däm\ — used as a form of polite address to a woman **2** *pl* **madams** **:** the female head of a house of prostitution

ma·dame \mə-'dam\ *n*, *pl* **mes·dames** \mā-'däm\ **:** MISTRESS — used as a title for a woman not of English-speaking nationality

mad·cap \'mad-,kap\ *adj* **:** WILD, RECKLESS — **madcap** *n*

mad·den \'mad-ᵊn\ *vb* **:** to make mad **:** ENRAGE

mad·der \'mad-ər\ *n* **:** a Eurasian plant with yellow flowers and fleshy red roots; *also* **:** its root or a dye prepared from it

mad·ding \'mad-iŋ\ *adj* **1 :** acting as if mad **:** FRENZIED 〈the ~ crowd〉 **2 :** MADDENING

made *past of* MAKE

Ma·dei·ra \mə-'dir-ə\ *n* **:** an amber-colored dessert wine

ma·de·moi·selle \,mad-ə-m(w)ə-'zel\ *n*, *pl* **mademoiselles** \-'zelz\ *or* **mes·de·moi·selles** \,mād-ə-m(w)ə-'zel\ **:** an unmarried girl or woman — used as a title for a woman not of English-speaking and esp. of French nationality

made-up \'mād-'əp\ *adj* **1 :** marked by the use of makeup 〈~ eyelids〉 **2 :** fancifully conceived or falsely devised 〈a ~ story〉

mad·house \'mad-,haůs\ *n* **1 :** a place for the detention and care of the insane **2 :** a place of great uproar or confusion

mad·man \-,man\ *n* **:** LUNATIC

ma·dras \mə-'dras, 'mad-rəs\ *n* **:** a fine usu. corded or striped cotton fabric

mad·ri·gal \'mad-ri-gəl\ *n* **:** a somewhat elaborate part-song esp. of the 16th century; *also* **:** a love poem suitable for a musical setting

mael·strom \'māl-strəm\ *n* **:** a violent whirlpool dangerous to ships

mae·nad \'mē-,nad\ *n* **1 :** a woman participating in bacchanalian rites **2 :** an unnaturally excited or distraught woman

mae·stro \'mī-strō\ *n*, *pl* **maestros** *or* **mae·stri** \-,strē\ **:** a master in an art; *esp* **:** an eminent composer, conductor, or teacher of music

mag·a·zine \'mag-ə-,zēn\ *n* **1 :** a storehouse esp. for military supplies **2 :** a place for keeping gunpowder in a fort or ship **3 :** a publication usu. containing stories, articles, or poems and issued periodically **4 :** a container in a gun for holding cartridges; *also* **:** a chamber (as on a camera) for film

mag·da·len \'mag-də-lən\ *or* **mag·da·lene** \-,lēn\ *n* **:** a reformed prostitute

ma·gen·ta \mə-'jent-ə\ *n* **:** a deep purplish red

mag·got \'mag-ət\ *n* **:** the legless worm-like larva of a two-winged fly — **mag·goty** *adj*

ma·gi \'mā-,jī\ *n pl, often cap* **:** the three wise men from the East who paid homage to the infant Jesus

mag·ic \'maj-ik\ *n* **1 :** the art of persons who claim to be able to do things by the help of supernatural powers or by their own knowledge of nature's secrets **2 :** a seemingly secret power **3 :** SLEIGHT OF HAND — **magic** *or*

ə abut; ᵊ kitten; ər further; a back; ā bake; ä cot, cart; aů out; ch chin; e less; ē easy; g gift; i trip; ī life; j joke; ŋ sing; ō flow; ȯ flaw; ȯi coin; th thin; <u>th</u> this; ü loot; ů foot; y yet; yü few; yů furious; zh vision

mag·i·cal \-i-kəl\ *adj* — **mag·i·cal·ly** *adv*

ma·gi·cian \mə-'jish-ən\ *n* **:** one skilled in magic

mag·is·te·ri·al \,maj-ə-'stir-ē-əl\ *adj* **1 :** AUTHORITATIVE **2 :** of or relating to a magistrate or his office or duties

mag·is·tral \'maj-ə-strəl\ *adj* **:** AUTHORITATIVE

mag·is·trate \'maj-ə-,strāt\ *n* **:** an official entrusted with administration of the laws — **mag·is·tra·cy** \-strə-sē\ *n*

mag·nan·i·mous \mag-'nan-ə-məs\ *adj* **1 :** showing or suggesting a lofty and courageous spirit **2 :** NOBLE, GENEROUS — **mag·na·nim·i·ty** \,mag-nə-'nim-ət-ē\ *n* — **mag·nan·i·mous·ly** \mag-'nan-ə-məs-lē\ *adv*

mag·nate \'mag-,nāt\ *n* **:** a person of rank, influence, or distinction

mag·ne·sia \mag-'nē-shə, -zhə\ *n* **:** a light white substance that is an oxide of magnesium and is used as a laxative

mag·ne·si·um \-'nē-zē-əm, -zhəm\ *n* **:** a silver-white light and easily worked metallic chemical element

mag·net \'mag-nət\ *n* **1 :** LODESTONE **2 :** a body having the property of attracting iron **3 :** something that attracts

mag·net·ic \mag-'net-ik\ *adj* **1 :** of or relating to a magnet or magnetism **2 :** magnetized or capable of being magnetized **3 :** having an unusual power or ability to attract ⟨a ~ personality⟩

magnetic north *n* **:** the northerly direction in the earth's magnetic field indicated by the north-seeking pole of the horizontal magnetic needle

magnetic tape *n* **:** a ribbon of thin material coated for use in recording by magnetic means

mag·ne·tism \'mag-nə-,tiz-əm\ *n* **1 :** the power to attract as possessed by a magnet **2 :** the property of a substance (as iron) that allows it to be magnetized **3 :** an ability to attract or charm

mag·ne·tize \'mag-nə-,tīz\ *vb* **1 :** to attract like a magnet **:** CHARM **2 :** to communicate magnetic properties to — **mag·ne·ti·za·tion** \,mag-nət-ə-'zā-shən\ *n*

mag·ne·to \mag-'nēt-ō\ *n* **:** a generator used to generate electricity for ignition in an internal-combustion engine

mag·nif·i·cent \mag-'nif-ə-sənt\ *adj* **1 :** great in deed or place **2 :** characterized by splendor or grandeur **3 :** strikingly beautiful or impressive **4 :** unusually fine ⟨a ~ day⟩ *syn* imposing, stately, noble — **mag·nif·i·cence** \-səns\ *n* — **mag·nif·i·cent·ly** *adv*

mag·nif·i·co \mag-'nif-i-,kō\ *n, pl* **-coes** *or* **-cos 1 :** a nobleman of Venice **2 :** a person of high position or distinguished appearance

mag·ni·fy \'mag-nə-,fī\ *vb* **1 :** EXTOL, LAUD; *also* **:** to cause to be held in greater esteem **2 :** INTENSIFY; *also* **:** EXAGGERATE **3 :** to enlarge in fact or in appearance — **mag·ni·fi·ca·tion** \,mag-nə-fə-'kā-shən\ *n* — **mag·ni·fi·er** \'mag-nə-,fī-(-ə)r\ *n*

mag·nil·o·quent \mag-'nil-ə-kwənt\ *adj* **:** GRANDILOQUENT — **mag·nil·o·quence** \-kwəns\ *n*

mag·ni·tude \'mag-nə-,t(y)üd\ *n* **1 :** greatness of size or extent **2 :** SIZE **3 :** QUANTITY; *also* **:** volume of sound

4 : degree of brightness of a star on a scale in which the fainter stars are indicated by higher numbers ⟨the naked eye can see stars up to ~ 6⟩

mag·no·lia \mag-'nōl-yə\ *n* **:** any of several spring-flowering shrubs and trees with large often fragrant flowers

mag·pie \'mag-,pī\ *n* **:** a long-tailed black-and-white bird related to the jays

Mag·yar \'mag-,yär, 'mäj-,är\ *n* **:** a member of the dominant people of Hungary — **Magyar** *adj*

ma·ha·ra·ja \,mä-hə-'räj-ə\ *n* **:** a Hindu prince ranking above a raja

ma·ha·ra·ni *or* **ma·ha·ra·nee** \,mä-hə-'rän-ē\ *n* **:** the wife of a maharaja; *also* **:** a Hindu princess ranking above a rani

ma·hat·ma \mə-'hät-mə\ *n* [Skt *mahāt-man* great-souled, fr. *mahā-* great + *ātman* soul, self] **:** a person revered for high-mindedness, wisdom, and selflessness

ma·hog·a·ny \mə-'häg-ə-nē\ *n* **:** any of various tropical trees with reddish wood used in furniture; *esp* **:** an American evergreen tree or its durable lustrous reddish brown wood

ma·hout \mə-'haút\ *n* **:** a keeper and driver of an elephant

maid \'mād\ *n* **1 :** an unmarried girl or young woman **2 :** a female servant

¹maid·en \'mād-ᵊn\ *n* **:** MAID 1 — **maid·en·ly** *adj*

²maiden *adj* **1 :** UNMARRIED; *also* **:** VIRGIN **2 :** of, relating to, or befitting a maiden **3 :** FIRST ⟨~ voyage⟩ **4 :** FRESH, UNTRIED

maid·en·hair \-,haər\ *n* **:** a fern with delicate feathery fronds

maid·en·hood \-,hùd\ *n* **:** the condition or time of being a maiden

maid-in-wait·ing *n, pl* **maids-in-wait·ing :** a young woman of a queen's or princess's household appointed to attend her

maid of honor : a bride's principal unmarried wedding attendant

maid·ser·vant \'mād-,sər-vənt\ *n* **:** a female servant

¹mail \'māl\ *n* **1 :** the bags of postal matter conveyed under public authority from one post office to another **2 :** a nation's postal system **3 :** postal matter

²mail *vb* **:** to send by mail

³mail \'māl\ *n* **:** armor made of metal links or plates

mail·box \-,bäks\ *n* **1 :** a public box for the collection of mail **2 :** a private box for the delivery of mail

mailed \'māld\ *adj* **:** protected or armed with or as if with mail ⟨a ~ fist⟩

mail·man \-,man\ *n* **:** a man who delivers mail

maim \'mām\ *vb* **:** to mutilate, disfigure, or wound seriously **:** CRIPPLE

¹main \'mān\ *n* **1 :** FORCE ⟨with might and ~⟩ **2 :** MAINLAND; *also* **:** HIGH SEA **3 :** the chief part **4 :** a principal pipe, duct, or circuit of a utility system

²main *adj* **1 :** OUTSTANDING, CONSPICUOUS; *also* **:** CHIEF, PRINCIPAL **2 :** fully exerted ⟨~ force⟩ **3 :** expressing the chief predication in a complex sentence ⟨~ clause⟩ — **main·ly** *adv*

main·land \-,land, -lənd\ *n* **:** a continuous body of land constituting the chief part of a country or continent

main·mast \-,mast, -məst\ *n* **:** the principal mast on a sailing ship

main·sail \'mān-,sāl, -səl\ *n* : the principal sail on the mainmast

main·sheet \-,shēt\ *n* : a rope by which the mainsail is trimmed and secured

main·spring \-,spriŋ\ *n* 1 : the chief spring in a mechanism (as of a watch) 2 : the chief motive, agent, or cause

main·stay \-,stā\ *n* 1 : a stay extending forward from the head of the mainmast to the foot of the foremast 2 : a chief support

main·stream \-,strēm\ *n* : a prevailing current or direction of activity or influence

main·tain \mān-'tān\ *vb* 1 : to keep in an existing state (as of repair) 2 : to sustain against opposition or danger 3 : to continue in : carry on 4 : to provide for : SUPPORT 5 : ASSERT — **main·tain·able** *adj* — **main·te·nance** \'mānt-(ə-)nəns\ *n*

mai·son·ette \,māz-ᵊn-'et\ *n* 1 : a small house 2 : an apartment often of two stories

maî·tre d'hô·tel \,mā-trə-dō-'tel\ *n* 1 : MAJORDOMO 2 : the head of a dining-room staff (as of a restaurant)

maize \'māz\ *n* : INDIAN CORN

maj·es·ty \'maj-ə-stē\ *n* 1 : sovereign power, authority, or dignity; also : the person of a sovereign — used as a title 2 : GRANDEUR, SPLENDOR — **ma·jes·tic** \mə-'jes-tik\ *or* **ma·jes·ti·cal** \-ti-kəl\ *adj* — **ma·jes·ti·cal·ly** *adv*

ma·jol·i·ca \mə-'jäl-i-kə\ *n* : any of several faiences; *esp* : an Italian tin-glazed pottery

¹ma·jor \'mā-jər\ *adj* 1 : greater in number, extent, or importance 2 : notable or conspicuous in effect or scope 3 : SERIOUS (a ~ illness) 4 : having half steps between the third and fourth and the seventh and eighth degrees (~ scale); *also* : based on a major scale (~ key) (~ chord)

²major *n* 1 : a commissioned officer (as in the army) ranking next below a lieutenant colonel 2 : a subject of academic study chosen as a field of specialization; *also* : a student specializing in such a field

³major *vb* : to pursue an academic major

ma·jor·do·mo \,mā-jər-'dō-mō\ *n* 1 : a head steward 2 : BUTLER

major general *n* : a commissioned officer (as in the army) ranking next below a lieutenant general

ma·jor·i·ty \mə-'jòr-ət-ē\ *n* 1 : the age at which full civil rights are accorded; *also* : the status of one who has attained this age 2 : a number greater than half of a total; *also* : the excess of this greater number over the remainder 3 : the military rank of a major

maj·us·cule \'maj-əs-,kyül, mə-'jəs-\ *n* : a large letter (as a capital)

¹make \'māk\ *vb* **made** \'mād\ **mak·ing** 1 : to cause to exist, occur, or appear; *also* : DESTINE 2 : FASHION; *also* : COMPOSE 3 : to formulate in the mind 4 : CONSTITUTE ⟨house *made* of stone⟩ 5 : to compute to be 6 : to set in order : PREPARE 7 : APPOINT 8 : ENACT; *also* : EXECUTE ⟨~ a will⟩

9 : CONCLUDE 10 : to carry out : PERFORM 11 : COMPEL 12 : to assure the success of 13 : to amount to in significance 14 : to be capable of developing or being fashioned into 15 : REACH, ATTAIN; *also* : GAIN 16 : to start out : GO 17 : to have weight or effect **syn** form, shape, fabricate, manufacture — **mak·er** *n*

²make *n* 1 : the manner or style of construction; *also* : the origin of a manufactured article 2 : MAKEUP 3 : the action or process of manufacturing

¹make-be·lieve \-bə-,lēv\ *n* : a pretending to believe : PRETENSE

²make-believe *adj* : FEIGNED

make-do \-,dü\ *adj* : MAKESHIFT

make·shift \-,shift\ *n* : a temporary expedient — **makeshift** *adj*

make·up \-,əp\ *n* 1 : the way in which something is put together; *also* : physical, mental, and moral constitution 2 : cosmetics esp. for the face

mal·adapt·ed \,mal-ə-'dap-təd\ *adj* : poorly suited to a particular use, purpose, or situation

mal·ad·just·ed \,mal-ə-'jəs-təd\ *adj* : poorly or inadequately adjusted (as to one's environment) — **mal·ad·just·ment** \'jəs(t)-mənt\ *n*

mal·ad·min·is·ter \,mal-əd-'min-ə-stər\ *vb* : to administer badly

mal·adroit \,mal-ə-'droit\ *adj* : not adroit : INEPT

mal·a·dy \'mal-əd-ē\ *n* : a disease or disorder of body or mind : AILMENT

mal·aise \ma-'lāz\ *n* : a sense of physical ill-being

mal·a·mute \'mal-ə-,myüt\ *n* : a sled dog of northern No. America

mal·a·pert \,mal-ə-'pərt\ *adj* : impudently bold : SAUCY

mal·a·prop·ism \'mal-ə-,präp-,iz-əm\ *n* [fr. Mrs. *Malaprop*, character in Sheridan's comedy *The Rivals*] : a usu. humorous misuse of a word

mal·ap·ro·pos \,mal-,ap-rə-'pō, mal-'ap-\ *adv* : in an inappropriate or inopportune way

ma·lar·ia \mə-'ler-ē-ə\ *n* : a disease marked by recurring chills and fever and caused by a parasite carried by a mosquito — **ma·lar·i·al** \-ē-əl\ *adj*

Ma·lay \mə-'lā, 'mā-,lā\ *n* : a member of a people of the Malay peninsula and archipelago — **Malay** *adj* — **Ma·lay·an** \-ən\ *n or adj*

mal·con·tent \,mal-kən-'tent\ *adj* : marked by a dissatisfaction with the existing state of affairs : DISCONTENTED — **malcontent** *n*

mal de mer \,mal-də-'meər\ *n* : SEASICKNESS

¹male \'māl\ *adj* 1 : of, relating to, or being the sex that fathers young; *also* : STAMINATE 2 : MASCULINE

²male *n* : a male individual

mal·e·dic·tion \,mal-ə-'dik-shən\ *n* : CURSE, EXECRATION

mal·e·fac·tor \'mal-ə-,fak-tər\ *n* : EVILDOER; *esp* : one who commits an offense against the law — **mal·e·fac·tion** \,mal-ə-'fak-shən\ *n*

ma·lef·ic \mə-'lef-ik\ *adj* 1 : BALEFUL 2 : MALICIOUS

ma·lef·i·cent \mə-'lef-ə-sənt\ *adj* : work-

ə abut; ᵊ kitten; ər further; a back; ā bake; ä cot, cart; aú out; ch chin; e less; ē easy; g gift; i trip; ī life; j joke; ŋ sing; ō flow; ò flaw; òi coin; th thin; th̲ this; ü loot; ù foot; y yet; yü few; yù furious; zh vision

ing or productive of harm or evil : HARMFUL — **mal·e·fi·cence** n

ma·lev·o·lent \mə-'lev-ə-lənt\ adj : having, showing, or arising from ill will, spite, or hatred syn malignant, malign, malicious, spiteful — **ma·lev·o·lence** \-ləns\ n

mal·fea·sance \mal-'fēz-³ns\ n : wrongful conduct esp. by a public official

mal·for·ma·tion \,mal-fôr-'mā-shən\ n : an irregular or faulty formation or structure — **mal·formed** \mal-'fôrmd\ adj

mal·func·tion \mal-'fəŋk-shən\ vb : to fail to operate in the normal or usual manner — **malfunction** n

mal·ice \'mal-əs\ n : ILL WILL — **ma·li·cious** \mə-'lish-əs\ adj — **ma·li·cious·ly** adv

¹ma·lign \mə-'līn\ adj 1 : evil in nature, influence, or effect; also : MALIGNANT 2 : MALEVOLENT

²malign vb : to speak evil of : DEFAME, SLANDER

ma·lig·nant \mə-'lig-nənt\ adj 1 : INJURIOUS, MALIGN 2 : tending or likely to cause death : VIRULENT — **ma·lig·nan·cy** \-nən-sē\ n — **ma·lig·nant·ly** adv — **ma·lig·ni·ty** \-nət-ē\ n

ma·lin·ger \mə-'liŋ-gər\ vb : to pretend illness so as to avoid duty — **ma·lin·ger·er** n

mal·i·son \'mal-ə-sən\ n : MALEDICTION

mall \'môl, 'mal\ n 1 : a shaded area designed esp. as a promenade 2 : a usu. paved or grassy strip esp. between two roadways

mal·lard \'mal-ərd\ n : a common wild duck that is the ancestor of domestic ducks

mal·le·a·ble \'mal-ē-ə-bəl\ adj 1 : capable of being extended or shaped by beating with a hammer or by the pressure of rollers 2 : susceptible of being fashioned into a different form or shape syn plastic, pliant, ductile — **mal·le·a·bil·i·ty** \,mal-ē-ə-'bil-ət-ē\ n

mal·let \'mal-ət\ n 1 : a tool with a large head for driving another tool or for striking a surface without marring it 2 : a hammerlike implement for striking a ball (as in polo or croquet)

mal·low \'mal-ō\ n : any of several tall herbs with lobed leaves and 5-petaled white, yellow, rose, or purplish flowers

malm·sey \'mä(l)m-zē\ n, often cap : a sweet aromatic dessert wine

mal·nour·ished \mal-'nər-isht\ adj : poorly nourished

mal·nu·tri·tion \,mal-n(y)ù-'trish-ən\ n : faulty and esp. inadequate nutrition

mal·oc·clu·sion \,mal-ə-'klü-zhən\ n : faulty coming together of teeth in biting

mal·odor·ous \mal-'ōd-ə-rəs\ adj : ill-smelling — **mal·odor·ous·ly** adv — **mal·odor·ous·ness** n

mal·prac·tice \-'prak-təs\ n : a dereliction from professional duty or a failure of professional skill that results in injury, loss, or damage

malt \'môlt\ n 1 : grain and esp. barley steeped in water until it has sprouted and used in brewing and distilling 2 : liquor made with malt — **malt·ster** \-stər\ n — **malty** adj

malted milk n : a powder prepared from dried milk and an extract from malt; also : a beverage of this powder in milk or other liquid

mal·treat \mal-'trēt\ vb : to treat cruelly or roughly : ABUSE — **mal·treat·ment** \-mənt\ n

mam·bo \'mäm-bō\ n : a dance of Haitian origin related to the rumba — **mambo** vb

mam·ma or **ma·ma** \'mäm-ə\ n : MOTHER

mam·mal \'mam-əl\ n : any of the group of vertebrate animals that includes man and all others which nourish their young with milk — **mam·ma·li·an** \mə-'mā-lē-ən, ma-'mā-\ adj or n

mam·ma·ry \'mam-ə-rē\ adj : of, relating to, or being the glands (**mammary glands**) that in female mammals secrete milk

mam·mon \'mam-ən\ n : material wealth or possessions having an esp. debasing influence — **mam·mon·ish** adj

¹mam·moth \'mam-əth\ n : any of various large hairy extinct elephants

²mammoth adj : of very great size : GIGANTIC syn colossal, enormous, immense, vast

¹man \'man\ n, pl men \'men\ 1 : a human being; esp : an adult male 2 : MANKIND 3 : one possessing in high degree the qualities considered distinctive of manhood; also : HUSBAND 4 : an adult male servant or employee 5 : one of the pieces with which various games (as chess) are played

²man vb manned; man·ning 1 : to supply with men (~ a fleet) 2 : FORTIFY, BRACE

man-about-town n, pl **men-about-town** : a worldly and socially active man

man·a·cle \'man-i-kəl\ n 1 : a shackle for the hand or wrist 2 : something used as a restraint — usu. used in pl. — **manacle** vb

man·age \'man-ij\ vb 1 : HANDLE, CONTROL; also : to direct or carry on business or affairs 2 : to make and keep submissive 3 : to treat with care : HUSBAND 4 : to achieve one's purpose : CONTRIVE — **man·age·abil·i·ty** \,man-ij-ə-'bil-ət-ē\ n — **man·age·able** \'man-ij-ə-bəl\ adj — **man·age·able·ness** n — **man·age·ably** adv

man·age·ment \'man-ij-mənt\ n 1 : the act or art of managing : CONTROL 2 : judicious use of means to accomplish an end 3 : executive ability 4 : the group of those who manage or direct an enterprise

man·ag·er \'man-ij-ər\ n : one that manages; esp : a person who directs a team or athlete — **man·a·ge·ri·al** \,man-ə-'jir-ē-əl\ adj

ma·ña·na \mən-'yän-ə\ n : an indefinite time in the future

man-at-arms \,man-ət-'ärmz\ n, pl **men-at-arms** \,men-\ : SOLDIER; esp : one who is heavily armed and mounted

man·ci·ple \'man-sə-pəl\ n : a steward or purveyor esp. for a college or monastery

man·da·mus \man-'dā-məs\ n : a writ issued by a superior court commanding that a specified official act or duty be performed

man·da·rin \'man-də-rən\ n 1 : a public official of high rank under the Chinese Empire 2 cap : the chief dialect of China 3 : a small loose-skinned citrus fruit : TANGERINE

man·date \'man-,dāt\ n 1 : an authoritative command **2** : an authorization to act given to a representative **3** : a commission granted by the League of Nations to a member nation for governing conquered territory; *also* : a territory so governed

man·da·to·ry \'man-də-ˌtōr-ē\ *adj* **1** : containing or constituting a command : OBLIGATORY **2** : of or relating to a League of Nations mandate

man·di·ble \'man-də-bəl\ *n* **1** : JAW; *esp* : a lower jaw **2** : either segment of a bird's bill

man·do·lin \ˌman-də-'lin, 'man-d'l-ən\ *n* : a stringed musical instrument with a pear-shaped body and a fretted neck

man·drag·o·ra \man-'drag-ə-rə\ *n* : MANDRAKE 1

man·drake \'man-ˌdrāk\ *n* **1** : an Old World herb of the nightshade group with a large forked root superstitiously credited with human and medicinal attributes **2** : MAYAPPLE

mane \'mān\ *n* : long heavy hair growing about the neck of some mammals (as a horse or lion)

ma·nege \ma-'nezh\ *n* : the art of horsemanship or of training horses

ma·nes \'män-ˌās, 'mā-ˌnēz\ *n pl, often cap* : the spirits of the dead and gods of the lower world in ancient Roman belief

ma·neu·ver \mə-'n(y)ü-vər\ *n* **1** : a military or naval movement; *also* : an armed forces training exercise — often used in pl. **2** : a procedure involving expert physical management **3** : an evasive movement or shift of tactics; *also* : an action taken to gain a tactical end — **maneuver** *vb* — **ma·neu·ver·abil·i·ty** \-ˌn(y)üv-(ə-)rə-'bil-ət-ē\ *n*

man·ful \'man-fəl\ *adj* : having or showing courage and resolution — **man·ful·ly** *adv*

man·ga·nese \'maŋ-gə-ˌnēz, -ˌnēs\ *n* : a grayish white metallic chemical element resembling iron but not magnetic

mange \'mānj\ *n* : a contagious itchy skin disease esp. of domestic animals — **mangy** \'mān-jē\ *adj*

man·gel-wur·zel \'maŋ-gəl-ˌwər-zəl\ *n* : a large coarse yellow to reddish orange beet extensively grown as food for cattle

man·ger \'mān-jər\ *n* : a trough or open box for livestock feed or fodder

¹**man·gle** \'maŋ-gəl\ *vb* **1** : to cut, bruise, or hack with repeated blows **2** : to spoil or injure in making or performing — **man·gler** \-g(ə-)lər\ *n*

²**mangle** *n* : a machine for ironing laundry by passing it between heated rollers

man·go \'maŋ-gō\ *n, pl* **-goes** *or* **-gos** : a yellowish red tropical fruit with juicy slightly acid pulp; *also* : an evergreen tree related to the sumacs that bears this fruit

man·grove \'man-ˌgrōv\ *n* : a tropical maritime tree that sends out many prop roots and forms dense thickets important in coastal land building

man·han·dle \'man-ˌhan-d'l\ *vb* : to handle roughly

man·hat·tan \man-'hat-ᵊn\ *n, often cap* : a cocktail made of whiskey and sweet vermouth

man·hole \'man-ˌhōl\ *n* : a hole (in a pavement, tank, or boiler) through which a man may go

man·hood \'man-ˌhùd\ *n* **1** : the condition of being a man and esp. an adult male **2** : manly qualities : COURAGE **3** : MEN

man·hour \'man-ˌaù(ə)r\ *n* : a unit of one hour's work by one man used esp. as a basis for wages and cost accounting

man·hunt \'man-ˌhənt\ *n* : an organized hunt for a person and esp. for one charged with a crime

ma·nia \'mā-nē-ə\ *n* **1** : insanity esp. when marked by extreme excitement **2** : excessive or unreasonable enthusiasm : CRAZE

¹**ma·ni·ac** \'mā-nē-ˌak\ *adj* **1** : affected with or suggestive of madness **2** : FRANTIC — **ma·ni·a·cal** \mə-'nī-ə-kəl\ *adj*

²**maniac** *n* : LUNATIC, MADMAN

man·ic-de·pres·sive \ˌman-ik-di-'pres-iv\ *adj* : characterized by alternating mania and depression — **manic-depressive** *n*

¹**man·i·cure** \'man-ə-ˌkyùr\ *n* [F, fr. L *manus* hand + *curare* to care for, fr. *cura* care] **1** : MANICURIST **2** : a treatment for the care of the hands and nails

²**manicure** *vb* **1** : to do manicure work on **2** : to trim closely and evenly

man·i·cur·ist \-ˌkyùr-əst\ *n* : a person who gives manicure treatments

¹**man·i·fest** \'man-ə-ˌfest\ *adj* **1** : readily perceived by the senses and esp by the sight **2** : easily understood : OBVIOUS — **man·i·fest·ly** *adv*

²**manifest** *vb* : to make evident or certain by showing or displaying syn evidence, evince, demonstrate

³**manifest** *n* : a list (as of passengers) or an invoice of cargo for a ship or plane

man·i·fes·ta·tion \ˌman-ə-fə-'stā-shən\ *n* : DISPLAY, DEMONSTRATION

man·i·fes·to \ˌman-ə-'fes-tō\ *n, pl* **-tos** *or* **-toes** : a public declaration of intentions, motives, or views

¹**man·i·fold** \'man-ə-ˌfōld\ *adj* **1** : marked by diversity or variety **2** : consisting of or operating many of one kind combined

²**manifold** *n* : a pipe fitting with several lateral outlets for connecting it with other pipes

³**manifold** *vb* **1** : to make several or many copies of (as a letter) **2** : MULTIPLY

man·i·kin *or* **man·ni·kin** \'man-i-kən\ *n* **1** : MANNEQUIN **2** : a little man : DWARF, PYGMY

Ma·nila hemp \mə-ˌnil-ə-\ *n* : a tough fiber from a Philippine banana plant used esp. for cordage

ma·nip·u·late \mə-'nip-yə-ˌlāt\ *vb* **1** : to treat or operate manually or mechanically esp. with skill **2** : to manage skillfully **3** : to control or change esp. by artful or unfair means so as to achieve a desired end — **ma·nip·u·la·tion** \mə-ˌnip-yə-'lā-shən\ *n* — **ma·nip·u·la·tive** \-'nip-yə-ˌlāt-iv\ *adj*—**ma·nip·u·la·tor** \-ˌlāt-ər\ *n*

man·kind *n* **1** \'man-'kīnd\ : the human race **2** \-ˌkīnd\ : men as distinguished from women

man·like \'man-ˌlīk\ *adj* : resembling or characteristic of a man

¹**man·ly** \'man-lē\ adj : having qualities appropriate to a man : BOLD, RESOLUTE — **man·li·ness** n

²**manly** adv : in a manly manner

man-made \'man-,mād\ adj : made by man rather than nature (~ systems); also : SYNTHETIC (~ fibers)

man·na \'man-ə\ n 1 : food miraculously supplied to the Israelites in their journey through the wilderness 2 : something of value that falls one's way : WINDFALL

manned \'mand\ adj : carrying or performed by a man (~ space flight)

man·ne·quin \'man-i-kən\ n 1 : an artist's, tailor's, or dressmaker's figure or model of the human body; also : a form representing the human figure used esp. for displaying clothes 2 : a woman who models clothing

man·ner \'man-ər\ n 1 : KIND, SORT 2 : a characteristic or customary mode of acting; also : MODE, FASHION 3 : a method of artistic execution 4 pl : social conduct; also : BEARING 5 pl : BEHAVIOR

man·ner·ism \-,iz-əm\ n 1 : ARTIFICIALITY, PRECIOSITY 2 : a characteristic mode or peculiarity of action, bearing, or treatment syn pose, air, affectation

man·ner·ly \-lē\ adj : showing good manners : POLITE — **man·ner·li·ness** n

man·nish \'man-ish\ adj 1 : resembling or suggesting a man rather than a woman 2 : suitable to or characteristic of a man syn male, masculine, manly, manlike, manful, virile — **man·nish·ly** adv — **man·nish·ness** n

ma·noeu·vre \mə-'n(y)ü-vər\ var of MANEUVER

man-of-war \,man-ə(v)-'wȯr\ n, pl **men-of-war** \,men-\ : a combatant warship

man·or \'man-ər\ n 1 : the house or hall of an estate; also : a landed estate 2 : an English estate of a feudal lord — **ma·no·ri·al** \mə-'nōr-ē-əl\ adj — **ma·no·ri·al·ism** \-,iz-əm\ n

man·qué \mäⁿ-'kā\ adj : short of or frustrated in the fulfillment of one's aspirations or talents (a poet ~)

man·sard \'man-,särd\ n : a roof having two slopes on all sides with the lower slope steeper than the upper one

manse \'mans\ n : the residence of a clergyman and esp. of a Presbyterian clergyman

man·ser·vant \'man-,sər-vənt\ n, pl **men·ser·vants** : a male servant

man·sion \'man-chən\ n : a large imposing residence; also : a separate apartment in a large structure

man·slaugh·ter \'man-,slȯt-ər\ n : the unlawful killing of a human being without express or implied malice

man·slay·er \-,slā-ər\ n : one that slays a man

man·sue·tude \'man-swi-,t(y)üd\ n : GENTLENESS

man·ta \'mant-ə\ n : a square piece of cloth or blanket used in southwestern U.S. and Latin America as a cloak or shawl

man·teau \man-'tō\ n : a loose cloak, coat, or robe

man·tel \'mant-ᵊl\ n : a beam, stone, or arch serving as a lintel to support the masonry above a fireplace; also : a shelf above a fireplace

man·te·let \'mant-lət\ n : a very short cape or cloak

man·tel·piece \'mant-ᵊl-,pēs\ n : the shelf of a mantel

man·til·la \man-'tē-(y)ə, -'til-ə\ n : a light scarf worn over the head and shoulders esp. by Spanish and Latin-American women

man·tis \'mant-əs\ n, pl **-tis·es** or **-tes** \'man-,tēz\ : a large insect related to the grasshoppers that feeds on other insects which it holds in forelimbs folded as if in prayer

¹**man·tle** \'mant-ᵊl\ n 1 : a loose sleeveless garment worn over other clothes 2 : something that covers, enfolds, or envelopes 3 : a lacy hood or sheath of some refractory material that gives light by incandescence when placed over a flame 4 : MANTEL

²**mantle** vb 1 : to cover with a mantle 2 : BLUSH

¹**man·u·al** \'man-yə-(wə)l\ adj 1 : of, relating to, or involving the hands; also : worked by hand (a ~ choke) 2 : requiring or using physical skill and energy (~ labor) — **man·u·al·ly** adv

²**manual** n 1 : a small book; esp : HANDBOOK 2 : the prescribed movements in the handling of a military item and esp. a weapon during a drill or ceremony 3 : a keyboard esp. of a pipe-organ console

man·u·fac·to·ry \,man-(y)ə-'fak-t(ə-)rē\ n : FACTORY

¹**man·u·fac·ture** \,man-(y)ə-'fak-chər\ n 1 : something made from raw materials 2 : the process of making wares by hand or by machinery; also : a productive industry using mechanical power and machinery

²**manufacture** vb 1 : to make from raw materials by hand or by machinery; also : to engage in manufacture 2 : INVENT, FABRICATE; also : CREATE — **man·u·fac·tur·er** n

man·u·mit \,man-yə-'mit\ vb **-mit·ted**; **-mit·ting** : to free from slavery — **man·u·mis·sion** \-'mish-ən\ n

¹**ma·nure** \mə-'n(y)ùr\ vb : to fertilize land with manure

²**manure** n : FERTILIZER; esp : refuse from stables and barnyards

man·u·script \'man-yə-,skript\ n 1 : a written or typewritten composition or document 2 : writing as opposed to print

Manx \'maŋks\ n pl : the people of the Isle of Man — **Manx** adj

¹**many** \'men-ē\ adj more \'mȯr\ most \'mōst\ : consisting of or amounting to a large but indefinite number

²**many** pron : a large number

³**many** n : a large but indefinite number

many·fold \,men-ē-'fōld\ adv : by many times

many-sid·ed \-'sīd-əd\ adj 1 : having many sides or aspects 2 : VERSATILE

Mao·ri \'maü(ə)r-ē\ n : a member of a Polynesian people native to New Zealand — **Maori** adj

¹**map** \'map\ n 1 : a representation usu. on a flat surface of the whole or part of an area 2 : a representation of the celestial sphere or part of it

²**map** vb **mapped**; **map·ping** 1 : to make a map of 2 : to plan in detail (~ out a program)

ma·ple \'mā-pəl\ n : any of various trees or shrubs with 2-winged dry fruit and opposite leaves; also : its hard light-colored wood used esp. for floors and furniture

mar \'mär\ vb **marred**; **mar·ring** : to

detract from the wholeness or perfection of : SPOIL   syn injure, hurt, harm, damage, impair

mar·a·schi·no \,mar-ə-'skē-nō\ *n* : a cherry preserved in or as if in a sweet cherry liqueur

mar·a·thon \'mar-ə-,thän\ *n* [fr. *Marathon*, Greece, site of a victory of Greeks over Persians in 490 B.C. news of which was carried to Athens by a long-distance runner] **1** : a long-distance race esp. on foot **2** : an endurance contest

ma·raud \mə-'rod\ *vb* : to roam about and raid in search of plunder : PILLAGE — **ma·raud·er** *n*

mar·ble \'mär-bəl\ *n* **1** : a limestone that can be polished and used in fine building work. **2** : something resembling marble (as in coldness or hardness) **3** : a small ball (as of glass) used by children in the game of **marbles** — **marble** *adj*

mar·bling \-b(ə-)liŋ\ *n* : an intermixture of fat through the lean of a cut of meat

mar·cel \mär-'sel\ *n* : a deep soft wave made in the hair by the use of a heated curling iron — **marcel** *vb*

¹march \'märch\ *n* : a border region : FRONTIER

²march *vb* **1** : to move along in or as if in military formation **2** : to walk in a direct purposeful manner; *also* : PROGRESS, ADVANCE **3** : TRAVERSE

³march *n* **1** : the action of marching; *also* : the distance covered (as by a military unit) in a march **2** : a regular measured stride or rhythmic step used in marching **3** : forward movement **4** : a piece of music with marked rhythm suitable for marching to — **march·er** *n*

March \'märch\ *n* : the 3d month of the year having 31 days

mar·chio·ness \'mär-shə-nəs\ *n* **1** : the wife or widow of a marquess **2** : a woman holding the rank of a marquess in her own right

march–past \'märch-,past\ *n* : a marching by esp. of troops in review

Mar·di Gras \,märd-ē-'grä\ *n* : the Tuesday before Ash Wednesday often observed with parades and merrymaking

mare \'maər\ *n* : a female of an animal (as a horse, zebra, or ass) of the horse group

mar·ga·rine \'märj-(ə-)rən, -ə-,rēn\ *n* : a food product made usu. from vegetable oils churned with skim milk and used as a spread and as a cooking fat

marge \'märj\ *n*, *archaic* : MARGIN

mar·gent \'mär-jənt\ *n*, *archaic* : MARGIN

mar·gin \'mär-jon\ *n* **1** : the part of a page outside the main body of printed or written matter **2** : EDGE **3** : a spare amount, measure, or degree allowed for contingencies **4** : measure or degree of difference — **mar·gin·al** \-ᵊl\ *adj*

mar·gi·na·lia \,mär-jə-'nā-lē-ə\ *n pl* : marginal notes

mar·grave \'mär-,gräv\ *n* : the military governor esp. of a medieval German border province

mar·i·gold \'mar-ə-,gōld, 'mer-\ *n* : a garden plant related to the daisies with

double yellow, orange, or reddish flower heads

mar·i·hua·na *or* **mar·i·jua·na** \,mar-ə-'(h)wän-ə\ *n* : an intoxicating drug obtained from the hemp plant and smoked by addicts in cigarettes; *also* : this plant

ma·ri·na \mə-'rē-nə\ *n* : a dock or basin providing secure moorings for motorboats and yachts

mar·i·nate \'mar-ə-,nāt\ *vb* : to steep (as meat or fish) in a brine or pickle

¹ma·rine \mə-'rēn\ *adj* **1** : of or relating to the sea, the navigation of the sea, or the commerce of the sea **2** : of or relating to marines

²marine *n* **1** : the mercantile and naval shipping of a country **2** : one of a class of soldiers serving on shipboard **3** : a picture representing marine scenery

mar·i·ner \'mar-ə-nər\ *n* : SEAMAN, SAILOR

mar·i·o·nette \,mar-ē-ə-'net, ,mer-\ *n* : a puppet moved by strings or by hand

mar·i·tal \'mar-ət-ᵊl\ *adj* : of or relating to marriage : CONJUGAL   syn matrimonial, connubial, nuptial

mar·i·time \'mar-ə-,tīm\ *adj* **1** : of or relating to navigation or commerce on the sea **2** : of, relating to, or bordering on the sea

mar·jo·ram \'märj-(ə-)rəm\ *n* : a fragrant aromatic mint used esp. as a seasoning

¹mark \'märk\ *n* **1** : TARGET; *also* : GOAL, OBJECT **2** : something (as a line or fixed object) designed to record position; *also* : the starting line or position in a track event **3** : BUTT **4** : the question under discussion **5** : NORM ⟨not up to the ∼⟩ **6** : a visible sign : INDICATION; *also* : CHARACTERISTIC **7** : a written or printed symbol **8** : GRADE ⟨a ∼ of B+⟩ **9** : IMPORTANCE, DISTINCTION **10** : a lasting impression

²mark *vb* **1** : to set apart by a line or boundary **2** : to designate by or make a mark on **3** : CHARACTERIZE; *also* : SIGNALIZE **4** : to take notice of : OBSERVE — **mark·er** *n*

³mark *n* **1** : the basic monetary unit of Germany **2** : a coin representing one mark

mark·down \'märk-,daùn\ *n* **1** : a lowering of price **2** : the amount by which an original price is reduced

marked \'märkt\ *adj* : NOTICEABLE — **mark·ed·ly** \'mär-kəd-lē\ *adv*

¹mar·ket \'mär-kət\ *n* **1** : a meeting together of people for trade by purchase and sale; *also* : a public place where such a meeting is held **2** : the rate or price offered for a commodity or security **3** : a geographical area of demand for commodities; *also* : extent of demand **4** : a retail establishment usu. of a specific kind ⟨a meat ∼⟩

²market *vb* : to go to a market to buy or sell; *also* : SELL — **mar·ket·able** \-ə-bəl\ *adj*

mar·ket·place \-,plās\ *n* **1** : an open square in a town where markets are held **2** : the world of trade or economic activity

mark·ka \'märk-,kä\ *n*, *pl* **mark·kaa** \-,kä\ *or* **markkas** — see MONEY table

marks·man \'märks-mən\ *n* : a person

skillful at hitting a target — **marks·man·ship** \-,ship\ n

mark·up \'märk-,əp\ n **1** : a raising of price **2** : an amount added to the cost price of an article to determine the selling price

marl \'märl\ n : an earthy deposit rich in lime used as fertilizer — **marly** adj

mar·lin \'mär-lən\ n : a large oceanic sport fish

mar·line·spike \'mär-lən-,spīk\ n : a pointed iron tool used to separate strands of rope or wire (as in splicing)

mar·ma·lade \'mär-mə-,lād\ n : a clear jelly holding in suspension pieces of fruit and fruit rind

mar·mo·re·al \mär-'mōr-ē-əl\ adj : of, relating to, or resembling marble or a marble statue

mar·mo·set \'mär-mə-,set\ n : any of various small bushy-tailed tropical American monkeys

mar·mot \'mär-mət\ n : a stout short-legged burrowing No. American rodent

¹ma·roon \mə-'rün\ vb **1** : to put ashore (as on a desolate island) and leave to one's fate **2** : to remain in isolation and without hope of escape

²maroon n : a dark red

mar·plot \'mär-,plät\ n : one who endangers the success of an enterprise by his meddling

mar·quee \mär-'kē\ n **1** : a large tent set up (as for an outdoor party) **2** : a usu. metal and glass canopy over an entrance (as of a theater)

mar·quess \'mär-kwəs\ n **1** : a nobleman of hereditary rank in Europe and Japan **2** : a member of the British peerage ranking below a duke and above an earl

mar·que·try \'mär-kə-trē\ n : inlaid work of wood, shell, or ivory (as in a table or cabinet)

mar·quis \'mär-kwəs, mär-'kē\ n : MARQUESS

mar·quise \mär-'kēz\ n : MARCHIONESS

mar·qui·sette \,mär-k(w)ə-'zet\ n : a sheer meshed fabric

mar·riage \'mar-ij\ n **1** : the state of being married : WEDLOCK **2** : a wedding ceremony and attendant festivities **3** : a close union — **mar·riage·able** \-ə-bəl\ adj

mar·row \'mar-ō\ n : a soft vascular tissue that fills the cavities of most bones

mar·row·bone \-,bōn\ n : a bone (as a shinbone) rich in marrow

mar·ry \'mar-ē\ vb **1** : to join as husband and wife according to law or custom **2** : to take as husband or wife : WED **3** : to enter into a close union — **mar·ried** adj or n

Mars \'märz\ n : the planet 4th in order of distance from the sun conspicuous for the redness of its light — **Mar·tian** \'mär-shən\ adj

marsh \'märsh\ n : a tract of soft wet land — **marshy** adj

¹mar·shal \'mär-shəl\ n **1** : a high official in a medieval household; also : a person in charge of the ceremonial aspects of a gathering **2** : a general officer of the highest military rank **3** : an administrative officer (as of a U.S. judicial district) having duties similar to a sheriff's **4** : the administrative head of a city police or fire department

²marshal vb -shaled or -shalled; -shal·ing or -shal·ling **1** : to arrange in order, rank, or position **2** : to lead

with ceremony : USHER

marsh·mal·low \'märsh-,mel-ō, -,mal-\ n : a light creamy confection made from corn syrup, sugar, albumen, and gelatin

mar·su·pi·al \mär-'sü-pē-əl\ n : any of a large group of mostly Australian primitive mammals that bear very immature young that are nourished in a pouch on the abdomen of the female — **marsupial** adj

mart \'märt\ n : MARKET

mar·ten \'märt-ᵊn\ n : a slender weasel-like mammal with fine gray or brown fur; also : this fur

mar·tial \'mär-shəl\ adj [L martialis of Mars, fr. Mart-, Mars Mars, Roman god of war] **1** : of, relating to, or suited for war or a warrior (~ music) **2** : of or relating to an army or military life **3** : WARLIKE

mar·tin \'märt-ᵊn\ n : any of several small swallows and flycatchers

mar·ti·net \,märt-ᵊn-'et\ n : a strict disciplinarian

mar·tin·gale \'märt-ᵊn-,gāl\ n : a strap connecting a horse's girth to the bit or reins so as to hold down its head

mar·ti·ni \mär-'tē-nē\ n : a cocktail made of gin or vodka and dry vermouth

mar·tyr \'märt-ər\ n **1** : a person who dies rather than renounce his religion; also : one who makes a great sacrifice for the sake of principle **2** : a great or constant sufferer — **martyr** vb — **mar·tyr·dom** \-ərd-əm\ n

¹mar·vel \'mär-vəl\ n **1** : something that causes wonder or astonishment **2** : intense surprise or interest

²marvel vb -veled or -velled; -vel·ing or -vel·ling **1** : to feel surprise, wonder, or amazed curiosity (~ed that they had been able to escape capture)

mar·vel·ous or **mar·vel·lous** \'märv-(ə-)ləs\ adj **1** : causing wonder : ASTONISHING **2** : of the highest kind or quality : SPLENDID — **mar·vel·ous·ly** adv — **mar·vel·ous·ness** n

Marx·ism \'märk-,siz-əm\ n : the political, economic, and social principles and policies advocated by Karl Marx — **Marx·ist** \-səst\ n or adj

mar·zi·pan \'märt-sə-,pän\ n : a confection of almond paste, sugar, and whites of eggs

mas·ca·ra \mas-'kar-ə\ n : a cosmetic for coloring the eyelashes and eyebrows

mas·cot \'mas-,kät\ n : a person, animal, or object believed to bring good luck

¹mas·cu·line \'mas-kyə-lən\ adj **1** : MALE; also : MANLY **2** : of, relating to, or constituting the gender that includes most words or grammatical forms referring to males — **mas·cu·lin·i·ty** \,mas-kyə-'lin-ət-ē\ n

²masculine n **1** : a male person **2** : a noun, pronoun, adjective, or inflectional form or class of the masculine gender; also : the masculine gender

¹mash \'mash\ n **1** : crushed malt or grain steeped in hot water to make wort **2** : a mixture of ground feeds for livestock **3** : a soft pulpy mass

²mash vb **1** : to reduce to a soft pulpy state **2** : CRUSH, SMASH

¹mask \'mask\ n **1** : a cover for the face usu. for disguise or protection **2** : MASQUE **3** : a figure of a head worn on the stage in antiquity **4** : a copy of a face made by means of a mold (death ~) **5** : something that conceals or disguises **6** : the face of an animal (as a fox)

²**mask** vb **1** : to take part in a masquerade **2** : to conceal from view — DIS-GUISE — **mask·er** n

mas·och·ism \'mas-ə-,kiz-əm, 'maz-\ n : abnormal sexual passion characterized by pleasure in being abused; also : any pleasure in being abused or dominated — **mas·och·ist** \-kəst\ n

ma·son \'mās-ᵊn\ n **1** : a skilled workman who builds with stone or similar material (as brick or concrete) **2** cap : FREEMASON

Ma·son·ic \mə-'sän-ik\ adj : of or relating to Freemasons or Freemasonry

ma·son·ry \'mās-ᵊn-rē\ n **1** : something constructed of materials used by masons **2** : the art, trade, or work of a mason **3** cap : FREEMASONRY

masque \'mask\ n **1** : MASQUERADE **2** : a short allegorical dramatic performance (as of the 17th century)

¹**mas·quer·ade** \,mas-kə-'rād\ n **1** : a social gathering of persons wearing masks; also : a costume for wear at such a gathering **2** : DISGUISE

²**masquerade** vb **1** : to disguise oneself : POSE **2** : to take part in a masquerade — **mas·quer·ad·er** n

¹**mass** \'mas\ n **1** : LUMP, HUNK **2** : EXPANSE, BULK; also : MASSIVENESS **3** : the principal part **4** : AGGREGATE, WHOLE **5** : the quantity of matter that a body possesses as evidenced by inertia **6** : a large quantity, amount, or number **7** : the great body of people — usu. used in pl. — **massy** adj

²**mass** vb : to form or collect into a mass

Mass \'mas\ n **1** : a sequence of prayers and ceremonies forming the eucharistic office of the Roman Catholic Church **2** often not cap : a celebration of the Eucharist

mas·sa·cre \'mas-i-kər\ n **1** : the killing of many persons under cruel or atrocious circumstances **2** : a wholesale slaughter — **massacre** vb

mas·sage \mə-'säzh, -'säj\ n : remedial or hygienic treatment of the body by manipulation (as rubbing and kneading) — **massage** vb

mas·seur \mas-'ər\ n : a man who practices massage

mas·seuse \mas-'ə(r)z, -'üz\ n : a woman who practices massage

mas·sif \mas-'ēf\ n : a principal mountain mass

mas·sive \'mas-iv\ adj **1** : forming or consisting of a large mass **2** : large in structure, scope, or degree — **mas·sive·ly** adv — **mas·sive·ness** n

mass-pro·duce \,mas-prə-'d(y)üs\ vb : to produce in quantity usu. by machinery — **mass production** n

¹**mast** \'mast\ n **1** : a long pole or spar rising from the keel or deck of a ship and supporting the yards, booms, and rigging **2** : a vertical pole

²**mast** n : nuts (as acorns) accumulated on the forest floor and often serving as food for hogs

¹**mas·ter** \'mas-tər\ n **1** : a male teacher; also : a person holding an academic degree higher than a bachelor's but lower than a doctor's **2** : one highly skilled (as in an art or profession)

3 : one having authority or control : RULER **4** : VICTOR, SUPERIOR **5** : the commander of a merchant ship **6** : a youth or boy too young to be called mister — used as a title **7** : an officer of court appointed to assist a judge

²**master** vb **1** : OVERCOME, SUBDUE **2** : to become skilled or proficient in

master chief petty officer n : a noncommissioned officer of the highest rating in the navy

mas·ter·ful \'mas-tər-fəl\ adj **1** : IMPERIOUS, DOMINEERING **2** : having or reflecting the skill of a master — **mas·ter·ful·ly** adv

mas·ter·ly \-tər-lē\ adj : indicating thorough knowledge or superior skill ⟨~ performance⟩

mas·ter·mind \-tər-,mīnd\ n : a person who provides the directing or creative intelligence for a project — **mastermind** vb

master of ceremonies : a person who acts as host at a formal event or a program of entertainment

mas·ter·piece \'mas-tər-,pēs\ n : a work done with extraordinary skill

master sergeant n **1** : a noncommissioned officer (as in the army) ranking next below a sergeant major **2** : a noncommissioned officer in the air force ranking next below a senior master sergeant

mas·ter·ship \'mas-tər-,ship\ n **1** : DOMINION, SUPERIORITY **2** : the status, office, or function of a master **3** : MASTERY

mas·ter·stroke \-,strōk\ n : a masterly performance or move

mas·ter·work \-,wərk\ n : MASTERPIECE

mas·tery \'mas-t(ə-)rē\ n **1** : DOMINION; also : SUPERIORITY **2** : possession or display of great skill or knowledge

mast·head \'mast-,hed\ n **1** : the top of a mast **2** : the printed matter in a newspaper giving details (as of ownership and rates)

mas·ti·cate \'mas-tə-,kāt\ vb : CHEW — **mas·ti·ca·tion** \,mas-tə-'kā-shən\ n

mas·tiff \'mas-təf\ n : a large smooth-coated dog used esp. as a guard dog

mas·to·don \'mas-tə-,dän\ n : a huge elephantlike extinct animal

mas·toid \'mas-,tòid\ n : a bony prominence behind the ear; also : an infection of this area — **mastoid** adj

mas·tur·ba·tion \,mas-tər-'bā-shən\ n : stimulation of the genital organs to a climax of excitement by contact (as manual) exclusive of sexual intercourse — **mas·tur·bate** \'mas-tər-,bāt\ vb

¹**mat** \'mat\ n **1** : a piece of coarse woven or plaited fabric **2** : something made up of many intertwined or tangled strands **3** : a large thick pad used as a surface for wrestling and gymnastics

²**mat** vb **mat·ted**; **mat·ting** : to form into a tangled mass

³**mat** adj : not shiny: DULL

⁴**mat** n **1** : a border going around a picture between picture and frame or serving as the frame **2** : a dull finish **3** : MATRIX

mat·a·dor \'mat-ə-,dòr\ n : a bullfighter whose role is to kill the bull in a bullfight

¹**match** \'mach\ *n* **1 :** a person or thing equal or similar to another **:** COUNTERPART **2 :** a pair of persons or objects that harmonize **3 :** a contest or game between two or more individuals **4 :** a marriage union; *also* **:** a prospective marriage partner — **match·less** \-ləs\ *adj*

²**match** *vb* **1 :** to meet as an antagonist; *also* **:** PIT, ARRAY **2 :** to provide with a worthy competitor; *also* **:** to set in comparison with **3 :** MARRY **4 :** to combine as being suitable or congenial; *also* **:** ADAPT, SUIT **5 :** to provide with a counterpart

³**match** *n* **:** a short slender piece of flammable material (as wood) tipped with a combustible mixture that ignites through friction

match·book \'mach-,bùk\ *n* **:** a small folder containing rows of paper matches

match·lock \-,läk\ *n* **:** a musket equipped with a slow-burning cord lowered over a hole in the breech to ignite the charge

match·mak·er \-,mā-kər\ *n* **:** one who arranges a match and esp. a marriage

match·wood \-,wùd\ *n* **:** small pieces of wood

¹**mate** \'māt\ *n* **1 :** ASSOCIATE, COMPANION; *also* **:** HELPER **2 :** a deck officer on a merchant ship ranking below the captain **3 :** one of a pair; *esp* **:** either member of a married couple

²**mate** *vb* **1 :** to join or fit together **:** COUPLE **2 :** to come or bring together as mates

³**ma·té** *or* **ma·te** \'mä-,tā\ *n* **:** an aromatic beverage used esp. in So. America

¹**ma·te·ri·al** \mə-'tir-ē-əl\ *adj* **1 :** PHYSICAL ⟨∼ world⟩; *also* **:** BODILY ⟨∼ needs⟩ **2 :** of or relating to matter rather than form ⟨∼ cause⟩; *also* **:** EMPIRICAL ⟨∼ knowledge⟩ **3 :** highly important **:** SIGNIFICANT **4 :** of a physical or worldly nature ⟨∼ progress⟩ — **ma·te·ri·al·ly** *adv*

²**material** *n* **1 :** the elements or substance of which something is composed or made **2 :** apparatus necessary for doing or making something ⟨writing ∼s⟩

ma·te·ri·al·ism \-,ē-ə-,liz-əm\ *n* **1 :** a theory that physical matter is the only reality and that all being and processes and phenomena can be explained as manifestations or results of matter **2 :** a preoccupation with material rather than intellectual or spiritual things — **ma·te·ri·al·ist** \-ləst\ *n or adj* — **ma·te·ri·al·is·tic** \mə-,tir-ē-ə-'lis-tik\ *adj* — **ma·te·ri·al·is·ti·cal·ly** *adv*

ma·te·ri·al·ize \mə-'tir-ē-ə-,līz\ *vb* **1 :** to give material form to; *also* **:** to assume bodily form **2 :** to make an often unexpected appearance — **ma·te·ri·al·i·za·tion** \mə-,tir-ē-ə-lə-'zā-shən\ *n*

ma·té·ri·el *or* **ma·te·ri·el** \mə-,tir-ē-'el\ *n* **:** equipment, apparatus, and supplies used by an organization or institution

ma·ter·nal \mə-'tərn-ᵊl\ *adj* **1 :** MOTHERLY **2 :** related through or inherited or derived from a mother — **ma·ter·nal·ly** *adv*

ma·ter·ni·ty \mə-'tər-nət-ē\ *n* **1 :** the quality or state of being a mother; *also* **:** MOTHERLINESS **2 :** a hospital facility for the care of women before and

during childbirth and for the care of newborn babies ⟨∼ ward⟩

math \'math\ *n* **:** MATHEMATICS

math·e·mat·ics \,math-ə-'mat-iks\ *n* **:** the science of numbers and their operations and the relations between them and of space configurations and their structure and measurement — **math·e·mat·i·cal** \-'mat-i-kəl\ *adj* — **math·e·mat·i·cal·ly** *adv* — **math·e·ma·ti·cian** \,math-ə-mə-'tish-ən\ *n*

mat·i·nee \,mat-ᵊn-'ā\ *n* **:** a musical or dramatic performance usu. in the afternoon

mat·ins \'mat-ᵊnz\ *n, often cap* **:** a morning service of liturgical prayer in Anglican churches

ma·tri·arch \'mā-trē-,ärk\ *n* **:** a woman who rules a family, group, or state — **ma·tri·ar·chal** \,mā-trē-'är-kəl\ *adj* — **ma·tri·ar·chy** \'mā-trē-,är-kē\ *n*

ma·tric·u·late \mə-'trik-yə-,lāt\ *vb* **:** to enroll as a member of a body and esp. of a college or university — **ma·tric·u·la·tion** \mə-,trik-yə-'lā-shən\ *n*

mat·ri·mo·ny \'mat-rə-,mō-nē\ *n* **:** MARRIAGE — **mat·ri·mo·ni·al** \,mat-rə-'mō-nē-əl\ *adj* — **mat·ri·mo·ni·al·ly** *adv*

ma·trix \'mā-triks\ *n, pl* **ma·tri·ces** \-trə-,sēz\ *or* **ma·trix·es 1 :** something within which something else originates or develops **2 :** a mold from which a relief surface (as a stereotype) is made

ma·tron \'mā-trən\ *n* **1 :** a married woman usu. of dignified maturity or social distinction **2 :** a woman supervisor (as in a school or police station) — **ma·tron·ly** *adj*

¹**mat·ter** \'mat-ər\ *n* **1 :** a subject of interest or concern **2 :** *pl* **:** events or circumstances of a particular situation; *also* **:** elements that constitute material for treatment (as in writing) **3 :** TROUBLE, DIFFICULTY ⟨what's the ∼⟩ **4 :** the substance of which a physical object is composed **5 :** PUS **6 :** the indeterminate subject of reality **7 :** a somewhat indefinite amount or quantity ⟨a ∼ of a few days⟩ **8 :** something written or printed **9 :** MAIL

²**matter** *vb* **1 :** to be of importance **:** SIGNIFY **2 :** to form or discharge pus

mat·ter-of-fact \adj **:** adhering to or concerned with fact **:** PRACTICAL — **mat·ter-of-fact·ness** *n*

mat·ting \'mat-iŋ\ *n* **1 :** material for mats **2 :** MATS

mat·tins *often cap, chiefly Brit var of* MATINS

mat·tock \'mat-ək\ *n* **:** a digging and grubbing implement with features of an adz, ax, and pick

mat·tress \'mat-rəs\ *n* **:** a fabric case filled with resilient material used as a bed or on a bedstead

mat·u·rate \'mach-ə-,rāt\ *vb* **:** MATURE

¹**ma·ture** \mə-'t(y)ùr\ *adj* **1 :** based on careful consideration ⟨∼ plan⟩ **2 :** fully grown and developed **:** RIPE **3 :** due for payment ⟨∼ loan⟩ — **ma·tu·ri·ty** \-'t(y)ùr-ət-ē\ *n*

²**mature** *vb* **:** to bring or come to maturity — **mat·u·ra·tion** \,mach-ə-'rā-shən\ *n*

mat·u·ti·nal \,mach-ù-'tīn-ᵊl\ *adj* **:** of, relating to, or occurring in the morning

mat·zo \'mät-sə,-,sō\ *n, pl* -**zoth** \-,tsōt\ *or* -**zos :** unleavened bread eaten at the Passover

maud·lin \'mòd-lən\ *adj* **1 :** tearfully

sentimental **2** : drunk enough to be emotionally silly

¹maul \'mol\ *n* : a heavy hammer often with a wooden head used esp. for driving wedges or piles

²maul *vb* **1** : BEAT, BRUISE; *also* : MANGLE **2** : to handle roughly

maun·der \'mon-dər\ *vb* **1** : to wander slowly and idly **2** : MUTTER

mau·so·le·um \,mo-sə-'lē-əm\ *n* : a large tomb usu. with places for entombment of the dead above ground

mauve \'mōv\ *n* : a moderate purple, violet, or lilac color

mav·er·ick \'mav-(ə-)rik\ *n* **1** : an unbranded range animal **2** : NONCONFORMIST

ma·vis \'mā-vəs\ *n* : an Old World thrush

maw \'mo\ *n* **1** : STOMACH; *also* : the crop of a bird **2** : the throat, gullet, or jaws usu. of a carnivore

mawk·ish \'mo-kish\ *adj* : nauseatingly sentimental — **mawk·ish·ly** *adv*

max·il·la \mak-'sil-ə\ *n, pl* **max·il·lae** \-'sil-(,)ē\ *or* **maxillas** : JAW; *esp* : an upper jaw

max·im \'mak-səm\ *n* : a proverbial saying

max·i·mal \'mak-sə-məl\ *adj* : MAXIMUM (~ development) — **max·i·mal·ly** *adv*

max·i·mum \'mak-sə-məm\ *n, pl* **-ma** \-mə\ *or* **-mums** **1** : the greatest quantity, value, or degree **2** : an upper limit allowed by authority **3** : the largest of a set of numbers — **maximum** *adj*

may \(')mā\ *vb* **1** : have permission or liberty to (you ~ go now) **2** : be in some degree likely to (you ~ be right) **3** — used as an auxiliary to express a wish or desire, purpose or expectation, or contingency or concession

May \'mā\ *n* : the 5th month of the year having 31 days

Ma·ya \'mī-ə\ *n* : a member of a group of peoples of the Yucatan peninsula and adjacent areas — **Ma·yan** *adj*

may·ap·ple \'mā-,ap-əl\ *n* : a No. American woodland herb with a poisonous root, large leaf, and edible but insipid yellow fruit

may·be \'mā-bē\ *adv* : PERHAPS

May Day *n* : May 1 celebrated as a springtime festival and in some countries as Labor Day

may·flow·er \'mā-,flaù(-ə)r\ *n* : any of several spring blooming herbs (as the trailing arbutus, hepatica, or anemone)

may·hem \'mā-,hem, 'mā-əm\ *n* : willful and permanent crippling, mutilation, or disfigurement of a person

may·on·naise \'mā-ə-,nāz\ *n* : a dressing of raw eggs or egg yolks, vegetable oil, and vinegar or lemon juice

may·or \'mā-ər\ *n* : an official elected to act as chief executive or nominal head of a city or borough — **may·or·al** \-əl\ *adj* — **may·or·al·ty** \-əl-tē\ *n*

may·pole \'mā-,pōl\ *n, often cap* : a tall flower-wreathed pole forming a center for May Day sports and dances

maze \'māz\ *n* : a confusing intricate network of passages — **mazy** \'mā-zē\ *adj*

ma·zur·ka \mə-'zər-kə\ *n* : a Polish dance in moderate triple measure

me \(')mē\ *pron, objective case of* I

¹mead \'mēd\ *n* : an alcoholic beverage brewed from water and honey, malt, and yeast

²mead *n, archaic* : MEADOW

mead·ow \'med-ō\ *n* : land in or mainly in grass; *esp* : a tract of moist low-lying usu. level grassland — **mead·owy** \'med-ə-wē\ *adj*

mead·ow·lark \'med-ō-,lärk\ *n* : any of a genus of largely brown and buff American birds noted for their long melodious songs

mea·ger *or* **mea·gre** \'mē-gər\ *adj* **1** : THIN **2** : lacking richness, fertility, or strength : POOR **syn** scanty, scant, spare, sparse — **mea·ger·ly** *adv* — **mea·ger·ness** *n*

¹meal \'mēl\ *n* **1** : the portion of food taken at one time : REPAST **2** : an act or the time of eating a meal

²meal *n* **1** : usu. coarsely ground seeds of a cereal (as Indian corn) **2** : a product resembling seed meal (as in texture) — **mealy** *adj*

meal·time \-,tīm\ *n* : the usual time at which a meal is served

mealy·mouthed \,mē-lē-'maùthd, -'maùtht\ *adj* : smooth, plausible, and insincere in speech; *also* : affectedly unwilling to use strong or coarse language

¹mean \'mēn\ *adj* **1** : HUMBLE **2** : lacking power or acumen : ORDINARY **3** : SHABBY, CONTEMPTIBLE **4** : IGNOBLE, BASE **5** : STINGY **6** : pettily selfish or malicious — **mean·ly** *adv* — **mean·ness** *n*

²mean *vb* **meant** \'ment\ **mean·ing 1** : to have in the mind as a purpose : INTEND **2** : to serve to convey, show, or indicate : SIGNIFY **3** : to direct to a particular individual **4** : to be of a specified degree of importance (music ~s little to him)

³mean *n* **1** : a middle point between extremes **2** *pl* : something helpful in achieving a desired end **3** *pl* : material resources affording a secure life **4** : a value computed by dividing the sum of a set of terms by the number of terms **5** : a value computed by dividing the sum of two extremes of a range of values by 2

⁴mean *adj* **1** : occupying a middle position (as in space, order, or time) **2** : being a mean (a ~ value)

¹me·an·der \mē-'an-dər\ *n* **1** : a turn or winding of a stream **2** : a winding course

²meander *vb* **1** : to follow a winding course **2** : to wander aimlessly or casually

mean·ing \'mē-niŋ\ *n* **1** : the thing one intends to convey esp. by language; *also* : the thing that is thus conveyed **2** : PURPOSE **3** : SIGNIFICANCE **4** : CONNOTATION; *also* : DENOTATION — **mean·ing·ful** \-fəl\ *adj* — **mean·ing·less** \-ləs\ *adj*

¹mean·time \'mēn-,tīm\ *n* : the intervening time

²meantime *adv* : MEANWHILE

¹mean·while \-,hwīl\ *n* : MEANTIME

²meanwhile *adv* : during the intervening time

mea·sles \'mē-zəlz\ *n sing or pl* : an

acute virus disease marked by fever and an eruption

mea·sly \'mēz-(ə-)lē\ *adj* : contemptibly small or insignificant

¹mea·sure \'mezh-ər\ *n* **1** : an adequate portion; *also* : a suitable limit **2** : the dimensions, capacity, or amount of something ascertained by measuring; *also* : an instrument or utensil for measuring **3** : a unit of measurement; *also* : a system of such units ⟨metric ~⟩ **4** : the act or process of measuring **5** : rhythmic structure or movement **6** : CRITERION **7** : a means to an end **8** : a legislative bill **9** : the part of a musical staff between two adjacent bars — **mea·sure·less** \-ləs\ *adj*

²measure *vb* **1** : to regulate esp. by a standard **2** : to apportion by measure **3** : to lay off by making measurements **4** : to ascertain the measurements of **5** : to bring into comparison or competition **6** : to serve as a measure of **7** : to have a specified measurement — **mea·sur·able** \'mezh-(ə-)rə-bəl\ *adj* — **mea·sur·ably** *adv* — **mea·sur·er** *n*

mea·sure·ment \'mezh-ər-mənt\ *n* **1** : the act or process of measuring **2** : a figure, extent, or amount obtained by measuring

meat \'mēt\ *n* **1** : FOOD; *esp* : solid food as distinguished from drink **2** : animal and esp. mammal flesh used as food **3** : the edible part inside a covering (as a shell or rind) — **meaty** *adj*

meat·ball \-,bȯl\ *n* : a small ball of chopped or ground meat ⟨spaghetti and ~s⟩

meat·man \-,man\ *n* : BUTCHER

mec·ca \'mek-ə\ *n, often cap* [fr. *Mecca,* Saudi Arabia, birthplace of Muhammad and place of pilgrimage for Muslims] : a place sought as a goal by numerous people

¹me·chan·ic \mi-'kan-ik\ *adj* **1** : of or relating to manual work or skill **2** : of the nature of or resembling a machine (as in automatic performance)

²mechanic *n* **1** : a manual worker **2** : MACHINIST

me·chan·i·cal \-i-kəl\ *adj* **1** : of or relating to machinery or tools, to manual operations, or to mechanics **2** : done as if by a machine : AUTOMATIC *syn* instinctive, impulsive, spontaneous — **me·chan·i·cal·ly** *adv*

me·chan·ics \-iks\ *n sing or pl* **1** : a branch of physical science that deals with energy and forces and their effect on bodies **2** : the practical application of mechanics (as to the operation of machines) **3** : mechanical or functional details

mech·a·nism \'mek-ə-,niz-əm\ *n* **1** : a piece of machinery; *also* : a process or technique for achieving a result **2** : mechanical operation or action **3** : the fundamental processes involved in or responsible for a natural phenomenon ⟨the visual ~⟩

mech·a·nis·tic \,mek-ə-'nis-tik\ *adj* **1** : mechanically determined ⟨~ universe⟩ **2** : MECHANICAL — **mech·a·nis·ti·cal·ly** *adv*

mech·a·nize \'mek-ə-,nīz\ *vb* **1** : to make mechanical **2** : to equip with machinery esp. to replace human or animal labor **3** : to equip with armed and armored motor vehicles — **mech·a·ni·za·tion** \,mek-ə-nə-'zā-shən\ *n*

med·al \'med-ᵊl\ *n* **1** : a metal disk

bearing a religious emblem or picture **2** : a piece of metal issued to commemorate a person or event or awarded for excellence or achievement

med·al·ist or **med·al·list** \-əst\ *n* **1** : a designer or maker of medals **2** : a recipient of a medal

me·dal·lion \mə-'dal-yən\ *n* **1** : a large medal **2** : a tablet or panel (as in a wall) bearing a portrait or an ornament

med·dle \'med-ᵊl\ *vb* : to interfere without right or propriety — **med·dler** \'med-lər\

med·dle·some \'med-ᵊl-səm\ *adj* : inclined to meddle in the affairs of others

me·di·al \'mēd-ē-əl\ *adj* **1** : occurring in or extending toward the middle : MEDIAN **2** : MEAN, AVERAGE

¹me·di·an \'mēd-ē-ən\ *n* **1** : a medial part **2** : a value in an ordered set of values below and above which there are an equal number of values

²median *adj* **1** : MEDIAL **2** : relating to or constituting a statistical median

me·di·ate \'mēd-ē-,āt\ *vb* : to act as an intermediary (as in settling a dispute or in carrying out a process) *syn* intercede, intervene, interpose — **me·di·a·tion** \,mēd-ē-'ā-shən\ *n* — **me·di·a·tor** \'mēd-ē-,āt-ər\ *n*

med·ic \'med-ik\ *n* : one engaged in medical work

med·i·ca·ble \'med-i-kə-bəl\ *adj* : CURABLE, REMEDIABLE — **med·i·ca·bly** *adv*

med·i·cal \-i-kəl\ *adj* : of or relating to the science or practice of medicine or the treatment of disease — **med·i·cal·ly** *adv*

me·dic·a·ment \mi-'dik-ə-mənt\ *n* : a medicine or healing application

med·i·cate \'med-ə-,kāt\ *vb* : to treat with medicine — **med·i·ca·tion** \,med-ə-'kā-shən\ *n*

me·dic·i·nal \mə-'dis-(ᵊ-)nəl\ *adj* : tending or used to relieve or cure disease or pain — **me·dic·i·nal·ly** *adv*

med·i·cine \'med-ə-sən\ *n* **1** : a substance or preparation used in treating disease : REMEDY **2** : a science or art dealing with the prevention or cure of disease

med·i·co \'med-i-,kō\ *n* : a medical practitioner or student

me·di·e·val or **me·di·ae·val** \,mēd-ē-'ē-vəl, ,med-\ *adj* : of, relating to, or characteristic of the Middle Ages — **me·di·e·val·ism** \-,iz-əm\ *n* — **me·di·e·val·ist** \-əst\ *n*

me·di·o·cre \,mēd-ē-'ō-kər\ *adj* : of moderate or low excellence : ORDINARY — **me·di·oc·ri·ty** \-'äk-rət-ē\ *n*

med·i·tate \'med-ə-,tāt\ *vb* **1** : to muse over : CONTEMPLATE, PONDER **2** : INTEND, PURPOSE — **med·i·ta·tion** \,med-ə-'tā-shən\ *n* — **med·i·ta·tive** \'med-ə-,tāt-iv\ *adj* — **med·i·ta·tive·ly** *adv*

¹me·di·um \'mēd-ē-əm\ *n, pl* **me·di·ums** or **me·dia** \-ē-ə\ **1** : something in a middle position; *also* : a middle position or degree **2** : a means of effecting or conveying something **3** : a surrounding or enveloping substance **4** : a channel of communication **5** : an individual held to be a channel of communication between the earthly world and a world of spirits **6** : material or technical means of artistic expression **7** : a condition in which something may function or flourish

²medium *adj* : intermediate in amount, quality, position, or degree

med·ley \'med-lē\ *n* **1** : HODGEPODGE

2 : a musical composition made up esp. of a series of songs

me·dul·la \mə-'dəl-ə\ n, pl -las or -lae \-(,)ē\ : an inner or deep anatomical part; also : the posterior part (medulla ob·lon·ga·ta \-,äb-,lȯŋ-'gät-ə\) of the brain

meed \'mēd\ n 1 archaic : REWARD 2 : a fitting return

meek \'mēk\ adj 1 : characterized by patience and long-suffering : MILD 2 : deficient in spirit and courage 3 : MODERATE — meek·ly adv — meek·ness n

meer·schaum \'miər-shəm, -,shȯm\ n : a tobacco pipe made of a light white clayey mineral

1meet \'mēt\ vb met \'met\ meet·ing 1 : to come upon : FIND 2 : JOIN, INTERSECT 3 : to appear to the perception of 4 : OPPOSE, FIGHT 5 : to join in conversation or discussion; also : AS-SEMBLE 6 : to conform to 7 : to pay fully 8 : to cope with 9 : to provide for 10 : to be introduced to

2meet n : an assembling esp. for a hunt or for competitive sports

3meet adj : SUITABLE, PROPER

meet·ing \'mēt-iŋ\ n 1 : an act of coming together : ASSEMBLY 2 : JUNC-TION, INTERSECTION

meet·ing·house \-,haús\ n : a building used for public assembly and esp. for Protestant worship

mega·cy·cle \'meg-ə-,sī-kəl\ n : one million cycles per second used as a unit of radio frequency

meg·a·lo·ma·nia \,meg-ə-lō-'mā-nē-ə\ n : a disorder of mind marked by feel-ings of personal omnipotence and grandeur

meg·a·lop·o·lis \,meg-ə-'läp-ə-ləs\ n : a very large urban unit

mega·phone \'meg-ə-,fōn\ n : a cone-shaped device used to intensify or direct the voice — megaphone vb

mega·ton \-,tən\ n : an explosive force equivalent to that of a million tons of TNT

mel·an·cho·lia \,mel-ən-'kō-lē-ə\ n : a mental condition marked by extreme depression often with delusions

mel·an·choly \'mel-ən-,käl-ē\ n [LL melancholia, fr. Gk, fr. melan-, melas black + cholē bile; so called fr. the former belief that it was caused by an excess in the system of black bile, a substance supposedly secreted by the kidneys or spleen] : depression of spirits : DEJECTION, GLOOM — melan-choly adj

Mel·a·ne·sian \,mel-ə-'nē-zhən\ n : a member of the dominant native group of Melanesia characterized by dark skin and frizzy hair — Melanesian adj

mé·lange \mā-'läⁿzh\ n : a mixture esp. of incongruous elements

1meld \'meld\ vb : to show or announce for a score in a card game

2meld n : a card or combination of cards that is or can be melded

me·lee \'mā-,lā, mā-'lā\ n : a confused struggle syn fracas, row, brawl

me·lio·rate \'mēl-yə-,rāt\ vb : to make or become better : IMPROVE — me·lio-ra·tion \,mēl-yə-'rā-shən\ n — me·lio·ra·tive \'mēl-yə-,rāt-iv\ adj

mel·lif·lu·ous \me-'lif-lə-wəs\ adj : sweetly flowing — mel·lif·lu·ous·ly adv — mel·lif·lu·ous·ness n

1mel·low \'mel-ō\ adj 1 : soft and sweet because of ripeness (~ apple); also : well aged and pleasingly mild (~ wine) 2 : made gentle by age or ex-perience 3 : of soft loamy consistency (~ soil) 4 : being rich and full but not garish or strident (~ colors) — mel·low·ness n

2mellow vb : to make or become mellow

me·lo·de·on \mə-'lōd-ē-ən\ n : a small reed organ in which a suction bellows draws air inward through the reeds

me·lo·di·ous \mə-'lōd-ē-əs\ adj : pleas-ing to the ear : TUNEFUL — me·lo·di·ous·ly adv — me·lo·di·ous·ness n

melo·dra·ma \'mel-ə-,dräm-ə, -,dram-\ n : an extravagantly theatrical play in which action and plot predominate over characterization — melo·dra·mat·ic \,mel-ə-drə-'mat-ik\ adj — melo·dram·a·tist \-'dram-ət-əst\ n

mel·o·dy \'mel-əd-ē\ n 1 : sweet or agreeable sound (birds making ~) 2 : a particular succession of notes : TUNE, AIR — me·lod·ic \mə-'läd-ik\ adj — me·lod·i·cal·ly \-i-k(ə-)lē\ adv

mel·on \'mel-ən\ n : any of certain gourds (as a muskmelon or watermelon) usu. eaten raw as fruits

melt \'melt\ vb 1 : to change from a solid to a liquid state usu. by heat 2 : DISSOLVE, DISINTEGRATE; also : to cause to disperse or disappear 3 : to make or become tender or gentle : SOFTEN

melt·wa·ter \-,wȯt-ər, -,wät-\ n : water derived from the melting of ice and snow

mem·ber \'mem-bər\ n 1 : a part (as an arm, leg, or branch) of a person, lower animal, or plant 2 : one of the individuals composing a group 3 : a constituent part of a whole

mem·ber·ship \-,ship\ n 1 : the state or status of being a member 2 : the body of members (as of a church)

mem·brane \'mem-,brān\ n : a thin pliable layer esp. of animal or plant tissue — mem·bra·nous \-brə-nəs\ adj

me·men·to \mi-'ment-ō\ n, pl -tos or -toes : something that serves to warn or remind : SOUVENIR

memo \'mem-ō\ n : MEMORANDUM

mem·oir \'mem-,wär\ n 1 : MEMORAN-DUM 2 : AUTOBIOGRAPHY — usu. used in pl. 3 : an account of something noteworthy; also, pl : the record of the proceedings of a learned society

mem·o·ra·bil·ia \,mem-ə-rə-'bil-yə\ n pl : things worthy of remembrance; also : a record of such things

mem·o·ra·ble \'mem-(ə-)rə-bəl\ adj : worth remembering : NOTABLE — mem·o·ra·ble·ness n — mem·o·ra·bly adv

mem·o·ran·dum \,mem-ə-'ran-dəm\ n, pl -dums or -da \-də\ 1 : an informal record; also : a written reminder 2 : an informal written note or communication

1me·mo·ri·al \mə-'mōr-ē-əl\ adj : serv-ing to preserve remembrance : COM-MEMORATIVE

2memorial n 1 : something designed to keep remembrance alive; esp : MONU-

MENT **2** : a statement of facts often accompanied with a petition — **me-mo-ri-al-ize** \-,īz\ vb

Memorial Day n : May 30 observed as a legal holiday in commemoration of dead servicemen

mem-o-rize \'mem-ə-,rīz\ vb : to learn by heart — **mem-o-riz-er** n

mem-o-ry \'mem-(ə-)rē\ n **1** : the power or process of remembering **2** : the store of things remembered; also : a particular act of recollection **3** : commemorative remembrance **4** : the time within which past events are remembered syn remembrance, recollection, reminiscence

men pl of MAN

1men-ace \'men-əs\ n **1** : THREAT **2** : DANGER; also : NUISANCE

2menace vb **1** : THREATEN **2** : EN-DANGER — **men-ac-ing-ly** adv

mé-nage \mā-'näzh\ n : HOUSEHOLD

me-nag-er-ie \mə-'naj-(ə-)rē\ n : a collection of wild animals esp. for exhibition

1mend \'mend\ vb **1** : to improve in manners or morals **2** : to put into good shape : REPAIR **3** : to restore to health : HEAL — **mend-er** n

2mend n : an act of mending **2** : a mended place

men-da-cious \men-'dā-shəs\ adj : given to deception or falsehood : UNTRUTH-FUL syn dishonest, deceitful — **men-da-cious-ly** adv — **men-dac-i-ty** \-'das-ət-ē\ n

men-di-cant \'men-di-kənt\ n **1** : BEG-GAR **2** often cap : FRIAR — **mendicant** adj

men-folk \'men-,fōk\ or **men-folks** n pl **1** : men in general **2** : the men of a family or community

1me-ni-al \'mē-nē-əl\ adj **1** : of or relating to servants **2** : HUMBLE; also : SERVILE — **me-ni-al-ly** adv

2menial n : a domestic servant

men-in-gi-tis \,men-ən-'jīt-əs\ n : in-flammation of the membranes enclosing the brain and spinal cord; also : a usu. bacterial disease marked by this

men-of-war pl of MAN-OF-WAR

meno-pause \'men-ə-,pòz\ n : the period of natural cessation of menstruation

men-ses \'men-,sēz\ n pl : the menstrual period or flow

men-stru-a-tion \,men-strə-'wā-shən, men-'strā-\ n : a discharging of bloody matter at approximately monthly in-tervals from the uterus of breeding-age primate females that are not pregnant — **men-stru-al** \'men-strə(-wə)l\ adj — **men-stru-ate** \'men-strə-,wāt, -,strāt\ vb

men-su-ra-ble \'men-sə-rə-bəl, 'men-chə-\ adj : MEASURABLE

men-su-ra-tion \,men-sə-'rā-shən, men-chə-\ n : MEASUREMENT

-ment \mənt\ n suffix **1** : concrete result, object, or agent of a (specified) action (embankment) (entanglement) **2** : concrete means or instrument of a (specified) action (entertainment) **3** : action : process (encirclement) (de-velopment) **4** : place of a (specified) action (encampment) **5** : state : condi-tion (amazement)

men-tal \'ment-ᵊl\ adj **1** : of or relating to the mind **2** : of, relating to, or af-fected with a disorder of the mind — **men-tal-ly** adv

men-tal-i-ty \men-'tal-ət-ē\ n : men-

tal power or capacity **2** : mode or way of thought

men-thol \'men-,thòl, -,thōl\ n : a white soothing substance from oil of peppermint — **men-tho-lat-ed** \-thə-,lāt-əd\ adj

1men-tion \'men-chən\ n **1** : a brief or casual reference **2** : a formal cita-tion for outstanding achievement

2mention vb **1** : to refer to : CITE **2** : to cite for outstanding achievement

men-tor \'men-,tòr, 'ment-ər\ n : a trusted counselor or guide; also : TUTOR, COACH

menu \'men-yü\ n : a list of the dishes available (as in a restaurant) for a meal; also : the dishes served

me-ow \mē-'aù\ vb : to make the char-acteristic cry of a cat — meow n

me-phit-ic \mə-'fit-ik\ adj : foul-smell-ing

mer-can-tile \'mər-kən-,tēl, -,tīl\ adj : of or relating to merchants or trading

1mer-ce-nary \'mərs-ᵊn-,er-ē\ n : one who serves merely for wages; esp : a soldier serving in a foreign army

2mercenary adj **1** : serving merely for pay or gain **2** : hired for service in a foreign army — **mer-ce-nar-i-ly** \,mərs-ᵊn-'er-ə-lē\ adv — **mer-ce-nar-i-ness** \'mərs-ᵊn-,er-ē-nəs\ n

mer-cer \'mər-sər\ n, Brit : a dealer in textile fabrics

mer-cer-ize \-,īz\ vb : to treat cotton yarn or cloth with alkali so that it looks silky or takes a better dye

1mer-chan-dise \'mər-chən-,dīz, -,dīs\ n : the commodities or goods that are bought and sold in business

2mer-chan-dise \-,dīz\ vb : to buy and sell in business : TRADE — **mer-chan-dis-er** n

mer-chant \'mər-chənt\ n **1** : a buyer and seller of commodities for profit **2** : STOREKEEPER

mer-chant-able \-ə-bəl\ adj : acceptable to buyers : MARKETABLE

mer-chant-man \-mən\ n : a ship used in commerce

merchant ship n : MERCHANTMAN

mer-cu-ri-al \,mər-'kyúr-ē-əl\ adj : un-predictably changeable — **mer-cu-ri-al-ly** adv — **mer-cu-ri-al-ness** n

mer-cu-ry \'mər-kyə-rē\ n **1** : a heavy silver-white liquid metallic chemical element used in thermometers and medicine **2** cap : the smallest of the planets and the one nearest the sun

mer-cy \'mər-sē\ n **1** : compassion shown to an offender; also : imprison-ment rather than death for first-degree murder **2** : a blessing resulting from divine favor or compassion; also : a fortunate circumstance **3** : compassion shown to victims of misfortune — **mer-ci-ful** \-si-fəl\ adj — **mer-ci-ful-ly** adv — **mer-ci-less** \-si-ləs\ adj : **mer-ci-less-ly** adv

1mere \'mir\ n : LAKE, POOL

2mere adj **1** : apart from anything else : BARE **2** : not diluted : PURE — **mere-ly** adv

mer-e-tri-cious \,mer-ə-'trish-əs\ adj : tawdrily attractive; esp : SPECIOUS — **mer-e-tri-cious-ly** adv — **mer-e-tri-cious-ness** n

merge \'mərj\ vb **1** : to combine, unite, or coalesce into one **2** : to blend gradually syn mingle, amalga-mate, fuse

merg-er \'mər-jər\ n **1** : absorption by

a corporation of one or more others **2** : the combination of two or more groups (as churches)

me·rid·i·an \mə-'rid-ē-ən\ *n* **1** : the highest point : CULMINATION **2** : one of the imaginary circles on the earth's surface passing through the north and south poles and any particular place — **meridian** *adj*

me·ringue \mə-'raŋ\ *n* : a dessert topping of baked beaten egg whites and powdered sugar

me·ri·no \mə-'rē-nō\ *n* **1** : any of a breed of sheep noted for fine soft wool; *also* : its wool or fleece **2** : a fine soft fabric or yarn of wool or wool and cotton

¹mer·it \'mer-ət\ *n* **1** : laudable or blameworthy traits or actions **2** : a praiseworthy quality; *also* : character or conduct deserving reward or honor **3** *pl* : the intrinsic rights and wrongs of a legal case; *also* : legal significance or standing

²merit *vb* : EARN, DESERVE

mer·i·to·ri·ous \,mer-ə-'tōr-ē-əs\ *adj* : deserving reward or honor — **mer·i·to·ri·ous·ly** *adv* — **mer·i·to·ri·ous·ness** *n*

mer·maid \'mər-,mād\ *n* : a legendary sea creature with a woman's body and a fish's tail

mer·man \-,man\ *n* : a legendary sea creature with a man's body and a fish's tail

mer·ri·ment \'mer-i-mənt\ *n* **1** : HILARITY **2** : FESTIVITY

mer·ry \'mer-ē\ *adj* **1** : full of gaiety or high spirits **2** : marked by festivity **3** : BRISK, INTENSE (a ~ pace) *syn* blithe, jocund, jovial, jolly — **mer·ri·ly** *adv*

mer·ry-go-round \'mer-ē-gō-,raůnd\ *n* **1** : a circular revolving platform with benches and figures of animals on which people sit for a ride **2** : a rapid round of activities

mer·ry·mak·ing \-,mā-kiŋ\ *n* **1** : CONVIVIALITY **2** : a festive occasion — **mer·ry·mak·er** *n*

me·sa \'mā-sə\ *n* : a flat-topped hill with steep sides

més·al·liance \,mā-,zal-'yäⁿs\ *n* : a marriage with a person of inferior social position

mesdames *pl of* MADAM *or of* MADAME

mesdemoiselles *pl of* MADEMOISELLE

¹mesh \'mesh\ *n* **1** : one of the openings between the threads or cords of a net; *also* : one of the similar spaces in a network **2** : the fabric of a net **3** : NETWORK **4** : working contact (as of the teeth of gears)

²mesh *vb* **1** : to catch in or as if in a mesh **2** : to be in or come into mesh : ENGAGE (the gears ~ed) **3** : to fit together properly : COORDINATE

mesh·work \-,wərk\ *n* : MESHES, NETWORK

mes·mer·ize \'mez-mə-,rīz\ *vb* : HYPNOTIZE — **mes·mer·ic** \mez-'mer-ik\ *adj* — **mes·mer·ism** \'mez-mə-,riz-əm\ *n*

mes·quite \mə-'skēt\ *n* : a thorny leguminous shrub of Mexico and the southwestern U.S. with sugar-rich pods important as fodder

¹mess \'mes\ *n* **1** : a quantity of food; *also* : enough food of a specified kind for a dish or meal (a ~ of beans) **2** : a group of persons who regularly eat together; *also* : a meal eaten by such a group **3** : a confused, dirty, or offensive state — **messy** *adj*

²mess *vb* **1** : to supply with meals; *also* : to take meals with a mess **2** : to make dirty or untidy; *also* : BUNGLE **3** : PUTTER, TRIFLE **4** : INTERFERE, MEDDLE

mes·sage \'mes-ij\ *n* : a communication sent by one person to another

messeigneurs *pl of* MONSEIGNEUR

mes·sen·ger \'mes-ⁿn-jər\ *n* : one who carries a message or does an errand

Mes·si·ah \mə-'sī-ə\ *n* **1** : the expected king and deliverer of the Jews **2** : Jesus **3** *not cap* : a professed or accepted leader — **mes·si·an·ic** \,mes-ē-'an-ik\ *adj*

messieurs *pl of* MONSIEUR

mess·mate \'mes-,māt\ *n* : a member of a group who eat regularly together (as on a ship)

mes·ti·zo \mes-'tē-zō\ *n* : a person of mixed blood

me·tab·o·lism \mə-'tab-ə-,liz-əm\ *n* : the sum of the processes in the building up and breaking down of the substance of plants and animals incidental to life; *also* : the processes by which a substance is handled in the body (~ of sugar) — **met·a·bol·ic** \,met-ə-'bäl-ik\ *adj* — **me·tab·o·lize** \mə-'tab-ə-,līz\ *vb*

met·al \'met-ⁿl\ *n* **1** : any of various opaque, fusible, ductile, and typically lustrous substances; *esp* : one that is a chemical element **2** : METTLE; *also* : the material out of which a person or thing is made — **me·tal·lic** \mə-'tal-ik\ *adj* — **met·al·lif·er·ous** \,met-ⁿl-'if-(ə-)rəs\ *adj* — **met·al·loid** \'met-ⁿl-,ȯid\ *n or adj*

met·al·lur·gy \'met-ⁿl-,ər-jē\ *n* : the science and technology of metals — **met·al·lur·gi·cal** \,met-ⁿl-'ər-ji-kəl\ *adj* — **met·al·lur·gist** \'met-ⁿl-,ər-jist\ *n*

met·al·ware \'met-ⁿl-,waər\ *n* : metal utensils for household use

met·al·work \-,wərk\ *n* **1** : the process or occupation of making things from metal **2** : work and esp. artistic work made of metal

met·a·mor·pho·sis \,met-ə-'mȯr-fə-səs\ *n, pl* **-pho·ses** \-,sēz\ **1** : a change of physical form, structure, or substance esp. by supernatural means; *also* : a striking alteration in appearance, character, or circumstances **2** : a fundamental change in form and often habits of an animal accompanying the transformation of a larva into an adult — **met·a·mor·phose** \-,fōz, -,fōs\ *vb*

met·a·phor \'met-ə-,fȯr, -fər\ *n* : a figure of speech in which a word denoting one object or idea is used in place of another to suggest a likeness between them (as in "the ship plows the sea") — **met·a·phor·i·cal** \,met-ə-'fȯr-i-kəl\ *adj*

meta·phys·ics \,met-ə-'fiz-iks\ *n* : the part of philosophy concerned with the study of the ultimate causes and the underlying nature of things — **meta-phys·i·cal** \-'fiz-i-kəl\ *adj* — **meta-phy·si·cian** \-fə-'zish-ən\ *n*

me·tas·ta·sis \mə-'tas-tə-səs\ *n, pl* **-ta·ses** \-tə-,sēz\ **1** : transfer of a health-impairing agency (as tumor cells) to a new site in the body; *also* : a secondary growth of a malignant tumor — **met·a-stat·ic** \,met-ə-'stat-ik\ *adj*

¹mete \'mēt\ *vb* **1** *archaic* : MEASURE **2** : ALLOT

²mete *n* : BOUNDARY ⟨∼s and bounds⟩

me·tem·psy·cho·sis \mə,-temp-sə-'kō-səs\ *n* : the passing of the soul at death into another body either human or animal

me·te·or \'mēt-ē-ər\ *n* **1** : a usu. small particle of matter in the solar system observable only when it falls into the earth's atmosphere where friction causes it to glow **2** : the streak of light produced by passage of a meteor

me·te·or·ic \,mēt-ē-'òr-ik\ *adj* **1** : of, relating to, or resembling a meteor **2** : transiently brilliant ⟨a ∼ career⟩ — **me·te·or·i·cal·ly** *adv*

me·te·or·ite \'mēt-ē-ə-,rīt\ *n* : a meteor that reaches the earth without being completely vaporized

me·te·or·oid \-ē-ə-,ròid\ *n* : METEOR 1

me·te·o·rol·o·gy \,mēt-ē-ə-'räl-ə-jē\ *n* : a science that deals with the atmosphere and its phenomena and esp. with weather and weather forecasting — **me·te·o·ro·log·i·cal** \-ē-,òr-ə-'läj-i-kəl\ *adj* — **me·te·o·rol·o·gist** \-ē-ə-'räl-ə-jəst\ *n*

¹me·ter \'mēt-ər\ *n* : rhythm in verse or music

²meter *n* : the basic metric unit of length equal to 39.37 inches

³meter *n* : a measuring and sometimes recording instrument ⟨a gas ∼⟩

⁴meter *vb* **1** : to measure by means of a meter **2** : to print postal indicia on by means of a postage meter ⟨∼ed mail⟩

meth·ane \'meth-,ān\ *n* : a colorless odorless flammable gas produced by decomposition of organic matter (as in marshes) or from coal and used as a fuel

meth·od \'meth-əd\ *n* **1** : a procedure or process for achieving an end ⟨the scientific ∼⟩ **2** : orderly arrangement : PLAN **syn** mode, manner, way, fashion, system — **me·thod·i·cal** \mə-'thäd-i-kəl\ *adj* — **me·thod·i·cal·ly** *adv* — **me·thod·i·cal·ness** *n*

Meth·od·ist \'meth-əd-əst\ *n* : a member of a Protestant denomination adhering to the doctrines of John Wesley — **Meth·od·ism** \-ə-,diz-əm\ *n*

meth·od·ize \-ə-,dīz\ *vb* : SYSTEMATIZE

meth·od·ol·o·gy \,meth-ə-'däl-ə-jē\ *n* **1** : a body of methods and rules followed in a science or discipline **2** : the study of the principles or procedures of inquiry in a particular field

me·tic·u·lous \mə-'tik-yə-ləs\ *adj* : extremely careful in attending to details — **me·tic·u·lous·ly** *adv* — **me·tic·u·lous·ness** *n*

mé·tier \mā-'tyā\ *n* : an area of activity in which one is expert or successful

me·tre \'mēt-ər\ *chiefly Brit var of* METER

met·ric \'met-rik\ *or* **met·ri·cal** \-ri-kəl\ *adj* **1** : of or relating to the meter; *esp* : of, relating to, or being a decimal system of weights and measures based

on the meter and the kilogram — **met·ri·cal·ly** *adv*

met·ri·cal *or* **met·ric** *adj* **1** : of, relating to, or composed in meter **2** : of or relating to measurement — **met·ri·cal·ly** *adv*

met·ro \'met-rō\ *n* : SUBWAY

met·ro·nome \'met-rə-,nōm\ *n* : an instrument for marking exact time by a regularly repeated tick

me·trop·o·lis \mə-'träp-(ə-)ləs\ *n* [Gk *mētropolis* mother city of a colony, fr. *mētēr* mother + *polis* city] : the chief or capital city of a country, state, or region — **met·ro·pol·i·tan** \,met-rə-'päl-ət-ᵊn\ *adj*

met·tle \'met-ᵊl\ *n* **1** : quality of temperament **2** : SPIRIT, COURAGE

met·tle·some \-səm\ *adj* : full of mettle

mew \'myü\ *vb* : CONFINE

mews \'myüz\ *n pl, chiefly Brit* : stables usu. with living quarters built around a court; *also* : a narrow street with dwellings converted from stables

Mex·i·can \'mek-si-kən\ *n* : a native or inhabitant of Mexico — **Mexican** *adj*

mez·za·nine \'mez-ᵊn-,ēn\ *n* **1** : a low-ceilinged story between two main stories of a building **2** : the lowest balcony in a theater; *also* : the first few rows of such a balcony

mez·zo-so·pra·no \,mets-ō-sə-'pran-ō, -me(d)z-\ *n* : a woman's voice having a full deep quality between that of the soprano and contralto; *also* : a singer having such a voice

mi·as·ma \mī-'az-mə\ *n, pl* **-mas** *or* **-ma·ta** \-mət-ə\ : an exhalation (as of a swamp) formerly held to cause disease : a noxious vapor — **mi·as·mal** \-məl\ *or* **mi·as·mic** \-mik\ *adj*

mi·ca \'mī-kə\ *n* : any of various minerals readily separable into thin transparent sheets

mice *pl of* MOUSE

mi·crobe \'mī-,krōb\ *n* : MICRO-ORGANISM; *esp* : one causing disease — **mi·cro·bi·al** \mī-'krō-bē-əl\ *adj*

mi·cro·copy \'mī-krō-,käp-ē\ *n* : a photographic copy (as of printed matter) on a reduced scale — **microcopy** *vb*

mi·cro·cosm \'mī-krə-,käz-əm\ *n* : a little world; *esp* : man or human nature that is an epitome of the world or the universe

mi·cro·film \-,film\ *n* : a film bearing a photographic record (as of printed matter) on a reduced scale — **microfilm** *vb*

mi·crom·e·ter \mī-'kräm-ət-ər\ *n* : an instrument used with a telescope or microscope for measuring minute distances

mi·cron \'mī-,krän\ *n* : a unit of length equal to one thousandth of a millimeter

mi·cro·or·ga·nism \,mī-krō-'òr-gə-,niz-əm\ *n* : a living being (as a bacterium) too tiny to be seen by the unaided eye

mi·cro·phone \'mī-krə-,fōn\ *n* : an instrument for converting sound waves into variations of an electric current for transmitting or recording sound

mi·cro·scope \-,skōp\ *n* : an optical instrument for making magnified images of minute objects — **mi·cros·co·py** \mī-'kräs-kə-pē\ *n*

mi·cro·scop·ic \,mī-krə-'skäp-ik\ *or* **mi·cro·scop·i·cal** \-i-kəl\ *adj* **1** : of, relating to, or involving the use of the microscope **2** : too tiny to be seen without the use of a microscope : very small — **mi·cro·scop·i·cal·ly** *adv* mid \'mid\ *adj* : MIDDLE

mid·day \'mid-,dā\ *n* : NOON

mid·den \'mid-ⁿn\ *n* : a refuse heap

¹mid·dle \'mid-ᵊl\ *adj* 1 : equally distant from the extremes : MEDIAL, CENTRAL   2 : being at neither extreme : INTERMEDIATE

²middle *n* 1 : a middle part, point, or position   2 : WAIST

Middle Ages *n pl* : the period of European history from about A.D. 500 to about 1500

mid·dle·brow \-,braù\ *n* : a person who is moderately but not highly cultivated

middle class *n* : a social class occupying a position between the upper class and the lower class — **middle-class** *adj*

mid·dle·man \'mid-ᵊl-,man\ *n* : INTERMEDIARY; *esp* : one intermediate between the producer of goods and the retailer or consumer

mid·dle·most \-,mōst\ *adj* : MIDMOST

mid·dle-of-the-road *adj* : standing for or following a course of action midway between extremes; *esp* : being neither liberal nor conservative in politics — mid·dle-of-the-road·er *n*

mid·dle·weight \'mid-ᵊl-,wāt\ *n* : one of average weight; *esp* : a boxer weighing more than 147 but not over 160 pounds

mid·dling \'mid-liŋ\ *adj* 1 : of middle, medium, or moderate size, degree, or quality   2 : MEDIOCRE, SECOND-RATE

mid·dy \'mid-ē\ *n* : MIDSHIPMAN

midge \'mij\ *n* : a very small fly : GNAT

midg·et \'mij-ət\ *n* : a very small person : DWARF

mid·land \'mid-lənd\ *n* : the interior or central region of a country

mid·most \-,mōst\ *adj* : being in the exact middle

mid·night \-,nīt\ *n* : twelve o'clock at night

mid·point \-,pòint\ *n* : a point at or near the center or middle

mid·riff \-,rif\ *n* 1 : DIAPHRAGM 1; *also* : the mid-region of the human torso

mid·ship·man \-,ship-mən\ *n* : a student naval officer

mid·ships \-,ships\ *adv* : AMIDSHIPS

¹midst \'midst\ *n* 1 : the interior or central part or point   2 : a position of proximity to the members of a group ⟨in our ∼⟩   3 : the condition of being surrounded or beset

²midst *prep* : in the midst of

mid·stream \'mid-'strēm\ *n* : the middle of a stream

mid·sum·mer \'mid-'səm-ər\ *n* : the middle of summer; *esp* : the summer solstice

¹mid·way \-,wā\ *n* : an avenue (as at a carnival) for concessions and light amusements

²midway *adv* (*or adj*) : in the middle of the way or distance : HALFWAY

mid·week \'mid-,wēk\ *n* : the middle of the week — mid·week·ly *adj or adv*

mid·wife \-,wīf\ *n* : a woman who helps other women in childbirth — mid·wife·ry \-,wī-f(ə-)rē\ *n*

mid·win·ter \-'wint-ər\ *n* : the middle of winter; *esp* : the winter solstice

mid·year \-,yiər\ *n* 1 : the middle of a year   2 : a midyear examination — midyear *adj*

mien \'mēn\ *n* 1 : air or bearing esp. as expressive of mood or personality : DEMEANOR   2 : APPEARANCE, ASPECT

miff \'mif\ *vb* : to put into an ill humor : OFFEND ⟨was ∼ed by his behavior⟩

¹might \(')mīt\ *past of* MAY — used as an auxiliary to express permission, liberty, probability, or possibility in the past, a present condition contrary to fact, less probability or possibility than *may*, or as a polite alternative to *may*, *ought*, or *should*

²might \'mīt\ *n* : the power, authority, or resources of an individual or a group : STRENGTH

mighty \'mīt-ē\ *adj* 1 : very strong : POWERFUL   2 : GREAT, NOTABLE — might·i·ly *adv* — might·i·ness *n* — mighty *adv*

mi·gnon·ette \,min-yə-'net\ *n* : a garden plant with spikes of tiny fragrant flowers

mi·graine \'mī-,grān\ *n* : a condition marked by recurrent headache and often nausea

mi·grant \'mī-grənt\ *n* : one that migrates; *esp* : a person who moves in order to find work (as in harvesting crops)

mi·grate \-'grāt\ *vb* 1 : to move from one country, place, or locality to another   2 : to pass usu. periodically from one region or climate to another for feeding or breeding — mi·gra·tion \mī-'grā-shən\ *n* — mi·gra·tion·al *adj* — mi·gra·to·ry \'mī-grə-,tōr-ē\ *adj*

mi·ka·do \mə-'käd-ō\ *n* : an emperor of Japan

mike \'mīk\ *n* : MICROPHONE

mil \'mil\ *n* — see MONEY table

milch \'milk, 'milch\ *adj* : giving milk ⟨∼ cow⟩

mild \'mīld\ *adj* 1 : gentle in nature or behavior   2 : moderate in action or effect   3 : TEMPERATE   *syn* soft, bland, lenient — mild·ly *adv* — mild·ness *n*

mil·dew \'mil-,d(y)ü\ *n* : a superficial usu. whitish growth produced on organic matter and on plants by a fungus; *also* : a fungus producing this growth — mildew *vb*

mile \'mīl\ *n* [OE *mīl*, fr. L *milia* miles, short for *milia passuum* thousands of paces] 1 : a unit of distance equal to 5280 feet   2 : NAUTICAL MILE

mile·age \'mī-lij\ *n* 1 : an allowance for traveling expenses at a certain rate per mile   2 : distance in miles traveled (as in a day); *also* : the amount of service yielded (as by a tire) expressed in terms of miles of travel

mile·post \'mīl-,pōst\ *n* : a post indicating the distance in miles from a given point

mile·stone \-,stōn\ *n* 1 : a stone serving as a milepost   2 : a significant point in development

mi·lieu \mēl-'yə(r), -'yü\ *n* : ENVIRONMENT, SETTING

mil·i·tant \'mil-ə-tənt\ *adj* 1 : engaged in warfare   2 : aggressively active — mil·i·tan·cy \-tən-sē\ *n* — mil·i·tant·ly *adv*

mil·i·ta·rism \'mil-ə-tə-,riz-əm\ *n* 1 : predominance of the military class or its ideals   2 : a policy of aggressive military preparedness — mil·i·ta·rist

\-rəst\ *n* — **mil·i·ta·ris·tic** \,mil-ə-tə-'ris-tik\ *adj*

mil·i·ta·rize \'mil-ə-tə-,rīz\ *vb* **1** : to equip with military forces and defenses **2** : to give a military character to

¹**mil·i·tary** \'mil-ə-,ter-ē\ *adj* **1** : of or relating to soldiers, arms, or war **2** : performed by armed forces; *also* : supported by armed force **3** : of or relating to the army **syn** martial, warlike — **mil·i·tar·i·ly** \,mil-ə-'ter-ə-lē\ *adv*

²**military** *n*, *pl* **military 1** : the military, naval, and air forces of a nation **2** : military persons

mil·i·tate \'mil-ə-,tāt\ *vb* **:** to have weight or effect

mi·li·tia \mə-'lish-ə\ *n* : a part of the organized armed forces of a country liable to call only in emergency

mi·li·tia·man \-mən\ *n* : a member of a militia

¹**milk** \'milk\ *n* **1** : a nutritive usu. whitish fluid secreted by female mammals for feeding their young **2** : a milklike liquid (as a plant juice) — **milk·i·ness** *n* — **milky** *adj*

²**milk** *vb* : to draw off the milk of ⟨∼ a cow⟩; *also* : to draw or yield milk ⟨a cow that ∼s 30 pounds⟩ — **milk·er** *n*

milk·maid \'milk-,mād\ *n* **:** DAIRYMAID

milk·man \-mən\ *n* : a man who sells or delivers milk

milk of magnesia : a milk-white mixture of hydroxide of magnesium and water used as an antacid and laxative

milk shake *n* : milk and flavoring syrup sometimes with ice cream blended thoroughly

milk·sop \'milk-,säp\ *n* : an unmanly man

milk·weed \-,wēd\ *n* : a coarse herb with milky juice and clustered flowers

Milky Way *n* : a broad irregular band of light that stretches across the sky and is caused by the light of myriads of faint stars

Milky Way galaxy *n* : the huge system of stars of which our sun is a member and which includes the myriads of stars that comprise the Milky Way

¹**mill** \'mil\ *n* **1** : a building with machinery for grinding grain into flour; *also* : a machine for grinding grain **2** : a building with machinery for manufacturing **3** : a machine used esp. for crushing, stamping, grinding, cutting, shaping, or polishing

²**mill** *vb* **1** : to subject to an operation or process in a mill **2** : to move in a circle or in an eddying mass — **mill·er** *n*

³**mill** *n* : a unit of monetary value equal to ¹⁄₁₀₀₀ U. S. dollar

mill·dam \'mil-,dam\ *n* : a dam to make a millpond; *also* : MILLPOND

mil·len·ni·um \mə-'len-ē-əm\ *n*, *pl* **-nia** \-ē-ə\ *or* **-ni·ums 1** : a period of 1000 years **2** : the 1000 years mentioned in Revelation 20 when holiness is to prevail and Christ is to reign on earth **3** : a period of great happiness or perfect government

mil·let \'mil-ət\ *n* : any of several small-seeded cereal and forage grasses long cultivated for grain or hay; *also* : the grain of a millet

mil·li·ard \'mil-ē-,ärd\ *n*, *Brit* : a thousand millions

mil·lieme \mē(l)-'yem\ *n* — see MONEY table

mil·li·gram \'mil-ə-,gram\ *n* : a unit of

weight equal to one thousandth of a gram

mil·li·me·ter \'mil-ə-,mēt-ər\ *n* : a unit of length equal to one thousandth of a meter

mil·li·ner \'mil-ə-nər\ *n* : one who designs, makes, trims, or sells women's hats

mil·li·nery \-,ner-ē\ *n* **1** : women's apparel for the head **2** : the business or work of a milliner

mill·ing \'mil-iŋ\ *n* : a corrugated edge on a coin

mil·lion \'mil-yən\ *n*, *pl* **millions** *or* **million** : a thousand thousands — **million** *adj* — **mil·lionth** \-yənth\ *adj or n*

mil·lion·aire \,mil-yə-'naər\ *n* : one whose wealth is estimated at a million or more (as of dollars)

mill·pond \'mil-,pänd\ *n* : a pond produced by damming a stream to produce a fall of water for operating a mill

mill·race \'mil-,rās\ *n* : a canal in which water flows to and from a mill wheel

mill·stone \-,stōn\ *n* : either of two round flat stones used for grinding grain

mill·stream \-,strēm\ *n* : the stream in a millrace

mill·wright \-,rīt\ *n* : one whose occupation is planning and building mills or setting up their machinery

mime \'mīm\ *n* **1** : MIMIC **2** : the art of characterization or of narration by body movement; *also* : a performance of mime — **mime** *vb*

mim·e·o·graph \'mim-ē-ə-,graf\ *n* : a machine for making many copies by means of a stencil through which ink is pressed — **mimeograph** *vb*

mi·met·ic \mə-'met-ik, mī-\ *adj* **1** : IMITATIVE **2** : relating to, characterized by, or exhibiting mimicry — **mi·me·sis** \-'mē-səs\ *n*

mim·ic \'mim-ik\ *n* : one who imitates esp. for amusement or ridicule — **mimic** *vb* — **mim·ic·ry** \-rē\ *n*

mi·mo·sa \mə-'mō-sə, mī-\ *n* : any of various leguminous trees, shrubs, and herbs of warm regions with globular heads of small white or pink flowers

min·a·ret \,min-ə-'ret\ *n* : a slender lofty tower attached to a mosque

min·a·to·ry \'min-ə-,tōr-ē, 'mī-nə-\ *adj* : THREATENING, MENACING

mince \'mins\ *vb* **1** : to cut into small pieces **2** : to utter or pronounce affectedly **3** : to walk in a prim affected manner — **minc·ing** *adj*

mince·meat \'mins-,mēt\ *n* : a finely chopped mixture esp. of raisins, apples, spices, and often meat used as a filling for a pie **(mince pie)**

¹**mind** \'mīnd\ *n* **1** : MEMORY **2** : the part of an individual that feels, perceives, wills, and esp. reasons **3** : INTENTION, DESIRE **4** : the normal condition of the mental faculties **5** : OPINION, VIEW **6** : a person or group embodying mental qualities **7** : intellectual ability — **mind·less** \-ləs\ *adj*

²**mind** *vb* **1** *chiefly dial* : REMEMBER **2** : to attend to ⟨∼ your own business⟩ **3** : HEED, OBEY **4** : to be concerned about : WORRY; *also* : DISLIKE **5** : to be careful or cautious : SEE **6** : to take charge of : TEND **7** : to regard with attention

mind·ful \-fəl\ *adj* **:** bearing in mind

: AWARE — **mind·ful·ly** *adv* — **mind·ful·ness** *n*

¹mine \'mīn\ *pron* : one or the ones belonging to me

²mine *n* **1** : an excavation in the earth from which mineral substances are taken; *also* : an ore deposit **2** : a subterranean passage under an enemy position; *also* : an encased explosive for destroying enemy personnel **3** : a rich source of supply

³mine *vb* **1** : to dig a mine **2** : UNDERMINE **3** : to get ore from the earth **4** : to place military mines in — **min·er** \'mī-nər\ *n*

mine·lay·er \'mīn-,lā-ər\ *n* : a naval vessel for laying underwater mines

min·er·al \'min-(ə-)rəl\ *n* **1** : a solid homogeneous crystalline substance (as diamond, gold, or quartz) not of animal or vegetable origin; *also* : ORE **2** : any of various naturally occurring homogeneous substances (as coal, salt, water, or gas) obtained for man's use usu. from the ground **3** *Brit* : MINERAL WATER — **mineral** *adj*

min·er·al·o·gy \,min-ə-'ral-ə-jē, -'räl-\ *n* : a science dealing with minerals — **min·er·al·og·i·cal** \-rə-'läj-i-kəl\ *adj* — **min·er·al·o·gist** \-'ral-ə-jəst, -'räl-\ *n*

mineral water *n* : water impregnated with mineral salts or gases

min·e·stro·ne \,min-ə-'strō-nē, -'strōn\ *n* : a rich thick vegetable soup

mine·sweep·er \'mīn-,swē-pər\ *n* : a warship designed for removing or neutralizing mines by dragging

min·gle \'miŋ-gəl\ *vb* **1** : to bring or combine together : MIX **2** : CONCOCT

min·ia·ture \'min-ē-(ə-),chùr, -chər\ *n* [ML *miniatura* illumination of manuscripts, fr. L *miniare* to paint with red lead, fr. *minium* red lead] **1** : a copy on a much reduced scale **2** : a small painting (as on ivory or metal) — **miniature** *adj* — **min·ia·tur·ist** \-əst\ *n*

min·i·mal \'min-ə-məl\ *adj* : relating to or being a minimum : LEAST

min·i·mize \'min-ə-,mīz\ *vb* **1** : to reduce to a minimum **2** : to estimate at a minimum; *also* : BELITTLE **syn** depreciate, decry, disparage

min·i·mum \'min-ə-məm\ *n, pl* **-ma** \-mə\ *or* **-mums** **1** : the least quantity, value, or degree **2** : a lower limit allowed by authority **3** : the least of a set of numbers — **minimum** *adj*

min·ion \'min-yən\ *n* **1** : a servile dependent **2** : one highly favored **3** : a subordinate official

min·is·cule \'min-əs-,kyül\ *var of* MINUSCULE

¹min·is·ter \'min-ə-stər\ *n* **1** : AGENT **2** : CLERGYMAN; *esp* : a Protestant clergyman **3** : a high officer of state entrusted with the management of a division of governmental activities **4** : a diplomatic representative to a foreign state — **min·is·te·ri·al** \,min-ə-'stir-ē-əl\ *adj*

²minister *vb* **1** : to perform the functions of a minister of religion **2** : to give aid — **min·is·tra·tion** \,min-ə-'strā-shən\ *n*

min·is·trant \'min-ə-strənt\ *adj* : performing service as a minister — **ministrant** *n*

min·is·try \'min-ə-strē\ *n* **1** : MINISTRATION **2** : the office, duties, or functions of a minister; *also* : his period of service or office **3** : CLERGY **4** : AGENCY **5** *often cap* : the body of ministers governing a nation or state; *also* : a government department headed by a minister

mink \'miŋk\ *n* : a slender mammal resembling the related weasels; *also* : its soft lustrous typically dark brown fur

min·ne·sing·er \'min-i-,siŋ-ər, -ə-,ziŋ-\ *n* : one of a class of German lyric poets and musicians of the 12th and 14th centuries

min·now \'min-ō\ *n* : any of numerous small freshwater fishes related to the carps

¹mi·nor \'mī-nər\ *n* **1** : a person who has not attained majority **2** : a subject of academic study chosen as a secondary field of specialization

²minor *adj* **1** : inferior in importance, size, or degree **2** : not having reached majority **3** : having the third, sixth, and sometimes the seventh degrees lowered by a half step ⟨∼ scale⟩; *also* : based on a minor scale ⟨∼ key⟩

³minor *vb* : to pursue an academic minor

mi·nor·i·ty \mə-'nor-ət-ē, mī-\ *n* **1** : the period or state of being a minor **2** : the smaller in number of two groups; *esp* : a group having less than the number of votes necessary for control **3** : a part of a population differing from others (as in race or religion)

min·ster \'min-stər\ *n* **1** : a church attached to a monastery **2** : a large or important church

min·strel \'min-strəl\ *n* **1** : a medieval singer of verses; *also* : MUSICIAN, POET **2** : one of a group of performers in a program usu. of Negro songs, jokes, and impersonations — **min·strel·sy** \-sē\ *n*

¹mint \'mint\ *n* **1** : a place where coins are made **2** : a vast sum — **mint** *vb* — **mint·age** \-ij\ *n* — **mint·er** *n*

²mint *adj* : unmarred as if fresh from a mint ⟨∼ coins⟩

³mint *n* : any of a large group of square-stemmed herbs and shrubs; *esp* : one (as spearmint or marjoram) with fragrant aromatic foliage used in flavoring — **minty** *adj*

min·u·end \'min-yə-,wend\ *n* : a number from which another is to be subtracted

min·u·et \,min-yə-'wet\ *n* : a slow graceful dance

¹mi·nus \'mī-nəs\ *prep* **1** : diminished by : LESS ⟨7 ∼ 3 equals 4⟩ **2** : LACKING, WITHOUT ⟨∼ his hat⟩

²minus *n* **1** : a sign — (minus sign) used in mathematics to require subtraction or designate a negative quantity **2** : a negative quantity

³minus *adj* **1** : requiring subtraction **2** : algebraically negative ⟨∼ quantity⟩ **3** : having negative qualities

¹min·us·cule \'min-əs-,kyül, mə-'nəs-\ *n* : a lowercase letter

²minuscule *adj* : very small

¹min·ute \'min-ət\ *n* **1** : the 60th part of an hour or of a degree **2** : a short space of time **3** *pl* : the official record of the proceedings of a meeting

²mi·nute \mī-'n(y)üt, mə-\ *adj* **1** : very

small **2** : of little importance : TRIFLING **3** : marked by close attention to details **syn** diminutive, tiny, miniature, wee — **mi·nute·ly** *adv* — **mi·nute·ness** *n*

min·ute·man \'min-ət-,man\ *n* : a member of a group of armed men pledged to take the field at a minute's notice during and immediately before the American Revolution

mi·nu·tia \mə-'n(y)ü-shē-ə, mī-\ *n, pl* **-ti·ae** \-shē-,ē\ : a minute or minor detail — usu. used in pl.

minx \'minks\ *n* : a pert girl

mir·a·cle \'mir-i-kəl\ *n* **1** : an extraordinary event manifesting a supernatural work of God **2** : an unusual event, thing, or accomplishment : WONDER, MARVEL — **mi·rac·u·lous** \mə-'rak-yə-ləs\ *adj* — **mi·rac·u·lous·ly** *adv*

mi·rage \mə-'räzh\ *n* **1** : a reflection visible at sea, in deserts, or above a hot pavement of some distant object often in distorted form as a result of atmospheric conditions **2** : something illusory and unattainable

¹**mire** \'mī(ə)r\ *n* : heavy and often deep mud, slush or dirt — **miry** *adj*

²**mire** *vb* : to stick or sink in or as if in mire

¹**mir·ror** \'mir-ər\ *n* **1** : a polished or smooth substance (as of glass) that forms images by reflection **2** : a true representation; *also* : MODEL

²**mirror** *vb* : to reflect in or as if in a mirror

mirth \'mərth\ *n* : gladness or gaiety accompanied with laughter **syn** glee, jollity, hilarity — **mirth·ful** \-fəl\ *adj* — **mirth·ful·ly** *adv* — **mirth·ful·ness** *n*

mis·ad·ven·ture \,mis-əd-'vench-ər\ *n* : MISFORTUNE, MISHAP

mis·an·thrope \'mis-ᵊn-,thrōp\ *n* : one who hates mankind — **mis·an·throp·ic** \,mis-ᵊn-'thräp-ik\ *adj* — **mis·an·throp·i·cal·ly** *adv* — **mis·an·thro·py** \mis-'an-thrə-pē\ *n*

mis·ap·ply \,mis-ə-'plī\ *vb* : to apply wrongly — **mis·ap·pli·ca·tion** \,mis-,ap-lə-'kā-shən\ *n*

mis·ap·pre·hend \,mis-,ap-ri-'hend\ *vb* : MISUNDERSTAND — **mis·ap·pre·hen·sion** \-'hen-chən\ *n*

mis·ap·pro·pri·ate \,mis-ə-'prō-prē-,āt\ *vb* : to appropriate wrongly; *esp* : to take dishonestly for one's own use — **mis·ap·pro·pri·a·tion** \-,prō-prē-'ā-shən\ *n*

mis·be·got·ten \,mis-bi-'gät-ᵊn\ *adj* : ILLEGITIMATE

mis·be·have \,mis-bi-'hāv\ *vb* : to behave improperly — **mis·be·hav·ior** \-'hā-vyər\ *n*

mis·be·liev·er \,mis-bə-'lē-vər\ *n* : one who holds a false or unorthodox belief

mis·cal·cu·late \mis-'kal-kyə-,lāt\ *vb* : to calculate wrongly — **mis·cal·cu·la·tion** \,mis-,kal-kyə-'lā-shən\ *n*

mis·call \mis-'kól\ *vb* : MISNAME

mis·car·ry \mis-'kar-ē\ *vb* **1** : to give birth prematurely and esp. before the fetus is capable of living independently **2** : to go wrong; *also* : to be unsuccessful — **mis·car·riage** \-'kar-ij\ *n*

mis·ce·ge·na·tion \,mis-,ej-ə-'nā-shən, ,mis-i-jə-\ *n* [L *miscēre* to mix + *genus* kind, race] : a mixture of races

mis·cel·la·ne·ous \,mis-ə-'lā-nē-əs\ *adj* **1** : consisting of diverse things or members; *also* : having various traits **2** : dealing with or interested in diverse subjects — **mis·cel·la·ne·ous·ly** *adv* —

mis·cel·la·ne·ous·ness *n*

mis·cel·la·ny \'mis-ə-,lā-nē\ *n* **1** : HODGEPODGE **2** : a collection of writings on various subjects

mis·chance \mis-'chans\ *n* : bad luck; *also* : MISHAP

mis·chief \'mis-chəf\ *n* **1** : injury caused by a human agency **2** : a cause of harm or irritation **3** : action that annoys; *also* : MISCHIEVOUSNESS

mis·chie·vous \'mis-chə-vəs\ *adj* **1** : HARMFUL, INJURIOUS **2** : causing annoyance or minor injury **3** : irresponsibly playful — **mis·chie·vous·ly** *adv* — **mis·chie·vous·ness** *n*

mis·ci·ble \'mis-ə-bəl\ *adj* : capable of being mixed; *esp* : soluble in each other

mis·con·ceive \,mis-kən-'sēv\ *vb* : to interpret incorrectly — **mis·con·cep·tion** \-'sep-shən\ *n*

mis·con·duct \mis-'kän-(,)dəkt\ *n* **1** : MISMANAGEMENT **2** : intentional wrongdoing **3** : improper behavior

mis·con·strue \,mis-kən-'strü\ *vb* : MISINTERPRET — **mis·con·struc·tion** \-'strək-shən\ *n*

mis·count \mis-'kaúnt\ *vb* : to count incorrectly : MISCALCULATE

mis·cre·ant \'mis-krē-ənt\ *n* : one who behaves criminally or viciously — **miscreant** *adj*

mis·cue \mis-'kyü\ *n* : MISTAKE, ERROR — **miscue** *vb*

mis·deed \-'dēd\ *n* : a wrong deed : OFFENSE

mis·de·mean·or \,mis-də-'mē-nər\ *n* **1** : a crime less serious than a felony **2** : MISDEED

mis·di·rect \,mis-də-'rekt, -dī-\ *vb* : to give a wrong direction to — **mis·di·rec·tion** \-'rek-shən\ *n*

mis·do·ing \mis-'dü-iŋ\ *n* **1** : WRONGDOING **2** : MISDEED — **mis·do·er** *n*

mise-en-scène \,mē-,zä[n]-'sen\ *n* **1** : the arrangement of the scenery, property, and actors on a stage **2** : SETTING; *also* : ENVIRONMENT

mi·ser \'mī-zər\ *n* : a person who hoards his money — **mi·ser·li·ness** *n* — **mi·ser·ly** *adj*

mis·er·a·ble \'miz-ər-(ə-)bəl\ *adj* **1** : wretchedly deficient; *also* : causing extreme discomfort **2** : extremely poor **3** : SHAMEFUL — **mis·er·a·ble·ness** *n* — **mis·er·a·bly** *adv*

mis·ery \'miz-(ə-)rē\ *n* **1** : a state of suffering and want caused by poverty or affliction **2** : a cause of suffering or discomfort **3** : a state of emotional distress

mis·fea·sance \mis-'fēz-ᵊns\ *n* : a wrong action : TRESPASS

mis·file \mis-'fīl\ *vb* : to file in an inappropriate place

mis·fire \-'fī(ə)r\ *vb* **1** : to fail to fire **2** : to miss an intended effect — **misfire** *n*

mis·fit \-'fit, *esp for 2* 'mis-,fit\ *n* **1** : an imperfect fit **2** : a person poorly adjusted to his environment

mis·for·tune \mis-'fór-chən\ *n* **1** : bad fortune **2** : MISHAP

mis·giv·ing \-'giv-iŋ\ *n* : a feeling of doubt or suspicion esp. concerning a future event

mis·gov·ern \-'gəv-ərn\ *vb* : to govern badly — **mis·gov·ern·ment** \-ər(n)-mənt\ *n*

mis·guid·ance \mis-'gīd-ᵊns\ *n* : faulty guidance : MISDIRECTION — **mis·guide** \-'gīd\ *vb*

mis·han·dle \-'han-dᵊl\ vb 1 : MALTREAT 2 : to manage wrongly
mis·hap \'mis-,hap\ n : an unfortunate accident
mish·mash \'mish-,mash, -,mäsh\ n : HODGEPODGE, JUMBLE
mis·in·form \,mis-ᵊn-'form\ vb : to give false or misleading information to — **mis·in·for·ma·tion** \,mis-,in-fər-'mā-shən\ n
mis·in·ter·pret \,mis-ᵊn-'tər-prət\ vb : to understand or explain wrongly — **mis·in·ter·pre·ta·tion** \-,tər-prə-'tā-shən\ n
mis·judge \mis-'jəj\ vb 1 : to estimate wrongly 2 : to have an unjust opinion of — **mis·judg·ment** \-mənt\ n
mis·lay \mis-'lā\ vb : MISPLACE, LOSE
mis·lead \-'lēd\ vb : to lead in a wrong direction or into a mistaken action or belief
mis·like \mis-'līk\ vb : DISLIKE — **mis·like** n
mis·man·age \-'man-ij\ vb : to manage badly — **mis·man·age·ment** \-mənt\ n
mis·match \-'mach\ vb : to match (as in marriage) unsuitably or badly — **mis·match** n
mis·name \-'nām\ vb : to name incorrectly : MISCALL
mis·no·mer \mis-'nō-mər\ n : a wrong name or designation
mi·sog·y·nist \mə-'säj-ə-nəst\ n : one who hates or distrusts women — **mi·sog·y·ny** \-nē\ n
mis·place \-'plās\ vb 1 : to put in a wrong place 2 : to set on a wrong object 〈~ trust〉
mis·play \-'plā\ n : a wrong or unskillful play — **misplay** vb
misprint \mis-'print\ vb : to print incorrectly — **misprint** n
mis·pri·sion \-'prizh-ən\ n : misconduct or corrupt administration esp. by a public official
mis·pro·nounce \,mis-prə-'naùns\ vb : to pronounce incorrectly — **mis·pro·nun·ci·a·tion** \-,nən-sē-'ā-shən\ n
mis·quote \mis-'kwōt\ vb : to quote incorrectly — **mis·quo·ta·tion** \,mis-kwō-'tā-shən\ n
mis·read \-'rēd\ vb : to read or interpret incorrectly
mis·rep·re·sent \,mis-,rep-ri-'zent\ vb : to represent falsely or unfairly — **mis·rep·re·sen·ta·tion** \-,zen-'tā-shən\ n
¹**mis·rule** \mis-'rül\ vb : MISGOVERN
²**misrule** n 1 : MISGOVERNMENT 2 : DISORDER
¹**miss** \'mis\ vb 1 : to fail to hit, reach, or contact 2 : to feel the absence of 3 : to fail to obtain 4 : AVOID 5 : OMIT 6 : to fail to understand 7 : to fail to perform or attend; also : MISFIRE
²**miss** n 1 : a failure to hit or to attain a result 2 : MISFIRE
³**miss** n 1 — used as a title prefixed to the name of an unmarried woman or girl 2 : a young unmarried woman or girl
mis·sal \'mis-əl\ n : a book containing all that is said or sung at mass during the entire year
mis·send \mis-'send\ vb : to send incorrectly 〈missent mail〉
mis·shape \mis(h)-'shāp\ vb : DEFORM — **mis·shap·en** \-'shā-pən\ adj
mis·sile \'mis-əl\ n [L, fr. neut. of

missilis capable of being thrown, fr. **mittere** to let go, send] 1 : an object (as a stone, bullet, or weapon) thrown or projected 2 : a self-propelled unmanned weapon (as a rocket)
mis·sile·man \-mən\ n : one who designs, manufactures, or uses a guided missile
mis·sile·ry \-rē\ n 1 : MISSILES 2 : the science of the making and use of guided missiles
miss·ing \'mis-iŋ\ adj : ABSENT; also : LOST
mis·sion \'mish-ən\ n 1 : a ministry commissioned by a church (as to propagate its faith); also : a place where such a ministry is carried out 2 : a group of envoys to a foreign country; also : a team of specialists or cultural leaders sent to a foreign country 3 : TASK, FUNCTION
¹**mis·sion·ary** \-,er-ē\ adj : of, relating to, or engaged in church missions
²**missionary** n : a person commissioned by a church to propagate its faith or carry on humanitarian work
mis·sion·er n : a person undertaking a mission and esp. a religious mission
mis·sive \'mis-iv\ n : LETTER
mis·spell \mis-'spel\ vb : to spell incorrectly — **mis·spell·ing** n
mis·state \-'stāt\ vb : to state incorrectly — **mis·state·ment** \-mənt\ n
mis·step \-'step\ n 1 : a wrong step 2 : MISTAKE, BLUNDER
mist \'mist\ n 1 : water in the form of particles suspended in the air 2 : something that dims or obscures : HAZE, FILM
mis·tak·able \mə-'stā-kə-bəl\ adj : capable of being misunderstood or mistaken
mis·take \mə-'stāk\ n 1 : a misunderstanding of the meaning or implication of something 2 : a wrong action or statement : ERROR, BLUNDER — **mistake** vb
mis·tak·en \-'stā-kən\ adj 1 : MISUNDERSTOOD 2 : having a wrong opinion or incorrect information 3 : ERRONEOUS — **mis·tak·en·ly** adv
mis·ter \'mis-tər\ n — used as a title prefixed to the name of a man or to a designation of occupation or office
mis·tle·toe \'mis-əl-,tō\ n : a parasitic green plant with yellowish flowers and waxy white berries that grows on trees (as oaks)
mis·tral \'mis-trəl, mi-'sträl\ n : a violent cold dry northerly wind of southern Europe
mis·treat \mis-'trēt\ vb : to treat badly : ABUSE — **mis·treat·ment** \-mənt\ n
mis·tress \'mis-trəs\ n 1 : a woman who has power, authority, or ownership 〈~ of the house〉 2 : a country or state having supremacy 〈~ of the seas〉 3 : a woman with whom a man cohabits without benefit of marriage; also, archaic : SWEETHEART 4 — used archaically as a title prefixed to the name of a married or unmarried woman
mis·tri·al \mis-'trī(-ə)l\ n : a trial that has no legal effect (as by reason of an error)
¹**mis·trust** \-'trəst\ n : a lack of confidence : DISTRUST — **mis·trust·ful**

\-fəl\ *adj* — **mis·trust·ful·ly** *adv* — **mis·trust·ful·ness** *n*

²**mistrust** *vb* **1** : to have no trust or confidence in **2** : SUSPECT

misty \'mis-tē\ *adj* **1** : obscured by or as if by mist : INDISTINCT — **mist·i·ly** *adv* — **mist·i·ness** *n*

mis·un·der·stand \,mis-ən-dər-'stand\ *vb* **1** : to fail to understand **2** : to interpret incorrectly

mis·un·der·stand·ing \-'stan-diŋ\ *n* **1** : MISINTERPRETATION **2** : DISAGREEMENT, QUARREL

mis·use \mis-'yüz\ *vb* **1** : to use incorrectly : MISAPPLY **2** : ABUSE, MISTREAT — **mis·use** \-'yüs\ *n*

mite \'mīt\ *n* **1** : any of various tiny animals related to the spiders that often live and feed on animals or plants **2** : a small coin or sum of money **3** : a small amount : BIT

mi·ter *or* **mi·tre** \'mīt-ər\ *n* **1** : a head-dress worn by bishops and abbots **2** : a joint or corner made by cutting two pieces of wood at an angle and fitting the cut edges together

mit·i·gate \'mit-ə-,gāt\ *vb* **1** : to make less harsh or hostile **2** : to make less severe or painful — **mit·i·ga·tion** \,mit-ə-'gā-shən\ *n* — **mit·i·ga·tive** \'mit-ə-,gāt-iv\ *adj* — **mit·i·ga·tor** \-,gāt-ər\ *n* — **mit·i·ga·to·ry** \-gə-,tōr-ē\ *adj*

mitt \'mit\ *n* : a baseball glove (as for a catcher)

mit·ten \'mit-ᵊn\ *n* : a covering for the hand having a separate section for the thumb only

¹**mix** \'miks\ *vb* **1** : to combine into one mass **2** : ASSOCIATE **3** : to form by mingling components **4** : CROSSBREED **5** : CONFUSE **6** : to become involved syn blend, merge, coalesce, amalgamate, fuse — **mix·able** \-ə-bəl\ *adj* — **mix·er** *n*

²**mix** *n* : a product of mixing

mix·ture \'miks-chər\ *n* **1** : the act or process of mixing; *also* : the state of being mixed **2** : a product of mixing **3** : COMBINATION

mix-up \'miks-,əp\ *n* : an instance of confusion ⟨a ∼ about who was to meet the train⟩

miz·zen *or* **miz·en** \'miz-ᵊn\ *n* : a fore-and-aft sail set on the mast aft or next aft of a mainmast

mne·mon·ic \ni-'män-ik\ *adj* : assisting or designed to assist memory ⟨∼ devices⟩

moan \'mōn\ *n* : a low prolonged sound indicative of pain or grief — **moan** *vb*

moat \'mōt\ *n* : a deep wide usu. water-filled trench around the rampart of a castle

¹**mob** \'mäb\ *n* **1** : MASSES, RABBLE **2** : a large disorderly crowd **3** : a criminal set : GANG

²**mob** *vb* **mobbed**; **mob·bing** : to crowd around and attack or annoy

¹**mo·bile** \'mō-bəl\ *adj* **1** : capable of moving or being moved **2** : changeable in appearance, mood, or purpose; *also* : ADAPTABLE **3** : using vehicles for transportation ⟨∼ warfare⟩

²**mo·bile** \-,bēl\ *n* : a construction or sculpture (as of wire and sheet metal) with parts that can be set in motion by air currents

mo·bi·lize \'mō-bə-,līz\ *vb* **1** : to put into movement or circulation **2** : to assemble and make ready for war duty; *also* : to marshal for action — **mo·bi·li-**

za·tion \,mō-bə-lə-'zā-shən\ *n* — **mo·bi·liz·er** \'mō-bə-,lī-zər\ *n*

mob·ster \'mäb-stər\ *n* : a member of a criminal gang

moc·ca·sin \'mäk-ə-sən\ *n* **1** : a soft leather heelless shoe **2** : a venomous snake of the southeastern U.S.

¹**mock** \'mäk\ *vb* **1** : to treat with contempt or ridicule **2** : DELUDE **3** : DEFY, CHALLENGE **4** : to mimic in sport or derision : IMITATE — **mock·er** *n* — **mock·ery** \-(ə-)rē\ *n* — **mock·ing·ly** *adv*

²**mock** *adj* : SHAM, PSEUDO

mock-he·ro·ic \,mäk-hi-'rō-ik\ *adj* : ridiculing or burlesquing the heroic style or heroic character or action ⟨a ∼ poem⟩

mock·ing·bird \-iŋ-,bərd\ *n* : a song-bird of the southern U.S. noted for its ability to mimic the calls of other birds

mock-up \-,əp\ *n* : a full-sized structural model built accurately to scale chiefly for study, testing, or display ⟨a ∼ of an airplane⟩

mode \'mōd\ *n* **1** : a particular form or variety of something; *also* : STYLE **2** : a manner of doing something : METHOD — **mod·al** \'mōd-ᵊl\ *adj*

¹**mod·el** \'mäd-ᵊl\ *n* **1** : structural design **2** : a miniature representation; *also* : a pattern of something to be made **3** : an example for imitation or emulation **4** : one who poses for an artist; *also* : MANNEQUIN **5** : TYPE, DESIGN — **model** *adj*

²**model** *vb* **-eled** *or* **-elled**; **-el·ing** *or* **-el·ling** **1** : SHAPE, FASHION, CONSTRUCT **2** : to work as a fashion model

¹**mod·er·ate** \'mäd-(ə-)rət\ *adj* **1** : avoiding extremes; *also* : TEMPERATE **2** : AVERAGE; *also* : MEDIOCRE **3** : limited in scope or effect **4** : not expensive — **moderate** *n* — **mod·er·ate·ly** *adv* — **mod·er·ate·ness** *n*

²**mod·er·ate** \'mäd-ə-,rāt\ *vb* **1** : to lessen the intensity of : TEMPER **2** : to act as a moderator — **mod·er·a·tion** \,mäd-ə-'rā-shən\ *n*

mod·er·a·tor \'mäd-ə-,rāt-ər\ *n* **1** : MEDIATOR **2** : a presiding officer

mod·ern \'mäd-ərn\ *adj* : of, relating to, or characteristic of the present or the immediate past : CONTEMPORARY — **mo·der·ni·ty** \mə-'dər-nət-ē\ *n* — **mod·ern·ly** \'mäd-ərn-lē\ *adv* — **mod·ern·ness** *n*

mod·ern·ism \'mäd-ər-,niz-əm\ *n* : a practice, movement, or belief peculiar to modern times

mod·ern·ize \-,nīz\ *vb* : to make or become modern — **mod·ern·i·za·tion** \,mäd-ər-nə-'zā-shən\ *n* — **mod·ern·iz·er** \'mäd-ər-,nī-zər\ *n*

mod·est \'mäd-əst\ *adj* **1** : having a moderate estimate of oneself; *also* : DIFFIDENT **2** : DECENT **3** : limited in size, amount, or aim : UNPRETENTIOUS — **mod·est·ly** *adv* — **mod·es·ty** \-ə-stē\ *n*

mod·i·cum \'mäd-i-kəm\ *n* : a small amount

mod·i·fy \'mäd-ə-,fī\ *vb* **1** : MODERATE **2** : to limit the meaning of esp. in a grammatical construction : QUALIFY **3** : CHANGE, ALTER — **mod·i·fi·ca·tion** \,mäd-ə-fə-'kā-shən\ *n* — **mod·i·fi·er** \'mäd-ə-,fī(-ə)r\ *n*

mod·ish \'mōd-ish\ *adj* : FASHIONABLE, STYLISH — **mod·ish·ly** *adv* — **mod·ish·ness** *n*

mo·diste \mō-'dēst\ *n* **:** a fashionable dressmaker

mod·u·lar \'mäj-ə-lər\ *adj* **:** constructed with standardized units 〈~ furniture〉

mod·u·late \'mäj-ə-,lāt\ *vb* **1 :** to tune to a key or pitch **2 :** to keep in proper measure or proportion **:** TEMPER **3 :** to vary the amplitude, frequency, or phase of a carrier wave for the transmission of intelligence (as in radio or television) — **mod·u·la·tion** \,mäj-ə-'lā-shən\ *n* — **mod·u·la·tor** \'mäj-ə-,lāt-ər\ *n* — **mod·u·la·to·ry** \-lə-,tōr-ē\ *adj*

mod·ule \'mäj-ül\ *n* **:** an assembly of wired electronic parts for use with other such assemblies

mo·gul \'mō-gəl, mō-'gəl\ *n* [fr. *Mogul*, one of the Mongol conquerors of India or their descendants, fr. Per *Mughul*, Mongol, fr. Mongolian *Mongol*] **:** an important person **:** MAGNATE

mo·hair \'mō-,haər\ *n* **:** a fabric or yarn made wholly or in part from the long silky hair of the Angora goat

Mo·ham·med·an *var of* MUHAMMADAN

moi·e·ty \'mói-ət-ē\ *n* **1 :** HALF **2 :** one of two approximately equal parts

moil \'mói(ə)l\ *vb* **:** to work hard **:** DRUDGE — **moil** *n* — **moil·er** *n*

moi·ré \mó-'rā, mwä-\ *or* **moire** *same or* 'mói(ə)r, 'mwär\ *n* **:** a fabric (as silk) having a watered appearance

moist \'móist\ *adj* **:** slightly or moderately wet — **moist·ly** *adv* — **moist·ness** *n*

moist·en \'mói·s-ən\ *vb* **:** to make or become moist — **moist·en·er** *n*

mois·ture \'mói·s-chər\ *n* **:** DAMPNESS

mo·lar \'mō-lər\ *n* **:** one of the broad teeth adapted to grinding food and located in the back of the jaw — **molar** *adj*

mo·las·ses \mə-'las-əz\ *n* **:** the thick brown syrup that is separated from raw sugar in sugar manufacture

¹**mold** \'mōld\ *n* **:** crumbly soil rich in organic matter

²**mold** *n* **1 :** distinctive nature or character **2 :** the frame in or around which something is constructed **3 :** a cavity in which something is shaped; *also* **:** an object so shaped **4 :** MOLDING

³**mold** *vb* **1 :** to shape in or as if in a mold **2 :** to ornament with molding — **mold·er** *n*

⁴**mold** *n* **:** a surface growth of fungus on damp or decaying matter; *also* **:** a fungus that forms molds — **mold·i·ness** *n* — **moldy** *adj*

⁵**mold** *vb* **:** to become moldy

mold·board \'mōl(d)-,bōrd\ *n* **:** a curved iron plate attached above the plowshare of a plow to lift and turn the soil

mold·er \'mōl-dər\ *vb* **:** to crumble into small pieces

mold·ing \'mōl-diŋ\ *n* **1 :** an act or process of shaping in a mold; *also* **:** an object so shaped **2 :** a decorative surface, plane, or curved strip

¹**mole** \'mōl\ *n* **:** a small often pigmented spot or protuberance on the skin

²**mole** *n* **:** a small burrowing mammal with tiny eyes, hidden ears, and soft fur

³**mole** *n* **:** a massive breakwater or jetty

mol·e·cule \'mäl-i-,kyül\ *n* **:** the smallest particle of matter that is the same chemi-

cally as the whole mass — **mo·lec·u·lar** \mə-'lek-yə-lər\ *adj*

mole·hill \'mōl-,hil\ *n* **:** a little ridge of earth thrown up by a mole

mole·skin \-,skin\ *n* **1 :** the skin of the mole used as fur **2 :** a heavy durable cotton fabric for industrial, medical, or clothing use

mo·lest \mə-'lest\ *vb* **1 :** ANNOY, DISTURB **2 :** to make indecent advances to — **mo·les·ta·tion** \,mō-,les-'tā-shən\ *n* — **mo·lest·er** \mə-'les-tər\ *n*

moll \'mäl\ *n* **:** a girl friend esp. of a gangster

mol·li·fy \'mäl-ə-,fī\ *vb* **1 :** APPEASE **2 :** SOFTEN **3 :** ASSUAGE — **mol·li·fi·ca·tion** \,mäl-ə-fə-'kā-shən\ *n*

mol·lusk *or* **mol·lusc** \'mäl-əsk\ *n* **:** any of a large group of mostly shelled and aquatic invertebrate animals including snails, clams, and squids

mol·ly·cod·dle \'mäl-ē-,käd-ᵊl\ *n* **:** a pampered man or boy — **mollycoddle** *vb*

molt \'mōlt\ *vb* **:** to shed hair, feathers, outer skin, or horns periodically with the parts being replaced by new growth — **molt·er** *n*

mol·ten \'mōlt-ᵊn\ *adj* **:** fused or liquefied by heat; *also* **:** GLOWING

mo·ly \'mō-lē\ *n* **:** a mythical herb with black root, white flowers, and magic powers

mo·lyb·de·num \mə-'lib-də-nəm\ *n* **:** a metallic chemical element used in strengthening and hardening steel

mo·ment \'mō-mənt\ *n* **1 :** a minute portion of time **:** INSTANT **2 :** a time of excellence 〈he has his ~s〉 **3 :** IMPORTANCE **syn** consequence, significance

mo·men·tary \'mō-mən-,ter-ē\ *adj* **1 :** continuing only a moment; *also* **:** EPHEMERAL **2 :** recurring at every moment — **mo·men·tar·i·ly** \,mō-mən-'ter-ə-lē\ *adv* — **mo·men·tar·i·ness** \'mō-mən-,ter-ē-nəs\ *n*

mo·men·tous \mō-'ment-əs\ *adj* **:** very important — **mo·men·tous·ly** *adv* — **mo·men·tous·ness** *n*

mo·men·tum \mō-'ment-əm\ *n, pl* **-men·ta** \-'ment-ə\ *or* **-men·tums :** the force which a moving body has because of its weight and motion

mon·arch \'män-ərk, -,ärk\ *n* **1 :** a person who reigns over a kingdom or an empire **2 :** one holding preeminent position or power — **mo·nar·chi·cal** \mə-'när-ki-kəl\ *or* **mo·nar·chic** \-'när-kik\ *adj*

mon·ar·chist \'män-ər-kəst\ *n* **:** a believer in monarchical government — **mon·ar·chism** \-,kiz-əm\ *n*

mon·ar·chy \'män-ər-kē\ *n* **:** a nation or state governed by a monarch

mon·as·tery \'män-ə-,ster-ē\ *n* **:** a house for persons under religious vows and esp. for monks — **mon·as·te·ri·al** \,män-ə-'stir-ē-əl\ *adj*

mo·nas·tic \mə-'nas-tik\ *adj* **:** of or relating to monasteries or to monks or nuns — **mo·nas·ti·cal·ly** *adv*

mo·nas·ti·cism \mə-'nas-tə-,siz-əm\ *n* **:** the monastic life, system, or condition

mon·au·ral \män-'ór-əl\ *adj* **:** MONOPHONIC

Mon·day \'mən-dē\ *n* **:** the 2d day of the week

mon·e·tary \\'män-ə-,ter-ē, 'mən-\\ *adj*
1 : of or relating to coinage or currency
2 : PECUNIARY
mon·ey \\'mən-ē\\ *n, pl* **-eys** *or* **-ies**
1 : something (as metal currency) accepted as a medium of exchange
2 : wealth reckoned in monetary terms
3 : the 1st, 2d, and 3d place in a horse or dog race (finished in the ~)

MONEY

COUNTRY	NAME	SUBDIVISIONS
Afghanistan	afghani	100 puls
Albania	lek	100 qintars
Algeria	franc	100 centimes
Andorra	peseta	100 centimos
Argentina	peso	100 centavos
Australia	pound	20 shillings / 240 pence
Austria	schilling	100 groschen
Belgium	franc	100 centimes
Bolivia	boliviano	100 centavos
Brazil	cruzeiro	100 centavos
British East Africa	shilling	100 cents
Bulgaria	lev	100 stotinki
Burma	kyat	100 pyas
Cambodia	riel	100 sen
Cameroun	franc	100 centimes
Canada	dollar	100 cents
Central African Republic	franc	100 centimes
Ceylon	rupee	100 cents
Chad	franc	100 centimes
Chile	escudo	100 centesimos
China (Formosa)	yuan	100 cents
China (mainland)	yuan	10 chiao / 100 fen
Colombia	peso	100 centavos
Congo (Brazzaville)	franc	100 centimes
Congo (Léopoldville)	franc	100 centimes
Costa Rica	colon	100 centimos
Cuba	peso	100 centavos
Cyprus	pound	1000 mils
Czechoslovakia	koruna	100 halers
Dahomey	franc	100 centimes
Denmark	krone	100 öre
Dominican Republic	peso	100 centavos
Ecuador	sucre	100 centavos
Egypt (United Arab Republic)	pound	100 piasters / 1000 milliemes
El Salvador	colon	100 centavos
Ethiopia	dollar	100 cents
Finland	markka	100 pennis
France	franc	100 centimes
Gabon	franc	100 centimes
Germany	deutsche mark	100 pfennigs
Ghana	pound	20 shillings / 240 pence
Greece	drachma	100 lepta
Guatemala	quetzal	100 centavos
Guinea	franc	100 centimes
Haiti	gourde	100 centimes
Honduras	lempira	100 centavos
Hong Kong	dollar	100 cents
Hungary	forint	100 fillers
Iceland	krona	100 aurar
India	rupee	100 naye paise
Indonesia	rupiah	100 sen
Iran	rial	100 dinars
Iraq	dinar	5 riyals / 20 dirhams / 1000 fils
Ireland	pound	20 shillings / 240 pence
Israel	pound	100 agorot
Italy	lira	100 centesimi
Ivory Coast	franc	100 centimes
Jamaica	pound	20 shillings / 240 pence
Japan	yen	100 sen
Jordan	dinar	1000 fils
Kenya	shilling	100 cents
Korea	won	100 chon
Kuwait	dinar	100 fils
Laos	kip	100 at
Lebanon	pound	100 piasters
Liberia	dollar	100 cents
Libya	pound	100 piasters / 1000 milliemes
Liechtenstein	franc	100 centimes
Luxembourg	franc	100 centimes
Malagasy Republic	franc	100 centimes
Malaysia	dollar	100 cents
Mali	franc	100 centimes
Mauritania	franc	100 centimes
Mexico	peso	100 centavos
Monaco	franc	100 centimes
Morocco	dirham	100 francs
Nepal	rupee	100 pice
Netherlands	gulden	100 cents
New Zealand	pound	20 shillings / 240 pence
Nicaragua	cordoba	100 centavos
Niger	franc	100 centimes
Nigeria	pound	20 shillings / 240 pence
Norway	krone	100 öre
Pakistan	rupee	100 pice
Panama	balboa	100 centesimos
Paraguay	guarani	100 centimos
Peru	sol	100 centavos
Philippines	peso	100 centavos
Poland	zloty	100 groszy
Portugal	escudo	100 centavos
Romania	leu	100 bani
San Marino	lira	100 centesimi
Saudi Arabia	riyal *or* rial	20 qurshes
Senegal	franc	100 centimes
Sierra Leone	pound	20 shillings / 240 pence
Somalia	somalo	100 centesimi
So. Africa	rand	100 cents
So. Vietnam	piaster	100 cents
Spain	peseta	100 centimos
Sudan	pound	10 rials / 100 piasters
Sweden	krona	100 öre
Switzerland	franc	100 centimes
Syria	pound	100 piasters
Tanganyika	shilling	100 cents
Thailand	baht	100 satangs
Togo	franc	100 centimes
Trinidad and Tobago	dollar	100 cents
Tunisia	dinar	1000 milliemes
Turkey	pound	100 piasters
Uganda	shilling	100 cents
United Kingdom	pound	20 shillings / 240 pence
United States	dollar	100 cents
Upper Volta	franc	100 centimes
Uruguay	peso	100 centesimos
U.S.S.R.	ruble	100 kopecks
Vatican City	lira	100 centesimi
Venezuela	bolivar	100 centimos
Yugoslavia	dinar	100 paras
Zanzibar	shilling	100 cents

mon·eyed *or* **mon·ied** \-ēd\ *adj* **1** : having money : WEALTHY **2** : consisting in or derived from money

mon·ey·mak·er \'mən-ē-,mā-kər\ *n* **1** : one who accumulates wealth **2** : a plan or product that produces profit

mon·ger \'məŋ-gər\ *n* : DEALER

Mon·go·lian \män-'gōl-yən\ *n* **1** : a native or inhabitant of Mongolia **2** : a member of a racial stock comprising chiefly the peoples of northern and eastern Asia — **Mon·gol** \'mäŋ-gol, 'män-,gōl\ *adj or n* — **Mongolian** *adj*

mon·grel \'məŋ-grəl, 'mäŋ-\ *n* : an offspring of parents of different breeds or uncertain ancestry

mo·nism \'mō-,niz-əm\ *n* : a view that a complex entity (as the universe) is basically one — **mo·nist** *n*

mo·ni·tion \mō-'nish-ən\ *n* : WARNING, CAUTION

¹mon·i·tor \'män-ət-ər\ *n* **1** : a student appointed to assist a teacher **2** : one that monitors; *esp* : a screen used by television personnel for viewing the picture being picked up by a camera **3** : a warship used esp. for coastal bombardment

²monitor *vb* **1** : to check or adjust the quality of (as a radio or television broadcast); *also* : to check for political, military, or criminal significance **2** : to test for intensity of radiation esp. from radioactivity (~ the upper air) **3** : to watch or observe for a special purpose ⟨the engineer ~ing the dials⟩ ⟨~ political gossip⟩

mon·i·to·ry \'män-ə-,tōr-ē\ *adj* : giving admonition : WARNING

monk \'məŋk\ *n* : a man belonging to a religious order and living in a monastery — **monk·ish** *adj* — **monk·ish·ly** *adv* — **monk·ish·ness** *n*

¹mon·key \'məŋ-kē\ *n* : a primate mammal other than man; *esp* : one of the smaller, longer-tailed, and usu. more arboreal primates as contrasted with the apes

²monkey *vb* **1** : FOOL, TRIFLE **2** : TAMPER

mon·key·shine \'məŋ-kē-,shīn\ *n* : PRANK

monkey wrench *n* : a wrench with one adjustable jaw

monks·hood \'məŋks-,hùd\ *n* : a poisonous herb related to the buttercups and often grown for its showy hood-shaped white or purple flowers

mon·o·cle \'män-ə-kəl\ *n* : an eyeglass for one eye

mon·o·dy \'män-əd-ē\ *n* : ELEGY, DIRGE — **mo·nod·ic** \mə-'näd-ik\ *adj* — **mon·o·dist** \'män-əd-əst\ *n*

mo·nog·a·my \mə-'näg-ə-mē\ *n* : marriage with but one person at a time — **mo·nog·a·mist** \-məst\ *n* — **mo·nog·a·mous** \-məs\ *adj*

mon·o·gram \'män-ə-,gram\ *n* : a sign of identity composed of the combined initials of a name — **monogram** *vb*

mon·o·graph \-,graf\ *n* : a learned treatise

mono·lin·gual \,män-ə-'liŋ-gwəl\ *adj* : expressed in or knowing or using only one language

mono·lith \'män-ᵊl-,ith\ *n* **1** : a single great stone often in the form of a monument or column **2** : something (as a social structure) held to be a single massive whole exhibiting solid uniformity — **mono·lith·ic** \,män-ᵊl-'ith-ik\ *adj*

mon·o·logue \'män-ᵊl-,óg\ *n* : a dramatic soliloquy; *also* : a long speech monopolizing conversation — **mon·o·logu·ist** \-,ò-gəst\ *or* **mo·nol·o·gist** \mə-'näl-ə-jəst\ *n*

mono·ma·nia \,män-ə-'mā-nē-ə\ *n* : mental derangement involving a single idea or area of mind — **mono·ma·ni·ac** \-nē-,ak\ *n or adj*

mono·phon·ic \,män-ə-'fän-ik\ *adj* : of or relating to sound transmission, recording, or reproduction by techniques that provide a single transmission path as contrasted with binaural techniques

mo·nop·o·ly \mə-'näp-ə-lē\ *n* **1** : exclusive ownership (as through command of supply) **2** : a commodity controlled by one party **3** : a person or group having a monopoly — **mo·nop·o·list** \-ləst\ *n* — **mo·nop·o·lis·tic** \mə-,näp-ə-'lis-tik\ *adj* — **mo·nop·o·li·za·tion** \-lə-'zā-shən\ *n* — **mo·nop·o·lize** \mə-'näp-ə-,līz\ *vb*

mono·rail \'män-ə-,rāl\ *n* : a single rail serving as a track for cars that are balanced on it or suspended from it

mono·syl·la·ble \'män-ə-,sil-ə-bəl\ *n* : a word of one syllable — **mono·syl·lab·ic** \,män-ə-sə-'lab-ik\ *adj* — **mono·syl·lab·i·cal·ly** *adv*

mono·the·ism \'män-ə-(,)thē-,iz-əm\ *n* : a doctrine or belief that there is only one deity — **mono·the·ist** \-thē-əst\ *n*

mono·tone \'män-ə-,tōn\ *n* : a succession of syllables, words, or sentences in one unvaried key or pitch

mo·not·o·nous \mə-'nät-ᵊn-əs\ *adj* **1** : uttered or sounded in one unvarying tone **2** : tediously uniform — **mo·not·o·nous·ly** *adv* — **mo·not·o·nous·ness** *n* — **mo·not·o·ny** \-ᵊn-ē\ *n*

mon·ox·ide \mə-'näk-,sīd\ *n* : an oxide containing one atom of oxygen in the molecule

mon·sei·gneur \,mōⁿ-,sān-'yər\ *n, pl* **mes·sei·gneurs** \,mā-,sān-'yər(z)\ : a French dignitary — used as a title

mon·sieur \məs(h)-'yə(r)\ *n, pl* **mes·sieurs** \-'yə(r)z, -'yə(r)\ : a Frenchman of high rank or station — used as a title equivalent to *Mister*

mon·si·gnor \män-'sēn-yər\ *n, pl* **mon·si·gnors** *or* **mon·si·gno·ri** \,män-,sēn-'yōr(-ē)\ : a Roman Catholic prelate — used as a title

mon·soon \män-'sün\ *n* : a periodic wind esp. in the Indian ocean and southern Asia; *also* : the season of the southwest monsoon esp. in India

mon·ster \'män-stər\ *n* **1** : an abnormally developed plant or animal **2** : an animal of strange or terrifying shape; *also* : one unusually large of its kind **3** : an extremely ugly, wicked, or cruel person — **mon·stros·i·ty** \män-'sträs-ət-ē\ *n* — **mon·strous** \'män-strəs\ *adj* — **mon·strous·ly** *adv*

mon·strance \'män-strəns\ *n* : a vessel in which the consecrated Host is exposed for the adoration of the faithful

mon·tage \män-'täzh\ *n* **1** : a composite photograph made by combining several separate pictures **2** : an artistic

---

ə abut; ᵊ kitten; ər further; a back; ā bake; ä cot, cart; aù out; ch chin; e less; ē easy; g gift; i trip; ī life; j joke; ŋ sing; ō flow; ò flaw; òi coin; th thin; t̲h̲ this; ü loot; ù foot; y yet; yü few; yù furious; zh vision

composition made up of several different kinds of items (as strips of newspaper, pictures, bits of wood) arranged together

month \'mənth\ *n* [OE *mōnath*, fr. *mōna* moon] **:** one of the twelve parts into which the year is divided — **month·ly** *adv or adj or n*

mon·u·ment \'män-yə-mənt\ *n* **1 :** a lasting reminder; *esp* **:** a structure erected in remembrance of a person or event **2 :** a natural feature or area of special interest set aside by the government as public property

mon·u·men·tal \,män-yə-'ment-ᵊl\ *adj* **1 :** MASSIVE; *also* **:** OUTSTANDING **2 :** of or relating to a monument **3 :** very great — **mon·u·men·tal·ly** *adv*

moo \'mü\ *vb* **:** to make the natural throat noise of a cow — **moo** *n*

¹mood \'müd\ *n* **1 :** a conscious state of mind or predominant emotion **:** FEELING **2 :** a prevailing attitude **:** DISPOSITION

²mood *n* **:** distinction of form of a verb to express whether its action or state is conceived as fact or in some other manner (as wish)

moody \'müd-ē\ *adj* **1 :** GLOOMY **2 :** subject to moods **:** TEMPERAMENTAL — **mood·i·ly** *adv* — **mood·i·ness** *n*

¹moon \'mün\ *n* **:** a celestial body that revolves around the earth

²moon *vb* **:** to engage in idle reverie **:** DREAM

moon·beam \-,bēm\ *n* **:** a ray of light from the moon

moon·light \-,līt\ *n* **:** the light of the moon — **moon·lit** \-,lit\ *adj*

moon·light·er \-,līt-ər\ *n* **:** a person holding two jobs at the same time — **moon·light·ing** *n*

moon·scape \-,skāp\ *n* **:** the surface of the moon as seen or as pictured

moon·shine \-,shīn\ *n* **1 :** MOONLIGHT **2 :** empty talk **3 :** intoxicating liquor usu. illegally distilled

moon·stone \-,stōn\ *n* **:** a transparent or translucent feldspar of pearly luster used as a gem

moon·struck \-,strək\ *adj* **1 :** mentally unbalanced **2 :** romantically sentimental; *also* **:** BEMUSED

¹moor \'mùr\ *n* **:** an area of open and usu. infertile and wet or peaty wasteland

²moor *vb* **:** to make fast with cables, lines, or anchors **:** tie up

Moor \'mùr\ *n* **:** one of the Muslim conquerors of Spain in the 8th century **2 :** MUSLIM — **Moor·ish** *adj*

moor·ing \'mùr-iŋ\ *n* **1 :** a place where or an object to which a craft can be made fast **2 :** moral or spiritual resources — usu. used in pl.

moor·land \'mùr-lənd, -,land\ *n* **:** land consisting of moors

moose \'müs\ *n, pl* **moose :** a large heavy-antlered American deer; *also* **:** the European elk

moot \'müt\ *adj* **1 :** open to question; *also* **:** DISPUTED **2 :** having no practical significance

¹mop \'mäp\ *n* **:** an implement made of absorbent material fastened to a handle and used esp. for cleaning floors

²mop *vb* **mopped; mop·ping :** to use a mop on **:** clean with a mop

mope \'mōp\ *vb* **1 :** to become dull, dejected, or listless **2 :** DAWDLE

mop·pet \'mäp-ət\ *n* **:** CHILD

mop-up \'mäp-,əp\ *n* **:** a final clearance or disposal

mo·raine \mə-'rān\ *n* **:** an accumulation of earth and stones left by a glacier

¹mor·al \'mòr-əl\ *adj* **1 :** of or relating to principles of right and wrong **2 :** conforming to a standard of right behavior; *also* **:** capable of right and wrong action **3 :** probable but not proved ⟨a ∼ certainty⟩ **4 :** PSYCHOLOGICAL ⟨a ∼ victory⟩ *syn* virtuous, righteous, noble — **mor·al·ly** *adv*

²mor·al \'mòr-əl, 3 *is* mə-'ral\ *n* **1 :** the practical meaning (as of a story) **:** LESSON **2** *pl* **:** moral practices or teachings **3 :** MORALE

mo·rale \mə-'ral\ *n* **1 :** MORALITY **2 :** the mental and emotional attitudes of an individual to the tasks expected of him; *also* **:** ESPRIT DE CORPS

mor·al·ist \'mòr-ə-ləst\ *n* **1 :** a teacher or student of morals **2 :** one concerned with regulating the morals of others — **mor·al·is·tic** \,mòr-ə-'lis-tik\ *adj* — **mor·al·is·ti·cal·ly** *adv*

mo·ral·i·ty \mə-'ral-ət-ē\ *n* **:** moral conduct **:** VIRTUE

mor·al·ize \'mòr-ə-,līz\ *vb* **:** to make moral reflections — **mor·al·i·za·tion** \,mòr-ə-lə-'zā-shən\ *n* — **mor·al·iz·er** \'mòr-ə-,lī-zər\ *n*

mo·rass \mə-'ras\ *n* **:** SWAMP

mor·a·to·ri·um \,mòr-ə-'tōr-ē-əm\ *n, pl* **-ri·ums** *or* **-ria** \-ē-ə\ **:** a suspension of activity

mor·bid \'mòr-bəd\ *adj* **1 :** of, relating to, or typical of disease; *also* **:** DISEASED, SICKLY **2 :** GRISLY, GRUESOME ⟨∼ details⟩ — **mor·bid·i·ty** \mòr-'bid-ət-ē\ *n* — **mor·bid·ly** \'mòr-bəd-lē\ *adv* — **mor·bid·ness** *n*

mor·dant \'mòrd-ᵊnt\ *adj* **1 :** INCISIVE **2 :** BURNING, PUNGENT — **mor·dant·ly** *adv*

more \'mōr\ *adj* **1 :** GREATER **2 :** ADDITIONAL — **more** *adv or n*

more·over \mōr-'ō-vər\ *adv* **:** in addition **:** FURTHER

mo·res \'mòr-,āz, -,(,)ēz\ *n pl* **1 :** the fixed morally binding customs of a group **2 :** HABITS, MANNERS

morgue \'mòrg\ *n* **:** a place where the bodies of persons found dead are kept until released for burial

mor·i·bund \'mòr-ə-,(,)bənd\ *adj* **:** being in a dying condition — **mor·i·bun·di·ty** \,mòr-ə-'bən-dət-ē\ *n*

Mor·mon \'mòr-mən\ *n* **:** a member of the Church of Jesus Christ of Latter Day Saints — **Mor·mon·ism** \-,iz-əm\ *n*

morn \'mòrn\ *n* **:** MORNING

morn·ing \'mòr-niŋ\ *n* **:** the early part of the day; *esp* **:** the time from sunrise to noon **2 :** BEGINNING

morning glory *n* **:** any of various twining plants related to the sweet potato that have often showy bell-shaped or funnel-shaped flowers

Mo·roc·can \mə-'räk-ən\ *n* **:** a native or inhabitant of Morocco

mo·roc·co \mə-'räk-ō\ *n* **:** a fine leather made of goatskins tanned with sumac

mo·ron \'mòr-,än\ *n* **:** a defective person having a mental capacity equivalent to that of a normal 8 to 12 year old and being able to do routine work under supervision; *also* **:** a stupid person — **mo·ron·ic** \mə-'rän-ik\ *adj* — **mo·ron·i·cal·ly** *adv*

mo·rose \mə-'rōs\ *adj* **:** having a sullen disposition; *also* **:** GLOOMY — **mo·rose·ly** *adv* — **mo·rose·ness** *n*

mor·pheme \'mȯr-ˌfēm\ n : a meaningful linguistic unit that contains no smaller meaningful parts — **mor·phe·mic** \mȯr-'fē-mik\ adj

mor·phia \'mȯr-fē-ə\ n : MORPHINE

mor·phine \'mȯr-ˌfēn\ n : an addictive drug obtained from opium and used to ease pain or induce sleep

mor·phol·o·gy \mȯr-'fäl-ə-jē\ n 1 : a branch of biology dealing with the form and structure of organisms 2 : a study and description of word formation in a language — **mor·pho·log·i·cal** \ˌmȯr-fə-'läj-i-kəl\ adj — **mor·phol·o·gist** \mȯr-'fäl-ə-jəst\ n

mor·ris \'mȯr-əs\ n : a vigorous English dance performed by men wearing costumes and bells

mor·row \'mär-ō\ n : TOMORROW

mor·sel \'mȯr-səl\ n 1 : a small piece or quantity 2 : a tasty dish

mor·tal \'mȯrt-ᵊl\ adj 1 : causing death : FATAL; also : exposing to spiritual death ⟨~ sin⟩ 2 : subject to death ⟨~ man⟩ 3 : implacably hostile ⟨~ foe⟩ 4 : very great : EXTREME ⟨~ fear⟩ 5 : HUMAN ⟨~ limitations⟩ — **mor·tal·i·ty** \mȯr-'tal-ət-ē\ n — **mor·tal·ly** \'mȯrt-ᵊl-ē\ adv

¹mor·tar \'mȯrt-ər\ n 1 : a strong bowl in which substances may be broken or powdered with a pestle 2 : a short-barreled cannon used to hurl projectiles at high angles

²mortar n : a plastic building material (as a mixture of cement, lime, or gypsum plaster with sand and water) that hardens and is used in masonry or plastering — **mortar** vb

mor·tar·board \-ˌbȯrd\ n 1 : a board or platform about 3 feet square for holding mortar 2 : an academic cap

mort·gage \'mȯr-gij\ n : a conveyance of property upon condition that becomes void on payment or performance according to stipulated terms — **mortgage** vb — **mort·gag·ee** \ˌmȯr-gi-'jē\ n — **mort·ga·gor** \ˌmȯr-gi-'jȯr\ n

mor·ti·cian \mȯr-'tish-ən\ n [L mort-, mors death + E -ician (as in physician)] : UNDERTAKER

mor·ti·fy \'mȯrt-ə-ˌfī\ vb 1 : to subdue (as the body) esp. by abstinence or self-inflicted pain 2 : HUMILIATE 3 : to become necrotic or gangrenous — **mor·ti·fi·ca·tion** \ˌmȯrt-ə-fə-'kā-shən\ n

mor·tise also **mor·tice** \'mȯrt-əs\ n : a hole cut in a piece of wood into which another piece fits to form a joint

mor·tu·ary \'mȯr-chə-ˌwer-ē\ n : a place in which dead bodies are kept until burial

mo·sa·ic \mō-'zā-ik\ n : a surface decoration made by inlaying small pieces (as of colored glass or stone) to form figures or patterns; also : a design made in mosaic

mo·sey \'mō-zē\ vb : SAUNTER

Mos·lem \'mäz-ləm\ var of MUSLIM

mosque \'mäsk\ n : a building used for public worship by Muslims

mos·qui·to \mə-'skēt-ō\ n, pl -toes : a two-winged fly the female of which sucks the blood of man and lower animals

moss \'mȯs\ n : any of a large group of green plants without flowers but with small leafy stems growing in clumps — **mossy** adj

moss·back \-ˌbak\ n : an extremely conservative person : FOGY

most \'mōst\ adj 1 : the majority of ⟨~ men⟩ 2 : GREATEST — **most** adv or n

-most \ˌmōst\ adj suffix : most toward ⟨headmost⟩

most·ly adv : MAINLY

mot \'mō\ n : a witty saying

mote \'mōt\ n : a small particle

mo·tel \mō-'tel\ n : a hotel for automobile tourists

mo·tet \mō-'tet\ n : a choral work on a sacred text for several voices usu. without instrumental accompaniment

moth \'mȯth\ n : any of various insects related to the butterflies but usu. night-flying and with a stouter body and smaller wings; esp : a small pale insect (clothes moth) whose larvae eat wool, fur, and feathers

moth·ball \-ˌbȯl\ n 1 : a ball (as of naphthalene) used to keep moths out of clothing 2 pl : protective storage ⟨ships put in ~s after the war⟩

¹moth·er \'məth-ər\ n 1 : a female parent 2 : a woman in authority 3 : SOURCE, ORIGIN — **moth·er·less** adj — **moth·er·li·ness** n — **moth·er·ly** adj

²mother vb 1 : to give birth to; also : PRODUCE 2 : to protect like a mother

moth·er·hood \-ˌhu̇d\ n : MATERNITY

mother-in-law n, pl **mothers-in-law** : the mother of one's spouse

moth·er·land \'məth-ər-ˌland\ n : the land of origin of something

mother-of-pearl n : the hard pearly substance forming the inner layer of a mollusk shell

mo·tif \mō-'tēf\ n : a dominant idea or central theme (as in a work of art)

mo·tile \'mōt-ᵊl\ adj : capable of spontaneous movement — **mo·til·i·ty** \mō-'til-ət-ē\ n

¹mo·tion \'mō-shən\ n 1 : a proposal for action (as by a deliberative body) 2 : an act, process, or instance of moving 3 pl : ACTIVITIES, MOVEMENTS — **mo·tion·less** \-ləs\ adj — **mo·tion·less·ly** adv — **mo·tion·less·ness** n

²motion vb : to direct or signal by a motion

motion picture n : a series of pictures thrown on a screen so rapidly that they produce a continuous picture in which persons and objects seem to move

mo·ti·vate \'mōt-ə-ˌvāt\ vb : to provide with a motive — **mo·ti·va·tion** \ˌmōt-ə-'vā-shən\ n

¹mo·tive \'mōt-iv\ n 1 : something (as a need or desire) that causes a person to act 2 : a recurrent theme in a musical composition — **mo·tive·less** \-ləs\ adj

²motive adj 1 : moving to action 2 : of or relating to motion

mot·ley \'mät-lē\ adj 1 : variegated in color 2 : made up of diverse elements syn heterogeneous, miscellaneous, assorted

¹mo·tor \'mōt-ər\ n 1 : one that imparts motion 2 : a small compact engine 3 : AUTOMOBILE

²motor vb : to travel or transport by automobile : DRIVE — **mo·tor·ist** \-əst\ n

mo·tor·boat \-ˌbōt\ n : a boat propelled

by an internal-combustion engine or an electric motor

mo·tor·cade \-ˌkād\ *n* **:** a procession of motor vehicles

mo·tor·car \-ˌkär\ *n* **:** AUTOMOBILE

motor court *n* **:** MOTEL

mo·tor·cy·cle \-ˌsī-kəl\ *n* **:** a 2-wheeled automotive vehicle

mo·tor·ize \-ˌīz\ *vb* **1 :** to equip with a motor **2 :** to equip with motor-driven vehicles — **mo·tor·i·za·tion** \ˌmōt-ər-ə-ˈzā-shən\ *n*

mo·tor·man \ˈmōt-ər-mən\ *n* **:** an operator of a motor-driven vehicle (as a streetcar or subway train)

mo·tor·truck \-ˌtrək\ *n* **:** an automotive truck for transporting freight

motor vehicle *n* **:** an automotive vehicle not operated on rails; *esp* **:** one with rubber tires for use on highways

mot·tle \ˈmät-ᵊl\ *vb* **:** to mark with spots of different color **:** BLOTCH

mot·to \ˈmät-ō\ *n, pl* **-toes** *also* **-tos** **1 :** a sentence, phrase, or word inscribed on something to indicate its character or use **2 :** MAXIM

moue \ˈmü\ *n* **:** a little grimace

mould *var of* MOLD

moult *var of* MOLT

¹mound \ˈmaund\ *n* **1 :** an artificial bank or hill of earth or stones **2 :** KNOLL

¹mount \ˈmaunt\ *n* **:** a high hill **:** MOUNTAIN

²mount *vb* **1 :** to increase in amount or extent; *also* **:** RISE, ASCEND **2 :** to get up on something above ground level; *esp* **:** to seat oneself on (as a horse) for riding **3 :** to put in position (~ artillery); *also* **:** to have as equipment **4 :** to set on something that elevates **5 :** to attach to a support **6 :** to prepare *esp.* for examination or display **:** ARRANGE — **mount·able** \-ə-bəl\ *adj* — **mount·er** *n*

³mount *n* **1 :** FRAME, SUPPORT **2 :** a means of conveyance; *esp* **:** a saddle horse

moun·tain \ˈmaunt-ᵊn\ *n* **:** a landmass higher than a hill — **moun·tain·ous** \-(ə-)nəs\ *adj*

moun·tain·eer \ˌmaunt-ᵊn-ˈiər\ *n* **1 :** a native or inhabitant of a mountainous region **2 :** one who climbs mountains for sport — **mountaineer** *vb*

moun·tain·side \ˈmaunt-ᵊn-ˌsīd\ *n* **:** the side of a mountain

moun·tain·top \-ˌtäp\ *n* **:** the summit of a mountain

moun·te·bank \ˈmaunt-i-ˌbaŋk\ *n* **:** QUACK, CHARLATAN

mount·ing \ˈmaunt-iŋ\ *n* **:** something that serves as a frame or support (a ~ for a diamond) (a ~ for an engine)

mourn \ˈmōrn\ *vb* **:** to feel or express grief or sorrow **:** LAMENT — **mourn·er** *n*

mourn·ful \-fəl\ *adj* **:** expressing, feeling, or causing sorrow — **mourn·ful·ly** *adv* — **mourn·ful·ness** *n*

mourn·ing \ˈmōr-niŋ\ *n* **1 :** an outward sign (as black clothes) of grief for a person's death **2 :** a period of time during which signs of grief are shown

mouse \ˈmaus\ *n, pl* **mice** \ˈmīs\ **:** any of various small rodents with pointed snout, long body, and slender tail

mous·er \ˈmau-zər\ *n* **:** a cat proficient at catching mice

mousse \ˈmüs\ *n* **:** a dessert of sweetened and flavored whipped cream or thin cream and gelatin frozen without stirring

mous·tache \ˈməs-ˌtash, (ˌ)məs-ˈtash\ *n* **:** the hair growing on the human upper lip

mousy *or* **mous·ey** \ˈmau-sē, -zē\ *adj* **1 :** QUIET **2 :** TIMID, COLORLESS

¹mouth \ˈmauth\ *n* **1 :** the opening through which an animal takes in food; *also* **:** the space between the mouth and the pharynx **2 :** something resembling a mouth (as in affording entrance) — **mouth·ful** \-ˌful\ *n*

²mouth \ˈmauth\ *vb* **:** SPEAK; *also* **:** DECLAIM

mouth·part \ˈmauth-ˌpärt\ *n* **:** a structure or appendage near the mouth

mouth·piece \ˈmauth-ˌpēs\ *n* **1 :** a part (as of a musical instrument) that goes in the mouth or to which the mouth is applied **2 :** SPOKESMAN

mouth·wash \-ˌwȯsh, -ˌwäsh\ *n* **:** a usu. antiseptic liquid preparation for cleaning the mouth and teeth

¹move \ˈmüv\ *vb* **1 :** to go or cause to go from one point to another **:** ADVANCE, *also* **:** DEPART **2 :** to change one's residence **3 :** to change or cause to change place, position, or posture **:** SHIFT **4 :** to show marked activity **5 :** to take or cause to take action **:** PROMPT **6 :** to make a formal request, application, or appeal **7 :** to stir the emotions **8 :** EVACUATE — **mov·able** *or* **move·able** \-ə-bəl\ *adj*

²move *n* **:** an act of moving **:** MOVEMENT **2 :** a calculated procedure **:** MANEUVER

move·ment \-mənt\ *n* **1 :** the act or process of moving **:** MOVE **2 :** TENDENCY, TREND; *also* **:** a series of organized activities working toward an objective **3 :** the moving parts of a mechanism (as of a watch) **4 :** RHYTHM, CADENCE **5 :** a unit or division of an extended musical composition **6 :** evacuation of or from the bowels

mov·er \ˈmü-vər\ *n* **:** one that moves; *esp* **:** a person or company that moves the belongings of others from one home or place of business to another

mov·ie \ˈmü-vē\ *n* **1 :** MOTION PICTURE **2** *pl* **:** a showing of a motion picture; *also* **:** the motion-picture industry

¹mow \ˈmau\ *n* **:** the part of a barn where hay or straw is stored

²mow \ˈmō\ *vb* **1 :** to cut (as grass) with a scythe or machine **2 :** to cut the standing herbage from (~ the lawn) — **mow·er** *n*

much \ˈməch\ *adj* **1 :** great in quantity, amount, extent, or degree (~ money) **2 :** very good (he's not ~ at sports) — **much** *adv or n*

mu·ci·lage \ˈmyü-s(ə-)lij\ *n* **:** a watery sticky solution (as of a gum) used esp. as an adhesive — **mu·ci·lag·i·nous** \ˌmyü-sə-ˈlaj-ə-nəs\ *adj*

muck \ˈmək\ *n* **1 :** soft moist barnyard manure **2 :** FILTH, DIRT **3 :** a dark richly organic soil; *also* **:** MUD, MIRE — **mucky** *adj*

muck·rak·er \-ˌrā-kər\ *n* **:** one who exposes publicly real or apparent misconduct of prominent individuals

mu·cus \ˈmyü-kəs\ *n* **:** a slimy slippery protective secretion of membranes lining various bodily cavities — **mu·cous** \-kəs\ *adj*

mud \ˈməd\ *n* **:** soft wet earth **:** MIRE — **mud·di·ly** *adv* — **mud·di·ness** *n* — **mud·dy** *adj or vb*

mud·dle \ˈməd-ᵊl\ *vb* **1 :** to make

muddy **2** : to confuse esp. with liquor **3** : BUNGLE — **muddle** n

mud·dle·head·ed \,məd-°l-'hed-əd\ adj **1** : mentally confused **2** : BUNGLING

mud·guard \'məd-,gärd\ n : a guard over a wheel of a vehicle to catch or deflect mud

mud·sling·er \'məd-,sliŋ-ər\ n : one who uses invective esp. against a political opponent — **mud·sling·ing** n

mu·ez·zin \m(y)ü-'ez-°n\ n : a Muslim crier who calls the hour of daily prayer

1muff \'məf\ n : a warm tubular covering for the hands

2muff n **1** : a bungling performance; esp : a failure to hold a ball in attempting a catch — **muff** vb

muf·fin \'məf-ən\ n : a small soft biscuit baked in a cup-shaped pan

muf·fle \'məf-əl\ vb **1** : to wrap up so as to conceal or protect **2** : to wrap or pad with something to dull the sound of **3** : to keep down : SUPPRESS

muf·fler \'məf-lər\ n **1** : a scarf worn around the neck **2** : a device to deaden noise

muf·ti \'məf-tē\ n : civilian clothes

1mug \'məg\ n : a usu. metal or earthenware cylindrical drinking cup

2mug vb **mugged; mug·ging 1** : to make faces esp. in order to attract the attention of an audience **2** : PHOTOGRAPH

3mug vb **mugged; mug·ging** : to assault esp. by garroting

mug·gy \'məg-ē\ adj : being warm, damp, and close — **mug·gi·ness** n₁

mug·wump \'məg-,wəmp\ n : an independent in politics

Mu·ham·mad·an \mō-'ham-əd-ən, mü-\ n : MUSLIM — **Mu·ham·mad·an·ism** \-,iz-əm\ n

muk·luk \'mək-,lək\ n **1** : an Eskimo boot of sealskin or reindeer skin **2** : a boot with a soft leather sole worn over several pairs of socks

mu·lat·to \m(y)ü-'lat-ō\ n, pl -toes : a first-generation offspring of a Negro and a white; also : a person of mixed Caucasian and Negro ancestry

mul·ber·ry \'məl-,ber-ē\ n : a tree grown for its leaves that are used as food for silkworms or for its edible berrylike fruit; also : this fruit

mulch \'məlch\ n : a protective covering (as of straw or leaves) spread on the ground esp. to reduce evaporation and erosion, control weeds, or improve the soil — **mulch** vb

1mulct \'məlkt\ n : FINE, PENALTY

2mulct vb **1** : FINE **2** : DEFRAUD

1mule \'myül\ n **1** : a hybrid offspring of a male ass and a female horse **2** : a very stubborn person — **mul·ish** \'myü-lish\ adj — **mul·ish·ly** adv — **mul·ish·ness** n

2mule n : a slipper without sidepieces

mu·le·teer \,myü-lə-'tiər\ n : one who drives mules

1mull \'məl\ vb : PONDER, MEDITATE

2mull vb : to sweeten, spice, and heat ⟨~ed wine⟩

mul·lein \'məl-ən\ n : a tall herb with coarse woolly leaves and flowers in spikes

mul·let \'məl-ət\ n **1** : any of various largely gray marine food fishes **2** : any

of various red or golden mostly tropical marine food fishes

mul·li·gan \'məl-i-gən\ n : a stew chiefly of vegetables and meat or fish

mul·li·ga·taw·ny \,məl-i-gə-'tô-nē\ n : a soup usu. of chicken stock seasoned with curry

mul·lion \'məl-yən\ n : a vertical strip separating lights of a window

mul·ti· \,məl-ti, -,tī\ comb form **1** : many : multiple ⟨multi-unit⟩ **2** : many times over ⟨multimillionaire⟩

mul·ti·col·ored \,məl-ti-'kəl-ərd\ adj : having many colors

mul·ti·far·i·ous \,məl-tə-'far-ē-əs\ adj : having great variety : DIVERSE — **mul·ti·far·i·ous·ly** adv

mul·ti·form \'məl-ti-,fôrm\ adj : having many forms or appearances — **mul·ti·for·mi·ty** \,məl-ti-'fôr-mət-ē\ n

mul·ti·mil·lion·aire \,məl-ti-,mil-yə-'naər\ n : a person worth several million dollars

1mul·ti·ple \'məl-tə-pəl\ adj **1** : more than one; also : MANY **2** : VARIOUS, COMPLEX

2multiple n : the product of a quantity by an integer ⟨35 is a ~ of 7⟩

mul·ti·pli·ca·tion \,məl-tə-plə-'kā-shən\ n **1** : INCREASE **2** : a short method of finding out what would be the result of adding a figure the number of times indicated by another figure

mul·ti·plic·i·ty \,məl-tə-'plis-ət-ē\ n : a great number or variety

mul·ti·ply \'məl-tə-,plī\ vb **1** : to increase in number (as by breeding or propagating) **2** : to find the product of by a process of multiplication — **mul·ti·pli·er** \-,plī-(ə)r\ n

mul·ti·tude \-,t(y)üd\ n : a great number : CROWD — **mul·ti·tu·di·nous** \,məl-tə-'t(y)üd-(°-)nəs\ adj

1mum \'məm\ adj : SILENT

2mum n : CHRYSANTHEMUM

mum·ble \'məm-bəl\ vb : to speak in a low indistinct manner : MUTTER — **mumble** n — **mum·bler** \-b(ə-)lər\ n

mum·ble·ty·peg \'məm-bəl-tē-,peg\ n : a game in which the players try to flip a knife from various positions so that the blade will stick into the ground

mum·bo jum·bo \,məm-bō-'jəm-bō\ n **1** : a complicated ritual with elaborate trappings **2** : complicated activity or language that obscures and confuses

mum·mer \'məm-ər\ n **1** : an actor esp. in a pantomime **2** : one who goes merrymaking in disguise during festivals — **mum·mery** n

mum·my \'məm-ē\ n : a body embalmed and preserved after the manner of the ancient Egyptians — **mum·mi·fi·ca·tion** \,məm-i-fə-'kā-shən\ n — **mum·mi·fy** \'məm-i-,fī\ vb

mumps \'məmps\ n sing or pl : a virus disease marked by fever and swelling esp. of the salivary glands

munch \'mənch\ vb : to chew with a crunching sound

mun·dane \,mən-'dān\ adj **1** : of or relating to the world : WORLDLY **2** : having no concern for the ideal or heavenly — **mun·dane·ly** adv

mu·nic·i·pal \myù-'nis-ə-pəl\ *adj* **1** : of, relating to, or characteristic of a municipality **2** : restricted to one locality — **mu·nic·i·pal·ly** *adv*

mu·nic·i·pal·i·ty \myù-,nis-ə-'pal-ət-ē\ *n* : an urban political unit with corporate status and usu. powers of self-government

mu·nif·i·cent \myù-'nif-ə-sənt\ *adj* : liberal in giving : GENEROUS — **mu·nif·i·cence** \-səns\ *n*

mu·ni·tion \myù-'nish-ən\ *n* : material used in war for defense or attack : ARMAMENT — usu. used in pl.

¹mu·ral \'myùr-əl\ *adj* : of, relating to, or resembling a wall

²mural *n* : a mural painting — **mu·ral·ist** \-əst\ *n*

¹mur·der \'mərd-ər\ *n* **1** : the crime of unlawfully killing a person esp. with malice aforethought **2** : something unusually difficult or dangerous — **mur·der·ous** \-əs\ *adj* — **mur·der·ous·ly** *adv*

²murder *vb* **1** : to commit a murder; *also* : to kill brutally **2** : to put an end to **3** : MUTILATE, MANGLE — **mur·der·er** *n* — **mur·der·ess** \-əs\ *n*

murk \'mərk\ *n* : DARKNESS, GLOOM — **murk·i·ly** *adv* — **murk·i·ness** *n* — **murky** *adj*

mur·mur \'mər-mər\ *n* **1** : a muttered complaint **2** : a low indistinct and often continuous sound — **murmur** *vb* — **mur·mur·er** *n* — **mur·mur·ous** \-əs\ *adj*

mur·rain \'mər-ən\ *n* : PLAGUE, PESTILENCE

mus·ca·tel \,məs-kə-'tel\ *n* : a sweet dessert wine

¹mus·cle \'məs-əl\ *n* [L *musculus*, lit., little mouse, fr. *mus* mouse] **1** : body tissue consisting of long cells that contract when stimulated; *also* : an organ consisting of this tissue and functioning in moving a body part **2** : STRENGTH, BRAWN — **mus·cu·lar** \'məs-kyə-lər\ *adj* — **mus·cu·lar·i·ty** \,məs-kyə-'lar-ət-ē\ *n*

²muscle *vb* : to force one's way (~ in on another racketeer)

mus·cle-bound \'məs-əl-,baùnd\ *adj* : having some of the muscles abnormally enlarged and lacking in elasticity (as from excessive athletic exercise)

mus·cu·la·ture \'məs-kyə-lə-,chùr\ *n* : the muscles of the body or one of its parts

¹muse \'myüz\ *vb* : MEDITATE — **mus·ing·ly** *adv*

²muse \'myüz\ *n* : a source of inspiration

mu·sette \myù-'zet\ *n* : a small knapsack (**musette bag**) with a shoulder strap used esp. by soldiers for carrying provisions and personal belongings

mu·se·um \myù-'zē-əm\ *n* : an institution devoted to the procurement, care, and display of objects of lasting interest or value

¹mush \'məsh\ *n* **1** : cornmeal boiled in water **2** : sentimental drivel

²mush *vb* : to travel esp. over snow with a sled drawn by dogs

¹mush·room \-,rüm, -,rùm\ *n* : the fleshy usu. caplike fruiting body of various fungi esp. when edible

²mushroom *vb* **1** : to grow rapidly **2** : to spread out : EXPAND

mushy *adj* **1** : soft like mush **2** : weakly sentimental

mu·sic \'myü-zik\ *n* **1** : the science or art of combining tones into a composition having structure and continuity; *also* : vocal or instrumental sounds having rhythm, melody, or harmony **2** : an agreeable sound **3** : punishment for a misdeed — **mu·si·cal** \-zi-kəl\ *adj* — **mu·si·cal·ly** *adv*

mu·si·cale \,myü-zi-'kal\ *n* : a usu. private social gathering featuring a concert of music

mu·si·cian \myù-'zish-ən\ *n* : a composer or performer of music — **mu·si·cian·ly** *adj* — **mu·si·cian·ship** \-,ship\ *n*

mu·si·col·o·gy \,myü-zi-'käl-ə-jē\ *n* : a study of music as a branch of knowledge or field of research — **mu·si·co·log·i·cal** \-kə-'läj-i-kəl\ *adj* — **mu·si·col·o·gist** \-'käl-ə-jəst\ *n*

musk \'məsk\ *n* : a substance obtained esp. from a small Asiatic deer and used as a perfume fixative — **musk·i·ness** *n* — **musky** *adj*

mus·kel·lunge \'məs-kə-,lənj\ *n* : a large No. American pike prized as a sport fish

mus·ket \'məs-kət\ *n* : a heavy large-caliber shoulder firearm — **mus·ke·teer** \,məs-kə-'tiər\ *n*

mus·ket·ry \'məs-kə-trē\ *n* **1** : MUSKETS; *also* : musket fire **2** : MUSKETEERS

musk·mel·on \'məsk-,mel-ən\ *n* : a small round to oval melon related to the cucumber that has usu. a sweet edible green or orange flesh

musk·rat \'məs-,krat\ *n* : a large No. American water rodent with webbed feet and dark brown fur; *also* : its fur

Mus·lim \'məz-ləm\ *n* : an adherent of the religion founded by the Arab prophet Muhammad

mus·lin \'məz-lən\ *n* : a plain-woven sheer to coarse cotton fabric

¹muss \'məs\ *n* : a state of disorder : MESS — **muss·i·ly** *adv* — **muss·i·ness** *n* — **mussy** *adj*

²muss *vb* : to make untidy : DISARRANGE

mus·sel \'məs-əl\ *n* **1** : a dark edible saltwater bivalve mollusk **2** : any of various freshwater bivalve mollusks of central U. S. having shells with a pearly lining

Mus·sul·man \'məs-əl-mən\ *n*, *pl* -**men** *or* -**mans** : MUSLIM

must \(')məst\ *vb* — used as an auxiliary esp. to express a command, requirement, obligation, or necessity

mus·tache *var of* MOUSTACHE

mus·tang \'məs-,taŋ\ *n* : a small hardy naturalized horse of the western plains of America

mus·tard \'məs-tərd\ *n* **1** : a pungent yellow powder obtained from the seeds of an herb related to the turnips and used as a condiment or in medicine **2** : the mustard plant; *also* : a closely related plant

¹mus·ter \'məs-tər\ *vb* **1** : CONVENE, ASSEMBLE; *also* : to call the roll of **2** : ACCUMULATE **3** : to call forth : ROUSE **4** : to amount to : COMPRISE

²muster *n* **1** : an act of assembling (as for military inspection); *also* : critical examination **2** : an assembled group

musty \'məs-tē\ *adj* : MOLDY, STALE; *also* : tasting or smelling of damp or decay — **must·i·ly** *adv* — **must·i·ness** *n*

mu·ta·ble \'myüt-ə-bəl\ *adj* **1** : prone to change : FICKLE **2** : liable to mutation : VARIABLE — **mu·ta·bil·i·ty**

\,myüt-ə-'bil-ət-ē\ *n* — **mu·ta·ble·ness**
\'myüt-ə-bəl-nəs\ *n* — **mu·ta·bly** *adv*
mu·tate \'myü-,tāt\ *vb* 1 : to undergo or
cause to undergo mutation
mu·ta·tion \myü-'tā-shən\ *n* 1 : CHANGE
2 : a sudden and relatively permanent
change in a hereditary character; *also*
: one marked by such a change — **mu·
ta·tion·al** \-ºl\ *adj* — **mu·ta·tion·
al·ly** *adv* — **mu·ta·tive** \'myü-,tāt-iv\
adj
¹**mute** \'myüt\ *adj* 1 : unable to speak
: DUMB 2 : SILENT — **mute·ly** *adv*
— **mute·ness** *n*
²**mute** *n* 1 : a person who cannot or
does not speak 2 : a device on a
musical instrument that reduces, softens,
or muffles the tone
³**mute** *vb* : to muffle or reduce the sound
of
mu·ti·late \'myüt-ºl-,āt\ *vb* 1 : MAIM,
CRIPPLE 2 : to cut up or alter radically
so as to make imperfect — **mu·ti·la·
tion** \,myüt-ºl-'ā-shən\ *n* — **mu·ti·
la·tor** \'myüt-ºl-,āt-ər\ *n*
mu·ti·ny \'myüt-ºn-ē\ *n* : willful refusal to obey constituted authority; *esp*
: revolt against a superior officer
— **mu·ti·neer** \,myüt-ºn-'iər\ *n* —
mu·ti·nous \'myüt-ºn-əs\ *adj* — **mu·
ti·nous·ly** *adv*
mutt \'mət\ *n* : MONGREL, CUR
mut·ter \'mət-ər\ *vb* 1 : to speak indistinctly or with a low voice and lips
partly closed 2 : GRUMBLE — **mutter** *n*
mut·ton \'mət-ºn\ *n* : the flesh of a mature sheep — **mut·tony** *adj*
mu·tu·al \'myü-chə(-wə)l\ *adj* 1 : given
and received in equal amount ⟨~ trust⟩
2 : having the same feelings one for the
other ⟨~ enemies⟩ 3 : COMMON, JOINT
⟨a ~ friend⟩ — **mu·tu·al·ly** *adv*
muu-muu \'mü-,mü\ *n* : a loose dress of
Hawaiian origin for informal wear
¹**muz·zle** \'məz-əl\ *n* 1 : the nose and
jaws of an animal; *also* : a covering for
the muzzle to prevent the animal from
biting or eating 2 : the mouth of a gun
²**muzzle** *vb* 1 : to put a muzzle on 2 : to
restrain from expression : GAG
my \(')mī, mə\ *adj* 1 : of or relating to
me or myself 2 — used interjectionally
esp. to express surprise
my·col·o·gy \mī-'käl-ə-jē\ *n* : the
study of fungi — **my·co·log·i·cal**
\,mī-kə-'läj-i-kəl\ *adj* — **my·col·o·gist**
\mī-'käl-ə-jəst\ *n*
my·na or **my·nah** \'mī-nə\ *n* : any of
several Asiatic starlings; *esp* : a brown
crested bird sometimes taught to
mimic speech
my·o·pia \mī-'ō-pē-ə\ *n* : SHORT-

SIGHTEDNESS — **my·o·pic** \-'ō-pik,
-'äp-ik\ *adj* — **my·o·pi·cal·ly** *adv*
¹**myr·i·ad** \'mir-ē-əd\ *n* : an indefinitely
large number
²**myriad** *adj* : consisting of a very great
but indefinite number ⟨the ~ grains of
sand in a single handful⟩
myr·mi·don \'mər-mə-,dän\ *n* : a
loyal follower; *esp* : one who executes
orders without protest or pity
myrrh \'mər\ *n* : a fragrant aromatic
plant gum used in perfumes and formerly for incense
myr·tle \'mərt-ºl\ *n* : an evergreen
shrub of southern Europe with shiny
leaves, fragrant flowers, and black berries; *also* : PERIWINKLE
my·self \mī-'self, mə-\ *pron* : I, ME —
used reflexively, for emphasis, or in absolute constructions ⟨I hurt ~⟩ ⟨I ~
did it⟩ ⟨~busy, I sent him instead⟩
mys·tery \'mis-t(ə-)rē\ *n* 1 : a religious truth known by revelation alone
2 : something not understood or beyond
understanding 3 : enigmatic quality or
character — **mys·te·ri·ous** \mis-'tir-
ē-əs\ *adj* — **mys·te·ri·ous·ly** *adv* —
mys·te·ri·ous·ness *n*
¹**mys·tic** \'mis-tik\ *adj* 1 : of or relating
to mystics or mysticism 2 : MYSTERI-
OUS; *also* : MYSTIFYING
²**mystic** *n* : a person who experiences
mystical union or direct communion
with God or ultimate reality
mys·ti·cal \'mis-ti-kəl\ *adj* 1 : SPIR-
ITUAL, SYMBOLICAL 2 : of or relating to
an intimate knowledge of or direct communion with God (as through con-
templation or visions)
mys·ti·cism \'mis-tə-,siz-əm\ *n* : the
belief that direct knowledge of God or
ultimate reality is attainable through
immediate intuition or insight
mys·ti·fy \'mis-tə-,fī\ *vb* 1 : to perplex
the mind of : BEWILDER 2 : to make
mysterious — **mys·ti·fi·ca·tion** \,mis-
tə-fə-'kā-shən\ *n*
mys·tique \mi-'stēk\ *n* : a set of beliefs
and attitudes developing around an object or associated with a particular
group : CULT
myth \'mith\ *n* 1 : a usu. legendary
narrative that presents part of the beliefs of a people or explains a practice
or natural phenomenon 2 : an imaginary or unverifiable person or thing —
myth·i·cal \-i-kəl\ *adj*
my·thol·o·gy \mith-'äl-ə-jē\ *n* : a body
of myths and esp. of those dealing with
the gods and heroes of a people —
myth·o·log·i·cal \,mith-ə-'läj-i-kəl\
adj — **my·thol·o·gist** \mith-'äl-əst\ *n*

---

n \'en\ *n, often cap* : the 14th letter of
the English alphabet
-n — see -EN
nab \'nab\ *vb* **nabbed; nab·bing**
: SEIZE; *esp* : ARREST
na·bob \'nā-,bäb\ *n* : a man of great
wealth or prominence
na·celle \nə-'sel\ *n* : an enclosed shelter
on an aircraft (as for an engine)

na·cre \'nā-kər\ *n* : MOTHER-OF-PEARL
na·dir \'nā-,diər, -dər\ *n* 1 : the point
of the celestial sphere that is directly
opposite the zenith and vertically downward from the observer 2 : the lowest
point ⟨our hopes had reached their ~⟩
¹**nag** \'nag\ *n* : HORSE; *esp* : an old or
decrepit horse
²**nag** *vb* **nagged; nag·ging** 1 : to find

ə **abut; ** º **kitten; ** ər **further; ** a **back; ** ā **bake; ** ä **cot, cart; ** aü **out; ** ch **chin;
** e **less; ** ē **easy; ** g **gift; ** i **trip; ** ī **life; ** j **joke; ** ŋ **sing; ** ō **flow; ** ȯ **flaw; ** ȯi **coin;
** th **thin; ** th **this; ** ü **loot; ** u **foot; ** y **yet; ** yü **few; ** yu **furious; ** zh **vision**

fault incessantly : COMPLAIN **2** : to irritate by constant scolding or urging **3** : to be a continuing source of annoyance ⟨a *nagging* toothache⟩

na·iad \'nā-əd\ *n, pl* **na·iads** *or* **na·ia·des** \-ə-ˌdēz\ : one of the nymphs in ancient mythology living in lakes, rivers, springs, and fountains

na·if \nä-'ēf\ *adj* : NAÏVE

¹nail \'nāl\ *n* **1** : a horny sheath protecting the end of each finger and toe in man and related primates **2** : a slender pointed and headed piece of metal driven into or through something for fastening

²nail *vb* : to fasten with or as if with a nail

nail down *vb* : to settle or establish clearly and unmistakably

nain·sook \'nān-ˌsůk\ *n* : a soft lightweight muslin

na·ive *also* **na·ïve** \nä-'ēv\ *adj* **1** : marked by unaffected simplicity : ARTLESS, INGENUOUS **2** : CREDULOUS — **na·ive·ly** *adv* — **na·ive·ness** *n*

na·ive·té *also* **na·ïve·té** \ˌnä-ˌēv(-ə)-'tā\ *n* **1** : the quality or state of being naïve **2** : a naïve remark or action

na·ive·ty *also* **na·ïve·ty** \nä-'ēv-(ə-)tē\ *n* : NAÏVETÉ

na·ked \'nā-kəd, 'nek-əd\ *adj* **1** : having no clothes on : NUDE **2** : UNSHEATHED ⟨a ~ sword⟩ **3** : lacking a usual or natural covering (as of foliage or feathers) **4** : PLAIN, UNADORNED ⟨the ~ truth⟩ **5** : not aided by artificial means ⟨seen by the ~ eye⟩ — **na·ked·ly** *adv* — **na·ked·ness** *n*

nam·by-pam·by \ˌnam-bē-'pam-bē\ *adj* **1** : INSIPID **2** : WEAK, INDECISIVE

¹name \'nām\ *n* **1** : a word or combination of words by which a person or thing is regularly known **2** : a descriptive often disparaging epithet ⟨call someone ~s⟩ **3** : REPUTATION; *esp* : distinguished reputation ⟨made a ~ for himself⟩ **4** : FAMILY, CLAN ⟨was a disgrace to his ~⟩ **5** : semblance as opposed to reality ⟨a friend in ~ only⟩

²name *vb* **1** : to give a name to : CALL **2** : to mention or identify by name **3** : NOMINATE, APPOINT **4** : to decide upon : CHOOSE **5** : to speak about : MENTION ⟨~ a price⟩ — **name·able** *adj*

³name *adj* **1** : of, relating to, or bearing a name ⟨~ tag⟩ **2** : having an established reputation ⟨~ brands⟩

name day *n* : the day of the saint whose name one bears

name·less \'nām-ləs\ *adj* **1** : having no name **2** : not marked with a name ⟨a ~ grave⟩ **3** : not known by name : UNKNOWN, ANONYMOUS ⟨a ~ hero⟩ **4** : not to be described ⟨~ fears⟩ ⟨~ indignities⟩ — **name·less·ly** *adv*

name·ly \-lē\ *adv* : that is to say : AS ⟨the cat family, ~, lions, tigers, and similar animals⟩

name·plate \-ˌplāt\ *n* : a plate or plaque bearing a name ⟨~ of a resident⟩

name·sake \-ˌsāk\ *n* : one that has the same name as another; *esp* : one named after another

nan·keen *also* **nan·kin** \nan-'kēn\ *n* : a durable brownish yellow cotton fabric orig. woven by hand in China

nan·ny goat \'nan-ē-\ *n* : a female domestic goat

¹nap \'nap\ *vb* **napped; nap·ping 1** : to sleep briefly esp. during the day : DOZE **2** : to be off guard ⟨was caught *napping*⟩

²nap *n* : a short sleep esp. during the day : SNOOZE

³nap *n* : a soft downy fibrous surface (as on yarn and cloth) — **nap·less** *adj*

na·palm \'nā-ˌpä(l)m\ *n* **1** : a thickener used in jelling gasoline esp. for incendiary bombs and flamethrowers **2** : fuel jelled with napalm

nape \'nāp, 'nap\ *n* : the back of the neck

na·pery \'nā-p(ə-)rē\ *n* : household linen esp. for the table

naph·tha \'naf-thə, 'nap-\ *n* **1** : PETROLEUM **2** : any of various liquids derived chiefly from petroleum and used in dry cleaning and in making varnish

naph·tha·lene \-ˌlēn\ *n* : a crystalline substance obtained from coal tar used in making dyes and chemicals and as a defense against moths

nap·kin \'nap-kən\ *n* **1** : a piece of material (as cloth or paper) used at table to wipe the lips or fingers and protect the clothes **2** : a small cloth or towel

na·po·leon \nə-'pōl-yən\ *n* **1** : a French 20-franc gold coin **2** : an oblong pastry with a filling of cream, custard, or jelly between layers of puff paste

Na·po·le·on·ic \nə-ˌpō-lē-'än-ik\ *adj* : of, relating to, or characteristic of Napoleon I or his family

nar·cis·sism \'när-sə-ˌsiz-əm\ *n* [fr. *Narcissus*, beautiful boy of Greek mythology who fell in love with his own image] : undue dwelling on one's own self or attainments — **nar·cis·sist** \-səst\ *n or adj*

nar·cis·sus \när-'sis-əs\ *n, pl* **-cis·sus** *or* **-cis·sus·es** *or* **-cis·si** \-'sis-ˌī, -ˌē\ : DAFFODIL; *esp* : one with short-tubed flowers usu. borne separately

nar·co·sis \när-'kō-səs\ *n, pl* **-co·ses** \-ˌsēz\ : a state of stupor, unconsciousness, or arrested activity produced by the influence of chemicals (as narcotics)

nar·cot·ic \när-'kät-ik\ *n* : a drug (as opium) that dulls the senses and induces sleep — **narcotic** *adj*

nar·co·tize \'när-kə-ˌtīz\ *vb* **1** : to treat with or subject to a narcotic; *also* : to put into a state of narcosis **2** : to soothe to unconsciousness or unawareness

nard \'närd\ *n* : a fragrant ointment of the ancients : SPIKENARD

nar·is \'nar-əs\ *n, pl* **nar·es** \-ˌēz\ : an opening of the nose : NOSTRIL

nar·rate \'nar-ˌāt\ *vb* : to recite the details of (as a story) : RELATE, TELL — **nar·ra·tion** \na-'rā-shən\ *n* — **nar·ra·tor** \'nar-ˌāt-ər\ *n*

nar·ra·tive \'nar-ət-iv\ *n* **1** : something that is narrated : STORY **2** : the art or practice of narrating

¹nar·row \'nar-ō\ *adj* **1** : of slender or less than standard width **2** : limited in size or scope : RESTRICTED **3** : not liberal in views : PREJUDICED **4** : interpreted or interpreting strictly ⟨a ~ view⟩ **5** : CLOSE ⟨a ~ escape⟩; *also* : barely successful ⟨won by a ~ margin⟩ — **nar·row·ly** *adv* — **nar·row·ness** *n*

²narrow *n* : a narrow passage : STRAIT — usu. used in pl.

³narrow *vb* : to lessen in width or extent

nar·row-mind·ed \ˌnar-ō-'mīn-dəd\ *adj* : not liberal or broad-minded : BIGOTED

nar·thex \'när-ˌtheks\ *n* : a vestibule in a church

nar·whal \'när-,hwäl, 'när-wəl\ *n* **:** an arctic sea animal about 20 feet long that is related to the dolphin and in the male has a long twisted ivory tusk

¹na·sal \'nā-zəl\ *n* **1 :** a nasal part **2 :** a nasal consonant or vowel

²nasal *adj* **1 :** of or relating to the nose **2 :** uttered through the nose — **na·sal·ly** *adv*

nas·cent \'nas-°nt, 'nās-\ *adj* **:** coming into existence **:** beginning to grow or develop — **nas·cence** \-°ns\ *n*

na·so·phar·ynx \,nā-zō-'far-iŋks\ *n* **:** the upper part of the pharynx continuous with the nasal passages — **na·so·pha·ryn·geal** \-fə-'rin-j(ē-)əl, -,far-ən-'jē-əl\ *adj*

nas·tur·tium \nə-'stər-shəm, na-\ *n* **:** a watery-stemmed herb with showy spurred flowers and pungent seeds

nas·ty \'nas-tē\ *adj* **1 :** FILTHY **2 :** INDECENT, OBSCENE **3 :** DISAGREEABLE ⟨~ weather⟩ **4 :** MEAN, ILL-NATURED ⟨a ~ temper⟩ **5 :** DISHONORABLE ⟨a ~ trick⟩ **6 :** HARMFUL, DANGEROUS ⟨took a ~ fall⟩ — **nas·ti·ly** *adv* — **nas·ti·ness** *n*

na·tal \'nāt-°l\ *adj* **1 :** NATIVE ⟨his ~ place⟩ **2 :** of, relating to, or present at birth ⟨~ defects⟩

na·tal·i·ty \nā-'tal-ət-ē\ *n* **:** BIRTHRATE

na·ta·to·ri·al \,nāt-ə-'tōr-ē-əl\ *or* **na·ta·to·ry** \'nāt-ə-,tōr-ē\ *adj* **1 :** of or relating to swimming **2 :** adapted to or characterized by swimming

na·ta·to·ri·um \,nāt-ə-'tōr-ē-əm\ *n* **:** a swimming pool esp. indoors

na·tion \'nā-shən\ *n* **1 :** NATIONALITY **5 ;** *also* **:** a politically organized nationality **2 :** a community of people composed of one or more nationalities with its own territory and government **3 :** a territorial division containing a body of people of one or more nationalities **4 :** a federation of tribes (as of American Indians) — **na·tion·hood** \-,hùd\ *n*

¹na·tion·al \'nash-(ə-)nəl\ *adj* **1 :** of or relating to a nation **2 :** comprising or characteristic of a nationality **3 :** FEDERAL **3** — **na·tion·al·ly** *adv*

²national *n* **1 :** one who is under the protection of a nation without regard to the more formal status of citizen or subject **2 :** an organization (as a labor union) having local units throughout a nation

National Guard *n* **:** a militia force recruited by each state, equipped by the federal government, and jointly maintained subject to the call of either

na·tion·al·ism \'nash-(ə-)nə-,liz-əm\ *n* **:** devotion to national interests, unity, and independence esp. of one nation above all others

na·tion·al·ist \-ləst\ *n* **1 :** an advocate of or believer in nationalism **2** *cap* **:** a member of a political party or group advocating national independence or strong national government — **nationalist** *adj, often cap* — **na·tion·al·is·tic** \,nash-(ə-)nə-'lis-tik\ *adj*

na·tion·al·i·ty \,nash-ə-'nal-ət-ē\ *n* **1 :** national character **2 :** national status; *esp* **:** a legal relationship involving allegiance of an individual and his protection by the state **3 :** membership in a particular nation **4 :** political

independence or existence as a separate nation **5 :** a people having a common origin, tradition, and language and capable of forming a state **6 :** an ethnic group within a larger unit (as a nation)

na·tion·al·ize \'nash-(ə-)nə-,līz\ *vb* **1 :** to make national **:** make a nation of **2 :** to remove from private ownership and place under government control ⟨~ the railroads⟩ — **na·tion·al·iza·tion** \,nash-(ə-)nə-'zā-shən\ *n*

na·tion·wide \,nā-shən-'wīd\ *adj* **:** extending throughout a nation

¹na·tive \'nāt-iv\ *adj* **1 :** INBORN, NATURAL **2 :** born in a particular place or country **3 :** belonging to a person because of the place or circumstances of his birth ⟨his ~ language⟩ **4 :** grown, produced, or originating in a particular place **:** INDIGENOUS

²native *n* **:** one that is native; *esp* **:** a person who belongs to a particular country by birth

Na·tiv·i·ty \nə-'tiv-ət-ē, nā-\ *n* **1 :** the birth of Christ **2 :** CHRISTMAS **3** *not cap* **:** the process or circumstances of being born **:** BIRTH

nat·ty \'nat-ē\ *adj* **:** trimly neat and tidy **:** SMART **2 :** SMART — **nat·ti·ly** *adv* — **nat·ti·ness** *n*

¹nat·u·ral \'nach-(ə-)rəl\ *adj* **1 :** determined by nature **:** INBORN, INNATE ⟨~ ability⟩ **2 :** BORN ⟨a ~ fool⟩ **3 :** ILLEGITIMATE **4 :** HUMAN **5 :** of or relating to nature **6 :** not artificial **7 :** being simple and sincere **:** not affected **8 :** LIFELIKE **9 :** having neither sharps nor flats in the key signature **syn** genuous, naive, unsophisticated, artless — **nat·u·ral·ness** *n*

²natural *n* **1 :** IDIOT **2 :** a character placed on a line or space of the musical staff to nullify the effect of a preceding sharp or flat **3 :** one obviously suitable for a specific purpose

natural history *n* **:** the study of natural objects esp. from an amateur or popular point of view

nat·u·ral·ism \-,iz-əm\ *n* **1 :** action, inclination, or thought based only on natural desires and instincts **2 :** a doctrine that denies a supernatural explanation of the origin, development, or end of the universe and holds that scientific laws account for everything in nature **3 :** realism in art and literature that emphasizes photographic exactness in portraying what actually exists — **nat·u·ral·is·tic** \,nach-(ə-)rəl-'is-tik\ *adj*

nat·u·ral·ist \'nach-(ə-)rəl-əst\ *n* **1 :** one that advocates or practices naturalism **2 :** a student of animals or plants esp. in the field

nat·u·ral·ize \-,īz\ *vb* **1 :** to become or cause to become established as if native ⟨~ new forage crops⟩ **2 :** to confer the rights and privileges of a native citizen on — **nat·u·ral·iza·tion** \,nach-(ə-)rəl-ə-'zā-shən\ *n*

nat·u·ral·ly \'nach-(ə-)rəl-ē, -ər-lē\ *adv* **1 :** by nature **:** by natural character or ability **2 :** as might be expected **3 :** without artificial aid; *also* **:** without affectation **4 :** REALISTICALLY

natural science *n* **:** a science (as physics, chemistry, or biology) that deals with matter, energy, and their interrelations and transformations or with objectively measurable phenomena

na·ture \'nā-chər\ *n* **1** : the peculiar quality or basic constitution of a person or thing **2** : KIND, SORT **3** : DISPOSITION, TEMPERAMENT **4** : the physical universe ⟨one's natural instincts or way of life ⟨quirks of human ∼⟩; *also* : primitive state ⟨a return to ∼⟩ **6** : natural scenery or environment ⟨beauties of ∼⟩

naught \'nȯt, 'nät\ *n* **1** : NOTHING **2** : the arithmetical symbol 0 : ZERO

naugh·ty \-ē\ *adj* **1** : guilty of disobedience or misbehavior **2** : lacking in taste or propriety — **naught·i·ly** *adv* — **naught·i·ness** *n*

nau·sea \'nȯ-zē-ə, 'nȯ-shə\ *n* **1** : sickness of the stomach with a desire to vomit **2** : extreme disgust — **nau·seous** \-shəs, -zē-əs\ *adj*

nau·se·ate \'nȯ-z(h)ē-,āt, -s(h)ē-\ *vb* : to affect or become affected with nausea — **nau·se·at·ing·ly** \-,āt-iŋ-lē\ *adv*

nautch \'nȯch\ *n* : an entertainment in India consisting chiefly of dancing by professional dancing girls

nau·ti·cal \'nȯt-i-kəl\ *adj* : of or relating to seamen, navigation, or ships — **nau·ti·cal·ly** *adv*

nautical mile *n* : an international unit of distance equal to about 6076.1 feet

nau·ti·lus \'nȯt-ᵊl-əs\ *n, pl* **-lus·es** *or* **-li** \-ᵊl-ī, -ᵊl-,ī\ : a sea mollusk related to the octopuses but having a spiral shell divided into chambers

Nav·a·ho *or* **Nav·a·jo** \'nav-ə-,hō, 'näv-\ *n* **1** : a member of an Indian people of northern New Mexico and Arizona **2** : the language of the Navaho people

na·val \'nā-vəl\ *adj* : of, relating to, or possessing a navy

naval stores *n pl* : products (as pitch, turpentine, or rosin) obtained from resinous conifers (as pines)

nave \'nāv\ *n* : the central part of a church running lengthwise

na·vel \'nā-vəl\ *n* : a depression in the middle of the abdomen that marks the point of attachment of fetus and mother

nav·i·ga·ble \'nav-i-gə-bəl\ *adj* **1** : capable of being navigated ⟨a ∼ river⟩ **2** : capable of being steered ⟨a ∼ balloon⟩ — **nav·i·ga·bil·i·ty** \,nav-i-gə-'bil-ət-ē\ *n*

nav·i·gate \'nav-ə-,gāt\ *vb* **1** : to sail on or through ⟨∼ the Atlantic ocean⟩ **2** : to steer or direct the course of a ship or aircraft **3** : MOVE; *esp* : WALK ⟨could hardly ∼⟩ — **nav·i·ga·tion** \,nav-ə-'gā-shən\ *n* — **nav·i·ga·tor** \'nav-ə-,gāt-ər\ *n*

na·vy \'nā-vē\ *n* **1** : the warships belonging to a nation ⟨*often cap* : a nation's organization for naval warfare

¹**nay** \'nā\ *adv* **1** : NO — used in oral voting **2** : INDEED, TRULY

²**nay** *n* : a negative vote; *also* : a person casting such a vote

na·ya pai·sa \nə-,yä-pī-'sä\ *n, pl* **na·ye pai·se** \-,yä-pī-'sä\ — see MONEY table

Na·zi \'nät-sē\ *n* : a member of a German fascist party controlling Germany from 1933 to 1945 under Adolf Hitler — **Nazi** *adj* — **Na·zism** \'nät-,siz-əm\ *or* **Na·zi·ism** \-sē-,iz-əm\ *n*

Ne·an·der·thal \nē-'an-dər-,t(h)ȯl\ *adj* : of, relating to, or being an extinct primitive Old World man; *also* : crudely primitive (as in manner or conduct)

neap \'nēp\ *adj* : being either of two tides **(neap tides)** that are the least in the lunar month

¹**near** \'niər\ *adv* **1** : at, within, or to a short distance or time **2** : ALMOST, NEARLY

²**near** *prep* : close to

³**near** *adj* **1** : closely related or associated; *also* : INTIMATE **2** : not far away; *also* : being the closer or left-hand member of a pair **3** : barely avoided ⟨a ∼ accident⟩ **4** : DIRECT, SHORT ⟨by the ∼*est* route⟩ **5** : STINGY **6** : not real but very like ⟨∼ silk⟩ — **near·ly** *adv* — **near·ness** *n*

⁴**near** *vb* : to draw near : APPROACH

near·by \niər-'bī\ *adv (or adj)* : close at hand

near·sight·ed \'niər-'sīt-əd\ *adj* : seeing distinctly at short distances only : SHORTSIGHTED — **near·sight·ed·ness** *n*

neat \'nēt\ *adj* **1** : not mixed or diluted ⟨∼ brandy⟩ **2** : marked by tasteful simplicity **3** : PRECISE, SYSTEMATIC **4** : SKILLFUL, ADROIT **5** : being orderly and clean **6** : CLEAR, NET ⟨∼ profit⟩ **7** *slang* : FINE, ADMIRABLE

neath \'nēth\ *prep, dial* : BENEATH

neat·herd \'nēt-,hərd\ *n* : HERDSMAN

neat's-foot oil \'nēts-,fut-\ *n* : a pale yellow fatty oil made esp. from the bones of cattle and used chiefly as a leather dressing

neb \'neb\ *n* **1** : the beak of a bird or tortoise : BILL; *also* : NOSE, SNOUT **2** : NIB, TIP

neb·u·la \'neb-yə-lə\ *n, pl* **-las** *or* **-lae** \-,lē\ **1** : any of many vast cloudlike masses of gas or dust among the stars **2** : GALAXY — **neb·u·lar** \-lər\ *adj*

neb·u·lize \-,līz\ *vb* : to reduce to a fine spray — **neb·u·liz·er** *n*

neb·u·los·i·ty \,neb-yə-'läs-ət-ē\ *n* **1** : the quality or state of being nebulous **2** : nebulous matter : NEBULA

neb·u·lous \'neb-yə-ləs\ *adj* **1** : HAZY, INDISTINCT ⟨a ∼ memory⟩ **2** : of or relating to a nebula

¹**nec·es·sary** \'nes-ə-,ser-ē\ *adj* **1** : INEVITABLE, INESCAPABLE; *also* : CERTAIN **2** : PREDETERMINED **3** : COMPULSORY **4** : positively needed : INDISPENSABLE *syn* requisite, essential — **nec·es·sar·i·ly** \,nes-ə-'ser-ə-lē\ *adv*

²**necessary** *n* : an indispensable item : ESSENTIAL ⟨the *necessaries* of life⟩

ne·ces·si·tate \ni-'ses-ə-,tāt\ *vb* : to make necessary : FORCE, COMPEL

ne·ces·si·tous \ni-'ses-ət-əs\ *adj* **1** : NEEDY, IMPOVERISHED **2** : URGENT **3** : NECESSARY

ne·ces·si·ty \ni-'ses-ət-ē\ *n* **1** : very great need **2** : something that is necessary **3** : WANT, POVERTY **4** : conditions that cannot be changed

neck \'nek\ *n* **1** : the part of the body connecting the head and the trunk **2** : the part of a garment covering or near to the neck **3** : something like a neck in shape or position : a relatively narrow part ⟨∼ of a bottle⟩ ⟨∼ of land⟩ **4** : a narrow margin esp. of victory ⟨won by a ∼⟩

neck and neck *adj (or adv)* : very close (as in a race)

neck·band \'nek-,band\ *n* **1** : a band worn around the neck **2** : a part of a garment that encircles the neck

neck·er·chief \'nek-ər-chəf, -,chēf\ *n, pl* **-chiefs** *also* **-chieves** \-,chēvz\ : a square of cloth worn folded about the neck like a scarf

neck·lace \'nek-ləs\ *n* : an ornamental chain or a string (as of jewels or beads) worn around the neck

neck·line \-,līn\ *n* : the outline of the neck opening of a garment

neck·piece \-,pēs\ *n* : an article of apparel (as a fur scarf) worn about the neck

neck·tie \-,tī\ *n* : a narrow length of material worn about the neck and tied in front

ne·crol·o·gy \nə-'kräl-ə-jē\ *n* 1 : a list of the dead 2 : OBITUARY

nec·ro·man·cy \'nek-rə-,man-sē\ *n* 1 : the art or practice of conjuring up the spirits of the dead for purposes of magically revealing the future 2 : MAGIC, SORCERY — **nec·ro·man·cer** \-sər\ *n*

ne·crop·o·lis \nə-'kräp-ə-ləs\ *n*, *pl* **-lis·es** *or* **-les** \-,lēz\ : CEMETERY; *esp* : a large elaborate cemetery of an ancient city

ne·cro·sis \nə-'krō-səs\ *n*, *pl* **-cro·ses** \-'krō-,sēz\ : usu. local death of body tissue — **ne·crot·ic** \-'krät-ik\ *adj*

nec·tar \'nek-tər\ *n* 1 : the drink of the Greek and Roman gods; *also* : any delicious drink 2 : a sweet plant secretion that is the raw material of honey

nec·tar·ine \,nek-tə-'rēn\ *n* : a smooth-skinned peach

née *or* **nee** \'nā\ *adj* : BORN — used to identify a woman by her maiden family name

¹need \'nēd\ *n* 1 : OBLIGATION ⟨no ~ to hurry⟩ 2 : a lack of something requisite, desirable, or useful 3 : a condition requiring supply or relief ⟨when the ~ arises⟩ 4 : POVERTY ⟨help those in ~⟩ **syn** necessity, exigency

²need *vb* 1 : to be in want 2 : to have cause or occasion for : REQUIRE ⟨he ~s advice⟩ 3 : to be under obligation or necessity ⟨we ~ to know the truth⟩

need·ful \-fəl\ *adj* : NECESSARY, REQUISITE

¹nee·dle \'nēd-⁷l\ *n* 1 : a slender pointed usu. steel implement used in sewing 2 : a slender rod (as for knitting, controlling a small opening, or transmitting vibrations to or from a recording) ⟨a phonograph ~⟩ 3 : a needle-shaped leaf (as of a pine) 4 : a slender bar of magnetized steel used in a compass; *also* : an indicator on a dial 5 : a slender hollow instrument by which material is introduced into or withdrawn from the body

²needle *vb* : PROD, GOAD; *esp* : to incite to action by repeated gibes

nee·dle·point \-,pȯint\ *n* 1 : lace worked with a needle over a paper pattern 2 : embroidery done on canvas across counted threads — **needlepoint** *adj*

need·less \'nēd-ləs\ *adj* : UNNECESSARY — **need·less·ly** *adv* — **need·less·ness** *n*

nee·dle·wom·an \'nēd-⁷l-,wu̇m-ən\ *n* : a woman who does needlework; *esp* : SEAMSTRESS

nee·dle·work \-,wərk\ *n* : work done with a needle; *esp* : work (as embroidery) other than plain sewing

needs \'nēdz\ *adv* : of necessity : NEC-

ESSARILY ⟨must ~ be recognized⟩

needy \'nēd-ē\ *adj* : being in want : POVERTY-STRICKEN

ne'er \'neər\ *adv* : NEVER

ne'er-do-well \'neərd-ü-,wel\ *n* : an idle worthless person — **ne'er-do-well** *adj*

ne·far·i·ous \ni-'far-ē-əs\ *adj* : very wicked : EVIL — **ne·far·i·ous·ly** *adv*

ne·gate \ni-'gāt\ *vb* 1 : to deny the existence or truth of 2 : to cause to be ineffective or invalid : NULLIFY

ne·ga·tion \ni-'gā-shən\ *n* 1 : the action of negating : DENIAL 2 : a negative doctrine or statement : CONTRADICTION

¹neg·a·tive \'neg-ət-iv\ *adj* 1 : marked by denial, prohibition, or refusal ⟨a ~ reply⟩ 2 : not positive or constructive; *esp* : not affirming the presence of what is sought or suspected to be present ⟨a ~ test⟩ 3 : less than zero ⟨a ~ number⟩ 4 : being or relating to the kind of electricity in silk when silk is used to rub glass; *also* : charged with negative electricity : having a preponderance of electrons ⟨a ~ particle⟩ 5 : having lights and shadows opposite to what they were in the original photographic subject — **neg·a·tive·ly** *adv*

²negative *n* 1 : a negative word or statement 2 : a negative vote or reply; *also* : REFUSAL 3 : something that is the opposite or negation of something else 4 : the side that votes or argues for the opposition (as in a debate) 5 : the platelike part to which the current flows from the external circuit in a discharging storage battery 6 : a negative photographic image on transparent material

³negative *vb* 1 : to refuse to accept or approve 2 : to vote against : VETO 3 : DISPROVE

neg·a·tiv·ism *n* : an attitude of skepticism and denial of nearly everything affirmed or suggested by others

¹ne·glect \ni-'glekt\ *vb* 1 : DISREGARD 2 : to leave undone or unattended to esp. through carelessness **syn** omit, ignore, overlook, slight, forget

²neglect *n* 1 : an act or instance of neglecting something 2 : the condition of being neglected — **ne·glect·ful** \-fəl\ *adj*

neg·li·gee *also* **neg·li·gé** \,neg-lə-'zhā\ *n* 1 : a woman's long flowing dressing gown 2 : carelessly informal or incomplete attire

neg·li·gent \'neg-li-jənt\ *adj* : marked by neglect **syn** neglectful, remiss — **neg·li·gence** \-jəns\ *n* — **neg·li·gent·ly** *adv*

neg·li·gi·ble \'neg-li-jə-bəl\ *adj* : fit to be neglected or disregarded : TRIFLING

ne·go·tiant \ni-'gō-sh(ē-)ənt\ *n* : NEGOTIATOR

ne·go·ti·ate \ni-'gō-shē-,āt\ *vb* 1 : to confer with another so as to arrive at the settlement of some matter; *also* : to arrange for or bring about by such conferences ⟨~ a treaty⟩ 2 : to transfer to another by delivery or endorsement in return for equivalent value ⟨~ a check⟩ 3 : to get through, around, or over successfully ⟨~ a turn⟩ — **ne·go·tia·ble** \-sh(ē-)ə-bəl\ *adj* — **ne·go·ti·a·tion**

ne·go·ti·a·tor \ni-'gō-s(h)ē-'ā-shən\ n — **ne·go·ti·a·tor** \-'gō-shē-,āt-ər\ n

Ne·gro \'nē-grō\ n, pl **-groes** : a member of the black race — **Negro** adj — **ne·groid** \-,groid\ n or adj, often cap

ne·gus \'nē-gəs\ n : a beverage of wine, hot water, sugar, lemon juice, and nutmeg

neigh \'nā\ n : a loud prolonged cry of a horse — **neigh** vb

¹neigh·bor \'nā-bər\ n [OE nēahgebūr, fr. nēah near, nigh + gebūr dweller] **1** : one living or located near another **2** : FELLOWMAN — often used as a term of address

²neighbor vb : to be next to or near to : border on

neigh·bor·hood \-,hùd\ n **1** : NEARNESS **2** : a place or region near : VICINITY; also : an approximate amount, extent, or degree (costs in the ~ of $10) **3** : the people living near one another **4** : a section lived in by neighbors and usu. having distinguishing characteristics

neigh·bor·ing \'nā-b(ə-)riŋ\ adj : living or being near : ADJOINING, ADJACENT

neigh·bor·ly \-bər-lē\ adj : befitting congenial neighbors; esp : FRIENDLY — **neigh·bor·li·ness** n

¹nei·ther \'nē-thər, 'nī-\ pron : neither one : not the one and not the other (~ of the two)

²neither conj **1** : not either (~ good nor bad) **2** : NOR (~ did I)

³neither adj : not either (~ hand)

nel·son \'nel-sən\ n : a wrestling hold marked by the application of leverage against an opponent's arm, neck, and head

nem·e·sis \'nem-ə-səs\ n, pl **-e·ses** \-ə-,sēz\ **1** : one that inflicts retribution or vengeance **2** : a formidable and usu. victorious rival **3** : an act or effect of retribution; also : CURSE

neo·clas·sic \,nē-ō-'klas-ik\ adj : of or relating to a revival or adaptation of the classical style esp. in literature, art, or music — **neo·clas·si·cal** \-i-kəl\ adj

neo·dym·i·um \,nē-ō-'dim-ē-əm\ n : a metallic chemical element

ne·ol·o·gism \nē-'äl-ə-,jiz-əm\ n : a new word or expression

ne·ol·o·gy \-jē\ n : the use of a new word or expression or of an established word in a new or different sense

ne·on \'nē-,än\ n : a gaseous chemical element that gives a reddish glow in a vacuum tube and is used in display signs

neo·na·tal \,nē-ō-'nāt-ᵊl\ adj : of, relating to, or affecting the newborn — **neo·na·tal·ly** adv — **ne·o·nate** \'nē-ō-,nāt\ n

ne·o·phyte \'nē-ə-,fīt\ n **1** : a new convert : PROSELYTE **2** : BEGINNER, NOVICE

neo·plasm \'nē-ə-,plaz-əm\ n : TUMOR — **neo·plas·tic** \,nē-ə-'plas-tik\ adj

ne·o·te·ny \,nē-ə-,tē-nē\ n : attainment of sexual maturity during the larval stage; also : retention of immature characters in adulthood

ne·pen·the \nə-'pen-thē\ n **1** : a potion used by the ancients to dull pain and sorrow **2** : something capable of making one forget grief or suffering

neph·ew \'nef-yü, chiefly Brit 'nev-\ n : a son of one's brother, sister, brother-in-law, or sister-in-law

ne·phri·tis \ni-'frīt-əs\ n : kidney inflammation

ne plus ul·tra \,nē-,pləs-'əl-trə\ n : the highest point capable of being attained : ACME

nep·o·tism \'nep-ə-,tiz-əm\ n : favoritism (as in the distribution of political offices) shown to a relative

Nep·tune \'nep-,t(y)ün\ n : the 4th largest of the planets and the one 8th in order of distance from the sun — **Nep·tu·ni·an** \nep-'t(y)ü-nē-ən\ adj

nep·tu·ni·um \nep-'t(y)ü-nē-əm\ n : a short-lived radioactive chemical element artificially produced as a by-product of plutonium

Ne·re·id \'nir-ē-əd\ n : any of the sea nymphs held in Greek mythology to be the daughters of the sea-god Nereus

¹nerve \'nərv\ n **1** : one of the strands of nervous tissue that carry nervous impulses to and fro between the brain and spinal cord and every part of the body **2** : power of endurance or control : FORTITUDE; also : BOLDNESS, DARING **3** pl : NERVOUSNESS, HYSTERIA **4** : a vein of a leaf or insect wing — **nerve·less** \-ləs\ adj

²nerve vb : to give strength or courage to

nerve gas n : a war gas damaging esp. to the nervous and respiratory systems

nerve-rack·ing or **nerve-wrack·ing** \-,rak-iŋ\ adj : extremely trying on the nerves

ner·vous \'nər-vəs\ adj **1** : FORCIBLE, SPIRITED **2** : of, relating to, or made up of nerve cells or nerves **3** : easily excited or annoyed : JUMPY **4** : TIMID, APPREHENSIVE (a ~ smile) **5** : UNEASY, UNSTEADY — **ner·vous·ly** adv — **ner·vous·ness** n

nervy adj **1** : showing calm courage : BOLD **2** : marked by impudence or presumption : BRASH (a ~ salesman) **3** : EXCITABLE, NERVOUS

-ness \nəs\ n suffix : state : condition : quality : degree (goodness)

¹nest \'nest\ n **1** : the bed or shelter prepared by a bird for its eggs and young **2** : a place where eggs (as of insects) are laid and hatched **3** : a place of rest, retreat, or lodging **4** : DEN, HANGOUT (a ~ of thieves) **5** : the occupants of a nest **6** : a series of objects (as bowls or tables) made to fit into or under the next larger one

²nest vb **1** : to build or occupy a nest **2** : to fit compactly together or within one another

nest egg n **1** : a natural or artificial egg left in a nest to induce a fowl to continue to lay there **2** : a fund of money accumulated as a reserve

nes·tle \'nes-əl\ vb **1** : to settle snugly or comfortably **2** : to settle, shelter, or house as if in a nest **3** : to press closely and affectionately : CUDDLE

nest·ling \'nest-liŋ\ n : a bird too young to leave its nest

¹net \'net\ n **1** : a meshed fabric twisted, knotted, or woven together at regular intervals; esp : a device of net used esp. to catch birds, fish, or insects **2** : something made of net used esp. for protecting, confining, carrying, or dividing (a tennis ~) **3** : SNARE, TRAP

²net vb **net·ted; net·ting 1** : to cover or enclose with or as if with a net **2** : to catch in or as if in a net

³net adj : free from all charges or deductions (~ profit) (~ weight)

⁴net vb **net·ted; net·ting** : to gain or

produce as profit : CLEAR, YIELD ⟨his business netted $8,000 a year⟩

⁵**net** *n* : a net amount, profit, weight, or price

neth·er \'neth-ər\ *adj* : situated down or below : LOWER ⟨the ~ regions of the earth⟩

neth·er·most \-,mōst\ *adj* : LOWEST

neth·er·world \-,wərld\ *n* **1** : the world of the dead **2** : UNDERWORLD

net·ting \'net-iŋ\ *n* **1** : NETWORK **2** : the act or process of making a net or network **3** : the act, process, or right of fishing with a net

¹**net·tle** \'net-ᵊl\ *n* : any of various coarse herbs with stinging hairs

²**nettle** *vb* : PROVOKE, VEX, IRRITATE

net·tle·some *adj* : causing vexation : IRRITATING

net·work \'net-,wərk\ *n* **1** : NET **2** : a system of elements (as lines or channels) that cross in the manner of the threads in a net **3** : a chain of radio or television stations

neu·ral \'n(y)ůr-əl\ *adj* : of, relating to, or involving a nerve or the nervous system

neu·ral·gia \n(y)ù-'ral-jə\ *n* : acute pain that follows the course of a nerve — **neu·ral·gic** \-jik\ *adj*

neur·as·the·nia \,n(y)ůr-əs-'thē-nē-ə\ *n* : a neurotic state marked by tension and malaise — **neu·ras·then·ic** \-'then-ik\ *adj or n*

neu·ri·tis \n(y)ù-'rīt-əs\ *n* : inflammation of a nerve : nervous inflammation — **neu·rit·ic** \-'rit-ik\ *adj or n*

neu·rol·o·gy \n(y)ù-'räl-ə-jē\ *n* : scientific study of the nervous system — **neu·ro·log·i·cal** \,n(y)ùr-ə-'läj-i-kəl\ *adj* — **neu·rol·o·gist** \n(y)ù-'räl-ə-jəst\ *n*

neu·ron \'n(y)ü-,rän\ *also* **neu·rone** \-,rōn\ *n* : a nerve cell with all of its processes

neu·ro·sis \n(y)ù-'rō-səs\ *n, pl* **-ro·ses** \-'rō-,sēz\ : a functional nervous disorder without demonstrable physical lesions

¹**neu·rot·ic** \n(y)ù-'rät-ik\ *adj* : of, relating to, being, or affected with a neurosis; *also* : NERVOUS

²**neurotic** *n* : an emotionally unstable or neurotic person

¹**neu·ter** \'n(y)üt-ər\ *adj* **1** : of, relating to, or constituting the gender that includes most words or grammatical forms referring to things classed as neither masculine nor feminine **2** : having imperfectly developed or no sex organs

²**neuter** *n* **1** : a noun, pronoun, adjective, or inflectional form or class of the neuter gender; *also* : the neuter gender **2** : WORKER 2; *also* : a spayed or castrated animal

¹**neu·tral** \'n(y)ü-trəl\ *adj* **1** : not favoring either side in a quarrel, contest, or war **2** : of or relating to a neutral state or power **3** : being neither one thing nor the other : MIDDLING, INDIFFERENT **4** : having no hue : GRAY; *also* : not decided in color **5** : neither acid nor basic ⟨a ~ solution⟩

²**neutral** *n* **1** : one that is neutral **2** : a neutral color **3** : the position of machine gears in which the motor imparts no motion

neu·tral·ism \-,iz-əm\ *n* : a policy or the advocacy of neutrality esp. in international affairs

neu·tral·i·ty \n(y)ü-'tral-ət-ē\ *n* **1** : the quality or state of being neutral **2** : the condition of being neutral in time of war that gives immunity from invasion or from use by belligerents

neu·tral·ize \'n(y)ü-trə-,līz\ *vb* : to render neutral; *esp* : COUNTERACT — **neu·tral·iza·tion** \,n(y)ü-trə-lə-'zā-shən\ *n*

neu·tri·no \n(y)ü-'trē-nō\ *n* : an uncharged elementary particle having less mass than the electron

neu·tron \'n(y)ü-,trän\ *n* : an uncharged elementary particle that is nearly equal in mass to the proton and that is present in all atomic nuclei except hydrogen

nev·er \'nev-ər\ *adv* **1** : not ever : at no time **2** : not in any degree, way, or condition

nev·er·more \,nev-ər-'mōr\ *adv* : never again

nev·er–nev·er land \,nev-ər-'nev-ər-\ *n* : an ideal or imaginary place

nev·er·the·less \,nev-ər-thə-'les\ *adv* : in spite of that : HOWEVER

ne·vus \'nē-vəs\ *n, pl* **ne·vi** \-,vī\ : a usu. pigmented birthmark

¹**new** \'n(y)ü\ *adj* **1** : not old : RECENT, MODERN **2** : different from the former **3** : recently discovered, recognized, or learned about ⟨~ drugs⟩ **4** : not formerly known or experienced : UNFAMILIAR **5** : not accustomed ⟨~ to the work⟩ **6** : beginning as a repetition of a previous act or thing ⟨a ~ year⟩ **7** : REFRESHED, REGENERATED ⟨rest made a ~ man of him⟩ **8** : being in a position or place for the first time ⟨a ~ member⟩ **9** *cap* : having been in use since medieval times : MODERN ⟨*New* Latin⟩ **syn** novel, original, fresh

²**new** *adv* : NEWLY, RECENTLY ⟨*new*-mown hay⟩

new·born \-'bórn\ *adj* **1** : recently born **2** : born anew : REBORN ⟨~ hope⟩

new·com·er \-,kəm-ər\ *n* **1** : one recently arrived **2** : BEGINNER

New Deal *n* : the legislative and administrative program of President F. D. Roosevelt designed to promote economic recovery and social reform during the 1930s — **New Deal·er** *n*

new·el \'n(y)ü-əl\ *n* : an upright post about which the steps of a circular staircase wind; *also* : a post at the foot of a stairway or one at a landing

new–fan·gled \'n(y)ü-'faŋ-gəld\ *adj* **1** : attracted to novelty **2** : of the newest style : NOVEL

new–fash·ioned \-'fash-ənd\ *adj* **1** : made in a new fashion or form **2** : UP-TO-DATE

new–found \'n(y)ü-'faùnd\ *adj* : newly found

new·ish \-ish\ *adj* : rather new

new·ly \'n(y)ü-lē\ *adv* **1** : LATELY, RECENTLY **2** : ANEW, AFRESH **3** : in a new way

new·ly·wed \-,wed\ *n* : one recently married

new moon *n* **1** : the phase of the moon with its dark side toward the earth **2** : the thin crescent moon seen for a few days after the new moon phase

ə abut; ᵊ kitten; ər further; a back; ā bake; ä cot, cart; aů out; ch chin; e less; ē easy; g gift; i trip; ī life; j joke; ŋ sing; ō flow; ó flaw; ói coin; th thin; t̲h̲ this; ü loot; ů foot; y yet; yü few; yů furious; zh vision

new·ness \'n(y)ü-nəs\ *n* : the quality or state of being new

news \'n(y)üz\ *n* **1** : a report of recent events : TIDINGS **2** : material reported in a newspaper or news periodical or on a newscast

news·boy \-,bȯi\ *n* : a person who delivers or sells newspapers

news·cast \-,kast\ *n* : a radio or television broadcast of news — **news·cast·er** *n*

news·let·ter \-,let-ər\ *n* : a newspaper containing news or information of interest chiefly to a special group

news·pa·per \-,pā-pər\ *n* : a paper that is printed and distributed at regular intervals and contains news, articles of opinion, features, and advertising

news·pa·per·man \-,man\ *n* : one who owns or is employed by a newspaper

news·print \'n(y)üz-,print\ *n* : cheap machine-finished paper made chiefly from wood pulp and used mostly for newspapers

news·reel \-,rēl\ *n* : a short motion picture portraying current events

news·stand \-,stand\ *n* : a place where newspapers and periodicals are sold

news·wor·thy \-,wər-thē\ *adj* : sufficiently interesting to the general public to warrant reporting (as in a newspaper)

newsy \'n(y)ü-zē\ *adj* : filled with news; *esp* : CHATTY

newt \'n(y)üt\ *n* : any of various small salamanders living chiefly in the water

New World *n* : the western hemisphere; *esp* : the continental landmass of No. and So. America

New Year *n* : NEW YEAR'S DAY; *also* : the first days of the year

New Year's Day *n* : January 1 observed as a legal holiday

New Zea·land·er \n(y)ü-'zē-lən-dər\ *n* : a native or inhabitant of New Zealand

¹next \'nekst\ *adj* : immediately preceding or following : NEAREST

²next *adv* **1** : in the time, place, or order nearest or immediately succeeding **2** : on the first occasion to come

³next *prep* : nearest or adjacent to

nex·us \'nek-səs\ *n*, *pl* **nex·us·es** or **nexus** : CONNECTION, LINK

ni·a·cin \'nī-ə-sən\ *n* : NICOTINIC ACID

nib \'nib\ *n* : POINT; *esp* : a pen point

¹nib·ble \'nib-əl\ *vb* : to bite gently or bit by bit

²nibble *n* : a small or cautious bite

nice \'nīs\ *adj* **1** : FASTIDIOUS, DISCRIMINATING **2** : marked by delicate discrimination or treatment **3** : PLEASING, AGREEABLE; *also* : well-executed **4** : WELL-BRED ⟨~ people⟩ **5** : VIRTUOUS, RESPECTABLE — **nice·ly** *adv* — **nice·ness** *n*

nice·ty \'nī-sət-ē\ *n* **1** : a dainty, delicate, or elegant thing ⟨enjoy the *niceties* of life⟩ **2** : a fine detail ⟨*niceties* of workmanship⟩ **3** : EXACTNESS, PRECISION, ACCURACY

niche \'nich\ *n* **1** : a recess (as for a statue) in a wall **2** : a place, work, or use for which a person or thing is best fitted

¹nick \'nik\ *n* **1** : a small groove : NOTCH **2** : CHIP ⟨a ~ in a cup⟩ **3** : the final critical moment ⟨in the ~ of time⟩

²nick *vb* : NOTCH, CHIP

nick·el \'nik-əl\ *n* **1** : a hard silver-white metallic chemical element capable of a high polish and used in alloys **2** : the U.S. 5-cent piece made of copper and nickel; *also* : the Canadian 5-cent piece

nick·el·ode·on \,nik-ə-'lōd-ē-ən\ *n* **1** : a theater presenting entertainment for an admission price of five cents **2** : JUKEBOX

nickel silver *n* : a silver-white alloy of copper, zinc, and nickel

nick·er \'nik-ər\ *vb* : NEIGH, WHINNY

nick·name \'nik-,nām\ *n* **1** : a usu. descriptive name given instead of or in addition to the one belonging to a person, place, or thing **2** : a familiar form of a proper name — **nickname** *vb*

nic·o·tine \'nik-ə-,tēn\ *n* : a poisonous substance found in tobacco and used as an insecticide

nic·o·tin·ic acid \,nik-ə-,tē-nik-, -,tin-ik-\ *n* : an organic acid of the vitamin B complex found in plants and animals and used against pellagra

niece \'nēs\ *n* : a daughter of one's brother, sister, brother-in-law, or sister-in-law

nif·ty \'nif-tē\ *adj* : FINE, SWELL

Ni·ge·ri·an \nī-'jir-ē-ən\ *n* : a native or inhabitant of Nigeria — **Nigerian** *adj*

nig·gard \'nig-ərd\ *n* : a stingy person : MISER — **nig·gard·li·ness** *n* — **nig·gard·ly** *adv*

nig·gling \'nig-(ə-)liŋ\ *adj* **1** : PETTY **2** : demanding meticulous care

¹nigh \'nī\ *adv* **1** : near in place, time, or relationship **2** : NEARLY, ALMOST

²nigh *adj* : CLOSE, NEAR

³nigh *prep* : NEAR

night \'nīt\ *n* **1** : the period between dusk and dawn **2** : NIGHTFALL **3** : the darkness of night — **night** *adj*

night blindness *n* : reduced visual capacity in faint light (as at night)

night·cap \'nīt-,kap\ *n* **1** : a cloth cap worn with nightclothes **2** : a usu. alcoholic drink taken at bedtime

night-clothes \-,klō(th)z\ *n pl* : garments worn in bed

night·club \-,kləb\ *n* : a place of entertainment open at night usu. serving food and liquor and providing music for dancing

night crawler *n* : EARTHWORM; *esp* : a large earthworm found on the soil surface at night

night·dress \-,dres\ *n* : NIGHTGOWN

night·fall \-,fȯl\ *n* : the coming of night

night·gown \-,gaún\ *n* : a loose garment designed for wear in bed

night·hawk \-,hȯk\ *n* **1** : any of several birds related to and resembling the whippoorwill **2** : a person who habitually stays up late at night

night·in·gale \'nīt-ən-,gāl\ *n* : any of several Old World thrushes noted for the sweet nocturnal song of the male

night·ly \'nīt-lē\ *adj* **1** : of or relating to the night or every night **2** : happening, done, or produced by night or every night — **nightly** *adv*

night·mare \-,maər\ *n* : a frightening oppressive dream or state occurring during sleep

night·shade \-,shād\ *n* : any of a large group of woody or herbaceous plants having alternate leaves, flowers in clusters, and fruits that are berries and including poisonous forms (as belladonna) and important food plants (as potato, tomato, or eggplant)

night·shirt \-,shərt\ *n* : a nightgown esp. for a man or a boy

night·stick \-,stik\ *n* : a policeman's club

night·time \'nīt-,tīm\ *n* : the time from dusk to dawn

nil \'nil\ *n* : NOTHING, ZERO

nim·ble \'nim-bəl\ *adj* **1** : quick and light in motion : AGILE ⟨a ~ dancer⟩ **2** : quick in understanding and learning : CLEVER ⟨a ~ mind⟩ — **nim·ble·ness** *n* — **nim·bly** \-ble\ *adv*

nim·bus \'nim-bəs\ *n, pl* **nim·bi** \-,bī, -,bē\ *or* **-bus·es 1** : a figure (as a disk) suggesting radiant light about the head of a drawn or sculptured divinity, saint, or sovereign **2** : a rain cloud that is of uniform grayness and extends over the entire sky **3** : a cloud from which rain is falling

Nim·rod \'nim-,räd\ *n* **1** : a mighty hunter and great-grandson of Noah **2** *often not cap* : HUNTER

nin·com·poop \'nin-kəm-,püp\ *n* : FOOL, SIMPLETON

nine \'nīn\ *n* **1** : one more than eight **2** : the 9th in a set or series **3** : something having nine units; *esp* : a baseball team — **nine** *adj or pron* — **ninth** \'nīnth\ *adj or adv or n*

nine·pins \'nīn-,pinz\ *n* : tenpins played without the headpin

nine·teen \'nīn-'tēn\ *n* : one more than 18 — **nineteen** *adj or pron* — **nineteenth** \-'tēnth\ *adj or n*

nine·ty \'nīnt-ē\ *n* : nine times 10 — **nine·ti·eth** \-ē-əth\ *adj or n* — **ninety** *adj or pron*

nin·ny \'nin-ē\ *n* : FOOL, SIMPLETON

nin·ny·ham·mer \-,ham-ər\ *n* : NINNY

ni·o·bi·um \nī-'ō-bē-əm\ *n* : a gray metallic chemical element used in alloys

nip \'nip\ *vb* **nipped; nip·ping 1** : to catch hold of and squeeze tightly between two surfaces, edges, or points : PINCH, BITE, CLAMP **2** : CLIP **3** : to destroy the growth, progress, or fulfillment of ⟨nipped in the bud⟩ **4** : to injure or make numb with cold : CHILL **5** : SNATCH, STEAL

²nip *n* **1** : a sharp stinging cold **2** : a biting or pungent flavor **3** : PINCH, BITE **4** : a small portion : BIT

³nip *n* : a small quantity of liquor ⟨takes a ~ now and then⟩

⁴nip *vb* **nipped; nip·ping 1** : to take liquor in nips : TIPPLE

nip and tuck \,nip-ən-'tək\ *adj (or adv)* : so close that the lead shifts rapidly from one contestant to another

nip·per \'nip-ər\ *n* **1** : one that nips **2** *pl* : PINCERS **3** : CHELA

nip·ple \'nip-əl\ *n* : the protuberance of a mammary gland through which milk is drawn off : TEAT; *also* : something resembling a nipple in form or function

nip·py \'nip-ē\ *adj* **1** : PUNGENT, SHARP **2** : CHILLY, CHILLING

nir·va·na \nir-'vän-ə\ *n, often cap* [Skt *nirvāṇa*, lit., extinction, fr. *nis-, nir-* out + *vāti* it blows] **1** : the final freeing of a soul from all that enslaves it; *esp* : the supreme happiness that according to Buddhism comes when all passion, hatred, and delusion die out and the soul is released from the necessity of further purification **2** : OBLIVION, PARADISE

ni·sei \'nē-'sā\ *n, pl* **nisei** *also* **niseis** : a

son or daughter of immigrant Japanese parents who is born and educated in America

nit \'nit\ *n* : the egg of a parasitic insect (as a louse); *also* : the young insect

ni·ter \'nīt-ər\ *also* **ni·tre** *n* **1** : POTASSIUM NITRATE **2** : SODIUM NITRATE

ni·trate \'nī-,trāt\ *n* **1** : a salt or ester of nitric acid **2** : sodium nitrate or potassium nitrate used as a fertilizer

ni·tric acid \,nī-trik-\ *n* : a corrosive liquid used in making dyes, explosives, and fertilizers

ni·tro·gen \'nī-trə-jən\ *n* : a tasteless odorless gaseous chemical element constituting 78 percent of the atmosphere by volume — **ni·tric** \'nī-trik\ *adj* — **ni·trog·e·nous** \nī-'träj-ə-nəs\ *adj* — **ni·trous** \'nī-trəs\ *adj*

ni·tro·glyc·er·in *or* **ni·tro·glyc·er·ine** \,nī-trō-'glis-(ə-)rən\ *n* : a heavy oily explosive liquid used in making dynamite and in medicine

nit·wit \'nit-,wit\ *n* : a flighty stupid person

¹nix \'niks\ *n, slang* : NOTHING

²nix *adv, slang* : NO — used to express disagreement or the withholding of permission

³nix *vb, slang* : VETO, FORBID

¹no \(')nō\ *adv* **1** — used to express the negative of an alternative choice or possibility ⟨shall we continue or ~⟩ **2** : in no respect or degree ⟨he is ~ better than the others⟩ **3** : not so ⟨~, I'm not ready⟩ **4** — used with a following adjective to imply a meaning expressed by the opposite positive statement ⟨in ~ uncertain terms⟩ **5** — used to emphasize a following negative or to introduce a more emphatic or explicit statement ⟨has the right, ~, the duty, to continue⟩ **6** — used as an interjection to express surprise or doubt ⟨~ — you don't say⟩

²no *adj* **1** : not any; *also* : hardly any **2** : not a ⟨he's ~ expert⟩

³no \'nō\ *n, pl* **noes** *or* **nos 1** : REFUSAL, DENIAL **2** : a negative vote or decision; *also, pl* : persons voting in the negative

no·bel·i·um \nō-'bel-ē-əm\ *n* : a radioactive chemical element produced artificially

No·bel prize \nō-'bel-\ *n* : any of various annual prizes (as in peace, literature, or medicine) established by the will of Alfred Nobel for the encouragement of persons who work for the interests of humanity

no·bil·i·ty \nō-'bil-ət-ē\ *n* **1** : NOBLENESS ⟨~ of character⟩ **2** : noble rank **3** : nobles considered as forming a class or group

¹no·ble \'nō-bəl\ *adj* **1** : ILLUSTRIOUS; *also* : FAMOUS, NOTABLE **2** : of high birth, rank, or station : ARISTOCRATIC **3** : EXCELLENT **4** : STATELY, IMPOSING ⟨a ~ edifice⟩ **5** : of a magnanimous nature — **no·ble·ness** *n* — **no·bly** \-blē\ *adv*

²noble *n* : a person of noble rank or birth

no·ble·man \'nō-bəl-mən\ *n* : a member of the nobility : PEER

¹no·body \'nō-,bäd-ē\ *pron* : no person

²nobody *n* : a person of no influence, importance, or worth

noc·tur·nal \näk-'tərn-ᵊl\ *adj* **1** : of,

relating to, or occurring in the night ⟨a ~ journey⟩ **2** : active at night ⟨a ~ bird⟩ — **noc·tur·nal·ly** adv

noc·turne \'näk-ˌtərn\ n : a work of art dealing with night; esp : a dreamy pensive instrumental composition

noc·u·ous \'näk-yə-wəs\ adj : likely to cause injury : HARMFUL

nod \'näd\ vb **nod·ded nod·ding 1** : to bend the head downward or forward (as in bowing or going to sleep or as a sign of assent) **2** : to move up and down ⟨the tulips nodded in the breeze⟩ **3** : to show by a nod of the head ⟨~ agreement⟩ **4** : to make a slip or error in a moment of abstraction — **nod** n

nod·dle \'näd-ʾl\ n : HEAD

nod·dy \'näd-ē\ n **1** : SIMPLETON **2** : a stout-bodied tropical tern

node \'nōd\ n : a thickened, swollen, or differentiated area (as of tissue); esp : the part of a stem from which a leaf arises

nod·ule \'näj-ül\ n : a small lump or swelling — **nod·u·lar** \'näj-ə-lər\ adj

nod·u·lose \'näj-ə-ˌlōs\ adj : having minute nodules : finely knobby

no·el \nō-'el\ n **1** : a Christmas carol **2** cap : the Christmas season

nog·gin \'näg-ən\ n **1** : a small mug or cup; also : a small quantity of drink usu. equivalent to a gill **2** : a person's head

no–good \'nō-ˌgùd\ adj : having no worth, use, or chance of success — **no-good** n

¹**noise** \'nòiz\ n **1** : loud, confused, or senseless shouting or outcry **2** : SOUND; esp : one that lacks agreeable musical quality or is noticeably unpleasant — **noise·less** \-ləs\ adj — **noise·less·ly** adv

²**noise** vb : to spread by rumor or report ⟨the story was noised abroad⟩

noise·mak·er \-ˌmā-kər\ n : one that makes noise; esp : a device used to make noise at parties

noi·some \'nòi-səm\ adj **1** : HARMFUL, UNWHOLESOME **2** : offensive to the senses (as smell) : DISGUSTING

noisy \'nòi-zē\ adj : making loud noises : full of noises : LOUD — **nois·i·ly** adv — **nois·i·ness** n

no·mad \'nō-ˌmad\ n **1** : one of a people that has no fixed location but wanders from place to place **2** : an individual who roams about aimlessly — **nomad** adj — **no·mad·ic** \nō-'mad-ik\ adj

no–man's–land \'nō-ˌmanz-ˌland\ n **1** : an area of unowned, unclaimed, or uninhabited land **2** : an unoccupied area between opposing troops

nom de guerre \ˌnäm-di-'geər\ n, pl **noms de guerre** \ˌnäm(z)-\ : PSEUDONYM

nom de plume \ˌnäm-di-'plüm\ n, pl **noms de plume** \ˌnäm(z)-di-\ : PSEUDONYM

no·men·cla·ture \'nō-mən-ˌklā-chər\ n **1** : NAME, DESIGNATION **2** : a system of names used in a science or art

nom·i·nal \'näm-ən-ʾl\ adj **1** : being something in name or form only ⟨~ head of a party⟩ **2** : TRIFLING, INSIGNIFICANT ⟨a ~ price⟩ — **nom·i·nal·ly** adv

nom·i·nate \'näm-ə-ˌnāt\ vb : to choose as a candidate for election, appointment, or honor : DESIGNATE, NAME — **nom·i·na·tion** \ˌnäm-ə-'nā-shən\ n

nom·i·na·tive \'näm-(ə-)nət-iv\ adj

: of, relating to, or constituting a grammatical case marking typically the subject of a verb — **nominative** n

nom·i·nee \ˌnäm-ə-'nē\ n : a person nominated for an office, duty, or position

non- \(')nän, ˌnän\ prefix : not : reverse of : absence of

nonabrasive	nonexistent
nonabsorbent	nonexplosive
nonacademic	nonfarm
nonacceptance	nonfattening
nonacid	nonfederated
nonactive	nonferrous
nonadherence	nonfiction
nonadhesive	nonfictional
nonadjacent	nonfilamentous
nonadjustable	nonfilterable
nonadministrative	nonflammable
nonaggression	nonflowering
nonalcoholic	nonfreezing
nonappearance	nonfulfillment
nonaromatic	nonfunctional
nonathletic	nonhereditary
nonattendance	nonhomogeneous
nonattributive	nonhomologous
nonbeliever	nonhuman
nonbelligerent	nonimportation
nonbreakable	nonindustrial
nonburning	noninfectious
noncellular	noninflammable
nonchargeable	nonintercourse
nonclerical	noninterference
noncollapsible	nonintoxicant
noncombat	nonintoxicating
noncombustible	nonionized
noncommercial	nonirritating
noncommunicable	nonlegal
noncommunist	nonlife
noncompeting	nonlinear
noncompetitive	nonliterary
noncompliance	nonliving
noncomplying	nonlogical
nonconcurrent	nonmagnetic
nonconducting	nonmalignant
nonconflicting	nonmarketable
nonconformance	nonmaterial
nonconforming	nonmember
nonconstructive	nonmembership
noncontagious	nonmigratory
noncontinuous	nonmilitary
noncontraband	nonmoral
noncontributing	nonmotile
noncorroding	nonmoving
noncorrosive	nonnegotiable
noncrystalline	nonobservance
nondeductible	nonoccurrence
nondelivery	nonofficial
nondemocratic	nonoily
nondenominational	nonorthodox
nondepartmental	nonparallel
nondevelopment	nonparasitic
nondiscrimination	nonparticipant
nondistinctive	nonparticipating
nondistribution	nonpathogenic
nondivided	nonpaying
nondrying	nonpayment
nondurable	nonperformance
noneducational	nonperishable
nonelastic	nonpermanent
nonelection	nonphysical
nonelective	nonpoisonous
nonelectric	nonpolar
nonemotional	nonpolitical
nonenforceable	nonporous
nonenforcement	nonproductive
nonessential	nonprofessional
nonethical	nonprotein
nonexchangeable	nonradioactive
nonexempt	nonrandom
nonexistence	(continued)

nonreactive
nonreciprocal
nonrecognition
nonrecoverable
nonrecurrent
nonrecurring
nonrefillable
nonreligious
nonremovable
nonrenewable
nonresidential
nonrestricted
nonreturnable
nonreversible
nonruminant
nonsalable
nonscientific
nonscientist
nonseasonal
nonsectarian
nonsegregated
nonselective
non-self-governing
nonseptate
nonsexual
nonshrinkable
nonsinkable
nonsmoker
nonsocial
nonspeaking
nonspecialized

nonsporting
nonstaining
nonstandard
nonstriated
nonstriker
nonsubscriber
nonsuccess
nonsustaining
nontaxable
nontechnical
nontemporal
nontheistic
nontoxic
nontransferable
nontransparency
nontransparent
nontypical
nonuniform
nonuser
nonvascular
nonvenomous
nonviable
nonviolation
nonviolent
nonvocal
nonvolatile
nonvoter
nonvoting
nonwhite
nonworker
nonworking

non·age \'nän-ij, 'nō-nij\ *n* **1** : legal minority **2** : a period of youth **3** : IMMATURITY

no·na·ge·nar·i·an \,nō-nə-jə-'ner-ē-ən, ,nän-ə-\ *n* : a person who is in his nineties

¹nonce \'näns\ *n* : the one, particular, or present occasion or purpose ⟨for the ~⟩

²nonce *adj* : occurring, used, or made only once or for a special occasion ⟨~ word⟩

non·cha·lant \,nän-shə-'länt\ *adj* [F, fr. OF, prp. of *nonchaloir* to disregard, fr. *non* not + *chaloir* to be important, fr. L *calēre* to be hot] : having a confident and easy manner : unconcerned about drawing attention to oneself : CASUAL — **non·cha·lance** \-'läns\ *n* — **non·cha·lant·ly** *adv*

non·com·bat·ant \,nän-kəm-'bat-°nt, nän-'käm-bət-ənt\ *n* : a member (as a chaplain) of the armed forces whose duties do not include fighting; *also* : CIVILIAN — **noncombatant** *adj*

non·com·mis·sioned officer \,nän-kə-mish-ənd-\ *n* : a subordinate officer in a branch of the armed forces appointed from enlisted personnel and holding one of various grades (as staff sergeant)

non·com·mit·tal \,nän-kə-'mit-°l\ *adj* : indicating neither consent nor dissent ⟨a ~ answer⟩

non com·pos men·tis \,nän-,käm-pəs-'ment-əs\ *adj* : not of sound mind

non·con·duc·tor \,nän-kən-'dək-tər\ *n* : a substance that is a very poor conductor of heat, electricity, or sound

non·con·form·ist \,nän-kən-'fȯr-məst\ *n* **1** *often cap* : a person who does not conform to an established church and esp. the Church of England **2** : a person who does not conform to a generally accepted pattern of thought or action — **non·con·for·mi·ty** \-'fȯr-mət-ē\ *n*

non·con·trib·u·to·ry \,nän-kən-'trib-yə-,tōr-ē\ *adj* : paid for entirely by an employer : not involving payments by employees ⟨~ pension plan⟩

non·co·op·er·a·tion \,nän-kō-,äp-ə-'rā-shən\ *n* : failure or refusal to cooperate; *esp* : refusal through civil disobedience of a people to cooperate with the government of a country

non·de·script \,nän-di-'skript\ *adj* : not belonging to any particular class or kind : not easily described

¹none \'nən\ *pron* **1** : not any ⟨~ of them went⟩ ⟨~ of it is needed⟩ **2** : not one ⟨~ of the family⟩ **3** : not any such thing or person ⟨half a loaf is better than ~⟩

²none *adj, archaic* : not any : NO

³none *adv* : by no means : not at all ⟨he got there ~ too soon⟩

non·en·ti·ty \nä-'nent-ət-ē\ *n* **1** : something that does not exist or exists only in the imagination **2** : one of no consequence or significance

nones \'nōnz\ *n sing or pl* : the 7th day of March, May, July, or October or the 5th day of any other month in the ancient Roman calendar

none·such \'nən-,səch\ *n* : a person or thing without an equal — **nonesuch** *adj*

none·the·less \,nən-thə-'les\ *adv* : NEVERTHELESS

non·in·ter·ven·tion \,nän-,int-ər-'ven-chən\ *n* : refusal or failure to intervene (as in the affairs of another state)

non·met·al \'nän-'met-°l\ *n* : a chemical element (as carbon, phosphorus, nitrogen, or oxygen) that lacks metallic properties — **non·me·tal·lic** \,nän-mə-'tal-ik\ *adj*

¹non·pa·reil \,nän-pə-'rel\ *adj* : having no equal : PEERLESS

²nonpareil *n* **1** : an individual of unequaled excellence : PARAGON **2** : a small flat disk of chocolate covered with white sugar pellets

non·par·ti·san \'nän-'pärt-ə-zən\ *adj* : not partisan; *esp* : not influenced by political party spirit or interests

non·plus \'nän-'pləs\ *vb* -plussed *also* -plused, -plus·sing *also* -plus·ing : PUZZLE, PERPLEX

non·prof·it \'nän-'präf-ət\ *adj* : not conducted or maintained for the purpose of making a profit ⟨a ~ organization⟩

non·res·i·dent \'nän-'rez-əd-ənt\ *adj* : not living in a specified or implied place — **non·res·i·dence** \-əd-əns\ *n* — **nonresident** *n*

non·re·sis·tance \,nän-ri-'zis-təns\ *n* : the principles or practice of passive submission to authority even when unjust or oppressive

non·re·stric·tive \,nän-ri-'strik-tiv\ *adj* **1** : not serving or tending to restrict **2** : not limiting the reference of the word or phrase modified ⟨a ~ clause⟩

non·sched·uled \'nän-'skej-üld\ *adj* : licensed to carry passengers or freight by air without a regular schedule ⟨~ airline⟩

non·sense \'nän-,sens, -səns\ *n* **1** : foolish or meaningless words or actions **2** : things of no importance or value : TRIFLES — **non·sen·si·cal** \nän-'sen-si-kəl\ *adj*

non sequi·tur \nän-'sek-wət-ər\ *n*

: an inference that does not follow from the premises

non·skid \'nän-'skid\ adj : having the tread corrugated or specially constructed to resist skidding

non·stop \'nän-'stäp\ adj : done or made without a stop — **nonstop** adv

non·sup·port \,nän-sə-'pōrt\ n : failure to support; esp : failure on the part of one under obligation to provide maintenance

non·union \nän-'yü-nyən\ adj 1 : not belonging to a trade union ⟨~ carpenters⟩ 2 : not recognizing or favoring trade unions or their members ⟨~ employers⟩

noo·dle \'nüd-ᵊl\ n : a food like macaroni but shaped into long flat strips and made with egg — usu. used in pl.

nook \'nuk\ n 1 : an interior angle or corner formed usu. by two walls ⟨a chimney ~⟩ 2 : a sheltered or hidden place ⟨a shady ~⟩

noon \'nün\ n : the middle of the day : 12 o'clock in the daytime — **noon** adj

noon·day \-,dā\ n : NOON, MIDDAY

no one pron : NOBODY

noon·tide \'nün-,tīd\ n : NOON

noon·time \-,tīm\ n : NOON

noose \'nüs\ n : a loop with a running knot (as in a lasso) that binds closer the more it is drawn

no-par \-,nō-,pär\ adj : having no nominal value ⟨~ stock⟩

nor \nər, (')nôr\ conj : and not ⟨not for you ~ for me⟩ — used esp. to introduce and negate the second member and each later member of a series of items preceded by neither ⟨neither here ~ there⟩

Nor·dic \'nôrd-ik\ adj 1 : of or relating to the Germanic peoples of northern Europe and esp. of Scandinavia 2 : of or relating to a physical type characterized by tall stature, long head, light skin and hair, and blue eyes — **Nordic** n

norm \'nôrm\ n : AVERAGE, STANDARD; esp : a set standard of development or achievement usu. derived from the average or median achievement of a large group

¹**nor·mal** \'nôr-məl\ adj 1 : REGULAR, STANDARD, NATURAL 2 : of average intelligence; also : sound in mind and body — **nor·mal·cy** \-sē\ n — **nor·mal·i·ty** \nôr-'mal-ət-ē\ n — **nor·mal·ly** \'nôr-mə-lē\ adv

²**normal** n 1 : one that is normal 2 : the usual condition, level, or quantity : AVERAGE

nor·mal·ize \'nôr-mə-,līz\ vb : to make normal or average

normal school n : a school for training chiefly elementary teachers

Norse \'nôrs\ n 1 pl **Norse** : SCANDINAVIANS; also : NORWEGIANS 2 : NORWEGIAN; also : any of the western Scandinavian dialects or languages

Norse·man \-mən\ n : one of the ancient Scandinavians

¹**north** \'nôrth\ adv : to or toward the north

²**north** adj 1 : situated toward or at the north 2 : coming from the north

³**north** n 1 : the direction to the left of one facing east 2 : the compass point directly opposite to south 3 cap : regions or countries north of a specified or implied point — **north·er·ly** \'nôrth-ər-lē\ adv or adj — **north·ern** \-ərn\ adj — **North·ern·er** \-ə(r)n-ər\ n —

north·ern·most \-ərn-,mōst\ adj — **north·ward** \'nôrth-wərd\ adv or adj — **north·wards** adv

north·east \nôrth-'ēst\ n 1 : the general direction between north and east 2 : the compass point midway between north and east 3 cap : regions or countries northeast of a specified or implied point — **northeast** adj or adv — **north·east·er·ly** \-ər-lē\ adv or adj — **north·east·ern** \-ərn\ adj

north·east·er \-ər\ n : a storm or strong wind from the northeast

north·er \'nôr-thər\ n : a storm or strong wind from the north

northern lights n pl : AURORA BOREALIS

north pole n, often cap N & P : the northernmost point of the earth

North Star n : the star toward which the northern end of the earth's axis very nearly points

north·west \nôrth-'west\ n 1 : the general direction between north and west 2 : the compass point midway between north and west 3 cap : regions or countries northwest of a specified or implied point — **northwest** adj or adv — **north·west·er·ly** \-ər-lē\ adv or adj — **north·west·ern** \-ərn\ adj

Nor·we·gian \nôr-'wē-jən\ n 1 : a native or inhabitant of Norway 2 : the language of Norway — **Norwegian** adj

¹**nose** \'nōz\ n 1 : the part of the face containing the nostrils and covering the front of the nasal cavity 2 : the organ or sense of smell 3 : something (as a point, edge, or projecting front part) that resembles a nose ⟨the ~ of a plane⟩

²**nose** vb 1 : to detect by or as if by smell : SCENT 2 : to push or move with the nose 3 : to touch or rub with the nose : NUZZLE 4 : to defeat by a narrow margin in a contest ⟨nosed out his opponent⟩ 5 : PRY 6 : to move ahead slowly ⟨the ship nosed into her berth⟩

nose·bleed \-,blēd\ n : a bleeding from the nose

nose cone n : a protective cone constituting the forward end of a rocket or missile

nose dive n 1 : a downward nose-first plunge (as of an airplane) 2 : a sudden extreme drop (as in prices)

nose·gay \'nōz-,gā\ n : a small bunch of flowers : POSY

nose·piece \-,pēs\ n 1 : a piece of armor for protecting the nose 2 : a fitting at the lower end of a microscope tube to which the objectives are attached

no-show \'nō-'shō\ n : a person who reserves space esp. on an airplane but neither uses nor cancels the reservation

nos·tal·gia \nä-'stal-jə, nə-\ n [NL, fr. Gk nostos return home + algos pain, grief] 1 : HOMESICKNESS 2 : a wistful yearning for something past or irrecoverable — **nos·tal·gic** \-jik\ adj

nos·tril \'näs-trəl\ n : an external naris usu. with the adjoining nasal wall and passage

nos·trum \'näs-trəm\ n : a questionable medicine or remedy

nosy \'nō-zē\ adj : INQUISITIVE, PRYING

not \(')nät\ adv 1 — used to make negative a group of words or a word ⟨the boys are ~ here⟩ 2 — used to stand for the negative of a preceding group of words ⟨sometimes hard to see and sometimes ~⟩

no·ta be·ne \ˌnōt-ə-'ben-ē\ — used to call attention to something important

no·ta·bil·i·ty \ˌnōt-ə-'bil-ət-ē\ *n* **1** : the quality or state of being notable **2** : a notable or prominent person

1no·ta·ble \'nōt-ə-bəl\ *adj* **1** : NOTE-WORTHY, REMARKABLE **2** : DISTIN-GUISHED, PROMINENT — **no·ta·bly** *adv*

2notable *n* : a person of note or of great reputation

no·tar·i·al \nō-'ter-ē-əl\ *adj* : of, relating to, or done by a notary public

no·ta·rize \'nōt-ə-ˌrīz\ *vb* : to acknowledge or make legally authentic as a notary public

no·ta·ry public \ˌnōt-ə-rē-\ *n, pl* **notaries public** *or* **notary publics** : a public official who attests or certifies writings (as deeds) to make them legally authentic

no·ta·tion \nō-'tā-shən\ *n* **1** : ANNO-TATION, NOTE **2** : the act, process, or method of representing data by marks, signs, figures, or characters; *also* : a system of symbols (as letters, numerals, or musical notes) used in such notation

1notch \'näch\ *n* **1** : a V-shaped hollow in an edge or surface **2** : a narrow pass between two mountains

2notch *vb* **1** : to cut or make notches in **2** : to score or record by or as if by cutting a series of notches ⟨~ed 20 points for the team⟩

1note \'nōt\ *vb* **1** : to notice or observe with care; *also* : to record or preserve in writing **2** : to make special mention of : REMARK

2note *n* **1** : a musical sound **2** : a cry, call, or sound esp. of a bird **3** : a special tone in a person's words or voice ⟨a ~ of fear⟩ **4** : a character in music used to indicate duration of a tone by its shapes and pitch by its position on the staff **5** : a characteristic feature : MOOD, QUALITY ⟨a ~ of optimism⟩ **6** : MEMORANDUM **7** : a brief and informal record; *also* : a written or printed comment or explanation **8** : a written promise to pay a debt **9** : a piece of paper money **10** : a short informal letter **11** : a formal diplomatic or official communication **12** : DIS-TINCTION, REPUTATION ⟨a man of ~⟩ **13** : OBSERVATION, NOTICE, HEED ⟨take ~ of the exact time⟩

note·book \-ˌbůk\ *n* : a book for notes or memoranda

not·ed \'nōt-əd\ *adj* : well known by reputation : EMINENT, CELEBRATED, FAMOUS

note·wor·thy \'nōt-ˌwər-thē\ *adj* : wor thy of note : REMARKABLE

1noth·ing \'nəth-iŋ\ *pron* **1** : no thing ⟨leaves ~ to the imagination⟩ **2** : no part **3** : one of no interest, value, or importance ⟨she's ~ to me⟩

2nothing *adv* : not at all : in no degree ⟨~ daunted by his fall, he got up and continued the race⟩

3nothing *n* **1** : something that does not exist **2** : ZERO **3** : a person or thing of little or no value or importance

noth·ing·ness \-nəs\ *n* **1** : the quality or state of being nothing **2** : NON-EXISTENCE; *also* : utter insignificance **3** : something insignificant or valueless

1no·tice \'nōt-əs\ *n* **1** : WARNING,

ANNOUNCEMENT **2** : notification of the termination of an agreement or contract at a specified time **3** : ATTENTION, HEED ⟨brought the matter to my ~⟩ **4** : a written or printed announcement ⟨see the ~ on the door⟩ ⟨obituary ~⟩ **5** : a short critical account or examination (as of a play) : REVIEW

2notice *vb* **1** : to make mention of : remark on : NOTE **2** : to take notice of : OBSERVE, MARK

no·tice·able \-ə-bəl\ *adj* **1** : worthy of notice **2** : capable of being or likely to be noticed — **no·tice·ably** \-blē\ *adv*

no·ti·fy \'nōt-ə-ˌfī\ *vb* **1** : to give notice of : report the occurrence of **2** : to give notice to : INFORM — **no·ti·fi·ca·tion** \ˌnōt-ə-fə-'kā-shən\ *n*

no·tion \'nō-shən\ *n* **1** : IDEA, CON-CEPTION ⟨have a ~ of what he means⟩ **2** : a belief held : OPINION, VIEW **3** : WHIM, FANCY ⟨a sudden ~ to go⟩ **4** *pl* : small useful articles (as pins, needles, or thread)

no·tion·al \'nō-sh(ə-)nəl\ *adj* **1** : existing in the mind only : IMAGINARY, UNREAL **2** : given to foolish or fanciful moods or ideas : WHIMSICAL

no·to·ri·ous \nō-'tōr-ē-əs\ *adj* : generally known and talked of; *esp* : widely and unfavorably known — **no·to·ri·ety** \ˌnōt-ə-'rī-ət-ē\ *n* — **no·to·ri·ous·ly** \nō-'tōr-ē-əs-lē\ *adv*

1not·with·stand·ing \ˌnät-with-'stan-diŋ\ *prep* : in spite of

2notwithstanding *adv* : NEVERTHELESS, HOWEVER

3notwithstanding *conj* : ALTHOUGH

nou·gat \'nü-gət\ *n* : a confection of nuts or fruit pieces in a sugar paste

nought *var of* NAUGHT

noun \'naůn\ *n* : a word that is the name of a subject of discourse (as a person or place)

nour·ish \'nər-ish\ *vb* : to cause to grow and develop (as by care and feeding)

nour·ish·ing *adj* : giving nourishment

nour·ish·ment \-ish-mənt\ *n* **1** : FOOD, NUTRIMENT **2** : the action or process of nourishing

nou·veau riche \ˌnü-ˌvō-'rēsh\ *n, pl* **nou·veaux riches** *same*\ : a person newly rich : PARVENU

no·va \'nō-və\ *n, pl* **novas** *or* **no·vae** \-(ˌ)vē\ : a star that suddenly increases greatly in brightness and then within a few months or years grows dim again

1nov·el \'näv-əl\ *adj* **1** : having no precedent : NEW **2** : STRANGE, UN-USUAL

2novel *n* : a long invented prose narrative dealing with human experience through a connected sequence of events — **nov·el·ist** \-ə-ləst\ *n*

nov·el·ette \ˌnäv-ə-'let\ *n* : a brief novel or long short story

nov·el·ize \'näv-ə-ˌlīz\ *vb* : to convert into the form of a novel — **nov·el·iza·tion** \ˌnäv-ə-lə-'zā-shən\ *n*

nov·el·ty \'näv-əl-tē\ *n* **1** : something new or unusual **2** : NEWNESS **3** : a small manufactured article intended mainly for personal or household adornment — usu. used in pl.

No·vem·ber \nō-'vem-bər\ *n* : the 11th month of the year having 30 days

ə abut; ᵊ kitten; ər further; a back; ā bake; ä cot, cart; aů out; ch chin; e less; ē easy; g gift; i trip; ī life; j joke; ŋ sing; ō flow; ȯ flaw; ȯi coin; th thin; th this; ü loot; ů foot; y yet; yü few; yů furious; zh vision

no·ve·na \nō-'vē-nə\ n : a Roman Catholic nine days' devotion

nov·ice \'näv-əs\ n 1 : a new member of a religious order who is preparing to take the vows of religion 2 : one who i inexperienced or untrained

no·vi·ti·ate \nō-'vish-ət\ n 1 : the period or state of being a novice 2 : NOVICE 3 : a house where novices are trained

¹now \(')naů\ adv 1 : at the present time or moment 2 : in the time immediately before the present 3 : FORTHWITH 4 — used with the sense of present time weakened or lost (as to express command, introduce an important point, or indicate a transition) 〈~ this would be treason〉 5 : SOMETIMES 〈~ one and ~ another〉 6 : under the present circumstances 7 : at the time referred to

²now conj : in view of the fact 〈~ that you're here, we'll start〉

³now \'naů\ n : the present time or moment : PRESENT

now·a·days \'naů-ə-ˌdāz\ adv : at the present time

no·way \'nō-ˌwā\ or **no·ways** \-ˌwāz\ adv : NOWISE

no·where \-ˌhweər\ adv : not anywhere : in, at, or to no place — **nowhere** n

nowhere near adv : not nearly

no·wise \'nō-ˌwīz\ adv : in no way : not at all

nox·ious \'näk-shəs\ adj : harmful esp. to health or morals

noz·zle \'näz-əl\ n : a projecting part with an opening for an outlet 〈the ~ of a gun〉; esp : a tube on a hose to direct flow of liquid

nth \'enth\ adj 1 : numbered with an unspecified or indefinitely large ordinal number 2 : EXTREME, UTMOST 〈to the ~ degree〉

nu·ance \'n(y)ü-ˌäns, n(y)ü-'äns\ n : a shade of difference : a delicate variation (as in color, tone, or meaning)

nub \'nəb\ n 1 : KNOB, LUMP 2 : GIST, POINT 〈the ~ of the story〉

nub·bin \'nəb-ən\ n 1 : a small shriveled or imperfect fruit (as an ear of Indian corn) 2 : a small projecting bit

nub·ble \'nəb-əl\ n : a small knob or lump : a projecting bit (as of yarn in a rough-textured fabric) — **nub·bly** \-(ə-)lē\ adj

nu·bile \'n(y)ü-bəl, -ˌbīl\ adj : of marriageable condition or age 〈~ girls〉

nu·cle·ar \'n(y)ü-klē-ər\ adj 1 : of, relating to, or constituting a nucleus 2 : of, relating to, or utilizing the atomic nucleus, atomic energy, the atom bomb, or atomic power

nu·cle·ic acid \(n)y)ü-ˌklē-ik-\ n : any of various complex organic acids found esp. in cell nuclei

nu·cle·us \'n(y)ü-klē-əs\ n, pl **-clei** \-klē-ˌī\ also **-cle·us·es** [L, kernel, fr. nuc-, nux nut] 1 : a central mass or part about which matter gathers or is collected : CORE 2 : the part of a cell that contains chromosomes and is the seat of the mechanisms of heredity 3 : the central part of an atom that comprises nearly all of the atomic mass

¹nude \'n(y)üd\ adj : BARE, NAKED, UNCLOTHED — **nu·di·ty** \'n(y)üd-ət-ē\ n

²nude n 1 : a nude human figure esp. as depicted in art 2 : the condition of being nude 〈in the ~〉

nudge \'nəj\ vb : to touch or push gently (as with the elbow) usu. in order to seek attention — **nudge** n

nud·ism \'n(y)üd-ˌiz-əm\ n : the cult or practice of living unclothed — **nud·ist** \'n(y)üd-əst\ n

nu·ga·to·ry \'n(y)ü-gə-ˌtōr-ē\ adj 1 : INCONSEQUENTIAL, WORTHLESS 2 : having no force : INOPERATIVE

nug·get \'nəg-ət\ n : a lump of precious metal (as gold)

nui·sance \'n(y)üs-ᵊns\ n : an annoying or troublesome person or thing

null \'nəl\ adj 1 : having no legal or binding force : INVALID, VOID 2 : amounting to nothing 3 : INSIGNIFICANT — **nul·li·ty** \'nəl-ət-ē\ n

null and void adj : having no force, binding power, or validity

nul·li·fy \'nəl-ə-ˌfī\ vb : to make null or valueless; also : ANNUL — **nul·li·fi·ca·tion** \ˌnəl-ə-fə-'kā-shən\ n

numb \'nəm\ adj : lacking sensation or emotion : BENUMBED — **numb** vb — **numb·ly** \'nəm-lē\ adv — **numb·ness** n

¹num·ber \'nəm-bər\ n 1 : the total of individuals or units taken together 2 : a group or aggregate not specif. enumerated 〈a small ~ of tickets remain unsold〉 3 : a numerable state 〈times without ~〉 4 : a distinction of word form to denote reference to one or more than one 5 : a unit belonging to a mathematical system and subject to its laws; also, pl : ARITHMETIC 6 : a symbol (as a character, letter, or word) used to represent a mathematical number; also : such a number used to identify or designate 〈~ 5 on the list〉 〈a phone ~〉 7 : one in a sequence or series 〈the best ~ on the program〉

²number vb 1 : COUNT, ENUMERATE 2 : to include with or be one of a group 3 : to restrict to a small or definite number 4 : to assign a number to 5 : to comprise in number : TOTAL

num·ber·less \-ləs\ adj : INNUMERABLE, COUNTLESS

nu·mer·a·ble \'n(y)üm-(ə-)rə-bəl\ adj : capable of being counted

nu·mer·al \'n(y)üm-(ə-)rəl\ n 1 : a word or symbol representing a number 2 pl : numbers designating by year a school or college class often awarded for distinction in an extracurricular activity — **numeral** adj

nu·mer·ate \'n(y)ü-mə-ˌrāt\ vb : ENUMERATE

nu·mer·a·tor \-ˌrāt-ər\ n : the part of a fraction above the line

nu·mer·i·cal \n(y)ü-'mer-i-kəl\ adj : of or relating to numbers : denoting a number or expressed in numbers — **nu·mer·i·cal·ly** adv

nu·mer·ol·o·gy \ˌn(y)ü-mə-'räl-ə-jē\ n : the study of the occult significance of numbers — **nu·mer·ol·o·gist** n

nu·mer·ous \'n(y)üm-(ə-)rəs\ adj : consisting of, including, or relating to a great number : MANY

nu·mis·mat·ics \ˌn(y)ü-məz-'mat-iks\ n : the study or collection of monetary objects (as coins, tokens, or paper money) — **nu·mis·ma·tist** \n(y)ü-'miz-mət-əst\ n

num·skull \'nəm-ˌskəl\ n : a stupid person : DUNCE

nun \'nən\ n : a woman belonging to a religious order; esp : one under solemn vows of poverty, chastity, and obedience — **nun·nery** \-(ə-)rē\ n

nun·cio \'nən-sē-,ō\ *n* : a papal representative of the highest rank permanently accredited to a civil government

¹**nup·tial** \'nəp-shəl\ *adj* : of or relating to marriage or a wedding

²**nuptial** *n* : MARRIAGE, WEDDING — usu. used in pl.

¹**nurse** \'nərs\ *n* **1** : a girl or woman employed to take care of children **2** : a person trained to care for sick people

²**nurse** *vb* **1** : SUCKLE **2** : to take charge of and watch over **3** : TEND ⟨~ an invalid⟩ **4** : to treat with special care ⟨~ a headache⟩ **5** : to hold in one's mind or consideration ⟨~ a grudge⟩ **6** : to act or serve as a nurse

nurse·maid \-,mād\ *n* : a girl employed to look after children

nur·sery \'nərs-(ə-)rē\ *n* **1** : a room for children **2** : a place where children are temporarily cared for in their parents' absence **3** : a place where young plants are grown usu. for transplanting

nur·sery·maid \-,mād\ *n* : NURSEMAID

nur·sery·man \-mən\ *n* : a man who keeps or works in a plant nursery

nursery school *n* : a school for children under kindergarten age

nurs·ling \'nərs-lin\ *n* **1** : one that is solicitously cared for **2** : a nursing child

¹**nur·ture** \'nər-chər\ *n* **1** : TRAINING, UPBRINGING; *also* : the influences that modify the hereditary potential of an individual **2** : FOOD, NOURISHMENT

²**nurture** *vb* **1** : to care for : FEED, NOURISH **2** : EDUCATE, TRAIN **3** : FOSTER

nut \'nət\ *n* **1** : a dry fruit or seed with a hard shell and a firm inner kernel; *also* : its kernel **2** : a metal block with a hole through it with the hole having a screw thread enabling the block to be screwed on a bolt or screw **3** : the ridge on the upper end of the fingerboard in a stringed musical instrument over which the strings pass **4** : a foolish, eccentric, or crazy person **5** : ENTHUSIAST

nut·crack·er \-,krak-ər\ *n* : an instru-

ment for cracking nuts

nut·hatch \'nət-,hach\ *n* : any of various small birds that creep on tree trunks in search of food and resemble titmice

nut·meg \-,meg\ *n* : the nutlike aromatic seed of a tropical tree that is ground for use as a spice; *also* : this spice

nut·pick \-,pik\ *n* : a small sharp-pointed table implement for extracting the kernels from nuts

nu·tria \'n(y)ü-trē-ə\ *n* **1** : COYPU **2** : the durable usu. light brown fur of the coypu

¹**nu·tri·ent** \'n(y)ü-trē-ənt\ *adj* : NOURISHING

²**nutrient** *n* : a nutritive substance or ingredient

nu·tri·ment \-trə-mənt\ *n* : NUTRIENT

nu·tri·tion \n(y)ü-'trish-ən\ *n* : the act or process of nourishing; *esp* : the processes by which an individual takes in and utilizes food material — **nu·tri·tion·al** \-'trish-(ə-)nəl\ *adj* — **nu·tri·tious** \-'trish-əs\ *adj* — **nu·tri·tive** \'n(y)ü-trət-iv\ *adj*

nuts \'nəts\ *adj* **1** : ENTHUSIASTIC, KEEN **2** : CRAZY, DEMENTED

nut·shell \'nət-,shel\ *n* : the shell of a nut — **in a nutshell** : in a small compass : in a few words ⟨that's the story *in a nutshell*⟩

nut·ty \'nət-ē\ *adj* **1** : containing or suggesting nuts ⟨~ flavor⟩ **2** : mentally unbalanced : ECCENTRIC

nuz·zle \'nəz-əl\ *vb* **1** : to root around, push, or touch with or as if with the nose **2** : NESTLE, SNUGGLE

ny·lon \'nī-,län\ *n* **1** : any of numerous strong tough elastic synthetic materials used esp. in textiles and plastics **2** *pl* : stockings made of nylon

nymph \'nimf\ *n* **1** : one of the lesser goddesses in ancient mythology represented as maidens living in the mountains, forests, meadows, and waters **2** : an immature insect; *esp* : one that resembles the adult but is smaller and less differentiated and usu. lacks wings

o \'ō\ *n, often cap* : the 15th letter of the English alphabet

oaf \'ōf\ *n* : a stupid or awkward person — **oaf·ish** \'ō-fish\ *adj*

oak \'ōk\ *n* : any of various trees or shrubs related to the beech and chestnut and having a rounded thin-shelled nut; *also* : the usu. tough hard durable wood of an oak — **oak·en** \'ō-kən\ *adj*

oa·kum \'ō-kəm\ *n* : loosely twisted hemp or jute fiber impregnated with tar and used esp. in caulking ships

oar \'ōr\ *n* : a long slender broad-bladed implement for propelling or steering a boat

oar·lock \-,läk\ *n* : a U-shaped device for holding an oar in place

oars·man \'ōrz-mən\ *n* : one who rows esp. in a racing crew

oa·sis \ō-'ā-səs\ *n, pl* **oa·ses** \-'ā-,sēz\ : a fertile or green area in an arid region

oat \'ōt\ *n* : a cereal grass widely grown for its edible seed; *also* : this seed — **oat·en** \-ᵊn\ *adj*

oat·cake \-,kāk\ *n* : a thin flat oatmeal cake

oath \'ōth\ *n* **1** : a solemn appeal to God to witness to the truth of a statement or the sacredness of a promise **2** : an irreverent or careless use of a sacred name

oat·meal \'ōt-,mēl\ *n* **1** : meal made from oats **2** : porridge made from ground or rolled oats

ob·bli·ga·to \,äb-lə-'gät-ō\ *n* : an accompanying part usu. played by a solo instrument ⟨violin ~⟩

ob·du·rate \'äb-d(y)ə-rət\ *adj* : stubbornly resistant : UNYIELDING **syn** inflexible, adamant — **ob·du·ra·cy** \-rə-sē\ *n*

obe·di·ent \ō-'bēd-ē-ənt\ *adj* : submissive to the restraint or command of authority **syn** docile, tractable, amenable — **obe·di·ence** \-əns\ n — **obe·dient·ly** adv

obei·sance \ō-'bās-əns, -'bēs-\ n : a bow made to show respect or submission; also : DEFERENCE, HOMAGE

ob·e·lisk \'äb-ə-,lisk\ n : a 4-sided pillar that tapers toward the top and ends in a pyramid

obese \ō-'bēs\ adj : extremely fat — **obe·si·ty** \-'bē-sət-ē\ n

obey \ō-'bā\ vb 1 : to follow the commands or guidance of : behave obediently 2 : to comply with ⟨~ orders⟩

ob·fus·cate \'äb-fə-,skāt\ vb 1 : to make dark or obscure 2 : CONFUSE — **ob·fus·ca·tion** \,äb-fə-'skā-shən\ n

obi \'ō-bē\ n : a broad sash worn with a Japanese kimono

obit \ō-'bit, 'ō-bət\ n : OBITUARY

obi·ter dic·tum \,ō-bət-ər-'dik-təm\ n, pl **obiter dic·ta** \-tə\ : an incidental remark or observation

obit·u·ary \ə-'bich-ə-,wer-ē\ n : a notice of a person's death usu. with a short biographical account

¹ob·ject \'äb-jikt\ n 1 : something that may be seen or felt; also : something that may be perceived or examined mentally 2 : something that arouses an emotional response (as of affection or pity) 3 : AIM, PURPOSE 4 : a word or word group denoting that on or toward which the action of a verb is directed; also : a noun or noun equivalent in a prepositional phrase

²ob·ject \əb-'jekt\ vb 1 : to offer in opposition 2 : to oppose something; also : DISAPPROVE **syn** protest, remonstrate, expostulate — **ob·jec·tion** \-'jek-shən\ n — **ob·jec·tion·able** \-sh(ə-)nə-bəl\ adj — **ob·jec·tor** \-'jek-tər\ n

ob·jec·ti·fy \əb-'jek-tə-,fī\ vb : to make objective

¹ob·jec·tive \əb-'jek-tiv\ adj 1 : of or relating to an object or end 2 : existing outside and independent of the mind 3 : treating or dealing with facts without distortion by personal feelings or prejudices 4 : of, relating to, or constituting a grammatical case marking typically the object of a verb or preposition — **ob·jec·tive·ly** adv — **ob·jec·tive·ness** n — **ob·jec·tiv·i·ty** \,äb-,jek-'tiv-ət-ē\ n

²objective n 1 : an aim or end of action : GOAL 2 : the objective case; also : a word in it 3 : the lens (as in a microscope) nearest the object and forming an image of it

ob·jet d'art \,ōb-,zhā-'där\ n, pl **objets d'art** \same\ : an article of artistic worth; also : CURIO

ob·jur·gate \'äb-jər-,gāt\ vb : to denounce harshly — **ob·jur·ga·tion** \,äb-jər-'gā-shən\ n

ob·late \äb-'lāt\ adj : flattened or depressed at the poles ⟨the earth is an ~ spheroid⟩

obla·tion \ə-'blā-shən\ n : a religious offering

ob·li·gate \'äb-lə-,gāt\ vb : to bind legally or morally; also : to bind by a favor

ob·li·ga·tion \,äb-lə-'gā-shən\ n 1 : an act of obligating oneself to a course of action 2 : something (as a promise or a contract) that binds one to a course of action 3 : DUTY 4 : INDEBTEDNESS; also : LIABILITY — **oblig·a·to·ry** \ə-

'blig-ə-,tōr-ē, 'äb-li-gə-\ adj

oblige \ə-'blīj\ vb 1 : FORCE, COMPEL 2 : to bind by a favor; also : to do a favor for or do something as a favor — **oblig·ing** adj — **oblig·ing·ly** adv

oblique \ō-'blēk, -'blīk\ adj 1 : neither perpendicular nor parallel : SLANTING 2 : not straightforward : INDIRECT — **oblique·ly** adv — **oblique·ness** n — **obliq·ui·ty** \-'blik-wət-ē\ n

oblit·er·ate \ə-'blit-ə-,rāt\ vb 1 : to make undecipherable by wiping out or covering over 2 : to remove from recognition or memory 3 : CANCEL — **oblit·er·a·tion** \-,blit-ə-'rā-shən\ n

obliv·i·on \ə-'bliv-ē-ən\ n 1 : FORGETFULNESS 2 : the quality or state of being forgotten

obliv·i·ous \-ē-əs\ adj 1 : lacking memory or mindful attention 2 : UNAWARE — **obliv·i·ous·ly** adv — **obliv·i·ous·ness** n

ob·long \'äb-,lȯŋ\ adj : longer in one direction than in the other with opposite sides parallel : RECTANGULAR — **oblong** n

ob·lo·quy \'äb-lə-kwē\ n 1 : strongly condemnatory utterance or language 2 : bad repute : DISGRACE **syn** dishonor, shame, infamy

ob·nox·ious \äb-'näk-shəs\ adj : REPUGNANT, OFFENSIVE — **ob·nox·ious·ly** adv — **ob·nox·ious·ness** n

oboe \'ō-bō\ n [It, fr. F hautbois, lit., high wood] : a woodwind instrument shaped like a slender conical tube with holes and keys and a reed mouthpiece — **o·bo·ist** \-,bō-əst\ n

ob·scene \äb-'sēn\ adj 1 : REPULSIVE 2 : deeply offensive to morality or decency; esp : designed to incite to lust or depravity **syn** gross, vulgar, coarse — **ob·scen·i·ty** \-'sen-ət-ē\ n

ob·scu·ran·tism \äb-'skyùr-ən-,tiz-əm, ,äb-skyù-'ran-\ n 1 : opposition to the spread of knowledge 2 : deliberate vagueness or abstruseness — **ob·scu·ran·tist** n or adj

¹ob·scure \äb-'skyùr\ adj 1 : DIM, GLOOMY 2 : REMOTE; also : HUMBLE 3 : not readily understood : VAGUE — **ob·scure·ly** adv — **ob·scu·ri·ty** \-'skyùr-ət-ē\ n

²obscure vb 1 : to make dark, dim, or indistinct 2 : to conceal or hide by or as if by covering

ob·se·qui·ous \əb-'sē-kwē-əs\ adj : excessively attentive : FAWNING, SYCOPHANTIC — **ob·se·qui·ous·ly** adv — **ob·se·qui·ous·ness** n

ob·se·quy \'äb-sə-kwē\ n : a funeral or burial rite — usu. used in pl.

ob·serv·able \əb-'zər-və-bəl\ adj 1 : necessarily or customarily observed 2 : NOTICEABLE

ob·ser·vance \-'zər-vəns\ n 1 : a customary practice or ceremony 2 : an act or instance of following a custom, rule, or law 3 : OBSERVATION

ob·ser·vant \-vənt\ adj 1 : ATTENTIVE 2 : MINDFUL 3 : quick to observe : KEEN

ob·ser·va·tion \,äb-sər-'vā-shən, -zər-\ n 1 : an act or the power of observing 2 : the gathering of information (as for scientific studies) by noting facts or occurrences 3 : a conclusion drawn from observing; also : REMARK, STATEMENT 4 : the fact of being observed

ob·ser·va·to·ry \əb-'zər-və-,tōr-ē\ n : a place or institution equipped for observation of natural phenomena (as in astronomy)

ob·serve \əb-'zərv\ vb 1 : to conform one's action or practice to 2 : CELEBRATE 3 : to see or sense with careful attention 4 : to come to realize esp. through consideration of noted facts 5 : REMARK 6 : to make a scientific observation — **ob·serv·er** n

ob·sess \əb-'ses\ vb : to preoccupy intensely or abnormally

ob·ses·sion \əb-'sesh-ən\ n : a persistent disturbing preoccupation with an idea or feeling; also : an emotion or idea causing such a preoccupation — **ob·ses·sive** \-'ses-iv\ adj

ob·sid·i·an \əb-'sid-ē-ən\ n : a dark natural glass formed by the cooling of molten lava

ob·so·les·cent \,äb-sə-'les-ᵊnt\ adj : going out of use : becoming obsolete — **ob·so·les·cence** \-ᵊns\ n

ob·so·lete \,äb-sə-'lēt\ adj : no longer in use : OUTMODED syn old, antiquated, ancient

ob·sta·cle \'äb-sti-kəl\ n : something that stands in the way or opposes : OBSTRUCTION

ob·stet·rics \əb-'stet-riks\ n : a branch of medicine that deals with childbirth — **ob·stet·ri·cal** \-ri-kəl\ also **ob·stet·ric** \-rik\ adj — **ob·ste·tri·cian** \,äb-stə-'trish-ən\ n

ob·sti·nate \'äb-stə-nət\ adj : fixed and unyielding (as in an opinion or course) despite reason or persuasion : STUBBORN — **ob·sti·na·cy** \-nə-sē\ n — **ob·sti·nate·ly** adv

ob·strep·er·ous \əb-'strep-(ə-)rəs\ adj 1 : uncontrollably noisy 2 : stubbornly defiant : UNRULY

ob·struct \əb-'strəkt\ vb 1 : to block by an obstacle 2 : to impede the passage, action, or operation of 3 : to shut off from sight — **ob·struc·tive** \-'strək-tiv\ adj — **ob·struc·tor** \-tər\ n

ob·struc·tion \-'strək-shən\ n 1 : an act of obstructing : the state of being obstructed 2 : something that obstructs : HINDRANCE

ob·struc·tion·ist n : a person who hinders progress or business esp. in a legislative body — **ob·struc·tion·ism** n

ob·tain \əb-tān\ vb 1 : to gain or attain usu. by planning or effort 2 : to be generally recognized or established syn procure, secure, win, earn — **ob·tain·able** \-'tā-nə-bəl\ adj

ob·trude \əb-'trüd\ vb 1 : to thrust out 2 : to thrust forward without warrant or request : INTRUDE — **ob·tru·sion** \-'trü-zhən\ n — **ob·tru·sive** \-'trü-siv\ adj

ob·tuse \äb-'t(y)üs\ adj 1 : not sharp or quick of wit 2 : exceeding 90 degrees but less than 180 degrees (~ angle) 3 : not pointed or acute : BLUNT — **ob·tuse·ly** adv — **ob·tuse·ness** n

¹**ob·verse** \äb-'vərs\ adj 1 : facing the observer or opponent 2 : having the base narrower than the top 3 : being a counterpart or complement — **ob·verse·ly** adv

²**ob·verse** \'äb-,vərs\ n 1 : the side (as of a coin) bearing the principal design and lettering 2 : a front or principal surface 3 : COUNTERPART

ob·vi·ate \'äb-vē-,āt\ vb : to anticipate and dispose of beforehand : make unnecessary syn prevent, avert — **ob·vi·a·tion** \,äb-vē-'ā-shən\ n

ob·vi·ous \'äb-vē-əs\ adj : easily discovered, seen, or understood : PLAIN syn evident, manifest, patent, clear — **ob·vi·ous·ly** adv — **ob·vi·ous·ness** n

oc·a·ri·na \,äk-ə-'rē-nə\ n : a simple wind instrument usu. of terra-cotta and with a mouthpiece and holes that may be opened or closed by the finger to vary the pitch

¹**oc·ca·sion** \ə-'kā-zhən\ n 1 : a favorable opportunity 2 : a direct or indirect cause 3 : the time of an event 4 : EXIGENCY 5 pl : AFFAIRS, BUSINESS 6 : a special event : CELEBRATION

²**occasion** vb : CAUSE

oc·ca·sion·al \ə-'kāzh-nəl, -ən-ᵊl\ adj 1 : happening or met with now and then (~ references to the war) 2 : used or designed for a special occasion (~ verse) syn infrequent, rare, sporadic — **oc·ca·sion·al·ly** \-ē\ adv

oc·ci·den·tal \,äk-sə-'dent-ᵊl\ adj, often cap : WESTERN — **Occidental** n

oc·clude \ə-'klüd\ vb 1 : OBSTRUCT 2 : to shut in or out 3 : to take up and hold by absorption or adsorption 4 : to come together with opposing surfaces in contact — **oc·clu·sion** \-'klü-zhən\ n — **oc·clu·sive** \-'klü-siv\ adj

oc·cult \ə-'kəlt, 'äk-,əlt\ adj 1 : not revealed : SECRET 2 : ABSTRUSE, MYSTERIOUS 3 : of or relating to supernatural agencies, their effects, or knowledge of them

oc·cu·pan·cy \'äk-yə-pən-sē\ n 1 : OCCUPATION 2 : an occupied building or part of a building

oc·cu·pant \-pənt\ n : one who occupies something; esp : RESIDENT

oc·cu·pa·tion \,äk-yə-'pā-shən\ n 1 : an activity in which one engages; esp : VOCATION 2 : the taking possession of property; also : the taking possession of an area by a foreign military force — **oc·cu·pa·tion·al** \-sh(ə-)nəl\ adj — **oc·cu·pa·tion·al·ly** adv

oc·cu·py \'äk-yə-,pī\ vb 1 : to engage the attention or energies of 2 : to fill up (an extent in space or time) 3 : to take or hold possession of 4 : to reside in as owner or tenant — **oc·cu·pi·er** \-,pī(-ə)r\ n

oc·cur \ə-'kər\ vb 1 : to be found or met with : APPEAR 2 : to take place 3 : to come to mind

oc·cur·rence \ə-'kər-əns\ n 1 : something that takes place : APPEARANCE

ocean \'ō-shən\ n 1 : the whole body of salt water that covers nearly three fourths of the surface of the earth 2 : one of the large bodies of water into which the great ocean is divided — **ocean·ic** \,ō-shē-'an-ik\ adj

ocean·go·ing \'ō-shən-,gō-iŋ\ adj : of, relating to, or suitable for ocean travel

oc·e·lot \'äs-ə-,lät, 'ō-sə-\ n : a medium-sized American wildcat ranging southward from Texas and having a tawny yellow or gray coat with black markings

ocher or **ochre** \'ō-kər\ n : an earthy usu. red or yellow iron ore used as a pigment; also : the color esp. of yellow ocher

o'clock \ə-ˈkläk\ *adv* : according to the clock

oc·ta·gon \ˈäk-tə-ˌgän\ *n* : a polygon of 8 angles and 8 sides — **oc·tag·o·nal** \äk-ˈtag-ən-ᵊl\ *adj* — **oc·tag·o·nal·ly** *adv*

oc·tave \ˈäk-tiv\ *n* **1** : a musical interval embracing eight degrees; *also* : a tone or note at this interval or the whole series of notes, tones, or keys within this interval **2** : a group of eight

oc·ta·vo \äk-ˈtä-vō, -ˈtäv-ō\ *n* **1** : the size of a piece of paper cut eight from a sheet **2** : a book printed on octavo pages

oc·tet \äk-ˈtet\ *n* **1** : a musical composition for eight voices or eight instruments; *also* : the performers of such a composition **2** : a group or set of eight

Oc·to·ber \äk-ˈtō-bər\ *n* : the 10th month of the year having 31 days

oc·to·ge·nar·i·an \ˌäk-tə-jə-ˈner-ē-ən\ *n* : a person who is in his eighties

oc·to·pus \ˈäk-tə-pəs\ *n* : any of various sea mollusks with eight long arms furnished with two rows of suckers by which it grasps and holds its prey — **oc·to·pod** \-ˌpäd\ *adj or n*

oc·to·roon \ˌäk-tə-ˈrün\ *n* : a person of one-eighth Negro ancestry

oc·to·syl·lab·ic \ˌäk-tə-sə-ˈlab-ik\ *adj* : having or composed of verses having eight syllables — **octosyllabic** *n*

oc·u·lar \ˈäk-yə-lər\ *adj* **1** : of or relating to the eye or the eyesight **2** : VISUAL

oc·u·list \-ləst\ *n* **1** : OPHTHALMOLOGIST **2** : OPTOMETRIST

odd \ˈäd\ *adj* **1** : being only one of a pair or set (an ~ shoe) **2** : not divisible by two without leaving a remainder (~ numbers) **3** : somewhat more than the number mentioned (forty ~ years ago) **4** : additional to what is usual : OCCASIONAL (~ jobs) **5** : UNCONVENTIONAL, STRANGE (an ~ way of behaving) — **odd·ly** *adv*

odd·ball \-ˌbȯl\ *n* : one whose behavior is eccentric

odd·i·ty \ˈäd-ət-ē\ *n* **1** : one that is odd **2** : the quality or state of being odd

odd·ment \-mənt\ *n* : something left over : REMNANT

odds \ˈädz\ *n pl* **1** : a difference by which one thing is favored over another **2** : an equalizing allowance made to one believed to have a smaller chance of winning **3** : DISAGREEMENT

odds and ends *n pl* : miscellaneous things or matters

odds-on \ˈädz-ˈȯn, -ˈän\ *adj* : having a better than even chance to win

ode \ˈōd\ *n* : a lyric poem marked by nobility of feeling and solemnity of style

odi·ous \ˈōd-ē-əs\ *adj* : causing or deserving hatred or repugnance — **odi·ous·ly** *adv* — **odi·ous·ness** *n*

odi·um \-ē-əm\ *n* **1** : merited loathing : HATRED **2** : DISGRACE, OPPROBRIUM

odom·e·ter \ō-ˈdäm-ət-ər\ *n* : an instrument for measuring distance traversed (as by a vehicle)

odor \ˈōd-ər\ *n* **1** : the quality of something that stimulates the sense of smell; *also* : a sensation resulting from such stimulation **2** : REPUTE, ESTIMATION — **odor·less** \-ləs\ *adj* — **odor·ous** \ˈōd-ə-rəs\ *adj*

od·ys·sey \ˈäd-ə-sē\ *n* : a long wandering marked usu. by many changes of fortune

o'er \ˈō(ə)r\ *adv or prep* : OVER

oe·soph·a·gus *var of* ESOPHAGUS

of \(ˈ)əv, ˈäv\ *prep* **1** : FROM (a man ~ the West) **2** : having as a significant background or character element (a man ~ noble birth) (a man ~ ability) **3** : owing to (died ~ flu) **4** : BY (the plays ~ Shakespeare) **5** : having as a component parts or material, contents, or members (a house ~ brick) (a glass ~ water) (a pack ~ fools) **6** : belonging to or included by (the front ~ the house) (a time ~ life) (one ~ you) (the best ~ his kind) (the son ~ a doctor) **7** : connected with : OVER (the king ~ England) **8** : marked by : having as a significant or the chief element (a day ~ reckoning) (a tale ~ woe) **9** : ABOUT (tales ~ the West) **10** : that is : signified as (the city ~ Rome) **11** — used to indicate apposition of the words it joins (that fool ~ a husband) **12** — as concerns : FOR (love ~ country) **13** — used to indicate the application of an adjective (fond ~ candy) **14** : BEFORE (five minutes ~ ten)

¹**off** \ˈȯf\ *adv* **1** : from a place or position (drove ~ in a new car); *also* : ASIDE (turned ~ into a side road) **2** : so as to be unattached or removed (the lid blew ~) (handle came ~) **3** : to a state of discontinuance, exhaustion, or completion (shut the radio ~) **4** : away from regular work (took time ~ for lunch) **5** : at a distance in time or space (stood ~ a few yards) (several years ~)

²**off** *prep* **1** : away from the surface or top of (take it ~ the table) (fell ~ the porch) **2** : FROM (borrowed a dollar ~ me) **3** : at the expense of (lives ~ his sister) **4** : to seaward of (sail ~ the Maine coast) **5** : not engaged in (~ duty) **6** : abstaining from (~ liquor) **7** : below the usual level of (~ his game) **8** : away from (just ~ the highway)

³**off** *adj* **1** : more removed or distant **2** : started on the way **3** : not operating **4** : not correct **5** : REMOTE, SLIGHT **6** : INFERIOR **7** : provided for (well ~)

of·fal \ˈȯ-fəl\ *n* : the waste or by-product of a process; *esp* : the viscera and trimmings of a butchered animal removed in dressing

¹**offbeat** \ˈȯf-ˌbēt\ *n* : the unaccented part of a musical measure

²**offbeat** *adj* : ECCENTRIC, UNCONVENTIONAL

off-col·or \ˈȯf-ˈkəl-ər\ *or* **off-col·ored** *adj* **1** : not having the right or standard color **2** : of doubtful propriety : RISQUÉ

offence *chiefly Brit var of* OFFENSE

of·fend \ə-ˈfend\ *vb* **1** : SIN, TRANSGRESS **2** : to cause discomfort or pain : HURT **3** : to cause dislike or vexation : ANNOY — *syn* affront, insult — **of·fend·er** *n*

of·fense \ə-ˈfens\ *n* **1** : something that outrages the senses **2** : ATTACK, ASSAULT **3** : DISPLEASURE **4** : SIN, MISDEED **5** : an infraction of law : CRIME

¹**of·fen·sive** \ə-ˈfen-siv\ *adj* **1** : AGGRESSIVE **2** : OBNOXIOUS **3** : INSULTING — **of·fen·sive·ly** *adv* — **of·fen·sive·ness** *n*

²**offensive** *n* : ATTACK

¹**of·fer** \ˈȯ-fər\ *vb* **1** : SACRIFICE **2** : to present for acceptance : TENDER; *also* : to propose as payment **3** : PROPOSE, SUGGEST; *also* : to declare one's readiness **4** : to put up (~ resistance) **5** : to place on sale — **of·fer·ing** \ˈȯ-f(ə-)riŋ\ *n*

²offer n **1** : PROPOSAL **2** : BID **3** : AT-TEMPT, TRY

of·fer·to·ry \'o-fər-ˌtōr-ē\ n : the presentation of offerings at a church service; also : the musical accompaniment during it

off·hand \'of-'hand\ adv (or adj) : without previous thought or preparation

of·fice \'of-əs\ n **1** : a special duty or position; esp : a position of authority in government (run for ~) **2** : a prescribed form or service of worship; also : RITE **3** : an assigned or assumed duty or role **4** : a place where a business is transacted or a service is supplied ⟨ticket ~⟩

of·fice·hold·er \-ˌhōl-dər\ n : one holding a public office

of·fi·cer \'o-fə-sər\ n **1** : one charged with the enforcement of law **2** : one who holds an office of trust or authority **3** : one who holds a commission in the armed forces

¹of·fi·cial \ə-'fish-əl\ n : OFFICER

²official adj **1** : of or relating to an office or to officers **2** : AUTHORIZED, AUTHORITATIVE **3** : FORMAL — **of·fi·cial·ly** adv

of·fi·cial·dom n : officials as a class

of·fi·cial·ism n : lack of flexibility and initiative combined with excessive adherence to regulations (as in the behavior of government officials)

of·fi·ci·ant \ə-'fish-ē-ənt\ n : an officiating clergyman

of·fi·ci·ate \ə-'fish-ē-ˌāt\ vb **1** : to perform a ceremony, function, or duty **2** : to act in an official capacity

of·fi·cious \ə-'fish-əs\ adj : volunteering one's services where they are neither asked for nor needed : MEDDLESOME — **of·fi·cious·ly** adv — **of·fi·cious·ness** n

off·ing \'o-fiŋ\ n **1** : the part of the deep sea seen from the shore **2** : the near or foreseeable future

off·ish \'o-fish\ adj : inclined to stand aloof

¹off·set \'of-ˌset\ n **1** : a sharp bend (as in a pipe) by which one part is turned aside out of line **2** : a printing process in which an inked impression is first made on a rubber-blanketed cylinder and then transferred to the paper

²offset vb **1** : to place over against : BALANCE **2** : to compensate for **3** : to form an offset in (as a wall)

off·shoot \'of-ˌshüt\ n **1** : a branch of a main stem (as of a plant) **2** : a collateral or derived branch, descendant, or member

¹off·shore \-'shōr\ adv : at a distance from the shore

²offshore adj **1** : moving away from the shore **2** : situated off the shore and esp. within a zone extending three miles from low-water line

off·spring \-ˌspriŋ\ n, pl **offspring** also **offsprings** : PROGENY, YOUNG

off·stage \-'stāj\ adv (or adj) : off or away from the stage

off-the-rec·ord adj : given or made in confidence and not for publication ⟨~ remarks⟩

oft \'oft\ adv : OFTEN

of·ten \'of-(t)ən\ adv : many times : FREQUENTLY

of·ten·times \-,tīmz\ adv : OFTEN

ogle \'ō-gəl\ vb : to stare in a flirtatious way : eye amorously — **ogle** n

ogre \'ō-gər\ n **1** : a monster of fairy tales and folklore that feeds on human beings **2** : a dreaded person or object

ohm \'ōm\ n [after George Simon Ohm d1854 German physicist] : a unit of electrical resistance equal to the resistance of a circuit in which a potential difference of one volt produces a current of one ampere — **ohm·ic** \'ō-mik\ adj

¹oil \'oil\ n **1** : a fatty or greasy liquid substance obtained from plants, animals, or minerals and used for fuel, lighting, food, medicines, and manufacturing **2** : PETROLEUM **3** : artists' colors made with oil; also : a painting in such colors — **oily** adj

²oil vb : to treat, furnish, or lubricate with oil

oil·cloth \-ˌklöth\ n : cloth treated with oil or paint and used for table and shelf coverings

oil·skin \-ˌskin\ n **1** : an oiled waterproof cloth **2** : clothing (as a raincoat) made of oilskin

oint·ment \'oint-mənt\ n : a medicinal or cosmetic preparation usu. with a fatty or greasy base for use on the skin

¹OK or okay \ō-'kā\ adv (or adj) : all right

²OK or okay vb **OK'd or okayed; OK'ing or okay·ing** : APPROVE, AUTHORIZE — **OK or okay** n

okra \'ō-krə\ n : a tall annual plant related to the hollyhocks and grown for its edible green pods used esp. in soups and stews; also : these pods

¹old \'ōld\ adj **1** : ANCIENT; also : of long standing **2** : having existed for a specified period of time **3** : of or relating to a past era **4** : advanced in years **5** : showing the effects of age or use **6** : no longer in use — **old·en** \'ōl-dən\ adj — **old·ish** \-dish\ adj

²old n : old or earlier time ⟨days of ~⟩

old·en \'ōl-dən\ adj : of or relating to a bygone era : ANCIENT

Old English n : the language of the English people from the time of the earliest documents in the 7th century to about 1100

old-fash·ioned \'ōl(d)-'fash-ənd\ adj **1** : ANTIQUATED **2** : CONSERVATIVE

old-line \-'līn\ adj **1** : ORIGINAL, ESTABLISHED ⟨an ~ business⟩ **2** : adhering to old policies or practices

old maid n **1** : SPINSTER **2** : a prim fussy person

old·ster \'ōl(d)-stər\ n : an old or elderly person

old-tim·er \-'tī-mər\ n : VETERAN; also : OLDSTER

Old World n : the eastern hemisphere; esp : continental Europe

old-world \'ōl(d)-'wərld\ adj : OLD-FASHIONED, PICTURESQUE

ole·ag·i·nous \ˌō-lē-'aj-ə-nəs\ adj : OILY

ole·an·der \'ō-lē-ˌan-dər\ n : a poisonous evergreen shrub often grown for its fragrant red or white flowers

oleo \'ō-lē-ˌō\ n : MARGARINE

oleo·mar·ga·rine \ˌō-lē-ō-'märj-(ə-)rən, -ə-ˌrēn\ n : MARGARINE

ol·fac·to·ry \äl-'fak-t(ə-)rē\ adj : of or relating to the sense of smell

ə abut; ᵉ kitten; ər further; a back; ā bake; ä cot, cart; au̇ out; ch chin; e less; ē easy; g gift; i trip; ī life; j joke; ŋ sing; ō flow; ȯ flaw; ȯi coin; th thin; t͟h this; ü loot; u̇ foot; y yet; yü few; yu̇ furious; zh vision

ol·i·gar·chy \'äl-ə-,gär-kē\ *n* **1** : a government in which the power is in the hands of a few **2** : a state having an oligarchy; *also* : the group holding power in such a state — **ol·i·garch** \-,gärk\ *n* — **ol·i·gar·chic** \,äl-ə-'gär-kik\ *or* **ol·i·gar·chi·cal** \-ki-kəl\ *adj*

olio \'ō-lē-,ō\ *n* : HODGEPODGE, MEDLEY

ol·ive \'äl-iv\ *n* : an Old World evergreen tree grown in warm regions for its fruit that is important as food and for its edible oil ⟨olive oil⟩

om·e·let *also* **om·e·lette** \'äm-(ə-)lət\ *n* : eggs beaten with milk or water, cooked without stirring until set, and folded over

omen \'ō-mən\ *n* : an event or phenomenon believed to be a sign or warning of a future occurrence

om·i·nous \'äm-ə-nəs\ *adj* : foretelling evil : THREATENING — **om·i·nous·ly** *adv* — **om·i·nous·ness** *n*

omit \ō-'mit\ *vb* **omit·ted; omit·ting** **1** : to leave out or leave unmentioned **2** : to fail to perform : NEGLECT — **omis·sion** \-'mish-ən\ *n*

¹**om·ni·bus** \'äm-ni-(,)bəs\ *n* [F, fr. L, for all] : BUS

²**omnibus** *adj* : of, relating to, or providing for many things at once ⟨an ~ bill⟩

om·nip·o·tent \äm-'nip-ət-ənt\ *adj* : having unlimited authority or influence : ALMIGHTY — **om·nip·o·tence** \-əns\ *n* — **om·nip·o·tent·ly** *adv*

om·ni·pres·ent \,äm-ni-'prez-ᵊnt\ *adj* : present in all places at all times — **om·ni·pres·ence** \-ᵊns\ *n*

om·ni·scient \äm-'nish-ənt\ *adj* : having infinite awareness, understanding, and insight — **om·ni·science** \-əns\ *n* — **om·ni·scient·ly** *adv*

om·ni·um-gath·er·um \,äm-nē-əm-'gath-ə-rəm\ *n* : a miscellaneous collection of persons or things

om·niv·o·rous \äm-'niv-(ə-)rəs\ *adj* : feeding on both animal and vegetable substances; *also* : AVID ⟨an ~ reader⟩ — **om·niv·o·rous·ly** *adv* — **om·niv·o·rous·ness** *n*

¹**on** \(')ȯn, ('ä)n\ *prep* **1** : in or to a position over and in contact with ⟨a book ~ the table⟩ ⟨jumped ~ his horse⟩ **2** : touching the surface of ⟨shadows ~ the wall⟩ **3** : in, ABOARD ⟨went ~ the train⟩ **4** : AT, TO ⟨~ the right were the mountains⟩ **5** : at or towards as an object ⟨crept up ~ him⟩ ⟨smiled ~ her⟩ **6** : ABOUT, CONCERNING ⟨a book ~ minerals⟩ **7** — used to indicate a basis, source, or standard of computation ⟨has it ~ good authority⟩ ⟨10 cents ~ the dollar⟩ **8** : with regard to ⟨a monopoly ~ wheat⟩ **9** : connected with as a member or participant ⟨~ a committee⟩ ⟨~ tour⟩ **10** : in a state or process of ⟨~ fire⟩ ⟨~ the wane⟩ **11** : during or at the time of ⟨came ~ Monday⟩ ⟨every hour ~ the hour⟩ **12** : through the agency of ⟨was cut ~ a tin can⟩

²**on** *adv* **1** : in or into a position of contact with or attachment to a surface **2** : FORWARD **3** : into operation

³**on** *adj* : being in operation or in progress

once \'wəns\ *adv* **1** : one time only **2** : at any one time : EVER **3** : FORMERLY **4** : by one degree of relationship

once-over \-,ō-vər\ *n* : a swift examination or survey

on·com·ing \'ȯn-,kəm-iŋ, 'än-\ *adj* : APPROACHING ⟨~ traffic⟩

¹**one** \'wən\ *adj* **1** : being a single unit

or thing ⟨~ man went⟩ **2** : being one in particular ⟨early ~ morning⟩ **3** : being the same in kind or quality ⟨members of ~ race⟩; *also* : UNITED **4** : being not specified or fixed ⟨at ~ time or another⟩

²**one** *pron* **1** : a single member or specimen ⟨saw ~ of his friends⟩ **2** : a person in general ⟨~ never knows⟩ **3** — used in place of a pronoun in the first person

³**one** *n* **1** : the number denoting unity **2** : the 1st in a set or series **3** : a single person or thing — **one·ness** \'wən-nəs\ *n*

on·er·ous \'än-ə-rəs, 'ō-nə-\ *adj* : imposing or constituting a burden : TROUBLESOME **syn** oppressive, exacting

one·self \(,)wən-'self\ *pron* : one's own self — usu. used reflexively or for emphasis

one-sid·ed \'wən-'sīd-əd\ *adj* **1** : having or occurring on one side only; *also* : having one side prominent or more developed **2** : UNEQUAL ⟨a ~ game⟩ **3** : PARTIAL ⟨a ~ attitude⟩

one-time \-,tīm\ *adj* : FORMER, SOMETIME

one-way \-'wā\ *adj* : moving, allowing movement, or functioning in only one direction ⟨~ streets⟩

on·go·ing \'ȯn-,gō-iŋ, 'än-\ *adj* : continuously moving forward

on·ion \'ən-yən\ *n* : a plant related to the lilies and grown for its pungent edible bulb; *also* : this bulb

on·ion·skin \-,skin\ *n* : a thin strong translucent paper of very light weight

on·look·er \'ȯn-,lùk-ər, 'än-\ *n* : SPECTATOR

¹**on·ly** \'ōn-lē\ *adj* **1** : unquestionably the best **2** : SOLE

²**only** *adv* **1** : MERELY, JUST ⟨~ two dollars⟩ **2** : SOLELY ⟨known ~ to me⟩ **3** : at the very least ⟨was ~ too true⟩ **4** : as a final result ⟨will ~ make you sick⟩

³**only** *conj* : except that

on·rush \'ȯn-,rəsh, 'än-\ *n* : a rushing onward

on·set \-,set\ *n* **1** : ATTACK **2** : BEGINNING

¹**on·shore** \-'shȯr\ *adv* : near the shore

²**onshore** *adj* **1** : moving toward the shore **2** : situated on or near the shore

on·slaught \'än-,slȯt, 'ȯn-\ *n* : a fierce attack

on·to \'ȯn-tü, 'än-, -tə\ *prep* : to a position or point on

onus \'ō-nəs\ *n* **1** : BURDEN; *also* : OBLIGATION **2** : BLAME

¹**on·ward** \'ȯn-wərd, 'än-\ *also* **on·wards** \-wərdz\ *adv* : FORWARD

²**onward** *adj* : directed or moving onward : FORWARD

on·yx \'än-iks\ *n* : chalcedony with parallel layers in different shades of color

oo·dles \'üd-ᵊlz\ *n pl* : a great quantity

¹**ooze** \'üz\ *n* **1** : a soft deposit ⟨as of mud⟩ on the bottom of a body of water **2** : MUD, SLIME — **oozy** \'ü-zē\ *adj*

²**ooze** *vb* **1** : to flow or leak out slowly or imperceptibly **2** : EXUDE

³**ooze** *n* : something that oozes

opal \'ō-pəl\ *n* : a noncrystalline silica mineral that is sometimes classed as a gem and has delicate changeable colors

opal·es·cent \,ō-pə-'les-ᵊnt\ *adj* : IRIDESCENT — **opal·es·cence** \-ᵊns\ *n*

opaque \ō-'pāk\ *adj* **1** : being neither transparent nor translucent **2** : not easily understood **3** : OBTUSE, STUPID — **opaque·ly** *adv* — **opaque·ness** *n*

ope \\'ōp\\ *vb* : OPEN
¹open \\'ō-pən\\ *adj* **1** : not shut or shut up ⟨~ door⟩ **2** : not secret or hidden; *also* : FRANK **3** : not enclosed or covered ⟨~ fire⟩; *also* : not protected **4** : free to be entered or used ⟨~ tournament⟩ **5** : easy to get through or see ⟨~ country⟩ **6** : spread out : EXTENDED **7** : free from restraints or controls ⟨~ season⟩ **8** : readily accessible and co-operative; *also* : GENEROUS **9** : not decided : UNCERTAIN ⟨~ question⟩ **10** : ready to operate ⟨stores are ~⟩ **11** : having components separated by a space in writing and printing ⟨the name *Spanish mackerel* is an ~ compound⟩ — **open·ly** *adv* — **open·ness** \\-pən-nəs\\ *n*
²open *vb* **1** : to change or move from a shut position; *also* : to make open by clearing away obstacles **2** : to make or become functional ⟨~ a store⟩ **3** : REVEAL; *also* : ENLIGHTEN **4** : to make openings in **5** : BEGIN **6** : to give access — **open·er** \\'ōp-(ə-)nər\\ *n*
³open *n* : OUTDOORS
open–air \\,ō-pən-'aər\\ *adj* : OUTDOOR ⟨~ theaters⟩
open–hand·ed \\,ō-pən-'han-dəd\\ *adj* : GENEROUS
open–hearth \\-'härth\\ *adj* : of, relating to, or being a process of making steel in a furnace that reflects the heat from the roof onto the material
open·ing \\'ōp-(ə-)niŋ\\ *n* **1** : an act or instance of making or becoming open **2** : something that is open **3** : BEGINNING **4** : OCCASION; *also* : an opportunity for employment
open–mind·ed \\,ō-pən-'mīn-dəd\\ *adj* : free from rigidly fixed preconceptions : UNPREJUDICED
open shop *n* : an establishment employing and retaining on the payroll members and nonmembers of a labor union
open·work \\'ō-pən-,wərk\\ *n* : work so made as to show openings through its substance ⟨a railing of wrought-iron ~⟩
¹opera *pl of* OPUS
²op·era \\'äp-(ə-)rə\\ *n* : a drama set to music — **op·er·at·ic** \\,äp-ə-'rat-ik\\ *adj*
op·er·a·ble \\'äp-(ə-)rə-bəl\\ *adj* **1** : fit, possible, or desirable to use **2** : suitable for surgical treatment ⟨an ~ cancer⟩
opera glass *n* : a small binocular adapted for use at an opera — often used in pl.
op·er·ate \\'äp-ə-,rāt\\ *vb* **1** : to perform work : FUNCTION **2** : to produce an effect **3** : to perform an operation **4** : to put or keep in operation — **op·er·a·tor** \\-,rāt-ər\\ *n*
op·er·a·tion \\,äp-ə-'rā-shən\\ *n* **1** : a doing or performing of a practical work **2** : an exertion of power or influence; *also* : method or manner of functioning **3** : a surgical procedure **4** : a process of deriving one mathematical expression from others according to a rule **5** : a military action, mission, or maneuver — **op·er·a·tion·al** \\-sh(ə-)nəl\\ *adj*
¹op·er·a·tive \\'äp-(ə-)rət-iv, 'äp-ə-,rāt-\\ *adj* **1** : producing an appropriate effect **2** : OPERATING **3** : having to do with physical operations; *also* : WORKING **4** : based on or consisting of an operation
²operative *n* : OPERATOR

op·er·et·ta \\,äp-ə-'ret-ə\\ *n* : a light musical-dramatic work with a romantic plot, spoken dialogue, and dancing scenes
oph·thal·mic \\äf-'thal-mik, äp-\\ *adj* : of, relating to, or located near the eye
oph·thal·mol·o·gy \\,äf-,thal-'mäl-ə-jē, ,äp-\\ *n* : a branch of medicine dealing with the structure, functions, and diseases of the eye — **oph·thal·mol·o·gist** \\-jəst\\ *n*
opi·ate \\'ō-pē-ət, -pē-,āt\\ *n* : a preparation or derivative of opium; *also* : NARCOTIC
opine \\ō-'pīn\\ *vb* : to express an opinion : STATE
opin·ion \\ə-'pin-yən\\ *n* **1** : a belief stronger than impression and less strong than positive knowledge **2** : JUDGMENT **3** : a formal statement by an expert after careful study
opin·ion·at·ed \\-yə-,nāt-əd\\ *adj* : obstinately adhering to personal opinions
opi·um \\'ō-pē-əm\\ *n* : an addictive narcotic drug that is the dried juice of a poppy
opos·sum \\ə-'päs-əm\\ *n* : any of various American marsupial mammals; *esp* : a common omnivorous tree-dwelling animal of the eastern U.S.
op·po·nent \\ə-'pō-nənt\\ *n* : one that opposes : ADVERSARY
op·por·tune \\,äp-ər-'t(y)ün\\ *adj* : SUITABLE, TIMELY — **op·por·tune·ly** *adv*
op·por·tun·ism \\-'t(y)ü-,niz-əm\\ *n* : a taking advantage of opportunities or circumstances esp. with little regard for principles or ultimate consequences — **op·por·tun·ist** \\-nəst\\ *n* — **op·por·tu·nis·tic** \\-t(y)ü-'nis-tik\\ *adj*
op·por·tu·ni·ty \\-'t(y)ü-nət-ē\\ *n* **1** : a favorable combination of circumstances, time, and place **2** : a chance for advancement or progress
op·pose \\ə-'pōz\\ *vb* **1** : to place opposite or against something (as to provide resistance or contrast) **2** : to strive against : RESIST — **op·po·si·tion** \\,äp-ə-'zish-ən\\ *n*
¹op·po·site \\'äp-ə-zət\\ *n* : one that is opposed or contrary
²opposite *adj* **1** : set over against something that is at the other end or side **2** : OPPOSED, HOSTILE; *also* : CONTRARY **3** : contrarily turned or moving — **op·po·site·ly** *adv* — **op·po·site·ness** *n*
³opposite *adv* : on opposite sides
⁴opposite *prep* : across from and usu. facing ⟨the house ~ ours⟩
op·press \\ə-'pres\\ *vb* **1** : to crush by abuse of power or authority **2** : to weigh down : BURDEN **syn** depress, wrong, persecute — **op·pres·sive** \\-'pres-iv\\ *adj* — **op·pres·sive·ly** *adv* — **op·pres·sor** \\-'pres-ər\\ *n*
op·pres·sion \\ə-'presh-ən\\ *n* **1** : unjust or cruel exercise of power or authority **2** : DEPRESSION
op·pro·bri·ous \\ə-'prō-brē-əs\\ *adj* : expressing or deserving opprobrium — **op·pro·bri·ous·ly** *adv*
op·pro·bri·um \\-brē-əm\\ *n* **1** : something that brings disgrace **2** : INFAMY
opt \\'äpt\\ *vb* : to make a choice
op·tic \\'äp-tik\\ *adj* : of or relating to vision or the eye

ə abut; ᵉ kitten; ər further; a back; ā bake; ä cot, cart; aů out; ch chin; e less; ē easy; g gift; i trip; ī life; j joke; ŋ sing; ō flow; ȯ flaw; ȯi coin; th thin; th̲ this; ü loot; ů foot; y yet; yü few; yů furious; zh vision

op·ti·cal \'äp-ti-kəl\ *adj* **1 :** relating to optics **2 :** OPTIC

op·ti·cian \äp-'tish-ən\ *n* **1 :** a maker of or dealer in optical items and instruments **2 :** one that grinds spectacle lenses to prescription and dispenses spectacles

op·tics \'äp-tiks\ *n* **:** a science that deals with the nature and properties of light and the effects that it undergoes and produces

op·ti·mal \'äp-tə-məl\ *adj* **:** most desirable or satisfactory — **op·ti·mal·ly** *adv*

op·ti·mism \'äp-tə-‚miz-əm\ *n* [F *optimisme*, fr. L *optimus* best] **1 :** a doctrine that this world is the best possible world **2 :** an inclination to anticipate the best possible outcome of actions or events — **op·ti·mist** \-məst\ *n* — **op·ti·mis·tic** \‚äp-tə-'mis-tik\ *adj* — **op·ti·mis·ti·cal·ly** \-ti-k(ə-)lē\ *adv*

op·ti·mum \'äp-tə-məm\ *n, pl* **-ma** \-mə\ *also* **-mums :** the amount or degree of something most favorable to an end; *also* **:** greatest degree attained under implied or specified conditions

op·tion \'äp-shən\ *n* **1 :** the power or right to choose **2 :** a right to buy or sell something at a specified price during a specified period **3 :** something offered for choice — **op·tion·al** \-sh(ə-)nəl\ *adj*

op·tom·e·try \äp-'täm-ə-trē\ *n* **:** the art or profession of examining the eyes for defects of refraction and of prescribing lenses to correct these — **op·tom·e·trist** \-trəst\ *n*

op·u·lent \'äp-yə-lənt\ *adj* **1 :** WEALTHY **2 :** richly abundant — **op·u·lence** \-ləns\ *n*

opus \'ō-pəs\ *n, pl* **opera** \'ō-pə-rə, 'äp-ə-\ *also* **opus·es :** WORK; *esp* **:** a musical composition

or \ər, (‚)ȯr\ *conj* — used as a function word to indicate an alternative ⟨sink ∼ swim⟩

-or \ər\ *n suffix* **:** one that does a (specified) thing ⟨calculator⟩ ⟨elevator⟩

or·a·cle \'ȯr-ə-kəl\ *n* **1 :** one held to give divinely inspired answers or revelations **2 :** an authoritative or wise utterance; *also* **:** a person of great authority or wisdom — **orac·u·lar** \ȯ-'rak-yə-lər\ *adj*

oral \'ȯr-əl, 'ȯr-\ *adj* **1 :** SPOKEN **2 :** of or relating to the mouth

or·ange \'ȯr-inj\ *n* **1 :** a juicy citrus fruit with reddish yellow rind; *also* **:** the evergreen tree with fragrant white flowers that bears this fruit **2 :** a color between red and yellow

or·ange·ade \‚ȯr-inj-'ād\ *n* **:** a beverage of orange juice, sugar, and water

or·ange·ry \'ȯr-inj-rē\ *n* **:** a protected place (as a greenhouse) for raising oranges in cool climates

orang·u·tan \ə-'raŋ-ə-‚taŋ, -‚tan\ *n* [Malay *orang hutan*, lit., man of the forest] **:** a reddish brown manlike tree-living ape of Borneo and Sumatra

orate \ȯ-'rāt\ *vb* **:** to speak in a declamatory manner

ora·tion \ə-'rā-shən\ *n* **:** an elaborate discourse delivered in a formal dignified manner

or·a·tor \'ȯr-ət-ər\ *n* **:** one noted for his skill and power as a public speaker

or·a·tor·i·cal \‚ȯr-ə-'tȯr-i-kəl\ *adj* **:** of, relating to, or characteristic of an orator or oratory

or·a·to·rio \‚ȯr-ə-'tȯr-ē-‚ō\ *n* **:** a choral work usu. on a scriptural subject

¹or·a·to·ry \'ȯr-ə-‚tȯr-ē\ *n* **:** a private or institutional chapel

²oratory *n* **:** the art of speaking eloquently and effectively in public **syn** eloquence, elocution — **or·a·tor·i·cal** \‚ȯr-ə-'tȯr-i-kəl\ *adj*

orb \'ȯrb\ *n* **:** a spherical body; *esp* **:** a celestial body (as a planet) — **or·bic·u·lar** \ȯr-'bik-yə-lər\ *adj*

¹or·bit \'ȯr-bət\ *n* [L *orbita*, lit., track, rut] **1 :** a path described by one body or object in its revolution about another **2 :** range or sphere of activity — **or·bit·al** \-ᵊl\ *adj*

²orbit *vb* **1 :** CIRCLE **2 :** to send up and make revolve in an orbit ⟨∼ a satellite⟩

or·chard \'ȯr-chərd\ *n* [OE *ortgeard*, fr. L *hortus* garden + OE *geard* yard, both fr. the same prehistoric IE noun meaning an enclosure] **:** a place where fruit trees or nut trees are grown; *also* **:** the trees of such a place — **or·chard·ist** \-əst\ *n*

or·ches·tra \'ȯr-kə-strə\ *n* **1 :** a group of instrumentalists organized to perform ensemble music **2 :** the front section of seats on the main floor of a theater — **or·ches·tral** \ȯr-'kes-trəl\ *adj*

or·ches·trate \'ȯr-kə-‚strāt\ *vb* **:** to compose or arrange for an orchestra — **or·ches·tra·tion** \‚ȯr-kə-'strā-shən\ *n*

or·chid \'ȯr-kəd\ *n* **:** any of numerous related plants having often showy flowers with three petals of which the middle one is enlarged into a lip; *also* **:** a flower of an orchid

or·dain \ȯr-'dān\ *vb* **1 :** to admit to the ministry or priesthood by the ritual of a church **2 :** DECREE, ENACT; *also* **:** DESTINE

or·deal \ȯr-'dē(-ə)l, 'ȯr-‚dē(-ə)l\ *n* **:** a severe trial or experience

¹or·der \'ȯrd-ər\ *n* **1 :** a group of people formally united; *also* **:** a badge or medal of such a group **2 :** any of the several grades of the Christian ministry; *also, pl* **:** ORDINATION **3 :** a rank, class, or special group of persons or things **4 :** ARRANGEMENT, SEQUENCE; *also* **:** the prevailing mode of things **5 :** a customary mode of procedure; *also* **:** the rule of law or proper authority **6 :** a specific rule, regulation, or authoritative direction **:** COMMAND **7 :** a style of building; *also* **:** an architectural column forming the unit of a style **8 :** condition esp. with regard to repair **9 :** a written direction to pay money or to buy or sell goods; *also* **:** goods bought or sold

²order *vb* **1 :** ARRANGE, REGULATE **2 :** COMMAND **3 :** to place an order

¹or·der·ly \'ȯrd-ər-lē\ *adj* **1 :** arranged according to some order; *also* **:** NEAT, TIDY **2 :** well behaved ⟨an ∼ crowd⟩ **syn** methodical, systematic — **or·der·li·ness** *n*

²orderly *n* **1 :** a soldier who attends a superior officer **2 :** a hospital attendant who does general work

¹or·di·nal \'ȯrd-ᵊn-əl, -ᵊnəl\ *adj* **:** indicating order or rank (as sixth) in a series

²ordinal *n* **:** an ordinal number

or·di·nance \'ȯrd-(ᵊ-)nəns\ *n* **:** an authoritative decree or law; *esp* **:** a municipal regulation

or·di·nary \'ȯrd-ᵊn-‚er-ē\ *adj* **1 :** to be expected **:** USUAL **2 :** of common quality, rank, or ability; *also* **:** POOR, INFERIOR **syn** customary, routine, normal — **or·di·nar·i·ly** \‚ȯrd-ᵊn-'er-ə-lē\ *adv*

or·di·na·tion \,ȯrd-ᵊn-'ā-shən\ *n* : the act or ceremony by which a person is ordained

ord·nance \'ȯrd-nəns\ *n* **1** : military supplies (as weapons, ammunition, or vehicles) **2** : CANNON, ARTILLERY

or·dure \'ȯr-jər\ *n* : EXCREMENT

¹ore \'ȯr\ *n* : a mineral containing a constituent for which it is mined and worked

²öre \'ər-ə\ *n, pl* öre — see MONEY table

or·gan \'ȯr-gən\ *n* **1** : a musical instrument having sets of pipes sounded by compressed air and controlled by keyboards; *also* : an instrument in which the sounds of the pipe organ are approximated by electronic devices **2** : a differentiated animal or plant structure made up of cells and tissues and performing some bodily function **3** : a means of performing a function or accomplishing an end **4** : PERIODICAL

or·gan·dy *also* **or·gan·die** \'ȯr-gən-dē\ *n* : a fine transparent muslin with a stiff finish

or·gan·ic \ȯr-'gan-ik\ *adj* **1** : of, relating to, or arising in a bodily organ **2** : ORGANIZED ⟨an ~ whole⟩ **3** : of, relating to, or derived from living things; *also* : containing carbon or its compounds **4** : of, relating to, or being a branch of chemistry dealing with carbon compounds formed or related to those formed by living things — **or·gan·i·cal·ly** *adv*

or·ga·nism \'ȯr-gə-,niz-əm\ *n* : a living person, animal, or plant

or·gan·ist \'ȯr-gə-nəst\ *n* : one who plays an organ

or·ga·ni·za·tion \,ȯr-gə-nə-'zā-shən\ *n* **1** : the act or process of organizing or of being organized; *also* : the condition or manner of being organized **2** : ASSOCIATION, SOCIETY **3** : MANAGEMENT

or·ga·nize \'ȯr-gə-,nīz\ *vb* **1** : to develop an organic structure **2** : to arrange or form into a complete and functioning whole **3** : to set up an administrative structure for **4** : to arrange by systematic planning and united effort **5** : to join in a union; *also* : UNIONIZE **syn** institute, found, establish — **or·ga·niz·er** *n*

or·gan·za \ȯr-'gan-zə\ *n* : a sheer dress fabric resembling organdy and usu. made of silk, rayon, or nylon

or·gasm \'ȯr-,gaz-əm\ *n* : a climax of sexual excitement

or·gi·as·tic \,ȯr-jē-'as-tik\ *adj* : of, relating to, or marked by orgies

or·gu·lous \'ȯr-g(y)ə-ləs\ *adj* : PROUD

or·gy \'ȯr-jē\ *n* : drunken revelry

ori·el \'ȯr-ē-əl\ *n* : a window built out from a wall and usu. supported by a bracket

ori·ent \'ȯr-ē-,ent\ *vb* **1** : to set or arrange in a definite position esp. in relation to the points of the compass **2** : to acquaint with an existing situation or environment — **ori·en·ta·tion** \,ȯr-ē-ən-'tā-shən\ *n*

ori·en·tal \,ȯr-ē-'ent-ᵊl\ *adj, often cap* : of or situated in the Orient — **Oriental** *n*

or·i·fice \'ȯr-ə-fəs\ *n* : OPENING, MOUTH

ori·flamme \'ȯr-ə-,flam\ *n* : a brightly colored banner used as a standard or ensign in battle

ori·ga·mi \,ȯr-ə-'gäm-ē\ *n* : the art or process of Japanese paper folding

or·i·gin \'ȯr-ə-jən\ *n* **1** : ANCESTRY **2** : rise, beginning, or derivation from a source; *also* : CAUSE

¹orig·i·nal \ə-'rij-ən-ᵊl\ *n* : something from which a copy, reproduction, or translation is made : PROTOTYPE

²original *adj* **1** : FIRST, INITIAL **2** : not copied from something else : FRESH **3** : INVENTIVE — **orig·i·nal·i·ty** \-,rij-ə-'nal-ət-ē\ *n* — **orig·i·nal·ly** \-'rij-ən-ᵊl-ē\ *adv*

orig·i·nate \ə-'rij-ə-,nāt\ *vb* **1** : to give rise to : INITIATE **2** : to come into existence : BEGIN — **orig·i·na·tor** *n*

ori·ole \'ȯr-ē-,ōl\ *n* : an American songbird about the size of a thrush with brilliant black and orange plumage in the male

or·i·son \'ȯr-ə-sən\ *n* : PRAYER

or·mo·lu \'ȯr-mə-,lü\ *n* : a brass made to imitate gold and used for decorative purposes

¹or·na·ment \'ȯr-nə-mənt\ *n* : something that lends grace or beauty : DECORATION — **or·na·men·tal** \,ȯr-nə-'ment-ᵊl\ *adj*

²ornament \'ȯr-nə-,ment\ *vb* : to provide with ornament : ADORN — **or·na·men·ta·tion** \,ȯr-nə-mən-'tā-shən\ *n*

or·nate \ȯr-'nāt\ *adj* : elaborately decorated — **or·nate·ly** *adv* — **or·nate·ness** *n*

or·nery \'ȯrn-(ə-)rē, 'än-\ *adj* : having an irritable disposition

or·ni·thol·o·gy \,ȯr-nə-'thäl-ə-jē\ *n* : a branch of zoology dealing with birds — **or·ni·tho·log·i·cal** \-thə-'läj-i-kəl\ *adj* — **or·ni·thol·o·gist** \-'thäl-ə-jəst\ *n*

oro·tund \'ȯr-ə-,tənd\ *adj* **1** : SONOROUS **2** : POMPOUS

or·phan \'ȯr-fən\ *n* : a child deprived by death of one or usu. both parents — **orphan** *vb*

or·phan·age \'ȯrf-(ə-)nij\ *n* : an institution for the care of orphans

or·ris \'ȯr-əs\ *n* : a European iris with a fragrant rootstock (**orrisroot**) used in perfume and sachets

or·tho·don·tia \,ȯr-thə-'dän-ch(ē-)ə\ *n* : ORTHODONTICS

or·tho·don·tics \-'dänt-iks\ *n* : a branch of dentistry dealing with faulty tooth occlusion and its correction — **or·tho·don·tist** \-'dänt-əst\ *n*

or·tho·dox \'ȯr-thə-,däks\ *adj* [LGk *orthodoxos*, fr. Gk *orthos* right + *doxa* opinion] **1** : conforming to established doctrine esp. in religion **2** : CONVENTIONAL **3** *cap* : of or relating to a Christian church originating in the church of the Eastern Roman Empire — **or·tho·doxy** \-,däk-sē\ *n*

or·tho·epy \'ȯr-thə-,wep-ē\ *n* : the customary pronunciation of a language — **or·tho·ep·ist** \-,wep-əst\ *n*

or·thog·ra·phy \ȯr-'thäg-rə-fē\ *n* : SPELLING — **or·tho·graph·ic** \,ȯr-thə-'graf-ik\ *adj*

or·tho·pe·dics \,ȯr-thə-'pēd-iks\ *n* : the correction or prevention of skeletal deformities — **or·tho·pe·dic** \-ik\ *adj* — **or·tho·pe·dist** \-'pēd-əst\ *n*

or·to·lan \'ȯr-tᵊl-ən\ *n* : a European bunting valued as a table delicacy

os·cil·late \'äs-ə-,lāt\ *vb* **1** : to swing

backward and forward like a pendulum
2 : VARY, FLUCTUATE 3 : to increase
and decrease in magnitude or reverse
direction periodically ⟨an *oscillating*
electric current⟩ — os·cil·la·tion \ˌäs-ə-'lā-shən\ n — os·cil·la·tor \'äs-ə-ˌlāt-ər\ n — os·cil·la·to·ry \'äs-il-ə-ˌtōr-ē\ adj

os·cil·lo·scope \ä-'sil-ə-ˌskōp\ n : an
instrument in which variations in current or voltage appear as visible waves
of light

os·cu·late \'äs-kyə-ˌlāt\ vb : KISS — os·cu·la·tion \ˌäs-kyə-'lā-shən\ n

osier \'ō-zhər\ n : a willow tree with
pliable twigs used esp. in making baskets
and furniture; *also* : a twig from an osier

os·mi·um \'äz-mē-əm\ n : a heavy hard
brittle metallic chemical element used in
alloys

os·mo·sis \äs-'mō-səs, äz-\ n : diffusion
through a partially permeable membrane
separating a solvent and a solution that
tends to equalize their concentrations —
os·mot·ic \-'mät-ik\ adj

os·prey \'äs-prē\ n : a large brown and
white fish-eating hawk

os·si·fy \'äs-ə-ˌfī\ vb : to change into
bone — os·si·fi·ca·tion \ˌäs-ə-fə-'kā-shən\ n

os·su·ary \'äsh-ə-ˌwer-ē, 'äs-(y)ə-\ n : a
depository for the bones of the dead

os·ten·si·ble \ä-'sten-sə-bəl\ adj : shown
outwardly : PROFESSED, APPARENT —
os·ten·si·bly \-blē\ adv

os·ten·ta·tion \ˌäs-tən-'tā-shən\ n : pre-
tentious or excessive display — os·ten·ta·tious \-shəs\ adj — os·ten·ta·tious·ly adv

os·te·op·a·thy \ˌäs-tē-'äp-ə-thē\ n : a
system of healing that emphasizes manipulation (as of joints) but does not exclude other agencies (as the use of medicine and surgery) — os·te·o·path
\'äs-tē-ə-ˌpath\ n — os·te·o·path·ic
\ˌäs-tē-ə-'path-ik\ adj

ostler *var of* HOSTLER

os·tra·cize \'äs-trə-ˌsīz\ vb : to exclude
from a group by common consent —
os·tra·cism \-ˌsiz-əm\ n

os·trich \'äs-trich\ n : a very large swift-
footed flightless bird of Africa and
Arabia

1oth·er \'əth-ər\ adj 1 : being the one
left; *also* : being the ones distinct from
those first mentioned 2 : ALTERNATE
⟨every ~ day⟩ 3 : DIFFERENT 4 : ADDI-
TIONAL 5 : recently past ⟨the ~ night⟩

2other pron 1 : remaining one or ones
⟨one foot and then the ~⟩ 2 : a different or additional one ⟨something or ~⟩

oth·er·wise \-ˌwīz\ adv 1 : in a different way 2 : in different circumstances
3 : in other respects — otherwise adj

oth·er·world \-ˌwərld\ n : a world beyond death or beyond present reality

oti·ose \'ō-shē-ˌōs\ adj 1 : IDLE
2 : STERILE 3 : USELESS

ot·ter \'ät-ər\ n : a web-footed fish-
eating mammal that is related to the
weasels and has dark brown fur; *also*
: its fur

ot·to·man \'ät-ə-mən\ n : an upholstered seat or couch; *also* : an over-
stuffed footstool

ou·bli·ette \ˌü-blē-'et\ n : a dungeon
with an opening only at the top

ought \'ȯt\ vb — used as an auxiliary to
express moral obligation, advisability,
natural expectation, or logical consequence

ounce \'aůns\ n : a weight equal to a
sixteenth part of a pound avoirdupois or
to a twelfth part of a pound troy

our \är, (')aů(ə)r\ adj : of or relating to
us or ourselves

ours \(')aů(ə)rz\ pron : one or the ones
belonging to us

our·selves \är-'selvz, aů(ə)r-\ pron
: our own selves — used reflexively, for
emphasis, or in absolute constructions
⟨we pleased ~⟩ ⟨we'll do it ~⟩ ⟨~
tourists, we avoided other tourists⟩

-ous \əs\ adj suffix : full of : abounding
in : having : possessing the qualities of
⟨clamorous⟩ ⟨poisonous⟩

oust \'aůst\ vb : to eject from or deprive
of property or position : EXPEL syn
evict, dismiss

oust·er \'aůs-tər\ n : REMOVAL, EX-
PULSION

1out \'aůt\ adv 1 : in a direction away
from the inside or center 2 : beyond
control 3 : to extinction, exhaustion, or
completion 4 : in or into the open
5 : so as to retire a batter or base runner;
also : so as to be retired

2out vb : to become public ⟨murder will
~⟩

3out adj 1 : situated outside or at a
distance 2 : not in : ABSENT; *also* : not
being in power 3 : not successful in
reaching base

4out prep 1 : out through ⟨looked ~ the
window⟩ 2 : outward on or along
⟨drive ~ the river road⟩

5out n : a batter or base runner who has
been retired

out-and-out \ˌaůt-ən(d)-'aůt\ adj
1 : OPEN, UNDISGUISED 2 : COMPLETE,
THOROUGHGOING

out·bal·ance \aůt-'bal-əns\ vb : OUT-
WEIGH

out·bid \-'bid\ vb -bid;-·bid·ding : to
make a higher bid than

1out·board \'aůt-ˌbōrd\ adj 1 : situated
outboard 2 : having or using an outboard motor

2outboard adv 1 : outside the lines of a
ship's hull : facing outward from the
median line 2 : in a position closer or
closest to either of the wing tips of an
airplane

outboard motor n : a small internal-
combustion engine with propeller attached for mounting at the stern of a
small boat

out·bound \'aůt-ˌbaůnd\ adj : outward
bound ⟨~ traffic⟩

out·break \'aůt-ˌbrāk\ n 1 : a sudden
or violent breaking out 2 : something
(as an epidemic) that breaks out

out·build·ing \'aůt-ˌbil-diŋ\ n : a
building separate from but accessory to
a main house

out·burst \'aůt-ˌbərst\ n : ERUPTION;
esp : a violent expression of feeling

out·cast \'aůt-ˌkast\ n : one who is
cast out by society : PARIAH

out·class \aůt-'klas\ vb : EXCEL, SUR-
PASS

out·come \'aůt-ˌkəm\ n : a final consequence : RESULT

out·crop \'aůt-ˌkräp\ n : the coming out
of a stratum to the surface of the
ground; *also* : the part of a stratum that
thus appears

out·cry \'aůt-ˌkrī\ n : a loud cry : CLAM-
OR

out·dat·ed \aůt-'dāt-əd\ adj : OBSOLETE

out·dis·tance \-'dis-təns\ vb : to go far
ahead of (as in a race) : OUTSTRIP

out·do \-'dü\ vb : to go beyond in action or performance : EXCEL

out·door \ˌaut-ˈdōr\ also **out·doors** \-ˌdōrz\ adj 1 : of or relating to the outdoors 2 : performed outdoors 3 : not enclosed (as by a roof)

¹**outdoors** \ˌaut-ˈdōrz\ adv : in or into the open air

²**outdoors** n 1 : the open air 2 : the world away from human habitation

out·er \ˈaut-ər\ adj 1 : EXTERNAL 2 : situated farther out; also : being away from a center

out·er·most \-ˌmōst\ adj : farthest out

out·face \aut-ˈfās\ vb 1 : to cause to waver or submit 2 : DEFY

out·field \ˈaut-ˌfēld\ n : the part of a baseball field beyond the infield and within the foul lines — **out·field·er** n

out·fight \aut-ˈfīt\ vb : to surpass in fighting : DEFEAT

¹**out·fit** \ˈaut-ˌfit\ n 1 : the equipment or apparel for a special purpose or occasion 2 : GROUP

²**outfit** vb : EQUIP — **out·fit·ter** n

out·flank \aut-ˈflaŋk\ vb : to get around the flank of (an opposing force)

out·flow \ˈaut-ˌflō\ n 1 : a flowing out 2 : something that flows out

out·fox \aut-ˈfäks\ vb : OUTSMART

out·gen·er·al \aut-ˈjen-(ə-)rəl\ vb -aled or -alled; -al·ing or -al·ling : to surpass in generalship

out·go \ˈaut-ˌgō\ n : EXPENDITURE, OUTLAY

out·go·ing \ˈaut-ˌgō-iŋ\ adj 1 : going out ⟨~ tide⟩ 2 : retiring from a place or position 3 : FRIENDLY

out·grow \aut-ˈgrō\ vb 1 : to grow faster than 2 : to grow too large for

out·growth \ˈaut-ˌgrōth\ n : a product of growing out : OFFSHOOT 1; also : CONSEQUENCE

out·guess \aut-ˈges\ vb : ANTICIPATE, OUTWIT

out·house \ˈaut-ˌhaus\ n : OUTBUILDING; esp : an outdoor toilet

out·ing \ˈaut-iŋ\ n 1 : EXCURSION 2 : a brief stay or trip in the open

out·land·ish \aut-ˈlan-dish\ adj 1 : of foreign appearance or manner; also : BIZARRE 2 : remote from civilization

out·last \-ˈlast\ vb : to last longer than : SURVIVE

¹**out·law** \ˈaut-ˌlȯ\ n 1 : a person excluded from the protection of the law 2 : a lawless person

²**outlaw** vb 1 : to deprive of the protection of the law 2 : to make illegal — **out·law·ry** \-rē\ n

out·lay \ˈaut-ˌlā\ n 1 : the act of spending 2 : EXPENDITURE

out·let \-ˌlet\ n 1 : EXIT, VENT 2 : a means of release (as for an emotion) 3 : a market for a commodity

¹**out·line** \-ˌlīn\ n 1 : a line marking the outer limits of an object or figure 2 : a drawing in which only contours are marked 3 : SUMMARY, SYNOPSIS 4 : PLAN

²**outline** vb 1 : to draw the outline of 2 : to indicate the chief features or parts of

out·live \aut-ˈliv\ vb : to live longer than : syn outlast, survive

out·look \ˈaut-ˌluk\ n 1 : a place offering a view; also : VIEW 2 : STANDPOINT

3 : the prospect for the future

out·ly·ing \-ˌlī-iŋ\ adj : distant from a center or main body

out·ma·neu·ver \ˌaut-mə-ˈn(y)ü-vər\ vb : to defeat by more skillful maneuvering

out·mod·ed \aut-ˈmōd-əd\ adj 1 : being out of style 2 : no longer acceptable or approved

out·num·ber \-ˈnəm-bər\ vb : to exceed in number

out of prep 1 : out from within ⟨walk out of the room⟩ or behind ⟨look out of the window⟩ 2 : from a state of ⟨wake up out of a deep sleep⟩ 3 : beyond the limits of ⟨out of sight⟩ 4 : from among ⟨one out of four⟩ 5 : in or into a state of loss or not having ⟨cheated him out of $5000⟩ ⟨we're out of matches⟩ 6 : because of ⟨came out of curiosity⟩ 7 : FROM, WITH ⟨built it out of scrap lumber⟩

out-of-bounds adv (or adj) : outside the prescribed area of play

out-of-date adj : no longer in fashion or in use : OUTMODED

out-of-door or **out-of-doors** adj : OUTDOOR

out-of-the-way adj 1 : being off the beaten track 2 : UNUSUAL

out·pa·tient \ˈaut-ˌpā-shənt\ n : a person not an inmate of a hospital who visits it for diagnosis or treatment

out·play \aut-ˈplā\ vb : to play more skillfully than

out·point \aut-ˈpȯint\ vb : to win more points than

out·post \ˈaut-ˌpōst\ n 1 : a military detachment stationed at some distance from a camp as a guard against enemy attack; also : a military base established (as by treaty) in a foreign country 2 : an outlying or frontier settlement

out·put \-ˌput\ n : the amount produced (as by a machine or factory) : PRODUCTION

¹**out·rage** \ˈaut-ˌrāj\ n : a violent or shameful act 2 : INJURY, INSULT

²**outrage** vb 1 : RAPE 2 : to subject to violent injury or gross insult 3 : to arouse to extreme resentment

out·ra·geous \aut-ˈrā-jəs\ adj : extremely offensive, insulting, or shameful : SHOCKING — **out·ra·geous·ly** adv

out·rank \aut-ˈraŋk\ vb : to rank higher than

ou·tré \ü-ˈtrā\ adj : violating convention or propriety : BIZARRE

out·reach \aut-ˈrēch\ vb 1 : to surpass in reach 2 : to get the better of by trickery

out·rid·er \ˈaut-ˌrīd-ər\ n : a mounted attendant

out·rig·ger \-ˌrig-ər\ n 1 : a projecting device (as a light spar with a log at the end) fastened at the side or sides of a boat to prevent upsetting 2 : a boat equipped with an outrigger

out·right \(ˈ)aut-ˈrīt\ adv 1 : COMPLETELY 2 : INSTANTANEOUSLY

out·run \aut-ˈrən\ vb : to run faster than; also : EXCEED

out·sell \-ˈsel\ vb : to exceed in sales

out·set \ˈaut-ˌset\ n : BEGINNING, START

out·shine \aut-ˈshīn\ vb 1 : to shine brighter than 2 : SURPASS

¹**out·side** \aut-ˈsīd, ˈaut-ˌsīd\ n 1 : a place or region beyond an enclosure or

boundary   **2** : EXTERIOR   **3** : the utmost limit or extent

²outside *adj* **1** : OUTER   **2** : coming from without ⟨~ influences⟩   **3** : being apart from one's regular duties ⟨~ activities⟩   **4** : REMOTE ⟨an ~ chance⟩

³outside *adv* : on or to the outside

⁴outside *prep* **1** : on or to the outside of   **2** : beyond the limits of   **3** : EXCEPT

outside of *prep* **1** : OUTSIDE   **2** : BESIDES

out·sid·er \'aut-'sīd-ər\ *n* : one who does not belong to a group

out-size \'aut-,sīz\ *n* : an unusual size; *esp* : a size larger than the standard

out-skirts \-,skərts\ *n pl* : the outlying parts (as of a city) : BORDERS

out·smart \aut-'smärt\ *vb* : OUTWIT

out·spo·ken \-'spō-kən\ *adj* : direct and open in speech or expression — **out·spo·ken·ness** *n*

out·spread \'aut-,spred\ *adj* : spread out : EXTENDED

out·stand·ing \(')aut-'stan-diŋ\ *adj* **1** : PROJECTING   **2** : UNPAID; *also* : UNRESOLVED   **3** : publicly issued and sold   **4** : CONSPICUOUS; *also* : DISTINGUISHED

out·stay \aut-'stā\ *vb* **1** : to stay longer than or beyond   **2** : to surpass in endurance

out·stretched \-'strecht\ *adj* : stretched out : EXTENDED

out·strip \-'strip\ *vb* **1** : to go faster than   **2** : EXCEL, SURPASS

¹out·ward \'aut-wərd\ *adj* **1** : moving or directed toward the outside   **2** : showing outwardly

²outward *or* **out·wards** \-wərdz\ *adv* : toward the outside

out·ward·ly *adv* : on the outside : EXTERNALLY

out·wear \aut-'waər\ *vb* : to wear longer than : OUTLAST

out·weigh \-'wā\ *vb* : to exceed in weight, value, or importance

out·wit \-'wit\ *vb* **-wit·ted; -wit·ting** : to get the better of by superior cleverness

¹out·work \aut-'wərk\ *vb* : to outdo in working

²out·work \'aut-,wərk\ *n* : a minor defensive position outside a fortified area

out·worn \aut-'wōrn\ *adj* : OUTMODED

ova *pl of* OVUM

oval \'ō-vəl\ *adj* : having the shape of an egg; *also* : broadly elliptical — **oval** *n*

ova·ry \'ōv-(ə-)rē\ *n* **1** : a usu. paired organ of a female animal in which eggs and often sex hormones are produced   **2** : the part of a flower in which seeds are produced — **ovar·i·an** \ō-'var-ē-ən, -'ver-\ *adj*

ova·tion \ō-'vā-shən\ *n* : an enthusiastic popular tribute : APPLAUSE

ov·en \'əv-ən\ *n* : a chamber (as in a stove) for baking, heating, or drying

ov·en·bird \-,bərd\ *n* : a large American warbler that builds its dome-shaped nest on the ground

¹over \'ō-vər\ *adv* **1** : across a barrier or intervening space   **2** : across the brim ⟨boil ~⟩   **3** : so as to bring the underside up   **4** : out of a vertical position   **5** : beyond some quantity, limit, or norm   **6** : ABOVE   **7** : at an end   **8** : THROUGH; *also* : THOROUGHLY   **9** : AGAIN

²over *prep* **1** : above in position ⟨towered ~ her⟩, authority ⟨obeyed those ~ him⟩, or scope ⟨the talk was ~ their heads⟩   **2** : more than ⟨paid ~ $100 for it⟩   **3** : ON, UPON ⟨a cape ~ his shoulders⟩   **4** : along the length of ⟨~ the road⟩

5 : through the medium of : ON ⟨spoke ~ TV⟩   **6** : all through ⟨showed me ~ the house⟩   **7** : on or above so as to cross ⟨walk ~ the bridge⟩ ⟨jump ~ a ditch⟩   **8** : DURING ⟨~ the past 25 years⟩   **9** : on account of ⟨fought ~ a woman⟩

³over *adj* **1** : UPPER, HIGHER   **2** : REMAINING   **3** : ENDED

over- *prefix* **1** : so as to exceed or surpass   **2** : excessive

overabundance	overindulgent
overabundant	overissue
overactive	overlarge
overambitious	overlearn
overanxious	overliberal
overbid	overload
overbold	overlong
overbuild	overman
overbuy	overmodest
overcapitalize	overnice
overcareful	overpay
overcautious	overpopulate
overcompensation	overpopulation
overconfidence	overpraise
overconfident	overprice
overconscientious	overproduce
overcooked	overproduction
overcritical	overproportion
overcrowd	overprotect
overdecorated	overproud
overdevelop	overrate
overdose	overrefinement
overdress	overripe
overdue	oversell
overeager	oversensitive
overeat	oversensitiveness
overemphasis	oversimplification
overemphasize	oversimplify
overenthusiastic	overspecialization
overestimate	overspecialize
overexcite	overspend
overexert	overstock
overexertion	overstrict
overextend	oversubtle
overfatigued	oversupply
overfeed	overtax
overfill	overtired
overgenerous	overtrain
overgraze	overuse
overhasty	overvalue
overheat	overweight
overindulge	overwork
overindulgence	overzealous

over·act \,ō-vər-'akt\ *vb* : to exaggerate in acting

¹over·age \,ō-vər-'āj\ *adj* **1** : too old to be useful   **2** : older than is normal for one's position, function, or grade ⟨~ students⟩

²over·age \'ōv-(ə-)rij\ *n* : SURPLUS, EXCESS

over·all \,ō-vər-'ȯl\ *adj* : including everything ⟨~ expenses⟩

over·alls \'ō-vər-,ȯlz\ *n pl* : trousers of strong material usu. with a piece extending up to cover the chest

over·arm \'ō-vər-,ärm\ *adj* : done with the arm raised above the shoulder ⟨~ pitching⟩

over·awe \,ō-vər-'ȯ\ *vb* : to restrain or subdue by awe

over·bal·ance \-'bal-əns\ *vb* **1** : OUTWEIGH   **2** : to cause to lose balance

over·bear·ing \-'ba(ə)r-iŋ\ *adj* : ARROGANT, DOMINEERING

over·board \'ō-vər-,bōrd\ *adv* **1** : over the side of a ship into the water   **2** : to extremes of enthusiasm

over·bur·den \,ō-vər-'bərd-°n\ *vb* : to burden too heavily

over·cast \'ō-vər-ˌkast\ *adj* : clouded over : GLOOMY

over·charge \ˌō-vər-'chärj\ *vb* 1 : to charge too much 2 : to fill or load too full — **over·charge** \'ō-vər-ˌchärj\ *n*

over·cloud \ˌō-vər-'klaůd\ *vb* : to overspread with clouds

over·coat \'ō-vər-ˌkōt\ *n* : a warm coat worn over indoor clothing

over·come \ˌō-vər-'kəm\ *vb* 1 : CONQUER 2 : to make helpless or exhausted

over·do \-'dü\ *vb* 1 : to do too much; *also* : to tire oneself 2 : EXAGGERATE 3 : to cook too long

over·draw \-'drȯ\ *vb* : to draw checks on a bank account for more than the balance — **over·draft** \'ō-vər-ˌdraft, -ˌdråft\ *n*

over·ex·pose \ˌō-vər-ik-'spōz\ *vb* : to expose (a photographic plate or film) for more time than is needed — **over·ex·po·sure** \-'spō-zhər\ *n*

¹**over·flow** \ˌō-vər-'flō\ *vb* 1 : INUNDATE; *also* : to pour forth in a flood 2 : to flow over the brim or top of

²**over·flow** \'ō-vər-ˌflō\ *n* 1 : FLOOD; *also* : SURPLUS 2 : an outlet for surplus liquid

over·grow \ˌō-vər-'grō\ *vb* 1 : to grow over so as to cover 2 : OUTGROW 3 : to grow excessively

over·hand \'ō-vər-ˌhand\ *adj* : made with the hand brought down from above — **overhand** *adv*

¹**over·hang** \ˌō-vər-'haŋ\ *vb* 1 : to project over : jut out 2 : to hang over threateningly

²**overhang** *n* : a part (as of a roof) that overhangs

over·haul \ˌō-vər-'hȯl\ *vb* 1 : to examine thoroughly and make necessary repairs and adjustments 2 : OVERTAKE

¹**over·head** \-'hed\ *adv* : ALOFT

²**over·head** \ˌō-vər-ˌhed\ *adj* : operating or lying above (~ door)

³**over·head** \'ō-vər-ˌhed\ *n* : business expenses not chargeable to a particular part of the work

over·hear \ˌō-vər-'hiər\ *vb* : to hear without the speaker's knowledge or intention

over·joy \ˌō-vər-'jȯi\ *vb* : to fill with great joy

over·kill \ˌō-vər-'kil\ *vb* : to obliterate (a target) with more nuclear force than required — **over·kill** \'ō-vər-ˌkil\ *n*

over·land \'ō-vər-ˌland, -lənd\ *adv* (or *adj*) : by, on, or across land

over·lap \ˌō-vər-'lap\ *vb* 1 : to lap over 2 : to have something in common

over·lay \-'lā\ *vb* : to lay or spread over or across — **over·lay** \'ō-vər-ˌlā\ *n*

over·leap \ˌō-vər-'lēp\ *vb* 1 : to leap over or across 2 : to defeat (oneself) by going too far

over·look \ˌō-vər-'lůk\ *vb* 1 : INSPECT 2 : to look down on from above 3 : to fail to see 4 : IGNORE; *also* : EXCUSE 5 : SUPERVISE

over·lord \'ō-vər-ˌlȯrd\ *n* : a lord who has supremacy over other lords

over·ly \'ō-vər-lē\ *adv* : EXCESSIVELY, TOO

over·mas·ter \ˌō-vər-'mas tər\ *vb* : OVERPOWER, SUBDUE

over·match \-'mach\ *vb* : to be more than a match for : DEFEAT

over·much \-'məch\ *adj* (or *adv*) : too much

¹**over·night** \-'nīt\ *adv* 1 : on or during the night 2 : SUDDENLY (became famous ~)

²**overnight** *adj* : of, lasting, or staying the night (~ guests)

over·pass \'ō-vər-ˌpas\ *n* : a crossing (as by means of a bridge) of two highways or of a highway and railroad at different levels

over·play \ˌō-vər-'plā\ *vb* 1 : EXAGGERATE; *also* : OVEREMPHASIZE 2 : to rely too much on the strength of

over·pow·er \-'pau̇-(ə)r\ *vb* 1 : to overcome by superior force 2 : OVERWHELM

over·reach \ˌō-və(r)-'rēch\ *vb* 1 : to reach above or beyond 2 : to defeat (oneself) by too great an effort

over·ride \-'rīd\ *vb* 1 : to ride over or across 2 : to prevail over; *also* : to set aside

over·rule \-'rül\ *vb* 1 : to prevail over 2 : to rule against 3 : to set aside : REVERSE

over·run \-'rən\ *vb* 1 : to defeat and occupy the positions of 2 : OVERSPREAD; *also* : INFEST 3 : to go beyond 4 : to flow over

over·seas \ˌō-vər-'sēz\ *adv or adj* : beyond or across the seas : ABROAD — **over·sea** \-'sē\ *adj* (or *adv*)

over·see \-'sē\ *vb* 1 : OVERLOOK 2 : INSPECT; *also* : SUPERVISE — **over·seer** \'ō-vər-ˌsiər\ *n*

over·shad·ow \ˌō-vər-'shad-ō\ *vb* 1 : DARKEN 2 : to exceed in importance

over·shoe \'ō-vər-ˌshü\ *n* : a protective outer shoe; *esp* : GALOSH

over·shoot \ˌō-vər-'shüt\ *vb* 1 : to pass swiftly beyond 2 : to shoot over or beyond (as a target)

over·sight \'ō-vər-ˌsīt\ *n* 1 : SUPERVISION 2 : an inadvertent omission or error

over·size \ˌō-vər-'sīz\ *or* **over·sized** \-'sīzd\ *adj* : of more than ordinary size

over·sleep \-'slēp\ *vb* : to sleep beyond the time for waking

over·spread \-'spred\ *vb* : to spread over or above

over·state \-'stāt\ *vb* : EXAGGERATE — **over·state·ment** \-mənt\ *n*

over·stay \-'stā\ *vb* : to stay beyond the time or limits of

over·step \-'step\ *vb* 1 : EXCEED, TRANSGRESS

over·stuffed \-'stəft\ *adj* 1 : stuffed too full 2 : covered completely and deeply with upholstery

over·sub·scribe \-səb-'skrīb\ *vb* : to subscribe for more of than is available, asked for, or offered for sale (~ a stock issue)

overt \ō-'vərt, 'ō-ˌvərt\ *adj* : not secret

over·take \ˌō-vər-'tāk\ *vb* : to catch up with

over·throw \-'thrō\ *vb* 1 : UPSET 2 : DEFEAT 3 : to throw over or past — **over·throw** \'ō-vər-ˌthrō\ *n*

over·time \'ō-vər-ˌtīm\ *n* : time beyond a set limit; *esp* : working time in excess of a standard day or week

over·tone \'ō-vər-ˌtōn\ *n* 1 : one of the higher tones in a complex musical tone 2 : IMPLICATION, SUGGESTION

ə abut; ᵊ kitten; ər further; a back; ā bake; ä cot, cart; au̇ out; ch chin; e less; ē easy; g gift; i trip; ī life; j joke; ŋ sing; ō flow; ȯ flaw; ȯi coin; th thin; t̲h̲ this; ü loot; u̇ foot; y yet; yü few; yu̇ furious; zh vision

over·top \,ō-vər-'täp\ *vb* **1** : to tower above   **2** : SURPASS

over·trick \'ō-vər-,trik\ *n* : a card trick won in excess of the number bid

over·ture \'ō-vər-,chúr, -chər\ *n* **1** : an opening offer : PROPOSAL   **2** : an orchestral introduction to a musical dramatic work

over·turn \,ō-vər-'tərn\ *vb* **1** : to turn over : UPSET   **2** : OVERTHROW

over·ween·ing \-'wē-niŋ\ *adj* **1** : ARROGANT   **2** : IMMODERATE

over·weigh \-'wā\ *vb* **1** : to exceed in weight   **2** : OPPRESS

over·whelm \-'hwelm\ *vb* **1** : OVERTHROW   **2** : SUBMERGE   **3** : to overcome completely

over·wrought \,ō-və(r)-'rót\ *adj* **1** : extremely excited   **2** : elaborated to excess

ovip·a·rous \ō-'vip-ə-rəs\ *adj* : reproducing by eggs that hatch outside the parent's body

ovoid \'ō-,vóid\ *adj* : egg-shaped : OVAL

ovule \'ō-,vyül\ *n* : any of the bodies in a plant ovary that after fertilization become seeds

ovum \'ō-vəm\ *n, pl* **ova** \-və\ : a female germ cell : EGG

owe \'ō\ *vb* **1** : to be under obligation to pay or render   **2** : to be indebted to or for; *also* : to be in debt

owing *to prep* : because of

owl \'aúl\ *n* : a nocturnal bird of prey with large head and eyes and strong talons — **owl·ish** \'aú-lish\ *adj* — **owl·ish·ly** *adv*

owl·et \'aú-lət\ *n* : a young or small owl

¹**own** \'ōn\ *adj* : belonging to oneself — used as an intensive after a possessive adjective ⟨his ~ car⟩

²**own** *vb* **1** : to have or hold as property : POSSESS   **2** : ACKNOWLEDGE; *also* : CONFESS — **own·er** *n* — **own·er·ship** \'ō-nər-,ship\ *n*

³**own** *pron* : own one or ones

ox \'äks\, *n, pl* **ox·en** \'äk-sən\ : an adult castrated male of the common domestic cattle

ox·blood \'äks-,bləd\ *n* : a moderate reddish brown

ox·bow \-,bō\ *n* **1** : a U-shaped collar worn by a draft ox   **2** : a U-shaped bend in a river

ox·cart \-,kärt\ *n* : a cart drawn by oxen

ox·ford \'äks-ford\ *n* : a low shoe laced or tied over the instep

ox·i·da·tion \,äk-sə-'dā-shən\ *n* : the act or process of oxidizing : the condition of being oxidized

ox·ide \'äk-,sīd\ *n* : a compound of oxygen with an element or radical

ox·i·dize \'äk-sə-,dīz\ *vb* : to combine with oxygen ⟨iron rusts because it is *oxidized* by exposure to the air⟩

oxy·acet·y·lene \,äk-sē-ə-'set-ᵊl-ən, -ᵊl-,en\ *adj* : of, relating to, or utilizing a mixture of oxygen and acetylene ⟨an ~ torch for welding or cutting through metal⟩

ox·y·gen \'äk-si-jən\ *n* : a colorless odorless gaseous chemical element that is found in the air, is essential to life, and is involved in combustion

oys·ter \'ói-stər\ *n* : any of various mollusks with an irregular 2-valved shell that live on stony bottoms in shallow seas and include edible shellfish and pearl producers

ozone \'ō-,zōn\ *n* **1** : a faintly blue form of oxygen that is produced by the silent discharge of electricity in air or oxygen, has a faint chlorinelike odor, and is used for sterilizing water, purifying air, and bleaching   **2** : pure and refreshing air

---

p \'pē\ *n, often cap* : the 16th letter of the English alphabet

pa \'pä, 'pó\ *n* : FATHER

pab·u·lum \'pab-yə-ləm\ *n* : usu. soft digestible food

¹**pace** \'pās\ *n* **1** : a step in walking; *also* : the length of such a step   **2** : rate of movement or progress (as in walking or working)   **3** : GAIT; *esp* : a horse's gait in which the legs on the same side move together

²**pace** *vb* **1** : to go or cover at a pace or with slow steps   **2** : to measure off by paces   **3** : to set or regulate the pace of

³**pa·ce** \'pā-sē\ *prep* : with due respect to

pace·mak·er \'pās-,mā-kər\ *n* : one that sets the pace for another

pac·er \'pā-sər\ *n* : a horse that paces   **2** : PACEMAKER

pach·y·derm \'pak-i-,dərm\ *n* : any of various thick-skinned hoofed mammals (as an elephant or hippopotamus)

pach·ys·an·dra \,pak-ə-'san-drə\ *n* : any of a genus of low evergreen plants used as a ground cover

pa·cif·ic \pə-'sif-ik\ *adj* **1** : tending to lessen conflict : PEACEABLE   **2** : CALM, PEACEFUL

pac·i·fi·er \'pas-ə-,fī(-ə)r\ *n* : one that pacifies; *esp* : a device for a baby to chew or suck on

pac·i·fism \-,fiz-əm\ *n* : opposition to war or violence as a means of settling disputes — **pac·i·fist** \-fəst\ *n*

pac·i·fy \'pas-ə-,fī\ *vb* **1** : to allay anger or agitation in : SOOTHE ⟨~ a weeping child⟩   **2** : SETTLE ⟨~ a quarrel⟩; *also* : SUBDUE ⟨~ a hostile population⟩ — **pac·i·fi·ca·tion** \,pas-ə-fə-'kā-shən\ *n*

¹**pack** \'pak\ *n* **1** : a compact bundle (as a packet or package)   **2** : a large amount or number : HEAP   **3** : a set of playing cards   **4** : a group or band of people or animals   **5** : wet absorbent material for application to the body

²**pack** *vb* **1** : to make into a pack   **2** : to put into a protective container   **3** : to fill completely : CRAM   **4** : to load with a pack ⟨~ a mule⟩   **5** : to stow goods for transportation   **6** : to crowd together   **7** : to cause to go without ceremony ⟨~ them off to school⟩   **8** : to fill in or surround so as to prevent passage of air, steam, or water   **9** : WEAR, CARRY ⟨~ a gun⟩

³**pack** *vb* : to make up fraudulently so as to secure a desired result ⟨~ a jury⟩

¹**pack·age** \'pak-ij\ *n* **1** : BUNDLE, PARCEL   **2** : something (as a group of related things offered as a whole) resembling a package

²**package** *vb* : to make into a package

pack·er \'pak-ər\ *n* : one that packs; *esp* : a wholesale dealer

pack·et \'pak-ət\ *n* **1 :** a small bundle or package **2 :** a passenger boat carrying mail and cargo on a regular schedule

pack·ing house *n* **:** an establishment for processing and packing foodstuffs and esp. meat and its by-products

pack·sad·dle \'pak-ˌsad-ᵊl\ *n* **:** a saddle for supporting packs on the back of an animal

pack·thread \-ˌthred\ *n* **:** strong thread for tying

pact \'pakt\ *n* **:** AGREEMENT, TREATY

¹pad \'pad\ *n* **1 :** a cushioning part or thing **:** CUSHION **2 :** the cushioned part of the foot of some mammals **3 :** the floating leaf of a water plant **4 :** a writing tablet

²pad *vb* **pad·ded; pad·ding 1 :** to furnish with a pad or padding **2 :** to expand with needless or fraudulent matter

pad·ding \'pad-iŋ\ *n* **:** the material with which something is padded

¹pad·dle \'pad-ᵊl\ *n* **1 :** an implement with a flat blade often shaped like an oar and used in propelling and steering a canoe **2 :** an implement used for stirring, mixing, or beating **3 :** a broad board on the outer rim of a waterwheel or a paddle wheel of a boat

²paddle *vb* **1 :** to move on or through water by or as if by using a paddle **2 :** to beat or stir with a paddle

³paddle *vb* **:** to move the hands and feet about in shallow water

paddle wheel *n* **:** a wheel with blades around its rim used to propel a boat

pad·dock \'pad-ək\ *n* **:** a usu. enclosed area for pasturing or exercising animals; *esp* **:** one where racehorses are saddled and paraded before a race

pad·dy \'pad-ē\ *n* **1 :** RICE **2 :** wet land where rice is grown

pad·lock \'pad-ˌläk\ *n* **:** a lock with a bow-shaped piece that can be snapped in or out of a catch by use of a key — **padlock** *vb*

pa·dre \'päd-rā\ *n* **1 :** PRIEST, CLERGYMAN **2 :** a military chaplain

pae·an \'pē-ən\ *n* **:** an exultant song esp. of joy or praise

pa·gan \'pā-gən\ *n* **:** HEATHEN — **pagan** *adj* — **pa·gan·ism** \-ˌiz-əm\ *n*

¹page \'pāj\ *n* **:** ATTENDANT; *esp* **:** one employed to deliver messages

²page *vb* **:** to summon by repeatedly calling out the name of

³page *n* **:** a single leaf (as of a book); *also* **:** a single side of such a leaf

⁴page *vb* **:** to mark or number the pages of

pag·eant \'paj-ənt\ *n* **:** an elaborate spectacle, show, or procession esp. with tableaux or floats — **pag·eant·ry** \-ən-trē\ *n*

page·boy \'pāj-ˌbói\ *n* **:** a woman's often shoulder-length bob with the ends of the hair turned under in a smooth roll

pag·i·na·tion \ˌpaj-ə-'nā-shən\ *n* **1 :** the paging of written or printed matter **2 :** the number and arrangement of pages (as of a book)

pa·go·da \pə-'gōd-ə\ *n* **:** a tower with roofs curving upward at the division of each of several stories (Chinese ~)

paid *past of* PAY

pail \'pāl\ *n* **:** a usu. cylindrical vessel with a handle — **pail·ful** \-ˌfùl\ *n*

¹pain \'pān\ *n* **1 :** PUNISHMENT, PENALTY **2 :** suffering or distress of body or mind; *also* **:** a basic sensation caused by harmful stimuli and marked by discomfort (as throbbing or aching) **3** *pl* **:** CARE, TROUBLE — **pain·ful** \-fəl\ *adj* — **pain·ful·ly** *adv* — **pain·less** \-ləs\ *adj*

²pain *vb* **:** to cause or experience pain **:** HURT

pains·tak·ing \'pān-ˌstā-kiŋ\ *adj* **:** taking pains **:** showing care — **painstaking** *n* — **pains·tak·ing·ly** *adv*

¹paint \'pānt\ *vb* **1 :** to apply color, pigment, or paint to **2 :** to produce or portray in lines or colors on a surface; *also* **:** to practice the art of painting **3 :** to decorate with colors **4 :** to use cosmetics **5 :** to describe vividly **6 :** SWAB — **paint·er** *n*

²paint *n* **1 :** something produced by painting **2 :** MAKEUP **3 :** a mixture of a pigment and a liquid that forms a thin adherent coating when spread on a surface; *also* **:** the dry pigment used in making this mixture **4 :** an applied coating of paint

paint·brush \-ˌbrəsh\ *n* **:** a brush for applying paint

paint·ing *n* **1 :** a work (as a picture) produced through the art of painting **2 :** the art or occupation of painting

¹pair \'paər\ *n* **1 :** two things of a kind designed for use together **2 :** something made up of two corresponding pieces ⟨a ~ of trousers⟩ **3 :** a set of two people or animals **:** COUPLE ⟨a carriage and ~⟩ ⟨a married ~⟩

²pair *vb* **1 :** to arrange in pairs **2 :** to form a pair **:** MATCH **3 :** to become associated with another

pais·ley \'pāz-lē\ *adj, often cap* **:** made typically of soft wool with colorful curved abstract figures ⟨a ~ shawl⟩

pa·ja·mas \pə-'jäm-əz, -'jam-\ *n pl* **:** a loose usu. 2-piece lightweight suit designed for sleeping or lounging

Pak·i·stani \ˌpak-ə-'stan-ē, ˌpäk-ə-'stän-ē\ *n* **:** a native or inhabitant of Pakistan — **Pakistani** *adj*

pal \'pal\ *n* **:** a close friend

pal·ace \'pal-əs\ *n* [OF *palais,* fr. L *palatium,* fr. *Palatium,* the Palatine Hill in Rome where the emperors' palaces were built] **1 :** the official residence of a sovereign **2 :** MANSION — **pa·la·tial** \pə-'lā-shəl\ *adj*

pal·a·din \'pal-əd-ən\ *n* **:** a knightly supporter of a medieval prince

pa·laes·tra \pə-'les-trə\ *n, pl* **-trae** \-ˌ()trē\ **:** a school in ancient Greece or Rome for sports (as wrestling)

pal·an·quin \ˌpal-ən-'kēn\ *n* **:** an enclosed couch for one person borne on the shoulders of men by means of poles

pal·at·able \'pal-ət-ə-bəl\ *adj* **:** agreeable to the taste **syn** appetizing, savory, tasty, toothsome

pal·ate \'pal-ət\ *n* **1 :** the roof of the mouth consisting of an anterior bony part (**hard palate**) and a posterior membranous fold (**soft palate**) **2 :** TASTE — **pal·a·tal** \-ət-ᵊl\ *adj*

pa·lat·i·nate \pə-'lat-ᵊn-ət\ *n* **:** the territory of a palatine

¹pal·a·tine \'pal-ə-ˌtīn\ *adj* **1 :** of or relating to a palace **:** PALATIAL **2 :** pos-

---

ə a**but**; ᵊ **kitten**; ər **furth**er; a **back**; ā **bake**; ä **cot**, **cart**; aù **out**; ch **chin**; e **less**; ē **easy**; g **gift**; i **trip**; ī **life**; j **joke**; ŋ **sing**; ō **flow**; ò **flaw**; òi **coin**; th **thin**; th̲ **this**; ü **loot**; ù **foot**; y **yet**; yü **few**; yù **furious**; zh **vision**

sessing royal privileges; *also* : of or relating to a palatine or a palatinate

²**palatine** *n* **1** : a high officer of an imperial palace **2** : a feudal lord having sovereign power within his domains

pa·lav·er \pə-'lav-ər, -'läv-\ *n* : a long parley : TALK — **palaver** *vb*

¹**pale** \'pāl\ *adj* **1** : deficient in color : WAN **2** : lacking in brightness : DIM ⟨~ star⟩ **3** : light in color or shade ⟨~ blue⟩ — **pale·ness** *n*

²**pale** *vb* : to make or become pale

³**pale** *vb* : to enclose with or as if with pales : FENCE

⁴**pale** *n* **1** : a stake or picket of a fence **2** : an enclosed place; *also* : a district or territory within certain bounds or under a particular jurisdiction **3** : LIMITS, BOUNDS ⟨conduct beyond the ~⟩

pale·face \'pāl-,fās\ *n* : a white person : CAUCASIAN

pa·le·og·ra·phy \,pā-lē-'äg-rə-fē\ *n* : the study of ancient writings and inscriptions — **pa·le·og·ra·pher** *n*

pa·le·on·tol·o·gy \,pā-lē-,än-'täl-ə-jē\ *n* : a science dealing with the life of past geologic periods esp. as known from fossil remains — **pa·le·on·tol·o·gist** \-jəst\ *n*

pal·ette \'pal-ət\ *n* : a thin often oval board or tablet on which a painter lays and mixes his colors; *also* : the colors on a palette

pal·frey \'pȯl-frē\ *n* : a saddle horse; *esp* : one suitable for a woman

pal·imp·sest \'pal-əmp-,sest\ *n* : writing material (as a parchment) used after the erasure of earlier writing

pal·in·drome \'pal-ən-,drōm\ *n* : a word, verse, or sentence (as "Able was I ere I saw Elba") that reads the same backward or forward

pal·ing \'pā-liŋ\ *n* **1** : a fence of pales **2** : material for pales **3** : PALE, PICKET

pal·in·ode \'pal-ə-,nōd\ *n* : an ode or song of recantation or retraction

pal·i·sade \,pal-ə-'sād\ *n* **1** : a high fence of stakes esp. for defense **2** : a line of bold cliffs

pall \'pȯl\ *vb* **1** : to lose in interest or attraction ⟨parties began to ~ on her⟩ **2** : SATIATE, CLOY

pal·la·di·um \pə-'lād-ē-əm\ *n* : a silver-white metallic chemical element used esp. as a catalyst and in alloys

pall·bear·er \'pȯl-,bar-ər\ *n* : a person who attends the coffin at a funeral

pal·let \'pal-ət\ *n* : a small, hard, or makeshift bed

pal·li·ate \'pal-ē-,āt\ *vb* **1** : to ease without curing **2** : to cover by excuses : EXTENUATE ⟨~ faults⟩ — **pal·li·a·tion** \,pal-ē-'ā-shən\ *n* — **pal·li·a·tive** \'pal-ē-,āt-iv\ *adj or n*

pal·lid \'pal-əd\ *adj* : PALE, WAN

pal·lor \'pal-ər\ *n* : PALENESS

¹**palm** \'päm\ *n* **1** : any of a group of mostly tropical trees, shrubs, or vines usu. with a tall unbranched stem topped by a crown of large leaves **2** : a symbol of victory; *also* : VICTORY **3** : the underpart of the hand between the fingers and the wrist

²**palm** *vb* **1** : to conceal in or with the hand ⟨~ a card⟩ **2** : to impose by fraud ⟨~ off a fake⟩

pal·mate \'pal-,māt\ *adj* : resembling a hand with the fingers spread

palm·er \'päm-ər\ *n* : a person wearing two crossed palm leaves as a sign of his pilgrimage to the Holy Land

pal·met·to \pal-'met-ō\ *n, pl* **-tos** or **-toes** : any of several usu. small palms with fan-shaped leaves

palm·ist·ry \'päm-ə-strē\ *n* : the practice of reading a person's character or future from the markings on his palms — **palm·ist** \-əst\ *n*

Palm Sunday *n* : the Sunday preceding Easter and commemorating Christ's triumphal entry into Jerusalem

palmy \'päm-ē\ *adj* **1** : abounding in or bearing palms **2** : FLOURISHING, PROSPEROUS ⟨during his ~ days⟩

pal·o·mi·no \,pal-ə-'mē-nō\ *n* : a light tan or cream-colored horse with lighter mane and tail

pal·pa·ble \'pal-pə-bəl\ *adj* **1** : capable of being touched or felt : TANGIBLE **2** : OBVIOUS, PLAIN syn perceptible, sensible, appreciable, evident, manifest — **pal·pa·bly** \-blē\ *adv*

pal·pate \'pal-,pāt\ *vb* : to examine by touch esp. medically — **pal·pa·tion** \pal-'pā-shən\ *n*

pal·pi·tate \'pal-pə-,tāt\ *vb* : to beat strongly and irregularly : THROB, QUIVER — **pal·pi·ta·tion** \,pal-pə-'tā-shən\ *n*

pal·sy \'pȯl-zē\ *n* **1** : PARALYSIS **2** : a condition marked by tremor — **pal·sied** \-zēd\ *adj*

pal·ter \'pȯl-tər\ *vb* **1** : to act insincerely : EQUIVOCATE **2** : HAGGLE, BARGAIN

pal·try \-trē\ *adj* **1** : TRASHY ⟨a ~ pamphlet⟩ **2** : VILE ⟨a ~ trick⟩ **3** : TRIVIAL ⟨~ excuses⟩

pam·pa \'pam-pə\ *n* : a large grassy So. American plain

pam·per \'pam-pər\ *vb* : to treat with excessive attention : INDULGE syn coddle, humor, baby, spoil

pam·phlet \'pam-flət\ *n* **1** : an unbound printed publication **2** : a controversial tract — **pam·phle·teer** \,pam-flə-'tiər\ *n*

¹**pan** \'pan\ *n* : a usu. broad, shallow, and open container for domestic use; *also* : something resembling such a container

²**pan** *vb* **panned; pan·ning** **1** : to wash earth or gravel in a pan in searching for gold **2** : to cook or wash in a pan **3** : to turn out; *esp* : SUCCEED ⟨an experiment that *panned* out⟩ **4** : to criticize severely ⟨a new play *panned* by the critics⟩

pan·a·cea \,pan-ə-'sē-ə\ *n* : a remedy for all ills or difficulties

pa·nache \pə-'nash\ *n* **1** : an ornamental tuft (as of feathers) esp. on a helmet **2** : dash or flamboyance in style and action

pan·a·ma \'pan-ə-,mä, -,mȯ\ *n* : a handmade hat braided from strips of the leaves from a tropical American tree

pan·a·tela \,pan-ə-'tel-ə\ *n* : a long slender cigar with straight sides rounded off at the sealed end

pan·cake \'pan-,kāk\ *n* **1** : a flat cake made of thin batter and fried on both sides **2** : a horizontal landing of an airplane with little run along the ground

pan·chro·mat·ic \,pan-krō-'mat-ik\ *adj* : sensitive to light of all colors ⟨~ film⟩

pan·cre·as \'paŋ-krē-əs, 'pan-\ *n* : a large gland that produces insulin and discharges enzymes into the intestine — **pan·cre·at·ic** \,paŋ-krē-'at-ik, ,pan-\ *adj*

pan·da \'pan-də\ *n* : either of two

Asiatic mammals related to the raccoon; *esp* : a large black-and-white animal resembling a bear

pan·dem·ic \pan-'dem-ik\ *n* : a widespread outbreak of disease — **pandemic** *adj*

pan·de·mo·ni·um \,pan-də-'mō-nē-əm\ *n* : a state of wild uproar : TUMULT

¹**pan·der** \'pan-dər\ *n* **1** : a go-between in love intrigues **2** : a man who solicits clients for a prostitute **3** : someone who caters to or exploits others' desires or weaknesses

²**pander** *vb* : to act as a pander

pan·dow·dy \pan-'daud-ē\ *n* : a deep-dish apple dessert spiced, sweetened, and covered with a rich crust

pane \'pān\ *n* : a sheet of glass (as in a door or window)

pan·e·gyr·ic \,pan-ə-'jir-ik\ *n* : a eulogistic oration or writing — **pan·e·gyr·ist** \-'jir-əst\ *n*

¹**pan·el** \'pan-ºl\ *n* **1** : a list of persons appointed for special duty (a jury ~) **2** : a group of people taking part in a discussion or quiz program **3** : a section of something (as a wall or door) often sunk below the level of the frame **4** : a flat piece of wood on which a picture is painted **5** : a board mounting instruments or controls

²**panel** *vb* : to decorate with panels

pan·el·ing *n* : decorative wood panels

pan·el·ist \'pan-ºl-əst\ *n* : a member of a discussion or quiz panel

pang \'paŋ\ *n* : a sudden sharp attack (as of pain)

¹**pan·han·dle** \'pan-,han-dºl\ *n* : a narrow projection of a larger territory (as a state)

²**panhandle** *vb* : to accost and beg from — **pan·han·dler** \-dlər\ *n*

¹**pan·ic** \'pan-ik\ *n* : a sudden overpowering fright **syn** terror, consternation, dismay, alarm, dread, fear — **pan·icky** \-i-kē\ *adj*

²**panic** *vb* **pan·icked**; **pan·ick·ing** : to affect or be affected with panic

pan·i·cle \'pan-i-kəl\ *n* : a loosely branched often pyramidal flower cluster (as of the oat)

pan·jan·drum \pan-'jan-drəm\ *n* : a powerful personage or pretentious official

pan·nier \'pan-yər\ *n* : a large basket esp. for bearing on the back

pan·ni·kin \'pan-i-kən\ *n, Brit* : a small pan or cup

pan·o·ply \'pan-ə-plē\ *n* **1** : a full suit of armor **2** : something forming a protective covering **3** : an impressive array

pan·o·rama \,pan-ə-'ram-ə, -'räm-\ *n* **1** : a view or picture unrolled before one's eyes **2** : a complete view in every direction — **pan·o·ram·ic** \-'ram-ik\ *adj*

pan·sy \'pan-zē\ *n* : a low-growing garden herb related to the violet; *also* : its showy flower

¹**pant** \'pant\ *vb* **1** : to breathe in a labored manner : GASP **2** : YEARN **3** : THROB

²**pant** *n* : a panting breath or sound

pan·ta·loons \,pant-ºl-'ünz\ *n pl* : TROUSERS

pan·the·ism \'pan-thē-,iz-əm\ *n* : a

doctrine that equates God with the forces and laws of the universe — **pan·the·ist** \-thē-əst\ *n* — **pan·the·is·tic** \,pan-thē-'is-tik\ *adj*

pan·the·on \'pan-thē-,än, -ən\ *n* **1** : a temple dedicated to all the gods **2** : a building serving as the burial place of or containing memorials to famous dead **3** : the gods of a people

pan·ther \'pan-thər\ *n* : a large wild cat (as a leopard or cougar)

pant·ie *or* **panty** \'pant-ē\ *n* : a woman's or child's undergarment covering the lower trunk and made with closed crotch and short legs — usu. used in pl.

pan·to·mime \'pant-ə-,mīm\ *n* **1** : a play in which the actors use no words **2** : expression of something by bodily or facial movements only — **pan·to·mim·ic** \,pant-ə-'mim-ik\ *adj*

pan·try \'pan-trē\ *n* : a room or closet used for storing provisions and dishes or for serving

pants \'pants\ *n pl* : TROUSERS; *also* : a woman's or child's short undergarment for the lower trunk

pap \'pap\ *n* : soft food for infants or invalids

pa·pa \'päp-ə\ *n* : FATHER

pa·pa·cy \'pā-pə-sē\ *n* **1** : the office of pope **2** : a succession of popes **3** : the term of a pope's reign **4** *cap* : the system of government of the Roman Catholic Church

pa·pal \'pā-pəl\ *adj* : of or relating to the pope or to the Roman Catholic Church

pa·paw **1** \pə-'pò\ : PAPAYA **2** \'päp-,ò\ : a No. American tree with yellow edible fruit; *also* : its fruit

pa·pa·ya \pə-'pī-ə\ *n* : a tropical American tree with large yellow black-seeded edible fruit; *also* : its fruit

pa·per \'pā-pər\ *n* **1** : a pliable substance made usu. of vegetable matter and used to write or print on, to wrap things in, or to cover walls; *also* : a single sheet of this substance **2** : a printed or written document **3** : NEWSPAPER **4** : WALLPAPER — **paper** *adj or vb* — **pa·pery** \'pā-p(ə-)rē\ *adj*

pa·per·back \'pā-pər-,bak\ *n* : a paper-covered book

pa·per·hang·er \-,haŋ-ər\ *n* : one that applies wallpaper — **pa·per·hang·ing** *n*

pa·per·weight \-,wāt\ *n* : an object used to hold down loose papers by its weight

pa·pier-mâ·ché \,pā-pər-mə-'shā\ *n* : a molding material of wastepaper and additives (as glue)

pa·pil·la \pə-'pil-ə\ *n* : a small projecting bodily part — **pap·il·lary** \'pap-ə-,ler-ē, pə-'pil-ə-rē\ *adj*

pa·pil·lote \'päp-ē-,(y)ōt\ *n* : a greased paper wrapper in which food is cooked

pa·pist \'pā-pəst\ *n, often cap* : ROMAN CATHOLIC — usu. used disparagingly

pa·poose \pa-'püs\ *n* : a young child of No. American Indian parents

pa·pri·ka \pə-'prē-kə\ *n* : a mild red spice made from the fruit of some sweet peppers

pa·py·rus \pə-'pī-rəs\ *n* **1** : a tall grassy Egyptian sedge **2** : paper made from papyrus pith

par \'pär\ *n* **1** : a stated value (as of

ə abut; ə kitten; ər further; a back; ā bake; ä cot, cart; aú out; ch chin; e less; ē easy; g gift; i trip; ī life; j joke; ŋ sing; ō flow; ò flaw; òi coin; th thin; <u>th</u> this; ü loot; ù foot; y yet; yü few; yù furious; zh vision

a security) **2** : a common level : EQUAL-ITY **3** : an accepted standard or normal condition **4** : the score standard set for each hole of a golf course — **par** adj

pa·ra \'pär-ä\ n — see MONEY table

par·a·ble \'par-ə-bəl\ n : a simple story told to illustrate a moral truth

pa·rab·o·la \pə-'rab-ə-lə\ n : a curve formed by the intersection of a cone with a plane parallel to its side — **par·a·bol·ic** \,par-ə-'bäl-ik\ adj

par·a·chute \'par-ə-,shüt\ n : a large umbrella-shaped device used esp. for making a descent from an airplane — **parachute** vb — **par·a·chut·ist** \-,shüt-əst\ n

¹pa·rade \pə-'rād\ n **1** : a pompous display : EXHIBITION ⟨a ~ of wealth⟩ **2** : MARCH, PROCESSION; esp : a ceremonial formation and march (as of troops) **3** : a place of promenade

²parade vb **1** : to march in a parade **2** : PROMENADE **3** : to show off **4** : MASQUERADE ⟨fiction parading as fact⟩

par·a·digm \'par-ə-,dīm\ n **1** : MODEL, PATTERN **2** : a systematic inflection of a verb or noun showing a complete conjugation or declension

par·a·dise \'par-ə-,dīs, -,dīz\ n [OF paradis, fr. LL paradisus, fr. Gk paradeisos, lit., enclosed park, of Iranian origin] **1** often cap : HEAVEN **2** : a place of bliss

par·a·di·si·a·cal \,par-ə-də-'sī-ə-kəl\ or **par·a·dis·i·ac** \-'diz-ē-,ak\ adj : of, relating to, or resembling paradise — **par·a·di·si·a·cal·ly** \-də-'sī-ə-k(ə-)lē\ adv

par·a·dox \'par-ə-,däks\ n : a statement that seems contrary to common sense and yet is perhaps true — **par·a·dox·i·cal** \,par-ə-'däk-si-kəl\ adj

par·af·fin \'par-ə-fən\ n **1** : a waxy substance used esp. for making candles and sealing foods **2** chiefly Brit : KEROSENE

par·a·gon \'par-ə-,gän, -gən\ n : a model of perfection : PATTERN

¹par·a·graph \'par-ə-,graf\ n : a subdivision of a written composition that consists of one or more sentences and deals with one point or gives the words of one speaker; also : a character (as ¶) marking the beginning of such a subdivision

²paragraph vb : to divide into paragraphs

par·a·keet var of PARRAKEET

par·al·lax \'par-ə-,laks\ n : the difference in apparent direction of an object as seen from two different points

¹par·al·lel \'par-ə-,lel\ adj **1** : lying or moving in the same direction but always the same distance apart **2** : similar in essential parts : LIKE — **par·al·lel·ism** \-,lel-,iz-əm\ n

²parallel n **1** : a parallel line, curve, or surface **2** : one of the imaginary circles on the earth's surface paralleling the equator and marking the latitude **3** : something essentially similar to another **4** : LIKENESS, SIMILARITY

³parallel vb **1** : COMPARE **2** : to correspond to **3** : to extend in a parallel direction with

par·al·lel·o·gram \,par-ə-'lel-ə-,gram\ n : a 4-sided geometrical figure with opposite sides equal and parallel

pa·ral·y·sis \pə-'ral-ə-səs\ n, pl **-y·ses** \-,sēz\ : loss of function and esp. of feeling or the power of voluntary motion

— **par·a·lyt·ic** \,par-ə-'lit-ik\ adj or n

par·a·lyze \'par-ə-,līz\ vb **1** : to affect with paralysis **2** : to make powerless or inactive

pa·ram·e·ter \pə-'ram-ət-ər\ n : a characteristic element; also : FACTOR

par·a·mount \'par-ə-,maünt\ adj : superior to all others : SUPREME **syn** preponderant, predominant, dominant, chief, sovereign

par·a·mour \'par-ə-,mùr\ n : an illicit lover; esp : MISTRESS

par·a·noia \,par-ə-'nȯi-ə\ n : mental disorder marked by delusions and irrational suspicion — **par·a·noid** \'par-ə-,nȯid\ adj or n

par·a·pet \'par-ə-pət, -,pet\ n **1** : a protecting rampart in a fort **2** : a low wall or railing (as at the edge of a platform or bridge)

par·a·pher·na·lia \,par-ə-fə(r)-'nāl-yə\ n sing or pl **1** : personal belongings **2** : EQUIPMENT, APPARATUS

par·a·phrase \'par-ə-,frāz\ n : a restatement of a text giving the meaning in different words — **paraphrase** vb

par·a·ple·gia \,par-ə-'plē-j(ē-)ə\ n : paralysis of the lower trunk and legs — **par·a·ple·gic** \-jik\ adj or n

par·a·site \'par-ə-,sīt\ n **1** : a plant or animal living in or on another organism usu. to its harm **2** : one depending on another and not making adequate return — **par·a·sit·ic** \,par-ə-'sit-ik\ adj — **par·a·sit·ism** \'par-ə-,sīt-,iz-əm\ n — **par·a·sit·ize** \-sə-,tīz\ vb

par·a·sol \'par-ə-,sȯl\ n : a lightweight umbrella used as a shield against the sun

par·a·thi·on \,par-ə-'thī-,än\ n : an extremely toxic insecticide

para·troop·er \'par-ə-,trü-pər\ n : a member of the paratroops

para·troops \-,trüps\ n pl : troops trained to parachute from an airplane

para·ty·phoid \,par-ə-'tī-,fȯid, -tī-'fȯid\ n : a food poisoning resembling typhoid fever

par·boil \'pär-,bȯil\ vb : to boil briefly

¹par·cel \'pär-səl\ n **1** : a tract or plot of land **2** : COLLECTION, LOT **3** : a wrapped bundle : PACKAGE

²parcel vb : to divide into portions : DISTRIBUTE

parch \'pärch\ vb **1** : to toast under dry heat : SCORCH **2** : to shrivel with heat

parch·ment \'pärch-mənt\ n : the skin of a sheep or goat prepared for writing on; also : a writing on such material

pard \'pärd\ n, archaic : LEOPARD

¹par·don \'pärd-ᵊn\ n : excuse of an offense without penalty : FORGIVENESS; esp : an official release from legal punishment

²pardon vb : to free from penalty : EXCUSE, FORGIVE — **par·don·able** \'pärd-(ᵊ-)nə-bəl\ adj

par·don·er \'pärd-(ᵊ-)nər\ n **1** : a medieval preacher delegated to raise money for religious works by soliciting offerings and granting indulgences **2** : one that pardons

pare \'paər\ vb **1** : to trim or shave off an outside part (as the skin or rind) of ⟨~ an apple⟩ **2** : to reduce as if by paring ⟨~ expenses⟩

par·e·gor·ic \,par-ə-'gȯr-ik\ n : an alcoholic preparation of opium and camphor

par·ent \'par-ənt\ n **1** : one that begets

or brings forth offspring : FATHER, MOTHER **2** : SOURCE, ORIGIN — **par·ent·age** \-ij\ *n* — **pa·ren·tal** \pə-'rent-ᵊl\ *adj* — **par·ent·hood** \'par-ənt-ˌhůd\ *n*

pa·ren·the·sis \pə-'ren-thə-səs\ *n, pl* **-the·ses** \-thə-ˌsēz\ **1** : a word, phrase, or sentence inserted in a passage to explain or modify the thought **2** : one of a pair of punctuation marks ( ) used esp. to enclose parenthetic matter — **par·en·thet·ic** \ˌpar-ən-'thet-ik\ *or* **par·en·thet·i·cal** *adj* — **par·en·thet·i·cal·ly** *adv*

pa·re·sis \pə-'rē-səs, 'par-ə-\ *n, pl* **-re·ses** \-ˌsēz\ : a usu. incomplete paralysis; *also* : a syphilitic disorder marked by mental and paralytic symptoms

par ex·cel·lence \ˌpär-ˌek-sə-'läⁿs\ *adv (or adj)* : in the highest degree : PREEMINENTLY

par·fait \pär-'fā\ *n* **1** : a flavored custard containing whipped cream and a syrup frozen without stirring **2** : a cold dessert made of layers of fruit, syrup, ice cream, and whipped cream

pa·ri·ah \pə-'rī-ə\ *n* : OUTCAST

pa·ri·e·tal \pə-'rī-ət-ᵊl\ *adj* : of, relating to, or forming the walls of an anatomical structure

pari·mu·tu·el \ˌpar-i-'myü-chə-(wə)l\ *n* : a system of betting in which those with winning bets share the total stakes minus a percentage for the management

par·ing \'par-iŋ\ *n* : something pared off ⟨potato ~s⟩

pa·ri pas·su \ˌpar-ē-'pas-ü\ *adv (or adj)* : at an equal rate or pace

par·ish \'par-ish\ *n* **1** : the ecclesiastical area in the charge of one pastor; *also* : the residents of such an area **2** : a local church community **3** : a civil division of the state of Louisiana : COUNTY

pa·rish·io·ner \pə-'rish-(ə-)nər\ *n* : a member or resident of a parish

par·i·ty \'par-ət-ē\ *n* : EQUALITY, EQUIVALENCE

¹park \'pärk\ *n* **1** : a tract of ground kept as a game preserve or recreation ground **2** : a place where vehicles (as automobiles) are parked **3** : an enclosed arena used esp. for ball games

²park *vb* **1** : to enclose in a park **2** : to keep (as an automobile) standing for a time at the edge of a public way or in a place reserved for the purpose

par·ka \'pär-kə\ *n* : a hooded fur pullover garment for arctic wear; *also* : a garment of similar style made of windproof fabric for sports or military wear

park·way \'pärk-ˌwā\ *n* : a broad landscaped thoroughfare

par·lance \'pär-ləns\ *n* **1** : SPEECH **2** : manner of speaking ⟨military ~⟩

par·lay \'pär-ˌlā\ *n* : a series of bets in which the original stake plus its winnings are risked on the successive wagers — **parlay** *vb*

par·ley \'pär-lē\ *n* : a conference usu. over matters in dispute : DISCUSSION — **parley** *vb*

par·lia·ment \'pär-lə-mənt\ *n* **1** : a formal governmental conference : COUNCIL **2** *cap* : an assembly that constitutes the supreme legislative body of a country (as the United Kingdom) — **par·lia-**

men·ta·ry \ˌpär-lə-'men-t(ə-)rē\ *adj*

par·lia·men·tar·i·an \ˌpär-lə-ˌmen-'ter-ē-ən\ *n* **1** *often cap* : an adherent of the parliament in opposition to the king during the English Civil War **2** : an expert in parliamentary procedure

par·lor \'pär-lər\ *n* **1** : a room for conversation or the reception of guests **2** : a place of business ⟨beauty ~⟩

par·lous \'pär-ləs\ *adj* : full of danger or risk : PRECARIOUS ⟨~ state of a country's finances⟩ — **par·lous·ly** *adv*

Par·me·san \'pär-mə-ˌzän, -ˌzan\ *n* : a hard dry cheese with a sharp flavor

pa·ro·chi·al \pə-'rō-kē-əl\ *adj* **1** : of or relating to a church parish **2** : limited in scope : NARROW, PROVINCIAL

par·o·dy \'par-əd-ē\ *n* : a composition (as a poem or song) that imitates another work humorously or satirically — **parody** *vb*

pa·role \pə-'rōl\ *n* **1** : pledged word; *esp* : the promise of a prisoner of war to fulfill stated conditions in return for release **2** : a conditional release of a prisoner before his sentence expires — **parole** *vb* — **pa·rol·ee** \-ˌrō-'lē\ *n*

par·ox·ysm \'par-ək-ˌsiz-əm\ *n* : a sudden sharp attack (as of pain or coughing) : SPASM **syn** convulsion, fit — **par·ox·ys·mal** \ˌpar-ək-'siz-məl\ *adj*

par·quet \'pär-ˌkā\ *n* **1** : a flooring of parquetry **2** : the lower floor of a theater; *esp* : the forward part of the orchestra

par·que·try \'pär-kə-trē\ *n* : fine woodwork inlaid in patterns

par·ra·keet \'par-ə-ˌkēt\ *n* : any of various small long-tailed parrots

par·ri·cide \'par-ə-ˌsīd\ *n* **1** : one that murders his father, mother, or a close relative **2** : the act of a parricide

par·rot \'par-ət\ *n* : a bright-colored tropical bird with a strong hooked bill

par·ry \'par-ē\ *vb* **1** : to ward off a weapon or blow **2** : to evade esp. by an adroit answer — **parry** *n*

parse \'pärs, 'pärz\ *vb* [L *pars orationis* part of speech, the first item to be given in parsing a word] : to give a grammatical description of a word or a group of words

par·si·mo·ny \'pär-sə-ˌmō-nē\ *n* : extreme or excessive frugality : STINGINESS — **par·si·mo·ni·ous** \ˌpär-sə-'mō-nē-əs\ *adj* — **par·si·mo·ni·ous·ly** *adv*

pars·ley \'pär-slē\ *n* : a garden plant with finely divided leaves used as a seasoning or garnish

pars·nip \'pär-snəp\ *n* : a garden plant with a long edible root; *also* : this root

par·son \'pärs-ᵊn\ *n* : a usu. Protestant clergyman

par·son·age \'pärs-(ᵊ)nij\ *n* : a house provided by a church for its pastor

¹part \'pärt\ *n* **1** : a division or portion of a whole **2** : a spare piece for a machine **3** : the melody or score for a particular voice or instrument ⟨the alto ~⟩ **4** : DUTY, FUNCTION **5** : one of the sides in a dispute ⟨took his friend's ~⟩ **6** : ROLE; *also* : an actor's lines in a play **7** *pl* : TALENTS, ABILITY **8** : the line where one's hair divides (as in combing)

ə abut; ᵊ kitten; ər further; a back; ā bake; ä cot, cart; aů out; ch chin; e less; ē easy; g gift; i trip; ī life; j joke; ŋ sing; ō flow; ȯ flaw; ȯi coin; th thin; t̲h̲ this; ü loot; ů foot; y yet; yü few; yů furious; zh vision

²part *vb* **1** : to take leave of someone **2** : to divide or break into parts : SEPARATE **3** : to go away : DEPART; *also* : DIE **4** : to give up possession ⟨~ed with her jewels⟩ **5** : APPORTION, SHARE

par·take \pär-'tāk, pər-\ *vb* **1** : to have a share or part : PARTICIPATE **2** : to take a portion (as of food) — **par·tak·er** *n*

par·terre \pär-'teər\ *n* **1** : an ornamental arrangement of flower beds **2** : the part of a theater floor behind the orchestra

par·the·no·gen·e·sis \,pär-thə-nō-'jen-ə-səs\ *n* : development of a new individual from an unfertilized egg

par·tial \'pär-shəl\ *adj* **1** : favoring one party over the other : BIASED **2** : markedly or foolishly fond — used with *to* **3** : not total or general : affecting a part only — **par·tial·i·ty** \,pärsh-(ē-)'al-ət-ē\ *n* — **par·tial·ly** \'pärsh-(ə-)lē\ *adv*

part·ible \'pärt-ə-bəl\ *adj* : capable of being parted

par·tic·i·pate \pär-'tis-ə-,pāt, pər-\ *vb* **1** : to take part in something ⟨~ in a game⟩ **2** : SHARE — **par·tic·i·pant** \-pənt\ *adj or n* — **par·tic·i·pa·tion** \-,tis-ə-'pā-shən\ *n* — **par·tic·i·pa·tor** \-'tis-ə-,pāt-ər\ *n*

par·ti·ci·ple \'pärt-ə-,sip-əl\ *n* : a word having the characteristics of both verb and adjective — **par·ti·cip·i·al** \,pärt-ə-'sip-ē-əl\ *adj*

par·ti·cle \'pärt-i-kəl\ *n* **1** : a very small bit of matter **2** : a unit of speech (as an article, preposition, or conjunction) expressing some general aspect of meaning or some connective or limiting relation

par·ti·col·ored \,pärt-ē-'kəl-ərd\ *adj* : showing different colors or tints : VARIEGATED ⟨~ beach balls⟩

¹par·tic·u·lar \pə(r)-'tik-yə-lər\ *adj* **1** : of or relating to a specific person or thing (the laws of a ~ state) **2** : DISTINCTIVE, SPECIAL ⟨the ~ point of his talk⟩ **3** : SEPARATE, INDIVIDUAL ⟨each ~ hair⟩ **4** : attentive to details : PRECISE **5** : hard to please : EXACTING *syn* single, sole, unique, lone, solitary, specific, concrete, fussy, squeamish, nice — **par·tic·u·lar·i·ty** \-,tik-yə-'lar-ət-ē\ *n* — **par·tic·u·lar·ly** \-'tik-yə-lər-lē\ *adv*

²particular *n* : an individual fact or detail

par·tic·u·lar·ize \pər-'tik-yə-lə-,rīz\ *vb* **1** : to state in detail : SPECIFY **2** : to go into details

¹part·ing \'pärt-iŋ\ *n* **1** : SEPARATION, DIVISION **2** : the action of leaving one another ⟨lovers' ~⟩ **3** : a place of separation or divergence

²parting *adj* **1** : DEPARTING; *esp* : DYING **2** : FAREWELL ⟨~ words⟩ **3** : serving to part : SEPARATING

par·ti pris \,pär-,tē-'prē\ *n* : a preconceived opinion : PREJUDICE

par·ti·san *or* **par·ti·zan** \'pärt-ə-zən\ *n* **1** : one that takes the part of another : ADHERENT **2** : GUERRILLA — **partisan** *adj* — **par·ti·san·ship** \-,ship\ *n*

par·ti·tion \pär-'tish-ən, pər-\ *n* **1** : DIVISION **2** : something that divides or separates; *esp* : an interior wall dividing one part of a house from another — **partition** *vb*

par·ti·tive \'pärt-ət-iv\ *adj* : of, relating

to, or denoting a part ⟨a ~ construction⟩

part·ly \'pärt-lē\ *adv* : in part : in some measure or degree

part·ner \'pärt-nər\ *n* **1** : ASSOCIATE, COLLEAGUE **2** : either of a couple who dance together **3** : one who plays on the same team with another **4** : HUSBAND, WIFE **5** : one of two or more persons contractually associated as joint principals in a business — **part·ner·ship** \-,ship\ *n*

part of speech : a traditional class of words distinguished according to the kind of idea denoted and the function performed in a sentence

par·tridge \'pär-trij\ *n* : any of various stout-bodied game birds

part-song \'pärt-,sȯŋ\ *n* : a song with two or more voice parts

par·tu·ri·tion \,pärt-ə-'rish-ən\ *n* : CHILDBIRTH

par·ty \'pärt-ē\ *n* **1** : a person or group taking one side of a question; *esp* : a group of persons organized for the purpose of directing the policies of a government **2** : a person or group concerned in an action or affair : PARTICIPANT **3** : a group of persons detailed for a common task **4** : a social gathering

par·ve·nu \'pär-və-,n(y)ü\ *n* : one who has recently or suddenly risen to wealth or power and has not yet secured the social position appropriate to it

pas \'pä\ *n, pl* **pas** \'pä(z)\ : a dance step or combination of steps

pa·sha \'päsh-ə, pə-'shä\ *n* : a man (as formerly a governor in Turkey) of high rank

¹pass \'pas\ *vb* **1** : MOVE, PROCEED **2** : to go away; *also* : DIE **3** : to go by : move past, beyond, or over **4** : to allow to elapse : ELAPSE, SPEND **5** : to go or make way through **6** : to go or allow to go unchallenged **7** : to undergo transfer : TRANSFER **8** : to render a legal judgment **9** : OCCUR **10** : to secure the approval of (as a legislature) **11** : to go or cause to go through an inspection, test, or course of study successfully **12** : to be regarded **13** : CIRCULATE **14** : VOID **15** : to transfer the ball or puck to another player **16** : to decline to bid or bet on one's hand in a card game **17** : to permit to reach first base by a base on balls — **pass·er** \-ər\ *n* — **pass·er·by** \,pas-ər-'bī\ *n*

²pass *n* : a gap in a mountain range ⟨the Brenner ~⟩

³pass *n* **1** : the act or an instance of passing **2** : REALIZATION, ACCOMPLISHMENT **3** : a state of affairs : CONDITION **4** : a written authorization to leave, enter, or move about freely **5** : a transfer of a ball or puck from one player to another **6** : BASE ON BALLS **7** : EFFORT, TRY

pass·able \'pas-ə-bəl\ *adj* **1** : capable of being passed or traveled on **2** : barely good enough : TOLERABLE — **pass·ably** *adv*

pas·sage \'pas-ij\ *n* **1** : the action or process of passing **2** : a means (as a road or corridor) of passing **3** : a voyage esp. by sea or air **4** : a right or permission to pass **5** : ENACTMENT **6** : a mutual act (as an exchange of blows) **7** : a usu. brief portion or section (as of a book)

pas·sage·way \-,wā\ *n* : a road or way

by which a person or thing may pass ⟨a ~ between buildings⟩

pass·book \'pas-,bůk\ *n* : BANKBOOK

pas·sé \pa-'sā\ *adj* **1** : past one's prime **2** : not up-to-date : OUTMODED

pas·sel \'pas-əl\ *n* : a large number : GROUP

pas·sen·ger \'pas-ᵊn-jər\ *n* : a traveler in a public or private conveyance

passe-par·tout \,pas-pər-'tü\ *n* : something that passes or enables one to pass everywhere

pas·ser·ine \'pas-ə-,rīn\ *adj* : of or relating to the great group of birds comprising singing birds that perch

pas·sim \'pas-əm\ *adv* : here and there : THROUGHOUT

pass·ing \'pas-iŋ\ *n* : the act of one that passes or causes to pass; *esp* : DEATH

pas·sion \'pash-ən\ *n* **1** *often cap* : the sufferings of Christ between the night of the Last Supper and his death **2** : strong feeling; *also, pl* : the emotions as distinguished from reason **3** : RAGE, ANGER **4** : LOVE; *also* : an object of affection or enthusiasm **5** : sexual desire — **pas·sion·ate** \'pash-(ə-)nət\ *adj* — **pas·sion·ate·ly** *adv* — **pas·sion·less** \-ən-ləs\ *adj*

pas·sive \'pas-iv\ *adj* **1** : not active : acted upon **2** : asserting that the grammatical subject is subjected to or affected by the action represented by the verb ⟨~ voice⟩ **3** : SUBMISSIVE, PATIENT — **passive** *n* — **pas·sive·ly** *adv* — **pas·siv·i·ty** \pa-'siv-ət-ē\ *n*

pass·key \'pas-,kē\ *n* : a key for opening two or more locks

Pass·over \'pas-,ō-vər\ *n* [so called fr. the exemption of the Israelites from the slaughter of the firstborn in Egypt, Exod 12:23–27] : a Jewish holiday celebrated in March or April in commemoration of the Hebrews' liberation from slavery in Egypt

pass·port \'pas-,pōrt\ *n* : an official document issued by a country upon request to a citizen requesting protection for him during travel abroad

pass·word \-,wərd\ *n* : a word or phrase that must be spoken by a person before he is allowed to pass a guard

¹past \'past\ *adj* **1** : AGO ⟨10 years ~⟩ **2** : just gone or elapsed ⟨the ~ month⟩ **3** : having existed or taken place in a period before the present : BYGONE ⟨~ history⟩ **4** : of, relating to, or constituting a verb tense that expresses time gone by

²past *prep or adv* : BEYOND

³past *n* **1** : time gone by **2** : something that happened or was done in former time **3** : the past tense; *also* : a verb form in it **4** : a secret past life or career

pas·ta \'päs-tə\ *n* **1** : a paste in processed form (as spaghetti) or in the form of fresh dough (as ravioli) **2** : a dish of cooked pasta

¹paste \'pāst\ *n* **1** : DOUGH **2** : a smooth food product made by evaporation or grinding ⟨almond ~⟩ **3** : a preparation (as of flour and water) for sticking things together **4** : a lead-glass composition of great brilliance used in imitation gems

²paste *vb* : to cause to adhere by paste : STICK

paste·board \'pās(t)-,bōrd\ *n* **1** : a stiff material made of sheets of paper pasted together **2** : medium-thick cardboard

¹pas·tel \pas-'tel\ *n* **1** : a paste made of ground color; *also* : a crayon of such paste **2** : a drawing in pastel **3** : a pale or light color

²pastel *adj* **1** : of or relating to a pastel **2** : pale and light in color

pas·tern \'pas-tərn\ *n* : the part of a horse's foot between the fetlock and the joint at the hoof

pas·teur·ize \'pas-chə-,rīz, 'pas-tə-\ *vb* : to heat (as milk) to a point where harmful germs are killed — **pas·teur·i·za·tion** \,pas-chə-rə-'zā-shən, ,pas-tə-\ *n* — **pas·teur·iz·er** *n*

pas·tiche \pas-'tēsh\ *n* : a composition (as in literature or music) made up of selections from different works

pas·tille \pas-'tēl\ *n* **1** : a small mass of aromatic paste for fumigating or scenting the air of a room **2** : an aromatic or medicated lozenge

pas·time \'pas-,tīm\ *n* : DIVERSION, RECREATION

pas·tor \'pas-tər\ *n* : a clergyman serving a local church or parish — **pas·tor·ate** \-t(ə-)rət\ *n*

¹pas·to·ral \'pas-t(ə-)rəl\ *adj* **1** : of or relating to shepherds or to rural life **2** : of or relating to spiritual guidance esp. of a congregation **3** : of or relating to the pastor of a church

²pastoral *n* : a literary work dealing with shepherds or rural life

pas·tra·mi \pə-'sträm-ē\ *n* : a highly seasoned smoked beef prepared esp. from shoulder cuts

pas·try \'pā-strē\ *n* : sweet baked goods made of dough or with a crust made of enriched dough

pas·tur·age \'pas-chə-rij\ *n* : PASTURE

¹pas·ture \'pas-chər\ *n* **1** : plants (as grass) for the feeding of grazing livestock **2** : land or a plot of land used for grazing

²pasture *vb* **1** : GRAZE **2** : to use as pasture

pasty \'pā-stē\ *adj* : resembling paste; *esp* : pallid and unhealthy in appearance

¹pat \'pat\ *n* **1** : a light tap esp. with the hand or a flat instrument; *also* : the sound made by it **2** : something (as butter) shaped into a small flat usu square individual portion

²pat *vb* **pat·ted**; **pat·ting 1** : to strike lightly with a flat instrument **2** : to flatten, smooth, or put into place or shape with a pat **3** : to tap gently or lovingly with the hand

³pat *adj (or adv)* **1** : exactly suited to the occasion **2** : memorized exactly **3** : UNYIELDING

¹patch \'pach\ *n* **1** : a piece of cloth used to cover a torn or worn place in a garment **2** : a small area (as of land) distinct from that about it

²patch *vb* **1** : to mend or cover with a patch **2** : to make of fragments **3** : to repair esp. insecurely ⟨~ up a quarrel⟩

patch·work \-,wərk\ *n* : something made of pieces of different materials, shapes, or colors

---

ə abut; ᵊ kitten; ər further; a back; ā bake; ä cot, cart; aů out; ch chin; e less; ē easy; g gift; i trip; ī life; j joke; ŋ sing; ō flow; ȯ flaw; ȯi coin; th thin; <u>th</u> this; ü loot; ů foot; y yet; yü few; yů furious; zh vision

pate \'pāt\ *n* : HEAD; *esp* : the crown of the head

pat·en \'pat-ᵊn\ *n* 1 : PLATE; *esp* : one of precious metal for the eucharistic bread 2 : a thin disk

¹**pa·tent** \1 & 4 are 'pat-, *Brit also* 'pāt-, 2 & 3 are 'pat-ᵊnt, 'pāt-\ *adj* 1 : open to public inspection ⟨letters ∼⟩ 2 : free from obstruction 3 : EVIDENT, OBVIOUS 4 : protected by a patent **syn** manifest, distinct, apparent, palpable, plain, clear

²**pat·ent** \'pat-ᵊnt, *Brit also* 'pāt-\ *n* 1 : an official document conferring a right or privilege 2 : a document securing to an inventor for a term of years exclusive right to his invention 3 : something patented — **pat·en·tee** \,pat-ᵊn-'tē, *Brit also* ,pāt-\ *n*

³**pat·ent** *vb* : to secure by patent

pa·ter·fa·mil·i·as \,pāt-ər-fə-'mil-ē-əs\ *n* : the father of a family : the male head of a household

pa·ter·nal \pə-'tərn-ᵊl\ *adj* 1 : FATHERLY 2 : related through or inherited or derived from a father — **pa·ter·nal·ly** *adv*

pa·ter·nal·ism \-,iz-əm\ *n* : a system under which an authority treats those under its control paternally (as by regulating their conduct and supplying their needs)

pa·ter·ni·ty \pə-'tər-nət-ē\ *n* 1 : FATHERHOOD 2 : descent from a father

path \'path, 'pàth\ *n* 1 : a trodden way 2 : ROUTE, COURSE — **path·less** \-ləs\ *adj*

pa·thet·ic \pə-'thet-ik\ *adj* : evoking tenderness, pity, or sorrow **syn** poignant, affecting, moving, touching, impressive — **pa·thet·i·cal·ly** *adv*

path·find·er \'path-,fīn-dər, 'pàth-\ *n* : one that discovers a way; *esp* : one that explores untraveled regions to mark out a new route

path·o·gen·ic \,path-ə-'jen-ik\ *adj* : causing disease — **path·o·ge·nic·i·ty** \-jə-'nis-ət-ē\ *n*

pa·thol·o·gy \pə-'thäl-ə-jē\ *n* 1 : the study of the essential nature of disease 2 : the abnormality of structure and function characteristic of a disease — **path·o·log·i·cal** \,path-ə-'läj-i-kəl\ *adj* — **pa·thol·o·gist** \pə-'thäl-ə-jəst\ *n*

pa·thos \'pā-,thäs\ *n* : an element in experience or artistic representation evoking pity or compassion

path·way \'path-,wā\ *n* : PATH, COURSE

pa·tience \'pā-shəns\ *n* 1 : the capacity, habit, or fact of being patient 2 *chiefly Brit* : SOLITAIRE 2

¹**pa·tient** \-shənt\ *adj* 1 : bearing pain or trials without complaint 2 : showing self-control : CALM 3 : STEADFAST, PERSEVERING — **pa·tient·ly** *adv*

²**patient** *n* : a person under medical care

pat·i·na \'pat-ə-nə, pə-'tē-nə\ *n* : a green film formed on copper and bronze by long exposure to moist air

pat·io \'pat-ē-,ō, 'pät-\ *n* 1 : COURTYARD 2 : a paved recreation area near a house

pa·tois \'pa-,twä\ *n, pl* **pa·tois** \-,twäz\ 1 : a dialect other than the standard or literary dialect; *esp* : illiterate or provincial speech 2 : JARGON 2

pa·tri·arch \'pā-trē-,ärk\ *n* 1 : a man revered as father or founder (as of a tribe or religion) 2 : a venerable old man : ELDER 3 : an ecclesiastical dignitary (as the bishop of an Eastern Orthodox see) — **pa·tri·ar·chal** \,pā-trē-'är-kəl\ *adj*

pa·tri·cian \pə-'trish-ən\ *n* : a person of high birth : ARISTOCRAT — **patrician** *adj*

pat·ri·mo·ny \'pa-trə-,mō-nē\ *n* : something (as an estate) inherited or derived esp. from one's father : HERITAGE — **pat·ri·mo·ni·al** \,pa-trə-'mō-nē-əl\ *adj*

pa·tri·ot \'pā-trē-ət, -,ät\ *n* : one who loves his country — **pa·tri·ot·ic** \,pā-trē-'ät-ik\ *adj* — **pa·tri·ot·i·cal·ly** *adv* — **pa·tri·o·tism** \'pā-trē-ə-,tiz-əm\ *n*

pa·tris·tic \pə-'tris-tik\ *adj* : of or relating to the church fathers or their writings

¹**pa·trol** \pə-'trōl\ *n* : the action of going the rounds (as of an area) for observation or the maintenance of security; *also* : a person or group performing such an action

²**patrol** *vb* **-trolled; -trol·ling** : to carry out a patrol

pa·trol·man \-'trōl-mən\ *n* : a policeman assigned to a beat

patrol wagon *n* : an enclosed police wagon or motortruck for carrying prisoners

pa·tron \'pā-trən\ *n* 1 : a person chosen or named as special protector 2 : a wealthy or influential supporter ⟨∼ of poets⟩; *also* : BENEFACTOR 3 : a regular client or customer **syn** sponsor, guarantor — **pa·tron·ess** \-trə-nəs\ *n*

pat·ron·age \'pat-rə-nij, 'pā-trə-\ *n* 1 : the support or influence of a patron 2 : the trade of customers 3 : control of appointment to government jobs

pa·tron·ize \'pā-trə-,nīz, 'pat-rə-\ *vb* 1 : to act as patron of; *esp* : to be a customer of 2 : to treat condescendingly

pat·ro·nym·ic \,pat-rə-'nim-ik\ *n* : a name derived from the name of one's father or paternal ancestor usu. by the addition of a prefix or suffix

pa·troon \pə-'trün\ *n* : the proprietor of a manorial estate esp. in New York under Dutch rule

pat·sy \'pat-sē\ *n* : one who is duped or victimized

¹**pat·ter** \'pat-ər\ *vb* : to talk glibly or mechanically **syn** chatter, prate, chat, prattle

²**patter** *n* 1 : a specialized lingo : CANT 2 : extremely rapid talk ⟨a comedian's ∼⟩

³**patter** *vb* : to strike, pat, or tap rapidly

⁴**patter** *n* : a quick succession of taps or pats ⟨the ∼ of rain⟩

¹**pat·tern** \'pat-ərn\ *n* 1 : an ideal model 2 : something used as a model for making things ⟨a dressmaker's ∼⟩ 3 : SAMPLE 4 : an artistic design 5 : CONFIGURATION

²**pattern** *vb* : to form according to a pattern

pat·ty \'pat-ē\ *n* 1 : a little pie 2 : a small flat cake esp. of chopped food

pau·ci·ty \'pò-sət-ē\ *n* : smallness of number or quantity

paunch \'pónch\ *n* : a usu. large belly : POTBELLY — **paunchy** *adj*

pau·per \'pò-pər\ *n* : a person without means of support except from charity — **pau·per·ism** \-pə-,riz-əm\ *n* — **pau·per·ize** \-pə-,rīz\ *vb*

¹**pause** \'pòz\ *n* 1 : a temporary stop; *also* : a period of inaction 2 : a brief

suspension of the voice **3** : a sign ⌒ or ‿ above or below a musical note or rest to show it is to be prolonged **4** : a reason for pausing

²**pause** vb : to stop, rest, or linger for a time

pave \'pāv\ vb : to cover (as a road) with hard material (as stone or asphalt) in order to smooth or firm the surface

pave·ment \-mənt\ n **1** : a paved surface **2** : the material with which something is paved

pa·vil·ion \pə-'vil-yən\ n **1** : a large tent **2** : a light structure (as in a park) used for entertainment or shelter

pav·ing \'pā-viŋ\ n : PAVEMENT

paw \'pò\ n : the foot of a quadruped (as a dog or lion) having claws

²**paw** vb **1** : to feel or handle clumsily or rudely **2** : to touch or strike with a paw; also : to scrape with a hoof **3** : to flail about or grab for with the hands

¹**pawn** \'pòn\ n **1** : goods deposited with another as security for a loan; also : HOSTAGE **2** : the state of being pledged

²**pawn** vb : to deposit as a pledge

³**pawn** n [MF poon, fr. ML pedon-, pedo foot soldier, fr. L ped-, pes foot] : a chessman of the least value

pawn·bro·ker \-,brō-kər\ n : one who loans money on goods pledged

pawn·shop \-,shäp\ n : a pawnbroker's place of business

¹**pay** \'pā\ vb paid \'pād\ also in sense 7 payed; pay·ing **1** : to make due return for goods or services **2** : to discharge indebtedness for : SETTLE (~ a bill) **3** : to give in forfeit (~ the penalty) **4** : REQUITE **5** : to give, offer, or make freely or as fitting (~ attention) **6** : to be profitable to : RETURN **7** : to make slack and allow to run out (~ out a rope) — **pay·able** \'pā-ə-bəl\ adj — **pay·ee** \pā-'ē\ n — **pay·er** \'pā-ər\ n

²**pay** n **1** : the status of being paid by an employer : EMPLOY **2** : something paid; esp : WAGES

³**pay** adj **1** : containing something valuable (as gold) (~ dirt) **2** : equipped to receive a fee for use (~ telephone)

pay·check \'pā-,chek\ n **1** : a check in payment of wages or salary **2** : WAGES, SALARY

pay·mas·ter \'pā-,mas-tər\ n : one who distributes the payroll

pay·ment \'pā-mənt\ n **1** : the act of paying **2** : something paid

pay·off \-,òf\ n **1** : payment at the outcome of an enterprise (a big ~ from an investment) **2** : the climax of an incident or enterprise (the ~ of a story)

pay·roll \-,rōl\ n : a list of persons entitled to receive pay; also : the money to pay those on such a list

pea \'pē\ n, pl peas also pease \'pēz\ **1** : the round edible protein-rich seed borne in the pod of a widely grown leguminous vine; also : this vine **2** : any of various plants resembling or related to the pea

peace \'pēs\ n **1** : a state of calm and quiet : TRANQUILLITY; esp : public security under law **2** : freedom from disturbing thoughts or emotions **3** : a state of concord (as between persons or governments); also : an agreement to end hostilities — **peace·able** \'pē-sə-bəl\ adj — **peace·ably** adv — **peace·ful** \-fəl\ adj — **peace·ful·ly** adv

peace·mak·er \'pēs-,mā-kər\ n : one who settles an argument or stops a fight

peace·time \-,tīm\ n : a time when a nation is not at war

peach \'pēch\ n : a sweet juicy fruit borne by a low tree with pink blossoms; also : this tree

pea·cock \'pē-,käk\ n : the male peafowl having long tail coverts which can be spread at will displaying brilliant colors

pea·fowl \-,faùl\ n : a very large domesticated Asiatic pheasant

pea·hen \-,hen\ n : the female peafowl

peak \'pēk\ n **1** : a pointed or projecting part **2** : the top of a hill or mountain; also : MOUNTAIN **3** : the front projecting part of a cap **4** : the narrow part of a ship's bow or stern **5** : the highest level or greatest degree

peaked \'pē-kəd\ adj : THIN, SICKLY

¹**peal** \'pēl\ n **1** : the loud ringing of bells **2** : a set of tuned bells **3** : a loud sound or succession of sounds

²**peal** vb : to give out peals : RESOUND

pea·nut \'pē-(,)nət\ n : an annual herb related to the pea but having pods that ripen underground; also : this pod or one of the edible seeds it bears

pear \'paər\ n : the fleshy fruit of a tree related to the apple; also : this tree

pearl \'pərl\ n **1** : a small hard often lustrous body formed within the shell of some mollusks and used as a gem **2** : one that is choice or precious (~s of wisdom) **3** : a slightly bluish medium gray — **pearly** adj

peas·ant \'pez-ªnt\ n **1** : one of a chiefly European class of tillers of the soil **2** : a person of low social or cultural status — **peas·ant·ry** \-ªn-trē\ n

pea·shoot·er \'pē-,shüt-ər\ n : a toy blowgun for shooting peas

peat \'pēt\ n : a dark substance formed by partial decay of plants (as mosses) in wet ground; also : a piece of this cut and dried for fuel — **peaty** adj

¹**peb·ble** \'peb-əl\ n : a small usu. round stone — **peb·bly** \-(ə-)lē\ adj

²**pebble** vb : to produce a rough surface texture in (~ leather)

pe·can \pi-'kän, -'kan\ n : a large American hickory tree bearing a smooth-shelled edible nut; also : this nut

pec·ca·dil·lo \,pek-ə-'dil-ō\ n, pl -loes or -los : a slight offense

pec·ca·ry \'pek-ə-rē\ n : an American chiefly tropical mammal resembling but smaller than the related pigs

pec·ca·vi \pe-'kä-,wē\ n : an acknowledgment of sin

¹**peck** \'pek\ n : a measure equal to 8 quarts or ¼ bushel

²**peck** vb **1** : to strike or pierce with or as if with the bill **2** : to pick up with or as if with the bill

³**peck** n **1** : an impression made by pecking **2** : a quick sharp stroke; also : KISS

pec·tin \'pek-tən\ n : any of various water-soluble substances found in plant tissues that cause fruit jellies to set — **pec·tic** \-tik\ adj

ə abut; ᵊ kitten; ər further; a back; ā bake; ä cot, cart; aù out; ch chin; e less; ē easy; g gift; i trip; ī life; j joke; ŋ sing; ō flow; ò flaw; òi coin; th thin; <u>th</u> this; ü loot; ù foot; y yet; yü few; yù furious; zh vision

pec·to·ral \'pek-t(ə-)rəl\ *adj* : of or relating to the breast or chest

pec·u·la·tion \,pek-yə-'lā-shən\ *n* : EMBEZZLEMENT

pe·cu·liar \pi-'kyül-yər\ *adj* 1 : belonging exclusively to one person or group 2 : CHARACTERISTIC, DISTINCTIVE 3 : QUEER, ODD **syn** individual, eccentric, singular, strange, unique — **pe·cu·liar·i·ty** \-,kyül-'yar-ət-ē, -ē-ar-\ *n* — **pe·cu·liar·ly** \-'kyül-yər-lē\ *adv*

pe·cu·ni·ary \pi-'kyü-nē,-er-ē\ *adj* : of or relating to money : MONETARY

ped·a·gogue *also* **ped·a·gog** \'ped-ə-,gäg\ *n* : TEACHER, SCHOOLMASTER

ped·a·gogy \-,gäj-ē,-,gō-jē\ *n* : the art or profession of teaching; *esp* : EDUCATION 2 — **ped·a·gog·ic** \,ped-ə-'gäj-ik\ *or* **ped·a·gog·i·cal** *adj*

¹**ped·al** \'ped-ᵊl\ *n* : a lever worked by the foot

²**pedal** *adj* : of or relating to the foot

³**pedal** *vb* -aled *also* -alled; -al·ing *also* -al·ling 1 : to use or work a pedal (as of a piano or bicycle) 2 : to ride a bicycle

ped·ant \'ped-ᵊnt\ *n* 1 : a person who makes a display of his learning 2 : a formal uninspired teacher — **pe·dan·tic** \pə-'dant-ik\ *adj* — **ped·ant·ry** \'ped-ᵊn-trē\ *n*

ped·dle \'ped-ᵊl\ *vb* : to sell or offer for sale from place to place — **ped·dler** *or* **ped·lar** \'ped-lər\ *n*

ped·es·tal \'ped-əst-ᵊl\ *n* 1 : the support or foot of something (as a column, statue, or vase) that is upright 2 : a raised platform or dais

¹**pe·des·tri·an** \pə-'des-trē-ən\ *adj* 1 : UNIMAGINATIVE, COMMONPLACE 2 : going on foot

²**pedestrian** *n* : WALKER

pe·di·at·rics \,pēd-ē-'at-riks\ *n* : a branch of medicine dealing with the care and diseases of children — **pe·di·at·ric** \-rik\ *adj* — **pe·di·a·tri·cian** \,pēd-ē-ə-'trish-ən\ *n*

pedi·cab \'ped-i-,kab\ *n* : a small 3-wheeled hooded passenger vehicle that is pedaled

ped·i·gree \'ped-ə-,grē\ *n* [MF *pie de grue* crane's foot; fr. the shape made by the lines of a genealogical chart] 1 : a record of a line of ancestors 2 : an ancestral line : LINEAGE

ped·i·ment \'ped-ə-mənt\ *n* : a low triangular gablelike decoration (as over a door or window) on a building

pe·dom·e·ter \pi-'däm-ət-ər\ *n* : an instrument that measures the distance one walks

pe·dun·cle \'pē-,dəŋ-kəl\ *n* : a narrow supporting stalk

peek \'pēk\ *vb* 1 : to look furtively 2 : to peer from a place of concealment 3 : GLANCE — **peek** *n*

¹**peel** \'pēl\ *vb* 1 : to strip the skin, bark, or rind from 2 : to strip off (as a coat); *also* : to come off 3 : to lose the skin, bark, or rind

²**peel** *n* : a skin or rind esp. of a fruit

peel·ing *n* : a peeled-off piece or strip (as of skin or rind)

peen \'pēn\ *n* : the usu. hemispherical or wedge-shaped end of the head of a hammer opposite the face

¹**peep** \'pēp\ *vb* : to utter a feeble shrill sound

²**peep** *n* : a feeble shrill sound

³**peep** *vb* 1 : to look slyly esp. through an aperture : PEEK 2 : to begin to emerge — **peep·er** *n*

⁴**peep** *n* 1 : the first faint appearance 2 : a brief or furtive look

peep·hole \'pēp-,hōl\ *n* : a hole to peep through

¹**peer** \'piər\ *n* 1 : one of equal standing with another : EQUAL 2 : NOBLE — **peer·age** \-ij\ *n* — **peer·ess** \-əs\ *n*

²**peer** *vb* 1 : to look intently or curiously 2 : to come slightly into view

peer·less \-ləs\ *adj* : having no equal : MATCHLESS **syn** supreme, superlative, incomparable

¹**peeve** \'pēv\ *vb* : to make resentful : AGGRIEVE

²**peeve** *n* 1 : a feeling or mood of resentment 2 : a particular grievance

pee·vish \'pē-vish\ *adj* : querulous in temperament : FRETFUL **syn** irritable, petulant, complaining — **pee·vish·ly** *adv* — **pee·vish·ness** *n*

pee·wee \'pē-(,)wē\ *n* : one that is diminutive or tiny

¹**peg** \'peg\ *n* 1 : a small pointed piece (as of wood) used to pin down or fasten things or to fit into holes 2 : a projecting piece used as a support or boundary marker 3 : SUPPORT, PRETEXT 4 : STEP, DEGREE 5 : THROW

²**peg** *vb* pegged; peg·ging 1 : to put a peg into : fasten, pin down, or attach with or as if with pegs 2 : to work hard and steadily : PLUG 3 : HUSTLE 4 : to mark by pegs (~ out a plot) 5 : to hold (as prices) at a set level 6 : THROW

pei·gnoir \pān-'wär\ *n* : NEGLIGEE

pe·jor·a·tive \pi-'jòr-ət-iv, 'pej-(ə-)rət-\ *adj* : having a tendency to make or become worse : DISPARAGING

Pe·king·ese \,pē-kə-'nēz, -kin-\ *n* : a small short-legged long-haired Chinese dog

pel·age \'pel-ij\ *n* : the hairy covering of a mammal

pe·lag·ic \pə-'laj-ik\ *adj* : OCEANIC

pelf \'pelf\ *n* : MONEY, RICHES

pel·i·can \'pel-i-kən\ *n* : a large web-footed bird having a pouched lower bill used to scoop in fish

pel·la·gra \pə-'lag-rə, -'läg-\ *n* : a chronic disease marked by skin and digestive disorder and nervous symptoms and caused by a faulty diet

pel·let \'pel-ət\ *n* 1 : a little ball (as of food or medicine) 2 : BULLET

pell-mell \'pel-'mel\ *adv* 1 : in mingled confusion 2 : in confused haste : HEADLONG

pel·lu·cid \pə-'lü-səd\ *adj* : extremely clear : LIMPID, TRANSPARENT **syn** translucent, lucid

¹**pelt** \'pelt\ *n* : a skin esp. of a fur-bearing animal

²**pelt** *vb* : to strike with a succession of blows or missiles

pel·vis \'pel-vəs\ *n* : a basin-shaped part of the vertebrate skeleton consisting chiefly of the two large bones of the hip — **pel·vic** \-vik\ *adj*

pem·mi·can \'pem-i-kən\ *n* : dried meat pounded fine and mixed with melted fat

¹**pen** \'pen\ *n* 1 : a small enclosure for animals 2 : a small place of confinement or storage

²**pen** *vb* penned; pen·ning : to shut in a pen : ENCLOSE

³**pen** *n* : an instrument with a split point to hold ink used for writing; *also* : a fluid-using writing instrument

⁴**pen** *vb* penned; pen·ning : WRITE

pe·nal \'pēn-°l\ *adj* : of or relating to punishment

pe·nal·ize \'pēn-°l-,īz, 'pen-\ *vb* : to put a penalty on

pen·al·ty \'pen-°l-tē\ *n* 1 : punishment for crime or offense 2 : something forfeited when a person fails to do what he agreed to do 3 : disadvantage, loss, or hardship due to some action

pen·ance \'pen-əns\ *n* 1 : an act performed to show sorrow or repentance for sin 2 : a sacrament (as in the Roman Catholic Church) consisting in repentance, confession, satisfaction as imposed by the confessor, and absolution

pe·na·tes \pə-'nāt-ēz\ *n pl* : the Roman gods of the household

pence *pl of* PENNY

pen·chant \'pen-chənt\ *n* : a strong inclination : LIKING   syn leaning, propensity, flair

¹pen·cil \'pen-səl\ *n* : an implement for writing or drawing consisting of or containing a slender cylinder of a solid marking substance

²pencil *vb* -ciled *or* -cilled; -cil·ing *or* -cil·ling : to paint, draw, or write with a pencil

pen·dant \'pen-dənt\ *n* : a hanging ornament (as an earring)

pen·dent *or* pen·dant \'pen-dənt\ *adj* : SUSPENDED, OVERHANGING

¹pend·ing \'pen-diŋ\ *prep* 1 : DURING 2 : while awaiting

²pending *adj* 1 : not yet decided 2 : IMMINENT

pen·du·lous \'pen-jə-ləs, -də-\ *adj* : hanging loosely : DROOPING

pen·du·lum \-ləm\ *n* : a body suspended from a fixed point so that it may swing freely

pen·e·trate \'pen-ə-,trāt\ *vb* 1 : to enter into : PIERCE 2 : PERMEATE 3 : to see into : UNDERSTAND, DISCOVER 4 : to affect deeply — pen·e·tra·ble \-trə-bəl\ *adj* — pen·e·tra·tion \,pen-ə-'trā-shən\ *n* — pen·e·tra·tive \'pen-ə-,trāt-iv\ *adj*

pen·e·trat·ing *adj* 1 : PIERCING ⟨a ~ shriek⟩ 2 : PERMEATING ⟨a ~ odor⟩ 3 : DISCERNING ⟨a ~ look⟩

pen·guin \'peŋ-gwən, 'pen-\ *n* : any of several erect short-legged flightless seabirds of the southern hemisphere

pen·hold·er \'pen-,hōl-dər\ *n* : a holder or handle for a pen

pen·i·cil·lin \,pen-ə-'sil-ən\ *n* : an antibiotic produced by a green mold and used against various bacteria

pen·in·su·la \pə-'nin-sə-lə, -'nin-chə-\ *n* [L *paeninsula*, fr. *paene* almost + *insula* island] : a long narrow portion of land extending out into the water from the main land body — pen·in·su·lar \-lər\ *adj*

pe·nis \'pē-nəs\ *n, pl* pe·nes \-,nēz\ *or* pe·nis·es : a male organ of copulation

¹pen·i·tent \'pen-ə-tənt\ *adj* : feeling sorrow for sins or offenses : REPENTANT — pen·i·tence \-təns\ *n* — pen·i·ten·tial \,pen-ə-'ten-chəl\ *adj*

²penitent *n* : a penitent person

pen·i·ten·tia·ry \,pen-ə-'tench-(ə-)rē\ *n* : a state or federal prison

penitentiary *adj* : of or relating to or incurring confinement in a penitentiary

pen·knife \'pen-,nīf\ *n* : a small pocketknife

pen·man \-mən\ *n* 1 : COPYIST 2 : one skilled in penmanship 3 : AUTHOR

pen·man·ship \'pen-mən-,ship\ *n* : the art or practice of writing with the pen

pen·nant \'pen-ənt\ *n* 1 : a small tapering nautical flag used for identification or signaling 2 : a long narrow flag 3 : a flag emblematic of championship

pen·ni \'pen-ē\ *n, pl* pen·nis *or* pen·nia \-ē-ə\ — see MONEY table

pen·non \'pen-ən\ *n* 1 : BANNER; *esp* : a long narrow ribbonlike flag borne on a lance 2 : WING

pen·ny \'pen-ē\ *n, pl* pennies \'pen-ēz\ *or* pence \'pens, *in compounds usu* pəns\ 1 : a British monetary unit equal to ¹⁄₁₂ shilling; *also* : a coin of this value — see MONEY table 2 *pl* pennies : a cent of the U.S. or Canada — pen·ni·less \'pen-i-ləs\ *adj*

pen·ny·roy·al \,pen-ē-'rȯi-əl, 'pen-i-,rȯil\ *n* : a hairy perennial mint with small pungently aromatic leaves

pen·ny·weight \'pen-ē-,wāt\ *n* : a unit of troy weight equal to ¹⁄₂₀ troy ounce

pen·ny·wise \-,wīz\ *adj* : wise or prudent only in small matters

pe·nol·o·gy \pi-'näl-ə-jē\ *n* : a branch of criminology dealing with prison management and the treatment of offenders

¹pen·sion \'pen-chən\ *n* : a fixed sum paid regularly esp. to a person retired from service

²pension *vb* : to pay a pension to — pen·sion·er *n*

pen·sive \'pen-siv\ *adj* : musingly, dreamily, or sadly thoughtful   syn reflective, speculative, contemplative, meditative — pen·sive·ly *adv*

pent \'pent\ *adj* : shut up : CONFINED

pen·ta·gon \'pen-ti-,gän\ *n* : a polygon of 5 angles and 5 sides — pen·tag·o·nal \pen-'tag-ən-°l\ *adj*

pen·tam·e·ter \pen-'tam-ət-ər\ *n* : a line consisting of five metrical feet

Pen·te·cost \'pent-i-,kȯst\ *n* : the 7th Sunday after Easter observed as a church festival commemorating the descent of the Holy Spirit on the apostles — Pen·te·cos·tal \,pent-i-'käst-°l\ *adj*

Pentecostal *n* : a member of a Christian religious body that is ardently evangelistic — Pen·te·cos·tal·ism \,pent-i-'käst-°l-,iz-əm\ *n*

pent·house \'pent-,haús\ *n* 1 : a shed or roof attached to and sloping from a wall or building 2 : an apartment built on the roof of a building

pen·tom·ic \pen-'täm-ik\ *adj* 1 : made up of five battle groups ⟨~ division⟩ 2 : organized into pentomic divisions ⟨~ army⟩

pen·ul·ti·mate \pə-'nəl-tə-mət\ *adj* : next to the last ⟨~ syllable⟩

pen·um·bra \pə-'nəm-brə\ *n, pl* -brae \-(,)brē\ *or* -bras : the partial shadow surrounding a complete shadow (as in an eclipse)

pe·nu·ri·ous \pə-'n(y)úr-ē-əs\ *adj* 1 : marked by penury 2 : MISERLY   syn stingy, close

pen·u·ry \'pen-yə-rē\ *n* : extreme poverty

pe·on \'pē-ˌän, -ən\ *n* **1** : a member of the landless laboring class in Spanish America **2** : one bound to service for payment of a debt — **pe·on·age** \-ə-nij\ *n*

pe·o·ny \'pē-ə-nē, 'pī-nē\ *n* : a garden plant with large usu. double red, pink, or white flowers; *also* : its flower

peo·ple \'pē-pəl\ *n, pl* **people 1** *pl* : human beings not individually known ⟨~ are funny⟩ **2** *pl* : human beings making up a group or linked by a common characteristic or interest **3** *pl* : the mass of persons in a community : POPULACE; *also* : ELECTORATE ⟨the ~'s choice⟩ **4** *pl* **peoples** : a body of persons (as a tribe, nation, or race) united by a common culture, sense of kinship, or political organization

²people *vb* : to supply or fill with or as if with people

¹pep \'pep\ *n* : brisk energy or initiative — **pep·py** *adj*

²pep *vb* **pepped; pep·ping** : to put pep into : STIMULATE

¹pep·per \'pep-ər\ *n* **1** : a pungent condiment from the berry of an East Indian climbing plant; *also* : this plant **2** : a plant related to the tomato and widely grown for its hot or mild sweet fruit used as a vegetable or in salads and pickles; *also* : this fruit

²pepper *vb* **1** : to sprinkle or season with or as if with pepper **2** : to shower with missiles or rapid blows

pep·per·corn \-ˌkȯrn\ *n* : a dried berry of the East Indian pepper

pep·per·mint \-ˌ(ˌ)mint\ *n* : a pungent aromatic mint; *also* : candy flavored with its oil

pep·pery \'pep-(ə-)rē\ *adj* **1** : having the qualities of pepper : PUNGENT, HOT **2** : having a hot temper : TOUCHY **3** : FIERY, STINGING

pep·sin \'pep-sən\ *n* : an enzyme of the stomach that begins the digestion of proteins; *also* : a preparation of this used medicinally

pep·tic \'pep-tik\ *adj* **1** : relating to or promoting digestion **2** : resulting from the action of digestive juices ⟨a ~ ulcer⟩

per \(')pər\ *prep* **1** : by means of : THROUGH **2** : to or for each **3** : according to

¹per·ad·ven·ture \'pər-əd-ˌven-chər\ *adv, archaic* : PERHAPS

²peradventure *n* : DOUBT, CHANCE

per·am·bu·late \pə-'ram-byə-ˌlāt\ *vb* : to travel over esp. on foot — **per·am·bu·la·tion** \-ˌram-byə-'lā-shən\ *n*

per·am·bu·la·tor \pə-'ram-byə-ˌlāt-ər\ *n, chiefly Brit* : a baby carriage

per an·num \(ˌ)pər-'an-əm\ *adv* : in or for each year : ANNUALLY

per·cale \(ˌ)pər-'kāl, -'kal\ *n* : a fine closely woven cotton cloth

per cap·i·ta \(ˌ)pər-'kap-ət-ə\ *adv (or adj)* : by or for each person

per·ceive \pər-'sēv\ *vb* **1** : to attain awareness of : REALIZE **2** : to become aware of through the senses : OBSERVE — **per·ceiv·able** \-'sē-və-bəl\ *adj*

¹per·cent \pər-'sent\ *adv* : in each hundred

²percent *n, pl* **percent 1** : one part in a hundred : HUNDREDTH **2** : PERCENTAGE

per·cent·age \-ij\ *n* **1** : a part of a whole expressed in hundredths **2** : ADVANTAGE, PROFIT

per·cen·tile \pər-'sen-ˌtīl\ *n* : a statistical measure expressing an individual's standing (as in a test) in terms of the percentage of individuals falling below him

per·cept \'pər-ˌsept\ *n* : a sense impression of an object accompanied by an understanding of what it is

per·cep·ti·ble \pər-'sep-tə-bəl\ *adj* : capable of being perceived — **per·cep·ti·bly** \-blē\ *adv*

per·cep·tion \pər-'sep-shən\ *n* **1** : an act or result of perceiving **2** : awareness of environment through physical sensation **3** : ability to perceive : INSIGHT, COMPREHENSION **syn** penetration, discernment, discrimination

per·cep·tive \pər-'sep-tiv\ *adj* : of or relating to perception : having perception; *also* : DISCERNING

per·cep·tu·al \-'sep-ch(ə-w)əl\ *adj* : of, relating to, or involving sensory stimulus as opposed to abstract concept — **per·cep·tu·al·ly** *adv*

¹perch \'pərch\ *n* **1** : a roost for birds **2** : a high station or vantage point

²perch *vb* : ROOST

³perch *n* : either of two small freshwater spiny-finned food fishes; *also* : any of various fishes resembling or related to these

per·chance \pər-'chans\ *adv* : PERHAPS

per·cip·i·ent \pər-'sip-ē-ənt\ *adj* : capable of or characterized by perception — **per·cip·i·ence** *n*

per·co·late \'pər-kə-ˌlāt\ *vb* **1** : to trickle or filter through a permeable substance **2** : to filter hot water through to extract the essence ⟨~ coffee⟩ — **per·co·la·tor** *n*

per con·tra \(ˌ)pər-'kän-trə\ *adv* **1** : on the contrary **2** : by way of contrast

per·cus·sion \pər-'kəsh-ən\ *n* **1** : a sharp blow : IMPACT; *esp* : a blow upon a cap (**percussion cap**) filled with powder and designed to explode the charge in a firearm **2** : the beating or striking of a musical instrument; *also* : percussion instruments ⟨woodwinds and ~⟩

per di·em \-'dē-əm\ *adv* : by the day — **per diem** *adj or n*

per·di·tion \pər-'dish-ən\ *n* **1** : eternal damnation **2** : HELL

per·du·ra·ble \(ˌ)pər-'d(y)ùr-ə-bəl\ *adj* : very durable — **per·du·ra·bil·i·ty** \-ˌd(y)ùr-ə-'bil-ət-ē\ *n*

per·e·gri·na·tion \ˌper-ə-grə-'nā-shən\ *n* : a journeying about from place to place

pe·remp·to·ry \pə-'remp-t(ə-)rē\ *adj* **1** : barring a right of action or delay : FINAL **2** : expressive of urgency or command : IMPERATIVE **3** : marked by self-assurance : DECISIVE **syn** imperious, masterful, domineering — **pe·remp·to·ri·ly** \-t(ə-)rə-lē\ *adv*

pe·ren·ni·al \pə-'ren-ē-əl\ *adj* **1** : present at all seasons of the year ⟨~ streams⟩ **2** : continuing to live from year to year ⟨~ plants⟩ **3** : recurring regularly : PERMANENT ⟨~ problems⟩ **syn** lasting, perpetual, stable, everlasting

¹per·fect \'pər-fikt\ *adj* **1** : being without fault or defect **2** : EXACT, PRECISE **3** : COMPLETE **4** : of, relating to, or constituting a verb tense that expresses an action or state completed at the time of speaking or at a time spoken of **syn** whole, entire, intact — **per·fect·ly** *adv* — **per·fect·ness** *n*

²per·fect \pər-'fekt, 'pər-fikt\ *vb* : to make perfect

³per·fect \'pər-fikt\ *n* **:** the perfect tense; *also* **:** a verb form in it

per·fect·ible \pər-'fek-tə-bəl, 'pər-fik-\ *adj* **:** capable of improvement or perfection — **per·fect·ibil·i·ty** \pər-,fek-tə-'bil-ət-ē, ,pər-fik-\ *n*

per·fec·tion \pər-'fek-shən\ *n* **1 :** the quality or state of being perfect **2 :** the highest degree of excellence **3 :** the act or process of perfecting **syn** virtue, merit

per·fec·tion·ist *n* **:** a person who will not accept or be content with anything less than perfection

per·fec·to \pər-'fek-tō\ *n* **:** a cigar that is thick in the middle and tapers almost to a point at each end

per·fi·dy \'pər-fəd-ē\ *n* **:** violation of faith or loyalty **:** TREACHERY — **per·fid·i·ous** \pər-'fid-ē-əs\ *adj*

per·fo·rate \'pər-fə-,rāt\ *vb* **:** to bore through **:** PIERCE; *esp* **:** to make a line of holes in to facilitate separation **syn** puncture, punch, prick — **per·fo·ra·tion** \,pər-fə-'rā-shən\ *n*

per·force \pər-'fōrs\ *adv* **:** of necessity

per·form \pər-'form\ *vb* **1 :** FULFILL **2 :** to carry out **:** ACCOMPLISH **3 :** to do in a set manner **4 :** FUNCTION **5 :** to give a performance **:** PLAY **syn** execute, discharge, achieve, effect — **per·form·er** *n*

per·for·mance \pər-'for-məns\ *n* **1 :** the act or process of performing **2 :** DEED, FEAT **3 :** a public presentation or exhibition

¹per·fume \'pər-,fyüm, pər-'fyüm\ *n* **1 :** a usu. pleasant odor **:** FRAGRANCE **2 :** a preparation used for scenting

²per·fume \pər-'fyüm\ *vb* **:** to treat with a perfume; *also* **:** SCENT

per·fum·ery \pər-'fyüm-(ə-)rē\ *n* **:** PERFUMES

per·func·to·ry \pər-'fəŋk-t(ə-)rē\ *adj* **:** done merely as a duty **:** INDIFFERENT, MECHANICAL — **per·func·to·ri·ly** *adv*

per·go·la \'pər-gə-lə\ *n* **:** a structure consisting of posts supporting an open roof in the form of a trellis

per·haps \pər-'(h)aps, 'praps\ *adv* **:** possibly but not certainly

per·i·gee \'per-ə-,jē\ *n* [fr. *perigee* point in the orbit of a satellite of the earth when it is nearest the earth, fr. NL *perigeum*, fr. Gk *perigeion*, fr. *peri* around, near + *gē* earth] **:** the point at which an orbiting object is nearest the body (as the earth or moon) being orbited

per·il \'per-əl\ *n* **:** DANGER; *also* **:** a source of danger **:** RISK **syn** jeopardy, hazard — **per·il·ous** \-əs\ *adj* — **per·il·ous·ly** *adv*

pe·rim·e·ter \pə-'rim-ət-ər\ *n* **:** the outer boundary of a body or figure

¹pe·ri·od \'pir-ē-əd\ *n* **1 :** a well-rounded sentence; *also* **:** the full pause closing the utterance of a sentence **2 :** END, STOP **3 :** a punctuation mark . used esp. to mark the end of a declarative sentence or an abbreviation **4 :** a portion or division of time in which something comes to an end and is ready to begin again **5 :** MENSES **6 :** an extent of time; *esp* **:** one regarded as a stage or division in a process or development **syn** epoch, era, age, aeon

²period *adj* **:** of or relating to a particular historical period

pe·ri·od·ic \,pir-ē-'äd-ik\ *adj* **1 :** occurring at regular intervals of time **2 :** happening repeatedly **:** INTERMITTENT **3 :** of or relating to a sentence that has no trailing elements following full grammatical statement of the essential idea

¹pe·ri·od·i·cal \-'äd-i-kəl\ *adj* **1 :** PERIODIC **2 :** published at regular intervals **3 :** of or relating to a periodical — **pe·ri·od·i·cal·ly** *adv*

²periodical *n* **:** a periodical publication

per·i·pa·tet·ic \,per-ə-pə-'tet-ik\ *adj* **:** performed or performing while moving about **:** ITINERANT

pe·riph·ery \pə-'rif-(ə-)rē\ *n* **1 :** the boundary of a rounded figure **:** PERIMETER **2 :** outward bounds **:** border area — **pe·riph·er·al** \-(ə-)rəl\ *adj*

pe·riph·ra·sis \pə-'rif-rə-səs\ *n, pl* **-ra·ses** \-,sēz\ **:** CIRCUMLOCUTION

pe·rique \pə-'rēk\ *n* **:** a strong-flavored Louisiana tobacco used in smoking mixtures

per·i·scope \'per-ə-,skōp\ *n* **:** an optical instrument enabling an observer (as in a submerged submarine or at the bottom of a deep trench) to get a view (as above the surface) that he could not otherwise get

per·ish \'per-ish\ *vb* **:** to become destroyed or ruined **:** pass away completely **:** DIE

per·ish·able \-ə-bəl\ *adj* **:** easily spoiled (~ foods)

per·i·stal·sis \,per-ə-'stȯl-səs, -'stal-\ *n, pl* **-stal·ses** \-,sēz\ **:** waves of contraction passing along the intestine and forcing its contents onward — **per·i·stal·tic** \-'stȯl-tik, -'stal-\ *adj*

per·i·style \'per-ə-,stīl\ *n* **:** a row of columns surrounding a building or court

per·i·to·ni·tis \,per-ət-ᵊn-'īt-əs\ *n* **:** inflammation of the membrane lining the cavity of the abdomen

peri·wig \'per-i-,wig\ *n* **:** WIG

¹per·i·win·kle \'per-i-,wiŋ-kəl\ *n* **:** a usu. blue-flowered creeping plant much grown as a ground cover

²periwinkle *n* **:** any of various small edible seashore snails

per·ju·ry \'pərj-(ə-)rē\ *n* **:** the voluntary violation of an oath to tell the truth **:** false swearing — **per·jure** \'pər-jər\ *vb* — **per·jur·er** *n*

perk \'pərk\ *vb* **1 :** to thrust (as the head) up impudently or jauntily **2 :** to make trim or brisk **:** FRESHEN **3 :** to regain vigor or spirit — **perky** *adj*

per·ma·frost \'pər-mə-,fròst\ *n* **:** a permanently frozen layer at variable depth below the earth's surface in frigid regions

per·ma·nent \'pər-mə-nənt\ *adj* **:** LASTING, STABLE — **per·ma·nence** \-nəns\ *or* **per·ma·nen·cy** \-nən-sē\ *n* — **per·ma·nent·ly** *adv*

per·me·a·ble \'pər-mē-ə-bəl\ *adj* **:** having pores or small openings that permit liquids or gases to seep through — **per·me·a·bil·i·ty** \,pər-mē-ə-'bil-ət-ē\ *n*

per·me·ate \'pər-mē-,āt\ *vb* **1 :** to seep through the pores of **2 :** PENETRATE

2 : PERVADE — per·me·a·tion \,pər-mē-'ā-shən\ n

per·mis·si·ble \pər-'mis-ə-bəl\ adj : that may be permitted : ALLOWABLE

per·mis·sion \pər-'mish-ən\ n : formal consent : AUTHORIZATION

per·mis·sive \pər-'mis-iv\ adj : granting permission; esp : INDULGENT

¹per·mit \pər-'mit\ vb -mit·ted; -mitting **1** : to consent to : ALLOW **2** : to make possible

²per·mit \'pər-,mit, pər-'mit\ n : a written permission : LICENSE

per·mu·ta·tion \,pər-myü-'tā-shən\ n **1** : TRANSFORMATION **2** : any one of the total number of changes in position or order possible among the units or members of a group (~s of the alphabet) syn alteration

per·ni·cious \pər-'nish-əs\ adj : very destructive or injurious

per·o·ra·tion \,per-ə-'rā-shən\ n : the concluding part of a speech

per·ox·ide \pə-'räk-,sīd\ n **1** : an oxide containing a large proportion of oxygen; esp : one in which oxygen is joined to oxygen **2** : HYDROGEN PEROXIDE

per·pen·dic·u·lar \,pər-pən-'dik-yə-lər\ adj **1** : standing at right angles to the plane of the horizon **2** : meeting another line at a right angle — perpendicular n — per·pen·dic·u·lar·ly adv

per·pe·trate \'pər-pə-,trāt\ vb : to be guilty of : COMMIT — per·pe·tra·tion \,pər-pə-'trā-shən\ n — per·pe·tra·tor \'pər-pə-,trāt-ər\ n

per·pet·u·al \pər-'pech-ə-(-wə)l\ adj **1** : continuing forever : EVERLASTING **2** : occurring continually : CONSTANT (~ annoyance) syn lasting, permanent, continual, continuous, incessant, perennial — per·pet·u·al·ly adv

per·pet·u·ate \pər-'pech-ə-,wāt\ vb : to make perpetual : cause to last indefinitely — per·pet·u·a·tion \-,pech-ə-'wā-shən\ n

per·pe·tu·i·ty \,pər-pə-'t(y)ü-ət-ē\ n : the quality or state of being perpetual

per·plex \pər-'pleks\ vb : to disturb mentally; esp : CONFUSE — per·plex·i·ty \-ət-ē\ n

per·plexed \-'plekst\ adj **1** : filled with uncertainty : PUZZLED **2** : full of difficulty : COMPLICATED — per·plex·ed·ly \-'plek-səd-lē\ adv

per·qui·site \'pər-kwə-zət\ n : a privilege or profit incidental to one's employment in addition to the regular pay

per se \,pər-'sā\ adv : by, of, or in itself : as such

per·se·cute \'pər-si-,kyüt\ vb : to pursue in such a way as to injure or afflict : HARASS; esp : to cause to suffer because of belief syn oppress, wrong, aggrieve — per·se·cu·tion \,pər-si-'kyü-shən\ n — per·se·cu·tor \'pər-si-,kyüt-ər\ n

per·se·vere \,pər-sə-'viər\ vb : to persist (as in an undertaking) in spite of difficulties — per·se·ver·ance \-'vir-əns\ n

Per·sian \'pər-zhən\ n : one of the people of Persia

per·si·flage \'pər-si-,fläzh, 'per-\ n : lightly jesting or mocking talk : RAILLERY

per·sim·mon \pər-'sim-ən\ n : a tree related to the ebony; also : its edible orange-red plumlike fruit

per·sist \pər-'sist, -'zist\ vb **1** : to go on

resolutely or stubbornly in spite of difficulties : PERSEVERE **2** : to continue to exist — per·sis·tence \-'sis-təns, -'zis-\ or per·sis·ten·cy \-tən-sē\ n — per·sis·tent \-tənt\ adj — per·sisttent·ly adv

per·snick·e·ty \pər-'snik-ət-ē\ adj : fussy about small details

per·son \'pərs-ən\ n [L persona actor's mask, character in a play, person, prob. fr. Etruscan *phersu* mask] **1** : a human being : INDIVIDUAL **2** : the body of a human being **3** : the individual personality of a human being : SELF **4** : reference of a segment of discourse to the speaker, to one spoken to, or to one spoken of esp. as indicated by certain pronouns **5** : one of the three modes of being in the Godhead as understood by Trinitarians

per·son·able \'pərs-(-ə)nə-bəl\ adj : pleasing in person : ATTRACTIVE

per·son·age \'pərs-(-ə)nij\ n : a person of rank, note, or distinction

¹per·son·al \'pərs-(-ə)nəl\ adj **1** : of, relating to, or affecting a person : PRIVATE (~ correspondence) **2** : done in person (a ~ inquiry) **3** : relating to the person or body (~ injuries) **4** : relating to an individual esp. in an offensive way (resented such ~ remarks) **5** : of or relating to temporary or movable property as distinguished from real estate (~ property) **6** : denoting grammatical person — per·son·al·ly adv

²personal n : a short newspaper paragraph relating to a person or group or to personal matters

per·son·al·i·ty \,pərs-ən-'al-ət-ē\ n **1** : an offensively personal remark (indulges in *personalities*) **2** : distinctive personal character **3** : distinction of personal and social traits; also : a person having such quality syn individuality, temperament, disposition

per·son·al·ize \'pərs-(-ə)nə-,līz\ vb : to make personal or individual; esp : to mark as belonging to a particular person

per·son·al·ty \'pərs-(-ə)nəl-tē\ n : personal property

per·so·na non gra·ta \pər-,sō-nə-,nän-'grat-ə, -'grät-\ n : a person who is not acceptable

per·son·ate \'pərs-ən-,āt\ vb : IMPERSONATE, REPRESENT

per·son·i·fy \pər-'sän-ə-,fī\ vb **1** : to think of or represent as a person (~ the forces of nature) **2** : to be the embodiment of : INCARNATE (~ the law) — per·son·i·fi·ca·tion \-,sän-ə-fə-'kā-shən\ n

per·son·nel \,pərs-ən-'el\ n : a body of persons employed in a service or an organization

per·spec·tive \pər-'spek-tiv\ n **1** : the science of painting and drawing so that objects represented have apparent depth and distance **2** : the aspect in which a subject or its parts are mentally viewed; esp : a view of things (as objects or events) in their true relationship or relative importance

per·spi·cac·i·ty \,pər-spə-'kas-ət-ē\ n : acuteness of mental vision or discernment — per·spi·ca·cious \-'kā-shəs\ adj

per·spic·u·ous \pər-'spik-yə-wəs\ adj : plain to the understanding : CLEAR (writes ~ prose) — per·spi·cu·i·ty \,pər-spə-'kyü-ət-ē\ n

per·spire \pər-'spīr\ vb : SWEAT —

per·spi·ra·tion \,pər-spə-'rā-shən\ *n*

per·suade \pər-'swād\ *vb* **:** to move by argument or entreaty to a belief or course of action — **per·sua·sive** \-'swā-siv, -ziv\ *adj* — **per·sua·sive·ly** *adv* — **per·sua·sive·ness** *n*

per·sua·sion \pər-'swā-zhən\ *n* **1 :** the act or process of persuading **2 :** OPINION, BELIEF

pert \'pərt\ *adj* **1 :** saucily free and forward **:** IMPUDENT **2 :** stylishly trim **:** JAUNTY **3 :** LIVELY

per·tain \pər-'tān\ *vb* **1 :** to belong to as a part, quality, or function ⟨duties ~ing to the office⟩ **2 :** to have reference **:** RELATE ⟨facts that ~ to the case⟩ **syn** bear, appertain, apply

per·ti·na·cious \,pərt-ᵊn-'ā-shəs\ *adj* **1 :** holding resolutely to an opinion or purpose ⟨a ~ opponent⟩ **2 :** obstinately persistent **:** TENACIOUS ⟨a ~ bill collector⟩ **syn** obstinate, dogged, mulish — **per·ti·nac·i·ty** \-'as-ət-ē\ *n*

per·ti·nent \'pərt-ᵊn-ənt\ *adj* **:** relating to the matter under consideration ⟨all ~ information⟩ **syn** relevant, germane, applicable, apropos

per·turb \pər-'tərb\ *vb* **:** to disturb greatly in mind **:** UPSET — **per·tur·ba·tion** \,pərt-ər-'bā-shən\ *n*

pe·ruke \pə-'rük\ *n* **:** WIG

pe·ruse \pə-'rüz\ *vb* **:** READ; *esp* **:** to read attentively — **pe·rus·al** \-'rü-zəl\ *n*

per·vade \pər-'vād\ *vb* **:** to spread through every part of **:** PERMEATE, PENETRATE — **per·va·sive** \-'vā-siv, -ziv\ *adj*

per·verse \pər-'vərs\ *adj* **1 :** turned away from what is right or good **:** CORRUPT **2 :** obstinate in opposing what is reasonable or accepted — **per·verse·ly** *adv* — **per·verse·ness** *n* — **per·ver·si·ty** \-'vər-sət-ē\ *n*

per·ver·sion \pər-'vər-zhən\ *n* **:** the action of perverting **:** the condition of being perverted **2 :** a perverted form of something; *esp* **:** abnormal sexual behavior

¹per·vert \pər-'vərt\ *vb* **1 :** to lead astray **:** CORRUPT ⟨~ the young⟩ **2 :** to divert to a wrong purpose **:** MISAPPLY ⟨~ evidence⟩ **3 :** to twist the meaning of ⟨~ a text⟩ **syn** deprave, debase

²per·vert \'pər-,vərt\ *n* **:** one that is perverted; *esp* **:** a person given to sexual perversion

pe·se·ta \pə-'sāt-ə\ *n* — see MONEY table

pes·ky \'pes-kē\ *adj* **:** causing annoyance **:** TROUBLESOME ⟨~ mosquitoes⟩

pe·so \'pā-sō\ *n* — see MONEY table

pes·si·mism \'pes-ə-,miz-əm\ *n* **:** an inclination to take the least favorable view (as of events) or to expect the worst possible outcome — **pes·si·mist** \-məst\ *n*

pest \'pest\ *n* **1 :** a destructive epidemic disease **:** PLAGUE **2 :** one that pesters **:** NUISANCE **3 :** a plant or animal detrimental to man

pes·ter \'pes-tər\ *vb* **:** to harass with petty irritations **:** ANNOY

pest·house \'pest-,haús\ *n* **:** a shelter or hospital for those infected with a contagious disease

pes·ti·cide \'pes-tə-,sīd\ *n* **:** an agent used to kill pests

pes·tif·er·ous \pes-'tif-(ə-)rəs\ *adj* **1 :** PESTILENT **2 :** ANNOYING

pes·ti·lence \'pes-tə-ləns\ *n* **:** a destructive infectious swiftly spreading disease; *esp* **:** PLAGUE — **pes·ti·len·tial** \,pes-tə-'len-chəl\ *adj*

pes·ti·lent \'pes-tə-lənt\ *adj* **1 :** dangerous to life **:** DEADLY; *also* **:** spreading or causing pestilence **2 :** PERNICIOUS, HARMFUL **3 :** TROUBLESOME

pes·tle \'pes-əl, 'pest-ᵊl\ *n* **:** an implement for grinding substances in a mortar

¹pet \'pet\ *n* **1 :** a domesticated animal kept for pleasure rather than utility **2 :** FAVORITE, DARLING

²pet *adj* **1 :** kept or treated as a pet ⟨~ dog⟩ **2 :** expressing fondness ⟨~ name⟩ **3 :** particularly liked or favored ⟨~ pupil⟩

³pet *vb* **pet·ted; pet·ting** **1 :** to stroke gently or lovingly **2 :** to make a pet of **:** PAMPER **3 :** to engage in amorous kissing and caressing with a member of the opposite sex

⁴pet *n* **:** a fit of peevishness, sulkiness, or anger

pet·al \'pet-ᵊl\ *n* **:** one of the modified leaves of a flower's corolla

pe·tard \pə-'tär(d)\ *n* **:** a case containing an explosive to break down a door or gate or breach a wall

pe·ter \'pēt-ər\ *vb* **:** to diminish gradually and come to an end ⟨stream ~s out⟩

pet·i·ole \'pet-ē-,ōl\ *n* **:** a stalk that supports a leaf

pe·tite \pə-'tēt\ *adj* **:** small and trim of figure ⟨a ~ woman⟩

pe·tit four \,pet-ē-'fȯr\ *n, pl* **petits fours** *or* **petit fours** \,pet-ē-'fȯrz\ **:** a small frosted and ornamented cake cut from pound cake or sponge cake

¹pe·ti·tion \pə-'tish-ən\ *n* **:** an earnest request **:** ENTREATY; *esp* **:** a formal written request made to a superior

²petition *vb* **:** to make a petition **:** ENTREAT — **pe·ti·tion·er** *n*

pet·rel \'pet-rəl\ *n* **:** any of various small seabirds that fly far from land

pet·ri·fy \'pet-rə-,fī\ *vb* **1 :** to change into stony material **2 :** to make rigid or inactive (as from fear or awe) — **pet·ri·fac·tion** \,pet-rə-'fak-shən\ *n*

pet·rol \'pet-rəl\ *n, Brit* **:** GASOLINE

pet·ro·la·tum \,pet-rə-'lāt-əm\ *n* **:** a tasteless, odorless, and oily or greasy substance from petroleum that is used esp. in ointments and dressings

pe·tro·le·um \pə-'trō-lē-əm\ *n* **:** a dark oily liquid found at places in the earth's upper strata and processed into useful products (as gasoline, kerosene, and oil)

¹pet·ti·coat \'pet-ē-,kōt\ *n* **1 :** a skirt worn under a dress **2 :** an outer skirt

²petticoat *adj* **:** FEMALE ⟨~ government⟩

pet·ti·fog \'pet-ē-,fȯg, -,fäg\ *vb* **-fogged; -fog·ging** **1 :** to engage in legal trickery **2 :** to quibble over insignificant details — **pet·ti·fog·ger** *n*

pet·tish \'pet-ish\ *adj* **:** PEEVISH **syn** irritable, petulant, fretful

pet·ty \'pet-ē\ *adj* **1 :** having secondary rank **:** MINOR ⟨~ prince⟩ **2 :** of little importance **:** TRIFLING ⟨~ faults⟩ **3 :** marked by narrowness or meanness

---

ə abut; ᵊ kitten; ər further; a back; ā bake; ä cot, cart; aú out; ch chin; e less; ē easy; g gift; i trip; ī life; j joke; ŋ sing; ō flow; ȯ flaw; ȯi coin; th thin; t͟h this; ü loot; ú foot; y yet; yü few; yú furious; zh vision

(~ attitude) — **pet·ti·ly** *adv* — **pet·ti·ness** *n*

petty officer *n* : an enlisted man in the navy of any of the three lowest non-commissioned ranks

pet·u·lant \'pech-ə-lənt\ *adj* : marked by capricious ill humor **syn** irritable, peevish, fretful — **pet·u·lance** \-ləns\ *n* — **pet·u·lant·ly** *adv*

pe·tu·nia \pə-'t(y)ü-nyə\ *n* : a garden plant with bright funnel-shaped flowers

pew \'pyü\ *n* : one of the benches with backs fixed in rows in a church

pew·ter \'pyüt-ər\ *n* : an alloy of tin usu. with lead and sometimes also copper or antimony used esp. for kitchen or table utensils

pfen·nig \'fen-ig\ *n* — see MONEY table

pha·eton \'fā-ət-ᵊn\ *n* **1** : a light 4-wheeled horse-drawn vehicle **2** : an open automobile with two cross seats

pha·lanx \'fā-,laṇks\ *n*, *pl* **pha·lanx·es** *or* **pha·lan·ges** \fə-'lan-,jēz\ : a group or body (as of troops) in compact formation

phal·a·rope \'fal-ə-,rōp\ *n* : any of several small shorebirds

phal·lus \'fal-əs\ *n*, *pl* **phal·li** \-,ī\ *or* **phal·lus·es** : PENIS; *also* : a symbolic representation of the penis

phan·tasm \'fan-,taz-əm\ *n* : a product of the imagination : ILLUSION, APPARITION

phan·tas·ma·go·ria \fan-,taz-mə-'gōr-ē-ə\ *n* : a constantly shifting complex succession of things seen or imagined; *also* : a scene that constantly changes or fluctuates

phantasy *var of* FANTASY

phan·tom \'fant-əm\ *n* **1** : something (as a specter) that is apparent to sense but has no substantial existence : APPARITION **2** : a mere show : SHADOW (~ of authority) **3** : a representation of something abstract, ideal, or incorporeal — **phantom** *adj*

phar·aoh \'fe(ə)r-ō, 'fā-rō\ *n*, *often cap* : a ruler of ancient Egypt

phar·i·sa·ical \,far-ə-'sā-ə-kəl\ *adj* : hypocritically self-righteous — **phar·i·sa·ical·ly** *adv*

phar·i·see \'far-ə-,sē\ *n* **1** *cap* : a member of an ancient Jewish sect noted for strict observance of rites and ceremonies of the traditional law **2** : a self-righteous or hypocritical person — **phar·i·sa·ic** \,far-ə-'sā-ik\ *adj*

phar·ma·ceu·ti·cal \,fär-mə-'süt-i-kəl\ *or* **phar·ma·ceu·tic** \-'süt-ik\ *adj* **1** : of or relating to pharmacy or pharmacists **2** : MEDICINAL — **pharmaceutical** *n*

phar·ma·col·o·gy \,fär-mə-'käl-ə-jē\ *n* **1** : the science of drugs esp. as related to medicinal uses **2** : the reactions and properties of a drug — **phar·ma·co·log·i·cal** \-kə-'läj-i-kəl\ *adj* — **phar·ma·col·o·gist** \-'käl-ə-jəst\ *n*

phar·ma·co·poe·ia \-kə-'pē-(y)ə\ *n* **1** : a book describing drugs and medicinal preparations **2** : a stock of drugs

phar·ma·cy \'fär-mə-sē\ *n* **1** : the art or practice of preparing and dispensing drugs **2** : DRUGSTORE — **phar·ma·cist** \-səst\ *n*

pha·ros \'faar-,äs\ *n* : a lighthouse or beacon to guide seamen

phar·ynx \'far-inks\ *n*, *pl* **pha·ryn·ges** \fə-'rin-,jēz\ *also* **phar·ynx·es** : the space just back of the mouth into which the nostrils, esophagus, and trachea open — **pha·ryn·ge·al** \fə-'rin-j(ē-)əl, ,far-ən-'jē-əl\ *adj*

phase \'fāz\ *n* **1** : a particular appearance in a recurring series of changes (~s of the moon) **2** : a stage or interval in a process or cycle (first ~ of an experiment) **3** : an aspect or part under consideration (~s of social work)

pheas·ant \'fez-ᵊnt\ *n* : any of various long-tailed brilliantly colored game birds related to the domestic fowl

phe·no·bar·bi·tal \,fē-nō-'bär-bə-,tól\ *n* : a crystalline drug used as a hypnotic and sedative

phe·nol \'fē-,nōl, fi-'nōl\ *n* : a caustic poisonous acidic compound in tar used as a disinfectant and in making plastics

phe·nom·e·non \fi-'näm-ə-,nän, -nən\ *n*, *pl* **-ena** \-nə\ [Gk *phainomenon*, fr. neut. of *phainomenos*, prp. of *phainesthai* to appear] **1** : an observable fact or event **2** : an outward sign of the working of a law of nature **3** *pl* **-enons** : an extraordinary person or thing : PRODIGY — **phe·nom·e·nal** \-'näm-ən-ᵊl\ *adj*

phi·al \'fī(-ə)l\ *n* : VIAL

phi·lan·der \fə-'lan-dər\ *vb* : to make love without serious intent : FLIRT — **phi·lan·der·er** *n*

phi·lan·thro·py \fə-'lan-thrə-pē\ *n* **1** : goodwill to fellowmen; *esp* : effort to promote human welfare **2** : a charitable act or gift; *also* : an organization that distributes or is supported by donated funds — **phil·an·throp·ic** \,fil-ən-'thräp-ik\ *adj* — **phi·lan·thro·pist** \fə-'lan-thrə-pəst\ *n*

phi·lat·e·ly \fə-'lat-ᵊl-ē\ *n* : the collection and study of postage and imprinted stamps — **phi·lat·e·list** \-ᵊl-əst\ *n*

phil·har·mon·ic \,fil-ər-'män-ik, ,fil-(h)är-\ *adj* : of or relating to a symphony orchestra

phi·lip·pic \fə-'lip-ik\ *n* : a speech full of bitter invective : TIRADE

phil·is·tine \'fil-ə-,stēn, fə-'lis-tən\ *n*, *often cap* : a materialistic person; *esp* : one who is smugly insensitive or indifferent to intellectual or artistic values — **philistine** *adj*

phil·o·den·dron \,fil-ə-'den-drən\ *n*, *pl* **-drons** *or* **-dra** \-drə\ : any of various arums grown for their showy foliage

phi·lol·o·gy \fə-'läl-ə-jē\ *n* **1** : the study of literature and relevant fields **2** : LINGUISTICS; *esp* : historical and comparative linguistics — **phil·o·log·i·cal** \,fil-ə-'läj-i-kəl\ *adj* — **phi·lol·o·gist** \fə-'läl-ə-jəst\ *n*

phi·los·o·pher \fə-'läs-ə-fər\ *n* **1** : a reflective thinker : SCHOLAR **2** : a student of or specialist in philosophy **3** : one whose philosophical perspective enables him to meet trouble calmly

phi·los·o·phize \-,fīz\ *vb* **1** : to reason like a philosopher : THEORIZE **2** : to expound a philosophy esp. superficially

phi·los·o·phy \fə-'läs-ə-fē\ *n* **1** : a critical study of fundamental beliefs and the grounds for them **2** : sciences and liberal arts exclusive of medicine, law, and theology (doctor of ~) **3** : a system of philosophical concepts (Aristotelian ~) **4** : a basic theory concerning a particular subject or sphere of activity (~ of education) **5** : the sum of the ideas and convictions of an individual or group (his ~ of life) **6** : calmness of temper and judgment —

phil·o·soph·ic \,fil-ə-'säf-ik\ *or* **phil·o·soph·i·cal** *adj* — **phil·o·soph·i·cal·ly** *adv*

phil·ter *or* **phil·tre** \'fil-tər\ *n* **1** : a potion, drug, or charm held to excite sexual love **2** : a magic potion

phiz \'fiz\ *n* : FACE

phle·bi·tis \fli-'bīt-əs\ *n* : inflammation of a vein

phle·bot·o·my \fli-'bät-ə-mē\ *n* : the letting of blood in the treatment of disease

phlegm \'flem\ *n* : thick mucus secreted in abnormal quantity esp. in the nose and throat

phleg·mat·ic \fleg-'mat-ik\ *adj* : having or showing a slow and stolid temperament **syn** impassive, apathetic, stoic

phlo·em \'flō-,em\ *n* : a vascular plant tissue external to the xylem that carries dissolved food material downward

phlox \'fläks\ *n* : any of several American herbs; *esp* : one grown for its tall stalks with showy spreading terminal clusters of flowers

pho·bia \'fō-bē-ə\ *n* : an irrational persistent fear or dread

phoe·nix \'fē-niks\ *n* : a legendary bird held to live for centuries and then to burn itself to death and rise fresh and young from its ashes

¹phone \'fōn\ *n* **1** : EARPHONE **2** : TELEPHONE

²phone *vb* : TELEPHONE

pho·neme \'fō-,nēm\ *n* : one of the smallest units of speech that distinguish one utterance from another — **pho·ne·mic** \fō-'nē-mik\ *adj*

pho·net·ics \fə-'net-iks\ *n* : the study and systematic classification of the sounds made in spoken utterance — **pho·net·ic** \-ik\ *adj* — **pho·ne·ti·cian** \,fō-nə-'tish-ən\ *n*

pho·no·graph \'fō-nə-,graf\ *n* : an instrument for reproducing sounds by means of the vibration of a needle following a spiral groove on a revolving disc — **pho·no·graph·ic** \,fō-nə-'graf-ik\ *adj*

pho·nol·o·gy \fə-'näl-ə-jē\ *n* : a study and description of the sound changes in a language — **pho·no·log·i·cal** \,fōn-ᵊl-'äj-i-kəl\ *adj* — **pho·nol·o·gist** \fə-'näl-ə-jəst\ *n*

pho·ny \'fō-nē\ *adj* : marked by empty pretension : FAKE — **phony** *n*

phos·phate \'fäs-,fāt\ *n* **1** : a chemical salt obtained esp. from various rocks and bones and widely used in fertilizers **2** : an effervescent drink of carbonated water flavored with fruit syrup — **phos·phat·ic** \fäs-'fat-ik\ *adj*

phos·pho·res·cence \,fäs-fə-'res-ᵊns\ *n* : the property (as of phosphorus) of emitting light without heat; *also* : light so produced — **phos·pho·res·cent** \-ᵊnt\ *adj*

phos·phor·ic acid \,fäs-,fòr-ik-, -,fär-\ *n* : a syrupy or crystalline acid obtained esp. from a rock and used in making fertilizers and flavoring soft drinks

phos·pho·rus \'fäs-f(ə-)rəs\ *n* : a waxy nonmetallic chemical element that is found combined with other elements in phosphates, soils, and bones and that has a faint glow in moist air — **phos·phor·ic** \fäs-'fòr-ik, -'fär-\ *adj* —

phos·pho·rous \'fäs-f(ə-)rəs; fäs-'fòr-əs, -'fòr-\ *adj*

pho·to \'fōt-ō\ *n* : PHOTOGRAPH — **photo** *vb*

pho·to·cell \'fōt-ə-,sel\ *n* : PHOTOELECTRIC CELL

pho·to·copy \-,käp-ē\ *n* : a photographic reproduction of graphic matter

pho·to·elec·tric \,fōt-ō-ə-'lek-trik\ *adj* : relating to an electrical effect due to the interaction of light with matter

photoelectric cell *n* : a device in which variations in light are converted into variations in an electric current

pho·to·en·grave \,fōt-ō-in-'grāv\ *vb* : to make a photoengraving of

pho·to·en·grav·ing *n* : a process by which an etched printing plate is made from a photograph or drawing; *also* : a print made from such a plate

photo finish *n* : a race finish so close that a photograph of the finish is used to determine the winner

pho·to·flash \'fōt-ə-,flash\ *n* : FLASHBULB

pho·to·gen·ic \,fōt-ə-'jen-ik\ *adj* : eminently suitable esp. aesthetically for being photographed

pho·to·graph \'fōt-ə-,graf\ *n* : a picture taken by photography — **pho·to·graph** *vb* — **pho·tog·ra·pher** \fə-'täg-rə-fər\ *n*

pho·tog·ra·phy \fə-'täg-rə-fē\ *n* : the art or process of producing images on a sensitized surface (as film in a camera) by the action of light — **pho·to·graph·ic** \,fōt-ə-'graf-ik\ *adj*

pho·to·mi·cro·graph \,fōt-ə-'mī-krə-,graf\ *n* : a photograph of a magnified image of a small object

pho·to·mu·ral \-'myúr-əl\ *n* : an enlarged photograph usu. several yards long used on walls esp. as decoration

pho·ton \'fō-,tän\ *n* : a quantum of radiant energy

pho·to·play \'fōt-ə-,plā\ *n* : MOTION PICTURE

pho·to·sen·si·tive \,fōt-ə-'sen-sət-iv\ *adj* : sensitive or sensitized to the action of radiant energy — **pho·to·sen·si·ti·za·tion** \-,sen-sət-ə-'zā-shən\ *n*

pho·to·syn·the·sis \,fōt-ə-'sin-thə-səs\ *n* : formation of carbohydrates by chlorophyll-containing plants exposed to sunlight

¹phrase \'frāz\ *n* **1** : a brief expression **2** : a group of two or more grammatically related words that form a sense unit expressing a thought

²phrase *vb* : to express in words

phra·se·ol·o·gy \,frā-zē-'äl-ə-jē\ *n* : a manner of phrasing : STYLE

phras·ing \'frā-ziŋ\ *n* : style of expression

phre·nol·o·gy \fri-'näl-ə-jē\ *n* : the study of the conformation of the skull as indicative of mental faculties and character traits

phy·lac·tery \fə-'lak-t(ə-)rē\ *n* **1** : one of two small square leather boxes containing slips inscribed with scripture passages and traditionally worn on the left arm and forehead by Jewish men during morning weekday prayers **2** : AMULET

phy·lum \'fī-ləm\ *n, pl* **-la** \-lə\ : a group (as of people or languages) apparently of common origin; *also* **:** a major division of the plant or animal kingdom

¹phys·ic \'fiz-ik\ *n* **1 :** the profession of medicine **2 :** MEDICINE; *esp* **:** CATHARTIC

²physic *vb* **-icked; -ick·ing :** PURGE

phys·i·cal \'fiz-i-kəl\ *adj* **1 :** of or relating to nature or the laws of nature **2 :** material as opposed to mental or spiritual **3 :** of or relating to physics **:** produced by the forces and operations of physics **4 :** of or relating to the body **:** BODILY — **phys·i·cal·ly** *adv*

physical science *n* **:** the sciences (as mineralogy and astronomy) that deal with physical objects and energy

phy·si·cian \fə-'zish-ən\ *n* **:** a doctor of medicine

phys·i·cist \'fiz-ə-səst\ *n* **:** a specialist in physics

phys·ics \'fiz-iks\ *n* **:** a science that deals with matter and motion and includes mechanics, heat, light, electricity, and sound

phys·i·og·no·my \,fiz-ē-'äg(g)-nə-mē\ *n* **:** facial appearance esp. as a reflection of inner character

phys·i·og·ra·phy \,fiz-ē-'äg-rə-fē\ *n* **:** geography dealing with physical features of the earth — **phys·i·o·graph·ic** \,fiz-ē-ə-'graf-ik\ *adj*

phys·i·ol·o·gy \,fiz-ē-'äl-ə-jē\ *n* **1 :** a science dealing with the functions and functioning of living matter and beings **2 :** functional processes in an organism or any of its parts — **phys·i·o·log·i·cal** \-ē-ə-'läj-i-kəl\ *adj* — **phys·i·o·log·i·cal·ly** *adv* — **phys·i·ol·o·gist** \-ē-'äl-ə-jəst\ *n*

phys·io·ther·a·py \,fiz-ē-ō-'ther-ə-pē\ *n* **:** treatment of disease by physical means (as massage or exercise)

phy·sique \fə-'zēk\ *n* **:** the build of a person's body **:** bodily constitution

¹pi \'pī\ *n* **:** the symbol *π* denoting the ratio of the circumference of a circle to its diameter; *also* **:** the ratio itself

²pi *n, pl* **pies :** jumbled type

pi·a·nis·si·mo \,pē-ə-'nis-ə-,mō\ *adv (or adj)* **:** very softly — used as a direction in music

pi·an·ist \pē-'an-əst, 'pē-ə-nəst\ *n* **:** one who plays the piano

pi·ano \pē-'an-ō\ *also* **pi·ano·forte** \-'an-ə-,fōrt, -,an-ə-'fōrt-ē\ *n* [It *pianoforte*, fr. *piano* soft (fr. L *planus* level, flat) + *forte* loud, fr. L *fortis* strong] **:** a musical instrument having steel strings sounded by felt-covered hammers operated from a keyboard

pi·as·ter \pē-'as-tər\ *n* — see MONEY table

pi·az·za \pē-'az-ə, *esp for 1* -'at-sə\ *n* **1 :** an open square esp. in an Italian town **2 :** an arcaded and roofed gallery; *also, chiefly North & Midland* **:** VERANDA

pi·broch \'pē-,bräk\ *n* **:** a set of martial or mournful variations for the Scottish bagpipe

pic·a·resque \,pik-ə-'resk\ *adj* **:** of or relating to rogues ⟨~ fiction⟩

pic·a·yune \,pik-ē-'(y)ün\ *adj* **:** of little value **:** TRIVIAL; *also* **:** PETTY

pic·ca·lil·li \,pik-ə-'lil-ē\ *n* **:** a pungent relish of chopped vegetables and spices

pic·co·lo \'pik-ə-,lō\ *n* **:** a small shrill flute pitched an octave higher than the ordinary flute

pice \'pīs\ *n, pl* **pice** — see MONEY table

¹pick \'pik\ *vb* **1 :** to pierce or break up with a pointed instrument **2 :** to remove bit by bit (~ meat from bones); *also* **:** to remove covering matter from **3 :** to gather by plucking (~ apples) **4 :** CULL, SELECT **5 :** ROB (~ a pocket) **6 :** PROVOKE (~ a quarrel) **7 :** to dig into or pull lightly at **8 :** to pluck with fingers or a plectrum **9 :** to loosen or pull apart with a sharp point (~ wool) **10 :** to unlock with a wire **11 :** to eat sparingly — **pick·er** *n*

²pick *n* **1 :** the act or privilege of choosing **:** CHOICE **2 :** the best or choicest one **3 :** the portion of a crop gathered at one time

³pick *n* **1 :** PICKAX **2 :** a pointed implement used for picking **3 :** PLECTRUM

pick·a·back \'pig-ē-,bak, 'pik-ə-\ *var of* PIGGYBACK

pick·a·nin·ny \'pik-ə-,nin-ē\ *n* **:** a Negro child

pick·ax *or* **pick·axe** \'pik-,aks\ *n* **:** a tool with a wooden handle and a blade pointed at one end or at both ends that is used by diggers and miners

pick·er·el \'pik-(ə-)rəl\ *n* **:** any of various small pikes; *also* **:** WALLEYE 3

¹pick·et \'pik-ət\ *n* **1 :** a pointed stake (as for a fence) **2 :** a detached body of soldiers on outpost duty; *also* **:** SENTINEL **3 :** a person posted by a labor union where workers are on strike; *also* **:** a person posted for a demonstration or protest

²picket *vb* **1 :** to guard with pickets **2 :** TETHER **3 :** to post pickets at (~ a factory) **4 :** to serve as a picket

pick·ings \'pik-iŋz\ *n pl* **1 :** gleanable or eatable fragments **:** SCRAPS **2 :** yield for effort expended **:** RETURN; *also* **:** share of spoils

pick·le \'pik-əl\ *n* **1 :** a brine or vinegar solution for preserving foods; *also* **:** a food preserved in a pickle **2 :** a difficult situation **:** PLIGHT — **pickle** *vb*

pick·lock \'pik-,läk\ *n* **1 :** a tool for picking locks **2 :** BURGLAR, THIEF

pick·pock·et \'pik-,päk-ət\ *n* **:** one who steals from pockets

pick·up \'pik-,əp\ *n* **1 :** a picking up **2 :** revival of activity **:** IMPROVEMENT **3 :** ACCELERATION **4 :** a temporary chance acquaintance **5 :** a light truck with open body and low sides

picky \'pik-ē\ *adj* **:** FUSSY, FINICKY

¹pic·nic \'pik-,nik\ *n* **:** an outing with food usu. provided by members of the group and eaten in the open

²picnic *vb* **-nicked; -nick·ing :** to go on a picnic **:** eat in picnic fashion

pi·cot \'pē-,kō\ *n* **:** one of a series of small loops forming an edging on ribbon or lace

pic·to·ri·al \pik-'tōr-ē-əl\ *adj* **1 :** of, relating to, or consisting of pictures **2 :** ILLUSTRATED

¹pic·ture \'pik-chər\ *n* **1 :** a representation made by painting, drawing, or photography **2 :** a vivid description in words **3 :** IMAGE, COPY ⟨the ~ of his father⟩ **4 :** a transitory visual image or reproduction **5 :** MOTION PICTURE **6 :** SITUATION ⟨the political ~⟩

²picture *vb* **1 :** to paint or draw a picture of **2 :** to describe vividly in words **3 :** to form a mental image of

pic·tur·esque \,pik-chə-'resk\ *adj* **1 :** resembling a picture or a painted scene ⟨a ~ landscape⟩ **2 :** CHARMING, QUAINT ⟨a ~ character⟩ **3 :** GRAPHIC, VIVID

⟨a ~ account⟩ — **pic·tur·esque·ness** n

pid·dle \'pid-ᵊl\ vb : to act or work idly : DAWDLE

pid·dling \-(ᵊ-)liŋ, -(ᵊ)liŋ\ adj : TRIVIAL, PALTRY

pid·gin \'pij-ən\ n : a simplified speech used for communication between people with different languages; esp : an English-based pidgin used in the Orient

¹pie \'pī\ n : a dish consisting of a pastry crust and a filling (as of fruit or meat)

²pie var of PI

¹pie·bald \'pī-,bȯld\ adj : of different colors; esp : blotched with white and black

²piebald n : a piebald animal (as a horse)

¹piece \'pēs\ n 1 : a part of a whole : FRAGMENT 2 : one of a group, set, or mass ⟨a ~ of mail⟩ ⟨chess ~⟩; also : a single item ⟨a ~ of news⟩ 3 : a length, weight, or size in which something is made or sold 4 : a product (as an essay or musical composition) of creative work 5 : FIREARM 6 : COIN

²piece vb 1 : to repair or complete by adding pieces : PATCH 2 : to join into a whole

pièce de ré·sis·tance \pē-,es-də-rə-,zē-'stäns\ n 1 : the chief dish of a meal 2 : an outstanding item

piece·meal \'pēs-,mēl\ adv (or adj) : one piece at a time : GRADUALLY

piece·work \-,wərk\ n : work done and paid for by the piece — **piece·work·er** n

pied \'pīd\ adj : of two or more colors in blotches : VARIEGATED

pied-à-terre \pē-,ād-ə-'tear\ n : a temporary or second lodging

pie·plant \'pī-,plant\ n : garden rhubarb

pier \'piər\ n 1 : a support for a bridge span 2 : a structure built out into the water for use as a landing place or a promenade or to protect or form a harbor 3 : PILLAR

pierce \'piərs\ vb 1 : to enter or thrust into sharply or painfully : STAB 2 : to make a hole in or through : PERFORATE 3 : to force or make a way into or through : PENETRATE 4 : to see through : DISCERN

pi·ety \'pī-ət-ē\ n 1 : fidelity to natural obligations (as to parents) 2 : dutifulness in religion : DEVOUTNESS 3 : a pious act syn allegiance, devotion, loyalty

pif·fle \'pif-əl\ n : trifling talk or action : NONSENSE

pig \'pig\ n 1 : SWINE; esp : a young swine 2 : PORK 3 : one resembling a pig (as in dirtiness or greed) 4 : a casting of metal (as iron or lead) run directly from a smelting furnace into a mold

pi·geon \'pij-ən\ n : any of numerous stout-bodied short-legged birds with smooth thick plumage; esp : a domesticated bird

¹pi·geon·hole \-,hōl\ n : a small open compartment (as in a desk) for keeping letters or documents

²pigeonhole vb 1 : to place in or as if in a pigeonhole : FILE 2 : to lay aside 3 : CLASSIFY

pi·geon-toed \,pij-ən-'tōd\ adj : having the toes turned in

pig·gish \'pig-ish\ adj : resembling a

pig esp. in greed, dirtiness, or stubbornness

pig·gy·back \'pig-ē-,bak\ adv (or adj) 1 : up on the back and shoulders 2 : on a railroad flatcar

pig·head·ed \'pig-'hed-əd\ adj : OBSTINATE, STUBBORN

pig·ment \'pig-mənt\ n 1 : coloring matter 2 : a powder mixed with a suitable liquid to give color (as in paints and enamels)

pig·men·ta·tion \,pig-mən-'tā-shən\ n : coloration with or deposition of pigment; esp : an excessive deposition of bodily pigment

pigmy var of PYGMY

pig·nut \'pig-,nət\ n : any of several bitter hickory nuts; also : a tree bearing these

pig·pen \-,pen\ n : STY; also : a dirty place

pig·skin \-,skin\ n 1 : the skin of a pig; also : leather made from it 2 : FOOTBALL

pig·sty \-,stī\ n : a pen for pigs

pig·tail \-,tāl\ n : a tight braid of hair

¹pike \'pīk\ n : a sharp point, spike, or tip

²pike n : a large slender greedy freshwater food fish; also : a related fish

³pike n : a long wooden shaft with a pointed steel head formerly used as a foot soldier's weapon

⁴pike n : TURNPIKE

pik·er \'pī-kər\ n 1 : one who does things in a small way or on a small scale 2 : TIGHTWAD, CHEAPSKATE

pike·staff \'pīk-,staf\ n : the staff of a foot soldier's pike

pi·las·ter \'pī-,las-tər, pə-'las-\ n : a slightly projecting upright column that ornaments or helps to support a wall

pil·chard \'pil-chərd\ n : any of several fishes related to the herrings and often packed as sardines

¹pile \'pīl\ n : a large pointed piece (as of wood or steel) driven into the ground to support a vertical load

²pile n 1 : a quantity of things heaped together 2 : PYRE 3 : a great number or quantity : LOT 4 : a large building or group of buildings

³pile vb 1 : to lay in a pile : STACK 2 : to heap up : ACCUMULATE 3 : to press forward in a mass : CROWD

⁴pile n : a velvety surface of fine short hairs or threads (as on cloth) — **piled** \'pīld\ adj

pil·fer \'pil-fər\ vb : to steal in small quantities

pil·grim \'pil-grəm\ n [OF pelegrin, fr. LL pelegrinus, modif. of L peregrinus, fr. peregre abroad, fr. per through + ager field, land] 1 : a traveler in alien lands : WAYFARER 2 : one who travels to a shrine or holy place as an act of devotion 3 cap : one of the English settlers founding Plymouth colony in 1620

pil·grim·age \-grə-mij\ n : a journey of a pilgrim esp. to a shrine or holy place

pil·ing \'pī-liŋ\ n : a structure of piles

pill \'pil\ n 1 : a medicine prepared in a little ball to be taken whole 2 : a disagreeable or tiresome person

pil·lage \'pil-ij\ vb : to take booty : LOOT, PLUNDER — **pillage** n

pil·lar \'pil-ər\ *n* : a column or shaft standing alone esp. as a monument; *also* : one used as an upright support in a building — **pil·lared** \-ərd\ *adj*

pill·box \'pil-,bäks\ *n* **1** : a low usu. round box to hold pills **2** : something (as a low concrete fortification containing machine guns) shaped like a pillbox

pil·lion \'pil-yən\ *n* **1** : a pad or cushion placed behind a saddle for an extra rider **2** : a motorcycle riding saddle for a passenger

¹pil·lo·ry \'pil-(ə-)rē\ *n* : a wooden frame for public punishment having holes in which the head and hands can be locked

²pillory *vb* **1** : to set in a pillory **2** : to expose to public scorn

¹pil·low \'pil-ō\ *n* : a case filled with springy material (as feathers) and used to support the head of a person resting

²pillow *vb* : to rest or place on or as if on a pillow; *also* : to serve as a pillow for

pil·low·case \-,kās\ *n* : a removable covering for a pillow

¹pi·lot \'pī-lət\ *n* **1** : HELMSMAN, STEERSMAN **2** : a person qualified and licensed to take ships into and out of a port **3** : GUIDE, LEADER **4** : one that flies an airplane — **pi·lot·less** *adj*

²pilot *vb* : CONDUCT, GUIDE; *esp* : to act as pilot of

³pilot *adj* : serving on a small scale as a guiding or activating device ⟨a ~ parachute⟩ or as a testing or trial unit ⟨a ~ factory⟩

pi·lot·age \-ij\ *n* : the act or business of piloting

pi·lot·house \-,haús\ *n* : an enclosed place forward on the upper deck of a ship that shelters the steering gear and the helmsman

pil·sner \'pilz-(ə-)nər\ *n* **1** : a light beer with a strong flavor of hops **2** : a tall slender footed glass for beer

pi·men·to \pə-'ment-ō\ *n* **1** : PIMIENTO **2** : ALLSPICE; *also* : the West Indian tree that yields allspice

pi·mien·to \pə-'m(y)ent-ō\ *n* : a mild red sweet pepper fruit that yields paprika

pimp \'pimp\ *n* : PANDER, PROCURER — **pimp** *vb*

pim·per·nel \'pim-pər-,nel\ *n* : a weedy herb related to the primroses with flowers that close in cloudy or rainy weather

pim·ple \'pim-pəl\ *n* : a small inflamed swelling on the skin often containing pus

¹pin \'pin\ *n* **1** : a piece of wood or metal used esp. for fastening articles together or as a support by which one article may be suspended from another **2** : a small pointed piece of wire with a head used for fastening clothes or attaching papers **3** : an ornament or emblem fastened to clothing with a pin **4** : one of the wooden pieces constituting the target (as in bowling); *also* : the staff of the flag marking a hole on a golf course **5** : LEG

²pin *vb* **pinned; pin·ning 1** : to fasten with a pin **2** : to press together and hold fast **3** : to make dependent ⟨*pinned* their hopes on one man⟩ **4** : to assign the blame for ⟨~ a crime on someone⟩ **5** : to define clearly : ESTABLISH ⟨~ down an idea⟩ **6** : to hold fast or immobile in a spot or position

pin·afore \'pin-ə-,fōr\ *n* : a sleeveless dress or apron tied or buttoned at the back

pince-nez \paⁿs-'nā, pans-\ *n* : eyeglasses clipped to the nose by a spring

pin·cer \'pin-sər\ *n* **1** *pl* : a gripping instrument with two handles and two grasping jaws **2** : a claw (as of a lobster) resembling pincers

¹pinch \'pinch\ *vb* **1** : to squeeze between the finger and thumb or between the jaws of an instrument **2** : to compress painfully : CRAMP **3** : CONTRACT, SHRIVEL **4** : to be miserly; *also* : to subject to strict economy **5** : STEAL **6** : ARREST

²pinch *n* **1** : a critical point : EMERGENCY **2** : painful effect : HARDSHIP **3** : an act of pinching : SQUEEZE **4** : a very small quantity **5** : ARREST

pinch-hit \(')pinch-'hit\ *vb* **1** : to bat in the place of another player esp. when a hit is particularly needed **2** : to act or serve in place of another — **pinch hit** *n* — **pinch hitter** *n*

pin·cush·ion \'pin-,kúsh-ən\ *n* : a cushion for pins not in use

¹pine \'pīn\ *vb* **1** : to lose vigor or health through distress **2** : to long for something intensely : YEARN

²pine *n* : any of numerous evergreen cone-bearing trees; *also* : the light durable resinous wood of pines

pine·ap·ple \'pīn-,ap-əl\ *n* : a tropical plant bearing an edible juicy fruit; *also* : its fruit

pin·feath·er \'pin-,feth-ər\ *n* : a new feather just coming through the skin

ping \'piŋ\ *n* **1** : a sharp sound like that of a bullet striking **2** : ignition knock ⟨heard a ~ in his car engine⟩

pin·hole \'pin-,hōl\ *n* : a small hole made by, for, or as if by a pin

¹pin·ion \'pin-yən\ *n* : the end section of a bird's wing; *also* : WING

²pinion *vb* : to restrain by binding the arms; *also* : SHACKLE

³pinion *n* : a gear with a small number of teeth designed to mesh with a larger wheel or rack

¹pink \'piŋk\ *vb* **1** : PIERCE, STAB **2** : to perforate in an ornamental pattern **3** : to cut a saw-toothed edge on

²pink *n* **1** : any of various plants with narrow leaves often grown for their showy flowers **2** : the highest degree ⟨the ~ of condition⟩

³pink *adj* : of the color pink **2** : holding socialistic views — **pink·ish** *adj*

⁴pink *n* **1** : a light tint of red **2** : a person who holds socialistic views

pink·eye \'piŋk-,ī\ *n* : an acute contagious eye inflammation

pin·kie *or* **pin·ky** \'piŋ-kē\ *n* : a little finger

pin·nace \'pin-əs\ *n* **1** : a light sailing ship **2** : a ship's boat

pin·na·cle \-,pin-i-kəl\ *n* **1** : a turret ending in a small spire **2** : a lofty peak **3** : the highest point : ACME

pin·nate \'pin-,āt\ *adj* : having similar parts arranged on each side of an axis

pi·noch·le \'pē-,nək-əl\ *n* : a card game played with a 48-card deck

pin·point \'pin-,pòint\ *vb* : to locate, hit, or aim with great precision

pin·prick \-,prik\ *n* **1** : a small puncture made by or as if by a pin **2** : a petty irritation or annoyance

pin·stripe \-,strīp\ *n* : a narrow stripe on a fabric; *also* : a suit with such stripes — **pin-striped** \-,strīpt\ *adj*

pint \'pīnt\ *n* **:** a measure of capacity equal to half a quart

pin·to \'pin-,tō\ *n* **:** a spotted horse

pin-up \'pin-,əp\ *adj* **:** suitable for pinning up on an admirer's wall (~ photo); *also* **:** suited (as by beauty) to be the subject of a pinup photograph (~ girl)

pin·wheel \-,hwēl\ *n* **1 :** a toy consisting of lightweight vanes that revolve at the end of a stick **2 :** a fireworks device in the form of a revolving wheel of colored fire

¹pi·o·neer \,pī-ə-'niər\ *n* **1 :** one that originates or helps open up a new line of thought or activity **2 :** an early settler in a territory

²pioneer *vb* **1 :** to act as a pioneer **2 :** to open or prepare for others to follow; *esp* **:** SETTLE

pi·ous \'pī-əs\ *adj* **1 :** marked by reverence for deity **:** DEVOUT **2 :** excessively or affectedly religious **3 :** SACRED, DEVOTIONAL **4 :** showing loyal reverence for a person or thing **:** DUTIFUL **5 :** marked by sham or hypocrisy — **pi·ous·ly** *adv*

¹pip \'pip\ *n* **1 :** a disease of birds **2 :** a usu. minor human ailment

²pip *n* **:** one of the dots or figures used chiefly to indicate numerical value (as of a playing card)

³pip *n* **:** a small fruit seed (as of an apple)

¹pipe \'pīp\ *n* **1 :** a musical instrument consisting of a tube played by forcing a blast of air through it **2 :** BAGPIPE **3 :** a long tube designed to conduct something (as water, steam, or oil) **4 :** a device for smoking consisting of a tube with a bowl at one end and a mouthpiece at the other

²pipe *vb* **1 :** to play on a pipe **2 :** to speak in a high or shrill voice **3 :** to convey by or as if by pipes — **pip·er** *n*

pipe·line \'pīp-,līn\ *n* **1 :** a line of pipe with pumps, valves, and control devices for conveying liquids, gases, or finely divided solids **2 :** a direct channel for information

pip·ing \'pī-piŋ\ *n* **1 :** the music of or as if of pipes **2 :** a narrow fold of material used to decorate edges or seams

pip·kin \'pip-kən\ *n* **:** a small earthenware or metal pot

pip·pin \'pip-ən\ *n* **:** any of several yellowish apples

pip–squeak \'pip-,skwēk\ *n* **:** a small or insignificant person

pi·quant \'pē-kənt\ *adj* **1 :** pleasantly savory **:** PUNGENT **2 :** engagingly provocative; *also* **:** having a lively charm — **pi·quan·cy** \-kən-sē\ *n*

¹pique \'pēk\ *n* **:** offense taken by one slighted; *also* **:** a fit of resentment

²pique *vb* **1 :** to offend esp. by slighting **2 :** to arouse by a provocation or challenge **:** GOAD

pi·quet \pi-'kā\ *n* **:** a two-handed card game played with 32 cards

pi·ra·cy \'pī-rə-sē\ *n* **1 :** robbery on the high seas **2 :** the unauthorized use of another's production or invention

pi·rate \'pī-rət\ *n* [L *pirata,* fr. Gk *peiratēs,* fr. *peiran* to attempt, attack] **:** one who commits piracy — **pirate** *vb* — **pi·rat·i·cal** \pə-'rat-i-kəl, pī-\ *adj*

pir·ou·ette \,pir-ə-'wet\ *n* **:** a full turn on the toe or ball of one foot in ballet; *also* **:** a rapid whirling about of the body — **pirouette** *vb*

pis·ca·to·ri·al \,pis-kə-'tōr-ē-əl\ *adj* **:** of or relating to fishing

pis·mire \'pis-,mī(ə)r\ *n* **:** ANT

pis·tach·io \pə-'stash-(ē-,)ō, -'stäsh-\ *n* **:** a small tree related to the sumac whose fruit contains a greenish edible seed; *also* **:** its seed

pis·til \'pist-ʾl\ *n* **:** the female reproductive organ in a flower — **pis·til·late** \'pis-tə-,lāt\ *adj*

pis·tol \'pist-ʾl\ *n* **:** a short firearm intended to be aimed and fired with one hand

pis·ton \'pis-tən\ *n* **:** a sliding piece that receives and transmits motion and that usu. consists of a short cylinder inside a larger cylinder

¹pit \'pit\ *n* **1 :** a hole, shaft, or cavity in the ground **2 :** an often sunken area designed for a particular use; *also* **:** an enclosed place (as for cockfights) **3 :** HELL **4 :** a hollow or indentation esp. in the surface of the body **5 :** a small indented scar (as from smallpox)

²pit *vb* **pit·ted; pit·ting 1 :** to form pits in or become marred with pits **2 :** to match (as cocks) for fighting **:** set in opposition

³pit *n* **:** the stony seed of some fruits (as the cherry, peach, and date)

⁴pit *vb* **pit·ted; pit·ting :** to remove the pit from

pit–a–pat \,pit-i-'pat\ *adv* (or *adj*) **:** PITTER-PATTER — **pit–a–pat** *n*

¹pitch \'pich\ *n* **1 :** a dark sticky substance left over esp. from distilling tar or petroleum **2 :** resin from various conifers — **pitchy** *adj*

²pitch *vb* **1 :** to erect and fix firmly in place (~ a tent) **2 :** THROW, FLING **3 :** to deliver a baseball to a batter **4 :** to toss (as coins) toward a mark **5 :** to set at a particular level (~ the voice low) **6 :** to fall headlong **7 :** to have the front end (as of a ship or airplane) alternately plunge and rise abruptly **8 :** to choose something casually (~ed on a likely spot) **9 :** to incline downward **:** SLOPE

³pitch *n* **1 :** the action or a manner of pitching **2 :** degree of slope (~ of a roof) **3 :** the relative level of some quality or state (a high ~ of excitement) **4 :** highness or lowness of sound **5 :** an often high-pressure sales talk **6 :** the delivery of a baseball to a batter; *also* **:** the baseball delivered

¹pitch·er \'pich-ər\ *n* **:** a container for holding and pouring liquids that usu. has a lip and a handle

²pitcher *n* **:** one that pitches esp. in a baseball game

pitch·fork \'pich-,fórk\ *n* **:** a long-handled fork used esp. in pitching hay

pitch·man \-mən\ *n* **:** SALESMAN; *esp* **:** one who vends novelties on the streets or from a concession

pit·e·ous \'pit-ē-əs\ *adj* **:** arousing pity **:** PITIFUL — **pit·e·ous·ly** *adv*

pit·fall \'pit-,fól\ *n* **1 :** TRAP, SNARE; *esp* **:** a flimsily covered pit used for capturing animals **2 :** a hidden danger or difficulty

ə abut; ᵉ kitten; ər further; a back; ā bake; ä cot, cart; aú out; ch chin; e less; ē easy; g gift; i trip; I life; j joke; ŋ sing; ō flow; ó flaw; ói coin; th thin; th̲ this; ü loot; ú foot; y yet; yü few; yú furious; zh vision

pith \'pith\ n 1 : loose spongy tissue esp. in the center of the stem of vascular plants 2 : the essential part : CORE

pith·ec·an·thro·pus \,pith-i-'kan-thrə-pəs\ n, pl **-thro·pi** \-,pī\ : any of several primitive extinct men from Java

pithy \'pith-ē\ adj 1 : consisting of or filled with pith 2 : being brief and to the point ⟨a ~ saying⟩

piti·able \'pit-ē-ə-bəl\ adj : PITIFUL

piti·ful \'pit-i-fəl\ adj 1 : arousing or deserving pity ⟨a ~ sight⟩ 2 : MEAN, MEAGER ⟨a ~ excuse⟩ — **pit·i·ful·ly** adv

piti·less \'pit-i-ləs\ adj : devoid of pity : MERCILESS

pi·ton \'pē-,tän\ n : a spike, wedge, or peg that can be driven into a rock or ice surface as a support often with an eye through which a rope may pass

pit·tance \'pit-ᵊns\ n : a small portion, amount, or allowance

pit·ter-pat·ter \'pit-ər-,pat-ər, 'pit-ē-,pat-\ n : a rapid succession of light taps or sounds — **pit·ter-pat·ter** \,pit-ər-'pat-ər, ,pit-ē-\ adv (or adj) — **pit·ter-patter** like adv\ vb

pi·tu·i·tary \pə-'t(y)ü-ə-,ter-ē\ adj : of, relating to, or being a small oval endocrine gland attached to the brain

pit viper n : any of various mostly New World specialized venomous snakes with a sensory pit on each side of the head and hollow perforated fangs

¹**pity** \'pit-ē\ n 1 : sympathetic sorrow : COMPASSION 2 : something to be regretted

²**pity** vb : to feel pity for

¹**piv·ot** \'piv-ət\ n : a fixed pin on the end of which something turns — **piv·ot·al** \-ᵊl\ adj

²**pivot** vb : to turn on or as if on a pivot

pix·ie or **pixy** \'pik-sē\ n : FAIRY; esp : a gay mischievous sprite

piz·za \'pēt-sə\ n : an open pie made typically of thinly rolled bread dough spread with a spiced mixture (as of tomatoes, cheese, and ground meat) and baked

piz·ze·ria \,pēt-sə-'rē-ə\ n : an establishment where pizzas are made and sold

¹**plac·ard** \'plak-ärd\ n : a notice posted in a public place : POSTER

²**placard** vb 1 : to cover with or as if with placards 2 : to announce by posting

pla·cate \'plā-,kāt, 'plak-,āt\ vb : to soothe esp. by concessions : APPEASE — **plac·a·ble** \'plak-ə-bəl, 'plā-kə-\ adj

¹**place** \'plās\ n [MF, open space, fr. L platea broad street, fr. Gk plateia, fem. of platys broad] 1 : SPACE, ROOM 2 : an indefinite region : AREA 3 : a building or locality used for a special purpose 4 : a center of population 5 : a particular part of a surface : SPOT 6 : relative position in a scale or sequence; also : high and esp. second position in a competition 7 : ACCOMMODATION; esp : SEAT 8 : JOB; esp : public office 9 : a public square : PLAZA

²**place** vb 1 : to distribute in an orderly manner : ARRANGE 2 : to put in a particular place : SET 3 : IDENTIFY 4 : to give an order for ⟨~ a bet⟩ 5 : to rank high and esp. second in a competition

pla·ce·bo \plə-'sē-bō\ n : an inert medication used for psychological reasons or as a control

place·ment \'plās-mənt\ n : an act or instance of placing

pla·cen·ta \plə-'sent-ə\ n : the structure by which a mammal is nourished and joined to the mother before birth — **pla·cen·tal** \-'sent-ᵊl\ adj

plac·er \'plas-ər\ n : a place where gold is obtained by washing sand and gravel containing particles of the metal

plac·id \'plas-əd\ adj : UNDISTURBED, PEACEFUL syn tranquil, serene, calm — **pla·cid·i·ty** \pla-'sid-ət-ē\ n — **plac·id·ly** \'plas-əd-lē\ adv

plack·et \'plak-ət\ n : a slit in a garment

pla·gia·rize \'plā-jə-,rīz\ vb : to pass off as one's own the ideas or words of another — **pla·gia·rism** \-,riz-əm\ n — **pla·gia·rist** \-rəst\ n

¹**plague** \'plāg\ n 1 : a disastrous evil or influx; also : NUISANCE 2 : PESTILENCE; esp : a destructive contagious bacterial disease (as bubonic plague)

²**plague** vb 1 : to afflict with or as if with disease or disaster 2 : TEASE, TORMENT, HARASS

plaid \'plad\ n 1 : a rectangular length of tartan worn esp. over the left shoulder in Scotland 2 : a twilled woolen fabric with a tartan pattern — **plaid** adj

¹**plain** \'plān\ n : an extensive area of level or rolling treeless country

²**plain** adj 1 : lacking ornament ⟨a ~ dress⟩ 2 : free of extraneous matter : PURE ⟨~ water⟩ 3 : OPEN, UNOBSTRUCTED ⟨~ view⟩ 4 : EVIDENT, OBVIOUS 5 : easily understood : CLEAR 6 : CANDID, BLUNT 7 : SIMPLE, UNCOMPLICATED ⟨~ cooking⟩ 8 : lacking beauty : HOMELY — **plain·ly** adv — **plain·ness** \'plān-nəs\ n

plain·clothes·man \'plān-'klō(th)z-mən\ n : a police officer who does not wear a uniform while on duty : DETECTIVE

plain·spo·ken \-'spō-kən\ adj : speaking or spoken plainly and esp. bluntly

plaint \'plānt\ n 1 : LAMENTATION, WAIL 2 : PROTEST, COMPLAINT

plain·tiff \'plānt-əf\ n : the complaining party in a lawsuit

plain·tive \'plānt-iv\ adj : expressive of suffering or woe : MELANCHOLY — **plain·tive·ly** adv

plait \'plāt, 'plat\ n 1 : PLEAT 2 : a braid esp. of hair or straw — **plait** vb

¹**plan** \'plan\ n 1 : a drawing or diagram drawn on a plane 2 : a method or program for accomplishing something : PROCEDURE 3 : GOAL, AIM — **plan·less** adj

²**plan** vb **planned; plan·ning** 1 : to form a plan of : DESIGN ⟨~ a new city⟩ 2 : to devise the accomplishment of ⟨~ the day's work⟩ 3 : INTEND ⟨planned to go⟩

¹**plane** \'plān\ vb : to smooth or level off with or as if with a plane — **plan·er** n

²**plane** n : any of several shade trees suggesting maples but having globular flower clusters

³**plane** n : a tool for smoothing or shaping a wood surface

⁴**plane** n 1 : a level or flat surface 2 : a level of existence, consciousness, or development 3 : AIRPLANE 4 : one of the main supporting surfaces of an airplane

⁵**plane** adj 1 : FLAT, LEVEL ⟨a ~ surface⟩ 2 : dealing with flat surfaces ⟨~ geometry⟩

plan·et \'plan-ət\ n [LL planeta, modif. of Gk planēt-, planēs, lit., wanderer, fr. planasthai to wander] : a celestial body other than a comet or meteor that revolves around the sun — **plan·e·tary** \-ə-,ter-ē\ *adj*

plan·e·tar·i·um \,plan-ə-'ter-ē-əm\ *n* **:** a room with a dome on which an optical device projects moving images of celestial bodies (as the moon and stars)

plan·gent \'plan-jənt\ *adj* **1 :** having a loud reverberating sound **2 :** having an expressive esp. plaintive quality — **plan·gen·cy** *n*

1plank \'plank\ *n* **1 :** a heavy thick board **2 :** an article in the platform of a political party

2plank *vb* **1 :** to cover with planks **2 :** to set or lay down forcibly **3 :** to cook and serve on a board

plank·ing *n* **:** a quantity or covering of planks

plank·ton \'plank-tən\ *n* **:** the passively floating or weakly swimming animal and plant life of a body of water

1plant \'plant\ *vb* **1 :** to set in the ground to grow **2 :** ESTABLISH, SETTLE **3 :** to stock or provide with something **4 :** to place firmly or forcibly **5 :** to hide or arrange with intent to deceive

2plant *n* **1 :** any of the great group of living things (as mushrooms, seaweeds, or trees) that usu. have no locomotor ability or obvious sense organs and have cellulose cell walls and usu. capacity for indefinite growth **2 :** the land, buildings, and machinery used in carrying on a trade or business

1plan·tain \'plant-ᵊn\ *n* **:** any of several short-stemmed weedy herbs with spikes of tiny greenish flowers

2plantain *n* **:** a banana plant with starchy greenish fruit; *also* **:** its fruit

plan·ta·tion \plan-'tā-shən\ *n* **1 :** a large group of trees under cultivation **2 :** an agricultural estate worked by resident laborers

plant·er \'plant-ər\ *n* **1 :** one that plants or sows; *esp* **:** an owner or operator of a plantation **2 :** a container for a plant

plaque \'plak\ *n* **1 :** an ornamental brooch **2 :** a flat thin piece (as of metal) used for decoration; *also* **:** a commemorative tablet

plash \'plash\ *n* **:** SPLASH — **plash** *vb*

plas·ma \'plaz-mə\ *n* **1 :** the watery part of blood, lymph, or milk **2 :** a gas composed of ionized particles

1plas·ter \'plas-tər\ *n* **1 :** a dressing consisting of a backing spread with an often medicated substance that clings to the skin (adhesive ~) **2 :** a paste that hardens as it dries and is used for coating walls and ceilings

2plaster *vb* **:** to cover with plaster — **plas·ter·er** *n*

plaster of Par·is \-'par-əs\ **:** a white powder made from gypsum and used as a quick-setting paste with water for casts and molds

1plas·tic \'plas-tik\ *adj* **1 :** CREATIVE (~ artist) **2 :** capable of being molded (~ clay) **3 :** characterized by or using modeling (~ arts) **syn** pliable, pliant, ductile, malleable, adaptable — **plas·tic·i·ty** \plas-'tis-ət-ē\ *n*

2plastic *n* **:** a plastic substance; *esp* **:** a synthetic or processed material that can

be formed into rigid objects or into films or filaments

plastic surgery *n* **:** surgery intended to repair or restore lost, mutilated, or deformed parts

1plat \'plat\ *n* **1 :** a small plot of ground **2 :** a plan of a piece of land (as a town site)

2plat *vb* **plat·ted; plat·ting :** to make a plat of

1plate \'plāt\ *n* **1 :** a flat thin piece of material **2 :** domestic hollow ware made of or plated with gold, silver, or base metals **3 :** DISH **4 :** a rubber slab at the apex of a baseball diamond that must be touched by a base runner in order to score **5 :** the molded metal or plastic cast of a page of type to be printed from **6 :** a thin sheet of material (as glass) that is coated with a chemical sensitive to light and is used in photography **7 :** the part of a denture that fits to the mouth and holds the teeth **8 :** something printed from an engraving

2plate *vb* **1 :** to arm with armor plate **2 :** to overlay with metal (as gold or silver) **3 :** to make a printing plate of

pla·teau \pla-'tō\ *n* **:** a large level area raised above adjacent land on at least one side **:** TABLELAND

plat·en \'plat-ᵊn\ *n* **1 :** a flat plate of metal; *esp* **:** one (as the part of a printing press which presses the paper against the type) that exerts or receives pressure **2 :** the roller of a typewriter

plat·form \'plat-,fȯrm\ *n* **1 :** a raised flooring or stage for speakers, performers, or workers **2 :** a declaration of the principles on which a group of persons (as a political party) stands

plat·ing \'plāt-iŋ\ *n* **:** a coating of metal plates or plate (the ~ of a ship)

plat·i·num \'plat-(ᵊ-)nəm\ *n* **:** a heavy silver-white metallic chemical element used esp. in jewelry

plat·i·tude \'plat-ə-,t(y)üd\ *n* **:** a flat or trite remark **:** COMMONPLACE

pla·ton·ic love \plə-,tän-ik-, plā-\ *n, often cap P* **:** a close relationship between two persons in which sexual desire has been excluded

pla·toon \plə-'tün\ *n* **:** a subdivision of a company-size military unit usu. consisting of two or more squads or sections

platoon sergeant *n* **:** SERGEANT FIRST CLASS

plat·ter \'plat-ər\ *n* **1 :** a large plate used esp. for serving meat **2 :** a phonograph record

plat·y·pus \'plat-i-pəs\ *n* **:** a small aquatic egg-laying mammal of Australia with webbed feet and a fleshy bill like a duck's

plau·dit \'plȯd-ət\ *n* **:** an act of applause

plau·si·ble \'plȯ-zə-bəl\ *adj* **:** seemingly worthy of belief **:** PERSUASIVE — **plau·si·bil·i·ty** \,plȯ-zə-'bil-ət-ē\ *n*

1play \'plā\ *n* **1 :** brisk handling of something (as a weapon) **2 :** the course of a game; *also* **:** a particular act or maneuver in a game **3 :** recreational activity; *esp* **:** the spontaneous activity of children **4 :** JEST (said in ~) **5 :** the act or an instance of punning **6 :** a stage representation of a drama;

also : a dramatic composition **7** : GAMBLING **8** : OPERATION (bring extra force into ~) **9** : a brisk, fitful, or light movement **10** : free motion (as of part of a machine); *also* : the length of such motion **11** : scope for action **12** : PUBLICITY **13** : an effort to arouse liking (made a ~ for her) — **play·ful** \-fəl\ *adj* — **play·ful·ly** *adv* — **play·ful·ness** *n* — **in play** : in condition or position to be played

²**play** *vb* **1** : to engage in recreation : take part in (a game) : FROLIC **2** : to move aimlessly about : TRIFLE (~s with a ring nervously) **3** : to deal in a light manner : JEST **4** : to make a pun (~ on words) **5** : to take advantage (~ on fears) **6** : to move or operate in a brisk, irregular, or alternating manner (a flashlight ~ed over the wall) **7** : to perform music (~ on a violin); *also* : to perform (music) on an instrument (~ a waltz) **8** : to perform music upon (~ the piano); *also* : to sound in performance (the organ is ~ing) **9** : to act in a dramatic medium; *also* : to act in the character of (~ the hero) **10** : GAMBLE **11** : to behave in a specified way (~ safe); *also* : COOPERATE (~ along with him) **12** : to deal with : MANAGE; *also* : EMPHASIZE (~ up the low price) **13** : to perform for amusement (~ a trick) **14** : WREAK (~ havoc) **15** : to contend with in a game; *also* : to fill (a certain position) on a team **16** : to make wagers on (~ the races) **17** : WIELD, PLY **18** : to keep in action — **play·er** *n*

play·act·ing \-,ak-tiŋ\ *n* **1** : performance in theatrical productions **2** : insincere or artificial behavior

play·back \-,bak\ *n* : an act of reproducing a sound recording often immediately after recording

play·bill \-,bil\ *n* : a poster advertising the performance of a play; *also* : a theater program

play·boy \-,bói\ *n* : a man whose chief interest is the pursuit of pleasure

play·go·er \-,gō(-ə)r\ *n* : a person who frequently attends plays

play·ground \-,graúnd\ *n* : a piece of ground used for games and recreation esp. by children

play·house \-,haús\ *n* **1** : THEATER **2** : a small house for children to play in

playing card *n* : one of a set of 24 to 78 cards marked to show its rank and suit and used to play a game of cards

play·mate \'plā-,māt\ *n* : a companion in play

play·off \'plā-,óf\ *n* : a contest or series of contests to break a tie or determine a championship

play·pen \-,pen\ *n* : a portable enclosure in which a baby or young child may play

play·suit \-,süt\ *n* : a sports and play outfit for women and children

play·thing \-,thiŋ\ *n* : TOY

play·wright \-,rīt\ *n* : a writer of plays

plaza \'plaz-ə, 'pläz-\ *n* : a public square in a city or town

plea \'plē\ *n* **1** : a defendant's answer in law to charges made against him **2** : something alleged as an excuse : PRETEXT **3** : ENTREATY, APPEAL

plead \'plēd\ *vb* **plead·ed** \'plēd-əd\ *or* **pled** \'pled\ **plead·ing 1** : to argue before a court or authority (~ a case) **2** : to answer to a charge or indictment

(~ guilty) **3** : to argue for or against something (~ for acquittal) **4** : to appeal earnestly : IMPLORE (~s for help) **5** : to offer as a plea usu. in defense or excuse (~ed illness) — **plead·er** *n*

pleas·ant \'plez-²nt\ *adj* **1** : giving pleasure : AGREEABLE (a ~ experience) **2** : marked by pleasing behavior or appearance (a ~ person) — **pleas·ant·ly** *adv* — **pleas·ant·ness** *n*

pleas·ant·ry \-²n-trē\ *n* : a playful or humorous act or speech : JEST

please \'plēz\ *vb* **1** : to give pleasure or satisfaction to : LIKE, WISH (do as you ~) **3** : to be the will or pleasure of (may it ~ your Majesty) **4** : to be willing to (~ come in)

pleas·ing *adj* : giving pleasure : AGREEABLE — **pleas·ing·ly** *adv*

plea·sur·able \'plezh-(ə-)rə-bəl\ *adj* : PLEASANT, GRATIFYING — **plea·sur·ably** *adv*

plea·sure \'plezh-ər\ *n* **1** : DESIRE, INCLINATION (await your ~) **2** : a state of gratification : ENJOYMENT **3** : a source of delight or joy

¹**pleat** \'plēt\ *vb* **1** : FOLD; *esp* : to arrange in pleats **2** : BRAID

²**pleat** *n* : a fold in cloth made by doubling material over on itself : PLAIT

plebe \'plēb\ *n* : a freshman at a military or naval academy

¹**ple·be·ian** \pli-'bē-ən\ *n* **1** : a member of the Roman plebs **2** : one of the common people

²**plebeian** *adj* **1** : of or relating to plebeians **2** : COMMON, VULGAR

pleb·i·scite \'pleb-ə-,sīt, -sət\ *n* : a vote of the people (as of a country) on a proposal officially submitted to them

plebs \'plebz\ *n, pl* **ple·bes** \'plē-bēz\ **1** : the common people of ancient Rome **2** : the general populace

plec·trum \'plek-trəm\ *n, pl* **-tra** \-trə\ : a small thin piece (as of ivory or metal) used to pluck a stringed instrument

¹**pledge** \'plej\ *n* **1** : something given as security for the performance of an act **2** : the state of being held as a security or guaranty **3** : TOAST **4** : PROMISE, VOW

²**pledge** *vb* **1** : to deposit as a pledge **2** : TOAST **3** : to bind by a pledge : PLIGHT **4** : PROMISE, UNDERTAKE

ple·na·ry \'plē-nə-rē, 'plen-ə-\ *adj* **1** : COMPLETE, FULL (~ power) **2** : including all entitled to attend (~ session)

pleni·po·ten·tia·ry \,plen-ə-pə-'tench-(ə-)rē\ *n* : a diplomatic agent having full authority — **plenipotentiary** *adj*

plen·i·tude \'plen-ə-,t(y)üd\ *n* **1** : COMPLETENESS **2** : ABUNDANCE

plen·te·ous \'plent-ē-əs\ *adj* **1** : FRUITFUL **2** : existing in plenty : ABUNDANT

plen·ti·ful \'plent-i-fəl\ *adj* **1** : containing or yielding plenty **2** : ABUNDANT, NUMEROUS — **plen·ti·ful·ly** *adv*

plen·ty \'plent-ē\ *n* : a more than adequate number or amount : ABUNDANCE

pleth·o·ra \'pleth-ə-rə\ *n* : an excessive quantity or fullness; *also* : PROFUSION

pleu·ri·sy \'plúr-ə-sē\ *n* : inflammation of the membrane that lines the chest and covers the lungs

plex·us \'plek-səs\ *n* : an interlacing network esp. of blood vessels or nerves

pli·a·ble \'plī-ə-bəl\ *adj* **1** : FLEXIBLE

2 : yielding easily to others **syn** plastic, pliant, ductile, malleable, adaptable

pli·ant \'plī-ənt\ *adj* **1** : FLEXIBLE **2** : easily influenced : PLIABLE — **pli·an·cy** \-ən-sē\ *n*

pli·ers \'plī-(ə)rz\ *n pl* : small pincers with long jaws for bending wire or handling small objects

¹plight \'plīt\ *vb* : to put or give in pledge : ENGAGE

²plight *n* : CONDITION, STATE; *esp* : a bad state

plinth \'plinth\ *n* : the lowest part of the base of an architectural column

plod \'pläd\ *vb* **plod·ded; plod·ding 1** : to walk heavily or slowly : TRUDGE **2** : to work laboriously and monotonously : DRUDGE — **plod·der** *n*

plop \'pläp\ *vb* **1** : to make or move with a sound like that of something dropping into water **2** : to allow the body to drop heavily **3** : to set, drop, or throw heavily — **plop** *n*

¹plot \'plät\ *n* **1** : a small area of ground **2** : a ground plan (as of an area) **3** : the main story of a literary work **4** : a secret scheme : INTRIGUE

²plot *vb* **plot·ted; plot·ting 1** : to make a plot or plan of **2** : to mark on or as if on a chart **3** : to plan or contrive (as something evil) esp. secretly — **plot·ter** *n*

plov·er \'pləv-ər, 'plō-vər\ *n* : any of various shorebirds related to the sandpipers but with shorter stouter bills

¹plow *or* **plough** \'plau\ *n* **1** : an implement used to cut, turn over, and partly break up soil **2** : a device operating like a plow; *esp* : SNOWPLOW

²plow *or* **plough** *vb* **1** : to open, break up, or work with a plow **2** : to cleave or move through like a plow ⟨a ship ~ing the waves⟩ **3** : to proceed laboriously — **plow·able** *adj* — **plow·er** *n*

plow·boy \'plau̇-,bȯi\ *n* : a boy who guides a plow or leads the horse drawing it

plow·man \-mən, -,man\ *n* **1** : a man who guides a plow **2** : a farm laborer

plow·share \-,shear\ *n* : the part of a plow that cuts the earth

ploy \'plȯi\ *n* : a tactic intended to embarrass or frustrate an opponent

¹pluck \'plək\ *vb* **1** : to pull off or out : PICK; *also* : to pull something from **2** : to pick, pull, or grasp at; *also* : to play (an instrument) in this manner **3** : TUG, TWITCH

²pluck *n* **1** : an act or instance of plucking **2** : SPIRIT, COURAGE

plucky \'plək-ē\ *adj* : COURAGEOUS, SPIRITED

¹plug \'pləg\ *n* **1** : STOPPER; *also* : an obstructing mass **2** : a cake of tobacco **3** : a poor or worn-out horse **4** : a device on the end of a cord for making an electrical connection **5** : a piece of favorable publicity

²plug *vb* **plugged; plug·ging 1** : to stop, make tight, or secure by inserting a plug **2** : HIT, SHOOT **3** : to publicize insistently **4** : PLOD, DRUDGE

plum \'pləm\ *n* **1** : a smooth-skinned juicy fruit borne by trees related to the peach and cherry; *also* : a tree bearing plums **2** : RAISIN **3** : something

excellent; *esp* : something given as recompense esp. for political service

plum·age \'plü-mij\ *n* : the feathers of a bird

¹plumb \'pləm\ *n* : a weight on the end of a line used esp. by builders to show vertical direction

²plumb *adv* **1** : VERTICALLY **2** : EXACTLY; *also* : IMMEDIATELY **3** : COMPLETELY

³plumb *vb* : to sound, adjust, or test with a plumb ⟨~ the depth of a well⟩ ⟨~ a wall⟩

⁴plumb *adj* **1** : VERTICAL **2** : DOWNRIGHT

plumb·er \'pləm-ər\ *n* : a workman who fits or repairs water and gas pipes and fixtures

plumb·ing \'pləm-iŋ\ *n* : a system of pipes in a building for supplying and carrying off water

¹plume \'plüm\ *n* : FEATHER; *esp* : a large, conspicuous, or showy feather — **plumy** \'plü-mē\ *adj*

²plume *vb* **1** : to provide or deck with feathers **2** : to indulge (oneself) in pride

plum·met \'pləm-ət\ *n* : PLUMB; *also* : a line with a plumb at one end

²plummet *vb* : to drop or plunge straight down

¹plump \'pləmp\ *vb* **1** : to drop or fall suddenly or heavily **2** : to favor something strongly ⟨~s for the new method⟩

²plump *adv* **1** : straight down : VERTICALLY; *also* : straight ahead **2** : UNQUALIFIEDLY, FLATLY

³plump *n* : a sudden heavy fall or blow; *also* : the sound made by it

⁴plump *adj* : having a full rounded usu. pleasing form : CHUBBY **syn** fleshy, stout — **plump·ness** *n*

¹plun·der \'plən-dər\ *vb* : to take the goods of by force or wrongfully : PILLAGE — **plun·der·er** *n*

²plunder *n* : something taken by force or theft : LOOT

¹plunge \'plənj\ *vb* **1** : IMMERSE, SUBMERGE **2** : to enter or cause to enter a state or course of action suddenly or violently ⟨~ into war⟩ **3** : to cast oneself into or as if into water **4** : to gamble heavily and recklessly **5** : to descend suddenly

²plunge *n* : an act or instance of plunging

plung·er \'plən-jər\ *n* **1** : one that plunges **2** : a sliding piece driven by or against fluid pressure : PISTON **3** : a rubber cup on a handle pushed against an opening to free a waste outlet of an obstruction

plunk \'pləŋk\ *vb* **1** : to make or cause to make a hollow metallic sound **2** : to drop heavily or suddenly — **plunk** *n*

¹plu·per·fect \(')plü-'pər-fikt\ *adj* : of, relating to, or constituting a verb tense that denotes an action or state as completed at or before a past time spoken of

²pluperfect *n* : the pluperfect tense; *also* : a verb form in it

plu·ral \'plur-əl\ *adj* : of, relating to, or constituting a word form used to denote more than one — **plural** *n*

plu·ral·i·ty \plu̇-'ral-ət-ē\ *n* **1** : the state of being plural **2** : an excess of votes over those cast for an opposing candidate **3** : a number of votes cast for one candidate that is greater than the number cast for any other in the contest but less than a majority

plu·ral·ize \'plùr-ə-,līz\ *vb* : to make plural or express in the plural form — **plu·ral·iza·tion** \,plùr-ə-lə-'zā-shən\ *n*

¹**plus** \'pləs\ *prep* [L, more] : increased by : with the addition of ⟨3 ∼ 4 equals 7⟩

²**plus** \'pləs\ *n* 1 : a sign + (plus sign) used in mathematics to require addition or designate a positive quantity 2 : an added quantity; *also* : a positive quantity 3 : ADVANTAGE

³**plus** *adj* 1 : requiring addition 2 : having or being in addition to what is anticipated or specified ⟨∼ values⟩

¹**plush** \'pləsh\ *n* : a fabric with a pile longer and less dense than velvet pile — **plushy** *adj*

²**plush** *adj* : notably luxurious — **plush·ly** *adv*

Plu·to \'plüt-ō\ *n* : the planet most remote from the sun

plu·toc·ra·cy \plü-'täk-rə-sē\ *n* 1 : government by the wealthy 2 : a controlling class of rich men — **plu·to·crat** \'plüt-ə-,krat\ *n* — **plu·to·crat·ic** \,plüt-ə-'krat-ik\ *adj*

plu·to·ni·um \plü-'tō-nē-əm\ *n* : a radioactive chemical element formed by the decay of neptunium

plu·vi·al \'plü-vē-əl\ *adj* 1 : of or relating to rain 2 : characterized by abundant rain

¹**ply** \'plī\ *vb* : to twist together ⟨∼ yarns⟩

²**ply** *n* : one of the folds, thicknesses, or strands of which something (as plywood or yarn) is made

³**ply** *vb* 1 : to use, practice, or work diligently ⟨*plies* her needle⟩ ⟨∼ a trade⟩ 2 : to keep furnishing to ⟨*plied* him with liquor⟩ 3 : to go or travel regularly esp. by sea

ply·wood \-,wùd\ *n* : material made of thin sheets of wood glued and pressed together

pneu·mat·ic \n(y)ù-'mat-ik\ *adj* 1 : of, relating to, or using air or wind 2 : moved by air pressure 3 : filled with compressed air

pneu·mo·nia \n(y)ù-'mō-nyə\ *n* : an inflammatory disease of the lungs

¹**poach** \'pōch\ *vb* : to cook (as an egg or fish) in simmering liquid

²**poach** *vb* : to hunt or fish unlawfully — **poach·er** *n*

pock \'päk\ *n* : a small swelling on the skin (as in smallpox); *also* : its scar

¹**pock·et** \'päk-ət\ *n* 1 : a small bag open at the top or side inserted in a garment 2 : supply of money : MEANS 3 : RECEPTACLE, CONTAINER 4 : a small isolated area or group 5 : a small body of ore — **pock·et·ful** \-,fùl\ *n*

²**pocket** *vb* 1 : to put in or as if in a pocket 2 : APPROPRIATE, STEAL 3 : to put up with : ACCEPT ⟨∼ an insult⟩

³**pocket** *adj* : small enough to fit in a pocket ⟨∼ dictionary⟩

pock·et·book \-,bùk\ *n* 1 : PURSE; *also* : HANDBAG 2 : financial resources

pock·et·knife \-,nīf\ *n* : a knife with a folding blade to be carried in the pocket

pock·mark \'päk-,märk\ *n* : the scar left by a pock — **pock-marked** \-,märkt\ *adj*

po·co a po·co \,pō-kō-ä-'pō-kō\ *adv* : little by little : by small degrees : GRADUALLY

po·co·sin \pə-'kōs-²n\ *n* : an upland

swamp of the coastal plain of the southeastern U.S.

pod \'päd\ *n* 1 : a dry fruit (as of a pea) that splits open when ripe 2 : a compartment (as for a jet engine) under an airplane

po·di·a·try \pə-'dī-ə-trē\ *n* : CHIROPODY — **po·di·a·trist** \-trəst\ *n*

po·di·um \'pōd-ē-əm\ *n* 1 : a dais esp. for an orchestral conductor 2 : LECTERN

po·em \'pō-əm\ *n* : a composition in verse

po·esy \'pō-ə-zē\ *n* : POETRY

po·et \'pō-ət\ *n* [L *poeta*, fr. Gk *poiētēs*, lit., maker, fr. *poiein* to make] : a writer of poetry; *also* : a creative artist of great sensitivity — **po·et·ess** \-əs\ *n*

po·et·as·ter \-,as-tər\ *n* : an inferior poet

po·et·ry \'pō-ə-trē\ *n* 1 : metrical writing 2 : POEMS — **po·et·ic** \pō-'et-ik\ *or* **po·et·i·cal** \-'et-i-kəl\ *adj*

po·grom \'pō-grəm, pō-'gräm\ *n* : an organized massacre of helpless people and esp. of Jews

poi·gnant \'pói-nyənt\ *adj* 1 : painfully affecting the feelings : PIERCING ⟨∼ grief⟩ 2 : deeply moving : TOUCHING ⟨∼ scene⟩ — **poi·gnan·cy** \-nyən-sē\ *n*

poi·lu \pwäl-'(y)ü\ *n* : a French soldier

poin·set·tia \pói̇n-'set-ē-ə\ *n* : a showy tropical American spurge that has scarlet bracts around its small greenish flowers

¹**point** \'pói̇nt\ *n* 1 : an individual detail; *also* : the most important essential 2 : PURPOSE 3 : a particular place : LOCALITY 4 : a particular stage or degree 5 : a sharp end : TIP 6 : a projecting piece of land 7 : a punctuation mark; *esp* : PERIOD 8 : a decimal mark 9 : one of the divisions of the compass 10 : a unit of counting (as in a game score) — **point·less** *adj*

²**point** *vb* 1 : to furnish with a point : give point to : SHARPEN 2 : PUNCTUATE 3 : to separate (a decimal fraction) from an integer by a decimal point 4 : to indicate the position of esp. by extending a finger 5 : to direct attention to ⟨∼ out an error⟩ 6 : AIM, DIRECT 7 : to lie extended, aimed, or turned in a particular direction : FACE, LOOK

point-blank \-'blaŋk\ *adj* 1 : so close to the target that a missile fired will travel in a straight line to the mark 2 : DIRECT, BLUNT

point·ed \'pói̇nt-əd\ *adj* 1 : having a point 2 : being to the point : DIRECT 3 : aimed at a particular person or group; *also* : CONSPICUOUS, MARKED — **point·ed·ly** *adv*

point·er \'pói̇nt-ər\ *n* 1 : one that points out : INDICATOR 2 : a large short-haired hunting dog 3 : HINT, TIP

¹**poise** \'pói̇z\ *vb* : BALANCE

²**poise** *n* 1 : BALANCE 2 : self-possessed composure of bearing; *also* : a particular way of carrying oneself

¹**poi·son** \'pói̇z-²n\ *n* : a substance that through its chemical action can injure or kill — **poi·son·ous** \-(-²-)nəs\ *adj*

²**poison** *vb* 1 : to injure or kill with poison 2 : to treat or taint with poison 3 : to affect destructively : CORRUPT ⟨∼ed her mind⟩ — **poi·son·er** \'pói̇z-(²-)nər\ *n*

poison ivy *n* : a usu. climbing plant related to sumac that has shiny 3-parted

leaves and may irritate the skin of one
who touches it

¹poke \'pōk\ n : BAG, SACK

²poke vb 1 : PROD; also : to stir up by
prodding 2 : to make a prodding or
jabbing movement esp. repeatedly
3 : HIT, PUNCH 4 : to thrust forward
obtrusively 5 : RUMMAGE 6 : MEDDLE,
PRY 7 : DAWDLE

³poke n : a quick thrust : JAB; also
: PUNCH

¹pok·er \'pō·kər\ n : a metal rod for
stirring a fire

²poker n : any of several card games
played with a deck of 52 cards in which
each player bets on the superiority of
his hand

poky or pok·ey \'pō·kē\ adj 1 : being
small and cramped 2 : SHABBY, DULL
3 : annoyingly slow

po·lar \'pō·lər\ adj 1 : of or relating to
a pole (as of a sphere or magnet) 2 : of
or relating to a geographical pole

Po·lar·is \pə·'lar·əs\ n : NORTH STAR

po·lar·i·ty \pō·'lar·ət·ē\ n : the quality
or state of having poles; esp : the quality
of having opposite negative and positive
charges of electricity or of having opposing magnetic poles

po·lar·i·za·tion \,pō·lə·rə·'zā·shən\ n
1 : the action of polarizing : the state of
being polarized 2 : concentration
about opposing extremes

po·lar·ize \'pō·lə·,rīz\ vb 1 : to cause to
have magnetic poles 2 : to cause (light
waves) to vibrate in a definite way

¹pole \'pōl\ n : a long slender piece of
wood or metal (telephone ~)

²pole n 1 : either end of an axis esp. of
the earth 2 : either of the terminals of
an electric battery 3 : one of two or
more regions in a magnetized body at
which the magnetism seems to be concentrated

Pole \'pōl\ n : a native or inhabitant of
Poland

pole·ax \'pōl·,aks\ n : a battle-ax with
a short handle and a cutting edge or
point opposite the blade

pole·cat \'pōl·,kat\ n 1 : a European
carnivorous mammal of which the ferret
is considered a domesticated variety
2 : SKUNK

po·lem·ic \pə·'lem·ik\ n : the art or
practice of disputation : CONTROVERSY
— usu. used in pl. — polemic or po·
lem·i·cal \-'lem·i·kəl\ adj

pole·star \'pōl·,stär\ n 1 : NORTH STAR
2 : a directing principle : GUIDE

pole vault n : a track-and-field contest
in which each contestant uses a pole to
vault for height — pole-vault vb —
pole-vault·er n

¹po·lice \pə·'lēs\ n 1 : the department
of government that keeps public order
and safety, enforces the laws, and detects and prosecutes lawbreakers; also
: the members of this department 2 : the
action or process of cleaning and putting
in order; also : military personnel detailed to perform this function

²police vb 1 : to control, regulate, or
keep in order esp. by use of police (~ a
highway) 2 : to make clean and put in
order (~ a camp)

po·lice·man \-mən\ n : a member of a
police force

¹pol·i·cy \'päl·ə·sē\ n 1 : wisdom in the
management of affairs 2 : a definite
course or method of action selected to
guide and determine present and future
decisions

²policy n : a writing whereby a contract
of insurance is made

pol·i·cy·hold·er \-,hōl·dər\ n : one
granted an insurance policy

po·lio \'pō·lē·,ō\ n : POLIOMYELITIS —
polio adj

po·lio·my·e·li·tis \-,mī·ə·'līt·əs\ n
: an acute virus disease marked by inflammation of the nerve cells of the
spinal cord

¹pol·ish \'päl·ish\ vb 1 : to make
smooth and glossy usu. by rubbing
2 : to refine or improve in manners or
condition 3 : to bring to a highly developed, finished, or refined state

²polish n 1 : a smooth glossy surface
: LUSTER 2 : REFINEMENT, CULTURE
3 : the action or process of polishing

Pol·ish \'pō·lish\ n : the language of
Poland — Polish adj

po·lite \pə·'līt\ adj 1 : REFINED, CUL-
TIVATED (~ society) 2 : marked by
correct social conduct : COURTEOUS;
also : CONSIDERATE, TACTFUL — po·lite·
ly adv — po·lite·ness n

po·li·tesse \,päl·i·'tes\ n : formal
politeness

pol·i·tic \'päl·ə·,tik\ adj 1 : wise in
promoting a policy (a ~ statesman)
2 : shrewdly tactful : EXPEDIENT (a ~
move)

po·lit·i·cal \pə·'lit·i·kəl\ adj : of or relating to government or politics — po·
lit·i·cal·ly adv

pol·i·ti·cian \,päl·ə·'tish·ən\ n : a person actively engaged in government or
politics

pol·i·tick \'päl·ə·,tik\ vb : to engage in
political discussion or activity

po·lit·i·co \pə·'lit·i·,kō\ n, pl -cos also
-coes : POLITICIAN

pol·i·tics \'päl·ə·,tiks\ n sing or pl
1 : the art or science of government, of
guiding or influencing governmental
policy, or of winning and holding control
over a government 2 : political affairs
or business; esp : competition between
groups or individuals for power and
leadership 3 : political opinions

pol·i·ty \'päl·ət·ē\ n : a politically organized unit; also : the form or constitution of such a unit

pol·ka \'pōl·kə\ n : a lively couple
dance of Bohemian origin; also : music
for this dance

¹poll \'pōl\ n 1 : HEAD 2 : the casting
and recording of votes; also : the total
vote cast 3 : the place where votes are
cast — usu. used in pl. 4 : a questioning of persons to obtain information or
opinions to be analyzed

²poll vb 1 : to cut off or shorten a growth
or part of : CLIP, SHEAR 2 : to receive
and record the votes of 3 : to receive
(as votes) in an election 4 : to question
in a poll

pol·lack or pol·lock \'päl·ək\ n : an important Atlantic food fish related to the
cods

pol·len \'päl·ən\ n : a mass of male
spores of a seed plant usu. appearing as
a yellow dust

ə abut; ᵊ kitten; ər further; a back; ā bake; ä cot, cart; au̇ out; ch chin;
e less; ē easy; g gift; i trip; ī life; j joke; ŋ sing; ō flow; ȯ flaw; ȯi coin;
th thin; t͟h this; ü loot; u̇ foot; y yet; yü few; yu̇ furious; zh vision

pol·li·na·tion \ˌpäl-ə-'nā-shən\ *n* : the carrying of pollen to the female part of a plant to fertilize the seed — **pol·li·nate** \'päl-ə-ˌnāt\ *vb* — **pol·li·na·tor** *n*

pol·li·wog *or* **pol·ly·wog** \'päl-ē-ˌwäg\ *n* : TADPOLE

poll·ster \'pōl-stər\ *n* : one that conducts a poll or compiles data obtained by a poll

pol·lute \pə-'lüt\ *vb* : to make impure : CONTAMINATE — **pol·lu·tion** \-'lü-shən\ *n*

po·lo \'pō-lō\ *n* : a game played by two teams of players on horseback using long-handled mallets to drive a wooden ball

po·lo·ni·um \pə-'lō-nē-əm\ *n* [NL, fr. ML *Polonia* Poland, birthplace of its discoverer, Mme. Curie] : a radioactive metallic chemical element

pol·ter·geist \'pōl-tər-ˌgīst\ *n* : a noisy usu. mischievous ghost held to be responsible for unexplained noises (as rappings)

pol·troon \päl-'trün\ *n* : COWARD

poly·clin·ic \ˌpäl-i-'klin-ik\ *n* : a clinic or hospital treating diseases of many sorts

po·lyg·a·my \pə-'lig-ə-mē\ *n* : the practice of having more than one wife or husband at one time — **po·lyg·a·mous** \-məs\ *adj*

pol·y·glot \'päl-i-ˌglät\ *adj* **1** : speaking or writing several languages **2** : containing or made up of several languages — **polyglot** *n*

pol·y·gon \'päl-i-ˌgän\ *n* : a closed plane figure bounded by straight lines — **po·lyg·o·nal** \pə-'lig-ən-ᵊl\ *adj*

pol·y·math \'päl-i-ˌmath\ *n* : a person of encyclopedic learning

pol·y·mer \'päl-ə-mər\ *n* : a substance formed by union of small molecules of the same kind — **pol·y·mer·ic** \ˌpäl-ə-'mer-ik\ *adj*

Pol·y·ne·sian \ˌpäl-ə-'nē-zhən\ *n* : a member of any of the native peoples of Polynesia — **Polynesian** *adj*

poly·no·mi·al \ˌpäl-i-'nō-mē-əl\ *n* : an algebraic expression having two or more terms

pol·yp \'päl-əp\ *n* **1** : an animal (as a coral) with a hollow cylindrical body closed at one end **2** : a projecting mass of overgrown membrane ⟨a rectal ∼⟩

po·lyph·o·ny \pə-'lif-ə-nē\ *n* : music consisting of two or more melodically independent but harmonizing voice parts — **poly·phon·ic** \ˌpäl-i-'fän-ik\ *adj*

poly·syl·lab·ic \ˌpäl-i-sə-'lab-ik\ *adj* **1** : having more than three syllables **2** : characterized by polysyllabic words ⟨∼ prose⟩

poly·syl·la·ble \'päl-i-ˌsil-ə-bəl\ *n* : a polysyllabic word

poly·tech·nic \ˌpäl-i-'tek-nik\ *adj* : of, relating to, or instructing in many technical arts or applied sciences

poly·the·ism \'päl-i-thē-ˌiz-əm\ *n* : belief in or worship of many gods — **poly·the·ist** \-thē-əst\ *adj or n* — **poly·the·is·tic** \ˌpäl-i-thē-'is-tik\ *adj*

poly·un·sat·u·rat·ed \ˌpäl-ē-ˌən-'sach-ə-ˌrāt-əd\ *adj* : rich in carbon atoms that can combine with other atoms to form a new compound ⟨a ∼ oil⟩

po·made \pō-'mäd, -'mād\ *n* : a perfumed ointment esp. for the hair

pome·gran·ate \'päm-(ə-)ˌgran-ət\ *n* : a tropical reddish fruit with many seeds and an edible crimson pulp; *also* : the tree that bears it

¹pom·mel \'pəm-əl, 'päm-\ *n* **1** : the knob on the hilt of a sword **2** : the knoblike bulge at the front and top of a saddlebow

²pom·mel \'pəm-əl\ *vb* **-meled** *or* **-melled; -mel·ing** *or* **-mel·ling** : PUMMEL

pomp \'pämp\ *n* **1** : brilliant display : SPLENDOR, PAGEANTRY **2** : OSTENTATION

pom·pa·dour \'päm-pə-ˌdōr\ *n* : a style of dressing the hair in which it is combed back to stand erect

pom·pa·no \'päm-pə-ˌnō, 'pəm-\ *n* : a food fish of the southern Atlantic coast

pom·pon \'päm-ˌpän\ *n* **1** : an ornamental ball or tuft used on a cap or costume **2** : a chrysanthemum or dahlia with small rounded flower heads

pomp·ous \'päm-pəs\ *adj* **1** : suggestive of pomp; *esp* : OSTENTATIOUS **2** : pretentiously dignified : SELF-IMPORTANT **3** : excessively elevated or ornate ⟨∼ showy, pretentious — **pom·pos·i·ty** \päm-'päs-ət-ē\ *n* — **pomp·ous·ly** *adv*

pon·cho \'pän-chō\ *n* **1** : a cloak resembling a blanket with a slit in the middle for the head **2** : a waterproof garment resembling a poncho

pond \'pänd\ *n* : a small body of water

pon·der \'pän-dər\ *vb* **1** : to weigh in the mind **2** : MEDITATE **3** : to deliberate over

pon·der·ous \-d(ə-)rəs\ *adj* **1** : of very great weight ⟨a ∼ stone⟩ **2** : UNWIELDY, CLUMSY ⟨a ∼ weapon⟩ **3** : oppressively dull ⟨a ∼ speech⟩ *syn* cumbrous, cumbersome, weighty

pone \'pōn\ *n, South and Midland* : an oval-shaped cornmeal cake; *also* : corn bread in the form of pones

pon·gee \pän-'jē\ *n* : a thin soft tan fabric

pon·iard \'pän-yərd\ *n* : DAGGER

pon·tiff \'pänt-əf\ *n* : BISHOP; *esp* : POPE — **pon·tif·i·cal** \pän-'tif-i-kəl\ *adj*

pon·tif·i·cals \pän-'tif-i-kəlz\ *n pl* : the insignia worn by a bishop when celebrating a pontifical mass

¹pon·tif·i·cate \pän-'tif-i-kət, -ə-ˌkāt\ *n* : the state, office, or term of office of a pontiff

²pon·tif·i·cate \-ə-ˌkāt\ *vb* : to deliver dogmatic opinions

pon·toon \pän-'tün\ *n* **1** : a flat-bottomed boat; *esp* : a flat-bottomed boat, float, or frame used in building bridges quickly for the passage of troops or vehicles **2** : a watertight structure attached to an aircraft so that it will float on water

po·ny \'pō-nē\ *n* : a small horse

po·ny·tail \-ˌtāl\ *n* : a style of arranging hair to resemble the tail of a pony

poo·dle \'püd-ᵊl\ *n* : an active dog with a heavy curly coat

pooh-pooh \'pü-ˌpü\ *also* **pooh** *vb* **1** : to express contempt or impatience **2** : DERIDE, SCORN

¹pool \'pül\ *n* **1** : a small and rather deep body of usu. fresh water **2** : a small body of standing liquid ⟨a ∼ of blood⟩

²pool *n* **1** : all the money bet on the result of a particular event **2** : any of several games of billiards played on a table (**pool table**) having six pockets **3** : the amount contributed by the participants in a joint venture **4** : a combination between competing firms for mutual profit **5 :** a readily available supply

³pool \'püp\ *vb* **:** to contribute to a common fund or effort

poop \'püp\ *n* **:** a raised deck above the open deck and at the rear of a ship

poor \'pu̇r\ *adj* **1 :** lacking material possessions ⟨~ people⟩ **2 :** less than adequate **:** MEAGER ⟨~ crop⟩ **3 :** arousing pity ⟨~ fellows⟩ **4 :** inferior in quality or value ⟨~ sportsmanship⟩ **5 :** UNPRODUCTIVE, BARREN ⟨~ soil⟩ **6 :** fairly unsatisfactory ⟨~ prospects⟩; *also* **:** UNFAVORABLE ⟨~ opinion⟩ *syn* bad, wrong — **poor·ly** *adv*

poor·house \-,hau̇s\ *n* **:** a publicly supported home for needy or dependent persons

¹pop \'päp\ *vb* **popped; pop·ping** **1 :** to go, come, enter, or issue forth suddenly or quickly ⟨~ into bed⟩ **2 :** to put or thrust suddenly ⟨~ questions⟩ **3 :** to burst with or make a sharp sound **4 :** to protrude from the sockets **5 :** SHOOT **6 :** to hit a pop-up

²pop *n* **1 :** a sharp explosive sound **2 :** SHOT **3 :** a flavored soft drink

pop·corn \'päp-,ko̍rn\ *n* **:** an Indian corn whose kernels burst open into a white starchy mass when heated; *also* **:** the burst kernels

pope \'pōp\ *n, often cap* **:** the head of the Roman Catholic Church

pop·eyed \'päp-'īd\ *adj* **:** having eyes that bulge (as from disease or excitement)

pop·gun \'päp-,gən\ *n* **:** a toy gun for shooting pellets with compressed air

pop·in·jay \'päp-ən-,jā\ *n* **:** a strutting supercilious person

pop·lar \'päp-lər\ *n* **:** any of various slender quick-growing trees related to the willows

pop·lin \'päp-lən\ *n* **:** a strong plain-woven fabric with crosswise ribs

pop·off \'päp-,òf\ *n* **:** one who talks loosely or loudly

pop·over \'päp-,ō-vər\ *n* **:** a biscuit made from a thin batter rich in egg and expanded by baking into a hollow shell

pop·py \'päp-ē\ *n* **:** any of several herbs that have showy flowers including one that yields opium

pop·py·cock \-,käk\ *n* **:** empty talk **:** NONSENSE

pop·u·lace \'päp-yə-ləs\ *n* **1 :** the common people **:** MASSES **2 :** POPULATION

pop·u·lar \'päp-yə-lər\ *adj* **1 :** of or relating to the general public ⟨~ government⟩ **2 :** easy to understand **:** PLAIN ⟨~ style⟩ **3 :** INEXPENSIVE ⟨~ rates⟩ **4 :** widely accepted **:** PREVALENT ⟨~ notion⟩ **5 :** commonly liked or approved ⟨~ teacher⟩ — **pop·u·lar·i·ty** \,päp-yə-'lar-ət-ē\ *n* — **pop·u·lar·ize** \'päp-yə-lə-,rīz\ *vb* — **pop·u·lar·ly** \-lər-lē\ *adv*

pop·u·late \'päp-yə-,lāt\ *vb* **1 :** to have a place in **:** INHABIT **2 :** PEOPLE

pop·u·la·tion \,päp-yə-'lā-shən\ *n* **1 :** the people or number of people in a country or area **2 :** the individuals under consideration (as in statistical sampling)

pop·u·lous \'päp-yə-ləs\ *adj* **1 :** densely populated **2 :** CROWDED — **pop·u·lous·ness** *n*

pop-up \'päp-,əp\ *n* **:** a short high fly in baseball

por·ce·lain \'pōr-s(ə-)lən\ *n* **:** a fine translucent ceramic ware

porch \'pōrch\ *n* **:** a covered entrance usu. with a separate roof **:** VERANDA

por·cine \'pōr-,sīn\ *adj* **:** of, relating to, or suggesting swine

por·cu·pine \'pōr-kyə-,pīn\ *n* **:** a mammal having stiff sharp easily detachable spines mingled with its hair

¹pore \'pōr\ *vb* **1 :** to read studiously or attentively ⟨~ over a book⟩ **2 :** PONDER, REFLECT

²pore *n* **:** a tiny hole or space (as in the skin or soil) — **pored** \'pōrd\ *adj*

pork \'pōrk\ *n* **:** the flesh of swine dressed for use as food

pork·er *n* **:** HOG; *esp* **:** a young pig suitable for use as fresh pork

por·nog·ra·phy \pōr-'näg-rə-fē\ *n* **:** the depiction (as in writing) of erotic behavior designed primarily to cause sexual excitement — **por·no·graph·ic** \,pōr-nə-'graf-ik\ *adj*

po·rous \'pōr-əs\ *adj* **1 :** full of pores **2 :** permeable to fluids **:** ABSORPTIVE — **po·ros·i·ty** \pə-'räs-ət-ē\ *n*

por·phy·ry \'pōr-f(ə-)rē\ *n* **:** a dark red or purple rock with white crystals embedded in it

por·poise \'pōr-pəs\ *n* [MF *porpois*, fr. ML *porcopiscis*, fr. L *porcus* pig + *piscis* fish] **1 :** any of several small bluntsnouted whales **2 :** any of several dolphins

por·ridge \'pōr-ij\ *n* **:** a soft food made by boiling meal of grains or legumes in milk or water

por·rin·ger \'pōr-ən-jər\ *n* **:** a low one-handled metal bowl or cup for children

¹port \'pōrt\ *n* **1 :** HARBOR **2 :** a city with a harbor **3 :** AIRPORT

²port *n* **1 :** an inlet or outlet (as in an engine) for a fluid **2 :** PORTHOLE

³port *n* **1 :** BEARING, CARRIAGE **2 :** the position of a ported weapon

⁴port *vb* **:** to carry (as a rifle) in a position sloping across the body from right to left with the barrel at the left shoulder

⁵port *n* **:** the left side of a ship or airplane looking forward — **port** *adj*

⁶port *vb* **:** to turn or put a helm or rudder to the left

⁷port *n* **:** a fortified sweet wine

por·ta·ble \'pōrt-ə-bəl\ *adj* **:** capable of being carried

por·tage \'pōrt-ij, pōr-'täzh\ *n* **:** the carrying of boats and goods overland between navigable bodies of water; *also* **:** a route for such carrying

por·tal \'pōrt-ᵊl\ *n* **:** DOOR, ENTRANCE; *esp* **:** a grand or imposing one

portal-to-portal *adj* **:** of or relating to the time spent by a workman in traveling from the entrance to his employer's property to his actual working place (as in a mine) and in returning after the work shift

port·cul·lis \pōrt-'kəl-əs\ *n* **:** a grating at the gateway of a castle or fortress that can be let down to stop entrance

porte co·chere \,pōrt-kō-'sheᵊr\ *n* **:** a roofed structure extending from the entrance of a building over an adjacent driveway and sheltering those getting in or out of vehicles

ə abut; ᵊ kitten; ər further; a back; ā bake; ä cot, cart; au̇ out; ch chin; e less; ē easy; g gift; i trip; ī life; j joke; ŋ sing; ō flow; ȯ flaw; òi coin; th thin; t̲h̲ this; ü loot; u̇ foot; y yet; yü few; yu̇ furious; zh vision

por·tend \pòr-'tend\ vb 1 : to give a sign or warning of beforehand 2 : INDICATE, SIGNIFY syn augur, prognosticate, foretell, predict, forecast, prophesy, forebode

por·tent \'pòr-,tent\ n 1 : something that foreshadows a coming event : OMEN 2 : MARVEL, PRODIGY

por·ten·tous \pòr-'tent-əs\ adj 1 : of, relating to, or constituting a portent 2 : PRODIGIOUS 3 : self-consciously weighty : POMPOUS

¹**por·ter** \'pòrt-ər\ n, chiefly Brit : DOOR-KEEPER

²**porter** n 1 : one that carries burdens; esp : one employed (as at a terminal) to carry baggage 2 : an attendant in a railroad car 3 : a dark heavy ale

por·ter·house \-,haüs\ n : a choice beefsteak with a large tenderloin

port·fo·lio \pòrt-'fō-lē-,ō\ n 1 : a portable case for papers or drawings 2 : the office and functions of a minister of state 3 : the securities held by an investor

port·hole \'pòrt-,hōl\ n : an opening in the side of a ship or airplane

por·ti·co \'pòrt-i-,kō\ n, pl -coes or -cos : a row of columns supporting a roof around or at the entrance of a building

por·ti·ere \,pòrt-ē-'eər, pòr-'tiər\ n : a curtain hanging across a doorway

¹**por·tion** \'pòr-shən\ n 1 : an individual's part or share (her ~ of worldly goods) 2 : DOWRY 3 : an individual's lot (sorrow was his ~) 4 : a part of a whole (~s of the book were interesting)

²**portion** vb 1 : to divide into portions : DISTRIBUTE 2 : to allot to as a portion : DOWER

por·tion·less adj : having no portion

port·ly \'pòrt-lē\ adj : somewhat stout

port·man·teau \pòrt-'man-,tō\ n, pl -teaus or -teaux \-,tōz\ : a large traveling bag

port of call : an intermediate port where ships customarily stop for supplies, repairs, or transshipment of cargo

port of entry 1 : a place where foreign goods may be cleared through a customhouse 2 : a place where an alien may enter a country

por·trait \'pòr-trət, -,trāt\ n : a picture (as a painting or photograph) of a person usu. showing the face

por·trait·ist n : a maker of portraits

por·trai·ture \'pòr-trə-,chür\ n : the practice or art of making portraits

por·tray \pòr-'trā\ vb 1 : to make a picture of : DEPICT 2 : to describe in words 3 : to play the role of — **por·tray·al** \-əl\ n

Por·tu·guese \,pòr-chə-'gēz\ n, pl Portuguese 1 : a native or inhabitant of Portugal 2 : the language of Portugal and Brazil — **Portuguese** adj

¹**pose** \'pōz\ vb 1 : to put or set in place 2 : to assume or cause to assume a posture usu. for artistic purposes 3 : to set forth : PROPOSE (~ a question) 4 : to affect an attitude or character

²**pose** n 1 : a sustained posture; esp : one assumed by a model 2 : an attitude assumed for effect : PRETENSE

¹**pos·er** \'pō-zər\ n : a puzzling question

²**poser** n : a person who poses

po·seur \pō-'zər\ n : an affected person

posh \'päsh\ adj : ELEGANT, FASHION-ABLE

pos·it \'päz-ət\ vb : to assume the existence of : POSTULATE

po·si·tion \pə-'zish-ən\ n 1 : an arranging in order 2 : the stand taken on a question 3 : the point or area occupied by something : SITUATION 4 : the arrangement of parts (as of the body) in relation to one another : POSTURE 5 : RANK, STATUS 6 : EMPLOYMENT, JOB

¹**pos·i·tive** \'päz-ət-iv\ adj 1 : expressed definitely (~ views) 2 : CONFIDENT, CERTAIN 3 : of, relating to, or constituting the degree of grammatical comparison that denotes no increase in quality, quantity, or relation 4 : not fictitious : REAL 5 : active and effective in function (~ leadership) 6 : having the light and shade as existing in the original subject (a ~ photograph) 7 : numerically greater than zero (a ~ number) 8 : being or relating to the kind of electricity in glass when glass is rubbed with silk; also : charged with positive electricity having a deficiency of electrons (~ particle) 9 : AFFIRMATIVE (a ~ response) — **pos·i·tive·ly** adv — **pos·i·tive·ness** n

²**positive** n 1 : the positive degree or a positive form in a language 2 : a positive photograph

pos·i·tron \'päz-ə-,trän\ n : a positively charged particle having the same mass and magnitude of charge as the electron

pos·se \'päs-ē\ n : a body of persons assigned to assist a sheriff in an emergency

pos·sess \pə-'zes\ vb 1 : to have as property : OWN 2 : to have as an attribute, knowledge, or skill 3 : to enter into and control firmly (~ed by a devil) — **pos·ses·sor** \-'zes-ər\ n

pos·ses·sion \pə-'zesh-ən\ n 1 : control or occupancy of property : OWNERSHIP 2 : something owned : PROPERTY 3 : domination by something 4 : SELF-CONTROL

pos·ses·sive \pə-'zes-iv\ adj 1 : of, relating to, or constituting a grammatical case denoting ownership 2 : showing the desire to possess (a ~ nature) — **possessive** n — **pos·ses·sive·ness** n

pos·si·ble \'päs-ə-bəl\ adj 1 : being within the limits of ability, capacity, or realization (a ~ task) 2 : being something that may or may not occur (~ dangers) 3 : able or fitted to become (a ~ site for a bridge) — **pos·si·bil·i·ty** \,päs-ə-'bil-ət-ē\ n — **pos·si·bly** \'päz-ə-blē\ adv

pos·sum \'päs-əm\ n : OPOSSUM

¹**post** \'pōst\ n 1 : an upright piece of timber or metal serving esp. as a support : PILLAR 2 : a pole or stake set up as a mark or indicator

²**post** vb 1 : to affix to a usual place (as a wall) for public notices (~ no bills) 2 : to publish or announce by or as if by a public notice (~ grades) 3 : to forbid (property) to trespassers by putting up a notice

³**post** n 1 obs : COURIER 2 chiefly Brit : MAIL; also : POST OFFICE

⁴**post** vb 1 : to ride or travel with haste : HURRY 2 : MAIL (~ a letter) 3 : INFORM (kept him ~ed on new developments)

⁵**post** n 1 : the place at which a soldier is stationed; esp : a sentry's beat or station 2 : a station or task to which a person is assigned 3 : the place at which a body of troops is stationed : CAMP 4 : OFFICE, POSITION 5 : a trading settlement or station

⁶**post** *vb* **1 :** to station in a given place **2 :** to put up (as bond)

post·age \'pō-stij\ *n* **:** the fee for postal service; *also* **:** stamps representing this fee

post·al \'pōst-²l\ *adj* **:** of or relating to the mails or the post office

postal card *n* **:** POSTCARD

post·boy \'pōs(t)-,bói\ *n* **:** POSTILION

post·card \'pōs(t)-,kärd\ *n* **:** a card on which a message may be written for mailing without an envelope

post chaise *n* **:** a 4-wheeled closed carriage for rapid travel

post·con·so·nan·tal \,pōst-,kän-sə-'nant-²l\ *adj* **:** immediately following a consonant

post·date \(')pōs(t)-'dāt\ *vb* **:** to date with a date later than that of execution

post·doc·tor·al \-'däk-t(ə-)rəl\ *adj* **:** of, relating to, or engaged in advanced academic or professional work beyond a doctor's degree ⟨~ students⟩

post·er \'pō-stər\ *n* **:** a bill or placard for posting in a public place

¹**pos·te·ri·or** \pä-'stir-ē-ər, pō-\ *adj* **1 :** later in time : SUBSEQUENT **2 :** situated behind

²**posterior** *n* **:** the hinder parts of the body : BUTTOCKS

pos·ter·i·ty \pä-'ster-ət-ē\ *n* **1 :** all the descendants from one ancestor **2 :** succeeding generations; *also* **:** future time

pos·tern \'pōs-tərn, 'päs-\ *n* **1 :** a back door or gate **2 :** a private or side entrance

post exchange *n* **:** a store at a military post that sells to military personnel and authorized civilians

post·grad·u·ate \(')pōs(t)-'graj-ə-wət, -,wāt\ *adj* **:** of or relating to studies beyond the bachelor's degree — **postgraduate** *n*

post·haste \'pōst-'hāst\ *n* **:** speed in traveling **:** great haste — **posthaste** *adj or adv*

post·hole \-,hōl\ *n* **:** a hole for a post and esp. a fence post

post·horse \-,hórs\ *n* **:** a horse for use esp. by couriers or mail carriers

post·hu·mous \'päs-chə-məs\ *adj* **1 :** born after the death of the father **2 :** published after the death of the author

pos·til·ion *or* **pos·til·lion** \pō-'stil-yən, pə-\ *n* **:** a rider on the left-hand horse of a pair drawing a coach

post·lude \'pōst-,lüd\ *n* **:** an organ solo played at the end of a church service

post·man \'pōs(t)-mən\ *n* **:** MAILMAN

post·mark \'pōs(t)-,märk\ *n* **:** an official postal marking on a piece of mail; *esp* **:** the mark canceling the postage stamp — **postmark** *vb*

post·mas·ter \-,mas-tər\ *n* **:** one who has charge of a post office

postmaster general *n, pl* **postmasters general :** an official in charge of a national post office department

post me·ri·di·em \,pōs(t)-mə-'rid-ē-əm\ *adj* **:** being after noon

post·mis·tress \'pōs(t)-,mis-trəs\ *n* **:** a woman in charge of a post office

¹**post·mor·tem** \'pōs(t)-'mórt-əm\ *adj* **1 :** occurring, made, or done after death **2 :** relating to a postmortem examination

²**postmortem** *n* **:** a postmortem examination of a body esp. to find the cause of death

post·na·sal \(')pōst-'nā-zəl\ *adj* **:** lying or occurring posterior to the nose ⟨~ drip⟩

post·na·tal \(')pōs(t)-'nāt-²l\ *adj* **:** subsequent to birth

post office *n* **1 :** a government department handling the transmission of mail **2 :** a local branch of a post office department

post·op·er·a·tive \(')pōst-'äp-(ə-)rət-iv, -'äp-ə-,rāt-\ *adj* **:** following a surgical operation ⟨~ care⟩

post·paid \'pōst-'pād\ *adj* **:** having postage paid by the seller and not included in the price to a buyer

post·pone \pōs(t)-'pōn\ *vb* **:** to hold back to a later time : DELAY — **postpone·ment** \-mənt\ *n*

post road *n* **:** a road over which mail is carried

post·script \'pōs-,skript\ *n* **:** a note added to a completed letter, article, or book

pos·tu·lant \'päs-chə-lənt\ *n* **:** a probationary candidate for membership in a religious house

¹**pos·tu·late** \-,lāt\ *vb* **:** to assume as true

²**pos·tu·late** \-lət, -,lāt\ *n* **:** a proposition taken for granted as true and made the starting point in a chain of reasoning

¹**pos·ture** \'päs-chər\ *n* **:** the position or bearing of the body or one of its parts

²**posture** *vb* **:** to strike a pose esp. for effect

post·war \'pōst-'wór\ *adj* **:** of or relating to the period after a war ⟨~ inflation⟩

po·sy \'pō-zē\ *n* **1 :** a brief sentiment **:** MOTTO **2 :** a bunch of flowers; *also* **:** FLOWER

¹**pot** \'pät\ *n* **1 :** a rounded metal or earthen container used chiefly for domestic purposes **2 :** the total of the bets at stake at one time

²**pot** *vb* **pot·ted; pot·ting 1 :** to preserve in a pot **2 :** SHOOT

po·ta·ble \'pōt-ə-bəl\ *adj* **:** suitable for drinking

po·tage \pò-'täzh\ *n* **:** a thick soup

pot·ash \'pät-,ash\ *n* **:** a potassium salt made orig. from wood ashes and used in making soap and glass; *also* **:** potassium or any of its various compounds

po·tas·si·um \pə-'tas-ē-əm\ *n* **:** a silver-white metallic chemical element used in making glass, gunpowder, and fertilizer

potassium nitrate *n* **:** a soluble salt that occurs in some soils and is used in making gunpowder, in preserving meat, and in medicine

po·ta·tion \pō-'tā-shən\ *n* **:** a usu. alcoholic drink; *also* **:** the act of drinking

po·ta·to \pə-'tāt-ō\ *n, pl* **-toes :** the edible starchy tuber of a plant related to the tomato; *also* **:** this plant

pot·bel·ly \'pät-,bel-ē\ *n* **:** a protruding abdomen — **pot·bel·lied** \-ēd\ *adj*

pot·boil·er \-,bói-lər\ *n* **:** a usu. inferior work of art or literature produced only to earn money

pot·boy \-,bói\ *n* **:** a boy who serves drinks in a tavern

---

ə abut; ᵊ kitten; ər further; a back; ā bake; ä cot, cart; aú out; ch chin; e less; ē easy; g gift; i trip; ī life; j joke; ŋ sing; ō flow; ò flaw; ói coin; th thin; t͟h this; ü loot; ú foot; y yet; yü few; yú furious; zh vision

po·teen \pə-'tēn\ *n* **:** illicitly distilled whiskey of Ireland

po·tent \'pōt-ᵊnt\ *adj* **1 :** having authority or influence — POWERFUL **2 :** chemically or medicinally effective **3 :** able to copulate *syn* forceful, forcible — **po·ten·cy** \-ⁿ-sē\ *n*

po·ten·tate \'pōt-ⁿ-,tāt\ *n* **:** one who wields controlling power **:** RULER

¹po·ten·tial \pə-'ten-chəl\ *adj* **:** existing in possibility **:** capable of becoming actual ⟨a ~ champion⟩ *syn* dormant, latent — **po·ten·ti·al·i·ty** \pə-,ten-chē-'al-ət-ē\ *n* — **po·ten·tial·ly** \-'tench-(ə-)lē\ *adv*

²potential *n* **1 :** something that can develop or become actual **2 :** degree of electrification with reference to a standard (as of the earth)

poth·er \'pät͟h-ər\ *n* **:** a noisy disturbance; *also* **:** FUSS

pot·herb \'pät-,(h)ərb\ *n* **:** an herb whose leaves or stems are boiled for greens or used to season food

pot·hole \-,hōl\ *n* **:** a pot-shaped hole in a road surface

pot·hook \-,hùk\ *n* **1 :** an S-shaped hook for hanging pots and kettles over an open fire **2 :** a written character resembling a pothook

po·tion \'pō-shən\ *n* **:** DRINK; *esp* **:** a dose of liquid medicine or poison

pot·luck \'pät-'lək\ *n* **:** the regular meal available to a guest for whom no special preparations have been made

pot·pie \-'pī\ *n* **:** meat or fowl stew served with a crust or dumplings

pot·pour·ri \,pō-pù-'rē\ *n* **:** a miscellaneous collection **:** MEDLEY

pot·sherd \'pät-,shərd\ *n* **:** a pottery fragment

pot·shot \-,shät\ *n* **1 :** a shot taken in a casual manner or at an easy target **2 :** a critical remark made in a random or sporadic manner

pot·tage \'pät-ij\ *n* **:** a thick soup of vegetables and vegetables and meat

¹pot·ter \'pät-ər\ *n* **:** one that makes pottery

²potter *vb* **:** PUTTER

pot·tery \'pät-ə-rē\ *n* **1 :** a place where earthen pots and dishes are made **2 :** the art of the potter **3 :** dishes, pots, and vases made from clay

¹pouch \'paùch\ *n* **1 :** a small bag (as for tobacco) carried on the person **2 :** a bag for storing or transporting goods ⟨mail ~⟩ ⟨diplomatic ~⟩ **3 :** an anatomical sac; *esp* **:** one in which a marsupial carries her young

²pouch *vb* **:** to make puffy or protuberant

poult \'pōlt\ *n* **:** a young fowl; *esp* **:** a young turkey

poul·ter·er \'pōl-tər-ər\ *n* **:** one that deals in poultry

poul·tice \'pōl-təs\ *n* **:** a soft usu. heated and medicated mass spread on cloth and applied to a sore or injury — **poultice** *vb*

poul·try \'pōl-trē\ *n* **:** domesticated birds kept for eggs or meat

poul·try·man \-mən\ *n* **1 :** one that raises domestic fowls esp. on a commercial scale **2 :** a dealer in poultry or poultry products

pounce \'paùns\ *vb* **:** to spring or swoop upon and seize something

¹pound \'paùnd\ *n* **1 :** a measure of weight equal to 16 ounces **2 —** see MONEY table

²pound *vb* **1 :** to crush to a powder or

pulp by beating **2 :** to strike or beat heavily or repeatedly **3 :** DRILL **4 :** to move or move along heavily

³pound *n* **:** a public enclosure where stray animals are kept

pound cake *n* **:** a rich cake made with a large amount of eggs and shortening in proportion to the flour used

pound-fool·ish \-'fü-lish\ *adj* **:** imprudent in dealing with large sums or large matters

pour \'pōr\ *vb* **1 :** to flow or cause to flow in a stream or flood **2 :** to rain hard **3 :** to supply freely and copiously

pour·boire \pùr-'bwär\ *n* **:** TIP, GRATUITY

pour·par·ler \,pùr-,pär-'lā\ *n* **:** a discussion preliminary to negotiations

pout \'paùt\ *vb* **:** to show displeasure by thrusting out the lips; *also* **:** to look sullen — **pout** *n*

pov·er·ty \'päv-ərt-ē\ *n* [OF *poverté*, fr. L *paupertai-, paupertas*, fr. *pauper* poor] **1 :** lack of money or material possessions **:** WANT **2 :** poor quality (as of soil)

pov·er·ty-strick·en \-,strik-ən\ *adj* **:** very poor **:** DESTITUTE

¹pow·der \'paùd-ər\ *n* **1 :** dry material made up of fine particles; *also* **:** a usu. medicinal or cosmetic preparation in this form **2 :** a solid explosive (as gunpowder) — **pow·dery** *adj*

²powder *vb* **1 :** to sprinkle or cover with or as if with powder **2 :** to reduce to powder

¹pow·er \'paù-(ə)r\ *n* **1 :** a position of ascendancy over others **:** AUTHORITY **2 :** the ability to act or produce an effect **3 :** one that has control or authority; *esp* **:** a sovereign state **4 :** physical might; *also* **:** mental or moral vigor **5 :** the number of times as indicated by an exponent a number is to be multiplied by itself **6 :** force or energy used to do work; *also* **:** the time rate at which work is done or energy transferred **7 :** the amount by which an optical lens magnifies — **pow·er·ful** \-fəl\ *adj* — **pow·er·ful·ly** *adv* — **pow·er·less** \-los\ *adj*

²power *vb* **:** to supply with power and esp. motive power

pow·er·boat \-,bōt\ *n* **:** MOTORBOAT

pow·er·house \-,haùs\ *n* **:** a building in which electric power is generated

pow-wow \'paù-,waù\ *n* **1 :** a No. American Indian ceremony (as for victory in war) **2 :** a meeting for discussion **:** CONFERENCE

pox \'päks\ *n* **:** any of various diseases (as smallpox or syphilis) marked by eruptions

prac·ti·ca·ble \'prak-ti-kə-bəl\ *adj* **:** capable of being put into practice, done, or accomplished **:** FEASIBLE — **prac·ti·ca·bil·i·ty** \,prak-ti-kə-'bil-ət-ē\ *n*

prac·ti·cal \'prak-ti-kəl\ *adj* **1 :** of, relating to, or shown in practice ⟨~ questions⟩ **2 :** VIRTUAL ⟨~ control⟩ **3 :** capable of being put to use or account ⟨a ~ knowledge of a language⟩ **4 :** inclined to action as opposed to speculation ⟨a ~ person⟩ **5 :** qualified by training but lacking the highest professional education ⟨~ nurse⟩ — **prac·ti·cal·i·ty** \,prak-ti-'kal-ət-ē\ *n* — **prac·ti·cal·ly** \'prak-ti-k(ə-)lē\ *adv*

¹prac·tice *or* **prac·tise** \'prak-təs\ *vb* **1 :** to perform or work at repeatedly so as to become proficient ⟨~ tennis strokes〉 **2** : to carry out : APPLY 〈*practices* what he preaches〉 **3** : to do or perform customarily or habitually 〈~ politeness〉 **4** : to be professionally engaged in 〈~ law〉

²**practice** *also* **practise** *n* **1** : actual performance or application **2** : customary action : HABIT **3** : systematic exercise for proficiency **4** : the exercise of a profession; *also* : a professional business

prac·ti·tion·er \prak-'tish-(ə-)nər\ *n* : one that practices a profession (as law or medicine)

prae·tor \'prēt-ər\ *n* : an ancient Roman magistrate ranking below a consul — **prae·to·ri·an** \prē-'tōr-ē-ən, -'tōr-\ *adj*

prag·mat·ic \prag-'mat-ik\ *adj* **1** : of or relating to practical affairs **2** : concerned with the practical consequences of actions or beliefs

prag·ma·tism \'prag-mə-,tiz-əm\ *n* : a practical approach to problems and affairs

prai·rie \'pre(ə)r-ē\ *n* : a broad tract of level or rolling land (as in the Mississippi valley) covered by coarse grass but with few trees

prairie schooner *n* : a covered wagon used by pioneers in cross-country travel

praise \'prāz\ *vb* **1** : to express approval of : COMMEND **2** : to glorify (a divinity or a saint) esp. in song — **praise** *n* — **praise·wor·thy** \-,wər-thē\ *adj*

pra·line \'prä-,lēn\ *n* : a candy of nut kernels embedded in boiled brown sugar or maple sugar

pram \'pram\ *n, chiefly Brit* : PERAMBULATOR

prance \'prans\ *vb* **1** : to spring from the hind legs (a *prancing* horse) **2** : SWAGGER; *also* : CAPER — **prance** *n* — **pranc·er** *n*

prank \'praŋk\ *n* : a playful or mildly mischievous act : TRICK — **prank·ster** \-stər\ *n*

pra·se·o·dym·i·um \,prā-zē-ō-'dim-ē-əm\ *n* : a white metallic chemical element

prate \'prāt\ *vb* : to talk long and idly : chatter foolishly

prat·fall \'prat-,fol\ *n* : a fall on the buttocks

pra·tique \pra-'tēk\ *n* : clearance given an incoming ship by the health authority of a port

¹**prat·tle** \'prat-ᵊl\ *vb* : PRATE, BABBLE

²**prattle** *n* : trifling or childish talk

prawn \'prȯn\ *n* : any of various edible shrimplike crustaceans

pray \'prā\ *vb* **1** : ENTREAT, IMPLORE **2** : to ask earnestly for something **3** : to address a divinity esp. with supplication

prayer \'praər\ *n* **1** : an earnest request **2** : the act or practice of addressing a divinity esp. in petition **3** *often pl* : a religious service consisting chiefly of prayers **4** : a form of words used in praying **5** : something prayed for

prayer book *n* : a book containing prayers and often directions for worship

prayer·ful \'praər-fəl\ *adj* **1** : DEVOUT **2** : EARNEST — **prayer·ful·ly** *adv*

preach \'prēch\ *vb* **1** : to deliver a sermon **2** : to set forth in a sermon **3** : to advocate earnestly — **preach·er** *n* — **preach·ment** \'prēch-mənt\ *n*

pre·ad·o·les·cence \,prē-,ad-ᵊl-'es-ᵊns\ *n* : the period of human development just preceding adolescence — **pre·ad·o·les·cent** *adj or n*

pre·am·ble \'prē-,am-bəl\ *n* : an introductory part : PREFACE 〈the ~ to a constitution〉

pre·ar·range \,prē-ə-'rānj\ *vb* : to arrange beforehand — **pre·ar·range·ment** \-mənt\ *n*

pre·as·signed \,prē-ə-'sīnd\ *adj* : assigned beforehand

preb·end \'preb-ənd\ *n* : an endowment held by a cathedral or collegiate church for the maintenance of a prebendary; *also* : the stipend paid from this endowment

preb·en·dary \-ən-,der-ē\ *n* **1** : a clergyman receiving a prebend for officiating and serving in the church **2** : an honorary canon

pre·can·cel \(')prē-'kan-səl\ *vb* : to cancel (a postage stamp) in advance of use — **pre·can·cel·la·tion** \,prē-,kan-sə-'lā-shən\ *n*

pre·can·cer·ous \'prē-'kans-(ə-)rəs\ *adj* : likely to become cancerous

pre·car·i·ous \pri-'kar-ē-əs\ *adj* : dependent on uncertain conditions : dangerously insecure : UNSTABLE 〈a ~ foothold〉 〈~ prosperity〉 **syn** dangerous, hazardous, perilous, jeopardous, risky — **pre·car·i·ous·ly** *adv* — **pre·car·i·ous·ness** *n*

pre·cau·tion \pri-'kȯ-shən\ *n* : a measure taken beforehand to prevent harm or secure good — **pre·cau·tion·ary** \-shə-,ner-ē\ *adj*

pre·cede \pri-'sēd\ *vb* : to be, go, or come ahead or in front of (as in rank, sequence, or time) — **prec·e·dence** \'pres-əd-əns, pri-'sēd-ᵊns\ *n*

¹**pre·ced·ent** \pri-'sēd-ᵊnt, 'pres-əd-ənt\ *adj* : prior in time, order, or significance

²**prec·e·dent** \'pres-əd-ənt\ *n* : something said or done that may serve to authorize or justify further words or acts of the same or a similar kind

pre·ced·ing \pri-'sēd-iŋ\ *adj* : that precedes : going before **syn** antecedent, foregoing, prior, former, anterior

pre·cen·tor \pri-'sent-ər\ *n* : a leader of the singing of a choir or congregation

pre·cept \'prē-,sept\ *n* : a command or principle intended as a general rule of action or conduct

pre·cep·tor \pri-'sep-tər\ *n* : TEACHER, TUTOR — **pre·cep·tress** \-trəs\ *n*

pre·cinct \'prē-,siŋkt\ *n* **1** : an administrative subdivision (as of a city) : DISTRICT 〈police ~〉 〈electoral ~〉 **2** *often pl* : an enclosure bounded by the limits of a building or place **3** *pl* : ENVIRONS

pre·ci·os·i·ty \,presh-ē-'äs-ət-ē\ *n* : fastidious refinement

pre·cious \'presh-əs\ *adj* **1** : of great value 〈~ jewels〉 **2** : greatly cherished : DEAR 〈~ memories〉 **3** : AFFECTED 〈~ language〉

prec·i·pice \'pres-ə-pəs\ *n* : a steep cliff

¹**pre·cip·i·tate** \pri-'sip-ə-,tāt\ *vb* **1** : to throw violently : HURL **2** : to throw down **3** : to cause to happen quickly or abruptly 〈~ a quarrel〉 **4** : to cause to separate out of a liquid and fall to the bottom **5** : to fall as rain, snow, or hail

syn speed, accelerate, quicken, hasten, hurry

²pre·cip·i·tate \-'sip-ət-ət, -ə-ˌtāt\ n : the solid matter that separates out and usu. falls to the bottom of a liquid

³pre·cip·i·tate \-ət-ət\ adj : showing extreme or unwise haste : RASH 2 : falling with steep descent; also : PRECIPITOUS — pre·cip·i·tate·ly adv — pre·cip·i·tate·ness n

pre·cip·i·ta·tion \pri-ˌsip-ə-'tā-shən\ n 1 : rash haste 2 : the causing of solid matter to separate from a liquid and usu. fall to the bottom 3 : water that falls as rain, snow, or hail; also : the quantity of this water

pre·cip·i·tous \pri-'sip-ət-əs\ adj 1 : PRECIPITATE 2 : having the character of a precipice : very steep ⟨a ~ slope⟩; also : containing precipices ⟨~ trails⟩ — pre·cip·i·tous·ly adv

pré·cis \prā-'sē\ n : a concise summary of essential points

pre·cise \pri-'sīs\ adj 1 : exactly defined or stated : DEFINITE 2 : highly accurate : EXACT 3 : conforming strictly to a standard : SCRUPULOUS — pre·cise·ly adv — pre·cise·ness n

pre·ci·sian \pri-'sizh-ən\ n : a person who stresses or practices scrupulous adherence to a strict standard esp. of religious observance or morality

pre·ci·sion \pri-'sizh-ən\ n : the quality or state of being precise : EXACTNESS

pre·clude \pri-'klüd\ vb : to make impossible : BAR, PREVENT

pre·co·cious \pri-'kō-shəs\ adj [L praecoc-, praecox early ripening, fr. prae- ahead + coquere to cook, ripen] : early in development and esp. in mental development — pre·co·cious·ly adv — pre·coc·i·ty \-'käs-ət-ē\ n

pre·con·ceive \ˌprē-kən-'sēv\ vb : to form an opinion of beforehand — pre·con·cep·tion \-'sep-shən\ n

pre·con·cert·ed \-'sərt-əd\ adj : arranged or agreed upon in advance ⟨a ~ plan of attack⟩

pre·con·di·tion \-'dish-ən\ vb : to put in proper or desired condition or frame of mind in advance

pre·cook \'prē-'kúk\ vb : to cook partially or entirely before final cooking or reheating

pre·cur·sor \pri-'kər-sər\ n : one that precedes and indicates the approach of another : FORERUNNER

pre·da·cious or pre·da·ceous \pri-'dā-shəs\ adj : living by preying on others : PREDATORY

pre·date \'prē-'dāt\ vb : ANTEDATE

pred·a·to·ry \'pred-ə-ˌtōr-ē\ adj 1 : of or relating to plunder ⟨~ warfare⟩ 2 : disposed to exploit others 3 : preying upon other animals — pred·a·tor \'pred-ət-ər\ n

pre·de·cease \ˌprē-di-'sēs\ vb : to die before another person

pred·e·ces·sor \'pred-ə-ˌses-ər, 'prēd-\ n : one who has previously held a position to which another has succeeded

pre·des·ig·nate \(')prē-'dez-ig-ˌnāt\ vb : to designate beforehand

pre·des·ti·na·tion \ˌprē-ˌdes-tə-'nā-shən\ n : the act of foreordaining to an earthly lot or eternal destiny by divine decree; also : the state of being so foreordained — pre·des·ti·nate \prē-'des-tə-ˌnāt\ vb

pre·des·tine \prē-'des-tən\ vb : to settle beforehand : FOREORDAIN

pre·de·ter·mine \ˌprē-di-'tər-mən\ vb : to determine beforehand

pred·i·ca·ble \'pred-i-kə-bəl\ adj : capable of being predicated or affirmed

pre·dic·a·ment \pri-'dik-ə-mənt\ n : a difficult or trying situation syn dilemma, quandary

¹pred·i·cate \'pred-i-kət\ n : the part of a sentence or clause that expresses what is said of the subject

²pred·i·cate \'pred-ə-ˌkāt\ vb 1 : AFFIRM, DECLARE 2 : to assert to be a quality or attribute ⟨~ intelligence of man⟩ 3 : FOUND, BASE — pred·i·ca·tion \ˌpred-ə-'kā-shən\ n

pre·dict \pri-'dikt\ vb : to declare in advance : FORECAST — pre·dic·tion \-'dik-shən\ n

pre·di·ges·tion \ˌprē-dī-'jes-chən, -də-\ n : artificial partial digestion of food esp. for use in illness — pre·di·gest \-'jest\ vb

pred·i·lec·tion \ˌpred-°l-'ek-shən, ˌprēd-\ n : favorable inclination : LIKING

pre·dis·pose \ˌprē-dis-'pōz\ vb : to incline in advance : make susceptible — pre·dis·po·si·tion \ˌprē-ˌdis-pə-'zish-ən\ n

pre·dom·i·nate \pri-'däm-ə-ˌnāt\ vb : to be superior esp. in power or numbers : PREVAIL — pre·dom·i·nance \-nəns\ n — pre·dom·i·nant \-nənt\ adj

pre·em·i·nent \prē-'em-ə-nənt\ adj : having highest rank : OUTSTANDING — pre·em·i·nence \-nəns\ n — pre·em·i·nent·ly adv

pre·empt \prē-'empt\ vb 1 : to settle upon (public land) with the right to purchase before others; also : to take by such right 2 : to seize upon before someone else can syn usurp, confiscate — pre·emp·tion \-'emp-shən\ n

preen \'prēn\ vb 1 : to trim or dress with the beak 2 : to dress or smooth up : PRIMP 3 : to pride (oneself) for achievement

pre·ex·ist \ˌprē-ig-'zist\ vb : to exist before — pre·ex·is·tence \-'zis-təns\ n — pre·ex·is·tent \-tənt\ adj

pre·fab \'prē-'fab\ n : a prefabricated structure

pre·fab·ri·cate \'prē-'fab-rə-ˌkāt\ vb : to fabricate the parts of (as a house) at the factory for rapid assembly elsewhere

¹pref·ace \'pref-əs\ n : introductory comments : FOREWORD ⟨author's ~ to his book⟩ — pref·a·to·ry \'pref-ə-ˌtōr-ē\ adj

²preface vb : to introduce with a preface

pre·fect \'prē-ˌfekt\ n 1 : a high official; esp : a chief officer or magistrate 2 : a student monitor — pre·fec·ture \-ˌfek-chər\ n

pre·fer \pri-'fər\ vb -ferred; -fer·ring 1 archaic : PROMOTE 2 : to like better : choose above another 3 : to bring (as a charge) against a person — pref·er·a·ble \'pref-(ə-)rə-bəl\ adj — pref·er·a·bly \'pref-(ə-)rə-blē\ adv

pref·er·ence \'pref-(ə-)rəns\ n 1 : a special liking for one thing over another 2 : CHOICE, SELECTION — pref·er·en·tial \ˌpref-ə-'ren-chəl\ adj

pre·fer·ment \pri-'fər-mənt\ n : PROMOTION, ADVANCEMENT

pre·fig·ure \prē-'fig-yər\ vb 1 : FORESHADOW 2 : to imagine beforehand

¹pre·fix \'prē-ˌfiks, prē-'fiks\ vb : to place before ⟨~ a title to a name⟩

²pre·fix \'prē-ˌfiks\ *n* : an affix occurring at the beginning of a word

pre·flight \'prē-ˈflīt\ *adj* : preparing for or preliminary to airplane flight (~ training)

pre·form \-ˈfȯrm\ *vb* : to form or shape beforehand

preg·nant \'preg-nənt\ *adj* **1** : containing unborn young **2** : rich in significance : MEANINGFUL — **preg·nan·cy** \-nən-sē\ *n*

pre·heat \'prē-ˈhēt\ *vb* : to heat beforehand; *esp* : to heat (an oven) to a designated temperature before placing food therein

pre·hen·sile \prē-ˈhen-səl, -ˌsīl\ *adj* : adapted for grasping esp. by wrapping around (a monkey with a ~ tail)

pre·his·tor·ic \ˌprē-(h)is-ˈtȯr-ik\ *adj* : of, relating to, or existing in the period before written history began

pre·judge \'prē-ˈjəj\ *vb* : to judge before full hearing or examination

¹prej·u·dice \'prej-əd-əs\ *n* **1** : DAMAGE; *esp* : detriment to one's rights or claims **2** : an opinion for or against something without adequate basis : BIAS — **prej·u·di·cial** \ˌprej-ə-ˈdish-əl\ *adj*

²prejudice *vb* **1** : to damage by a judgment or action esp. at law **2** : to cause to have prejudice

prel·ate \'prel-ət\ *n* : an ecclesiastic (as a bishop) of high rank — **prel·a·cy** \-ə-sē\ *n*

¹pre·lim·i·nary \pri-ˈlim-ə-ˌner-ē\ *n* : something that precedes or introduces the main business or event

²preliminary *adj* : preceding the main discourse or business

prel·ude \'prel-ˌyüd, 'prā-ˌlüd\ *n* **1** : an introductory performance or event **2** : a musical section or movement introducing the main theme; *also* : an organ solo played at the beginning of a church service

pre·ma·ture \ˌprē-mə-ˈt(y)u̇r\ *adj* : happening, coming, born, or done before the usual or proper time *syn* untimely, advanced — **pre·ma·ture·ly** *adv*

pre·med \'prē-ˈmed\ *adj* : PREMEDICAL — **premed** *n*

pre·med·i·cal \(ˈ)prē-ˈmed-i-kəl\ *adj* : preceding and preparing for the professional study of medicine

pre·med·i·tate \pri-ˈmed-ə-ˌtāt\ *vb* : to consider and plan beforehand — **pre·med·i·ta·tion** \-ˌmed-ə-ˈtā-shən\ *n*

¹pre·mier \pri-ˈm(y)iər, 'prē-mē-ər\ *adj* **1** : first in rank or importance : CHIEF; *also* : first in time : EARLIEST

²premier *n* : the first minister of state : the prime minister — **pre·mier·ship** \-ˌship\ *n*

pre·miere \pri-ˈmyeər, -ˈmiər\ *n* **1** : a first performance **2** : the leading lady of a group (as a theatrical cast)

prem·ise \'prem-əs\ *n* **1** : a statement of fact made or implied as a basis of argument **2** *pl* : a piece of land with the structures on it; *also* : the place of business of an enterprise

pre·mi·um \'prē-mē-əm\ *n* **1** : REWARD, PRIZE **2** : a sum over and above the stated value **3** : something paid over and above a fixed wage or price : BONUS **4** : something given with a purchase **5** : the sum paid for a contract of

insurance **6** : an exceptionally high value

pre·mix \'prē-ˈmiks\ *vb* : to mix before use

pre·mo·ni·tion \ˌprē-mə-ˈnish-ən, ˌprem-ə-\ *n* : previous notice : FOREWARNING; *also* : PRESENTIMENT — **pre·mon·i·to·ry** \pri-ˈmän-ə-ˌtȯr-ē\ *adj*

pre·na·tal \'prē-ˈnāt-ᵊl\ *adj* : occurring or existing before birth

pre·oc·cu·pa·tion \prē-ˌäk-yə-ˈpā-shən\ *n* : complete absorption of the mind or interests; *also* : something that causes such absorption

pre·oc·cu·pied \prē-ˈäk-yə-ˌpīd\ *adj* **1** : lost in thought : ENGROSSED **2** : already occupied *syn* abstracted, absent, absentminded, distraught

pre·oc·cu·py \-ˌpī\ *vb* **1** : to occupy the attention of beforehand **2** : to take possession of before another

pre·op·er·a·tive \(ˈ)prē-ˈäp-(ə-)rət-iv, -ˈäp-ə-ˌrāt-\ *adj* : occurring during the period preceding a surgical operation

pre·or·dain \ˌprē-ȯr-ˈdān\ *vb* : FOREORDAIN

pre·par·a·to·ry school \pri-ˈpar-ə-ˌtȯr-ē\ *n* **1** : a usu. private school preparing students primarily for college **2** *Brit* : a private elementary school preparing students primarily for public schools

pre·pare \pri-ˈpaər\ *vb* **1** : to make or get ready (~ dinner) (~ a boy for college) **2** : to get ready beforehand : PROVIDE (~ equipment for a trip) **3** : to put together : COMPOUND (~ a vaccine) **4** : to put into written form (~ a document) — **prep·a·ra·tion** \ˌprep-ə-ˈrā-shən\ *n* — **pre·par·a·to·ry** \pri-ˈpar-ə-ˌtȯr-ē\ *adj*

pre·par·ed·ness \pri-ˈpar-əd-nəs\ *n* : a state of adequate preparation esp. for war

pre·pay \'prē-ˈpā\ *vb* : to pay or pay the charge on in advance

pre·pon·der·ate \pri-ˈpän-də-ˌrāt\ *vb* [L *praeponderare,* fr. *prae-* ahead + *ponder-, pondus* weight] : to exceed in weight, power, importance, or numbers : PREDOMINATE — **pre·pon·der·ance** \-d(ə-)rəns\ *n* — **pre·pon·der·ant** \-d(ə-)rənt\ *adj*

prep·o·si·tion \ˌprep-ə-ˈzish-ən\ *n* : a word that combines with a noun or pronoun to form a phrase — **prep·o·si·tion·al** \-ˈzish-(ə-)nəl\ *adj*

pre·pos·sess \ˌprē-pə-ˈzes\ *vb* **1** : to influence beforehand for or against someone or something : PREJUDICE **2** : to induce to a favorable opinion beforehand

pre·pos·sess·ing *adj* : tending to create a favorable impression : ATTRACTIVE (a ~ manner)

pre·pos·ses·sion \-ˈzesh-ən\ *n* **1** : PREJUDICE **2** : an exclusive concern with one idea or object

pre·pos·ter·ous \pri-ˈpäs-t(ə-)rəs\ *adj* : contrary to nature or reason : ABSURD (a story too ~ to believe)

pre·puce \'prē-ˌpyüs\ *n* : FORESKIN

pre·re·cord \ˌprē-ri-ˈkȯrd\ *vb* : to record (as a radio or television program) in advance of presentation or use

pre·req·ui·site \prē-ˈrek-wə-zət\ *n* : something that is required beforehand or for the end in view — **prerequisite** *adj*

pre·rog·a·tive \pri-'räg-ət-iv\ *n* : an exclusive or special right, power, or privilege

¹pres·age \'pres-ij\ *n* **1** : something that foreshadows a future event : OMEN **2** : FOREBODING

²pres·age \'pres-ij, pri-'sāj\ *vb* **1** : to give an omen or warning of : FORE-SHADOW **2** : FORETELL, PREDICT

pres·by·o·pia \,prez-bē-'ō-pē-ə\ *n* : FAR-SIGHTEDNESS — **pres·by·op·ic** \-'äp-ik, -'ōp-\ *adj*

pres·by·ter \'prez-bət-ər\ *n* **1** : PRIEST, MINISTER **2** : an elder in a Presbyterian church

¹Pres·by·te·ri·an \,prez-bə-'tir-ē-ən\ *adj* **1** *often not cap* : characterized by a graded system of representative ecclesiastical bodies (as presbyteries) exercising legislative and judicial powers **2** : of or relating to a group of Protestant Christian bodies that are presbyterian in government

²Presbyterian *n* : a member of a Protestant denomination that traditionally adheres to the doctrines of John Calvin — **Pres·by·te·ri·an·ism** \-,iz-əm\ *n*

pres·by·tery \'prez-bə-,ter-ē\ *n* **1** : the part of a church reserved for the officiating clergy **2** : a ruling body in Presbyterian churches consisting of the ministers and representative elders of a district

pre·school \'prē-'skül\ *adj* : of, relating to, or constituting the period in a child's life from infancy to the age of five or six

pre·science \'prē-sh(ē-)əns\ *n* : foreknowledge of events; *also* : FORESIGHT — **pre·sci·ent** \-sh(ē-)ənt\ *adj*

pre·scribe \pri-'skrīb\ *vb* **1** : to lay down as a guide or rule of action **2** : to direct the use of something as a remedy

pre·scrip·tion \pri-'skrip-shən\ *n* **1** : the action of prescribing **2** : a written direction for the preparation and use of a medicine: *also* : a medicine prescribed

pres·ence \'prez-³ns\ *n* **1** : the fact or condition of being present (noted his ~) **2** : the space immediately around a person (stood in her ~) **3** : one that is present **4** : the bearing of a person; *esp* : stately bearing

¹pres·ent \'prez-³nt\ *n* : something presented : GIFT

²pre·sent \pri-'zent\ *vb* **1** : to bring into the presence or acquaintance of : INTRODUCE **2** : to bring before the public (~ a play) **3** : to make a gift to **4** : to give formally **5** : to lay (as a charge) before a court for inquiry **6** : to aim or direct (as a weapon) so as to face in a particular direction — **pre·sent·able** \-ə-bəl\ *adj* — **pre·sen·ta·tion** \,prē-,zen-'tā-shən, ,prez-³n-\ *n* — **pre·sent·ment** \pri-'zent-mənt\ *n*

³pres·ent \'prez-³nt\ *adj* **1** : now existing or in progress (~ conditions) **2** : being in view or at hand (~ at the meeting) **3** : constituting the one actually involved (the ~ writer) **4** : of, relating to, or constituting a verb tense that expresses present time or the time of speaking — **pres·ent·ly** *adv*

⁴pres·ent \'prez-³nt\ *n* **1** *pl* : the present legal document **2** : the present tense; *also* : a verb form in it **3** : the present time

pres·ent–day \,prez-³nt-,dā\ *adj* : now existing or occurring : CURRENT

pre·sen·ti·ment \pri-'zent-ə-mənt\ *n* : a feeling that something is about to happen : PREMONITION

¹pre·serve \pri-'zərv\ *vb* **1** : to keep safe : GUARD, PROTECT **2** : to keep from decaying; *esp* : to process food (as by canning or pickling) to prevent spoilage **3** : MAINTAIN (~ silence) — **pres·er·va·tion** \,prez-ər-'vā-shən\ *n* — **pre·ser·va·tive** \pri-'zər-vət-iv\ *adj or n* — **pre·serv·er** \-'zər-vər\ *n*

²preserve *n* **1** : preserved fruit **2** : an area for the protection of natural resources (as animals or plants)

pre·set \'prē-'set\ *vb* : to set beforehand

pre·shrunk \-'shrəŋk\ *adj* : of, relating to, or constituting a fabric subjected to a shrinking process during manufacture usu. to reduce later shrinking

pre·side \pri-'zīd\ *vb* **1** : to occupy the place of authority; *esp* : to act as chairman **2** : to exercise guidance or control

pres·i·dent \'prez-əd-ənt\ *n* **1** : one chosen to preside (~ of the assembly) **2** : the chief officer of an organization (as a corporation or society) **3** : an elected official serving as both chief of state and chief political executive; *also* : a chief of state often with only minimal political powers — **pres·i·den·cy** \-ən-sē\ *n* — **pres·i·den·tial** \,prez-ə-'den-chəl\ *adj*

pre·si·dio \pri-'sēd-ē-,ō\ *n* : a garrisoned place; *esp* : a military post or fortified settlement in areas currently or orig. under Spanish control

pre·sid·i·um \pri-'sid-ē-əm\ *n, pl* **-ia** \-ē-ə\ *or* **-i·ums** : a permanent executive committee selected in Communist countries to act for a larger body

¹press \'pres\ *n* **1** : a crowded condition : THRONG **2** : a machine for exerting pressure (as for stamping, pushing a tool, or expressing a liquid); *esp* : PRINTING PRESS **3** : CLOSET, CUP-BOARD **4** : PRESSURE **5** : the properly creased condition of a freshly pressed garment **6** : the act or process of printing **7** : a printing or publishing establishment **8** : the media (as newspapers) of public news and comment; *also* : persons (as reporters) employed in these media **9** : comment in newspapers and periodicals **10** : a pressure device (as for keeping a tennis racket from warping)

²press *vb* **1** : to bear down upon : push steadily against **2** : ASSAIL, COMPEL **3** : to squeeze out the juice or contents of (~ grapes) **4** : to squeeze to a desired density, shape, or smoothness; *esp* : IRON **5** : to try hard to persuade : URGE **6** : to follow through : PROSE-CUTE **7** : CROWD **8** : to make (a phonograph record) from a matrix — **press·er** *n*

press agent *n* : an agent employed to maintain good public relations through publicity

press·man \-mən\ *n* : the operator of a press and *esp.* a printing press

press·room \-,rüm, -,rum\ *n* : a room in a printing plant containing the printing presses; *also* : a room for the use of reporters

¹pres·sure \'presh-ər\ *n* **1** : the burden of physical or mental distress : OP-PRESSION **2** : the action of pressing;

esp : the application of force to something by something else in direct contact with it **3** : the condition of being pressed or of exerting force over a surface **4** : the stress or urgency of matters demanding attention **syn** stress, strain, tension

²pressure *vb* : to apply pressure to : CONSTRAIN

pres·sur·ize \'presh-ə-,rīz\ *vb* 1 : to maintain normal atmospheric pressure within (an airplane cabin) during high-level flight

pres·ti·dig·i·ta·tion \,pres-tə-,dij-ə-'tā-shən\ *n* : SLEIGHT OF HAND

pres·tige \pres-'tēzh, -'tēj\ *n* : standing or estimation in the eyes of people : REPUTATION **syn** influence, authority

pres·to \'pres-tō\ *adv* : at once : QUICKLY

pre·sume \pri-'züm\ *vb* 1 : to take upon oneself without leave or warrant : DARE **2** : to take for granted : ASSUME **3** : to act or behave with undue boldness — **pre·sum·able** \-'zü-mə-bəl\ *adj* — **pre·sum·ably** \-blē\ *adv*

pre·sump·tion \pri-'zəmp-shən\ *n* 1 : presumptuous attitude or conduct : AUDACITY **2** : an attitude or belief dictated by probability; *also* : the grounds lending probability to a belief — **pre·sump·tive** \-tiv\ *adj*

pre·sump·tu·ous \pri-'zəmp-chə-(wə)s\ *adj* : overstepping due bounds : taking liberties : OVERBOLD

pre·sup·pose \,prē-sə-'pōz\ *vb* 1 : to suppose beforehand **2** : to require beforehand as a necessary condition **syn** presume, assume — **pre·sup·po·si·tion** \,prē-,səp-ə-'zish-ən\ *n*

pre·tend \pri-'tend\ *vb* 1 : PROFESS (doesn't ~ to be scientific) **2** : FEIGN (~ to be angry) **3** : to lay claim (~ allege a title (~ to a throne) — **pre·tend·er** *n*

pre·tense *or* **pre·tence** \'prē-,tens, pri-'tens\ *n* 1 : CLAIM; *esp* : one not supported by fact **2** : mere display : SHOW **3** : an attempt to attain a certain condition (made a ~ at discipline) **4** : false show : PRETEXT — **pre·ten·sion** \pri-'ten-chən\ *n*

pre·ten·tious \pri-'ten-chəs\ *adj* 1 : making or possessing claims (as to excellence) : OSTENTATIOUS (~ furniture) **2** : making demands on one's ability or means : AMBITIOUS (too ~ an undertaking) — **pre·ten·tious·ly** *adv* — **pre·ten·tious·ness** *n*

pret·er·it *or* **pret·er·ite** \'pret-ə-rət\ *adj* : PAST **4** — preterit *n*

pre·ter·mi·nal \(')prē-'tər-mən-ᵊl\ *adj* : occurring before death

pre·ter·nat·u·ral \,prēt-ər-'nach-(ə-)rəl\ *adj* 1 : exceeding what is natural : ABNORMAL **2** : inexplicable by ordinary means : STRANGE

pre·text \'prē-,tekst\ *n* : a purpose stated or assumed to cloak the real intention or state of affairs

pret·ti·fy \'prit-i-,fī, 'pùrt-\ *vb* 1 : to make pretty — **pret·ti·fi·ca·tion** \,prit-i-fə-'kā-shən, ,pùrt-\ *n*

¹pret·ty \'prit-ē, 'pùrt-\ *adj* 1 : pleasing by delicacy or grace : superficially appealing rather than strikingly beautiful (~ flowers) (a ~ girl) (~ verses) **2** : FINE, GOOD (a ~ profit) — often

used ironically (a ~ state of affairs) **syn** comely, fair — **pret·ti·ly** *adv* — **pret·ti·ness** *n*

²pret·ty \'pùrt-ē, pərt-, ,prit-\ *adv* : in some degree : MODERATELY

³pret·ty \'prit-ē, 'pùrt-\ *vb* : to make pretty (~ up the place)

pret·zel \'pret-səl\ *n* : a brittle, glazed, salted, and usu. twisted cracker

pre·vail \pri-'vāl\ *vb* 1 : to win mastery : TRIUMPH **2** : to be or become effective : SUCCEED **3** : to urge successfully (~ed upon her to sing) **4** : to be frequent : PREDOMINATE

prev·a·lent \'prev-ə-lənt\ *adj* : generally or widely existent : WIDESPREAD — **prev·a·lence** \-ləns\ *n*

pre·var·i·cate \pri-'var-ə-,kāt\ *vb* : to deviate from the truth : EQUIVOCATE — **pre·var·i·ca·tion** \-,var-ə-'kā-shən\ *n*

pre·vent \pri-'vent\ *vb* 1 : to keep from happening or existing (steps to ~ war) **2** : to hold back : HINDER, STOP (tried to ~ us from going) — **pre·vent·able** \-ə-bəl\ *adj* — **pre·ven·tion** \-'ven-chən\ *n* — **pre·ven·tive** \-'vent-iv\ *or* **pre·ven·ta·tive** \-'vent-ət-iv\ *adj or n*

¹pre·view \'prē-,vyü\ *vb* : to see beforehand; *esp* : to view or show in advance of public presentation

²preview *n* 1 : an advance showing or viewing **2** *also* **pre·vue** \-,vyü\ : a showing of snatches from a motion picture advertised for future appearance **3** : FORETASTE

pre·vi·ous \'prē-vē-əs\ *adj* : going before : EARLIER, FORMER **syn** foregoing, prior, preceding — **pre·vi·ous·ly** *adv*

pre·vi·sion \prē-'vizh-ən\ *n* 1 : FORESIGHT, PRESCIENCE **2** : FORECAST, PREDICTION

pre·war \'prē-'wȯr\ *adj* : occurring or existing before a war

¹prey \'prā\ *n* 1 : an animal taken for food by another; *also* : VICTIM **2** : the act or habit of preying

²prey *vb* 1 : to raid for booty : PLUNDER **2** : to seize and devour something as prey **3** : to have a harmful or wearing effect (fears that ~ on the mind)

¹price \'prīs\ *n* 1 *archaic* : VALUE (a pearl of great ~) **2** : the amount of money paid or asked for the sale of a specified thing; *also* : the cost at which something is obtained

²price *vb* 1 : to set a price on **2** : to ask the price of

price·cut·ting \-,kət-iŋ\ *n* : the lowering of prices esp. in order to cripple competition

price·less \'prīs-ləs\ *adj* : having a value beyond any price : INVALUABLE **syn** precious, costly, expensive

¹prick \'prik\ *n* 1 : a mark or small wound made by a pointed instrument **2** : something sharp or pointed **3** : an instance of pricking; *also* : a sensation of being pricked

²prick *vb* 1 : to pierce slightly with a sharp point; *also* : to have or cause a sensation of this **2** : to affect with anguish or remorse (~s his conscience) **3** : to outline with punctures (~ out a pattern) **4** : to cause to stand erect (the dog ~ed up his ears) **syn** punch, puncture, perforate, bore, drill

---

ə abut; ᵉ kitten; ər further; a back; ā bake; ä cot, cart; aù out; ch chin; e less; ē easy; g gift; i trip; ī life; j joke; ŋ sing; ō flow; ȯ flaw; ȯi coin; th thin; t̲h̲ this; ü loot; ù foot; y yet; yü furious; zh vision

¹**prick·le** \'prik-əl\ *n* **1** : a small sharp point (as on a plant) **2** : a slight stinging pain — **prick·ly** \'prik-lē\ *adj*

²**prickle** *vb* **1** : to prick lightly **2** : TINGLE

¹**pride** \'prīd\ *n* **1** : CONCEIT **2** : justifiable self-respect **3** : elation over an act or possession **4** : haughty behavior — **pride·ful** \-fəl\ *adj*

²**pride** *vb* : to indulge in pride : PLUME

prie-dieu \'prē-'dyə(r)\ *n, pl* **prie-dieux** \-'dyə(r)(z)\ : a small kneeling bench designed for use by a person at prayer and fitted with a raised shelf on which the elbows or a book may be rested

priest \'prēst\ *n* [OE *prēost*, fr. LL *presbyter*, fr. Gk *presbyteros* elder, priest, fr. compar. of *presbys* old, old man] : a person having authority to perform the sacred rites of a religion; *esp* : an Anglican, Eastern, or Roman Catholic clergyman ranking below a bishop and above a deacon — **priest·ess** \-əs\ *n* — **priest·hood** \-.húd\ *n* — **priest·li·ness** \-lē-nəs\ *n* — **priest·ly** *adj*

prig \'prig\ *n* : one who irritates by rigid or pointed observance of proprieties — **prig·gish** *adj* — **prig·gish·ly** *adv*

prim \'prim\ *adj* : stiffly formal and precise : DECOROUS

pri·ma·cy \'prī-mə-sē\ *n* **1** : the state of being first (as in rank) **2** : the office, rank, or character of an ecclesiastical primate

pri·ma don·na \,prim-ə-'dän-ə\ *n* **1** : a principal female singer (as in an opera) **2** : an extremely sensitive, vain, or undisciplined performer

pri·ma fa·cie \,prī-mə-'fā-shə, -shē\ *adj (or adv)* **1** : based on immediate impression : APPARENT **2** : SELF-EVIDENT

pri·mal \'prī-məl\ *adj* **1** : ORIGINAL, PRIMITIVE **2** : first in importance : FUNDAMENTAL

pri·mar·i·ly \prī-'mer-ə-lē\ *adv* **1** : FUNDAMENTALLY, MAINLY **2** : ORIGINALLY

¹**pri·ma·ry** \'prī-,mer-ē, 'prim-(ə-)rē\ *adj* **1** : first in order of time or development; *also* : PREPARATORY **2** : of first rank or importance : PRINCIPAL; *also* : FUNDAMENTAL **3** : not derived from or dependent on something else ⟨~ sources⟩ ⟨a ~ color⟩

²**primary** *n* **1** : something that stands first in order or importance : FUNDAMENTAL — usu. used in pl. **2** : a preliminary election in which voters nominate or express a preference among candidates usu. of their own party

pri·mate \'prī-,māt, -mət\ *n* **1** *often cap* : the highest-ranking bishop of a province or nation **2** : any of the group of mammals that includes man, the apes, and monkeys

¹**prime** \'prīm\ *n* **1** : the earliest stage of something; *esp* : SPRINGTIME **2** : the most active, thriving, or successful stage or period (as of one's life) **3** : the best individual; *also* : the best part of something

²**prime** *adj* **1** : standing first (as in time, rank, significance, or quality) ⟨~ requisite⟩ ⟨~ beef⟩ **2** : not capable of being divided by any number except itself or 1 ⟨a ~ number⟩

³**prime** *vb* **1** : FILL, LOAD **2** : to lay a preparatory coating upon (as in painting) **3** : to put in working condition **4** : to instruct beforehand : COACH

¹**prim·er** \'prim-ər\ *n* **1** : a small book for teaching children to read **2** : an introductory book on a subject

²**prim·er** \'prī-mər\ *n* **1** : one that primes **2** : a device for igniting an explosive **3** : material for priming a surface

pri·me·val \prī-'mē-vəl\ *adj* : of or relating to the earliest ages : PRIMITIVE

prim·i·tive \'prim-ət-iv\ *adj* **1** : ORIGINAL, PRIMEVAL **2** : of, relating to, or characteristic of an early stage of development or a relatively simple people or culture **3** : ELEMENTAL, NATURAL

pri·mo·gen·i·tor \,prī-mō-'jen-ət-ər\ *n* : ANCESTOR, FOREFATHER

pri·mo·gen·i·ture \,prī-mō-'jen-ə-,chúr, -'jen-i-chər\ *n* **1** : the state of being the firstborn of a family **2** : an exclusive right of inheritance belonging to the eldest son

pri·mor·di·al \prī-'mórd-ē-əl\ *adj* : first created or developed : existing in its original state : RUDIMENTARY, PRIMEVAL, PRIMARY

primp \'primp\ *vb* : to dress in a careful or finicky manner

prim·rose \'prim-,rōz\ *n* : any of several low herbs with clusters of showy flowers

prince \'prins\ *n* **1** : MONARCH, KING **2** : a male member of a royal family; *esp* : a son of the king **3** : a person of high standing (as in a class) ⟨a ~ of poets⟩ — **prince·dom** \-dəm\ *n* — **prince·ly** *adj*

prince·ling \-liŋ\ *n* : a petty prince

prin·cess \'prin-səs, -,ses\ *n* **1** : a female member of a royal family **2** : the consort of a prince

¹**prin·ci·pal** \'prin-sə-pəl\ *adj* : most important : CHIEF, MAIN — **prin·ci·pal·ly** *adv*

²**principal** *n* **1** : a leading person (as in a play) **2** : the chief officer of an educational institution **3** : the person from whom an agent's authority derives **4** : a capital sum placed at interest or used as a fund

prin·ci·pal·i·ty \,prin-sə-'pal-ət-ē\ *n* : the position, territory, or jurisdiction of a prince

prin·ci·ple \'prin-sə-pəl\ *n* **1** : a general or fundamental law, doctrine, or assumption **2** : a rule or code of conduct; *also* : devotion to such a code **3** : the laws or facts of nature underlying the working of an artificial device **4** : a primary source : ORIGIN; *also* : an underlying faculty or endowment **5** : the active part (as of a drug)

prin·ci·pled *adj* : exhibiting, based on, or characterized by principle ⟨highprincipled⟩

prink \'priŋk\ *vb* : PRIMP

¹**print** \'print\ *n* **1** : a mark made by pressure **2** : something stamped with an impression **3** : printed state or form **4** : printed matter **5** : a copy made by printing **6** : cloth upon which a figure is stamped

²**print** *vb* **1** : to stamp (as a mark) in or on something **2** : to produce impressions of (as from type or engraved plates) **3** : to write in letters like those of printer's type **4** : to make (a positive picture) from a photographic negative — **print·er** *n*

print·able *adj* **1** : capable of being printed or of being printed from **2** : worthy or fit to be published

print·ing n **1 :** reproduction in printed form **2 :** the art, practice, or business of a printer **3 :** IMPRESSION 5

printing press n **:** a machine by which printing is done from type or plates

¹pri·or \'prī(-ə)r\ n **:** the superior of a religious house — **pri·or·ess** \'prī-ə-rəs\ n

²prior adj **1 :** earlier in time or order **2 :** taking precedence logically or in importance — **pri·or·i·ty** \prī-'ȯr-ət-ē\ n

pri·o·ry \'prī-ə-rē\ n **:** a religious house under a prior or prioress

prism \'priz-əm\ n **1 :** a solid whose sides are parallelograms and whose ends are parallel and alike in shape and size **2 :** a 3-sided glass or crystal object of prism shape that breaks up light into rainbow colors — **pris·mat·ic** \priz-'mat-ik\ adj

pris·on \'priz-ᵊn\ n **:** a place or state of confinement esp. for criminals

pris·on·er \'priz-(ᵊ-)nər\ n **:** a person deprived of his liberty; esp **:** one on trial or in prison

pris·sy \'pris-ē\ adj **:** being prim and precise — **pris·si·ness** n

pris·tine \'pris-,tēn\ adj **1 :** PRIMITIVE **2 :** having the purity of its original state **:** UNSPOILED

prith·ee \'prith-ē\ interj, archaic — used to express a wish or request

pri·va·cy \'prī-və-sē\ n **1 :** the quality or state of being apart from others **2 :** SECRECY

¹pri·vate \'prī-vət\ adj **1 :** belonging to or intended for a particular individual or group ⟨~ property⟩ ⟨a ~ beach⟩ **2 :** restricted to the individual ⟨~ : PERSONAL ⟨~ opinion⟩ **3 :** carried on by the individual independently ⟨~ study⟩ **4 :** not holding public office ⟨a ~ citizen⟩ **5 :** withdrawn from company or observation ⟨a ~ place⟩ **6 :** not known publicly **:** SECRET ⟨~ dealings⟩ — **pri·vate·ly** adv

²private n **1 :** PRIVACY **2 :** an enlisted man of the lowest rank in the marine corps and of the next to lowest rank in the army

pri·va·teer \,prī-və-'tiər\ n **:** an armed private ship commissioned to cruise against enemy ships and commerce; also **:** the commander or one of the crew of such a ship

private first class n **:** an enlisted man ranking next below a corporal in the army and next below a lance corporal in the marine corps

pri·va·tion \prī-'vā-shən\ n **1 :** DEPRIVATION **2 :** the state of being deprived; esp **:** lack of what is needed for existence

priv·et \'priv-ət\ n **:** a nearly evergreen shrub related to the olive and widely used for hedges

¹priv·i·lege \'priv-(ə-)lij\ n **:** a right or immunity granted as an advantage or favor esp. to some and not others

²privilege vb **:** to grant a privilege to

priv·i·leged adj **1 :** having or enjoying one or more privileges ⟨~ classes⟩ **2 :** not subject to disclosure in a court of law ⟨a ~ communication⟩

¹pri·vy \'priv-ē\ adj **1 :** PERSONAL, PRIVATE **2 :** SECRET, CONFIDENTIAL

3 : admitted as one sharing in a secret ⟨~ to the conspiracy⟩ — **priv·i·ly** adv

²privy n **:** TOILET; esp **:** OUTHOUSE

¹prize \'prīz\ n **1 :** something offered or striven for in competition or in contests of chance **2 :** something exceptionally desirable

²prize adj **1 :** awarded or worthy of a prize ⟨a ~ essay⟩; also **:** awarded as a prize ⟨a ~ medal⟩ **2 :** OUTSTANDING

³prize vb **:** to value highly **:** ESTEEM syn treasure, cherish, appreciate

⁴prize n **:** property (as a ship) lawfully captured in time of war

⁵prize or **prise** \'prīz\ vb **:** PRY

prize·fight \-,fīt\ n **:** a professional boxing match — **prize·fight·er** n — **prizefighting** n

prize·win·ner \-,win-ər\ n **:** a winner of a prize — **prize-win·ning** adj

¹pro \'prō\ n **:** a favorable argument, person, or position

²pro adv **:** in favor **:** FOR

³pro n or adj **:** PROFESSIONAL

prob·a·ble \'präb-ə-bəl\ adj **1 :** apparently or presumably true ⟨a ~ hypothesis⟩ **2 :** likely to be or become true or real ⟨a ~ result⟩ — **prob·a·bil·i·ty** \,präb-ə-'bil-ət-ē\ n — **prob·a·bly** \'präb-ə-blē\ adv

¹pro·bate \'prō-,bāt\ n **:** the judicial determination of the validity of a will

²probate vb **:** to establish (a will) by probate as genuine and valid

pro·ba·tion \prō-'bā-shən\ n **1 :** subjection of an individual to a period of testing and trial to ascertain fitness (as for a job) **2 :** the action of giving a convicted offender freedom during good behavior under the supervision of a probation officer — **pro·ba·tion·ary** \-shə-,ner-ē\ adj

pro·ba·tion·er \-sh(ə-)nər\ n **1 :** one (as a newly admitted student nurse) whose fitness is being tested during a trial period **2 :** a convicted offender on probation

pro·ba·tive \'prō-bət-iv\ adj **1 :** serving to test or try **2 :** serving to prove

¹probe \'prōb\ n **1 :** a slender instrument for examining a cavity (as a wound) **2 :** a penetrating investigation **3 :** an information-gathering device sent high into the air or into outer space syn inquiry, inquest, research

²probe vb **1 :** to examine with a probe **2 :** to investigate thoroughly

pro·bi·ty \'prōb-ət-ē, 'präb-\ n **:** UPRIGHTNESS, HONESTY

prob·lem \'präb-ləm\ n **1 :** a question raised for consideration or solution **2 :** an intricate unsettled question **3 :** a source of perplexity or vexation

prob·lem·at·ic \,präb-lə-'mat-ik\ or **prob·lem·at·i·cal** \-i-kəl\ adj **1 :** difficult to solve or decide **:** PUZZLING **2 :** DUBIOUS, QUESTIONABLE

pro·bos·cis \prə-'bäs-əs\ n **:** a long flexible snout (as the trunk of an elephant)

pro·ca·the·dral \,prō-kə-'thē-drəl\ n **:** a parish church used as a cathedral

pro·ce·dure \prə-'sē-jər\ n **1 :** a particular way of doing something (democratic ~) **2 :** a series of steps followed in a regular order (surgical ~)

pro·ceed \prō-'sēd\ vb **1 :** to come

ə abut; ᵊ kitten; ər further; a back; ā bake; ä cot, cart; aů out; ch chin; e less; ē easy; g gift; i trip; ī life; j joke; ŋ sing; ō flow; ȯ flaw; ȯi coin; th thin; t̲h̲ this; ü loot; ů foot; y yet; yü few; yů furious; zh vision

forth : ISSUE **2 :** to go on in an orderly way; *also* : CONTINUE **3 :** to begin and carry on an action **4 :** to take legal action **5 :** to go forward : ADVANCE

pro·ceed·ing *n* **1 :** PROCEDURE **2** *pl* : DOINGS **3** *pl* : legal action **4 :** TRANSACTION **5** *pl* : an official record of things said or done

pro·ceeds \'prō-ˌsēdz\ *n pl* : the total amount or the profit arising from a business deal : RETURN

1proc·ess \'präs-ˌes, 'prŏs-\ *n* **1 :** PROGRESS, ADVANCE **2 :** something going on : PROCEEDING **3 :** a natural phenomenon marked by gradual changes that lead toward a particular result ⟨the ∼ of growth⟩ **4 :** a series of actions or operations directed toward a particular result ⟨a manufacturing ∼⟩ **5 :** legal action **6 :** a mandate issued by a court; *esp* : SUMMONS **7 :** a projecting part of an organism or organic structure

2process *vb* **:** to subject to a special process or treatment

pro·ces·sion \prə-'sesh-ən\ *n* **:** a group of individuals moving along in an orderly often ceremonial way : PARADE

pro·ces·sion·al \-'sesh-(ə-)nəl\ *n* **1 :** a musical composition designed for a procession **2 :** a ceremonial procession

pro·claim \prō-'klām\ *vb* **:** to make known publicly : DECLARE, ANNOUNCE — **proc·la·ma·tion** \ˌpräk-lə-'māshən\ *n*

pro·cliv·i·ty \prō-'kliv-ət-ē\ *n* **:** an inherent inclination esp. toward something objectionable

pro·cras·ti·nate \prə-'kras-tə-ˌnāt\ *vb* [L *procrastinare*, fr. *pro-* forward + *crastinus* of tomorrow, fr. *cras* tomorrow] **:** to put off usu. habitually the doing of something that should be done **syn** dawdle, delay, loiter — **pro·cras·ti·na·tion** \-ˌkras-tə-'nā-shən\ *n*

pro·cre·ate \'prō-krē-ˌāt\ *vb* **:** to beget or bring forth offspring **syn** reproduce — **pro·cre·ation** \ˌprō-krē-'ā-shən\ *n* — **pro·cre·ative** \'prō-krē-ˌāt-iv\ *adj* — **pro·cre·ator** \-ˌāt-ər\ *n*

proc·tor \'präk-tər\ *n* **:** one appointed to supervise students (as at an examination) — **proctor** *vb* — **proc·to·ri·al** \präk-'tōr-ē-əl\ *adj*

proc·u·ra·tor \'präk-yə-ˌrāt-ər\ *n* **:** ADMINISTRATOR; *esp* : an official of ancient Rome administering a province

pro·cure \prə-'kyūr\ *vb* **1 :** to get possession of : OBTAIN **2 :** to make women available for promiscuous sexual intercourse **3 :** to bring about : ACHIEVE **syn** secure, acquire, gain, win, earn — **pro·cur·able** \-'kyūr-ə-bəl\ *adj* — **pro·cur·er** *n*

prod \'präd\ *vb* **prod·ded; prod·ding 1 :** to thrust a pointed instrument into : GOAD **2 :** INCITE, STIR — **prod** *n*

prod·i·gal \'präd-i-gəl\ *adj* **1 :** recklessly extravagant; *also* : LUXURIANT **2 :** WASTEFUL, LAVISH **syn** profuse — **prodigal** *n* — **prod·i·gal·i·ty** \ˌpräd-ə-'gal-ət-ē\ *n*

pro·di·gious \prə-'dij-əs\ *adj* **:** exciting wonder : EXTRAORDINARY in size or degree : ENORMOUS **syn** monstrous, tremendous, stupendous, monumental

prod·i·gy \'präd-ə-jē\ *n* **1 :** something extraordinary : WONDER **2 :** a highly talented child

1pro·duce \prə-'d(y)üs\ *vb* **1 :** to present to view : EXHIBIT **2 :** to give birth or rise to : YIELD **3 :** EXTEND,

PROLONG **4 :** to give being or form to : bring about : MAKE; *esp* : MANUFACTURE **5 :** to accrue or cause to accrue ⟨∼ a profit⟩ — **pro·duc·er** *n*

2prod·uce \'präd-ˌüs, 'prōd-\ *n* **:** PRODUCT **1**; *also* : agricultural products and esp. fresh fruits and vegetables

prod·uct \'präd-(ˌ)əkt\ *n* **1 :** something produced (as by labor, thought, or growth) **2 :** the number resulting from multiplication

pro·duc·tion \prə-'dək-shən\ *n* **1 :** something produced : PRODUCT **2 :** the act or process of producing — **pro·duc·tive** \-'dək-tiv\ *adj* — **pro·duc·tive·ness** *n* — **pro·duc·tiv·i·ty** \ˌ(ˌ)prō-ˌdək-'tiv-ət-ē, ˌpräd-(ˌ)ək-\ *n*

pro·em \'prō-ˌem\ *n* **1 :** preliminary comment : PREFACE **2 :** PRELUDE

1pro·fane \prō-'fān\ *vb* **1 :** to treat (something sacred) with irreverence or contempt : DESECRATE **2 :** to debase by an unworthy use — **prof·a·na·tion** \ˌpräf-ə-'nā-shən\ *n*

2profane *adj* **1 :** not concerned with religion : SECULAR **2 :** not holy because unconsecrated, impure, or defiled **3 :** serving to debase what is holy : IRREVERENT ⟨∼ language⟩ — **pro·fane·ly** *adv*

pro·fan·i·ty \prō-'fan-ət-ē\ *n* **1 :** the quality or state of being profane **2 :** the use of profane language

pro·fess \prə-'fes\ *vb* **1 :** to declare or admit openly : AFFIRM **2 :** to declare in words only : PRETEND **3 :** to confess one's faith in : PRACTICE **4 :** to practice or claim to be versed in (a calling or occupation) — **pro·fess·ed·ly** \-'fes-əd-lē\ *adv*

pro·fes·sion \prə-'fesh-ən\ *n* **1 :** an open declaration or avowal of a belief or opinion **2 :** a calling requiring specialized knowledge and often long academic preparation **3 :** the whole body of persons engaged in a calling

1pro·fes·sion·al \prə-'fesh-(ə-)nəl\ *adj* **1 :** of, relating to, or characteristic of a profession **2 :** engaged in one of the learned professions **3 :** participating for gain in an activity often engaged in by amateurs — **pro·fes·sion·al·ly** *adv*

2professional *n* **:** one that engages in an activity professionally

pro·fes·sion·al·ism *n* **1 :** the conduct, aims, or qualities that characterize or mark a profession or a professional person **2 :** the following of a profession (as athletics) for gain or livelihood

pro·fes·sion·al·ize *vb* **:** to give a professional character to

pro·fes·sor \prə-'fes-ər\ *n* **:** a teacher at a university or college; *also* : a faculty member of the highest academic rank at such an institution — **pro·fes·so·ri·al** \ˌprōf-ə-'sōr-ē-əl, ˌpräf-ə-\ *adj* — **pro·fes·sor·ship** \prə-'fes-ər-ˌship\ *n*

prof·fer \'präf-ər\ *vb* **:** to present for acceptance : OFFER, TENDER — **proffer** *n*

pro·fi·cient \prə-'fish-ənt\ *adj* **:** well advanced in an art, occupation, or branch of knowledge **syn** adept, skillful — **pro·fi·cien·cy** \-ən-sē\ *n* — **proficient** *n* — **pro·fi·cient·ly** *adv*

pro·file \'prō-ˌfīl\ *n* **1 :** a representation of something in outline; *esp* : a human head seen in a side view **2 :** a concise biographical sketch **syn** contour, silhouette

1prof·it \'präf-ət\ *n* **1 :** a valuable return : GAIN **2 :** the excess of the selling price of goods over their cost — **prof·it·less** \-ləs\ *adj*

²**profit** *vb* **1** : to be of use : BENEFIT **2** : to derive benefit : GAIN — **prof·it·able** \-ə-bəl\ *adj* — **prof·it·ably** *adv*

prof·i·teer \ˌpräf-ə-ˈtiər\ *n* : one who makes what is considered an unreasonable profit — **profiteer** *vb*

prof·li·gate \ˈpräf-li-gət, -lə-ˌgāt\ *adj* **1** : completely given up to dissipation and licentiousness **2** : wildly extravagant — **prof·li·ga·cy** \-li-gə-sē\ *n* — **profligate** *n* — **prof·li·gate·ly** *adv*

pro for·ma \prō-ˈför-mə\ *adj* : as a matter of form

pro·found \prə-ˈfaund\ *adj* **1** : marked by intellectual depth or insight ⟨a ~ thought⟩ **2** : coming from or reaching to a depth : DEEP-SEATED ⟨a ~ sigh⟩ **3** : deeply felt : INTENSE ⟨~ sympathy⟩ — **pro·found·ly** *adv* — **pro·fun·di·ty** \-ˈfən-dət-ē\ *n*

pro·fuse \prə-ˈfyüs\ *adj* : pouring forth liberally : ABUNDANT **syn** lavish, prodigal, luxuriant, exuberant — **pro·fuse·ly** *adv* — **pro·fu·sion** \-ˈfyü-zhən\ *n*

pro·gen·i·tor \prō-ˈjen-ət-ər\ *n* **1** : a direct ancestor : FOREFATHER **2** : ORIGINATOR, PRECURSOR

prog·e·ny \ˈpräj-ə-nē\ *n* : OFFSPRING, CHILDREN, DESCENDANTS

prog·na·thous \ˈpräg-nə-thəs\ *adj* : having the jaws projecting beyond the upper part of the face

prog·no·sis \präg-ˈnō-səs\ *n, pl* **-no·ses** \-ˌsēz\ : a forecast esp. of the course of a disease

prog·nos·tic \-ˈnäs-tik\ *n* **1** : PORTENT **2** : PROPHECY — **prognostic** *adj*

prog·nos·ti·cate \präg-ˈnäs-tə-ˌkāt\ *vb* : to foretell from signs or symptoms : PREDICT — **prog·nos·ti·ca·tion** \-ˌnäs-tə-ˈkā-shən\ *n* — **prog·nos·ti·ca·tor** \-ˈnäs-tə-ˌkāt-ər\ *n*

¹**pro·gram** *or* **pro·gramme** \ˈprō-ˌgram, -grəm\ *n* **1** : a brief outline of the order to be pursued at the subjects included (as in a public entertainment); *also* : PERFORMANCE **2** : a plan of procedure **3** : coded instructions for a computer

²**program** *vb* **-grammed** *or* **-gramed; -gram·ming** *or* **-gram·ing** **1** : to enter in a program **2** : to provide (an electronic computer) with a program

¹**prog·ress** \ˈpräg-rəs, -ˌres\ *n* **1** : a forward movement : ADVANCE **2** : a gradual betterment

²**pro·gress** \prə-ˈgres\ *vb* **1** : to move forward : PROCEED **2** : to develop to a move advanced stage : IMPROVE

pro·gres·sion \prə-ˈgresh-ən\ *n* **1** : an act of progressing : ADVANCE **2** : a continuous and connected series : SEQUENCE

¹**pro·gres·sive** \prə-ˈgres-iv\ *adj* **1** : of, relating to, or characterized by progress ⟨a ~ city⟩ **2** : advancing by stages ⟨~ worsening of a condition⟩ — **pro·gres·sive·ly** *adv*

²**progressive** *n* **1** : one that is progressive **2** *cap* : a member of a Progressive Party (as in the presidential campaigns of 1912, 1924, and 1948) in the U.S.

pro·hib·it \prō-ˈhib-ət\ *vb* **1** : to forbid by authority **2** : to prevent from doing something

pro·hi·bi·tion \ˌprō-ə-ˈbish-ən\ *n* **1** : the act of prohibiting **2** : the forbidding by

law of the sale or manufacture of alcoholic liquors as beverages — **pro·hi·bi·tion·ist** \-ˈbish-(ə-)nəst\ *n* — **pro·hib·i·tive** \prō-ˈhib-ət-iv\ *adj* — **pro·hib·i·to·ry** \prō-ˈhib-ə-ˌtōr-ē\ *adv*

¹**proj·ect** \ˈpräj-ˌekt, -ikt\ *n* **1** : a specific plan or design : SCHEME **2** : a planned undertaking ⟨a research ~⟩ ⟨housing ~s⟩

²**pro·ject** \prə-ˈjekt\ *vb* **1** : to devise in the mind : DESIGN **2** : to throw forward **3** : to cause to protrude **4** : to cause (light or shadow) to fall into space or (an image) upon a surface ⟨~ a beam of light⟩ ⟨~ motion pictures on a screen⟩ — **pro·jec·tion** \-ˈjek-shən\ *n*

pro·jec·tile \prə-ˈjek-t°l\ *n* **1** : a body hurled or projected by external force; *esp* : a missile for a firearm **2** : a self-propelling weapon

pro·jec·tion·ist \-ˈjek-sh(ə-)nəst\ *n* : one that makes projections; *esp* : one that operates a motion-picture projector or television equipment

pro·jec·tor \-ˈjek-tər\ *n* : one that projects; *esp* : a device for projecting pictures on a screen (a motion-picture ~)

pro·le·gom·e·non \ˌprō-li-ˈgäm-ə-ˌnän\ *n, pl* **-na** \-nə\ : prefatory remarks

pro·le·tar·i·an \ˌprō-lə-ˈter-ē-ən\ *n* : a member of the proletariat — **proletarian** *adj*

pro·le·tar·i·at \-ˈter-ē-ət\ *n* : the laboring class : wage earners

pro·lif·er·ate \prə-ˈlif-ə-ˌrāt\ *vb* : to grow or increase by rapid production of new units (as cells or offspring) — **pro·lif·er·a·tion** \-ˌlif-ə-ˈrā-shən\ *n*

pro·lif·ic \prə-ˈlif-ik\ *adj* **1** : producing young or fruit abundantly **2** : marked by abundant inventiveness or productivity ⟨a ~ writer⟩ — **pro·lif·i·cal·ly** *adv*

pro·lix \prō-ˈliks, ˈprō-ˌliks\ *adj* : marked by wordiness : VERBOSE **syn** wordy, diffuse, redundant — **pro·lix·i·ty** \prō-ˈlik-sət-ē\ *n*

pro·logue \ˈprō-ˌlóg\ *n* : PREFACE, INTRODUCTION ⟨~ of a play⟩

pro·long \prə-ˈlóŋ\ *vb* **1** : to lengthen in time : CONTINUE ⟨~ a meeting⟩ **2** : to lengthen in extent or range ⟨~ a line⟩ **syn** protract, extend, elongate — **pro·lon·ga·tion** \ˌprō-ˌlóŋ-ˈgā-shən\ *n*

prom \ˈpräm\ *n* : a formal dance given by a high school or college class

¹**prom·e·nade** \ˌpräm-ə-ˈnād, -ˈnäd\ *n* **1** : a leisurely walk for pleasure or display **2** : a place for strolling **3** : an opening grand march at a formal ball

²**promenade** *vb* **1** : to take a promenade **2** : to walk about, in, or on

pro·me·thi·um \prə-ˈmē-thē-əm\ *n* : a metallic chemical element obtained from uranium or neodymium

prom·i·nent \ˈpräm-ə-nənt\ *adj* **1** : jutting out : PROJECTING **2** : readily noticeable : CONSPICUOUS **3** : DISTINGUISHED, EMINENT **syn** remarkable, outstanding, striking — **prom·i·nence** \-nəns\ *n* — **prom·i·nent·ly** *adv*

pro·mis·cu·ous \prə-ˈmis-kyə-wəs\ *adj* **1** : consisting of various sorts and kinds : MIXED **2** : not restricted to one class or person; *esp* : not restricted to one sexual partner **syn** miscellaneous — **prom·is-**

cu·i·ty \,präm-is-'kyü-ət-ē, ,prō-,mis-\ *n* — **pro·mis·cu·ous·ly** \prə-'mis-kyə-wəs-lē\ *adv*

¹**prom·ise** \'präm-əs\ *n* **1** : a pledge to do or not to do something specified **2** : ground for expectation usu. of success or improvement **3** : something that is promised

²**promise** *vb* **1** : to engage to do, bring about, or provide ⟨~ help⟩ **2** : to suggest beforehand ⟨dark clouds ~ rain⟩ **3** : to give ground for expectation ⟨the book ~s to be good⟩

prom·is·ing *adj* : full of promise : AUSPICIOUS — **prom·is·ing·ly** *adv*

prom·is·so·ry \'präm-ə-,sōr-ē\ *adj*: containing a promise

prom·on·to·ry \'präm-ən-,tōr-ē\ *n* : a point of land jutting into the sea : HEADLAND

pro·mote \prə-'mōt\ *vb* **1** : to advance in station, rank, or honor **2** : to contribute to the growth or prosperity of : FURTHER **3** : LAUNCH — **pro·mo·tion** \-'mō-shən\ *n* — **pro·mo·tion·al** \-'mōsh-(ə-)nəl\ *adj*

pro·mot·er \prə-'mōt-ər\ *n* **1** : one that promotes; *esp* : one that takes the first steps in launching an enterprise **2** : one that assumes the financial responsibilities of a sports event

¹**prompt** \'prämpt\ *vb* **1** : INCITE **2** : to assist (one acting or reciting) by suggesting the next words **3** : INSPIRE, URGE — **prompt·er** *n*

²**prompt** *adj* **1** : being ready and quick to act; *also* : PUNCTUAL **2** : performed readily or immediately ⟨~ service⟩ — **prompt·ly** *adv* — **prompt·ness** *n*

prompt·book \-,buk\ *n* : a copy of a play with directions for performance used by a theater prompter

promp·ti·tude \'prämp-tə-,t(y)üd\ *n* : the quality or habit of being prompt : PROMPTNESS

prom·ul·gate \'präm-əl-,gāt, prō-'məl-\ *vb* : to make known by open declaration : PROCLAIM — **prom·ul·ga·tion** \,präm-əl-'gā-shən, prō-(,)məl-\ *n*

prone \'prōn\ *adj* **1** : having a tendency or inclination : DISPOSED **2** : lying face downwards; *also* : lying flat or prostrate **syn** subject, exposed, open, liable, susceptible — **prone·ness** *n*

prong \'prȯŋ\ *n* : one of the sharp points of a fork : TINE; *also* : a slender projecting part (as of an antler or a tooth)

pro·noun \'prō-,naun\ *n* : a word used as a substitute for a noun

pro·nounce \prə-'naùns\ *vb* **1** : to utter officially or as an opinion ⟨~ sentence⟩ ⟨~ the book a success⟩ **2** : to employ the organs of speech in order to produce ⟨~ a word⟩; *esp* : to say or speak correctly ⟨she can't ~ his name⟩ — **pro·nounce·able** *adj* — **pro·nun·ci·a·tion** \-,nən-sē-'ā-shən\ *n*

pro·nounced *adj* : strongly marked : DECIDED

pro·nounce·ment \prə-'naùns-mənt\ *n* **1** : a formal declaration of opinion; *also* : ANNOUNCEMENT

pron·to \'prän-,tō\ *adv* : QUICKLY, PROMPTLY

pro·nun·ci·a·men·to \prō-,nən-sē-ə-'ment-ō\ *n, pl* **-tos** *or* **-toes** : PROCLAMATION, MANIFESTO

¹**proof** \'prüf\ *n* **1** : the evidence that compels acceptance by the mind of a truth or fact **2** : a process or operation

that establishes validity or truth : TEST **3** : a trial print from a photographic negative **4** : a trial impression (as from type) **5** : alcoholic content (as of a beverage) indicated by a number that is about twice the percent by volume of alcohol present ⟨whiskey of 90 ~ is about 45% alcohol⟩

²**proof** *adj* **1** : successful in resisting or repelling ⟨~ against tampering⟩ **2** : of standard strength or quality or alcoholic content

proof·read \-,rēd\ *vb* : to read and mark corrections in (printer's proof) — **proof·read·er** *n*

¹**prop** \'präp\ *n* : something that props : SUPPORT

²**prop** *vb* **prop·ped; prop·ping 1** : to support by placing something under or against ⟨~ up a wall⟩ **2** : SUSTAIN, STRENGTHEN

³**prop** *n* : PROPERTY 4

⁴**prop** *n* : PROPELLER

prop·a·gan·da \,präp-ə-'gan-də, ,prō-pə-\ *n* : the spreading of ideas or information deliberately to further one's cause or damage an opposing cause; *also* : ideas, facts, or allegations spread for such a purpose — **prop·a·gan·dist** \-dəst\ *n*

prop·a·gan·dize \-,dīz\ *vb* : to subject to or carry on propaganda

prop·a·gate \'präp-ə-,gāt\ *vb* **1** : to reproduce or cause to reproduce biologically : MULTIPLY **2** : to cause to spread — **prop·a·ga·tion** \,präp-ə-'gā-shən\ *n*

pro·pane \'prō-,pān\ *n* : a heavy flammable gas found in petroleum and natural gas and used as a fuel

pro·pel \prə-'pel\ *vb* **-pelled; -pel·ling 1** : to drive forward or onward **2** : to urge on : MOTIVATE **syn** push, shove, thrust

pro·pel·lant *also* **pro·pel·lent** \-'pel-ənt\ *n* : something (as an explosive or fuel) that propels — **propellant** *or* **propellent** *adj*

pro·pel·ler \prə-'pel-ər\ *n* : a device consisting of a hub fitted with revolving blades that imparts motion to a vehicle (as a motorboat or an airplane)

pro·pen·si·ty \prə-'pen-sət-ē\ *n* : a particular disposition of mind or character : BENT

prop·er \'präp-ər\ *adj* **1** : marked by suitability or rightness ⟨~ punishment⟩ **2** : referring to one individual only ⟨~ noun⟩ **3** : belonging characteristically to a species or individual : PECULIAR **4** : very satisfactory : EXCELLENT **5** : strictly limited to a specified thing ⟨the city ~⟩ **6** : CORRECT ⟨the ~ way to proceed⟩ **7** : strictly decorous : GENTEEL **syn** meet, appropriate, fitting, seemly — **prop·er·ly** *adv*

prop·er·tied \'präp-ərt-ēd\ *adj* : owning property and esp. much property

prop·er·ty \'präp-ərt-ē\ *n* **1** : a quality peculiar to an individual or thing **2** : something owned; *esp* : a piece of real estate **3** : OWNERSHIP **4** : an article or object used in a play other than painted scenery and actors' costumes

proph·e·cy \'präf-ə-sē\ *n* **1** : an inspired utterance of a prophet **2** : PREDICTION

proph·e·sy \-,sī\ *vb* **1** : to speak or utter by divine inspiration **2** : PREDICT — **proph·e·si·er** \-,sī-(ə)r\ *n*

proph·et \'präf-ət\ n [L *propheta*, fr. Gk *prophētēs*, fr. *pro-* for, forth + *phanai* to speak] **1** : one who utters divinely inspired revelations — **proph·et·ess** \-əs\ n **2** : one who foretells future events — **proph·et·ess** \-əs\ n

pro·phet·ic \prə-'fet-ik\ adj : of, relating to, or characteristic of a prophet or prophecy — **pro·phet·i·cal** adj — **pro·phet·i·cal·ly** adv

1pro·phy·lac·tic \‚prō-fə-'lak-tik, ‚präf-ə-\ adj **1** : preventing or guarding from disease **2** : PROTECTIVE, PREVENTIVE

2prophylactic n : something (as a drug or device) that protects from disease

pro·pin·qui·ty \prō-'piŋ-kwət-ē\ n **1** : KINSHIP **2** : nearness in place or time : PROXIMITY

pro·pi·ti·ate \prō-'pish-ē-‚āt\ vb : to make favorable : APPEASE, CONCILIATE — **pro·pi·ti·a·tion** \-‚pis(h)-ē-'ā-shən\ n — **pro·pi·tia·to·ry** \-'pish-(ē-)ə-‚tōr-ē\ adj

pro·pi·tious \prə-'pish-əs\ adj **1** : favorably disposed ‹~ deities› **2** : being of good omen : FAVORABLE ‹~ circumstances›

prop·jet engine \‚präp-‚jet-\ n : TURBO-PROPELLER ENGINE

prop·man \'präp-‚man\ n : one who is in charge of theater or motion-picture stage properties

pro·po·nent \prə-'pō-nənt\ n : one who argues in favor of something : ADVOCATE

1pro·por·tion \prə-'pōr-shən\ n **1** : the relation of one part to another or to the whole with respect to magnitude, quantity, or degree : RATIO **2** : BALANCE, SYMMETRY **3** : SHARE, QUOTA **4** : SIZE, DEGREE — **pro·por·tion·al** \-sh(ə-)nəl\ adj — **pro·por·tion·ate** \-sh(ə-)nət\ adj — **pro·por·tion·ate·ly** adv

2proportion vb **1** : to adjust (a part or thing) in size relative to other parts or things **2** : to make the parts of harmonious

pro·pose \prə-'pōz\ vb **1** : PLAN, INTEND ‹*proposes* to buy a house› **2** : to make an offer of marriage **3** : to offer for consideration : SUGGEST ‹~ a policy› — **pro·pos·al** \-'pō-zəl\ n — **pro·pos·er** n

prop·o·si·tion \‚präp-ə-'zish-ən\ n **1** : something proposed for consideration : PROPOSAL **2** : a statement of something to be discussed, proved, or explained **3** : SITUATION, AFFAIR ‹a tough ~›

pro·pound \prə-'paůnd\ vb : to set forth for consideration or debate ‹~ a doctrine›

pro·pri·e·tary \prə-'prī-ə-‚ter-ē\ adj **1** : of, relating to, or characteristic of a proprietor ‹~ control› **2** : made and sold by one with the sole right to do so ‹~ medicines›

pro·pri·e·tor \prə-'prī-ət-ər\ n : OWNER — **pro·pri·e·tor·ship** \-‚ship\ n — **pro·pri·e·tress** \-'prī-ə-trəs\ n

pro·pri·e·ty \prə-'prī-ət-ē\ n **1** : the standard of what is socially acceptable in conduct or speech **2** pl : the customs of polite society

pro·pul·sion \prə-'pəl-shən\ n **1** : the action or process of propelling : a driving forward **2** : driving power — **pro·pul·sive** \-'pəl-siv\ adj

pro ra·ta \prō-'rāt-ə, -'rät-\ adv : in proportion : PROPORTIONATELY

pro·rate \'prō-'rāt\ vb : to divide, distribute, or assess proportionally

pro·rogue \prə-'rōg\ vb : to suspend or end a session of (a legislative body) syn adjourn, dissolve

pro·sa·ic \prō-'zā-ik\ adj : lacking imagination or excitement : DULL, COMMONPLACE

pro·sce·ni·um \prō-'sē-nē-əm\ n : the wall that separates the stage from the auditorium and provides the arch that frames it

pro·scribe \prō-'skrīb\ vb **1** : OUTLAW **2** : to condemn or forbid as harmful : PROHIBIT — **pro·scrip·tion** \-'skrip-shən\ n

prose \'prōz\ n : the ordinary language of men in speaking or writing

pros·e·cute \'präs-i-‚kyüt\ vb **1** : to follow to the end ‹~ an investigation› **2** : to pursue before a legal tribunal for punishment of (a violation of law ‹~ a forger› — **pros·e·cu·tion** \‚präs-i-'kyü-shən\ n — **pros·e·cu·tor** \'präs-i-‚kyüt-ər\ n

1pros·e·lyte \'präs-ə-‚līt\ n : a person newly converted esp. to a religion or party — **pros·e·lyt·ism** \-‚līt-‚iz-əm\ n

2proselyte vb : to convert from one religion, belief, or party to another

pros·o·dy \'präs-əd-ē\ n : the study of versification and esp. of metrical structure

1pros·pect \'präs-‚pekt\ n **1** : an extensive view; also : OUTLOOK **2** : the act of looking forward : ANTICIPATION **3** : a mental vision of something to come **4** : something that is awaited or expected : POSSIBILITY **5** : a potential buyer or customer; also : a likely candidate — **pro·spec·tive** \prə-'spek-tiv, 'präs-‚pek-\ adj — **pro·spec·tive·ly** adv

2prospect vb : to explore esp. for mineral deposits — **pros·pec·tor** \'präs-‚pek-tər\ n

pro·spec·tus \prə-'spek-təs\ n : a preliminary printed statement that describes an enterprise and is distributed to prospective buyers or participants

pros·per \'präs-pər\ vb : SUCCEED, THRIVE; esp : to achieve economic success

pros·per·i·ty \präs-'per-ət-ē\ n **1** : thriving condition : SUCCESS; esp : economic well-being

pros·per·ous \'präs-p(ə-)rəs\ adj **1** : FAVORABLE ‹~ winds› **2** : marked by success or economic well-being ‹a ~ business›

pros·tate \'präs-‚tāt\ n : a glandular body about the base of the male urethra — **prostate** adj

pros·the·sis \präs-'thē-səs, 'präs-thə-\ n, pl -ses \-‚sēz\ : an artificial device to replace a missing part of the body — **pros·thet·ic** \präs-'thet-ik\ adj

1pros·ti·tute \'präs-tə-‚t(y)üt\ vb **1** : to offer indiscriminately for sexual intercourse esp. for money **2** : to devote to corrupt or unworthy purposes — **pros·ti·tu·tion** \‚präs-tə-'t(y)ü-shən\ n

2prostitute n : a woman who engages in promiscuous sexual intercourse esp. for pay

1pros·trate \'präs-‚trāt\ adj **1** : stretched

pros·trate out with face on the ground in adoration or submission **2** : extended in a horizontal position : FLAT ⟨a ~ shrub⟩ **3** : laid low ⟨OVERCOME ~ with a cold⟩

²**prostrate** *vb* **1** : to throw or put into a prostrate position **2** : to reduce to submission, helplessness, or exhaustion — **pros·tra·tion** \präs-'trā-shən\ *n*

prosy \'prō-zē\ *adj* **1** : PROSAIC **2** : TEDIOUS

pro·tag·o·nist \prō-'tag-ə-nəst\ *n* **1** : one who takes the leading part in a drama or story **2** : a spokesman for a cause : CHAMPION

pro·tect \prə-'tekt\ *vb* : to shield from injury : GUARD

pro·tec·tion \prə-'tek-shən\ *n* **1** : the act of protecting : the state of being protected **2** : one that protects ⟨wear a helmet as a ~⟩ **3** : the oversight or support of one that is smaller and weaker **4** : the freeing of the producers of a country from foreign competition in their home market by high duties on foreign competitive goods — **pro·tec·tive** \-'tek-tiv\ *adj*

pro·tec·tion·ist *n* : an advocate of government economic protection for domestic producers through restrictions on foreign competitors — **pro·tec·tion·ism** *n*

pro·tec·tor \prə-'tek-tər\ *n* **1** : one that protects : GUARDIAN **2** : a device used to prevent injury : GUARD **3** : REGENT — **pro·tec·tress** \-trəs\ *n*

pro·tec·tor·ate \-t(ə-)rət\ *n* **1** : government by a protector **2** : the relationship of superior authority assumed by one power over a dependent one; *also* : the dependent political unit in such a relationship

pro·té·gé \'prōt-ə-,zhā\ *n* : one who is under the care and protection of an influential person — **pro·té·gée** \-,zhā\ *n*

pro·tein \'prō-,tēn, 'prōt-ē-ən\ *n* : any of a great class of chemicals that contain carbon, hydrogen, nitrogen, oxygen, and sometimes other elements, are present in all living matter, and are an essential food item

pro tem \prō-'tem\ *adv* : for the time being

pro tem·po·re \prō-'tem-pə-rē\ *adv* : for the present : TEMPORARILY

¹**pro·test** \'prō-,test\ *n* **1** : the act of protesting **2** : a complaint or objection against an idea, an act, or a course of action

²**pro·test** \prə-'test\ *vb* **1** : to assert positively : make solemn declaration of ⟨~s his innocence⟩ **2** : to object strongly : make a protest against ⟨~ a ruling⟩ — **prot·es·ta·tion** \,prät-əs-'tā-shən\ *n*

Prot·es·tant \'prät-əs-tənt, *3 also* prə-'tes-\ *n* **1** : a member or adherent of one of the Christian churches deriving from the Reformation **2** : a Christian not of a Catholic or Orthodox church **3** *not cap* : one who makes a protest — **Prot·es·tant·ism** \-,iz-əm\ *n*

pro·tha·la·mi·on \,prō-thə-'lā-mē-ən\ *or* **pro·tha·la·mi·um** \-mē-əm\ *n, pl* **-mia** \-mē-ə\ : a song in celebration of a marriage

pro·to·col \'prōt-ə-,kȯl\ *n* **1** : an original draft or record **2** : a preliminary memorandum of diplomatic negotiation **3** : a code of diplomatic or military etiquette and precedence

pro·to·mar·tyr \'prōt-ō-,märt-ər\ *n* : the first martyr in a cause or region

pro·ton \'prō-,tän\ *n* [Gk *prōton*, neut. of *prōtos* first] : an elementary particle that is present in all atomic nuclei and carries a positive charge of electricity

pro·to·plasm \'prōt-ə-,plaz-əm\ *n* : the complex colloidal largely protein living substance of plant and animal cells — **pro·to·plas·mic** \,prōt-ə-'plaz-mik\ *adj*

pro·to·type \'prōt-ə-,tīp\ *n* : an original model : ARCHETYPE

pro·to·zo·an \,prōt-ə-'zō-ən\ *n* : any of a great group of lowly animals that are essentially single cells

pro·tract \prō-'trakt\ *vb* : to prolong in time or space *syn* extend, lengthen

pro·trac·tor \-'trak-tər\ *n* : an instrument for constructing and measuring angles

pro·trude \prō-'trüd\ *vb* : to stick out or cause to stick out : jut out — **pro·tru·sion** \-'trü-zhən\ *n*

pro·tu·ber·ance \prō-'t(y)ü-b(ə-)rəns\ *n* : something that is protuberant : BULGE, SWELLING

pro·tu·ber·ant \-b(ə-)rənt\ *adj* : extending beyond the surrounding surface in a bulge

proud \'praud\ *adj* **1** : having or showing excessive self-esteem : HAUGHTY **2** : highly pleased : EXULTANT **3** : having proper self-respect ⟨too ~ to beg⟩ **4** : GLORIOUS ⟨a ~ occasion⟩ **5** : SPIRITED ⟨a ~ steed⟩ *syn* arrogant, insolent, overbearing, disdainful — **proud·ly** *adv*

prove \'prüv\ *vb* **proved; proved** *or* **prov·en** \'prü-vən\ **prov·ing 1** : to test by experiment or by a standard **2** : to establish the truth of by argument or evidence **3** : to show to be correct, valid, or genuine — **prov·able** \'prü-və-bəl\ *adj*

prov·e·nance \'präv-ə-nəns\ *n* : ORIGIN, SOURCE

Pro·ven·çal \,präv-ən-'säl\ *n* : a native or inhabitant of Provence — **Provençal** *adj*

prov·en·der \'präv-ən-dər\ *n* **1** : dry food for domestic animals : FEED **2** : FOOD, VICTUALS

pro·ve·nience \prə-'vē-nyəns\ *n* : ORIGIN, SOURCE

prov·erb \'präv-,ərb\ *n* : a pithy popular saying : ADAGE — **prov·er·bi·al** \prə-'vər-bē-əl\ *adj*

pro·vide \prə-'vīd\ *vb* **1** : to take measures beforehand ⟨~ against inflation⟩ **2** : to make a proviso or stipulation **3** : to supply what is needed ⟨~ for a family⟩ **4** : EQUIP **5** : to supply for use : YIELD — **pro·vid·er** *n*

prov·i·dence \'präv-əd-əns\ *n* **1** *often cap* : divine guidance or care **2** *cap* : ²GOD **3** : the quality or state of being provident

prov·i·dent \-əd-ənt\ *adj* **1** : making provision for the future : PRUDENT **2** : FRUGAL, SAVING — **prov·i·dent·ly** *adv*

prov·i·den·tial \,präv-ə-'den-chəl\ *adj* **1** : of, relating to, or determined by Providence **2** : OPPORTUNE, LUCKY

prov·ince \'präv-əns\ *n* **1** : an administrative district or division of a country **2** *pl* : all of a country except the metropolis **3** : proper business or scope : SPHERE

pro·vin·cial \prə-'vin-chəl\ adj 1 : of or relating to a province 2 : confined to a region : NARROW ⟨~ ideas⟩ — pro·vin·cial·ism \-,iz-əm\ n

¹pro·vi·sion \prə-'vizh-ən\ n 1 : the act or process of providing; also : a measure taken beforehand 2 : a stock of needed supplies; esp : a stock of food — usu. used in pl. 3 : PROVISO, STIPULATION

²provision vb : to supply with provisions

pro·vi·sion·al \-'vizh-(ə-)nəl\ adj : provided for a temporary need : CONDITIONAL

pro·vi·so \prə-'vī-zō\ n, pl -sos or -soes : an article or clause that introduces a condition : STIPULATION

pro·voke \prə-'vōk\ vb 1 : to incite to anger : INCENSE 2 : to bring on : EVOKE ⟨a sally that provoked laughter⟩ 3 : to stir up on purpose ⟨~ an argument⟩ syn irritate, exasperate, excite, stimulate, pique — prov·o·ca·tion \,präv-ə-'kā-shən\ n — pro·voc·a·tive \prə-'väk-ət-iv\ adj

pro·vost \'prō-,vōst, 'präv-əst\ n : a high official : DIGNITARY; esp : a high-ranking university administrative officer

pro·vost mar·shal \,prō-,vō-'mär-shəl\ n : an officer who supervises the military police of a command

prow \'prau\ n : the bow of a ship

prow·ess \'prau-əs\ n 1 : military valor and skill 2 : extraordinary ability

prowl \'praul\ vb : to roam about stealthily — prowl n — prowl·er n

prox·i·mate \'präk-sə-mət\ adj 1 : very near 2 : DIRECT ⟨the ~ cause⟩

prox·im·i·ty \präk-'sim-ət-ē\ n : NEARNESS

prox·i·mo \'präk-sə-,mō\ adj : of or occurring in the next month after the present

proxy \'präk-sē\ n : the authority or power to act for another; also : a document giving such authorization

prude \'prüd\ n : one who shows or affects extreme modesty — prud·ery \'prüd-ə-rē\ n — prud·ish \'prüd-ish\ adj

pru·dent \'prüd-ənt\ adj 1 : shrewd in the management of practical affairs 2 : CAUTIOUS, DISCREET 3 : PROVIDENT, FRUGAL syn judicious, foresighted, sensible, sane — pru·dence \-ə⁰ns\ n — pru·den·tial \prü-'den-chəl\ adj — pru·dent·ly \'prüd-ənt-lē\ adv

¹prune \'prün\ n : a plum dried or capable of being dried without fermentation

²prune vb : to cut off unwanted parts (as of a tree) : remove as superfluous : TRIM

pru·ri·ent \'prur-ē-ənt\ adj : LASCIVIOUS; also : exciting to lasciviousness — pru·ri·ence \-ē- əns\ n

¹pry \'prī\ vb : to look closely or inquisitively; esp : SNOOP

²pry vb 1 : to raise, move, or pull apart with a pry or lever 2 : to detach or open with difficulty

³pry n : a tool for prying

psalm \'säm\ n, often cap : a sacred song or poem; esp : one of the hymns collected in the Book of Psalms — psalm·ist \-əst\ n

psalm·o·dy \'-əd-ē\ n : the singing of psalms in worship; also : a collection of psalms

Psal·ter \'sol-tər\ n : the Book of Psalms; also : a collection of the Psalms arranged for devotional use

pseu·do \'süd-ō\ adj : SPURIOUS, SHAM ⟨a ~ intellectual⟩

pseud·onym \'süd-ⁿn-,im\ n : a fictitious name

psy·che \'sī-kē\ n : SOUL, SELF; also : MIND

psy·chi·a·try \sə-'kī-ə-trē, sī-\ n : a branch of medicine dealing with mental disorders — psy·chi·at·ric \,sī-kē-'at-rik\ adj — psy·chi·a·trist \sə-'kī-ə-trəst, sī-\ n

psy·chic \'sī-kik\ adj 1 : of or relating to the psyche 2 : lying outside the sphere of physical science 3 : sensitive to nonphysical or supernatural forces — psy·chi·cal adj — psy·chi·cal·ly adv

psy·cho·anal·y·sis \,sī-kō-ə-'nal-ə-səs\ n : a method of dealing with psychic disorders by study of the normally hidden content of the mind esp. to resolve conflicts — psy·cho·an·a·lyst \-'an-ⁿl-əst\ n — psy·cho·an·a·lyt·ic \-,an-ⁿl-'it-ik\ adj — psy·cho·an·a·lyze \-'an-ⁿl-,īz\ vb

psy·chol·o·gy \sī-'käl-ə-jē\ n 1 : the science of mind and behavior 2 : the mental and behavioral aspect (as of an individual) — psy·cho·log·i·cal \,sī-kə-'läj-i-kəl\ adj — psy·cho·log·i·cal·ly adv — psy·chol·o·gist \sī-'käl-ə-jəst\ n

psy·cho·path \'sī-kə-,path\ n : a person seriously defective in mental stability and social adjustment — psy·cho·path·ic \,sī-kə-'path-ik\ adj

psy·cho·so·mat·ic \,sī-kə-sə-'mat-ik\ adj : of, relating to, or caused by the interaction of mental and bodily phenomena ⟨~ ulcers⟩

pto·maine \'tō-,mān\ n : a chemical substance formed by bacteria in decaying matter (as meat)

ptomaine poisoning n : a disorder of the stomach and intestines caused by food contaminated usu. with bacteria or their products

pub \'pəb\ n, chiefly Brit : PUBLIC HOUSE, TAVERN

pu·ber·ty \'pyü-bərt-ē\ n : the condition of being or period of becoming capable of reproducing sexually — pu·ber·tal \-bərt-ⁿl\ adj

¹pub·lic \'pəb-lik\ adj 1 : of, relating to, or affecting the people as a whole ⟨~ opinion⟩ 2 : CIVIC, GOVERNMENTAL ⟨~ expenditures⟩ 3 : not private : SOCIAL ⟨~ morality⟩ 4 : of, relating to, or serving the community ⟨~ officials⟩ 5 : open to all ⟨~ library⟩ 6 : exposed to general view : not kept secret ⟨the story became ~⟩ 7 : well known : PROMINENT ⟨~ figures⟩ — pub·lic·ly adv

²public n 1 : the people as a whole : POPULACE 2 : a group of people having common interests ⟨wrote for his ~⟩

pub·li·can \'pəb-li-kən\ n 1 : a Jewish tax collector for the ancient Romans 2 chiefly Brit : the licensee of a public house

---

ə abut; ᵊ kitten; ər further; a back; ā bake; ä cot, cart; au̇ out; ch chin; e less; ē easy; g gift; i trip; ī life; j joke; ŋ sing; ō flow; ȯ flaw; ȯi coin; th thin; t͟h this; ü loot; u̇ foot; y yet; yü few; yu̇ furious; zh vision

pub·li·ca·tion \ˌpəb-lə-ˈkā-shən\ n 1 : the act or process of publishing 2 : a published work

public house n 1 : INN 2 chiefly Brit : a licensed saloon or bar

pub·li·cist \ˈpəb-lə-səst\ n : one that publicizes; esp : PRESS AGENT

pub·lic·i·ty \(ˌ)pə-ˈblis-ət-ē\ n 1 : information with news value issued to gain public attention or support 2 : public attention or acclaim

pub·li·cize \ˈpəb-lə-ˌsīz\ vb : to give publicity to : ADVERTISE

public school n 1 : an endowed secondary boarding school in Great Britain offering a classical curriculum and preparation for the universities or public service 2 : a free tax-supported school controlled by a local governmental authority

pub·lic–spir·it·ed \ˌpəb-lik-ˈspir-ət-əd\ adj : motivated by devotion to the general or national welfare

pub·lish \ˈpəb-lish\ vb 1 : to make generally known : announce publicly 2 : to produce or release for sale to the public — **pub·lish·er** n

¹**puck** \ˈpək\ n : a mischievous sprite — **puck·ish** adj

²**puck** n : a disk used in ice hockey

¹**puck·er** \ˈpək-ər\ vb : to contract into folds or wrinkles

²**pucker** n : FOLD, WRINKLE

pud·ding \ˈpu̇d-iŋ\ n : a dessert of a soft, spongy, or thick creamy consistency

pud·dle \ˈpəd-ᵊl\ n : a very small pool of usu. dirty or muddy water

pud·dling \ˈpəd-ᵊliŋ\ n : the process of converting pig iron into wrought iron by subjecting it to heat and stirring in the presence of oxidizing substances

pudgy \ˈpəj-ē\ adj : being short and plump : CHUBBY

pueb·lo \ˈpü-ˈeb-lō\ n : an Indian village of Arizona or New Mexico consisting of flat-roofed stone or adobe houses

pu·er·ile \ˈpyü-ə-rəl\ adj : CHILDISH, SILLY — **pu·er·il·i·ty** \ˌpyü-ə-ˈril-ət-ē\ n

Puer·to Ri·can \ˌpwert-ə-ˈrē-kən, ˌpȯrt-\ n : a native or inhabitant of Puerto Rico — **Puerto Rican** adj

¹**puff** \ˈpəf\ vb 1 : to blow in short gusts 2 : PANT 3 : to emit small whiffs or clouds 4 : BLUSTER, BRAG 5 : INFLATE, SWELL 6 : to make proud or conceited 7 : to praise extravagantly

²**puff** n 1 : a short discharge (as of air or smoke); also : a slight explosive sound accompanying it 2 : a light fluffy pastry 3 : a slight swelling 4 : a fluffy mass; esp : a small pad for applying cosmetic powder 5 : a laudatory notice or review — **puffy** adj

pug \ˈpəg\ n 1 : a small stocky short-haired dog 2 : a short nose turned up at the tip 3 : a tight wad of hair

pu·gi·lism \ˈpyü-jə-ˌliz-əm\ n : BOXING — **pu·gi·list** \-ləst\ n — **pu·gi·lis·tic** \ˌpyü-jə-ˈlis-tik\ adj

pug·na·cious \ˌpəg-ˈnā-shəs\ adj : fond of fighting : COMBATIVE syn belligerent, quarrelsome — **pug·nac·i·ty** \-ˈnas-ət-ē\ n

puis·sance \ˈpwis-ᵊns, ˈpyü-ə-səns\ n : POWER, STRENGTH — **puis·sant** adj

puke \ˈpyük\ vb : VOMIT

puk·ka \ˈpək-ə\ adj : GENUINE, AUTHENTIC; also : FIRST-CLASS, COMPLETE

pul \ˈpül\ n — see MONEY table

pul·chri·tude \ˈpəl-krə-ˌt(y)üd\ n : BEAUTY

pule \ˈpyül\ vb : WHINE, WHIMPER ⟨a puling infant⟩

¹**pull** \ˈpu̇l\ vb 1 : PLUCK; also : EXTRACT ⟨~ a tooth⟩ 2 : to exert force so as to draw (something) toward the force; also : MOVE ⟨~ out of a driveway⟩ 3 : STRETCH, STRAIN ⟨~ a tendon⟩ 4 : to draw apart : TEAR 5 : to make (as a proof) by printing 6 : REMOVE 7 : DRAW ⟨~ a gun⟩ 8 : to carry out esp. with daring ⟨~ a robbery⟩ 9 : to be guilty of : PERPETRATE 10 : ATTRACT 11 : to express strong sympathy — **pull·er** n

²**pull** n 1 : the act or an instance of pulling 2 : the effort expended in moving ⟨a long ~ uphill⟩ 3 : ADVANTAGE; esp : special influence 4 : a device for pulling something or for operating by pulling 5 : a force ,that attracts or compels

pul·let \ˈpu̇l-ət\ n : a young hen

pul·ley \ˈpu̇l-ē\ n 1 : a wheel with a grooved rim that forms part of a tackle for hoisting or for changing the direction of a force 2 : a wheel used to transmit power by means of a band, belt, rope, or chain

Pull·man \ˈpu̇l-mən\ n : a railroad passenger car with specially comfortable furnishings; esp : one with berths

pull·over \ˈpu̇l-ˌō-vər\ adj : put on by being pulled over the head ⟨~ sweater⟩

pul·mo·nary \ˈpu̇l-mə-ˌner-ē, ˈpəl-\ adj : of or relating to the lungs

pul·mo·tor \-ˌmōt-ər\ n : an apparatus for pumping oxygen or air into and out of the lungs (as of an asphyxiated person)

pulp \ˈpəlp\ n 1 : the soft juicy or fleshy part of a fruit or vegetable 2 : a soft moist mass 3 : a material (as from wood or rags) used in making paper 4 : a magazine using rough-surfaced paper and often dealing with sensational material — **pulpy** adj

pul·pit \ˈpu̇l-ˌpit\ n : a raised platform or high reading desk used in preaching or conducting a worship service

pulp·wood \ˈpəlp-ˌwu̇d\ n : wood suitable for paper pulp

pul·sate \ˈpəl-ˌsāt\ vb : to expand and contract rhythmically : BEAT — **pul·sa·tion** \ˌpəl-ˈsā-shən\ n

pulse \ˈpəls\ n 1 : the regular throbbing in the arteries caused by the contractions of the heart 2 : a brief change in electrical current or voltage — **pulse** vb

pul·ver·ize \ˈpəl-və-ˌrīz\ vb 1 : to reduce (as by crushing or grinding) or be reduced to very small particles 2 : DEMOLISH

pu·ma \ˈp(y)ü-mə\ n : COUGAR

pum·ice \ˈpəm-əs\ n : a light porous volcanic glass used in polishing and erasing

pum·mel \ˈpəm-əl\ vb -meled or -melled; -mel·ing or -mel·ling : POUND, BEAT

¹**pump** \ˈpəmp\ n : a device for raising, transferring, or compressing fluids or gases esp. by suction or pressure

²**pump** vb 1 : to raise (as water) with a pump 2 : to draw water or air from by means of a pump; also : to fill by means of a pump ⟨~ up a tire⟩ 3 : to force or propel in the manner of a pump

pum·per·nick·el \ˈpəm-pər-ˌnik-əl\ n

: a dark coarse somewhat sour rye bread

pump·kin \'pəŋ-kən, 'pəm(p)-\ *n* : the large yellow fruit of a vine related to the gourd grown for food; *also* : this vine

pun \'pən\ *n* : the humorous use of a word in a way that suggests two interpretations — **pun** *vb*

¹**punch** \'pənch\ *vb* **1** : PROD, POKE; *also* : to drive or herd (cattle) **2** : to strike with the fist **3** : to make a hole through or to cut or make with a punch — **punch·er** *n*

²**punch** *n* **1** : a quick blow with or as if with the fist **2** : energy that commands attention : EFFECTIVENESS

³**punch** *n* : a tool for piercing, stamping, cutting, or forming

⁴**punch** *n* [perh. fr. Hindi *pāc* five, fr. Skt *pañca*; fr. the number of ingredients] : a beverage usu. composed of wine or alcoholic liquor, citrus juice, spices, tea, and water; *also* : a beverage composed of nonalcoholic liquids (as fruit juices)

pun·cheon \'pən-chən\ *n* : a large cask

punc·til·io \ˌpəŋk-'til-ē-ˌō\ *n* **1** : a nice detail of conduct in a ceremony or in observance of a code **2** : careful observance of forms (as in social conduct)

punc·til·i·ous \ˌpəŋk-'til-ē-əs\ *adj* : marked by precise accordance with the details of codes or conventions **syn** meticulous, scrupulous, careful, punctual

punc·tu·al \'pəŋk-chə-(wə)l\ *adj* : acting or habitually acting at an appointed time : not late : PROMPT — **punc·tu·al·i·ty** \ˌpəŋk-chə-'wal-ət-ē\ *n* — **punc·tu·al·ly** \'pəŋk-chə-(wə)-lē\ *adv*

punc·tu·ate \'pəŋk-chə-ˌwāt\ *vb* **1** : to mark or divide (written matter) with punctuation marks **2** : to break into at intervals **3** : EMPHASIZE

punc·tu·a·tion \ˌpəŋk-chə-'wā-shən\ *n* : the act, practice, or system of inserting standardized marks in written matter to clarify the meaning and separate structural units

¹**punc·ture** \'pəŋk-chər\ *n* **1** : an act of puncturing **2** : a small hole made by puncturing

²**puncture** *vb* **1** : to make a hole in : PIERCE **2** : to make useless as if by a puncture

pun·dit \'pən-dət\ *n* **1** : a learned man : TEACHER **2** : AUTHORITY

pun·gent \'pən-jənt\ *adj* **1** : sharply stimulating : POINTED, BITING (a ~ editorial) **2** : causing a sharp or irritating sensation; *esp* : ACRID (~ smell of burning leaves) — **pun·gen·cy** \-jən-sē\ *n* — **pun·gent·ly** *adv*

pun·ish \'pən-ish\ *vb* **1** : to impose a penalty upon for a fault or crime (~ an offender) **2** : to inflict a penalty for (~ treason with death) **3** : to inflict injury upon : HURT (~ed his man with body blows) **syn** chastise, castigate, chasten, discipline, correct — **pun·ish·able** \-ə-bəl\ *adj*

pun·ish·ment \-mənt\ *n* **1** : retributive suffering, pain, or loss : PENALTY **2** : rough treatment

pu·ni·tive \'pyü-nət-iv\ *adj* : inflicting, involving, or aiming at punishment

punk \'pəŋk\ *n* : dry crumbly wood useful for tinder; *also* : a substance made from fungi for use as tinder

pun·kin *var of* PUMPKIN

pun·ster \'pən-stər\ *n* : one who is given to punning

¹**punt** \'pənt\ *n* : a long narrow flat-bottomed boat

²**punt** *vb* : to propel (as a punt) by pushing with a pole against the bottom

³**punt** *vb* : to kick a football dropped from the hands before it touches the ground

⁴**punt** *n* : the act or an instance of punting a ball

pu·ny \'pyü-nē\ *adj* [MF *puisné* younger, fr. *puis* afterwards (fr. L *post*) + *né* born, fr. L *natus*] : slight in power, size, or importance : WEAK

pup \'pəp\ *n* : a young dog; *also* : one of the young of some other animals

pu·pa \'pyü-pə\ *n, pl* **-pae** \-(ˌ)pē, -ˌpī\ *or* **-pas** : an insect (as a bee, moth, or beetle) in an intermediate stage of its growth when it is in a case or cocoon — **pu·pal** *adj*

¹**pu·pil** \'pyü-pəl\ *n* **1** : a child or young person in school or in the charge of a tutor **2** : DISCIPLE

²**pupil** *n* : the dark central opening of the iris of the eye

pup·pet \'pəp-ət\ *n* **1** : a small figure of a person or animal moved by hand or by strings or wires **2** : DOLL **3** : one whose acts are controlled by an outside force

pup·py \'pəp-ē\ *n* : a young dog

pur·blind \'pər-ˌblīnd\ *adj* **1** : partly blind **2** : lacking in insight : OBTUSE

¹**pur·chase** \'pər-chəs\ *vb* : to obtain by paying money or its equivalent : BUY — **pur·chas·er** *n*

²**purchase** *n* **1** : an act or instance of purchasing **2** : something purchased **3** : a secure hold or grasp; *also* : advantageous leverage

pur·dah \'pərd-ə\ *n* : seclusion of women from public observation among Muslims and some Hindus esp. in India

pure \'pyùr\ *adj* **1** : unmixed with any other matter (~ gold) : free from taint (~ water) : free from harshness (a ~ tone) **2** : SHEER, ABSOLUTE (~ nonsense) **3** : ABSTRACT, THEORETICAL (~ mathematics) **4** : free from what vitiates, weakens, or pollutes (speaks a ~ French) **5** : free from moral fault : INNOCENT **6** : CHASTE, CONTINENT — **pure·ly** *adv*

pure·bred \-'bred\ *adj* : bred from members of a recognized breed, strain, or kind without admixture of other blood over many generations

pu·ree \pyù-'rā\ *n* : a paste or thick liquid suspension usu. produced by rubbing cooked food through a sieve; *also* : a thick soup having vegetables so prepared as a base

¹**pur·ga·tive** \'pər-gət-iv\ *adj* : purging or tending to purge; *also* : being a purgative

²**purgative** *n* : a vigorously laxative drug : CATHARTIC

pur·ga·to·ry \'pər-gə-ˌtōr-ē\ *n* **1** : an intermediate state after death for expiatory purification **2** : a place or state of temporary punishment — **pur·ga·tor·i·al** \ˌpər-gə-'tōr-ē-əl\ *adj*

¹purge \'pərj\ *vb* **1** : to cleanse or purify esp. from sin **2** : to have or cause free evacuation from the bowels **3** : to rid (as a political party) by a purge

²purge *n* **1** : an act or result of purging; *esp* : a ridding of persons regarded as treacherous or disloyal **2** : something that purges; *esp* : PURGATIVE

pu·ri·fy \'pyùr-ə-ˌfī\ *vb* : to make or become pure — **pu·ri·fi·ca·tion** \ˌpyùr-ə-fə-'kā-shən\ *n* — **pu·rif·i·ca·to·ry** \pyù-'rif-i-kə-ˌtōr-ē\ *adj* — **pu·ri·fi·er** \'pyùr-ə-ˌfī-(-ə)r\ *n*

pur·ism \'pyùr-ˌiz-əm\ *n* : rigid adherence to or insistence on purity or nicety esp. in use of words — **pur·ist** \'pyùr-əst\ *n*

pu·ri·tan \'pyùr-ət-ᵊn\ *n* **1** *cap* : a member of a 16th and 17th century Protestant group in England and New England opposing formal usages of the Church of England **2** : one who practices or preaches a stricter or professedly purer moral code than that which prevails — **pu·ri·tan·i·cal** \ˌpyùr-ə-'tan-i-kəl\ *adj*

pu·ri·ty \'pyùr-ət-ē\ *n* : the quality or state of being pure

¹purl \'pərl\ *n* : a stitch in knitting

²purl *vb* : to knit in purl stitch

³purl *n* : a gentle murmur or movement (as of purling water)

⁴purl *vb* **1** : EDDY, SWIRL **2** : to make a soft murmuring sound

pur·lieu \'pərl-(y)ü\ *n* **1** : an outlying district : SUBURB **2** *pl* : ENVIRONS, NEIGHBORHOOD

pur·loin \(ˌ)pər-'lóin\ *vb* : to appropriate wrongfully : FILCH

¹pur·ple \'pər-pəl\ *adj* **1** : of the color purple **2** : highly rhetorical (a ~ passage) **3** : PROFANE (~ language) — **pur·plish** \'pər-p(ə-)lish\ *adj*

²purple *n* **1** : a bluish red color **2** : a purple robe emblematic of esp. regal rank or authority

¹pur·port \'pər-ˌpōrt\ *n* : meaning conveyed or implied; *also* : GIST

²pur·port \(ˌ)pər-'pōrt\ *vb* : to convey or profess outwardly as the meaning or intention : CLAIM

¹pur·pose \'pər-pəs\ *n* **1** : an object or result aimed at : INTENTION **2** : RESOLUTION, DETERMINATION — **pur·pose·ful** \-fəl\ *adj* — **pur·pose·ful·ly** *adv* — **pur·pose·less** \-pəs-ləs\ *adj* — **pur·pose·ly** *adv*

²purpose *vb* : to propose as an aim to oneself

purr \'pər\ *n* : a low murmur typical of a contented cat — **purr** *vb*

¹purse \'pərs\ *n* **1** : a receptacle (as a pouch) to carry money and often other small objects in **2** : RESOURCES, FUNDS **3** : a sum of money offered as a prize or present

²purse *vb* : PUCKER

purs·er \'pər-sər\ *n* : an official on a ship who keeps accounts and attends to the comfort of passengers

pur·su·ance \pər-'sü-əns\ *n* : the act of pursuing or carrying into effect

pur·su·ant to \-'sü-ənt-\ *prep* : in carrying out : according to ⟨*pursuant to* your instructions⟩

pur·sue \pər-'sü\ *vb* **1** : to follow in order to overtake or overcome : CHASE **2** : to seek to accomplish ⟨~ his aims⟩ **3** : to proceed along : FOLLOW (~ a course) **4** : to engage in (~ a vocation) — **pur·su·er** *n*

pur·suit \pər-'süt\ *n* **1** : the act of pursuing **2** : OCCUPATION, BUSINESS

pu·ru·lent \'pyùr-(y)ə-lənt\ *adj* : containing or accompanied by pus — **pu·ru·lence** \-ləns\ *n*

pur·vey \(ˌ)pər-'vā\ *vb* : to supply (as provisions) usu. as a business — **pur·vey·or** *n*

pur·view \'pər-ˌvyü\ *n* **1** : the range or limit esp. of authority, responsibility, or intention **2** : range of vision, understanding, or cognizance

pus \'pəs\ *n* : thick yellowish fluid (as in a boil) containing germs, blood cells, and tissue debris

¹push \'push\ *vb* **1** : to press against with force in order to drive or impel **2** : to thrust forward, downward, or outward **3** : to urge on : press forward

²push *n* **1** : a vigorous effort : DRIVE **2** : an act of pushing : SHOVE **3** : vigorous enterprise : ENERGY

push·cart \-ˌkärt\ *n* : a cart or barrow pushed by hand

push·over \-ˌō-vər\ *n* **1** : an opponent easy to defeat **2** : SUCKER **3** : something accomplished without difficulty

pu·sil·lan·i·mous \ˌpyü-sə-'lan-ə-məs\ *adj* : contemptibly timid : COWARDLY — **pu·sil·la·nim·i·ty** \ˌpyü-sə-lə-'nim-ət-ē\ *n*

pussy \'pùs-ē\ *n* : CAT

pussy·foot \'pùs-ē-ˌfùt\ *vb* **1** : to tread or move warily or stealthily **2** : to refrain from committing oneself

pus·tule \'pəs-chül\ *n* : a pus-filled pimple

put \'pùt\ *vb* **put**; **put·ting** **1** : to bring into a specified position : PLACE (~ the book on the table) **2** : SEND, THRUST **3** : to throw with an upward pushing motion (~ the shot) **4** : to bring into a specified state (~ the matter right) **5** : SUBJECT (~ him to expense) **6** : IMPOSE **7** : to set before one for decision (~ the question) **8** : EXPRESS, STATE **9** : TRANSLATE, ADAPT **10** : APPLY, ASSIGN (~ them to work) **11** : to give as an estimate (~ the number at 20) **12** : ATTACH, ATTRIBUTE (~ a high value on it) **13** : to take a specified course (the ship ~ out to sea)

pu·ta·tive \'pyüt-ət-iv\ *adj* **1** : commonly accepted : REPUTED **2** : INFERRED

put·out \'pùt-ˌaùt\ *n* : the retiring of a base runner or batter in baseball

pu·tre·fy \'pyü-trə-ˌfī\ *vb* : to make or become putrid : ROT — **pu·tre·fac·tion** \ˌpyü-trə-'fak-shən\ *n* — **pu·tre·fac·tive** \-'fak-tiv\ *adj*

pu·trid \'pyü-trəd\ *adj* **1** : ROTTEN, DECAYED **2** : VILE, CORRUPT — **pu·trid·i·ty** \pyü-'trid-ət-ē\ *n*

putsch \'pùch\ *n* : a secretly plotted and suddenly executed attempt to overthrow a government

putt \'pət\ *n* : a golf stroke made on the green to cause the ball to roll into the hole — **putt** *vb*

put·tee \ˌpə-'tē, 'pət-ē\ *n* **1** : a cloth strip wrapped around the lower leg **2** : a leather legging

¹put·ter \'pùt-ər\ *n* : one that puts

²put·ter \'pət-ər\ *n* **1** : a golf club used in putting **2** : one that putts

³put·ter \'pət-ər\ *vb* : to move or act aimlessly or idly **2** : TINKER

put·ty \'pət-ē\ *n* : a doughlike cement usu. of whiting and linseed oil used to fasten glass in sashes — **putty** *vb*

¹**puz·zle** \'pəz-əl\ *vb* **1 :** to bewilder mentally **:** CONFUSE, PERPLEX **2 :** to solve with difficulty or ingenuity ⟨~ out a mystery⟩ **3 :** to be in a quandary ⟨~ over what to do⟩ **4 :** to attempt a solution of a puzzle ⟨~ over a person's words⟩ **syn** mystify, bewilder, nonplus, confound

²**puzzle** *n* **1 :** something that puzzles **2 :** a question, problem, or contrivance designed for testing ingenuity

pya \pē-ä\ *n* — see MONEY table

pyg·my \'pig-mē\ *n* [L *Pygmaei* Pygmies, fr. Gk *Pygmaioi*, fr. pl. of *pygmaios* dwarfish, fr. *pygmē* fist, a measure of length] **1** *cap* **:** one of a small people of equatorial Africa **2 :** DWARF

py·ja·mas \pə-\ *var of* PAJAMAS

py·lon \'pī-,län, -lən\ *n* **1 :** a usu. massive gateway; *esp* **:** an Egyptian one flanked by flat-topped pyramids **2 :** a tower that serves as a support for a long span of wire **3 :** a post or tower marking a prescribed course of flight for an airplane

py·or·rhea \,pī-ə-'rē-ə\ *n* **:** an inflammation of the sockets of the teeth

¹**pyr·a·mid** \'pir-ə-,mid\ *n* **1 :** a massive structure with a square base and four triangular faces meeting at a point **2 :** a geometrical figure having for its base a polygon and for its sides several triangles meeting at a common point — **py·ram·i·dal** \pə-'ram-əd-²l\ *adj*

²**pyramid** *vb* **1 :** to build up in the form of a pyramid **:** heap up **2 :** to increase rapidly on a broadening base

pyre \'pī(ə)r\ *n* **:** a combustible heap for burning a dead body

py·ro·ma·nia \,pī-rō-'mā-nē-ə\ *n* **:** an irresistible impulse to start fires — **py·ro·ma·ni·ac** \-nē-,ak\ *n*

py·ro·tech·nics \,pī-rə-'tek-niks\ *n pl* **1 :** a display of fireworks **2 :** a spectacular display (as of oratory) — **py·ro·tech·nic** *or* **py·ro·tech·ni·cal** *adj*

py·thon \'pī-,thän, -thən\ *n* **:** any of several very large Old World constricting snakes

pyx \'piks\ *n* **:** a small case used to carry the Eucharist to the sick

q \'kyü\ *n, often cap* **:** the 17th letter of the English alphabet

qin·tar \kin-'tär\ *n* — see MONEY table

¹**quack** \'kwak\ *vb* **:** to make the characteristic cry of a duck

²**quack** *n* **:** the cry of a duck

³**quack** *n* **1 :** a pretender to medical skill **2 :** CHARLATAN **syn** faker, impostor — **quack** *adj* — **quack·ery** \-ə-rē\ *n* — **quack·ish** \-ish\ *adj*

quack·sal·ver \'kwak-,sal-vər\ *n* **:** CHARLATAN, QUACK

¹**quad** \'kwäd\ *n* **:** QUADRANGLE

²**quad** *n* **:** QUADRUPLET

quad·ran·gle \'kwäd-,raŋ-gəl\ *n* **1 :** a flat geometrical figure having 4 angles and 4 sides **2 :** a 4-sided courtyard or enclosure — **qua·dran·gu·lar** \kwä-'draŋ-gyə-lər\ *adj*

quad·rant \'kwäd-rənt\ *n* **1 :** one quarter of a circle **:** an arc of 90° **2 :** an instrument for measuring heights used esp. in astronomy and surveying **3 :** any of the 4 quarters into which something is divided by 2 lines intersecting each other at right angles

qua·drat·ic \kwä-'drat-ik\ *adj* **:** involving no higher power of terms than a square ⟨a ~ equation⟩

qua·drat·ics *n* **:** a branch of algebra dealing with quadratic equations

qua·dren·ni·al \kwä-'dren-ē-əl\ *adj* **1 :** consisting of or lasting for 4 years **2 :** occurring every 4 years

qua·dren·ni·um \-ē-əm\ *n, pl* **-ni·ums** *or* **-nia** \-ē-ə\ **:** a period of 4 years

quad·ri·lat·er·al \,kwäd-rə-'lat-ə-rəl\ *adj* **:** QUADRANGULAR — **quadrilateral** *n*

qua·drille \kwä-'dril, k(w)ə-\ *n* **:** a square dance made up of 5 or 6 figures in various rhythms

quad·ri·par·tite \,kwäd-rə-'pär-,tīt\ *adj* **1 :** consisting of four parts **2 :** shared by four parties or persons

qua·driv·i·um \kwä-'driv-ē-əm\ *n* **:** the

4 liberal arts of arithmetic, music, geometry, and astronomy in a medieval university

qua·droon \kwä-'drün\ *n* **:** a person of quarter Negro ancestry

quad·ru·ped \'kwäd-rə-,ped\ *n* **:** an animal having 4 feet — **qua·dru·pe·dal** \kwä-'drü-pəd-²l\ *adj*

¹**qua·dru·ple** \kwä-'drüp-əl, -'drəp-\ *vb* **1 :** to multiply by 4 **:** increase fourfold **2 :** to total 4 times as many

²**quadruple** *adj* **:** FOURFOLD

qua·dru·plet \kwä-'drüp-lət, -'drəp-\ *n* **1** *pl* **:** four offspring born at one birth **2 :** a group of four of a kind

quaff \'kwäf, 'kwaf\ *vb* **:** to drink deeply or repeatedly — **quaff** *n*

quag·mire \'kwag-,mī(ə)r, 'kwäg-\ *n* **:** soft miry land that yields under the foot

qua·hog \'kwò-,hòg, 'k(w)ō-, -,häg\ *n* **:** a round thick-shelled American clam

quai \'kä\ *n* **:** QUAY

¹**quail** \'kwāl\ *n* **:** any of various shortwinged stout-bodied game birds related to the grouse

²**quail** *vb* **:** to lose heart **:** COWER **syn** recoil, shrink, flinch, wince

quaint \'kwānt\ *adj* **1 :** unusual or different in character or appearance **2 :** pleasingly old-fashioned or unfamiliar **syn** odd, queer, outlandish — **quaint·ly** *adv* — **quaint·ness** *n*

¹**quake** \'kwāk\ *vb* **1 :** to shake usu. from shock or instability **2 :** to tremble usu. from cold or fear

²**quake** *n* **:** a tremulous agitation; *esp* **:** EARTHQUAKE

Quak·er \'kwā-kər\ *n* **:** FRIEND 4

Quaker meeting *n* **1 :** a meeting of Friends for worship marked often by long periods of silence **2 :** a social gathering marked by many periods of silence

qual·i·fi·ca·tion \,kwäl-ə-fə-'kā-shən\

ə abut; ᵊ kitten; ər further; a back; ā bake; ä cot, cart; aú out; ch chin; e less; ē easy; g gift; i trip; ī life; j joke; ŋ sing; ō flow; ò flaw; òi coin; th thin; t͟h this; ü loot; u̇ foot; y yet; yü few; yu̇ furious; zh vision

n **1 :** LIMITATION, MODIFICATION **2 :** a special skill that fits a person for some work or position

qual·i·fy \'kwäl-ə-,fī\ *vb* **1 :** to reduce from a general to a particular form **:** MODIFY **2 :** to make less harsh **3 :** to fit by skill or training for some purpose **4 :** to give or have a legal right to do something **5 :** to demonstrate the necessary ability (as in a preliminary race) **6 :** to limit the meaning of (as a noun) **syn** moderate, temper — **qual·i·fied** *adj*

qual·i·ta·tive \'kwäl-ə-,tāt-iv\ *adj* **:** of, relating to, or involving quality — **qual·i·ta·tive·ly** *adv*

qual·i·ty \'kwäl-ət-ē\ *n* **1 :** peculiar and essential character **:** NATURE **2 :** degree of excellence **3 :** high social status **4 :** a distinguishing attribute

qualm \'kwäm, 'kwóm\ *n* **1 :** a sudden attack (as of nausea) **2 :** a sudden misgiving **3 :** SCRUPLE

quan·da·ry \'kwän-d(ə-)rē\ *n* **:** a state of perplexity or doubt **syn** predicament, dilemma, plight

quan·ti·ta·tive \'kwän-tə-,tāt-iv\ *adj* **:** of, relating to, or involving quantity — **quan·ti·ta·tive·ly** *adv*

quan·ti·ty \'kwän-tət-ē\ *n* **1 :** AMOUNT, NUMBER **2 :** a considerable amount

quan·tum \'kwänt-əm\ *n, pl* **quan·ta** \-ə\ **1 :** QUANTITY, AMOUNT **2 :** an elemental unit of energy

quar·an·tine \'kwór-ən-,tēn\ *n* [It *quarantina*, lit., period of 40 days, fr. F *quarantaine*, fr. *quarante* 40, fr. L *quadraginta*] **1 :** a term during which a ship arriving in port and suspected of carrying contagious disease is forbidden contact with the shore **2 :** a restraint on the movements of persons or goods intended to prevent the spread of pests or disease **3 :** a place or period of quarantine — **quarantine** *vb*

¹quar·rel \'kwór-(ə)l\ *n* **1 :** a ground of dispute **2 :** a verbal clash **:** CONFLICT — **quar·rel·some** \-səm\ *adj*

²quarrel *vb* -reled *or* -relled; -rel·ing *or* -rel·ling **1 :** to find fault **2 :** to dispute angrily **:** WRANGLE

¹quar·ry \'kwór-ē\ *n* **1 :** game hunted with hawks **2 :** PREY

²quarry *n* **:** an open excavation usu. for obtaining building stone, slate, or limestone — **quarry** *vb*

quart \'kwórt\ *n* **:** a measure of capacity that equals 2 pints

¹quar·ter \'kwórt-ər\ *n* **1 :** a fourth part **2 :** a fourth of a dollar; *also* **:** a coin of this value **3 :** a district of a city **4** *pl* **:** LODGINGS (moved into new ~*s*) **5 :** MERCY, CLEMENCY (gave no ~) — **at close quarters :** at close range or in immediate contact

²quarter *vb* **1 :** to divide into 4 equal parts **2 :** to provide with lodgings or shelter

quar·ter·back \-,bak\ *n* **:** a football player who calls the signals for his team

quarter day *n, chiefly Brit* **:** the day which begins a quarter of the year and on which a quarterly payment falls due

quar·ter·deck \'kwórt-ər-,dek\ *n* **:** the stern area of a ship's upper deck

quarter horse *n* **:** an alert stocky muscular horse capable of high speed for short distances and of great endurance under the saddle

¹quar·ter·ly \'kwórt-ər-lē\ *adv* **:** at 3-month intervals

²quarterly *adj* **:** occurring, issued, or payable at 3-month intervals

³quarterly *n* **:** a periodical published 4 times a year

quar·ter·mas·ter \-,mas-tər\ *n* **1 :** a petty officer who attends to a ship's helm, binnacle, and signals **2 :** an army officer who provides clothing and subsistence for troops

quar·ter·staff \-,staf\ *n* **:** a long stout staff formerly used as a weapon

quar·tet *also* **quar·tette** \kwór-'tet\ *n* **1 :** a musical composition for four instruments or voices **2 :** a group of four and esp. of four musicians

quar·to \'kwórt-ō\ *n* **1 :** the size of a piece of paper cut four from a sheet **2 :** a book printed on quarto pages

quartz \'kwórts\ *n* **:** a common often transparent crystalline mineral that is a form of silica

¹quash \'kwäsh\ *vb* **:** to set aside by judicial action **:** VOID

²quash *vb* **:** to suppress completely **:** QUELL

¹qua·si \'kwā-,zī, -,sī; 'kwäz-ē\ *adv* **:** in some sense or degree (*quasi-historical*)

²quasi *adj* **:** SEEMING, VIRTUAL

qua·train \'kwä-,trān\ *n* **:** a unit of 4 lines of verse

qua·ver \'kwā-vər\ *vb* **1 :** to TREMBLE, SHAKE **2 :** TRILL **3 :** to speak in tremulous tones **syn** shudder, quake, totter, quiver, shiver — **quaver** *n*

quay \'kē, 'k(w)ā\ *n* **:** WHARF

quean \'kwēn\ *n* **:** a disreputable woman

quea·sy \'kwē-zē\ *adj* **:** NAUSEATED

queen \'kwēn\ *n* **1 :** the wife or widow of a king **2 :** a female monarch **3 :** a woman notable for rank, power, or attractiveness **4 :** the most privileged piece in the game of chess **5 :** a playing card bearing the figure of a queen **6 :** the fertile female of a social insect (as a bee or termite) — **queen·ly** *adj*

queen consort *n, pl* **queens consort** **:** the wife of a reigning king

queen mother *n* **:** a dowager queen who is mother of the reigning sovereign

¹queer \'kwir\ *adj* **:** differing from the usual or normal **:** PECULIAR, STRANGE **syn** erratic, eccentric, curious — **queer·ly** *adv*

²queer *vb* **:** DISRUPT (the rain ~ed our plans)

quell \'kwel\ *vb* **:** to put down **:** CRUSH (~ a riot)

quench \'kwench\ *vb* **1 :** to put out **:** EXTINGUISH **2 :** SUBDUE **3 :** SLAKE, SATISFY (~ed his thirst) **4 :** to cool (as heated steel) suddenly by immersion esp. in water or oil — **quench·able** *adj* — **quench·less** *adj*

quer·u·lous \'kwer-(y)ə-ləs\ *adj* **1 :** constantly complaining **:** FRETFUL, WHINING **syn** petulant, pettish, irritable, peevish

que·ry \'kwi(ə)r-ē\ *n* **:** QUESTION — **query** *vb*

quest \'kwest\ *n* **:** SEARCH

¹ques·tion \'kwes-chən\ *n* **1 :** an interrogative expression **:** QUERY **2 :** a subject for discussion or debate; *also* **:** a proposition to be voted on in a meeting **3 :** INQUIRY **4 :** OBJECTION, DISPUTE

²question *vb* **1 :** to ask questions **2 :** DOUBT, DISPUTE **3 :** to subject to analysis **:** EXAMINE **syn** ask, interrogate, quiz

ques·tion·able \-ə-bəl\ adj **1** : not certain or exact : DOUBTFUL **2** : not believed to be true, sound, or moral syn dubious, problematical

question mark n : a punctuation mark ? used esp. at the end of a sentence to indicate a direct question

ques·tion·naire \ˌkwes-chə-'na(ə)r\ n : a set of questions for obtaining information

quet·zal \ket-'säl\ n, pl **quetzals** or **quet·za·les** \-'säl-ās\ — see MONEY table

queue \'kyü\ n **1** : a braid of hair usu. worn hanging at the back of the head **2** : a line esp. of persons or vehicles

quib·ble \'kwib-əl\ n **1** : an evasion of or shifting from the point at issue : EQUIVOCATION **2** : a minor objection — **quibble** vb

¹quick \'kwik\ adj **1** archaic : LIVING **2** : RAPID, SPEEDY ⟨~ steps⟩ **3** : prompt to understand, think, or perceive : ALERT **4** : easily aroused ⟨a ~ temper⟩ **5** : turning or bending sharply ⟨a ~ turn in the road⟩ syn fleet, fast, prompt, ready — **quick** adv — **quick·ly** adv — **quick·ness** n

²quick n **1** : sensitive living flesh **2** : a vital part : HEART

quick bread n : a bread made with a leavening agent that permits immediate baking of the dough or batter mixture

quick·en \'kwik-ən\ vb **1** : to come to life : REVIVE **2** : AROUSE, STIMULATE **3** : to increase in speed : HASTEN **4** : to show vitality (as by growing or moving) syn animate, enliven, excite, provoke

quick-freeze \'kwik-'frēz\ vb : to freeze (food) for preservation so rapidly that ice crystals formed are too small to rupture the cells

quick·ie \'kwik-ē\ n : something hurriedly done or made

quick·sand \-ˌsand\ n : a deep mass of loose sand mixed with water

quick·sil·ver \-ˌsil-vər\ n : MERCURY

quick·step \-ˌstep\ n : a spirited march tune esp. accompanying a march in quick time

quick time n : a rate of marching in which 120 steps each 30 inches in length are taken in one minute

quick-wit·ted \-'wit-əd\ adj : mentally alert syn clever, bright, smart, intelligent

quid \'kwid\ n : a cut or wad of something chewable ⟨~ of tobacco⟩

quid pro quo \ˌkwid-ˌprō-'kwō\ n : something given or received for something else

qui·es·cent \kwī-'es-ᵊnt\ adj **1** : being at rest : QUIET **2** : INACTIVE syn latent, dormant, potential — **qui·es·cence** \-ᵊns\ n

¹quiet \'kwī-ət\ n : REPOSE, TRANQUILITY

²quiet adj **1** : marked by little motion or activity : CALM **2** : GENTLE, MILD ⟨a man of ~ disposition⟩ **3** : PEACEFUL ⟨a ~ cup of tea⟩ **4** : free from noise or uproar **5** : not showy : MODEST ⟨~ clothes⟩ **6** : SECLUDED ⟨a ~ nook⟩ — **quiet** adv — **qui·et·ly** adv — **qui·et·ness** n

³quiet vb **1** : CALM, PACIFY **2** : to become quiet ⟨~ down⟩

qui·etude \'kwī-ə-ˌt(y)üd\ n : QUIETNESS, REPOSE

qui·etus \kwī-'ēt-əs\ n **1** : final settlement (as of a debt) **2** : DEATH

quill \'kwil\ n **1** : a large stiff feather; also : the hollow barrel of a feather **2** : a spine of a hedgehog or porcupine

quilt \'kwilt\ n **1** : a padded bed coverlet

quince \'kwins\ n : a hard yellow applelike fruit; also : a tree related to the roses that bears this fruit

qui·nine \'kwī-ˌnīn\ n : a bitter white salt obtained from cinchona bark and used esp. in treating malaria

quin·sy \'kwin-zē\ n : a severe inflammation of the throat or adjacent parts with swelling and fever

quint \'kwint\ n : QUINTUPLET

quin·tes·sence \kwin-'tes-ᵊns\ n **1** : the purest essence of something **2** : the most typical example or representative

quin·tet also **quin·tette** \kwin-'tet\ n **1** : a musical composition for five instruments or voices **2** : a group of five and esp. of five musicians; also : a male basketball team

quin·tup·let \kwin-'təp-lət, -'t(y)üp-\ n **1** : a group of five of a kind **2** pl : five offspring born at one birth

¹quip \'kwip\ n : a clever remark : GIBE

²quip vb **quipped; quip·ping 1** : to make quips : GIBE **2** : to jest or gibe at

quire \'kwī(ə)r\ n : a set of 24 or sometimes 25 sheets of paper of the same size and quality

quirk \'kwərk\ n : a peculiarity of action or behavior : IDIOSYNCRASY

quirt \'kwərt\ n : a riding whip with a short handle and a rawhide lash

quis·ling \'kwiz-liŋ\ n : a traitor who collaborates with the invaders of his country esp. by serving in a puppet government

quit \'kwit\ vb **quit** also **quit·ted; quit·ting 1** : CONDUCT, BEHAVE ⟨~ themselves well⟩ **2** : to depart from : LEAVE, ABANDON syn acquit, comfort, deport, demean — **quit·ter** n

quite \'kwīt\ adv **1** : COMPLETELY, WHOLLY **2** : to an extreme : POSITIVELY **3** : to a considerable extent : RATHER

quits \'kwits\ adj : even or equal with another (as by repaying a debt, returning a favor, or retaliating for an injury)

quit·tance \'kwit-ᵊns\ n : RECOMPENSE, REQUITAL

¹quiv·er \'kwiv-ər\ n : a case for carrying arrows

²quiver vb : to shake with a slight trembling motion syn shiver, shudder, quaver, quake

³quiver n : TREMOR

quix·ot·ic \kwik-'sät-ik\ adj [fr. Don Quixote, hero of the novel Don Quixote de la Mancha by Cervantes] : idealistic to an impractical degree

¹quiz \'kwiz\ n, pl **quiz·zes 1** : an eccentric person **2** : a practical joke **3** : a short oral or written test

²quiz vb **quizzed; quiz·zing 1** : MOCK **2** : to look at inquisitively **3** : to question closely : EXAMINE syn ask, interrogate, query

quiz·zi·cal \'kwiz-i-kəl\ adj **1** : slightly eccentric : ODD **2** : BANTERING, TEASING **3** : INQUISITIVE

ə abut; ᵊ kitten; ər further; a back; ā bake; ä cot, cart; au̇ out; ch chin; e less; ē easy; g gift; i trip; ī life; j joke; ŋ sing; ō flow; o̊ flaw; o̊i coin; th thin; t͟h this; ü loot; u̇ foot; y yet; yü few; yu̇ furious; zh vision

quoit \\kwāt, 'k(w)oit\\ *n* **:** a flattened ring (as of iron) or circle (as of rope) used in a game (**quoits**)

quon·dam \\'kwän-dəm, -,dam\\ *adj* **:** FORMER

quo·rum \\'kwŏr-əm\\ *n* **:** the number of members of a body required to be present for business to be legally transacted

quo·ta \\'kwŏt-ə\\ *n* **:** a proportional part **:** SHARE

quo·ta·tion mark \\kwŏ-'tā-shən-\\ *n* **:** one of a pair of punctuation marks " " or ' ' used esp. to indicate the beginning and the end of a quotation in which the exact phraseology of another is directly cited

quote \\'kwŏt\\ *vb* **1 :** to speak or write a passage from another usu. with acknowledgment; *also* **:** to repeat a passage in substantiation or illustration **2 :** to state the market price of a commodity, stock, or bond — **quo·ta·tion** \\kwŏ-'tā-shən\\ *n*

quoth \\'kwŏth\\ *vb, archaic* **:** SAID — usu. used in the 1st and 3d persons with the subject following

quo·tid·i·an \\kwŏ-'tid-ē-ən\\ *adj* **1 :** DAILY **2 :** COMMONPLACE, ORDINARY

quo·tient \\'kwŏ-shənt\\ *n* **:** the number resulting from the division of one number by another

qursh \\'kûrsh\\ *or* **qu·rush** \\'kûr-əsh\\ *n* — see MONEY table

---

r \\'är\\ *n, often cap* **:** the 18th letter of the English alphabet

¹rab·bet \\'rab-ət\\ *n* **:** a groove in the edge or face of a board esp. to receive another piece

²rabbet *vb* **:** to cut a rabbet in; *also* **:** to joint by means of a rabbet

rab·bi \\'rab-,ī\\ *n* **1 :** MASTER, TEACHER — used by Jews as a term of address **2 :** a Jew trained and ordained for professional religious leadership — **rab·bin·ic** \\rə-'bin-ik\\ *or* **rab·bin·i·cal** \\-i-kəl\\ *adj*

rab·bin·ate \\'rab-ə-nət, -,nāt\\ *n* **1 :** the office of a rabbi **2 :** RABBIS

rab·bit \\'rab-ət\\ *n* **:** a long-eared burrowing mammal related to the hare

rab·ble \\'rab-əl\\ *n* **1 :** MOB **2 :** the lowest class of people

rab·id \\'rab-əd\\ *adj* **1 :** VIOLENT, FURIOUS **2 :** being fanatical or extreme (as in opinion or partisanship) **3 :** affected with rabies — **rab·id·ly** *adv*

ra·bies \\'rā-bēz\\ *n* **:** an acute deadly virus disease transmitted by the bite of a rabid animal

rac·coon \\ra-'kün\\ *n* **:** a tree-dwelling gray No. American mammal with a bushy ringed tail; *also* **:** its fur

¹race \\'rās\\ *n* **1 :** a strong current of running water; *also* **:** its channel **2 :** an onward course (as of time or life) **3 :** a contest in speed **4 :** a contest for a desired end (as election to office)

²race *vb* **1 :** to run in a race **2 :** to run swiftly **:** RUSH **3 :** to engage in a race with **4 :** to drive at high speed — **rac·er** *n*

³race *n* **1 :** a family, tribe, people, or nation of the same stock; *also* **:** MANKIND **2 :** a group of individuals within a biological species able to breed together — **ra·cial** \\'rā-shəl\\ *adj*

race·course \\'rās-,kŏrs\\ *n* **:** a course for racing (as horses or dogs)

race·horse \\-,hŏrs\\ *n* **:** a horse bred or kept for racing

ra·ceme \\rā-'sēm\\ *n* **:** a flower cluster with flowers borne along a stem and blooming from the base toward the tip — **rac·e·mose** \\'ras-ə-,mōs\\ *adj*

rac·ism \\'rās-,iz-əm\\ *n* **:** a belief that some races are by nature superior to others; *also* **:** discrimination based on such belief — **rac·ist** \\-əst\\ *n*

¹rack \\'rak\\ *n* **1 :** a framework on or in which something may be placed (as for display or storage) **2 :** an instrument of torture on which a body is stretched **3 :** a bar fitted with teeth to gear with a pinion or worm

²rack *vb* **1 :** to torture with or as if with a rack **2 :** to stretch or strain by force **3 :** TORMENT, HARASS **4 :** to place on or in a rack

¹rack·et *also* **rac·quet** \\'rak-ət\\ *n* **:** a light bat made of netting stretched across an oval open frame and used for striking a ball (as in tennis)

²racket *n* **1 :** confused noise **:** DIN **2 :** a fraudulent or dishonest scheme or activity (as a system for obtaining money by threats of violence)

³racket *vb* **1 :** to make a racket **2 :** to engage in active social life (~ around)

rack·e·teer \\,rak-ə-'tiər\\ *n* **:** a person who extorts money or advantages esp. from businessmen by threats of violence or unlawful interference — **rack·e·teer·ing** *n*

rack up \\(')rak-'əp\\ *vb* **:** SCORE

ra·con·teur \\,rak-,än-'tər\\ *n* **:** one good at telling anecdotes

racy \\'rā-sē\\ *adj* **1 :** having the distinctive quality of something in its original or most characteristic form (~ vernacular of the islanders) **2 :** full of zest **3 :** PUNGENT, SPICY **4 :** RISQUÉ, SUGGESTIVE — **rac·i·ly** *adv* — **rac·i·ness** *n*

ra·dar \\'rā-,där\\ *n* [*r*adio *d*etecting *a*nd *r*anging] **:** a detecting device that establishes through reception and timing of reflected radio waves the distance, height, and direction of motion of an object in the path of the beam

ra·dar·scope \\-,skōp\\ *n* **:** a device that gives the visual indication in a radar receiver

ra·di·al \\'rād-ē-əl\\ *adj* **:** arranged or having parts arranged like rays coming from a common center — **ra·di·al·ly** *adv*

ra·di·ant \\'rād-ē-ənt\\ *adj* **1 :** SHINING, GLOWING **2 :** beaming with happiness **3 :** transmitted by radiation *syn* brilliant, bright, luminous, lustrous — **ra·di·ance** \\-əns\\ *also* **ra·di·an·cy** \\-ən-sē\\ *n* — **ra·di·ant·ly** *adv*

radiant energy *n* **:** energy transmitted as electromagnetic waves (heat, light, and radio waves are *radiant energy*)

ra·di·ate \\'rād-ē-,āt\\ *vb* **1 :** to send out rays **:** SHINE, GLOW **2 :** to issue in rays (light ~s) (heat ~s) **3 :** to spread around as from a center — **ra·di·a·tion** \\,rād-ē-'ā-shən\\ *n*

ra·di·a·tor \'rād-ē-ˌāt-ər\ n : a device to heat air (as in a room) or to cool an object (as an automobile engine)

¹rad·i·cal \'rad-i-kəl\ adj [L radic-, radix root] 1 : FUNDAMENTAL, EXTREME, THOROUGHGOING 2 : of or relating to radicals in politics — **rad·i·cal·ism** \-ˌiz-əm\ n — **rad·i·cal·ly** adv

²radical n 1 : a person who favors rapid and sweeping changes in laws and methods of government 2 : a group of atoms that is replaceable by a single atom or remains unchanged during reactions 3 : the indicated root of a mathematical expression; also : the sign √ placed before an expression to indicate that its root is to be taken ⟨the ∛̄ indicates the square root of 2 and ∛27 indicates the cube root of 27⟩

radii pl of RADIUS

¹ra·dio \'rād-ē-ˌō\ n 1 : transmission or reception of signals and esp. sound by means of electric waves without a connecting wire 2 : a radio receiving set 3 : the radio broadcasting industry — **radio** adj

²radio vb : to communicate or send a message to by radio

ra·dio·ac·tiv·i·ty \ˌrād-ē-ō-ˌak-'tiv-ət-ē\ n : the property that some elements (as radium) have of spontaneously emitting rays of radiant energy by the disintegration of the nuclei of atoms — **ra·dio·ac·tive** \-'ak-tiv\ adj

radio astronomy n : astronomy dealing with radio waves received from outside the earth's atmosphere

ra·dio·car·bon \-'kär-bən\ n : CARBON 14

ra·dio·gram \'rād-ē-ō-ˌgram\ n : a message transmitted by radiotelegraphy

¹ra·dio·graph \-ˌgraf\ n : a photograph made by some form of radiation other than light; esp : an X-ray photograph

²radiograph vb : to make a radiograph of

ra·dio·iso·tope \ˌrād-ē-ō-'ī-sə-ˌtōp\ n : a radioactive isotope

ra·di·ol·o·gy \ˌrād-ē-'äl-ə-jē\ n : the science of high-energy radiations; esp : the use of radiant energy (as X rays and radium radiations) in medicine — **ra·di·ol·o·gist** \-jist\ n

ra·dio·tel·e·graph \ˌrād-ē-ō-'tel-ə-ˌgraf\ n : wireless telegraphy — **ra·dio·te·leg·ra·phy** \-tə-'leg-rə-fē\ n

ra·dio·tel·e·phone \-'tel-ə-ˌfōn\ n : a telephone that utilizes radio waves wholly or partly instead of connecting wires

radio telescope n : a radio receiver-antenna combination used in radio astronomy

ra·dio·ther·a·py \-'ther-ə-pē\ n : treatment of disease by radiation (as X rays) — **ra·dio·ther·a·pist** \-pəst\ n

rad·ish \'rad-ish\ n : a pungent fleshy root usu. eaten raw; also : a plant related to the mustards that produces this root

ra·di·um \'rād-ē-əm\ n : a metallic chemical element that is notable for its emission of radiant energy by the disintegration of the nuclei of atoms and is used in luminous materials and in the treatment of cancer

ra·di·us \'rād-ē-əs\ n, pl **ra·dii** \-ē-ˌī\

1 : a straight line extending from the center of a circle or a sphere to the circumference or surface 2 : a circular area defined by the length of its radius ⟨within a ~ of 10 miles of home⟩ syn range, reach, scope, compass

ra·don \'rā-ˌdän\ n : a heavy radioactive gaseous chemical element

raf·fia \'raf-ē-ə\ n : fiber used esp. for baskets and hats and obtained from the stalks of the leaves of a Madagascar palm (**raffia palm**)

¹raf·fle \'raf-əl\ n : a lottery in which the prize is won by one of a number of persons buying chances

²raffle vb : to dispose of by means of a raffle

¹raft \'raft\ n 1 : a number of logs or timbers fastened together to form a float 2 : a flat structure for support or transportation on water

²raft vb 1 : to travel or transport by raft 2 : to make into a raft

³raft n : a large amount or number

raf·ter \'raf-tər\ n : a usu. sloping timber of a roof

rag \'rag\ n : a waste piece of cloth

rag·a·muf·fin \'rag-ə-ˌməf-ən\ n : a ragged dirty man or child

¹rage \'rāj\ n 1 : violent and uncontrolled anger : FURY 2 : VOGUE, FASHION ⟨was all the ~⟩

²rage vb 1 : to be furiously angry : RAVE 2 : to be violent ⟨the storm raged⟩ 3 : to continue out of control ⟨for weeks the plague raged⟩

rag·ged \'rag-əd\ adj 1 : TORN, TATTERED; also : wearing tattered clothes 2 : done in an uneven way ⟨a ~ performance⟩ — **rag·ged·ly** adv — **rag·ged·ness** n

rag·lan \'rag-lən\ n : an overcoat with sleeves (**raglan sleeves**) sewn in with seams slanting from neck to underarm

ra·gout \ra-'gü\ n : a highly seasoned meat stew with vegetables

rag·tag and bob·tail \ˌrag-ˌtag-ən-'bäb-ˌtāl\ n : RABBLE

rag·time \'rag-ˌtīm\ n : rhythm in which there is more or less continuous syncopation in the melody

rag·weed \-ˌwēd\ n : any of several coarse weedy herbs with allergenic pollen

¹raid \'rād\ n : a sudden usu. surprise attack or invasion : FORAY

²raid vb : to make a raid on — **raid·er** n

¹rail \'rāl\ n 1 : a bar extending from one support to another as a guard, barrier, or support 2 : a bar forming a track for wheeled vehicles 3 : RAILROAD

²rail vb : to provide with a railing : FENCE

³rail n : any of several small wading birds related to the cranes

⁴rail vb : to complain angrily : SCOLD, REVILE — **rail·er** n

rail·ing \'rā-liŋ\ n : a barrier of rails

rail·lery \'rā-lə-rē\ n : good-natured ridicule : BANTER

¹rail·road \'rāl-ˌrōd\ n : a permanent road with rails providing a track for cars; also : such a road with all the lands, buildings, and rolling stock belonging with it

²railroad vb 1 : to send by rail 2 : to work on a railroad 3 : to put through (as a law) too hastily **4 :** to convict hastily or with insufficient or improper evidence — **rail·road·er** n — **rail·road·ing** n

rail·way \-ˌwā\ n **1 :** RAILROAD **2 :** a line of track providing a runway for wheels ⟨a cash or parcel ~⟩

rai·ment \'rā-mənt\ n **:** CLOTHING, GARMENTS

¹rain \'rān\ n **1 :** water falling in drops from the clouds **2 :** a shower of objects ⟨a ~ of bullets⟩ — **rainy** \'rā-nē\ adj

²rain vb **1 :** to fall as or like rain **2 :** to send down rain **3 :** to pour down **:** bestow abundantly

rain·bow \-ˌbō\ n **:** an arc of colors formed opposite the sun by the refraction and reflection of the sun's rays in rain, spray, or mist

rain·coat \-ˌkōt\ n **:** a waterproof or water-resistant coat

rain·drop \-ˌdräp\ n **:** a drop of rain

rain·fall \-ˌfȯl\ n **:** a fall of rain; esp **:** the amount that falls measured by depth in inches

rain out vb **:** to interrupt or prevent by rain

rain·storm \'rān-ˌstȯrm\ n **:** a storm of or with rain

¹raise \'rāz\ vb **1 :** to cause or help to rise **:** LIFT ⟨~ a window⟩ **2 :** AWAKEN, AROUSE ⟨enough to ~ the dead⟩ **3 :** BUILD, ERECT ⟨~ a monument⟩ **4 :** ELEVATE, PROMOTE ⟨was raised to captain⟩ **5 :** COLLECT ⟨~ money⟩ **6 :** BREED ⟨~ cattle⟩ **:** GROW ⟨~ corn⟩ **:** bring up ⟨~ a family⟩ **7 :** PROVOKE ⟨~ a laugh⟩ **8 :** to bring to notice ⟨~ an objection⟩ **9 :** INCREASE ⟨~ prices⟩ ⟨~ a bet⟩; also **:** to bet more than **10 :** to make light and spongy ⟨~ dough⟩ **11 :** END ⟨~ a siege⟩ **12 :** to cause to form ⟨~ a blister⟩ **syn** lift, hoist, boost — **rais·er** n

²raise n **:** an increase in amount (as of a bid or bet); also **:** an increase in pay

rai·sin \'rāz-ᵊn\ n **:** a grape usu. of a special kind dried for food

rai·son d'être \ˌrā-ˌzōⁿ-'detrᵊ\ n **:** reason or justification for being

ra·ja or **ra·jah** \'räj-ə\ n **:** an Indian prince

¹rake \'rāk\ n **:** a long-handled garden tool having a crossbar with teeth or prongs

²rake vb **1 :** to gather, loosen, or smooth with or as if with a rake **2 :** to sweep the length of (as a trench or ship) with gunfire

³rake n **:** inclination from either perpendicular or horizontal **:** SLANT, SLOPE

⁴rake n **:** a dissolute man **:** LIBERTINE, ROUÉ

rake-off \'rāk-ˌȯf\ n **:** an often unlawful commission or profit received by one party to a transaction

¹rak·ish \'rā-kish\ adj **:** DISSOLUTE — **rak·ish·ly** adv — **rak·ish·ness** n

²rakish adj **1 :** having a smart appearance indicative of speed ⟨a ~ sloop⟩ ⟨~ masts⟩ **2 :** JAUNTY, SPORTY — **rak·ish·ly** adv — **rak·ish·ness** n

¹ral·ly \'ral-ē\ vb **1 :** to call together and reduce to order (as troops) **2 :** to arouse to activity or from depression or weakness **:** REVIVE, RECOVER **3 :** to come together again to renew an effort **syn** stir, rouse, awaken, waken

²rally n **1 :** an act of rallying **2 :** a mass meeting to arouse enthusiasm

³rally vb **:** BANTER, TEASE

¹ram \'ram\ n **1 :** a male sheep **2 :** a wooden beam or metal bar used in battering down (as in a siege) walls or doors

²ram vb **rammed; ram·ming 1 :** to force or drive in or through **2 :** CRAM, CROWD, STUFF **3 :** to strike against violently

¹ram·ble \'ram-bəl\ vb **:** to go about aimlessly **:** ROAM, WANDER

²ramble n **:** a leisurely excursion; esp **:** an aimless walk

ram·bler \'ram-blər\ n **:** one that rambles; esp **:** a hardy climbing rose with large clusters of small flowers

ram·bunc·tious \ram-'bəŋk-shəs\ adj **:** UNRULY

ra·mie \'ram-ē, 'rā-mē\ n **:** a strong lustrous textile fiber from an Asiatic nettle

ram·i·fy \'ram-ə-ˌfī\ vb **:** to branch out — **ram·i·fi·ca·tion** \ˌram-ə-fə-'kā-shən\ n

ramp \'ramp\ n **:** a sloping passageway connecting different levels

¹ram·page \'ram-ˌpāj\ vb **:** to rush about wildly

²rampage n **:** riotous behavior — **ram·pa·geous** \ram-'pā-jəs\ adj

ram·pant \'ram-pənt\ adj **:** unchecked in growth or spread **:** RIFE ⟨fear was ~ in the town⟩ — **ram·pant·ly** adv

ram·part \'ram-ˌpärt\ n **1 :** a fortification embankment **2 :** a protective barrier **3 :** a ridge like a wall

ram·rod \'ram-ˌräd\ n **1 :** a rod used to ram a charge into a muzzle-loading gun **2 :** a cleaning rod for small arms

ram·shack·le \-ˌshak-əl\ adj **:** RICKETY, TUMBLEDOWN

ran past of RUN

¹ranch \'ranch\ n **1 :** an establishment for the raising and grazing of cattle, sheep, or horses **2 :** a large farm devoted to a specialty — **ranch·er** n

²ranch vb **:** to live or work on a ranch

ran·cid \'ran-səd\ adj **1 :** having a rank smell or taste **2 :** ROTTEN, SPOILED — **ran·cid·i·ty** \ran-'sid-ət-ē\ n — **ran·cid·ness** \-səd-nəs\ n

ran·cor \'raŋ-kər\ n **:** deep hatred **:** intense ill will **syn** antagonism, animosity, antipathy, enmity, hostility — **ran·cor·ous** \-əs\ adj

rand \'rand\ n — see MONEY table

ran·dom \'ran-dəm\ adj **:** CHANCE, HAPHAZARD — **ran·dom·ly** adv — **at random :** without definite aim or method

rang past of RING

¹range \'rānj\ n **1 :** a series of things in a row **2 :** the act of ranging or roaming **3 :** open land where cattle may roam and graze **4 :** a cooking stove **5 :** a variation within limits **6 :** the distance a gun will shoot **7 :** a place where shooting is practiced ⟨a rifle ~⟩; also **:** a course over which missiles are tested **8 :** the space or extent included, covered, or used **:** SCOPE, DISTANCE **syn** reach, compass, radius

²range vb **1 :** to set in a row or in proper order **2 :** to set in place among others of the same kind **3 :** to roam over or through **:** EXPLORE **4 :** to roam at large or freely **5 :** to correspond in direction or line **6 :** to vary within limits

rang·er \'rān-jər\ n **1 :** a warden who patrols forest lands **2 :** one that ranges

3 : a member of a body of troops who range over a region **4** : an expert in close-range fighting and raiding attached to a special unit of assault troops

rangy \'jē\ *adj* : being long-limbed and slender — **rang·i·ness** *n*

ra·ni *or* **ra·nee** \rä-'nē\ *n* : a raja's wife

¹rank \'raŋk\ *adj* **1** : strong and vigorous and usu. coarse in growth ⟨~ weeds⟩ ⟨a ~ meadow⟩ **2** : unpleasantly strong-smelling : RANCID — **rank·ly** *adv* — **rank·ness** *n*

²rank *n* **1** : ROW **2** : a line of soldiers ranged side by side **3** *pl* : the body of enlisted men ⟨rose from the ~*s*⟩ **4** : an orderly arrangement **5** : CLASS, DIVISION **6** : a grade of official standing (as in an army) **7** : position in a group **8** : superior position

³rank *vb* **1** : to arrange in lines or in regular formation **2** : to arrange according to classes **3** : to take or have a relative position **4** : to rate above (as in official standing)

rank and file *n* **1** : the enlisted men of an armed force **2** : the general membership of a body as contrasted with its leaders

rank·ing *adj* **1** : having a high position : FOREMOST, OUTSTANDING **2** : being next to the chairman in seniority

ran·kle \'raŋ-kəl\ *vb* **1** : to become inflamed : FESTER **2** : to cause anger, irritation, or bitterness

ran·sack \'ran-,sak\ *vb* **1** : to search thoroughly **2** : PILLAGE, PLUNDER

¹ran·som \'ran-səm\ *n* [OF *rançon*, fr. L *redemption-, redemptio* act of buying back, fr *redimere* to buy back, redeem] **1** : something paid or demanded for the freedom of a captive **2** : the act of ransoming

²ransom *vb* : to free from captivity or punishment by paying a price — **ran·som·er** *n*

rant \'rant\ *vb* **1** : to talk loudly and wildly **2** : to scold violently : RAIL — **rant·er** *n*

¹rap \'rap\ *n* **1** : a sharp blow : KNOCK **2** : a sharp rebuke **3** *slang* : responsibility for or consequences of an action

²rap *vb* **rapped; rap·ping 1** : to strike sharply : KNOCK **2** : to utter sharply ⟨~ out an order⟩ **3** : to criticize sharply

ra·pa·cious \rə-'pā-shəs\ *adj* **1** : excessively greedy or covetous **2** : living on prey **3** : RAVENOUS — **ra·pa·cious·ly** *adv* — **ra·pa·cious·ness** *n* — **ra·pac·i·ty** \-'pas-ət-ē\ *n*

¹rape \'rāp\ *vb* : to commit rape on : RAVISH — **rap·er** *n* — **rap·ist** \'rā-pəst\ *n*

²rape *n* **1** : a carrying away by force **2** : unlawful sexual intercourse with a woman without her consent and chiefly by force or deception

¹rap·id \'rap-əd\ *adj* : very fast : SWIFT *syn* fleet, quick, speedy — **ra·pid·i·ty** \rə-'pid-ət-ē\ *n* — **rap·id·ly** \'rap-əd-lē\ *adv*

²rapid *n* : a place in a stream where the current flows very fast usu. over obstructions — usu. used in pl.

ra·pi·er \'rā-pē-ər\ *n* : a straight 2-edged sword with a narrow pointed blade

rap·ine \'rap-ən\ *n* : PILLAGE, PLUNDER

rap·port \ra-'pōr\ *n* : RELATION; *esp* : relation characterized by harmony or accord

rap·proche·ment \,rap-,rōsh-'mäⁿ\ *n* : the establishment or a state of cordial relations

rap·scal·lion \rap-'skal-yən\ *n* : RASCAL, SCAMP

rapt \'rapt\ *adj* : carried away (as in thoughts or spirit) : ABSORBED, ENGROSSED — **rapt·ly** *adv*

rap·ture \'rap-chər\ *n* : spiritual or emotional ecstasy — **rap·tur·ous** \-chə-rəs\ *adj*

ra·ra avis \,rar-ə-'ā-vəs\ *n* : a rare person or thing : RARITY

¹rare \'ra(ə)r\ *adj* : not thoroughly cooked

²rare *adj* **1** : not thick or dense : THIN ⟨~ air⟩ **2** : unusually fine : EXCELLENT, SPLENDID **3** : seldom met with : very uncommon — **rare·ly** *adv* — **rare·ness** *n* — **rar·i·ty** \'rar-ət-ē\ *n*

rare·bit \'ra(ə)r-bət\ *n* : WELSH RABBIT

rar·efy \'rar-ə-,fī\ *vb* : to make or become rare, thin, or less dense — **rar·efac·tion** \,rar-ə-'fak-shən\ *n*

ras·cal \'ras-kəl\ *n* **1** : a mean or dishonest person **2** : a mischievous person — **ras·cal·i·ty** \ras-'kal-ət-ē\ *n* — **ras·cal·ly** \'ras-kə-lē\ *adj*

¹rash \'rash\ *adj* : having or showing little regard for consequences : too hasty in decision, action, or speech : RECKLESS *syn* daring, foolhardy, adventurous, venturesome — **rash·ly** *adv* — **rash·ness** *n*

²rash *n* : an eruption on the body

rash·er \'rash-ər\ *n* : a thin slice of bacon or ham broiled or fried

¹rasp \'rasp\ *vb* **1** : to rub with or as if with a rough file **2** : to grate harshly upon (as one's nerves) **3** : to speak in a grating tone

²rasp *n* : a coarse file with cutting points instead of ridges

rasp·ber·ry \'raz-,ber-ē\ *n* **1** : an edible red or black berry produced by some brambles; *also* : such a bramble **2** : a sound of contempt made through protruded lips

¹rat \'rat\ *n* **1** : a scaly-tailed destructive rodent larger than the mouse **2** : one that betrays his associates

²rat *vb* **rat·ted; rat·ting 1** : to betray one's associates **2** : to hunt or catch rats

ratch·et \'rach-ət\ *n* : a device that consists of a notched wheel held or moved by a separate projection and is used esp. in a hand tool (as a drill or screwdriver) for giving motion in one direction

¹rate \'rāt\ *vb* : to scold violently

²rate *n* **1** : quantity, amount, or degree measured by some standard **2** : an amount (as of payment) measured by its relation to some other amount (as of time) **3** : a charge, payment, or price fixed according to a ratio, scale, or standard ⟨tax ~⟩ **4** : RANK, CLASS

³rate *vb* **1** : CONSIDER, REGARD **2** : ESTIMATE **3** : to settle the relative rank or class of **4** : to be classed : RANK **5** : to be of consequence **6** : to have a right to : DESERVE — **rat·er** *n*

rath·er \'rath-ər, 'räth-\ *adv* **1** : PREFERABLY **2** : on the other hand **3** : more properly **4** : more correctly speaking **5** : SOMEWHAT

rat·i·fy \'rat-ə-,fī\ *vb* : to approve and accept esp. formally : CONFIRM — **rat·i·fi·ca·tion** \,rat-ə-fə-'kā-shən\ *n*

rat·ing \'rāt-iŋ\ *n* **1** : a classification according to grade : RANK **2** *Brit* : a naval enlisted man **3** : an estimate of the credit standing and business responsibility of a person or firm

ra·tio \'rā-sh(ē-)ō\ *n* **1** : the quotient of one quantity divided by another ⟨the ~ of 6 to 3 may be expressed as 6:3, 6/3, or 2⟩ **2** : the relation in number, quantity, or degree between things ⟨women outnumbered men in the ~ of 3 to 1⟩

rat·i·o·ci·na·tion \,rat-ē-,ōs-³n-'ā-shən, ,rash-, -,äs-\ *n* : exact thinking : REASONING — **ra·ti·o·ci·nate** \-'ōs-³n-,āt, -'äs-\ *vb* — **ra·ti·o·ci·na·tive** \-,āt-iv\ *adj* — **ra·ti·o·ci·na·tor** \-,āt-ər\ *n*

¹ra·tion \'rash-ən, 'rā-shən\ *n* **1** : a food allowance for one day **2** : FOOD, PROVISIONS, DIET — usu. used in pl. **3** : SHARE, ALLOTMENT

²ration *vb* **1** : to supply with or allot as rations **2** : to use or allot sparingly **syn** apportion, portion

ra·tio·nal \'rash-(ə-)nəl\ *adj* **1** : having reason or understanding; *also* : SANE **2** : of or relating to reason **3** : being an integer or the quotient of two integers (as ⅔) — **ra·tio·nal·ly** *adv*

ra·tio·nale \,rash-ə-'nal\ *n* **1** : an explanation of controlling principles of belief or practice **2** : an underlying reason

ra·tio·nal·ism \'rash-(ə)nə-,liz-əm\ *n* : the practice of guiding one's actions and opinions solely by what seems reasonable — **ra·tio·nal·ist** \-ləst\ *n* — **ra·tio·nal·is·tic** \,rash-(ə)nə-'lis-tik\ *adj*

ra·tio·nal·i·ty \,rash-ə-'nal-ət-ē\ *n* : the quality or state of being rational

ra·tio·nal·ize \'rash-(ə-)nə-,līz\ *vb* **1** : to make (something irrational) rational or reasonable **2** : to provide a natural explanation of (as a myth) **3** : to justify (as one's behavior or weaknesses) esp. to oneself **4** : to find plausible but untrue reasons for conduct

rat·line \'rat-lən\ *n* : one of the small ropes fastened to and running across the shrouds and forming a rope ladder; *also* : the tarred line used in these ropes

rat·tan \ra-'tan\ *n* : an Asiatic climbing palm with long stems used esp. for canes and wickerwork

¹rat·tle \'rat-³l\ *vb* **1** : to make or cause to make a series of clattering sounds **2** : to move with a clattering sound ⟨~ down the road⟩ **3** : to say or do in a brisk lively fashion ⟨~ off the answers⟩ **4** : CONFUSE, UPSET ⟨~ a witness⟩

²rattle *n* **1** : a series of clattering and knocking sounds **2** : a toy that produces a rattle when shaken **3** : one of the horny pieces on a rattlesnake's tail or the organ made of these

rat·tler \'rat-lər\ *n* : RATTLESNAKE

rat·tle·snake \'rat-³l-,snāk\ *n* : any of various American venomous snakes with a rattle at the end of the tail

rat·tle·trap \-,trap\ *n* : something rickety and full of rattles; *esp* : an old car

rat·tling \'rat-liŋ\ *adj* **1** : LIVELY, BRISK **2** : FIRST-RATE, SPLENDID

rat·trap \'rat-,trap\ *n* **1** : a trap for rats **2** : a dilapidated building **3** : a hopeless situation

rau·cous \'ro·kəs\ *adj* **1** : HARSH, HOARSE, STRIDENT **2** : boisterously disorderly — **rau·cous·ly** *adv* — **rau·cous·ness** *n*

rau·wol·fia \raù-'wùl-fē-ə, ro·\ *n* : a medicinal extract from the root of an Indian tree; *also* : this tree

¹rav·age \'rav-ij\ *n* : an act or result of ravaging : DEVASTATION

²ravage *vb* : to lay waste : DEVASTATE, PLUNDER — **rav·ag·er** *n*

rave \'rāv\ *vb* **1** : to talk wildly in or as if in delirium : STORM, RAGE **2** : to talk with extreme enthusiasm

¹rav·el \'rav-əl\ *vb* -eled *or* -elled; -el·ing *or* -el·ling : UNRAVEL, UNTWIST

²ravel *n* **1** : something tangled **2** : something raveled out; *esp* : a loose thread

¹ra·ven \'rā-vən\ *n* : a large black bird related to the crow

²raven *adj* : black and glossy like a raven's feathers

rav·en·ing \'rav-(ə-)niŋ\ *adj* : greedily devouring : RAPACIOUS, VORACIOUS

rav·en·ous \'rav-ə-nəs\ *adj* : RAPACIOUS, VORACIOUS **2** : eager for food : very hungry — **rav·en·ous·ly** *adv*

ra·vine \rə-'vēn\ *n* : a small narrow steep-sided valley larger than a gully and smaller than a canyon

rav·i·o·li \,rav-ē-'ō-lē\ *n* : small shells of noodle dough with a savory filling

rav·ish \'rav-ish\ *vb* **1** : to carry away by violence **2** : to overcome with emotion and esp. with joy or delight **3** : RAPE — **rav·ish·er** *n* — **rav·ish·ment** *n*

¹raw \'ro\ *adj* **1** : not cooked **2** : changed little from the original form : not processed ⟨~ materials⟩ **3** : not trained or experienced ⟨~ recruits⟩ **4** : having the skin abraded or irritated ⟨a ~ sore⟩ **5** : disagreeably cold and damp : BLEAK ⟨a ~ day⟩ **6** : VULGAR, COARSE ⟨~ joke⟩ **7** : UNFAIR ⟨~ deal⟩ — **raw·ness** *n*

²raw *n* : a raw place or state; *esp* : NUDITY

raw-boned \-'bōnd\ *adj* : THIN, LEAN, GAUNT

raw·hide \-,hīd\ *n* : the untanned skin of cattle; *also* : a whip made of this

¹ray \'rā\ *n* : any of various large flat fishes that are related to the sharks and have the hind end of the body slender and taillike

²ray *n* [MF *rai*, fr. L *radius* rod, spoke, radius, ray] **1** : one of the lines of light that appear to radiate from a bright object **2** : a thin beam of radiant energy (as light) **3** : light from a beam **4** : a tiny bit : PARTICLE ⟨~ of hope⟩ **5** : a thin line like a beam of light **6** : an animal or plant structure resembling a ray

ray·on \'rā-,än\ *n* : a shiny fabric that resembles silk and is made from fibers produced chemically from cellulose

raze \'rāz\ *vb* **1** : to destroy to the ground : DEMOLISH **2** : to scrape, cut, or shave off

ra·zor \'rā-zər\ *n* : a sharp cutting instrument used to shave off hair

ra·zor-backed \,rā-zər-'bakt\ *or* **ra·zor·back** \'rā-zər-,bak\ *adj* : having a sharp narrow back ⟨~ horse⟩

¹razz \'raz\ *n* : RASPBERRY 2

²razz *vb* : RIDICULE, TEASE

re- \rē, ˌrē, 'rē\ *prefix* **1** : again : anew **2** : back : backward

reabsorb	recapitalization	redirect
reaccommodate	recapitalize	rediscount
reacquire	recapture	rediscover
reactuate	recast	rediscovery
readapt	rechannel	redissolve
readdress	recharge	redistill
readjust	recharter	redistillation
readjustment	recheck	redistribute
readmission	rechristen	redistribution
readmit	reclean	redo
readmittance	recoat	redomesticate
readopt	recoin	redouble
readoption	recolonization	redraw
reaffirm	recolonize	reecho
reaffirmation	recolor	reeducate
realign	recomb	reeducation
realignment	recombination	reelect
reallocate	recombine	reelection
reallocation	recommence	reembark
reanalysis	recommission	reembodiment
reanalyze	recompile	reembody
reanimate	recomplete	reemerge
reanimation	recompose	reemergence
reannex	recompound	reemphasis
reannexation	recompress	reemphasize
reappear	recompression	reemploy
reappearance	recomputation	reemployment
reapplication	recompute	reenact
reapply	reconceive	reenactment
reappoint	reconcentrate	reenlist
reappointment	reconception	reenlistment
reapportion	recondensation	reenter
reapportionment	recondense	reequip
reappraisal	recondition	reestablish
reappraise	reconfine	reestablishment
rearm	reconfirm	reevaluate
rearmament	reconfirmation	reevaluation
rearouse	reconnect	reevoke
rearrange	reconquer	reexamination
rearrangement	reconquest	reexamine
rearrest	reconsecrate	reexchange
reascend	reconsecration	reexport
reassail	reconsign	refasten
reassemble	reconsignment	refight
reassembly	reconstructive	refigure
reassert	reconsult	refilm
reassess	reconsultation	refilter
reassessment	recontact	refinish
reassign	recontaminate	refit
reassignment	recontamination	refix
reassort	recontract	refloat
reassume	reconvene	reflow
reattach	reconvert	reflower
reattachment	recook	refly
reattack	recopy	refocus
reattain	recouple	refold
reattainment	recross	reforge
reattempt	recrystallize	reformulate
reauthorization	recurve	reformulation
reauthorize	recut	refortify
reawake	redecorate	refound
reawaken	redecoration	refreeze
rebaptism	rededicate	refuel
rebaptize	rededication	refurnish
rebid	redefine	regather
rebind	redefinition	regild
reboil	redemand	regive
rebroadcast	redeposit	reglow
rebuild	redesign	reglue
reburial	redetermination	regrade
rebury	redetermine	regrind
recalculate	redigest	regrow
recalculation	redip	rehandle
		rehear
		reheat
		rehouse
		reimpose

reimposition
reincorporate
reinsert
reinsertion
reinterpret
reinterpretation
reintroduce
reintroduction
reinvest
reinvestment
reinvigorate
reinvigoration
reissue
rejudge
rekindle
reknit
relearn
relet
reletter
relight
relive
reload
relocate
relocation
remake
remanufacture
remarriage
remarry
remelt
remigrate
remix
remold
rename
renegotiate
renegotiation
renominate
renomination
renumber
reoccupy
reopen
reorient
reorientation
repack
repackage
repaint
repass
repeople
rephotograph
rephrase
replant
replay
reprice
reprint
republication
republish
repurchase
reradiate
reread
rerecord
rerun
resay
rescore
rescreen
reseal
reseed
resell
reset
resettle
resettlement
resew
reshow
resilver
resitting
resmooth
resow
respell
(continued)

(continued)

ə abut; ᵊ kitten; ər further; a back; ā bake; ä cot, cart; aȯ out; ch chin; e less; ē easy; g gift; i trip; ī life; j joke; ŋ sing; ō flow; ȯ flaw; ȯi coin; th thin; t̲h̲ this; ü loot; u̇ foot; y yet; yü few; yu̇ furious; zh vision

respring
restaff
restate
restatement
restock
restraighten
restrengthen
restrike
restring
restudy
restuff
restyle
resubmit
resummon
resurface
resurvey
resynthesis
resynthesize
retaste
retell
retest
rethink
retool
retrain
retransmission

retransmit
retraverse
retrial
reunification
reunify
reunite
reuse
revaluate
revaluation
revalue
reverification
reverify
revictual
revisit
rewarm
rewash
rewater
reweave
rewed
reweigh
reweld
rewind
rewire
rework
rewrite

¹reach \'rēch\ *vb* 1 : to stretch out : EXTEND 2 : to touch or move to touch or seize 3 : to extend to : stretch as far as 4 : to arrive at 5 : to communicate with **syn** gain, compass, achieve, attain — **reach·er** *n*

²reach *n* 1 : the act of reaching 2 : the distance or extent of reaching or of ability to reach 3 : an unbroken stretch or expanse; *esp* : a straight part of a river 4 : power to grasp

re·act \rē-'akt\ *vb* 1 : to exert a return or counteracting influence 2 : to respond to a stimulus 3 : to act in opposition to a force or influence 4 : to turn back or revert to a former condition 5 : to undergo chemical reaction

re·act \'rē-'akt\ *vb* : to perform again

re·ac·tion \rē-'ak-shən\ *n* 1 : a return or reciprocal action 2 : a counter tendency; *esp* : a tendency toward a former esp. outmoded political or social order or policy 3 : bodily, mental, or emotional response to a stimulus 4 : chemical change

¹re·ac·tion·ary \-shə-ˌner-ē\ *adj* : relating to, marked by, or favoring esp. political reaction

²reactionary *n* : a reactionary person

re·ac·tive \rē-'ak-tiv\ *adj* : reacting or tending to react

re·ac·tor \-tər\ *n* 1 : one that reacts 2 : a vat for a chemical reaction 3 : an apparatus in which a chain reaction of fissionable material is initiated and controlled

¹read \'rēd\ *vb* read \'red\ read·ing \'rēd-iŋ\ 1 : to understand language by interpreting written symbols for speech sounds 2 : to utter aloud written or printed words 3 : to learn by observing 〈~ nature's signs〉 4 : to discover the meaning of 〈~ the future〉 5 : to attribute (a meaning) to something 〈~ guilt in the boy's manner〉 6 : to study by a course of reading 〈~ law〉 7 : to consist in phrasing or meaning 〈the two versions ~ quite differently〉 — **read·a·bil·i·ty** \ˌrēd-ə-'bil-ət-ē\ *n* — **read·a·ble** \'rēd-ə-bəl\ *adj* — **read·a·bly** \-blē\ *adv* — **read·er** *n*

²read \'red\ *adj* : informed by reading 〈a widely ~ man〉

read·ing \'rēd-iŋ\ *n* 1 : something read or for reading 2 : a public recital 3 : the form in which something is written : VERSION 4 : the study of books or literature 5 : manner of rendering something written; *also* : INTERPRETATION 6 : something that is indicated so as to be read 〈a thermometer ~〉

read out *vb* : to expel from an organization

¹ready \'red-ē\ *adj* 1 : prepared for use or action 2 : likely to do something indicated; *also* : willingly disposed : INCLINED 3 : spontaneously prompt 4 : notably dexterous, adroit, or skilled 5 : immediately available : HANDY — **read·i·ly** *adv* — **read·i·ness** *n*

²ready *vb* : to make ready : PREPARE

³ready *n* : the state of being ready 〈guns at the ~〉

ready-made \ˌred-ē-'mād\ *adj* : already made up for general sale : not made to special order

re·agent \rē-'ā-jənt\ *n* : a substance that takes part in or brings about a particular chemical reaction

re·al \'rē(-ə)l\ *adj* 1 : actually being or existent : not imaginary : ACTUAL 2 : not artificial : GENUINE — **re·al·ness** *n*

real estate *n* : property in houses and land

re·al·ism \'rē-ə-ˌliz-əm\ *n* 1 : the disposition to face facts and to deal with them practically 2 : true and faithful portrayal of nature and of men in art or literature — **re·al·ist** \-ləst\ *n* — **re·al·is·tic** \ˌrē-ə-'lis-tik\ *adj* — **re·al·is·ti·cal·ly** \-ti-k(ə-)lē\ *adv*

re·al·i·ty \rē-'al-ət-ē\ *n* 1 : the quality or state of being real 2 : something real 3 : the totality of real things and events

re·al·ize \'rē-ə-ˌlīz\ *vb* 1 : to make a reality : ACCOMPLISH 2 : OBTAIN, GAIN 〈~ a profit〉 3 : to convert into money 〈~ assets〉 4 : to be aware of : UNDERSTAND — **re·al·iz·able** \-ˌlī-zə-bəl\ *adj* — **re·al·i·za·tion** \ˌrē-ə-lə-'zā-shən\ *n*

re·al·ly \'rē-(ə-)lē\ *adv* : in truth : in fact : ACTUALLY

realm \'relm\ *n* 1 : KINGDOM 2 : SPHERE, DOMAIN

re·al·tor \'rē(-ə)l-tər\ *n* : a real estate agent who is a member of the National Association of Real Estate Boards

re·al·ty \'rē(-ə)l-tē\ *n* : REAL ESTATE

¹ream \'rēm\ *n* : a quantity of paper usu. 480, 500, or 516 sheets

²ream *vb* 1 : to enlarge or shape with a reamer 2 : to clean or clear with a reamer

ream·er \'rē-mər\ *n* : a tool with cutting edges that is used to enlarge or shape a hole

reap \'rēp\ *vb* 1 : to cut or clear with a scythe, sickle, or machine 2 : to gather by or as if by cutting : HARVEST 〈~ a reward〉 — **reap·er** *n*

¹rear \'riər\ *vb* 1 : to set or raise upright 2 : to erect by building 3 : to breed and rear for use or market 〈~ livestock〉 4 : to bring up (as offspring) : FOSTER 5 : to lift or rise up; *esp* : to rise on the hind legs 〈a ~ing horse〉

²rear *n* 1 : the unit (as of an army) or area farthest from the enemy 2 : BACK; *also* : position at the back of something

³rear *adj* : being at the back

rear admiral *n* : a commissioned officer

in the navy ranking next below a vice admiral

1rear·ward \'riər-wərd\ *adj* **1 :** being at or toward the rear **2 :** directed to the rear

2rearward *also* **rear·wards** *adv* **:** at or to the rear

1rea·son \'rēz-ᵊn\ *n* **1 :** a statement offered in explanation or justification **2 :** GROUND, CAUSE **3 :** the power to think **:** INTELLECT **4 :** a sane or sound mind **5 :** due exercise of the faculty of logical thought

2reason *vb* **1 :** to use the faculty of reason **:** THINK **2 :** to talk with another so as to influence his actions or opinions **3 :** to discover or formulate by the use of reason — **rea·son·er** *n* — **rea·son·ing** *n*

rea·son·able \'rēz-(ᵊ-)nə-bəl\ *adj* **1 :** being within the bounds of reason **:** not extreme **:** MODERATE, FAIR **2 :** INEXPENSIVE **3 :** able to reason **:** RATIONAL — **rea·son·a·ble·ness** *n* — **rea·son·a·bly** *adv*

re·as·sure \,rē-ə-'shu̇r\ *vb* **1 :** to assure again **2 :** to restore confidence to **:** free from fear — **re·as·sur·ance** \-'shu̇r-əns\ *n*

1re·bate \'rē-,bāt\ *vb* **:** to make or give a rebate

2rebate *n* **:** a return of part of a payment **syn** deduction, abatement, discount

1reb·el \'reb-əl\ *adj* **:** of or relating to rebels **:** REBELLIOUS

2rebel *n* **:** one that rebels against authority

3re·bel \ri-'bel\ *vb* **-belled; -bel·ling** **1 :** to resist the authority of one's government **2 :** to act in or show disobedience

re·bel·lion \ri-'bel-yən\ *n* **:** resistance to authority; *esp* **:** open defiance of established government through uprising or revolt

re·bel·lious \-yəs\ *adj* **:** given to or engaged in rebellion **:** INSUBORDINATE — **re·bel·lious·ly** *adv* — **re·bel·lious·ness** *n*

re·birth \'rē-'bərth\ *n* **1 :** a new or second birth **2 :** RENAISSANCE, REVIVAL

re·born \-'bȯrn\ *adj* **:** born again **:** having a rebirth

1re·bound \'rē-'bau̇nd, ri-\ *vb* **1 :** to spring back on or as if on striking another body **2 :** to recover from a setback or frustration

2re·bound \'rē-,bau̇nd\ *n* **1 :** the action of rebounding **2 :** a rebounding ball (as in basketball) **3 :** immediate spontaneous reaction to setback or frustration

1re·buff \ri-'bəf\ *vb* **1 :** to refuse or repulse curtly **:** SNUB **2 :** to drive or beat back **:** REPULSE

2rebuff *n* **1 :** a curt rejection of an offer or advance **:** SNUB **2 :** a sharp check or setback **:** REPULSE

1re·buke \ri-'byük\ *vb* **:** to reprimand sharply **:** REPROVE

2rebuke *n* **:** a sharp reprimand

re·bus \'rē-bəs\ *n* **:** a representation of syllables or words by means of pictures; *also* **:** a riddle composed of such pictures

re·but \ri-'bət\ *vb* **-but·ted; -but·ting** **:** to refute esp. formally (as in debate) by evidence and arguments **syn** disprove, controvert — **re·but·ter** *n*

re·but·tal \ri-'bət-ᵊl\ *n* **:** the act of rebutting

re·cal·ci·trant \ri-'kal-sə-trənt\ *adj* **1 :** stubbornly resisting authority **2 :** resistant to handling or treatment **syn** refractory, headstrong, willful, unruly, ungovernable — **re·cal·ci·trance** \-trəns\ *n*

1re·call \ri-'kȯl\ *vb* **1 :** to call back **2 :** REMEMBER, RECOLLECT **3 :** REVOKE, ANNUL **4 :** RESTORE, REVIVE

2re·call \ri-'kȯl, 'rē-,kȯl\ *n* **1 :** a summons to return **2 :** the right or procedure of removing an official by popular vote **3 :** remembrance of things learned or experienced **4 :** the act of revoking

re·cant \ri-'kant\ *vb* **:** to take back (something one has said) publicly **:** make an open confession of error — **re·can·ta·tion** \,rē-,kan-'tā-shən\ *n*

1re·cap \'rē-,kap\ *vb* **:** to vulcanize a strip of rubber upon the outer surface of (a worn tire) — **re·cap·pa·ble** *adj*

2re·cap \'rē-,kap\ *n* **:** a recapped tire

re·ca·pit·u·late \,rē-kə-'pich-ə-,lāt\ *vb* **:** to restate briefly **:** SUMMARIZE — **re·ca·pit·u·la·tion** \-,pich-ə-'lā-shən\ *n*

re·cede \ri-'sēd\ *vb* **1 :** to move back or away **:** WITHDRAW **2 :** to slant backward **3 :** DIMINISH, CONTRACT

re·ceipt \ri-'sēt\ *n* **1 :** RECIPE **2 :** the act of receiving **3 :** something received — usu. used in pl. **4 :** a writing acknowledging the receiving of money or goods

2receipt *vb* **1 :** to give a receipt for **2 :** to mark as paid

re·ceiv·able \ri-'sē-və-bəl\ *adj* **1 :** capable of being received; *esp* **:** acceptable as legal (~ certificates) **2 :** subject to call for payment **:** PAYABLE (accounts ~)

re·ceive \ri-'sēv\ *vb* **1 :** to take in or accept (as something sent or paid) **:** come into possession of **:** GET **2 :** CONTAIN, HOLD **3 :** to permit to enter **:** GREET, WELCOME **4 :** to be at home to visitors **5 :** to accept as true or authoritative **6 :** to be the subject of **:** UNDERGO, EXPERIENCE (~ a shock) **7 :** to change incoming radio waves into sounds or pictures

re·ceiv·er *n* **1 :** one that receives **2 :** a person legally appointed to receive and have charge of property or money involved in a lawsuit **3 :** an apparatus for receiving and changing an electrical signal into an audible or visible effect (telephone ~) (radio or television ~)

re·ceiv·er·ship \-,ship\ *n* **1 :** the office or function of a receiver **2 :** the condition of being in the hands of a receiver

re·cen·cy \'rēs-ᵊn-sē\ *n* **:** the quality or state of being recent

re·cent \'rēs-ᵊnt\ *adj* **1 :** lately made or used **:** NEW, FRESH **2 :** of the present time or time just past (~ history) — **re·cent·ly** *adv* — **re·cent·ness** *n*

re·cep·ta·cle \ri-'sep-ti-kəl\ *n* **1 :** something used to receive and hold something else **:** CONTAINER **2 :** the enlarged end of a stalk bearing a flower **3 :** an electrical fitting containing the live parts of a circuit

re·cep·tion \ri-'sep-shən\ *n* **1 :** the act

of receiving **2 :** a social gathering; *esp* **:** one at which guests are formally welcomed

re·cep·tion·ist \-sh(ə-)nəst\ *n* **:** one employed to greet callers

re·cep·tive \ri-'sep-tiv\ *adj* **:** able or inclined to take in or apply (as ideas or stimuli) — **re·cep·tive·ly** *adv* — **re·cep·tive·ness** *n* — **re·cep·tiv·i·ty** \,rē-,sep-'tiv-ət-ē\ *n*

re·cep·tor \ri-'sep-tər\ *n* **:** one that receives; *esp* **:** SENSE ORGAN

¹re·cess \'rē-,ses, ri-'ses\ *n* **1 :** an indentation in a line or surface (as a niche in a wall or an alcove in a room) **2 :** a secret or secluded place **:** RETREAT **3 :** an intermission between work periods **:** a usu. brief suspension of any regular procedure

²recess *vb* **1 :** to put into a recess **2 :** to make a recess in **3 :** to interrupt for a recess **4 :** to take a recess

re·ces·sion \ri-'sesh-ən\ *n* **1 :** the act of receding **:** WITHDRAWAL **2 :** a return procession **3 :** a period of reduced economic activity

re·ces·sion·al \-(ə-)nəl\ *n* **1 :** a hymn or musical piece at the conclusion of a service or program **2 :** a return processional

re·ces·sive \ri-'ses-iv\ *adj* **:** tending to go back **:** RECEDING

rec·i·pe \'res-ə-(,)pē\ *n* [L, take, imperative of *recipere* to receive, fr. *re-* back + *capere* to take] **1 :** a set of instructions for making something (as a food dish) from various ingredients **2 :** a method of procedure **:** FORMULA ⟨a ~ for happiness⟩

re·cip·i·ent \ri-'sip-ē-ənt\ *n* **:** one that receives

re·cip·ro·cal \ri-'sip-rə-kəl\ *adj* **1 :** MUTUAL, JOINT, SHARED **2 :** so related to each other that one completes the other or is equivalent to the other **syn** common, correspondent, complementary — **re·cip·ro·cal·ly** *adv*

re·cip·ro·cate \-,kāt\ *vb* **1 :** to move backward and forward alternately ⟨a *reciprocating* mechanical part⟩ **2 :** to make a return for something done or given **3 :** to give and take mutually — **re·cip·ro·ca·tion** \-,sip-rə-'kā-shən\ *n*

rec·i·proc·i·ty \,res-ə-'präs-ət-ē\ *n* **1 :** the quality or state of being reciprocal **2 :** mutual exchange of privileges; *esp* **:** a trade policy by which special advantages are granted by one country in return for special advantages granted it by another

re·cit·al \ri-'sīt-ºl\ *n* **1 :** an act or instance of reciting **:** ACCOUNT, NARRATIVE, STORY **2 :** a public reading or recitation ⟨a poetry ~⟩ **3 :** a program of music given by one musician ⟨song ~⟩ ⟨piano ~⟩ **4 :** an exhibition concert by music pupils **5 :** a public performance by a dancer or dance troupe

rec·i·ta·tion \,res-ə-'ta-shən\ *n* **1 :** RECITING, RECITAL **2 :** delivery before an audience of something memorized **3 :** a classroom exercise in which pupils answer questions on a lesson they have studied; *also* **:** a class period

re·cite \ri-'sīt\ *vb* **1 :** to repeat verbatim (as something memorized) **2 :** to recount in some detail **:** RELATE **3 :** to reply to a teacher's questions on a lesson — **re·cit·er** *n*

reck·less \'rek-ləs\ *adj* **:** lacking due

caution **:** RASH **syn** hasty, headlong, impetuous — **reck·less·ly** *adv* — **reck·less·ness** *n*

reck·on \'rek-ən\ *vb* **1 :** COUNT, CALCULATE, COMPUTE **2 :** CONSIDER, REGARD **3** *chiefly dial* **:** THINK, SUPPOSE, GUESS — **reck·on·er** *n*

reck·on·ing *n* **1 :** an act or instance of reckoning **2 :** calculation of a ship's position **3 :** a settling of accounts ⟨day of ~⟩

re·claim \ri-'klām\ *vb* **1 :** to recall from wrong conduct **:** REFORM **2 :** to put into a desired condition (as by labor or discipline) ⟨~ marshy land⟩ **3 :** to obtain (as rubber) from a waste product or by-product **syn** save, redeem, rescue — **re·claim·able** *adj* — **rec·la·ma·tion** \,rek-lə-'mā-shən\ *n*

re·cline \ri-'klīn\ *vb* **1 :** to lean or incline backward **2 :** to lie down **:** REST

rec·luse \'rek-,lüs, ri-'klüs\ *n* **:** a person who lives in seclusion or leads a solitary life **:** HERMIT

rec·og·ni·tion \,rek-ig-'nish-ən\ *n* **1 :** the act of recognizing **:** the state of being recognized **:** ACKNOWLEDGMENT **2 :** special notice or attention

re·cog·ni·zance \ri-'kä(g)-nə-zəns\ *n* **:** a promise recorded before a court or magistrate to do something (as to appear in court or to keep the peace)

rec·og·nize \'rek-ig-,nīz\ *vb* **1 :** to identify as previously known **2 :** to perceive clearly **:** REALIZE, UNDERSTAND **3 :** to take notice of **4 :** to take approving notice of **:** acknowledge with appreciation **5 :** to acknowledge acquaintance with **6 :** to acknowledge (as a speaker in a meeting) as one entitled to be heard at the time **7 :** to acknowledge the existence or the independence of (a country or government) — **rec·og·niz·able** *adj* — **rec·og·niz·ably** *adv*

¹re·coil \ri-'kȯil\ *vb* **1 :** to draw back **:** RETREAT **2 :** to spring back to or as if to a starting point **syn** shrink, flinch, wince

²re·coil \ri-'kȯil, 'rē-,kȯil\ *n* **:** the action of recoiling (as by a gun or spring)

re·coil·less \ri-'kȯil-ləs, 'rē-,kȯil-\ *adj* **:** having a minimum of recoil ⟨~ gun⟩

rec·ol·lect \,rek-ə-'lekt\ *vb* **:** to recall to mind **:** REMEMBER **syn** recall, remind, reminisce, bethink

rec·ol·lec·tion \-'lek-shən\ *n* **1 :** the act of recollecting **2 :** the power of recollecting **3 :** the time within which things can be recollected **:** MEMORY **4 :** something recollected

rec·om·mend \,rek-ə-'mend\ *vb* **1 :** to present as deserving of acceptance or trial **2 :** to give in charge **:** COMMIT, ENTRUST **3 :** to cause to receive favorable attention **4 :** ADVISE, COUNSEL — **rec·om·men·da·to·ry** \-'men-də-,tȯr-ē\ *adj* — **rec·om·mend·er** *n*

rec·om·men·da·tion \-mən-'dā-shən\ *n* **1 :** the act of recommending **2 :** something that recommends **3 :** a thing or a course of action recommended

¹rec·om·pense \'rek-əm-,pens\ *vb* **1 :** to give compensation to **:** pay for **2 :** to return in kind **:** REQUITE **syn** reimburse, indemnify, repay

²recompense *n* **:** COMPENSATION

rec·on·cile \'rek-ən-,sīl\ *vb* **1 :** to cause to be friendly or harmonious again **2 :** ADJUST, SETTLE ⟨~ differences⟩

3 : to bring to quiet submission or acceptance **syn** conform, accommodate, adapt — rec·on·cil·able \-sĭ-lə-bəl\ *adj* — rec·on·cile·ment \-,sīl-mənt\ *n* — rec·on·cil·er \ — rec·on·cil·i·a·tion \,rek-ən-,sil-ē-'ā-shən\ *n*

rec·on·dite \'rek-ən-,dīt\ *adj* 1 : hard to understand : PROFOUND, ABSTRUSE 2 : little known : OBSCURE

re·con·nais·sance \ri-'kän-ə-zəns\ *n* : a preliminary survey of an area to get information; *esp* : an exploratory military survey of enemy territory

rec·on·noi·ter \,rē-kə-'nóit-ər\ *vb* : to make a reconnaissance of : engage in reconnaissance

re·con·sid·er \,rē-kən-'sid-ər\ *vb* : to consider again with a view to changing or reversing; *esp* : to take up again in a meeting — re·con·sid·er·a·tion \-,sid-ə-'rā-shən\ *n*

re·con·sti·tute \'rē-'kän-stə-,t(y)üt\ *vb* 1 : to constitute again 2 : to restore to former condition by adding water (~ powdered milk)

re·con·struct \,rē-kən-'strəkt\ *vb* : to construct again : REBUILD

re·con·struc·tion \-'strək-shən\ *n* : the action of reconstructing : the state of being reconstructed 2 *often cap* : the reorganization and reestablishment of the seceded states in the Union after the American Civil War 3 : something reconstructed

¹re·cord \ri-'kórd\ *vb* 1 : to set down (as proceedings in a meeting) in writing 2 : to register permanently 3 : INDICATE, READ 4 : to cause (as sound or visual images) to be registered (as on a phonograph disc or magnetic tape) in a form that permits reproduction 5 : to give evidence of

²rec·ord \'rek-ərd\ *n* 1 : the act of recording 2 : a written account of proceedings 3 : known facts about a person 4 : the best that has been done in any competition 5 : something (as a phonograph disc) on which sound or visual images have been recorded

re·cord·er \ri-'kórd-ər\ *n* 1 : a person who records (transactions) officially (~ of deeds) 2 : a judge in some city courts 3 : an early vertical flute 4 : a recording instrument or device

re·cord·ing \ri-'kórd-iŋ\ *n* : RECORD 5

¹re·count \ri-'kaúnt\ *vb* 1 : to relate in detail : TELL 2 : ENUMERATE **syn** recite, rehearse, narrate, describe, state, report

²re·count \'rē-'kaúnt\ *vb* : to count again

³re·count \'rē-'kaúnt, -,kaúnt\ *n* : a second or fresh count

re·coup \ri-'küp\ *vb* : to get an equivalent or compensation for : make up for something lost **syn** retrieve, regain, recover

re·course \'rē-,kórs, ri-'kórs\ *n* 1 : a turning to someone or something for assistance or protection : RESORT 2 : a source of aid

re·cov·er \ri-'kəv-ər\ *vb* 1 : to get back again : REGAIN, RETRIEVE 2 : to regain normal health, poise, or status 3 : RECLAIM (~ land from the sea) 4 : to make up for : RECOUP (~ed all his losses) 5 : to obtain a legal judg-

ment in one's favor — re·cov·er·able *adj* — re·cov·ery \-'kəv-(ə-)rē\ *n*

re·cov·er \'rē-'kəv-ər\ *vb* : to cover again

¹rec·re·ant \'rek-rē-ənt\ *adj* 1 : COWARDLY, CRAVEN 2 : UNFAITHFUL, FALSE

²recreant *n* 1 : COWARD 2 : DESERTER

rec·re·ate \'rek-rē-,āt\ *vb* : to give new life or freshness to

re·cre·ate \,rē-krē-'āt\ *vb* : to create again — re·cre·a·tion \-krē-'ā-shən\ *n* — re·cre·ative \-'āt-iv\ *adj*

rec·re·ation \,rek-rē-'ā-shən\ *n* : a refreshing of strength or spirits after work or anxiety; *also* : a means of refreshment **syn** diversion, relaxation — rec·re·ation·al \-sh(ə-)nəl\ *adj* — rec·re·ative \'rek-rē-,āt-iv\ *adj*

re·crim·i·nate \ri-'krim-ə-,nāt\ *vb* : to make an accusation against an accuser — re·crim·i·na·tion \-,krim-ə-'nā-shən\ *n* — re·crim·i·na·to·ry \-'krim-ə-nə-,tōr-ē\ *adj*

¹re·cruit \ri-'krüt\ *n* [obs. F *recrute* fresh growth, new levy of soldiers, fr. MF *recroistre* to grow up again, fr. L *recrescere*, fr. *re-* again + *crescere* to grow] : a newcomer to an activity; *esp* : an enlisted man of the lowest rank in the army

²recruit *vb* 1 : to form or strengthen with new members (~ an army) 2 : to secure the services of (~ engineers) 3 : to restore or increase in health or vigor (resting to ~ his strength) — re·cruit·er *n* — re·cruit·ment *n*

rec·tal \'rek-t°l\ *adj* : of or relating to the rectum

rect·an·gle \'rek-,taŋ-gəl\ *n* : a 4-sided figure with 4 right angles — rect·an·gu·lar \rek-'taŋ-gyə-lər\ *adj*

rec·ti·fy \'rek-tə-,fī\ *vb* : to make or set right : CORRECT **syn** amend, remedy, redress — rec·ti·fi·ca·tion \,rek-tə-fə-'kā-shən\ *n* — rec·ti·fi·er \'rek-tə-,fī(-ə)r\ *n*

rec·ti·lin·ear \,rek-tə-'lin-ē-ər\ *adj* 1 : moving in a straight line 2 : characterized by straight lines

rec·ti·tude \'rek-tə-,t(y)üd\ *n* 1 : moral integrity 2 : correctness of procedure **syn** virtue, goodness, morality

rec·to \'rek-tō\ *n* : a right-hand page

rec·tor \'rek-tər\ *n* 1 : a clergyman in charge of a parish 2 : the head of a university or school — rec·tor·ate \-t(ə-)rət\ *n* — rec·to·ri·al \rek-'tōr-ē-əl\ *adj*

rec·to·ry \'rek-t(ə-)rē\ *n* : the residence of a rector

rec·tum \'rek-təm\ *n, pl* -tums *or* -ta \-tə\ : the last part of the intestine joining colon and anus

re·cum·bent \ri-'kəm-bənt\ *adj* : lying down : RECLINING

re·cu·per·ate \ri-'k(y)ü-pə-,rāt\ *vb* : to get back (as health, strength, or losses) : RECOVER — re·cu·per·a·tion \-,k(y)ü-pə-'rā-shən\ *n* — re·cu·per·a·tive \-'k(y)ü-pə-,rāt-iv\ *adj*

re·cur \ri-'kər\ *vb* -curred; -curring 1 : to go or come back in thought or discussion 2 : to occur or appear again *esp*. after an interval — re·cur·rence \-'kər-əns\ *n* — re·cur·rent \-ənt\ *adj*

ə abut; ᵊ kitten; ər further; a back; ā bake; ä cot, cart; aù out; ch chin; e less; ē easy; g gift; i trip; ī life; j joke; ŋ sing; ō flow; ó flaw; ói coin; th thin; th̲ this; ü loot; ù foot; y yet; yü few; yù furious; zh vision

¹**red** \'red\ adj 1 : of the color red 2 : endorsing radical social or political change esp. by force 3 : of or relating to the U.S.S.R. or its allies — **red·ly** adv — **red·ness** n

²**red** n 1 : the color of blood or of the ruby 2 : a revolutionary in politics 3 cap : COMMUNIST 4 : the condition of showing a loss (in the ~)

red·breast \'red-,brest\ n : ROBIN

red·cap \-,kap\ n : a baggage porter at a railroad station

red·coat \-,kōt\ n : a British soldier esp. during the Revolutionary War

red·den \'red-ªn\ vb : to make or become red or reddish : FLUSH, BLUSH

red·dish \'red-ish\ adj : tinged with red — **red·dish·ness** n

re·deem \ri-'dēm\ vb [L redimere to buy back, fr. re-, red- back + emere to buy] 1 : to recover (property) by discharging an obligation 2 : to ransom, free, or rescue by paying a price 3 : to atone for 4 : to make good (a promise) by performing : FULFILL 5 : to free from the bondage of sin — **re·deem·able** adj — **re·deem·er** n

re·demp·tion \ri-'demp-shən\ n : the act of redeeming : the state of being redeemed — **re·demp·tive** \-tiv\ adj — **re·demp·to·ry** \-t(ə-)rē\ adj

red-hand·ed \'red-'han-dəd\ adv (or adj) : in the act of committing a crime or misdeed

red·head \-,hed\ n : a person having red hair — **red·head·ed** \-'hed-əd\ adj

red-hot \-'hät\ adj 1 : glowing red with heat (~ iron) 2 : EXCITED, FURIOUS 3 : very new

re·dis·trict \'rē-'dis-(,)trikt\ vb : to organize into new territorial and esp. political divisions

red-let·ter \'red-'let-ər\ adj : of special significance : MEMORABLE

red·o·lent \'red-ªl-ənt\ adj 1 : FRAGRANT, AROMATIC 2 : having a specified fragrance; also : IMPREGNATED, IMBUED 3 : REMINISCENT, SUGGESTIVE — **red·o·lence** n — **red·o·lent·ly** adv

re·doubt \ri-'daut\ n : a small usu. temporary fortification

re·doubt·able \ri-'daut-ə-bəl\ adj : arousing dread or fear : FORMIDABLE, DOUGHTY

re·dound \ri-'daund\ vb 1 : to have an effect : CONDUCE 2 : to become added or transferred : ACCRUE

¹**re·dress** \ri-'dres\ vb 1 : to set right : REMEDY 2 : COMPENSATE 3 : to remove the cause of (a grievance) 4 : AVENGE

²**redress** n 1 : relief from distress 2 : a means or possibility of seeking a remedy 3 : compensation for loss or injury 4 : an act or instance of redressing

red·skin \'red-,skin\ n : a No. American Indian

re·duce \ri-'d(y)üs\ vb 1 : LESSEN 2 : to put in a lower rank or grade 3 : CONQUER (~ a fort) 4 : to bring into a certain order or classification 5 : to bring to a specified state or condition (~ chaos to order) 6 : to correct (as a fracture) by restoration of displaced parts 7 : to lessen one's weight syn decrease, diminish, abate, dwindle, vanquish, defeat, subjugate, beat — **re·duc·er** n — **re·duc·ible** \-'d(y)üs-ə-bəl\ adj

re·duc·tion \ri-'dək-shən\ n 1 : the act of reducing : the state of being re-

duced 2 : the amount taken off in reducing something 3 : something made by reducing

re·dun·dan·cy \ri-'dən-dən-sē\ n 1 : the quality or state of being redundant : SUPERFLUITY 2 : something redundant or in excess 3 : the use of surplus words

re·dun·dant \-dənt\ adj : exceeding what is needed or normal : SUPERFLUOUS; esp : using more words than necessary — **re·dun·dant·ly** adv

red·wood \'red-,wud\ n : a tall coniferous timber tree of California or its durable wood

reed \'rēd\ n 1 : any of various tall slender grasses of wet areas; also : a stem or growth of reed 2 : a musical instrument made from the hollow stem of a reed 3 : an elastic tongue of cane, wood, or metal by which tones are produced in organ pipes and certain other wind instruments — **reedy** adj

¹**reef** \'rēf\ n 1 : a part of a sail taken in or let out in regulating the size of the sail 2 : the reduction in sail area made by reefing

²**reef** vb 1 : to reduce the area of a sail by rolling or folding part of it 2 : to lower or bring inboard a spar

³**reef** n : a ridge of rocks or sand at or near the surface of the water

¹**reef·er** \'rē-fər\ n 1 : one that reefs 2 : a close-fitting thick jacket

²**reefer** n : a marihuana cigarette

¹**reek** \'rēk\ n : a strong or disagreeable fume or odor — **reeky** adj

²**reek** vb 1 : to give off or become permeated with a strong or offensive odor 2 : to give a strong impression of some constituent quality — **reek·er** n

¹**reel** \'rēl\ n : a revolvable device on which something flexible (as yarn, thread, or wire) may be wound; also : a quantity of something (as motion-picture film) wound on such a device

²**reel** vb 1 : to wind on or as if on a reel 2 : to pull or draw (as a fish) by reeling a line — **reel·able** adj — **reel·er** n

³**reel** vb 1 : WHIRL; also : to be giddy 2 : to waver or fall back from a blow : RECOIL 3 : to walk or move unsteadily

⁴**reel** n : a reeling motion

⁵**reel** n : a lively Scottish dance or its music

re·en·force var of REINFORCE

reeve \'rēv\ vb rove \'rōv\ or reeved \'rēvd\ **reev·ing** : to pass (as a rope) through a hole in a block or cleat

re·fec·tion \ri-'fek-shən\ n 1 : refreshment esp. after hunger or fatigue 2 : food and drink together : REPAST

re·fec·to·ry \ri-'fek-t(ə-)rē\ n : a dining hall esp. in a monastery

re·fer \ri-'fər\ vb **-ferred; -fer·ring** 1 : to assign to a certain source, cause, or relationship 2 : to direct or send to some person or place (as for treatment, information, or help) 3 : to submit to someone else for consideration or action 4 : to have recourse (as for information or aid) 5 : to have connection : RELATE 6 : to direct attention : speak of : MENTION, ALLUDE syn credit, accredit, ascribe, attribute, resort, apply, go, turn — **re·fer·able** \'ref-(ə-)rə-bəl, ri-'fər-ə-\ adj

¹**ref·er·ee** \,ref-ə-'rē\ n 1 : a person to whom an issue esp. in law is referred for investigation or settlement 2 : an umpire in certain games

²**referee** vb : to act as referee

ref·er·ence \'ref-(ə-)rəns\ n 1 : the act of referring 2 : RELATION, RESPECT 3 : a direction of the attention to another passage or book 4 : ALLUSION, MENTION 5 : consultation esp. for obtaining information (~ books) 6 : a person of whom inquiries can be made about the character or ability of another person 7 : a written recommendation of a person for employment

ref·er·en·dum \,ref-ə-'ren-dəm\ n, pl -da \-də\ or -dums : the principle or practice of referring legislative measures to the voters for approval or rejection; also : a vote on a measure so submitted

re·fill \'rē-'fil\ vb 1 : to fill again : REPLENISH — re·fill·able adj

re·fine \ri-'fīn\ vb 1 : to free from impurities or waste matter : reduce to a pure state 2 : IMPROVE, PERFECT 3 : to free or become free of what is coarse or uncouth 4 : to make improvements by introducing subtle changes — re·fin·er n

re·fined adj 1 : freed from impurities 2 : CULTURED, CULTIVATED 3 : SUBTLE

re·fine·ment \ri-'fīn-mənt\ n 1 : the action of refining 2 : the quality or state of being refined 3 : a refined feature or method; also : a device or contrivance intended to improve or perfect

re·fin·ery \ri-'fīn-(ə-)rē\ n : a building and equipment for refining metals, oil, or sugar

re·flect \ri-'flekt\ vb 1 : to bend or cast back (as light, heat, or sound) 2 : to give back a likeness or image of as a mirror does 3 : to bring as a result (~ed credit on him) 4 : to cast reproach or blame 5 : PONDER, MEDITATE — re·flec·tion \-'flek-shən\ n — re·flec·tive \-tiv\ adj — re·flec·tor n

¹**re·flex** \'rē-,fleks\ n : an automatic and usu. inborn response to a stimulus not involving higher mental centers

²**reflex** adj 1 : bent or directed back 2 : of or relating to a psychic reflex — re·flex·ly adv

¹**re·flex·ive** \ri-'flek-siv\ adj : of or relating to an action directed back upon the doer or the grammatical subject (a ~ verb) (the ~ pronoun himself) — re·flex·ive·ly adv — re·flex·ive·ness n

²**reflexive** n : a reflexive verb or pronoun

re·for·est \rē-'fȯr-əst\ vb : to renew forest cover on by seeding or planting — re·for·es·ta·tion \,rē-,fȯr-ə-'stā-shən\ n

¹**re·form** \ri-'fȯrm\ vb 1 : to make or become better by removal of faults : IMPROVE, AMEND 2 : to induce to abandon evil ways syn correct, rectify, emend, remedy, redress, revise — re·form·able adj — re·for·ma·tive \-'fȯr-mət-iv\ adj

²**reform** n : improvement or correction of what is corrupt or defective

re-form \'rē-'fȯrm\ vb : to form again — re·for·ma·tion \,rē-fȯr-'mā-shən\ n

ref·or·ma·tion \,ref-ər-'mā-shən\ n 1 : the act of reforming : the state of being reformed : IMPROVEMENT 2 cap : a 16th century religious movement marked by the establishment of the Protestant churches

¹**re·for·ma·to·ry** \ri-'fȯr-mə-,tōr-ē\ adj : aiming at or tending toward reformation : REFORMATIVE

²**reformatory** n : a penal institution for reforming young or first offenders or women

re·form·er \ri-'fȯr-mər\ n 1 : one that works for or urges reform 2 cap : a leader of the Protestant Reformation

re·fract \ri-'frakt\ vb : to subject (as rays of light) to refraction — re·frac·tor n

re·frac·tion \ri-'frak-shən\ n : the bending of a ray of light, heat, or sound when it passes obliquely from one medium into another in which its velocity is different — re·frac·tive \-tiv\ adj

re·frac·to·ry \ri-'frak-t(ə-)rē\ adj 1 : OBSTINATE, STUBBORN, UNMANAGEABLE 2 : difficult to melt, corrode, or draw out; esp : capable of enduring high temperature (~ bricks) syn recalcitrant, intractable, ungovernable, unruly, headstrong, willful — re·frac·to·ri·ly adv — re·frac·to·ri·ness n

¹**re·frain** \ri-'frān\ vb : to hold oneself back : FORBEAR, ABSTAIN — re·frain·ment n

²**refrain** n : a phrase or verse recurring regularly in a poem or song

re·fresh \ri-'fresh\ vb 1 : to make or become fresh or fresher 2 : to revive by or as if by renewal of supplies (~ one's memory) 3 : to freshen up 4 : to supply or take refreshment syn restore, rejuvenate, renovate, refurbish — re·fresh·er n

re·fresh·ment \-mənt\ n 1 : the act of refreshing : the state of being refreshed 2 : something that refreshes 3 pl : a light meal

re·frig·er·ate \ri-'frij-ə-,rāt\ vb : to make cool; esp : to chill or freeze (food) for preservation — re·frig·er·ant \-(ə-)rənt\ adj or n — re·frig·er·a·tion \-,frij-ə-'rā-shən\ n — re·frig·er·a·tor \-'frij-ə-,rāt-ər\ n

ref·uge \'ref-,yüj\ n 1 : shelter or protection from danger or distress 2 : a place that provides protection : SHELTER, ASYLUM

ref·u·gee \,ref-yü-'jē\ n : one who flees for safety esp. to a foreign country

re·ful·gence \ri-'fùl-jəns, -'fəl-\ n : radiant or shining quality or state : BRILLIANCE, BRIGHTNESS — re·ful·gent adj

¹**re·fund** \ri-'fənd, 'rē-,fənd\ vb : to give or put back (money) : REPAY — re·fund·able adj

²**re·fund** \'rē-,fənd\ n 1 : the act of refunding 2 : a sum refunded

re·fur·bish \rē-'fər-bish\ vb : to brighten or freshen up : RENOVATE

¹**re·fuse** \ri-'fyüz\ vb 1 : to decline to accept 2 : to decline to do, give, or grant : DENY — re·fus·al \-'fyüz-əl\ n

²**ref·use** \'ref-,yüs, -,yüz\ n : rejected or worthless matter : RUBBISH, TRASH

re·fute \ri-'fyüt\ vb : to prove to be false by argument or evidence — re·fu·ta·tion \,ref-yü-'tā-shən\ n — re·fut·er \-'fyüt-ər\ n

re·gain \rē-'gān\ vb 1 : to gain or get again : get back (~ed his health) 2 : to get back to : reach again (~ the shore) syn recover, retrieve

---

re·gal \'rē-gəl\ adj 1 : of, relating to, or befitting a king : ROYAL 2 : STATELY, SPLENDID — **re·gal·ly** adv

re·gale \ri-'gāl\ vb 1 : to entertain richly or agreeably 2 : to give pleasure or amusement to syn gratify, delight, please, rejoice, gladden — **re·gale·ment** n

re·ga·lia \ri-'gāl-yə\ n pl 1 : the emblems, symbols, or paraphernalia of royalty (as the crown and scepter) 2 : the insignia of an office or order 3 : special costume : FINERY

¹re·gard \ri-'gärd\ n 1 : CONSIDERATION, HEED; also : CARE, CONCERN 2 : GAZE, GLANCE, LOOK 3 : RESPECT, ESTEEM 4 pl : friendly greetings implying respect and esteem 5 : an aspect to be considered : PARTICULAR — **re·gard·ful** adj — **re·gard·less** adj

²regard vb 1 : to pay attention to 2 : to show respect for : HEED 3 : to hold in high esteem : care for 4 : to look at : gaze upon 5 : to relate to : touch on 6 : to think of : CONSIDER, JUDGE

re·gard·ing prep : CONCERNING, RESPECTING

regardless of prep : in spite of

re·gat·ta \ri-'gät-ə, -'gat-\ n : a rowing, speedboat, or sailing race or a series of such races

re·gen·cy \'rē-jən-sē\ n 1 : the office or government of a regent or body of regents 2 : a body of regents 3 : the period during which a regent governs

¹re·gen·er·ate \ri-'jen-ə-rət\ adj 1 : formed or created again 2 : spiritually reborn or converted

²re·gen·er·ate \-ə-,rāt\ vb 1 : to reform completely 2 : to give or gain new life; also : to renew by a new growth of tissue 3 : to subject to spiritual renewal — **re·gen·er·a·tion** \-,jen-ə-'rā-shən\ n — **re·gen·er·a·tive** \-'jen-ə-,rāt-iv\ adj — **re·gen·er·a·tor** \-,rāt-ər\ n

re·gent \'rē-jənt\ n 1 : a person who rules during the childhood, absence, or incapacity of the sovereign 2 : a member of a governing board (as of a state university)

reg·i·cide \'rej-ə-,sīd\ n 1 : one who murders a king 2 : murder of a king — **reg·i·ci·dal** \,rej-ə-'sīd-ᵊl\ adj

re·gime \rā-'zhēm\ n 1 : REGIMEN 2 : a form or system of government or administration

reg·i·men \'rej-ə-mən\ n 1 : a systematic course of treatment or behavior (a strict dietary ~) 2 : GOVERNMENT, RULE

¹reg·i·ment \'rej-ə-mənt\ n : a military unit consisting of a variable number of units (as battalions) — **reg·i·men·tal** \,rej-ə-'ment-ᵊl\ adj

²reg·i·ment \'rej-ə-,ment\ vb : to organize rigidly esp. for regulation or central control : subject to order or uniformity — **reg·i·men·ta·tion** \,rej-ə-mən-'tā-shən\ n

reg·i·men·tals \,rej-ə-'ment-ᵊlz\ n pl 1 : a regimental uniform 2 : military dress

re·gion \'rē-jən\ n : an often indefinitely defined part or area; also : VICINITY (the ~ of the lungs)

re·gion·al \'rē-jə-)nəl\ adj 1 : of or relating to a geographical region 2 : of or relating to a bodily region : LOCALIZED — **re·gion·al·ly** adv

¹reg·is·ter \'rej-ə-stər\ n 1 : a record of

items or details; also : a book or system for keeping such a record 2 : a device (as in a floor or wall) to regulate ventilation or flow of heat from a furnace 3 : a mechanical device which records items 4 : the range of a voice or instrument

²register vb 1 : to enter or enroll in a register (as in a list of voters, students, or guests) 2 : to record automatically 3 : to secure special care for (mail matter) by paying additional postage 4 : to show (emotions) by facial expression or gestures 5 : to correspond or adjust so as to correspond exactly

reg·is·trar \-,strär\ n : an official recorder or keeper of records

reg·is·tra·tion \,rej-ə-'strā-shən\ n 1 : the act of registering 2 : an entry in a register 3 : the number of persons registered : ENROLLMENT 4 : a document certifying an act of registering

reg·is·try \'rej-ə-strē\ n 1 : ENROLLMENT, REGISTRATION 2 : the state or fact of being entered in a register 3 : a place of registration 4 : an official record book or an entry in one

reg·nal \'reg-nᵊl\ adj : of or relating to a king or his reign (~ year)

reg·nant \-nənt\ adj 1 : REIGNING 2 : DOMINANT 3 : of common or widespread occurrence : PREVALENT

¹re·gress \'rē-,gres\ n 1 : WITHDRAWAL 2 : RETROGRESSION

²re·gress \ri-'gres\ vb : to go or cause to go back or to a lower level — **re·gression** n — **re·gres·sive** adj — **re·gressor** n

¹re·gret \ri-'gret\ vb -gret·ted; -gret·ting 1 : to mourn the loss or death of 2 : to be keenly sorry for 3 : to experience regret — **re·gret·ta·ble** adj — **re·gret·ta·bly** adv — **re·gret·ter** n

²regret n 1 : distress of mind on account of something past 2 : an expression of sorrow 3 pl : a note or oral message politely declining an invitation — **re·gret·ful** adj — **re·gret·ful·ly** adv

¹reg·u·lar \'reg-yə-lər\ adj [LL regularis of a rule, fr. L regula straightedge, ruler, rule, fr. regere to guide straight, rule] 1 : belonging to a religious order 2 : made, built, or arranged according to a rule, standard, or type; also : even or symmetrical in form or structure 3 : ORDERLY, METHODICAL (~ habits); also : not varying : STEADY (a ~ pace) 4 : made, selected, or conducted according to rule or custom 5 : properly qualified (not a ~ lawyer) 6 : conforming to the normal or usual manner of inflection 7 : belonging to a permanent standing army and esp. to one maintained by a federal government syn systematic, typical, natural — **reg·u·lar·i·ty** \,reg-yə-'lar-ət-ē\ n — **reg·u·lar·ize** \'reg-yə-lə-,rīz\ vb — **reg·u·lar·ly** \-lər-lē\ adv

²regular n 1 : one that is regular (as in attendance) 2 : a member of the regular clergy 3 : a soldier in a regular army 4 : a player on an athletic team who usu. starts every game

reg·u·late \'reg-yə-,lāt\ vb 1 : to govern or direct according to rule : CONTROL 2 : to bring under the control of law or authority 3 : to put in good order 4 : to fix or adjust the time, amount, degree, or rate of — **reg·u·la·tive** \-,lāt-iv\ adj — **reg·u·la·tor** \-,lāt-ər\ n — **reg·u·la·to·ry** \-lə-,tōr-ē\ adj

reg·u·la·tion \ˌreg-yə-'lā-shən\ *n* **1** : the act of regulating : the state of being regulated **2** : a rule dealing with details of procedure **3** : an order issued by executive authority of a government and having the force of law

re·gur·gi·tate \rē-'gər-jə-ˌtāt\ *vb* : to throw or be thrown back or out; *esp* : VOMIT — **re·gur·gi·ta·tion** \-ˌgər-jə-'tā-shən\ *n*

re·ha·bil·i·tate \ˌrē-(h)ə-'bil-ə-ˌtāt\ *vb* **1** : to restore to a former capacity, rank, or right : REINSTATE **2** : to put into good condition again — **re·ha·bil·i·ta·tion** \-ˌbil-ə-'tā-shən\ *n* — **re·ha·bil·i·ta·tive** \-'bil-ə-ˌtāt-iv\ *adj*

¹**re·hash** \'rē-ˌhash\ *vb* : to present again in another form without real change or improvement

²**re·hash** \'rē-ˌhash\ *n* : a product or an act of rehashing

re·hear·ing \'rē-'hi(ə)r-iŋ\ *n* : a second or new hearing by the same tribunal

re·hears·al \ri-'hərs\ *n* **1** : something told again : RECITAL **2** : a private performance or practice session preparatory to a public appearance

re·hearse \ri-'hərs\ *vb* **1** : to say again : REPEAT **2** : to recount in order : ENUMERATE **3** : to give a rehearsal of ⟨∼ a play⟩ **4** : to train by rehearsal ⟨∼ an actor⟩ **5** : to engage in a rehearsal — **re·hears·er** *n*

¹**reign** \'rān\ *n* **1** : the authority or rule of a sovereign **2** : the time during which a sovereign rules

²**reign** *vb* **1** : to rule as a sovereign **2** : to be predominant or prevalent

re·im·burse \ˌrē-əm-'bərs\ *vb* : to pay back : make restitution : REPAY **syn** indemnify, recompense, requite — **re·im·burs·able** *adj* — **re·im·burse·ment** *n*

¹**rein** \'rān\ *n* **1** : a line of a bridle by which a rider or driver directs an animal **2** : a restraining influence : CHECK **3** : position of control or command ⟨the ∼s of government⟩ **4** : complete freedom : SCOPE — *usu* used in the phrase *give rein to*

²**rein** *vb* : to check or direct by or as if by reins

re·in·car·na·tion \ˌrē-ˌin-ˌkär-'nā-shən\ *n* : rebirth of the soul in a new body — **re·in·car·nate** \ˌrē-in-ˈkär-ˌnāt\ *vb*

rein·deer \'rān-ˌdiər\ *n* : any of several large deers of northern regions used for draft and meat

re·in·force \ˌrē-ən-'fōrs\ *vb* **1** : to strengthen with new force, aid, material, or support **2** : to strengthen with additional forces (as troops or ships) — **re·in·force·ment** *n* — **re·in·forc·er** *n*

re·in·state \ˌrē-ən-'stāt\ *vb* **1** : to place again **2** : to restore to a previous effective state — **re·in·state·ment** *n*

re·it·er·ate \rē-'it-ə-ˌrāt\ *vb* : to say or do over again or repeatedly **syn** repeat, iterate — **re·it·er·a·tion** \-ˌit-ə-'rā-shən\ *n*

¹**re·ject** \ri-'jekt\ *vb* **1** : to refuse to acknowledge or submit to **2** : to refuse to take or accept **3** : to refuse to grant, consider, or accede to **4** : to throw back or out esp. as useless or unsatis-

factory : DISCARD — **re·jec·tion** \-'jek-shən\ *n*

²**re·ject** \'rē-ˌjekt\ *n* : a rejected person or thing

re·joice \ri-'jȯis\ *vb* **1** : to give joy to : GLADDEN **2** : to feel joy or great delight — **re·joic·er** *n* — **re·joic·ing** *n*

re·join \'rē-'jȯin *for 1*, ri- *for 2*\ *vb* **1** : to join again : come together again : REUNITE **2** : to say in answer (as to a plaintiff's plea in court) : REPLY

re·join·der \ri-'jȯin-dər\ *n* : REPLY; *esp* : an answer to a reply

re·ju·ve·nate \ri-'jü-və-ˌnāt\ *vb* : to make young or youthful again : give new vigor to **syn** renew, refresh — **re·ju·ve·na·tion** \-ˌjü-və-'nā-shən\ *n*

¹**re·lapse** \ri-'laps\ *vb* : to slip back into a former condition (as of illness) after a change for the better

²**re·lapse** \ri-'laps, 'rē-ˌlaps\ *n* : the action or process of relapsing; *esp* : a recurrence of illness after a period of improvement

re·late \ri-'lāt\ *vb* **1** : to give an account of : TELL, NARRATE **2** : to show or establish logical or causal connection between **3** : to be connected : have reference **4** : to have meaningful social relationships — **re·lat·able** *adj* — **re·lat·er** *n*

re·lat·ed *adj* **1** : connected by some understood relationship ⟨pneumonia and ∼ diseases⟩ **2** : connected through membership in the same family

re·la·tion \ri-'lā-shən\ *n* **1** : NARRATION, ACCOUNT **2** : CONNECTION, RELATIONSHIP **3** : connection by blood or marriage : KINSHIP **4** : REFERENCE, RESPECT ⟨in ∼ to this matter⟩ **5** : the state of being mutually interested or involved (as in social or commercial matters) **6** *pl* : DEALINGS, AFFAIRS **7** *pl* : sexual intercourse

re·la·tion·ship \-ˌship\ *n* : the state of being related or interrelated

¹**rel·a·tive** \'rel-ət-iv\ *n* **1** : a word referring grammatically to an antecedent **2** : a thing having a relation to or a dependence upon another thing **3** : a person connected with another by blood or marriage; *also* : an animal or plant related to another by common descent

²**relative** *adj* **1** : introducing a subordinate clause qualifying an expressed or implied antecedent ⟨∼ pronoun⟩; *also* : introduced by such a connective ⟨∼ clause⟩ **2** : PERTINENT, RELEVANT **3** : not absolute or independent : COMPARATIVE **4** : expressed as the ratio of the specified quantity to the total magnitude or to the mean of all quantities involved **syn** dependent, contingent, conditional — **rel·a·tive·ly** *adv* — **rel·a·tive·ness** *n*

rel·a·tiv·i·ty \ˌrel-ə-'tiv-ət-ē\ *n* **1** : the quality or state of being relative **2** : a theory leading to the assertion of the equivalence of mass and energy and of the increase of the mass of a body with increased velocity

re·la·tor \ri-'lāt-ər\ *n* : NARRATOR

re·lax \ri-'laks\ *vb* **1** : to make or become less firm, tense, or rigid **2** : to make less severe or strict **3** : to seek rest or recreation — **re·lax·er** *n* re·lax·a·tion \ˌrē-ˌlak-ˈsā-shən\ n 1 : the act or fact of relaxing or of being relaxed : a lessening of tension 2 : DIVERSION, RECREATION syn rest, repose, leisure, ease, comfort

¹re·lay \ˈrē-ˌlā\ n 1 : a fresh supply (as of horses or men) arranged beforehand to relieve or replace others at various stages 2 : a race between teams in which each team member covers a specified part of a course 3 : an electromagnetic device for remote or automatic control of other devices (as switches) in the same or a different circuit 4 : the act of passing along by stages

²re·lay \ˈrē-ˌlā, ri-ˈlā\ vb 1 : to place in or provide with relays 2 : to pass along by relays 3 : to control or operate by a relay

³re·lay \ˈrē-ˈlā\ vb : to lay again

¹re·lease \ri-ˈlēs\ vb 1 : to set free from confinement or restraint 2 : to relieve from something (as pain, trouble, or penalty) that oppresses or burdens 3 : RELINQUISH (~ a claim) 4 : to permit publication or performance (as of a news story or a motion picture) on but not before a specified date syn emancipate, discharge

²release n 1 : relief or deliverance from sorrow, suffering, or trouble 2 : discharge from an obligation or responsibility 3 : an act of setting free : the state of being freed 4 : a document effecting a legal release 5 : a device for holding or releasing a mechanism as required 6 : a releasing for performance or publication; also : the matter released (as a statement prepared for the press)

rel·e·gate \ˈrel-ə-ˌgāt\ vb 1 : to send into exile : BANISH 2 : to remove or dismiss (a person or thing) to some less prominent position 3 : to assign to a particular class or sphere 4 : to submit or refer for judgment, decision, or execution : DELEGATE syn commit, entrust, consign — rel·e·ga·tion \ˌrel-ə-ˈgā-shən\ n

re·lent \ri-ˈlent\ vb 1 : to become less stern, severe, or harsh 2 : SLACKEN

re·lent·less \-ləs\ adj : mercilessly hard or harsh : immovably stern or persistent — re·lent·less·ly adv — re·lent·less·ness n

rel·e·vance \ˈrel-ə-vəns\ also rel·e·van·cy \-vən-sē\ n : the state of being relevant

rel·e·vant \-vənt\ adj : bearing upon the matter at hand : having reference to the case under consideration : PERTINENT syn germane, material, applicable, apropos — rel·e·vant·ly adv

re·li·able \ri-ˈlī-ə-bəl\ adj : fit to be trusted or relied on : DEPENDABLE, TRUSTWORTHY — re·li·a·bil·i·ty \-ˌlī-ə-ˈbil-ət-ē\ n — re·li·able·ness \-ˈlī-ə-bəl-nəs\ n — re·li·ably \-ə-blē\ adv

re·li·ance \ri-ˈlī-əns\ n 1 : the act of relying 2 : the state or attitude of one that relies : CONFIDENCE, DEPENDENCE, FAITH 3 : something or someone relied on — re·li·ant \-ənt\ adj

rel·ic \ˈrel-ik\ n 1 : an object venerated because of its association with a saint or martyr 2 pl : REMAINS, RUINS 3 : a remaining trace : SURVIVAL, VESTIGE 4 : SOUVENIR, MEMENTO

rel·ict \ˈrel-ikt\ n 1 : WIDOW 2 : something left unchanged in a process of change

re·lief \ri-ˈlēf\ n 1 : removal or lightening of something oppressive, painful, or distressing 2 : aid in the form of money or necessities (as for the aged or handicapped) 3 : military assistance in or rescue from a position of difficulty 4 : release from a post or from performance of a duty; also : one that relieves another by taking his place 5 : legal remedy or redress 6 : projection of figures or ornaments from the background (as in sculpture) 7 : elevations of a land surface (map showing ~)

re·lieve \ri-ˈlēv\ vb 1 : to free partly or wholly from a burden or from distress 2 : to remove or lessen (as pain or trouble) : MITIGATE 3 : to release from a post or duty; also : to take the place of 4 : to break the monotony of (as by contrast in color) 5 : to raise in relief syn alleviate, lighten, assuage, allay — re·liev·er n

re·li·gion \ri-ˈlij-ən\ n 1 : the service and worship of God or the supernatural 2 : devotion to a religious faith 3 : an organized system of faith and worship; also : a personal set of religious beliefs and practices 4 : a cause, principle, or belief held to with faith and ardor — re·li·gion·ist n

¹re·li·gious \ri-ˈlij-əs\ adj 1 : relating or devoted to the divine or that which is held to be of ultimate importance 2 : of or relating to religious beliefs or observances 3 : scrupulously and conscientiously faithful 4 : FERVENT, ZEALOUS — re·li·gious·ly adv

²religious n, pl religious : one (as a monk) bound by vows and devoted to a life of piety

re·lin·quish \ri-ˈliŋ-kwish\ vb 1 : to withdraw or retreat from : ABANDON, QUIT 2 : RENOUNCE 3 : to let go of : RELEASE syn yield, leave, resign, surrender, cede, waive — re·lin·quish·ment n

rel·i·quary \ˈrel-ə-ˌkwer-ē\ n : a container for holding religious relics

re·lique \ri-ˈlēk, ˈrel-ik\ archaic var of RELIC

¹rel·ish \ˈrel-ish\ n [ME reles aftertaste, fr. OF, release, something left over, fr. relessier to relax, release, fr. L relaxare] 1 : a characteristic flavor (as of food) : SAVOR 2 : keen enjoyment or delight in something : GUSTO 3 : APPETITE, INCLINATION 4 : a food eaten with other food to add flavor

²relish vb 1 : to add relish to 2 : to take pleasure in : be gratified by : ENJOY 3 : to eat with relish — rel·ish·able adj

re·luc·tance \ri-ˈlək-təns\ n 1 : the quality or state of being reluctant 2 : the opposition offered by a magnetic substance to magnetic flux

re·luc·tant \-tənt\ adj : holding back (as from acting, giving, or serving) : UNWILLING; also : showing unwillingness syn disinclined, indisposed, hesitant, loath, averse — re·luc·tant·ly adv

re·ly \ri-ˈlī\ vb : to place faith or confidence : DEPEND syn trust, count

re·main \ri-ˈmān\ vb 1 : to be left after others have been removed, subtracted, or destroyed 2 : to be left as yet to be done or considered 3 : to stay after others have gone 4 : to continue unchanged

re·main·der \-dər\ n 1 : that which is

left over **:** a remaining group, part, or trace **2 :** the number left after subtraction **3 :** a book sold at a reduced price by the publisher after sales have slowed syn leavings, rest, balance, remnant, residue

re·mains \ri-'mānz\ *n pl* **1 :** a remaining part or trace (the ∼ of a meal) **2 :** writings left unpublished at an author's death **3 :** a dead body

re·mand \ri-'mand\ *vb* **:** to order back; *esp* **:** to return to custody pending trial or for further detention

¹re·mark \ri-'märk\ *vb* **1 :** to take notice of **:** OBSERVE **2 :** to express as an observation or comment **:** SAY

²remark *n* **1 :** the act of remarking **:** OBSERVATION, NOTICE **2 :** a passing observation or comment **:** a casual statement

re·mark·able \ri-'mär-kə-bəl\ *adj* **:** worthy of being or likely to be noticed **:** UNUSUAL, EXTRAORDINARY, NOTEWORTHY — **re·mark·able·ness** *n* — **re·mark·ably** *adv*

re·me·di·al \ri-'mēd-ē-əl\ *adj* **:** intended to remedy or improve — **re·me·di·al·ly** *adv*

¹rem·e·dy \'rem-əd-ē\ *n* **1 :** a medicine or treatment that cures or relieves **2 :** something that corrects or counteracts an evil or compensates for a loss

²remedy *vb* **:** to provide or serve as a remedy for — **re·me·di·a·ble** \ri-'mēd-ē-ə-bəl\ *adj*

re·mem·ber \ri-'mem-bər\ *vb* **1 :** to have come into the mind again **:** think of again **:** RECOLLECT **2 :** to keep from forgetting **:** keep in mind **:** retain in the memory **3 :** to recall to another's mind; *esp* **:** to convey greetings from **4 :** COMMEMORATE

re·mem·brance \-brəns\ *n* **1 :** an act of remembering **:** RECOLLECTION **2 :** the state of being remembered **:** MEMORY **3 :** the power of remembering; *also* **:** the period over which one's memory extends **4 :** a memory of a person, thing, or event **5 :** something that serves to bring to mind **:** REMINDER, MEMENTO **6 :** a greeting or gift recalling or expressing friendship or affection

re·mind \ri-'mīnd\ *vb* **:** to put in mind of someone or something **:** cause to remember — **re·mind·er** *n*

rem·i·nisce \,rem-ə-'nis\ *vb* **:** to indulge in reminiscence

rem·i·nis·cence \-'nis-°ns\ *n* **1 :** a recalling or telling of a past experience **2 :** an account of a memorable experience **3 :** something so like another as to suggest unconscious repetition or imitation

rem·i·nis·cent \-°nt\ *adj* **1 :** of or relating to reminiscence **2 :** marked by or given to reminiscence **3 :** serving to remind **:** SUGGESTIVE — **rem·i·nis·cent·ly** *adv*

re·miss \ri-'mis\ *adj* **1 :** negligent or careless in the performance of work or duty **2 :** showing neglect or inattention syn lax, neglectful — **re·miss·ly** *adv* — **re·miss·ness** *n*

re·mis·sion \ri-'mish-ən\ *n* **:** the act or process of remitting (as from sin)

re·mit \ri-'mit\ *vb* **-mit·ted; -mit·ting** **1 :** FORGIVE, PARDON **2 :** to give or gain

relief from (as pain) **3 :** to refer for consideration, report, or decision **4 :** to refrain from exacting or enforcing (as a penalty) **5 :** to send (money) in payment of a bill syn excuse, condone

re·mit·tance \ri-'mit-°ns\ *n* **1 :** a sum of money remitted **2 :** a sending of money esp. to a distance

rem·nant \'rem-nənt\ *n* **1 :** a usu. small part or trace remaining **2 :** an unsold or unused end of fabrics that are sold by the yard syn remainder, residue, rest

re·mod·el \'rē-'mäd-°l\ *vb* **:** to alter the structure of **:** make over

re·mon·strance \ri-'män-strəns\ *n* **:** an act or instance of remonstrating **:** EXPOSTULATION

re·mon·strant \-strənt\ *adj* **:** vigorously objecting or opposing — **re·mon·strant** *n* — **re·mon·strant·ly** *adv*

re·mon·strate \ri-'män-,strāt\ *vb* **:** to give or urge reasons in opposition **:** speak in protest or reproof syn expostulate, object — **re·mon·stra·tion** \ri-,män-'strā-shən, ,rem-ən-\ *n* — **re·mon·stra·tive** \ri-'män-strət-iv\ *adj* — **re·mon·stra·tor** \ri-'män-,strāt-ər\

re·morse \ri-'mórs\ *n* **:** regret for one's sins or for acts that wrong others **:** distress arising from a sense of guilt syn penitence, repentance, contrition — **re·morse·ful** *adj* — **re·morse·less** *adj*

re·mote \ri-'mōt\ *adj* **1 :** far off in place or time **:** not near **2 :** not closely related **:** DISTANT **3 :** located out of the way **:** SECLUDED **4 :** small in degree **:** SLIGHT ⟨a ∼ chance⟩ **5 :** distant in manner **:** ALOOF — **re·mote·ly** *adv* — **re·mote·ness** *n*

¹re·mount \'rē-'maúnt\ *vb* **1 :** to mount again **2 :** to furnish remounts to

²re·mount \'rē-,maúnt\ *n* **:** a fresh horse to replace one disabled or exhausted

¹re·move \ri-'müv\ *vb* **1 :** to move from one place to another **:** TRANSFER **2 :** to move by lifting or taking off or away **3 :** DISMISS, DISCHARGE **4 :** to get rid of **:** ELIMINATE ⟨∼ a fire hazard⟩ **5 :** to change one's residence or location **6 :** to go away **:** DEPART **7 :** to be capable of being removed — **re·mov·able** \-'mü-və-bəl\ *adj* — **re·mov·al** \-vəl\ *n* — **re·mov·er** *n*

²remove *n* **1 :** a transfer from one location to another **:** MOVE **2 :** a degree or stage of separation

re·mu·ner·ate \ri-'myü-nə-,rāt\ *vb* **:** to pay an equivalent for or to **:** RECOMPENSE — **re·mu·ner·a·tor** \-,rāt-ər\ *n* — **re·mu·ner·a·to·ry** \-rə-,tōr-ē\ *adj*

re·mu·ner·a·tion \-,myü-nə-'rā-shən\ *n* **:** COMPENSATION, PAYMENT

re·mu·ner·a·tive \-'myü-nə-,rāt-iv, -rət-\ *adj* **:** serving to remunerate **:** GAINFUL, PROFITABLE — **re·mu·ner·a·tive·ly** *adv* — **re·mu·ner·a·tive·ness** *n*

re·nais·sance \,ren-ə-'säns, -'zäns\ *n* **1** *cap* **:** the revival in art and literature in Europe in the 14th–17th centuries; *also* **:** the period of the Renaissance **2** *often cap* **:** a movement or period of vigorous artistic and intellectual activity **3 :** REBIRTH, REVIVAL

re·nal \'rēn-°l\ *adj* **:** of, relating to, or located in or near the kidneys

ə abut; ° kitten; ər further; a back; ā bake; ä cot, cart; aú out; ch chin; e less; ē easy; g gift; i trip; ī life; j joke; ŋ sing; ō flow; ó flaw; ói coin; th thin; th this; ü loot; ú foot; y yet; yü few; yú furious; zh vision

re·nas·cence \ri-'nas-ᵊns, -'näs-\ *n*, often cap **:** RENAISSANCE

ren·con·tre \räⁿ-kōⁿtr², ren-'känt-ər\ *or* **ren·coun·ter** \ren-'kaunt-ər\ *n* **1 :** a hostile meeting or contest **:** COMBAT **2 :** a casual meeting

rend \'rend\ *vb* rent \'rent\ rend·ing **1 :** to remove by violence **:** WREST **2 :** to tear forcibly apart **:** SPLIT, CLEAVE, RIP

ren·der \'ren-dər\ *vb* **1 :** to extract (as lard) by heating **2 :** DELIVER, GIVE; *also* **:** YIELD **3 :** to give in return as retribution **4 :** to do (a service) for another (~ aid) **5 :** to cause to be or become **:** MAKE **6 :** to represent by artistic or verbal means (as by a singing performance or by playing or singing) **7 :** TRANSLATE (~ into English)

¹ren·dez·vous \'rän-di-ˌvü\ *n* **1 :** a place appointed for a meeting; *also* **:** a meeting at an appointed place **2 :** a place of popular resort **syn** tryst, engagement, appointment

²rendezvous *vb* **-voused** \-ˌvüd\ **-vous·ing** \-ˌvü-iŋ\ **:** to come or bring together at a rendezvous

ren·di·tion \ren-'dish-ən\ *n* **:** an act or a result of rendering (demanded the ~ of the fugitives) (first ~ of the work into English)

ren·e·gade \'ren-i-ˌgād\ *n* **:** one who deserts a faith, cause, principle, or party for another **:** TURNCOAT, TRAITOR

re·nege \ri-'nig, -'neg, -'nēg\ *vb* **1 :** to fail to follow suit when able in a card game in violation of the rules **2 :** to go back on a promise or commitment — **re·neg·er** *n*

re·new \ri-'n(y)ü\ *vb* **1 :** to make or become new, fresh, or strong again **2 :** to restore to existence **:** RECREATE, REVIVE **3 :** to make or do again **:** REPEAT (~ a complaint) **4 :** to begin again **:** RESUME (~ed his efforts) **5 :** REPLACE (~ the lining of a coat) **6 :** to grant or obtain an extension of or on (~ a lease) (~ a subscription) — **re·new·able** *adj* — **re·new·er** *n*

re·new·al \-əl\ *n* **1 :** the act of renewing **:** the state of being renewed **2 :** something renewed

re·nounce \ri-'nauns\ *vb* **1 :** to give up, refuse, or resign use, by formal declaration **2 :** to cast off **:** REPUDIATE **syn** abdicate, forswear — **re·nounce·ment** *n*

ren·o·vate \'ren-ə-ˌvāt\ *vb* **1 :** to restore to vigor or activity **2 :** to make like new again **:** put in good condition **:** REPAIR — **ren·o·va·tion** \ˌren-ə-'vā-shən\ *n* — **ren·o·va·tor** \'ren-ə-ˌvāt-ər\ *n*

re·nown \ri-'naun\ *n* **:** a state of being widely acclaimed and honored **:** FAME, CELEBRITY **syn** honor, glory, reputation, repute — **re·nowned** \-'naund\ *adj*

¹rent \'rent\ *n* **:** money or the amount of money paid or due (as weekly or monthly) for the use of another's property

²rent *vb* **1 :** to take and hold under an agreement to pay rent **2 :** to give possession and use of in return for rent **3 :** to be for or bring in as rent (~s for $100 a month)

³rent *n* **1 :** a tear in cloth **2 :** a split in a party or organized group **:** SCHISM

¹rent·al \'rent-ᵊl\ *n* **1 :** an amount paid or collected as rent **2 :** a property rented **3 :** an act of renting

²rental *adj* **:** of or relating to rent (~ value) (~ property)

re·nun·ci·a·tion \ri-ˌnən-sē-'ā-shən\ *n* **:** the act of renouncing **:** REPUDIATION, DISAVOWAL

re·or·ga·nize \rē-'ȯr-gə-ˌnīz\ *vb* **:** to organize again or anew — **re·or·ga·ni·za·tion** \-ˌȯr-gə-nə-'zā-shən\ *n*

¹re·pair \ri-'paər\ *vb* **:** to betake oneself **:** GO (~ed to his den)

²repair *vb* **1 :** to restore to good condition esp. by replacing parts or putting together something torn or broken **:** FIX, MEND **2 :** to restore to a healthy state **:** HEAL **3 :** REMEDY (~ a wrong) — **re·pair·er** *n*

³repair *n* **1 :** an act of repairing **2 :** an instance or result of repairing **3 :** condition with respect to soundness or need of repairing (in bad ~)

rep·a·ra·tion \ˌrep-ə-'rā-shən\ *n* **1 :** the act of making amends for a wrong **2 :** amends made for a wrong; *esp* **:** money paid by a defeated nation in compensation for damages caused during hostilities — usu. used in pl. **syn** redress, restitution, indemnity

re·par·a·tive \ri-'par-ət-iv\ *adj* **1 :** of, relating to, or effecting repairs **2 :** serving to make amends

rep·ar·tee \ˌrep-ər-'tē\ *n* **1 :** a witty retort **2 :** a succession of clever retorts; *also* **:** adroitness in making such retorts

re·past \ri-'past\ *n* **:** something taken as food; *esp* **:** a supply of food and drink served as a meal

re·pay \rē-'pā\ *vb* **1 :** to pay back **:** REFUND **2 :** to give or do in return or requital **3 :** to make a return payment to **:** RECOMPENSE, REQUITE **syn** remunerate, satisfy, reimburse, indemnify — **re·pay·able** *adj* — **re·pay·ment** *n*

re·peal \ri-'pēl\ *vb* **:** to rescind or annul by authoritative and esp. legislative action — **repeal** *n* — **re·peal·er** *n*

¹re·peat \ri-'pēt\ *vb* **1 :** to say again **2 :** to do again **3 :** to say over from memory **syn** iterate, reiterate — **re·peat·able** *adj* — **re·peat·er** *n*

²repeat *n* **1 :** the act of repeating **2 :** something repeated or to be repeated (as a passage in music or a radio or television rebroadcast)

re·peat·ed *adj* **:** done or recurring again and again **:** FREQUENT — **re·peat·ed·ly** *adv*

re·pel \ri-'pel\ *vb* **-pelled; -pel·ling 1 :** to drive away **:** REPULSE **2 :** REJECT **3 :** to ward off or keep out **:** RESIST **4 :** to cause aversion in **:** DISGUST — **re·pel·lent** \-'pel-ənt\ *adj or n*

re·pent \ri-'pent\ *vb* **1 :** to turn from sin and resolve to reform one's life **2 :** to feel sorry for (something done) **:** REGRET (~ a decision) — **re·pen·tance** \-'pent-ᵊns\ *n* — **re·pen·tant** \-'pent-ᵊnt\ *adj*

re·per·cus·sion \ˌrē-pər-'kəsh-ən, ˌrep-ər-\ *n* **1 :** REVERBERATION **2 :** a reciprocal action or effect **3 :** a widespread, indirect, or unforeseen effect of something done or said

rep·er·toire \'rep-ə(r)-ˌtwär\ *n* **1 :** a list of plays, operas, pieces, or parts which a company or performer is prepared to present **2 :** a list of the skills or devices possessed by a person or needed in his occupation

rep·er·tory \'rep-ə(r)-ˌtōr-ē\ *n* **1 :** REPOSITORY **2 :** REPERTOIRE **3 :** the practice of presenting several plays successively or alternately in the same season

rep·e·ti·tion \,rep-ə-'tish-ən\ n 1 : the act or an instance of repeating 2 : the fact of being repeated

rep·e·ti·tious \-'tish-əs\ adj : marked by repetition; esp : tediously repeating — **rep·e·ti·tious·ly** adv — **rep·e·ti·tious·ness** n

re·pet·i·tive \ri-'pet-ət-iv\ adj : REPETITIOUS — **re·pet·i·tive·ly** adv — **re·pet·i·tive·ness** n

re·pine \ri-'pīn\ vb : to feel or express discontent or dejection : COMPLAIN, FRET

re·place \ri-'plās\ vb 1 : to restore to a former place or position 2 : to take the place of : SUPPLANT 3 : to fill the place of : supply an equivalent for — **re·place·able** adj — **re·plac·er** n

re·place·ment \ri-'plās-mənt\ n 1 : the act of replacing : the state of being replaced : SUBSTITUTION 2 : one that replaces; esp : one assigned to a military unit to replace a loss or fill a quota

re·plen·ish \ri-'plen-ish\ vb : to fill or build up again : stock or supply anew — **re·plen·ish·ment** n

re·plete \ri-'plēt\ adj 1 : fully provided 2 : FULL; esp : full of food — **re·plete·ness** n

re·ple·tion \ri-'plē-shən\ n : the state of being replete

rep·li·ca \'rep-li-kə\ n 1 : a close reproduction (as of a painting or statue) esp. by the maker of the original 2 : FACSIMILE 3 : COPY, DUPLICATE

¹re·ply \ri-'plī\ vb : to say or do in answer : RESPOND

²reply n : ANSWER, RESPONSE

¹re·port \ri-'pōrt\ n 1 : common talk or an account spread by common talk : RUMOR 2 : FAME, REPUTATION 3 : a usu. detailed account or statement 4 : an explosive noise

²report vb 1 : to give an account of : RELATE, TELL 2 : to describe as being in a specified state (~ed ill) 3 : to serve as carrier of (a message) 4 : to make a written record or summary of (as a meeting or debate) 5 : to prepare or present an account of (an event) for a newspaper or for broadcast 6 : to make a charge of misconduct against 7 : to present oneself (as for work) 8 : to make known to the proper authorities (~ a fire) — **re·port·able** adj

re·port·ed·ly adv : according to report

re·port·er n : one that reports; esp : a person who gathers and reports news for a newspaper — **rep·or·to·ri·al** \,rep-ər-'tōr-ē-əl\ adj

¹re·pose \ri-'pōz\ vb 1 : to place (as trust or hope) unquestioningly 2 : to place for control, management, or use

²repose vb 1 : to lay at rest 2 : to lie at rest 3 : to lie dead 4 : to take rest 5 : to rest for support : LIE

³repose n 1 : a state of resting (as after exertion); esp : SLEEP 2 : CALM, PEACE 3 : cessation or absence of activity, movement, or animation 4 : quiet ease and dignity of bearing : COMPOSURE — **re·pose·ful** adj

re·pos·i·to·ry \ri-'päz-ə-,tōr-ē\ n 1 : a place where something is deposited or

stored 2 : a person to whom something is entrusted

re·pos·sess \,rē-pə-'zes\ vb : to regain possession of — **re·pos·ses·sion** \-'zesh-ən\ n

rep·re·hend \,rep-ri-'hend\ vb : to express disapproval of : CENSURE syn criticize, condemn, denounce, blame, reprimand — **rep·re·hen·sion** \-'hen-chən\ n

rep·re·hen·si·ble \-'hen-sə-bəl\ adj : deserving blame or censure : CULPABLE — **rep·re·hen·si·bly** adv

rep·re·sent \,rep-ri-'zent\ vb 1 : to present a picture or a likeness of : PORTRAY, DEPICT 2 : to serve as a sign or symbol of 3 : to act the role of 4 : to stand in the place of : act or speak for 5 : to be a member or example of : TYPIFY 6 : to describe as having a specified quality or character 7 : to state with the purpose of affecting judgment or action 8 : to serve as an elected representative of (~ed his district in congress)

rep·re·sen·ta·tion \-,zen-'tā-shən\ n 1 : the act of representing 2 : one (as a picture, image, symbol, or emblem) that represents something else 3 : the state of being represented in a legislative body; also : the body of persons representing a constituency 4 : a usu. formal statement made to effect a change : PROTEST

¹rep·re·sen·ta·tive \-'zent-ət-iv\ adj 1 : serving to represent 2 : standing or acting for another 3 : founded on the principle of representation : carried on by elected representatives (~ government) — **rep·re·sen·ta·tive·ly** adv — **rep·re·sen·ta·tive·ness** n

²representative n 1 : a typical example of a group, class, or quality 2 : one that represents another; esp : one representing a district or a state in a legislative body usu. as a member of a lower house

re·press \ri-'pres\ vb 1 : CURB, SUBDUE 2 : RESTRAIN, SUPPRESS (~ed an angry retort); esp : to exclude from consciousness (childhood fears ~ed but not wholly lost) — **re·pres·sion** \-'presh-ən\ n — **re·pres·sive** \-'pres-iv\ adj

¹re·prieve \ri-'prēv\ vb 1 : to delay the punishment or execution of 2 : to give temporary relief to

²reprieve n 1 : the act of reprieving : the state of being reprieved 2 : a formal temporary suspension of a sentence esp. of death 3 : a temporary respite

¹rep·ri·mand \'rep-rə-,mand\ n : a severe or formal reproof

²reprimand vb : to reprove severely or formally

re·pri·sal \ri-'prī-zəl\ n : action or an act in retaliation for something done by another person

¹re·proach \ri-'prōch\ n 1 : a cause or occasion of blame or disgrace 2 : DISGRACE, DISCREDIT 3 : the act of reproaching : REBUKE — **re·proach·ful** adj — **re·proach·ful·ly** adv

²reproach vb 1 : CENSURE, REBUKE 2 : to cast discredit upon syn chide, admonish, reprove, reprimand — **reproach·able** adj

rep·ro·bate \'rep-rə-ˌbāt\ n : a thoroughly bad person : SCOUNDREL — **rep·robate** adj

rep·ro·ba·tion \ˌrep-rə-'bā-shən\ n : strong disapproval : CONDEMNATION

re·pro·duce \ˌrē-prə-'d(y)üs\ vb 1 : to produce again or anew (as by repeating or portraying) 2 : to bear offspring — **re·pro·duc·tion** \-'dək-shən\ n — **re·pro·duc·tive** \-'dək-tiv\ adj

re·proof \ri-'prüf\ n : blame or censure for a fault

re·prove \ri-'prüv\ vb 1 : to administer a rebuke to 2 : to express disapproval of syn reprimand, admonish, reproach, chide — **re·prov·er** n

rep·tile \'rep-t'l, -ˌtīl\ n [LL reptile, fr. L repere to creep] : any of a large group of air-breathing scaly vertebrates including snakes, lizards, alligators, and turtles — **rep·til·i·an** \rep-'til-ē-ən\ adj or n

re·pub·lic \ri-'pəb-lik\ n 1 : a government having a chief of state who is not a monarch and is usu. a president; also : a nation or other political unit having such a government 2 : a government in which supreme power is held by the citizens entitled to vote and is exercised by elected officers and representatives governing according to law; also : a nation or other political unit having such a form of government

¹**re·pub·li·can** \-li-kən\ adj 1 : of, relating to, or resembling a republic 2 : favoring or supporting a republic 3 cap : of, relating to, or constituting one of the two major political parties in the U.S. evolving in the mid-19th century — **re·pub·li·can·ism** n, often cap

²**republican** n 1 : one that favors or supports a republican form of government 2 cap : a member of a republican party and esp. of the Republican party of the U.S.

re·pu·di·ate \ri-'pyüd-ē-ˌāt\ vb 1 : to cast off : DISOWN 2 : to refuse to have anything to do with : refuse to acknowledge, accept, or pay (~ a charge) (~ a debt) syn spurn, reject, decline — **re·pu·di·a·tion** \-ˌpyüd-ē-'ā-shən\ n — **re·pu·di·a·tor** \-'pyüd-ē-ˌāt-ər\ n

re·pug·nance \ri-'pəg-nəns\ n 1 : the quality or fact of being opposed esp. reciprocally 2 : strong dislike, distaste, or antagonism

re·pug·nant \-nənt\ adj 1 : marked by repugnance 2 : contrary to a person's tastes or principles : exciting distaste or aversion syn repellent, abhorrent, distasteful, obnoxious, revolting, offensive, loathsome — **re·pug·nant·ly** adv

¹**re·pulse** \ri-'pəls\ vb 1 : to drive or beat back : REPEL 2 : to repel by discourtesy or denial : REBUFF 3 : to cause a feeling of repulsion in : DISGUST

²**repulse** n 1 : REBUFF, REJECTION 2 : a repelling or being repelled in hostile encounter

re·pul·sion \ri-'pəl-shən\ n 1 : the action of repulsing : the state of being repulsed 2 : the force with which bodies, particles, or like forces repel one another 3 : a feeling of aversion : REPUGNANCE

re·pul·sive \ri-'pəl-siv\ adj 1 : serving or tending to repel or reject 2 : arousing aversion or disgust syn repugnant, revolting, loathsome — **re·pul·sive·ly** adv — **re·pul·sive·ness** n

rep·u·ta·ble \'rep-yət-ə-bəl\ adj : bearing a good reputation : ESTIMABLE — **rep·u·ta·bly** adv

rep·u·ta·tion \ˌrep-yə-'tā-shən\ n 1 : character commonly ascribed to a person 2 : FAME, RENOWN (a national ~) 3 : place in public esteem (lost his ~)

¹**re·pute** \ri-'pyüt\ vb : to hold in thought : CONSIDER, ACCOUNT

²**repute** n 1 : the character commonly ascribed to one : REPUTATION 2 : the state of being favorably known or spoken of

re·put·ed \ri-'pyüt-əd\ adj 1 : REPUTABLE 2 : according to reputation : SUPPOSED — **re·put·ed·ly** adv

¹**re·quest** \ri-'kwest\ n 1 : an act or instance of asking for something 2 : a thing asked for 3 : the fact or condition of being asked for (available on ~)

²**request** vb 1 : to make a request to or of 2 : to ask for — **re·quest·er** n

req·ui·em \'rek-wē-əm, 'rāk-\ n 1 : a mass for a dead person; also : a musical setting for this 2 : a musical service or hymn in honor of the dead

re·quire \ri-'kwī(ə)r\ vb 1 : to insist upon : DEMAND, COMPEL 2 : to call for as essential : NEED

re·quire·ment \-mənt\ n 1 : something (as a condition or quality) required (entrance ~) 2 : NECESSITY, NEED

¹**req·ui·site** \'rek-wə-zət\ adj : REQUIRED, NECESSARY, ESSENTIAL

²**requisite** n : REQUIREMENT

¹**req·ui·si·tion** \ˌrek-wə-'zish-ən\ n 1 : formal application or demand (as for supplies) 2 : the state of being in demand or use

²**requisition** vb : to make a requisition for or on : press into service

re·quite \ri-'kwīt\ vb 1 : to make return for : REPAY 2 : to make retaliation for : AVENGE 3 : to make return to for a benefit or service or for an injury — **re·quit·al** \-'kwīt-°l\ n

re·run \'rē-ˌrən, -'rən\ n : the act or an instance of running again or anew; esp : showing of a moving picture or television film after its first run — **re·run** \'rē-'rən\ vb

re·sale \'rē-ˌsāl, -'sāl\ n : the act of selling again usu. to a new party — **re·sal·able** \'rē-'sā-lə-bəl\ adj

re·scind \ri-'sind\ vb : REPEAL, CANCEL, ANNUL — **re·scind·er** n — **re·scis·sion** \-'sizh-ən\ n

re·script \'rē-ˌskript\ n : official or authoritative order or decree

res·cue \'res-kyü\ vb : to free from danger, harm, or confinement syn deliver, redeem, ransom, reclaim, save — **rescue** n — **res·cu·er** n

re·search \ri-'sərch, 'rē-ˌsərch\ n 1 : careful or diligent search 2 : studious and critical inquiry and examination aimed at the discovery and interpretation of new knowledge — **research** vb — **re·search·er** n

re·sem·blance \ri-'zem-bləns\ n : the quality or state of resembling : LIKENESS, SIMILARITY

re·sem·ble \-bəl\ vb : to be like or similar to

re·sent \ri-'zent\ vb : to feel or exhibit annoyance or indignation at — **re·sent·ful** adj — **re·sent·ful·ly** adv — **re·sent·ment** n

re·ser·pine \ri-'sər-pən\ n : a drug obtained from rauwolfia and used in treating high blood pressure and nervous tensions

res·er·va·tion \,rez-ər-'vā-shən\ *n* **1** : an act of reserving **2** : something reserved; *esp* : a tract of public land set aside for a special use **3** : something (as a room in a hotel) arranged for in advance **4** : a limiting condition

¹re·serve \ri-'zərv\ *vb* **1** : to store for future or special use **2** : to hold back for oneself **3** : to set aside or arrange to have set aside or held for special use ⟨~ a table⟩

²reserve *n* **1** : something reserved : STOCK, STORE **2** : a tract set apart : RESERVATION **3** : a military force withheld from action for later decisive use — usu. used in pl. **4** : the military forces of a country not part of the regular services; *also* : RESERVIST **5** : an act of reserving **6** : restraint, caution, or closeness in one's words or bearing **7** : money or its equivalent kept in hand or set apart to meet liabilities

re·served \ri-'zərvd\ *adj* **1** : restrained in words and actions **2** : set aside for future or special use — **re·serv·ed·ly** \-'zər-vəd-lē\ *adv* — **re·serv·ed·ness** \-vəd-nəs\ *n*

re·serv·ist \ri-'zər-vəst\ *n* : a member of a military reserve

res·er·voir \'rez-ə(r)v-,wär, -,(w)ȯr\ *n* : a place where something is kept in store; *esp* : a place where water is collected and kept for use when wanted (as by a city)

re·side \ri-'zīd\ *vb* **1** : to make one's home : DWELL **2** : to be present as a quality or vested as a right

res·i·dence \'rez-əd-əns\ *n* **1** : the act or fact of residing in a place as a dweller or in discharge of a duty or an obligation **2** : the place where one actually lives **3** : DWELLING **4** : the period of living in a place

res·i·den·cy \-ən-sē\ *n* **1** : the residence of or the territory under a diplomatic resident **2** : a period of advanced training in a medical specialty

¹res·i·dent \-ənt\ *adj* **1** : RESIDING **2** : being in residence **3** : not migratory

²resident *n* **1** : one who resides in a place **2** : a diplomatic representative with governing powers (as in a protectorate) **3** : a physician serving a residency

res·i·den·tial \,rez-ə-'den-chəl\ *adj* **1** : used as a residence or by residents ⟨~ hotel⟩ **2** : occupied by or restricted to residences ⟨~ neighborhood⟩ — **res·i·den·tial·ly** *adv*

re·sid·u·al \ri-'zij-(ə-w)əl\ *adj* : being a residue or remainder

re·sid·u·ary \ri-'zij-ə-,wer-ē\ *adj* : of, relating to, or constituting a residue esp. of an estate

res·i·due \'rez-ə-,d(y)ü\ *n* : a part remaining after another part has been taken away : REMAINDER

re·sid·u·um \ri-'zij-ə-wəm\ *n, pl* **-ua** \-wə\ **1** : something remaining or residual after certain deductions are made : RESIDUE **2** : a residual product : BY-PRODUCT **syn** remainder, rest, balance, remnant

re·sign \ri-'zīn\ *vb* **1** : to give up deliberately (as one's position) esp. by a formal act **2** : to give (oneself) over (as to grief or despair) without resistance

res·ig·na·tion \,rez-ig-'nā-shən\ *n* **1** : an act or instance of resigning; *also* : a formal notification of such an act **2** : the quality or state of being resigned : SUBMISSION

re·signed \ri-'zīnd\ *adj* : SUBMISSIVE, ACQUIESCENT — **re·sign·ed·ly** \-'zī-nəd-lē\ *adv*

re·sil·ient \ri-'zil-yənt\ *adj* : ELASTIC, SPRINGY ⟨~ flexible, supple⟩ — **re·sil·ience** *or* **re·sil·ien·cy** *n*

res·in \'rez-ᵊn\ *n* : a substance obtained from the gum or sap of some trees and used esp. in varnishes, plastics, and medicine; *also* : a comparable synthetic product — **res·in·ous** *adj*

re·sist \ri-'zist\ *vb* **1** : to withstand the force or effect of ⟨~ disease⟩ **2** : to fight against : OPPOSE ⟨~ aggression⟩ **syn** combat, withstand, antagonize — **re·sis·tance** *n* — **re·sis·tant** *adj* — **re·sist·less** *adj*

re·sis·tor \ri-'zis-tər\ *n* : a device used to provide resistance to the flow of an electric current

res·o·lute \'rez-ə-,lüt\ *adj* : firmly determined in purpose : RESOLVED **syn** steadfast, staunch, faithful, true, loyal — **res·o·lute·ly** *adv* — **res·o·lute·ness** *n*

res·o·lu·tion \,rez-ə-'lü-shən\ *n* **1** : the act or process of resolving **2** : the action of solving; *also* : SOLUTION **3** : the quality of being resolute : FIRMNESS, DETERMINATION **4** : a formal statement expressing the opinion, will, or intent of a body of persons

¹re·solve \ri-'zälv\ *vb* **1** : to break up into constituent parts : ANALYZE **2** : to find an answer to : SOLVE **3** : DETERMINE, DECIDE **4** : to make or pass a formal resolution — **re·solv·able** *adj*

²resolve *n* **1** : something resolved : DETERMINATION, RESOLUTION **2** : fixity of purpose

re·solved *adj* : having a fixed purpose : DETERMINED

res·o·nance \'rez-ᵊn-əns\ *n* **1** : the quality or state of being resonant **2** : a prolongation or increase of sound in one body caused by sound waves from another vibrating body (the ~ of the body of a violin responding to the vibration of the strings)

res·o·nant \-ənt\ *adj* **1** : continuing to sound : RESOUNDING **2** : relating to or exhibiting resonance **3** : intensified and enriched by or as if by resonance ⟨a voice having ~ quality⟩ — **res·o·nant·ly** *adv*

res·o·na·tor \-'rez-ᵊn-,āt-ər\ *n* : something that resounds or exhibits resonance

¹re·sort \ri-'zȯrt\ *n* **1** : one looked to for help : REFUGE, RESOURCE **2** : RECOURSE **3** : frequent or general visiting (place of ~) **4** : a frequently visited place : HAUNT **5** : a place providing recreation esp. to vacationers

²resort *vb* **1** : to go often or habitually **2** : to have recourse (as if for aid)

re·sound \ri-'zaùnd\ *vb* **1** : to become filled with sound : REVERBERATE, RING

2 : to sound loudly — **re·sound·ing·ly** *adv*

re·source \'rē-,sōrs, ri-'sōrs\ *n* **1 :** a new or a reserve source of supply or support **2** *pl* **:** available funds **3 :** a possibility of relief or recovery **4 :** a means of spending leisure time **5 :** ability to meet and handle situations — **re·source·ful** *adj* — **re·source·ful·ness** *n*

¹re·spect \ri-'spekt\ *n* **1 :** relation to something usu. specified **:** REFERENCE, REGARD **2 :** high or special regard **:** ESTEEM **3** *pl* **:** an expression of respect or deference **4 :** DETAIL, PARTICULAR — **re·spect·ful** *adj* — **re·spect·ful·ly** *adv* — **re·spect·ful·ness** *n*

²respect *vb* **1 :** to consider deserving of high regard **:** ESTEEM **2 :** to refrain from interfering with ⟨∼ another's privacy⟩ **3 :** to have reference to **:** CONCERN — **re·spect·er** *n*

re·spect·able \ri-'spek-tə-bəl\ *adj* **1 :** worthy of respect **:** ESTIMABLE **2 :** decent or correct in conduct **:** PROPER **3 :** fair in size, quantity, or quality **:** MODERATE, TOLERABLE **4 :** fit to be seen **:** PRESENTABLE — **re·spect·a·bil·i·ty** \-,spek-tə-'bil-ət-ē\ *n* — **re·spect·ably** \-'spek-tə-blē\ *adv*

re·spect·ing \-'spek-tiŋ\ *prep* **:** with regard to

re·spec·tive \ri-'spek-tiv\ *adj* **:** relating to particular persons or things each to each ⟨returned to their ∼ homes⟩ *syn* individual, special, specific — **re·spec·tive·ly** *adv*

res·pi·ra·tion \,res-pə-'rā-shən\ *n* **1 :** an act or the process of breathing **2 :** an energy-yielding oxidation in living matter — **res·pi·ra·to·ry** \'res-p(ə-)rə-,tōr-ē, ri-'spī-rə-\ *adj* — **re·spire** \ri-'spī(ə)r\ *vb*

res·pi·ra·tor \'res-pə-,rāt-ər\ *n* **1 :** a device covering the mouth or nose esp. to prevent the inhaling of harmful vapors **2 :** a device for artificial respiration

re·spite \'res-pət\ *n* **1 :** a temporary delay **:** POSTPONEMENT, REPRIEVE **2 :** an interval of rest or relief

re·splen·dent \ri-'splen-dənt\ *adj* **:** shining brilliantly **:** gloriously bright **:** SPLENDID — **re·splen·dence** *n* — **re·splen·dent·ly** *adv*

re·spond \ri-'spänd\ *vb* **1 :** ANSWER, REPLY **2 :** REACT ⟨∼ to a stimulus⟩ **3 :** to show favorable reaction ⟨∼ to medication⟩ — **re·spond·er** *n*

re·spon·dent \ri-'spän-dənt\ *n* **:** one who responds; *esp* **:** one who answers in various legal proceedings — **respondent** *adj*

re·sponse \ri-'späns\ *n* **1 :** an act of responding **2 :** something constituting a reply or a reaction

re·spon·si·bil·i·ty \ri-,spän-sə-'bil-ət-ē\ *n* **1 :** the quality or state of being responsible **2 :** something for which one is responsible **:** CARE, DUTY

re·spon·si·ble \ri-'spän-sə-bəl\ *adj* **1 :** liable to be called upon to answer for one's acts or decisions **:** ANSWERABLE **2 :** able to fulfill one's obligations **:** RELIABLE, TRUSTWORTHY **3 :** being a free moral agent **4 :** involving accountability or important duties ⟨∼ position⟩ — **re·spon·si·ble·ness** *n* — **re·spon·si·bly** *adv*

re·spon·sive \-siv\ *adj* **1 :** RESPONDING **2 :** quick to respond **:** SENSITIVE **3 :** using responses ⟨∼ readings⟩ — **re·**

spon·sive·ly *adv* — **re·spon·sive·ness** *n*

¹rest \'rest\ *n* **1 :** REPOSE, SLEEP **2 :** freedom from work or activity **3 :** a state of motionlessness or inactivity **4 :** a place of shelter or lodging ⟨a sailors' ∼⟩ **5 :** something used as a support **6 :** a silence in music equivalent in duration to a note of the same name; *also* **:** a character indicating this — **rest·ful** *adj* — **rest·ful·ly** *adv*

²rest *vb* **1 :** to get rest by lying down; *esp* **:** SLEEP **2 :** to cease from action or motion **3 :** to give rest to **:** set at rest **4 :** to sit or lie fixed or supported **5 :** to place on or against a support **6 :** to remain based or founded **7 :** to cause to be firmly fixed **:** GROUND **8 :** to remain for action **:** DEPEND ⟨the next move ∼s with him⟩

³rest *n* **:** something that remains over

res·tau·rant \'res-t(ə-)rənt, -tə-,ränt\ *n* **:** a public eating house

res·tau·ra·teur \,res-tə-rə-'tər\ *n* **:** a restaurant keeper

res·ti·tu·tion \,res-tə-'t(y)ü-shən\ *n* **:** the act of restoring **:** the state of being restored; *esp* **:** restoration of something to its rightful owner *syn* amends, redress, reparation, indemnity

res·tive \'res-tiv\ *adj* [MF *restif*, fr. *rester* to stop behind, fr. L *restare*, fr. *re-* back + *stare* to stand] **1 :** BALKY **2 :** UNEASY, FIDGETY *syn* restless, impatient, nervous — **res·tive·ly** *adv* — **res·tive·ness** *n*

rest·less \'rest-ləs\ *adj* **1 :** lacking rest **2 :** giving no rest **3 :** never resting or ceasing **:** UNQUIET ⟨the ∼ sea⟩ **4 :** lacking in repose **:** averse to inaction **:** DISCONTENTED *syn* restive, impatient, nervous, fidgety — **rest·less·ly** *adv* — **rest·less·ness** *n*

res·to·ra·tion \,res-tə-'rā-shən\ *n* **1 :** an act of restoring **:** the state of being restored **2 :** something that is restored; *esp* **:** a reconstruction or representation of an original form (as of a fossil animal or a building)

re·stor·a·tive \ri-'stōr-ət-iv\ *n* **:** something that restores esp. to consciousness or health — **restorative** *adj*

re·store \ri-'stōr\ *vb* **1 :** to give back **:** RETURN **2 :** to put back into use or service **3 :** to put or bring back into a former or original state **:** REPAIR, RENEW **4 :** to put back into possession — **re·stor·er** *n*

re·strain \ri-'strān\ *vb* **1 :** to prevent from doing something **2 :** to limit, restrict, or keep under control **:** CURB, CHECK, REPRESS **3 :** to place under restraint or arrest — **re·strain·able** *adj* — **re·strain·er** *n*

re·strained \-'strānd\ *adj* **:** marked by restraint **:** DISCIPLINED — **re·strain·ed·ly** \-'strā-nəd-lē\ *adv*

re·straint \ri-'strānt\ *n* **1 :** an act of restraining **:** the state of being restrained **2 :** a restraining force or agency **3 :** deprivation or limitation of liberty **:** CONFINEMENT **4 :** control over one's feelings **:** RESERVE

re·strict \ri-'strikt\ *vb* **1 :** to confine within bounds **:** LIMIT **2 :** to place under restriction as to use — **re·stric·tive** *adj* — **re·stric·tive·ly** *adv*

re·stric·tion \ri-'strik-shən\ *n* **1 :** something (as a law or rule) that restricts **2 :** an act of restricting **:** the state of being restricted

¹re·sult \ri-'zəlt\ *vb* **:** to proceed or come about as an effect or consequence — **re·sul·tant** \-'zəlt-ᵊnt\ *adj or n*

²result *n* **1 :** something that results **:** EFFECT, CONSEQUENCE **2 :** beneficial or discernible effect **3 :** something obtained by calculation or investigation

¹re·sume \ri-'züm\ *vb* **1 :** to take or assume again **2 :** to return to or begin again after interruption **3 :** to take back to oneself — **re·sump·tion** \-'zəmp-shən\ *n*

²ré·su·mé *or* **re·su·me** \'rez-ə-,mā\ *n* **:** a summing up (as of something said) **:** SUMMARY

res·ur·rect \,rez-ə-'rekt\ *vb* **1 :** to raise from the dead **2 :** to bring to attention or use again

res·ur·rec·tion \-'rek-shən\ *n* **1** *cap* **:** the rising of Christ from the dead **2** *often cap* **:** the rising to life of all human dead before the final judgment **3 :** REVIVAL

re·sus·ci·tate \ri-'səs-ə-,tāt\ *vb* **:** to revive from a condition resembling death — **re·sus·ci·ta·tion** \-,səs-ə-'tā-shən\ *n* — **re·sus·ci·ta·tive** \-'səs-ə-,tāt-iv\ *adj* — **re·sus·ci·ta·tor** \-,tāt-ər\ *n*

¹re·tail \'rē-,tāl, ri-'tāl\ *vb* **1 :** to sell in small quantities or directly to the ultimate consumer **2 :** to tell in detail or to one person after another — **re·tail·er** *n*

²re·tail \'rē-,tāl\ *n* **:** the sale of goods in small amounts to ultimate consumers — **retail** *adj or adv*

re·tain \ri-'tān\ *vb* **1 :** to keep in a fixed place or position **2 :** to hold in possession or use **3 :** to engage (as a lawyer) by paying a fee in advance *syn* detain, withhold, reserve

re·tain·er *n* **1 :** one that retains **2 :** a servant or follower in a wealthy household **3 :** a fee paid to secure services (as of a lawyer)

¹re·take \'rē-'tāk\ *vb* **1 :** to take or seize again **2 :** to photograph again

²re·take \'rē-,tāk\ *n* **:** a second photograph of a motion-picture scene

re·tal·i·ate \ri-'tal-ē-,āt\ *vb* **:** to return like for like; *esp* **:** to get revenge — **re·tal·i·a·tion** \-,tal-ē-'ā-shən\ *n* — **re·tal·ia·to·ry** \-'tal-yə-,tōr-ē\ *adj*

re·tard \ri-'tärd\ *vb* **:** to hold back **:** delay the progress of *syn* slow, slacken, detain — **retard** *n* — **re·tar·da·tion** *n* — **re·tard·er** *n*

retch \'rech, 'rēch\ *vb* **:** to try to vomit **:** VOMIT

re·ten·tion \ri-'ten-chən\ *n* **1 :** the act of retaining **:** the state of being retained **2 :** power of retaining esp. in the mind **:** RETENTIVENESS

re·ten·tive \ri-'tent-iv\ *adj* **:** having the power of retaining; *esp* **:** retaining knowledge easily — **re·ten·tive·ness** *n*

ret·i·cent \'ret-ə-sənt\ *adj* **:** inclined to be silent or secretive **:** UNCOMMUNICATIVE *syn* reserved, taciturn — **ret·i·cence** *n* — **ret·i·cent·ly** *adv*

ret·i·na \'ret-ᵊn-ə\ *n, pl* **-nas** *or* **-nae** \-ᵊn-,ē\ **:** the sensory membrane lining the eye and receiving the image formed by the lens

ret·i·nue \'ret-ᵊn-,(y)ü\ *n* **:** the body of attendants or followers of a distinguished person

re·tire \ri-'tī(ə)r\ *vb* **1 :** RETREAT **2 :** to withdraw esp. for privacy **3 :** to withdraw from one's occupation or position **4 :** to go to bed **5 :** to withdraw from circulation or from the market or from usual use or service **6 :** to cause to be out in baseball — **re·tire·ment** *n*

re·tired *adj* **1 :** SECLUDED, QUIET **2 :** withdrawn from active duty or from one's occupation **3 :** received by or due to one who has retired (~ pay)

re·tir·ing *adj* **:** SHY, RESERVED

¹re·tort \ri-'tȯrt\ *vb* **1 :** to say in reply **:** answer back usu. sharply **2 :** to answer (an argument) by a counter argument **3 :** RETALIATE

²retort *n* **:** a quick, witty, or cutting reply

³retort *n* **:** a vessel in which substances are distilled or broken up by heat

re·touch \'rē-'təch\ *vb* **:** to touch or treat again (as a picture, play, or essay) in an effort to improve

re·trace \(')rē-'trās\ *vb* **1 :** to trace over again **2 :** to go over again in a reverse direction (retraced his steps)

re·tract \ri-'trakt\ *vb* **1 :** to draw back or in **2 :** to withdraw (as a charge or promise) **:** DISAVOW — **re·tract·able** *adj* — **re·trac·tile** \-'trak-tᵊl\ *adj* — **re·trac·tion** \-'trak-shən\ *n*

re·tread \'rē-'tred\ *vb* **:** to put a new tread upon the bare cord fabric of (a worn pneumatic tire)

¹re·treat \ri-'trēt\ *n* **1 :** an act of withdrawing esp. from something dangerous, difficult, or disagreeable **2 :** a military signal for withdrawal; *also* **:** a military flag-lowering ceremony **3 :** a place of privacy or safety **:** REFUGE, ASYLUM **4 :** a period of group withdrawal for prayer, meditation, and study

²retreat *vb* **:** to make a retreat **:** WITHDRAW; *also* **:** to slope backward

re·trench \ri-'trench\ *vb* **1 :** to cut down or pare away **:** REDUCE, CURTAIL **2 :** to cut down expenses **:** ECONOMIZE — **re·trench·ment** *n*

ret·ri·bu·tion \,ret-rə-'byü-shən\ *n* **:** something administered or exacted in recompense; *esp* **:** PUNISHMENT *syn* reprisal, vengeance, revenge, retaliation — **re·trib·u·tive** \ri-'trib-yət-iv\ *or* **re·trib·u·to·ry** \-yə-,tōr-ē\ *adj*

re·trieve \ri-'trēv\ *vb* **1 :** to search about for and bring in (killed or wounded game) **2 :** RECOVER, RESTORE — **re·triev·able** *adj* — **re·triev·al** \-'trē-vəl\ *n*

re·triev·er *n* **:** one that retrieves; *esp* **:** a dog bred or trained for retrieving game

¹ret·ro·grade \'ret-rə-,grād\ *adj* **:** moving or tending backward or from a better to a worse condition

²retrograde *vb* **:** RETREAT; *also* **:** DETERIORATE, DEGENERATE — **ret·ro·gres·sion** \,ret-rə-'gresh-ən\ *n*

ret·ro·spect \'ret-rə-,spekt\ *n* **:** a looking backward **:** a review of past events — **ret·ro·spec·tion** \,ret-rə-'spek-shən\ *n* — **ret·ro·spec·tive** \-'spek-tiv\ *adj* — **ret·ro·spec·tive·ly** *adv*

¹re·turn \ri-'tərn\ *vb* **1 :** to go or come back **2 :** to pass, give, or send back to an earlier possessor **3 :** to put back to or in a former place or state **4 :** REPLY, ANSWER **5 :** to report esp. officially **6 :** to elect (a candidate) as shown by

---

ə abut; ᵊ kitten; ər further; a back; ā bake; ä cot, cart; aů out; ch chin; e less; ē easy; g gift; i trip; ī life; j joke; ŋ sing; ō flow; ȯ flaw; ȯi coin; th thin; <u>th</u> this; ü loot; ů foot; y yet; yü few; yů furious; zh vision

an official report **7 :** to bring in (as profit) **:** YIELD **8 :** to give or perform in return — **re·turn·able** *adj* — **re·turn·er** *n*

²return *n* **1 :** an act of coming or going back to or from a former place or state **2 :** RECURRENCE **3 :** a report of the results of balloting **4 :** a formal statement of taxable income **5 :** the act of returning something **6 :** something that returns or is returned; *also* **:** a means (as a pipe) of returning **7 :** the profit from labor, investment, or business **:** YIELD **8 :** something given in repayment or reciprocation (as an answer or an answering or retaliatory play) — **return** *adj*

re·union \rē-'yü-nyən\ *n* **1 :** an act of reuniting **:** the state of being reunited **2 :** a meeting again of persons who have been separated

rev \'rev\ *vb* **revved; rev·ving :** to increase the number of revolutions per minute of (a motor)

re·vamp \(')rē-'vamp\ *vb* **:** RECONSTRUCT, REVISE; *esp* **:** to give a new form to old materials

re·veal \ri-'vēl\ *vb* **1 :** to make known **:** DIVULGE **2 :** to show plainly **:** open up to view **:** DISCLOSE

re·veil·le \'rev-ə-lē\ *n* **:** a military signal sounded at sunrise

¹rev·el \'rev-əl\ *vb* **-eled** *or* **-elled; -el·ing** *or* **-el·ling** **1 :** to take part in a revel **2 :** to take great delight — **rev·el·er** *or* **rev·el·ler** *n* — **rev·el·ry** \-əl-rē\ *n*

²revel *n* **:** a usu. wild party or celebration

rev·e·la·tion \,rev-ə-'lā-shən\ *n* **1 :** an act of revealing **2 :** something revealed; *esp* **:** an enlightening or astonishing disclosure

¹re·venge \ri-'venj\ *vb* **:** to inflict harm or injury in return for (a wrong) **:** AVENGE — **re·veng·er** *n*

²revenge *n* **1 :** the act of revenging **2 :** a desire to return evil for evil **3 :** an opportunity for getting satisfaction **syn** vengeance, retaliation, retribution — **re·venge·ful** *adj*

rev·e·nue \'rev-ə-n(y)ü\ *n* [MF, fr. *revenir* to return, fr. L *revenire*, fr. *re-* back + *venire* to come] **1 :** investment income **2 :** money collected by a government (as through taxes and duties)

re·ver·ber·ate \ri-'vər-bə-,rāt\ *vb* **1 :** REFLECT (~ light or heat) **2 :** to resound in or as if in a series of echoes — **re·ver·ber·a·tion** \-,vər-bə-'rā-shən\ *n*

¹re·vere \ri-'viər\ *vb* **:** to show honor and devotion to **:** VENERATE **syn** reverence, worship, adore

²re·vere \ri-'viər\ *n* **:** REVERS

¹rev·er·ence \'rev-(ə)-rəns\ *n* **1 :** honor and respect mixed with love and awe **2 :** a sign (as a bow or curtsy) of respect

²reverence *vb* **:** to regard or treat with reverence

rev·er·end \-rənd\ *adj* **1 :** worthy of reverence **:** REVERED **2 :** being a member of the clergy — used as a title

rev·er·ent \-rənt\ *adj* **:** expressing reverence — **rev·er·ent·ly** *adv*

rev·er·en·tial \,rev-ə-'ren-chəl\ *adj* **:** REVERENT

rev·er·ie *or* **rev·ery** \'rev-(ə)-rē\ *n* **1 :** DAYDREAM **2 :** the state of being lost in thought

re·vers \ri-'viər, -'veər\ *n, pl* **revers** \-'viərz, -'veərz\ **:** a lapel esp. on a woman's garment

re·ver·sal \ri-'vər-səl\ *n* **:** an act or process of reversing

¹re·verse \ri-'vərs\ *adj* **1 :** opposite to a previous or normal condition **2 :** acting or operating in a manner opposite to contrary **3 :** effecting reverse movement — **re·verse·ly** *adv*

²reverse *vb* **1 :** to turn upside down or completely about in position or direction **2 :** to set aside or change (as a legal decision) **3 :** to change to the contrary (~ a policy) **4 :** to turn or move in the opposite direction **5 :** to put a mechanism (as an engine) in reverse — **re·vers·ible** *adj*

³reverse *n* **1 :** something contrary to something else **:** OPPOSITE **2 :** an act or instance of reversing; *esp* **:** a change for the worse **3 :** the back of something **4 :** an adjustment of gears causing movement backwards

re·ver·sion \ri-'vər-zhən\ *n* **1 :** the right of succession or future possession (as to a title or property) **2 :** return toward some former or ancestral condition; *also* **:** a product of this — **re·ver·sion·ary** \-zhə-,ner-ē\ *adj*

re·vert \ri-'vərt\ *vb* **1 :** to come or go back (~ed to savagery) **2 :** to return to a proprietor or his heirs **3 :** to return to an ancestral type

¹re·view \ri-'vyü\ *n* **1 :** an act of revising **2 :** a formal military inspection **3 :** a general survey **:** INSPECTION, EXAMINATION; *esp* **:** REEXAMINATION **5 :** a critical evaluation (as of a book) **6 :** a magazine devoted to reviews and essays **7 :** a renewed study of previously studied material **3 :** REVUE

²review *vb* **1 :** to examine or study again; *esp* **:** to reexamine judicially **2 :** to view retrospectively **:** look back over (~ed his life) **3 :** to write a critical examination of (~ a novel) **4 :** to hold a review of (~ troops) **5 :** to study material again (~ for a test)

re·view·er *n* **:** one that reviews; *esp* **:** a writer of critical reviews

re·vile \ri-'vīl\ *vb* **:** to abuse verbally **:** rail at **syn** vituperate, berate, rate, upbraid, scold — **re·vile·ment** *n* — **re·vil·er** *n*

re·vise \ri-'vīz\ *vb* **1 :** to look over something written in order to correct or improve (~ a manuscript) (~ a proof) **2 :** to make a new version of (~ a textbook) (~ the tax laws) — **re·vis·able** *adj* — **revise** *n* — **re·vis·er** *or* **re·vi·sor** \-'vī-zər\ *n* — **re·vi·sion** \-'vizh-ən\ *n*

re·vi·tal·ize \'rē-'vīt-'l-,īz\ *vb* **:** to give new life or vigor to — **re·vi·tal·i·za·tion** \,rē-,vīt-'l-ə-'zā-shən\ *n*

re·viv·al \ri-'vī-vəl\ *n* **1 :** an act of reviving **:** the state of being revived **2 :** a new publication or presentation (as of a book or play) **3 :** an evangelistic meeting or series of meetings **:** REVITALIZATION

re·vive \ri-'vīv\ *vb* **1 :** to return or restore to consciousness or life **:** become or make active or flourishing again **2 :** to bring back into use **3 :** to renew mentally **:** RECALL — **re·viv·er** *n*

re·viv·i·fy \rē-'viv-ə-,fī\ *vb* **:** REVIVE — **re·viv·i·fi·ca·tion** \-,viv-ə-fə-'kā-shən\ *n*

rev·o·ca·ble \'rev-ə-kə-bəl\ *adj* **:** capable of being revoked

rev·o·ca·tion \,rev-ə-'kā-shən\ *n* **:** an act or instance of revoking

re·voke \ri-'vōk\ vb **1 :** to annul by recalling or taking back **:** REPEAL, RESCIND **2 :** RENEGE 1 — **re·vok·er** n

¹re·volt \ri-'vōlt\ vb **1 :** to throw off allegiance to a ruler or government **:** REBEL **2 :** to experience disgust or shock **3 :** to turn or cause to turn away with disgust or abhorrence — **re·volt·er** n

²revolt n **:** REBELLION, INSURRECTION

re·volt·ing adj **:** extremely offensive **:** DISGUSTING — **re·volt·ing·ly** adv

rev·o·lu·tion \,rev-ə-'lü-shən\ n **1 :** RO-TATION **2 :** progress (as that of a planet) around in an orbit **3 :** CYCLE **4 :** a sudden, radical, or complete change; esp **:** the overthrow or renun-ciation of one ruler or government and substitution of another by the governed

¹rev·o·lu·tion·ary \-shə-,ner-ē\ adj **1 :** of or relating to revolution **2 :** tend-ing to or promoting revolution **3 :** RAD-ICAL

²revolutionary n **:** REVOLUTIONIST

rev·o·lu·tion·ist \-sh(ə-)nəst\ n **:** one who takes part in a revolution or who advocates revolutionary doctrines — **revolutionist** adj

rev·o·lu·tion·ize \-shə-,nīz\ vb **:** to change fundamentally or completely **:** make revolutionary — **rev·o·lu·tion·iz·er** n

re·volve \ri-'välv\ vb **1 :** to turn over in the mind **:** reflect upon **:** PONDER **2 :** to move or cause to move in an orbit; also **:** ROTATE — **re·volv·able** adj

re·volv·er n **:** a pistol with a revolving cylinder of several chambers

re·vue \ri-'vyü\ n **:** a theatrical produc-tion consisting typically of brief often satirical sketches and songs

re·vul·sion \ri-'vəl-shən\ n **1 :** a strong sudden reaction or change of feeling **2 :** a feeling of complete distaste or repugnance

¹re·ward \ri-'wórd\ vb **1 :** to give a reward to or for **2 :** RECOMPENSE

²reward n **:** something given in return for good or evil done or received; esp **:** something given or offered for some service or attainment   syn premium, prize, award

rhap·so·dy \'rap-səd-ē\ n **1 :** a highly emotional utterance or literary composi-tion **:** extravagantly rapturous discourse **2 :** an instrumental composition of ir-regular form — **rhap·sod·ic** \rap-'säd-ik\ adj — **rhap·sod·i·cal·ly** adv — **rhap·so·dize** \'rap-sə-,dīz\ vb

rhe·ni·um \'rē-nē-əm\ n **:** a heavy hard metallic chemical element

rhe·o·stat \'rē-ə-,stat\ n **:** a device that controls the flow of electric current

rhe·sus \'rē-səs\ n **:** a pale brown In-dian monkey

rhet·o·ric \'ret-ə-rik\ n [Gk *rhētorikē* art of the orator, fr. *rhētōr* orator] **:** the art of speaking or writing effectively — **rhe·tor·i·cal** \ri-'tór-i-kəl\ adj — **rhe·to·ri·cian** \,ret-ə-'rish-ən\ n

rheum \'rüm\ n **:** a watery discharge from the mucous membranes esp. of the eyes or nose — **rheumy** adj

rheu·ma·tism \'rü-mə-,tiz-əm\ n **:** a disorder marked by inflammation or pain in muscles or joints — **rheu·mat·ic** \rù-'mat-ik\ adj

Rh factor \är-'āch-\ n [fr. *rhesus* mon-key (in which it was first detected)] **:** a substance in blood cells that may cause dangerous reactions in some infants or in transfusions

rhine·stone \'rīn-,stōn\ n **:** a colorless imitation stone of high luster made of glass, paste, or gem quartz

rhi·noc·er·os \rī-'näs-(ə-)rəs\ n **:** a large thick-skinned mammal of Africa and Asia with one or two upright horns on the snout

rhi·zome \'rī-,zōm\ n **:** a specialized rootlike plant stem that forms shoots above and roots below — **rhi·zom·a·tous** \rī-'zäm-ət-əs\ adj

rho·di·um \'rōd-ē-əm\ n **:** a hard ductile metallic chemical element

rho·do·den·dron \,rōd-ə-'den-drən\ n **:** any of various shrubs or trees related to the heaths and grown for their clusters of large bright flowers

rhom·boid \'räm-,bóid\ n **:** a parallelo-gram with unequal adjacent sides and oblique angles

rhom·bus \'räm-bəs\ n **:** a parallelo-gram with equal sides and usu oblique angles

rhu·barb \'rü-,bärb\ n **:** a garden plant with edible juicy petioles

¹rhyme \'rīm\ n **1 :** correspondence in terminal sounds (as of two lines of verse) **2 :** a composition in verse that rhymes; also **:** POETRY

²rhyme vb **1 :** to make rhymes; also **:** to write poetry **2 :** to have rhymes **:** be in rhyme

rhythm \'rith-əm\ n **1 :** regular rise and fall in the flow of sound in speech **2 :** a movement or activity in which some action or element recurs regularly — **rhyth·mic** \'rith-mik\ or **rhyth·mi·cal** adj — **rhyth·mi·cal·ly** adv

ri·al \rē-'ól, -'äl\ n — see MONEY table

¹rib \'rib\ n **1 :** one of the series of curved paired bony rods that are joined to the spine and stiffen the body wall of most vertebrates **2 :** something resem-bling a rib in shape or function **3 :** an elongated ridge

²rib vb **ribbed; rib·bing 1 :** to furnish or strengthen with ribs **2 :** to mark with ridges (*ribbed* fabrics) **3 :** to make fun of **:** TEASE — **rib·ber** n

rib·ald \'rib-əld\ adj **:** coarse or in-decent esp. in language (~ jokes) — **rib·ald·ry** \-əl-drē\ n

rib·and \'rib-ənd\ n **:** RIBBON

rib·bon \'rib-ən\ n **1 :** a narrow fabric typically of silk or velvet used for trim-ming and for badges **2 :** a narrow strip or shred (torn to ~s) **3 :** a strip of inked cloth (as in a typewriter)

ri·bo·fla·vin \,rī-bə-'flā-vən\ n **:** a growth-promoting vitamin of the B complex occurring in milk and liver

rice \'rīs\ n **:** an annual cereal grass grown in warm wet areas for its edible seed; also **:** this seed

rich \'rich\ adj **1 :** possessing or con-trolling great wealth **:** WEALTHY **2 :** COSTLY, VALUABLE **3 :** containing much sugar, fat, or seasoning; also **:** high in combustible content **4 :** deep and pleasing in color or tone **5 :** ABUN-DANT **6 :** FRUITFUL, FERTILE — **rich·ly** adv — **rich·ness** n

rich·es \'rich-əz\ *n pl* [ME *richesse* richness, fr. OF, fr. *riche* rich, of Gmc origin] : things that make one rich : WEALTH

rick \'rik\ *n* : a large stack (as of hay) in the open air

rick·ets \'rik-əts\ *n* : a children's disease marked esp. by soft deformed bones and caused by vitamin D deficiency

rick·ety \-ət-ē\ *adj* 1 : affected with rickets 2 : SHAKY, FEEBLE

¹**ric·o·chet** \'rik-ə-,shā, *Brit also* -,shet\ *n* : a glancing rebound or skipping (as of a bullet off a wall)

²**ricochet** *vb* **-cheted** *or* **-chet·ted**; **-chet·ing** *or* **-chet·ting** : to skip with or as if with glancing rebounds

rid \'rid\ *vb* **rid** *also* **rid·ded**; **rid·ding** : to make free : CLEAR, RELIEVE — **rid·dance** \'rid-ᵊns\ *n*

¹**rid·dle** \'rid-ᵊl\ *n* : a puzzling question to be solved or answered by guessing : ENIGMA, CONUNDRUM

²**riddle** *vb* 1 : EXPLAIN, SOLVE 2 : to speak in riddles

³**riddle** *n* : a coarse sieve

⁴**riddle** *vb* 1 : to sift with a riddle 2 : to fill as full of holes as a sieve

¹**ride** \'rīd\ *vb* **rode** \'rōd\ **rid·den** \'rid-ᵊn\ **rid·ing** \'rīd-iŋ\ 1 : to go on an animal's back or in a conveyance (as a boat, car, or airplane); *also* : to sit on and control so as to be carried along ⟨∼ a bicycle⟩ 2 : to float or move on water ⟨∼ at anchor⟩; *also* : to move like a floating object 3 : to travel over a surface ⟨car ∼s well⟩ 4 : to proceed over on horseback 5 : to bear along : CARRY ⟨rode him on their shoulders⟩ 6 : OBSESS, OPPRESS ⟨ridden with anxiety⟩ 7 : to torment by nagging or teasing

²**ride** *n* 1 : an act of riding; *esp* : a trip on horseback or by vehicle 2 : a way (as a lane) suitable for riding 3 : a mechanical device (as a merry-go-round) for riding on 4 : a means of transportation

rid·er \'rīd-ər\ *n* 1 : one that rides 2 : an addition to a document often attached on a separate piece of paper 3 : a clause dealing with an unrelated matter attached to a legislative bill during passage — **rid·er·less** *adj*

¹**ridge** \'rij\ *n* 1 : a range of hills 2 : a raised line or strip 3 : the line made where two sloping surfaces meet — **ridgy** *adj*

²**ridge** *vb* 1 : to form into a ridge 2 : to extend in ridges

ridge·pole \'rij-,pōl\ *n* : the highest horizontal timber in a sloping roof to which the upper ends of the rafters are fastened

¹**rid·i·cule** \'rid-ə-,kyül\ *n* : the act of exposing to laughter : remarks or actions intended to make people laugh at another person : MOCKERY, DERISION

²**ridicule** *vb* : to laugh at or make fun of mockingly or contemptuously **syn** deride, taunt, twit, mock

ri·dic·u·lous \rə-'dik-yə-ləs\ *adj* : arousing or deserving ridicule : ABSURD, PREPOSTEROUS **syn** laughable, ludicrous — **ri·dic·u·lous·ly** *adv* — **ri·dic·u·lous·ness** *n*

ri·el \rē-'el\ *n* — see MONEY table

rife \'rīf\ *adj* : WIDESPREAD, PREVALENT, ABOUNDING — **rife** *adv* — **rife·ness** *n*

riff·raff \'rif-,raf\ *n* 1 : RABBLE 2 : REFUSE, TRASH

¹**ri·fle** \'rī-fəl\ *vb* 1 : to ransack esp. in order to steal 2 : STEAL — **ri·fler** *n*

²**rifle** *vb* : to groove the inside of (a gun barrel) to increase accuracy of fire

³**rifle** *n* 1 : a firearm with a rifled barrel intended for being fired from the shoulder 2 *pl* : a body of soldiers armed with rifles — **ri·fle·man** \-mən\ *n*

rift \'rift\ *n* 1 : CLEFT, FISSURE 2 : ESTRANGEMENT, SEPARATION — **rift** *vb*

¹**rig** \'rig\ *vb* **rigged**; **rig·ging** 1 : to fit out (as a ship) with rigging 2 : CLOTHE, DRESS 3 : EQUIP 4 : to set up esp. as a makeshift ⟨∼ up a shelter⟩

²**rig** *n* 1 : the distinctive arrangement of sails and masts that differentiate different types of vessels 2 : CLOTHING, DRESS 3 : EQUIPMENT 4 : a carriage with its horse or horses 5 : APPARATUS

³**rig** *vb* **rigged**; **rig·ging** 1 : to manipulate esp. by dishonest means 2 : to fix in advance for a desired result

rig·ger *n* 1 : one that rigs 2 : a ship of a specified rig

rig·ging \'rig-iŋ\ *n* 1 : the lines (as ropes and chains) that hold and move masts, sails, and spars of a ship 2 : a network (as in theater scenery) used for support and manipulation

¹**right** \'rīt\ *adj* 1 : RIGHTEOUS, UPRIGHT 2 : JUST, PROPER 3 : conforming to truth or fact : CORRECT 4 : APPROPRIATE, SUITABLE 5 : STRAIGHT ⟨a ∼ line⟩ 6 : GENUINE, REAL ⟨∼ deer⟩ 7 : NORMAL, SOUND ⟨not in his ∼ mind⟩ 8 : of, relating to, or being the stronger hand in most persons 9 : located nearer to the right hand; *esp* : being on the right when facing in the same direction as the observer 10 : made to be placed or worn outward ⟨∼ side of a rug⟩ **syn** good, accurate, exact, precise, nice — **right·ness** *n*

²**right** *n* 1 : something that is correct, just, proper, or honorable 2 : just action or decision : the cause of justice 3 : something (as a power or privilege) to which one has a just or lawful claim 4 : the side or part that is on or toward the right side 5 *often cap* : political conservatives; *also* : the beliefs they hold — **right·ward** \-wərd\ *adj*

³**right** *adv* 1 : according to what is right ⟨live ∼⟩ 2 : EXACTLY, PRECISELY ⟨∼ here and now⟩ 3 : DIRECTLY ⟨went ∼ home⟩ 4 : according to fact or truth ⟨guess ∼⟩ 5 : all the way : COMPLETELY ⟨∼ to the end⟩ 6 : IMMEDIATELY ⟨∼ after lunch⟩ 7 : on or to the right ⟨looked ∼ and left⟩ 8 : QUITE, VERY ⟨∼ nice weather⟩

⁴**right** *vb* 1 : to relieve from wrong 2 : to adjust or restore to a proper state or position 3 : to bring or restore to an upright position 4 : to become upright — **right·er** *n*

right angle *n* : an angle bounded by two lines perpendicular to each other

righ·teous \'rī-chəs\ *adj* : acting or being in accordance with what is just, honorable, and free from guilt or wrong : UPRIGHT **syn** virtuous, noble, moral, ethical — **righ·teous·ly** *adv* — **righ·teous·ness** *n*

right·ful \'rīt-fəl\ *adj* 1 : JUST; *also* : FITTING 2 : having or held by a legally just claim — **right·ful·ly** *adv* — **right·ful·ness** *n*

right-hand \'rīt-,hand\ *adj* 1 : situated on the right 2 : RIGHT-HANDED

3 : chiefly relied on ⟨his ~ man⟩

right-hand·ed \-'han-dəd\ *adj* 1 : using the right hand habitually or better than the left 2 : designed for or done with the right hand 3 : CLOCKWISE ⟨a ~ twist⟩ — **right-handed** *adv* — **right-hand·ed·ly** *adv* — **right-handed·ness** *n*

right·ly *adv* 1 : FAIRLY, JUSTLY 2 : PROPERLY 3 : CORRECTLY, EXACTLY

rig·id \'rij-əd\ *adj* 1 : lacking flexibility : STIFF 2 : STRICT **syn** tense, rigorous, stringent — **ri·gid·i·ty** \rə-'jid-ət-ē\ *n* — **rig·id·ly** \'rij-əd-lē\ *adv*

rig·ma·role \'rig-(ə-)mə-,rōl\ *n* 1 : confused or senseless talk 2 : a complex largely meaningless procedure

rig·or \'rig-ər\ *n* 1 : the quality of being inflexible or unyielding : STRICTNESS 2 : HARSHNESS, SEVERITY 3 : a tremor caused by a chill 4 : strict precision : EXACTNESS **syn** difficulty, hardship — **rig·or·ous** *adj* — **rig·or·ous·ly** *adv*

rile \'rīl\ *vb* 1 : ROIL 1 2 : to make angry

rill \'ril\ *n* : a very small brook : RIVULET

¹**rim** \'rim\ *n* 1 : an outer edge esp. of something curved : BORDER, MARGIN 2 : the outer part of a wheel

²**rim** *vb* **rimmed; rim·ming** 1 : to furnish with a rim 2 : to run around the rim of

¹**rime** \'rīm\ *n* 1 : FROST 2 : frostlike ice tufts formed from fog or cloud on the windward side of exposed objects — **rimy** \'rī-mē\ *adj*

²**rime** *var of* RHYME

rind \'rīnd\ *n* : a usu. hard or tough outer layer (as of skin) ⟨bacon ~⟩

¹**ring** \'riŋ\ *n* 1 : a circular band worn as an ornament or token or used for holding or fastening ⟨wedding ~⟩ ⟨key ~⟩ 2 : something circular in shape ⟨smoke ~⟩ 3 : a place for contest or display ⟨boxing ~⟩; *also* : PRIZEFIGHTING 4 : a group of people who work together for selfish or dishonest purposes ⟨gambling ~⟩ — **ring·like** *adj*

²**ring** *vb* **ringed; ring·ing** 1 : ENCIRCLE 2 : to move in a ring or spirally 3 : to throw a ring over (a mark) in a game (as quoits)

³**ring** *vb* **rang** \'raŋ\ **rung** \'rəŋ\ **ring·ing** 1 : to sound resonantly when struck; *also* : to feel as if filled with such sound 2 : to cause to make a clear metallic sound by striking 3 : to sound a bell ⟨~ for the maid⟩ 4 : to announce or call by or as if by striking a bell ⟨~ an alarm⟩ 5 : to repeat loudly and persistently 6 : to call on the telephone

⁴**ring** *n* 1 : a set of bells 2 : the clear resonant sound of vibrating metal 3 : resonant tone : SONORITY 4 : a sound or character expressive of a particular quality ⟨the ~ of truth⟩ 5 : an act or instance of ringing; *esp* : a telephone call

¹**ring·er** *n* 1 : one that sounds by ringing 2 : one that enters a competition under false representations 3 : one that closely resembles another

²**ringer** *n* : one that encircles or puts a ring around

ring·lead·er \'riŋ-,lēd-ər\ *n* : a leader esp. of a group of troublemakers

ring·let \'riŋ-lət\ *n* : a long curl

ring·worm \-,wərm\ *n* : a contagious skin disease caused by fungi

rink \'riŋk\ *n* : a level extent of ice marked off for skating or various games; *also* : a similar surface (as of wood) marked off or enclosed for a sport or game ⟨roller-skating ~⟩

¹**rinse** \'rins\ *vb* 1 : to wash lightly or in water only 2 : to cleanse (as of soap) with clear water 3 : to treat (hair) with a rinse — **rins·er** *n*

²**rinse** *n* 1 : an act of rinsing 2 : a liquid used for rinsing 3 : a solution that temporarily tints hair

ri·ot \'rī-ət\ *n* 1 : disorderly behavior 2 : disturbance of the public peace; *esp* : a violent public disorder 3 : random or disorderly profusion ⟨a ~ of color⟩ — **riot** *vb* — **ri·ot·er** *n* — **ri·ot·ous** *adj*

¹**rip** \'rip\ *vb* **ripped; rip·ping** 1 : to cut or tear open 2 : to saw or split (wood) with the grain — **rip·per** *n*

²**rip** *n* : a rent made by ripping

ri·par·i·an \rə-'per-ē-ən\ *adj* : of or relating to the bank of a stream or lake

ripe \'rīp\ *adj* 1 : fully grown and developed : MATURE ⟨~ fruit⟩ 2 : fully prepared : READY ⟨~ for action⟩ — **ripe·ly** *adv* — **ripe·ness** *n*

rip·en \'rī-pən\ *vb* : to grow or make ripe

ri·poste \ri-'pōst\ *n* 1 : a fencer's return thrust after a parry 2 : a retaliatory maneuver or response; *esp* : a quick retort — **riposte** *vb*

rip·ple \'rip-əl\ *vb* 1 : to become lightly ruffled on the surface 2 : to make a sound like that of rippling water — **ripple** *n*

rip·saw \'rip-,sȯ\ *n* : a saw with coarse teeth used for cutting wood in the direction of the grain

¹**rise** \'rīz\ *vb* **rose** \'rōz\ **ris·en** \'riz-ªn\ **ris·ing** \'rī-ziŋ\ 1 : to get up from sitting, kneeling, or lying 2 : to get up from sleep or from one's bed 3 : to return from death 4 : to end a session : ADJOURN 5 : to take up arms : go to war; *also* : REBEL 6 : to appear above the horizon 7 : to move upward : ASCEND 8 : to extend above other objects 9 : to attain a higher level or rank 10 : to increase in quantity or in intensity 11 : to come into being : HAPPEN, BEGIN, ORIGINATE

²**rise** *n* 1 : an act of rising or a state of being risen 2 : BEGINNING, ORIGIN, SOURCE 3 : the elevation of one point above another 4 : an increase in amount, number, or volume 5 : an upward slope 6 : a spot higher than surrounding ground 7 : an angry reaction

ris·er \'rī-zər\ *n* 1 : one that rises ⟨an early ~⟩ 2 : the upright part between stair treads

ris·i·bil·i·ty \,riz-ə-'bil-ət-ē\ *n* : the ability or inclination to laugh — often used in pl.

ris·i·ble \'riz-ə-bəl\ *adj* 1 : able or inclined to laugh 2 : of or relating to laughter ⟨~ muscles⟩

¹**risk** \'risk\ *n* : exposure to possible

loss or injury : DANGER, PERIL — **risk·i·ness** *n* — **risky** *adj*

²**risk** *vb* **1** : to expose to danger ⟨∼ed his life⟩ **2** : to incur the danger of ⟨∼ infection⟩

ris·qué \ris-'kā\ *adj* : verging on impropriety or indecency

rite \'rīt\ *n* **1** : a set form of conducting a ceremony **2** : the liturgy of a church **3** : a ceremonial act or action

rit·u·al \'rich-(ə-w)əl\ *n* **1** : the established form esp. for a religious ceremony **2** : a system of rites **3** : a ceremonial act or action — **ritual** *adj* — **rit·u·al·ism** \-,iz-əm\ *n* — **rit·u·al·is·tic** \,rich-(ə-w)əl-'is-tik\ *adj* — **rit·u·al·is·ti·cal·ly** *adv* — **rit·u·al·ly** \'rich-(ə-w)ə-lē\ *adv*

¹**ri·val** \'rī-vəl\ *n* **1** : one of two or more trying to get what only one can have **2** : one who tries to excel another **3** : one that equals another esp. in desired qualities : MATCH, PEER

²**rival** *adj* : COMPETING

³**rival** *vb* **-valed** *or* **-valled; -val·ing** *or* **-val·ling** **1** : to be in competition with **2** : to try to equal or excel **3** : to have qualities that equal another's : MATCH

ri·val·ry \'rī-vəl-rē\ *n* : COMPETITION

rive \'rīv\ *vb* **rived; riv·en** \'riv-ən\ *also* **rived; riv·ing** \'rī-viŋ\ **1** : SPLIT, REND **2** : SHATTER

riv·er \'riv-ər\ *n* : a natural stream larger than a brook

riv·er·side \-,sīd\ *n* : the side or bank of a river

¹**riv·et** \'riv-ət\ *n* : a headed metal bolt or pin for fastening things together by being put through holes in them and then being flattened on the plain end to make another head

²**rivet** *vb* : to fasten with a rivet — **riv·et·er** *n*

riv·u·let \'riv-(y)ə-lət\ *n* : a small stream

ri·yal \rē-'(y)ȯl, -'(y)äl\ *n* — see MONEY table

¹**roach** \'rōch\ *n* : a European freshwater fish related to the carp

²**roach** *n* : COCKROACH

road \'rōd\ *n* **1** : an anchorage for ships usu. less sheltered than a harbor — often used in pl. **2** : an open way for vehicles, persons, and animals : HIGHWAY **3** : ROUTE, PATH

road·a·bil·i·ty \,rōd-ə-'bil-ət-ē\ *n* : the qualities wanted in an automobile on the road

road·bed \'rōd-,bed\ *n* **1** : the foundation of a road or railroad **2** : the traveled surface of a road

road·side \-,sīd\ *n* : the strip of land along a road — **roadside** *adj*

road·stead \-,sted\ *n* : ROAD 1

road·ster \-stər\ *n* **1** : a driving horse **2** : an open automobile with one cross seat

road·way \-,wā\ *n* : ROAD; *esp* : ROADBED

roam \'rōm\ *vb* **1** : WANDER, ROVE **2** : to range or wander over or about ⟨∼ the streets⟩

¹**roan** \'rōn\ *adj* : having a dark (as bay or black) coat with white hairs interspersed ⟨a ∼ steer⟩

²**roan** *n* : an animal with a roan coat; *also* : its color

¹**roar** \'rōr\ *vb* **1** : to utter a full loud prolonged sound **2** : to make a loud confused sound (as of wind or waves) — **roar·er** *n*

²**roar** *n* : a sound of roaring : a prolonged shout, bellow, or loud confused noise

¹**roast** \'rōst\ *vb* **1** : to cook by dry heat (as before a fire or in an oven) **2** : to criticize severely — **roast·er** *n*

²**roast** *n* **1** : a piece of meat suitable for roasting **2** : an outing for roasting food ⟨corn ∼⟩

³**roast** *adj* : ROASTED

rob \'räb\ *vb* **robbed; rob·bing** **1** : to steal from **2** : to deprive of something due or expected **3** : to commit robbery — **rob·ber** *n*

rob·bery \'räb-(ə-)rē\ *n* : the act or practice of robbing; *esp* : theft of something from a person by use of violence or threat

robe \'rōb\ *n* **1** : a long flowing outer garment; *esp* : one used for ceremonial occasions **2** : a wrap or covering for the lower body (as for sitting outdoors)

²**robe** *vb* **1** : to clothe with or as if with a robe **2** : DRESS ⟨robed in white⟩

rob·in \'räb-ən\ *n* **1** : a small European thrush with a yellowish red breast **2** : a large No. American thrush with blackish head and tail and reddish breast

ro·bot \'rō-,bät, -bət\ *n* **1** : a machine that looks and acts like a human being **2** : an efficient but insensitive person **3** : an automatic apparatus **4** : something guided by automatic controls

ro·bust \rō-'bəst, 'rō-(,)bəst\ *adj* : strong and vigorously healthy — **ro·bust·ly** *adv* — **ro·bust·ness** *n*

¹**rock** \'räk\ *vb* **1** : to move back and forth in or as if in a cradle **2** : to sway or cause to sway back and forth — **rock** *n*

²**rock** *n* **1** : a mass of stony material; *also* : broken pieces of stone **2** : solid mineral deposits **3** : something like a rock in firmness : SUPPORT, DEFENSE, REFUGE — **rock·like** *adj* — **rocky** *adj*

rock·bound \-,baùnd\ *adj* : fringed or covered with rocks

rock·er \'räk-ər\ *n* **1** : one of the curved pieces on which something (as a chair or cradle) rocks **2** : a device that works with a rocking motion

rock·et \'räk-ət\ *n* [It *rocchetta*, fr. dim. of *rocca* distaff] **1** : a firework consisting of a case containing a combustible substance that is propelled through the air by the reaction to the rearward discharge of gases produced by burning **2** : a jet engine that operates on the same principle as a firework rocket but carries the oxygen needed for burning its fuel **3** : a rocket-propelled bomb or missile

rock·et·ry \-ə-trē\ *n* : the study or use of rockets

rock salt *n* : common salt in rocklike masses or large crystals

rock wool *n* : woollike insulation made from molten rock or slag

rod \'räd\ *n* **1** : a straight slender stick **2** : a stick or bundle of twigs used in punishing a person; *also* : PUNISHMENT **3** : a staff borne to show rank **4** : a measure of length that equals 16½ feet **5** *slang* : PISTOL

rode *past of* RIDE

ro·dent \'rōd-²nt\ *n* : any of a large group of small gnawing mammals (as mice, squirrels, and beavers)

ro·deo \'rōd-ē-,ō, rə-'dā-ō\ *n* **1** : ROUNDUP 1 **2** : a public performance representing features of cowboy life

1roe \'rō\ *n* **1** : a small nimble European deer **2** : DOE

2roe *n* : the eggs of a fish esp. while bound together in a mass

roe·buck \'rō-,bək\ *n* : a male roe deer

roent·gen ray \,rent-gən-\ *n, often cap 1st R* : X RAY

ro·ga·tion \rō-'gā-shən\ *n* : SUPPLICATION

rog·er \'räj-ər\ *interj* — used esp. in radio and signaling to indicate that a message has been received and understood

rogue \'rōg\ *n* **1** : a dishonest person : SCOUNDREL **2** : a mischievous person : SCAMP — **rogu·ery** \'rō-gə-rē\ *n* — **rogu·ish** \'rō-gish\ *adj* — **rogu·ish·ly** *adv* — **rogu·ish·ness** *n*

roil \'roil *for 2 also* 'ril\ *vb* **1** : to make cloudy or muddy by stirring up **2** : RILE 2

rois·ter \'roi-stər\ *vb* : to engage in noisy revelry : CAROUSE — **rois·ter·er** *n*

role *also* **rôle** \'rōl\ *n* **1** : an assigned or assumed character; *also* : a part played (as by an actor) **2** : FUNCTION

1roll \'rōl\ *n* **1** : a document containing an official record **2** : an official list of names **3** : something (as a bun) that is rolled up or rounded as if rolled **4** : something that rolls : ROLLER

roll *vb* **1** : to move by turning over and over **2** : to move on wheels **3** : to move onward as if by completing a revolution (years ~ed by) **4** : to flow or seem to flow in a continuous stream or with a rising and falling motion **5** : to swing or sway from side to side **6** : to shape or become shaped in rounded form **7** : to press with a roller **8** : to sound with a full reverberating tone **9** : to make a continuous beating sound (as on a drum) **10** : to utter with a trill (~ed his r's)

3roll *n* **1** : a sound produced by rapid strokes on a drum **2** : a heavy reverberating sound **3** : a rolling movement or action **4** : a swaying movement (as of the body, a train, or a ship) **5** : SOMERSAULT

roll call *n* : the act or an instance of calling off a list of names (as of soldiers); *also* : a time for a roll call

roll·er \'rō-lər\ *n* **1** : a revolving cylinder used for moving, pressing, shaping, or smoothing **2** : a rod on which something is rolled up **3** : a long heavy wave on a coast **4** : a tumbler pigeon

roller skate *n* : a skate with wheels instead of a runner for skating on a surface other than ice — **roll·er-skate** \'rō-lər-,skāt\ *vb* — **roller skater** *n*

rol·lick \'räl-ik\ *vb* : ROMP, FROLIC

rol·lick·ing *adj* **1** : BOISTEROUS, SWAGGERING **2** : lightheartedly gay — **rol·lick·ing·ly** *adv*

1Ro·man \'rō-mən\ *n* **1** : a native or resident of Rome **2** : a citizen of the Roman Empire

2Roman *adj* **1** : of or relating to Rome or the Romans **2** : of or relating to the Roman Catholic Church

Roman candle *n* : a cylindrical firework that discharges balls or stars of fire

Roman Catholic *adj* : of or relating to the body of Christians in communion with the pope and having a liturgy centered in the Mass — **Roman Catholic** *n*

1ro·mance \rō-'mans\ *n* **1** : a medieval tale of knightly adventure **2** : a prose narrative dealing with heroic or mysterious events set in a remote time or place **3** : a love story **4** : a love affair — **ro·manc·er** *n*

2romance *vb* **1** : to exaggerate or invent detail or incident **2** : to have romantic fancies **3** : to carry on a love affair with

Ro·mance \rō-'mans\ *adj* : of or relating to the languages developed from Latin

Ro·ma·ni·an \ru̇-'mā-nē-ən, rō-\ *n* **1** : a native or inhabitant of Romania **2** : the language of Romania — **Romanian** *adj*

ro·man·tic \rō-'mant-ik\ *adj* **1** : IMAGINARY **2** : VISIONARY **3** : having an imaginative or emotional appeal **4** : ARDENT, FERVENT — **ro·man·ti·cal·ly** *adv*

ro·man·ti·cism \rō-'mant-ə-,siz-əm\ *n, often cap* : a literary movement (as in early 19th century England) marked esp. by emphasis on the imagination and the emotions and by the use of autobiographical material — **ro·man·ti·cist** \-səst\ *n, often cap*

romp \'rämp\ *vb* **1** : to play actively and noisily **2** : to run or play so as to win easily — **romp** *n*

romp·er *n* **1** : one that romps **2** : a child's one-piece garment with the lower part shaped like bloomers — usu. used in pl.

rood \'rüd\ *n* **1** : CROSS, CRUCIFIX **2** : a unit of area equal to ¼ acre

1roof \'rüf, 'ru̇f\ *n* **1** : the upper covering part of a building **2** : something suggesting a roof of a building — **roof·ing** *n* — **roof·less** *adj*

2roof *vb* : to cover with a roof

roof·top \-,täp\ *n* : a roof esp. of a house

roof·tree \-,trē\ *n* : RIDGEPOLE

1rook \'ru̇k\ *n* : an Old World bird resembling the related crow — **rook·ery** \-ə-rē\ *n*

2rook *vb* : CHEAT, SWINDLE

3rook *n* : a chess piece that can move parallel to the sides of the board across any number of unoccupied squares

rook·ie \'ru̇k-ē\ *n* : RECRUIT; *also* : NOVICE

1room \'rüm, 'ru̇m\ *n* **1** : unoccupied area : SPACE **2** : sufficient unoccupied space **3** : a partitioned part of a building : CHAMBER, APARTMENT; *also* : the people in a room **4** : OPPORTUNITY, CHANCE (~ to develop his talents) — **roomy** *adj*

2room *vb* : to occupy lodgings : LODGE — **room·er** *n*

room·ette \rüm-'et, ru̇m-\ *n* : a small private room on a sleeping car

room·mate \'rüm-,māt, 'ru̇m-\ *n* : one of two or more persons occupying the same room

1roost \'rüst\ *n* : a support on which or place where birds perch

2roost *vb* : to settle on or as if on a roost

roost·er *n* : an adult male domestic fowl : COCK

1root \'rüt, 'ru̇t\ *n* **1** : the leafless usu.

underground part of a seed plant that functions in absorption, aeration, and storage or as a means of anchorage; *also* : an underground plant part **2** : something (as the basal part of a tooth or hair) resembling a root **3** : SOURCE, ORIGIN **4** : the essential core 〈HEART 〈get to the ~ of the matter〉 **5** : a number that when taken as a factor an indicated number of times gives a specified number **6** : the lower part : BASIS, BASE — **root·less** *adj* — **root·like** *adj*

²**root** *vb* **1** : to form roots **2** : to fix or become fixed by or as if by roots : ESTABLISH **3** : UPROOT

³**root** *vb* **1** : to turn up or dig with the snout 〈pigs ~*ing*〉 **2** : to poke or dig around (as in search of something)

⁴**root** \'rüt\ *vb* **1** : to applaud or encourage noisily : CHEER **2** : to wish success or lend support to — **root·er** *n*

root·let \'rüt-lət, 'rüt-\ *n* : a small root

root·stock \-'stäk\ *n* : a rootlike underground stem : RHIZOME

¹**rope** \'rōp\ *n* **1** : a large strong cord made of strands of fiber **2** : a hangman's noose **3** : a thick string (as of pearls) made by twisting or braiding

²**rope** *vb* **1** : to bind, tie, or fasten together with a rope **2** : to separate or divide off by means of a rope **3** : LASSO

ro·sa·ry \'rō-zə-rē\ *n* **1** : a string of beads used in counting prayers **2** *often cap* : a Roman Catholic devotion consisting of meditation on sacred mysteries during recitation of Ave Marias

¹**rose** *past of* RISE

²**rose** \'rōz\ *n* **1** : any of various prickly shrubs with divided leaves and bright often fragrant flowers; *also* : one of these flowers **2** : something resembling a rose in form **3** : a variable color averaging a moderate purplish red

³**ro·sé** \rō-'zā\ *n* : a light pink table wine

ro·se·ate \'rō-zē-ət, -zē-,āt\ *adj* **1** : resembling a rose esp. in color **2** : OPTIMISTIC 〈a ~ view of the future〉

rose·mary \'rōz-,mer-ē\ *n* [L *rosmarinus*, fr. *ros* dew + *marinus* of the sea, fr. *mare* sea] : a fragrant shrubby mint with evergreen leaves used in perfumery and cooking

ro·sette \rō-'zet\ *n* **1** : a usu. small badge or ornament of ribbon gathered in the shape of a rose **2** : a circular architectural ornament filled with representations of leaves

rose water *n* : a watery solution of the fragrant constituents of the rose used as a perfume

rose·wood \'rōz-,wùd\ *n* **:** any of various tropical trees with dark red wood streaked with black; *also* : this wood

Rosh Ha·sha·nah \,rōsh-hə-'shō-nə\ *n* : the Jewish New Year observed as a religious holiday in September or October

ros·in \'räz-ᵊn\ *n* : a hard brittle resin obtained esp. from pine trees and used in varnishes and on violin bows

ros·ter \'räs-tər\ *n* **1** : a list of personnel : ROLL **2** : an itemized list

ros·trum \'räs-trəm\ *n, pl* -trums *or* -tra \-trə\ : a stage or platform for public speaking

rosy \'rō-zē\ *adj* **1** : of the color rose **2** : HOPEFUL, PROMISING — **ros·i·ly** *adv* — **ros·i·ness** *n*

¹**rot** \'rät\ *vb* rot·ted; rot·ting : to undergo decomposition : DECAY

²**rot** *n* **1** : DECAY **2** : a disease of plants or animals in which tissue breaks down

¹**ro·ta·ry** \'rōt-ə-rē\ *adj* **1** : turning on its axis like a wheel **2** : having a rotating part

²**rotary** *n* **1** : a rotary machine **2** : a circular road at a road junction

ro·tate \'rō-,tāt\ *vb* **1** : to turn about an axis or a center : REVOLVE **2** : to alternate in a series syn turn, circle, spin, whirl, twirl — **ro·ta·tion** \rō-'tā-shən\ *n* — **ro·ta·tor** \'rō-,tāt-ər\ *n* — **ro·ta·to·ry** \'rōt-ə-,tōr-ē\ *adj*

rote \'rōt\ *n* **1** : repetition from memory of forms or phrases often without attention to meaning **2** : fixed routine or repetition

ro·to·gra·vure \,rōt-ə-grə-'vyùr\ *n* : a process by which pictures and text are printed from etched plates affixed to the rollers of a rotary printing press; *also* : an illustration so printed

ro·tor \'rō-tər\ *n* **1** : a part that rotates **2** : a system of rotating horizontal blades for supporting a helicopter

rot·ten \'rät-ᵊn\ *adj* **1** : having rotted **2** : SPOILED, UNSOUND **2** : CORRUPT **3** : extremely unpleasant or inferior — **rot·ten·ness** *n*

ro·tund \rō-'tənd\ *adj* : round or rounded out syn plump, chubby, portly, stout — **ro·tun·di·ty** \-'tən-dət-ē\ *n*

ro·tun·da \rō-'tən-də\ *n* **1** : a round building; *esp* : one covered by a dome **2** : a large round room

rou·ble \'rü-bəl\ *var of* RUBLE

roué \rù-'ā\ *n* **:** a man given to debauched living : RAKE

rouge \'rüzh, 'rüj\ *n* **1** : a cosmetic used to give a red color to cheeks and lips **2** : a red powder used in polishing glass, gems, and metal — **rouge** *vb*

¹**rough** \'rəf\ *adj* **1** : uneven in surface : not smooth **2** : SHAGGY **3** : not calm : TURBULENT, TEMPESTUOUS **4** : marked by harshness or violence : not gentle **5** : DIFFICULT, TRYING **6** : coarse or rugged in character or appearance **7** : marked by lack of refinement **8** : UNCOUTH **8** : CRUDE, UNFINISHED **9** : done or made hastily or tentatively : not exact — **rough·ly** *adv* — **rough·ness** *n*

²**rough** *n* **1** : uneven ground covered with high grass esp. along a golf fairway **2** : a crude, unfinished, or preliminary state; *also* : something in such a state **3** : ROWDY, TOUGH

³**rough** *vb* **1** : ROUGHEN **2** : MANHANDLE 〈~*ed* him up〉 **3** : to make or shape roughly esp. in a preliminary way 〈~ out a scheme〉 — **rough·er** *n*

rough·age \'rəf-ij\ *n* : coarse bulky food (as bran) whose bulk stimulates the activity of the intestines

rough-and-ready \,rəf-ᵊn-'red-ē\ *adj* : rude or unpolished in nature, method, or manner but effective in action or use

rough·en \'rəf-ən\ *vb* : to make or become rough

rough·hew \'rəf-'hyü\ *vb* **1** : to hew (as timber) coarsely without smoothing **2** : to form crudely or roughly

rough·house \-,haùs\ *n* : an outbreak of rough noisy behavior — **roughhouse** *vb*

rough·neck \-,nek\ *n* : ROWDY, TOUGH

rough·shod \-'shäd\ *adv* : in a dominating, tyrannizing, or cavalier manner 〈ride ~ over〉

rou·lette \rü-'let\ *n* **1** : a gambling

game in which a whirling wheel is used **2** : a toothed wheel or disk for making rows of dots or small holes

Rou·ma·ni·an \rü-'mā-nē-ən\ *var of* ROMANIAN

¹round \'raůnd\ *adj* **1** : having every part of the surface or circumference the same distance from the center **2** : CYLINDRICAL **3** : COMPLETE, FULL **4** : approximately correct : being in even units : being without fractions **5** : liberal or ample in size or amount **6** : BLUNT, OUTSPOKEN **7** : moving in or forming a circle **8** : curved or predominantly curved rather than angular — **round·ish** *adj* — **round·ly** *adv* — **round·ness** *n*

²round *prep or adv* : AROUND

³round *n* **1** : something round (as a circle, globe, or ring) **2** : a curved or rounded part (as a rung of a ladder) **3** : a circuitous path or course; *also* : a habitually covered route (as of a watchman) **4** : a series or cycle of recurring actions or events **5** : a period of time or a unit of play in a game or contest **6** : one shot fired by a soldier or a gun; *also* : ammunition for one shot **7** : a cut of beef esp. between the rump and the lower leg — **in the round** **1** : FREESTANDING **2** : with a center stage surrounded by an audience on all sides ⟨theater *in the round*⟩

⁴round *vb* **1** : to make or become round **2** : to go or pass around or part way around **3** : to follow a winding course : BEND **4** : COMPLETE, FINISH **5** : to become plump or shapely **6** : to express as a round number

¹round·about \'raůn-də-‚baůt\ *n, Brit* : MERRY-GO-ROUND

²roundabout *adj* : INDIRECT, CIRCUITOUS

roun·de·lay \'raůn-də-‚lā\ *n* **1** : a simple song with refrain **2** : a poem with a refrain recurring frequently or at fixed intervals

round·house \'raůnd-‚haůs\ *n* **1** : a circular building for housing and repairing locomotives **2** : a cabin on the after part of the quarterdeck of an old sailing ship

round-up \'raůnd-‚əp\ *n* **1** : the gathering together of cattle on the range by riding around them and driving them in; *also* : the men and horses engaged in a roundup **2** : a gathering in of scattered persons or things ⟨a ~ of criminals⟩ **3** : SUMMARY, RÉSUMÉ ⟨news ~⟩ — **round up** \'raůnd-'əp\ *vb*

rouse \'raůz\ *vb* **1** : to wake from sleep **2** : to excite to activity : stir up

roust·about \'raůs-tə-‚baůt\ *n* : one who does heavy unskilled labor (as on a dock or in an oil field)

¹rout \'raůt\ *n* **1** : MOB 1, 2 **2** : DISTURBANCE **3** : a fashionable gathering : RECEPTION

²rout *vb* **1** : RUMMAGE **2** : to gouge out **3** : to turn out by compulsion ⟨~ed him out of bed⟩

³rout *n* **1** : a state of wild confusion or disorderly retreat **2** : a disastrous defeat

⁴rout *vb* **1** : to put to flight **2** : to defeat decisively

¹route \'rüt, 'raůt\ *n* **1** : a traveled way **2** : CHANNEL **3** : a line of travel

²route *vb* **1** : to send by a selected route **2** : to arrange and direct the order of (as a series of operations)

rou·tine \rü-'tēn\ *n* **1** : a round (as of work or play) regularly followed **2** : any regular course of action — **routine** *adj* — **rou·tine·ly** *adv* — **rou·tin·ize** \-'tēn-‚īz\ *vb*

rove \'rōv\ *vb* : to wander over or through : RAMBLE, ROAM

rove *past of* REEVE

ro·ver \'rō-vər\ *n* : PIRATE

¹row \'rō\ *vb* **1** : to propel a boat with oars **2** : to travel or convey in a rowboat **3** : to match rowing skill against — **row·er** *n*

²row *n* : an act or instance of rowing

³row *n* **1** : a number of objects in an orderly sequence **2** : WAY, STREET

⁴row \'raů\ *n* : a noisy quarrel

⁵row \'raů\ *vb* : to engage in a row

row·boat \'rō-‚bōt\ *n* : a boat designed to be rowed

row·dy \'raůd-ē\ *adj* : coarse or boisterous in behavior : ROUGH — **row·di·ness** *n* — **rowdy** *n* — **row·dy·ish** *adj* — **row·dy·ism** *n*

row·el \'raů(-ə)l\ *n* : a small pointed wheel on a spur used to urge on a horse — **rowel** *vb*

roy·al \'rói-əl\ *adj* **1** : of or relating to a king or sovereign : KINGLY, REGAL **2** : resembling or befitting a king : MAJESTIC, MAGNIFICENT — **roy·al·ly** *adv*

roy·al·ist \-ə-ləst\ *n* : an adherent of a king or of monarchical government

roy·al·ty \-əl-tē\ *n* **1** : the state of being royal **2** : a royal person : royal persons **3** : a share of a product or profit (as of a mine or oil well) claimed by the owner for allowing another person to use the property **4** : payment made to the owner of a patent or copyright for the use of it

¹rub \'rəb\ *vb* **rubbed; rub·bing** **1** : to use pressure and friction on a body or object **2** : to scour, polish, erase, or smear by pressure and friction **3** : to fret or chafe with friction

²rub *n* **1** : an act or instance of rubbing **2** : a place roughened or injured by rubbing **3** : DIFFICULTY, OBSTRUCTION **4** : something grating to the feelings

¹rub·ber \'rəb-ər\ *n* **1** : one that rubs **2** : ERASER **3** : a flexible waterproof elastic substance made from the juice of various tropical plants or synthetically; *also* : something made of this material — **rub·ber·ize** \-‚īz\ *vb* — **rub·bery** *adj*

²rubber *n* : an extra game or hand played to decide a tie in a game

rub·bish \'rəb-ish\ *n* : something worthless : TRASH

rub·ble \'rəb-əl\ *n* : broken stones or bricks used in masonry; *also* : a mass of such material ⟨the ~ of a bombed building⟩

ru·bi·cund \'rü-bi-(‚)kənd\ *adj* : RED, RUDDY

ru·bid·i·um \rü-'bid-ē-əm\ *n* : a soft silvery metallic chemical element

ru·ble \'rü-bəl\ *n* — see MONEY table

ru·bric \'rü-brik\ *n* : a rule esp. for the conduct of a religious service

ru·by \'rü-bē\ *n* : a precious stone of a clear red color

rud·der \'rəd-ər\ *n* : a movable flat

---

piece attached vertically at the rear of a boat or aircraft for steering

rud·dy \'rəd-ē\ *adj* : REDDISH; *esp* : of a healthy reddish complexion — **rud·di·ness** *n*

rude \'rüd\ *adj* 1 : roughly made : CRUDE 2 : UNDEVELOPED, PRIMITIVE 3 : UNSKILLED 4 : IMPOLITE, DISCOURTEOUS — **rude·ly** *adv* — **rude·ness** *n*

ru·di·ment \'rüd-ə-mənt\ *n* 1 : something not fully developed 2 : an elementary principle or basic skill — **ru·di·men·ta·ry** \,rüd-ə-'men-t(ə-)rē\ *adj*

¹**rue** \'rü\ *vb* : to feel regret, remorse, or penitence for

²**rue** *n* : REGRET, SORROW — **rue·ful** *adj* — **rue·ful·ly** *adv* — **rue·ful·ness** *n*

³**rue** *n* : a European strong-scented woody herb with bitter-tasting leaves

ruff \'rəf\ *n* 1 : a wheel-shaped frilled collar worn about 1600 2 : a fringe of hair or feathers around the neck of an animal — **ruffed** \'rəft\ *adj*

ruf·fi·an \'rəf-ē-ən\ *n* : a brutal cruel fellow — **ruf·fi·an·ly** *adj*

¹**ruf·fle** \'rəf-əl\ *vb* 1 : to draw into or provide with plaits or folds 2 : to roughen the surface of 3 : to erect (as hair or feathers) in or like a ruff 4 : IRRITATE, VEX 5 : to flip through (as pages)

²**ruffle** *n* 1 : RIPPLE 2 : a strip of fabric gathered or pleated on one edge 3 : RUFF 2

rug \'rəg\ *n* 1 : a piece of heavy fabric usu. with a nap or pile used as a floor covering 2 : a lap robe

Rug·by \'rəg-bē\ *n* : a football game in which play is continuous

rug·ged \'rəg-əd\ *adj* 1 : having a rough uneven surface 2 : TURBULENT, STORMY 3 : HARSH, STERN 4 : ROBUST, STURDY — **rug·ged·ly** *adv* — **rug·ged·ness** *n*

¹**ru·in** \'rü-ən\ *n* 1 : complete collapse or destruction 2 : the remains of something destroyed — usu. used in pl. 3 : a cause of destruction 4 : the action of destroying

²**ruin** *vb* 1 : to reduce to ruins : DESTROY 2 : to damage beyond repair 3 : BANKRUPT

ru·in·a·tion \,rü-ə-'nā-shən\ *n* : RUIN, DESTRUCTION

ru·in·ous \'rü-ə-nəs\ *adj* 1 : RUINED, DILAPIDATED 2 : causing ruin — **ru·in·ous·ly** *adv*

¹**rule** \'rül\ *n* 1 : a guide or principle for governing action : REGULATION 2 : the usual way of doing something 3 : GOVERNMENT, CONTROL 4 : a straight strip of material (as wood or metal) marked off in units and used for measuring or as a guide in drawing straight lines

²**rule** *vb* 1 : CONTROL, GOVERN 2 : to be preeminent in : DOMINATE, PREVAIL 3 : to give or state as a considered decision 4 : to mark on paper with or as if with a rule

rul·er \'rü-lər\ *n* 1 : SOVEREIGN 2 : RULE 4

rum \'rəm\ *n* 1 : a liquor distilled from a fermented cane product (as molasses) 2 : alcoholic liquor

Ru·ma·ni·an \rù-'mā-nē-ən\ *var of* ROMANIAN

rum·ba \'rəm-bə, 'rüm-\ *n* : a Cuban Negro dance or an imitation of it

¹**rum·ble** \'rəm-bəl\ *vb* : to make a low heavy rolling sound; *also* : to travel or move along with such a sound — **rum·bler** \-b(ə-)lər\ *n*

²**rumble** *n* 1 : a low heavy rolling sound 2 : a seat behind and outside a carriage body; *also* : a folding seat located behind the regular seating space in the back of an automobile and not covered by the top 3 *slang* : a street fight esp. among teen-age gangs

ru·mi·nant \'rü-mə-nənt\ *n* : any of a great group of hoofed mammals (as cattle, deer, and camels) that chew the cud — **ruminant** *adj*

ru·mi·nate \'rü-mə-,nāt\ *vb* 1 : MEDITATE, MUSE 2 : to chew the cud — **ru·mi·na·tion** \,rü-mə-'nā-shən\ *n*

¹**rum·mage** \'rəm-ij\ *n* 1 : an act of rummaging 2 : things found by rummaging : miscellaneous old things

²**rummage** *vb* : to poke around in all corners looking for something — **rum·mag·er** *n*

rum·my \'rəm-ē\ *n* : any of several card games for two or more players

ru·mor \'rü-mər\ *n* 1 : common talk : HEARSAY 2 : a statement or report current but not authenticated

rump \'rəmp\ *n* 1 : the rear part of an animal; *also* : a cut of beef between the upper sirloin 2 : FAG END, REMNANT

rum·ple \'rəm-pəl\ *vb* : TOUSLE, MUSS, WRINKLE — **rumple** *n* — **rum·ply** *adj*

rum·pus \'rəm-pəs\ *n* : DISTURBANCE, FRACAS

rum·run·ner \'rəm-,rən-ər\ *n* : a person or ship engaged in transporting liquor into a country or state in which it is prohibited — **rum·run·ning** *n*

¹**run** \'rən\ *vb* ran \'ran\ run; running 1 : to go at a pace faster than a walk 2 : to take to flight : FLEE 3 : to go without restraint ⟨lets his children ∼⟩ 4 : to go rapidly or hurriedly : HASTEN, RUSH 5 : to make a quick or casual trip or visit 6 : to contend in a race; *esp* : to enter an election 7 : to move on or as if on wheels : pass freely 8 : to go back and forth : PLY 9 : FUNCTION, OPERATE 10 : to continue in force ⟨two years to ∼⟩ 11 : to flow rapidly or under pressure : MELT, FUSE, SPREAD, DISSOLVE; *also* : DISCHARGE 12 : to tend to produce or to recur ⟨family ∼s to blonds⟩ 13 : to take a certain direction : EXTEND, SPREAD 14 : to be current : CIRCULATE ⟨rumors running wild⟩ 15 : to move in schools esp. to a spawning ground ⟨shad are running⟩ 16 : to be worded or written 17 : to cause to run 18 : to perform or bring about by running 19 : TRACE ⟨∼ down a rumor⟩ 20 : to put forward as a candidate for office 21 : to cause to pass 22 : to cause to collide 23 : SMUGGLE 24 : MANAGE, CONDUCT, OPERATE 25 : INCUR ⟨∼ a risk⟩ 26 : to permit to accumulate before settling ⟨∼ a charge account⟩ — **run·ner** *n*

²**run** *n* 1 : an act or the action of running 2 : BROOK, CREEK 3 : a continuous series esp. of similar things 4 : persistent heavy demands from depositors, creditors, or customers 5 : the quantity of work turned out in a continuous operation; *also* : a period of operation (as of a machine or plant) 6 : the usual or normal kind ⟨the ordinary ∼ of men⟩ 7 : the distance covered in continuous travel or sailing 8 : a regular course or route; *also* : TRIP, JOURNEY 9 : a school of migrating fish 10 : an enclosure for animals 11 : a lengthwise ravel (as in a stocking) 12 : a score in baseball

made by a base runner reaching home
13 : an inclined course (as for skiing)

run·about \'rən-ə-ˌbaút\ n : a light
wagon, automobile, or motorboat

run·a·gate \'rən-ə-ˌgāt\ n **1** : RUN-
AWAY, FUGITIVE **2** : VAGABOND

run·around \'rən-ə-ˌraúnd\ n : evasive
or delaying action esp. in reply to a
request

¹run·away \'rən-ə-ˌwā\ n **1** : FUGITIVE
2 : the act of running away or out of
control

²runaway adj **1** : FUGITIVE **2** : accomplished by elopement (~ marriage)
3 : won by a long lead **4** : subject to
rapid changes (~ inflation)

run down \'rən-'daún\ vb **1** : to collide
with and knock down **2** : to chase
until exhausted or captured **3** : to find
by search **4** : DISPARAGE **5** : to cease
to operate for lack of motive power
6 : to decline in physical condition

run-down \'rən-ˌdaún\ adj **1** : being in
poor repair : DILAPIDATED **2** : worn
out **3** : completely unwound

run-down \'rən-ˌdaún\ n : an item-by-
item report : SUMMARY

rune \'rün\ n **1** : a character of an
alphabet formerly used by the Germanic peoples **2** : MYSTERY, MAGIC
3 : a poem esp. in Finnish or Old Norse
— **ru·nic** \'rü-nik\ adj

¹rung past of RING

²rung \'rəŋ\ n : a round of a chair or
ladder **2** : a spoke of a wheel

run in \'rən-'in\ vb **1** : to insert as additional matter **2** : to arrest for a
minor offense **3** : to pay a casual visit

run-in \'rən-ˌin\ n **1** : something run in
2 : ALTERCATION, QUARREL

run·let \'rən-lət\ n : RUNNEL, BROOK

run·nel \'rən-ᵊl\ n : BROOK, RIVULET,
STREAMLET

run·ner-up \'rən-ər-ˌəp\ n : the competitor in a contest who finishes next to
the winner

¹run·ning \'rən-iŋ\ adj **1** : FLUID,
RUNNY **2** : CONTINUOUS, INCESSANT
3 : measured in a straight line (cost per
~ foot) **4** : FLOWING (~ handwriting)
5 : of or relating to an act of running
(~ start) (~ time) **6** : fitted or trained
for running (~ horse)

²running adv : in succession

run·ny \'rən-ē\ adj : having a tendency
to run

run·off \'rən-ˌóf\ n : a final contest to a
previous indecisive contest

run on \'rən-'ón, -'än\ vb **1** : to continue (matter in type) without a break
or a new paragraph **2** : to place or add
(as an entry in a dictionary) at the end
of a paragraphed item — **run-on** \-ˌón,
-ˌän\ n

runt \'rənt\ n : an unusually small person or animal : DWARF — **runty** adj

run·way \'rən-ˌwā\ n **1** : a beaten path
made by animals; also : a passage for
animals **2** : a surfaced strip of ground
for the landing and takeoff of airplanes
3 : a narrow platform from a stage into
an auditorium **4** : a support (as a track,
pipe, or trough) on which something
runs

ru·pee \rü-'pē\ n — see MONEY table

ru·pi·ah \rü-'pē-ə\ n, pl **rupiah** or
rupiahs — see MONEY table

¹rup·ture \'rəp-chər\ n : a breaking or
tearing apart; also : HERNIA

²rupture vb : to cause or undergo rupture

ru·ral \'rúr-əl\ adj : of or relating to the
country, country people, or agriculture

ruse \'rüs, 'rüz\ n : TRICK, ARTIFICE

¹rush \'rəsh\ n : a hollow-stemmed
grasslike marsh plant — **rushy** adj

²rush vb **1** : to move forward or act with
too great haste or eagerness or without
preparation **2** : to perform in a short
time or at high speed **3** : ATTACK,
CHARGE — **rush·er** n

³rush n **1** : a violent forward motion
2 : a crowding of people to one place
3 : unusual demand or activity

rusk \'rəsk\ n : a sweet or plain bread
baked, sliced, and baked again until dry
and crisp

rus·set \'rəs-ət\ n **1** : a variable reddish brown or yellowish brown color
2 : a coarse cloth of the color russet
3 : any of various winter apples with
rough russet skins — **russet** adj

Rus·sian \'rəsh-ən\ n **1** : a native or
inhabitant of Russia or the U.S.S.R.
2 : the chief language of the U.S.S.R.
— **Russian** adj

rust \'rəst\ n **1** : a reddish coating
formed on metal (as iron) when it is
exposed to air **2** : the reddish orange
color of rust **3** : any of various diseases causing reddish spots on plants —
rusty adj

¹rus·tic \'rəs-tik\ adj **1** : RURAL
2 : AWKWARD, BOORISH **3** : PLAIN,
SIMPLE **4** : made of the rough limbs of
trees (~ furniture) — **rus·ti·cal·ly**
\'rəs-ti-k(ə-)lē\ adv — **rus·tic·i·ty**
\ˌrəs-'tis-ət-ē\ n

²rustic n : a rustic person

rus·ti·cate \'rəs-ti-ˌkāt\ vb **1** : to go or
to force to go into the country for
residence : banish or be banished to the
country **2** : to become or cause to become rustic — **rus·ti·ca·tion** \ˌrəs-ti-
'kā-shən\ n — **rus·ti·ca·tor** \'rəs-ti-
ˌkāt-ər\ n

¹rus·tle \'rəs-əl\ vb **1** : to make or
cause a rustle **2** : to cause to rustle (~
a newspaper) **3** : to act or move with
energy or speed; also : to procure in this
way **4** : to forage food **5** : to steal
cattle from the range

²rustle n : a quick succession or confusion of small sounds (~ of leaves)

¹rut \'rət\ n : state or period of sexual
excitement esp. in male deer — **rut** vb

²rut n **1** : a track worn by wheels or by
habitual passage of something **2** : a
usual way of doing something from
which one is not easily stirred —
rut·ted adj

ru·ta·ba·ga \ˌrüt-ə-'bā-gə\ n : a turnip
with a large yellowish root

ru·the·ni·um \rü-'thē-nē-əm\ n : a hard
brittle metallic chemical element

ruth·less \'rüth-ləs\ adj : having no
pity : MERCILESS, CRUEL — **ruth·less-
ness** n

-ry \rē\ n suffix : -ERY (bigotry)
(citizenry)

rye \'rī\ n **1** : a hardy cereal grass
grown for grain or as a cover crop;
also : its seed **2** : a whiskey distilled
from a rye mash

ə abut; ᵊ kitten; ər further; a back; ā bake; ä cot, cart; aú out; ch chin;
e less; ē easy; g gift; i trip; ī life; j joke; ŋ sing; ō flow; ó flaw; ói coin;
th thin; t̲h̲ this; ü loot; ú foot; y yet; yü few; yú furious; zh vision

s \'es\ *n, often cap* : the 19th letter of the English alphabet

1-s \s *after sounds* f, k, k̯, p, t, th; əz *after sounds* ch, j, s, sh, z, zh; z *after other sounds*\ *n pl suffix* **1** — used to form the plural of most nouns that do not end in *s, z, sh, ch,* or postconsonantal *y* ⟨heads⟩ ⟨books⟩ ⟨boys⟩ ⟨beliefs⟩, to form the plural of proper nouns that end in postconsonantal *y* ⟨Marys⟩, and with or without a preceding apostrophe to form the plural of abbreviations, numbers, letters, and symbols used as nouns ⟨MCs⟩ ⟨4s⟩ ⟨#s⟩ ⟨B's⟩ **2** — used to form adverbs denoting usual or repeated action or state ⟨goes to school nights⟩

2-s *vb suffix* — used to form the third person singular present of most verbs that do not end in *s, z, sh, ch,* or postconsonantal *y* ⟨falls⟩ ⟨takes⟩ ⟨plays⟩

Sab·bath \'sab-əth\ *n* **1** : the 7th day of the week observed as a day of worship by Jews and some Christians **2** : Sunday observed among Christians as a day of worship

sa·ber *or* **sa·bre** \'sā-bər\ *n* : a cavalry sword with a curved blade and thick back

Sa·bin vaccine \,sā-bən-\ *n* [after Albert B. Sabin †1906 American pediatrician] : a polio vaccine taken by mouth

sa·ble \'sā-bəl\ *n* **1** : the color black **2** *pl* : mourning garments **3** : a dark brown mammal of northern Europe and Asia valued for its fur; *also* : this fur

1sab·o·tage \'sab-ə-,täzh\ *n* **1** : deliberate destruction of an employer's property or hindering of production by workmen **2** : destructive or hampering action by enemy agents or sympathizers in time of war

2sabotage *vb* : to practice sabotage on : WRECK

sac \'sak\ *n* : a baglike part of an animal or plant

sac·cha·rin \'sak-(ə-)rən\ *n* : a very sweet white crystalline substance made from coal tar

sac·cha·rine \-(ə-)rən\ *adj* : nauseatingly sweet ⟨~ poetry⟩

sac·er·do·tal \,sas-ər-'dōt-°l\ *adj* : PRIESTLY — **sac·er·do·tal·ism** *n* — **sac·er·do·tal·ly** *adv*

sa·chem \'sā-chəm\ *n* : a No. American Indian chief

sa·chet \sa-'shā\ *n* : a small bag filled with perfumed powder (**sachet powder**) for scenting clothes

1sack \'sak\ *n* **1** : a large coarse bag; *also* : a small container esp. of paper **2** : a loose jacket or short coat

2sack *vb* : DISMISS, FIRE

3sack *n* : a white wine popular in England in the 16th and 17th centuries

4sack *vb* : to plunder a captured town

sack·cloth \-,klȯth\ *n* : a garment worn as a sign of mourning or penitence

sac·ra·ment \'sak-rə-mənt\ *n* **1** : a formal religious act or rite; *esp* : one (as baptism or the Eucharist) held to have been instituted by Christ **2** : the elements of the Eucharist — **sac·ra·men·tal** \,sak-rə-'ment-°l\ *adj*

sa·cred \'sā-krəd\ *adj* **1** : set apart for the service or worship of deity **2** : de- voted exclusively to one service or use **3** : worthy of veneration or reverence **4** : of or relating to religion : RELIGIOUS syn blessed, divine, hallowed, holy, spiritual — **sa·cred·ly** *adv* — **sa·cred·ness** *n*

1sac·ri·fice \'sak-rə-,fīs\ *n* **1** : the offering of something precious to deity **2** : something offered in sacrifice **3** : LOSS, DEPRIVATION **4** : a bunt allowing a base runner to advance while the batter is put out; *also* : a fly ball allowing a runner to score after the catch — **sac·ri·fi·cial** \,sak-rə-'fish-əl\ *adj* — **sac·ri·fi·cial·ly** *adv*

2sacrifice *vb* **1** : to offer up or kill as a sacrifice **2** : to accept the loss or destruction of for an end, cause, or ideal **3** : to make a sacrifice in baseball

sac·ri·lege \'sak-rə-lij\ *n* **1** : violation of something consecrated to deity **2** : gross irreverence toward a hallowed person, place, or thing — **sac·ri·le·gious** \,sak-rə-'lij-əs, -'lē-jəs\ *adj* — **sac·ri·le·gious·ly** *adv*

sac·ris·tan \'sak-rə-stən\ *n* **1** : a church officer in charge of the sacristy **2** : SEXTON

sac·ris·ty \-stē\ *n* : VESTRY

sac·ro·sanct \'sak-rō-,saŋkt\ *adj* : SACRED, INVIOLABLE

sad \'sad\ *adj* **1** : GRIEVING, MOURNFUL, DOWNCAST **2** : causing sorrow : DEPRESSING **3** : DULL, SOMBER — **sad·ly** *adv* — **sad·ness** *n*

sad·den \'sad-°n\ *vb* : to make sad

1sad·dle \'sad-°l\ *n* **1** : a usu. padded leather-covered seat (as for a rider on horseback or on a bicycle) **2** : the upper back portion of a carcass (as of mutton)

2saddle *vb* **1** : to put a saddle on **2** : BURDEN

sad·dle·bow \-,bō\ *n* : the arch in the front of a saddle

Sad·du·cee \'saj-ə-,sē\ *n* : a member of an ancient Jewish sect opposed to the Pharisees — **Sad·du·ce·an** \,saj-ə-'sē-ən\ *adj*

sad·iron \'sad-,ī-(ə)rn\ *n* : a flatiron with a removable handle

sa·dism \'sād-,iz-əm, 'sad-\ *n* : abnormal delight in cruelty — **sa·dist** *n* — **sa·dis·tic** \sə-'dis-tik\ *adj*

1safe \'sāf\ *adj* **1** : freed from injury or risk **2** : affording safety; *also* : secure from danger or loss **3** : RELIABLE, TRUSTWORTHY — **safe·ly** *adv*

2safe *n* : a container for keeping articles (as valuables) safe

safe-con·duct \-'kän-(,)dəkt\ *n* : a pass permitting a person to go through enemy lines

1safe·guard \-,gärd\ *n* : a measure or device for preventing accident or injury

2safeguard *vb* : to provide a safeguard for : PROTECT

safe·keep·ing \-'kē-piŋ\ *n* : a keeping or being kept in safety

safe·ty \'sāf-tē\ *n* **1** : freedom from danger : SECURITY **2** : a protective device **3** : a football play in which the ball is downed by the offensive team behind its own goal line **4** : a player whose position is in the deepest position — **safety** *adj*

saf·fron \'saf-rən\ *n* : an aromatic deep

orange powder from the flower of a crocus used to color and flavor foods

sag \'sag\ *vb* **sagged; sag·ging 1 :** to bend down at the middle **2 :** to become flabby **:** DROOP — **sag** *n*

sa·ga \'sä·g·ə\ *n* **:** a narrative of heroic deeds; *esp* **:** one recorded in Iceland in the 12th and 13th centuries

sa·ga·cious \sə-'gā-shəs\ *adj* **:** of keen mind **:** SHREWD — **sa·gac·i·ty** \-'gas-ət-ē\ *n*

sag·a·more \'sag-ə-,mŏr\ *n* **:** a subordinate chief of the No. American Indians

¹sage \'sāj\ *adj* **:** WISE, PRUDENT — **sage·ly** *adv*

²sage *n* **:** a wise man **:** PHILOSOPHER

³sage *n* **1 :** a shrublike mint with leaves used in flavoring **2 :** SAGEBRUSH

sage·brush \-,brəsh\ *n* **:** a low shrub of the western U.S. with a sagelike odor

sa·go \'sā-gō\ *n* **:** a dry granulated starch esp. from the pith of an East Indian palm

said *past of* SAY

¹sail \'sāl\ *n* **1 :** a piece of fabric by means of which the wind is used to propel a ship **2 :** a sailing ship **3 :** something resembling a sail **4 :** a trip on a sailboat

²sail *vb* **1 :** to travel on a sailing ship **2 :** to pass over in a ship **3 :** to manage or direct the course of a ship **4 :** to glide through the air

sail·boat \-,bōt\ *n* **:** a boat propelled by wind

sail·ing *n* **:** the action, fact, or pastime of cruising or racing in a sailboat

sail·or \'sā-lər\ *n* **:** one that sails; *esp* **:** a member of a ship's crew

saint \'sānt\ *n* **1 :** one officially recognized as preeminent for holiness **2 :** one of the spirits of the departed in heaven **3 :** a holy or godly person — **saint·ed** *adj* — **saint·hood** *n*

saint·ly *adj* **:** relating to, resembling, or befitting a saint — **saint·li·ness** *n*

¹sake \'sāk\ *n* **1 :** MOTIVE, PURPOSE **2 :** personal or social welfare, safety, or well-being ⟨died for the ~ of his country⟩

²sa·ke *or* **sa·ki** \'säk-ē\ *n* **:** a Japanese alcoholic beverage of fermented rice

sa·la·cious \sə-'lā-shəs\ *adj* **:** OBSCENE, PORNOGRAPHIC

sal·ad \'sal-əd\ *n* **:** a cold dish (as of lettuce, vegetables, or fruit) served with dressing

sal·a·man·der \'sal-ə-,man-dər\ *n* **:** a small lizardlike animal related to the frogs

sa·la·mi \sə-'läm-ē\ *n* **:** highly seasoned sausage of pork and beef

sal·a·ry \'sal-(ə-)rē\ *n* **:** payment made at regular intervals for services

sale \'sāl\ *n* **1 :** transfer of ownership of property from one person to another in return for money **2 :** ready market **:** DEMAND **3 :** AUCTION **4 :** a selling of goods at bargain prices — **sal·able** *or* **sale·able** *adj*

sales·girl \'sālz-,gərl\ *n* **:** SALESWOMAN

sales·man \-mən\ *n* **:** a person who sells in a store or to outside customers — **sales·man·ship** *n*

sales·wom·an \-,wùm-ən\ *n* **:** a woman who sells merchandise

sal·i·cyl·ic acid \,sal-ə-,sil-ik-\ *n* **:** a crystalline organic acid used in the form of its salts to relieve pain and fever

¹sa·lient \'sāl-yənt\ *adj* **:** jutting forward beyond a line; *also* **:** OUTSTANDING, PROMINENT **syn** conspicuous, striking, noticeable

²salient *n* **:** a projecting part in a line of defense

¹sa·line \'sā-,lēn, -,līn\ *adj* **:** consisting of or containing salt **:** SALTY

²saline *n* **1 :** a metallic salt esp. with a purgative action **2 :** a saline solution

sa·li·va \sə-'lī-və\ *n* **:** a liquid secreted into the mouth that helps digestion — **sal·i·vary** \'sal-ə-,ver-ē\ *adj*

Salk vaccine \(,)sò(l)k-\ *n* [after Jonas *Salk* b1914 American physician] **:** a polio vaccine taken by injection

sal·low \'sal-ō\ *adj* **:** of a yellowish sickly color (a ~ liverish skin)

sal·ly \'sal-ē\ *n* **1 :** a rushing attack on besiegers by troops of a besieged place **2 :** a witty remark or retort **3 :** a brief excursion **:** JAUNT — **sally** *vb*

salm·on \'sam-ən\ *n* **1 :** any of several soft-finned food fishes with pinkish flesh **2 :** a strong yellowish pink

sa·lon \sa-'lōⁿ, -'län\ *n* **:** an elegant drawing room; *also* **:** a fashionable shop (beauty ~)

sa·loon \sə-'lün\ *n* **1 :** a large drawing room or ballroom esp. on a passenger ship **2 :** a place where liquors are sold and drunk **:** BARROOM **3** *Brit* **:** SEDAN

sal so·da \'sal-'sōd-ə\ *n* **:** WASHING SODA

¹salt \'sòlt\ *n* **1 :** a white crystalline substance that consists of sodium and chlorine and is used in seasoning foods **2 :** a saltlike cathartic substance **3 :** a compound formed usu. by action of an acid on metal — **salt·i·ness** *n* — **salty** *adj*

²salt *vb* **:** to preserve, season, or feed with salt

³salt *adj* **:** preserved or treated with salt; *also* **:** SALTY

salt·pe·ter *also* **salt·pe·tre** \'sòlt-'pēt-ər\, *n* **:** a chemical salt found in the earth and used in making explosives, in fertilizers, and in curing meat

salt·wa·ter \,sòlt-,wòt-ər, -,wät-\ *adj* **:** of, relating to, or living in salt water

sa·lu·bri·ous \sə-'lü-brē-əs\ *adj* **:** favorable to health

sal·u·tary \'sal-yə-,ter-ē\ *adj* **:** health-giving; *also* **:** BENEFICIAL

sal·u·ta·tion \,sal-yə-'tā-shən\ *n* **:** an expression of greeting, goodwill, or courtesy usu. by word or gesture

¹sa·lute \sə-'lüt\ *vb* **1 :** GREET **2 :** to honor by special ceremonies **3 :** to show respect to (a superior officer) by a formal position of hand, rifle, or sword

²salute *n* **1 :** GREETING **2 :** the formal position assumed in saluting a superior

¹sal·vage \'sal-vij\ *n* **1 :** money paid for saving a ship, its cargo, or passengers when the ship is wrecked or in danger **2 :** the saving of a ship **3 :** the saving of possessions in danger of being lost **4 :** things saved from loss or destruction (as by fire or wreck)

²salvage *vb* **:** to rescue from destruction

sal·va·tion \sal-'vā-shən\ *n* **1 :** the

ə abut; ᵊ kitten; ər further; a back; ā bake; ä cot, cart; aù out; ch chin; e less; ē easy; g gift; i trip; ī life; j joke; ŋ sing; ō flow; ò flaw; òi coin; th thin; t̷h this; ü loot; ù foot; y yet; yü few; yù furious; zh vision

saving of a person from sin or its consequences esp. in the life after death **2** : the saving from danger, difficulty, or evil **3** : something that saves or redeems

¹**salve** \'sav, 'sȧv\ n : a medicinal ointment

²**salve** vb : EASE, SOOTHE

sal·ver \'sal-vər\ n : a small serving tray

sal·vo \'sal-vō\ n, pl -vos or -voes : a simultaneous discharge of guns at the same target or as a salute

sa·mar·i·um \sə-'mer-ē-əm\ n : a pale gray lustrous metallic chemical element

¹**same** \'sām\ adj **1** : being the one referred to : not different **2** : SIMILAR syn identical, equivalent, equal — **sameness** n

²**same** pron : the same one or ones (sighted sub, same ~)

³**same** adv : in the same manner

¹**sam·ple** \'sam-pəl\ n : a piece or item that shows the quality of the whole from which it was taken : EXAMPLE, SPECIMEN

²**sample** vb : to judge the quality of by a sample

sam·pler \-plər\ n : a piece of needlework; esp : one testing skill in embroidering

san·a·to·ri·um \,san-ə-'tōr-ē-əm\ n : an establishment for the care esp. of convalescents or the chronically ill : a health resort

sanc·ti·fy \'saŋk-tə-ˌfī\ vb **1** : to make holy : CONSECRATE, HALLOW **2** : to free from sin : PURIFY — **sanc·ti·fi·ca·tion** \,saŋk-tə-fə-'kā-shən\ n

sanc·ti·mo·ni·ous \,saŋk-tə-'mō-nē-əs\ adj : hypocritically pious — **sanc·ti·mo·ni·ous·ly** adv

¹**sanc·tion** \'saŋk-shən\ n : authoritative approval

²**sanction** vb : to give approval to : RATIFY syn endorse, accredit, certify

sanc·ti·ty \'saŋk-tət-ē\ n **1** : GODLINESS **2** : SACREDNESS

sanc·tu·ary \'saŋk-chə-ˌwer-ē\ n **1** : a consecrated place (as the part of a church in which the altar is placed) **2** : a place of refuge (bird ~)

sanc·tum \'saŋk-təm\ n : a private office or study : DEN (an editor's ~)

¹**sand** \'sand\ n : loose particles of hard broken rock — **sandy** adj

²**sand** vb **1** : to cover or fill with sand **2** : to scour, smooth, or polish with sand or sandpaper

san·dal \'san-d'l\ n : a shoe consisting of a sole strapped to the foot; also : a low or open slipper or rubber overshoe

sand·bank \'san(d)-ˌbaŋk\ n : a deposit of sand in a mound, hillside, bar, or shoal

sand·blast \-ˌblast\ n : sand blown (as for cleaning stone) by air or steam

sand·hog \'sand-ˌhȯg, -ˌhäg\ n : a laborer who drives underwater tunnels

sand·man \'san(d)-ˌman\ n : the genie of folklore who makes children sleepy

sand·pa·per \-ˌpā-pər\ n : paper with sand glued on one side used in smoothing and polishing surfaces — **sandpaper** vb

sand·pip·er \-ˌpī-pər\ n : a long-billed shorebird related to the plovers

sand·stone \-ˌstōn\ n : rock made of sand held together by some natural cement

sand·wich \'sand-(ˌ)wich\ n : two or more slices of bread with a layer (as of meat or cheese) spread between them

sane \'sān\ adj **1** : mentally sound and healthy; also : SENSIBLE, RATIONAL — **sane·ly** adv

sang past of SING

san·gui·nary \'saŋ-gwə-ˌner-ē\ adj : BLOODY (~ battle)

san·guine \'saŋ-gwən\ adj **1** : RUDDY (a ~ complexion) **2** : CHEERFUL, HOPEFUL

san·i·tar·i·um \,san-ə-'ter-ē-əm\ n : SANATORIUM

san·i·tary \'san-ə-ˌter-ē\ adj **1** : of or relating to health : HYGIENIC **2** : free from filth or infective matter

san·i·ta·tion \,san-ə-'tā-shən\ n : a making sanitary; also : protection of health by maintenance of sanitary conditions

san·i·tize \'san-ə-ˌtīz\ vb : to make sanitary (as by sterilizing)

san·i·ty \'san-ət-ē\ n : soundness of mind

sank past of SINK

sans \(ˌ)sanz\ prep : WITHOUT

San·skrit \'san-ˌskrit\ n : an ancient language that is the classical language of India and of Hinduism — **Sanskrit** adj

¹**sap** \'sap\ n : a vital fluid; esp : a watery fluid that circulates through a vascular plant — **sap·less** adj

²**sap** vb sapped; sap·ping **1** : UNDERMINE **2** : to weaken or exhaust gradually

sa·pi·ent \'sāp-ē-ənt, 'sap-\ adj : WISE, DISCERNING — **sa·pi·ence** n

sap·ling \'sap-liŋ\ n : a young tree

sap·phire \'saf-ˌī(ə)r\ n : a hard transparent bright blue precious stone

sap·py \'sap-ē\ adj **1** : full of sap **2** : SILLY, FOOLISH

sap·suck·er \'sap-ˌsək-ər\ n : any of several small American woodpeckers

sap·wood \-ˌwùd\ n : the younger active and usu. lighter and softer outer layer of wood (as of a tree trunk)

sar·casm \'sär-ˌkaz-əm\ n **1** : a cutting or contemptuous remark **2** : ironical criticism or reproach — **sar·cas·tic** \sär-'kas-tik\ adj — **sar·cas·ti·cal·ly** adv

sar·coph·a·gus \sär-'käf-ə-gəs\ n, pl -gi \-ˌgī, -ˌjī\ or -gus·es : a large coffin displayed in the open air or in a tomb

sar·dine \sär-'dēn\ n : a young or very small fish (as a pilchard) preserved esp. in oil for use as food

sar·don·ic \sär-'dän-ik\ adj : expressing scorn or mockery : bitterly disdainful syn ironical, satirical, sarcastic — **sar·don·i·cal·ly** adv

sar·sa·pa·ril·la \ˌsas-(ə-)pə-'ril-ə, ˌsärs-\ n : the root of a tropical American smilax used esp. for flavoring

¹**sash** \'sash\ n : a broad band (as of silk) worn around the waist or over the shoulder

²**sash** n : a frame for a pane of glass in a door or window; also : the movable part of a window

sas·sa·fras \'sas-ə-ˌfras\ n : a No. American tree related to the laurel; also : its dried bark used in medicine and as flavoring

sassy \'sas-ē\ adj : SAUCY

sat past of SIT

Sa·tan \'sāt-ən\ n : DEVIL

sa·tang \sə-'täŋ\ n — see MONEY table

sa·tan·ic \sə-'tan-ik, sā-\ adj **1** : of or resembling Satan **2** : extremely malicious or wicked — **sa·tan·i·cal·ly** adv

satch·el \'sach-əl\ n : VALISE

sate \'sāt\ *vb* **:** to satisfy to the full; *also* **:** SURFEIT, GLUT

sa·teen \sa-'tēn\ *n* **:** a cotton cloth finished to resemble satin

sat·el·lite \'sat-ᵊl-ˌīt\ *n* **1 :** an obsequious follower of a prince or distinguished person **:** TOADY **2 :** a smaller celestial body that revolves around a larger body; *also* **:** a man-made object that orbits the earth or a celestial body

sa·ti·ate \'sā-shē-ˌāt\ *vb* **1 :** to satisfy fully **2 :** SURFEIT, CLOY

sa·ti·e·ty \sə-'tī-ət-ē\ *n* **:** fullness to the point of disgust

sat·in \'sat-ᵊn\ *n* **:** a silk fabric with a glossy surface — **sat·iny** *adj*

sat·in·wood \-ˌwu̇d\ *n* **:** a hard yellowish brown wood of satiny luster; *also* **:** a tree yielding this wood

sat·ire \'sa-ˌtī(ə)r\ *n* **:** biting wit, irony, or sarcasm used to expose vice or folly; *also* **:** a literary work having these qualities — **sa·tir·ic** \sə-'tir-ik\ *or* **sa·tir·i·cal** \-i-kəl\ *adj* — **sat·i·rist** \'sat-ə-rəst\ *n* — **sat·i·rize** \-ə-ˌrīz\ *vb*

sat·is·fac·tion \ˌsat-əs-'fak-shən\ *n* **1 :** payment through penance of sin incurred by sin **2 :** CONTENTMENT, GRATIFICATION **3 :** reparation (as by a duel) for an insult **4 :** settlement of a claim

sat·is·fac·to·ry \-'fak-t(ə-)rē\ *adj* **:** giving satisfaction **:** ADEQUATE

sat·is·fy \'sat-əs-ˌfī\ *vb* **1 :** to make happy **:** GRATIFY **2 :** to pay what is due **3 :** to answer or discharge (a claim) in full **4 :** CONVINCE **5 :** to meet the requirements of

sa·trap \'sā-ˌtrap, 'sa-\ *n* **:** a petty prince **:** subordinate ruler

sat·u·rate \'sach-ə-ˌrāt\ *vb* **1 :** to soak thoroughly **2 :** to treat or charge with something to the point (**saturation point**) where no more can be absorbed, dissolved, or retained ⟨water *saturated* with salt⟩ ⟨air *saturated* with water vapor⟩ — **sat·u·ra·tion** \ˌsach-ə-'rā-shən\ *n*

Sat·ur·day \'sat-ərd-ē\ *n* **:** the 7th day of the week **:** the Jewish Sabbath

Sat·urn \'sat-ərn\ *n* **:** the 2d largest of the planets and the one 6th in order of distance from the sun

sat·ur·nine \'sat-ər-ˌnīn\ *adj* **:** SULLEN, SARDONIC

sa·tyr \'sāt-ər, 'sat-\ *n* **1 :** a woodland deity of Greek mythology with a horse's ears and tail **2 :** a lecherous man

¹sauce \'sȯs, *3 usu* 'sas\ *n* **1 :** a dressing for salads, meats, or puddings **2 :** stewed fruit **3 :** IMPUDENCE

²sauce *vb* **1 :** to add zest to **2 :** to be impudent to

sauce·pan \'sȯs-ˌpan\ *n* **:** a cooking pan with a long handle

sau·cer \'sȯ-sər\ *n* **:** a rounded shallow dish for use under a cup

saucy \'sas-ē, 'sȯs-\ *adj* **:** IMPUDENT, PERT — **sauc·i·ly** *adv*

sau·er·kraut \'sau̇(-ə)r-ˌkrau̇t\ *n* [G, lit., sour cabbage] **:** finely cut cabbage fermented in brine

saun·ter \'sȯnt-ər\ *vb* **:** STROLL

sau·sage \'sȯ-sij\ *n* **:** minced and highly seasoned meat (as pork) usu. enclosed in a tubular casing

sau·té \sȯ-'tā, sō-\ *vb* **-téed; -té·ing :** to fry lightly and quickly in a little fat — **sauté** *n*

sau·terne \sō-'tərn\ *n* **:** a usu. semisweet white table wine

¹sav·age \'sav-ij\ *adj* **1 :** WILD, UNTAMED **2 :** UNCIVILIZED, BARBAROUS **3 :** CRUEL, FIERCE — **sav·age·ly** *adv* — **sav·age·ness** *n* — **sav·age·ry** *n*

²savage *n* **1 :** a member of a primitive human society **2 :** a rude, unmannerly, or brutal person

sa·vant \sa-'vänt, 'sav-ənt\ *n* **:** a learned man **:** SCHOLAR

¹save \'sāv\ *vb* **1 :** to rescue from danger **2 :** to preserve or guard from destruction or loss **3 :** to redeem from sin **4 :** to put by **:** HOARD — **sav·er** *n*

²save *n* **:** a play that prevents an opponent from scoring or winning

³save \(ˌ)sāv\ *prep* **:** EXCEPT ⟨no hope ~ one⟩

⁴save \(ˌ)sāv\ *conj* **:** BUT ⟨no one knew ~ she⟩

sav·ior *or* **sav·iour** \'sāv-yər\ *n* **1 :** one who saves or delivers **2** *cap* **:** Jesus

sa·voir–faire \ˌsav-ˌwär-'faər\ *n* **:** readiness in knowing how to act **:** TACT

¹sa·vor \'sā-vər\ *n* **1 :** the taste and odor of something **2 :** a special flavor or quality — **sa·vory** *adj*

²savor *vb* **1 :** to have a specified taste, smell, or quality **2 :** to taste with pleasure

¹saw \'sȯ\ *past of* SEE

²saw *n* **:** a cutting tool with a thin flat blade having a line of teeth along its edge

³saw *vb* **:** to cut or divide with or as if with a saw — **saw·yer** \-yər\ *n*

⁴saw *n* **:** a common saying **:** MAXIM

saw·dust \'sȯ-(ˌ)dəst\ *n* **:** fine particles made by a saw in cutting

saw·horse \-ˌhȯrs\ *n* **:** a frame or rack on which wood is rested while being sawed by hand

saw·mill \-ˌmil\ *n* **:** a mill for sawing logs

sax·o·phone \'sak-sə-ˌfōn\ *n* **:** a wind instrument with reed mouthpiece and metal body

¹say \'sā\ *vb* **said** \'sed\ **say·ing 1 :** to express in words ⟨~ what you mean⟩; *also* **:** PRONOUNCE ⟨still can't ~ her r's⟩ **2 :** ALLEGE ⟨*said* to be rich⟩ **3 :** to state positively ⟨can't ~ what will happen⟩ **4 :** RECITE ⟨~ your prayers⟩

²say *n* **1 :** an expression of opinion ⟨have your ~⟩ **2 :** power of decision ⟨no ~ in the matter⟩

say·ing *n* **:** a commonly repeated statement

¹scab \'skab\ *n* **1 :** a disease of plants or animals marked by crusted lesions **2 :** a protective crust over a sore or wound **3 :** a worker who replaces a striker or who works under conditions not authorized by a trade union — **scab·by** *adj*

²scab *vb* **scabbed; scab·bing 1 :** to become covered with a scab **2 :** to work as a scab

scab·bard \'skab-ərd\ *n* **:** a sheath for the blade of a weapon (as a sword or dagger)

scaf·fold \'skaf-əld\ *n* **1 :** a raised platform for workmen to sit or stand on **2 :** a platform on which a criminal is

---

ə abut; ᵊ kitten; ər further; a back; ā bake; ä cot, cart; au̇ out; ch chin; e less; ē easy; g gift; i trip; ī life; j joke; ŋ sing; ō flow; ȯ flaw; ȯi coin; th thin; t͟h this; ü loot; u̇ foot; y yet; yü few; yu̇ furious; zh vision

executed (as by hanging or beheading)

scaf·fold·ing \'skȯl-diŋ\ *n* : a system of scaffolds; *also* : materials for scaffolds

¹**scald** \'skȯld\ *vb* 1 : to burn with or as if with hot liquid or steam 2 : to heat up to the boiling point

²**scald** *n* : a burn caused by scalding

¹**scale** \'skāl\ *n* 1 : either pan of a balance 2 : BALANCE — usu. used in pl. 3 : a weighing machine

²**scale** *vb* : WEIGH

³**scale** *n* 1 : one of the small thin plates that cover the body esp. of a fish or reptile 2 : a thin plate 3 : a thin coating, layer, or incrustation — **scaled** *adj* — **scale·less** \'skāl-ləs\ *adj* — **scaly** *adj*

⁴**scale** *vb* : to strip of scales

⁵**scale** *n* [LL *scala* ladder, staircase, fr. L *scalae* (pl.) stairs, rungs, ladder] 1 : something divided into regular spaces as a help in drawing or measuring 2 : a graduated series (a ~ of prices) 3 : the size of a sample (as a model) in proportion to the size of the actual thing 4 : a standard of estimation or judgment (~ of values) 5 : a series of musical tones going up or down in pitch according to a specified scheme

⁶**scale** *vb* 1 : to go up by or as if by a ladder 2 : to arrange in a graded series

scale insect *n* : any of numerous small insects that live on plants and have wingless scale-covered females

scal·lion \'skal-yən\ *n* : an onion without an enlarged bulb

¹**scal·lop** \'skäl-əp, 'skal-\ *n* 1 : a marine mollusk with radially ridged shell valves; *also* : a large edible muscle of this mollusk 2 : one of a continuous series of rounded projections forming an edge (as in lace)

²**scallop** *vb* 1 : to edge (as lace) with scallops 2 : to bake in a casserole (~ed potatoes)

¹**scalp** \'skalp\ *n* : the part of the skin and flesh of the head usu. covered with hair

²**scalp** *vb* 1 : to tear the scalp from 2 : to obtain for the sake of reselling at greatly increased prices (~ing theater tickets)

scal·pel \'skal-pəl\ *n* : a small straight knife with a thin blade used esp. in surgery

scamp \'skamp\ *n* : RASCAL

scam·per \'skam-pər\ *vb* : to run nimbly and playfully — **scamper** *n*

scan \'skan\ *vb* **scanned; scan·ning** 1 : to read (verses) so as to show metrical structure 2 : to examine closely **syn** scrutinize, inspect

scan·dal \'skan-d'l\ *n* 1 : DISGRACE, DISHONOR 2 : malicious gossip : SLANDER — **scan·dal·ize** *vb* — **scan·dal·ous** *adj*

scan·dal·mon·ger \-,məŋ-gər\ *n* : a person who circulates scandal

Scan·di·na·vi·an \,skan-də-'nā-vē-ən\ *n* : a native or inhabitant of Scandinavia — **Scandinavian** *adj*

scan·di·um \'skan-dē-əm\ *n* : a white metallic chemical element

¹**scant** \'skant\ *adj* 1 : barely sufficient 2 : having scarcely enough **syn** scanty, skimpy, meager, sparse

²**scant** *vb* 1 : STINT 2 : SKIMP

scant·ling \-liŋ\ *n* : a piece of lumber; *esp* : one used for an upright in building

scanty *adj* : barely sufficient : SCANT — **scant·i·ly** *adv* — **scant·i·ness** *n*

scape·goat \'skāp-,gōt\ *n* : one that bears the blame for others

scape·grace \-,grās\ *n* : a reckless rascal

scar \'skär\ *n* : a mark left after injured tissue has healed — **scar** *vb*

scar·ab \'skar-əb\ *n* : a large dark beetle; *also* : an ornament (as a gem) representing such a beetle

scarce \'skeərs\ *adj* 1 : not plentiful 2 : RARE — **scarce·ci·ty** \'sker-sət-ē\ *n*

scarce·ly \'skeərs-lē\ *adv* 1 : BARELY 2 : almost not 3 : very probably not

¹**scare** \'skeər\ *vb* : FRIGHTEN, STARTLE

²**scare** *n* : FRIGHT — **scary** *adj*

scare·crow \'skeər-,krō\ *n* : a crude figure set up to scare birds away from crops

scarf \'skärf\ *n, pl* **scarves** \'skärvz\ *or* **scarfs** *n* 1 : a broad band (as of cloth) worn about the shoulders, around the neck, over the head, or about the waist 2 : a long narrow strip of fabric (as for use on a sideboard)

scar·la·ti·na \,skär-lə-'tē-nə\ *n* : a usu. mild scarlet fever

scar·let \'skär-lət\ *n* : a bright red — **scarlet** *adj*

scarlet fever *n* : an acute contagious disease marked by fever, sore throat, and red rash

scat·ter \'skat-ər\ *vb* 1 : to distribute or strew about irregularly 2 : DISPERSE

scav·enge \'skav-ənj\ *vb* : to work or function as a scavenger

scav·en·ger \'skav-ən-jər\ *n* : a person or animal that collects or disposes of refuse or waste

sce·nar·io \sə-'nar-ē-,ō\ *n* : the story of the plot of a motion picture

scene \'sēn\ *n* 1 : a division of one act of a play 2 : a single situation or sequence in a play or motion picture 3 : a stage setting 4 : VIEW, PROSPECT 5 : the place of an occurrence or action 6 : a display of strong feeling and esp. anger — **sce·nic** \'sē-nik\ *adj*

sce·nery \'sēn-(ə-)rē\ *n* 1 : the painted scenes or hangings of a stage and the fittings that go with them 2 : picturesque views or landscape

¹**scent** \'sent\ *vb* 1 : SMELL 2 : to imbue or fill with odor

²**scent** *n* 1 : ODOR, SMELL (the ~ of roses) 2 : sense of smell 3 : course of pursuit : TRACK 4 : PERFUME 2 — **scent·less** *adj*

scep·ter \'sep-tər\ *n* : a staff borne by a sovereign as an emblem of authority

sceptic \'skep-tik\, **sceptical**, **scepticism** *var of* SKEPTIC, SKEPTICAL, SKEPTICISM

¹**sched·ule** \'skej-ül, *esp Brit* 'shed-yül\ *n* 1 : a list of items or details 2 : TIMETABLE

²**schedule** *vb* : to make a schedule of; *also* : to enter on a schedule

sche·mat·ic \ski-'mat-ik\ *adj* : of or relating to a scheme or diagram : DIAGRAMMATIC — **schematic** *n*

¹**scheme** \'skēm\ *n* 1 : a plan for doing something; *esp* : a crafty plot 2 : a systematic design

²**scheme** *vb* : to form a plot : INTRIGUE — **schem·er** *n* — **schem·ing** *adj*

schil·ling \'shil-iŋ\ *n* — see MONEY table

schism \'siz-əm, 'skiz-\ *n* 1 : DIVISION, SPLIT; *also* : DISCORD, DISSENSION 2 : a formal division in or separation from a religious body 3 : the offence of promoting schism

schis·mat·ic \siz-'mat-ik, skiz-\ n : one who creates or takes part in schism — **schismatic** adj

schizo·phre·nia \,skit-sə-'frē-nē-ə\ n [NL, fr. Gk schizein to split + phrēn diaphragm, mind] : mental disorder marked by loss of contact with reality, personality disintegration, and often hallucination — **schiz·oid** \'skit-,sóid\ adj or n — **schizo·phren·ic** \,skit-sə-'fren-ik\ adj or n

schol·ar \'skäl-ər\ n 1 : STUDENT, PUPIL 2 : a learned man : SAVANT — **schol·ar·ly** adj

schol·ar·ship n 1 : the qualities or learning of a scholar 2 : money given to a student to help him pay for his education

scho·las·tic \skə-'las-tik\ adj : of or relating to schools, scholars, or scholarship

¹**school** \'skül\ n 1 : an institution for teaching and learning; also : the pupils in attendance 2 : a body of persons of like opinions or beliefs ⟨the radical ∼⟩

²**school** vb : TEACH, TRAIN, DRILL

³**school** n : a large number of one kind of water animal and esp. of fish swimming and feeding together

school·boy \-,bói\ n : a boy attending school

school·fel·low \-,fel-ō\ n : SCHOOLMATE

school·girl \-,gərl\ n : a girl attending school

school·house \-,haus\ n : a building used as a school

school·marm \-,mä(r)m\ or **school·ma'am** \-,mäm, -,mam\ n 1 : a woman schoolteacher 2 : a person who exhibits characteristics (as pedantry) popularly attributed to schoolteachers

school·mas·ter \-,mas-tər\ n : a male schoolteacher

school·mate \-,māt\ n : a school companion

school·mis·tress \-,mis-trəs\ n : a woman schoolteacher

school·room \-,rüm, -,rùm\ n : a room in a school in which classes meet

school·teach·er \-,tē-chər\ n : a person who teaches in a school

schoo·ner \'skü-nər\ n : a fore-and-aft rigged sailing ship

sci·at·i·ca \sī-'at-i-kə\ n : pain in the region of the hips or along the course of the nerve at the back of the thigh

sci·ence \'sī-əns\ n 1 : a branch of study concerned with observation and classification of facts and esp. with the establishment of verifiable general laws 2 : accumulated systematized knowledge esp. when it relates to the physical world — **sci·en·tif·ic** \,sī-ən-'tif-ik\ adj — **sci·en·tif·i·cal·ly** adv — **sci·en·tist** \'sī-ənt-əst\ n

scim·i·tar \'sim-ət-ər\ n : a curved sword used chiefly by Arabs

scin·til·la \sin-'til-ə\ n : SPARK, TRACE

scin·til·late \'sint-ᵊl-,āt\ vb : SPARKLE, GLEAM — **scin·til·la·tion** \,sint-ᵊl-'ā-shən\ n

sci·on \'sī-ən\ n 1 : a shoot of a plant joined to a stock in grafting 2 : DESCENDANT

scis·sors \'siz-ərz\ n pl : a cutting instrument like shears but usu. smaller

scissors kick n : a swimming kick (as in

a sidestroke) in which the legs move like scissors

scle·ro·sis \sklə-'rō-səs\ n : a usu. abnormal hardening of tissue (as of an artery) — **scle·rot·ic** \-'rät-ik\ adj

scoff \'skäf\ vb : MOCK, JEER — **scoff·er** n

¹**scold** \'skōld\ n : a person who scolds

²**scold** vb : to censure severely or angrily

scone \'skōn, 'skän\ n : a biscuit of oatmeal or barley flour baked on a griddle

¹**scoop** \'sküp\ n 1 : a large shovel; also : a shovellike utensil (a sugar ∼) 2 : a bucket of a dredge or grain elevator 3 : an act or the action of scooping 4 : publication of a news story ahead of a competitor

²**scoop** vb 1 : to take out or up or empty with or as if with a scoop 2 : to dig out : make hollow 3 : to gather in as if with a scoop 4 : to get a scoop on (a rival newspaper)

¹**scope** \'skōp\ n 1 : mental range 2 : extent covered : RANGE 3 : room for development

²**scope** n : an instrument (as a microscope or radarscope) for viewing

scorch \'skórch\ vb : to burn the surface of; also : to dry or shrivel with heat ⟨∼ed lawns⟩

¹**score** \'skōr\ n 1 : DEBT 2 : CUT, SCRATCH, SLASH 3 : REASON (absent on the ∼ of illness) 4 : a record of points made (as in a game) 5 : TWENTY 6 : the music of a composition or arrangement with different parts indicated

²**score** vb 1 : RECORD 2 : to mark with lines, grooves, scratches, or notches 3 : to keep score in a game 4 : to gain or tally in or as if in a game ⟨scored a point⟩ 5 : to assign a grade or score to ⟨∼ the tests⟩

¹**scorn** \'skórn\ n : an emotion involving both anger and disgust : CONTEMPT — **scorn·ful** adj — **scorn·ful·ly** adv

²**scorn** vb : to hold in contempt : DISDAIN — **scorn·er** n

scor·pi·on \'skór-pē-ən\ n : a spiderlike animal with a poisonous sting at the tip of its long jointed tail

Scot \'skät\ n : a native or inhabitant of Scotland

Scotch \'skäch\ n 1 Scotch pl : the people of Scotland 2 : SCOTS 3 : a whiskey distilled in Scotland esp. from malted barley — **Scotch** adj — **Scotch·man** \-mən\ n

scot-free \'skät-'frē\ adj : free from obligation, harm, or penalty

Scots \'skäts\ n : the English language of Scotland

Scot·tish \'skät-ish\ adj : SCOTCH

scoun·drel \'skaun-drəl\ n : a mean worthless fellow : VILLAIN

¹**scour** \'skaù(ə)r\ vb 1 : to move rapidly through : RUSH 2 : to examine thoroughly

²**scour** vb 1 : to rub (as with a gritty substance) in order to clean 2 : to cleanse by or as if by rubbing 3 : to suffer from diarrhea

¹**scourge** \'skərj\ n 1 : LASH, WHIP 2 : PUNISHMENT; also : a cause of affliction (as a plague)

²**scourge** vb 1 : LASH, FLOG 2 : to punish severely

¹**scout** \'skaut\ vb 1 : to look around

: RECONNOITER   2 : to inspect or observe to get information

²scout n 1 : a person sent out to get information; also : a soldier, airplane, or ship sent out to reconnoiter 2 : a member of either of two youth organizations (**Boy Scouts, Girl Scouts**) — **scout·mas·ter** \-,mas-tər\ n

³scout vb : SCORN, SCOFF

scow \'skaù\ n : a large flat-bottomed boat with square ends

scowl \'skaùl\ vb : to lower the face muscles in displeasure — **scowl** n

scrab·ble \'skrab-əl\ vb 1 : SCRAPE, SCRATCH   2 : CLAMBER, SCRAMBLE 3 : to work hard and long 4 : SCRIBBLE — **scrabble** n

scram·ble \'skram-bəl\ vb 1 : to clamber clumsily around 2 : to struggle for or as if for possession of something 3 : to spread irregularly 4 : to mix together 5 : to fry (eggs) after mixing the yolks and whites — **scramble** n

¹scrap \'skrap\ n 1 : FRAGMENT, PIECE 2 : discarded material : REFUSE

²scrap vb scrapped; scrap·ping 1 : to make into scrap (∼ a battleship) 2 : to get rid of as useless

scrap·book \-,bùk\ n : a blank book in which printed items or pictures are kept

¹scrape \'skrāp\ vb 1 : to remove by drawing a knife over; also : to clean or smooth by rubbing off the covering 2 : GRATE; also : to damage or injure the surface of by contact with something rough 3 : to scrape anything with a grating sound 4 : to get together (money) by scratching or by strict economy 5 : to hoard money little by little 6 : to get along with difficulty — **scrap·er** n

²scrape n 1 : the act or the effect of scraping 2 : a bow accompanied by a drawing back of the foot 3 : an unpleasant predicament

¹scratch \'skrach\ vb 1 : to scrape, dig, or rub with or as if with claws or nails (a dog ∼ing at the door) (∼ed his arm on thorns) 2 : to cause to move or strike roughly and gratingly (∼ed his nails across the blackboard) 3 : to scrape (as money) together 4 : to cancel or erase by or as if by drawing a line through (∼ out a word) (∼ed his horse from the race)

²scratch n 1 : a mark made by or as if by scratching; also : a sound so made 2 : the starting line in a race

³scratch adj 1 : made as or used for a trial attempt (∼ paper) 2 : made or done by chance (a ∼ hit)

scrawl \'skròl\ vb : to write hastily and carelessly — **scrawl** n

scraw·ny \'skrò-nē\ adj : very thin : SKINNY

¹scream \'skrēm\ vb : to cry out loudly and shrilly

²scream n : a loud shrill cry

screech \'skrēch\ vb : SHRIEK — **screech** n

¹screen \'skrēn\ n 1 : a device or partition used to hide, restrain, protect, or decorate (a wire-mesh window ∼); also : something that shelters, protects, or conceals 2 : a sieve or perforated material for separating finer from coarser parts (as of sand) 3 : a surface upon which pictures appear (as in movies or television); also : the motion-picture industry

²screen vb 1 : to shield with or as if with a screen 2 : to separate with or as if

with a screen 3 : to present (as a motion picture) on the screen — syn hide, conceal, secrete

¹screw \'skrü\ n 1 : a naillike metal piece with a spiral groove and a head with a slot twisted into or through pieces of solid material to hold them together; also : a device with a spirally grooved cylinder used as a machine 2 : a wheel-like device with a central hub and radiating blades for propelling vehicles (as motorboats or airplanes)

²screw vb 1 : to fasten or close by means of a screw 2 : to operate or adjust by means of a screw 3 : to move or cause to move spirally; also : to close or set in position by such an action

screw·ball \-,bòl\ n 1 : a baseball pitch breaking in a direction opposite to a curve 2 : a whimsical, eccentric, or crazy person

screw·driv·er \-,drī-vər\ n 1 : a tool for turning screws 2 : a drink made of vodka and orange juice

¹scrib·ble \'skrib-əl\ vb : to write hastily or carelessly — **scrib·bler** \-(ə-)lər\ n

²scribble n : hasty or careless writing

scribe \'skrīb\ n 1 : one of a learned class in ancient Palestine serving as copyists, teachers, and jurists 2 : a person whose business is the copying of writing 3 : AUTHOR; esp : JOURNALIST

scrim \'skrim\ n : a light loosely woven cotton or linen cloth

scrim·mage \'skrim-ij\ n : the play between two football teams beginning with the snap of the ball; also : practice play between a team's squads

scrimp \'skrimp\ vb : to be niggardly : economize greatly (∼ and save to buy a house)

scrip \'skrip\ n 1 : paper money for an amount less than one dollar 2 : a certificate showing its holder is entitled to something (as stock or land)

script \'skript\ n : written matter (as lines for a play or broadcast)

scrip·ture \'skrip-chər\ n 1 cap : BIBLE — often used in pl. 2 : the sacred writings of a religion — **scrip·tur·al** adj — **scrip·tur·al·ly** adv

scriv·en·er \'skriv-(ə-)nər\ n : SCRIBE, WRITER, AUTHOR

scroll \'skrōl\ n : a roll of paper or parchment for writing a document; also : a spiral or coiled ornamental form suggesting a loosely or partly rolled scroll

scro·tum \'skrōt-əm\ n : a pouch that in most mammals contains the testes

¹scrub \'skrəb\ n 1 : a stunted tree or shrub; also : a growth of these 2 : an inferior domestic animal 3 : a person of insignificant size or standing; esp : a player not on the first team — **scrub** adj — **scrub·by** adj

²scrub vb scrubbed; scrub·bing 1 : to rub in washing (∼ clothes) 2 : to wash by rubbing (∼ out a spot) — **scrub** n

scruff \'skrəf\ n : the loose skin of the back of the neck : NAPE

¹scru·ple \'skrü-pəl\ n 1 : a point of conscience or honor 2 : hesitation due to ethical considerations — **scru·pu·lous** \-pyə-ləs\ adj — **scru·pu·lous·ly** adv

²scruple vb : to be reluctant on grounds of conscience : HESITATE

scru·ti·nize \'skrüt-²n-,īz\ vb : to examine closely : make a scrutiny

scru·ti·ny \'skrüt-²n-ē\ n : a careful

looking over : close examination **syn** inspection

scu·ba \\'sk(y)ü-bə\\ *n* [*self-contained underwater breathing apparatus*] : an apparatus for breathing while swimming under water

1scud \\'skəd\\ *vb* **scud·ded; scud·ding** : to move speedily

2scud *n* : loose vaporlike clouds driven by the wind

scuf·fle \\'skəf-əl\\ *vb* **1** : to struggle confusedly at close quarters **2** : to shuffle one's feet — **scuffle** *n*

1scull \\'skəl\\ *n* **1** : an oar for use in sculling; *also* : one of a pair of short oars for a single oarsman

2scull *vb* : to propel (a boat) by an oar over the stern

scul·lery \\'skəl-(ə-)rē\\ *n* : a small room near the kitchen used for cleaning dishes, culinary utensils, and vegetables

scul·lion \\'skəl-yən\\ *n* : a kitchen menial

sculp·tor \\'skəlp-tər\\ *n* : one who produces works of sculpture

1sculp·ture \\'skəlp-chər\\ *n* : the act, process, or art of carving or molding material (as stone, wood, or plastic); *also* : work produced this way

2sculpture *vb* : to form or alter as or as if a work of sculpture ⟨~ a face on the side of a mountain⟩

scum \\'skəm\\ *n* **1** : a foul filmy covering on the surface of a liquid (as a stagnant pool) **2** : waste matter **3** : the lowest class : RABBLE

scup·per \\'skəp-ər\\ *n* : an opening in the side of a ship through which water on deck is drained overboard

scurf \\'skərf\\ *n* : thin dry scales of skin (as dandruff); *also* : a scaly deposit or covering — **scurfy** *adj*

scur·ri·lous \\'skər-ə-ləs\\ *adj* : coarsely jesting : OBSCENE, VULGAR

scur·ry \\'skər-ē\\ *vb* : SCAMPER

1scur·vy \\'skər-vē\\ *adj* : MEAN, CONTEMPTIBLE — **scur·vi·ly** *adv*

2scurvy *n* : a vitamin-deficiency disease marked by spongy gums, loosened teeth, and bleeding into the tissues

scutch·eon \\'skəch-ən\\ *n* : ESCUTCHEON

1scut·tle \\'skət-ᵊl\\ *n* : a pail for carrying coal

2scuttle *n* : a small opening with a lid esp. in the deck, side, or bottom of a ship

3scuttle *vb* : to cut a hole in the deck, side, or bottom of (a ship) in order to sink

4scuttle *vb* : SCURRY, SCAMPER

scythe \\'sīth\\ *n* : an implement for mowing (as grass or grain) by hand — **scythe** *vb*

sea \\'sē\\ *n* **1** : a large body of salt water **2** : OCEAN **3** : rough water; *also* : a heavy wave **4** : something like or likened to a large body of water — **sea** *adj*

sea·bird \\-,bərd\\ *n* : a bird (as a gull) frequenting the open ocean

sea·board \\-,bōrd\\ *n* : a seacoast with the country bordering it

sea·coast \\-,kōst\\ *n* : land at and near the edge of a sea

sea·far·er \\-,far-ər\\ *n* : SEAMAN

sea·far·ing *n* : a mariner's calling — **seafaring** *adj*

sea·food \\-,füd\\ *n* : edible marine fish and shellfish

sea·go·ing \\-,gō-iŋ\\ *adj* : used, working, or operating on the open sea

sea horse *n* : a small sea fish with a head suggesting that of a horse

1seal \\'sēl\\ *n* **1** : any of various large sea mammals of cold regions with limbs adapted for swimming **2** : the pelt of a seal

2seal *vb* : to hunt seals — **seal·er** *n*

3seal *n* **1** : a device having a raised design that can be stamped on clay or wax; *also* : the impression made by stamping with such a device **2** : something that fastens or secures as a stamped wax impression fastens a letter; *specif* : GUARANTY, PLEDGE **3** : a mark acceptable as having the legal effect of an official seal

4seal *vb* **1** : to affix a seal to; *also* : AUTHENTICATE **2** : to fasten with a seal; *esp* : to enclose securely **3** : to determine irrevocably — **seal·er** *n*

sea level *n* : the level of the surface of the sea esp. at its mean position midway between mean high and low water

seal·skin \\'sēl-,skin\\ *n* : ¹SEAL 2

1seam \\'sēm\\ *n* **1** : the line of junction of two edges and esp. of edges of fabric sewn together **2** : WRINKLE **3** : a layer of mineral matter ⟨coal ~s⟩ — **seam·less** *adj*

2seam *vb* **1** : to join by or as if by sewing **2** : WRINKLE, FURROW

sea·man \\'sē-mən\\ *n* **1** : one who assists in the handling of ships : MARINER **2** : an enlisted man in the navy ranking next below a petty officer third class

seaman apprentice *n* : an enlisted man in the navy ranking next below a seaman

seaman recruit *n* : an enlisted man of the lowest rank in the navy

sea·man·ship *n* : the art or skill of handling a ship

seam·stress \\'sēm-strəs\\ *n* : a woman who does sewing

seamy \\'sē-mē\\ *adj* **1** : UNPLEASANT **2** : DEGRADED, SORDID

sea·plane \\'sē-,plān\\ *n* : an airplane so made that it can rise from or alight on the water

sea·port \\-,pōrt\\ *n* : a port for seagoing ships

sear \\'siər\\ *vb* **1** : to dry up : WITHER **2** : to burn or scorch esp. on the surface; *also* : BRAND

1search \\'sərch\\ *vb* **1** : to look through in trying to find something **2** : SEEK **3** : PROBE — **search·er** *n*

2search *n* **1** : the act of searching **2** : critical examination **3** : an act of boarding and inspecting a ship on the high seas in exercise of right of search

search·light \\-,līt\\ *n* **1** : an apparatus for projecting a beam of light; *also* : the light projected **2** : FLASHLIGHT 2

sea·shore \\'sē-,shōr\\ *n* : the shore of a sea

sea·sick \\-,sik\\ *adj* : nauseated by or as if by the motion of a ship — **sea·sick·ness** *n*

sea·side \\-,sīd\\ *n* : SEASHORE

1sea·son \\'sēz-ᵊn\\ *n* **1** : one of the divisions of the year (as spring, summer, autumn, or winter) **2** : a special period ⟨the Easter ~⟩ — **sea·son·al** *adj*

²**season** vb **1** : to make pleasant to the taste by use of salt, pepper, or spices **2** : FLAVOR **3** : to make (as by aging or drying) suitable for use **4** : to accustom or habituate to something (as hardship or misfortune) syn harden, inure, acclimatize

sea·son·able \'sēz-(ᵊ-)nə-bəl\ adj : occurring at a fit time : OPPORTUNE syn timely

sea·son·ing \-(ᵊ-)niŋ\ n : something that seasons : CONDIMENT

¹**seat** \'sēt\ n **1** : a place on or at which a person sits **2** : a chair, bench, or stool for sitting on **3** : a place which serves as a capital or center

²**seat** vb **1** : to place in or on a seat **2** : to provide seats for

¹**sea·ward** \'sē-wərd\ also **sea·wards** \-wərdz\ adv (or adj) : toward the sea

²**seaward** n : the direction or side away from land and toward the open sea

sea·way \-,wā\ n : an inland waterway that admits ocean shipping

sea·weed \-,wēd\ n : a marine alga : a mass of marine algae

sea·wor·thy \-,wər-thē\ adj : fit for a sea voyage

se·ba·ceous \si-'bā-shəs\ adj : of, relating to, or secreting fatty material (~ glands of the skin)

se·cede \si-'sēd\ vb : to withdraw from an organized body and esp. from a political body

se·ces·sion \-'sesh-ən\ n : the act of seceding — **se·ces·sion·ist** n

se·clude \si-'klüd\ vb : to shut off by oneself : ISOLATE

se·clu·sion \-'klü-zhən\ n : the act of secluding : the state of being secluded

¹**sec·ond** \'sek-ənd\ adj **1** : being number two in a countable series **2** : next after the first — **second** adv — **sec·ond·ly** adv

²**second** n **1** : one that is second **2** : one who assists another (as in a duel) **3** : an inferior or flawed article (as of merchandise) **4** : the 2d forward gear in an automotive vehicle

³**second** n **1** : a 60th part of a minute either of time or of a degree **2** : an instant of time

⁴**second** vb **1** : to act as a second to **2** : to encourage or give support to (as a person or plan) **3** : to support (a motion) by adding one's voice to that of a proposer

sec·ond·ary \'sek-ən-,der-ē\ adj **1** : second in rank, value, or occurrence : INFERIOR, LESSER **2** : coming after the primary : higher than the elementary (~ schools) (~ education) **3** : belonging to a second or later stage of development syn subordinate

sec·ond·hand \,sek-ən-'hand\ adj **1** : not original (~ information) **2** : not new : USED (~ clothes) **3** : dealing in used goods

second lieutenant n : a commissioned officer (as in the army) ranking next below a first lieutenant

sec·ond-rate \,sek-ən(d)-'rāt\ adj : INFERIOR

se·cre·cy \'sē-krə-sē\ n **1** : the habit or practice of being secretive **2** : the quality or state of being secret

¹**se·cret** \'sē-krət\ adj **1** : HIDDEN, CONCEALED (a ~ panel) **2** : COVERT, STEALTHY; also : engaged in detecting or spying (a ~ agent) **3** : kept from general knowledge (a ~ password) — **se·cret·ly** adv

²**secret** n **1** : something kept from the knowledge of others **2** : MYSTERY **3** : CONCEALMENT

sec·re·tar·i·at \,sek-rə-'ter-ē-ət\ n **1** : the office of a secretary **2** : the body of secretaries in an office **3** : the administrative department of a governmental organization (the UN ~)

sec·re·tary \'sek-rə-,ter-ē\ n **1** : a confidential clerk **2** : a corporation or business official who is in charge of correspondence or records **3** : an official at the head of a department of government **4** : a writing desk — **sec·re·tar·i·al** \,sek-rə-'ter-ē-əl\ adj — **sec·re·tary·ship** \'sek-rə-,ter-ē-,ship\ n

¹**se·crete** \si-'krēt\ vb : to produce and emit as a secretion

²**se·crete** \si-'krēt, 'sē-krət\ vb : HIDE, CONCEAL

se·cre·tion \si-'krē-shən\ n **1** : an act or process of secreting **2** : a product of glandular activity; esp : one (as a hormone or enzyme) useful in the organism — **se·cre·to·ry** \-'krēt-ə-rē\ adj

se·cre·tive \'sē-krət-iv, si-'krēt-\ adj : tending to keep secrets or to act secretly — **se·cre·tive·ly** adv — **se·cre·tive·ness** n

sect \'sekt\ n **1** : a dissenting religious body **2** : a religious denomination **3** : a group adhering to a distinctive doctrine or to a leader

¹**sec·tar·i·an** \sek-'ter-ē-ən\ adj **1** : of or relating to a sect or sectarian **2** : limited in character or scope — **sec·tar·i·an·ism** n

²**sectarian** n **1** : an adherent of a sect **2** : a narrow or bigoted person

sec·ta·ry \'sek-tə-rē\ n : a member of a sect

sec·tion \'sek-shən\ n **1** : a cutting apart; also : a part cut off or separated **2** : a distinct part (as of a book, a country, or a community) **3** : the appearance that a thing has or would have if cut straight through

sec·tion·al \-sh(ə-)nəl\ adj **1** : of, relating to, or characteristic of a section **2** : local or regional rather than general in character **3** : divided into sections — **sec·tion·al·ism** n

sec·tor \'sek-tər\ n **1** : a part of a circle between two radii **2** : a definite part of a region assigned to a military leader as his area of operations

sec·u·lar \'sek-yə-lər\ adj **1** : not sacred or ecclesiastical : NONRELIGIOUS **2** : not bound by monastic vows : not belonging to a religious order (~ priest)

sec·u·lar·ism n : indifference to or exclusion of religion — **sec·u·lar·ist** n or adj

¹**se·cure** \si-'kyùr\ adj **1** : easy in mind : free from fear **2** : free from danger or risk of loss : SAFE **3** : CERTAIN, SURE — **se·cure·ly** adv

²**secure** vb **1** : to make safe : GUARD **2** : to assure payment of by giving a pledge or collateral **3** : to fasten safely (~ a door) **4** : GET, ACQUIRE

se·cu·ri·ty \si-'kyùr-ət-ē\ n **1** : SAFETY **2** : CERTAINTY **3** : freedom from worry **4** : PROTECTION, SHELTER **5** : something (as collateral) given as pledge of payment **6** pl : bond or stock certificates

se·dan \si-'dan\ n **1** : a covered chair borne on poles by two men **2** : an enclosed automobile usu. with front and back seats **3** : a motorboat with one passenger compartment

se·date \si-'dāt\ *adj* : quiet and dignified in behavior **syn** staid, sober, serious, solemn — **se·date·ly** *adv*

¹sed·a·tive \'sed-ət-iv\ *adj* : serving or tending to relieve tension — **se·da·tion** \si-'dā-shən\ *n*

²sedative *n* : a sedative drug

sed·en·tary \'sed-ᵊn-ter-ē\ *adj* : characterized by or requiring much sitting (~ work)

sedge \'sej\ *n* : a grasslike plant with solid stems growing in tufts in marshes — **sedgy** *adj*

sed·i·ment \'sed-ə-mənt\ *n* **1** : the material that settles to the bottom of a liquid : LEES, DREGS **2** : material (as stones and sand) deposited by water, wind, or a glacier — **sed·i·men·ta·ry** \,sed-ə-'men-t(ə-)rē\ *adj*

se·di·tion \si-'dish-ən\ *n* : the causing of discontent, insurrection, or resistance against a government — **se·di·tious** *adj*

se·duce \si-'d(y)üs\ *vb* **1** : to persuade to disobedience or disloyalty **2** : to lead astray (*seduced* into crime) **3** : to entice (a person) into unchastity **syn** tempt, entice, inveigle, lure — **se·duc·er** *n* — **se·duc·tion** \-'dək-shən\ *n* — **se·duc·tive** \-'dək-tiv\ *adj*

sed·u·lous \'sej-ə-ləs\ *adj* : DILIGENT, PAINSTAKING

¹see \'sē\ *vb* **saw** \'sȯ\ **seen** \'sēn\ **see·ing 1** : to perceive by the eye : have the power of sight **2** : EXPERIENCE **3** : NOTICE, HEED **4** : UNDERSTAND **5** : to meet with **syn** behold, descry, espy, view, observe, note, discern

²see *n* : the authority or jurisdiction of a bishop

¹seed \'sēd\ *n* **1** : a ripened ovule of a plant that may develop into a new plant **2** : a part (as a small seedlike fruit) by which a plant is propagated **3** : DESCENDANTS (the ~ of David) **4** : SOURCE, ORIGIN — **seed·less** *adj* — **seedy** *adj*

²seed *vb* **1** : SOW, PLANT (~ land to grass) **2** : to bear or shed seeds **3** : to remove seeds from (~ raisins) — **seed·er** *n*

seed·ling \-liŋ\ *n* **1** : a plant grown from seed **2** : a young plant; *esp* : a tree smaller than a sapling

seed·time \-,tīm\ *n* : the season for sowing

seek \'sēk\ *vb* **sought** \'sȯt\ **seek·ing 1** : to search for **2** : to try to reach or obtain **3** : ATTEMPT — **seek·er** *n*

seem \'sēm\ *vb* **1** : to give the impression of being : APPEAR **2** : to appear to the observation or understanding; *also* : to appear to one's own mind or opinion **3** : to give evidence of existing or being present

seem·ing *adj* : outwardly apparent : OSTENSIBLE — **seem·ing·ly** *adv*

seem·ly \'sēm-lē\ *adj* : PROPER, DECENT

seep \'sēp\ *vb* : to leak through fine pores or cracks : percolate slowly — **seep·age** *n*

seer \'siər\ *n* : a person who foresees or predicts events : PROPHET

see·saw \'sē-,sȯ\ *n* **1** : a children's sport of riding up and down on the ends of a plank supported in the middle; *also* : the plank so used **2** : a contest in which now one side now the other has the lead — **seesaw** *vb*

---

seethe \'sēth\ *vb* : to make or become violently agitated

seg·ment \'seg-mənt\ *n* **1** : a division of a thing : SECTION (~ of an orange) **2** : a part cut off from a geometrical figure (as a circle) by a line

seg·re·gate \'seg-ri-,gāt\ *vb* [L *segregare,* fr. *se-* apart + *greg-, grex* herd, flock] : to cut off from others : ISOLATE — **seg·re·ga·tion** \,seg-ri-'gā-shən\ *n*

seg·re·ga·tion·ist *n* : one who believes in or practices the segregation of races

sei·gneur \sān-'yər\ *n* : a feudal lord

¹seine \'sān\ *n* : a large weighted fishing net

²seine *vb* : to fish or catch with a seine

seis·mic \'sīz-mik, 'sīs-\ *adj* : of, relating to, resembling, or caused by an earthquake — **seis·mi·cal·ly** *adv*

seis·mo·graph \-mə-,graf\ *n* : an apparatus for recording the intensity, direction, and duration of earthquakes — **seis·mo·graph·ic** \,sīz-mə-'graf-ik, ,sīs-\ *adj*

seize \'sēz\ *vb* **1** : to lay hold of or take possession of by force **2** : ARREST **3** : UNDERSTAND **syn** take, grasp, clutch, snatch, grab — **sei·zure** \'sē-zhər\ *n*

sel·dom \'sel-dəm\ *adv* : not often : RARELY

¹se·lect \sə-'lekt\ *adj* **1** : CHOSEN, PICKED; *also* : CHOICE **2** : judicious or restrictive in choice : DISCRIMINATING

²select *vb* : to take by preference from a number or group : pick out : CHOOSE — **se·lec·tive** *adj*

se·lec·tion \sə-'lek-shən\ *n* **1** : the act of selecting : CHOICE **2** : something selected **3** : a natural or artificial process that increases the chance of propagation of some organisms and decreases that of others

se·lect·man \si-'lekt-,man, -mən\ *n* : one of the town officials chosen annually in most New England states to administer town affairs

se·le·ni·um \sə-'lē-nē-əm\ *n* : a nonmetallic chemical element that varies in electrical conductivity with the intensity of its illumination

self \'self\ *n, pl* **selves** \'selvz\ **1** : the essential person distinct from all other persons in identity **2** : a particular side of a person's character **3** : personal interest : SELFISHNESS

self- *comb form* **1** : oneself : itself **2** : of oneself or itself **3** : by oneself; *also* : automatic **4** : to, for, or toward oneself

self-abasement	self-complacent
self-accusation	self-conceit
self-acting	self-concerned
self-addressed	self-condemned
self-adjusting	self-confidence
self-administered	self-confident
self-advancement	self-constituted
self-analysis	self-contradiction
self-appointed	self-control
self-assertion	self-created
self-assertive	self-criticism
self-assurance	self-cultivation
self-assured	self-deception
self-awareness	self-defeating
self-betrayal	self-defense
self-closing	self-delusion
self-command	(continued)

ə abut; ᵊ kitten; ər further; a back; ā bake; ä cot, cart; au̇ out; ch chin; e less; ē easy; g gift; i trip; ī life; j joke; ŋ sing; ō flow; ȯ flaw; ȯi coin; th thin; t̲h̲ this; ü loot; u̇ foot; y yet; yü few; yu̇ furious; zh vision

self-denial
self-denying
self-destruction
self-determination
self-discipline
self-distrust
self-doubt
self-driven
self-educated
self-employed
self-employment
self-esteem
self-evident
self-examination
self-explaining
self-explanatory
self-expression
self-forgetful
self-giving
self-governing
self-government
self-help
self-importance
self-important
self-imposed
self-improvement
self-induced
self-indulgence
self-inflicted
self-interest
self-limiting
self-love

self-luminous
self-mastery
self-perpetuating
self-pity
self-portrait
self-possessed
self-possession
self-preservation
self-propelled
self-propelling
self-protection
self-regard
self-regulating
self-reliance
self-reliant
self-reproach
self-respect
self-respecting
self-restraint
self-sacrifice
self-satisfaction
self-satisfied
self-seeking
self-service
self-starting
self-sufficiency
self-sufficient
self-supporting
self-sustaining
self-taught
self-will

self-cen·tered \'self-'sent-ərd\ *adj* : concerned only with one's own desires or interests : SELFISH — **self-cen·tered·ness** *n*

self-con·scious \-'kän-chəs\ *adj* **1** : aware of oneself as an individual **2** : uncomfortably conscious of oneself as an object of the observation of others : ill at ease — **self-con·scious·ly** *adv* — **self-con·scious·ness** *n*

self-con·tained \,self-kən-'tānd\ *adj* **1** : showing self-command; *also* : reserved in manner **2** : complete in itself (~ machine)

self-ef·fac·ing \,self-ə-'fā-siŋ\ *adj* : keeping oneself in the background : RETIRING

self·ish \'sel-fish\ *adj* : taking care of one's own comfort, pleasure, or interest excessively or without regard for others — **self·ish·ly** *adv* — **self·ish·ness** *n*

self·less \'self-ləs\ *adj* : UNSELFISH — **self·less·ness** *n*

self-made \'self-'mād\ *adj* : rising from poverty or obscurity by one's own efforts (~ man)

self-righ·teous \-'rī-chəs\ *adj* : strongly convinced of one's own righteousness

self·same \-,sām\ *adj* : precisely the same : IDENTICAL

sell \'sel\ *vb* **sold** \'sōld\ **sell·ing 1** : to transfer (property) in return for money or something else of value **2** : to deal in as a business **3** : to be sold : find buyers (cars are ~ing well) — **sell·er** *n*

sel·vage *or* **sel·vedge** \'sel-vij\ *n* : the edge of a woven fabric so formed as to prevent raveling

selves *pl of* SELF

se·man·tic \si-'mant-ik\ *adj* : of or relating to meaning

se·man·tics *n* : the study of meanings in language

sem·a·phore \'sem-ə-,fōr\ *n* **1** : a visual signaling apparatus with movable arms **2** : signaling by hand-held flags

sem·blance \'sem-bləns\ *n* **1** : outward appearance **2** : IMAGE, LIKENESS

se·men \'sē-mən\ *n* : male reproductive

fluid consisting of secretions and germ cells

se·mes·ter \sə-'mes-tər\ *n* : half a year; *esp* : one of the two terms into which many colleges divide the school year

semi- \'sem-ē, -i, -,ī\ *prefix* **1** : precisely half of **2** : half in quantity or value; *also* : half of or occurring halfway through a specified period **3** : partly : incompletely **4** : partial : incomplete **5** : having some of the characteristics of

semiannual
semiarid
semicircle
semicircular
semicivilized
semiconscious
semidarkness
semidivine
semiformal
semi-independent
semiliquid
semiliterate

semimonthly
semiofficial
semipermanent
semipolitical
semiprecious
semiprofessional
semireligious
semiskilled
semisweet
semitransparent
semitropical
semiweekly

semi·co·lon \'sem-i-,kō-lən\ *n* : a punctuation mark ; used esp. in a coordinating function between major sentence elements

semi·con·duc·tor \,sem-i-kən-'dək-tər, -,ī-\ *n* : a substance whose electrical conductivity is between that of a conductor and an insulator and increases with temperature increase

1semi·fi·nal \,sem-i-'fīn-ᵊl\ *adj* : being next to the last in an elimination tournament

2semi·fi·nal \'sem-i-,fīn-ᵊl\ *n* : a semifinal round or match

semi·flu·id \,sem-i-'flü-əd, -,ī-\ *adj* : having the qualities of both a fluid and a solid

semi·lu·nar \,sem-i-'lü-nər, -,ī-\ *adj* : crescent-shaped

sem·i·nar \'sem-ə-,när\ *n* **1** : a course of study pursued by a group of advanced students doing original research under a professor **2** : CONFERENCE

sem·i·nary \'sem-ə-,ner-ē\ *n* : an educational institution; *esp* : one that gives theological training — **sem·i·nar·i·an** \,sem-ə-'ner-ē-ən\ *n*

Sem·ite \'sem-,īt\ *n* : a member of any of a group of peoples (as the Jews or Arabs) of southwestern Asia — **Se·mit·ic** \sə-'mit-ik\ *adj*

semp·stress \'semp-strəs\ *var of* SEAMSTRESS

sen \'sen\ *n, pl* **sen** — see MONEY table

sen·ate \'sen-ət\ *n* : the upper and generally smaller branch of various state and national legislatures

sen·a·tor \'sen-ət-ər\ *n* : a member of a senate — **sen·a·to·ri·al** \,sen-ə-'tōr-ē-əl\ *adj*

send \'send\ *vb* **sent** \'sent\ **send·ing 1** : to cause to go : DISPATCH **2** : EMIT **3** : to propel or drive esp. with force (~ a rocket to the moon) — **send·er** *n*

Sen·e·ga·lese \,sen-i-gə-'lēz\ *n, pl* **Senegalese** : a native or inhabitant of Senegal — **Senegalese** *adj*

se·nile \'sē-,nīl\ *adj* : OLD, AGED; *also* : DODDERING — **se·nil·i·ty** \si-'nil-ət-ē\ *n*

1se·nior \'sē-nyər\ *n* **1** : a person older or of higher rank than another **2** : a member of the graduating class of a high school or college

2senior *adj* **1** : ELDER **2** : more advanced in dignity or rank **3** : belonging to the final year of a school or college course

senior chief petty officer *n* : a noncommissioned officer in the navy ranking next below a master chief petty officer

se·nior·i·ty \sēn-'yȯr-ət-ē\ *n* **1** : the quality or state of being senior **2** : a privileged status owing to length of continuous service

senior master sergeant *n* : a noncommissioned officer in the air force ranking next below a chief master sergeant

sen·na \'sen-ə\ *n* **1** : any of various cassias **2** : the dried leaflets of a cassia used as a purgative

sen·sa·tion \sen-'sā-shən\ *n* **1** : awareness (as of noise or heat) or a mental process (as seeing or hearing) due to stimulation of a sense organ; *also* : an indefinite bodily feeling **2** : a condition of excitement; *also* : the thing that causes this condition

sen·sa·tion·al *adj* **1** : of or relating to sensation or the senses **2** : arousing an intense and usu. superficial interest or emotional reaction — **sen·sa·tion·al·ly** *adv*

sen·sa·tion·al·ism *n* : the use or effect of sensational subject matter or treatment

¹sense \'sens\ *n* **1** : the faculty of perceiving by means of sense organs; *also* : a bodily function or mechanism based on this (the pain ~) **2** : JUDGMENT, UNDERSTANDING **3** : semantic content (as of a word or phrase) : MEANING **4** : OPINION (the ~ of the meeting) — **sense·less** *adj*

²sense *vb* : to be or become aware of : perceive by the senses

sense organ *n* : a bodily structure that responds to a stimulus (as heat or light) and sends impulses to the brain where they are interpreted as corresponding sensations

sen·si·bil·i·ty \,sen-sə-'bil-ət-ē\ *n* : delicacy of feeling : SENSITIVITY, RESPONSIVENESS

sen·si·ble \'sen-sə-bəl\ *adj* **1** : capable of being perceived by the senses or by reason; *also* : capable of receiving sense impressions **2** : AWARE, CONSCIOUS **3** : REASONABLE, INTELLIGENT — **sen·si·bly** *adv*

sen·si·tive \'sen-sət-iv\ *adj* **1** : subject to excitation by or responsive to stimuli : SENSORY **2** : having power of feeling **3** : of such a nature as to be easily affected : SUSCEPTIBLE — **sen·si·tive·ness** *n* — **sen·si·tiv·i·ty** \,sen-sə-'tiv-ət-ē\ *n*

sen·si·tize \'sen-sə-,tīz\ *vb* : to make or become sensitive or hypersensitive — **sen·si·ti·za·tion** \,sen-sət-ə-'zā-shən\ *n*

sen·sor \'sen-,sȯr, -sər\ *n* : a device that responds to a physical stimulus

sen·so·ry \'sens-(ə-)rē\ *adj* : of or relating to sensation or the senses

sen·su·al \'sen-chə-wəl\ *adj* **1** : relating to the pleasing of the senses **2** : devoted to the pleasures of the senses — **sen·su·al·ist** *n* — **sen·su·al·i·ty** \,sen-chə-'wal-ət-ē\ *n* — **sen·su·al·ly** \'sen-chə-wə-lē\ *adv*

sen·su·ous \'sen-chə-wəs\ *adj* : relating to the senses or to things that can be perceived by the senses

sent *past of* SEND

¹sen·tence \'sent-°ns, -°nz\ *n* **1** : DE-

CISION, JUDGMENT (pass ~) **2** : a grammatically self-contained speech unit that expresses an assertion, a question, a command, a wish, or an exclamation

²sentence *vb* : to pronounce sentence on

sen·ten·tious \sen-'ten-chəs\ *adj* : using wise sayings or proverbs; *also* : using pompous language

sen·tient \'sen-ch(ē-)ənt\ *adj* : capable of feeling : having perception

sen·ti·ment \'sent-ə-mənt\ *n* **1** : FEELING; *also* : thought and judgment influenced by feeling : emotional attitude **2** : OPINION, NOTION

sen·ti·men·tal \,sent-ə-'ment-°l\ *adj* **1** : influenced by tender feelings **2** : affecting the emotions **syn** romantic — **sen·ti·men·tal·ism** *n* — **sen·ti·men·tal·ist** *n* — **sen·ti·men·tal·i·ty** \,men-'tal-ət-ē\ *n* — **sen·ti·men·tal·ly** \-'ment-°l-ē\ *adv*

sen·ti·nel \'sent-(°-)nəl\ *n* : one that watches or guards

sen·try \'sen-trē\ *n* : SENTINEL, GUARD

se·pal \'sēp-əl, 'sep-\ *n* : one of the modified leaves comprising a flower calyx

sep·a·ra·ble \'sep-(ə-)rə-bəl\ *adj* : capable of being separated

¹sep·a·rate \'sep-ə-,rāt\ *vb* **1** : to set or keep apart : DISUNITE, DISCONNECT, SEVER **2** : to keep apart by something intervening **3** : to cease to be together : PART

²sep·a·rate \-(ə-)rət\ *adj* **1** : not connected **2** : divided from each other : APART **3** : SINGLE, PARTICULAR (the ~ pieces of the puzzle) — **sep·a·rate·ly** *adv*

sep·a·ra·tion \,sep-ə-'rā-shən\ *n* **1** : the act or process of separating : the state of being separated **2** : a point, line, means, or area of division

sep·a·ra·tist \'sep-(ə-)rət-əst, -ə-,rāt-\ *n* : an advocate of separation (as from a political or religious body)

sep·a·ra·tor \-ə-,rāt-ər\ *n* : one that separates; *esp* : a device for separating cream from milk

se·pia \'sē-pē-ə\ *n* : a brownish gray to dark brown

sep·sis \'sep-səs\ *n, pl* **sep·ses** \'sep-,sēz\ : a poisoned condition due to spread of bacteria or their products in the body

Sep·tem·ber \sep-'tem-bər\ *n* : the 9th month of the year having 30 days

sep·tic \'sep-tik\ *adj* **1** : PUTREFACTIVE **2** : relating to or characteristic of sepsis

septic tank *n* : a tank in which sewage is disintegrated by bacteria

Sep·tu·a·gint \sep-'t(y)ü-ə-jənt, 'sep-tə-wə-,jint\ *n* : a Greek version of the Old Testament used by Greek-speaking Christians

¹sep·ul·cher *or* **sep·ul·chre** \'sep-əl-kər\ *n* : burial vault : TOMB

²sepulcher *or* **sepulchre** *vb* : BURY, ENTOMB

se·pul·chral \sə-'pəl-krəl\ *adj* **1** : relating to burial or the grave **2** : GLOOMY

sep·ul·ture \'sep-əl-,chūr\ *n* **1** : BURIAL, INTERMENT **2** : SEPULCHER

se·quel \'sē-kwəl\ *n* **1** : logical consequence **2** : EFFECT, RESULT **3** : a literary work continuing a story begun in a preceding issue

se·quence \'sē-kwəns\ n 1 : the condition or fact of following something else 2 : SERIES 3 : RESULT, SEQUEL 4 : chronological order of events syn succession, set — **se·quen·tial** \si-'kwen-chəl\ adj

se·quent \-kwənt\ adj 1 : SUCCEEDING, CONSECUTIVE 2 : RESULTANT

se·ques·ter \si-'kwes-tər\ vb : to set apart : SEGREGATE

se·ques·trate \si-'kwes-,trāt\ vb : SEQUESTER — **se·ques·tra·tion** \,sē-kwə-'strā-shən\ n

se·quin \'sē-kwən\ n 1 : an obsolete gold coin of Turkey and Italy 2 : SPANGLE

se·quoia \si-'kwòi-ə\ n : either of two huge California coniferous trees

sera pl of SERUM

se·ra·glio \sə-'ral-yō\ n : HAREM

ser·aph \'ser-əf\ n, pl ser·a·phim \-ə-,fim\ or seraphs : an angel of a high order of celestial beings — **se·raph·ic** \sə-'raf-ik\ adj

sere \'siər\ adj : DRY, WITHERED

¹ser·e·nade \,ser-ə-'nād\ n : music sung or played as a compliment; esp : such music performed outdoors at night for a lady

²serenade vb : to entertain with or perform a serenade

se·rene \sə-'rēn\ adj 1 : CLEAR ⟨~ skies⟩ 2 : QUIET, CALM syn tranquil, peaceful, placid — **se·rene·ly** adv

se·ren·i·ty \-'ren-ət-ē\ n : the quality or state of being serene

serf \'sərf\ n : a peasant bound to the land and subject in some degree to the owner — **serf·dom** n

serge \'sərj\ n : a twilled woolen cloth

ser·geant \'sär-jənt\ n [OF sergent, serjant servant, attendant, officer who keeps order, fr. L servient-, serviens, prp. of servire to serve] 1 : a noncommissioned officer (as in the army) ranking next below a staff sergeant 2 : an officer in a police force

sergeant first class n : a noncommissioned officer in the army ranking next below a master sergeant

sergeant major n : a noncommissioned officer (as in the army) of the highest rank

¹se·ri·al \'sir-ē-əl\ adj : appearing in parts that follow regularly ⟨a ~ story⟩

²serial n : a serial story or other writing

se·ries \'si(ə)r-ēz\ n, pl series : a number of things or events arranged in order and connected by being alike in some way syn succession, progression, sequence, set, suit, chain, train, string

se·ri·ous \'sir-ē-əs\ adj 1 : thoughtful or subdued in appearance or manner : SOBER 2 : requiring much thought or work 3 : DANGEROUS, HARMFUL syn grave, sedate, sober — **se·ri·ous·ly** adv — **se·ri·ous·ness** n

ser·mon \'sər-mən\ n 1 : a religious discourse esp. as part of a worship service 2 : a lecture on conduct or duty

ser·pent \'sər-pənt\ n : SNAKE

ser·pen·tine \-pən-,tēn, -,tīn\ adj 1 : SLY, CRAFTY 2 : WINDING, DEVIOUS

ser·rate \'ser-,āt\ or ser·rat·ed \-'rāt-əd\ adj : having a saw-toothed edge

ser·ried \'ser-ēd\ adj : CROWDED, DENSE

se·rum \'sir-əm\ n, pl serums or se·ra \-ə\ : the watery part of an animal fluid (as blood) remaining after coagulation; esp : blood serum that contains specific immune bodies (as antitoxins) — **se·rous** adj

ser·vant \'sər-vənt\ n : a person employed by another esp. for domestic work

¹serve \'sərv\ vb 1 : to work as a servant 2 : to render obedience and worship to (God) 3 : to comply with the commands or demands of 4 : to work through or perform a term of service (as in the army) 5 : to put in ⟨served 5 years in jail⟩ 6 : to be of use : ANSWER ⟨pine boughs served for a bed⟩ 7 : BENEFIT 8 : to prove adequate or satisfactory for ⟨a pie that ~s 8 people⟩ 9 : to make ready and pass out ⟨~ drinks⟩ 10 : to wait on ⟨~ a customer⟩ 11 : to furnish or supply with something ⟨one power company serving the whole state⟩ 12 : to put the ball in play (as in tennis) 13 : to treat or act toward in a specified way ⟨he served me ill⟩ — **serv·er** n

²serve n : the act of serving a ball (as in tennis)

¹ser·vice \'sər-vəs\ n 1 : the occupation of a servant 2 : the act, fact, or means of serving 3 : required duty 4 : a meeting for worship; also : a form followed in worship or in a ceremony ⟨burial ~⟩ 5 : performance of official or professional duties 6 : a branch of public employment; also : the persons in it ⟨civil ~⟩ 7 : military or naval duty 8 : a set of dishes or silverware 9 : HELP, BENEFIT 10 : a serving of the ball (as in tennis) syn use, advantage, profit, account, avail

²service vb : to do maintenance or repair work on or for

ser·vice·able adj : prepared for service : USEFUL, USABLE

ser·vice·man \-,man\ n 1 : a male member of the armed forces 2 : a man employed to repair or maintain equipment

ser·vile \'sər-vəl, -,vīl\ adj 1 : befitting a slave or servant 2 : behaving like a slave : SUBMISSIVE

ser·vil·i·ty \,sər-'vil-ət-ē\ n : the quality or state of being servile

ser·vi·tor \'sər-vət-ər\ n : a male servant

ser·vi·tude \'sər-və-,t(y)üd\ n : SLAVERY, BONDAGE

ses·a·me \'ses-ə-mē\ n : an East Indian annual herb; also : its seeds that yield an edible oil (**sesame oil**) and are used in flavoring

ses·sile \'ses-əl, -,īl\ adj : attached by the base

ses·sion \'sesh-ən\ n 1 : a meeting or series of meetings of a body (as a court or legislature) for the transaction of business 2 : a meeting or period devoted to a particular activity

¹set \'set\ vb set; set·ting 1 : to cause to sit 2 : PLACE 3 : SETTLE, DECREE 4 : to cause to be or do 5 : ARRANGE, ADJUST 6 : to fix in a frame 7 : ESTIMATE 8 : WAGER, STAKE 9 : to make fast or rigid 10 : to adapt (as words) to something (as music) 11 : BROOD 12 : FIT 13 : to pass below the horizon 14 : to have a certain direction : TEND, INCLINE 15 : to become fixed or firm or solid 16 : to defeat in bridge

²set adj 1 : fixed by authority or custom : PRESCRIBED 2 : DELIBERATE 3 : RIGID 4 : PERSISTENT 5 : FORMED, MADE

³set n 1 : a setting or a being set 2 : FORM, BUILD 3 : DIRECTION, COURSE; also : TENDENCY 4 : the fit of something (as a coat) 5 : a group of persons or things of the same kind or having a common characteristic usu. classed together **6 :** an artificial setting for the scene of a play or motion picture **7 :** an electronic apparatus ⟨a television ∼⟩ **8 :** a group of tennis games in which one side wins at least 6 to an opponent's 4 or less

set·back \'set-,bak\ *n* **:** REVERSE

set·tee \se-'tē\ *n* **:** a bench or sofa with a back and arms

set·ter \'set-ər\ *n* **:** a large long-coated hunting dog

set·ting *n* **1 :** the act of setting ⟨the ∼ of type⟩ **2 :** that in which something is mounted **3 :** BACKGROUND, ENVIRONMENT; *also* **:** SCENERY **4 :** music written for a text (as of a poem) **5 :** the eggs that a fowl sits on for hatching at one time

set·tle \'set-ʾl\ *vb* **1 :** to put in place **2 :** to locate permanently **3 :** to make compact **4 :** to sink gradually to a lower level **5 :** to establish in life, business, or a home **6 :** to direct one's efforts **7 :** to fix by agreement **8 :** to give legally **9 :** ADJUST, ARRANGE **10 :** QUIET, CALM **11 :** DECIDE, DETERMINE **12 :** to make a final disposition of ⟨∼ an account⟩ **13 :** to reach an agreement on **14 :** to become clear by depositing sediment **syn** set, fix — **set·tler** \-(ʾ)lər\ *n*

set·tle·ment \'set-ʾl-mənt\ *n* **1 :** the act or process of settling **2 :** establishment in life, business, or a home **3 :** something that settles or is settled **4 :** BESTOWAL ⟨a marriage ∼⟩ **5 :** payment of an account **6 :** adjustment of doubts and differences **7 :** COLONIZATION; *also* **:** COLONY **8 :** a small village **9 :** an institution in a poor district of a city to give aid to the community

sev·en \'sev-ən\ *n* **1 :** one more than six **2 :** the 7th in a set or series **3 :** something having seven units — **seven** *adj or pron* — **sev·enth** *adj or n*

sev·en·teen \,sev-ən-'tēn\ *n* **:** one more than 16 — **seventeen** *adj or pron* — **sev·en·teenth** *adj or n*

sev·en·ty \'sev-ən-tē\ *n* **:** seven times 10 — **sev·en·ti·eth** *adj or n* — **seventy** *adj or pron*

sev·er \'sev-ər\ *vb* **:** DIVIDE; *esp* **:** to separate by force (as by cutting or tearing) — **sev·er·ance** *n*

sev·er·al \'sev-(ə-)rəl\ *adj* **1 :** INDIVIDUAL, DISTINCT ⟨federal union of the ∼ states⟩ **2 :** consisting of an indefinite number but yet not very many

sev·er·al·ly *adv* **1 :** one at a time **2 :** RESPECTIVELY

severance pay *n* **:** extra pay given an employee upon his leaving a job permanently

se·vere \sə-'vior\ *adj* **1 :** marked by strictness or sternness **:** AUSTERE **2 :** strict in discipline **3 :** causing distress and esp. physical discomfort or pain ⟨∼ weather⟩ ⟨a ∼ wound⟩ **4 :** hard to endure ⟨∼ trials⟩ **syn** stern — **se·vere·ly** *adv* — **se·ver·i·ty** \-'ver-ət-ē\ *n*

sew \'sō\ *vb* **sewed;** **sewed** *or* **sewn** \'sōn\ **sew·ing 1 :** to fasten by stitches made with thread and needle **2 :** to practice sewing esp. as an occupation

sew·age \'sü-ij\ *n* **:** matter (as refuse liquids) carried off by sewers

¹**sew·er** \'sō-(ə)r\ *n* **:** one that sews

²**sew·er** \'sü-ər\ *n* **:** an artificial pipe or channel to carry off waste matter (as refuse water)

sew·er·age *n* **1 :** SEWAGE **2 :** a system of sewers

sew·ing \'sō-iŋ\ *n* **1 :** the occupation of one who sews **2 :** material that has been or is to be sewed

sex \'seks\ *n* **1 :** either of two divisions of organisms distinguished respectively as male and female; *also* **:** the qualities by which these sexes are differentiated and which directly or indirectly function in biparental reproduction **2 :** sexual activity or intercourse — **sexed** *adj*

sex·tant \'sek-stənt\ *n* **:** an instrument for measuring angular distances of celestial bodies which is used esp. at sea to ascertain latitude and longitude

sex·tet \sek-'stet\ *n* **1 :** a musical composition for 6 voices or 6 instruments; *also* **:** the 6 performers of such a composition **2 :** a group or set of 6

sex·ton \'sek-stən\ *n* **:** one who takes care of church property

sex·u·al \'sek-sh(ə-w)əl\ *adj* **:** of, relating to, or involving sex or the sexes ⟨a ∼ spore⟩ ⟨∼ relations⟩ — **sex·u·al·i·ty** \,sek-shə-'wal-ət-ē\ *n* — **sex·u·al·ly** \'sek-shə-(wə-)lē\ *adv*

shab·by \'shab-ē\ *adj* **1 :** threadbare and faded from wear **2 :** dressed in worn clothes **3 :** MEAN ⟨∼ treatment⟩

shack \'shak\ *n* **:** HUT, SHANTY

¹**shack·le** \'shak-əl\ *n* **1 :** something (as a manacle or fetter) that confines the legs or arms **2 :** a check on free action made as if by fetters **3 :** a device for making something fast or secure

²**shackle** *vb* **:** to fasten with or as if with shackles **:** CHAIN

shad \'shad\ *n* **:** a No. American food fish of the Atlantic coast that ascends rivers to spawn

¹**shade** \'shād\ *n* **1 :** partial obscurity **2 :** space sheltered from the light esp. of the sun **3 :** a dark color or a variety of a color **4 :** a small difference ⟨various ∼s of meaning⟩ **5 :** PHANTOM **6 :** something that shelters from or intercepts light or heat — **shady** *adj*

²**shade** *vb* **1 :** to shelter from light and heat **2 :** DARKEN, OBSCURE **3 :** to mark with degrees of light or color **4 :** to show slight differences esp. in color or meaning

shad·ing \'shād-iŋ\ *n* **:** the color and lines representing darkness or shadow in a drawing or painting

¹**shad·ow** \'shad-ō\ *n* **1 :** partial darkness in a space from which light rays are cut off **2 :** SHELTER **3 :** a small portion or degree **:** TRACE ⟨a ∼ of doubt⟩ **4 :** influence that casts a gloom **5 :** shade cast upon a surface by something intercepting rays from a light ⟨the ∼ of a tree⟩ **6 :** PHANTOM **7 :** a shaded portion of a picture — **shad·owy** *adj*

²**shadow** *vb* **1 :** to cast a shadow on **:** DARKEN, DIM **2 :** to represent faintly or vaguely **3 :** to follow and watch closely **:** TRAIL

shaft \'shaft\ *n* **1 :** the long handle of a spear or lance **2** *or pl* **shaves**

\'shavz\ : POLE; *esp* : one of two poles between which a horse is hitched to pull a vehicle **3** : SPEAR, LANCE **4** : something (as a column) long and slender **5** : a bar to support a rotating piece or to transmit power by rotation **6** : a vertical opening (as for an elevator) through the floors of a building **7** : an inclined opening (as in a mine for raising ore) in the ground

shag \'shag\ *n* **1** : a shaggy tangled mat (as of wool) **2** : a strong finely shredded tobacco

shag·gy *adj* **1** : rough with or as if with long hair or wool **2** : tangled or rough in surface

¹shake \'shāk\ *vb* **shook** \'shùk\ **shak·en** \'shā-kən\ **shak·ing** **1** : to move or cause to move jerkily or irregularly : QUIVER (the explosion *shook* the house) **2** : BRANDISH, WAVE (*shaking* his fist) **3** : to disturb emotionally (*shaken* by her death) **4** : WEAKEN (*shook* his faith) **5** : to bring or come into a certain position, condition, or arrangement by or as if by moving jerkily (~ flour out of a can) (the radiator cap *shook* off) **6** : to clasp (hands) in greeting or as a sign of goodwill or agreement *syn* tremble, quake, totter, shiver, rock, convulse — **shak·able** *adj*

²shake *n* **1** : the act or a result of shaking **2** : DEAL, TREATMENT (a fair ~)

shak·er *n* **1** : one that shakes (pepper ~) **2** *cap* : a member of a religious sect founded in England in 1747

shaky \'shā-kē\ *adj* : UNSOUND, WEAK — **shak·i·ly** *adv* — **shak·i·ness** *n*

shale \'shāl\ *n* : a rock formed of densely packed clay, mud, or silt that splits easily into layers

shall \shəl, (')shal\ *vb, past* **should** \shəd, (')shùd\ — used as an auxiliary to express a command, what seems inevitable or likely in the future, simple futurity, or determination

shal·lop \'shal-əp\ *n* : a light open boat

¹shal·low \'shal-ō\ *adj* **1** : not deep **2** : not intellectually profound *syn* superficial

²shallow *n* : a shallow place in a body of water — usu. used in pl.

¹sham \'sham\ *n* **1** : COUNTERFEIT, IMITATION **2** : something resembling an article of household linen and used in its place as a decoration (a pillow ~)

²sham *vb* **shammed; sham·ming** : FEIGN, PRETEND — **sham·mer** *n*

³sham *adj* : FALSE

sham·ble \'sham-bəl\ *vb* : to walk clumsily : shuffle along — **shamble** *n*

sham·bles \-bəlz\ *n* **1** : a scene of great slaughter **2** : a scene or state of great destruction or disorder

¹shame \'shām\ *n* **1** : a painful sense of guilt **2** : DISGRACE, DISHONOR — **shame·ful** *adj* — **shame·ful·ly** *adv* — **shame·less** *adj* — **shame·less·ly** *adv*

²shame *vb* **1** : to make ashamed **2** : DISGRACE

shame·faced \-'fāst\ *adj* : ASHAMED, ABASHED — **shame·fac·ed·ly** \-'fā-səd-lē\ *adv*

¹sham·poo \sham-'pü\ *vb* : to wash (as the hair) with soap and water or with a special preparation; *also* : to wash or clean (as a rug) with soap or a dry-cleaning preparation

²shampoo *n* **1** : the act or process of shampooing **2** : a preparation designed for use in shampooing

sham·rock \'sham-ˌräk\ *n* [IrGael *seamrōg*] : a plant with three leaflets used as an Irish floral emblem

shang·hai \shaŋ-'hī\ *vb* : to force aboard a ship for service as a sailor; *also* : to trick or force into something

shank \'shaŋk\ *n* **1** : the part of the leg between the knee and ankle in man or a corresponding part of a quadruped **2** : a cut of meat from the leg **3** : the part of a tool or instrument (as a key or anchor) connecting the functioning part with the handle

shan·ty \'shant-ē\ *n* : a small roughly built shelter or dwelling : HUT

¹shape \'shāp\ *vb* **1** : to form esp. in a particular shape **2** : DESIGN **3** : ADAPT, ADJUST **4** : REGULATE *syn* make, fashion, fabricate, manufacture

²shape *n* **1** : APPEARANCE **2** : surface configuration : FORM **3** : bodily contour apart from the head and face : FIGURE **4** : PHANTOM **5** : CONDITION (he's in pretty good ~)

shape·less *adj* **1** : having no definite shape **2** : not shapely — **shape·less·ly** *adv* — **shape·less·ness** *n*

shape·ly *adj* : having a pleasing shape — **shape·li·ness** *n*

shard \'shärd\ *n* : a broken piece : FRAGMENT

¹share \'shear\ *n* **1** : a portion belonging to one person **2** : any of the equal interests, each represented by a certificate, into which the capital stock of a corporation is divided

²share *vb* **1** : APPORTION **2** : to use or enjoy together with others **3** : PARTICIPATE — **shar·er** *n*

³share *n* : PLOWSHARE

share·crop·per \-ˌkräp-ər\ *n* : a farmer who works another's land in return for a share of the crop — **share·crop** *vb*

share·hold·er \-ˌhōl-dər\ *n* : STOCKHOLDER

shark \'shärk\ *n* **1** : any of various active, greedy, and mostly large sea fishes with skeletons of cartilage **2** : a greedy crafty person

shark·skin \-ˌskin\ *n* **1** : the hide of a shark or leather made from it **2** : a fabric (as of cotton or rayon) woven from strands of many fine threads and having a sleek appearance and silky feel

¹sharp \'shärp\ *adj* **1** : having a thin cutting edge or fine point : not dull or blunt **2** : COLD, NIPPING (a ~ wind) **3** : keen in intellect, perception, or attention **4** : BRISK, ENERGETIC **5** : IRRITABLE (a ~ temper) **6** : causing intense distress (a ~ pain) **7** : HARSH, CUTTING (~ words) **8** : affecting the senses as if cutting or piercing (a ~ sound) (a ~ smell) **9** : not smooth or rounded : ANGULAR (~ features) **10** : involving an abrupt or extreme change (a ~ turn) (a ~ drop in prices) **11** : CLEAR, DISTINCT (mountains in ~ relief); *also* : easy to perceive (a ~ contrast) **12** : higher than the true pitch; *also* : raised by a half step *syn* keen, acute — **sharp·ly** *adv* — **sharp·ness** *n*

²sharp *vb* : to raise in pitch by a half step

³sharp *adv* **1** : in a sharp manner : SHARPLY **2** : EXACTLY, PRECISELY (left at 8 ~)

⁴sharp *n* **1** : a sharp edge or point **2** : a character # indicating a note a half step higher than the note named

sharp·en \'shär-pən\ *vb* : to make or become sharp

shat·ter \'shat-ər\ *vb* : to dash or burst into fragments

¹**shave** \'shāv\ *vb* **shaved**; **shaved** *or* **shav·en** \'shā-vən\ **shav·ing 1 :** to cut or pare off by the sliding movement of a razor **2 :** to make bare or smooth by cutting the hair from **3 :** to slice in thin pieces **4 :** to skim along or near the surface of

²**shave** *n* **1 :** any of various tools for cutting thin slices **2 :** an act or process of shaving **3 :** an act of passing very near so as almost to graze

shav·ing *n* **1 :** the act of one that shaves **2 :** a thin slice pared off

shawl \'shȯl\ *n* **:** a square or oblong piece of fabric used esp. by women as a loose covering for the head or shoulders

she \(')shē\ *pron* **:** that female one (who is ~); *also* **:** that one regarded as feminine (~'s a fine ship)

sheaf \'shēf\ *n, pl* **sheaves** \'shēvz\ **1 :** a bundle of stalks and ears of grain **2 :** a group of things bound together (a ~ of arrows)

¹**shear** \'shiər\ *vb* **sheared**; **sheared** *or* **shorn** \'shȯrn\ **shear·ing 1 :** to cut the hair or wool from **2 : CLIP, TRIM 2 :** to cut or break sharply **3 :** to deprive of or as if by cutting

²**shear** *n* **1 :** the act, an instance, or the result of shearing **2 :** a machine for cutting metal

shears \'shiərz\ *n pl* **:** any of various instruments used for cutting that consist of two blades fastened together so that the edges slide one by the other

sheath \'shēth\ *n, pl* **sheaths** \'shēthz, 'shēths\ **:** a case for a blade (as of a knife); *also* **:** an anatomical covering suggesting such a case

sheathe \'shēth\ *vb* **1 :** to put into a sheath **2 :** to cover with something that guards or protects

sheave \'shiv, 'shēv\ *n* **:** a grooved wheel or pulley (as on a pulley block)

¹**shed** \'shed\ *vb* **shed**; **shed·ding 1 :** to pour down in drops (~ tears) **2 :** to cause to flow from a cut or wound (~ blood) **3 :** to give out (as light) : DIFFUSE **4 :** to throw off (as a natural covering) : DISCARD

²**shed** *n* **:** a slight structure built for shelter or storage

sheen \'shēn\ *n* **:** a subdued luster : GLOSS

sheep \'shēp\ *n* **1 :** a domesticated mammal related to the goat and raised for meat, wool, and hide **2 :** a timid or defenseless person **3 : SHEEPSKIN**

sheep·fold \-ˌfōld\ *n* **:** a pen or shelter for sheep

sheep·ish *adj* **: BASHFUL, TIMID;** *esp* **:** embarrassed by consciousness of a fault

sheep·skin \'shēp-ˌskin\ *n* **1 :** the hide of a sheep or leather prepared from it; *also* **: PARCHMENT 2 : DIPLOMA**

¹**sheer** \'shiər\ *adj* **1 : UNQUALIFIED** (~ folly) **2 :** very steep **3 :** of very thin or transparent texture **syn** pure, simple, absolute, precipitous, abrupt — **sheer** *adv*

²**sheer** *vb* **:** to turn from a course : SWERVE

¹**sheet** \'shēt\ *n* **1 :** a broad piece of plain cloth (as for a bed) **2 :** a single piece of paper (as for writing or printing) **3 :** a broad flat surface (a ~ of

water) **4 :** something broad and long and relatively thin (a ~ of iron)

²**sheet** *n* **1 :** a rope that regulates the angle at which a sail is set to catch the wind **2** *pl* **:** spaces at either end of an open boat

sheet·ing *n* **:** material (as linen or cotton cloth) in the form of sheets or suitable for forming into sheets

sheik *or* **sheikh** \'shēk, 'shāk\ *n* **:** an Arab chief

shelf \'shelf\ *n, pl* **shelves** \'shelvz\ **1 :** a thin flat usu. long and narrow structure fastened against a wall above the floor to hold things **2 :** a sandbank or ledge of rocks usu. partially submerged

¹**shell** \'shel\ *n* **1 :** a hard or tough outer covering of an animal (as a beetle, turtle, or mollusk) or of an egg or a seed or fruit (as a nut); *also* **:** something that resembles a shell (a pastry ~) **2 :** a case holding an explosive and designed to be fired from a cannon; *also* **:** a case holding the charge of powder and shot or bullet for small arms **3 :** a light narrow racing boat propelled by oarsmen — **shell·y** *adj*

²**shell** *vb* **1 :** to remove from a shell or husk : SHUCK **2 : BOMBARD** — **shell·er** *n*

¹**shel·lac** \shə-'lak\ *n* **:** a purified resin used in varnishes and sealing wax; *also* **:** this resin dissolved in alcohol and used as a varnish

²**shellac** *vb* **-lacked**; **-lack·ing 1 :** to coat or treat with shellac **2 :** to defeat decisively

shell·fish \'shel-ˌfish\ *n* **:** a water animal (as an oyster, crab, or lobster) with a shell

shell shock *n* **:** a nervous disorder appearing in soldiers exposed to modern warfare — **shell–shock** *vb*

¹**shel·ter** \'shel-tər\ *n* **:** something that gives protection : REFUGE

²**shelter** *vb* **:** to give protection or refuge to : PROTECT **syn** harbor, lodge, house

shelve \'shelv\ *vb* **1 :** to slope gradually **2 :** to store on shelves **3 :** to dismiss from service or use

¹**shep·herd** \'shep-ərd\ *n* **:** one that tends and guards sheep — **shep·herd·ess** *n*

²**shepherd** *vb* **:** to tend as or in the manner of a shepherd

sher·bet \'shər-bət\ *n* [Turk *şerbet*, fr. Per *sharbat*, fr. Ar *sharbah* drink] **1 :** a drink of sweetened diluted fruit juice **2 :** a frozen dessert of fruit juices, sugar, milk or water, and egg whites or gelatin

sher·iff \'sher-əf\ *n* **:** a county officer charged with the execution of the law and the preservation of order

sher·ry \'sher-ē\ *n* **:** a fortified wine with a nutty flavor

shew \'shō\ *archaic var of* SHOW

shib·bo·leth \'shib-ə-ləth\ *n* **1 :** a pet phrase : CATCHWORD, SLOGAN **2 :** language that is a criterion for distinguishing members of a group

¹**shield** \'shēld\ *n* **1 :** a broad piece of defensive armor carried on the arm **2 :** something that protects or hides

²**shield** *vb* **:** to protect or hide with a shield **syn** protect, guard, safeguard

¹**shift** \'shift\ *vb* **1 : EXCHANGE, REPLACE 2 :** to change place, position, or

direction : MOVE; *also* : to change the arrangement of gears transmitting power in an automobile 3 : to get along : MANAGE syn remove

²**shift** *n* 1 : TRANSFER 2 : SCHEME, TRICK 3 : a group working together alternating with other groups 4 : GEAR-SHIFT

shift·less *adj* : LAZY, INEFFICIENT — **shift·less·ness** *n*

shifty \'shif-tē\ *adj* 1 : TRICKY; *also* : ELUSIVE 2 : indicative of a tricky nature ⟨∼ eyes⟩

shill \'shil\ *n* : one who acts as a decoy (as for a cheater)

shil·ling \'shil-iŋ\ *n* — see MONEY table

shim·mer \'shim-ər\ *vb* : to shine waveringly or tremulously : GLIMMER syn flash, gleam, glint, sparkle, glitter — **shimmer** *n* — **shim·mery** *adj*

shim·my \'shim-ē\ *n* : an abnormal vibration (as in the front wheels of an automobile)

¹**shin** \'shin\ *n* : the front part of the leg below the knee

²**shin** *vb* **shinned; shin·ning** : to climb (as a pole) by gripping alternately with arms or hands and legs

shin·bone \-'bōn\ *n* : TIBIA

¹**shine** \'shīn\ *vb* **shone** \'shōn\ *or* **shined; shin·ing** 1 : to give light 2 : GLEAM, GLITTER 3 : to be eminent 4 : to cause to shed light 5 : POLISH

²**shine** *n* 1 : BRIGHTNESS, RADIANCE 2 : LUSTER, BRILLIANCE 3 : SUNSHINE

shin·er \'shī-nər\ *n* 1 : a small silvery fish : MINNOW 2 : a bruised eye

¹**shin·gle** \'shiŋ-gəl\ *n* 1 : a small thin piece of building material (as wood or an asbestos composition) used in overlapping rows for covering a roof or outside wall 2 : a small sign (as on a doctor's or lawyer's office)

²**shingle** *vb* : to cover with shingles

³**shingle** *n* : a beach strewn with gravel; *also* : coarse gravel (as on a beach)

Shin·to \'shin-tō\ *n* : the indigenous religion of Japan consisting esp. in reverence of the spirits of natural forces and imperial ancestors — **Shin·to·ism** *n* — **Shin·to·ist** *adj or n* — **Shin·to·is·tic** \,shin-tō-'is-tik\ *adj*

shiny \'shī-nē\ *adj* : BRIGHT, RADIANT; *also* : POLISHED

¹**ship** \'ship\ *n* 1 : a large seagoing boat 2 : AIRSHIP, AIRPLANE 3 : a ship's officers and crew

²**ship** *vb* **shipped; ship·ping** 1 : to put or receive on board a ship for transportation 2 : to have transported by a carrier ⟨∼ grain by rail⟩ 3 : to take or draw into a boat ⟨∼ oars⟩ ⟨∼ water⟩ 4 : to engage to serve on a ship — **ship·per** *n*

-**ship** \,ship\ *n suffix* 1 : state : condition : quality ⟨friendship⟩ 2 : office : dignity : profession ⟨lordship⟩ ⟨clerkship⟩ 3 : art : skill ⟨horsemanship⟩ 4 : something showing, exhibiting, or embodying a quality or state ⟨township⟩ 5 : one entitled to a (specified) rank, title, or appellation ⟨his Lordship⟩

ship·board \'ship-bōrd\ *n* : SHIP ⟨met on ∼⟩

ship·mate \-,māt\ *n* : a fellow sailor

ship·ment *n* : the process of shipping; *also* : the goods shipped

ship·ping *n* 1 : SHIPS; *esp* : ships in one port or belonging to one country 2 : transportation of goods

ship·shape \'ship-'shāp\ *adj* : TRIM, TIDY

ship·worm \-,wərm\ *n* : a wormlike sea clam that burrows in wood and damages wooden ships and wharves

¹**ship·wreck** \-,rek\ *n* 1 : a wrecked ship 2 : destruction or loss of a ship (as by sinking or being driven on rocks) 3 : total loss or failure : RUIN

²**shipwreck** *vb* : to cause or meet disaster at sea through destruction or foundering

ship·yard \-,yärd\ *n* : a place where ships are built or repaired

shire \'shī(ə)r, *as suffix* ,shior *or* shər\ *n* : a county in Great Britain

shirk \'shərk\ *vb* : to avoid performing (duty or work) — **shirk·er** *n*

shirr \'shər\ *vb* 1 : to make shirring in 2 : to bake (eggs) in a dish with cream or bread crumbs

shirr·ing *n* : a decorative gathering in cloth made by drawing up parallel lines of stitches

shirt \'shərt\ *n* 1 : a loose cloth garment usu. having a collar, sleeves, a front opening, and a tail long enough to be tucked inside trousers or a skirt 2 : UNDERSHIRT — **shirt·less** *adj*

shirt·ing *n* : cloth suitable for making shirts

¹**shiv·er** \'shiv-ər\ *vb* : TREMBLE, QUIVER syn shudder, quaver, shake, quake

²**shiver** *n* : an instance of shivering : QUIVER — **shiv·er·er** *n* — **shiv·ery** *adj*

¹**shoal** \'shōl\ *n* 1 : a shallow place in a sea, lake, or river 2 : a sandbank or bar creating a shallow

²**shoal** *n* : a large group (as of fish) : SCHOOL, CROWD

shoat \'shōt\ *n* : a weaned young pig

¹**shock** \'shäk\ *n* : a pile of sheaves of grain set up in the field

²**shock** *n* 1 : a sharp impact or violent shake or jar 2 : a sudden violent mental or emotional disturbance 3 : the effect of a charge of electricity passing through the body 4 : a depressed bodily condition caused esp. by crushing wounds, blood loss, or burns 5 : an attack of apoplexy or heart disease

³**shock** *vb* 1 : to strike with surprise, horror, or disgust 2 : to subject (a body) to the action of an electrical discharge

shock·ing *adj* : extremely startling and offensive — **shock·ing·ly** *adv*

¹**shod·dy** \'shäd-ē\ *n* 1 : wool reclaimed from old rags; *also* : a fabric made from it 2 : inferior or imitation material 3 : pretentious vulgarity

²**shod·dy** \'shäd-ē\ *adj* 1 : made of shoddy 2 : cheaply imitative : INFERIOR, SHAM — **shod·di·ly** *adv* — **shod·di·ness** *n*

¹**shoe** \'shü\ *n* 1 : a covering for the human foot 2 : HORSESHOE 3 : the part of a brake that presses on the wheel 4 : the casing of an automobile tire

²**shoe** *vb* **shod** \'shäd\ *also* **shoed; shoe·ing** : to put a shoe or shoes on

shoe·mak·er \'shü-,mā-kər\ *n* : one who sells or repairs shoes

shone *past of* SHINE

shook *past of* SHAKE

¹**shoot** \'shüt\ *vb* **shot** \'shät\ **shoot·ing** 1 : to drive (as an arrow or bullet) forward quickly or forcibly 2 : to hit, kill, or wound with a missile 3 : to cause a missile to be driven forth or forth from ⟨∼ a gun⟩ ⟨∼ an arrow⟩ 4 : to send forth (as a ray of light) 5 : to thrust forward or out 6 : to pass rapidly along ⟨∼ the rapids⟩ 7 : PHO-

TOGRAPH, FILM ⟨∼ a motion picture⟩ **8** : to drive or rush swiftly : DART **9** : to grow by or as if by sending out shoots; *also* : MATURE, DEVELOP — **shoot·er** *n*

²shoot *n* **1** : a shooting match **2** : the aerial part of a plant; *also* : a plant part (as a branch) developed from one bud

shooting star *n* : METEOR

¹shop \'shäp\ *n* **1** : a place where things are made or worked on : FACTORY, MILL **2** : a retail store ⟨dress ∼⟩

²shop *vb* **shopped**; **shop·ping** : to visit stores for purchasing or examining goods — **shop·per** *n*

shop·keep·er \-‚kē-pər\ *n* : a retail merchant

shop·worn \-‚wōrn\ *adj* : soiled or frayed from much handling in a store

¹shore \'shōr\ *n* : land along the edge of a body of water — **shore·less** *adj*

²shore *vb* : to give support to : BRACE, PROP

shore·bird \-‚bərd\ *n* : any of a large group of birds (as the plovers and sandpipers) mostly found along the seashore

shorn *past part of* SHEAR

¹short \'shōrt\ *adj* **1** : not long or tall **2** : not great in distance **3** : brief in time **4** : CURT, ABRUPT **5** : not coming up to standard or to an expected amount **6** : insufficiently supplied : not having enough **7** : made with shortening : FLAKY **8** : not having goods or property that one has sold in anticipation of a fall in prices; *also* : consisting of or relating to a sale of securities or commodities that the seller does not possess or has not contracted for at the time of the sale ⟨∼ sale⟩ — **short·ness** *n*

²short *adv* **1** : ABRUPTLY, CURTLY **2** : at some point before a goal or limit aimed at ⟨fell ∼ of the target⟩

³short *n* **1** : something shorter than normal or standard **2** *pl* : drawers or trousers of less than knee length

short·age *n* : a deficiency in the amount required : DEFICIT

short·cake \'shōrt-‚kāk\ *n* : a dessert consisting of short biscuit spread with sweetened fruit

short circuit *n* : a connection of comparatively low resistance accidentally or intentionally made between points in an electric circuit — **short-circuit** *vb*

short·com·ing \'shōrt-‚kəm-iŋ\ *n* : FAILING, DEFECT

short·cut \-‚kət\ *n* **1** : a route more direct than that usu. taken **2** : a quicker way of doing something

short·en \'shōrt-ᵊn\ *vb* : to make or become short **syn** curtail, abbreviate, abridge, retrench

short·en·ing \-(ᵊ-)niŋ\ *n* : a substance (as lard or butter) that makes pastry crisp and flaky

short·hand \'shōrt-‚hand\ *n* : a method of writing rapidly by using symbols and abbreviations for letters, words, or phrases : STENOGRAPHY

short·hand·ed \-'han-dəd\ *adj* : short of the regular or needed number of workers

short·horn \-‚hōrn\ *n* : any of a breed of mostly red cattle of English origin

short-lived \-'līvd, -'livd\ *adj* : of short life or duration

short·ly *adv* **1** : in a few words : BRIEFLY,

CURTLY 2 : in a short time : SOON

short-sight·ed \-'sīt-əd\ *adj* **1** : NEARSIGHTED **2** : lacking foresight — **short·sight·ed·ness** *n*

short·stop \'shōrt-‚stäp\ *n* : a baseball player defending the area between second and third base

short story *n* : a short invented prose narrative usu. dealing with a few characters and aiming at unity of effect

short-term \'shōrt-'tərm\ *adj* **1** : occurring over or involving a relatively short period of time **2** : of or relating to a financial transaction based on a term usu. of less than a year

short-wave \-'wāv\ *n* : a radio wave of 60-meter wavelength or less used esp. in long-distance broadcasting

shot \'shät\ *n* **1** : an act of shooting **2** : a stroke in some games **3** : something that is shot : MISSILE, PROJECTILE; *esp* : small pellets forming a charge for a shotgun **4** : a metal sphere that is thrown for distance in a field sport ⟨**shot put**⟩ **5** : RANGE, REACH **6** : MARKSMAN **7** : a single photographic exposure **8** : a single sequence of a motion picture or a television program made by one camera **9** : an injection (as of medicine) into the body **10** : a portion (as of liquor or medicine) taken at one time

shot·gun \-‚gən\ *n* : a gun with a smooth bore used to fire small shot at short range

should \shəd, (‚)shud\ *past of* SHALL — used as an auxiliary to express condition, obligation or propriety, probability, or futurity from a point of view in the past

¹shoul·der \'shōl-dər\ *n* **1** : the part of the human body formed by the bones and muscles where the arm joins the trunk; *also* : a corresponding part of a lower animal **2** : a projecting part resembling a human shoulder

²shoulder *vb* **1** : to push or thrust with the shoulder **2** : to take upon the shoulder **3** : to take the responsibility of

shoulder blade *n* : the flat triangular bone at the back of the shoulder

shout \'shaut\ *vb* : to utter a sudden loud cry — **shout** *n*

shove \'shəv\ *vb* : to push along, aside, or away — **shove** *n*

¹shov·el \'shəv-əl\ *n* **1** : a broad long-handled scoop used to lift and throw loose material (as earth, coal, or snow) **2** : the amount of something held by a shovel

²shovel *vb* **-eled** *or* **-elled**; **-el·ing** *or* **-el·ling 1** : to take up and throw with a shovel **2** : to dig or clean out with a shovel

¹show \'shō\ *vb* **showed**; **shown** \'shōn\ *or* **showed**; **show·ing 1** : to cause or permit to be seen : EXHIBIT ⟨∼ anger⟩ **2** : CONFER, BESTOW ⟨∼ mercy⟩ **3** : REVEAL, DISCLOSE ⟨∼ed courage in battle⟩ **4** : INSTRUCT ⟨∼ed me how to do it⟩ **5** : PROVE ⟨∼s he was guilty⟩ **6** : APPEAR **7** : to be noticeable **8** : to be third in a horse race

²show *n* **1** : a demonstrative display **2** : outward appearance ⟨a ∼ of resistance⟩ **3** : SPECTACLE **4** : a theatrical presentation **5** : a radio or television program **6** : third place in a horse race

---

1show·er \\'shaú-(-)r\\ *n* **1** : a brief fall of rain **2** : a bath in which water is showered on the person **3** : a party given by friends who bring gifts — **show·ery** *adj*

2shower *vb* **1** : to fall in a shower **2** : to bathe in a shower

show·man \\'shō-mən\\ *n* : one having a gift for dramatization and visual effectiveness

showy \\'shō-ē\\ *adj* : superficially impressive or striking : OSTENTATIOUS, GAUDY — **show·i·ly** *adv* — **show·i·ness** *n*

shrap·nel \\'shrap-n°l\\ *n* **1** : a case filled with shot and having a bursting charge which explodes it in flight **2** : bomb, mine, or shell fragments

1shred \\'shred\\ *n* : a narrow strip cut or torn off : a small fragment

2shred *vb* **shred·ded; shred·ding** : to cut or tear into shreds

shrew \\'shrü\\ *n* **1** : a scolding woman **2** : a very small mouselike mammal

shrewd \\'shrüd\\ *adj* : KEEN, ASTUTE — **shrewd·ly** *adv* — **shrewd·ness** *n*

shrew·ish *adj* : having an irritable disposition : ILL-TEMPERED

shriek \\'shrēk\\ *n* : a shrill cry : SCREAM, YELL — **shriek** *vb*

shrift \\'shrift\\ *n, archaic* : the act of shriving

shrike \\'shrīk\\ *n* : a grayish or brownish bird that often impales its usu. insect prey upon thorns before devouring it

1shrill \\'shril\\ *vb* : to make a high-pitched piercing sound

2shrill *adj* : high-pitched : PIERCING (~ whistle) — **shril·ly** \\'shril-lē\\ *adv*

shrimp \\'shrimp\\ *n* **1** : any of various small sea crustaceans related to the lobsters **2** : a small or puny person

shrine \\'shrīn\\ *n* [OE *scrīn* receptacle for the relics of a saint, fr. L *scrinium* box, case] **1** : the tomb of a saint; *also* : a place where devotion is paid to a saint or deity **2** : a place or object hallowed by its associations

shrink \\'shrink\\ *vb* **shrank** \\'shrank\\ *or* **shrunk** \\'shrank\\ **shrunk** *or* **shrunk·en** \\-ən\\ **shrink·ing 1** : to draw back or away : COWER, HUDDLE **2** : to become smaller in width or length or both (~ from wetting and drying out) **3** : to lessen in value **syn** recoil, flinch, quail, contract, constrict, compress, condense, deflate — **shrink·able** *adj*

shrink·age *n* **1** : the act of shrinking **2** : a decrease in value **3** : the amount by which something contracts or lessens in extent

shrive \\'shrīv\\ *vb* **shrived** *or* **shrove** \\'shrōv\\ **shriv·en** \\'shriv-ən\\ *or* **shrived; shriv·ing** \\'shrī-viŋ\\ : to minister the sacrament of penance to

shriv·el \\'shriv-əl\\ *vb* **-eled** *or* **-elled; -el·ing** *or* **-el·ling** : to shrink and draw together into wrinkles : wither up

1shroud \\'shraüd\\ *n* **1** : a cloth placed over a dead body **2** : something that covers or screens **3** : one of the ropes leading usu. in pairs from the masthead of a ship to the side to support the mast

2shroud *vb* : to veil or screen from view ⟨plans ~ed in secrecy⟩

shrub \\'shrəb\\ *n* : a low usu. several-stemmed woody plant — **shrub·by** *adj*

shrub·bery \\-(-)rē\\ *n* : a planting or growth of shrubs

shrug \\'shrəg\\ *vb* **shrugged; shrug·ging** : to hunch (the shoulders) up to express doubt, indifference, or dislike — **shrug** *n*

1shuck \\'shək\\ *n* : SHELL, HUSK

2shuck *vb* : to strip of shucks

shud·der \\'shəd-ər\\ *vb* : TREMBLE, QUAKE — **shudder** *n*

shuf·fle \\'shəf-əl\\ *vb* **1** : to mix in a disorderly mass **2** : to rearrange the order of (cards in a pack) by mixing two parts of the pack together **3** : to move with a sliding or dragging gait **4** : to shift from place to place **5** : to dance in a slow lagging manner — **shuffle** *n*

shun \\'shən\\ *vb* **shunned; shun·ning** : to avoid deliberately or habitually **syn** evade, elude, escape

1shunt \\'shənt\\ *vb* : to turn off to one side; *esp* : to switch (a train) from one track to another

2shunt *n* **1** : a means for turning or thrusting aside **2** *chiefly Brit* : a railroad switch

shut \\'shət\\ *vb* **shut; shut·ting 1** : CLOSE **2** : to forbid entrance into **3** : to lock up : CONFINE (~ in prison) **4** : to fold together (~ a penknife)

shut·ter \\'shət-ər\\ *n* **1** : a movable cover for a door or window for privacy or to keep out light or air : BLIND **2** : the part of a camera that opens or closes to expose the film

1shut·tle \\'shət-°l\\ *n* **1** : an instrument used in weaving for passing the horizontal threads between the vertical threads **2** : a vehicle traveling back and forth over a short route (a ~ bus)

2shuttle *vb* : to move back and forth rapidly or frequently

shut·tle·cock \\-ˌkäk\\ *n* : a light feathered object (as of cork or plastic) used in badminton

1shy \\'shī\\ *adj* **1** : TIMID, DISTRUSTFUL **2** : WARY **3** : BASHFUL **4** : DEFICIENT, LACKING (this coat is ~ a button) — **shy·ly** *adv* — **shy·ness** *n*

2shy *vb* **1** : to shrink back : RECOIL **2** : to start suddenly aside through fright ⟨the horse *shied*⟩

Shy·lock \\'shī-ˌläk\\ *n* [after Shylock, moneylender in Shakespeare's *Merchant of Venice*] : a hardhearted greedy person; *esp* : an extortionate moneylender

Si·a·mese \\ˌsī-ə-'mēz\\ *n, pl* **Siamese** : THAI — **Siamese** *adj*

Siamese twins *n pl* : twins with bodies united at birth

sib·yl \\'sib-əl\\ *n* : PROPHETESS — **sib·yl·line** \\-ə-ˌlīn\\ *adj*

sick \\'sik\\ *adj* **1** : not in good health : ILL; *also* : of, relating to, or intended for the sick (~ pay) **2** : NAUSEATED **3** : LANGUISHING, PINING **4** : DISGUSTED — **sick·ly** *adj*

sick·en \\'sik-ən\\ *vb* : to make or become sick

sick·le \\'sik-əl\\ *n* : a curved metal blade with a short handle used esp. for cutting grass

sick·ness *n* **1** : ill health; *also* : a specific disease **2** : NAUSEA

side \\'sīd\\ *n* **1** : a border of an object; *esp* : one of the longer borders as contrasted with an end **2** : an outer surface of an object **3** : the right or left part of the trunk of a body **4** : a place away from a central point or line **5** : a position regarded as opposite to another **6** : a body of contestants — **side** *adj*

side·arm \\-ˌärm\\ *adj* : made with a sideways sweep of the arm — **sidearm** *adv*

side·board \\-ˌbōrd\\ *n* : a piece of dining-room furniture for holding articles of table service

¹**side·long** \-ˌlȯ̇ŋ\ *adv* : in the direction along the side : OBLIQUELY

²**sidelong** *adj* : directed to one side : SLANTING ⟨~ look⟩

side·piece \'sīd-ˌpēs\ *n* : a piece forming or contained in the side of something

si·de·re·al \sī-'dir-ē-əl\ *adj* 1 : of or relating to the stars 2 : measured by the apparent motion of the fixed stars ⟨~ time⟩

side·stroke \'sīd-ˌströk\ *n* : a stroke made by a swimmer while lying on his side in which the arms are moved without breaking water while the legs do a scissors kick

¹**side·track** \-ˌtrak\ *n* : SIDING

²**sidetrack** *vb* 1 : to switch from a main railroad line to a siding 2 : to turn aside from a purpose

side·walk \-ˌwȯk\ *n* : a paved walk at the side of a road or street

side·ways \-ˌwāz\ *or* **side·wise** \-ˌwīz\ *adv* (*or adj*) 1 : from the side 2 : with one side to the front 3 : to, toward, or at one side

sid·ing \'sīd-iŋ\ *n* 1 : a short railroad track connected with the main track 2 : material (as boards) covering the outside of frame buildings

si·dle \'sīd-ᵊl\ *vb* : to move sideways or side foremost

siege \'sēj\ *n* 1 : the placing of an army around or before a fortified place to force its surrender 2 : a persistent attack (as of illness)

si·er·ra \sē-'er-ə\ *n* [Sp, lit., saw, fr. L *serra*] : a range of mountains whose peaks make a jagged outline

si·es·ta \sē-'es-tə\ *n* : a midday rest or nap

sieve \'siv\ *n* : a utensil with meshes or holes to separate the finer particles of a substance from the coarser or solids from liquids

sift \'sift\ *vb* 1 : to pass through a sieve 2 : to separate with or as if with a sieve 3 : to examine carefully 4 : to scatter by or as if by passing through a sieve — **sift·er** *n*

sigh \'sī\ *vb* 1 : to make a long audible respiration (as to express weariness or sorrow) 2 : GRIEVE, YEARN — **sigh** *n*

¹**sight** \'sīt\ *n* 1 : something seen 2 : the process, function, or power of seeing; *esp* : the special sense of which the eye is the receptor and by which qualities of appearance (as position, shape, and color) are perceived 3 : INSPECTION 4 : a device (as a small bead on a gun barrel) that aids the eye in aiming 5 : VIEW, GLIMPSE 6 : the range of vision — **sight·less** *adj*

²**sight** *vb* 1 : to get sight of 2 : to aim by means of a sight

sight·ed *adj* : having sight

sight·ly *adj* : pleasing to the sight

sight-see·ing \'sīt-ˌsē-iŋ\ *adj* : engaged in or used for seeing sights of interest ⟨a ~ tour⟩ — **sight·seer** *n*

¹**sign** \'sīn\ *n* 1 : SYMBOL 2 : a gesture expressing a command, wish, or thought 3 : a lettered notice publicly displayed for advertising purposes or for giving direction or warning 4 : OMEN, PORTENT 5 : TRACE, VESTIGE

²**sign** *vb* 1 : to mark with a sign 2 : to represent by a sign 3 : to make a sign or signal 4 : to write one's name on in token of assent or obligation 5 : to assign legally — **sign·er** *n*

¹**sig·nal** \'sig-nᵊl\ *n* 1 : a sign agreed upon as the start of some joint action 2 : a sign giving warning or notice of something 3 : the message, sound, or image transmitted in electronic communication (as radio)

²**signal** *vb* -**naled** *or* -**nalled**; -**nal·ing** *or* -**nal·ling** 1 : to communicate by signals 2 : to notify by a signal

³**signal** *adj* 1 : DISTINGUISHED, OUTSTANDING ⟨a ~ honor⟩ 2 : used in signaling ⟨~ flare⟩ — **sig·nal·ly** *adv*

sig·nal·ize \'sig-nᵊl-ˌīz\ *vb* : to point out or make conspicuous

sig·na·to·ry \'sig-nə-ˌtōr-ē\ *n* : a person or government that signs jointly with others — **signatory** *adj*

sig·na·ture \'sig-nə-ˌchùr\ *n* 1 : the name of a person written by himself 2 : the sign placed after the clef to indicate the key or the meter of a piece of music 3 : a tune or sound effect or in television a visual effect to identify a program, entertainer, or orchestra

sign·board \'sīn-ˌbȯrd\ *n* : a board bearing a sign or notice

sig·net \'sig-nət\ *n* : a small intaglio seal (as in a ring)

sig·nif·i·cance \sig-'nif-i-kəns\ *n* 1 : something signified : MEANING 2 : SUGGESTIVENESS 3 : CONSEQUENCE, IMPORTANCE

sig·nif·i·cant \-kənt\ *adj* 1 : having meaning; *esp* : having a hidden or special meaning 2 : having or likely to have considerable influence or effect : IMPORTANT — **sig·nif·i·cant·ly** *adv*

sig·ni·fy \'sig-nə-ˌfī\ *vb* 1 : to show by a sign 2 : MEAN, IMPORT 3 : to have significance — **sig·ni·fi·ca·tion** \ˌsig-nə-fə-'kā-shən\ *n*

sign·post \'sīn-ˌpōst\ *n* : a post bearing a sign

Sikh \'sēk\ *n* : an adherent of a religion of India marked by rejection of caste — **Sikh·ism** *n*

si·lage \'sī-lij\ *n* : chopped fodder stored in silos to ferment for use as animal feed

¹**si·lence** \'sī-ləns\ *n* 1 : the state of being silent 2 : SECRECY 3 : STILLNESS

²**silence** *vb* 1 : to reduce to silence : STILL 2 : to cause to cease hostile firing by one's own fire or by bombing

si·lenc·er *n* : a device for muffling the noise of the discharge of a firearm

si·lent \'sī-lənt\ *adj* 1 : not speaking : MUTE; *also* : TACITURN 2 : STILL, QUIET 3 : performed or borne without utterance **syn** reticent, reserved, secretive, close — **si·lent·ly** *adv*

¹**sil·hou·ette** \ˌsil-ə-'wet\ *n* 1 : a representation of the outlines of an object filled in with black or some other uniform color 2 : OUTLINE ⟨~ of a ship⟩

²**silhouette** *vb* : to represent by a silhouette; *also* : to show against a light background

sil·i·ca \'sil-i-kə\ *n* : a mineral that consists of silicon and oxygen and is found as quartz and opal

ə abut; ᵊ kitten; ər further; a back; ā bake; ä cot, cart; aù out; ch chin; e less; ē easy; g gift; i trip; ī life; j joke; ŋ sing; ō flow; ȯ flaw; ȯi coin; th thin; t̲h̲ this; ü loot; ù foot; y yet; yü few; yù furious; zh vision

sil·i·cate \'sil-ə-ˌkāt, -i-kət\ *n* : a compound formed from silica and any of various oxides of metals

si·li·ceous *or* **si·li·cious** \sə-'lish-əs\ *adj* : of, relating to, or containing silica or a silicate

sil·i·con \'sil-i-kən\ *n* : a nonmetallic chemical element that is found in nature always combined with some other substance and that is the most abundant element next to oxygen in the earth's crust

sil·i·cone \'sil-ə-ˌkōn\ *n* : an organic silicon compound obtained as oil, grease, or plastic

sil·i·co·sis \ˌsil-ə-'kō-səs\ *n* : a lung disease caused by prolonged inhaling of silica dusts

silk \'silk\ *n* **1** : a fine strong lustrous protein fiber produced by insect larvae for their cocoons; *esp* : one from moth larvae (**silk·worms** \-ˌwərmz\) used for cloth **2** : thread or cloth made from silk — **silk·en** *adj* — **silky** *adj*

sill \'sil\ *n* : a heavy crosspiece (as of wood or stone) that forms the bottom member of a window frame or a doorway; *also* : a horizontal supporting piece at the base of a structure

sil·ly \'sil-ē\ *adj* : FOOLISH, ABSURD, STUPID — **sil·li·ness** *n*

si·lo \'sī-lō\ *n* : a trench, pit, or tall cylinder (as of wood or brick) where silage is stored

¹silt \'silt\ *n* **1** : fine earth; *esp* : particles of such soil floating in rivers, ponds, or lakes **2** : a deposit (as by a river) of silt

²silt *vb* : to choke, obstruct, or cover with silt 〈~ up a channel〉

¹sil·ver \'sil-vər\ *n* **1** : a white ductile metallic chemical element that takes a high polish and is used for money, jewelry, and table utensils **2** : coin made of silver **3** : SILVERWARE **4** : a grayish white color — **sil·very** *adj*

²silver *adj* **1** : relating to, made of, or coated with silver **2** : SILVERY

³silver *vb* : to coat with or as if with silver

silver nitrate *n* : a soluble salt of silver used in photography and as an antiseptic

sil·ver·ware \'sil-vər-ˌwaȯr\ *n* : articles (as knives, forks, and spoons) made of silver, silver-plated metal, or stainless steel

sim·i·an \'sim-ē-ən\ *n* : MONKEY, APE — **simian** *adj*

sim·i·lar \'sim-ə-lər\ *adj* : marked by correspondence or resemblance **syn** alike, akin, comparable, parallel — **sim·i·lar·i·ty** \ˌsim-ə-'lar-ət-ē\ *n* — **sim·i·lar·ly** \'sim-ə-lər-lē\ *adv*

sim·i·le \'sim-ə-(ˌ)lē\ *n* [L, likeness, comparison, fr. neut. of *similis* like, similar] : a figure of speech in which two dissimilar things are compared by the use of *like* or *as* (as in "cheeks like roses")

si·mil·i·tude \sə-'mil-ə-ˌt(y)üd\ *n* : LIKENESS, RESEMBLANCE **syn** similarity

sim·mer \'sim-ər\ *vb* **1** : to stew at or just below the boiling point **2** : to be on the point of bursting out with violence or emotional disturbance

si·mo·nize \'sī-mə-ˌnīz\ *vb* : to polish with or as if with wax

si·mo·ny \'sīm-ə-nē, 'sim-\ *n* : the buying or selling of a church office

sim·per \'sim-pər\ *n* : a silly affected smile : SMIRK — **simper** *vb*

¹sim·ple \'sim-pəl\ *adj* **1** : not com-

bined with anything else **2** : not other than : MERE **3** : not complex : PLAIN **4** : ABSOLUTE 〈land held in fee ~〉 **5** : STRAIGHTFORWARD; *also* : ARTLESS **6** : UNADORNED **7** : lacking education, experience, or intelligence **syn** pure, sheer, easy, facile, light, effortless, natural, ingenuous, naïve, unsophisticated, foolish, silly — **sim·ple·ness** *n* — **sim·ply** \-plē\ *adv*

²simple *n* **1** : a person of humble birth : COMMONER **2** : a medicinal plant

sim·ple·ton \'sim-pəl-tən\ *n* : FOOL

sim·plic·i·ty \sim-'plis-ət-ē\ *n* **1** : lack of complication : CLEARNESS **2** : CANDOR, ARTLESSNESS **3** : plainness in manners or way of life **4** : IGNORANCE, FOOLISHNESS

sim·pli·fy \'sim-plə-ˌfī\ *vb* : to make simple : make less complex : CLARIFY — **sim·pli·fi·ca·tion** \ˌsim-plə-fə-'kā-shən\ *n*

sim·u·late \'sim-yə-ˌlāt\ *vb* : to create the effect or appearance of : FEIGN — **sim·u·la·tion** \ˌsim-yə-'lā-shən\ *n*

si·mul·ta·ne·ous \ˌsīm-əl-'tā-nē-əs, ˌsim-\ *adj* : occurring or operating at the same time — **si·mul·ta·ne·ous·ly** *adv*

¹sin \'sin\ *n* **1** : an offense esp. against God **2** : FAULT **3** : a weakened state of human nature in which the self is estranged from God — **sin·less** *adj*

²sin *vb* sinned; sin·ning : to commit a sin — **sin·ner** *n*

¹since \(')sins\ *adv* **1** : from a past time until now 〈have lived there ever ~〉 **2** : backward in time : AGO 〈died long ~〉

²since *prep* **1** : in the period after 〈changes made ~ the war〉 **2** : continuously from 〈has been here ~ 1955〉

³since *conj* **1** : from the time when **2** : seeing that : BECAUSE

sin·cere \sin-'siər\ *adj* **1** : free from hypocrisy : HONEST **2** : GENUINE, REAL — **sin·cere·ly** *adv* — **sin·cer·i·ty** \-'ser-ət-ē\ *n*

si·ne·cure \'sī-ni-ˌkyur, 'sin-i-\ *n* : a well-paid job that requires little work

si·ne die \ˌsī-nē-'dī-ē, ˌsin-\ *adv* : INDEFINITELY 〈the council adjourned *sine die*〉

sin·ew \'sin-yü\ *n* **1** : TENDON **2** : physical strength — **sin·ewy** *adj*

sin·ful *adj* : marked by or full of sin : WICKED — **sin·ful·ly** *adv* — **sin·ful·ness** *n*

sing \'siŋ\ *vb* sang \'saŋ\ *or* sung \'səŋ\; sung; sing·ing **1** : to produce musical tones with the voice; *also* : to utter with musical tones **2** : to produce harmonious sustained sounds 〈birds ~ing〉 **3** : CHANT, INTONE **4** : to make a prolonged shrill sound 〈locusts ~ing〉 **5** : to write poetry; *also* : to celebrate in song or verse **6** : to give information or evidence — **sing·er** *n*

singe \'sinj\ *vb* singed; singe·ing : to scorch lightly the outside of; *esp* : to remove the hair or down from (a plucked fowl) with flame

singing bird *n* : any of numerous mostly small perching birds many of which have pleasing songs : SONGBIRD

¹sin·gle \'siŋ-gəl\ *adj* **1** : one only **2** : ALONE **3** : UNMARRIED **4** : having only one feature or part **5** : made for one person or family **syn** sole, unique, lone, solitary, separate, particular — **sin·gle·ness** *n* — **sin·gly** \-glē\ *adv*

²single *n* **1** : a separate person or thing **2** : a hit in baseball that enables the batter to reach first base **3** *pl* : a tennis match with one player on each side

³single *vb* **1** : to select (one) from a group **2** : to hit a single

sin·gle·ton \'siŋ-gəl-tən\ *n* : a card that is the only one of its suit *orig.* held in a hand

sin·gle·tree \-(,)trē\ *n* : WHIFFLETREE

sin·gu·lar \'siŋ-gyə-lər\ *adj* **1** : of, relating to, or constituting a word form denoting one person, thing, or instance **2** : of unusual quality **3** : OUTSTANDING, EXCEPTIONAL **4** : ODD, STRANGE — **singular** *n* — **sin·gu·lar·i·ty** \,siŋ-gyə-'lar-ət-ē\ *n* — **sin·gu·lar·ly** \'siŋ-gyə-lor-lē\ *adv*

sin·is·ter \'sin-ə-stər\ *adj* **1** : threatening or foreboding evil or disaster **2** : indicative of lurking evil *syn* baleful, malign

¹sink \'siŋk\ *vb* sank \'saŋk\ *or* sunk \'səŋk\ sunk; sink·ing **1** : SUBMERGE **2** : to descend lower and lower **3** : to grow less in volume or height **4** : to slope downward **5** : to penetrate downward **6** : to fail in health or strength **7** : LAPSE, DEGENERATE **8** : to cause (a ship) to plunge to the bottom **9** : to make (a hole or shaft) by digging, boring, or cutting **10** : INVEST — **sink·able** *adj*

²sink *n* **1** : DRAIN, SEWER **2** : a basin connected with a drain for washing **3** : an extensive depression in the land surface

sink·er *n* : a weight for sinking a fishing line or net

sin·u·ous \'sin-yə-wəs\ *adj* : bending in and out : WINDING — **sin·u·os·i·ty** \,sin-yə-'wäs-ət-ē\ *n*

si·nus \'sī-nəs\ *n* **1** : any of several cavities of the skull mostly connecting with the nostrils **2** : a space forming a channel (as for the passage of blood or pus)

sip \'sip\ *vb* sipped; sip·ping : to drink in small quantities — **sip** *n*

¹si·phon \'sī-fən\ *n* **1** : a bent tube through which a liquid can be transferred by means of air pressure up and over the edge of one container and into another container placed at a lower level **2** *usu* **sy·phon** : a bottle that ejects soda water through a tube when a valve is opened

³siphon *vb* : to draw off by means of a siphon

sir \(')sər\ *n* [ME *sire* sire, fr. OF, fr. L *senior*, compar. of *senex* old, old man] **1** : a man of rank or position — used as a title before the given name of a knight or baronet **2** — used in addressing a man without using his name

¹sire \'sī(ə)r\ *n* **1** : FATHER; *also*, *archaic* : FOREFATHER **2** : the male parent of an animal (as a horse or dog) **3** *archaic* : LORD — used as a title of respect esp. in addressing a sovereign

²sire *vb* : BEGET, PROCREATE

si·ren \'sī-rən\ *n* **1** : a seductive or alluring woman **2** : a loud wailing often electrically operated whistle used to sound warning signals (ambulance ~) (air-raid ~) — **siren** *adj*

sir·loin \'sər-,lóin\ *n* : a cut of beef taken from the part in front of the round

si·roc·co \sə-'räk-ō\ *n* **1** : a hot wind blowing north from the Libyan deserts **2** : a hot southerly wind

sirup *var of* SYRUP

si·sal \'sī-səl\ *n* : a strong cordage fiber from an agave

sis·ter \'sis-tər\ *n* **1** : a female person or lower animal viewed in relation to another individual having the same parents (**whole sister**) or one parent in common (**half sister**) **2** : a member of a religious order of women : NUN **3** *chiefly Brit* : NURSE — **sis·ter·ly** *adj*

sis·ter·hood \-,húd\ *n* **1** : the state of being sisters or a sister **2** : a community or society of sisters

sister-in-law *n*, *pl* **sisters-in-law** : the sister of one's husband or wife; *also* : the wife of one's brother

sit \'sit\ *vb* sat \'sat\ sit·ting **1** : to rest upon the buttocks or haunches **2** : ROOST, PERCH **3** : to occupy a seat **4** : to hold a session **5** : to cover eggs for hatching : BROOD **6** : to pose for a portrait **7** : to remain quiet or inactive **8** : FIT **9** : to cause (oneself) to be seated **10** : to place in position **11** : to keep one's seat upon (~ a horse) — **sit·ter** *n*

site \'sīt\ *n* **1** : LOCATION (~ of a building) (battle ~)

sit·u·at·ed \'sich-ə-,wāt-əd\ *adj* **1** : LOCATED, PLACED **2** : placed in a particular place or environment or in certain circumstances

sit·u·a·tion \,sich-ə-'wā-shən\ *n* **1** : LOCATION, SITE **2** : CONDITION, CIRCUMSTANCES **3** : place of employment : JOB, POST

six \'siks\ *n* **1** : one more than five **2** : the 6th in a set or series **3** : something having six units; *esp* : a 6-cylinder engine or automobile — **six** *adj or pron* — **sixth** *adj or adv or n*

six·pence \-pəns\ *n* : the sum of six pence; *also* : an English silver coin of this value — **six·pen·ny** \-,pen-ē\ *adj*

six·teen \'siks-'tēn\ *n* : one more than 15 — **sixteen** *adj or pron* — **six·teenth** *adj or n*

six·ty \'siks-tē\ *n* : six times 10 — **six·ti·eth** *adj or n* — **sixty** *adj or pron*

siz·able *or* **size·able** \'sī-zə-bəl\ *adj* : somewhat large : CONSIDERABLE — **siz·ably** *adv*

¹size \'sīz\ *n* : physical extent or bulk : DIMENSIONS; *also* : MAGNITUDE

²size *vb* : to grade or classify according to size

³size *n* : a gluey material used for filling the pores in paper, plaster, or textiles — **siz·ing** *n*

⁴size *vb* : to cover, stiffen, or glaze with size

siz·zle \'siz-əl\ *vb* : to fry or shrivel up with a hissing sound — **sizzle** *n*

¹skate \'skāt\ *n* : any of numerous rays with thick broad fins

²skate *n* **1** : a metal runner with a frame fitting on a shoe used for gliding over ice **2** : ROLLER SKATE — **skate** *vb* — **skat·er** *n*

skein \'skān\ *n* : a loosely twisted quantity (as of yarn) as it is taken from the reel

skel·e·ton \'skel-ət-°n\ *n* **1** : the usu. bony supporting framework of an animal body **2** : FRAMEWORK — **skel·e·tal** \-ət-ᵊl\ *adj*

skep·tic \'skep-tik\ *n* **1** : one who believes in skepticism as a doctrine **2** : one having a critical or doubting attitude **3** : one who doubts or disbelieves in religious tenets — **skep·ti·cal** *adj*

skep·ti·cism \-tə-,siz-əm\ *n* **1** : a doctrine that certainty of knowledge cannot be attained **2** : a doubting state of mind **3** : unbelief in religion

sketch \'skech\ *n* **1** : a rough drawing or outline **2** : a short or slight literary composition (as a story or essay); *also* : a vaudeville act — **sketch** *vb* — **sketchy** *adj*

1skew \'skyü\ *vb* : SWERVE

2skew *n* : SLANT

skew·er \'skyü-ər\ *n* : a pin for holding meat in form while roasting — **skewer** *vb*

1ski \'skē\ *n* : one of a pair of long strips (as of wood) bound one on each foot and used for gliding over snow

2ski *vb* : to glide on skis

1skid \'skid\ *n* **1** : a plank for supporting something above the ground **2** : a device placed under a wheel to prevent turning **3** : a timber or rail over or on which something is slid or rolled **4** : a runner on the landing gear of an airplane **5** : the action of skidding

2skid *vb* **skid·ded; skid·ding 1** : to slide without rotating ⟨a *skidding* wheel⟩ **2** : to slide sideways on the road ⟨the car *skidded* on ice⟩

skiff \'skif\ *n* : a small open boat

skill \'skil\ *n* **1** : ability to use one's knowledge effectively in doing something **2** : developed or acquired ability **syn** art, craft — **skilled** *adj*

skil·let \'skil-ət\ *n* : a frying pan

skill·ful *or* **skil·ful** \'skil-fəl\ *adj* **1** : having or displaying skill : EXPERT **2** : accomplished with skill — **skill·ful·ly** *adv* — **skill·ful·ness** *n*

skim \'skim\ *vb* **skimmed; skim·ming 1** : to take off from the top of a liquid; *also* : to remove (scum or cream) from ⟨~ milk⟩ **2** : to read rapidly and superficially **3** : to pass swiftly over

skimp \'skimp\ *vb* : to give insufficient attention, effort, or funds; *also* : to save by skimping

skimpy *adj* : deficient in supply or execution : SCANTY

1skin \'skin\ *n* **1** : the outer limiting layer of an animal body; *also* : the usu. thin tough tissue of which this is made **2** : an outer or surface layer (as a rind or peel)

2skin *vb* **skinned; skin·ning** : to free from skin : remove the skin of

skin dive *vb* : to swim below the surface of water with a face mask and portable breathing device

skin·flint \'skin-,flint\ *n* : a very stingy person

skin·ny *adj* **1** : resembling skin **2** : very thin : LEAN

skin·tight \'skin-'tīt\ *adj* : closely fitted to the figure

1skip \'skip\ *vb* **skipped; skip·ping 1** : to move with leaps and bounds **2** : to pass from point to point (as in reading) disregarding what is in between **3** : to leap lightly over **4** : to pass over without notice or mention

2skip *n* : a light bound; *also* : a gait of alternate hops and steps

skip·per \'skip-ər\ *n* [MD *schipper* boatman, skipper, fr. *schip* ship] : the master of a ship

skir·mish \'skər-mish\ *n* : a minor or preliminary engagement in war — **skirmish** *vb*

1skirt \'skərt\ *n* : a garment or part of a garment that hangs below the waist

2skirt *vb* **1** : BORDER **2** : to pass around the outer edge of

skit \'skit\ *n* : a brief dramatic sketch

skit·tish \'skit-ish\ *adj* **1** : CAPRICIOUS, IRRESPONSIBLE **2** : easily frightened ⟨a ~ horse⟩

skulk \'skəlk\ *vb* : to move furtively : SNEAK, LURK — **skulk·er** *n*

skull \'skəl\ *n* : the bony or cartilaginous case that protects the brain and supports the jaws

skull·cap \-,kap\ *n* : a close-fitting brimless cap

skunk \'skəŋk\ *n* **1** : a No. American mammal related to the weasels that can forcibly eject an ill-smelling fluid when startled **2** : a contemptible person

sky \'skī\ *n* **1** : the upper air : the great vault that seems to extend over the earth **2** : HEAVEN — **sky·ey** *adj*

1sky·lark \-,lärk\ *n* : a European lark noted for its song and its steep upward flight

2skylark *vb* : to frolic boisterously or recklessly

sky·light \-,līt\ *n* : a window in a roof or ceiling

sky·line \-,līn\ *n* **1** : HORIZON **2** : an outline against the sky ⟨buildings forming the ~⟩

sky·rock·et \-,räk-ət\ *n* : a firework that flies upward and explodes high in the air : ROCKET

sky·scrap·er \-,skrā-pər\ *n* : a very tall building

sky·ward \-wərd\ *adv* (*or adj*) : toward the sky

sky·writ·ing \-,rīt-iŋ\ *n* : writing in the sky formed by smoke emitted from an airplane — **sky·writ·er** *n*

slab \'slab\ *n* **1** : a thick plate or slice **2** : the outside piece taken from a log in sawing it

1slack \'slak\ *adj* **1** : CARELESS, NEGLIGENT **2** : SLUGGISH, LISTLESS **3** : not taut : LOOSE **4** : not busy or active **syn** lax, remiss, neglectful — **slack·ly** *adv* — **slack·ness** *n*

2slack *vb* **1** : to make or become slack : LOOSEN, RELAX **2** : SLAKE

3slack *n* **1** : cessation of movement or flow : LETUP **2** : a part that hangs loose without strain ⟨~ of a rope⟩ **3** *pl* : trousers for casual wear

slack·en \'slak-ən\ *vb* : to make or become slack

slack·er \'slak-ər\ *n* : one that shirks work or evades military duty

slag \'slag\ *n* : the waste left after the melting of ores and the separation of metal from them

slain *past part of* SLAY

slake \'slāk, *for 2 also* 'slak\ *vb* **1** : to cause to subside with or as if with refreshing drink ⟨~ thirst⟩ **2** : to cause (lime) to crumble by mixture with water

sla·lom \'släl-əm\ *n* : skiing in a zigzag course between obstacles

1slam \'slam\ *n* : the winning of every trick ⟨grand slam⟩ or of all tricks but one ⟨little slam⟩ in bridge

2slam *n* : a heavy jarring impact : BANG

3slam *vb* **slammed; slam·ming 1** : to

shut violently and noisily : BANG 2 : to throw or strike with a loud impact

1slan·der \'slan-dər\ *n* **:** a false report maliciously uttered and tending to injure the reputation of a person — **slan·der·ous** *adj*

2slander *vb* **:** to utter slander against **: DEFAME — slan·der·er** *n*

slang \'slaŋ\ *n* **:** an informal nonstandard vocabulary composed typically of coinages, arbitrarily changed words, and extravagant figures of speech

1slant \'slant\ *vb* **1 : SLOPE 2 :** to interpret or present in accordance with a special viewpoint **syn** incline, lean — **slant·ing** *adj* — **slant·ing·ly** *adv*

2slant *n* **1 :** a sloping direction, line, or plane **2 :** a particular or personal viewpoint — **slant** *adj* — **slant·wise** *adv*

slap \'slap\ *vb* **slapped; slap·ping 1 :** to strike sharply with the open hand **2 : REBUFF, INSULT — slap** *n*

1slash \'slash\ *vb* **1 :** to cut with sweeping strokes **2 :** to cut slits in (a garment) **3 :** to reduce sharply (~ a budget)

2slash *n* **1 : GASH 2 :** an ornamental slit in a garment **3 :** a clearing in a forest littered with debris; *also* **:** the debris present

slat \'slat\ *n* **:** a thin narrow flat strip (the ~s of a blind)

1slate \'slāt\ *n* **1 :** a dense fine-grained rock that splits into thin layers **2 :** a roofing tile or a writing tablet made from this rock **3 :** a list of candidates for election

2slate *vb* **1 :** to cover with slate **2 :** to designate for action or appointment

slat·tern \'slat-ərn\ *n* **:** a slovenly woman — **slat·tern·ly** *adv or adj*

1slaugh·ter \'slȯt-ər\ *n* **1 :** the butchering of livestock for market **2 :** great destruction of lives esp. in battle

2slaughter *vb* **1 :** to kill (animals) for food **: BUTCHER 2 :** to kill in large numbers or in a bloody way **: MASSACRE**

slaugh·ter·house \-,haús\ *n* **:** an establishment where animals are butchered

Slav \'släv, 'slav\ *n* **:** a person speaking a Slavic language

1slave \'slāv\ *n* [OF *esclave*, fr. ML *sclavus*, fr. *Sclavus* Slav; fr. the reduction to slavery of many Slavic peoples of Europe] **:** a person held in servitude as property — **slave** *adj*

2slave *vb* **:** to work like a slave **: DRUDGE**

1slav·er \'slav-ər, 'släv-\ *n* **: SLOBBER — slavery** *vb*

2slav·er \'slāv-ər\ *n* **:** a ship or a person engaged in transporting slaves

slav·ery \'slāv-(ə-)rē\ *n* **1 :** wearisome drudgery **2 :** the condition of being a slave **3 :** the custom or practice of owning slaves **syn** servitude, bondage

1Slav·ic \'slav-ik, 'släv-\ *adj* **:** of or relating to the Slavs or their languages

2Slavic *n* **:** a branch of the Indo-European language family including various languages (as Russian or Polish) of eastern Europe

slav·ish \'slāv-ish\ *adj* **1 : SERVILE 2 :** obeying or imitating with no freedom of judgment or choice — **slav·ish·ly** *adv*

slaw \'slȯ\ *n* **: COLESLAW**

slay \'slā\ *vb* **slew** \'slü\ **slain** \'slān\ **slay·ing : KILL — slay·er** *n*

slea·zy \'slē-zē, 'slā-\ *adj* **: FLIMSY, SHODDY**

1sled \'sled\ *n* **:** a vehicle on runners adapted esp. for sliding on snow

2sled *vb* **sled·ded; sled·ding :** to ride or carry on a sled

1sledge \'slej\ *n* **: SLEDGEHAMMER**

2sledge *n* **:** a strong heavy vehicle with low runners for carrying heavy loads over snow or ice

sledge·ham·mer \-,ham-ər\ *n* **:** a large heavy hammer usu. wielded with both hands

1sleek \'slēk\ *vb* **1 :** to make smooth or glossy **2 :** to gloss over

2sleek *adj* **:** having a smooth well-groomed look

1sleep \'slēp\ *n* **1 :** a natural periodic suspension of consciousness **2 :** a state (as death or coma) suggesting sleep — **sleep·less** *adj* — **sleep·less·ness** *n*

2sleep *vb* **slept** \'slept\ **sleep·ing 1 :** to rest or be in a state of sleep; *also* **:** to spend or get rid of in sleep (~ cares away) **2 :** to lie in a state of inactivity or stillness

sleep·er *n* **1 :** one that sleeps **2 :** a horizontal beam to support something on or near the ground level **3 :** a railroad car with berths for sleeping

sleeping car *n* **: SLEEPER 3**

sleepy \'slē-pē\ *adj* **1 :** ready for sleep **: DROWSY 2 :** quietly inactive — **sleep·i·ly** *adv* — **sleep·i·ness** *n*

sleet \'slēt\ *n* **1 :** partly frozen rain; *also* **:** a mixture of rain and snow **2 : GLAZE — sleet** *vb* — **sleety** *adj*

sleeve \'slēv\ *n* **1 :** the part of a garment covering the arm **2 :** a tubular part fitting over another part — **sleeveless** *adj*

1sleigh \'slā\ *n* **:** a vehicle on runners for use on snow or ice

2sleigh *vb* **:** to drive or travel in a sleigh

sleight \'slīt\ *n* **1 : TRICK 2 : DEXTERITY**

sleight of hand : a trick requiring skillful manual manipulation

slen·der \'slen-dər\ *adj* **1 : SLIM, THIN 2 : WEAK, SLIGHT 3 : MEAGER, INADEQUATE**

sleuth \'slüth\ *n* **: DETECTIVE**

slew *past of* **SLAY**

1slice \'slīs\ *n* **1 :** a thin flat piece cut from something **2 :** a wedge-shaped blade (as for serving fish) **3 :** a flight of a ball (as in golf) that curves in the direction of the dominant hand of the player propelling it

2slice *vb* **1 :** to cut a slice from; *also* **:** to cut into slices **2 :** to hit (a ball) so that a slice results

1slick \'slik\ *vb* **:** to make smooth or sleek

2slick *adj* **1 :** very smooth **: SLIPPERY 2 : CLEVER, SMART**

3slick *n* **1 :** a smooth patch of water covered with a film of oil **2 :** a popular magazine printed on coated stock

slick·er \'slik-ər\ *n* **1 :** a long loose raincoat **2 :** a clever crook

1slide \'slīd\ *vb* **slid** \'slid\ **slid·ing** \'slīd-iŋ\ **1 :** to move or cause to move smoothly along a surface **2 :** to fall by a loss of support **3 :** to slip along quietly

---

ə abut; ᵉ kitten; ər further; a back; ā bake; ä cot, cart; aú out; ch chin; e less; ē easy; g gift; i trip; ī life; j joke; ŋ sing; ō flow; ȯ flaw; ȯi coin; th thin; th this; ü loot; ú foot; y yet; yü few; yú furious; zh vision

²**slide** n **1** : an act or instance of sliding **2** : a fall of a mass of earth or snow down a hillside **3** : something (as a cover or fastener) that operates by sliding **4** : a surface on which something slides **5** : a plate from which a picture may be projected **6** : a glass plate on which a specimen can be placed for examination under a microscope

slid·er n **1** : one that slides **2** : a baseball pitch that looks like a fast ball but curves slightly

slide rule n : an instrument for rapid calculation consisting of a ruler and a medial slide graduated with logarithmic scales

¹**slight** \'slīt\ adj **1** : SLENDER; also : FRAIL **2** : SCANTY, MEAGER **3** : UNIMPORTANT — **slight·ly** adv

²**slight** vb **1** : to treat as unimportant **2** : to ignore discourteously **3** : to perform or attend to carelessly syn neglect, overlook, disregard

³**slight** n : a humiliating discourtesy

¹**slim** \'slim\ adj **1** : SLENDER, SLIGHT, THIN **2** : SCANTY, MEAGER

²**slim** vb **slimmed**; **slim·ming** : to make or become slender

slime \'slīm\ n **1** : sticky mud **2** : a slippery substance (as on the skin of a slug or catfish) — **slimy** adj

¹**sling** \'sliŋ\ vb **slung** \'sləŋ\ **slinging 1** : to hurl with a sling **2** : to throw forcibly : FLING **3** : to place in a sling for hoisting or carrying

²**sling** n **1** : a short strap with strings attached for hurling stones or shot **2** : a strap, rope, or chain for holding securely something being lifted, lowered, or carried

sling·shot \-,shät\ n : a forked stick with elastic bands for shooting small stones or shot

slink \'sliŋk\ vb **slunk** \'sləŋk\ **slinking** : to move stealthily or furtively

¹**slip** \'slip\ vb **slipped**; **slip·ping 1** : to escape quietly or secretly **2** : to slide along or cause to slide along smoothly **3** : to make a mistake **4** : to pass unnoticed or undone **5** : to fall off from a standard or level ⟨*slipping* prices⟩

²**slip** n **1** : a ramp for repairing ships **2** : a ship's berth between two piers **3** : secret or hurried departure, escape, or evasion **4** : a sudden mishap **5** : BLUNDER **6** : PILLOWCASE **7** : a woman's one-piece garment worn under a dress

³**slip** n **1** : a shoot or twig from a plant for planting or grafting **2** : a long narrow strip; esp : one of paper used for a record ⟨deposit ~⟩

⁴**slip** vb **slipped**; **slip·ping** : to take slips from (a plant)

slip·knot \'slip-,nät\ n : a knot that slips along the rope around which it is made

slip·per \'slip-ər\ n : a light low shoe that may be easily slipped on and off

slip·pery \'slip-(ə-)rē\ adj **1** : icy, wet, or greasy enough to cause one to fall or lose one's hold **2** : TRICKY, UNRELIABLE — **slip·peri·ness** n

slip·shod \'slip-'shäd\ adj : SLOVENLY, CARELESS ⟨~ work⟩

¹**slit** \'slit\ vb **slit**; **slit·ting 1** : SLASH **2** : to cut off or away

²**slit** n : a long narrow cut or opening

slith·er \'slith-ər\ vb : to slip or glide along like a snake — **slith·ery** adj

sliv·er \'sliv-ər\ n : SPLINTER

slob·ber \'släb-ər\ vb : to dribble saliva : SLAVER — **slobber** n

sloe \'slō\ n : the fruit of the blackthorn

slo·gan \'slō-gən\ n [Gael *sluag-ghairm* army cry, war cry] : a word or phrase expressing the spirit or aim of a party, group, or cause

sloop \'slüp\ n : a sailing boat with one mast, a fore-and-aft rig, and a single jib

¹**slop** \'släp\ n **1** : thin tasteless drink or liquid food — usu. used in pl. **2** : food waste or gruel for animal feed **3** : body and toilet waste — usu. used in pl.

²**slop** vb **slopped**; **slop·ping 1** : SPILL **2** : to feed with slop ⟨~ hogs⟩

¹**slope** \'slōp\ vb : SLANT, INCLINE

²**slope** n **1** : ground that forms an incline **2** : upward or downward slant or degree of slant **3** : the part of a landmass draining into a particular ocean ⟨the Pacific ~⟩

slop·py \'släp-ē\ adj **1** : MUDDY, SLUSHY **2** : SLOVENLY, MESSY

slot \'slät\ n **1** : a long narrow opening or groove **2** : a position in a sequence

sloth \'slóth, 'slŏth\ n **1** : LAZINESS, INDOLENCE **2** : a slow-moving So. and Central American mammal related to the armadillos — **sloth·ful** adj

slot machine n : a machine whose operation is begun by dropping a coin into a slot

¹**slouch** \'slauch\ n **1** : a loose or drooping gait or posture **2** : a lazy or incompetent person

²**slouch** vb : to walk, stand, or sit with a slouch : SLUMP

¹**slough** \'slü, 3 usu 'slau\ n **1** : SWAMP **2** : a muddy place **3** : a discouraged state of mind

²**slough** \'sləf\ or **sluff** n : something (as dead tissue or a snake's skin) that may be shed

³**slough** \'sləf\ or **sluff** vb : to cast off : DISCARD

slov·en \'sləv-ən\ n : an untidy person

slov·en·ly adj **1** : untidy in dress or person **2** : lazily or carelessly done : SLIPSHOD

¹**slow** \'slō\ adj **1** : SLUGGISH; also : dull in mind : STUPID **2** : moving, flowing, or proceeding at less than the usual speed **3** : taking more than the usual time **4** : registering behind the correct time **5** : not lively : BORING syn dilatory, laggard, deliberate, leisurely — **slow** adv — **slow·ly** adv — **slow·ness** n

²**slow** vb **1** : to make slow : hold back **2** : to go slower

sludge \'sləj\ n : a slushy mass : OOZE; esp : solid matter produced by sewage treatment processes

¹**slug** \'sləg\ n : a slimy wormlike mollusk related to the snails

²**slug** n **1** : a small mass of metal; esp : BULLET **2** : a metal disk for use (as in a slot machine) in place of a coin **3** : a single drink of liquor

³**slug** vb **slugged**; **slug·ging** : to strike forcibly and heavily — **slug·ger** n

slug·gard \'sləg-ərd\ n : a lazy person

slug·gish \-ish\ adj **1** : SLOTHFUL, LAZY **2** : slow in movement or flow **3** : STAGNANT, DULL ⟨~ market⟩ — **slug·gish·ly** adv — **slug·gish·ness** n

¹**sluice** \'slüs\ n **1** : an artificial passage for water with a gate for controlling the flow; also : the gate so used **2** : a channel that carries off surplus water **3** : an inclined trough or flume for washing ore or floating logs

²**sluice** vb **1** : to draw off through a

sluice **2 :** to wash with running water **:** FLUSH **3 :** to transport (as logs) in a sluice

¹slum \'sləm\ *n* **:** a thickly populated area marked by poverty and dirty or deteriorated houses

²slum *vb* slummed; slum·ming **:** to visit slums esp. out of curiosity

¹slum·ber \'sləm-bər\ *vb* **1 :** to sleep lightly **:** DOZE **2 :** to be in a sluggish or torpid state

²slumber *n* **:** SLEEP

slum·ber·ous *or* slum·brous \-b(ə-)rəs\ *adj* **1 :** SLUMBERING, SLEEPY **2 :** PEACEFUL, INACTIVE

slump \'sləmp\ *vb* **1 :** to sink down suddenly **:** fall in a heap **:** COLLAPSE **2 :** SLOUCH **3 :** to decline sharply ⟨~ing prices⟩ — slump *n*

slung *past of* SLING

slunk *past of* SLINK

¹slur \'slər\ *vb* slurred; slur·ring **1 :** to slide or slip over without due mention or emphasis **2 :** to perform two or more successive notes of different pitch in a smooth or connected way

²slur *n* **:** a curved line ⌣ or ⌢ connecting notes to be slurred; *also* **:** a group of slurred notes

³slur *n* **:** a slighting remark **:** ASPERSION

slush \'sləsh\ *n* **1 :** partly melted or watery snow **2 :** soft mud — slushy *adj*

slut \'slət\ *n* **1 :** a slovenly woman **2 :** PROSTITUTE — slut·tish *adj*

sly \'slī\ *adj* **1 :** CRAFTY, CUNNING **2 :** SECRETIVE, FURTIVE **3 :** ROGUISH *syn* tricky, wily, artful — sly·ly *adv* — sly·ness *n*

¹smack \'smak\ *n* **1 :** a sharp noise (as in appreciation of some taste) made by the lips **2 :** a noisy slap

²smack *vb* **1 :** to move (the lips) so as to make a sharp noise **2 :** to kiss or slap with a loud noise

³smack *n* **:** a sailing ship used in fishing

small \'smol\ *adj* **1 :** little in size or amount **2 :** few in number **3 :** TRIFLING, UNIMPORTANT **4 :** operating on a limited scale **5 :** MEAN, PETTY **6 :** made up of little things *syn* diminutive, petite, wee, tiny, minute — small·ish *adj* — small·ness *n*

small·pox \-,päks\ *n* **:** a contagious virus disease marked by fever and eruption

¹smart \'smärt\ *vb* **1 :** to cause or feel a stinging pain **2 :** to feel or endure distress — smart *n*

²smart *adj* **1 :** making one smart ⟨a ~ blow⟩ **2 :** mentally quick **:** BRIGHT **3 :** WITTY, CLEVER **4 :** STYLISH, FASHIONABLE *syn* knowing, quick-witted, intelligent, dapper — smart·ly *adv* — smart·ness *n*

¹smash \'smash\ *vb* **1 :** to break or be broken into pieces **2 :** to move forward with force and shattering effect **3 :** to destroy utterly **:** WRECK

²smash *n* **1 :** a smashing blow; *esp* **:** a hard overhand stroke in tennis **2 :** the act or sound of smashing **3 :** a collision of vehicles **:** CRASH **4 :** COLLAPSE, RUIN; *esp* **:** BANKRUPTCY

smat·ter·ing \'smat-ə-riŋ\ *n* **:** superficial knowledge

¹smear \'smiər\ *n* **:** a spot left by an oily or sticky substance

²smear *vb* **1 :** to overspread with something oily or sticky **2 :** SMUDGE, SOIL **3 :** to injure by slander or insults

¹smell \'smel\ *vb* smelled \'smeld\ *or* smelt \'smelt\ smell·ing **1 :** to perceive the odor of by sense organs of the nose; *also* **:** to detect or seek with or as if with these organs **2 :** to have or give off an odor

²smell *n* **1 :** the process or power of perceiving odor; *also* **:** the special sense by which one perceives odor **2 :** ODOR, SCENT **3 :** an act of smelling — smelly *adj*

smelling salts *n pl* **:** an aromatic preparation used as a stimulant and restorative (as to relieve faintness)

¹smelt \'smelt\ *n* **:** any of several small food fishes of coastal or fresh waters

²smelt *vb* **:** to melt or fuse (ore) in order to separate the metal; *also* **:** REFINE

smelt·er *n* **1 :** one that smelts **2 :** an establishment for smelting

smi·lax \'smī-,laks\ *n* **1 :** any of various mostly climbing and prickly plants related to the lilies **2 :** an ornamental asparagus

¹smile \'smīl\ *vb* **1 :** to look with a smile **2 :** to be favorable **3 :** to express by a smile

²smile *n* **:** a change of facial expression to express amusement, pleasure, or affection

smirch \'smərch\ *vb* **1 :** to make dirty or stained **2 :** to bring disgrace on — smirch *n*

smirk \'smərk\ *vb* **:** to wear a self-conscious or conceited smile **:** SIMPER — smirk *n*

smite \'smīt\ *vb* smote \'smōt\ smit·ten \'smit-ᵊn\ *or* smote; smit·ing \'smīt-iŋ\ **1 :** to strike heavily; *also* **:** to kill by striking **2 :** to affect as if by a heavy blow ⟨*smitten* with smallpox⟩

smith \'smith\ *n* **:** a worker in metals; *esp* **:** BLACKSMITH

smith·er·eens \,smith-ə-'rēnz\ *n pl* **:** FRAGMENTS, BITS

smithy \'smith-ē\ *n* **:** a smith's workshop

¹smock \'smäk\ *n* **:** a long loose garment worn over other clothes as a protection

²smock *vb* **:** to gather (cloth) in regularly spaced tucks — smock·ing *n*

smog \'smäg\ *n* **:** a fog made heavier and darker by smoke and chemical fumes

¹smoke \'smōk\ *n* **1 :** the gas from burning material (as coal, wood, or tobacco) in which are suspended particles of soot **2 :** a suspension of solid or liquid particles in a gas **3 :** vapor resulting from action of heat on moisture — smoke·less *adj* — smoky *adj*

²smoke *vb* **1 :** to emit smoke **2 :** to inhale and exhale the fumes of burning tobacco; *also* **:** to use in smoking ⟨~ a pipe⟩ **3 :** to stupefy or drive away by smoke **4 :** to discolor with smoke **5 :** to cure (as meat) with smoke

smoke·stack \-,stak\ *n* **:** a chimney or funnel through which smoke and gases are discharged (as from a ship or factory)

smol·der *or* smoul·der \'smōl-dər\ *vb* **1 :** to burn and smoke without flame **2 :** to burn inwardly — smolder *n*

¹smooth \'smüth\ *adj* **1 :** not rough or

ə abut; ° kitten; ər further; a back; ā bake; ä cot, cart; aù out; ch chin; e less; ē easy; g gift; i trip; ī life; j joke; ŋ sing; ō flow; ò flaw; òi coin; th thin; th̸ this; ü loot; ù foot; y yet; yü few; yù furious; zh vision

uneven 2 : not jarring or jolting
3 : BLAND, MILD, AGREEABLE 4 : fluent
in speech and agreeable in manner syn
even, flat, level, diplomatic, suave,
urbane — smooth·ly adv — smoothness n

²smooth vb 1 : to make smooth 2 : to
free from trouble or difficulty

smor·gas·bord \'smȯr-gəs-ˌbȯrd\ n [Sw
smörgåsbord, fr. smörgås open sandwich + bord table] : a luncheon or
supper buffet consisting of many foods
(as hot and cold meats, smoked and
pickled fish, cheeses, salads, and relishes)

smote past of SMITE

¹smoth·er \'smə̇th-ər\ n 1 : thick
stifling smoke 2 : dense fog, spray,
foam, or dust 3 : a confused multitude
of things : WELTER

²smother vb 1 : to kill by depriving of
air : SUFFOCATE 2 : SUPPRESS 3 : to
cover thickly

¹smudge \'sməj\ vb : to soil or blur by
rubbing or smearing

²smudge n 1 : thick stifling smoke 2 : a
dirty or blurred spot — smudgy adj

smug \'sməg\ adj : conscious of one's
virtue and importance : SELF-SATISFIED,
COMPLACENT — smug·ly adv — smug-
ness n

smug·gle \'sməg-əl\ vb 1 : to import
or export secretly, illegally, or without
paying the duties required by law 2 : to
convey secretly — smug·gler \-(ə-)lər\
n

smut \'smət\ n 1 : something (as soot)
that smudges; also : SMUDGE, SPOT
2 : indecent language or jokes 3 : any
of various destructive fungous diseases
of plants — smut·ty adj

smutch \'sməch\ n : SMUDGE

snack \'snak\ n : a light meal : BITE

snaf·fle \'snaf-əl\ n : a simple jointed
bit for a horse's bridle

¹snag \'snag\ n 1 : a stump or piece
of a tree esp. when under water 2 : an
unexpected difficulty syn obstacle,
obstruction, impediment, bar

²snag vb snagged; snag·ging 1 : to
become caught on or as if on a snag
2 : to seize quickly : SNATCH

snail \'snāl\ n : a small mollusk with a
spiral shell into which it can withdraw

snake \'snāk\ n 1 : a long-bodied
limbless crawling reptile : SERPENT 2 : a
contemptible or treacherous person —
snaky adj

¹snap \'snap\ vb snapped; snap·ping
1 : to grasp or slash at something with
the teeth 2 : to utter sharp or angry
words 3 : to get or buy quickly 4 : to
break suddenly with a sharp sound
5 : to give a sharp cracking noise 6 : to
throw with a quick motion 7 : FLASH
⟨her eyes snapped⟩ 8 : to put a football
into play — snap·per n — snap·pish
adj — snap·py adj

²snap n 1 : the act or sound of snapping
2 : a short period of cold weather 3 : a
catch or fastening that closes with a
click 4 : a thin brittle cookie 5 : EN-
ERGY, VIM; also : smartness of movement
6 : the putting of the ball into play in
football

snap·drag·on \'snap-ˌdrag-ən\ n : a
garden plant with long spikes of showy
2-lipped flowers

snap·shot \-ˌshät\ n : a photograph
made by rapid exposure with a hand-
held camera

snare \'snaər\ n : a trap often consisting
of a noose — snare vb

¹snarl \'snärl\ n or vb : TANGLE

²snarl vb : to growl angrily or threateningly

³snarl n : an angry ill-tempered growl

¹snatch \'snach\ vb 1 : to try to grasp
something suddenly 2 : to seize or take
away suddenly syn clutch, seize

²snatch n 1 : an act of snatching 2 : a
short period 3 : something brief or
fragmentary ⟨~es of song⟩

¹sneak \'snēk\ vb : to move, act, or take
in a furtive manner — sneak·ing·ly
adv

²sneak n 1 : one who acts in a furtive
or shifty manner 2 : a stealthy or furtive move or escape — sneaky adj

sneak·er \'snē-kər\ n : a canvas sports
shoe with pliable rubber sole

sneer \'snior\ vb : to show scorn or contempt by curling the lip or by a jeering
tone — sneer n

sneeze \'snēz\ vb : to force the breath
out with sudden and involuntary violence — sneeze n

snick·er \'snik-ər\ or snig·ger \'snig-
ər\ n : a partly suppressed laugh —
snicker vb

snide \'snīd\ adj 1 : MEAN, LOW ⟨a ~
trick⟩ 2 : slyly disparaging ⟨a ~
remark⟩

sniff \'snif\ vb 1 : to draw air audibly
up the nose 2 : to show disdain or
scorn 3 : to detect by or as if by
smelling — sniff n

snif·fle \'snif-əl\ n : SNUFFLE — sniffle
vb

snip \'snip\ vb snipped; snip·ping
: to cut off by bits : CLIP; also : to remove by cutting off

²snip n 1 : a fragment snipped off 2 : a
simple stroke of the scissors or shears

¹snipe \'snīp\ n : any of several game
birds esp. of marshes that resemble the
related woodcocks

²snipe vb : to shoot at an exposed enemy
from a concealed position usu. at long
range

snip·py \'snip-ē\ adj : CURT, SNAPPISH

snitch \'snich\ vb : PILFER, SNATCH

sniv·el \'sniv-əl\ vb -eled or -elled;
-el·ing or -el·ling 1 : to have a running
nose; also : SNUFFLE 2 : to whine in a
snuffling manner — snivel n

snob \'snäb\ n : one who seeks association with persons of higher social
position than himself and looks down
on those he considers inferior — snobbish adj — snob·bish·ly adv — snob-
bish·ness n

snob·bery \-(ə-)rē\ n : snobbish conduct

¹snoop \'snüp\ vb : to pry in a furtive
or meddlesome way

²snoop n : a prying meddlesome person

snooze \'snüz\ vb : to take a nap : DOZE
— snooze n

snore \'snōr\ vb : to breathe with a
rough hoarse noise while sleeping —
snore n

snor·kel \'snȯr-kəl\ n : a tube projecting above the water used by swim-
mers for breathing with the head under
water

snort \'snȯrt\ vb : to force air violently
and noisily through the nose ⟨his horse
~ed⟩ — snort n

snout \'snaut\ n 1 : a long projecting
nuzzle (as of a swine) 2 : a usu. large
or grotesque nose

¹snow \'snō\ n : crystals of ice formed
from the vapor of water in the air;
also : a fall of such crystals — snowy
adj

²snow vb **1** : to fall or cause to fall in or as snow **2** : to cover or shut in with or as if with snow

snow–drop \-,dräp\ n : a plant with narrow leaves and a nodding white flower that blooms early in the spring

snow–fall \-,fȯl\ n : a fall of snow

snow–plow \-,plaů\ n : a device for clearing away snow

¹snow–shoe \-,shü\ n : a light frame of wood strung with rawhide leather worn under the shoe to prevent sinking down into soft snow

²snowshoe vb : to travel on snowshoes

snow–storm \-,stȯrm\ n : a storm of falling snow

snub \'snəb\ vb **snubbed; snub·bing 1** : to treat with disdain : SLIGHT **2** : to slow up or check the motion of : snub n

snub–nosed \-'nōzd\ adj : having a nose slightly turned up at the end

¹snuff \'snəf\ vb **1** : to pinch off the charred end of (a candle) **2** : to put out (a candle) — **snuff·er** n

²snuff vb **1** : to draw forcibly into or through the nose **2** : SMELL

³snuff n **1** : SNIFF **2** : pulverized tobacco

snuf·fle \'snəf-əl\ vb **1** : to snuff or sniff audibly and repeatedly **2** : to breathe with a sniffing sound — **snuffle** n

snug \'snəg\ adj **1** : COMFORTABLE, COZY **2** : CONCEALED (lie ~ till they go) **3** : fitting closely : TIGHT — **snug·ly** adv — **snug·ness** n

snug·gle \'snəg-əl\ vb : to curl up or draw close comfortably : NESTLE

¹so \(')sō\ adv **1** : in the manner indicated **2** : in the same way **3** : to the extent indicated **4** : THEREFORE **5** : FINALLY **6** : THUS

²so conj : for that reason (he wanted it, ~ he took it)

³so pron **1** : the same (became chairman and remained ~) **2** : approximately that (I'd like a dozen or ~)

¹soak \'sōk\ vb **1** : to remain in a liquid **2** : WET, SATURATE **3** : to draw in by or as if by absorption **syn** drench, steep, impregnate

²soak n **1** : the act of soaking **2** : the liquid in which something is soaked **3** : DRUNKARD

soap \'sōp\ n : a cleansing substance made usu. by action of alkali on fat — **soapy** adj

soap opera n [so called fr. its frequently being sponsored by soap manufacturers] : a radio or television daytime serial drama

soap·stone \'sōp-,stōn\ n : a soft stone with a soapy feel containing talc

soar \'sōr\ vb : to fly upward or at a height on or as if on wings

sob \'säb\ vb **sobbed; sob·bing** : to weep with convulsive heavings of the chest or contractions of the throat — **sob** n

so·ber \'sō-bər\ adj **1** : temperate in the use of liquor **2** : not drunk **3** : serious or grave in mood or disposition **4** : not affected by passion or prejudice **syn** solemn, earnest — **so·ber·ly** adv — **so·ber·ness** n

so·bri·ety \sə-'brī-ət-ē\ n : the quality

or state of being sober : SOBERNESS

so·bri·quet \'sō-bri-,kā, -,ket\ n : NICK-NAME

so–called \'sō-'kȯld\ adj : commonly or popularly but often inaccurately so termed (the ~ pocket veto) (his ~ friend)

soc·cer \'säk-ər\ n : a football game played on a field by two teams with a round inflated ball

¹so·cia·ble \'sō-shə-bəl\ adj **1** : liking companionship : FRIENDLY **2** : characterized by pleasant social relations **syn** gracious, cordial, affable, genial — **so·cia·bil·i·ty** \,sō-shə-'bil-ət-ē\ n — **so·cia·bly** \'sō-shə-blē\ adv

²sociable n : an informal social gathering

¹so·cial \'sō-shəl\ adj **1** : marked by pleasant companionship with one's friends **2** : naturally living or growing in groups or communities (~ insects) **3** : of or relating to human society, the interaction of the group and its members, and the welfare of these members (~ legislation) (~ behavior) **4** : of, relating to, or based on rank in a particular society (different ~ circles); also : of or relating to fashionable society (a ~ leader) **5** : SOCIALIST — **so·cial·ly** adv

²social n : a social gathering

so·cial·ism n : a theory of social organization based on government ownership, management, or control of the means of production and the distribution and exchange of goods — **so·cial·ist** n or adj — **so·cial·is·tic** \,sō-shə-'lis-tik\ adj

so·cial·ize \'sō-shə-,līz\ vb **1** : to regulate according to the theory and practice of socialism **2** : to adapt to social needs or uses : organize on a social basis — **so·cial·iza·tion** \,sō-shə-lə-'zā-shən\ n

so·ci·ety \sə-'sī-ət-ē\ n **1** : COMPANIONSHIP **2** : community life **3** : a part of a community bound together by common interests and standards; esp : a leisure class indulging in social affairs **4** : a voluntary association of persons for common ends

so·ci·ol·o·gy \,sō-s(h)ē-'äl-ə-jē\ n : the study of the development and structure of society and social relationships — **so·ci·o·log·i·cal** \-ə-'läj-i-kəl\ adj — **so·ci·ol·o·gist** \-'äl-ə-jəst\ n

¹sock \'säk\ n, pl **socks 1** or pl **sox 1** : a stocking with a short leg **2** : comic drama

²sock vb : to hit, strike, or apply forcefully

³sock n : a vigorous blow : PUNCH

sock·et \'säk-ət\ n : an opening or hollow that receives and holds something (an eye ~) (an electric light ~)

¹sod \'säd\ n : the surface layer of the soil filled with roots (as of grass)

²sod vb **sod·ded; sod·ding** : to cover with sod or turfs

so·da \'sōd-ə\ n **1** : a powdery saltlike substance used in washing and making glass **2** : SODIUM BICARBONATE **3** : SODIUM **4** : SODA WATER **5** : a sweet drink of soda water, flavoring, and often ice cream

soda pop n : SODA WATER 2

soda water n **1** : a beverage of water

charged with carbon dioxide **2** : a soft
drink of soda water with flavoring and
a sweet syrup

sod·den \'säd-ən\ *adj* **1** : lacking
spirit : DULLED **2** : SOAKED, DRENCHED
3 : heavy or doughy from being improperly cooked (~ biscuits)

so·di·um \'sōd-ē-əm\ *n* : a soft waxy
silver-white metallic chemical element
occurring in nature in combined form
(as in salt)

sodium bicarbonate *n* : BICARBONATE OF
SODA

sodium carbonate *n* : a carbonate of
sodium used esp. in washing and bleaching textiles

sodium chloride *n* : SALT 1

sodium hydroxide *n* : a white brittle
caustic substance used in making soap
and rayon and in bleaching

sodium nitrate *n* : a crystalline salt found
in rock in Chile and used as a fertilizer
and in curing meat

so·ev·er \sō-'ev-ər\ *adv* **1** : in any degree or manner (how bad ~) **2** : at all
: of any kind (any help ~)

so·fa \'sō-fə\ *n* [Ar *ṣuffah* long bench]
: a couch usu. with upholstered back and
arms

soft \'sȯft\ *adj* **1** : not hard or rough
: NONVIOLENT **2** : RESTFUL, GENTLE,
SOOTHING **3** : emotionally susceptible
4 : not prepared to endure hardship
5 : not containing certain salts that
prevent lathering (~ water) **6** : not
alcoholic **7** : BITUMINOUS (~ coal)
syn bland, mild — **soft·ly** *adv* — **soft·
ness** *n*

soft·ball \'sȯf(t)-ˌbȯl\ *n* : a game similar
to baseball played with a ball larger and
softer than a baseball; *also* : the ball
used in this game

soft·en \'sȯ-fən\ *vb* **1** : to make or become soft — **soft·en·er** *n*

sog·gy \'säg-ē\ *adj* : heavy with moisture : SOAKED, SODDEN — **sog·gi·ly** *adv*
— **sog·gi·ness** *n*

¹soil \'sȯil\ *vb* **1** : CORRUPT, POLLUTE
2 : to make or become dirty **3** : STAIN,
DISGRACE

²soil *n* **1** : STAIN, DEFILEMENT **2** : EXCRE-
MENT, WASTE

³soil *n* **1** : firm land : EARTH **2** : the
loose surface material of the earth in
which plants grow **3** : COUNTRY,
REGION

soi·ree *or* **soi·rée** \swä-'rā\ *n* : an evening party

so·journ \'sō-ˌjərn, sō-'jərn\ *vb* **1** : to
dwell in a place temporarily — **sojourn**
n — **so·journ·er** *n*

sol \'säl, 'sōl\ *n, pl* **so·les** \'sō-ˌläs\ :
see MONEY table

Sol \'säl\ *n* : SUN

¹sol·ace \'säl-əs\ *n* : relief from grief or
anxiety : COMFORT

²solace *vb* : to give solace to : CONSOLE

so·lar \'sō-lər\ *adj* **1** : of, from, or relating to the sun (~ heat) **2** : measured
by the earth's course in relation to the
sun (the ~ year) **3** : operated by or
utilizing the sun's heat (~ battery) (~
house)

so·lar·i·um \sō-'lar-ē-əm\ *n, pl* **-ia**
\-ē-ə\ *also* **-i·ums** : a room exposed to
the sun; *esp* : a room in a hospital for
exposure of the body to sunshine

solar plex·us \-'plek-səs\ *n* **1** : a network of nerves situated behind the
stomach **2** : the hollow below the lower
end of the breastbone

solar system *n* : the sun with the group

of celestial bodies that revolve about it

sold *past of* SELL

¹sol·der \'säd-ər\ *n* : a metallic alloy
used when melted to mend or join metallic surfaces

²solder *vb* **1** : to unite or repair with
solder **2** : to join securely : CEMENT

¹sol·dier \'sōl-jər\ *n* : a person in military service; *esp* : an enlisted man as
distinguished from a commissioned officer — **sol·dier·ly** *adj or adv*

²soldier *vb* **1** : to serve as a soldier
2 : to pretend to work while actually
doing nothing

soldier of fortune : ADVENTURER

sol·diery *n* **1** : a body of soldiers **2** : the
profession of soldiering

¹sole \'sōl\ *n* **1** : the undersurface of
the foot **2** : the bottom of a shoe

²sole *vb* : to furnish (a shoe) with a sole

³sole *n* : any of various mostly small-
mouthed flatfishes valued as food

⁴sole *adj* : ONLY, SINGLE — **sole·ly**
\'sō(l)-lē\ *adv*

sol·e·cism \'säl-ə-ˌsiz-əm\ *n* **1** : a mistake in grammar **2** : a breach of etiquette

sol·emn \'säl-əm\ *adj* **1** : marked by or
observed with full religious ceremony
2 : FORMAL, CEREMONIOUS **3** : highly
serious **4** : GRAVE **5** : SOMBER, GLOOMY
syn ceremonial, conventional, sober —
so·lem·ni·ty \sə-'lem-nət-ē\ *n* — **sol·
emn·ly** \'säl-əm-lē\ *adv* — **sol·emn·
ness** *n*

sol·em·nize \'säl-əm-ˌnīz\ *vb* **1** : to
observe or honor with solemnity **2** : to
perform (as a marriage ceremony) with
solemn rites — **sol·em·ni·za·tion** \ˌsäl-
əm-nə-'zā-shən\ *n*

so·lic·it \sə-'lis-ət\ *vb* **1** : ENTREAT, BEG
2 : to approach with a request or plea
3 : TEMPT, LURE **syn** ask, request —
so·lic·i·ta·tion \-ˌlis-ə-'tā-shən\ *n*

so·lic·i·tor \-'lis-ət-ər\ *n* **1** : one that
solicits (as subscriptions or contributions) **2** : LAWYER; *esp* : a legal official
of a city or state

so·lic·i·tous \-ət-əs\ *adj* **1** : WORRIED,
CONCERNED **2** : EAGER, WILLING **syn**
careful, anxious — **so·lic·i·tous·ly** *adv*

so·lic·i·tude \-ə-ˌt(y)üd\ *n* : CONCERN,
ANXIETY

¹sol·id \'säl-əd\ *adj* **1** : not hollow;
also : written as one word without a
hyphen (a ~ compound) **2** : having,
involving, or dealing with three dimensions or with solids (~ geometry)
3 : not loose or spongy : COMPACT (a ~
mass of rock); *also* : neither gaseous nor
liquid : HARD, RIGID (~ ice) **4** : of
good substantial quality or kind (~
comfort) **5** : UNANIMOUS, UNITED (~
for pay increases) **6** : thoroughly dependable : RELIABLE (a ~ citizen);
also : serious in purpose or character
(~ reading) **7** : of one substance or
character — **solid** *adv* — **so·lid·i·ty**
\sə-'lid-ət-ē\ *n* — **sol·id·ly** \'säl-əd-lē\
adv — **sol·id·ness** *n*

²solid *n* **1** : a geometrical figure (as a
cube or sphere) having 3 dimensions
2 : a solid substance

sol·i·dar·i·ty \ˌsäl-ə-'dar-ət-ē\ *n* : a
unity of interest or purpose among a
group

so·lid·i·fy \sə-'lid-ə-ˌfī\ *vb* : to make
or become solid — **so·lid·i·fi·ca·tion**
\-ˌlid-ə-fə-'kā-shən\ *n*

so·lil·o·quize \sə-'lil-ə-ˌkwīz\ *vb* : to
talk to oneself : utter a soliloquy

so·lil·o·quy \-kwē\ *n* **1** : the act of

talking to oneself **2** : a dramatic monologue that gives the illusion of being a series of unspoken reflections

sol·i·taire \'säl-ə-ˌtaər\ n **1** : a single gem (as a diamond) set alone **2** : a card game played by one person alone

sol·i·tary \-ˌter-ē\ adj **1** : being or living apart from others **2** : LONELY, SECLUDED **3** : SOLE, ONLY

sol·i·tude \-ˌt(y)üd\ n **1** : the state of being alone : SECLUSION **2** : a lonely place syn isolation

¹so·lo \'sō-lō\ n **1** : a piece of music for a single voice or instrument with or without accompaniment **2** : an action in which there is only one performer — **solo** adj or vb — **so·lo·ist** n

²solo adv : without a companion : ALONE

sol·stice \'säl-stəs\ n : the time of the year when the sun is farthest north (**summer solstice**) about June 22 or south (**winter solstice**) about Dec. 22 of the equator — **sol·sti·tial** \säl-'stish-əl\ adj

sol·u·ble \'säl-yə-bəl\ adj **1** : capable of being dissolved in liquid **2** : capable of being solved or explained — **sol·u·bil·i·ty** \ˌsäl-yə-'bil-ət-ē\ n

so·lu·tion \sə-'lü-shən\ n **1** : an action or process of solving a problem; also : an answer to a problem **2** : an act or the process by which one substance is mixed with another usu. liquid substance forming a mixture consisting apparently of only one substance; also : a mixture thus formed

solve \'sälv\ vb : to find the answer to or a solution for — **solv·able** adj

sol·ven·cy \'säl-vən-sē\ n : the condition of being solvent

¹sol·vent \-vənt\ adj **1** : able or sufficient to pay all legal debts **2** : dissolving or able to dissolve

²solvent n : a usu. liquid substance capable of dissolving or dispersing one or more other substances

so·ma·lo \sə-'mäl-ō\ n, pl **so·ma·li** \-ē\ — see MONEY table

som·ber \'säm-bər\ adj **1** : DARK, GLOOMY **2** : GRAVE, MELANCHOLY — **som·ber·ly** adv

som·bre·ro \səm-'bre(ə)r-ō\ n : a broadbrimmed felt hat worn esp. in the Southwest and in Spanish America

¹some \(')səm\ adj **1** : one unspecified ⟨~ man called⟩ **2** : an unspecified or indefinite number of ⟨~ berries are ripe⟩ **3** : at least a few or a little ⟨~ years ago⟩

²some pron : a certain number or amount ⟨~ of them are here⟩ ⟨~ of it's missing⟩

¹-some \səm\ adj suffix : characterized by a (specified) thing, quality, state, or action ⟨awesome⟩ ⟨burdensome⟩

²-some \səm\ n suffix : a group of (so many) members and esp. persons ⟨foursome⟩

¹some·body \'səm-ˌbäd-ē\ pron : some person

²somebody n : a person of importance

some·day \-ˌdā\ adv : at some future time

some·how \-ˌhaú\ adv : by some means

some·one \-(ˌ)wən\ pron : some person

som·er·sault \'səm-ər-ˌsólt\ n : a leap or roll in which a person turns his heels over his head — **somersault** vb

som·er·set \-ˌset\ n or vb : SOMERSAULT

some·thing \'səm-thiŋ\ pron : some undetermined or unspecified thing

some·time \-ˌtīm\ adv **1** : at a future time **2** : at an unknown or unnamed time

some·times \-ˌtīmz\ adv : OCCASIONALLY

¹some·what \-ˌhwät, -ˌhwət\ pron **1** : a certain part or amount : SOME ⟨told them ~ of his adventures⟩ **2** : one with certain qualities

²somewhat adv : by a little : in some degree

some·where \-ˌhweər\ adv : in, at, or to an unknown or unnamed place

som·nam·bu·lism \säm-'nam-byə-ˌliz-əm\ n : activity (as walking about) during sleep — **som·nam·bu·list** n

som·no·lent \'säm-nə-lənt\ adj : SLEEPY, DROWSY — **som·no·lence** n

son \'sən\ n **1** : a male offspring or descendant **2** cap : Jesus Christ **3** : a person deriving from a particular source (as a country, race, or school)

so·nar \'sō-ˌnär\ n : an apparatus that detects the presence and location of submerged objects (as submarines) by reflected vibrations

so·na·ta \sə-'nät-ə\ n : an instrumental composition with three or four movements differing in rhythm and mood but related in key

song \'sóŋ\ n **1** : vocal music; also : a short composition of words and music **2** : poetic composition **3** : a small amount ⟨sold for a ~⟩

song·bird \-ˌbərd\ n : a bird with musical tones; also : SINGING BIRD

song·ster \-stər\ n : one that sings — **song·stress** \-strəs\ n

son·ic \'sän-ik\ adj : of or relating to sound waves or the speed of sound

son-in-law n, pl **sons-in-law** : the husband of one's daughter

son·net \'sän-ət\ n : a poem of 14 lines usu. in iambic pentameter with a definite rhyme scheme

so·no·rous \sə-'nōr-əs, 'sän-ə-rəs\ adj **1** : giving out sound when struck **2** : loud, deep, or rich in sound : RESONANT **3** : high-sounding : IMPRESSIVE — **so·nor·i·ty** \sə-'nór-ət-ē\ n

soon \'sün\ adv **1** : before long **2** : PROMPTLY, QUICKLY **3** : EARLY **4** : WILLINGLY, READILY

soot \'sút, 'sət\ n : a black substance that is formed when something burns, that colors smoke, and that sticks to the sides of the chimney carrying the smoke — **sooty** adj

sooth \'süth\ n, archaic : TRUTH

soothe \'süth\ vb **1** : to please by flattery or attention **2** : to calm down : REASSURE, COMFORT — **sooth·er** n — **sooth·ing·ly** adv

sooth·say·er \'süth-ˌsā-ər\ n : one that foretells events — **sooth·say·ing** n

¹sop \'säp\ vb sopped; sop·ping **1** : to steep or dip in or as if in a liquid **2** : to wet thoroughly : SOAK; also : to mop up (a liquid)

²sop n : a conciliatory bribe, gift, or concession

soph·ism \'säf-ˌiz-əm\ n **1** : an argument correct in form but embodying a subtle fallacy **2** : SOPHISTRY

ə abut; ᵉ kitten; ər further; a back; ā bake; ä cot, cart; aú out; ch chin; e less; ē easy; g gift; i trip; ī life; j joke; ŋ sing; ō flow; ó flaw; ói coin; th thin; th this; ü loot; ú foot; y yet; yü few; yú furious; zh vision

soph·ist \-əst\ *n* **:** PHILOSOPHER; *esp* **:** a captious or fallacious reasoner

so·phis·tic \sə-'fis-tik\ *or* **so·phis·ti·cal** *adj* **:** of or characteristic of sophists or sophistry **syn** fallacious

so·phis·ti·cat·ed \sə-'fis-tə-ˌkāt-əd\ *adj* **1 :** made wise or worldly-wise by experience or disillusionment **:** not innocent or naïve **2 :** intellectually appealing (~ novel) **3 :** COMPLEX (~ instruments) — **so·phis·ti·ca·tion** \-ˌfis-tə-'kā-shən\ *n*

soph·ist·ry \'säf-ə-strē\ *n* **:** subtly fallacious reasoning or argument

soph·o·more \'säf-(ˌ)ə-ˌmōr\ *n* **:** a student in his 2d year of college or secondary school

sop·o·rif·ic \ˌsäp-ə-'rif-ik, ˌsōp-\ *adj* **1 :** causing sleep or drowsiness **2 :** LETHARGIC

so·pra·no \sə-'pran-ō\ *n* **1 :** the highest singing voice; *also* **:** a part for this voice **2 :** a singer with a soprano voice — **soprano** *adj*

sor·cery \'sȯrs-(ə-)rē\ *n* **:** the use of magic **:** WITCHCRAFT — **sor·cer·er** \-rər\ *n* — **sor·cer·ess** \-rəs\ *n*

sor·did \'sȯrd-əd\ *adj* **1 :** FILTHY, DIRTY **2 :** marked by baseness or grossness **:** VILE — **sor·did·ly** *adv* — **sor·did·ness** *n*

¹sore \'sōr\ *adj* **1 :** causing pain or distress (~ news) (a ~ bruise) **2 :** painfully sensitive **:** TENDER (~ eyes) **3 :** SEVERE, INTENSE **4 :** IRRITATED, ANGRY — **sore·ly** *adv* — **sore·ness** *n*

²sore *n* **1 :** a sore spot on the body; *esp* **:** one (as an ulcer) with the tissues broken and usu. infected **2 :** a source of pain or vexation

sor·ghum \'sȯr-gəm\ *n* **:** a tall variable Old World tropical grass grown widely for its edible seed, for forage, or for its sweet juice which yields a syrup

so·ror·i·ty \sə-'rȯr-ət-ē\ *n* [ML *sororitas* sisterhood, fr. L *soror* sister] **:** a club of girls or women esp. at a college

sor·rel \'sȯr-əl\ *n* **:** any of several sour-juiced herbs

sor·row \'sär-ō\ *n* **1 :** pain of mind caused by some loss **:** SADNESS **2 :** repentance for having done something wrong **3 :** a cause of grief — **sor·row·ful** *adj* — **sor·row·ful·ly** *adv*

sor·ry \'sär-ē\ *adj* **1 :** feeling sorrow, regret, or penitence **2 :** WORTHLESS, CONTEMPTIBLE **3 :** DISMAL, GLOOMY

¹sort \'sȯrt\ *n* **1 :** a group of persons or things that have similar characteristics **:** CLASS **2 :** WAY, MANNER **3 :** QUALITY, NATURE

²sort *vb* **1 :** to put in a certain place according to kind, class, or nature **2** *archaic* **:** to be in accord **:** AGREE

sor·tie \'sȯrt-ē, sȯr-'tē\ *n* **1 :** an assault by troops from a besieged place against the besiegers **2 :** one mission or attack by one airplane

so-so \'sō-ˌsō\ *adv (or adj)* **:** PASSABLY

sot \'sät\ *n* **1 :** a habitual drunkard — **sot·tish** *adj*

sou·brette \sü-'bret\ *n* **:** a coquettish maidservant or a frivolous young woman in a comedy; *also* **:** an actress playing such a part

souf·flé \sü-'flā\ *n* **:** a spongy hot dish made light in baking by stiffly beaten egg whites

sough \'saú, 'səf\ *n* **:** a murmuring sighing sound (as of the wind through trees) — **sough** *vb*

sought *past of* SEEK

soul \'sōl\ *n* **1 :** the immaterial essence of an individual life **2 :** the spiritual principle embodied in human beings or the universe **3 :** an active or essential part **4 :** man's moral and emotional nature **5 :** spiritual or moral force **6 :** PERSON (a kindly ~) — **soul·less** \'sōl-ləs\ *adj*

soul·ful \-fəl\ *adj* **:** full of or expressing deep feeling — **soul·ful·ly** *adv*

¹sound \'saúnd\ *adj* **1 :** free from flaw or defect **2 :** not diseased or sickly **:** HEALTHY **3 :** FIRM, STRONG **4 :** SOLID **5 :** free from error **:** RIGHT **6 :** showing good judgment **7 :** THOROUGH **8 :** UNDISTURBED (~ sleep) **9 :** LEGAL, VALID — **sound·ly** *adv* — **sound·ness** *n*

²sound *n* **1 :** the sensation experienced through the sense of hearing; *also* **:** mechanical energy transmitted by longitudinal pressure waves (as in air) that is the stimulus to hearing **2 :** something heard **:** NOISE, TONE; *also* **:** hearing distance **:** EARSHOT — **sound·less** *adj* — **sound·less·ly** *adv*

³sound *vb* **1 :** to make or cause to make a noise **2 :** to order or proclaim by a sound (~ the alarm) **3 :** to convey a certain impression **:** SEEM **4 :** to examine the condition of by causing to give out sounds — **sound·er** *n*

⁴sound *n* **1 :** a long passage of water wider than a strait often connecting two larger bodies of water (Long Island ~) **2 :** the air bladder of a fish

⁵sound *vb* **1 :** to measure the depth of (water) esp. by a weighted line dropped from the surface **:** FATHOM **2 :** PROBE **3 :** to dive down suddenly (the hooked fish ~ed)

¹soup \'süp\ *n* **1 :** a liquid food with a meat, fish, or vegetable stock as a base and often containing pieces of solid food **2 :** something having the consistency of soup **3 :** an unfortunate predicament (in the ~)

²soup *vb* **:** to increase the power of (~ up an engine) — **souped-up** \'süpt-'əp\ *adj*

¹sour \'saú(ə)r\ *adj* **1 :** having an acid or tart taste (~ as vinegar) **2 :** SPOILED, PUTRID (a ~ odor) **3 :** UNPLEASANT, DISAGREEABLE (~ disposition) — **sour·ish** *adj* — **sour·ly** *adv* — **sour·ness** *n*

²sour *vb* **:** to become or make sour

source \'sōrs\ *n* **1 :** the beginning of a stream of water **2 :** ORIGIN, BEGINNING **3 :** a supplier of information

¹souse \'saús\ *vb* **1 :** PICKLE **2 :** to plunge into a liquid **3 :** DRENCH **4 :** to make drunk

²souse *n* **1 :** something (as pigs' feet) steeped in pickle **2 :** BRINE **3 :** a soaking in liquid **4 :** DRUNKARD

¹south \'saúth\ *adv* **:** to or toward the south

²south *adj* **1 :** situated toward or at the south **2 :** coming from the south

³south *n* **1 :** the direction to the right of one facing east **2 :** the compass point directly opposite to north **3** *cap* **:** regions or countries south of a specified or implied point; *esp* **:** the part of the U.S. that lies south of the Mason-Dixon line, the Ohio river, and the southern boundaries of Missouri and Kansas — **south·er·ly** \'səth-ər-lē\ *adv or adj* — **south·ern** \'səth-ərn\ *adj* — **Southern·er** *n* — **south·ern·most** *adj* — **south·ward** \'saúth-wərd\ *adv or adj* — **south·wards** *adv*

south·east \saúth-'ēst\ *n* **1 :** the general direction between south and east 2 : the compass point midway between south and east 3 *cap* : regions or countries southeast of a specified or implied point — southeast *adj or adv* — south-east·er·ly *adv or adj* — south·east·ern *adj*

south·east·er *n* : a storm or strong wind coming from the southeast

south pole *n, often cap S & P* : the southernmost point of the earth

south·west \saùth-'west\ *n* 1 : the general direction between south and west 2 : the compass point midway between south and west 3 *cap* : regions or countries southwest of a specified or implied point — southwest *adj or adv* — south·west·er·ly *adv or adj* — south·west·ern *adj*

sou·ve·nir \'sü-və-,niər\ *n* : something serving as a reminder

sou'·west·er \saù-'wes-tər\ *n* : a waterproof hat worn at sea in stormy weather, *also* : a long waterproof coat

¹**sov·er·eign** \'säv-(ə-)rən\ *n* 1 : one possessing the supreme power and authority in a state 2 : a gold coin of Great Britain worth 1 pound

²**sovereign** *adj* 1 : CHIEF, HIGHEST 2 : supreme in power or authority 3 : having independent authority 4 : EXCELLENT, FINE **syn** dominant, predominant, paramount, free

sov·er·eign·ty \-tē\ *n* 1 : supremacy in rule or power 2 : power to govern without external control 3 : the supreme political power in a state

so·vi·et \'sōv-ē-,et, 'säv-, -ē-ət\ *n* 1 : an elected governmental council in a Communist country 2 *pl, cap* : the people and esp. the leaders of the U.S.S.R. — **so·vi·et·ism** *n, often cap* — **so·vi·et·ize** *vb, often cap*

¹**sow** \'saù\ *n* : a female swine

²**sow** \'sō\ *vb* **sowed; sown** \'sōn\ or **sowed; sow·ing** 1 : to plant seed for growing esp. by scattering 2 : to strew with or as if with seed 3 : to scatter abroad — **sow·er** *n*

sox *pl of* SOCK

soy \'sói\ *n* : a sauce made from soybeans fermented in brine

soy·bean \-,bēn\ *n* : an Asiatic legume widely grown for forage and for its edible seeds that yield a valuable oil (soybean oil); *also* : its seed

spa \'spä\ *n* [fr. *Spa*, watering place in Belgium] : a mineral spring; *also* : a resort with mineral springs

¹**space** \'spās\ *n* 1 : the limitless area in which all things exist and move 2 : some small measurable part of space 3 : the region beyond the earth's atmosphere 4 : a definite place (as a seat or stateroom on a train or ship) 5 : a period of time 6 : an empty place

²**space** *vb* : to place at intervals : arrange with spaces in between

space·man \-,man\ *n* : one concerned with traveling beyond the earth's atmosphere

space·ship \'spās(h)-,ship\ *n* : a man-carrying vehicle for travel beyond the earth's atmosphere

space station *n* : a manned artificial satellite in a fixed orbit serving as a base (as for refueling spaceships)

space suit *n* : a suit with provisions to make life beyond the earth's atmosphere possible for its wearer

spa·cious \'spā-shəs\ *adj* : very large in extent : ROOMY **syn** commodious, capacious, ample — **spa·cious·ly** *adv* — **spa·cious·ness** *n*

¹**spade** \'spād\ *n* : a shovel with a flat blade — **spade·ful** *n*

²**spade** *vb* : to dig with a spade

³**spade** *n* : any of a suit of playing cards marked with a black figure resembling an inverted heart with a short stem at the bottom

spa·ghet·ti \spə-'get-ē\ *n* : a dough made chiefly from wheat flour and formed in thin solid strings

¹**span** \'span\ *n* 1 : an English unit of length equal to 9 inches 2 : a limited portion of time 3 : the spread of an arch, beam, truss, or girder from one support to another 4 : a pair of animals (as mules) driven together

²**span** *vb* **spanned; span·ning** 1 : MEASURE 2 : to extend over or reach across

span·gle \'spaŋ-gəl\ *n* : a small disk of shining metal used esp. on a dress for ornament — **spangle** *vb*

Span·iard \'span-yərd\ *n* : a native or inhabitant of Spain

span·iel \'span-yəl\ *n* : any of several mostly small and short-legged dogs with long silky hair and drooping ears

Span·ish \'span-ish\ *n* 1 **Spanish** *pl* : the people of Spain 2 : the chief language of Spain and of many countries colonized by the Spanish — **Spanish** *adj*

Spanish American *n* : a native or inhabitant of a country colonized by Spain in South or Central America; *also* : a resident of the U.S. whose native language is Spanish — **Spanish-American** *adj*

Spanish fly *n* : a green European beetle containing a substance irritating to the skin; *also* : a dried preparation of these beetles

spank \'spaŋk\ *vb* : to strike the buttocks of with the open hand — **spank** *n*

spank·ing *adj* : BRISK, LIVELY (~ breeze)

¹**spar** \'spär\ *n* : a rounded wood or metal piece (as a mast, yard, boom, or gaff) for supporting sail rigging

²**spar** *vb* **sparred; spar·ring** 1 : to box scientifically without serious hitting; *also* : SKIRMISH, WRANGLE

¹**spare** \'spaər\ *vb* 1 : to use frugally or rarely 2 : to exempt from something 3 : to get along without 4 : to refrain from punishing or injuring : show mercy to

²**spare** *adj* 1 : held in reserve : SUPERFLUOUS 3 : not liberal or profuse 4 : LEAN, THIN 5 : SCANTY **syn** extra, lanky, scrawny, meager, sparse, skimpy

³**spare** *n* 1 : a duplicate kept in reserve; *esp* : a spare tire 2 : the knocking down of all the bowling pins with the first two balls

spar·ing \'spa(ə)r-iŋ\ *adj* : SAVING, FRUGAL **syn** thrifty, economical — **spar·ing·ly** *adv*

¹**spark** \'spärk\ *n* 1 : a small particle of a burning substance or a hot glowing particle struck from a mass (as by steel on flint) 2 : SPARKLE 3 : a particle

ə abut; ᵊ kitten; ər further; a back; ā bake; ä cot, cart; aù out; ch chin; e less; ē easy; g gift; i trip; ī life; j joke; ŋ sing; ō flow; ò flaw; ói coin; th thin; th̲ this; ü loot; ù foot; y yet; yü few; yù furious; zh vision

capable of being kindled or developed : GERM   4 : a luminous electrical discharge of short duration between two conductors

³**spark** *vb* 1 : to emit or produce sparks   2 : to stir to activity : INCITE

³**spark** *n* : DANDY, GALLANT

¹**spar·kle** \'spär-kəl\ *vb* 1 : FLASH, GLEAM   2 : EFFERVESCE   3 : to perform brilliantly — **spark·ler** \-k(ə-)lər\ *n*

³**sparkle** *n* 1 : a little spark : GLEAM   2 : ANIMATION

spark plug *n* : a device that produces a spark for combustion in an engine cylinder

spar·row \'spar-ō\ *n* : any of several small dull singing birds

sparse \'spärs\ *adj* : thinly scattered : SCANTY   **syn** meager, spare, skimpy — **sparse·ly** *adv*

spasm \'spaz-əm\ *n* 1 : an involuntary and abnormal muscular contraction   2 : a sudden, violent, and temporary effort or feeling — **spas·mod·ic** \spaz-'mäd-ik\ *adj* — **spas·mod·i·cal·ly** *adv*

spas·tic \'spas-tik\ *adj* : of, relating to, or marked by muscular spasm (~ paralysis) — **spastic** *n*

¹**spat** \'spat\ *past of* SPIT

²**spat** *n* : the young of a bivalve mollusk (as the oyster)

³**spat** *n* : a gaiter covering instep and ankle

⁴**spat** *n* : a brief petty quarrel : DISPUTE

⁵**spat** *vb* **spat·ted; spat·ting** : to quarrel briefly

spate \'spāt\ *n* : a sudden outburst : RUSH

spa·tial \'spā-shəl\ *adj* : of or relating to space — **spa·tial·ly** *adv*

spat·ter \'spat-ər\ *vb* 1 : to splash with drops of liquid   2 : to sprinkle around — **spatter** *n*

spat·u·la \'spach-ə-lə\ *n* : a flexible knifelike implement for scooping, spreading, or mixing soft substances (as paints or drugs)

spav·in \'spav-ən\ *n* : a bony enlargement of the hock of a horse — **spav·ined** *adj*

¹**spawn** \'spȯn\ *vb* 1 : to produce eggs or offspring esp. in large numbers   2 : to bring forth : GENERATE

²**spawn** *n* 1 : the eggs of water animals (as fishes or oysters) that lay many small eggs   2 : offspring esp. when produced in great quantities

spay \'spā\ *vb* : to remove the ovaries from (an animal)

speak \'spēk\ *vb* **spoke** \'spōk\ **spoken** \'spō-kən\ **speak·ing** 1 : to utter words   2 : to express orally : make known one's thoughts, feelings, or opinions in words   3 : to address an audience   4 : to use or be able to use (a language) in speech — **speak·er** *n*

speak·easy \-‚ē-zē\ *n* : an illicit drinking place

¹**spear** \'spiər\ *n* 1 : a long-shafted weapon with a sharp point for thrusting or throwing   2 : a sharp-pointed instrument with barbs (as for spearing fish)   3 : a young shoot (as of grass) — **spear·man** \-mən\ *n*

²**spear** *vb* : to strike or pierce with or as if with a spear

spear·mint \-‚(‚)mint\ *n* : a common highly aromatic garden mint

spe·cial \'spesh-əl\ *adj* 1 : UNCOMMON, NOTEWORTHY   2 : INDIVIDUAL, UNIQUE   3 : particularly favored   4 : EXTRA, ADDITIONAL   5 : confined to or designed

for a definite field of action, purpose, or occasion — **special** *n* — **spe·cial·ly** *adv*

spe·cial·ist *n* 1 : one who devotes himself to some special branch of learning or activity   2 : an army enlisted man holding any of several ranks that correspond to the ranks of noncommissioned officers

spe·cial·ize *vb* : to concentrate one's efforts in a special activity or field; *also* : to change in an adaptive manner — **spe·cial·iza·tion** \‚spesh-ə-lə-'zā-shən\ *n*

spe·cial·ty \'spesh-əl-tē\ *n* 1 : a particular quality or detail   2 : a product of a special kind or of special excellence   3 : a branch of knowledge, business, or professional work in which one specializes

spe·cie \'spē-shē\ *n* : money in coin usu. of gold or silver

spe·cies \'spē-shēz\ *n, pl* **species** [L, appearance, kind, species, fr. *specere* to look] 1 : SORT, KIND   2 : a taxonomic group comprising closely related organisms potentially able to breed with one another

¹**spe·cif·ic** \spi-'sif-ik\ *adj* 1 : of, relating to, or constituting a species   2 : DEFINITE, EXACT   3 : having a unique relation to something (~ antibodies); *esp* : exerting a distinctive and usu. curative or causative influence — **spe·cif·i·cal·ly** *adv*

²**specific** *n* : a specific remedy

spec·i·fi·ca·tion \‚spes-ə-fə-'kā-shən\ *n* 1 : something specified : ITEM   2 : a description of work to be done and materials to be used (as in building) — usu. used in pl.

specific gravity *n* : the ratio of the weight of any volume of a substance to the weight of an equal volume of another substance (as water for solids and liquids or air or hydrogen for gases) taken as the standard

spec·i·fy \'spes-ə-‚fī\ *vb* : to mention or name explicitly or in detail

spec·i·men \'spes-ə-mən\ *n* : a part or a single thing that shows what the whole thing or group is like : SAMPLE

spe·cious \'spē-shəs\ *adj* : seeming to be genuine, correct, or beautiful but not really so (~ reasoning)

speck \'spek\ *n* 1 : a small spot or blemish   2 : a small particle : BIT — **speck** *vb*

speck·le \-əl\ *n* : a little speck — **speck·le** *vb*

spec·ta·cle \'spek-ti-kəl\ *n* 1 : something exhibited to view; *esp* : an impressive public display   2 *pl* : GLASS 3; *esp* : glasses held in place by pieces passing over the ears — **spec·ta·cled** *adj*

spec·tac·u·lar \spek-'tak-yə-lər\ *adj* : SENSATIONAL, STRIKING, SHOWY

spec·ta·tor \'spek-‚tāt-ər\ *n* : one who looks on (as at a sports event)   **syn** observer, witness

spec·ter *or* **spec·tre** \'spek-tər\ *n* : a visible disembodied spirit : APPARITION, GHOST

spec·tral \-trəl\ *adj* 1 : of, relating to, or resembling a specter   2 : of, relating to, or made by a spectrum (~ analysis)

spec·tro·scope \'spek-trə-‚skōp\ *n* : an optical instrument for forming and examining spectra — **spec·tro·scop·ic** \‚spek-trə-'skäp-ik\ *adj*

spec·trum \'spek-trəm\ *n, pl* **-tra** \-trə\ *or* **-trums** 1 : a series of colors formed when a beam of white light is dispersed (as by a prism) so that its parts are arranged in the order of their wavelengths **2** : a series of radiations arranged in regular order **3** : a continuous sequence or range ⟨a wide ∼ of political opinions⟩

spec·u·late \'spek-yə-ˌlāt\ *vb* **1** : REFLECT, MEDITATE **2** : to engage in a business deal where a good profit may be made at considerable risk **syn** reason, think, deliberate — **spec·u·la·tion** \ˌspek-yə-'lā-shən\ *n* — **spec·u·la·tive** \'spek-yə-ˌlāt-iv\ *adj* — **spec·u·la·tive·ly** *adv* — **spec·u·la·tor** \-ˌlāt-ər\ *n*

speech \'spēch\ *n* **1** : the power of speaking **2** : act or manner of speaking **3** : TALK, CONVERSATION **4** : a public discourse **5** : LANGUAGE, DIALECT — **speech·less** *adj*

¹speed \'spēd\ *n* **1** *archaic* : SUCCESS **2** : SWIFTNESS, RAPIDITY **3** : rate of motion or performance **4** : a transmission gear in an automobile **syn** haste, hurry, dispatch, momentum, pace — **speed·i·ly** *adv* — **speedy** *adj*

²speed *vb* **sped** \'sped\ *or* **speed·ed**; **speed·ing** **1** : to get along : FARE, PROSPER **2** : to go fast **3** : to cause to go faster : ACCELERATE

speed·boat \-ˌbōt\ *n* : a fast launch or motorboat

speed·om·e·ter \spi-'däm-ət-ər\ *n* : an instrument for indicating speed or speed and distance traveled

speed·way \'spēd-ˌwā\ *n* : a road on which speeding is allowed; *also* : a racecourse for motor vehicles

speed·well \-ˌwel\ *n* : a low creeping plant with spikes of small usu. bluish flowers

¹spell \'spel\ *n* **1** : a magic formula : INCANTATION **2** : a controlling influence

²spell *vb* **1** : to name, write, or print in order the letters of a word **2** : MEAN, SIGNIFY

³spell *n* **1** : the relief of one person by another in any work or duty : one's turn at work or duty **3** : a period of rest from work or duty **4** : a stretch of a specified kind of weather **5** : a period of bodily or mental distress or disorder : ATTACK

⁴spell *vb* : to take the place of for a time in work or duty : RELIEVE

spell·bind·er \-ˌbīn-dər\ *n* : a speaker of compelling eloquence

spell·bound \-'baund\ *adj* : held by or as if by a spell : FASCINATED

spell·er \ \ *n* **1** : one who spells **2** : a book with exercises for teaching spelling

spe·lunk·er \spi-'ləŋ-kər\ *n* : one who makes a hobby of exploring caves — **spe·lunk·ing** *n*

spend \'spend\ *vb* **spent** \'spent\ **spend·ing** **1** : to use up or pay out **2** : to wear out : EXHAUST; *also* : to consume wastefully **3** : to cause or permit to elapse : PASS **4** : to make use of

spend·thrift \'spen(d)-ˌthrift\ *n* : one who spends wastefully or recklessly : PRODIGAL

spent \'spent\ *adj* : drained of energy : EXHAUSTED

sperm \'spərm\ *n* : SEMEN; *also* : SPERMATOZOON

sper·ma·to·zo·on \ˌspər-mət-ə-'zō-ˌän\ *n, pl* **-zoa** \-'zō-ə\ : a male germ cell

sperm whale *n* : a large whale with conical teeth and no whalebone

spew \'spyü\ *vb* : VOMIT

sphere \'sfiər\ *n* **1** : a figure so shaped that every point on its surface is an equal distance from the center : BALL **2** : a globular body : GLOBE; *esp* : a celestial body **3** : range of action or influence : FIELD — **spher·i·cal** \'sfir-i-kəl, 'sfer-\ *adj* — **spher·i·cal·ly** *adv*

spher·oid \'sfi(ə)r-ˌoid, 'sfe(ə)r-\ *n* : a figure similar to a sphere but not perfectly round — **sphe·roi·dal** \sfir-'oid-°l\ *adj*

sphinc·ter \'sfiŋk-tər\ *n* : a muscular ring that closes a bodily opening

sphinx \'sfiŋks\ *n* **1** : a monster in Greek mythology with the head and bust of a woman, the body of a lion, and wings; *esp* : one who asks a riddle of persons who pass and destroys those who cannot answer it **2** : a person whose character and motives are hard to understand

spice \'spīs\ *n* **1** : any of various aromatic plant products (as pepper or nutmeg) used to season or flavor foods **2** : something that adds interest and relish — **spice** *vb* — **spicy** *adj*

spick-and-span \ˌspik-ən-'span\ *adj* : quite new; *also* : spotlessly clean

spic·ule \'spik-yül\ *n* : a slender pointed body esp. of bony material (sponge ∼s)

spi·der \'spīd-ər\ *n* **1** : any of numerous small wingless animals that resemble insects but have eight legs and a body divided into two parts **2** : a cast-iron frying pan — **spi·dery** *adj*

spig·ot \'spig-ət, 'spik-\ *n* : FAUCET, COCK

¹spike \'spīk\ *n* **1** : a very large nail **2** : any of various pointed projections (as on the sole of a shoe to prevent slipping) — **spiky** *adj*

²spike *vb* **1** : to fasten with spikes **2** : to put an end to : QUASH (∼ a rumor) **3** : to pierce with or impale on a spike **4** : to add alcoholic liquor to (a drink)

³spike *n* **1** : an ear of grain **2** : a long cluster of usu. stemless flowers

¹spill \'spil\ *vb* **spilled** \'spild\ *also* **spilt** \'spilt\ **spill·ing** **1** : to cause or allow unintentionally to fall, flow, or run out (∼ water from a glass) **2** : to lose or allow to be scattered **3** : to cause (blood) to flow **4** : to run out or over with resulting loss or waste

²spill *n* **1** : an act of spilling; *also* : a fall from a horse or vehicle or in running **2** : something spilled : SPILLWAY

spill·way \-ˌspil-ˌwā\ *n* : a passage for surplus water to run over or around an obstruction (as a dam)

¹spin \'spin\ *vb* **spun** \'spən\ **spin·ning** **1** : to draw out (fiber) and twist into thread; *also* : to form (thread) by such means **2** : to form thread by extruding a sticky quickly hardening fluid; *also* : to construct from such thread (spiders *spun* their webs) **3** : to produce slowly and by degrees (∼ a story) **4** : TWIRL **5** : WHIRL, REEL (my head is

ə abut; ᵉ kitten; ər further; a back; ā bake; ä cot, cart; aù out; ch chin; e less; ē easy; g gift; i trip; ī life; j joke; ŋ sing; ō flow; ò flaw; òi coin; th thin; t͟h this; ü loot; ù foot; y yet; yü few; yù furious; zh vision

spinning⟩ 6 : to move rapidly along — **spin·ner** *n*

²**spin** *n* 1 : a rapid rotating motion 2 : an excursion in a wheeled vehicle

spin·ach \'spin-ich\ *n* : a garden herb grown for its edible leaves

spi·nal \'spīn-ᵊl\ *adj* : of or relating to the backbone or spinal cord — **spi·nal·ly** *adv*

spinal column *n* : BACKBONE

spinal cord *n* : the thick strand of nervous tissue that extends from the brain along the back in the cavity of the backbone

spin·dle \'spin-dᵊl\ *n* 1 : a round tapering stick or rod by which fibers are twisted in spinning 2 : a turned part of a piece of furniture ⟨the ∼s of a chair⟩ 3 : a slender pin or rod which turns or on which something else turns

spin·dling \'spin-dliŋ\ *adj* : being long or tall and thin and usu. weak

spin·dly \-dlē\ *adj* : SPINDLING

spine \'spīn\ *n* 1 : BACKBONE 2 : a stiff sharp process on a plant or animal; *esp* : one that is a modified leaf — **spine·less** *adj* — **spiny** *adj*

spin·et \'spin-ᵊt\ *n* : a small upright piano

spinning wheel *n* : a small domestic machine for spinning thread or yarn in which a large wheel drives a single spindle

spin·ster \'spin-stər\ *n* : an unmarried woman past the common age for marrying — **spin·ster·hood** *n*

spiny lobster *n* : an edible crustacean differing from the related lobster in lacking the large front claws and in having a very spiny carapace

¹**spi·ral** \'spī-rəl\ *adj* 1 : circling around a center like the thread of a screw 2 : winding or coiling around a center or pole in gradually enlarging circles — **spi·ral·ly** *adv*

²**spiral** *n* 1 : something that has a spiral form; *also* : a single turn in a spiral object 2 : a continuously spreading and accelerating increase or decrease ⟨wage ∼⟩

³**spiral** *vb* -raled *or* -ralled; -ral·ing *or* -ral·ling 1 : to move in a spiral course 2 : to rise or fall in a spiral ⟨the cost of living ∼ed upward⟩

spire \'spī(ə)r\ *n* 1 : a slender tapering stalk (as of grass) 2 : a pointed tip (as of a tree or antler) 3 : STEEPLE — **spiry** *adj*

¹**spir·it** \'spir-ət\ *n* 1 : a life-giving force; *also* : the animating principle : SOUL 2 *cap* : the active presence of God in human life : the third person of the Trinity 3 : SPECTER, GHOST 4 : PERSON 5 : DISPOSITION, MOOD 6 : VIVACITY, ARDOR 7 : LOYALTY ⟨school ∼⟩ 8 : essential or real meaning : INTENT 9 : distilled alcoholic liquor — **spir·it·less** *adj*

²**spirit** *vb* : to carry off secretly or mysteriously

spir·it·ed *adj* 1 : ANIMATED, LIVELY 2 : COURAGEOUS

¹**spir·i·tu·al** \'spir-i-ch(ə-w)əl\ *adj* 1 : of, relating to, or consisting of spirit : INCORPOREAL 2 : of or relating to sacred matters 3 : ecclesiastical rather than lay or temporal — **spir·i·tu·al·i·ty** \,spir-i-chə-'wal-ət-ē\ *n* — **spir·i·tu·al·ize** \'spir-i-ch(ə-w)ə-,līz\ *vb* — **spir·i·tu·al·ly** *adv*

²**spiritual** *n* : a religious song originating among Negroes of the southern U.S.

spir·i·tu·al·ism \'spir-i-ch(ə-w)ə-,liz-əm\ *n* : the belief that spirits of the dead hold intercourse with the living through physical phenomena (as table rappings) or the trances of mediums — **spir·i·tu·al·ist** *n* — **spir·i·tu·al·is·tic** \,spir-i-ch(ə-w)ə-'lis-tik\ *adj*

spir·i·tu·ous \'spir-ich-(ə-w)əs\ *adj* : containing alcohol ⟨∼ liquors⟩

spi·ro·chete \'spī-rə-,kēt\ *n* : any of various spiral bacteria including one that causes syphilis

spirt *var of* SPURT

¹**spit** \'spit\ *n* 1 : a thin pointed rod for holding meat over a fire 2 : a point of land that runs out into the water

²**spit** *vb* **spit·ted; spit·ting** : to pierce with or as if with a spit

³**spit** *vb* **spit** *or* **spat** \'spat\ **spit·ting** 1 : to eject (saliva) from the mouth 2 : to send forth forcefully, defiantly, or disgustedly

⁴**spit** *n* 1 : SALIVA; *also* : an act of spitting 2 : perfect likeness ⟨∼ and image of his father⟩ 3 : a flurry of rain or snow

spit·ball \-,bȯl\ *n* 1 : paper chewed and rolled into a ball to be thrown as a missile 2 : a baseball pitch delivered after the ball has been moistened with saliva or sweat

¹**spite** \'spīt\ *n* : ill will with a wish to annoy, anger, or defeat : petty malice syn malignity, spleen, grudge, malevolence — **spite·ful** *adj* — **spite·ful·ly** *adv* — **spite·ful·ness** *n* — in spite of : in defiance or contempt of : NOTWITHSTANDING

²**spite** *vb* : to treat maliciously (as by insulting or thwarting)

spit·tle \'spit-ᵊl\ *n* : SALIVA

spit·toon \spi-'tün\ *n* : a receptacle for spit

splash \'splash\ *vb* 1 : to dash a liquid about 2 : to scatter a liquid upon : SPATTER 3 : to fall or strike with a splashing noise syn sprinkle, bespatter — **splash** *n*

splat·ter \'splat-ər\ *vb* : SPATTER — **splatter** *n*

¹**splay** \'splā\ *vb* 1 : to spread out 2 : to slope or slant outwards ⟨∼ed doorway⟩ — **splay** *n*

²**splay** *adj* 1 : spread out : turned outward 2 : AWKWARD, CLUMSY

spleen \'splēn\ *n* 1 : a vascular organ located near the stomach in most vertebrates concerned esp. with the storage, formation, and destruction of blood cells 2 : SPITE, MALICE syn malignity, grudge, malevolence

splen·did \'splen-dəd\ *adj* 1 : SHINING, BRILLIANT 2 : SHOWY, GORGEOUS 3 : ILLUSTRIOUS 4 : EXCELLENT syn resplendent, glorious, sublime, superb — **splen·did·ly** *adv*

splen·dor \'splen-dər\ *n* 1 : BRILLIANCE 2 : POMP, MAGNIFICENCE

sple·net·ic \spli-'net-ik\ *adj* 1 : SPLENIC 2 : SPITEFUL, MALICIOUS 3 : IRRITABLE

sple·nic \'splē-nik, 'splen-ik\ *adj* : of, relating to, or located in the spleen

splice \'splīs\ *vb* 1 : to unite (as two ropes) by weaving the strands together 2 : to unite (as two timbers) by lapping the ends and making them fast — **splice** *n*

splint \'splint\ *n* 1 : a thin strip of wood interwoven with others to make something (as a basket or a chair seat) 2 : material or a device used to protect and keep in place an injured body part (as a broken arm)

¹splin·ter \'splint-ər\ n : a thin piece of something split off lengthwise : SLIVER

²splinter vb : to split into splinters

split \'split\ vb split; split·ting 1 : to divide lengthwise or along a grain or seam 2 : to burst or break in pieces 3 : to divide into parts or sections syn rend, cleave, rip, tear — split n

split·ting adj : causing a feeling of breaking or bursting (~ headache)

splotch \'spläch\ n : BLOTCH

splurge \'splərj\ n : a showy display or expense — splurge vb

splut·ter \'splət-ər\ n : SPUTTER — splutter vb

¹spoil \'spȯil\ n : PLUNDER, BOOTY

²spoil vb spoiled \'spȯild\ or spoilt \'spȯilt\ spoil·ing 1 : ROB, PILLAGE 2 : to damage seriously : RUIN 3 : to impair the quality or effect of 4 : to damage the disposition of by pampering; also : INDULGE, CODDLE 5 : DECAY, ROT 6 : to have an eager desire (~ing for a fight) syn injure, harm, hurt, mar — spoil·age n — spoil·er n

¹spoke \'spōk\ past of SPEAK

²spoke n 1 : any of the rods extending from the hub of a wheel to the rim 2 : a rung of a ladder

spoken past part of SPEAK

spokes·man \'spōks-mən\ n : one who speaks as the representative of another or others

spo·li·a·tion \,spō-lē-'ā-shən\ n : the act of plundering : the state of being plundered

¹sponge \'spənj\ n 1 : the elastic porous mass of fibers that forms the skeleton of any of a group of lowly sea animals; also : one of the animals 2 : the act of washing or wiping with a sponge 3 : a spongelike or porous mass or material (as used for sponging) — spong·er n — spongy adj

²sponge vb 1 : to gather sponges 2 : to bathe or wipe with a sponge 3 : to live at another's expense

sponge cake n : a cake made without shortening

spon·sor \'spän-sər\ n [L, fr. spons-, spondēre to pledge, promise] 1 : one who takes the responsibility for some other person or thing : SURETY 2 : GOD-PARENT 3 : a business firm who pays a broadcaster and performer for a radio or television program that allots some time to advertising its product syn patron, guarantor — sponsor vb — spon·sor·ship n

spon·ta·ne·ous \spän-'tā-nē-əs\ adj 1 : done or produced freely, naturally, and without constraint 2 : acting or taking place without external force or cause syn impulsive, instinctive, automatic, mechanical — spon·ta·ne·i·ty \,spänt-ə-'nē-ət-ē\ n — spon·ta·ne·ous·ly \spän-'tā-nē-əs-lē\ adv

spontaneous combustion n : a bursting into flame of combustible material through heat produced within itself by chemical action (as oxidation)

spoof \'spüf\ vb 1 : DECEIVE, HOAX 2 : to make good-natured fun of — spoof n

spook \'spük\ n : GHOST, APPARITION

spool \'spül\ n : a cylinder on which flexible material (as thread, wire, or tape) is wound

spoon \'spün\ n 1 : an eating or cooking implement consisting of a shallow bowl with a handle 2 : a metal piece used on a fishing line as a lure — spoon vb — spoon·ful n

spoor \'spu̇r, 'spȯr\ n : a track or trail esp. of a wild animal

spo·rad·ic \spə-'rad-ik\ adj : occurring in scattered single instances syn occasional, rare, scarce, infrequent, uncommon — spo·rad·i·cal·ly adv

spore \'spȯr\ n : a primitive usu. one-celled resistant or reproductive body produced by plants and some lower animals

¹sport \'spȯrt\ vb 1 : to amuse oneself : FROLIC 2 : to wear or display ostentatiously — sport·ive adj

²sport n 1 : a source of diversion : PASTIME 2 : physical activity engaged in for pleasure 3 : JEST 4 : MOCKERY (make ~ of his efforts) 5 : BUTT, LAUGHINGSTOCK 6 : one who accepts results cheerfully whether favoring his interests or not 7 : a person devoted to a gay easy life 8 : an individual distinguished by a mutation syn play, frolic, fun — sporty adj

³sport or sports adj : of, relating to, or suitable for sport (~ fish) (~ coats)

sports·man \'spȯrts-mən\ n 1 : one who engages in field sports 2 : one who plays fairly and wins or loses gracefully — sports·man·ship n

¹spot \'spät\ n 1 : STAIN, BLEMISH 2 : a small part different (as in color) from the main part 3 : LOCATION, SITE — spot·less adj — spot·less·ly adv

²spot vb spot·ted; spot·ting 1 : to mark or disfigure with spots 2 : to pick out : RECOGNIZE, IDENTIFY

spot·light \-,līt\ n 1 : a circle of brilliant light projected upon a particular area, person, or object (as on a stage); also : the device that produces this light 2 : public notice

spot·ter n 1 : one that watches for approaching airplanes 2 : one that locates enemy targets

spot·ty adj : uneven in quality

spou·sal \'spau̇-zəl\ n : NUPTIALS — usu. used in pl.

spouse \'spau̇s\ n : one's husband or wife

¹spout \'spau̇t\ vb 1 : to eject or issue forth forcibly and freely (wells ~ing oil) (blood ~ing from a wound) 2 : to declaim pompously

²spout n 1 : a pipe or hole through which liquid spouts 2 : a jet of liquid; esp : WATERSPOUT

¹sprain \'sprān\ n : a sudden or severe twisting of a joint with stretching and tearing of ligaments; also : a sprained condition

²sprain vb : to subject to sprain

sprang past of SPRING

sprat \'sprat\ n : a small European herring; also : a young herring

sprawl \'sprȯl\ vb 1 : to lie or sit with limbs spread out awkwardly 2 : to spread out irregularly (a ~ing vine) — sprawl n

¹spray \'sprā\ n : a usu. flowering

branch or a decorative arrangement of flowers and foliage

²**spray** *n* **1** : liquid flying in small drops like water blown from a wave **2** : a jet of fine vapor (as from an atomizer) **3** : an instrument (as an atomizer) for scattering fine liquid

³**spray** *vb* **1** : to scatter or let fall in a spray **2** : to discharge spray on or into — **spray·er** *n*

¹**spread** \'spred\ *vb* spread; spread·ing **1** : to scatter over a surface **2** : to flatten out : open out **3** : to stretch, force, or push apart **4** : to distribute over a period of time or among many persons **5** : to pass on from person to person **6** : to cover with something (~ a floor with rugs) **7** : to prepare for a meal (~ a table) — **spread·er** *n*

²**spread** *n* **1** : act of spreading : EXPANSION **2** : EXPANSE, EXTENT **3** : distance or difference between two points : GAP **4** : a cloth cover for a bed **5** : a food to be spread on bread or crackers **6** : a prominent display in a magazine or newspaper

spree \'sprē\ *n* : an unrestrained outburst (buying ~); *esp* : a drinking bout

sprig \'sprig\ *n* : a small shoot or twig

spright·ly \'sprīt-lē\ *adj* : LIVELY, SPIRITED **syn** animated, vivacious, gay

¹**spring** \'sprin\ *vb* sprang \'spran\ *or* sprung \'sprən\ sprung; spring·ing **1** : to move suddenly upward or forward : LEAP, BOUND **2** : to shoot up (weeds ~ up overnight) **3** : to move quickly by elastic force **4** : to make lame : STRAIN **5** : WARP **6** : to develop (a leak) through the seams **7** : to make known suddenly (~ a surprise) **8** : to cause to close suddenly (~ a trap)

²**spring** *n* **1** : a source of supply; *esp* : an issuing of water from the ground **2** : SOURCE, ORIGIN; *also* : MOTIVE **3** : the season between winter and summer **4** : an elastic body or device that recovers its original shape when it is released after being distorted **5** : the act or an instance of leaping up or forward : JUMP **6** : elastic power — **springy** *adj*

spring·board \-,bōrd\ *n* : a springy board used in jumping or vaulting or for diving

spring tide *n* : either of two tides in the lunar month at new moon or full moon when the range is the greatest

spring·time \'sprin-,tīm\ *n* : the season of spring

¹**sprin·kle** \'sprin-kəl\ *vb* : to scatter in small drops or particles — **sprin·kler** \-k(ə-)lər\ *n*

²**sprinkle** *n* : a light rainfall

sprin·kling \-klin\ *n* : a small scattered quantity or number

¹**sprint** \'sprint\ *vb* : to run at top speed esp. for a short distance — **sprint·er** *n*

²**sprint** *n* **1** : a short run at top speed **2** : a short distance race

sprite \'sprīt\ *n* **1** : GHOST, SPIRIT **2** : ELF, FAIRY

sprock·et \'spräk-ət\ *n* : a tooth on a wheel (**sprocket wheel**) shaped so as to interlock with a chain

¹**sprout** \'spraut\ *vb* : to send out new growth esp. rapidly (~ing seeds)

²**sprout** *n* : a usu. young and growing plant shoot

¹**spruce** \'sprüs\ *n* : any of various conical evergreen trees related to the pines

²**spruce** *adj* : neat and smart in appearance **syn** stylish, fashionable, modish

³**spruce** *vb* : to make or become spruce (~ up for a party)

sprung *past of* SPRING

spry \'sprī\ *adj* : NIMBLE, ACTIVE **syn** agile, brisk

spud \'spəd\ *n* **1** : a sharp narrow spade **2** : POTATO

spume \'spyüm\ *n* : frothy matter on liquids : FOAM

spun *past of* SPIN

spunk \'spənk\ *n* : PLUCK, COURAGE — **spunky** *adj*

¹**spur** \'spər\ *n* **1** : a pointed device fastened to a rider's boot and used to urge on a horse **2** : something that urges to action **3** : a stiffly projecting part or process (as on the leg of a cock or on some flowers) **4** : a ridge extending sideways from a mountain **5** : a branch of railroad track extending from the main line **syn** goad, motive, impulse, incentive, inducement — **on the spur of the moment** : on hasty impulse

²**spur** *vb* spurred; spur·ring **1** : to urge a horse on with spurs **2** : INCITE, STIMULATE

spurge \'spərj\ *n* : any of various herbs and woody plants with milky often poisonous juice

spu·ri·ous \'spyür-ē-əs\ *adj* : not genuine : FALSE

spurn \'spərn\ *vb* **1** : to kick away or trample on **2** : to reject with disdain **syn** repudiate, refuse, decline

¹**spurt** \'spərt\ *n* **1** : a sudden brief burst of effort or speed **2** : a sharp increase of activity (~ in sales)

²**spurt** *vb* : to make a spurt

³**spurt** *vb* : to gush out : spout forth : JET

⁴**spurt** *n* : a sudden gushing or spouting

sput·ter \'spət-ər\ *vb* **1** : to spit small scattered particles : SPLUTTER **2** : to utter words hastily or explosively in excitement or confusion **3** : to make small popping sounds — **sputter** *n*

spu·tum \'spyüt-əm\ *n* : expectorated material consisting of saliva and mucus

¹**spy** \'spī\ *vb* **1** : to watch secretly usu. for hostile purposes : SCOUT **2** : to get a momentary or quick glimpse of : SEE **3** : to search for information secretly

²**spy** *n* **1** : one who secretly watches others **2** : one who secretly tries to obtain information for his own country in the territory of an enemy country

spy-glass \-,glas\ *n* : a small telescope

squab \'skwäb\ *n* : a young pigeon

squab·ble \'skwäb-əl\ *n* : a noisy altercation : WRANGLE **syn** quarrel, spat — **squabble** *vb*

squad \'skwäd\ *n* **1** : a small organized group of military personnel **2** : a small group engaged in some common effort

squad·ron \'skwäd-rən\ *n* **1** : a body of men in regular formation **2** : any of several units of military organization

squal·id \'skwäl-əd\ *adj* **1** : filthy or degraded through neglect or poverty **2** : SORDID, DEBASED **syn** nasty, foul

squall \'skwol\ *n* : a sudden violent gust of wind often with rain or snow — **squally** *adj*

squal·or \'skwäl-ər\ *n* : the quality or state of being squalid

squan·der \'skwän-dər\ *vb* : to spend wastefully or foolishly

¹**square** \'skwaer\ *n* **1** : an instrument used to lay out or test right angles **2** : a flat figure that has four equal sides and four right angles **3** : something

square **4** : an area bounded by four streets **5** : an open area in a city where streets meet **6** : the product of a number multiplied by itself **7** : a highly conventional person

²square adj **1** : having 4 equal sides and 4 right angles **2** : forming a right angle ⟨cut a ~ corner⟩ **3** : multiplied by itself : SQUARED ⟨X² is the symbol for X ~⟩ **4** : converted from a linear unit into a square unit of area having the same length of side ⟨a ~ foot is the area of a square each side of which is a foot⟩ **5** : being of a specified length in each of 2 dimensions ⟨an area 10 feet ~⟩ **6** : exactly adjusted **7** : JUST, FAIR ⟨a ~ deal⟩ **8** : leaving no balance : EVEN ⟨make accounts ~⟩ **9** : SUBSTANTIAL, SATISFYING ⟨a ~ meal⟩ — **square·ly** ⟨~ an account⟩ adv

³square vb **1** : to form with 4 equal sides and right angles or with flat surfaces ⟨~ a timber⟩ **2** : to multiply a number by itself **3** : CONFORM, AGREE ⟨the story does not ~ with fact⟩ **4** : BALANCE, SETTLE ⟨~ an account⟩

square dance n : a dance for 4 couples arranged to form a square

square–rigged \'skwaər-'rigd\ adj : having the chief sails extended on yards that are fastened to the masts horizontally and at their center ⟨a ~ ship⟩

square root n : a factor of a number that when multiplied by itself gives the number ⟨the *square root* of 9 is ± 3⟩

¹squash \'skwäsh\ vb **1** : to beat or press into a pulp or flat mass **2** : QUASH, SUPPRESS

²squash n **1** : the impact of something soft and heavy; *also* : the sound of such impact **2** : a crushed mass **3** : SQUASH RACQUETS

³squash n : a fruit of any of various plants related to the gourds that are used esp. as a vegetable; *also* : a plant bearing squashes

squash racquets n : a game played on a 4-wall court with a racket and rubber ball

¹squat \'skwät\ vb **squat·ted** or **squat; squat·ting** **1** : to sit down upon the hams or heels **2** : to settle on land without right or title; *also* : to settle on public land with a view to acquiring title — **squat·ter** n

²squat n : the act or posture of squatting

³squat adj : low to the ground; *also* : short and thick in stature **syn** thickset, stocky

squaw \'skwo\ n : an American Indian woman

squawk \'skwok\ n : a harsh loud cry; *also* : a noisy protest — **squawk** vb

squeak \'skwēk\ vb **1** : to utter or speak in a weak shrill tone **2** : to make a thin high-pitched sound — **squeak** n — **squeaky** adj

¹squeal \'skwēl\ vb **1** : to make a shrill sound or cry **2** : COMPLAIN, PROTEST **3** : to betray a secret or turn informer

²squeal n : a shrill sharp somewhat prolonged cry

squea·mish \'skwē-mish\ adj **1** : easily nauseated; *also* : NAUSEATED **2** : easily disgusted **syn** fussy, nice, dainty — **squea·mish·ness** n

squee·gee \'skwē-jē\ n : a blade crosswise on a handle used for spreading or wiping liquid on, across, or off a surface — **squeegee** vb

¹squeeze \'skwēz\ vb **1** : to exert pressure on the opposite sides or parts of **2** : to obtain by pressure ⟨~ juice from a lemon⟩ **3** : to force, thrust, or cause to pass by pressure — **squeez·er** n

²squeeze n **1** : an act of squeezing : COMPRESSION **2** : a quantity squeezed out

squelch \'skwelch\ vb **1** : to suppress completely : CRUSH **2** : to move in soft mud — **squelch** n

squib \'skwib\ n **1** : a small firecracker; *esp* : one that fizzes instead of exploding **2** : a brief witty writing or speech

squid \'skwid\ n : a 10-armed long-bodied sea mollusk with no shell

squint \'skwint\ vb **1** : to look or aim obliquely **2** : to close the eyes partly ⟨the glare made him ~⟩ **3** : to be cross-eyed — **squint** n or adj

¹squire \'skwīr\ n [OF *esquier*, fr. LL *scutarius*, fr. L *scutum* shield] **1** : an armor-bearer of a knight **2** : a member of the British gentry ranking below a knight and above a gentleman; *also* : a prominent landowner **3** : a local magistrate **4** : a man gallantly devoted to a lady

²squire vb : to accompany a lady as an escort

squirm \'skwərm\ vb : to twist about like a worm : WRIGGLE

squir·rel \'skwər(-ə)l\ n : any of various rodents usu. with a long bushy tail and strong hind legs; *also* : the fur of a squirrel

¹squirt \'skwərt\ vb : to eject liquid in a thin spurt

²squirt n **1** : an instrument (as a syringe) for squirting **2** : a small forcible jet of liquid

-st — see **-EST**

¹stab \'stab\ vb **stabbed; stab·bing** : to pierce or wound with or as if with a pointed weapon; *also* : THRUST, DRIVE

²stab n **1** : a wound given by a pointed weapon **2** : a quick thrust; *also* : a brief attempt

sta·bile \'stā-,bēl\ n : a stable abstract sculpture or construction typically made of sheet metal, wire, and wood

sta·bi·lize \'stā-bə-,līz\ vb **1** : to make stable **2** : to hold steady ⟨~ prices⟩ **syn** balance — **sta·bi·li·za·tion** \,stā-bə-lə-'zā-shən\ n — **sta·bi·liz·er** \'stā-bə-,lī-zər\ n

¹sta·ble \'stā-bəl\ n : a building in which livestock is sheltered and fed — **sta·ble·man** \-mən\ n

²stable adj **1** : firmly established; *also* : mentally healthful and well-balanced **2** : steady in purpose : CONSTANT **3** : DURABLE, ENDURING **4** : resistant to chemical or physical change **syn** lasting, permanent, perpetual — **sta·bil·i·ty** \stə-'bil-ə-t-ē\ n

stac·ca·to \stə-'kät-ō\ adj : cut short or apart in performing ⟨~ notes⟩

¹stack \'stak\ n **1** : a large pile (as of hay, grain, or straw) **2** : a large quantity **3** : a vertical pipe : SMOKESTACK, CHIMNEY **4** : an orderly pile (as of poker chips) **5** : a rack with shelves for storing books

²**stack** \\vb **1 :** to pile up **2 :** to arrange (cards) secretly for cheating

sta·di·um \\'stād-ē-əm\\ n **:** a structure with tiers of seats for spectators built around a field for sports events

staff \\'staf\\ n, pl **staves** \\'stāvz\\ or in senses 3 & 4 **staffs 1 :** a pole, stick, rod, or bar used for supporting, for measuring, or as a symbol of authority; also **:** CLUB, CUDGEL **2 :** something that sustains \\bread is the ~ of life\\ **3 :** a body of assistants to an executive **4 :** a group of officers holding no command but having duties concerned with planning and managing **5 :** the five horizontal lines on which music is written

staff sergeant n **:** a noncommissioned officer ranking in the army next below a sergeant first class, in the air force next below a technical sergeant, and in the marine corps next below a gunnery sergeant

stag \\'stag\\ n **:** an adult male of various large deer

¹**stage** \\'stāj\\ n **1 :** a raised platform on which an orator may speak or a play may be presented **2 :** the acting profession **:** THEATER **3 :** the scene of a notable action or event **4 :** a station or resting place on a traveled road **5 :** STAGECOACH **6 :** a degree of advance in an undertaking, process, or development **7 :** a propulsion unit in a rocket — **stagy** \\'stā-jē\\ adj

²**stage** vb **:** to produce or perform on or as if on a stage

stage-coach \\-,kōch\\ n **:** a coach that runs regularly between stations

¹**stag·ger** \\'stag-ər\\ vb **1 :** to reel from side to side **:** TOTTER **2 :** to begin to doubt **:** WAVER **3 :** to cause to reel or waver **4 :** to arrange (working hours) in overlapping or alternating positions or times

²**stagger** n **1** pl **:** an abnormal condition of domestic mammals and birds associated with damage to the central nervous system and marked by lack of coordination and a reeling unsteady gait **2 :** a reeling or unsteady gait or stance

stag·ing \\'stā-jiŋ\\ n **:** SCAFFOLDING

stag·nant \\'stag-nənt\\ adj **1 :** not flowing **:** MOTIONLESS \\~ water in a pond\\ **2 :** DULL, INACTIVE \\~ business\\

stag·nate \\'stag-,nāt\\ vb **:** to be or become stagnant — **stag·na·tion** \\stag-'nā-shən\\ n

staid \\'stād\\ adj **:** SOBER, SEDATE syn grave, serious, earnest

¹**stain** \\'stān\\ vb **1 :** DISCOLOR, SOIL **2 :** to color (as wood, paper, or cloth) by processes affecting the material itself **3 :** TAINT, CORRUPT **4 :** DISGRACE

²**stain** n **1 :** SPOT, DISCOLORATION **2 :** a taint of guilt **:** STIGMA **3 :** a preparation (as a dye or pigment) used in staining — **stain·less** adj

stainless steel n **:** steel alloyed with chromium that is highly resistant to stain, rust, and corrosion

stair \\'staər\\ n **1 :** any one step of a series for ascending or descending from one level to another **2** pl **:** a flight of steps

stair·case \\-,kās\\ n **:** a flight of steps with their supporting framework, casing, and balusters

stair·way \\-,wā\\ n **:** one or more flights of stairs with connecting landings

¹**stake** \\'stāk\\ n **1 :** a pointed piece of material (as of wood) driven into the ground as a marker or a support **2 :** a post to which a person who is to be burned is bound; also **:** death by such burning **3 :** something that is staked for gain or loss **4 :** the prize in a contest

²**stake** vb **1 :** to mark the limits of with stakes **2 :** to tether to a stake **3 :** to support or secure with stakes **4 :** to place as a bet

sta·lac·tite \\stə-'lak-,tīt\\ n **:** an icicle-shaped deposit hanging from the roof or sides of a cavern

sta·lag·mite \\-'lag-,mīt\\ n **:** a deposit resembling an inverted stalactite rising from the floor of a cavern

stale \\'stāl\\ adj **1 :** flat and tasteless from age \\~ beer\\ **2 :** not freshly made \\~ bread\\ **3 :** COMMONPLACE, TRITE — **stale** vb

¹**stalk** \\'stòk\\ vb **1 :** to walk stiffly or haughtily **2 :** to approach (game) stealthily

²**stalk** n **:** a plant stem; also **:** any slender usu. upright supporting or connecting part — **stalked** \\'stòkt\\ adj

¹**stall** \\'stòl\\ n **1 :** a compartment in a stable for one animal **2 :** a booth or counter where articles may be displayed for sale **3 :** a seat in a church choir; also **:** a church pew **4** Brit **:** a seat in the front part of the orchestra

²**stall** vb **:** to bring or come to a standstill unintentionally \\~ an engine\\

stal·lion \\'stal-yən\\ n **:** a male horse

stal·wart \\'stòl-wərt\\ adj **:** STOUT, STRONG; also **:** BRAVE, VALIANT

sta·men \\'stā-mən\\ n **:** an organ of a flower that produces pollen — **sta·mi·nate** \\'stā-mə-nət, 'stam-ə-\\ adj

stam·i·na \\'stam-ə-nə\\ n **:** VIGOR, ENDURANCE

stam·mer \\'stam-ər\\ vb **:** to hesitate or stumble in speaking **:** STUTTER — **stammer** n — **stam·mer·er** n

¹**stamp** \\'stamp\\ vb **1 :** to pound or crush with a heavy instrument **2 :** to strike or beat with the bottom of the foot **3 :** to impress or imprint with a mark **4 :** to cut out or indent with a stamp or die **5 :** to put a postage stamp upon

²**stamp** n **1 :** a device or instrument for stamping **2 :** the mark made by stamping; also **:** a distinctive mark or quality **3 :** a paper or a mark put on a thing to show that a required charge (as a tax) has been paid \\a postage ~\\ **4 :** the act of stamping

¹**stam·pede** \\stam-'pēd\\ n **:** a wild headlong rush or flight esp. of frightened animals

²**stampede** vb **1 :** to flee or cause to flee in panic **2 :** to act or cause to act together suddenly and heedlessly

stance \\'stans\\ n **:** a way of standing **:** POSTURE

¹**stanch** \\'stònch\\ vb **:** to check the flowing of (as blood); also **:** to cease flowing or bleeding

²**stanch** var of STAUNCH

stan·chion \\'stan-chən\\ n **:** an upright bar, post, or support

¹**stand** \\'stand\\ vb **stood** \\'stud\\ **standing 1 :** to take or be at rest in an upright or firm position **2 :** to assume a (specified) position **3 :** to remain stationary or unchanged **4 :** to be steadfast **5 :** to act in resistance \\~ against a foe\\ **6 :** to maintain a relative position or rank **7 :** to gather slowly and remain briefly \\tears stood in her eyes\\ **8 :** to set upright **9 :** ENDURE,

TOLERATE **10** : to submit to ⟨~ trial⟩

²**stand** n **1** : an act of standing, staying, or resisting **2** : a place taken by a witness to testify in court **3** : a structure for a small retail business **4** : a raised platform (as for speakers or performers) **5** : a structure for supporting or holding something upright ⟨umbrella ~⟩ ⟨music ~⟩ **6** : a group of plants growing in a continuous area **7** pl : tiered seats for spectators **8** : a stop made to give a performance

stan·dard \'stan-dərd\ n **1** : a figure adopted as an emblem by a people **2** : the personal flag of a ruler; also : FLAG **3** : something set up as a rule for measuring or as a model to be followed **4** : an upright support ⟨lamp ~⟩ — **standard** adj

stan·dard-bear·er \-,bar-ər\ n : the leader of a cause

stan·dard·ize \'stan-dər-,dīz\ vb : to make standard or uniform — **stand·ard·iza·tion** \,stan dərd-ə-'zā-shən\ n

standard time n : the time established by law or by general usage over a region or country

stand·by \'stan(d)-,bī\ n : one that can be relied upon

¹**stand·ing** adj **1** : ERECT **2** : not flowing : STAGNANT **3** : remaining at the same level or amount for an indefinite period ⟨~ offer⟩ **4** : PERMANENT **5** : done from a standing position ⟨a ~ jump⟩

²**standing** n **1** : length of service; also : relative position : RANK **2** : DURATION ⟨a friend of long ~⟩

stand·pipe \'stan(d)-,pīp\ n : a high vertical pipe or reservoir for water used to produce a uniform pressure

stand·point \-,point\ n : a position from which objects or principles are judged

stand·still \-,stil\ n : a state of rest : STOP

stank past of STINK

stan·za \'stan-zə\ n : a group of lines forming a division of a poem

staph·y·lo·coc·cus \,staf-ə-lō-'käk-əs\ n : any of various spherical bacteria including some that cause purulent infections

¹**sta·ple** \'stā-pəl\ n : a U-shaped piece of metal with sharp points to be driven into a surface to hold something (as a hook or wire); also : a similarly shaped piece of wire driven through papers and bent over at the ends to fasten them together or through thin material to fasten it to a surface ⟨fasten cardboard to wood with ~s⟩ — **staple** vb — **sta·pler** \-p(ə-)lər\ n

²**staple** n **1** : a chief commodity or product **2** : the main part of a thing : chief item **3** : unmanufactured or raw material **4** : a textile fiber suitable for spinning into yarn

³**staple** adj **1** : regularly produced in large quantities **2** : PRINCIPAL, MAIN ⟨~ crop⟩

¹**star** \'stär\ n **1** : a natural celestial body that is visible as an apparently fixed point of light; esp : such a body that is gaseous, self-luminous, and of great mass **2** : a planet or configuration of planets that is held in astrology to

influence one's fortune — usu. used in pl. **3** : DESTINY, FORTUNE **4** : a conventional figure representing a star **5** : ASTERISK **6** : a brilliant performer **7** : an actor or actress playing the leading role — **star·less** adj — **star·like** adj — **star·ry** adj

²**star** vb **starred; star·ring 1** : to adorn with stars or spangles **2** : to mark with an asterisk **3** : to play the leading role

star·board \'stär-bərd\ n : the right side of a ship or airplane looking forward — **starboard** adj

¹**starch** \'stärch\ n : a complex carbohydrate that is stored in plants, is an important foodstuff, and is used in adhesives and sizes, in laundering, and in pharmacy — **starchy** adj

²**starch** vb : to stiffen with starch

stare \'staər\ vb **1** : to look fixedly with wide-open eyes **2** : to be conspicuous ⟨staring colors⟩ — **stare** n — **star·er** n

star·fish \'stär-,fish\ n : a star-shaped sea animal that feeds on mollusks

stark \'stärk\ adj **1** : STRONG, ROBUST **2** : rigid as if in death; also : STRICT **3** : SHEER, UTTER **4** : BARREN, DESOLATE ⟨~ landscape⟩; also : UNADORNED ⟨~ realism⟩ **5** : sharply delineated — **stark** adv — **stark·ly** adv

star·ling \'stär-liŋ\ n : a dark brown or greenish black European bird related to the crows that is naturalized and often a pest in the U.S.

¹**start** \'stärt\ vb **1** : to give an involuntary twitch or jerk (as from surprise) **2** : BEGIN, COMMENCE **3** : to set going : help to begin **4** : to enter (as a horse) in a contest **5** : TAP ⟨~ a cask⟩ — **start·er** n

²**start** n **1** : a sudden involuntary motion : LEAP **2** : a spasmodic and brief effort or action **3** : BEGINNING; also : the place of beginning

star·tle \'stärt-ᵊl\ vb : to frighten or surprise suddenly : cause to start

star·tling \-(ᵊ-)liŋ\ adj : causing sudden fear, surprise, or anxiety

starve \'stärv\ vb **1** : to perish from hunger **2** : to suffer extreme hunger **3** : to kill with hunger; also : to distress or subdue by famine — **star·va·tion** \stär-'vā-shən\ n

starve·ling \'stärv-liŋ\ n : one that is thin from lack of nourishment

¹**state** \'stāt\ n [L status, fr stare to stand] **1** : mode or condition of being ⟨gaseous ~ of water⟩ **2** : condition of mind **3** : social position; esp : high rank **4** : a body of people occupying a definite territory and politically organized under one government; also : the government of such a body of people **5** : one of the constituent units of a nation having a federal government — **state·hood** n

²**state** vb **1** : to express in words : TELL, DECLARE **2** : SETTLE, FIX ⟨stated intervals⟩

state·craft \-,kraft\ n : state management : STATESMANSHIP

state·ly adj **1** : having lofty dignity : HAUGHTY **2** : IMPRESSIVE, MAJESTIC syn magnificent, imposing, august — **state·li·ness** n

state·ment n **1** : the act or result of

ə abut; ᵊ kitten; ər further; a back; ā bake; ä cot, cart; aù out; ch chin; e less; ē easy; g gift; i trip; ī life; j joke; ŋ sing; ō flow; ȯ flaw; ȯi coin; th thin; th this; ü loot; ù foot; y yet; yü few; yù furious; zh vision

presenting in words : ACCOUNT, REPORT
2 : a summary of a financial account

state·room \'stāt-,rüm, -,rum\ n : a private room on a ship or on a railroad car

states·man \'stāts-mən\ n : one skilled in government and wise in handling public affairs; also : one influential in shaping public policy — **states·man·like** adj — **states·man·ship** n

1stat·ic \'stat-ik\ adj **1** : acting by mere weight without motion ⟨∼ pressure⟩ **2** : relating to bodies or forces at rest or in equilibrium **3** : not moving : not active **4** : of or relating to stationary charges of electricity **5** : of, relating to, or caused by radio static

2static n : noise produced in a radio or television receiver by atmospheric or other electrical disturbances

1sta·tion \'stā-shən\ n **1** : the place where a person or thing stands or is appointed to remain **2** : a regular stopping place on a transportation route ⟨a railroad ∼⟩ ⟨a bus ∼⟩; also : DEPOT **3** : a stock farm or ranch in Australia or New Zealand **4** : a place where a fleet is assigned for duty **5** : a military post **6** : social standing **7** : a complete assemblage of radio or television equipment for sending or receiving

2station vb : to assign to a station or position

sta·tion·ary \'stā-shə-,ner-ē\ adj **1** : fixed in a certain place or position **2** : not changing condition : neither improving nor getting worse

sta·tio·ner \'stā-sh(ə-)nər\ n : one that sells stationery

sta·tio·nery \'stā-shə-,ner-ē\ n : materials (as paper, pens, or ink) for writing; esp : letter paper with envelopes

station wagon n : an automobile having an interior longer than a sedan's, one or more folding or removable seats to facilitate trucking, and no separate luggage compartment

sta·tis·tics \stə-'tis-tiks\ n sing or pl **1** : a branch of mathematics dealing with the analysis and interpretation of masses of numerical data **2** : facts collected and arranged in an orderly way (as in tables of figures) for study — **sta·tis·ti·cal** \-ti-kəl\ adj — **stat·is·ti·cian** \,stat-ə-'stish-ən\ n

stat·u·ary \'stach-ə-,wer-ē\ n **1** : a branch of sculpture dealing with figures in the round **2** : a collection of statues

stat·ue \'stach-ü\ n : a likeness of a living being sculptured in a solid substance

stat·u·esque \,stach-ə-'wesk\ adj : resembling a statue esp. in well-proportioned or massive dignity

stat·u·ette \,stach-ə-'wet\ n : a small statue

stat·ure \'stach-ər\ n **1** : natural height (as of a person) **2** : quality or status gained (as by growth or achievement)

sta·tus \'stāt-əs, 'stat-\ n **1** : the state or condition of a person in the eyes of the law or of others **2** : condition of affairs

sta·tus quo \-'kwō\ n : the existing state of affairs

stat·ute \'stach-üt\ n : a law enacted by a legislative body

stat·u·to·ry \'stach-ə-,tōr-ē\ adj : imposed by statute : LAWFUL

1staunch \'stȯnch\ var of STANCH

2staunch adj **1** : WATERTIGHT ⟨a ∼ ship⟩ **2** : FIRM, STRONG; also : STEADFAST,

LOYAL syn resolute, constant, true; faithful — **staunch·ly** adv

1stave \'stāv\ n **1** : CUDGEL, STAFF **2** : any of several narrow strips of wood placed edge to edge to make something (as a barrel or bucket) **3** : STANZA

2stave vb staved or stove \'stōv\ stav·ing **1** : to break in the staves of (as a barrel or boat); also : to break a hole in **2** : to drive or thrust away ⟨∼ off trouble⟩

staves pl of STAFF

1stay \'stā\ vb **1** : PAUSE, WAIT **2** : LIVE, DWELL **3** : to stand firm **4** : STOP, CHECK **5** : DELAY, POSTPONE **6** : to last out (as a race) syn remain, abide, linger, sojourn, lodge, reside

2stay n **1** : STOP, HALT **2** : a residence or sojourn in a place

3stay n **1** : a strong rope or wire used to support or steady something (as a ship's mast) **2** : a holding or stiffening part in a structure (as a bridge) **3** : PROP, SUPPORT **4** pl : CORSET

4stay vb **1** : to hold up : PROP **2** : to satisfy (as hunger) for a time

stead \'sted\ n [OE stede place] **1** : the place or function that another person has ⟨his brother served in his ∼⟩ **2** : ADVANTAGE, AVAIL ⟨his cudgel stood him in good ∼⟩

stead·fast \-,fast\ adj **1** : firmly fixed in place **2** : not subject to change **3** : firm in belief, determination, or adherence **2** : LOYAL syn resolute, true, faithful, staunch — **stead·fast·ly** adv — **stead·fast·ness** n

1steady \'sted-ē\ adj **1** : STABLE, FIRM **2** : not faltering or swerving; also : CALM **3** : CONSTANT, RESOLUTE **4** : REGULAR **5** : RELIABLE, SOBER syn uniform, even — **stead·i·ly** adv — **stead·i·ness** n — steady adv

2steady vb : to make or become steady

steak \'stāk\ n : a slice of meat cut from a fleshy part esp. of a beef carcass

1steal \'stēl\ vb stole \'stōl\ sto·len \'stō-lən\ steal·ing **1** : to take and carry away without right or permission **2** : to get for oneself slyly or secretly **3** : to come or go secretly or gradually **4** : to gain a base in baseball by running without the aid of a hit or an error syn pilfer, filch, purloin

2steal n **1** : an act of stealing **2** : BARGAIN

stealth \'stelth\ n : secret or underhand procedure : FURTIVENESS

stealthy adj : done by stealth : FURTIVE, SLY syn secret, covert, clandestine, surreptitious, underhanded — **stealth·i·ly** adv

1steam \'stēm\ n **1** : the vapor into which water is changed when heated to the boiling point **2** : water vapor when compressed so that it supplies heat and power **3** : POWER, FORCE, ENERGY — steamy adj

2steam vb **1** : to emit vapor **2** : to pass off as vapor **3** : to move by or as if by the agency of steam — **steam·er** n

steam fitter n : a workman who puts in or repairs equipment (as steam pipes) for heating, ventilating, or refrigerating systems

steed \'stēd\ n : HORSE

steel \'stēl\ n **1** : iron treated with intense heat and mixed with carbon to make it hard and tough **2** : an instrument or implement made of steel **3** : steellike quality : HARDNESS, COLDNESS — steely adj

²steel *adj* **1** : made of steel **2** : resembling steel

³steel *vb* **1** : to sheathe, point, or edge with steel **2** : to make able to resist : HARDEN

steel wool *n* : long fine steel shavings used esp. for scouring and smoothing

steel·yard \'stēl-ˌyärd\ *n* : a weighing device in which the object to be weighed is hung from the shorter arm of a lever and is balanced by a weight that slides along the longer arm

¹steep \'stēp\ *adj* **1** : having a very sharp slope : PRECIPITOUS **2** : too great or too high (~ prices) — **steep·ly** *adv* — **steep·ness** *n*

²steep *n* : a steep slope

³steep *vb* **1** : to soak in a liquid; *esp* : to extract the essence of by soaking (~ tea) **2** : SATURATE (~ed in learning)

stee·ple \'stē-pəl\ *n* : a tall tapering structure built on top of a church tower; *also* : a church tower

stee·ple·chase \-ˌchās\ *n* : a race across country by horsemen; *also* : a race over a course obstructed by hurdles (as hedges, walls, or ditches)

¹steer \'stiər\ *n* : an ox castrated before sexual maturity and usu. raised for beef

²steer *vb* **1** : to direct the course of (as by a rudder or wheel) **2** : GUIDE, CONTROL **3** : to obey the helm **4** : to pursue a course of action — **steers·man** \'stiərz-mən\ *n*

steer·age \'sti(ə)r-ij\ *n* **1** : DIRECTION, GUIDANCE **2** : a section in a passenger ship for passengers paying the lowest fares

stein \'stīn\ *n* : an earthenware mug

stel·lar \'stel-ər\ *adj* : of or relating to stars : resembling a star

¹stem \'stem\ *n* **1** : the main shaft of a plant; *also* : a plant part that supports another part (as a leaf or fruit) **2** : a line of ancestry : STOCK **3** : something resembling the stem of a plant **4** : the prow of a ship **5** : that part of an inflected word which remains unchanged throughout a given inflection — **stem·less** *adj*

²stem *vb* **stemmed; stem·ming** : to have a specified source : DERIVE

³stem *vb* **stemmed; stem·ming** : to make headway against (~ the tide)

⁴stem *vb* **stemmed; stem·ming** : to stop or check by or as if by damming (~ a flow of blood)

stench \'stench\ *n* : STINK

sten·cil \'sten-səl\ *n* : a piece of thin impervious material (as metal or paper) that is perforated with lettering or a design through which a substance (as ink or paint) is applied to a surface to be printed — **stencil** *vb*

ste·nog·ra·phy \stə-'näg-rə-fē\ *n* : the art or process of writing in shorthand — **ste·nog·ra·pher** *n* — **sten·o·graph·ic** \ˌsten-ə-'graf-ik\ *adj*

sten·to·ri·an \sten-'tōr-ē-ən\ *adj* : extremely loud

¹step \'step\ *n* **1** : an advance made by raising one foot and putting it down in a different spot **2** : a rest for the foot in ascending or descending : STAIR **3** : a degree, rank, or plane in a series **4** : a small space or distance **5** : manner of walking **6** : a sequential measure leading to a result

²step *vb* **stepped; step·ping 1** : to advance or recede by steps **2** : to go on foot : WALK **3** : to move along briskly **4** : to measure by steps **5** : to press down with the foot **6** : to construct or arrange in or as if in steps

step·broth·er \'step-ˌbrəth-ər\ *n* : the son of one's stepparent by a former marriage

step·child \-ˌchīld\ *n* : a child of one's husband or wife by a former marriage

step·fa·ther \-ˌfäth-ər\ *n* : the husband of one's mother by a subsequent marriage

step·lad·der \-ˌlad-ər\ *n* : a light portable set of steps in a hinged frame

step·moth·er \-ˌməth-ər\ *n* : the wife of one's father by a subsequent marriage

step·par·ent \-ˌpar-ənt\ *n* : the husband or wife of one's mother or father by a subsequent marriage

steppe \'step\ *n* : dry grass-covered land in regions of wide temperature range esp. in southeastern Europe and Asia

step·sis·ter \'step-ˌsis-tər\ *n* : the daughter of one's stepparent by a former marriage

ster·eo \'ster-ē-ˌō, 'stir-\ *n* **1** : a stereoscopic method or effect **2** : a stereoscopic photograph **3** : stereophonic reproduction **4** : a stereophonic sound system

ster·e·o·phon·ic \ˌster-ē-ə-'fän-ik, ˌstir-\ *adj* : giving, relating to, or being a three-dimensional effect of reproduced sound

ster·e·o·scope \'ster-ē-ə-ˌskōp, 'stir-\ *n* [Gk *stereos* solid + *skopein* to look at] : an optical instrument with 2 eyeglasses through which a person looks at 2 photographs of the same scene taken a little way apart so that the 2 pictures blend into one and give the effect of solidity and depth

ster·e·o·scop·ic \ˌster-ē-ə-'skäp-ik, ˌstir-\ *adj* **1** : of or relating to the stereoscope **2** : characterized by stereoscopy (~ vision)

ster·e·os·co·py \ˌster-ē-'äs-kə-pē, ˌstir-\ *n* : the seeing of objects in three dimensions

ster·e·o·type \'ster-ē-ə-ˌtīp, 'stir-\ *n* **1** : a metal printing plate cast from a mold made from set type **2** : repeated without variation : lacking originality or individuality (~ response) *syn* trite

ster·e·o·typed *adj* : repeated without variation : lacking originality or individuality (~ response) *syn* trite

ster·ile \'ster-əl\ *adj* **1** : unable to bear fruit, crops, or offspring **2** : free from infectious matter — **ste·ril·i·ty** \stə-'ril-ət-ē\ *n*

ster·il·ize \'ster-ə-ˌlīz\ *vb* : to make sterile; *esp* : to free from germs — **ster·il·iza·tion** \ˌster-ə-lə-'zā-shən\ *n* — **ster·il·iz·er** \'ster-ə-ˌlī-zər\ *n*

¹ster·ling \'stər-liŋ\ *n* **1** : British money **2** : sterling silver

²sterling *adj* **1** : of, relating to, or calculated in terms of British sterling **2** : having a fixed standard of purity represented by an alloy of 925 parts of silver with 75 parts of copper (~ silver) **3** : made of sterling silver **4** : GENUINE (~ merit)

¹stern \'stərn\ *adj* **1** : SEVERE, AUSTERE **2** : STOUT, STURDY (~ resolve) — **stern·ly** *adv* — **stern·ness** *n*

²stern *n* : the rear end of a boat

ster·num \'stər-nəm\ *n* : a long flat

bone or cartilage at the center front of the chest connecting the ribs of the two sides — **ster·nal** \'stərn-ᵊl\ adj

steth·o·scope \'steth-ə-ˌskōp\ n : an instrument used for listening to sounds produced in the body and esp. in the chest

ste·ve·dore \'stē-və-ˌdōr\ n [Sp estibador, fr. estibar to pack, fr. L stipare] : one who works at loading and unloading ships in port

¹**stew** \'st(y)ü\ vb : to boil slowly : SIMMER

²**stew** n : a dish of stewed meat and vegetables served in gravy

stew·ard \'st(y)ü-ərd\ n 1 : one employed on a large establishment to manage domestic concerns (as collecting rents, keeping accounts, and directing servants) 2 : one actively concerned with the direction of the affairs of an organization 3 : one who supervises the provision and distribution of food (as on a ship); also : an employee on a ship or airplane who serves passengers generally — **stew·ard·ess** n — **stew·ard·ship** n

¹**stick** \'stik\ n 1 : a cut or broken branch or twig; also : a long slender piece of wood 2 : ROD, STAFF 3 : something like a stick in being rigid, slender, and rigid 4 : a dull uninteresting person

²**stick** vb **stuck** \'stək\ **stick·ing** 1 : STAB, PRICK 2 : to thrust or project in some direction or manner 3 : IMPALE 4 : to hold fast by or as if by gluing : ADHERE 5 : ATTACH, FASTEN 6 : to hold to something firmly or closely : CLING 7 : to become jammed or blocked 8 : to be unable to proceed or move freely

stick·er \'stik-ər\ n : one that sticks (as a bur) or causes sticking (as glue); esp : a gummed label

stick·ler \'stik-(ə-)lər\ n : one who insists on exactness or completeness

sticky \'stik-ē\ adj 1 : ADHESIVE 2 : VISCOUS, GLUEY 3 : tending to stick (~ valve)

stiff \'stif\ adj 1 : not pliant : RIGID 2 : not limber (~ joints) 3 : TENSE, TAUT 4 : not flowing or working easily (~ paste) 5 : not natural and easy : FORMAL 6 : STRONG, FORCEFUL (~ breeze) 7 : HARSH, SEVERE 8 : DIFFICULT syn inflexible — **stiff·ly** adv — **stiff·ness** n

stiff·en vb : to make or become stiff — **stiff·en·er** n

stiff-necked \'stif-'nekt\ adj : STUBBORN, HAUGHTY

sti·fle \'stī-fəl\ vb 1 : SUFFOCATE 2 : QUENCH, SUPPRESS 3 : SMOTHER, MUFFLE 4 : to die because of obstruction of the breath

stig·ma \'stig-mə\ n, pl **stig·ma·ta** \stig-'mät-ə, 'stig-mət-ə\ or **stigmas** 1 : a mark of disgrace or discredit : BRAND, STAIN 2 pl : bodily marks resembling the wounds of the crucified Christ 3 : the part of the pistil of a flower that receives the pollen in fertilization — **stig·mat·ic** \stig-'mat-ik\ adj

stig·ma·tize \'stig-mə-ˌtīz\ vb 1 : to mark with a stigma 2 : to set a mark of disgrace upon : CENSURE

stile \'stīl\ n : steps used for crossing a fence or wall

sti·let·to \stə-'let-ō\ n, pl **-tos** or **-toes** : a slender dagger

¹**still** \'stil\ adj 1 : MOTIONLESS 2 : making no sound : QUIET, SILENT — **stillness** n

²**still** n 1 : STILLNESS, SILENCE 2 : a static photograph esp. of an instant in a motion picture

³**still** vb : to make or become still : QUIET

⁴**still** adv 1 : without motion (sit ~) 2 : up to and during this or that time 3 : in spite of that : NEVERTHELESS 4 : EVEN, YET (~ more difficult problem) (ran ~ faster)

still-born \'stil-'bórn\ adj : born dead

still life n, pl **still lifes** : a picture of inanimate objects

stilt \'stilt\ n : one of a pair of poles for walking with each having a step or loop for the foot; also : a polelike support of a structure above ground or water level

stilt·ed \'stil-təd\ adj : FORMAL, POMPOUS (~ writing)

Stil·ton \'stilt-ᵊn\ n : a blue-veined cheese with wrinkled rind

stim·u·lant \'stim-yə-lənt\ n 1 : an agent (as a drug) that temporarily increases the activity of an organism or any of its parts 2 : STIMULUS 3 : an alcoholic beverage — **stimulant** adj

stim·u·late \-ˌlāt\ vb : to make active or more active : ANIMATE, AROUSE syn excite, provoke — **stim·u·la·tion** \ˌstim-yə-'lā-shən\ n — **stim·u·la·tive** \'stim-yə-ˌlāt-iv\ adj

stim·u·lus \'stim-yə-ləs\ n, pl **-li** \-ˌlī\ : something that stimulates : SPUR

¹**sting** \'stiŋ\ vb **stung** \'stəŋ\ **stinging** 1 : to prick painfully esp. with a sharp or poisonous process 2 : to cause to suffer acutely

²**sting** n 1 : an act of stinging; also : a resultant sore, pain, or mark 2 : a pointed often venom-bearing organ (as of a bee or scorpion) used esp. in defense

stin·gy \'stin-jē\ adj : not generous : SPARING, NIGGARDLY — **stin·gi·ness** n

stink \'stiŋk\ vb **stank** \'staŋk\ or **stunk** \'stəŋk\ **stunk; stink·ing** : to give forth a strong and offensive smell; also : to be extremely bad in quality or repute — **stink** n

¹**stint** \'stint\ vb 1 : to restrict to a scant allowance : cut short in amount 2 : to be sparing or frugal

²**stint** n 1 : RESTRAINT, LIMITATION 2 : an assigned amount of work

sti·pend \'stī-ˌpend, -pənd\ n : a fixed sum of money paid periodically for services or to defray expenses

stip·ple \'stip-əl\ vb 1 : to engrave by means of dots and light strokes instead of by lines 2 : to apply (as paint or ink) with small short touches that together produce an even and softly graded shadow — **stipple** n

stip·u·late \'stip-yə-ˌlāt\ vb : to make an agreement; esp : to make a special demand for something as a condition in an agreement — **stip·u·la·tion** \ˌstip-yə-'lā-shən\ n

¹**stir** \'stər\ vb **stirred; stir·ring** 1 : to move slightly 2 : to move to activity (as by pushing, beating, or prodding) 3 : to mix, dissolve, or make by a continued circular movement (~ eggs into cake batter) 4 : AROUSE, EXCITE

²**stir** n 1 : a state of agitation or activity 2 : an act of stirring

³**stir** n, slang : PRISON

stir·ring adj 1 : ACTIVE, BUSTLING 2 : ROUSING, INSPIRING

stir·rup \'stər-əp\ n [OE stigrāp, lit., mounting rope] : a light frame hung from a saddle to support the foot of a horseback rider

¹stitch \'stich\ *n* **1** : one of the series of loops formed by or over a needle in sewing **2** : a particular method of stitching **3** : a sudden sharp pain esp. in the side *syn* twinge

²stitch *vb* **1** : to fasten or join with stitches **2** : to decorate with stitches **3** : SEW

stoat \'stōt\ *n* : the European ermine esp. in its brown summer coat

¹stock \'stäk\ *n* **1** : a block of wood **2** : a stupid person **3** : a wooden part of a thing serving as its support, frame, or handle **4** : the original from which others derive : SOURCE; *also* : a group having a common origin : FAMILY, STRAIN **5** : farm animals : LIVESTOCK **6** : the supply of goods kept by a merchant **7** : the sum of money invested in a large business **8** *pl* : PILLORY **9** : a company of actors playing at a particular theater and presenting a series of plays **10** : raw material

²stock *vb* : to provide with stock or a stock

³stock *adj* : kept regularly for sale or use; *also* : used regularly : STANDARD

stock·ade \stä-'kād\ *n* : an enclosure of posts and stakes for defense or confinement

stock·bro·ker \'stäk-,brō-kər\ *n* : one who executes orders to buy and sell securities

stock exchange *n* **1** : an association of stockbrokers **2** : a place where trading in securities is accomplished under an organized system

stock·hold·er \'stäk-,hōl-dər\ *n* : one who owns stock

stock·i·net \,stäk-ə-'net\ *n* : an elastic knitted textile fabric used esp. for infants' wear and bandages

stock·ing \'stäk-iŋ\ *n* : a close-fitting knitted covering for the foot and leg

stock market *n* **1** : STOCK EXCHANGE 1 **2** : a market for stocks or for a particular stock

stock·pile \'stäk-,pīl\ *n* : a reserve supply esp. of something essential — **stockpile** *vb*

stocky \'stäk-ē\ *adj* : being short and relatively thick : STURDY *syn* thickset, squat

stock·yard \'stäk-,yärd\ *n* : a yard for stock; *esp* : one for livestock about to be slaughtered or shipped

stodgy \'stäj-ē\ *adj* : HEAVY, DULL, UNINSPIRED

¹sto·ic \'stō-ik\ *n* : one who suffers silently and without complaining

³stoic *adj* : not affected by passion or feeling; *esp* : showing indifference to pain *syn* impassive, phlegmatic, apathetic, stolid — **sto·i·cal** \'stō-i-kəl\ *adj* — **sto·i·cal·ly** *adv* — **sto·i·cism** \'stō-ə-,siz-əm\ *n*

stoke \'stōk\ *vb* **1** : to stir up a fire **2** : to tend and supply fuel to a furnace — **stok·er** *n*

¹stole \'stōl\ *past of* STEAL

²stole *n* **1** : a long narrow band worn round the neck by some clergymen **2** : a long wide scarf or similar covering worn by women usu. across the shoulders

stolen *past part of* STEAL

stol·id \'stäl-əd\ *adj* : not easily aroused or excited : showing little or no emotion *syn* phlegmatic, apathetic — **sto·lid·i·ty** \stä-'lid-ət-ē\ *n* — **stol·id·ly** \'stäl-əd-lē\ *adv*

¹stom·ach \'stəm-ək, -ik\ *n* **1** : a sac-like digestive organ into which food goes from the mouth by way of the throat and which opens below into the intestine **2** : ABDOMEN, BELLY **3** : APPETITE

²stomach *vb* : to bear without overt resentment : BROOK

stom·ach·er \'stəm-i-kər, -chər\ *n* : the front of a bodice often appearing between the laces of an outer garment (as in 16th century costume)

¹stone \'stōn\ *n* **1** : hardened earth or mineral matter : ROCK **2** : a small piece of rock **3** : a precious stone : GEM **4** *pl usu* **stone** : a British unit of weight equal to 14 pounds **5** : a hard stony seed or one (as of a plum) with a stony covering **6** : a hard abnormal mass in a bodily cavity or duct — **stony** *adj*

²stone *vb* **1** : to pelt or kill with stones **2** : to remove the stones of (a fruit)

stood *past of* STAND

stooge \'stüj\ *n* **1** : an actor whose function is to feed lines to the chief comedian **2** : a person who plays a subordinate or compliant role to a principal

stool \'stül\ *n* **1** : a seat without back or arms **2** : FOOTSTOOL **3** : a discharge of fecal matter

¹stoop \'stüp\ *vb* **1** : to bend over **2** : CONDESCEND **3** : to humiliate or lower oneself socially or morally

²stoop *n* **1** : an act of bending over **2** : a bent position of head and shoulders

³stoop *n* : a small porch or platform at a house door

¹stop \'stäp\ *vb* **stopped; stop·ping** **1** : to close (an opening or hole) by filling or covering closely **2** : BLOCK, HALT **3** : to cease to go on **4** : to cease activity or operation **5** : STAY, TARRY *syn* quit, discontinue, desist, lodge, sojourn

²stop *n* **1** : CHECK, OBSTRUCTION **2** : END, CESSATION **3** : a set of organ pipes of one tone quality; *also* : a control knob for such a set **4** : PLUG, STOPPER **5** : an act of stopping **6** : a delay in a journey : STAY **7** : a place for stopping **8** *chiefly Brit* : any of several punctuation marks

stop·page *n* : the act of stopping : the state of being stopped

stop·per *n* : something (as a cork or plug) for sealing an opening

stop·watch \'stäp-,wäch\ *n* : a watch having a hand that can be started or stopped at will for exact timing (as of a race)

stor·age \'stōr-ij\ *n* **1** : the act of storing; *esp* : the safekeeping of goods (as in a warehouse) **2** : space for storing; *also* : cost of storing

storage battery *n* : a group of connected cells that converts chemical energy into electrical energy by reversible chemical reactions and that may be recharged by electrical means

¹store \'stōr\ *vb* **1** : to provide esp. for

a future need **2** : to collect and keep for future use **3** : to deposit in a safe place (as a warehouse)

²store n **1** : something accumulated and kept for future use **2** : a large or ample quantity **3** : STOREHOUSE **4** : a retail business establishment

store·house \-,haus\ n : a building for storing goods or supplies; *also* : an abundant source or supply

store·keep·er \-,kē-pər\ n : one who operates a retail store

store·room \'stōr-,rüm, -,rùm\ n : a room for storing goods or supplies

sto·ried \'stōr-ēd\ adj : celebrated in story or history

stork \'stórk\ n : a large stout-billed Old World wading bird related to the herons

¹storm \'stórm\ n **1** : a heavy fall of rain, snow, or hail with high wind **2** : a violent outbreak or disturbance **3** : a mass attack ⟨capture a position by ∼⟩ — **storm·i·ly** adv — **storm·i·ness** n — **stormy** adj

²storm vb **1** : to blow with violence; *also* : to rain, snow, or hail heavily **2** : to be violently angry : RAGE **3** : to rush along furiously **4** : to make a mass attack against

¹sto·ry \'stōr-ē\ n **1** : NARRATIVE, ACCOUNT **2** : REPORT, STATEMENT **3** : ANECDOTE **4** : FIB syn chronicle, lie, falsehood, untruth

²story *also* **sto·rey** n : a floor of a building or the habitable space between two floors

sto·ry·tell·er \-,tel-ər\ n : a teller of stories — **sto·ry·tell·ing** adj or n

sto·tin·ka \stō-'ting-kə\ n, pl **sto·tin·ki** \-kē\ — see MONEY table

¹stout \'staút\ adj **1** : BRAVE **2** : STURDY, STAUNCH **3** : FIRM, SOLID **4** : FORCEFUL **5** : BULKY, THICKSET syn strong, stalwart, tough, tenacious, fleshy, fat, portly, corpulent, obese, plump — **stout·ly** adv — **stout·ness** n

²stout n : a dark heavy alcoholic beverage brewed from roasted malt and hops

¹stove \'stōv\ n : an apparatus that burns fuel or uses electricity to provide heat (as for cooking or room heating)

²stove *past of* STAVE

stow \'stō\ vb **1** : to pack in a compact mass **2** : HIDE, STORE

stow·away \-ə-,wā\ n : one who conceals himself on a ship or airplane to obtain a passage

strad·dle \'strad-²l\ vb **1** : to stand, sit, or walk with legs spread apart **2** : to favor or seem to favor two apparently opposite sides — **straddle** n

strafe \'strāf\ vb : to fire upon with machine guns from a low-flying airplane

strag·gle \'strag-əl\ vb **1** : to wander from the direct course : ROVE **2** : to become separated from others of the same kind : STRAY — **strag·gler** \-(ə-)lər\ n — **strag·gly** \-(ə-)lē\ adj

¹straight \'strāt\ adj **1** : following the same direction throughout its length : not curved : not crooked or bent : not irregular : DIRECT **2** : not wandering from the main point or proper course ⟨∼ thinking⟩ **3** : HONEST, UPRIGHT **4** : not in confusion : correctly arranged or ordered **5** : UNMIXED, UNDILUTED ⟨∼ whisky⟩

²straight adv : in a straight manner

³straight n **1** : a straight line, course, or arrangement **2** : the part of a race track between the last turn and the

finish **3** : a sequence of five cards in a poker hand

straight·edge \-,ej\ n : a bar with a straight edge for testing straight lines and surfaces or drawing straight lines

straight·en \'strāt-²n\ vb : to make or become straight

straight·for·ward \strāt-'fór-wərd\ adj **1** : proceeding in a straight course or manner **2** : CANDID, HONEST

straight·way \'strāt-,wā, -'wā\ adv : IMMEDIATELY

¹strain \'strān\ n **1** : LINEAGE, ANCESTRY **2** : a group (as of people or plants) of presumed common ancestry; *also* : a distinctive quality shared by its members **3** : STREAK, TRACE **4** : the general style or tone **5** : MELODY

²strain vb **1** : to draw taut **2** : to exert to the utmost **3** : to filter or remove by filtering **4** : to stretch beyond a proper limit **5** : to injure by improper or excessive use ⟨∼ed his heart⟩ ⟨a ∼ed back⟩ **6** : to strive violently — **strain·er** n

³strain n **1** : excessive tension or exertion (as of body or mind) **2** : bodily injury from excessive tension, effort, or use; *esp* : one in which muscles or ligaments are unduly stretched usu. from a wrench or twist **3** : deformation of a material body under the action of applied forces

¹strait \'strāt\ adj **1** *archaic* : NARROW, CONSTRICTED **2** *archaic* : STRICT **3** : DIFFICULT, STRAITENED

²strait n **1** : a narrow channel connecting two bodies of water **2** pl : DISTRESS, NEED

strait·en \'strāt-²n\ vb **1** : to hem in : CONFINE **2** : to make distressing or difficult

strait-laced \-'lāst\ adj : strict in observing moral or religious laws

¹strand \'strand\ n : SHORE; *esp* : a shore of a sea or ocean

²strand vb **1** : to run, drift, or drive upon the shore ⟨a ∼ed ship⟩ **2** : to place or leave in a helpless position

³strand n **1** : one of the fibers twisted or plaited together into a cord, rope, or cable; *also* : a cord, rope, or cable made up of such fibers **2** : a twisted or plaited ropelike mass ⟨a ∼ of pearls⟩

strange \'strānj\ adj [OF *estrange*, fr. L *extraneus*, fr. *extra* outside] **1** : of external origin, kind, or character **2** : UNUSUAL; *also* : UNNATURAL **3** : NEW, UNFAMILIAR **4** : SHY **5** : UNACCUSTOMED, INEXPERIENCED syn singular, unique, peculiar, eccentric, erratic, odd, queer, quaint, curious — **strange·ly** adv — **strange·ness** n

strang·er \'strān-jər\ n **1** : FOREIGNER **2** : INTRUDER **3** : a person with whom one is unacquainted

stran·gle \'strang-gəl\ vb **1** : to choke to death : THROTTLE **2** : STIFLE, SUFFOCATE — **stran·gler** \-g(ə-)lər\ n

stran·gu·late \'stran-gyə-,lāt\ vb : to become so constricted as to stop circulation ⟨a *strangulated* rupture⟩

stran·gu·la·tion \,stran-gyə-'lā-shən\ n : the act or process of strangling or strangulating : the state of being strangled or strangulated

¹strap \'strap\ n : a narrow strip of flexible material used esp. for fastening, holding together, or wrapping

²strap vb **strapped**; **strap·ping** **1** : to secure with a strap **2** : BIND, CONSTRICT **3** : to flog with a strap **4** : STROP

strap·less *adj* **:** having no straps and esp. no shoulder straps

strap·ping \'strap-iŋ\ *adj* **:** LARGE, STRONG, HUSKY

strat·a·gem \'strat-ə-jəm\ *n* 1 **:** a trick in war to deceive or outwit the enemy; *also* **:** a deceptive scheme 2 **:** skill in deception

strat·e·gy \'strat-ə-jē\ *n* 1 **:** the science and art of military command employed with the object of meeting the enemy under conditions advantageous to one's own force 2 **:** a careful plan or method esp. for achieving an end — **stra·te·gic** \strə-'tē-jik\ *adj* — **strat·e·gist** \'strat-ə-jəst\ *n*

strat·i·fy \'strat-ə-ˌfī\ *vb* 1 **:** to form or arrange in layers — **strat·i·fi·ca·tion** \ˌstrat-ə-fə-'kā-shən\ *n*

strat·o·sphere \'strat-ə-ˌsfiər\ *n* **:** a portion of the earth's atmosphere from about 7 to 31 miles above the earth's surface — **strat·o·spher·ic** \ˌstrat-ə-'sfi(ə)r-ik, -'sfer-\ *adj*

stra·tum \'strāt-əm, 'strat-\ *n, pl* **stra·ta** \-ə\, 1 **:** a bed, layer, or sheetlike mass (as of one kind of rock lying between layers of other kinds of rock) 2 **:** a level of culture; *also* **:** a group of people representing one stage in cultural development

¹**straw** \'strò\ *n* 1 **:** stalks of grain after threshing; *also* **:** a single coarse dry stem (as of a grass) 2 **:** a thing of small worth **:** TRIFLE 3 **:** a prepared tube for sucking up a beverage

²**straw** *adj* 1 **:** made of straw 2 **:** having no real value, force, or validity ⟨a ~ vote⟩

straw·ber·ry \'stro-ˌber-ē, -b(ə-)rē\ *n* **:** an edible juicy red pulpy fruit borne by a low herb related to the roses; *also* **:** this plant

¹**stray** \'strā\ *vb* 1 **:** to wander from a course **:** DEVIATE 2 **:** ROVE, ROAM

²**stray** *n* 1 **:** a domestic animal wandering at large or lost **:** WAIF

³**stray** *adj* 1 **:** having strayed **:** separated from the group or the main body 2 **:** occurring at random **:** UNRELATED ⟨~ remarks⟩

¹**streak** \'strēk\ *n* 1 **:** a line or mark of a different color or texture from its background 2 **:** a narrow band of light; *also* **:** a lightning bolt 3 **:** a slight admixture **:** TRACE 4 **:** a brief run (as of luck); *also* **:** an unbroken series ⟨winning ~⟩

²**streak** *vb* 1 **:** to form streaks in or on 2 **:** to move very swiftly

¹**stream** \'strēm\ *n* 1 **:** a body of water (as a brook or river) flowing on the earth 2 **:** a course of running liquid 3 **:** a steady flow (as of water, air, or gas) 4 **:** a continuous procession (the ~ of history)

²**stream** *vb* 1 **:** to flow in or as if in a stream 2 **:** to pour out streams of liquid 3 **:** to stretch or trail out in length 4 **:** to move forward in a steady stream

stream·er *n* 1 **:** a long narrow ribbon-like flag 2 **:** a long ribbon on a dress or hat 3 **:** a column of light (as from the aurora borealis) 4 **:** a newspaper headline that runs across the entire sheet

stream·let *n* **:** a small stream

stream·lined \'strēm-ˌlīnd\ *also*

stream·line *adj* 1 **:** made with contours to reduce resistance to motion through water or air 2 **:** SIMPLIFIED 3 **:** MODERNIZED — **streamline** *vb*

street \'strēt\ *n* [OE *strǣt*, fr. LL *strata* paved road, fr. L, fem. of *stratus*, pp. of *sternere* to spread flat] 1 **:** a thoroughfare esp. in a city, town, or village 2 **:** the occupants of the houses on a street

street·car \-ˌkär\ *n* **:** a passenger vehicle running on rails on the public streets

strength \'streŋth\ *n* 1 **:** the quality of being strong **:** ability to do or endure **:** POWER 2 **:** TOUGHNESS, SOLIDITY 3 **:** power to resist attack 4 **:** INTENSITY 5 **:** force as measured in numbers ⟨~ of an army⟩

strength·en \'streŋ-thən\ *vb* **:** to make, grow, or become stronger — **strength·en·er** *n*

stren·u·ous \'stren-yə-wəs\ *adj* 1 **:** VIGOROUS, ENERGETIC 2 **:** requiring energetic effort or stamina — **stren·u·ous·ly** *adv*

strep·to·coc·cus \ˌstrep-tə-'käk-əs\ *n* **:** any of various spherical bacteria that usu. grow in chains and include causers of serious diseases

strep·to·my·cin \-'mīs-ⁿn\ *n* **:** an antibiotic produced by soil bacteria and used esp. in treating tuberculosis

¹**stress** \'stres\ *n* 1 **:** PRESSURE, STRAIN; *esp* **:** a force that tends to distort a body 2 **:** URGENCY, EMPHASIS 3 **:** intense effort 4 **:** prominence of sound **:** ACCENT; *also* **:** any syllable carrying the accent 5 **:** a factor that induces bodily or mental tension; *also* **:** a state induced by such a factor

²**stress** *vb* 1 **:** to put pressure or strain on 2 **:** to put emphasis on **:** ACCENT

¹**stretch** \'strech\ *vb* 1 **:** to spread or reach out **:** EXTEND 2 **:** to draw out in length or breadth **:** EXPAND 3 **:** to make tense **:** STRAIN 4 **:** EXAGGERATE 5 **:** to become extended without breaking ⟨rubber ~es easily⟩

²**stretch** *n* 1 **:** an act of extending or drawing out beyond ordinary or normal limits 2 **:** a continuous extent in length, area, or time 3 **:** the extent to which something may be stretched 4 **:** either of the straight sides of a racecourse

³**stretch** *adj* **:** easily stretched ⟨~ pants⟩

stretch·er *n* 1 **:** one that stretches 2 **:** a litter (as of canvas) esp. for carrying a disabled person

strew \'strü\ *vb* **strewed**; **strewed** *or* **strewn** \'strün\ **strew·ing** 1 **:** to spread by scattering 2 **:** to cover by or as if by scattering something over or on 3 **:** DISSEMINATE

stria \'strī-ə\ *n, pl* **stri·ae** \-ˌē\ **:** a threadlike line or narrow band (as of color) esp. when one of a series of parallel lines — **stri·at·ed** \-ˌāt-əd\ *adj* — **stri·a·tion** \strī-'ā-shən\ *n*

strick·en \'strik-ən\ *adj* 1 **:** WOUNDED 2 **:** afflicted with disease, misfortune, or sorrow

strict \'strikt\ *adj* 1 **:** allowing no evasion or escape **:** RIGOROUS ⟨~ discipline⟩ 2 **:** ACCURATE, PRECISE **syn** stringent, rigid — **strict·ly** *adv* — **strict·ness** *n*

stric·ture \'strik-chər\ *n* 1 **:** hostile criticism **:** a critical remark 2 **:** an abnormal narrowing of a bodily passage; *also* : the narrowed part

¹stride \'strīd\ *vb* strode \'strōd\ strid·den \'strid-ᵊn\ strid·ing \'strīd-iŋ\ : to walk or run with long regular steps — strid·er *n*

²stride *n* 1 : a long step; *also* : the distance covered by such a step 2 : manner of striding : GAIT

stri·dent \'strīd-ᵊnt\ *adj* : of loud harsh sound : SHRILL

strife \'strīf\ *n* : CONFLICT, FIGHT, STRUGGLE **syn** discord, contention, dissension

¹strike \'strīk\ *vb* struck \'strək\ struck *or* strick·en \'strik-ən\ strik·ing 1 : to take a course : GO ⟨~ out for home⟩ 2 : to touch or hit sharply; *also* : to deliver a blow 3 : to cause by or as if by a blow ⟨*struck* terror in the foe⟩ 4 : to lower (as a flag or sail) usu. in salute or surrender 5 : to collide with; *also* : to injure or destroy by collision 6 : DELETE, CANCEL 7 : to produce by impressing ⟨*struck* a medal⟩; *also* : COIN ⟨a new cent⟩ 8 : to cause to sound ⟨~ a bell⟩ 9 : to afflict suddenly : lay low ⟨*stricken* with a high fever⟩ 10 : to appear to; *also* : to appear to as remarkable : IMPRESS 11 : to reach by reckoning ⟨~ an average⟩ 12 : to stop work in order to obtain a change in conditions of employment 13 : to cause (a match) to ignite by rubbing 14 : to come upon : meet with ⟨~ a detour from the main road⟩ 15 : to take on : ASSUME ⟨~ a pose⟩ — strik·er *n*

²strike *n* 1 : an act or instance of striking 2 : a sudden discovery of rich ore or oil deposits 3 : a pitched baseball recorded against a batter 4 : the knocking down of all the bowling pins with the first ball 5 : a military attack

strike out \'strīk-'aut\ *vb* 1 : to enter upon a course of action 2 : to start out vigorously 3 : to make an out in baseball by a strikeout

strike·out \-,aut\ *n* : an out in baseball as a result of a batter's being charged with three strikes

strike zone *n* : the area over home plate through which a pitched baseball must pass to be called a strike

strik·ing *adj* : attracting attention : very noticeable **syn** arresting, salient, conspicuous, outstanding, remarkable, prominent — strik·ing·ly *adv*

¹string \'striŋ\ *n* 1 : a line usu. composed of twisted threads 2 : a series of things arranged as if strung on a cord 3 : a natural fiber (as that joining the halves of a bean pod) 4 *pl* : the stringed instruments of an orchestra **syn** succession, progression, sequence, set

²string *vb* strung \'strəŋ\ string·ing 1 : to provide with strings ⟨~ a racket⟩ 2 : to thread on or as if on a string ⟨~ pearls⟩ 3 : to take the strings out of ⟨~ beans⟩ 4 : to hang, tie, or fasten by a string 5 : to make taut 6 : to extend like a string

strin·gen·cy \'strin-jən-sē\ *n* 1 : STRICTNESS, SEVERITY 2 : SCARCITY ⟨~ of money⟩ — strin·gent *adj*

string·er \'striŋ-ər\ *n* : a long horizontal member in a framed structure or a bridge

stringy \'striŋ-ē\ *adj* 1 : resembling string esp. in tough, fibrous, or disordered quality ⟨~ meat⟩ ⟨~ hair⟩

2 : lean and sinewy in build

¹strip \'strip\ *vb* stripped; strip·ping 1 : to take the covering or clothing from 2 : to take off one's clothes 3 : to pull or tear off 4 : to make bare or clear (as by cutting or grazing) 5 : PLUNDER, PILLAGE **syn** divest, denude

²strip *n* 1 : a long narrow flat piece 2 : AIRSTRIP

¹stripe \'strīp\ *n* 1 : a line or long narrow division having a different color from the background 2 : a strip of braid (as on a sleeve) indicating military rank or length of service 3 : TYPE, CHARACTER **syn** description, nature, kind, sort

²stripe *vb* : to make stripes upon

strip·ling \'strip-liŋ\ *n* : YOUTH, LAD

strive \'strīv\ *vb* strove \'strōv\ striv·en \'striv-ən\ *or* strived; striv·ing \'strī-viŋ\ 1 : to struggle in opposition : CONTEND 2 : to make effort : labor hard **syn** endeavor, attempt, try

stro·bo·scope \'strō-bə-,skōp\ *n* : an instrument for studying rapid motion by means of a rapidly flashing light — stro·bo·scop·ic \,strō-bə-'skäp-ik\ *adj*

strode *past of* STRIDE

¹stroke \'strōk\ *n* 1 : the act of striking : BLOW, KNOCK 2 : a sudden action or process producing an impact ⟨~ of lightning⟩ ⟨a ~ of luck⟩; *also* : APOPLEXY 3 : a vigorous effort 4 : the sound of striking (as of a clock) 5 : one of a series of movements against air or water to get through or over it ⟨the ~ of a bird's wing⟩ 6 : a single movement with or as if with a tool or implement ⟨a ~ of the pen⟩ 7 : an oarsman who sets the tempo for a crew

²stroke *vb* 1 : to set gently 2 : to set the stroke for (a racing crew)

stroll \'strōl\ *vb* : to walk in a leisurely or idle manner **syn** saunter, amble — stroll *n* — stroll·er *n*

strong \'strȯŋ\ *adj* stron·ger \'strȯŋ-gər\ stron·gest \-gəst\ 1 : POWERFUL, VIGOROUS 2 : HEALTHY, ROBUST 3 : of a specified number ⟨an army 10 thousand ~⟩ 4 : not mild or weak 5 : VIOLENT ⟨~ wind⟩ 6 : ZEALOUS 7 : not easily broken 8 : FIRM, SOLID **syn** stout, sturdy, stalwart, tough — strong·ly \'strȯŋ-lē\ *adv*

strong·hold \'strȯŋ-,hōld\ *n* : a fortified place : FORTRESS

stron·tium \'strän-ch(ē-)əm, 'stränt-ē-əm\ *n* : a soft malleable metallic chemical element

¹strop \'sträp\ *n* : STRAP; *esp* : one for sharpening a razor

²strop *vb* stropped; strop·ping : to sharpen a razor on a strop

stro·phe \'strō-fē\ *n* : a division of a poem — stroph·ic \'sträf-ik\ *adj*

strove *past of* STRIVE

struck *past of* STRIKE

struc·ture \'strək-chər\ *n* 1 : the manner of building : CONSTRUCTION 2 : something built (as a house or a dam); *also* : something made up of interdependent parts in a definite pattern of organization 3 : arrangement or relationship of elements (as particles, parts, or organs) in a substance, body, or system — struc·tur·al *adj*

strug·gle \'strəg-əl\ *vb* 1 : to make strenuous efforts against opposition : STRIVE 2 : to proceed with difficulty or with great effort **syn** endeavor, attempt, try

²**struggle** *n* **1** : a violent effort or exertion **2** : CONTEST, STRIFE

strum \'strəm\ *vb* **strummed; strumming** : to play on a stringed instrument by brushing the strings with the fingers ⟨~ a guitar⟩

strum·pet \'strəm-pət\ *n* : PROSTITUTE

strung *past of* STRING

¹**strut** \'strət\ *vb* **strut·ted; strut·ting** : to walk with an affectedly proud gait **syn** swagger

²**strut** *n* **1** : a haughty or pompous gait **2** : a bar or rod for resisting lengthwise pressure

strych·nine \'strik-,nīn, -nən\ *n* : a bitter poisonous alkaloid from some plants used to kill vermin and in small doses as a stimulant

¹**stub** \'stəb\ *n* **1** : STUMP 1 **2** : a short blunt end **3** : a small part of each leaf (as of a checkbook) kept as a memorandum of the items on the detached part

²**stub** *vb* **stubbed; stub·bing** : to strike (as one's toe) against something

stub·ble \'stəb-əl\ *n* : the stumps of herbs and esp. grasses left in the soil after harvest — **stub·bly** \-(ə-)lē\ *adj*

stub·born \'stəb-ərn\ *adj* **1** : FIRM, DE-TERMINED **2** : not easily controlled or remedied ⟨a ~ fever⟩ **3** : done or continued in a willful, unreasonable, or persistent manner — **stub·born·ly** *adv* — **stub·born·ness** *n*

stub·by \'stəb-ē\ *adj* : short, blunt, and thick like a stub

¹**stuc·co** \'stək-ō\ *n* : plaster for coating exterior walls

²**stucco** *vb* **stuc·coed; stuc·co·ing** : to coat or decorate with stucco

stuck *past of* STICK

stuck-up \'stək-'əp\ *adj* : CONCEITED, VAIN

¹**stud** \'stəd\ *n* **1** : one of the smaller uprights in a building to which sheathing, paneling, or laths are fastened **2** : a removable device like a button used as a fastener or ornament ⟨shirt ~s⟩ **3** : a projecting nail, pin, or rod

²**stud** *vb* **stud·ded; stud·ding 1** : to supply with or adorn with studs **2** : DOT ⟨rocks *studded* the field⟩

stud·ding *n* **1** : material for studs **2** : STUDS

stu·dent \'st(y)üd-ᵊnt\ *n* : SCHOLAR, PUPIL; *esp* : one who attends a school

stud·ied \'stəd-ēd\ *adj* : INTENTIONAL ⟨a ~ insult⟩ **syn** deliberate, considered, premeditated, designed

stu·dio \'st(y)üd-ē-,ō\ *n* **1** : a place where an artist works; *also* : a place for the study of an art **2** : a place where motion pictures are made **3** : a place equipped for the transmission of radio or television programs

stu·di·ous \'st(y)üd-ē-əs\ *adj* : devoted to study; given to reading — **stu·di·ous·ly** *adv*

¹**study** \'stəd-ē\ *n* **1** : the use of the mind to gain knowledge **2** : the act or process of learning about something **3** : a branch of learning **4** : INTENT, PURPOSE **5** : careful examination **6** : a room esp. for reading and writing

²**study** *vb* **1** : to apply the attention and mind to a subject : examine closely **2** : MEDITATE, PONDER **syn** consider, contemplate, weigh

¹**stuff** \'stəf\ *n* **1** : personal property

2 : raw material **3** : a finished textile fabric; *esp* : a worsted fabric **4** : writing, talk, or ideas of little or transitory worth **5** : an aggregate of matter; *also* : matter of a particular often unspecified kind **6** : fundamental material : SUBSTANCE **7** : special knowledge or capability

²**stuff** *vb* **1** : to fill by packing something into : CRAM **2** : to stop up : PLUG **3** : to prepare (as meat) by filling with seasoned bread crumbs and spices **4** : to eat greedily : GORGE

stuff·ing *n* : material used to fill tightly; *esp* : a mixture of bread crumbs and spices used to stuff meat and poultry

stuffy \'stəf-ē\ *adj* : lacking fresh air : CLOSE; *also* : blocked up (a ~ nose)

stul·ti·fy \'stəl-tə-,fī\ *vb* **1** : to cause to appear foolish or stupid **2** : make untrustworthy; *also* : DISGRACE, DIS-HONOR — **stul·ti·fi·ca·tion** \,stəl-tə-fə-'kā-shən\ *n*

stum·ble \'stəm-bəl\ *vb* **1** : to trip in walking or running **2** : to walk unsteadily; *also* : to speak or act in a blundering or clumsy manner **3** : to blunder morally; *also* : to come or happen by chance ⟨~ onto the truth⟩ — **stumble** *n*

¹**stump** \'stəmp\ *n* **1** : the part of a plant and esp. a tree remaining when the root after the top is cut off **2** : the base of a bodily part (as a leg or tooth) left after the rest is removed **3** : a place or occasion for political public speaking — **stumpy** *adj*

²**stump** *vb* **1** : to clear (land) of stumps **2** : to tour (a region) making political speeches **3** : BAFFLE, PERPLEX **4** : to walk clumsily and heavily

stun \'stən\ *vb* **stunned; stun·ning 1** : to make senseless or dizzy by or as if by a blow **2** : BEWILDER, STUPEFY

stung *past of* STING

stunk *past of* STINK

stun·ning *adj* : strikingly pretty or attractive

stunt \'stənt\ *vb* : to hinder the normal growth of : DWARF

²**stunt** *n* : an unusual or spectacular feat

stu·pe·fy \'st(y)ü-pə-,fī\ *vb* : to make dull, torpid, or numb by or as if by drugs; *also* : AMAZE, BEWILDER — **stu·pe·fac·tion** \,st(y)ü-pə-'fak-shən\ *n*

stu·pen·dous \st(y)ü-'pen-dəs\ *adj* : causing astonishment esp. because of great size or height **syn** tremendous, prodigious, monumental, monstrous — **stu·pen·dous·ly** *adv*

stu·pid \'st(y)ü-pəd\ *adj* **1** : very dull in mind **2** : lacking in understanding **2** : showing or resulting from dullness of mind — **stu·pid·i·ty** \st(y)ü-'pid-ət-ē\ *n* — **stu·pid·ly** \'st(y)ü-pəd-lē\ *adv*

stu·por \'st(y)ü-pər\ *n* **1** : a condition marked by great dulling or suspension of sense or feeling **2** : a torpid state often following stress or shock — **stu·por·ous** *adj*

stur·dy \'stərd-ē\ *adj* [ME, reckless, brave, fr. OF *estourdi* stunned, fr. pp. of *estourdir* to stun, fr. (assumed) VL *exturdire* to be dizzy like a thrush drunk from eating grapes, fr. L *ex-*, intensive prefix +‖*turdus* thrush] **1** : RESOLUTE, UNYIELDING **2** : STRONG, ROBUST **syn**

ə abut; ᵊ kitten; ər further; a back; ā bake; ä cot, cart; aú out; ch chin; e less; ē easy; g gift; i trip; I life; j joke; ŋ sing; ō flow; ó flaw; ói coin; th thin; t͟h this; ü loot; ú foot; y yet; yü few; yú furious; zh vision

stout, stalwart, tough, tenacious —
stur·di·ly adv — **stur·di·ness** n
stur·geon \'stər-jən\ n : any of various
large food fishes whose roe is made into
caviar
stut·ter \'stət-ər\ vb : to speak haltingly
: STAMMER — **stutter** n
¹**sty** \'stī\ n : a pen or housing for swine
²**sty** or **stye** \'stī\ n : an inflamed swelling on the edge of an eyelid
¹**style** \'stīl\ n 1 : a slender pointed
instrument or process; esp : STYLUS
2 : a way of speaking or writing; esp
: one characteristic of an individual,
period, school, or nation ⟨ornate ~⟩
3 : the custom or plan followed in
spelling, capitalization, punctuation,
and typographic arrangement and display 4 : mode of address : TITLE
5 : manner or method of acting or performing esp. as sanctioned by some
standard; also : a distinctive or characteristic manner 6 : a fashionable
manner or mode ⟨her dress is out of ~⟩
7 : overall excellence, skill, or grace in
performance, manner, or appearance
²**style** vb 1 : NAME, DESIGNATE 2 : to
make or design in accord with a prevailing mode
styl·ish \'stī-lish\ adj : conforming to
an accepted standard of style : FASH-
IONABLE syn modish, smart, chic ~
styl·ish·ly adv — **styl·ish·ness** n
styl·ist \'stī-ləst\ n : a master of style
esp. in writing
sty·lus \'stī-ləs\ n, pl **sty·li** \-,lī\ also
sty·lus·es 1 : a pointed implement
used by the ancients for writing on wax
2 : a phonograph needle
¹**sty·mie** \'stī-mē\ n : a position in golf
when the ball nearer the hole lies in the
line of play of another ball
²**stymie** vb **sty·mied; sty·mie·ing** n
: BLOCK, FRUSTRATE
styp·tic \'stip-tik\ adj : tending to check
bleeding
suave \'swäv\ adj : persuasively pleasing : smoothly agreeable syn urbane,
diplomatic, bland — **suave·ly** adv —
sua·vi·ty \'swäv-ət-ē\ n
sub \'səb\ n : SUBMARINE
sub- \,səb, 'səb\ prefix 1 : under : beneath 2 : subordinate : secondary
3 : subordinate portion of : subdivision
of 4 : with repetition of a process
described in a simple verb so as to form,
stress, or deal with subordinate parts or
relations 5 : somewhat 6 : falling
nearly in the category of : bordering
upon

subacute	subcommission
subagency	subcontract
subagent	subcortical
subangular	subcrystalline
subaqueous	subculture
subarctic	subdeacon
subarea	subdean
subarid	subdepot
subatmospheric	subentry
subaverage	subepidermal
subbasement	subequal
subcaliber	subequatorial
subcaption	suberect
subcaste	subessential
subcellar	subfamily
subchairman	subfauna
subchief	subflora
subcivilized	subfossil
subclass	subfreezing
subclassify	subgenus
subclause	subgroup
subclinical	subhorizontal

subhuman	subprofessional
subindex	subrational
subinterval	subregion
subirrigate	subsaturated
subkingdom	subscience
sublateral	subsense
sublease	subsexual
sublethal	subsocial
subliterate	subspecialty
submaximal	subspecies
subminimal	substage
suboblique	subsystem
suboceanic	subtemperate
subocular	subthreshold
subopaque	subtidal
suboptimal	subtopic
suborbicular	subtotal
subparagraph	subtreasury
subparallel	subtype
subpermanent	subunit
subplot	subvisible
subpolar	subvocal
subprincipal	

sub·al·tern \,sə-'bȯl-tərn\ n : SUBORDI-
NATE; also : a commissioned officer in
the British army below the rank of captain
sub·atom·ic \,səb-ə-'täm-ik\ adj : of
or relating to the inside of the atom or
particles smaller than atoms
sub·com·mit·tee \'səb-kə-,mit-ē\ n : a
subordinate division of a committee
sub·con·scious \'səb-'kän-chəs\ adj
: existing in the mind and affecting
thought and behavior without entering
conscious awareness — **subconscious**
n — **sub·con·scious·ly** adv
sub·con·ti·nent \'səb-'känt-(ə-)nənt\ n
: a vast subdivision of a continent
sub·cu·ta·ne·ous \,səb-kyu̇-'tā-nē-əs\
adj : located, made, or used under the
skin ⟨~ fat⟩ ⟨a ~ needle⟩
sub·di·vide \,səb-də-'vīd\ vb : to divide
into several parts; esp : to divide (a
tract of land) into building lots — **sub-
di·vi·sion** \-'vizh-ən\ n
sub·due \səb-'d(y)ü\ vb 1 : to bring
into subjection : VANQUISH 2 : to bring
under control : CURB 3 : to reduce the
intensity of
¹**sub·ject** \'səb-jikt\ n 1 : a person
under the authority of another 2 : a
person subject to a sovereign 3 : an
individual subjected to an operation or
process 4 : the person or thing discussed or treated : TOPIC, THEME 5 : a
word or word group denoting that of
which something is affirmed or declared
²**subject** adj 1 : being under the power
or rule of another 2 : LIABLE, EXPOSED
⟨~ to floods⟩ 3 : dependent on some
act or condition ⟨appointment ~ to
senate approval⟩ syn subordinate,
secondary, tributary, open, prone,
susceptible
³**sub·ject** \səb-'jekt\ vb 1 : to bring
under control : CONQUER 2 : to make
liable : EXPOSE 3 : to cause to undergo
or submit to — **sub·jec·tion** \-'jek-
shən\ n
sub·jec·tive \səb-'jek-tiv\ adj 1 : of,
relating to, or of the nature of a subject
2 : of, relating to, or arising within one's
self or mind in contrast to what is outside : PERSONAL — **sub·jec·tive·ly** adv
— **sub·jec·tiv·i·ty** \-,jek-'tiv-ət-ē\ n
sub·ject matter \'səb-jikt-\ n : matter
presented for consideration, discussion,
or study
sub·join \(,)səb-'jȯin\ vb : ANNEX, AP-
PEND
sub ju·di·ce \sub-'yüd-i-,kā\ adv : be-

fore a judge or court **:** not yet legally decided

sub·ju·gate \'səb-ji-ˌgāt\ *vb* **:** CONQUER, SUBDUE; *also* **:** ENSLAVE **syn** reduce, overcome, overthrow, rout, vanquish, defeat, beat — **sub·ju·ga·tion** \ˌsəb-ji-'gā-shən\ *n*

sub·junc·tive \səb-'jəŋk-tiv\ *adj* **:** of, relating to, or constituting a verb form that represents a denoted act or state as contingent or possible or viewed emotionally (as with desire) ⟨∼ mood⟩ — **subjunctive** *n*

sub·let \'səb-'let\ *vb* **:** to let all or a part of (a leased property) to another; *also* **:** to rent (a property) from a lessee

sub·li·mate \'səb-lə-ˌmāt\ *vb* **1 :** to cause to pass from a solid to a vapor state by the action of heat and then condense to solid form without apparently liquefying **2 :** to direct the energy of (as desires) toward higher ends — **sub·li·ma·tion** \ˌsəb-lə-'mā-shən\ *n*

¹sub·lime \sə-'blīm\ *adj* **1 :** EXALTED, NOBLE **2 :** having awe-inspiring beauty or grandeur **syn** glorious, splendid, superb, resplendent, gorgeous — **sub·lim·i·ty** \-'blim-ət-ē\ *n*

²sublime *vb* **:** SUBLIMATE

sub·lu·nar \'səb-'lü-nər\ *adj* **:** SUBLUNARY

sub·lu·na·ry \-nə-rē\ *adj* **:** situated beneath the moon **:** TERRESTRIAL

sub·ma·chine gun \ˌsəb-mə-'shēn-ˌgən\ *n* **:** an automatic or partly automatic firearm fired from the shoulder or hip

¹sub·ma·rine \'səb-mə-ˌrēn\ *adj* **:** existing, acting, or growing under the sea

²submarine *n* **:** a naval boat capable of operation either on or below the surface of the water

sub·merge \səb-'mərj\ *vb* **1 :** to put or plunge under the surface of water **2 :** INUNDATE **syn** immerse, duck, dip — **sub·mer·gence** *n*

sub·merse \-'mərs\ *vb* **:** SUBMERGE — **sub·mer·sion** \-'mər-zhən\ *n*

sub·mit \səb-'mit\ *vb* **-mit·ted; -mit·ting 1 :** to commit to the discretion or decision of another or of others **2 :** YIELD, SURRENDER **3 :** to put forward as an opinion — **sub·mis·sion** \-'mish-ən\ *n* — **sub·mis·sive** \-'mis-iv\ *adj*

sub·nor·mal \'səb-'nȯr-məl\ *adj* **:** falling below what is normal (mentally ∼) ⟨a ∼ rainfall⟩ — **sub·nor·mal·i·ty** \ˌsəb-nȯr-'mal-ət-ē\ *n*

¹sub·or·di·nate \sə-'bȯrd-(ˑ-)nət\ *adj* **1 :** of lower class or rank **2 :** INFERIOR **3 :** submissive to authority **4 :** subordinated to other elements in a sentence **:** DEPENDENT ⟨∼ clause⟩ **syn** secondary, subject, tributary

²subordinate *n* **:** one that is subordinate

³sub·or·di·nate \-ˑn-ˌāt\ *vb* **1 :** to place in a lower rank or class **2 :** SUBDUE — **sub·or·di·na·tion** \-ˌbȯrd-ˑn-'ā-shən\ *n*

sub·orn \sə-'bȯrn\ *vb* **1 :** to incite secretly **:** INSTIGATE **2 :** to induce to commit perjury — **sub·or·na·tion** \ˌsəb-ˌȯr-'nā-shən\ *n*

¹sub·poe·na \sə-'pē-nə\ *n* [L *sub poena* under penalty] **:** a writ commanding the person named in it to attend court under penalty for failure to do so

²subpoena *vb* **:** to summon with a subpoena

sub·scribe \səb-'skrīb\ *vb* **1 :** to sign one's name to a document **2 :** to give consent by or as if by signing one's name **3 :** to promise to contribute by signing one's name with the amount promised **4 :** to place an order by signing **5 :** FAVOR, APPROVE **syn** agree, acquiesce — **sub·scrib·er** *n*

sub·scrip·tion \-'skrip-shən\ *n* **1 :** the act of subscribing **:** SIGNATURE **2 :** a purchase by signed order

sub·se·quent \'səb-si-kwənt, -ˌkwent\ *adj* **:** following after **:** SUCCEEDING — **sub·se·quent·ly** *adv*

sub·ser·vi·ence \səb-'sər-vē-əns\ *n* **1 :** a subordinate place or condition; *also* **:** willingness to serve in a subordinate capacity **2 :** SERVILITY — **sub·ser·vi·en·cy** *n* — **sub·ser·vi·ent** *adj*

sub·side \səb-'sīd\ *vb* **1 :** to settle to the bottom of a liquid **2 :** to tend downward **:** DESCEND **3 :** SINK, SUBMERGE **4 :** to become quiet and tranquil **syn** abate, wane — **sub·sid·ence** \səb-'sīd-ˑns, 'səb-səd-əns\ *n*

¹sub·sid·i·ary \səb-'sid-ē-ˌer-ē\ *adj* **1 :** furnishing aid or support; *also* **:** owned or controlled by some main company **2 :** of or relating to a subsidy **syn** auxiliary, contributory, subservient

²subsidiary *n* **:** one that is subsidiary; *esp* **:** a company controlled by another

sub·si·dize \'səb-sə-ˌdīz\ *vb* **:** to aid or furnish with a subsidy

sub·si·dy \'səb-səd-ē\ *n* **:** a gift of public money to another country or to private enterprise **syn** grant, appropriation

sub·sist \səb-'sist\ *vb* **1 :** EXIST, PERSIST **2 :** to receive the means (as food and clothing) of maintaining life

sub·sis·tence \-'sis-təns\ *n* **1 :** EXISTENCE **2 :** means of subsisting **:** the minimum (as of food and clothing) necessary to support life

sub·soil \'səb-ˌsȯil\ *n* **:** a layer of weathered material just under the surface soil

sub·son·ic \səb-'sän-ik\ *adj* **1 :** being or relating to a speed less than that of sound; *also* **:** moving at such a speed **2 :** INFRASONIC

sub·stance \'səb-stəns\ *n* **1 :** essential nature **:** ESSENCE ⟨divine ∼⟩; *also* **:** the fundamental or essential part or quality ⟨the ∼ of his speech⟩ **2 :** physical material from which something is made or which has discrete existence; *also* **:** matter of particular or definite chemical constitution **3 :** material possessions **:** PROPERTY, WEALTH

sub·stan·dard \'səb-'stan-dərd\ *adj* **:** falling short of a standard or norm ⟨∼ housing⟩

sub·stan·tial \səb-'stan-chəl\ *adj* **1 :** existing as or in substance **:** MATERIAL; *also* **:** not illusory **:** REAL **2 :** IMPORTANT, ESSENTIAL **3 :** NOURISHING, SATISFYING ⟨∼ meal⟩ **4 :** having means **:** WELL-TO-DO **5 :** CONSIDERABLE ⟨∼ profit⟩ **6 :** STRONG, FIRM — **sub·stan·tial·ly** *adv*

sub·stan·ti·ate \səb-'stan-chē-ˌāt\ *vb* **1 :** VERIFY, PROVE **2 :** to give substance or body to **:** EMBODY — **sub·stan·ti·a·tion** \-ˌstan-chē-'ā-shən\ *n*

sub·stan·tive \'səb-stən-tiv\ *n* **:** NOUN

also : a word or phrase used as a noun

sub·sta·tion \'səb-₁stā-shən\ *n* : a station (as a post-office branch) subordinate to another station

¹**sub·sti·tute** \'səb-stə-₁t(y)üt\ *n* : a person or thing replacing another

²**substitute** *vb* **1** : to put in the place of another **2** : to serve as a substitute — **sub·sti·tu·tion** \₁səb-stə-'t(y)ü-shən\ *n*

sub·stra·tum \'səb-₁strāt-əm, -₁strat-\ *n, pl* **-ta** \-ə\ : the layer or structure lying underneath

sub·struc·ture \'səb-₁strək-chər\ *n* : the structure underneath : FOUNDATION

sub·ter·fuge \'səb-tər-₁fyüj\ *n* : a trick or device used in order to conceal, escape, or evade **syn** fraud, deception, trickery

sub·ter·ra·ne·an \₁səb-tə-'rā-nē-ən\ *adj* **1** : lying or being underground **2** : SECRET, HIDDEN

sub·tile \'sət-ºl, ₁səb-tºl\ *adj* : SUBTLE

sub·ti·tle \'səb-₁tīt-ºl\ *n* **1** : a secondary or explanatory title (as of a book) **2** : printed matter projected on a motion-picture screen during or between the scenes

sub·tle \'sət-ºl\ *adj* **1** : hardly noticeable : DELICATE, REFINED **2** : SHREWD, KEEN **3** : CLEVER, SLY — **sub·tle·ty** \-tē\ *n* — **sub·tly** \'sət-(º)lē\ *adv*

sub·tract \səb-'trakt\ *vb* : to take away (as one number from another) — **sub·trac·tion** \-'trak-shən\ *n*

sub·tra·hend \'səb-trə-₁hend\ *n* : the quantity to be subtracted in mathematics

sub·trop·i·cal \₁səb-'träp-i-kəl\ *adj* : of, relating to, or being regions bordering on the tropical zone

sub·urb \'səb-₁ərb\ *n* **1** : an outlying part of a city; *also* : a small community adjacent to a city **2** *pl* : a residential area adjacent to a city — **sub·ur·ban** \sə-'bər-bən\ *adj*

sub·ur·ban·ite \sə-'bər-bə-₁nīt\ *n* : one living in a suburb

sub·ven·tion \səb-'ven-chən\ *n* : SUBSIDY, ENDOWMENT

sub·vert \səb-'vərt\ *vb* **1** : OVERTHROW, RUIN **2** : CORRUPT **syn** overturn, upset — **sub·ver·sion** \-'vər-zhən\ *n* — **sub·ver·sive** \-'vər-siv\ *adj*

sub·way \'səb-₁wā\ *n* : an underground way; *esp* : an underground electric railway

suc·ceed \sək-'sēd\ *vb* **1** : to follow next in order or next after some other person or thing; *esp* : to inherit sovereignty **2** : to attain a desired object or end : be successful

suc·cess \-'ses\ *n* **1** : satisfactory completion of something **2** : the gaining of wealth and fame **3** : a person or thing that succeeds — **suc·cess·ful** *adj* — **suc·cess·ful·ly** *adv*

suc·ces·sion \-'sesh-ən\ *n* **1** : the order, act, or right of succeeding to a property, title, or throne **2** : a repeated following of one person or thing after another **3** : a series of persons or things that follow one after another **syn** progression, sequence, set, chain, train, string

suc·ces·sive \-'ses-iv\ *adj* : following in order : CONSECUTIVE — **suc·ces·sive·ly** *adv*

suc·ces·sor \-'ses-ər\ *n* : one that succeeds to a throne, title, estate, or office

suc·cinct \sə(k)-'siŋkt\ *adj* : BRIEF, CONCISE **syn** terse, laconic, summary — suc-

cinct·ly *adv* — **suc·cinct·ness** *n*

suc·cor \'sək-ər\ *n* **1** : AID, HELP, RELIEF — **succor** *vb*

suc·co·tash \'sək-ə-₁tash\ *n* : beans and kernels of sweet corn cooked together

suc·cu·lent \'sək-yə-lənt\ *adj* : full of juice : JUICY; *also* : having fleshy tissues that conserve moisture — **suc·cu·lence** *n*

suc·cumb \sə-'kəm\ *vb* **1** : to give up : YIELD **2** : DIE **syn** submit, capitulate, relent

¹**such** \(')səch\ *adj* **1** : of this or that kind **2** : having a quality just specified or to be specified

²**such** *pron* **1** : such a one or ones ⟨he's the boss, and had the right to act as ~⟩ **2** : that or those similar or related thereto ⟨bought boards and nails and ~⟩

³**such** *adv* : to that degree : so ⟨~ fine clothes⟩

such·like \'səch-₁līk\ *adj* : SIMILAR

¹**suck** \'sək\ *vb* **1** : to draw in liquid and esp. mother's milk with the mouth **2** : to draw liquid from by action of the mouth ⟨~ an orange⟩ **3** : to take in or up or remove by or as if by suction

²**suck** *n* : the act of sucking : SUCTION

suck·er *n* **1** : one that sucks **2** : a part of an animal's body used for sucking or for clinging **3** : a fish with thick soft lips that suck in food **4** : a shoot from the roots or lower part of a plant **5** : a person easily cheated or deceived

suck·le \'sək-əl\ *vb* : to give or draw milk from the breast or udder; *also* : NURTURE, REAR

suck·ling \'sək-liŋ\ *n* : a young unweaned mammal

su·cre \'sü-krā\ *n* — see MONEY table

su·crose \'sü-₁krōs\ *n* : cane or beet sugar

suc·tion \'sək-shən\ *n* **1** : the act of sucking **2** : the act or process of drawing something (as liquid or dust) into a space (as in a vacuum cleaner or a pump) by partially exhausting the air in the space

sud·den \'səd-ºn\ *adj* **1** : happening or coming quickly or unexpectedly ⟨~ shower⟩; *also* : come upon unexpectedly ⟨~ turn in the road⟩ **2** : ABRUPT, STEEP ⟨~ descent to the sea⟩ **3** : marked by or showing hastiness : RASH ⟨~ decision⟩ **4** : made or brought about in a short time : PROMPT ⟨~ cure⟩ **syn** precipitate, headlong, impetuous — **sud·den·ly** *adv* — **sud·den·ness** *n*

suds \'sədz\ *n pl* : soapy water esp. when frothy

sue \'sü\ *vb* **1** : PETITION, SOLICIT **2** : to seek justice or right by bringing legal action **syn** pray, plead

suede or **suède** \'swād\ *n* [F *gants de Suède* Swedish gloves] **1** : leather with a napped surface **2** : a fabric with a suedelike nap

su·et \'sü-ət\ *n* : the hard fat from beef and mutton that yields tallow

suf·fer \'səf-ər\ *vb* **1** : to feel or endure pain : EXPERIENCE, UNDERGO **3** : to bear loss, damage, or injury **4** : ALLOW, PERMIT **syn** endure, abide, tolerate, stand, brook, let, leave — **suf·fer·er** *n*

suf·fer·ance \-(ə-)rəns\ *n* **1** : consent or approval implied by lack of interference or resistance **2** : ENDURANCE, PATIENCE

suf·fer·ing \-(ə-)riŋ\ *n* : PAIN, MISERY, HARDSHIP

suf·fice \sə-'fīs\ *vb* **1** : to satisfy a

need : be sufficient **2** : to be capable or competent

suf·fi·cien·cy \sə-'fish-ən-sē\ n **1** : a sufficient quantity to meet one's needs **2** : ADEQUACY **3** : SELF-CONFIDENCE

suf·fi·cient \sə-'fish-ənt\ adj : adequate to accomplish a purpose or meet a need : ENOUGH — **suf·fi·cient·ly** adv

¹**suf·fix** \'səf-,iks\ n : an affix occurring at the end of a word

²**suf·fix** \'səf-,iks, (,)sə-'fiks\ vb : to attach as a suffix

suf·fo·cate \'səf-ə-,kāt\ vb : STIFLE, SMOTHER, CHOKE — **suf·fo·ca·tion** \,səf-ə-'kā-shən\ n

suf·fra·gan \'səf-ri-gən\ n : an assistant bishop; esp : one not having the right of succession — **suffragan** adj

suf·frage \'səf-rij\ n **1** : VOTE **2** : the right to vote : FRANCHISE

suf·frag·ette \,səf-ri-'jet\ n : a woman who advocates suffrage for her sex

suf·frag·ist \'səf-ri-jəst\ n : one who advocates extension of the suffrage esp. to women

suf·fuse \sə-'fyüz\ vb : to spread over or through in the manner of a fluid or light syn infuse, imbue, ingrain — **suf·fu·sion** \-'fyü-zhən\ n

¹**sug·ar** \'shug-ər\ n **1** : a sweet substance that is colorless or white when pure and is chiefly derived from sugarcane or sugar beets **2** : a water-soluble compound (as glucose) that varies widely in sweetness — **sug·ary** adj

²**sugar** vb **1** : to mix, cover, or sprinkle with sugar **2** : SWEETEN ⟨~ advice with flattery⟩ **3** : to form sugar ⟨a syrup that ~s⟩ **4** : GRANULATE

sugar beet n : a large beet with a white root from which sugar is made

sug·ar·cane \'shug-ər-,kān\ n : a tall grass widely grown in warm regions for the sugar in its stalks

sug·ar·plum \-,pləm\ n : a small ball of candy

sug·gest \sə(g)-'jest\ vb **1** : to put (as a thought, plan, or desire) into a person's mind **2** : to remind or evoke by association of ideas syn imply, hint, intimate, insinuate — **sug·gest·ible** adj

sug·ges·tion \-'jes-chən\ n **1** : an act or instance of suggesting; also : something suggested **2** : a slight indication : TRACE ⟨a ~ of blue in the gray⟩

sug·ges·tive \-'jes-tiv\ adj : tending to suggest something; esp : suggesting something improper or indecent — **sug·ges·tive·ly** adv — **sug·ges·tive·ness** n

su·i·cide \'sü-ə-,sīd\ n **1** : the act of killing oneself purposely **2** : a person who kills himself purposely — **su·i·cid·al** \,sü-ə-'sīd-ə¹\ adj

sui ge·ner·is \,sü-,ī-'jen-ə-rəs, ,sü-ē-\ adj : being in a class by itself : UNIQUE

¹**suit** \'süt\ n **1** : an action in court to recover a right or claim **2** : an act of suing or entreating; esp : COURTSHIP **3** : a number of things used together ⟨~ of clothes⟩ **4** : one of the four sets of playing cards in a pack syn prayer, plea, petition, appeal

²**suit** vb **1** : to be appropriate or fitting **2** : to be becoming to **3** : to meet the needs or desires of : PLEASE

suit·able \'süt-ə-bəl\ adj : FITTING, PROPER, APPROPRIATE syn fit, meet, apt — **suit·abil·i·ty** \,süt-ə-'bil-ət-ē\ n —

suit·able·ness \'süt-ə-bəl-nəs\ n — **suit·ably** adv

suit·case \'süt-,kās\ n : a flat rectangular traveling bag

suite \'swēt\ n **1** : a personal staff attending a dignitary or ruler : RETINUE **2** : a group of rooms occupied as a unit : APARTMENT **3** : a modern instrumental composition free in its character and number of movements; also : a long orchestral concert arrangement in suite form of material drawn from a longer work (as a ballet) **4** : a set of matched furniture for a room

suit·ing \'süt-iŋ\ n : fabric for suits of clothes

suit·or \'süt-ər\ n **1** : one who sues or petitions **2** : one who seeks to marry a woman

sul·fa \'səl-fə\ adj **1** : related chemically to sulfanilamide **2** : of, relating to, or using sulfa drugs ⟨~ therapy⟩

sul·fa·nil·a·mide \,səl-fə-'nil-ə-,mīd\ n : a sulfur-containing organic compound used in the treatment of various infections

sul·fate or **sul·phate** \'səl-,fāt\ n : a salt or ester of sulfuric acid

sul·fide or **sul·phide** \-,fīd\ n : a compound of sulfur with an element or radical

sul·fur or **sul·phur** \'səl-fər\ n : a nonmetallic element that occurs in nature combined or free in the form of yellow crystals and in masses, crusts, and powder and is used in making gunpowder and matches, in vulcanizing rubber, and in medicine — **sul·fu·re·ous** \,səl-'fyúr-ē-əs\ adj

sul·fu·ric or **sul·phu·ric** \,səl-'fyúr-ik\ adj : of, relating to, or containing sulfur

sulfuric acid n : a heavy corrosive oily liquid used esp. in making fertilizers, chemicals, and petroleum products

sul·fu·rous or **sul·phu·rous** \'səl-f(y)ə-rəs, ,səl-'fyúr-əs\ adj **1** : of, relating to, or containing sulfur **2** : of or relating to brimstone or the fire of hell : INFERNAL **3** : FIERY, SCORCHING

¹**sulk** \'səlk\ vb : to be or become moodily silent

²**sulk** n : a sulky mood or spell

¹**sulky** adj : inclined to sulk : MOROSE, MOODY syn surly, glum, sullen, gloomy — **sulk·i·ly** adv — **sulk·i·ness** n

²**sulky** n : a light 2-wheeled vehicle with a seat for the driver and usu. no body

sul·len \'səl-ən\ adj **1** : gloomily silent : MOROSE **2** : DISMAL, GLOOMY ⟨a ~ sky⟩ syn glum, surly, surly — **sul·len·ly** adv — **sul·len·ness** n

sul·ly \'səl-ē\ vb : to SOIL, SMIRCH, DEFILE

sul·phur var of SULFUR

sul·tan \'səlt-ⁿn\ n : a sovereign esp. of a Muslim state — **sul·tan·ate** \-,āt\ n

sul·ta·na \,səl-'tan-ə\ n **1** : the wife of the mother, sister, or daughter of a sultan **2** : a pale seedless grape; also : a raisin of this grape

sul·try \'səl-trē\ adj : very hot and moist : SWELTERING; also : burning hot : TORRID

¹**sum** \'səm\ n **1** : a quantity of money **2** : the whole amount **3** : GIST **4** : the result obtained by adding numbers **5** : a problem in arithmetic syn aggregate, total, whole

²**sum** vb **summed**; **sum·ming 1** : to find the sum of by adding or counting

2 : SUMMARIZE — usu. used with *up*

su·mac *or* **su·mach** \'s(h)ü-,mak\ *n* : any of various shrubs or small trees with feathery compound leaves and spikes of red or whitish berries

sum·ma·rize \'səm-ə-,rīz\ *vb* : to tell in a summary : present briefly

¹sum·ma·ry \'səm-ə-rē\ *adj* 1 : covering the main points briefly : CONCISE 2 : done without delay or formality ⟨∼ punishment⟩ **syn** terse, succinct, laconic — **sum·mar·i·ly** \(,)sə-'mer-ə-lē, 'səm-ə-rə-lē\ *adv*

²summary *n* : a concise statement of the main points

sum·ma·tion \(,)sə-'mā-shən\ *n* : a summing up; *esp* : a speech in court summing up the arguments in a case

sum·mer \'səm-ər\ *n* : the season of the year in a region in which the sun shines most directly : the warmest period of the year — **sum·mery** *adj*

sum·mer·house \-,haus\ *n* : a rustic covered structure in a garden to provide a shady retreat

sum·mit \'səm-ət\ *n* : the highest point : PEAK

sum·mon \'səm-ən\ *vb* 1 : to call to a meeting : CONVOKE 2 : to send for; *also* : to order to appear in court 3 : to evoke esp. by an act of the will ⟨∼ up courage⟩ — **sum·mon·er** *n*

sum·mons \'səm-ənz\ *n, pl* **-mons·es** 1 : an authoritative call to appear at a designated place or to attend to a duty 2 : a warning or citation to appear in court at a specified time to answer charges

sump·tu·ous \'səmp-ch(ə-w)əs\ *adj* [L *sumptuosus* expensive, fr. *sumptus* expense, fr. *sumere* to take, spend] : LAVISH, LUXURIOUS

¹sun \'sən\ *n* 1 : the shining celestial body around which the earth and other planets revolve and from which they receive light and heat 2 : a celestial body that like the sun is the center of a system of planets 3 : SUNSHINE — **sun·less** *adj* — **sun·ny** *adj*

²sun *vb* **sunned; sun·ning** 1 : to expose to or as if to the rays of the sun 2 : to sun oneself

sun·bon·net \-,bän-ət\ *n* : a bonnet with a wide brim to shield the face and neck from the sun

¹sun·burn \-,bərn\ *vb* : to burn or discolor by the sun

²sunburn *n* : a skin inflammation caused by exposure to sunlight

sun·dae \'sən-dē\ *n* : ice cream served with topping (as crushed fruit and syrups)

Sun·day \'sən-dē\ *n* : the 1st day of the week : the Christian Sabbath

sun·der \'sən-dər\ *vb* : to force apart : separate with violence **syn** sever, part

sun·di·al \'sən-,dī(-ə)l\ *n* : a device for showing the time of day from the shadow cast by an upright pin on a plate

sun·down \-,daun\ *n* : the time of the setting of the sun

sun·dries \'sən-drēz\ *n pl* : various small articles or items

sun·dry \-drē\ *adj* : SEVERAL, DIVERS, VARIOUS **syn** many, numerous

sun·fish \-,fish\ *n* 1 : a huge sea fish with a deep flattened body 2 : any of various American freshwater fishes resembling the perches

sun·flow·er \-,flau(-ə)r\ *n* : a tall plant related to the daisies and often grown for the oil-rich seeds of its yellow-petaled dark-centered flower heads

sung *past of* SING

sunk *past of* SINK

sunk·en \'sən-kən\ *adj* 1 : SUBMERGED ⟨∼ ships⟩ 2 : fallen in : HOLLOW ⟨∼ cheeks⟩ 3 : lying in a depression ⟨∼ garden⟩; *also* : constructed below the general floor level ⟨∼ living room⟩

sun·light \'sən-,līt\ *n* : SUNSHINE

sun·lit \-,lit\ *adj* : lighted by direct sunshine

sun·rise \-,rīz\ *n* : the apparent rising of the sun above the horizon; *also* : the time of this rising

sun·set \-,set\ *n* : the apparent descent of the sun below the horizon; *also* : the time of this descent

sun·shade \-,shād\ *n* : something (as a parasol or awning) used as a protection from the sun's rays

sun·shine \'sən-,shīn\ *n* : the direct light of the sun — **sun·shiny** *adj*

sun·spot \-,spät\ *n* : one of the dark spots that appear from time to time on the sun's surface

sun·stroke \-,strōk\ *n* : heatstroke caused by exposure to the sun

sun·up \-,əp\ *n* : the time of the rising of the sun

¹sup \'səp\ *vb* **supped; sup·ping** : to take or drink in swallows or gulps

²sup *n* : a mouthful esp. of liquor or broth : SIP; *also* : a small quantity of liquid

³sup *vb* **supped; sup·ping** 1 : to eat the evening meal 2 : to make one's supper ⟨*supped* on roast beef⟩

su·per- \,sü-pər, 'sü-\ *prefix* 1 : over and above : higher in quantity, quality, or degree than 2 : more than 3 : in addition : extra 3 : exceeding a norm 4 : in excessive degree or intensity 5 : surpassing all or most others of its kind 6 : situated above, on, or at the top of 7 : next above or higher 8 : more inclusive than 9 : superior in status or position

superacid	supersalesman
superalkaline	supersalesmanship
superbomb	supersecret
supereminent	supersize
superendurance	supersized
superfine	superspectacle
supergalaxy	superspeed
supergene	superstate
superglacial	superstratum
supergovernment	superstrength
superheat	supersubtle
superhuman	supersubtlety
superhumanly	supersystem
superindividual	supertanker
superliner	supertax
supermicroscope	supertemporal
supernormal	supertower
superpatriot	supervoltage
superpatriotism	superwoman
superphysical	superzealot
superpower	

su·per·abun·dant \,sü-pər-ə-'bən-dənt\ *adj* : more than ample : EXCESSIVE — **su·per·abun·dance** *n*

su·per·an·nu·ate \-'an-yə-,wāt\ *vb* : to retire and pension because of old age — **su·per·an·nu·at·ed** *adj*

su·perb \su̇-'pərb\ *adj* 1 : LORDLY, MAJESTIC 2 : RICH, SPLENDID 3 : of highest quality **syn** resplendent, glorious, gorgeous, sublime — **su·perb·ly** *adv*

su·per·car·go \,sü-pər-'kär-gō\ *n* : an officer on a merchant ship who manages the business part of the voyage

su·per·cil·i·ous \,sü-pər-'sil-ē-əs\ *adj* [L *supercilium* eyebrow, haughtiness] : haughtily contemptuous **syn** disdainful, overbearing, arrogant

su·per·ego \,sü-pər-'ē-gō\ *n* : a largely unconscious part of the psyche significant in character formation

su·per·fi·cial \,sü-pər-'fish-əl\ *adj* 1 : of or relating to the surface or appearance only 2 : not thorough : SHALLOW \ns cursory — **su·per·fi·ci·al·i·ty** \,fish-ē-'al-ət-ē\ *n* — **su·per·fi·cial·ly** \-'fish-(ə-)lē\ *adv*

su·per·flu·ous \sù-'pər-flə-wəs\ *adj* : exceeding what is sufficient or necessary : SURPLUS **syn** extra, spare — **su·per·flu·i·ty** \,sù-pər-'flü-ət-ē\ *n*

su·per·high·way \,sü-pər-'hī-,wā\ *n* : a broad highway designed for high-speed traffic

su·per·im·pose \-im-'pōz\ *vb* : to lay (one thing) over and above something else **syn** superpose

su·per·in·tend \,sü-p(ə-)rin-'tend\ *vb* : to have or exercise the charge and oversight of : DIRECT — **su·per·in·ten·dence** *n* — **su·per·in·ten·den·cy** *n* — **su·per·in·ten·dent** *n*

¹**su·pe·ri·or** \sù-'pir-ē-ər\ *adj* 1 : situated higher up; *also* : higher in rank or numbers 2 : better than most others of its kind 3 : of greater value or importance 4 : courageously indifferent (as to pain or misfortune) 5 : ARROGANT, HAUGHTY — **su·pe·ri·or·i·ty** \-,pir-ē-'ȯr-ət-ē\ *n*

²**superior** *n* 1 : one who is above another in rank, office, or station; *esp* : the head of a religious house or order 2 : one higher in quality or merit

¹**su·per·la·tive** \sù-'pər-lət-iv\ *adj* 1 : of, relating to, or constituting the degree of grammatical comparison that denotes an extreme or unsurpassed level or extent 2 : surpassing others : SUPREME **syn** peerless, incomparable

²**superlative** *n* 1 : the superlative degree or a superlative form in a language 2 : the utmost degree : ACME

su·per·nal \sù-'pərn-ᵊl\ *adj* 1 : of or from on high : high in position : TOWERING 2 : of heavenly or spiritual character : ETHEREAL

su·per·nat·u·ral \,sü-pər-'nach-(ə-)rəl\ *adj* : of or relating to phenomena beyond or outside of nature; *esp* : relating to or attributed to a divinity, ghost, or infernal spirit — **su·per·nat·u·ral·ly** *adv*

¹**su·per·nu·mer·ary** \-'n(y)ü-mə-,rer-ē\ *adj* : exceeding the number stated or required : EXTRA **syn** surplus, superfluous

²**supernumerary** *n* : an extra person or thing; *esp* : an actor hired for a nonspeaking part

su·per·pose \,sü-pər-'pōz\ *vb* : SUPERIMPOSE — **su·per·po·si·tion** \-pə-'zish-ən\ *n*

su·per·scribe \'sü-pər-,skrīb\ *vb* : to write on the top or outside : write a name or address on the outside or cover of : ADDRESS — **su·per·scrip·tion** \,sü-pər-'skrip-shən\ *n*

su·per·sede \,sü-pər-'sēd\ *vb* : to take the place or position of : REPLACE **syn** displace, supplant

su·per·son·ic \-'sän-ik\ *adj* 1 : having a frequency above the human ear's audibility limit (~ vibrations) 2 : relating to supersonic waves or vibrations 3 : being or relating to speeds from one to five times the speed of sound; *also* : capable of moving at such a speed (a ~ airplane)

su·per·sti·tion \-'stish-ən\ *n* 1 : beliefs or practices resulting from ignorance, fear of the unknown, or trust in magic or chance 2 : an irrationally abject attitude of mind toward nature, the unknown, or God resulting from superstition — **su·per·sti·tious** *adj*

su·per·struc·ture \'sü-pər-,strək-chər\ *n* : something built on a base or as a vertical extension

su·per·vene \,sü-pər-'vēn\ *vb* : to occur as something additional or unexpected **syn** follow, succeed, ensue

su·per·vise \'sü-pər-,vīz\ *vb* : OVERSEE, SUPERINTEND — **su·per·vi·sion** \,sü-pər-'vizh-ən\ *n* — **su·per·vi·sor** \'sü-pər-,vī-zər\ *n* — **su·per·vi·so·ry** \,sü-pər-'vīz-(ə-)rē\ *adj*

su·pine \sù-'pīn\ *adj* 1 : lying on the back with face upward 2 : LETHARGIC, SLUGGISH; *also* : ABJECT **syn** inactive, inert, passive, idle

sup·per \'səp-ər\ *n* : the evening meal when dinner is taken at midday — **sup·per·less** *adj* — **sup·per·time** \-,tīm\ *n*

sup·plant \sə-'plant\ *vb* 1 : to take the place of (another) esp. by force or trickery 2 : REPLACE **syn** displace, supersede

sup·ple \'səp-əl\ *adj* 1 : capable of bending without breaking or creasing : LIMBER, PLIANT 2 : COMPLIANT, ADAPTABLE **syn** resilient, elastic

¹**sup·ple·ment** \'səp-lə-mənt\ *n* 1 : something that supplies a want or makes an addition 2 : a continuation of a book or periodical containing corrections or additional material — **sup·ple·men·tal** \,səp-lə-'ment-ᵊl\ *adj* — **sup·ple·men·ta·ry** \-'ment-(ə-)rē\ *adj*

²**sup·ple·ment** \'səp-lə-,ment\ *vb* : to fill up the deficiencies of : add to

sup·pli·ant \'səp-lē-ənt\ *n* : one who supplicates : PETITIONER, PLEADER

sup·pli·cant \'səp-li-kənt\ *n* : SUPPLIANT

sup·pli·cate \'səp-lə-,kāt\ *vb* 1 : to make a humble entreaty; *esp* : to pray to God 2 : to ask earnestly and humbly : BESEECH **syn** implore, beg — **sup·pli·ca·tion** \,səp-lə-'kā-shən\ *n*

¹**sup·ply** \sə-'plī\ *vb* 1 : to add as a supplement 2 : to satisfy the needs of 3 : FURNISH, PROVIDE — **sup·pli·er** *n*

²**supply** *n* 1 : the quantity or amount (as of a commodity) needed or available; *also* : PROVISIONS, STORES — usu. used in pl. 2 : the act or process of filling a want or need : PROVISION 3 : the quantities of goods or services offered for sale at a particular time or at one price

¹**sup·port** \sə-'pōrt\ *vb* 1 : BEAR, TOLERATE 2 : to take sides with : BACK, ASSIST 3 : to provide with food, clothing, and shelter 4 : to hold up or serve as a foundation for : keep from sinking or falling **syn** uphold, advocate, champion — **sup·port·able** *adj* — **sup·port·er** *n*

²**support** *n* 1 : the act of supporting : the state of being supported 2 : one that supports : PROP, BASE

sup·pose \sə-'pōz\ *vb* 1 : to assume to be true (as for the sake of argument)

ə abut; ᵊ kitten; ər further; a back; ā bake; ä cot, cart; aù out, chin; e less; ē easy; g gift; i trip; ī life; j joke; ŋ sing; ō flow; ȯ flaw; ȯi coin; th thin; th this; ü loot; ù foot; y yet; yü few; yù furious; zh vision

2 : EXPECT ⟨I am *supposed* to go⟩ **3** : to think probable : incline to believe

sup-posed \sə-'pōzd\ *adj* : BELIEVED; *also* : mistakenly supposed — **sup-pos-ed-ly** \-'pō-zəd-lē\ *adv*

sup-pos-ing *conj* : if by way of hypothesis : on the assumption that

sup-po-si-tion \ˌsəp-ə-'zish-ən\ *n* **1** : something that is supposed : HYPOTHESIS **2** : the act of supposing

sup-pos-i-to-ry \sə-'päz-ə-ˌtōr-ē\ *n* : a small easily melted mass of usu. medicated material for insertion (as into the rectum)

sup-press \sə-'pres\ *vb* **1** : to put down by authority or force : SUBDUE ⟨~ a revolt⟩ **2** : to keep from being known; *also* : to stop the publication or circulation of **3** : to exclude from consciousness : REPRESS — **sup-press-ible** *adj* — **sup-pres-sion** \-'presh-ən\ *n*

sup-pu-rate \'səp-yə-ˌrāt\ *vb* : to form or give off pus — **sup-pu-ra-tion** \ˌsəp-yə-'rā-shən\ *n*

su-prem-a-cy \su̇-'prem-ə-sē\ *n* : supreme rank, power, or authority

su-preme \su̇-'prēm\ *adj* **1** : highest in rank or authority **2** : UTMOST **3** : most excellent ⟨he is ~ among poets⟩ **4** : ULTIMATE ⟨the ~ sacrifice⟩ **syn** superlative, surpassing, peerless, incomparable — **su-preme-ly** *adv*

Supreme Being *n* : ²GOD

sur-cease \'sər-ˌsēs\ *n* : CESSATION, RESPITE

¹sur-charge \'sər-ˌchärj\ *vb* **1** : to fill to excess : OVERCHARGE, OVERLOAD **2** : to print or write a surcharge on (postage stamps)

²surcharge *n* **1** : an excessive load or burden **2** : an extra fee or cost **3** : something officially printed on a postage stamp to give it a new value or use

sur-cin-gle \'sər-ˌsiŋ-gəl\ *n* : a band passing around a horse's body to make something (as a saddle or pack) fast

¹sure \'shu̇r\ *adj* **1** : firmly established : not likely to be overthrown or displaced **2** : CONFIDENT, CERTAIN **3** : TRUSTWORTHY, RELIABLE **4** : not to be disputed : UNDOUBTED **5** : bound to happen **syn** assured, positive — **sure-ly** *adv* — **sure-ness** *n*

²sure *adv* : SURELY

sure-fire \-'fī(ə)r\ *adj* : certain to get results : DEPENDABLE

sure-ty \'shu̇r-(ə)t-ē\ *n* **1** : SURENESS, CERTAINTY **2** : something that makes sure : GUARANTEE **3** : one who becomes a guarantor for another person **syn** security, bond, bail, sponsor, backer

surf \'sərf\ *n* : the swell of the sea as it breaks on the shore; *also* : the sound or foam caused by breaking waves

¹sur-face \'sər-fəs\ *n* **1** : the outside of an object or body **2** : outward aspect or appearance

²surface *vb* **1** : to give a surface to : make smooth **2** : to rise to the surface

surf-board \'sərf-ˌbōrd\ *n* : a buoyant board used in riding the crests of waves

¹sur-feit \'sər-fət\ *n* **1** : EXCESS, SUPERABUNDANCE **2** : excessive indulgence (as in food or drink); *also* : bodily distress caused by such indulgence **3** : disgust caused by excess in eating and drinking : SATIETY

²surfeit *vb* : to feed, supply, or indulge to the point of surfeit : CLOY

¹surge \'sərj\ *vb* **1** : to rise and fall actively : TOSS **2** : to move in waves

3 : to rise suddenly to a high value **syn** arise, mount, soar

²surge *n* **1** : a large billow **2** : a sweeping onward like a wave of the sea ⟨a ~ of emotion⟩ **3** : a transient sudden increase of current in an electrical circuit

sur-geon \'sər-jən\ *n* [OF *cirurgien*, fr. *cirurgie* surgery, fr. L *chirurgia*, fr Gk *cheirourgia*, fr. *cheir* hand + *ergon* work] : a physician who specializes in surgery

sur-gery \'sərj-(ə-)rē\ *n* **1** : a branch of medicine concerned with the correction of physical defects, the repair of injuries, and the treatment of disease esp. by operation **2** : a surgeon's operating room or laboratory **3** : work done by a surgeon

sur-gi-cal \'sər-ji-kəl\ *adj* : of, relating to, or associated with surgeons or surgery — **sur-gi-cal-ly** *adv*

sur-ly \'sər-lē\ *adj* : ILL-NATURED, CRABBED **syn** morose, glum, sullen, sulky, gloomy — **sur-li-ness** *n*

sur-mise \sər-'mīz\ *vb* : GUESS **syn** conjecture — **surmise** *n*

sur-mount \sər-'mau̇nt\ *vb* **1** : to rise superior to : OVERCOME ⟨~ a difficulty⟩ **2** : to get to or lie at the top of **syn** overthrow, rout, vanquish, defeat, subdue

sur-name \'sər-ˌnām\ *n* **1** : NICKNAME **2** : the name borne in common by members of a family

sur-pass \sər-'pas\ *vb* **1** : to be superior in quality, degree, or performance : EXCEL **2** : to be beyond the reach or powers of **syn** transcend, outdo, outstrip, exceed

sur-plice \'sər-pləs\ *n* : a loose white knee-length outer vestment worn at services by some clergymen

sur-plus \'sər-(ˌ)pləs\ *n* **1** : quantity left over : EXCESS **2** : the excess of assets over liabilities **syn** superfluity

¹sur-prise \sə(r)-'prīz\ *n* **1** : an attack made without warning **2** : a taking unawares **3** : something that surprises **4** : AMAZEMENT, ASTONISHMENT

²surprise *vb* **1** : to come upon and attack unexpectedly **2** : to take unawares **3** : to strike with amazement : AMAZE **4** : to effect or accomplish by means of a surprise **syn** waylay, ambush, astonish, astound — **sur-pris-ing** *adj* — **sur-pris-ing-ly** *adv*

¹sur-ren-der \sə-'ren-dər\ *vb* **1** : to yield to the power of another : give up under compulsion **2** : RELINQUISH

²surrender *n* : the act of giving up or yielding oneself or the possession of something into another's possession or control **syn** submission, capitulation

sur-rep-ti-tious \ˌsər-əp-'tish-əs\ *adj* : done, made, or acquired by stealth : SECRET, CLANDESTINE **syn** underhand, covert, furtive — **sur-rep-ti-tious-ly** *adv*

sur-rey \'sər-ē\ *n* : a 4-wheeled 2-seated horse-drawn carriage

sur-ro-gate \'sər-ə-ˌgāt, -gət\ *n* **1** : DEPUTY, SUBSTITUTE **2** : a law officer in some states with authority in the probate of wills, the settlement of estates, and the appointment of guardians

sur-round \sə-'rau̇nd\ *vb* **1** : to enclose on all sides : ENCOMPASS, ENCIRCLE **2** : to enclose so as to cut off retreat or escape

sur-round-ings *n pl* : conditions by which one is surrounded : ENVIRONMENT

sur-tax \'sər-ˌtaks\ *n* : an additional

tax over and above a normal tax

sur·tout \(,)sər-'tü\ *n* **:** a man's long close-fitting overcoat

sur·veil·lance \sər-'vāl-(y)əns\ *n* **:** close watch; *also* **:** SUPERVISION

¹**sur·vey** \sər-'vā\ *vb* **1 :** to look over and examine closely **2 :** to make a survey of (as a tract of land) **3 :** to view or study something as a whole **syn** behold, see, observe, remark — **sur·vey·or** *n*

²**sur·vey** \'sər-,vā\ *n* **1 :** INSPECTION, EXAMINATION **2 :** a wide general view ⟨a ∼ of English literature⟩ **3 :** the process of finding and representing the contours, measurements, and position of a part of the earth's surface; *also* **:** a measured plan and description of a region

sur·vey·ing \sər-'vā-iŋ\ *n* **:** the branch of mathematics that teaches the art of making surveys

sur·vive \sər-'vīv\ *vb* **1 :** to remain alive or existent **2 :** OUTLIVE, OUTLAST — **sur·viv·al** *n* — **sur·vi·vor** *n*

sus·cep·ti·ble \sə-'sep-tə-bəl\ *adj* **1 :** of such a nature as to permit ⟨words ∼ of being misunderstood⟩ **2 :** having little resistance to a stimulus or agency ⟨∼ to colds⟩ **3 :** easily affected or emotionally moved **:** RESPONSIVE **syn** sensitive, subject, exposed, prone, liable, open — **sus·cep·ti·bil·i·ty** \-,sep-tə-'bil-ət-ē\ *n*

¹**sus·pect** \sə-'spekt\ *vb* **1 :** to have doubts of **:** MISTRUST **2 :** to imagine to be guilty without proof **3 :** SURMISE

²**sus·pect** \'səs-,pekt\ *n* **:** one who is suspected (as of a crime)

³**sus·pect** \'səs-,pekt, sə-'spekt\ *adj* **:** regarded with suspicion

sus·pend \sə-'spend\ *vb* **1 :** to bar temporarily from a privilege, office, or function **2 :** to stop temporarily **:** make inactive for a time **3 :** to withhold (judgment) for a time **4 :** HANG; *esp* **:** to hang so as to be free except at one point **5 :** to fail to meet obligations **syn** exclude, eliminate, stay, postpone, defer

sus·pend·er *n* **1 :** one of two supporting straps which pass over the shoulders and to which the trousers are fastened **2** *Brit* **:** GARTER

sus·pense \sə-'spens\ *n* **1 :** SUSPENSION **2 :** mental uncertainty **:** ANXIETY

sus·pen·sion \-'spen-chən\ *n* **1 :** the act of suspending **:** the state or period of being suspended **2 :** the state of a substance when its particles are mixed with but undissolved in a fluid or solid; *also* **:** a substance in this state **3 :** something suspended **4 :** a device by which something is suspended

sus·pi·cion \sə-'spish-ən\ *n* **1 :** the act or an instance of suspecting something wrong without proof **2 :** a slight trace **syn** mistrust, uncertainty

sus·pi·cious \-'spish-əs\ *adj* **1 :** open to or arousing suspicion **2 :** inclined to suspect **3 :** showing suspicion — **sus·pi·cious·ly** *adv*

sus·tain \sə-'stān\ *vb* **1 :** to provide with nourishment **2 :** to keep going **:** PROLONG ⟨∼ed effort⟩ **3 :** to hold up **:** PROP **4 :** to hold up under **:** ENDURE **5 :** SUFFER ⟨∼ a broken arm⟩ **6 :** to support as true, legal, or valid **7 :** PROVE, CORROBORATE

sus·te·nance \'səs-tə-nəns\ *n* **1 :** FOOD, NOURISHMENT **2 :** a supplying with the necessities of life **3 :** something that sustains or supports

su·ture \'sü-chər\ *n* **1 :** a seam or line along which two things or parts are joined by or as if by sewing ⟨the ∼s of the skull⟩ **2 :** material or a stitch for sewing a wound together

su·zer·ain \'süz-(ə-)rən, -ə-,rān\ *n* **1 :** a feudal lord **2 :** a nation that has political control over another nation — **su·zer·ain·ty** *n*

svelte \'sfelt\ *adj* **:** SLENDER, LITHE

¹**swab** \'swäb\ *n* **1 :** MOP **2 :** a wad of absorbent material esp. for applying medicine or for cleaning (as a wound) **3 :** SAILOR

²**swab** *vb* **swabbed; swab·bing :** to use a swab on **:** MOP

swad·dle \'swäd-ᵊl\ *vb* **1 :** to bind (an infant) in bands of cloth **2 :** to wrap up **:** SWATHE

swad·dling clothes \-(-ᵊ-)liŋ-\ *n pl* **1 :** bands of cloth wrapped around an infant **2 :** period of infancy; *also* **:** restrictions placed on the young

swag \'swag\ *n* **:** stolen goods **:** BOOTY, LOOT

swage \'swāj, 'swej\ *n* **:** a tool used by metal workers for shaping their work — **swage** *vb*

swag·ger \'swag-ər\ *vb* **1 :** to walk with a conceited swing or strut **2 :** BOAST, BRAG — **swagger** *n*

Swa·hi·li \swä-'hē-lē\ *n* **:** a language that is a trade and governmental language over much of East Africa and the Congo region

swain \'swān\ *n* **1 :** RUSTIC; *esp* **:** SHEPHERD **2 :** ADMIRER, SUITOR

¹**swal·low** \'swäl-ō\ *n* **:** any of various small long-wing fork-tailed migratory birds

²**swallow** *vb* **1 :** to take into the stomach through the throat **2 :** to envelop or take in as if by swallowing **3 :** to accept or believe too easily **4 :** ENDURE, BEAR

³**swallow** *n* **1 :** an act of swallowing **2 :** as much as can be swallowed at one time

swal·low·tail \-,tāl\ *n* **1 :** a deeply forked and tapering tail like that of a swallow **2 :** TAILCOAT **3 :** any of various large butterflies with the border of the hind wing drawn out into a process resembling a tail — **swal·low·tailed** *adj*

swam *past of* SWIM

¹**swamp** \'swämp\ *n* **:** wet spongy land; *also* **:** a tract of this — **swampy** *adj*

²**swamp** *vb* **1 :** to plunge or sink in or as if in a swamp **2 :** to deluge with or as if with water; *also* **:** to sink by filling with water

swan \'swän\ *n* **:** any of several heavy-bodied, long-necked, mostly pure white swimming birds related to the geese

¹**swank** \'swaŋk\ *n* **1 :** PRETENTIOUSNESS **2 :** ELEGANCE

²**swank** \'swaŋk\ *or* **swanky** *adj* **:** showily smart and dashing; *also* **:** fashionably elegant

swans·down \'swänz-,daun\ *n* **1 :** the very soft down of a swan used esp. for trimming or powder puffs **2 :** a soft thick cotton flannel

swap \'swäp\ *vb* **swapped; swap·ping :** TRADE, EXCHANGE — **swap** *n*

ə abut; ⁹ kitten; ər further; a back; ā bake; ä cot, cart; au̇ out; ch chin; e less; ē easy; g gift; i trip; ī life; j joke; ŋ sing; ō flow; ȯ flaw; ȯi coin; th thin; t͟h this; ü loot; u̇ foot; y yet; yü few; yu̇ furious; zh vision

sward \'swȯrd\ *n* : the grassy surface of land

¹swarm \'swȯrm\ *n* **1** : a great number of honeybees including a queen and leaving a hive to start a new colony; *also* : a hive of bees **2** : a large crowd : THRONG

²swarm *vb* **1** : to form in a swarm and depart from a hive **2** : to throng together : gather in great numbers

swart \'swȯrt\ *adj* : SWARTHY

swarthy \'swȯr-thē, -thē\ *adj* : dark in color or complexion : dark-skinned

swash \'swȯsh\ *vb* : to move about with a splashing sound : SPLASH — **swash** *n*

swash·buck·ler \-,bək-lər\ *n* : a boasting blustering soldier or daredevil — **swash·buck·ling** \-liŋ\ *adj*

swas·ti·ka \'swȯs-ti-kə, swä-'stē-\ *n* [Skt *svastika*, fr. *svasti* welfare, fr. *su-* well + *-asti* being] : a symbol or ornament in the form of a Greek cross with the arms bent at right angles

swat \'swȯt\ *vb* **swat·ted; swat·ting** : to hit sharply ⟨~ a fly⟩ ⟨~ a ball⟩ — **swat** *n*

swath \'swȯth, 'swȯth\ *or* **swathe** \'swäth, 'swȯth, 'swāth\ *n* **1** : the sweep of a scythe or mowing machine or the path cut in mowing **2** : a row of cut grass or grain

swathe \'swäth, 'swȯth, 'swāth\ *vb* : to bind or wrap with or as if with a bandage

¹sway \'swā\ *vb* **1** : to swing gently from side to side **2** : RULE, GOVERN **3** : to cause to swing from side to side **4** : BEND, SWERVE; *also* : INFLUENCE **syn** oscillate, fluctuate, vibrate, waver

²sway *n* **1** : a gentle swinging from side to side **2** : sovereign power : DOMINION; *also* : a controlling influence : DOMINANCE

swear \'swaar\ *vb* **swore** \'swȯr\ **sworn** \'swȯrn\ **swear·ing 1** : to make a solemn statement or promise under oath : VOW **2** : to use profane or obscene language **3** : to assert emphatically as true with an appeal to God or one's honor **4** : to charge or confirm under oath; *also* : to bind by or as if by an oath **5** : to administer an oath to — **swear·er** *n* — **swear·ing** *n*

¹sweat \'swet\ *vb* **sweat** *or* **sweat·ed; sweat·ing 1** : to excrete salty moisture from glands of the skin : PERSPIRE **2** : to form drops of moisture on the surface **3** : to work so that one sweats : TOIL **4** : to cause to sweat **5** : to draw out or get rid of by perspiring **6** : to make a person overwork ⟨a factory that ~s its employees⟩

²sweat *n* **1** : perceptible liquid exuded through pores from glands (**sweat glands**) of the skin : PERSPIRATION **2** : moisture issuing from or gathering on a surface in drops — **sweaty** *adj*

sweat·er \'swet-ər\ *n* **1** : one that sweats **2** : a knitted or crocheted jacket or pullover

Swede \'swēd\ *n* : a native or inhabitant of Sweden

Swed·ish \'swēd-ish\ *n* **1 Swedish** *pl* : the people of Sweden **2** : the language of Sweden — **Swedish** *adj*

¹sweep \'swēp\ *vb* **swept** \'swept\ **sweep·ing 1** : to remove or clean by brushing **2** : to remove or destroy by vigorous continuous action **3** : to strip or clear by gusts of wind or rain **4** : to move over with speed and force ⟨the tide *swept* over the shore⟩ **5** : to gather in with a single swift movement **6** : to move or extend in a wide curve —

sweep·er *n* — **sweep·ing** *adj*

²sweep *n* **1** : a clearing off or away **2** : a sweeping movement ⟨~ of a scythe⟩ **3** : RANGE, SCOPE **4** : CURVE, BEND **5** : something (as a long oar) that operates with a sweeping motion

sweep·ing *n* **1** : the act or action of one that sweeps ⟨gave the room a good ~⟩ **2** *pl* : things collected by sweeping : REFUSE

sweep·stakes \'swēp-,stāks\ *also* **sweep·stake** \-,stāk\ *n, pl* **sweepstakes 1** : a race or contest in which the entire prize may go to the winner; *esp* : a horse race in which the stakes are contributed at least in part by the owners of the horses **2** : any of various lotteries

¹sweet \'swēt\ *adj* **1** : being or causing the primary taste sensation that is typical of sugars; *also* : pleasing to the taste **2** : not stale or spoiled : WHOLESOME ⟨~ milk⟩ **3** : not salted ⟨~ butter⟩ **4** : pleasing to a sense other than taste ⟨a ~ smell⟩ ⟨~ music⟩ **5** : KINDLY, MILD — **sweet·ish** *adj* — **sweet·ly** *adv* — **sweet·ness** *n*

²sweet *n* **1** : something sweet : CANDY **2** : DARLING

sweet·bread \'swet-,bred\ *n* : the pancreas or thymus of an animal (as a calf or lamb) used for food

sweet·bri·er \-,brī-(ə)r\ *n* : a thorny European rose with fragrant white to deep pink flowers

sweet corn *n* : an Indian corn with kernels rich in sugar and suitable for table use when young

sweet·en \'swet-ᵊn\ *vb* : to make sweet

sweet·heart \'swet-,härt\ *n* : a loved person : LOVER

sweet·meat \-,mēt\ *n* : CANDY

sweet pea *n* : a garden plant with climbing stems and fragrant flowers of many colors; *also* : its flower

sweet potato *n* : a tropical vine related to the morning glory; *also* : its sweet yellow edible root

¹swell \'swel\ *vb* **swelled; swelled** *or* **swol·len** \'swō-lən\ **swell·ing 1** : to grow big or make bigger : increase in size, quantity, or value **2** : to expand or distend abnormally or excessively ⟨a *swollen* joint⟩; *also* : BULGE **3** : to fill or be filled with pride, anger, or some other emotion **syn** expand, amplify, distend, inflate, dilate — **swell·ing** *n*

²swell *adj* **1** : FASHIONABLE, STYLISH; *also* : socially prominent **2** : EXCELLENT, FIRST-RATE

³swell *n* **1** : sudden increase in size or value **2** : a long crestless wave or series of waves in the open sea **3** : a person dressed in the height of fashion; *also* : a person of high social position or outstanding competence

swel·ter \'swel-tər\ *vb* : to be faint or oppressed with the heat

swept *past of* SWEEP

swept·wing \'swept-'wiŋ\ *adj* : having wings that slant backwards ⟨~ airplane⟩

swerve \'swȯrv\ *vb* : to move abruptly aside from a straight line or course **syn** veer, deviate, diverge — **swerve** *n*

¹swift \'swift\ *adj* **1** : moving or capable of moving with great speed **2** : occurring suddenly **3** : READY, ALERT — **swift·ly** *adv* — **swift·ness** *n*

²swift *n* : a small insect-eating bird with long narrow wings

swig \'swig\ *vb* **swigged; swig·ging** : to drink in long drafts : GULP — **swig** *n*

¹swill \'swil\ *vb* **1** : to swallow greedily

: GUZZLE 2 : to feed (as hogs) on swill

²swill n 1 : food for animals composed of edible refuse mixed with liquid 2 : GARBAGE

¹swim \'swim\ vb **swam** \'swam\ **swum** \'swəm\ **swim·ming** 1 : to propel oneself along in water by natural means (as by hands and legs, by tail, or by fins) 2 : to glide smoothly along 3 : FLOAT 4 : to be covered with or as if with a liquid 5 : to cross or go over by swimming 6 : to be dizzy ⟨his head *swam*⟩ – **swim·mer** n

²swim n 1 : an act of swimming 2 : the main current of activity or fashion ⟨in the social ∼⟩

swim·ming n : the action, art, or sport of swimming and diving

swin·dle \'swin-d°l\ vb : CHEAT, DEFRAUD — **swindle** n — **swin·dler** \-d(°)lər\ n

swine \'swīn\ n, pl **swine** 1 : any of various stout short-legged hoofed mammals with bristly skin and flexible snout; esp : one widely raised as a meat animal 2 : a contemptible person — **swin·ish** adj

¹swing \'swin\ vb **swung** \'swəŋ\ **swing·ing** 1 : to move rapidly in an arc 2 : to sway or cause to sway back and forth 3 : to hang so as to move freely back and forth or in a curve 4 : to be executed by hanging 5 : to move or turn on a hinge or pivot 6 : to march or walk with free swaying movements 7 : to manage or handle successfully 8 : to have a steady pulsing rhythm syn wave, flourish, brandish, thrash, oscillate, vibrate, fluctuate, wield, manipulate, ply

²swing n 1 : the act of swinging 2 : a swinging blow, movement, or rhythm 3 : the distance through which something swings : FLUCTUATION 4 : a seat suspended by a rope or chain for swinging back and forth for pleasure 5 : music marked by lively rhythm and improvisation

¹swipe \'swīp\ n : a strong sweeping blow

²swipe vb 1 : to strike or wipe with a sweeping motion 2 : PILFER, SNATCH

swirl \'swərl\ vb : WHIRL, EDDY — **swirl** n

swish \'swish\ n 1 : a prolonged hissing sound (as of a whip cutting the air) 2 : a light sweeping or brushing sound (as of a full silk skirt in motion) — **swish** vb

Swiss \'swis\ n, pl **Swiss** : a native or inhabitant of Switzerland 2 : a hard cheese with large holes that form during ripening

¹switch \'swich\ n 1 : a slender flexible whip, rod, or twig 2 : a blow with a switch 3 : a shift from one thing to another 4 : a device for adjusting the rails of a track so that a locomotive or train may be turned from one track to another; also : a railroad siding 5 : a device for making, breaking, or changing the connections in an electrical circuit 6 : a heavy strand of hair often used in addition to a person's own hair for some coiffures

²switch vb 1 : to punish or urge on with a switch ⟨a cow ∼ing her

tail⟩ 3 : to shift or turn by operating a switch 4 : CHANGE, EXCHANGE

switch·board \-,bōrd\ n : a panel on which is mounted a group of electric switches so arranged that a number of circuits may be connected, combined, and controlled

switch·man \-mən\ n : one who attends a railroad switch

¹swiv·el \'swiv-əl\ n : a part that turns on or as if on a headed bolt or pin; also : a system of links joined by such a part so as to permit rotation

²swivel vb -eled or -elled; -el·ing or -el·ling : to swing or turn on or as if on a swivel

swollen past part of SWELL

swoon \'swün\ n : FAINT — **swoon** vb

swoop \'swüp\ vb : to descend or pounce swiftly like a hawk on its prey — **swoop** n

sword \'sōrd\ n 1 : a weapon with a long pointed blade and sharp cutting edges 2 : a symbol of authority or military power 3 : the use of force : WAR

sword·fish \-,fish\ n : a very large ocean food fish with the bones of the upper jaw prolonged in a long swordlike beak

sword·play \-,plā\ n : the art or skill of wielding a sword

swords·man \'sōrdz-mən\ n : one skilled in wielding a sword; esp : FENCER

swore past of SWEAR

sworn past part of SWEAR

swum past part of SWIM

swung past of SWING

syb·a·rite \'sib-ə-,rīt\ n : a lover of luxury : VOLUPTUARY

syc·a·more \'sik-ə-,mōr\ n : any of several shade trees (as an Old World maple or an American plane tree)

syc·o·phant \'sik-ə-fənt\ n : a servile flatterer — **syc·o·phan·tic** \,sik-ə-'fant-ik\ adj

syl·lab·i·ca·tion \sə-,lab-ə-'kā-shən\ n : the dividing of words into syllables

syl·lab·i·fy \sə-'lab-ə-,fī\ vb : to form or divide into syllables — **syl·lab·i·fi·ca·tion** \-,lab-ə-fə-'kā-shən\ n

syl·la·ble \'sil-ə-bəl\ n : a unit of spoken language consisting of an uninterrupted utterance and forming either a whole word (as *man*) or a commonly recognized division of a word (as *syl* in *syl·la·ble*); also : one or more letters representing such a unit — **syl·lab·ic** \sə-'lab-ik\ adj

syl·la·bus \'sil-ə-bəs\ n, pl -**bi** \-,bī\ or -**bus·es** : a summary containing the heads or main topics of a speech, book, or course of study

syl·lo·gism \'sil-ə-,jiz-əm\ n : a logical scheme of a formal argument consisting of a major and a minor premise and a conclusion which must logically be true if the premises are true — **syl·lo·gis·tic** \,sil-ə-'jis-tik\ adj

sylph \'silf\ n 1 : an imaginary being inhabiting the air 2 : a slender graceful woman

syl·van \'sil-vən\ adj 1 : living or located in a wooded area; also : of, relating to, or characteristic of forest 2 : abounding in woods or trees : WOODED

sym·bol \'sim-bəl\ n 1 : something that stands for something else; esp : something concrete that represents or suggests another thing that cannot in itself be

---

ə abut; ⁰ kitten; ər further; a back; ā bake; ä cot, cart; aù out; ch chin; e less; ē easy; g gift; i trip; ī life; j joke; ŋ sing; ō flow; ò flaw; òi coin; th thin; t̲h̲ this; ü loot; ù foot; y yet; yü few; yù furious; zh vision

represented or visualized **2** : a letter, character, or sign used in writing or printing relating to a particular field (as mathematics, physics, or music) to represent operations, quantities, elements, sounds, or other ideas — **sym·bol·ic** \sim-'bäl-ik\ *or* **sym·bol·i·cal** *adj* — **sym·bol·i·cal·ly** *adv*

sym·bol·ism \ sim-bə-,liz-əm\ *n* : representation of abstract or intangible things by means of symbols or emblems

sym·bol·ize \'sim-bə-,līz\ *vb* **1** : to serve as a symbol of **2** : to represent by symbols — **sym·bol·iza·tion** \,sim-bə-lə-'zā-shən\ *n*

sym·me·try \'sim-ə-trē\ *n* **1** : correspondence in size, shape, and position of parts that are on opposite sides of a dividing line or center **2** : an arrangement marked by regularity and balanced proportions **syn** proportion, balance, harmony — **sym·met·ri·cal** \sə-'met-ri-kəl\ *adj* — **sym·met·ri·cal·ly** *adv*

sym·pa·thize \'sim-pə-,thīz\ *vb* : to feel or show sympathy — **sym·pa·thiz·er** *n*

sym·pa·thy \'sim-pə-thē\ *n* **1** : a relationship between persons or things wherein whatever affects one similarly affects the others **2** : harmony of interests and aims **3** : the ability of entering into and sharing the feelings or interests of another; *also* : COMPASSION, PITY **4** : FAVOR, SUPPORT **5** : an expression of sorrow for another's loss, grief, or misfortune — **sym·pa·thet·ic** \,sim-pə-'thet-ik\ *adj* — **sym·pa·thet·i·cal·ly** *adv*

sym·pho·ny \'sim-fə-nē\ *n* **1** : harmony of sounds **2** : a large and complex composition for a full orchestra **3** : a large orchestra of a kind that plays symphonies — **sym·phon·ic** \sim-'fän-ik\ *adj*

sym·po·si·um \sim-'pō-zē-əm\ *n, pl* **-sia** \-zē-ə\ *or* **-si·ums** [L, drinking party after a banquet, fr. Gk *symposion*, fr. *sympinein* to drink together, fr. *syn-* together + *pinein* to drink] : a conference at which a particular topic is discussed by various speakers; *also* : a collection of opinions about a subject

symp·tom \'simp-təm\ *n* **1** : a change in an organism indicative of disease or abnormality; *esp* : one (as headache) directly perceptible only to the victim **2** : SIGN, INDICATION — **symp·tom·at·ic** \,simp-tə-'mat-ik\ *adj*

syn·a·gogue \'sin-i-,gäg\ *n* **1** : a Jewish congregation **2** : the house of worship of a Jewish congregation

sync \'siŋk\ *vb* : SYNCHRONIZE — **sync** *n*

syn·chro·nize \'siŋ-krə-,nīz\ *vb* **1** : to occur or cause to occur at the same instant **2** : to represent, arrange, or tabulate according to dates or time **3** : to cause to agree in time ⟨~ two watches⟩ **4** : to make synchronous in operation ⟨~ two machines⟩ — **syn·chro·nism** \-,niz-əm\ *n*

syn·chro·nous \-nəs\ *adj* **1** : happening at the same time : CONCURRENT **2** : working, moving, or occurring together at the same rate and at the proper time

syn·co·pa·tion \,siŋ-kə-'pā-shən\ *n* : a shifting of the regular musical accent : occurrence of accented notes on the weak beat — **syn·co·pate** \'siŋ-kə-,pāt\ *vb*

syn·co·pe \'siŋ-kə-(,)pē\ *n* : the loss of one or more sounds or letters in the interior of a word (as in *fo'c's'le* from *forecastle*)

[1]syn·di·cate \'sin-di-kət\ *n* **1** : a group of persons who combine to carry out a financial or industrial undertaking **2** : a business concern that sells materials for publication in many newspapers and periodicals at the same time

[2]syn·di·cate \-də-,kāt\ *vb* **1** : to combine into or manage as a syndicate **2** : to publish through a syndicate — **syn·di·ca·tion** \,sin-də-'kā-shən\ *n*

syn·drome \'sin-,drōm\ *n* : a group of signs and symptoms that occur together and characterize a particular abnormality

syn·er·gism \'sin-ər-,jiz-əm\ *n* : joint action of discrete agencies (as drugs) in which the total effect is greater than the sum of their effects when acting independently — **syn·er·gist** *n* — **syn·er·gis·ti·cal·ly** \,sin-ər-'jis-ti-k(ə-)lē\ *adv*

syn·od \'sin-əd\ *n* **1** : COUNCIL, ASSEMBLY; *esp* : a religious governing body — **syn·od·al** \'sin-ə-d°l\ *adj* — **syn·od·i·cal** \sə-'näd-i-kəl\ *adj*

syn·onym \'sin-ə-,nim\ *n* : one of two or more words in the same language which have the same or very nearly the same meaning — **syn·on·y·mous** \sə-'nän-ə-məs\ *adj*

syn·op·sis \sə-'näp-səs\ *n, pl* **-op·ses** \-,sēz\ : a condensed statement or outline (as of a narrative or treatise) : ABSTRACT

syn·tax \'sin-,taks\ *n* : the way in which words are put together to form phrases, clauses, or sentences — **syn·tac·ti·cal** \sin-'tak-ti-kəl\ *adj*

syn·the·sis \'sin-thə-səs\ *n, pl* **-the·ses** \-,sēz\ : the combination of parts or elements into a whole — **syn·the·size** \-,sīz\ *vb*

syn·thet·ic \sin-'thet-ik\ *adj* : produced artificially esp. by chemical means; *also* : not genuine — **synthetic** *n* — **syn·thet·i·cal·ly** *adv*

syph·i·lis \'sif-(ə-)ləs\ *n* : a destructive contagious usu. venereal disease caused by a bacterium — **syph·i·lit·ic** \,sif-ə-'lit-ik\ *adj or n*

sy·phon *var of* SIPHON

[1]sy·ringe \sə-'rinj, 'sir-inj\ *n* : a device used esp. for injecting liquids into or withdrawing them from the body

[2]syringe *vb* : to inject or cleanse with or as if with a syringe

syr·up \'sər-əp, 'sir-\ *n* **1** : a thick sticky solution of sugar and water **2** : the concentrated juice of a fruit or plant — **syr·upy** *adj*

sys·tem \'sis-təm\ *n* **1** : a group of units so combined as to form a whole and to operate in unison : an organized whole **2** : the body as a functioning whole; *also* : a group of bodily organs that together carry on some vital function (the nervous ~) **3** : a definite scheme or method of procedure or classification **4** : regular method or order : ORDERLINESS — **sys·tem·at·ic** \,sis-tə-'mat-ik\ *adj* — **sys·tem·at·i·cal** *adj* — **sys·tem·at·i·cal·ly** *adv*

sys·tem·a·tize \'sis-tə-mə-,tīz\ *vb* : to make into a system : arrange methodically : ORGANIZE, CLASSIFY

sys·tem·ic \sis-'tem-ik\ *adj* : of or relating to the whole body (~ disease)

sys·tem·ize \'sis-tə-,mīz\ *vb* : SYSTEMATIZE

sys·to·le \'sis-tə-(,)lē\ *n* : a rhythmically recurrent contraction esp. of the heart — **sys·tol·ic** \sis-'täl-ik\ *adj*

t \'tē\ *n, often cap* : the 20th letter of the English alphabet

tab \'tab\ *n* **1** : a short projecting flap, loop, or tag; *also* : a small insert or addition **2** : close surveillance : WATCH (keep ~ on him) **3** : BILL, CHECK

tab·by \'tab-ē\ *n* : a usu. striped or mottled domestic cat; *also* : a female cat

tab·er·na·cle \'tab-ər-,nak-əl\ *n* **1** *often cap* : a tent sanctuary used by the Israelites during the Exodus **2** : a receptacle for the consecrated elements of the Eucharist **3** : a house of worship

¹**ta·ble** \'tā-bəl\ *n* **1** : a flat slab or plaque : TABLET **2** : a piece of furniture consisting of a smooth flat slab fixed on legs **3** : a supply of food : BOARD, FARE **4** : a group of people assembled at or as if at a table **5** : a systematic arrangement of data for ready reference **6** : a condensed enumeration : LIST

²**table** *vb* **1** *Brit* : to place on the agenda **2** : to remove (a parliamentary motion) from consideration indefinitely

tab·leau \'tab-,lō\ *n, pl* **-leaux** \-,lōz\ *also* **-leaus 1** : a graphic description : PICTURE **2** : a striking or artistic grouping **3** : a static depiction of a scene usu. presented on a stage by costumed participants

ta·ble·cloth \'tā-bəl-,klòth\ *n* : a covering spread over a dining table before the places are set

ta·ble d'hôte \,tāb-əl-'dōt\ *n* : a complete meal of several courses offered at a fixed price

ta·ble·land \'tā-bəl(l)-,land\ *n* : PLATEAU

ta·ble·spoon \'tā-bəl-,spün\ *n* : a large spoon used esp. for serving — **ta·ble·spoon·ful** \,tā-bəl-'spün-,fùl\ *n*

tab·let \'tab-lət\ *n* **1** : a flat slab or plaque suited for or bearing an inscription **2** : a collection of sheets of paper glued together at one edge (a writing ~) **3** : a compressed or molded block of material; *esp* : a usu. disk-shaped medicated mass

ta·ble·ware \'tā-bəl-,waər\ *n* : utensils (as of china, glass, or silver) for table use

¹**tab·loid** \'tab-,lòid\ *adj* : condensed into small scope

²**tabloid** *n* : a newspaper of small page size marked by condensation of the news and usu. much photographic matter; *esp* : one characterized by sensationalism

¹**ta·boo** *or* **ta·bu** \ta-'bü, tə-\ *adj* **1** : set apart as charged with a dangerous supernatural power : INVIOLABLE **2** : banned esp. as immoral or dangerous

²**taboo** *or* **tabu** *n* **1** : an act or object avoided as taboo **2** : a prohibition imposed by social usage or as a protection

ta·bor *also* **ta·bour** \'tā-bər\ *n* : a small drum used to accompany a pipe or fife played by the same person

tab·u·lar \'tab-yə-lər\ *adj* **1** : having a flat surface **2** : arranged in a table; *esp* : set up in rows and columns **3** : computed by means of a table

tab·u·late \-,lāt\ *vb* : to put into tabular form — **tab·u·la·tion** \,tab-yə-'lā-

shən\ *n* — **tab·u·la·tor** \'tab-yə-,lāt-ər\ *n*

ta·chom·e·ter \tə-'käm-ət-ər\ *n* : a device to indicate speed of rotation

tac·it \'tas-ət\ *adj* **1** : expressed without words or speech (~ sympathy) **2** : implied or indicated but not actually expressed (~ consent) — **tac·it·ly** *adv*

tac·i·turn \'tas-ə-,tərn\ *adj* : disinclined to talk : habitually silent **syn** uncommunicative, reserved, reticent, secretive — **tac·i·tur·ni·ty** \,tas-ə-'tər-nət-ē\ *n*

¹**tack** \'tak\ *n* **1** : a small sharp nail with a broad flat head **2** : the direction a ship is sailing as shown by the way the sails are trimmed; *also* : the run of a ship trimmed in one way **3** : a change of course from one tack to another **4** : a zigzag course **5** : a course of action

²**tack** *vb* **1** : to fasten with tacks; *also* : to add on : ATTACH **2** : to change the direction of (a sailing ship) from one tack to another **3** : to follow a zigzag course

¹**tack·le** \'tak-əl\ *n* **1** : GEAR, APPARATUS, EQUIPMENT **2** : the rigging of a ship **3** : an arrangement of ropes and pulleys for hoisting or pulling heavy objects **4** : the act or an instance of tackling; *also* : a football lineman playing between guard and end

²**tackle** *vb* **1** : to attach and secure with or as if with tackle **2** : to seize, grapple with, or throw down with the intention of subduing or stopping **3** : to set about dealing with (~ a problem)

tacky \'tak-ē\ *adj* : sticky to the touch (a ~ varnished surface)

tact \'takt\ *n* : a keen sense of what to do or say to keep good relations with others or avoid offense — **tact·ful** *adj* — **tact·ful·ly** *adv* — **tact·less** *adj* — **tact·less·ly** *adv*

tac·tic \'tak-tik\ *n* : a device for accomplishing an end

tac·tics \'tak-tiks\ *n sing or pl* **1** : the science and art of disposing and maneuvering forces in combat **2** : the art or skill of employing available means to accomplish an end — **tac·ti·cal** \-ti-kəl\ *adj* — **tac·ti·cian** \tak-'tish-ən\ *n*

tac·tile \'tak-t'l, -,tīl\ *adj* : of, relating to, or perceptible through the sense of touch

tad·pole \'tad-,pōl\ *n* : a larval frog or toad with tail and gills

taf·fe·ta \'taf-ət-ə\ *n* : a crisp lustrous fabric of various fibers

taff·rail \'taf-,rāl\ *n* : the rail around a ship's stern

taf·fy \'taf-ē\ *n* : a candy usu. of molasses or brown sugar stretched until porous and light-colored

¹**tag** \'tag\ *n* **1** : a metal or plastic binding on an end of a shoelace **2** : a piece of hanging or attached material (as of cardboard, plastic, or metal) (price ~) (identification ~) **3** : a hackneyed quotation or saying : CLICHÉ **4** : a descriptive or identifying epithet

²**tag** *vb* **tagged; tag·ging 1** : to provide or mark with or as if with a tag; *esp* : IDENTIFY **2** : to attach as an addition

---

ə abut; ᵊ kitten; ər further; a back; ā bake; ä cot, cart; aù out; ch chin; e less; ē easy; g gift; i trip; ī life; j joke; ŋ sing; ō flow; ò flaw; òi coin; th thin; th this; ü loot; ù foot; y yet; yü few; yù furious; zh vision

3 : to follow closely and persistently ⟨~*s* along everywhere we go⟩ **4 :** to hold responsible for something

3tag *n* **:** a game in which one player chases others and tries to touch one of them

4tag *vb* **tagged; tag·ging 1 :** to touch in or as if in a game of tag **2 :** SELECT

1tail \'tāl\ *n* **1 :** the rear end or a process extending from the rear end of an animal **2 :** something resembling an animal's tail **3** *pl* **:** full evening dress for men **4 :** the back, last, lower, or inferior part of something; *esp* **:** the reverse of a coin — **tail·less** \'tāl-ləs\ *adj*

2tail *vb* **:** FOLLOW; *esp* **:** to follow for the purposes of surveillance **syn** pursue, chase, trail, tag

tail·coat \-'kōt\ *n* **:** a coat with tails; *esp* **:** a man's full-dress coat with two long tapering skirts at the back

1tai·lor \'tā-lər\ *n* [OF *tailleur*, lit., cutter, fr. *taillier* to cut, fr. LL *taliare*] **:** one whose occupation is making or altering outer garments

2tailor *vb* **1 :** to make or fashion as the work of a tailor **2 :** to make or adapt to suit a special purpose

1taint \'tānt\ *vb* **1 :** to affect or become affected with something bad and esp. putrefaction **2 :** CORRUPT, CONTAMI-NATE **syn** pollute, defile

2taint *n* **1 :** a result of tainting **:** BLEMISH, FLAW **2 :** a contaminating influence

1take \'tāk\ *vb* **took** \'tuk\ **tak·en** \'tā-kən\ **tak·ing 1 :** to get into one's hands or possession **:** GRASP, SEIZE **2 :** CAPTURE; *also* **:** DEFEAT **3 :** to catch or attack through the effect of a sudden force or influence ⟨*taken* ill⟩ **4 :** CAP-TIVATE, DELIGHT **5 :** to receive into one's body (as by eating) ⟨~ a pill⟩ **6 :** to bring into a relation ⟨~ a wife⟩ **7 :** RECEIVE, ACCEPT **8 :** to obtain or secure for use; *also* **:** to take when bestowed ⟨~ a degree⟩ **9 :** ASSUME, UNDERTAKE **10 :** to pick out **:** CHOOSE **11 :** to use for transportation ⟨~ a bus⟩ **12 :** NEED, REQUIRE **13 :** to obtain as the result of a special procedure ⟨~ a snapshot⟩ **14 :** ENDURE, UNDERGO **15 :** to become impregnated with **:** ABSORB ⟨~*s* a dye⟩ **16 :** to lead, carry, or cause to go along to another place **17 :** REMOVE, SUBTRACT **18 :** to undertake and do, make, or perform ⟨~ a walk⟩ **19 :** to take effect **:** ACT, OPERATE **syn** grab, clutch, snatch, en-chant, fascinate, allure, attract — **tak·er** *n*

2take *n* **1 :** an act or the action of taking **2 :** the number or quantity taken **:** CATCH; *also* **:** PROCEEDS, RECEIPTS **3 :** mental response **:** REACTION

take off \'tāk-'of\ *vb* **1 :** REMOVE **2 :** to set out **:** go away **:** WITHDRAW **3 :** COPY, REPRODUCE; *esp* **:** MIMIC **4 :** to leave the surface; *esp* **:** to begin flight

take-off \-,of\ *n* **:** an act or instance of taking off

1tak·ing *n* **1 :** SEIZURE **2** *pl* **:** receipts esp. of money

2taking *adj* **1 :** ATTRACTIVE, CAPTIVAT-ING **2 :** CONTAGIOUS ⟨measles is a ~ disease⟩ **syn** charming, enchanting, fascinating, bewitching, alluring

talc \'talk\ *n* **:** a soft mineral of a soapy feel used esp. in making toilet powder (**tal·cum powder** \'tal-kəm-\)

tale \'tāl\ *n* **1 :** a relation of a series of events **:** ACCOUNT **2 :** a report of a confidential matter **3 :** idle talk; *esp*

: harmful gossip **4 :** a usu. imaginative narrative **:** STORY **5 :** FALSEHOOD **6 :** COUNT, TALLY

tal·ent \'tal-ənt\ *n* **1 :** an ancient unit of weight and value **2 :** the natural endowments of a person **3 :** a special often creative or artistic aptitude **4 :** mental power **:** ABILITY **5 :** a person of talent in a field or activity **syn** genius, gift, faculty, aptitude, knack — **tal-ent·ed** *adj*

tales·man \'tālz-mən\ *n* **:** a person summoned for jury duty

tal·is·man \'tal-əs-mən, -əz-\ *n* **:** an object thought to act as a charm to avert evil and bring good fortune

1talk \'tok\ *vb* **1 :** to express in speech **:** utter words **:** SPEAK **2 :** DISCUSS ⟨~ business⟩ **3 :** to influence or cause by talking ⟨~*ed* him into agreeing⟩ **4 :** to use (a language) for communicating **5 :** CONVERSE **6 :** to reveal confidential information; *also* **:** GOSSIP **7 :** to give a talk **:** LECTURE — **talk·er** *n*

2talk *n* **1 :** the act of talking **:** SPEECH, CONVERSATION **2 :** a way of speaking **:** LANGUAGE **3 :** a formal discussion **:** CONFERENCE **4 :** REPORT, RUMOR **5 :** the topic of comment or gossip ⟨the ~ of the town⟩ **6 :** an informal address or lecture

talk·ative \'to-kət-iv\ *adj* **:** given to talking **syn** loquacious, voluble, gar-rulous — **talk·ative·ly** *adv*

tall \'tol\ *adj* **1 :** high in stature; *also* **:** of a specified height ⟨six feet ~⟩ **2 :** LARGE, FORMIDABLE ⟨a ~ order⟩ **3 :** UNBELIEVABLE, IMPROBABLE ⟨a ~ story⟩ **syn** lofty

tal·low \'tal-ō\ *n* **1 :** animal fat; *esp* **:** SUET **2 :** a hard white fat rendered usu. from cattle or sheep tissues and used esp. in soap, margarine, and lubricants

1tal·ly \'tal-ē\ *n* **1 :** a device (as a mechanical counter or a sheet) for visibly recording or accounting esp. business transactions **2 :** a recorded account **:** RECKONING, SCORE **3 :** a cor-responding part **:** COUNTERPART; *also* **:** CORRESPONDENCE, AGREEMENT

2tally *vb* **1 :** to mark on or as if on a tally **:** TABULATE **2 :** to make a count of **:** RECKON; *also* **:** SCORE **3 :** COR-RESPOND, MATCH **syn** square, accord, harmonize, conform, jibe

tal·ly·ho \,tal-ē-'hō\ *n* **:** a 4-horse coach used for show and sport

Tal·mud \'täl-,mud, 'tal-məd\ *n* **:** the authoritative body of Jewish tradition — **tal·mu·dic** \tal-'m(y)üd-ik, -'məd-\ *adj*, *often cap* — **tal·mud·ist** \'täl-,mud-əst, 'tal-məd-\ *n*, *often cap*

tal·on \'tal-ən\ *n* **:** the claw of an ani-mal and esp. of a bird of prey

tam \'tam\ *n* **:** TAM-O'-SHANTER

tam·a·rack \'tam-ə-,rak\ *n* **:** an Ameri-can larch; *also* **:** its hard resinous wood

tam·a·rind \'tam-ə-,rind\ *n* **:** a tropical tree with hard yellowish wood and feathery leaves; *also* **:** its acid brown fruit

tam·bou·rine \,tam-bə-'rēn\ *n* **:** a small shallow drum with loose disks at the sides played by shaking or striking with the hand

1tame \'tām\ *adj* **1 :** reduced from a state of native wildness so. so as to be useful to man **:** DOMESTICATED **2 :** made docile **:** SUBDUED **3 :** lacking spirit or interest **:** INSIPID **syn** submissive — **tame·ly** *adv* — **tame·ness** *n*

¹**tame** vb **1** : to make or become tame; also : to subject (land) to cultivation **2** : HUMBLE, SUBDUE — **tam·able** or **tame·able** adj — **tame·less** adj — **tam·er** n

tam-o'-shan·ter \'tam-ə-,shant-ər\ n : a Scottish woolen cap with a wide flat circular crown and usu. a pompon in the center

tamp \'tamp\ vb : to drive down or in by a series of light blows ⟨~ the earth over the grave⟩

tam·per \'tam-pər\ vb **1** : to carry on underhand negotiations (as by bribery) ⟨~ with a witness⟩ **2** : to interfere so as to weaken or change for the worse ⟨~ with a document⟩ **3** : to try foolish or dangerous experiments : MEDDLE

¹**tan** \'tan\ vb **tanned**; **tan·ning 1** : to change (hide) into leather esp. by soaking in a liquid containing tannin **2** : to make or become brown (as by exposure to the sun) **3** : WHIP, THRASH

²**tan** n **1** : TANBARK; also : a tanning material **2** : a brown skin color induced by sun or weather **3** : a light yellowish brown color

tan·bark \'tan-,bärk\ n : bark (as of oak or sumac) that is rich in tannin and used in tanning

¹**tan·dem** \'tan-dəm\ n **1** : a 2-seated carriage with horses hitched tandem; also : its team (or adj) : one behind the other

²**tandem** adv (or adj) : one behind another

tang \'taŋ\ n **1** : a part in a tool that connects the blade with the handle **2** : a sharp distinctive flavor; also : a pungent odor — **tangy** \-ē\ adj

tan·gent \'tan-jənt\ adj [L tangent-, tangens, prp. of tangere to touch] : TOUCHING; esp : meeting a curve or surface and not cutting it if extended

tangent n **1** : a tangent line, curve, or surface **2** : an abrupt change of course : DIGRESSION — **tan·gen·tial** \tan-'jen-chəl\ adj

tan·ger·ine \'tan-jə-,rēn\ n : a deep orange loose-skinned citrus fruit

tan·gi·ble \'tan-jə-bəl\ adj **1** : perceptible esp. by the sense of touch : PALPABLE **2** : substantially real : MATERIAL ⟨~ rewards⟩ **3** : capable of being appraised syn appreciable — **tan·gi·bil·i·ty** \,tan-jə-'bil-ət-ē\ n

tangible n : something tangible; esp : a tangible asset

tan·gle \'taŋ-gəl\ vb **1** : to involve so as to hamper or embarrass; also : ENTRAP **2** : to unite or knit together in intricate confusion : ENTANGLE

tangle n **1** : a tangled twisted mass (as of vines) **2** : a confusedly complicated state : MUDDLE

tan·go \'taŋ-gō\ n : a dance of Spanish-American origin — **tango** vb

tank \'taŋk\ n **1** : a large artificial receptacle for liquids **2** : an armored and armed tractor for military use

tan·kard \'taŋ-kərd\ n : a tall one-handled drinking vessel; esp : a silver or pewter mug with a lid

tank·er \'taŋ-kər\ n : a vehicle (as a ship, airplane, truck, or trailer) equipped with one or more tanks for transporting a liquid (as fuel)

tan·ner \'tan-ər\ n : one that tans hides

tan·nery \-(ə-)rē\ n : a place where tanning is carried on

tan·nic acid \,tan-ik-\ n : TANNIN

tan·nin \'tan-ən\ n : any of various substances of plant origin used in tanning and dyeing, in inks, and as astringents

tan·ta·lize \'tant-ºl-,īz\ vb [fr. Tantalus, mythical Greek king punished in Hades by having to stand up to his chin in water that receded whenever he bent to drink] : to tease or torment by presenting something desirable to the view but continually keeping it out of reach — **tan·ta·liz·er** n

tan·ta·lum \'tant-ºl-əm\ n : a hard ductile acid-resisting chemical element

tan·ta·mount \'tant-ə-,maùnt\ adj : equivalent in value or meaning syn same, selfsame, identical

tan·trum \'tan-trəm\ n : a fit of bad temper

Tao·ism \'taù-,iz-əm, 'daù-\ n : a religion developed from a Chinese mystic philosophy and Buddhist religion — **Tao·ist** adj or n

¹**tap** \'tap\ n **1** : FAUCET, COCK **2** : liquor drawn through a tap **3** : the removing of fluid from a container or cavity by tapping **4** : a tool for forming an internal screw thread **5** : a point in an electric circuit where a connection may be made

²**tap** vb **tapped**; **tap·ping 1** : to release or cause to flow by piercing or by drawing a plug from a container or cavity **2** : to pierce so as to let out or draw off a fluid **3** : to draw from ⟨~ resources⟩ **4** : to connect into (a telephone wire) to get information or to connect into (an electrical circuit) **5** : to connect (as a gas or water main) with a local supply

³**tap** vb **tapped**; **tap·ping 1** : to rap lightly **2** : to make (as a hole) by repeated light blows **3** : to repair by putting a half sole on **4** : SELECT; esp : to elect to membership

⁴**tap** n **1** : a light blow or stroke; also : its sound **2** : a small metal plate for the sole or heel of a shoe

¹**tape** \'tāp\ n **1** : a narrow band of woven fabric **2** : a narrow flexible strip (as of paper, plastic, or metal) **3** : MAGNETIC TAPE **4** : TAPE MEASURE

²**tape** vb **1** : to fasten or support with tape **2** : to measure with a tape measure **3** : to record on magnetic tape

tape measure n : a long flexible measuring instrument made of tape

¹**ta·per** \'tā-pər\ n **1** : a slender wax candle or a long waxed wick **2** : a gradual lessening of thickness or width in a long object ⟨the ~ of a steeple⟩

²**taper** vb **1** : to make or become gradually smaller toward one end **2** : to diminish gradually

tape·re·cord \,tāp-ri-'kòrd\ vb : to make a recording of (as sounds) on magnetic tape — **tape recorder** n

tap·es·try \'tap-ə-strē\ n : a heavy handwoven reversible textile characterized by complicated pictorial designs and used esp. as a wall hanging

tape·worm \'tāp-,wərm\ n : a long flat segmented worm that lives in the intestines

tap·i·o·ca \,tap-ē-'ō-kə\ n : a usu.

granular preparation of cassava starch used esp. in puddings

ta·pir \'tā-pər\ *n* : any of several large harmless hoofed mammals of tropical America and southeast Asia

tap·room \'tap-,rüm, -,rum\ *n* : BARROOM

tap·root \-,rüt, -,rut\ *n* : a large main root growing vertically downward and giving off small lateral roots

taps \'taps\ *n sing or pl* : the last bugle call at night blown as a signal that lights are to be put out; *also* : a similar call blown at military funerals and memorial services

tap·ster \'tap-stər\ *n* : one employed to dispense liquors in a barroom

¹tar \'tär\ *n* **1** : a thick dark sticky liquid distilled from organic material (as wood, coal, or peat) **2** : SAILOR, SEAMAN

²tar *vb* **tarred; tar·ring** : to treat or smear with tar

ta·ran·tu·la \tə-'ran-chə-lə, -'rant-ºl-ə\ *n* **1** : a large European spider once thought very dangerous **2** : any of various large hairy American spiders essentially harmless to man

tar·dy \'tärd-ē\ *adj* **1** : moving slowly : SLUGGISH **2** : LATE; *also* : DILATORY **syn** behindhand, overdue — **tar·di·ly** *adv* — **tar·di·ness** *n*

¹tare \'taər\ *n* : a weed of fields where grain is grown

²tare *n* : a deduction from the gross weight of a substance and its container made in allowance for the weight of the container

tar·get \'tär-gət\ *n* **1** : a mark to shoot at **2** : an object of ridicule or criticism **3** : a goal to be achieved

tar·iff \'tar-əf\ *n* **1** : a schedule of duties imposed by a government esp. on imported goods; *also* : a duty or rate of duty imposed in such a schedule **2** : a schedule of rates or charges **syn** customs, toll, tax, levy, assessment

tarn \'tärn\ *n* : a small mountain lake or pool

tar·nish \'tär-nish\ *vb* : to make or become dull, dim, or discolored : SULLY — **tarnish** *n*

ta·ro \'tär-ō, 'tar-\ *n* : a tropical plant grown for its edible fleshy root; *also* : this root

tar·pau·lin \tär-'pò-lən, 'tär-pə-\ *n* : waterproof material and esp. canvas used in sheets for protecting exposed objects (as goods)

tar·pon \'tär-pən\ *n* : a large silvery sport fish common off the Florida coast

¹tar·ry \'tar-ē\ *vb* **1** : to be tardy : DELAY; *esp* : to be slow in leaving **2** : to stay in or at a place : SOJOURN **syn** remain, wait

²tar·ry \'tär-ē\ *adj* : of, resembling, or smeared with tar

¹tart \'tärt\ *adj* **1** : agreeably sharp to the taste : PUNGENT **2** : BITING, CAUSTIC **syn** sour, acid — **tart·ly** *adv* — **tart·ness** *n*

²tart *n* **1** : a small pie or pastry shell containing jelly, custard, or fruit **2** : PROSTITUTE

tar·tan \'tärt-ºn\ *n* : a twilled woolen fabric with a plaid design of Scottish origin consisting of stripes of varying width and color against a solid ground

tar·tar \'tärt-ər\ *n* **1** : a substance in the juice of grapes deposited (as in wine casks) as a reddish crust or sediment **2** : a hard crust of saliva, debris,

and calcium salts on the teeth — **tar·tic** \tär-'tar-ik\ *adj*

¹task \'task\ *n* : a usu. assigned piece of work often to be finished within a certain time **syn** job, duty, chore, stint, assignment

²task *vb* : to oppress with great labor : BURDEN

task·mas·ter \-,mas-tər\ *n* : one that imposes a task or labor upon another

¹tas·sel \'tas-əl, 'täs-\ *n* **1** : a pendent ornament made by laying parallel a bunch of cords of even length and fastening them at one end **2** : something suggesting a tassel; *esp* : a male flower cluster of Indian corn

²tassel *vb* **-seled** *or* **-selled; -sel·ing** *or* **-sel·ling** : to adorn with or put forth tassels

¹taste \'tāst\ *vb* **1** : to try or determine the flavor of by taking a bit into the mouth **2** : to eat or drink esp. in small quantities : SAMPLE **3** : EXPERIENCE, UNDERGO **4** : to have a specific flavor

²taste *n* **1** : a small amount tasted **2** : BIT; *esp* : a sample of experience **3** : the special sense that identifies sweet, sour, bitter, or salty qualities and is mediated by receptors in the tongue **4** : a quality perceptible to the sense of taste; *also* : a complex sensation involving true taste, smell, and touch : FLAVOR **5** : individual preference : INCLINATION **6** : critical judgment, discernment, or appreciation; *also* : aesthetic quality **syn** tang, relish — **taste·ful** *adj* — **taste·ful·ly** *adv* — **taste·less** *adj* — **taste·less·ly** *adv*

tasty \'tā-stē\ *adj* : pleasing to the taste : SAVORY **syn** palatable, appetizing, toothsome, flavorsome — **tast·i·ness** *n*

tat \'tat\ *vb* **tat·ted; tat·ting** : to work at or make by tatting

¹tat·ter \'tat-ər\ *n* **1** : a part torn and left hanging : SHRED **2** *pl* : tattered clothing : RAGS

²tatter *vb* : to make or become ragged

tat·ter·de·ma·lion \,tat-ərd-i-'māl-yən\ *n* : one that is ragged or disreputable

tat·ting \'tat-iŋ\ *n* : a delicate handmade lace; *also* : the act or process of making such lace

tat·tle \'tat-ºl\ *vb* **1** : CHATTER, PRATE **2** : to tell secrets; *also* : to inform against another

tat·tle·tale \-,tāl\ *n* : one that tattles : INFORMER

¹tat·too \ta-'tü\ *n* [alter. of earlier *taptoo*, fr. D *taptoe*, fr. the phrase *tap toe!* *taps* shut] **1** : a call sounded before taps as notice to go to quarters **2** : a rapid rhythmic rapping

²tattoo *n* : an indelible figure fixed upon the body esp. by insertion of pigment under the skin

³tattoo *vb* : to mark (the skin) with tattoos

taught *past of* TEACH

¹taunt \'tònt\ *vb* : to reproach or challenge in a mocking manner : jeer at **syn** mock, deride, ridicule, twit — **taunt·er** *n*

²taunt *n* : a sarcastic challenge or insult

taupe \'tōp\ *n* : a brownish gray

taut \'tòt\ *adj* **1** : tightly drawn : not slack **2** : extremely nervous : TENSE **3** : TRIM, TIDY ⟨a ~ ship⟩ — **taut·ly** *adv* — **taut·ness** *n*

tav·ern \'tav-ərn\ *n* **1** : an establishment where alcoholic liquors are sold to be drunk on the premises **2** : INN

taw \'tò\ *n* : a marble used as a

shooter **2 :** the line from which players shoot at marbles

taw·dry \'tȯ-drē\ *adj* **:** cheap and gaudy in appearance and quality **syn** garish, flashy — **taw·dri·ly** *adv*

taw·ny \'tȯ-nē\ *adj* **:** of a brownish orange color

1tax \'taks\ *vb* **1 :** to levy a tax on **2 :** CHARGE, ACCUSE **3 :** to put under pressure **:** STRAIN **syn** assessment, customs, duty, tariff

2tax *n* **1 :** a usu. pecuniary charge imposed by authority upon persons or property for public purposes **2 :** a heavy charge **:** STRAIN **syn** assessment, customs, duty, tariff — **tax·able** *adj* — **tax·a·tion** \tak-'sā-shən\ *n*

1taxi \'tak-sē\ *n* **:** TAXICAB; *also* **:** a similarly operated boat or airplane

2taxi *vb* **tax·ied; taxi·ing** *or* **taxy·ing 1 :** to go by taxicab **2 :** to run along the ground or on the water under an airplane's own power when starting or when coming in after a landing

taxi·cab \'tak-sē-,kab\ *n* **:** a chauffeur-driven automobile for hire that usu. carries a device (**taxi·me·ter** \-,mēt-ər\) for automatic registering of the fare due

tax·i·der·my \'tak-sə-,dər-mē\ *n* **:** the art of preparing, stuffing, and mounting skins of animals — **tax·i·der·mist** *n*

tax·on·o·my \tak-'sän-ə-mē\ *n* **:** classification esp. of animals or plants according to natural relationships — **tax·o·nom·ic** \,tak-sə-'näm-ik\ *adj*

tax·pay·er \'taks-,pā-ər\ *n* **:** one who pays or is liable for a tax

TB \(')tē-'bē\ *n* **:** TUBERCULOSIS

tea \'tē\ *n* **1 :** the cured leaves and leaf buds of a shrub grown chiefly in China, Japan, India, and Ceylon; *also* **:** this shrub **2 :** a drink made by steeping tea in boiling water **3 :** refreshments usu. including tea served in late afternoon; *also* **:** a reception at which tea is served

teach \'tēch\ *vb* **taught** \'tȯt\ **teach·ing 1 :** to cause to know a subject **:** act as a teacher **2 :** to show how ⟨~ a child to swim⟩ **3 :** to guide the studies of **4 :** to make to know the disagreeable consequences of an action **5 :** to impart the knowledge of ⟨~ algebra⟩ — **teach·able** *adj* — **teach·er** *n*

teach·ing *n* **1 :** the act, practice, or profession of a teacher **2 :** something taught; *esp* **:** DOCTRINE

teak \'tēk\ *n* **:** a tall East Indian timber tree; *also* **:** its hard durable yellowish brown wood

teal \'tēl\ *n* **:** any of several small short-necked wild ducks

1team \'tēm\ *n* **1 :** two or more draft animals harnessed to the same vehicle or implement **2 :** a number of persons associated in work or activity; *esp* **:** a group on one side in a match — **team·mate** \'tēm-,māt\ *n*

2team *vb* **1 :** to haul with or drive a team **2 :** to form a team **:** join forces ⟨~ up together⟩

3team *adj* **:** of or performed by a team

team·ster \'tēm-stər\ *n* **:** one that drives a team or motortruck esp. as an occupation

team·work \-,wərk\ *n* **:** the work or activity of a number of persons acting in close association as members of a unit

1tear \'tiər\ *n* **:** a drop of the salty liquid that moistens the eye and inner side of the eyelids — **tear·ful** *adj* — **tear·ful·ly** *adv*

2tear \'taər\ *vb* **tore** \'tōr\ **torn** \'tȯrn\ **tear·ing 1 :** to separate parts of or pull apart by force **:** REND **2 :** LACERATE **3 :** to disrupt by the pull of contrary forces **4 :** to break off **:** WRENCH **5 :** to move or act with violence, haste, or force **syn** rip, split, cleave

3tear \'taər\ *n* **1 :** the act of tearing **2 :** a hole or flaw made by tearing **:** RENT

1tease \'tēz\ *vb* **1 :** to disentangle and lay parallel by combing or carding ⟨~ wool⟩ **2 :** to scratch the surface of (cloth) so as to raise a nap **3 :** to annoy persistently esp. in fun by goading, coaxing, or tantalizing **syn** harass, worry, pester

2tease *n* **1 :** a teasing or being teased **2 :** one that teases

tea·sel \'tē-zəl\ *n* **:** a prickly herb or its flower head covered with stiff bracts and used to raise the nap on cloth; *also* **:** an artificial device used for this purpose

tea·spoon \'tē-,spün\ *n* **:** a small spoon suitable for stirring and sipping tea or coffee and holding one third of a tablespoon — **tea·spoon·ful** \-,fu̇l\ *n*

teat \'tit, 'tēt\ *n* **:** NIPPLE

tech·nic \'tek-nik\ *n* **:** TECHNIQUE

tech·ni·cal \'tek-ni-kəl\ *adj* [Gk *technikos*, fr. *technē* art, craft] **1 :** having special knowledge esp. of a mechanical or scientific subject ⟨~ experts⟩ **2 :** of or relating to a particular and esp. a practical or scientific subject ⟨~ training⟩ **3 :** according to a strict interpretation of the rules ⟨a ~ victory⟩ **4 :** of or relating to technique ⟨an artist's ~ skill⟩ — **tech·ni·cal·ly** *adv*

tech·ni·cal·i·ty \,tek-nə-'kal-ət-ē\ *n* **1 :** the quality or state of being technical **2 :** a detail meaningful only to a specialist

technical sergeant *n* **:** a noncommissioned officer in the air force ranking next below a master sergeant

tech·ni·cian \tek-'nish-ən\ *n* **:** a person who has acquired the technique of a specialized skill or standard

tech·nique \tek-'nēk\ *n* **:** the manner in which technical details are treated or used in accomplishing a desired aim **:** technical methods

tech·noc·ra·cy \tek-'näk-rə-sē\ *n* **:** management of society by technical experts — **tech·no·crat** \'tek-nə-,krat\ *n* — **tech·no·crat·ic** \,tek-nə-'krat-ik\ *adj*

tech·nol·o·gy \tek-'näl-ə-jē\ *n* **:** applied science; *also* **:** a technical method of achieving a practical purpose — **tech·no·log·i·cal** \,tek-nə-'läj-i-kəl\ *adj*

te·dious \'tēd-ē-əs, 'tē-jəs\ *adj* **:** tiresome because of length or dullness **syn** boring, wearisome, irksome — **te·dious·ly** *adv* — **te·dious·ness** *n*

te·di·um \'tēd-ē-əm\ *n* **:** TEDIOUSNESS; *also* **:** BOREDOM

1tee \'tē\ *n* **:** a small mound or peg on which a golf ball is placed before the beginning of play on a hole; *also* **:** the area from which the ball is hit to begin play

2tee *vb* **:** to place (a ball) on a tee

teem \'tēm\ *vb* **:** to become filled to

overflowing **:** ABOUND **syn** swarm

teen-age \'tēn-,āj\ *or* **teen-aged** \-,ājd\ *adj* **:** of, being, or relating to people in their teens — **teen-ag·er** *n*

teens \'tēnz\ *n pl* **:** the numbers 13 to 19 inclusive; *esp* **:** the years 13 to 19 in a person's life

tee·ny \'tē-nē\ *adj* **:** TINY

tee·pee *var of* TEPEE

tee·ter \'tēt-ər\ *vb* **1 :** to move unsteadily **:** WOBBLE **2 :** SEESAW — **teeter** *n*

teeth *pl of* TOOTH

teethe \'tēth\ *vb* **:** to grow teeth **:** cut one's teeth

tee·to·tal \'tē-'tōt-ºl\ *adj* **:** of or relating to the practice of complete abstinence from alcoholic drinks — **tee·to·tal·er** *or* **tee·to·tal·ler** *n* — **tee·to·tal·ism** *n*

tele·cast \'tel-i-,kast\ *vb* **-cast** *also* **-cast·ed; -cast·ing :** to broadcast by television — **telecast** *n* — **tele·cast·er** *n*

tele·com·mu·ni·ca·tion \,tel-i-kə-,myü-nə-'kā-shən\ *n* **:** communication at a distance (as by telephone or radio)

tel·e·gram \'tel-ə-,gram\ *n* **:** a message sent by telegraph

¹tel·e·graph \-,graf\ *n* **:** an apparatus or system for communication at a distance by electrical transmission of coded signals

²telegraph *vb* **:** to send or communicate by telegraph — **te·leg·ra·pher** \tə-'leg-rə-fər\ *n* — **te·leg·ra·phist** \-fəst\ *n*

te·leg·ra·phy \tə-'leg-rə-fē\ *n* **:** the use or operation of a telegraph apparatus or system — **tel·e·graph·ic** \,tel-ə-'graf-ik\ *adj*

tele·me·ter \'tel-ə-,mēt-ər\ *n* **:** an electrical apparatus for measuring something (as temperature) and transmitting the result by radio to a distant station — **tele·met·ric** \,tel-ə-'met-rik\ *adj* — **te·lem·e·try** \tə-'lem-ə-trē\ *n*

te·lep·a·thy \tə-'lep-ə-thē\ *n* **:** apparent communication from one mind to another without speech or signs — **tel·e·path·ic** \,tel-ə-'path-ik\ *adj* — **tel·e·path·i·cal·ly** *adv*

¹tel·e·phone \'tel-ə-,fōn\ *n* **:** an instrument for reproducing sounds and esp. spoken words transmitted from a distance by electrical means over wires

²telephone *vb* **1 :** to send or communicate by telephone **2 :** to speak to (a person) by telephone

te·leph·o·ny \tə-'lef-ə-nē, 'tel-ə,fō-\ *n* **:** use or operation of apparatus for electrical transmission of sounds and esp. speech between distant points with or without connecting wires — **tele·phon·ic** \,tel-ə-'fän-ik\ *adj*

tele·pho·to \,tel-ə-'fōt-ō\ *adj* **:** being a camera lens giving a large image of a distant object — **tele·pho·to·graph** \-'fōt-ə,graf\ *n or vb* — **tele·pho·tog·ra·phy** \,fə-'täg-rə-fē\ *n*

¹tel·e·scope \'tel-ə-,skōp\ *n* **:** a long tube-shaped instrument equipped with lenses for viewing objects at a distance and esp for observing celestial bodies

²telescope *vb* **:** to slide, pass, or force or cause to slide, pass, or force one within another like the sections of a hand telescope

tel·e·scop·ic \,tel-ə-'skäp-ik\ *adj* **1 :** of or relating to a telescope **2 :** seen only by a telescope **3 :** able to discern objects at a distance **4 :** having parts that telescope

tele·view \'tel-ə-,vyü\ *vb* **:** to watch by means of a television receiver — **tele·view·er** *n*

tel·e·vise \'tel-ə-,vīz\ *vb* **:** to pick up and broadcast by television

tele·vi·sion \'tel-ə-,vizh-ən\ *n* [F *télévision*, fr. Gk *tēle* far, at a distance + F *vision* vision] **:** transmission and reproduction of a rapid series of images by a device that converts light waves into radio waves and then converts these back into visible light rays

tell \'tel\ *vb* **told** \'tōld\ **tell·ing 1 :** COUNT, ENUMERATE **2 :** to relate in detail **:** NARRATE **3 :** SAY, UTTER **4 :** to make known **:** REVEAL **5 :** to report to **:** INFORM **6 :** ORDER, DIRECT **7 :** to ascertain by observing **8 :** to have a marked effect **9 :** to serve as evidence **syn** reveal, disclose, discover, betray

tell·er *n* **1 :** one that relates **:** NARRATOR **2 :** one that counts (appoint ∼s to tally the votes) **3 :** a bank employee handling money received or paid out

tell·ing *adj* **:** producing a marked effect **:** EFFECTIVE **syn** cogent, convincing, sound

tell·tale \'tel-,tāl\ *n* **1 :** INFORMER, TATTLETALE **2 :** something that serves to disclose **:** INDICATION — **telltale** *adj*

tel·lu·ri·um \tə-'lùr-ē-əm\ *n* **:** a chemical element that resembles sulfur in properties

tem·blor \'tem-blər, -,blȯr\ *n* **:** EARTHQUAKE

te·mer·i·ty \tə-'mer-ət-ē\ *n* **:** rash or presumptuous daring **:** BOLDNESS **syn** audacity, effrontery, gall, nerve, cheek, gall

¹tem·per \'tem-pər\ *vb* **1 :** to dilute or soften by the addition of something else (∼ justice with mercy) **2 :** to bring to a desired consistency or texture (as clay by moistening and kneading, paints by mixing with oil, steel by gradual heating and cooling) **3 :** TOUGHEN **4 :** TUNE

²temper *n* **1 :** characteristic tone **:** TENDENCY **2 :** the state of a metal or other substance with respect to various qualities (as hardness) (∼ of a knife blade) **3 :** frame of mind **:** DISPOSITION **4 :** calmness of mind **:** COMPOSURE **5 :** MOOD, HUMOR **6 :** heat of mind or emotion **:** proneness to anger **syn** temperament, character, personality

tem·per·a·ment \'tem-p(ə-)rə-mənt\ *n* **1 :** characteristic or habitual inclination or mode of emotional response **:** DISPOSITION (nervous ∼) **2 :** excessive sensitiveness or irritability **syn** character, personality — **tem·per·a·men·tal** \,tem-p(ə-)rə-'ment-ºl\ *adj*

tem·per·ance \'tem-p(ə-)rəns\ *n* **:** habitual moderation in the indulgence of the appetites or passions; *esp* **:** moderation in or abstinence from the use of intoxicating drink

tem·per·ate \'tem-p(ə)rət\ *adj* **1 :** not extreme or excessive **:** MILD, RESTRAINED **2 :** moderate in indulgence of appetite or desire **3 :** moderate in the use of intoxicating liquors **4 :** having a moderate climate **syn** sober, continent

temperate zone *n* **:** the region between the tropic of Cancer and the arctic circle or between the tropic of Capricorn and the antarctic circle

tem·per·a·ture \'tem-pər-,chùr, -p(ə-)rə-,chùr, -chər\ *n* **1 :** degree of hotness or coldness of something (as air, water, or the body) as shown by a thermometer **2** : FEVER ⟨the patient had a ~⟩

tem·pest \'tem-pəst\ *n* **:** a violent wind; *esp* : one with rain, hail, or snow

tem·pes·tu·ous \tem-'pes-chə-wəs\ *adj* : of, involving, or resembling a tempest **:** STORMY — **tem·pes·tu·ous·ly** *adv*

tem·plate *or* **tem·plet** \'tem-plət\ *n* : a gauge, mold, or pattern used as a guide to the form of a piece being made

¹**tem·ple** \'tem-pəl\ *n* **1** : an edifice for the worship of a deity **2** : a place devoted to a special or exalted purpose

²**temple** *n* : the flattened space on each side of the forehead esp. of man

tem·po \'tem-pō\ *n*, *pl* -**pi** \-pē\ *or* -**pos 1** : the rate of speed of a musical piece or passage **2** : rate of motion or activity **:** PACE

¹**tem·po·ral** \'tem-p(ə-)rəl\ *adj* **1** : of, relating to, or limited by time ⟨~ and spatial bounds⟩ **2** : of or relating to earthly life or secular concerns ⟨~ power⟩ **syn** temporary, secular, lay

²**temporal** *adj* : of or relating to the temples or to the sides of the skull

tem·po·rary \'tem-pə-ˌrer-ē\ *adj* : lasting for a time only **:** TRANSITORY **syn** provisional, impermanent — **tem·po·rar·i·ly** \ˌtem-pə-'rer-ə-lē\ *adv*

tem·po·rize \'tem-pə-ˌrīz\ *vb* **1** : to adapt one's actions to the time or the dominant opinion **:** COMPROMISE **2** : to draw out matters so as to gain time **:** DELAY — **tem·po·riz·er** *n*

tempt \'tempt\ *vb* **1** : to entice to do wrong by promise of pleasure or gain **2** : PROVOKE **3** : to risk the dangers of **4** : to induce to do something **:** INCITE **syn** inveigle, decoy, seduce — **tempt·er** *n* — **tempt·ress** \'temp-trəs\ *n*

temp·ta·tion \temp-'tā-shən\ *n* **1** : a tempting or a being tempted **2** : something that tempts

ten \'ten\ *n* **1** : one more than nine **2** : the 10th in a set or series **3** : something having 10 units — **ten** *adj or pron* — **tenth** *adj or adv or n*

ten·a·ble \'ten-ə-bəl\ *adj* : capable of being held, maintained, or defended **:** DEFENSIBLE, REASONABLE — **ten·a·bil·i·ty** \ˌten-ə-'bil-ət-ē\ *n*

te·na·cious \tə-'nā-shəs\ *adj* **1** : not easily pulled apart **:** COHESIVE, TOUGH ⟨steel is a ~ metal⟩ **2** : holding fast **:** PERSISTENT, STUBBORN ⟨~ of his rights⟩ **3** : RETENTIVE ⟨~ memory⟩ — **te·na·cious·ly** *adv* — **te·nac·i·ty** \tə-'nas-ət-ē\ *n*

ten·an·cy \'ten-ən-sē\ *n* : the temporary possession or occupancy of something (as a house) that belongs to another; *also* : the period of a tenant's occupancy

ten·ant \'ten-ənt\ *n* **1** : one who rents or leases (as a house) from a landlord **2** : DWELLER, OCCUPANT — **tenant** *vb* — **ten·ant·less** *adj*

ten·ant·ry *n* : the body of tenants esp. on a great estate

¹**tend** \'tend\ *vb* **1** : to apply oneself ⟨~ to your affairs⟩ **2** : to take care of ⟨~ a plant⟩ **3** : to manage the operations of ⟨~ a machine⟩ **syn** mind, watch

²**tend** *vb* **1** : to move or develop one's course in a particular direction **2** : to show an inclination or tendency

ten·den·cy \'ten-dən-sē\ *n* **1** : DRIFT, TREND **2** : a proneness to or readiness

for a particular kind of thought or action **:** PROPENSITY **syn** tenor, current, bent, leaning

¹**ten·der** \'ten-dər\ *adj* **1** : having a soft texture **:** easily broken, chewed, or cut **2** : physically weak **:** DELICATE; *also* **:** IMMATURE **3** : expressing or responsive to love or sympathy **:** LOVING, COMPASSIONATE **4** : SENSITIVE, TOUCHY **syn** sympathetic, warm, warmhearted — **ten·der·ly** *adv* — **ten·der·ness** *n*

²**tend·er** \'ten-dər\ *n* **1** : one that tends or takes care **2** : a vehicle attached to a locomotive to carry fuel and water **3** : a boat carrying passengers and freight to a larger ship

³**ten·der** *n* **1** : an offer or proposal made for acceptance; *esp* : an offer of a bid for a contract **2** : something (as money) that may be offered in payment

⁴**ten·der** *vb* : to present for acceptance **:** OFFER

ten·der·foot \'ten-dər-ˌfu̇t\ *n* **1** : one not hardened to frontier or rough outdoor life **2** : an inexperienced beginner **:** NEOPHYTE

ten·der·heart·ed \ˌten-dər-'härt-əd\ *adj* : easily moved to love, pity, or sorrow **:** COMPASSIONATE

ten·der·ize \'ten-də-ˌrīz\ *vb* : to make (meat) tender

ten·der·loin \'ten-dər-ˌlȯin\ *n* **1** : a strip of very tender meat on each side of the backbone in beef or pork **2** : a district of a city marked by extensive vice, crime, and corruption

ten·don \'ten-dən\ *n* : a tough cord of dense tissue uniting a muscle with another part (as a bone) — **ten·di·nous** \-də-nəs\ *adj*

ten·dril \'ten-drəl\ *n* : a slender coiling organ by which some climbing plants attach themselves to a support

ten·e·ment \'ten-ə-mənt\ *n* **1** : a house used as a dwelling **2** : a dwelling house divided into separate apartments for rent to families; *esp* : one meeting only minimum standards of safety and comfort **3** : APARTMENT, FLAT

ten·et \'ten-ət\ *n* : one of the principles or doctrines held in common by members of an organized group (as a church or profession) **syn** doctrine, dogma, belief

ten·fold \'ten-ˈfōld\ *adj* : being ten times as great or as many — **tenfold** *adv*

ten·nis \'ten-əs\ *n* : a game played with a ball and racket on a court divided by a net

ten·on \'ten-ən\ *n* : the shaped end of one piece of wood that fits into the hole in another piece and thus joins the two pieces together

ten·or \'ten-ər\ *n* **1** : the general drift of something spoken or written **:** PURPORT **2** : the highest natural adult male voice **:** TREND, TENDENCY

ten·pen·ny \ˌten-ˌpen-ē\ *adj* : amounting to, worth, or costing 10 pennies

ten·pin \'ten-ˌpin\ *n* : a bottle-shaped bowling pin set in groups of ten and bowled at in a game (**tenpins**)

¹**tense** \'tens\ *n* [MF *tens* time, tense, fr. L *tempus*] **:** distinction of form of a verb to indicate the time of the action or state

²**tense** *adj* **1** : stretched tight **:** TAUT **2** : feeling or marked by nervous tension

---

ə abut; ᵊ kitten; ər further; a back; ā bake; ä cot, cart; au̇ out; ch chin; e less; ē easy; g gift; i trip; ī life; j joke; ŋ sing; ō flow; ȯ flaw; ȯi coin; th thin; t͟h this; ü loot; u̇ foot; y yet; yü few; yu̇ furious; zh vision

syn stiff, rigid, inflexible — **tense·ly**
adv — **tense·ness** *n* — **ten·si·ty** \'ten-sət-ē\ *n*
ten·sile \'ten-səl, -ˌsīl\ *adj* : of or relating to tension ⟨~ strength⟩
ten·sion \'ten-chən\ *n* **1** : the act of straining or stretching; *also* : the condition of being strained or stretched **2** : a state of mental unrest often with signs of bodily stress **3** : a state of latent hostility or opposition ⟨~ between parents and children⟩
¹tent \'tent\ *n* **1** : a collapsible shelter of canvas or other material stretched and supported by poles **2** : a canopy placed over the head and shoulders to retain vapors or oxygen being medically administered
²tent *vb* **1** : to lodge in tents **2** : to cover with or as if with a tent
ten·ta·cle \'tent-i-kəl\ *n* : a long flexible projection about the head or mouth (as of an insect, mollusk, or fish) — **ten·ta·cled** *adj* — **ten·tac·u·lar** \ten-'tak-yə-lər\ *adj*
ten·ta·tive \'tent-ət-iv\ *adj* : of the nature of an experiment or hypothesis : not final : PROVISIONAL — **ten·ta·tive·ly** *adv*
ten·u·ous \'ten-yə-wəs\ *adj* **1** : not dense : RARE ⟨a ~ fluid⟩ **2** : not thick : SLENDER ⟨a ~ rope⟩ **3** : having little substance : FLIMSY, WEAK ⟨~ influences⟩ **syn** thin, slim, slight — **te·nu·i·ty** \te-'n(y)ü-ət-ē, tə-\ *n* — **ten·u·ous·ly** \'ten-yə-wəs-lē\ *adv* — **ten·u·ous·ness** *n*
ten·ure \'ten-yər\ *n* : the act, right, manner, or period of holding something (as a landed property or a position)
te·pee \'tē-(ˌ)pē\ *n* : an American Indian conical tent usu. of skins
tep·id \'tep-əd\ *adj* **1** : moderately warm : LUKEWARM **2** : HALFHEARTED
te·qui·la \tə-'kē-lə\ *n* : a Mexican liquor
ter·bi·um \'tər-bē-əm\ *n* : a metallic chemical element
ter·cen·ten·a·ry \ˌtər-ˌsen-'ten-ə-rē, tər-'sent-ᵊn-ˌer-ē\ *n* : a 300th anniversary; *also* : its celebration — **tercentenary** *adj*
te·re·do \tə-'rēd-ō\ *n, pl* **-dos** *or* **-red·i·nes** \-'red-ᵊn-ˌēz\ : SHIPWORM
¹term \'tərm\ *n* **1** : END, TERMINATION **2** : DURATION; *esp* : a period of time fixed esp. b. law or custom **3** : a mathematical expression connected with another by a plus or minus sign; *also* : any of the members of a ratio or of a series **4** : a word or expression that has a precise meaning in some uses or is peculiar to a subject or field **5** *pl* : PROVISIONS, CONDITIONS ⟨~s of a contract⟩ **6** *pl* : mutual relationship ⟨on good ~s with his neighbors⟩ **7** : AGREEMENT, CONCORD
²term *vb* : to apply a term to : CALL, NAME
ter·ma·gant \'tər-mə-gənt\ *n* : an overbearing or nagging woman : SHREW **syn** virago, vixen
¹ter·mi·nal \'tər-mən-ᵊl\ *adj* : of, relating to, or forming an end, limit, or terminus **syn** final, concluding, last, latest, extreme
²terminal *n* **1** : EXTREMITY, END **2** : a device at the end of a wire or on an apparatus for making an electrical connection **3** : either end of a carrier line (as a railroad or trucking line) with its handling and storage facilities and stations; *also* : a freight or passenger station
ter·mi·nate \'tər-mə-ˌnāt\ *vb* : to bring

or come to an end : CLOSE **syn** conclude, finish, complete — **ter·mi·na·ble** \-nə-bəl\ *adj* — **ter·mi·na·tion** \ˌtər-mə-'nā-shən\ *n*
ter·mi·nol·o·gy \ˌtər-mə-'näl-ə-jē\ *n* : the technical or special terms used in a business, art, science, or special subject
ter·mi·nus \'tər-mə-nəs\ *n* **1** : final goal : finishing point : END **2** : either end of a transportation line, travel route, pipeline, or canal; *also* : the station or city at such a place
ter·mite \'tər-ˌmīt\ *n* : any of a large group of pale soft-bodied social insects that feed on wood
tern \'tərn\ *n* : any of various small sea gulls with narrow wings and a black cap and light body
¹ter·race \'ter-əs\ *n* **1** : a flat roof or open platform **2** : a level paved or planted area next to a building **3** : an embankment with level top **4** : a bank or ridge on a slope to conserve moisture and soil **5** : a row of houses on raised land; *also* : a street with such a row of houses **6** : a strip of park in the middle of a street
²terrace *vb* : to form into a terrace or supply with terraces
ter·ra·cot·ta \ˌter-ə-'kät-ə\ *n* : a reddish brown earthenware used for vases and small statues
ter·ra fir·ma \-'fər-mə\ *n* : firm earth
ter·rain \tə-'rān\ *n* : a tract of ground considered with reference to its surface features ⟨a rough ~⟩
ter·ra·pin \'ter-ə-pən\ *n* : any of various No. American edible turtles of fresh or brackish water
ter·res·tri·al \tə-'res-t(r)ē-əl\ *adj* **1** : of or relating to the earth or its inhabitants : EARTHLY **2** : living or growing on land ⟨~ plants⟩ **syn** mundane, mortal
ter·ri·ble \'ter-ə-bəl\ *adj* **1** : exciting terror : FEARFUL, DREADFUL ⟨~ weapons⟩ **2** : hard to bear : DISTRESSING ⟨a ~ situation⟩ **3** : extreme in degree : INTENSE ⟨~ heat⟩ **4** : of very poor quality : AWFUL ⟨a ~ play⟩ **syn** frightful, horrible, shocking, appalling — **ter·ri·bly** \-blē\ *adv*
ter·ri·er \'ter-ē-ər\ *n* : any of various usu. small dogs orig. used by hunters to drive small game from holes
ter·rif·ic \tə-'rif-ik\ *adj* **1** : exciting terror : AWESOME **2** : EXTRAORDINARY, ASTOUNDING ⟨~ speed⟩ **3** : unusually fine : MAGNIFICENT **syn** terrible, frightful, dreadful, fearful, horrible, awful
ter·ri·fy \'ter-ə-ˌfī\ *vb* : to fill with terror : FRIGHTEN **syn** scare, terrorize, startle, intimidate
¹ter·ri·to·ri·al \ˌter-ə-'tōr-ē-əl\ *adj* **1** : of or relating to a territory ⟨~ government⟩ **2** : of or relating to an assigned area ⟨~ commanders⟩
²territorial *n* : a member of a territorial military unit
ter·ri·to·ry \'ter-ə-ˌtōr-ē\ *n* **1** : a geographical area belonging to or under the jurisdiction of a governmental authority **2** : a part of the U.S. not included within any state but organized with a separate legislature **3** : REGION, DISTRICT **4** : a field of knowledge or interest **5** : an assigned area ⟨a salesman's ~⟩
ter·ror \'ter-ər\ *n* **1** : a state of intense fear : FRIGHT **2** : one that inspires fear : SCOURGE **syn** panic, consternation, dread, alarm, dismay, horror, trepidation
ter·ror·ism *n* : the systematic use of ter-

ror esp. as a means of coercion — **ter·ror·ist** n

ter·ror·ize \'ter-ər- īz\ vb 1 : to fill with terror : SCARE 2 : to coerce by threat or violence syn terrify, frighten, alarm, startle

terse \'tərs\ adj : effectively brief : CONCISE — **terse·ly** adv

ter·ti·ary \'tər-shē-,er-ē\ adj 1 : of 3d rank, importance, or value 2 : occurring or being in the 3d stage

tes·sel·late \'tes-ə-,lāt\ vb : to form into or adorn with mosaic

¹test \'test\ n 1 : a critical examination or evaluation : TRIAL 2 : a means or result of testing

²test vb 1 : to put to test : TRY, EXAMINE 2 : to undergo or score on tests (an ore that ~s high in gold)

tes·ta·ment \'tes-tə-mənt\ n 1 cap : either of two main divisions (Old Testament, New Testament) of the Bible 2 : EVIDENCE, WITNESS 3 : CREDO 4 : an act by which a person determines the disposition of his property after his death : WILL — **tes·ta·men·ta·ry** \,tes-tə-'men-t(ə-)rē\ adj

tes·ta·tor \'tes-,tāt-ər, tes-'tāt-\ n : a person who leaves a will in force at his death — **tes·ta·trix** \tes-'tā-triks\ n

¹tes·ter \'tes-tər, 'tes-\ n : a canopy over a bed, pulpit, or altar

²test·er \'tes-tor\ n : one that tests

tes·ti·cle \'tes-ti-kəl\ n : TESTIS

tes·ti·fy \'tes-tə-,fī\ vb 1 : to make a statement based on personal knowledge or belief : bear witness 2 : to serve as evidence or proof syn swear, affirm

tes·ti·mo·ni·al \,tes-tə-'mō-nē-əl\ n 1 : a statement testifying to a person's good character or to the worth of something : TRIBUTE 2 : an expression of appreciation

tes·ti·mo·ny \'tes-tə-,mō-nē\ n 1 : a solemn declaration made by a witness under oath esp. in a court 2 : authoritative statement : WITNESS 3 : an outward sign : SYMBOL syn evidence, affidavit

tes·tis \'tes-təs\ n, pl tes·tes \'tes-,tēz\ : a male reproductive gland

test tube n : a thin glass tube closed at one end and used esp. in chemistry and biology

tes·ty \'tes-tē\ adj : marked by ill humor : easily annoyed

tet·a·nus \'tet-'n-əs\ n : a disease caused by bacterial poisons and marked by violent muscular spasm esp. of the jaw — **te·tan·ic** \te-'tan-ik\ adj

tête-à-tête \,tāt-ə-'tāt\ adv (or adj) [F, lit., head to head] : being face to face : PRIVATE

²tête-à-tête n : a private conversation between two persons

¹teth·er \'teth-ər\ n 1 : a line (as of rope or chain) by which an animal is fastened so as to restrict its range 2 : the limit of one's strength or resources

²tether vb : to fasten or restrain by or as if by a tether

te·tram·e·ter \te-'tram-ət-ər\ n : a line consisting of four metrical feet

Teu·ton·ic \t(y)ü-'tän-ik\ adj : GERMANIC

text \'tekst\ n 1 : the actual words of an author's work 2 : the main body of printed or written matter on a page 3 : a scriptural passage chosen as the subject esp. of a sermon 4 : TEXTBOOK 5 : THEME, TOPIC — **tex·tu·al** \'teks-ch(ə-w)əl\ adj

text·book \'teks(t)-,búk\ n : a book used in the study of a subject

tex·tile \'teks-,tīl, -t²l\ n : CLOTH; esp : a woven or knit cloth

tex·ture \'teks-chər\ n 1 : the visual or tactile surface characteristics and appearance of something (a coarse ~) 2 : essential part : SUBSTANCE, NATURE 3 : basic scheme or structure : FABRIC 4 : overall structure : BODY

¹-th \th\ — see -ETH

²-th \th\ or -eth \əth\ adj suffix — used in forming ordinal numbers (hundredth) (fortieth)

³-th n suffix 1 : act or process 2 : state or condition (dearth)

Thai \'tī\ n : a native or inhabitant of Thailand — **Thai** adj

thal·li·um \'thal-ē-əm\ n : a poisonous metallic chemical element

than \thən, (')than\ conj : when compared to the way, manner, extent, or degree in or to which (he's older ~ I am) (it works better ~ the other one did)

thane \'thān\ n 1 : a free retainer of an Anglo-Saxon lord 2 : a Scottish feudal lord

¹thank \'thank\ n : an expression of gratitude — usu. used in pl. (~s for the ride) — **thank·ful** adj — **thank·ful·ly** adv — **thank·ful·ness** n — **thank·less** adj

²thank vb : to express gratitude to (~ed him for the present)

thanks·giv·ing \thanks-'giv-in\ n 1 : the act of giving thanks 2 : prayer expressing gratitude 3 cap : the 4th Thursday in November observed as a legal holiday for giving thanks for divine goodness

¹that \(')that\ pron, pl those \(')thōz\ 1 : the one indicated, mentioned, or understood (~'s my wife) 2 : the one farther away or first mentioned (this is an elm, ~'s a maple) 3 : what has been indicated or mentioned (after ~, we left) 4 : the one or ones : IT, THEY (those who wish to leave may do so) (the richest ore is ~ found higher up)

²that adj, pl those 1 : being the one mentioned, indicated, or understood (~ boy) (those people) 2 : being the one farther away or first mentioned (this chair or ~ one)

³that \thət, (,)that\ conj 1 : the following, namely (he said ~ he would); also : which is, namely (there's a chance ~ it may fail) 2 : to this end or purpose (shouted ~ all might hear) 3 : as to result in the following, namely (so heavy ~ it can't be moved) 4 : for this reason, namely (we're glad ~ you came) 5 : I wish this, or I am surprised or indignant at this, namely (~ it should come to this)

⁴that \thət, (,)that\ pron 1 : WHO, WHOM, WHICH (the man ~ saw you) (the man ~ you saw) (the money ~ was spent) 2 : in, on, or at which (the way ~ he drives) (the day ~ it rained) (tell me the moment ~ he comes in)

ə abut; ᵊ kitten; ər further; a back; ā bake; ä cot, cart; aú out; ch chin; e less; ē easy; g gift; i trip; ī life; j joke; ŋ sing; ō flow; ò flaw; òi coin; th thin; th this; ü loot; ú foot; y yet; yü few; yú furious; zh vision

⁵**that** \'that\ *adv* **:** to such an extent or degree ⟨I like it, but not ∼ much⟩

¹**thatch** \'thach\ *vb* **:** to cover with thatch

²**thatch** *n* **1 :** plant material (as straw) for use as roofing **2 :** a covering of or as if of thatch ⟨a ∼ of white hair⟩

thaw \'thò\ *vb* **1 :** to melt or cause to melt **2 :** to become so warm or mild as to melt ice or snow **3 :** to abandon aloofness or hostility **syn** liquefy — **thaw** *n*

¹**the** \thə, *before vowel sounds usu* thē\ *definite article* **1 :** that in particular **2** — used before adjectives functioning as nouns ⟨a word to ∼ wise⟩ ⟨nothing but ∼ best⟩

²**the** *adv* **1 :** to what extent ⟨∼ sooner, the better⟩ **2 :** to that extent ⟨the sooner, ∼ better⟩

the·a·ter *or* **the·a·tre** \'thē-ət-ər\ *n* **1 :** a building for dramatic performances; *also* **:** a building or area for showing motion pictures **2 :** a place (as a lecture room) similar to such a building **3 :** a place of enactment of significant events **4 :** dramatic literature or performance

the·at·ri·cal \thē-'at-ri-kəl\ *adj* **1 :** of or relating to the theater **2 :** marked by artificiality of emotion **:** HISTRIONIC **3 :** marked by extravagant display **:** SHOWY **syn** dramatic, melodramatic

thee \(')thē\ *pron, objective case of* THOU

theft \'theft\ *n* **:** the act of stealing **:** LARCENY

thegn \'thān\ *n* **:** THANE 1

their \thər, (,)theər\ *adj* **:** of or relating to them or themselves

theirs \'theərz\ *pron* **:** one or the ones belonging to them

the·ism \'thē-,iz-əm\ *n* **:** belief in the existence of a god or gods — **the·ist** \-əst\ *n* — **the·is·tic** \thē-'is-tik\ *adj*

them \(th)əm, (')them\ *pron, objective case of* THEY

theme \'thēm\ *n* **1 :** a subject or topic of discourse or of artistic representation **2 :** a written exercise **:** COMPOSITION **3 :** a melodic subject of a musical composition or movement

them·selves \thəm-'selvz, them-\ *pron pl* **:** THEY, THEM — used reflexively, for emphasis, or in absolute constructions ⟨they govern ∼⟩ ⟨they ∼ couldn't come⟩ ⟨∼ busy, they sent me⟩

¹**then** \(')then\ *adv* **1 :** at that time **2 :** soon after that **:** NEXT **3 :** in addition **:** BESIDES **4 :** in that case **5 :** CONSEQUENTLY

²**then** \'then\ *n* **:** that time

³**then** \'then\ *adj* **:** existing or acting at that time ⟨the ∼ king⟩

thence \'thens\ *adv* **1 :** from that place **2** *archaic* **:** THENCEFORTH **3 :** from that fact **:** THEREFROM

thence·forth \-,fōrth\ *adv* **:** from that time forward **:** THEREAFTER

thence·for·ward \thens-'fōr-wərd\ *also* **thence·for·wards** *adv* **:** onward from that place or time **:** THENCEFORTH

the·oc·ra·cy \thē-'äk-rə-sē\ *n* **1 :** government of a state by immediate divine guidance or by officials regarded as divinely inspired **2 :** a state governed by a theocracy — **the·o·crat·ic** \,thē-ə-'krat-ik\ *adj*

the·ol·o·gy \thē-'äl-ə-jē\ *n* **1 :** the study of religion and of religious ideas and beliefs; *esp* **:** a branch of theology treating of God and his relation to the world **2 :** a theory or system of theology — **the·o·lo·gian** \,thē-ə-'lō-jən\ *n* — **the·o·log·i·cal** \-'läj-i-kəl\ *adj*

the·o·rem \'thē-ə-rəm, 'thir-əm\ *n* **1 :** a statement in mathematics that has been or is to be proved **2 :** an idea accepted or proposed as a demonstrable truth **:** PROPOSITION

the·o·ret·i·cal \,thē-ə-'ret-i-kəl\ *adj* **1 :** relating to or having the character of theory **:** ABSTRACT, SPECULATIVE **2 :** existing only in theory **:** HYPOTHETICAL — **the·o·ret·i·cal·ly** *adv*

the·o·rize \'thē-ə-,rīz\ *vb* **:** to form a theory **:** SPECULATE — **the·o·rist** *n*

the·o·ry \'thē-ə-rē, 'thir-ē\ *n* **1 :** the general principles drawn from any body of facts (as in science); *also* **:** the principles governing practice (as in a profession or art) **2 :** a more or less plausible or scientifically acceptable general principle offered to explain observed facts **3 :** HYPOTHESIS, GUESS **4 :** abstract thought

the·os·o·phy \thē-'äs-ə-fē\ *n* **:** belief about God and the world held to be based on mystical insight — **the·o·soph·i·cal** \,thē-ə-'säf-i-kəl\ *adj* — **the·os·o·phist** \thē-'äs-ə-fəst\ *n*

ther·a·peu·tic \,ther-ə-'pyüt-ik\ *adj* **:** of, relating to, or dealing with healing and esp. with remedies for diseases **:** MEDICINAL — **ther·a·peu·ti·cal·ly** *adv*

ther·a·peu·tics *n* **:** a branch of medical science dealing with the use of remedies

ther·a·py \'ther-ə-pē\ *n* **:** remedial treatment of bodily, mental, or social disorders or maladjustment — **ther·a·pist** \-pəst\ *n*

¹**there** \'theər\ *adv* **1 :** in or at that place — often used interjectionally **2 :** to or into that place **:** THITHER **3 :** in that matter or respect

²**there** \(,)tha(ə)r, ther\ *pron* — used as an anticipatory subject before copulas, auxiliaries, and certain other verbs ⟨∼'s a man here⟩ ⟨∼'s trouble brewing⟩ ⟨∼ comes a time⟩ ⟨∼'s no use⟩

³**there** \'theər\ *n* **:** that place ⟨get away from ∼⟩

there·abouts *or* **there·about** \,thar-ə-'baut(s)\ *adv* **1 :** near that place or time **2 :** near that number, degree, or quantity

there·af·ter \thar-'af-tər\ *adv* **:** after that **:** AFTERWARD

there·at \-'at\ *adv* **1 :** at that place **2 :** at that occurrence **:** on that account

there·by \tha(ə)r-'bī\ *adv* **1 :** by that **:** by that means **2 :** connected with or with reference to that

there·for \-'fōr\ *adv* **:** for or in return for that

there·fore \'theər-,fōr\ *adv* **:** for that reason **:** CONSEQUENTLY

there·from \tha(ə)r-'from, -'främ\ *adv* **:** from that or it

there·in \thar-'in\ *adv* **1 :** in or into that place, time, or thing **2 :** in that respect

there·of \-'əv, -'äv\ *adv* **1 :** of that or it **2 :** from that **:** THEREFROM

there·on \-'ón, -'än\ *adv* **1 :** on that **2** *archaic* **:** THEREUPON 3

there·to \tha(ə)r-'tü\ *adv* **:** to that

there·un·to \thar-'ən-tü\ *adv, archaic* **:** THERETO

there·upon \'thar-ə-,pón, -,pän\ *adv* **1 :** on that matter **:** THEREON **2 :** THEREFORE **3 :** immediately after that **:** at once

there·with \tha(ə)r-'with, -'with\ *adv* **1 :** with that **2** *archaic* **:** THEREUPON, FORTHWITH there·with·al \ˌtha(ə)r-wə-ˌthȯl, ˌthȯl\ adv 1 archaic : BESIDES 2 : THEREWITH

ther·mal \ˈthər-məl\ adj : of, relating to, or caused by heat : WARM, HOT

ther·mo·dy·nam·ics \ˌthər-mō-dī-ˈnam-iks\ n : physics that deals with the mechanical action or relations of heat — ther·mo·dy·nam·ic adj — ther·mo·dy·nam·i·cal·ly adv

ther·mom·e·ter \thə(r)-ˈmäm-ət-ər\ n : an instrument for measuring temperature commonly by means of the expansion or contraction of mercury or alcohol as indicated by its rise or fall in a thin glass tube — ther·mo·met·ric \ˌthər-mə-ˈmet-rik\ adj

ther·mo·nu·cle·ar \ˌthər-mō-ˈn(y)ü-klē-ər\ adj 1 : of or relating to changes in the nucleus of atoms of low atomic weight (as hydrogen) that require a very high temperature (as in the hydrogen bomb) 2 : utilizing or relating to a thermonuclear bomb (~ war)

ther·mo·plas·tic \ˌthər-mə-ˈplas-tik\ adj : having the property of softening when heated and of hardening when cooled (~ resins) — thermoplastic n

ther·mo·set·ting \ˈthər-mō-ˌset-iŋ\ adj : having the property of becoming permanently rigid when heated (~ resins)

ther·mo·stat \ˈthər-mə-ˌstat\ n : a device that automatically controls temperature (as by regulating a flow of oil or electricity) — ther·mo·stat·ic \ˌthər-mə-ˈstat-ik\ adj — ther·mo·stat·i·cal·ly adv

the·sau·rus \thi-ˈsȯr-əs\ n, pl -sau·ri \-ˈsȯr-ˌī\ or -sau·rus·es : a book of words; esp : a dictionary of synonyms

these pl of THIS

the·sis \ˈthē-səs\ n, pl the·ses \-ˌsēz\ 1 : a proposition that a person advances and offers to maintain by argument 2 : an essay embodying results of original research; esp : one written by a candidate for an academic degree

thes·pi·an \ˈthes-pē-ən\ adj, often cap [fr. Thespis, 6th cent. B.C. Greek poet and reputed originator of tragedy] : relating to the drama : DRAMATIC

²thespian n : ACTOR

thew \ˈth(y)ü\ n : MUSCLE, SINEW — usu. used in pl.

they \(ˈ)thā\ pron 1 : those individuals under discussion : the ones previously mentioned or referred to 2 : unspecified persons : PEOPLE

thi·a·mine \ˈthī-ə-ˌmēn\ n : a vitamin essential to normal metabolism and nerve function

¹thick \ˈthik\ adj 1 : having relatively great depth or extent from one surface to its opposite (a ~ plank); also : heavily built : THICKSET 2 : densely massed : CROWDED; also : FREQUENT, NUMEROUS 3 : dense or viscous in consistency (~ syrup) 4 : marked by haze, fog, or mist (~ weather) 5 : measuring in thickness (12 inches ~) 6 : imperfectly articulated : INDISTINCT (~ speech) 7 : STUPID, OBTUSE 8 : associated on close terms : INTIMATE 9 : EXCESSIVE syn stocky, compact, close, confidential — thick·ly adv — thick·ness n

²thick n 1 : the most crowded or active part 2 : the part of greatest thickness

thick·en \ˈthik-ən\ vb : to make or become thick — thick·en·er \-(ə-)nər\ n

thick·et \ˈthik-ət\ n : a dense local growth of bushes or small trees

thick·set \ˈthik-ˈset\ adj 1 : closely placed or planted 2 : of short stout build : STOCKY

thick-skinned \-ˈskind\ adj 1 : having a thick skin 2 : INSENSITIVE, CALLOUS

thief \ˈthēf\ n, pl thieves \ˈthēvz\ : one that steals esp. secretly

thieve \ˈthēv\ vb : STEAL, ROB syn plunder, rifle, loot, burglarize

thiev·ery \ˈthēv-(ə-)rē\ n : the act of stealing : THEFT

thigh \ˈthī\ n : the part of the vertebrate hind limb between the knee and the hip

thim·ble \ˈthim-bəl\ n : a cap or guard used in sewing to protect the finger when pushing the needle — thim·ble·ful n

¹thin \ˈthin\ adj 1 : having little extent from one surface through to its opposite : not thick : SLENDER 2 : not closely set or placed : SPARSE (~ hair) 3 : not dense or not dense enough : more fluid or rarefied than normal (~ air) (~ syrup) 4 : lacking substance, fullness, or strength (~ broth) 5 : FLIMSY syn slim, slight, tenuous — thin·ly adv — thin·ness n

²thin vb thinned; thin·ning : to make or become thin

thine \(ˈ)thīn\ pron, archaic : one or the ones belonging to thee

thing \ˈthiŋ\ n 1 : a matter of concern : AFFAIR (~s to do) 2 pl : state of affairs (~s are improving) 3 : EVENT, CIRCUMSTANCE (the crime was a terrible ~) 4 : DEED, ACT (expected great ~s of him) 5 : a distinct entity : OBJECT 6 : an inanimate object distinguished from a living being 7 pl : POSSESSIONS, EFFECTS (packed his ~s) 8 : an article of clothing 9 : DETAIL, POINT 10 : IDEA, NOTION

think \ˈthiŋk\ vb thought \ˈthȯt\ think·ing 1 : to form or have in the mind 2 : to have as an opinion : BELIEVE 3 : to reflect on : PONDER 4 : to call to mind : REMEMBER 5 : to devise by thinking 6 : to form a mental picture of : IMAGINE 7 : REASON syn conceive, fancy, realize, cogitate, reflect, speculate, deliberate — think·er n

thin·ner \ˈthin-ər\ n : a volatile liquid (as turpentine) used to thin paint

thin-skinned \ˈthin-ˈskind\ adj 1 : having a thin skin 2 : sensitive esp. to criticism

¹third \ˈthərd\ adj 1 : being number three in a countable series 2 : next after the second — third or third·ly adv

²third n 1 : one that is third 2 : one of three equal parts of something : the 3rd forward gear in an automotive vehicle

third degree n : the subjection of a prisoner to mental or physical torture to force a confession

¹thirst \ˈthərst\ n 1 : a feeling of dryness in the mouth and throat associated with a wish to drink; also : a bodily condition producing this 2 : an ardent desire : CRAVING (a ~ for knowledge) — thirsty adj

²thirst vb 1 : to need drink : suffer thirst 2 : to have a strong desire : CRAVE

thir·teen \ˈthər-ˈtēn\ n : one more than

12 — thirteen *adj or pron* — thirteenth *adj or n*

thir·ty \'thərt-ē\ *n* : three times 10 — thir·ti·eth *adj or n* — thirty *adj or pron*

¹this \(')this\ *pron, pl* these \(')thēz\ 1 : the one close or closest in time or space ⟨~ is your book⟩ 2 : what is in the present or under immediate observation or discussion ⟨~ is a mess⟩; *also* : what is happening or being done now ⟨after ~ we'll leave⟩

²this *adj, pl* these 1 : being the one near, present, just mentioned, or more immediately under observation ⟨~ book⟩ ⟨~ morning⟩ 2 : constituting the immediate past or future ⟨friends all *these* years⟩

³this \'this\ *adv* : to such an extent or degree ⟨we need a book about ~ big⟩

this·tle \'this-əl\ *n* : any of several tall prickly herbs

this·tle·down \-,daůn\ *n* : the down from the ripe flower head of a thistle

¹thith·er \'thith-ər\ *adv* : to that place : THERE

²thither *adj* : being on the farther side : more remote

thith·er·ward *adv* : toward that place : THITHER

thole \'thōl\ *n* : a pin set in the gunwale of a boat against which an oar pivots in rowing

thong \'thỏŋ\ *n* : a strip of leather used esp. to fasten something

tho·rax \'thōr,aks\ *n, pl* tho·rax·es *or* tho·ra·ces \'thōr-ə-,sēz, 'thōr-ə-\ 1 : the part of the body of a mammal between the neck and the abdomen; *also* : its cavity 2 : the middle of the three divisions of the body of an insect — tho·rac·ic \thə-'ras-ik\ *adj*

tho·ri·um \'thōr-ē-əm\ *n* : a radioactive metallic chemical element

thorn \'thỏrn\ *n* 1 : a woody plant bearing sharp processes 2 : a sharp rigid plant process that is usu. a modified leafless branch 3 : something that causes irritation or distress — thorny *adj*

thor·ough \'thər-ō\ *adj* 1 : COMPLETE, EXHAUSTIVE ⟨a ~ search⟩ 2 : very careful : PAINSTAKING ⟨a ~ scholar⟩ 3 : having full mastery ⟨a ~ musician⟩ — thor·ough·ly *adv* — thor·ough·ness *n*

¹thor·ough·bred \'thər-ə-,bred\ *adj* 1 : bred from the best blood through a long line 2 *cap* : of or relating to the Thoroughbred breed of horses 3 : marked by high-spirited grace

²thoroughbred *n* 1 *cap* : any of an English breed of light speedy horses kept chiefly for racing 2 : one ⟨as a pedigreed animal⟩ of excellent quality

thor·ough·fare \-,faər\ *n* : a public road or street

thor·ough·go·ing \,thər-ə-'gō-iŋ\ *adj* : marked by thoroughness or zeal

thorp \'thỏrp\ *n, archaic* : VILLAGE, HAMLET

those *pl of* THAT

thou \(')thaů\ *pron, archaic* : the person addressed

¹though \'thō\ *adv* : HOWEVER, NEVERTHELESS ⟨failed to convince him, ~⟩

²though \(,)thō\ *conj* 1 : despite the fact that ⟨~ the odds are hopeless, they fight on⟩ 2 : granting that ⟨~ it may look bad, still, all is not lost⟩

¹thought \'thỏt\ *past of* THINK

²thought *n* 1 : the process of thinking 2 : serious consideration : REGARD

3 : reasoning power 4 : the power to imagine : CONCEPTION 5 : IDEA, NOTION 6 : OPINION, BELIEF 7 : a slight amount : BIT

thought·ful *adj* 1 : absorbed in thought 2 : marked by careful thinking ⟨a ~ essay⟩ 3 : considerate of others ⟨a ~ host⟩ — thought·ful·ly *adv* — thought·ful·ness *n*

thought·less *adj* 1 : insufficiently alert : CARELESS ⟨a ~ worker⟩ 2 : RECKLESS ⟨a ~ act⟩ 3 : lacking concern for others : INCONSIDERATE ⟨~ remarks⟩ — thought·less·ly *adv* — thought·less·ness *n*

thou·sand \'thaůz-ᵊnd\ *n, pl* thousands *or* thousand : 10 times 100 — thousand *adj* — thou·sandth *adj or n*

thrall \'thrỏl\ *n* 1 : SLAVE, BONDMAN 2 : THRALLDOM

thrall·dom *or* thral·dom *n* : the condition of a thrall : SLAVERY, BONDAGE

thrash \'thrash\ *vb* 1 : THRESH 1 2 : BEAT, WHIP; *also* : DEFEAT 3 : to move about violently : toss about 4 : to go over again and again ⟨~ over the matter⟩; *also* : to hammer out ⟨~ out a plan⟩

thrash·er *n* 1 : THRESHER 2 : a long-tailed bird resembling a thrush

thread \'thred\ *n* 1 : a thin fine cord formed by spinning and twisting short textile fibers into a continuous strand 2 : something felt to resemble a textile thread 3 : a train of thought 4 : a continuing element 5 : the ridge or groove that winds around a screw

thread·bare \-,baər\ *adj* 1 : worn so that the thread shows : SHABBY 2 : TRITE, HACKNEYED

thready *adj* 1 : consisting of or bearing fibers or filaments ⟨a ~ bark⟩ 2 : lacking in fullness, body, or vigor : THIN

threat \'thret\ *n* 1 : an expression of intention to do harm 2 : something that threatens

threat·en \-ᵊn\ *vb* 1 : to utter threats against 2 : to give signs or warning of : PORTEND 3 : to hang over as a threat : MENACE — threat·en·ing·ly \-(ᵊ-)niŋ-lē\ *adv*

three \'thrē\ *n* 1 : one more than two 2 : the 3d in a set or series 3 : something having three units — three *adj or pron*

3–D \'thrē-'dē\ *n* : three-dimensional form

three-di·men·sion·al *adj* 1 : relating to or having three dimensions 2 : giving the illusion of varying distances ⟨a ~ picture⟩

three·fold \'thrē-'fōld\ *adj* 1 : having three parts : TRIPLE 2 : being three times as great or as many — threefold *adv*

three·pence \'thrip-əns, 'thrəp-\ *n* 1 : the sum of three usu. British pennies 2 : a coin worth three pennies

three-score \'thrē-'skōr\ *adj* : being three times twenty : SIXTY

thren·o·dy \'thren-əd-ē\ *n* : a song of lamentation : ELEGY

thresh \'thrash, 'thresh\ *vb* 1 : to separate ⟨as grain from straw⟩ by beating 2 : THRASH — thresh·er *n*

thresh·old \'thresh-,ōld\ *n* 1 : the sill of a door 2 : a point or place of beginning or entering : OUTSET, ENTRANCE

threw *past of* THROW

thrice \'thrīs\ *adv* 1 : three times 2 : in a threefold manner or degree

thrift \'thrift\ *n* : careful management

esp. of money : FRUGALITY — **thrift·i·ly** *adv* — **thrift·less** *adj* — **thrifty** *adj*

thrill \'thril\ *vb* **1** : to have or cause to have a sudden sharp feeling of excitement; *also* : TINGLE, SHIVER **2** : TREMBLE, VIBRATE — **thrill** *n* — **thrill·er** *n*

thrive \'thrīv\ *vb* **throve** \'thrōv\ *or* **thrived**; **thriv·en** \'thriv-ən\ *also* **thrived**; **thriv·ing** \'thrī-viŋ\ **1** : to grow luxuriantly : FLOURISH **2** : to gain in wealth or possessions : PROSPER

throat \'thrōt\ *n* **1** : the part of the neck in front of the spinal column; *also* : the passage through it to the stomach and lungs — **throat·ed** *adj*

throaty *adj* **1** : uttered or produced from low in the throat (a ~ voice) **2** : heavy, thick, or deep as if from the throat (~ notes of a horn) — **throat·i·ly** *adv* — **throat·i·ness** *n*

1throb \'thräb\ *vb* **throbbed**; **throb·bing** : to pulsate or pound esp. with abnormal force or rapidity : BEAT, VIBRATE

2throb *n* : BEAT, PULSE

throe \'thrō\ *n* **1** : PANG, SPASM **2** *pl* : a hard or painful struggle

throm·bo·sis \thräm-'bō-səs\ *n* : the formation or presence of a clot in a blood vessel during life — **throm·bot·ic** \-'bät-ik\ *adj*

throne \'thrōn\ *n* **1** : the chair of state esp. of a king or bishop **2** : royal power : SOVEREIGNTY

1throng \'thröŋ\ *n* **1** : a crowding together of many persons **2** : MULTITUDE

2throng *vb* : CROWD

1throt·tle \'thrät-ᵊl\ *vb* **1** : CHOKE, STRANGLE **2** : SUPPRESS **3** : to obstruct the flow of (fuel) to an engine; *also* : to reduce the speed of (an engine) by such means

2throttle *n* **1** : THROAT, TRACHEA **2** : a valve regulating the volume of steam or fuel charge delivered to the cylinders of an engine; *also* : the lever controlling this valve

1through \(')thrü\ *prep* **1** : into at one side and out at the other side of (go ~ the door) **2** : by way of (entered ~ a skylight) **3** : AMONG (a path ~ the trees) **4** : by means of (succeeded ~ hard work) **5** : over the whole of (rumors swept ~ the office) **6** : during the whole of (~ the night)

2through \'thrü\ *adv* **1** : from one end or side to the other **2** : from beginning to end : to completion (see it ~) **3** : to the core : THOROUGHLY **4** : into the open : OUT (break ~)

3through \'thrü\ *adj* **1** : permitting free or continuous passage : DIRECT (a ~ road) **2** : going from point of origin to destination without change or reshipment (~ train) **3** : FINISHED (~ with the job)

through·out \thrü-'aüt\ *adv* **1** : EVERYWHERE **2** : from beginning to end

throughout *prep* **1** : in or to every part of **2** : during the whole period of

through·way \'thrü-,wā\ *n* : EXPRESSWAY

throve *past of* THRIVE

1throw \'thrō\ *vb* **threw** \'thrü\ **thrown** \'thrōn\ **throw·ing** **1** : to propel through the air with a forward motion of the hand and arm (~ a ball)

2 : HURL, CAST **3** : to cause to fall or fall off **4** : to fling precipitately or violently : DASH **5** : to put in some position or condition (~ into panic) **6** : to give up : ABANDON; *also* : to lose intentionally **7** : to move (a lever) so as to connect or disconnect parts of something (as a clutch or switch) **syn** toss, fling, pitch, sling

2throw *n* **1** : an act of throwing, hurling, or flinging; *also* : CAST **2** : the distance a missile may be thrown **3** : a light coverlet **4** : a woman's scarf or light wrap

thrum \'thrəm\ *vb* **thrummed**; **thrumming** : to play or pluck a stringed instrument idly : STRUM

thrush \'thrəsh\ *n* : any of numerous songbirds usu. of a plain color but sometimes with spotted underparts

1thrust \'thrəst\ *vb* **thrust**; **thrust·ing** **1** : to push or drive with force : SHOVE **2** : STAB, PIERCE **3** : INTERJECT **4** : to press the acceptance of upon someone

2thrust *n* **1** : a lunge with a pointed weapon **2** : a violent push : SHOVE **3** : ATTACK **4** : force exerted endwise through a propeller shaft (as of a ship or airplane); *also* : forward force produced (as in a rocket) by a high-speed jet of fluid discharged rearward **5** : the pressure of one part of a construction against another (as of an arch against an abutment)

1thud \'thəd\ *vb* **thud·ded**; **thud·ding** : to move or strike so as to make a thud

2thud *n* **1** : BLOW **2** : a dull sound : THUMP

thug \'thəg\ *n* : a brutal ruffian; *also* : ASSASSIN

thu·li·um \'th(y)ü-lē-əm\ *n* : a rare metallic chemical element

1thumb \'thəm\ *n* **1** : the short thick first digit of the human hand or a corresponding digit of a lower animal **2** : the part of a glove that covers the thumb

2thumb *vb* **1** : to leaf through (pages) with the thumb **2** : to wear or soil with the thumb by frequent handling **3** : to request or obtain (a ride) in a passing automobile by signaling with the thumb

thumb·screw \-,skrü\ *n* **1** : a screw with a head that may be turned by the thumb and forefinger **2** : an old instrument of torture for squeezing the thumb

thumb·tack \-,tak\ *n* : a tack with a broad flat head for pressing with one's thumb into a board or wall

1thump \'thəmp\ *vb* **1** : to strike with or as if with something thick or heavy so as to cause a dull heavy sound **2** : POUND

2thump *n* : a blow with or as if with something blunt or heavy; *also* : the sound made by such a blow

1thun·der \'thən-dər\ *n* **1** : the sound following a flash of lightning; *also* : a noise like such a sound **2** : a loud utterance or threat

2thunder *vb* **1** : to produce thunder **2** : ROAR, SHOUT

thun·der·bolt \-,bōlt\ *n* : a single discharge of lightning with its accompanying thunder

thun·der·clap \-ˌklap\ n : a crash of thunder

thun·der·cloud \-ˌklau̇d\ n : a cloud producing lightning and thunder

thun·der·head \-ˌhed\ n : a rounded mass of clouds often appearing before a thunderstorm

thun·der·ous \'thən-d(ə-)rəs\ adj : producing thunder; also : making a noise like thunder — **thun·der·ous·ly** adv

thun·der·show·er \'thən-dər-ˌshau̇(-ə)r\ n : a shower accompanied by thunder and lightning

thun·der·storm \-ˌstȯrm\ n : a storm accompanied by thunder and lightning

thun·der·struck \-ˌstrək\ adj : struck dumb : ASTONISHED

Thurs·day \'thərz-dē\ n : the 5th day of the week

thus \'thəs\ adv 1 : in this or that manner 2 : to this degree or extent : SO 3 : because of this or that : HENCE

¹thwack \'thwak\ vb : to strike with something flat or heavy

²thwack n : a heavy blow : WHACK

¹thwart \'thwȯrt\ adv : ATHWART

²thwart adj : situated or placed across something else

³thwart vb 1 : BAFFLE 2 : BLOCK, DEFEAT syn foil, outwit, frustrate

⁴thwart \'th(w)ȯrt\ n : a rower's seat extending across a boat

thy \(ˌ)thī\ adj, archaic : of, relating to, or done by or to thee or thyself

thyme \'tīm, 'thīm\ n : any of several mints with aromatic leaves used esp. in seasoning

thy·mus \'thī-məs\ n : a glandular organ of the neck that in lambs and calves is a sweetbread

thy·roid \'thī-ˌrȯid\ adj : of, relating to, or being a large endocrine gland that lies at the base of the neck and produces a hormone with a profound influence on growth and metabolism — **thyroid** n

thy·self \thī-'self\ pron, archaic : YOURSELF

ti·ara \tē-'ar-ə, -'är-\ n 1 : the pope's triple crown 2 : a decorative headband or semicircle for formal wear by women

Ti·bet·an \tə-'bet-²n\ n : a native or inhabitant of Tibet — **Tibetan** adj

tib·ia \'tib-ē-ə\ n, pl **tib·i·ae** \-ē-ˌē\ also **tib·i·as** : the inner of the two bones of the vertebrate hind limb between the knee and the ankle

tic \'tik\ n : a local and habitual twitching of muscles esp. of the face

¹tick \'tik\ n : any of numerous small 8-legged blood-sucking animals

²tick n 1 : a light rhythmic audible tap or beat 2 : a small mark used to draw attention to or check something

³tick vb 1 : to make a tick or series of ticks (loud ∼ing of a clock) 2 : to mark or check with a tick 3 : to mark, count, or announce by or as if by the ticks of a clock or of a telegraph instrument 4 : to function as an operating mechanism : RUN

⁴tick n : the fabric case of a mattress or pillow; also : a mattress consisting of a tick and its filling

⁵tick n : CREDIT; also : a credit account

tick·er \'tik-ər\ n 1 : something (as a watch) that ticks 2 : a telegraph instrument that prints off news (as stock quotations) on paper tape

¹tick·et \'tik-ət\ n 1 : CERTIFICATE, LICENSE, PERMIT; esp : a certificate or token showing that a fare or admission fee has been paid 2 : TAG, LABEL

3 : a summons issued to a traffic offender 4 : SLATE 3

²ticket vb 1 : to attach a ticket to : LABEL 2 : to furnish with a ticket : BOOK

tick·ing \'tik-iŋ\ n : a strong fabric used in upholstering and as a mattress covering

tick·le \'tik-əl\ vb 1 : to have a tingling sensation 2 : to excite or stir up agreeably : PLEASE, AMUSE 3 : to touch (as a body part) lightly so as to cause uneasiness, laughter, or spasmodic movements syn gratify, delight, regale — **tickle** n

tick·lish \-(ə-)lish\ adj 1 : sensitive to tickling 2 : OVERSENSITIVE, TOUCHY 3 : UNSTABLE ⟨a ∼ foothold⟩ 4 : requiring delicate handling ⟨∼ subject⟩

tid·al wave \ˌtīd-²l-\ n 1 : a high sea wave that sometimes follows an earthquake 2 : the great rise of water alongshore due to exceptionally strong winds

tid·bit \'tid-ˌbit\ n : a choice morsel

¹tide \'tīd\ n [OE tīd time] 1 : the alternate rising and falling of the surface of the ocean 2 : something that fluctuates like the tides of the sea — **tid·al** \'tīd-²l\ adj

²tide vb : to carry through or help along as if by the tide ⟨a loan to ∼ him over⟩

tide·land \-ˌland\ n 1 : land overflowed during flood tide 2 : land under the ocean within a nation's territorial waters — often used in pl.

tide·wa·ter \-ˌwȯt-ər, -ˌwät-\ n 1 : water overflowing land at flood tide 2 : low-lying coastal land

tid·ings \'tīd-iŋz\ n pl : NEWS, MESSAGE

¹ti·dy \'tīd-ē\ adj 1 : well ordered and cared for : NEAT 2 : LARGE, SUBSTANTIAL ⟨a ∼ sum⟩ — **ti·di·ness** n

tidy vb 1 : to put in order ⟨∼ up a room⟩ 2 : to make things tidy

³tidy n : a piece of decorated cloth or needlework used to protect the back or arms of a chair from wear or soil

¹tie \'tī\ n 1 : a line, ribbon, or cord used for fastening, uniting, or closing 2 : a structural element (as a beam or rod) holding two pieces together 3 : one of the cross supports to which railroad rails are fastened 4 : a connecting link : BOND ⟨family ∼s⟩ 5 : an equality in number (as of votes or scores); also : an undecided or deadlocked contest 6 : NECKTIE

²tie vb **tied**; **ty·ing** or **tie·ing** 1 : to fasten, attach, or close by means of a tie 2 : to bring together firmly : UNITE 3 : to form a knot or bow in ⟨∼ a scarf⟩ 4 : to restrain from freedom of action : CONSTRAIN 5 : to make or have an equal score with

tier \'tiər\ n : ROW, LAYER; esp : one of two or more rows arranged one above another

tie-up \'tī-ˌəp\ n 1 : a suspension of traffic or business 2 : CONNECTION, ASSOCIATION

tiff \'tif\ n : a petty quarrel — **tiff** vb

tif·fin \'tif-ən\ n : LUNCHEON

ti·ger \'tī-gər\ n : a large tawny black-striped Asiatic flesh-eating mammal related to the cat — **ti·ger·ish** \'tī-g(ə-)rish\ adj — **ti·gress** \-grəs\ n

¹tight \'tīt\ adj 1 : so close in structure as not to permit passage of a liquid or gas 2 : fixed or held very firmly in place 3 : TAUT 4 : fitting usu. too closely ⟨∼ shoes⟩ 5 : set close together : COMPACT ⟨a ∼ formation⟩

6 : difficult to get out of ⟨get in a ~ spot⟩ **7 :** STINGY, MISERLY **8 :** evenly contested **:** CLOSE **9 :** INTOXICATED **10 :** low in supply **:** hard to get **:** SCARCE ⟨money is ~⟩ — **tight·ly** *adv* — **tight·ness** *n*

²tight *adv* **1 :** TIGHTLY, FIRMLY **2 :** SOUNDLY ⟨sleep ~⟩

tight·en \'tīt-°n\ *vb* **:** to make or become tight

tight·fist·ed \'tīt-'fis-təd\ *adj* **:** STINGY

tight·rope \-,rōp\ *n* **:** a taut rope or wire for acrobats to perform on

tights \'tīts\ *n pl* **:** skintight garments covering the body esp. from the waist down

tight·wad \'tīt-,wäd\ *n* **:** a stingy person

¹tile \'tīl\ *n* **1 :** a thin piece of fired clay, stone, or concrete used for roofs, floors, or walls; *also* **:** a hollow or concave earthenware or concrete piece used for a drain **2 :** a thin piece (as of a rubber composition) used for covering walls or floors — **til·ing** *n*

²tile *vb* **1 :** to cover with tiles **2 :** to install drainage tile in

¹till \(,)til\ *prep or conj* **:** UNTIL

²till \'til\ *vb* **:** to work by plowing, sowing, and raising crops from **:** CULTIVATE — **till·able** *adj*

³till \'til\ *n* **:** DRAWER; *esp* **:** a money drawer in a store or bank

till·age \'til-ij\ *n* **1 :** the work of tilling land **2 :** cultivated land

til·ler \'til-ər\ *n* **:** a lever used for turning a boat's rudder from side to side

¹tilt \'tilt\ *vb* **1 :** to move or shift so as to incline **:** TIP **2 :** to engage in or as if in a combat with lances **:** JOUST

²tilt *n* **1 :** a military exercise in which two combatants charging usu. with lances try to unhorse each other **:** JOUST; *also* **:** a tournament of tilts **2 :** a verbal contest **:** CONTENTION **3 :** SLANT, TIP

tilth \'tilth\ *n* **1 :** TILLAGE **2 :** the state or degree of being tilled ⟨land in good ~⟩

¹tim·ber \'tim-bər\ *n* **1 :** wood for use in making something **2 :** a usu. large squared or dressed piece of wood **3 :** wooded land or growing trees from which timber may be obtained — **tim·ber·ing** *n* — **tim·ber·land** \-bər-,land\ *n*

²timber *vb* **:** to cover, frame, or support with timbers — **tim·bered** *adj*

tim·ber·line \'tim-bər-,līn\ *n* **:** the upper limit of tree growth on mountains or in high latitudes

timber wolf *n* **:** a large usu. gray No. American wolf

tim·bre \'tam-bər, 'tim-\ *n* **:** the distinctive quality given to a sound by its overtones

tim·brel \'tim-brəl\ *n* **:** a small hand drum or tambourine

¹time \'tīm\ *n* **1 :** a period during which an action, process, or condition exists or continues ⟨gone a long ~⟩ **2 :** LEISURE ⟨found ~ to read⟩ **3 :** a point or period when something occurs **:** OCCASION ⟨the last ~ we met⟩ **4 :** a set or customary moment or hour for something to occur ⟨arrived on ~⟩ **5 :** AGE, ERA **6** *pl* **:** state of affairs **:** CONDITIONS ⟨hard ~s⟩ **7 :** rate of

speed **:** TEMPO **8 :** a moment, hour, day, or year as indicated by a clock or calendar ⟨what ~ is it⟩ **9 :** a system of reckoning time ⟨solar ~⟩ **10 :** one of a series of recurring instances; *also*, *pl* **:** multiplied instances ⟨five ~s greater⟩ **11 :** a person's experience during a particular period ⟨had a good ~ at the beach⟩

²time *vb* **1 :** to arrange or set the time of **:** SCHEDULE ⟨~s his calls conveniently⟩ **2 :** to set the tempo or duration of ⟨~ a performance⟩ **3 :** to cause to keep time with ⟨~s her steps to the music⟩ **4 :** to determine or record the time, duration, or rate of ⟨~ a sprinter⟩ — **tim·er** *n*

time clock *n* **:** a clock that records the times of arrival and departure of workers

time-hon·ored \'tīm-,än-ərd\ *adj* **:** honored because of age or long usage

time-keep·er \-,kē-pər\ *n* **1 :** a clerk who keeps records of the time worked by employees **2 :** one appointed to mark and announce the time in an athletic game or contest

time·less *adj* **1 :** UNENDING **2 :** not limited or affected by time ⟨~ works of art⟩ — **time·less·ly** *adv*

time·ly *adj* **1 :** coming early or at the right time **:** OPPORTUNE ⟨~ arrival⟩ **2 :** appropriate to the time ⟨a ~ book⟩ — **time·li·ness** *n*

time·piece \'tīm-,pēs\ *n* **:** a device (as a clock or watch) to show the passage of time

times \,tīmz\ *prep* **:** multiplied by ⟨2 ~ 2 is 4⟩

time·ta·ble \'tīm-,tā-bəl\ *n* **1 :** a table of the departure and arrival times of scheduled conveyances **2 :** a schedule showing a planned order or sequence

time·worn \-,wōrn\ *adj* **1 :** worn by time **2 :** HACKNEYED, STALE

tim·id \'tim-əd\ *adj* **:** lacking in courage or self-confidence **:** FEARFUL — **ti·mid·i·ty** \tə-'mid-ət-ē\ *n* — **tim·id·ly** \'tim-əd-lē\ *adv*

tim·o·rous \'tim-(ə-)rəs\ *adj* **:** of a timid disposition **:** AFRAID — **tim·o·rous·ly** *adv* — **tim·o·rous·ness** *n*

tim·o·thy \'tim-ə-thē\ *n* **:** a grass with long cylindrical spikes widely grown for hay

tim·pa·ni \'tim-pə-nē\ *n pl* **:** a set of kettledrums played by one performer in an orchestra — **tim·pa·nist** \-nəst\ *n*

¹tin \'tin\ *n* **1 :** a soft white crystalline metallic chemical element malleable at ordinary temperatures but brittle when heated that is used in solders and alloys **2 :** a container (as a can) made of tinplate

²tin *vb* **tinned; tin·ning 1 :** to cover or plate with tin **2** *chiefly Brit* **:** to pack in tins **:** CAN

tinct \'tiŋkt\ *n* **:** TINCTURE, TINGE

¹tinc·ture \'tiŋk-chər\ *n* **1 :** a substance that colors or dyes **2 :** a slight admixture **:** TRACE **3 :** an alcoholic solution of a medicinal substance **syn** touch, suggestion, suspicion

²tincture *vb* **:** COLOR, TINGE

tin·der \'tin-dər\ *n* **:** something that catches fire easily; *esp* **:** a substance used to kindle a fire from a slight spark

---

ə abut; ° kitten; ər further; a back; ā bake; ä cot, cart; aú out; ch chin; e less; ē easy; g gift; i trip; ī life; j joke; ŋ sing; ō flow; ó flaw; ói coin; th thin; <u>th</u> this; ü loot; ú foot; y yet; yü few; yú furious; zh vision

tin·der·box \-ˌbäks\ *n* : a metal box for holding tinder and usu. flint and steel for striking a spark

tine \'tīn\ *n* : a slender pointed part (as of a fork or an antler) : PRONG

tin·foil \'tin-ˌfȯil\ *n* : a thin metal sheeting usu. of aluminum or tin-lead alloy

¹tinge \'tinj\ *vb* tinged; tinge·ing or ting·ing **1** : to color slightly : TINT **2** : to affect or modify esp. with a slight odor or taste

²tinge *n* : a slight coloring, flavor, or quality : TRACE **syn** touch, suggestion

tin·gle \'tin-gəl\ *vb* **1** : to feel a pricking or thrilling sensation **2** : TINKLE — tingle *n*

¹tin·ker \'tin-kər\ *n* **1** : a usu. itinerant mender of household utensils **2** : an unskillful mender : BUNGLER

²tinker *vb* : to repair or adjust something in an unskillful or experimental manner

¹tin·kle \'tin-kəl\ *vb* : to make or cause to make a tinkle

²tinkle *n* : a series of short high ringing or clinking sounds

tin·ny \'tin-ē\ *adj* **1** : of or yielding tin **2** : resembling tin (as in being thin, hard, and brittle or as in sounding metallic) **3** : tasting of tin (~ canned food)

tin·plate \'tin-ˌplāt\ *n* : thin sheet iron or steel coated with tin

tin·sel \'tin-səl\ *n* **1** : a thread, strip, or sheet of metal, paper, or plastic used to produce a glittering appearance (as in fabrics or decorations) **2** : something superficially attractive but of little worth

tin·smith \'tin-ˌsmith\ *n* : one that works with tin or other metal

¹tint \'tint\ *n* **1** : a slight or pale coloration : HUE **2** : any of various shades of a color

²tint *vb* : to impart a tint to : COLOR

tin·tin·nab·u·la·tion \ˌtin-tə-ˌnab-yə-ˈlā-shən\ *n* **1** : the ringing of bells **2** : a jingling sound as if of bells

tin·type \'tin-ˌtīp\ *n* : a photograph made on a thin darkened iron plate

tin·ware \-ˌwaər\ *n* : articles made of tinplate

ti·ny \'tī-nē\ *adj* : very small : MINUTE **syn** miniature, diminutive, wee, little

¹tip \'tip\ *n* **1** : the usu. pointed end of something **2** : a small piece or part serving as an end, cap, or point

²tip *vb* tipped; tip·ping **1** : to furnish with a tip **2** : to cover or adorn the tip of

³tip *vb* tipped; tip·ping **1** : OVERTURN, UPSET **2** : LEAN, SLANT; *also* : TILT

⁴tip *n* : the act or an instance of tipping : TILT

⁵tip *vb* tipped; tip·ping : to strike lightly : TAP

⁶tip *vb* tipped; tip·ping : to give a gratuity to

⁷tip *n* : a gift or small sum given for a service performed or anticipated : GRATUITY

⁸tip *n* : a piece of expert or confidential information : HINT

⁹tip *vb* tipped; tip·ping : to impart a piece of information about or to

tip·pet \'tip-ət\ *n* : a long scarf or shoulder cape

tip·ple \'tip-əl\ *vb* : to drink intoxicating liquor esp. habitually or excessively — tip·pler \-(ə-)lər\ *n*

tip·ster \'tip-stər\ *n* : one who gives or sells tips esp. for gambling

tip·sy \'tip-sē\ *adj* : unsteady or foolish from the effects of alcohol

¹tip·toe \'tip-ˌtō\ *n* : the end of the toes

²tiptoe *adv* (*or adj*) : on or as if on tiptoe

³tiptoe *vb* : to walk or proceed on or as if on tiptoe

¹tip·top \'tip-'täp\ *n* : the highest point : SUMMIT

²tip–top *adj* : EXCELLENT, FIRST-RATE

ti·rade \'tī-ˌrād\ *n* : a prolonged speech of abuse or condemnation

¹tire \'tī(ə)r\ *vb* **1** : to make or become weary : FATIGUE **2** : to wear out the patience of : BORE

²tire *n* **1** : a metal band that forms the tread of a wheel **2** : a rubber cushion usu. containing compressed air that encircles a wheel (as of an automobile)

tired \'tī(ə)rd\ *adj* **1** : WEARY, FATIGUED **2** : HACKNEYED

tire·less \'tī(ə)r-ləs\ *adj* : not tiring : UNTIRING, INDEFATIGABLE — tire·less·ly *adv* — tire·less·ness *n*

tire·some *adj* : tending to bore : WEARISOME, TEDIOUS — tire·some·ly *adv* — tire·some·ness *n*

tis·sue \'tish-ü\ *n* **1** : a fine lightweight often sheer fabric **2** : NETWORK, WEB **3** : a soft absorbent paper **4** : a mass or layer of cells forming a basic structural element of an animal or plant body

¹tit \'tit\ *n* : TEAT

²tit *n* : TITMOUSE

ti·tan \'tīt-ᵊn\ *n* : one gigantic in size or power

ti·tan·ic \tī-'tan-ik\ *adj* : enormous in size, force, or power **syn** immense, huge, vast, gigantic, giant, colossal, mammoth

ti·ta·ni·um \tī-'tā-nē-əm, tə-\ *n* : a gray light strong metallic chemical element used in alloys

tit·bit \'tit-ˌbit\ *var of* TIDBIT

tithe \'tīth\ *n* : a tenth part paid or given esp. for support of the church — tithe *vb* — tith·er *n*

tit·il·late \'tit-ᵊl-ˌāt\ *vb* **1** : TICKLE **2** : to excite pleasurably — tit·il·la·tion \ˌtit-ᵊl-'ā-shən\ *n*

tit·i·vate *or* tit·ti·vate \'tit-ə-ˌvāt\ *vb* : to dress up : spruce up

ti·tle \'tīt-ᵊl\ *n* **1** : CLAIM, RIGHT; *esp* : a legal right to the ownership of property **2** : the distinguishing name esp. of an artistic production (as a book) **3** : an appellation of honor, rank, or office **4** : CHAMPIONSHIP **syn** designation, denomination

ti·tled \'tīt-ᵊld\ *adj* : having a title esp. of nobility

title page *n* : a page of a book bearing the title and usu. the names of the author and publisher

tit·mouse \'tit-ˌmaús\ *n*, *pl* tit·mice \-ˌmīs\ : any of numerous small long-tailed songbirds

tit·ter \'tit-ər\ *vb* : to laugh in an affected or in a nervous or half-suppressed manner — titter *n*

tit·tle \'tit-ᵊl\ *n* : a tiny piece : PARTICLE, JOT

tit·tle-tat·tle \-ˌtat-ᵊl\ *n* : idle talk : GOSSIP

tit·u·lar \'tich-ə-lər\ *adj* **1** : existing in title only : NOMINAL (~ ruler) **2** : of, relating to, or bearing a title (~ role)

TNT \ˌtē-ˌen-'tē\ *n* : a high explosive used in artillery shells and bombs and in blasting

¹to \tə, (')tü\ *prep* **1** : in the direction of and reaching ⟨drove ~ town⟩ **2** : in the direction of : TOWARDS ⟨walking ~ school⟩ **3** : ON, AGAINST ⟨apply salve ~ a burn⟩ **4** : as far as ⟨can pay up ~

a dollar⟩ **5 :** and thus brought into the state of or changed into ⟨beaten ~ death⟩ ⟨broken ~ pieces⟩ **6 :** BEFORE ⟨it's five minutes ~ six⟩ **7 :** UNTIL ⟨from May ~ December⟩ **8 :** fitting or being a part of **:** FOR ⟨key ~ the lock⟩ **9 :** with the accompaniment of ⟨sing ~ the music⟩ **10 :** in relation or comparison with ⟨similar ~ that one⟩ ⟨won ten ~ six⟩ **11 :** in accordance with ⟨add salt ~ taste⟩ **12 :** within the range of ⟨~ my knowledge⟩ **13 :** contained, occurring, or included in ⟨two pints ~ a quart⟩ **14 :** as regards ⟨attitude ~ our friends⟩ **15 :** affecting as the receiver or beneficiary ⟨whispered ~ her⟩ ⟨gave it ~ me⟩ **16 :** for no one except ⟨a room ~ myself⟩ **17 :** into the action of ⟨we got ~ talking⟩ **18 :** used for marking the following verb as an infinitive ⟨wants ~ go⟩ ⟨easy ~ like⟩ ⟨the man ~ beat⟩ and often used by itself at the end of a clause in place of an infinitive suggested by the preceding context ⟨goes to town whenever he wants ~⟩ ⟨can leave if you'd like ~⟩ ⟨knows more than he seems ~⟩

²to \'tü\ *adv* **1 :** in a direction toward ⟨run ~ and fro⟩ ⟨wrong side ~⟩ **2 :** into contact esp. with the frame of a door ⟨the door snapped ~⟩ **3 :** to the matter in hand ⟨fell ~ and ate heartily⟩ **4 :** to a state of consciousness or awareness ⟨came ~ hours after the accident⟩

toad \'tōd\ *n* **:** a tailless leaping amphibian differing typically from the related frogs in shorter stockier build, rough dry warty skin, and less aquatic habits

toad·stool \-,stül\ *n* **:** MUSHROOM; *esp* **:** one that is poisonous or inedible

toady \'tōd-ē\ *n* **:** one who flatters in the hope of gaining favors **:** SYCOPHANT — **toady** *vb*

¹toast \'tōst\ *vb* **1 :** to make (as bread) crisp, hot, and brown by heat **2 :** to warm thoroughly

²toast *n* **1 :** sliced toasted bread **2 :** someone or something in whose honor persons drink **3 :** an act of drinking in honor of a toast

³toast *vb* **:** to propose or drink to as a toast

toast·er *n* **:** one that toasts; *esp* **:** an electrical appliance for toasting

toast·mas·ter \'tōst-,mas-tər\ *n* **:** one that presides at a banquet and introduces the after-dinner speakers

to·bac·co \tə-'bak-ō\ *n* **1 :** a tall broad-leaved herb related to the potato; *also* **:** its leaves prepared for smoking or chewing or as snuff **2 :** manufactured tobacco products (as cigars)

to·bac·co·nist \-'bak-ə-nəst\ *n* **:** a dealer in tobacco

¹to·bog·gan \tə-'bäg-ən\ *n* **:** a long flat-bottomed light sled made of thin boards curved up at one end

²toboggan *vb* **1 :** to coast on a toboggan **2 :** to decline suddenly (as in value)

toc·sin \'täk-sən\ *n* **1 :** an alarm bell **2 :** a warning signal

¹to·day \tə-'dā\ *adv* **1 :** on or for this day **2 :** at the present time

²today *n* **:** the present day, time, or age

tod·dle \'täd-ᵊl\ *vb* **:** to walk with short tottering steps in the manner of a young

child — **toddle** *n* — **tod·dler** \-(ᵊ)lər\ *n*

tod·dy \'täd-ē\ *n* **:** a drink made of liquor, sugar, spices, and hot water

to-do \tə-'dü\ *n* **:** BUSTLE, STIR

¹toe \'tō\ *n* **1 :** one of the terminal jointed members of the foot **2 :** the front part of a foot or hoof

²toe *vb* **toed; toe·ing :** to touch, reach, or drive with the toes

toe·nail \'tō-,nāl\ *n* **:** a nail of a toe

tof·fee *or* **tof·fy** \'tàf-ē\ *n* **:** TAFFY

tog \'täg\ *vb* **togged; tog·ging :** to put togs on **:** DRESS

to·ga \'tō-gə\ *n* **:** the loose outer garment worn in public by citizens of ancient Rome — **to·gaed** \-gād\ *adj*

to·geth·er \tə-'geth-ər\ *adv* **1 :** in or into one place or group **2 :** in or into contact or association ⟨mix ~⟩ **3 :** at one time **:** SIMULTANEOUSLY ⟨talk and work ~⟩ **4 :** in succession ⟨for days ~⟩ **5 :** in or into harmony or coherence ⟨get ~ on a plan⟩ **6 :** as a group **:** JOINTLY — **to·geth·er·ness** *n*

tog·gery \'täg-(ə-)rē\ *n* **:** CLOTHING

togs \'tägz\ *n pl* **:** CLOTHING; *esp* **:** clothes for a specified use ⟨riding ~⟩

¹toil \'tòil\ *n* **1 :** laborious effort **2 :** long fatiguing labor **:** DRUDGERY — **toil·some** *adj*

²toil *vb* **1 :** to work hard and long **2 :** to proceed with laborious effort **:** PLOD — **toil·er** *n*

³toil *n* **:** NET, TRAP — usu. used in pl.

toi·let \'tòi-lət\ *n* **1 :** the act or process of dressing and grooming oneself **2 :** BATHROOM **3 :** a fixture for use in urinating and defecating; *esp* **:** one consisting essentially of a hopper that can be flushed with water

toi·let·ry \'tòi-lə-trē\ *n* **:** an article or preparation used in making one's toilet — usu. used in pl.

toi·lette \twä-'let\ *n* **1 :** TOILET 1 **2 :** formal attire; *also* **:** a particular costume

toil·worn \'tòil-,wōrn\ *adj* **:** showing the effects of toil

to·ken \'tō-kən\ *n* **1 :** an outward sign **2 :** SYMBOL **3 :** SOUVENIR, KEEPSAKE **4 :** a small part representing the whole **:** INDICATION **5 :** a piece resembling a coin issued as money or for use by a particular group on specified terms — **token** *adj*

told *past of* TELL

tol·er·a·ble \'täl-(ə-)rə-bəl\ *adj* **1 :** capable of being borne or endured **2 :** moderately good **:** PASSABLE — **tol·er·a·bly** *adv*

tol·er·ance \'täl-(ə-)rəns\ *n* **1 :** the act or practice of tolerating; *esp* **:** sympathy or indulgence for beliefs or practices differing from one's own **2 :** capacity for enduring or adapting (as to a poor environment) **3 :** the allowable deviation from a standard (as of size) **syn** forbearance, leniency, clemency — **tol·er·ant** *adj* — **tol·er·ant·ly** *adv*

tol·er·ate \'täl-ə-,rāt\ *vb* **1 :** to allow to be or to be done without hindrance **2 :** to endure or resist the action of (as a drug) **syn** abide, bear, suffer, stand — **tol·er·a·tion** \,täl-ə-'rā-shən\ *n*

¹toll \'tōl\ *n* **1 :** a tax paid for a privilege (as for passing over a bridge) **2 :** a charge for a service (as for a long-

---

ə abut; ᵊ kitten; ər further; a back; ā bake; ä cot, cart; aù out; ch chin; e less; ē easy; g gift; i trip; ī life; j joke; ŋ sing; ō flow; ò flaw; òi coin; th thin; th̶ this; ü loot; ù foot; y yet; yü few; yù furious; zh vision

distance telephone call) **3** : the cost in loss or suffering at which something is achieved *syn* levy, assessment

²**toll** *vb* **1** : to give signal of : SOUND ⟨the clock ∼s the hour⟩ **2** : to cause the slow regular sounding of (a bell) esp. by pulling a rope **3** : to sound with slow measured strokes **4** : to announce by tolling

³**toll** *n* : the sound of a tolling bell

toll-gate \-ˌgāt\ *n* : a point where vehicles stop to pay toll

¹**tom·a·hawk** \'täm-i-ˌhók\ *n* : a light ax used as a missile and as a hand weapon by No. American Indians

²**tomahawk** *vb* : to strike or kill with a tomahawk

to·ma·to \tə-'māt-ō, -'mät-\ *n, pl* **-toes** : a tropical American herb related to the potato and widely grown for its usu. large, rounded, and red or yellow pulpy edible berry; *also* : this fruit

tomb \'tüm\ *n* **1** : a place of burial : GRAVE **2** : a house, chamber, or vault for the dead

tom·boy \'täm-ˌbói\ *n* : a girl of boyish behavior

tomb·stone \'tüm-ˌstōn\ *n* : a stone marking a grave

tom·cat \'täm-ˌkat\ *n* : a male cat

tome \'tōm\ *n* : BOOK; *esp* : a large or weighty one

tom·fool·ery \täm-'fül-(ə-)rē\ *n* : foolish trifling : NONSENSE

to·mor·row \tə-'mär-ō\ *adv* : on or for the day after today — **tomorrow** *n*

tom·tit \(')täm-'tit\ *n* : any of several small active birds

tom-tom \'täm-ˌtäm\ *n* **1** : a small-headed drum beaten with the hands **2** : a monotonous beating

ton \'tən\ *n* **1** : a unit of weight that equals 2240 lbs. avoirdupois (**long ton**) or 2000 lbs. avoirdupois (**short ton**) **2** : a unit of internal capacity for ships equal to 100 cubic feet **3** : a unit equal to the volume of a long-ton weight of sea water or 35 cubic feet used in reckoning the displacement of ships **4** : a unit of volume for a ship's cargo freight usu. reckoned at 40 cubic feet

to·nal·i·ty \tō-'nal-ət-ē\ *n* : tonal quality

¹**tone** \'tōn\ *n* [L *tonus*, fr. Gk *tonos*, lit., stretching, tension; fr. the dependence of the pitch of a musical string on its tension] **1** : vocal or musical sound; *esp* : sound quality **2** : a sound of definite pitch **3** : WHOLE STEP **4** : accent or inflection expressive of an emotion **5** : style or manner of expression **6** : color quality; *also* : SHADE, TINT **7** : the effect in painting of light and shade together with color **8** : the healthy and vigorous condition of a living body or bodily part **9** : general character, quality, or trend *syn* atmosphere, feeling, savor — **ton·al** \'tōn-ᵊl\ *adj*

²**tone** *vb* **1** : to give a particular intonation or inflection to **2** : to impart tone to : STRENGTHEN **3** : SOFTEN, MELLOW **4** : to harmonize in color : BLEND

tong \'täŋ, 'tóŋ\ *n* : a Chinese secret society

tongs \'täŋz, 'tóŋz\ *n pl* : an instrument for holding, gripping, or lifting commonly resembling in general appearance a pair of scissors

¹**tongue** \'təŋ\ *n* **1** : a fleshy movable process of the floor of the mouth used in tasting and in taking and swallowing food and in man as a speech organ **2** : the flesh of a tongue (as of the ox) used as food **3** : the power of communication : SPEECH **4** : LANGUAGE **1 5** : manner or quality of utterance; *also* : intended meaning **6** : something resembling an animal's tongue in being elongated and fastened at one end only — **tongue·less** *adj*

²**tongue** *vb* **tongued; tongu·ing 1** : to touch or lick with the tongue **2** : to articulate notes on a wind instrument

tongue–tied \-ˌtīd\ *adj* : unable to speak clearly or freely usu. from shortness of the membrane under the tongue or from shyness

¹**ton·ic** \'tän-ik\ *adj* **1** : of, relating to, or producing a healthy physical or mental condition : INVIGORATING **2** : of or relating to tones **3** : relating to or based on the first tone of a scale

²**tonic** *n* **1** : something (as a drug) that invigorates, restores, or refreshes **2** : the first degree of a musical scale

¹**to·night** \tə-'nīt\ *adv* : on this present night or the night following this present day

²**tonight** *n* : the present or the coming night

ton·nage \'tən-ij\ *n* **1** : a duty on ships based on tons carried **2** : ships in terms of the number of tons registered or carried **3** : the cubical content of a ship in units of 100 cubic feet **4** : total weight in tons shipped, carried, or mined

ton·neau \tə-'nō\ *n* : the rear seating compartment of an automobile body

ton·sil \'tän-səl\ *n* : either of a pair of oval masses of spongy tissue in the throat at the back of the mouth

ton·sil·lec·to·my \ˌtän-sə-'lek-tə-mē\ *n* : the surgical removal of the tonsils

ton·sil·li·tis \-'līt-əs\ *n* : inflammation of the tonsils

ton·so·ri·al \tän-'sōr-ē-əl\ *adj* : of or relating to a barber or his work

ton·sure \'tän-chər\ *n* **1** : the rite of admission to the clerical state by the clipping or shaving of the head **2** : the shaven crown or patch worn by clerics (as monks)

too \(')tü\ *adv* **1** : ALSO, BESIDES **2** : EXCESSIVELY **3** : to such a degree as to be regrettable **4** : VERY *syn* besides, moreover, furthermore

took *past of* TAKE

¹**tool** \'tül\ *n* **1** : a hand instrument used to aid in mechanical operations **2** : the cutting or shaping part in a machine; *also* : a machine for shaping metal in any way **3** : an instrument or apparatus used in performing an operation or necessary in the practice of a vocation or profession ⟨a scholar's books are ∼s⟩; *also* : a means to an end **4** : a person used by another : DUPE

²**tool** *vb* **1** : to shape, form, or finish with a tool; *esp* : to letter or decorate (as a book cover) by means of hand tools **2** : to equip a plant or industry with machines and tools for production

¹**toot** \'tüt\ *vb* **1** : to sound or cause to sound esp. in short blasts **2** : to blow a wind instrument (as a horn)

²**toot** *n* : a short blast (as on a horn)

tooth \'tüth\ *n, pl* **teeth** \'tēth\ **1** : one of the hard bony structures borne esp. on the jaws of vertebrates and used for seizing and chewing food and as weapons **2** : something resembling an animal's tooth in shape, sharpness, or action **3** : one of the projections on the edge of a wheel that fits into existing projections on another wheel — **toothed** \'tütht\ *adj* — **tooth·less** \'tüth-ləs\ *adj*

tooth·ache \'tüth-ˌāk\ *n* : pain in or about a tooth

tooth·brush \-ˌbrəsh\ *n* : a brush for cleaning the teeth

tooth·pick \-ˌpik\ *n* : a pointed instrument for removing substances lodged between the teeth

tooth·some *adj* : pleasing to the taste : DELICIOUS **syn** palatable, appetizing, savory, tasty

¹**top** \'täp\ *n* **1** : the highest part, point, or level of something **2** : the stalks and leaves of a plant with edible roots (beet ~s) **3** : the upper end, edge, or surface ⟨the ~ of a page⟩ **4** : an upper piece, lid, or covering **5** : a platform around the head of the lower mast **6** : the highest degree, pitch, or rank : ACME

²**top** *vb* **topped; top·ping 1** : to remove or trim the top of : PRUNE ⟨~ a tree⟩ **2** : to cover with a top or on the top : CROWN, CAP **3** : to be superior to : EXCEL, SURPASS **4** : to go over the top of : SURMOUNT **5** : to strike (a golf ball) above the center **6** : to make an end or conclusion ⟨~ off a meal with coffee⟩

³**top** *adj* : of, relating to, or at the top : HIGHEST

⁴**top** *n* : a child's toy that has a tapering point on which it is made to spin

to·paz \'tō-ˌpaz\ *n* : a hard silicate mineral that when occurring as perfect yellow crystals is valued as a gem

top·coat \'täp-ˌkōt\ *n* : a lightweight overcoat

tope \'tōp\ *vb* : to drink intoxicating liquor to excess

top·er \'tō-pər\ *n* : one that topes; *esp* : DRUNKARD

top flight \'täp-'flīt\ *n* : the highest level of excellence or rank — **top-flight** *adj*

top-heavy \'täp-ˌhev-ē\ *adj* : having the top part too heavy for the lower part

top·ic \'täp-ik\ *n* **1** : a heading in an outlined argument **2** : the subject of a discourse or a section of it : THEME

top·i·cal *adj* **1** : of, relating to, or arranged by topics ⟨a ~ outline⟩ **2** : relating to current or local events ⟨a ~ skit⟩ — **top·i·cal·ly** *adv*

top·knot \'täp-ˌnät\ *n* **1** : an ornament (as a knot of ribbons) forming a headdress **2** : a crest of feathers or hair on the top of the head

top·mast \-ˌmast, -məst\ *n* : the second mast above a ship's deck

top·most \-ˌmōst\ *adj* : highest of all : UPPERMOST

top-notch \-'näch\ *adj* : of the highest quality : FIRST-RATE

to·pog·ra·phy \tə-'päg-rə-fē\ *n* **1** : the art of showing in detail on a map or chart the physical features of a place or region **2** : the outline of the form of a place showing its relief and the position of features (as rivers, roads, or cities) — **to·pog·ra·pher** *n* — **top·o·graph·ic** \ˌtäp-ə-'graf-ik\ *adj* — **top·o·graph·i·cal** *adj*

top·ping \'täp-iŋ\ *n* : something (as a

garnish or sauce) that forms a top

top·ple \'täp-əl\ *vb* **1** : to fall from or as if from being top-heavy **2** : to push over : OVERTURN **3** : OVERTHROW

tops \'täps\ *adj* : topmost in quality or eminence ⟨is considered ~ in his field⟩

top·sail \'täp-ˌsāl, -səl\ *n* : the sail next above the lowest sail on a mast in a square-rigged ship

top·soil \-ˌsȯil\ *n* : surface soil; *esp* : the organic layer in which plants have most of their roots

top·sy-tur·vy \ˌtäp-sē-'tər-vē\ *adv* (or *adj*) **1** : upside down **2** : in utter confusion

toque \'tōk\ *n* : a woman's small hat without a brim

tor \'tȯr\ *n* : a high craggy hill

To·rah \'tōr-ə\ *n, pl* **To·roth** \tō-'rōt(h)\ *or* **Torahs 1** : a scroll of the first five books of the Old Testament used in a synagogue; *also* : these five books **2** : the body of divine knowledge and law found in the Jewish scriptures and tradition

torch \'tȯrch\ *n* **1** : a flaming light made of something that burns brightly and usu. carried in the hand **2** : something that resembles a torch in giving light, heat, or guidance **3** *chiefly Brit* : FLASHLIGHT — **torch·bear·er** \-ˌbar-ər\ *n* — **torch·light** \-ˌlīt\ *n*

tore *past of* TEAR

tor·e·ador \'tȯr-ē-ə-ˌdȯr\ *n* : BULLFIGHTER

¹**tor·ment** \'tȯr-ˌment\ *n* **1** : extreme pain or anguish of body or mind **2** : a source of vexation or pain

²**tor·ment** \tȯr-'ment\ *vb* **1** : to cause severe suffering of body or mind to **2** : VEX, HARASS **syn** rack, afflict, try, torture — **tor·men·tor** *n*

torn *past part of* TEAR

tor·na·do \tȯr-'nād-ō\ *n, pl* **-does** or **-dos** [modif. of Sp *tronada* thunderstorm, fr. *tronar* to thunder, modif. of L *tonare*] : a violent destructive whirling wind accompanied by a funnel-shaped cloud that moves over a narrow path

¹**tor·pe·do** \tȯr-'pēd-ō\ *n, pl* **-does** : a self-propelling cigar-shaped submarine missile filled with explosive

²**torpedo** *vb* : to hit with or destroy by a torpedo

tor·pid \'tȯr-pəd\ *adj* **1** : having lost motion or the power of exertion : SLUGGISH **2** : lacking vigor : DULL — **tor·pid·i·ty** \tȯr-'pid-ət-ē\ *n*

tor·por \'tȯr-pər\ *n* **1** : extreme sluggishness : STAGNATION **2** : DULLNESS, APATHY **syn** stupor, lethargy, languor, lassitude

torque \'tȯrk\ *n* : a force that produces or tends to produce rotation or torsion

tor·rent \'tȯr-ənt\ *n* **1** : a rushing stream (as of water or lava) **2** : a tumultuous outburst

tor·ren·tial \tȯ-'ren-chal\ *adj* **1** : relating to or having the character of a torrent ⟨~ rains⟩ **2** : resembling a torrent ⟨~ abuse⟩

tor·rid \'tȯr-əd\ *adj* **1** : parched with heat esp. of the sun : HOT **2** : ARDENT, PASSIONATE

torrid zone *n* : the region of the earth between the tropics over which the sun is vertical at some time of the year

---

ə abut; ᵉ kitten; ər further; a back; ā bake; ä cot, cart; aú out; ch chin; e less; ē easy; g gift; i trip; ī life; j joke; ŋ sing; ō flow; ȯ flaw; ȯi coin; th thin; t͟h this; ü loot; u̇ foot; y yet; yü few; yu̇ furious; zh vision

tor·sion \'tȯr-shən\ *n* : a twisting or being twisted : a wrenching by which one part of a body is under pressure to turn about a longitudinal axis while the other part is held fast or is under pressure to turn in the opposite direction

tor·so \'tȯr-sō\ *n, pl* **torsos** *or* **tor·si** \-,sē\ : the trunk of the human body

tort \'tȯrt\ *n* : a wrongful act except one involving a breach of contract for which the injured party can recover damages in a civil action

tor·til·la \tȯr-'tē-(y)ə\ *n* : a round thin cake of unleavened cornmeal bread usu. eaten hot with a topping of ground meat or cheese

tor·toise \'tȯrt-əs\ *n* : TURTLE; *esp* : a sea turtle whose shell yields horny mottled brown-and-yellow plates (**tortoise-shell**) used for various ornamental objects

tor·tu·ous \'tȯr-chə-wəs\ *adj* **1** : marked by twists or turns : WINDING **2** : DEVIOUS, TRICKY

¹tor·ture \'tȯr-chər\ *n* **1** : the infliction of severe pain esp. to punish or coerce **2** : anguish of body or mind : AGONY

²torture *vb* **1** : to punish or coerce by inflicting severe pain **2** : to cause intense suffering to : TORMENT **3** : TWIST, DISTORT *syn* rack, grill, afflict, try — **tor·tur·er** *n*

To·ry \'tȯr-ē\ *n* **1** : a member of a chiefly 18th century British party upholding the established church and the traditional political structure **2** : an American supporter of the British during the American Revolution **3** : a member of the Conservative party in the United Kingdom **4** *often not cap* : an extreme conservative — **Tory** *adj*

¹toss \'tȯs, 'täs\ *vb* **1** : to fling to and fro or up and down **2** : to throw with a quick light motion; *also* : BANDY **3** : to fling or lift with a sudden motion (~ed her head angrily) **4** : to move restlessly or turbulently (~es on the waves) **5** : to twist and turn repeatedly **6** : FLOUNCE **7** : to accomplish readily (~ off an article) **8** : to decide an issue by flipping a coin

²toss *n* : an act or instance of tossing

¹tot \'tät\ *n* **1** : a small child **2** : a small drink of alcoholic liquor : SHOT

²tot *vb* **tot·ted; tot·ting** : to add up : TOTAL

¹to·tal \'tōt-ᵊl\ *adj* **1** : making up a whole : ENTIRE (~ amount) **2** : COMPLETE, UTTER (a ~ failure) **3** : concentrating all personnel and resources on an objective : THOROUGHGOING (~ war) — **to·tal·ly** *adv*

²total *n* : the entire amount : SUM *syn* aggregate, whole, quantity

³total *vb* **-taled** *or* **-talled; -tal·ing** *or* **-tal·ling** **1** : to add up : COMPUTE **2** : to amount to : NUMBER

to·tal·i·tar·i·an \tō-,tal-ə-'ter-ē-ən\ *adj* : of or relating to a political regime based on subordination of the individual to the state and strict control of all aspects of life esp. by coercive measures; *also* : advocating, constituting, or characteristic of such a regime — **totalitarian** *n*

to·tal·i·ty \tō-'tal-ət-ē\ *n* **1** : an aggregate amount : SUM, WHOLE **2** : ENTIRETY, WHOLENESS

to·tal·iza·tor *or* **to·tal·isa·tor** \'tōt-ᵊl-ə-,zāt-ər\ *n* : a machine for registering and indicating the nature and number of bets made on a horse or dog race

tote \'tōt\ *vb* : CARRY, HAUL

to·tem \'tōt-əm\ *n* : an object (as an animal or plant) serving as the emblem of a family or clan and often as a reminder of its ancestry; *also* : a usu. carved or painted representation of such an object (as on a **totem pole**)

tot·ter \'tät-ər\ *vb* **1** : to tremble or rock as if about to fall : SWAY **2** : to move unsteadily : STAGGER

tou·can \'tü-,kan\ *n* : a brilliantly colored fruit-eating tropical American bird with a very large bill

¹touch \'təch\ *vb* **1** : to bring a bodily part (as the hand) into contact with so as to feel **2** : to be or cause to be in contact **3** : to strike or push lightly esp. with the hand or foot **4** : to make use of (never ~es alcohol) **5** : DISTURB, HARM **6** : to induce to give or lend **7** : to get to : REACH **8** : to refer to in passing : MENTION **9** : to affect the interest of : CONCERN **10** : to leave a mark on; *also* : BLEMISH **11** : to improve with or as if with a brush (~ up a portrait) **12** : to move to sympathetic feeling **13** : to come close : VERGE **14** : to have a bearing : RELATE **15** : to make a usu. brief or incidental stop in port (~ed at several coastal towns) *syn* affect, influence, impress, strike, sway

²touch *n* **1** : a light stroke or tap **2** : the act or fact of touching or being touched **3** : the sense by which pressure or traction is felt; *also* : a particular sensation conveyed by this sense **4** : mental or moral sensitiveness : TACT (has a fine ~ with children) **5** : a small quantity : TRACE **6** : a manner of striking or touching an instrument **7** : an improving detail (add a few ~es to the painting) **8** : distinctive manner or skill (~ of a master) **9** : the state of being in contact (keep in ~) *syn* suggestion, suspicion, tincture, tinge

touch·down \'təch-,daûn\ *n* : the act of scoring six points in American football by being lawfully in possession of the ball on, above, or behind an opponent's goal line

touch·ing *adj* : capable of stirring emotions : PATHETIC *syn* moving, impressive, poignant

touch·stone \'təch-,stōn\ *n* : a test or criterion of genuineness or quality *syn* standard, gauge

touchy \'təch-ē\ *adj* **1** : easily offended : PEEVISH **2** : calling for tact in treatment (a ~ subject) *syn* irascible, cranky, cross

tough \'təf\ *adj* **1** : strong or firm in texture but flexible and not brittle **2** : not easily chewed **3** : characterized by severity and determination (a ~ policy) **4** : capable of enduring strain or hardship : ROBUST **5** : hard to influence : STUBBORN **6** : difficult to cope with (a ~ problem) **7** : ROWDYISH, RUFFIANLY *syn* tenacious, stout, sturdy, stalwart — **tough·ly** *adv* — **tough·ness** *n*

tough·en \-ən\ *vb* : to make or become tough

tou·pee \tü-'pā\ *n* : a small wig for a bald spot

¹tour \'túr\ *n* **1** : one's turn : SHIFT **2** : a journey in which one returns to the starting point

²tour *vb* : to travel or travel over as a tourist

tour de force \,túrd-ə-'fōrs\ *n* : a feat of strength, skill, or ingenuity

tour·ist \'túr-əst\ *n* : one that makes a tour for pleasure or culture

tourist class *n* : economy accommodation on a ship, airplane, or train

tour·ma·line \'túr-mə-lən, -,lēn\ *n* : a mineral that when transparent is valued as a gem

tour·na·ment \'túr-nə-mənt, 'tər-\ *n* 1 : a medieval sport in which mounted armored knights contended with blunted lances or swords; *also* : the whole series of knightly sports, jousts, and tilts occurring at one time and place. 2 : a championship series of games or athletic contests

tour·ney \-nē\ *n* : TOURNAMENT

tour·ni·quet \'túr-ni-kət, 'tər-\ *n* : a device (as a bandage twisted tight with a stick) for stopping bleeding or blood flow

tou·sle \'taú-zəl\ *vb* : to disorder by rough handling : DISHEVEL, MUSS

¹tout \'taút\ *vb* : to give a tip or solicit bets on a racehorse — **tout** *n*

²tout *vb* : to praise or publicize loudly

¹tow \'tō\ *vb* : to draw or pull along behind **syn** tug, haul, drag

²tow *n* 1 : an act of towing or condition of being towed 2 : something (as a barge) that is towed

³tow *n* : short broken fiber from hemp, flax, or jute used esp. for twine or stuffing

to·ward *or* **to·wards** \(')tō(-ə)rd(z), tə-'wórd(z)\ *prep* 1 : in the direction of ⟨heading ~ the river⟩ 2 : along a course leading to ⟨efforts ~ reconciliation⟩ 3 : in regard to ⟨tolerance ~ minorities⟩ 4 : FACING ⟨the gun's muzzle was ~ him⟩ 5 : close upon : NEAR ⟨it was getting along ~ sundown⟩ 6 : for part payment of ⟨paid $100 ~ his tuition⟩

tow·el \'taú(-ə)l\ *n* : an absorbent cloth or paper for wiping or drying

tow·el·ing *or* **tow·el·ling** *n* : a cotton or linen fabric often used for making towels

¹tow·er \'taú(-ə)r\ *n* 1 : a tall structure either isolated or built upon a larger structure ⟨a bell ~ of a church⟩ ⟨an observation ~⟩ 2 : a towering citadel : FORTRESS

²tower *vb* : to reach or rise to a great height **syn** soar, mount, ascend, surge

tow·er·ing *adj* 1 : LOFTY, IMPOSING ⟨~ pines⟩ 2 : reaching high intensity ⟨a ~ rage⟩ 3 : EXCESSIVE ⟨~ ambition⟩

tow·head \'tō-,hed\ *n* : a person having soft whitish hair — **tow·head·ed** \-'hed-əd\ *adj*

to wit \tə-'wit\ *adv* : that is to say : NAMELY

town \'taún\ *n* 1 : a compactly settled area usu. larger than a village but smaller than a city 2 : CITY 3 : a New England territorial and political unit usu. containing both rural and urban areas; *also* : a New England community in which matters of local government are decided by a general assembly ⟨town meeting⟩ of qualified voters

towns·folk \'taúnz-,fōk\ *n pl* : TOWNSPEOPLE

town·ship \'taún-,ship\ *n* 1 : TOWN 3 2 : a unit of local government in some states · 3 : an unorganized subdivision of a county; *also* : an administrative division 4 : a division of territory in surveys of U.S. public land containing 36 square miles

towns·man \'taúnz-mən\ *n* 1 : a native or resident of a town or city 2 : a fellow citizen of a town

towns·peo·ple \-,pē-pəl\ *n pl* 1 : the inhabitants of a town or city 2 : townbred persons

tow·path \'tō-,path, -,páth\ *n* : a path (as along a canal) traveled by men or animals towing boats

tox·emia \täk-'sē-mē-ə\ *n* : abnormality associated with the presence of toxic matter in the blood

tox·ic \'täk-sik\ *adj* [L *toxicum*, n., poison, fr. Gk *toxikon* arrow poison, fr. *toxa* bow and arrows, fr. pl. of *toxon* bow] : of, relating to, or caused by poison or a toxin : POISONOUS

tox·i·col·o·gy \,täk-si-'käl-ə-jē\ *n* : a science that deals with poisons and esp. with problems of their use and control — **tox·i·co·log·ic** \,täk-si-kə-'läj-ik\ *or* **tox·i·co·log·i·cal** \-i-kəl\ *adj* — **tox·i·col·o·gist** \,täk-sə-'käl-ə-jəst\ *n*

tox·in \'täk-sən\ *n* : a substance produced by a living organism that is very poisonous when introduced into the tissues but is usu. destroyed by digestive processes when taken by mouth

¹toy \'tói\ *n* 1 : something trifling 2 : a small ornament : BAUBLE 3 : something for a child to play with : PLAYTHING

²toy *vb* 1 : FLIRT 2 : to deal lightly : TRIFLE 3 : to amuse oneself as if with a plaything

³toy *adj* 1 : designed for use as a toy 2 : DIMINUTIVE

¹trace \'trās\ *n* 1 : a mark (as a footprint or track) left by something that has passed : VESTIGE 2 : a minute or barely detectable amount

²trace *vb* 1 : to mark out : SKETCH 2 : to form (as letters) carefully 3 : to copy (a drawing) by marking lines on transparent paper laid over the drawing to be copied 4 : to follow the trail of : track down 5 : to study out and follow the development of ⟨traced his ancestors⟩ — **trace·able** *adj* — **trac·er** *n*

³trace *n* : either of two lines of a harness for fastening a draft animal to a vehicle

trac·ery \'trās-(ə-)rē\ *n* : ornamental work having a design with branching or interlacing lines

tra·chea \'trā-kē-ə\ *n, pl* **-che·ae** \-kē-,ē\ : the main tube by which air enters the lungs : WINDPIPE — **tra·che·al** \-kē-əl\ *adj*

trac·ing *n* 1 : the act of one that traces 2 : something that is traced 3 : a graphic record made by an instrument for measuring vibrations or pulsations

¹track \'trak\ *n* 1 : a mark left in passing 2 : PATH, ROUTE, TRAIL 3 : a course laid out for racing; *also* : track-and-field sports 4 : a way for various wheeled vehicles; *esp* : a way made by two parallel lines of metal rails 5 : awareness of a fact or progression ⟨lost ~ of his movements⟩ 6 : either of two endless metal belts on which a vehicle (as a tractor) travels

²track *vb* 1 : to follow the tracks or traces of : TRAIL 2 : to make tracks upon — **track·er** *n*

track-and-field *adj* : of or relating to

athletic contests held on a running track or on the adjacent field

¹**tract** \'trakt\ *n* **:** a pamphlet of political or religious propaganda

²**tract** *n* **1 :** a stretch of land without precise boundaries ⟨broad ∼s of prairie⟩ **2 :** a defined area of land ⟨a garden ∼⟩ **3 :** a system of body parts or organs together serving some special purpose ⟨the digestive ∼⟩

trac·ta·ble \'trak-tə-bəl\ *adj* **1 :** easily controlled **:** DOCILE **2 :** easily wrought **:** MALLEABLE *syn* amenable, obedient

trac·tate \'trak-ˌtāt\ *n* **:** TREATISE

trac·tion \'trak-shən\ *n* **1 :** the act of drawing or condition of being drawn **2 :** the drawing of a vehicle by motive power; *also* **:** the particular form of motive power used **3 :** the adhesive friction of a body on a surface on which it moves (as of a wheel on a rail) — **trac·tive** \'trak-tiv\ *adj*

trac·tor \'trak-tər\ *n* **1 :** an automotive vehicle that is borne on four wheels or beltlike metal tracks and used for drawing, pushing, or bearing implements or vehicles **2 :** a motortruck with short chassis for hauling a trailer

¹**trade** \'trād\ *n* **1 :** one's regular business or work **:** OCCUPATION **2 :** an occupation requiring manual or mechanical skill **3 :** the persons engaged in a business or industry **4 :** the business of buying and selling or bartering commodities **5 :** an act of trading **:** TRANSACTION *syn* craft, profession, commerce, industry

²**trade** *vb* **1 :** to give in exchange for another commodity **:** BARTER **2 :** to engage in the exchange, purchase, or sale of goods **3 :** to deal regularly as a customer **4 :** EXPLOIT ⟨∼s on his family name⟩

¹**trade·mark** \-ˌmärk\ *n* **:** a device (as a word or mark) that points distinctly to the origin or ownership of merchandise or service to which it is applied and that is legally reserved for the exclusive use of the owner

²**trademark** *vb* **1 :** to label with a trademark **2 :** to secure the trademark rights for

trad·er \'trād-ər\ *n* **1 :** a person whose business is buying or selling **2 :** a ship engaged in trade

trades·man \'trādz-mən\ *n* **1 :** one who runs a retail store **:** SHOPKEEPER **2 :** CRAFTSMAN

trades·peo·ple \-ˌpē-pəl\ *n pl* **:** TRADESMEN I

trade wind *n* **:** a wind blowing regularly from northeast to southwest north of the equator and from southeast to northwest south of the equator

tra·di·tion \trə-'dish-ən\ *n* **1 :** the handing down of beliefs and customs by word of mouth or by example without written instruction; *also* **:** a belief or custom thus handed down **2 :** an inherited pattern of thought or action — **tra·di·tion·al** *adj* — **tra·di·tion·al·ly** *adv* — **tra·di·tion·ary** *adj*

tra·duce \trə-'d(y)üs\ *vb* **:** to lower the reputation of **:** DEFAME, SLANDER *syn* malign, libel — **tra·duc·er** *n*

¹**traf·fic** \'traf-ik\ *n* **1 :** the business of bartering or buying and selling **2 :** INTERCOURSE, BUSINESS **3 :** the movement (as of vehicles) along a route **4 :** the passengers or cargo carried by a transportation system

²**traffic** *vb* **-ficked; -fick·ing :** to carry

on traffic — **traf·fick·er** *n*

tra·ge·di·an \trə-'jēd-ē-ən\ *n* **1 :** a writer of tragedies **2 :** an actor who plays tragic roles

tra·ge·di·enne \trə-ˌjēd-ē-'en\ *n* **:** an actress who plays tragic roles

trag·e·dy \'traj-əd-ē\ *n* **1 :** a serious drama describing a conflict between the protagonist and a superior force (as destiny) and having a sad end that excites pity or terror **2 :** a disastrous event **:** CALAMITY; *also* **:** MISFORTUNE **3 :** tragic quality or element

trag·ic \'traj-ik\ *adj* **1 :** of, relating to, or expressive of tragedy **2 :** appropriate to tragedy **3 :** LAMENTABLE, UNFORTUNATE — **trag·i·cal** *adj* — **trag·i·cal·ly** *adv*

¹**trail** \'trāl\ *vb* **1 :** to hang down so as to drag along or sweep the ground **2 :** to draw or drag along behind **3 :** to extend over a surface in a straggling manner **4 :** to follow slowly **:** lag behind ⟨∼s his competitors⟩ **5 :** to follow upon the track of **:** PURSUE **6 :** DWINDLE ⟨her voice ∼ed off⟩ *syn* chase, tag, tail

²**trail** *n* **1 :** something that trails or is trailed ⟨a ∼ of smoke⟩ **2 :** a trace or mark left by something that has passed or been drawn along **:** TRACK ⟨a ∼ of blood⟩ **3 :** a beaten path; *also* **:** a marked path through woods **4 :** SCENT

trail·er \'trā-lər\ *n* **1 :** one that trails; *esp* **:** a creeping plant (as an ivy) **2 :** a vehicle that is hauled by another (as by a tractor) **3 :** a vehicle equipped to serve wherever parked as a dwelling or as a place of business

¹**train** \'trān\ *n* **1 :** a part of a gown that trails behind the wearer **2 :** RETINUE **3 :** a moving file of persons, vehicles, or animals **4 :** a connected series ⟨a ∼ of thought⟩ **5 :** a connected line of railroad cars usu. hauled by a locomotive **6 :** AFTERMATH *syn* succession, sequence, procession, chain

²**train** *vb* **1 :** to cause to grow as desired ⟨∼ a vine on a trellis⟩ **2 :** to form by instruction, discipline, or drill **3 :** to make or become prepared (as by exercise) for a test of skill **4 :** to aim or point at an object ⟨∼ guns on a fort⟩ *syn* discipline, school, educate, direct, level — **train·er** *n*

¹**train·ing** *n* **1 :** the act or process of one who trains **2 :** the state of being trained

²**training** *adj* **:** used in or for training; *also* **:** providing training

train·load \-'lōd\ *n* **:** the full freight or passenger capacity of a railroad train

train·man \-mən\ *n* **:** a member of a train crew

trait \'trāt\ *n* **:** a distinguishing quality (as of personality or physical makeup) **:** CHARACTERISTIC

trai·tor \'trāt-ər\ *n* **1 :** one who betrays another's trust or is false to an obligation **2 :** one who commits treason — **trai·tor·ous** *adj* — **trai·tress** \'trā-trəs\

tra·jec·to·ry \trə-'jek-t(ə-)rē\ *n* **:** the curve that a body (as a planet in its orbit, a projectile in flight, or a missile passing through the air) describes in space

tram \'tram\ *n* **1** *chiefly Brit* **:** STREETCAR **2 :** a boxlike car running on a railway (**tram·way** \-ˌwā\) in a mine or a logging camp

¹**tram·mel** \'tram-əl\ *n* **:** something

impeding activity, progress, or freedom
²**trammel** vb **-meled** or **-melled; -mel-ing** or **-mel-ling 1 :** to catch and hold in or as if in a net **2 :** HAMPER **syn** clog, fetter, shackle

¹**tramp** \'tramp\ vb **1 :** to walk, tread, or step heavily **2 :** to walk about or through; also **:** HIKE **3 :** to tread on forcibly and repeatedly

²**tramp** n **1 :** a foot traveler **2 :** a begging or thieving vagrant **3 :** an immoral woman; esp **:** PROSTITUTE **4 :** a walking trip **:** HIKE **5 :** the succession of sounds made by the beating of feet on a road **6 :** a ship that does not follow a regular course but takes cargo to any port

tram·ple \'tram-pəl\ vb **1 :** to tread heavily so as to bruise, crush, or injure **2 :** to inflict injury or destruction **3 :** to press down or crush by or as if by treading **:** STAMP **— trample** n **— tram·pler** \-p(ə-)lər\ n

trance \'trans\ n **1 :** DAZE, STUPOR **2 :** a prolonged and profound sleeplike condition (as of deep hypnosis) **3 :** a state of mystical absorption **:** RAPTURE

tran·quil \'traŋ-kwəl\ adj **:** free from agitation or disturbance **:** QUIET **syn** serene, placid, peaceful **— tran·quil·li·ty** or **tran·quil·i·ty** \traŋ-'kwil-ət-ē\ n **— tran·quil·ly** \'traŋ-kwə-lē\ adv

tran·quil·ize or **tran·quil·lize** \'traŋ-kwə-‚līz\ vb **:** to make or become tranquil; esp **:** to relieve of mental tension and anxiety

tran·quil·iz·er n **:** a drug used to relieve tension and anxiety

trans·act \trans-'akt, tranz-\ vb **:** to carry out **:** PERFORM; esp **:** to carry on ⟨~ business⟩

trans·ac·tion \-'ak-shən\ n **1 :** an act or process of transacting **2 :** something transacted; esp **:** a business deal **3** pl **:** the records of the proceedings of a society or organization

trans·at·lan·tic \‚trans-ət-'lant-ik, ‚tranz-\ adj **1 :** crossing or extending across or situated beyond the Atlantic ocean

tran·scend \trans-'end\ vb **1 :** to rise above the limits of **2 :** SURPASS **syn** exceed, outdo

tran·scen·dent \trans-'en-dənt\ adj **1 :** exceeding usual limits **:** SURPASSING **2 :** transcending material existence **syn** superlative, supreme, peerless, incomparable

tran·scen·den·tal \‚trans-‚en-'dent-ᵊl\ adj **1 :** TRANSCENDENT **2 :** of, relating to, or characteristic of transcendentalism; also **:** ABSTRUSE, ABSTRACT

tran·scen·den·tal·ism n **:** a philosophy holding that ultimate reality is unknowable and asserting the primacy of the spiritual over the material and empirical

trans·con·ti·nen·tal \‚trans-‚känt-ᵊn-'ent-ᵊl\ adj **1 :** extending or going across a continent **2 :** situated on the farther side of a continent

tran·scribe \trans-'krīb\ vb **1 :** to write a copy of **2 :** to make a copy of (shorthand notes or recorded matter) in longhand or on a typewriter **3 :** to represent (speech sounds) by means of phonetic symbols; also **:** to make a musical transcription of **4 :** to record

on a phonograph record or magnetic tape for later radio broadcast; also **:** to broadcast recorded matter

tran·script \'trans-‚kript\ n **1 :** a written, printed, or typed copy **2 :** an official copy esp. of a student's educational record

tran·scrip·tion \trans-'krip-shən\ n **1 :** an act or process of transcribing **2 :** COPY, TRANSCRIPT **3 :** an arrangement of a musical composition for some instrument or voice other than the original **4 :** radio broadcasting from a phonograph record; also **:** the record itself

tran·sept \'trans-‚ept\ n **:** the part of a cruciform church that crosses at right angles to the greatest length; also **:** either of the projecting ends

¹**trans·fer** \'trans-fər\ vb **-ferred; -fer·ring 1 :** to pass or cause to pass from one person, place, or situation to another **:** TRANSPORT, TRANSMIT **2 :** to make over the possession of **:** CONVEY **3 :** to print or copy from one surface to another by contact **4 :** to change from one vehicle or transportation line to another **— trans·fer·able** adj **— trans·fer·al** n

²**trans·fer** \'trans-fər\ n **1 :** conveyance of right, title, or interest in property from one person to another **2 :** an act or process of transferring **3 :** one that transfers or is transferred **4 :** a ticket entitling a passenger on a public conveyance to continue his journey on another route

trans·fer·ence \trans-'fər-əns\ n **:** an act, process, or instance of transferring

trans·fig·ure \trans-'fig-yər\ vb **1 :** to change the form or appearance of **2 :** EXALT, GLORIFY **— trans·fig·u·ra·tion** \‚trans-‚fig-(y)ə-'rā-shən\ n

trans·fix \trans-'fiks\ vb **1 :** to pierce through with or as if with a pointed weapon **2 :** to hold motionless by or as if by piercing

trans·form \trans-'fórm\ vb **1 :** to change in structure, appearance, or character **2 :** to change (an electric current) in potential or type **syn** transmute, transfigure **— trans·for·ma·tion** \‚trans-fər-'mā-shən\ n **— trans·form·er** \trans-'fór-mər\ n

trans·fuse \trans-'fyüz\ vb **1 :** to cause to pass from one to another **2 :** to diffuse into or through **3 :** to transfer (as blood) into a vein of a man or animal **— trans·fu·sion** \-'fyü-zhən\ n

trans·gress \trans-'gres, tranz-\ vb [L transgress-, transgredi to cross beyond, fr. trans- across + gradi to step, go] **1 :** to go beyond the limits set by ⟨~ the divine law⟩ **2 :** to go beyond **:** EXCEED **3 :** SIN **— trans·gres·sion** \-'gresh-ən\ n **— trans·gres·sor** \-'gres-ər\ n

¹**tran·sient** \'tran-chənt\ adj **1 :** not lasting long **:** SHORT-LIVED **2 :** passing through a place with only a brief stay **syn** transitory, passing, momentary, fleeting **— tran·sient·ly** adv

²**transient** n **:** one that is transient; esp **:** a transient guest

tran·sis·tor \tranz-'is-tər, trans-\ n **1 :** a small electronic device to control electrons **2 :** a radio having transistors

tran·sit \'trans-ət, 'tranz-\ n **1 :** a

passing through or across **:** PASSAGE **2 :** conveyance of persons or things from one place to another **3 :** usu. local transportation esp. of people by public conveyance **4 :** a surveyor's instrument for measuring angles

tran·si·tion \trans-'ish-ən, tranz-\ *n* **:** passage from one state, place, stage, or subject to another **:** CHANGE — **tran·si·tion·al** *adj*

tran·si·tive \'trans-ət-iv, 'tranz-\ *adj* **1 :** having or containing an object required to complete its meaning **2 :** TRANSITIONAL — **tran·si·tive·ly** *adv* — **tran·si·tive·ness** *n*

tran·si·to·ry \'trans-ə-ˌtōr-ē, 'tranz-\ *adj* **:** of brief duration **:** SHORT-LIVED, TEMPORARY **syn** transient, passing, momentary, fleeting

trans·lat·a·ble \trans-'lāt-ə-bəl, tranz-\ *adj* **:** capable of being translated

trans·late \trans-'lāt, tranz-\ *vb* **1 :** to bear or change from one place, state, or form to another **2 :** to convey to heaven without death **3 :** to transfer (a bishop) from one see to another **4 :** to turn into one's own or another language — **trans·la·tion** \-'lā-shən\ *n* — **trans·la·tor** \-'lāt-ər\ *n*

trans·lu·cent \-'lüs-ᵊnt\ *adj* **:** admitting and diffusing light so that objects beyond cannot be clearly distinguished **:** partly transparent — **trans·lu·cence** *n* — **trans·lu·cen·cy** *n*

trans·mi·grate \-'mī-ˌgrāt\ *vb* **:** to pass at death from one body or being to another — **trans·mi·gra·tion** \ˌtrans-mī-'grā-shən, ˌtranz-\ *n* — **trans·mi·gra·to·ry** \trans-'mī-grə-ˌtōr-ē, tranz-\ *adj*

trans·mis·sion \-'mish-ən\ *n* **1 :** an act or process of transmitting **2 :** the passage of radio waves between transmitting stations and receiving stations **3 :** the gears by which power is transmitted from the engine of an automobile to the axle that propels the vehicle **4 :** something transmitted

trans·mit \-'mit\ *vb* **1 :** to transfer from one person or place to another **:** FORWARD **2 :** to pass on by or as if by inheritance **3 :** to cause (as light, electricity, or force) to pass through space or a medium **4 :** to send out (radio or television signals) **syn** carry, bear, convey, transport — **trans·mis·si·ble** \-'mis-ə-bəl\ *adj* — **trans·mit·ta·ble** \-'mit-ə-bəl\ *adj*

trans·mit·ter *n* **1 :** one that transmits **2 :** the part of a telephone into which one speaks **3 :** a set of apparatus for transmitting telegraph, radio, or television signals

trans·mute \-'myüt\ *vb* **:** to change or alter in form, appearance, or nature **syn** transform, convert — **trans·mu·ta·tion** \ˌtrans-myü-'tā-shən, ˌtranz-\ *n*

trans·oce·an·ic \ˌtrans-ˌō-shē-'an-ik, ˌtranz-\ *adj* **1 :** lying or dwelling beyond the ocean **2 :** crossing or extending beyond the ocean

tran·som \'tran-səm\ *n* **1 :** a piece (as a crossbar in the frame of a window or door) that lies crosswise in a structure **2 :** a window above an opening (as a door) built on and often hinged to a horizontal crossbar

tran·son·ic \tran(s)-'sän-ik\ *adj* **:** being, relating to, or moving at a speed that is about that of sound in air or about 741 miles per hour

trans·pa·cif·ic \ˌtrans-pə-'sif-ik\ *adj* **:** crossing or extending across or situated beyond the Pacific ocean

trans·par·ent \trans-'par-ənt\ *adj* **1 :** transmitting light **:** clear enough to be seen through **2 :** SHEER, DIAPHANOUS ⟨a ~ fabric⟩ **3 :** readily understood **:** CLEAR; *also* **:** easily detected ⟨a ~ lie⟩ **syn** lucid — **trans·par·en·cy** *n* — **trans·par·ent·ly** *adv*

tran·spire \trans-'pī(ə)r\ *vb* **1 :** to pass off (as watery vapor) through pores or a membrane **2 :** to become known **:** come to light **3 :** to take place **:** OCCUR — **tran·spi·ra·tion** \ˌtrans-pə-'rā-shən\ *n*

¹**trans·plant** \trans-'plant\ *vb* **1 :** to take up and set again in another soil or location **2 :** to remove from one place and settle or introduce elsewhere **:** TRANSPORT **3 :** to transfer (an organ or tissue) from one part or individual to another **4 :** to admit of being transplanted — **trans·plan·ta·tion** \ˌtrans-ˌplan-'tā-shən\ *n*

²**trans·plant** \'trans-ˌplant\ *n* **1 :** the act or process of transplanting **2 :** something transplanted

¹**trans·port** \trans-'pōrt\ *vb* **1 :** to convey from one place to another **:** CARRY **2 :** to carry away by strong emotion **:** ENRAPTURE **3 :** to send to a penal colony overseas **syn** transmit, deport, exile — **trans·por·ta·tion** \ˌtrans-pər-'tā-shən\ *n* — **trans·port·er** \trans-'pōrt-ər\ *n*

²**trans·port** \'trans-ˌpōrt\ *n* **1 :** act of transporting **:** TRANSPORTATION **2 :** strong or intensely pleasurable emotion **:** RAPTURE **3 :** a ship used in transporting troops or supplies; *also* **:** a vehicle (as a truck or plane) used to transport persons or goods

trans·pose \trans-'pōz\ *vb* **1 :** to change the position or sequence of ⟨~ the letters in a word⟩ **2 :** to write or perform (a musical composition) in a different key **syn** reverse, invert — **trans·po·si·tion** \ˌtrans-pə-'zish-ən\ *n*

trans·ship \tran(s)-'ship\ *vb* **:** to transfer for further transportation from one ship or conveyance to another — **trans·ship·ment** *n*

tran·sub·stan·ti·a·tion \ˌtrans-əb-ˌstan-chē-'ā-shən\ *n* **:** the change in the eucharistic elements from the substance of bread and wine to the substance of the body of Christ with only the accidents (as taste and color) remaining

trans·verse \trans-'vərs, tranz-\ *adj* **:** lying across **:** set crosswise — **transverse** \'trans-ˌvərs, 'tranz-\ *n* — **trans·verse·ly** *adv*

¹**trap** \'trap\ *n* **1 :** a device (as a snare) for catching animals **2 :** something by which one is caught unawares **3 :** a machine for throwing objects into the air to be targets for shooters; *also* **:** a hazard on a golf course consisting of a depression containing sand **4 :** a light 2-wheeled or 4-wheeled one-horse carriage on springs **5 :** a device to allow some one thing to pass through while keeping other things out ⟨a ~ in a drainpipe⟩

²**trap** *vb* **trapped; trap·ping 1 :** to catch in or as if in a trap; *also* **:** CONFINE **2 :** to provide or set (a place) with traps **3 :** to set traps for animals esp. as a business **syn** snare, entrap, ensnare, bag, lure, decoy — **trap·per** *n*

³**trap** *also* **trap·rock** \-'räk\ *n* **:** any of

various dark fine-grained igneous rocks used esp. in road making

trap·door \'trap-'dōr\ n : a lifting or sliding door covering an opening in a floor or roof

tra·peze \tra-'pēz\ n : a gymnastic apparatus consisting of a horizontal bar suspended by two parallel ropes

trap·e·zoid \'trap-ə-,zóid\ n : a plane 4-sided figure with two parallel sides — **trap·e·zoi·dal** \,trap-ə-'zóid-°l\ adj

trap·pings \'trap-iŋz\ n pl : ornamental covering esp. for a horse; also : ORNAMENTS, DRESS

traps \'traps\ n pl : personal belongings : LUGGAGE

trap·shoot·ing \'trap-,shüt-iŋ\ n : shooting at clay pigeons sprung into the air from a trap

trash \'trash\ n 1 : something of little worth : RUBBISH 2 : a worthless person; also : such persons as a group : RIFFRAFF — **trashy** adj

trau·ma \'traú-mə, 'tró-\ n, pl -ma·ta \-mət-ə\ or -mas : a bodily or mental injury usu. caused by an external agent; also : a cause of trauma — **trau·mat·ic** \trə-'mat-ik, tró-, traú-\ adj

¹**tra·vail** \trə-'vāl, 'trav-,āl\ n 1 : painful work or exertion : TOIL 2 : AGONY, TORMENT 3 : CHILDBIRTH, LABOR syn work, drudgery

²**travail** vb : to labor hard : TOIL

¹**trav·el** \'trav-əl\ vb -eled or -elled; -el·ing or -el·ling 1 : to go on or as if on a trip or tour : JOURNEY 2 : to move as if by traveling : PASS 3 : ASSOCIATE 4 : to go from place to place as a salesman 5 : to move from point to point ⟨light waves ~ very fast⟩ 6 : to journey over or through — **trav·el·er** or **trav·el·ler** n

²**travel** n 1 : the act of traveling : PASSAGE 2 : JOURNEY, TRIP—often used in pl. 3 : the number traveling : TRAFFIC 4 : the motion of a piece of machinery and esp. when to and fro; also : length of motion (as of a piston)

traveling bag n : a bag carried by hand and designed to hold a traveler's clothing and personal articles

trav·el·ogue also **trav·el·og** \-,óg\ n : a usu. illustrated lecture on travel

¹**trav·erse** \'trav-ərs\ n : something (as a crosswise beam) that crosses or lies across

²**tra·verse** \trə-'vərs\ vb 1 : to pass through : PENETRATE 2 : to go or travel across or over 3 : to extend over 4 : SWIVEL

³**trav·erse** \'trav-ərs\ adj : lying across : TRANSVERSE

trav·er·tine \'trav-ər-,tēn\ n : a crystalline mineral formed by deposition from spring waters

¹**trav·es·ty** \'trav-ə-stē\ n : a burlesque and usu. grotesque translation or imitation

²**travesty** vb : to make a travesty of

¹**trawl** \'tról\ vb : to fish or catch with a trawl — **trawl·er** n

²**trawl** n 1 : a large conical net dragged along the sea bottom in fishing 2 : a long fishing line anchored at both ends and equipped with many hooks

tray \'trā\ n : an open receptacle with flat bottom and low rim for holding,

carrying, or exhibiting articles

treach·er·ous \'trech-(ə-)rəs\ adj 1 : characterized by treachery 2 : UNTRUSTWORTHY, UNRELIABLE 3 : providing insecure footing or support syn traitorous, faithless, false, disloyal — **treach·er·ous·ly** adv

treach·ery \-rē\ n : violation of allegiance or trust : TREASON, PERFIDY

trea·cle \'trē-kəl\ n, chiefly Brit : MOLASSES

¹**tread** \'tred\ vb trod \'träd\ trod·den \'träd-°n\ or trod; tread·ing 1 : to step or walk on or over 2 : to move on foot : WALK; also : DANCE 3 : to beat or press with the feet : TRAMPLE

²**tread** n 1 : a mark made by or as if by treading 2 : manner of stepping 3 : the sound of treading 4 : the part of something that is trodden upon ⟨the ~ of a step in a flight of stairs⟩ 5 : the part of a thing on which it runs ⟨the ~ of a tire⟩

trea·dle \'tred-°l\ n : a lever device pressed by the foot to drive a machine

tread·mill \'tred-,mil\ n 1 : a mill worked by persons who tread steps around the edge of a wheel or by animals that walk on an endless belt 2 : a wearisome routine

trea·son \'trēz-°n\ n : the offense of attempting by overt acts to overthrow the government of the state to which one owes allegiance or to kill or injure the sovereign or his family — **trea·son·able** \-(°-)nə-bəl\ adj — **trea·son·ous** \-(°-)nəs\ adj

¹**trea·sure** \'trezh-ər\ n 1 : wealth (as money or jewels) stored up or held in reserve 2 : something of great value

²**treasure** vb 1 : HOARD 2 : to keep as precious : CHERISH syn prize, value, appreciate

trea·sur·er \-ər-ər\ n : an officer entrusted with the receipt, care, and disbursement of funds

treasure trove \-,trōv\ n 1 : treasure (as money in gold) that is found hidden and whose ownership is unknown 2 : a valuable discovery

trea·sury \'trezh-(ə-)rē\ n 1 : a place in which stores of wealth are kept 2 : the place of deposit and disbursement of collected funds; esp : one where public revenues are deposited, kept, and disbursed 3 cap : a governmental department in charge of finances

¹**treat** \'trēt\ vb 1 : NEGOTIATE 2 : to deal with esp. in writing; also : HANDLE 3 : to pay for the food or entertainment of 4 : to bear oneself toward ⟨~ them well⟩ 5 : to regard in a specified manner ⟨~ as inferiors⟩ 6 : to care for medically or surgically ⟨~ a wound⟩ ⟨~ patients⟩ 7 : to subject to some action (as of a chemical) ⟨~ soil with lime⟩

²**treat** n 1 : food or entertainment paid for by another 2 : a source of joy or amusement

trea·tise \'trēt-əs\ n : a systematic written exposition or argument on a subject

treat·ment \-mənt\ n : the act or manner or an instance of treating someone or something; also : a substance or method used in treating

trea·ty \'trēt-ē\ n : an agreement made

by negotiation or diplomacy esp. between two or more states or governments **syn** contract, bargain, pact

¹tre·ble \'treb-əl\ *n* **1** : the highest of the four voice parts in vocal music : SOPRANO **2** : a high-pitched or shrill voice or sound **3** : the upper half of the musical pitch range

²treble *adj* **1** : triple in number or amount **2** : relating to or having the range of a musical treble **3** : high-pitched : SHRILL — **tre·bly** \'treb-lē\ *adv*

³treble *vb* : to make or become three times the size, amount, or number

¹tree \'trē\ *n* **1** : a woody perennial plant usu. with a single main stem and a head of branches and leaves at the top **2** : a piece of wood adapted to a particular use ⟨a shoe ~⟩ **3** : something in the form of or felt to resemble a tree ⟨a genealogical ~⟩ — **tree·less** *adj*

²tree *vb* **treed; tree·ing** : to drive to or up a tree ⟨~ a raccoon⟩

tre·foil \'trē-,fȯil\ *n* **1** : a clover or related herb with leaves with 3 leaflets **2** : a decorative design with 3 leaflike parts

¹trek \'trek\ *n* **1** : a migration esp. of settlers by ox wagon **2** : TRIP; *esp* : one involving difficulties or complex organization

²trek *vb* **trekked; trek·king 1** : to travel or migrate by ox wagon **2** : to make one's way arduously

¹trel·lis \'trel-əs\ *n* : a structure of latticework

²trellis *vb* : to train (as a vine) on a trellis

¹trem·ble \'trem-bəl\ *vb* **1** : to shake involuntarily (as with fear or cold) : SHIVER **2** : to move, sound, pass, or come to pass as if shaken or tremulous **3** : to be affected with fear or doubt

²tremble *n* : a spell of shaking or quivering : TREMOR

tre·men·dous \tri-'men-dəs\ *adj* **1** : fitted to excite trembling : TERRIFYING **2** : astonishingly large, powerful, or great **syn** stupendous, monumental, monstrous — **tre·men·dous·ly** *adv*

trem·o·lo \'trem-ə-,lō\ *n* : a rapid fluttering of a tone or alternating tones to produce a tremulous effect

trem·or \'trem-ər\ *n* **1** : a trembling or shaking esp. from weakness or disease **2** : a quivering motion of the earth (as during an earthquake)

trem·u·lous \'trem-yə-ləs\ *adj* **1** : marked by trembling or tremors : QUIVERING **2** : TIMOROUS, TIMID **3** : UNSTEADY ⟨~ handwriting⟩ — **trem·u·lous·ly** *adv*

¹trench \'trench\ *n* **1** : a long narrow cut in land : DITCH; *also* : a similar depression in an ocean floor **2** : a ditch protected by banks of earth and used to shelter soldiers

²trench *vb* **1** : to cut or dig trenches in; *also* : to drain by trenches **2** : to protect (troops) with trenches **3** : to come close : VERGE

tren·chant \'tren-chənt\ *adj* **1** : vigorously effective; *esp* : CAUSTIC **2** : sharply perceptive : KEEN **3** : CLEAR-CUT, DISTINCT **syn** incisive, biting, crisp

tren·cher \-chər\ *n* : a wooden platter for serving food

tren·cher·man \-mən\ *n* : a hearty eater

¹trend \'trend\ *vb* **1** : to have or take a general direction : TEND **2** : to show a tendency : INCLINE

²trend *n* **1** : general direction taken (as by a stream or mountain range) **2** : a prevailing tendency : DRIFT

tre·pan \tri-'pan\ *vb* **-panned; -panning** : to remove surgically a disk of bone from (the skull)

trep·i·da·tion \,trep-ə-'dā-shən\ *n* : nervous agitation : APPREHENSION **syn** horror, terror, panic, consternation, dread, fright, dismay

¹tres·pass \'tres-pəs, -,pas\ *n* **1** : SIN, OFFENSE **2** : wrongful entry on real property **syn** transgression, violation, infraction, infringement

²trespass *vb* **1** : to commit an offense : ERR, SIN **2** : INTRUDE, ENCROACH; *also* : to enter unlawfully upon the land of another — **tres·pass·er** *n*

tress \'tres\ *n* : a long lock of hair — usu. used in pl.

tres·tle \'tres-əl\ *n* **1** : a supporting framework consisting usu. of a horizontal piece with spreading legs at each end **2** : a braced framework of timbers, piles, or steel for carrying a road or railroad over a depression

trey \'trā\ *n* : a card or dice with three spots

tri·ad \'trī-,ad,-əd\ *n* : a union of three esp. closely related persons or things : TRINITY

¹tri·al \'trī(-ə)l\ *n* **1** : the action or process of trying or putting to the proof : TEST **2** : the hearing and judgment of a matter in issue before a competent tribunal **3** : a source of vexation or annoyance **4** : a temporary use or experiment to test quality or usefulness **5** : EFFORT, ATTEMPT **syn** proof, demonstration, tribulation, affliction

²trial *adj* **1** : of, relating to, or used in a trial **2** : made or done as a test **3** : used in a test

tri·an·gle \'trī-,aŋ-gəl\ *n* : a plane figure that is bounded by 3 straight lines and has 3 angles; *also* : something shaped like such a figure — **tri·an·gu·lar** \trī-'aŋ-gyə-lər\ *adj* — **tri·an·gu·lar·ly** *adv*

tri·an·gu·late \trī-'aŋ-gyə-,lāt\ *vb* : to divide into triangles (as in making a survey of an area) — **tri·an·gu·la·tion** \-,aŋ-gyə-'lā-shən\ *n*

tribe \'trīb\ *n* **1** : a social group comprising numerous families, clans, or generations **2** : a group of persons having a common character, occupation, or interest **3** : a group of related plants or animals ⟨the cat ~⟩ — **trib·al** \'trī-bəl\ *adj*

tribes·man \'trībz-mən\ *n* : a member of a tribe

trib·u·la·tion \,trib-yə-'lā-shən\ *n* : distress or suffering resulting from oppression or persecution; *also* : a trying experience **syn** trial, affliction

tri·bu·nal \trī-'byün-ᵊl, trib-'yün-\ *n* **1** : the seat of a judge **2** : a court of justice **3** : something that decides or determines

trib·une \'trib-,yün, trib-'yün\ *n* **1** : an official in ancient Rome with the function of protecting the interests of plebeian citizens from the patricians **2** : a defender of the people

¹trib·u·tary \'trib-yə-,ter-ē\ *adj* **1** : paying tribute : SUBJECT **2** : flowing into a larger stream or a lake **syn** subordinate, secondary, dependent

²tributary *n* **1** : a ruler or state that pays tribute **2** : a tributary stream

trib·ute \'trib-yüt\ *n* **1** : a payment

by one ruler or nation to another as acknowledgment of submission or price of protection **2** : a usu. excessive tax, rental, or levy exacted by a sovereign or superior **3** : a gift or service showing respect, gratitude, or affection; *also* : PRAISE **syn** assessment, rate, eulogy, citation

trice \'trīs\ *n* : INSTANT, MOMENT

tri·ceps \'trī-ˌseps\ *n* : a 3-headed muscle along the back of the upper arm

trich·i·no·sis \ˌtrik-ə-'nō-səs\ *n* : a disease caused by infestation of muscle tissue by small worms (**tri·chi·nae** \'trik-ˌnē\) and marked by pain, fever, and swelling

¹**trick** \'trik\ *n* **1** : a crafty procedure meant to deceive **2** : a mischievous action : PRANK **3** : a childish action **4** : a deceptive or ingenious feat designed to puzzle or amuse **5** : PECULIARITY, MANNERISM **6** : an artful expedient : KNACK **7** : the cards played in one round of a card game **8** : a tour of duty : SHIFT **syn** ruse, maneuver, artifice, wile, feint

²**trick** *vb* **1** : to deceive by cunning or artifice : CHEAT **2** : to dress ornately : ORNAMENT

trick·ery \-(ə-)rē\ *n* : deception by tricks and stratagems

trick·le \'trik-əl\ *vb* **1** : to run or fall in drops **2** : to flow in a thin gentle stream — **trickle** *n*

trick·ster \'trik-stər\ *n* : one who tricks or cheats

tricky *adj* **1** : inclined to trickery ⟨a ~ person⟩ **2** : requiring skill or caution : DELICATE ⟨a ~ situation to handle⟩ **3** : UNRELIABLE

tri·col·or \'trī-ˌkəl-ər\ *n* : a flag of three colors ⟨the French ~⟩

tri·cus·pid \trī-'kəs-pəd\ *n* : a tooth with three cusps

tri·cy·cle \'trī-ˌsik-əl\ *n* : a 3-wheeled vehicle propelled by pedals, hand levers, or motor

tri·dent \'trīd-ənt\ *n* [L *trident-, tridens*, fr. *tres* three + *dent-, dens* tooth] : a 3-pronged spear

tried \'trīd\ *adj* **1** : found trustworthy through testing **2** : subjected to trials **syn** reliable, dependable, trusty

tri·en·ni·al \trī-'en-ē-əl\ *adj* **1** : lasting for three years **2** : occurring or being done every three years — **triennial** *n*

¹**tri·fle** \'trī-fəl\ *n* : something of little value or importance; *esp* : an insignificant amount (as of money)

²**trifle** *vb* **1** : to talk in a jesting or mocking manner **2** : to act frivolously or playfully **3** : DALLY, FLIRT **4** : to handle something idly : TOY — **tri·fler** \-f(ə-)lər\ *n*

tri·fling \-f(ə-)liŋ\ *adj* **1** : FRIVOLOUS **2** : TRIVIAL, INSIGNIFICANT **syn** petty, paltry

tri·fo·cals \trī-'fō-kəlz\ *n pl* : eyeglasses with lenses having one part for close focus, one for intermediate focus, and one for distant focus

trig \'trig\ *adj* : stylishly trim : SMART **syn** tidy, spruce

¹**trig·ger** \'trig-ər\ *n* : the part of a firearm lock moved by the finger to release the hammer in firing

²**trigger** *vb* **1** : to fire by pulling a trigger

2 : to initiate, actuate, or set off as if by a trigger

trig·o·nom·e·try \ˌtrig-ə-'näm-ə-trē\ *n* : the branch of mathematics dealing with the relations of the sides and angles of triangles and of methods of deducing from given parts other required parts — **trig·o·no·met·ric** \-nə-'met-rik\ *or* **trig·o·no·met·ri·cal** *adj*

¹**trill** \'tril\ *n* **1** : the alternation of two musical tones a scale degree apart **2** : WARBLE **3** : the rapid vibration of one speech organ against another (as of the tip of the tongue against the ridge of the teeth)

²**trill** *vb* : to utter as or with a trill

tril·lion \'tril-yən\ *n, pl* **trillions** *or* **trillion** **1** : a thousand billions **2** *Brit* : a million billions — **trillion** *adj* — **tril·lionth** *adj or n*

tril·o·gy \'tril-ə-jē\ *n* : a series of three dramas or literary or musical compositions that although each is complete in itself are mutually related and develop one theme

¹**trim** \'trim\ *vb* **trimmed; trim·ming** **1** : to put ornaments on : ADORN **2** : to defeat esp. resoundingly **3** : CHEAT **4** : to make trim, neat, regular, or less bulky by or as if by cutting ⟨~ a beard⟩ ⟨~ a budget⟩ **5** : to cause (a boat) to assume a desired position in the water by arrangement of ballast, cargo, or passengers; *also* : to adjust (as a submarine or airplane) for motion and esp. for horizontal motion **6** : to adjust (a sail) to a desired position **7** : to change one's views for safety or expediency **syn** stabilize, steady, poise, balance, ballast — **trim·ly** *adv* — **trim·mer** *n* — **trim·ness** *n*

²**trim** *adj* : showing neatness, good order, or compactness ⟨~ houses⟩ ⟨~ figure⟩ **syn** tidy, trig

³**trim** *n* **1** : the readiness of a ship for sailing; *also* : the position of a ship in the water **2** : good condition : FITNESS **3** : material used for ornament or trimming; *esp* : the woodwork in the finish of a house esp. around doors and windows **4** : something that is trimmed off

trim·e·ter \'trim-ət-ər\ *n* : a line consisting of three metrical feet

trine \'trīn\ *adj* : THREEFOLD, TRIPLE

Trin·i·tar·i·an \ˌtrin-ə-'ter-ē-ən\ *n* : a believer in the doctrine of the Trinity — **Trin·i·tar·i·an·ism** *n*

trin·i·ty \'trin-ət-ē\ *n* **1** *cap* : the unity of Father, Son, and Holy Spirit as three persons in one godhead **2** : a union of three in one : TRIAD

trin·ket \'triŋ-kət\ *n* **1** : a small ornament (as a jewel or ring) **2** : TRIFLE

trio \'trē-ō\ *n* **1** : a musical composition for three voices or three instruments **2** : the performers of a musical or dance trio **3** : a group or set of three

¹**trip** \'trip\ *vb* **tripped; trip·ping** **1** : to move with light quick steps **2** : to catch the foot against something so as to stumble or cause to stumble **3** : to make a mistake : SLIP; *also* : to detect in a misstep : EXPOSE **4** : to release (as a spring or switch) by moving a catch; *also* : ACTIVATE

²**trip** *n* **1** : JOURNEY, VOYAGE **2** : a quick light step **3** : a false step : STUMBLE; *also* : ERROR **4** : the action of tripping

---

ə abut; ᵊ kitten; ᵊr further; a back; ā bake; ä cot, cart; aů out; ch chin; e less; ē easy; g gift; i trip; I life; j joke; ŋ sing; ō flow; ȯ flaw; ȯi coin; th thin; t͟h this; ü loot; ů foot; y yet; yü few; yů furious; zh vision

mechanically; *also* **:** a device for tripping

tri·par·tite \\trī-'pär-,tīt\ *adj* **1 :** divided into three parts **2 :** having three corresponding parts or copies **3 :** made between three parties ⟨a ~ treaty⟩

tripe \'trīp\ *n* **:** stomach tissue of a ruminant and esp. an ox for use as food

¹tri·ple \'trip-əl\ *vb* **1 :** to make or become three times as great or as many **2 :** to hit a triple

²triple *n* **1 :** a triple quantity **2 :** a group of three **3 :** a hit in baseball that enables the batter to reach third base

³triple *adj* **1 :** having three units or members **2 :** being three times as great or as many **3 :** three times repeated

trip·let \'trip-lət\ *n* **1 :** a unit of three lines of verse **2 :** a group of three of a kind **3** *pl* **:** three offspring born at one birth

trip·lex \'trip-,leks, 'trīp-\ *adj* **:** THREEFOLD, TRIPLE

¹trip·li·cate \'trip-li-kət\ *adj* **:** made in three identical copies

²trip·li·cate \-ə-,kāt\ *vb* **1 :** TRIPLE **2 :** to provide three copies of ⟨~ a document⟩

³trip·li·cate \-li-kət\ *n* **:** one of three identical copies

tri·pod \'trī-,päd\ *n* **:** something (as a caldron, stool, or camera stand) that rests on three legs

trip·tych \'trip-tik\ *n* **:** a picture or carving (as an altarpiece) in three panels side by side

tri·reme \'trī-,rēm\ *n* **:** an ancient galley having three banks of oars

tri·sect \'trī-,sekt\ *vb* **:** to divide into 3 usu. equal parts

trite \'trīt\ *adj* [L *tritus,* fr. pp. of *terere* to rub, wear away] **:** used so commonly that the novelty is worn off **:** STALE **syn** hackneyed, stereotyped, commonplace

trit·i·um \'trit-ē-əm\ *n* **:** a radioactive form of hydrogen with atoms of three times the mass of ordinary hydrogen atoms

trit·u·rate \'trich-ə-,rāt\ *vb* **:** to rub or grind to a fine powder

¹tri·umph \'trī-əmf\ *n* **1 :** the joy or exultation of victory or success **2 :** VICTORY, CONQUEST — **tri·um·phal** \trī-'əm-fəl\ *adj*

²triumph *vb* **1 :** to celebrate victory or success exultantly **2 :** to obtain victory **:** PREVAIL — **tri·um·phant** \trī-'əm-fənt\ *adj* — **tri·um·phant·ly** *adv*

tri·um·vir \trī-'əm-vər\ *n* **:** one of a commission or ruling body (**tri·um·vi·rate** \-ə-rət\) of three

tri·une \'trī-,(y)ün\ *adj* **:** being three in one (the ~ God)

triv·et \'triv-ət\ *n* **1 :** a 3-legged stand **:** TRIPOD **2 :** a metal stand with short feet for use under a hot dish

triv·i·al \'triv-ē-əl\ *adj* [L *trivialis* commonplace, fr. *trivium* meeting of three roads, street corner, fr. *tres* three + *via* way, road] **:** of little importance **:** TRIFLING — **triv·i·al·i·ty** \,triv-ē-'al-ət-ē\ *n*

triv·i·um \'triv-ē-əm\ *n* **:** the three liberal arts of grammar, rhetoric, and logic in a medieval university

tro·che \'trō-kē\ *n* **:** a medicinal lozenge

tro·chee \'trō-,kē\ *n* **:** a metrical foot of one accented syllable followed by one unaccented syllable — **tro·cha·ic** \trō-'kā-ik\ *adj*

trod *past of* TREAD

trodden *past part of* TREAD

¹troll \'trōl\ *vb* **1 :** to sing the parts of (a song) in succession **2 :** to angle for with a hook and line drawn through the water **3 :** to sing or play in a jovial manner

²troll *n* **:** a lure used in trolling; *also* **:** the line with its lure

³troll *n* **:** a supernatural being of Teutonic folklore inhabiting caves or hills

trol·ley *or* **trol·ly** \'träl-ē\ *n* **1 :** a device (as a grooved wheel on the end of a pole) to carry current from a wire to an electrically driven vehicle **2 :** a passenger car that runs on tracks and gets its electric power through a trolley **3 :** a wheeled carriage running on an overhead rail or track (as on a parcel railway in a store)

trolley bus *n* **:** a bus powered by electric power from two overhead wires

trol·lop \'träl-əp\ *n* **1 :** a slovenly woman **:** SLATTERN **2 :** a loose woman **:** WANTON

trom·bone \träm-'bōn\ *n* [It, lit., fr. *tromba* trumpet] **:** a brass wind instrument that consists of a long metal tube bent twice upon itself and flaring at the end and that has a movable slide to vary the pitch

¹troop \'trüp\ *n* **1 :** a cavalry unit corresponding to an infantry company **2 :** an armed force **:** SOLDIERS — usu. used in pl. **3 :** a collection of people or things **4 :** a unit of boy or girl scouts under a leader **syn** band, troupe, party

²troop *vb* **:** to move or gather in crowds or groups

troop·er *n* **1 :** an enlisted cavalryman; *also* **:** a cavalry horse **2 :** a mounted policeman

troop·ship \'trüp-,ship\ *n* **:** a ship for carrying troops

trope \'trōp\ *n* **:** the use of a word or expression in a figurative sense

tro·phy \'trō-fē\ *n* **:** something gained or given in conquest or victory esp. when mounted as a memorial

trop·ic \'träp-ik\ *n* [Gk *tropikos* of the solstice, fr. *tropē* turn] **1 :** either of the two parallels of latitude one 23° 27′ north of the equator (**tropic of Can·cer** \-'kan-sər\) and one 23° 27′ south of the equator (**tropic of Cap·ri·corn** \-'kap-rə-,kȯrn\) where the sun is directly overhead when apparently at its greatest distance north or south of the equator **2** *pl, often cap* **:** the region lying between the tropics of Cancer and Capricorn — **trop·ic** *or* **trop·i·cal** *adj*

tro·po·sphere \'trōp-ə-,sfiər, 'träp-\ *n* **:** the portion of the atmosphere that is below the stratosphere and extends outward about 10 miles from the earth's surface

¹trot \'trät\ *n* **1 :** a moderately fast gait of a 4-footed animal (as a horse) in which the legs move in diagonal pairs **2 :** a jogging gait of a man between a walk and a run

²trot *vb* **trot·ted; trot·ting 1 :** to ride, drive, or go at a trot **2 :** to proceed briskly **:** HURRY — **trot·ter** *n*

troth \'trȯth, 'trōth\ *n* **1 :** pledged faithfulness **:** FIDELITY **2 :** one's pledged word; *also* **:** BETROTHAL

trou·ba·dour \'trü-bə-,dȯr\ *n* **:** one of a class of poet-musicians flourishing esp. in southern France and northern Italy during the 11th, 12th, and 13th centuries

¹trou·ble \'trəb-əl\ vb 1 : to agitate mentally or spiritually : DISTURB, WORRY 2 : to produce physical disorder in : AFFLICT 3 : to put to inconvenience 4 : to make an effort 5 : RUFFLE ⟨~ the waters⟩ syn distress, discommode, molest — trou·ble·some adj — trou·ble·some·ly adv — trou·blous \-(ə-)ləs\ adj

²trouble n 1 : the quality or state of being troubled : MISFORTUNE 2 : an instance of distress or annoyance 3 : a cause of disturbance or distress 4 : EXERTION, PAINS ⟨took the ~ to phone⟩ 5 : ill health : AILMENT

trou·ble·mak·er \-,mā-kər\ n : a person who causes dissension

trough \'trof\ n 1 : a long shallow open boxlike container esp. for water or feed for livestock 2 : a gutter along the eaves of a house 3 : a long channel or depression (as between waves or hills)

trounce \'traúns\ vb 1 : to thrash or punish severely 2 : to defeat decisively

troupe \'trüp\ n : COMPANY; esp : a group of performers on the stage — troup·er n

trou·sers \'traú-zərz\ n pl : an outer garment extending from the waist to the ankle or sometimes only to the knee, covering each leg separately, and worn esp. by men and boys — trouser adj

trous·seau \'trü-sō, trü-'sō\ n : the personal outfit of a bride

trout \'traút\ n, pl trout also trouts : any of various mostly freshwater food and game fishes usu. smaller than the related salmons

trow \'trō\ vb, archaic : THINK, SUPPOSE

trow·el \'traú(-ə)l\ n 1 : any of various hand implements used for spreading, shaping, or smoothing loose or plastic material (as mortar or plaster) 2 : a small flat or scooplike implement used in gardening

troy \'troi\ adj : of or relating to a system of weights (troy weights) based on a pound of 12 ounces and one ounce of 480 grains

tru·ant \'trü-ənt\ n : one who shirks duty; esp : one who stays out of school without permission — tru·an·cy n

truce \'trüs\ n 1 : ARMISTICE 2 : a respite esp. from a disagreeable state or action

¹truck \'trək\ vb 1 : EXCHANGE, BARTER 2 : to have dealings : TRAFFIC

²truck n 1 : BARTER 2 : small goods or merchandise; esp : vegetables grown for market 3 : close association : DEALINGS

³truck n 1 : a vehicle (as a small flat-topped car on small wheels, a 2-wheeled barrow with long handles, or a strong heavy wagon or automobile) designed for carrying heavy articles 2 : a swiveling frame with springs and one or more pairs of wheels used to carry and guide one end of a locomotive or of a railroad or electric car

⁴truck vb 1 : to transport on a truck 2 : to be employed in driving a truck — truck·er n

truck·age n : transportation by truck; also : the cost of such transportation

¹truck·le \'trək-əl\ n : a small wheel : PULLEY, CASTER

²truckle vb : to yield slavishly to the

will of another : SUBMIT   syn fawn, toady, cringe, cower

truckle bed n : TRUNDLE BED

truck·load \'trək-'lōd\ n 1 : a load that fills a truck 2 : the minimum weight required for shipping at truck-load rates

truck-trail·er n : a combination of a trailer and the truck that draws it

truc·u·lent \'trək-yə-lənt\ adj 1 : feeling or showing ferocity : SAVAGE 2 : aggressively self-assertive : PUGNACIOUS — truc·u·lence also truc·u·len·cy n — truc·u·lent·ly adv

trudge \'trəj\ vb 1 : to walk or march steadily and usu. laboriously

¹true \'trü\ adj 1 : STEADFAST, LOYAL 2 : conformable to fact or reality ⟨a ~ description⟩ 3 : CORRECT, ACCURATE; also : placed or formed accurately 4 : GENUINE, REAL; also : properly so called ⟨the ~ stomach⟩ 5 : CONSISTENT ⟨~ to expectations⟩ 6 : RIGHTFUL ⟨~ and lawful king⟩ syn constant, staunch, resolute, actual — tru·ly adv

²true n 1 : something that is true : REALITY ⟨the good, the beautiful, and the ~⟩ 2 : the state of being accurate (as in alignment) ⟨out of ~⟩

³true vb trued; tru·ing also tru·ing : to bring to exactly correct condition as to place, position, or shape

⁴true adv 1 : TRUTHFULLY 2 : ACCURATELY ⟨the bullet flew straight and ~⟩; also : without variation from type ⟨breed ~⟩

true-blue adj : marked by unswerving loyalty

truf·fle \'trəf-əl, 'trüf-\ n : a European underground fungus or its dark wrinkled fruit esteemed as a delicacy

tru·ism \'trü-,iz-əm\ n : an undoubted or self-evident truth syn commonplace, platitude, bromide, cliché

¹trump \'trəmp\ n : TRUMPET

²trump n : a card of a suit designated (as by declaration) any of whose cards will win over a card that is not a trump; also : the suit itself — often used in pl.

³trump vb : to take with a trump

trum·pery \'trəm-p(ə-)rē\ n 1 : trivial articles : JUNK 2 : NONSENSE

¹trum·pet \'trəm-pət\ n 1 : a wind instrument consisting of a long curved metal tube flaring at one end and with a cup-shaped mouthpiece at the other 2 : a funnel-shaped instrument for collecting, directing, or intensifying sound 3 : something that resembles a trumpet or its tonal quality

²trumpet vb 1 : to blow a trumpet 2 : to proclaim on or as if on a trumpet — trum·pet·er n

¹trun·cate \'trəŋ-,kāt\ vb : to shorten by or as if by cutting : LOP — trun·ca·tion \,trəŋ-'kā-shən\ n

²truncate adj : having the end square or blunt

trun·cheon \'trən-chən\ n : a policeman's club

trun·dle \'trən-d'l\ vb : to roll along : WHEEL

trundle bed n : a low bed that can be slid under a higher bed

¹trunk \'trəŋk\ n 1 : the main stem of a tree 2 : the body of a man or animal apart from the head and limbs 3 : the main or basal part of something 4 : the

ə abut; ⁰ kitten; ər further; a back; ā bake; ä cot, cart; aú out; ch chin; e less; ē easy; g gift; i trip; ī life; j joke; ŋ sing; ō flow; ò flaw; òi coin; th thin; tẖ this; ü loot; ú foot; y yet; yü few; yú furious; zh vision

long muscular nose of an elephant **5** : a box or chest used to hold usu. clothes or personal effects (as of a traveler); *also* : the enclosed luggage space in the rear of an automobile **6** *pl* : men's shorts worn chiefly for sports **7** : a passage or duct serving as a conduit or conveyor **8** : a circuit between telephone exchanges for making connections between subscribers

²**trunk** *adj* : being or relating to a main line (as of a railroad, telegraph, or telephone system)

¹**truss** \'trəs\ *vb* **1** : to secure tightly : BIND **2** : to arrange for cooking by binding close the wings or legs of (a fowl) **3** : to support by a truss : strengthen or stiffen (as a girder) by braces

²**truss** *n* **1** : a collection of structural parts (as beams, bars, or rods) so put together as to form a rigid framework (as in bridge or building construction) **2** : an appliance worn to hold a hernia in place

¹**trust** \'trəst\ *n* **1** : assured reliance on the character, strength, or truth of someone or something **2** : one in which confidence is placed **3** : confident hope **4** : financial credit **5** : a property interest held by one person for the benefit of another **6** : a combination of firms formed by a legal agreement; *esp* : one that reduces competition **7** : something entrusted to one to be cared for in the interest of another **8** : CARE, CUSTODY **syn** confidence, dependence, faith, monopoly, corner, pool

²**trust** *vb* **1** : to place confidence : DEPEND **2** : to be confident : expect confidently : HOPE **3** : ENTRUST **4** : to permit to stay or go or to act without fear or misgiving **5** : to rely on or on the truth of : BELIEVE **6** : to extend credit to

trust-ee \ˌtrəs-'tē\ *n* : a person to whom property is legally committed in trust

trust-ful \'trəst-fəl\ *adj* : full of trust : CONFIDING — **trust-ful-ly** *adv* — **trust-ful-ness** *n*

trust-wor-thy \-ˌwər-thē\ *adj* : worthy of confidence : DEPENDABLE **syn** trusty, tried, reliable — **trust-wor-thi-ness** *n*

¹**trusty** *adj* : TRUSTWORTHY, DEPENDABLE

²**trusty** *n* : a trusted person; *esp* : a convict considered trustworthy and allowed special privileges

truth \'trüth\ *n* **1** : TRUTHFULNESS, HONESTY **2** : the state of being true : FACT **3** : the body of real events or facts : ACTUALITY **4** : a true or accepted statement or proposition **5** : agreement with fact or reality : CORRECTNESS **syn** veracity, verity, verisimilitude

truth-ful *adj* : telling or disposed to tell the truth — **truth-ful-ly** *adv* — **truth-ful-ness** *n*

¹**try** \'trī\ *vb* **tried; try-ing 1** : to examine or investigate judicially **2** : to conduct the trial of **3** : to put to test or trial 〈*tried* on several dresses〉 **4** : to subject to strain, affliction, or annoyance **5** : to extract or clarify (as lard) by melting **6** : to make an effort to do something : ATTEMPT, ENDEAVOR **syn** essay, assay, strive, struggle

²**try** *n* : an experimental trial : ATTEMPT

try-ing *adj* : severely straining the powers of endurance

tryst \'trist, 'trīst\ *n* : an agreement (as between lovers) to meet; *also* : an appointed place of meeting **syn** rendezvous, engagement

tsar \'zär, '(t)sär\ *var of* CZAR

tub \'təb\ *n* **1** : a wide low bucketlike vessel **2** : BATHTUB; *also* : BATH **3** : the amount that a tub will hold

tu-ba \'t(y)üb\ *n* : a large low-pitched brass wind instrument

tube \'t(y)üb\ *n* **1** : a hollow cylinder to convey fluids : CHANNEL, DUCT **2** : any of various usu. cylindrical structures or devices **3** : a round metal container from which a paste is squeezed **4** : a tunnel for vehicular or rail travel — **tube-less** *adj*

tu-ber \'t(y)ü-bər\ *n* : a short fleshy usu. underground stem (as of a potato plant) bearing minute scalelike leaves each with a bud at its base

tu-ber-cle \-kəl\ *n* **1** : a small knobby prominence or outgrowth esp. on an animal or plant **2** : a small abnormal lump in an organ or the skin; *esp* : one caused by tuberculosis

tu-ber-cu-lar \t(y)u̇-'bər-kyə-lər\ *adj* **1** : of, resembling, or being a tubercle **2** : TUBERCULATE 1 **3** : TUBERCULOUS

tu-ber-cu-late \-lət\ *adj* **1** : having or covered with tubercles **2** : TUBERCULAR 1

tu-ber-cu-lo-sis \t(y)u̇-ˌbər-kyə-'lō-səs\ *n* : a communicable bacterial disease typically marked by wasting, fever, and formation of cheesy tubercles often in the lungs — **tu-ber-cu-lous** \-'bər-kyə-ləs\ *adj*

tube-rose \'t(y)üb-ˌrōz\ *n* : a bulbous herb related to the amaryllis and often grown for its spike of fragrant waxy-white flowers

tu-ber-ous \'t(y)ü-b(ə-)rəs\ *adj* : of, resembling, or being a plant tuber

tub-ing \'t(y)ü-biŋ\ *n* **1** : material in the form of a tube; *also* : a length of tube **2** : a series of tubes

tu-bu-lar \'t(y)ü)b-lər\ *adj* : having the form of or consisting of a tube; *also* : made with tubes

tu-bule \'t(y)ü-byül\ *n* : a small tube

¹**tuck** \'tək\ *vb* **1** : to pull up into a fold 〈~ed up her skirt〉 **2** : to make tucks in **3** : to put into a snug often concealing place 〈~ a book under the arm〉 **4** : to secure in place by pushing the edges under 〈~ in a blanket〉 **5** : to cover by tucking in bedclothes

²**tuck** *n* : a fold stitched into cloth to shorten, decorate, or control fullness

tuck-er \'tək-ər\ *vb* : EXHAUST, FATIGUE

Tues-day \'t(y)üz-dē\ *n* : the 3d day of the week

tu-fa \'t(y)ü-fə\ *n* : a porous rock formed as a deposit from springs or streams

¹**tuft** \'təft\ *n* **1** : a small cluster of long flexible outgrowths (as hairs or feathers); *also* : a bunch of soft fluffy threads cut off short and used as ornament **2** : CLUMP, CLUSTER

²**tuft** *vb* **1** : to provide or adorn with a tuft **2** : to make (as a mattress) firm by stitching at intervals and sewing on tufts

¹**tug** \'təg\ *vb* **tugged; tug-ging 1** : to pull hard **2** : to struggle in opposition : CONTEND **3** : to move by pulling hard : HAUL **4** : to tow with a tugboat

²**tug** *n* **1** : a harness trace **2** : an act of tugging : PULL **3** : a straining effort **4** : a struggle between opposing people or forces **5** : a strongly built boat used for towing or pushing

tug-boat \'təg-ˌbōt\ *n* : TUG

tug-of-war *n*, *pl* **tugs-of-war 1** : a

struggle for supremacy **2** : an athletic contest in which two teams pull against each other at opposite ends of a rope

tu·i·tion \t(y)ù-'ish-ən\ *n* **1** : INSTRUCTION **2** : the price of or payment for instruction

tu·lip \'t(y)ü-ləp\ *n* [NL *tulipa*, fr. Turk *tülbend* turban] : any of various Old World bulbous herbs related to the lilies and grown for their large showy erect cup-shaped flowers; *also* : a flower or bulb of a tulip

tulip tree *n* : a tall American timber tree with greenish tuliplike flowers and soft white wood

tulle \'tül\ *n* : a sheer silk, rayon, or nylon net ⟨a bridal veil of ∼⟩

tum·ble \'təm-bəl\ *vb* **1** : to perform gymnastic feats of rolling and turning **2** : to fall or cause to fall suddenly and helplessly **3** : to fall into ruin : COLLAPSE **4** : to roll over and over : TOSS **5** : to issue forth hurriedly and confusedly **6** : to come to understand : catch on **7** : to throw together in a confused mass

2tumble *n* **1** : a disorderly state **2** : an act or instance of tumbling

tum·ble·down \-,daún\ *adj* : DILAPIDATED, RAMSHACKLE

tum·bler \'təm-blər\ *n* **1** : one that tumbles; *esp* : ACROBAT **2** : a drinking glass without foot or stem **3** : a domestic pigeon having the habit of somersaulting backward in flight **4** : a movable obstruction in a lock that must be adjusted to a particular position (as by a key) before the bolt can be thrown

tum·ble·weed \'təm-bəl-,wēd\ *n* : a plant that breaks away from its roots in autumn and is driven about by the wind

tum·brel *or* **tum·bril** \'təm-brəl\ *n* **1** : CART **2** : a vehicle carrying condemned persons (as political prisoners during the French Revolution) to a place of execution

tu·mid \'t(y)ü-məd\ *adj* **1** : SWOLLEN, DISTENDED **2** : BOMBASTIC, TURGID — **tu·mid·i·ty** \t(y)ü-'mid-ət-ē\ *n*

tu·mor \'t(y)ü-mər\ *n* : an abnormal and functionless mass of tissue that is not inflammatory and arises without obvious cause from preexistent tissue — **tu·mor·ous** *adj*

tu·mult \'t(y)ü-,məlt\ *n* **1** : disorderly agitation of a crowd usu. with uproar and confusion of voices **2** : DISTURBANCE, RIOT **3** : a confusion of loud noise and usu. turbulent movement **4** : violent agitation of mind or feelings

tu·mul·tu·ous \t(y)ü-'məl-chə-wəs\ *adj* **1** : marked by tumult ⟨a ∼ reception⟩ **2** : tending to incite a tumult ⟨a ∼ faction⟩ **3** : marked by violent upheaval ⟨∼ passions⟩

tun \'tən\ *n* **1** : a large cask **2** : the capacity of a tun; *esp* : a unit of 252 gallons

tu·na \'t(y)ü-nə\ *n* : any of several mostly large sea fishes related to the mackerels and important for food and sport

tun·able *also* **tune·able** \'t(y)ü-nə-bəl\ *adj* : capable of being tuned

tun·dra \'tən-drə\ *n* : a treeless plain of northern arctic regions

1tune \'t(y)ün\ *n* **1** : an easily remembered melody **2** : correct musical pitch **3** : harmonious relationship : AGREEMENT ⟨in ∼ with the times⟩ **4** : general attitude ⟨changed his ∼⟩ **5** : AMOUNT, EXTENT ⟨in debt to the ∼ of millions⟩

2tune *vb* **1** : to bring or come into harmony : ATTUNE **2** : to adjust in musical pitch **3** : to adjust a radio or television receiver so as to receive a broadcast **4** : to put in first-class working order ⟨∼ up a motor⟩ — **tun·er** *n*

tune·ful *adj* : MELODIOUS, MUSICAL — **tune·ful·ly** *adv*

tune·less *adj* **1** : UNMELODIOUS **2** : not producing music

tune-up \'t(y)ün-,əp\ *n* : an adjustment to ensure efficient functioning ⟨a motor ∼⟩

tung·sten \'təŋ-stən\ *n* : a white hard heavy ductile metallic element used for electrical purposes and in an alloy (**tungsten steel**) noted for its strength and hardness

tu·nic \'t(y)ü-nik\ *n* **1** : a usu. knee-length belted under or outer garment worn by ancient Greeks and Romans **2** : a hip-length or longer blouse or jacket

tuning fork *n* : a 2-pronged metal implement that gives a fixed tone when struck and is useful for tuning musical instruments

Tu·ni·sian \t(y)ü-'nēzh-ən, -'nizh-\ *n* : a native or inhabitant of Tunisia — **Tunisian** *adj*

1tun·nel \'tən-ºl\ *n* : an underground passageway excavated esp. for a road, railroad, water system, or sewer; *also* : a horizontal passage in a mine

2tunnel *vb* **-neled** *or* **-nelled**; **-nel·ing** *or* **-nel·ling** : to make a tunnel through or under

tun·ny \'tən-ē\ *n* : TUNA

tuque \'t(y)ük\ *n* : a warm knitted cone-shaped cap with a tassel or pompon worn esp. for winter sports or play

tur·ban \'tər-bən\ *n* **1** : a headdress worn esp. by Muslims and made of a cap around which is wound a long cloth **2** : a headdress resembling a Muslim turban; *esp* : a woman's close-fitting hat without a brim

tur·bid \'tər-bəd\ *adj* **1** : thick with roiled sediment ⟨a ∼ stream⟩ **2** : heavy with smoke or mist : DENSE **3** : CONFUSED, MUDDLED

tur·bine \'tər-bən\ *n* : an engine whose central driving shaft is fitted with curved vanes whirled by the pressure of water, steam, or gas

tur·bo·jet \'tər-bō-,jet\ *n* : an airplane powered by a jet engine (**turbojet engine**) having a turbine-driven air compressor supplying compressed air to the combustion chamber

tur·bo·prop \-,präp\ *n* : an airplane powered by a jet engine (**turbo-propeller engine**) having a turbine-driven propeller but usu. obtaining additional thrust from the discharge of a jet of hot gases

tur·bot \'tər-bət\ *n* : a European flatfish esteemed as food; *also* : any of several flatfishes resembling this

tur·bu·lence \'tər-byə-ləns\ *n* : the quality or state of being turbulent **:** violent agitation **:** COMMOTION

tur·bu·lent *adj* **1 :** causing violence or disturbance **2 :** marked by agitation or tumult **:** TEMPESTUOUS — **tur·bu·lent·ly** *adv*

tu·reen \t(y)ù-'rēn\ *n* **:** a deep bowl from which foods (as soup) are served at table

¹**turf** \'tərf\ *n, pl* **turfs** *or* **turves** \'tərvz\ **1 :** the upper layer of soil bound by grass and roots into a close mat; *also* **:** a piece of this **:** SOD **2 :** a piece of peat dried for fuel **3 :** a track or course for horse racing; *also* **:** horse racing as a sport or business

²**turf** *vb* **:** to cover with turf

tur·gid \'tər-jəd\ *adj* **1 :** marked by distention **:** SWOLLEN **2 :** excessively embellished in style or language **:** BOMBASTIC — **tur·gid·i·ty** \,tər-'jid-ət-ē\ *n*

Turk \'tərk\ *n* **:** a native or inhabitant of Turkey

tur·key \'tər-kē\ *n* **:** a large American bird related to the common fowl and widely raised for food; *also* **:** either of these plants

turkey buzzard *n* **:** BUZZARD 2

Turk·ish *n* **:** the language of Turkey — **Turkish** *adj*

tur·moil \'tər-,moil\ *n* **:** an extremely confused or agitated condition

¹**turn** \'tərn\ *vb* **1 :** to move or cause to move around an axis or center **:** ROTATE, REVOLVE ⟨~ a wheel⟩ **2 :** to twist so as to effect a desired end ⟨~ a key⟩ **3 :** WRENCH ⟨~ an ankle⟩ **4 :** to change or cause to change position by moving through an arc of a circle ⟨~ed his chair to the fire⟩ **5 :** to cause to move around a center so as to show another side of ⟨~ a page⟩ **6 :** to revolve mentally **:** PONDER **7 :** to become dizzy **:** REEL **8 :** to reverse the sides or surfaces of ⟨~ a pancake⟩ **9 :** UPSET, DISORDER ⟨things ~ed topsy-turvy⟩ ⟨~ed his stomach⟩ **10 :** to set in another esp. contrary direction **11 :** to change one's course or direction **12 :** TRANSFER ⟨~ the task over to him⟩ **13 :** to go around ⟨~ a corner⟩ **14 :** to reach or pass beyond ⟨~ed twenty-one⟩ **15 :** to direct toward or away from something; *also* **:** DEVOTE, APPLY **16 :** to have recourse **:** RESORT ⟨~ to an agency for help⟩ **17 :** to become or make hostile **18 :** to make or become spoiled **:** SOUR **19 :** to cause to become of a specified nature or appearance ⟨~s the leaves yellow⟩ **20 :** to pass from one state to another ⟨water ~s to ice⟩ **21 :** CONVERT, TRANSFORM **22 :** TRANSLATE, PARAPHRASE **23 :** to give a rounded form to; *esp* **:** to shape by means of a lathe **24 :** to gain by passing in trade ⟨~ a quick profit⟩

²**turn** *n* **1 :** a turning about a center or axis **:** REVOLUTION, ROTATION **2 :** the action or an act of giving or taking a different direction ⟨make a left ~⟩ **3 :** a change of course or tendency ⟨a ~ for the better⟩ **4 :** a place at which something turns **:** BEND, CURVE **5 :** a short walk or trip round about ⟨take a ~ around the deck⟩ **6 :** an act affecting another ⟨did him a good ~⟩ **7 :** a place, time, or opportunity accorded in a scheduled order ⟨waited his ~ to be served⟩ **8 :** a period of duty **:** SHIFT **9 :** a short act esp. in a variety show **10 :** a special purpose or requirement ⟨the job serves his ~⟩ **11 :** a skillful fashioning ⟨neat ~ of phrase⟩ **12 :** a

single round (as of rope passed around an object) **13 :** natural or special aptitude **:** BENT **14 :** a usu. sudden and brief disorder of body or spirits; *esp* **:** a spell of nervous shock or faintness

turn·buck·le \'tərn-,bək-əl\ *n* **:** a link with a screw thread at one or both ends for tightening a rod or stay

turn·coat \-,kōt\ *n* **:** one who forsakes his party or principles **:** RENEGADE

turn·er *n* **1 :** one that turns or is used for turning **2 :** one that forms articles with a lathe

turn·ery \'tər-nə-rē\ *n* **:** the work, products, or shop of a turner

turn in *vb* **1 :** to deliver up **2 :** to inform on **3 :** to acquit oneself of ⟨*turn in* a good job⟩ **4 :** to go to bed

turn·ing *n* **1 :** the act or course of one that turns **2 :** a place of a change of direction

tur·nip \'tər-nəp\ *n* **:** the thick edible root of either of two herbs related to the mustards; *also* **:** either of these plants

turn·key \'tərn-,kē\ *n* **:** one who has charge of a prison's keys **:** JAILER

turn out \'tərn-'aùt\ *vb* **1 :** EXPEL, EVICT **2 :** PRODUCE **3 :** to come forth and assemble ⟨*turn out* for drill⟩ **4 :** to get out of bed **5 :** to prove to be in the end

turn·out \'tərn-,aùt\ *n* **1 :** an act of turning out **2 :** a gathering of people for a special purpose **3 :** a widened place in a highway for vehicles to pass or park **4 :** manner of dress **5 :** net yield **:** OUTPUT

¹**turn·over** \-,ō-vər\ *n* **1 :** UPSET **2 :** SHIFT, REVERSAL **3 :** a filled pastry made by turning half of the crust over the other half **4 :** the volume of business done **5 :** movement (as of goods or people) into, through, and out of a place; *esp* **:** a cycle of purchase, sale, and replacement of a stock of goods **6 :** the number of persons hired within a period to replace those leaving or dropped; *also* **:** the ratio of this number to that of the average force maintained

²**turnover** *adj* **:** capable of being turned over

turn·pike \'tərn-,pīk\ *n* **1 :** TOLLGATE; *also* **:** a road having a tollgate **2 :** a main road

turn·spit \-,spit\ *n* **:** a device for turning a spit

turn·stile \-,stīl\ *n* **1 :** a post with four arms pivoted on the top set in a passageway so that persons can pass through but cattle cannot **2 :** a similar device set in an entrance for controlling or counting the persons entering

turn·ta·ble \-,tā-bəl\ *n* **:** a circular platform that revolves (as for turning a locomotive or a phonograph record)

turn up *vb* **1 :** to come to light or bring to light **:** DISCOVER, APPEAR **2 :** to arrive at an appointed time or place **3 :** to happen unexpectedly

tur·pen·tine \'tər-pən-,tīn\ *n* **1 :** a mixture of oil and resin obtained from various cone-bearing trees (as pines) as a substance that oozes from cuts in the trunk **2 :** a colorless or yellowish oil obtained from various turpentines by distillation and used as a solvent and thinner (as in paint); *also* **:** a similar oil obtained from distillation of pine wood

tur·pi·tude \'tər-pə-,t(y)üd\ *n* **:** inherent baseness **:** DEPRAVITY

tur·quoise \'tər-,k(w)óiz\ *n* **1 :** a blue,

bluish green, or greenish gray mineral that contains a little copper and is valued as a gem **2 :** a light greenish blue color

tur·ret \'tər-ət\ *n* **1 :** a little tower often at an angle of a larger structure and merely ornamental **2 :** a revolable holder in a machine tool **3 :** a tower-like armored and usu. revolving structure within which guns are mounted in a warship or tank; *also* **:** a similar structure in an airplane

¹**tur·tle** \'tərt-ᵊl\ *n, archaic* **:** TURTLE-DOVE

²**turtle** *n* **:** any of a group of horny-beaked land, freshwater, or sea reptiles with the trunk enclosed in a bony shell

tur·tle·dove \-,dəv\ *n* **:** any of several small wild pigeons; *esp* **:** an Old World bird noted for plaintive cooing

turves *pl of* TURF

tusk \'təsk\ *n* **1 :** a long enlarged protruding tooth (as of an elephant, walrus, or boar) used to dig up food or as a weapon **2 :** a long projecting tooth — **tusked** \'təskt\ *adj*

¹**tus·sle** \'təs-əl\ *vb* **:** to struggle roughly **:** SCUFFLE

²**tussle** *n* **1 :** a physical struggle **:** SCUFFLE **2 :** a rough controversy or struggle against difficult odds

tus·sock \'təs-ək\ *n* **:** a dense tuft esp. of grass or sedge; *also* **:** a hummock in marsh bound together by roots — **tussocky** *adj*

tu·te·lage \'t(y)üt-ᵊl-ij\ *n* **1 :** an act of guarding or protecting **:** GUARDIANSHIP **2 :** the state of being under a guardian or tutor **3 :** instruction esp. of an individual

tu·te·lar \-ᵊl-ər\ *adj* **:** TUTELARY

tu·te·lary \-ᵊl-,er-ē\ *adj* **:** acting as a guardian ⟨~ deity⟩ ⟨a ~ power⟩

¹**tu·tor** \'t(y)üt-ər\ *n* **1 :** a person charged with the instruction and guidance of another **2 :** a private teacher **3 :** a college or university teacher ranking below an instructor

²**tutor** *vb* **1 :** to have the guardianship of **2 :** to teach or guide individually **:** COACH ⟨~ed the boy in Latin⟩ **3 :** to receive instruction esp. privately

tu·to·ri·al \t(y)ü-'tōr-ē-əl\ *n* **:** a class conducted by a tutor for one student or a small number of students

tux·e·do \,tək-'sēd-ō\ *n* **1 :** a usu. black or blackish blue jacket **2 :** semiformal evening clothes for men

TV \'tē-'vē\ *n* **:** TELEVISION

¹**twad·dle** \'twäd-ᵊl\ *n* **:** silly idle talk **:** DRIVEL — **twaddle** *vb* — **twad·dler** \-(ᵊ)lər\ *n*

twain \'twān\ *n* **1 :** TWO **:** COUPLE, PAIR

¹**twang** \'twaŋ\ *n* **1 :** a harsh quick ringing sound like that of a plucked bowstring **2 :** nasal speech or resonance **3 :** the characteristic speech of a region

²**twang** *vb* **1 :** to sound or cause to sound with a twang **2 :** to speak with a nasal twang

tweak \'twēk\ *vb* **:** to pinch and pull with a sudden jerk and twitch — **tweak** *n*

tweed \'twēd\ *n* **1 :** a rough woolen fabric made usu. in twill weaves **2** *pl* **:** tweed clothing; *esp* **:** a tweed suit

tweet \'twēt\ *n* **:** a chirping note — **tweet** *vb*

tweez·ers \'twē-zərz\ *n pl* **:** a small pincerlike implement held between the thumb and forefinger for grasping or extracting something

twelve \'twelv\ *n* **1 :** one more than 11 **2 :** the 12th in a set or series **3 :** something having 12 units — **twelve** \'twelfth\ *adj or n* — **twelve** *adj or pron*

twelve·month \-,mənth\ *n* **:** YEAR

twen·ty \'twent-ē\ *n* **:** two times 10 — **twen·ti·eth** *adj or n* — **twenty** *adj or pron*

twice \'twīs\ *adv* **1 :** on two occasions ⟨absent ~⟩ **2 :** two times ⟨~ two is four⟩

¹**twid·dle** \'twid-ᵊl\ *vb* **1 :** to be busy with trifles; *also* **:** to play idly with something **:** FIDDLE **2 :** to rotate lightly or idly **:** TWIRL

²**twiddle** *n* **:** TURN, TWIST

twig \'twig\ *n* **:** a small branch — **twig·gy** *adj*

twi·light \'twī-,līt\ *n* **1 :** the light from the sky between full night and sunrise or between sunset and full night **2 :** a state of imperfect clarity; *also* **:** a period of decline — **twilight** *adj*

twilight sleep *n* **:** a state produced by injection of drugs in which awareness and memory of pain is dulled

¹**twill** \'twil\ *n* **1 :** a fabric with a twill weave **2 :** a textile weave that gives an appearance of diagonal lines in the fabric

²**twill** *vb* **:** to make cloth with a twill weave

¹**twin** \'twin\ *adj* **1 :** born with one another or as a pair at one birth ⟨~ brother⟩ ⟨~ girls⟩ **2 :** made up of two similar or related members or parts **:** DOUBLE **3 :** being one of a pair ⟨~ city⟩

²**twin** *n* **1 :** either of two offspring produced at a birth **2 :** one of two persons or things closely related to or resembling each other

³**twin** *vb* **twinned; twin·ning 1 :** to bring forth twins **2 :** to be coupled with another

¹**twine** \'twīn\ *n* **1 :** a strong thread of two or three strands twisted together **2 :** an act of entwining or interlacing — **twiny** *adj*

²**twine** *vb* **1 :** to twist together; *also* **:** to form by twisting **2 :** INTERLACE, WEAVE **3 :** to coil about a support **4 :** to stretch or move in a sinuous manner **:** MEANDER — **twin·er** *n*

¹**twinge** \'twinj\ *vb* **:** to affect with or feel a sharp sudden pain

²**twinge** *n* **:** a sudden sharp stab (as of pain or distress)

¹**twin·kle** \'twiŋ-kəl\ *vb* **1 :** to shine or cause to shine with a flickering or sparkling light **2 :** to flutter or flit rapidly **3 :** to appear bright with merriment — **twin·kler** \-k(ə-)lər\ *n*

²**twinkle** *n* **1 :** a wink of the eyelids; *also* **:** the duration of a wink **2 :** an intermittent radiance **3 :** a rapid flashing motion

twin·kling \-kliŋ\ *n* **1 :** a wink of the eyelids **2 :** the time occupied by a single wink **syn** instant, moment, minute, second, flash

¹**twirl** \'twərl\ *vb* **1 :** to whirl round

2 : to pitch in a baseball game **syn** turn, revolve, rotate, circle, spin, swirl, pirouette

²twirl n **1** : an act of twirling **2** : COIL, WHORL

¹twist \'twist\ vb **1** : to unite by winding one thread or strand round another **2** : WREATHE, TWINE **3** : to turn so as to hurt ⟨~ed her ankle⟩ **4** : to twirl into spiral shape **5** : to subject (as a shaft) to torsion **6** : to pull off or break by torsion **7** : to turn from the true form or meaning **8** : to follow a winding course **9** : to turn around

²twist n **1** : something formed by twisting or winding **2** : an act of twisting : the state of being twisted **3** : a spiral turn or curve; also : SPIN **4** : a turning aside : DEFLECTION **5** : ECCENTRICITY, IDIOSYNCRASY **6** : a distortion of meaning **7** : an unexpected turn or development **8** : a variant approach or method **9** : DEVICE, TRICK

twist·er n **1** : one that twists; esp : a ball with a forward and spinning motion **2** : a tornado or waterspout in which the rotary ascending column of air is apparent

twit \'twit\ vb **twit·ted; twit·ting** : to reproach, taunt, or tease esp. by reminding of a fault or defect **syn** ridicule, deride, mock

¹twitch \'twich\ vb **1** : to move or pull with a sudden motion : JERK **2** : to move jerkily : QUIVER

²twitch n **1** : an act or movement of twitching **2** : a short sharp contraction of muscle fibers

¹twit·ter \'twit-ər\ vb **1** : to make a succession of chirping noises **2** : to talk in a chattering fashion; also : TITTER **3** : to have a slight trembling of the nerves : FLUTTER

²twitter n **1** : a small tremulous intermittent noise (as made by a swallow) **2** : a light chattering; also : TITTER **3** : a slight agitation of the nerves

two \'tü\ n **1** : one more than one **2** : the 2d in a set or series **3** : something having two units — **two** adj or pron

two-faced \-'fāst\ adj **1** : having two faces **2** : DOUBLE-DEALING, FALSE — **two·fac·ed·ly** \-'fā-səd-lē\ adv

two·fold \-'fōld\ adj **1** : having two units or members **2** : being twice as much or as many — **twofold** adv

two·pence \'təp-əns\ n, pl **twopence or two·penc·es** : the sum of two pence

two·pen·ny \'təp-ə-nē\ adj : of the value of or costing twopence

two-ply \'tü-'plī\ adj **1** : woven as a double cloth **2** : consisting of two strands or thicknesses

two·some \-səm\ n **1** : a group of two persons or things : COUPLE **2** : a golf match between two players

two-step \-,step\ n : a ballroom dance performed with a sliding step in march or polka time; also : a piece of music for this dance — **two-step** vb

two-way adj : involving two elements or allowing movement or use in two directions or manners

two-winged fly \,tü-,wiŋd-\ n : any of a large group of insects mostly with one pair of functional wings and another pair that if present are reduced to balancing organs

-ty \tē\ n suffix : quality : condition : degree ⟨realty⟩

ty·coon \tī-'kün\ n **1** : a powerful businessman or industrialist **2** : a masterful leader (as in politics)

tying pres part of TIE

tyke \'tīk\ n **1** : DOG, CUR **2** : a small child

tym·pa·num \'tim-pə-nəm\ n, pl **-nums or -na** \-nə\ : the cavity of the middle part of the ear closed externally by the eardrum; also : EARDRUM — **tym·pan·ic** \tim-'pan-ik\ adj

¹type \'tīp\ n **1** : a distinctive stamp, mark, or sign : EMBLEM **2** : a person, thing, or event that foreshadows another to come : TOKEN, SYMBOL **3** : general character or form common to a number of individuals and setting them off as a distinguishable class (horses of draft ~) **4** : a class, kind, or group set apart by common characteristics ⟨ a seedless ~ of orange⟩; also : something distinguishable as a variety (reactions of this ~) **5** : MODEL, EXAMPLE **6** : a rectangular block usu. of metal or wood having its face so shaped as to produce in printing a character (as a letter or figure); also : such blocks or the letters or characters printed from them **syn** sort, nature, character, description

²type vb **1** : to represent beforehand as a type **2** : to produce a copy of; also : REPRESENT, TYPIFY **3** : TYPEWRITE **4** : to identify as belonging to a type **5** : TYPECAST

type·cast \-,kast\ vb **1** : to cast (an actor) in a part calling for characteristics possessed by the actor himself **2** : to cast repeatedly in the same type of role

type·face \-,fās\ n : all type of a single design

type·script \-,skript\ n : typewritten matter

type·set·ter \-,set-ər\ n : one that sets type — **type·set** vb

type·write \-,rīt\ vb : to write with a typewriter

type·writ·er \-,rīt-ər\ n **1** : a machine for writing in characters similar to those produced by printers' types by means of types striking through an inked ribbon **2** : a person who operates a typewriter

type·writ·ing n : the use of a typewriter (teach ~); also : the printing done with a typewriter

¹ty·phoid \'tī-,fóid, tī-'fóid\ adj : of, relating to, or being a communicable bacterial disease (typhoid fever) marked by fever, diarrhea, prostration, and intestinal inflammation

²typhoid n : TYPHOID FEVER

ty·phoon \tī-'fün\ n : a tropical cyclone in the region of the Philippines or the China Sea

ty·phus \'tī-fəs\ n : a severe disease transmitted esp. by body lice and marked by high fever, stupor and delirium, intense headache, and a dark red rash

typ·i·cal \'tip-i-kəl\ adj **1** : having the nature of a type : SYMBOLIC **2** : exhibiting the essential characteristics of a group **3** : conforming to a type — **typ·i·cal·ly** adv — **typ·i·cal·ness** n

typ·i·fy \'tip-ə-,fī\ vb **1** : to represent by an image, form, model, or resemblance **2** : to embody the essential or common characteristics of

typ·ist \'tī-pəst\ n : one who operates a typewriter

ty·pog·ra·pher \tī-'päg-rə-fər\ n **1** : PRINTER **2** : one who designs or arranges printing

ty·pog·ra·phy \-fē\ n : the art of printing with type; also : the style, arrangement, or appearance of matter printed from type — **ty·po·graph·ic** \ˌtī-pə-'graf-ik\ *or* **ty·po·graph·i·cal** *adj* — **ty·po·graph·i·cal·ly** *adv*

ty·ran·ni·cal \tə-'ran-i-kəl, tī-\ *also* **ty·ran·nic** *adj* **:** of or relating to a tyrant **:** unjustly severe in governing : DESPOTIC *syn* arbitrary, absolute, autocratic — **ty·ran·ni·cal·ly** *adv*

tyr·an·nize \'tir-ə-,nīz\ *vb* **:** to act as a tyrant **:** rule with unjust severity — **tyr·an·niz·er** *n*

tyr·an·nous \'tir-ə-nəs\ *adj* **:** TYRANNI-CAL, DESPOTIC — **tyr·an·nous·ly** *adv*

tyr·an·ny \-nē\ *n* **1 :** the rule or authority of a tyrant **:** government in which absolute power is vested in a single ruler **2 :** despotic use of power **:** DESPOTISM **3 :** a tyrannical act

ty·rant \'tī-rənt\ *n* **1 :** an absolute ruler **:** DESPOT **2 :** a ruler who governs oppressively or brutally **3 :** one who uses authority or power harshly

ty·ro \'tī-rō\ *n* **:** a beginner in learning **:** NOVICE

tzar \'zär, '(t)sär\ *var of* CZAR

---

u \'yü\ *n; often cap* **:** the 21st letter of the English alphabet

ubiq·ui·tous \yü-'bik-wət-əs\ *adj* **:** existing or being everywhere at the same time **:** OMNIPRESENT — **ubiq·ui·tous·ly** *adv* — **ubiq·ui·ty** \-wət-ē\ *n*

U-boat \'yü-ˌbōt\ *n* **:** a German submarine

ud·der \'əd-ər\ *n* **:** an organ (as of a cow) consisting of two or more milk glands enclosed in a large hanging sac and each provided with a nipple

ug·ly \'əg-lē\ *adj* **1 :** FRIGHTFUL, DIRE **2 :** offensive to the sight **:** HIDEOUS **3 :** offensive or unpleasing to any sense **4 :** morally objectionable **:** REPULSIVE **5 :** likely to cause inconvenience or discomfort **:** TROUBLESOME **6 :** SURLY, QUARRELSOME (an ~ disposition) — **ug·li·ness** *n*

ukase \yü-'kās\ *n* **:** an edict esp. of a Russian emperor or government

Ukrai·ni·an \yü-'krā-nē-ən\ *n* **:** a native or inhabitant of the Ukraine

uku·le·le \ˌyü-kə-'lā-lē\ *n* **:** a small usu. 4-stringed guitar popularized in Hawaii and played with the fingers or a pick

ul·cer \'əl-sər\ *n* **1 :** an eroded sore often discharging pus **2 :** something that festers and corrupts like an open sore — **ul·cer·ous** *adj*

ul·cer·ate \'əl-sə-,rāt\ *vb* **:** to cause or become affected with an ulcer — **ul·cer·a·tion** \ˌəl-sə-'rā-shən\ *n*

ul·lage \'əl-ij\ *n* **:** the amount that a container (as a cask) lacks of being full

ul·ster \'əl-stər\ *n* **:** a long loose overcoat

ul·te·ri·or \ˌəl-'tir-ē-ər\ *adj* **1 :** situated beyond or on the farther side **2 :** lying farther away **:** more remote **3 :** going beyond what is openly said or shown **:** HIDDEN (~ motives)

1ul·ti·mate \'əl-tə-mət\ *adj* **1 :** most remote in space or time **:** FARTHEST **2 :** last in a progression **:** FINAL **3 :** EXTREME, UTMOST **4 :** finally reckoned **5 :** FUNDAMENTAL, ABSOLUTE, SUPREME (~ reality) **6 :** incapable of further analysis or division **:** ELEMENTAL **7 :** MAXIMUM — **ul·ti·mate·ly** *adv*

2ultimate *n* **:** something ultimate

ul·ti·ma·tum \ˌəl-tə-'māt-əm, -'mät-\ *n, pl* **-tums** *or* **-ta** \-ə\ **:** a final proposition, condition, or demand; *esp* **:** one whose rejection will bring about an end of negotiations

ul·ti·mo \'əl-tə-,mō\ *adj* **:** of or occurring the month preceding the present

1ul·tra \'əl-trə\ *adj* **:** going beyond others or beyond due limits **:** EXTREME

2ultra *n* **:** EXTREMIST

ul·tra·con·ser·va·tive \ˌəl-trə-kən-'sər-vət-iv\ *adj* **:** extremely conservative

ul·tra·fash·ion·able \-'fash-(ə-)nə-bəl\ *adj* **:** extremely fashionable

ul·tra·high frequency \ˌəl-trə-,hī-\ *n* **:** a frequency of a radio wave between 300 and 3000 megacycles

1ul·tra·ma·rine \ˌəl-trə-mə-'rēn\ *n* **1 :** a deep blue pigment **2 :** a very bright deep blue color

2ultramarine *adj* **:** situated beyond the sea

ul·tra·mod·ern \-'mäd-ərn\ *adj* **:** extremely or excessively modern in idea, style, or tendency

ul·tra·mon·tane \-ˌmän-,tān\ *adj* **1 :** of or relating to countries or peoples beyond the mountains (as the Alps) **2 :** favoring greater or absolute supremacy over national or diocesan authority in the Roman Catholic Church — **ultramontane** *n, often cap* — **ul·tra·mon·tan·ism** \-'mänt-ˀn-,iz-əm\ *n*

ul·tra·son·ic \-'sän-ik\ *adj* **:** SUPERSONIC — **ultrasonic** *n*

ul·tra·vi·o·let \-'vī-ə-lət\ *adj* **:** having a wavelength shorter than those of visible light (~ radiation); *also* **:** producing or employing ultraviolet radiation — **ultraviolet** *n*

ul·tra vi·res \ˌəl-trə-'vī-rēz\ *adv* (*or adj*) **:** beyond the scope of legal power or authority

ul·u·late \'əl-yə-,lāt, '(y)ül-\ *vb* **:** HOWL, WAIL

um·bel \'əm-bəl\ *n* **:** a flat or rounded flower cluster in which the individual flower stalks all arise at one point on the main stem — **um·bel·late** \-bə-,lāt\ *adj*

um·ber \'əm-bər\ *n* **:** a brown earthy substance valued as a pigment either in its raw state or burnt — **umber** *adj*

um·bil·i·cus \ˌəm-'bil-i-kəs, əm-bə-'lī-\ *n, pl* **-bil·i·ci** \-,kī\ *or* **-bil·i·cus·es** **:** a small depression on the abdominal wall marking the site of the cord (**umbilical cord**) that joins the unborn fetus to its mother — **um·bil·i·cal** \əm-'bil-i-kəl\ *adj*

um·bra \'əm-brə\ *n, pl* **-bras** *or* **-brae** \-(,)brē\ **1 :** SHADE, SHADOW **2 :** the shadow which is thrown by a planet or satellite on the side away from the sun

---

ə abut; ᵊ kitten; ər further; a back; ā bake; ä cot, cart; aù out; ch chin; e less; ē easy; g gift; i trip; ī life; j joke; ŋ sing; ō flow; ȯ flaw; ȯi coin; th thin; t͟h this; ü loot; u̇ foot; y yet; yü few; yu̇ furious; zh vision

and within which a spectator could see no part of the sun's disk

um·brage \\'əm-brij\ *n* **1** : SHADE; *also* : FOLIAGE **2** : RESENTMENT, OFFENSE ⟨take ~ at a remark⟩

um·brel·la \\,əm-'brel-ə\ *n* **1** : a collapsible shade for protection against weather consisting of fabric stretched over hinged ribs radiating from a center pole **2** : the saucer-shaped transparent body of a jellyfish

umi·ak \\'ü-mē-,ak\ *n* : an open Eskimo boat made of a wooden frame covered with skins

um·pire \\'əm-,pī(ə)r\ *n* [ME *oumpere*, alter. of *noumpere* (the phrase *a noumpere* being understood as *an oumpere*), fr. MF *nomper* not equal, not paired, fr. *non* not + *per* equal, fr. L *par*] **1** : one having authority to decide finally a controversy or question between parties **2** : an official in a sport who rules on plays — **umpire** *vb*

ump·teen \\'əmp-'tēn\ *adj* : very many : indefinitely numerous

un- \\,ən, 'ən\ *prefix* **1** : not : IN-, NON- **2** : opposite of : contrary to

unabashed	unattended
unabated	unattested
unabbreviated	unattractive
unabsolved	unauthentic
unabsorbed	unauthenticated
unacademic	unauthorized
unaccented	unavailable
unacceptable	unavenged
unacclimatized	unavowed
unaccommodating	unawakened
unaccomplished	unbaked
unaccredited	unbaptized
unacknowledged	unbefitting
unacquainted	unblamed
unadapted	unbleached
unadjusted	unblemished
unadorned	unblinking
unadvertised	unbound
unaffiliated	unbranched
unafraid	unbranded
unaided	unbreakable
unaimed	unbridgeable
unaired	unbrotherly
unalarmed	unbruised
unalike	unbrushed
unallied	unburied
unallowable	unburned
unalterable	unburnished
unaltered	uncanceled
unambiguous	uncanonical
unambitious	uncapitalized
unanchored	uncared-for
unanimated	uncataloged
unannounced	uncaught
unanswerable	uncensored
unanswered	uncensured
unanticipated	unchallenged
unapologetic	unchangeable
unappalled	unchanged
unapparent	unchanging
unappealing	unchaperoned
unappeased	uncharged
unappetizing	uncharted
unappreciated	unchastened
unappreciative	unchecked
unapproachable	unchivalrous
unappropriated	unchristened
unapproved	unclaimed
unartistic	unclassified
unashamed	uncleaned
unasked	unclear
unassertive	uncleared
unassisted	unclosed
unattainable	unclothed
unattempted	unclouded

uncluttered	undimmed
uncoated	undiplomatic
uncollected	undirected
uncolored	undiscerning
uncombed	undisciplined
uncombined	undisclosed
uncomely	undiscovered
uncomforted	undiscriminating
uncompensated	undisguised
uncomplaining	undismayed
uncompleted	undisputed
uncomplicated	undissolved
uncomplimentary	undistinguished
uncompounded	undistributed
uncomprehending	undisturbed
unconcealed	undivided
unconfined	undivulged
unconfirmed	undogmatic
unconformable	undomesticated
uncongealed	undone
uncongenial	undoubled
unconnected	undramatic
unconquered	undraped
unconscientious	undrawn
unconsecrated	undressed
unconsolidated	undrinkable
unconstrained	undulled
unconsumed	undutiful
uncontaminated	undyed
uncontested	uneatable
uncontradicted	uneaten
uncontrolled	uneconomic
unconverted	uneconomical
unconvincing	unedifying
uncooked	uneducated
uncooperative	unembarrassed
uncoordinated	unemotional
uncordial	unemphatic
uncorrected	unenclosed
uncorroborated	unencumbered
uncorrupted	unendorsed
uncountable	unendurable
uncovered	unenforceable
uncredited	unenforced
uncropped	unengaged
uncrowded	unenjoyable
uncrowned	unenlightened
uncrystallized	unenterprising
uncultivated	unentertaining
uncultured	unenthusiastic
uncurbed	unenviable
uncured	unequipped
uncurtained	unessential
undamaged	unethical
undamped	unexaggerated
undated	unexcelled
undazzled	unexceptional
undecipherable	unexchangeable
undecked	unexcited
undeclared	unexciting
undecorated	unexecuted
undefeated	unexperienced
undefended	unexpired
undefiled	unexplained
undefinable	unexploded
undefined	unexplored
undemanding	unexposed
undemocratic	unexpressed
undenominational	unexpurgated
undependable	unextended
undeserved	unextinguished
undeserving	unfading
undetachable	unfaltering
undetected	unfashionable
undetermined	unfathomable
undeterred	unfavored
undeveloped	unfeasible
undifferentiated	unfed
undigested	unfeminine
undignified	unfenced
undiluted	unfermented
undiminished	(continued)

unfertilized
unfilled
unfiltered
unfinished
unfitted
unfitting
unflagging
unflattering
unflavored
unforced
unforeseeable
unforeseen
unforgivable
unformulated
unfortified
unframed
unfulfilled
unfunded
unfurnished
ungentle
ungentlemanly
unglazed
ungoverned
ungraded
ungrammatical
ungrudging
unguided
unhackneyed
unhampered
unhardened
unharmed
unhatched
unhealthful
unheeded
unheralded
unheroic
unhesitating
unhindered
unhonored
unhoused
unhurried
unhurt
unhygienic
unidentified
unidiomatic
unimaginable
unimaginative
unimpaired
unimpassioned
unimpeded
unimportant
unimposing
unimpressive
unimproved
unincorporated
uninflammable
uninfluenced
uninformed
uninhabitable
uninhabited
uninitiated
uninjured
uninspired
uninstructed
uninsured
unintended
uninteresting
uninvested
uninvited
uninviting
unjointed
unjustifiable
unjustified
unkept
unknowable
unknowledgeable
unlabeled
unlabored

unlamented
unleavened
unlicensed
unlighted
unlikable
unlimited
unlined
unlisted
unlit
unlivable
unlobed
unlovable
unloved
unmanageable
unmanufactured
unmapped
unmarked
unmarketable
unmarred
unmarried
unmastered
unmatched
unmeant
unmeasured
unmeditated
unmelodious
unmelted
unmentioned
unmerited
unmethodical
unmilitary
unmilled
unmixed
unmolested
unmounted
unmovable
unmusical
unnameable
unnamed
unnaturalized
unnavigable
unnecessary
unneighborly
unnoticeable
unnoticed
unobjectionable
unobliging
unobscured
unobservant
unobserved
unobserving
unobstructed
unobtainable
unoffending
unofficial
unopened
unopposed
unordained
unoriginal
unorthodox
unostentatious
unowned
unpaid
unpainted
unpaired
unpalatable
unpardonable
unpasteurized
unpatriotic
unpaved
unpedigreed
unpeopled
unperceived
unperceptive
unperformed
unperturbed
unpitied
unplanned

unplanted
unpleasing
unplowed
unpoetic
unpolished
unpolluted
unposed
unpractical
unpracticed
unprejudiced
unpremeditated
unprepared
unprepossessing
unpresentable
unpressed
unpretending
unpreventable
unprivileged
unprocessed
unproductive
unprofessed
unprogressive
unpromising
unprompted
unpronounceable
unpropitious
unprotected
unproven
unprovided
unprovoked
unpublished
unpunished
unquenchable
unquestioned
unraised
unratified
unreadable
unready
unrealistic
unrealized
unrecognizable
unrecompensed
unrecorded
unredeemable
unrefined
unreflecting
unregarded
unregistered
unregulated
unrehearsed
unrelated
unreliable
unrelieved
unremembered
unremunerative
unrented
unrepentant
unreported
unrepresentative
unrepressed
unreproved
unrequited
unresisting
unresolved
unresponsive
unrestful
unrestricted
unreturned
unrewarding
unrhymed
unromantic
unsafe
unsaid
unsalable
unsalted
unsanitary
unsatisfactory
unsatisfied

unscented
unscheduled
unscholarly
unsealed
unseasoned
unseen
unsentimental
unserviceable
unshaded
unshakable
unshaken
unshapely
unshaven
unshed
unshorn
unsifted
unsigned
unsinkable
unsmiling
unsociable
unsoiled
unsold
unsoldierly
unsolicited
unsolvable
unsolved
unsorted
unspecified
unspoiled
unspoken
unstained
unstinting
unstressed
unsubdued
unsubstantiated
unsuccessful
unsuited
unsullied
unsupervised
unsupported
unsuppressed
unsure
unsurpassed
unsuspected
unsuspecting
unsuspicious
unswayed
unsweetened
unswept
unswerving
unsymmetrical
unsympathetic
unsystematic
untactful
untainted
untalented
untamed
untanned
untarnished
untaxed
unteachable
untenable
untenanted
unterrified
untested
unthankful
unthoughtful
untidy
untilled
untiring
untouched
untraceable
untrained
untrammeled
untranslatable
untraveled
untraversed
(continued)

ə abut; ə kitten; ər further; a back; ā bake; ä cot, cart; aù out; ch chin;
e less; ē easy; g gift; i trip; ī life; j joke; ŋ sing; ō flow; o flaw; oi coin;
th thin; th this; ü loot; u foot; y yet; yü few; yu furious; zh vision

untrimmed	unwatched
untrod	unwavering
untroubled	unweaned
untrustworthy	unwearable
untruthful	unwearied
unusable	unweathered
unvaried	unwed
unvarying	unwelcome
unventilated	unwifely
unverifiable	unwished
unverified	unwitnessed
unversed	unwomanly
unvexed	unworkable
unvisited	unworn
unwanted	unworried
unwarranted	unwounded
unwary	unwrinkled
unwashed	unwrought

un·a·ble \'ən-'ā-bəl\ *adj* 1 : not able : INCAPABLE 2 : UNQUALIFIED, INCOMPETENT, INEFFICIENT

un·abridged \,ən-ə-'brijd\ *adj* 1 : not abridged : COMPLETE ⟨an ~ edition of Shakespeare⟩ 2 : complete of its class : not based on one larger ⟨an ~ dictionary⟩

un·ac·com·pa·nied \,ən-ə-'kəmp-(ə-)nēd\ *adj* : not accompanied; *esp* : being without instrumental accompaniment

un·ac·count·able \-'kaůnt-ə-bəl\ *adj* 1 : not to be accounted for : INEXPLICABLE, STRANGE 2 : not responsible — **un·ac·count·ably** *adv*

un·ac·count·ed \-'kaůnt-əd\ *adj* : not accounted : UNEXPLAINED ⟨the loss was ~ for⟩

un·ac·cus·tomed \-'kəs-təmd\ *adj* 1 : not customary : not usual or common 2 : not accustomed or habituated ⟨~ to noise⟩

un·adorned \,ən-ə-'dórnd\ *adj* : not adorned : lacking embellishment or decoration : BARE, PLAIN, SIMPLE

un·adul·ter·at·ed \,ən-ə-'dəl-tə-,rāt-əd\ *adj* : PURE, UNMIXED

un·ad·vised \,ən-əd-'vīzd\ *adj* 1 : done without due consideration : RASH 2 : not prudent — **un·ad·vis·ed·ly** \-'vī-zəd-lē\ *adv*

un·af·fect·ed \,ən-ə-'fek-təd\ *adj* 1 : not influenced or changed mentally, physically, or chemically 2 : free from affectation : NATURAL, GENUINE — **un·af·fect·ed·ly** *adv*

un·alien·able \'ən-āl-yə-nə-bəl\ *adj* : INALIENABLE

un·al·loyed \,ən-ə-'lóid\ *adj* : UNMIXED, UNQUALIFIED, PURE ⟨~ metals⟩ ⟨~ happiness⟩

un-Amer·i·can \,ən-ə-'mer-ə-kən\ *adj* : not characteristic of or consistent with American customs, principles, or traditions

unan·i·mous \yů-'nan-ə-məs\ *adj* [L *unanimus*, fr. *unus* one + *animus* spirit, mind] 1 : being of one mind : AGREEING 2 : formed with or indicating the agreement of all — **una·nim·i·ty** \,yů-nə-'nim-ət-ē\ *n* — **unan·i·mous·ly** \yů-'nan-ə-məs-lē\ *adv*

un·arm \'ən-'ärm\ *vb* : DISARM

un·armed \-'ärmd\ *adj* : not armed or armored

un·as·sail·able \,ən-ə-'sā-lə-bəl\ *adj* : not assailable : not liable to doubt, attack, or question

un·as·sum·ing \-'sü-miŋ\ *adj* : MODEST, RETIRING

un·at·tached \,ən-ə-'tacht\ *adj* 1 : not attached 2 : not married or engaged

un·avail·ing \,ən-ə-'vā-liŋ\ *adj* : being

of no avail : not successful : VAIN — **un·avail·ing·ly** *adv*

un·avoid·able \-'vóid-ə-bəl\ *adj* : not avoidable : INEVITABLE — **un·avoid·ably** *adv*

¹un·aware \,ən-ə-'waər\ *adv* : UNAWARES

²unaware *adj* : not aware : IGNORANT — **un·aware·ness** *n*

un·awares \-'waərz\ *adv* 1 : without warning : by surprise ⟨taken ~⟩ 2 : without knowing : UNINTENTIONALLY

un·bal·anced \'ən-'bal-ənst\ *adj* 1 : not equally poised or balanced 2 : mentally disordered 3 : not adjusted so as to make credits equal to debits ⟨an ~ account⟩

un·bar \-'bär\ *vb* : UNBOLT, OPEN

un·bear·able \-'bar-ə-bəl\ *adj* : greater than can be borne ⟨~ pain⟩ — **un·bear·ably** *adv*

un·beat·able \-'bēt-ə-bəl\ *adj* : not capable of being defeated

un·beat·en \-'bēt-'n\ *adj* 1 : not pounded, beaten, or whipped 2 : UNTROD 3 : UNDEFEATED

un·be·com·ing \,ən-bi-'kəm-iŋ\ *adj* : not becoming : UNSUITABLE, IMPROPER — **un·be·com·ing·ly** *adv*

un·be·known \-'nōn\ *or* **un·be·knownst** \-'nōnst\ *adj* : happening without one's knowledge : UNKNOWN ⟨~ to his parents⟩

un·be·lief \,ən-bə-'lēf\ *n* : the withholding or absence of belief : DOUBT — **un·be·liev·ing** *adj*

un·be·liev·able \-'lē-və-bəl\ *adj* : too improbable for belief : INCREDIBLE — **un·be·liev·ably** *adv*

un·be·liev·er \-'lē-vər\ *n* 1 : DOUBTER 2 : INFIDEL

un·bend \-'bend\ *vb* 1 : to free from being bent : make or become straight 2 : UNTIE 3 : to make or become less stiff or more affable : RELAX

un·bend·ing \-'ben-diŋ\ *adj* : formal and distant in manner : INFLEXIBLE

un·bi·ased \'ən-'bī-əst\ *adj* : free from bias; *esp* : UNPREJUDICED, IMPARTIAL

un·bid·den \-'bid-'n\ *also* **un·bid** \-'bid\ *adj* : not bidden : UNASKED, UNINVITED

un·bind \-'bīnd\ *vb* 1 : to remove bindings from : UNTIE, UNFASTEN, LOOSE 2 : RELEASE

un·blessed *also* **un·blest** \-'ən-'blest\ *adj* 1 : not blessed 2 : EVIL

un·blush·ing \-'bləsh-iŋ\ *adj* 1 : not blushing 2 : SHAMELESS — **un·blush·ing·ly** *adv*

un·bod·ied \-'bäd-ēd\ *adj* 1 : having no body; *also* : DISEMBODIED 2 : FORMLESS

un·bolt \-'bōlt\ *vb* : to open or unfasten by withdrawing a bolt

un·born \-'bórn\ *adj* : not yet born : FUTURE ⟨~ generations⟩

un·bo·som \-'bůz-əm\ *vb* 1 : DISCLOSE, REVEAL ⟨~ed his secrets⟩ 2 : to disclose the thoughts or feelings of oneself

un·bound·ed \-'baůn-dəd\ *adj* : having no bounds or limits ⟨~ enthusiasm⟩

un·bowed \-'baůd\ *adj* 1 : not bowed down 2 : UNSUBDUED

un·bri·dled \-'brīd-'ld\ *adj* 1 : not confined by a bridle 2 : UNRESTRAINED, UNGOVERNED

un·bro·ken \'ən-'brō-kən\ *adj* 1 : not damaged : WHOLE 2 : not subdued or tamed 3 : not interrupted : CONTINUOUS ⟨~ sleep⟩

un·buck·le \-'bək-əl\ vb : to loose the buckle of : UNFASTEN \~ a belt)

un·bur·den \-'bərd-ᵊn\ vb 1 : to free or relieve from a burden 2 : to relieve oneself of (as cares or worries) : cast off

un·but·ton \-'bət-ᵊn\ vb : to unfasten the buttons of \~ your coat)

un·called-for \,ən-'kȯld-,fȯr\ adj : not called for, needed, or wanted : not proper

un·can·ny \'ən-'kan-ē\ adj 1 : GHOSTLY, MYSTERIOUS, EERIE 2 : suggesting superhuman or supernatural powers — un·can·ni·ly adv

un·cap \-'kap\ vb : to remove a cap or covering from

un·ceas·ing \-'sē-siŋ\ adj : never ceasing : CONTINUOUS, INCESSANT — un·ceas·ing·ly adv

un·cer·e·mo·ni·ous \,ən-,ser-ə-'mō-nē-əs\ adj : acting without or lacking ordinary courtesy : ABRUPT — un·cer·e·mo·ni·ous·ly adv

un·cer·tain \'ən-'sərt-ᵊn\ adj 1 : not determined or fixed \an \~ quantity) 2 : subject to chance or change : not dependable 3 : not sure \~ of the truth) 4 : not definitely known — un·cer·tain·ly adv

un·cer·tain·ty \-ᵊn-tē\ n 1 : lack of certainty : DOUBT 2 : something that is uncertain

un·chain \'ən-'chān\ vb : to free by or as if by removing a chain : set loose

un·char·i·ta·ble \-'char-ət-ə-bəl\ adj : not charitable; esp : severe in judging others — un·char·i·ta·ble·ness n — un·char·i·ta·bly adv

un·chaste \-'chāst\ adj : not chaste : lacking in chastity — un·chaste·ly adv — un·chaste·ness n — un·chas·ti·ty \-'chas-tət-ē\ n

un·chris·tian \-'kris-chən\ adj 1 : not of the Christian faith 2 : contrary to the Christian spirit

un·cial \'ən-chəl\ adj : relating to or written in a form of script with rounded letters used esp. in early Greek and Latin manuscripts — uncial n

un·cir·cum·cised \'ən-'sər-kəm-,sīzd\ adj : not circumcised; also : HEATHEN

un·civ·il \-'siv-əl\ adj 1 : not civilized 2 : DISCOURTEOUS, ILL-MANNERED, IMPOLITE

un·civ·i·lized \-'siv-ə-,līzd\ adj 1 : not civilized : BARBAROUS 2 : remote from civilization : WILD

un·clad \-'klad\ adj : not clothed : UNDRESSED, NAKED

un·clasp \-'klasp\ vb : to loose the clasp of : open by or as if by loosing the clasp

un·cle \'əŋ-kəl\ n : the brother of one's father or mother; also : the husband of one's aunt

un·clean \'ən-'klēn\ adj 1 : morally or spiritually impure 2 : prohibited by ritual law for use or contact 3 : DIRTY, FILTHY — un·clean·ness \-'klēn-nəs\ n

un·clean·ly \-'klen-lē\ adj : morally or physically unclean — un·clean·li·ness n

un·clench \-'klench\ vb : to open from a clenched position : RELAX

un·cloak \-'klōk\ vb 1 : to remove a cloak or cover from 2 : UNMASK, REVEAL

un·close \'ən-'klōz\ vb : OPEN

un·clothe \-'klōth\ vb : to strip of clothes or a covering

un·coil \-'kȯil\ vb : to release or become released from a coiled state : UNWIND

un·com·fort·able \-'kəm(f)-tə-bəl, -'kəm-fərt-ə-bəl\ adj 1 : causing discomfort 2 : feeling discomfort : UNEASY — un·com·fort·ably adv

un·com·mit·ted \,ən-kə-'mit-əd\ adj : not committed; esp : not pledged to a particular belief, allegiance, or program

un·com·mon \'ən-'käm-ən\ adj 1 : not ordinarily encountered : UNUSUAL, RARE 2 : REMARKABLE, EXCEPTIONAL — un·com·mon·ly adv

un·com·mu·ni·ca·tive \,ən-kə-'myü-nə-,kāt-iv, -ni-kət-\ adj : not inclined to talk or impart information : RESERVED

un·com·pro·mis·ing \'ən-'käm-prə-,mī-ziŋ\ adj : not making or accepting a compromise : UNYIELDING

un·con·cern \,ən-kən-'sərn\ n 1 : lack of care or interest : INDIFFERENCE 2 : freedom from excessive concern or anxiety

un·con·cerned \-'sərnd\ adj 1 : not having any part or interest 2 : not anxious or upset : free of worry — un·con·cern·ed·ly \-'sər-nəd-lē\ adv

un·con·di·tion·al \,ən-kən-'dish-(ə-)nəl\ adj : not limited in any way : ABSOLUTE, UNQUALIFIED — un·con·di·tion·al·ly adv

un·con·di·tioned \-'dish-ənd\ adj 1 : not subject to conditions : not acquired or learned : INHERENT, NATURAL 2 : UNCONDITIONAL

un·con·quer·able \'ən-'käŋ-k(ə-)rə-bəl\ adj : incapable of being conquered or overcome : INDOMITABLE

un·con·scio·na·ble \-'känch-(ə-)nə-bəl\ adj 1 : not in accordance with what is right or just : UNREASONABLE, EXCESSIVE 2 : not guided or controlled by conscience — un·con·scio·na·bly adv

¹un·con·scious \-'kän-chəs\ adj 1 : deprived of consciousness or awareness 2 : not realized by oneself : not consciously done — un·con·scious·ly adv — un·con·scious·ness n

²unconscious n : the part of one's mental life not ordinarily available to consciousness but revealed esp. in spontaneous behavior (as slips of the tongue) or in dreams

un·con·sti·tu·tion·al \,ən-,kän-stə-'t(y)ü-sh(ə-)nəl\ adj : not according to or consistent with the constitution of a state or society — un·con·sti·tu·tion·al·i·ty \-,t(y)ü-shə-'nal-ət-ē\ n — un·con·sti·tu·tion·al·ly \-'t(y)ü-sh(ə-)nə-lē\ adv

un·con·trol·la·ble \,ən-kən-'trō-lə-bəl\ adj : incapable of being controlled : UNGOVERNABLE — un·con·trol·la·bly adv

un·con·ven·tion·al \-'vench-(ə-)nəl\ adj : not conventional : being out of the ordinary — un·con·ven·tion·al·i·ty \-,ven-chə-'nal-ət-ē\ n — un·con·ven·tion·al·ly \-'vench-(ə-)nə-lē\ adv

un·cork \'ən-'kȯrk\ vb 1 : to draw a cork from 2 : to release from a sealed or pent-up state; also : to let go

un·count·ed \-'kaúnt-əd\ adj : not counted; also : INNUMERABLE

ə abut; ᵊ kitten; ər further; a back; ā bake; ä cot, cart; aú out; ch chin; e less; ē easy; g gift; i trip; ī life; j joke; ŋ sing; ō flow; ȯ flaw; ȯi coin; th thin; th this; ü loot; ú foot; y yet; yü few; yú furious; zh vision

un·cou·ple \-'kəp-əl\ vb : DISCONNECT ⟨~ railroad cars⟩

un·couth \-'küth\ adj [OE *uncūth* unknown, unfamiliar, fr. *un-* + *cūth* known] 1 : strange, awkward, and clumsy in shape or appearance 2 : vulgar in conduct or speech : RUDE

un·cov·er \-'kəv-ər\ vb 1 : to make known : DISCLOSE, REVEAL 2 : to expose to view by removing some covering 3 : to take the cover from 4 : to remove the hat from; *also* : to take off the hat as a token of respect

un·crit·i·cal \-'krit-i-kəl\ adj 1 : not critical : lacking in discrimination 2 : showing lack or improper use of critical standards or procedures — **un·crit·i·cal·ly** adv

un·cross \-'krós\ vb : to change from a crossed position ⟨~ed his legs⟩

unc·tion \'əŋk-shən\ n 1 : the act of anointing as a rite of consecration or healing 2 : exaggerated, assumed, or superficial earnestness of language or manner

unc·tu·ous \'əŋk-chə(-w)əs\ adj 1 : FATTY, OILY 2 : full of unction in speech and manner; *esp* : insincerely smooth — **unc·tu·ous·ly** adv

un·curl \ˌən-'kərl\ vb : to make or become straightened out from a curled or coiled position

un·cut \-'kət\ adj 1 : not cut down or into 2 : not shaped by cutting ⟨an ~ diamond⟩ 3 : not having the folds of the leaves slit 4 : not abridged or curtailed

un·daunt·ed \'ən-'dónt-əd\ adj : not daunted : not discouraged or dismayed : FEARLESS — **un·daunt·ed·ly** adv

un·de·ceive \ˌən-di-'sēv\ vb : to free from deception, illusion, or error

un·de·cid·ed \-'sīd-əd\ adj 1 : not yet determined : UNSETTLED 2 : uncertain what to do : WAVERING

un·de·mon·stra·tive \ˌən-di-'män-strət-iv\ adj : restrained in expression of feeling : RESERVED

un·de·ni·able \-'nī-ə-bəl\ adj 1 : plainly true : INCONTESTABLE 2 : unquestionably excellent or genuine — **un·de·ni·ably** adv

¹**un·der** \'ən-dər\ adv 1 : in or into a position below or beneath something 2 : below some quantity, level, or norm ⟨$10 or ~⟩ 3 : in or into a condition of subjection, subordination, or unconsciousness ⟨the ether put him ~⟩

²**under** prep 1 : lower than and overhung, surmounted, or sheltered by ⟨~ a tree⟩ 2 : below the surface of ⟨~ the sea⟩ 3 : in or into such a position as to be covered or concealed by ⟨a vest ~ his jacket⟩ ⟨the moon went ~ a cloud⟩ 4 : subject to the authority or guidance of ⟨served ~ him⟩ ⟨had the man ~ contract⟩ 5 : with the guarantee of ⟨~ the royal seal⟩ 6 : controlled, limited, or oppressed by ⟨~ lock and key⟩ ⟨brave ~ trials⟩ 7 : subject to the action or effect of ⟨~ an anesthetic⟩ 8 : within the division or grouping of ⟨items ~ this head⟩ 9 : less or lower than ⟨as in size, amount, or rank⟩ ⟨makes ~ $5000⟩ ⟨nobody ~ 21⟩

³**under** adj 1 : lying below, beneath, or on the ventral side 2 : facing or protruding downward 3 : SUBORDINATE 4 : lower than usual, proper, or desired in amount, quality, or degree

un·der·act \ˌən-dər-'akt\ vb : to perform feebly or with restraint

un·der·age \-'āj\ adj : of less than mature or legal age

un·der·arm \-'ärm\ adj 1 : placed under or on the underside of the arm ⟨~ seams⟩ 2 : performed with the hand kept below the level of the shoulder : UNDERHAND ⟨an ~ throw⟩ — **underarm** adv or n

un·der·bel·ly \'ən-dər-ˌbel-ē\ n : the under surface of a body or mass; *also* : a vulnerable area

un·der·bid \ˌən-dər-'bid\ vb 1 : to bid less than another 2 : to bid too low ⟨as in cards⟩

un·der·bred \-'bred\ adj 1 : marked by lack of good breeding : ILL-BRED 2 : of inferior or mixed breeding

un·der·brush \'ən-dər-ˌbrəsh\ n : shrubs and small trees growing beneath large trees

un·der·car·riage \-ˌkar-ij\ n 1 : a supporting framework ⟨as of an automobile⟩ 2 : the landing structure of an airplane

un·der·charge \ˌən-dər-'chärj\ vb : to charge ⟨as a person⟩ too little — **un·der·charge** \'ən-dər-ˌchärj\ n

un·der·class·man \ˌən-dər-'klas-mən\ n : a member of the freshman or sophomore class

un·der·clothes \'ən-dər-ˌklō(th)z\ n pl : UNDERWEAR

un·der·cloth·ing \-ˌklō-thiŋ\ n : UNDERWEAR

un·der·coat \-ˌkōt\ n 1 : a coat worn under another 2 : a growth of short hair or fur partly concealed by a longer growth ⟨a dog's ~⟩ 3 : a coat of paint under another

un·der·coat·ing n : a special waterproof coating applied to the undersurfaces of a vehicle

un·der·cov·er \ˌən-dər-'kəv-ər\ adj : acting or executed in secret; *esp* : employed or engaged in secret investigation ⟨~ agent⟩

un·der·croft \'ən-dər-ˌkróft\ n : a vaulted chamber under a church

un·der·cur·rent \-ˌkər-ənt\ n 1 : a current below the surface 2 : a hidden tendency of feeling or opinion

un·der·cut \ˌən-dər-'kət\ vb 1 : to cut away the underpart of 2 : to offer to sell or to work at a lower rate than 3 : to strike ⟨the ball⟩ in golf, tennis, or hockey obliquely downward so as to give a backward spin or elevation to the shot — **un·der·cut** \'ən-dər-ˌkət\ n

un·der·de·vel·oped \-di-'vel-əpt\ adj 1 : not normally or adequately developed ⟨~ muscles⟩ 2 : failing to reach a potential level of economic development ⟨as from lack of capital⟩ ⟨the ~ nations⟩

un·der·dog \'ən-dər-ˌdóg\ n 1 : the losing dog in a fight 2 : the loser or predicted loser in a struggle

un·der·done \ˌən-dər-'dən\ adj : not thoroughly done or cooked : RARE ⟨~ steak⟩

un·der·draw·ers \'ən-dər-ˌdró(-ə)rz\ n pl : an article of underwear covering the lower body and the legs ⟨calf-length ~⟩

un·der·es·ti·mate \ˌən-dər-'es-tə-ˌmāt\ vb : to set too low a value on : estimate below the truth

un·der·ex·pose \-ik-'spōz\ vb : to expose ⟨a photographic plate or film⟩ for less time than is needed — **un·der·ex·po·sure** \-'spō-zhər\ n

un·der·feed \-'fēd\ vb 1 : to feed inadequately 2 : to feed ⟨as a furnace⟩

with fuel admitted from below

un·der·foot \\'ən-dər-'fut\ *adv* **1** : under the feet ⟨flowers trampled ~⟩ **2** : close about one's feet : in the way ⟨a puppy always ~⟩

un·der·gar·ment \\'ən-dər-ˌgär-mənt\ *n* : a garment to be worn under another

un·der·gird \\ən-dər-'gərd\ *vb* **1** : to make secure underneath **2** : to brace up : STRENGTHEN

un·der·go \\-'gō\ *vb* **1** : to be subjected to : ENDURE **2** : to pass through : EXPERIENCE

un·der·grad·u·ate \\-'graj-(ə-)wət\ *n* : a student at a university or college who has not taken a first degree

¹**un·der·ground** \\ən-dər-'graund\ *adv* **1** : beneath the surface of the earth **2** : in secret

²**un·der·ground** \\'ən-dər-ˌgraund\ *adj* **1** : being or growing under the surface of the ground ⟨~ stems⟩ **2** : conducted by secret means

³**un·der·ground** \\'ən-dər-ˌgraund\ *n* **1** : a space under the surface of the ground; *esp* : an underground railway **2** : a secret political movement or group; *esp* : an organized body working in secret to overthrow a government or an occupying power

un·der·growth \\'ən-dər-ˌgrōth\ *n* : low growth (as of herbs and shrubs) on the floor of a forest

¹**un·der·hand** \\'ən-dər-ˌhand\ *adv* **1** : in an underhand or secret manner **2** : with an underhand motion

²**underhand** *adj* **1** : marked by secrecy and deception : SLY **2** : made with the hand kept below the level of the shoulder

un·der·hand·ed \\ˌən-dər-'han-dəd\ *adj* (*or adv*) : UNDERHAND — **un·der·hand·ed·ly** *adv* — **un·der·hand·ed·ness** *n*

un·der·lie \\-'lī\ *vb* **1** : to lie or be situated under **2** : to be at the basis of : form the foundation of : SUPPORT

un·der·line \\'ən-dər-ˌlīn\ *vb* **1** : to draw a line under **2** : EMPHASIZE, STRESS — **underline** *n*

un·der·ling \\'ən-dər-lin\ *n* : SUBORDINATE, INFERIOR

un·der·lip \\ˌən-dər-'lip\ *n* : the lower lip

un·der·ly·ing \\-'lī-iŋ\ *adj* **1** : lying under or below **2** : FUNDAMENTAL, BASIC ⟨~ principles⟩

un·der·mine \\-'mīn\ *vb* **1** : to excavate beneath **2** : to weaken or wear away secretly or gradually ⟨~ a government⟩

un·der·most \\'ən-dər-ˌmōst\ *adj* : lowest in relative position — **undermost** *adv*

¹**un·der·neath** \\ˌən-dər-'nēth\ *prep* **1** : directly under **2** : under subjection to

²**underneath** *adv* **1** : below a surface or object : BENEATH **2** : on the lower side

un·der·nour·ished \\-'nər-isht\ *adj* : supplied with insufficient nourishment — **un·der·nour·ish·ment** *n*

un·der·pants \\'ən-dər-ˌpants\ *n pl* : short or long pants worn under an outer garment : DRAWERS

un·der·part \\-ˌpärt\ *n* **1** : a part lying on the lower side esp. of a bird or mammal **2** : a subordinate or auxiliary part or role

un·der·pass \\-ˌpas\ *n* : a passage underneath ⟨a railroad ~⟩

un·der·pay \\ˌən-dər-'pā\ *vb* : to pay too little

un·der·pin·ning \\'ən-dər-ˌpin-iŋ\ *n* : the material and construction (as a foundation) used for support of a structure

un·der·play \\ˌən-dər-'plā\ *vb* : to treat or handle with restraint; *esp* : to play a role with subdued force

un·der·priv·i·leged \\-'priv-(ə-)lijd\ *adj* : having fewer esp. economic and social privileges than others : POOR

un·der·pro·duc·tion \\ˌən-dər-prə-'dək-shən\ *n* : the production of less than enough to satisfy the demand or of less than the usual supply

un·der·rate \\ˌən-də(r)-'rāt\ *vb* : to rate or value too low

un·der·score \\'ən-dər-ˌskōr\ *vb* **1** : to draw a line under : UNDERLINE **2** : EMPHASIZE — **underscore** *n*

¹**un·der·sea** \\ˌən-dər-'sē\ *adj* : being, carried on, or used beneath the surface of the sea

²**undersea** *or* **un·der·seas** \\-'sēz\ *adv* : beneath the surface of the sea

un·der·sec·re·tary \\'sek-rə-ˌter-ē\ *n* : a secretary immediately subordinate to a principal secretary ⟨~ of state⟩

un·der·sell \\-'sel\ *vb* : to sell articles cheaper than ⟨~ a competitor⟩

un·der·shirt \\'ən-dər-ˌshərt\ *n* : a collarless undergarment with or without sleeves

un·der·shot \\ˌən-dər-'shät\ *adj* **1** : having the lower front teeth projecting beyond the upper when the mouth is closed **2** : moved by water passing beneath ⟨an ~ waterwheel⟩

un·der·side \\'ən-dər-ˌsīd\ *n* : the side or surface lying underneath

un·der·signed \\-'sīnd\ *n, pl* **undersigned** : one who signs his name at the end of a document ⟨the ~ agree⟩

un·der·sized \\ˌən-dər-'sīzd\ *adj* : of a size less than is common, proper, normal, or average ⟨~ trout⟩

un·der·skirt \\'ən-dər-ˌskərt\ *n* : a skirt worn under an outer skirt; *esp* : PETTICOAT

un·der·slung \\ˌən-dər-'sləŋ\ *adj* : suspended so as to extend below the axles ⟨an ~ automobile frame⟩

un·der·stand \\ˌən-dər-'stand\ *vb* **1** : to grasp the meaning of : COMPREHEND **2** : to have thorough or technical acquaintance with or expertness in ⟨~ finance⟩ **3** : GATHER, INFER ⟨I ~ that you spread this rumor⟩ **4** : INTERPRET ⟨we ~ this to be a refusal⟩ **5** : to have a sympathetic attitude **6** : to accept as settled ⟨it is *understood* that he will pay the expenses⟩ — **un·der·stand·able** *adj* — **un·der·stand·ably** *adv*

un·der·stand·ing *n* **1** : knowledge and ability to apply judgment : INTELLIGENCE **2** : ability to comprehend and judge ⟨a man of ~⟩ **3** : agreement of opinion or feeling **4** : a mutual agreement informally or tacitly entered into (as between two nations)

²**understanding** *adj* : endowed with understanding : TOLERANT, SYMPATHETIC

un·der·state \\ˌən-dər-'stāt\ *vb* **1** : to represent as less than is the case **2** : to state with restraint esp. for greater effect — un·der·state·ment *n*

un·der·stood \-'stůd\ *adj* **1** : agreed upon **2** : IMPLICIT

1un·der·study \'ən-dər-,stəd-ē\ *vb* : to study another actor's part in order to be his substitute in an emergency — understudy *n*

un·der·sur·face \-,sər-fəs\ *n* : UNDERSIDE

un·der·take \,ən-dər-'tāk\ *vb* **1** : to take upon oneself as a task : set about **2** : to put oneself under obligation : AGREE, CONTRACT **3** : GUARANTEE, PROMISE

un·der·tak·er \'ən-dər-,tā-kər\ *n* : one whose business is to prepare the dead for burial and to take charge of funerals

un·der·tak·ing \-,tā-kiŋ\ *n* **1** : the act of one who undertakes or engages in any project or business **2** : the business of an undertaker **3** : something undertaken **4** : PROMISE, GUARANTEE

un·der-the-count·er *adj* : UNLAWFUL, ILLICIT (~ sale of drugs)

un·der·tone \'ən-dər-,tōn\ *n* **1** : a low or subdued tone or utterance **2** : a subdued color (as seen through and modifying another color)

un·der·tow \-,tō\ *n* : the current beneath the surface that sets seaward when waves are breaking upon the shore

un·der·trick \-,trik\ *n* : a trick by which a declarer in bridge falls short of making his contract

un·der·val·ue \,ən-dər-'val-yü\ *vb* **1** : to value or estimate below the real worth **2** : to esteem lightly

un·der·waist \'ən-dər-,wāst\ *n* : a waist for wear under another garment

un·der·wa·ter \,ən-dər-,wòt-ər, -,wät-\ *adj* : lying, growing, worn, or operating below the surface of the water — underwater *adv*

under way *adv* **1** : into motion from a standstill **2** : in progress : AFOOT (preparations were *under way*)

un·der·wear \'ən-dər-,wa(ə)r\ *n* : a garment worn next to the skin and under other clothing

un·der·weight \,ən-dər-'wāt\ *n* : weight below what is normal, average, or necessary — underweight *adj*

un·der·world \'ən-dər-,world\ *n* **1** : the place of departed souls : HADES **2** : a social sphere below the level of ordinary life; *esp* : the world of organized crime

un·der·writ· \'ən-də(r)-,rīt\ *vb* **1** : to write under or at the end of something else **2** : to set one's name to an insurance policy and thereby become answerable for a designated loss or damage : insure life or property **3** : to subscribe to : agree to **4** : to agree to purchase (as bonds) usu. on a fixed date at a fixed price; *also* : to guarantee financial support of — un·der·writ·er *n*

un·de·sir·able \,ən-di-'zī-rə-bəl\ *adj* : not desirable : UNWANTED — undesirable *n*

un·de·vi·at·ing \'ən-dē-vē-,āt-iŋ\ *adj* : keeping a true course : UNSWERVING

un·dies \'ən-dēz\ *n pl* : UNDERWEAR; *esp* : women's underwear

un·do \,ən-'dü\ *vb* **1** : to make or become unfastened or loosened : OPEN **2** : to make null or as if not done : REVERSE **3** : to bring to ruin; *also* : UPSET

un·do·ing *n* **1** : LOOSING, UNFASTENING **2** : RUIN; *also* : a cause of ruin **3** : REVERSAL

un·doubt·ed \'ən-'daůt-əd\ *adj* : not doubted or called into question : CERTAIN — un·doubt·ed·ly *adv*

1un·dress \-'dres\ *vb* : to remove the clothes or covering of : STRIP, DISROBE

2undress *n* **1** : informal dress; *esp* : a loose robe or dressing gown **2** : ordinary dress **3** : NUDITY

un·due \-'d(y)ü\ *adj* **1** : not due **2** : INAPPROPRIATE, UNSUITABLE **3** : EXCESSIVE, IMMODERATE (~ severity)

un·du·lant \'ən-jə-lənt, -d(y)ə-\ *adj* : UNDULATING

un·du·late \-,lāt\ *vb* **1** : to have a wavelike motion or appearance **2** : to rise and fall in pitch or volume *syn* waver, swing, sway, oscillate, vibrate, fluctuate

un·du·la·tion \,ən-jə-'lā-shən, -d(y)ə-\ *n* **1** : wavy or wavelike motion **2** : pulsation of sound **3** : a wavy appearance or outline — un·du·la·to·ry \-jə-lə-,tōr-ē, -d(y)ə-\ *adj*

un·du·ly \'ən-'d(y)ü-lē\ *adv* : in an undue manner; *esp* : EXCESSIVELY

un·dy·ing \-'dī-iŋ\ *adj* : not dying : IMMORTAL, PERPETUAL

un·earned \-'ərnd\ *adj* : not earned by labor, service, or skill (~ income)

un·earth \-'ərth\ *vb* **1** : to drive or draw from the earth : dig up (~ buried treasure) **2** : to bring to light : DISCOVER (~ a secret)

un·earth·ly \-lē\ *adj* **1** : not of or belonging to the earth **2** : SUPERNATURAL, WEIRD, TERRIFYING

un·easy \'ən-'ē-zē\ *adj* **1** : AWKWARD, EMBARRASSED (~ among strangers) **2** : disturbed by pain or worry; *also* : RESTLESS — un·eas·i·ly *adv* — un·eas·i·ness *n*

un·em·ployed \,ən-im-'plóid\ *adj* : not employed; *esp* : not engaged in a gainful occupation

un·em·ploy·ment \-'plói-mənt\ *n* : lack of employment

un·end·ing \'ən-'en-diŋ\ *adj* : having no ending : ENDLESS

un·equal \-'ē-kwəl\ *adj* **1** : not alike (as in size, amount, number, or value) **2** : not uniform : VARIABLE, UNEVEN **3** : badly balanced or matched **4** : INADEQUATE, INSUFFICIENT (timber ~ to the strain) — un·equal·ly *adv*

un·equaled *adj* : not equaled : UNPARALLELED

un·equiv·o·cal \,ən-i-'kwiv·ə-kəl\ *adj* : leaving no doubt : CLEAR — un·equiv·o·cal·ly *adv*

un·err·ing \'ən-'e(ə)r-iŋ, -'ər-\ *adj* : making no errors : CERTAIN, UNFAILING — un·err·ing·ly *adv*

un·even \-'ē-vən\ *adj* **1** : ODD **2** : not even : not level or smooth : RUGGED, RAGGED **3** : IRREGULAR; *also* : varying in quality — un·even·ly *adv* — un·even·ness \-vən-nəs\ *n*

un·event·ful \,ən-i-'vent-fəl\ *adj* : not eventful : lacking interesting or noteworthy incidents

un·ex·am·pled \,ən-ig-'zam-pəld\ *adj* : UNPRECEDENTED, UNPARALLELED

un·ex·cep·tion·able \,ən-ik-'sep-sh(ə-)nə-bəl\ *adj* : not open to exception or objection : beyond reproach

un·ex·pect·ed \,ən-ik-'spek-təd\ *adj* : not expected : UNFORESEEN — un·ex·pect·ed·ly *adv*

un·fail·ing \'ən-'fā-liŋ\ *adj* **1** : not failing, flagging, or waning : CONSTANT **2** : INEXHAUSTIBLE **3** : INFALLIBLE

un·fair \-'faər\ *adj* **1** : marked by injustice, partiality, or deception : UNJUST,

DISHONEST **2 :** not equitable in business dealings — **un·fair·ly** \-\ adv — **un·fair·ness** n

un·faith·ful \-'fāth-fəl\ adj **1 :** not observant of vows, allegiance, or duty **:** DISLOYAL **2 :** INACCURATE, UNTRUSTWORTHY — **un·faith·ful·ly** adv — **un·faith·ful·ness** n

un·fa·mil·iar \-,ən-fə-'mil-yər\' adj **1 :** not well known **:** STRANGE ⟨an ~ place⟩ **2 :** not well acquainted ⟨~ with the subject⟩ — **un·fa·mil·iar·i·ty** \-,mil-'yar-ət-ē\ n

un·fas·ten \'ən-'fas-ən\ vb **:** to make or become loose **:** UNDO, DETACH, UNTIE

un·fa·vor·able \-'fāv-(ə-)rə-bəl\ adj **:** not favorable — **un·fa·vor·ably** adv

un·feel·ing \-'fē-liŋ\ adj **1 :** lacking feeling **:** INSENSATE **2 :** HARDHEARTED, CRUEL — **un·feel·ing·ly** adv

un·feigned \-'fānd\ adj **:** not feigned **:** not hypocritical **:** GENUINE

un·fet·ter \-'fet-ər\ vb **1 :** to free from fetters **2 :** LIBERATE

¹un·fit \'ən-'fit\ adj **:** not fit or suitable; esp **:** physically or mentally unsound — **un·fit·ness** n

²unfit vb **:** DISABLE, DISQUALIFY

un·fix \'ən-'fiks\ vb **1 :** to loosen from a fastening **:** DETACH **2 :** UNSETTLE

un·fledged \-'flejd\ adj **:** not feathered or ready for flight; also **:** IMMATURE, CALLOW

un·flinch·ing \-'flin-chiŋ\ adj **:** not flinching or shrinking **:** STEADFAST

un·fold \-'fōld\ vb **1 :** to open the folds of **:** open up **2 :** to lay open to view **:** REVEAL, DISCLOSE ⟨~ a plan⟩ **3 :** BLOSSOM, DEVELOP

un·fold·ed \-'fōl-dəd\ adj **:** not folded

un·for·get·ta·ble \-,ən-fər-'get-ə-bəl\ adj **:** not to be forgotten **:** lasting in memory — **un·for·get·ta·bly** adv

un·formed \'ən-'fôrmd\ adj **:** not regularly formed **:** SHAPELESS

un·for·tu·nate \-'fôrch-(ə-)nət\ adj **1 :** not fortunate **:** UNLUCKY **2 :** attended with misfortune **3 :** UNSUITABLE — **unfortunate** n — **un·for·tu·nate·ly** adv

un·found·ed \-'faûn-dəd\ adj **:** lacking a sound basis **:** GROUNDLESS ⟨an ~ rumor⟩

un·fre·quent·ed \,ən-fri-'kwent-əd\ adj **:** seldom visited or traveled over

un·friend·ly \'ən-'frend-lē\ adj **1 :** not friendly or kind **:** HOSTILE **2 :** UNFAVORABLE — **un·friend·li·ness** n

un·frock \-'fräk\ vb **:** to divest of a frock; esp **:** to deprive (as a priest) of the right to exercise the functions of his office

un·fruit·ful \-'früt-fəl\ adj **1 :** not producing fruit or offspring **:** UNPRODUCTIVE **2 :** yielding no desired or valuable result ⟨~ efforts⟩

un·furl \-'fərl\ vb **:** to loose from a furled state **:** UNFOLD

un·gain·ly \-'gān-lē\ adj **:** CLUMSY, AWKWARD — **un·gain·li·ness** n

un·gen·er·ous \'ən-'jen-(ə-)rəs\ adj **:** not generous or liberal **:** PETTY, MEAN, STINGY

un·gird \'gərd\ vb **:** to divest of a restraining band or girdle **:** UNBIND

un·god·ly \'gäd-lē\ adj **1 :** IMPIOUS, IRRELIGIOUS **2 :** SINFUL, WICKED **3 :** OUTRAGEOUS — **un·god·li·ness** n

un·gov·ern·able \-'gəv-ər-nə-bəl\ adj **:** not capable of being governed, guided, or restrained **:** UNRULY

un·grace·ful \-'grās-fəl\ adj **:** not graceful **:** AWKWARD — **un·grace·ful·ly** adv

un·gra·cious \-'grā-shəs\ adj **1 :** not courteous **:** RUDE **2 :** not pleasing **:** DISAGREEABLE

un·grate·ful \'ən-'grāt-fəl\ adj **1 :** not thankful for favors **2 :** not pleasing **:** DISAGREEABLE — **un·grate·ful·ly** adv — **un·grate·ful·ness** n

un·ground·ed \-'graün-dəd\ adj **1 :** UNFOUNDED, BASELESS **2 :** not instructed or informed

un·guard·ed \-'gärd-əd\ adj **1 :** UNPROTECTED **2 :** DIRECT, INCAUTIOUS

un·guent \'əŋ-gwənt\ n **:** a soothing or healing salve **:** OINTMENT

¹un·gu·late \'əŋ-gyə-lət\ adj **:** having hoofs

²ungulate n **:** a hoofed mammal (as a cow, horse, or rhinoceros)

un·hal·lowed \'ən-'hal-ōd\ adj **1 :** not consecrated **:** UNHOLY **2 :** IMPIOUS, PROFANE

un·hand \-'hand\ vb **:** to remove the hand from **:** let go

un·hand·some \-'han-səm\ adj **1 :** not beautiful or handsome **:** HOMELY **2 :** UNBECOMING **3 :** DISCOURTEOUS, RUDE

un·handy \-'han-dē\ adj **:** INCONVENIENT; also **:** AWKWARD

un·hap·py \-'hap-ē\ adj **1 :** UNLUCKY, UNFORTUNATE **2 :** SAD, MISERABLE **3 :** INAPPROPRIATE ⟨~ color combination⟩ — **un·hap·pi·ly** adv — **un·hap·pi·ness** n

un·har·ness \'ən-'här-nəs\ vb **:** to remove the harness from (as a horse)

un·healthy \-'hel-thē\ adj **1 :** not conducive to health **:** UNWHOLESOME **2 :** SICKLY, DISEASED

un·heard \-'hərd\ adj **1 :** not heard **2 :** not granted a hearing

un·heard-of \-,ˌəv, -,äv\ adj **:** previously unknown **:** UNPRECEDENTED

un·hinge \'ən-'hinj\ vb **1 :** to take from the hinges **2 :** to make unstable (as one's mind)

un·hitch \-'hich\ vb **:** UNFASTEN, LOOSE

un·ho·ly \-'hō-lē\ adj **:** not holy **:** PROFANE, WICKED — **un·ho·li·ness** n

un·hook \-'hük\ vb **:** to loose or become loosed from a hook

un·horse \-'hôrs\ vb **:** to dislodge from or as if from a horse **:** UNSEAT

uni·cam·er·al \,yü-ni-'kam-(ə-)rəl\ adj **:** having a single legislative house or chamber

uni·cel·lu·lar \-'sel-yə-lər\ adj **:** of or having a single cell — **uni·cel·lu·lar·i·ty** \-,sel-yə-'lar-ət-ē\ n

uni·corn \'yü-nə-,kôrn\ n [OF unicorne, fr. LL unicornis, fr. L, having one horn, fr. unus one + cornu horn] **:** a legendary animal with one horn in the middle of the forehead

uni·cy·cle \'yü-ni-,sī-kəl\ n **:** a vehicle that has a single wheel and is usu. propelled by pedals

uni·fi·ca·tion \,yü-nə-fə-'kā-shən\ n **:** the act, process, or result of unifying **:** the state of being unified

¹uni·form \'yü-nə-,fôrm\ adj **:** having always the same form, manner, or degree **:** not varying **2 :** of the same form with others **:** conforming to one rule — **u·ni·form·ly** adv

²uniform vb **:** to clothe with a uniform

³uniform n **:** distinctive dress worn by members of a particular group (as an army or a police force)

uni·for·mi·ty \ˌyü-nə-ˈfȯr-mət-ē\ n **:** the state of being uniform **:** absence of variation

uni·fy \ˈyü-nə-ˌfī\ vb **:** to make into a unit or a coherent whole **:** UNITE

uni·lat·er·al \ˌyü-nə-ˈlat-(ə-)rəl\ adj **:** of, having, affecting, or done by one side only — **uni·lat·er·al·ly** adv

un·im·peach·able \ˌən-im-ˈpē-chə-bəl\ adj **:** exempt from liability to accusation **:** BLAMELESS

un·in·hib·it·ed \ˌən-in-ˈhib-ət-əd\ adj **:** free from inhibition; also **:** boisterously informal

un·in·tel·li·gent \-ˈtel-ə-jənt\ adj **:** lacking intelligence **:** UNWISE, IGNORANT

un·in·tel·li·gi·ble \-jə-bəl\ adj **:** not intelligible **:** OBSCURE — **un·in·tel·li·gi·bly** adv

un·in·ten·tion·al \ˌən-in-ˈtench-(ə-)nəl\ adj **:** not intentional — **un·in·ten·tion·al·ly** adv

un·in·ter·est·ed \ˈən-ˈin-t(ə-)rəs-təd, -tə-ˌres-\ adj **1 :** having no interest and esp. no property interest in **2 :** not having the mind or feelings engaged **:** not having the curiosity or sympathy aroused

un·in·ter·rupt·ed \ˌən-ˌint-ə-ˈrəp-təd\ adj **:** not interrupted **:** CONTINUOUS

union \ˈyü-nyən\ n **1 :** an act or instance of uniting two or more things into one **:** the state of being so united **:** COMBINATION, JUNCTION **2 :** a uniting in marriage **3 :** something formed by a combining of parts or members; esp **:** a confederation of independent individuals (as nations or persons) for some common purpose **4 :** an organization of workers (labor union, trade union) formed to advance its members' interests esp. in respect to wages and working conditions **5 :** a device emblematic of union used on or as a national flag; also **:** the upper inner corner of a flag **6 :** any of various devices for connecting parts (as of a machine); esp **:** a coupling for pipes

Union adj **:** of, relating to, or being the side favoring the federal union in the U.S. Civil War (the ~ army)

union·ism n **1 :** the principle or policy of forming or adhering to a union; esp, cap **:** adherence to the policy of a firm federal union prior to or during the U.S. Civil War **2 :** the principles or system of trade unions — **union·ist** n, often cap

union·ize vb **:** to form into or cause to become a member of a labor union — **union·iza·tion** \ˌyü-nyən-ə-ˈzā-shən\ n

union jack n **1 :** a flag consisting of the part of a national flag that signifies union **2** cap U & J **:** the national flag of the United Kingdom

unique \yu̇-ˈnēk\ adj **1 :** being the only one of its kind **:** SINGLE, SOLE **2 :** very unusual **:** NOTABLE

uni·son \ˈyü-nə-sən\ n **1 :** sameness or identity in pitch **2 :** the condition of being tuned or sounded at the same pitch or at an octave (sing **in** ~ rather than in harmony) **3 :** exact agreement **:** ACCORD

unit \ˈyü-nət\ n **1 :** the least whole number **:** ONE **2 :** a definite amount or quantity used as a standard of measure-

ment **3 :** a single thing or person or group that is a constituent of a whole (the family is the ~ of a nation); also **:** a part of a military establishment that has a prescribed organization

Uni·tar·i·an \ˌyü-nə-ˈter-ē-ən\ n **:** a member of a religious denomination stressing individual freedom of belief — **Uni·tar·i·an·ism** n

uni·tary \ˈyü-nə-ˌter-ē\ adj **1 :** of or relating to a unit **:** characterized by unity **2 :** not divided

unite \yu̇-ˈnīt\ vb **1 :** to put or join together so as to make one **:** COMBINE, COALESCE **2 :** to join by a legal or moral bond (as nations by treaty); also **:** to join in interest or fellowship **3 :** AMALGAMATE, CONSOLIDATE **4 :** to join in an act (~ in prayer)

unit·ed \yu̇-ˈnīt-əd\ adj **1 :** made one **:** COMBINED **2 :** relating to or produced by joint action **3 :** being in agreement **:** HARMONIOUS

uni·ty \ˈyü-nət-ē\ n **1 :** the quality or state of being one **:** ONENESS, SINGLENESS **2 :** a definite quantity or combination of quantities taken as one or for which 1 is made to stand in calculation **3 :** CONCORD, ACCORD, HARMONY **4 :** continuity without change (~ of purpose) **5 :** reference of all the parts of a literary or artistic composition to a single main idea **:** singleness of effect or style **6 :** totality of related parts **syn** solidarity, union

uni·valve \ˈyü-ni-ˌvalv\ n **:** a mollusk (as a snail or whelk) having a shell with one valve

uni·ver·sal \ˌyü-nə-ˈvər-səl\ adj **1 :** including, covering, or affecting the whole without limit or exception **:** UNLIMITED, GENERAL (a ~ rule) **2 :** present or occurring everywhere **3 :** used or for use among all (a ~ language) **4 :** affirming or denying something of all members of a class ("No man knows everything" is a ~ negative) — **uni·ver·sal·ly** adv

uni·ver·sal·i·ty \-vər-ˈsal-ət-ē\ n **:** the quality or state of being universal (as in range, occurrence, or appeal)

uni·verse \ˈyü-nə-ˌvərs\ n **:** all created things and phenomena viewed as constituting one system or whole

uni·ver·si·ty \ˌyü-nə-ˈvər-s(ə-)tē\ n **:** an institution of higher learning authorized to confer degrees in various special fields (as theology, law, and medicine) as well as in the arts and sciences generally

un·just \ˈən-ˈjəst\ adj **:** characterized by injustice **:** WRONGFUL — **un·just·ly** adv

un·kempt \-ˈkempt\ adj **1 :** not combed **:** DISHEVELED **2 :** ROUGH, UNPOLISHED

un·kind \-ˈkīnd\ adj **:** wanting in kindness or sympathy **:** CRUEL, HARSH — **un·kind·ly** adv — **un·kind·ness** n

un·kind·ly adj **:** UNKIND

un·know·ing \ˈən-ˈnō-iŋ\ adj **:** not knowing **:** IGNORANT — **un·know·ing·ly** adv

un·known \ˈən-ˈnōn\ adj **:** not known **:** UNFAMILIAR; also **:** not ascertained — **unknown** n

un·lace \-ˈlās\ vb **:** to loose by undoing a lacing

un·lade \-ˈlād\ vb **:** to take the load or cargo from **:** UNLOAD

un·latch \-ˈlach\ vb **1 :** to open or loose by lifting the latch **2 :** to become loosed or opened

un·law·ful \ˈən-ˈlȯ-fəl\ adj **1 :** not law-

ful : ILLEGAL **2 :** ILLEGITIMATE — **un-law-ful-ly** adv

un-learn \-'lərn\ vb **:** to put out of one's knowledge or memory

un-learned adj **1** \-'lər-nəd\ **:** UNEDUCATED, ILLITERATE **2** \-'lərnd\ **:** not learned by study **:** not known **3** \-'lərnd\ **:** not learned by previous experience

un-leash \-'lēsh\ vb **:** to free from or as if from a leash

un-less \ən-,les\ conj **:** except on condition that ⟨won't go ~ you do⟩

un-let-tered \'ən-'let-ərd\ adj **:** not educated **:** ILLITERATE

un-like \-'līk\ prep **1 :** different from ⟨he's quite ~ his brother⟩ **2 :** unusual for ⟨it's ~ him to be late⟩ **3 :** differently from ⟨behaves ~ his brother⟩

unlike adj **1 :** not like **:** DISSIMILAR, DIFFERENT **2 :** UNEQUAL — **un-like-ness** n

un-like-li-hood \-lē-,hu̇d\ n **:** IMPROBABILITY

un-like-ly \-lē\ adj **1 :** not likely **:** IMPROBABLE **2 :** likely to fail **:** UNPROMISING

un-lim-ber \'ən-'lim-bər\ vb **:** to get ready for action

un-load \-'lōd\ vb **1 :** to take away or off **:** REMOVE ⟨~ cargo from a hold⟩; also **:** to get rid of **2 :** to take a load from; also **:** to relieve or set free **:** UNBURDEN ⟨~ one's mind of worries⟩ **3 :** to get rid of or be relieved of a burden **4 :** to sell in volume ⟨~ surplus goods⟩

un-lock \-'läk\ vb **1 :** to unfasten through release of a lock **2 :** RELEASE ⟨~ed her emotions⟩ **3 :** DISCLOSE, REVEAL

un-looked–for \-'lu̇kt-,fȯr\ adj **:** UNEXPECTED

un-loose \'ən-'lüs\ vb **:** to relax the strain of **:** set free; also **:** UNTIE

un-loos-en \-'lüs-ᵊn\ vb **:** UNLOOSE

un-love-ly \-'ləv-lē\ adj **:** having no charm or appeal **:** not amiable **:** DISAGREEABLE

un-lucky \-'lək-ē\ adj **1 :** UNFORTUNATE, ILL-FATED **2 :** likely to bring misfortune **:** INAUSPICIOUS **3 :** REGRETTABLE — **un-luck-i-ly** adv

un-man \'ən-'man\ vb **1 :** to deprive of manly courage **2 :** to deprive of men

un-man-ly \-'man-lē\ adj **:** not manly **:** COWARDLY; also **:** EFFEMINATE

un-manned \-'mand\ adj **:** having no men aboard

un-man-ner-ly \-'man-ər-lē\ adj **:** RUDE, IMPOLITE — **unmannerly** adv

un-mask \-'mask\ vb **1 :** to strip of a mask or a disguise **:** EXPOSE **2 :** to remove one's own disguise (as at a masquerade)

un-mean-ing \-'mē-niŋ\ adj **:** having no meaning **:** SENSELESS

un-meet \-'mēt\ adj **:** not meet or fit **:** UNSUITABLE, IMPROPER

un-men-tion-able \-'mench-(ə-)nə-bəl\ adj **:** not fit or proper to be talked about

un-mer-ci-ful \-'mər-si-fəl\ adj **:** not merciful **:** CRUEL, MERCILESS

un-mind-ful \-'mīnd-fəl\ adj **:** not mindful **:** CARELESS, UNAWARE

un-mis-tak-able \,ən-mə-'stā-kə-bəl\ adj **:** not capable of being mistaken or misunderstood **:** CLEAR, OBVIOUS — **un-mis-tak-ably** adv

un-mit-i-gat-ed \'ən-'mit-ə-,gāt-əd\ adj **1 :** not softened or lessened **2 :** ABSOLUTE, DOWNRIGHT ⟨an ~ liar⟩

un-moor \-'mu̇r\ vb **1 :** to loose from or as if from moorings **2 :** to cast off moorings

un-mor-al \-'mȯr-əl\ adj **:** having no moral perception or quality **:** being neither moral nor immoral — **un-mo-ral-i-ty** \,ən-mə-'ral-ət-ē\ n

un-moved \'ən-'müvd\ adj **1 :** not moved **2 :** FIRM, RESOLUTE, UNSHAKEN; also **:** CALM, UNDISTURBED

un-nat-u-ral \-'nach-(ə-)rəl\ adj **:** contrary to or acting contrary to nature or natural instincts **:** ARTIFICIAL, IRREGULAR; also **:** ABNORMAL — **un-nat-u-ral-ly** adv — **un-nat-u-ral-ness** n

un-nec-es-sar-i-ly \,ən-,nes-ə-'ser-ə-lē\ adv **1 :** not by necessity ⟨spent more money ~⟩ **2 :** to an unnecessary degree ⟨~ harsh⟩

un-nerve \'ən-'nərv\ vb **:** to deprive of nerve, courage, or self-control

un-num-bered \-'nəm-bərd\ adj **:** not numbered or counted **:** INNUMERABLE

un-ob-tru-sive \,ən-əb-'trü-siv\ adj **:** not obtrusive or forward **:** not bold **:** INCONSPICUOUS

un-oc-cu-pied \'ən-'äk-yə-,pīd\ adj **1 :** not busy **:** UNEMPLOYED **2 :** not occupied **:** EMPTY, VACANT

un-or-ga-nized \-'ȯr-gə-,nīzd\ adj **1 :** not formed or brought into an integrated or ordered whole **2 :** not organized into unions ⟨~ labor⟩

un-pack \-'pak\ vb **1 :** to separate and remove things packed **2 :** to open and remove the contents of ⟨~ a trunk⟩

un-par-al-leled \-'par-ə-,leld\ adj **:** having no parallel; esp **:** having no equal or match **:** UNSURPASSED

un-par-lia-men-ta-ry \,ən-,pär-lə-'ment(ə-)rē\ adj **:** contrary to parliamentary practice

un-peg \'ən-'peg\ vb **:** to remove a peg from **:** UNFASTEN

un-pile \-'pīl\ vb **:** to take or disentangle from a pile; also **:** to become disentangled from a pile

un-pin \-'pin\ vb **:** to remove a pin from **:** UNFASTEN

un-pleas-ant \-'plez-ᵊnt\ adj **:** not pleasant **:** DISAGREEABLE, DISPLEASING — **un-pleas-ant-ly** adv — **un-pleas-ant-ness** n

un-plumbed \-'pləmd\ adj **1 :** not tested with a plumb line **2 :** not measured with a plumb **3 :** not explored in depth, intensity, or significance

un-pop-u-lar \-'päp-yə-lər\ adj **:** not popular **:** looked upon or received unfavorably — **un-pop-u-lar-i-ty** \,ən-,päp-yə-'lar-ət-ē\ n

un-prec-e-dent-ed \-'pres-ə-,dent-əd\ adj **:** having no precedent **:** NOVEL, NEW

un-pre-dict-able \,ən-pri-'dik-tə-bəl\ adj **:** not predictable — **un-pre-dict-abil-i-ty** \-,dik-tə-'bil-ət-ē\ n — **un-pre-dict-ably** \-'dik-tə-blē\ adv

un-pre-ten-tious \-'ten-chəs\ adj **:** not pretentious or pompous **:** SIMPLE, MODEST

un-prin-ci-pled \'ən-'prin-sə-pəld\ adj **:** lacking sound or honorable principles **:** UNSCRUPULOUS

un·print·able \-'print-ə-bəl\ *adj* : unfit to be printed

un·pro·fes·sion·al \,ən-prə-'fesh-(ə-)nəl\ *adj* : not conforming to the technical or ethical standards of a profession

un·prof·it·able \'ən-'präf-ət-ə-bəl\ *adj* : not profitable : USELESS

un·qual·i·fied \-'kwäl-ə-,fīd\ *adj* 1 : not having requisite qualifications 2 : not modified or restricted by reservations — **un·qual·i·fied·ly** \-,fī-(ə)d-lē\ *adv*

un·ques·tion·able \-'kwes-chə-nə-bəl\ *adj* 1 : acknowledged as beyond doubt 2 : INDISPUTABLE — **un·ques·tion·a·bly** *adv*

un·ques·tion·ing \-chə-niŋ\ *adj* : not questioning : accepting without examination or hesitation — **un·ques·tion·ing·ly** *adv*

un·qui·et \-'kwī-ət\ *adj* : AGITATED, DISTURBED, RESTLESS, UNEASY

un·quote \'ən-,kwōt\ *vb* : to inform a hearer or reader that the matter preceding is quoted

un·rav·el \-'rav-əl\ *vb* 1 : to separate the threads of : DISENTANGLE 2 : SOLVE (~ a mystery) 3 : to become unraveled

un·read \-'red\ *adj* 1 : not read 2 : not well informed through reading 3 : UNEDUCATED

un·re·al \'ən-'rē-(ə)l\ *adj* : lacking in reality, substance, or genuineness : ARTIFICIAL — **un·re·al·i·ty** \,ən-rē-'al-ət-ē\ *n*

un·rea·son·able \-'rēz-(ə-)nə-bəl\ *adj* 1 : not governed by or acting according to reason; *also* : not conformable to reason : ABSURD 2 : exceeding the bounds of reason or moderation — **un·rea·son·able·ness** *n* — **un·rea·son·ably** *adv*

un·rea·soned \-'rēz-°nd\ *adj* : not based on reason or reasoning

un·rea·son·ing \-'rēz(-)niŋ\ *adj* : not using or showing the use of reason as a guide or control

un·re·con·struct·ed \,ən-,rē-kən-'strək-təd\ *adj* : not reconciled to some political, economic, or social change; *esp* : holding stubbornly to principles, beliefs, or views that are or are held to be outmoded

un·reel \'ən-'rēl\ *vb* : to unwind from or as if from a reel

un·re·gen·er·ate \,ən-ri-'jen-(ə-)rət\ *adj* : not regenerated or reformed

un·re·lent·ing \-'lent-iŋ\ *adj* 1 : not yielding in determination : HARD, STERN 2 : not letting up or weakening in vigor or pace — **un·re·lent·ing·ly** *adv*

un·re·mit·ting \-'mit-iŋ\ *adj* : CONTINUOUS, INCESSANT, PERSEVERING — **un·re·mit·ting·ly** *adv*

un·re·served \-'zərvd\ *adj* 1 : not held in reserve : not kept back 2 : having or showing no reserve in manner or speech — **un·re·serv·ed·ly** \-'zər-vəd-lē\ *adv*

un·rest \'ən-'rest\ *n* : want of rest : a disturbed or uneasy state : TURMOIL

un·re·strained \,ən-ri-'strānd\ *adj* 1 : IMMODERATE, UNCONTROLLED 2 : SPONTANEOUS

un·rid·dle \'ən-'rid-°l\ *vb* : to read the riddle of : SOLVE

un·righ·teous \-'rī-chəs\ *adj* 1 : SINFUL, WICKED 2 : UNJUST — **un·righ·teous·ness** *n*

un·ripe \-'rīp\ *adj* : not ripe : IMMATURE

un·ri·valed *or* **un·ri·valled** \-'rī-vəld\ *adj* : having no rival : INCOMPARABLE, UNEQUALED

un·robe \-'rōb\ *vb* : DISROBE, UNDRESS

un·roll \-'rōl\ *vb* 1 : to unwind a roll of : open out 2 : DISPLAY, DISCLOSE 3 : to become unrolled or spread out : UNFOLD

un·roof \-'rüf, -'rùf\ *vb* : to strip off the roof or covering of

un·ruf·fled \-'rəf-əld\ *adj* 1 : not agitated or upset 2 : not ruffled : SMOOTH (~ water)

un·ru·ly \ən-'rü-lē\ *adj* : not submissive to rule or restraint : TURBULENT, UNCONTROLLABLE, UNGOVERNABLE

un·sad·dle \-'sad-°l\ *vb* 1 : to remove the saddle from a horse 2 : UNHORSE

un·saved \-'sāvd\ *adj* : not saved; *esp* : not rescued from eternal punishment

un·sa·vory \-'sāv-(ə-)rē\ *adj* 1 : TASTELESS 2 : unpleasant to taste or smell 3 : morally offensive

un·say \-'sā\ *vb* : to take back (something said) : RETRACT, WITHDRAW

un·scathed \-'skāthd\ *adj* : wholly unharmed : not injured

un·schooled \-'sküld\ *adj* : not schooled : UNTAUGHT, UNTRAINED

un·sci·en·tif·ic \,ən-,sī-ən-'tif-ik\ *adj* : not scientific : not in accord with the principles and methods of science

un·scram·ble \'ən-'skram-bəl\ *vb* 1 : RESOLVE, CLARIFY 2 : to restore (as a radio message) to intelligible form

un·screw \-'skrü\ *vb* 1 : to draw the screws from 2 : to loosen by turning

un·scru·pu·lous \-'skrü-pyə-ləs\ *adj* : not scrupulous : UNPRINCIPLED

un·seal \-'sēl\ *vb* : to break or remove the seal of : OPEN

un·search·able \-'sər-chə-bəl\ *adj* : not to be searched or explored : INSCRUTABLE

un·sea·son·able \-'sēz-(°)nə-bəl\ *adj* : not seasonable : happening or coming at the wrong time : UNTIMELY — **un·sea·son·ably** *adv*

un·seat \'ən-'sēt\ *vb* 1 : to throw from one's seat esp. on horseback 2 : to remove from political office

un·seem·ly \-'sēm-lē\ *adj* : not according with established standards of good form or taste; *also* : not suitable

un·seg·re·gat·ed \-'seg-ri-,gāt-əd\ *adj* : not segregated; *esp* : free from racial segregation

un·self·ish \-'sel-fish\ *adj* : not selfish : GENEROUS — **un·self·ish·ly** *adv* — **un·self·ish·ness** *n*

un·set·tle \-'set-°l\ *vb* : to move or loosen from a settled position : DISPLACE, DISTURB

un·set·tled *adj* 1 : not settled : not fixed (as in position or character) 2 : not calm : DISTURBED 3 : not decided in mind : UNDETERMINED (~ what to do) 4 : not paid (~ accounts) 5 : not occupied by settlers

un·shack·le \-'shak-əl\ *vb* : to free from shackles

un·shaped \'ən-'shāpt\ *adj* : not shaped : not perfectly shaped : RUDE (~ ideas) (~ timber)

un·sheathe \-'shēth\ *vb* : to draw from or as if from a sheath

un·ship \-'ship\ *vb* 1 : to remove from a ship 2 : to remove or become removed from position (~ an oar)

un·shod \-'shäd\ *adj* : not shod : not wearing shoes

un·sight·ly \-'sīt-lē\ *adj* : unpleasant to the sight : UGLY

un·skilled \-'skild\ *adj* 1 : not skilled;

esp : not skilled in a specified branch of work **2** : not requiring skill

un·skill·ful \-'skil-fəl\ *adʲ* : lacking in skill or proficiency

un·snap \-'snap\ *vb* : to loosen or free by or as if by undoing a snap

un·snarl \-'snärl\ *vb* : to remove snarls from : UNTANGLE

un·so·phis·ti·cat·ed \ˌən-sə-'fis-tə-ˌkāt-əd\ *adj* **1** : not worldly-wise : lacking sophistication **2** : PLAIN, SIMPLE

un·sought \'ən-'sȯt\ *adj* : not sought : not searched for or asked for : not obtained by effort

un·sound \-'saund\ *adj* **1** : not healthy or whole; *also* : not mentally normal **2** : not valid **3** : not firmly made or fixed — **un·sound·ly** *adv* — **un·sound·ness** *n*

un·spar·ing \-'spa(ə)r-iŋ\ *adj* **1** : HARD, RUTHLESS **2** : LIBERAL, PROFUSE

un·speak·able \-'spē-kə-bəl\ *adj* **1** : impossible to express in words **2** : extremely bad — **un·speak·ably** *adv*

un·spot·ted \-'spät-əd\ *adj* : free from spot or stain; *esp* : free from moral stain

un·sta·ble \'ən-'stā-bəl\ *adj* **1** : not stable **2** : FLUCTUATING, IRREGULAR **2** : FICKLE, VACILLATING; *also* : having defective emotional control **3** : readily changing chemically or physically; *esp* : tending to decompose spontaneously ⟨an ~ atomic nucleus⟩

un·steady \-'sted-ē\ *adj* : not steady : UNSTABLE — **un·stead·i·ly** *adv* — **un·stead·i·ness** *n*

un·stop \-'stäp\ *vb* **1** : to free from an obstruction : OPEN **2** : to remove a stopper from

un·strap \-'strap\ *vb* : to remove or loose a strap from

un·strung \-'strəŋ\ *adj* **1** : having the strings loose or detached **2** : nervously tired or anxious

un·stud·ied \-'stəd-ēd\ *adj* **1** : not acquired by study **2** : NATURAL, UNFORCED

un·sub·stan·tial \ˌən-səb-'stan-chəl\ *adj* : lacking substance, firmness, or strength

un·suit·able \'ən-'süt-ə-bəl\ *adj* : not suitable or fitting : UNBECOMING, INAPPROPRIATE — **un·suit·ably** *adv*

un·sung \-'səŋ\ *adj* **1** : not sung **2** : not celebrated in song or verse ⟨~ heroes⟩

un·tan·gle \-'taŋ-gəl\ *vb* **1** : DISENTANGLE **2** : to straighten out : RESOLVE ⟨~ a problem⟩

un·taught \-'tȯt\ *adj* **1** : not instructed or taught : IGNORANT **2** : NATURAL, SPONTANEOUS

un·think·able \-'thiŋ-kə-bəl\ *adj* : not to be thought of or considered as possible : INCREDIBLE

un·think·ing \-kiŋ\ *adj* : not thinking; *esp* : THOUGHTLESS, HEEDLESS, CARELESS — **un·think·ing·ly** *adv*

un·thought-of \'ən-'thȯt-ˌəv, -ˌäv\ *adj* : not thought of : not considered

un·tie \'ən-'tī\ *vb* **1** : to free from something that ties, fastens, or restrains : UNBIND **2** : DISENTANGLE, RESOLVE **3** : to become loosened or unbound

¹un·til \(ˌ)ən-'til\ *prep* : up to the time of ⟨worked ~ 5 o'clock⟩

²until *conj* **1** : up to the time that ⟨wait ~ he calls⟩ **2** : to the point or degree that ⟨ran ~ he was breathless⟩

¹un·time·ly \'ən-'tīm-lē\ *adv* : at an inopportune time : UNSEASONABLY; *also* : PREMATURELY

²untimely *adj* : PREMATURE ⟨~ death⟩; *also* : INOPPORTUNE, UNSEASONABLE

un·to \'ən-tə, -tü\ *prep* : TO

un·told \'ən-'tōld\ *adj* **1** : not told : not revealed **2** : not counted : VAST, NUMBERLESS

¹un·touch·able \-'təch-ə-bəl\ *adʲ* : forbidden to the touch

²untouchable *n* : a member of the lowest social class in India having in traditional Hindu belief the quality of defiling by contact a member of a higher caste

un·to·ward \'ən-'tō(-ə)rd\ *adj* **1** : difficult to manage : STUBBORN, WILLFUL ⟨an ~ child⟩ **2** : INCONVENIENT, TROUBLESOME, UNLUCKY ⟨an ~ encounter⟩

un·tried \-'trīd\ *adj* : not tested or proved by experience or trial; *also* : not tried in court

un·true \-'trü\ *adj* **1** : not faithful : DISLOYAL **2** : not according with a standard of correctness : INEXACT **3** : FALSE

un·truth \-'trüth\ *n* **1** : lack of truthfulness : FALSITY **2** : FALSEHOOD

un·tune \-'t(y)ün\ *vb* **1** : to put out of tune **2** : DISARRANGE, DISCOMPOSE

un·tu·tored \-'t(y)üt-ərd\ *adj* **1** : UNTAUGHT, UNLEARNED, IGNORANT

un·twine \'ən-'twīn\ *vb* : UNWIND, DISENTANGLE

un·twist \-'twist\ *vb* **1** : to separate the twisted parts of : UNTWINE **2** : to become untwined

un·used *adj* **1** \-'yüst, -'yüzd\ : UNACCUSTOMED **2** \-'yüzd\ : not used

un·usu·al \-'yü-zh(ə-w)əl\ *adj* : not usual : UNCOMMON, RARE — **un·usu·al·ly** *adv*

un·ut·ter·able \-'ət-ə-rə-bəl\ *adj* **1** : not pronounceable **2** : INEXPRESSIBLE — **un·ut·ter·ably** *adv*

un·var·nished \'ən-'vär-nisht\ *adj* **1** : not varnished **2** : not embellished : PLAIN ⟨the ~ truth⟩

un·veil \-'vāl\ *vb* **1** : to remove a veil or covering from : DISCLOSE **2** : to remove a veil : reveal oneself

un·voiced \-'vȯist\ *adj* **1** : not verbally expressed : UNSPOKEN **2** : VOICELESS **2**

un·war·rant·able \-'wȯr-ənt-ə-bəl\ *adj* : not justifiable : INEXCUSABLE

un·weave \-'wēv\ *vb* : DISENTANGLE, RAVEL

un·well \-'wel\ *adj* **1** : SICK, AILING **2** : MENSTRUATING

un·wept \'ən-'wept\ *adj* : not mourned : UNLAMENTED ⟨died ~ and unsung⟩

un·whole·some \-'hōl-səm\ *adj* : harmful to physical, mental, or moral well-being

un·wieldy \-'wēl-dē\ *adj* : not easily managed or handled because of size or weight : AWKWARD, CLUMSY, CUMBERSOME ⟨an ~ tool⟩

un·will·ing \-'wil-iŋ\ *adj* : not willing — **un·will·ing·ly** *adv* — **un·will·ing·ness** *n*

un·wind \-'wīnd\ *vb* **1** : to undo something that is wound : loose from coils **2** : to become unwound : be capable of being unwound

un·wise \-'wīz\ *adj* : not wise : FOOLISH — **un·wise·ly** *adv*

un·wit·ting \'ən-'wit-iŋ\ *adj* **1** : not

intended **:** INADVERTENT **2 :** not knowing **:** UNAWARE — **un·wit·ting·ly** adv

un·wont·ed \-'wȯnt-əd, -'wȯnt-, -'wənt-\ adj **1 :** RARE, UNUSUAL **2** archaic **:** not accustomed by experience — **un·wont·ed·ly** adv

un·world·ly \-'wərld-lē\ adj **1 :** not of this world; esp **:** SPIRITUAL **2 :** NAÏVE **3 :** not swayed by worldly considerations — **un·world·li·ness** n

un·wor·thy \-'wər-thē\ adj **1 :** BASE, DISHONORABLE **2 :** not meritorious **:** not worthy **:** UNDESERVING — **un·wor·thi·ness** n

un·wrap \-'rap\ vb **:** to free from wrappings **:** DISCLOSE

un·writ·ten \-'rit-ᵊn\ adj **1 :** not in writing **:** ORAL, TRADITIONAL ⟨an ~ law⟩ **2 :** containing no writing **:** BLANK

un·yield·ing \-'yēl-diŋ\ adj **1 :** characterized by lack of softness or flexibility **2 :** characterized by firmness or obduracy

un·yoke \-'yōk\ vb **:** to free from a yoke; also **:** SEPARATE, DISCONNECT

un·zip \-'zip\ vb **:** to zip open **:** open by means of a zipper

¹up \'əp\ adv **1 :** in or to a higher position or level **:** away from the center of the earth **2 :** from beneath a surface (as ground or water) **3 :** from below the horizon **4 :** in or into an upright position **5 :** out of bed **6 :** with greater intensity ⟨speak ~⟩ **7 :** in or into a better or more advanced state or a state of greater intensity or activity ⟨stir ~ a fire⟩ **8 :** into existence, evidence, or knowledge ⟨the missing book turned ~⟩ **9 :** into consideration ⟨bring the matter ~⟩ **10 :** to or at bat **11 :** into possession or custody ⟨gave himself ~⟩ **12 :** ENTIRELY, COMPLETELY ⟨eat it ~⟩ **13** — used for emphasis ⟨clean ~ a room⟩ **14 :** ASIDE, BY ⟨lay ~ supplies⟩ **15 :** into a state of tightness or confinement ⟨wrap ~ the bread⟩ **16 :** so as to arrive or approach ⟨ran ~ the path⟩ **17 :** in a direction opposite to down **18 :** so as to be even with, overtake, or arrive at ⟨catch ~⟩ **19 :** in or into parts ⟨tear ~ paper⟩ **20 :** to a stop ⟨pull ~ at the curb⟩ **21 :** in advance ⟨one ~ on his opponent⟩ **22 :** for each side ⟨the score was 15 ~⟩

²up adj **1 :** risen above the horizon **2 :** being out of bed **3 :** relatively high ⟨prices are ~⟩ **4 :** RAISED, LIFTED **5 :** BUILT ⟨the house is ~⟩ **6 :** grown above a surface **7 :** moving, inclining, or directed upward **8 :** marked by agitation, excitement, or activity **9 :** READY; esp **:** highly prepared **10 :** going on **:** taking place ⟨find out what is ~⟩ **11 :** EXPIRED, ENDED ⟨the time is ~⟩ **12 :** well informed ⟨~ on the news⟩ **13 :** being ahead or in advance of an opponent ⟨one hole ~ in a match⟩ **14 :** presented for or being under consideration **15 :** charged before a court ⟨~ for robbery⟩

³up vb upped; up·ping **1 :** to act abruptly or surprisingly ⟨she upped and left home⟩ **2 :** to rise from a lying or sitting position **3 :** to move or cause to move upward **:** ASCEND

⁴up prep **1 :** to, toward, or at a higher point of ⟨~ a ladder⟩ **2 :** to or toward the source of ⟨~ the river⟩ **3 :** to or toward the northern part of ⟨~ the coast⟩ **4 :** to or toward the interior of ⟨traveling ~ the country⟩ **5 :** ALONG ⟨walk ~ the street⟩

⁵up n **1 :** an upward course or slope **2 :** a period or state of prosperity or success ⟨he had his ~s and downs⟩

up·beat \'əp-,bēt\ n **:** an unaccented beat in a musical measure; esp **:** the last beat of the measure

up·braid \əp-'brād\ vb **:** to criticize, reproach, or scold severely ⟨~ed him for his careless writing⟩

up·bring·ing \'əp-,briŋ-iŋ\ n **:** the process of bringing up and training

up·com·ing \'əp-'kəm-iŋ\ adj **:** FORTHCOMING, APPROACHING

up·coun·try \'əp-'kən-trē\ adj **:** of or relating to the interior of a country or a region — **up·country** adv

up·date \əp-'dāt\ vb **:** to bring up to date

up·draft \'əp-,draft, -,dràft\ n **:** an upward movement of gas (as air)

up·end \,əp-'end\ vb **:** to set, stand, or rise on end

¹up·grade \'əp-,grād\ n **1 :** an upward grade or slope **2 :** INCREASE, RISE **3 :** a rise toward a better state or position ⟨trade is on the ~⟩

²upgrade vb **:** to raise to a higher grade or position

up·growth \'əp-,grōth\ n **:** the process or result of growing up **:** upward growth **:** DEVELOPMENT

up·heav·al \əp-'hē-vəl\ n **1 :** the action or an instance of uplifting esp. of part of the earth's crust **2 :** a violent agitation or change

¹up·hill \'əp-'hil\ adv **:** upward on a hill or incline; also **:** against difficulties

²uphill adj **1 :** situated on elevated ground **2 :** ASCENDING **3 :** DIFFICULT, LABORIOUS

up·hold \,əp-'hōld\ vb **1 :** to give support to **2 :** to support against an opponent **3 :** to keep elevated **:** lift up — **up·hold·er** n

up·hol·ster \,əp-'hōl-stər\ vb **:** to furnish with or as if with upholstery; esp **:** to cover with padding and fabric that is fastened over the padding ⟨~ a chair⟩ — **up·hol·ster·er** n

up·hol·stery \-st(ə-)rē\ n **:** materials (as fabrics, padding, and springs) used to make a soft covering esp. for a seat

up·keep \'əp-,kēp\ n **:** the act or cost of keeping up or maintaining **:** MAINTENANCE; also **:** the state of being maintained

up·land \'əp-lənd, -,land\ n **:** high land esp. at some distance from the sea — **upland** adj

¹up·lift \,əp-'lift\ vb **1 :** to lift or raise up **:** ELEVATE **2 :** to improve the condition of esp. morally, socially, or intellectually ⟨~ the drama⟩

²up·lift \'əp-,lift\ n **1 :** an upheaval of the earth's surface **2 :** moral or social improvement; also **:** a movement to make such improvement

up·most \'əp-,mōst\ adj **:** UPPERMOST

up·on \ə-'pȯn, -'pän\ prep **:** ON

¹up·per \'əp-ər\ adj **1 :** higher in physical position, rank, or order **2 :** constituting the smaller and more restricted branch of a bicameral legislature **3** cap **:** being a later part or formation of a specific geological period **4 :** being toward the interior **:** further inland ⟨the ~ Amazon⟩ **5 :** NORTHERN ⟨~ New York State⟩

²upper n **:** one that is upper; esp **:** the parts of a shoe or boot above the sole

upper class n **:** a social class occupying a position above the middle class and having the highest status in a society — **upper-class** adj

up·per·class·man \,əp-ər-'klas-mən\ n : a junior or senior in a college or high school

up·per·cut \'əp-ər-,kət\ n : a short swinging punch delivered in an upward direction

upper hand n : MASTERY, ADVANTAGE

up·per·most \'əp-ər-,mōst\ adv : in or into the highest or most prominent position — **uppermost** adj

up·pish \'əp-ish\ adj : UPPITY

up·pi·ty \'əp-ət-ē\ adj : ARROGANT, PRESUMPTUOUS

up·raise \,əp-'rāz\ vb : to lift up : ELEVATE

up·rear \,əp-'riər\ vb 1 : to lift up : RAISE, ERECT 2 : RISE

¹**up·right** \'əp-,rīt\ adj 1 : PERPENDICULAR, VERTICAL 2 : erect in carriage or posture 3 : morally correct : JUST — **up·right·ly** adv — **up·right·ness** n

²**upright** n 1 : the state of being upright : a vertical position 2 : something upright

upright piano n : a piano whose strings run vertically

up·ris·ing \'əp-,rī-ziŋ\ n : INSURRECTION, REVOLT, REBELLION

up·roar \'əp-,rōr\ n : a state of commotion, excitement, or violent disturbance

up·roar·i·ous \,əp-'rōr-ē-əs\ adj 1 : marked by uproar 2 : extremely funny — **up·roar·i·ous·ly** adv

up·root \,əp-'rüt\ vb : to remove by or as if by pulling up the roots

¹**up·set** \,əp-'set\ vb 1 : to force or be forced out of the usual upright, level, or proper position : OVERTURN, CAPSIZE 2 : to disturb emotionally : WORRY; also : to make somewhat ill 3 : UNSETTLE, DISARRANGE 4 : to defeat unexpectedly

²**up·set** \'əp-,set\ n 1 : an upsetting or being upset; esp : a minor physical disorder 2 : a derangement of plans or ideas

up·shot \'əp-,shät\ n : final result : OUTCOME

up·side \'əp-,sīd\ n : the upper side

upside down adv 1 : with the upper and the lower parts reversed in position 2 : in or into confusion or disorder

¹**up·stage** \'əp-'stāj\ adv (or adj) : toward or at the rear of a theatrical stage

²**upstage** vb 1 : to force (as an actor) to face away from the audience by staying upstage 2 : to treat snobbishly

¹**up·stairs** \'əp-'staərz\ adv 1 : up the stairs : to or on a higher floor 2 : to or at a higher position

²**upstairs** adj : situated above the stairs; also : of or relating to the upper floors ⟨~ maid⟩

³**upstairs** n sing or pl : the part of a building above the ground floor

up·stand·ing \,əp-'stan-diŋ\ adj 1 : ERECT 2 : STRAIGHTFORWARD, HONEST

¹**up·start** \,əp-'stärt\ vb : to jump up suddenly

²**up·start** \'əp-,stärt\ n : one that has risen suddenly (as from a low position to wealth or power); esp : one that claims more personal importance than he warrants — **upstart** adj

¹**up·state** \'əp-'stāt\ adj : of, relating

to, or characteristic of a part of a state away from a large city and esp. to the north

²**upstate** n : an upstate region

up·stream \'əp-'strēm\ adv : at or toward a location nearer the source of a stream — **upstream** adj

up·stroke \-,strōk\ n : an upward stroke (as of a pen)

up·surge \-,sərj\ n : a rapid or sudden rise

up·swept \-,swept\ adj : swept upward ⟨~ hairdo⟩

up·swing \'əp-,swiŋ\ n : an upward swing; esp : a marked increase or rise (as in activity)

up·take \-,tāk\ n 1 : UNDERSTANDING, COMPREHENSION ⟨quick on the ~⟩ 2 : the process of absorbing and incorporating esp. into a living organism ⟨~ of iodine by the thyroid gland⟩

up-to-date adj 1 : extending up to the present time 2 : abreast of the times (as in style or technique) : MODERN — **up-to-date·ness** n

up·town \'əp-'taün\ adv : toward, to, or in the upper part of a town or city — **uptown** adj

¹**up·turn** \'əp-,tərn\ vb 1 : to turn (as earth) up or over 2 : to turn or direct upward

²**upturn** n : an upward turn esp. toward better conditions or higher prices

¹**up·ward** \'əp-wərd\ or **up·wards** \-wərdz\ adv 1 : in a direction from lower to higher 2 : toward a higher or better condition 3 : toward a greater amount or higher number, degree, or rate

²**upward** adj : directed or moving toward or situated in a higher place or level : ASCENDING

upwards of also **upward of** adv : more than : in excess of

up·wind \'əp-'wind\ adv (or adj) : in the direction from which the wind is blowing

ura·ni·um \yu̇-'rā-nē-əm\ n : a heavy white metallic radioactive chemical element used as a source of atomic energy

Ura·nus \'yu̇r-ə-nəs, yu̇-'rā-\ n : the 3d largest planet and the one 7th in order of distance from the sun

ur·ban \'ər-bən\ adj : of, relating to, characteristic of, or constituting a city

ur·bane \,ər-'bān\ adj : COURTEOUS, POLITE, POLISHED, SUAVE

ur·ban·ite \'ər-bə-,nīt\ n : one living in a city

ur·ban·i·ty \,ər-'ban-ət-ē\ n : the quality or state of being urbane

ur·ban·ize \'ər-bə-,nīz\ vb : to cause to take on urban characteristics ⟨urbanized areas⟩ — **ur·ban·iza·tion** \,ər-bə-nə-'zā-shən\ n

ur·chin \'ər-chən\ n : a pert or mischievous youngster

Ur·du \'ur-dü, 'ər-\ n : a language that is an official literary language of Pakistan and is widely used in India

urea \yu̇-'rē-ə\ n : a soluble nitrogenous compound that is the chief solid constituent of mammalian urine

ure·mia \yu̇-'rē-mē-ə\ n : accumulation in the blood of materials normally passed off in the urine resulting in a poisoned condition — **ure·mic** adj

ure·ter \'yu̇r-ət-ər, yu̇-'rēt-\ n : a duct

ə abut; ᵊ kitten; ər further; a back; ā bake; ä cot, cart; au̇ out; ch chin; e less; ē easy; g gift; i trip; ī life; j joke; ŋ sing; ō flow; ȯ flaw; ȯi coin; th thin; t͟h this; ü loot; u̇ foot; y yet; yü few; yu̇ furious; zh vision

that carries the urine from a kidney to the bladder

ure·thra \yu̇-'rē-thrə\ n, pl **-thras** or **-thrae** \-'thrē\ : the canal that in most mammals carries off the urine from the bladder and in the male also serves as a genital duct — **ure·thral** adj

1urge \'ərj\ vb **1** : to present, advocate, or demand earnestly **2** : to try to persuade or sway ⟨∼ a guest to stay⟩ **3** : to serve as a motive or reason for **4** : to impress or impel to some course or activity ⟨the dog urged the sheep onward⟩

2urge n **1** : the act or process of urging **2** : a force or impulse that urges or drives

ur·gent \'ər-jənt\ adj **1** : calling for immediate attention : PRESSING **2** : urging insistently — **ur·gen·cy** n — **ur·gent·ly** adv

uric \'yu̇r-ik\ adj : of, relating to, or found in urine

uric acid n : a nearly insoluble acid that is the chief nitrogenous excretion of birds and present in small amounts in mammalian urine

uri·nal \'yu̇r-ən-ᵊl\ n **1** : a receptacle for urine **2** : a place for urinating

uri·nal·y·sis \ˌyu̇r-ə-'nal-ə-səs\ n : analysis of urine usu. for medical purposes

uri·nary \'yu̇r-ə-ˌner-ē\ adj **1** : relating to, occurring in, or being organs for the formation and discharge of urine **2** : of, relating to, or found in urine

uri·nate \-ˌnāt\ vb : to discharge urine — **uri·na·tion** \ˌyu̇r-ə-'nā-shən\ n

urine \'yu̇r-ən\ n : a usu. yellowish and liquid waste material from the kidneys

urn \'ərn\ n **1** : a vessel that typically has the form of a vase on a pedestal and often is used to hold the ashes of the dead **2** : a closed vessel usu. with a spout for serving a hot beverage ⟨coffee ∼⟩

Ur·sa Ma·jor \ˌər-sə-'mā-jər\ n : the most conspicuous of the northern constellations that contains the stars which form the Big Dipper

Ur·sa Mi·nor \-'mī-nər\ n : the constellation including the north pole of the heavens and the stars that form the Little Dipper with the North Star at the tip of the handle

ur·sine \'ər-ˌsīn\ adj : of, relating to, or resembling a bear

ur·ti·car·ia \ˌərt-ə-'kar-ē-ə\ n : HIVES

us \(ˌ)əs\ pron, objective case of WE

us·able \'yü-zə-bəl\ adj : suitable or fit for use — **us·abil·i·ty** \ˌyü-zə-'bil-ət-ē\ n

us·age \'yü-sij, -zij\ n **1** : habitual or customary practice or procedure **2** : the way in which words and phrases are actually used **3** : the action or mode of using **4** : manner of treating

1use \'yüs\ n **1** : the act or practice of using or employing something : EMPLOYMENT, APPLICATION **2** : the fact or state of being used ⟨a book in daily ∼⟩ **3** : the way of using **4** : USAGE, CUSTOM **5** : the privilege or benefit of using something **6** : the ability or power to use something (as a limb) **7** : the legal enjoyment of property that consists in its employment, occupation, or exercise; also : the benefit or profit esp. from property held in trust **8** : USEFULNESS, UTILITY; also : the end served : OBJECT, FUNCTION **9** : the occasion or need to employ ⟨he had no more ∼ for it⟩ **10** : ESTEEM, LIKING ⟨had no ∼ for modern art⟩

2use \'yüz; "used to" usu 'yüs-tə\ vb **1** : ACCUSTOM, HABITUATE ⟨he was used to the heat⟩ **2** : to put into action or service : EMPLOY **3** : to consume or take (as drugs) regularly **4** : UTILIZE ⟨∼ tact⟩ **5** : to expend or consume by putting to use **6** : to behave toward : TREAT ⟨used the horse cruelly⟩ **7** — used in the past with to to indicate a former practice, fact, or state ⟨we used to work harder⟩ — **us·er** n

use·ful \'yüs-fəl\ adj : capable of being put to use : ADVANTAGEOUS; esp : serviceable for a beneficial end ⟨∼ ideas⟩ — **use·ful·ly** adv — **use·ful·ness** n

use·less \'yüs-ləs\ adj : having or being of no use : UNSERVICEABLE, WORTHLESS — **use·less·ly** adv — **use·less·ness** n

1ush·er \'əsh-ər\ n **1** : an officer who walks before a person of rank **2** : one who escorts people to their seats (as in a church or theater)

2usher vb **1** : to conduct to a place **2** : to precede as an usher, forerunner, or harbinger **3** : INAUGURATE, INTRODUCE ⟨∼ in a new era⟩

usu·al \'yü-zh(ə-w)əl\ adj **1** : accordant with usage, custom, or habit : NORMAL **2** : commonly or ordinarily used **3** : ORDINARY syn customary, habitual, accustomed — **usu·al·ly** adv

usu·fruct \'yü-zə-ˌfrəkt\ n : the legal right to use and enjoy the benefits and profits of something belonging to another

usu·rer \'yü-zhər-ər\ n : one that lends money esp. at an excessively high rate of interest

usu·ri·ous \yu̇-'zhu̇r-ē-əs\ adj : practicing, involving, or constituting usury ⟨a ∼ rate of interest⟩

usurp \yu̇-'sərp, -'zərp\ vb : to seize and hold by force or without right ⟨∼ a throne⟩ — **usur·pa·tion** \ˌyü-sər-'pā-shən, -zər-\ n — **usurp·er** \yu̇-'sər-pər, -'zər-\ n

usu·ry \'yüzh-(ə-)rē\ n **1** : the lending of money with an interest charge for its use **2** : an excessive rate or amount of interest charged; esp : interest above an established legal rate

uten·sil \yu̇-'ten-səl\ n **1** : an instrument or vessel used in a household and esp. a kitchen **2** : an article serving a useful purpose

uter·us \'yüt-ə-rəs\ n, pl **uteri** \-ˌrī\ : an organ of a female mammal for containing and usu. for nourishing the young during the development previous to birth — **uter·ine** \-ˌrīn, -rən\ adj

utile \'yüt-ᵊl\ adj : USEFUL

1util·i·tar·i·an \yu̇-ˌtil-ə-'ter-ē-ən\ n : a person who believes in utilitarianism

2utilitarian adj **1** : of or relating to utilitarianism **2** : of or relating to utility : aiming at usefulness rather than beauty; also : serving a useful purpose

util·i·tar·i·an·ism n : a doctrine that one's conduct should be determined by the usefulness of its results; esp : a theory that the greatest good of the greatest number should be the main consideration in making a choice of actions

util·i·ty \yu̇-'til-ət-ē\ n **1** : USEFULNESS **2** : something useful or designed for use **3** : a business organization performing a public service and subject to special governmental regulation **4** : a public service or a commodity provided by a public utility; also : equipment (as plumbing) to provide such or a similar service

uti·lize \'yüt-ᵊl-ˌīz\ vb : to make use of : turn to profitable account or use — **uti·li·za·tion** \ˌyüt-ᵊl-ə-'zā-shən\ n

ut·most \'ət-ˌmōst\ adj 1 : situated at the farthest or most distant point : EXTREME 2 : of the greatest or highest degree, quantity, number, or amount — **utmost** n

uto·pia \yu̇-'tō-pē-ə\ n [fr. Utopia, imaginary island described in St. Thomas More's Utopia, fr. Gk ou not, no + topos place] 1 often cap : a place of ideal perfection esp. in laws, government, and social conditions 2 : an impractical scheme for social improvement

¹uto·pi·an \-pē-ən\ adj, often cap 1 : of, relating to, or resembling a utopia 2 : proposing ideal social and political schemes that are impractical : VISIONARY

²utopian n 1 : a believer in the perfectibility of human society 2 : one that proposes or advocates utopian schemes

¹ut·ter \'ət-ər\ adj : ABSOLUTE, TOTAL ⟨~ ruin⟩ — **ut·ter·ly** adv

²utter vb 1 : to send forth usu. as a sound : express in usu. spoken words : PRONOUNCE, SPEAK 2 : to put (as currency) into circulation

ut·ter·ance n 1 : something uttered; esp : an oral or written statement 2 : the action of uttering with the voice : SPEECH 3 : power, style, or manner of speaking

ut·ter·most \'ət-ər-ˌmōst\ adj : EXTREME, UTMOST ⟨the ~ parts of the earth⟩ — **uttermost** n

uvu·la \'yü-vyə-lə\ n, pl **-las** or **-lae** \-ˌlē\ : the fleshy lobe hanging at the back of the palate — **uvu·lar** \-lər\ adj

uxo·ri·ous \ˌək-'sōr-ē-əs, ˌəg-'zōr-\ adj : excessively devoted or submissive to a wife

v \'vē\ n, often cap : the 22d letter of the English alphabet

va·can·cy \'vā-kən-sē\ n 1 : a vacating esp. of an office, position, or piece of property 2 : the state of being vacant 3 : a vacant office, position, or tenancy; also : the period during which it stands vacant 4 : empty space : VOID

va·cant \'vā-kənt\ adj 1 : not occupied ⟨~ seat⟩ ⟨~ room⟩ 2 : EMPTY ⟨~ space⟩ 3 : free from business or care : LEISURE 4 : FOOLISH, STUPID ⟨~ laugh⟩; also : EXPRESSIONLESS ⟨~ stare⟩ — **va·cant·ly** adv

va·cate \'vā-ˌkāt\ vb 1 : to make void : ANNUL 2 : to make vacant (as an office or house); also : to give up the occupancy of

¹va·ca·tion \vā-'kā-shən\ n : a period of rest from work : HOLIDAY

²vacation vb : to take or spend a vacation — **va·ca·tion·er** \-sh(ə-)nər\ n

va·ca·tion·ist \-'kā-sh(ə-)nəst\ n : a person taking a vacation

va·ca·tion·land \-shən-ˌland\ n : an area with recreational attractions and facilities for vacationists

vac·ci·nate \'vak-sə-ˌnāt\ vb : to inoculate with a related harmless virus to produce immunity to smallpox; also : to administer a vaccine to usu. by injection

vac·ci·na·tion \ˌvak-sə-'nā-shən\ n : the act of or the scar left by vaccinating

vac·cine \vak-'sēn\ n [L vaccinus of or from cows; so called from the derivation of smallpox vaccine from cows] : material (as a preparation of killed or weakened virus or bacteria) used in vaccinating to induce immunity to a disease — **vaccine** adj

vac·il·late \'vas-ə-ˌlāt\ vb 1 : SWAY, TOTTER; also : FLUCTUATE 2 : to incline first to one course or opinion and then to another : WAVER — **vac·il·la·tion** \ˌvas-ə-'lā-shən\ n

va·cu·i·ty \va-'kyü-ət-ē, və-\ n 1 : an empty space 2 : EMPTINESS, HOLLOWNESS 3 : vacancy of mind 4 : a foolish remark

vac·u·ous \'vak-yə-wəs\ adj 1 : EMPTY; VACANT, BLANK 2 : DULL, STUPID, INANE

¹vac·u·um \'vak-yə-(ˌw)əm, -ˌyüm\ n, pl **vac·u·ums** or **vac·ua** \-yə-wə\ 1 : a space entirely empty of matter 2 : a space almost exhausted of air (as by a special pump) 3 : VOID, GAP

²vacuum vb : to use a vacuum device (as a cleaner) on

vacuum bottle n : a double-walled bottle with a vacuum between outer and inner walls used to keep liquids hot or cold

vacuum cleaner n : an electrical appliance for cleaning (as floors or rugs) by suction

vacuum tube n : an electron tube having a high degree of vacuum

va·de me·cum \ˌvād-ē-'mē-kəm\ n : something (as a handbook or manual) carried as a constant companion

¹vag·a·bond \'vag-ə-ˌbänd\ adj 1 : WANDERING, HOMELESS 2 : of, characteristic of, or leading the life of a vagrant or tramp 3 : leading an unsettled or irresponsible life

²vagabond n : one leading a vagabond life; esp : TRAMP

va·ga·ry \'vā-gə-rē, və-'ge(ə)r-ē\ n : an odd or eccentric idea or action : WHIM, CAPRICE

va·gi·na \və-'jī-nə\ n, pl **-nae** \-(ˌ)nē\ or **-nas** : a canal that leads out from the uterus

va·gran·cy \'vā-grən-sē\ n 1 : the quality or state of being vagrant; also : a vagrant act or notion 2 : the offense of being a vagrant

¹va·grant \'vā-grənt\ n : one who wanders idly with no residence and no visible means of support

²vagrant adj 1 : of, relating to, or characteristic of a vagrant 2 : following no fixed course : RANDOM, CAPRICIOUS ⟨~ thoughts⟩ — **va·grant·ly** adv

va·grom \'vāg\ adj : VAGRANT

vague \'vāg\ adj 1 : not clear : not definite or exact : not distinct 2 : not clearly felt or analyzed ⟨a ~ unrest⟩

ə abut; ᵊ kitten; ər further; a back; ā bake; ä cot, cart; au̇ out; ch chin; e less; ē easy; g gift; i trip; ī life; j joke; ŋ sing; ō flow; ȯ flaw; ȯi coin; th thin; th this; ü loot; u̇ foot; y yet; yü few; yu̇ furious; zh vision

syn obscure, dark, enigmatic, ambiguous, equivocal — **vague·ly** *adv* — **vague·ness** *n*

vail \'vāl\ *vt* : to lower esp. as a sign of respect or submission

vain \'vān\ *adj* **1** : of no real value : IDLE, WORTHLESS **2** : FUTILE, UNSUCCESSFUL **3** : CONCEITED syn empty, hollow, fruitless, proud, vainglorious — **vain·ly** *adv*

vain·glo·ri·ous \(')vān-'glōr-ē-əs\ *adj* : marked by vainglory : BOASTFUL

vain·glo·ry \'vān-ˌglōr-ē\ *n* **1** : excessive or ostentatious pride esp. in one's own achievements **2** : vain display : VANITY

val·ance \'val-əns, 'vāl-\ *n* **1** : drapery hanging from an edge (as of an altar table, bed, or shelf) **2** : a drapery or a decorative frame across the top of a window

1vale \'vāl\ *n* : VALLEY, DALE

2va·le \'väl-(ˌ)ā, 'wäl-\ *interj* : FAREWELL

val·e·dic·tion \ˌval-ə-'dik-shən\ *n* : an act or utterance of leave-taking : FAREWELL

val·e·dic·to·ri·an \ˌval-ə-ˌdik-'tōr-ē-ən\ *n* : the student of the graduating class who pronounces the valedictory oration at commencement

val·e·dic·to·ry \ˌval-ə-'dik-t(ə-)rē\ *adj* : bidding farewell : delivered as a valediction (a ~ address) — **valedictory** *n*

va·lence \'vā-ləns\ *n* : the degree of combining power of a chemical element or radical as shown by the number of atomic weights of hydrogen, chlorine, or sodium with which the atomic weight of the element will combine or for which it can be substituted

Va·len·ci·ennes \və-ˌlen-sē-'enz, ˌval-ən-sē-\ *n* : a fine handmade lace

va·len·cy \'vā-lən-sē\ *n* : VALENCE

val·en·tine \'val-ən-ˌtīn\ *n* : a sweetheart to whom one pays his respects on St. Valentine's Day; *also* : a greeting card sent often anonymously on this day

1val·et \'val-ət, va-'lā\ *n* **1** : a male servant who takes care of a man's clothes and performs personal services **2** : an attendant in a hotel who performs for patrons the services of a manservant

2valet *vb* : to serve as a valet

val·e·tu·di·nar·i·an \ˌval-ə-ˌt(y)üd-ᵊn-'er-ē-ən\ *n* : a person of a weak or sickly constitution; *esp* : one whose chief concern is his invalidism — **val·e·tu·di·nar·i·an·ism** \-ē-ə-ˌniz-əm\ *n*

val·iant \'val-yənt\ *adj* : having or showing valor : BRAVE, HEROIC syn valorous, doughty, courageous, bold, audacious, dauntless, undaunted, intrepid — **val·iant·ly** *adv*

val·id \'val-əd\ *adj* **1** : having legal force (a ~ contract) **2** : founded on truth or fact : capable of being justified or defended : SOUND (a ~ argument) (~ reasons) — **val·id·ly** *adv* — **val·id·ness** *n*

val·i·date \'val-ə-ˌdāt\ *vb* **1** : to make legally valid **2** : to confirm the validity of **3** : VERIFY, SUBSTANTIATE — **val·i·da·tion** \ˌval-ə-'dā-shən\ *n*

va·lid·i·ty \və-'lid-ət-ē\ *n* : the quality or state of being valid

va·lise \və-'lēs\ *n* : a traveling bag

val·ley \'val-ē\ *n* **1** : a long depression between ranges of hills or mountains **2** : a channel at the meeting place of two slopes of a roof

val·or \'val-ər\ *n* : personal bravery syn heroism, prowess, gallantry — **val-**

or·ous \'val-ə-rəs\ *adj*

val·o·ri·za·tion \ˌval-ə-rə-'zā-shən\ *n* : the support of commodity prices by any of various forms of government subsidy — **val·o·rize** \'val-ə-ˌrīz\ *vb*

valse \vȧls\ *n* : WALTZ; *esp* : a concert waltz

1valu·able \'val-yə-(-wə)-bəl\ *adj* **1** : having money value **2** : having great money value **3** : of great use or service syn invaluable, priceless, costly, expensive, dear, precious

2valuable *n* : a usu. personal possession of considerable value

val·u·ate \'val-yə-ˌwāt\ *vb* **1** : to place a value on : APPRAISE — **val·u·a·tor** \-ˌwāt-ər\ *n*

val·u·a·tion \ˌval-yə-'wā-shən\ *n* **1** : the act or process of valuing; *esp* : appraisal of property **2** : the estimated or determined market value of a thing

1val·ue \'val-yü\ *n* **1** : a fair return or equivalent in money, goods, or services for something exchanged **2** : the worth of a thing : market price, purchasing power, or estimated worth **3** : assigned or computed numerical quantity (the ~ of *x* in an equation) : AMOUNT **4** : precise meaning (~ of a word) **5** : distinctive quality of sound in speech **6** : luminosity of a color : BRILLIANCE; *also* : the relation of one detail in a picture to another with respect to lightness or darkness **7** : the relative length of a tone or note **8** : something (as a principle or ideal) intrinsically valuable or desirable (instill a sense of ~s) — **val·ue·less** \-ləs\ *adj*

2value *vb* **1** : to estimate the monetary worth of : APPRAISE **2** : to rate in usefulness, importance, or general worth **3** : to consider or rate highly : PRIZE, ESTEEM — **val·u·er** *n*

val·ued *adj* : highly esteemed : PRIZED

valve \'valv\ *n* **1** : a structure (as in a vein) that temporarily closes a passage or that permits movement in one direction only **2** : one of the pieces in which a ripe seed capsule or pod separates **3** : a device by which the flow of liquid or gas may be regulated by a movable part that either opens or obstructs passage; *also* : the movable part of such a device **4** : a device in a brass wind instrument for quickly varying the tube length in order to change the fundamental tone by some definite interval **5** : ELECTRON TUBE **6** : one of the separable usu. hinged pieces of which the shell of some animals and esp. bivalve mollusks consists — **valved** \'valvd\ *adj* — **valve·less** *adj*

val·vu·lar \'val-vyə-lər\ *adj* **1** : resembling or functioning as a valve; *also* : opening by valves **2** : of or relating to a valve esp. of the heart

va·moose \va-'müs, və-\ *vb, slang* : to leave or go away quickly

1vamp \'vamp\ *n* : the part of a boot or shoe upper covering esp. the front part of the foot

2vamp *vb* **1** : to provide with a new vamp **2** : to patch up with a new part **3** : INVENT, IMPROVISE

3vamp *n* : a woman who uses her charm and allurements to seduce and exploit men

4vamp *vb* : to practice seductive wiles on

vam·pire \'vam-ˌpī(ə)r\ *n* **1** : a nightwandering bloodsucking ghost or a person who preys on other people; *esp*

: a woman who exploits and ruins her lover 3 : a So. American bat that sucks the blood of animals including man; *also* : any of several bats believed to suck blood

1van \'van\ *n* : VANGUARD

2van *n* : a usu. enclosed wagon or motortruck for moving goods or animals; *also* : a closed railroad freight or baggage car

va·na·di·um \və-'nād-ē-əm\ *n* : a soft ductile metallic chemical element used to form alloys

van·dal \'van-d°l\ *n* 1 *cap* : a member of a Germanic people charged with sacking Rome in A.D. 455 2 : one who willfully or ignorantly mars or destroys property belonging to another or to the public

van·dal·ism \-,iz-əm\ *n* : willful or malicious destruction or defacement of public or private property

van·dal·ize \-,īz\ *vb* : to subject to vandalism : DAMAGE

Van·dyke \van-'dīk\ *n* : a trim pointed beard

vane \'vān\ *n* 1 : a movable device attached to a high object to show the way the wind blows 2 : a flat extended surface attached to an axis and moved by air or wind ⟨the ∼s of a windmill⟩; *also* : a fixture revolving in a manner resembling this and moving in or by water or air ⟨the ∼s of a propeller⟩

van·guard \'van-,gärd\ *n* 1 : the troops moving at the front of an army : VAN 2 : the forefront of an action or movement

va·nil·la \və-'nil-ə\ *n* : a tropical American climbing orchid with beanlike pods; *also* : its pods or a flavoring extract made from these

van·ish \'van-ish\ *vb* : to pass from sight or existence : disappear completely — **van·ish·er** *n*

van·i·ty \'van-ət-ē\ *n* 1 : something that is vain, empty, or useless 2 : the quality or fact of being useless or futile : FUTILITY 3 : undue pride in oneself or one's appearance : CONCEIT 4 : a small box for cosmetics : COMPACT

van·quish \'van̄-kwish, 'van-\ *vb* 1 : to overcome in battle or in a contest 2 : CONQUER

van·tage \'vant-ij\ *n* 1 : superiority in a contest 2 : a position or condition of affairs giving a strategic advantage or a commanding perspective

van·ward \'van-wərd\ *adj* : being in or toward the vanguard : ADVANCED — **vanward** *adv*

vap·id \'vap-əd\ *adj* : lacking spirit, liveliness, or zest : FLAT, INSIPID — **va·pid·i·ty** \va-'pid-ət-ē\ *n* — **vap·id·ly** \'vap-əd-lē\ *adv* — **vap·id·ness** *n*

1va·por \'vā-pər\ *n* 1 : fine separated particles (as fog or smoke) floating in the air and clouding it 2 : a substance in the gaseous state; *esp* : one that is liquid under ordinary conditions 3 : something unsubstantial or fleeting 4 *pl, archaic* : a depressed or hysterical nervous condition

2vapor *vb* 1 : to rise or pass off in vapor 2 : to emit vapor

va·por·ing *n* : an idle, boastful, or highflown expression or speech — usu. used in *pl*

va·por·ize \'vā-pə-,rīz\ *vb* : to convert into vapor either naturally or artificially — **va·por·iza·tion** \,vā-pə-rə-'zā-shən\ *n*

va·por·iz·er *n* : a device that vaporizes something (as a fuel oil or a medicated liquid)

va·por·ous \'vā-p(ə-)rəs\ *adj* 1 : consisting of or characteristic of vapor 2 : producing vapors : VOLATILE 3 : full of vapors : FOGGY, MISTY — **va·por·ous·ly** *adv* — **va·por·ous·ness** *n*

va·po·ry \-p(ə-)rē\ *adj* : VAPOROUS, VAGUE

va·que·ro \vä-'ke(ə)r-ō\ *n* : a ranch hand : COWBOY

var·ia \'ver-ē-ə\ *n pl* : MISCELLANY; *esp* : a literary miscellany

1vari·able \'ver-ē-ə-bəl\ *adj* 1 : able or apt to vary : CHANGEABLE 2 : FICKLE 3 : not true to type : not breeding true ⟨a ∼ wheat⟩ — **vari·abil·i·ty** \,ver-ē-ə-'bil-ət-ē\ *n* — **vari·able·ness** \'ver-ē-ə-bəl-nəs\ *n* — **vari·ably** *adv*

2variable *n* 1 : something that is variable 2 : a quantity that may assume a succession of values; *also* : a symbol standing for any one of a class of things

vari·ance \'ver-ē-əns\ *n* 1 : variation or a degree of variation : DEVIATION 2 : DISAGREEMENT, DISPUTE 3 : a license to do something contrary to the usual rule ⟨a zoning ∼⟩ **syn** discord, contention, dissension, strife, conflict

1vari·ant \'ver-ē-ənt\ *adj* 1 : differing from others of its kind or class 2 : varying usu. slightly from the standard or type 3 : VARYING, DISCREPANT

2variant *n* 1 : one that exhibits variation from a type or norm 2 : one of two or more different spellings or pronunciations of a word

vari·a·tion \,ver-ē-'ā-shən\ *n* 1 : an act or instance of varying : a change in form, position, or condition : MODIFICATION, ALTERATION 2 : extent of change or difference 3 : divergence in qualities from those typical or usual to a group; *also* : one exhibiting such variation 4 : repetition of a musical theme with modifications in rhythm, tune, harmony, or key

vari·col·ored \'ver-i-,kəl-ərd\ *adj* : having various colors : VARIEGATED

var·i·cose \'var-ə-,kōs\ *adj* : abnormally and irregularly swollen ⟨∼ veins⟩

var·ied \'ver-ēd\ *adj* 1 : CHANGED, ALTERED 2 : of different kinds : VARIOUS 3 : VARIEGATED — **var·ied·ly** *adv*

var·ie·gate \'ver-ē-(ə-),gāt\ *vb* 1 : to diversify in external appearance esp. with different colors 2 : to introduce variety into : DIVERSIFY — **var·ie·gat·ed** *adj* — **var·ie·ga·tion** \,ver-ē-(ə-)'gā-shən\ *n*

va·ri·etal \və-'rī-ət-°l\ *adj* : of or relating to a variety; *also* : being a variety rather than an individual or species — **va·ri·etal·ly** *adv*

va·ri·ety \və-'rī-ət-ē\ *n* 1 : the state of being varied or various : DIVERSITY 2 : VARIATION, DIFFERENCE 3 : a collection of different things 4 : something varying from other things of the same general kind 5 : entertainment such as is given in a stage presentation comprising a series of performances (as songs, dances, or acrobatic acts) 6 : any of various groups of animals or plants ranking lower than the species

var·i·o·rum \,ver-ē-'ōr-əm\ *n* : an edition or text of a work containing notes by various persons or variant readings of the text

var·i·ous \'ver-ē-əs\ *adj* **1** : VARICOLORED **2** : of differing kinds : MULTIFARIOUS **3** : UNLIKE **4** : having a number of different aspects **5** : NUMEROUS, MANY **6** : DIVERSE, SEPARATE **syn** divergent, disparate, sundry, divers, manifold, multifold— **var·i·ous·ly** *adv*

var·let \'vär-lət\ *n* **1** *archaic* : ATTENDANT **2** : SCOUNDREL, KNAVE

¹var·nish \'vär-nish\ *n* **1** : a liquid preparation that is spread on a surface and dries into a hard glossy coating; *also* : the glaze of this coating **2** : something suggesting varnish by its gloss **3** : outside show : GLOSS

²varnish *vb* **1** : to cover with varnish **2** : to cover or conceal with something that gives a fair appearance : gloss over

var·si·ty \'värs-(ə-)tē\ *n* **1** *chiefly Brit* : UNIVERSITY **2** : a first team representing a college, school, or club

vary \'ver-ē\ *vb* **1** : ALTER, CHANGE **2** : to make or be of different kinds : introduce or have variety : DIVERSIFY, DIFFER **3** : DEVIATE, SWERVE **4** : to diverge structurally or physiologically from typical members of a group

vas·cu·lar \'vas-kyə-lər\ *adj* [L *vasculum* small vessel, dim. of *vas* vase, vessel] : of or relating to a channel for the conveyance of a body fluid (as blood or sap) to a system of such channels; *also* : supplied with or containing such vessels an esp. blood vessels

vase \'vās, 'vāz\ *n* : a usu. round vessel of greater depth than width used chiefly for ornament or for flowers

vaso·mo·tor \,vas-ə-'mōt-ər, ,vāz-\ *adj* : of, relating to, or being nerves controlling the size of the blood vessels

vas·sal \'vas-əl\ *n* **1** : a person acknowledging another as his feudal lord and protector to whom he owes homage and loyalty : a feudal tenant **2** : one occupying a dependent or subordinate position — **vassal** *adj*

vas·sal·age \-ij\ *n* **1** : the state of being a vassal **2** : the homage and loyalty due from a vassal to his lord **3** : SERVITUDE, SUBJECTION **4** : a politically dependent territory

¹vast \'vast\ *adj* : very great in size, amount, degree, intensity, or esp. extent **syn** enormous, huge, gigantic, colossal, mammoth — **vast·ly** *adv* — **vast·ness** *n*

²vast *n* : a great expanse : IMMENSITY

vasty \'vas-tē\ *adj* **1** : VAST, IMMENSE

vat \'vat\ *n* : a large vessel (as a tub or barrel) esp. for holding liquids in manufacturing processes

vat·ic \'vat-ik\ *adj* : PROPHETIC, ORACULAR

Vat·i·can \'vat-i-kən\ *n* **1** : the papal headquarters in Rome **2** : the papal government

vaude·ville \'vȯd-(ə-)vəl, 'vōd-, -,vil\ *n* : a stage entertainment consisting of unrelated acts (as of acrobats, comedians, dancers, or singers)

¹vault \'vȯlt\ *n* **1** : an arched masonry structure usu. forming a ceiling or roof **2** : a room or space covered by a vault esp. when underground and used for a special purpose (as for storage of valuables or wine supplies) **3** : the canopy

of heaven : SKY **4** : a burial chamber; *also* : a usu. metal or concrete case in which a casket is enclosed at burial — **vaulty** *adj*

²vault *vb* : to form or cover with a vault

³vault *vb* : to leap vigorously esp. by aid of the hands or a pole — **vault·er** *n*

⁴vault *n* : an act of vaulting : LEAP

vault·ed *adj* **1** : built in the form of a vault : ARCHED **2** : covered with a vault

vault·ing *adj* : leaping upwards : reaching for the heights (~ ambition)

vaunt \'vȯnt\ *vb* : BRAG, BOAST — **vaunt** *n*

veal \'vēl\ *n* : the flesh of a young calf

vec·tor \'vek-tər\ *n* : an organism (as a fly) that transmits disease germs

Ve·da \'vād-ə\ *n* : any of a class of Hindu sacred writings — **Ve·dic** \'vād-ik\ *adj*

veer \'viər\ *vb* : to shift from one direction or course to another **syn** swerve, deviate, depart, digress, diverge — **veer** *n*

vee·ry \'vi(ə)r-ē\ *n* : a tawny brown thrush of the woods of the eastern U. S.

¹veg·e·ta·ble \'vej-(ə-)tə-bəl\ *adj* **1** : of, relating to, or made up of plants **2** : obtained from plants (~ oils) (the ~ kingdom) **3** : suggesting that of a plant (a ~ existence)

²vegetable *n* **1** : PLANT 1 **2** : a usu. herbaceous plant grown for an edible part that is usu. eaten with the principal course of a meal; *also* : such an edible part

veg·e·tal \'vej-ət-ᵊl\ *adj* **1** : VEGETABLE **2** : VEGETATIVE

veg·e·tar·i·an \,vej-ə-'ter-ē-ən\ *n* : one that believes in or practices living solely on plant products — **vegetarian** *adj* — **veg·e·tar·i·an·ism** \-ē-ə,niz-əm\ *n*

veg·e·tate \'vej-ə-,tāt\ *vb* : to grow in the manner of a plant; *esp* : to lead a dull inert life

veg·e·ta·tion \,vej-ə-'tā-shən\ *n* **1** : the act or process of vegetating; *also* : a dull inert existence **2** : plant life or cover (as of an area) **3** : an abnormal bodily outgrowth — **veg·e·ta·tion·al** \-'tā-sh(ə-)nəl\ *adj*

veg·e·ta·tive \'vej-ə-,tāt-iv\ *adj* **1** : of or relating to nutrition and growth esp. as contrasted with reproduction **2** : leading or marked by a passive, stupid, and dull existence **3** : VEGETATIONAL

ve·he·mence \'vē-ə-məns\ *n* : the quality or state of being vehement : INTENSITY, VIOLENCE

ve·he·ment \-mənt\ *adj* **1** : marked by great force or energy **2** : marked by strong feeling or expression : PASSIONATE **3** : strong in effect : INTENSE — **ve·he·ment·ly** *adv*

ve·hi·cle \'vē-,(h)ik-əl\ *n* **1** : a medium through or by means of which something is conveyed or expressed **2** : a medium by which a thing is applied or administered (linseed oil is a ~ for pigments) **3** : a means of carrying or transporting something : CONVEYANCE **syn** means, instrument, agent, agency, organ, channel — **ve·hic·u·lar** \vē-'hik-yə-lər\ *adj*

¹veil \'vāl\ *n* **1** : a piece of often sheer or diaphanous material used to screen or curtain something or to cover the head or face **2** : the state accepted or the vows made when a woman becomes a nun (take the ~) **3** : something that hides or obscures like a veil

2veil *vb* **:** to cover with or as if with a veil ; wear a veil

veil·ing \'vā-liŋ\ *n* **1 :** VEIL **2 :** any of various sheer fabrics (as net or chiffon)

1vein \'vān\ *n* **1 :** a fissure in rock filled with mineral matter; *also* **:** a bed of useful mineral matter **2 :** one of the tubular branching vessels that carry blood toward the heart **3 :** one of the vascular bundles forming the framework of a leaf **4 :** one of the thickened ribs that stiffen the wings of an insect **5 :** something (as a wavy variegation in marble) suggesting veins **6 :** something of distinctive character considered as running through something else **:** STRAIN **7 :** a distinctive mode of expression **:** STYLE **8 :** MOOD, HUMOR — **veined** \'vānd\ *adj*

2vein *vb* **:** to form or mark with or as if with veins — **vein·ing** *n*

ve·lar \'vē-lər\ *adj* **:** of or relating to a velum and esp. that of the soft palate

veld *or* **veldt** \'felt, 'velt\ *n* **:** open grassland esp. in Africa usu. with scattered shrubs or trees

vel·le·i·ty \ve-'lē-ət-ē\ *n* **1 :** the lowest degree of volition **2 :** a slight wish or tendency

vel·lum \'vel-əm\ *n* **1 :** a fine-grained lambskin, kidskin, or calfskin prepared for writing on or for binding books **2 :** a paper manufactured to resemble vellum — **vellum** *adj*

ve·loc·i·pede \və-'läs-ə-,pēd\ *n* **:** a light vehicle propelled by the rider; *esp* **:** a child's tricycle

ve·loc·i·ty \və-'läs-(ə-)tē\ *n* **:** quickness of motion **:** SPEED ⟨the ~ of light⟩ **syn** momentum, impetus, pace

ve·lour *or* **ve·lours** \və-'lùr\ *n, pl* **ve·lours** \-'lùrz\ **:** any of various textile fabrics with pile like that of velvet

ve·lum \'vē-ləm\ *n, pl* **ve·la** \-lə\ **:** a membranous partition (as the soft back part of the palate) resembling a veil

1vel·vet \'vel-vət\ *n* **1 :** a fabric of silk, rayon, cotton, nylon, or wool characterized by a short soft dense pile **2 :** something resembling or suggesting velvet (as in softness or luster) **3 :** soft skin covering the growing antlers of deer **4 :** the amount a player is ahead in a gambling game **:** WINNINGS — **vel·vety** *adj*

2velvet *adj* **1 :** made of or covered with velvet **2 :** resembling or suggesting velvet **:** SMOOTH, SOFT, SLEEK

vel·ve·teen \,vel-və-'tēn\ *n* **1 :** a fabric woven usu. of cotton in imitation of velvet **2** *pl* **:** clothes made of velveteen

ve·nal \'vēn-ᵊl\ *adj* **:** capable of being bought esp. by underhand means **:** MERCENARY, CORRUPT — **ve·nal·i·ty** \vi-'nal-ət-ē\ *n* — **ve·nal·ly** \'vēn-ᵊl-ē\ *adv*

ve·na·tion \vā-'nā-shən, vē-\ *n* **:** an arrangement or system of veins ⟨the ~ of the hand⟩ ⟨leaf ~⟩

vend \'vend\ *vb* **:** SELL; *esp* **:** to sell as a hawker or peddler — **vend·ible** *adj*

vend·ee \ven-'dē\ *n* **:** one to whom a thing is sold **:** BUYER

vend·er \'ven-dər\ *n* **:** VENDOR

ven·det·ta \ven-'det-ə\ *n* **:** a feud between clans or families

ven·dor \'ven-dər, ven-'dòr\ *n* **1 :** one that vends **:** SELLER **2 :** a vending machine

1ve·neer \və-'niər\ *n* **1 :** a thin usu. superficial layer of material ⟨brick ~⟩; *esp* **:** a thin layer of fine wood glued over a cheaper wood **2 :** superficial display **:** GLOSS

2veneer *vb* **:** to overlay with a veneer

ven·er·a·ble \'ven-ər-(ə-)bəl, 'ven-rə-bəl\ *adj* **1 :** deserving to be venerated — often used as a religious title **2 :** made sacred by association

ven·er·ate \'ven-ə-,rāt\ *vb* **:** to regard with reverential respect **syn** adore, revere, reverence, worship — **ven·er·a·tion** \,ven-ə-'rā-shən\ *n*

ve·ne·re·al \və-'nir-ē-əl\ *adj* **:** of or relating to sexual intercourse or to diseases transmitted by it

ve·ne·tian blind \və-,nē-shən-\ *n* **:** a blind having thin horizontal parallel wooden slats that can be set to overlap to keep out light or tipped to let light come in between them

ven·geance \'ven-jəns\ *n* **:** punishment inflicted in retaliation for an injury or offense **:** RETRIBUTION

venge·ful \'venj-fəl\ *adj* **:** filled with a desire for revenge **:** VINDICTIVE — **venge·ful·ly** *adv*

ve·ni·al \'vē-nē-əl, -nyəl\ *adj* **:** capable of being forgiven **:** EXCUSABLE ⟨~ sin⟩

ven·i·son \'ven-ə-sən, -zən\ *n* **:** the edible flesh of a deer

ven·om \'ven-əm\ *n* **1 :** poisonous material secreted by some animals (as snakes, spiders, or bees) and transmitted usu. by biting or stinging **2 :** something that poisons or embitters the mind or spirit **:** MALIGNITY, MALICE

ven·om·ous \'ven-ə-məs\ *adj* **1 :** full of venom **:** POISONOUS **2 :** MALIGNANT, SPITEFUL, MALICIOUS **3 :** secreting and using venom ⟨~ snakes⟩ — **ven·om·ous·ly** *adv*

ve·nous \'vē-nəs\ *adj* **1 :** of, relating to, or full of veins **2 :** being purplish red oxygen-deficient blood present in most veins

1vent \'vent\ *vb* **1 :** to provide with a vent **2 :** to serve as a vent for **3 :** to let out at a vent **:** EXPEL, DISCHARGE **4 :** to give expression to

2vent *n* **1 :** an opportunity or way of escape or passage **:** OUTLET **2 :** an opening for passage or escape (as of a fluid, gas, or smoke) or for relieving pressure **3 :** ANUS

3vent *n* **:** a slit in a garment esp. in the lower part of a seam (as of a jacket or skirt)

ven·ti·late \'vent-ᵊl-,āt\ *vb* **1 :** to cause fresh air to circulate through (as a room or mine) so as to replace foul air **2 :** to give vent to ⟨~ one's grievances⟩ **3 :** to discuss freely and openly ⟨~ a question⟩ **4 :** to provide with a vent or outlet **syn** aerate, express, vent, air, utter, voice, broach — **ven·ti·la·tor** *n*

ven·ti·la·tion \,vent-ᵊl-'ā-shən\ *n* **1 :** the act or process of ventilating **2 :** circulation of air (as in a room) **3 :** a system or means of providing fresh air

ven·tral \'ven-trəl\ *adj* **1 :** of or relating to the belly **:** ABDOMINAL **2 :** of, relating to, or located on or near the surface of the body that in man is the front but in most other animals is the lower surface — **ven·tral·ly** *adv*

ven·tri·cle \'ven-tri-kəl\ n 1 : a chamber of the heart that receives blood from the atrium of the same side and pumps it into the arteries 2 : one of the communicating cavities of the brain that are continuous with the central canal of the spinal cord

ven·tril·o·quism \ven-'tril-ə-,kwiz-əm\ n : the production of the voice in such a manner that the sound appears to come from a source other than the speaker — **ven·tril·o·quist** \-ə-kwəst\ n

ven·tril·o·quy \-ə-kwē\ n : VENTRILO-QUISM

1ven·ture \'ven-chər\ vb 1 : to expose to hazard : RISK 2 : to undertake the risks of : BRAVE 3 : to advance or put forward or expose to criticism or argument (~ an opinion) 4 : to make a venture : run a risk : proceed despite danger : DARE

2venture n 1 : an undertaking involving chance or risk; esp : a speculative business enterprise 2 : something risked in a speculative venture : STAKE

ven·ture·some \-səm\ adj 1 : inclined to venture : BOLD, DARING 2 : involving risk : DANGEROUS, HAZARDOUS syn adventurous, venturous, rash, reckless, foolhardy — **ven·ture·some·ly** adv — **ven·ture·some·ness** n

ven·tur·ous \'vench-(ə-)rəs\ adj : VEN-TURESOME — **ven·tur·ous·ly** adv — **ven·tur·ous·ness** n

ven·ue \'ven-yü\ n : the place in which the alleged events from which a legal action arises took place; also : the place from which the jury is taken and where the trial is held

Ve·nus \'vē-nəs\ n : the brightest planet and the one 2d in order of distance from the sun

Ve·nu·sian \vi-'n(y)ü-zhən\ adj : of or relating to the planet Venus — Venusian n

ve·ra·cious \və-'rā-shəs\ adj 1 : TRUTH-FUL, HONEST 2 : TRUE, ACCURATE — **ve·ra·cious·ly** adv

ve·rac·i·ty \və-'ras-ət-ē\ n 1 : devotion to truth : TRUTHFULNESS 2 : CORRECT-NESS 3 : conformity with fact : ACCU-RACY 4 : something true

ve·ran·da or **ve·ran·dah** \və-'ran-də\ n : a usu. roofed open gallery or portico attached to the exterior of a building : PORCH

verb \'vərb\ n : a word that is the grammatical center of a predicate and expresses an act, occurrence, or mode of being

1ver·bal \'vər-bəl\ adj 1 : of, relating to, or consisting of words; esp : having to do with words rather than with the ideas to be conveyed 2 : expressed in usu. spoken words : not written : ORAL (a ~ contract) 3 : LITERAL, VERBATIM 4 : of, relating to, or formed from a verb — **ver·bal·ly** adv

2verbal n : a word that combines characteristics of a verb with those of a noun or adjective

ver·bal·ize \'vər-bə-,līz\ vb 1 : to speak, write, or express in wordy or empty fashion 2 : to express something in words : describe verbally 3 : to convert into a verb — **ver·bal·iza·tion** \,vər-bə-lə-'zā-shən\ n

verbal noun n : a noun derived directly from a verb or verb stem and in some uses having the sense and constructions of a verb

ver·ba·tim \(,)vər-'bāt-əm\ adv (or adj) : in the same words : word for word

ver·be·na \(,)vər-'bē-nə\ n : VERVAIN; esp : any of several garden plants known for their showy spikes of bright, long-lasting, and often fragrant flowers

ver·bi·age \'vər-bē-ij\ n 1 : superfluity of words or words with little meaning : WORDINESS 2 : DICTION, WORDING

ver·bose \(,)vər-'bōs\ adj : using more words than are needed to convey a meaning : WORDY syn prolix, diffuse, redundant — **ver·bos·i·ty** \-'bäs-ət-ē\ n

ver·bo·ten \vər-'bōt-ᵊn\ adj : forbidden usu. by authority and often unreasonably

ver·dant \'vərd-ᵊnt\ adj 1 : green with growing plants 2 : unripe in experience : GREEN — **ver·dant·ly** adv

ver·dict \'vər-(,)dikt\ n 1 : the finding or decision of a jury on the matter submitted in trial 2 : DECISION, JUDGMENT

ver·di·gris \'vərd-ə-,grēs, -,gris\ n : a green or bluish deposit that forms on copper, brass, or bronze surfaces when exposed to the weather

ver·dure \'vər-jər\ n : the greenness of growing vegetation; also : green vegetation

1verge \'vərj\ n 1 : a staff carried as an emblem of authority or office 2 : something that borders or bounds : EDGE, MARGIN 3 : BRINK, THRESHOLD

2verge vb : to be on the verge, edge, or margin : be contiguous : APPROACH, BORDER

3verge vb 1 : to incline toward the horizon : SINK 2 : to move or incline in a particular direction 3 : to be in transition or change

verg·er n 1 Brit : an attendant who carries a verge (as before a bishop) 2 : SEXTON

ver·i·fy \'ver-ə-,fī\ vb 1 : to confirm in law by oath 2 : to establish the truth, accuracy, or reality of syn authenticate, confirm, corroborate, substantiate, validate — **ver·i·fi·able** adj — **ver·i·fi·ca·tion** \,ver-ə-fə-'kā-shən\ n

ver·i·ly \'ver-ə-lē\ adv 1 : in very truth : CERTAINLY 2 : TRULY, CONFI-DENTLY

veri·si·mil·i·tude \,ver-ə-sə-'mil-ə-,t(y)üd\ n : the quality or state of appearing to be true : PROBABILITY; also : a statement that is apparently true syn truth, veracity, verity

ver·i·ta·ble \'ver-ət-ə-bəl\ adj : ACTUAL, GENUINE, TRUE — **ver·i·ta·bly** adv

ver·i·ty \'ver-ət-ē\ n 1 : the quality or state of being true or real : TRUTH, REALITY 2 : a true fact or statement 3 : HONESTY, VERACITY

ver·meil n 1 \'vər-məl, -,māl\ : VER-MILION 2 \ver-'mā\ : gilded silver, bronze, or copper

ver·mi·cel·li \,vər-mə-'chel-ē, -'sel-\ n : a dough made in long solid strings smaller in diameter than spaghetti

ver·mi·form \'vər-mə-,form\ adj : long and slender like a worm

vermiform appendix n : the intestinal appendix

ver·mi·fuge \'vər-mə-,fyüj\ n : a medicine for destroying or expelling intestinal worms

ver·mil·ion \vər-'mil-yən\ n : any of a number of very bright red colors not quite as bright as scarlet; also : a pigment yielding one of these colors

ver·min \'vər-mən\ n, pl **vermin** : small

common harmful or disgusting animals (as lice or mice) that are difficult to get rid of — **ver·min·ous** \-mə-nəs\ *adj*

ver·mouth \vər-'müth\ *n* [F *vermout*, fr. G *wermut* wormwood] **:** a white wine flavored with herbs

1ver·nac·u·lar \və(r)-'nak-yə-lər\ *adj* **1 :** of, relating to, or being a language or dialect native to a region or country rather than a literary, cultured, or foreign language **2 :** of, relating to, or being the normal spoken form of a language

2vernacular *n* **1 :** a vernacular language **2 :** the mode of expression of a group or class **3 :** a vernacular name of a plant or animal

ver·nal \'vərn-ᵊl\ *adj* **:** of, relating to, or occurring in the spring of the year

ver·ni·er \'vər-nē-ər\ *n* **:** a short scale made to slide along the divisions of a graduated instrument to indicate parts of divisions

ve·ron·i·ca \və-'rän-i-kə\ *n* **:** SPEEDWELL

ver·sa·tile \'vər-sət-ᵊl\ *adj* **:** turning with ease from one thing or position to another; *esp* **:** having many aptitudes ⟨a ~ genius⟩ — **ver·sa·til·i·ty** \,vər-sə-'til-ət-ē\ *n*

verse \'vərs\ *n* **1 :** a line of poetry; *also* **:** STANZA **2 :** metrical language **3 :** POETRY; *also* **:** POEM **4 :** one of the short divisions of a chapter in the Bible

versed \'vərst\ *adj* **:** familiar from experience, study, or practice **:** SKILLED, PRACTICED

ver·si·cle \'vər-si-kəl\ *n* **:** a verse or sentence said or sung by a clergyman and followed by a response from the people

ver·si·fi·ca·tion \,vər-sə-fə-'kā-shən\ *n* **1 :** the making of verses **2 :** metrical structure

ver·si·fy \'vər-sə-,fī\ *vb* **1 :** to write verse **2 :** to turn into verse — **ver·si·fi·er** \-,fī(-ə)r\ *n*

ver·sion \'vər-zhən\ *n* **1 :** TRANSLATION; *esp* **:** a translation of the Bible **2 :** an account or description from a particular point of view esp. as contrasted with another **3 :** a form or variant of a type or original

vers li·bre \ve(ə)r-'lēbrᵊ\ *n*, *pl* **vers li·bres** *same*\ **:** FREE VERSE

ver·so \'vər-sō\ *n* **:** a left-hand page

verst \'vərst\ *n* **:** a Russian measure of length equal to 0.6629 mile

ver·sus \'vər-səs\ *prep* **1 :** AGAINST ⟨John Doe ~ Richard Roe⟩ **2 :** in contrast or as an alternative to ⟨free trade ~ protection⟩

ver·te·bra \'vərt-ə-brə\ *n*, *pl* **-brae** \-(,)brē, -,brā\ *or* **-bras :** one of the segments making up the backbone

ver·te·bral \'vərt-ə-brəl\ *adj* **:** of, relating to, or made up of vertebrae **:** SPINAL ⟨the ~ column or backbone⟩

1ver·te·brate \'vərt-ə-brət, -,brāt\ *adj* **1 :** having a backbone **2 :** of or relating to the vertebrates

2vertebrate *n* **:** any of a large group of animals (as mammals, birds, reptiles, amphibians, or fishes) distinguished by possession of a backbone

ver·tex \'vər-,teks\ *n*, *pl* **ver·tex·es** *or* **ver·ti·ces** \'vərt-ə-,sēz\ **1 :** the point opposite to and farthest from the base of a geometrical figure **2 :** ZENITH

3 : the highest point **:** TOP, SUMMIT

ver·ti·cal \'vərt-i-kəl\ *adj* **1 :** of, relating to, or located at the vertex **:** directly overhead **2 :** rising perpendicularly from a level surface **:** UPRIGHT — **vertical** *n* — **ver·ti·cal·ly** *adv* — **ver·ti·cal·ness** *n*

ver·ti·cil·late \,vərt-ə-'sil-ət\ *adj* **:** arranged in whorls about a stem ⟨~ leaves⟩

ver·tig·i·nous \(,)vər-'tij-ə-nəs\ *adj* **1 :** marked by, suffering from, or tending to cause dizziness **2 :** marked by turning **:** WHIRLING, ROTARY

ver·ti·go \'vərt-i-,gō\ *n*, *pl* **vertigoes** *or* **ver·tig·i·nes** \(,)vər-'tij-ə-,nēz\ **:** DIZZINESS, GIDDINESS

ver·vain \'vər-,vān\ *n* **:** any of a group of herbs or low woody plants with often showy heads or spikes of 5-parted regular flowers

verve \'vərv\ *n* **:** liveliness of imagination; *also* **:** VIVACITY

1very \'ver-ē\ *adj* **1 :** EXACT, PRECISE ⟨the ~ heart of the city⟩ **2 :** exactly suitable ⟨the ~ tool for the job⟩ **3 :** ABSOLUTE, UTTER ⟨the *veriest* nonsense⟩ **4 :** MERE, BARE ⟨the ~ idea scared him⟩ **5 :** SELFSAME, IDENTICAL ⟨the ~ man I saw⟩ **6 :** even the **:** EVEN ⟨made the ~ walls shake⟩

2very *adv* **1 :** to a high degree **:** EXTREMELY **2 :** in actual fact **:** TRULY

very high frequency *n* **:** a frequency of a radio wave between 30 and 300 megacycles

ves·i·cant \'ves-i-kənt\ *n* **:** an agent that causes blistering — **vesicant** *adj*

ves·i·cle \'ves-i-kəl\ *n* **:** a membranous and usu. fluid-filled cavity in a plant or animal; *also* **:** BLISTER — **ve·sic·u·lar** \və-'sik-yə-lər\ *adj*

1ves·per \'ves-pər\ *n* **1** *cap* **:** the evening star **2 :** a vesper bell **3** *archaic* **:** EVENING, EVENTIDE

2vesper *adj* **:** of or relating to vespers or to the evening

ves·pers \-pərz\ *n pl*, *often cap* **:** a late afternoon or evening worship service

ves·per·tine \'ves-pər-,tīn\ *adj* **1 :** of, relating to, or taking place in the evening **2 :** active or flourishing in the evening

ves·sel \'ves-əl\ *n* **1 :** a hollow or concave utensil (as a barrel, bottle, bowl, or cup) for holding something **2 :** a craft bigger than a rowboat for navigation of the water **3 :** a person regarded as one into whom some quality is infused **4 :** a tube in which a body fluid (as blood) is contained and circulated

1vest \'vest\ *vb* **1 :** to place or give into the possession or discretion of some person or authority **2 :** to clothe with a particular authority, right, or property **3 :** to become legally vested **4 :** to clothe with or as if with a garment; *esp* **:** to garb in ecclesiastical vestments

2vest *n* **1 :** a man's sleeveless garment worn under a suit coat; *also* **:** a similar garment for women **2 :** UNDERSHIRT **3 :** a front piece of a dress resembling the front of a vest

1ves·tal \'vest-ᵊl\ *adj* **1 :** of or relating to Vesta **2 :** relating to, characteristic of, or befitting a vestal virgin **:** CHASTE — **ves·tal·ly** *adv*

2vestal *n* **1 :** a virgin consecrated to Vesta and to watching the sacred fire

ə abut; ᵊ kitten; ər further; a back; ā bake; ä cot, cart; au̇ out; ch chin; e less; ē easy; g gift; i trip; ī life; j joke; ŋ sing; ō flow; ȯ flaw; ȯi coin; th thin; th this; ü loot; u̇ foot; y yet; yü few; yu̇ furious; zh vision

kept burning on her altar **2** : VIRGIN; *also* : NUN

vest·ee \ve-'stē\ *n* : an ornamental piece showing the open edges on the front of a woman's jacket or blouse

ves·ti·bule \'ves-tə-,byül\ *n* **1** : a passage or room between the outer door and the interior of a building **2** : the enclosed entrance to a railroad passenger car **3** : a bodily cavity forming or suggesting an entrance to some other part — **ves·tib·u·lar** \ve-'stib-yə-lər\ *adj*

ves·tige \'ves-tij\ *n* : a trace or visible sign left by something lost or vanished; *also* : a minute remaining amount — **ves·ti·gial** \ve-'stij-(ē-)əl\ *adj* — **ves·ti·gial·ly** *adv*

vest·ment \'ves(t)-mənt\ *n* **1** : an outer garment; *esp* : a ceremonial or official robe **2** *pl* : CLOTHING, GARB **3** : a garment or insignia worn by a clergyman when officiating or assisting at a religious service

ves·try \'ves-trē\ *n* **1** : a room in a church for vestments, altar linens, and sacred vessels **2** : a room used for church meetings and classes **3** : a body administering the temporal affairs of an Episcopal parish

ves·try·man \-mən\ *n* : a member of a vestry

ves·ture \'ves-chər\ *n* **1** : a covering garment (as a robe) **2** : CLOTHING, APPAREL

vet \'vet\ *n* : VETERINARIAN, VETERINARY

vetch \'vech\ *n* : any of several herbs related to the pea including some valued for fodder

vet·er·an \'vet-(ə-)rən\ *n* **1** : an old soldier of long service **2** : a former member of the armed forces **3** : a person of long experience in an occupation or skill — **veteran** *adj*

Veterans Day *n* : November 11 observed as a legal holiday in commemoration of the end of hostilities in 1918 and 1945

vet·er·i·nar·i·an \,vet-(ə-)rən-'er-ē-ən, ,vet-ᵊn-\ *n* : one qualified and authorized to treat injuries and diseases of animals

¹vet·er·i·nary \'vet-(ə-)rən-,er-ē, 'vet-ᵊn-\ *adj* : of, relating to, or being the medical care of animals and esp. domestic animals

²veterinary *n* : VETERINARIAN

¹ve·to \'vēt-ō\ *n, pl* **-toes** [L, I forbid] **1** : an authoritative prohibition **2** : a power of one part of a government to forbid the carrying out of projects attempted by another part; *esp* : a power vested in a chief executive to prevent the carrying out of measures adopted by a legislature **3** : the exercise of the power of veto; *also* : a document or message stating the reasons for a specific use of this power

²veto *vb* **1** : FORBID, PROHIBIT **2** : to refuse assent to (a legislative bill) so as to prevent enactment or cause reconsideration — **ve·to·er** *n*

¹vex \'veks\ *vb* **1** : to bring trouble, distress, or agitation to **2** : to irritate or annoy by petty provocations **3** : to debate or discuss at length : DISPUTE (a ~ed question) **4** : to shake or toss about

vex·a·tion \vek-'sā-shən\ *n* **1** : the quality or state of being vexed : IRRITATION **2** : the act of vexing : a cause of trouble or annoyance

vex·a·tious \-shəs\ *adj* **1** : causing vexation : ANNOYING, DISTRESSING **2** : full of distress or annoyance : TROUBLED — **vex·a·tious·ly** *adv* — **vex·a·tious·ness** *n*

via \,vī-ə, ,vē-ə\ *prep* : by way of (goods shipped ~ the Panama Canal)

vi·a·ble \'vī-ə-bəl\ *adj* **1** : capable of living or growing; *esp* : born alive and sufficiently developed physically as to be normally capable of living (a ~ infant) **2** : capable of being put into practice : WORKABLE — **vi·a·bil·i·ty** \,vī-ə-'bil-ət-ē\ *n* — **vi·a·bly** \'vī-ə-blē\ *adv*

via·duct \'vī-ə-,dəkt\ *n* : a bridge with high supporting towers or piers for carrying a road or railroad over something (as a valley, river, or road)

vi·al \'vī(-ə)l\ *n* : a small vessel for liquids

vi·and \'vī-ənd\ *n* : an article of food — usu. used in pl.

vi·at·i·cum \vī-'at-i-kəm\ *n, pl* **-cums** or **-ca** \-kə\ **1** : an allowance esp. in money for traveling needs and expenses **2** : the Christian Eucharist given to a person in danger of death

vi·brant \'vī-brənt\ *adj* **1** : VIBRATING, PULSING **2** : pulsing with vigor or activity **3** : readily set in vibration : RESPONSIVE, SENSITIVE **4** : sounding from vibration — **vi·bran·cy** *n*

vi·brate \'vī-,brāt\ *vb* **1** : OSCILLATE **2** : to set in vibration **3** : to be in vibration **4** : to respond sympathetically : THRILL **5** : WAVER, FLUCTUATE — **vi·bra·tor** *n*

vi·bra·tion \vī-'brā-shən\ *n* **1** : an act of vibrating : a state of being vibrated : OSCILLATION **2** : a rapid to-and-fro motion of the particles of an elastic body or medium (as a stretched cord) that produces sound **3** : a trembling motion **4** : VACILLATION

vi·bra·to·ry \'vī-brə-,tōr-ē\ *adj* : consisting of, capable of, or causing vibration

vi·bur·num \vī-'bər-nəm\ *n* : any of several shrubs or trees related to the honeysuckle with small usu. white flowers in broad clusters

vic·ar \'vik-ər\ *n* **1** : an administrative deputy **2** : an Anglican clergyman in charge of a dependent parish — **vi·car·i·al** \vī-'kar-ē-əl\ *adj* — **vi·car·i·ate** \-ē-ət\ *n*

vic·ar·age \'vik-ə-rij\ *n* : the benefice or house of a vicar

vicar-general *n, pl* **vicars-general** : an administrative deputy (as of a Roman Catholic bishop)

vi·car·i·ous \vī-'kar-ē-əs\ *adj* **1** : acting for another **2** : done or suffered by one person on behalf of another or others (a ~ sacrifice) **3** : realized or experienced by one person through sympathetic sharing in the experience of another — **vi·car·i·ous·ly** *adv* — **vi·car·i·ous·ness** *n*

¹vice \'vīs\ *n* **1** : a moral fault; *esp* : an immoral habit : DEPRAVITY, WICKEDNESS **3** : a physical imperfection : BLEMISH **4** : an undesirable behavior pattern in a domestic animal

²vice *n, chiefly Brit* : VISE

³vi·ce \'vī-sē\ *prep* : in the place of : SUCCEEDING (appointed chairman ~ J.W.Doe, resigned)

vice admiral *n* : a commissioned officer in the navy ranking next below an admiral

vice·ge·rent \'vīs-'jir-ənt\ *n* : an administrative deputy of a king or magistrate — **vice·ge·ren·cy** n

vi·cen·ni·al \vī-'sen-ē-əl\ adj : happening once every twenty years

vice-pres·i·den·cy \,vīs-'prez-əd-ən-sē\ n : the office of vice-president

vice-pres·i·dent n 1 : an officer ranking next to a president and usu. empowered to act for him during an absence or disability 2 : a president's deputy in charge of a particular location or function

vice·re·gal \'vīs-'rē-gəl\ adj : of or relating to a viceroy

vice·roy \'vīs-,roi\ n : the governor of a country or province who rules as representative of his sovereign — **vice·roy·al·ty** \-əl-tē\ n

vice ver·sa \,vīs-(i-)'vər-sə\ adv : with the order reversed : CONVERSELY

vi·chys·soise \,vish-ē-'swäz, ,vēsh-\ n : a thick soup made esp. from leeks or onions and potatoes and usu. served cold

vi·chy water \'vish-ē-\ n : water impregnated with carbon dioxide

vic·i·nage \'vis-ᵊn-ij\ n : a neighboring or surrounding district : VICINITY

vic·i·nal \-ᵊn-əl\ adj : of or relating to a limited district : LOCAL

vi·cin·i·ty \və-'sin·ət-ē\ n 1 : NEARNESS, PROXIMITY 2 : a surrounding area : NEIGHBORHOOD

vi·cious \'vish-əs\ adj 1 : addicted to vice : WICKED, DEPRAVED 2 : DEFECTIVE, FAULTY; also : INVALID 3 : IMPURE, FOUL 4 : having a savage disposition 5 : MALICIOUS, SPITEFUL 6 : worsened by internal causes that augment each other (~ wage-price spiral) — **vi·cious·ly** adv — **vi·cious·ness** n

vi·cis·si·tude \və-'sis-ə-,t(y)üd, vī-\ n 1 : the quality or state of being changeable 2 : a change or succession from one thing to another; esp : an irregular, unexpected, or surprising change — usu. used in pl.

vic·tim \'vik-təm\ n 1 : a living being offered as a sacrifice in a religious rite 2 : an individual injured or killed (as by disease or accident) 3 : a person cheated, fooled, or injured (a ~ of circumstances)

vic·tim·ize \'vik-tə-,mīz\ vb : to make a victim of — **vic·tim·iza·tion** \,vik-tə-mə-'zā-shən\ n — **vic·tim·iz·er** \'vik-tə-,mī-zər\ n

vic·tor \'vik-tər\ n : WINNER, CONQUEROR

vic·to·ria \vik-'tōr-ē-ə\ n : a low 4-wheeled carriage with a folding top and a raised seat in front for the driver

¹**Vic·to·ri·an** \-ē-ən\ adj 1 : of or relating to the reign of Queen Victoria of England or the art, letters, or taste of her time 2 : typical of the standards or conduct of the age of Victoria esp. when prudish or narrow

²**Victorian** n : a person and esp. an author of the Victorian period

vic·to·ri·ous \vik-'tōr-ē-əs\ adj 1 : having won a victory : CONQUERING 2 : of, relating to, or characteristic of victory — **vic·to·ri·ous·ly** adv

vic·to·ry \'vik-t(ə-)rē\ n 1 : the overcoming of an enemy or an antagonist 2 : achievement of success in a struggle or endeavor against odds

¹**vict·ual** \'vit-ᵊl\ n 1 : food usable by man 2 pl : food supplies : PROVISIONS

²**victual** vb -ualed or -ualled; -ual·ing or -ual·ling 1 : to supply with food 2 : to lay in provisions

vict·ual·er or **vict·ual·ler** n 1 : the keeper of a restaurant or tavern 2 : one that supplies an army, a navy, or a ship with food

vi·cu·ña \vī-'k(y)ü-nə, vi-'kün-yə\ n 1 : a So. American wild mammal related to the llama and alpaca; also : its wool 2 : a soft fabric woven from the wool of the vicuña; also : a sheep's wool imitation of this

vi·de \'vīd-ē\ imperative verb : SEE — used to direct a reader to another item

vi·de·li·cet \və-'del-ə-,set, vī-\ adv : that is to say : NAMELY

¹**vid·eo** \'vid-ē-,ō\ adj : relating to or used in transmission or reception of the television image

²**video** n : TELEVISION

vie \'vī\ vb vied; vy·ing : to strive for superiority : CONTEND — **vi·er** \'vī(-ə)r\ n

Viet·nam·ese \vē-,et-nə-'mēz\ n, pl **Vietnamese** : a native or inhabitant of Vietnam — **Vietnamese** adj

¹**view** \'vyü\ n 1 : the act of seeing or examining : INSPECTION; also : SURVEY 2 : ESTIMATE, JUDGMENT (stated his ~s) 3 : a sight (as of a landscape) regarded for its pictorial quality (a beautiful ~) 4 : extent or range of vision (within ~) 5 : a picture of a scene (~s of Paris) 6 : OBJECT, PURPOSE (done with a ~ to promotion)

²**view** vb 1 : SEE, BEHOLD 2 : to look at attentively : EXAMINE 3 : to examine mentally : CONSIDER — **view·er** n

view·point \'vyü-,point\ n : a position from which something is considered : point of view : STANDPOINT

vi·ges·i·mal \vī-'jes-ə-mal\ adj : based on the number 20

vig·il \'vij-əl\ n 1 : a religious observance formerly held on the night before a religious feast 2 : the day before a religious feast observed as a day of spiritual preparation 3 : evening or nocturnal devotions or prayers — usu. used in pl. 4 : an act or a time of keeping awake when sleep is customary; esp : an act of wakeful watching

vig·i·lance \'vij-ə-ləns\ n : the quality or state of being vigilant

vig·i·lant adj : alertly watchful esp. to avoid danger — **vig·i·lant·ly** adv

vig·i·lan·te \,vij-ə-'lant-ē\ n : a member of a volunteer committee (**vigilance committee**) of citizens organized to suppress and punish crime summarily (as when the processes of law appear inadequate)

¹**vi·gnette** \vin-'yet\ n 1 : a small decorative design on or just before the title page of a book or at the beginning or end of a chapter 2 : a picture (as an engraving or a photograph) that shades off gradually into the surrounding ground 3 : a brief word picture

²**vignette** vb : to finish (as a photograph) in the manner of a vignette

vig·or \'vig-ər\ n 1 : active strength or energy of body or mind 2 : INTENSITY, FORCE

vig·or·ous \'vig-(ə)-rəs\ adj 1 : having vigor : ROBUST 2 : done with vigor : carried out forcefully and energetically — **vig·or·ous·ly** adv

Vi·king \'vī-kiŋ\ n : one of the pirate Northmen plundering the coasts of Europe from the 8th to the 10th century

vile \'vīl\ adj 1 : WORTHLESS, MEAN, BASE 2 : morally base : WICKED 3 : UNCLEAN, REPULSIVE, ODIOUS — **vile·ly** \'vīl-lē\ adv — **vile·ness** n

vil·i·fy \'vil-ə-ˌfī\ vb : to blacken the character of with abusive language : DEFAME syn malign, calumniate, slander, libel, traduce — **vil·i·fi·ca·tion** \ˌvil-ə-fə-ˈkā-shən\ n — **vil·i·fi·er**, \'vil-ə-ˌfī(-ə)r\ n

vil·la \'vil-ə\ n 1 : a country estate 2 : a usu. somewhat pretentious rural or suburban residence

vil·lage \'vil-ij\ n 1 : a settlement usu. larger than a hamlet and smaller than a town 2 : an incorporated minor municipality 3 : the people of a village

vil·lag·er n : an inhabitant of a village

vil·lain \'vil-ən\ n 1 : VILLEIN 2 : a deliberate scoundrel or criminal

vil·lain·ous adj 1 : befitting a villain : WICKED, EVIL 2 : highly objectionable : DETESTABLE syn vicious, iniquitous, nefarious, infamous, corrupt, degenerate — **vil·lain·ous·ly** adv — **vil·lain·ous·ness** n

vil·lainy n 1 : villainous conduct; also : a villainous act 2 : villainous character or nature : DEPRAVITY

vil·lein \'vil-ən, -ˌān\ n 1 : a free villager of Anglo-Saxon times 2 : a serf of a class gradually changing its status to that of free peasants

vil·len·age \'vil-ə-nij\ n 1 : the holding of land at the will of a feudal lord 2 : the status of a villein

vil·lous \'vil-əs\ adj : covered with fine hairs or villi

vil·lus \'vil-əs\ n, pl **vil·li** \'vil-ˌī\ : a slender usu. vascular process; esp : one of the tiny projections of the mucous membrane of the small intestine that function in the absorption of food

vim \'vim\ n : robust energy and enthusiasm : VITALITY

vin·ai·grette \ˌvin-i-ˈgret\ n : a small box or bottle for holding aromatic preparations (as smelling salts)

vin·ci·ble \'vin-sə-bəl\ adj : capable of being overcome or subdued

vin·di·cate \'vin-də-ˌkāt\ vb 1 : AVENGE 2 : EXONERATE, ABSOLVE 3 : CONFIRM, SUBSTANTIATE 4 : to provide defense for : JUSTIFY 5 : to maintain a right to : ASSERT — **vin·di·ca·tor** n

vin·di·ca·tion \ˌvin-də-ˈkā-shən\ n : a vindicating or being vindicated; esp : justification against denial or censure

vin·dic·tive \vin-ˈdik-tiv\ adj 1 : disposed to revenge 2 : intended for or involving revenge 3 : VICIOUS, SPITEFUL — **vin·dic·tive·ly** adv — **vin·dic·tive·ness** n

vine \'vīn\ n 1 : GRAPE 2 2 : a plant whose stem requires support and which climbs (as by tendrils) or trails along the ground; also : the stem of such a plant

vin·e·gar \'vin-i-gər\ n [OF vinaigre, fr. vin wine + aigre sour] : a sour liquid obtained by fermentation (as of cider, wine, or malt) and used in cookery and pickling

vin·e·gary adj 1 : resembling vinegar : SOUR 2 : disagreeable in manner or disposition : CRABBED

vine·yard \'vin-yərd\ n : a plantation of grapevines; also : an area of physical or mental occupation

vi·nous \'vī-nəs\ adj 1 : of, relating to, or made with wine ⟨~ medications⟩ 2 : showing the effects of the use of wine

vin·tage \'vint-ij\ n 1 : a season's yield of grapes or wine 2 : the act or period of gathering grapes or making wine 3 : WINE; esp : a wine of a particular type, region, and year and usu. of superior quality 4 : a period of origin ⟨clothes of the ~ of 1890⟩

vint·ner \'vint-nər\ n : a dealer in wines

vi·nyl \'vīn-ʾl\ n : any of various tough plastics used esp. for coatings, sheeting, tile, flooring, and molded objects

vi·ol \'vī-əl\ n : a bowed stringed instrument chiefly of the 16th and 17th centuries having a fretted neck and usu. 6 strings

vi·o·la \vē-ˈō-lə\ n : an instrument of the violin family slightly larger and tuned lower than a violin

vi·o·la·ble \'vī-ə-lə-bəl\ adj : capable of being violated

vi·o·late \'vī-ə-ˌlāt\ vb 1 : BREAK, DISREGARD ⟨~ a law⟩ ⟨~ a frontier⟩ 2 : RAPE 3 : PROFANE, DESECRATE 4 : INTERRUPT, DISTURB ⟨violated his privacy⟩ — **vi·o·la·tor** n

vi·o·la·tion \ˌvī-ə-ˈlā-shən\ n : an act or instance of violating : the state of being violated syn breach, infraction, trespass, infringement

vi·o·lence \'vī-ə-ləns\ n 1 : exertion of physical force so as to injure or abuse 2 : injury by or as if by infringement or profanation 3 : intense or furious often destructive action or force 4 : vehement feeling or expression : INTENSITY 5 : jarring quality : DISCORDANCE syn compulsion, coercion, duress, constraint, restraint

vi·o·lent adj 1 : marked by extreme force or sudden intense activity; esp : marked by improper use of such force 2 : EXTREME, INTENSE 3 : caused by force : not natural ⟨~ death⟩ 4 : caused by or showing strong feeling ⟨~ words⟩ — **vi·o·lent·ly** adv

vi·o·let \'vī-ə-lət\ n 1 : any of numerous low plants with mostly heart-shaped leaves and both aerial and underground flowers; esp : one with small solid-colored flowers 2 : a variable color averaging a reddish blue — **violet** adj

vi·o·lin \ˌvī-ə-ˈlin\ n : a bowed stringed instrument with four strings that has a shallower body and a more curved bridge than a viol

vi·o·lin·ist n : one who plays the violin

vi·o·list \vē-ˈō-ləst\ n : one who plays the viola

vi·o·lon·cel·list \ˌvī-ə-lən-ˈchel-əst, ˌvē-\ n : CELLIST

vi·o·lon·cel·lo \ˌvī-ə-lən-ˈchel-ō\ n : CELLO

vi·os·ter·ol \vī-ˈäs-tə-ˌrȯl\ n : a vitamin D preparation usu. in a vegetable oil

vi·per \'vī-pər\ n 1 : any of a group of sluggish heavy-bodied Old World venomous snakes 2 : PIT VIPER 3 : a venomous or reputedly venomous snake 4 : a treacherous or malignant person

vi·ra·go \və-ˈrä-gō, ˈvir-ə-ˌgō\ n, pl **-goes** or **-gos** : a scolding, quarrelsome, or loud overbearing woman syn amazon, termagant, scold, shrew, vixen

vi·ral \'vī-rəl\ adj : of, relating to, or caused by a virus

vir·eo \'vir-ē-ˌō\ n : any of various small

insect-eating American songbirds mostly olive green and grayish in color

¹vir·gin \'vər-jən\ *n* **1 :** an unmarried woman devoted to religion **2** *cap* **:** the mother of Jesus **3 :** an unmarried woman **4 :** a person who has not had sexual intercourse

²virgin *adj* **1 :** free from stain **:** PURE, SPOTLESS **2 :** CHASTE **3 :** befitting a virgin **:** MODEST **4 :** FRESH, UNSPOILED; *esp* **:** not altered by human activity ⟨~ forest⟩ **5 :** INITIAL, FIRST

¹vir·gin·al *adj* **:** of, relating to, or characteristic of a virgin or virginity — **vir·gin·al·ly** *adv*

²virginal *n* **:** a small rectangular spinet without legs popular in the 16th and 17th centuries

Vir·gin·ia creeper \vər-ˌjin-yə-\ *n* **:** a No. American vine having leaves with five leaflets and bluish black berries

Virginia reel *n* **:** an American country-dance

vir·gin·i·ty \vər-'jin-ət-ē\ *n* **1 :** the quality or state of being virgin; *esp* **:** MAIDENHOOD **2 :** the unmarried life **:** CELIBACY

vir·gule \'vər-ˌgyül\ *n* **:** a mark / used typically to denote "or" (as in and/or) or "per" (as in *feet/second*)

vir·i·des·cent \ˌvir-ə-'des-°nt\ *adj* **:** slightly green **:** GREENISH

vir·ile \'vir-əl\ *adj* **1 :** having the nature, powers, or qualities of a man **2 :** MASTERFUL, FORCEFUL **3 :** MASCULINE, MALE — **vi·ril·i·ty** \və-'ril-ət-ē\ *n*

vir·tu \ˌvər-'tü, vir-\ *n* **1 :** a love of or taste for objects of art **2 :** objects of art (as curios and antiques)

vir·tu·al \'vər-ch(ə-w)əl\ *adj* **:** being in essence or in effect though not formally recognized or admitted ⟨a ~ dictator⟩ — **vir·tu·al·ly** *adv*

vir·tue \'vər-chü\ *n* **1 :** conformity to a standard of right **:** MORALITY **2 :** a particular moral excellence **3 :** active power to accomplish a given effect **:** POTENCY, EFFICACY **4 :** manly strength or courage **:** VALOR **5 :** a commendable quality **:** MERIT **6 :** chastity esp. in a woman

vir·tu·os·i·ty \ˌvər-chə-'wäs-ət-ē\ *n* **:** great technical skill in the practice of the fine arts

vir·tu·o·so \ˌvər-chə-'wō-sō, -zō\ *n, pl* -sos *or* -si \-(ˌ)sē, -(ˌ)zē\ **1 :** one skilled in or having a taste for the fine arts **2 :** one who excels in the technique of an art; *esp* **:** a musical performer syn connoisseur, aesthete, dilettante, expert, adept, artist — **virtuoso** *adj*

vir·tu·ous \'vər-chə-wəs\ *adj* **:** having or showing virtue and esp. moral virtue **2 :** CHASTE — **vir·tu·ou·ly** *adv*

vir·u·lent \'vir-(y)ə-lənt\ *adj* **1 :** extremely poisonous or venomous **:** NOXIOUS **2 :** bitterly hostile **:** MALIGNANT **3 :** highly infectious ⟨a ~ germ⟩; *also* **:** marked by a rapid and very severe course ⟨a ~ disease⟩ — **vir·u·lence** *or* **vir·u·len·cy** *n* — **vir·u·lent·ly** *adv*

vi·rus \'vī-rəs\ *n* **1 :** an infective agent too small to be seen with a light microscope and active after passage through a filter too fine for a bacterium to pass; *also* **:** a disease caused by a virus **2 :** something (as a corrupting influence) that poisons the mind or spirit

¹vi·sa \'vē-zə\ *n* **1 :** an endorsement by the proper authorities on a passport to show that it has been examined and the bearer may proceed **2 :** a signature by a superior official signifying approval of a document

²visa *vb* **vi·saed; vi·sa·ing :** to give a visa to (a passport)

vis·age \'viz-ij\ *n* **:** the face or countenance of a person or sometimes an animal; *also* **:** LOOK, APPEARANCE

¹vis-à-vis \ˌvē-zə-'vē\ *n, pl* **vis-à-vis** \-zə-'vē(z)\ **1 :** one that is face to face with another **2 :** ESCORT **3 :** COUNTERPART **4 :** TÊTE-À-TÊTE

²vis-à-vis *prep* **1 :** face to face with **:** OPPOSITE **2 :** in relation to **:** as compared with

³vis-à-vis *adv* **:** in company **:** TOGETHER

viscera *pl of* VISCUS

vis·cer·al \'vis-ə-rəl\ *adj* **1 :** felt in or as if in the viscera **2 :** of or relating to the viscera — **vis·cer·al·ly** *adv*

vis·cid \'vis-əd\ *adj* **:** VISCOUS — **vis·cid·i·ty** \vis-'id-ət-ē\ *n* — **vis·cid·ly** \'vis-əd-lē\

vis·cose \'vis-ˌkōs\ *n* **:** a syruplike solution made by chemically treating cellulose and used in making rayon and transparent films

vis·cos·i·ty \vis-'käs-ət-ē\ *n* **:** the quality of being viscous; *esp* **:** the property of fluids that causes them not to flow easily because of the friction of their molecules ⟨the ~ of oil⟩

vis·count \'vī-ˌkaůnt\ *n* **:** a member of the British peerage ranking below an earl and above a baron

vis·count·ess *n* **1 :** the wife or widow of a viscount **2 :** a woman holding the rank of a viscount in her own right

vis·cous \'vis-kəs\ *adj* **1 :** having the sticky consistency of glue **2 :** having or characterized by viscosity **:** THICK

vis·cus \'vis-kəs\ *n, pl* **vis·cera** \'vis-ə-rə\ **:** an internal organ of the body; *esp* **:** one (as the heart or liver) located in the cavity of the trunk

¹vise \'vīs\ *n* **:** a device for holding or clamping work typically having two jaws closed by a screw or lever

²vise \'vē-ˌzā\ *n* **:** VISA — **visé** *vb*

vis·i·bil·i·ty \ˌviz-ə-'bil-ət-ē\ *n* **1 :** the quality, condition, or degree of being visible **2 :** the degree of clearness of the atmosphere

vis·i·ble \'viz-ə-bəl\ *adj* **:** capable of being seen ⟨~ stars⟩; *also* **:** MANIFEST, APPARENT ⟨has no ~ means of support⟩ — **vis·i·bly** *adv*

¹vi·sion \'vizh-ən\ *n* **1 :** something seen otherwise than by ordinary sight (as in a dream or trance) **2 :** a vivid picture created by the imagination **3 :** the act or power of imagination **4 :** unusual wisdom in foreseeing what is going to happen **5 :** the act or power of seeing **:** SIGHT **6 :** something seen; *esp* **:** a lovely sight

²vision *vb* **:** to see in or as if in a vision **:** IMAGINE, ENVISION

¹vi·sion·ary \'vizh-ə-ˌner-ē\ *adj* **1 :** seeing or likely to see visions **:** given to dreaming or imagining **2 :** of the nature of a vision **:** ILLUSORY, UNREAL **3 :** not practical **:** UTOPIAN syn imaginary, fantastic, chimerical, quixotic

²visionary *n* **1 :** one who sees visions

2 **:** one whose ideas or projects are impractical **:** DREAMER

¹vis·it \'viz-ət\ *vb* 1 **:** to go to see in order to comfort or help 2 **:** to call upon either as an act of courtesy or in a professional capacity 3 **:** to dwell with for a time as a guest 4 **:** to come to or upon as a reward, affliction, or punishment 5 **:** INFLICT 6 **:** to make a visit or regular or frequent visits 7 **:** CHAT, CONVERSE — **vis·it·able** *adj*

²visit *n* 1 **:** a short stay **:** CALL 2 **:** a brief residence as a guest 3 **:** a journey to and stay at a place 4 **:** a formal or professional call (as by a doctor)

vis·i·tant \'viz-ə-tənt\ *n* **:** VISITOR

vis·i·ta·tion \,viz-ə-'tā-shən\ *n* 1 **:** VIS-IT; *esp* **:** an official visit 2 **:** a special dispensation of divine favor or wrath; *also* **:** a severe trial

vis·i·tor \'viz-ə-tər\ *n* **:** one that visits

vi·sor \'vī-zər\ *n* 1 **:** the front piece of a helmet; *esp* **:** a movable upper piece 2 **:** VIZARD 3 **:** a projecting part (as on a cap or an automobile windshield) to shade the eyes

vis·ta \'vis-tə\ *n* 1 **:** a distant view through or along an avenue or opening 2 **:** an extensive mental view over a series of years or events

vi·su·al \'vizh-(ə-w)əl\ *adj* 1 **:** of, relating to, or used in sight (~ organs) 2 **:** perceived by vision (a ~ impression) 3 **:** attained or performed by sight (~ tests) 4 **:** done by sight only (~ navigation) 5 **:** VISIBLE 6 **:** of or relating to instruction by means of sight (~ aids) — **vi·su·al·ly** *adv*

vi·su·al·ize \'vizh-ə-(wə-),līz\ *vb* **:** to make visible; *esp* **:** to form a mental image of — **vi·su·al·iza·tion** \,vizh-ə-(wə-)lə-'zā-shən\ *n* — **vi·su·al·iz·er** \'vizh-ə-(wə-),lī-zər\ *n*

vi·ta \'vīt-ə, 'wē-,tä\ *n*, *pl* **vi·tae** \'vīt-ē, 'wē-,tī\ **:** a brief autobiographical sketch

vi·tal \'vīt-ʰl\ *adj* 1 **:** of, relating to, or characteristic of life 2 **:** concerned with or necessary to the maintenance of life 3 **:** full of life and vigor **:** ANIMATED 4 **:** FATAL, MORTAL (~ wound) 5 **:** FUNDAMENTAL, BASIC, INDISPENSABLE 6 **:** dealing with births, deaths, marriages, health, and disease (~ statistics) — **vi·tal·ly** *adv*

vi·tal·i·ty \vī-'tal-ət-ē\ *n* 1 **:** the peculiarity distinguishing the living from the nonliving; *also* **:** capacity to live **:** mental and physical vigor 2 **:** enduring quality 3 **:** ANIMATION, LIVELINESS

vi·tal·ize \'vīt-ʰl-,īz\ *vb* **:** to impart life or vigor to **:** ANIMATE, ENERGIZE — **vi·tal·iza·tion** \,vīt-ʰl-ə-'zā-shən\ *n* — **vi·tal·iz·er** *n*

vi·tals \'vīt-ʰlz\ *n pl* 1 **:** vital organs 2 **:** essential parts

vi·ta·min \'vīt-ə-mən\ *n* **:** any of various organic substances that are essential in tiny amounts to most animals and some plants and are mostly obtained from foods

vitamin A *n* **:** a vitamin (as from egg yolk or fish-liver oils) required for healthy epithelium and sight

vitamin B *n* **:** any of various vitamins important in metabolic reactions and as growth factors; *esp* **:** THIAMINE

vitamin C *n* **:** a vitamin esp. from fruits and leafy vegetables that functions chiefly as a cellular enzyme and is used to prevent scurvy

vitamin D *n* **:** a vitamin esp. from fish-

liver oils that is essential to normal bone formation

vi·ti·ate \'vish-ē-,āt\ *vb* 1 **:** CONTAMINATE, POLLUTE; *also* **:** DEBASE, PERVERT 2 **:** to make legally without force **:** INVALIDATE — **vi·ti·a·tion** \,vish-ē-'ā-shən\ *n* — **vi·ti·a·tor** \'vish-ē-,āt ər\ *n*

vit·re·ous \'vi-trē-əs\ *adj* 1 **:** of, relating to, or resembling glass 2 **:** GLASSY (~ rocks) 3 **:** of, relating to, or being the clear colorless transparent jelly (**vitreous humor**) behind the lens in the eyeball

vit·ri·fy \'vi-rə-,fī\ *vb* **:** to change into glass or a glassy substance by heat and fusion

vit·ri·ol \-ē-əl\ *n* 1 **:** a sulfate of any of various metals (as copper, iron, or zinc) 2 **:** SULFURIC ACID 3 **:** something resembling vitriol in being caustic, corrosive, or biting — **vit·ri·ol·ic** \,vit-rē-'äl-ik\ *adj* 1 **:** derived from vitriol 2 **:** CAUSTIC, BITING (~ speech)

vit·tle \'vit-ʰl\ *n* **:** VICTUAL

vi·tu·per·ate \vī-'t(y)ü-pə-,rāt, və-\ *vb* **:** to abuse in words **:** SCOLD syn revile, berate, rate, upbraid, rail — **vi·tu·per·a·tion** \-,t(y)ü-pə-'rā-shən\ *n* — **vi·tu·per·a·tive** \-'t(y)ü-p(ə-)rət-iv, -,pə-,rāt-\ *adj* — **vi·tu·per·a·tive·ly** *adv*

vi·va \'vē-və\ *interj* — used to express goodwill

vi·va·ce \vē-'väch-ā\ *adv* (*or adj*) **:** in a brisk spirited manner — used as a direction in music

vi·va·cious \və-'vā-shəs, vī-\ *adj* **:** lively in temper or conduct **:** ANIMATED, SPRIGHTLY — **vi·va·cious·ly** *adv* — **vi·va·cious·ness** *n*

vi·vac·i·ty \-'vas-ət-ē\ *n* **:** the quality or state of being vivacious

vi·va vo·ce \,vī-və-'vō-sē\ *adj* **:** expressed or conducted by word of mouth **:** ORAL (*viva voce* examination) (*viva voce* voting) — **viva voce** *adv*

viv·id \'viv-əd\ *adj* 1 **:** having the appearance of vigorous life or freshness **:** LIVELY 2 **:** BRILLIANT, INTENSE (a ~ red) 3 **:** producing a strong impression on the senses **:** SHARP 4 **:** calling forth lifelike mental images (a ~ description) — **viv·id·ly** *adv* — **viv·id·ness** *n*

viv·i·fy \'viv-ə-,fī\ *vb* 1 **:** to endue with life **:** ANIMATE 2 **:** to make vivid — **viv·i·fi·ca·tion** \,viv-ə-fə-'kā-shən\ *n* — **viv·i·fi·er** \'viv-ə-,fī(-ə)r\ *n*

vi·vip·a·rous \vī-'vip-(ə-)rəs\ *adj* **:** producing living young from within the body rather than from eggs

vivi·sec·tion \,viv-ə-'sek-shən\ *n* **:** the cutting of or operation on a living animal; *also* **:** animal experimentation

vix·en \'vik-sən\ *n* 1 **:** a female fox 2 **:** an ill-tempered scolding woman **:** syn shrew, scold, termagant, virago

viz·ard \'viz-ərd\ *n* **:** a mask for disguise or protection

vi·zier \və-'zior\ *n* **:** a high executive officer of many Muslim countries and esp. of the former Turkish empire

vizor *var of* VISOR

vo·ca·ble \'vō-kə-bəl\ *n* **:** TERM, NAME; *esp* **:** a word composed of various sounds or letters without regard to its meaning

vo·cab·u·lary \vō-'kab-yə-,ler-ē\ *n* 1 **:** a list or collection of words usu. alphabetically arranged and defined or explained **:** LEXICON 2 **:** a stock of words used in a language by a class or individual or in relation to a subject

vocabulary entry n : a word (as the noun *book*), hyphened or open compound (as the verb *cross-refer* or the noun *boric acid*), word element (as the affix *-an*), abbreviation (as *agt*), verbalized symbol (as *Na*), or term (as *master of ceremonies*) entered alphabetically in a dictionary for the purpose of definition or identification or expressly included as an inflectional form (as the noun *mice* or the verb *saw*) or as a derived form (as the noun *godlessness* or the adverb *globally*) or related phrase (as *in spite of*) run on at its base word and usu. set in a type (as boldface) readily distinguishable from that of the lightface running text which defines, explains, or identifies the entry

¹**vo·cal** \'vō-kəl\ *adj* 1 : uttered by the voice : ORAL 2 : relating to, composed or arranged for, or sung by the human voice (~ *music*) 3 : of, relating to, or having the power of producing voice 4 : full of voices : RESOUNDING 5 : given to expressing one's feelings or opinions in speech : TALKATIVE; *also* : OUTSPOKEN **syn** articulate, fluent, eloquent, voluble, glib

²**vocal** n 1 : a vocal sound 2 : a vocal solo (in a dance number)

vo·cal·ic \vō-'kal-ik\ *adj* : of, relating to, or functioning as a vowel

vo·cal·ist \'vō-kə-ləst\ n : SINGER

vo·cal·ize \'vō-kə-,līz\ *vb* 1 : to give vocal expression to : UTTER; *esp* : SING 2 : to make voiced rather than voiceless — **vo·cal·iz·er** n

vo·ca·tion \vō-'kā-shən\ n 1 : a summons or strong inclination to a particular state or course of action (religious ~) 2 : the work to which one feels he is called or specially fitted 3 : regular employment : OCCUPATION, PROFESSION — **vo·ca·tion·al** *adj*

vo·ca·tion·al·ism n : emphasis on vocational training in education

voc·a·tive \'väk-ət-iv\ *adj* : of, relating to, or constituting a grammatical case marking the one addressed — **vocative** n

vo·cif·er·ate \vō-'sif-ə-,rāt\ *vb* : to cry out loudly : CLAMOR, SHOUT — **vo·cif·er·a·tion** \-,sif-ə-'rā-shən\ n

vo·cif·er·ous \vō-'sif-(ə-)rəs\ *adj* : making or given to loud outcry : CLAMOROUS — **vo·cif·er·ous·ly** *adv* — **vo·cif·er·ous·ness** n

vod·ka \'väd-kə\ n [Russ. fr. *yoda* water] : a liquor that is distilled from a grain mash and has no color, aroma, or taste

vogue \'vōg\ n 1 : popular acceptance or favor : POPULARITY 2 : a period of popularity 3 : something or someone in fashion at a particular time **syn** mode, fad, rage

vogu·ish \'vō-gish\ *adj* 1 : FASHIONABLE, SMART 2 : suddenly or temporarily popular

¹**voice** \'vois\ n 1 : sound produced through the mouth by vertebrates and esp. by human beings in speaking or shouting 2 : musical sound produced by the vocal cords : the power to produce such sound; *also* : one of the melodic parts in a vocal or instrumental composition 3 : the vocal organs as a means of tone production (train the ~) 4 : sound produced by vibration of the vocal cords as heard in vowels and some consonants 5 : the faculty of speech 6 : a sound suggesting vocal utterance (the ~ of the sea) 7 : an instrument or medium of expression 8 : a choice, opinion, or wish openly expressed; *also* : right of expression 9 : distinction of form of a verb to indicate the relation of the subject to the action expressed by the verb

²**voice** *vb* 1 : to give voice or expression to : UTTER; *also* : ANNOUNCE 2 : to regulate the tone of (~ the pipes of an organ) **syn** express, vent, air, ventilate

voiced \'voist\ *adj* 1 : furnished with a voice (soft-*voiced*) 2 : expressed by the voice 3 : uttered with voice — **voiced·ness** n

voice·less *adj* 1 : having no voice 2 : not pronounced with voice — **voice·less·ly** *adv* — **voice·less·ness** n

¹**void** \'void\ *adj* 1 : containing nothing : EMPTY 2 : UNOCCUPIED, VACANT 3 : LACKING, DEVOID (proposals ~ of sense) 4 : VAIN, USELESS 5 : of no legal force or effect : NULL

²**void** n 1 : empty space : EMPTINESS, VACUUM 2 : a feeling of want or hollowness

³**void** *vb* 1 : to make or leave empty; *also* : VACATE, LEAVE 2 : DISCHARGE, EMIT (~ urine) 3 : to render void : ANNUL, NULLIFY — **void·able** *adj* — **void·er** n

voile \'voil\ n : a sheer fabric from various fibers used for women's clothing and curtains

vol·a·tile \'väl-ət-ºl\ *adj* 1 : readily becoming a vapor at a relatively low temperature (a ~ liquid) 2 : LIGHTHEARTED 3 : easily erupting into violent action 4 : CHANGEABLE — **vol·a·til·i·ty** \,väl-ə-'til-ət-ē\ n — **vol·a·til·ize** \'väl-ət-ºl-,īz\ *vb*

vol·can·ic \väl-'kan-ik\ *adj* 1 : of or relating to a volcano 2 : explosively violent : VOLATILE (~ emotions)

volcanic glass n : natural glass produced by cooling of molten lava

vol·ca·no \väl-'kā-nō\ n, *pl* **-noes** or **-nos** : an opening in the earth's crust from which molten rock and steam issue; *also* : a hill or mountain composed of the ejected material

vole \'vōl\ n : any of various mouselike or ratlike rodents

vo·li·tion \vō-'lish-ən\ n 1 : the act or the power of making a choice or decision : WILL 2 : a choice or decision made — **vo·li·tion·al** *adj*

¹**vol·ley** \'väl-ē\ n 1 : a flight of missiles (as arrows or bullets) 2 : simultaneous discharge of a number of missile weapons 3 : a pouring forth of many things at the same instant (a ~ of oaths) 4 : the act of volleying

²**volley** *vb* 1 : to discharge or become discharged in or as if in a volley 2 : to hit an object of play in the air before it touches the ground

vol·ley·ball \-,bol\ n : a game played by volleying an inflated ball over a net

vol·plane \'väl-,plān\ *vb* : to glide in an airplane

volt \'vōlt\ n : the unit of electromotive

ə abut; ə kitten; ər further; a back; ā bake; ä cot, cart; aủ out; ch chin; e less; ē easy; g gift; i trip; ī life; j joke; ŋ sing; ō flow; ȯ flaw; ȯi coin; th thin; th this; ü loot; ủ foot; y yet; yü few; yủ furious; zh vision force equal to a force that when steadily applied to a conductor whose resistance is one ohm will produce a current of one ampere

volt·age n : electromotive force measured in volts

vol·ta·ic \väl-'tā-ik, vōl-\ adj : of, relating to, or producing direct electric current by chemical action ⟨~ current⟩

volte-face \vȯlt-(ə-)'fäs\ n : a facing about esp. in policy

volt·me·ter \'vōlt-,mēt-ər\ n : an instrument for measuring in volts the differences of potential between different points of an electrical circuit

vol·u·ble \'väl-yə-bəl\ adj : fluent and smooth in speech : GLIB syn eloquent, vocal, articulate, garrulous, loquacious, talkative — **vol·u·bil·i·ty** \,väl-yə-'bil-ət-ē\ n — **vol·u·bly** \'väl-yə-blē\ adv

vol·ume \'väl-yəm\ n 1 : a series of printed sheets bound typically in book form; also : an arbitrary number of issues of a periodical 2 : sufficient matter to fill a book ⟨his glance spoke ~s⟩ 3 : space occupied as measured by cubic units ⟨the ~ of a cylinder⟩ 4 : AMOUNT ⟨increasing ~ of business⟩; also : MASS, BULK 5 : the degree of loudness or the intensity of a sound syn magnitude, size, extent, dimensions, area

vol·u·met·ric \,väl-yu-'met-rik\ adj : of or relating to the measurement of volume

vo·lu·mi·nous \və-'lü-mə-nəs\ adj 1 : consisting of many folds or windings 2 : BULKY, LARGE, SWELLING 3 : filling or sufficient to fill a large volume or several volumes — **vo·lu·mi·nos·i·ty** \-,lü-mə-'näs-ət-ē\ n — **vo·lu·mi·nous·ly** \-'lü-mə-nəs-lē\ adv — **vo·lu·mi·nous·ness** n

1vol·un·tary \'väl-ən-,ter-ē\ adj 1 : done, made, or given freely and without compulsion ⟨a ~ sacrifice⟩ 2 : not accidental : INTENTIONAL ⟨a ~ slight⟩ 3 : of, relating to, or controlled by the will ⟨~ muscles⟩ 4 : having power of free choice ⟨man is a ~ agent⟩ 5 : supported by gifts rather than by the state ⟨~ churches⟩ syn deliberate, willful, willing — **vol·un·tar·i·ly** \,väl-ən-'ter-ə-lē\ adv

2voluntary n : an organ solo played in a religious service

1vol·un·teer \,väl-ən-'tiər\ n : a person who of his own free will offers himself for a service or duty — **volunteer** adj

2volunteer vb 1 : to offer or give voluntarily 2 : to offer oneself as a volunteer

vo·lup·tu·ary \və-'ləp-chə-,wer-ē\ n : one whose chief interest in life is the indulgence of sensual appetites

vo·lup·tu·ous \və-'ləp-ch(ə-w)əs\ adj 1 : giving sensual gratification ⟨~ furnishings⟩ 2 : given to or spent in enjoyment of luxury or pleasure syn luxurious, epicurean, sensuous, sensual — **vo·lup·tu·ous·ness** n

vo·lute \və-'lüt\ n : a spiral or scroll-shaped decoration

1vom·it \'väm-ət\ n : an act or instance of discharging the stomach contents through the mouth; also : the matter discharged

2vomit vb 1 : to discharge the stomach contents as vomit 2 : to belch forth : GUSH

voo·doo \'vüd-ü\ n 1 : VOODOOISM 2 : one who practices voodooism 3 : a charm or a fetish used in voodooism — **voodoo** adj

voo·doo·ism n 1 : a religion derived from African ancestor worship and consisting largely of sorcery 2 : the practice of sorcery

vo·ra·cious \vȯ-'rā-shəs, və-\ adj 1 : greedy in eating : RAVENOUS 2 : excessively eager : INSATIABLE ⟨a ~ reader⟩ syn gluttonous, ravening, rapacious — **vo·ra·cious·ly** adv — **vo·ra·cious·ness** n — **vo·rac·i·ty** \-'ras-ət-ē\ n

vor·tex \'vȯr-,teks\ n, pl **vor·ti·ces** \'vȯrt-ə-,sēz\ also **vor·tex·es** : a mass of liquid in whirling motion forming in the center of the mass a depression or cavity toward which things are drawn : WHIRLPOOL — **vor·ti·cal** \'vȯrt-i-kəl\ adj

vo·ta·ry \'vōt-ə-rē\ n 1 : ENTHUSIAST, DEVOTEE; also : a devoted adherent or admirer 2 : a devout or zealous worshiper

1vote \'vōt\ n 1 : a choice or opinion of a person or body of persons expressed usu. by a ballot, spoken word, or raised hand; also : the ballot, word, or gesture used to express a choice or opinion 2 : the decision reached by voting 3 : the right of suffrage 4 : a group of voters with some common characteristics ⟨the big city ~⟩

2vote vb 1 : to cast a vote 2 : to choose, endorse, authorize, or defeat by vote 3 : to express an opinion 4 : to adjudge by general agreement : DECLARE 5 : to offer as a suggestion : PROPOSE 6 : to cause to vote esp. in a given way — **vot·er** n

vo·tive \'vōt-iv\ adj : offered or performed in fulfillment of a vow or in petition, gratitude, or devotion ⟨~ lights⟩

vouch \'vauch\ vb 1 : PROVE, SUBSTANTIATE 2 : to verify by examining documentary evidence 3 : to give a guarantee 4 : to supply supporting evidence or testimony; also : to give personal assurance

vouch·er n 1 : an act of vouching 2 : one that vouches for another 3 : a documentary record of a business transaction 4 : a written affidavit or authorization

vouch·safe \vauch-'sāf\ vb 1 : to grant or give often in a condescending manner 2 : to grant as a privilege or as a special favor — **vouch·safe·ment** n

1vow \'vau\ n : a solemn promise or assertion; esp : one by which a person binds himself to an act, service, or condition

2vow vb 1 : to make a vow or as a vow 2 : to bind or commit by a vow — **vow·er** n

vow·el \'vau(-ə)l\ n 1 : a speech sound produced without obstruction or friction in the mouth 2 : a letter representing such a sound

vox po·pu·li \'väks-'päp-yə-,lī\ n : popular sentiment

1voy·age \'vȯi-ij\ n 1 : JOURNEY 2 : a journey by water from one place or country to another 3 : a journey through air or space

2voyage vb : to take or make a voyage — **voy·ag·er** n

voya·geur \,vwä-yä-'zhər\ n : a boatman and trapper in the Northwest; esp : one employed by a fur company

vul·can·ite \'vəl-kə-,nīt\ n : a hard vulcanized rubber

vul·can·ize \'vəl-kə-,nīz\ vb : to subject to or undergo a process of treating rubber or rubberlike material chemically to give useful properties (as elasticity and strength) — **vul·can·iza·tion** \ˌvəl-kə-nə-ˈzā-shən\ *n* — **vul·can·iz·er** \ˈvəl-kə-ˌnī-zər\ *n*

vul·gar \ˈvəl-gər\ *adj* **1** : of or relating to the common people : GENERAL, COMMON **2** : VERNACULAR ⟨the ~ tongue⟩ **3** : lacking cultivation or refinement : BOORISH; *also* : offensive to good taste or refined feelings **syn** common, ordinary, familiar, popular, gross, obscene, ribald — **vul·gar·ly** *adv*

vul·gar·i·an \ˌvəl-ˈgar-ē-ən\ *n* : a vulgar person

vul·gar·ism \ˈvəl-gə-ˌriz-əm\ *n* **1** : a word or expression originated or used chiefly by illiterate persons : OBSCENITY **3** : VULGARITY

vul·gar·i·ty \ˌvəl-ˈgar-ət-ē\ *n* **1** : the quality or state of being vulgar **2** : an instance of coarseness of manners or language

vul·gar·ize \ˈvəl-gə-ˌrīz\ *vb* : to make vulgar — **vul·gar·iza·tion** \ˌvəl-gə-rə-ˈzā-shən\ *n* — **vul·gar·iz·er** \ˈvəl-gə-ˌrī-zər\ *n*

Vul·gate \ˈvəl-ˌgāt\ *n* : a Latin version of the Bible used by the Roman Catholic Church

vul·ner·a·ble \ˈvəl-nə-rə-bəl\ *adj* **1** : capable of being wounded : susceptible to wounds **2** : open to attack **3** : liable to increased penalties in contract bridge — **vul·ner·a·bil·i·ty** \ˌvəl-nə-rə-ˈbil-ət-ē\ *n*—**vul·ner·a·bly** \ˈvəl-nə-rə-blē\ *adv*

vul·pine \ˈvəl-ˌpīn\ *adj* : of, relating to, or resembling a fox esp. in cunning

vul·ture \ˈvəl-chər\ *n* : any of various large birds related to hawks and eagles but having weaker claws and the head usu. naked and living chiefly on carrion

vul·va \ˈvəl-və\ *n* : the external genital parts of the female or their opening — **vul·val** *adj*

vy·ing *pres part of* VIE

---

w \ˈdəb-əl-(ˌ)yü\ *n, often cap* : the 23d letter of the English alphabet

wab·ble \ˈwäb-əl\ *var of* WOBBLE

wacky \ˈwak-ē\ *adj* : ECCENTRIC, CRAZY

¹wad \ˈwäd\ *n* **1** : a little mass, bundle, or tuft ⟨~*s* of clay⟩ **2** : a soft mass of usu. light fibrous material **3** : a pliable plug (as of felt) used to retain a powder charge (as in a cartridge) **4** : a roll of paper money **5** : a considerable amount (as of money)

²wad *vb* **wad·ded; wad·ding 1** : to form into a wad **2** : to push a wad into ⟨~ a gun⟩ **3** : to hold in by a wad ⟨~ a bullet in a gun⟩ **4** : to stuff or line with a wad : PAD

wad·able *or* **wade·able** \ˈwād-ə-bəl\ *adj* : capable of being waded ⟨a ~ stream⟩

wad·ding \ˈwäd-iŋ\ *n* **1** : WADS; *also* : material for making wads **2** : a soft mass or sheet of short loose fibers used for stuffing or padding

wad·dle \ˈwäd-ᵊl\ *vb* : to walk with short steps swaying from side to side like a duck — **waddle** *n*

wade \ˈwād\ *vb* **1** : to step in or through a medium (as water) more resistant than air **2** : to move or go with difficulty or labor and often with determined vigor ⟨~ through a dull book⟩ — **wade** *n*

wad·er \ˈwād-ər\ *n* **1** : one that wades **2** : WADING BIRD **3** *pl* : high waterproof rubber boots or trousers for wading

wa·di \ˈwäd-ē\ *n* : a watercourse dry except in the rainy season esp. in the Near East and northern Africa

wading bird *n* : a long-legged bird (as a sandpiper or heron) that wades in water in search of food

wa·fer \ˈwā-fər\ *n* **1** : a thin crisp cake or cracker **2** : a thin round piece of unleavened bread used in the Eucharist **3** : something (as a piece of candy or an adhesive seal) that resembles a wafer

waf·fle \ˈwäf-əl\ *n* : a soft but crisped cake of pancake batter cooked in a special hinged metal utensil (**waffle iron**)

¹waft \ˈwäft, ˈwaft\ *vb* : to cause to

move or go lightly by or as if by the impulse of wind or waves

²waft *n* **1** : a slight breeze : PUFF **2** : the act of waving

¹wag \ˈwag\ *vb* **wagged; wag·ging 1** : to sway or swing shortly from side to side or to and fro ⟨the dog *wagged* his tail⟩ **2** : to move in chatter or gossip ⟨scandal caused tongues to ~⟩

²wag *n* **1** : WIT, JOKER **2** : an act of wagging : a wagging movement

¹wage \ˈwāj\ *vb* **1** : to engage in : carry on ⟨~ a war⟩ **2** : to be in process of being waged

²wage *n* **1** : payment for labor or services usu. according to contract **2** *pl* : RECOMPENSE, REWARD

¹wa·ger \ˈwā-jər\ *n* **1** : BET, STAKE **2** : an act of betting : GAMBLE

²wager *vb* : RISK, VENTURE; *esp* : to risk usu. money on the outcome of an uncertain event — **wa·ger·er** *n*

wag·gery \ˈwag-ə-rē\ *n* **1** : mischievous merriment : PLEASANTRY **2** : JEST, TRICK

wag·gish \ˈwag-ish\ *adj* **1** : resembling or characteristic of a wag : MISCHIEVOUS, ROGUISH, FROLICSOME **2** : SPORTIVE, HUMOROUS

wag·gle \ˈwag-əl\ *vb* : to move backward and forward or from side to side : WAG — **waggle** *n*

wag·on \ˈwag-ən\ *n* **1** : a 4-wheeled vehicle; *esp* : one drawn by animals and used for freight or merchandise **2** : a child's 4-wheeled cart **3** : STATION WAGON **4** : PATROL WAGON

wag·on·er *n* : the driver of a wagon

wag·on·ette \ˌwag-ə-ˈnet\ *n* : a light wagon with two facing seats along the sides behind a cross seat in front

wa·gon-lit \və-gō̃-ˈlē\ *n, pl* **wagons-lits** *or* **wagon-lits** *same*\ : a railroad sleeping car

wagon train *n* : a group of wagons traveling overland

wag·tail \ˈwag-ˌtāl\ *n* : any of various slender-bodied mostly Old World birds with a long tail that jerks up and down

---

ə abut; ᵉ kitten; ər further; a back; ā bake; ä cot, cart; au̇ out; ch chin; e less; ē easy; g gift; i trip; ī life; j joke; ŋ sing; ō flow; ȯ flaw; ȯi coin; th thin; tẖ this; ü loot; u̇ foot; y yet; yü few; yu̇ furious; zh vision

wa·hoo \'wä-ˌhü\ n : any of several American trees or shrubs

waif \'wāf\ n 1 : something found without an owner and esp. by chance 2 : a stray person or animal; esp : a homeless child

wail \'wāl\ vb 1 : LAMENT, WEEP 2 : to make a sound suggestive of a mournful cry 3 : COMPLAIN — **wail** n

wail·ful adj : SORROWFUL, MOURNFUL — **wail·ful·ly** adv

wain \'wān\ n : a usu. large heavy farm wagon

wain·scot \'wān-ˌskŏt, -ˌskŭt, -skət\ n 1 : a usu. paneled wooden lining of an interior wall of a room 2 : the lower part of an interior wall when finished differently from the rest — **wainscot** vb

wain·scot·ing or **wain·scot·ting** n : material for a wainscot; also : WAINSCOT

wain·wright \'wān-ˌrīt\ n : a builder and repairer of wagons

waist \'wāst\ n 1 : the narrowed part of the body between the chest and hips 2 : a part resembling the human waist esp. in narrowness or central position (the ~ of a ship) 3 : a garment (as a blouse or bodice) for the upper part of the body 4 : a child's undergarment to which other garments may be buttoned

waist·band \'wās(t)-ˌband\ n : a band (as on trousers or a skirt) that fits around the waist

waist·coat \'wās(t)-ˌkŏt, 'wes-kət\, chiefly Brit : VEST

waist·line \'wāst-ˌlīn\ n 1 : a line thought of as surrounding the waist at its narrowest part; also : the length of this 2 : the line at which the waist and skirt of a dress meet

¹wait \'wāt\ vb 1 : to remain inactive in readiness or expectation : AWAIT (~ for orders) 2 : POSTPONE, DELAY (~ dinner for late guests) 3 : to act as attendant or servant (~ on customers) 4 : to attend as a waiter : SERVE (~ tables) (~ at a banquet) 5 : to be ready

²wait n 1 : a position of concealment usu. with intent to attack or surprise (lie in ~) 2 : an act or period of waiting

wait·er n 1 : one that waits upon another; esp : a man who waits on table 2 : TRAY

waiting room n : a room (as at a railroad station or in the office suite of a doctor) for the use of persons waiting

wait·ress \'wā-trəs\ n : a girl or woman who waits on table

waive \'wāv\ vb 1 : to give up claim to (waived his right to a trial) 2 : POSTPONE

waiv·er \'wā-vər\ n : the act of waiving right, claim, or privilege; also : a document containing a declaration of such an act

¹wake \'wāk\ vb **waked** or **woke** \'wōk\ **waked** or **wo·ken** \'wō-kən\ **wak·ing** 1 : to be or remain awake; esp : to keep watch (as over a corpse) 2 : AWAKE, AWAKEN (the baby waked up early) (the thunder waked him up)

²wake n 1 : the state of being awake 2 : a watch held over the body of a dead person prior to burial

³wake n : the track left by a ship in the water; also : a track left behind

wake·ful adj : not sleeping or able to sleep : SLEEPLESS, ALERT — **wake·ful·ness** n

wak·en \'wā-kən\ vb : WAKE; also : to rouse to action

¹wale \'wāl\ n 1 : a streak or ridge made on the skin usu. by a rod or whip : WHEAL 2 : a ridge esp. on cloth; also : TEXTURE

²wale vb : to mark with wales or stripes

¹walk \'wȯk\ vb 1 : to move or cause to move along on foot usu. at a natural unhurried gait (~ to town) (~ a horse) 2 : to pass over, through, or along by walking (~ the streets) 3 : to perform or accomplish by walking (~ guard) 4 : to follow a course of action or way of life (~ humbly in the sight of God) 5 : to receive a base on balls; also : to give a base on balls to — **walk·er** n

²walk n 1 : a going on foot (go for a ~) 2 : a place, path, or course for walking 3 : distance to be walked (a 10-minute ~ from here) 4 : manner of living : CONDUCT, BEHAVIOR; also : social or economic status (various ~s of life) 5 : manner of walking : GAIT; esp : a slow 4-beat gait of a horse 6 : BASE ON BALLS

walk·ie-talk·ie \'wȯ-kē-'tȯ-kē\ n : a small portable radio sending and receiving set

walk-in \'wȯk-ˌin\ adj : large enough to be walked into (a ~ refrigerator)

walk-on \-ˌȯn, -ˌin\ n : a small usu. nonspeaking part in a dramatic production

walk·out \-ˌaut\ n : a labor strike

walk·over \-ˌō-vər\ n : a one-sided contest : an easy victory

walk-up \-ˌəp\ n : a building or apartment house without an elevator — **walk-up** adj

walk·way \-ˌwā\ n : a passage for walking

¹wall \'wȯl\ n 1 : a structure (as of stone or brick) intended for defense or security or for enclosing something 2 : one of the upright enclosing parts of a building or room 3 : something like a wall in appearance or function (a tariff ~) 4 : the inside surface of a cavity or vessel (the ~ of a boiler)

²wall vb 1 : to provide, separate, or surround with or as if with a wall (~ in a garden) 2 : to close (an opening) with or as if with a wall (~ up a door)

wal·la·by \'wäl-ə-bē\ n : any of various small or medium-sized kangaroos

wall·board \'wȯl-ˌbȯrd\ n : a structural material (as of wood pulp or plaster) made in large sheets and used for sheathing interior walls and ceilings

wal·let \'wäl-ət\ n 1 : a bag or sack for carrying things on a journey 2 : a pocketbook with compartments (as for cards and photographs) : BILLFOLD

wall·eye \'wȯl-ˌī\ n 1 : an eye with whitish iris or an opaque white cornea 2 : an eye that turns outward 3 : a large No. American food and sport fish related to the perches — **wall·eyed** \-ˌīd\ adj

wall·flow·er \'wȯl-ˌflaú(-ə)r\ n 1 : any of several Old World plants related to the mustards; esp : one widely grown for its showy fragrant flowers 2 : a person who usu. from shyness or unpopularity remains on the sidelines of a social activity

Wal·loon \wä-'lün\ n : a member of a chiefly Celtic people of southern and southeastern Belgium and adjacent parts of France — **Walloon** adj

¹wal·lop \'wäl-əp\ n 1 : a powerful

blow or impact **2 :** the ability to hit hard

¹**wallop** *vb* **1 :** to beat soundly **: TROUNCE 2 :** to hit hard **: SOCK**

¹**wal·low** \'wäl-ō\ *vb* **1 :** to roll oneself about in or as if in deep mud **: FLOUNDER** ⟨hogs *~ing* in the mire⟩ **2 :** to live or be filled with excessive pleasure in some condition ⟨*~* in luxury⟩

²**wallow** *n* **:** a muddy or dust-filled area where animals wallow

wall·pa·per \'wȯl-‚pā-pər\ *n* **:** decorative paper for the walls of a room — **wallpaper** *vb*

wal·nut \'wȯl-(‚)nət\ *n* [OE *wealhhnutu*, fr. *wealh* foreigner, Welshman + *hnutu* nut] **1 :** an edible nut with a furrowed usu. rough shell and an adherent husk; *also* **:** any of several trees related to the hickories that produce such nuts **2 :** the usu. reddish to dark brown wood of a walnut used esp. in cabinetwork and veneers **3 :** a hickory nut or tree

wal·rus \'wȯl-rəs, 'wäl-\ *n* **:** either of two large mammals of northern seas related to the seals and hunted esp. for hides, the ivory tusks of the male, and oil

¹**waltz** \'wȯlts\ *n* **1 :** a gliding dance done to music having three beats to the measure **2 :** music for or suitable for waltzing

²**waltz** *vb* **1 :** to dance a waltz **2 :** to move or advance easily, successfully, or conspicuously ⟨he *~ed* through customs⟩

wam·pum \'wäm-pəm\ *n* **1 :** beads made of shells strung in strands, belts, or sashes used by No. American Indians as money and ornaments **2** *slang* **: MONEY**

wan \'wän\ *adj* **1 : SICKLY, PALLID;** *also* **: FEEBLE 2 : DIM, FAINT 3 : LANGUID** ⟨a *~* smile⟩ — **wan·ly** *adv*

¹**wand** \'wänd\ *n* **1 :** a slender staff carried in a procession **2 :** the staff of a fairy, diviner, or magician

wan·der \'wän-dər\ *vb* **1 :** to move about aimlessly or without a fixed course or goal **: RAMBLE 2 : STRAY 3 :** to go astray in conduct or thought; *esp* **:** to become delirious — **wan·der·er** *n*

wan·der·ing Jew *n* **:** any of several trailing or creeping plants some of which are often planted in hanging baskets

wan·der·lust \'wän-dər-‚ləst\ *n* **:** strong longing for or impulse toward wandering

¹**wane** \'wän\ *vb* **1 :** to grow gradually smaller or less after being at the full ⟨the moon *~s*⟩ ⟨his strength *waned*⟩ **2 :** to lose power, prosperity, or influence **3 :** to draw near an end ⟨summer *~s* away⟩

²**wane** *n* **:** a waning (as in size or power); *also* **:** a period in which something is waning

wan·gle \'waŋ-gəl\ *vb* **1 :** to obtain by sly or roundabout means; *also* **:** to use trickery or questionable means to achieve an end **2 : MANIPULATE;** *also* **: FINAGLE**

¹**want** \'wȯnt\ *vb* **1 :** to fail to possess **: LACK** ⟨the necessities of life⟩ **2 :** to fall short by ⟨it *~s* three minutes to six⟩ **3 :** to feel or suffer the need of **4 : NEED, REQUIRE** ⟨the house *~s*

painting⟩ **5 :** to desire earnestly **: WISH** ⟨*~s* to go home⟩

²**want** *n* **1 :** a lack of a required or usual amount **: SHORTAGE 2 :** dire need **: DESTITUTION 3 :** something wanted **: DESIRE 4 : FAULT**

¹**want·ing** *adj* **1 :** not present or in evidence **: ABSENT 2 :** falling below standards or expectations **3 :** lacking in ability or capacity **: DEFICIENT** ⟨*~* in common sense⟩

²**wanting** *prep* **1 : LESS, MINUS** ⟨a book *~* a cover⟩ ⟨a month *~* two days⟩

¹**wan·ton** \'wȯnt-ᵊn\ *adj* **1 :** excessively merry **: FROLICSOME** ⟨*~* holidays⟩ ⟨a *~* breeze⟩ **2 : UNCHASTE, LEWD, LUSTFUL;** *also* **: SENSUAL 3 :** having no regard for justice or for other persons' feelings, rights, or safety **: MERCILESS, INHUMANE** ⟨*~* cruelty⟩ **4 :** having no just cause ⟨a *~* attack⟩ — **wan·ton·ly** *adv* — **wan·ton·ness** *n*

²**wanton** *n* **:** a wanton individual; *esp* **:** a lewd or immoral person

³**wanton** *vb* **1 :** to be wanton **:** act wantonly **2 :** to pass or waste wantonly

wap·i·ti \'wäp-ət-ē\ *n* **:** the American elk

¹**war** \'wȯr\ *n* **1 :** a state or period of usu. open and declared armed fighting between states or nations **2 :** the art or science of warfare **3 :** a state of hostility, conflict, or antagonism **4 :** a struggle between opposing forces or for a particular end ⟨*~* against disease⟩

²**war** *vb* **warred; war·ring 1 :** to engage in warfare **:** be in conflict

¹**war·ble** \'wȯr-bəl\ *n* **1 :** a melodious succession of low pleasing sounds **2 :** a musical trill

²**warble** *vb* **1 :** to sing or utter in a trilling manner or with variations **2 :** to express by or as if by warbling

war·bler \'wȯr-blər\ *n* **1 : SONGSTER 2 :** any of various small slender-billed Old World singing birds related to the thrushes and noted for their song **3 :** any of various small bright-colored American insect-eating birds with a usu. weak and unmusical song

war·bon·net \'wȯr-‚bän-ət\ *n* **:** an Indian ceremonial headdress with a feathered extension down the back

war cry *n* **1 :** a cry used by fighters in war **2 :** a slogan used esp. to rally people to a cause

¹**ward** \'wȯrd\ *n* **1 :** a guarding or being under guard or guardianship; *esp* **: CUSTODY 2 :** a body of guards **3 :** a division of a prison **4 :** a division in a hospital **5 :** a division of a city for electoral or administrative purposes **6 :** a person (as a child) under the protection of a guardian or a law court **7 :** a person or body of persons under the protection or tutelage of a government **8 :** means of defense **: PROTECTION**

²**ward** *vb* **:** to turn aside **: DEFLECT —** usu. used with *off* ⟨*~* off a blow⟩

¹**-ward** \wȯrd\ *also* **-wards** \wȯrdz\ *adj suffix* **1 :** that moves, tends, faces, or is directed toward ⟨wind*ward*⟩ **2 :** that occurs or is situated in the direction of ⟨left*ward*⟩

²**-ward** *or* **-wards** *adv suffix* **1 :** in a (specified) direction ⟨up*wards*⟩ ⟨after-

ward⟩ **2 :** toward a (specified) point, position, or area ⟨earth*ward*⟩

war dance *n* **:** a dance performed by primitive peoples before going to war or in celebration of victory

war·den \'wȯrd-ᵊn\ *n* **1 :** GUARDIAN, KEEPER **2 :** the governor of a town, district, or fortress **3 :** an official charged with special supervisory duties or with the enforcement of specified laws or regulations ⟨game ~⟩ ⟨air raid ~⟩ **4 :** an official in charge of the operation of a prison **5 :** one of two ranking lay officers of an Episcopal parish **6 :** any of various British college officials

ward·er \'wȯrd-ər\ *n* **:** WATCHMAN, WARDEN

ward·robe \'wȯrd-‚rōb\ *n* **1 :** a room or closet where clothes are kept; *also* **:** CLOTHESPRESS **2 :** a collection of wearing apparel ⟨his summer ~⟩

ward·room \-‚rüm, -‚rum\ *n* **:** the quarters in a warship allotted to the commissioned officers except the captain; *esp* **:** the room allotted to these officers for meals

ward·ship \-‚ship\ *n* **1 :** GUARDIANSHIP **2 :** the state of being under care of a guardian

ware \'waər\ *n* **1 :** manufactured articles or products of art or craft **:** GOODS **2 :** an article of merchandise ⟨a peddler hawking his ~s⟩ **3 :** items (as dishes) of fired clay **:** POTTERY

ware·house \-‚haús\ *n* **:** place for the storage of merchandise or commodities **:** STOREHOUSE

ware·room \'waər-‚rüm, -‚rum\ *n* **:** a room in which goods are exhibited for sale

war·fare \'wȯr-‚faər\ *n* **1 :** military operations between enemies **:** WAR; *also* **:** an activity undertaken by one country to weaken or destroy another ⟨economic ~⟩ **2 :** STRUGGLE, CONFLICT

war·head \-‚hed\ *n* **:** the section of a missile (as a bomb) containing the charge

war·horse \-‚hȯrs\ *n* **1 :** a horse for use in war **2 :** a veteran soldier or public person (as a politician)

war·i·ly \'war-ə-lē\ *adv* **:** in a wary manner **:** CAUTIOUSLY

war·i·ness \'war-ē-nəs\ *n* **:** WATCHFULNESS, CAUTION

war·less \'wȯr-ləs\ *adj* **:** free from war

war·like \-‚līk\ *adj* **1 :** fond of war ⟨~ peoples⟩ **2 :** of, relating to, or having to do with war **:** MILITARY, MARTIAL ⟨~ supplies⟩ **3 :** threatening war **:** HOSTILE ⟨~ attitudes⟩

war·lock \-‚läk\ *n* **:** SORCERER, WIZARD

war·lord \-‚lȯrd\ *n* **1 :** a high military leader **2 :** a military commander exercising local civil power by force ⟨former Chinese ~s⟩

¹**warm** \'wȯrm\ *adj* **1 :** having or giving out heat to a moderate or adequate degree ⟨~ milk⟩ ⟨a ~ stove⟩ **2 :** serving to retain heat ⟨~ clothes⟩ **3 :** feeling or inducing sensations of heat ⟨~ from exercise⟩ ⟨a ~ climb⟩ **4 :** showing or marked by strong feeling **:** ARDENT ⟨~ support⟩ **5 :** marked by tense excitement or hot anger ⟨a ~ campaign⟩ **6 :** marked by or tending toward injury, distress, or pain ⟨made things ~ for the enemy⟩ **7 :** newly made **:** FRESH ⟨a ~ scent⟩ **8 :** near to a goal ⟨getting ~ in a search⟩ **9 :** giving a pleasant impression of warmth, cheer-

fulness, or friendliness ⟨~ colors⟩ ⟨a ~ tone of voice⟩ — **warm·ly** *adv*

²**warm** *vb* **1 :** to make or become warm **2 :** to give a feeling of warmth or vitality to **3 :** to experience feelings of affection or pleasure ⟨she ~ed to her guest⟩ **4 :** to reheat for eating ⟨~ed over the roast⟩ **5 :** to make or become ready for operation or performance by preliminary exercise or operation ⟨~ up the motor⟩ **6 :** to become increasingly ardent, interested, or competent ⟨the speaker ~ed to his topic⟩

warm-blood·ed \-'bləd-əd\ *adj* **:** able to maintain a relatively high and constant body temperature essentially independent of that of the surroundings

warmed-over \'wȯrmd-'ō-vər\ *adj* **1 :** REHEATED ⟨~ cabbage⟩ **2 :** not fresh or new ⟨~ ideas⟩

warm-heart·ed \'wȯrm-'härt-əd\ *adj* **:** marked by warmth of feeling **:** CORDIAL

war·mon·ger \'wȯr-‚məŋ-gər, -‚mäŋ-\ *n* **:** one who urges or attempts to stir up war

warmth \'wȯrmth\ *n* **1 :** the quality or state of being warm **2 :** ZEAL, ARDOR, FERVOR

warn \'wȯrn\ *vb* **1 :** to put on guard **:** CAUTION; *also* **:** ADMONISH, COUNSEL **2 :** to notify esp. in advance **:** INFORM **3 :** to order to go or keep away

¹**warn·ing** *n* **1 :** the act of warning **:** the state of being warned **2 :** something that warns or serves to warn

²**warning** *adj* **:** serving as an alarm, signal, summons, or admonition ⟨~ bell⟩ — **warn·ing·ly** *adv*

¹**warp** \'wȯrp\ *n* **1 :** the lengthwise threads on a loom or in a woven fabric **2 :** a warping or being warped **:** a twist out of a true plane or straight line ⟨a ~ in a board⟩

²**warp** *vb* **1 :** to turn or twist out of shape; *also* **:** to become so twisted **2 :** to lead astray **:** PERVERT; *also* **:** FALSIFY, DISTORT **3 :** to move (a ship) by hauling on a line attached to some fixed object (as a buoy, anchor, or dock)

war paint *n* **:** paint put on the face and body by savages on going to war

war·path \'wȯr-‚path, -‚páth\ *n* **1 :** the course taken by a party of American Indians going on a hostile expedition **2 :** a hostile course of action or frame of mind

war·plane \-‚plān\ *n* **:** a military airplane; *esp* **:** one armed for combat

¹**war·rant** \'wȯr-ənt\ *n* **1 :** AUTHORIZATION; *also* **:** JUSTIFICATION, GROUND **2 :** evidence (as a document) of authorization; *esp* **:** a legal writ authorizing an officer to take action (as in making an arrest, seizure, or search) **3 :** a certificate of appointment issued to an officer of lower rank than a commissioned officer

²**warrant** *vb* **1 :** to declare or maintain positively ⟨I ~ this is so⟩ **2 :** to assure (a person) of the truth of what is said **3 :** to guarantee to be as it appears or as it is represented ⟨~ goods as of the first quality⟩ **4 :** to guarantee security or immunity to **:** SECURE **5 :** SANCTION, AUTHORIZE **6 :** to give proof of **:** ATTEST; *also* **:** GUARANTEE **7 :** JUSTIFY ⟨his need ~s the expenditure⟩

warrant officer *n* **:** an officer in the armed forces ranking next below a commissioned officer

war·ran·ty \'wȯr-ənt-ē\ *n* **:** an expressed or implied statement that some situation or thing is as it appears or is represented to be; *esp* : a usu. written guarantee of the integrity of a product and of the maker's responsibility for the repair or replacement of defective parts

war·ren \'wȯr-ən\ *n* 1 : an area for the keeping and rearing of small game and esp. rabbits; *also* : an area where rabbits breed 2 : a crowded tenement or district

war·rior \'wȯr-yər, 'wär-ē-ər\ *n* : a man engaged or experienced in warfare

war·ship \'wȯr-,ship\ *n* : a government ship used for war purposes

wart \'wȯrt\ *n* 1 : a small usu. horny projection on the skin; *esp* : one caused by a virus 2 : a protuberance resembling a wart (as on a plant) — **warty** *adj*

wart·hog \'wȯrt-,hȯg, -,häg\ *n* : an African wild hog with large tusks and two pairs of rough warty protuberances below the eyes

war·time \'wȯr-,tīm\ *n* : a period during which a war is in progress

wary \'wa(ə)r-ē\ *adj* : very cautious; *esp* : careful in guarding against danger or deception

was *past 1st & 3d sing of* BE

¹**wash** \'wȯsh, 'wäsh\ *vb* 1 : to cleanse with or as if with a liquid (as water) 2 : to wet thoroughly with water or other liquid 3 : to flow along the border of 〈waves ~ the shore〉 4 : to pass (a gas or gaseous mixture) through or over a liquid for purifying 5 : to pour or flow in a stream or current 6 : to move or remove by or as if by the action of water 7 : to cover or daub lightly with a liquid (as whitewash) 8 : to run water over (as gravel or ore) in order to separate valuable matter from refuse 〈~ sand for gold〉 9 : to bear washing without injury 〈some materials do not ~〉 10 : to stand a test 〈that story will not ~〉 11 : to be worn away by water

²**wash** *n* 1 : the act or process or an instance of washing or being washed 2 : articles to be washed or being washed 3 : the flow, sound, or action of a mass of water (as a wave) 4 : water or waves thrown back (as by oars or paddles) 5 : erosion by waves (as of the sea) 6 *West* : the dry bed of a stream 7 : worthless esp. liquid waste : REFUSE, SWILL 8 : the liquid with which something is washed or tinted 9 : a disturbance in the air caused by the passage of an airplane wing or propeller

³**wash** *adj* : WASHABLE

wash·able *adj* : capable of being washed without damage

wash·ba·sin \'wȯsh-,bās-ᵊn, 'wäsh-\ *n* : WASHBOWL

wash·board \-,bȯrd\ *n* : a grooved board to scrub clothes on

wash·bowl \-,bōl\ *n* : a large bowl for water for washing hands and face

wash·cloth \-,klȯth\ *n* : a cloth used for washing one's face and body

washed-out \'wȯsht-'aut, 'wäsht-\ *adj* 1 : faded in color 2 : EXHAUSTED 〈felt ~ after working all night〉

wash·er \'wȯsh-ər, 'wäsh-\ *n* 1 : one that washes; *esp* : a machine for washing 2 : a ring or perforated plate used

around a bolt or screw to ensure tightness or relieve friction

wash·er·wom·an \-,wùm-ən\ *n* : a woman who works at washing clothes

wash·house \'wȯsh-,haus, 'wäsh-\ *n* : a house or building used or equipped for washing and esp. for washing clothes

wash·ing *n* 1 : material obtained by washing 2 : a thin covering or coat 〈a ~ of silver〉 3 : articles washed or to be washed

washing soda *n* : a form of sodium carbonate used in washing and bleaching textiles

Wash·ing·ton pie \,wȯsh-iŋ-tən-, -wäsh-\ *n* : layer cake with a filling of jam or jelly

Washington's Birthday *n* : February 22 observed as a legal holiday

wash·out \'wȯsh-,aut, 'wäsh-\ *n* 1 : the washing out or away of earth esp. in a roadbed by a freshet; *also* : a place where earth is washed away 2 : FAILURE; *esp* : one who fails in a course of training or study

wash·room \-,rüm, -,rum\ *n* : a room equipped with washing and toilet facilities : LAVATORY

wash·stand \-,stand\ *n* 1 : a stand holding articles needed for washing face and hands 2 : a washbowl permanently set in place

wash·tub \-,təb\ *n* : a tub for washing clothes or for soaking them before washing

wash·wom·an \-,wùm-ən\ *n* : WASHERWOMAN

washy \'wȯsh-ē, 'wäsh-\ *adj* 1 : WEAK, WATERY 2 : PALLID 3 : lacking in vigor, individuality, or definiteness

wasp \'wȯsp\ *n* : a slender-bodied winged insect related to the bees and ants with biting mouthparts and in females and workers a formidable sting

wasp·ish *adj* 1 : SNAPPISH, IRRITABLE 2 : resembling a wasp in form; *esp* : slightly built

¹**was·sail** \'wäs-əl, wä-'sāl\ *n* [ME *wæs hæil*, a salutation used in toasting, fr. ON *ves heill* be in good health] 1 : an early English toast to someone's health 2 : a liquor formerly drunk in England on festive occasions 3 : riotous drinking : REVELRY

²**wassail** *vb* 1 : CAROUSE 2 : to drink to the health or thriving of — **was·sail·er** *n*

Was·ser·mann test \,wäs-ər-mən-, ,väs-\ *n* : a blood test for infection with syphilis

wast·age \'wā-stij\ *n* : loss by use, decay, erosion, or leakage or through wastefulness

¹**waste** \'wāst\ *n* 1 : a sparsely settled or barren region : DESERT; *also* : uncultivated land 2 : the act or an instance of wasting : the state of being wasted 3 : gradual loss or decrease by use, wear, or decay 4 : damaged, defective, or superfluous material; *esp* : refuse matter of cotton or wool used for wiping machinery or absorbing oil 5 : refuse (as garbage or rubbish) that accumulates about habitations; *also* : material (as feces) produced but not used by a living body — **waste·ful** *adj* — **waste·ful·ly** *adv* — **waste·ful·ness** *n*

²waste vb **1 :** DEVASTATE **2 :** to wear away or diminish gradually **:** CONSUME **3 :** to spend money or use property carelessly or uselessly **:** SQUANDER; also **:** to allow to be used inefficiently or become dissipated **4 :** to lose or cause to lose weight, strength, or vitality ⟨*wasting* away from fever⟩ **5 :** to become diminished in bulk or substance **:** DWINDLE

³waste adj **1 :** being wild and uninhabited **:** BARREN, DESOLATE; also **:** UNCULTIVATED **2 :** RUINED, DEVASTATED ⟨bombs laid ～ the city⟩ **3 :** discarded as worthless after being used ⟨～ water⟩ **4 :** of no further use to a person, animal, or plant ⟨～ matter thrown off by the body⟩ **5 :** serving to conduct or hold refuse material; esp **:** carrying off superfluous water

waste·land \-ˌland\ n **:** barren or uncultivated land

waste·pa·per \ˈwās(t)-ˈpā-pər\ n **:** paper discarded as used, superfluous, or not fit for use

wast·rel \ˈwā-strəl\ n **:** one that wastes **:** SPENDTHRIFT

¹watch \ˈwäch\ vb **1 :** to be or stay awake intentionally **:** keep vigil ⟨～ed by the patient's bedside⟩ ⟨～ and pray⟩ **2 :** to be on the lookout for danger **:** be on one's guard **3 :** to keep guard ⟨～ outside the door⟩ **4 :** OBSERVE ⟨～ a game⟩ **5 :** to keep in view so as to prevent harm or warn of danger ⟨～ a brush fire carefully⟩ **6 :** to keep oneself informed about ⟨～ his progress⟩ **7 :** to lie in wait for esp. so as to take advantage of ⟨～ed his opportunity⟩ — **watch·er** n

²watch n **1 :** the act of keeping awake to guard, protect, or attend; also **:** a state of alert and continuous attention **2 :** close observation **3 :** one that watches **:** LOOKOUT, WATCHMAN, GUARD **4 :** an allotted period of usu. 4 hours for being on nautical duty; also **:** the members of a ship's company operating the vessel during such a period **5 :** a portable timepiece carried on the person

watch·band \-ˌband\ n **:** the bracelet or strap of a wristwatch

watch·case \-ˌkās\ n **:** the outside metal covering of a watch

watch·dog \-ˌdȯg\ n **1 :** a dog kept to guard property **2 :** one that guards or protects

watch·ful \-fəl\ adj **:** steadily attentive and alert esp. to danger **:** VIGILANT — **watch·ful·ly** adv — **watch·ful·ness** n

watch·mak·er \-ˌmā-kər\ n **:** one that makes or repairs watches — **watch·mak·ing** n

watch·man \-mən\ n **:** a person assigned to watch **:** GUARD

watch·tow·er \-ˌtau̇-(ə)r\ n **:** a tower for a lookout

watch·word \-ˌwərd\ n **1 :** a secret word used as a signal or sign of recognition **2 :** a motto used as a slogan or rallying cry

¹wa·ter \ˈwȯt-ər, ˈwät-\ n **1 :** the liquid that descends as rain and forms rivers, lakes, and seas **2 :** mineral waters **3** pl **:** the water occupying or flowing in a particular bed; also **:** a band of seawater bordering on and under the control of a country ⟨sailing Canadian ～s⟩ **4 :** any of various liquids containing or resembling water; esp **:** a watery fluid (as tears, urine, or sap) formed in a living body **5 :** the clearness and luster of a precious stone ⟨a diamond of the purest ～⟩ **6 :** a specified degree of thoroughness or completeness ⟨a scoundrel of the first ～⟩ **7 :** a wavy lustrous pattern such as is given to some silks and metals

²water vb **1 :** to supply with or get or take water ⟨～ horses⟩ ⟨the ship ～ed at each port⟩ **2 :** to treat (as cloth) so as to give a lustrous appearance in wavy lines **3 :** to dilute by or as if by adding water to **4 :** to form or secrete water or watery matter ⟨his eyes ～ed⟩ ⟨my mouth ～ed⟩

wa·ter·borne \-ˌbȯrn\ adj **:** supported or carried by water

water buffalo n **:** a common oxlike often domesticated Asiatic buffalo

water closet n **:** a compartment or room containing a device for flushing a toilet bowl with water **:** BATHROOM; also **:** such a toilet with its accessories

wa·ter·col·or \ˈwȯt-ər-ˌkəl-ər, ˈwät-\ n **1 :** a paint whose liquid part is water **2 :** the art of painting with watercolors **3 :** a picture made with watercolors

wa·ter·course \-ˌkȯrs\ n **:** a stream of water; also **:** the bed of a stream

wa·ter·cress \-ˌkres\ n **:** a perennial cress with white flowers growing mostly in clear running water and used esp. in salads

wa·ter·fall \-ˌfȯl\ n **:** a very steep descent of the water of a stream

water flea n **:** any of various tiny active freshwater crustaceans

wa·ter·fowl \-ˌfau̇l\ n **1 :** a bird that frequents the water **2** pl **:** swimming game birds

wa·ter·front \-ˌfrənt\ n **:** land or a section of a town fronting or abutting on a body of water

water gas n **:** a gas made by forcing air and steam over glowing hot coke or coal to give a mixture of hydrogen and carbon monoxide used as a fuel

water glass n **1 :** a drinking glass **2 :** a whitish powdery substance that is a silicate of sodium or potassium or of both and forms a syrupy liquid when dissolved in water that is used as a cement and a protective coating and in preserving eggs

watering place n **:** a resort that features mineral springs or bathing

water lily n **:** an aquatic plant with floating roundish leaves and showy solitary flowers

wa·ter·line \ˈwȯt-ər-ˌlīn, ˈwät-\ n **:** any of several lines that are marked on the outside of a ship and correspond with the surface of the water when it is afloat on an even keel

wa·ter·logged \-ˌlȯgd, -ˌlägd\ adj **:** so filled or soaked with water as to be heavy or unmanageable ⟨a ～ boat⟩ ⟨～ timbers⟩

wa·ter·loo \ˌwȯt-ər-ˈlü, ˌwät-\ n **:** a decisive defeat

¹wa·ter·mark \ˈwȯt-ər-ˌmärk, ˈwät-\ n **1 :** a mark indicating height to which water has risen **2 :** a marking in paper visible when the paper is held up to the light

²watermark vb **:** to mark (paper) with a watermark

wa·ter·mel·on \-ˌmel-ən\ n **:** a large roundish or oblong fruit with sweet juicy usu. red pulp; also **:** an African vine related to the gourds that produces watermelons

water moccasin n **:** a venomous snake

of the southern U.S. related to the copperhead

water polo *n* : a team game played in a swimming pool with a ball resembling a soccer ball

wa·ter-pow·er \'wȯt-ər-,paù(-ə)r, 'wät-\ *n* : the power of moving water used to run machinery

¹**wa·ter-proof** \,wȯt-ər-'prüf, ,wät-\ *adj* : not letting water through; *esp* : covered or treated with a material to prevent permeation by water

²**wa·ter-proof** \'wȯt-ər-,prüf, 'wät-\ *n* 1 : a waterproof fabric 2 *chiefly Brit* : RAINCOAT

³**wa·ter-proof** \,wȯt-ər-'prüf, ,wät-\ *vb* : to make waterproof

wa·ter-shed \'wȯt-ər-,shed, 'wät-\ *n* 1 : a dividing ridge between two drainage areas 2 : the region or area drained by a particular body of water

wa·ter-side \-,sīd\ *n* : the land bordering a body of water

water ski *n* : a ski used on water when the wearer is towed — **wa·ter-ski** *vb*

wa·ter-spout \'wȯt-ər-,spaùt, 'wät-\ *n* 1 : a pipe from which water is spouted 2 : a funnel-shaped column of rotating cloud-filled wind extending from a cumulus cloud down to a cloud of spray torn up by whirling winds from an ocean or lake

water table *n* : the upper limit of the ground wholly saturated with water

wa·ter-tight \,wȯt-ər-'tīt, ,wät-\ *adj* 1 : so tight as not to let water in 2 : so worded that its meaning cannot be misunderstood or its purpose defeated ⟨a ~ contract⟩

wa·ter-way \'wȯt-ər-,wā, 'wät-\ *n* : a navigable body of water

wa·ter-wheel \-,hwēl\ *n* : a wheel rotated by direct action of water flowing against it

water wings *n pl* : an air-filled device to give support to a person's body while he is swimming or learning to swim

wa·ter-works \-,wərks\ *n pl* : a system including reservoirs, pipes, and machinery by which water is supplied (as to a city)

wa·tery \'wȯt-ə-rē, 'wät-\ *adj* 1 : of or relating to water 2 : containing, full of, or giving out water ⟨~ clouds⟩ 3 : being like water : THIN, WEAK ⟨~ lemonade⟩ 4 : being soft and soggy ⟨~ turnips⟩

watt \'wät\ *n* [after James *Watt* d1819 Scottish engineer and inventor] : a unit of electric power equal to the power produced in a circuit when a pressure of one volt causes a current of one ampere to flow

watt·age *n* : amount of electric power expressed in watts

wat·tle \'wät-ᵊl\ *n* 1 : a framework of rods with flexible branches or reeds interlaced used for fencing and esp. formerly in building; *also* : material for this framework 2 : a naked fleshy process hanging usu. about the head or neck (as of a bird) — **wat·tled** *adj*

¹**wave** \'wāv\ *vb* 1 : FLUTTER ⟨flags *waving* in the breeze⟩ 2 : to motion with the hands or with something held in them in signal or salute 3 : to become moved or brandished to and fro; *also* : BRANDISH, FLOURISH ⟨~ a sword⟩

4 : to move before the wind with a wavelike motion ⟨fields of *waving* grain⟩ 5 : to curve up and down like a wave : UNDULATE

²**wave** *n* 1 : a moving ridge or swell on the surface of water 2 : a wavelike formation or shape ⟨a ~ in the hair⟩ 3 : the action or process of making wavy or curly 4 : a waving motion; *esp* : a signal made by waving something 5 : FLOW, GUSH ⟨a ~ of color swept her face⟩ 6 : a rapid increase : SURGE ⟨a ~ of buying⟩ ⟨a heat ~⟩ 7 : a disturbance somewhat similar to a wave in water that transfers energy progressively from point to point ⟨a light ~⟩ ⟨a sound ~⟩ ⟨a radio ~⟩

wave-length \-,leŋth\ *n* : the distance in the line of advance of a wave from any one point (as a crest) to the next corresponding point

wave-let \-lət\ *n* : a little wave : RIPPLE

wa·ver \'wā-vər\ *vb* 1 : to vacillate between choices : fluctuate in opinion, allegiance, or direction : HESITATE 2 : REEL, TOTTER; *also* : QUIVER, FLICKER ⟨~*ing* flames⟩ 3 : FALTER 4 : to give an unsteady sound : QUAVER — **waver** *n* — **wa·ver·er** *n* — **wa·ver·ing·ly** *adv*

wavy \'wā-vē\ *adj* : having waves : moving in waves

¹**wax** \'waks\ *n* 1 : a yellowish plastic substance secreted by bees for constructing the honeycomb : BEESWAX 2 : any of various substances resembling beeswax; *esp* : a solid mixture of higher hydrocarbons

²**wax** *vb* : to treat or rub with wax

³**wax** *vb* 1 : to increase in size, numbers, strength, volume, or duration 2 : to increase in apparent size ⟨the moon ~*es* toward the full⟩ 3 : to pass from one state to another : BECOME ⟨~*ed* indignant⟩ ⟨the party ~*ed* merry⟩

wax·en *adj* 1 : made of or covered with wax 2 : resembling wax (as in color or consistency)

wax myrtle *n* : any of various shrubs or trees with aromatic leaves; *esp* : an American shrub bearing small hard berries coated with a white wax used for candles

wax·wing \'waks-,wiŋ\ *n* : any of several singing birds that are mostly brown with a showy crest and velvety plumage

wax·work \-,wərk\ *n* 1 : an effigy usu. of a person in wax 2 *pl* : an exhibition of wax figures

waxy *adj* 1 : made of or full of wax 2 : resembling wax 3 : PLASTIC, IMPRESSIONABLE

way \'wā\ *n* 1 : a thoroughfare for travel or passage : ROAD, PATH, STREET; *also* : an opening for passage ⟨make ~ for the ambulance⟩ 2 : ROUTE 3 : a course of action ⟨chose the easy ~⟩; *also* : opportunity, capability, or fact of doing as one pleases ⟨always had his own ~⟩ 4 : a possible course : POSSIBILITY ⟨no two ~s about it⟩ 5 : METHOD, MODE ⟨this ~ of thinking⟩ ⟨a new ~ of painting⟩ 6 : FEATURE, RESPECT ⟨a good worker in many ~s⟩ 7 : the usual or characteristic state of affairs ⟨as is the ~ with old people⟩ 8 : STATE, CONDITION ⟨that is the ~ things are⟩

9 : individual characteristic or peculiarity (used to his ~s) **10 :** a regular continued course (as of life or action) (the American ~) **11 :** DISTANCE (a short ~ from here) (a long ~ from success) **12 :** progress along a course **:** HEADWAY (earned his ~ through college) **13 :** something having direction **:** LOCALITY (out our ~) **14 :** room or chance to progress or advance (make ~ for youth) **15 :** place for something else **16** *pl* **:** an inclined structure upon which a ship is built or is supported in launching **17 :** CATEGORY, KIND (get what you need in the ~ of supplies) **18 :** motion or speed of a boat through the water — **by way of 1 :** for the purpose of (by way of illustration) **2 :** by the route through **:** VIA — **out of the way 1 :** WRONG, IMPROPER **2 :** SECLUDED, REMOTE — **under way 1 :** in motion through the water **2 :** in progress

way·bill \'wā-,bil\ *n* **:** a paper that accompanies a freight shipment and gives details of goods, route, and charges

way·far·er \-,far-ər\ *n* **:** a traveler esp. on foot — **way·far·ing** *adj*

way·lay \-,lā\ *vb* **1 :** to lie in wait for often in order to seize, rob, or kill **2 :** to stop or attempt to stop so as to speak with

-ways \,wāz\ *adv suffix* **:** in (such) a way, course, direction, or manner (sideways) (flatways)

way·side \'wā-,sīd\ *n* **:** the side of or land adjacent to a road or path

way·ward \-word\ *adj* **1 :** taking one's own and usu. irregular or improper way **:** DISOBEDIENT (~ children) **2 :** UNPREDICTABLE, IRREGULAR **3 :** opposite to what is desired or expected (~ fate)

way·worn \-,wōrn\ *adj* **:** wearied by traveling

we \(')wē\ *pron* **1 —** used of a group that includes the speaker or writer **2 —** used for the singular *I* by sovereigns and by writers (as of editorials)

weak \'wēk\ *adj* **1 :** lacking strength or vigor **:** FEEBLE **2 :** not able to sustain or resist much weight, pressure, or strain **3 :** deficient in vigor of mind or character; *also* **:** resulting from or indicative of such deficiency (a ~ policy) (a ~ will) (weak-minded) **4 :** deficient in the usual or required ingredients **:** of less than usual strength (~ tea) **5 :** not supported by truth or logic (a ~ argument) **6 :** not able to function properly **7 :** lacking skill or proficiency; *also* **:** indicative of a lack of skill or aptitude **8 :** wanting in vigor of expression or effect **9 :** not having or exerting authority (~ government); *also* **:** INEFFECTIVE, IMPOTENT **10 :** of, relating to, or constituting a verb or verb conjugation that forms the past tense and past participle by adding *-ed* or *-d* or *-t* — **weak·ly** *adv*

weak·en *vb* **:** to make or become weak **syn** enfeeble, debilitate, undermine, sap, cripple, disable

weak·fish \'wēk ,fish\ *n* **:** any of several food fishes related to the perches; *esp* **:** a common sport and market fish of the Atlantic coast of the U.S.

weak-kneed \-'nēd\ *adj* **:** lacking willpower or resolution

weak·ling \-liŋ\ *n* **:** a person that is physically, mentally, or morally weak

weak·ly *adj* **:** FEEBLE, WEAK

weak·ness *n* **1 :** the quality or state of being weak; *also* **:** an instance or period

of being weak (in a moment of ~ he agreed to go) **2 :** FAULT, DEFECT **3 :** an object of special desire or fondness (coffee is her ~)

¹weal \'wēl\ *n* **:** WELL-BEING, PROSPERITY

²weal *n* **:** WHEAL, WELT

weald \'wēld\ *n* **1 :** FOREST **2 :** a wild or uncultivated usu. upland region **:** WOLD

wealth \'welth\ *n* **1 :** large possessions or resources **:** AFFLUENCE, RICHES **2 :** abundant supply **:** PROFUSION (a ~ of detail) **3 :** all property that has a money or an exchange value; *also* **:** all objects or resources that have usefulness for man

wealthy *adj* **:** having wealth **:** RICH, AFFLUENT, OPULENT

wean \'wēn\ *vb* **1 :** to accustom (a young mammal) to take food otherwise than by nursing **2 :** to turn (one) away from something long desired or followed (~ a boy from smoking)

weap·on \'wep-ən\ *n* **1 :** something (as a gun, knife, or club) that may be used to fight with **2 :** a means by which one contends against another

weap·on·less *adj* **:** lacking weapons **:** UNARMED

¹wear \'waor\ *vb* **wore** \'wōr\ **worn** \'wōrn\ **wear·ing 1 :** to bear on the person or use habitually for clothing or adornment (~ a coat) (~ a wig); *also* **:** to carry on the person (~ a sword) **2 :** to have or show an appearance of (~ a smile) **3 :** to impair, diminish, or decay by use or by scraping or rubbing (clothes worn to shreds) (letters on the stone worn away by weathering); *also* **:** to produce gradually by friction, rubbing, or wasting away (~ a hole in the rug) **4 :** to exhaust or lessen the strength of **:** WEARY, FATIGUE (worn by care and toil) **5 :** to endure use **:** last under use or the passage of time (this cloth ~s well) **6 :** to diminish or fail with the passage of time (the day ~s on) **7 :** to grow or become by attrition, use, or age (the coin was worn thin) — **wear·a·ble** \'war-ə-bəl\ *adj* — **wear·er** \'war-ər\ *n*

²wear *n* **1 :** the act of wearing **:** the state of being worn **:** USE (clothes for everyday ~) **2 :** clothing usu. of a particular kind or for a special occasion or use (men's ~) **3 :** wearing or lasting quality (the coat still has lots of ~ in it) **4 :** the result of wearing or use **:** impairment resulting from use (her suit shows ~)

wea·ri·some \'wir-ē-səm\ *adj* **:** causing weariness **:** TIRESOME — **wea·ri·some·ly** *adv*

wear out *vb* **1 :** to make or become useless by wear **2 :** TIRE

¹wea·ry \'wi(ə)r-ē\ *adj* **1 :** worn out in strength, endurance, vigor, or freshness **2 :** expressing or characteristic of weariness (a ~ sigh) **3 :** having one's patience, tolerance, or pleasure exhausted (~ of war) — **wea·ri·ly** *adv* — **wea·ri·ness** *n*

²weary *vb* **:** to become or make weary **:** TIRE

wea·sand \'wēz-ᵊnd\ *n* **:** WINDPIPE; *also* **:** THROAT

wea·sel \'wē-zəl\ *n* **:** any of various small slender bloodthirsty flesh-eating mammals related to the minks

¹weath·er \'weth-ər\ *n* **1 :** condition of the atmosphere with respect to heat or cold, wetness or dryness, calm or storm, clearness or cloudiness **2** : a particular and esp a disagreeable atmospheric state : RAIN, STORM

²**weather** vb **1** : to expose to or endure the action of weather; *also* : to alter (as in color or texture) by such exposure **2** : to sail or pass to the windward of **3** : to bear up against successfully ⟨~ a storm⟩ ⟨~ troubles⟩

weath·er·abil·i·ty \‚weth-ə-rə-'bil-ət-ē\ *n* : capability of withstanding weather ⟨~ of a plastic⟩

weath·er·beat·en \'weth-ər-‚bēt-ᵊn\ *adj* : altered by exposure to the weather; *also* : toughened or tanned by the weather ⟨~ face⟩

weath·er·board \-‚bōrd\ *n* : CLAPBOARD

weath·er·bound \-‚baund\ *adj* : kept in port or at anchor or from travel or sport by bad weather

weath·er·cock \-‚käk\ *n* **1** : a vane often in the figure of a cock that turns with the wind to show the wind's direction **2** : a fickle person

weath·er·glass \-‚glas\ *n* : an instrument (as a barometer) that shows atmospheric conditions

weath·er·ing \'weth-(ə-)riŋ\ *n* : the action of the weather in altering the color, texture, composition, or form of exposed objects; *also* : alteration thus effected

weath·er·man \'weth-ər-‚man\ *n* : one who reports and forecasts the weather : METEOROLOGIST

weath·er·proof \‚weth-ər-'prüf\ *adj* : able to withstand exposure to weather without appreciable harm — **weatherproof** vb

weather strip *n* : a strip of material to make a seal where a door or window joins the sill or casing — **weather·strip** vb

weath·er·tight \‚weth-ər-'tīt\ *adj* : proof against wind and rain ⟨~ storage bin⟩

weather vane *n* : VANE 1

weath·er·worn \'weth-ər-‚wōrn\ *adj* : worn by exposure to the weather

¹**weave** \'wēv\ *vb* **wove** \'wōv\ **wov·en** \'wō-vən\ **weav·ing 1** : to form by interlacing strands of material; *esp* : to make on a loom by interlacing warp and filling threads ⟨~ cloth⟩ **2** : to interlace (as threads) into a fabric and esp. cloth **3** : SPIN **2 4** : CONTRIVE **5** : to unite in a coherent whole **6** : to work in ⟨wove the episodes into a story⟩ **7** : to direct or move in a winding or zigzag course esp. to avoid obstacles ⟨we wove our way through the crowd⟩ — **weav·er** *n*

²**weave** *n* : a pattern or method of weaving ⟨a coarse loose ~⟩

¹**web** \'web\ *n* **1** : a fabric on a loom or coming from a loom **2** : COBWEB; *also* : SNARE, ENTANGLEMENT **3** : an animal or plant membrane; *esp* : one uniting the toes (as in many birds) **4** : a thin metal sheet or strip (as used in machinery or engineering between stiffening ribs or girders) **5** : NETWORK ⟨a ~ of highways⟩ **6** : the series of barbs on each side of the shaft of a feather

²**web** vb **webbed**; **web·bing 1** : to cover or provide with webs or a network **2** : ENTANGLE, ENSNARE **3** : to make a web

webbed \'webd\ *adj* : having or being toes or fingers united by a web ⟨a ~ foot⟩

web·bing *n* : a strong closely woven tape used esp. for straps, harness, or upholstery

web-foot·ed \'web-'fut-əd\ *adj* : having webbed feet

wed \'wed\ *vb* **wed·ded** *also* **wed**; **wed·ding 1** : to take, give, or join in marriage : enter into matrimony : MARRY **2** : to unite firmly

wed·ding \'wed-iŋ\ *n* **1** : a marriage ceremony usu. with accompanying festivities : NUPTIALS **2** : a joining in close association **3** : a wedding anniversary or its celebration

¹**wedge** \'wej\ *n* **1** : a solid triangular piece of wood or metal that tapers to a thin edge and is used to split logs or rocks or to raise heavy weights **2** : a wedge-shaped object or part ⟨a ~ of pie⟩ **3** : something (as an action or policy) that serves to open up a way for a breach, change, or intrusion

²**wedge** vb **1** : to hold firm by or as if by driving in a wedge **2** : to force (something) into a narrow space **3** : to split apart with or as if with a wedge

wed·lock \'wed-‚läk\ *n* : the state of being married : MARRIAGE, MATRIMONY

Wednes·day \'wenz-dē\ *n* : the 4th day of the week

wee \'wē\ *adj* **1** : very small : TINY **2** : very early ⟨~ hours of the morning⟩

¹**weed** \'wēd\ *n* : a plant of no value and usu. of rank growth; *esp* : one growing in cultivated ground to the damage of the crop

²**weed** vb **1** : to clear of or remove weeds or something harmful, inferior, or superfluous ⟨~ a garden⟩ **2** : to get rid of (unwanted items) ⟨~ out the loafers from the crew⟩ — **weed·er** *n*

³**weed** *n* : GARMENT; *esp* : dress worn (as by a widow) as a sign of mourning — usu. used in pl.

weedy *adj* **1** : full of weeds **2** : resembling a weed esp. in vigor of growth or spread **3** : noticeably lean and scrawny : LANK

week \'wēk\ *n* **1** : seven successive days; *esp* : a calendar period of 7 days beginning with Sunday and ending with Saturday **2** : the working or school days of the calendar week

week·day \-‚dā\ *n* : a day of the week except Sunday or sometimes except Saturday and Sunday

¹**week·end** \-‚end\ *n* : the period between the close of one working or business or school week and the beginning of the next

²**weekend** vb : to spend the weekend

¹**week·ly** \-lē\ *adj* **1** : occurring, done, produced, or issued every week **2** : computed in terms of one week — **weekly** adv

²**weekly** *n* : a weekly publication

ween \'wēn\ *vb*, *archaic* : IMAGINE, SUPPOSE

wee·ny \'wē-nē\ *adj* : exceptionally small

weep \'wēp\ *vb* **wept** \'wept\ **weep·ing 1** : to express emotion and esp. sorrow by shedding tears : BEWAIL, CRY **2** : to drip or exude (liquid) — **weep·er** *n*

weep·ing adj 1 : TEARFUL; also : RAINY 2 : having slender drooping branches (a ~ willow)

wee·vil \'wē-vəl\ n : any of numerous mostly small beetles with a long head usu. curved into a snout and larvae that feed esp. in fruits or seeds — **wee·vily** or **wee·vil·ly** adj

weft \'weft\ n 1 : WOOF 2 : WEB; also : something woven

¹weigh \'wā\ vb 1 : to ascertain the heaviness of by a balance 2 : to have weight or a specified weight 3 : to consider carefully : PONDER 4 : to merit consideration as important : COUNT (evidence ~ing against him) 5 : to heave up (an anchor) 6 : to press down with or as if with a heavy weight

²weigh n : WAY — used in the phrase *under weigh*

¹weight \'wāt\ n 1 : quantity as determined by weighing 2 : the property of a body measurable by weighing 3 : the amount that something weighs 4 : relative heaviness (as of a textile) 5 : a unit (as a pound or kilogram) of weight or mass; also : a system of such units 6 : a heavy object for holding or pressing something down 7 : BURDEN (a ~ of grief) 8 : PRESSURE (~ of an attack) 9 : IMPORTANCE; also : INFLUENCE syn significance, moment, consequence, import, authority, prestige, credit

²weight vb 1 : to load with or as if with a weight 2 : to oppress with a burden (~ed down with cares)

weight·less adj 1 : having little weight 2 : lacking apparent gravitational pull — **weight·less·ness** n

weighty adj 1 : of much importance or consequence : MOMENTOUS, SERIOUS (~ problems) 2 : SOLEMN (a ~ manner) 3 : HEAVY 4 : BURDENSOME, GRIEVOUS 5 : exerting force, influence, or authority (~ arguments)

weir \'waər, 'wiər\ n 1 : a dam in a river for the purpose of directing water to a mill or making a pond 2 : a fence (as of brush) set in a stream or waterway for catching fish

weird \'wiərd\ adj 1 : MAGICAL 2 : UNEARTHLY, MYSTERIOUS 3 : ODD, UNUSUAL, FANTASTIC syn eerie, uncanny

Welch \'welch\ var of WELSH

¹wel·come \'wel-kəm\ vb 1 : to greet cordially or courteously 2 : to accept, meet, or face with pleasure (he ~s criticism)

²welcome adj 1 : received gladly (a ~ visitor) 2 : giving pleasure : PLEASING (~ news) 3 : willingly permitted or admitted (all are ~ to use the books)

³welcome n : a cordial greeting or reception

¹weld \'weld\ vb 1 : to unite (metal or plastic parts) either by heating and allowing the parts to flow together or by hammering or pressing together 2 : to unite closely or intimately (~ed together in friendship)

²weld n 1 : a welded joint 2 : union by welding

wel·fare \'wel-,faər\ n 1 : the state of doing well esp. in respect to happiness, well-being, or prosperity 2 : organized efforts for the social betterment of a group in society 3 : RELIEF 2

wel·kin \'wel-kən\ n : SKY; also : AIR

¹well \'wel\ n 1 : a spring with its pool : FOUNTAIN 2 : a hole sunk in the earth to obtain a natural deposit (as of water, oil, or gas) 3 : a source of supply (a ~ of information) 4 : something (as a container or space) suggesting a well 5 : the reservoir of a fountain pen 6 : an open space (as for a staircase or elevator) extending vertically through floors 7 : an enclosure in the middle of a ship's hold around the pumps

²well vb : to rise up and flow forth : RUN (tears ~ed from her eyes)

³well adv bet·ter \'bet-ər\ best \'best\ 1 : in a good or proper manner : RIGHTLY; also : EXCELLENTLY, SKILLFULLY 2 : SATISFACTORILY, FORTUNATELY (the party turned out ~) 3 : ABUNDANTLY (eat ~) 4 : with reason or courtesy : PROPERLY (I cannot ~ refuse) 5 : COMPLETELY, FULLY, QUITE (~ worth the price) (~ hidden) 6 : INTIMATELY, CLOSELY (I know him ~) 7 : CONSIDERABLY, FAR (~ over a million) (~ ahead) 8 : without trouble or difficulty (he could ~ have gone) 9 : EXACTLY, DEFINITELY (remember it ~)

⁴well adj 1 : SATISFACTORY, PLEASING (all is ~) 2 : PROSPEROUS; also : being in satisfactory condition or circumstances 3 : ADVISABLE, DESIRABLE (it is not ~ to anger him) 4 : free or recovered from infirmity or disease : HEALTHY 5 : FORTUNATE (it is ~ that this has happened)

well-ad·vised \,wel-əd-'vīzd\ adj 1 : PRUDENT 2 : resulting from, based on, or showing careful deliberation or wise counsel (~ plans)

well-ap·point·ed \-ə-'point-əd\ adj : having good and complete equipment

well-be·ing \'wel-'bē-iŋ\ n : the state of being happy, healthy, or prosperous : WELFARE

well-born \-'bôrn\ adj : born of good stock either socially or physically

well-bred \-'bred\ adj : having or indicating good breeding : REFINED

well-de·fined \,wel-di-'fīnd\ adj : having clearly distinguishable limits or boundaries (a ~ scar)

well-dis·posed \,wel-dis-'pōzd\ adj : disposed to be friendly, favorable, or sympathetic

well-done \'wel-'dən\ adj 1 : rightly or properly performed 2 : cooked thoroughly

well-fa·vored \-'fā-vərd\ adj : GOOD-LOOKING, HANDSOME

well-fixed \-'fikst\ adj : well-off financially

well-found·ed \-'faun-dəd\ adj : based on sound information, reasoning, judgment, or grounds (~ rumors)

well-groomed \-'grümd, -'grümd\ adj : well and neatly dressed or cared for (~ men) (a ~ lawn)

well-ground·ed \'wel-'graun-dəd\ adj : having a firm foundation

well-knit \-'nit\ adj : well and firmly formed or framed (a ~ argument)

well-mean·ing \-'mē-niŋ\ adj : having or based on good intentions

well-nigh \-'nī\ adv : ALMOST, NEARLY

well-off \-'òf\ adj : being in good condition or circumstances; esp : WELL-TO-DO

well-or·dered \'wel-'ôrd-ərd\ adj : having an orderly procedure or arrangement

well-read \-'red\ adj : well informed through reading

well-spring \-,spriŋ\ n : FOUNTAINHEAD, SPRING

well-timed \-'tīmd\ adj : coming or

happening at an opportune moment : TIMELY

well-to-do \,wel-tə-'dü\ *adj* : having more than adequate material resources : PROSPEROUS

well-turned \'wel-'tərnd\ *adj* 1 : pleasingly rounded : SHAPELY ⟨a ~ ankle⟩ 2 : pleasingly and appropriately expressed ⟨a ~ phrase⟩

well-wish-er \-,wish-ər\ *n* : one that wishes well to another

well-worn \-'wōrn\ *adj* 1 : worn by much use ⟨~ shoes⟩ 2 : TRITE 3 : worn well or properly ⟨~ honors⟩

welsh \'welsh, 'welch\ *vb* 1 : to cheat by avoiding payment of bets 2 : to avoid dishonorably the fulfillment of an obligation ⟨~ed on his promises⟩

Welsh \'welsh\ *n* 1 **Welsh** *pl* : the people of Wales 2 : the Celtic language of Wales — **Welsh** *adj* — **Welsh·man** \-mən\ *n*

Welsh rabbit *n* : melted often seasoned cheese poured over toast or crackers

Welsh rare·bit \-'raər-bət\ *n* : WELSH RABBIT

¹welt \'welt\ *n* 1 : the narrow strip of leather between a shoe upper and sole to which other parts are stitched 2 : a doubled edge, strip, insert, or seam for ornament or reinforcement 3 : a ridge or lump raised on the skin usu. by a blow; *also* : a heavy blow

²welt *vb* 1 : to furnish with a welt 2 : to hit hard

¹wel·ter \'wel-tər\ *vb* 1 : WRITHE, TOSS; *also* : WALLOW 2 : to rise and fall or toss about in or with waves 3 : to lie soaked or drenched ⟨~ing in his gore⟩ 4 : to become deeply sunk or involved ⟨~ed in misery⟩ 5 : to be in turmoil

²welter *n* 1 : TURMOIL 2 : a chaotic mass or jumble

wel·ter·weight \'wel-tər-,wāt\ *n* : a boxer weighing more than 135 but not over 147 pounds

wen \'wen\ *n* : a cyst formed by blocking of a skin gland and filled with fatty material

wench \'wench\ *n* 1 : a young woman : GIRL 2 : a female servant

wend \'wend\ *vb* : to direct one's course : proceed on (one's way)

went *past of* GO

wept *past of* WEEP

were *past 2d sing, past pl,* or *past subjunctive of* BE

were·wolf \'wiər-,wůlf, 'weər-, 'weər-\ *n* [OE *werwulf,* fr. *wer* man + *wulf* wolf] : a person held to be transformed or able to transform into a wolf

¹west \'west\ *adv* : to or toward the west

²west *adj* 1 : situated toward or at the west 2 : coming from the west

³west *n* 1 : the general direction of sunset 2 : the compass point directly opposite to east 3 *cap* : regions or countries west of a specified or implied point 4 *cap* : Europe and the Americas — **west·er·ly** \-ər-lē\ *adv* or *adj* — **west·ward** *adv* or *adj* — **west·wards** *adv*

¹west·ern \'wes-tərn\ *adj* 1 *often cap* : of, relating to, or characteristic of a region conventionally designated West 2 : lying toward or coming from the west 3 *cap* : of or relating to the Roman Catholic or Protestant segment of Christianity — **West·ern·er** *n*

²western *n* 1 : one that is produced in or is characteristic of a western region and esp. the western U.S. 2 *often cap* : a novel, story, motion picture, or broadcast dealing with life in the western U.S. during the latter half of the 19th century

west·ern·ize *vb* : to give western characteristics to

¹wet \'wet\ *adj* 1 : consisting of or covered or soaked with liquid (as water) 2 : RAINY 3 : not dry ⟨~ paint⟩ 4 : permitting or advocating the manufacture and sale of intoxicating liquor ⟨a ~ town⟩ ⟨a ~ candidate⟩ — **syn** damp, dank, moist, humid — **wet·ness** *n*

²wet *n* 1 : WATER; *also* : WETNESS, MOISTURE 2 : rainy weather : RAIN 3 : an advocate of a wet liquor policy

³wet *vb* **wet** or **wet·ted; wet·ting** : to make or become wet

wet blanket *n* : one that quenches or dampens enthusiasm or pleasure

weth·er \'weth-ər\ *n* : a male sheep castrated while immature

wet·land \'wet-,land\ *n* : land containing much soil moisture : swampy or boggy land

wet nurse *n* : one who cares for and suckles young not her own

¹whack \'hwak\ *vb* 1 : to strike with a smart or resounding blow 2 : CHOP

²whack *n* 1 : a smart or resounding blow; *also* : the sound of such a blow 2 : PORTION, SHARE 3 : CONDITION; *esp* : proper working order ⟨the machine is out of ~⟩ 4 : an opportunity or attempt to do something : CHANCE 5 : a single action or occasion : TIME ⟨made 3 pies at a ~⟩

¹whale \'hwāl\ *n* 1 : a large sea mammal that superficially resembles a fish but breathes air and suckles its young 2 : a person or thing impressive in size or quality ⟨a ~ of a story⟩

²whale *vb* : to fish or hunt for whales

³whale *vb* 1 : THRASH 2 : to strike or hit vigorously

whale·boat \-,bōt\ *n* : a long narrow rowboat made with both ends sharp and sloping and used by whalers

whale·bone \-,bōn\ *n* : a horny substance attached in plates to the upper jaw of some large whales (whalebone whales) and used esp. for ribs in corsets or fans

whal·er \'hwā-lər\ *n* 1 : a person or ship employed in the whale fishery 2 : WHALEBOAT

wharf \'hwórf\ *n, pl* **wharves** \'hwórvz\ *also* **wharfs** : a structure alongside which ships lie to load and unload

wharf·age *n* : the provision or use of a wharf; *also* : the charge for using a wharf

wharf·in·ger \'hwór-fən-jər\ *n* : the operator or manager of a wharf

¹what \(')hwät\ *pron* 1 — used to inquire the identity or nature of a being, an object, or some matter or situation ⟨~ is he, a salesman⟩ ⟨~'s that⟩ ⟨~ happened⟩ 2 : that which ⟨I know ~ you want⟩ 3 : WHATEVER 1 ⟨take ~ you want⟩

²what *adv* 1 : in what respect : HOW; *also* : how much ⟨~ does he care⟩

ə abut; ᵊ kitten; ər further; a back; ā bake; ä cot, cart; aù out; ch chin; e less; ē easy; g gift; i trip; ī life; j joke; ŋ sing; ō flow; ò flaw; òi coin; th thin; t͟h this; ü loot; ů foot; y yet; yü few; yů furious; zh vision

2 — used with *with* to introduce a prepositional phrase that expresses cause ⟨kept busy ~ with school and work⟩

³**what** *adj* **1** : used to inquire about the identity or nature of a person, object, or matter ⟨~ books does he read⟩ **2** : how remarkable or surprising ⟨~ an idea⟩ **3** : WHATEVER

¹**what·ev·er** \hwät-'ev-ər\ *pron* **1** : anything or everything that ⟨does ~ he wants to⟩ **2** : no matter what ⟨~ you do, don't cheat⟩ **3** : WHAT **1** — used as an intensive ⟨~ happened⟩

²**whatever** *adj* : of any kind at all ⟨no food ~⟩

what·not \'hwät-,nät\ *n* : a light open set of shelves for small ornaments

what·so·ev·er \,hwät-sə-'wev-ər\ *pron or adj* : WHATEVER

wheal \'hwēl\ *n* : a wale or welt on the skin; *also* : a suddenly-appearing itching or burning raised patch of skin

wheat \'hwēt\ *n* : a cereal grain that yields a fine white flour and is the chief breadstuff of temperate regions; *also* : any of several grasses whose white to dark red grains are wheat — **wheat·en** *adj*

wheat germ *n* : the vitamin-rich wheat embryo separated in milling

whee·dle \'hwēd-ºl\ *vb* **1** : to coax or entice by flattery **2** : to gain or get by wheedling

¹**wheel** \'hwēl\ *n* **1** : a disk or circular frame capable of turning on a central axis **2** : something resembling a wheel in shape, use, or method of turning; *esp* : a circular frame with handles for controlling a ship's rudder **3** : a device the chief part of which is a wheel or wheels; *esp* : BICYCLE **4** : a former wheellike instrument of torture to which a victim was bound **5** : a revolution or rotation : a turn around an axis; *esp* : a turning movement of troops or ships in line in which units preserve alignment and relative position as they change direction **6** : machinery that imparts motion : moving power ⟨the ~s of government⟩ **7** : a directing or controlling person; *esp* : a political leader — **wheeled** *adj*

²**wheel** *vb* **1** : to convey or move on wheels or in a vehicle having wheels **2** : ROTATE, REVOLVE **3** : to turn so as to change direction

wheel·bar·row \-,bar-ō\ *n* : a vehicle with handles and usu. one wheel for conveying small loads

wheel·base \-,bās\ *n* : the distance in inches between the front and rear axles of an automotive vehicle

wheel·chair \-,cheər\ *n* : a chair mounted on wheels esp. for the use of invalids

wheel·er *n* **1** : one that wheels **2** : something that has wheels — used in combination ⟨a 4-*wheeler* carriage⟩ **3** : WHEELHORSE

wheel·horse \'hwēl-,hórs\ *n* **1** : a horse in a position nearest the wheels in a tandem or similar arrangement **2** : a steady and effective worker esp. in a political body

wheel·house \-,haús\ *n* : a small house on or above the deck of a ship and containing the steering wheel

wheel·wright \-,rīt\ *n* : a man whose occupation is to make or repair wheels and wheeled vehicles

¹**wheeze** \'hwēz\ *vb* : to breathe with difficulty usu. with a whistling sound

²**wheeze** *n* **1** : a sound of wheezing

2 : GAG, JOKE **3** : a trite saying

wheezy *adj* **1** : inclined to wheeze **2** : having a wheezing sound

whelk \'hwelk\ *n* : a large sea snail; *esp* : one much used as food in Europe

whelm \'hwelm\ *vb* : to overcome or engulf completely : OVERWHELM

¹**whelp** \'hwelp\ *n* **1** : one of the young of various carnivorous mammals (as a dog) **2** : a low contemptible fellow

²**whelp** *vb* : to give birth to (whelps) : bring forth whelps

¹**when** \(')hwen, hwən\ *adv* **1** : at what time ⟨~ did it happen⟩ **2** : the time at which ⟨that's ~ it happened⟩ ⟨unsure of ~ they would come⟩ **3** : at, in, or during which ⟨at a time ~ things were upset⟩ **4** : at which time ⟨come at night, ~ things will be quiet⟩

²**when** *conj* **1** : at or during the time that ⟨leave ~ I do⟩ **2** : every time that ⟨they all laughed ~ he sang⟩ **3** : in the event that : IF ⟨the batter is out ~ he bunts foul with two strikes⟩ **4** : ALTHOUGH

³**when** \,hwen\ *pron* : what or which time ⟨since ~ have you been the boss⟩

⁴**when** \'hwen\ *n* : the time of a happening

whence \(')hwens\ *adv* **1** : from what place, source, or cause ⟨~ come all these questions⟩ **2** : from or out of which ⟨the land ~ he came⟩

when·ev·er \hwen-'ev-ər, hwən-\ *conj or adv* : at whatever time

when·so·ev·er \'hwen-sə-,wev-ər\ *conj* : at whatever time

¹**where** \(')hweər\ *adv* **1** : at, in, or to what place ⟨~ is he⟩ ⟨~ did he go⟩ **2** : the place to or in which ⟨he knows ~ we went⟩ ⟨spoke of ~ they'd been⟩ **3** : at or in which ⟨this is the dock ~ you get the ferry⟩ ⟨the restaurant ~ we eat⟩ **4** : in or at which place ⟨went to New York, ~ they had a wonderful time⟩ **5** : in what way or particular ⟨~ is he wrong⟩

²**where** *conj* **1** : in, at, or to the place or point in, at, or to which ⟨sit ~ the light's better⟩ ⟨went ~ he had promised to go⟩ ⟨it's cold ~ you're going⟩ ⟨won't go ~ I'm not wanted⟩ **2** : every place that : WHEREVER ⟨goes ~ he likes⟩ **3** : in the situation or respect in which ⟨outstanding ~ endurance is called for⟩

³**where** \'hweər\ *n* : PLACE, LOCATION ⟨the ~ and how of the accident⟩

⁴**where** \,hweər\ *pron* : what place ⟨~ is he from⟩

¹**where·abouts** \'hwer-ə-,baúts\ *also* **where·about** *adv* : about where ⟨~ does he live⟩

²**whereabouts** *n sing or pl* : the place where a person or thing is

where·as \hwer-'az\ *conj* **1** : in view of the fact that : SINCE **2** : when in fact : while on the contrary

where·at \-'at\ *conj* **1** : at or toward which **2** : in consequence of which : WHEREUPON

where·by \-'bī\ *adv* : by or through which ⟨the means ~ he achieved his goal⟩

¹**where·fore** \'hweər-,fōr\ *adv* **1** : for what reason or purpose : WHY **2** : THEREFORE

²**wherefore** *n* : CAUSE, REASON

where·in \hwer-'in\ *adv* **1** : in what place, point, or particular ⟨~ was he wrong⟩ **2** : in which ⟨the place ~ he resides⟩ **3** : during which ⟨a period ~ nothing was done⟩ **4** : the point or particular in which ⟨showed me ~ I was wrong⟩

where·of \-'əv, -'äv\ conj 1 : of what ⟨knows ~ he speaks⟩ 2 : of which or whom ⟨books ~ the best are lost⟩

where·on \-'òn, -'än\ adv : on which ⟨the base ~ it rests⟩

where·so·ev·er \'hwer-sə-,wev-ər\ conj, archaic : WHEREVER

where·to \'hwer-,tü\ conj : to which

¹where·up·on \'hwer-ə-,pòn, -,pän\ adv : WHEREON

²whereupon conj : because of or after which ⟨she hit him in the eye, ~ he hit her⟩

¹wher·ev·er \hwer-'ev-ər\ adv : where in the world ⟨~ did she get that hat⟩

²wherever conj : at, in, or to whatever place 2 : in any circumstance in which

where·with \'hweər-,with, -,with\ adv : with or by means of which

where·with·al \'hwer-with-,òl, -,with-\ n : MEANS, RESOURCES; esp : MONEY ⟨the ~ for a dinner⟩

wher·ry \'hwer-ē\ n : a light boat; esp : a long light rowboat sharp at both ends

whet \'hwet\ vb whet·ted; whet·ting 1 : to sharpen by rubbing against or with a hard substance (as a whetstone) 2 : to make keen : STIMULATE ⟨~ the appetite⟩

wheth·er \'hweth-ər\ conj 1 : IF ⟨ask ~ he's going⟩ 2 : if the following be the case ⟨ask ~ or not he's going⟩ 3 : which is the better or best course, namely ⟨uncertain ~ to go or stay⟩ 4 : no matter if ⟨~ you like it or not, you're going⟩

whet·stone \'hwet-,stōn\ n : a stone for whetting sharp-edged tools

whey \'hwā\ n : the watery part of milk that separates after the milk sours and thickens

¹which \('hwich\ adj 1 : being what one or ones out of a group ⟨~ tie should I wear⟩ 2 : WHICHEVER

²which pron 1 : which one or ones ⟨~ is yours⟩ ⟨~ are his⟩ ⟨he's a Swede or a Dane, I don't remember ~⟩ 2 : WHICHEVER ⟨we have all kinds of them; take ~ you like⟩ 3 — used to introduce a relative clause and to serve as a substitute therein for the substantive modified by the clause ⟨give me the money ~ is coming to me⟩

¹which·ev·er \hwich-'ev-ər\ pron : whatever one or ones

²whichever adj : no matter which ⟨~ way you go⟩

which·so·ev·er pron or adj \,hwich-sə-'wev-ər\ : WHICHEVER

whick·er \'hwik-ər\ vb : NEIGH, WHINNY — whicker n

¹whiff \'hwif\ n 1 : a quick puff or slight gust esp. of air, gas, smoke, or spray 2 : an inhalation of odor, gas, or smoke ⟨a ~ of perfume⟩ 3 : a slight trace : HINT

²whiff vb : to expel, puff out, or blow away in or as if in whiffs 2 : to inhale an odor

whif·fle·tree \'hwif-əl-(,)trē\ n : the pivoted swinging bar to which the traces of a harness are fastened

Whig \'hwig\ n 1 : a member or supporter of a British political group of the 18th and early 19th centuries seeking to limit royal authority and increase par-

liamentary power 2 : an American favoring independence from Great Britain during the American Revolution 3 : a member or supporter of an American political party formed about 1834 to oppose the Democrats

¹while \'hwīl\ n 1 : a period of time ⟨stay a ~⟩ 2 : the time and effort used ⟨worth your ~⟩ : TROUBLE

²while \(,)hwīl\ conj 1 : during the time that ⟨she called ~ you were out⟩ 2 : as long as ⟨~ there's life there's hope⟩ 3 : ALTHOUGH ⟨~ he's respected, he's not liked⟩

³while \'hwīl\ vb : to cause to pass esp. pleasantly ⟨~ away an hour⟩

whi·lom \'hwī-ləm\ adv, archaic : FORMERLY

²whilom adj : FORMER ⟨his ~ friends⟩

whilst \'hwīlst\ conj, chiefly Brit : WHILE

whim \'hwim\ n : a sudden wish, desire, or change of mind : NOTION, FANCY, CAPRICE

whim·per \'hwim-pər\ vb : to make a low whining plaintive or broken sound — whimper n

whim·si·cal \'hwim-zi-kəl\ adj : full of whims : CAPRICIOUS 2 : resulting from or characterized by whim or caprice : ERRATIC — whim·si·cal·i·ty \,hwim-zə-'kal-ət-ē\ n — whim·si·cal·ly \'hwim-zi-k(ə-)lē\ adv

whim·sy or whim·sey \'hwim-zē\ n 1 : WHIM, CAPRICE 2 : a fanciful or fantastic device, object, or creation esp. in writing or art

whine \'hwīn\ vb 1 : to utter a usu. high-pitched plaintive or distressed cry; also : to make a sound similar to such a cry 2 : to utter a complaint with or as if with a whine — whine n

¹whin·ny \'hwin-ē\ vb : to neigh usu. in a low or gentle manner

²whinny n : NEIGH

¹whip \'hwip\ vb whipped; whip·ping 1 : to move, snatch, or jerk quickly or forcefully ⟨~ out a gun⟩ 2 : to strike with a slender lithe implement (as a lash) esp. as a punishment; also : SPANK 3 : to drive or urge on by or as if by using a whip 4 : to bind or wrap (as a rope or rod) with cord in order to protect and strengthen; also : to wind or wrap around something 5 : DEFEAT 6 : to stir up : INCITE ⟨~ up enthusiasm⟩ 7 : to produce in a hurry ⟨~ up a meal⟩ 8 : to beat (as eggs or cream) into a froth 9 : to gather together or hold together for united action 10 : to move nimbly or briskly; also : to thrash about like a whiplash

²whip n 1 : an instrument used for whipping 2 : a stroke or cut with or as if with a whip 3 : a dessert made by whipping a portion of the ingredients (prune ~) 4 : a person who handles a whip; esp : a driver of horses 5 : a member of a legislative body appointed to enforce party discipline and to secure the attendance of party members at important sessions 6 : a whipping or thrashing motion ⟨a ~ of his tail⟩

whip·cord \-,kòrd\ n 1 : a thin tough cord made of braided or twisted hemp or catgut 2 : a cloth that is made of hard-twisted yarns and has fine diagonal cords or ribs

---

ə abut; ᵉ kitten; ər further; a back; ā bake; ä cot, cart; aù out; ch chin; e less; ē easy; g gift; i trip; ī life; j joke; ŋ sing; ō flow; ò flaw; òi coin; th thin; th̲ this; ü loot; ù foot; y yet; yü few; yù furious; zh vision

whip hand *n* : positive control : ADVANTAGE

whip·lash \'hwip-,lash\ *n* : the lash of a whip

whip·per·snap·per \'hwip-ər-,snap-ər\ *n* : a small, insignificant, or presumptuous person

whip·pet \'hwip-ət\ *n* : a small swift dog of greyhound type often used for racing

whip·ple·tree \'hwip-əl-(,)trē\ *n* : WHIFFLETREE

whip·poor·will \'hwip-ər-,wil\ *n* : an American bird with dull variegated plumage whose call is heard at nightfall and just before dawn

¹**whip·saw** \'hwip-,sȯ\ *n* 1 : a narrow tapering saw that has hook teeth and is from 5 to 7½ feet long 2 : a 2-man crosscut saw

²**whipsaw** *vb* 1 : to saw with a whipsaw 2 : to worst in two opposite ways at once, by a two-phase operation, or by the collusive action of two opponents

¹**whir** *also* **whirr** \'hwər\ *vb* **whirred; whir·ring** : to move, fly, or revolve with a whizzing sound : WHIZ

²**whir** *also* **whirr** *n* : a continuous fluttering or vibratory sound made by something in rapid motion

¹**whirl** \'hwərl\ *vb* 1 : to move or drive in a circle or similar curve esp. with force or speed 2 : to turn or cause to turn on or around an axis : SPIN 3 : to turn abruptly : WHEEL 4 : to pass, move, or go quickly 5 : to become dizzy or giddy : REEL

²**whirl** *n* 1 : a rapid rotating or circling movement; *also* : something undergoing such a movement 2 : COMMOTION, BUSTLE 3 : a state of mental confusion

whirl·i·gig \'hwər-li-,gig\ *n* 1 : a child's toy having a whirling motion 2 : MERRY-GO-ROUND 3 : something that continuously whirls or changes; *also* : a whirling course

whirl·pool \'hwərl-,pül\ *n* : water moving rapidly in a circle so as to produce a depression in the center into which floating objects may be drawn

whirl·wind \-,wind\ *n* 1 : a small whirling windstorm 2 : a confused rush : WHIRL

whirly·bird \'hwər-lē-,bərd\ *n* : HELICOPTER

¹**whish** \'hwish\ *vb* : to move with a whizzing or swishing sound

²**whish** *n* : a rushing sound : SWISH

¹**whisk** \'hwisk\ *n* 1 : a quick light sweeping or brushing motion 2 : a small usu. wire kitchen implement for hand beating of food 3 : a flexible bunch (as of twigs, feathers, or straw) attached to a handle for use as a brush

²**whisk** *vb* 1 : to move nimbly and quickly 2 : to move or convey briskly ⟨~ out a knife⟩ ⟨~ed the children off to bed⟩ 3 : to beat or whip lightly ⟨~ eggs⟩ 4 : to brush or wipe off lightly ⟨~ a coat⟩

whisk broom *n* : a small broom with a short handle used esp. as a clothes brush

whisk·er \'hwis-kər\ *n* 1 *pl* : the part of the beard that grows on the sides of the face or on the chin 2 : one hair of the beard 3 : one of the long bristles or hairs growing near the mouth of an animal (as a cat or bird) — **whisk·ered** *adj*

whis·key *or* **whis·ky** \'hwis-kē\ *n* [IrGael *uisce beathadh* & ScGael *uisge beatha*, lit., water of life] : a liquor distilled from a fermented mash of grain (as rye, corn, or barley)

¹**whis·per** \'hwis-pər\ *vb* 1 : to speak very low or under the breath; *also* : to tell or utter by whispering ⟨~ a secret⟩ 2 : to make a low rustling sound ⟨~ing leaves⟩

²**whisper** *n* 1 : an act or instance of whispering; *esp* : speech without vibration of the vocal cords 2 : something communicated by or as if by whispering : HINT, RUMOR

whist \'hwist\ *n* : a card game played by 4 players in 2 partnerships with a deck of 52 cards

¹**whis·tle** \'hwis-əl\ *n* 1 : a device by which a shrill sound is produced ⟨steam ~⟩ ⟨tin ~⟩ 2 : a shrill clear sound made by forcing breath out or air in through the puckered lips 3 : the sound or signal produced by a whistle or as if by whistling 4 : the shrill clear note of an animal (as a bird)

²**whistle** *vb* 1 : to utter a shrill clear sound by blowing or drawing air through the puckered lips 2 : to utter a shrill note or call resembling a whistle 3 : to make a shrill clear sound esp. by rapid movement ⟨bullets *whistled* by him⟩ 4 : to blow or sound a whistle 5 : to signal or call by a whistle 6 : to produce, utter, or express by whistling ⟨~ a tune⟩ — **whis·tler** \-(ə-)lər\ *n*

whit \'hwit\ *n* : the smallest part or particle imaginable : BIT

¹**white** \'hwīt\ *adj* 1 : free from color 2 : of the color of new snow or milk; *esp* : of the color white 3 : light or pallid in color ⟨lips ~ with fear⟩ 4 : SILVERY; *also* : made of silver 5 : of, relating to, or being a member of a group or race characterized by light-colored skin 6 : free from spot or blemish : PURE, INNOCENT 7 : BLANK ⟨~ space in printed matter⟩ 8 : not intended to cause harm ⟨a ~ lie⟩ 9 : wearing white ⟨~ friars⟩ 10 : SNOWY ⟨~ Christmas⟩ 11 : ARDENT, PASSIONATE ⟨~ fury⟩ 12 : conservative or reactionary in politics

²**white** *n* 1 : the color of maximal lightness that characterizes objects which both reflect and transmit light : the opposite of black 2 : a white or light-colored part or thing ⟨the ~ of an egg⟩; *also, pl* : white garments 3 : the light-colored pieces in a 2-handed board game; *also*; the person by whom these are played 4 : one that is or approaches the color white 5 : a member of a light-skinned race 6 : a member of a conservative or reactionary political group

white ant *n* : TERMITE

white·bait \'hwīt-,bāt\ *n* : the young of a herring or a similar small fish esteemed a delicacy

white blood cell *n* : a blood cell that does not contain hemoglobin : LEUKOCYTE

white·cap \'hwīt-,kap\ *n* : a wave crest breaking into foam

white–col·lar *adj* : of, relating to, or constituting the class of salaried workers whose duties require a well-groomed appearance

white elephant *n* [so called because white elephants were venerated in parts of Asia and maintained without being required to work] 1 : something requiring much care and expense and yielding little profit 2 : an object no longer wanted by its owner though not without value to others

white-faced \'hwīt-'fāst\ *adj* **:** having a wan pale face

white feather *n* **:** a mark or symbol of cowardice

white-fish \'hwīt-,fish\ *n* **:** any of various freshwater food fishes related to the salmons and trouts

white flag *n* **:** a flag of plain white used as a flag of truce or as a token of surrender

White-hall \'hwīt-,hȯl\ *n* **:** the British government

white heat *n* **:** a temperature higher than red heat at which a body becomes brightly incandescent so as to appear white — **white–hot** *adj*

White House *n* **1 :** the presidential mansion in Washington **2 :** the executive department of the U.S. government

white lead *n* **:** a heavy white powder that is a carbonate of lead and is used as a pigment

white matter *n* **:** the whitish part of nervous tissue consisting mostly of nerve-cell processes

whit-en \'hwīt-ᵊn\ *vb* **:** to make or become white **syn** blanch, bleach

white-ness \'hwīt-nəs\ *n* **:** the quality or state of being white

white slave *n* **:** a woman or girl held unwillingly for purposes of prostitution

white-wall \'hwīt-,wȯl\ *n* **:** an automobile tire having white sides

1white-wash \-,wȯsh, -,wäsh\ *vb* **1 :** to whiten with whitewash **2 :** to clear of a charge of wrongdoing by offering excuses, hiding facts, or conducting a perfunctory investigation **3 :** to defeat (an opponent) so that he fails to score

2whitewash *n* **1 :** a liquid preparation (as of lime and water or of whiting, size, and water) for whitening structural surfaces **2 :** WHITEWASHING

white-wood \-,wu̇d\ *n* **:** any of various trees (as a tulip tree or cottonwood) having light-colored wood; *also* **:** the wood of such a tree

whith-er \'hwith-ər\ *adv* **1 :** to what place **2 :** to what situation, position, degree, or end 〈~ will this drive him〉 **3 :** to the place at, in, or to which; *also* **:** to which place **4 :** to whatever place

whith-er-so-ev-er \,hwith-ər-sə-'wev-ər\ *conj* **:** to whatever place

1whit-ing \'hwīt-iŋ\ *n* **:** any of several usu. light or silvery food fishes (as a hake) found mostly near seacoasts

2whiting *n* **:** pulverized chalk or limestone used as a pigment and in putty

whit-ish \'hwīt-ish\ *adj* **:** somewhat white

whit-low \'hwit-,lō\ *n* **:** FELON

Whit-sun-day \'hwit-,sən-dē\ *n* **:** PENTECOST

whit-tle \'hwit-ᵊl\ *vb* **1 :** to pare or cut off chips from the surface of (wood) with a knife; *also* **:** to cut or shape by such paring **2 :** to reduce, remove, or destroy gradually as if by paring down **:** PARE 〈~ down expenses〉

1whiz *or* **whizz** \'hwiz\ *vb* **whizzed**; **whiz-zing :** to hum, whir, or hiss like a speeding object (as an arrow or ball) passing through air

2whiz *or* **whizz** *n, pl* **whiz-zes :** a hissing, buzzing, or whirring sound

who \('hü\ *pron* **1 :** — used to inquire the identity of an indicated person or group 〈~ did it〉 〈~ is he〉 〈~ are they〉 **2 :** the person or persons that 〈knows ~ did it〉 **3 :** \(,)hü, ü\ — used to introduce a relative clause and to serve as a substitute therein for the substantive modified by the clause 〈the man ~ lives there is rich〉 〈the people ~ did it were caught〉

who-dun-it \hü-'dən-ət\ *n* **:** a detective story or mystery story presented as a novel, play, or motion picture

who-ev-er \hü-'ev-ər\ *pron* **:** whatever person or persons **:** no matter who

1whole \'hōl\ *adj* **1 :** being in healthy or sound condition **:** free from defect or damage **:** WELL, INTACT **2 :** having all its proper parts or elements 〈~ milk〉 **3 :** constituting the total sum of **:** INTEGRAL **4 :** each or all of the 〈the ~ family〉 **5 :** not scattered or divided **:** CONCENTRATED 〈gave me his ~ attention〉 **6 :** seemingly complete or total **syn** entire, perfect — **whole-ness** *n*

2whole *n* **1 :** a complete amount or sum **:** a number, aggregate, or totality lacking no part, member, or element **2 :** something constituting a complex unity **:** a coherent system or organization of parts fitting or working together as one — **on the whole 1 :** in view of all the circumstances or conditions **2 :** in general

whole-heart-ed \-'härt-əd\ *adj* **:** undivided in purpose, enthusiasm, or will **:** HEARTY, ZESTFUL, SINCERE

whole number *n* **:** INTEGER

1whole-sale \'hōl-,sāl\ *n* **:** the sale of goods in quantity usu. for resale by a retail merchant

2wholesale *adj* **:** of, relating to, or engaged in wholesaling **2 :** performed on a large scale without discrimination 〈~ slaughter〉 — **wholesale** *adv*

3wholesale *vb* **:** to sell at wholesale — **whole-sal-er** *n*

whole-some \'hōl-səm\ *adj* **1 :** promoting mental, spiritual, or bodily health or well-being 〈~ advice〉 〈a ~ environment〉 **2 :** not detrimental to health or well-being; *esp* **:** fit for food **3 :** sound in body, mind, or morals **:** HEALTHY **4 :** PRUDENT 〈~ respect for the champion's right hand〉 — **whole-some-ness** *n*

whole step *n* **:** a musical interval comprising two half steps (as C–D or F♯–G♯)

whole wheat *adj* **:** made of ground entire wheat kernels

whol-ly \'hō(l)-lē\ *adv* **1 :** COMPLETELY, TOTALLY **2 :** SOLELY, EXCLUSIVELY

whom \(')hüm\ *pron, objective case of* WHO

whom-ev-er \hüm-'ev-ər\ *pron, objective case of* WHOEVER

whom-so-ev-er \,hüm-sə-'wev-ər\ *pron, objective case of* WHOSOEVER

1whoop \'h(w)üp, 'h(w)u̇p\ *vb* **1 :** to shout or call loudly and vigorously **2 :** to make the sound that follows a fit of coughing in whooping cough **3 :** to go or pass with a loud noise **4 :** to utter or express with a whoop; *also* **:** to urge, drive, or cheer with a whoop

2whoop *n* **1 :** a whooping sound or utterance **:** SHOUT, HOOT **2 :** a crowing sound accompanying the intake of breath after a fit of coughing in whooping cough

---

ə abut; ᵊ kitten; ər further; a back; ā bake; ä cot, cart; au̇ out; ch chin; e less; ē easy; g gift; i trip; ī life; j joke; ŋ sing; ō flow; ȯ flaw; ȯi coin; th thin; t͟h this; ü loot; u̇ foot; y yet; yü few; yu̇ furious; zh vision

whooping cough *n* : an infectious disease esp. of children marked by convulsive coughing fits sometimes followed by a whoop

whop·per \'hwäp-ər\ *n* : something unusually large or extreme of its kind; *esp* : a monstrous lie

whore \'hōr\ *n* : PROSTITUTE

whorl \'hwȯrl, 'hwȯrl\ *n* **1** : a row of parts (as leaves or petals) encircling an axis and esp. a plant stem **2** : something that whirls or coils or whose form suggests such movement : COIL, SPIRAL **3** : one of the turns of a snail shell

1whose \(')hüz\ *adj* : of or relating to whom or which esp. as possessor or possessors, agent or agents, or object or objects of an action (asked ~ bag it was)

2whose *pron* : whose one or ones (~ is this car) (~ are those books)

who·so \'hü-ˌsō\ *pron* : WHOEVER

who·so·ev·er \ˌhü-sə-'wev-ər\ *pron* : WHOEVER

1why \(')hwī\ *adv* **1** : for what reason, cause, or purpose (~ did you do it) **2** : the reason for or because of which (knows ~ he did it) (spoke of ~ he'd done it) **3** : for or because of which (the reason ~ it happened was that he was careless)

2why \'hwī\ *n, pl* **whys** : REASON, CAUSE (the ~ of race prejudice)

3why \(ˌ)wī\ *interj* — used to express surprise, hesitation, approval, disapproval, or impatience (~, here's what I was looking for)

wick \'wik\ *n* : a loosely bound bundle of soft fibers that draws up oil, tallow, or wax to be burned in a candle, oil lamp, or stove

wick·ed \'wik-əd\ *adj* **1** : morally bad : EVIL, SINFUL **2** : FIERCE, VICIOUS **3** : HARMFUL, DANGEROUS (a ~ attack) **4** : REPUGNANT, VILE (a ~ odor) **5** : ROGUISH — **wick·ed·ly** *adv* — **wick·ed·ness** *n*

wick·er \'wik-ər\ *n* **1** : a small pliant branch (as an osier or a withe) **2** : WICKERWORK — **wicker** *adj*

wick·er·work \-ˌwərk\ *n* : work made of osiers, twigs, or rods : BASKETRY

wick·et \'wik-ət\ *n* **1** : a small gate or door; *esp* : one forming a part of or placed near a larger one **2** : a window-like opening usu. with a grille or grate (as at a ticket office) **3** : a small gate for regulating the amount of water in a canal lock **4** : a set of three upright rods topped by two crosspieces bowled at in cricket **5** : an arch through which the ball is driven in croquet

wick·i·up \'wik-ē-ˌəp\ *n* : a rough frame hut covered with reed mats, grass, or brushwood and used by nomadic Indians of the western and southwestern U.S.

1wide \'wīd\ *adj* **1** : covering a vast area **2** : measured across or at right angles to the length **3** : not narrow : BROAD; *also* : ROOMY **4** : opened to full width (eyes ~ with wonder) **5** : not limited : EXTENSIVE (~ experience) **6** : far from the goal, mark, or truth (a ~ guess) — **wide·ly** *adv*

2wide *adv* **1** : over a great distance or extent : WIDELY (searched far and ~) **2** : over a specified distance, area, or extent **3** : so as to leave a wide space between (~ apart) **4** : so as to clear by a considerable distance (ran ~ around left end) **5** : COMPLETELY, FULLY

(opened her eyes ~) **6** : ASTRAY, AFIELD (the bullet went ~)

wide-awake \ˌwīd-ə-'wāk\ *adj* : fully awake; *also* : KNOWING, ALERT (a group of ~ young men)

wide-eyed \'wīd-'īd\ *adj* **1** : having the eyes wide open **2** : AMAZED **3** : NAIVE

wid·en \'wīd-ᵊn\ *vb* : to make or become wide : BROADEN

wide·spread \'wīd-'spred\ *adj* **1** : widely extended or spread out (~ wings) **2** : widely scattered or prevalent (~ fear)

wid·geon *also* **wi·geon** \'wij-ən\ *n* : any of several freshwater ducks between the teal and the mallard in size

1wid·ow \'wid-ō\ *n* : a woman who has lost her husband by death; *esp* : one who has not married again — **wid·ow·hood** *n*

2widow *vb* : to cause to become a widow

wid·ow·er \'wid-ə-wər\ *n* : a man who has lost his wife by death and has not married again

width \'width\ *n* **1** : a distance from side to side : the measurement taken at right angles to the length : BREADTH **2** : largeness of extent or scope; *also* : FULLNESS **3** : a measured and cut piece of material (a ~ of calico) (a ~ of lumber)

wield \'wēld\ *vb* **1** : to use or handle esp. effectively (~ a broom) (~ a pen) **2** : to exert authority by means of : EMPLOY (~ influence) — **wield·er** *n*

wie·ner \'wē-nər\ *n* [short for *wiener-wurst*, fr. G, *lit.*, Vienna sausage] : FRANKFURTER

wife \'wīf\ *n, pl* **wives** \'wīvz\ **1** *dial* : WOMAN **2** : a woman acting in a specified capacity — used in combination **3** : a married woman — **wife·hood** \'wīf-ˌhud\ *n* — **wife·ly** *adj*

wife·less *adj* : having no wife

wig \'wig\ *n* : a manufactured covering of hair for the head often made of human hair; *also* : TOUPEE

wig·gle \'wig-əl\ *vb* **1** : to move to and fro with quick jerky or shaking movements : JIGGLE **2** : WRIGGLE — **wiggle** \-(ə-)lər\ *n*

wig·gly \-(ə-)lē\ *adj* **1** : tending to wiggle (a ~ worm) **2** : WAVY (~ lines)

wight \'wīt\ *n* : a living being : CREATURE

1wig·wag \'wig-ˌwag\ *vb* **1** : to signal by or as if by a flag or light waved according to a code **2** : to make or cause to make a signal (as with the hand or arm)

2wigwag *n* **1** : the art or practice of wigwagging **2** : a wigwagged message

wig·wam \'wig-ˌwäm\ *n* : a hut of the Indians of the eastern U.S. having typically an arched framework of poles overlaid with bark, rush mats, or hides

1wild \'wīld\ *adj* **1** : living in a state of nature and not ordinarily tamed (~ ducks) **2** : growing or produced without human aid or care (~ honey) (~ plants) **3** : WASTE, DESOLATE (~ country) **4** : UNCONTROLLED, UNRESTRAINED, UNRULY (~ passions) (a ~ young stallion) **5** : TURBULENT, STORMY (a ~ night) **6** : EXTRAVAGANT, FANTASTIC, CRAZY (~ ideas) **7** : indicative of strong passion, desire, or emotion (a ~ stare) **8** : UNCIVILIZED, SAVAGE **9** : deviating from the natural or expected course : ERRATIC (a ~ price increase) **10** : having a denomination determined by the holder ⟨deuces ∼⟩ — **wild·ly** *adv* — **wild·ness** *n*

²wild *n* **1** : WILDERNESS **2** : a natural or undomesticated state or existence

³wild *adv* **1** : WILDLY **2** : without regulation or control ⟨running ∼⟩

¹wild·cat \'wīl(d)-ˌkat\ *n* **1** : any of various small or medium-sized cats (as a lynx or ocelot) **2** : a quick-tempered hard-fighting person **3** : a well drilled for oil or gas in a region not known to be productive

²wildcat *adj* : not sound or safe ⟨∼ banks⟩ ⟨∼ schemes⟩

³wildcat *vb* **-cat·ted; -cat·ting** : to drill an oil or gas well in a region not known to be productive

wil·der·ness \'wil-dər-nəs\ *n* : an uncultivated and uninhabited region

wild·fire \'wīl(d)-ˌfī(ə)r\ *n* : a sweeping and destructive fire ⟨the news spread like ∼⟩

wild·fowl \-ˌfaůl\ *n* : a game bird; *esp* : a game waterfowl (as a wild duck or goose)

wild·life \-ˌlīf\ *n* : creatures that are neither human nor domesticated; *esp* : mammals, birds, and fishes hunted by man

wild rice *n* : a No. American aquatic grass; *also* : its edible seed

wild·wood \'wīld-ˌwůd\ *n* : a wild or unfrequented wood

¹wile \'wīl\ *n* **1** : a trick or stratagem intended to ensnare or deceive; *also* : a playful trick **2** : TRICKERY, GUILE

²wile *vb* : LURE, ENTICE

wil·i·ness \'wī-lē-nəs\ *n* : the quality or state of being wily

¹will \wəl, (ˈ)wil\ (ˈ)will\ *vb, past* **would** \wəd, (ə)d, (ˈ)wůd\ *1* : WISH, DESIRE ⟨call it what you ∼⟩ **2** — used as an auxiliary to express desire or consent, habitual action or natural disposition, simple futurity, capability, probability, determination, inevitability, or a command

²will \'wil\ *n* **1** : wish or desire often combined with determination ⟨the ∼ to win⟩ **2** : something desired; *esp* : a choice or determination of one having authority or power **3** : the act, process, or experience of willing : VOLITION **4** : the mental powers manifested as wishing, choosing, desiring, or intending **5** : a disposition to act according to principles or ends **6** : SELF-CONTROL ⟨a man of iron ∼⟩ **7** : a legal document in which a person declares to whom his possessions are to go after his death

³will \'wil\ *vb* **1** : to dispose of by or as if by a will : BEQUEATH **2** : to determine by an act of choice; *also* : DECREE, ORDAIN **3** : INTEND, PURPOSE; *also* : CHOOSE

will·ful *or* **wil·ful** \'wil-fəl\ *adj* **1** : governed by will without regard to reason : OBSTINATE, STUBBORN **2** : INTENTIONAL ⟨∼ murder⟩ — **will·ful·ly** *adv* — **will·ful·ness** *n*

wil·lies \'wil-ēz\ *n pl* : a fit of nervousness : JITTERS

will·ing \'wil-iŋ\ *adj* **1** : inclined or favorably disposed in mind : READY ⟨∼ to go⟩ **2** : prompt to act or respond ⟨∼ workers⟩ **3** : done, borne, or accepted voluntarily or without reluctance : VOLUNTARY **4** : VOLITIONAL — **will·ing·ly** *adv* — **will·ing·ness** *n*

wil·li·waw \'wil-ē-ˌwó\ *n* : a sudden violent gust of cold land air common along mountainous coasts of high latitudes

will-o'-the-wisp \ˌwil-ə-thə-'wisp\ *n* **1** : a light that appears at night over marshy grounds **2** : a misleading or elusive goal or hope

wil·low \'wil-ō\ *n* **1** : any of numerous quick-growing shrubs and trees with tough pliable shoots used in basketry **2** : the wood of a willow **3** : an object made of willow wood

wil·low·ware \-ˌwaǒr\ *n* : dinnerware that is usu. blue and white and that is decorated with a storytelling design featuring a large willow tree by a little bridge

wil·lowy \'wil-ə-wē\ *adj* : PLIANT; *also* : gracefully tall and slender ⟨a ∼ young woman⟩

will·pow·er \'wil-ˌpaů(-ə)r\ *n* : energetic determination : RESOLUTENESS

wil·ly-nil·ly \ˌwil-ē-'nil-ē\ *adv* (*or adj*) : without regard for one's choice : by compulsion ⟨they rushed us along ∼⟩

¹wilt \'wilt\ *vb* **1** : to lose or cause to lose freshness and become limp : DROOP **2** : to grow weak or faint : LANGUISH **3** : to lose courage or spirit **4** : to lower the spirit, force, or vigor of

²wilt *n* : any of various plant disorders marked by wilting and often shriveling

Wil·ton \'wilt-°n\ *n* : a carpet or rug with a pile or velvetlike surface

wily \'wī-lē\ *adj* : full of guile : TRICKY ⟨a ∼ player⟩

¹wim·ple \'wim-pəl\ *n* : a cloth covering worn outdoors over the head and around the neck and chin by women esp. in the late medieval period and by some nuns

²wimple *vb* **1** : to cover with or as if with a wimple **2** : to ripple or cause to ripple **3** : to fall or lie in folds

¹win \'win\ *vb* **won** \'wən\ **win·ning** **1** : to gain the victory in or as if in a contest : SUCCEED **2** : to get possession of esp. by effort : GAIN **3** : to gain in or as if in battle or contest; *also* : to be the victor in ⟨won the war⟩ **4** : to obtain by work : EARN **5** : to solicit and gain the favor of; *esp* : to induce to accept oneself in marriage

²win *n* : VICTORY; *esp* : first place at the finish of a horse race

wince \'wins\ *vb* : to shrink back involuntarily (as from pain) : FLINCH — **wince** *n*

winch \'winch\ *n* **1** : a machine to hoist, haul, turn, or strain something forcibly **2** : a crank with a handle for giving motion to a machine (as a grindstone)

¹wind \'wind\ *n* **1** : a movement of the air of any velocity **2** : a force or agency that carries along or influences : TENDENCY, TREND **3** : BREATH ⟨he had the ∼ knocked out of him⟩ **4** : gas generated in the stomach or intestines **5** : something insubstantial; *esp* : idle words **6** : air carrying a scent (as of game) **7** : INTIMATION ⟨they got ∼ of our plans⟩ **8** : WIND INSTRUMENTS; *also, pl* : players of wind instruments

²wind \'wind\ *vb* **1** : to get a scent of ⟨the dogs ∼ed the game⟩ **2** : to cause to be out of breath ⟨he was ∼ed from the climb⟩

ə abut; ᵊ kitten; ər further; a back; ā bake; ä cot, cart; aů out; ch chin; e less; ē easy; g gift; i trip; ī life i joke; ŋ sing; ō flow; ȯ flaw; ȯi coin; th thin; ᵗʰ this; ü loot; ů foot; y yet; yü few; yů furious; zh vision

3 : to allow (as a horse) to rest so as to recover breath

³wind \'wind, 'wind\ *vb* **wound** \'waúnd\ **wind·ing :** to sound by blowing 〈~ a horn〉

⁴wind \'wind\ *vb* **wound** \'waúnd\ *also* **wind·ed; wind·ing :** to have a curving course or shape 〈a river ~ing through the valley〉 **2 :** to move or lie so as to encircle **3 :** ENTANGLE, INVOLVE **4 :** to introduce stealthily **:** INSINUATE **5 :** to encircle or cover with something pliable **:** WRAP, COIL, TWINE, TWIST 〈~ a bobbin〉 **6 :** to hoist or haul up by a rope or chain 〈~ a ship to the wharf〉 **7 :** to tighten the spring of; *also* **:** CRANK **8 :** to raise to a high level (as of excitement) **9 :** to cause to move in a curving line or path **10 :** TURN **11 :** to traverse on a curving course

⁵wind \'wind\ *n* **:** COIL, TURN

wind·age \'win-dij\ *n* **:** the influence of the wind in deflecting the course of a projectile through the air; *also* **:** the amount of such deflection

wind·bag \-(d)-,bag\ *n* **:** an idly talkative person

wind-blown \-,blōn\ *adj* **:** blown by the wind; *also* **:** having the appearance of being blown by the wind

wind-break \-,brāk\ *n* **:** something serving to break the force of the wind; *esp* **:** a growth of trees and shrubs

wind-bro·ken \-,brō-kən\ *adj* **:** having the power of breathing impaired by disease 〈a ~ horse〉

wind-burn \-,bərn\ *n* **:** skin irritation caused by wind

wind·er \'wīn-dər\ *n* **:** one that winds

wind·fall \'win(d)-,fȯl\ *n* **1 :** something (as a tree or fruit) blown down by the wind **2 :** an unexpected or sudden gift, gain, or advantage

wind-flow·er \-,flaú(-ə)r\ *n* **:** ANEMONE

¹wind·ing \'wīn-diŋ\ *n* **:** material (as wire) wound or coiled about an object

²winding *adj* **1 :** having a pronounced curve; *esp* **:** SPIRAL 〈~ stairs〉 **2 :** having a course that winds 〈a ~ road〉

wind·ing-sheet \-,shēt\ *n* **:** SHROUD

wind instrument \'wind-\ *n* **:** a musical instrument (as a flute or horn) sounded by wind and esp. by the breath

wind-jam·mer \'win(d)-,jam-ər\ *n* **:** a sailing ship; *also* **:** one of its crew

wind-lass \'win-dləs\ *n* **:** a machine for hoisting or hauling that consists in its simple form of a horizontal barrel wound with the hoisting rope and supported in vertical frames and that has a crank with a handle for turning it

wind·mill \'win(d)-,mil\ *n* **:** a mill or machine worked by the wind turning sails or vanes that radiate from a central shaft

win·dow \'win-dō\ *n* **1 :** an opening in the wall of a building to let in light and air; *also* **:** the framework with fittings that closes such an opening **2 :** WINDOWPANE **3 :** an opening resembling or suggesting that of a window in a building

win·dow·pane \-,pān\ *n* **:** a pane in a window

win·dow-shop \-,shäp\ *vb* **:** to look at the displays in store windows without going inside the stores to make purchases — **win·dow-shop·per** *n*

win·dow·sill \-,sil\ *n* **:** the horizontal member at the bottom of a window opening

wind·pipe \'win(d)-,pīp\ *n* **:** the passage

for the breath from the larynx to the lungs

wind-proof \-'prüf\ *adj* **:** proof against the wind 〈a ~ jacket〉

wind-row \'win-,(d)rō\ *n* **1 :** hay raked up into a row to dry **2 :** a row of something (as dry leaves) swept up by or as if by the wind

wind-shield \'win(d)-,shēld\ *n* **:** a transparent screen in front of the occupants of a vehicle to protect them from wind and rain

wind-storm \-,stȯrm\ *n* **:** a storm with high wind and little or no precipitation

wind-swept \-,swept\ *adj* **:** swept by or as if by wind 〈~ plains〉

wind up \'win-'dəp\ *vb* **1 :** END **2 :** SETTLE **3 :** to arrive in a place, situation, or condition at the end or as a result of a course of action 〈wound up as paupers〉 **4 :** to give a preliminary swing to the arm

wind-up \-,dəp\ *n* **1 :** CONCLUSION, FINISH **2 :** a pitcher's motion preliminary to delivering a pitch

¹wind·ward \'win-dwərd\ *adj* **:** moving toward or situated on the side toward the direction from which the wind is blowing

²windward *n* **:** the point or side from which the wind is blowing

windy \'win-dē\ *adj* **1 :** having wind **:** exposed to winds 〈a ~ day〉 〈a ~ prairie〉 **2 :** STORMY **3 :** FLATULENT **4 :** indulging in or characterized by useless talk **:** VERBOSE

¹wine \'wīn\ *n* **1 :** fermented grape juice **2 :** the usu. fermented juice of a plant product (as fruit) used as a beverage 〈rice ~〉 〈cherry ~〉

²wine *vb* **:** to treat to or drink wine

wine cellar *n* **:** a room for storing wines; *also* **:** a stock of wines

wine-grow·er \'wīn-,grō(-ə)r\ *n* **:** one that cultivates a vineyard and makes wine

wine-press \-,pres\ *n* **:** a vat in which juice is expressed from grapes by treading or by means of a plunger

wine-shop \-,shäp\ *n* **:** a tavern that specializes in serving wine

¹wing \'wiŋ\ *n* **1 :** one of the movable feathered or membranous paired appendages by means of which a bird, bat, or insect is able to fly **2 :** something suggesting a wing in shape, position, or appearance **3 :** a plant or animal appendage or part likened to a wing; *esp* **:** one that is flat or broadly extended **4 :** a turned-back or extended edge on an article of clothing **5 :** a unit in military aviation consisting of a varying number of airplanes **6 :** a means of flight or rapid progress **7 :** the act or manner of flying **:** FLIGHT **8 :** ARM; *esp* **:** a throwing or pitching arm **9 :** a part of a building projecting from the main part **10** *pl* **:** the area at the side of the stage out of sight **11 :** the right or left division of an army, fleet, or command as it faces an enemy **12 :** a position or player on each side of the center (as in hockey) **13 :** either of two opposing groups within an organization **:** FACTION — **wing·less** *adj* — **on the wing :** in flight **:** FLYING — **under one's wing :** in one's charge or care

²wing *vb* **1 :** to fit with wings; *also* **:** to enable to fly easily **2 :** to pass through in flight **:** FLY 〈~ the air〉 〈swallows ~ing southward〉 **3 :** to achieve or accomplish by flying **4 :** to let fly **:** DIS-

PATCH ⟨~ an arrow through the air⟩ **5** : to wound in the wing ⟨~ a bird⟩; *also* : to wound without killing

winged \'wiŋd, *also except for "esp." sense of 1* 'wiŋ-əd\ *adj* **1** : having wings *esp.* of a specified character **2** : soaring with or as if with wings : ELEVATED **3** : SWIFT, RAPID

wing·span \'wiŋ-,span\ *n* : WINGSPREAD; *esp* : the distance between the tips of an airplane's wings

wing·spread \-,spred\ *n* : the spread of the wings; *esp* : the distance between the tips of the fully extended wings of a winged animal

¹**wink** \'wiŋk\ *vb* **1** : to close and open the eyes quickly : BLINK **2** : to avoid seeing or noticing something ⟨~ at a violation of the law⟩ **3** : TWINKLE, FLICKER **4** : to close and open one eye quickly as a signal or hint **5** : to affect or influence by or as if by blinking the eyes ⟨he ~ed back his tears⟩

²**wink** *n* **1** : a brief period of sleep : NAP **2** : an act of winking; *esp* : a hint or sign given by winking **3** : INSTANT ⟨dries in a ~⟩

wink·er *n* **1** : one that winks **2** : EYELASH

win·kle \'wiŋ-kəl\ *n* **1** : PERIWINKLE **2** : any of various whelks

win·ner *n* : one that wins

win·ning *n* **1** : VICTORY **2** : something won; *esp* : money won at gambling ⟨large ~s⟩

²**winning** *adj* **1** : successful in competition **2** : ATTRACTIVE, CHARMING

win·now \'win-ō\ *vb* **1** : to remove (as chaff from grain) by a current of air; *also* : to free (as grain) from waste in this manner **2** : to get rid of (something unwanted) or to separate, sift, or sort (something) as if by winnowing

win·some \'win-səm\ *adj* **1** : causing joy or pleasure : PLEASANT, WINNING ⟨a ~ lass⟩ **2** : CHEERFUL, GAY — **win·some·ly** *adv* — **win·some·ness** *n*

¹**win·ter** \'wint-ər\ *n* **1** : the season of the year in any region in which the noonday sun shines most obliquely : the coldest period of the year **2** : YEAR ⟨a man of 70 ~s⟩ **3** : a time or season of inactivity or decay

²**winter** *vb* **1** : to pass or survive the winter **2** : to keep, feed, or manage through the winter ⟨~ cattle on silage⟩

³**winter** *adj* **1** : occurring in or surviving winter; *esp* : sown in autumn for harvesting in the following spring or summer ⟨~ wheat⟩

win·ter·green \'wint-ər-,grēn\ *n* **1** : any of several low evergreen plants related to the heaths; *esp* : one with spicy red berries **2** : an aromatic oil from the common wintergreen or its flavor or something flavored with it

win·ter·ize \-,īz\ *vb* : to make ready or safe for use in winter conditions

win·ter·kill \-,kil\ *vb* : to kill or die by exposure to winter weather

win·ter·tide \-,tīd\ *n* : the season of winter : WINTERTIME

win·ter·time \-,tīm\ *n* : WINTER

win·try \'win-t(ə-)rē\ *adj* **1** : of or characteristic of winter : coming in winter ⟨~ weather⟩ **2** : CHILLING, COLD, CHEERLESS ⟨a ~ welcome⟩

¹**wipe** \'wīp\ *vb* **1** : to clean or dry by rubbing ⟨~ dishes⟩ **2** : to remove by or as if by rubbing or cleaning ⟨~ away tears⟩ **3** : to erase completely : OBLITERATE, DESTROY ⟨the regiment was *wiped* out⟩ **4** : to pass or draw over a surface ⟨*wiped* his hand across his face⟩ — **wip·er** *n*

²**wipe** *n* **1** : an act or instance of wiping; *also* : BLOW, STRIKE, SWIPE **2** : something used for wiping

¹**wire** \'wī(ə)r\ *n* **1** : metal in the form of a thread or slender rod; *also* : a thread or rod of metal **2** : work made of wire threads or rods and esp. of wire netting **3** : a telegraph or telephone wire or system **4** : TELEGRAM, CABLEGRAM **5** *usu pl* : hidden or secret influences controlling the action of a person or body of persons ⟨pull ~s to get a nomination⟩ **6** : the finish line of a race

²**wire** *vb* **1** : to provide or equip with wire ⟨~ a house for electricity⟩ **2** : to bind, string, or mount with wire **3** : to telegraph or telegraph to

wire·draw \'wī(ə)r-,dró\ *vb* **1** : to draw (metal) into wire **2** : to draw or spin out to great length, tenuity, or overrefinement

wire·haired \-'haərd\ *adj* : having a stiff wiry outer coat of hair

¹**wire·less** \-ləs\ *adj* **1** : having or using no wire or wires *chiefly Brit* : RADIO

²**wireless** *n* **1** : a system for communicating by code signals and radio waves and without connecting wires **2** *chiefly Brit* : RADIO — **wireless** *vb*

wire·tap \-,tap\ *vb* : to tap a telephone or telegraph wire to get information — **wiretap** *n*

wire·worm \-,wərm\ *n* : the slender hard-coated larva of certain beetles often destructive to plant roots

wir·ing \'wī(ə)r-iŋ\ *n* : a system of wires; *esp* : one for distributing electricity through a building

wiry \-ē\ *adj* **1** : of, relating to, or resembling wire **2** : slender yet strong and sinewy — **wir·i·ness** *n*

wis·dom \'wiz-dəm\ *n* **1** : accumulated learning : KNOWLEDGE; *also* : INSIGHT **2** : good sense : JUDGMENT **3** : a wise attitude or course of action

wisdom tooth *n* : the last tooth of the full set on each half of each jaw in man

¹**wise** \'wīz\ *n* : WAY, MANNER, FASHION ⟨in no ~⟩ ⟨in this ~⟩

²**wise** *adj* **1** : having wisdom : SAGE **2** : having or showing good sense or good judgment : SENSIBLE, SOUND, PRUDENT **3** : aware of what is going on : KNOWING, INFORMED; *also* : CRAFTY, SHREWD — **wise·ly** *adv*

wise·acre \'wīz-,ā-kər\ *n* : one who pretends to knowledge or cleverness

¹**wise·crack** \-,krak\ *n* : a clever, smart, or flippant remark

²**wisecrack** *vb* : to make a wisecrack

¹**wish** \'wish\ *vb* **1** : to have a desire : long for : CRAVE, WANT ⟨~ you were here⟩ ⟨~ for a puppy⟩ **2** : to form or express a wish concerning ⟨~ed him a happy birthday⟩ **3** : BID ⟨he ~ed me good morning⟩ **4** : to request by expressing a desire ⟨I ~ you to go now⟩

²**wish** *n* **1** : an act or instance of wishing

ə abut; ⁹ kitten; ər further; a back; ā bake; ä cot, cart; aù out; ch chin; e less; ē easy; g gift; i trip; I life; j joke; ŋ sing; ō flow; ò flaw; òi coin; th thin; t̲h̲ this; ü loot; ù foot; y yet; yü few; yù furious; zh vision

or desire : WANT; *also* : GOAL **2** : an expressed will or desire : MANDATE

wish·bone \-ˌbōn\ *n* : a forked bone in front of the breastbone in most birds

wish·ful *adj* **1** : expressive of a wish : HOPEFUL, LONGING; *also* : DESIROUS **2** : according with wishes rather than fact ⟨~ thinking⟩

wishy–washy \'wish-ē-ˌwȯsh-ē, -ˌwäsh-\ *adj* : WEAK, INSIPID; *also* : morally feeble

wisp \'wisp\ *n* **1** : a small bunch of hay or straw **2** : a thin strand, strip, or fragment ⟨a ~ of hair⟩; *also* : a thready streak ⟨a ~ of smoke⟩ **3** : something frail, slight, or fleeting ⟨a ~ of a girl⟩ ⟨a ~ of a smile⟩

wis·te·ria \wis-'tir-ē-ə\ *or* **wis·tar·ia** \-'tir-, -'ter-\ *n* : any of various Asiatic woody vines related to the peas and widely grown for their long showy clusters of blue, white, purple, or rose flowers

wist·ful \'wist-fəl\ *adj* : full of unfulfilled longing or desire : YEARNING ⟨a ~ expression⟩ — **wist·ful·ly** *adv* — **wist·ful·ness** *n*

wit \'wit\ *n* **1** : reasoning power : INTELLIGENCE **2** : mental soundness : SANITY — usu. used in pl. **3** : RESOURCEFULNESS, INGENUITY; *esp* : quickness and cleverness in handling words and ideas **4** : a talent for making clever remarks; *also* : one noted for making witty remarks — **at one's wit's end** : at a loss for a means of solving a problem

¹witch \'wich\ *n* **1** : a person believed to have magic power; *esp* : SORCERESS **2** : an ugly old woman : HAG **3** : a charming or unusually attractive girl or woman

²witch *vb* : BEWITCH

witch·craft \-ˌkraft\ *n* : the power or practices of a witch : SORCERY

witch doctor *n* : a practitioner of magic in a primitive society

witch·ery \'wich-(ə-)rē\ *n* **1** : SORCERY **2** : FASCINATION, CHARM

witch ha·zel \'wich-ˌhā-zəl\ *n* **1** : a No. American shrub having small yellow flowers after the leaves have fallen **2** : an alcoholic solution of material from witch hazel bark used as a soothing astringent lotion

witch–hunt \-ˌhənt\ *n* **1** : a searching out and persecution of persons accused of witchcraft **2** : the searching out and deliberate harassment of those (as political opponents) with unpopular views

witch·ing *adj* **1** : of, relating to, or suitable for sorcery or supernatural occurrences **2** : BEWITCHING, FASCINATING

wi·te·na·ge·mot *or* **wi·te·na·ge·mote** \'wit-ᵊn-ə-gə-ˌmōt\ *n* : an Anglo-Saxon council of nobles, prelates, and officials to advise the king on administrative and judicial matters

with \(ˈ)with, (ˈ)with\ *prep* **1** : AGAINST ⟨a fight ~ his wife⟩ **2** : in mutual relation to ⟨talk ~ a friend⟩ **3** : as regards : TOWARD ⟨patient ~ children⟩ **4** : compared to ⟨on equal terms ~ another⟩ **5** : in support of ⟨I'm ~ you all the way⟩ **6** : in the opinion of : as judged by ⟨their arguments had weight ~ him⟩ **7** : because of : THROUGH ⟨pale ~ anger⟩ **8** : in a manner indicating ⟨work ~ a will⟩ **9** : GIVEN, GRANTED ⟨~ your permission I'll leave⟩ **10** : in the company of ⟨a professor ~ his students⟩ **11** : HAVING ⟨came ~ good news⟩ ⟨stood

there ~ his mouth open⟩ **12** : DESPITE ⟨~ all his cleverness, he failed⟩ **13** : at the time of : right after ⟨~ that he paused⟩ **14** : CONTAINING ⟨tea ~ sugar⟩ **15** : FROM ⟨parting ~ friends⟩ **16** : by means of ⟨hit him ~ a club⟩ **17** : so as not to cross or oppose ⟨swim ~ the tide⟩

with·al \with-'ȯl, with-\ *adv* **1** : together with this : BESIDES **2** *archaic* : THEREWITH **3** : on the other hand : NEVERTHELESS

with·draw \with-'drȯ, with-\ *vb* **1** : to take back or away : draw away : REMOVE **2** : to call back (as from consideration) : RECALL, RESCIND; *also* : RETRACT ⟨~ an accusation⟩ **3** : to go away : RETREAT, LEAVE **4** : to terminate one's participation in or use of something — **with·draw·al** \-'drȯ-(ə)l\ *n*

with·drawn \-'drȯn\ *adj* **1** : ISOLATED, SECLUDED **2** : socially detached and unresponsive

withe \'with\ *n* : a slender flexible twig or branch; *esp* : one used as a band or rope

with·er \'with-ər\ *vb* **1** : to become dry and shrunken; *esp* : to shrivel from or as if from loss of bodily moisture **2** : to lose or cause to lose vitality, force, or freshness **3** : to cause to feel shriveled or blighted : STUN ⟨~ed him with a glance⟩

with·ers \'with-ərz\ *n pl* : the ridge between the shoulder bones of a horse

with·hold \with-'hōld, with-\ *vb* **1** : to hold back : RESTRAIN; *also* : RETAIN **2** : to refrain from granting, giving, or allowing ⟨~ permission⟩ ⟨~ names⟩

withholding tax *n* : a tax on income withheld at the source

¹with·in \with-'in, with-\ *adv* **1** : in or into the interior : INSIDE **2** : inside oneself : INWARDLY ⟨calm without but furious ~⟩

²within *prep* **1** : in or to the inner part of ⟨~ the room⟩ **2** : in the limits or compass of ⟨~ a mile⟩ **3** : inside the limits or influence of ⟨~ call⟩

¹with·out \with-'aut, with-\ *prep* **1** : at, to, or on the outside of ⟨~ the gate⟩ **2** : out of the limits of **3** : LACKING ⟨he's ~ hope⟩; *also* : unaccompanied or unmarked by ⟨spoke ~ thinking⟩ ⟨took his punishment ~ flinching⟩

²without *adv* **1** : on the outside : EXTERNALLY **2** : with something lacking or absent ⟨has learned to do ~⟩

with·stand \with-'stand, with-\ *vb* : to stand against : RESIST; *esp* : to oppose (as an attack or bad influence) successfully

withy \'with-ē\ *n* : WITHE

wit·less \'wit-ləs\ *adj* : lacking wit or understanding : mentally defective : FOOLISH — **wit·less·ly** *adv* — **wit·less·ness** *n*

¹wit·ness \'wit-nəs\ *n* **1** : TESTIMONY ⟨bear ~ to the fact⟩ **2** : one that gives evidence; *esp* : one who testifies in a cause or before a court **3** : one present at a transaction so as to be able to testify that it has taken place **4** : one who has personal knowledge or experience of something **5** : something serving as evidence or proof : SIGN

²witness *vb* **1** : to bear witness : ATTEST, TESTIFY **2** : to act as legal witness of **3** : to furnish proof of : BETOKEN **4** : to be a witness of **5** : to be the scene of ⟨this region has ~ed many wars⟩

wit·ted \'wit-əd\ *adj* : having wit or understanding ⟨dull-*witted*⟩

wit·ti·cism \'wit-ə-,siz-əm\ *n* : a witty saying or phrase

wit·ting \'wit-iŋ\ *adj* : done knowingly : INTENTIONAL — **wit·ting·ly** *adv*

wit·ty \'wit-ē\ *adj* : marked by or full of wit : AMUSING ⟨a ~ writer⟩ ⟨a ~ remark⟩ **syn** humorous, facetious, jocular, jocose

wive \'wīv\ *vb* 1 : to marry a woman 2 : to take for a wife

wives *pl of* WIFE

wiz·ard \'wiz-ərd\ *n* [ME *wysard* wise man, fr. *wys* wise] 1 : MAGICIAN, SORCERER 2 : a very clever or skillful person ⟨a ~ at chess⟩

wiz·ard·ry *n* : magic skill : SORCERY, WITCHCRAFT

wiz·ened \'wiz-ʰnd\ *adj* : dried up : SHRIVELED, WITHERED

woad \'wōd\ *n* : a European herb related to the mustards; *also* : a blue dye-stuff made from its leaves

wob·ble \'wäb-əl\ *vb* 1 : to move or cause to move with an irregular rocking or side-to-side motion 2 : TREMBLE, QUAVER 3 : WAVER, VACILLATE — **wob·ble** *n* — **wob·bly** \-(ə-)lē\ *adj*

woe \'wō\ *n* 1 : a condition of deep suffering from misfortune, affliction, or grief 2 : CALAMITY, MISFORTUNE ⟨economic ~*s*⟩

woe·be·gone \'wō-bi-,gòn\ *adj* : exhibiting woe, sorrow, or misery; *also* : DISMAL, DESOLATE

woe·ful *also* **wo·ful** \'wō-fəl\ *adj* 1 : full of woe : AFFLICTED 2 : involving, bringing, or relating to woe ⟨~ poverty⟩ 3 : PALTRY, DEPLORABLE — **woe·ful·ly** *adv*

woke *past of* WAKE

woken *past part of* WAKE

wold \'wōld\ *n* : an upland plain or stretch of rolling land without woods

¹wolf \'wùlf\ *n, pl* **wolves** \'wùlvz\ 1 : any of several large erect-eared bushy-tailed doglike mammals that are crafty, greedy, and destructive to game and livestock 2 : a fierce or destructive person 3 : a man forward, direct, and zealous in amatory attentions to women — **wolf·ish** *adj*

²wolf *vb* : to eat greedily : DEVOUR

wolf·hound \-,haùnd\ *n* : any of several large dogs orig. used in hunting wolves

wol·fram \'wùl-frəm\ *n* : TUNGSTEN

wolfs·bane \'wùlfs-,bān\ *n* : ACONITE 1; *esp* : a poisonous yellow-flowered Eurasian herb

wol·ver·ine \,wùl-və-'rēn\ *n* : a dark shaggy-coated American flesh-eating mammal related to the sables and noted for cunning and gluttony

wom·an \'wùm-ən\ *n, pl* **wom·en** \'wim-ən\ [OE *wīfman*, fr. *wīf* woman, wife + *man* man] 1 : an adult female person 2 : WOMANKIND 3 : feminine nature : WOMANLINESS 4 : a female servant or attendant

wom·an·hood \-,hùd\ *n* 1 : the state of being a woman : the distinguishing qualities of a woman or of womankind 2 : WOMEN, WOMANKIND

wom·an·ish *adj* 1 : of, relating to, or characteristic of a woman 2 : suitable to a woman rather than to a man : EFFEMINATE

wom·an·kind \'wùm-ən-,kīnd\ *n* : the females of the human race : WOMEN

wom·an·like *adj* : WOMANLY

wom·an·ly *adj* : having the qualities characteristic of a woman — **wom·an·li·ness** *n*

woman suffrage *n* : the possession and exercise of suffrage by women

womb \'wüm\ *n* 1 : UTERUS 2 : a place where something is generated or developed

wom·bat \'wäm-,bat\ *n* : an Australian burrowing marsupial mammal resembling a small bear

wom·en·folk \'wim-ən-,fōk\ *or* **wom·en·folks** \-,fōks\ *n pl* : WOMEN

¹won *past of* WIN

²won \'wòn\ *n, pl* **won** — see MONEY table

¹won·der \'wən-dər\ *n* 1 : a cause of astonishment or surprise : MARVEL; *also* : MIRACLE 2 : a feeling (as of awed astonishment or uncertainty) aroused by something extraordinary or affecting 3 : the quality of exciting wonder ⟨the charm and ~ of the scene⟩

²wonder *vb* 1 : to feel surprise or amazement 2 : to feel curiosity or doubt

wonder drug *n* : a medicinal substance of outstanding effectiveness

won·der·ful \'wən-dər-fəl\ *adj* 1 : exciting wonder : MARVELOUS, ASTONISHING 2 : unusually good : ADMIRABLE — **won·der·ful·ly** *adv*

won·der·land \-,land, -lənd\ *n* 1 : a fairylike imaginary realm 2 : a place that excites admiration or wonder

won·der·ment \-mənt\ *n* 1 : ASTONISHMENT, SURPRISE 2 : a cause of or occasion for wonder 3 : curiosity about something

won·drous \'wən-drəs\ *adj* : WONDERFUL, MARVELOUS — **wondrous** *adv, archaic* — **won·drous·ly** *adv*

¹wont \'wònt, 'wōnt\ *adj* 1 : ACCUSTOMED, USED ⟨as he was ~ to do⟩ 2 : INCLINED, APT

²wont *n* : CUSTOM, USAGE, HABIT ⟨according to her ~⟩

wont·ed *adj* : ACCUSTOMED, CUSTOMARY ⟨his ~ courtesy⟩

woo \'wü\ *vb* 1 : to sue for the affection of and usu. marriage with : COURT 2 : SOLICIT, ENTREAT 3 : to try to gain or bring about ⟨~ public favor⟩

¹wood \'wùd\ *n* 1 : a dense growth of trees usu. larger than a grove and smaller than a forest — often used in pl. 2 : a hard fibrous substance that forms the bulk of trees and shrubs beneath the bark; *also* : this material fit or prepared for some use (as burning or building) 3 : something made of wood

²wood *adj* 1 : WOODEN 2 : suitable for holding, cutting, or working with wood 3 *or* **woods** \'wùdz\ : living or growing in woods

³wood *vb* 1 : to supply or load with wood esp. for fuel 2 : to cover with a growth of trees

wood alcohol *n* : a flammable liquid that resembles ordinary alcohol but is very poisonous and is used as a solvent and an antifreeze

wood·bine \'wùd-,bīn\ *n* : any of several climbing vines (as a honeysuckle)

wood block *n* 1 : a block of wood 2 : a

ə abut; ᵊ kitten; ər further; a back; ā bake; ä cot, cart; aù out; ch chin; e less; ē easy; g gift; i trip; ī life; j joke; ŋ sing; ō flow; ò flaw; òi coin; th thin; th this; ü loot; ù foot; y yet; yü few; yù furious; zh vision

die for printing cut in relief on wood; *also* : a print from such a die

wood·chop·per \'wud-ˌchäp-ər\ *n* : one engaged esp. in chopping down trees

wood·chuck \-ˌchək\ *n* : a thickset grizzled marmot of the northeastern U. S. and Canada

wood·cock \-ˌkäk\ *n* : either of two long-billed mottled birds related to the snipe; *esp* : an American upland game bird

wood·craft \-ˌkraft\ *n* 1 : skill and practice in matters relating to the woods esp. in maintaining oneself and making one's way in or hunting or trapping 2 : skill in shaping or constructing articles from wood

wood·cut \-ˌkət\ *n* : an engraving on wood; *also* : a print from such an engraving

wood·cut·ter \-ˌkət-ər\ *n* : a person who cuts wood esp. as an occupation

wood·ed \-əd\ *adj* : covered with woods or trees 〈~ slopes〉

wood·en \'wud-ᵊn\ *adj* 1 : made of wood 2 : lacking resilience : STIFF 3 : AWKWARD, CLUMSY — **wood·en·ly** *adv*

wood·en·ware \-ˌwaər\ *n* : articles made of wood for domestic use

wood·land \'wud-lənd, -ˌland\ *n* : land covered with trees : FOREST

wood·lot \-ˌlät\ *n* : a relatively small area of trees kept usu. to meet fuel and timber needs 〈a farm ~〉

wood louse *n* : a small flat grayish crustacean that lives esp. under stones and bark

wood·man \'wud-mən\ *n* : WOODSMAN

wood·note \-ˌnōt\ *n* : a sound or call (as of a bird) natural in a wood

wood nymph *n* : a nymph living in the woods

wood·peck·er \'wud-ˌpek-ər\ *n* : any of various usu. brightly marked climbing birds with stiff spiny tail feathers and a chisellike bill used to drill into trees for insects

wood·pile \-ˌpīl\ *n* : a pile of wood and esp. firewood

wood·ruff \-ˌ(ˌ)rəf\ *n* : a small European sweet-scented herb used in perfumery and in flavoring wine

wood·shed \-ˌshed\ *n* : a shed for storing wood and esp. firewood

woods·man \'wudz-mən\ *n* : one who frequents or works in the woods; *esp* : one skilled in woodcraft

woodsy \'wud-zē\ *adj* : relating to or suggestive of woods

wood·wind \'wud-ˌwind\ *n* : one of a group of wind instruments including flutes, clarinets, oboes, bassoons, and sometimes saxophones

wood·work \-ˌwərk\ *n* : work made of wood; *esp* : interior fittings (as moldings or stairways) of wood

woody \-ē\ *adj* 1 : abounding or overgrown with woods 2 : of or containing wood or wood fibers 3 : resembling or characteristic of wood

wood·yard \-ˌyärd\ *n* : a yard for storing or sawing wood

woo·er \'wü-ər\ *n* : one that woos; *esp* : SUITOR

woof \'wüf, 'wuf\ *n* 1 : the threads in a woven fabric that cross the warp 2 : a woven fabric; *also* : its texture

wool \'wul\ *n* 1 : the soft wavy or curly hair of some mammals and esp. the sheep; *also* : something (as a textile or garment) made of wool 2 : short thick often crisply curled human hair 3 : a

light and fleecy woollike substance — **wooled** *adj*

¹wool·en *or* **wool·len** *adj* 1 : made of wool 2 : of or relating to the manufacture or sale of woolen products 〈~ mills〉

²woolen *or* **woollen** *n* 1 : a fabric made of wool 2 : garments of woolen fabric — usu. used in pl.

wool·gath·er·ing \'wul-ˌgath-(ə-)riŋ\ *n* : the act of indulging in stray fancies

¹wool·ly *also* **wooly** \'wul-ē\ *adj* 1 : of, relating to, or bearing wool 2 : consisting of or resembling wool 3 : CONFUSED, BLURRY 〈~ thinking〉 4 : marked by a lack of order or restraint 〈the wild and ~ West of frontier times〉

²woolly *also* **wooly** *n* : a garment made from wool; *esp* : underclothing of knitted wool

wool·sack \'wul-ˌsak\ *n* 1 : a sack of or for wool 2 : the seat of the Lord Chancellor in the House of Lords

woo·zy \'wü-zē\ *adj* 1 : BEFUDDLED 2 : somewhat dizzy, nauseated, or weak

¹word \'wərd\ *n* 1 : something that is said; *esp* : a brief remark 2 : a speech sound or series of speech sounds that communicates a meaning; *also* : a graphic representation of such a sound or series of sounds 3 : ORDER, COMMAND 4 *often cap* : the second person of the Trinity; *also* : GOSPEL 5 : NEWS, INFORMATION 6 : PROMISE 7 *pl* : QUARREL, DISPUTE 8 : a verbal signal : PASSWORD — **word·less** *adj*

²word *vb* : to express in words : PHRASE

word·book \-ˌbuk\ *n* : VOCABULARY, DICTIONARY

word·ing *n* : verbal expression : PHRASEOLOGY

word·play \'wərd-ˌplā\ *n* : verbal wit

wordy *adj* : using many words : VERBOSE syn prolix, diffuse, redundant — **word·i·ness** *n*

wore *past of* WEAR

¹work \'wərk\ *n* 1 : TOIL, LABOR; *also* : EMPLOYMENT 〈out of ~〉 2 : TASK, JOB 〈have ~ to do〉 3 : DEED, ACHIEVEMENT 4 : material in the process of manufacture 5 : something produced by mental effort or physical labor; *esp* : an artistic production (as a book or needlework) 6 *pl* : engineering structures 7 *pl* : the buildings, grounds, and machinery of a factory 8 *pl* : the moving parts of a mechanism 9 : WORKMANSHIP 〈careless ~〉 10 : a fortified structure of any kind 11 : the transference of energy when a force produces movement of a body 12 *pl* : everything possessed, available, or belonging 〈the whole ~s went overboard〉; *also* : subjection to drastic treatment 〈gave him the ~s〉 syn occupation, employment, business, pursuit, calling, travail, grind, drudgery

²work *adj* 1 : suitable or styled for wear while working 〈~ clothes〉 2 : used for work 〈~ elephants〉

³work *vb* **worked** *or* **wrought** \'rȯt\ **work·ing** 1 : to bring to pass : EFFECT 2 : to fashion or create by expending labor or exertion upon 3 : to prepare for use esp. by stirring or kneading 4 : to bring into a desired form by a gradual process of cutting, hammering, scraping, pressing, or stretching 〈~ cold steel〉 5 : to set or keep in operation : OPERATE 〈a pump ~ed by hand〉 6 : to solve by reasoning or calculation 〈~ a problem〉 7 : to cause to toil or labor ⟨~ed his men hard⟩; *also* : EXPLOIT **8** : to pay for with labor or service ⟨~ off a debt⟩ **9** : to bring into some (specified) position or condition by stages ⟨the stream ~ed itself clear⟩ **10** : CONTRIVE, ARRANGE ⟨we'll go if we can ~ it⟩ **11** : to practice trickery or cajolery on for some end ⟨~ed the management for a free ticket⟩ **12** : EXCITE, PROVOKE ⟨~ed himself into a rage⟩ **13** : to exert oneself physically or mentally; *esp* : to perform work regularly for wages **14** : to function according to plan or design **15** : to produce a desired effect : SUCCEED **16** : to make way slowly and with difficulty ⟨he ~ed forward through the crowd⟩ **17** : to permit of being worked ⟨this wood ~s easily⟩ **18** : to be in restless motion; *also* : FERMENT 1 **19** : to move slightly in relation to another part; *also* : to get into a specified condition slowly or imperceptibly ⟨the knot ~ed loose⟩ — **work on 1** : AFFECT **2** : to try to influence or persuade — **work upon** : to have effect upon : operate on : PERSUADE, INFLUENCE

work·a·ble *adj* **1** : capable of being worked **2** : PRACTICABLE, FEASIBLE

work·a·day \'wərk-ə-,dā\ *adj* **1** : relating to or suited for working days **2** : PROSAIC, ORDINARY

work·bag \'wərk-,bag\ *n* : a bag for holding implements or materials for work; *esp* : a bag for needlework

work·bas·ket \-,bas-kət\ *n* : a basket for needlework

work·bench \-,bench\ *n* : a bench on which work esp. of mechanics, machinists, and carpenters is performed

work·book \-,bŭk\ *n* **1** : a booklet outlining a course of study **2** : a workman's manual **3** : a record book of work done **4** : a student's individual book of problems to be solved directly on the pages

work·box \-,bäks\ *n* : a box for work instruments and materials

work·day \-,dā\ *n* **1** : a day on which work is done as distinguished from Sunday or a holiday **2** : the period of time in a day when work is performed

work·er *n* **1** : one that works; *esp* : a person who works for wages **2** : one of the sexually undeveloped individuals of a colony of social insects (as bees, ants, or termites) that perform the work of the community

work·horse \'wərk-,hòrs\ *n* **1** : a horse used chiefly for labor **2** : a person who undertakes arduous labor

work·house \-,haủs\ *n* **1** *Brit* : POORHOUSE **2** : a house of correction where persons who have committed a minor offense are confined

¹work·ing \'wər-kiŋ\ *adj* **1** : adequate to allow work to be done ⟨a ~ majority⟩ ⟨a ~ knowledge of French⟩ **2** : adopted or assumed to help further work or activity ⟨a ~ draft of a peace treaty⟩

²working *n* **1** : manner of functioning : OPERATION **2** *pl* : an excavation made in mining or tunneling

work·ing·man \-,man\ *n* : one who works for wages usu. at manual labor or in industry

work·man \'wərk-mən\ *n* **1** : WORKINGMAN **2** : ARTISAN, CRAFTSMAN

work·man·like *adj* : worthy of a good workman : SKILLFUL

work·man·ship *n* : the art or skill of a workman : CRAFTSMANSHIP; *also* : the quality imparted to something in the process of making it ⟨a vase of exquisite ~⟩

work·out \'wərk-,aủt\ *n* **1** : a practice or exercise to test or improve one's fitness esp. for athletic competition, ability, or performance **2** : a test or trial to determine ability or capacity or suitability

work·room \-,rüm, -,rủm\ *n* : a room used esp. for manual work

work·shop \-,shäp\ *n* **1** : a small establishment where manufacturing or handicrafts are carried on **2** : a seminar emphasizing exchange of ideas and practical methods and given mainly for adults already employed in the field

work·ta·ble \-,tā-bəl\ *n* : a table for holding working materials and implements (as for needlework)

world \'wərld\ *n* **1** : UNIVERSE, CREATION **2** : the earth with its inhabitants and all things upon it **3** : people in general : MANKIND **4** : a state of existence : scene of life and action ⟨the ~ of the future⟩ **5** : a great number or quantity ⟨a ~ of troubles⟩ **6** : a part or section of the earth or its inhabitants by itself **7** : the affairs of men ⟨withdraw from the ~⟩ **8** : a heavenly body esp. if inhabited **9** : a distinctive class of persons or their sphere of interest ⟨the musical ~⟩

world–beat·er \-,bēt-ər\ *n* : one that excels all others of its kind

world·ling \-liŋ\ *n* : a person absorbed in the affairs and pleasures of the present world

world·ly \'wərld-lē\ *adj* **1** : of, relating to, or devoted to this world and its pursuits rather than to religion or spiritual affairs **2** : WORLDLY-WISE, SOPHISTICATED — **world·li·ness** *n*

world·ly–wise \-,wīz\ *adj* : wise as to things and ways of this world

world–wide \'wərld-'wīd\ *adj* : extended throughout the entire world ⟨~ fame⟩

¹worm \'wərm\ *n* **1** : an earthworm or a closely related and similar animal; *also* : any of various small long usu. naked and soft-bodied creeping animals (as a maggot) **2** : a human being who is an object of contempt, loathing, or pity : WRETCH **3** : something that inwardly torments or devours **4** : a spiral or wormlike thing (as the thread of a screw) **5** *pl* : infestation with or disease caused by parasitic worms — **wormy** *adj*

²worm *vb* **1** : to move or cause to move or proceed slowly and deviously **2** : to insinuate or introduce (oneself) by devious or subtle means **3** : to free from worms ⟨~ a dog⟩ **4** : to obtain or extract by artful or insidious pleading, asking, or persuading ⟨~ed the truth out of him⟩

worm–eat·en \'wərm-,ēt-ʼn\ *adj* **1** : eaten or burrowed by worms **2** : PITTED **3** : WORN-OUT, ANTIQUATED ⟨tried to update the ~ regulations⟩

worm gear *n* **1** : WORM WHEEL **2** : a gear consisting of a short threaded revolving

ə abut; ᵊ kitten; ər further; a back; ā bake; ä cot, cart; aủ out; ch chin; e less; ē easy; g gift; i trip; ī life; j joke; ŋ sing; ō flow; ȯ flaw; ȯi coin; th thin; <u>th</u> this; ü loot; ủ foot; y yet; yü few; yủ furious; zh vision

screw and a worm wheel meshing and working together

worm·hole \'wərm-ˌhōl\ *n* : a hole or passage burrowed by a worm

worm wheel *n* : a toothed wheel gearing with the threads of a revolving threaded screw

worm·wood \'wərm-ˌwu̇d\ *n* **1** : any of several aromatic woody herbs related to the daisies; *esp* : a European plant used in making absinthe **2** : something bitter or grievous : BITTERNESS

worn *past part of* WEAR

worn–out \'wōrn-'au̇t\ *adj* : exhausted or used up by or as if by wear ⟨an old ~ suit⟩ ⟨a ~ automobile⟩

wor·ri·some \'wər-ē-səm\ *adj* **1** : causing distress or worry **2** : inclined to worry or fret

¹wor·ry \'wər-ē\ *vb* **1** : to shake and mangle with the teeth ⟨a terrier ~ing a rat⟩ **2** : TROUBLE, PLAGUE ⟨his poor health *worries* his parents⟩ **3** : to feel or express great care or anxiety : FRET — **wor·ri·er** *n*

²worry *n* **1** : ANXIETY **2** : a cause of anxiety : TROUBLE

wor·ry·wart \-ˌwȯrt\ *n* : one who is inclined to worry unduly

¹worse \'wərs\ *adj, comparative of* BAD *or of* ILL **1** : bad or evil in a greater degree : less good; *esp* : more unwell **2** : more unfavorable, unpleasant, or painful

²worse *n* **1** : one that is worse **2** : a greater degree of ill or badness

³worse *adv, comparative of* BAD *or of* ILL : in a worse manner : to a worse extent or degree

wors·en \'wərs-ᵊn\ *vb* : to make or become worse

¹wor·ship \'wər-shəp\ *n* [OE *weorthscipe* honor, respect, fr. *weorth* worth, worthy + *-scipe* -ship, suffix denoting quality or condition] **1** *chiefly Brit* : a person of importance — used as a title for officials (as magistrates and some mayors) **2** : reverence toward God, a god, or a sacred object; *also* : the expression of such reverence **3** : extravagant respect or admiration for or devotion to an object of esteem ⟨~ of the dollar⟩

²worship *vb* **-shiped** *or* **-shipped**; **-ship·ing** *or* **-ship·ping** **1** : to honor or reverence as a divine being or supernatural power **2** : IDOLIZE **3** : to perform or take part in worship — **wor·ship·er** *or* **wor·ship·per** *n*

wor·ship·ful *adj* **1** *archaic* : NOTABLE, DISTINGUISHED **2** *chiefly Brit* — used as a title for various persons or groups of rank or distinction **3** : VENERATING, WORSHIPING

¹worst \'wərst\ *adj, superlative of* BAD *or of* ILL **1** : most bad, evil, ill, or corrupt **2** : most unfavorable, unpleasant, or painful; *also* : most unsuitable, faulty, or unattractive **3** : least skillful or efficient **4** : most wanting in quality, value, or condition

²worst *n* **1** : one that is worst **2** : the greatest degree of ill or badness

³worst *adv, superlative of* ILL *or of* BAD *or* BADLY : to the extreme degree of badness or inferiority : in the worst manner

⁴worst *vb* : DEFEAT

wor·sted \'wu̇s-təd, 'wər-\ *n* : a smooth compact yarn from long wool fibers used esp. for firm napless fabrics, carpeting, or knitting; *also* : a fabric made from such yarn

¹wort \'wərt, 'wȯrt\ *n* : PLANT; *esp* : an herbaceous plant

²wort *n* : a solution obtained by infusion from malt and fermented to form beer

¹worth \'wərth\ *prep* **1** : equal in value to; *also* : having possessions or income equal to **2** : deserving of ⟨well ~ the effort⟩ **3** : capable of ⟨ran for all he was ~⟩

²worth *n* **1** : monetary value : the equivalent of a specified amount or figure **2** : the value of something measured by its qualities or by the esteem in which it is held **3** : moral or personal value : MERIT, EXCELLENCE **4** : WEALTH, RICHES

worth·less *adj* **1** : lacking worth : VALUELESS; *also* : USELESS **2** : LOW, DESPICABLE — **worth·less·ness** *n*

worth·while \'wərth-'hwīl\ *adj* : being worth the time or effort spent

¹wor·thy \'wər-thē\ *adj* **1** : having worth or value : ESTIMABLE **2** : HONORABLE, MERITORIOUS **3** : having sufficient worth ⟨a man ~ of the honor⟩ — **wor·thi·ly** *adv* — **wor·thi·ness** *n*

²worthy *n* : a worthy person

would \wəd, (ə)d, (')wu̇d\ *past of* WILL **1** *archaic* : wish for : WANT ⟨he ~ a word with you⟩ **2** : strongly desire : WISH ⟨I ~ I were young again⟩ **3** — used as an auxiliary to express preference, wish or desire, intention, habitual action, a contingency or possibility, probability, capability, a request, or simple futurity from a point of view in the past **4** : COULD **5** : SHOULD

would–be \'wu̇d-ˌbē\ *adj* : desiring or professing to be ⟨a ~ artist⟩

¹wound \'wu̇nd\ *n* **1** : an injury in which the skin is broken (as by violence or by surgery) **2** : an injury or hurt to feelings or reputation

²wound *vb* : to inflict a wound to or in

³wound \'wau̇nd\ *past of* WIND

wove *past of* WEAVE

woven *past part of* WEAVE

¹wrack \'rak\ *n* **1** : RUIN, DESTRUCTION **2** : a remnant of something destroyed

²wrack *n* **1** : a wrecked ship; *also* : WRECKAGE, WRECK **2** : sea vegetation (as kelp) esp. when cast up upon the shore

wraith \'rāth\ *n* **1** : APPARITION; *also* : GHOST, SPECTER **2** : an insubstantial appearance : SHADOW

¹wran·gle \'raŋ-gəl\ *vb* **1** : to quarrel angrily or peevishly : BICKER **2** : ARGUE **3** : to obtain by persistent arguing **4** : to herd and care for (livestock) on the range — **wran·gler** *n*

²wrangle *n* : an angry, noisy, or prolonged dispute or quarrel; *also* : CONTROVERSY

¹wrap \'rap\ *vb* **wrapped**; **wrap·ping** **1** : to cover esp. by winding or folding **2** : to envelop and secure for transportation or storage : BUNDLE **3** : to enclose wholly : ENFOLD **4** : to coil, fold, draw, or twine about something **5** : SURROUND, ENVELOP; *also* : SUFFUSE **6** : INVOLVE, ENGROSS ⟨*wrapped* up in a hobby⟩ **7** : to conceal as if by enveloping or enfolding : HIDE **8** : to put on clothing : DRESS **9** : to be subject to covering or enclosing ⟨~s up into a small package⟩

²wrap *n* **1** : WRAPPER, WRAPPING **2** : an article of clothing that may be wrapped around a person; *esp* : an outer garment (as a coat or shawl)

wrap·around \'rap-ə-ˌrau̇nd\ *n* : a garment (as a dress) made with a full-length opening and adjusted to the figure by wrapping around

wrap·per n 1 : that in which something is wrapped 2 : one that wraps 3 : an article of clothing worn wrapped around the body; *also* : a loose outer garment

wrap·ping n : something used to wrap an object : WRAPPER

wrap up \\'rap-'əp\\ vb 1 : END, CONCLUDE 2 : to make a single comprehensive report of

wrap-up \\-,əp\\ n : a summarizing news report

wrasse \\'ras\\ n : any of various usu. brightly colored spiny-finned sea fishes including many food fishes

wrath \\'rath\\ n 1 : violent anger : RAGE 2 : retributory punishment for an offense or a crime : divine chastisement syn indignation, ire, fury

wrath·ful adj 1 : filled with wrath : very angry 2 : showing, marked by, or arising from anger — **wrath·ful·ly** adv

wreak \\'rēk\\ vb 1 : to exact as a punishment : INFLICT ⟨~ vengeance on an enemy⟩ 2 : to give free scope or rein to ⟨~ed his wrath⟩

wreath \\'rēth\\ n : something (as boughs or flowers) intertwined into a circular shape

wreathe \\'rēth\\ vb 1 : to twist or become twisted esp. so as to show folds or creases ⟨a face *wreathed* in smiles⟩ 2 : to shape or take on the shape of a wreath : move or extend in circles or spirals 3 : to fold or coil around : ENTWINE

¹**wreck** \\'rek\\ n 1 : something (as goods) cast up on the land by the sea after a shipwreck 2 : broken remains (as of a ship or vehicle after heavy damage) 3 : something disabled or in a state of ruin; *also* : an individual broken in health or strength 4 : SHIPWRECK 5 : the action of breaking up or destroying something : WRECKING

²**wreck** vb 1 : SHIPWRECK 2 : to ruin or damage by breaking up : involve in disaster or ruin

wreck·age n 1 : the act of wrecking : the state of being wrecked : RUIN 2 : the remains of a wreck

wreck·er n 1 : one that wrecks; *esp* : one occupied with tearing down and removing buildings 2 : one who searches for or works upon the wrecks of ships 3 : an automotive vehicle equipped to remove disabled cars

wren \\'ren\\ n : any of various small mostly brown singing birds with short wings and tail

¹**wrench** \\'rench\\ vb 1 : to move with a violent twist 2 : to pull, strain, or tighten with violent twisting or force 3 : to injure or disable by a violent twisting or straining 4 : to change (as the meaning of a word) violently : DISTORT 5 : to snatch forcibly : WREST 6 : to cause to suffer anguish

²**wrench** n 1 : a forcible twisting; *also* : an injury (as to one's ankle) by twisting 2 : a tool for exerting a twisting force (as on a nut or bolt)

¹**wrest** \\'rest\\ vb 1 : to pull or move by a forcible twisting movement 2 : to gain with difficulty by or as if by force or violence ⟨~ a living⟩ ⟨~ the power

from the usurper⟩ 3 : to wrench (a word or passage) from its proper meaning or use

²**wrest** n : a forcible twist : WRENCH

¹**wres·tle** \\'res-əl\\ vb 1 : to scuffle with an opponent in an attempt to trip him or throw him down 2 : to contend against in wrestling 3 : to struggle for mastery (as with something difficult) ⟨~ with a problem⟩ — **wres·tler** n

²**wrestle** n : the action or an instance of wrestling : STRUGGLE

wres·tling \\'res-liŋ\\ n : the sport of hand-to-hand combat between two opponents who seek to throw and pin each other

wretch \\'rech\\ n 1 : a miserable unhappy person 2 : a base, despicable, or vile person

wretch·ed \\'rech-əd\\ adj 1 : deeply afflicted, dejected, or distressed : MISERABLE 2 : WOEFUL, GRIEVOUS ⟨a ~ accident⟩ 3 : DESPICABLE ⟨a ~ trick⟩ 4 : poor in quality or ability : INFERIOR ⟨~ workmanship⟩ — **wretch·ed·ness** n

wrig·gle \\'rig-əl\\ vb 1 : to twist and turn restlessly : SQUIRM ⟨*wriggled* in his chair⟩; *also* : to move or advance by twisting and turning ⟨a snake *wriggled* along the path⟩ 2 : to extricate oneself or bring into a state or place by maneuvering, twisting, or dodging ⟨~ out of a difficulty⟩ — **wriggle** n

wrig·gler \\-(ə-)lər\\ n 1 : one that wriggles 2 : the larva or pupa of a mosquito

wring \\'riŋ\\ vb **wrung** \\'rəŋ\\ **wringing** 1 : to squeeze or twist esp. so as to make dry or to extract moisture or liquid ⟨~ clothes⟩ 2 : to get by or as if by forcible exertion of pressure : EXTORT ⟨~ the truth out of him⟩ 3 : to twist so as to strain or sprain : CONTORT ⟨~ his neck⟩ 4 : to twist together as a sign of anguish ⟨*wrung* her hands⟩ 5 : to affect painfully as if by wringing : TORMENT ⟨her plight *wrung* my heart⟩ 6 : to shake (a hand) vigorously in greeting

wring·er n : one that wrings; *esp* : a device for squeezing out liquid or moisture ⟨clothes ~⟩

¹**wrin·kle** \\'riŋ-kəl\\ n 1 : a crease or small fold on a surface (as in the skin or in cloth) 2 : METHOD, TECHNIQUE; *also* : information about a method 3 : an innovation in method, technique, or equipment : NOVELTY ⟨the latest ~ in hairdos⟩ — **wrin·kly** adj

²**wrinkle** vb : to develop or cause to develop wrinkles

wrist \\'rist\\ n : the joint or region between the hand and the arm; *also* : a corresponding part in a lower animal

wrist·band \\'ris(t)-,band\\ n 1 : the part of a sleeve covering the wrist 2 : a band encircling the wrist

wrist·let \\'rist-lət\\ n : a band encircling the wrist; *esp* : a close-fitting knitted band worn for warmth

wrist·watch \\-,wäch\\ n : a small watch attached to a bracelet or strap to fasten about the wrist

writ \\'rit\\ n 1 : WRITING 2 : a legal order in writing issued in the name of the sovereign power or in the name of a court or judicial authority commanding the performance or nonperformance of a specified act 3 : a written order constituting a symbol of the power and authority of the issuer

write \'rīt\ vb **wrote** \'rōt\ **writ·ten** \'rit-ᵊn\ also **writ** \'rit\ **writ·ing** \'rīt-iŋ\ 1 : to form characters, letters, or words on a surface (as with a pen) ⟨learn to read and ∼⟩ 2 : to form the letters or the words of (as on paper) : INSCRIBE ⟨wrote his name⟩ 3 : to put down on paper : give expression to in writing 4 : to make up and set down for others to read : COMPOSE ⟨∼ music⟩ 5 : to pen, typewrite, or dictate a letter to 6 : to communicate by letter : CORRESPOND 7 : to be fitted for writing ⟨this pen ∼s easily⟩

write off vb 1 : to reduce the estimated value of : DEPRECIATE 2 : CANCEL ⟨write off a bad debt⟩

writ·er \'rīt-ər\ n : one that writes esp. as a business or occupation : AUTHOR

write-up \'rīt-ˌəp\ n : a written account (as in a newspaper); esp : a flattering article

writhe \'rīth\ vb 1 : to move or proceed with twists and turns ⟨∼ in pain⟩ 2 : to suffer with shame or confusion : SQUIRM

writ·ing \'rīt-iŋ\ n 1 : the act of one that writes; also : HANDWRITING 2 : something (as a letter, book, or document) that is written or printed 3 : INSCRIPTION 4 : a style or form of composition 5 : the occupation of a writer

¹wrong \'rȯŋ\ n 1 : an injurious, unfair, or unjust act 2 : something that is contrary to justice, goodness, equity, or law ⟨know right from ∼⟩ 3 : the state, position, or fact of being or doing wrong; also : the state of being guilty ⟨in the ∼⟩ 4 : a violation of the legal rights of another person

²wrong adj 1 : SINFUL, IMMORAL 2 : not right according to a standard or code : IMPROPER 3 : UNSUITABLE, INAPPROPRIATE 4 : INCORRECT ⟨a ∼ solution⟩

5 : UNSATISFACTORY 6 : constituting a surface that is considered the back, bottom, inside, or reverse of something ⟨iron only on the ∼ side of the fabric⟩ syn false, bad, poor

³wrong adv 1 : in a wrong direction, manner, position, or relation 2 : INCORRECTLY

⁴wrong vb 1 : to do wrong to : INJURE, HARM 2 : to treat unjustly : DISHONOR, MALIGN syn oppress, persecute, aggrieve

wrong·do·er \'rȯŋ-ˌdü-ər\ n : a person who does wrong and esp. moral wrong — **wrong·do·ing** n

wrong·ful \-fəl\ adj 1 : WRONG, UNJUST 2 : UNLAWFUL — **wrong·ful·ly** adv

wrong·head·ed \-'hed-əd\ adj : obstinately wrong : PERVERSE

wrong·ly \'rȯŋ-lē\ adv 1 : in an improper or inappropriate way 2 : UNFAIRLY, UNJUSTLY 3 : INCORRECTLY 4 : in error : by mistake ⟨rightly or ∼⟩

wrote past of WRITE

wroth \'rȯth, 'rōth\ adj : filled with wrath : ANGRY

wrought \'rȯt\ adj 1 : FASHIONED, FORMED 2 : ORNAMENTED 3 : beaten into shape : HAMMERED ⟨∼ silver dishes⟩ 4 : deeply stirred : EXCITED ⟨gets easily ∼ up over nothing⟩

wrought iron n : a commercial form of iron that contains less than 0.3 percent carbon and is tough, malleable, and relatively soft — **wrought-iron** adj

wrung past of WRING

wry \'rī\ adj 1 : turned abnormally to one side : CONTORTED; also : made by twisting the facial muscles ⟨a ∼ smile⟩ 2 : cleverly and often ironically humorous — **wry·ly** adv

wry·neck \-ˌnek\ n 1 : a disorder marked by a twisting of the neck and head 2 : any of several birds related to the woodpeckers that have a peculiar manner of writhing the head and neck

wurst \'wərst, 'wu̇rst\ n : SAUSAGE

X \'eks\ n, often cap : the 24th letter of the English alphabet

Xan·thip·pe \zan-'t(h)ip-ē\ or **Xan·tip·pe** \-'tip-\ n : an ill-tempered woman

X-dis·ease \'eks-diz-ˌēz\ n : a virus disease of uncertain origin and relationships; esp : an encephalitis first encountered in Australia

xe·bec \'zē-ˌbek\ n : a usu. 3-masted Mediterranean sailing ship with long overhanging bow and stern

xe·nia \'zē-nē-ə\ n : the effect of the pollen on fruit tissues other than the embryo

xe·non \'zēn-ˌän, 'zen-\ n : a heavy gaseous chemical element occurring in minute quantities in air

xeno·pho·bia \ˌzen-ə-'fō-bē-ə\ n : fear and hatred of strangers or foreigners or of what is strange or foreign — **xeno·phobe** \'zen-ə-ˌfōb\ n

xe·ric \'zi(ə)r-ik\ adj : low or deficient in moisture for the support of life

xe·roph·i·lous \zə-'räf-ə-ləs\ adj : tolerant of drought ⟨∼ plants⟩

xe·roph·thal·mia \ˌzir-ˌäf-'thal-mē-ə, -ˌäp-\ n : an eye disease resulting from

severe lack of vitamin A — **xe·roph·thal·mic** adj

xe·ro·phyte \'zir-ə-ˌfīt\ n : a plant adapted for growth with a limited water supply

Xmas \'kris-məs\ n : CHRISTMAS

X ray \'eks-ˌrā\ n 1 : a radiation of the same nature as light rays but of extremely short wavelength that is generated by the striking of a stream of electrons against a metal surface in a vacuum and that is able to penetrate through various thicknesses of solids 2 : a photograph taken with X rays

x-ray vb, often cap X : to examine, treat, or photograph with X rays

xy·lem \'zī-ləm\ n : woody tissue of higher plants that transports water and dissolved materials upward, functions also in support and storage, and lies central to the phloem

xy·lo·phone \'zī-lə-ˌfōn\ n [Gk xylon wood + phōnē voice, sound] : a musical instrument consisting of a series of wooden bars graduated in length to sound the musical scale, supported on belts of straw or felt, and sounded by striking with two small wooden hammers

y \'wī\ *n, often cap* : the 25th letter of the English alphabet

1-y *also* **-ey** \ē\ *adj suffix* **-i·er** \ē-ər\ **-i·est** \ē-əst\ **1** : characterized by : full of ⟨dirt*y*⟩ ⟨clay*ey*⟩ **2** : having the character of : composed of ⟨ic*y*⟩ **3** : like : like that of ⟨home*y*⟩ ⟨wintr*y*⟩ ⟨stag*y*⟩ **4** : devoted to : addicted to : enthusiastic over ⟨hors*y*⟩ **5** : tending or inclined to ⟨sleep*y*⟩ ⟨chatt*y*⟩ **6** : giving occasion for (specified) action ⟨tear*y*⟩ **7** : performing (specified) action ⟨curl*y*⟩ **8** : somewhat : rather : -ISH ⟨chill*y*⟩ **9** : having (such) characteristics to a marked degree or in an affected or superficial way ⟨French*y*⟩

2-y \ē\ *n suffix, pl* **-ies** \ēz\ **1** : state : condition : quality ⟨beggar*y*⟩ **2** : activity, place of business, or goods dealt with ⟨laundr*y*⟩ **3** : whole body or group ⟨soldier*y*⟩

3-y *n suffix, pl* **-ies** : instance of a (specified) action ⟨entreat*y*⟩ ⟨inquir*y*⟩

1yacht \'yät\ *n* : any of various relatively small sailing or mechanically driven ships that usu. have a sharp prow and graceful lines and are used esp. for pleasure cruising and racing

2yacht *vb* : to race or cruise in a yacht

yacht·ing *n* : the action, fact, or pastime of racing or cruising in a yacht

yachts·man \'yäts-mən\ *n* : one who owns or sails a yacht

ya·hoo \'yä-hü, 'yä-\ *n* : an uncouth or rowdy person

Yah·weh \'yä-,wā\ *n* : the God of the Hebrews

1yak \'yak\ *n* : a large long-haired blackish brown ox of Tibet and adjacent Asiatic uplands

2yak *n* : persistent or voluble talk — yak *vb*

yam \'yam\ *n* **1** : the edible starchy root of a twining vine that largely replaces the potato as food in the tropics **2** : a usu. deep orange sweet potato

yam·mer \'yam-ər\ *vb* **1** : WHIMPER **2** : CHATTER — yammer *n*

1yank \'yaŋk\ *n* : a strong sudden pull : JERK

2yank *vb* : to pull with a quick vigorous movement

Yank \'yaŋk\ *n* : YANKEE

Yan·kee \'yaŋ-kē\ *n* **1** : a native or inhabitant of New England; *also* : a native or inhabitant of the northern U.S. **2** : AMERICAN **2** — Yankee *adj*

yan·qui \'yän-kē\ *n, often cap* : a citizen of the U.S. as distinguished from a Latin American

1yap \'yap\ *vb* **yapped; yap·ping 1** : BARK, YELP **2** : GAB

2yap *n* **1** : a quick sharp bark **2** : CHATTER

1yard \'yärd\ *n* **1** : a measure of length equaling 3 feet or 0.9144 meter **2** : a long spar tapered toward the ends that supports and spreads the head of a sail

2yard *n* **1** : a small enclosed area open to the sky and adjacent to a building **2** : the grounds of a building **3** : an enclosure for livestock **4** : an area set aside for a particular business or activity ⟨a navy ~⟩ **5** : a system of railroad tracks for storing cars and making up trains

yard·age *n* : an aggregate number of yards; *also* : the length, extent, or volume of something as measured in yards

yard·arm \'yärd-,ärm\ *n* : either end of the yard of a square-rigged ship

yard·man \-mən\ *n* : a man employed in or about a yard

yard·mas·ter \-,mas-tər\ *n* : the man in charge of operations in a railroad yard

yard·stick \-,stik\ *n* **1** : a graduated measuring stick 3 feet long **2** : a standard for making a critical judgment : CRITERION **syn** gauge, touchstone

yarn \'yärn\ *n* **1** : a continuous often plied strand composed of fibers or filaments and used in weaving and knitting to form cloth **2** : STORY; *esp* : a tall tale

yar·row \'yar-ō\ *n* : a strong-scented herb related to the daisies that has white or pink flowers in flat clusters

yaw \'yo\ *vb* : to deviate erratically from side to side of a course ⟨the ship ~ed in the heavy seas⟩ — yaw *n*

yawl \'yol\ *n* **1** : a ship's small boat **2** : a fore-and-aft-rigged sailboat carrying a mainsail and one or more jibs

1yawn \'yon\ *vb* : to open wide; *esp* : to open the mouth wide usu. as an involuntary reaction to fatigue or boredom — yawn·er *n*

2yawn *n* : a deep usu. involuntary intake of breath through the wide-open mouth

yaws \'yoz\ *n sing or pl* : a tropical disease related to syphilis but not venereal

yclept \i-'klept\ *adj, archaic* : NAMED, CALLED

1ye \(')yē\ *pron, archaic* : YOU 1

2ye \yē, yə, *or like* THE\ *definite article, archaic* : THE — used by early printers to represent the manuscript word þe (*the*)

1yea \'yā\ *adv* **1** : YES — used in oral voting **2** : INDEED, TRULY

2yea *n* : an affirmative vote; *also* : a person casting such a vote

yean \'yēn\ *vb* : to bring forth young — used of a sheep or goat

yean·ling *n* : LAMB, KID

year \'yior\ *n* **1** : the period of about 365¼ solar days required for one revolution of the earth around the sun **2** : a cycle in the Gregorian calendar of 365 or 366 days beginning with January 1; *also* : a calendar year specified usu. by a number **3** *pl* : a time of special significance ⟨~s of plenty⟩ **4** *pl* : AGE ⟨advanced in ~s⟩ **5** : a period of time other than a calendar year ⟨the school ~⟩

year·book \-,bùk\ *n* **1** : a book published annually esp. as a report **2** : a school publication recording the history and activities of a graduating class

year·ling \'yior-liŋ, 'yor-lən\ *n* : one that is or is rated as a year old

year·long \'yior-'loŋ\ *adj* : lasting through a year

1year·ly \-lē\ *adj* : ANNUAL

2yearly *adv* : every year

yearn \'yərn\ *vb* **1** : to feel a longing or craving **2** : to feel tenderness or com-

---

ə abut; ᵊ kitten; ər further; a back; ā bake; ä cot, cart; aù out; ch chin; e less; ē easy; g gift; i trip; ī life; j joke; ŋ sing; ō flow; ò flaw; òi coin; th thin; <u>th</u> this; ü loot; ù foot; y yet; yü few; yù furious; zh vision

passion syn long, pine, hanker, hunger, thirst

yearn·ing n : a tender or urgent longing

year-round \'yiər-'raùnd\ adj 1 : effective, employed, or operating for the full year : not seasonal ⟨a ~ resort⟩

yeast \'yēst\ n 1 : a surface froth or a sediment in sugary liquids (as fruit juices) that consists largely of cells of a tiny fungus and is used in making alcoholic liquors and as a leaven in baking 2 : any of various usu. one-celled fungi that reproduce by budding and promote alcoholic fermentation 3 : a commercial product containing yeast plants in a moist or dry medium 4 : the foam of waves : SPUME 5 : something that causes ferment or activity

yeasty adj 1 : of, relating to, or resembling yeast 2 : UNSETTLED 3 : EXUBERANT; also : FRIVOLOUS

¹**yell** \'yel\ vb : to utter a loud cry or scream : SHOUT

²**yell** n 1 : SHOUT 2 : a cheer used esp. to encourage an athletic team (as at a college)

¹**yel·low** \'yel-ō\ adj 1 : of the color yellow 2 : having a yellow complexion or skin 3 : SENSATIONAL ⟨~ journalism⟩ 4 : COWARDLY

²**yellow** vb : to make or turn yellow

³**yellow** n 1 : a color between green and orange in the spectrum : the color of ripe lemons or sunflowers 2 : something yellow; esp : the yolk of an egg 3 pl : JAUNDICE 4 pl : any of several plant virus diseases marked by stunted growth and yellowing of foliage

yellow fever n : an acute destructive virus disease marked by prostration, jaundice, fever, and often hemorrhage and transmitted by a mosquito

yel·low·ish adj : somewhat yellow

yel·low jack \'yel-ō-,jak\ n 1 : YELLOW FEVER 2 : a flag raised on ships in quarantine

yellow jacket n : an American social wasp having the body barred with bright yellow

yelp \'yelp\ vb : to utter a sharp quick shrill cry — yelp n

¹**yen** \'yen\ n, pl yen — see MONEY table

²**yen** n : a strong desire : LONGING

yeo·man \'yō-mən\ n 1 : an attendant or officer in a royal or noble household 2 : a small farmer who cultivates his own land; esp : one of a class of English freeholders below the gentry 3 : a naval petty officer who performs clerical duties

yeo·man·ry n : the body of yeomen and esp. of small landed proprietors

-yer — see -ER

¹**yes** \'yes\ adv — used as a function word esp. to express assent or agreement or to introduce a more emphatic or explicit phrase

²**yes** n : an affirmative reply

yes-man \-,man\ n : a person who endorses uncritically every opinion or proposal of a superior

yes·ter·day \'yes-tərd-ē\ adv 1 : on the day preceding today 2 : only a short time ago

²**yesterday** n 1 : the day last past 2 : time not long past

yes·ter·year \-tər-,yiər\ n 1 : last year 2 : the recent past

¹**yet** \(')yet\ adv 1 : in addition : BESIDES; also : EVEN 2 : up to now; also : STILL 3 : so soon as now (not time

to go ~⟩ 4 : EVENTUALLY 5 : NEVERTHELESS, HOWEVER

²**yet** conj : despite the fact that : BUT

yew \'yü\ n 1 : any of various evergreen trees or shrubs with dark stiff poisonous needles and fleshy fruits 2 : the fine-grained wood of a yew; esp : that of an Old World yew valued for bows, hoops, and cabinetwork

Yid·dish \'yid-ish\ n [Yiddish yidish, short for yidish daytsh, lit., Jewish German] : a language derived from German and spoken by Jews esp. of eastern Europe — **Yiddish** adj

¹**yield** \'yēld\ vb 1 : to give as fitting, owed, or required 2 : to give up; esp : to give up possession of on claim or demand 3 : to bear as a natural product 4 : PRODUCE, SUPPLY 5 : to bring in : RETURN 6 : to give way (as to force or influence) 7 : to give place syn relinquish, cede, waive, submit, capitulate, defer

²**yield** n : something yielded; esp : the amount or quantity produced or returned

yield·ing adj 1 : not rigid or stiff : FLEXIBLE 2 : SUBMISSIVE, COMPLIANT

yo·del \'yōd-ʾl\ vb -deled or -delled; -del·ing or -del·ling : to sing by suddenly changing from chest voice to falsetto and the reverse; also : to shout or call in this manner — yodel n — **yo·del·er** n

yo·ga \'yō-gə\ n 1 cap : a Hindu theistic philosophy teaching the suppression of all activity of body, mind, and will in order that the self may realize its distinction from them and attain liberation 2 : a system of exercises for attaining bodily or mental control and well-being

yo·gi \'yō-gē\ or **yo·gin** \-gən\ n 1 : a person who practices yoga 2 cap : an adherent of Yoga philosophy

yo·gurt or **yo·ghurt** \'yō-gərt\ n : a fermented slightly acid semifluid milk food made of skimmed cow's milk and milk solids to which cultures of bacteria have been added

¹**yoke** \'yōk\ n 1 : a wooden bar or frame by which two draft animals (as oxen) are coupled at the heads or necks for working together; also : a frame fitted to a person's shoulders to carry a load in two equal portions 2 : a clamp that embraces two parts to hold or unite them in position 3 pl yoke : two animals yoked together 4 : SERVITUDE, BONDAGE 5 : TIE, LINK ⟨the ~ of matrimony⟩ 6 : a fitted or shaped piece esp. at the shoulder of a garment syn couple, pair, brace

²**yoke** vb 1 : to put a yoke on : couple with a yoke 2 : to attach a draft animal to ⟨~ a plow⟩ 3 : JOIN; esp : MARRY

yo·kel \'yō-kəl\ n : BUMPKIN

yolk \'yō(l)k\ n 1 : the yellow rounded inner mass of the egg of a bird or reptile : the stored food material of an egg 2 : oily matter in sheep's wool

Yom Kip·pur \,yöm-'kip-ər, -ki-'pùr\ n : a Jewish holiday observed in September or October with fasting and prayer as a day of atonement

¹**yon** \'yän\ adj : YONDER

²**yon** adv 1 : YONDER 2 : THITHER ⟨ran hither and ~⟩

yon·der \'yän-dər\ adv : at or to that place

²**yonder** adj 1 : more distant ⟨the ~ side

of the river⟩ **2 :** being at a distance within view ⟨~ hills⟩

yore \'yōr\ *n* **:** time long past ⟨in days of ~⟩

you \(')yü, yə\ *pron* **1 :** the person or persons addressed ⟨~ are a nice person⟩ ⟨~ are nice people⟩ **2 :** ONE **2** ⟨~ turn this knob to open it⟩

1young \'yəŋ\ *adj* **1 :** being in the first or an early stage of life, growth, or development **2 :** INEXPERIENCED **3 :** recently come into being **4 :** YOUTHFUL **5** *cap* **:** belonging to or representing a new or revived usu. political group or movement

2young *n pl* **:** young persons or lower animals

young·ish \'yəŋ-ish\ *adj* **:** somewhat young

young·ling \-liŋ\ *n* **:** one that is young — **youngling** *adj*

young·ster \-stər\ *n* **1 :** a young person **2 :** CHILD

youn·ker \'yəŋ-kər\ *n* **1 :** a young man **2 :** YOUNGSTER

your \yər, 'yu̇r, (')yōr\ *adj* **:** of or relating to you or yourself

yours \'yu̇rz, 'yōrz\ *pron* **:** one or the ones belonging to you

your·self \yər-'self\ *pron, pl* **your·selves** \-'selvz\ **:** YOU — used reflexively, for emphasis, or in absolute constructions ⟨you'll hurt ~⟩ ⟨do it ~⟩ ⟨~ a man, you should understand⟩

youth \'yüth\ *n* **1 :** the period of life between childhood and maturity **2 :** a young man; *also* **:** young persons **3 :** YOUTHFULNESS

youth·ful *adj* **1 :** of, relating to, or appropriate to youth **2 :** being young and not yet mature **3 :** FRESH, VIGOROUS — **youth·ful·ly** *adv* — **youth·ful·ness** *n*

yowl \'yau̇l\ *vb* **:** to utter a loud long mournful cry **:** WAIL — **yowl** *n*

yt·ter·bi·um \i-'tər-bē-əm\ *n* **:** a rare metallic chemical element

yt·tri·um \'it-rē-əm\ *n* **:** a rare metallic chemical element

yu·an \'yü-ən, yü-'än\ *n, pl* **yuan** — see MONEY table

yuc·ca \'yək-ə\ *n* **:** any of several plants related to the lilies that grow in dry regions and have white cup-shaped flowers in erect clusters; *also* **:** the flower of this plant

Yu·go·slav \,yü-gō-'släv, -'slav\ *n* **:** a native or inhabitant of Yugoslavia — **Yugoslav** *adj* — **Yu·go·sla·vi·an** \-'släv-ē-ən\ *adj or n*

yule \'yül\ *n, often cap* **:** CHRISTMAS

yule log *n, often cap* Y **:** a large log formerly put on the hearth on Christmas Eve as the foundation of the fire

yule·tide \'yül-,tīd\ *n, often cap* **:** CHRISTMASTIDE

yum·my \'yəm-ē\ *adj* **:** highly attractive or pleasing

---

z \'zē\ *n, often cap* **:** the 26th letter of the English alphabet

1za·ny \'zā-nē\ *n* **1 :** CLOWN, BUFFOON **2 :** a silly or foolish person

3zany *adj* **1 :** characteristic of a zany **2 :** CRAZY, FOOLISH — **za·ni·ly** *adv* — **za·ni·ness** *n*

zeal \'zēl\ *n* **:** eager and ardent interest in the pursuit of something **:** FERVOR **syn** enthusiasm, passion

zeal·ot \'zel-ət\ *n* **:** a zealous person; *esp* **:** a fanatical partisan **syn** enthusiast, bigot

zeal·ous \'zel-əs\ *adj* **:** filled with, characterized by, or due to zeal — **zeal·ous·ly** *adv* — **zeal·ous·ness** *n*

ze·bra \'zē-brə\ *n* **:** any of several African mammals related to the horse and ass but conspicuously striped with black or brown and white or buff

ze·bu \'zē-b(y)ü\ *n* **:** an Asiatic ox occurring in many domestic breeds and differing from European cattle esp. in the presence of a fleshy hump on the shoulders and a loose folded skin

zed \'zed\ *n, chiefly Brit* **:** the letter z

zeit·geist \'tsīt-,gīst\ *n* **:** the general intellectual, moral, and cultural state of an era

Zen \'zen\ *n* **:** a Japanese Buddhist sect that teaches self-discipline, meditation, and attainment of enlightenment through direct intuitive insight

ze·na·na \zə-'nän-ə\ *n* **:** HAREM, SERAGLIO

ze·nith \'zē-nəth\ *n* **1 :** the point in the heavens directly overhead **2 :** the

highest point **:** ACME **syn** culmination, pinnacle, apex

zeph·yr \'zef-ər\ *n* **1 :** a breeze from the west; *also* **:** a gentle breeze **2 :** any of various lightweight fabrics and articles of clothing

zep·pe·lin \'zep-(ə-)lən\ *n* **:** a rigid airship consisting of a cylindrical trussed and covered frame supported by internal gas cells

1ze·ro \'zē-rō\ *n, pl* **-ros** *also* **-roes** **1 :** CIPHER, NAUGHT **2 :** the point at which the graduated degrees or measurements on a scale (as of a thermometer) begin **3 :** the lowest point

2zero *vb* **:** TRAIN ⟨~ in artillery on the crossroads⟩

zero hour *n* **1 :** the hour at which a previously planned military operation is started **2 :** the scheduled time for an action or operation to begin

zest \'zest\ *n* **1 :** a quality of enhancing enjoyment **:** PIQUANCY **2 :** keen enjoyment **:** RELISH, GUSTO — **zest·ful** *adj* — **zest·ful·ly** *adv* — **zest·ful·ness** *n*

1zig·zag \'zig-,zag\ *n* **:** one of a series of short sharp turns, angles, or alterations in a course; *also* **:** something marked by such a series

2zigzag *adv* **:** in or by a zigzag path or course

3zigzag *adj* **:** having short sharp turns or angles

4zigzag *vb* **-zagged; -zag·ging :** to form into or proceed along a zigzag

zinc \'ziŋk\ *n* **:** a bluish white crystalline metallic chemical element that tar-

---

nishes only slightly in moist air at ordinary temperatures and is used to make alloys and as a protective coating for iron

zinc ointment *n* : an ointment containing 20 percent of zinc oxide and used for skin disorders

zinc oxide *n* : an infusible white solid used as a pigment, in compounding rubber, and in ointments

zing \'ziŋ\ *n* **1** : a shrill humming noise **2** : VITALITY — **zing** *vb*

zin·nia \'zin-ē-ə, 'zēn-yə\ *n* : an American herb related to the daisies and widely grown for its showy long-lasting flower heads

Zi·on \'zī-ən\ *n* **1** : the Jewish people **2** : the Jewish homeland as a symbol of Judaism or of Jewish national aspiration **3** : HEAVEN **4** : UTOPIA

Zi·on·ism *n* : a theory, plan, or movement for setting up a Jewish national or religious community in Palestine — **Zi·on·ist** *n*

¹zip \'zip\ *vb* **zipped**; **zip·ping** : to move or act with speed or vigor

²zip *n* **1** : a sudden sharp hissing sound **2** : ENERGY, VIM

³zip *vb* **zipped**; **zip·ping** : to close or open with a zipper

zip·per \'zip-ər\ *n* : a fastener consisting of two rows of metal or plastic teeth on strips of tape and a sliding piece that closes an opening by drawing the teeth together

zip·py \-ē\ *adj* : BRISK, SNAPPY

zir·con \'zər-ˌkän\ *n* : a zirconium-containing mineral several transparent varieties of which are used as gems

zir·co·ni·um \ˌzər-'kō-nē-əm\ *n* : a heat-resistant and corrosion-resistant metallic element used in alloys and ceramics

zith·er \'zith-ər, 'zith-\ *n* : a musical instrument having 30 to 40 strings played with plectrum and fingers

zlo·ty \'zlot-ē\ *n, pl* **zlotys** *also* **zloty** — see MONEY table

zo·di·ac \'zōd-ē-ˌak\ *n* [Gk *zōidiakos, fr. zōidion* small figure, sign of the zodiac, fr. dim. of *zōion* animal] **1** : an imaginary elongated region in the heavens that encompasses the paths of all the principal planets except Pluto, that has the ecliptic as its central line, and that is divided into 12 signs (Ar·i·es \'ar-ē-ˌēz\ the Ram, Tau·rus \'tȯr-əs\ the Bull, Gem·i·ni \'jem-ə-nē, -ˌnī\ the Twins, Can·cer \'kan-sər\ the Crab, Leo \'lē-ō\ the Lion, Vir·go \'vər-gō\ the Virgin, Li·bra \'lī-brə\ the Balance, Scor·pio \'skȯr-pē-ˌō\ the Scorpion, Sag·it·tar·i·us \ˌsaj-ə-'ter-ē-əs\ the Archer, Cap·ri·corn \'kap-rə-ˌkȯrn\ the Goat, Aquar·i·us \ə-'kwar-ē-əs\ the Water Bearer, Pi·sces \'pīs-ˌēz, 'pis-\ the Fishes) with each taken for astrological purposes to extend 30 degrees of longitude **2** : a figure representing the signs of the zodiac and their symbols — **zo·di·a·cal** \zō-'dī-ə-kəl\ *adj*

zom·bi *or* **zom·bie** \'zäm-bē\ *n* **1** : the voodoo snake deity **2** : the supernatural power held in voodoo belief to enter into and reanimate a dead body

zon·al \'zōn-ᵊl\ *adj* : of, relating to, or having the form of a zone — **zon·al·ly** *adv*

¹zone \'zōn\ *n* **1** : any of five great divisions of the earth's surface that is made according to latitude and temperature and includes the torrid zone extending 23°27′ on each side of the equator, the two temperate zones lying between the torrid zone and the polar circles which are 23°27′ from the poles, and the two frigid zones lying between the polar circles and the poles **2** *archaic* : GIRDLE, BELT **3** : an encircling band or girdle ⟨a ~ of trees⟩ **4** : an area or region set off or distinguished in some way from adjoining parts

²zone *vb* **1** : ENCIRCLE **2** : to arrange in or mark off into zones; *esp* : to divide (as a city) into sections reserved for different purposes — **zo·na·tion** \zō-'nā-shən\ *n* — **zoned** \'zōnd\ *adj*

zoo \'zü\ *n* : a zoological garden or collection of living animals usu. for public display

zoo·ge·og·ra·phy \ˌzō-ə-jē-'äg-rə-fē\ *n* : a branch of biogeography concerned with the geographical distribution of animals — **zoo·ge·og·ra·pher** \-fər\ *n* — **zoo·ge·o·graph·ic** \-ˌjē-ə-'graf-ik\ *or* **zoo·ge·o·graph·i·cal** *adj* — **zoo·ge·o·graph·i·cal·ly** *adv*

zo·oid \'zō-ˌoid\ *n* : an entity (as a blood cell) with some but not all of the properties of a complete organism; *esp* : one of the members of a colonial animal (as a coral) produced by other than direct sexual means

zo·o·log·i·cal garden \ˌzō-ə-'läj-i-kəl-\ *n* : a garden or park where wild animals are kept for exhibition

zo·ol·o·gy \zō-'äl-ə-jē\ *n* : a science that deals with animals and the animal kingdom — **zo·o·log·i·cal** \ˌzō-ə-'läj-i-kəl\ *adj* — **zo·o·log·i·cal·ly** *adv* — **zo·ol·o·gist** \zō-'äl-ə-jəst\ *n*

zoom \'züm\ *vb* **1** : to move with a loud hum or buzz **2** : to climb sharply and briefly by means of momentum (the airplane ~ed) — **zoom** *n*

zoo·mor·phism \ˌzō-ə-'mȯr-ˌfiz-əm\ *n* **1** : the representation of a deity in the form or with the attributes of an animal **2** : the use of animal forms in art — **zoo·mor·phic** *adj*

zoo·phyte \'zō-ə-ˌfīt\ *n* : any of numerous invertebrate animals (as a coral or sponge) suggesting plants esp. in growth

zoo·spore \-ˌspȯr\ *n* : a motile spore

zoot suit \'züt-\ *n* : a flashy suit of extreme cut — **zoot-suit·er** *n*

Zo·ro·as·tri·an·ism \ˌzōr-ə-'was-trē-ən-ˌiz-əm\ *n* : a religion founded by the Persian prophet Zoroaster — **Zo·ro·as·tri·an** *adj or n*

Zou·ave \zü-'äv\ *n* : a member of a French infantry unit orig. composed of Algerians wearing a brilliant uniform and conducting a quick spirited drill; *also* : a member of a military unit modeled on the Zouaves

zounds \'zaün(d)z\ *interj* — used as a mild oath

zuc·chet·to \zü-'ket-ō, tsü-\ *n* : a small round skullcap worn by Roman Catholic ecclesiastics

zwie·back \'swē-ˌbak, 'swī-\ *n* : a usu. sweetened bread that is baked and then sliced and toasted until dry and crisp

Zwing·li·an \'zwiŋ-(g)lē-ən, 'swiŋ-\ *n* : a follower or adherent of the Swiss religious reformer Ulrich Zwingli or his teachings — **Zwinglian** *adj*

zy·gote \'zī-ˌgōt\ *n* : a cell formed by the union of two sexual cells

zy·mase \'zī-ˌmās\ *n* : an enzyme or enzyme complex that promotes fermentation of simple sugars

ABBREVIATIONS

Most of these abbreviations have been normalized to one form. Variation in use of periods, in typeface, and in capitalization is frequent and widespread (as *mph*, *MPH*, *m.p.h.*, *Mph*)

a acre, alto, answer
A ace, argon, assists
AA Alcoholics Anonymous, associate in arts
AAA American Automobile Association
A and M agricultural and mechanical
ab about
AB able-bodied seaman, at bats, bachelor of arts
abbr abbreviation
ABC American Broadcasting Company
abl ablative
abp archbishop
abr abridged, abridgment
abs absolute
abstr abstract
ac account
Ac actinium
AC alternating current; ante Christum (L, before Christ), ante cibum (L, before meals)
acad academic, academy
accel accelerando
acct account
ack acknowledge, acknowledgment
act active, actual
A.C.T. Australian Capital Territory
actg acting
A.D. after date, anno Domini (L, in the year of our Lord)
addn addition
addnl additional
ad int ad interim
adj adjective, adjutant
ad loc ad locum (L, to [at] the place)
adm admiral
admin administration
adv adverb, advertisement
ad val ad valorem (L, according to value)
advg advertising
advt advertisement
AEF American Expeditionary Force
aeq aequales (L, equal)
aet, aetat aetatis (L, of age)
AF air force, audio frequency
AFB air force base
afft affidavit
AFL-CIO American Federation of Labor and Congress of Industrial Organization
Afr Africa, African
Ag argentum (L, silver)
AG adjutant general, attorney general
agcy agency
agric, agr agricultural, agriculture
agt agent
AID Agency for International Development
Al aluminum
Ala Alabama
ALA Automobile Legal Association
alc alcohol
ald alderman
alg algebra
alk alkaline
alt alternate, altitude
Alta Alberta
alter alteration
a.m. ante meridiem (L, before noon)
Am America, American, americium
AM amplitude modulation, master of arts

AMA American Medical Association
amb ambassador
amdt amendment
AME African Methodist Episcopal
Amer America, American
AmerInd American Indian
amp ampere
amt amount
anal analogy, analysis, analytic
anat anatomy
anc ancient
and andante
ann annals, annual
anon anonymous
ans answer
ant antonym
anthrop anthropology
a/o account of
ap apothecaries'
AP additional premium, Associated Press
APO army post office
app apparatus, appendix
appl applied
appnt appointment
approx approximate, approximately
appt appoint, appointment
Apr April
apt apartment
aq aqueous
ar arrival, arrive
Ar Arabic, argon
ARC American Red Cross
arch, archit architecture
archeol archeology
arith arithmetic
Ariz Arizona
Ark Arkansas
arr arranged, arrival, arrive
art article, artificial, artillery
ARV American Revised Version
As arsenic
AS Anglo-Saxon, antisubmarine
assn association
assoc associate, association
ASSR Autonomous Soviet Socialist Republic
asst assistant
astrol astrology
astron astronomer, astronomy
ASV American Standard Version
At astatine
Atl Atlantic
atm atmosphere, atmospheric
att attached, attention, attorney
attn attention
attrib attributive
atty attorney
Au aurum (L, gold)
aud audit, auditor
Aug August
AUS Army of the United States
Austral Australian
auth authentic, author, authorized
aux auxiliary
av avenue, average, avoirdupois
AV ad valorem (L, according to value); audiovisual, Authorized Version
avdp avoirdupois
ave avenue
avg average

b bass, book, born
B bachelor, bishop, boron
Ba barium
BA bachelor of arts

bal balance
bar barometer
Bart baronet
BB bases on balls, best of breed
BBA bachelor of business administration
BBB Better Business Bureau
BBC British Broadcasting Corporation
bbl barrel
B.C. before Christ, British Columbia
BCS bachelor of commercial science
bd board, bound
BD bachelor of divinity, bank draft, bills discounted, brought down
bdl bundle
Be beryllium
BE bill of exchange
BEF British Expeditionary Force
Belg Belgian, Belgium
bet between
bf boldface
BF brought forward
bg bag
bhd bulkhead
Bi bismuth
bib Bible, biblical
bibliog bibliographer, bibliography
BID bis in die (L, twice a day)
biochem biochemistry
biog biographical, biography
biol biologic, biological, biology
bk bank, book
Bk berkelium
bkg banking
bkgd background
bkt basket, bracket
bl bale, blue
B/L bill of lading
bldg building
bldr builder
blk black, block
blvd boulevard
BM basal metabolism, bowel movement
B/M bill of material
BMR basal metabolic rate
BO body odor, branch office, buyer's option
BOD biochemical oxygen demand
BOQ bachelor officers' quarters
bor borough
bot botanical, botany
bp bishop, boiling point
BP bills payable, blood pressure, British Pharmacopoeia
bpl birthplace
BPOE Benevolent and Protective Order of Elks
br branch, brass, brown
Br British, bromine
BR bills receivable
brig brigade, brigadier
Brit Britain, British
bro brother
bros brothers
BS bachelor of science, balance sheet, bill of sale
BSA Boy Scouts of America
BSc bachelor of science
bskt basket
Bt baronet
Btu British thermal unit
bu bushel
bull bulletin
bur bureau
bus business
BV Blessed Virgin
BWI British West Indies
bx box

c cape, carat, cent, centimeter, century, chapter, circa, copyright, cup
C carbon, centigrade
ca circa
Ca calcium
CA chartered accountant, chief accountant, chronological age
CAF, C and F cost and freight
cal calendar, caliber, calorie
calc calculating
Calif, Cal California
Can, Canad Canada, Canadian
canc canceled
cap capacity, capital, capitalize, capitalized
caps capitals, capsule
capt captain
card cardinal
CARE Co-operative for American Remittances to Everywhere
cat catalog
CBC Canadian Broadcasting Corporation
CBD cash before delivery
CBS Columbia Broadcasting System
cc cubic centimeter
CC carbon copy
CCC Civilian Conservation Corps
ccw counterclockwise
cd cord
Cd cadmium
cdr commander
Ce cerium
CE chemical engineer, civil engineer
cen central
cent centigrade, central, century
cert certificate, certification, certified, certify
cf confer (L, compare)
Cf californium
CF carried forward, cost and freight
CFI cost, freight, and insurance
cg, cgm centigram
CG coast guard, commanding general
ch chain, champion, chapter, church
CH clearinghouse, courthouse, customhouse
chap chapter
chem chemical, chemist, chemistry
chg change, charge
Chin Chinese
chm, chmn chairman
chron chronicle, chronological, chronology
Chron Chronicles
CI cost and insurance
cía compañía (Sp, company)
cie compagnie (F, company)
CIF cost, insurance, and freight
C in C commander in chief
cir circle, circular
circ circular
cit citation, cited, citizen
civ civil, civilian
ck cask, check
cl class
Cl chlorine
CL carload
cld called, cleared
clk clerk
clo clothing
clr clear
cm centimeter
CM Congregation of the Mission
cml commercial
CN credit note
CNO chief of naval operations
CNS central nervous system

co company, county
c/o care of
Co cobalt
CO cash order, commanding officer, conscientious objector
COD cash on delivery, collect on delivery
C of C Chamber of Commerce
C of S chief of staff
cog cognate
col colonel, colony, column
Col Colossians
coll college
collat collateral
colloq colloquial
Colo Colorado
com commander, commerce, commissioner, committee, common
comb combination, combining
comdg commanding
comdr commander
comdt commandant
coml commercial
comm commission, commonwealth
commo commodore
comp comparative, compiled, compiler, composition, compound
compar comparative
comr commissioner
con consul, contra (L, against)
conc concentrated
conf conference
Confed Confederate
cong congress
conj conjunction
Conn Connecticut
cons consonant
consol consolidated
const constant, constitution, constitutional
constr construction
cont containing, contents, continent, continental, continued, control
contd continued
contg containing
contr contract, contraction
contrib contribution, contributor
cor corner
Cor Corinthians
CORE Congress of Racial Equality
corp corporal, corporation
corr corrected, correction, correspondence, corresponding, corrugated
cos companies, counties
COS cash on shipment, chief of staff
cp compare, coupon
CP chemically pure, Communist party
CPA certified public accountant
cpd compound
CPFF cost plus fixed fee
cpl corporal
CPO chief petty officer
CPS cycles per second
CQ charge of quarters
cr credit, creditor, crown
Cr chromium
cresc crescendo
crit critical, criticism
cryst crystalline
cs case, cases
c/s cycles per second
Cs cesium
CS chief of staff, civil service
CSA Confederate States of America
C SS R Congregatio Sanctissimi Redemptoris (L, Congregation of the Most Holy Redeemer)
CST Central standard time
ct carat, cent, count, court
CT Central time

ctge cartage
ctn carton
ctr center
cu cubic
Cu cuprum (L, copper)
cum cumulative
cur currency, current
cw clockwise
CWO cash with order, chief warrant officer
cwt hundredweight
cyc, cycl cyclopedia
cyl cylinder
CYO Catholic Youth Organization
CZ Canal Zone

d date, daughter, day, degree, died, penny
D Democrat, Democratic, diameter, doctor, dollar, Dutch
DA days after acceptance, deposit account, district attorney, don't answer
Dan Daniel, Danish
DAR Daughters of the American Revolution
dat dative
dau daughter
db decibel
dbl double
DC da capo (It, fr. the beginning), decimal classification, direct current, District of Columbia, double crochet
DD days after date, demand draft, dishonorable discharge, doctor of divinity
DDD direct distance dialing
DDS doctor of dental science, doctor of dental surgery
dec deceased, decrease
Dec December
def definite, definition
deg degree
del delegate, delegation
Del Delaware
dely delivery
Dem Democrat, Democratic
Den Denmark
dep depart, departure, deposit, deputy
depr depreciation
dept department
deriv derivation, derivative
det detached, detachment, detail
Deut Deuteronomy
dev deviation
DEW distant early warning
DF damage free
DFC distinguished flying cross
DFM distinguished flying medal
DG Dei gratia (LL, by the grace of God); director general
dia, diam diameter
diag diagonal, diagram
dial dialect
dict dictionary
diff difference
dig digest
dil dilute
dim dimension, diminished, diminutive
dir director
disc discount
dist distance, district
distn distillation
distr distribute, distribution, distributor
div divided, dividend, division
dk dark, deck, dock
DLitt, DLit doctor of letters, doctor of literature
DLO dead letter office
dn down
do ditto

DOA dead on arrival
doc document
dol dollar
dom domestic, dominant, dominion
doz dozen
DP domestic prelate, double play
dpt department
dr debit, debtor, dram, drive, drum
Dr doctor
DR dead reckoning, dining room
DS dal segno (It, fr. the sign), days after sight
DSC distinguished service cross, doctor of surgical chiropody
DSM distinguished service medal
DSO distinguished service order
dsp decessit sine prole (L, died without issue)
DST daylight saving time
Du Dutch
dup, dupl duplicate
DV Deo volente (L, God willing), Douay Version
DVM doctor of veterinary medicine
dwt pennyweight
DX distance
dz dozen

E east, eastern, einsteinium, English, errors, excellent
ea each
E and OE errors and omissions excepted
EC east central
eccl ecclesiastic, ecclesiastical
Eccles Ecclesiastes
Ecclus Ecclesiasticus
ecol ecological, ecology
econ economics, economist, economy
Ecua Ecuador
ed edited, edition, editor, education
EDT Eastern daylight time
educ education, educational
EE electrical engineer
eff efficiency
e.g. exempli gratia (L, for example)
Eg Egypt, Egyptian
ehf extremely high frequency
el, elev elevation
elec, elect electric, electrical, electricity
elem elementary
embryol embryology
emer emeritus
EMF electromotive force
emp emperor, empress
emu electromagnetic unit
enc, encl enclosure
ency, encyc encyclopedia
ENE east-northeast
eng engine, engineer, engineering
Eng England, English
engr engineer, engraved, engraving
enl enlarged, enlisted
ens ensign
entom, entomol entomology
env envelope
EOM end of month
Eph Ephesians
eq equal, equation
equip equipment
equiv equivalent
ER earned runs
ERA earned run average
erron erroneous
Es einsteinium
ESE east-southeast
esp especially
ESP extrasensory perception

esq esquire
est established, estimate, estimated
EST Eastern standard time
Esth Esther
ET Eastern time
ETA estimated time of arrival
et al et alii (L, and others)
etc et cetera (L, and so forth)
ETD estimated time of departure
ethnol ethnology
et seq et sequens (L, and the following one), et sequentes or et sequentia (L, and those that follow)
ety etymology
Eu europium
Eur Europe, European
EV electron volt
evap evaporate
ex example, express, extra
exc excellent, except
exch exchange, exchanged
ex div without dividend
exec executive, executor
Exod Exodus
exor executor
exp expense, export, exported, express
expt experiment
exptl experimental
ext extension, exterior, external, extra, extract
Ezek Ezekiel

f female, feminine, filly, focal length, folio, following, forte, frequency
F Fahrenheit, fair, false, fellow, fluorine, French, Friday, furlong
fac facsimile, faculty
FAdm fleet admiral
Fahr Fahrenheit
FAO Food and Agricultural Organization of the United Nations
FAS free alongside
fath fathom
FB freight bill
FBI Federal Bureau of Investigation
fcp foolscap
fcy fancy
FDIC Federal Deposit Insurance Corporation
Fe ferrum (L, iron)
Feb February
fec fecit (L, he [she] made it)
fed federal, federation
fedl federal
fedn federation
fem feminine
FEPC Fair Employment Practices Commission
ff folios, following
FICA Federal Insurance Contributions Act
FIFO first in, first out
fig figurative, figuratively, figure
fin finance, financial, finish
Finn Finnish
FIO free in and out
fisc fiscal
fl flourished, fluid
Fla Florida
Flem Flemish
fm fathom
Fm fermium
FM frequency modulation
fn footnote
fo, fol folio
FOB free on board
FOC free of charge

for foreign, forestry
FOR free on rail
FOS free on steamer
FOT free on truck
fp freezing point
fpm feet per minute
FPO fleet post office
fr father, friar, from
Fr francium, French, Friday
freq frequent, frequently
Fri Friday
front frontispiece
FRS Federal Reserve System
frt freight
frwy freeway
FSLIC Federal Savings and Loan Insurance Corporation
ft feet, foot, fort
fur furlong
furn furnished, furniture
fut future
fwd forward
FYI for your information

g acceleration of gravity, gauge, gram, gravity
G German, good
ga gauge
Ga gallium, Georgia
GA general agent, general assembly, general average
Gael Gaelic
gal gallon
Gal Galatians
galv galvanized
gar garage
GAR Grand Army of the Republic
GAW guaranteed annual wage
gaz gazette, gazetteer
GB games behind, Great Britain
GCA ground-controlled approach
GCT Greenwich civil time
Gd gadolinium
gds goods
Ge germanium
gen general, genitive
Gen Genesis
genl general
geog geographic, geographical, geography
geol geologic, geological, geology
geom geometrical, geometry
ger gerund
Ger German, Germany
GHQ general headquarters
gi gill
GI general issue, government issue
Gk Greek
gloss glossary
gm gram
GM general manager
Gmc Germanic
GNP gross national product
GOP Grand Old Party (Republican)
Goth Gothic
gov governor
govt government
gp group
GP general practitioner
GPO general post office, Government Printing Office
GQ general quarters
gr grade, grain, gram, gravity, gross
grad graduate
gram grammar
gro gross
GSA Girl Scouts of America

gt great, gutta (L, drop)
GT gross ton
Gt Brit Great Britain
gtd guaranteed

h hard, hardness, hour, husband
H hits, hydrogen
ha hectare
Hab Habakkuk
Hag Haggai
handbk, hdbk handbook
Hb hemoglobin
HBM Her Britannic Majesty, His Britannic Majesty
HC Holy Communion, House of Commons
HCL high cost of living
hd head
HD heavy-duty
hdbk handbook
hdkf handkerchief
hdqrs headquarters
hdwe, hdwre hardware
He helium
HE high explosive, His Eminence, His Excellency
Heb Hebrew, Hebrews
hf half, high frequency
Hf hafnium
Hg hydrargyrum (L, mercury)
HG High German
hgt height
HH Her Highness, His Highness, His Holiness
hhd hogshead
hist historian, historical, history
HJ hic jacet (L, here lies)—used in epitaphs
HL House of Lords
HM Her Majesty, His Majesty
HMS Her Majesty's Ship, His Majesty's Ship
Ho holmium
hon honor, honorable, honorary
hor horizontal
hort horticultural, horticulture
Hos Hosea
hosp hospital
hp horsepower
HP high pressure
HQ headquarters
hr hour
HR home run, House of Representatives
HRH Her Royal Highness, His Royal Highness
HS high school, house surgeon
hse house
ht height
HT high-tension
Hung Hungarian, Hungary
HV high voltage
hvy heavy
hwy highway
hyp, hypoth hypothesis, hypothetical

I iodine, island, isle
Ia Iowa
ib, ibid ibidem (L, in the same place)
ICJ International Court of Justice
id idem (L, the same)
ID identification
i.e. id est (L, that is)
IE Indo-European
IF intermediate frequency
IGY International Geophysical Year

IHP indicated horsepower
IHS Iesus Hominum Salvator (L, Jesus, Savior of Men)
ill, illus, illust illustrated, illustration
Ill Illinois
ILS instrument landing system
imit imitative
imp imperative, imperfect, imperial, import, imported
imperf imperfect
in inch
In indium
inc incorporated, increase
incl including, inclusive
incog incognito
incr increase
ind independent, index, industrial, industry
Ind Indiana
indef indefinite
indic indicative
inf infantry, infinitive, information
infl influenced
INP International News Photo
INRI Iesus Nazarenus Rex Iudaeorum (L, Jesus of Nazareth, King of the Jews)
ins inches, insurance
insol insoluble
insp inspector
inst instant, institute, institution
instr instructor, instrument
int interest, interior, internal, international
interj interjection
interrog interrogative
intl international
intrans intransitive
introd introduction
inv invoice
IOOF Independent Order of Odd Fellows
IP innings pitched
IPA International Phonetic Alphabet
i.q. idem quod (L, the same as)
IQ intelligence quotient
Ir iridium, Irish
IRBM intermediate range ballistic missile
Ire Ireland
IrGael Irish Gaelic
irreg irregular
Isa Isaiah
isl island
Isr Israel, Israeli
It, Ital Italian
ital italic, italicized
IV intravenous
IW Isle of Wight
IWW Industrial Workers of the World

J jack, journal
Jam Jamaica
Jan January
Jap Japan, Japanese
Jas James
JCC Junior Chamber of Commerce
JCS joint chiefs of staff
jct junction
Je June
Jer Jeremiah
jg junior grade
Jn John
jnt, jt joint
Josh Joshua
jour journal
JP jet propulsion, justice of the peace
jr, jun junior
JRC Junior Red Cross

Judg Judges
Jul July
Jun June
junc junction
juv juvenile
JV junior varsity

k karat, knit
K kalium (L, potassium), king
Kans Kansas
kc kilocycle
KC king's counsel, Knights of Columbus
kc/s kilocycles per second
KD kiln-dried, knocked down
kg, kgm kilogram
KKK Ku Klux Klan
km kilometer
kn knot
K of C Knights of Columbus
kt karat, knight
kw kilowatt
Ky Kentucky

l left, length, line, liter
L lake, large, Latin, libra (L, pound)
La Louisiana
LA law agent, Los Angeles
Lab Labrador
lam laminated
Lam Lamentations
lang language
lat latitude
Lat Latin
lb pound
LC letter of credit, Library of Congress
LCD lowest common denominator
lcdr lieutenant commander
LCL less than carload
LCM least common multiple
ld load, lord
LD lethal dose
ldg landing, loading
lect lecture
leg legal, legislative, legislature
legis legislative, legislature
Lev Leviticus
lf low frequency
lg, lge large
LG Low German
LGk Late Greek
LH left hand, lower half
li link
Li lithium
LI Long Island
lib liberal, librarian, library
lieut lieutenant
LIFO last in, first out
lin lineal, linear
liq liquid, liquor
lit liter, literal, literally, literary, literature
lith, litho lithography
LittD, LitD doctor of letters, doctor of literature
Lk Luke
ll lines
LL Late Latin
LLD doctor of laws
LOB left on bases
loc cit loco citato (L, in the place cited)
log logarithm
Lond London
long longitude
loq loquitur (L, he [she] speaks)
LP low pressure
LS left side, letter signed, locus sigilli (L, place of the seal)

lt lieutenant, light
LT long ton, low-tension
ltd limited
LTL less than truckload
ltr letter
lub lubricant, lubricating
lv leave

m male, mare, married, masculine, meridian, meridies (L, noon), meter, mile, mill, minute, month, moon
M master, medium, mille (L, thousand), Monday, monsieur
MA master of arts, mental age
mach machine, machinery, machinist
mag magazine, magnetism, magneto, magnitude
maj major
Mal Malachi
man manual
Man Manitoba
manuf manufacture, manufacturing
mar maritime
Mar March
masc masculine
Mass Massachusetts
math mathematical, mathematician, mathematics
MATS Military Air Transport Service
max maximum
mc megacycle
MC master of ceremonies, member of congress
Md Maryland
MD doctor of medicine, months after date
mdnt midnight
mdse merchandise
Me Maine
ME mechanical engineer, Middle English, mining engineer
meas measure
mech mechanical, mechanics
med medical, medicine, medieval, medium
mem member, memoir, memorial
mer meridian
Messrs messieurs
met metropolitan
meteorol meteorology
MEV million electron volts
Mex Mexican, Mexico
mf medium frequency
MF Middle French
mfd manufactured
mfg manufacturing
mfr manufacture, manufacturer
mg milligram
Mg magnesium
MG machine gun, military government
MGk Middle Greek
mgr manager, monseigneur, monsignor
mgt management
mi mile, mill
MI military intelligence
MIA missing in action
Mic Micah
Mich Michigan
mid middle
mil military
min minimum, mining, minister, minor, minute
mineral mineralogy
Minn Minnesota
misc miscellaneous
Miss Mississippi
mixt mixture
mk mark

Mk Mark
ML Middle Latin
MLD minimum lethal dose
Mlle mademoiselle
mm millimeter
MM Maryknoll Missioners, messieurs
Mme madame
Mn manganese
mo month
Mo Missouri, molybdenum
MO mail order, medical officer, money order
mod moderate, modern
modif modification
mol molecular, molecule
mol wt molecular weight
MOM middle of month
Mon Monday
Mont Montana
mos months
mp melting point
MP member of parliament, metropolitan police, military police, military policeman
mpg miles per gallon
mph miles per hour
Mr mister
Mrs mistress
MS manuscript, master of science, motor ship
msg message
msgr monseigneur, monsignor
MSgt master sergeant
msl mean sea level
MSS manuscripts
MST Mountain standard time
mt mount, mountain
Mt Matthew
MT metric ton, Mountain time
mtg, mtge mortgage
mtl metal
mtn mountain
mun, munic municipal
mus museum, music
MV mean variation, motor vessel
mythol mythology

n net, neuter, new, noon, note, noun, number
N knight, nitrogen, normal, north, northern
Na natrium (L, sodium)
NA no account
NAACP National Association for the Advancement of Colored People
Nah Nahum
NAS naval air station
nat national, native, natural
natl national
NATO North Atlantic Treaty Organization
naut nautical
nav naval, navigable, navigation
Nb niobium
NB nota bene (L, note well)
N.B. New Brunswick
NBC National Broadcasting Company
NBS National Bureau of Standards
NC no charge
N.C. North Carolina
NCE New Catholic Edition
NCO noncommissioned officer
Nd neodymium
ND no date
N.Dak., N.D. North Dakota
Ne neon

NE New England, northeast
NEB New English Bible
Nebr, Neb Nebraska
NED New English Dictionary
neg negative
Neh Nehemiah
NEI not elsewhere included, not else-
where indicated
NES not elsewhere specified
Neth Netherlands
neurol neurology
neut neuter
Nev Nevada
NF no funds
Nfld Newfoundland
NG National Guard, no good
NGk New Greek
N.H. New Hampshire
NHG New High German
NHI national health insurance (Brit.)
Ni nickel
N.J. New Jersey
nk neck
NL New Latin, night letter, non liquet
(L, it is not clear)
NLT night letter
NM nautical mile, night message, no
mark, not marked
N.Mex, N.M. New Mexico
NNE north-northeast
NNW north-northwest
no north, northern, nose, number
No nobelium
NOIBN not otherwise indexed by name
nol pros nolle prosequi (L, to be unwill-
ing to prosecute)
nom nominative
non seq non sequitur
Norw Norway, Norwegian
NOS not otherwise specified
Nov November
Np neptunium
NP no protest, notary public
NPN nonprotein nitrogen
nr near, number
NS not specified
N.S. Nova Scotia
NSF not sufficient funds
N.S.W. New South Wales
NT New Testament
N.T. Northern Territory
NTP normal temperature and pressure
nt wt net weight
NU name unknown
Num Numbers
numis numismatic, numismatics
NW northwest
NWT Northwest Territories
N.Y. New York
NYC New York City
N.Z. New Zealand

o ocean, ohm
O oxygen
o/a on account
OAS Organization of American States
ob obiit (L, he [she] died)
Obad Obadiah
obj object, objective
obl oblique, oblong
obs obsolete
obv obverse
OC overcharge
occas occasionally
OCS officer candidate school

oct octavo
Oct October
o/d on demand
OD officer of the day, olive drab, over-
draft, overdrawn
OE Old English
OED Oxford English Dictionary
OES Order of the Eastern Star
OF Old French
ofc office
off office, officer, official
OFM Order of Friars Minor
O.F.S. Orange Free State
OG original gum
Okla Oklahoma
ON Old Norse
Ont Ontario
op opus, out of print
OP Order of Preachers
op cit opere citato (L, in the work cited)
opp opposite
opt optical, optician, optional
OR owner's risk
orch orchestra
ord order, ordnance
Oreg, Ore Oregon
org organization, organized
orig original, originally
ornith ornithology
o/s out of stock
Os osmium
OS ordinary seaman
OS and D over, short, and damaged
OSB Order of St. Benedict
OT Old Testament, overtime
OTS officers' training school
oz ounce

p page, participle, past, penny, per, pint,
purl
P pawn, phosphorus, pressure
pa per annum
Pa Pennsylvania
PA passenger agent, power of attorney,
press agent, private account, public
address, purchasing agent
Pac Pacific
paleon paleontology
pam pamphlet
Pan Panama
P and L profit and loss
par paragraph, parallel, parish
parl parliament, parliamentary
part participial, participle, particular
pass passenger, passive
pat patent
path, pathol pathology
payt payment
Pb plumbum (L, lead)
pc percent, percentage, piece, postcard,
post cibum (L, after meals)
PC petty cash, privy council, privy
councillor
pct percent
pd paid, pond
Pd palladium
PD per diem, potential difference
PE professional engineer, Protestant
Episcopal
ped pedal
P.E.I. Prince Edward Island
penin, pen peninsula
Penn, Penna Pennsylvania
per period
Per Persian
perf perfect, perforated
perh perhaps

perm permanent
perp perpendicular
pers person, personal
Pers Persia, Persian
pert pertaining
Pet Peter
pf, pfd preferred
pfc private first class
pg page
PG postgraduate
pharm pharmaceutical, pharmacist, pharmacy
PhD doctor of philosophy
Phil Philippians
Phila Philadelphia
Philem Philemon
philos philosopher, philosophy
phon phonetics
photog photographic, photography
phr phrase
phys physical, physician, physics
physiol physiologist, physiology
pinx pinxit (L, he [she] painted it)
pk park, peak, peck
pkg package
pkt packet
pkwy parkway
pl place, plate, plural
pm premium
p.m. post meridiem (L, afternoon)
Pm promethium
PM paymaster, police magistrate, postmaster, postmortem, prime minister, provost marshal
pmk postmark
pmt payment
PN promissory note
pnxt pinxit (L, he [she] painted it)
Po polonium
PO petty officer, postal order, post office, putouts
POC port of call
POD pay on delivery
POE port of embarkation, port of entry
Pol Poland, Polish
polit political, politician
polytech polytechnic
pop popular, population
POR pay on return
Port Portugal, Portuguese
pos position, positive
poss possessive
POW prisoner of war
pp pages, past participle, pianissimo
PP parcel post, post position
PPC pour prendre congé (F, to take leave)
ppd postpaid, prepaid
PPS post postscriptum (L, an additional postscript)
ppt precipitate
pptn precipitation
PQ Province of Quebec
pr pair, price
Pr praseodymium
PR payroll, public relations, Puerto Rico
prec preceding
pred predicate
pref preface, preference, preferred, prefix
prelim preliminary
prem premium
prep preparatory, preposition
pres present, president
prev previous
prf proof
prim primary, primitive
prin principal
PRN pro re nata (L, for an occasion

that has arisen) as occasion arises
PRO public relations officer
prob probable, probably, problem
proc proceedings
prod production
prof professor
pron pronoun, pronounced, pronunciation
prop propeller, property, proprietor, proposition
pros prosody
Prot Protestant
prov province, provincial, provisional
Prov Proverbs
prp present participle
Ps Psalms
PS postscriptum (L, postscript), public school
pseud pseudonym
psi pounds per square inch
PST Pacific standard time
psych psychology
psychol psychologist, psychology
pt part, payment, pint, point, port
Pt platinum
PT Pacific time, physical therapy, physical training
PTA Parent-Teacher Association
pte private (Brit.)
ptg printing
PTO please turn over
Pu plutonium
pub public, publication, published, publisher, publishing
publ publication, published
pvt private
PW prisoner of war
PX post exchange

q quart, quarto, query, question, quire
Q queen
QC Queen's Counsel
qd quaque die (L, daily)
qda quantity discount agreement
QED quod erat demonstrandum (L, which was to be demonstrated)
QEF quod erat faciendum (L, which was to be done)
QEI quod erat inveniendum (L, which was to be found out)
QID quater in die (L, four times a day)
Qld, Q'land Queensland
QM quartermaster
QMC quartermaster corps
QMG quartermaster general
qq v quae vide (L, which [pl] see)
qr quarter, quire
qt quart
q.t. quiet
qto quarto
qty quantity
quad quadrant
Que Quebec
quot quotation
q.v. quod vide (L, which see)
qy query

r rare, right, river, roentgen
R rabbi, radius, Republican, resistance, rook, runs
Ra radium
RA regular army, royal academy
RAAF Royal Australian Air Force
rad radical, radio, radius
RAdm rear admiral
RAF Royal Air Force
Rb rubidium

RBC red blood cells, red blood count
RBI runs batted in
RC Red Cross, Roman Catholic
RCAF Royal Canadian Air Force
RCMP Royal Canadian Mounted Police
rd road, rod, round
RD rural delivery
re reference, regarding
Re rhenium
REA Railway Express Agency
rec receipt, record, recording, recreation
recd received
recip reciprocal, reciprocity
rec sec recording secretary
rect rectangle, rectangular, receipt, rectified
ref referee, reference, referred, reformed, refunding
refl reflex, reflexive
refr refraction
refrig refrigerating, refrigeration
reg region, register, registered, regular, regulation
regt regiment
rel relating, relative
relig religion
rep report, reporter, representative, republic
Rep Republican
repl replace, replacement
rept report
req require, required, requisition
res research, reserve, residence, resolution
resp respective, respectively
retd retained, retired, returned
rev revenue, reverend, reverse, review, reviewed, revised, revision, revolution
Rev Revelation
RF radio frequency
RFD rural free delivery
Rh rhodium
RH right hand
R.I. Rhode Island
RIP requiescat in pace (L, may he [she] rest in peace)
riv river
rm ream, room
RMA Royal Military Academy (Sandhurst)
Rn radon
RN registered nurse, Royal Navy
rnd round
RNZAF Royal New Zealand Air Force
ROG receipt of goods
Rom Roman, Romance, Romania, Romanian, Romans
ROTC Reserve Officers' Training Corps
rpm revolutions per minute
RPO railway post office
rps revolutions per second
rpt repeat, report
rr rear
RR railroad, rural route
RS recording secretary, revised statutes, right side, Royal Society
RSV Revised Standard Version
RSVP répondez s'il vous plait (Fr, please reply)
RSWC right side up with care
rt right, route
RT radiotelephone
rte route
Ru ruthenium
Rum Rumania, Rumanian
Russ Russia, Russian
RW right worshipful, right worthy
rwy, ry railway

s second, section, semi, series, shilling, singular, son, soprano
S sacrifice, saint, Saturday, senate, small, south, southern, sulfur, Sunday
Sa Saturday
SA Salvation Army, sex appeal, sine anno (L, without date), South Africa, subject to approval
SAC Strategic Air Command
Sam Samuel
sanit sanitary, sanitation
SAR Sons of the American Revolution
Sask Saskatchewan
sat saturate, saturated, saturation
Sat Saturday
S. Aust, S.A. South Australia
sb substantive
SB bachelor of science, stolen base
sc scale, scene, science, scilicet (L, that is to say), small capitals
Sc scandium, Scots
S.C. South Carolina
Scand Scandinavia, Scandinavian
ScD doctor of science
ScGael Scottish Gaelic
sch school
sci science, scientific
scil scilicet (L, that is to say)
Scot Scotland, Scottish
script scripture
sculp, sculpt sculpsit (L, he [she] carved it), sculptor, sculpture
SD sea-damaged, sine die, special delivery
S. Dak, S.D. South Dakota
Se selenium
SE southeast
SEATO Southeast Asia Treaty Organization
sec second, secondary, secretary, section, secundum (L, according to)
sect section
secy secretary
sel select, selected, selection
sem seminary
sen senate, senator, senior
sep separate
sepn separation
Sept, Sep September
seq sequens (L, the following)
seqq sequentia (L, the following [pl])
ser serial, series
serg, sergt sergeant
serv service
sf science fiction
SF sacrifice fly
sfc sergeant first class
sg senior grade, singular, specific gravity
SG solicitor general, surgeon general
sgd signed
sgt sergeant
sh share, show
Shak Shakespeare
shpt, shipt shipment
shr share
sht sheet
shtg shortage
Si silicon
S.I. Sandwich Islands, Staten Island (N.Y.)
sig signal, signature
sigill sigillum (L, seal)
sing singular
SJ Society of Jesus
Skt Sanskrit
SL salvage loss
s.l.a.n. sine loco, anno, vel nomine (L, without place, year, or name)
sld sailed, sealed

sm small
Sm samarium
SM master of science, Society of Mary
Sn stannum (LL, tin)
so south, southern
SO seller's option, strikeouts
soc social, society
sociol sociology
sol solicitor, soluble, solution
Sol Solomon
soln solution
sop soprano
SOP standard operating procedure
soph sophomore
sp special, species, specimen, spelling, spirit
Sp Spain, Spanish
SP shore patrol, sine prole (L, without issue)
Span Spanish
SPCA Society for the Prevention of Cruelty to Animals
SPCC Society for the Prevention of Cruelty to Children
spec special, specialist
specif specific, specifically
sp. gr. specific gravity
spp species (pl)
sq squadron, square
sr senior
Sr sister, strontium
SR shipping receipt
SRO standing room only
SS saints, steamship, Sunday school, sworn statement
SSE south-southeast
SSgt staff sergeant
ssp subspecies
SSR Soviet Socialist Republic
SSS Selective Service System
SSW south-southwest
st saint, stanza, start, state, stitch, stone, straight, strait, street
ST short ton
sta station
stat statute
stbd starboard
std standard
STD doctor of sacred theology
stg, ster sterling
stk stock
STP standard temperature and pressure
str stretch
stud student
subj subject, subjunctive
suff sufficient, suffix
suffr suffragan
Sun Sunday
sup superior, supplement, supplementary, supply, supra (L, above)
superl superlative
supp, suppl supplement, supplementary
supt superintendent
surg surgeon, surgery, surgical
surv survey, surveying, surveyor
SV sub verbo or sub voce (L, under the word)
SW shipper's weight, shortwave, south-west
S.W.A. South-West Africa
Switz Switzerland
syll syllable
sym symbol, symmetrical
syn synonym, synonymous, synonymy
syst system

t teaspoon, temperature, tenor, ton, troy

T tablespoon, Thursday, true, Tuesday
Ta tantalum
tan tangent
Tas, Tasm Tasmania
taxon taxonomy
Tb terbium
TB trial balance, tuberculosis
tbs, tbsp tablespoon
TC teachers college
TD touchdown
Te tellurium
tech technical, technically, technician, technological, technology
tel telegram, telegraph, telephone
teleg telegraphy
temp temperature, temporary, tempore (L, in the time of)
ten tenor
Tenn Tennessee
ter terrace, territory
terr territory
Tex Texas
Th thorium, Thursday
ThD doctor of theology
theat theatrical
theol theological, theology
therm thermometer
Thess Thessalonians
thou thousand
Thurs, Thur, Thu Thursday
Ti titanium
TID ter in die (L, three times a day)
Tim Timothy
tinct tincture
Tit Titus
tk tank, truck
TKO technical knockout
tkt ticket
Tl thallium
TL total loss
TLC tender loving care
Tm thulium
TM trademark
TMO telegraph money order
tn ton, town
tnpk turnpike
TO telegraph office, turn over
topog topography
tot total
tp title page, township
tpk turnpike
tr translated, translation, translator, transpose
trans transaction, transitive, translated, translation, translator, transportation, transverse
transl translated, translation
transp transportation
treas treasurer, treasury
trib tributary
trig trigonometry
TSgt technical sergeant
tsp teaspoon
Tues, Tue, Tu Tuesday
Turk Turkey, Turkish
TV television
TVA Tennessee Valley Authority

u unit
U university, uranium
UAR United Arab Republic
UFO unidentified flying object
UH upper half
uhf ultrahigh frequency
UK United Kingdom
ult ultimate
UMT Universal Military Training

UN United Nations
UNESCO United Nations Educational, Scientific, and Cultural Organization
univ universal, university
UNRWA United Nations Relief and Works Agency
UPI United Press International
u.s. ubi supra (L, where above [mentioned], ut supra (L, as above)
US United States
USA United States Army, United States of America
USAF United States Air Force
USCG United States Coast Guard
USES United States Employment Service
USM United States mail, United States Marines
USMA United States Military Academy
USMC United States Marine Corps
USN United States Navy
USNA United States Naval Academy
USNG United States National Guard
USNR United States Naval Reserve
USO United Service Organizations
USP United States Pharmacopeia
USS United States Ship
USSR Union of Soviet Socialist Republics
usu usual, usually
UV ultraviolet
UW underwriter

v vector, velocity, verb, verse, versus, vide (L, see), voice, volume, vowel
V vanadium, victory, volt, voltage
Va Virginia
VA Veterans Administration, vice admiral
VAdm vice admiral
val value
var variable, variant, variation, variety, various
vb verb
VC vice-chancellor, vice-consul
VD venereal disease
veg vegetable
vel vellum, velocity
ven venerable
vert vertical
vet veterinarian, veterinary
VF video frequency, visual field
VFD volunteer fire department
VFW Veterans of Foreign Wars
VG very good, vicar-general
vhf very high frequency
vi verb intransitive, vide infra (L, see below)
VI Virgin Islands
vic vicinity
Vic Victoria
vil village
VIP very important person
vis visibility, visual
viz videlicet (L, namely)
VL Vulgar Latin
vlf very low frequency
VNA Visiting Nurse Association
VOA Voice of America
voc vocative
vocab vocabulary
vol volume, volunteer
vou voucher
VP vice-president
vs verse, versus, vide supra (L, see above)
vss verses, versions
vt verb transitive

Vt Vermont
VTOL vertical takeoff and landing
Vulg Vulgate
vv verses, vice versa

w water, watt, week, weight, wide, width, wife, with
W Wednesday, Welsh, west, western, wolfram
war warrant
Wash Washington
W. Aust. Western Australia
WB water ballast, waybill
WBC white blood cells, white blood count
WC water closet, west central, without charge
WCTU Women's Christian Temperance Union
Wed Wednesday
wf wrong font
wh which
whf wharf
WHO World Health Organization
whol wholesale
whs, whse warehouse
whsle wholesale
W.I. West Indies
wid widow, widower
Wis, Wisc Wisconsin
wk week, work
WL wavelength
wmk watermark
WNW west-northwest
w/o without
WO warrant officer
wpm words per minute
wrnt warrant
WSW west-southwest
wt weight
W. Va. West Virginia
WW World War
Wyo Wyoming

xd, x div without dividend
Xe xenon
x in, x int without interest
XL extra large
Xn Christian
Xnty Christianity

y yard, year
Y YMCA, yttrium
Yb ytterbium
yd yard
yld yield
YMCA Young Men's Christian Association
YMHA Young Men's Hebrew Association
YO yarn over, year-old
yr year, your
yrbk yearbook
Yt yttrium
YT Yukon Territory
YWCA, YW Young Women's Christian Association
YWHA Young Women's Hebrew Association

z zero
Zech Zechariah
Zeph Zephaniah
ZIP Zone Improvement Plan
Zn zinc
zool zoological, zoology
Zr zirconium

POPULATION OF URBAN PLACES
IN THE UNITED STATES
HAVING 10,000 OR MORE INHABITANTS IN 1960

Places over 1,000,000

Chicago, Ill.	3,550,404
Detroit, Mich.	1,670,144
Los Angeles, Calif.	2,479,015
New York City, N. Y.	7,781,984
Philadelphia, Pa.	2,002,512

Places 500,000–1,000,000

Baltimore, Md.	939,024
Boston, Mass.	697,197
Buffalo, N. Y.	532,759
Cincinnati, Ohio	502,550
Cleveland, Ohio	876,050
Dallas, Tex.	679,684
Houston, Tex.	938,219
Milwaukee, Wis.	741,324
New Orleans, La.	627,525
Pittsburgh, Pa.	604,332
St. Louis, Mo.	750,026
San Antonio, Tex.	587,718
San Diego, Calif.	573,224
San Francisco, Calif.	740,316
Seattle, Wash.	557,087
Washington, D. C.	763,956

Places 250,000–500,000

Akron, Ohio	290,351
Atlanta, Ga.	487,455
Birmingham, Ala.	340,887
Columbus, Ohio	471,316
Dayton, Ohio	262,332
Denver, Colo.	493,887
El Paso, Tex.	276,687
Fort Worth, Tex.	356,268
Honolulu. Hawaii	294,194
Indianapolis, Ind.	476,258
Jersey City, N. J.	276,101
Kansas City, Mo.	475,539
Long Beach, Calif.	344,168
Louisville, Ky.	390,639
Memphis, Tenn.	497,524
Miami, Fla.	291,688
Minneapolis, Minn.	482,872
Newark, N. J.	405,220
Norfolk, Va.	304,869
Oakland, Calif.	367,548
Oklahoma City, Okla.	324,253
Omaha, Nebr.	301,598
Phoenix, Ariz.	439,170
Portland, Oreg.	372,676
Rochester, N. Y.	318,611
St. Paul, Minn.	313,411
Tampa, Fla.	274,970
Toledo, Ohio	318,003
Tulsa, Okla.	261,685
Wichita, Kans.	254,698

Places 100,000–250,000

Albany, N. Y.	129,726
Albuquerque, N. Mex.	201,189
Allentown, Pa.	108,347
Amarillo, Tex.	137,969
Anaheim, Calif.	104,184
Arlington County, Va.	163,401
Austin, Tex.	186,545
Baton Rouge, La	152,419
Beaumont, Tex.	119,175
Berkeley, Calif.	111,268
Bridgeport, Conn.	156,748
Cambridge, Mass.	107,716
Camden, N. J.	117,159
Canton, Ohio	113,631
Charlotte, N. C.	201,564
Chattanooga, Tenn.	130,009
Columbus, Ga.	116,779
Corpus Christi, Tex.	167,690
Dearborn, Mich.	112,007
Des Moines, Iowa	208,982
Duluth, Minn.	106,884
East Los Angeles, Calif.	104,270
Elizabeth, N. J.	107,698
Erie, Pa.	138,440
Evansville, Ind.	141,543
Flint, Mich.	196,940
Fort Wayne, Ind.	161,776
Fresno, Calif.	133,929
Gary, Ind.	178,320
Glendale, Calif.	119,442
Grand Rapids, Mich.	177,313
Greensboro, N. C.	119,574
Hammond, Ind.	111,698
Hartford, Conn.	162,178
Jackson, Miss.	144,422
Jacksonville, Fla.	201,030
Kansas City, Kans.	121,901
Knoxville, Tenn.	111,827
Lansing, Mich.	107,807
Lincoln, Nebr.	128,521
Little Rock, Ark.	107,813
Lubbock, Tex.	128,691
Madison, Wis.	126,706
Mobile, Ala.	202,779
Montgomery, Ala.	134,393
Nashville, Tenn.	170,874
New Bedford, Mass.	102,477
New Haven, Conn.	152,048
Newport News, Va.	113,662
Niagara Falls, N. Y.	102,394
Pasadena, Calif.	116,407
Paterson, N. J.	143,663
Peoria, Ill.	103,162
Portsmouth, Va.	114,773
Providence, R. I.	207,498
Richmond, Va.	219,958
Rockford, Ill.	126,706
Sacramento, Calif.	191,667
St. Petersburg, Fla.	181,298
Salt Lake City, Utah	189,454
San Jose, Calif.	204,196
Santa Ana, Calif.	100,350
Savannah, Ga.	149,245
Scranton, Pa.	111,443
Shreveport, La.	164,372
South Bend, Ind.	132,445
Spokane, Wash.	181,608
Springfield, Mass.	174,463
Syracuse, N. Y.	216,038
Tacoma, Wash.	147,979
Topeka, Kans.	119,484
Torrance, Calif.	100,991
Trenton, N. J.	114,167
Tucson, Ariz.	212,892
Utica, N. Y.	100,410
Waterbury, Conn.	107,130
Wichita Falls, Tex.	101,724
Winston-Salem, N. C.	111,135
Worcester, Mass.	186,587
Yonkers, N. Y.	190,634

Youngstown, Ohio 166,689

Places 50,000–100,000

Abilene, Tex.	90,368
Abington, Pa.	55,831
Alameda, Calif.	63,855
Albany, Ga.	55,890
Alexandria, Va.	91,023
Alhambra, Calif.	54,807
Altoona, Pa.	69,407
Ann Arbor, Mich.	67,340
Arden—Arcade, Calif.	73,352
Asheville, N. C.	60,192
Atlantic City, N. J.	59,544
Augusta, Ga.	70,626
Aurora, Ill.	63,715
Bakersfield, Calif.	56,848
Bay City, Mich.	53,604
Bayonne, N. J.	74,215
Berwyn, Ill.	54,224
Bethesda, Md.	56,527
Bethlehem, Pa.	75,408
Billings, Mont.	52,851
Binghamton, N. Y.	75,941
Bloomfield, N. J.	51,867
Bloomington, Minn.	50,498
Brockton, Mass.	72,813
Brookline, Mass.	54,044
Burbank, Calif.	90,155
Cedar Rapids, Iowa	92,035
Charleston, S. C.	65,925
Charleston, W. Va.	85,796
Cheektowaga-Northwest, N. Y.	52,362
Chester, Pa.	63,658
Chicopee, Mass.	61,533
Cicero, Ill.	69,130
Cleveland Heights, Ohio ...	61,813
Clifton, N. J.	82,084
Colorado Springs, Colo. ...	70,194
Columbia, S. C.	97,433
Compton, Calif.	71,812
Council Bluffs, Iowa	55,641
Covington, Ky.	60,376
Cranston, R. I.	66,766
Davenport, Iowa	88,981
Decatur, Ill.	78,004
Downey, Calif.	82,505
Dubuque, Iowa	56,606
Dundalk, Md.	82,428
Durham, N. C.	78,302
East Chicago, Ind.	57,669
East Orange, N. J.	77,259
East St. Louis, Ill.	81,712
Euclid, Ohio	62,998
Eugene, Oreg.	50,977
Evanston, Ill.	79,283
Fall River, Mass.	99,942
Fort Lauderdale, Fla.	83,648
Fort Smith, Ark.	52,991
Fullerton, Calif.	56,180
Gadsden, Ala.	58,088
Galveston, Tex.	67,175
Garden Grove, Calif.	84,238
Great Falls, Mont.	55,244
Green Bay, Wis.	62,888
Greenville, S. C.	66,188
Greenwich, Conn.	53,793
Hamilton, N. J.	65,035
Hamilton, Ohio	72,354
Hampton, Va.	89,258
Harrisburg, Pa.	79,697
Haverford, Pa.	54,019
Hayward, Calif	72,700
Hialeah, Fla.	66,972
Hicksville, N. Y.	50,405
High Point, N. C.	62,063
Holyoke, Mass.	52,689
Huntington, W. Va.	83,627
Huntsville, Ala.	72,365

Independence, Mo.	62,328
Inglewood, Calif.	63,390
Irvington, N. J.	59,379
Jackson, Mich.	50,720
Johnstown, Pa.	53,949
Joliet, Ill.	66,780
Kalamazoo, Mich.	82,089
Kenosha, Wis.	67,899
Kettering, Ohio	54,462
Lake Charles, La.	63,392
Lakewood, Calif.	67,126
Lakewood, Ohio	66,154
Lancaster, Pa.	61,055
Laredo, Tex.	60,678
Las Vegas, Nev.	64,405
Lawrence, Mass.	70,933
Lawton, Okla.	61,697
Levittown, N. Y.	65,276
Lexington, Ky.	62,810
Lima, Ohio	51,037
Lincoln Park, Mich.	53,933
Livonia, Mich.	66,702
Lorain, Ohio	68,932
Lowell, Mass.	92,107
Lower Merion, Pa.	59,420
Lynchburg, Va.	54,790
Lynn, Mass.	94,478
Macon, Ga.	69,764
Malden, Mass.	57,676
Manchester, N. H.	88,282
Medford, Mass.	64,971
Meriden, Conn.	51,850
Miami Beach, Fla.	63,145
Midland, Tex.	62,625
Monroe, La.	52,219
Mount Vernon, N. Y.	76,010
Muncie, Ind.	68,603
New Britain, Conn.	82,201
New Rochelle, N. Y.	76,812
Newton, Mass.	92,384
North Little Rock, Ark.	58,032
Norwalk, Calif.	88,739
Norwalk, Conn.	67,775
Oak Park, Ill.	61,093
Odessa, Tex.	80,338
Ogden, Utah	70,197
Orlando, Fla.	88,135
Palo Alto, Calif.	52,287
Parma, Ohio	82,845
Pasadena, Tex.	58,737
Passaic, N. J.	53,963
Pawtucket, R. I.	81,001
Penn Hills, Pa.	51,512
Pensacola, Fla.	56,752
Pittsfield, Mass.	57,879
Pomona, Calif.	67,157
Pontiac, Mich.	82,233
Port Arthur, Tex.	66,676
Portland, Me.	72,566
Pueblo, Colo.	91,181
Quincy, Mass.	87,409
Racine, Wis.	89,144
Raleigh, N. C.	93,931
Reading, Pa.	98,177
Reno, Nev.	51,470
Richmond, Calif.	71,854
Riverside, Calif.	84,332
Roanoke, Va.	97,110
Rock Island, Ill.	51,863
Rome, N. Y.	51,646
Roseville, Mich.	50,195
Royal Oak, Mich.	80,612
Saginaw, Mich.	98,265
St. Clair Shores, Mich.	76,657
St. Joseph, Mo.	79,673
San Angelo, Tex.	58,815
San Bernardino, Calif.	91,922
San Leandro, Calif.	65,962
San Mateo, Calif.	69,870
Santa Barbara, Calif.	58,768

Santa Clara, Calif.	58,880	Bellingham, Wash.	34,688
Santa Monica, Calif.	83,249	Belmont, Mass.	28,715
Schenectady, N. Y.	81,682	Beloit, Wis.	32,846
Silver Spring, Md.	66,348	Bergenfield, N. J.	27,203
Sioux City, Iowa	89,159	Bessemer, Ala.	33,054
Sioux Falls, S. Dak.	65,466	Beverly, Mass.	36,108
Skokie, Ill.	59,364	Beverly Hills, Calif.	30,817
Somerville, Mass.	94,697	Big Spring, Tex.	31,230
South Gate, Calif.	53,831	Biloxi, Miss.	44,053
Springfield, Ill.	83,271	Birmingham, Mich.	25,525
Springfield, Mo.	95,865	Bismarck, N. Dak.	27,670
Springfield, Ohio	82,723	Bloomington, Ill.	36,271
Stamford, Conn.	92,713	Bloomington, Ind.	31,357
Stockton, Calif.	86,321	Boise, Idaho	34,481
Sunnyvale, Calif.	52,898	Bossier City, La.	32,776
Terre Haute, Ind.	72,500	Boulder, Colo.	37,718
Troy, N. Y.	67,492	Bowling Green, Ky.	28,338
Tuscaloosa, Ala.	63,370	Braintree, Mass.	31,069
Tyler, Tex.	51,230	Bremerton, Wash.	28,922
Union, N. J.	51,499	Bristol, Conn.	45,499
Union City, N. J.	52,180	Brownsville, Fla.	38,417
University City, Mo.	51,249	Brownsville, Tex.	48,040
Upper Darby, Pa.	93,158	Bryan, Tex.	27,542
Vallejo, Calif.	60,877	Buena Park, Calif.	46,401
Waco, Tex.	97,808	Burlington, Iowa	32,430
Waltham, Mass.	55,413	Burlington, N. C.	33,199
Warren, Mich.	89,246	Burlington, Vt.	35,531
Warren, Ohio	59,648	Butte, Mont.	27,877
Warwick, R. I.	68,504	Calumet City, Ill.	25,000
Waterloo, Iowa	71,755	Carlsbad, N. Mex.	25,541
Waukegan, Ill.	55,719	Carson, Calif.	38,059
Wauwatosa, Wis.	56,923	Casper, Wyo.	38,930
West Allis, Wis.	68,157	Castro Valley, Calif.	37,120
West Covina, Calif.	50,645	Catonsville, Md.	37,372
West Hartford, Conn.	62,382	Champaign, Ill.	49,583
West Palm Beach, Fla.	56,208	Charlottesville, Va.	29,427
Wheaton, Md.	54,635	Chelsea, Mass.	33,749
Wheeling, W. Va.	53,400	Cheltenham, Pa.	35,990
White Plains, N. Y.	50,485	Cheyenne, Wyo.	43,505
Wilkes-Barre, Pa.	63,551	Chicago Heights, Ill.	34,331
Wilmington, Del.	95,827	Chula Vista, Calif.	42,034
Woodbridge, N. J.	78,846	Clarksburg, W. Va.	28,112
York, Pa.	54,504	Clearwater, Fla.	34,653
		Clinton, Iowa	33,589
Places 25,000–50,000		Columbia, Mo.	36,650
Aberdeen, S. Dak.	25,073	Concord, Calif.	36,208
Alexandria, La.	40,279	Concord, N. H.	28,991
Aliquippa, Pa.	26,369	Coral Gables, Fla.	34,793
Allen Park, Mich.	37,052	Costa Mesa, Calif.	37,550
Alliance, Ohio	28,362	Cranford, N. J.	26,424
Altadena, Calif.	40,568	Culver City, Calif.	32,163
Alton, Ill.	43,047	Cumberland, Md.	33,415
Ames, Iowa	27,003	Cuyahoga Falls, Ohio	47,922
Amsterdam, N. Y.	28,772	Daly City, Calif.	44,791
Anchorage, Alaska	44,237	Danville, Ill.	41,856
Anderson, Ind.	49,061	Danville, Va.	46,577
Anderson, S. C.	41,316	Daytona Beach, Fla.	37,395
Anniston, Ala.	33,657	Decatur, Ala.	29,217
Appleton, Wis.	48,411	Delaware, N. J.	31,522
Arcadia, Calif.	41,005	Denton, Tex.	26,844
Arlington, Mass.	49,953	Des Plaines, Ill.	34,886
Arlington, Tex.	44,775	Dothan, Ala.	31,440
Arlington Heights, Ill.	27,878	East Cleveland, Ohio	37,991
Ashland, Ky.	31,283	East Detroit, Mich.	45,756
Athens, Ga.	31,355	East Hartford, Conn.	43,977
Attleboro, Mass.	27,118	East Lansing, Mich.	30,198
Auburn, N. Y.	35,249	East Meadow, N. Y.	46,036
Aurora, Colo.	48,548	Easton, Pa.	31,955
Austin, Minn.	27,908	East Point, Ga.	35,633
Baldwin, N. Y.	30,204	East Providence, R. I.	41,955
Baldwin Park, Calif.	33,951	Eau Claire, Wis.	37,987
Bangor, Me.	38,912	Edina, Minn.	28,501
Barberton, Ohio	33,805	Edison, N. J.	44,799
Bartlesville, Okla.	27,893	Eggertsville, N. Y.	44,807
Battle Creek, Mich.	44,169	El Cajon, Calif.	37,618
Baytown, Tex.	28,159	El Cerrito, Calif.	25,437
Belleville, Ill.	37,264	El Dorado, Ark.	25,292
Belleville, N. J.	35,005	Elgin, Ill.	49,447
Bellflower, Calif.	45,909	Elkhart, Ind.	40,274
Bell Gardens, Calif.	26,467	Elmhurst, Ill.	36,991

City	Population	City	Population
Mount Lebanon, Pa.	35,361	Rockville Centre, N. Y.	26,355
Muskegon, Mich.	46,485	Rocky Mount, N. C.	32,147
Muskogee, Okla.	38,059	Rome, Ga.	32,226
Nashua, N. H.	39,096	Ross, Pa.	25,952
Natick, Mass.	28,831	Roswell, N. Mex.	39,593
National City, Calif.	32,771	St. Cloud, Minn.	33,815
Needham, Mass.	25,793	St. Louis Park, Minn.	43,310
New Albany, Ind.	37,812	Salem, Mass.	39,211
Newark, Ohio	41,790	Salem, Oreg.	49,142
New Brunswick, N. J.	40,139	Salina, Kans.	43,202
Newburgh, N. Y.	30,979	Salinas, Calif.	28,957
New Castle, Pa.	44,790	San Bruno, Calif.	29,063
New Hanover, N. J.	28,528	San Buenaventura, Calif. (see Ventura)	
New Iberia, La.	29,062	Sandusky, Ohio	31,989
New London, Conn.	34,182	Santa Cruz, Calif.	25,596
Newport, Ky.	30,070	Santa Fe, N. Mex.	34,676
Newport, R. I.	47,049	Santa Rosa, Calif.	31,027
Newport Beach, Calif.	26,564	Sarasota, Fla.	34,083
Norman, Okla.	33,412	Selma, Ala.	28,385
Norristown, Pa.	38,925	Shaker Heights, Ohio	36,460
Northampton, Mass.	30,058	Sharon, Pa.	25,267
North Bergen, N. J.	42,387	Sheboygan, Wis.	45,747
North Miami, Fla.	28,708	South Euclid, Ohio	27,569
North Tonawanda, N. Y.	34,757	Southfield, Mich.	31,501
Norwich, Conn.	38,506	Southgate, Mich.	29,404
Norwood, Ohio	34,580	South San Francisco, Calif.	39,418
Nutley, N. J.	29,513	South San Gabriel, Calif.	26,213
Oak Lawn, Ill.	27,471	Spartanburg, S. C.	44,352
Oak Park, Mich.	36,632	Springfield (Delaware Co.),	
Oak Ridge, Tenn.	27,169	Pa.	26,733
Oceanside, N. Y.	30,448	Steubenville, Ohio	32,495
Ontario, Calif.	46,617	Stratford, Conn.	45,012
Orange, Calif.	26,444	Superior, Wis.	33,563
Orange, N. J.	35,789	Tallahassee, Fla.	48,174
Orange, Tex.	25,605	Taunton, Mass.	41,132
Oshkosh, Wis.	45,110	Teaneck, N. J.	42,085
Ottumwa, Iowa	33,871	Temple, Tex.	30,419
Owensboro, Ky.	42,471	Temple City, Calif.	31,838
Oxnard, Calif.	40,265	Texarkana, Tex.	30,218
Paducah, Ky.	34,479	Texas City, Tex.	32,065
Panama City, Fla.	33,275	Torrington, Conn.	30,045
Paramount, Calif.	27,249	Upper Arlington, Ohio	28,486
Parkersburg, W. Va.	44,797	Urbana, Ill.	27,294
Park Forest, Ill.	29,993	Valdosta, Ga.	30,652
Park Ridge, Ill.	32,659	Valley Stream, N. Y.	38,629
Parkville—Carney, Md.	27,236	Vancouver, Wash.	32,464
Parsippany—Troy Hills, N. J.	25,557	Ventura, Calif.	29,114
Peabody, Mass.	32,202	Vicksburg, Miss.	29,143
Pekin, Ill.	28,146	Victoria, Tex.	33,047
Pennsauken, N. J.	33,771	Vineland, N. J.	37,685
Perth Amboy, N. J.	38,007	Wallingford, Conn.	29,920
Petersburg, Va.	36,750	Wantagh, N. Y.	34,172
Phenix City, Ala.	27,630	Watertown, Mass.	39,092
Pico Rivera, Calif.	49,150	Watertown, N. Y.	33,306
Pine Bluff, Ark.	44,037	Waukesha, Wis.	30,004
Plainfield, N. J.	45,330	Wausau, Wis.	31,943
Plainview, N. Y.	27,710	Wayne, N. J.	29,353
Pocatello, Idaho	28,534	Webster Groves, Mo.	28,990
Port Huron, Mich.	36,084	Weirton, W. Va.	28,201
Portsmouth, N. H.	26,900	Wellesley, Mass.	26,071
Portsmouth, Ohio	33,637	Westfield, Mass.	26,302
Pottstown, Pa.	26,144	Westfield, N. J.	31,447
Poughkeepsie, N. Y.	38,330	West Haven, Conn.	43,002
Prairie Village, Kans.	25,356	West Hollywood, Calif.	28,870
Prichard, Ala.	47,371	West Mifflin, Pa.	27,289
Provo, Utah	36,047	Westminster, Calif.	25,750
Quincy, Ill.	43,793	West New York, N. J.	35,547
Rahway, N. J.	27,699	West Orange, N. J.	39,895
Rapid City, S. Dak.	42,399	Weymouth, Mass.	48,177
Redlands, Calif.	26,829	Whittier, Calif.	33,663
Redondo Beach, Calif.	46,986	Wilkinsburg, Pa.	30,066
Redwood City, Calif.	46,290	Williamsport, Pa.	41,967
Revere, Mass.	40,080	Wilmette, Ill.	28,268
Richfield, Minn.	42,523	Wilmington, N. C.	44,013
Richmond, Ind.	44,149	Wilson, N. C.	28,753
Ridgewood, N. J.	25,391	Winona, Mass.	31,214
Ridley, Pa.	35,738	Woonsocket, R. I.	47,080
Rochester, Minn.	40,663	Wyandotte, Mich.	43,519
Rock Hill, S. C.	29,404	Wyoming, Mich.	45,829
Rockville, Md.	26,090	Yakima, Wash.	43,284

Zanesville, Ohio	39,077	

Place	Population	Place	Population
Bellaire, Tex.	19,872		
Bellefontaine, Ohio	11,424		
Bellefontaine Neighbors, Mo.	13,650		
Abbeville, La.	10,414	Belle Glade, Fla.	11,273
Aberdeen, Wash.	18,741	Bellevue, Pa.	11,412
Ada, Okla.	14,347	Bellevue, Wash.	12,809
Adams, Mass.	11,949	Bellmawr, N. J.	11,853
Adrian, Mich.	20,347	Bellmore, N. Y.	12,784
Aiea, Hawaii	11,826	Bellwood, Ill.	20,729
Aiken, S. C.	11,243	Belmont, Calif.	15,996
Alameda, Idaho	10,660	Belvidere, Ill.	11,223
Alamogordo, N. Mex.	21,723	Bend, Oreg.	11,936
Albany, Calif.	14,804	Benton, Ark.	10,399
Albany, Oreg.	12,926	Benton Harbor, Mich.	19,136
Albemarle, N. C.	12,261	Berea, Ohio	16,592
Albert Lea, Minn.	17,108	Berkeley, Mo.	18,676
Albion, Mich.	12,749	Berkley, Mich.	23,275
Alexander City, Ala.	13,140	Berlin, N. H.	17,821
Alice, Tex.	20,861	Berwick, Pa.	13,353
Alisal, Calif.	16,473	Bethany, Okla.	12,342
Alpena, Mich.	14,682	Bethel, Pa.	23,650
Altamont, Oreg.	10,811	Bethpage—Old Bethpage,	
Altus, Okla.	21,225	N. Y.	20,515
Alum Rock, Calif.	18,942	Bettendorf, Iowa	11,534
Ambridge, Pa.	13,865	Bexley, Ohio	14,319
Americus, Ga.	13,472	Biddeford, Me.	19,255
Amherst, Mass.	10,306	Bloomsburg, Pa.	10,655
Anaconda, Mont.	12,054	Bluefield, W. Va.	19,256
Andalusia, Ala.	10,263	Blue Island, Ill.	19,618
Andrews, Tex.	11,135	Blytheville, Ark.	20,797
Annapolis, Md.	23,385	Bogalusa, La.	21,423
Anoka, Minn.	10,562	Boone, Iowa	12,468
Ansonia, Conn.	19,819	Borger, Tex.	20,911
Antioch, Calif.	17,305	Bound Brook, N. J.	10,263
Arbutus—Halethorpe—		Bountiful, Utah	17,039
Relay, Md.	22,402	Bowling Green, Ohio	13,574
Ardmore, Okla.	20,184	Boynton Beach, Fla.	10,467
Arkansas City, Kans.	14,262	Bozeman, Mont.	13,361
Artesia, N. Mex.	12,000	Braddock, Pa.	12,337
Arvada, Colo.	19,242	Bradenton, Fla.	19,380
Asbury Park, N. J.	17,366	Bradford, Pa.	15,061
Ashland, Ohio	17,419	Brainerd, Minn.	12,898
Ashland, Wis.	10,132	Brawley, Calif.	12,703
Ashtabula, Ohio	24,559	Brentwood, Mo.	12,250
Aston, Pa.	10,595	Brentwood, N. Y.	15,387
Astoria, Oreg.	11,239	Brentwood, Pa.	13,706
Atchison, Kans.	12,529	Bridgeton, N. J.	20,966
Athens, Ohio	16,470	Brigham City, Utah	11,728
Athens, Tenn.	12,103	Bristol, Pa.	12,364
Athol, Mass.	10,161	Bristol, R. I.	14,570
Auburn, Ala.	16,261	Bristol, Tenn.	17,582
Auburn, Me.	24,449	Bristol, Va.	17,144
Auburn, Wash.	11,933	Brookfield, Ill.	20,429
Audubon, N. J.	10,440	Brookfield, Wis.	19,812
Augusta, Me.	21,680	Brookings, S. Dak.	10,558
Azusa, Calif.	20,497	Brooklyn, Ohio	10,733
Babylon, N. Y.	11,062	Brooklyn Center, Minn.	24,356
Bainbridge, Ga.	12,714	Brooklyn Park, Minn.	10,197
Baldwin, Pa.	24,489	Brook Park, Ohio	12,856
Banning, Calif.	10,250	Brown Deer, Wis.	11,280
Barre, Vt.	10,387	Brownfield, Tex.	10,286
Barrington, R. I.	13,826	Brownwood, Tex.	16,974
Barstow, Calif.	11,644	Brunswick, Ga.	21,703
Bartow, Fla.	12,849	Brunswick, Ohio	11,725
Bastrop, La.	15,193	Bucyrus, Ohio	12,276
Batavia, N. Y.	18,210	Burlingame, Calif.	24,036
Bath, Me.	10,717	Burlington, N. J.	12,687
Bay, Ohio	14,489	Butler, Pa.	20,975
Bay City, Tex.	11,656	Cadillac, Mich.	10,112
Beacon, N. Y.	13,922	Cahokia, Ill.	15,829
Beatrice, Nebr.	12,132	Caldwell, Idaho	12,230
Beaver Dam, Wis.	13,118	Cambridge, Md.	12,239
Beaver Falls, Pa.	16,240	Cambridge, Ohio	14,562
Beckley, W. Va.	18,642	Camden, Ark.	15,823
Bedford, Ind.	13,024	Campbell, Calif.	11,863
Bedford, Ohio	15,223	Campbell, Ohio	13,406
Beech Grove, Ind.	10,973	Canonsburg, Pa.	11,877
Beeville, Tex.	13,811	Canton, Ill.	13,588
Bell, Calif.	19,450	Cape Girardeau, Mo.	24,947
Bellaire, Ohio	11,502	Carbondale, Ill.	14,670

Carbondale, Pa.	13,595	Crawfordsville, Ind.	14,231
Carlisle, Pa.	16,623	Crestwood, Mo.	11,106
Carmichael, Calif.	20,455	Crowley, La.	15,617
Carnegie, Pa.	11,887	Crystal, Minn.	24,283
Carol City, Fla.	21,749	Cudahy, Wis.	17,975
Carpentersville, Ill.	17,424	Cullman, Ala.	10,883
Carrollton, Ga.	10,973	Dalles, Oreg.	10,493
Carteret, N. J.	20,502	Dalton, Ga.	17,868
Carthage, Mo.	11,264	Danbury, Conn.	22,928
Castle Shannon, Pa.	11,836	Danvers, Mass.	21,926
Cedar Falls, Iowa	21,195	Darby, Pa.	14,059
Cedar Grove, N. J.	14,603	Decatur, Ga.	22,026
Center Line, Mich.	10,164	Dedham, Mass.	23,869
Central Falls, R. I.	19,858	Deerfield, Ill.	11,786
Centralia, Ill.	13,904	Deer Park, N. Y.	16,726
Centreville, Ill.	12,869	Defiance, Ohio	14,553
Chambersburg, Pa.	17,670	De Kalb, Ill.	18,486
Chanute, Kans.	10,849	De Land, Fla.	10,775
Chapel Hill, N. C.	12,573	Delano, Calif.	11,913
Charleston, Ill.	10,505	Delaware, Ohio	13,282
Cheektowaga-Southwest, N. Y.	12,766	Del City, Okla.	12,934
Cheviot, Ohio	10,701	Del Paso Heights— Robla, Calif.	11,495
Chickasaw, Ala.	10,002	Delray Beach, Fla.	12,230
Chickasha, Okla.	14,866	Del Rio, Tex.	18,612
Chico, Calif.	14,757	Denison, Tex.	22,748
Chillicothe, Ohio	24,957	De Pere, Wis.	10,045
Chino, Calif.	10,305	Depew, N. Y.	13,580
Chippewa Falls, Wis.	11,708	Derby, Colo.	10,124
Circleville, Ohio	11,059	Derby, Conn.	12,132
Clairton, Pa.	18,389	Dixon, Ill.	19,565
Claremont, Calif.	12,633	Dodge City, Kans.	13,520
Claremont, N. H.	13,563	Dolton, Ill.	18,746
Clark, N. J.	12,195	Donelson, Tenn.	17,195
Clarksdale, Miss.	21,105	Donora, Pa.	11,131
Clarksville, Tenn.	22,021	Dormont, Pa.	13,098
Clawson, Mich.	14,795	Douglas, Ariz.	11,925
Clayton, Mo.	15,245	Dover, N. H.	19,131
Cleburne, Tex.	15,381	Dover, N. J.	13,034
Cleveland, Miss.	10,172	Dover, Ohio	11,300
Cleveland, Tenn.	16,196	Downers Grove, Ill.	21,154
Cliffside Park, N. J.	17,642	Duarte, Calif.	13,962
Clinton, Mass.	12,848	Dublin, Ga.	13,814
Clovis, N. Mex.	23,713	Du Bois, Pa.	10,667
Coatesville, Pa.	12,971	Dumont, N. J.	18,882
Cocoa, Fla.	12,294	Dunbar, W. Va.	11,006
Coeur d'Alene, Idaho	14,291	Duncan, Okla.	20,009
Coffeyville, Kans.	17,382	Dunkirk, N. Y.	18,205
Cohoes, N. Y.	20,129	Dunmore, Pa.	18,917
College Park, Ga.	23,469	Duquesne, Pa.	15,019
College Park, Md.	18,482	Durango, Colo.	10,530
College Station, Tex.	11,396	Durant, Okla.	10,467
Collingdale, Pa.	10,268	Dyersburg, Tenn.	12,499
Collingswood, N. J.	17,370	Eagle Pass, Tex.	12,094
Collinsville, Ill.	14,217	East Grand Rapids, Mich.	10,924
Colton, Calif.	18,666	East Haven, Conn.	21,388
Columbia, Pa.	12,075	Eastlake, Ohio	12,467
Columbia, Tenn.	17,624	Eastlawn, Mich.	17,652
Columbia Heights, Minn.	17,533	East Liverpool, Ohio	22,306
Columbus, Ind.	20,778	East Massapequa, N. Y.	14,779
Columbus, Miss.	24,771	East Moline, Ill.	16,732
Columbus, Nebr.	12,476	East Paterson, N. J.	19,344
Concord, N. C.	17,799	East Peoria, Ill.	12,310
Conneaut, Ohio	10,557	East Ridge, Tenn.	19,570
Connellsville, Pa.	12,814	East Rockaway, N. Y.	10,721
Connersville, Ind.	17,698	East Whittier, Calif.	19,884
Conshohocken, Pa.	10,259	Eatontown, N. J.	10,334
Coon Rapids, Minn.	14,931	Eau Gallie, Fla.	12,300
Copiague, N. Y.	14,081	Ecorse, Mich.	17,328
Cordele, Ga.	10,609	Edinburg, Tex.	18,706
Corinth, Miss.	11,453	El Centro, Calif.	16,811
Corning, N. Y.	17,085	El Dorado, Kans.	12,523
Corona, Calif.	13,336	Elizabeth City, N. C.	14,062
Coronado, Calif.	18,039	Elizabethton, Tenn.	10,896
Corsicana, Tex.	20,344	Ellwood City, Pa.	12,413
Cortland, N. Y.	19,181	El Monte, Calif.	13,163
Corvallis, Oreg.	20,669	Elmwood Park, Ill.	23,866
Coshocton, Ohio	13,106	El Reno, Okla.	11,015
Covina, Calif.	20,124	El Segundo, Calif.	14,219
Covington, Va.	11,062	Elwood, Ind.	11,793

Emmaus, Pa.	10,262	Grants, N. Mex.	10,274
Emporia, Kans.	18,190	Grants Pass, Oreg.	10,118
Endicott, N. Y.	18,775	Great Bend, Kans.	16,670
Enterprise, Ala.	11,410	Great Neck, N. Y.	10,171
Escanaba, Mich.	15,391	Greeneville, Tenn.	11,759
Escondido, Calif.	16,377	Greenfield, Mass.	14,389
Eunice, La.	11,326	Greenfield, Wis.	17,636
Evergreen Park, Ill.	24,178	Greensburg, Pa.	17,383
Fairbanks, Alaska	13,311	Greenville, N. C.	22,860
Fairborn, Ohio	19,453	Greenville, Ohio	10,585
Fairfax, Va.	13,585	Greenville, Tex.	19,087
Fairfield, Ala.	15,816	Greenwood, Miss.	20,436
Fairfield, Calif.	14,968	Greenwood, S. C.	16,644
Fairview Park, Ohio	14,624	Gretna, La.	21,967
Falls Church, Va.	10,192	Griffin, Ga.	21,735
Faribault, Minn.	16,926	Grosse Pointe Farms, Mich.	12,172
Farmers Branch, Tex.	13,441	Grosse Pointe Park, Mich.	15,457
Farmington, N. Mex.	23,786	Grosse Pointe Woods, Mich.	18,580
Farrell, Pa.	13,793	Groton, Conn.	10,111
Fayetteville, Ark.	20,274	Groves, Tex.	17,304
Fergus Falls, Minn.	13,733	Haddon, N. J.	17,099
Ferguson, Mo.	22,149	Haddonfield, N. J.	13,201
Flagstaff, Ariz.	18,214	Hagginwood, Calif.	11,469
Floral Park, N. Y.	17,499	Hallandale, Fla.	10,483
Florence, S. C.	24,722	Haltom City, Tex.	23,133
Fontana, Calif.	14,659	Hamburg—Lake Shore, N. Y.	11,527
Forest Park, Ga.	14,201	Hammond, La.	10,563
Forest Park, Ill.	14,452	Hanford, Calif.	10,133
Forrest City, Ark.	10,544	Hannibal, Mo.	20,028
Fort Lee, N. J.	21,815	Hanover, Pa.	15,538
Fort Madison, Iowa	15,247	Hapeville, Ga.	10,082
Fort Myers, Fla.	22,523	Harper Woods, Mich.	19,995
Fort Thomas, Ky.	14,896	Harrison, N. J.	11,743
Fort Walton Beach, Fla.	12,147	Harrison, Pa.	15,710
Fostoria, Ohio	15,732	Harrisonburg, Va.	11,916
Fountain City, Tenn.	10,365	Hasbrouck Heights, N. J.	13,046
Frankfort, Ind.	15,302	Hastings, Nebr.	21,412
Frankfort, Ky.	18,365	Havre, Mont.	10,740
Franklin, Wis.	10,006	Hawthorne, N. J.	17,735
Franklin Park, Ill.	18,322	Hays, Kans.	11,947
Frederick, Md.	21,744	Helena, Ark.	11,500
Fredericksburg, Va.	13,639	Helena, Mont.	20,227
Freeport, Tex.	11,619	Henderson, Ky.	16,892
Fremont, Nebr.	19,698	Henderson, Nev.	12,525
Fremont, Ohio	17,573	Henderson, N. C.	12,740
Fridley, Minn.	15,173	Hermosa Beach, Calif.	16,115
Fulton, Mo.	11,131	Hibbing, Minn.	17,731
Fulton, N. Y.	14,261	Hickory, N. C.	19,328
Gaffney, S. C.	10,435	Highland, Ind.	16,284
Gainesville, Ga.	16,523	Highland Park, N. J.	11,049
Gainesville, Tex.	13,083	Highland Park, Tex.	10,411
Galena Park, Tex.	10,852	Hillcrest Heights, Md.	15,295
Galion, Ohio	12,650	Hillgrove, Calif.	14,669
Gallup, N. Mex.	14,089	Hillside, N. J.	22,304
Garden City, Kans.	11,811	Hinsdale, Ill.	12,859
Garden City, N. Y.	23,948	Hobart, Ind.	18,680
Garden City Park—		Holland, Mich.	24,777
Herricks, N. Y.	15,364	Homewood, Ala.	20,289
Gardner, Mass.	19,038	Homewood, Ill.	13,371
Geneva, N. Y.	17,286	Hopewell, Va.	17,895
Georgetown, S. C.	12,261	Hopkins, Minn.	11,370
Girard, Ohio	12,997	Hopkinsville, Ky.	19,465
Gladstone, Mo.	14,502	Hoquiam, Wash.	10,762
Glasgow, Ky.	10,069	Hornell, N. Y.	13,907
Glassboro, N. J.	10,253	Houma, La.	22,561
Glencoe, Ill.	10,472	Hudson, N. Y.	11,075
G'en Cove, N. Y.	23,817	Huntington, Ind.	16,185
Glendale, Ariz.	15,696	Huntington, N. Y.	11,255
Glendora, Calif.	20,752	Huntington Beach, Calif.	11,492
Glen Ellyn, Ill.	15,972	Huntington Station, N. Y.	23,438
Glen Rock, N. J.	12,896	Huntsville, Tex.	11,999
Glens Falls, N. Y.	18,580	Huron, S. Dak.	14,180
G.enview, Ill.	18,132	Hurst, Tex.	10,165
Gloucester City, N. J.	15,511	Hyattsville, Md.	15,168
Gloversville, N. Y.	21,741	Ilion, N. Y.	10,199
Golden Valley, Minn.	14,559	Imperial Beach, Calif.	17,713
Goosport, La.	16,778	Independence, Kans.	11,222
Goshen, Ind.	13,718	Indiana, Pa.	13,005
Grand Haven, Mich.	11,066	Inwood, N. Y.	10,362
Grand Junction, Colo.	18,694	Ironton, Ohio	15,745

Ironwood, Mich.	10,265	Loch Raven, Md.	23,278
Ivywild, Colo.	11,065	Lock Haven, Pa.	11,748
Jacksonville, Ark.	14,488	Locust Grove, N. Y.	11,558
Jacksonville, Ill.	21,690	Lodi, Calif.	22,229
Jacksonville, N. C.	13,491	Lodi, N. J.	23,502
Jacksonville Beach, Fla.	12,049	Logan, Utah	18,731
Jamestown, N. Dak.	15,163	Logansport, Ind.	21,106
Jasper, Ala.	10,799	Lombard, Ill.	22,561
Jeannette, Pa.	16,565	Lomita, Calif.	14,983
Jefferson Heights, La.	19,353	Lompoc, Calif.	14,415
Jeffersonville, Ind.	19,522	Longmont, Colo.	11,489
Jennings, La.	11,887	Longview, Wash.	23,349
Jennings, Mo.	19,965	Los Alamos, N. Mex.	12,584
Jericho, N. Y.	10,795	Los Altos, Calif.	19,696
Johnson City, N. Y.	19,118	Lower Burrell, Pa.	11,952
Johnstown, N. Y.	10,390	Lower Southampton, Pa.	12,619
Jonesboro, Ark.	21,418	Lufkin, Tex.	17,641
Junction City, Kans.	18,700	Lumberton, N. C.	15,305
Kalispell, Mont.	10,151	Lynbrook, N. Y.	19,881
Kaneohe, Hawaii	14,414	Lyndhurst, N. J.	21,867
Kaukauna, Wis.	10,096	Lyndhurst, Ohio	16,805
Kearney, Nebr.	14,210	McAlester, Okla.	17,419
Kearns, Utah	17,172	McComb, Miss.	12,020
Keene, N. H.	17,562	McKees Rocks, Pa.	13,185
Kenmore, N. Y.	21,261	McKinney, Tex.	13,763
Kenner, La.	17,037	Macomb, Ill.	12,135
Kennewick, Wash.	14,244	Madera, Calif.	14,430
Kent, Ohio	17,836	Madison, Ind.	10,097
Keokuk, Iowa	16,316	Madison, N. J.	15,122
Kermit, Tex.	10,465	Madison, Tenn.	13,583
Kewanee, Ill.	16,324	Madisonville, Ky.	13,110
Kilgore, Tex.	10,092	Magnolia, Ark.	10,651
Killeen, Tex.	23,377	Mamaroneck, N. Y.	17,673
Kingston, Pa.	20,261	Mandan, N. Dak.	10,525
Kinston, N. C.	24,819	Manhattan, Kans.	22,993
Kirksville, Mo.	13,123	Mankato, Minn.	23,797
Klamath Falls, Oreg.	16,949	Manville, N. J.	10,995
La Canada—Flintridge, Calif.	18,338	Maple Shade, N. J.	12,947
Laconia, N. H.	15,288	Maplewood, Minn.	18,519
La Grange, Ga.	23,632	Maplewood, Mo.	12,552
La Grange, Ill.	15,285	Maplewood, N. J.	23,977
La Grange Park, Ill.	13,793	Marblehead, Mass.	18,521
Lake Forest, Ill.	10,687	Marietta, Ohio	16,847
Lakeview, Mich.	10,384	Marinette, Wis.	13,329
Lakewood, Colo.	19,338	Marion, Ill.	11,274
Lakewood, N. J.	13,004	Marion, Iowa	10,882
Lake Worth, Fla.	20,758	Markham, Ill.	11,704
La Marque, Tex.	13,969	Marlborough, Mass.	18,819
Lamesa, Tex.	12,438	Marple, Pa.	19,722
Lancaster, N. Y.	12,254	Marquette, Mich.	19,824
Langley Park, Md.	11,510	Marshalltown, Iowa	22,521
Lansdale, Pa.	12,612	Marshfield, Wis.	14,153
Lansdowne, Pa.	12,601	Martinsburg, W. Va.	15,179
Lansdowne—Baltimore Highlands, Md.	13,134	Martins Ferry, Ohio	11,919
		Martinsville, Va.	18,798
Lansing, Ill.	18,098	Maryville, Tenn.	10,348
La Porte, Ind.	21,157	Massapequa Park, N. Y.	19,904
La Puente, Calif.	24,723	Massena, N. Y.	15,478
Laramie, Wyo.	17,520	Mattoon, Ill.	19,088
La Salle, Ill.	11,897	Maumee, Ohio	12,063
Latrobe, Pa.	11,932	Mayfield, Ky.	10,762
Lawndale, Calif.	21,740	Mayfield Heights, Ohio	13,478
Lawrence, Ind.	10,103	Maywood, Calif.	14,588
Leavenworth, Kans.	22,052	Maywood, N. J.	11,460
Lebanon, Tenn.	10,512	Meadville, Pa.	16,671
Leesburg, Fla.	11,172	Medford, Oreg.	24,425
Lemon Grove, Calif.	19,348	Melbourne, Fla.	11,982
Lenoir, N. C.	10,257	Melrose Park, Ill.	22,291
Levelland, Tex.	10,153	Melvindale, Mich.	13,089
Levittown, N. J. (see Willingboro)		Menasha, Wis.	14,647
Lewiston, Idaho	12,691	Menominee, Mich.	11,289
Lewistown, Pa.	12,640	Menomonee Falls, Wis.	18,276
Lexington, N. C.	16,093	Merced, Calif.	20,068
Liberal, Kans.	13,813	Mercedes, Tex.	10,943
Lincoln, Ill.	16,890	Merrick, N. Y.	18,789
Lincolnwood, Ill.	11,744	Metuchen, N. J.	14,041
Lindenhurst, N. Y.	20,905	Mexico, Mo.	12,889
Littleton, Colo.	13,670	Miami, Okla.	12,869
Livermore, Calif.	16,058	Miami Springs, Fla.	11,229
Livingston, N. J.	23,124	Middle River, Md.	10,825

Middlesborough, Ky.	12,607	Niles, Mich.	13,842
Middlesex, N. J.	10,520	Niles, Ohio	19,545
Middletown, N. Y.	23,475	Norfolk, Nebr.	13,111
Middletown, Pa. (Dauphin		Normal, Ill.	13,357
Co.)	11,182	Norridge, Ill.	14,087
Midway—Hardwick, Ga.	16,909	North Adams, Mass.	19,905
Milford, Mass.	13,722	North Arlington, N. J.	17,477
Millbrae, Calif.	15,873	North Atlanta, Ga.	12,661
Millburn, N. J.	18,799	North Augusta, S. C.	10,348
Milledgeville, Ga.	11,117	North Bellmore, N. Y.	19,639
Mill Valley, Calif.	10,411	North Braddock, Pa.	13,204
Millville, N. J.	19,096	Northbrook, Ill.	11,635
Minden, La.	12,785	North Chicago, Ill.	20,517
Mineola, N. Y.	20,519	North College Hill, Ohio	12,035
Mineral Wells, Tex.	11,053	North Highlands, Calif.	21,271
Mirada Hills, Calif.	22,444	Northlake, Ill.	12,318
Mission, Tex.	14,081	North Las Vegas, Nev.	18,422
Mitchell, S. Dak.	12,555	North Merrick, N. Y.	12,976
Moberly, Mo.	13,170	North Miami Beach, Fla.	21,405
Monessen, Pa.	18,424	North New Hyde Park, N. Y.	17,929
Monmouth, Ill.	10,372	North Olmsted, Ohio	16,290
Monroe, Mich.	22,968	North Plainfield, N. J.	16,993
Monroe, N. C.	10,882	North Platte, Nebr.	17,184
Monroeville, Pa.	22,446	North Providence, R. I.	18,220
Montclair, Calif.	13,546	North Sacramento, Calif.	12,922
Monterey, Calif.	22,618	North Valley Stream, N. Y.	17,239
Moorhead, Minn.	22,934	North Versailles, Pa.	13,583
Morgan City, La.	13,540	Norwalk, Ohio	12,900
Morgantown, W. Va.	22,487	Norwood, Mass.	24,898
Morristown, N. J.	17,712	Novato, Calif.	17,881
Morristown, Tenn.	21,267	Oakwood, Ohio	10,493
Morton Grove, Ill.	20,533	Ocala, Fla.	13,598
Moscow, Idaho	11,183	Oceanside, Calif.	24,971
Moses Lake, Wash.	11,299	Ogdensburg, N. Y.	16,122
Moultrie, Ga.	15,764	Oil City, Pa.	17,692
Moundsville, W. Va.	15,163	Okmulgee, Okla.	15,951
Mountain Brook, Ala.	12,680	Olathe, Kans.	10,987
Mount Carmel, Pa.	10,760	Olean, N. Y.	21,868
Mount Clemens, Mich.	21,016	Olympia, Wash.	18,273
Mount Holly, N. J.	13,271	Oneida, N. Y.	11,677
Mount Pleasant, Mich.	14,875	Oneonta, N. Y.	13,412
Mount Prospect, Ill.	18,906	Opelika, Ala.	15,678
Mount Vernon, Ill.	15,566	Opelousas, La.	17,417
Mount Vernon, Ohio	13,284	Opportunity, Wash.	12,465
Mundelein, Ill.	10,526	Orangeburg, S. C.	13,852
Munhall, Pa.	17,312	Oregon, Ohio	13,319
Munster, Ind.	10,313	Orem, Utah	18,394
Murfreesboro, Tenn.	18,991	Oskaloosa, Iowa	11,053
Murray, Utah	16,806	Ossining, N. Y.	18,662
Muscatine, Iowa	20,997	Oswego, N. Y.	22,155
Muskegon Heights, Mich.	19,552	Ottawa, Ill.	19,408
Nacogdoches, Tex.	12,674	Ottawa, Kans.	10,673
Nampa, Idaho	18,013	Overland, Mo.	22,763
Nanticoke, Pa.	15,601	Overland Park, Kans.	21,110
Napa, Calif.	22,170	Overlea, Md.	10,795
Naperville, Ill.	12,933	Owatonna, Minn.	13,409
Natchez, Miss.	23,791	Owosso, Mich.	17,006
Natchitoches, La.	13,924	Pacifica, Calif.	20,995
Naugatuck, Conn.	19,511	Pacific Grove, Calif.	12,121
Nederland, Tex.	12,036	Painesville, Ohio	16,116
Neenah, Wis.	18,057	Palatine, Ill.	11,504
Neptune, N. J.	21,487	Palatka, Fla.	11,028
Nether Providence, Pa.	10,380	Palestine, Tex.	13,974
Newark, Del.	11,404	Palisades Park, N. J.	11,943
Newark, N. Y.	12,868	Palmdale, Calif.	11,522
New Berlin, Wis.	15,788	Palm Springs, Calif.	13,468
New Bern, N. C.	15,717	Pampa, Tex.	24,664
New Braunfels, Tex.	15,631	Paramus, N. J.	23,238
Newburyport, Mass.	14,004	Paris, Tex.	20,977
New Castle, Pa.	20,349	Parma Heights, Ohio	18,100
New Hyde Park, N. Y.	10,808	Parsons, Kans.	13,929
New Kensington, Pa.	23,485	Pascagoula, Miss.	17,155
New Milford, N. J.	18,810	Pasco, Wash.	14,522
Newnan, Ga.	12,169	Pecos, Tex.	12,728
New Philadelphia, Ohio	14,241	Peekskill, N. Y.	18,737
New Providence, N. J.	10,243	Pendleton, Oreg.	14,434
Newton, Iowa	15,381	Peru, Ill.	10,460
Newton, Kans.	14,877	Peru, Ind.	14,453
New Ulm, Minn.	11,114	Petaluma, Calif.	14,035
Niles, Ill.	20,393	Pharr, Tex.	14,106

South Portland, Me.	22,788	Upland, Calif.	15,918
South River, N. J.	13,397	Upper Moreland, Pa.	21,032
South Sacramento—		Urbana, Ohio	10,461
Fruitridge, Calif.	16,443	Uvalde, Tex.	10,293
South St. Paul, Minn.	22,032	Vacaville, Calif.	10,898
South Westbury, N. Y.	11,977	Valley Station, Ky.	10,553
Sparks, Nev.	16,618	Valparaiso, Ind.	15,227
Sparrows Point—Fort		Van Wert, Ohio	11,323
Howard—Edgmere, Md.	11,775	Vernon, Tex.	12,141
Springdale, Ark.	10,076	Verona, N. J.	13,782
Springfield, N. J.	14,467	Vienna, Va.	11,440
Springfield, Oreg.	19,616	Villa Park, Ill.	20,391
Springfield (Montgomery		Vincennes, Ind.	18,046
Co.), Pa.	20,652	Virginia, Minn.	14,034
Springfield, Va.	10,783	Visalia, Calif.	15,791
Spring Garden, Pa.	11,387	Vista, Calif.	14,795
Stanton, Calif.	11,163	Wabash, Ind.	12,621
State College, Pa.	22,409	Wadsworth, Ohio	10,635
Statesville, N. C.	19,844	Wahiawa, Hawaii	15,512
Staunton, Va.	22,232	Wakefield, Mass.	24,295
Steelton, Pa.	11,266	Waldwick, N. J.	10,495
Sterling, Colo.	10,751	Walla Walla, Wash.	24,536
Sterling, Ill.	15,688	Warminster, Pa.	15,994
Stevens Point, Wis.	17,837	Warner Robins, Ga.	18,633
Stillwater, Okla.	23,965	Warren, Pa.	14,505
Stoneham, Mass.	17,821	Warrensville Heights, Ohio	10,609
Stoneleigh—Rodgers Forge,		Warrington, Fla.	16,752
Md.	15,645	Washington, Ind.	10,846
Stow, Ohio	12,194	Washington, Ohio	12,388
Stowe, Pa.	11,730	Washington, Pa.	23,545
Streator, Ill.	16,868	Watertown, S. Dak.	14,077
Struthers, Ohio	15,631	Watertown, Wis.	13,943
Suffolk, Va.	12,609	Waterville, Me.	18,695
Suitland—Silver Hills, Md.	10,300	Watervliet, N. Y.	13,917
Sulphur, La.	11,429	Watsonville, Calif.	13,293
Summit, Ill.	10,374	Waxahachie, Tex.	12,749
Summit, N. J.	23,677	Waycross, Ga.	20,944
Sumter, S. C.	23,062	Wayne, Mich.	16,034
Sunbury, Pa.	13,687	Waynesboro, Pa.	10,427
Swampscott, Mass.	13,294	Waynesboro, Va.	15,694
Sweetwater, Tex.	13,914	Webster, Mass.	12,072
Swissvale, Pa.	15,089	Weehawken, N. J.	13,504
Sylacauga, Ala.	12,857	Wenatchee, Wash.	16,726
Takoma Park, Md.	16,799	Weslaco, Tex.	15,649
Talladega, Ala.	17,742	Westbrook, Me.	13,820
Tallmadge, Ohio	10,246	Westbury, N. Y.	14,757
Tamaqua, Pa.	10,173	Westchester, Ill.	18,092
Tarrytown, N. Y.	11,109	West Chester, Pa.	15,705
Tempe, Ariz.	24,897	West Des Moines, Iowa	11,949
Tenafly, N. J.	14,264	Western Springs, Ill.	10,838
Terrell, Tex.	13,803	West Hempstead—Lakeview,	
Texarkana, Ark.	19,788	N. Y.	24,783
The Village, Okla.	12,118	West Lafayette, Ind.	12,680
Thibodaux, La.	13,403	Westlake, Ohio	12,906
Thomasville, Ga.	18,246	West Memphis, Ark.	19,374
Thomasville, N. C.	15,190	Westminster, Colo.	13,850
Thornton, Colo.	11,353	West Monroe, La.	15,215
Tiffin, Ohio	21,478	West St. Paul, Minn.	13,101
Timonium—Lutherville, Md.	12,265	West Seneca, N. Y.	23,138
Tonawanda, N. Y.	21,561	West University Place, Tex.	14,628
Totowa, N. J.	10,897	West Warwick, R. I.	21,414
Towson, Md.	19,090	Westwood Lakes, Fla.	22,517
Tracy, Calif.	11,289	Wethersfield, Conn.	20,561
Traverse City, Mich.	18,432	Wheaton, Ill.	24,312
Trenton, Mich.	18,439	Wheat Ridge, Colo.	21,619
Trinidad, Colo.	10,691	White Bear Lake, Minn.	12,849
Troy, Ala.	10,234	Whitefish Bay, Wis.	18,390
Troy, Mich.	19,058	Whitehall, Ohio	20,818
Troy, Ohio	13,685	Whitehall, Pa.	16,075
Tulare, Calif.	13,824	Whitehaven, Tenn.	13,894
Tullahoma, Tenn.	12,242	White Settlement, Tex.	11,513
Tupelo, Miss.	17,221	Whitman, Mass.	10,485
Turtle Creek, Pa.	10,607	Whitney, Idaho	13,603
Twin Falls, Idaho	20,126	Wickliffe, Ohio	15,760
Two Rivers, Wis.	12,393	Willimantic, Conn.	13,881
Union, S. C.	10,191	Willingboro (Levittown), N.J.	11,861
Uniondale, N. Y.	20,081	Williston, N. Dak.	11,866
Uniontown, Pa.	17,942	Willmar, Minn.	10,417
University Heights, Ohio	16,641	Willoughby, Ohio	15,058
University Park, Tex.	23,202	Willowick, Ohio	18,749

Winchester, Ky.	10,187	Woodlawn—Rockdale—	
Winchester, Mass.	19,376	Milford Mills, Md.	19,254
Winchester, Va.	15,110	Woodmere, N. Y.	14,011
Winfield, Kans.	11,117	Woodmont—Green Hills—	
Winnetka, Ill.	13,368	Glendale, Tenn.	23,161
Winona, Minn.	24,895	Wood River, Ill.	11,694
Winter Haven, Fla.	16,277	Wooster, Ohio	17,046
Winter Park, Fla.	17,162	Wyckoff, N. J.	11,205
Winthrop, Mass.	20,303	Xenia, Ohio	20,445
Wisconsin Rapids, Wis.	15,042	Yazoo City, Miss.	11,236
Woodbine—Radnor—		Yeadon, Pa.	11,610
Glencliff, Tenn.	14,485	Ypsilanti, Mich.	20,957
Woodbury, N. J.	12,453	Yuba City, Calif.	11,507
Woodland, Calif.	13,524	Yuma, Ariz.	23,974
		Zion, Ill.	11,941

POPULATION OF UNITED STATES IN 1960

SUMMARY BY STATES AND DEPENDENCIES

(Figure in parentheses gives rank in population.)

THE STATES AND THE DISTRICT OF COLUMBIA

Alabama	(19)	3,266,740	New Mexico	(37)	951,023
Alaska	(51)	226,167	New York	(1)	16,782,304
Arizona	(35)	1,302,161	North Carolina	(12)	4,556,155
Arkansas	(31)	1,786,272	North Dakota	(45)	632,446
California	(2)	15,717,204	Ohio	(5)	9,706,397
Colorado	(33)	1,753,947	Oklahoma	(27)	2,328,284
Connecticut	(25)	2,535,234	Oregon	(32)	1,768,687
Delaware	(47)	446,292	Pennsylvania	(3)	11,319,366
District of			Rhode Island	(39)	859,488
Columbia	(40)	763,956	South Carolina	(26)	2,382,594
Florida	(10)	4,951,560	South Dakota	(41)	680,514
Georgia	(16)	3,943,116	Tennessee	(17)	3,567,089
Hawaii	(44)	632,772	Texas	(6)	9,579,677
Idaho	(43)	667,191	Utah	(38)	890,627
Illinois	(4)	10,081,158	Vermont	(48)	389,881
Indiana	(11)	4,662,498	Virginia	(14)	3,966,949
Iowa	(24)	2,757,537	Washington	(23)	2,853,214
Kansas	(28)	2,178,611	West Virginia	(30)	1,860,421
Kentucky	(22)	3,038,156	Wisconsin	(15)	3,951,777
Louisiana	(20)	3,257,022	Wyoming	(49)	330,066
Maine	(36)	969,265			
Maryland	(21)	3,100,689			**179,323,175**
Massachusetts	(9)	5,148,578			
Michigan	(7)	7,823,194	**DEPENDENCIES**		
Minnesota	(18)	3,413,864			
Mississippi	(29)	2,178,141	American Samoa		20,051
Missouri	(13)	4,319,813	Canal Zone		42,122
Montana	(42)	674,767	Guam		67,044
Nebraska	(34)	1,411,330	Puerto Rico		2,349,544
Nevada	(50)	285,278	Virgin Islands of the U. S.		32,099
New Hampshire	(46)	606,921	Total		2,510,860
New Jersey	(8)	6,066,782	Total U. S. &		
			Dependencies		181,834,035

POPULATION OF PLACES
IN CANADA
HAVING 10,000 OR MORE INHABITANTS IN 1961

ALBERTA
Bonnyville	10,209
Calgary	249,641
Edmonton	281,027
Forest Lawn	12,263
Jasper Place	30,530
Leduc	10,647
Lethbridge	35,454
Medicine Hat	24,484
Red Deer	19,612
Rocky View	10,748
Strathcona	12,075

BRITISH COLUMBIA
Burnaby	100,157
Chilliwack	18,296
Coquitlam	29,053
Dawson Creek	10,946
Delta	14,597
Esquimalt	12,048
Kamloops	10,076
Kelowna	13,188
Langley	14,585
Maple Ridge	16,748
Matsqui	14,293
Nanaimo	14,135
New Westminster	33,654
North Vancouver	23,656
Oak Bay	16,935
Penticton	13,859
Port Alberni	11,560
Prince George	13,877
Prince Rupert	11,987
Powell River	10,748
Richmond	43,323
Saanich	48,876
Surrey	70,838
Trail	11,580
Vancouver	384,522
Vernon	10,250
Victoria	54,941
West Vancouver	25,454

MANITOBA
Brandon	28,166
East Kildonan	27,305
Flin Flon	11,104
Fort Garry	17,528
Portage la Prairie	12,388
Saint Boniface	37,600
Saint James	33,977
Saint Vital	27,269
Transcona	14,248
West Kildonan	20,077
Winnipeg	265,429

NEW BRUNSWICK
Edmundston	12,791
Fredericton	19,683
Lancaster	13,848
Moncton	43,840
Oromocto	12,170
Saint John	55,153

NEWFOUNDLAND
Corner Brook	25,185
Saint John's	63,633

NOVA SCOTIA
Amherst	10,788
Annapolis	18,885
Cape Breton	39,644
Colchester	20,666
Cumberland	17,838
Dartmouth	46,966
East Hants	10,419
Glace Bay	24,186
Halifax	92,511
Inverness	15,072
Kings	33,385
Lunenburg	18,416
New Waterford	10,592
Pictou	16,817
Richmond	11,250
Sydney	33,617
Truro	12,421
West Hants	10,374

ONTARIO
Barrie	21,169
Belleville	30,655
Brampton	18,467
Brantford	55,201
Brockville	17,744
Burlington	47,008
Chatham	29,826
Cobourg	10,646
Cornwall	43,639
Dundas	12,912
Eastview	24,555
Elliot Lake	13,179
Forest Hill	20,489
Fort William	45,214
Galt	27,830
Georgetown	10,298
Guelph	39,838
Hamilton	273,991
Kenora	10,904
Kingston	53,526
Kitchener	74,485
Leaside	18,579
Lindsay	11,399
London	169,569
Long Branch	11,039
Mimico	18,212
New Toronto	13,384
Niagara Falls	22,351
North Bay	23,781
Oakville	10,366
Orillia	15,345
Oshawa	62,415
Ottawa	268,206
Owen Sound	17,421
Pembroke	16,791
Peterborough	47,185
Port Arthur	45,276
Port Colborne	14,886
Preston	11,577
Richmond Hill	16,446
Riverside	18,089
Saint Catharines	84,472
Saint Thomas	22,469
Sarnia	50,976
Sault Sainte Marie	43,088
Stratford	20,467
Sudbury	80,120
Timmins	29,270
Toronto	672,407
Trenton	13,183
Waterloo	21,366

Welland	36,079
Whitby	14,685
Windsor	114,367
Woodstock	20,486

PRINCE EDWARD ISLAND

Charlottetown	18,318

QUEBEC

Alma	13,309
Arvida	14,460
Asbestos	11,083
Beaconsfield	10,064
Cap-de-la-Madeleine	26,925
Charlesbourg	14,308
Chicoutimi	31,657
Chicoutimi-Nord	11,229
Chomedey	30,445
Côte-Saint-Luc	13,266
Dorval	18,592
Drummondville	27,909
Duvernay	10,939
Gatineau	13,022
Giffard	10,129
Granby	31,463
Grand'Mère	15,806
Hull	56,929
Jacques-Cartier	40,807
Joliette	18,088
Jonquière	28,588
Kénogami	11,816
Lachine	38,630
Laflèche	10,984
LaSalle	30,904
La Tuque	13,023
Lauzon	11,533
Laval-des-Rapides	19,227
Levis	15,112
Longueuil	24,131
Magog	13,139
Montreal	1,191,062
Montreal-Nord	48,433
Mount Royal (Mont-Royal)	21,182

Noranda	11,477
Outremont	30,753
Pierrefonds	12,171
Pointe-aux-Trembles	21,926
Pointe-Claire	22,709
Pont-Viau	16,077
Quebec	171,979
Rimouski	17,739
Rivière-des-Prairies	10,054
Rivière-du-Loup	10,835
Rouyn	18,716
Sainte-Foy	29,716
Sainte Thérèse	11,771
Saint Hubert	14,380
Saint Hyacinthe	22,354
Saint Jean (Saint John)	26,988
Saint Jérôme	24,546
Saint Lambert	14,531
Saint Laurent	49,805
Saint Michel	55,978
Saint-Vincent-de-Paul	11,214
Sept-Îles	14,196
Shawinigan	32,169
Shawinigan-Sud	12,683
Sherbrooke	66,554
Sillery	14,109
Sorel	17,147
Thetford Mines	21,618
Trois-Rivières (Three Rivers)	53,477
Val-d'Or	10,983
Valleyfield	27,297
Verdun	78,317
Victoriaville	18,720
Westmount	25,012

SASKATCHEWAN

Moose Jaw	33,206
North Battleford	11,230
Prince Albert	24,168
Regina	112,141
Saskatoon	95,526
Swift Current	12,186

POPULATION OF CANADA IN 1961
SUMMARY BY PROVINCES AND TERRITORIES

Alberta	1,331,944	**TERRITORIES**	
British Columbia	1,629,082	Yukon Territory	14,628
Manitoba	921,686	Northwest Territories	22,998
New Brunswick	597,936	Total	37,626
Newfoundland	457,853		
Nova Scotia	737,007	Total of Provinces and	
Ontario	6,236,092	Territories	18,238,247
Prince Edward Island	104,629		
Quebec	5,259,211		
Saskatchewan	925,181		
Total	18,200,621		

FOREIGN WORDS AND PHRASES

INCLUDING STATE AND NATIONAL MOTTOES

ab·eunt stu·dia in mo·res \'äb-e-‚únt-'stüd-ē-‚ä-‚in-'mō-‚rās\ [L] : practices zealously pursued pass into habits

ab in·cu·na·bu·lis \‚äb-‚in-kə-'näb-ə-‚lēs\ [L] : from the cradle : from infancy

à bon chat, bon rat \à-bōⁿ-'shà bōⁿ-'rà\ [F] : to a good cat, a good rat : retaliation in kind

à bouche ou·verte \à-bü-shü-vert\ [F] : with open mouth : eagerly : uncritically

ab ovo us·que ad ma·la \‚äb-'ō-vō-‚üs-kwe-‚äd-'mäl-ä\ [L] : from egg to apples : from soup to nuts : from beginning to end

à bras ou·verts \à-brá-zü-ver\ [F] : with open arms : cordially

ab·sit in·vi·dia \'äb-‚sit-in-'wid-ē-‚ä\ [L] : let there be no envy or ill will

ab uno dis·ce om·nes \‚äb-'ü-nō-‚dis-ke-'ōm-‚nās\ [L] : from one learn to know all

ab ur·be con·di·ta \‚äb-'ür-be-'kòn-də-‚tä\ [L] : from the founding of the city (Rome, founded 753 B.C.) — used by the Romans in reckoning dates

ab·usus non tol·lit usum \'äb-‚ü-səs-‚nōn-‚tò-lət-'ü-səm\ [L] : abuse does not take away use, i.e., is not an argument against proper use

à compte \à-kōⁿt\ [F] : on account

à coup sûr \à-kü-sü̅r\ [F] : with sure stroke : surely

ad ar·bi·tri·um \ad-är-'bit-rē-əm\ [L] : at will : arbitrarily

ad as·tra per as·pera \ad-'as-trə-‚pər-'as-pə-rə\ [L] : to the stars by hard ways — motto of Kansas

ad ex·tre·mum \ad-ik-'strē-məm\ [L] : to the extreme : at last

ad ka·len·das Grae·cas \‚äd-kə-'len-dəs-'grī-‚käs\ [L] : at the Greek calends : never (since the Greeks had no calends)

ad pa·tres \äd-'pä-‚trās\ [L] : (gathered) to his fathers : deceased

à droite \à-drwät\ [F] : to or on the right hand

ad un·guem \äd-'üⁿ-‚gwem\ [L] : to the fingernail : to a nicety : exactly (from the use of the fingernail to test the smoothness of marble)

ad utrum·que pa·ra·tus \‚äd-ü-'trüm-kwe-pə-'rät-əs\ [L] : prepared for either (event)

ad vi·vum \äd-'wē-‚wüm\ [L] : to the life

ae·gri som·nia \‚ī-grē-'sòm-nē-‚ä\ [L] : a sick man's dreams

ae·quam ser·va·re men·tem \'ī-‚kwäm-sər-‚wä-rē-'men-‚tem\ [L] : to preserve a calm mind

ae·quo ani·mo \‚ī-‚kwō-'än-ə-‚mō\ [L] : with even mind : calmly

ae·re per·en·ni·us \‚ī-rā-pə-'ren-ē-‚üs\ [L] : more lasting than bronze

à gauche \à-gōsh\ [F] : to or on the left hand

age quod agis \'äg-e-‚kwòd-'äg-‚is\ [L] : do what you are doing : to the business at hand

à grands frais \à-gräⁿ-fre\ [F] : at great expense

à huis clos \à-w^yē-klō\ [F] : with closed doors

aide-toi, le ciel t'aidera \ed-twà lə-'syel-te-drà\ [F] : help yourself (and) heaven will help you

aî·né \e-nā\ [F] : elder : senior (masc.)

aî·née \e-nā\ [F] : elder : senior (fem.)

à l'aban·don \à-là-bäⁿ-dōⁿ\ [F] : carelessly : in disorder

à la belle étoile \à-là-bel-ā-twàl\ [F] : under the beautiful star : in the open air at night

à la bonne heure \à-là-bò-nœr\ [F] : at a good time : well and good : all right

à la fran·çaise \à-là-fräⁿ-sez\ [F] : in the French style

à l'an·glaise \à-läⁿ-glez\ [F] : in the English style

alea jac·ta est \'äl-ē-‚ä-‚yäk-tə-'est\ [L] : the die is cast

à l'im·pro·viste \à-laⁿ-prò-vēst\ [F] : unexpectedly

ali·quan·do bo·nus dor·mi·tat Home·rus \‚äl-ə-‚kwän-dō-'bò-nəs-‚dòr-mə-‚tät-hō-'mer-əs\ [L] : sometimes (even) good Homer nods

alis vo·lat pro·pri·is \'äl-‚ēs-'wò-‚lät-'prō-prē-‚ēs\ [L] : she flies with her own wings — motto of Oregon

al·ki \'al-‚kī-‚kē\ [Chinook Jargon] : by and by — motto of Washington

alo·ha oe \à-‚lō-hä-'òi‚-ō-ē\ [Hawaiian] : love to you : greetings : farewell

al·ter idem \‚òl-tər-'ī-‚dem, ‚äl-tər-ē-\ [L] : second self

a max·i·mis ad mi·ni·ma \ä-'mäk-sə-‚mēs-‚äd-'min-ə-‚mä\ [L] : from the greatest to the least

ami·cus hu·ma·ni ge·ner·is \ä-'mē-kəs-hü-‚män-ē-'gen-ə-rəs\ [L] : friend of the human race

ami·cus us·que ad aras \-‚ùs-kwe-‚äd-'är-‚äs\ [L] : a friend as far as to the altars, i.e., except in what is contrary to one's religion; also : a friend to the last extremity

ami de cour \à-‚mēd-ə-'kúr\ [F] : court friend : insincere friend

amor pa·tri·ae \‚äm-‚òr-'pä-trē-‚ī\ [L] : love of one's country

amor vin·cit om·nia \'ä-‚mòr-‚win-kət-'òm-nē-ə\ [L] : love conquers all things

an·cienne no·blesse \äⁿ-syen-nò-bles\ [F] : old-time nobility : the French nobility before the Revolution of 1789

an·guis in her·ba \‚äⁿ-gwəs-in-'her-‚bä\ [L] : snake in the grass

ani·mal bi·pes im·plu·me \'än-i-‚mäl-‚bip-‚äs-im-'plü-me\ [L] : two-legged animal without feathers (i.e., man)

ani·mis opi·bus·que pa·ra·ti \'än-ə-‚mēs-‚ò-pə-'bùs-kwe-pə-'rät-ē\ [L] : prepared in spirits and resources — one of the mottoes of South Carolina

an·no ae·ta·tis su·ae \'än-ō-ī-‚tät-əs-'sü-‚ī\ [L] : in the (specified) year of his (or her) age

an·no mun·di \,än-ō-'mùn-dē\ [L] : in the year of the world — used in reckoning dates from the supposed period of the creation of the world, esp. as fixed by James Ussher at 4004 B.C. or by the Jews at 3761 B.C.

an·no ur·bis con·di·tae \,än-ō-,ùr-bəs-'kòn-də-,tī\ [L] : in the year of the founded city (Rome, founded 753 B.C.)

an·nu·it coep·tis \,än-ə-,wit-'kòip-,tēs\ [L] : He (God) has smiled on our undertakings — motto on the reverse of the great seal of the United States

à peu près \a-pœ-pre\ [F] : nearly : approximately

à pied \a-pyā\ [F] : on foot

après moi le dé·luge \a-pre-mwà-lə-dä-lüezh\ [F] : after me the deluge (attributed to Louis XV)

à pro·pos de bottes \a-prə-pōd-ə-bòt\ [F] : apropos of boots — used to change the subject

à propos de rien \-ryaⁿ\ [F] : apropos of nothing

aqua et ig·ni in·ter·dic·tus \,äk-wä-et-'ig-nē-,int-ər-'dik-təs\ [L] : forbidden to be furnished with water and fire : outlawed

Ar·ca·des am·bo \är-kə-,des-'äm-bō\ [L] : both Arcadians : two persons of like occupations or tastes; *also* : two rascals

a ri·ve·der·ci \är-ē-vä-'der-chē\ [It] : till we meet again — used as a formula of farewell

ar·rec·tis au·ri·bus \ä-'rek-,tēs-'aù-ri-,bùs\ [L] : with ears pricked up : attentively

ars est ce·la·re ar·tem \,ärs-,est-kā-,lär-ē-'är-,tem\ [L] : it is (true) art to conceal art

ars lon·ga, vi·ta bre·vis \ärs-'lòⁿ-,gä,wē-,tä-'bre-wəs\ [L] : art is long, life is short

à tort et à tra·vers \a-tòr-tā-à-trà-ver\ [F] : wrong and crosswise : at random : without rhyme or reason

au bout de son la·tin \ō-büd-(ə-)sōⁿ-là-taⁿ\ [F] : at the end of one's Latin : at the end of one's mental resources

au con·traire \ō-kōⁿ-'trer\ [F] : on the contrary

au·de·mus ju·ra no·stra de·fen·dere \aù-'dā-məs-,yùr-ə-'nò-strə-dā-'fen-də-rē\ [L] : we dare defend our rights — motto of Alabama

au·den·tes for·tu·na ju·vat \aù-'den-,tās-fòr-,tü-nə-'yü-,wät\ [L] : fortune favors the bold

au fond \ō-fōⁿ\ [F] : at bottom : fundamentally

au grand sé·rieux \ō-grän-sā-ryœ\ [F] : in all seriousness

au pays des aveugles les borgnes sont rois \ō-pā-ē-dā-zä-vœglᵊ là-bórnᵊ-ə-sōⁿ-rwä\ [F] : in the country of the blind the one-eyed men are kings

au·rea me·di·o·cri·tas \'aù-rē-ə-,med-ē-'ó-krə-,täs\ [L] : the golden mean

au reste \ō-rest\ [F] : for the rest : besides

au·spi·ci·um me·li·o·ris ae·vi \aù-'spik-ē-,üm-,mel-ē-,ōr-əs-'ī-,wē\ [L] : an omen of a better age — motto of the Order of St. Michael and St. George

aus·si·tôt dit, aus·si·tôt fait \ō-sē-tō-dē-'ō-sē-tō-fe\ [F] : no sooner said than done

aut Cae·sar aut ni·hil \aùt-'kī-sär-,aùt-'ni-,hil\ [L] : either a Caesar or nothing

aut Caesar aut nul·lus \-'nùl-əs\ [L] : either a Caesar or a nobody

au·tres temps, au·tres mœurs \ō-trə-täⁿ-ō-trə-mœrs\ [F] : other times, other customs

aut vin·ce·re aut mo·ri \aùt-'wiŋ-kə-rē-,aùt-'mó-,rē\ [L] : either to conquer or to die

aux armes \ō-zàrm\ [F] : to arms

ave at·que va·le \'ä-,wä-,ät-kwe-'wä-,lā\ [L] : hail and farewell

à vo·tre sau·té \a-vòt-sä"-tā, -vò-trə-\ [F] : to your health — used as a toast

beaux yeux \bō-zyœ\ [F] : beautiful eyes : beauty of face

bien en·ten·du \byaⁿ-näⁿ-täⁿ-dü\ [F] : well understood : of course

bien·sé·ance \byaⁿ-sā-äⁿs\ [F] : propriety

bis dat qui ci·to dat \,bis-,dät-kwē-'ki-tō-,dät\ [L] : he gives twice who gives promptly

bon gré, mal gré \'bōⁿ-,grä-'màl-,grä\ [F] : whether with good grace or bad : willy-nilly

bo·nis avi·bus \,bó-,nēs-'ä-wi-,bùs\ [L] : under good auspices

bon jour \bōⁿ-zhür\ [F] : good day : good morning

bonne foi \bòn-fwä\ [F] : good faith

bon soir \bōⁿ-swàr\ [F] : good evening

bru·tum ful·men \,brüt-əm-'fùl-mən\ [L] : insensible thunderbolt : a futile threat or display of force

ca·dit quae·stio \,käd-ət-'kwī-stē-,ō\ [L] : the question drops : the argument collapses

cau·sa si·ne qua non \'kaù-,sä-,sin-ē-kwä-'nōn\ [L] : an indispensable cause or condition

ca·ve ca·nem \,kä-wā-'kän-,em\ [L] : beware the dog

ce·dant ar·ma to·gae \'kā-,dänt-,är-mə-'tō-,gī\ [L] : let arms yield to the toga : let military power give way to civil power — motto of Wyoming

c'est à dire \se-tà-dēr\ [F] : that is to say : namely

c'est au·tre chose \se-tōt-shōz, -tō-trə-\ [F] : that's a different thing

c'est plus qu'un crime, c'est une faute \se-plē-kœⁿ-krēm se-tüⁿ-fōt\ [F] : it is worse than a crime, it is a blunder

ce·te·ra de·sunt \,kāt-ə-,rä-'dā-,sùnt\ [L] : the rest is missing

cha·cun à son gout \shà-kœⁿ-nä-sōⁿ-gü\ [F] : everyone to his taste

châ·teau en Es·pagne \shä-tō-äⁿ-nes-pánᵃ\ [F] : castle in Spain : a visionary project

cher·chez la femme \sher-shā-là-fàm\ [F] : look for the woman

che sa·rà, sa·rà \kä-sä-,rä-sä-'rä\ [It] : what will be, will be

che·val de ba·taille \shə-vál-də-bà-täⁱᵃ\ [F] : war-horse : argument constantly relied on : favorite subject

co·gi·to, er·go sum \'kō-gə-,tō-,er-gō-'süm\ [L] : I think, therefore I exist

com·pa·gnon de voy·age \kōⁿ-pà-nᵊō²-də-vwà-yàzh\ [F] : traveling companion

compte ren·du \kōⁿt-räⁿ-dü\ [F] : report (as of proceedings in an investigation)

coup de maî·tre \küd-(ə-)metrᵃ\ [F] : master stroke

coup d'es·sai \kü-dä-se\ [F] : experiment : trial

coûte que coûte \küt-kə-küt\ [F]: cost what it may

cre·do quia ab·sur·dum est \,krād-ō-'kwē-ä-äp-,sùrd-əm-'est\ [L] : I believe it because it is absurd

cres·cit eun·do \,kres-kət-'eùn-dō\ [L] : it grows as it goes — motto of New Mexico

crux cri·ti·co·rum \'krúks-,krit-ə-'kōr-əm\ [L] : crux of critics

cum gra·no sa·lis \,kùm-,grän-ō-'säl-əs\ [L] : with a grain of salt

cus·tos mo·rum \,kùs-tōs-'mōr-əm\ [L] : guardian of manners or morals : censor

d'ac·cord \dȧ-kôr\ [F] : in accord : agreed

dame d'hon·neur \dȧm-dȯ-nœr\ [F] : lady-in-waiting

dam·nant quod non in·tel·li·gunt \'däm-,nänt-,kwód-,nōn-in-'tel-ə-,gùnt\ [L] : they condemn what they do not understand

de bonne grâce \də-bȯn-gräs\ [F] : with good grace : willingly

de gus·ti·bus non est dis·pu·tan·dum \dā-'gùs-tə-,bùs-,nōn-,est-,dis-pü-'tän-,dúm\ [L] : there is no disputing about tastes

de in·te·gro \dā-'int-ə-,grō\ [L] : anew : afresh

de l'au·dace, en·core de l'au·dace, et tou·jours de l'au·dace \də-lō-däs-ä°-,kōr-də-lō-däs-ä-tü-'zhùr-də-lō-däs\ [F] : audacity, more audacity, and ever more audacity

de·len·da est Car·tha·go \dā-'len-dä-,est-kär-'täg-ō\ [L] : Carthage must be destroyed

de·li·ne·a·vit \dā-,lē-nā-'ä-wit\ [L] : he (or she) drew it

de mal en pis \də-mȧl-ä°-pē\ [F]: from bad to worse

de mi·ni·mis non cu·rat lex \dā-'min-ə-,mēs-,nōn-,kü-,rät-'leks\ [L] : the law takes no account of trifles

de mor·tu·is nil ni·si bo·num \dā-'mort-ə-,wēs-,nēl-,nis-ē-'bō-,nùm\ [L] : of the dead (say) nothing but good

Deo fa·ven·te \,dā-ō-fə-'vent-ē\ [L] : with God's favor

Deo gra·ti·as \,dā-ō-'grät-ē-,äs\ [L] : thanks (be) to God

de pro·fun·dis \,dā-prō-'fùn-dēs, -'fən-\ [L] : out of the depths

der Geist der stets ver·neint \dər-'gīst-dər-,shtäts-fer-'nīnt\ [G] : the spirit that ever denies — applied originally to Mephistopheles

de·si·pere in lo·co \dā-'sip-ə-rē-in-'lō-kō\ [L] : to indulge in trifling at the proper time

Deus vult \,dā-əs-'wùlt\ [L] : God wills it — rallying cry of the First Crusade

di·es fau·stus \'dē-,äs-'faù-stəs\ [L] : lucky day

dies in·fau·stus \-'in-,faù-stəs\ [L] : unlucky day

di·es irae \-'ē-,rī, -,rā\ [L] : day of wrath — used of the Judgment Day

Dieu et mon droit \dyœ-ā-mō°-drwä\ [F] : God and my right — motto on the British royal arms

Dieu vous garde \dyœ-vü-gȧrd\ [F] : God keep you

di·ri·go \'dē-ri-gō\ [L] : I direct — motto of Maine

dis ali·ter vi·sum \,dēs-,al-ə-,ter-'wē-,sùm\ [L] : the gods decreed otherwise

di·tat De·us \'dē-,tät-'dā-,ùs\ [L] : God enriches — motto of Arizona

di·vi·de et im·pe·ra \'dē-wi-,de-,et-'im-pə-,rä\ [L] : divide and rule

do·cen·do dis·ci·mus \dō-,ken-dō-'dis-ki-,mus\ [L] : we learn by teaching

Domine, dirige nos \'dō-mi-,ne-,dē-ri-,ge-'nōs\ [L] : Lord, direct us — motto of the City of London

Do·mi·nus vo·bis·cum \,dó-mi-,nùs-wō-'bēs-,kùm\ [L] : the Lord be with you

dul·ce et de·co·rum est pro pa·tria mo·ri \,dúl-,ket-de-'kōr-,əst-prō-,pä-trē-,ä-'mó-,rē\ [L] : it is sweet and seemly to die for one's country

dum spi·ro, spe·ro \,dúm-'spē-rō-'spār-ō\ [L] : while I breathe I hope — one of the mottoes of South Carolina

dum vi·vi·mus vi·va·mus \,dúm-'wē-wē-,mùs-wē-'wäm-ùs\ [L] : while we live, let us live

dux fe·mi·na fac·ti \,dùks-,fā-mi-nä-'fäk-,tē\ [L] : a woman was leader of the exploit

ec·ce sig·num \,ek-e-'sig-,nùm\ [L] : behold the sign : look at the proof

e con·tra·rio \,ā-kōn-'trär-ē-,ō\ [L] : on the contrary

écra·sez l' in·fâme \ā-krä-zā-la°-'fäm\ [F]: crush the infamous thing

eheu fu·ga·ces la·bun·tur an·ni \,ā-,heù-fü-gä-,käs-lä-,bùn-,túr-'än-,ē\ [L] : alas! the fleeting years glide on

ein fes·te Burg ist un·ser Gott \īn-,fes-tə-'bùrk-ist-,ùn-zər-'gót\ [G] : a mighty fortress is our God

em·bar·ras de ri·chesses \ä°-bȧ-räd-(ə-)rē-shes\ [F] : embarrassing surplus of riches : confusing abundance

em·bar·ras du choix \ä°-bȧ-rä-dü-shwä\ [F] : embarrassing variety of choice

en ami \ä°-nȧ-mē\ [F] : as a friend

en ef·fet \ä°-nā-fe\ [F] : in fact : indeed

en fa·mille \ä°-fȧ-mēy\ [F] : in one's family : at home

en·fant gâ·té \ä°-fä°-gä-tā\ [F] : spoiled child

en·fants per·dus \ä°-fä°-per-dᴜ̄\ [F] : lost children : soldiers sent to a dangerous post

en·fin \ä°-fa°\ [F] : in conclusion : in a word

en gar·çon \ä°-gȧr-sō°\ [F] : as or like a bachelor

en pan·tou·fles \ä°-pä°-tüfl°\ [F] : in slippers : at ease : informally

en plein air \ä°-plen-er\ [F] : in the open air

en plein jour \ä°-pla°-zhür\ [F] : in broad day

en rè·gle \ä°-regl°\ [F] : in order : in due form

en re·tard \ä°r-(ə-)tȧr\ [F] : behind time : late

en re·traite \ä°-rə-tret\ [F] : in retreat : in retirement

en re·vanche \ä°-rə-(və)vä°sh\ [F] : in return : in compensation

en·se pe·tit pla·ci·dam sub li·ber·ta·te qui·e·tem \,en-se-,pet-ət-'pläk-i-,däm-,sùb-,lē-ber-,tä-te-kwē-'ā-,tem\ [L] : with the sword she seeks calm repose under liberty — motto of Massachusetts

e plu·ri·bus unum \,ē-,plùr-ə-bəs-'(y)ü-,nəm, ,ā-,plùr-\ [L] : one out of many — motto of the United States

e pur si muo·ve \ā-,pür-sē-'mwȯ-vā\

[It] : and yet it does move — attributed to Galileo after recanting his assertion of the earth's motion

er·ra·re hu·ma·num est \e-ˈrär-e-hü-ˌmän-əm-ˈest\ [L] : to err is human

es·prit de l'es·ca·lier \es-prēd-les-kȧ-lyä\ *or* **es·prit d'es·ca·lier** \-prē-des-\ [F] : spirit of the staircase : repartee thought of only too late, on the way home

es·se quam vi·de·ri \ˈes-ē-ˌkwäm-wi-ˈdā-rē\ [L] : to be rather than to seem — motto of North Carolina

est mo·dus in re·bus \est-ˈmȯ-ˌdüs-in-ˈrā-ˌbus\ [L] : there is a proper measure in things, i.e., the golden mean should always be observed

es·to per·pe·tua \ˈes-ˌto-pər-ˈpet-ə-wä\ [L] : may she endure forever — motto of Idaho

et hoc ge·nus om·ne \et-ˌhōk-ˌgen-əs-ˈom-ne\ *or* **et id ge·nus om·ne** \et-ˌid-\ [L] : and everything of this kind

et in Ar·ca·dia ego \et-in-är-ˌkād-ē-ə-ˈeg-ō\ [L] : I too (lived) in Arcadia

et sic de si·mil·i·bus \et-ˌsēk-dā-sə-ˈmil-ə-ˌbus\ [L] : and so of like things

et tu Bru·te \et-ˈtü-ˈbrü-te\ [L] : thou too, Brutus   exclamation attributed to Julius Caesar on seeing his friend Brutus among his assassins

eu·re·ka \yu̇-ˈrē-kə\ [Gk] : I have found it   motto of California

Ewig-Weib·li·che \ˌā-vik-ˈvīp-li-kə\ [G] : eternal feminine

ex ani·mo \ek-ˈsän-ə-ˌmō\ [L] : from the heart : sincerely

ex·cel·si·or \ik-ˈsel-sē-ər, eks-ˈkel-sē-ˌȯr\ [L] : still higher — motto of New York

ex·cep·tio pro·bat re·gu·lam de re·bus non ex·cep·tis \eks-ˈkep-tē-ˌō-ˌprō-ˌbät-ˈrā-gə-ˌläm-dā-ˈrā-ˌbüs-ˌnōn-eks-ˈkep-ˌtēs\ [L] : an exception establishes the rule as to things not excepted

ex·cep·tis ex·ci·pi·en·dis \eks-ˌkep-ˌtēs-eks-ˌkip-ē-ˈen-ˌdēs\ [L] : with the proper or necessary exceptions

ex·i·tus ac·ta pro·bat \ˈek-sə-ˌtüs-ˌäk-tə-ˈprō-ˌbät\ [L] : the event justifies the deed

ex li·bris \eks-ˈlē-brəs\ [L] : from the books of - used on bookplates

ex me·ro mo·tu \ˌeks-ˌmer-ō-ˈmō-tü\ [L] : out of mere impulse : of one's own accord

ex ne·ces·si·ta·te rei \ˌeks-nə-ˌkes-ə-ˈtä-te-ˈrā(-ˌē)\ [L] : from the necessity of the case

ex ni·hi·lo ni·hil fit \eks-ˈnī-hi-ˌlō-ˌni-ˌhil-ˈfit\ [L] : from nothing nothing is produced

ex pe·de Her·cu·lem \eks-ˌped-e-ˈher-kə-ˌlem\ [L] : from the foot (we may judge of the size of) Hercules : from a part we may judge of the whole

ex·per·to cre·di·te \eks-ˌpert-ō-ˈkrād-ə-ˌte\ [L] : believe one who has had experience

ex un·gue le·o·nem \eks-ˈüŋ-gwe-le-ˈō-ˌnem\ [L] : from the claw (we may judge of) the lion : from a part we may judge of the whole

ex vi termini \eks-ˌwē-ˈter-mə-ˌnē\ [L] : from the force of the term

fa·ci·le prin·ceps \ˌfäk-i-le-ˈpriŋ-ˌkeps\ [L] : easily first

fa·ci·lis de·scen·sus Aver·no \ˈfäk-i-lis-dā-ˌskän-ˌsüs-ä-ˈwer-nō\ *or* **facilis descensus Aver·ni** \-(ˌ)nē\ [L] : the descent to Avernus is easy : the road to evil is easy

faire suivre \fer-swᵉēvrᵃ\ [F] : have forwarded : please forward

fas est et ab ho·ste do·ce·ri \fäs-ˈest-ät-ˌhȯ-ste-dȯ-ˈkä-(ˌ)rē\ [L] : it is right to learn even from an enemy

Fa·ta vi·am in·ve·ni·ent \fä-tä-ˈwē-ˌäm-in-ˈwen-ē-ˌent\ [L] : the Fates will find a way

fat·ti mas·chii, pa·ro·le fe·mi·ne \ˌfät-ē-ˈmäs-ˌkē pä-ˌrō-lā-ˈfā-mē-ˌnä\ [It] : deeds are males, words are females : deeds are more effective than words   motto of Maryland, where it is generally interpreted as meaning "manly deeds, womanly words"

femme de cham·bre \ˌfäm-də-shäⁿbrᵃ\ [F] : chambermaid : lady's maid

fe·sti·na len·te \fe-ˌstē-nə-ˈlen-ˌtä\ [L] : make haste slowly

feux d'ar·ti·fice \fœ-där-tē-fēs\ [F] : fireworks : display of wit

fi·at ex·per·i·men·tum in cor·po·re vi·li \ˈfē-ˌät-ek-ˌsper-ē-ˈmen-ˌtüm-in-ˌkȯr-pə-rē-ˈwē-lē\ [L] : let experiment be made on a worthless body

fi·at ju·sti·tia, ru·at cae·lum \ˌfē-ˌät-ˌyüs-ˈtit-ē-ä ˌrü-ˌät-ˈkī-ˌlüm\ [L] : let justice be done though the heavens fall

fi·at lux \ˌfē-ˌät-ˈlüks\ [L] : let there be light

Fi·dei De·fen·sor \ˌfid-e-ˌē-dā-ˈfän-ˌsȯr\ [L] : Defender of the Faith — a title of the sovereigns of England

fi·dus Acha·tes \ˌfēd-əs-ä-ˈkā-ˌtäs\ [L] : faithful Achates : trusty friend

fille de cham·bre \fēy-də-shäⁿbrᵃ\ [F] : lady's maid

fille d'hon·neur \fēy-dȯ-nœr\ [F] : maid of honor

fils \fēs\ [F] : son — used after French proper names to distinguish a son from his father

fi·nem re·spi·ce \ˌfē-nem-ˈrä-spi-ˌke\ [L] : consider the end

fi·nis co·ro·nat opus \ˌfē-nəs-kə-ˌrō-ˌnät-ˈō-ˌpus\ [L] : the end crowns the work

fluc·tu·at nec mer·gi·tur \ˈflük-tə-ˌwät-ˌnek-ˈmer-gə-ˌtùr\ [L] : it is tossed by the waves but does not sink — motto of Paris

fors·an et haec olim me·mi·nis·se ju·va·bit \ˌfȯr-ˌsän-ˌet-ˈhīk-ˌō-lim-ˌmem-ə-ˈnis-e-yü-ˈwä-bit\ [L] : perhaps this too will be a pleasure to look back on one day

for·tes for·tu·na ju·vat \ˈfȯr-ˌtäs-fȯr-ˌtü-nə-ˈyü-ˌwät\ [L] : fortune favors the brave

fron·ti nul·la fi·des \ˌfrȯn-ˌtē-ˌnül-ə-ˈfid-ˌās\ [L] : no reliance can be placed on appearance

fu·it Il·i·um \ˈfü-ət-ˈil-ē-əm\ [L] : Troy has been (i.e., is no more)

fu·ror lo·quen·di \ˌfür-ˌȯr-lō-ˈkwen-(ˌ)dē\ [L] : rage for speaking

fu·ror po·e·ti·cus \-pō-ˈät-i-kùs\ [L] : poetic frenzy

furor scri·ben·di \-skrē-ˈben-(ˌ)dē\ [L] : rage for writing

Gal·li·ce \ˈgäl-ə-ˌke\ [L] : in French : after the French manner

gar·çon d'hon·neur \gȧr-sōⁿ-dȯ-nœr\ [F] : bridegroom's attendant

garde du corps \gȧrd-dü̃-kȯr\ [F] : bodyguard

gar·dez la foi \gȧr-dā-là-fwä\ [F] : keep faith

gau·de·a·mus igi·tur \,gaùd-ē-'äm-əs-'ig-ə-,tùr\ [L] : let us then be merry

gens d'é·glise \zhä-dā-glēz\ [F] : church people; clergy

gens de guerre \zhä-də-ger\ [F] : military people; soldiery

gens du monde \zhä-d̄ū̄-mōd\ [F] : people of the world : fashionable people

gno·thi se·au·ton \gə-'nō-thē-,se·aù-'tón\ [Gk] : know thyself

grand monde \grä-mōd\ [F] : great world : high society

guerre à ou·trance \ger-à-ü-träs\ [F] : war to the uttermost

haut goût \ō-gü\ [F] : high flavor : slight taint of decay

hic et ubi·que \,hēk-et-ù-'bē-kwe\ [L] : here and everywhere

hic ja·cet \hik-'jā-sət, hēk-'yäk-ət\ [L] : here lies — used preceding a name on a tombstone

hinc il·lae la·cri·mae \,hink-,il-,ī-'läk-ri-,mī\ [L] : hence those tears

hoc age \hōk-'äg-e\ [L] : do this : apply yourself to what you are about

hoc opus, hic labor est \hōk-'ō-,pùs-,hēk-,lä-,bór-'est\ [L] : this is the hard work, this is the toil

homme d'af·faires \òm-dà-fer\ [F] : man of business : business agent

homme d'es·prit \-des-prē\ [F] : man of wit

ho·mo sum: hu·ma·ni nil a me ali·e·num pu·to \'hò-mō-,sùm hü-,män-ē-'nēl-il-,mä,-äl-ē-'ä-nəm-'pü-tō\ [L] : I am a man; I regard nothing that concerns man as foreign to my interests

ho·ni soit qui mal y pense \ò-nē-swà-kē-mál-ē-päs\ [F] : shamed be he who thinks evil of it — motto of the Order of the Garter

hô·tel-Dieu \ō-tel-dyȳ\ [F] : hospital

hu·ma·num est er·ra·re \hü-,män-əm-,est-e-'rär-e\ [L] : to err is human

ich dien \ik-'dēn\ [G] : I serve — motto of the Prince of Wales

ici on parle français \ē-sē-ō-párl(-ə)-frä-se\ [F] : French is spoken here

id est \id-'est\ [L] : that is

ig·no·ran·tia ju·ris ne·mi·nem ex·cu·sat \,ig-nə-,ränt-ē-ä-'yür-əs-'nä-mə-,nem-eks-'kü-,sät\ [L] : ignorance of the law excuses no one

ig·no·tum per ig·no·ti·us \ig-'nōt-əm-,per-ig-'nōt-ē-,ùs\ [L] : (explaining) the unknown by means of the more unknown

il faut cul·ti·ver no·tre jar·din \ēl-fō-kuel-tē-vā-,nót-zhär-da, -nō-trə-zhàr-\ [F] : we must cultivate our garden : we must tend to our own affairs

in ae·ter·num \,in-ī-'ter-,nùm\ [L] : forever

in du·bio \in-'dùb-ē-,ō\ [L] : in doubt : undetermined

in fu·tu·ro \,in-fə-'tùr-ō\ [L] : in the future

in hoc sig·no vin·ces \in-hōk-'sig-nō-'vin,-kās\ [L] : by this sign (the Cross) thou shalt conquer

in li·mi·ne \in-'lē-mə-,ne\ [L] : on the threshold : at the beginning

in om·ni·a pa·ra·tus \in-'òm-nē-ə-pə-'rä-,tùs\ [L] : ready for all things

in par·ti·bus in·fi·de·li·um \in-'pärt-ə-,bùs-,in-fə-'dā-lē-,ùm\ [L] : in the regions of the infidels — used of a titular bishop having no diocesan jurisdic-

tion, usu. in non-Christian countries

in prae·sen·ti \,in-prī-'sen-,tē\ [L] : at the present time

in sae·cu·la sae·cu·lo·rum \in-'sī-kù-,lä-,sī-kə-'lōr-əm, -'sā-kù-,lä,-sā-\ [L] : for ages of ages : forever and ever

in sta·tu quo an·te bel·lum \in-'stä-,tü-kwō-,änt-ē-'bel-əm\ [L] : in the same state as before the war

in·te·ger vi·tae sce·le·ris·que pu·rus \,in-tə-,ger-'wē-,tī-,skel-ə-'ris-kwe-'pü-rəs\ [L] : upright of life and free from wickedness

in·ter nos \,int-ər-'nōs\ [L] : between ourselves

in·tra mu·ros \,in-trä-'mü,-rōs\ [L] : within the walls

in usum Del·phi·ni \in-'ü-səm-del-'fē-nē\ [L] : for the use of the Dauphin : expurgated

in utrum·que pa·ra·tus \,in-ü-'trùm-kwe-pə-'rä-,tùs\ [L] : prepared for either (event)

in·ve·nit \in-'wä-nit\ [L] : he (or she) devised it

in vi·no ve·ri·tas \in-,wē-nō-'wä-rə-,täs\ [L] : there is truth in wine

in·vi·ta Mi·ner·va \in-'wē-,tä-mi-'ner-,wä\ [L] : Minerva being unwilling : without natural talent or inspiration

ip·sis·si·ma ver·ba \ip-,sis-ə-,mä-'wer-,bä\ [L] : the very words

ira fu·ror bre·vis est \,ē-rä-'für-,ór-bre-wəs-,est\ [L] : anger is a brief madness

jac·ta alea est \'yäk-,tä-,ä-lē-,ä-'est\ [L] : the die is cast

j'adoube \zhà-düb\ [F] : I adjust — used in chess when touching a piece without intending to move it

ja·nu·is clau·sis \,yän-ə-,wēs-'klaù-,sēs\ [L] : with closed doors

je main·tien·drai \zhə-ma-'tya-drä\ [F] : I will maintain — motto of the Netherlands

je ne sais quoi \zhən-(ə-)sä-kwà\ [F] : I don't know what : an inexpressible something

jeu de mots \zhȳd-(ə-)mō\ [F] : play on words : pun

Jo·an·nes est no·men eius \yō-'än-äs-est-,nō-men-'ā-yùs\ [L] : John is his name — motto of Puerto Rico

jour·nal in·time \zhür-nál-a-tēm\ [F] : intimate journal : private diary

jus di·vi·num \,yüs-di-'wē-,nùm\ [L] : divine law

jus·ti·tia om·ni·bus \yùs-,tit-ē-,ä-'òm-ni-,bùs\ [L] : justice for all — motto of the District of Columbia

j'y suis, j'y reste \zhē-swȳē-zhē-rest\ [F] : here I am, here I remain

kte·ma es aei \(kə-)'tä-,mä-,es-ä-'ā\ [Gk] : a possession for ever — applied to a work of art or literature of enduring significance

la belle dame sans mer·ci \là-bel-dàm-sä-mer-sē\ [F] : the beautiful lady without mercy

la·bo·ra·re est ora·re \'läb-ō-,rär-e-,est-'ō-,rär-e\ [L] : to work is to pray

la·bor om·nia vin·cit \'lä-,bór-,òm-nē-,ä-'win,-kit\ [L] : labor conquers all things — motto of Oklahoma

la·cri·mae re·rum \,läk-ri-,mī-'rä,-rùm\ [L] : tears for things : pity for misfortune; also : tears in things : tragedy of life

lais·ser·al·ler \le-sā-ä-lā\ [F]: letting go : lack of restraint

lap·sus ca·la·mi \läp-səs-'käl-ə-,mē, ,lap-səs-'kal-ə-,mī\ [L]: slip of the pen

lap·sus lin·guae \,lap-səs-'liŋ-,gwī, ,läp-,sùs-\ [L]: slip of the tongue

la reine le veut \lä-ren-lə-'vœ\ [F]: the queen wills it

la·scia·te ogni spe·ran·za, voi ch'en·tra·te \läsh-'shä-tä ,ō-nē-spä-'rän-tsä-vō-ē-kän-'trä-tä\ [It]: abandon all hope, ye who enter

lau·da·tor tem·po·ris ac·ti \laù-'dä-,tòr,-tem-pə-ris-'äk,-tē\ [L]: one who praises past times

laus Deo \laùs-'dā-ō\ [L]: praise (be) to God

le roi est mort, vive le roi \lə-rwä-e-mór vēv-lə-rwä\ [F]: the king is dead, long live the king

le roi le veut \lə-və̄\ [F]: the king wills it

le roi s'avi·se·ra \-sä-vēz-rä\ [F]: the king will consider

le style, c'est l'homme \lə-stēl-se-lóm\ [F]: the style is the man

l'état, c'est moi \lä-tà-se-mwà\ [F]: the state, it is I

l'étoile du nord \lä-twàl-dē-nòr\ [F]: the star of the north — motto of Minnesota

Lie·der·kranz \'lēd-ər-,kräns\ [G]: wreath of songs : German singing society

lit·tera scrip·ta ma·net \,lit-ə-,rä-,skrip-tə-'män-et\ [L]: the written letter abides

lo·cus in quo \,lō-kəs-in-'kwō\ [L]: place in which

l'union fait la force \lē-nyōⁿ-fe-là-fórs\ [F]: union makes strength — motto of Belgium

lu·sus na·tu·rae \,lü-səs-nə-'tùr-ē, -'tùr-,ī\ [L]: freak of nature

ma foi \mà-fwà\ [F]: my faith! : indeed

mag·na est ve·ri·tas et prae·va·le·bit \,mäg-nä-,est-'wä-ri-,täs-et-,prī-wä-'lä-bit\ [L]: truth is mighty and will prevail

mag·ni no·mi·nis um·bra \,mäg-nē-,nō-mə-nis-'ùm-brä\ [L]: the shadow of a great name

mai·son de san·té \mā-zō⁴d-(ə-)sän-'tā\ [F]: private hospital : asylum

ma·lis avi·bus \,mäl-,ēs-'ä-wi-,bùs\ [L]: under evil auspices

man spricht Deutsch \män-shprikt-'dóich\ [G]: German spoken

ma·riage de con·ve·nance \mà-ryàzh-də-kōⁿv-nä⁴s\ [F]: marriage of convenience

mau·vaise honte \mō-vez-ō⁴t\ [F]: bad shame : bashfulness

me·den agan \(,)mä-,den-'äg,än\ [Gk]: nothing in excess

me·dio tu·tis·si·mus ibis \'med-ē-,ō-tü-,tis-ə-mus-'ē-bəs\ [L]: you will go most safely by the middle course

me ju·di·ce \mā-'yüd-ə-ke\ [L]: I being judge : in my judgment

mens sa·na in cor·po·re sa·no \mäns-'sän-ə-in-,kór-pə-re-'sän-ō\ [L]: a sound mind in a sound body

me·um et tu·um \,mē-əm-,et-'tü-əm, ,me-əm-\ [L]: mine and thine: distinction of private property

mi·ra·bi·le vi·su \mə-,räb-ə-lē-'wē-sü\ [L]: wonderful to behold

mi·ra·bi·lia \,mir-ə-'bil-ē-ə\ [L]: wonders : miracles

mo·le ru·it sua \'mō-le-,rù-it,-sù-ä\ [L]: it collapses from its own bigness

monde \mō⁴d\ [F]: world : fashionable world : society

mon·ta·ni sem·per li·be·ri \mòn-'tän-ē,-sem-por-'lē-bə-,rē\ [L]: mountaineers are always free men — motto of West Virginia

mo·nu·men·tum ae·re per·en·ni·us \,mó-nə-'men-tùm-,ī-re-pə-'ren-ē-ùs\ [L]: a monument more lasting than bronze — used of an immortal work of art or literature

mo·ri·tu·ri te sa·lu·ta·mus \,mór-ə-'tùr-ē,-tä,-säl-ə-'täm-ùs\ [L]: we who are about to die salute thee

mul·tum in par·vo \,mùl-təm-in-'pär-vō\ [L]: much in little

mu·ta·to no·mi·ne de te fa·bu·la nar·ra·tur \mü-,tät-ō-'nō-mə-ne-dä-'tä-,fäb-ə-lä-nä-'rä-,tür\ [L]: with the name changed the story applies to you

na·tu·ra non fa·cit sal·tum \nä-'tü-rä-,nòn-,fäk-ət-'säl-,tùm\ [L]: nature makes no leap

ne ce·de ma·lis \nā-,kā-de-'mäl-ēs\ [L]: yield not to misfortunes

ne·mo me im·pu·ne la·ces·sit \'nā-mō-'mä-im-,pü-nä-lä-'kes-ət\ [L]: no one attacks me with impunity — motto of Scotland and of the Order of the Thistle

ne quid ni·mis \nā-,kwid-'nim-əs\ [L]: not anything in excess

n'est-ce pas? \nes-pä\ [F]: isn't it so?

nil ad·mi·ra·ri \'nēl,-äd-mə-'rär-ē\ [L]: to be excited by nothing : equanimity

nil de·spe·ran·dum \'nēl,-dä-spä-'rän-dùm\ [L]: never despair

nil si·ne nu·mi·ne \'nēl,-sin-e-'nü-mə-ne\ [L]: nothing without the divine will — motto of Colorado

n'im·porte \na⁴-'pórt\ [F]: it's no matter

no·lens vo·lens \,nō-,lenz-'vō-,lenz\ [L]: unwilling (or) willing : willy-nilly

non om·nia pos·su·mus om·nes \nōn-,òm-ē-ä,-pò-sə-mùs-'óm,-näs\ [L]: we can't all (do) all things

non om·nis mo·ri·ar \nōn-,òm-nəs-,mór-ē-,är\ [L]: I shall not wholly die

non sans droict \nō⁴-sä⁴-drwä\ [OF]: not without right — motto on Shakespeare's coat of arms

non sum qua·lis eram \,nōn-,sùm-,kwäl-əs-'er-,äm\ [L]: I am not what I used to be

nos·ce te ip·sum \,nós-ke-,tä-'ip-,sùm\ [L]: know thyself

nos·tal·gie de la boue \nós-tàl-zhēd-(ə-)là-bü\ [F]: nostalgia for the mud : homesickness for the gutter

nous avons chan·gé tout ce·la \nü-zà-vō⁴-shä⁴-zhä-tü-s(l)à\ [F]: we have changed all that

nous ver·rons ce que nous ver·rons \nü-ve-rō⁴s-(ə-)kə-nü-ve-rō⁴\ [F]: we shall see what we shall see

no·vus ho·mo \,nō-wəs-'hó-mō\ [L]: new man : man newly ennobled : upstart

no·vus or·do se·clo·rum \-'ór-,dō-sä-'klór-əm\ [L]: a new cycle of the ages — motto on the reverse of the great seal of the United States

nu·gae \'nü-,gī\ [L]: trifles

nyet \'nyet\ [Russ]: no

ob·iit \'ò-bē-,it\ [L]: he (or she) died

ob·scu·rum per ob·scu·ri·us \əb-

'sky·ùr-əm-, per-əb-'skyùr-ē-əs\ [L]: (explaining) the obscure by means of the more obscure

om·ne ig·no·tum pro mag·ni·fi·co \,ȯm-ne-ig-'nō-,tùm-prō-mäg-'nif-i-,kō\ [L]: everything unknown (is taken) as grand : the unknown tends to be exaggerated in importance or difficulty

om·nia mu·tan·tur, nos et mu·ta·mur in il·lis \,ȯm-nē-ä-mü-'tän-,tùr ,nōs-,et-mü-,täm-ȯr-in-'il-,ēs\ [L]: all things are changing, and we are changing with them

om·nia vin·cit amor \'ȯm-nē-ä-,wiŋ-kət-'äm-,ȯr\ [L]: love conquers all

onus pro·ban·di \,ō-nəs-prō-'ban-,dī, -dē\ [L]: burden of proof

ora pro no·bis \,ō-rä-prō-'nō-,bēs\ [L]: pray for us

ore ro·tun·do \,ōr-ē-rō-'tən-dō\ [L]: with round mouth : eloquently

oro y pla·ta \,ōr-ō-ē-'plät-ə\ [Sp] gold and silver — motto of Montana

o tem·po·ra! o mo·res! \ō-'tem-pə-rä-ō-'mō-,räs\ [L]: oh the times! oh the manners!

oti·um cum dig·ni·ta·te \'ōt-ē-,ùm-kùm-,dig-nə-'tä-te\ [L]: leisure with dignity

où sont les neiges d'an·tan? \ü-sōⁿ-lā-nezh-däⁿ-'täⁿ\ [F]: where are the snows of yesteryear?

pal·li·da Mors \,pal-əd-ə-'mȯrz\ [L]: pale Death

pa·nem et cir·cen·ses \'pän-,em-et-kir-'kän-,sēs\ [L]: bread and circuses : provision of the means of life and recreation by government to appease discontent

par avance \pär-à-väⁿs\ [F]: in advance : by anticipation

par avion \pär-à-vyōⁿ\ [F]: by airplane — used on airmail

par ex·em·ple \pär-āg-zäⁿpl⁾\ [F]: for example

par·tu·ri·unt mon·tes, nas·ce·tur ri·di·cu·lus mus \pär-,tùr-ē-,ùnt-'mȯn-,tās näs-'kā-,tùr-ri-,dik-ə-ləs-'mùs\ [L]: the mountains are in labor, and a ridiculous mouse will be brought forth

pa·ter pa·tri·ae \,pä-,ter-'pä-trē-,ī\ [L]: father of his country

pau·cis ver·bis \,paù-,kēs-'wer-,bēs\ [L]: in a few words

pax vo·bis·cum \,päks-wō-'bēs-,kùm\ [L]: peace (be) with you

peine forte et dure \pen-fȯr-tā-d̄ēr\ [F]: strong and hard punishment : torture

per an·gus·ta ad au·gus·ta \per-'äŋ-,gùs-tə-äd-'aù-,gùs-tə, per-'äŋ-\ [L]: through difficulties to honors

père \per\ [F]: father — used after French proper names to distinguish a father from his son

per·eant qui an·te nos nos·tra dix·e·runt \'per-e-,änt-kwē-,än-te-'nōs-'nōs-trä-dēk-'sā-,rùnt\ [L]: may they perish who have expressed our bright ideas before us

per·eunt et im·pu·tan·tur \'per-e-,ùnt-et-,im-pə-'tän-,tùr\ [L]: they (the hours) pass away and are reckoned to (our) account

per·fide Al·bion \per-fēd-àl-byōⁿ\ [F]: perfidious Albion (England)

peu à peu \pœ-à-pœ\ [F]: little by little

peu de chose \pœd-(ə-)shōz\ [F]: a trifle

pièce d'oc·ca·sion \pyes-dȯ-kä-zyōⁿ\ [F]: piece for a special occasion

pinx·it \'piŋk-sət\ [L]: he (or she) painted it

place aux dames \plàs-ō-dàm\ [F]: (make) room for the ladies

ple·no ju·re \plä-nō-'yür-e\ [L]: with full right

plus ça change, plus c'est la même chose \pl ǖ-sà-shä⁼zh pl ǖ-se-là-mem-shōz\ [F]: the more that changes, the more it's the same thing

po·cas pa·la·bras \,pō-käs-pä-'läv-räs\ [Sp]: few words

po·eta nas·ci·tur, non fit \pȯ-,ä-tä-'näs-kə-,tùr nōn-'fit\ [L]: a poet is born, not made

pol·li·ce ver·so \,pȯ-li-ke-'ver-sō\ [L]: with thumb turned : with a gesture or expression of condemnation

post hoc, er·go prop·ter hoc \'pȯst-,hōk ,er-gō-'prȯp-ter-,hōk\ [L]: after this, therefore on account of it (a fallacy of argument)

post ob·itum \pȯst-'ȯ-bə-,tùm\ [L]: after death

pour ac·quit \pür-à-kē\ [F]: received payment

pour le mé·rite \pür-lə-mā-rēt\ [F]: for merit

pro aris et fo·cis \prō-,ä-,rēs-et-'fō-,kēs\ [L]: for altars and firesides

pro bo·no pu·bli·co \,prō-,bō-nō-'pù-bli-,kō\ [L]: for the public good

pro hac vi·ce \,prō-,häk-'wik-e\ [L]: for this occasion

pro pa·tria \,prō-'pä-trē-,ä\ [L]: for one's country

pro re·ge, le·ge, et gre·ge \prō-'rā-,ge-lā-,ge-et-'greg-,e\ [L]: for the king, the law, and the people

pro re na·ta \,prō-,rā-'nät-ə\ [L]: for an occasion that has arisen : as needed — used in medical prescriptions

quand même \käⁿ-mem\ [F]: even though : whatever may happen

quan·tum mu·ta·tus ab il·lo \,kwänt-əm-mü-'tät-əs-äb-'il-ō\ [L]: how changed from what he once was

quan·tum suf·fi·cit \,kwänt-əm-'səf-ə-,kit\ [L]: as much as suffices : a sufficient quantity — used in medical prescriptions

¿quien sa·be? \kyän-'sä-vä\ [Sp]: who knows?

qui fa·cit per ali·um fa·cit per se \kwē-,fäk-it-,per-'äl-ē-,ùm-,fäk-it-,per-'sā\ [L]: he who does (anything) through another does it through himself

quis cus·to·di·et ip·sos cus·to·des? \,kwis-kùs-'tōd-ē-,et-,ip-,sōs-kùs-'tō-dās\ [L]: who will keep the keepers themselves?

qui s'ex·cuse s'ac·cuse \kē-'sek-,sküez-'sä-,kǖz\ [F]: he who excuses himself accuses himself

quis se·pa·ra·bit? \,kwis-,sā-pə-'räb-it\ [L]: who shall separate (us)? — motto of the Order of St. Patrick

qui trans·tu·lit sus·ti·net \kwē-'träns-tə-,lit-'sùs-tə-,net\ [L]: He who transplanted sustains (us) — motto of Connecticut

qui va là? \kē-vä-là\ [F]: who goes there?

quo·ad hoc \,kwȯ-,äd-'hōk\ [L]: as far as this : to this extent

quod erat de·mon·stran·dum \,kwȯd-'er-,ät-,dem-ən-'stran-dəm, -,dä-,mȯn-

'strän-,dŭm\ [L] : which was to be
proved

quod erat fa·ci·en·dum \-,fäk-ē-'en-
,dŭm\ [L] : which was to be done

quod vi·de \kwŏd-'wid-,e\ [L] : which
see

quos de·us vult per·de·re pri·us de-
men·tat \kwōs-'de-ŭs-,wŭlt-'perd-ə-,re,
,pri-ŭs-dā-'men-,tät\ [L] : those whom
a god wishes to destroy he first drives
mad

quot ho·mi·nes, tot sen·ten·ti·ae
\kwŏt-'hō-mə-,nās,-,tŏt-sen-'ten-tē-,ī\
[L] : there are as many opinions as there
are men

quo va·dis? \kwō-'wäd-əs\ [L] : whither
are you going?

rai·son d'état \re-zōⁿ-dā-tȧ\ [F] : reason of state

re·cu·ler pour mieux sau·ter \rə-kū̇-
lā-pür-myœ̄-sō-tā\ [F] : to draw back
in order to make a better jump

reg·nat po·pu·lus \,reg-,nät-'pò-pə-
,lŭs\ [L] : the people rule — motto of
Arkansas

re in·fec·ta \,rā-in-'fek-tä\ [L] : the
business being unfinished : without accomplishing one's purpose

re·li·gio lo·ci \re-,lig-ē-,ō-'lō-,kē\ [L]
: religious sanctity of a place

ré·pon·dez s'il vous plaît \rā-pōⁿ-dā-
sēl-vü-ple\ [F] : reply, if you please

re·qui·es·cat in pa·ce \,rek-wē-'es-
,kät-in-'päk-,e, ,rā-kwē-'es-,kät-in-
'päch-,ā\ [L] : may he (or she) rest in
peace — used on tombstones

re·spi·ce fi·nem \,rā-spi-,ke-'fē-,nem\
[L] : look to the end : consider the outcome

re·sur·gam \re-'sŭr-,gäm\ [L] : I shall
rise again

re·te·nue \rət-nū̇e\ [F] : self-restraint
: reserve

re·ve·nons à nos mou·tons \rəv-nōⁿ-ȧ-
nō-mü-tōⁿ\ [F] : let us return to our
sheep : let us get back to the subject

ruse de guerre \rüz-də-ger\ [F] : war
stratagem

rus in ur·be \,rüs-in-'ùr,be\ [L] : country in the city

sal At·ti·cum \sal-'at-i-kəm\ [L]
: Attic salt : wit

salle à man·ger \sȧl-ȧ-mäⁿ-zhā\ [F]
: dining room

sa·lus po·pu·li su·pre·ma lex es·to
\,säl-,ùs-'pò-pə-,lē-sù-,prā-mə-,leks-'es-
tō\ [L] : let the welfare of the people be
the supreme law — motto of Missouri

sans doute \säⁿ-düt\ [F] : without
doubt

sans gêne \säⁿ-zhen\ [F] : without embarrassment or constraint

sans peur et sans re·proche \säⁿ-pœr-
ā-säⁿ-rə-'prōsh\ [F] : without fear and
without reproach

sans sou·ci \säⁿ-sü-sē\ [F] : without
worry

sculp·sit \'skŏlp-sət, 'skŭlp-\ [L] : he
(or she) carved it

scu·to bo·nae vo·lun·ta·tis tu·ae co-
ro·nas·ti nos \'skü-,tō-'bò-,nī-,ō-,vŭln-
,tät-əs-'tü,-ī-,kòr-ə-,näs-tē-'nōs\ [L]
: Thou hast crowned us with the shield
of Thy good will — a motto on the
Great Seal of Maryland

se·cun·dum ar·tem \se-,kùn-dəm-'är-
,tem\ [L] : according to the art : according to the accepted practice of a
profession or trade

se·cun·dum na·tu·ram \-nə-'tü-,räm\
[L] : according to nature : naturally

se de·fen·den·do \'sā-,dā-,fen'den-dō\
[L] : in self-defense

se ha·bla es·pa·ñol \sā-,äv-lä-,äs-pä-
'n'òl\ [Sp] : Spanish spoken

sem·per ea·dem \,sem-,per'e-ä-,dem\
[L] : always the same (fem.) — motto of
Queen Elizabeth I

sem·per fi·de·lis \,sem-pər-fə-'dā-ləs\
[L] : always faithful — motto of the
U. S. Marine Corps

sem·per idem \,sem-,per-'ē-,dem\ [L]
: always the same (masc.)

sem·per pa·ra·tus \,sem-pər-pə-'rät-əs\
[L] : always prepared — motto of the
U. S. Coast Guard

se non è ve·ro, è ben tro·va·to \sä-
,nōn-e-'vā-rō-e,-ben-trō-'vä-tō\ [It]
: even if it is not true, it is well conceived

sic itur ad as·tra \sēk-'i-,tŭr-,äd-'as-
trə\ [L] : thus one goes to the stars
: such is the way to immortality

sic pas·sim \sēk-'päs-im\ [L] : so
everywhere

sic sem·per ty·ran·nis \,sik-,sem-pər-
tə-'ran-əs\ [L] : thus ever to tyrants —
motto of Virginia

sic tran·sit glo·ria mun·di \sēk-'trän-
sət-,glōr-ē-ä-'mùn-dē\ [L] : so passes
away the glory of the world

sic·ut pa·tri·bus sit De·us no·bis \,sē-
,kŭt-'pä-tri-,büs-sit-,De-ùs-'nō-,bēs\ [L]
: as to our fathers may God be to us —
motto of Boston

si jeu·nesse sa·vait, si vieil·lesse pou-
vait! \sē-'zhœ-nes-,sȧ-ve sē-'vye-yes-
'pü-ve\ [F] : if youth only knew, if age
only could!

si·lent le·ges in·ter ar·ma \,sil-,ent-
'lā-,gäs,-,int-ər-'är-mä\ [L] : the laws
are silent in the midst of arms

s'il vous plaît \sēl-vü-ple\ [F] : if you
please

si·mi·lia si·mi·li·bus cu·ran·tur \sim-
'il-ē-ä-,sim-'il-ə-bùs-kü-'rän-,tùr\ [L]
: like is cured by like

si·mi·lis si·mi·li gau·det \sim-ə-ləs-
'sim-ə-,lē-'gaù-,det\ [L] : like takes
pleasure in like

si mo·nu·men·tum re·qui·ris, cir-
cum·spi·ce \,sē-,mò-nə-,ment-əm-re-
'kwē-rəs kir-'kùm-spi-ke\ [L] : if you
seek his monument, look around — epi-
taph of Sir Christopher Wren in St.
Paul's, London, of which he was archi-
tect

si quae·ris pen·in·su·lam amoe·nam,
cir·cum·spi·ce \sē-,kwī-rəs-pā-,nin-sə-
,läm-ə-'mòi-,näm kir-'kùm-spi-ke\ [L]
: if you seek a beautiful peninsula, look
around — motto of Michigan

sis·te vi·a·tor \,sis-te-wē-'ā,-tòr\ [L]
: stop, traveler — used on roadside
tombs

sol·vi·tur am·bu·lan·do \'sòl-wə-,tùr-
,äm-bə-'län-dō\ [L] : it is solved by
walking : the problem is solved by a
practical experiment

splen·di·de men·dax \,splen-də-,dā-
'men-,däks\ [L] : nobly untruthful

spo·lia opi·ma \,spō-lē-ə-ō-'pē-mə\ [L]
: rich spoils : the arms taken by the victorious from the vanquished general

sta·tus in quo \,stät-əs-,in-'kwō\ [L]
: state in which : the existing state

sta·tus quo an·te bel·lum \'stät-əs-
kwō,-änt-e-'bel-ùm\ [L] : the state existing before the war

sua·vi·ter in mo·do, for·ti·ter in re

\'swä-wə-,ter-in-'mŏd-ō 'fŏrt-ə-,ter-in-'rä\ [L] : gently in manner, strongly in deed

sub ver·bo \,sùb-'wer-bō\ or sub vo·ce \,sùb-'wō-ke\ [L] : under the word — introducing a cross-reference in a dictionary or index

sunt la·cri·mae re·rum \sùnt-,läk-ri-,mī-'rä-rùm\ [L] : there are tears for things

suo ju·re \,sù-ō-'yùr-e\ [L] : in his (or her) own right

suo lo·co \-'lō-kō\ [L] : in its proper place

suo Mar·te \-'när-te\ [L] : by one's own exertions

su·um cui·que \,sù-əm-'kwik-we\ [L] : to each his own

tant mieux \täⁿ-myœ̄\ [F] : so much the better

tant pis \-pē\ [F] : so much the worse

tem·po·ra mu·tan·tur, nos et mu·ta·mur in il·lis \,tem-pə-rä-mü-'tän-,tùr ,nŏs,-et-mü-,täm-ər-in-'il-,ēs\ [L] : the times are changing, and we are changing with them

tem·pus edax re·rum \'tem-pùs,-ed-,äks-'rä-rùm\ [L] : time, that devours all things

tem·pus fu·git \,tem-pəs-'fyü-jət, -'fü-git\ [L] : time flies

ti·meo Da·na·os et do·na fe·ren·tes \,tim-ē-,ō-'dän-ä-,ōs,-et-,dō-nä-fe-'ren-,täs\ [L] : I fear the Greeks even when they bring gifts

to·ti·dem ver·bis \,tōt-ə-,dem-'wer-,bēs\ [L] : in so many words

to·tis vi·ri·bus \,tō-,tēs-'wē-ri-,bùs\ [L] : with all one's might

to·to cae·lo \-,tō-tō-'kī-lō\ or toto coe·lo \-'kòi-lō\ [L] : by the whole extent of the heavens; diametrically

tou·jours per·drix \tü-zhür-per-drē\ [F] : always partridge : too much of a good thing

tous frais faits \tü-fre-fe\ [F] : all expenses defrayed

tout à fait \tü-ta-fe\ [F] : altogether : quite

tout au con·traire \tü-tō-kōⁿ-trer\ [F] : quite the contrary

tout à vous \tü-ta-vü\ [F] : wholly yours : at your service

tout bien ou rien \tü-'byaⁿ-nü-'ryaⁿ\ [F] : everything well (done) or nothing (attempted)

tout com·pren·dre c'est tout par·don·ner \'tü-kōⁿ-präⁿ-drə se-'tü-pàr-dó-nä\ [F] : to understand all is to forgive all

tout court \tü-kür\ [F] : quite short : simply; also : brusquely

tout de même \tüt-mem\ [F] : all the same : nevertheless

tout de suite \tüt-swēt\ [F] : immediately; also : at once : consecutively

tout en·sem·ble \tü-täⁿ-säⁿblᵊ\ [F] : all together : general effect

tout est per·du fors l'hon·neur \tü-te-per-dü-fōr-lō-ner\ or tout est perdu hors l'honneur \-dü-òr-\ [F] : all is lost save honor

tout le monde \tül-mōⁿd\ [F] : all the world : everybody

tria junc·ta in uno \,tri-ä-'yùⁿk-tä-in-'ü-nō\ [L] : three joined in one — motto of the Order of the Bath

tru·di·tur di·es die \'trüd-ə-,tùr-,di-,äs-'di-,ä\ [L] : day is pushed forth by day : one day hurries on another

tu·e·bor \tù-'ä-,bòr\ [L] : I will defend

— a motto on the Great Seal of Michigan

ua mau ke ea o ka ai·na i ka po·no \,ù-ä-'mä-ù-ke-'e-ä-ō-kä-'ä-ē-nä-,ē-kä-'pō-nō\ [Hawaiian] : the life of the land is established in righteousness — motto of Hawaii

ul·ti·ma ra·tio re·gum \'ùl-ti-mä-,rät-ē-ō-'rä-gùm\ [L] : the final argument of kings, i.e., war

und so wei·ter \ùnt-zō-'vī-tər\ [G] : and so on

uno ani·mo \,ü-nō-'än-ə-,mō\ [L] : with one mind : unanimously

ur·bi et or·bi \,ùr-bē-,et-'òr-bē\ [L] : to the city (Rome) and the world

uti·le dul·ci \,üt-ᵊl-e-'dùl,-kē\ [L] : the useful with the agreeable

ut in·fra \ùt-'in-frä\ [L] : as below

ut su·pra \ùt-'sü-prä\ [L] : as above

va·de re·tro me, Sa·ta·na \,wä-de-'rä-trō-,mä-'sä-tə-,nä\ [L] : get thee behind me, Satan

vae vic·tis \wī-'wik-,tēs\ [L] : woe to the vanquished

va·ria lec·tio \,wär-ē-ä-'lek-tē-,ō\ pl va·ri·ae lec·ti·o·nes \'wär-ē-,ī-,lek-tē-'ō-,näs\ [L] : variant reading

va·ri·um et mu·ta·bi·le sem·per fe·mi·na \,wär-ē-,et-,mü-'tä-bə-le-,sem-per-'fä-mə-nä\ [L] : woman is ever a fickle and changeable thing

ve·di Na·po·li e poi mo·ri \,vä-dē-'nä-pō-lē-ä-,pò-ē-'mò-rē\ [It] : see Naples, and then die

ve·ni, vi·di, vi·ci \,wä-nē-,wēd-ē-'wē-kē\ [L] : I came, I saw, I conquered

ven·tre à terre \väⁿ-trà-ter\ [F] : belly to the ground : at very great speed

ver·ba·tim ac lit·te·ra·tim \wer-'bä-tim-,äk-,lit-ə-'rä-tim\ [L] : word for word and letter for letter

ver·bum sat sa·pi·en·ti est \,wer-bùm-'sät-,säp-ē-'ent-ē-,est\ [L] : a word to the wise is sufficient

vin·cit om·nia ve·ri·tas \,wiⁿ-kət-'òm-nē-ä-'wä-rə-,täs\ [L] : truth conquers all things

vin·cu·lum ma·tri·mo·nii \,wiⁿ-kə-lùm-,mä-trə-'mō-nē-,ē\ [L] : bond of marriage

vir·gin·i·bus pu·er·is·que \,wir-'gin-ə-bùs-,pù-ə-'rēs-kwe\ [L] : for girls and boys

vir·tu·te et ar·mis \wir-'tü-te,-et-'är-mēs\ [L] : by valor and arms — motto of Mississippi

vive la reine \vēv-là-ren\ [F] : long live the queen

vive le roi \vēv-lə-rwä\ [F] : long live the king

vix·e·re for·tes an·te Aga·mem·no·na \wik-,sā-re-'fòr-,täs-,änt-,äg-ə-'mem-nə-,nä\ [L] : brave men lived before Agamemnon

vogue la ga·lère \vòg-là-gà-ler\ [F] : let the galley be kept rowing : keep on, whatever may happen

voi·là tout \vwà-là-tü\ [F] : that's all

vox et prae·te·rea ni·hil \'wōks-et-prī-,ter-ē-ä-'ni,-hil\ [L] : voice and nothing more

vox po·pu·li vox Dei \wōks-'pò-pə-,lē-,wōks-'dē-ē\ [L] : the voice of the people is the voice of God

Wan·der·jahr \'vän-dər-,yär\ [G] : year of wandering

wie geht's? \vē-'gāts\ [G] : how goes it?

MERRIAM-WEBSTER DICTIONARIES

WEBSTER'S THIRD NEW INTERNATIONAL DICTIONARY, *Unabridged*

The completely new authority of our language. Includes 100,000 new words and new meanings with 200,000 demonstrations of word usage. Every definition given in a single phrase of precise meaning. 3,000 illustrations; 20 plates in glorious color. 450,000 entries; 2,728 pages.

WEBSTER'S SEVENTH NEW COLLEGIATE DICTIONARY

This new desk dictionary is the latest in the famous Merriam-Webster Collegiate series, the outstanding favorite in schools, homes, and offices. 130,000 entries include 20,000 new words and new meanings for more complete coverage than any other desk dictionary. Precise, clear definitions with 10,000 usage examples assure full understanding and accurate use of words. 1,244 pages.

WEBSTER'S DICTIONARY OF SYNONYMS

A valuable book for anyone who strives for clear expression and correct usage in speech and in writing. The most useful, modern, comprehensive treatment of synonyms ever published.

WEBSTER'S BIOGRAPHICAL DICTIONARY

Concise biographies of more than 40,000 noteworthy men and women of every historical period, every nationality, all walks of life.

WEBSTER'S GEOGRAPHICAL DICTIONARY

A quick-reference source of information about 40,000 of the world's important places. The greatest fund of current geographical information obtainable in a single volume to aid in a clear understanding of the vital news of the day.

WEBSTER'S ELEMENTARY DICTIONARY

The only dictionary written specifically for boys and girls in the fourth, fifth, sixth, and seventh grades. 18,000 vocabulary entries selected for school needs in the elementary grades.

G. & C. Merriam Co., Springfield, Mass. 01101, U. S. A.

MERRIAM-WEBSTER DICTIONARIES

In 1831 George and Charles Merriam, printers in Springfield, Massachusetts, U.S.A., began publishing in a modest way. Twelve years later, following Noah Webster's death, the Merriams obtained all unbound sheets of Webster's Dictionary. Thus began an alliance of business and scholarship which has continued for more than a hundred years. Since 1847 the Merriam-Webster editorial staff has produced six complete revisions of the unabridged dictionary, the latest of which is entitled WEBSTER'S THIRD NEW INTERNATIONAL DICTIONARY.

The preparation of this latest edition absorbed 757 editor years and required a capital outlay of $3,500,000. It now serves as the final word authority for schools, colleges, libraries, and courts. It provides a prime linguistic aid to interpreting the culture and civilization of today, as the first edition served the America of 1828.

WEBSTER'S
THIRD
NEW INTERNATIONAL
DICTIONARY
UNABRIDGED

CAUTION: The Merriam series of Webster's dictionaries can be identified by a circular trademark on the cover, and also by the trademark *a Merriam-Webster* REG. U.S. PAT. OFF. on the title page. Only in this series are to be found the most authoritative dictionaries, based on the experience of more than a century of dictionary making. These trademarks insure accuracy, reliability, and up-to-dateness. GET THE BEST.

G. & C. Merriam Co., Springfield, Mass. 01101, U. S. A.